SACRED
SCRIPTURES

2nd Edition 2020

Presented To

_____

On this day

_____

From

_____

Date of Water Baptism: _____

Date of Holy Spirit Baptism: _____

SACRED

SCRIPTURES

2nd Edition 2020

Yahwah Apostolic Ministries
Ohio USA

Psalm 119:105
Thy word is a lamp unto my feet, and a light unto my path.

נר לרגלי דברך ואור לנתיבתי

PARTRIDGE

Library of Congress Control Number: 2019915520
ISBN: Hardcover   978-1-5437-5439-1
                 Softcover   978-1-5437-5437-7
                 eBook   978-1-5437-5438-4

Print information available on the last page.

To order additional copies of this book, contact
Toll Free +65 3165 7531 (Singapore)
Toll Free +60 3 3099 4412 (Malaysia)
orders.singapore@partridgepublishing.com

www.partridgepublishing.com/singapore

Introduction

This book as it is named: יהוה **Sacred Scriptures**, is a revised English translation Scriptures using the KJV 1769 bible as the main reference and many other references from different version of English and Hebrew bibles. This book of the Scriptures consists of two volumes: The title for the first volume is "First Blood Covenant" which is called "Tanakh" in Hebrew. "First Blood Covenant" – the "Tanakh" is commonly known as "Old Testament" of the English translated Bible. Tanakh is a canonical collection of 39 books of Hebrew Scriptures, an acronym of the first Hebrew letter of each of the Masoretic Text's three traditional subdivisions: **T**orah (also known as "Five Books of Moses –Pentateuch"), **N**evi'im (Prophets) and **K**etuvim (Writings) — hence called "**TaNaKh**".

The title for the second volume of the Scriptures is "New Blood Covenant" which is called "Dam haBerit Chadashah" in Hebrew. The "New Blood Covenant" was commonly known as "New Testament (NT)" of the English translated Bibles. It is a collection of the texts of Messiah's followers (Mashiachim) at different times by various authors. The New Blood Covenant (NT) volume consists of 27 books: The four canonical gospels (Matthew, Mark, Luke, and John), the Acts of the Apostles, the twenty-one epistles of Apostles, and the Book of Revelation.

In the Old Testament (OT) and New Testament (NT) of the English translated Holy Bible, the sacred name of the everlasting God (Elohim) which appear in the Scriptures nearly 7000 times has been replaced with titles such as "the LORD / the Lord", "GOD", "ADONAI" and many other mis-transliterated names.

In the third commandment of יהוה (Exodus 20:7), it was written:
You shalt not take the name of יהוה your God (YHWH Eloheikha) in vain; for יהוה will not hold him guiltless that taketh His name in vain.

לא תשא את־שם־יהוה אלהיך לשוא כי לא ינקה יהוה את אשר־ישא את־שמו לשוא:

In obeying the commandment of God (Elohim, יהוה (YHWH)), thus in this book of the Scriptures: The sacred name of the one true living God (Elohim) the Creator and Savior of mankind in Hebrew Script: יהוה was restored to its rightful place in the First Blood Covenant volume, as it was found originally written in the Hebrew Tanakh. In the New Blood Covenant (NT) volume, the name of the Messiah (haMashiach) was written in Latin script as "Yahwah" which is the transliteration of יהוה (YHWH). Also in the New Blood Covenant (NT) volume, the sacred and everlasting name of God (Elohim) was written in three different form of scripts: יהוה/**YHWH/Yahwah**. These are not three different names of God (Elohim) but One God (Elohim, Eph. 4:6); One Lord (Adonai, Eph. 4:5); and One Name (Zech. 14:9): יהוה/**YHWH/Yahwah: "The Name Above Every Name (Phil. 2:9)"** who has three attributes and manifestation as expressed distinctly by apostle John in *1 John 5:7: For there are three that bear witness in heaven: the Father, the Word (Son), and the Holy Spirit; and these three are one;*
(1) יהוה – Sacred name of God (Elohim) in Hebrew script.
(2) YHWH – Sacred name of God (Elohim) transliterated in Latin script (Tetragrammaton).
(3) Yahwah – Sacred name of God (Elohim) transliterated in Latin script with vowel.

Also in the New Blood Covenant (NT) volume where God (Elohim)'s name should have been written instead of title "the Lord" or "God", the name Yahwah/YHWH was written in parenthesis next to "the Lord"; and "God" was substituted by God (Elohim, יהוה (YHWH)). As for the title used in addressing to God (Elohim, יהוה (YHWH)), Hebrew title "Adonai" or "Adon" was written in parenthesis next to the English title "Lord".

In order for reader to have the correct understanding of the Apostles' epistles in the New Blood Covenant (NT) volume concerning the Messiah (haMashiach) who is God (Elohim, יהוה (YHWH)) the Savior of mankind: the word "Son" was substituted by "Humanity" or "Humanity of El" in most contexts. The phrase "Son of God" was also appropriately substituted by "Humanity of El (YHWH)" which reveal the truth that God (Elohim, יהוה (YHWH)) manifested Himself in human flesh (1 Tim.

3:16, John 1:14), and became the "Son/Son of Man" who bears the Father's name (John 5:43): YHWH (Yahwah).

The Hebrew transliterated names for the main characters and some Hebrew key words in this Scriptures were also written in parenthesis next to the English scripts. All the Hebrew names having letter "Y" for "Yod (י)" which had been written with letter "J" in English also have the correct transliteration according to the Hebrew scripts. An article entitled "**The Plan of Salvation in יהוה (YHWH)'s Sacred Name**" – a teaching about salvation according to the Scriptures, is attached to this Scriptures to help readers to have a clear understanding about the importance of having faith and believe in the true sacred name of God (Elohim, יהוה (YHWH)) and how they shall receive salvation and everlasting life from the one and only true living God (Elohim) and Savior.

Study Guides for Readers – The Appendixes

There are three Appendixes attached at the end of this Scriptures as study guides for readers. Appendix I contained the Hebrew Alphabet (22 abjad of consonant letters) and the Niqqud (a system of vowel points). Appendix II has two sections: Appendix II-A and Appendix II-B. Appendix II-A consists a list of names or attribute names with commentary. Appendix II-B consists a list of study notes on words or verses in the Scriptures. Whenever reader sees in the Scriptures, a superscript number start with the capital-letter A, refers to Appendix II-A for reference; and for superscript number start with the capital-letter B, refers to Appendix II-B for reference.

Translation of LORD, GOD and Jehovah/Yehovah

In the Jewish (Yehudim) tradition, it is forbidden to pronouce the sacred name of God (Elohim) – יהוה (YHWH). The prohibition of pronouncing the Name יהוה (YHWH) as written is sometimes called the "Ineffable", "Unutterable", or "Distinctive Name". The utterance of the Name (HaShem) is denounced in the Mishnah (which is the first major written collection of the Jewish (Yehudim) oral traditions known as the "Oral Torah".) Due to such prohibition, Hakadosh Baruch Hu ("The Holy One, Blessed Be He"), Adonai ("LORD/the Lord") or Hashem ("The Name") became the common Hebrew forms of substitutions for the sacred name of יהוה (YHWH).

To prohibit the readers from pronouncing the actual biblical name of יהוה while reading the Hebrew Scriptures, Masoretic vowel points were added to the name יהוה which direct the reader to read in title "Adonai" or "Elohim". When the name יהוה is preceded by Adonai, it receives the vowels from the title Elohim instead. This is why אדני יהוה is read as "Adonai Elohim" and thus translated as "Lord GOD" in English. The transliteration name of "Jehovah/Yehovah" was also derived from Masoretic punctuation, which has the vowel points for Adonai: יְהֹוָה.

The table below illustrates the English translation or transliteration for the sacred name יהוה from the Masoretic punctuation of Hebrew text and its transliteration:

Hebrew Script		Reading by Jewish (Yehudim)	Translation / Transliteration in English Bibles	Transliteration in this Scriptures
יְהֹוָה		Adonai אֲדֹנָי	LORD	יהוה (YHWH)
			Jehovah / Yehovah	Yahwah
יֱהֹוִה	יְהֹוִה	Elohim אֱלֹהִים	GOD	יהוה (YHWH)
אֲדֹנָי יְהֹוִה		Adonai Elohim	Lord GOD	Adonai YHWH

The Sacred Name of יהוה (YHWH) and Its Pronunciation

יהוה (yod hey waw hey) are 4-Hebrew consonant letters written in the Hebrew block letter, represented by the Latin script as YHWH (called the Tetragrammaton, meaning four letters). יהוה (**YHWH**) is the sacred name of the God (Elohim) of Yisrael, which was found originally written in the form of Pictograph: 𝌖𝘠𝌖⌐, Phoenesian: ⺈𝖄⺕⺜ and Paleo-Hebrew: ⺝𝖄⺝⺎.

Each of the Hebrew letters has a unique meaning. יהוה (Pictograph: 𝌖𝘠𝌖⌐) properly read from right to left for Hebrew letters, are:

1st letter	Y	י	⌐	yod	the Hand	Anciently portrayed by the symbol of a hand.
2nd letter	H	ה	𝌖	hey	Behold	Anciently portrayed by the symbol of a man which means 'behold, to show or to reveal'.
3rd letter	W	ו	𝘠	waw	the Nail	Signifies a nail, peg or hook which means 'nailed or bound together'.
4th letter	H	ה	𝌖	hey	Behold	Same as the 2nd letter.

Reading from left to right in English, יהוה (**YHWH**) is revealed as:
"**Behold the Nail, Behold the Hand.**" i.e. "**Behold the Nailed Hand.**"

יהוה is derived from the Hebrew triconsonantal root: היה (H1961 ha.yah), an archaic form of which is הוה (H1934 ha.wah). Thus: יה (**YH**) and וה (**WH**) for יהוה (**YHWH**) is pronounced **YaHWaH** in Hebrew and similar phonetic sound when transliterated to all other languages.

Purpose of Printing יהוה Sacred Scriptures

The purpose of printing יהוה **Sacred Scriptures** is to restore the sacred name of the true Creator, Redeemer and Savior – יהוה (YHWH) back into the Scriptures, to give יהוה (YHWH) glory due to His name (Psa. 96:8).

It was written in the Tanakh: Deuteronomy 6:5, "And you shall love יהוה your God (YHWH Eloheikha) with all your heart, and with all your soul, and with all your might." Thus, as faithful believers of God (Elohim) and Savior, we show our true love for Adonai יהוה by loving, revering, worshiping and glorifying His sacred name; for Adonai יהוה has spoken and declared in the Scriptures through His prophets:
Exodus (Shemot) 3:15 " יהוה ..... *This is My Name forever, and this is My memorial to all generation.*"
Isaiah (Yeshayahu) 42:8 "*I am יהוה, that is My name; and I will not give My glory to another, neither My praise to graven images.*"
Isaiah (Yeshayahu) 43:10:11 "*You are My witnesses,*" saith יהוה, "*And My servant whom I have chosen, that you may know and believe Me, and understand that I am He; before Me there was no God (El) formed, nor shall there be after Me. I, even I, am יהוה; and besides Me there is no Savior.*
Micah (Mikhah) 4:5 For all people will walk every one in the name of his god (elohim), but we will walk in the name of יהוה our God (YHWH Eloheinu) forever and ever.
Malachi (Malakhi) 3:1 "*Behold, I will send My messenger (John the Baptist), and he shall prepare the way before Me (YHWH); and the Lord (Adon) whom you seek, shall suddenly come to His temple, even the messenger of the covenant, whom you delight in; behold, He shall come,*" saith יהוה of hosts (YHWH Tsevaot).*

The Scriptures show evidences that believing and baptising in the true name of God (Elohim) and Savior יהוה (YHWH) is the only promise for remission of sins and salvation:

Joel (Yoel) 2:32
"And it shall come to pass, that whosoever shall call on the name of יהוה (YHWH) shall be delivered; for in Mount Zion and in Yerushalayim shall be deliverance, as יהוה (YHWH) hath said, and in the remnant whom יהוה (YHWH) shall call."

Acts 2:38
Then Peter (Kefa) said unto them, "Repent, and be baptized every one of you in the name of Yahwah haMashiach for the remission of sins, and you shall receive the gift of the Holy Spirit (Ruach haQodesh)."

Acts 4:12
Neither is there salvation in any other, for there is none other name under heaven given among men, whereby we must be saved.

Acts 10:43
To Him give all the prophets witness, that through His name (YHWH, Yahwah) whosoever believe in Him shall receive remission of sins.

A Message for Readers

We believe the truth of the Scriptures is solely by the revelation of the Holy Spirit of יהוה (YHWH) – the Creator of heavens and earth, Redeemer and Savior of mankind. We are sharing the truth in love and we certainly do not mean to offend, neither do we make any accusation to any one or any group or any organization for the differences in opinions and beliefs.

All commentaries written in the Appendixes of יהוה **Sacred Scriptures** are study notes for scriptures' truth and knowledge sharing purposes, to all who loves truth and righteousness of Adonai יהוה (YHWH) - the true living God (Elohim). As apostle Paul encourages us in 2 Timothy 2:15: Study to show yourself approved unto God (Elohim, יהוה (YHWH)), a workman that need not to be ashamed, rightly dividing the word of truth.

All readers are encouraged to pray earnestly and seek the counsel of the Holy Spirit by themselves for complete guidance in reading and understanding this book of the Sacred Scriptures.

Our Contacts:

Yahwah Apostolic Ministries
P.O. Box 132,
1271 Main Street,
Smithfield, Ohio 43948
USA

Email: yam543238@gmail.com
Facebook Links: https://web.facebook.com/
Yahwah-Apostolic-Ministries-Ohio-619817078189119/

An Article Written By: Pastor John Anderson, Yahwah Apostolic Ministries Ohio

THERE IS SO MANY DOCTRINES OF MEN .... **BUT THERE IS ONLY ONE DORTRINE OF THE GOSPEL OF TRUTH THAT WILL SAVE YOU AND ME!**

Rom. 1:16 For I am not ashamed of the gospel of haMashiach, for it is the power of יהוה (YHWH) unto salvation to everyone who believed; to the Jew first, and also to the Greek.

Eph. 1:13 In Him you also trusted, after that you heard the word of truth, the gospel of your salvation; in whom also after that you believed, you were sealed with the Holy Spirit of promise;

Gal. 1:8 But though we, or an angel from heaven, preach any other gospel unto you than that which we have preached unto you, let him be accursed.

2 Cor. 11:4 For if he that comes preaches another Yahwah (YHWH), whom we have not preached, or if you receive another spirit, which you have not received, or another gospel, which you have not accepted, you might well bear with him.

Mat. 25:32 And before Him shall be gathered all nations: and He shall separate them one from another, as a shepherd divides his sheep from the goats:

Mat. 25:33 And He shall set the sheep on His right hand, but the goats on the left.

THE KINGDOM OF יהוה (YHWH)
&
THE GOSPEL OF TRUTH INTO SALVATION
IN THE NEW BLOOD COVENANT (NEW TESTAMENT)

Zec. 14:9 And יהוה (YHWH) shall be king over all the earth; in that day shall there be one יהוה (YHWH, Yahwah), and His name one.

Dan. 2:44 And in the days of these kings shall the God (Elohim) of heaven set up a kingdom, which shall never be destroyed: and the kingdom shall not be left to other people, but it shall break in pieces and consume all these kingdoms, and it shall stand forever.

Rev. 11:15 And the seventh angel sounded; and there were great voices in heaven, saying, "The kingdoms of this world have become the kingdoms of our Lord (Adonai), and of His Anointed (Mashiach); and He shall reign forever and ever.

Mat. 3:1 In those days came John the Baptist, preaching in the wilderness of Judea,

Mat. 3:2 And saying, "Repent you: for the kingdom of heaven is at hand."

Mat. 3:3 For this is he that was spoken of by the prophet Isaiah, saying, "The voice of one crying in the wilderness: Prepare you the way of יהוה (Yahwah, YHWH), make His paths straight.

Isa. 40:3 The voice of him that cries in the wilderness, "Prepare you the way of יהוה (Yahwah, YHWH), make straight in the desert a highway for our God (Elohim).

YAHWAH (YHWH) MINISTERS TO GREAT CROWDS

Mat. 4:23 And Yahwah went about all Galilee, teaching in their synagogues, and preaching the gospel of the kingdom, and healing all manner of sickness and all manner of disease among the people.

Luk. 9:2 And He sent them to preach the kingdom of God (Elohim, יהוה (YHWH)), and to heal the sick.

Mat. 28:18 And Yahwah came and spoke unto them, saying, "All power is given unto Me in heaven and in earth."

Why did Yahwah said: "All heaven and earth"?... Because God (Elohim, יהוה (YHWH)) is Spirit everywhere at the same time as He is in the human form as a man, therefore we can now see the invisbible God (Elohim) through His Humanity: the Messiah (haMashiach) Yahwah.

BAPTISM IN THE NAME OF יהוה (YHWH, YAHWAH) FOR SALVATION

Mat. 28:19   Go you therefore, and teach all nations, baptizing them in the name of the Father, and of the Son, and of the Holy Spirit;

Mat. 28:20   Teaching them to observe all things whatsoever I have commanded you: and, behold, I am with you always, even unto the end of the world. Amen.

Notice it's written: "Go you therefore"..that means to go and be done; and "baptizing them in the Name..." The question is: Baptizing in what Name? Notice it's written: ***"In the Name of the Father..."*** What is the Father's Name? Note that there is no New Testament (New Blood Covenant) writing (yet to be written at the time of the Messiah (haMashiach)). So it has to be the Name from the Tanakh Scriptures (Genesis to Malachi). The Only Name found in the Tanakh Scriptures is the Father's Name: יהוה (YHWH) (Isa.63:16, 64:8). So Matthew understood that the Name of the Father, Son and Holy Spirit is יהוה (YHWH) alone, not any other names. The Scriptures testify that the Father, Son and Holy Spirit are the three manifestation of the one and only true living God (Elohim) with one holy name - יהוה (YHWH) (Deu. 6:4, Isa. 45:5, Jer. 10:10, Zec. 14:9, 1 John 5:7, 1 Tim. 3:16).

Matthew was present when Apostle Peter preached the gospel as written in Acts chapter 2. And in Acts 2:38 we see that they were going to do what was commanded by Yahwah (YHWH). If baptism should be done using title "Father, Son and Holy Spirit", then it would contradict with the doctrine of Apostle Peter in Acts 2:38 who preached saying: "...repent and let everyone of you be baptized **in the name of Yahwah haMaschiach...".** But the Word of truth is: The name of the Father, Son and Holy Spirit is יהוה (YHWH, Yahwah); therefore Matthew 28:19 and Acts 2:38 agrees to one another. The Words spoken by the Messiah (haMashiach) Himself in John 5:39 and 5:43 as written in Book of John also testified that Yahwah (YHWH) is the Name of the Messiah (haMashiach).

John 5:39   Search the scriptures, for in them you think you have eternal life; and they are they which testify of Me.

John 5:43   I am come in My Father's name, and you receive Me not; if another shall come in his own name, him ye will receive.

The Scriptures revealed that salvation belongs to the one and only true living God (Elohim) – יהוה **(YHWH),** the same name to call on for deliverance and the same name to believe and be baptized for remission of sins; not many different names or titles:

Psa. 3:8   Salvation belongth unto יהוה. Your blessing is upon Your people.

Jer. 10:10   But יהוה is the true God (Elohim), He is the living God (Elohim chayim), and an everlasting King;

Acts 2:21   (Yoel 2:32a) And it shall come to pass, that whosoever shall call on the name of יהוה (YHWH) shall be saved.

Acts 2:38   "Repent and let everyone of you be baptized in the name of Yahwah haMaschiah for the remission of sin..."

According to Mat. 5:18, one jot or tittle shall in no wise pass from the Torah ...so if you removed even one jot or tittle, you changed יהוה (YHWH)'s name and there is no salvation if God (Elohim)'s name is changed, for it is written in **Acts 4:12: Neither is there salvation in any other, for there is none other name under heaven given among men, whereby we must be saved.**

YOU MUST BE BORN AGAIN

John 3:1   There was a man of the Pharisees, named Nicodemus, a ruler of the Jews:

John 3:2   The same came to Yahwah by night, and said unto him, Rabbi, we know that thou art a teacher come from God (Elohim); for no man can do these miracles that you do, except God (Elohim) be with him.

John 3:3   Yahwah answered and said unto him, "Verily, verily, I say unto you, except a man be born again, he cannot see the kingdom of God (Elohim, יהוה (YHWH))."

John 3:4   Nicodemus saith unto him, "How can a man be born when he is old? Can he enter the second time into his mother's womb, and be born?

John 3:5   Yahwah answered, "Verily, verily, I say unto thee, except a man be born of water and of the Spirit, he cannot enter into the kingdom of God (Elohim, יהוה (YHWH))."

John 3:6   That which is born of the flesh is flesh; and that which is born of the Spirit is spirit.

John 3:7   Marvel not that I said unto you, "You must be born again."

John 3:8   The wind bloweth where it listeth, and thou hearest the sound thereof, but canst not tell whence it cometh, and whither it goeth: so is every one that is born of the Spirit.

BORN AGAIN OF THE HOLY SPIRIT

Acts 2:1   And when the day of Pentecost was fully come, they were all with one accord in one place.

Acts 2:2   And suddenly there came a sound from heaven as of a rushing mighty wind, and it filled all the house where they were sitting.

Acts 2:3   And there appeared unto them cloven tongues like as of fire, and it sat upon each of them.

Acts 2:4   And they were all filled with the Holy Spirit, and began to speak with other tongues, as the Spirit gave them utterance.

2The 1:7   And to you who are troubled rest with us, when the Lord Yahwah (Adonai YHWH) shall be revealed from heaven with His mighty angels,

2The 1:8   In flaming fire taking vengeance on them that know not God (Elohim, יהוה (YHWH)), and that obey not the gospel of our Lord (Adonai) Yahwah haMaschiach;

THERE ARE 4 PARTS OF THE GOSPEL (GOOD NEWS)
1. BELIEVE ... 2. REPENT ... 3. BAPTIZE ... 4. RECEIVE HOLY SPIRIT

1. Yahwah haMashiach came to save mankind: We are to believe in His name for remission of sins;
2. Yahwah haMashiach died on the stake: We are to repent, die to flesh daily;
3. Yahwah haMashiach was buried: We are to be fully immersed in water and baptized in His name;
4. Yahwah haMashiach was resurrected: We are to receive His Holy Spirit to be born again.

1 Cor 15:1   Moreover, brethren, I declare unto you the gospel which I preached unto you, which also you have received, and wherein you stand;

1 Cor 15:2   By which also you are saved, if you keep in memory what I preached unto you, unless you have believed in vain.

1 Cor 15:3   For I delivered unto you first of all that which I also received, how that haMashich died for our sins according to the scriptures;

1 Cor 15:4   And that he was buried, and that he rose again the third day according to the scriptures.

Rom 6:3   Know ye not, that so many of us as were baptized into Yahwah haMashiach were baptized into His death?

Rom 6:4   Therefore we are (buried) with him by baptism into death: that just as haMashiach was raised up from the dead by the glory of the Father, even so we also should walk in newness of life.

Rom 8:11   But if the Spirit of Him that raised up Yahwah's flesh from the dead dwell in you, he that raised up haMashiach from the dead shall also quicken your mortal bodies by his Spirit that dwells in you.

1 John 5:8   And there are three that bear witness in earth, the Spirit, and the water, and the blood; and these three agree as one:

1.(Spirit: HOLY SPIRIT) 2.(Water: BAPTISM) 3.(Blood: REPENTANCE).

Apostle Peter preached from the book of Yoel chapter 2 to prick their hearts in Acts 2:37. So what Name did Peter says was the Messiah (haMashiach), if he preached using the Scriptures (Genesis to Malachi) and knowing that there is no New Testament writing? The truth is revealed in the Hebrew Scriptures written in the book of Yoel as preached by Apostle Peter in the book of Acts Chapter 2:

Act 2:16	But this is that which was spoken by the prophet Yoel:
Act 2:17	(Yoel 2:28) And it shall come to pass in the last days, saith God (Elohim), I will pour out of my Spirit upon all flesh: and your sons and your daughters shall prophesy, and your young men shall see visions, and your old men shall dream dreams:
Act 2:18	(Yoel 2:29) And on my servants and on my handmaidens I will pour out in those days of my Spirit; and they shall prophesy:
Act 2:19	(Yoel 2:30) And I will shew wonders in heaven above, and signs in the earth beneath; blood, and fire, and vapour of smoke:
Act 2:20	(Yoel 2:31) The sun shall be turned into darkness, and the moon into blood, before that great and notable day of יהוה (YHWH) come:
Act 2:21	(Yoel 2:32a) And it shall come to pass, that **whosoever shall call on the name of יהוה (YHWH) shall be saved.**
Yoel 2:32	And it shall come to pass, **that whosoever shall call on the name of the יהוה (YHWH) shall be delivered (saved);** for in Mount Zion and in Jerusalem (Yerushalayim) shall be deliverance, as the יהוה (YHWH) has said, and in the remnant whom יהוה (YHWH) shall call.

Acts 2:37 - 39

Now when they heard this, they were pricked in their heart, and said unto Peter and to the rest of the apostles, "Men and brethren, what shall we do?" Then Peter said unto them, 'Repent, and be baptized every one of you in the name of Yahwah haMashiach for the remission of sins, and you shall receive the gift of the Holy Spirit. For the promise is unto you, and to your children, and to all that are afar off, even as many as YHWH our God (Elohim) shall call.'

Why were they pricked in their hearts?... Because Peter told them that on that stake was God (Elohim, יהוה (YHWH)) as a human form our Savior and they killed Him... they destroyed the flesh and the flesh died...not God (Elohim, Who is Spirit); and in that flesh dwells all the fulness of Godhead bodily (Col 2:9).

GOD (ELOHIM) YHWH BLESSED AND ADDED
TO THE ASSEMBLY AS PETER CONTINUES PREACHING
THE GOSPEL OF TRUTH FOR SALVATION

Act 2:41	Then they that gladly received his word were baptized: and the same day there were added unto them about three thousand souls...
Act 2:47	Praising God (Elohim), and having favor with all the people. And YHWH added to the assembly daily such as should be saved...

Acts 8:12 -17

But when they believed Philip preaching the things concerning the kingdom of God (Elohim, יהוה (YHWH)), and the name of Yahwah haMashiach, they were baptized, both men and women. Then Simon himself believed also; and when he was baptized, he continued with Philip, and wondered, beholding the miracles and signs which were done. Now when the apostles which were at Jerusalem (Yerushalayim) heard that Samaria had received the word of God (Elohim, יהוה (YHWH)), they sent unto them Peter and John; who, when they were come down, prayed for them, that they might receive the Holy Spirit; for as yet He was fallen upon none of them; only they were baptized in the name of the Lord Yahwah (Adonai YHWH). Then laid they their hands on them, and they received the Holy Spirit.

Acts 10:43 - 48

To Him give all the prophets witness, that through his name whosoever believed in Him shall receive remission of sins. While Peter yet spoke these words, the Holy Spirit fell on all them which heard the word. And they of the circumcision which believed were astonished, as many as came with Peter, because that on the Gentiles also was poured out the gift of the Holy Spirit. For they heard them speak with tongues, and magnify יהוה (YHWH). Then answered Peter: "Can any man forbid water, that these should not be baptized, which have received the Holy Spirit as well as we? And he commanded them to be baptized in the name of Yahwah (YHWH). Then prayed they him to tarry certain days.

4 PARTS OF THE GOSPEL OF SALVATION THAT WE MUST BELIEVED AND OBEYED:

1. Believed in the name of God (Elohim): יהוה/YHWH/Yahwah.
2. Repent and turn away from our sinful ways.
3. Be baptized in the name of the Messiah (haMashiach): Yahwah (YHWH)
4. Received the Holy Spirit of יהוה (YHWH).

FIRST BLOOD COVENANT
TANAKH

FIRST
BLOOD COVENANT

תָּנָ"ךְ

Tanakh

GENESIS
BERESHIT בְּרֵאשִׁית
(In the Beginning)

1 In the beginning God ([B1a]Elohim) created the heavens and the earth.

2 And the earth was without form, and void; and darkness was upon the face of the deep. And the Spirit of God (Elohim) moved upon the face of the waters.

3 And God (Elohim) said, "Let there be light"; and there was light.

4 And God (Elohim) saw the light, that it was good; and God (Elohim) divided the light from the darkness.

5 And God (Elohim) called the light Day (Yom), and the darkness he called Night (Layelah). And the evening and the morning were the first day.

6 And God (Elohim) said, "Let there be a firmament in the midst of the waters, and let it divide the waters from the waters."

7 And God (Elohim) made the firmament, and divided the waters which were under the firmament from the waters which were above the firmament; and it was so.

8 And God (Elohim) called the firmament Heaven (Shamayim). And the evening and the morning were the second day.

9 And God (Elohim) said, "Let the waters under the heavens be gathered together unto one place, and let the dry land appear"; and it was so.

10 And God (Elohim) called the dry land Earth (Erets); and the gathering together of the waters He called Seas (Yam). And God (Elohim) saw that it was good.

11 And God (Elohim) said, "Let the earth bring forth grass, the herb yielding seed, and the fruit tree yielding fruit after its kind, whose seed is in itself, upon the earth"; and it was so.

12 And the earth brought forth grass, and herb yielding seed after its kind, and the tree yielding fruit, whose seed was in itself, after its kind; and God (Elohim) saw that it was good.

13 And the evening and the morning were the third day.

14 And God (Elohim) said, "Let there be lights in the firmament of the heaven to divide the day from the night; and let them be for signs, and for seasons, and for days, and years;

15 And let them be for lights in the firmament of the heaven to give light upon the earth"; and it was so.

16 And God (Elohim) made two great lights; the greater light to rule the day, and the lesser light to rule the night. He made the stars also.

17 And God (Elohim) set them in the firmament of the heaven to give light upon the earth,

18 And to rule over the day and over the night, and to divide the light from the darkness; and God (Elohim) saw that it was good.

19 And the evening and the morning were the fourth day.

20 And God (Elohim) said, "Let the waters bring forth abundantly the moving creature that hath life, and fowl that may fly above the earth in the open firmament of heaven."

21 And God (Elohim) created great whales, and every living creature that moveth, which the waters brought forth abundantly, after their kind, and every winged fowl after its kind. And God (Elohim) saw that it was good.

22 And God (Elohim) blessed them, saying, "Be fruitful, and multiply, and fill the waters in the seas, and let fowl multiply in the earth."

23 And the evening and the morning were the fifth day.

24 And God (Elohim) said, "Let the earth bring forth the living creature after its kind, cattle, and creeping thing, and beast of the earth after its kind"; and it was so.

25 And God (Elohim) made the beast of the earth after its kind, and cattle after their kind, and every thing that creepeth upon the earth after its kind. And God (Elohim) saw that it was good.

26 And God (Elohim) said, "[B3]Let Us make mankind (adam) in Our image, after Our likeness; and let them have dominion over the fish of the sea, and over the fowl of the air, and over the cattle, and over all the earth, and over every creeping thing that creepeth upon the earth."

27 So God (Elohim) created mankind (adam) in [B4]His own image, in the image of God (Elohim) created He him; male and female created He them.

28 And God (Elohim) blessed them, and God (Elohim) said unto them, "Be fruitful, and multiply, and replenish the earth, and subdue it; and have dominion over the fish of the sea, and over the fowl of the air, and over every living thing that moveth upon the earth."

29 And God (Elohim) said, "Behold, I have given you every herb bearing seed, which is upon the face of all the earth, and every tree, in the which is the fruit of a tree yielding seed; to you it shall be for food."

30 And to every beast of the earth, and to every fowl of the air, and to every thing that creepeth upon the earth, wherein there is life, I have given every green herb for meat: and it was so.

31 And God (Elohim) saw every thing that he had made, and, behold, it was very good. And the evening and the morning were the sixth day.

2 Thus the heavens and the earth were finished, and all the host of them.

2 And on the seventh day God (Elohim) ended His work which He had made; and He rested on the seventh day from all His work which He had made.

3 And God (Elohim) blessed the seventh day and sanctified it, because that in it He had rested from all His work which God (Elohim) created and made.

4 These are the generations of the heavens and of the earth when they were created, in the day that God (Elohim) ^{A1} יהוה made the earth and the heavens,

5 And every plant of the field before it was in the earth, and every herb of the field before it grew; for God (Elohim) יהוה had not caused it to rain upon the earth, and there was not a man to till the ground.

6 But there went up a mist from the earth, and watered the whole face of the ground.

7 And God (Elohim) יהוה formed man of the dust of the ground, and breathed into his nostrils the breath of life; and man became a living soul.

8 And God (Elohim) יהוה planted a garden eastward in Eden; and there He put the man whom He had formed.

9 And out of the ground made God (Elohim) יהוה to grow every tree that is pleasant to the sight, and good for food; the tree of life also in the midst of the garden, and the tree of knowledge of good and evil.

10 And a river went out of Eden to water the garden; and from thence it was parted, and became into four heads.

11 The name of the first is Pishon; that is it which compasseth the whole land of Havilah, where there is gold;

12 And the gold of that land is good; there is bdellium and the onyx stone.

13 And the name of the second river is Gihon: the same is it that compasseth the whole land of Ethiopia (Kush).

14 And the name of the third river is Hiddekel; that is it which goeth toward the east of Assyria (Ashshur). And the fourth river is Euphrates.

15 And God (Elohim) יהוה took the man, and put him into the garden of Eden to dress it and to keep it.

16 And God (Elohim) יהוה commanded the man, saying, "Of every tree of the garden you mayest freely eat;

17 But of the tree of the knowledge of good and evil, you shalt not eat of it; for in the day that you eatest thereof you shalt surely die."

18 And God (Elohim) יהוה said, "It is not good that the man should be alone; I will make him a help meet for him."

19 And out of the ground God (Elohim) יהוה formed every beast of the field, and every fowl of the air; and brought them unto Adam to see what he would call them; and whatsoever Adam called every living creature, that was the name thereof.

20 And Adam gave names to all cattle, and to the fowl of the air, and to every beast of the field; but for Adam there was not found a help meet for him.

21 And God (Elohim) יהוה caused a deep sleep to fall upon Adam, and he slept; and he took one of his ribs, and closed up the flesh instead thereof;

22 And the rib, which God (Elohim) יהוה had taken from man, made He a woman, and brought her unto the man.

23 And Adam said, "This is now bone of my bones, and flesh of my flesh; she shall be called Woman (Ishshah), because she was taken out of Man (Ish).

24 Therefore shall a man leave his father and his mother, and shall cleave unto his wife, and they shall be one flesh.

25 And they were both naked, the man and his wife, and were not ashamed.

3 Now the serpent (nachash) was more subtil than any beast of the field which God (Elohim) יהוה had made. And he said unto the woman, "Yea, hath God (Elohim) said, 'You shall not eat of every tree of the garden'?"

2 And the woman said unto the serpent, "We

may eat of the fruit of the trees of the garden;

3 But of the fruit of the tree which is in the midst of the garden, God (Elohim) hath said, 'You shall not eat of it, neither shall you touch it, lest you die.'"

4 And the serpent said unto the woman, "You shall not surely die;

5 For God (Elohim) doth know that in the day you eat thereof, then your eyes shall be opened, and you shall be as God (Elohim), knowing good and evil."

6 And when the woman saw that the tree was good for food, and that it was pleasant to the eyes, and a tree to be desired to make one wise, she took of the fruit thereof, and did eat, and gave also unto her husband with her; and he did eat.

7 And the eyes of them both were opened, and they knew that they were naked; and they sewed fig leaves together, and made themselves aprons.

8 And they heard the voice of God (Elohim) יהוה walking in the garden in the cool of the day; and Adam and his wife hid themselves from the presence of God (Elohim) יהוה amongst the trees of the garden.

9 And God (Elohim) יהוה called unto Adam, and said unto him, "Where are you?"

10 And he said, "I heard Your voice in the garden, and I was afraid, because I was naked; and I hid myself."

11 And He said, "Who told you that you wast naked? Have you eaten of the tree, whereof I commanded you that you shouldest not eat?"

12 And the man said, "The woman whom You gavest to be with me, she gave me of the tree, and I did eat."

13 And God (Elohim) יהוה said unto the woman, "What is this that you have done?" And the woman said, "The serpent beguiled me, and I did eat."

14 And God (Elohim) יהוה said unto the serpent, "Because you have done this, you are cursed above all cattle, and above every beast of the field; upon your belly shalt you go, and dust shalt you eat all the days of your life;

15 And I will put enmity between you and the woman, and between your seed and her seed; it shall bruise your head, and you shalt bruise his heel."

16 Unto the woman He said, "I will greatly multiply your sorrow and your conception; in sorrow you shalt bring forth children; and your desire shall be to your husband, and he shall rule over you."

17 And unto Adam He said, "Because you have hearkened unto the voice of your wife, and hast eaten of the tree, of which I commanded you, saying, 'You shalt not eat of it'; cursed is the ground for your sake; in sorrow shalt you eat of it all the days of your life.

18 Thorns also and thistles shall it bring forth to you; and you shalt eat the herb of the field;

19 In the sweat of your face shalt you eat bread, till you return unto the ground; for out of it wast you taken; for dust you are, and unto dust shalt you return."

20 And Adam called his wife's name [A9]Eve (Chawah), because she was the mother of all living.

21 Unto Adam also and to his wife did God (Elohim) יהוה make coats of skins, and clothed them.

22 And God (Elohim) יהוה said, "Behold, the man is become as one of Us, to know good and evil. And now, lest he put forth his hand, and take also of the tree of life, and eat, and live forever."

23 Therefore God (Elohim) יהוה sent him forth from the garden of Eden, to till the ground from whence he was taken.

24 So He drove out the man; and He placed at the east of the garden of Eden cherubims (keruvim), and a flaming sword which turned every way, to keep the way of the tree of life.

4 And Adam knew Eve (Chawah) his wife; and she conceived, and bare Cain (Qayin), and said, "I have gotten a man from יהוה."

2 And she again bare his brother Abel (Hevel). And Abel (Hevel) was a keeper of sheep, but Cain (Qayin) was a tiller of the ground.

3 And in process of time it came to pass, that Cain (Qayin) brought of the fruit of the ground an offering unto יהוה.

4 And Abel (Hevel), he also brought of the firstlings of his flock and of the fat thereof. And יהוה had respect unto Abel (Hevel) and to his offering:

5 But unto Cain (Qayin) and to his offering He had not respect. And Cain (Qayin) was very wroth, and his countenance fell.

6 And יהוה said unto Cain (Qayin), "Why are you

wroth? And why is your countenance fallen?

7 If you doest well, shalt you not be accepted? And if you doest not well, sin lieth at the door. And unto you shall be his desire, and you shalt rule over him."

8 And Cain (Qayin) talked with Abel (Hevel) his brother; and it came to pass, when they were in the field, that Cain (Qayin) rose up against Abel (Hevel) his brother, and slew him.

9 And יהוה said unto Cain (Qayin), "Where is Abel (Hevel) your brother?" And he said, "I know not. Am I my brother's keeper?"

10 And He said, "What have you done? The voice of your brother's blood crieth unto Me from the ground.

11 And now are you cursed from the earth, which hath opened her mouth to receive your brother's blood from your hand;

12 When you tillest the ground, it shall not henceforth yield unto you her strength; a fugitive and a vagabond shalt you be in the earth."

13 And Cain (Qayin) said unto יהוה, "My punishment is greater than I can bear.

14 Behold, you have driven me out this day from the face of the earth; and from your face shall I be hidden; and I shall be a fugitive and a vagabond in the earth; and it shall come to pass, that every one that findeth me shall slay me."

15 And יהוה said unto him, "Therefore whosoever slayeth Cain (Qayin), vengeance shall be taken on him sevenfold." And יהוה set a mark upon Cain (Qayin), lest any finding him should kill him.

16 And Cain (Qayin) went out from the presence of יהוה, and dwelt in the land of Nod, on the east of Eden.

17 And Cain (Qayin) knew his wife; and she conceived, and bare Enoch (Chanok). And he builded a city, and called the name of the city, after the name of his son, Enoch (Chanok).

18 And unto Enoch (Chanok) was born Irad; and Irad begat Mechuyael, and Mechuyael begat Metushael, and Metushael begat Lamech.

19 And Lamech took unto him two wives: the name of the one was Adah, and the name of the other Zillah.

20 And Adah bare Yaval. He was the father of such as dwell in tents, and of such as have cattle.

21 And his brother's name was Yuval. He was the father of all such as handle the harp and organ.

22 And Zillah, she also bare Tubalcain, an instructer of every artificer in brass and iron; and the sister of Tubalcain was Naamah.

23 And Lamech said unto his wives, "Adah and Zillah, hear my voice; you wives of Lamech, hearken unto my speech; for I have slain a man to my wounding, and a young man to my hurt.

24 If Cain (Qayin) shall be avenged sevenfold, truly Lamech seventy and sevenfold."

25 And Adam knew his wife again; and she bare a son, and called his name Shet: "For God (Elohim)", said she, "hath appointed me another seed instead of Abel (Hevel), whom Cain (Qayin) slew."

26 And to Shet, to him also there was born a son; and he called his name Enosh. Then began men to call upon the name of יהוה.

5 This is the book of the generations of Adam. In the day that God (Elohim) created man, in the likeness of God (Elohim) made He him;

2 Male and female created He them; and blessed them, and called them mankind (adam), in the day when they were created.

3 And Adam lived a hundred and thirty years, and begat a son in his own likeness, after his image; and called his name Shet:

4 And the days of Adam after he had begotten Shet were eight hundred years; and he begat sons and daughters.

5 And all the days that Adam lived were nine hundred and thirty years; and he died.

6 And Shet lived a hundred and five years, and begat Enosh.

7 And Shet lived after he begat Enosh eight hundred and seven years, and begat sons and daughters.

8 And all the days of Shet were nine hundred and twelve years; and he died.

9 And Enosh lived ninety years, and begat Cainan (Kenan).

10 And Enosh lived after he begat Cainan (Kenan) eight hundred and fifteen years, and begat sons and daughters.

11 And all the days of Enosh were nine hundred and five years; and he died.

12 And Cainan (Kenan) lived seventy years, and begat Mahalalel.

13 And Cainan (Kenan) lived after he begat Mahalalel eight hundred and forty years, and begat sons and daughters.

14 And all the days of Cainan (Kenan) were nine hundred and ten years; and he died.

15 And Mahalalel lived sixty and five years, and begat Jared (Yered).

16 And Mahalalel lived after he begat Jared (Yered) eight hundred and thirty years, and begat sons and daughters.

17 And all the days of Mahalalel were eight hundred ninety and five years; and he died.

18 And Jared (Yered) lived a hundred sixty and two years, and he begat Enoch (Chanok).

19 And Jared (Yered) lived after he begat Enoch (Chanok) eight hundred years, and begat sons and daughters.

20 And all the days of Jared (Yered) were nine hundred sixty and two years; and he died.

21 And Enoch (Chanok) lived sixty and five years, and begat Metushelach.

22 And Enoch (Chanok) walked with God (Elohim) after he begat Metushelach three hundred years, and begat sons and daughters.

23 And all the days of Enoch (Chanok) were three hundred sixty and five years.

24 And Enoch (Chanok) walked with God (Elohim); and he was not, for God (Elohim) took him.

25 And Metushelach lived a hundred eighty and seven years, and begat Lamech.

26 And Metushelach lived after he begat Lamech seven hundred eighty and two years, and begat sons and daughters.

27 And all the days of Metushelach were nine hundred sixty and nine years; and he died.

28 And Lamech lived a hundred eighty and two years, and begat a son.

29 And he called his name Noach, saying, "This same shall comfort us concerning our work and toil of our hands, because of the ground which יהוה hath cursed."

30 And Lamech lived after he begat Noach five hundred ninety and five years, and begat sons and daughters.

31 And all the days of Lamech were seven hundred seventy and seven years; and he died.

32 And Noach was five hundred years old; and Noach begat Shem, Ham, and Japheth (Yefet).

6 And it came to pass, when men began to multiply on the face of the earth, and daughters were born unto them,

2 That the sons of God (Elohim) saw the daughters of men that they were fair; and they took them wives of all which they chose.

3 And יהוה said, "My Spirit shall not always strive with man, for that he also is flesh; yet his days shall be a hundred and twenty years."

4 There were giants in the earth in those days; and also after that, when the sons of God (Elohim) came in unto the daughters of men, and they bare children to them, the same became mighty men which were of old, men of renown.

5 And יהוה saw that the wickedness (raah) of man was great in the earth, and that every imagination of the thoughts of his heart was only evil continually.

6 And it regretted יהוה that He had made man on the earth, and it grieved Him at His heart.

7 And יהוה said, "I will destroy man whom I have created from the face of the earth; both man, and beast, and the creeping thing, and the fowls of the air; for it regretted Me that I have made them."

8 But Noach found grace in the eyes of יהוה.

9 These are the generations of Noach: Noach was a just man and perfect in his generations, and Noach walked with God (Elohim).

10 And Noach begat three sons, Shem, Ham, and Japheth (Yefet).

11 The earth also was corrupt before God (Elohim), and the earth was filled with violence.

12 And God (Elohim) looked upon the earth, and, behold, it was corrupt; for all flesh had corrupted his way upon the earth.

13 And God (Elohim) said unto Noach, "The end of all flesh has come before Me; for the earth is filled with violence through them; and, behold, I will destroy them with the earth.

14 Make you an ark of gopher wood; rooms shalt you make in the ark, and shalt pitch it inside and outside with pitch.

15 And this is the fashion which you shalt make it of: The length of the ark shall be three hundred cubits, the breadth of it fifty cubits, and the height of it thirty cubits.

16 A window shalt you make to the ark, and in a cubit shalt you finish it above; and the door of the ark shalt you set in the side thereof; with lower, second, and third stories shalt you make it.

17 And, behold, I, even I, do bring a flood of waters upon the earth, to destroy all flesh, wherein is the breath of life, from under heaven; and every thing that is in the earth shall die.

18 But with you will I establish My covenant (berit); and you shalt come into the ark, you,

and your sons, and your wife, and your sons'
wives with you.

19 And of every living thing of all flesh, two
of every sort shalt you bring into the ark, to
keep them alive with you; they shall be male
and female.

20 Of fowls after their kind, and of cattle after
their kind, of every creeping thing of the earth
after its kind, two of every sort shall come unto
you, to keep them alive.

21 And take you unto you of all food that is
eaten, and you shalt gather it to you; and it shall
be for food for you, and for them."

22 Thus did Noach; according to all that God
(Elohim) commanded him, so did he.

7 And יהוה said unto Noach, "Come you and
all your house into the ark; for you have I
seen righteous before Me in this generation.

2 Of every clean beast you shalt take to you by
sevens, the male and his female: and of beasts
that are not clean by two, the male and his
female.

3 Of fowls also of the air by sevens, the male
and the female; to keep seed alive upon the face
of all the earth.

4 For yet seven days, and I will cause it to rain
upon the earth forty days and forty nights; and
every living substance that I have made will I
destroy from off the face of the earth."

5 And Noach did according unto all that יהוה
commanded him.

6 And Noach was six hundred years old when
the flood of waters was upon the earth.

7 And Noach went in, and his sons, and his
wife, and his sons' wives with him, into the ark,
because of the waters of the flood.

8 Of clean beasts, and of beasts that are not
clean, and of fowls, and of every thing that
creepeth upon the earth,

9 There went in two and two unto Noach into the
ark, the male and the female, as God (Elohim)
had commanded Noach.

10 And it came to pass after seven days, that the
waters of the flood were upon the earth.

11 In the six hundredth year of Noach's life, in
the second month, the seventeenth day of the
month, the same day were all the fountains of
the great deep broken up, and the windows of
heaven were opened.

12 And the rain was upon the earth forty days
and forty nights.

13 In the selfsame day entered Noach, and
Shem, and Ham, and Japheth (Yefet), the sons
of Noach, and Noach's wife, and the three wives
of his sons with them, into the ark;

14 They, and every beast after its kind, and all the
cattle after their kind, and every creeping thing
that creepeth upon the earth after its kind, and
every fowl after its kind, every bird of every sort.

15 And they went in unto Noach into the ark,
two and two of all flesh, wherein is the breath
of life.

16 And they that went in, went in male and
female of all flesh, as God (Elohim) had
commanded him; and יהוה shut him in.

17 And the flood was forty days upon the earth;
and the waters increased, and bare up the ark,
and it was lift up above the earth.

18 And the waters prevailed, and were increased
greatly upon the earth; and the ark went upon
the face of the waters.

19 And the waters prevailed exceedingly upon
the earth; and all the high hills, that were under
the whole heaven, were covered.

20 Fifteen cubits upward did the waters prevail;
and the mountains were covered.

21 And all flesh died that moved upon the earth,
both of fowl, and of cattle, and of beast, and
of every creeping thing that creepeth upon the
earth, and every man.

22 All in whose nostrils was the breath of life,
of all that was in the dry land, died.

23 And every living substance was destroyed
which was upon the face of the ground: both
man, and cattle, and the creeping things, and
the fowl of the heaven; and they were destroyed
from the earth and Noach only remained alive,
and they that were with him in the ark.

24 And the waters prevailed upon the earth a
hundred and fifty days.

8 And God (Elohim) remembered Noach, and
every living thing, and all the cattle that was
with him in the ark. And God (Elohim) made
a wind to pass over the earth, and the waters
asswaged;

2 The fountains also of the deep and the
windows of heaven were stopped, and the rain
from heaven was restrained.

3 And the waters returned from off the earth
continually; and after the end of the hundred
and fifty days the waters were abated.

4 And the ark rested in the seventh month, on

the seventeenth day of the month, upon the mountains of Ararat.

5 And the waters decreased continually until the tenth month. In the tenth month, on the first day of the month, were the tops of the mountains seen.

6 And it came to pass at the end of forty days, that Noach opened the window of the ark which he had made.

7 And he sent forth a raven, which went forth to and fro, until the waters were dried up from off the earth.

8 Also he sent forth a dove from him, to see if the waters were abated from off the face of the ground;

9 But the dove found no rest for the sole of her foot, and she returned unto him into the ark, for the waters were on the face of the whole earth. Then he put forth his hand, and took her, and pulled her in unto him into the ark.

10 And he stayed yet other seven days; and again he sent forth the dove out of the ark;

11 And the dove came in to him in the evening; and, behold, in her mouth was an olive leaf pluckt off. So Noach knew that the waters were abated from off the earth.

12 And he stayed yet other seven days; and sent forth the dove; which returned not again unto him any more.

13 And it came to pass in the six hundredth and first year, in the first month, the first day of the month, the waters were dried up from off the earth; and Noach removed the covering of the ark, and looked, and, behold, the face of the ground was dry.

14 And in the second month, on the seven and twentieth day of the month, was the earth dried.

15 And God (Elohim) spake unto Noach, saying,

16 "Go forth of the ark, you, and your wife, and your sons, and your sons' wives with you.

17 Bring forth with you every living thing that is with you, of all flesh, both of fowl, and of cattle, and of every creeping thing that creepeth upon the earth; that they may breed abundantly in the earth, and be fruitful, and multiply upon the earth."

18 And Noach went forth, and his sons, and his wife, and his sons' wives with him.

19 Every beast, every creeping thing, and every fowl, and whatsoever creepeth upon the earth, after their kinds, went forth out of the ark.

20 And Noach builded an altar unto יהוה; and took of every clean beast, and of every clean fowl, and offered burnt offerings on the altar.

21 And יהוה smelled a sweet savour; and יהוה said in His heart, "I will not again curse the ground any more for man's sake; for the imagination of man's heart is evil from his youth; neither will I again smite anymore every thing living, as I have done.

22 While the earth remaineth, seedtime and harvest, and cold and heat, and summer and winter, and day and night shall not cease."

9 And God (Elohim) blessed Noach and his sons, and said unto them, "Be fruitful, and multiply, and replenish the earth.

2 And the fear of you and the dread of you shall be upon every beast of the earth, and upon every fowl of the air, upon all that moveth upon the earth, and upon all the fishes of the sea; into your hand are they delivered.

3 Every moving thing that liveth shall be foodt for you; even as the green herb have I given you all things.

4 But flesh with the life thereof, which is the blood thereof, shall you not eat.

5 And surely your blood of your lives will I require; at the hand of every beast will I require it, and at the hand of man; at the hand of every man's brother will I require the life of man.

6 Whoso sheddeth man's blood, by man shall his blood be shed; for in the image of God (Elohim) made He man.

7 And you, be you fruitful, and multiply; bring forth abundantly in the earth, and multiply therein."

8 And God (Elohim) spake unto Noach, and to his sons with him, saying,

9 "And I, behold, I establish My covenant with you, and with your seed after you;

10 And with every living creature that is with you, of the fowl, of the cattle, and of every beast of the earth with you; from all that go out of the ark, to every beast of the earth.

11 And I will establish My covenant with you; neither shall all flesh be cut off any more by the waters of a flood; neither shall there any more be a flood to destroy the earth."

12 And God (Elohim) said, "This is the token of the covenant which I make between Me and you and every living creature that is with you, for perpetual generations:

13 I do set My rainbow in the cloud, and it shall be for a token of a covenant between Me and the earth.

14 And it shall come to pass, when I bring a cloud over the earth, that the rainbow shall be seen in the cloud:

15 And I will remember My covenant, which is between Me and you and every living creature of all flesh; and the waters shall no more become a flood to destroy all flesh.

16 And the rainbow shall be in the cloud; and I will look upon it, that I may remember the everlasting covenant between God (Elohim) and every living creature of all flesh that is upon the earth."

17 And God (Elohim) said unto Noach, "This is the token of the covenant, which I have established between Me and all flesh that is upon the earth."

18 And the sons of Noach, that went forth of the ark, were Shem, and Ham, and Japheth (Yefet); and Ham is the father of Canaan.

19 These are the three sons of Noach; and of them was the whole earth overspread.

20 And Noach began to be a husbandman, and he planted a vineyard.

21 And he drank of the wine, and was drunken; and he was uncovered within his tent.

22 And Ham, the father of Canaan, saw the nakedness of his father, and told his two brethren outside.

23 And Shem and Japheth (Yefet) took a garment, and laid it upon both their shoulders, and went backward, and covered the nakedness of their father; and their faces were backward, and they saw not their father's nakedness.

24 And Noach awoke from his wine, and knew what his younger son had done unto him.

25 And he said: "Cursed be Canaan; a servant of servants shall he be unto his brethren."

26 And he said: "Blessed be יהוה God (Elohim) of Shem; and Canaan shall be his servant.

27 God (Elohim) shall enlarge Japheth (Yefet), and he shall dwell in the tents of Shem; and Canaan shall be his servant."

28 And Noach lived after the flood three hundred and fifty years.

29 And all the days of Noach were nine hundred and fifty years; and he died.

10 Now these are the generations of the sons of Noach: Shem, Ham, and Japheth

(Yefet). And unto them were sons born after the flood.

2 The sons of Japheth (Yefet): Gomer, and Magog, and Madai, and Yawan, and Tubal, and Meshech, and Tiras.

3 And the sons of Gomer: Ashkenaz, and Riphath, and Togarmah.

4 And the sons of Yawan: Elishah, and Tarshish, Kittim, and Dodanim.

5 By these were the isles of the Gentiles (Goyim) divided in their lands; every one after his tongue, after their families, in their nations.

6 And the sons of Ham: Cush, and Mitsrayim, and Phut, and Canaan.

7 And the sons of Cush: Seba, and Havilah, and Sabtah, and Raamah, and Sabtecha; and the sons of Raamah: Sheva, and Dedan.

8 And Cush begat Nimrod; he began to be a mighty one on the earth.

9 He was a mighty hunter before יהוה; therefore it is said, "Even as Nimrod the mighty hunter before יהוה."

10 And the beginning of his kingdom was Babel, and Erech, and Accad, and Calneh, in the land of Shinar.

11 Out of that land went forth Asshur, and builded Nineveh, and the city Rehoboth, and Calah,

12 And Resen between Nineveh and Calah; the same is a great city.

13 And Mitsrayim begat Ludim, and Anamim, and Lehabim, and Naphtuhim,

14 And Pathrusim, and Casluhim, (out of whom came Philistim,) and Caphtorim.

15 And Canaan begat Sidon his firstborn, and Heth,

16 And the Jebusite (Yevusi), and the Amorite, and the Girgasite,

17 And the Hivite, and the Arkite, and the Sinite,

18 And the Arvadite, and the Zemarite, and the Hamathite: and afterward were the families of the Canaanites spread abroad.

19 And the border of the Canaanites was from Sidon, as you comest to Gerar, unto Gaza (Azzah); as you goest, unto Sodom, and Gomorrah, and Admah, and Zeboim, even unto Lasha.

20 These are the sons of Ham, after their families, after their tongues, in their countries, and in their nations.

21 Unto Shem also, the father of all the children of Eber, the brother of Japheth (Yefet) the elder, even to him were children born.

22 The children of Shem: Elam, and Asshur, and Arphaxad, and Lud, and Aram.

23 And the children of Aram: Uz, and Hul, and Gether, and Mash.

24 And Arphaxad begat Salah; and Salah begat Eber.

25 And unto Eber were born two sons: the name of one was Peleg, for in his days was the earth divided; and his brother's name was Yoktan.

26 And Yoktan begat Almodad, and Sheleph, and Hazarmaveth, and Yerah,

27 And Hadoram, and Uzal, and Diklah,

28 And Obal, and Abimael, and Sheva,

29 And Ophir, and Havilah, and Yovav. All these were the sons of Yoktan.

30 And their dwelling was from Mesha, as you goest unto Sephar a mount of the east.

31 These are the sons of Shem, after their families, after their tongues, in their lands, after their nations.

32 These are the families of the sons of Noach, after their generations, in their nations; and from these were the nations divided in the earth after the flood.

11 And the whole earth was of one language, and of one speech.

2 And it came to pass, as they journeyed from the east, that they found a plain in the land of Shinar; and they dwelt there.

3 And they said one to another, "Go to, let us make brick, and burn them throughly. And they had brick for stone, and slime had they for morter."

4 And they said, "Come, let us build us a city and a tower, whose top may reach unto heaven; and let us make us a name, lest we be scattered abroad upon the face of the whole earth."

5 And יהוה came down to see the city and the tower, which the children of men builded.

6 And יהוה said, "Behold, the people is one, and they have all one language; and this they begin to do; and now nothing will be restrained from them, which they have imagined to do.

7 Come, let Us go down, and there confound their language, that they may not understand one another's speech."

8 So יהוה scattered them abroad from there upon the face of all the earth, and they left off to build the city.

9 Therefore is the name of it called Babylon (Bavel), because יהוה did there confound the language of all the earth; and from there did יהוה scatter them abroad upon the face of all the earth.

10 These are the generations of Shem: Shem was a hundred years old, and begat Arphaxad two years after the flood;

11 And Shem lived after he begat Arphaxad five hundred years, and begat sons and daughters.

12 And Arphaxad lived five and thirty years, and begat Salah.

13 And Arphaxad lived after he begat Salah four hundred and three years, and begat sons and daughters.

14 And Salah lived thirty years, and begat Eber;

15 And Salah lived after he begat Eber four hundred and three years, and begat sons and daughters.

16 And Eber lived four and thirty years, and begat Peleg;

17 And Eber lived after he begat Peleg four hundred and thirty years, and begat sons and daughters.

18 And Peleg lived thirty years, and begat Reu;

19 And Peleg lived after he begat Reu two hundred and nine years, and begat sons and daughters.

20 And Reu lived two and thirty years, and begat Serug;

21 And Reu lived after he begat Serug two hundred and seven years, and begat sons and daughters.

22 And Serug lived thirty years, and begat Nahor;

23 And Serug lived after he begat Nahor two hundred years, and begat sons and daughters.

24 And Nahor lived nine and twenty years, and begat Terah;

25 And Nahor lived after he begat Terah a hundred and nineteen years, and begat sons and daughters.

26 And Terah lived seventy years, and begat A10Avram, Nahor, and Haran.

27 Now these are the generations of Terah: Terah begat Avram, Nahor, and Haran; and Haran begat Lot.

28 And Haran died before his father Terah in the land of his nativity, in Ur of the Chaldees.

29 And Avram and Nahor took them wives: the

name of Avram's wife was Sarai; and the name of Nahor's wife, Milcah, the daughter of Haran, the father of Milcah, and the father of Iscah.

30 But Sarai was barren; she had no child.

31 And Terah took Avram his son, and Lot the son of Haran his son's son, and Sarai his daughter in law, his son Avram's wife; and they went forth with them from Ur of the Chaldees, to go into the land of Canaan; and they came unto Haran, and dwelt there.

32 And the days of Terah were two hundred and five years; and Terah died in Haran.

12 Now יהוה had said unto Avram, "Get you out of your country, and from your kindred, and from your father's house, unto a land that I will shew you.

2 And I will make of you a great nation, and I will bless you, and make your name great; and you shalt be a blessing.

3 And I will bless them that bless you, and curse him that curseth you; and in you shall all families of the earth be blessed."

4 So Avram departed, as יהוה had spoken unto him; and Lot went with him. And Avram was seventy and five years old when he departed out of Haran.

5 And Avram took Sarai his wife, and Lot his brother's son, and all their substance that they had gathered, and the souls that they had gotten in Haran; and they went forth to go into the land of Canaan; and into the land of Canaan they came.

6 And Avram passed through the land unto the place of Sichem, unto the plain of Moreh. And the Canaanite was then in the land.

7 And יהוה appeared unto Avram, and said, "Unto your seed will I give this land." And there builded he an altar unto יהוה, who appeared unto him.

8 And he removed from there unto a mountain on the east of Bethel (Beit-El), and pitched his tent, having Bethel (Beit-El) on the west, and Hai on the east; and there he builded an altar unto יהוה, and called upon the name of יהוה.

9 And Avram journeyed, going on still toward the south.

10 And there was a famine in the land; and Avram went down into Egypt (Mitsrayim) to sojourn there; for the famine was grievous in the land.

11 And it came to pass, when he was come near to enter into Egypt (Mitsrayim), that he said unto Sarai his wife, "Behold now, I know that you are a fair woman to look upon.

12 Therefore it shall come to pass, when the Egyptians (Mitsrayim) shall see you, that they shall say, 'This is his wife'; and they will kill me, but they will save you alive.

13 Please say you are my sister, that it may be well with me for your sake; and my soul shall live because of you."

14 And it came to pass, that, when Avram was come into Egypt (Mitsrayim), the Egyptians (Mitsrayim) beheld the woman that she was very fair.

15 The princes also of Pharaoh (Paroh) saw her, and commended her before Pharaoh (Paroh); and the woman was taken into Pharaoh (Paroh)'s house.

16 And he entreated Avram well for her sake; and he had sheep, and oxen, and he asses, and menservants, and maidservants, and she asses, and camels.

17 And יהוה plagued Pharaoh (Paroh) and his house with great plagues because of Sarai Avram's wife.

18 And Pharaoh (Paroh) called Avram, and said, "What is this that you have done unto me? Why didst you not tell me that she was your wife?

19 Why saidst you, 'She is my sister'? So I might have taken her to me to wife. Now therefore behold your wife, take her, and go your way."

20 And Pharaoh (Paroh) commanded his men concerning him; and they sent him away, and his wife, and all that he had.

13 And Avram went up out of Egypt (Mitsrayim), he, and his wife, and all that he had, and Lot with him, into the south.

2 And Avram was very rich in cattle, in silver, and in gold.

3 And he went on his journeys from the south even to Bethel (Beit-El), unto the place where his tent had been at the beginning, between Bethel (Beit-El) and Hai;

4 Unto the place of the altar, which he had made there at the first; and there Avram called on the name of יהוה.

5 And Lot also, which went with Avram, had flocks, and herds, and tents.

6 And the land was not able to bear them, that they might dwell together; for their substance was great, so that they could not dwell together.

7 And there was a strife between the herdmen of Avram's cattle and the herdmen of Lot's cattle; and the Canaanite and the Perizzite dwelled then in the land.

8 And Avram said unto Lot, "Please et there be no strife, between me and you, and between my herdmen and your herdmen; for we be brethren.

9 Is not the whole land before you? Please separate yourself from me. If you wilt take the left hand, then I will go to the right; or if you depart to the right hand, then I will go to the left."

10 And Lot lifted up his eyes, and beheld all the plain of Jordan (Yarden), that it was well watered every where, before יהוה destroyed Sodom and Gomorrah, even as the garden of יהוה, like the land of Egypt (Mitsrayim), as you comest unto Zoar.

11 Then Lot chose him all the plain of Jordan (Yarden); and Lot journeyed east; and they separated themselves the one from the other.

12 Avram dwelled in the land of Canaan, and Lot dwelled in the cities of the plain, and pitched his tent toward Sodom.

13 But the men of Sodom were wicked and sinners before יהוה exceedingly.

14 And יהוה said unto Avram, after that Lot was separated from him, "Lift up now your eyes, and look from the place where you are northward, and southward, and eastward, and westward;

15 For all the land which you seest, to you will I give it, and to your seed forever.

16 And I will make your seed as the dust of the earth; so that if a man can number the dust of the earth, then shall your seed also be numbered.

17 Arise, walk through the land in the length of it and in the breadth of it, for I will give it unto you."

18 Then Avram removed his tent, and came and dwelt in the plain of Mamre, which is in Hebron, and built there an altar unto יהוה.

14 And it came to pass in the days of Amraphel king of Shinar, Arioch king of Ellasar, Chedorlaomer king of Elam, and Tidal king of nations;

2 That these made war with Bera king of Sodom, and with Birsha king of Gomorrah, Shinab king of Admah, and Shemeber king of Zeboiim, and the king of Bela, which is Zoar.

3 All these were joined together in the vale of Siddim, which is the salt sea.

4 Twelve years they served Chedorlaomer, and in the thirteenth year they rebelled.

5 And in the fourteenth year came Chedorlaomer, and the kings that were with him, and smote the Rephaims in Ashteroth Karnaim, and the Zuzims in Ham, and the Emims in Shaveh Qiryatayim,

6 And the Horites in their mount Seir, unto Elparan, which is by the wilderness.

7 And they returned, and came to Enmishpat, which is Qadesh, and smote all the country of the Amalekites, and also the Amorites, that dwelt in Hazezontamar.

8 And there went out the king of Sodom, and the king of Gomorrah, and the king of Admah, and the king of Zeboiim, and the king of Bela (the same is Zoar;) and they joined battle with them in the vale of Siddim;

9 With Chedorlaomer the king of Elam, and with Tidal king of nations, and Amraphel king of Shinar, and Arioch king of Ellasar; four kings with five.

10 And the vale of Siddim was full of slimepits; and the kings of Sodom and Gomorrah fled, and fell there; and they that remained fled to the mountain.

11 And they took all the goods of Sodom and Gomorrah, and all their victuals, and went their way.

12 And they took Lot, Avram's brother's son, who dwelt in Sodom, and his goods, and departed.

13 And there came one that had escaped, and told Avram the Hebrew (Ivri); for he dwelt in the plain of Mamre the Amorite, brother of Eshcol, and brother of Aner; and these were confederate with Avram.

14 And when Avram heard that his brother was taken captive, he armed his trained servants, born in his own house, three hundred and eighteen, and pursued them unto Dan.

15 And he divided himself against them, he and his servants, by night, and smote them, and pursued them unto Hobah, which is on the left hand of Damascus (Dammeseq).

16 And he brought back all the goods, and also brought again his brother Lot, and his goods, and the women also, and the people.

17 And the king of Sodom went out to meet him after his return from the slaughter of Chedorlaomer, and of the kings that were with

him, at the valley of Shaveh, which is the king's dale.

18 And Melchizedek king of Salem brought forth bread and wine: and he was the priest (kohen) of the [B6a]Most High God (El Elyon).

19 And he blessed him, and said: "Blessed be Avram of the Most High God (El Elyon), possessor of heavens and earth;

20 And blessed be the Most High God (El Elyon), Who hath delivered your enemies into your hand." And he gave him tithes of all.

21 And the king of Sodom said unto Avram, "Give me the persons, and take the goods to yourself."

22 And Avram said to the king of Sodom, "I have lift up mine hand unto יהוה, the Most High God (El Elyon), the possessor of heavens and earth,

23 That I will not take from a thread even to a shoelatchet, and that I will not take any thing that is yours, lest you shouldest say, 'I have made Avram rich';

24 Except only that which the young men have eaten, and the portion of the men which went with me: Aner, Eshcol, and Mamre; let them take their portion."

15 After these things the word of יהוה came unto Avram in a vision, saying, "Fear not, Avram. I am your shield, and your exceeding great reward."

2 And Avram said, "[B12]My Lord (Adonai) יהוה, what wilt You give me, seeing I go childless, and the steward of my house is this Eliezer of Damascus (Dammeseq)?"

3 And Avram said, "Behold, to me You have given no seed; and, behold, one born in my house is mine heir."

4 And, behold, the word of יהוה came unto him, saying, "This shall not be your heir, but he that shall come forth out of your own bowels shall be your heir."

5 And He brought him forth abroad, and said, "Look now toward heaven, and tell the stars, if you be able to number them." And He said unto him, "So shall your seed be."

6 And he believed in יהוה; and He counted it to him for righteousness.

7 And He said unto him, "I am יהוה who brought you out of Ur of the Chaldees, to give you this land to inherit it."

8 And he said, "My Lord (Adonai) יהוה, whereby shall I know that I shall inherit it?"

9 And He said unto him, "Take Me a heifer of three years old, and a she goat of three years old, and a ram of three years old, and a turtledove, and a young pigeon."

10 And he took unto Him all these, and divided them in the midst, and laid each piece one against another; but the birds divided he not.

11 And when the fowls came down upon the carcases, Avram drove them away.

12 And when the sun was going down, a deep sleep fell upon Avram; and, behold, a horror of great darkness fell upon him.

13 And He said unto Avram, "Know of a surety that your seed shall be a stranger in a land that is not theirs, and shall serve them; and they shall afflict them four hundred years.

14 And also that nation, whom they shall serve, will I judge; and afterward shall they come out with great substance.

15 And you shalt go to your fathers in peace; you shalt be buried in a good old age.

16 But in the fourth generation they shall come hither again: for the iniquity of the Amorites is not yet full.

17 And it came to pass, that, when the sun went down, and it was dark, behold a smoking furnace, and a burning lamp that passed between those pieces.

18 In the same day יהוה made a covenant with Avram, saying, "Unto your seed have I given this land, from the river of Egypt (Mitsrayim) unto the great river, the river Euphrates:

19 The Kenites, and the Kenizzites, and the Kadmonites,

20 And the Hittites, and the Perizzites, and the Rephaims,

21 And the Amorites, and the Canaanites, and the Girgashites, and the Jebusites (Yevusi)."

16 Now Sarai Avram's wife bare him no children. And she had a handmaid, an Egyptian (Mitsri), whose name was Hagar.

2 And Sarai said unto Avram, "Behold now, יהוה hath restrained me from bearing. Please, go in unto my maid; it may be that I may obtain children by her." And Avram hearkened to the voice of Sarai.

3 And Sarai Avram's wife took Hagar her maid the Egyptian (Mitsri), after Avram had dwelt ten years in the land of Canaan, and gave her to her husband Avram to be his wife.

4 And he went in unto Hagar, and she conceived; and when she saw that she had conceived, her mistress was despised in her eyes.

5 And Sarai said unto Avram, "My wrong be upon you: I have given my maid into your bosom; and when she saw that she had conceived, I was despised in her eyes. יהוה judge between me and you."

6 But Avram said unto Sarai, "Behold, your maid is in your hand; do to her as it pleaseth you." And when Sarai dealt hardly with her, she fled from her face.

7 And the angel of יהוה found her by a fountain of water in the wilderness, by the fountain in the way to Shur.

8 And he said, "Hagar, Sarai's maid, whence camest you? And whither wilt you go?" And she said, "I flee from the face of my mistress Sarai."

9 And the angel of יהוה said unto her, "Return to your mistress, and submit yourself under her hands."

10 And the angel of יהוה said unto her, "I will multiply your seed exceedingly, that it shall not be numbered for multitude."

11 And the angel of יהוה said unto her, "Behold, you are with child, and shalt bear a son, and shalt call his name Yishmael, because יהוה hath heard your affliction.

12 And he will be a wild man; his hand will be against every man, and every man's hand against him; and he shall dwell in the presence of all his brethren."

13 And she called the name of יהוה who spake unto her, "B8Thou God Seeth Me (Attah El Roi)"; for she said, "Have I also here looked after Him who seeth me?"

14 Therefore the well was called 'Well of the Living One Seeth Me (Beer la-Chai Roi)'; behold, it is between Qadesh and Bered.

15 And Hagar bare Avram a son; and Avram called his son's name, which Hagar bare, Yishmael.

16 And Avram was fourscore and six years old, when Hagar bare Yishmael to Avram.

17 And when Avram was ninety years old and nine, יהוה appeared to Avram, and said unto him, "I am B7bAlmighty God (El Shaddai); walk before Me, and be you perfect.

2 And I will make My covenant between Me and you, and will multiply you exceedingly."

3 And Avram fell on his face; and God (Elohim) talked with him, saying,

4 "As for Me, behold, My covenant (berit) is with you, and you shalt be a father of many nations.

5 Neither shall your name anymore be called Avram, but your name shall be A11Avraham; for a father of many nations have I made you.

6 And I will make you exceeding fruitful, and I will make nations of you, and kings shall come out of you.

7 And I will establish My covenant between Me and you and your seed after you in their generations for an everlasting covenant, to be a God (Elohim) unto you, and to your seed after you.

8 And I will give unto you, and to your seed after you, the land wherein you are a stranger, all the land of Canaan, for an everlasting possession; and I will be their God (Elohim)."

9 And God (Elohim) said unto Avraham, "You shalt keep My covenant therefore, you, and your seed after you in their generations.

10 This is My covenant, which you shall keep, between Me and you and your seed after you: Every man child among you shall be circumcised.

11 And you shall circumcise the flesh of your foreskin; and it shall be a token of the covenant between Me and you.

12 And he that is eight days old shall be circumcised among you, every man child in your generations, he that is born in the house, or bought with money of any stranger, which is not of your seed.

13 He that is born in your house, and he that is bought with your money, must needs be circumcised; and My covenant shall be in your flesh for an everlasting covenant.

14 And the uncircumcised man child whose flesh of his foreskin is not circumcised, that soul shall be cut off from his people; he hath broken My covenant."

15 And God (Elohim) said unto Avraham, "As for Sarai your wife, you shalt not call her name Sarai, but Sarah shall her name be.

16 And I will bless her, and give you a son also of her: yea, I will bless her, and she shall be a mother of nations; kings of people shall be of her."

17 Then Avraham fell upon his face, and laughed, and said in his heart, "Shall a child

be born unto him that is a hundred years old? And shall Sarah, that is ninety years old, bear?"

18 And Avraham said unto God (Elohim), "O that Yishmael might live before you!"

19 And God (Elohim) said, "Sarah your wife shall bear you a son indeed; and you shalt call his name [A12]Isaac (Yitschaq); and I will establish My covenant with him for an everlasting covenant, and with his seed after him.

20 And as for Yishmael, I have heard you. Behold, I have blessed him, and will make him fruitful, and will multiply him exceedingly; twelve princes shall he beget, and I will make him a great nation.

21 But My covenant will I establish with Isaac (Yitschaq), which Sarah shall bear unto you at this set time in the next year."

22 And he left off talking with him, and God (Elohim) went up from Avraham.

23 And Avraham took Yishmael his son, and all that were born in his house, and all that were bought with his money, every male among the men of Avraham's house; and circumcised the flesh of their foreskin in the selfsame day, as God (Elohim) had said unto him.

24 And Avraham was ninety years old and nine, when he was circumcised in the flesh of his foreskin.

25 And Yishmael his son was thirteen years old, when he was circumcised in the flesh of his foreskin.

26 In the selfsame day was Avraham circumcised, and Yishmael his son.

27 And all the men of his house, born in the house, and bought with money of the stranger, were circumcised with him.

18 And יהוה appeared unto him in the plains of Mamre; and he sat in the tent door in the heat of the day.

2 And he lifted up his eyes and looked, and, behold, three men stood by him: and when he saw them, he ran to meet them from the tent door, and bowed himself toward the ground,

3 And said, "My Lord (Adonai), if now I have found favor in Your sight, please pass not away from Your servant.

4 Please let a little water be fetched, and wash your feet, and rest yourselves under the tree.

5 And I will fetch a morsel of bread, and comfort you your hearts; after that you shall pass on; for therefore are you come to your servant." And

they said, "So do, as you have said."

6 And Avraham hastened into the tent unto Sarah, and said, "Make ready quickly three measures of fine meal, knead it, and make cakes upon the hearth."

7 And Avraham ran unto the herd, and fetcht a calf tender and good, and gave it unto a young man; and he hasted to dress it.

8 And he took butter, and milk, and the calf which he had dressed, and set it before them; and he stood by them under the tree, and they did eat.

9 And they said unto him, "Where is Sarah your wife?" And he said, "Behold, in the tent."

10 And he said, "I will certainly return unto you according to the time of life; and, behold, Sarah your wife shall have a son." And Sarah heard it in the tent door, which was behind him.

11 Now Avraham and Sarah were old and well stricken in age; and it ceased to be with Sarah after the manner of women.

12 Therefore Sarah laughed within herself, saying, "After I am waxed old shall I have pleasure, [B13]my lord (adoni) being old also?"

13 And יהוה said unto Avraham, "Wherefore did Sarah laugh, saying, 'Shall I of a surety bear a child, which am old?'

14 Is any thing too hard for יהוה? At the time appointed I will return unto you, according to the time of life, and Sarah shall have a son."

15 Then Sarah denied, saying, "I laughed not;" for she was afraid. And He said, "Nay; but you didst laugh."

16 And the men rose up from thence, and looked toward Sodom and Avraham went with them to bring them on the way.

17 And יהוה said, "Shall I hide from Avraham that thing which I do;

18 Seeing that Avraham shall surely become a great and mighty nation, and all the nations of the earth shall be blessed in him?

19 For I know him, that he will command his children and his household after him, and they shall keep the way of יהוה, to do justice and judgment; that יהוה may bring upon Avraham that which He hath spoken of him."

20 And יהוה said, "Because the cry of Sodom and Gomorrah is great, and because their sin is very grievous;

21 I will go down now, and see whether they have done altogether according to the cry of it,

which is come unto Me; and if not, I will know."

22 And the men turned their faces from thence, and went toward Sodom; but Avraham stood yet before יהוה.

23 And Avraham drew near, and said, "Wilt You also destroy the righteous with the wicked?

24 Suppose there be fifty righteous within the city; wilt You also destroy and not spare the place for the fifty righteous that are therein?

25 That be far from You to do after this manner, to slay the righteous with the wicked; and that the righteous should be as the wicked, that be far from You. Shall not the Judge of all the earth do right?"

26 And יהוה said, "If I find in Sodom fifty righteous within the city, then I will spare all the place for their sakes."

27 And Avraham answered and said, "Behold now, I have taken upon me to speak unto [12]my Lord (Adonai), who am but dust and ashes:

28 Suppose there shall lack five of the fifty righteous: wilt You destroy all the city for lack of five?" And He said, "If I find there forty and five, I will not destroy it."

29 And he spake unto Him yet again, and said, "Suppose there shall be forty found there." And He said, "I will not do it for forty's sake."

30 And he said unto Him, "Oh let not my Lord (Adonai) be angry, and I will speak: Suppose there shall thirty be found there." And He said, "I will not do it, if I find thirty there."

31 And he said, "Behold now, I have taken upon me to speak unto my Lord (Adonai): Suppose there shall be twenty found there." And He said, "I will not destroy it for twenty's sake."

32 And he said, "Oh let not my Lord (Adonai) be angry, and I will speak yet but this once: Suppose ten shall be found there." And He said, "I will not destroy it for ten's sake."

33 And יהוה went His way, as soon as He had left communing with Avraham; and Avraham returned unto his place.

19 And there came two angels to Sodom at even; and Lot sat in the gate of Sodom; and Lot seeing them rose up to meet them; and he bowed himself with his face toward the ground;

2 And he said, "Behold now, my lords (adonai), please turn in into your servant's house, and tarry all night, and wash your feet, and you shall rise up early, and go on your ways." And they said; "Nay; but we will abide in the street all night."

3 And he pressed upon them greatly; and they turned in unto him, and entered into his house; and he made them a feast, and did bake unleavened bread, and they did eat.

4 But before they lay down, the men of the city, even the men of Sodom, compassed the house round, both old and young, all the people from every quarter:

5 And they called unto Lot, and said unto him, "Where are the men who came in to you this night? Bring them out unto us, that we may know them."

6 And Lot went out at the door unto them, and shut the door after him,

7 And said, "Please, brethren, do not so wickedly.

8 Behold now, I have two daughters which have not known man; please let me bring them out unto you, and do you to them as is good in your eyes; only unto these men do nothing, for therefore came they under the shadow of my roof."

9 And they said, "Stand back." And they said again, "This one fellow came in to sojourn, and he will needs be a judge; now will we deal worse with you, than with them." And they pressed sore upon the man, even Lot, and came near to break the door.

10 But the men put forth their hand, and pulled Lot into the house to them, and shut to the door.

11 And they smote the men that were at the door of the house with blindness, both small and great, so that they wearied themselves to find the door.

12 And the men said unto Lot, "Have you here any besides? Son in law, and your sons, and your daughters, and whatsoever you have in the city, bring them out of this place;

13 For we will destroy this place, because the cry of them is waxen great before the face of יהוה; and יהוה hath sent us to destroy it."

14 And Lot went out, and spake unto his sons in law, who married his daughters, and said, "Up, get you out of this place; for יהוה will destroy this city." But he seemed as one that mocked unto his sons in law.

15 And when the morning arose, then the angels hastened Lot, saying, "Arise, take your wife, and your two daughters, which are here; lest you be consumed in the iniquity of the city."

16 And while he lingered, the men laid hold upon his hand, and upon the hand of his wife, and upon the hand of his two daughters; יהוה being merciful unto him; and they brought him forth, and set him outside the city.

17 And it came to pass, when they had brought them forth abroad, that he said, "Escape for your life; look not behind you, neither stay you in all the plain; escape to the mountain, lest you be consumed."

18 And Lot said unto them, "Oh, not so, my lord (adoni)!

19 Behold now, your servant hath found grace in your sight, and you have magnified your mercy, which you have shewed unto me in saving my life; and I cannot escape to the mountain, lest the disaster (B36raah) overtake me, and I die.

20 Behold now, this city is near to flee unto, and it is a little one; Oh, let me escape thither, (is it not a little one?) and my soul shall live."

21 And he said unto him, "See, I have accepted you concerning this thing also, that I will not overthrow this city, for which you have spoken.

22 Haste you, escape thither; for I cannot do any thing till you arrive there." Therefore the name of the city was called Zoar.

23 The sun was risen upon the earth when Lot entered into Zoar.

24 Then יהוה rained upon Sodom and upon Gomorrah brimstone and fire from יהוה out of heaven;

25 And He overthrew those cities, and all the plain, and all the inhabitants of the cities, and that which grew upon the ground.

26 But his wife looked back from behind him, and she became a pillar of salt.

27 And Avraham gat up early in the morning to the place where he stood before יהוה.

28 And he looked toward Sodom and Gomorrah, and toward all the land of the plain, and beheld, and, behold, the smoke of the country went up as the smoke of a furnace.

29 And it came to pass, when God (Elohim) destroyed the cities of the plain, that God (Elohim) remembered Avraham, and sent Lot out of the midst of the overthrow, when he overthrew the cities in the which Lot dwelt.

30 And Lot went up out of Zoar, and dwelt in the mountain, and his two daughters with him; for he feared to dwell in Zoar; and he dwelt in a cave, he and his two daughters.

31 And the firstborn said unto the younger, "Our father is old, and there is not a man in the earth to come in unto us after the manner of all the earth.

32 Come, let us make our father drink wine, and we will lie with him, that we may preserve seed of our father."

33 And they made their father drink wine that night; and the firstborn went in, and lay with her father; and he perceived not when she lay down, nor when she arose.

34 And it came to pass on the next day, that the firstborn said unto the younger, "Behold, I lay last night with my father; let us make him drink wine this night also; and go you in, and lie with him, that we may preserve seed of our father."

35 And they made their father drink wine that night also; and the younger arose, and lay with him; and he perceived not when she lay down, nor when she arose.

36 Thus were both the daughters of Lot with child by their father.

37 And the firstborn bare a son, and called his name Moav; the same is the father of the Moavites unto this day.

38 And the younger, she also bare a son, and called his name Benammi; the same is the father of the children of Ammon unto this day.

20 And Avraham journeyed from thence toward the south country, and dwelled between Qadesh and Shur, and sojourned in Gerar.

2 And Avraham said of Sarah his wife, "She is my sister;" and Abimelech (Avimelekh) king of Gerar sent, and took Sarah.

3 But God (Elohim) came to Abimelech (Avimelekh) in a dream by night, and said to him, "Behold, you are but a dead man, for the woman which you have taken; for she is a man's wife."

4 But Abimelech (Avimelekh) had not come near her: and he said, "Lord (Adonai), wilt You slay also a righteous nation?

5 Said he not unto me, 'She is my sister'? And she, even she herself said, 'He is my brother'; in the integrity of my heart and innocency of my hands have I done this."

6 And God (Elohim) said unto him in a dream, "Yea, I know that you didst this in the integrity of your heart; for I also withheld you from sinning against Me; therefore allowed I you not

to touch her.

7 Now therefore restore the man his wife; for he is a prophet, and he shall pray for you, and you shalt live. And if you restore her not, know you that you shalt surely die, you, and all that are yours."

8 Therefore Abimelech (Avimelekh) rose early in the morning, and called all his servants, and told all these things in their ears; and the men were sore afraid.

9 Then Abimelech (Avimelekh) called Avraham, and said unto him, "What have you done unto us? And what have I offended you, that you have brought on me and on my kingdom a great sin? You have done deeds unto me that ought not to be done."

10 And Abimelech (Avimelekh) said unto Avraham, "What sawest you, that you have done this thing?"

11 And Avraham said, "Because I thought, surely the fear of God (Elohim) is not in this place; and they will slay me for my wife's sake.

12 And yet indeed she is my sister; she is the daughter of my father, but not the daughter of my mother; and she became my wife.

13 And it came to pass, when God (Elohim) caused me to wander from my father's house, that I said unto her, 'This is your kindness which you shalt shew unto me; at every place whither we shall come, say of me, "He is my brother."

14 And Abimelech (Avimelekh) took sheep, and oxen, and menservants, and womenservants, and gave them unto Avraham, and restored him Sarah his wife.

15 And Abimelech (Avimelekh) said, "Behold, my land is before you; dwell where it pleaseth you."

16 And unto Sarah he said, "Behold, I have given your brother a thousand pieces of silver; behold, he is to you a covering of the eyes, unto all that are with you, and with all other." Thus she was reproved.

17 So Avraham prayed unto God (Elohim); and God (Elohim) healed Abimelech (Avimelekh), and his wife, and his maidservants; and they bare children.

18 For יהוה had fast closed up all the wombs of the house of Abimelech (Avimelekh), because of Sarah Avraham's wife.

21 And יהוה visited Sarah as He had said, and יהוה did unto Sarah as He had spoken.

2 For Sarah conceived, and bare Avraham a son in his old age, at the set time of which God (Elohim) had spoken to him.

3 And Avraham called the name of his son that was born unto him, whom Sarah bare to him, Isaac (Yitschaq).

4 And Avraham circumcised his son Isaac (Yitschaq) being eight days old, as God (Elohim) had commanded him.

5 And Avraham was a hundred years old, when his son Isaac (Yitschaq) was born unto him.

6 And Sarah said, "God (Elohim) hath made me to laugh, so that all who hear will laugh with me."

7 And she said, "Who would have said unto Avraham, that Sarah should have given children suck? For I have born him a son in his old age."

8 And the child grew, and was weaned. And Avraham made a great feast the same day that Isaac (Yitschaq) was weaned.

9 And Sarah saw the son of Hagar the Egyptian (Mitsri), whom she had born unto Avraham, mocking.

10 Therefore she said unto Avraham, "Cast out this bondwoman and her son; for the son of this bondwoman shall not be heir with my son, even with Isaac (Yitschaq)."

11 And the thing was very grievous in Avraham's sight because of his son.

12 And God (Elohim) said unto Avraham, "Let it not be grievous in your sight because of the lad, and because of your bondwoman; in all that Sarah hath said unto you, hearken unto her voice; for in Isaac (Yitschaq) shall your seed be called.

13 And also of the son of the bondwoman will I make a nation, because he is your seed."

14 And Avraham rose up early in the morning, and took bread, and a bottle of water, and gave it unto Hagar, putting it on her shoulder, and the child, and sent her away; and she departed, and wandered in the wilderness of Beer-Sheva.

15 And the water was spent in the bottle, and she cast the child under one of the shrubs.

16 And she went, and sat her down opposite him a good way off, as it was a bowshot; for she said, "Let me not see the death of the child." And she sat opposite him, and lift up her voice, and wept.

17 And God (Elohim) heard the voice of the lad; and the angel of God (Elohim) called to Hagar out of heaven, and said unto her, "What aileth

you, Hagar? Fear not, for God (Elohim) hath heard the voice of the lad where he is.

18 Arise, lift up the lad, and hold him in your hand; for I will make him a great nation."

19 And God (Elohim) opened her eyes, and she saw a well of water; and she went, and filled the bottle with water, and gave the lad drink.

20 And God (Elohim) was with the lad; and he grew, and dwelt in the wilderness, and became an archer.

21 And he dwelt in the wilderness of Paran; and his mother took him a wife out of the land of Egypt (Mitsrayim).

22 And it came to pass at that time, that Abimelech (Avimelekh) and Phichol the chief captain of his host spake unto Avraham, saying, "God (Elohim) is with you in all that you doest.

23 Now therefore swear unto me here by God (Elohim) that you wilt not deal falsely with me, nor with my son, nor with my son's son; but according to the kindness that I have done unto you, you shalt do unto me, and to the land wherein you have sojourned."

24 And Avraham said, "I will swear."

25 And Avraham reproved Abimelech (Avimelekh) because of a well of water, which Abimelech (Avimelekh)'s servants had violently taken away.

26 And Abimelech (Avimelekh) said, "I do not know who hath done this thing; neither didst you tell me, neither yet heard I of it, but today."

27 And Avraham took sheep and oxen, and gave them unto Abimelech (Avimelekh); and both of them made a covenant.

28 And Avraham set seven ewe lambs of the flock by themselves.

29 And Abimelech (Avimelekh) said unto Avraham, "What mean these seven ewe lambs which you have set by themselves?"

30 And he said, "For these seven ewe lambs shalt you take of my hand, that they may be a witness unto me, that I have digged this well."

31 Therefore he called that place Beer-Sheva, because there they sware both of them.

32 Thus they made a covenant at Beer-Sheva; then Abimelech (Avimelekh) rose up, and Phichol the chief captain of his host, and they returned into the land of the Philistines.

33 And Avraham planted a tamarisk tree in Beer-Sheva, and called there on the name of יהוה, the everlasting God (El Olam).

34 And Avraham sojourned in the Philistines' land many days.

22 And it came to pass after these things, that God (Elohim) tested Avraham, and said unto him, "Avraham"; and he said, "Behold, here I am."

2 And He said, "Take now your son, your only son Isaac (Yitschaq), whom you lovest, and get you into the land of Moriah; and offer him there for a burnt offering upon one of the mountains which I will tell you of."

3 And Avraham rose up early in the morning, and saddled his ass, and took two of his young men with him, and Isaac (Yitschaq) his son, and clave the wood for the burnt offering, and rose up, and went unto the place of which God (Elohim) had told him.

4 Then on the third day Avraham lifted up his eyes, and saw the place afar off.

5 And Avraham said unto his young men, "Abide you here with the ass; and I and the lad will go yonder and worship, and come again to you."

6 And Avraham took the wood of the burnt offering, and laid it upon Isaac (Yitschaq) his son; and he took the fire in his hand, and a knife; and they went both of them together.

7 And Isaac (Yitschaq) spake unto Avraham his father, and said, "My father"; and he said, "Here am I, my son." And he said, "Behold the fire and the wood; but where is the lamb for a burnt offering?"

8 And Avraham said, "My son, God (Elohim) will provide Himself a lamb for a burnt offering." So they went both of them together.

9 And they came to the place which God (Elohim) had told him of; and Avraham built an altar there, and laid the wood in order, and bound Isaac (Yitschaq) his son, and laid him on the altar upon the wood.

10 And Avraham stretched forth his hand, and took the knife to slay his son.

11 And the angel of יהוה called unto him out of heaven, and said, "Avraham, Avraham!" And he said, "Here am I."

12 And He said, "Lay not your hand upon the lad, neither do you any thing unto him; for now I know that you fearest God (Elohim), seeing you have not withheld your son, your only son from Me."

13 And Avraham lifted up his eyes, and looked,

and behold behind him a ram caught in a thicket by his horns; and Avraham went and took the ram, and offered him up for a burnt offering in the stead of his son.

14 And Avraham called the name of that place A3יהוה Yireh (YHWH Sees, YHWH Provides); as it is said to this day: "In the mountain of יהוה it shall be seen (provided)."

15 And the angel of יהוה called unto Avraham out of heaven the second time,

16 And said, "By Myself have I sworn", saith יהוה, "for because you have done this thing, and hast not withheld your son, your only son;

17 That in blessing I will bless you, and in multiplying I will multiply your seed as the stars of the heaven, and as the sand which is upon the sea shore; and your seed shall possess the gate of his enemies;

18 And in your seed shall all the nations of the earth be blessed, because you have obeyed My voice."

19 So Avraham returned unto his young men, and they rose up and went together to Beer-Sheva; and Avraham dwelt at Beer-Sheva.

20 And it came to pass after these things, that it was told Avraham, saying, "Behold, Milcah, she hath also born children unto your brother Nahor:

21 Huz his firstborn, and Buz his brother, and Kemuel the father of Aram,

22 And Chesed, and Hazo, and Pildash, and Yidlaf, and Bethuel.

23 And Bethuel begat Rebekah: these eight Milcah did bear to Nahor, Avraham's brother.

24 And his concubine, whose name was Reumah, she bare also Tebah, and Gaham, and Thahash, and Maachah.

23 And Sarah was a hundred and twenty seven years old; these were the years of the life of Sarah.

2 And Sarah died in Qiryat-Arba; the same is Hebron in the land of Canaan: and Avraham came to mourn for Sarah, and to weep for her.

3 And Avraham stood up from before his dead, and spake unto the sons of Heth, saying,

4 "I am a stranger and a sojourner with you; give me a possession of a buryingplace with you, that I may bury my dead out of my sight."

5 And the children of Heth answered Avraham, saying unto him,

6 "Hear us, my lord (adoni): you are a mighty prince among us; in the choice of our sepulchres bury your dead; none of us shall withhold from you his sepulchre, but that you mayest bury your dead."

7 And Avraham stood up, and bowed himself to the people of the land, even to the children of Heth.

8 And he communed with them, saying, "If it be your mind that I should bury my dead out of my sight; hear me, and intreat for me to Ephron the son of Zohar,

9 That he may give me the cave of Machpelah, which he hath, which is in the end of his field; for as much money as it is worth he shall give it me for a possession of a buryingplace amongst you."

10 And Ephron dwelt among the children of Heth; and Ephron the Hittite answered Avraham in the audience of the children of Heth, even of all that went in at the gate of his city, saying,

11 "Nay, my lord (adoni), hear me: the field give I you, and the cave that is therein, I give it you; in the presence of the sons of my people give I it you; bury your dead."

12 And Avraham bowed down himself before the people of the land.

13 And he spake unto Ephron in the audience of the people of the land, saying, "But if you wilt give it, please hear me: I will give you money for the field; take it of me, and I will bury my dead there."

14 And Ephron answered Avraham, saying unto him,

15 "My lord (Adoni), hearken unto me: the land is worth four hundred shekels of silver; what is that betwixt me and you? Bury therefore your dead."

16 And Avraham hearkened unto Ephron; and Avraham weighed to Ephron the silver, which he had named in the audience of the sons of Heth, four hundred shekels of silver, current money with the merchant.

17 And the field of Ephron, which was in Machpelah, which was before Mamre, the field, and the cave which was therein, and all the trees that were in the field, that were in all the borders round about, were made sure

18 Unto Avraham for a possession in the presence of the children of Heth, before all that went in at the gate of his city.

19 And after this, Avraham buried Sarah his

wife in the cave of the field of Machpelah before Mamre; the same is Hebron in the land of Canaan.

20 And the field, and the cave that is therein, were made sure unto Avraham for a possession of a buryingplace by the sons of Heth.

24 And Avraham was old, and well stricken in age; and יהוה had blessed Avraham in all things.

2 And Avraham said unto his eldest servant of his house, that ruled over all that he had, "Please put your hand under my thigh;

3 And I will make you swear by יהוה, the God of the heaven (Elohei hashamayim), and the God of the earth (Elohei haerets), that you shalt not take a wife unto my son of the daughters of the Canaanites, among whom I dwell;

4 But you shalt go unto my country, and to my kindred, and take a wife unto my son Isaac (Yitschaq)."

5 And the servant said unto him, "Suppose the woman will not be willing to follow me unto this land; must I needs bring your son again unto the land from whence you camest?"

6 And Avraham said unto him, "Beware you that you bring not my son thither again.

7 יהוה God of heaven (YHWH Elohei shamayim), who took me from my father's house, and from the land of my kindred, and which spake unto me, and that sware unto me, saying, "Unto your seed will I give this land; he shall send his angel before you, and you shalt take a wife unto my son from thence.

8 And if the woman will not be willing to follow you, then you shalt be clear from this my oath; only bring not my son thither again."

9 And the servant put his hand under the thigh of Avraham his master, and sware to him concerning that matter.

10 And the servant took ten camels of the camels of his master, and departed; for all the goods of his master were in his hand: and he arose, and went to Mesopotamia, unto the city of Nahor.

11 And he made his camels to kneel down outside the city by a well of water at the time of the evening, even the time that women go out to draw water.

12 And he said, "O יהוה God (Elohim) of my master Avraham, please send me good speed this day, and shew kindness unto my master Avraham.

13 Behold, I stand here by the well of water; and the daughters of the men of the city come out to draw water.

14 And let it come to pass, that the damsel to whom I shall say, 'Please down your pitcher, that I may drink'; and she shall say, 'Drink, and I will give your camels drink also'; let the same be she that you have appointed for your servant Isaac (Yitschaq); and thereby shall I know that you have shewed kindness unto my master."

15 And it came to pass, before he had done speaking, that, behold, Rebekah came out, who was born to Bethuel, son of Milcah, the wife of Nahor, Avraham's brother, with her pitcher upon her shoulder.

16 And the damsel was very fair to look upon, a virgin, neither had any man known her: and she went down to the well, and filled her pitcher, and came up.

17 And the servant ran to meet her, and said, "Please let me drink a little water of your pitcher."

18 And she said, "Drink, my lord (adoni)"; and she hasted, and let down her pitcher upon her hand, and gave him drink.

19 And when she had done giving him drink, she said, "I will draw water for your camels also, until they have done drinking."

20 And she hasted, and emptied her pitcher into the trough, and ran again unto the well to draw water, and drew for all his camels.

21 And the man wondering at her held his peace, to know whether יהוה had made his journey prosperous or not.

22 And it came to pass, as the camels had done drinking, that the man took a golden earring of half a shekel weight, and two bracelets for her hands of ten shekels weight of gold;

23 And said, "Whose daughter are you? Please tell me, is there room in your father's house for us to lodge in?"

24 And she said unto him, "I am the daughter of Bethuel the son of Milcah, whom she bare unto Nahor."

25 She said moreover unto him, "We have both straw and provender enough, and room to lodge in."

26 And the man bowed down his head, and worshipped יהוה.

27 And he said, "Blessed be יהוה God (Elohim) of my master Avraham, who hath not left

destitute my master of his mercy and his truth; I being in the way, יהוה led me to the house of my master's brethren."

28 And the damsel ran, and told them of her mother's house these things.

29 And Rebekah had a brother, and his name was Lavan; and Lavan ran out unto the man, unto the well.

30 And it came to pass, when he saw the earring and bracelets upon his sister's hands, and when he heard the words of Rebekah his sister, saying, "Thus spake the man unto me"; that he came unto the man; and, behold, he stood by the camels at the well.

31 And he said, "Come in, you blessed of יהוה; wherefore standest you outside? For I have prepared the house, and room for the camels."

32 And the man came into the house; and he ungirded his camels, and gave straw and provender for the camels, and water to wash his feet, and the men's feet that were with him.

33 And there was set meat before him to eat: but he said, I will not eat, until I have told mine errand. And he said, "Speak on."

34 And he said, "I am Avraham's servant.

35 And יהוה hath blessed my master greatly; and he has become great; and he hath given him flocks, and herds, and silver, and gold, and menservants, and maidservants, and camels, and asses.

36 And Sarah my master's wife bare a son to my master when she was old; and unto him hath he given all that he hath.

37 And my master made me swear, saying, 'You shalt not take a wife to my son of the daughters of the Canaanites, in whose land I dwell;

38 But you shalt go unto my father's house, and to my kindred, and take a wife unto my son.'

39 And I said unto my master, 'Suppose the woman will not follow me.'

40 And he said unto me, 'יהוה, before whom I walk, will send his angel with you, and prosper your way; and you shalt take a wife for my son of my kindred, and of my father's house:

41 Then shalt you be clear from this my oath, when you comest to my kindred; and if they give not you one, you shalt be clear from my oath.'

42 And I came this day unto the well, and said, 'O יהוה God (Elohim) of my master Avraham, if now you do prosper my way which I go;

43 Behold, I stand by the well of water; and it shall come to pass, that when the virgin cometh forth to draw water, and I say to her, "Please give me a little water of your pitcher to drink";

44 And she says to me, "Both drink you, and I will also draw for your camels"; let the same be the woman whom יהוה hath appointed out for my master's son.'

45 And before I had done speaking in mine heart, behold, Rebekah came forth with her pitcher on her shoulder; and she went down unto the well, and drew water; and I said unto her, 'Please let me drink.'

46 And she made haste, and let down her pitcher from her shoulder, and said, 'Drink, and I will give your camels drink also.' So I drank, and she made the camels drink also.

47 And I asked her, and said, 'Whose daughter are you?' And she said, 'The daughter of Bethuel, Nahor's son, whom Milcah bare unto him.' And I put the earring upon her face, and the bracelets upon her hands.

48 And I bowed down my head, and worshipped יהוה, and blessed יהוה God (Elohim) of my master Avraham, who had led me in the right way to take my master's brother's daughter unto his son.

49 And now if you will deal kindly and truly with my master, tell me: and if not, tell me; that I may turn to the right hand, or to the left."

50 Then Lavan and Bethuel answered and said, "The thing proceedeth from יהוה; we cannot speak unto you bad or good.

51 Behold, Rebekah is before you, take her, and go, and let her be your master's son's wife, as יהוה hath spoken."

52 And it came to pass, that, when Avraham's servant heard their words, he worshipped יהוה, bowing himself to the earth.

53 And the servant brought forth jewels of silver, and jewels of gold, and raiment, and gave them to Rebekah; he gave also to her brother and to her mother precious things.

54 And they did eat and drink, he and the men that were with him, and tarried all night; and they rose up in the morning, and he said, "Send me away unto my master."

55 And her brother and her mother said, "Let the damsel abide with us a few days, at the least ten; after that she shall go."

56 And he said unto them, "Hinder me not,

seeing יהוה hath prospered my way; send me away that I may go to my master."

57 And they said, "We will call the damsel, and enquire at her mouth."

58 And they called Rebekah, and said unto her, "Wilt you go with this man?" And she said, "I will go."

59 And they sent away Rebekah their sister, and her nurse, and Avraham's servant, and his men.

60 And they blessed Rebekah, and said unto her, "You are our sister, be you the mother of thousands of millions, and let your seed possess the gate of those which hate them."

61 And Rebekah arose, and her damsels, and they rode upon the camels, and followed the man; and the servant took Rebekah, and went his way.

62 And Isaac (Yitschaq) came from the way of the well Lahai-Roi; for he dwelt in the south country.

63 And Isaac (Yitschaq) went out to meditate in the field at the eventide; and he lifted up his eyes, and saw, and, behold, the camels were coming.

64 And Rebekah lifted up her eyes, and when she saw Isaac (Yitschaq), she lighted off the camel.

65 For she had said unto the servant, "What man is this that walketh in the field to meet us?" And the servant had said, "It is my master." Therefore she took a vail, and covered herself.

66 And the servant told Isaac (Yitschaq) all things that he had done.

67 And Isaac (Yitschaq) brought her into his mother Sarah's tent, and took Rebekah, and she became his wife; and he loved her. And Isaac (Yitschaq) was comforted after his mother's death.

25 Then again Avraham took a wife, and her name was Keturah.

2 And she bare him Zimran, and Yokshan, and Medan, and Midian, and Ishbak, and Shuah.

3 And Yokshan begat Sheva, and Dedan. And the sons of Dedan were Asshurim, and Letushim, and Leummim.

4 And the sons of Midian: Ephah, and Epher, and Hanoch, and Abida, and Eldaah. All these were the children of Keturah.

5 And Avraham gave all that he had unto Isaac (Yitschaq).

6 But unto the sons of the concubines, which Avraham had, Avraham gave gifts, and sent them away from Isaac (Yitschaq) his son, while he yet lived, eastward, unto the east country.

7 And these are the days of the years of Avraham's life which he lived, a hundred threescore and fifteen years.

8 Then Avraham gave up the spirit, and died in a good old age, an old man, and full of years; and was gathered to his people.

9 And his sons Isaac (Yitschaq) and Yishmael buried him in the cave of Machpelah, in the field of Ephron the son of Zohar the Hittite, which is before Mamre;

10 The field which Avraham purchased of the sons of Heth; there was Avraham buried, and Sarah his wife.

11 And it came to pass after the death of Avraham, that God (Elohim) blessed his son Isaac (Yitschaq); and Isaac (Yitschaq) dwelt by the well Lahairoi.

12 Now these are the generations of Yishmael, Avraham's son, whom Hagar the Egyptian (Mitsri), Sarah's handmaid, bare unto Avraham.

13 And these are the names of the sons of Yishmael, by their names, according to their generations: the firstborn of Yishmael, Nevayot; and Kedar, and Adbeel, and Mibsam,

14 And Mishma, and Dumah, and Massa,

15 Hadar, and Tema, Yetur, Naphish, and Kedemah:

16 These are the sons of Yishmael, and these are their names, by their towns, and by their castles; twelve princes according to their nations.

17 And these are the years of the life of Yishmael, a hundred and thirty and seven years; and he gave up the spirit and died; and was gathered unto his people.

18 And they dwelt from Havilah unto Shur, that is before Egypt (Mitsrayim), as you goest toward Assyria (Ashshur); and he died in the presence of all his brethren.

19 And these are the generations of Isaac (Yitschaq), Avraham's son: Avraham begat Isaac (Yitschaq).

20 And Isaac (Yitschaq) was forty years old when he took Rebekah to wife, the daughter of Bethuel the Arammi (Syrian) of Padanaram, the sister to Lavan the Arammi (Syrian).

21 And Isaac (Yitschaq) intreated יהוה for his wife, because she was barren: and יהוה was intreated of him, and Rebekah his wife

conceived.

22 And the children struggled together within her; and she said, "If it be so, why am I thus?" And she went to enquire of יהוה.

23 And יהוה said unto her, "Two nations are in your womb, and two manner of people shall be separated from your bowels; and the one people shall be stronger than the other people; and the elder shall serve the younger."

24 And when her days to be delivered were fulfilled, behold, there were twins in her womb.

25 And the first came out red, all over like a hairy garment; and they called his name [A13]Esaw.

26 And after that came his brother out, and his hand took hold on Esaw's heel; and his name was called [A14]Jacob (Yaaqov); and Isaac (Yitschaq) was threescore years old when she bare them.

27 And the boys grew; and Esaw was a cunning hunter, a man of the field; and Jacob (Yaaqov) was a plain man, dwelling in tents.

28 And Isaac (Yitschaq) loved Esaw, because he did eat of his venison; but Rebekah loved Jacob (Yaaqov).

29 And Jacob (Yaaqov) cooked pottage; and Esaw came from the field, and he was faint.

30 And Esaw said to Jacob (Yaaqov), "Please feed me with that same red pottage; for I am faint"; therefore was his name called Edom.

31 And Jacob (Yaaqov) said, "Sell me this day your birthright."

32 And Esaw said, "Behold, I am at the point to die; and what profit shall this birthright do to me?"

33 And Jacob (Yaaqov) said, "Swear to me this day"; and he sware unto him; and he sold his birthright unto Jacob (Yaaqov).

34 Then Jacob (Yaaqov) gave Esaw bread and pottage of lentiles; and he did eat and drink, and rose up, and went his way. Thus Esaw despised his birthright.

26 And there was a famine in the land, beside the first famine that was in the days of Avraham. And Isaac (Yitschaq) went unto Abimelech (Avimelekh) king of the Philistines unto Gerar.

2 And יהוה appeared unto him, and said, "Go not down into Egypt (Mitsrayim); dwell in the land which I shall tell you of.

3 Sojourn in this land, and I will be with you, and will bless you; for unto you, and unto your seed, I will give all these countries, and I will perform the oath which I sware unto Avraham your father;

4 And I will make your seed to multiply as the stars of heaven, and will give unto your seed all these countries; and in your seed shall all the nations of the earth be blessed;

5 Because that Avraham obeyed My voice, and kept My charge, My commandments, My statutes, and My laws."

6 And Isaac (Yitschaq) dwelt in Gerar.

7 And the men of the place asked him of his wife; and he said, "She is my sister: for he feared to say, "She is my wife; lest," said he, "the men of the place should kill me for Rebekah, because she was fair to look upon."

8 And it came to pass, when he had been there a long time, that Abimelech (Avimelekh) king of the Philistines looked out at a window, and saw, and, behold, Isaac (Yitschaq) was sporting with Rebekah his wife.

9 And Abimelech (Avimelekh) called Isaac (Yitschaq), and said, "Behold, of a surety she is your wife; and how saidst you, 'She is my sister'?" And Isaac (Yitschaq) said unto him, "Because I said, 'Lest I die for her.'"

10 And Abimelech (Avimelekh) said, "What is this you have done unto us? One of the people might lightly have lien with your wife, and you shouldest have brought guiltiness upon us."

11 And Abimelech (Avimelekh) charged all his people, saying, "He that toucheth this man or his wife shall surely be put to death."

12 Then Isaac (Yitschaq) sowed in that land, and received in the same year a hundredfold; and יהוה blessed him.

13 And the man waxed great, and went forward, and grew until he became very great;

14 For he had possession of flocks, and possession of herds, and great store of servants; and the Philistines envied him.

15 For all the wells which his father's servants had digged in the days of Avraham his father, the Philistines had stopped them, and filled them with earth.

16 And Abimelech (Avimelekh) said unto Isaac (Yitschaq), "Go from us; for you are much mightier than we."

17 And Isaac (Yitschaq) departed thence, and pitched his tent in the valley of Gerar, and dwelt

there.

18 And Isaac (Yitschaq) digged again the wells of water, which they had digged in the days of Avraham his father; for the Philistines had stopped them after the death of Avraham; and he called their names after the names by which his father had called them.

19 And Isaac (Yitschaq)'s servants digged in the valley, and found there a well of springing water.

20 And the herdmen of Gerar did strive with Isaac (Yitschaq)'s herdmen, saying, "The water is ours." And he called the name of the well Esek, because they strove with him.

21 And they digged another well, and strove for that also; and he called the name of it Sitnah.

22 And he removed from thence, and digged another well; and for that they strove not: and he called the name of it Rehoboth; and he said, "For now יהוה hath made room for us, and we shall be fruitful in the land."

23 And he went up from thence to Beer-Sheva.

24 And יהוה appeared unto him the same night, and said, "I am the God (Elohim) of Avraham your father; fear not, for I am with you, and will bless you, and multiply your seed for My servant Avraham's sake."

25 And he builded an altar there, and called upon the name of יהוה, and pitched his tent there; and there Isaac (Yitschaq)'s servants digged a well.

26 Then Abimelech (Avimelekh) went to him from Gerar, and Ahuzzath one of his friends, and Phichol the chief captain of his army.

27 And Isaac (Yitschaq) said unto them, "Wherefore come you to me, seeing you hate me, and have sent me away from you?"

28 And they said, "We saw certainly that יהוה was with you; and we said, 'Let there be now an oath betwixt us, even betwixt us and you, and let us make a covenant with you;

29 That you wilt do us no hurt, as we have not touched you, and as we have done unto you nothing but good, and have sent you away in peace. You are now the blessed of יהוה.'"

30 And he made them a feast, and they did eat and drink.

31 And they rose up betimes in the morning, and sware one to another: and Isaac (Yitschaq) sent them away, and they departed from him in peace.

32 And it came to pass the same day, that Isaac (Yitschaq)'s servants came, and told him concerning the well which they had digged, and said unto him, "We have found water."

33 And he called it Shevah. Therefore the name of the city is Beer-Sheva unto this day.

34 And Esaw was forty years old when he took to wife Yudit the daughter of Beeri the Hittite, and Bashemath the daughter of Elon the Hittite;

35 Which were a grief of mind unto Isaac (Yitschaq) and to Rebekah.

27 And it came to pass, that when Isaac (Yitschaq) was old, and his eyes were dim, so that he could not see, he called Esaw his eldest son, and said unto him, "My son"; and he said unto him, "Behold, here am I."

2 And he said, "Behold now, I am old, I know not the day of my death.

3 Now therefore please take your weapons, your quiver and your bow, and go out to the field, and take me some venison;

4 And make me savoury meat, such as I love, and bring it to me, that I may eat; that my soul may bless you before I die."

5 And Rebekah heard when Isaac (Yitschaq) spake to Esaw his son. And Esaw went to the field to hunt for venison, and to bring it.

6 And Rebekah spake unto Jacob (Yaaqov) her son, saying, "Behold, I heard your father speak unto Esaw your brother, saying,

7 'Bring me venison, and make me savoury meat, that I may eat, and bless you before יהוה before my death.'

8 Now therefore, my son, obey my voice according to that which I command you.

9 Go now to the flock, and fetch me from thence two good kids of the goats; and I will make them savoury meat for your father, such as he loveth;

10 And you shalt bring it to your father, that he may eat, and that he may bless you before his death."

11 And Jacob (Yaaqov) said to Rebekah his mother, "Behold, Esaw my brother is a hairy man, and I am a smooth man.

12 My father perhaps will feel me, and I shall seem to him as a deceiver; and I shall bring a curse upon me, and not a blessing."

13 And his mother said unto him, "Upon me be your curse, my son; only obey my voice, and go fetch me them."

14 And he went, and fetched, and brought them to his mother: and his mother made savoury meat, such as his father loved.

15 And Rebekah took goodly raiment of her eldest son Esaw, which were with her in the house, and put them upon Jacob (Yaaqov) her younger son:

16 And she put the skins of the kids of the goats upon his hands, and upon the smooth of his neck.

17 And she gave the savoury meat and the bread, which she had prepared, into the hand of her son Jacob (Yaaqov).

18 And he came unto his father, and said, "My father"; and he said, "Here am I; who are you, my son?"

19 And Jacob (Yaaqov) said unto his father, "I am Esaw your firstborn; I have done according as you badest me; please arise, sit and eat of my venison, that your soul may bless me."

20 And Isaac (Yitschaq) said unto his son, "How is it that you have found it so quickly, my son?" And he said, "Because ᴮ¹¹יהוה your God (YHWH Eloheikha) brought it to me."

21 And Isaac (Yitschaq) said unto Jacob (Yaaqov), "Please come near that I may feel you, my son, whether you be my very son Esaw or not."

22 And Jacob (Yaaqov) went near unto Isaac (Yitschaq) his father; and he felt him, and said, "The voice is Jacob (Yaaqov)'s voice, but the hands are the hands of Esaw."

23 And he discerned him not, because his hands were hairy, as his brother Esaw's hands; so he blessed him.

24 And he said, "Are you my very son Esaw?" And he said, "I am."

25 And he said, "Bring it near to me, and I will eat of my son's venison, that my soul may bless you." And he brought it near to him, and he did eat; and he brought him wine, and he drank.

26 And his father Isaac (Yitschaq) said unto him, "Come near now, and kiss me, my son."

27 And he came near, and kissed him; and he smelled the smell of his raiment, and blessed him, and said, "See, the smell of my son is as the smell of a field which יהוה hath blessed.

28 Therefore God (Elohim) give you of the dew of heaven, and the fatness of the earth, and plenty of corn and wine.

29 Let people serve you, and nations bow down to you; be lord (gevir) over your brethren, and let your mother's sons bow down to you. Cursed be every one that curseth you, and blessed be he that blesseth you."

30 And it came to pass, as soon as Isaac (Yitschaq) had made an end of blessing Jacob (Yaaqov), and Jacob (Yaaqov) was yet scarce gone out from the presence of Isaac (Yitschaq) his father, that Esaw his brother came in from his hunting.

31 And he also had made savoury meat, and brought it unto his father, and said unto his father, "Let my father arise, and eat of his son's venison, that your soul may bless me."

32 And Isaac (Yitschaq) his father said unto him, "Who are you?" And he said, "I am your son, your firstborn Esaw."

33 And Isaac (Yitschaq) trembled very exceedingly, and said, "Who? Where is he that hath taken venison, and brought it me, and I have eaten of all before you camest, and have blessed him? Yea, and he shall be blessed."

34 And when Esaw heard the words of his father, he cried with a great and exceeding bitter cry, and said unto his father, "Bless me, even me also, O my father."

35 And he said, "Your brother came with subtilty, and hath taken away your blessing."

36 And he said, "Is not he rightly named Jacob (Yaaqov)? For he hath supplanted me these two times: he took away my birthright; and, behold, now he hath taken away my blessing." And he said, "Have you not reserved a blessing for me?"

37 And Isaac (Yitschaq) answered and said unto Esaw, "Behold, I have made him your lord (gevir), and all his brethren have I given to him for servants; and with corn and wine have I sustained him; and what shall I do now unto you, my son?"

38 And Esaw said unto his father, "Have you but one blessing, my father? Bless me, even me also, O my father." And Esaw lifted up his voice, and wept.

39 And Isaac (Yitschaq) his father answered and said unto him, "Behold, your dwelling shall be the fatness of the earth, and of the dew of heaven from above;

40 And by your sword shalt you live, and shalt serve your brother; and it shall come to pass when you shalt have the dominion, that you shalt break his yoke from off your neck."

41 And Esaw hated Jacob (Yaaqov) because of the blessing wherewith his father blessed him; and Esaw said in his heart, "The days of mourning for my father are at hand; then will I slay my brother Jacob (Yaaqov)."

42 And these words of Esaw her elder son were told to Rebekah; and she sent and called Jacob (Yaaqov) her younger son, and said unto him, "Behold, your brother Esaw, as touching you, doth comfort himself, purposing to kill you.

43 Now therefore, my son, obey my voice; and arise, flee you to Lavan my brother to Haran;

44 And tarry with him a few days, until your brother's fury turns away;

45 Until your brother's anger turns away from you, and he forget that which you have done to him; then I will send, and fetch you from thence. Why should I be deprived also of you both in one day?"

46 And Rebekah said to Isaac (Yitschaq), "I am weary of my life because of the daughters of Heth; if Jacob (Yaaqov) take a wife of the daughters of Heth, such as these which are of the daughters of the land, what good shall my life do me?"

28 And Isaac (Yitschaq) called Jacob (Yaaqov), and blessed him, and charged him, and said unto him, "You shalt not take a wife of the daughters of Canaan.

2 Arise, go to Padanaram, to the house of Bethuel your mother's father; and take you a wife from thence of the daughters of Lavan your mother's brother.

3 And Almighty God (El Shaddai) bless you, and make you fruitful, and multiply you, that you mayest be a multitude of people;

4 And give you the blessing of Avraham, to you, and to your seed with you; that you mayest inherit the land wherein you are a stranger, which God (Elohim) gave unto Avraham."

5 And Isaac (Yitschaq) sent away Jacob (Yaaqov); and he went to Padanaram unto Lavan, son of Bethuel the Syrian (Arammi), the brother of Rebekah, Jacob (Yaaqov)'s and Esaw's mother.

6 When Esaw saw that Isaac (Yitschaq) had blessed Jacob (Yaaqov), and sent him away to Padanaram, to take him a wife from thence; and that as he blessed him he gave him a charge, saying, "You shalt not take a wife of the daughters of Canaan";

7 And that Jacob (Yaaqov) obeyed his father and his mother, and was gone to Padanaram;

8 And Esaw seeing that the daughters of Canaan pleased not Isaac (Yitschaq) his father;

9 Then went Esaw unto Yishmael, and took unto the wives which he had Mahalath the daughter of Yishmael Avraham's son, the sister of Nebajoth, to be his wife.

10 And Jacob (Yaaqov) went out from Beer-Sheva, and went toward Haran.

11 And he lighted upon a certain place, and tarried there all night, because the sun was set; and he took of the stones of that place, and put them for his pillows, and lay down in that place to sleep.

12 And he dreamed, and behold a ladder set up on the earth, and the top of it reached to heaven; and behold the angels of God (Elohim) ascending and descending on it.

13 And, behold, יהוה stood above it, and said, "I am יהוה God (Elohim) of Avraham your father, and the God (Elohim) of Isaac (Yitschaq); the land whereon you liest, to you will I give it, and to your seed;

14 And your seed shall be as the dust of the earth, and you shalt spread abroad to the west, and to the east, and to the north, and to the south: and in you and in your seed shall all the families of the earth be blessed.

15 And, behold, I am with you, and will keep you in all places whither you goest, and will bring you again into this land; for I will not leave you, until I have done that which I have spoken to you of."

16 And Jacob (Yaaqov) awaked out of his sleep, and he said, "Surely יהוה is in this place; and I knew it not."

17 And he was afraid, and said, "How dreadful is this place! This is none other but the house of God (Elohim), and this is the gate of heaven.

18 And Jacob (Yaaqov) rose up early in the morning, and took the stone that he had put for his pillows, and set it up for a pillar, and poured oil upon the top of it.

19 And he called the name of that place Bethel (Beit-El); but the name of that city was called Luz at the first.

20 And Jacob (Yaaqov) vowed a vow, saying, "If God (Elohim) will be with me, and will keep me in this way that I go, and will give me bread to eat, and raiment to put on,

21 So that I come again to my father's house in peace; then shall יהוה be my God (Elohim).

22 And this stone, which I have set for a pillar, shall be God (Elohim)'s house; and of all that you shalt give me I will surely give the tenth unto You."

29 Then Jacob (Yaaqov) went on his journey, and came into the land of the people of the east.

2 And he looked, and behold a well in the field, and, behold, there were three flocks of sheep lying by it; for out of that well they watered the flocks: and a great stone was upon the well's mouth.

3 And thither were all the flocks gathered; and they rolled the stone from the well's mouth, and watered the sheep, and put the stone again upon the well's mouth in his place.

4 And Jacob (Yaaqov) said unto them, "My brethren, whence be you?" And they said, "Of Haran are we."

5 And he said unto them, "Know you Lavan the son of Nahor?" And they said, "We know him."

6 And he said unto them, "Is he well?" And they said, "He is well"; and, behold, Rachel his daughter cometh with the sheep.

7 And he said, "Behold, it is yet high day, neither is it time that the cattle should be gathered together; water you the sheep, and go and feed them."

8 And they said, "We cannot, until all the flocks be gathered together, and till they roll the stone from the well's mouth; then we water the sheep."

9 And while he yet spake with them, Rachel came with her father's sheep; for she kept them.

10 And it came to pass, when Jacob (Yaaqov) saw Rachel the daughter of Lavan his mother's brother, and the sheep of Lavan his mother's brother, that Jacob (Yaaqov) went near, and rolled the stone from the well's mouth, and watered the flock of Lavan his mother's brother.

11 And Jacob (Yaaqov) kissed Rachel, and lifted up his voice, and wept.

12 And Jacob (Yaaqov) told Rachel that he was her father's brother, and that he was Rebekah's son; and she ran and told her father.

13 And it came to pass, when Lavan heard the tidings of Jacob (Yaaqov) his sister's son, that he ran to meet him, and embraced him, and kissed him, and brought him to his house. And he told Lavan all these things.

14 And Lavan said to him, "Surely you are my bone and my flesh." And he aboded with him the space of a month.

15 And Lavan said unto Jacob (Yaaqov), "Because you are my brother, shouldest you therefore serve me for nought? Tell me, what shall your wages be?"

16 And Lavan had two daughters: the name of the elder was Leah, and the name of the younger was Rachel.

17 Leah was tender eyed; but Rachel was beautiful and well favoured.

18 And Jacob (Yaaqov) loved Rachel; and said, "I will serve you seven years for Rachel your younger daughter."

19 And Lavan said, "It is better that I give her to you, than that I should give her to another man; abide with me."

20 And Jacob (Yaaqov) served seven years for Rachel; and they seemed unto him but a few days, for the love he had to her.

21 And Jacob (Yaaqov) said unto Lavan, "Give me my wife, for my days are fulfilled, that I may go in unto her."

22 And Lavan gathered together all the men of the place, and made a feast.

23 And it came to pass in the evening, that he took Leah his daughter, and brought her to him; and he went in unto her.

24 And Lavan gave unto his daughter Leah Zilpah his maid for a handmaid.

25 And it came to pass, that in the morning, behold, it was Leah; and he said to Lavan, "What is this you have done unto me? Did not I serve with you for Rachel? Wherefore then have you beguiled me?"

26 And Lavan said, "It must not be so done in our country, to give the younger before the firstborn.

27 Fulfil her week, and we will give you this also for the service which you shalt serve with me yet seven other years."

28 And Jacob (Yaaqov) did so, and fulfilled her week; and he gave him Rachel his daughter to wife also.

29 And Lavan gave to Rachel his daughter Bilhah his handmaid to be her maid.

30 And he went in also unto Rachel, and he loved also Rachel more than Leah, and served with him yet seven other years.

31 And when יהוה saw that Leah was hated, he

opened her womb; but Rachel was barren.

32 And Leah conceived, and bare a son, and she called his name [A16]Reuven; for she said, "Surely יהוה hath looked upon my affliction; now therefore my husband will love me."

33 And she conceived again, and bare a son; and said, "Because יהוה hath heard that I was hated, He hath therefore given me this son also"; and she called his name [A17]Shimon.

34 And she conceived again, and bare a son; and said, "Now this time will my husband be joined unto me, because I have born him three sons." Therefore was his name called [A18]Lewi.

35 And she conceived again, and bare a son; and she said, "Now will I praise יהוה"; therefore she called his name [A19]Judah (Yehudah); and left bearing.

30 And when Rachel saw that she bare Jacob (Yaaqov) no children, Rachel envied her sister; and said unto Jacob (Yaaqov), Give me children, or else I die.

2 And Jacob (Yaaqov)'s anger was kindled against Rachel; and he said, "Am I in God (Elohim)'s stead, who hath withheld from you the fruit of the womb?"

3 And she said, "Behold my maid Bilhah, go in unto her; and she shall bear upon my knees, that I may also have children by her."

4 And she gave him Bilhah her handmaid to wife; and Jacob (Yaaqov) went in unto her.

5 And Bilhah conceived, and bare Jacob (Yaaqov) a son.

6 And Rachel said, "God (Elohim) hath judged me, and hath also heard my voice, and hath given me a son." Therefore called she his name [A20]Dan.

7 And Bilhah Rachel's maid conceived again, and bare Jacob (Yaaqov) a second son.

8 And Rachel said, "With great wrestlings have I wrestled with my sister, and I have prevailed." And she called his name [A21]Naftali.

9 When Leah saw that she had left bearing, she took Zilpah her maid, and gave her Jacob (Yaaqov) to wife.

10 And Zilpah Leah's maid bare Jacob (Yaaqov) a son.

11 And Leah said, "A troop cometh!" And she called his name [A22]Gad.

12 And Zilpah Leah's maid bare Jacob (Yaaqov) a second son.

13 And Leah said, "Happy am I, for the daughters will call me blessed." And she called his name [A23]Asher.

14 And Reuven went in the days of wheat harvest, and found mandrakes in the field, and brought them unto his mother Leah. Then Rachel said to Leah, "Please give me of your son's mandrakes."

15 And she said unto her, "Is it a small matter that you have taken my husband? And wouldest you take away my son's mandrakes also?" And Rachel said, "Therefore he shall lie with you tonight for your son's mandrakes."

16 And Jacob (Yaaqov) came out of the field in the evening, and Leah went out to meet him, and said, "You must come in unto me; for surely I have hired you with my son's mandrakes." And he lay with her that night.

17 And God (Elohim) hearkened unto Leah, and she conceived, and bare Jacob (Yaaqov) the fifth son.

18 And Leah said, "God (Elohim) hath given me my hire, because I have given my maiden to my husband." And she called his name [A24]Issachar (Yissaskhar).

19 And Leah conceived again, and bare Jacob (Yaaqov) the sixth son.

20 And Leah said, "God (Elohim) hath endued me with a good dowry; now will my husband dwell with me, because I have born him six sons." And she called his name [A25]Zevulun.

21 And afterwards she bare a daughter, and called her name Dinah.

22 And God (Elohim) remembered Rachel, and God (Elohim) hearkened to her, and opened her womb.

23 And she conceived, and bare a son; and said, "God (Elohim) hath taken away my reproach."

24 And she called his name [A26]Joseph (Yosef); and said, "יהוה shall add to me another son."

25 And it came to pass, when Rachel had born Joseph (Yosef), that Jacob (Yaaqov) said unto Lavan, "Send me away, that I may go unto mine own place, and to my country.

26 Give me my wives and my children, for whom I have served you, and let me go; for you knowest my service which I have done you."

27 And Lavan said unto him, "Please, if I have found favor in your eyes, tarry; for I have learned by experience that יהוה hath blessed me for your sake."

28 And he said, "Appoint me your wages, and

I will give it."

29 And he said unto him, "You knowest how I have served you, and how your cattle was with me.

30 For it was little which you hadst before I came, and it is now increased unto a multitude; and יהוה hath blessed you since my coming: and now when shall I provide for mine own house also?"

31 And he said, "What shall I give you?" And Jacob (Yaaqov) said, "You shalt not give me any thing; if you wilt do this thing for me, I will again feed and keep your flock.

32 I will pass through all your flock today, removing from thence all the speckled and spotted cattle, and all the brown cattle among the sheep, and the spotted and speckled among the goats; and of such shall be my hire.

33 So shall my righteousness answer for me in time to come, when it shall come for my hire before your face: every one that is not speckled and spotted among the goats, and brown among the sheep, that shall be counted stolen with me."

34 And Lavan said, "Behold, I would it might be according to your word."

35 And he removed that day the he goats that were ringstraked and spotted, and all the she goats that were speckled and spotted, and every one that had some white in it, and all the brown among the sheep, and gave them into the hand of his sons.

36 And he set three days' journey betwixt himself and Jacob (Yaaqov); and Jacob (Yaaqov) fed the rest of Lavan's flocks.

37 And Jacob (Yaaqov) took him rods of green poplar, and of the hazel and chesnut tree; and pilled white strakes in them, and made the white appear which was in the rods.

38 And he set the rods which he had pilled before the flocks in the gutters in the watering troughs when the flocks came to drink, that they should conceive when they came to drink.

39 And the flocks conceived before the rods, and brought forth cattle ringstraked, speckled, and spotted.

40 And Jacob (Yaaqov) did separate the lambs, and set the faces of the flocks toward the ringstraked, and all the brown in the flock of Lavan; and he put his own flocks by themselves, and put them not unto Lavan's cattle.

41 And it came to pass, whensoever the stronger cattle did conceive, that Jacob (Yaaqov) laid the rods before the eyes of the cattle in the gutters, that they might conceive among the rods.

42 But when the cattle were feeble, he put them not in; so the feebler were Lavan's, and the stronger Jacob (Yaaqov)'s.

43 And the man increased exceedingly, and had much cattle, and maidservants, and menservants, and camels, and asses.

31 And he heard the words of Lavan's sons, saying, Jacob (Yaaqov) hath taken away all that was our father's; and of that which was our father's hath he gotten all this glory.

2 And Jacob (Yaaqov) beheld the countenance of Lavan, and, behold, it was not toward him as before.

3 And יהוה said unto Jacob (Yaaqov), "Return unto the land of your fathers, and to your kindred; and I will be with you."

4 And Jacob (Yaaqov) sent and called Rachel and Leah to the field unto his flock,

5 And said unto them, "I see your father's countenance, that it is not toward me as before; but the God (Elohim) of my father hath been with me.

6 And you know that with all my power I have served your father.

7 And your father hath deceived me, and changed my wages ten times; but God (Elohim) suffered him not to hurt me.

8 If he said thus: 'The speckled shall be your wages;' then all the cattle bare speckled; and if he said thus: 'The ringstraked shall be your hire;' then bare all the cattle ringstraked.

9 Thus God (Elohim) hath taken away the cattle of your father, and given them to me.

10 And it came to pass at the time that the cattle conceived, that I lifted up mine eyes, and saw in a dream, and, behold, the rams which leaped upon the cattle were ringstraked, speckled, and grisled.

11 And the angel of God (Elohim) spake unto me in a dream, saying, 'Jacob (Yaaqov).' And I said, 'Here am I.'

12 And he said, 'Lift up now your eyes, and see, all the rams which leap upon the cattle are ringstraked, speckled, and grisled; for I have seen all that Lavan doeth unto you.

13 I am the God (Elohim) of Bethel (Beit-El), where you anointedst the pillar, and where you vowedst a vow unto me. Now arise, get you out

from this land, and return unto the land of your kindred.'"

14 And Rachel and Leah answered and said unto him, "Is there yet any portion or inheritance for us in our father's house?

15 Are we not counted of him strangers? for he hath sold us, and hath quite devoured also our money.

16 For all the riches which God (Elohim) hath taken from our father, that is ours, and our children's; now then, whatsoever God (Elohim) hath said unto you, do."

17 Then Jacob (Yaaqov) rose up, and set his sons and his wives upon camels;

18 And he carried away all his cattle, and all his goods which he had gotten, the cattle of his getting, which he had gotten in Padanaram, for to go to Isaac (Yitschaq) his father in the land of Canaan.

19 And Lavan went to shear his sheep; and Rachel had stolen the images that were her father's.

20 And Jacob (Yaaqov) stole away unawares to Lavan the Arammi (Syrian), in that he told him not that he fled.

21 So he fled with all that he had; and he rose up, and passed over the river, and set his face toward the mount Gilad.

22 And it was told Lavan on the third day that Jacob (Yaaqov) was fled.

23 And he took his brethren with him, and pursued after him seven days' journey; and they overtook him in the mount Gilad.

24 And God (Elohim) came to Lavan the Arammi (Syrian) in a dream by night, and said unto him, "Take heed that you speak not to Jacob (Yaaqov) either good or bad."

25 Then Lavan overtook Jacob (Yaaqov). Now Jacob (Yaaqov) had pitched his tent in the mountain; and Lavan with his brethren pitched in the mount of Gilad.

26 And Lavan said to Jacob (Yaaqov), "What have you done, that you have stolen away unawares to me, and carried away my daughters, as captives taken with the sword?

27 Wherefore didst you flee away secretly, and steal away from me; and didst not tell me, that I might have sent you away with mirth, and with songs, with tabret, and with harp?

28 And hast not suffered me to kiss my sons and my daughters? You have now done foolishly in

so doing.

29 It is in the power of my hand to do you hurt; but the God (Elohim) of your father spake unto me yesternight, saying, 'Take you heed that you speak not to Jacob (Yaaqov) either good or bad.'

30 And now, though you wouldest needs be gone, because you sore longedst after your father's house, yet wherefore have you stolen my gods (B1belohim)?"

31 And Jacob (Yaaqov) answered and said to Lavan, "Because I was afraid: for I said, 'Perhaps you wouldest take by force your daughters from me.'

32 With whomsoever you findest your gods (elohim), let him not live; before our brethren discern you what is your with me, and take it to you." For Jacob (Yaaqov) knew not that Rachel had stolen them.

33 And Lavan went into Jacob (Yaaqov)'s tent, and into Leah's tent, and into the two maidservants' tents; but he found them not. Then went he out of Leah's tent, and entered into Rachel's tent.

34 Now Rachel had taken the images, and put them in the camel's furniture, and sat upon them. And Lavan searched all the tent, but found them not.

35 And she said to her father, "Let it not displease my lord (adoni) that I cannot rise up before you; for the custom of women is upon me." And he searched, but found not the images.

36 And Jacob (Yaaqov) was wroth, and chode with Lavan; and Jacob (Yaaqov) answered and said to Lavan: "What is my trespass? What is my sin, that you have so hotly pursued after me?

37 Whereas you have searched all my stuff, what have you found of all your household stuff? set it here before my brethren and your brethren, that they may judge betwixt us both!

38 These twenty years have I been with you; your ewes and your she goats have not cast their young, and the rams of your flock have I not eaten.

39 That which was torn of beasts I brought not unto you; I bare the loss of it; of my hand didst you require it, whether stolen by day, or stolen by night.

40 Thus I was; in the day the drought consumed me, and the frost by night; and my sleep departed from mine eyes.

41 Thus have I been twenty years in your

house; I served you fourteen years for your two daughters, and six years for your cattle; and you have changed my wages ten times.

42 Except the God (Elohim) of my father, the God (Elohim) of Avraham, and the fear of Isaac (Yitschaq), had been with me, surely you hadst sent me away now empty. God (Elohim) hath seen mine affliction and the labour of my hands, and rebuked you yesternight."

43 And Lavan answered and said unto Jacob (Yaaqov), "These daughters are my daughters, and these children are my children, and these cattle are my cattle, and all that you seest is mine; and what can I do this day unto these my daughters, or unto their children which they have born?

44 Now therefore come you, let us make a covenant, I and you; and let it be for a witness between me and you."

45 And Jacob (Yaaqov) took a stone, and set it up for a pillar.

46 And Jacob (Yaaqov) said unto his brethren, "Gather stones;" and they took stones, and made a heap; and they did eat there upon the heap.

47 And Lavan called it Yegarsahaduta, but Jacob (Yaaqov) called it Galeed.

48 And Lavan said, "This heap is a witness between me and you this day. Therefore was the name of it called Galeed,

49 And Mizpah; for he said, 'יהוה watch between me and you, when we are absent one from another.

50 If you shalt afflict my daughters, or if you shalt take other wives besides my daughters, no man is with us; see, God (Elohim) is witness betwixt me and you."

51 And Lavan said to Jacob (Yaaqov), "Behold this heap, and behold this pillar, which I have cast betwixt me and you;

52 This heap be witness, and this pillar be witness, that I will not pass over this heap to you, and that you shalt not pass over this heap and this pillar unto me, for harm.

53 The God (Elohim) of Avraham, and the God (Elohim) of Nahor, the God (Elohim) of their father, judge betwixt us." And Jacob (Yaaqov) sware by the fear of his father Isaac (Yitschaq).

54 Then Jacob (Yaaqov) offered sacrifice upon the mount, and called his brethren to eat bread; and they did eat bread, and tarried all night in the mountain.

55 And early in the morning Lavan rose up, and kissed his sons and his daughters, and blessed them; and Lavan departed, and returned unto his place.

32 And Jacob (Yaaqov) went on his way, and the angels of God (Elohim) met him.

2 And when Jacob (Yaaqov) saw them, he said, "This is God (Elohim)'s host." And he called the name of that place Mahanaim.

3 And Jacob (Yaaqov) sent messengers before him to Esaw his brother unto the land of Seir, the country of Edom.

4 And he commanded them, saying, "Thus shall you speak unto my lord (adoni) Esaw: 'Your servant Jacob (Yaaqov) saith thus, I have sojourned with Lavan, and stayed there until now.

5 And I have oxen, and asses, flocks, and menservants, and womenservants: and I have sent to tell my lord (adoni), that I may find grace in your sight.'"'

6 And the messengers returned to Jacob (Yaaqov), saying, "We came to your brother Esaw, and also he cometh to meet you, and four hundred men with him."

7 Then Jacob (Yaaqov) was greatly afraid and distressed; and he divided the people that was with him, and the flocks, and herds, and the camels, into two bands;

8 And said, "If Esaw come to the one company, and smite it, then the other company which is left shall escape."

9 And Jacob (Yaaqov) said, "O God (Elohim) of my father Avraham, and God (Elohim) of my father Isaac (Yitschaq), יהוה which saidst unto me, 'Return unto your country, and to your kindred, and I will deal well with you':

10 I am not worthy of the least of all the mercies, and of all the truth, which you have shewed unto your servant; for with my staff I passed over this Jordan (Yarden); and now I am become two bands.

11 Deliver me, please, from the hand of my brother, from the hand of Esaw; for I fear him, lest he will come and smite me, and the mother with the children.

12 And you saidst, 'I will surely do you good, and make your seed as the sand of the sea, which cannot be numbered for multitude.'"

13 And he lodged there that same night; and took of that which came to his hand a present

for Esaw his brother:

14 Two hundred she goats, and twenty he goats, two hundred ewes, and twenty rams,

15 Thirty milch camels with their colts, forty kine, and ten bulls, twenty she asses, and ten foals.

16 And he delivered them into the hand of his servants, every drove by themselves; and said unto his servants, "Pass over before me, and put a space betwixt drove and drove."

17 And he commanded the foremost, saying, "When Esaw my brother meeteth you, and asketh you, saying, 'Whose are you? And whither goest you? And whose are these before you?'

18 Then you shalt say, 'They be your servant Jacob (Yaaqov)'s; it is a present sent unto my lord (adoni) Esaw; and, behold, also he is behind us.'"

19 And so commanded he the second, and the third, and all that followed the droves, saying, "On this manner shall you speak unto Esaw, when you find him.

20 And say you moreover, 'Behold, your servant Jacob (Yaaqov) is behind us.' For he said, "I will appease him with the present that goeth before me, and afterward I will see his face; perhaps he will accept of me."

21 So went the present over before him; and himself lodged that night in the company.

22 And he rose up that night, and took his two wives, and his two womenservants, and his eleven sons, and passed over the ford Yabok.

23 And he took them, and sent them over the brook, and sent over that he had.

24 And Jacob (Yaaqov) was left alone; and there wrestled a man with him until the breaking of the day.

25 And when he saw that he prevailed not against him, he touched the hollow of his thigh; and the hollow of Jacob (Yaaqov)'s thigh was out of joint, as he wrestled with him.

26 And he said, "Let me go, for the day breaketh." And he said, "I will not let you go, except you bless me."

27 And he said unto him, "What is your name?" And he said, "Jacob (Yaaqov)."

28 And he said, "Your name shall be called no more Jacob (Yaaqov), but [A15]Yisrael; for as a prince have you power with God (Elohim) and with men, and hast prevailed."

29 And Jacob (Yaaqov) asked him, and said, "Tell me, please, your name." And he said, "Wherefore is it that you dost ask after my name?" And he blessed him there.

30 And Jacob (Yaaqov) called the name of the place Peniel; for I have seen God (Elohim) face to face, and my life is preserved.

31 And as he passed over Penuel the sun rose upon him, and he halted upon his thigh.

32 Therefore the children of Yisrael eat not of the sinew which shrank, which is upon the hollow of the thigh, unto this day; because he touched the hollow of Jacob (Yaaqov)'s thigh in the sinew that shrank.

33 And Jacob (Yaaqov) lifted up his eyes, and looked, and, behold, Esaw came, and with him four hundred men. And he divided the children unto Leah, and unto Rachel, and unto the two handmaids.

2 And he put the handmaids and their children foremost, and Leah and her children after, and Rachel and Joseph (Yosef) hindermost.

3 And he passed over before them, and bowed himself to the ground seven times, until he came near to his brother.

4 And Esaw ran to meet him, and embraced him, and fell on his neck, and kissed him; and they wept.

5 And he lifted up his eyes, and saw the women and the children; and said, "Who are those with you?" And he said, "The children which God (Elohim) hath graciously given your servant."

6 Then the handmaidens came near, they and their children, and they bowed themselves.

7 And Leah also with her children came near, and bowed themselves; and after came Joseph (Yosef) near and Rachel, and they bowed themselves.

8 And he said, "What meanest you by all this drove which I met?" And he said, "These are to find grace in the sight of my lord (adoni)."

9 And Esaw said, "I have enough, my brother; keep that you have unto yourself."

10 And Jacob (Yaaqov) said, "Nay, I please, if now I have found grace in your sight, then receive my present at my hand; for therefore I have seen your face, as though I had seen the face of God (Elohim), and you wast pleased with me.

11 Take, please, my blessing that is brought to you; because God (Elohim) hath dealt graciously

with me, and because I have enough." And he urged him, and he took it.

12 And he said, "Let us take our journey, and let us go, and I will go before you."

13 And he said unto him, "My lord (Adoni) knoweth that the children are tender, and the flocks and herds with young are with me; and if men should overdrive them one day, all the flock will die.

14 Please let my lord (adoni) pass over before his servant; and I will lead on softly, according as the cattle that goeth before me and the children be able to endure, until I come unto my lord (adoni) unto Seir."

15 And Esaw said, "Let me now leave with you some of the folk that are with me." And he said, "What needeth it? Let me find grace in the sight of my lord (adoni)."

16 So Esaw returned that day on his way unto Seir.

17 And Jacob (Yaaqov) journeyed to Sukkot, and built him a house, and made booths for his cattle; therefore the name of the place is called Succoth.

18 And Jacob (Yaaqov) came to Shalem, a city of Shechem, which is in the land of Canaan, when he came from Padanaram; and pitched his tent before the city.

19 And he bought a parcel of a field, where he had spread his tent, at the hand of the children of Hamor, Shechem's father, for a hundred pieces of money.

20 And he erected there an altar, and called it 'Mighty God of Yisrael (El Elohei Yisrael)'.

34 And Dinah the daughter of Leah, which she bare unto Jacob (Yaaqov), went out to see the daughters of the land.

2 And when Shechem the son of Hamor the Hivite, prince of the country, saw her, he took her, and lay with her, and defiled her.

3 And his soul clave unto Dinah the daughter of Jacob (Yaaqov), and he loved the damsel, and spake kindly unto the damsel.

4 And Shechem spake unto his father Hamor, saying, "Get me this damsel as wife."

5 And Jacob (Yaaqov) heard that he had defiled Dinah his daughter. Now his sons were with his cattle in the field; and Jacob (Yaaqov) held his peace until they were come.

6 And Hamor the father of Shechem went out unto Jacob (Yaaqov) to commune with him.

7 And the sons of Jacob (Yaaqov) came out of the field when they heard it; and the men were grieved, and they were very wroth, because he had wrought folly in Yisrael in lying with Jacob (Yaaqov)'s daughter; which thing ought not to be done.

8 And Hamor communed with them, saying, "The soul of my son Shechem longeth for your daughter; please give her him as wife.

9 And make you marriages with us, and give your daughters unto us, and take our daughters unto you.

10 And you shall dwell with us; and the land shall be before you; dwell and trade you therein, and get you possessions therein."

11 And Shechem said unto her father and unto her brethren, "Let me find grace in your eyes, and what you shall say unto me I will give.

12 Ask me never so much dowry and gift, and I will give according as you shall say unto me; but give me the damsel as wife."

13 And the sons of Jacob (Yaaqov) answered Shechem and Hamor his father deceitfully, and said, because he had defiled Dinah their sister.

14 And they said unto them, "We cannot do this thing, to give our sister to one that is uncircumcised; for that were a reproach unto us;

15 But in this will we consent unto you: If you will be as we be, that every male of you be circumcised,

16 Then will we give our daughters unto you, and we will take your daughters to us, and we will dwell with you, and we will become one people.

17 But if you will not hearken unto us, to be circumcised; then will we take our daughter, and we will be gone."

18 And their words pleased Hamor, and Shechem Hamor's son.

19 And the young man deferred not to do the thing, because he had delight in Jacob (Yaaqov)'s daughter; and he was more honourable than all the house of his father.

20 And Hamor and Shechem his son came unto the gate of their city, and communed with the men of their city, saying:

21 "These men are peaceable with us; therefore let them dwell in the land, and trade therein; for the land, behold, it is large enough for them; let us take their daughters to us for wives, and let us give them our daughters.

22 Only herein will the men consent unto us for to dwell with us, to be one people, if every male among us be circumcised, as they are circumcised.

23 Shall not their cattle and their substance and every beast of theirs be ours? Only let us consent unto them, and they will dwell with us."

24 And unto Hamor and unto Shechem his son hearkened all that went out of the gate of his city; and every male was circumcised, all that went out of the gate of his city.

25 And it came to pass on the third day, when they were sore, that two of the sons of Jacob (Yaaqov), Shimon and Lewi, Dinah's brethren, took each man his sword, and came upon the city boldly, and slew all the males.

26 And they slew Hamor and Shechem his son with the edge of the sword, and took Dinah out of Shechem's house, and went out.

27 The sons of Jacob (Yaaqov) came upon the slain, and spoiled the city, because they had defiled their sister.

28 They took their sheep, and their oxen, and their asses, and that which was in the city, and that which was in the field,

29 And all their wealth, and all their little ones, and their wives took they captive, and spoiled even all that was in the house.

30 And Jacob (Yaaqov) said to Shimon and Lewi, "You have troubled me to make me to stink among the inhabitants of the land, among the Canaanites and the Perizzites; and I being few in number, they shall gather themselves together against me, and slay me; and I shall be destroyed, I and my house."

31 And they said, "Should he deal with our sister as with a harlot?"

35 And God (Elohim) said unto Jacob (Yaaqov), "Arise, go up to Bethel (Beit-El), and dwell there; and make there an altar unto God (Elohim), that appeared unto you when you fleddest from the face of Esaw your brother."

2 Then Jacob (Yaaqov) said unto his household, and to all that were with him, "Put away the strange gods (elohim) that are among you, and be clean, and change your garments;

3 And let us arise, and go up to Bethel (Beit-El); and I will make there an altar unto God (Elohim), who answered me in the day of my distress, and was with me in the way which I went.

4 And they gave unto Jacob (Yaaqov) all the strange gods (elohim) which were in their hand, and all their earrings which were in their ears; and Jacob (Yaaqov) hid them under the oak which was by Shechem.

5 And they journeyed; and the terror of God (Elohim) was upon the cities that were round about them, and they did not pursue after the sons of Jacob (Yaaqov).

6 So Jacob (Yaaqov) came to Luz, which is in the land of Canaan, that is, Bethel (Beit-El), he and all the people that were with him.

7 And he built there an altar, and called the place El Beit-El; because there God (Elohim) appeared unto him, when he fled from the face of his brother.

8 But Deborah Rebekah's nurse died, and she was buried beneath Bethel (Beit-El) under an oak; and the name of it was called Allon Bakhut.

9 And God (Elohim) appeared unto Jacob (Yaaqov) again, when he came out of Padanaram, and blessed him.

10 And God (Elohim) said unto him, "Your name is Jacob (Yaaqov); your name shall not be called anymore Jacob (Yaaqov), but [A15]Yisrael shall be your name; and He called his name Yisrael.

11 And God (Elohim) said unto him, "I am Almighty God (El Shaddai); be fruitful and multiply; a nation and a company of nations shall be of you, and kings shall come out of your loins;

12 And the land which I gave Avraham and Isaac (Yitschaq), to you I will give it, and to your seed after you will I give the land."

13 And God (Elohim) went up from him in the place where He talked with him.

14 And Jacob (Yaaqov) set up a pillar in the place where He talked with him, even a pillar of stone; and he poured a drink offering thereon, and he poured oil thereon.

15 And Jacob (Yaaqov) called the name of the place where God (Elohim) spake with him, Bethel (Beit-El).

16 And they journeyed from Bethel (Beit-El); and there was but a little way to come to Ephrath; and Rachel travailed, and she had hard labour.

17 And it came to pass, when she was in hard labour, that the midwife said unto her, "Fear not; you shalt have this son also."

18 And it came to pass, as her soul was in departing, (for she died) that she called his name Benoni; but his father called him Binyamin.

19 And Rachel died, and was buried in the way to Ephrath, which is Bethlehem (Beit-Lechem).

20 And Jacob (Yaaqov) set a pillar upon her grave; that is the pillar of Rachel's grave unto this day.

21 And Yisrael journeyed, and spread his tent beyond the tower of Edar.

22 And it came to pass, when Yisrael dwelt in that land, that Reuven went and lay with Bilhah his father's concubine; and Yisrael heard it. Now the sons of Jacob (Yaaqov) were twelve:

23 The sons of Leah: Reuven, Jacob (Yaaqov)'s firstborn, and Shimon, and Lewi, and Judah (Yehudah), and Yissaskhar, and Zevulun;

24 The sons of Rachel: Joseph (Yosef), and A27Benjamin (Binyamin);

25 And the sons of Bilhah, Rachel's handmaid: Dan, and Naftali;

26 And the sons of Zilpah, Leah's handmaid: Gad, and Asher; these are the sons of Jacob (Yaaqov), who were born to him in Padanaram.

27 And Jacob (Yaaqov) came unto Isaac (Yitschaq) his father unto Mamre, unto the city of Arbah, which is Hebron, where Avraham and Isaac (Yitschaq) sojourned.

28 And the days of Isaac (Yitschaq) were a hundred and fourscore years.

29 And Isaac (Yitschaq) gave up the spirit, and died, and was gathered unto his people, being old and full of days; and his sons Esaw and Jacob (Yaaqov) buried him.

36 Now these are the generations of Esaw, who is Edom.

2 Esaw took his wives of the daughters of Canaan; Adah the daughter of Elon the Hittite, and Aholibamah the daughter of Anah the daughter of Zibeon the Hivite;

3 And Bashemath Yishmael's daughter, sister of Nevayot.

4 And Adah bare to Esaw Eliphaz; and Bashemath bare Reuel;

5 And Aholibamah bare Yeush, and Yaalam, and Korah (Qorach); these are the sons of Esaw, which were born unto him in the land of Canaan.

6 And Esaw took his wives, and his sons, and his daughters, and all the persons of his house, and his cattle, and all his beasts, and all his substance, which he had got in the land of Canaan; and went into the country from the face of his brother Jacob (Yaaqov).

7 For their riches were more than that they might dwell together; and the land wherein they were strangers could not bear them because of their cattle.

8 Thus dwelt Esaw in mount Seir; Esaw is Edom.

9 And these are the generations of Esaw the father of the Edomites in Mount Seir.

10 These are the names of Esaw's sons: Eliphaz the son of Adah the wife of Esaw, Reuel the son of Bashemath the wife of Esaw.

11 And the sons of Eliphaz were Teman, Omar, Zepho, and Gatam, and Kenaz.

12 And Timna was concubine to Eliphaz Esaw's son; and she bare to Eliphaz Amalek: these were the sons of Adah Esaw's wife.

13 And these are the sons of Reuel: Nahath, and Zerah, Shammah, and Mizzah; these were the sons of Bashemath Esaw's wife.

14 And these were the sons of Aholibamah, the daughter of Anah the daughter of Zibeon, Esaw's wife; and she bare to Esaw Yeush, and Yaalam, and Korah (Qorach).

15 These were dukes of the sons of Esaw: the sons of Eliphaz the firstborn son of Esaw: duke Teman, duke Omar, duke Zepho, duke Kenaz,

16 Duke Korah (Qorach), duke Gatam, and duke Amalek: these are the dukes that came of Eliphaz in the land of Edom; these were the sons of Adah.

17 And these are the sons of Reuel Esaw's son: duke Nahath, duke Zerah, duke Shammah, duke Mizzah; these are the dukes that came of Reuel in the land of Edom; these are the sons of Bashemath Esaw's wife.

18 And these are the sons of Aholibamah Esaw's wife: duke Yeush, duke Yaalam, duke Korah (Qorach); these were the dukes that came of Aholibamah the daughter of Anah, Esaw's wife.

19 These are the sons of Esaw, who is Edom, and these are their dukes.

20 These are the sons of Seir the Horite, who inhabited the land: Lotan, and Shobal, and Zibeon, and Anah,

21 And Dishon, and Ezer, and Dishan; these are the dukes of the Horites, the children of Seir in the land of Edom.

22 And the children of Lotan were Hori and

Hemam; and Lotan's sister was Timna.

23 And the children of Shobal were these: Alvan, and Manahath, and Ebal, Shepho, and Onam.

24 And these are the children of Zibeon: both Ayah, and Anah; this was that Anah that found the mules in the wilderness, as he fed the asses of Zibeon his father.

25 And the children of Anah were these: Dishon, and Aholibamah the daughter of Anah.

26 And these are the children of Dishon: Hemdan, and Eshban, and Ithran, and Cheran.

27 The children of Ezer are these: Bilhan, and Zaavan, and Akan.

28 The children of Dishan are these: Uz, and Aran.

29 These are the dukes that came of the Horites: duke Lotan, duke Shobal, duke Zibeon, duke Anah,

30 Duke Dishon, duke Ezer, duke Dishan; these are the dukes that came of Hori, among their dukes in the land of Seir.

31 And these are the kings that reigned in the land of Edom, before there reigned any king over the children of Yisrael.

32 And Bela the son of Beor reigned in Edom; and the name of his city was Dinhabah.

33 And Bela died, and Yovav the son of Zerah of Bozrah reigned in his stead.

34 And Yovav died, and Husham of the land of Temani reigned in his stead.

35 And Husham died, and Hadad the son of Bedad, who smote Midian in the field of Moav, reigned in his stead: and the name of his city was Avith.

36 And Hadad died, and Samlah of Masrekah reigned in his stead.

37 And Samlah died, and Shaul of Rehoboth by the river reigned in his stead.

38 And Shaul died, and Baalhanan the son of Achbor reigned in his stead.

39 And Baalhanan the son of Achbor died, and Hadar reigned in his stead; and the name of his city was Pau; and his wife's name was Mehetabel, the daughter of Matred, the daughter of MezAchav.

40 And these are the names of the dukes that came of Esaw, according to their families, after their places, by their names: duke Timnah, duke Alvah, duke Yetet,

41 Duke Aholibamah, duke Ela, duke Pinon,

42 Duke Kenaz, duke Teman, duke Mibzar,

43 Duke Magdiel, duke Iram; these be the dukes of Edom, according to their habitations in the land of their possession; he is Esaw the father of the Edomites.

37 And Jacob (Yaaqov) dwelt in the land wherein his father was a stranger, in the land of Canaan.

2 These are the generations of Jacob (Yaaqov). Joseph (Yosef), being seventeen years old, was feeding the flock with his brethren; and the lad was with the sons of Bilhah, and with the sons of Zilpah, his father's wives; and Joseph (Yosef) brought unto his father their evil report.

3 Now Yisrael loved Joseph (Yosef) more than all his children, because he was the son of his old age; and he made him a coat of many colours.

4 And when his brethren saw that their father loved him more than all his brethren, they hated him, and could not speak peaceably unto him.

5 And Joseph (Yosef) dreamed a dream, and he told it his brethren: and they hated him yet the more.

6 And he said unto them, "Please hear this dream which I have dreamed:

7 For, behold, we were binding sheaves in the field, and, behold, my sheaf arose, and also stood upright; and, behold, your sheaves stood round about, and made obeisance to my sheaf."

8 And his brethren said to him, "Shalt you indeed reign over us? Or shalt you indeed have dominion over us?" And they hated him yet the more for his dreams, and for his words.

9 And he dreamed yet another dream, and told it his brethren, and said, "Behold, I have dreamed a dream more; and, behold, the sun and the moon and the eleven stars made obeisance to me."

10 And he told it to his father, and to his brethren; and his father rebuked him, and said unto him, "What is this dream that you have dreamed? Shall I and your mother and your brethren indeed come to bow down ourselves to you to the earth?"

11 And his brethren envied him; but his father observed the saying.

12 And his brethren went to feed their father's flock in Shechem.

13 And Yisrael said unto Joseph (Yosef), "Do not your brethren feed the flock in Shechem?

Come, and I will send you unto them." And he said to him, "Here am I."

14 And he said to him, "Please go, see whether it be well with your brethren, and well with the flocks; and bring me word again." So he sent him out of the vale of Hebron, and he came to Shechem.

15 And a certain man found him, and, behold, he was wandering in the field: and the man asked him, saying, "What seekest you?"

16 And he said, "I seek my brethren. Please tell me, where they feed their flocks."

17 And the man said, "They are departed hence; for I heard them say, 'Let us go to Dothan.'" And Joseph (Yosef) went after his brethren, and found them in Dothan.

18 And when they saw him afar off, even before he came near unto them, they conspired against him to slay him.

19 And they said one to another, "Behold, this dreamer cometh.

20 Come now therefore, and let us slay him, and cast him into some pit, and we will say, 'Some evil beast hath devoured him.' And we shall see what will become of his dreams!"

21 And Reuven heard it, and he delivered him out of their hands; and said, "Let us not kill him."

22 And Reuven said unto them, "Shed no blood, but cast him into this pit that is in the wilderness, and lay no hand upon him; that he might rid him out of their hands, to deliver him to his father again."

23 And it came to pass, when Joseph (Yosef) was come unto his brethren, that they stript Joseph (Yosef) out of his coat, his coat of many colours that was on him;

24 And they took him, and cast him into a pit; and the pit was empty, there was no water in it.

25 And they sat down to eat bread; and they lifted up their eyes and looked, and, behold, a company of Yishmaelites came from Gilad with their camels bearing spicery and balm and myrrh, going to carry it down to Egypt (Mitsrayim).

26 And Judah (Yehudah) said unto his brethren, "What profit is it if we slay our brother, and conceal his blood?

27 Come, and let us sell him to the Ismaelites (Yishmaelim), and let not our hand be upon him; for he is our brother and our flesh." And

his brethren were content.

28 Then there passed by Midianites merchantmen; and they drew and lifted up Joseph (Yosef) out of the pit, and sold Joseph (Yosef) to the Yishme-elites for twenty pieces of silver; and they brought Joseph (Yosef) into Egypt (Mitsrayim).

29 And Reuven returned unto the pit; and, behold, Joseph (Yosef) was not in the pit; and he rent his clothes.

30 And he returned unto his brethren, and said, "The child is not there; and I, whither shall I go?"

31 And they took Joseph (Yosef)'s coat, and killed a kid of the goats, and dipped the coat in the blood;

32 And they sent the coat of many colours, and they brought it to their father; and said, "This have we found; know now whether it be your son's coat or not."

33 And he knew it, and said, "It is my son's coat; an evil beast hath devoured him; Joseph (Yosef) is without doubt rent in pieces."

34 And Jacob (Yaaqov) rent his clothes, and put sackcloth upon his loins, and mourned for his son many days.

35 And all his sons and all his daughters rose up to comfort him; but he refused to be comforted; and he said, "For I will go down into the grave unto my son mourning." Thus his father wept for him.

36 And the Midianites sold him into Egypt (Mitsrayim) unto Potiphar, an officer of Pharaoh (Paroh)'s, and captain of the guard.

38 And it came to pass at that time, that Judah (Yehudah) went down from his brethren, and turned in to a certain Adullamite, whose name was Hirah.

2 And Judah (Yehudah) saw there a daughter of a certain Canaanite, whose name was Shuah; and he took her, and went in unto her.

3 And she conceived, and bare a son; and he called his name Er.

4 And she conceived again, and bare a son; and she called his name Onan.

5 And she yet again conceived, and bare a son; and called his name Shelah: and he was at Chezib, when she bare him.

6 And Judah (Yehudah) took a wife for Er his firstborn, whose name was Tamar.

7 And Er, Judah (Yehudah)'s firstborn, was

wicked in the sight of יהוה; and יהוה slew him.

8 And Judah (Yehudah) said unto Onan, "Go in unto your brother's wife, and marry her, and raise up seed to your brother."

9 And Onan knew that the seed should not be his; and it came to pass, when he went in unto his brother's wife, that he spilled it on the ground, lest that he should give seed to his brother.

10 And the thing which he did displeased יהוה; therefore He slew him also.

11 Then said Judah (Yehudah) to Tamar his daughter in law, "Remain a widow at your father's house, till Shelah my son be grown." For he said, "Lest suppose he dies also, as his brethren did." And Tamar went and dwelt in her father's house.

12 And in process of time the daughter of Shuah, Judah (Yehudah)'s wife died; and Judah (Yehudah) was comforted, and went up unto his sheepshearers to Timnath, he and his friend Hirah the Adullamite.

13 And it was told Tamar, saying, "Behold your father in law goeth up to Timnath to shear his sheep."

14 And she put her widow's garments off from her, and covered her with a vail, and wrapped herself, and sat in an open place, which is by the way to Timnath; for she saw that Shelah was grown, and she was not given unto him to wife.

15 When Judah (Yehudah) saw her, he thought her to be a harlot; because she had covered her face.

16 And he turned unto her by the way, and said, "Please come, let me come in unto you"; (for he knew not that she was his daughter in law.) and she said, "What wilt you give me, that you mayest come in unto me?"

17 And he said, "I will send you a kid from the flock." And she said, "Wilt you give me a pledge, till you send it?"

18 And he said, "What pledge shall I give you?" And she said, "Your signet, and your bracelets, and your staff that is in your hand." And he gave it her, and came in unto her, and she conceived by him.

19 And she arose, and went away, and laid by her vail from her, and put on the garments of her widowhood.

20 And Judah (Yehudah) sent the kid by the hand of his friend the Adullamite, to receive his pledge from the woman's hand, but he found her not.

21 Then he asked the men of that place, saying, "Where is the harlot, that was openly by the way side?" And they said, "There was no harlot in this place."

22 And he returned to Judah (Yehudah), and said, "I cannot find her; and also the men of the place said, that there was no harlot in this place."

23 And Judah (Yehudah) said, "Let her take it to her, lest we be shamed; behold, I sent this kid, and you have not found her."

24 And it came to pass about three months after, that it was told Judah (Yehudah), saying, "Tamar your daughter in law hath played the harlot; and also, behold, she is with child by whoredom." And Judah (Yehudah) said, "Bring her forth, and let her be burned!"

25 When she was brought forth, she sent to her father in law, saying, "By the man, whose these are, am I with child." And she said, "Please discern, whose are these, the signet, and bracelets, and staff."

26 And Judah (Yehudah) acknow-ledged them, and said, "She hath been more righteous than I; because that I gave her not to Shelah my son." And he knew her again no more.

27 And it came to pass in the time of her travail, that, behold, twins were in her womb.

28 And it came to pass, when she travailed, that the one put out his hand; and the midwife took and bound upon his hand a scarlet thread, saying, "This came out first."

29 And it came to pass, as he drew back his hand, that, behold, his brother came out; and she said, "How have you broken forth? This breach be upon you!" Therefore his name was called Pharez (Perets).

30 And afterward came out his brother, that had the scarlet thread upon his hand; and his name was called Zarah.

39 And Joseph (Yosef) was brought down to Egypt (Mitsrayim); and Potiphar, an officer of Pharaoh (Paroh), captain of the guard, an Egyptian (Mitsri), bought him of the hands of the Yishmaelites, who had brought him down thither.

2 And יהוה was with Joseph (Yosef), and he was a prosperous man; and he was in the house of his master the Egyptian (Mitsri).

3 And his master saw that יהוה was with him,

and that יהוה made all that he did to prosper in his hand.

4 And Joseph (Yosef) found grace in his sight, and he served him; and he made him overseer over his house, and all that he had he put into his hand.

5 And it came to pass from the time that he had made him overseer in his house, and over all that he had, that יהוה blessed the Egyptian (Mitsri)'s house for Joseph (Yosef)'s sake; and the blessing of יהוה was upon all that he had in the house, and in the field.

6 And he left all that he had in Joseph (Yosef)'s hand; and he knew not ought he had, save the bread which he did eat. And Joseph (Yosef) was a goodly person, and well favoured.

7 And it came to pass after these things, that his master's wife cast her eyes upon Joseph (Yosef); and she said, "Lie with me."

8 But he refused, and said unto his master's wife, "Behold, my master knows not what is with me in the house, and he hath committed all that he hath to my hand;

9 There is none greater in this house than I; neither hath he kept back any thing from me but you, because you are his wife; how then can I do this great wickedness, and sin against God (Elohim)?"

10 And it came to pass, as she spake to Joseph (Yosef) day by day, that he hearkened not unto her, to lie by her, or to be with her.

11 And it came to pass about this time, that Joseph (Yosef) went into the house to do his business; and there was none of the men of the house there within.

12 And she caught him by his garment, saying, "Lie with me." And he left his garment in her hand, and fled, and got him out.

13 And it came to pass, when she saw that he had left his garment in her hand, and was fled forth,

14 That she called unto the men of her house, and spake unto them, saying, "See, he hath brought in a Hebrew (Ivri) unto us to mock us; he came in unto me to lie with me, and I cried with a loud voice.

15 And it came to pass, when he heard that I lifted up my voice and cried, that he left his garment with me, and fled, and got him out."

16 And she laid up his garment by her, until his master came home.

17 And she spake unto him according to these words, saying, "The Hebrew (Ivri) servant, whom you have brought unto us, came in unto me to mock me;

18 And it came to pass, as I lifted up my voice and cried, that he left his garment with me, and fled out."

19 And it came to pass, when his master heard the words of his wife, which she spake unto him, saying, "After this manner did your servant to me;" that his wrath was kindled.

20 And Joseph (Yosef)'s master took him, and put him into the prison, a place where the king's prisoners were bound; and he was there in the prison.

21 But יהוה was with Joseph (Yosef), and shewed him mercy, and gave him favor in the sight of the keeper of the prison.

22 And the keeper of the prison committed to Joseph (Yosef)'s hand all the prisoners that were in the prison; and whatsoever they did there, he was the doer of it.

23 The keeper of the prison looked not to anything that was under his hand; because יהוה was with him, and that which he did, יהוה made it to prosper.

40 And it came to pass after these things, that the butler of the king of Egypt (Mitsrayim) and his baker had offended their [B13]lord (adon) the king of Egypt (Mitsrayim).

2 And Pharaoh (Paroh) was wroth against two of his officers, against the chief of the butlers, and against the chief of the bakers.

3 And he put them in ward in the house of the captain of the guard, into the prison, the place where Joseph (Yosef) was bound.

4 And the captain of the guard charged Joseph (Yosef) with them, and he served them; and they continued a season in ward.

5 And they dreamed a dream both of them, each man his dream in one night, each man according to the interpretation of his dream, the butler and the baker of the king of Egypt (Mitsrayim), which were bound in the prison.

6 And Joseph (Yosef) came in unto them in the morning, and looked upon them, and, behold, they were sad.

7 And he asked Pharaoh (Paroh)'s officers that were with him in the ward of his master's house, saying, "Wherefore look you so sadly today?"

8 And they said unto him, "We have dreamed

a dream, and there is no interpreter of it." And Joseph (Yosef) said unto them, "Do not interpretations belong to God (Elohim)? Please tell them to me."

9 And the chief butler told his dream to Joseph (Yosef), and said to him, "In my dream, behold, a vine was before me;

10 And in the vine were three branches; and it was as though it budded, and her blossoms shot forth; and the clusters thereof brought forth ripe grapes.

11 And Pharaoh (Paroh)'s cup was in my hand; and I took the grapes, and pressed them into Pharaoh (Paroh)'s cup, and I gave the cup into Pharaoh (Paroh)'s hand."

12 And Joseph (Yosef) said unto him, "This is the interpretation of it: The three branches are three days.

13 Yet within three days shall Pharaoh (Paroh) lift up your head, and restore you unto your place; and you shalt deliver Pharaoh (Paroh)'s cup into his hand, after the former manner when you wast his butler.

14 But think on me when it shall be well with you, and please shew kindness unto me, and make mention of me unto Pharaoh (Paroh), and bring me out of this house;

15 For indeed I was stolen away out of the land of the Hebrews (Ivrim); and here also have I done nothing that they should put me into the dungeon."

16 When the chief baker saw that the interpretation was good, he said unto Joseph (Yosef), "I also was in my dream, and, behold, I had three white baskets on my head.

17 And in the uppermost basket there was of all manner of bakemeats for Pharaoh (Paroh); and the birds did eat them out of the basket upon my head."

18 And Joseph (Yosef) answered and said, "This is the interpretation thereof: The three baskets are three days.

19 Yet within three days shall Pharaoh (Paroh) lift up your head from off you, and shall hang you on a tree; and the birds shall eat your flesh from off you."

20 And it came to pass the third day, which was Pharaoh (Paroh)'s birthday, that he made a feast unto all his servants; and he lifted up the head of the chief butler and of the chief baker among his servants.

21 And he restored the chief butler unto his butlership again; and he gave the cup into Pharaoh (Paroh)'s hand;

22 But he hanged the chief baker, as Joseph (Yosef) had interpreted to them.

23 Yet did not the chief butler remember Joseph (Yosef), but forgat him.

41 And it came to pass at the end of two full years, that Pharaoh (Paroh) dreamed: and, behold, he stood by the river.

2 And, behold, there came up out of the river seven well favoured kine and fatfleshed; and they fed in a meadow.

3 And, behold, seven other kine came up after them out of the river, ill favoured and leanfleshed; and stood by the other kine upon the brink of the river.

4 And the ill favoured and leanfleshed kine did eat up the seven well favoured and fat kine. So Pharaoh (Paroh) awoke.

5 And he slept and dreamed the second time; and, behold, seven ears of corn came up upon one stalk, rank and good.

6 And, behold, seven thin ears and blasted with the east wind sprung up after them.

7 And the seven thin ears devoured the seven rank and full ears. And Pharaoh (Paroh) awoke, and, behold, it was a dream.

8 And it came to pass in the morning that his spirit was troubled; and he sent and called for all the magicians of Egypt (Mitsrayim), and all the wise men thereof. And Pharaoh (Paroh) told them his dream; but there was none that could interpret them unto Pharaoh (Paroh).

9 Then spake the chief butler unto Pharaoh (Paroh), saying, "I do remember my faults this day.

10 Pharaoh (Paroh) was wroth with his servants, and put me in ward in the captain of the guard's house, both me and the chief baker;

11 And we dreamed a dream in one night, I and he; we dreamed each man according to the interpretation of his dream.

12 And there was there with us a young man, a Hebrew (Ivri), servant to the captain of the guard; and we told him, and he interpreted to us our dreams; to each man according to his dream he did interpret.

13 And it came to pass, as he interpreted to us, so it was; me he restored unto mine office, and him he hanged."

14 Then Pharaoh (Paroh) sent and called Joseph (Yosef), and they brought him hastily out of the dungeon; and he shaved himself, and changed his raiment, and came in unto Pharaoh (Paroh).

15 And Pharaoh (Paroh) said unto Joseph (Yosef), "I have dreamed a dream, and there is none that can interpret it; and I have heard say of you, that you canst understand a dream to interpret it."

16 And Joseph (Yosef) answered Pharaoh (Paroh), saying, "It is not in me; God (Elohim) shall give Pharaoh (Paroh) an answer of peace."

17 And Pharaoh (Paroh) said unto Joseph (Yosef), "In my dream, behold, I stood upon the bank of the river.

18 And, behold, there came up out of the river seven kine, fatfleshed and well favoured; and they fed in a meadow.

19 And, behold, seven other kine came up after them, poor and very ill favoured and leanfleshed, such as I never saw in all the land of Egypt (Mitsrayim) for badness.

20 And the lean and the ill favoured kine did eat up the first seven fat kine.

21 And when they had eaten them up, it could not be known that they had eaten them; but they were still ill favoured, as at the beginning. So I awoke.

22 And I saw in my dream, and, behold, seven ears came up in one stalk, full and good.

23 And, behold, seven ears, withered, thin, and blasted with the east wind, sprung up after them.

24 And the thin ears devoured the seven good ears; and I told this unto the magicians; but there was none that could declare it to me."

25 And Joseph (Yosef) said unto Pharaoh (Paroh), "The dream of Pharaoh is one: God (Elohim) hath shewed Pharaoh what He is about to do.

26 The seven good kine are seven years; and the seven good ears are seven years; the dream is one.

27 And the seven thin and ill favoured kine that came up after them are seven years; and the seven empty ears blasted with the east wind shall be seven years of famine.

28 This is the thing which I have spoken unto Pharaoh (Paroh): What God (Elohim) is about to do He sheweth unto Pharaoh (Paroh).

29 Behold, there come seven years of great plenty throughout all the land of Egypt (Mitsrayim);

30 And there shall arise after them seven years of famine; and all the plenty shall be forgotten in the land of Egypt (Mitsrayim); and the famine shall consume the land;

31 And the plenty shall not be known in the land by reason of that famine following; for it shall be very grievous.

32 And for that the dream was doubled unto Pharaoh (Paroh) twice; it is because the thing is established by God (Elohim), and God (Elohim) will shortly bring it to pass.

33 Now therefore let Pharaoh (Paroh) look out a man discreet and wise, and set him over the land of Egypt (Mitsrayim).

34 Let Pharaoh (Paroh) do this, and let him appoint officers over the land, and take up the fifth part of the land of Egypt (Mitsrayim) in the seven plenteous years.

35 And let them gather all the food of those good years that come, and lay up corn under the hand of Pharaoh (Paroh), and let them keep food in the cities.

36 And that food shall be for store to the land against the seven years of famine, which shall be in the land of Egypt (Mitsrayim); that the land perishes not through the famine."

37 And the thing was good in the eyes of Pharaoh (Paroh), and in the eyes of all his servants.

38 And Pharaoh (Paroh) said unto his servants, "Can we find such a one as this is, a man in whom the Spirit of God (Elohim) is?"

39 And Pharaoh (Paroh) said unto Joseph (Yosef), "Forasmuch as God (Elohim) hath shewed you all this, there is none so discreet and wise as you are.

40 You shalt be over my house, and according unto your word shall all my people be ruled; only in the throne will I be greater than you.

41 And Pharaoh (Paroh) said unto Joseph (Yosef), "See, I have set you over all the land of Egypt (Mitsrayim)."

42 And Pharaoh (Paroh) took off his ring from his hand, and put it upon Joseph (Yosef)'s hand, and arrayed him in vestures of fine linen, and put a gold chain about his neck;

43 And he made him to ride in the second chariot which he had; and they cried before him, "Bow the knee!" And he made him ruler over all the land of Egypt (Mitsrayim).

44 And Pharaoh (Paroh) said unto Joseph (Yosef), "I am Pharaoh (Paroh), and without you shall no man lift up his hand or foot in all the land of Egypt (Mitsrayim)."

45 And Pharaoh (Paroh) called Joseph (Yosef)'s name Zaphnath-Paaneah; and he gave him as wife Asenath the daughter of Potipherah priest (kohen) of On. And Joseph (Yosef) went out over all the land of Egypt (Mitsrayim).

46 And Joseph (Yosef) was thirty years old when he stood before Pharaoh (Paroh) king of Egypt (Mitsrayim). And Joseph (Yosef) went out from the presence of Pharaoh (Paroh), and went throughout all the land of Egypt (Mitsrayim).

47 And in the seven plenteous years the earth brought forth by handfuls.

48 And he gathered up all the food of the seven years, which were in the land of Egypt (Mitsrayim), and laid up the food in the cities; the food of the field, which was round about every city, laid he up in the same.

49 And Joseph (Yosef) gathered corn as the sand of the sea, very much, until he left numbering; for it was without number.

50 And unto Joseph (Yosef) were born two sons before the years of famine came, which Asenath the daughter of Potipherah priest (kohen) of On bare unto him.

51 And Joseph (Yosef) called the name of the firstborn [A28]Manasseh (Menashsheh): "For God (Elohim)", said he, "hath made me forget all my toil, and all my father's house."

52 And the name of the second called he [A29]Efrayim: "For God (Elohim) hath caused me to be fruitful in the land of my affliction."

53 And the seven years of plenteousness, that was in the land of Egypt (Mitsrayim), were ended.

54 And the seven years of dearth began to come, according as Joseph (Yosef) had said; and the dearth was in all lands; but in all the land of Egypt (Mitsrayim) there was bread.

55 And when all the land of Egypt (Mitsrayim) was famished, the people cried to Pharaoh (Paroh) for bread; and Pharaoh (Paroh) said unto all the Egyptians (Mitsrayim), "Go unto Joseph (Yosef); what he saith to you, do."

56 And the famine was over all the face of the earth. And Joseph (Yosef) opened all the storehouses, and sold unto the Egyptians (Mitsrayim); and the famine waxed sore in the land of Egypt (Mitsrayim).

57 And all countries came into Egypt (Mitsrayim) to Joseph (Yosef) for to buy corn, because that the famine was so sore in all lands.

42 Now when Jacob (Yaaqov) saw that there was corn in Egypt (Mitsrayim), Jacob (Yaaqov) said unto his sons, "Why do you look one upon another?"

2 And he said, "Behold, I have heard that there is corn in Egypt (Mitsrayim); get you down thither, and buy for us from thence; that we may live, and not die."

3 And Joseph (Yosef)'s ten brethren went down to buy corn in Egypt (Mitsrayim).

4 But Binyamin, Joseph (Yosef)'s brother, Jacob (Yaaqov) sent not with his brethren; for he said, "Lest peradventure mischief befall him."

5 And the sons of Yisrael came to buy corn among those that came, for the famine was in the land of Canaan.

6 And Joseph (Yosef) was the governor over the land, and he it was that sold to all the people of the land; and Joseph (Yosef)'s brethren came, and bowed down themselves before him with their faces to the earth.

7 And Joseph (Yosef) saw his brethren, and he knew them, but made himself strange unto them, and spake roughly unto them; and he said unto them, "Whence come you?" And they said, "From the land of Canaan to buy food."

8 And Joseph (Yosef) knew his brethren, but they knew not him.

9 And Joseph (Yosef) remembered the dreams which he dreamed of them, and said unto them, "You are spies; to see the nakedness of the land you are come."

10 And they said unto him, "Nay, my lord (adoni), but to buy food are your servants come."

11 We are all one man's sons; we are true men, your servants are not spies."

12 And he said unto them, "Nay, but to see the nakedness of the land you are come."

13 And they said, "Your servants are twelve brethren, the sons of one man in the land of Canaan; and, behold, the youngest is this day with our father, and one is not."

14 And Joseph (Yosef) said unto them, "That is it that I spake unto you, saying, 'You are spies!'

15 Hereby you shall be proved: By the life of Pharaoh (Paroh) you shall not go forth hence,

except your youngest brother come hither.

16 Send one of you, and let him fetch your brother, and you shall be kept in prison, that your words may be proved, whether there be any truth in you; or else by the life of Pharaoh (Paroh) surely you are spies!"

17 And he put them all together into ward three days.

18 And Joseph (Yosef) said unto them the third day, "This do, and live; for I fear God (Elohim);

19 If you be true men, let one of your brethren be bound in the house of your prison: go you, carry corn for the famine of your houses;

20 But bring your youngest brother unto me; so shall your words be verified, and you shall not die." And they did so.

21 And they said one to another, "We are verily guilty concerning our brother, in that we saw the anguish of his soul, when he besought us, and we would not hear; therefore is this distress come upon us."

22 And Reuven answered them, saying, "Spake I not unto you, saying, 'Do not sin against the child; and you would not hear?' Therefore, behold, also his blood is required."

23 And they knew not that Joseph (Yosef) understood them; for he spake unto them by an interpreter.

24 And he turned himself about from them, and wept; and returned to them again, and communed with them, and took from them Shimon, and bound him before their eyes.

25 Then Joseph (Yosef) commanded to fill their sacks with corn, and to restore every man's money into his sack, and to give them provision for the way; and thus did he unto them.

26 And they laded their asses with the corn, and departed thence.

27 And as one of them opened his sack to give his ass provender in the inn, he espied his money; for, behold, it was in his sack's mouth.

28 And he said unto his brethren, "My money is restored; and, behold, it is even in my sack!" And their heart failed them, and they were afraid, saying one to another, "What is this that God (Elohim) hath done unto us?"

29 And they came unto Jacob (Yaaqov) their father unto the land of Canaan, and told him all that befell unto them; saying,

30 "The man, who is the owner (adon) of the land, spake roughly to us, and took us for spies of the country.

31 And we said unto him, 'We are true men; we are not spies.

32 We be twelve brethren, sons of our father; one is not, and the youngest is this day with our father in the land of Canaan.'

33 And the man, the ruler (adon) of the country, said unto us, 'Hereby shall I know that you are true men: Leave one of your brethren here with me, and take food for the famine of your households, and be gone.

34 And bring your youngest brother unto me; then shall I know that you are not spies, but that you are true men; so will I deliver you your brother, and you shall traffick in the land.'"

35 And it came to pass as they emptied their sacks, that, behold, every man's bundle of money was in his sack; and when both they and their father saw the bundles of money, they were afraid.

36 And Jacob (Yaaqov) their father said unto them, "Me have you bereaved of my children; Joseph (Yosef) is gone, and Shimon is gone, and you will take Binyamin away; all these things are against me."

37 And Reuven spake unto his father, saying, "Slay my two sons, if I bring him not to you; deliver him into my hand, and I will bring him to you again."

38 And he said, "My son shall not go down with you; for his brother is dead, and he is left alone. If mischief befall him by the way in the which you go, then shall you bring down my gray hairs with sorrow to the grave."

43 And the famine was sore in the land.

2 And it came to pass, when they had eaten up the corn which they had brought out of Egypt (Mitsrayim), their father said unto them, "Go again, buy us a little food."

3 And Judah (Yehudah) spake unto him, saying, "The man did solemnly protest unto us, saying, 'You shall not see my face, except your brother be with you.'

4 If you wilt send our brother with us, we will go down and buy you food;

5 But if you wilt not send him, we will not go down, for the man said unto us, 'You shall not see my face, except your brother be with you.'"

6 And Yisrael said, "Wherefore dealt you so ill with me, as to tell the man whether you had yet a brother?"

7 And they said, "The man asked us straitly of our state, and of our kindred, saying, 'Is your father yet alive? Have you another brother?' And we told him according to the tenor of these words. Could we certainly know that he would say, 'Bring your brother down'?"

8 And Judah (Yehudah) said unto Yisrael his father, "Send the lad with me, and we will arise and go; that we may live, and not die, both we, and you, and also our little ones.

9 I will be surety for him; of my hand shalt you require him; if I bring him not unto you, and set him before you, then let me bear the blame forever;

10 For except we had lingered, surely now we had returned this second time."

11 And their father Yisrael said unto them, "If it must be so now, do this; take of the best fruits in the land in your vessels, and carry down the man a present, a little balm, and a little honey, spices, and myrrh, nuts, and almonds:

12 And take double money in your hand; and the money that was brought again in the mouth of your sacks, carry it again in your hand; peradventure it was an oversight:

13 Take also your brother, and arise, go again unto the man:

14 And Almighty God (El Shaddai) give you mercy before the man, that he may send away your other brother, and Binyamin. If I be bereaved of my children, I am bereaved."

15 And the men took that present, and they took double money in their hand, and Binyamin; and rose up, and went down to Egypt (Mitsrayim), and stood before Joseph (Yosef).

16 And when Joseph (Yosef) saw Binyamin with them, he said to the ruler of his house, "Bring these men home, and slay, and make ready; for these men shall dine with me at noon."

17 And the man did as Joseph (Yosef) bade; and the man brought the men into Joseph (Yosef)'s house.

18 And the men were afraid, because they were brought into Joseph (Yosef)'s house; and they said, "Because of the money that was returned in our sacks at the first time are we brought in; that he may seek occasion against us, and fall upon us, and take us for bondmen, and our asses."

19 And they came near to the steward of Joseph (Yosef)'s house, and they communed with him at the door of the house,

20 And said, "O sir, we came indeed down at the first time to buy food;

21 And it came to pass, when we came to the inn, that we opened our sacks, and, behold, every man's money was in the mouth of his sack, our money in full weight; and we have brought it again in our hand.

22 And other money have we brought down in our hands to buy food. We cannot tell who put our money in our sacks."

23 And he said, "Peace be to you, fear not. Your God (Elohim), and the God (Elohim) of your father, hath given you treasure in your sacks; I had your money." And he brought Shimon out unto them.

24 And the man brought the men into Joseph (Yosef)'s house, and gave them water, and they washed their feet; and he gave their asses provender.

25 And they made ready the present for Joseph (Yosef)'s coming at noon, for they heard that they should eat bread there.

26 And when Joseph (Yosef) came home, they brought him the present which was in their hand into the house, and bowed themselves to him to the earth.

27 And he asked them of their welfare, and said, "Is your father well, the old man of whom you spake? Is he yet alive?"

28 And they answered, "Your servant our father is in good health, he is yet alive." And they bowed down their heads, and made obeisance.

29 And he lifted up his eyes, and saw his brother Binyamin, his mother's son, and said, "Is this your younger brother, of whom you spake unto me?" And he said, "God (Elohim) be gracious unto you, my son."

30 And Joseph (Yosef) made haste; for his bowels did yearn upon his brother; and he sought where to weep; and he entered into his chamber, and wept there.

31 And he washed his face, and went out, and refrained himself, and said, "Set on bread."

32 And they set on for him by himself, and for them by themselves, and for the Egyptians (Mitsrayim), which did eat with him, by themselves, because the Egyptians (Mitsrayim) might not eat bread with the Hebrews (Ivrim); for that is an abomination unto the Egyptians (Mitsrayim).

33 And they sat before him, the firstborn according to his birthright, and the youngest according to his youth; and the men marvelled one at another.

34 And he took and sent messes unto them from before him, but Binyamin's mess was five times so much as any of theirs. And they drank, and were merry with him.

44 And he commanded the steward of his house, saying, "Fill the men's sacks with food, as much as they can carry, and put every man's money in his sack's mouth.

2 And put my cup, the silver cup, in the sack's mouth of the youngest, and his corn money." And he did according to the word that Joseph (Yosef) had spoken.

3 As soon as the morning was light, the men were sent away, they and their asses.

4 And when they were gone out of the city, and not yet far off, Joseph (Yosef) said unto his steward, "Up, follow after the men; and when you dost overtake them, say unto them, 'Wherefore have you rewarded evil for good?

5 Is not this it in which my lord (adoni) drinketh, and whereby indeed he divineth? You have done evil in so doing.'"

6 And he overtook them, and he spake unto them these same words.

7 And they said unto him, "Wherefore saith my lord (adoni) these words? God (Elohim) forbid that your servants should do according to this thing.

8 Behold, the money, which we found in our sacks' mouths, we brought again unto you out of the land of Canaan; how then should we steal out of your lord (adon)'s house silver or gold?

9 With whomsoever of your servants it be found, both let him die, and we also will be my lord (adoni)'s bondmen."

10 And he said, "Now also let it be according unto your words: he with whom it is found shall be my servant; and you shall be blameless."

11 Then they speedily took down every man his sack to the ground, and opened every man his sack.

12 And he searched, and began at the eldest, and left at the youngest; and the cup was found in Binyamin's sack.

13 Then they rent their clothes, and laded every man his ass, and returned to the city.

14 And Judah (Yehudah) and his brethren came to Joseph (Yosef)'s house, for he was yet there; and they fell before him on the ground.

15 And Joseph (Yosef) said unto them, "What deed is this that you have done? Know you not that such a man as I can certainly divine?"

16 And Judah (Yehudah) said, "What shall we say unto my lord (adoni)? What shall we speak? Or how shall we clear ourselves? God (Elohim) hath found out the iniquity of your servants; behold, we are my lord (adoni)'s servants, both we, and he also with whom the cup is found."

17 And he said, "God (Elohim) forbid that I should do so; but the man in whose hand the cup is found, he shall be my servant; and as for you, get you up in peace unto your father."

18 Then Judah (Yehudah) came near unto him, and said, "Oh my lord (adoni), please let your servant speak a word in my lord (adoni)'s ears, and let not your anger burn against your servant; for you are even as Pharaoh (Paroh).

19 My lord (Adoni) asked his servants, saying, "Have you a father, or a brother?"

20 And we said unto my lord (adoni), 'We have a father, an old man, and a child of his old age, a little one; and his brother is dead, and he alone is left of his mother, and his father loveth him.'

21 And you saidst unto your servants, 'Bring him down unto me, that I may set mine eyes upon him.'

22 And we said unto my lord (adoni), 'The lad cannot leave his father: for if he should leave his father, his father would die.'

23 And you saidst unto your servants, 'Except your youngest brother come down with you, you shall see my face no more.'

24 And it came to pass when we came up unto your servant my father, we told him the words of my lord (adoni).

25 And our father said, 'Go again, and buy us a little food.'

26 And we said, 'We cannot go down; if our youngest brother be with us, then will we go down; for we may not see the man's face, except our youngest brother be with us.'

27 And your servant my father said unto us, 'You know that my wife bare me two sons;

28 And the one went out from me, and I said, "Surely he is torn in pieces"; and I saw him not since;

29 And if you take this also from me, and mischief befall him, you shall bring down my

gray hairs with sorrow to the grave.'

30 Now therefore when I come to your servant my father, and the lad be not with us; seeing that his life is bound up in the lad's life;

31 It shall come to pass, when he seeth that the lad is not with us, that he will die: and your servants shall bring down the gray hairs of your servant our father with sorrow to the grave.

32 For your servant became surety for the lad unto my father, saying, 'If I bring him not unto you, then I shall bear the blame to my father forever.'

33 Now therefore, please let your servant abide instead of the lad a bondman to my lord (adoni); and let the lad go up with his brethren.

34 For how shall I go up to my father, and the lad be not with me? Lest perhaps I see the evil that shall come on my father?"

45 Then Joseph (Yosef) could not refrain himself before all them that stood by him; and he cried, "Make every man to go out from me!" And there stood no man with him, while Joseph (Yosef) made himself known unto his brethren.

2 And he wept aloud; and the Egyptians (Mitsrayim) and the house of Pharaoh (Paroh) heard.

3 And Joseph (Yosef) said unto his brethren, "I am Joseph (Yosef); doth my father yet live?" And his brethren could not answer him; for they were troubled at his presence.

4 And Joseph (Yosef) said unto his brethren, "Please come near to me." And they came near. And he said, "I am Joseph (Yosef) your brother, whom you sold into Egypt (Mitsrayim).

5 Now therefore be not grieved, nor angry with yourselves, that you sold me hither; for God (Elohim) did send me before you to preserve life.

6 For these two years hath the famine been in the land: and yet there are five years, in the which there shall neither be earing nor harvest.

7 And God (Elohim) sent me before you to preserve you a posterity in the earth, and to save your lives by a great deliverance.

8 So now it was not you that sent me hither, but God (Elohim); and He hath made me a father to Pharaoh (Paroh), and lord (adon) of all his house, and a ruler throughout all the land of Egypt (Mitsrayim).

9 Haste you, and go up to my father, and say unto him, 'Thus saith your son Joseph (Yosef): "God (Elohim) hath made me lord (adon) of all Egypt (Mitsrayim); come down unto me, tarry not;

10 And you shalt dwell in the land of Goshen, and you shalt be near unto me, you, and your children, and your children's children, and your flocks, and your herds, and all that you have:

11 And there will I nourish you; for yet there are five years of famine; lest you, and your household, and all that you have, come to poverty."'

12 And, behold, your eyes see, and the eyes of my brother Binyamin, that it is my mouth that speaketh unto you.

13 And you shall tell my father of all my glory in Egypt (Mitsrayim), and of all that you have seen; and you shall haste and bring down my father hither.

14 And he fell upon his brother Binyamin's neck, and wept; and Binyamin wept upon his neck.

15 Moreover he kissed all his brethren, and wept upon them; and after that his brethren talked with him.

16 And the fame thereof was heard in Pharaoh (Paroh)'s house, saying, "Joseph (Yosef)'s brethren are come." And it pleased Pharaoh (Paroh) well, and his servants.

17 And Pharaoh (Paroh) said unto Joseph (Yosef), "Say unto your brethren, 'This do you; lade your beasts, and go, get you unto the land of Canaan;

18 And take your father and your households, and come unto me: and I will give you the good of the land of Egypt (Mitsrayim), and you shall eat the fat of the land.

19 Now you are commanded, this do you; take you wagons out of the land of Egypt (Mitsrayim) for your little ones, and for your wives, and bring your father, and come.

20 Also regard not your stuff; for the good of all the land of Egypt (Mitsrayim) is yours.'"

21 And the children of Yisrael did so; and Joseph (Yosef) gave them wagons, according to the commandment of Pharaoh (Paroh), and gave them provision for the way.

22 To all of them he gave each man changes of raiment; but to Binyamin he gave three hundred pieces of silver, and five changes of raiment.

23 And to his father he sent after this manner;

ten asses laden with the good things of Egypt (Mitsrayim), and ten she asses laden with corn and bread and meat for his father by the way.

24 So he sent his brethren away, and they departed; and he said unto them, "See that you fall not out by the way."

25 And they went up out of Egypt (Mitsrayim), and came into the land of Canaan unto Jacob (Yaaqov) their father,

26 And told him, saying, "Joseph (Yosef) is yet alive, and he is governor over all the land of Egypt (Mitsrayim)." And Jacob (Yaaqov)'s heart fainted, for he believed them not.

27 And they told him all the words of Joseph (Yosef), which he had said unto them; and when he saw the wagons which Joseph (Yosef) had sent to carry him, the spirit of Jacob (Yaaqov) their father revived;

28 And Yisrael said, "It is enough; Joseph (Yosef) my son is yet alive; I will go and see him before I die."

46 And Yisrael took his journey with all that he had, and came to Beer-Sheva, and offered sacrifices unto the God (Elohim) of his father Isaac (Yitschaq).

2 And God (Elohim) spake unto Yisrael in the visions of the night, and said, "Jacob (Yaaqov), Jacob (Yaaqov)." And he said, "Here am I."

3 And He said, "I am the [B5a]Mighty One (El), God (Elohim) of your father; fear not to go down into Egypt (Mitsrayim), for I will there make of you a great nation;

4 I will go down with you into Egypt (Mitsrayim); and I will also surely bring you up again; and Joseph (Yosef) shall put his hand upon your eyes."

5 And Jacob (Yaaqov) rose up from Beer-Sheva; and the sons of Yisrael carried Jacob (Yaaqov) their father, and their little ones, and their wives, in the wagons which Pharaoh (Paroh) had sent to carry him.

6 And they took their cattle, and their goods, which they had gotten in the land of Canaan, and came into Egypt (Mitsrayim), Jacob (Yaaqov), and all his seed with him.

7 His sons, and his sons' sons with him, his daughters, and his sons' daughters, and all his seed brought he with him into Egypt (Mitsrayim).

8 And these are the names of the children of Yisrael, which came into Egypt (Mitsrayim),

Jacob (Yaaqov) and his sons: Reuven, Jacob (Yaaqov)'s firstborn.

9 And the sons of Reuven: Hanoch, and Phallu, and Hezron, and Carmi.

10 And the sons of Shimon: Yemuel, and Yamin, and Ohad, and Yakhin, and Zohar, and Shaul the son of a Canaanitish woman.

11 And the sons of Lewi: Gershon, Kohath, and Merari.

12 And the sons of Judah (Yehudah): Er, and Onan, and Shelah, and Pharez, and Zerah; but Er and Onan died in the land of Canaan. And the sons of Pharez were Hezron and Hamul.

13 And the sons of Yissaskhar: Tola, and Phuvah, and Job (Iyov), and Shimron.

14 And the sons of Zevulun: Sered, and Elon, and Yahleel.

15 These be the sons of Leah, which she bare unto Jacob (Yaaqov) in Padanaram, with his daughter Dinah; all the souls of his sons and his daughters were thirty-three.

16 And the sons of Gad: Ziphion, and Haggi, Shuni, and Ezbon, Eri, and Arodi, and Areli.

17 And the sons of Asher: Yimnah, and Ishuah, and Isui, and Beriyah, and Serah their sister: and the sons of Beriyah: Heber, and Malchiel.

18 These are the sons of Zilpah, whom Lavan gave to Leah his daughter, and these she bare unto Jacob (Yaaqov), even sixteen souls.

19 The sons of Rachel Jacob (Yaaqov)'s wife: Joseph (Yosef), and Binyamin.

20 And unto Joseph (Yosef) in the land of Egypt (Mitsrayim) were born Menashsheh and Efrayim, which Asenath the daughter of Potipherah priest (kohen) of On bare unto him.

21 And the sons of Binyamin were Belah, and Becher, and Ashbel, Gera, and Naaman, Ehi, and Rosh, Muppim, and Huppim, and Ard.

22 These are the sons of Rachel, which were born to Jacob (Yaaqov); all the souls were fourteen.

23 And the sons of Dan: Hushim.

24 And the sons of Naftali: Yahzeel, and Guni, and Yezer, and Shillem.

25 These are the sons of Bilhah, which Lavan gave unto Rachel his daughter, and she bare these unto Jacob (Yaaqov); all the souls were seven.

26 All the souls that came with Jacob (Yaaqov) into Egypt (Mitsrayim), which came out of his loins, besides Jacob (Yaaqov)'s sons' wives, all

the souls were threescore and six.

27 And the sons of Joseph (Yosef), which were born him in Egypt (Mitsrayim), were two souls; all the souls of the house of Jacob (Yaaqov), which came into Egypt (Mitsrayim), were threescore and ten.

28 And he sent Judah (Yehudah) before him unto Joseph (Yosef), to direct his face unto Goshen; and they came into the land of Goshen.

29 And Joseph (Yosef) made ready his chariot, and went up to meet Yisrael his father, to Goshen, and presented himself unto him; and he fell on his neck, and wept on his neck a good while.

30 And Yisrael said unto Joseph (Yosef), "Now let me die, since I have seen your face, because you are yet alive."

31 And Joseph (Yosef) said unto his brethren, and unto his father's house, "I will go up, and shew Pharaoh (Paroh), and say unto him, 'My brethren, and my father's house, who were in the land of Canaan, are come unto me;

32 And the men are shepherds, for their trade hath been to feed cattle; and they have brought their flocks, and their herds, and all that they have.'

33 And it shall come to pass, when Pharaoh (Paroh) shall call you, and shall say, 'What is your occupation?'

34 That you shall say, 'Your servants' trade hath been about cattle from our youth even until now, both we, and also our fathers,' that you may dwell in the land of Goshen; for every shepherd is an abomination unto the Egyptians (Mitsrayim)."

47 Then Joseph (Yosef) came and told Pharaoh (Paroh), and said, "My father and my brethren, and their flocks, and their herds, and all that they have, are come out of the land of Canaan; and, behold, they are in the land of Goshen."

2 And he took some of his brethren, even five men, and presented them unto Pharaoh (Paroh).

3 And Pharaoh (Paroh) said unto his brethren, "What is your occupation?" And they said unto Pharaoh (Paroh), "Your servants are shepherds, both we, and also our fathers."

4 They said moreover unto Pharaoh (Paroh), "For to sojourn in the land are we come; for your servants have no pasture for their flocks; for the famine is sore in the land of Canaan. Now therefore, please let your servants dwell in the land of Goshen."

5 And Pharaoh (Paroh) spake unto Joseph (Yosef), saying, "Your father and your brethren are come unto you.

6 The land of Egypt (Mitsrayim) is before you; in the best of the land make your father and brethren to dwell; in the land of Goshen let them dwell; and if you knowest any men of activity among them, then make them rulers over my cattle."

7 And Joseph (Yosef) brought in Jacob (Yaaqov) his father, and set him before Pharaoh (Paroh); and Jacob (Yaaqov) blessed Pharaoh (Paroh).

8 And Pharaoh (Paroh) said unto Jacob (Yaaqov), "How old are you?"

9 And Jacob (Yaaqov) said unto Pharaoh (Paroh), "The days of the years of my pilgrimage are a hundred and thirty years: few and unpleasant have the days of the years of my life been, and have not attained unto the days of the years of the life of my fathers in the days of their pilgrimage."

10 And Jacob (Yaaqov) blessed Pharaoh (Paroh), and went out from before Pharaoh (Paroh).

11 And Joseph (Yosef) placed his father and his brethren, and gave them a possession in the land of Egypt (Mitsrayim), in the best of the land, in the land of Rameses, as Pharaoh (Paroh) had commanded.

12 And Joseph (Yosef) nourished his father, and his brethren, and all his father's household, with bread, according to their families.

13 And there was no bread in all the land; for the famine was very sore, so that the land of Egypt (Mitsrayim) and all the land of Canaan fainted by reason of the famine.

14 And Joseph (Yosef) gathered up all the money that was found in the land of Egypt (Mitsrayim), and in the land of Canaan, for the corn which they bought; and Joseph (Yosef) brought the money into Pharaoh (Paroh)'s house.

15 And when money failed in the land of Egypt (Mitsrayim), and in the land of Canaan, all the Egyptians (Mitsrayim) came unto Joseph (Yosef), and said, "Give us bread, for why should we die in your presence? For the money faileth."

16 And Joseph (Yosef) said, "Give your cattle; and I will give you for your cattle, if money fail."

17 And they brought their cattle unto Joseph

(Yosef); and Joseph (Yosef) gave them bread in exchange for horses, and for the flocks, and for the cattle of the herds, and for the asses; and he fed them with bread for all their cattle for that year.

18 When that year was ended, they came unto him the second year, and said unto him, "We will not hide it from my lord (adoni), how that our money is spent; my lord (adoni) also hath our herds of cattle; there is not ought left in the sight of my lord (adoni), but our bodies, and our land.

19 Wherefore shall we die before your eyes, both we and our land? Buy us and our land for bread, and we and our land will be servants unto Pharaoh (Paroh); and give us seed, that we may live, and not die, that the land be not desolate."

20 And Joseph (Yosef) bought all the land of Egypt (Mitsrayim) for Pharaoh (Paroh); for the Egyptians (Mitsrayim) sold every man his field, because the famine prevailed over them; so the land became Pharaoh (Paroh)'s.

21 And as for the people, he removed them to cities from one end of the borders of Egypt (Mitsrayim) even to the other end thereof.

22 Only the land of the priests (kohanim) bought he not; for the priests (kohanim) had a portion assigned them of Pharaoh (Paroh), and did eat their portion which Pharaoh (Paroh) gave them; wherefore they sold not their lands.

23 Then Joseph (Yosef) said unto the people, "Behold, I have bought you this day and your land for Pharaoh (Paroh); behold, here is seed for you, and you shall sow the land.

24 And it shall come to pass in the increase, that you shall give the fifth part unto Pharaoh (Paroh), and four parts shall be your own, for seed of the field, and for your food, and for them of your households, and for food for your little ones."

25 And they said, "You have saved our lives; let us find grace in the sight of my lord (adoni), and we will be Pharaoh (Paroh)'s servants."

26 And Joseph (Yosef) made it a law over the land of Egypt (Mitsrayim) unto this day, that Pharaoh (Paroh) should have the fifth part; except the land of the priests (kohanim) only, which became not Pharaoh (Paroh)'s.

27 And Yisrael dwelt in the land of Egypt (Mitsrayim), in the country of Goshen; and they had possessions therein, and grew, and multiplied exceedingly.

28 And Jacob (Yaaqov) lived in the land of Egypt (Mitsrayim) seventeen years; so the whole age of Jacob (Yaaqov) was a hundred forty and seven years.

29 And the time drew near that Yisrael must die; and he called his son Joseph (Yosef), and said unto him, "If now I have found grace in your sight, please put your hand under my thigh, and deal kindly and truly with me; please bury me not in Egypt (Mitsrayim);

30 But I will lie with my fathers, and you shalt carry me out of Egypt (Mitsrayim), and bury me in their burying place." And he said, "I will do as you have said."

31 And he said, "Swear unto me." And he sware unto him. And Yisrael bowed himself upon the bed's head.

48 And it came to pass after these things, that one told Joseph (Yosef), "Behold, your father is sick; and he took with him his two sons, Menashsheh and Efrayim.

2 And one told Jacob (Yaaqov), and said, "Behold, your son Joseph (Yosef) cometh unto you"; and Yisrael strengthened himself, and sat upon the bed.

3 And Jacob (Yaaqov) said unto Joseph (Yosef), "Almighty God (El Shaddai) appeared unto me at Luz in the land of Canaan, and blessed me,

4 And said unto me, 'Behold, I will make you fruitful, and multiply you, and I will make of you a multitude of people; and will give this land to your seed after you for an everlasting possession.'

5 And now your two sons, Efrayim and Menashsheh, who were born unto you in the land of Egypt (Mitsrayim) before I came unto you into Egypt (Mitsrayim), are mine; as Reuven and Shimon, they shall be mine.

6 And your issue, whom you begettest after them, shall be yours, and shall be called after the name of their brethren in their inheritance.

7 And as for me, when I came from Padan, Rachel died by me in the land of Canaan in the way, when yet there was but a little way to come unto Ephrath: and I buried her there in the way of Ephrath; the same is Bethlehem (Beit-Lechem)."

8 And Yisrael beheld Joseph (Yosef)'s sons, and said, "Who are these?"

9 And Joseph (Yosef) said unto his father,

"They are my sons, whom God (Elohim) hath given me in this place." And he said, "Please bring them unto me, and I will bless them."

10 Now the eyes of Yisrael were dim for age, so that he could not see. And he brought them near unto him; and he kissed them, and embraced them.

11 And Yisrael said unto Joseph (Yosef), "I had not thought to see your face; and, behold, God (Elohim) hath shewed me also your seed!"

12 And Joseph (Yosef) brought them out from between his knees, and he bowed himself with his face to the earth.

13 And Joseph (Yosef) took them both, Efrayim in his right hand toward Yisrael's left hand, and Menashsheh in his left hand toward Yisrael's right hand, and brought them near unto him.

14 And Yisrael stretched out his right hand, and laid it upon Efrayim's head, who was the younger, and his left hand upon Menashsheh's head, guiding his hands wittingly; for Menashsheh was the firstborn.

15 And he blessed Joseph (Yosef), and said, "God (Elohim), before whom my fathers Avraham and Isaac (Yitschaq) did walk, the God (Elohim) who fed me all my life long unto this day,

16 The Angel who redeemed me from all evil, bless the lads; and let my name be named on them, and the name of my fathers Avraham and Isaac (Yitschaq); and let them grow into a multitude in the midst of the earth."

17 And when Joseph (Yosef) saw that his father laid his right hand upon the head of Efrayim, it displeased him; and he held up his father's hand, to remove it from Efrayim's head unto Menashsheh's head.

18 And Joseph (Yosef) said unto his father, "Not so, my father, for this is the firstborn; put your right hand upon his head."

19 And his father refused, and said, "I know it, my son, I know it; he also shall become a people, and he also shall be great; but truly his younger brother shall be greater than he, and his seed shall become a multitude of nations."

20 And he blessed them that day, saying, "In you shall Yisrael bless, saying, 'God (Elohim) make you as Efrayim and as Menashsheh!'" And he set Efrayim before Menashsheh.

21 And Yisrael said unto Joseph (Yosef), "Behold, I die; but God (Elohim) shall be with you, and bring you again unto the land of your fathers.

22 Moreover I have given to you one portion above your brethren, which I took out of the hand of the Amorite with my sword and with my bow."

49 And Jacob (Yaaqov) called unto his sons, and said, "Gather yourselves together, that I may tell you that which shall befall you in the last days.

2 Gather yourselves together, and hear, you sons of Jacob (Yaaqov); and hearken unto Yisrael your father.

3 Reuven, you are my firstborn, my might, and the beginning of my strength, the excellency of dignity, and the excellency of power.

4 Unstable as water, you shalt not excel; because you wentest up to your father's bed; then defiledst you it; he went up to my couch.

5 Shimon and Lewi are brethren; instruments of cruelty are in their habitations.

6 O my soul, come not you into their secret; unto their assembly, mine honor, be not you united: for in their anger they slew a man, and in their selfwill they digged down a wall.

7 Cursed be their anger, for it was fierce; and their wrath, for it was cruel! I will divide them in Jacob (Yaaqov), and scatter them in Yisrael.

8 Judah (Yehudah), you are he whom your brethren shall praise: your hand shall be in the neck of your enemies; your father's children shall bow down before you.

9 Judah (Yehudah) is a lion's whelp; from the prey, my son, you are gone up; he stooped down, he couched as a lion, and as an old lion; who shall rouse him up?

10 The sceptre shall not depart from Judah (Yehudah), nor a lawgiver from between his feet, until Shiloh come; and unto him shall the gathering of the people be.

11 Binding his foal unto the vine, and his ass's colt unto the choice vine; he washed his garments in wine, and his clothes in the blood of grapes.

12 His eyes shall be red with wine, and his teeth white with milk.

13 Zevulun shall dwell at the haven of the sea; and he shall be for a haven of ships; and his border shall be unto Zidon.

14 Yissaskhar is a strong ass couching down between two burdens;

15 And he saw that rest was good, and the land that it was pleasant; and bowed his shoulder to bear, and became a servant unto tribute.

16 Dan shall judge his people, as one of the tribes of Yisrael.

17 Dan shall be a serpent by the way, an adder in the path, that biteth the horse heels, so that his rider shall fall backward.

18 I have waited for Your salvation, O יהוה.

19 Gad, a troop shall overcome him; but he shall overcome at the last.

20 Out of Asher his bread shall be fat, and he shall yield royal dainties.

21 Naftali is a hind let loose; he giveth goodly words.

22 Joseph (Yosef) is a fruitful bough, even a fruitful bough by a well; whose branches run over the wall.

23 The archers have sorely grieved him, and shot at him, and hated him;

24 But his bow abode in strength, and the arms of his hands were made strong by the hands of the mighty God (Elohim) of Jacob (Yaaqov); (from thence is the shepherd, the stone of Yisrael;)

25 Even by the God (Elohim) of your father, who shall help you; and by [B7a]Almighty (Shaddai), who shall bless you with blessings of heaven above, blessings of the deep that lieth under, blessings of the breasts, and of the womb.

26 The blessings of your father have prevailed above the blessings of my progenitors unto the utmost bound of the everlasting hills; they shall be on the head of Joseph (Yosef), and on the crown of the head of him that was separate from his brethren.

27 Binyamin shall ravin as a wolf; in the morning he shall devour the prey, and at night he shall divide the spoil."

28 All these are the twelve tribes of Yisrael: and this is it that their father spake unto them, and blessed them; every one according to his blessing he blessed them.

29 And he charged them, and said unto them, I am to be gathered unto my people: bury me with my fathers in the cave that is in the field of Ephron the Hittite,

30 In the cave that is in the field of Machpelah, which is before Mamre, in the land of Canaan, which Avraham bought with the field of Ephron the Hittite for a possession of a buryingplace.

31 There they buried Avraham and Sarah his wife; there they buried Isaac (Yitzchaq) and Rebekah his wife; and there I buried Leah.

32 The purchase of the field and of the cave that is therein was from the children of Heth."

33 And when Jacob (Yaaqov) had made an end of commanding his sons, he gathered up his feet into the bed, and yielded up the spirit, and was gathered unto his people.

50 And Joseph (Yosef) fell upon his father's face, and wept upon him, and kissed him.

2 And Joseph (Yosef) commanded his servants the physicians to embalm his father; and the physicians embalmed Yisrael.

3 And forty days were fulfilled for him; for so are fulfilled the days of those which are embalmed; and the Egyptians (Mitsrayim) mourned for him three-score and ten days.

4 And when the days of his mourning were past, Joseph (Yosef) spake unto the house of Pharaoh (Paroh), saying, "If now I have found grace in your eyes, please speak in the ears of Pharaoh (Paroh), saying,

5 'My father made me swear, saying, "Behold, I die; in my grave which I have digged for me in the land of Canaan, there shalt you bury me." Now therefore please let me go up, and bury my father, and I will come again.'"

6 And Pharaoh (Paroh) said, "Go up, and bury your father, according as he made you swear."

7 And Joseph (Yosef) went up to bury his father; and with him went up all the servants of Pharaoh (Paroh), the elders of his house, and all the elders of the land of Egypt (Mitsrayim),

8 And all the house of Joseph (Yosef), and his brethren, and his father's house. Only their little ones, and their flocks, and their herds, they left in the land of Goshen.

9 And there went up with him both chariots and horsemen; and it was a very great company.

10 And they came to the threshingfloor of Atad, which is beyond Jordan (Yarden), and there they mourned with a great and very sore lamentation; and he made a mourning for his father seven days.

11 And when the inhabitants of the land, the Canaanites, saw the mourning in the floor of Atad, they said, "This is a grievous mourning to the Egyptians (Mitsrayim)." Therefore the name of it was called Avel Mitsrayim, which is beyond Jordan (Yarden).

12 And his sons did unto him according as he commanded them;

13 For his sons carried him into the land of Canaan, and buried him in the cave of the field of Machpelah, which Avraham bought with the field for a possession of a buryingplace of Ephron the Hittite, before Mamre.

14 And Joseph (Yosef) returned into Egypt (Mitsrayim), he, and his brethren, and all that went up with him to bury his father, after he had buried his father.

15 And when Joseph (Yosef)'s brethren saw that their father was dead, they said, "Joseph (Yosef) will perhaps hate us, and will certainly requite us all the evil which we did unto him."

16 And they sent a messenger unto Joseph (Yosef), saying, "Your father did command before he died, saying,

17 'So shall you say unto Joseph (Yosef), "I beg you, please forgive the trespass of your brethren, and their sin; for they did unto you evil."' And now, please forgive the trespass of the servants of the God (Elohim) of your father." And Joseph (Yosef) wept when they spake unto him.

18 And his brethren also went and fell down before his face; and they said, "Behold, we be your servants."

19 And Joseph (Yosef) said unto them, "Fear not, for am I in the place of God (Elohim)?

20 But as for you, you thought evil against me; but God (Elohim) meant it unto good, to bring to pass, as it is this day, to save much people alive.

21 Now therefore fear you not; I will nourish you, and your little ones." And he comforted them, and spake kindly unto them.

22 And Joseph (Yosef) dwelt in Egypt (Mitsrayim), he, and his father's house; and Joseph (Yosef) lived a hundred and ten years.

23 And Joseph (Yosef) saw Efrayim's children of the third generation. The children also of Machir the son of Menashsheh were brought up upon Joseph (Yosef)'s knees.

24 And Joseph (Yosef) said unto his brethren, "I die; and God (Elohim) will surely visit you, and bring you out of this land unto the land which he sware to Avraham, to Isaac (Yitschaq), and to Jacob (Yaaqov)."

25 And Joseph (Yosef) took an oath of the children of Yisrael, saying, "God (Elohim) will surely visit you, and youshall carry up my bones from hence."

26 So Joseph (Yosef) died, being a hundred and ten years old; and they embalmed him, and he was put in a coffin in Egypt (Mitsrayim).

EXODUS
SHEMOT שְׁמוֹת
(Names)

1 Now these are the names of the children of Yisrael, who came into Egypt (Mitsrayim); every man and his household came with Jacob (Yaaqov):

2 Reuven, Shimon, Lewi, and Judah (Yehudah),

3 Yissaskhar, Zevulun, and Binyamin,

4 Dan, and Naftali, Gad, and Asher.

5 And all the souls that came out of the loins of Jacob (Yaaqov) were seventy souls; for Joseph (Yosef) was in Egypt (Mitsrayim) already.

6 And Joseph (Yosef) died, and all his brethren, and all that generation.

7 And the children of Yisrael were fruitful, and increased abundantly, and multiplied, and waxed exceeding mighty; and the land was filled with them.

8 Now there arose up a new king over Egypt (Mitsrayim), which knew not Joseph (Yosef).

9 And he said unto his people, "Behold, the people of the children of Yisrael are more and mightier than we.

10 Come on, let us deal wisely with them; lest they multiply, and it come to pass, that, when there falleth out any war, they join also unto our enemies, and fight against us, and so get them up out of the land."

11 Therefore they did set over them taskmasters to afflict them with their burdens. And they built for Pharaoh (Paroh) treasure cities, Pithom and Raamses.

12 But the more they afflicted them, the more they multiplied and grew. And they were grieved because of the children of Yisrael.

13 And the Egyptians (Mitsrayim) made the children of Yisrael to serve with rigour.

14 And they made their lives bitter with hard bondage, in morter, and in brick, and in all manner of service in the field: all their service, wherein they made them serve, was with rigour.

15 And the king of Egypt (Mitsrayim) spake to the Hebrew (Ivri) midwives, of which the name of the one was Shiphrah, and the name of the other Puah;

16 And he said, "When you do the office of a midwife to the Hebrew (Ivri) women, and see them upon the stools; if it be a son, then you shall kill him; but if it be a daughter, then she shall live."

17 But the midwives feared God (Elohim), and did not as the king of Egypt (Mitsrayim) commanded them, but saved the men children alive.

18 And the king of Egypt (Mitsrayim) called for the midwives, and said unto them, "Why have you done this thing, and have saved the men children alive?"

19 And the midwives said unto Pharaoh (Paroh), "Because the Hebrew (Ivri) women are not as the Egyptian (Mitsri) women; for they are lively, and are delivered ere the midwives come in unto them."

20 Therefore God (Elohim) dealt well with the midwives; and the people multiplied, and waxed very mighty.

21 And it came to pass, because the midwives feared God (Elohim), that He made them households.

22 And Pharaoh (Paroh) charged all his people, saying, "Every son that is born you shall cast into the river, and every daughter you shall save alive."

2 And there went a man of the house of Lewi, and took to wife a daughter of Lewi.

2 And the woman conceived, and bare a son; and when she saw him that he was a goodly child, she hid him three months.

3 And when she could no longer hide him, she took for him an ark of bulrushes, and daubed it with slime and with pitch, and put the child therein; and she laid it in the flags by the river's brink.

4 And his sister stood afar off, to know what would be done to him.

5 And the daughter of Pharaoh (Paroh) came down to wash herself at the river; and her maidens walked along by the river's side; and when she saw the ark among the flags, she sent her maid to fetch it.

6 And when she had opened it, she saw the child; and, behold, the babe wept. And she had compassion on him, and said, "This is one of the Hebrews' children."

7 Then said his sister to Pharaoh (Paroh)'s daughter, "Shall I go and call to you a nurse of the Hebrew (Ivri) women, that she may nurse the child for you?"

8 And Pharaoh (Paroh)'s daughter said to her,

"Go." And the maid went and called the child's mother.

9 And Pharaoh (Paroh)'s daughter said unto her, "Take this child away, and nurse it for me, and I will give you your wages." And the woman took the child, and nursed it.

10 And the child grew, and she brought him unto Pharaoh (Paroh)'s daughter, and he became her son. And she called his name [A30]Moses (Mosheh); and she said, "Because I drew him out of the water."

11 And it came to pass in those days, when Moses (Mosheh) was grown, that he went out unto his brethren, and looked on their burdens; and he spied an Egyptian (Mitsri) smiting a Hebrew (Ivri), one of his brethren.

12 And he looked this way and that way, and when he saw that there was no man, he slew the Egyptian (Mitsri), and hid him in the sand.

13 And when he went out the second day, behold, two men of the Hebrews (Ivrim) strove together; and he said to him that did the wrong, "Wherefore smitest you your fellow?"

14 And he said, "Who made you a prince and a judge over us? Intendest you to kill me, as you killedst the Egyptian (Mitsri)?" And Moses (Mosheh) feared, and said, "Surely this thing is known."

15 Now when Pharaoh (Paroh) heard this thing, he sought to slay Moses (Mosheh). But Moses (Mosheh) fled from the face of Pharaoh (Paroh), and dwelt in the land of Midian; and he sat down by a well.

16 Now the priest (kohen) of Midian had seven daughters; and they came and drew water, and filled the troughs to water their father's flock.

17 And the shepherds came and drove them away; but Moses (Mosheh) stood up and helped them, and watered their flock.

18 And when they came to Reuel their father, he said, "How is it that you are come so soon today?"

19 And they said, "An Egyptian (Mitsri) delivered us out of the hand of the shepherds, and also drew water enough for us, and watered the flock."

20 And he said unto his daughters, "And where is he? Why is it that you have left the man? Call him, that he may eat bread."

21 And Moses (Mosheh) was content to dwell with the man; and he gave Moses (Mosheh) Zipporah his daughter.

22 And she bares him a son, and he called his name Gershom, for he said, "I have been a stranger in a strange land."

23 And it came to pass in process of time, that the king of Egypt (Mitsrayim) died; and the children of Yisrael sighed by reason of the bondage, and they cried, and their cry came up unto God (Elohim) by reason of the bondage.

24 And God (Elohim) heard their groaning, and God (Elohim) remembered His covenant with Avraham, with Isaac (Yitschaq), and with Jacob (Yaaqov).

25 And God (Elohim) looked upon the children of Yisrael, and God (Elohim) had respect unto them.

3 Now Moses (Mosheh) kept the flock of Yetro his father in law, the priest (kohen) of Midian; and he led the flock to the backside of the desert, and came to the mountain of God (Elohim), even to Horeb (Chorev).

2 And the angel of יהוה appeared unto him in a flame of fire out of the midst of a bush; and he looked, and, behold, the bush burned with fire, and the bush was not consumed.

3 And Moses (Mosheh) said, "I will now turn aside, and see this great sight, why the bush is not burnt."

4 And when יהוה saw that he turned aside to see, God (Elohim) called unto him out of the midst of the bush, and said, "Moses, Moses (Mosheh)." And he said, "Here am I."

5 And He said, "Draw not near hither; put off your shoes from off your feet, for the place whereon you standest is holy ground."

6 Moreover He said, "I am the God (Elohim) of your father, the God (Elohim) of Avraham, the God (Elohim) of Isaac (Yitschaq), and the God (Elohim) of Jacob (Yaaqov)." And Moses (Mosheh) hid his face; for he was afraid to look upon God (Elohim).

7 And יהוה said, "I have surely seen the affliction of My people who are in Egypt (Mitsrayim), and have heard their cry by reason of their taskmasters; for I know their sorrows;

8 And I am come down to deliver them out of the hand of the Egyptians (Mitsrayim), and to bring them up out of that land unto a good land and a large, unto a land flowing with milk and honey; unto the place of the Canaanites, and the Hittites, and the Amorites, and the Perizzites,

and the Hivites, and the Jebusites (Yevusi).

9 Now therefore, behold, the cry of the children of Yisrael is come unto Me; and I have also seen the oppression wherewith the Egyptians (Mitsrayim) oppress them.

10 Come now therefore, and I will send you unto Pharaoh (Paroh), that you mayest bring forth My people the children of Yisrael out of Egypt (Mitsrayim).''

11 And Moses (Mosheh) said unto God (Elohim), "Who am I, that I should go unto Pharaoh (Paroh), and that I should bring forth the children of Yisrael out of Egypt (Mitsrayim)?"

12 And He said, "Certainly I will be with you; and this shall be a token unto you, that I have sent you. When you have brought forth the people out of Egypt (Mitsrayim), you shall serve God (Elohim) upon this mountain."

13 And Moses (Mosheh) said unto God (Elohim), "Behold, when I come unto the children of Yisrael, and shall say unto them, 'The God (Elohim) of your fathers hath sent me unto you'; and they shall say to me, 'What is His name?' What shall I say unto them?"

14 And God (Elohim) said unto Moses (Mosheh), "ᴮ¹⁵ᵃI Am Who I Am (Ehyeh Asher Ehyeh)." And He said, "Thus shalt you say unto the children of Yisrael, 'ᴮ¹⁵ᵇI AM (Ehyeh) hath sent me unto you.'"

15 And God (Elohim) said moreover unto Moses (Mosheh), "Thus shalt you say unto the children of Yisrael: ᴮ¹⁶יהוה, God (Elohim) of your fathers, God (Elohim) of Avraham, God (Elohim) of Isaac (Yitschaq), and God (Elohim) of Jacob (Yaaqov), hath sent me unto you. This is My name forever, and this is My memorial unto all generations.'

16 Go, and gather the elders of Yisrael together, and say unto them, 'יהוה God (Elohim) of your fathers, God (Elohim) of Avraham, of Isaac (Yitschaq), and of Jacob (Yaaqov), appeared unto me, saying, "I have surely visited you, and seen that which is done to you in Egypt (Mitsrayim):

17 And I have said, I will bring you up out of the affliction of Egypt (Mitsrayim) unto the land of the Canaanites, and the Hittites, and the Amorites, and the Perizzites, and the Hivites, and the Jebusites (Yevusi), unto a land flowing with milk and honey.'"

18 And they shall hearken to your voice; and

you shalt come, you and the elders of Yisrael, unto the king of Egypt (Mitsrayim), and you shall say unto him, 'יהוה God (Elohim) of the Hebrews (Ivrim) hath met with us; and now let us go, we beseech you, three days' journey into the wilderness, that we may sacrifice to יהוה our God (YHWH Eloheinu).'

19 And I am sure that the king of Egypt (Mitsrayim) will not let you go, no, not by a mighty hand.

20 And I will stretch out My hand, and smite Egypt (Mitsrayim) with all My wonders which I will do in the midst thereof; and after that he will let you go.

21 And I will give this people favor in the sight of the Egyptians (Mitsrayim); and it shall come to pass, that, when you go, you shall not go empty;

22 But every woman shall borrow of her neighbour, and of her that sojourneth in her house, jewels of silver, and jewels of gold, and raiment; and you shall put them upon your sons, and upon your daughters; and you shall spoil the Egyptians (Mitsrayim)."

4 And Moses (Mosheh) answered and said, "But, behold, they will not believe me, nor hearken unto my voice; for they will say, 'יהוה hath not appeared unto you.'"

2 And יהוה said unto him, "What is that in your hand?" And he said, "A rod."

3 And He said, "Cast it on the ground." And he cast it on the ground, and it became a serpent; and Moses (Mosheh) fled from before it.

4 And יהוה said unto Moses (Mosheh), "Put forth your hand, and take it by the tail." And he put forth his hand, and caught it, and it became a rod in his hand;

5 That they may believe that יהוה God (Elohim) of their fathers, God (Elohim) of Avraham, God (Elohim) of Isaac (Yitschaq), and God (Elohim) of Jacob (Yaaqov), hath appeared unto you.

6 And יהוה said furthermore unto him, "Put now your hand into your bosom." And he put his hand into his bosom: and when he took it out, behold, his hand was leprous as snow.

7 And He said, "Put your hand into your bosom again." And he put his hand into his bosom again; and plucked it out of his bosom, and, behold, it was turned again as his other flesh.

8 And it shall come to pass, if they will not believe you, neither hearken to the voice of the

first sign, that they will believe the voice of the latter sign.

9 "And it shall come to pass, if they will not believe also these two signs, neither hearken unto your voice, that you shalt take of the water of the river, and pour it upon the dry land: and the water which you takest out of the river shall become blood upon the dry land."

10 And Moses (Mosheh) said unto יהוה, "O Lord (Adonai), I am not eloquent, neither before, nor since You have spoken unto your servant; but I am slow of speech, and of a slow tongue."

11 And יהוה said unto him, "Who hath made man's mouth? Or who maketh the dumb, or deaf, or the seeing, or the blind? Have not I יהוה?

12 Now therefore go, and I will be with your mouth, and teach you what you shalt say."

13 And he said, "O my Lord (Adonai), please send by the hand of him whom You wilt send."

14 And the anger of יהי was kindled against Moses (Mosheh), and He said, "Is not ᴬ³¹Aaron (Aharon) the Lewite your brother? I know that he can speak well. And also, behold, he cometh forth to meet you; and when he seeth you, he will be glad in his heart.

15 And you shalt speak unto him, and put words in his mouth; and I will be with your mouth, and with his mouth, and will teach you what you shall do.

16 And he shall be your spokesman unto the people; and he shall be, even he shall be to you as a mouth, and you shalt be to him as God (Elohim).

17 And you shalt take this rod in your hand, wherewith you shalt do signs."

18 And Moses (Mosheh) went and returned to Yetro his father in law, and said unto him, "Please let me go and return unto my brethren which are in Egypt (Mitsrayim), and see whether they be yet alive." And Yetro said to Moses (Mosheh), "Go in peace."

19 And יהוה said unto Moses (Mosheh) in Midian, "Go, return into Egypt (Mitsrayim); for all the men are dead who sought your life."

20 And Moses (Mosheh) took his wife and his sons, and set them upon an ass, and he returned to the land of Egypt (Mitsrayim); and Moses (Mosheh) took the rod of God (Elohim) in his hand.

21 And יהוה said unto Moses (Mosheh), "When you goest to return into Egypt (Mitsrayim), see that you do all those wonders before Pharaoh (Paroh), which I have put in your hand; but I will harden his heart, that he shall not let the people go.

22 And you shalt say unto Pharaoh (Paroh), 'Thus saith יהוה, Yisrael is My son, even My firstborn;

23 And I say unto you, "Let My son go, that he may serve Me; and if you refuse to let him go, behold, I will slay your son, even your firstborn."'"

24 And it came to pass by the way in the inn, that יהוה met him, and sought to kill him.

25 Then Zipporah took a sharp stone, and cut off the foreskin of her son, and cast it at his feet, and said, "Surely a bloody husband are you to me."

26 So He let him go; then she said, "A bloody husband you are, because of the circumcision!"

27 And יהוה said to Aaron (Aharon), "Go into the wilderness to meet Moses (Mosheh)." And he went, and met him in the mount of God (Elohim), and kissed him.

28 And Moses (Mosheh) told Aaron (Aharon) all the words of יהוה who had sent him, and all the signs which He had commanded him.

29 And Moses (Mosheh) and Aaron (Aharon) went and gathered together all the elders of the children of Yisrael;

30 And Aaron (Aharon) spake all the words which יהוה had spoken unto Moses (Mosheh), and did the signs in the sight of the people.

31 And the people believed; and when they heard that יהוה had visited the children of Yisrael, and that He had looked upon their affliction, then they bowed their heads and worshipped.

5 And afterward Moses (Mosheh) and Aaron (Aharon) went in, and told Pharaoh (Paroh), "Thus saith יהוה God of Israel (Elohei Yisrael), 'Let My people go, that they may hold a feast unto Me in the wilderness.'"

2 And Pharaoh (Paroh) said, "Who is יהוה, that I should obey His voice to let Yisrael go? I know not יהוה, neither will I let Yisrael go."

3 And they said, "The God (Elohim) of the Hebrews (Ivrim) hath met with us. Please, let us go three days' journey into the desert and sacrifice unto יהוה our God (YHWH Eloheinu); lest He fall upon us with pestilence, or with the

sword."

4 And the king of Egypt (Mitsrayim) said unto them, "Wherefore do you, Moses (Mosheh) and Aaron (Aharon), let the people from their works? Get back unto your labors."

5 And Pharaoh (Paroh) said, "Behold, the people of the land now are many, and you make them rest from their labors!"

6 And Pharaoh (Paroh) commanded the same day the taskmasters of the people, and their officers, saying,

7 "You shall no more give the people straw to make brick as before; let them go and gather straw for themselves.

8 And the tale of the bricks, which they did make before, you shall lay upon them; you shall not diminish ought thereof: for they be idle; therefore they cry, saying, 'Let us go and sacrifice to our God (Elohim).'

9 Let there more work be laid upon the men, that they may labour therein; and let them not regard vain words."

10 And the taskmasters of the people went out, and their officers, and they spake to the people, saying, "Thus saith Pharaoh (Paroh), 'I will not give you straw.

11 Go you, get you straw where you can find it; yet none of your work shall be diminished.'"

12 So the people were scattered abroad throughout all the land of Egypt (Mitsrayim) to gather stubble instead of straw.

13 And the taskmasters hasted them, saying, "Fulfill your works, your daily tasks, as when there was straw."

14 And the officers of the children of Yisrael, whom Pharaoh (Paroh)'s taskmasters had set over them, were beaten, and demanded, "Wherefore have you not fulfilled your task in making brick both yesterday and today, as before?"

15 Then the officers of the children of Yisrael came and cried unto Pharaoh (Paroh), saying, "Wherefore dealest you thus with your servants?

16 There is no straw given unto your servants, and they say to us, 'Make brick'; and, behold, your servants are beaten; but the fault is in your own people."

17 But he said, "You are idle, you are idle! Therefore you say, 'Let us go and do sacrifice to יהוה.'

18 Go therefore now, and work; for there shall no straw be given you, yet shall you deliver the tale of bricks."

19 And the officers of the children of Yisrael did see that they were in evil case, after it was said, "You shall not reduce any bricks from your daily task."

20 And they met Moses (Mosheh) and Aaron (Aharon), who stood in the way, as they came forth from Pharaoh (Paroh);

21 And they said unto them, "יהוה look upon you, and judge; because you have made our savour to be abhorred in the eyes of Pharaoh (Paroh), and in the eyes of his servants, to put a sword in their hand to slay us."

22 And Moses (Mosheh) returned unto יהוה, and said, "Lord (Adonai), wherefore have You so evil entreated this people? Why is it that You have sent me?

23 For since I came to Pharaoh (Paroh) to speak in Your name, he hath done evil to this people; neither have You delivered Your people at all."

6 Then יהוה said unto Moses (Mosheh), "Now shalt you see what I will do to Pharaoh (Paroh), for with a strong hand shall he let them go; and with a strong hand shall he drive them out of his land."

2 And God (Elohim) spake unto Moses (Mosheh), and said unto him, "I am יהוה:

3 And I appeared unto Avraham, unto Isaac (Yitschaq), and unto Jacob (Yaaqov) as Almighty God (El Shaddai), but [B39]by My name [A1] יהוה (YHWH) was I not known to them?

4 And I have also established My covenant with them, to give them the land of Canaan, the land of their pilgrimage, wherein they were strangers.

5 And I have also heard the groaning of the children of Yisrael, whom the Egyptians (Mitsrayim) keep in bondage; and I have remembered My covenant.

6 Therefore say unto the children of Yisrael, I am יהוה, and I will bring you out from under the burdens of the Egyptians (Mitsrayim), and I will rid you out of their bondage, and I will redeem you with a stretched-out arm, and with great judgments;

7 And I will take you to Me for a people, and I will be to you a God (Elohim); and you shall know that I am יהוה your God (YHWH Eloheikhem), who bringeth you out from under the burdens of the Egyptians (Mitsrayim).

8 And I will bring you in unto the land, concerning which I did swear to give it to Avraham, to Isaac (Yitschaq), and to Jacob (Yaaqov); and I will give it you for a heritage: I am יהוה.'"

9 And Moses (Mosheh) spake so unto the children of Yisrael; but they hearkened not unto Moses (Mosheh) for anguish of spirit, and for cruel bondage.

10 And יהוה spake unto Moses (Mosheh), saying,

11 "Go in, speak unto Pharaoh (Paroh) king of Egypt (Mitsrayim), that he let the children of Yisrael go out of his land."

12 And Moses (Mosheh) spake before יהוה, saying, "Behold, the children of Yisrael have not hearkened unto Me; how then shall Pharaoh (Paroh) hear me, who am of uncircumcised lips?"

13 And יהוה spake unto Moses (Mosheh) and unto Aaron (Aharon), and gave them a command unto the children of Yisrael, and unto Pharaoh (Paroh) king of Egypt (Mitsrayim), to bring the children of Yisrael out of the land of Egypt (Mitsrayim).

14 These be the heads of their fathers' houses: The sons of Reuven the firstborn of Yisrael: Hanoch, and Pallu, Hezron, and Carmi; these be the families of Reuven.

15 And the sons of Shimon: Yemuel, and Yamin, and Ohad, and Yakhin, and Zohar, and Shaul the son of a Canaanitish woman; these are the families of Shimon.

16 And these are the names of the sons of Lewi according to their generations: Gershon, and Kohath, and Merari; and the years of the life of Lewi were a hundred thirty and seven years.

17 The sons of Gershon: Libni and Shimi, according to their families.

18 And the sons of Kohath: Amram, and Izhar, and Hebron, and Uzziel; and the years of the life of Kohath were a hundred thirty and three years.

19 And the sons of Merari: Mahali and Mushi; these are the families of Lewi according to their generations.

20 And Amram took him Jochebed (Yokheved) his father's sister to wife; and she bare him Aaron (Aharon) and Moses (Mosheh): and the years of the life of Amram were a hundred and thirty and seven years.

21 And the sons of Izhar: Korah (Qorach), and Nepheg, and Zichri.

22 And the sons of Uzziel: Mishael, and Elzaphan, and Zithri.

23 And Aaron (Aharon) took him Elisheba, daughter of Amminadab, sister of Naashon, to wife; and she bare him Nadav, and Avihu, Eleazar, and Ithamar.

24 And the sons of Korah (Qorach): Assir, and Elkanah, and Aviyahsaph; these are the families of the Korhites.

25 And Eleazar Aaron (Aharon)'s son took him one of the daughters of Putiel to wife; and she bare him Phinehas; these are the heads of the fathers of the [A18]Levites (Lewiyim) according to their families.

26 These are that Aaron (Aharon) and Moses (Mosheh), to whom יהוה said, "Bring out the children of Yisrael from the land of Egypt (Mitsrayim) according to their armies."

27 These are they who spake to Pharaoh (Paroh) king of Egypt (Mitsrayim), to bring out the children of Yisrael from Egypt (Mitsrayim); these are that Moses (Mosheh) and Aaron (Aharon).

28 And it came to pass on the day when יהוה spake unto Moses (Mosheh) in the land of Egypt (Mitsrayim),

29 That יהוה spake unto Moses (Mosheh), saying, "I am יהוה. Speak you unto Pharaoh (Paroh) king of Egypt (Mitsrayim) all that I say unto you."

30 And Moses (Mosheh) said before יהוה, "Behold, I am of uncircumcised lips, and how shall Pharaoh (Paroh) hearken unto me?"

7 And יהוה said unto Moses (Mosheh), "See, I have made you [4]God (Elohim) to Pharaoh (Paroh); and Aaron (Aharon) your brother shall be your prophet.

2 You shalt speak all that I command you; and Aaron (Aharon) your brother shall speak unto Pharaoh (Paroh), that he sends the children of Yisrael out of his land.

3 And I will harden Pharaoh (Paroh)'s heart, and multiply my signs and my wonders in the land of Egypt (Mitsrayim).

4 But Pharaoh (Paroh) shall not hearken unto you, that I may lay My hand upon Egypt (Mitsrayim), and bring forth Mine armies, and My people the children of Yisrael, out of the land of Egypt (Mitsrayim) by great judgments.

5 And the Egyptians (Mitsrayim) shall know that I am יהוה, when I stretch forth Mine hand upon Egypt (Mitsrayim), and bring out the children of Yisrael from among them."

6 And Moses (Mosheh) and Aaron (Aharon) did as יהוה commanded them, so did they.

7 And Moses (Mosheh) was fourscore (eighty) years old, and Aaron (Aharon) fourscore (eighty) and three years old, when they spake unto Pharaoh (Paroh).

8 And יהוה spake unto Moses (Mosheh) and unto Aaron (Aharon), saying,

9 "When Pharaoh (Paroh) shall speak unto you, saying, 'Shew a miracle for yourselves,' then you shalt say unto Aaron (Aharon), 'Take your rod, and cast it before Pharaoh (Paroh), and it shall become a serpent.'"

10 And Moses (Mosheh) and Aaron (Aharon) went in unto Pharaoh (Paroh), and they did so as יהוה had commanded. And Aaron (Aharon) cast down his rod before Pharaoh (Paroh), and before his servants, and it became a serpent.

11 Then Pharaoh (Paroh) also called the wise men and the sorcerers; now the magicians of Egypt (Mitsrayim), they also did in like manner with their enchantments.

12 For they cast down every man his rod, and they became serpents; but Aaron (Aharon)'s rod swallowed up their rods.

13 And Pharaoh (Paroh)'s heart was hardened, that he hearkened not unto them, as יהוה had said.

14 And יהוה said unto Moses (Mosheh), "Pharaoh (Paroh)'s heart is hardened, he refuseth to let the people go.

15 Get you unto Pharaoh (Paroh) in the morning; behold, he goeth out unto the water; and you shalt stand by the river's brink against he come; and the rod which was turned to a serpent shalt you take in your hand.

16 And you shalt say unto him, 'יהוה God (Elohim) of the Hebrews (Ivrim) hath sent me unto you, saying, "Let My people go, that they may serve Me in the wilderness"; but, behold, until now you wouldest not hear!

17 Thus saith יהוה: "In this you shalt know that I am יהוה. Behold, I will smite with the rod that is in Mine hand upon the waters which are in the river, and they shall be turned to blood.

18 And the fish that is in the river shall die, and the river shall stink; and the Egyptians (Mitsrayim) shall lothe to drink of the water of the river."'"

19 And יהוה spake unto Moses (Mosheh), "Say unto Aaron (Aharon), 'Take your rod, and stretch out your hand upon the waters of Egypt (Mitsrayim), upon their streams, upon their rivers, and upon their ponds, and upon all their pools of water, that they may become blood; and that there may be blood throughout all the land of Egypt (Mitsrayim), both in vessels of wood, and in vessels of stone.'"

20 And Moses (Mosheh) and Aaron (Aharon) did so, as יהוה commanded; and he lifted up the rod, and smote the waters that were in the river, in the sight of Pharaoh (Paroh), and in the sight of his servants; and all the waters that were in the river were turned to blood.

21 And the fish that was in the river died; and the river stank, and the Egyptians (Mitsrayim) could not drink of the water of the river; and there was blood throughout all the land of Egypt (Mitsrayim).

22 And the magicians of Egypt (Mitsrayim) did so with their enchantments; and Pharaoh (Paroh)'s heart was hardened, neither did he hearken unto them, as יהוה had said.

23 And Pharaoh (Paroh) turned and went into his house, neither did he set his heart to this also.

24 And all the Egyptians (Mitsrayim) digged round about the river for water to drink; for they could not drink of the water of the river.

25 And seven days were fulfilled, after that יהוה had smitten the river.

8 And יהוה spake unto Moses (Mosheh), "Go unto Pharaoh (Paroh), and say unto him, 'Thus saith יהוה, "Let My people go, that they may serve Me.

2 And if you refuse to let them go, behold, I will smite all your borders with frogs.

3 And the river shall bring forth frogs abundantly, which shall go up and come into your house, and into your bedchamber, and upon your bed, and into the house of your servants, and upon your people, and into your ovens, and into your kneadingtroughs.

4 And the frogs shall come up both on you, and upon your people, and upon all your servants."'"

5 And יהוה spake unto Moses (Mosheh), "Say unto Aaron (Aharon), 'Stretch forth your hand with your rod over the streams, over the rivers,

and over the ponds, and cause frogs to come up upon the land of Egypt (Mitsrayim).'"

6 And Aaron (Aharon) stretched out his hand over the waters of Egypt (Mitsrayim); and the frogs came up, and covered the land of Egypt (Mitsrayim).

7 And the magicians did so with their enchantments, and brought up frogs upon the land of Egypt (Mitsrayim).

8 Then Pharaoh (Paroh) called for Moses (Mosheh) and Aaron (Aharon), and said, "Intreat יהוה, that He may take away the frogs from me, and from my people; and I will let the people go, that they may do sacrifice unto יהוה."

9 And Moses (Mosheh) said unto Pharaoh (Paroh), "Glory over me; when shall I intreat for you, and for your servants, and for your people, to destroy the frogs from you and your houses, that they may remain in the river only?"

10 And he said, "Tomorrow." And he said, "Be it according to your word, that you mayest know that there is none like unto יהוה our God (YHWH Eloheinu).

11 And the frogs shall depart from you, and from your houses, and from your servants, and from your people; they shall remain in the river only."

12 And Moses (Mosheh) and Aaron (Aharon) went out from Pharaoh (Paroh); and Moses (Mosheh) cried unto יהוה because of the frogs which he had brought against Pharaoh (Paroh).

13 And יהוה did according to the word of Moses (Mosheh); and the frogs died out of the houses, out of the villages, and out of the fields.

14 And they gathered them together upon heaps: and the land stank.

15 But when Pharaoh (Paroh) saw that there was respite, he hardened his heart, and hearkened not unto them, as יהוה had said.

16 And יהוה said unto Moses (Mosheh), "Say unto Aaron (Aharon), 'Stretch out your rod, and smite the dust of the land, that it may become lice throughout all the land of Egypt (Mitsrayim).'"

17 And they did so; for Aaron (Aharon) stretched out his hand with his rod, and smote the dust of the earth, and it became lice in man, and in beast; all the dust of the land became lice throughout all the land of Egypt (Mitsrayim).

18 And the magicians did so with their enchantments to bring forth lice, but they could not; so there were lice upon man, and upon beast.

19 Then the magicians said unto Pharaoh (Paroh), "This is the finger of God (Elohim)." And Pharaoh (Paroh)'s heart was hardened, and he hearkened not unto them, as יהוה had said.

20 And יהוה said unto Moses (Mosheh), "Rise up early in the morning, and stand before Pharaoh (Paroh); behold, he cometh forth to the water; and say unto him, 'Thus saith יהוה, "Let My people go, that they may serve Me.

21 Else, if you wilt not let My people go, behold, I will send swarms of flies upon you, and upon your servants, and upon your people, and into your houses: and the houses of the Egyptians (Mitsrayim) shall be full of swarms of flies, and also the ground whereon they are.

22 And I will sever in that day the land of Goshen, in which My people dwell, that no swarms of flies shall be there; to the end you mayest know that I am יהוה in the midst of the earth.

23 And I will put a division between My people and your people; tomorrow shall this sign be.""'"

24 And יהוה did so; and there came a grievous swarm of flies into the house of Pharaoh (Paroh), and into his servants' houses, and into all the land of Egypt (Mitsrayim); the land was corrupted by reason of the swarm of flies.

25 And Pharaoh (Paroh) called for Moses (Mosheh) and for Aaron (Aharon), and said, "Go you, sacrifice to your God (Elohim) in the land."

26 And Moses (Mosheh) said, "It is not right so to do; for we shall sacrifice the abomination of the Egyptians (Mitsrayim) to יהוה our God (YHWH Eloheinu); behold, shall we sacrifice the abomination of the Egyptians (Mitsrayim) before their eyes, and will they not stone us?

27 We will go three days' journey into the wilderness, and sacrifice to יהוה our God (YHWH Eloheinu), as He shall command us."

28 And Pharaoh (Paroh) said, "I will let you go, that you may sacrifice to יהוה your God (YHWH Eloheikhem) in the wilderness; only you shall not go very far away. Intreat for me."

29 And Moses (Mosheh) said, "Behold, I go out from you, and I will intreat יהוה that the swarms of flies may depart from Pharaoh (Paroh), from his servants, and from his people, tomorrow; but let not Pharaoh (Paroh) deal deceitfully

anymore in not letting the people go to sacrifice to יהוה."

30 And Moses (Mosheh) went out from Pharaoh (Paroh), and intreated יהוה.

31 And יהוה did according to the word of Moses (Mosheh); and He removed the swarms of flies from Pharaoh (Paroh), from his servants, and from his people; there remained not one.

32 And Pharaoh (Paroh) hardened his heart at this time also, neither would he let the people go.

9 Then יהוה said unto Moses (Mosheh), "Go in unto Pharaoh (Paroh), and tell him, 'Thus saith יהוה God (Elohim) of the Hebrews (Ivrim), "Let My people go, that they may serve Me."

2 For if you refuse to let them go, and wilt hold them still,

3 Behold, the hand of יהוה is upon your cattle which is in the field, upon the horses, upon the asses, upon the camels, upon the oxen, and upon the sheep; there shall be a very grievous murrain.

4 And יהוה shall sever between the cattle of Yisrael and the cattle of Egypt (Mitsrayim); and there shall nothing die of all that is the children's of Yisrael.""

5 And יהוה appointed a set time, saying, "Tomorrow יהוה shall do this thing in the land."

6 And יהוה did that thing on the next day, and all the cattle of Egypt (Mitsrayim) died; but of the cattle of the children of Yisrael died not one.

7 And Pharaoh (Paroh) sent, and, behold, there was not one of the cattle of the Yisraelites dead. But the heart of Pharaoh (Paroh) was hardened, and he did not let the people go.

8 And יהוה said unto Moses (Mosheh) and unto Aaron (Aharon), "Take to you handfuls of ashes of the furnace, and let Moses (Mosheh) sprinkle it toward the heaven in the sight of Pharaoh (Paroh).

9 And it shall become small dust in all the land of Egypt (Mitsrayim), and shall be a boil breaking forth with blains upon man, and upon beast, throughout all the land of Egypt (Mitsrayim)."

10 And they took ashes of the furnace, and stood before Pharaoh (Paroh); and Moses (Mosheh) sprinkled it up toward heaven; and it became a boil breaking forth with blains upon man, and upon beast.

11 And the magicians could not stand before Moses (Mosheh) because of the boils; for the boil was upon the magicians, and upon all the

Egyptians (Mitsrayim).

12 And יהוה hardened the heart of Pharaoh (Paroh), and he hearkened not unto them, as יהוה had spoken unto Moses (Mosheh).

13 And יהוה said unto Moses (Mosheh), "Rise up early in the morning, and stand before Pharaoh (Paroh), and say unto him, 'Thus saith יהוה God (Elohim) of the Hebrews (Ivrim), "Let My people go, that they may serve Me.

14 For I will at this time send all My plagues upon your heart, and upon your servants, and upon your people; that you mayest know that there is none like Me in all the earth.

15 For now I will stretch out My hand, that I may smite you and your people with pestilence; and you shalt be cut off from the earth.

16 And in very deed for this cause have I raised you up, for to shew in you My power; and that My name may be declared throughout all the earth.

17 As yet exaltest you yourself against My people, that you wilt not let them go.

18 Behold, tomorrow about this time I will cause it to rain a very grievous hail, such as hath not been in Egypt (Mitsrayim) since the foundation thereof even until now.

19 Send therefore now, and gather your cattle, and all that you have in the field; for upon every man and beast which shall be found in the field, and shall not be brought home, the hail shall come down upon them, and they shall die.""

20 He that feared the word of יהוה among the servants of Pharaoh (Paroh) made his servants and his cattle flee into the houses;

21 And he that regarded not the word of יהוה left his servants and his cattle in the field.

22 And יהוה said unto Moses (Mosheh), "Stretch forth your hand toward heaven, that there may be hail in all the land of Egypt (Mitsrayim), upon man, and upon beast, and upon every herb of the field, throughout the land of Egypt (Mitsrayim)."

23 And Moses (Mosheh) stretched forth his rod toward heaven; and יהוה sent thunder and hail, and the fire ran along upon the ground; and יהוה rained hail upon the land of Egypt (Mitsrayim).

24 So there was hail, and fire mingled with the hail, very grievous, such as there was none like it in all the land of Egypt (Mitsrayim) since it became a nation.

25 And the hail smote throughout all the land of

Egypt (Mitsrayim) all that was in the field, both man and beast; and the hail smote every herb of the field, and broke every tree of the field.

26 Only in the land of Goshen, where the children of Yisrael were, was there no hail.

27 And Pharaoh (Paroh) sent, and called for Moses (Mosheh) and Aaron (Aharon), and said unto them, "I have sinned this time; יהוה is righteous, and I and my people are wicked.

28 Intreat יהוה (for it is enough) that there be no more mighty thunderings and hail; and I will let you go, and you shall stay no longer."

29 And Moses (Mosheh) said unto him, "As soon as I am gone out of the city, I will spread abroad my hands unto יהוה; and the thunder shall cease, neither shall there be any more hail; that you mayest know how that the earth is יהוה's.

30 But as for you and your servants, I know that you will not yet fear God (Elohim) יהוה."

31 Now the flax and the barley was smitten, for the barley was in the ear, and the flax was bolled.

32 But the wheat and the rie were not smitten, for they were not grown up.

33 And Moses (Mosheh) went out of the city from Pharaoh (Paroh), and spread abroad his hands unto יהוה; and the thunders and hail ceased, and the rain was not poured upon the earth.

34 And when Pharaoh (Paroh) saw that the rain and the hail and the thunders were ceased, he sinned yet more, and hardened his heart, he and his servants.

35 And the heart of Pharaoh (Paroh) was hardened, neither would he let the children of Yisrael go, as יהוה had spoken by Moses (Mosheh).

10 And יהוה said unto Moses (Mosheh), "Go in unto Pharaoh (Paroh); for I have hardened his heart, and the heart of his servants, that I might shew these My signs before him:

2 And that you mayest tell in the ears of your son, and of your son's son, what things I have wrought in Egypt (Mitsrayim), and My signs which I have done among them, that you may know how that I am יהוה."

3 And Moses (Mosheh) and Aaron (Aharon) came in unto Pharaoh (Paroh), and said unto him, "Thus saith יהוה God (Elohim) of the Hebrews (Ivrim), 'How long wilt you refuse to humble yourself before Me? Let My people go, that they may serve Me.

4 Else, if you refuse to let My people go, behold, tomorrow will I bring the locusts into your coast;

5 And they shall cover the face of the earth, that one cannot be able to see the earth; and they shall eat the residue of that which is escaped, which remaineth unto you from the hail, and shall eat every tree which groweth for you out of the field;

6 And they shall fill your houses, and the houses of all your servants, and the houses of all the Egyptians (Mitsrayim); which neither your fathers, nor your fathers' fathers have seen, since the day that they were upon the earth unto this day.'" And he turned himself, and went out from Pharaoh (Paroh).

7 And Pharaoh (Paroh)'s servants said unto him, "How long shall this man be a snare unto us? Let the men go, that they may serve יהוה their God (YHWH Eloheihem); knowest you not yet that Egypt (Mitsrayim) is destroyed?"

8 And Moses (Mosheh) and Aaron (Aharon) were brought again unto Pharaoh (Paroh); and he said unto them, "Go, serve יהוה your God (YHWH Eloheikhem); but who are they that shall go?"

9 And Moses (Mosheh) said, "We will go with our young and with our old, with our sons and with our daughters, with our flocks and with our herds will we go; for we must hold a feast unto יהוה."

10 And he said unto them, "Let יהוה be so with you, as I will let you go, and your little ones. Look to it, for evil is before you.

11 Not so! Go now you that are men, and serve יהוה, for that you did desire." And they were driven out from Pharaoh (Paroh)'s presence.

12 And יהוה said unto Moses (Mosheh), "Stretch out your hand over the land of Egypt (Mitsrayim) for the locusts, that they may come up upon the land of Egypt (Mitsrayim), and eat every herb of the land, even all that the hail hath left."

13 And Moses (Mosheh) stretched forth his rod over the land of Egypt (Mitsrayim), and יהוה brought an east wind upon the land all that day, and all that night; and when it was morning, the east wind brought the locusts.

14 And the locusts went up over all the land of Egypt (Mitsrayim), and rested in all the coasts

of Egypt (Mitsrayim); very grievous were they; before them there were no such locusts as they, neither after them shall be such.

15 For they covered the face of the whole earth, so that the land was darkened; and they did eat every herb of the land, and all the fruit of the trees which the hail had left; and there remained not any green thing in the trees, or in the herbs of the field, through all the land of Egypt (Mitsrayim).

16 Then Pharaoh (Paroh) called for Moses (Mosheh) and Aaron (Aharon) in haste; and he said, "I have sinned against יהוה your God (YHWH Eloheikhem), and against you.

17 Now therefore please forgive my sin only this once, and intreat יהוה your God (YHWH Eloheikhem), that He may take away from me this death only."

18 And he went out from Pharaoh (Paroh), and intreated יהוה.

19 And יהוה turned a mighty strong west wind, which took away the locusts, and cast them into the Red sea; there remained not one locust in all the coasts of Egypt (Mitsrayim).

20 But יהוה hardened Pharaoh (Paroh)'s heart, so that he would not let the children of Yisrael go.

21 And יהוה said unto Moses (Mosheh), "Stretch out your hand toward heaven, that there may be darkness over the land of Egypt (Mitsrayim), even darkness which may be felt."

22 And Moses (Mosheh) stretched forth his hand toward heaven; and there was a thick darkness in all the land of Egypt (Mitsrayim) three days.

23 They saw not one another, neither rose any from his place for three days; but all the children of Yisrael had light in their dwellings.

24 And Pharaoh (Paroh) called unto Moses (Mosheh), and said, "Go you, serve יהוה; only let your flocks and your herds be stayed; let your little ones also go with you."

25 And Moses (Mosheh) said, "You must give us also sacrifices and burnt offerings, that we may sacrifice unto יהוה our God (YHWH Eloheinu).

26 Our cattle also shall go with us; there shall not a hoof be left behind; for thereof must we take to serve יהוה our God (YHWH Eloheinu); and we know not with what we must serve יהוה, until we come thither."

27 But יהוה hardened Pharaoh (Paroh)'s heart, and he would not let them go.

28 And Pharaoh (Paroh) said unto him, "Get you from me, take heed to yourself, see my face no more; for in that day you seest my face you shalt die."

29 And Moses (Mosheh) said, "You have spoken well, I will see your face again no more."

11 And יהוה said unto Moses (Mosheh), "Yet will I bring one plague more upon Pharaoh (Paroh), and upon Egypt (Mitsrayim); afterwards he will let you go hence; when he shall let you go, he shall surely thrust you out hence altogether.

2 Speak now in the ears of the people, and let every man borrow of his neighbour, and every woman of her neighbour, jewels of silver, and jewels of gold."

3 And יהוה gave the people favor in the sight of the Egyptians (Mitsrayim). Moreover the man Moses (Mosheh) was very great in the land of Egypt (Mitsrayim), in the sight of Pharaoh (Paroh)'s servants, and in the sight of the people.

4 And Moses (Mosheh) said, "Thus saith יהוה, 'About midnight will I go out into the midst of Egypt (Mitsrayim).

5 And all the firstborn in the land of Egypt (Mitsrayim) shall die, from the firstborn of Pharaoh (Paroh) that sitteth upon his throne, even unto the firstborn of the maidservant that is behind the mill; and all the firstborn of beasts.

6 And there shall be a great cry throughout all the land of Egypt (Mitsrayim), such as there was none like it, nor shall be like it anymore.

7 But against any of the children of Yisrael shall not a dog move his tongue, against man or beast, that you may know how that יהוה doth put a difference between the Egyptians (Mitsrayim) and Yisrael.

8 And all these your servants shall come down unto me, and bow down themselves unto me, saying, 'Get you out, and all the people that follow you!' And after that I will go out." And he went out from Pharaoh (Paroh) in a great anger.

9 And יהוה said unto Moses (Mosheh), "Pharaoh (Paroh) shall not hearken unto you; that My wonders may be multiplied in the land of Egypt (Mitsrayim)."

10 And Moses (Mosheh) and Aaron (Aharon) did all these wonders before Pharaoh (Paroh); and יהוה hardened Pharaoh (Paroh)'s heart, so

that he would not let the children of Yisrael go out of his land.

12 And יהוה spake unto Moses (Mosheh) and Aaron (Aharon) in the land of Egypt (Mitsrayim), saying,

2 "This month shall be unto you the beginning of months; it shall be the first month of the year to you.

3 Speak you unto all the congregation of Yisrael, saying, "In the tenth day of this month they shall take to them every man a lamb, according to the house of their fathers, a lamb for a house;

4 And if the household be too little for the lamb, let him and his neighbour next unto his house take it according to the number of the souls; every man according to his eating shall make your count for the lamb.

5 Your lamb shall be without blemish, a male of the first year; you shall take it out from the sheep, or from the goats;

6 And you shall keep it up until the fourteenth day of the same month; and the whole assembly of the congregation of Yisrael shall kill it in the evening.

7 And they shall take of the blood, and strike it on the two side posts and on the upper door post of the houses, wherein they shall eat it.

8 And they shall eat the flesh in that night, roast with fire, and unleavened bread (matstsah); and with bitter herbs they shall eat it.

9 Eat not of it raw, nor sodden at all with water, but roast with fire; his head with his legs, and with the purtenance thereof.

10 And you shall let nothing of it remain until the morning; and that which remaineth of it until the morning you shall burn with fire.

11 And thus shall you eat it: with your loins girded, your shoes on your feet, and your staff in your hand; and you shall eat it in haste; it is יהוה's [B19]Passover (Pesach).

12 For I will pass through the land of Egypt (Mitsrayim) this night, and will smite all the firstborn in the land of Egypt (Mitsrayim), both man and beast; and against all the gods (elohim) of Egypt (Mitsrayim) I will execute judgment: I am יהוה.

13 And the blood shall be to you for a token upon the houses where you are; and when I see the blood, I will pass over you, and the plague shall not be upon you to destroy you, when I smite the land of Egypt (Mitsrayim).

14 And this day shall be unto you for a memorial; and you shall keep it a feast to יהוה throughout your generations; you shall keep it a feast by an ordinance forever.

15 Seven days shall you eat unleavened bread (matstsah); even the first day you shall put away leaven out of your houses, for whosoever eateth leavened bread from the first day until the seventh day, that soul shall be cut off from Yisrael.

16 And in the first day there shall be a holy convocation, and in the seventh day there shall be a holy convocation to you; no manner of work shall be done in them, except that which every man must eat, that only may be done of you.

17 And you shall observe the [B20]Feast of Unleavened Bread (Chag HaMatzot); for in this selfsame day have I brought your armies out of the land of Egypt (Mitsrayim); therefore shall you observe this day in your generations by an ordinance forever.

18 In the first month, on the fourteenth day of the month at even, you shall eat unleavened bread, until the one and twentieth day of the month at even.

19 Seven days shall there be no leaven found in your houses, for whosoever eateth that which is leavened, even that soul shall be cut off from the congregation of Yisrael, whether he be a stranger, or born in the land.

20 You shall eat nothing leavened; in all your habitations shall you eat unleavened bread.

21 Then Moses (Mosheh) called for all the elders of Yisrael, and said unto them, "Draw out and take you a lamb according to your families, and kill the [B19]passover lamb (pesach).

22 And you shall take a bunch of hyssop, and dip it in the blood that is in the bason, and strike the lintel and the two side posts with the blood that is in the bason; and none of you shall go out at the door of his house until the morning.

23 For יהוה will pass through to smite the Egyptians (Mitsrayim); and when He seeth the blood upon the lintel, and on the two side posts, יהוה will pass over the door, and will not allow the destroyer to come in unto your houses to smite you.

24 And you shall observe this thing for an ordinance to you and to your sons forever.

25 And it shall come to pass, when you come to

the land which יהוה will give you, according as He hath promised, that you shall keep this service.

26 And it shall come to pass, when your children shall say unto you, 'What mean you by this service?'

27 That you shall say, 'It is the sacrifice of יהוה's Passover (Pesach), who passed over the houses of the children of Yisrael in Egypt (Mitsrayim), when He smote the Egyptians (Mitsrayim), and delivered our households.'" And the people bowed the head and worshipped.

28 And the children of Yisrael went away, and did as יהוה had commanded Moses (Mosheh) and Aaron (Aharon), so did they.

29 And it came to pass, that at midnight יהוה smote all the firstborn in the land of Egypt (Mitsrayim), from the firstborn of Pharaoh (Paroh) that sat on his throne unto the firstborn of the captive that was in the dungeon; and all the firstborn of cattle.

30 And Pharaoh (Paroh) rose up in the night, he, and all his servants, and all the Egyptians (Mitsrayim); and there was a great cry in Egypt (Mitsrayim); for there was not a house where there was not one dead.

31 And he called for Moses (Mosheh) and Aaron (Aharon) by night, and said, "Rise up, and get you forth from among my people, both you and the children of Yisrael; and go, serve יהוה, as you have said.

32 Also take your flocks and your herds, as you have said, and be gone; and bless me also."

33 And the Egyptians (Mitsrayim) urged upon the people, that they might send them out of the land in haste; for they said, "We be all dead men."

34 And the people took their dough before it was leavened, their kneadingtroughs being bound up in their clothes upon their shoulders.

35 And the children of Yisrael did according to the word of Moses (Mosheh); and they borrowed of the Egyptians (Mitsrayim) jewels of silver, and jewels of gold, and raiment;

36 And יהוה gave the people favor in the sight of the Egyptians (Mitsrayim), so that they lent unto them such things as they required. And they plundered the Egyptians (Mitsrayim).

37 And the children of Yisrael journeyed from Rameses to Sukkot, about six hundred thousand on foot that were men, besides children.

38 And a mixed multitude went up also with them; and flocks, and herds, even very much cattle.

39 And they baked unleavened cakes of the dough which they brought forth out of Egypt (Mitsrayim), for it was not leavened, because they were thrust out of Egypt (Mitsrayim), and could not tarry, neither had they prepared for themselves any victual.

40 Now the sojourning of the children of Yisrael, who dwelt in Egypt (Mitsrayim), was four hundred and thirty years.

41 And it came to pass at the end of the four hundred and thirty years, even the selfsame day it came to pass, that all the hosts of יהוה went out from the land of Egypt (Mitsrayim).

42 It is a night to be much observed unto יהוה for bringing them out from the land of Egypt (Mitsrayim). This is that night of יהוה to be observed of all the children of Yisrael in their generations.

43 And יהוה said unto Moses (Mosheh) and Aaron (Aharon), "This is the ordinance of the [B19]Passover (Pesach): There shall no stranger eat thereof;

44 But every man's servant that is bought for money, when you have circumcised him, then shall he eat thereof.

45 A foreigner and a hired servant shall not eat thereof.

46 In one house shall it be eaten; you shalt not carry forth ought of the flesh abroad out of the house; neither shall you break a bone thereof.

47 All the congregation of Yisrael shall keep it.

48 And when a stranger shall sojourn with you, and will keep the Passover (Pesach) to יהוה, let all his males be circumcised, and then let him come near and keep it; and he shall be as one that is born in the land; for no uncircumcised person shall eat thereof.

49 One law shall be to him that is homeborn, and unto the stranger that sojourneth among you.

50 Thus did all the children of Yisrael, as יהוה commanded Moses (Mosheh) and Aaron (Aharon), so did they.

51 And it came to pass the selfsame day, that יהוה did bring the children of Yisrael out of the land of Egypt (Mitsrayim) by their armies.

13 And יהוה spake unto Moses (Mosheh), saying,

2 "Sanctify unto Me all the firstborn,

whatsoever openeth the womb among the children of Yisrael, both of man and of beast: it is Mine."

3 And Moses (Mosheh) said unto the people, "Remember this day, in which you came out from Egypt (Mitsrayim), out of the house of bondage, for by strength of hand יהוה brought you out from this place; there shall no leavened bread be eaten.

4 This day came you out in the month Aviv.

5 And it shall be when יהוה shall bring you into the land of the Canaanites, and the Hittites, and the Amorites, and the Hivites, and the Jebusites (Yevusi), which He sware unto your fathers to give you, a land flowing with milk and honey, that you shalt keep this service in this month.

6 Seven days you shalt eat unleavened bread, and in the seventh day shall be a feast to יהוה.

7 Unleavened bread shall be eaten seven days; and there shall no leavened bread be seen with you, neither shall there be leaven seen with you in all your quarters.

8 And you shalt shew your son in that day, saying, 'This is done because of that which יהוה did unto me when I came forth out of Egypt (Mitsrayim).'

9 And it shall be for a sign unto you upon your hand, and for a memorial between your eyes, that יהוה's [B28a]Torah may be in your mouth; for with a strong hand hath יהוה brought you out of Egypt (Mitsrayim).

10 You shalt therefore keep this ordinance in its season from year to year.

11 And it shall be when יהוה shall bring you into the land of the Canaanites, as He sware unto you and to your fathers, and shall give it you,

12 That you shalt set apart unto יהוה all that openeth the matrix, and every firstling that cometh of a beast which you have; the males shall be יהוה's.

13 And every firstling of an ass you shalt redeem with a lamb; and if you wilt not redeem it, then you shalt break his neck; and all the firstborn of man among your children shalt you redeem.

14 And it shall be when your son asketh you in time to come, saying, 'What is this?' that you shalt say unto him, 'By strength of hand יהוה brought us out from Egypt (Mitsrayim), from the house of bondage.

15 And it came to pass, when Pharaoh (Paroh) would hardly let us go, that יהוה slew all the firstborn in the land of Egypt (Mitsrayim), both the firstborn of man, and the firstborn of beast; therefore I sacrifice to יהוה all that openeth the matrix, being males; but all the firstborn of my children I redeem.'

16 And it shall be for a token upon your hand, and for frontlets between your eyes; for by strength of hand יהוה brought us forth out of Egypt (Mitsrayim).

17 And it came to pass, when Pharaoh (Paroh) had let the people go, that God (Elohim) led them not through the way of the land of the Philistines, although that was near; for God (Elohim) said, "Lest perhaps the people regret when they see war, and they return to Egypt (Mitsrayim)."

18 But God (Elohim) led the people about, through the way of the wilderness of the Red sea; and the children of Yisrael went up harnessed out of the land of Egypt (Mitsrayim).

19 And Moses (Mosheh) took the bones of Joseph (Yosef) with him: for he had straitly sworn the children of Yisrael, saying, "God (Elohim) will surely visit you; and you shall carry up my bones away hence with you."

20 And they took their journey from Sukkoth, and encamped in Etham, in the edge of the wilderness.

21 And יהוה went before them by day in a pillar of a cloud, to lead them the way; and by night in a pillar of fire, to give them light; to go by day and night.

22 He took not away the pillar of the cloud by day, nor the pillar of fire by night, from before the people.

14 And יהוה spake unto Moses (Mosheh), saying,

2 "Speak unto the children of Yisrael, that they turn and encamp before Pihahiroth, between Migdol and the sea, opposite Baalzephon; before it shall you encamp by the sea.

3 For Pharaoh (Paroh) will say of the children of Yisrael, 'They are entangled in the land, the wilderness hath shut them in.'

4 And I will harden Pharaoh (Paroh)'s heart, that he shall follow after them; and I will be honored upon Pharaoh (Paroh), and upon all his host, that the Egyptians (Mitsrayim) may know that I am יהוה." And they did so.

5 And it was told the king of Egypt (Mitsrayim) that the people fled; and the heart of Pharaoh

(Paroh) and of his servants was turned against the people, and they said, "Why have we done this, that we have let Yisrael go from serving us?"

6 And he made ready his chariot, and took his people with him.

7 And he took six hundred chosen chariots, and all the chariots of Egypt (Mitsrayim), and captains over every one of them.

8 And יהוה hardened the heart of Pharaoh (Paroh) king of Egypt (Mitsrayim), and he pursued after the children of Yisrael; and the children of Yisrael went out with a high hand (boldly).

9 But the Egyptians (Mitsrayim) pursued after them, all the horses and chariots of Pharaoh (Paroh), and his horsemen, and his army, and overtook them encamping by the sea, beside Pihahiroth, before Baalzephon.

10 And when Pharaoh (Paroh) drew near, the children of Yisrael lifted up their eyes, and, behold, the Egyptians (Mitsrayim) marched after them; and they were sore afraid; and the children of Yisrael cried out unto יהוה.

11 And they said unto Moses (Mosheh), "Because there were no graves in Egypt (Mitsrayim), have you taken us away to die in the wilderness? Wherefore have you dealt thus with us, to carry us forth out of Egypt (Mitsrayim)?

12 Is not this the word that we did tell you in Egypt (Mitsrayim), saying, 'Let us alone, that we may serve the Egyptians (Mitsrayim)?' For it had been better for us to serve the Egyptians (Mitsrayim), than that we should die in the wilderness."

13 And Moses (Mosheh) said unto the people, "Fear you not, stand still, and see the salvation of יהוה, which He will shew to you today; for the Egyptians (Mitsrayim) whom you have seen today, you shall see them again no more forever."

14 יהוה shall fight for you, and you shall hold your peace.

15 And יהוה said unto Moses (Mosheh), "Wherefore criest you unto Me? Speak unto the children of Yisrael, that they go forward;

16 But lift you up your rod, and stretch out your hand over the sea, and divide it; and the children of Yisrael shall go on dry ground through the midst of the sea.

17 And I, behold, I will harden the hearts of the Egyptians (Mitsrayim), and they shall follow them; and I will get My honor upon Pharaoh (Paroh), and upon all his army, upon his chariots, and upon his horsemen.

18 And the Egyptians (Mitsrayim) shall know that I am יהוה, when I have gotten My honor upon Pharaoh (Paroh), upon his chariots, and upon his horsemen."

19 And the angel of God (Elohim), who went before the camp of Yisrael, moved and went behind them; and the pillar of the cloud went from before their face, and stood behind them.

20 And it came between the camp of the Egyptians (Mitsrayim) and the camp of Yisrael; and it was a cloud and darkness to them, but it gave light by night to these, so that the one came not near the other all the night.

21 And Moses (Mosheh) stretched out his hand over the sea; and יהוה caused the sea to go back by a strong east wind all that night, and made the sea dry land, and the waters were divided.

22 And the children of Yisrael went into the midst of the sea upon the dry ground; and the waters were a wall unto them on their right hand, and on their left.

23 And the Egyptians (Mitsrayim) pursued, and went in after them to the midst of the sea, even all Pharaoh (Paroh)'s horses, his chariots, and his horsemen.

24 And it came to pass, that in the morning watch, יהוה looked unto the army of the Egyptians (Mitsrayim) through the pillar of fire and of the cloud, and troubled the army of the Egyptians (Mitsrayim),

25 And took off their chariot wheels, that they drave them heavily; so that the Egyptians (Mitsrayim) said, "Let us flee from the face of Yisrael; for יהוה fighteth for them against the Egyptians (Mitsrayim)."

26 And יהוה said unto Moses (Mosheh), "Stretch out your hand over the sea, that the waters may come again upon the Egyptians (Mitsrayim), upon their chariots, and upon their horsemen."

27 And Moses (Mosheh) stretched forth his hand over the sea, and the sea returned to its strength when the morning appeared; and the Egyptians (Mitsrayim) fled against it; and יהוה overthrew the Egyptians (Mitsrayim) in the midst of the sea.

28 And the waters returned, and covered the

chariots, and the horsemen, and all the army of Pharaoh (Paroh) that came into the sea after them; there remained not so much as one of them.

29 But the children of Yisrael walked upon dry land in the midst of the sea; and the waters were a wall unto them on their right hand, and on their left.

30 Thus יהוה saved Yisrael that day out of the hand of the Egyptians (Mitsrayim); and Yisrael saw the Egyptians (Mitsrayim) dead upon the sea shore.

31 And Yisrael saw that great work which יהוה did upon the Egyptians (Mitsrayim); and the people feared יהוה, and believed יהוה, and His servant Moses (Mosheh).

15 Then sang Moses (Mosheh) and the children of Yisrael this song unto יהוה, and spake, saying, "I will sing unto יהוה, for He hath triumphed gloriously; the horse and its rider hath He thrown into the sea.

2 [A2]יה (Yah) is my strength and song, and He has become my salvation; He is my God (Elohim), and I will prepare Him a habitation; my father's God (Elohim), and I will exalt Him.

3 יהוה is a man of war; יהוה is His name.

4 Pharaoh (Paroh)'s chariots and his army hath He cast into the sea; his chosen captains also are drowned in the Red sea.

5 The depths have covered them; they sank into the bottom as a stone.

6 Your right hand, O יהוה, has become glorious in power; Your right hand, O יהוה, hath dashed in pieces the enemy.

7 And in the greatness of Your excellency You have overthrown them that rose up against You; You sentest forth Your wrath, which consumed them as stubble.

8 And with the blast of Your nostrils the waters were gathered together, the floods stood upright as a heap, and the depths were congealed in the heart of the sea.

9 The enemy said, 'I will pursue, I will overtake, I will divide the spoil; my lust shall be satisfied upon them; I will draw my sword, my hand shall destroy them.'

10 You didst blow with Your wind, the sea covered them; they sank as lead in the mighty waters.

11 Who is like unto You, O יהוה, among the mighty ones ([B1]elohim)? Who is like You,

glorious in holiness, fearful in praises, doing wonders?

12 You stretchedst out Your right hand, the earth swallowed them.

13 You in Your mercy have led forth the people whom You have redeemed; You have guided them in Your strength unto Your holy habitation.

14 The people shall hear, and be afraid; sorrow shall take hold on the inhabitants of Palestina.

15 Then the dukes of Edom shall be amazed; the mighty men of Moav, trembling shall take hold upon them; all the inhabitants of Canaan shall melt away.

16 Fear and dread shall fall upon them; by the greatness of Your arm they shall be as still as a stone, till Your people pass over, O יהוה, till the people pass over, whom You have purchased.

17 You shalt bring them in, and plant them in the mountain of Your inheritance, in the place, O יהוה, which You have made for You to dwell in, in the sanctuary, O Lord (Adonai), which Your hands have established.

18 יהוה shall reign forever and ever."

19 For the horse of Pharaoh (Paroh) went in with his chariots and with his horsemen into the sea, and יהוה brought again the waters of the sea upon them; but the children of Yisrael went on dry land in the midst of the sea.

20 And Miryam the prophetess (neviah), the sister of Aaron (Aharon), took a timbrel in her hand; and all the women went out after her with timbrels and with dances.

21 And Miryam answered them, "Sing you to יהוה, for He hath triumphed gloriously; the horse and its rider hath He thrown into the sea."

22 So Moses (Mosheh) brought Yisrael from the Red sea, and they went out into the wilderness of Shur; and they went three days in the wilderness, and found no water.

23 And when they came to Marah, they could not drink of the waters of Marah, for they were bitter; therefore the name of it was called Marah.

24 And the people murmured against Moses (Mosheh), saying, "What shall we drink?"

25 And he cried unto יהוה; and יהוה shewed him a tree, which when he had cast into the waters, the waters were made sweet; there He made for them a statute and an ordinance, and there He proved them,

26 And said, "If you wilt diligently hearken to the voice of יהוה your God (YHWH Eloheikha),

and wilt do that which is right in His sight, and wilt give ear to His commandments, and keep all His statutes, I will put none of these diseases upon you, which I have brought upon the Egyptians (Mitsrayim) for I am יהוה who healeth you."

27 And they came to Elim, where were twelve wells of water, and threescore and ten palm trees; and they encamped there by the waters.

16 And they took their journey from Elim, and all the congregation of the children of Yisrael came unto the wilderness of Ciyn, which is between Elim and Sinai, on the fifteenth day of the second month after their departing out of the land of Egypt (Mitsrayim).

2 And the whole congregation of the children of Yisrael murmured against Moses (Mosheh) and Aaron (Aharon) in the wilderness;

3 And the children of Yisrael said unto them, "Would that we had died by the hand of יהוה in the land of Egypt (Mitsrayim), when we sat by the flesh pots, and when we did eat bread to the full; for you have brought us forth into this wilderness, to kill this whole assembly with hunger."

4 Then said יהוה unto Moses (Mosheh), "Behold, I will rain bread from heaven for you; and the people shall go out and gather a certain rate every day, that I may prove them, whether they will walk in My [B28a]Torah, or no.

5 And it shall come to pass, that on the sixth day they shall prepare that which they bring in; and it shall be twice as much as they gather daily."

6 And Moses (Mosheh) and Aaron (Aharon) said unto all the children of Yisrael, "At even, then you shall know that יהוה hath brought you out from the land of Egypt (Mitsrayim);

7 And in the morning, then you shall see the glory of יהוה; for that He heareth your murmurings against יהוה; but what are we, that you murmur against us?"

8 And Moses (Mosheh) said, "This shall be, when יהוה shall give you in the evening meat to eat, and in the morning bread to the full; for that יהוה heareth your murmurings which you murmur against Him; and what are we? Your murmurings are not against us, but against יהוה."

9 And Moses (Mosheh) spake unto Aaron (Aharon), "Say unto all the congregation of the children of Yisrael, 'Come near before יהוה, for He hath heard your murmurings.'"

10 And it came to pass, as Aaron (Aharon) spake unto the whole congregation of the children of Yisrael, that they looked toward the wilderness, and, behold, the glory of יהוה appeared in the cloud.

11 And יהוה spake unto Moses (Mosheh), saying,

12 "I have heard the murmurings of the children of Yisrael; speak unto them, saying, 'At even you shall eat meat, and in the morning you shall be filled with bread; and you shall know that I am יהוה your God (YHWH Eloheikhem).'"

13 And it came to pass, that at even the quails came up, and covered the camp; and in the morning the dew lay round about the host.

14 And when the dew that lay was gone up, behold, upon the face of the wilderness there lay a small round thing, as small as the hoar frost on the ground.

15 And when the children of Yisrael saw it, they said one to another, "What is it (Man hu)?" for they knew not what it was. And Moses (Mosheh) said unto them, "This is the bread which יהוה hath given you to eat.

16 This is the thing which יהוה hath commanded, 'Gather of it every man according to his eating, an omer for every man, according to the number of your persons; take you every man for them which are in his tents.'"

17 And the children of Yisrael did so, and gathered, some more, some less.

18 And when they did measure it with an omer, he that gathered much had nothing over, and he that gathered little had no lack; they gathered every man according to his eating.

19 And Moses (Mosheh) said, "Let no man leave of it till the morning."

20 Notwithstanding they hearkened not unto Moses (Mosheh); but some of them left of it until the morning, and it bred worms, and stank; and Moses (Mosheh) was wroth with them.

21 And they gathered it every morning, every man according to his eating; and when the sun waxed hot, it melted.

22 And it came to pass, that on the sixth day they gathered twice as much bread, two omers for one man; and all the rulers of the congregation came and told Moses (Mosheh).

23 And he said unto them, "This is that which יהוה hath said, 'Tomorrow is [B17]Shabbaton,

B18Shabbat of holiness unto יהוה: bake that which you will bake today, and seethe that you will seethe; and that which remaineth over lay up for you to be kept until the morning.'"

24 And they laid it up till the morning, as Moses (Mosheh) bade; and it did not stink, neither was there any worm therein.

25 And Moses (Mosheh) said, "Eat that today; for today is a Shabbat unto יהוה; today you shall not find it in the field.

26 Six days you shall gather it; but on the seventh day, which is the Shabbat, in it there shall be none."

27 And it came to pass, that there went out some of the people on the seventh day for to gather, and they found none.

28 And יהוה said unto Moses (Mosheh), "How long refuse you to keep My commandments (mitswot) and My instructions (torot)?

29 See, for that יהוה hath given you the Shabbat, therefore He giveth you on the sixth day the bread for two days; abide you every man in his place, let no man go out of his place on the seventh day."

30 So the people rested on the seventh day.

31 And the house of Yisrael called the name thereof Manna; and it was like coriander seed, white; and the taste of it was like wafers made with honey.

32 And Moses (Mosheh) said, "This is the thing which יהוה commandeth, 'Fill an omer of it to be kept for your generations, that they may see the bread wherewith I have fed you in the wilderness, when I brought you forth from the land of Egypt (Mitsrayim).'"

33 And Moses (Mosheh) said unto Aaron (Aharon), "Take a pot, and put an omer full of manna therein, and lay it up before יהוה, to be kept for your generations."

34 As יהוה commanded Moses (Mosheh), so Aaron (Aharon) laid it up before the Testimony, to be kept.

35 And the children of Yisrael did eat manna forty years, until they came to a land inhabited; they did eat manna, until they came unto the borders of the land of Canaan.

36 Now an omer is the tenth part of an ephah.

17 And all the congregation of the children of Yisrael journeyed from the wilderness of Sin, after their journeys, according to the commandment of יהוה, and pitched in Rephidim;

and there was no water for the people to drink.

2 Wherefore the people did contend with Moses (Mosheh), and said, "Give us water that we may drink." And Moses (Mosheh) said unto them, "Why contend you with me? Wherefore do you tempt יהוה?"

3 And the people thirsted there for water; and the people murmured against Moses (Mosheh), and said, "Wherefore is this that you have brought us up out of Egypt (Mitsrayim), to kill us and our children and our cattle with thirst?"

4 And Moses (Mosheh) cried unto יהוה, saying, "What shall I do unto this people? They are almost ready to stone me."

5 And יהוה said unto Moses (Mosheh), "Go on before the people, and take with you of the elders of Yisrael; and your rod, wherewith you smotest the river, take in your hand, and go.

6 Behold, I will stand before you there upon the rock in Horeb (Chorev); and you shalt smite the rock, and there shall come water out of it, that the people may drink." And Moses (Mosheh) did so in the sight of the elders of Yisrael.

7 And he called the name of the place Massah, and Meribah, because of the contention of the children of Yisrael, and because they tempted יהוה, saying, "Is יהוה among us, or not?"

8 Then came Amalek, and fought with Yisrael in Rephidim.

9 And Moses (Mosheh) said unto A32Joshua (Yehoshua), "Choose us out men, and go out, fight with Amalek; tomorrow I will stand on the top of the hill with the rod of God (Elohim) in mine hand."

10 So Joshua (Yehoshua) did as Moses (Mosheh) had said to him, and fought with Amalek; and Moses (Mosheh), Aaron (Aharon), and Hur went up to the top of the hill.

11 And it came to pass, when Moses (Mosheh) held up his hand, that Yisrael prevailed; and when he let down his hand, Amalek prevailed.

12 But Moses (Mosheh)' hands were heavy; and they took a stone, and put it under him, and he sat thereon; and Aaron (Aharon) and Hur stayed up his hands, the one on the one side, and the other on the other side; and his hands were steady until the going down of the sun.

13 And Joshua (Yehoshua) discomfited Amalek and his people with the edge of the sword.

14 And יהוה said unto Moses (Mosheh), "Write this for a memorial in a book, and rehearse it in

the ears of Joshua (Yehoshua); for I will utterly put out the remembrance of Amalek from under heaven.

15 And Moses (Mosheh) built an altar, and called the name of it A4"יהוה Nissi (YHWH Is My Banner)";

16 For he said, "Because יהוה hath sworn that יהוה will have war with Amalek from generation to generation."

18 When Yetro, the priest (kohen) of Midian, Moses (Mosheh)'s father in law, heard of all that God (Elohim) had done for Moses (Mosheh), and for Yisrael His people, and that יהוה had brought Yisrael out of Egypt (Mitsrayim);

2 Then Yetro, Moses (Mosheh)'s father in law, took Zipporah, Moses (Mosheh)'s wife, after he had sent her back,

3 And her two sons; of whom the name of the one was Gershom; for he said, "I have been an alien in a strange land";

4 And the name of the other was Eliezer; for said he, "The God (Elohim) of my father was my help, and delivered me from the sword of Pharaoh (Paroh)".

5 And Yetro, Moses (Mosheh)'s father in law, came with his sons and his wife unto Moses (Mosheh) into the wilderness, where he encamped at the mount of God (Elohim).

6 And he said unto Moses (Mosheh), "I, your father in law Yetro am come unto you, and your wife, and her two sons with her."

7 And Moses (Mosheh) went out to meet his father in law, and did obeisance, and kissed him; and they asked each other of their welfare; and they came into the tent.

8 And Moses (Mosheh) told his father in law all that יהוה had done unto Pharaoh (Paroh) and to the Egyptians (Mitsrayim) for Yisrael's sake, and all the travail that had come upon them by the way, and how יהוה delivered them.

9 And Yetro rejoiced for all the goodness which יהוה had done to Yisrael, whom He had delivered out of the hand of the Egyptians (Mitsrayim).

10 And Yetro said, "Blessed be יהוה, who hath delivered you out of the hand of the Egyptians (Mitsrayim), and out of the hand of Pharaoh (Paroh), who hath delivered the people from under the hand of the Egyptians (Mitsrayim).

11 Now I know that יהוה is greater than all rulers (B1belohim); for in the thing wherein they dealt proudly He was above them.

12 And Yetro, Moses (Mosheh)'s father in law, took a burnt offering and sacrifices for God (Elohim); and Aaron (Aharon) came, and all the elders of Yisrael, to eat bread with Moses (Mosheh)'s father in law before God (Elohim).

13 And it came to pass on the next day, that Moses (Mosheh) sat to judge the people; and the people stood by Moses (Mosheh) from the morning unto the evening.

14 And when Moses (Mosheh)'s father in law saw all that he did to the people, he said, "What is this thing that you doest to the people? Why sittest you yourself alone, and all the people stand by you from morning unto even?"

15 And Moses (Mosheh) said unto his father in law, "Because the people come unto me to enquire of God (Elohim);

16 When they have a matter, they come unto me; and I judge between one and another, and I do make them know the statutes of God (Elohim), and His laws (torot)."

17 And Moses (Mosheh)'s father in law said unto him, "The thing that you doest is not good.

18 You wilt surely wear away, both you, and this people that is with you; for this thing is too heavy for you; you are not able to perform it yourself alone.

19 Hearken now unto my voice, I will give you counsel, and God (Elohim) shall be with you: Be you for the people before God (Elohim), that you mayest bring the causes unto God (Elohim);

20 And you shalt teach them ordinances and the laws (torot), and shalt shew them the way wherein they must walk, and the work that they must do.

21 Moreover you shalt provide out of all the people able men, such as fear God (Elohim), men of truth, hating covetousness; and place such over them, to be rulers of thousands, and rulers of hundreds, rulers of fifties, and rulers of tens.

22 And let them judge the people at all seasons; and it shall be, that every great matter they shall bring unto you, but every small matter they shall judge; so shall it be easier for yourself, and they shall bear the burden with you.

23 If you shalt do this thing, and God (Elohim) command you so, then you shalt be able to endure, and all this people shall also go to their place in peace."

24 So Moses (Mosheh) hearkened to the voice of his father in law, and did all that he had said.
25 And Moses (Mosheh) chose able men out of all Yisrael, and made them heads over the people, rulers of thousands, rulers of hundreds, rulers of fifties, and rulers of tens.
26 And they judged the people at all seasons; the hard causes they brought unto Moses (Mosheh), but every small matter they judged themselves.
27 And Moses (Mosheh) let his father in law depart; and he went his way into his own land.

19 In the third month, when the children of Yisrael were gone forth out of the land of Egypt (Mitsrayim), the same day came they into the wilderness of Sinai.
2 For they were departed from Rephidim, and were come to the desert of Sinai, and had pitched in the wilderness; and there Yisrael camped before the mount.
3 And Moses (Mosheh) went up unto God (Elohim), and יהוה called unto him out of the mountain, saying, "Thus shalt you say to the house of Jacob (Yaaqov), and tell the children of Yisrael:
4 'You have seen what I did unto the Egyptians (Mitsrayim), and how I bare you on eagles' wings, and brought you unto Myself.
5 Now therefore, if you will obey My voice indeed, and keep My covenant, then you shall be a peculiar treasure unto Me above all people; for all the earth is Mine.
6 And you shall be unto Me a kingdom of priests (kohanim), and a holy nation.' These are the words which you shalt speak unto the children of Yisrael."
7 And Moses (Mosheh) came and called for the elders of the people, and laid before their faces all these words which יהוה commanded him.
8 And all the people answered together, and said, "All that יהוה hath spoken we will do." And Moses (Mosheh) returned the words of the people unto יהוה.
9 And יהוה said unto Moses (Mosheh), "Lo, I come unto you in a thick cloud, that the people may hear when I speak with you, and believe you forever." And Moses (Mosheh) told the words of the people unto יהוה.
10 And יהוה said unto Moses (Mosheh), "Go unto the people, and sanctify them today and tomorrow, and let them wash their clothes,
11 And be ready for the third day; for the third day יהוה will come down in the sight of all the people upon Mount Sinai.
12 And you shalt set bounds unto the people round about, saying, 'Take heed to yourselves, that you go not up into the mount, or touch the border of it; whosoever toucheth the mount shall be surely put to death.
13 There shall not a hand touch it, but he shall surely be stoned, or shot through; whether it be beast or man, it shall not live.' When the trumpet soundeth long, they shall come up to the mountain."
14 And Moses (Mosheh) went down from the mountain unto the people, and sanctified the people; and they washed their clothes.
15 And he said unto the people, "Be ready for the third day; come not near your wives."
16 And it came to pass on the third day in the morning, that there were thunders and lightnings, and a thick cloud upon the mount, and the voice of the trumpet exceeding loud; so that all the people that was in the camp trembled.
17 And Moses (Mosheh) brought forth the people out of the camp to meet with God (Elohim); and they stood at the nether part of the mount.
18 And Mount Sinai was altogether on a smoke, because יהוה descended upon it in fire; and the smoke thereof ascended as the smoke of a furnace, and the whole mount quaked greatly.
19 And when the voice of the trumpet sounded long, and waxed louder and louder, Moses (Mosheh) spake, and God (Elohim) answered him by a voice.
20 And יהוה came down upon Mount Sinai, on the top of the mount; and יהוה called Moses (Mosheh) up to the top of the mountain; and Moses (Mosheh) went up.
21 And יהוה said unto Moses (Mosheh), "Go down, warn the people, lest they break through unto יהוה to gaze, and many of them perish.
22 And let the priests (kohanim) also, which come near to יהוה, sanctify themselves, lest יהוה break forth upon them."
23 And Moses (Mosheh) said unto יהוה, "The people cannot come up to Mount Sinai, for You warned us, saying, 'Set bounds about the mountain, and sanctify it.'"
24 And יהוה said unto him, "Away, get you down, and you shalt come up, you, and Aaron

(Aharon) with you; but let not the priests (kohanim) and the people break through to come up unto יהוה, lest He break forth upon them."

25 So Moses (Mosheh) went down unto the people, and spake unto them.

20 And God (Elohim) spake all these words, saying,

2 "I am יהוה your God (YHWH Eloheikha), who brought you out of the land of Egypt (Mitsrayim), out of the house of bondage.

3 You shalt have no other gods (elohim) before Me.

4 You shalt not make unto you any graven image, or any likeness of any thing that is in heaven above, or that is in the earth beneath, or that is in the water under the earth.

5 You shalt not bow down yourself to them, nor serve them; for I יהוה your God (YHWH Eloheikha) am a jealous God (El), visiting the iniquity of the fathers upon the children unto the third and fourth generation of them that hate Me;

6 And shewing mercy unto thousands of them who love Me, and keep My commandments (mitswot).

7 You shalt not take the name of יהוה your God (YHWH Eloheikha) in vain; for יהוה will not hold him guiltless who taketh His name in vain.

8 Remember the Shabbat day, to keep it holy.

9 Six days shalt you labor, and do all your work;

10 But the seventh day is the Shabbat of יהוה your God (YHWH Eloheikha); in it you shalt not do any work, you, nor your son, nor your daughter, your manservant, nor your maidservant, nor your cattle, nor your stranger that is within your gates;

11 For in six days יהוה made heaven and earth, the sea, and all that in them is, and rested the seventh day. Therefore יהוה blessed the Shabbat day, and hallowed it.

12 Honor your father and your mother, that your days may be long upon the land which יהוה your God (YHWH Eloheikha) giveth you.

13 You shalt not kill.

14 You shalt not commit adultery.

15 You shalt not steal.

16 You shalt not bear false witness against your neighbor.

17 You shalt not covet your neighbour's house, you shalt not covet your neighbour's wife, nor his manservant, nor his maidservant, nor

his ox, nor his ass, nor any thing that is your neighbour's."

18 And all the people saw the thunderings, and the lightnings, and the noise of the trumpet, and the mountain smoking; and when the people saw it, they trembled, and stood afar off.

19 And they said unto Moses (Mosheh), "Speak you with us, and we will hear; but let not God (Elohim) speak with us, lest we die."

20 And Moses (Mosheh) said unto the people, "Fear not; for God (Elohim) has come to prove you, and that His fear may be before your faces, that you sin not."

21 And the people stood afar off, and Moses (Mosheh) drew near unto the thick darkness where God (Elohim) was.

22 And יהוה said unto Moses (Mosheh), "Thus you shalt say unto the children of Yisrael, 'You have seen that I have talked with you from heaven.

23 You shall not make besides Me, gods (elohim) of silver, neither shall you make gods (elohim) of gold unto you.

24 An altar of earth you shalt make unto Me, and shalt sacrifice thereon your burnt offerings, and your peace offerings, your sheep, and your oxen; in all places where I record My name I will come unto you, and I will bless you.

25 And if you wilt make Me an altar of stone, you shalt not build it of hewn stone; for if you lift up your tool upon it, you have polluted it.

26 Neither shalt you go up by steps unto Mine altar, that your nakedness be not discovered thereon.'

21 Now these are the judgments which you shalt set before them.

2 If you buy a Hebrew (Ivri) servant, six years he shall serve; and in the seventh he shall go out free for nothing.

3 If he came in by himself, he shall go out by himself; if he was married, then his wife shall go out with him.

4 If his master has given him a wife, and she has born him sons or daughters; the wife and her children shall be her master's, and he shall go out by himself.

5 And if the servant shall plainly say, 'I love my master, my wife, and my children; I will not go out free,'

6 Then his master shall bring him unto the judges; he shall also bring him to the door, or

unto the door post; and his master shall bore his ear through with an aul; and he shall serve him forever.

7 And if a man sells his daughter to be a maidservant, she shall not go out as the menservants do.

8 If she pleases not her master, who hath betrothed her to himself, then shall he let her be redeemed; to sell her unto a strange nation he shall have no power, seeing he hath dealt deceitfully with her.

9 And if he has betrothed her unto his son, he shall deal with her after the manner of daughters.

10 If he takes him another wife; her food, her raiment, and her duty of marriage, shall he not diminish.

11 And if he does not these three unto her, then shall she go out free without money.

12 He that smiteth a man, so that he dies, shall be surely put to death.

13 And if a man lies not in wait, but God (Elohim) deliver him into his hand; then I will appoint you a place whither he shall flee.

14 But if a man come presumptuously upon his neighbour, to slay him with guile; you shalt take him from mine altar, that he may die.

15 And he that smiteth his father, or his mother, shall be surely put to death.

16 And he that stealeth a man, and selleth him, or if he be found in his hand, he shall surely be put to death.

17 And he that curseth his father, or his mother, shall surely be put to death.

18 And if men strive together, and one smite another with a stone, or with his fist, and he die not, but keepeth his bed;

19 If he rises again, and walk abroad upon his staff, then shall he that smote him be quit; only he shall pay for the loss of his time, and shall cause him to be thoroughly healed.

20 And if a man smites his servant, or his maid, with a rod, and he die under his hand; he shall be surely punished.

21 Notwithstanding, if he continues a day or two, he shall not be punished; for he is his property.

22 If men strive, and hurt a woman with child, so that her fruit depart from her, and yet no mischief follow; he shall be surely punished, according as the woman's husband will lay upon him; and he shall pay as the judges determine.

23 And if any mischief follows, then you shalt give life for life,

24 Eye for eye, tooth for tooth, hand for hand, foot for foot,

25 Burning for burning, wound for wound, stripe for stripe.

26 And if a man smites the eye of his servant, or the eye of his maid, that it perishes; he shall let him go free for his eye's sake.

27 And if he smites out his manservant's tooth, or his maidservant's tooth; he shall let him go free for his tooth's sake.

28 If an ox gores a man or a woman, that they die; then the ox shall be surely stoned, and his flesh shall not be eaten; but the owner of the ox shall be quit.

29 But if the ox were wont to push with his horn in time past, and it hath been testified to his owner, and he hath not kept him in, but that he hath killed a man or a woman; the ox shall be stoned, and his owner also shall be put to death.

30 If there be laid on him a sum of money, then he shall give for the ransom of his life whatsoever is laid upon him.

31 Whether he has gored a son, or have gored a daughter, according to this judgment shall it be done unto him.

32 If the ox shall push a manservant or a maidservant; he shall give unto their master thirty shekels of silver, and the ox shall be stoned.

33 And if a man shall open a pit, or if a man shall dig a pit, and not cover it, and an ox or an ass fall therein;

34 The owner of the pit shall make it good, and give money unto the owner of them; and the dead beast shall be his.

35 And if one man's ox hurt another's, that he dies; then they shall sell the live ox, and divide the money of it; and the dead ox also they shall divide.

36 Or if it be known that the ox hath used to push in time past, and his owner hath not kept him in; he shall surely pay ox for ox; and the dead shall be his own.

22 If a man shall steal an ox, or a sheep, and kill it, or sell it; he shall restore five oxen for an ox, and four sheep for a sheep.

2 If a thief be found breaking up, and be smitten that he dies, there shall no blood be shed for him.

3 If the sun be risen upon him, there shall be blood shed for him; for he should make full restitution; if he has nothing, then he shall be sold for his theft.

4 If the theft be certainly found in his hand alive, whether it be ox, or ass, or sheep; he shall restore double.

5 If a man shall cause a field or vineyard to be eaten, and shall put in his beast, and shall feed in another man's field; of the best of his own field, and of the best of his own vineyard, shall he make restitution.

6 If fire break out, and catch in thorns, so that the stacks of corn, or the standing corn, or the field, be consumed therewith; he that kindled the fire shall surely make restitution.

7 If a man shall deliver unto his neighbour money or stuff to keep, and it be stolen out of the man's house; if the thief be found, let him pay double.

8 If the thief be not found, then the master of the house shall be brought unto the judges, to see whether he has put his hand unto his neighbour's goods.

9 For all manner of trespass, whether it be for ox, for ass, for sheep, for raiment, or for any manner of lost thing, which another challengeth to be his, the cause of both parties shall come before the judges; and whom the judges shall condemn, he shall pay double unto his neighbour.

10 If a man delivers unto his neighbour an ass, or an ox, or a sheep, or any beast, to keep; and it die, or be hurt, or driven away, no man seeing it;

11 Then shall an oath of יהוה be between them both, that he hath not put his hand unto his neighbour's goods; and the owner of it shall accept thereof, and he shall not make it good.

12 And if it be stolen from him, he shall make restitution unto the owner thereof.

13 If it be torn in pieces, then let him bring it for witness, and he shall not make good that which was torn.

14 And if a man borrow ought of his neighbour, and it be hurt, or die, the owner thereof being not with it, he shall surely make it good.

15 But if the owner thereof be with it, he shall not make it good; if it be a hired thing, it came for his hire.

16 And if a man entices a maid that is not betrothed, and lie with her, he shall surely endow her to be his wife.

17 If her father utterly refuses to give her unto him, he shall pay money according to the dowry of virgins.

18 You shalt not suffer a witch to live.

19 Whosoever lieth with a beast shall surely be put to death.

20 He that sacrificeth unto any god (Blbelohim), except unto יהוה only, he shall be utterly destroyed.

21 You shalt neither vex a stranger, nor oppress him, for you were strangers in the land of Egypt (Mitsrayim).

22 You shall not afflict any widow, or fatherless child.

23 If you afflict them in any wise, and they cry at all unto Me, I will surely hear their cry;

24 And My wrath shall wax hot, and I will kill you with the sword; and your wives shall be widows, and your children fatherless.

25 If you lend money to any of My people that is poor by you, you shalt not be to him as a usurer, neither shalt you lay upon him usury.

26 If you at all take your neighbour's raiment to pledge, you shalt deliver it unto him by that the sun goeth down.

27 For that is his covering only, it is his raiment for his skin; wherein shall he sleep? And it shall come to pass, when he crieth unto Me, that I will hear; for I am gracious.

28 You shalt not revile God (Elohim), nor curse the ruler of your people.

29 You shalt not delay to offer the first of your ripe fruits, and of your liquors; the firstborn of your sons shalt you give unto Me.

30 Likewise shalt you do with your oxen, and with your sheep; seven days it shall be with his dam; on the eighth day you shalt give it Me.

31 And you shall be holy men unto Me; neither shall you eat any flesh that is torn of beasts in the field; you shall cast it to the dogs.

23 You shalt not raise a false report. Put not your hand with the wicked to be an unrighteous witness.

2 You shalt not follow a multitude to do evil; neither shalt you speak in a cause to decline after many to wrest judgment.

3 Neither shalt you countenance a poor man in his cause.

4 If you meet your enemy's ox or his ass going astray, you shalt surely bring it back to him again.

5 If you see the ass of him that hateth you lying under his burden, and wouldest forbear to help him, you shalt surely help with him.

6 You shalt not wrest the judgment of your poor in his cause.

7 Keep you far from a false matter; and the innocent and righteous slay you not, for I will not justify the wicked.

8 And you shalt take no gift, for the gift blindeth the wise, and perverteth the words of the righteous.

9 Also you shalt not oppress a stranger, for you know the heart of a stranger, seeing you were strangers in the land of Egypt (Mitsrayim).

10 And six years you shalt sow your land, and shalt gather in the fruits thereof;

11 But the seventh year you shalt let it rest and lie still; that the poor of your people may eat; and what they leave the beasts of the field shall eat. In like manner you shalt deal with your vineyard, and with your oliveyard.

12 Six days you shalt do your work, and on the seventh day you shalt rest; that your ox and your ass may rest, and the son of your handmaid, and the stranger, may be refreshed.

13 And in all things that I have said unto you be circumspect; and make no mention of the name of other [4]gods (elohim), neither let it be heard out of your mouth.

14 Three times you shalt keep a feast unto Me in the year.

15 You shalt keep the [B20]Feast of Unleavened Bread (Chag HaMatzot); (you shalt eat unleavened bread seven days, as I commanded you, in the time appointed of the month Aviv; for in it you camest out from Egypt (Mitsrayim) and none shall appear before Me empty.)

16 And the Feast of Harvest, the firstfruits of your labors, which you have sown in the field; and the Feast of Ingathering, which is in the end of the year, when you have gathered in your labors out of the field.

17 Three times in the year all your males shall appear before Lord (Adonai) יהוה.

18 You shalt not offer the blood of My sacrifice with leavened bread; neither shall the fat of My sacrifice remain until the morning.

19 The first of the firstfruits of your land you shalt bring into the house of יהוה your God (YHWH Eloheikha). You shalt not seethe a kid in his mother's milk.

20 Behold, I send an Angel before you, to keep you in the way, and to bring you into the place which I have prepared.

21 Beware of him, and obey his voice, provoke him not; for he will not pardon your transgressions; for My name is in him.

22 But if you shalt indeed obey his voice, and do all that I speak; then I will be an enemy unto your enemies, and an adversary unto your adversaries.

23 For mine Angel shall go before you, and bring you in unto the Amorites, and the Hittites, and the Perizzites, and the Canaanites, the Hivites, and the Jebusites (Yevusi): and I will cut them off.

24 You shalt not bow down to their gods (elohim), nor serve them, nor do after their works; but you shalt utterly overthrow them, and quite break down their images.

25 And you shall serve יהוה your God (YHWH Eloheikhem), and He shall bless your bread, and your water; and I will take sickness away from the midst of you.

26 There shall nothing cast their young, nor be barren, in your land; the number of your days I will fulfil.

27 I will send My fear before you, and will destroy all the people to whom you shalt come, and I will make all your enemies turn their backs unto you.

28 And I will send hornets before you, which shall drive out the Hivite, the Canaanite, and the Hittite, from before you.

29 I will not drive them out from before you in one year; lest the land become desolate, and the beast of the field multiply against you.

30 By little and little I will drive them out from before you, until you be increased, and inherit the land.

31 And I will set your bounds from the Red sea even unto the sea of the Philistines, and from the desert unto the river; for I will deliver the inhabitants of the land into your hand; and you shalt drive them out before you.

32 You shalt make no covenant with them, nor with their gods (elohim).

33 They shall not dwell in your land, lest they make you sin against Mel for if you serve their gods (elohim), it will surely be a snare unto you.

24 And He said unto Moses (Mosheh), "Come up unto יהוה, you, and Aaron

(Aharon), Nadav, and Avihu, and seventy of the elders of Yisrael; and worship you afar off.

2 And Moses (Mosheh) alone shall come near יהוה; but they shall not come near; neither shall the people go up with him."

3 And Moses (Mosheh) came and told the people all the words of יהוה, and all the judgments; and all the people answered with one voice, and said, "All the words which יהוה hath said will we do."

4 And Moses (Mosheh) wrote all the words of יהוה, and rose up early in the morning, and builded an altar under the hill, and twelve pillars, according to the twelve tribes of Yisrael.

5 And he sent young men of the children of Yisrael, who offered burnt offerings, and sacrificed peace offerings of oxen unto יהוה.

6 And Moses (Mosheh) took half of the blood, and put it in basons; and half of the blood he sprinkled on the altar.

7 And he took the Book of the Covenant (Sefer haBerith), and read in the audience of the people; and they said, "All that יהוה hath said will we do, and be obedient."

8 And Moses (Mosheh) took the blood, and sprinkled it on the people, and said, "Behold the blood of the covenant, which יהוה hath made with you concerning all these words."

9 Then went up Moses (Mosheh), and Aaron (Aharon), Nadav, and Avihu, and seventy of the elders of Yisrael;

10 And they saw the God of Israel (Elohei Yisrael); and there was under His feet as it was a paved work of a sapphire stone, and as it was the body of heaven in its clearness.

11 And upon the nobles of the children of Yisrael He laid not His hand; also they saw God (Elohim), and did eat and drink.

12 And יהוה said unto Moses (Mosheh), "Come up to Me into the mountain, and be there; and I will give you tablets of stone with the [B28a]Law (Torah) and the commandments (mitswot) which I have written; that you mayest teach them."

13 And Moses (Mosheh) rose up, and his minister Joshua (Yehoshua); and Moses (Mosheh) went up into the mountain of God (Elohim).

14 And he said unto the elders, "Tarry you here for us, until we come again unto you. And, behold, Aaron (Aharon) and Hur are with you;

if any man has any matters to do, let him come unto them."

15 And Moses (Mosheh) went up into the mountain, and a cloud covered the mountain.

16 And the glory of יהוה abode upon Mount Sinai, and the cloud covered it six days; and the seventh day He called unto Moses (Mosheh) out of the midst of the cloud.

17 And the sight of the glory of יהוה was like devouring fire on the top of the mountain in the eyes of the children of Yisrael.

18 And Moses (Mosheh) went into the midst of the cloud, and gat him up into the mountain; and Moses (Mosheh) was on the mountain forty days and forty nights.

25 And יהוה spake unto Moses (Mosheh), saying,

2 "Speak unto the children of Yisrael, that they bring Me an offering: of every man that giveth it willingly with his heart you shall take My offering.

3 And this is the offering which you shall take of them: gold, and silver, and brass,

4 And blue, and purple, and scarlet, and fine linen, and goats' hair,

5 And rams' skins dyed red, and badgers' skins, and shittim wood,

6 Oil for the light, spices for anointing oil, and for sweet incense,

7 Onyx stones, and stones to be set in the ephod, and in the breastplate.

8 And let them make Me a sanctuary, that I may dwell among them.

9 According to all that I shew you, after the pattern of the tabernacle, and the pattern of all the instruments thereof, even so shall you make it.

10 And they shall make an ark of shittim wood: two cubits and a half shall be the length thereof, and a cubit and a half the breadth thereof, and a cubit and a half the height thereof.

11 And you shalt overlay it with pure gold, inside and outside shalt you overlay it, and shalt make upon it a crown of gold round about.

12 And you shalt cast four rings of gold for it, and put them in the four corners thereof; and two rings shall be in the one side of it, and two rings in the other side of it.

13 And you shalt make staves of shittim wood, and overlay them with gold.

14 And you shalt put the staves into the rings by

the sides of the ark, that the ark may be borne with them.

15 The staves shall be in the rings of the ark; they shall not be taken from it.

16 And you shalt put into the ark the testimony which I shall give you.

17 And you shalt make a mercy seat of pure gold: two cubits and a half shall be the length thereof, and a cubit and a half the breadth thereof.

18 And you shalt make two cherubims (keruvim) of gold, of beaten work shalt you make them, in the two ends of the mercy seat.

19 And make one cherub (keruv) on the one end, and the other cherub (keruv) on the other end; even of the mercy seat shall you make the cherubims (keruvim) on the two ends thereof.

20 And the cherubims (keruvim) shall stretch forth their wings on high, covering the mercy seat with their wings, and their faces shall look one to another; toward the mercy seat shall the faces of the cherubims (keruvim) be.

21 And you shalt put the mercy seat above upon the ark; and in the ark you shalt put the testimony that I shall give you.

22 And there I will meet with you, and I will commune with you from above the mercy seat, from between the two cherubims (keruvim) which are upon the ark of the testimony, of all things which I will give you in commandment unto the children of Yisrael.

23 You shalt also make a table of shittim wood: two cubits shall be the length thereof, and a cubit the breadth thereof, and a cubit and a half the height thereof.

24 And you shalt overlay it with pure gold, and make thereto a crown of gold round about.

25 And you shalt make unto it a border of a hand breadth round about, and you shalt make a golden crown to the border thereof round about.

26 And you shalt make for it four rings of gold, and put the rings in the four corners that are on the four feet thereof.

27 Over against the border shall the rings be for places of the staves to bear the table.

28 And you shalt make the staves of shittim wood, and overlay them with gold, that the table may be borne with them.

29 And you shalt make the dishes thereof, and spoons thereof, and covers thereof, and bowls thereof, to cover withal: of pure gold shalt you make them.

30 And you shalt set upon the table shewbread before Me alway.

31 And you shalt make a candlestick (menorah) of pure gold; of beaten work shall the candlestick (menorah) be made: his shaft, and his branches, his bowls, his knops, and his flowers, shall be of the same.

32 And six branches shall come out of the sides of it; three branches of the candlestick (menorah) out of the one side, and three branches of the candlestick (menorah) out of the other side:

33 Three bowls made like unto almonds, with a knop and a flower in one branch; and three bowls made like almonds in the other branch, with a knop and a flower; so in the six branches that come out of the candlestick (menorah).

34 And in the candlestick (menorah) shall be four bowls made like unto almonds, with their knops and their flowers.

35 And there shall be a knop under two branches of the same, and a knop under two branches of the same, and a knop under two branches of the same, according to the six branches that proceed out of the candlestick (menorah).

36 Their knops and their branches shall be of the same: all it shall be one beaten work of pure gold.

37 And you shalt make the seven lamps thereof; and they shall light the lamps thereof, that they may give light opposite it.

38 And the tongs thereof, and the snuffdishes thereof, shall be of pure gold.

39 Of a talent of pure gold shall he make it, with all these vessels.

40 And look that you make them after their pattern, which was shewed you in the mountain.

26 Moreover you shalt make the tabernacle with ten curtains of fine twined linen, and blue, and purple, and scarlet; with cherubims (keruvim) of cunning work shalt you make them.

2 The length of one curtain shall be eight and twenty cubits, and the breadth of one curtain four cubits: and every one of the curtains shall have one measure.

3 The five curtains shall be coupled together one to another; and other five curtains shall be coupled one to another.

4 And you shalt make loops of blue upon the edge of the one curtain from the selvedge in the coupling; and likewise shalt you make in

the uttermost edge of another curtain, in the coupling of the second.

5 Fifty loops shalt you make in the one curtain, and fifty loops shalt you make in the edge of the curtain that is in the coupling of the second; that the loops may take hold one of another.

6 And you shalt make fifty taches of gold, and couple the curtains together with the taches; and it shall be one tabernacle.

7 And you shalt make curtains of goats' hair to be a covering upon the tabernacle; eleven curtains shalt you make.

8 The length of one curtain shall be thirty cubits, and the breadth of one curtain four cubits: and the eleven curtains shall be all of one measure.

9 And you shalt couple five curtains by themselves, and six curtains by themselves, and shalt double the sixth curtain in the forefront of the tabernacle.

10 And you shalt make fifty loops on the edge of the one curtain that is outmost in the coupling, and fifty loops in the edge of the curtain which coupleth the second.

11 And you shalt make fifty taches of brass, and put the taches into the loops, and couple the tent together, that it may be one.

12 And the remnant that remaineth of the curtains of the tent, the half curtain that remaineth, shall hang over the backside of the tabernacle.

13 And a cubit on the one side, and a cubit on the other side of that which remaineth in the length of the curtains of the tent, it shall hang over the sides of the tabernacle on this side and on that side, to cover it.

14 And you shalt make a covering for the tent of rams' skins dyed red, and a covering above of badgers' skins.

15 And you shalt make boards for the tabernacle of shittim wood standing up.

16 Ten cubits shall be the length of a board, and a cubit and a half shall be the breadth of one board.

17 Two tenons shall there be in one board, set in order one against another. Thus shalt you make for all the boards of the tabernacle.

18 And you shalt make the boards for the tabernacle, twenty boards on the south side southward.

19 And you shalt make forty sockets of silver under the twenty boards; two sockets under one

board for his two tenons, and two sockets under another board for his two tenons.

20 And for the second side of the tabernacle on the north side there shall be twenty boards:

21 And their forty sockets of silver; two sockets under one board, and two sockets under another board.

22 And for the sides of the tabernacle westward you shalt make six boards.

23 And two boards shalt you make for the corners of the tabernacle in the two sides.

24 And they shall be coupled together beneath, and they shall be coupled together above the head of it unto one ring; thus shall it be for them both; they shall be for the two corners.

25 And they shall be eight boards, and their sockets of silver, sixteen sockets; two sockets under one board, and two sockets under another board.

26 And you shalt make bars of shittim wood; five for the boards of the one side of the tabernacle,

27 And five bars for the boards of the other side of the tabernacle, and five bars for the boards of the side of the tabernacle, for the two sides westward.

28 And the middle bar in the midst of the boards shall reach from end to end.

29 And you shalt overlay the boards with gold, and make their rings of gold for places for the bars; and you shalt overlay the bars with gold.

30 And you shalt rear up the tabernacle according to the fashion thereof which was shewed you in the mountain.

31 And you shalt make a vail of blue, and purple, and scarlet, and fine twined linen of cunning work: with cherubims (keruvim) shall it be made.

32 And you shalt hang it upon four pillars of shittim wood overlaid with gold; their hooks shall be of gold, upon the four sockets of silver.

33 And you shalt hang up the vail under the taches, that you mayest bring in thither within the vail the ark of the testimony; and the vail shall divide unto you between the holy place and the most holy.

34 And you shalt put the mercy seat upon the ark of the testimony in the most holy place.

35 And you shalt set the table without the vail, and the [B29]candlestick (menorah) opposite the table on the side of the tabernacle toward the

south; and you shalt put the table on the north side.

36 And you shalt make a hanging for the door of the tent, of blue, and purple, and scarlet, and fine twined linen, wrought with needlework.

37 And you shalt make for the hanging five pillars of shittim wood, and overlay them with gold, and their hooks shall be of gold; and you shalt cast five sockets of brass for them.

27 And you shalt make an altar of shittim wood, five cubits long, and five cubits broad; the altar shall be foursquare; and the height thereof shall be three cubits.

2 And you shalt make the horns of it upon the four corners thereof; its horns shall be of the same; and you shalt overlay it with brass.

3 And you shalt make its pans to receive its ashes, and its shovels, and its basons, and its fleshhooks, and its firepans; all the vessels thereof you shalt make of brass.

4 And you shalt make for it a grate of network of brass; and upon the net shalt you make four brasen rings in the four corners thereof.

5 And you shalt put it under the compass of the altar beneath, that the net may be even to the midst of the altar.

6 And you shalt make staves for the altar, staves of shittim wood, and overlay them with brass.

7 And the staves shall be put into the rings, and the staves shall be upon the two sides of the altar, to bear it.

8 Hollow with boards shalt you make it; as it was shewed you in the mount, so shall they make it.

9 And you shalt make the court of the tabernacle; for the south side southward there shall be hangings for the court of fine twined linen of a hundred cubits long for one side.

10 And the twenty pillars thereof and their twenty sockets shall be of brass; the hooks of the pillars and their fillets shall be of silver.

11 And likewise for the north side in length there shall be hangings of a hundred cubits long, and his twenty pillars and their twenty sockets of brass; the hooks of the pillars and their fillets of silver.

12 And for the breadth of the court on the west side shall be hangings of fifty cubits; their pillars ten, and their sockets ten.

13 And the breadth of the court on the east side eastward shall be fifty cubits.

14 The hangings of one side of the gate shall be fifteen cubits: their pillars three, and their sockets three.

15 And on the other side shall be hangings fifteen cubits: their pillars three, and their sockets three.

16 And for the gate of the court shall be a hanging of twenty cubits, of blue, and purple, and scarlet, and fine twined linen, wrought with needlework; and their pillars shall be four, and their sockets four.

17 All the pillars round about the court shall be filleted with silver; their hooks shall be of silver, and their sockets of brass.

18 The length of the court shall be a hundred cubits, and the breadth fifty every where, and the height five cubits of fine twined linen, and their sockets of brass.

19 All the vessels of the tabernacle in all the service thereof, and all the pins thereof, and all the pins of the court, shall be of brass.

20 And you shalt command the children of Yisrael, that they bring you pure oil olive beaten for the light, to cause the lamp to burn always.

21 In the tabernacle of the congregation outside the vail, which is before the Testimony, Aaron (Aharon) and his sons shall order it from evening to morning before יהוה. It shall be a statute forever unto their generations on the behalf of the children of Yisrael.

28 And take you unto you Aaron (Aharon) your brother, and his sons with him, from among the children of Yisrael, that he may minister unto me as priests (kohanim), even Aaron (Aharon), Nadav and Avihu, Eleazar and Ithamar, Aaron (Aharon)'s sons.

2 And you shalt make holy garments for Aaron (Aharon) your brother for glory and for beauty.

3 And you shalt speak unto all that are wise hearted, whom I have filled with the spirit of wisdom, that they may make Aaron (Aharon)'s garments to consecrate him, that he may minister unto Me as priests (kohanim).

4 And these are the garments which they shall make; a breastplate, and an ephod, and a robe, and a broidered coat, a mitre, and a girdle: and they shall make holy garments for Aaron (Aharon) your brother, and his sons, that he may minister unto Me as priests (kohanim).

5 And they shall take gold, and blue, and purple, and scarlet, and fine linen.

6 And they shall make the ephod of gold, of blue, and of purple, of scarlet, and fine twined linen, with cunning work.

7 It shall have the two shoulderpieces thereof joined at the two edges thereof; and so it shall be joined together.

8 And the curious girdle of the ephod, which is upon it, shall be of the same, according to the work thereof; even of gold, of blue, and purple, and scarlet, and fine twined linen.

9 And you shalt take two onyx stones, and grave on them the names of the children of Yisrael;

10 Six of their names on one stone, and the other six names of the rest on the other stone, according to their birth.

11 With the work of an engraver in stone, like the engravings of a signet, shalt you engrave the two stones with the names of the children of Yisrael. You shalt make them to be set in ouches of gold.

12 And you shalt put the two stones upon the shoulders of the ephod for stones of memorial unto the children of Yisrael; and Aaron (Aharon) shall bear their names before יהוה upon his two shoulders for a memorial.

13 And you shalt make ouches of gold;

14 And two chains of pure gold at the ends; of wreathen work shalt you make them, and fasten the wreathen chains to the ouches.

15 And you shalt make the breastplate of judgment with cunning work; after the work of the ephod you shalt make it; of gold, of blue, and of purple, and of scarlet, and of fine twined linen, shalt you make it.

16 Foursquare it shall be being doubled; a span shall be the length thereof, and a span shall be the breadth thereof.

17 And you shalt set in it settings of stones, even four rows of stones: the first row shall be a sardius, a topaz, and a carbuncle; this shall be the first row.

18 And the second row shall be an emerald, a sapphire, and a diamond.

19 And the third row a ligure, an agate, and an amethyst.

20 And the fourth row a beryl, and an onyx, and a jasper; they shall be set in gold in their inclosings.

21 And the stones shall be with the names of the children of Yisrael, twelve, according to their names, like the engravings of a signet; every

one with his name shall they be according to the twelve tribes.

22 And you shalt make upon the breastplate chains at the ends of wreathen work of pure gold.

23 And you shalt make upon the breastplate two rings of gold, and shalt put the two rings on the two ends of the breastplate.

24 And you shalt put the two wreathen chains of gold in the two rings which are on the ends of the breastplate.

25 And the other two ends of the two wreathen chains you shalt fasten in the two ouches, and put them on the shoulderpieces of the ephod before it.

26 And you shalt make two rings of gold, and you shalt put them upon the two ends of the breastplate in the border thereof, which is in the side of the ephod inward.

27 And two other rings of gold you shalt make, and shalt put them on the two sides of the ephod underneath, toward the forepart thereof, opposite the other coupling thereof, above the curious girdle of the ephod.

28 And they shall bind the breastplate by the rings thereof unto the rings of the ephod with a lace of blue, that it may be above the curious girdle of the ephod, and that the breastplate be not loosed from the ephod.

29 And Aaron (Aharon) shall bear the names of the children of Yisrael in the breastplate of judgment upon his heart, when he goeth in unto the holy place, for a memorial before יהוה continually.

30 And you shalt put in the breastplate of judgment the Urim and the Thummim; and they shall be upon Aaron (Aharon)'s heart, when he goeth in before יהוה. And Aaron (Aharon) shall bear the judgment of the children of Yisrael upon his heart before יהוה continually.

31 And you shalt make the robe of the ephod all of blue.

32 And there shall be a hole in the top of it, in the midst thereof; it shall have a binding of woven work round about the hole of it, as it was the hole of a habergeon, that it be not rent.

33 And beneath upon the hem of it you shalt make pomegranates of blue, and of purple, and of scarlet, round about the hem thereof; and bells of gold between them round about:

34 A golden bell and a pomegranate, a golden

bell and a pomegranate, upon the hem of the robe round about.

35 And it shall be upon Aaron (Aharon) to minister; and its sound shall be heard when he goeth in unto the holy place before יהוה, and when he cometh out, that he dies not.

36 And you shalt make a plate of pure gold, and engrave upon it, like the engravings of a signet: B10Holiness unto יהוה (Qodesh la-YHWH).

37 And you shalt put it on a blue lace, that it may be upon the mitre; upon the forefront of the mitre it shall be.

38 And it shall be upon Aaron (Aharon)'s forehead, that Aaron (Aharon) may bear the iniquity of the holy things, which the children of Yisrael shall hallow in all their holy gifts; and it shall be always upon his forehead, that they may be accepted before יהוה.

39 And you shalt embroider the coat of fine linen, and you shalt make the mitre of fine linen, and you shalt make the girdle of needlework.

40 And for Aaron (Aharon)'s sons you shalt make coats, and you shalt make for them girdles, and bonnets shalt you make for them, for glory and for beauty.

41 And you shalt put them upon Aaron (Aharon) your brother, and his sons with him; and shalt anoint them, and consecrate them, and sanctify them, that they may minister unto Me as priests (kohanim).

42 And you shalt make them linen breeches to cover their nakedness; from the loins even unto the thighs they shall reach:

43 And they shall be upon Aaron (Aharon), and upon his sons, when they come in unto the tabernacle of the congregation, or when they come near unto the altar to minister in the holy place; that they bear not iniquity, and die. It shall be a statute forever unto him and his seed after him."

29 "And this is the thing that you shalt do unto them to hallow them, to minister unto Me as priests (kohanim): Take one young bullock, and two rams without blemish,

2 And unleavened bread, and cakes unleavened tempered with oil, and wafers unleavened anointed with oil, of wheaten flour shalt you make them.

3 And you shalt put them into one basket, and bring them in the basket, with the bullock and the two rams.

4 And Aaron (Aharon) and his sons you shalt bring unto the door of the tabernacle of the congregation, and shalt wash them with water.

5 And you shalt take the garments, and put upon Aaron (Aharon) the coat, and the robe of the ephod, and the ephod, and the breastplate, and gird him with the curious girdle of the ephod.

6 And you shalt put the mitre upon his head, and put the holy crown upon the mitre.

7 Then shalt you take the anointing oil, and pour it upon his head, and anoint him.

8 And you shalt bring his sons, and put coats upon them.

9 And you shalt gird them with girdles, Aaron (Aharon) and his sons, and put the bonnets on them; and the priest's office (kehunnah) shall be theirs for a perpetual statute. And you shalt consecrate Aaron (Aharon) and his sons.

10 And you shalt cause a bullock to be brought before the tabernacle of the congregation; and Aaron (Aharon) and his sons shall put their hands upon the head of the bullock.

11 And you shalt kill the bullock before יהוה, by the door of the tabernacle of the congregation.

12 And you shalt take of the blood of the bullock, and put it upon the horns of the altar with your finger, and pour all the blood beside the bottom of the altar.

13 And you shalt take all the fat that covereth the inwards, and the caul that is above the liver, and the two kidneys, and the fat that is upon them, and burn them upon the altar.

14 But the flesh of the bullock, and his skin, and his dung, shalt you burn with fire outside the camp: it is a sin offering.

15 You shalt also take one ram; and Aaron (Aharon) and his sons shall put their hands upon the head of the ram.

16 And you shalt slay the ram, and you shalt take his blood, and sprinkle it round about upon the altar.

17 And you shalt cut the ram in pieces, and wash the inwards of him, and his legs, and put them unto his pieces, and unto his head.

18 And you shalt burn the whole ram upon the altar. It is a burnt offering unto יהוה; it is a sweet savour, an offering made by fire unto יהוה.

19 And you shalt take the other ram; and Aaron (Aharon) and his sons shall put their hands upon the head of the ram.

20 Then shalt you kill the ram, and take of his

blood, and put it upon the tip of the right ear of Aaron (Aharon), and upon the tip of the right ear of his sons, and upon the thumb of their right hand, and upon the great toe of their right foot, and sprinkle the blood upon the altar round about.

21 And you shalt take of the blood that is upon the altar, and of the anointing oil, and sprinkle it upon Aaron (Aharon), and upon his garments, and upon his sons, and upon the garments of his sons with him; and he shall be hallowed, and his garments, and his sons, and his sons' garments with him.

22 Also you shalt take of the ram the fat and the rump, and the fat that covereth the inwards, and the caul above the liver, and the two kidneys, and the fat that is upon them, and the right shoulder; for it is a ram of consecration;

23 And one loaf of bread, and one cake of oiled bread, and one wafer out of the basket of the unleavened bread that is before יהוה;

24 And you shalt put all in the hands of Aaron (Aharon), and in the hands of his sons; and shalt wave them for a wave offering before יהוה.

25 And you shalt receive them of their hands, and burn them upon the altar for a burnt offering, for a sweet savour before יהוה; it is an offering made by fire unto יהוה.

26 And you shalt take the breast of the ram of Aaron (Aharon)'s consecration, and wave it for a wave offering before יהוה; and it shall be your part.

27 And you shalt sanctify the breast of the wave offering, and the shoulder of the heave offering, which is waved, and which is heaved up, of the ram of the consecration, even of that which is for Aaron (Aharon), and of that which is for his sons.

28 And it shall be Aaron (Aharon)'s and his sons' by a statute forever from the children of Yisrael; for it is a heave offering; and it shall be a heave offering from the children of Yisrael of the sacrifice of their peace offerings, even their heave offering unto יהוה.

29 And the holy garments of Aaron (Aharon) shall be his sons' after him, to be anointed therein, and to be consecrated in them.

30 And that son that is priest (kohen) in his stead shall put them on seven days, when he cometh into the tabernacle of the congregation to minister in the holy place.

31 And you shalt take the ram of the consecration, and seethe his flesh in the holy place.

32 And Aaron (Aharon) and his sons shall eat the flesh of the ram, and the bread that is in the basket, by the door of the tabernacle of the congregation.

33 And they shall eat those things wherewith the atonement was made, to consecrate and to sanctify them; but a stranger shall not eat thereof, because they are holy.

34 And if ought of the flesh of the consecrations, or of the bread, remain unto the morning, then you shalt burn the remainder with fire. It shall not be eaten, because it is holy.

35 And thus shalt you do unto Aaron (Aharon), and to his sons, according to all things which I have commanded you; seven days shalt you consecrate them.

36 And you shalt offer every day a bullock for a sin offering for atonement. And you shalt cleanse the altar, when you have made an atonement for it, and you shalt anoint it, to sanctify it.

37 Seven days you shalt make an atonement for the altar, and sanctify it; and it shall be an altar most holy; whatsoever toucheth the altar shall be holy.

38 Now this is that which you shalt offer upon the altar; two lambs of the first year day by day continually.

39 The one lamb you shalt offer in the morning; and the other lamb you shalt offer at even.

40 And with the one lamb a tenth deal of flour mingled with the fourth part of an hin of beaten oil; and the fourth part of an hin of wine for a drink offering.

41 And the other lamb you shalt offer at even, and shalt do thereto according to the meat offering of the morning, and according to the drink offering thereof, for a sweet savour, an offering made by fire unto יהוה.

42 This shall be a continual burnt offering throughout your generations at the door of the tabernacle of the congregation before יהוה, where I will meet you, to speak there unto you.

43 And there I will meet with the children of Yisrael, and the tabernacle shall be sanctified by My glory.

44 And I will sanctify the tabernacle of the congregation, and the altar. I will sanctify also both Aaron (Aharon) and his sons, to minister

to Me as priests (kohanim).

45 And I will dwell among the children of Yisrael, and will be their God (Elohim).

46 And they shall know that I am יהוה their God (YHWH Eloheihem), that brought them forth out of the land of Egypt (Mitsrayim), that I may dwell among them. I am יהוה their God (YHWH Eloheihem)."

30 "And you shalt make an altar to burn incense upon; of shittim wood shalt you make it.

2 A cubit shall be the length thereof, and a cubit the breadth thereof; foursquare shall it be; and two cubits shall be the height thereof. The horns thereof shall be of the same.

3 And you shalt overlay it with pure gold, the top thereof, and the sides thereof round about, and the horns thereof; and you shalt make unto it a crown of gold round about.

4 And two golden rings shalt you make to it under the crown of it, by the two corners thereof, upon the two sides of it shalt you make it; and they shall be for places for the staves to bear it withal.

5 And you shalt make the staves of shittim wood, and overlay them with gold.

6 And you shalt put it before the vail that is by the ark of the testimony, before the mercy seat that is over the testimony, where I will meet with you.

7 And Aaron (Aharon) shall burn thereon sweet incense every morning; when he dresseth the lamps, he shall burn incense upon it.

8 And when Aaron (Aharon) lighteth the lamps at even, he shall burn incense upon it, a perpetual incense before יהוה throughout your generations.

9 You shall offer no strange incense thereon, nor burnt sacrifice, nor meat offering; neither shall you pour drink offering thereon.

10 And Aaron (Aharon) shall make an atonement upon the horns of it once in a year with the blood of the sin offering of atonements; once in the year shall he make atonement upon it throughout your generations. It is most holy unto יהוה"

11 And יהוה spake unto Moses (Mosheh), saying:

12 "When you takest the sum of the children of Yisrael after their number, then shall they give every man a ransom for his soul unto יהוה, when you numberest them; that there be no plague among them, when you numberest them.

13 This they shall give, every one that passeth among them that are numbered, half a shekel after the shekel of the sanctuary: (a shekel is twenty gerahs:) a half shekel shall be the offering of יהוה.

14 Every one that passeth among them that are numbered, from twenty years old and above, shall give an offering unto יהוה.

15 The rich shall not give more, and the poor shall not give less than half a shekel, when they give an offering unto יהוה, to make an atonement for your souls.

16 And you shalt take the atonement money of the children of Yisrael, and shalt appoint it for the service of the tabernacle of the congregation; that it may be a memorial unto the children of Yisrael before יהוה, to make an atonement for your souls.

17 And יהוה spake unto Moses (Mosheh), saying,

18 You shalt also make a laver of brass, and his foot also of brass, to wash withal; and you shalt put it between the tabernacle of the congregation and the altar, and you shalt put water therein.

19 For Aaron (Aharon) and his sons shall wash their hands and their feet thereat.

20 When they go into the tabernacle of the congregation, they shall wash with water, that they die not; or when they come near to the altar to minister, to burn offering made by fire unto יהוה:

21 So they shall wash their hands and their feet, that they die not; and it shall be a statute forever to them, even to him and to his seed throughout their generations.

22 Moreover יהוה spake unto Moses (Mosheh), saying,

23 "Take you also unto you principal spices, of pure myrrh five hundred shekels, and of sweet cinnamon half so much, even two hundred and fifty shekels, and of sweet calamus two hundred and fifty shekels,

24 And of cassia five hundred shekels, after the shekel of the sanctuary, and of oil olive an hin;

25 And you shalt make it an oil of holy ointment, an ointment compound after the art of the apothecary; it shall be a holy anointing oil.

26 And you shalt anoint the tabernacle of the congregation therewith, and the ark of the

testimony,

27 And the table and all his vessels, and the candlestick (menorah) and his vessels, and the altar of incense,

28 And the altar of burnt offering with all his vessels, and the laver and his foot.

29 And you shalt sanctify them, that they may be most holy; whatsoever toucheth them shall be holy.

30 And you shalt anoint Aaron (Aharon) and his sons, and consecrate them, that they may minister unto Me as priests (kohanim).

31 And you shalt speak unto the children of Yisrael, saying, 'This shall be a holy anointing oil unto Me throughout your generations.

32 Upon man's flesh shall it not be poured, neither shall you make any other like it, after the composition of it. It is holy, and it shall be holy unto you.

33 Whosoever compoundeth any like it, or whosoever putteth any of it upon a stranger, shall even be cut off from his people.'"

34 And יהוה said unto Moses (Mosheh), Take unto you sweet spices, stacte, and onycha, and galbanum; these sweet spices with pure frankincense; of each shall there be a like weight;

35 And you shalt make it a perfume, a confection after the art of the apothecary, tempered together, pure and holy;

36 And you shalt beat some of it very small, and put of it before the testimony in the tabernacle of the congregation, where I will meet with you; it shall be unto you most holy.

37 And as for the perfume which you shalt make, you shall not make to yourselves according to the composition thereof; it shall be unto you holy for יהוה.

38 Whosoever shall make like unto that, to smell thereto, shall even be cut off from his people."

31 And יהוה spake unto Moses (Mosheh), saying,

2 "See, I have called by name Bezaleel the son of Uri, the son of Hur, of the tribe of Judah (Yehudah).

3 And I have filled him with the spirit of God (Elohim), in wisdom, and in understanding, and in knowledge, and in all manner of workmanship,

4 To devise cunning works, to work in gold, and

in silver, and in brass,

5 And in cutting of stones, to set them, and in carving of timber, to work in all manner of workmanship.

6 And I, behold, I have given with him Aholiab, the son of Ahisamach, of the tribe of Dan; and in the hearts of all that are wise hearted I have put wisdom, that they may make all that I have commanded you;

7 The tabernacle of the congregation, and the ark of the testimony, and the mercy seat that is thereupon, and all the furniture of the tabernacle,

8 And the table and its furniture, and the pure candlestick (menorah) with all its furniture, and the altar of incense,

9 And the altar of burnt offering with all its furniture, and the laver and its foot,

10 And the cloths of service, and the holy garments for Aaron (Aharon) the priest (kohen), and the garments of his sons, to minister as priests (kohanim).,

11 And the anointing oil, and sweet incense for the holy place; according to all that I have commanded you shall they do.

12 And יהוה spake unto Moses (Mosheh), saying,

13 "Speak you also unto the children of Yisrael, saying, 'Verily My Shabbats you shall keep, for it is a sign between Me and you throughout your generations; that you may know that I am יהוה that doth sanctify you.

14 You shall keep the Shabbat therefore; for it is holy unto you; every one that defileth it shall surely be put to death; for whosoever doeth any work therein, that soul shall be cut off from among his people.

15 Six days may work be done; but in the seventh is the Shabbat of rest, holy to יהוה; whosoever doeth any work in the Shabbat day, he shall surely be put to death.

16 Wherefore the children of Yisrael shall keep the Shabbat, to observe the Shabbat throughout their generations, for a perpetual covenant.

17 It is a sign between Me and the children of Yisrael forever; for in six days יהוה made heaven and earth, and on the seventh day He rested, and was refreshed.'"

18 And He gave unto Moses (Mosheh), when He had made an end of communing with him upon Mount Sinai, two tablets of Testimony,

tablets of stone, written with the finger of God (Elohim).

32 And when the people saw that Moses (Mosheh) delayed to come down out of the mountain, the people gathered themselves together unto Aaron (Aharon), and said unto him, "Up, make us ⁴god (elohim), which shall go before us; for as for this Moses (Mosheh), the man that brought us up out of the land of Egypt (Mitsrayim), we know not what is become of him."

2 And Aaron (Aharon) said unto them, "Break off the golden earrings, which are in the ears of your wives, of your sons, and of your daughters, and bring them unto me."

3 And all the people broke off the golden earrings which were in their ears, and brought them unto Aaron (Aharon).

4 And he received them at their hand, and fashioned it with an engraving tool, after he had made it a molten calf; and they said, "These be your god (ᴮ¹ᵇelohim), O Yisrael, who brought you up out of the land of Egypt (Mitsrayim).

5 And when Aaron (Aharon) saw it, he built an altar before it; and Aaron (Aharon) made proclamation, and said, "Tomorrow is a feast to יהוה."

6 And they rose up early on the next day, and offered burnt offerings, and brought peace offerings; and the people sat down to eat and to drink, and rose up to play.

7 And יהוה said unto Moses (Mosheh), "Go, get you down; for your people, whom you broughtest out of the land of Egypt (Mitsrayim), have corrupted themselves.

8 They have turned aside quickly out of the way which I commanded them. They have made themselves a molten calf, and have worshipped it, and have sacrificed thereunto, and said, 'These be your god (elohim), O Yisrael, who have brought you up out of the land of Egypt (Mitsrayim)!'"

9 And יהוה said unto Moses (Mosheh), "I have seen this people, and, behold, it is a stiffnecked people!

10 Now therefore let Me alone, that My wrath may wax hot against them, and that I may consume them; and I will make of you a great nation."

11 And Moses (Mosheh) besought יהוה his God (Elohim), and said, "יהוה, why doth Your wrath wax hot against Your people, whom You have brought forth out of the land of Egypt (Mitsrayim) with great power, and with a mighty hand?

12 Wherefore should the Egyptians (Mitsrayim) speak, and say, 'For mischief did He bring them out, to slay them in the mountains, and to consume them from the face of the earth?' Turn from Your fierce wrath, and regret of this disaster against Your people.

13 Remember Avraham, Isaac (Yitschaq), and Yisrael, Your servants, to whom You swarest by Your own self, and saidst unto them, 'I will multiply your seed as the stars of heaven, and all this land that I have spoken of will I give unto your seed, and they shall inherit it forever.'"

14 And יהוה regretted of the disaster which He thought to do unto His people.

15 And Moses (Mosheh) turned, and went down from the mountain, and the two tablets of the Testimony were in his hand: the tablets were written on both their sides; on the one side and on the other were they written.

16 And the tablets were the work of God (Elohim), and the writing was the writing of God (Elohim), graven upon the tablets.

17 And when Joshua (Yehoshua) heard the noise of the people as they shouted, he said unto Moses (Mosheh), "There is a noise of war in the camp."

18 And he said, "It is not the voice of them that shout for mastery, neither is it the voice of them that cry for being overcome; but the noise of them that sing do I hear."

19 And it came to pass, as soon as he came near unto the camp, that he saw the calf, and the dancing; and Moses (Mosheh)'s anger waxed hot, and he cast the tablets out of his hands, and broke them beneath the mountain.

20 And he took the calf which they had made, and burnt it in the fire, and ground it to powder, and strawed it upon the water, and made the children of Yisrael drink of it.

21 And Moses (Mosheh) said unto Aaron (Aharon), "What did this people unto you, that you have brought so great a sin upon them?"

22 And Aaron (Aharon) said, "Let not the anger of my lord (adoni) wax hot; you knowest the people, that they are set on mischief.

23 For they said unto me, 'Make us god (ᴮ¹ᵇelohim), which shall go before us; for as for

this Moses (Mosheh), the man that brought us up out of the land of Egypt (Mitsrayim), we know not what is become of him.'

24 And I said unto them, 'Whosoever hath any gold, let them break it off.' So they gave it me; then I cast it into the fire, and there came out this calf."

25 And when Moses (Mosheh) saw that the people were naked; (for Aaron (Aharon) had made them naked unto their shame among their enemies);

26 Then Moses (Mosheh) stood in the gate of the camp, and said, "Who is on יהוה's side? Let him come unto me." And all the sons of Lewi gathered themselves together unto him.

27 And he said unto them, "Thus saith יהוה God of Israel (Elohei Yisrael), 'Put every man his sword by his side, and go in and out from gate to gate throughout the camp, and slay every man his brother, and every man his companion, and every man his neighbour.'"

28 And the children of Lewi did according to the word of Moses (Mosheh); and there fell of the people that day about three thousand men.

29 For Moses (Mosheh) had said, "Consecrate yourselves today to יהוה, even every man upon his son, and upon his brother; that he may bestow upon you a blessing this day."

30 And it came to pass on the next day, that Moses (Mosheh) said unto the people, "You have sinned a great sin; and now I will go up unto יהוה; perhaps I shall make an atonement for your sin."

31 And Moses (Mosheh) returned unto יהוה, and said, "Oh, this people have sinned a great sin, and have made them god (elohim) of gold.

32 Yet now, if You wilt forgive their sin--and if not, please blot me out of Your book which You have written."

33 And יהוה said unto Moses (Mosheh), "Whosoever hath sinned against Me, him will I blot out of My book.

34 Therefore now go, lead the people unto the place of which I have spoken unto you. Behold, My Angel shall go before you; nevertheless in the day when I visit I will visit their sin upon them."

35 And יהוה plagued the people, because they made the calf, which Aaron (Aharon) made.

33 And יהוה said unto Moses (Mosheh), "Depart, and go up hence, you and the people whom you have brought up out of the land of Egypt (Mitsrayim), unto the land which I sware unto Avraham, to Isaac (Yitschaq), and to Jacob (Yaaqov), saying, 'Unto your seed will I give it.'

2 And I will send an angel before you; and I will drive out the Canaanite, the Amorite, and the Hittite, and the Perizzite, the Hivite, and the Jebusite (Yevusi).

3 Unto a land flowing with milk and honey; for I will not go up in the midst of you; for you are a stiffnecked people; lest I consume you in the way."

4 And when the people heard these evil tidings, they mourned; and no man did put on his ornaments.

5 For יהוה had said unto Moses (Mosheh), "Say unto the children of Yisrael, 'You are a stiffnecked people. I will come up into the midst of you in a moment, and consume you; therefore now put off your ornaments from you, that I may know what to do unto you.'"

6 And the children of Yisrael stripped themselves of their ornaments by the Mount Horeb (Chorev).

7 And Moses (Mosheh) took the tabernacle, and pitched it outside the camp, afar off from the camp, and called it the Tabernacle of the congregation. And it came to pass, that every one who sought יהוה went out unto the tabernacle of the congregation, which was outside the camp.

8 And it came to pass, when Moses (Mosheh) went out unto the tabernacle, that all the people rose up, and stood every man at his tent door, and looked after Moses (Mosheh), until he was gone into the tabernacle.

9 And it came to pass, as Moses (Mosheh) entered into the tabernacle, the cloudy pillar descended, and stood at the door of the tabernacle, and יהוה talked with Moses (Mosheh).

10 And all the people saw the cloudy pillar stand at the tabernacle door; and all the people rose up and worshipped, every man in his tent door.

11 And יהוה spake unto Moses (Mosheh) face to face, as a man speaketh unto his friend. And he turned again into the camp; but his servant Joshua (Yehoshua), the son of Nun, a young man, departed not out of the tabernacle.

12 And Moses (Mosheh) said unto יהוה, "See,

You sayest unto me, 'Bring up this people; and You have not let me know whom You wilt send with me. Yet You have said, 'I know you by name, and you have also found grace in My sight.'

13 Now therefore, please, if I have found grace in Your sight, shew me now Your way, that I may know You, that I may find grace in Your sight; and consider that this nation is Your people."

14 And He said, "My presence shall go with you, and I will give you rest."

15 And he said unto Him, "If Your presence goes not with me, carry us not up here.

16 For wherein shall it be known here that I and Your people have found grace in Your sight? Is it not in that You goest with us? So shall we be separated, I and Your people, from all the people that are upon the face of the earth."

17 And יהוה said unto Moses (Mosheh), "I will do this thing also that you have spoken; for you have found grace in My sight, and I know you by name."

18 And he said, "I beseech You, shew me Your glory."

19 And He said, "I will make all My goodness pass before you, and I will proclaim the name of יהוה before you; and will be gracious to whom I will be gracious, and will shew mercy on whom I will shew mercy."

20 And He said, "You canst not see My face; for there shall no man see Me, and live."

21 And יהוה said, "Behold, there is a place by Me, and you shalt stand upon a rock.

22 And it shall come to pass, while My glory passeth by, that I will put you in a clift of the rock, and will cover you with My hand while I pass by.

23 And I will take away Mine hand, and you shalt see My back parts; but My face shall not be seen."

34 And יהוה said unto Moses (Mosheh), "Hew you two tablets of stone like unto the first; and I will write upon these tablets the words that were in the first tablets, which you brakest.

2 And be ready in the morning, and come up in the morning unto Mount Sinai, and present yourself there to Me on the top of the mountain.

3 And no man shall come up with you, neither let any man be seen throughout all the mountain;

neither let the flocks nor herds feed before that mountain."

4 And he hewed two tablets of stone like unto the first; and Moses (Mosheh) rose up early in the morning, and went up unto Mount Sinai, as יהוה had commanded him, and took in his hand the two tablets of stone.

5 And יהוה descended in the cloud, and stood with him there, and proclaimed the name of יהוה.

6 And יהוה passed by before him, and proclaimed, "יהוה, God (El) יהוה, merciful and gracious, longsuffering, and abundant in goodness and truth,

7 Keeping mercy for thousands, forgiving iniquity and transgression and sin, and that will by no means clear the guilty; visiting the iniquity of the fathers upon the children, and upon the children's children, unto the third and to the fourth generation."

8 And Moses (Mosheh) made haste, and bowed his head toward the earth, and worshipped.

9 And he said, "If now I have found grace in Your sight, O Lord (Adonai), please let my Lord (Adonai) go among us; for it is a stiffnecked people; and pardon our iniquity and our sin, and take us for Your inheritance."

10 And He said, "Behold, I make a covenant; before all your people I will do marvels, such as have not been done in all the earth, nor in any nation; and all the people among whom you are shall see the work of יהוה, for it is an awesome thing that I will do with you.

11 Observe you that which I command you this day. Behold, I drive out before you the Amorite, and the Canaanite, and the Hittite, and the Perizzite, and the Hivite, and the Jebusite (Yevusi).

12 Take heed to yourself, lest you make a covenant with the inhabitants of the land whither you goest, lest it be for a snare in the midst of you;

13 But you shall destroy their altars, break their pillars, and cut down their [B34b]Asherahs (Asherim);

14 For you shalt worship no other God (Elohim); for יהוה, whose name (shem) is Jealous (Qanna), is a jealous God (El);

15 Lest you make a covenant with the inhabitants of the land, and they go a whoring after their gods (elohim), and do sacrifice unto

their gods (elohim), and one call you, and you eat of his sacrifice;

16 And you take of their daughters unto your sons, and their daughters go a whoring after their gods (elohim), and make your sons go a whoring after their gods (elohim).

17 You shalt make you no molten gods (elohim).

18 The Feast of Unleavened Bread (Chag HaMatzot) shalt you keep. Seven days you shalt eat unleavened bread, as I commanded you, in the time of the month Aviv; for in the month Aviv you camest out from Egypt (Mitsrayim).

19 All that openeth the matrix is Mine; and every firstling among your cattle, whether ox or sheep, that is male.

20 But the firstling of an ass you shalt redeem with a lamb; and if you redeem him not, then shalt you break his neck. All the firstborn of your sons you shalt redeem. And none shall appear before Me empty.

21 Six days you shalt work, but on the seventh day you shalt rest; in earing time and in harvest you shalt rest.

22 And you shalt observe the [B21]Feast of Weeks (Chag Shavuot), of the firstfruits of wheat harvest, and the Feast of Ingathering at the year's end.

23 Thrice in the year shall all your men children appear before Lord (Adonai) יהוה, the God of Israel (Elohei Yisrael).

24 For I will cast out the nations before you, and enlarge your borders; neither shall any man desire your land, when you shalt go up to appear before יהוה your God (YHWH Eloheikha) thrice in the year.

25 You shalt not offer the blood of My sacrifice with leaven; neither shall the sacrifice of the [B19]Feast of Passover (Pesach) be left unto the morning.

26 The first of the firstfruits of your land you shalt bring unto the house of יהוה your God (YHWH Eloheikha). You shalt not seethe a kid in his mother's milk.

27 And יהוה said unto Moses (Mosheh), "Write you these words; for after the tenor of these words I have made a covenant with you and with Yisrael."

28 And he was there with יהוה forty days and forty nights; he did neither eat bread, nor drink water. And he wrote upon the tablets the words of the covenant, the Ten Commandments.

29 And it came to pass, when Moses (Mosheh) came down from Mount Sinai with the two tablets of Testimony in Moses (Mosheh)'s hand, when he came down from the mountain, that Moses (Mosheh) knew not that the skin of his face shone while he talked with Him.

30 And when Aaron (Aharon) and all the children of Yisrael saw Moses (Mosheh), behold, the skin of his face shone; and they were afraid to come near him.

31 And Moses (Mosheh) called unto them; and Aaron (Aharon) and all the rulers of the congregation returned unto him; and Moses (Mosheh) talked with them.

32 And afterward all the children of Yisrael came near; and he gave them in commandment all that יהוה had spoken with him in Mount Sinai.

33 And till Moses (Mosheh) had done speaking with them, he put a vail on his face.

34 But when Moses (Mosheh) went in before יהוה to speak with Him, he took the vail off, until he came out. And he came out, and spake unto the children of Yisrael that which he was commanded.

35 And the children of Yisrael saw the face of Moses (Mosheh), that the skin of Moses (Mosheh)'s face shone; and Moses (Mosheh) put the vail upon his face again, until he went in to speak with Him.

35 And Moses (Mosheh) gathered all the congregation of the children of Yisrael together, and said unto them, "These are the words which יהוה hath commanded, that you should do them:

2 Six days shall work be done, but on the seventh day there shall be to you a holy day, a Shabbat [B17]Shabbaton to יהוה; whosoever doeth work therein shall be put to death.

3 You shall kindle no fire throughout your habitations upon the Shabbat day."

4 And Moses (Mosheh) spake unto all the congregation of the children of Yisrael, saying, "This is the thing which יהוה commanded, saying,

5 'Take you from among you an offering unto יהוה; whosoever is of a willing heart, let him bring it, an offering of יהוה; gold, and silver, and brass;

6 And blue, and purple, and scarlet, and fine linen, and goats' hair;

7 And rams' skins dyed red, and badgers' skins, and shittim wood;

8 And oil for the light, and spices for anointing oil, and for the sweet incense;

9 And onyx stones, and stones to be set for the ephod, and for the breastplate.

10 And every wise hearted among you shall come, and make all that יהוה hath commanded:

11 The tabernacle, its tent, and its covering, its taches, and its boards, its bars, its pillars, and its sockets;

12 The ark, and the staves thereof, with the mercy seat, and the vail of the covering;

13 The table, and its staves, and all its vessels, and the shewbread;

14 The candlestick (menorah) also for the light, and its furniture, and its lamps, with the oil for the light;

15 And the incense altar, and its staves, and the anointing oil, and the sweet incense, and the hanging for the door at the entering in of the tabernacle;

16 The altar of burnt offering, with its brasen grate, its staves, and all its vessels, the laver and its foot;

17 The hangings of the court, its pillars, and their sockets, and the hanging for the door of the court;

18 The pins of the tabernacle, and the pins of the court, and their cords;

19 The cloths of service, to do service in the holy place, the holy garments for Aaron (Aharon) the priest (kohen), and the garments of his sons, to minister as priests (kohanim).'"

20 And all the congregation of the children of Yisrael departed from the presence of Moses (Mosheh).

21 And they came, every one whose heart stirred him up, and every one whom his spirit made willing, and they brought יהוה's offering to the work of the tabernacle of the congregation, and for all his service, and for the holy garments.

22 And they came, both men and women, as many as were willing hearted, and brought bracelets, and earrings, and rings, and tablets, all jewels of gold; and every man that offered offered an offering of gold unto יהוה.

23 And every man, with whom was found blue, and purple, and scarlet, and fine linen, and goats' hair, and red skins of rams, and badgers' skins, brought them.

24 Every one that did offer an offering of silver and brass brought יהוה's offering; and every man, with whom was found shittim wood for any work of the service, brought it.

25 And all the women that were wise hearted did spin with their hands, and brought that which they had spun, both of blue, and of purple, and of scarlet, and of fine linen.

26 And all the women whose heart stirred them up in wisdom spun goats' hair.

27 And the rulers brought onyx stones, and stones to be set, for the ephod, and for the breastplate;

28 And spice, and oil for the light, and for the anointing oil, and for the sweet incense.

29 The children of Yisrael brought a willing offering unto יהוה, every man and woman, whose heart made them willing to bring for all manner of work, which יהוה had commanded to be made by the hand of Moses (Mosheh).

30 And Moses (Mosheh) said unto the children of Yisrael, "See, יהוה hath called by name Bezaleel the son of Uri, the son of Hur, of the tribe of Judah (Yehudah);

31 And He hath filled him with the Spirit of God (Elohim), in wisdom, in understanding, and in knowledge, and in all manner of workmanship;

32 And to devise curious works, to work in gold, and in silver, and in brass,

33 And in the cutting of stones, to set them, and in carving of wood, to make any manner of cunning work.

34 And He hath put in his heart that he may teach, both he, and Aholiab, the son of Ahisamach, of the tribe of Dan.

35 Them hath He filled with wisdom of heart, to work all manner of work, of the engraver, and of the cunning workman, and of the embroiderer, in blue, and in purple, in scarlet, and in fine linen, and of the weaver, even of them that do any work, and of those that devise cunning work.

36 Then wrought Bezaleel and Aholiab, and every wise hearted man, in whom יהוה put wisdom and understanding to know how to work all manner of work for the service of the sanctuary, according to all that יהוה had commanded.

2 And Moses (Mosheh) called Bezaleel and Aholiab, and every wise hearted man, in whose heart יהוה had put wisdom, even every one

whose heart stirred him up to come unto the work to do it.

3 And they received of Moses (Mosheh) all the offering, which the children of Yisrael had brought for the work of the service of the sanctuary, to make it withal. And they brought yet unto him free offerings every morning.

4 And all the wise men, that wrought all the work of the sanctuary, came every man from his work which they made;

5 And they spake unto Moses (Mosheh), saying, "The people bring much more than enough for the service of the work, which יהוה commanded to make."

6 And Moses (Mosheh) gave commandment, and they caused it to be proclaimed throughout the camp, saying, "Let neither man nor woman make any more work for the offering of the sanctuary." So the people were restrained from bringing.

7 For the stuff they had was sufficient for all the work to make it, and too much.

8 And every wise hearted man among them that wrought the work of the tabernacle made ten curtains of fine twined linen, and blue, and purple, and scarlet; with cherubims (keruvim) of cunning work made he them.

9 The length of one curtain was twenty and eight cubits, and the breadth of one curtain four cubits; the curtains were all of one size.

10 And he coupled the five curtains one unto another; and the other five curtains he coupled one unto another.

11 And he made loops of blue on the edge of one curtain from the selvedge in the coupling; likewise he made in the uttermost side of another curtain, in the coupling of the second.

12 Fifty loops made he in one curtain, and fifty loops made he in the edge of the curtain which was in the coupling of the second; the loops held one curtain to another.

13 And he made fifty taches of gold, and coupled the curtains one unto another with the taches; so it became one tabernacle.

14 And he made curtains of goats' hair for the tent over the tabernacle: eleven curtains he made them.

15 The length of one curtain was thirty cubits, and four cubits was the breadth of one curtain; the eleven curtains were of one size.

16 And he coupled five curtains by themselves, and six curtains by themselves.

17 And he made fifty loops upon the uttermost edge of the curtain in the coupling, and fifty loops made he upon the edge of the curtain which coupleth the second.

18 And he made fifty taches of brass to couple the tent together, that it might be one.

19 And he made a covering for the tent of rams' skins dyed red, and a covering of badgers' skins above that.

20 And he made boards for the tabernacle of shittim wood, standing up.

21 The length of a board was ten cubits, and the breadth of a board one cubit and a half.

22 One board had two tenons, equally distant one from another. Thus did he make for all the boards of the tabernacle.

23 And he made boards for the tabernacle; twenty boards for the south side southward.

24 And forty sockets of silver he made under the twenty boards; two sockets under one board for his two tenons, and two sockets under another board for his two tenons.

25 And for the other side of the tabernacle, which is toward the north corner, he made twenty boards;

26 And their forty sockets of silver; two sockets under one board, and two sockets under another board.

27 And for the sides of the tabernacle westward he made six boards.

28 And two boards made he for the corners of the tabernacle in the two sides.

29 And they were coupled beneath, and coupled together at the head thereof, to one ring. Thus he did to both of them in both the corners.

30 And there were eight boards; and their sockets were sixteen sockets of silver, under every board two sockets.

31 And he made bars of shittim wood; five for the boards of the one side of the tabernacle,

32 And five bars for the boards of the other side of the tabernacle, and five bars for the boards of the tabernacle for the sides westward.

33 And he made the middle bar to shoot through the boards from the one end to the other.

34 And he overlaid the boards with gold, and made their rings of gold to be places for the bars, and overlaid the bars with gold.

35 And he made a vail of blue, and purple, and scarlet, and fine twined linen: with cherubims

(keruvim) made he it of cunning work.

36 And he made thereunto four pillars of shittim wood, and overlaid them with gold; their hooks were of gold; and he cast for them four sockets of silver.

37 And he made a hanging for the tabernacle door of blue, and purple, and scarlet, and fine twined linen, of needlework;

38 And the five pillars of it with their hooks; and he overlaid their chapiters and their fillets with gold; but their five sockets were of brass.

37 And Bezaleel made the ark of shittim wood; two cubits and a half was the length of it, and a cubit and a half the breadth of it, and a cubit and a half the height of it.

2 And he overlaid it with pure gold inside and outside, and made a crown of gold to it round about.

3 And he cast for it four rings of gold, to be set by the four corners of it; even two rings upon the one side of it, and two rings upon the other side of it.

4 And he made staves of shittim wood, and overlaid them with gold.

5 And he put the staves into the rings by the sides of the ark, to bear the ark.

6 And he made the mercy seat of pure gold; two cubits and a half were the length thereof, and one cubit and a half the breadth thereof.

7 And he made two cherubims (keruvim) of gold, beaten out of one piece made he them, on the two ends of the mercy seat;

8 One cherub (keruv) on the end on this side, and another cherub (keruv) on the other end on that side; out of the mercy seat made he the cherubims (keruvim) on the two ends thereof.

9 And the cherubims (keruvim) spread out their wings on high, and covered with their wings over the mercy seat, with their faces one to another; even to the mercy seatward were the faces of the cherubims (keruvim).

10 And he made the table of shittim wood: two cubits was the length thereof, and a cubit the breadth thereof, and a cubit and a half the height thereof.

11 And he overlaid it with pure gold, and made thereunto a crown of gold round about.

12 Also he made thereunto a border of a handbreadth round about; and made a crown of gold for the border thereof round about.

13 And he cast for it four rings of gold, and put the rings upon the four corners that were in the four feet thereof.

14 Over against the border were the rings, the places for the staves to bear the table.

15 And he made the staves of shittim wood, and overlaid them with gold, to bear the table.

16 And he made the vessels which were upon the table, its dishes, and its spoons, and its bowls, and its covers to cover withal, of pure gold.

17 And he made the candlestick (menorah) of pure gold: of beaten work made he the candlestick (menorah); its shaft, and its branch, its bowls, its knops, and its flowers, were of the same:

18 And six branches going out of the sides thereof; three branches of the candlestick (menorah) out of the one side thereof, and three branches of the candlestick (menorah) out of the other side thereof.

19 Three bowls made after the fashion of almonds in one branch, a knop and a flower; and three bowls made like almonds in another branch, a knop and a flower: so throughout the six branches going out of the candlestick (menorah).

20 And in the candlestick (menorah) were four bowls made like almonds, its knops, and its flowers:

21 And a knop under two branches of the same, and a knop under two branches of the same, and a knop under two branches of the same, according to the six branches going out of it.

22 Their knops and their branches were of the same: all of it was one beaten work of pure gold.

23 And he made its seven lamps, and its snuffers, and its snuffdishes, of pure gold.

24 Of a talent of pure gold made he it, and all the vessels thereof.

25 And he made the incense altar of shittim wood: the length of it was a cubit, and the breadth of it a cubit; it was foursquare; and two cubits was the height of it; the horns thereof were of the same.

26 And he overlaid it with pure gold, both the top of it, and the sides thereof round about, and the horns of it: also he made unto it a crown of gold round about.

27 And he made two rings of gold for it under the crown thereof, by the two corners of it, upon the two sides thereof, to be places for the staves to bear it withal.

28 And he made the staves of shittim wood, and overlaid them with gold.

29 And he made the holy anointing oil, and the pure incense of sweet spices, according to the work of the apothecary.

38 And he made the altar of burnt offering of shittim wood: five cubits was the length thereof, and five cubits the breadth thereof; it was foursquare; and three cubits the height thereof.

2 And he made the horns thereof on the four corners of it; the horns thereof were of the same; and he overlaid it with brass.

3 And he made all the vessels of the altar, the pots, and the shovels, and the basons, and the fleshhooks, and the firepans: all the vessels thereof made he of brass.

4 And he made for the altar a brasen grate of network under the compass thereof beneath unto the midst of it.

5 And he cast four rings for the four ends of the grate of brass, to be places for the staves.

6 And he made the staves of shittim wood, and overlaid them with brass.

7 And he put the staves into the rings on the sides of the altar, to bear it withal; he made the altar hollow with boards.

8 And he made the laver of brass, and the foot of it of brass, of the lookingglasses of the women assembling, which assembled at the door of the tabernacle of the congregation.

9 And he made the court: on the south side southward the hangings of the court were of fine twined linen, a hundred cubits;

10 Their pillars were twenty, and their brasen sockets twenty; the hooks of the pillars and their fillets were of silver.

11 And for the north side the hangings were a hundred cubits, their pillars were twenty, and their sockets of brass twenty; the hooks of the pillars and their fillets of silver.

12 And for the west side were hangings of fifty cubits, their pillars ten, and their sockets ten; the hooks of the pillars and their fillets of silver.

13 And for the east side eastward fifty cubits.

14 The hangings of the one side of the gate were fifteen cubits; their pillars three, and their sockets three.

15 And for the other side of the court gate, on this hand and that hand, were hangings of fifteen cubits; their pillars three, and their sockets three.

16 All the hangings of the court round about were of fine twined linen.

17 And the sockets for the pillars were of brass; the hooks of the pillars and their fillets of silver; and the overlaying of their chapiters of silver; and all the pillars of the court were filleted with silver.

18 And the hanging for the gate of the court was needlework, of blue, and purple, and scarlet, and fine twined linen: and twenty cubits was the length, and the height in the breadth was five cubits, answerable to the hangings of the court.

19 And their pillars were four, and their sockets of brass four; their hooks of silver, and the overlaying of their chapiters and their fillets of silver.

20 And all the pins of the tabernacle, and of the court round about, were of brass.

21 This is the sum of the tabernacle, even of the tabernacle of testimony, as it was counted, according to the commandment of Moses (Mosheh), for the service of the Levites (Lewiyim), by the hand of Ithamar, son to Aaron (Aharon) the priest (kohen).

22 And Bezaleel the son of Uri, the son of Hur, of the tribe of Judah (Yehudah), made all that יהוה commanded Moses (Mosheh).

23 And with him was Aholiab, son of Ahisamach, of the tribe of Dan, an engraver, and a cunning workman, and an embroiderer in blue, and in purple, and in scarlet, and fine linen.

24 All the gold that was occupied for the work in all the work of the holy place, even the gold of the offering, was twenty and nine talents, and seven hundred and thirty shekels, after the shekel of the sanctuary.

25 And the silver of them that were numbered of the congregation was a hundred talents, and a thousand seven hundred and threescore and fifteen shekels, after the shekel of the sanctuary:

26 A bekah for every man, that is, half a shekel, after the shekel of the sanctuary, for every one that went to be numbered, from twenty years old and upward, for six hundred thousand and three thousand and five hundred and fifty men.

27 And of the hundred talents of silver were cast the sockets of the sanctuary, and the sockets of the vail; a hundred sockets of the hundred talents, a talent for a socket.

28 And of the thousand seven hundred seventy and five shekels he made hooks for the pillars, and overlaid their chapiters, and filleted them.

29 And the brass of the offering was seventy talents, and two thousand and four hundred shekels.

30 And therewith he made the sockets to the door of the tabernacle of the congregation, and the brasen altar, and the brasen grate for it, and all the vessels of the altar,

31 And the sockets of the court round about, and the sockets of the court gate, and all the pins of the tabernacle, and all the pins of the court round about.

39 And of the blue, and purple, and scarlet, they made cloths of service, to do service in the holy place, and made the holy garments for Aaron (Aharon), as יהוה commanded Moses (Mosheh).

2 And he made the ephod of gold, blue, and purple, and scarlet, and fine twined linen.

3 And they did beat the gold into thin plates, and cut it into wires, to work it in the blue, and in the purple, and in the scarlet, and in the fine linen, with cunning work.

4 They made shoulderpieces for it, to couple it together; by the two edges was it coupled together.

5 And the curious girdle of his ephod, that was upon it, was of the same, according to the work thereof; of gold, blue, and purple, and scarlet, and fine twined linen, as יהוה commanded Moses (Mosheh).

6 And they wrought onyx stones inclosed in ouches of gold, graven, as signets are graven, with the names of the children of Yisrael.

7 And he put them on the shoulders of the ephod, that they should be stones for a memorial to the children of Yisrael, as יהוה commanded Moses (Mosheh).

8 And he made the breastplate of cunning work, like the work of the ephod; of gold, blue, and purple, and scarlet, and fine twined linen.

9 It was foursquare; they made the breastplate double: a span was the length thereof, and a span the breadth thereof, being doubled.

10 And they set in it four rows of stones: the first row was a sardius, a topaz, and a carbuncle: this was the first row.

11 And the second row, an emerald, a sapphire, and a diamond.

12 And the third row, a ligure, an agate, and an amethyst.

13 And the fourth row, a beryl, an onyx, and a jasper: they were inclosed in ouches of gold in their inclosings.

14 And the stones were according to the names of the children of Yisrael, twelve, according to their names, like the engravings of a signet, every one with his name, according to the twelve tribes.

15 And they made upon the breastplate chains at the ends, of wreathen work of pure gold.

16 And they made two ouches of gold, and two gold rings; and put the two rings in the two ends of the breastplate.

17 And they put the two wreathen chains of gold in the two rings on the ends of the breastplate.

18 And the two ends of the two wreathen chains they fastened in the two ouches, and put them on the shoulderpieces of the ephod, before it.

19 And they made two rings of gold, and put them on the two ends of the breastplate, upon the border of it, which was on the side of the ephod inward.

20 And they made two other golden rings, and put them on the two sides of the ephod underneath, toward the forepart of it, opposite the other coupling thereof, above the curious girdle of the ephod.

21 And they did bind the breastplate by his rings unto the rings of the ephod with a lace of blue, that it might be above the curious girdle of the ephod, and that the breastplate might not be loosed from the ephod, as יהוה commanded Moses (Mosheh).

22 And he made the robe of the ephod of woven work, all of blue.

23 And there was a hole in the midst of the robe, as the hole of a habergeon, with a band round about the hole, that it should not rend.

24 And they made upon the hems of the robe pomegranates of blue, and purple, and scarlet, and twined linen.

25 And they made bells of pure gold, and put the bells between the pomegranates upon the hem of the robe, round about between the pomegranates;

26 A bell and a pomegranate, a bell and a pomegranate, round about the hem of the robe to minister in, as יהוה commanded Moses (Mosheh).

27 And they made coats of fine linen of woven work for Aaron (Aharon), and for his sons,

28 And a mitre of fine linen, and goodly bonnets of fine linen, and linen breeches of fine twined linen,

29 And a girdle of fine twined linen, and blue, and purple, and scarlet, of needlework, as יהוה commanded Moses (Mosheh).

30 And they made the plate of the holy crown of pure gold, and wrote upon it a writing, like to the engravings of a signet: [B10]Holiness unto יהוה (Qodesh la-YHWH).

31 And they tied unto it a lace of blue, to fasten it on high upon the mitre, as יהו׳ commanded Moses (Mosheh).

32 Thus was all the work of the tabernacle of the tent of the congregation finished; and the children of Yisrael did according to all that יהוה commanded Moses (Mosheh), so did they.

33 And they brought the tabernacle unto Moses (Mosheh), the tent, and all its furniture, its taches, its boards, its bars, and its pillars, and its sockets,

34 And the covering of rams' skins dyed red, and the covering of badgers' skins, and the vail of the covering,

35 The ark of the testimony, and the staves thereof, and the mercy seat,

36 The table, and all the vessels thereof, and the shewbread,

37 The pure candlestick (menorah), with the lamps thereof, even with the lamps to be set in order, and all the vessels thereof, and the oil for light,

38 And the golden altar, and the anointing oil, and the sweet incense, and the hanging for the tabernacle door,

39 The brasen altar, and its grate of brass, its staves, and all its vessels, the laver and its foot,

40 The hangings of the court, its pillars, and its sockets, and the hanging for the court gate, its cords, and its pins, and all the vessels of the service of the tabernacle, for the tent of the congregation,

41 The cloths of service to do service in the holy place, and the holy garments for Aaron (Aharon) the priest (kohen), and his sons' garments, to minister as priests (kohanim).

42 According to all that יהוה commanded Moses (Mosheh), so the children of Yisrael made all the work.

43 And Moses (Mosheh) did look upon all the work, and, behold, they had done it as יהוה had commanded, even so had they done it; and Moses (Mosheh) blessed them.

40 And יהוה spake unto Moses (Mosheh), saying,

2 "On the first day of the first month shalt you set up the tabernacle of the tent of the congregation.

3 And you shalt put therein the ark of the testimony, and cover the ark with the vail.

4 And you shalt bring in the table, and set in order the things that are to be set in order upon it; and you shalt bring in the candlestick (menorah), and light the lamps thereof.

5 And you shalt set the altar of gold for the incense before the ark of the testimony, and put the hanging of the door to the tabernacle.

6 And you shalt set the altar of the burnt offering before the door of the tabernacle of the tent of the congregation.

7 And you shalt set the laver between the tent of the congregation and the altar, and shalt put water therein.

8 And you shalt set up the court round about, and hang up the hanging at the court gate.

9 And you shalt take the anointing oil, and anoint the tabernacle, and all that is therein, and shalt hallow it, and all the vessels thereof; and it shall be holy.

10 And you shalt anoint the altar of the burnt offering, and all its vessels, and sanctify the altar: and it shall be an altar most holy.

11 And you shalt anoint the laver and its foot, and sanctify it.

12 And you shalt bring Aaron (Aharon) and his sons unto the door of the tabernacle of the congregation, and wash them with water.

13 And you shalt put upon Aaron (Aharon) the holy garments, and anoint him, and sanctify him; that he may minister unto Me as priests (kohanim).

14 And you shalt bring his sons, and clothe them with coats;

15 And you shalt anoint them, as you didst anoint their father, that they may minister unto Me as priests (kohanim); for their anointing shall surely be an everlasting priesthood (kehunnah) throughout their generations.

16 Thus did Moses (Mosheh); according to all that יהוה commanded him, so did he.

17 And it came to pass in the first month in the second year, on the first day of the month, that the tabernacle was reared up.

18 And Moses (Mosheh) reared up the tabernacle, and fastened its sockets, and set up the boards thereof, and put in the bars thereof, and reared up its pillars.

19 And he spread abroad the tent over the tabernacle, and put the covering of the tent above upon it, as יהוה commanded Moses (Mosheh).

20 And he took and put the testimony into the ark, and set the staves on the ark, and put the mercy seat above upon the ark:

21 And he brought the ark into the tabernacle, and set up the vail of the covering, and covered the ark of the testimony, as יהוה commanded Moses (Mosheh).

22 And he put the table in the tent of the congregation, upon the side of the tabernacle northward, without the vail.

23 And he set the bread in order upon it before יהוה, as יהוה had commanded Moses (Mosheh).

24 And he put the candlestick (menorah) in the tent of the congregation, opposite the table, on the side of the tabernacle southward.

25 And he lighted the lamps before יהוה, as יהוה commanded Moses (Mosheh).

26 And he put the golden altar in the tent of the congregation before the vail;

27 And he burnt sweet incense thereon; as יהוה commanded Moses (Mosheh).

28 And he set up the hanging at the door of the tabernacle.

29 And he put the altar of burnt offering by the door of the tabernacle of the tent of the congregation, and offered upon it the burnt offering and the meat offering, as יהוה commanded Moses (Mosheh).

30 And he set the laver between the tent of the congregation and the altar, and put water there, to wash withal

31 And Moses (Mosheh) and Aaron (Aharon) and his sons washed their hands and their feet thereat;

32 When they went into the tent of the congregation, and when they came near unto the altar, they washed; as יהוה commanded Moses (Mosheh).

33 And he reared up the court round about the tabernacle and the altar, and set up the hanging of the court gate. So Moses (Mosheh) finished the work.

34 Then a cloud covered the tent of the congregation, and the glory of יהוה filled the tabernacle.

35 And Moses (Mosheh) was not able to enter into the tent of the congregation, because the cloud abode thereon, and the glory of יהוה filled the tabernacle.

36 And when the cloud was taken up from over the tabernacle, the children of Yisrael went onward in all their journeys;

37 But if the cloud were not taken up, then they journeyed not till the day that it was taken up.

38 For the cloud of יהוה was upon the tabernacle by day, and fire was on it by night, in the sight of all the house of Yisrael, throughout all their journeys.

LEVITICUS
WAYIQRA וַיִּקְרָא
(And He Called)

1 And יהוה called unto Moses (Mosheh), and spake unto him out of the tabernacle of the congregation, saying,

2 "Speak unto the children of Yisrael, and say unto them: 'If any man of you bring an offering unto יהוה, you shall bring your offering of the cattle, even of the herd, and of the flock.

3 If his offering be a burnt sacrifice of the herd, let him offer a male without blemish; he shall offer it of his own voluntary will at the door of the tabernacle of the congregation before יהוה.

4 And he shall put his hand upon the head of the burnt offering; and it shall be accepted for him to make atonement for him.

5 And he shall kill the bullock before יהוה: and the priests (kohanim), Aaron (Aharon)'s sons, shall bring the blood, and sprinkle the blood round about upon the altar that is by the door of the tabernacle of the congregation.

6 And he shall flay the burnt offering, and cut it into his pieces.

7 And the sons of Aaron (Aharon) the priest (kohen) shall put fire upon the altar, and lay the wood in order upon the fire;

8 And the priests (kohanim), Aaron (Aharon)'s sons, shall lay the parts, the head, and the fat, in order upon the wood that is on the fire which is upon the altar;

9 But his inwards and his legs shall he wash in water; and the priest (kohen) shall burn all on the altar, to be a burnt sacrifice, an offering made by fire, of a sweet savour unto יהוה.

10 And if his offering be of the flocks, namely, of the sheep, or of the goats, for a burnt sacrifice; he shall bring it a male without blemish.

11 And he shall kill it on the side of the altar northward before יהוה; and the priests (kohanim), Aaron (Aharon)'s sons, shall sprinkle his blood round about upon the altar.

12 And he shall cut it into his pieces, with his head and his fat; and the priest (kohen) shall lay them in order on the wood that is on the fire which is upon the altar;

13 But he shall wash the inwards and the legs with water; and the priest (kohen) shall bring it all, and burn it upon the altar: it is a burnt sacrifice, an offering made by fire, of a sweet savour unto יהוה.

14 And if the burnt sacrifice for his offering to יהוה be of fowls, then he shall bring his offering of turtledoves, or of young pigeons.

15 And the priest (kohen) shall bring it unto the altar, and wring off his head, and burn it on the altar; and the blood thereof shall be wrung out at the side of the altar;

16 And he shall pluck away his crop with his feathers, and cast it beside the altar on the east part, by the place of the ashes;

17 And he shall cleave it with the wings thereof, but shall not divide it asunder; and the priest (kohen) shall burn it upon the altar, upon the wood that is upon the fire: it is a burnt sacrifice, an offering made by fire, of a sweet savour unto יהוה.

2 And when any will offer a meat offering unto יהוה, his offering shall be of fine flour; and he shall pour oil upon it, and put frankincense thereon;

2 And he shall bring it to Aaron (Aharon)'s sons the priests (kohanim): and he shall take thereout his handful of the flour thereof, and of the oil thereof, with all the frankincense thereof; and the priest (kohen) shall burn the memorial of it upon the altar, to be an offering made by fire, of a sweet savour unto יהוה;

3 And the remnant of the meat offering shall be Aaron (Aharon)'s and his sons'; it is a thing most holy of the offerings of יהוה made by fire.

4 And if you bring an oblation of a meat offering baken in the oven, it shall be unleavened cakes of fine flour mingled with oil, or unleavened wafers anointed with oil.

5 And if your oblation be a meat offering baken in a pan, it shall be of fine flour unleavened, mingled with oil.

6 You shalt part it in pieces, and pour oil thereon: it is a meat offering.

7 And if your oblation be a meat offering baken in the fryingpan, it shall be made of fine flour with oil.

8 And you shalt bring the meat offering that is made of these things unto יהוה; and when it is presented unto the priest (kohen), he shall bring it unto the altar.

9 And the priest (kohen) shall take from the meat offering a memorial thereof, and shall burn it upon the altar: it is an offering made by

fire, of a sweet savour unto יהוה.

10 And that which is left of the meat offering shall be Aaron (Aharon)'s and his sons': it is a thing most holy of the offerings of יהוה made by fire.

11 No meat offering, which you shall bring unto יהוה, shall be made with leaven; for you shall burn no leaven, nor any honey, in any offering of יהוה made by fire.

12 As for the oblation of the firstfruits, you shall offer them unto יהוה; but they shall not be burnt on the altar for a sweet savour.

13 And every oblation of your meat offering shalt you season with salt; neither shalt you allow the salt of the covenant of your God (Elohim) to be lacking from your meat offering; with all your offerings you shalt offer salt.

14 And if you offer a meat offering of your firstfruits unto יהוה, you shalt offer for the meat offering of your firstfruits green ears of corn dried by the fire, even corn beaten out of full ears.

15 And you shalt put oil upon it, and lay frankincense thereon; it is a meat offering.

16 And the priest (kohen) shall burn the memorial of it, part of the beaten corn thereof, and part of the oil thereof, with all the frankincense thereof; it is an offering made by fire unto יהוה.

3 And if his oblation be a sacrifice of peace offering, if he offer it of the herd; whether it be a male or female, he shall offer it without blemish before יהוה.

2 And he shall lay his hand upon the head of his offering, and kill it at the door of the tabernacle of the congregation; and Aaron (Aharon)'s sons the priests (kohanim) shall sprinkle the blood upon the altar round about.

3 And he shall offer of the sacrifice of the peace offering an offering made by fire unto יהוה; the fat that covereth the inwards, and all the fat that is upon the inwards,

4 And the two kidneys, and the fat that is on them, which is by the flanks, and the caul above the liver, with the kidneys, it shall he take away.

5 And Aaron (Aharon)'s sons shall burn it on the altar upon the burnt sacrifice, which is upon the wood that is on the fire: it is an offering made by fire, of a sweet savour unto יהוה.

6 And if his offering for a sacrifice of peace offering unto יהוה be of the flock; male or female, he shall offer it without blemish.

7 If he offers a lamb for his offering, then shall he offer it before יהוה.

8 And he shall lay his hand upon the head of his offering, and kill it before the tabernacle of the congregation; and Aaron (Aharon)'s sons shall sprinkle the blood thereof round about upon the altar.

9 And he shall offer of the sacrifice of the peace offering an offering made by fire unto יהוה; the fat thereof, and the whole rump, it shall he take off hard by the backbone; and the fat that covereth the inwards, and all the fat that is upon the inwards,

10 And the two kidneys, and the fat that is upon them, which is by the flanks, and the caul above the liver, with the kidneys, it shall he take away.

11 And the priest (kohen) shall burn it upon the altar: it is the food of the offering made by fire unto יהוה.

12 And if his offering be a goat, then he shall offer it before יהוה.

13 And he shall lay his hand upon the head of it, and kill it before the tabernacle of the congregation; and the sons of Aaron (Aharon) shall sprinkle the blood thereof upon the altar round about.

14 And he shall offer thereof his offering, even an offering made by fire unto יהוה; the fat that covereth the inwards, and all the fat that is upon the inwards,

15 And the two kidneys, and the fat that is upon them, which is by the flanks, and the caul above the liver, with the kidneys, it shall he take away.

16 And the priest (kohen) shall burn them upon the altar; it is the food of the offering made by fire for a sweet savour; all the fat is יהוה's.

17 It shall be a perpetual statute for your generations throughout all your dwellings, that you eat neither fat nor blood.'"

4 And יהוה spake unto Moses (Mosheh), saying,

2 "Speak unto the children of Yisrael, saying: 'If a soul shall sin through ignorance against any of the commandments of יהוה concerning things which ought not to be done, and shall do against any of them;

3 If the priest (kohen) that is anointed do sin according to the sin of the people; then let him bring for his sin, which he hath sinned, a young bullock without blemish unto יהוה for a sin

offering.

4 And he shall bring the bullock unto the door of the tabernacle of the congregation before יהוה; and shall lay his hand upon the bullock's head, and kill the bullock before יהוה.

5 And the priest (kohen) that is anointed shall take of the bullock's blood, and bring it to the tabernacle of the congregation;

6 And the priest (kohen) shall dip his finger in the blood, and sprinkle of the blood seven times before יהוה, before the vail of the sanctuary.

7 And the priest (kohen) shall put some of the blood upon the horns of the altar of sweet incense before יהוה, which is in the tabernacle of the congregation; and shall pour all the blood of the bullock at the bottom of the altar of the burnt offering, which is at the door of the tabernacle of the congregation.

8 And he shall take off from it all the fat of the bullock for the sin offering; the fat that covereth the inwards, and all the fat that is upon the inwards,

9 And the two kidneys, and the fat that is upon them, which is by the flanks, and the caul above the liver, with the kidneys, it shall he take away,

10 As it was taken off from the bullock of the sacrifice of peace offerings; and the priest (kohen) shall burn them upon the altar of the burnt offering.

11 And the skin of the bullock, and all his flesh, with his head, and with his legs, and his inwards, and his dung,

12 Even the whole bullock shall he carry forth without the camp unto a clean place, where the ashes are poured out, and burn him on the wood with fire; where the ashes are poured out shall he be burnt.

13 And if the whole congregation of Yisrael sin through ignorance, and the thing be hidden from the eyes of the assembly, and they have done somewhat against any of the commandments of יהוה concerning things which should not be done, and are guilty;

14 When the sin, which they have sinned against it, is known, then the congregation shall offer a young bullock for the sin, and bring him before the tabernacle of the congregation.

15 And the elders of the congregation shall lay their hands upon the head of the bullock before יהוה: and the bullock shall be killed before יהוה.

16 And the priest (kohen) that is anointed shall bring of the bullock's blood to the tabernacle of the congregation:

17 And the priest (kohen) shall dip his finger in some of the blood, and sprinkle it seven times before יהוה, even before the vail.

18 And he shall put some of the blood upon the horns of the altar which is before יהוה, that is in the tabernacle of the congregation, and shall pour out all the blood at the bottom of the altar of the burnt offering, which is at the door of the tabernacle of the congregation.

19 And he shall take all his fat from him, and burn it upon the altar.

20 And he shall do with the bullock as he did with the bullock for a sin offering, so shall he do with this; and the priest (kohen) shall make an atonement for them, and it shall be forgiven them.

21 And he shall carry forth the bullock without the camp, and burn him as he burned the first bullock: it is a sin offering for the congregation.

22 When a ruler hath sinned, and done somewhat through ignorance against any of the commandments of יהוה his God (Elohim) concerning things which should not be done, and is guilty;

23 Or if his sin, wherein he hath sinned, come to his knowledge; he shall bring his offering, a kid of the goats, a male without blemish;

24 And he shall lay his hand upon the head of the goat, and kill it in the place where they kill the burnt offering before יהוה: it is a sin offering.

25 And the priest (kohen) shall take of the blood of the sin offering with his finger, and put it upon the horns of the altar of burnt offering, and shall pour out his blood at the bottom of the altar of burnt offering.

26 And he shall burn all his fat upon the altar, as the fat of the sacrifice of peace offerings: and the priest (kohen) shall make an atonement for him as concerning his sin, and it shall be forgiven him.

27 And if any one of the common people sin through ignorance, while he doeth somewhat against any of the commandments of יהוה concerning things which ought not to be done, and be guilty;

28 Or if his sin, which he hath sinned, come to his knowledge; then he shall bring his offering, a kid of the goats, a female without blemish, for his sin which he hath sinned.

29 And he shall lay his hand upon the head of the sin offering, and slay the sin offering in the place of the burnt offering.

30 And the priest (kohen) shall take of the blood thereof with his finger, and put it upon the horns of the altar of burnt offering, and shall pour out all the blood thereof at the bottom of the altar.

31 And he shall take away all the fat thereof, as the fat is taken away from off the sacrifice of peace offerings; and the priest (kohen) shall burn it upon the altar for a sweet savour unto יהוה; and the priest (kohen) shall make an atonement for him, and it shall be forgiven him.

32 And if he brings a lamb for a sin offering, he shall bring it a female without blemish.

33 And he shall lay his hand upon the head of the sin offering, and slay it for a sin offering in the place where they kill the burnt offering.

34 And the priest (kohen) shall take of the blood of the sin offering with his finger, and put it upon the horns of the altar of burnt offering, and shall pour out all the blood thereof at the bottom of the altar:

35 And he shall take away all the fat thereof, as the fat of the lamb is taken away from the sacrifice of the peace offerings; and the priest (kohen) shall burn them upon the altar, according to the offerings made by fire unto יהוה; and the priest (kohen) shall make an atonement for his sin that he hath committed, and it shall be forgiven him.

5 And if a soul sin, and hear the voice of swearing, and is a witness, whether he hath seen or known of it; if he do not utter it, then he shall bear his iniquity.

2 Or if a soul touches any unclean thing, whether it be a carcase of an unclean beast, or a carcase of unclean cattle, or the carcase of unclean creeping things, and if it be hidden from him; he also shall be unclean, and guilty.

3 Or if he touches the uncleanness of man, whatsoever uncleanness it be that a man shall be defiled withal, and it be hidden from him; when he knoweth of it, then he shall be guilty.

4 Or if a soul swears, pronouncing with his lips to do evil, or to do good, whatsoever it be that a man shall pronounce with an oath, and it be hidden from him; when he knoweth of it, then he shall be guilty in one of these.

5 And it shall be, when he shall be guilty in one of these things, that he shall confess that he hath sinned in that thing:

6 And he shall bring his trespass offering unto יהוה for his sin which he hath sinned, a female from the flock, a lamb or a kid of the goats, for a sin offering; and the priest (kohen) shall make an atonement for him concerning his sin.

7 And if he be not able to bring a lamb, then he shall bring for his trespass, which he hath committed, two turtledoves, or two young pigeons, unto יהוה; one for a sin offering, and the other for a burnt offering.

8 And he shall bring them unto the priest (kohen), who shall offer that which is for the sin offering first, and wring off his head from his neck, but shall not divide it asunder:

9 And he shall sprinkle of the blood of the sin offering upon the side of the altar; and the rest of the blood shall be wrung out at the bottom of the altar: it is a sin offering.

10 And he shall offer the second for a burnt offering, according to the manner; and the priest (kohen) shall make an atonement for him for his sin which he hath sinned, and it shall be forgiven him.

11 But if he be not able to bring two turtledoves, or two young pigeons, then he that sinned shall bring for his offering the tenth part of an ephah of fine flour for a sin offering; he shall put no oil upon it, neither shall he put any frankincense thereon; for it is a sin offering.

12 Then shall he bring it to the priest (kohen), and the priest (kohen) shall take his handful of it, even a memorial thereof, and burn it on the altar, according to the offerings made by fire unto יהוה: it is a sin offering.

13 And the priest (kohen) shall make an atonement for him as touching his sin that he hath sinned in one of these, and it shall be forgiven him; and the remnant shall be the priest (kohen)'s, as a meat offering.'"

14 And יהוה spake unto Moses (Mosheh), saying:

15 "If a soul commits a trespass, and sin through ignorance, in the holy things of יהוה; then he shall bring for his trespass unto יהוה a ram without blemish out of the flocks, with your estimation by shekels of silver, after the shekel of the sanctuary, for a trespass offering;

16 And he shall make amends for the harm that he hath done in the holy thing, and shall add the fifth part thereto, and give it unto the priest

(kohen); and the priest (kohen) shall make an atonement for him with the ram of the trespass offering, and it shall be forgiven him.

17 And if a soul sin, and commit any of these things which are forbidden to be done by the commandments of יהוה; though he wist it not, yet is he guilty, and shall bear his iniquity.

18 And he shall bring a ram without blemish out of the flock, with your estimation, for a trespass offering, unto the priest (kohen); and the priest (kohen) shall make an atonement for him concerning his ignorance wherein he erred and wist it not, and it shall be forgiven him.

19 It is a trespass offering; he hath certainly trespassed against יהוה."

6 And יהוה spake unto Moses (Mosheh), saying:

2 "If a soul sins, and commits a trespass against יהוה, and lies unto his neighbour in that which was delivered him to keep, or in fellowship, or in a thing taken away by violence, or hath deceived his neighbour;

3 Or have found that which was lost, and lieth concerning it, and sweareth falsely; in any of all these that a man doeth, sinning therein;

4 Then it shall be, because he hath sinned, and is guilty, that he shall restore that which he took violently away, or the thing which he hath deceitfully gotten, or that which was delivered him to keep, or the lost thing which he found,

5 Or all that about which he hath sworn falsely; he shall even restore it in the principal, and shall add the fifth part more thereto, and give it unto him to whom it appertaineth, in the day of his trespass offering.

6 And he shall bring his trespass offering unto יהוה, a ram without blemish out of the flock, with your estimation, for a trespass offering, unto the priest (kohen).

7 And the priest (kohen) shall make an atonement for him before יהוה; and it shall be forgiven him for any thing of all that he hath done in trespassing therein."

8 And יהוה spake unto Moses (Mosheh), saying,

9 "Command Aaron (Aharon) and his sons, saying: 'This is the [B28a]law (torah) of the burnt offering: It is the burnt offering, because of the burning upon the altar all night unto the morning, and the fire of the altar shall be burning in it.

10 And the priest (kohen) shall put on his linen garment, and his linen breeches shall he put upon his flesh, and take up the ashes which the fire hath consumed with the burnt offering on the altar, and he shall put them beside the altar.

11 And he shall put off his garments, and put on other garments, and carry forth the ashes without the camp unto a clean place.

12 And the fire upon the altar shall be burning in it; it shall not be put out: and the priest (kohen) shall burn wood on it every morning, and lay the burnt offering in order upon it; and he shall burn thereon the fat of the peace offerings.

13 The fire shall ever be burning upon the altar; it shall never go out.

14 And this is the law (torah) of the meat offering: the sons of Aaron (Aharon) shall offer it before יהוה, before the altar.

15 And he shall take of it his handful, of the flour of the meat offering, and of the oil thereof, and all the frankincense which is upon the meat offering, and shall burn it upon the altar for a sweet savour, even the memorial of it, unto יהוה.

16 And the remainder thereof shall Aaron (Aharon) and his sons eat; with unleavened bread shall it be eaten in the holy place; in the court of the tabernacle of the congregation they shall eat it.

17 It shall not be baken with leaven. I have given it unto them for their portion of my offerings made by fire; it is most holy, as is the sin offering, and as the trespass offering.

18 All the males among the children of Aaron (Aharon) shall eat of it. It shall be a statute forever in your generations concerning the offerings of יהוה made by fire; every one that toucheth them shall be holy.'"

19 And יהוה spake unto Moses (Mosheh), saying:

20 "This is the offering of Aaron (Aharon) and of his sons, which they shall offer unto יהוה in the day when he is anointed; the tenth part of an ephah of fine flour for a meat offering perpetual, half of it in the morning, and half thereof at night.

21 In a pan it shall be made with oil; and when it is baken, you shalt bring it in: and the baken pieces of the meat offering shalt you offer for a sweet savour unto יהוה.

22 And the priest (kohen) of his sons that is anointed in his stead shall offer it; it is a statute forever unto יהוה; it shall be wholly burnt.

23 For every meat offering for the priest (kohen) shall be wholly burnt; it shall not be eaten."

24 And יהוה spake unto Moses (Mosheh), saying,

25 "Speak unto Aaron (Aharon) and to his sons, saying: 'This is the law (torah) of the sin offering: In the place where the burnt offering is killed shall the sin offering be killed before יהוה: it is most holy.

26 The priest (kohen) that offereth it for sin shall eat it; in the holy place shall it be eaten, in the court of the tabernacle of the congregation.

27 Whatsoever shall touch the flesh thereof shall be holy; and when there is sprinkled of the blood thereof upon any garment, you shalt wash that whereon it was sprinkled in the holy place.

28 But the earthen vessel wherein it is sodden shall be broken: and if it be sodden in a brasen pot, it shall be both scoured, and rinsed in water.

29 All the males among the priests (kohanim) shall eat thereof: it is most holy.

30 And no sin offering, whereof any of the blood is brought into the tabernacle of the congregation to reconcile withal in the holy place, shall be eaten; it shall be burnt in the fire.

7 Likewise this is the law (torah) of the trespass offering: it is most holy.

2 In the place where they kill the burnt offering shall they kill the trespass offering; and the blood thereof shall he sprinkle round about upon the altar.

3 And he shall offer of it all the fat thereof; the rump, and the fat that covereth the inwards,

4 And the two kidneys, and the fat that is on them, which is by the flanks, and the caul that is above the liver, with the kidneys, it shall he take away;

5 And the priest (kohen) shall burn them upon the altar for an offering made by fire unto יהוה: it is a trespass offering.

6 Every male among the priests (kohanim) shall eat thereof: it shall be eaten in the holy place: it is most holy.

7 As the sin offering is, so is the trespass offering; there is one law (torah) for both; the priest (kohen) that maketh atonement therewith shall have it.

8 And the priest (kohen) that offereth any man's burnt offering, even the priest (kohen) shall have to himself the skin of the burnt offering which he hath offered.

9 And all the meat offering that is baken in the oven, and all that is dressed in the fryingpan, and in the pan, shall be the priest (kohen)'s that offereth it.

10 And every meat offering, mingled with oil, and dry, shall all the sons of Aaron (Aharon) have, one as much as another.

11 And this is the law (torah) of the sacrifice of peace offerings, which he shall offer unto יהוה:

12 If he offers it for a thanksgiving, then he shall offer with the sacrifice of thanksgiving unleavened cakes mingled with oil, and unleavened wafers anointed with oil, and cakes mingled with oil, of fine flour, fried.

13 Besides the cakes, he shall offer for his offering leavened bread with the sacrifice of thanksgiving of his peace offerings.

14 And of it he shall offer one out of the whole oblation for a heave offering unto יהוה, and it shall be the priest (kohen)'s that sprinkleth the blood of the peace offerings.

15 And the flesh of the sacrifice of his peace offerings for thanksgiving shall be eaten the same day that it is offered; he shall not leave any of it until the morning.

16 But if the sacrifice of his offering be a vow, or a voluntary offering, it shall be eaten the same day that he offereth his sacrifice; and on the next day also the remainder of it shall be eaten;

17 But the remainder of the flesh of the sacrifice on the third day shall be burnt with fire.

18 And if any of the flesh of the sacrifice of his peace offerings be eaten at all on the third day, it shall not be accepted, neither shall it be imputed unto him that offereth it. It shall be an abomination, and the soul that eateth of it shall bear his iniquity.

19 And the flesh that toucheth any unclean thing shall not be eaten; it shall be burnt with fire; and as for the flesh, all that be clean shall eat thereof.

20 But the soul that eateth of the flesh of the sacrifice of peace offerings, that pertain unto יהוה, having his uncleanness upon him, even that soul shall be cut off from his people.

21 Moreover the soul that shall touch any unclean thing, as the uncleanness of man, or any unclean beast, or any abominable unclean thing, and eat of the flesh of the sacrifice of peace offerings, which pertain unto יהוה, even that

soul shall be cut off from his people.'"

22 And יהוה spake unto Moses (Mosheh), saying,

23 "Speak unto the children of Yisrael, saying: 'You shall eat no manner of fat, of ox, or of sheep, or of goat.

24 And the fat of the beast that dieth of itself, and the fat of that which is torn with beasts, may be used in any other use: but you shall in no wise eat of it.

25 For whosoever eateth the fat of the beast, of which men offer an offering made by fire unto יהוה, even the soul that eateth it shall be cut off from his people.

26 Moreover you shall eat no manner of blood, whether it be of fowl or of beast, in any of your dwellings.

27 Whatsoever soul it be that eateth any manner of blood, even that soul shall be cut off from his people.'"

28 And יהוה spake unto Moses (Mosheh), saying,

29 "Speak unto the children of Yisrael, saying: 'He that offereth the sacrifice of his peace offerings unto יהוה shall bring his oblation unto יהוה of the sacrifice of his peace offerings.

30 His own hands shall bring the offerings of יהוה made by fire, the fat with the breast, it shall he bring, that the breast may be waved for a wave offering before יהוה.

31 And the priest (kohen) shall burn the fat upon the altar; but the breast shall be Aaron (Aharon)'s and his sons'.

32 And the right shoulder shall you give unto the priest (kohen) for a heave offering of the sacrifices of your peace offerings.

33 He among the sons of Aaron (Aharon), that offereth the blood of the peace offerings, and the fat, shall have the right shoulder for his part.

34 For the wave breast and the heave shoulder have I taken of the children of Yisrael from off the sacrifices of their peace offerings, and have given them unto Aaron (Aharon) the priest (kohen) and unto his sons by a statute forever from among the children of Yisrael.'"

35 This is the portion of the anointing of Aaron (Aharon), and of the anointing of his sons, out of the offerings of יהוה made by fire, in the day when he presented them to minister unto יהוה as priests (kohanim);

36 Which יהוה commanded to be given them of the children of Yisrael, in the day that he anointed them, by a statute forever throughout their generations.

37 This is the law (torah) of the burnt offering, of the meat offering, and of the sin offering, and of the trespass offering, and of the consecrations, and of the sacrifice of the peace offerings;

38 Which יהוה commanded Moses (Mosheh) in Mount Sinai, in the day that he commanded the children of Yisrael to offer their oblations unto יהוה, in the wilderness of Sinai.

8 And יהוה spake unto Moses (Mosheh), saying:

2 "Take Aaron (Aharon) and his sons with him, and the garments, and the anointing oil, and a bullock for the sin offering, and two rams, and a basket of unleavened bread;

3 And gather you all the congregation together unto the door of the tabernacle of the congregation."

4 And Moses (Mosheh) did as יהוה commanded him; and the assembly was gathered together unto the door of the tabernacle of the congregation.

5 And Moses (Mosheh) said unto the congregation, "This is the thing which יהוה commanded to be done."

6 And Moses (Mosheh) brought Aaron (Aharon) and his sons, and washed them with water.

7 And he put upon him the coat, and girded him with the girdle, and clothed him with the robe, and put the ephod upon him, and he girded him with the curious girdle of the ephod, and bound it unto him therewith.

8 And he put the breastplate upon him: also he put in the breastplate the Urim and the Thummim.

9 And he put the mitre upon his head; also upon the mitre, even upon his forefront, did he put the golden plate, the holy crown; as יהוה commanded Moses (Mosheh).

10 And Moses (Mosheh) took the anointing oil, and anointed the tabernacle and all that was therein, and sanctified them.

11 And he sprinkled thereof upon the altar seven times, and anointed the altar and all his vessels, both the laver and his foot, to sanctify them.

12 And he poured of the anointing oil upon Aaron (Aharon)'s head, and anointed him, to sanctify him.

13 And Moses (Mosheh) brought Aaron

(Aharon)'s sons, and put coats upon them, and girded them with girdles, and put bonnets upon them; as יהוה commanded Moses (Mosheh).

14 And he brought the bullock for the sin offering; and Aaron (Aharon) and his sons laid their hands upon the head of the bullock for the sin offering.

15 And he slew it; and Moses (Mosheh) took the blood, and put it upon the horns of the altar round about with his finger, and purified the altar, and poured the blood at the bottom of the altar, and sanctified it, to make reconciliation upon it.

16 And he took all the fat that was upon the inwards, and the caul above the liver, and the two kidneys, and their fat, and Moses (Mosheh) burned it upon the altar.

17 But the bullock, and his hide, his flesh, and his dung, he burnt with fire without the camp; as יהוה commanded Moses (Mosheh).

18 And he brought the ram for the burnt offering: and Aaron (Aharon) and his sons laid their hands upon the head of the ram.

19 And he killed it; and Moses (Mosheh) sprinkled the blood upon the altar round about.

20 And he cut the ram into pieces; and Moses (Mosheh) burnt the head, and the pieces, and the fat.

21 And he washed the inwards and the legs in water; and Moses (Mosheh) burnt the whole ram upon the altar; it was a burnt sacrifice for a sweet savour, and an offering made by fire unto יהוה; as יהוה commanded Moses (Mosheh).

22 And he brought the other ram, the ram of consecration; and Aaron (Aharon) and his sons laid their hands upon the head of the ram.

23 And he slew it; and Moses (Mosheh) took of the blood of it, and put it upon the tip of Aaron (Aharon)'s right ear, and upon the thumb of his right hand, and upon the great toe of his right foot.

24 And he brought Aaron (Aharon)'s sons, and Moses (Mosheh) put of the blood upon the tip of their right ear, and upon the thumbs of their right hands, and upon the great toes of their right feet; and Moses (Mosheh) sprinkled the blood upon the altar round about.

25 And he took the fat, and the rump, and all the fat that was upon the inwards, and the caul above the liver, and the two kidneys, and their fat, and the right shoulder;

26 And out of the basket of unleavened bread, that was before יהוה, he took one unleavened cake, and a cake of oiled bread, and one wafer, and put them on the fat, and upon the right shoulder:

27 And he put all upon Aaron (Aharon)'s hands, and upon his sons' hands, and waved them for a wave offering before יהוה.

28 And Moses (Mosheh) took them from off their hands, and burnt them on the altar upon the burnt offering: they were consecrations for a sweet savour: it is an offering made by fire unto יהוה.

29 And Moses (Mosheh) took the breast, and waved it for a wave offering before יהוה; for of the ram of consecration it was Moses (Mosheh)' part; as יהוה commanded Moses (Mosheh).

30 And Moses (Mosheh) took of the anointing oil, and of the blood which was upon the altar, and sprinkled it upon Aaron (Aharon), and upon his garments, and upon his sons, and upon his sons' garments with him; and sanctified Aaron (Aharon), and his garments, and his sons, and his sons' garments with him.

31 And Moses (Mosheh) said unto Aaron (Aharon) and to his sons, "Boil the flesh at the door of the tabernacle of the congregation; and there eat it with the bread that is in the basket of consecrations, as I commanded, saying, 'Aaron (Aharon) and his sons shall eat it.'

32 And that which remaineth of the flesh and of the bread shall you burn with fire.

33 And you shall not go out of the door of the tabernacle of the congregation in seven days, until the days of your consecration be at an end; for seven days shall he consecrate you.

34 As he hath done this day, so יהוה hath commanded to do, to make an atonement for you.

35 Therefore shall you abide at the door of the tabernacle of the congregation day and night seven days, and keep the charge of יהוה, that you die not; for so I am commanded."

36 So Aaron (Aharon) and his sons did all things which יהוה commanded by the hand of Moses (Mosheh).

9 And it came to pass on the eighth day, that Moses (Mosheh) called Aaron (Aharon) and his sons, and the elders of Yisrael;

2 And he said unto Aaron (Aharon), "Take you a young calf for a sin offering, and a ram for a

burnt offering, without blemish, and offer them before יהוה.

3 And unto the children of Yisrael you shalt speak, saying, 'Take you a kid of the goats for a sin offering; and a calf and a lamb, both of the first year, without blemish, for a burnt offering;

4 Also a bullock and a ram for peace offerings, to sacrifice before יהי; and a meat offering mingled with oil; for today יהוה will appear unto you.'"

5 And they brought that which Moses (Mosheh) commanded before the tabernacle of the congregation; and all the congregation drew near and stood before יהוה.

6 And Moses (Mosheh) said, "This is the thing which יהוה commanded that you should do; and the glory of יהי shall appear unto you."

7 And Moses (Mosheh) said unto Aaron (Aharon), "Go unto the altar, and offer your sin offering, and your burnt offering, and make an atonement for yourself, and for the people; and offer the offering of the people, and make an atonement for them; as יהי commanded."

8 Aaron (Aharon) therefore went unto the altar, and slew the calf of the sin offering, which was for himself.

9 And the sons of Aaron (Aharon) brought the blood unto him; and he dipped his finger in the blood, and put it upon the horns of the altar, and poured out the blood at the bottom of the altar:

10 But the fat, and the kidneys, and the caul above the liver of the sin offering, he burnt upon the altar; as יהי commanded Moses (Mosheh).

11 And the flesh and the hide he burnt with fire outside the camp.

12 And he slew the burnt offering; and Aaron (Aharon)'s sons presented unto him the blood, which he sprinkled round about upon the altar.

13 And they presented the burnt offering unto him, with the pieces thereof, and the head; and he burnt them upon the altar.

14 And he did wash the inwards and the legs, and burnt them upon the burnt offering on the altar.

15 And he brought the people's offering, and took the goat, which was the sin offering for the people, and slew it, and offered it for sin, as the first.

16 And he brought the burnt offering, and offered it according to the manner.

17 And he brought the meat offering, and took a handful thereof, and burnt it upon the altar, beside the burnt sacrifice of the morning.

18 He slew also the bullock and the ram for a sacrifice of peace offerings, which was for the people; and Aaron (Aharon)'s sons presented unto him the blood, which he sprinkled upon the altar round about,

19 And the fat of the bullock and of the ram, the rump, and that which covereth the inwards, and the kidneys, and the caul above the liver;

20 And they put the fat upon the breasts, and he burnt the fat upon the altar:

21 And the breasts and the right shoulder Aaron (Aharon) waved for a wave offering before יהוה, as Moses (Mosheh) commanded.

22 And Aaron (Aharon) lifted up his hand toward the people, and blessed them, and came down from offering of the sin offering, and the burnt offering, and peace offerings.

23 And Moses (Mosheh) and Aaron (Aharon) went into the tabernacle of the congregation, and came out, and blessed the people; and the glory of יהוה appeared unto all the people.

24 And there came a fire out from before יהוה, and consumed upon the altar the burnt offering and the fat, which when all the people saw, they shouted, and fell on their faces.

10 And Nadav and Avihu, the sons of Aaron (Aharon), took either of them his censer, and put fire therein, and put incense thereon, and offered strange fire before יהי, which he commanded them not.

2 And there went out fire from יהוה, and devoured them, and they died before יהוה.

3 Then Moses (Mosheh) said unto Aaron (Aharon), "This is it that יהוה spake, saying: 'I will be sanctified in them that come near me, and before all the people I will be glorified.'" And Aaron (Aharon) held his peace.

4 And Moses (Mosheh) called Mishael and Elzaphan, the sons of Uzziel the uncle of Aaron (Aharon), and said unto them, "Come near, carry your brethren from before the sanctuary out of the camp."

5 So they went near, and carried them in their coats out of the camp; as Moses (Mosheh) had said.

6 And Moses (Mosheh) said unto Aaron (Aharon), and unto Eleazar and unto Ithamar, his sons, "Uncover not your heads, neither rend your clothes; lest you die, and lest wrath come

upon all the people; but let your brethren, the whole house of Yisrael, bewail the burning which יהוה hath kindled.

7 And you shall not go out from the door of the tabernacle of the congregation, lest you die; for the anointing oil of יהוה is upon you." And they did according to the word of Moses (Mosheh).

8 And יהוה spake unto Aaron (Aharon), saying:

9 "Do not drink wine nor strong drink, you, nor your sons with you, when you go into the tabernacle of the congregation, lest you die; it shall be a statute forever throughout your generations;

10 And that you may put difference between holy and unholy, and between unclean and clean;

11 And that you may teach the children of Yisrael all the statutes which יהוה hath spoken unto them by the hand of Moses (Mosheh)."

12 And Moses (Mosheh) spake unto Aaron (Aharon), and unto Eleazar and unto Ithamar, his sons that were left: "Take the meat offering that remaineth of the offerings of יהוה made by fire, and eat it without leaven beside the altar; for it is most holy.

13 And you shall eat it in the holy place, because it is your due, and your sons' due, of the sacrifices of יהוה made by fire; for so I am commanded.

14 And the wave breast and heave shoulder shall you eat in a clean place; you, and your sons, and your daughters with you; for they be your due, and your sons' due, which are given out of the sacrifices of peace offerings of the children of Yisrael.

15 The heave shoulder and the wave breast shall they bring with the offerings made by fire of the fat, to wave it for a wave offering before יהוה; and it shall be yours, and your sons' with you, by a statute forever; as יהוה hath commanded."

16 And Moses (Mosheh) diligently sought the goat of the sin offering, and, behold, it was burnt; and he was angry with Eleazar and Ithamar, the sons of Aaron (Aharon) which were left alive, saying,

17 "Wherefore have you not eaten the sin offering in the holy place, seeing it is most holy, and God (Elohim) hath given it you to bear the iniquity of the congregation, to make atonement for them before יהוה?

18 Behold, the blood of it was not brought in within the holy place; you should indeed have eaten it in the holy place, as I commanded."

19 And Aaron (Aharon) said unto Moses (Mosheh), "Behold, this day have they offered their sin offering and their burnt offering before יהוה; and such things have befallen me: and if I had eaten the sin offering today, should it have been accepted in the sight of יהוה?"

20 And when Moses (Mosheh) heard that, he was content.

11 And יהוה spake unto Moses (Mosheh) and to Aaron (Aharon), saying unto them,

2 "Speak unto the children of Yisrael, saying: 'These are the beasts which you shall eat among all the beasts that are on the earth:

3 Whatsoever parteth the hoof, and is clovenfooted, and cheweth the cud, among the beasts, that shall you eat.

4 Nevertheless these shall you not eat of them that chew the cud, or of them that divide the hoof; as the camel, because he cheweth the cud, but divideth not the hoof; he is unclean unto you.

5 And the coney, because he cheweth the cud, but divideth not the hoof; he is unclean unto you.

6 And the hare, because he cheweth the cud, but divideth not the hoof; he is unclean unto you.

7 And the swine, though he divides the hoof, and be clovenfooted, yet he cheweth not the cud; he is unclean to you.

8 Of their flesh shall you not eat, and their carcase shall you not touch; they are unclean to you.

9 These shall you eat of all that are in the waters: whatsoever hath fins and scales in the waters, in the seas, and in the rivers, them shall you eat.

10 And all that have not fins and scales in the seas, and in the rivers, of all that move in the waters, and of any living thing which is in the waters, they shall be an abomination unto you:

11 They shall be even an abomination unto you; you shall not eat of their flesh, but you shall have their carcases in abomination.

12 Whatsoever hath no fins nor scales in the waters, that shall be an abomination unto you.

13 And these are they which you shall have in abomination among the fowls; they shall not be eaten, they are an abomination: the eagle, and the ossifrage, and the ospray,

14 And the vulture, and the kite after its kind;

15 Every raven after its kind;

16 And the owl, and the night hawk, and the cuckow, and the hawk after its kind,

17 And the little owl, and the cormorant, and the great owl,

18 And the swan, and the pelican, and the gier eagle,

19 And the stork, the heron after her kind, and the lapwing, and the bat.

20 All fowls that creep, going upon all four, shall be an abomination unto you.

21 Yet these may you eat of every flying creeping thing that goeth upon all four, which have legs above their feet, to leap withal upon the earth;

22 Even these of them you may eat; the locust after its kind, and the bald locust after its kind, and the beetle after its kind, and the grasshopper after its kind.

23 But all other flying creeping things, which have four feet, shall be an abomination unto you.

24 And for these you shall be unclean: whosoever toucheth the carcase of them shall be unclean until the even.

25 And whosoever beareth ought of the carcase of them shall wash his clothes, and be unclean until the even:

26 The carcases of every beast which divideth the hoof, and is not clovenfooted, nor cheweth the cud, are unclean unto you; every one that toucheth them shall be unclean.

27 And whatsoever goeth upon his paws, among all manner of beasts that go on all four, those are unclean unto you; whoso toucheth their carcase shall be unclean until the even.

28 And he that beareth the carcase of them shall wash his clothes, and be unclean until the even; they are unclean unto you.

29 These also shall be unclean unto you among the creeping things that creep upon the earth; the weasel, and the mouse, and the tortoise after its kind,

30 And the ferret, and the chameleon, and the lizard, and the snail, and the mole.

31 These are unclean to you among all that creep: whosoever doth touch them, when they be dead, shall be unclean until the even.

32 And upon whatsoever any of them, when they are dead, doth fall, it shall be unclean; whether it be any vessel of wood, or raiment, or skin, or sack, whatsoever vessel it be, wherein any work is done, it must be put into water, and it shall be unclean until the even; so it shall be cleansed.

33 And every earthen vessel, whereinto any of them falleth, whatsoever is in it shall be unclean; and you shall break it.

34 Of all meat which may be eaten, that on which such water cometh shall be unclean: and all drink that may be drunk in every such vessel shall be unclean.

35 And every thing whereupon any part of their carcase falleth shall be unclean; whether it be oven, or ranges for pots, they shall be broken down; for they are unclean, and shall be unclean unto you.

36 Nevertheless a fountain or pit, wherein there is plenty of water, shall be clean; but that which toucheth their carcase shall be unclean.

37 And if any part of their carcase fall upon any sowing seed which is to be sown, it shall be clean.

38 But if any water be put upon the seed, and any part of their carcase fall thereon, it shall be unclean unto you.

39 And if any beast, of which you may eat, die; he that toucheth the carcase thereof shall be unclean until the even.

40 And he that eateth of the carcase of it shall wash his clothes, and be unclean until the even; he also that beareth the carcase of it shall wash his clothes, and be unclean until the even.

41 And every creeping thing that creepeth upon the earth shall be an abomination; it shall not be eaten.

42 Whatsoever goeth upon the belly, and whatsoever goeth upon all four, or whatsoever hath more feet among all creeping things that creep upon the earth, them you shall not eat; for they are an abomination.

43 You shall not make yourselves abominable with any creeping thing that creepeth, neither shall you make yourselves unclean with them, that you should be defiled thereby.

44 For I am יהוה your God (YHWH Eloheikhem). You shall therefore sanctify yourselves, and you shall be holy; for I am holy. Neither shall you defile yourselves with any manner of creeping thing that creepeth upon the earth.

45 For I am יהוה that bringeth you up out of the land of Egypt (Mitsrayim), to be your God (Elohim); you shall therefore be holy, for I am holy.

46 This is the [B28a]Torah of the beasts, and of the fowl, and of every living creature that moveth in the waters, and of every creature that creepeth upon the earth:

47 To make a difference between the unclean and the clean, and between the beast that may be eaten and the beast that may not be eaten.'"

12 And יהוה spake unto Moses (Mosheh), saying,

2 "Speak unto the children of Yisrael, saying: 'If a woman has conceived seed, and born a man child; then she shall be unclean seven days; according to the days of the separation for her infirmity shall she be unclean.

3 And in the eighth day the flesh of his foreskin shall be circumcised.

4 And she shall then continue in the blood of her purifying three and thirty days; she shall touch no hallowed thing, nor come into the sanctuary, until the days of her purifying be fulfilled.

5 But if she bears a maid child, then she shall be unclean two weeks, as in her separation; and she shall continue in the blood of her purifying threescore and six days.

6 And when the days of her purifying are fulfilled, for a son, or for a daughter, she shall bring a lamb of the first year for a burnt offering, and a young pigeon, or a turtledove, for a sin offering, unto the door of the tabernacle of the congregation, unto the priest (kohen);

7 Who shall offer it before יהוה, and make an atonement for her; and she shall be cleansed from the issue of her blood. This is the law (torah) for her that hath born a male or a female.

8 And if she be not able to bring a lamb, then she shall bring two turtledoves, or two young pigeons; the one for the burnt offering, and the other for a sin offering; and the priest (kohen) shall make an atonement for her, and she shall be clean.'"

13 And יהוה spake unto Moses (Mosheh) and Aaron (Aharon), saying:

2 "When a man shall have in the skin of his flesh a rising, a scab, or bright spot, and it be in the skin of his flesh like the plague of leprosy; then he shall be brought unto Aaron (Aharon) the priest (kohen), or unto one of his sons the priests (kohanim):

3 And the priest (kohen) shall look on the plague in the skin of the flesh; and when the hair in the plague is turned white, and the plague in sight be deeper than the skin of his flesh, it is a plague of leprosy: and the priest (kohen) shall look on him, and pronounce him unclean.

4 If the bright spot be white in the skin of his flesh, and in sight be not deeper than the skin, and the hair thereof be not turned white; then the priest (kohen) shall shut up him that hath the plague seven days.

5 And the priest (kohen) shall look on him the seventh day; and, behold, if the plague in his sight be at a stay, and the plague spread not in the skin; then the priest (kohen) shall shut him up seven days more.

6 And the priest (kohen) shall look on him again the seventh day; and, behold, if the plague be somewhat dark, and the plague spread not in the skin, the priest (kohen) shall pronounce him clean; it is but a scab. And he shall wash his clothes, and be clean.

7 But if the scab spread much abroad in the skin, after that he hath been seen of the priest (kohen) for his cleansing, he shall be seen of the priest (kohen) again.

8 And if the priest (kohen) sees that, behold, the scab spreadeth in the skin, then the priest (kohen) shall pronounce him unclean; it is a leprosy.

9 When the plague of leprosy is in a man, then he shall be brought unto the priest (kohen);

10 And the priest (kohen) shall see him; and, behold, if the rising be white in the skin, and it have turned the hair white, and there be quick raw flesh in the rising;

11 It is an old leprosy in the skin of his flesh, and the priest (kohen) shall pronounce him unclean, and shall not shut him up, for he is unclean.

12 And if a leprosy breaks out abroad in the skin, and the leprosy cover all the skin of him that hath the plague from his head even to his foot, wheresoever the priest (kohen) looketh;

13 Then the priest (kohen) shall consider; and, behold, if the leprosy has covered all his flesh, he shall pronounce him clean that hath the plague; it is all turned white, he is clean.

14 But when raw flesh appeareth in him, he shall be unclean.

15 And the priest (kohen) shall see the raw flesh, and pronounce him to be unclean; for the raw flesh is unclean: it is a leprosy.

16 Or if the raw flesh turns again, and be changed unto white, he shall come unto the

priest (kohen);

17 And the priest (kohen) shall see him; and, behold, if the plague be turned into white; then the priest (kohen) shall pronounce him clean that hath the plague: he is clean.

18 The flesh also, in which, even in the skin thereof, was a boil, and is healed,

19 And in the place of the boil there be a white rising, or a bright spot, white, and somewhat reddish, and it be shewed to the priest (kohen);

20 And if, when the priest (kohen) seeth it, behold, it be in sight lower than the skin, and the hair thereof be turned white; the priest (kohen) shall pronounce him unclean: it is a plague of leprosy broken out of the boil.

21 But if the priest (kohen) looks on it, and, behold, there be no white hairs therein, and if it be not lower than the skin, but be somewhat dark; then the priest (kohen) shall shut him up seven days.

22 And if it spread much abroad in the skin, then the priest (kohen) shall pronounce him unclean; it is a plague.

23 But if the bright spot stays in his place, and spread not, it is a burning boil; and the priest (kohen) shall pronounce him clean.

24 Or if there be any flesh, in the skin whereof there is a hot burning, and the quick flesh that burneth have a white bright spot, somewhat reddish, or white;

25 Then the priest (kohen) shall look upon it; and, behold, if the hair in the bright spot be turned white, and it be in sight deeper than the skin; it is a leprosy broken out of the burning; wherefore the priest (kohen) shall pronounce him unclean: it is the plague of leprosy.

26 But if the priest (kohen) looks on it, and, behold, there be no white hair in the bright spot, and it be no lower than the other skin, but be somewhat dark; then the priest (kohen) shall shut him up seven days.

27 And the priest (kohen) shall look upon him the seventh day; and if it be spread much abroad in the skin, then the priest (kohen) shall pronounce him unclean: it is the plague of leprosy.

28 And if the bright spot stays in his place, and spread not in the skin, but it be somewhat dark; it is a rising of the burning, and the priest (kohen) shall pronounce him clean; for it is an inflammation of the burning.

29 If a man or woman have a plague upon the head or the beard;

30 Then the priest (kohen) shall see the plague: and, behold, if it be in sight deeper than the skin; and there be in it a yellow thin hair; then the priest (kohen) shall pronounce him unclean: it is a dry scall, even a leprosy upon the head or beard.

31 And if the priest (kohen) looks on the plague of the scall, and, behold, it be not in sight deeper than the skin, and that there is no black hair in it; then the priest (kohen) shall shut up him that hath the plague of the scall seven days.

32 And in the seventh day the priest (kohen) shall look on the plague; and, behold, if the scall spread not, and there be in it no yellow hair, and the scall be not in sight deeper than the skin;

33 He shall be shaven, but the scall shall he not shave; and the priest (kohen) shall shut up him that hath the scall seven days more.

34 And in the seventh day the priest (kohen) shall look on the scall; and, behold, if the scall be not spread in the skin, nor be in sight deeper than the skin; then the priest (kohen) shall pronounce him clean; and he shall wash his clothes, and be clean.

35 But if the scall spread much in the skin after his cleansing;

36 Then the priest (kohen) shall look on him; and, behold, if the scall be spread in the skin, the priest (kohen) shall not seek for yellow hair; he is unclean.

37 But if the scall be in his sight at a stay, and that there is black hair grown up therein; the scall is healed, he is clean: and the priest (kohen) shall pronounce him clean.

38 If a man also or a woman have in the skin of their flesh bright spots, even white bright spots;

39 Then the priest (kohen) shall look; and, behold, if the bright spots in the skin of their flesh be darkish white; it is a freckled spot that groweth in the skin; he is clean.

40 And the man whose hair is fallen off his head, he is bald; yet is he clean.

41 And he that hath his hair fallen off from the part of his head toward his face, he is forehead bald: yet is he clean.

42 And if there be in the bald head, or bald forehead, a white reddish sore; it is a leprosy sprung up in his bald head, or his bald forehead.

43 Then the priest (kohen) shall look upon it;

and, behold, if the rising of the sore be white reddish in his bald head, or in his bald forehead, as the leprosy appeareth in the skin of the flesh;

44 He is a leprous man, he is unclean; the priest (kohen) shall pronounce him utterly unclean; his plague is in his head.

45 And the leper in whom the plague is, his clothes shall be rent, and his head bare, and he shall put a covering upon his upper lip, and shall cry, 'Unclean, unclean!'

46 All the days wherein the plague shall be in him he shall be defiled; he is unclean, he shall dwell alone; without the camp shall his habitation be.

47 The garment also that the plague of leprosy is in, whether it be a woollen garment, or a linen garment;

48 Whether it be in the warp, or woof; of linen, or of woollen; whether in a skin, or in any thing made of skin;

49 And if the plague be greenish or reddish in the garment, or in the skin, either in the warp, or in the woof, or in any thing of skin; it is a plague of leprosy, and shall be shewed unto the priest (kohen).

50 And the priest (kohen) shall look upon the plague, and shut up it that hath the plague seven days.

51 And he shall look on the plague on the seventh day; if the plague be spread in the garment, either in the warp, or in the woof, or in a skin, or in any work that is made of skin; the plague is a fretting leprosy; it is unclean.

52 He shall therefore burn that garment, whether warp or woof, in woollen or in linen, or any thing of skin, wherein the plague is; for it is a fretting leprosy; it shall be burnt in the fire.

53 And if the priest (kohen) shall look, and, behold, the plague be not spread in the garment, either in the warp, or in the woof, or in any thing of skin;

54 Then the priest (kohen) shall command that they wash the thing wherein the plague is, and he shall shut it up seven days more;

55 And the priest (kohen) shall look on the plague, after that it is washed: and, behold, if the plague has not changed his colour, and the plague be not spread; it is unclean; you shalt burn it in the fire; it is fret inward, whether it be bare inside or outside.

56 And if the priest (kohen) look, and, behold, the plague be somewhat dark after the washing of it; then he shall rend it out of the garment, or out of the skin, or out of the warp, or out of the woof.

57 And if it appears still in the garment, either in the warp, or in the woof, or in any thing of skin; it is a spreading plague; you shalt burn that wherein the plague is with fire.

58 And the garment, either warp, or woof, or whatsoever thing of skin it be, which you shalt wash, if the plague be departed from them, then it shall be washed the second time, and shall be clean.

59 This is the law (torah) of the plague of leprosy in a garment of woollen or linen, either in the warp, or woof, or any thing of skins, to pronounce it clean, or to pronounce it unclean."

14 And יהוה spake unto Moses (Mosheh), saying:

2 "This shall be the law (torah) of the leper in the day of his cleansing: He shall be brought unto the priest (kohen).

3 And the priest (kohen) shall go forth out of the camp; and the priest (kohen) shall look, and, behold, if the plague of leprosy be healed in the leper;

4 Then shall the priest (kohen) command to take for him that is to be cleansed two birds alive and clean, and cedar wood, and scarlet, and hyssop.

5 And the priest (kohen) shall command that one of the birds be killed in an earthen vessel over running water.

6 As for the living bird, he shall take it, and the cedar wood, and the scarlet, and the hyssop, and shall dip them and the living bird in the blood of the bird that was killed over the running water;

7 And he shall sprinkle upon him that is to be cleansed from the leprosy seven times, and shall pronounce him clean, and shall let the living bird loose into the open field.

8 And he that is to be cleansed shall wash his clothes, and shave off all his hair, and wash himself in water, that he may be clean; and after that he shall come into the camp, and shall tarry abroad out of his tent seven days.

9 But it shall be on the seventh day, that he shall shave all his hair off his head and his beard and his eyebrows, even all his hair he shall shave off; and he shall wash his clothes, also he shall wash his flesh in water, and he shall be clean.

10 And on the eighth day he shall take two he

lambs without blemish, and one ewe lamb of the first year without blemish, and three tenth deals of fine flour for a meat offering, mingled with oil, and one log of oil.

11 And the priest (kohen) that maketh him clean shall present the man that is to be made clean, and those things, before יהוה, at the door of the tabernacle of the congregation.

12 And the priest (kohen) shall take one he lamb, and offer him for a trespass offering, and the log of oil, and wave them for a wave offering before יהוה.

13 And he shall slay the lamb in the place where he shall kill the sin offering and the burnt offering, in the holy place; for as the sin offering is the priest (kohen)'s, so is the trespass offering: it is most holy.

14 And the priest (kohen) shall take some of the blood of the trespass offering, and the priest (kohen) shall put it upon the tip of the right ear of him that is to be cleansed, and upon the thumb of his right hand, and upon the great toe of his right foot.

15 And the priest (kohen) shall take some of the log of oil, and pour it into the palm of his own left hand.

16 And the priest (kohen) shall dip his right finger in the oil that is in his left hand, and shall sprinkle of the oil with his finger seven times before יהוה.

17 And of the rest of the oil that is in his hand shall the priest (kohen) put upon the tip of the right ear of him that is to be cleansed, and upon the thumb of his right hand, and upon the great toe of his right foot, upon the blood of the trespass offering.

18 And the remnant of the oil that is in the priest (kohen)'s hand he shall pour upon the head of him that is to be cleansed; and the priest (kohen) shall make an atonement for him before יהוה.

19 And the priest (kohen) shall offer the sin offering, and make an atonement for him that is to be cleansed from his uncleanness; and afterward he shall kill the burnt offering.

20 And the priest (kohen) shall offer the burnt offering and the meat offering upon the altar; and the priest (kohen) shall make an atonement for him, and he shall be clean.

21 And if he be poor, and cannot get so much; then he shall take one lamb for a trespass offering to be waved, to make an atonement for

him, and one tenth deal of fine flour mingled with oil for a meat offering, and a log of oil;

22 And two turtledoves, or two young pigeons, such as he is able to get; and the one shall be a sin offering, and the other a burnt offering.

23 And he shall bring them on the eighth day for his cleansing unto the priest (kohen), unto the door of the tabernacle of the congregation, before יהוה.

24 And the priest (kohen) shall take the lamb of the trespass offering, and the log of oil, and the priest (kohen) shall wave them for a wave offering before יהוה.

25 And he shall kill the lamb of the trespass offering, and the priest (kohen) shall take some of the blood of the trespass offering, and put it upon the tip of the right ear of him that is to be cleansed, and upon the thumb of his right hand, and upon the great toe of his right foot.

26 And the priest (kohen) shall pour of the oil into the palm of his own left hand.

27 And the priest (kohen) shall sprinkle with his right finger some of the oil that is in his left hand seven times before יהוה.

28 And the priest (kohen) shall put of the oil that is in his hand upon the tip of the right ear of him that is to be cleansed, and upon the thumb of his right hand, and upon the great toe of his right foot, upon the place of the blood of the trespass offering.

29 And the rest of the oil that is in the priest (kohen)'s hand he shall put upon the head of him that is to be cleansed, to make an atonement for him before יהוה.

30 And he shall offer the one of the turtledoves, or of the young pigeons, such as he can get;

31 Even such as he is able to get, the one for a sin offering, and the other for a burnt offering, with the meat offering: and the priest (kohen) shall make an atonement for him that is to be cleansed before יהוה.

32 This is the law (torah) of him in whom is the plague of leprosy, whose hand is not able to get that which pertaineth to his cleansing."

33 And יהוה spake unto Moses (Mosheh) and unto Aaron (Aharon), saying:

34 "When you be come into the land of Canaan, which I give to you for a possession, and I put the plague of leprosy in a house of the land of your possession;

35 And he that owneth the house shall come and

tell the priest (kohen), saying, 'It seemeth to me there is as it was a plague in the house;'

36 Then the priest (kohen) shall command that they empty the house, before the priest (kohen) go into it to see the plague, that all that is in the house be not made unclean; and afterward the priest (kohen) shall go in to see the house.

37 And he shall look on the plague, and, behold, if the plague be in the walls of the house with hollow strakes, greenish or reddish, which in sight are lower than the wall;

38 Then the priest (kohen) shall go out of the house to the door of the house, and shut up the house seven days.

39 And the priest (kohen) shall come again the seventh day, and shall look; and, behold, if the plague be spread in the walls of the house;

40 Then the priest (kohen) shall command that they take away the stones in which the plague is, and they shall cast them into an unclean place outside the city.

41 And he shall cause the house to be scraped within round about, and they shall pour out the dust that they scrape off outside the city into an unclean place.

42 And they shall take other stones, and put them in the place of those stones; and he shall take other morter, and shall plaister the house.

43 And if the plague come again, and break out in the house, after that he hath taken away the stones, and after he hath scraped the house, and after it is plaistered;

44 Then the priest (kohen) shall come and look, and, behold, if the plague be spread in the house, it is a fretting leprosy in the house: it is unclean.

45 And he shall break down the house, the stones of it, and the timber thereof, and all the morter of the house; and he shall carry them forth out of the city into an unclean place.

46 Moreover he that goeth into the house all the while that it is shut up shall be unclean until the even.

47 And he that lieth in the house shall wash his clothes; and he that eateth in the house shall wash his clothes.

48 And if the priest (kohen) shall come in, and look upon it, and, behold, the plague hath not spread in the house, after the house was plaistered; then the priest (kohen) shall pronounce the house clean, because the plague is healed.

49 And he shall take to cleanse the house two birds, and cedar wood, and scarlet, and hyssop.

50 And he shall kill the one of the birds in an earthen vessel over running water;

51 And he shall take the cedar wood, and the hyssop, and the scarlet, and the living bird, and dip them in the blood of the slain bird, and in the running water, and sprinkle the house seven times.

52 And he shall cleanse the house with the blood of the bird, and with the running water, and with the living bird, and with the cedar wood, and with the hyssop, and with the scarlet.

53 But he shall let go the living bird out of the city into the open fields, and make an atonement for the house; and it shall be clean.

54 This is the law (torah) for all manner of plague of leprosy, and scall,

55 And for the leprosy of a garment, and of a house,

56 And for a rising, and for a scab, and for a bright spot,

57 To teach when it is unclean, and when it is clean. This is the law (torah) of leprosy."

15 And יהוה spake unto Moses (Mosheh) and to Aaron (Aharon), saying,

2 "Speak unto the children of Yisrael, and say unto them: 'When any man hath a running issue out of his flesh, because of his issue he is unclean.

3 And this shall be his uncleanness in his issue; whether his flesh run with his issue, or his flesh be stopped from his issue, it is his uncleanness.

4 Every bed, whereon he lieth that hath the issue, is unclean; and every thing, whereon he sitteth, shall be unclean.

5 And whosoever toucheth his bed shall wash his clothes, and bathe himself in water, and be unclean until the even.

6 And he that sitteth on any thing whereon he sat that hath the issue shall wash his clothes, and bathe himself in water, and be unclean until the even.

7 And he that toucheth the flesh of him that hath the issue shall wash his clothes, and bathe himself in water, and be unclean until the even.

8 And if he that hath the issue spit upon him that is clean; then he shall wash his clothes, and bathe himself in water, and be unclean until the even.

9 And what saddle soever he rideth upon that

hath the issue shall be unclean.

10 And whosoever toucheth anything that was under him shall be unclean until the even; and he that beareth any of those things shall wash his clothes, and bathe himself in water, and be unclean until the even.

11 And whomsoever he toucheth that hath the issue, and hath not rinsed his hands in water, he shall wash his clothes, and bathe himself in water, and be unclean until the even.

12 And the vessel of earth, that he toucheth which hath the issue, shall be broken, and every vessel of wood shall be rinsed in water.

13 And when he that hath an issue is cleansed of his issue; then he shall number to himself seven days for his cleansing, and wash his clothes, and bathe his flesh in running water, and shall be clean.

14 And on the eighth day he shall take to him two turtledoves, or two young pigeons, and come before יהוה unto the door of the tabernacle of the congregation, and give them unto the priest (kohen).

15 And the priest (kohen) shall offer them, the one for a sin offering, and the other for a burnt offering; and the priest (kohen) shall make an atonement for him before יהוה for his issue.

16 And if any man's seed of copulation go out from him, then he shall wash all his flesh in water, and be unclean until the even.

17 And every garment, and every skin, whereon is the seed of copulation, shall be washed with water, and be unclean until the even.

18 The woman also with whom man shall lie with seed of copulation, they shall both bathe themselves in water, and be unclean until the even.

19 And if a woman has an issue, and her issue in her flesh be blood, she shall be put apart seven days; and whosoever toucheth her shall be unclean until the even.

20 And every thing that she lieth upon in her separation shall be unclean; every thing also that she sitteth upon shall be unclean.

21 And whosoever toucheth her bed shall wash his clothes, and bathe himself in water, and be unclean until the even.

22 And whosoever toucheth anything that she sat upon shall wash his clothes, and bathe himself in water, and be unclean until the even.

23 And if it be on her bed, or on any thing whereon she sitteth, when he toucheth it, he shall be unclean until the even.

24 And if any man lies with her at all, and her flowers be upon him, he shall be unclean seven days; and all the bed whereon he lieth shall be unclean.

25 And if a woman has an issue of her blood many days out of the time of her separation, or if it run beyond the time of her separation; all the days of the issue of her uncleanness shall be as the days of her separation: she shall be unclean.

26 Every bed whereon she lieth all the days of her issue shall be unto her as the bed of her separation; and whatsoever she sitteth upon shall be unclean, as the uncleanness of her separation.

27 And whosoever toucheth those things shall be unclean, and shall wash his clothes, and bathe himself in water, and be unclean until the even.

28 But if she be cleansed of her issue, then she shall number to herself seven days, and after that she shall be clean.

29 And on the eighth day she shall take unto her two turtles, or two young pigeons, and bring them unto the priest (kohen), to the door of the tabernacle of the congregation.

30 And the priest (kohen) shall offer the one for a sin offering, and the other for a burnt offering; and the priest (kohen) shall make an atonement for her before יהוה for the issue of her uncleanness.

31 Thus shall you separate the children of Yisrael from their uncleanness; that they die not in their uncleanness, when they defile my tabernacle that is among them.

32 This is the law (torah) of him that hath an issue, and of him whose seed goeth from him, and is defiled therewith;

33 And of her that is sick of her flowers, and of him that hath an issue, of the man, and of the woman, and of him that lieth with her that is unclean.'"

16 And יהוה spake unto Moses (Mosheh) after the death of the two sons of Aaron (Aharon), when they offered before יהוה, and died;

2 And יהוה said unto Moses (Mosheh): "Speak unto Aaron (Aharon) your brother, that he come not at all times into the holy place within the vail before the mercy seat, which is upon the

ark; that he dies not: for I will appear in the cloud upon the mercy seat.

3 Thus shall Aaron (Aharon) come into the Holy Place: with a young bullock for a sin offering, and a ram for a burnt offering.

4 He shall put on the holy linen coat, and he shall have the linen breeches upon his flesh, and shall be girded with a linen girdle, and with the linen mitre shall he be attired; these are holy garments; therefore shall he wash his flesh in water, and so put them on.

5 And he shall take of the congregation of the children of Yisrael two kids of the goats for a sin offering, and one ram for a burnt offering.

6 And Aaron (Aharon) shall offer his bullock of the sin offering, which is for himself, and make an atonement for himself, and for his house.

7 And he shall take the two goats, and present them before יהוה at the door of the tabernacle of the congregation.

8 And Aaron (Aharon) shall cast lots upon the two goats; one lot for יהוה, and the other lot for the scapegoat.

9 And Aaron (Aharon) shall bring the goat upon which יהוה's lot fell, and offer him for a sin offering.

10 But the goat, on which the lot fell to be the scapegoat, shall be presented alive before יהוה, to make an atonement with him, and to let him go for a scapegoat into the wilderness.

11 And Aaron (Aharon) shall bring the bullock of the sin offering, which is for himself, and shall make an atonement for himself, and for his house, and shall kill the bullock of the sin offering which is for himself.

12 And he shall take a censer full of burning coals of fire from off the altar before יהוה, and his hands full of sweet incense beaten small, and bring it within the vail.

13 And he shall put the incense upon the fire before יהוה, that the cloud of the incense may cover the mercy seat that is upon the testimony, that he dies not.

14 And he shall take of the blood of the bullock, and sprinkle it with his finger upon the mercy seat eastward; and before the mercy seat shall he sprinkle of the blood with his finger seven times.

15 Then shall he kill the goat of the sin offering, that is for the people, and bring his blood within the vail, and do with that blood as he did with the blood of the bullock, and sprinkle it upon the mercy seat, and before the mercy seat;

16 And he shall make an atonement for the holy place, because of the uncleanness of the children of Yisrael, and because of their transgressions in all their sins; and so shall he do for the tabernacle of the congregation, that remaineth among them in the midst of their uncleanness.

17 And there shall be no man in the tabernacle of the congregation when he goeth in to make an atonement in the holy place, until he come out, and have made an atonement for himself, and for his household, and for all the congregation of Yisrael.

18 And he shall go out unto the altar that is before יהוה, and make an atonement for it; and shall take of the blood of the bullock, and of the blood of the goat, and put it upon the horns of the altar round about.

19 And he shall sprinkle of the blood upon it with his finger seven times, and cleanse it, and hallow it from the uncleanness of the children of Yisrael.

20 And when he hath made an end of reconciling the holy place, and the tabernacle of the congregation, and the altar, he shall bring the live goat;

21 And Aaron (Aharon) shall lay both his hands upon the head of the live goat, and confess over him all the iniquities of the children of Yisrael, and all their transgressions in all their sins, putting them upon the head of the goat, and shall send him away by the hand of a fit man into the wilderness.

22 And the goat shall bear upon him all their iniquities unto a land not inhabited; and he shall let go the goat in the wilderness.

23 And Aaron (Aharon) shall come into the tabernacle of the congregation, and shall put off the linen garments, which he put on when he went into the holy place, and shall leave them there.

24 And he shall wash his flesh with water in the holy place, and put on his garments, and come forth, and offer his burnt offering, and the burnt offering of the people, and make an atonement for himself, and for the people.

25 And the fat of the sin offering shall he burn upon the altar.

26 And he that let go the goat for the scapegoat

shall wash his clothes, and bathe his flesh in water, and afterward come into the camp.

27 And the bullock for the sin offering, and the goat for the sin offering, whose blood was brought in to make atonement in the holy place, shall one carry forth outside the camp; and they shall burn in the fire their skins, and their flesh, and their dung.

28 And he that burneth them shall wash his clothes, and bathe his flesh in water, and afterward he shall come into the camp.

29 And this shall be a statute forever unto you: that in the seventh month, on the tenth day of the month, you shall afflict your souls, and do no work at all, whether it be one of your own country, or a stranger that sojourneth among you.

30 For on that day shall the priest (kohen) make an atonement for you, to cleanse you, that you may be clean from all your sins before יהוה.

31 It shall be a Shabbat of rest unto you, and you shall afflict your souls, by a statute forever.

32 And the priest (kohen), whom he shall anoint, and whom he shall consecrate to minister in the priest's office (kehunnah) in his father's stead, shall make the atonement, and shall put on the linen clothes, even the holy garments;

33 And he shall make an atonement for the holy sanctuary, and he shall make an atonement for the tabernacle of the congregation, and for the altar, and he shall make an atonement for the priests (kohanim), and for all the people of the congregation.

34 And this shall be an everlasting statute unto you, to make an atonement for the children of Yisrael for all their sins once a year." And he did as יהוה commanded Moses (Mosheh).

17 And יהוה spake unto Moses (Mosheh), saying,

2 "Speak unto Aaron (Aharon), and unto his sons, and unto all the children of Yisrael, and say unto them: 'This is the thing which יהוה hath commanded, saying,

3 What man soever there be of the house of Yisrael, that killeth an ox, or lamb, or goat, in the camp, or that killeth it out of the camp,

4 And bringeth it not unto the door of the tabernacle of the congregation, to offer an offering unto יהוה before the tabernacle of יהוה; blood shall be imputed unto that man; he hath shed blood; and that man shall be cut off from among his people,

5 To the end that the children of Yisrael may bring their sacrifices, which they offer in the open field, even that they may bring them unto יהוה, unto the door of the tabernacle of the congregation, unto the priest (kohen), and offer them for peace offerings unto יהוה.

6 And the priest (kohen) shall sprinkle the blood upon the altar of יהוה at the door of the tabernacle of the congregation, and burn the fat for a sweet savour unto יהוה.

7 And they shall no more offer their sacrifices unto devils, after whom they have gone a whoring. This shall be a statute forever unto them throughout their generations.

8 And you shalt say unto them, Whatsoever man there be of the house of Yisrael, or of the strangers which sojourn among you, that offereth a burnt offering or sacrifice,

9 And bringeth it not unto the door of the tabernacle of the congregation, to offer it unto יהוה; even that man shall be cut off from among his people.

10 And whatsoever man there be of the house of Yisrael, or of the strangers that sojourn among you, that eateth any manner of blood; I will even set my face against that soul that eateth blood, and will cut him off from among his people.

11 For the life of the flesh is in the blood; and I have given it to you upon the altar to make an atonement for your souls; for it is the blood that maketh an atonement for the soul.'

12 Therefore I said unto the children of Yisrael, 'No soul of you shall eat blood, neither shall any stranger that sojourneth among you eat blood.'

13 And whatsoever man there be of the children of Yisrael, or of the strangers that sojourn among you, which hunteth and catcheth any beast or fowl that may be eaten; he shall even pour out the blood thereof, and cover it with dust.

14 For it is the life of all flesh; the blood of it is for the life thereof. Therefore I said unto the children of Yisrael, 'You shall eat the blood of no manner of flesh, for the life of all flesh is the blood thereof; whosoever eateth it shall be cut off.'

15 And every soul that eateth that which died of itself, or that which was torn with beasts, whether it be one of your own country, or a stranger, he shall both wash his clothes, and bathe himself in water, and be unclean until the

even, then shall he be clean.

16 But if he washes them not, nor bathe his flesh; then he shall bear his iniquity."

18 And יהוה spake unto Moses (Mosheh), saying,

2 "Speak unto the children of Yisrael, and say unto them: 'I am יהוה your God (YHWH Eloheikhem).

3 After the doings of the land of Egypt (Mitsrayim), wherein you dwelt, shall you not do: and after the doings of the land of Canaan, whither I bring you, shall you not do; neither shall you walk in their ordinances.

4 You shall do my judgments, and keep Mine ordinances, to walk therein: I am יהוה your God (YHWH Eloheikhem).

5 You shall therefore keep My statutes, and My judgments, which if a man does, he shall have life through them: I am יהוה.

6 None of you shall approach to any that is near of kin to him, to uncover their nakedness: I am יהוה.

7 The nakedness of your father, or the nakedness of your mother, shalt you not uncover. She is your mother; you shalt not uncover her nakedness.

8 The nakedness of your father's wife shalt you not uncover; it is your father's nakedness.

9 The nakedness of your sister, the daughter of your father, or daughter of your mother, whether she be born at home, or born abroad, even their nakedness you shalt not uncover.

10 The nakedness of your son's daughter, or of your daughter's daughter, even their nakedness you shalt not uncover; for theirs is your own nakedness.

11 The nakedness of your father's wife's daughter, begotten of your father, she is your sister, you shalt not uncover her nakedness.

12 You shalt not uncover the nakedness of your father's sister; she is your father's near kinswoman.

13 You shalt not uncover the nakedness of your mother's sister, for she is your mother's near kinswoman.

14 You shalt not uncover the nakedness of your father's brother, you shalt not approach to his wife; she is your aunt.

15 You shalt not uncover the nakedness of your daughter in law; she is your son's wife; you shalt not uncover her nakedness.

16 You shalt not uncover the nakedness of your brother's wife; it is your brother's nakedness.

17 You shalt not uncover the nakedness of a woman and her daughter, neither shalt you take her son's daughter, or her daughter's daughter, to uncover her nakedness; for they are her near kinswomen: it is wickedness.

18 Neither shalt you take a wife to her sister, to vex her, to uncover her nakedness, beside the other in her life time.

19 Also you shalt not approach unto a woman to uncover her nakedness, as long as she is put apart for her uncleanness.

20 Moreover you shalt not lie carnally with your neighbour's wife, to defile yourself with her.

21 And you shalt not let any of your seed pass through the fire to Molech, neither shalt you profane the name of your God (Elohim): I am יהוה.

22 You shalt not lie with mankind, as with womankind: it is abomination.

23 Neither shalt you lie with any beast to defile yourself therewith; neither shall any woman stand before a beast to lie down thereto: it is perversion.

24 Defile not you yourselves in any of these things: for in all these the nations are defiled which I cast out before you.

25 And the land is defiled; therefore I do visit the iniquity thereof upon it, and the land itself vomiteth out her inhabitants.

26 You shall therefore keep My statutes and My judgments, and shall not commit any of these abominations; neither any of your own nation, nor any stranger that sojourneth among you;

27 (For all these abominations have the men of the land done, which were before you, and the land is defiled;)

28 That the land spue not you out also, when you defile it, as it spued out the nations that were before you.

29 For whosoever shall commit any of these abominations, even the souls that commit them shall be cut off from among their people.

30 Therefore shall you keep Mine ordinance, that you commit not any one of these abominable customs, which were committed before you, and that you defile not yourselves therein: I am יהוה your God (YHWH Eloheikhem).'"

19 And יהוה spake unto Moses (Mosheh), saying,

2 "Speak unto all the congregation of the children of Yisrael, and say unto them: 'You shall be holy, for I יהוה your God (YHWH Eloheikhem) am holy.

3 You shall fear every man his mother, and his father, and keep My Shabbats: I am יהוה your God (YHWH Eloheikhem).

4 Turn you not unto idols, nor make to yourselves molten gods (elohim): I am יהוה your God (YHWH Eloheikhem).

5 And if you offer a sacrifice of peace offerings unto יהוה, you shall offer it at your own will.

6 It shall be eaten the same day you offer it, and on the next day; and if any remains until the third day, it shall be burnt in the fire.

7 And if it be eaten at all on the third day, it is abominable; it shall not be accepted.

8 Therefore every one that eateth it shall bear his iniquity, because he hath profaned the hallowed thing of יהוה; and that soul shall be cut off from among his people.

9 And when you reap the harvest of your land, you shalt not wholly reap the corners of your field, neither shalt you gather the gleanings of your harvest.

10 And you shalt not glean your vineyard, neither shalt you gather every grape of your vineyard; you shalt leave them for the poor and stranger: I am יהוה your God (YHWH Eloheikhem).

11 You shall not steal, neither deal falsely, neither lie one to another.

12 And you shall not swear by My name falsely, neither shalt you profane the name of your God (Elohim): I am יהוה.

13 You shalt not defraud your neighbour, neither rob him; the wages of him that is hired shall not abide with you all night until the morning.

14 You shalt not curse the deaf, nor put a stumblingblock before the blind, but shalt fear your God (Elohim): I am יהוה.

15 You shall do no unrighteousness in judgment. You shalt not be partial to the poor, nor honor the person of the mighty; but in righteousness shalt you judge your neighbour.

16 You shalt not go up and down as a talebearer among your people; neither shalt you stand against the blood of your neighbour: I am יהוה.

17 You shalt not hate your brother in your heart; you shalt in any wise rebuke your neighbour, and not allow sin upon him.

18 You shalt not avenge, nor bear any grudge against the children of your people, but you shalt love your neighbour as yourself: I am יהוה.

19 You shall keep My statutes. You shalt not let your cattle gender with a diverse kind. You shalt not sow your field with mingled seed; neither shall a garment mingled of linen and woollen come upon you.

20 And whosoever lieth carnally with a woman, that is a bondmaid, betrothed to a husband, and not at all redeemed, nor freedom given her; she shall be scourged; they shall not be put to death, because she was not free.

21 And he shall bring his trespass offering unto יהוה, unto the door of the tabernacle of the congregation, even a ram for a trespass offering.

22 And the priest (kohen) shall make an atonement for him with the ram of the trespass offering before יהוה for his sin which he hath done; and the sin which he hath done shall be forgiven him.

23 And when you shall come into the land, and shall have planted all manner of trees for food, then you shall count the fruit thereof as uncircumcised. Three years shall it be as uncircumcised unto you; it shall not be eaten of.

24 But in the fourth year all the fruit thereof shall be holy to praise יהוה withal.

25 And in the fifth year shall you eat of the fruit thereof, that it may yield unto you the increase thereof: I am יהוה your God (YHWH Eloheikhem).

26 You shall not eat anything with the blood; neither shall you use enchantment, nor observe times.

27 You shall not round the corners of your heads, neither shalt you mar the corners of your beard.

28 You shall not make any cuttings in your flesh for the dead, nor print any marks upon you: I am יהוה.

29 Do not prostitute your daughter, to cause her to be a whore; lest the land fall to whoredom, and the land become full of wickedness.

30 You shall keep My Shabbats, and reverence My sanctuary: I am יהוה.

31 Regard not them that have familiar spirits, neither seek after wizards, to be defiled by them: I am יהוה your God (YHWH Eloheikhem).

32 You shalt rise up before the hoary head, and honor the face of the old man, and fear your God

(Elohim): I am יהוה.

33 And if a stranger sojourn with you in your land, you shall not vex him.

34 But the stranger that dwelleth with you shall be unto you as one born among you, and you shalt love him as yourself; for you were strangers in the land of Egypt (Mitsrayim): I am יהוה your God (YHWH Eloheikhem).

35 You shall do no unrighteousness in judgment, in meteyard, in weight, or in measure.

36 Just balances, just weights, a just ephah, and a just hin, shall you have: I am יהוה your God (YHWH Eloheikhem), which brought you out of the land of Egypt (Mitsrayim).

37 Therefore shall you observe all My statutes, and all My judgments, and do them: I am יהוה.'"

20 And יהוה spake unto Moses (Mosheh), saying,

2 "Again, you shalt say to the children of Yisrael: 'Whosoever he be of the children of Yisrael, or of the strangers that sojourn in Yisrael, that giveth any of his seed unto Molech; he shall surely be put to death: the people of the land shall stone him with stones.

3 And I will set my face against that man, and will cut him off from among his people; because he hath given of his seed unto Molech, to defile My sanctuary, and to profane My holy name.

4 And if the people of the land do any ways hide their eyes from the man, when he giveth of his seed unto Molech, and kill him not;

5 Then I will set My face against that man, and against his family, and will cut him off, and all that go a whoring after him, to commit whoredom with Molech, from among their people.

6 And the soul that turneth after such as have familiar spirits, and after wizards, to go a whoring after them, I will even set My face against that soul, and will cut him off from among his people.

7 Sanctify yourselves therefore, and be you holy, for I am יהוה your God (YHWH Eloheikhem).

8 And you shall keep My statutes, and do them: I am יהוה which sanctify you.

9 For every one that curseth his father or his mother shall be surely put to death. He hath cursed his father or his mother; his blood shall be upon him.

10 And the man that committeth adultery with another man's wife, even he that committeth

adultery with his neighbour's wife, the adulterer and the adulteress shall surely be put to death.

11 And the man that lieth with his father's wife hath uncovered his father's nakedness: both of them shall surely be put to death; their blood shall be upon them.

12 And if a man lies with his daughter in law, both of them shall surely be put to death; they have wrought perversion; their blood shall be upon them.

13 If a man also lies with a male, as he lieth with a woman, both of them have committed an abomination. They shall surely be put to death; their blood shall be upon them.

14 And if a man takes a wife and her mother, it is wickedness. They shall be burnt with fire, both he and they, that there be no wickedness among you.

15 And if a man lies with a beast, he shall surely be put to death; and you shall slay the beast.

16 And if a woman approach unto any beast, and lie down thereto, you shalt kill the woman, and the beast. They shall surely be put to death; their blood shall be upon them.

17 And if a man shall take his sister, his father's daughter, or his mother's daughter, and see her nakedness, and she see his nakedness; it is a wicked thing; and they shall be cut off in the sight of their people. He hath uncovered his sister's nakedness; he shall bear his iniquity.

18 And if a man shall lie with a woman having her sickness, and shall uncover her nakedness; he hath discovered her fountain, and she hath uncovered the fountain of her blood; and both of them shall be cut off from among their people.

19 And you shalt not uncover the nakedness of your mother's sister, nor of your father's sister, for he uncovereth his near kin. They shall bear their iniquity.

20 And if a man shall lie with his uncle's wife, he hath uncovered his uncle's nakedness. They shall bear their sin; they shall die childless.

21 And if a man shall take his brother's wife, it is an unclean thing. He hath uncovered his brother's nakedness; they shall be childless.

22 You shall therefore keep all My statutes, and all My judgments, and do them; that the land, whither I bring you to dwell therein, spue you not out.

23 And you shall not walk in the manners of the nation, which I cast out before you; for they

committed all these things, and therefore I abhorred them.

24 But I have said unto you, "You shall inherit their land, and I will give it unto you to possess it, a land that floweth with milk and honey." I am יהוה your God (YHWH Eloheikhem), who has separated you from other people.

25 You shall therefore put difference between clean beasts and unclean, and between unclean fowls and clean; and you shall not make your souls abominable by beast, or by fowl, or by any manner of living thing that creepeth on the ground, which I have separated from you as unclean.

26 And you shall be holy unto Me, for I יהוה am holy, and have separated you from other people, that you should be Mine.

27 A man also or woman who hath a familiar spirit, or that is a wizard, shall surely be put to death. They shall stone them with stones; their blood shall be upon them.'"

21 And יהוה said unto Moses (Mosheh), "Speak unto the priests (kohanim) the sons of Aaron (Aharon), and say unto them: 'There shall none be defiled for the dead among his people;

2 But for his kin, that is near unto him, that is, for his mother, and for his father, and for his son, and for his daughter, and for his brother,

3 And for his sister a virgin, that is near unto him, who hath had no husband; for her may he be defiled.

4 But he shall not defile himself, being a chief man among his people, to profane himself.

5 They shall not make baldness upon their head, neither shall they shave off the corner of their beard, nor make any cuttings in their flesh.

6 They shall be holy unto their God (Elohim), and not profane the name of their God (Elohim), for the offerings of יהוה made by fire, and the bread of their God (Elohim), they do offer; therefore they shall be holy.

7 They shall not take a wife that is a whore, or profane; neither shall they take a woman put away from her husband; for he is holy unto his God (Elohim).

8 You shalt sanctify him therefore; for he offereth the bread of your God (Elohim). He shall be holy unto you, for I יהוה, who sanctify you, am holy.

9 And the daughter of any priest (kohen), if she profanes herself by playing the whore, she profaneth her father; she shall be burnt with fire.

10 And he that is the high priest (kohen hagadol) among his brethren, upon whose head the anointing oil was poured, and that is consecrated to put on the garments, shall not uncover his head, nor rend his clothes;

11 Neither shall he go in to any dead body, nor defile himself for his father, or for his mother;

12 Neither shall he go out of the sanctuary, nor profane the sanctuary of his God (Elohim); for the crown of the anointing oil of his God (Elohim) is upon him: I am יהוה.

13 And he shall take a wife in her virginity.

14 A widow, or a divorced woman, or profane, or a harlot, these shall he not take; but he shall take a virgin of his own people to wife.

15 Neither shall he profane his seed among his people, for I יהוה do sanctify him.'"

16 And יהוה spake unto Moses (Mosheh), saying,

17 "Speak unto Aaron (Aharon), saying: 'Whosoever he be of your seed in their generations that hath any blemish, let him not approach to offer the bread of his God (Elohim).

18 For whatsoever man he be that hath a blemish, he shall not approach: a blind man, or a lame, or he that hath a flat nose, or any thing superfluous,

19 Or a man that is brokenfooted, or brokenhanded,

20 Or crookbackt, or a dwarf, or that hath a blemish in his eye, or be scurvy, or scabbed, or hath his stones broken;

21 No man that hath a blemish of the seed of Aaron (Aharon) the priest (kohen) shall come near to offer the offerings of יהוה made by fire. He hath a blemish; he shall not come near to offer the bread of his God (Elohim).

22 He shall eat the bread of his God (Elohim), both of the most holy, and of the holy.

23 Only he shall not go in unto the vail, nor come near unto the altar, because he hath a blemish; that he profanes not My sanctuaries; for I יהוה do sanctify them.'"

24 And Moses (Mosheh) told it unto Aaron (Aharon), and to his sons, and unto all the children of Yisrael.

22 And יהוה spake unto Moses (Mosheh), saying,

2 "Speak unto Aaron (Aharon) and to his sons,

that they separate themselves from the holy things of the children of Yisrael, and that they profane not My holy name in those things which they hallow unto Me: I am יהוה.

3 Say unto them: 'Whosoever he be of all your seed among your generations, that goeth unto the holy things, which the children of Yisrael hallow unto יהוה, having his uncleanness upon him, that soul shall be cut off from My presence: I am יהוה.

4 Whatever man of the seed of Aaron (Aharon) is a leper, or hath a running issue; he shall not eat of the holy things, until he be clean. And whoso toucheth any thing that is unclean by the dead, or a man whose seed goeth from him;

5 Or whosoever toucheth any creeping thing, whereby he may be made unclean, or a man of whom he may take uncleanness, whatsoever unclean-ness he hath;

6 The soul who hath touched any such shall be unclean until even, and shall not eat of the holy things, unless he washes his flesh with water.

7 And when the sun is down, he shall be clean, and shall afterward eat of the holy things, because it is his food.

8 That which dieth of itself, or is torn with beasts, he shall not eat to defile himself therewith: I am יהוה.

9 They shall therefore keep Mine ordinance, lest they bear sin for it, and die therefore, if they profane it: I יהוה do sanctify them.

10 There shall no stranger eat of the holy thing; a sojourner of the priest (kohen), or a hired servant, shall not eat of the holy thing.

11 But if the priest (kohen) buys any soul with his money, he shall eat of it, and he that is born in his house; they shall eat of his meat.

12 If the priest (kohen)'s daughter also be married unto a stranger, she may not eat of an offering of the holy things.

13 But if the priest (kohen)'s daughter be a widow, or divorced, and have no child, and is returned unto her father's house, as in her youth, she shall eat of her father's food; but there shall no stranger eat thereof.

14 And if a man eats of the holy thing unwittingly, then he shall put the fifth part thereof unto it, and shall give it unto the priest (kohen) with the holy thing.

15 And they shall not profane the holy things of the children of Yisrael, which they offer unto יהוה;

16 Or allow them to bear the iniquity of trespass, when they eat their holy things; for I יהוה do sanctify them.'"

17 And יהוה spake unto Moses (Mosheh), saying,

18 "Speak unto Aaron (Aharon), and to his sons, and unto all the children of Yisrael, and say unto them: 'Whatsoever he be of the house of Yisrael, or of the strangers in Yisrael, that will offer his oblation for all his vows, and for all his freewill offerings, which they will offer unto יהוה for a burnt offering;

19 You shall offer at your own will a male without blemish, of the beeves, of the sheep, or of the goats.

20 But whatsoever hath a blemish, that shall you not offer, for it shall not be acceptable for you.

21 And whosoever offereth a sacrifice of peace offerings unto יהוה to accomplish his vow, or a freewill offering in beeves or sheep, it shall be perfect to be accepted; there shall be no blemish therein.

22 Blind, or broken, or maimed, or having a wen, or scurvy, or scabbed, you shall not offer these unto יהוה, nor make an offering by fire of them upon the altar unto יהוה.

23 Either a bullock or a lamb that hath any thing superfluous or lacking in his parts, that mayest you offer for a freewill offering; but for a vow it shall not be accepted.

24 You shall not offer unto יהוה that which is bruised, or crushed, or broken, or cut; neither shall you make any offering thereof in your land.

25 Neither from a stranger's hand shall you offer the bread of your God (Elohim) of any of these; because their corruption is in them, and blemishes be in them. They shall not be accepted for you.'"

26 And יהוה spake unto Moses (Mosheh), saying:

27 "When a bullock, or a sheep, or a goat, is brought forth, then it shall be seven days under the dam; and from the eighth day and thenceforth it shall be accepted for an offering made by fire unto יהוה.

28 And whether it be cow or ewe, you shall not kill it and her young both in one day.

29 And when you will offer a sacrifice of thanksgiving unto יהוה, offer it at your own will.

30 On the same day it shall be eaten up; you shall leave none of it until the next day: I am יהוה.

31 Therefore shall you keep My, and do them: I am יהוה.

32 Neither shall you profane My holy name; but I will be hallowed among the children of Yisrael: I am יהוה who sanctifies you,

33 Who brought you out of the land of Egypt (Mitsrayim), to be your God (Elohim): I am יהוה."

23 And יהוה spake unto Moses (Mosheh), saying,

2 "Speak unto the children of Yisrael, and say unto them: 'Concerning the feasts of יהוה, which you shall proclaim to be holy convocations, even these are My feasts.

3 Six days shall work be done, but the seventh day is the Shabbat Shabbaton, a holy convocation; you shall do no work therein; it is the Shabbat of יהוה in all your dwellings.

4 These are the feasts of יהוה, even holy convocations, which you shall proclaim in their seasons:

5 In the fourteenth day of the first month at even is יהוה's [B19]Passover (Pesach).

6 And on the fifteenth day of the same month is the [B20]Feast of Unleavened Bread (Chag HaMatzot) unto יהוה; seven days you must eat unleavened bread (matstsah).

7 In the first day you shall have a holy convocation; you shall do no servile work therein.

8 But you shall offer an offering made by fire unto יהוה seven days. The seventh day is a holy convocation; you shall do no servile work therein.'"

9 And יהוה spake unto Moses (Mosheh), saying,

10 "Speak unto the children of Yisrael, and say unto them: 'When you be come into the land which I give unto you, and shall reap the harvest thereof, then you shall bring a sheaf of the firstfruits of your harvest unto the priest (kohen):

11 And he shall wave the sheaf before יהוה, to be accepted for you; on the next day after the Shabbat the priest (kohen) shall wave it.

12 And you shall offer that day when you wave the sheaf an he lamb without blemish of the first year for a burnt offering unto יהוה.

13 And the meat offering thereof shall be two tenth deals of fine flour mingled with oil, an offering made by fire unto יהוה for a sweet savour; and the drink offering thereof shall be of wine, the fourth part of an hin.

14 And you shall eat neither bread, nor parched corn, nor green ears, until the selfsame day that you have brought an offering unto your God (Elohim); it shall be a statute forever throughout your generations in all your dwellings.

15 And you shall count unto you from the next day after the Shabbat, from the day that you brought the sheaf of the wave offering; seven Shabbats shall be completed.

16 Unto the next day after the seventh Shabbat shall you number fifty days; and you shall offer a new meat offering unto יהוה.

17 You shall bring out of your habitations two wave loaves of two tenth deals; they shall be of fine flour; they shall be baken with leaven; they are the firstfruits unto יהוה.

18 And you shall offer with the bread seven lambs without blemish of the first year, and one young bullock, and two rams: they shall be for a burnt offering unto יהוה, with their meat offering, and their drink offerings, even an offering made by fire, of sweet savour unto יהוה.

19 Then you shall sacrifice one kid of the goats for a sin offering, and two lambs of the first year for a sacrifice of peace offerings.

20 And the priest (kohen) shall wave them with the bread of the firstfruits for a wave offering before יהוה, with the two lambs. They shall be holy to יהוה for the priest (kohen).

21 And you shall proclaim on the selfsame day, that it may be a holy convocation unto you. You shall do no servile work therein; it shall be a statute forever in all your dwellings throughout your generations.

22 And when you reap the harvest of your land, you shalt not make clean riddance of the corners of your field when you reapest, neither shalt you gather any gleaning of your harvest. You shalt leave them unto the poor, and to the stranger: I am יהוה your God (YHWH Eloheikhem).'"

23 And יהוה spake unto Moses (Mosheh), saying,

24 "Speak unto the children of Yisrael, saying: 'In the seventh month, in the first day of the month, shall you have a Shabbat, a memorial of [B22]blowing of trumpets (Teruah), a holy convocation.

25 You shall do no servile work therein; but you shall offer an offering made by fire unto יהוה.'"

26 And יהוה spake unto Moses (Mosheh), saying:

27 "Also on the tenth day of this seventh month there shall be a [B23]Day of the Atonements (Yom haKippurim); it shall be a holy convocation unto you; and you shall afflict your souls, and offer an offering made by fire unto יהוה.

28 And you shall do no work in that same day, for it is Day of the Atonements (Yom HaKippurim), to make an atonement (kippur) for you before יהוה your God (YHWH Eloheikhem).

29 For whatsoever soul it be that shall not be afflicted in that same day, he shall be cut off from among his people.

30 And whatsoever soul it be that doeth any work in that same day, the same soul will I destroy from among his people.

31 You shall do no manner of work: it shall be a statute forever throughout your generations in all your dwellings.

32 It shall be unto you a Shabbat of solemn rest ([B17]Shabbat Shabbatton), and you shall afflict your souls. On the ninth day of the month at even, from even unto even, shall you celebrate your Shabbat.

33 And יהוה spake unto Moses (Mosheh), saying,

34 "Speak unto the children of Yisrael, saying: 'The fifteenth day of this seventh month shall be the [B24]Feast of Tabernacles (Chag Sukkot) for seven days unto יהוה.

35 On the first day shall be a holy convocation. You shall do no servile work therein.

36 Seven days you shall offer an offering made by fire unto יהוה. On the eighth day shall be a holy convocation unto you; and you shall offer an offering made by fire unto יהוה: it is a solemn assembly; and you shall do no servile work therein.

37 These are the feasts of יהוה, which you shall proclaim to be holy convocations, to offer an offering made by fire unto יהוה, a burnt offering, and a meat offering, a sacrifice, and drink offerings, everything upon its day;

38 Besides the Shabbats of יהוה, and besides your gifts, and besides all your vows, and beside all your freewill offerings, which you give unto יהוה.

39 Also on the fifteenth day of the seventh month, when you have gathered in the fruit of the land, you shall keep a feast unto יהוה seven days; on the first day shall be a Shabbat, and on the eighth day shall be a Shabbat.

40 And you shall take you on the first day the boughs of goodly trees, branches of palm trees, and the boughs of thick trees, and willows of the brook; and you shall rejoice before יהוה your God (YHWH Eloheikhem) seven days.

41 And you shall keep it a feast unto יהוה seven days in the year. It shall be a statute forever in your generations: you shall celebrate it in the seventh month.

42 You shall dwell in booths seven days; all that are Israelites (Yisraelis) born shall dwell in booths (sukkot);

43 That your generations may know that I made the children of Yisrael to dwell in booths (sukkot), when I brought them out of the land of Egypt (Mitsrayim): I am יהוה your God (YHWH Eloheikhem).'"

44 And Moses (Mosheh) declared unto the children of Yisrael the feasts of יהוה.

24 And יהוה spake unto Moses (Mosheh), saying:

2 "Command the children of Yisrael, that they bring unto you pure oil olive beaten for the light, to cause the lamps to burn continually.

3 Outside the vail of the testimony, in the tabernacle of the congregation, shall Aaron (Aharon) order it from the evening unto the morning before יהוה continually; it shall be a statute forever in your generations.

4 He shall order the lamps upon the pure candlestick (menorah) before יהוה continually.

5 And you shalt take fine flour, and bake twelve cakes thereof. Two tenth deals shall be in one cake.

6 And you shalt set them in two rows, six on a row, upon the pure table before יהוה.

7 And you shalt put pure frankincense upon each row, that it may be on the bread for a memorial, even an offering made by fire unto יהוה.

8 Every Shabbat he shall set it in order before יהוה continually, being taken from the children of Yisrael by an everlasting covenant.

9 And it shall be Aaron (Aharon)'s and his sons'; and they shall eat it in the holy place; for it is

most holy unto him of the offerings of יהוה made by fire by a perpetual statute."

10 And the son of a Yisraeli woman, whose father was an Egyptian (Mitsri), went out among the children of Yisrael; and this son of the Yisraeli woman and a man of Yisrael strove together in the camp;

11 And the Yisraeli woman's son blasphemed the name of יהוה, and cursed. And they brought him unto Moses (Mosheh). (His mother's name was Shelomith, the daughter of Dibri, of the tribe of Dan.)

12 And they put him in ward, that the mind of יהוה might be shewed them.

13 And יהוה spake unto Moses (Mosheh), saying,

14 "Bring forth him that hath cursed outside the camp; and let all that heard him lay their hands upon his head, and let all the congregation stone him.

15 And you shalt speak unto the children of Yisrael, saying: 'Whosoever curseth his God (Elohim) shall bear his sin.

16 And he that blasphemeth the name of יהוה, he shall surely be put to death, and all the congregation shall certainly stone him; as well the stranger, as he who is born in the land, when he blasphemeth the name of יהוה, shall be put to death.

17 And he who killeth any man shall surely be put to death.

18 And he who killeth a beast shall make it good; beast for beast.

19 And if a man causes a blemish in his neighbour; as he hath done, so shall it be done to him;

20 Breach for breach, eye for eye, tooth for tooth; as he hath caused a blemish in a man, so shall it be done to him.

21 And he who killeth a beast, he shall restore it; and he who killeth a man, he shall be put to death.

22 You shall have one manner of law (torah), as well for the stranger, as for one of your own country; for I am יהוה your God (YHWH Eloheikhem).'"

23 And Moses (Mosheh) spake to the children of Yisrael, that they should bring forth him who had cursed out of the camp, and stone him with stones. And the children of Yisrael did as יהוה commanded Moses (Mosheh).

25 And יהוה spake unto Moses (Mosheh) in Mount Sinai, saying,

2 "Speak unto the children of Yisrael, and say unto them: 'When you come into the land which I give you, then shall the land keep a Shabbat unto יהוה.

3 Six years you shalt sow your field, and six years you shalt prune your vineyard, and gather in the fruit thereof;

4 But in the seventh year shall be a Shabbat of rest (Shabbat Shabbaton) unto the land, a Shabbat for יהוה. You shalt neither sow your field, nor prune your vineyard.

5 That which groweth of its own accord of your harvest you shalt not reap, neither gather the grapes of your vine undressed, for it is a year of rest unto the land.

6 And the Shabbat produce of the land shall be food for you; for you, and for your servant, and for your maid, and for your hired servant, and for your stranger that sojourneth with you,

7 And for your cattle, and for the beast that are in your land, shall all the increase thereof be for food.

8 And you shalt number seven Shabbats of years unto you, seven times seven years; and the space of the seven Shabbats of years shall be unto you forty-nine years.

9 Then shalt you cause the trumpet of the [B25]Jubilee (Yovel) to sound on the tenth day of the seventh month, on the day of atonement (yom kippur) shall you make the trumpet sound throughout all your land.

10 And you shall consecrate the fiftieth year, and proclaim liberty throughout all the land unto all the inhabitants thereof. It shall be a Jubilee (Yovel) unto you; and you shall return every man unto his possession, and you shall return every man unto his family.

11 A Jubilee (Yovel) shall that fiftieth year be unto you; you shall not sow, neither reap that which groweth of itself in it, nor gather the grapes in it of your vine undressed.

12 For it is the Jubilee (Yovel); it shall be holy unto you; you shall eat the increase thereof out of the field.

13 In the year of this Jubilee (Yovel) you shall return every man unto his possession.

14 And if you sell anything unto your neighbour, or buyest from your neighbour's hand, you shall not oppress one another.

15 According to the number of years after the Jubilee (Yovel) you shalt buy from your neighbour, and according unto the number of years of the fruits he shall sell unto you.

16 According to the multitude of years you shalt increase the price thereof, and according to the fewness of years you shalt diminish the price of it; for according to the number of the years of the fruits doth he sells unto you.

17 You shall not therefore oppress one another; but you shalt fear your God (Elohim); for I am יהוה your God (YHWH Eloheikhem).

18 Therefore you shall do My statutes, and keep My judgments, and do them; and you shall dwell in the land in safety.

19 And the land shall yield its fruit, and you shall eat your fill, and dwell therein in safety.

20 And if you shall say, "What shall we eat the seventh year, since we shall not sow, nor gather in our produce?"

21 Then I will command My blessing upon you in the sixth year, and it shall bring forth fruit for three years.

22 And you shall sow the eighth year, and eat yet of old fruit until the ninth year; until its produce come in, you shall eat of the old store.

23 The land shall not be sold forever; for the land is Mine; for you are strangers and sojourners with Me.

24 And in all the land of your possession you shall grant a redemption for the land.

25 If your brother be waxen poor, and hath sold away some of his possession, and if any of his kin come to redeem it, then shall he redeem that which his brother sold.

26 And if the man has none to redeem it, and himself be able to redeem it;

27 Then let him count the years of the sale thereof, and restore the overplus unto the man to whom he sold it; that he may return unto his possession.

28 But if he be not able to restore it to him, then that which is sold shall remain in the hand of him that hath bought it until the year of Jubilee (Yovel); and in the Jubilee (Yovel) it shall go out, and he shall return unto his possession.

29 And if a man sells a dwelling house in a walled city, then he may redeem it within a whole year after it is sold; within a full year may he redeem it.

30 And if it be not redeemed within the space of a full year, then the house that is in the walled city shall be established forever to him that bought it throughout his generations. It shall not go out in the Jubilee (Yovel).

31 But the houses of the villages which have no wall round about them shall be counted as the fields of the country. They may be redeemed, and they shall go out in the Jubilee (Yovel).

32 Notwithstanding the cities of the Levites (Lewiyim), and the houses of the cities of their possession, may the Levites (Lewiyim) redeem at any time.

33 And if a man purchases of the Levites (Lewiyim), then the house that was sold, and the city of his possession, shall go out in the year of Jubilee (Yovel); for the houses of the cities of the Levites (Lewiyim) are their possession among the children of Yisrael.

34 But the field of the suburbs of their cities may not be sold; for it is their perpetual possession.

35 And if your brother be waxen poor, and fallen in decay with you; then you shalt relieve him; yea, though he be a stranger, or a sojourner; that he may live with you.

36 Take you no usury of him, or increase but fear your God (Elohim), that your brother may live with you.

37 You shalt not give him your money upon usury, nor lend him your victuals for increase.

38 I am יהוה your God (YHWH Eloheikhem), who brought you forth out of the land of Egypt (Mitsrayim), to give you the land of Canaan, and to be your God (Elohim).

39 And if your brother who dwelleth by you be waxen poor, and be sold unto you; you shalt not compel him to serve as a bondservant;

40 But as a hired servant, and as a sojourner, he shall be with you, and shall serve you unto the year of Jubilee (Yovel).

41 And then shall he depart from you, both he and his children with him, and shall return unto his own family, and unto the possession of his fathers shall he return.

42 For they are My servants, whom I brought forth out of the land of Egypt (Mitsrayim); they shall not be sold as bondmen.

43 You shalt not rule over him with rigour; but shalt fear your God (Elohim).

44 Both your bondmen, and your bondmaids, which you shalt have, shall be of the heathen that are round about you; of them shall you buy

bondmen and bondmaids.

45 Moreover of the children of the strangers that do sojourn among you, of them shall you buy, and of their families that are with you, which they begat in your land; and they shall be your possession.

46 And you shall take them as an inheritance for your children after you, to inherit them for a possession; they shall be your bondmen forever. But over your brethren the children of Yisrael, you shall not rule one over another with rigour.

47 And if a sojourner or stranger wax rich by you, and your brother who dwelleth by him wax poor, and sell himself unto the stranger or sojourner by you, or to the stock of the stranger's family;

48 After that he is sold he may be redeemed again; one of his brethren may redeem him;

49 Either his uncle, or his uncle's son, may redeem him, or any that is near of kin unto him of his family may redeem him; or if he be able, he may redeem himself.

50 And he shall reckon with him that bought him from the year that he was sold to him unto the year of Jubilee (Yovel); and the price of his sale shall be according unto the number of years, according to the time of a hired servant shall it be with him.

51 If there be yet many years behind, according unto them he shall give again the price of his redemption out of the money that he was bought for.

52 And if there remain but few years unto the year of Jubilee (Yovel), then he shall count with him, and according unto his years shall he give him again the price of his redemption.

53 And as a yearly hired servant shall he be with him; and the other shall not rule with rigour over him in your sight.

54 And if he be not redeemed in these years, then he shall go out in the year of Jubilee (Yovel), both he, and his children with him.

55 For unto Me the children of Yisrael are servants; they are My servants whom I brought forth out of the land of Egypt (Mitsrayim): I am יהוה your God (YHWH Eloheikhem).

26 You shall make you no idols nor graven image, neither rear you up a standing pillar, neither shall you set up any image of stone in your land, to bow down unto it; for I am יהוה your God (YHWH Eloheikhem).

2 You shall keep My Shabbats, and reverence My sanctuary: I am יהוה.

3 If you walk in My statutes, and keep My commandments, and do them;

4 Then I will give you rain in due season, and the land shall yield her increase, and the trees of the field shall yield their fruit.

5 And your threshing shall reach unto the vintage, and the vintage shall reach unto the sowing time; and you shall eat your bread to the full, and dwell in your land safely.

6 And I will give peace in the land, and you shall lie down, and none shall make you afraid; and I will rid evil beasts out of the land, neither shall the sword go through your land.

7 And you shall chase your enemies, and they shall fall before you by the sword.

8 And five of you shall chase a hundred, and a hundred of you shall put ten thousand to flight; and your enemies shall fall before you by the sword.

9 For I will have respect unto you, and make you fruitful, and multiply you, and establish My covenant with you.

10 And you shall eat old store, and bring forth the old because of the new.

11 And I will set My tabernacle among you; and My soul shall not abhor you.

12 And I will walk among you, and will be your God (Elohim), and you shall be My people.

13 I am יהוה your God (YHWH Eloheikhem), who brought you forth out of the land of Egypt (Mitsrayim), that you should not be their bondmen; and I have broken the bands of your yoke, and made you go upright.

14 But if you will not hearken unto Me, and will not do all these commandments;

15 And if you shall despise My statutes, or if your soul abhors My judgments, so that you will not do all My commandments, but that you break My covenant;

16 I also will do this unto you; I will even appoint over you terror, consumption, and the burning ague, that shall consume the eyes, and cause sorrow of heart; and you shall sow your seed in vain, for your enemies shall eat it.

17 And I will set My face against you, and you shall be slain before your enemies; they that hate you shall reign over you; and you shall flee when none pursueth you.

18 And if you will not yet for all this hearken

unto Me, then I will punish you seven times more for your sins.

19 And I will break the pride of your power; and I will make your heaven as iron, and your earth as brass:

20 And your strength shall be spent in vain; for your land shall not yield her increase, neither shall the trees of the land yield their fruits.

21 And if you walk contrary unto Me, and will not hearken unto Me; I will bring seven times more plagues upon you according to your sins.

22 I will also send wild beasts among you, which shall rob you of your children, and destroy your cattle, and make you few in number; and your high ways shall be desolate.

23 And if you will not be reformed by Me by these things, but will walk contrary unto Me;

24 Then will I also walk contrary unto you, and will punish you yet seven times for your sins.

25 And I will bring a sword upon you, that shall avenge the quarrel of my covenant; and when you are gathered together within your cities, I will send the pestilence among you; and you shall be delivered into the hand of the enemy.

26 And when I have broken the staff of your bread, ten women shall bake your bread in one oven, and they shall deliver you your bread again by weight; and you shall eat, and not be satisfied.

27 And if you will not for all this hearken unto Me, but walk contrary unto Me;

28 Then I will walk contrary unto you also in fury; and I, even I, will chastise you seven times for your sins.

29 And you shall eat the flesh of your sons, and the flesh of your daughters shall you eat.

30 And I will destroy your high places, and cut down your sun-pillars, and cast your carcasses upon the carcasses of your idols, and My soul shall abhor you.

31 And I will make your cities waste, and bring your sanctuaries unto desolation, and I will not smell the savour of your sweet odours.

32 And I will bring the land into desolation; and your enemies who dwell therein shall be astonished at it.

33 And I will scatter you among the heathen, and will draw out a sword after you; and your land shall be desolate, and your cities waste.

34 Then shall the land enjoy her Shabbats, as long as it lieth desolate, and you be in your enemies' land; even then shall the land rest, and enjoy her Shabbats.

35 As long as it lieth desolate it shall rest; because it did not rest in your Shabbats, when you dwelt upon it.

36 And upon them that are left alive of you I will send a faintness into their hearts in the lands of their enemies; and the sound of a shaken leaf shall chase them; and they shall flee, as fleeing from a sword; and they shall fall when none pursueth.

37 And they shall fall one upon another, as it was before a sword, when none pursueth; and you shall have no power to stand before your enemies.

38 And you shall perish among the heathen, and the land of your enemies shall eat you up.

39 And they that are left of you shall pine away in their iniquity in your enemies' lands; and also in the iniquities of their fathers shall they pine away with them.

40 If they shall confess their iniquity, and the iniquity of their fathers, with their trespass which they trespassed against Me, and that also they have walked contrary unto Me;

41 And that I also have walked contrary unto them, and have brought them into the land of their enemies; if then their uncircumcised hearts be humbled, and they then accept of the punishment of their iniquity;

42 Then will I remember My covenant with Jacob (Yaaqov), and also My covenant with Isaac (Yitschaq), and also my covenant with Avraham will I remember; and I will remember the land.

43 The land also shall be left of them, and shall enjoy her Shabbats, while she lieth desolate without them; and they shall accept of the punishment of their iniquity; because, even because they despised My judgments, and because their soul abhorred My statutes.

44 And yet for all that, when they be in the land of their enemies, I will not cast them away, neither will I abhor them, to destroy them utterly, and to break My covenant with them; for I am יהוה their God (YHWH Eloheihem).

45 But I will for their sakes remember the covenant of their ancestors, whom I brought forth out of the land of Egypt (Mitsrayim) in the sight of the heathen, that I might be their God (Elohim): I am יהוה.'"

46 These are the statutes and judgments and laws (torot), which יהוה made between Him and the children of Yisrael in Mount Sinai by the hand of Moses (Mosheh).

27 And יהוה spake unto Moses (Mosheh), saying,

2 "Speak unto the children of Yisrael, and say unto them: 'When a man shall make a singular vow, the persons shall be for יהוה by your estimation.

3 And your estimation shall be of the male from twenty years old even unto sixty years old, even your estimation shall be fifty shekels of silver, after the shekel of the sanctuary.

4 And if it be a female, then your estimation shall be thirty shekels.

5 And if it be from five years old even unto twenty years old, then your estimation shall be of the male twenty shekels, and for the female ten shekels.

6 And if it be from a month old even unto five years old, then your estimation shall be of the male five shekels of silver, and for the female your estimation shall be three shekels of silver.

7 And if it be from sixty years old and above; if it be a male, then your estimation shall be fifteen shekels, and for the female ten shekels.

8 But if he be poorer than your estimation, then he shall present himself before the priest (kohen), and the priest (kohen) shall value him; according to his ability that vowed shall the priest (kohen) value him.

9 And if it be a beast, whereof men bring an offering unto יהוה, all that any man giveth of such unto יהוה shall be holy.

10 He shall not alter it, nor change it, a good for a bad, or a bad for a good; and if he shall at all change beast for beast, then it and the exchange thereof shall be holy.

11 And if it be any unclean beast, of which they do not offer a sacrifice unto יהוה, then he shall present the beast before the priest (kohen);

12 And the priest (kohen) shall value it, whether it be good or bad; as you valuest it, who art the priest (kohen), so shall it be.

13 But if he will at all redeem it, then he shall add a fifth part thereof unto your estimation.

14 And when a man shall sanctify his house to be holy unto יהוה, then the priest (kohen) shall estimate it, whether it be good or bad: as the priest (kohen) shall estimate it, so shall it stand.

15 And if he that sanctified it will redeem his house, then he shall add the fifth part of the money of your estimation unto it, and it shall be his.

16 And if a man shall sanctify unto יהוה some part of a field of his possession, then your estimation shall be according to the seed thereof. A homer of barley seed shall be valued at fifty shekels of silver.

17 If he sanctifies his field from the year of Jubilee (Yovel), according to your estimation it shall stand.

18 But if he sanctifies his field after the Jubilee (Yovel), then the priest (kohen) shall reckon unto him the money according to the years that remain, even unto the year of the Jubilee (Yovel), and it shall be abated from your estimation.

19 And if he that sanctified the field will in any wise redeem it, then he shall add the fifth part of the money of your estimation unto it, and it shall be assured to him.

20 And if he will not redeem the field, or if he has sold the field to another man, it shall not be redeemed any more.

21 But the field, when it goeth out in the Jubilee (Yovel), shall be holy unto יהוה, as a field devoted; the possession thereof shall be the priest (kohen)'s.

22 And if a man sanctifies unto יהוה a field which he hath bought, which is not of the fields of his possession;

23 Then the priest (kohen) shall reckon unto him the worth of your estimation, even unto the year of the Jubilee (Yovel); and he shall give your estimation in that day, as a holy thing unto יהוה.

24 In the year of the Jubilee (Yovel) the field shall return unto him of whom it was bought, even to him to whom the possession of the land did belong.

25 And all your estimations shall be according to the shekel of the sanctuary: twenty gerahs shall be the shekel.

26 Only the firstling of the beasts, which should be יהוה's firstling, no man shall sanctify it; whether it be ox, or sheep; it is יהוה's.

27 And if it be of an unclean beast, then he shall redeem it according to your estimation, and shall add a fifth part of it thereto; or if it be not redeemed, then it shall be sold according to your estimation.

28 Notwithstanding no devoted thing, that a man shall devote unto יהוה of all that he hath, both of man and beast, and of the field of his possession, shall be sold or redeemed; every devoted thing is most holy unto יהוה.

29 None devoted, which shall be devoted of men, shall be redeemed; but shall surely be put to death.

30 And all the tithe of the land, whether of the seed of the land, or of the fruit of the tree, is יהוה's; it is holy unto יהוה.

31 And if a man will at all redeem ought of his tithes, he shall add thereto the fifth part thereof.

32 And concerning the tithe of the herd, or of the flock, even of whatsoever passeth under the rod, the tenth shall be holy unto יהוה.

33 He shall not search whether it be good or bad, neither shall he change it; and if he changes it at all, then both it and the change thereof shall be holy; it shall not be redeemed.'"

34 These are the commandments, which יהוה commanded Moses (Mosheh) for the children of Yisrael in Mount Sinai.

NUMBERS
BEMIDBAR בְּמִדְבַּר
(In the Wilderness)

1 And יהוה spake unto Moses (Mosheh) in the wilderness of Sinai, in the tabernacle of the congregation, on the first day of the second month, in the second year after they were come out of the land of Egypt (Mitsrayim), saying:

2 "Take you the sum of all the congregation of the children of Yisrael, after their families, by the house of their fathers, with the number of their names, every male by their polls;

3 From twenty years old and upward, all that are able to go forth to war in Yisrael; you and Aaron (Aharon) shall number them by their armies.

4 And with you there shall be a man of every tribe; every one head of the house of his fathers.

5 And these are the names of the men who shall stand with you: of the tribe of Reuven: Elizur the son of Shedeur.

6 Of Shimon, Shelumiel the son of Zurishaddai.

7 Of Judah (Yehudah), Nahshon the son of Amminadab.

8 Of Yissaskhar, Nethaneel the son of Zuar.

9 Of Zevulun, Eliav the son of Helon.

10 Of the children of Joseph (Yosef): of Efrayim, Elishama the son of Ammihud; of Menashsheh, Gamaliel the son of Pedahzur.

11 Of Binyamin, Abidan the son of Gideoni.

12 Of Dan, Ahiezer the son of Ammishaddai.

13 Of Asher, Pagiel the son of Ocran.

14 Of Gad, Elijahaph (Elyasaf) the son of Deuel.

15 Of Naftali, Ahira the son of Enan."

16 These were the renowned of the congregation, princes of the tribes of their fathers, heads of thousands in Yisrael.

17 And Moses (Mosheh) and Aaron (Aharon) took these men who are expressed by their names,

18 And they assembled all the congregation together on the first day of the second month, and they declared their pedigrees after their families, by the house of their fathers, according to the number of the names, from twenty years old and upward, by their polls.

19 As יהוה commanded Moses (Mosheh), so he numbered them in the wilderness of Sinai.

20 And the children of Reuven, Yisrael's eldest son, by their generations, after their families, by the house of their fathers, according to the number of the names, by their polls, every male from twenty years old and upward, all that were able to go forth to war;

21 Those that were numbered of them, even of the tribe of Reuven, were forty and six thousand and five hundred.

22 Of the children of Shimon, by their generations, after their families, by the house of their fathers, those that were numbered of them, according to the number of the names, by their polls, every male from twenty years old and upward, all that were able to go forth to war;

23 Those that were numbered of them, even of the tribe of Shimon, were fifty and nine thousand and three hundred.

24 Of the children of Gad, by their generations, after their families, by the house of their fathers, according to the number of the names, from twenty years old and upward, all that were able to go forth to war:

25 Those that were numbered of them, even of the tribe of Gad, were forty and five thousand six hundred and fifty.

26 Of the children of Judah (Yehudah), by their generations, after their families, by the house of their fathers, according to the number of the names, from twenty years old and upward, all that were able to go forth to war:

27 Those that were numbered of them, even of the tribe of Judah (Yehudah), were threescore and fourteen thousand and six hundred.

28 Of the children of Yissaskhar, by their generations, after their families, by the house of their fathers, according to the number of the names, from twenty years old and upward, all that were able to go forth to war:

29 Those that were numbered of them, even of the tribe of Yissaskhar, were fifty and four thousand and four hundred.

30 Of the children of Zevulun, by their generations, after their families, by the house of their fathers, according to the number of the names, from twenty years old and upward, all that were able to go forth to war:

31 Those that were numbered of them, even of the tribe of Zevulun, were fifty and seven thousand and four hundred.

32 Of the children of Joseph (Yosef), namely, of the children of Efrayim, by their generations, after their families, by the house of their fathers,

according to the number of the names, from twenty years old and upward, all that were able to go forth to war:

33 Those that were numbered of them, even of the tribe of Efrayim, were forty thousand and five hundred.

34 Of the children of Menashsheh, by their generations, after their families, by the house of their fathers, according to the number of the names, from twenty years old and upward, all that were able to go forth to war:

35 Those that were numbered of them, even of the tribe of Menashsheh, were thirty and two thousand and two hundred.

36 Of the children of Binyamin, by their generations, after their families, by the house of their fathers, according to the number of the names, from twenty years old and upward, all that were able to go forth to war:

37 Those that were numbered of them, even of the tribe of Binyamin, were thirty and five thousand and four hundred.

38 Of the children of Dan, by their generations, after their families, by the house of their fathers, according to the number of the names, from twenty years old and upward, all that were able to go forth to war:

39 Those that were numbered of them, even of the tribe of Dan, were threescore and two thousand and seven hundred.

40 Of the children of Asher, by their generations, after their families, by the house of their fathers, according to the number of the names, from twenty years old and upward, all that were able to go forth to war:

41 Those that were numbered of them, even of the tribe of Asher, were forty and one thousand and five hundred.

42 Of the children of Naftali, throughout their generations, after their families, by the house of their fathers, according to the number of the names, from twenty years old and upward, all that were able to go forth to war:

43 Those that were numbered of them, even of the tribe of Naftali, were fifty and three thousand and four hundred.

44 These are those that were numbered, whom Moses (Mosheh) and Aaron (Aharon) numbered, and the princes of Yisrael, being twelve men, each one was for the house of his fathers.

45 So were all those that were numbered of the children of Yisrael, by the house of their fathers, from twenty years old and upward, all that were able to go forth to war in Yisrael;

46 Even all they that were numbered were six hundred thousand and three thousand and five hundred and fifty.

47 But the Levites (Lewiyim) after the tribe of their fathers were not numbered among them.

48 For יהוה had spoken unto Moses (Mosheh), saying:

49 "Only you shalt not number the tribe of Lewi, neither take the sum of them among the children of Yisrael;

50 But you shalt appoint the Levites (Lewiyim) over the tabernacle of testimony, and over all the vessels thereof, and over all things that belong to it; they shall bear the tabernacle, and all the vessels thereof; and they shall minister unto it, and shall encamp round about the tabernacle.

51 And when the tabernacle setteth forward, the Levites (Lewiyim) shall take it down; and when the tabernacle is to be pitched, the Levites (Lewiyim) shall set it up. And the stranger that cometh near shall be put to death.

52 And the children of Yisrael shall pitch their tents, every man by his own camp, and every man by his own standard, throughout their armies.

53 But the Levites (Lewiyim) shall pitch round about the tabernacle of testimony, that there be no wrath upon the congregation of the children of Yisrael; and the Levites (Lewiyim) shall keep the charge of the tabernacle of Testimony."

54 And the children of Yisrael did according to all that יהוה commanded Moses (Mosheh), so did they.

2 And יהוה spake unto Moses (Mosheh) and unto Aaron (Aharon), saying:

2 "Every man of the children of Yisrael shall pitch by his own standard, with the ensign of their father's house; far off about the tabernacle of the congregation shall they pitch.

3 And on the east side toward the rising of the sun shall they of the standard of the camp of Judah (Yehudah) pitch throughout their armies; and Nahshon the son of Amminadab shall be captain of the children of Judah (Yehudah).

4 And his army, and those that were numbered of them, were threescore and fourteen thousand and six hundred.

5 And those that do pitch next unto him shall be the tribe of Yissaskhar; and Nethaneel the son of Zuar shall be captain of the children of Yissaskhar.

6 And his army, and those that were numbered thereof, were fifty and four thousand and four hundred.

7 Then the tribe of Zevulun, and Eliav the son of Helon shall be captain of the children of Zevulun.

8 And his army, and those that were numbered thereof, were fifty and seven thousand and four hundred.

9 All that were numbered in the camp of Judah (Yehudah) were a hundred thousand and fourscore thousand and six thousand and four hundred, throughout their armies. These shall first set forth.

10 On the south side shall be the standard of the camp of Reuven according to their armies; and the captain of the children of Reuven shall be Elizur the son of Shedeur.

11 And his army, and those that were numbered thereof, were forty and six thousand and five hundred.

12 And those who pitch by him shall be the tribe of Shimon; and the captain of the children of Shimon shall be Shelumiel the son of Zurishaddai.

13 And his army, and those that were numbered of them, were fifty and nine thousand and three hundred.

14 Then the tribe of Gad, and the captain of the sons of Gad shall be Elijahaph (Elyasaf) the son of Reuel.

15 And his army, and those that were numbered of them, were forty and five thousand and six hundred and fifty.

16 All that were numbered in the camp of Reuven were a hundred thousand and fifty and one thousand and four hundred and fifty, throughout their armies. And they shall set forth in the second rank.

17 Then the tabernacle of the congregation shall set forward with the camp of the Levites (Lewiyim) in the midst of the camp; as they encamp, so shall they set forward, every man in his place by their standards.

18 On the west side shall be the standard of the camp of Efrayim according to their armies; and the captain of the sons of Efrayim shall be Elishama the son of Ammihud.

19 And his army, and those that were numbered of them, were forty thousand and five hundred.

20 And by him shall be the tribe of Menashsheh; and the captain of the children of Menashsheh shall be Gamaliel the son of Pedahzur.

21 And his army, and those that were numbered of them, were thirty and two thousand and two hundred.

22 Then the tribe of Binyamin, and the captain of the sons of Binyamin shall be Abidan the son of Gideoni.

23 And his army, and those that were numbered of them, were thirty and five thousand and four hundred.

24 All that were numbered of the camp of Efrayim were a hundred thousand and eight thousand and a hundred, throughout their armies. And they shall go forward in the third rank.

25 The standard of the camp of Dan shall be on the north side by their armies: and the captain of the children of Dan shall be Ahiezer the son of Ammishaddai.

26 And his army, and those that were numbered of them, were threescore and two thousand and seven hundred.

27 And those that encamp by him shall be the tribe of Asher; and the captain of the children of Asher shall be Pagiel the son of Ocran.

28 And his army, and those that were numbered of them, were forty and one thousand and five hundred.

29 Then the tribe of Naftali, and the captain of the children of Naftali shall be Ahira the son of Enan.

30 And his army, and those that were numbered of them, were fifty and three thousand and four hundred.

31 All they that were numbered in the camp of Dan were a hundred thousand and fifty and seven thousand and six hundred. They shall go hindmost with their standards."

32 These are those which were numbered of the children of Yisrael by the house of their fathers. All those that were numbered of the camps throughout their hosts were six hundred thousand and three thousand and five hundred and fifty.

33 But the Levites (Lewiyim) were not numbered among the children of Yisrael; as

יהוה commanded Moses (Mosheh).

34 And the children of Yisrael did according to all that יהוה commanded Moses (Mosheh); so they pitched by their standards, and so they set forward, every one after their families, according to the house of their fathers.

3 These also are the generations of Aaron (Aharon) and Moses (Mosheh) in the day that יהוה spake with Moses (Mosheh) in Mount Sinai.

2 And these are the names of the sons of Aaron (Aharon): Nadav the firstborn, and Avihu, Eleazar, and Ithamar.

3 These are the names of the sons of Aaron (Aharon), the priests (kohanim) who were anointed, whom he consecrated to minister as priests (kohanim).

4 And Nadav and Avihu died before יהוה, when they offered strange fire before יהוה, in the wilderness of Sinai, and they had no children. And Eleazar and Ithamar ministered as priests (kohanim) in the sight of Aaron (Aharon) their father.

5 And יהוה spake unto Moses (Mosheh), saying:

6 "Bring the tribe of Lewi near, and present them before Aaron (Aharon) the priest (kohen), that they may minister unto him.

7 And they shall keep his charge, and the charge of the whole congregation before the tabernacle of the congregation, to do the service of the tabernacle.

8 And they shall keep all the instruments of the tabernacle of the congregation, and the charge of the children of Yisrael, to do the service of the tabernacle.

9 And you shalt give the Levites (Lewiyim) unto Aaron (Aharon) and to his sons; they are wholly given unto him out of the children of Yisrael.

10 And you shalt appoint Aaron (Aharon) and his sons, and they shall wait on their priest (kohen)'s office; and the stranger that cometh near shall be put to death."

11 And יהוה spake unto Moses (Mosheh), saying:

12 "And I, behold, I have taken the Levites (Lewiyim) from among the children of Yisrael instead of all the firstborn that openeth the matrix among the children of Yisrael; therefore the Levites (Lewiyim) shall be Mine;

13 Because all the firstborn are mine; for on the day that I smote all the firstborn in the land of Egypt (Mitsrayim) I hallowed unto Me all the firstborn in Yisrael, both man and beast; Mine shall they be: I am יהוה."

14 And יהוה spake unto Moses (Mosheh) in the wilderness of Sinai, saying:

15 "Number the children of Lewi after the house of their fathers, by their families; every male from a month old and upward shalt you number them."

16 And Moses (Mosheh) numbered them according to the word of יהוה, as he was commanded.

17 And these were the sons of Lewi by their names: Gershon, and Kohath, and Merari.

18 And these are the names of the sons of Gershon by their families: Libni, and Shimei.

19 And the sons of Kohath by their families: Amram, and Izehar, Hebron, and Uzziel.

20 And the sons of Merari by their families: Mahli, and Mushi. These are the families of the Levites (Lewiyim) according to the house of their fathers.

21 Of Gershon was the family of the Libnites, and the family of the Shimites; these are the families of the Gershonites.

22 Those that were numbered of them, according to the number of all the males, from a month old and upward, even those that were numbered of them were seven thousand and five hundred.

23 The families of the Gershonites shall pitch behind the tabernacle westward.

24 And the chief of the house of the father of the Gershonites shall be Elijahaph (Elyasaf) the son of Lael.

25 And the charge of the sons of Gershon in the tabernacle of the congregation shall be the tabernacle, and the tent, the covering thereof, and the hanging for the door of the tabernacle of the congregation,

26 And the hangings of the court, and the curtain for the door of the court, which is by the tabernacle, and by the altar round about, and the cords of it for all the service thereof.

27 And of Kohath was the family of the Amramites, and the family of the Izeharites, and the family of the Hebronites, and the family of the Uzzielites; these are the families of the Kohathites.

28 In the number of all the males, from a month old and upward, were eight thousand and six

hundred, keeping the charge of the sanctuary.

29 The families of the sons of Kohath shall pitch on the side of the tabernacle southward.

30 And the chief of the house of the father of the families of the Kohathites shall be Elizaphan the son of Uzziel.

31 And their charge shall be the ark, and the table, and the candlestick (menorah), and the altars, and the vessels of the sanctuary wherewith they minister, and the hanging, and all the service thereof.

32 And Eleazar the son of Aaron (Aharon) the priest (kohen) shall be chief over the chief of the Levites (Lewiyim), and have the oversight of them that keep the charge of the sanctuary.

33 Of Merari was the family of the Mahlites, and the family of the Mushites; these are the families of Merari.

34 And those that were numbered of them, according to the number of all the males, from a month old and upward, were six thousand and two hundred.

35 And the chief of the house of the father of the families of Merari was Zuriel the son of Avihail; these shall pitch on the side of the tabernacle northward.

36 And under the custody and charge of the sons of Merari shall be the boards of the tabernacle, and the bars thereof, and the pillars thereof, and the sockets thereof, and all the vessels thereof, and all that serveth thereto,

37 And the pillars of the court round about, and their sockets, and their pins, and their cords.

38 But those that encamp before the tabernacle toward the east, even before the tabernacle of the congregation eastward, shall be Moses (Mosheh), and Aaron (Aharon) and his sons, keeping the charge of the sanctuary for the charge of the children of Yisrael; and the stranger that cometh near shall be put to death.

39 All that were numbered of the Levites (Lewiyim), which Moses (Mosheh) and Aaron (Aharon) numbered at the commandment of יהוה, throughout their families, all the males from a month old and upward, were twenty and two thousand.

40 And יהוה said unto Moses (Mosheh): "Number all the firstborn of the males of the children of Yisrael from a month old and upward, and take the number of their names.

41 And you shalt take the Levites (Lewiyim) for

Me (I am יהוה) instead of all the firstborn among the children of Yisrael; and the cattle of the Levites (Lewiyim) instead of all the firstlings among the cattle of the children of Yisrael."

42 And Moses (Mosheh) numbered, as יהוה commanded him, all the firstborn among the children of Yisrael.

43 And all the firstborn males by the number of names, from a month old and upward, of those that were numbered of them, were twenty and two thousand two hundred and threescore and thirteen.

44 And יהוה spake unto Moses (Mosheh), saying:

45 "Take the Levites (Lewiyim) instead of all the firstborn among the children of Yisrael, and the cattle of the Levites (Lewiyim) instead of their cattle; and the Levites (Lewiyim) shall be Mine: I am יהוה.

46 And for those that are to be redeemed of the two hundred and threescore and thirteen of the firstborn of the children of Yisrael, which are more than the Levites (Lewiyim);

47 You shalt even take five shekels apiece by the poll, after the shekel of the sanctuary shalt you take them; (the shekel is twenty gerahs;)

48 And you shalt give the money, wherewith the odd number of them is to be redeemed, unto Aaron (Aharon) and to his sons."

49 And Moses (Mosheh) took the redemption money of them that were over and above them that were redeemed by the Levites (Lewiyim).

50 Of the firstborn of the children of Yisrael took he the money; a thousand three hundred and threescore and five shekels, after the shekel of the sanctuary.

51 And Moses (Mosheh) gave the money of them that were redeemed unto Aaron (Aharon) and to his sons, according to the word of יהוה, as יהוה commanded Moses (Mosheh).

4 And יהוה spake unto Moses (Mosheh) and unto Aaron (Aharon), saying:

2 "Take the sum of the sons of Kohath from among the sons of Lewi, after their families, by the house of their fathers,

3 From thirty years old and upward even until fifty years old, all that enter into the army, to do the work in the tabernacle of the congregation.

4 This shall be the service of the sons of Kohath in the tabernacle of the congregation, about the

most holy things:

5 And when the camp setteth forward, Aaron (Aharon) shall come, and his sons, and they shall take down the covering vail, and cover the ark of Testimony with it.

6 And shall put thereon the covering of badgers' skins, and shall spread over it a cloth wholly of blue, and shall put in the staves thereof.

7 And upon the table of shewbread they shall spread a cloth of blue, and put thereon the dishes, and the spoons, and the bowls, and covers to cover withal; and the continual bread shall be thereon:

8 And they shall spread upon them a cloth of scarlet, and cover the same with a covering of badgers' skins, and shall put in the staves thereof.

9 And they shall take a cloth of blue, and cover the candlestick (menorah) of the light, and his lamps, and his tongs, and his snuffdishes, and all the oil vessels thereof, wherewith they service unto it.

10 And they shall put it and all the vessels thereof within a covering of badgers' skins, and shall put it upon a bar.

11 And upon the golden altar they shall spread a cloth of blue, and cover it with a covering of badgers' skins, and shall put to the staves thereof.

12 And they shall take all the instruments of service, wherewith they minister in the sanctuary, and put them in a cloth of blue, and cover them with a covering of badgers' skins, and shall put them on a bar.

13 And they shall take away the ashes from the altar, and spread a purple cloth thereon.

14 And they shall put upon it all the vessels thereof, wherewith they minister about it, even the censers, the fleshhooks, and the shovels, and the basons, all the vessels of the altar; and they shall spread upon it a covering of badgers' skins, and put to the staves of it.

15 And when Aaron (Aharon) and his sons have made an end of covering the sanctuary, and all the vessels of the sanctuary, as the camp is to set forward; after that, the sons of Kohath shall come to bear it; but they shall not touch any holy thing, lest they die. These things are the burden of the sons of Kohath in the tabernacle of the congregation.

16 And to the office of Eleazar the son of Aaron (Aharon) the priest (kohen) pertaineth the oil for the light, and the sweet incense, and the daily meat offering, and the anointing oil, and the oversight of all the tabernacle, and of all that therein is, in the sanctuary, and in the vessels thereof."

17 And יהוה spake unto Moses (Mosheh) and unto Aaron (Aharon), saying:

18 "Cut you not off the tribe of the families of the Kohathites from among the Levites (Lewiyim);

19 But thus do unto them, that they may live, and not die, when they approach unto the most holy things: Aaron (Aharon) and his sons shall go in, and appoint them every one to his service and to his burden.

20 But they shall not go in to see when the holy things are covered, lest they die."

21 And יהוה spake unto Moses (Mosheh), saying:

22 "Take also the sum of the sons of Gershon, throughout the houses of their fathers, by their families.

23 From thirty years old and upward until fifty years old shalt you number them; all that enter in to perform the service, to do the work in the tabernacle of the congregation.

24 This is the service of the families of the Gershonites, to serve, and for burdens:

25 And they shall bear the curtains of the tabernacle, and the tabernacle of the congregation, his covering, and the covering of the badgers' skins that is above upon it, and the hanging for the door of the tabernacle of the congregation,

26 And the hangings of the court, and the hanging for the door of the gate of the court, which is by the tabernacle and by the altar round about, and their cords, and all the instruments of their service, and all that is made for them: so shall they serve.

27 At the appointment of Aaron (Aharon) and his sons shall be all the service of the sons of the Gershonites, in all their burdens, and in all their service; and you shall appoint unto them in charge all their burdens.

28 This is the service of the families of the sons of Gershon in the tabernacle of the congregation; and their charge shall be under the hand of Ithamar the son of Aaron (Aharon) the priest (kohen).

29 As for the sons of Merari, you shalt number them after their families, by the house of their fathers.

30 From thirty years old and upward even unto fifty years old shalt you number them, every one that entereth into the service, to do the work of the tabernacle of the congregation.

31 And this is the charge of their burden, according to all their service in the tabernacle of the congregation; the boards of the tabernacle, and the bars thereof, and the pillars thereof, and sockets thereof,

32 And the pillars of the court round about, and their sockets, and their pins, and their cords, with all their instruments, and with all their service; and by name you shall reckon the instruments of the charge of their burden.

33 This is the service of the families of the sons of Merari, according to all their service, in the tabernacle of the congregation, under the hand of Ithamar the son of Aaron (Aharon) the priest (kohen)."

34 And Moses (Mosheh) and Aaron (Aharon) and the chief of the congregation numbered the sons of the Kohathites after their families, and after the house of their fathers,

35 From thirty years old and upward even unto fifty years old, every one that entereth into the service, for the work in the tabernacle of the congregation;

36 And those that were numbered of them by their families were two thousand seven hundred and fifty.

37 These were they that were numbered of the families of the Kohathites, all that might do service in the tabernacle of the congregation, which Moses (Mosheh) and Aaron (Aharon) did number according to the commandment of יהוה by the hand of Moses (Mosheh).

38 And those that were numbered of the sons of Gershon, throughout their families, and by the house of their fathers,

39 From thirty years old and upward even unto fifty years old, every one that entereth into the service, for the work in the tabernacle of the congregation,

40 Even those that were numbered of them, throughout their families, by the house of their fathers, were two thousand and six hundred and thirty.

41 These are they that were numbered of the families of the sons of Gershon, of all that might do service in the tabernacle of the congregation, whom Moses (Mosheh) and Aaron (Aharon) did number according to the commandment of יהוה.

42 And those that were numbered of the families of the sons of Merari, throughout their families, by the house of their fathers,

43 From thirty years old and upward even unto fifty years old, every one that entereth into service, for the work in the tabernacle of the congregation,

44 Even those that were numbered of them after their families, were three thousand and two hundred.

45 These be those that were numbered of the families of the sons of Merari, whom Moses (Mosheh) and Aaron (Aharon) numbered according to the word of יהוה by the hand of Moses (Mosheh).

46 All those that were numbered of the Levites (Lewiyim), whom Moses (Mosheh) and Aaron (Aharon) and the chief of Yisrael numbered, after their families, and after the house of their fathers,

47 From thirty years old and upward even unto fifty years old, every one that came to do the service of the ministry, and the service of the burden in the tabernacle of the congregation,

48 Even those that were numbered of them, were eight thousand and five hundred and fourscore.

49 According to the commandment of יהוה they were numbered by the hand of Moses (Mosheh), every one according to his service, and according to his burden; thus were they numbered of him, as יהוה commanded Moses (Mosheh).

5 And יהוה spake unto Moses (Mosheh), saying:

2 "Command the children of Yisrael, that they put out of the camp every leper, and every one that hath an issue, and whosoever is defiled by the dead;

3 Both male and female shall you put out, outside the camp shall you put them; that they defile not their camps, in the midst whereof I dwell."

4 And the children of Yisrael did so, and put them outside the camp; as יהוה spake unto Moses (Mosheh), so did the children of Yisrael.

5 And יהוה spake unto Moses (Mosheh), saying,

6 "Speak unto the children of Yisrael: 'When a

man or woman shall commit any sin that men commit, to do a trespass against יהוה, and that person be guilty;

7 Then they shall confess their sin which they have done; and he shall recompense his trespass with the principal thereof, and add unto it the fifth part thereof, and give it unto him against whom he hath trespassed.

8 But if the man has no kinsman to recompense the trespass unto, let the trespass be recompensed unto יהוה, even to the priest (kohen); besides the ram of the atonement, whereby an atonement shall be made for him.

9 And every offering of all the holy things of the children of Yisrael, which they bring unto the priest (kohen), shall be his.

10 And every man's hallowed things shall be his; whatsoever any man giveth the priest (kohen), it shall be his.'"

11 And יהוה spake unto Moses (Mosheh), saying,

12 "Speak unto the children of Yisrael and say unto them: 'If any man's wife goes aside, and commit a trespass against him,

13 And a man lies with her carnally, and it be hiddden from the eyes of her husband, and be kept close, and she be defiled, and there be no witness against her, neither she be taken with the manner;

14 And the spirit of jealousy come upon him, and he be jealous of his wife, and she be defiled; or if the spirit of jealousy come upon him, and he be jealous of his wife, and she be not defiled:

15 Then shall the man bring his wife unto the priest (kohen), and he shall bring her offering for her, the tenth part of an ephah of barley meal; he shall pour no oil upon it, nor put frankincense thereon; for it is an offering of jealousy, an offering of memorial, bringing iniquity to remembrance.

16 And the priest (kohen) shall bring her near, and set her before יהוה.

17 And the priest (kohen) shall take holy water in an earthen vessel; and of the dust that is in the floor of the tabernacle the priest (kohen) shall take, and put it into the water:

18 And the priest (kohen) shall set the woman before יהוה, and uncover the woman's head, and put the offering of memorial in her hands, which is the jealousy offering; and the priest (kohen) shall have in his hand the bitter water that causeth the curse.

19 And the priest (kohen) shall charge her by an oath, and say unto the woman, "If no man has lain with you, and if you have not gone aside to uncleanness with another instead of your husband, be you free from this bitter water that causeth the curse.

20 But if you have gone aside to another instead of your husband, and if you be defiled, and some man have lain with you besides your husband;"

21 Then the priest (kohen) shall charge the woman with an oath of cursing, and the priest (kohen) shall say unto the woman, "יהוה make you a curse and an oath among your people, when יהוה doth make your thigh to rot, and your belly to swell;

22 And this water that causeth the curse shall go into your bowels, to make your belly to swell, and your thigh to rot." And the woman shall say, "So be it (Amen)! So be it (Amen)!"

23 And the priest (kohen) shall write these curses in a book, and he shall blot them out with the bitter water.

24 And he shall cause the woman to drink the bitter water that causeth the curse; and the water that causeth the curse shall enter into her, and become bitter.

25 Then the priest (kohen) shall take the jealousy offering out of the woman's hand, and shall wave the offering before יהוה, and offer it upon the altar;

26 And the priest (kohen) shall take a handful of the offering, even the memorial thereof, and burn it upon the altar, and afterward shall cause the woman to drink the water.

27 And when he hath made her to drink the water, then it shall come to pass, that, if she be defiled, and have done trespass against her husband, that the water that causeth the curse shall enter into her, and become bitter, and her belly shall swell, and her thigh shall rot; and the woman shall be a curse among her people.

28 And if the woman be not defiled, but be clean; then she shall be free, and shall conceive seed.

29 This is the law (torah) of jealousies, when a wife goeth aside to another instead of her husband, and is defiled;

30 Or when the spirit of jealousy cometh upon him, and he be jealous over his wife, and shall set the woman before יהוה, and the priest

(kohen) shall execute upon her all this law (torah).

31 Then shall the man be guiltless from iniquity, and this woman shall bear her iniquity.'"

6 And יהוה spake unto Moses (Mosheh), saying,

2 "Speak unto the children of Yisrael and say unto them: 'When either man or woman shall separate themselves to vow a vow of a B30Nazarite (Nazir), to separate themselves unto יהוה.

3 He shall separate himself from wine and strong drink, and shall drink no vinegar of wine, or vinegar of strong drink, neither shall he drink any liquor of grapes, nor eat moist grapes, or dried.

4 All the days of his separation shall he eat nothing that is made of the vine tree, from the kernels even to the husk.

5 All the days of the vow of his separation there shall no razor come upon his head; until the days be fulfilled, in the which he separateth himself unto יהוה, he shall be holy, and shall let the locks of the hair of his head grow.

6 All the days that he separateth himself unto יהוה he shall come at no dead body.

7 He shall not make himself unclean for his father, or for his mother, for his brother, or for his sister, when they die, because the consecration of his God (Elohim) is upon his head.

8 All the days of his separation he is holy unto יהוה.

9 And if any man dies very suddenly by him, and he hath defiled the head of his consecration; then he shall shave his head in the day of his cleansing, on the seventh day shall he shave it.

10 And on the eighth day he shall bring two turtles, or two young pigeons, to the priest (kohen), to the door of the tabernacle of the congregation;

11 And the priest (kohen) shall offer the one for a sin offering, and the other for a burnt offering, and make an atonement for him, for that he sinned by the dead, and shall hallow his head that same day.

12 And he shall consecrate unto יהוה the days of his separation, and shall bring a lamb of the first year for a trespass offering: but the days that were before shall be lost, because his separation was defiled.

13 And this is the law (torah) of the Nazarite (Nazir), when the days of his separation are fulfilled; he shall be brought unto the door of the tabernacle of the congregation.

14 And he shall offer his offering unto יהוה, one he lamb of the first year without blemish for a burnt offering, and one ewe lamb of the first year without blemish for a sin offering, and one ram without blemish for peace offerings,

15 And a basket of unleavened bread, cakes of fine flour mingled with oil, and wafers of unleavened bread anointed with oil, and their meat offering, and their drink offerings.

16 And the priest (kohen) shall bring them before יהוה, and shall offer his sin offering, and his burnt offering:

17 And he shall offer the ram for a sacrifice of peace offerings unto יהוה, with the basket of unleavened bread; the priest (kohen) shall offer also his meat offering, and his drink offering.

18 And the Nazarite (Nazir) shall shave the head of his separation at the door of the tabernacle of the congregation, and shall take the hair of the head of his separation, and put it in the fire which is under the sacrifice of the peace offerings.

19 And the priest (kohen) shall take the sodden shoulder of the ram, and one unleavened cake out of the basket, and one unleavened wafer, and shall put them upon the hands of the Nazarite (Nazir), after the hair of his separation is shaven;

20 And the priest (kohen) shall wave them for a wave offering before יהוה; this is holy for the priest (kohen), with the wave breast and heave shoulder. And after that the Nazarite (Nazir) may drink wine.'

21 This is the law (torah) of the Nazarite (Nazir) who hath vowed, and of his offering unto יהוה for his separation, besides that what his hand shall get; according to the vow which he vowed, so he must do after the law (torah) of his separation."

22 And יהוה spake unto Moses (Mosheh), saying,

23 "Speak unto Aaron (Aharon) and unto his sons, saying: 'On this wise you shall bless the children of Yisrael, saying unto them:

24 "יהוה bless you, and keep you;

25 יהוה make His face shine upon you, and be gracious unto you;

26 יהוה lift up His countenance upon you, and give you peace.'"

27 And they shall put My name upon the children of Yisrael; and I will bless them."

7 And it came to pass on the day that Moses (Mosheh) had fully set up the tabernacle, and had anointed it, and sanctified it, and all the instruments thereof, both the altar and all the vessels thereof, and had anointed them, and sanctified them;

2 That the princes of Yisrael, heads of the house of their fathers, who were the princes of the tribes, and were over them that were numbered, offered.

3 And they brought their offering before יהוה, six covered wagons, and twelve oxen; a wagon for two of the princes, and for each one an ox; and they brought them before the tabernacle.

4 And יהוה spake unto Moses (Mosheh), saying,

5 "Take it of them, that they may be to do the service of the tabernacle of the congregation; and you shalt give them unto the Levites (Lewiyim), to every man according to his service."

6 And Moses (Mosheh) took the wagons and the oxen, and gave them unto the Levites (Lewiyim).

7 Two wagons and four oxen he gave unto the sons of Gershon, according to their service;

8 And four wagons and eight oxen he gave unto the sons of Merari, according unto their service, under the hand of Ithamar the son of Aaron (Aharon) the priest (kohen).

9 But unto the sons of Kohath he gave none, because the service of the sanctuary belonging unto them was that they should bear upon their shoulders.

10 And the princes offered for dedicating of the altar in the day that it was anointed, even the princes offered their offering before the altar.

11 And יהוה said unto Moses (Mosheh), "They shall offer their offering, each prince on his day, for the dedicating of the altar."

12 And he that offered his offering the first day was Nahshon the son of Amminadab, of the tribe of Judah (Yehudah).

13 And his offering was one silver charger, the weight thereof was a hundred and thirty shekels, one silver bowl of seventy shekels, after the shekel of the sanctuary; both of them were full of fine flour mingled with oil for a meat offering;

14 One spoon of ten shekels of gold, full of incense;

15 One young bullock, one ram, one lamb of the first year, for a burnt offering;

16 One kid of the goats for a sin offering;

17 And for a sacrifice of peace offerings, two oxen, five rams, five he goats, five lambs of the first year. This was the offering of Nahshon the son of Amminadab.

18 On the second day Nethaneel the son of Zuar, prince of Yissaskhar, did offer.

19 He offered for his offering one silver charger, the weight whereof was a hundred and thirty shekels, one silver bowl of seventy shekels, after the shekel of the sanctuary; both of them full of fine flour mingled with oil for a meat offering;

20 One spoon of gold of ten shekels, full of incense;

21 One young bullock, one ram, one lamb of the first year, for a burnt offering;

22 One kid of the goats for a sin offering;

23 And for a sacrifice of peace offerings, two oxen, five rams, five he goats, five lambs of the first year. This was the offering of Nethaneel the son of Zuar.

24 On the third day Eliav the son of Helon, prince of the children of Zevulun, did offer.

25 His offering was one silver charger, the weight whereof was a hundred and thirty shekels, one silver bowl of seventy shekels, after the shekel of the sanctuary; both of them full of fine flour mingled with oil for a meat offering;

26 One golden spoon of ten shekels, full of incense;

27 One young bullock, one ram, one lamb of the first year, for a burnt offering;

28 One kid of the goats for a sin offering;

29 And for a sacrifice of peace offerings: two oxen, five rams, five he goats, five lambs of the first year. This was the offering of Eliav the son of Helon.

30 On the fourth day Elizur the son of Shedeur, prince of the children of Reuven, did offer.

31 His offering was one silver charger of the weight of a hundred and thirty shekels, one silver bowl of seventy shekels, after the shekel of the sanctuary; both of them full of fine flour mingled with oil for a meat offering;

32 One golden spoon of ten shekels, full of incense;

33 One young bullock, one ram, one lamb of the first year, for a burnt offering;

34 One kid of the goats for a sin offering;

35 And for a sacrifice of peace offerings, two oxen, five rams, five he goats, five lambs of the first year. This was the offering of Elizur the son of Shedeur.

36 On the fifth day Shelumiel the son of Zurishaddai, prince of the children of Shimon, did offer.

37 His offering was one silver charger, the weight whereof was a hundred and thirty shekels, one silver bowl of seventy shekels, after the shekel of the sanctuary; both of them full of fine flour mingled with oil for a meat offering;

38 One golden spoon of ten shekels, full of incense;

39 One young bullock, one ram, one lamb of the first year, for a burnt offering;

40 One kid of the goats for a sin offering;

41 And for a sacrifice of peace offerings, two oxen, five rams, five he goats, five lambs of the first year. This was the offering of Shelumiel the son of Zurishaddai.

42 On the sixth day Elijahaph the son of Deuel, prince of the children of Gad, offered.

43 His offering was one silver charger of the weight of a hundred and thirty shekels, a silver bowl of seventy shekels, after the shekel of the sanctuary; both of them full of fine flour mingled with oil for a meat offering;

44 One golden spoon of ten shekels, full of incense:

45 One young bullock, one ram, one lamb of the first year, for a burnt offering;

46 One kid of the goats for a sin offering;

47 And for a sacrifice of peace offerings, two oxen, five rams, five he goats, five lambs of the first year. This was the offering of Elijahaph the son of Deuel.

48 On the seventh day Elishama the son of Ammihud, prince of the children of Efrayim, offered.

49 His offering was one silver charger, the weight whereof was a hundred and thirty shekels, one silver bowl of seventy shekels, after the shekel of the sanctuary; both of them full of fine flour mingled with oil for a meat offering;

50 One golden spoon of ten shekels, full of incense;

51 One young bullock, one ram, one lamb of the first year, for a burnt offering;

52 One kid of the goats for a sin offering;

53 And for a sacrifice of peace offerings, two oxen, five rams, five he goats, five lambs of the first year: this was the offering of Elishama the son of Ammihud.

54 On the eighth day offered Gamaliel the son of Pedahzur, prince of the children of Menashsheh.

55 His offering was one silver charger of the weight of a hundred and thirty shekels, one silver bowl of seventy shekels, after the shekel of the sanctuary; both of them full of fine flour mingled with oil for a meat offering;

56 One golden spoon of ten shekels, full of incense;

57 One young bullock, one ram, one lamb of the first year, for a burnt offering;

58 One kid of the goats for a sin offering;

59 And for a sacrifice of peace offerings, two oxen, five rams, five he goats, five lambs of the first year. This was the offering of Gamaliel the son of Pedahzur.

60 On the ninth day Abidan the son of Gideoni, prince of the children of Binyamin, offered.

61 His offering was one silver charger, the weight whereof was a hundred and thirty shekels, one silver bowl of seventy shekels, after the shekel of the sanctuary; both of them full of fine flour mingled with oil for a meat offering;

62 One golden spoon of ten shekels, full of incense;

63 One young bullock, one ram, one lamb of the first year, for a burnt offering;

64 One kid of the goats for a sin offering;

65 And for a sacrifice of peace offerings, two oxen, five rams, five he goats, five lambs of the first year. This was the offering of Abidan the son of Gideoni.

66 On the tenth day Ahiezer the son of Ammishaddai, prince of the children of Dan, offered.

67 His offering was one silver charger, the weight whereof was a hundred and thirty shekels, one silver bowl of seventy shekels, after the shekel of the sanctuary; both of them full of fine flour mingled with oil for a meat offering;

68 One golden spoon of ten shekels, full of incense;

69 One young bullock, one ram, one lamb of the first year, for a burnt offering;

70 One kid of the goats for a sin offering;

71 And for a sacrifice of peace offerings, two

oxen, five rams, five he goats, five lambs of the first year. This was the offering of Ahiezer the son of Ammishaddai.

72 On the eleventh day Pagiel the son of Ocran, prince of the children of Asher, offered.

73 His offering was one silver charger, the weight whereof was a hundred and thirty shekels, one silver bowl of seventy shekels, after the shekel of the sanctuary; both of them full of fine flour mingled with oil for a meat offering;

74 One golden spoon of ten shekels, full of incense;

75 One young bullock, one ram, one lamb of the first year, for a burnt offering;

76 One kid of the goats for a sin offering;

77 And for a sacrifice of peace offerings, two oxen, five rams, five he goats, five lambs of the first year. This was the offering of Pagiel the son of Ocran.

78 On the twelfth day Ahira the son of Enan, prince of the children of Naftali, offered.

79 His offering was one silver charger, the weight whereof was a hundred and thirty shekels, one silver bowl of seventy shekels, after the shekel of the sanctuary; both of them full of fine flour mingled with oil for a meat offering;

80 One golden spoon of ten shekels, full of incense;

81 One young bullock, one ram, one lamb of the first year, for a burnt offering;

82 One kid of the goats for a sin offering;

83 And for a sacrifice of peace offerings, two oxen, five rams, five he goats, five lambs of the first year. This was the offering of Ahira the son of Enan.

84 This was the dedication of the altar, in the day when it was anointed, by the princes of Yisrael; twelve chargers of silver, twelve silver bowls, twelve spoons of gold.

85 Each charger of silver weighing a hundred and thirty shekels, each bowl seventy: all the silver vessels weighed two thousand and four hundred shekels, after the shekel of the sanctuary.

86 The golden spoons were twelve, full of incense, weighing ten shekels apiece, after the shekel of the sanctuary; all the gold of the spoons was a hundred and twenty shekels.

87 All the oxen for the burnt offering were twelve bullocks, the rams twelve, the lambs of the first year twelve, with their meat offering;

and the kids of the goats for sin offering twelve.

88 And all the oxen for the sacrifice of the peace offerings were twenty and four bullocks, the rams sixty, the he goats sixty, the lambs of the first year sixty. This was the dedication of the altar, after that it was anointed.

89 And when Moses (Mosheh) was gone into the tabernacle of the congregation to speak with Him, then he heard the voice of one speaking unto him from off the mercy seat that was upon the ark of Testimony, from between the two cherubims (keruvim); and He spake unto him.

8 And יהוה spake unto Moses (Mosheh), saying,

2 "Speak unto Aaron (Aharon), and say unto him: 'When you lightest the lamps, the seven lamps shall give light opposite the candlestick (menorah).'"

3 And Aaron (Aharon) did so; he lighted the lamps thereof opposite the candlestick (menorah), as יהוה commanded Moses (Mosheh).

4 And this work of the candlestick (menorah) was of beaten gold, unto the shaft thereof, unto the flowers thereof, was beaten work; according unto the pattern which יהוה had shewed Moses (Mosheh), so he made the candlestick (menorah).

5 And יהוה spake unto Moses (Mosheh), saying:

6 "Take the Levites (Lewiyim) from among the children of Yisrael, and cleanse them.

7 And thus shalt you do unto them, to cleanse them: Sprinkle water of purifying upon them, and let them shave all their flesh, and let them wash their clothes, and so make themselves clean.

8 Then let them take a young bullock with his meat offering, even fine flour mingled with oil, and another young bullock shalt you take for a sin offering.

9 And you shalt bring the Levites (Lewiyim) before the tabernacle of the congregation: and you shalt gather the whole assembly of the children of Yisrael together.

10 And you shalt bring the Levites (Lewiyim) before יהוה; and the children of Yisrael shall put their hands upon the Levites (Lewiyim);

11 And Aaron (Aharon) shall offer the Levites (Lewiyim) before יהוה for an offering of the children of Yisrael, that they may execute the service of יהוה.

12 And the Levites (Lewiyim) shall lay their

hands upon the heads of the bullocks; and you shalt offer the one for a sin offering, and the other for a burnt offering, unto יהוה, to make an atonement for the Levites (Lewiyim).

13 And you shalt set the Levites (Lewiyim) before Aaron (Aharon), and before his sons, and offer them for an offering unto יהוה.

14 Thus shalt you separate the Levites (Lewiyim) from among the children of Yisrael; and the Levites (Lewiyim) shall be Mine.

15 And after that shall the Levites (Lewiyim) go in to do the service of the tabernacle of the congregation: and you shalt cleanse them, and offer them for an offering.

16 For they are wholly given unto me from among the children of Yisrael; instead of such as open every womb, even instead of the firstborn of all the children of Yisrael, have I taken them unto Me.

17 For all the firstborn of the children of Yisrael are Mine, both man and beast; on the day that I smote every firstborn in the land of Egypt (Mitsrayim) I sanctified them for Myself.

18 And I have taken the Levites (Lewiyim) for all the firstborn of the children of Yisrael.

19 And I have given the Levites (Lewiyim) as a gift to Aaron (Aharon) and to his sons from among the children of Yisrael, to do the service of the children of Yisrael in the tabernacle of the congregation, and to make an atonement for the children of Yisrael, that there be no plague among the children of Yisrael, when the children of Yisrael come near unto the sanctuary."

20 And Moses (Mosheh), and Aaron (Aharon), and all the congregation of the children of Yisrael, did to the Levites (Lewiyim) according unto all that יהוה commanded Moses (Mosheh) concerning the Levites (Lewiyim), so did the children of Yisrael unto them.

21 And the Levites (Lewiyim) were purified, and they washed their clothes; and Aaron (Aharon) offered them as an offering before יהוה; and Aaron (Aharon) made an atonement for them to cleanse them.

22 And after that went the Levites (Lewiyim) in to do their service in the tabernacle of the congregation before Aaron (Aharon), and before his sons; as יהוה had commanded Moses (Mosheh) concerning the Levites (Lewiyim), so did they unto them.

23 And יהוה spake unto Moses (Mosheh), saying,

24 "This is it that belongeth unto the Levites (Lewiyim): From twenty and five years old and upward they shall go in to wait upon the service of the tabernacle of the congregation;

25 And from the age of fifty years they shall cease waiting upon the service thereof, and shall serve no more;

26 But shall minister with their brethren in the tabernacle of the congregation, to keep the charge, and shall do no service. Thus shalt you do unto the Levites (Lewiyim) concerning their charge."

9 And יהוה spake unto Moses (Mosheh) in the wilderness of Sinai, in the first month of the second year after they had come out of the land of Egypt (Mitsrayim), saying:

2 "Let the children of Yisrael also keep the Passover (Pesach) at its appointed season.

3 In the fourteenth day of this month, at even, you shall keep it in his appointed season. According to all the rites of it, and according to all the ceremonies thereof, shall you keep it."

4 And Moses (Mosheh) spake unto the children of Yisrael, that they should keep the Passover (Pesach).

5 And they kept the Passover (Pesach) on the fourteenth day of the first month at even in the wilderness of Sinai; according to all that יהוה commanded Moses (Mosheh), so did the children of Yisrael.

6 And there were certain men, who were defiled by the dead body of a man, that they could not keep the Passover (Pesach) on that day; and they came before Moses (Mosheh) and before Aaron (Aharon) on that day.

7 And those men said unto him, "We are defiled by the dead body of a man. Wherefore are we kept back, that we may not offer an offering of יהוה in his appointed season among the children of Yisrael?"

8 And Moses (Mosheh) said unto them, "Stand still, and I will hear what יהוה will command concerning you."

9 And יהוה spake unto Moses (Mosheh), saying,

10 "Speak unto the children of Yisrael, saying: 'If any man of you or of your posterity shall be unclean by reason of a dead body, or be in a journey afar off, yet he shall keep the Passover (Pesach) unto יהוה.

11 The fourteenth day of the second month

at even they shall keep it, and eat it with unleavened bread and bitter herbs.

12 They shall leave none of it unto the morning, nor break any bone of it; according to all the ordinances of the Passover (Pesach) they shall keep it.

13 But the man that is clean, and is not in a journey, and forbeareth to keep the Passover (Pesach), even the same soul shall be cut off from among his people, because he brought not the offering of יהוה in his appointed season, that man shall bear his sin.

14 And if a stranger shall sojourn among you, and will keep the Passover (Pesach) unto יהוה; according to the ordinance of the Passover (Pesach), and according to the manner thereof, so shall he do; you shall have one ordinance, both for the stranger, and for him that was born in the land.'"

15 And on the day that the tabernacle was reared up the cloud covered the tabernacle, namely, the tent of the Testimony; and at even there was upon the tabernacle as it was the appearance of fire, until the morning.

16 So it was always; the cloud covered it by day, and the appearance of fire by night.

17 And when the cloud was taken up from the tabernacle, then after that the children of Yisrael journeyed: and in the place where the cloud abode, there the children of Yisrael pitched their tents.

18 At the commandment of יהוה the children of Yisrael journeyed, and at the commandment of יהוה they pitched; as long as the cloud abode upon the tabernacle they rested in their tents.

19 And when the cloud tarried long upon the tabernacle many days, then the children of Yisrael kept the charge of יהוה, and journeyed not.

20 And so it was, when the cloud was a few days upon the tabernacle; according to the commandment of יהוה they abode in their tents, and according to the commandment of יהוה they journeyed.

21 And so it was, when the cloud abode from even unto the morning, and that the cloud was taken up in the morning, then they journeyed: whether it was by day or by night that the cloud was taken up, they journeyed.

22 Or whether it was two days, or a month, or a year, that the cloud tarried upon the tabernacle,

remaining thereon, the children of Yisrael abode in their tents, and journeyed not; but when it was taken up, they journeyed.

23 At the commandment of יהוה they rested in the tents, and at the commandment of יהוה they journeyed: they kept the charge of יהוה, at the commandment of יהוה by the hand of Moses (Mosheh).

10 And יהוה spake unto Moses (Mosheh), saying:

2 "Make you two trumpets of silver; of a whole piece shalt you make them; that you mayest use them for the calling of the assembly, and for the journeying of the camps.

3 And when they shall blow with them, all the assembly shall assemble themselves to you at the door of the tabernacle of the congregation.

4 And if they blow but with one trumpet, then the princes, which are heads of the thousands of Yisrael, shall gather themselves unto you.

5 When you blow an alarm, then the camps that lie on the east parts shall go forward.

6 When you blow an alarm the second time, then the camps that lie on the south side shall take their journey; they shall blow an alarm for their journeys.

7 But when the congregation is to be gathered together, you shall blow, but you shall not sound an alarm.

8 And the sons of Aaron (Aharon), the priests (kohanim), shall blow with the trumpets; and they shall be to you for an ordinance forever throughout your generations.

9 And if you go to war in your land against the enemy that oppresseth you, then you shall blow an alarm with the trumpets; and you shall be remembered before יהוה your God (YHWH Eloheikhem), and you shall be saved from your enemies.

10 Also in the day of your gladness, and in your solemn days, and in the beginnings of your months, you shall blow with the trumpets over your burnt offerings, and over the sacrifices of your peace offerings; that they may be to you for a memorial before your God (Elohim): I am יהוה your God (YHWH Eloheikhem)."

11 And it came to pass on the twentieth day of the second month, in the second year, that the cloud was taken up from off the tabernacle of the Testimony.

12 And the children of Yisrael took their

journeys out of the wilderness of Sinai; and the cloud rested in the wilderness of Paran.

13 And they first took their journey according to the commandment of יהוה by the hand of Moses (Mosheh).

14 In the first place went the standard of the camp of the children of Judah (Yehudah) according to their armies; and over his army was Nahshon the son of Amminadab.

15 And over the army of the tribe of the children of Yissaskhar was Nethaneel the son of Zuar.

16 And over the army of the tribe of the children of Zevulun was Eliav the son of Helon.

17 And the tabernacle was taken down; and the sons of Gershon and the sons of Merari set forward, bearing the tabernacle.

18 And the standard of the camp of Reuven set forward according to their armies; and over his army was Elizur the son of Shedeur.

19 And over the army of the tribe of the children of Shimon was Shelumiel the son of Zurishaddai.

20 And over the army of the tribe of the children of Gad was Elijahaph the son of Deuel.

21 And the Kohathites set forward, bearing the sanctuary; and the other did set up the tabernacle before they came.

22 And the standard of the camp of the children of Efrayim set forward according to their armies; and over his army was Elishama the son of Ammihud.

23 And over the army of the tribe of the children of Menashsheh was Gamaliel the son of Pedahzur.

24 And over the army of the tribe of the children of Binyamin was Abidan the son of Gideoni.

25 And the standard of the camp of the children of Dan set forward, which was the rereward of all the camps throughout their armies; and over his army was Ahiezer the son of Ammishaddai.

26 And over the army of the tribe of the children of Asher was Pagiel the son of Ocran.

27 And over the army of the tribe of the children of Naftali was Ahira the son of Enan.

28 Thus were the journeyings of the children of Yisrael according to their armies, when they set forward.

29 And Moses (Mosheh) said unto Hobab, the son of Raguel the Midianite, Moses (Mosheh)'s father in law, "We are journeying unto the place of which יהוה said: 'I will give it you.' Come you

with us, and we will do you good; for יהוה hath spoken good concerning Yisrael."

30 And he said unto him, I will not go; but I will depart to mine own land, and to my kindred.

31 And he said: "Please leave us not, forasmuch as you knowest how we are to encamp in the wilderness, and you mayest be to us instead of eyes.

32 And it shall be, if you go with us, yea, it shall be, that what goodness יהוה shall do unto us, the same will we do unto you."

33 And they departed from the mount of יהוה three days' journey; and the ark of the covenant of יהוה went before them in the three days' journey, to search out a resting place for them.

34 And the cloud of יהוה was upon them by day, when they went out of the camp.

35 And it came to pass, when the ark set forward, that Moses (Mosheh) said: "Rise up, O יהוה! And let your enemies be scattered; and let them that hate You flee before You."

36 And when it rested, he said: "Return, O יהוה, unto the many thousands of Yisrael."

11 And when the people complained, it displeased יהוה; and יהוה heard it, and His anger was kindled; and the fire of יהוה burnt among them, and consumed them who were in the uttermost parts of the camp.

2 And the people cried unto Moses (Mosheh); and when Moses (Mosheh) prayed unto יהוה, the fire was quenched.

3 And he called the name of the place Taberah, because the fire of יהוה burnt among them.

4 Now the mixt multitude that was among them fell a lusting; and the children of Yisrael also wept again, and said, "Who shall give us flesh to eat?

5 We remember the fish, which we did eat in Egypt (Mitsrayim) freely; the cucumbers, and the melons, and the leeks, and the onions, and the garlick;

6 But now our soul is dried away; there is nothing at all, besides this manna, before our eyes!"

7 And the manna was as coriander seed, and the colour thereof as the colour of bdellium.

8 And the people went about, and gathered it, and ground it in mills, or beat it in a mortar, and baked it in pans, and made cakes of it; and the taste of it was as the taste of fresh oil.

9 And when the dew fell upon the camp in the

night, the manna fell upon it.

10 Then Moses (Mosheh) heard the people weep throughout their families, every man in the door of his tent; and the anger of יהוה was kindled greatly; Moses (Mosheh) also was displeased.

11 And Moses (Mosheh) said unto יהוה, "Wherefore have you afflicted your servant? And wherefore have I not found favor in Your sight, that You layest the burden of all this people upon me?

12 Have I conceived all this people? Have I begotten them, that You shouldest say unto me, 'Carry them in your bosom, as a nursing father beareth the sucking child, unto the land which you swarest unto their fathers?'

13 Whence should I have flesh to give unto all this people? For they weep unto me, saying, 'Give us flesh, that we may eat.'

14 I am not able to bear all this people alone, because it is too heavy for me.

15 And if You deal thus with me, please kill me out of hand, if I have found favor in Your sight; and let me not see my wretchedness!"

16 And יהוה said unto Moses (Mosheh), "Gather unto Me seventy men of the elders of Yisrael, whom you knowest to be the elders of the people, and officers over them; and bring them unto the tabernacle of the congregation, that they may stand there with you.

17 And I will come down and talk with you there; and I will take of the Spirit which is upon you, and will put it upon them; and they shall bear the burden of the people with you, that you bear it not yourself alone.

18 And say you unto the people, 'Sanctify yourselves for tomorrow, and you shall eat flesh; for you have wept in the ears of יהוה, saying, "Who shall give us flesh to eat? For it was well with us in Egypt (Mitsrayim).' Therefore יהוה will give you flesh, and you shall eat.

19 You shall not eat one day, nor two days, nor five days, neither ten days, nor twenty days;

20 But even a whole month, until it come out at your nostrils, and it be loathsome unto you, because that you have despised יהוה who is among you, and have wept before Him, saying, "Why came we forth out of Egypt (Mitsrayim)?"'"

21 And Moses (Mosheh) said, "The people, among whom I am, are six hundred thousand footmen; and You have said, 'I will give them flesh, that they may eat a whole month.'

22 Shall the flocks and the herds be slain for them, to suffice them? Or shall all the fish of the sea be gathered together for them, to suffice them?"

23 And יהוה said unto Moses (Mosheh), "Is יהוה's hand waxed short? You shalt see now whether My word shall come to pass unto you or not."

24 And Moses (Mosheh) went out, and told the people the words of יהוה, and gathered the seventy men of the elders of the people, and set them round about the tabernacle.

25 And יהוה came down in a cloud, and spake unto him, and took of the Spirit that was upon him, and gave it unto the seventy elders; and it came to pass, that, when the Spirit rested upon them, they prophesied, and did not cease.

26 But there remained two of the men in the camp, the name of the one was Eldad, and the name of the other Medad; and the Spirit rested upon them; and they were of them that were written, but went not out unto the tabernacle; and they prophesied in the camp.

27 And there ran a young man, and told Moses (Mosheh), and said, "Eldad and Medad do prophesy in the camp."

28 And Joshua (Yehoshua) the son of Nun, the servant of Moses (Mosheh), one of his young men, answered and said, "My lord (Adoni) Moses (Mosheh), forbid them!"

29 And Moses (Mosheh) said unto him, "Enviest you for my sake? Would that all יהוה's people were prophets, and that יהוה would put His Spirit upon them!"

30 And Moses (Mosheh) gat him into the camp, he and the elders of Yisrael.

31 And there went forth a wind from יהוה, and brought quails from the sea, and let them fall by the camp, as it was a day's journey on this side, and as it was a day's journey on the other side, round about the camp, and as it was two cubits high upon the face of the earth.

32 And the people stood up all that day, and all that night, and all the next day, and they gathered the quails; he that gathered least gathered ten homers; and they spread them all abroad for themselves round about the camp.

33 And while the flesh was yet between their teeth, ere it was chewed, the wrath of יהוה was

kindled against the people, and יהוה smote the people with a very great plague.

34 And he called the name of that place 'Qivrot Hattaavah (Graves of Lust)', because there they buried the people who lusted.

35 And the people journeyed from Qivrot Hattaavah unto Hazeroth; and abode at Hazeroth.

12 And Miryam and Aaron (Aharon) spake against Moses (Mosheh) because of the Ethiopian (Kushi) woman whom he had married; for he had married an Ethiopian (Kushi) woman.

2 And they said, "Hath יהוה indeed spoken only by Moses (Mosheh)? Hath he not spoken also by us?" And יהוה heard it.

3 (Now the man Moses (Mosheh) was very meek, above all the men who were upon the face of the earth.)

4 And יהוה spake suddenly unto Moses (Mosheh), and unto Aaron (Aharon), and unto Miryam, "Come out you three unto the tabernacle of the congregation." And they three came out.

5 And יהוה came down in the pillar of the cloud, and stood in the door of the tabernacle, and called Aaron (Aharon) and Miryam; and they both came forth.

6 And He said, "Hear now My words: If there be a prophet among you, I יהוה will make Myself known unto him in a vision, and will speak unto him in a dream.

7 My servant Moses (Mosheh) is not so, who is faithful in all Mine house.

8 With him will I speak mouth to mouth, even apparently, and not in dark speeches; and the similitude of יהוה shall he behold. Wherefore then were you not afraid to speak against My servant Moses (Mosheh)?"

9 And the anger of יהוה was kindled against them, and He departed.

10 And the cloud departed from off the tabernacle; and, behold, Miryam became leprous, white as snow; and Aaron (Aharon) looked upon Miryam, and, behold, she was leprous.

11 And Aaron (Aharon) said unto Moses (Mosheh), "Alas, my lord (adoni), I beseech you, lay not the sin upon us, wherein we have done foolishly, and wherein we have sinned.

12 Let her not be as one dead, of whom the flesh is half consumed when he cometh out of his mother's womb!"

13 And Moses (Mosheh) cried unto יהוה, saying, "Heal her now, O God (Elohim), I beseech You."

14 And יהוה said unto Moses (Mosheh), "If her father had but spit in her face, should she not be ashamed seven days? Let her be shut out from the camp seven days, and after that let her be received in again."

15 And Miryam was shut out from the camp seven days; and the people journeyed not till Miryam was brought in again.

16 And afterward the people moved from Hazeroth, and pitched in the wilderness of Paran.

13 And יהוה spake unto Moses (Mosheh), saying:

2 "Send you men, that they may search the land of Canaan, which I give unto the children of Yisrael; of every tribe of their fathers shall you send a man, every one a ruler among them.

3 And Moses (Mosheh) by the commandment of יהוה sent them from the wilderness of Paran; all those men were heads of the children of Yisrael.

4 And these were their names: of the tribe of Reuven, Shammua the son of Zaccur.

5 Of the tribe of Shimon, Shaphat the son of Hori.

6 Of the tribe of Judah (Yehudah), Caleb the son of Yefunneh.

7 Of the tribe of Yissaskhar, Igal the son of Joseph (Yosef).

8 Of the tribe of Efrayim, [A32]Joshua (Hoshea) the son of Nun.

9 Of the tribe of Binyamin, Palti the son of Raphu.

10 Of the tribe of Zevulun, Gaddiel the son of Sodi.

11 Of the tribe of Joseph (Yosef), namely, of the tribe of Menashsheh, Gaddi the son of Susi.

12 Of the tribe of Dan, Ammiel the son of Gemalli.

13 Of the tribe of Asher, Sethur the son of Mikhael.

14 Of the tribe of Naftali, Nahbi the son of Vophsi.

15 Of the tribe of Gad, Geuel the son of Machi.

16 These are the names of the men whom Moses (Mosheh) sent to spy out the land. And Moses (Mosheh) called [A32]Hoshea the son of Nun Joshua (Yehoshua).

17 And Moses (Mosheh) sent them to spy out the land of Canaan, and said unto them, "Get you up this way southward, and go up into the mountain,

18 And see the land, what it is; and the people that dwelleth therein, whether they be strong or weak, few or many;

19 And what the land is that they dwell in, whether it be good or bad; and what cities they be that they dwell in, whether in tents, or in strong holds;

20 And what the land is, whether it be fat or lean, whether there be wood therein, or not. And be you of good courage, and bring of the fruit of the land. Now the time was the time of the firstripe grapes.

21 So they went up, and searched the land from the wilderness of Zin unto Rehob, as men come to Hamath.

22 And they ascended by the south, and came unto Hebron; where Ahiman, Sheshai, and Talmai, the children of Anak, were. (Now Hebron was built seven years before Zoan in Egypt (Mitsrayim).)

23 And they came unto the Brook of Eshcol, and cut down from thence a branch with one cluster of grapes, and they bare it between two upon a staff; and they brought of the pomegranates, and of the figs.

24 The place was called the brook Eshcol, because of the cluster of grapes which the children of Yisrael cut down from thence.

25 And they returned from searching of the land after forty days.

26 And they went and came to Moses (Mosheh), and to Aaron (Aharon), and to all the congregation of the children of Yisrael, unto the wilderness of Paran, to Qadesh; and brought back word unto them, and unto all the congregation, and shewed them the fruit of the land.

27 And they told him, and said, "We came unto the land whither you sentest us, and surely it floweth with milk and honey; and this is the fruit of it.

28 Nevertheless the people be strong that dwell in the land, and the cities are walled, and very great; and moreover we saw the children of Anak there.

29 The Amalekites dwell in the land of the south; and the Hittites, and the Yevus, and

the Amorites, dwell in the mountains; and the Canaanites dwell by the sea, and by the coast of Jordan (Yarden)."

30 And Caleb stilled the people before Moses (Mosheh), and said, "Let us go up at once, and possess it; for we are well able to overcome it."

31 But the men that went up with him said, "We be not able to go up against the people, for they are stronger than we."

32 And they brought up an evil report of the land which they had searched unto the children of Yisrael, saying, "The land, through which we have gone to search it, is a land that eateth up the inhabitants thereof; and all the people that we saw in it are men of a great stature.

33 And there we saw the giants (Nefilim), the sons of Anaq, who come of the giants (Nefilim); and we were in our own sight as grasshoppers, and so we were in their sight."

14 And all the congregation lifted up their voice, and cried; and the people wept that night.

2 And all the children of Yisrael murmured against Moses (Mosheh) and against Aaron (Aharon), and the whole congregation said unto them, "If only that we had died in the land of Egypt (Mitsrayim)! Or if only we had died in this wilderness!

3 And wherefore hath יהוה brought us unto this land, to fall by the sword, that our wives and our children should be a prey? Was it not better for us to return into Egypt (Mitsrayim)?"

4 And they said one to another, "Let us make a captain, and let us return into Egypt (Mitsrayim)."

5 Then Moses (Mosheh) and Aaron (Aharon) fell on their faces before all the assembly of the congregation of the children of Yisrael.

6 And Joshua (Yehoshua) the son of Nun, and Caleb the son of Yefunneh, which were of them that searched the land, rent their clothes;

7 And they spake unto all the company of the children of Yisrael, saying, "The land, which we passed through to search it, is an exceeding good land.

8 If יהוה delight in us, then He will bring us into this land, and give it us; 'a land which floweth with milk and honey.'

9 Only rebel not you against יהוה, neither fear you the people of the land; for they are bread for us; their defence is departed from them, and

יהוה is with us; fear them not.

10 But all the congregation bade stone them with stones. And the glory of יהוה appeared in the tabernacle of the congregation before all the children of Yisrael.

11 And יהוה said unto Moses (Mosheh), "How long will this people provoke Me? And how long will it be ere they believe Me, for all the signs which I have shewed among them?

12 I will smite them with the pestilence, and disinherit them, and will make of you a greater nation and mightier than they."

13 And Moses (Mosheh) said unto יהוה, "Then the Egyptians (Mitsrayim) shall hear it, (for You broughtest up this people in Your might from among them;)

14 And they will tell it to the inhabitants of this land; for they have heard that You יהוה art among this people, that You יהוה art seen face to face, and that Your cloud standeth over them, and that You goest before them, by day time in a pillar of a cloud, and in a pillar of fire by night.

15 Now if You shalt kill all this people as one man, then the nations which have heard the fame of You will speak, saying,

16 'Because יהוה was not able to bring this people into the land which He sware unto them, therefore He hath slain them in the wilderness.'

17 And now, I beseech You, let the power of my Lord (Adonai) be great, according as You have spoken, saying,

18 'יהוה is longsuffering, and of great mercy, forgiving iniquity and transgression, and by no means clearing the guilty, visiting the iniquity of the fathers upon the children unto the third and fourth generation.'

19 Pardon, I beseech You, the iniquity of this people according unto the greatness of Your mercy, and as You have forgiven this people, from Egypt (Mitsrayim) even until now."

20 And יהוה said, "I have pardoned according to your word;

21 But as truly as I live, all the earth shall be filled with the glory of יהוה.

22 Because all those men who have seen My glory, and My miracles, which I did in Egypt (Mitsrayim) and in the wilderness, and have tempted Me now these ten times, and have not hearkened to My voice,

23 Surely they shall not see the land which I sware unto their fathers, neither shall any of them who provoked Me, see it;

24 But My servant Caleb, because he had another spirit with him, and hath followed Me fully, him will I bring into the land whereinto he went; and his seed shall possess it."

25 (Now the Amalekites and the Canaanites dwelt in the valley.) To morrow turn you, and get you into the wilderness by the way of the Red sea."

26 And יהוה spake unto Moses (Mosheh) and unto Aaron (Aharon), saying,

27 "How long shall I bear with this evil congregation, who murmur against Me? I have heard the murmurings of the children of Yisrael, which they murmur against Me.

28 Say unto them, 'As truly as I live', saith יהוה, 'as you have spoken in Mine ears, so will I do to you:

29 Your carcasses shall fall in this wilderness; and all that were numbered of you, according to your whole number, from twenty years old and upward, which have murmured against Me,

30 Doubtless you shall not come into the land, concerning which I sware to make you dwell therein, except Caleb the son of Yefunneh, and Joshua (Yehoshua) the son of Nun.

31 But your little ones, which you said should be a prey, them will I bring in, and they shall know the land which you have despised.

32 But as for you, your carcasses, they shall fall in this wilderness.

33 And your children shall wander in the wilderness forty years, and bear your whoredoms, until your carcasses be wasted in the wilderness.

34 After the number of the days in which you searched the land, even forty days, each day for a year, shall you bear your iniquities, even forty years, and you shall know My breach of promise.

35 I יהוה have said, I will surely do it unto all this evil congregation, who are gathered together against Me; in this wilderness they shall be consumed, and there they shall die.'"

36 And the men, whom Moses (Mosheh) sent to search the land, who returned, and made all the congregation to murmur against him, by bringing up a slander upon the land,

37 Even those men who did bring up the evil report upon the land, died by the plague before יהוה.

38 But Joshua (Yehoshua) the son of Nun, and Caleb the son of Yefunneh, which were of the men that went to search the land, lived still.

39 And Moses (Mosheh) told these sayings unto all the children of Yisrael: and the people mourned greatly.

40 And they rose up early in the morning, and gat them up into the top of the mountain, saying, Lo, we be here, and will go up unto the place which יהוה hath promised, for we have sinned!'

41 And Moses (Mosheh) said, "Wherefore now do you transgress the commandment of יהוה? But it shall not prosper.

42 Go not up, for יהוה is not among you; that you be not smitten before your enemies.

43 For the Amalekites and the Canaanites are there before you, and you shall fall by the sword; because you are turned away from יהוה, therefore יהוה will not be with you."

44 But they presumed to go up unto the hill top; nevertheless the ark of the covenant of יהוה, and Moses (Mosheh), departed not out of the camp.

45 Then the Amalekites, and the Canaanites who dwelt in that hill, came down and smote them, and discomfited them, even unto Hormah.

15 And יהוה spake unto Moses (Mosheh), saying,

2 "Speak unto the children of Yisrael, and say unto them: 'When you have come into the land of your habitations, which I give unto you,

3 And will make an offering by fire unto יהוה, a burnt offering, or a sacrifice in performing a vow, or in a freewill offering, or in your solemn feasts, to make a sweet savour unto יהוה, of the herd, or of the flock,

4 Then shall he who offereth his offering unto יהוה bring a meat offering of a tenth deal of flour mingled with the fourth part of an hin of oil.

5 And the fourth part of an hin of wine for a drink offering shalt you prepare with the burnt offering or sacrifice, for one lamb.

6 Or for a ram, you shalt prepare for a meat offering two tenth deals of flour mingled with the third part of an hin of oil.

7 And for a drink offering you shalt offer the third part of an hin of wine, for a sweet savour unto יהוה.

8 And when you preparest a bullock for a burnt offering, or for a sacrifice in performing a vow, or peace offerings unto יהוה.

9 Then shall he bring with a bullock a meat offering of three tenth deals of flour mingled with half an hin of oil.

10 And you shalt bring for a drink offering half an hin of wine, for an offering made by fire, of a sweet savour unto יהוה.

11 Thus shall it be done for one bullock, or for one ram, or for a lamb, or a kid.

12 According to the number that you shall prepare, so shall you do to every one according to their number.

13 All that are born of the country shall do these things after this manner, in offering an offering made by fire, of a sweet savour unto יהוה.

14 And if a stranger sojourn with you, or whosoever be among you in your generations, and will offer an offering made by fire, of a sweet savour unto יהוה; as you do, so he shall do.

15 One ordinance shall be both for you of the congregation, and also for the stranger that sojourneth with you, an ordinance forever in your generations; as you are, so shall the stranger be before יהוה.

16 One law (torah) and one manner shall be for you, and for the stranger that sojourneth with you.

17 And יהוה spake unto Moses (Mosheh), saying,

18 "Speak unto the children of Yisrael, and say unto them: 'When you come into the land whither I bring you,

19 Then it shall be, that, when you eat of the bread of the land, you shall offer up a heave offering unto יהוה.

20 You shall offer up a cake of the first of your dough for a heave offering; as you do the heave offering of the threshingfloor, so shall you heave it.

21 Of the first of your dough you shall give unto יהוה an heave offering in your generations.

22 And if you have erred, and not observed all these commandments, which יהוה hath spoken unto Moses (Mosheh),

23 Even all that יהוה hath commanded you by the hand of Moses (Mosheh), from the day that יהוה commanded Moses (Mosheh), and henceforward among your generations;

24 Then it shall be, if it is committed by ignorance without the knowledge of the congregation, that all the congregation shall offer one young bullock for a burnt offering, for

a sweet savour unto יהוה, with his meat offering, and his drink offering, according to the manner, and one kid of the goats for a sin offering.

25 And the priest (kohen) shall make an atonement for all the congregation of the children of Yisrael, and it shall be forgiven them; for it is ignorance; and they shall bring their offering, a sacrifice made by fire unto יהוה, and their sin offering before יהוה, for their ignorance.

26 And it shall be forgiven all the congregation of the children of Yisrael, and the stranger that sojourneth among them; seeing all the people were in ignorance.

27 And if any soul sin through ignorance, then he shall bring a she goat of the first year for a sin offering.

28 And the priest (kohen) shall make an atonement for the soul that sinneth ignorantly, when he sinneth by ignorance before יהוה, to make an atonement for him; and it shall be forgiven him.

29 You shall have one law (torah) for him that sinneth through ignorance, both for him that is born among the children of Yisrael, and for the stranger that sojourneth among them.

30 But the soul that doeth ought presumptuously, whether he be born in the land, or a stranger, the same reproacheth יהוה; and that soul shall be cut off from among his people.

31 Because he hath despised the word of יהוה, and hath broken His commandment, that soul shall utterly be cut off; his iniquity shall be upon him.'"

32 And while the children of Yisrael were in the wilderness, they found a man that gathered sticks upon the Shabbat day.

33 And they that found him gathering sticks brought him unto Moses (Mosheh) and Aaron (Aharon), and unto all the congregation.

34 And they put him in ward, because it was not declared what should be done to him.

35 And יהוה said unto Moses (Mosheh), "The man shall be surely put to death; all the congregation shall stone him with stones outside the camp.

36 And all the congregation brought him outside the camp, and stoned him with stones, and he died, as יהוה commanded Moses (Mosheh).

37 And יהוה spake unto Moses (Mosheh), saying,

38 "Speak unto the children of Yisrael, and bid them that they make them tassels in the corners of their garments throughout their generations, and that they put upon the tassels of the corners a ribband of blue.

39 And it shall be unto you for a tassel, that you may look upon it, and remember all the commandments of יהוה, and do them; and that you seek not after your own heart and your own eyes, after which you use to go a whoring,

40 That you may remember, and do all My commandments, and be holy unto your God (Elohim).

41 I am יהוה your God (YWH Eloheikhem), who brought you out of the land of Egypt (Mitsrayim), to be your God (Elohim): I am יהוה your God (YHWH Eloheikhem)."

16 Now Korah (Qorach), the son of Izhar, the son of Kohath, the son of Lewi, and Dathan and Aviram, the sons of Eliav, and On, the son of Peleth, sons of Reuven, took men;

2 And they rose up before Moses (Mosheh), with certain of the children of Yisrael, two hundred and fifty princes of the assembly, famous in the congregation, men of renown.

3 And they gathered themselves together against Moses (Mosheh) and against Aaron (Aharon), and said unto them, "You take too much upon you, seeing all the congregation are holy, every one of them, and יהוה is among them. Wherefore then lift you up yourselves above the congregation of יהוה?"

4 And when Moses (Mosheh) heard it, he fell upon his face;

5 And he spake unto Korah (Qorach) and unto all his company, saying, "Tomorrow יהוה will shew who are His, and who is holy; and will cause him to come near unto Him; him whom he hath chosen will He cause to come near unto Him.

6 This do: Take you censers, Korah (Qorach), and all his company;

7 And put fire therein, and put incense in them before יהוה tomorrow; and it shall be that the man whom יהוה doth choose, he shall be holy. You take too much upon you, you sons of Lewi!"

8 And Moses (Mosheh) said unto Korah (Qorach), "Please hear, you sons of Lewi:

9 Seemeth it but a small thing unto you, that the God of Israel (Elohei Yisrael) hath separated you from the congregation of Yisrael, to bring

you near to Himself to do the service of the tabernacle of יהוה, and to stand before the congregation to minister unto them?

10 And He hath brought you near to Him, and all your brethren the sons of Lewi with you; and seek you the priesthood (kehunnah) also?

11 For which cause both you and all your company are gathered together against יהוה. And what is Aaron (Aharon), that you murmur against him?"

12 And Moses (Mosheh) sent to call Dathan and Abiram, the sons of Eliav, who said, "We will not come up!

13 Is it a small thing that you have brought us up out of a land that floweth with milk and honey, to kill us in the wilderness, except you make yourself altogether a prince over us?

14 Moreover you have not brought us into a land that floweth with milk and honey, or given us inheritance of fields and vineyards. Wilt you put out the eyes of these men? We will not come up!"

15 And Moses (Mosheh) was very wroth, and said unto יהוה, "Respect not You their offering. I have not taken one ass from them, neither have I hurt one of them."

16 And Moses (Mosheh) said unto Korah (Qorach), "Be you and all your company present before יהוה, you, and they, and Aaron (Aharon), tomorrow.

17 And take every man his censer, and put incense in them, and bring you before יהוה every man his censer, two hundred and fifty censers; you also, and Aaron (Aharon), each of you his censer.

18 And they took every man his censer, and put fire in them, and laid incense thereon, and stood in the door of the tabernacle of the congregation with Moses (Mosheh) and Aaron (Aharon).

19 And Korah (Qorach) gathered all the congregation against them unto the door of the tabernacle of the congregation; and the glory of יהוה appeared unto all the congregation.

20 And יהוה spake unto Moses (Mosheh) and unto Aaron (Aharon), saying,

21 "Separate yourselves from among this congregation, that I may consume them in a moment."

22 And they fell upon their faces, and said, "O God (El), God (Elohim) of the spirits of all flesh, shall one man sin, and wilt You be wroth with all the congregation?"

23 And יהוה spake unto Moses (Mosheh), saying,

24 "Speak unto the congregation, saying, 'Get you up from about the tabernacle of Korah (Qorach), Dathan, and Abiram.'"

25 And Moses (Mosheh) rose up and went unto Dathan and Abiram; and the elders of Yisrael followed him.

26 And he spake unto the congregation, saying, "Please depart from the tents of these wicked men, and touch nothing of theirs, lest you be consumed in all their sins."

27 So they gat up from the tabernacle of Korah (Qorach), Dathan, and Abiram, on every side; and Dathan and Abiram came out, and stood in the door of their tents, and their wives, and their sons, and their little children.

28 And Moses (Mosheh) said, "Hereby you shall know that יהוה hath sent me to do all these works; for I have not done them of mine own mind.

29 If these men die the common death of all men, or if they be visited after the visitation of all men; then יהוה hath not sent me.

30 But if יהוה make a new thing, and the earth open her mouth, and swallow them up, with all that appertain unto them, and they go down quick into the pit; then you shall understand that these men have provoked יהוה."

31 And it came to pass, as he had made an end of speaking all these words, that the ground that was under them split apart;

32 And the earth opened her mouth, and swallowed them up, and their houses, and all the men that appertained unto Korah (Qorach), and all their goods.

33 They, and all that appertained to them, went down alive into the pit, and the earth closed upon them, and they perished from among the congregation.

34 And all Yisrael who were round about them fled at the cry of them, for they said, "Lest the earth swallow us up also."

35 And there came out a fire from יהוה, and consumed the two hundred and fifty men who offered incense.

36 And יהוה spake unto Moses (Mosheh), saying,

37 Speak unto Eleazar the son of Aaron (Aharon) the priest (kohen), that he takes up

the censers out of the burning, and scatter you the fire yonder; for they are sanctified.

38 The censers of these sinners against their own souls, let them make them broad plates for a covering of the altar, for they offered them before יהוה, therefore they are sanctified; and they shall be a sign unto the children of Yisrael."

39 And Eleazar the priest (kohen) took the brasen censers, wherewith they that were burnt had offered; and they were made broad plates for a covering of the altar,

40 To be a memorial unto the children of Yisrael, that no stranger, who is not of the seed of Aaron (Aharon), come near to offer incense before יהוה; that he be not as Korah (Qorach), and as his company, as יהוה said to him by the hand of Moses (Mosheh).

41 But on the next day all the congregation of the children of Yisrael murmured against Moses (Mosheh) and against Aaron (Aharon), saying, "You have killed the people of יהוה"

42 And it came to pass, when the congregation was gathered against Moses (Mosheh) and against Aaron (Aharon), that they looked toward the tabernacle of the congregation; and, behold, the cloud covered it, and the glory of יהוה appeared.

43 And Moses (Mosheh) and Aaron (Aharon) came before the tabernacle of the congregation.

44 And יהוה spake unto Moses (Mosheh), saying,

45 "Get you up from among this congregation, that I may consume them as in a moment." And they fell upon their faces.

46 And Moses (Mosheh) said unto Aaron (Aharon), "Take a censer, and put fire therein from off the altar, and put on incense, and go quickly unto the congregation, and make an atonement for them; for there is wrath gone out from יהוה; the plague has begun."

47 And Aaron (Aharon) took as Moses (Mosheh) commanded, and ran into the midst of the congregation; and, behold, the plague had begun among the people. And he put on incense, and made an atonement for the people.

48 And he stood between the dead and the living; and the plague was stopped.

49 Now they who died in the plague were fourteen thousand and seven hundred, besides them who died about the matter of Korah (Qorach).

50 And Aaron (Aharon) returned unto Moses (Mosheh) unto the door of the tabernacle of the congregation; for the plague had stopped.

17 And יהוה spake unto Moses (Mosheh), saying:

2 "Speak unto the children of Yisrael, and take of every one of them a rod according to the house of their fathers, of all their princes according to the house of their fathers twelve rods: write you every man's name upon his rod.

3 And you shalt write Aaron (Aharon)'s name upon the rod of Lewi; for one rod shall be for the head of the house of their fathers.

4 And you shalt lay them up in the tabernacle of the congregation before the Testimony, where I will meet with you.

5 And it shall come to pass, that the man's rod, whom I shall choose, shall blossom; and I will make to cease from me the murmurings of the children of Yisrael, whereby they murmur against you.

6 And Moses (Mosheh) spake unto the children of Yisrael, and every one of their princes gave him a rod apiece, for each prince one, according to their fathers' houses, even twelve rods; and the rod of Aaron (Aharon) was among their rods.

7 And Moses (Mosheh) laid up the rods before יהוה in the tabernacle of witness.

8 And it came to pass, that on the next day Moses (Mosheh) went into the tabernacle of witness; and, behold, the rod of Aaron (Aharon) for the house of Lewi was budded, and brought forth buds, and bloomed blossoms, and yielded almonds.

9 And Moses (Mosheh) brought out all the rods from before יהוה unto all the children of Yisrael; and they looked, and took every man his rod.

10 And יהוה said unto Moses (Mosheh), "Bring Aaron (Aharon)'s rod again before the Testimony, to be kept for a token against the rebels; and you shalt quite take away their murmurings from Me, that they die not."

11 And Moses (Mosheh) did so; as יהוה commanded him, so did he.

12 And the children of Yisrael spake unto Moses (Mosheh), saying, "Behold, we die, we perish, we all perish!

13 Whosoever cometh anything near unto the tabernacle of יהוה shall die: shall we perish completely?"

18

And יהוה said unto Aaron (Aharon): "You and your sons and your father's house with you shall bear the iniquity of the sanctuary; and you and your sons with you shall bear the iniquity of your priesthood (kehunnah).

2 And your brethren also of the tribe of Lewi, the tribe of your father, bring you with you, that they may be joined unto you, and minister unto you; but you and your sons with you shall minister before the tabernacle of witness.

3 And they shall keep your charge, and the charge of all the tabernacle; only they shall not come near the vessels of the sanctuary and the altar, that neither they, nor you also, die.

4 And they shall be joined unto you, and keep the charge of the tabernacle of the congregation, for all the service of the tabernacle; but a stranger shall not come near unto you.

5 And you shall keep the charge of the sanctuary, and the charge of the altar, that there be no wrath anymore upon the children of Yisrael.

6 And I, behold, I have taken your brethren the Levites (Lewiyim) from among the children of Yisrael; to you they are given as a gift for יהוה, to do the service of the tabernacle of the congregation.

7 Therefore you and your sons with you shall keep your priest's office (kehunnah) for everything of the altar, and within the vail; and you shall serve. I have given your priest's office (kehunnah) unto you as a service of gift; and the stranger that cometh near shall be put to death.

8 And יהוה spake unto Aaron (Aharon), Behold, I also have given you the charge of Mine heave offerings of all the hallowed things of the children of Yisrael; unto you have I given them by reason of the anointing, and to your sons, by an ordinance forever.

9 This shall be your of the most holy things, reserved from the fire; every oblation of theirs, every meat offering of theirs, and every sin offering of theirs, and every trespass offering of theirs, which they shall render unto me, shall be most holy for you and for your sons.

10 In the most holy place shalt you eat it; every male shall eat it. It shall be holy unto you.

11 And this is yours: the heave offering of their gift, with all the wave offerings of the children of Yisrael; I have given them unto you, and to your sons and to your daughters with you, by a statute forever. Everyone who is clean in your house shall eat of it.

12 All the best of the oil, and all the best of the wine, and of the wheat, the firstfruits of them which they shall offer unto יהוה, them have I given you.

13 And whatsoever is first ripe in the land, which they shall bring unto יהוה, shall be yours; everyone who is clean in your house shall eat of it.

14 Every thing devoted in Yisrael shall be yours.

15 Every thing that openeth the matrix in all flesh, which they bring unto יהוה, whether it be of men or beasts, shall be yours; nevertheless the firstborn of man shalt you surely redeem, and the firstling of unclean beasts shalt you redeem.

16 And those that are to be redeemed from a month old shalt you redeem, according to your estimation, for the money of five shekels, after the shekel of the sanctuary, which is twenty gerahs.

17 But the firstling of a cow, or the firstling of a sheep, or the firstling of a goat, you shalt not redeem; they are holy. You shalt sprinkle their blood upon the altar, and shalt burn their fat for an offering made by fire, for a sweet savour unto יהוה.

18 And the flesh of them shall be yours, as the wave breast and as the right shoulder are yours.

19 All the heave offerings of the holy things, which the children of Yisrael offer unto יהוה, have I given you, and your sons and your daughters with you, by a statute forever; it is a covenant of salt forever before יהוה unto you and to your seed with you.

20 And יהוה spake unto Aaron (Aharon): "You shalt have no inheritance in their land, neither shalt you have any part among them; I am your part and your inheritance among the children of Yisrael.

21 And, behold, I have given the children of Lewi all the tenth in Yisrael for an inheritance, for their service which they serve, even the service of the tabernacle of the congregation.

22 Neither must the children of Yisrael henceforth come near the tabernacle of the congregation, lest they bear sin, and die.

23 But the Levites (Lewiyim) shall do the service of the tabernacle of the congregation, and they shall bear their iniquity; it shall be

a statute forever throughout your generations, that among the children of Yisrael they have no inheritance.

24 But the tithes of the children of Yisrael, which they offer as a heave offering unto יהוה, I have given to the Levites (Lewiyim) to inherit; therefore I have said unto them, 'Among the children of Yisrael they shall have no inheritance.'"

25 And יהוה spake unto Moses (Mosheh), saying,

26 "Thus speak unto the Levites (Lewiyim), and say unto them: 'When you take of the children of Yisrael the tithes which I have given you from them for your inheritance, then you shall offer up a heave offering of it for יהוה, even a tenth part of the tithe.

27 And this your heave offering shall be reckoned unto you, as though it was the corn of the threshingfloor, and as the fulness of the winepress.

28 Thus you also shall offer a heave offering unto יהוה of all your tithes, which you receive of the children of Yisrael; and you shall give thereof יהוה's heave offering to Aaron (Aharon) the priest (kohen).

29 Out of all your gifts you shall offer every heave offering of יהוה, of all the best thereof, even the hallowed part thereof out of it.'

30 Therefore you shalt say unto them: 'When you have heaved the best thereof from it, then it shall be counted unto the Levites (Lewiyim) as the increase of the threshingfloor, and as the increase of the winepress.

31 And you shall eat it in every place, you and your households, for it is your reward for your service in the tabernacle of the congregation.

32 And you shall bear no sin by reason of it, when you have heaved from it the best of it; neither shall you pollute the holy things of the children of Yisrael, lest you die.'"

19 And יהוה spake unto Moses (Mosheh) and unto Aaron (Aharon), saying,

2 "This is the ordinance of the law (torah) which יהוה hath commanded, saying: 'Speak unto the children of Yisrael, that they bring you a red heifer without spot, wherein is no blemish, and upon which never came yoke.

3 And you shall give her unto Eleazar the priest (kohen), that he may bring her forth outside the camp, and one shall slay her before his face;

4 And Eleazar the priest (kohen) shall take of her blood with his finger, and sprinkle of her blood directly before the tabernacle of the congregation seven times.

5 And one shall burn the heifer in his sight; her skin, and her flesh, and her blood, with her dung, shall he burn.

6 And the priest (kohen) shall take cedar wood, and hyssop, and scarlet, and cast it into the midst of the burning of the heifer.

7 Then the priest (kohen) shall wash his clothes, and he shall bathe his flesh in water, and afterward he shall come into the camp, and the priest (kohen) shall be unclean until the even.

8 And he that burneth her shall wash his clothes in water, and bathe his flesh in water, and shall be unclean until the even.

9 And a man that is clean shall gather up the ashes of the heifer, and lay them up outside the camp in a clean place, and it shall be kept for the congregation of the children of Yisrael for a water of separation; it is a purification for sin.

10 And he that gathereth the ashes of the heifer shall wash his clothes, and be unclean until the even. And it shall be unto the children of Yisrael, and unto the stranger that sojourneth among them, for a statute forever.

11 He that toucheth the dead body of any man shall be unclean seven days.

12 He shall purify himself with it on the third day, and on the seventh day he shall be clean; but if he purifies not himself the third day, then the seventh day he shall not be clean.

13 Whosoever toucheth the dead body of any man that is dead, and purifieth not himself, defileth the tabernacle of יהוה; and that soul shall be cut off from Yisrael, because the water of separation was not sprinkled upon him, he shall be unclean; his uncleanness is yet upon him.

14 This is the law (torah): when a man dieth in a tent: All that come into the tent, and all that is in the tent, shall be unclean seven days.

15 And every open vessel, which hath no covering bound upon it, is unclean.

16 And whosoever toucheth one that is slain with a sword in the open fields, or a dead body, or a bone of a man, or a grave, shall be unclean seven days.

17 And for an unclean person they shall take of the ashes of the burnt heifer of purification

for sin, and running water shall be put thereto in a vessel.

18 And a clean person shall take hyssop, and dip it in the water, and sprinkle it upon the tent, and upon all the vessels, and upon the persons that were there, and upon him that touched a bone, or one slain, or one dead, or a grave.

19 And the clean person shall sprinkle upon the unclean on the third day, and on the seventh day; and on the seventh day he shall purify himself, and wash his clothes, and bathe himself in water, and shall be clean at even.

20 But the man that shall be unclean, and shall not purify himself, that soul shall be cut off from among the congregation, because he hath defiled the sanctuary of יהוה. The water of separation hath not been sprinkled upon him; he is unclean.

21 And it shall be a perpetual statute unto them, that he that sprinkleth the water of separation shall wash his clothes; and he that toucheth the water of separation shall be unclean until even.

22 And whatsoever the unclean person toucheth shall be unclean; and the soul that toucheth it shall be unclean until even.'"

20 Then came the children of Yisrael, even the whole congregation, into the desert of Zin in the first month, and the people abode in Qadesh; and Miryam died there, and was buried there.

2 And there was no water for the congregation; and they gathered themselves together against Moses (Mosheh) and against Aaron (Aharon).

3 And the people chode with Moses (Mosheh), and spake, saying: "If only we had died when our brethren died before יהוה!

4 And why have you brought up the congregation of יהוה into this wilderness, that we and our cattle should die there?

5 And wherefore have you made us to come up out of Egypt (Mitsrayim), to bring us in unto this evil place? It is no place of seed, or of figs, or of vines, or of pomegranates; neither is there any water to drink."

6 And Moses (Mosheh) and Aaron (Aharon) went from the presence of the assembly unto the door of the tabernacle of the congregation, and they fell upon their faces. And the glory of יהוה appeared unto them.

7 And יהוה spake unto Moses (Mosheh), saying,

8 "Take the rod, and gather you the assembly together, you, and Aaron (Aharon) your brother, and speak you unto the rock before their eyes; and it shall give forth his water, and you shalt bring forth to them water out of the rock; so you shalt give the congregation and their beasts drink.

9 And Moses (Mosheh) took the rod from before יהוה, as He commanded him.

10 And Moses (Mosheh) and Aaron (Aharon) gathered the congregation together before the rock, and he said unto them, "Hear now, you rebels! Must we fetch you water out of this rock?"

11 And Moses (Mosheh) lifted up his hand, and with his rod he smote the rock twice; and the water came out abundantly, and the congregation drank, and their beasts also.

12 And יהוה spake unto Moses (Mosheh) and Aaron (Aharon), "Because you believed Me not, to sanctify Me in the eyes of the children of Yisrael, therefore you shall not bring this congregation into the land which I have given them."

13 This is the water of Meribah, because the children of Yisrael strove with יהוה, and He was sanctified in them.

14 And Moses (Mosheh) sent messengers from Qadesh unto the king of Edom, "Thus saith your brother Yisrael: 'You knowest all the travail that hath befallen us;

15 How our fathers went down into Egypt (Mitsrayim), and we have dwelt in Egypt (Mitsrayim) a long time; and the Egyptians (Mitsrayim) vexed us, and our fathers.

16 And when we cried unto יהוה, He heard our voice, and sent an angel, and hath brought us forth out of Egypt (Mitsrayim); and, behold, we are in Qadesh, a city in the uttermost of your border.

17 Please let us pass through your country. We will not pass through the fields, or through the vineyards, neither will we drink of the water of the wells; we will go by the king's high way, we will not turn to the right hand nor to the left, until we have passed your borders.'"

18 And Edom said unto him, "You shalt not pass by me, lest I come out against you with the sword."

19 And the children of Yisrael said unto him, "We will go by the high way; and if I and my cattle drink of your water, then I will pay for

it; I will only, without doing anything else, go through on my feet."

20 And he said, "You shalt not go through." And Edom came out against him with much people, and with a strong hand.

21 Thus Edom refused to give Yisrael passage through his border; wherefore Yisrael turned away from him.

22 And the children of Yisrael, even the whole congregation, journeyed from Qadesh, and came unto Mount Hor.

23 And יהוה spake unto Moses (Mosheh) and Aaron (Aharon) in Mount Hor, by the coast of the land of Edom, saying:

24 "Aaron (Aharon) shall be gathered unto his people, for he shall not enter into the land which I have given unto the children of Yisrael, because you rebelled against My word at the water of Meribah.

25 Take Aaron (Aharon) and Eleazar his son, and bring them up unto Mount Hor;

26 And strip Aaron (Aharon) of his garments, and put them upon Eleazar his son; and Aaron (Aharon) shall be gathered unto his people, and shall die there."

27 And Moses (Mosheh) did as יהוה commanded; and they went up into Mount Hor in the sight of all the congregation.

28 And Moses (Mosheh) stripped Aaron (Aharon) of his garments, and put them upon Eleazar his son; and Aaron (Aharon) died there in the top of the mountain. And Moses (Mosheh) and Eleazar came down from the mountain.

29 And when all the congregation saw that Aaron (Aharon) was dead, they mourned for Aaron (Aharon) thirty days, even all the house of Yisrael.

21 And when king Arad the Canaanite, who dwelt in the south, heard that Yisrael came by the way of the spies; then he fought against Yisrael, and took some of them prisoners.

2 And Yisrael vowed a vow unto יהוה, and said, "If You wilt indeed deliver this people into my hand, then I will utterly destroy their cities.

3 And יהוה hearkened to the voice of Yisrael, and delivered up the Canaanites; and they utterly destroyed them and their cities. And he called the name of the place Hormah.

4 And they journeyed from Mount Hor by the way of the Red sea, to compass the land of Edom; and the soul of the people was much discouraged because of the way.

5 And the people spake against God (Elohim), and against Moses (Mosheh), Wherefore have you brought us up out of Egypt (Mitsrayim) to die in the wilderness? For there is no bread, neither is there any water; and our soul loatheth this light bread."

6 And יהוה sent fiery serpents among the people, and they bit the people; and much people of Yisrael died.

7 Therefore the people came to Moses (Mosheh), and said, "We have sinned, for we have spoken against יהוה, and against you; pray unto יהוה, that He take away the serpents from us. And Moses (Mosheh) prayed for the people.

8 And יהוה said unto Moses (Mosheh), "Make you a fiery serpent, and set it upon a pole; and it shall come to pass, that everyone who is bitten, when he looketh upon it, shall live."

9 And Moses (Mosheh) made a serpent of brass, and put it upon a pole, and it came to pass, that if a serpent had bitten any man, when he beheld the serpent of brass, he lived.

10 And the children of Yisrael set forward, and pitched in Oboth.

11 And they journeyed from Oboth, and pitched at Iye-haAvarim, in the wilderness which is before Moav, toward the sunrising.

12 From thence they moved, and pitched in the valley of Zared.

13 From thence they removed, and pitched on the other side of Arnon, which is in the wilderness that cometh out of the coasts of the Amorites; for Arnon is the border of Moav, between Moav and the Amorites.

14 Wherefore it is said in the book of the Wars of יהוה: "Wahev in Sufah, and in the brooks of Arnon,

15 And at the stream of the brooks that goeth down to the dwelling of Ar, and lieth upon the border of Moav."

16 And from thence they went to Beer, that is the well whereof יהוה spake unto Moses (Mosheh), "Gather the people together, and I will give them water."

17 Then Yisrael sang this song: "Spring up, O well! Sing you unto it.

18 The princes digged the well, the nobles of the people digged it, by the direction of the lawgiver, with their staves." And from the wilderness they went to Mattanah,

19 And from Mattanah to Nahaliel, and from Nahaliel to Bamoth,

20 And from Bamoth in the valley, that is in the country of Moav, to the top of Pisgah, which looketh toward Yeshimon.

21 And Yisrael sent messengers unto Sihon king of the Amorites, saying,

22 "Let me pass through your land; we will not turn into the fields, or into the vineyards; we will not drink of the waters of the well; but we will go along by the king's high way, until we be past your borders."

23 But Sihon would not allow Yisrael to pass through his border. So Sihon gathered all his people together, and went out against Yisrael into the wilderness; and he came to Yahats, and fought against Yisrael.

24 And Yisrael smote him with the edge of the sword, and possessed his land from Arnon unto Yabok, even unto the children of Ammon; for the border of the children of Ammon was strong.

25 And Yisrael took all these cities, and Yisrael dwelt in all the cities of the Amorites, in Heshbon, and in all the villages thereof.

26 For Heshbon was the city of Sihon the king of the Amorites, who had fought against the former king of Moav, and taken all his land out of his hand, even unto Arnon.

27 Wherefore they that speak in proverbs say, "Come into Heshbon, let the city of Sihon be built and be established.

28 For there is a fire gone out of Heshbon, a flame from the city of Sihon: it hath consumed Ar of Moav, and B33athe lords (Baalei) of the high places of Arnon.

29 Woe to you, Moav! You are undone, O people of Chemosh! He hath given his sons that escaped, and his daughters, into captivity unto Sihon king of the Amorites.

30 We have shot at them; Heshbon is perished even unto Dibon, and we have laid them waste even unto Nophah, which reacheth unto Medeba."

31 Thus Yisrael dwelt in the land of the Amorites.

32 And Moses (Mosheh) sent to spy out Yaazer, and they took the villages thereof, and drove out the Amorites that were there.

33 And they turned and went up by the way of Bashan; and Og the king of Bashan went out against them, he, and all his people, to the battle at Edrei.

34 And יהוה said unto Moses (Mosheh), "Fear him not, for I have delivered him into your hand, and all his people, and his land; and you shalt do to him as you didst unto Sihon king of the Amorites, which dwelt at Heshbon."

35 So they smote him, and his sons, and all his people, until there was none left him alive; and they possessed his land.

22 And the children of Yisrael set forward, and pitched in the plains of Moav on this side Jordan (Yarden) by Yericho.

2 And Balak the son of Zippor saw all that Yisrael had done to the Amorites.

3 And Moav was sore afraid of the people, because they were many; and Moav was distressed because of the children of Yisrael.

4 And Moav said unto the elders of Midian, "Now shall this company lick up all that are round about us, as the ox licketh up the grass of the field." And Balak the son of Zippor was king of the Moavites at that time.

5 He sent messengers therefore unto Balaam the son of Beor to Pethor, which is by the river of the land of the children of his people, to call him, saying, "Behold, there is a people come out from Egypt (Mitsrayim). Behold, they cover the face of the earth, and they abide opposite me!

6 Please come now therefore, curse this people for me; for they are too mighty for me: peradventure I shall prevail, that we may smite them, and that I may drive them out of the land, for I know that he whom you blessest is blessed, and he whom you cursest is cursed."

7 And the elders of Moav and the elders of Midian departed with the rewards of divination in their hand; and they came unto Balaam, and spake unto him the words of Balak.

8 And he said unto them, "Lodge here this night, and I will bring you word again, as יהוה shall speak unto me." And the princes of Moav abode with Balaam.

9 And God (Elohim) came unto Balaam, and said, "What men are these with you?"

10 And Balaam said unto God (Elohim), "Balak the son of Zippor, king of Moav, hath sent unto me, saying,

11 'Behold, there is a people come out of Egypt (Mitsrayim), who covereth the face of the earth. Come now, curse them for me; perhaps I shall

be able to overcome them, and drive them out."

12 And God (Elohim) said unto Balaam, "You shalt not go with them; you shalt not curse the people, for they are blessed."

13 And Balaam rose up in the morning, and said unto the princes of Balak, "Get you into your land, for יהוה refuseth to give me leave to go with you."

14 And the princes of Moav rose up, and they went unto Balak, and said, "Balaam refuseth to come with us."

15 And Balak sent yet again princes, more, and more honourable than they.

16 And they came to Balaam, and said to him, "Thus saith Balak the son of Zippor, 'Please let nothing hinder you from coming unto me;

17 For I will promote you unto very great honor, and I will do whatsoever you sayest unto me. Please come therefore, curse this people for me.'"

18 And Balaam answered and said unto the servants of Balak, "If Balak would give me his house full of silver and gold, I cannot go beyond the word of יהוה my God (YHWH Elohai), to do less or more.

19 Now therefore, please tarry you also here this night, that I may know what יהוה will say unto me more."

20 And God (Elohim) came unto Balaam at night, and said unto him, "If the men come to call you, rise up, and go with them; but yet the word which I shall say unto you, that shalt you do."

21 And Balaam rose up in the morning, and saddled his ass, and went with the princes of Moav.

22 And God (Elohim)'s anger was kindled because he went, and the angel of יהוה stood in the way for an adversary against him. Now he was riding upon his ass, and his two servants were with him.

23 And the ass saw the angel of יהוה standing in the way, and his sword drawn in his hand; and the ass turned aside out of the way, and went into the field. And Balaam smote the ass, to turn her into the way.

24 But the angel of יהוה stood in a path of the vineyards, a wall being on this side, and a wall on that side.

25 And when the ass saw the angel of יהוה, she thrust herself unto the wall, and crushed

Balaam's foot against the wall; and he smote her again.

26 And the angel of יהוה went further, and stood in a narrow place, where was no way to turn either to the right hand or to the left.

27 And when the ass saw the angel of יהוה, she fell down under Balaam; and Balaam's anger was kindled, and he smote the ass with a staff.

28 And יהוה opened the mouth of the ass, and she said unto Balaam, "What have I done unto you, that you have smitten me these three times?"

29 And Balaam said unto the ass, "Because you have mocked me. I would there were a sword in mine hand, for now would I kill you!"

30 And the ass said unto Balaam, "Am not I your ass, upon which you have ridden ever since I was yours unto this day? Was I ever been accustomed to do so unto you?" And he said, "Nay."

31 Then יהוה opened the eyes of Balaam, and he saw the angel of יהוה standing in the way, and his sword drawn in his hand; and he bowed down his head, and fell flat on his face.

32 And the angel of יהוה said unto him, "Wherefore have you smitten your ass these three times? Behold, I went out to withstand you, because your way is perverse before me.

33 And the ass saw me, and turned from me these three times; unless she had turned from me, surely now also I had slain you, and saved her alive."

34 And Balaam said unto the angel of יהוה, "I have sinned, for I knew not that you stoodest in the way against me; now therefore, if it displeases you, I will get me back again."

35 And the angel of יהוה said unto Balaam, "Go with the men; but only the word that I shall speak unto you, that you shalt speak." So Balaam went with the princes of Balak.

36 And when Balak heard that Balaam was come, he went out to meet him unto a city of Moav, which is in the border of Arnon, which is in the utmost coast.

37 And Balak said unto Balaam, "Did I not earnestly send unto you to call you? Wherefore camest you not unto me? Am I not able indeed to promote you to honor?"

38 And Balaam said unto Balak, "Lo, I am come unto you; have I now power at all to say anything? The word that God (Elohim) putteth

in my mouth, that shall I speak."

39 And Balaam went with Balak, and they came unto Qiryat-Chutsot.

40 And Balak offered oxen and sheep, and sent to Balaam, and to the princes that were with him.

41 And it came to pass on the next day, that Balak took Balaam, and brought him up into the high places of the Bamot-Baal, that thence he might see the utmost part of the people.

23 And Balaam said unto Balak, "Build me here seven altars, and prepare me here seven oxen and seven rams."

2 And Balak did as Balaam had spoken; and Balak and Balaam offered on every altar a bullock and a ram.

3 And Balaam said unto Balak, "Stand by your burnt offering, and I will go; perhaps יהוה will come to meet me; and whatsoever He sheweth me I will tell you." And he went to a high place.

4 And God (Elohim) met Balaam, and He said unto him, "I have prepared seven altars, and I have offered upon every altar a bullock and a ram."

5 And יהוה put a word in Balaam's mouth, and said, "Return unto Balak, and thus you shalt speak."

6 And he returned unto him, and, behold, he stood by his burnt sacrifice, he, and all the princes of Moav.

7 And he took up his parable, and said, "Balak the king of Moav hath brought me from Aram, out of the mountains of the east, saying, 'Come, curse Jacob (Yaaqov) for me, and come, defy Yisrael!'

8 How shall I curse, whom God (Elohim) hath not cursed? Or how shall I defy, whom יהוה hath not defied?

9 For from the top of the rocks I see him, and from the hills I behold him; behold, the people shall dwell alone, and shall not be reckoned among the nations.

10 Who can count the dust of Jacob (Yaaqov), and the number of the fourth part of Yisrael? Let me die the death of the righteous, and let my last end be like his!"

11 And Balak said unto Balaam, "What have you done unto me? I took you to curse mine enemies, and, behold, you have blessed them altogether."

12 And he answered and said, "Must I not take

heed to speak that which יהוה hath put in my mouth?"

13 And Balak said unto him, "Please come with me unto another place, from whence you mayest see them; you shalt see but the utmost part of them, and shalt not see them all; and curse them from thence for me."

14 And he brought him into the field of Zophim, to the top of Pisgah, and built seven altars, and offered a bullock and a ram on every altar.

15 And he said unto Balak, "Stand here by your burnt offering, while I meet יהוה over there."

16 And יהוה met Balaam, and put a word in his mouth, and said, "Go again unto Balak, and say thus."

17 And when he came to him, behold, he stood by his burnt offering, and the princes of Moav with him. And Balak said unto him, "What hath יהוה spoken?"

18 And he took up his parable, and said, "Rise up, Balak, and hear! Hearken unto me, you son of Zippor!

19 God (Elohim) is not a man, that He should lie; neither the son of man, that He should repent. hath He said, and shall He not do it? Or hath He spoken, and shall He not make it good?

20 Behold, I have received commandment to bless; and He hath blessed; and I cannot reverse it.

21 He hath not beheld iniquity in Jacob (Yaaqov), neither hath He seen perverseness in Yisrael. יהוה his God (Elohim) is with him, and the shout of a king is among them.

22 God (Elohim) brought them out of Egypt (Mitsrayim); He hath as it was the strength of a unicorn.

23 Surely there is no enchantment against Jacob (Yaaqov), neither is there any divination against Yisrael. According to this time it shall be said of Jacob (Yaaqov) and of Yisrael, 'What hath God (Elohim) wrought!'

24 Behold, the people shall rise up as a great lion, and lift up himself as a young lion; he shall not lie down until he eats of the prey, and drink the blood of the slain."

25 And Balak said unto Balaam, "Neither curse them at all, nor bless them at all."

26 But Balaam answered and said unto Balak, "Told not I you, saying, 'All that יהוה speaketh, that I must do?'"

27 And Balak said unto Balaam, "Please come,

I will bring you unto another place; perhaps it will please God (Elohim) that you mayest curse them for me from thence."

28 And Balak brought Balaam unto the top of Peor, that looketh toward Yeshimon.

29 And Balaam said unto Balak, "Build me here seven altars, and prepare me here seven bullocks and seven rams."

30 And Balak did as Balaam had said, and offered a bullock and a ram on every altar.

24 And when Balaam saw that it pleased יהוה to bless Yisrael, he went not, as at other times, to seek for enchantments, but he set his face toward the wilderness.

2 And Balaam lifted up his eyes, and he saw Yisrael abiding in his tents according to their tribes; and the Spirit of God (Elohim) came upon him.

3 And he took up his parable, and said: "Balaam the son of Beor hath said, and the man whose eyes are open hath said;

4 He hath said, who heard the words of God (Elohim), who saw the vision of the Almighty, falling into a trance, but having his eyes open:

5 How goodly are your tents, O Jacob (Yaaqov), and your tabernacles, O Yisrael!

6 As the valleys are they spread forth, as gardens by the river's side, as the trees of lign aloes which יהוה hath planted, and as cedar trees beside the waters.

7 He shall pour the water out of his buckets, and his seed shall be in many waters, and his king shall be higher than Agag, and his kingdom shall be exalted.

8 God (Elohim) brought him forth out of Egypt (Mitsrayim); he hath as it was the strength of a unicorn; he shall eat up the nations his enemies, and shall break their bones, and pierce them through with his arrows.

9 'He couched, he lay down as a lion, and as a great lion; who shall stir him up?' "Blessed is he that blesseth you, and cursed is he that curseth you."

10 And Balak's anger was kindled against Balaam, and he smote his hands together; and Balak said unto Balaam, "I called you to curse mine enemies, and, behold, you have altogether blessed them these three times!

11 Therefore now flee you to your place. I thought to promote you unto great honor; but, behold, יהוה hath kept you back from honor."

12 And Balaam said unto Balak, "Spake I not also to your messengers whom you sentest unto me, saying,

13 'If Balak would give me his house full of silver and gold, I cannot go beyond the commandment of יהוה, to do either good or bad of mine own mind; but what יהוה saith, that will I speak'?

14 And now, behold, I go unto my people. Come therefore, and I will advertise you what this people shall do to your people in the latter days."

15 And he took up his parable, and said, "Balaam the son of Beor hath said, and the man whose eyes are open hath said:

16 He hath said, which heard the words of God (Elohim), and knew the knowledge of the B6bMost High (Elyon), who saw the vision of the Almighty (Shaddai), falling into a trance, but having his eyes open:

17 I shall see Him, but not now; I shall behold Him, but not near; there shall come a Star out of Jacob (Yaaqov), and a Sceptre shall rise out of Yisrael, and shall smite the corners of Moav, and destroy all the children of Shet.

18 And Edom shall be a possession, Seir also shall be a possession for his enemies; and Yisrael shall do valiantly.

19 Out of Jacob (Yaaqov) shall come he that shall have dominion, and shall destroy him that remaineth of the city."

20 And when he looked on Amalek, he took up his parable, and said: "Amalek was the first of the nations; but his latter end shall be that he perishes forever."

21 And he looked on the Kenites, and took up his parable, and said, "Strong is your dwellingplace, and you puttest your nest in a rock;

22 Nevertheless the Kenite shall be wasted, until Asshur shall carry you away captive.

23 And he took up his parable, and said: "Alas, who shall live when God (Elohim) doeth this!

24 And ships shall come from the coast of Chittim, and shall afflict Asshur, and shall afflict Eber, and he also shall perish forever."

25 And Balaam rose up, and went and returned to his place; and Balak also went his way.

25 And Yisrael abode in Shittim, and the people began to commit whoredom with the daughters of Moav.

2 And they called the people unto the sacrifices of their gods (elohim). And the people did eat,

and bowed down to their gods (elohim).

3 And Yisrael joined himself unto Baalpeor; and the anger of יהוה was kindled against Yisrael.

4 And יהוה said unto Moses (Mosheh), "Take all the heads of the people, and hang them up before יהוה against the sun, that the fierce anger of יהוה may be turned away from Yisrael.

5 And Moses (Mosheh) said unto the judges of Yisrael, "Slay you everyone his men that were joined unto Baalpeor."

6 And, behold, one of the children of Yisrael came and brought unto his brethren a Midianitish woman in the sight of Moses (Mosheh), and in the sight of all the congregation of the children of Yisrael, who were weeping before the door of the tabernacle of the congregation.

7 And when Phinehas, the son of Eleazar, the son of Aaron (Aharon) the priest (kohen), saw it, he rose up from among the congregation, and took a javelin in his hand;

8 And he went after the man of Yisrael into the tent, and thrust both of them through, the man of Yisrael, and the woman through her belly. So the plague was stayed from the children of Yisrael.

9 And those that died in the plague were twenty and four thousand.

10 And יהוה spake unto Moses (Mosheh), saying,

11 Phinehas, the son of Eleazar, the son of Aaron (Aharon) the priest (kohen), hath turned My wrath away from the children of Yisrael, while he was zealous for My sake among them, that I consumed not the children of Yisrael in My jealousy.

12 Wherefore say, 'Behold, I give unto him My covenant of peace;

13 And he shall have it, and his seed after him, even the covenant of an everlasting priesthood (kehunnah); because he was zealous for his God (Elohim), and made an atonement for the children of Yisrael.'"

14 Now the name of the Yisraeli that was slain, even that was slain with the Midianitish woman, was Zimri, the son of Salu, a prince of a chief house among the Shimonites.

15 And the name of the Midianitish woman that was slain was Cozbi, the daughter of Zur; he was head over a people, and of a chief house in Midian.

16 And יהוה spake unto Moses (Mosheh), saying:

17 "Vex the Midianites, and smite them;

18 For they vex you with their wiles, wherewith they have beguiled you in the matter of Peor, and in the matter of Cozbi, the daughter of a prince of Midian, their sister, which was slain in the day of the plague for Peor's sake."

26 And it came to pass after the plague, that יהוה spake unto Moses (Mosheh) and unto Eleazar the son of Aaron (Aharon) the priest (kohen), saying:

2 "Take the sum of all the congregation of the children of Yisrael, from twenty years old and upward, throughout their fathers' house, all that are able to go to war in Yisrael.

3 And Moses (Mosheh) and Eleazar the priest (kohen) spake with them in the plains of Moav by Jordan (Yarden) near Yericho, saying,

4 Take the sum of the people, from twenty years old and upward, as יהוה commanded Moses (Mosheh) and the children of Yisrael, which went forth out of the land of Egypt (Mitsrayim).

5 Reuven, the eldest son of Yisrael; the children of Reuven: Hanoch, of whom cometh the family of the Hanochites: of Pallu, the family of the Palluites:

6 Of Hezron, the family of the Hezronites: of Carmi, the family of the Carmites.

7 These are the families of the Reubenites (Reuveni); and they that were numbered of them were forty and three thousand and seven hundred and thirty.

8 And the sons of Pallu: Eliav.

9 And the sons of Eliav: Nemuel, and Dathan, and Abiram. This is that Dathan and Abiram, who were famous in the congregation, who strove against Moses (Mosheh) and against Aaron (Aharon) in the company of Korah (Qorach), when they strove against יהוה;

10 And the earth opened her mouth, and swallowed them up together with Korah (Qorach), when that company died, what time the fire devoured two hundred and fifty men; and they became a sign.

11 Notwithstanding the children of Korah (Qorach) died not.

12 The sons of Shimon after their families: of Nemuel, the family of the Nemuelites: of Yamin, the family of the Yaminites; of Yakhin, the family of the Yakhinites;

13 Of Zerah, the family of the Zarhites; of

Shaul, the family of the Shaulites.

14 These are the families of the Shimonites, twenty and two thousand and two hundred.

15 The children of Gad after their families: of Zephon, the family of the Zephonites; of Haggi, the family of the Haggites; of Shuni, the family of the Shunites;

16 Of Ozni, the family of the Oznites; of Eri, the family of the Erites;

17 Of Arod, the family of the Arodites; of Areli, the family of the Arelites.

18 These are the families of the children of Gad according to those that were numbered of them, forty thousand and five hundred.

19 The sons of Judah (Yehudah) were Er and Onan; and Er and Onan died in the land of Canaan.

20 And the sons of Judah (Yehudah) after their families were: of Shelah, the family of the Shelanites: of Pharez, the family of the Pharzites: of Zerah, the family of the Zarhites.

21 And the sons of Pharez were: of Hezron, the family of the Hezronites; of Hamul, the family of the Hamulites.

22 These are the families of Judah (Yehudah) according to those that were numbered of them, threescore and sixteen thousand and five hundred.

23 Of the sons of Yissaskhar after their families: of Tola, the family of the Tolaites; of Pua, the family of the Punites;

24 Of Yashuv, the family of the Yashuvites; of Shimron, the family of the Shimronites.

25 These are the families of Yissaskhar according to those that were numbered of them, threescore and four thousand and three hundred.

26 Of the sons of Zevulun after their families: of Sered, the family of the Sardites; of Elon, the family of the Elonites; of Yahleel, the family of the Yahleelites.

27 These are the families of the Zevulunites according to those that were numbered of them, threescore thousand and five hundred.

28 The sons of Joseph (Yosef) after their families were Menashsheh and Efrayim.

29 Of the sons of Menashsheh: of Machir, the family of the Machirites: and Machir begat Gilad; of Gilad come the family of the Giladites.

30 These are the sons of Gilad: of Iezer, the family of the Iezerites; of Helek, the family of the Helekites;

31 And of Asriel, the family of the Asrielites: and of Shechem, the family of the Shechemites;

32 And of Shemida, the family of the Shemidaites; and of Hepher, the family of the Hepherites.

33 And Zelophehad the son of Hepher had no sons, but daughters; and the names of the daughters of Zelophehad were Mahlah, and Noach, Hoglah, Milcah, and Tirzah.

34 These are the families of Menashsheh, and those that were numbered of them, fifty and two thousand and seven hundred.

35 These are the sons of Efrayim after their families: of Shuthelah, the family of the Shuthalhites; of Becher, the family of the Bachrites; of Tahan, the family of the Tahanites.

36 And these are the sons of Shuthelah: of Eran, the family of the Eranites.

37 These are the families of the sons of Efrayim according to those that were numbered of them, thirty and two thousand and five hundred. These are the sons of Joseph (Yosef) after their families.

38 The sons of Binyamin after their families: of Bela, the family of the Belaites; of Ashbel, the family of the Ashbelites; of Ahiram, the family of the Ahiramites;

39 Of Shupham, the family of the Shuphamites; of Hupham, the family of the Huphamites.

40 And the sons of Bela were Ard and Naaman; of Ard, the family of the Ardites; and of Naaman, the family of the Naamites.

41 These are the sons of Binyamin after their families; and they that were numbered of them were forty and five thousand and six hundred.

42 These are the sons of Dan after their families: of Shuham, the family of the Shuhamites. These are the families of Dan after their families.

43 All the families of the Shuhamites, according to those that were numbered of them, were threescore and four thousand and four hundred.

44 Of the children of Asher after their families: of Yimna, the family of the Yimnites; of Yishvi, the family of the Yishvites; of Beriyah, the family of the Beriites.

45 Of the sons of Beriyah: of Heber, the family of the Heberites; of Malchiel, the family of the Malchielites.

46 And the name of the daughter of Asher was Sarah.

47 These are the families of the sons of Asher according to those that were numbered of them; who were fifty and three thousand and four hundred.

48 Of the sons of Naftali after their families: of Yahzeel, the family of the Yahzeelites; of Guni, the family of the Gunites;

49 Of Yezer, the family of the Yezerites; of Shillem, the family of the Shillemites.

50 These are the families of Naftali according to their families: and they that were numbered of them were forty and five thousand and four hundred.

51 These were the numbered of the children of Yisrael, six hundred thousand and a thousand seven hundred and thirty.

52 And יהוה spake unto Moses (Mosheh), saying:

53 "Unto these the land shall be divided for an inheritance according to the number of names.

54 To many you shalt give the more inheritance, and to few you shalt give the less inheritance; to every one shall his inheritance be given according to those that were numbered of him.

55 Notwithstanding the land shall be divided by lot; according to the names of the tribes of their fathers they shall inherit.

56 According to the lot shall the possession thereof be divided between many and few."

57 And these are they that were numbered of the Levites (Lewiyim) after their families: of Gershon, the family of the Gershonites; of Kohath, the family of the Kohathites; of Merari, the family of the Merarites.

58 These are the families of the Levites (Lewiyim): the family of the Libnites, the family of the Hebronites, the family of the Mahlites, the family of the Mushites, the family of the Korathites. And Kohath begat Amram.

59 And the name of Amram's wife was Yokheved, the daughter of Lewi, whom her mother bare to Lewi in Egypt (Mitsrayim); and she bare unto Amram Aaron (Aharon) and Moses (Mosheh), and Miryam their sister.

60 And unto Aaron (Aharon) was born Nadav, and Avihu, Eleazar, and Ithamar.

61 And Nadav and Avihu died, when they offered strange fire before יהוה.

62 And those that were numbered of them were twenty and three thousand, all males from a month old and upward; for they were not numbered among the children of Yisrael, because there was no inheritance given them among the children of Yisrael.

63 These are they that were numbered by Moses (Mosheh) and Eleazar the priest (kohen), who numbered the children of Yisrael in the plains of Moav by Jordan (Yarden) near Yericho.

64 But among these there was not a man of them whom Moses (Mosheh) and Aaron (Aharon) the priest (kohen) numbered, when they numbered the children of Yisrael in the wilderness of Sinai.

65 For יהוה had said of them, "They shall surely die in the wilderness." And there was not left a man of them, save Caleb the son of Yefunneh, and Joshua (Yehoshua) the son of Nun.

27 Then came the daughters of Zelophehad, the son of Hepher, the son of Gilad, the son of Machir, the son of Menashsheh, of the families of Menashsheh the son of Joseph (Yosef); and these are the names of his daughters: Mahlah, Noach, and Hoglah, and Milcah, and Tirzah.

2 And they stood before Moses (Mosheh), and before Eleazar the priest (kohen), and before the princes and all the congregation, by the door of the tabernacle of the congregation, saying:

3 "Our father died in the wilderness, and he was not in the company of them that gathered themselves together against יהוה in the company of Korah (Qorach); but died in his own sin, and had no sons.

4 Why should the name of our father be done away from among his family, because he hath no son? Give unto us therefore a possession among the brethren of our father."

5 And Moses (Mosheh) brought their cause before יהוה.

6 And יהוה spake unto Moses (Mosheh), saying:

7 "The daughters of Zelophehad speak right; you shalt surely give them a possession of an inheritance among their father's brethren; and you shalt cause the inheritance of their father to pass unto them.

8 And you shalt speak unto the children of Yisrael, saying: 'If a man dies, and have no son, then you shall cause his inheritance to pass unto his daughter.

9 And if he has no daughter, then you shall give his inheritance unto his brethren.

10 And if he has no brethren, then you shall give

his inheritance unto his father's brethren.

11 And if his father has no brethren, then you shall give his inheritance unto his kinsman that is next to him of his family, and he shall possess it.'" And it shall be unto the children of Yisrael a statute of judgment, as יהוה commanded Moses (Mosheh).

12 And יהוה said unto Moses (Mosheh): "Get you up into this mount Abarim, and see the land which I have given unto the children of Yisrael.

13 And when you have seen it, you also shalt be gathered unto your people, as Aaron (Aharon) your brother was gathered.

14 For you rebelled against my commandment in the desert of Zin, in the strife of the congregation, to sanctify me at the water before their eyes." That is the water of Meribah in Qadesh in the wilderness of Zin.

15 And Moses (Mosheh) spake unto יהוה, saying:

16 "Let יהוה, God (Elohim) of the spirits of all flesh, set a man over the congregation,

17 Who may go out before them, and which may go in before them, and which may lead them out, and who may bring them in, that the congregation of יהוה be not as sheep which have no shepherd.

18 And יהוה said unto Moses (Mosheh): "Take you Joshua (Yehoshua) the son of Nun, a man in whom is the spirit, and lay your hand upon him;

19 And set him before Eleazar the priest (kohen), and before all the congregation; and give him a charge in their sight.

20 And you shalt put some of your honor upon him, that all the congregation of the children of Yisrael may be obedient.

21 And he shall stand before Eleazar the priest (kohen), who shall ask counsel for him after the judgment of Urim before יהוה; at his word shall they go out, and at his word they shall come in, both he, and all the children of Yisrael with him, even all the congregation."

22 And Moses (Mosheh) did as יהוה commanded him. And he took Joshua (Yehoshua), and set him before Eleazar the priest (kohen), and before all the congregation.

23 And he laid his hands upon him, and gave him a charge, as יהוה commanded by the hand of Moses (Mosheh).

28 And יהוה spake unto Moses (Mosheh), saying:

2 "Command the children of Yisrael, and say unto them, 'My offering, and My bread for My sacrifices made by fire, for a sweet savour unto Me, shall you observe to offer unto Me in their due season.'

3 And you shalt say unto them, 'This is the offering made by fire which you shall offer unto יהוה: two lambs of the first year without spot day by day, for a continual burnt offering.

4 The one lamb shalt you offer in the morning, and the other lamb shalt you offer at even;

5 And a tenth part of an ephah of flour for a meat offering, mingled with the fourth part of an hin of beaten oil.

6 It is a continual burnt offering, which was ordained in Mount Sinai for a sweet savour, a sacrifice made by fire unto יהוה.

7 And the drink offering thereof shall be the fourth part of an hin for the one lamb; in the holy place shalt you cause the strong wine to be poured unto יהוה for a drink offering.

8 And the other lamb shalt you offer at even; as the meat offering of the morning, and as the drink offering thereof, you shalt offer it, a sacrifice made by fire, of a sweet savour unto יהוה.

9 And on the Shabbat day two lambs of the first year without spot, and two tenth deals of flour for a meat offering, mingled with oil, and the drink offering thereof.

10 This is the burnt offering of every Shabbat, besides the continual burnt offering, and his drink offering.

11 And in the beginnings of your months you shall offer a burnt offering unto יהוה: two young bullocks, and one ram, seven lambs of the first year without spot;

12 And three tenth deals of flour for a meat offering, mingled with oil, for one bullock; and two tenth deals of flour for a meat offering, mingled with oil, for one ram;

13 And a several tenth deal of flour mingled with oil for a meat offering unto one lamb; for a burnt offering of a sweet savour, a sacrifice made by fire unto יהוה.

14 And their drink offerings shall be half an hin of wine unto a bullock, and the third part of an hin unto a ram, and a fourth part of an hin unto a lamb; this is the burnt offering of every month throughout the months of the year.

15 And one kid of the goats for a sin offering unto יהוה shall be offered, besides the continual

burnt offering, and his drink offering.

16 And in the fourteenth day of the first month is the Passover (Pesach) of יהוה.

17 And in the fifteenth day of this month is the feast; seven days shall unleavened bread be eaten.

18 In the first day shall be a holy convocation; you shall do no manner of servile work therein.

19 But you shall offer a sacrifice made by fire for a burnt offering unto יהוה; two young bullocks, and one ram, and seven lambs of the first year. They shall be unto you without blemish.

20 And their meat offering shall be of flour mingled with oil; three tenth deals shall you offer for a bullock, and two tenth deals for a ram;

21 A several tenth deal shalt you offer for every lamb, throughout the seven lambs;

22 And one goat for a sin offering, to make an atonement for you.

23 You shall offer these besides the burnt offering in the morning, which is for a continual burnt offering.

24 After this manner you shall offer daily, throughout the seven days, the meat of the sacrifice made by fire, of a sweet savour unto יהוה; it shall be offered beside the continual burnt offering, and his drink offering.

25 And on the seventh day you shall have a holy convocation; you shall do no servile work.

26 Also in the day of the firstfruits, when you bring a new meat offering unto יהוה, after your weeks be out, you shall have a holy convocation; you shall do no servile work.

27 But you shall offer the burnt offering for a sweet savour unto יהוה; two young bullocks, one ram, seven lambs of the first year;

28 And their meat offering of flour mingled with oil, three tenth deals unto one bullock, two tenth deals unto one ram,

29 A several tenth deal unto one lamb, throughout the seven lambs;

30 And one kid of the goats, to make an atonement for you.

31 You shall offer them beside the continual burnt offering, and his meat offering, (they shall be unto you without blemish) and their drink offerings.

29 And in the seventh month, on the first day of the month, you shall have an holy convocation; you shall do no servile work. It is a day of blowing the trumpets [B22](Yom Teruah) unto you.

2 And you shall offer a burnt offering for a sweet savour unto יהוה; one young bullock, one ram, and seven lambs of the first year without blemish:

3 And their meat offering shall be of flour mingled with oil, three tenth deals for a bullock, and two tenth deals for a ram,

4 And one tenth deal for one lamb, throughout the seven lambs;

5 And one kid of the goats for a sin offering, to make an atonement for you;

6 Besides the burnt offering of the month, and its meat offering, and the daily burnt offering, and its meat offering, and their drink offerings, according unto their manner, for a sweet savour, a sacrifice made by fire unto יהוה.

7 And you shall have on the tenth day of this seventh month a holy convocation; and you shall afflict your souls; you shall not do any work therein;

8 But you shall offer a burnt offering unto יהוה for a sweet savour; one young bullock, one ram, and seven lambs of the first year; they shall be unto you without blemish.

9 And their meat offering shall be of flour mingled with oil, three tenth deals to a bullock, and two tenth deals to one ram,

10 A several tenth deal for one lamb, throughout the seven lambs;

11 One kid of the goats for a sin offering; besides the sin offering of atonement, and the continual burnt offering, and the meat offering of it, and their drink offerings.

12 And on the fifteenth day of the seventh month you shall have a holy convocation; you shall do no servile work, and you shall keep a feast unto יהוה seven days.

13 And you shall offer a burnt offering, a sacrifice made by fire, of a sweet savour unto יהוה: thirteen young bullocks, two rams, and fourteen lambs of the first year; they shall be without blemish.

14 And their meat offering shall be of flour mingled with oil, three tenth deals unto every bullock of the thirteen bullocks, two tenth deals to each ram of the two rams,

15 And a several tenth deal to each lamb of the fourteen lambs;

16 And one kid of the goats for a sin offering;

besides the continual burnt offering, his meat offering, and his drink offering.

17 And on the second day you shall offer twelve young bullocks, two rams, fourteen lambs of the first year without spot;

18 And their meat offering and their drink offerings for the bullocks, for the rams, and for the lambs, shall be according to their number, after the manner;

19 And one kid of the goats for a sin offering; besides the continual burnt offering, and the meat offering thereof, and their drink offerings.

20 And on the third day eleven bullocks, two rams, fourteen lambs of the first year without blemish;

21 And their meat offering and their drink offerings for the bullocks, for the rams, and for the lambs, shall be according to their number, after the manner;

22 And one goat for a sin offering; besides the continual burnt offering, and its meat offering, and its drink offering.

23 And on the fourth day ten bullocks, two rams, and fourteen lambs of the first year without blemish;

24 Their meat offering and their drink offerings for the bullocks, for the rams, and for the lambs, shall be according to their number, after the manner;

25 And one kid of the goats for a sin offering; besides the continual burnt offering, its meat offering, and its drink offering.

26 And on the fifth day nine bullocks, two rams, and fourteen lambs of the first year without spot;

27 And their meat offering and their drink offerings for the bullocks, for the rams, and for the lambs, shall be according to their number, after the manner;

28 And one goat for a sin offering; besides the continual burnt offering, and its meat offering, and its drink offering.

29 And on the sixth day eight bullocks, two rams, and fourteen lambs of the first year without blemish;

30 And their meat offering and their drink offerings for the bullocks, for the rams, and for the lambs, shall be according to their number, after the manner;

31 And one goat for a sin offering; besides the continual burnt offering, his meat offering, and his drink offering.

32 And on the seventh day seven bullocks, two rams, and fourteen lambs of the first year without blemish;

33 And their meat offering and their drink offerings for the bullocks, for the rams, and for the lambs, shall be according to their number, after the manner;

34 And one goat for a sin offering; besides the continual burnt offering, his meat offering, and his drink offering.

35 On the eighth day you shall have a solemn assembly. You shall do no servile work therein.

36 But you shall offer a burnt offering, a sacrifice made by fire, of a sweet savour unto יהוה: one bullock, one ram, seven lambs of the first year without blemish;

37 Their meat offering and their drink offerings for the bullock, for the ram, and for the lambs, shall be according to their number, after the manner:

38 And one goat for a sin offering; beside the continual burnt offering, and its meat offering, and its drink offering.

39 These things you shall do unto יהוה in your set feasts, beside your vows, and your freewill offerings, for your burnt offerings, and for your meat offerings, and for your drink offerings, and for your peace offerings.'"

40 And Moses (Mosheh) told the children of Yisrael according to all that יהוה commanded Moses (Mosheh).

30 And Moses (Mosheh) spake unto the heads of the tribes concerning the children of Yisrael, saying: "This is the thing which יהוה hath commanded:

2 If a man vows a vow unto יהוה, or swear an oath to bind his soul with a bond; he shall not break his word, he shall do according to all that proceedeth out of his mouth.

3 If a woman also vows a vow unto יהוה, and bind herself by a bond, being in her father's house in her youth;

4 And her father hears her vow, and her bond wherewith she hath bound her soul, and her father shall hold his peace at her: then all her vows shall stand, and every bond wherewith she hath bound her soul shall stand.

5 But if her father disallows her in the day that he heareth; not any of her vows, or of her bonds wherewith she hath bound her soul, shall stand:

and יהוה shall forgive her, because her father disallowed her.

6 And if she had at all a husband, when she vowed, or uttered ought out of her lips, wherewith she bound her soul;

7 And her husband heard it, and held his peace at her in the day that he heard it: then her vows shall stand, and her bonds wherewith she bound her soul shall stand.

8 But if her husband disallowed her on the day that he heard it; then he shall make her vow which she vowed, and that which she uttered with her lips, wherewith she bound her soul, of none effect, and יהוה shall forgive her.

9 But every vow of a widow, and of her that is divorced, wherewith they have bound their souls, shall stand against her.

10 And if she vowed in her husband's house, or bound her soul by a bond with an oath;

11 And her husband heard it, and held his peace at her, and disallowed her not; then all her vows shall stand, and every bond wherewith she bound her soul shall stand.

12 But if her husband hath utterly made them void on the day he heard them; then whatsoever proceeded out of her lips concerning her vows, or concerning the bond of her soul, shall not stand; her husband hath made them void; and יהוה shall forgive her.

13 Every vow, and every binding oath to afflict the soul, her husband may establish it, or her husband may make it void.

14 But if her husband altogether holds his peace at her from day today; then he establisheth all her vows, or all her bonds, which are upon her; he confirmeth them, because he held his peace at her in the day that he heard them.

15 But if he shall any ways make them void after that he hath heard them; then he shall bear her iniquity."

16 These are the statutes, which יהוה commanded Moses (Mosheh), between a man and his wife, between the father and his daughter, being yet in her youth in her father's house.

31 And יהוה spake unto Moses (Mosheh), saying:

2 "Avenge the children of Yisrael of the Midianites. Afterward shalt you be gathered unto your people."

3 And Moses (Mosheh) spake unto the people, saying, "Arm some of yourselves unto the war, and let them go against the Midianites, and avenge יהוה of Midian.

4 Of every tribe a thousand, throughout all the tribes of Yisrael, shall you send to the war."

5 So there were delivered out of the thousands of Yisrael, a thousand of every tribe, twelve thousand armed for war.

6 And Moses (Mosheh) sent them to the war, a thousand of every tribe, them and Phinehas the son of Eleazar the priest (kohen), to the war, with the holy instruments, and the trumpets to blow in his hand.

7 And they warred against the Midianites, as יהוה commanded Moses (Mosheh); and they slew all the males.

8 And they slew the kings of Midian, beside the rest of them that were slain; namely: Evi, and Rekem, and Zur, and Hur, and Reba, five kings of Midian. Balaam also the son of Beor they slew with the sword.

9 And the children of Yisrael took all the women of Midian captives, and their little ones, and took the spoil of all their cattle, and all their flocks, and all their goods.

10 And they burnt all their cities wherein they dwelt, and all their goodly castles, with fire.

11 And they took all the spoil, and all the prey, both of men and of beasts.

12 And they brought the captives, and the prey, and the spoil, unto Moses (Mosheh), and Eleazar the priest (kohen), and unto the congregation of the children of Yisrael, unto the camp at the plains of Moav, which are by Jordan (Yarden) near Yericho.

13 And Moses (Mosheh), and Eleazar the priest (kohen), and all the princes of the congregation, went forth to meet them outside the camp.

14 And Moses (Mosheh) was wroth with the officers of the army, with the captains over thousands, and captains over hundreds, which came from the battle.

15 And Moses (Mosheh) said unto them, "Have you saved all the women alive?

16 Behold, these caused the children of Yisrael, through the counsel of Balaam, to commit trespass against יהוה in the matter of Peor, and there was a plague among the congregation of יהוה.

17 Now therefore kill every male among the little ones, and kill every woman that hath known man by lying with him.

18 But all the women children, that have not known a man by lying with him, keep alive for yourselves.

19 And do you abide outside the camp seven days; whosoever hath killed any person, and whosoever hath touched any slain, purify both yourselves and your captives on the third day, and on the seventh day.

20 And purify all your raiment, and all that is made of skins, and all work of goats' hair, and all things made of wood."

21 And Eleazar the priest (kohen) said unto the men of war which went to the battle, "This is the ordinance of the [B28a]law (torah) which יהוה commanded Moses (Mosheh):

22 Only the gold, and the silver, the brass, the iron, the tin, and the lead,

23 Everything that may abide the fire, you shall make it go through the fire, and it shall be clean; nevertheless it shall be purified with the water of separation; and all that abideth not the fire you shall make go through the water.

24 And you shall wash your clothes on the seventh day, and you shall be clean, and afterward you shall come into the camp."

25 And יהוה spake unto Moses (Mosheh), saying:

26 "Take the sum of the prey that was taken, both of man and of beast, you, and Eleazar the priest (kohen), and the chief fathers of the congregation;

27 And divide the prey into two parts; between them that took the war upon them, who went out to battle, and between all the congregation.

28 And levy a tribute unto יהוה of the men of war which went out to battle: one soul of five hundred, both of the persons, and of the beeves, and of the asses, and of the sheep;

29 Take it of their half, and give it unto Eleazar the priest (kohen), for a heave offering of יהוה.

30 And of the children of Yisrael's half, you shalt take one portion of fifty, of the persons, of the beeves, of the asses, and of the flocks, of all manner of beasts, and give them unto the Levites (Lewiyim), which keep the charge of the tabernacle of יהוה."

31 And Moses (Mosheh) and Eleazar the priest (kohen) did as יהוה commanded Moses (Mosheh).

32 And the booty, being the rest of the prey which the men of war had caught, was six hundred thousand and seventy thousand and five thousand sheep,

33 And threescore and twelve thousand beeves,

34 And threescore and one thousand asses,

35 And thirty and two thousand persons in all, of women that had not known man by lying with him.

36 And the half, which was the portion of them that went out to war, was in number three hundred thousand and seven and thirty thousand and five hundred sheep;

37 And יהוה's tribute of the sheep was six hundred and threescore and fifteen.

38 And the beeves were thirty and six thousand; of which יהוה's tribute was threescore and twelve.

39 And the asses were thirty thousand and five hundred; of which יהוה's tribute was threescore and one.

40 And the persons were sixteen thousand; of which יהוה's tribute was thirty and two persons.

41 And Moses (Mosheh) gave the tribute, which was יהוה's heave offering, unto Eleazar the priest (kohen), as יהוה commanded Moses (Mosheh).

42 And of the children of Yisrael's half, which Moses (Mosheh) divided from the men that warred,

43 (Now the half that pertained unto the congregation was three hundred thousand and thirty thousand and seven thousand and five hundred sheep,

44 And thirty and six thousand beeves,

45 And thirty thousand asses and five hundred,

46 And sixteen thousand persons;)

47 Even of the children of Yisrael's half, Moses (Mosheh) took one portion of fifty, both of man and of beast, and gave them unto the Levites (Lewiyim), who kept the charge of the tabernacle of יהוה, as יהוה commanded Moses (Mosheh).

48 And the officers which were over thousands of the army, the captains of thousands, and captains of hundreds, came near unto Moses (Mosheh);

49 And they said unto Moses (Mosheh), "Your servants have taken the sum of the men of war which are under our charge, and there lacketh not one man of us.

50 We have therefore brought an oblation for יהוה, what every man hath gotten, of jewels of

gold: chains, and bracelets, rings, earrings, and tablets, to make an atonement for our souls before יהוה"

51 And Moses (Mosheh) and Eleazar the priest (kohen) took the gold of them, even all wrought jewels.

52 And all the gold of the offering that they offered up to יהוה, of the captains of thousands, and of the captains of hundreds, was sixteen thousand seven hundred and fifty shekels.

53 (For the men of war had taken spoil, every man for himself.)

54 And Moses (Mosheh) and Eleazar the priest (kohen) took the gold of the captains of thousands and of hundreds, and brought it into the tabernacle of the congregation, for a memorial for the children of Yisrael before יהוה.

32 Now the children of Reuven and the children of Gad had a very great multitude of cattle; and when they saw the land of Yazer, and the land of Gilad, that, behold, the place was a place for cattle;

2 The children of Gad and the children of Reuven came and spake unto Moses (Mosheh), and to Eleazar the priest (kohen), and unto the princes of the congregation, saying:

3 "Ataroth, and Dibon, and Yazer, and Nimrah, and Heshbon, and Elealeh, and Shebam, and Nebo, and Beon,

4 Even the country which יהוה smote before the congregation of Yisrael, is a land for cattle, and your servants have cattle."

5 Wherefore, said they, "If we have found grace in your sight, let this land be given unto your servants for a possession, and bring us not over Jordan (Yarden)."

6 And Moses (Mosheh) said unto the children of Gad and to the children of Reuven: "Shall your brethren go to war, and shall you sit here?

7 And wherefore discourage you the heart of the children of Yisrael from going over into the land which יהוה hath given them?

8 Thus did your fathers, when I sent them from Qadesh Barnea to see the land.

9 For when they went up unto the valley of Eshcol, and saw the land, they discouraged the heart of the children of Yisrael, that they should not go into the land which יהוה had given them.

10 And יהוה's anger was kindled the same time, and He sware, saying,

11 'Surely none of the men that came up out of Egypt (Mitsrayim), from twenty years old and upward, shall see the land which I sware unto Avraham, unto Isaac (Yitschaq), and unto Jacob (Yaaqov); because they have not wholly followed Me,

12 Except Caleb the son of Yefunneh the Kenezite, and Joshua (Yehoshua) the son of Nun; for they have wholly followed יהוה'

13 And יהוה's anger was kindled against Yisrael, and He made them wander in the wilderness forty years, until all the generation, that had done evil in the sight of יהוה, was consumed.

14 And, behold, you are risen up in your fathers' stead, an increase of sinful men, to augment yet the fierce anger of יהוה toward Yisrael.

15 For if you turn away from after Him, He will yet again leave them in the wilderness; and you shall destroy all this people."

16 And they came near unto him, and said: "We will build sheepfolds here for our cattle, and cities for our little ones;

17 But we ourselves will go ready armed before the children of Yisrael, until we have brought them unto their place; and our little ones shall dwell in the fenced cities because of the inhabitants of the land.

18 We will not return unto our houses, until the children of Yisrael have inherited every man his inheritance.

19 For we will not inherit with them on yonder side Jordan (Yarden), or forward; because our inheritance is fallen to us on this side Jordan (Yarden) eastward."

20 And Moses (Mosheh) said unto them: "If you will do this thing, if you will go armed before יהוה to war,

21 And will go all of you armed over Jordan (Yarden) before יהוה, until He hath driven out his enemies from before Him,

22 And the land be subdued before יהוה: then afterward you shall return, and be guiltless before יהוה, and before Yisrael; and this land shall be your possession before יהוה.

23 But if you will not do so, behold, you have sinned against יהוה; and be sure your sin will find you out.

24 Build you cities for your little ones, and folds for your sheep; and do that which hath proceeded out of your mouth."

25 And the children of Gad and the children of Reuven spake unto Moses (Mosheh), saying:

"Your servants will do as my lord (adoni) commandeth.

26 Our little ones, our wives, our flocks, and all our cattle, shall be there in the cities of Gilad;

27 But your servants will pass over, every man armed for war, before יהוה to battle, as my lord (adoni) saith."

28 So concerning them Moses (Mosheh) commanded Eleazar the priest (kohen), and Joshua (Yehoshua) the son of Nun, and the chief fathers of the tribes of the children of Yisrael:

29 And Moses (Mosheh) said unto them: "If the children of Gad and the children of Reuven will pass with you over Jordan (Yarden), every man armed to battle, before יהוה, and the land shall be subdued before you; then you shall give them the land of Gilad for a possession.

30 But if they will not pass over with you armed, they shall have possessions among you in the land of Canaan."

31 And the children of Gad and the children of Reuven answered, saying: "As יהוה hath said unto your servants, so will we do.

32 We will pass over armed before יהוה into the land of Canaan, that the possession of our inheritance on this side Jordan (Yarden) may be ours."

33 And Moses (Mosheh) gave unto them, even to the children of Gad, and to the children of Reuven, and unto half the tribe of Menashsheh the son of Joseph (Yosef), the kingdom of Sihon king of the Amorites, and the kingdom of Og king of Bashan, the land, with the cities thereof in the coasts, even the cities of the country round about.

34 And the children of Gad built Dibon, and Ataroth, and Aroer,

35 And Atroth, Shophan, and Yaazer, and Yogbehah,

36 And Bethnimrah, and Bethharan, fenced cities, and folds for sheep.

37 And the children of Reuven built Heshbon, and Elealeh, and Qiryataim,

38 And Nebo, and Baal-Meon, (their names being changed,) and Shibmah; and gave other names unto the cities which they builded.

39 And the children of Machir the son of Menashsheh went to Gilad, and took it, and dispossessed the Amorite which was in it.

40 And Moses (Mosheh) gave Gilad unto Machir the son of Menashsheh; and he dwelt therein.

41 And Yair the son of Menashsheh went and took the small towns thereof, and called them Chawot-Yair.

42 And Nobah went and took Kenath, and the villages thereof, and called it Nobah, after his own name.

33 These are the journeys of the children of Yisrael, who went forth out of the land of Egypt (Mitsrayim) with their armies under the hand of Moses (Mosheh) and Aaron (Aharon).

2 And Moses (Mosheh) wrote their goings out according to their journeys by the commandment of יהוה. And these are their journeys according to their goings out;

3 And they departed from Rameses in the first month, on the fifteenth day of the first month; on the next day after the Passover (Pesach) the children of Yisrael went out with a high hand (boldly) in the sight of all the Egyptians (Mitsrayim).

4 For the Egyptians (Mitsrayim) buried all their firstborn, which יהוה had smitten among them. Upon their gods (elohim) also יהוה executed judgments.

5 And the children of Yisrael moved from Rameses, and pitched in Sukkot.

6 And they departed from Sukkot, and pitched in Etham, which is in the edge of the wilderness.

7 And they removed from Etham, and turned again unto Pihahiroth, which is before Baal-Zephon; and they pitched before Migdol.

8 And they departed from before Pihahiroth, and passed through the midst of the sea into the wilderness, and went three days' journey in the wilderness of Etham, and pitched in Marah.

9 And they moved from Marah, and came unto Elim; and in Elim were twelve fountains of water, and threescore and ten palm trees; and they pitched there.

10 And they moved from Elim, and encamped by the Red sea.

11 And they moved from the Red sea, and encamped in the wilderness of Sin.

12 And they took their journey out of the wilderness of Sin, and encamped in Dophkah.

13 And they departed from Dophkah, and encamped in Alush.

14 And they moved from Alush, and encamped at Rephidim, where was no water for the people to drink.

15 And they departed from Rephidim, and pitched in the wilderness of Sinai.

16 And they moved from the desert of Sinai, and pitched at Qivrot-hattaavah.

17 And they departed from Qivrot-hattaavah, and encamped at Hazeroth.

18 And they departed from Hazeroth, and pitched in Rithmah.

19 And they departed from Rithmah, and pitched at Rimmonparez.

20 And they departed from Rimmonparez, and pitched in Libnah.

21 And they moved from Libnah, and pitched at Rissah.

22 And they journeyed from Rissah, and pitched in Kehelathah.

23 And they went from Kehelathah, and pitched in mount Shapher.

24 And they removed from mount Shapher, and encamped in Haradah.

25 And they moved from Haradah, and pitched in Makheloth.

26 And they moved from Makheloth, and encamped at Tahath.

27 And they departed from Tahath, and pitched at Tarah.

28 And they moved from Tarah, and pitched in Mithcah.

29 And they went from Mithcah, and pitched in Hashmonah.

30 And they departed from Hashmonah, and encamped at Moseroth.

31 And they departed from Moseroth, and pitched in Beneyaakan.

32 And they moved from Benejaakan, and encamped at Horhagidgad.

33 And they went from Horhagidgad, and pitched in Yotbathah.

34 And they moved from Yotbathah, and encamped at Ebronah.

35 And they departed from Ebronah, and encamped at Eziongaber.

36 And they moved from Eziongaber, and pitched in the wilderness of Zin, which is Qadesh.

37 And they moved from Qadesh, and pitched in Mount Hor, in the edge of the land of Edom.

38 And Aaron (Aharon) the priest (kohen) went up into Mount Hor at the commandment of יהוה, and died there, in the fortieth year after the children of Yisrael were come out of the land of Egypt

(Mitsrayim), in the first day of the fifth month.

39 And Aaron (Aharon) was a hundred and twenty and three years old when he died in Mount Hor.

40 And king Arad the Canaanite, which dwelt in the south in the land of Canaan, heard of the coming of the children of Yisrael.

41 And they departed from Mount Hor, and pitched in Zalmonah.

42 And they departed from Zalmonah, and pitched in Punon.

43 And they departed from Punon, and pitched in Oboth.

44 And they departed from Oboth, and pitched in Iye-Avarim, in the border of Moav.

45 And they departed from Iim, and pitched in Dibongad.

46 And they moved from Dibongad, and encamped in Almondiblathaim.

47 And they moved from Almondiblathaim, and pitched in the mountains of Avarim, before Nebo.

48 And they departed from the mountains of Avarim, and pitched in the plains of Moav by Jordan (Yarden) near Yericho.

49 And they pitched by Jordan (Yarden), from Beit-Hayshimot even unto Avelshittim in the plains of Moav.

50 And יהוה spake unto Moses (Mosheh) in the plains of Moav by Jordan (Yarden) near Yericho, saying,

51 "Speak unto the children of Yisrael, and say unto them, 'When you are passed over Jordan (Yarden) into the land of Canaan;

52 Then you shall drive out all the inhabitants of the land from before you, and destroy all their engraved stones, and destroy all their molten images, and pluck down all their high places;

53 And you shall dispossess the inhabitants of the land, and dwell therein, for I have given you the land to possess it.

54 And you shall divide the land by lot for an inheritance among your families; and to the more you shall give the more inheritance, and to the fewer you shall give the less inheritance; every man's inheritance shall be in the place where his lot falleth; according to the tribes of your fathers you shall inherit.

55 But if you will not drive out the inhabitants of the land from before you; then it shall come to pass, that those which you let remain of them

shall be pricks in your eyes, and thorns in your sides, and shall vex you in the land wherein you dwell.

56 Moreover it shall come to pass, that I shall do unto you, as I thought to do unto them.'"

34 And יהוה spake unto Moses (Mosheh), saying,

2 "Command the children of Yisrael, and say unto them: 'When you come into the land of Canaan; (this is the land that shall fall unto you for an inheritance, even the land of Canaan with the coasts thereof.)

3 Then your south quarter shall be from the wilderness of Zin along by the coast of Edom, and your south border shall be the outmost coast of the Salt Sea eastward;

4 And your border shall turn from the south to the ascent of Akrabbim, and pass on to Zin, and the going forth thereof shall be from the south to Qadesh Barnea, and shall go on to Hazaraddar, and pass on to Azmon;

5 And the border shall fetch a compass from Azmon unto the river of Egypt (Mitsrayim), and the goings out of it shall be at the sea.

6 And as for the western border, you shall even have the great sea for a border; this shall be your west border.

7 And this shall be your north border: From the great sea you shall point out for you Mount Hor;

8 From mount Hor you shall point out your border unto the entrance of Hamath; and the goings forth of the border shall be to Zedad;

9 And the border shall go on to Ziphron, and the goings out of it shall be at Hazarenan; this shall be your north border.

10 And you shall point out your east border from Hazarenan to Shepham;

11 And the coast shall go down from Shepham to Riblah, on the east side of Ain; and the border shall descend, and shall reach unto the side of the sea of Chinnereth eastward;

12 And the border shall go down to Jordan (Yarden), and the goings out of it shall be at the Salt Sea; this shall be your land with the coasts thereof round about.

13 And Moses (Mosheh) commanded the children of Yisrael, saying: "This is the land which you shall inherit by lot, which יהוה commanded to give unto the nine tribes, and to the half tribe.

14 For the tribe of the children of Reuven according to the house of their fathers, and the tribe of the children of Gad according to the house of their fathers, have received their inheritance; and half the tribe of Menashsheh have received their inheritance.

15 The two tribes and the half tribe have received their inheritance on this side Jordan (Yarden) near Yericho eastward, toward the sunrising."

16 And יהוה spake unto Moses (Mosheh), saying,

17 "These are the names of the men which shall divide the land unto you: Eleazar the priest (kohen), and Joshua (Yehoshua) the son of Nun.

18 And you shall take one prince of every tribe, to divide the land by inheritance.

19 And the names of the men are these: Of the tribe of Judah (Yehudah), Caleb the son of Yefunneh.

20 And of the tribe of the children of Shimon, Shemuel the son of Ammihud.

21 Of the tribe of Binyamin, Elidad the son of Chislon.

22 And the prince of the tribe of the children of Dan, Bukki the son of Yogli.

23 The prince of the children of Joseph (Yosef), for the tribe of the children of Menashsheh, Hanniel the son of Ephod.

24 And the prince of the tribe of the children of Efrayim, Kemuel the son of Shiphtan.

25 And the prince of the tribe of the children of Zevulun, Elizaphan the son of Parnach.

26 And the prince of the tribe of the children of Yissaskhar, Paltiel the son of Azzan.

27 And the prince of the tribe of the children of Asher, Ahihud the son of Shelomi.

28 And the prince of the tribe of the children of Naftali, Pedahel the son of Ammihud."

29 These are they whom יהוה commanded to divide the inheritance unto the children of Yisrael in the land of Canaan.

35 And יהוה spake unto Moses (Mosheh) in the plains of Moav by Jordan (Yarden) near Yericho, saying,

2 "Command the children of Yisrael, that they give unto the Levites (Lewiyim) of the inheritance of their possession cities to dwell in; and you shall give also unto the Levites (Lewiyim) suburbs for the cities round about them.

3 And the cities shall they have to dwell in; and

the suburbs of them shall be for their cattle, and for their goods, and for all their beasts.

4 And the suburbs of the cities, which you shall give unto the Levites (Lewiyim), shall reach from the wall of the city and outward a thousand cubits round about.

5 And you shall measure from outside the city on the east side two thousand cubits, and on the south side two thousand cubits, and on the west side two thousand cubits, and on the north side two thousand cubits; and the city shall be in the midst; this shall be to them the suburbs of the cities.

6 And among the cities which you shall give unto the Levites (Lewiyim) there shall be six cities for refuge, which you shall appoint for the manslayer, that he may flee thither; and to them you shall add forty and two cities.

7 So all the cities which you shall give to the Levites (Lewiyim) shall be forty and eight cities; them shall you give with their suburbs.

8 And the cities which you shall give shall be of the possession of the children of Yisrael; from them that have many you shall give many; but from them that have few you shall give few; every one shall give of his cities unto the Levites (Lewiyim) according to his inheritance which he inheriteth."

9 And יהוה spake unto Moses (Mosheh), saying,

10 "Speak unto the children of Yisrael, and say unto them: 'When you be come over Jordan (Yarden) into the land of Canaan;

11 Then you shall appoint cities to be cities of refuge for you, that the slayer may flee thither, which killeth any person at unawares.

12 And they shall be unto you cities for refuge from the avenger, that the manslayer die not, until he stand before the congregation in judgment.

13 And of these cities which you shall give six cities shall you have for refuge.

14 You shall give three cities on this side Jordan (Yarden), and three cities shall you give in the land of Canaan, which shall be cities of refuge.

15 These six cities shall be a refuge, both for the children of Yisrael, and for the stranger, and for the sojourner among them, that every one that killeth any person unawares may flee thither.

16 And if he smites him with an instrument of iron, so that he dies, he is a murderer; the murderer shall surely be put to death.

17 And if he smites him with throwing a stone, wherewith he may die, and he die, he is a murderer; the murderer shall surely be put to death.

18 Or if he smites him with a hand weapon of wood, wherewith he may die, and he die, he is a murderer; the murderer shall surely be put to death.

19 The revenger of blood himself shall slay the murderer; when he meeteth him, he shall slay him.

20 But if he thrust him of hatred, or hurl at him by laying of wait, that he dies;

21 Or in enmity smite him with his hand, that he dies, he that smote him shall surely be put to death; for he is a murderer; the revenger of blood shall slay the murderer, when he meeteth him.

22 But if he thrust him suddenly without enmity, or have cast upon him any thing without laying of wait,

23 Or with any stone, wherewith a man may die, seeing him not, and cast it upon him, that he dies, and was not his enemy, neither sought his harm;

24 Then the congregation shall judge between the slayer and the revenger of blood according to these judgments.

25 And the congregation shall deliver the slayer out of the hand of the revenger of blood, and the congregation shall restore him to the city of his refuge, whither he was fled: and he shall abide in it unto the death of the high priest (kohen hagadol), which was anointed with the holy oil.

26 But if the slayer shall at any time come outside the border of the city of his refuge, whither he was fled;

27 And the revenger of blood finds him outside the borders of the city of his refuge, and the revenger of blood kill the slayer; he shall not be guilty of blood,

28 Because he should have remained in the city of his refuge until the death of the high priest (kohen hagadol); but after the death of the high priest (kohen hagadol) the slayer shall return into the land of his possession.

29 So these things shall be for a statute of judgment unto you throughout your generations in all your dwellings.

30 Whoso killeth any person, the murderer shall be put to death by the mouth of witnesses; but one witness shall not testify against any person

to cause him to die.

31 Moreover you shall take no satisfaction for the life of a murderer, which is guilty of death, but he shall be surely put to death.

32 And you shall take no satisfaction for him that is fled to the city of his refuge, that he should come again to dwell in the land, until the death of the priest (kohen).

33 So you shall not pollute the land wherein you are, for blood it defileth the land; and the land cannot be cleansed of the blood that is shed therein, but by the blood of him that shed it.

34 Defile not therefore the land which you shall inhabit, wherein I dwell; for I יהוה dwell among the children of Yisrael.'"

36 And the chief fathers of the families of the children of Gilad, the son of Machir, the son of Menashsheh, of the families of the sons of Joseph (Yosef), came near, and spake before Moses (Mosheh), and before the princes, the chief fathers of the children of Yisrael;

2 And they said: "יהוה commanded my lord (adoni) to give the land for an inheritance by lot to the children of Yisrael, and my lord (adoni) was commanded by יהוה to give the inheritance of Zelophehad our brother unto his daughters.

3 And if they be married to any of the sons of the other tribes of the children of Yisrael, then shall their inheritance be taken from the inheritance of our fathers, and shall be put to the inheritance of the tribe whereunto they are received; so shall it be taken from the lot of our inheritance.

4 And when the [B25]Jubilee (Yovel) of the children of Yisrael shall be, then shall their inheritance be put unto the inheritance of the tribe whereunto they are received; so shall their inheritance be taken away from the inheritance of the tribe of our fathers."

5 And Moses (Mosheh) commanded the children of Yisrael according to the word of יהוה, saying: "The tribe of the sons of Joseph (Yosef) hath said well.

6 This is the thing which יהוה doth command concerning the daughters of Zelophehad, saying, 'Let them marry to whom they think best; only to the family of the tribe of their father shall they marry.'

7 So shall not the inheritance of the children of Yisrael remove from tribe to tribe, for every one of the children of Yisrael shall keep himself to the inheritance of the tribe of his fathers.

8 And every daughter, that possesseth an inheritance in any tribe of the children of Yisrael, shall be wife unto one of the family of the tribe of her father, that the children of Yisrael may enjoy every man the inheritance of his fathers.

9 Neither shall the inheritance remove from one tribe to another tribe; but every one of the tribes of the children of Yisrael shall keep himself to his own inheritance."

10 Even as יהוה commanded Moses (Mosheh), so did the daughters of Zelophehad;

11 For Mahlah, Tirzah, and Hoglah, and Milcah, and Noach, the daughters of Zelophehad, were married unto their father's brothers' sons.

12 And they were married into the families of the sons of Menashsheh the son of Joseph (Yosef), and their inheritance remained in the tribe of the family of their father.

13 These are the commandments and the judgments, which יהוה commanded by the hand of Moses (Mosheh) unto the children of Yisrael in the plains of Moav by Jordan (Yarden) near Yericho.

DEUTERONOMY
DEVARIM דְּבָרִים
(Words)

1 These be the words which Moses (Mosheh) spake unto all Yisrael on this side Jordan (Yarden) in the wilderness, in the plain opposite the Red sea, between Paran, and Tophel, and Lavan, and Hazeroth, and Di Zahav.

2 There are eleven days' journey from Horeb (Chorev) by the way of Mount Seir unto Qadesh Barnea.

3 And it came to pass in the fortieth year, in the eleventh month, on the first day of the month, that Moses (Mosheh) spake unto the children of Yisrael, according unto all that יהוה had given him in commandment unto them;

4 After he had slain Sihon the king of the Amorites, which dwelt in Heshbon, and Og the king of Bashan, which dwelt at Astaroth in Edrei.

5 On this side Jordan (Yarden), in the land of Moav, began Moses (Mosheh) to declare this instruction, saying,

6 "יהוה our God (YHWH Eloheinu) spake unto us in Horeb (Chorev), saying: 'You have dwelt long enough in this mountain.

7 Turn and take your journey, and go to the mount of the Amorites, and unto all the places near thereunto, in the plain, in the hills, and in the vale, and in the south, and by the sea side, to the land of the Canaanites, and unto Lebanon, unto the great river, the river Euphrates.

8 Behold, I have set the land before you; go in and possess the land which יהוה sware unto your fathers, Avraham, Isaac (Yitschaq), and Jacob (Yaaqov), to give unto them and to their seed after them.'

9 And I spake unto you at that time, saying: 'I am not able to bear you myself alone.

10 יהוה your God (YHWH Eloheikhem) hath multiplied you, and, behold, you are this day as the stars of heaven for multitude.

11 יהוה God (Elohim) of your fathers make you a thousand times so many more as you are, and bless you, as He hath promised you!

12 How can I myself alone bear your cumbrance, and your burden, and your strife?

13 Take you wise men, and understanding, and known among your tribes, and I will make them rulers over you.'

14 And you answered me, and said, 'The thing which you have spoken is good for us to do.'

15 So I took the chief of your tribes, wise men, and known, and made them heads over you, captains over thousands, and captains over hundreds, and captains over fifties, and captains over tens, and officers among your tribes.

16 And I charged your judges at that time, saying, 'Hear the causes between your brethren, and judge righteously between every man and his brother, and the stranger that is with him.

17 You shall not respect persons in judgment; but you shall hear the small as well as the great; you shall not be afraid of the face of man; for the judgment is God (Elohim)'s; and the cause that is too hard for you, bring it unto me, and I will hear it.'

18 And I commanded you at that time all the things which you should do.

19 And when we departed from Horeb (Chorev), we went through all that great and terrible wilderness, which you saw by the way of the mountain of the Amorites, as יהוה our God (YHWH Eloheinu) commanded us; and we came to Qadesh Barnea.

20 And I said unto you, 'You have come unto the mountain of the Amorites, which יהוה our God (YHWH Eloheinu) doth give unto us.

21 Behold, יהוה your God (Eloheikha) hath set the land before you; go up and possess it, as יהוה God (Elohim) of your fathers hath said unto you; fear not, neither be discouraged.'

22 And you came near unto me every one of you, and said, 'We will send men before us, and they shall search us out the land, and bring us word again by what way we must go up, and into what cities we shall come.'

23 And the saying pleased me well; and I took twelve men of you, one of a tribe.

24 And they turned and went up into the mountain, and came unto the valley of Eshcol, and searched it out.

25 And they took of the fruit of the land in their hands, and brought it down unto us, and brought us word again, and said, 'It is a good land which יהוה our God (YHWH Eloheinu) doth give us.'

26 Notwithstanding you would not go up, but rebelled against the commandment of יהוה your God (YHWH Eloheikhem);

27 And you murmured in your tents, and said, 'Because יהוה hated us, He hath brought us forth

out of the land of Egypt (Mitsrayim), to deliver us into the hand of the Amorites, to destroy us. 28 Whither shall we go up? Our brethren have discouraged our heart, saying, "The people is greater and taller than we; the cities are great and walled up to heaven; and moreover we have seen the sons of the Anakims there."

29 Then I said unto you, 'Dread not, neither be afraid of them.

30 יהוה your God (YHWH Eloheikhem) who goeth before you, He shall fight for you, according to all that He did for you in Egypt (Mitsrayim) before your eyes;

31 And in the wilderness, where you have seen how that יהוה your God (YHWH Eloheikha) bare you, as a man doth bear his son, in all the way that you went, until you came into this place.'

32 Yet in this thing you did not believe יהוה your God (YHWH Eloheikhem),

33 Who went in the way before you, to search you out a place to pitch your tents in, in fire by night, to shew you by what way you should go, and in a cloud by day.

34 And יהוה heard the voice of your words, and was wroth, and sware, saying,

35 'Surely there shall not one of these men of this evil generation see that good land, which I sware to give unto your fathers,

36 Except Caleb the son of Yefunneh; he shall see it, and to him will I give the land that he hath trodden upon, and to his children, because he hath wholly followed יהוה'

37 Also יהוה was angry with me for your sakes, saying, 'You also shalt not go in thither;

38 But Joshua (Yehoshua) the son of Nun, who standeth before you, he shall go in thither. Encourage him, for he shall cause Yisrael to inherit it.

39 Moreover your little ones, which you said should be a prey, and your children, which in that day had no knowledge between good and evil, they shall go in thither, and unto them will I give it, and they shall possess it.

40 But as for you, turn you, and take your journey into the wilderness by the way of the Red sea.'

41 Then you answered and said unto me, 'We have sinned against יהוה, we will go up and fight, according to all that יהוה our God (YHWH Eloheinu) commanded us.' And when you had

girded on every man his weapons of war, you were ready to go up into the hill.

42 And יהוה said unto me, 'Say unto them, "Go not up, neither fight; for I am not among you; lest you be smitten before your enemies."'

43 So I spake unto you; and you would not hear, but rebelled against the commandment of יהוה, and went presumptuously up into the mountain.

44 And the Amorites, who dwelt in that mountain, came out against you, and chased you, as bees do, and destroyed you in Seir, even unto Hormah.

45 And you returned and wept before יהוה; but יהוה would not hearken to your voice, nor give ear unto you.

46 So you abode in Qadesh many days, according unto the days that you abode there."

2 "Then we turned, and took our journey into the wilderness by the way of the Red sea, as יהוה spake unto me, and we compassed mount Seir many days.

2 And יהוה spake unto me, saying:

3 'You have compassed this mountain long enough; turn northward.

4 And command you the people, saying, "You are to pass through the coast of your brethren the children of Esaw, which dwell in Seir; and they shall be afraid of you; take you good heed unto yourselves therefore.

5 Meddle not with them, for I will not give you of their land, no, not so much as a foot breadth, because I have given Mount Seir unto Esaw for a possession.

6 You shall buy meat of them for money, that you may eat; and you shall also buy water of them for money, that you may drink.

7 For יהוה your God (YHWH Eloheikha) hath blessed you in all the works of your hand. He knoweth your walking through this great wilderness. These forty years יהוה your God (YHWH Eloheikha) hath been with you; you have lacked nothing."'

8 And when we passed by from our brethren the children of Esaw, which dwelt in Seir, through the way of the plain from Elath, and from Eziongaber, we turned and passed by the way of the wilderness of Moav.

9 And יהוה said unto me, 'Distress not the Moavites, neither contend with them in battle; for I will not give you of their land for a possession; because I have given Ar unto the

children of Lot for a possession.'"

10 The Emims dwelt therein in times past, a people great, and many, and tall, as the Anakims.

11 Which also were accounted giants, as the Anakims; but the Moavites call them Emims.

12 The Horims also dwelt in Seir beforetime; but the children of Esaw succeeded them, when they had destroyed them from before them, and dwelt in their stead; as Yisrael did unto the land of his possession, which יהוה gave unto them.

13 Now rise up, said I, and get you over the brook Zered. And we went over the brook Zered.

14 And the space in which we came from Qadesh Barnea, until we were come over the brook Zered, was thirty and eight years; until all the generation of the men of war were wasted out from among the army, as יהוה sware unto them.

15 For indeed the hand of יהוה was against them, to destroy them from among the army, until they were consumed.

16 So it came to pass, when all the men of war were consumed and dead from among the people,

17 That יהוה spake unto me, saying:

18 'You are to pass over through Ar, the coast of Moav, this day.

19 And when you comest near opposite the children of Ammon, distress them not, nor meddle with them, for I will not give you of the land of the children of Ammon any possession; because I have given it unto the children of Lot for a possession.

20 (That also was accounted a land of giants; giants dwelt therein in old time; and the Ammonites call them Zamzummims,

21 A people great, and many, and tall, as the Anakims; but יהוה destroyed them before them; and they succeeded them, and dwelt in their stead,

22 As he did to the children of Esaw, which dwelt in Seir, when he destroyed the Horims from before them; and they succeeded them, and dwelt in their stead even unto this day.

23 And the Avims which dwelt in Hazerim, even unto Azzah, the Caphtorims, which came forth out of Caphtor, destroyed them, and dwelt in their stead.)

24 'Rise you up, take your journey, and pass over the river Arnon. Behold, I have given into your hand Sihon the Amorite, king of Heshbon, and his land. Begin to possess it, and contend with him in battle.

25 This day will I begin to put the dread of you and the fear of you upon the nations that are under the whole heaven, who shall hear report of you, and shall tremble, and be in anguish because of you.'

26 And I sent messengers out of the wilderness of Kedemoth unto Sihon king of Heshbon with words of peace, saying,

27 'Let me pass through your land; I will go along by the high way, I will neither turn unto the right hand nor to the left.

28 You shalt sell me meat for money, that I may eat; and give me water for money, that I may drink; only I will pass through on my feet;

29 (As the children of Esaw which dwell in Seir, and the Moavites which dwell in Ar, did unto me;) until I shall pass over Jordan (Yarden) into the land which יהוה our God (YHWH Eloheinu) giveth us.'

30 But Sihon king of Heshbon would not let us pass by him, for יהוה your God (YHWH Eloheikha) hardened his spirit, and made his heart obstinate, that he might deliver him into your hand, as appeareth this day.

31 And יהוה said unto me, 'Behold, I have begun to give Sihon and his land before you; begin to possess, that you mayest inherit his land.'

32 Then Sihon came out against us, he and all his people, to fight at Yahats.

33 And יהוה our God (YHWH Eloheinu) delivered him before us; and we smote him, and his sons, and all his people.

34 And we took all his cities at that time, and utterly destroyed the men, and the women, and the little ones, of every city, we left none to remain.

35 Only the cattle we took for a prey unto ourselves, and the spoil of the cities which we took.

36 From Aroer, which is by the brink of the river of Arnon, and from the city that is by the river, even unto Gilad, there was not one city too strong for us; יהוה our God (YHWH Eloheinu) delivered all unto us.

37 Only unto the land of the children of Ammon you camest not, nor unto any place of the river Yabok, nor unto the cities in the mountains, nor

unto whatsoever יהוה our God (YHWH Eloheinu) forbad us.

3 Then we turned, and went up the way to Bashan; and Og the king of Bashan came out against us, he and all his people, to battle at Edrei.

2 And יהוה said unto me, 'Fear him not, for I will deliver him, and all his people, and his land, into your hand; and you shalt do unto him as you didst unto Sihon king of the Amorites, which dwelt at Heshbon.'

3 So יהוה our God (YHWH Eloheinu) delivered into our hands Og also, the king of Bashan, and all his people; and we smote him until none was left to him remaining.

4 And we took all his cities at that time, there was not a city which we took not from them, threescore cities, all the region of Argob, the kingdom of Og in Bashan.

5 All these cities were fenced with high walls, gates, and bars; besides unwalled towns a great many.

6 And we utterly destroyed them, as we did unto Sihon king of Heshbon, utterly destroying the men, women, and children, of every city.

7 But all the cattle, and the spoil of the cities, we took for a prey to ourselves.

8 And we took at that time out of the hand of the two kings of the Amorites the land that was on this side Jordan (Yarden), from the river of Arnon unto Mount Hermon;

9 (Which Hermon the Sidonians call Sirion; and the Amorites call it Shenir;)

10 All the cities of the plain, and all Gilad, and all Bashan, unto Salchah and Edrei, cities of the kingdom of Og in Bashan.

11 For only Og king of Bashan remained of the remnant of giants; behold, his bedstead was a bedstead of iron; is it not in Rabbath of the children of Ammon? Nine cubits was the length thereof, and four cubits the breadth of it, after the cubit of a man.

12 And this land, which we possessed at that time, from Aroer, which is by the river Arnon, and half mount Gilad, and the cities thereof, gave I unto the Reubenites (Reuveni) and to the Gadites.

13 And the rest of Gilad, and all Bashan, being the kingdom of Og, gave I unto the half tribe of Menashsheh; all the region of Argob, with all Bashan, which was called the land of giants.

14 Yair the son of Menashsheh took all the country of Argob unto the coasts of Geshuri and Maachathi; and called them after his own name, Bashanhavothyair, unto this day.

15 And I gave Gilad unto Machir.

16 And unto the Reubenites (Reuveni) and unto the Gadites I gave from Gilad even unto the river Arnon half the valley, and the border even unto the river Yabok, which is the border of the children of Ammon;

17 The plain also, and Jordan (Yarden), and the coast thereof, from Chinnereth even unto the sea of the plain, even the salt sea, under Ashdothpisgah eastward.

18 And I commanded you at that time, saying: 'יהוה your God (YHWH Eloheikhem) hath given you this land to possess it; you shall pass over armed before your brethren the children of Yisrael, all that are meet for the war.

19 But your wives, and your little ones, and your cattle, (for I know that you have much cattle,) shall abide in your cities which I have given you;

20 Until יהוה have given rest unto your brethren, as well as unto you, and until they also possess the land which יהוה your God (YHWH Eloheikhem) hath given them beyond Jordan (Yarden). And then shall you return every man unto his possession, which I have given you.'

21 And I commanded Joshua (Yehoshua) at that time, saying, 'Your eyes have seen all that יהוה your God (YHWH Eloheikhem) hath done unto these two kings; so shall יהוה do unto all the kingdoms whither you passest.

22 You shall not fear them, for יהוה your God (YHWH Eloheikhem), He shall fight for you.'

23 And I besought יהוה at that time, saying:

24 'O Lord (Adonai) יהוה, You have begun to shew Your servant Your greatness, and Your mighty hand, for what God (Elohim) is there in heaven or in earth, that can do according to Your works, and according to Your might?

25 I pray, let me go over, and see the good land that is beyond Jordan (Yarden), that goodly mountain, and Lebanon.'

26 But יהוה was wroth with me for your sakes, and would not hear me. And יהוה said unto me: 'Let it suffice you; speak no more unto Me of this matter.

27 Get you up into the top of Pisgah, and lift up your eyes westward, and northward, and

southward, and eastward, and behold it with your eyes, for you shalt not go over this Jordan (Yarden).

28 But charge Joshua (Yehoshua), and encourage him, and strengthen him; for he shall go over before this people, and he shall cause them to inherit the land which you shalt see.'

29 So we abode in the valley opposite Beit-Peor.

4 Now therefore hearken, O Yisrael, unto the statutes and unto the judgments, which I teach you, for to do them, that you may live, and go in and possess the land which יהוה God (Elohim) of your fathers giveth you.

2 You shall not add unto the word which I command you, neither shall you diminish ought from it, that you may keep the commandments of יהוה your God (YHWH Eloheikhem) which I command you.

3 Your eyes have seen what יהוה did because of Baalpeor; for all the men that followed Baalpeor, יהוה your God (YHWH Eloheikhem) hath destroyed them from among you.

4 But you that did cleave unto יהוה your God (YHWH Eloheikhem) are alive every one of you this day.

5 Behold, I have taught you statutes and judgments, even as יהוה my God (YHWH Elohai) commanded me, that you should do so in the land whither you go to possess it.

6 Keep therefore and do them; for this is your wisdom and your understanding in the sight of the nations, which shall hear all these statutes, and say, 'Surely this great nation is a wise and understanding people.'

7 For what nation is there so great, who hath God (Elohim) so near unto them, as יהוה our God (YHWH Eloheinu) is in all things that we call upon Him for?

8 And what nation is there so great, that hath statutes and judgments so righteous as this whole Torah, which I set before you this day?

9 Only take heed to yourself, and keep your soul diligently, lest you forget the things which your eyes have seen, and lest they depart from your heart all the days of your life; but teach them your sons, and your sons' sons;

10 Specially the day that you stoodest before יהוה your God (YHWH Eloheikha) in Horeb, when יהוה said unto me, 'Gather Me the people together, and I will make them hear My words, that they may learn to fear Me all the days that

they shall live upon the earth, and that they may teach their children.'

11 And you came near and stood under the mountain; and the mountain burned with fire unto the midst of heaven, with darkness, clouds, and thick darkness.

12 And יהוה spake unto you out of the midst of the fire. You heard the voice of the words, but saw no similitude; only you heard a voice.

13 And He declared unto you His covenant, which He commanded you to perform, even ten commandments; and He wrote them upon two tables of stone.

14 And יהוה commanded me at that time to teach you statutes and judgments, that you might do them in the land whither you go over to possess it.

15 Take you therefore good heed unto yourselves; for you saw no manner of similitude on the day that יהוה spake unto you in Horeb (Chorev) out of the midst of the fire;

16 Lest you corrupt yourselves, and make you a graven image, the similitude of any figure, the likeness of male or female,

17 The likeness of any beast that is on the earth, the likeness of any winged fowl that flieth in the air,

18 The likeness of any thing that creepeth on the ground, the likeness of any fish that is in the waters beneath the earth.

19 And lest you lift up your eyes unto heaven, and when you seest the sun, and the moon, and the stars, even all the host of heaven, shouldest be driven to worship them, and serve them, which יהוה your God (YHWH Eloheikhem) hath divided unto all nations under the whole heaven.

20 But יהוה hath taken you, and brought you forth out of the iron furnace, even out of Egypt (Mitsrayim), to be unto Him a people of inheritance, as you are this day.

21 Furthermore יהוה was angry with me for your sakes, and sware that I should not go over Jordan (Yarden), and that I should not go in unto that good land, which יהוה your God (YHWH Eloheikha) giveth you for an inheritance.

22 But I must die in this land, I must not go over Jordan (Yarden); but you shall go over, and possess that good land.

23 Take heed unto yourselves, lest you forget the covenant of יהוה your God (YHWH

Eloheikhem), which He made with you, and make you a graven image, or the likeness of any thing, which יהוה your God (YHWH Eloheikhem) hath forbidden you.

24 For יהוה your God (YHWH Eloheikha) is a consuming fire, even a jealous God (El).

25 When you shalt beget children, and children's children, and you shall have remained long in the land, and shall corrupt yourselves, and make a graven image, or the likeness of any thing, and shall do evil in the sight of יהוה your God (YHWH Eloheikha), to provoke Him to anger;

26 I call heaven and earth to witness against you this day, that you shall soon utterly perish from off the land whereunto you go over Jordan (Yarden) to possess it; you shall not prolong your days upon it, but shall utterly be destroyed.

27 And יהוה shall scatter you among the nations, and you shall be left few in number among the heathen, whither יהוה shall lead you.

28 And there you shall serve gods (elohim), the work of men's hands, wood and stone, which neither see, nor hear, nor eat, nor smell.

29 But if from thence you shalt seek יהוה your God (YHWH Eloheikha), you shalt find Him, if you seek Him with all your heart and with all your soul.

30 When you are in tribulation, and all these things are come upon you, even in the latter days, if you turn to יהוה your God (YHWH Eloheikha), and shalt be obedient unto His voice;

31 (For יהוה your God (YHWH Eloheikha) is a merciful God (Elohim);) He will not forsake you, neither destroy you, nor forget the covenant of your fathers which He sware unto them.

32 For ask now of the days that are past, which were before you, since the day that God (Elohim) created man upon the earth, and ask from the one side of heaven unto the other, whether there hath been any such thing as this great thing is, or hath been heard like it?

33 Did ever people hear the voice of God (Elohim) speaking out of the midst of the fire, as you have heard, and live?

34 Or hath God (Elohim) assayed to go and take Him a nation from the midst of another nation, by temptations, by signs, and by wonders, and by war, and by a mighty hand, and by a stretched- out arm, and by great terrors, according to all that יהוה your God (YHWH

Eloheikhem) did for you in Egypt (Mitsrayim) before your eyes?

35 Unto you it was shewed, that you mightest know that יהוה He is God (Elohim); there is none else besides Him.

36 Out of heaven He made you to hear His voice, that He might instruct you; and upon earth He shewed you His great fire; and you heardest His words out of the midst of the fire.

37 And because He loved your fathers, therefore He chose their seed after them, and brought you out in His sight with His mighty power out of Egypt (Mitsrayim);

38 To drive out nations from before you greater and mightier than you are, to bring you in, to give you their land for an inheritance, as it is this day.

39 Know therefore this day, and consider it in your heart, that יהוה He is God (Elohim) in heaven above, and upon the earth beneath; there is none else.

40 You shalt keep therefore His statutes, and His commandments, which I command you this day, that it may go well with you, and with your children after you, and that you mayest prolong your days upon the earth, which יהוה your God (YHWH Eloheikha) giveth you, forever."

41 Then Moses (Mosheh) separated three cities on this side Jordan (Yarden) toward the sunrising;

42 That the slayer might flee thither, which should kill his neighbour unawares, and hated him not in times past; and that fleeing unto one of these cities he might live;

43 Namely: Bezer in the wilderness, in the plain country, of the Reubenites (Reuveni); and Ramot in Gilad, of the Gadites; and Golan in Bashan, of the Manassites.

44 And this is the teaching which Moses (Mosheh) set before the children of Yisrael.

45 These are the testimonies, and the statutes, and the judgments, which Moses (Mosheh) spake unto the children of Yisrael, after they came forth out of Egypt (Mitsrayim),

46 On this side Jordan (Yarden), in the valley opposite Beit-Peor, in the land of Sihon king of the Amorites, who dwelt at Heshbon, whom Moses (Mosheh) and the children of Yisrael smote, after they were come forth out of Egypt (Mitsrayim).

47 And they possessed his land, and the land of

Og king of Bashan, two kings of the Amorites, which were on this side Jordan (Yarden) toward the sunrising;

48 From Aroer, which is by the bank of the river Arnon, even unto mount Sion, which is Hermon,

49 And all the plain on this side Jordan (Yarden) eastward, even unto the sea of the plain (Aravah), under the springs of Pisgah.

5 And Moses (Mosheh) called all Yisrael, and said unto them: "Hear, O Yisrael, the statutes and judgments which I speak in your ears this day, that you may learn them, and keep, and do them.

2 יהוה our God (YHWH Eloheinu) made a covenant with us in Horeb (Chorev).

3 יהוה made not this covenant with our fathers, but with us, even us, who are all of us here alive this day.

4 יהוה talked with you face to face in the mount out of the midst of the fire,

5 (I stood between יהוה and you at that time, to shew you the word of יהוה; for you were afraid by reason of the fire, and went not up into the mountain;) saying:

6 'I am יהוה your God (YHWH Eloheikha), who brought you out of the land of Egypt (Mitsrayim), from the house of bondage.

7 You shalt have none other gods (elohim) before Me.

8 You shalt not make you any graven image, or any likeness of anything that is in heaven above, or that is in the earth beneath, or that is in the waters beneath the earth;

9 You shalt not bow down yourself unto them, nor serve them; for I יהוה your God (YHWH Eloheikha) am a jealous God (El), visiting the iniquity of the fathers upon the children unto the third and fourth generation of them that hate Me,

10 And shewing mercy unto thousands of them that love Me and keep My commandments.

11 You shalt not take the name of יהוה your God (YHWH Eloheikha) in vain, for יהוה will not hold Him guiltless that taketh His name in vain.

12 Keep the Shabbat day to sanctify it, as יהוה your God (YHWH Eloheikha) hath commanded you.

13 Six days you shalt labor, and do all your work:

14 But the seventh day is the Shabbat of יהוה your God (YHWH Eloheikha). In it you shalt not do any work, you, nor your son, nor your daughter, nor your manservant, nor your maidservant, nor your ox, nor your ass, nor any of your cattle, nor your stranger that is within your gates, that your manservant and your maidservant may rest as well as you.

15 And remember that you wast a servant in the land of Egypt (Mitsrayim), and that יהוה your God (YHWH Eloheikha) brought you out thence through a mighty hand and by an outstretched arm; therefore יהוה your God (YHWH Eloheikha) commanded you to keep the Shabbat day.

16 Honor your father and your mother, as יהוה your God (YHWH Eloheikha) hath commanded you, that your days may be prolonged, and that it may go well with you, in the land which יהוה your God (YHWH Eloheikha) giveth you.

17 You shalt not kill.

18 Neither shalt you commit adultery.

19 Neither shalt you steal.

20 Neither shalt you bear false witness against your neighbour.

21 Neither shalt you desire your neighbour's wife, neither shalt you covet your neighbour's house, his field, or his manservant, or his maidservant, his ox, or his ass, or anything that is your neighbour's.'

22 These words יהוה spake unto all your assembly in the mount out of the midst of the fire, of the cloud, and of the thick darkness, with a great voice: and He added no more. And He wrote them in two tables of stone, and delivered them unto me.

23 And it came to pass, when you heard the voice out of the midst of the darkness, (for the mountain did burn with fire,) that you came near unto me, even all the heads of your tribes, and your elders;

24 And you said: 'Behold, יהוה our God (YHWH Eloheinu) hath shewed us His glory and His greatness, and we have heard His voice out of the midst of the fire. We have seen this day that God (Elohim) doth talk with man, yet he liveth.

25 Now therefore why should we die? For this great fire will consume us; if we hear the voice of יהוה our God (YHWH Eloheinu) anymore, then we shall die.

26 For who is there of all flesh, that hath heard

the voice of the [B2]living God (Elohim chayim) speaking out of the midst of the fire, as we have, and lived?

27 Go you near, and hear all that יהוה our God (YHWH Eloheinu) shall say: and speak you unto us all that יהוה our God (YHWH Eloheinu) shall speak unto you; and we will hear it, and do it.'

28 And יהוה heard the voice of your words, when you spake unto me; and יהוה said unto me: 'I have heard the voice of the words of this people, which they have spoken unto you: they have well said all that they have spoken.

29 O that there was such a heart in them, that they would fear Me, and keep all My commandments always, that it might be well with them, and with their children forever!

30 Go say to them, "Get you into your tents again."

31 But as for you, stand you here by Me, and I will speak unto you all the commandments, and the statutes, and the judgments, which you shalt teach them, that they may do them in the land which I give them to possess it.'

32 You shall observe to do therefore as יהוה your God (YHWH Eloheikhem) hath commanded you; you shall not turn aside to the right hand or to the left.

33 You shall walk in all the ways which יהוה your God (YHWH Eloheikhem) hath commanded you, that you may live, and that it may be well with you, and that you may prolong your days in the land which you shall possess.

6 Now these are the commandments, the statutes, and the judgments, which יהוה your God (YHWH Eloheikha) commanded to teach you, that you might do them in the land whither you go to possess it;

2 That you mightest fear יהוה your God (YHWH Eloheikha), to keep all His statutes and His commandments, which I command you, you, and your son, and your son's son, all the days of your life; and that your days may be prolonged.

3 Hear therefore, O Yisrael, and observe to do it, that it may be well with you, and that you may increase mightily, as יהוה God (Elohim) of your fathers hath promised you, in the land that floweth with milk and honey.

4 [B40]Hear, O Yisrael: יהוה our God, יהוה is one. (Shema Yisrael: YHWH Eloheinu YHWH echad).

5 And you shalt love יהוה your God (YHWH Eloheikha) with all your heart, and with all your soul, and with all your might.

6 And these words, which I command you this day, shall be in your heart;

7 And you shalt teach them diligently unto your children, and shalt talk of them when you sittest in your house, and when you walkest by the way, and when you liest down, and when you risest up.

8 And you shalt bind them for a sign upon your hand, and they shall be as frontlets between your eyes.

9 And you shalt write them upon the posts of your house, and on your gates.

10 And it shall be, when יהוה your God (YHWH Eloheikha) shall have brought you into the land which He sware unto your fathers, to Avraham, to Isaac (Yitschaq), and to Jacob (Yaaqov), to give you great and goodly cities, which you buildedst not,

11 And houses full of all good things, which you filledst not, and wells digged, which you diggedst not, vineyards and olive trees, which you plantedst not; when you shalt have eaten and be full;

12 Then beware lest you forget יהוה, which brought you forth out of the land of Egypt (Mitsrayim), from the house of bondage.

13 You shalt fear יהוה your God (YHWH Eloheikha), and serve Him, and shalt swear by His name.

14 You shall not go after other gods (elohim), of the gods (elohim) of the people which are round about you;

15 (For יהוה your God (YHWH Eloheikha) is a jealous God (El) among you) lest the anger of יהוה your God (YHWH Eloheikha) be kindled against you, and destroy you from off the face of the earth.

16 You shall not tempt יהוה your God (YHWH Eloheikhem), as you tempted Him in Massah.

17 You shall diligently keep the commandments of יהוה your God (YHWH Eloheikhem), and His testimonies, and His statutes, which He hath commanded you.

18 And you shalt do that which is right and good in the sight of יהוה, that it may be well with you, and that you mayest go in and possess the good land which יהוה sware unto your fathers,

19 To cast out all your enemies from before you, as יהוה hath spoken.

20 And when your son asketh you in time to come, saying, 'What mean the testimonies, and the statutes, and the judgments, which יהוה our God (YHWH Eloheinu) hath commanded you?'

21 Then you shalt say unto your son: 'We were Pharaoh (Paroh)'s bondmen in Egypt (Mitsrayim); and יהוה brought us out of Egypt (Mitsrayim) with a mighty hand;

22 And יהוה shewed signs and wonders, great and sore, upon Egypt (Mitsrayim), upon Pharaoh (Paroh), and upon all his household, before our eyes.

23 And He brought us out from thence, that He might bring us in, to give us the land which He sware unto our fathers.

24 And יהוה commanded us to do all these statutes, to fear יהוה our God (YHWH Eloheinu), for our good always, that He might preserve us alive, as it is at this day.

25 And it shall be our righteousness, if we observe to do all these commandments before יהוה our God (YHWH Eloheinu), as He hath commanded us.'

7 When יהוה your God (YHWH Eloheikha) shall bring you into the land whither you goest to possess it, and hath cast out many nations before you, the Hittites, and the Girgashites, and the Amorites, and the Canaanites, and the Perizzites, and the Hivites, and the Yevusis, seven nations greater and mightier than you;

2 And when יהוה your God (YHWH Eloheikha) shall deliver them before you; you shalt smite them, and utterly destroy them; you shalt make no covenant with them, nor shew mercy unto them.

3 Neither shalt you make marriages with them; your daughter you shalt not give unto his son, nor his daughter shalt you take unto your son.

4 For they will turn away your son from following Me, that they may serve other gods (elohim); so will the anger of יהוה be kindled against you, and destroy you suddenly.

5 But thus shall you deal with them; you shall destroy their altars, and break down their images, and cut down their B34bAsherahs (Asherim), and burn their graven images with fire.

6 For you are a holy people unto יהוה your God (YHWH Eloheikha); יהוה your God (YHWH Eloheikha) hath chosen you to be a special people unto himself, above all people that are upon the face of the earth.

7 יהוה did not set His love upon you, nor choose you, because you were more in number than any people; for you were the fewest of all people;

8 But because יהוה loved you, and because He would keep the oath which He had sworn unto your fathers, hath יהוה brought you out with a mighty hand, and redeemed you out of the house of bondmen, from the hand of Pharaoh (Paroh) king of Egypt (Mitsrayim).

9 Know therefore that יהוה your God (YHWH Eloheikha), He is the God (Elohim), the faithful God (El), which keepeth covenant and mercy with them that love Him and keep His commandments to a thousand generations;

10 And repayeth them that hate Him to their face, to destroy them. He will not be slack to him who hateth Him, He will repay him to his face.

11 You shalt therefore keep the commandments, and the statutes, and the judgments, which I command you this day, to do them.

12 Wherefore it shall come to pass, if you hearken to these judgments, and keep, and do them, that יהוה your God (YHWH Eloheikha) shall keep unto you the covenant and the mercy which He sware unto your fathers.

13 And He will love you, and bless you, and multiply you; He will also bless the fruit of your womb, and the fruit of your land, your corn, and your wine, and your oil, the increase of your kine, and the flocks of your sheep, in the land which he sware unto your fathers to give you.

14 You shalt be blessed above all people; there shall not be male or female barren among you, or among your cattle.

15 And יהוה will take away from you all sickness, and will put none of the evil diseases of Egypt (Mitsrayim), which you knowest, upon you; but will lay them upon all them that hate you.

16 And you shalt consume all the people whom יהוה your God (YHWH Eloheikha) shall deliver you; your eye shall have no pity upon them; neither shalt you serve their gods (elohim); for that will be a snare unto you.

17 If you shalt say in your heart, 'These nations are more than I; how can I dispossess them?'

18 You shalt not be afraid of them, but shalt well remember what יהוה your God (YHWH Eloheikha) did unto Pharaoh (Paroh), and unto all Egypt (Mitsrayim);

19 The great temptations which your eyes saw, and the signs, and the wonders, and the mighty hand, and the outstretched arm, whereby יהוה your God (YHWH Eloheikha) brought you out; so shall יהוה your God (YHWH Eloheikha) do unto all the people of whom you are afraid.

20 Moreover יהוה your God (YHWH Eloheikha) will send the hornet among them, until they that are left, and hide themselves from you, be destroyed.

21 You shalt not be affrighted at them: for יהוה your God (YHWH Eloheikha) is among you, B41a mighty and awesome God (El).

22 And יהוה your God (YHWH Eloheikha) will put out those nations before you by little and little; you mayest not consume them at once, lest the beasts of the field increase upon you.

23 But יהוה your God (YHWH Eloheikha) shall deliver them unto you, and shall destroy them with a mighty destruction, until they be destroyed.

24 And he shall deliver their kings into your hand, and you shalt destroy their name from under heaven; there shall no man be able to stand before you, until you have destroyed them.

25 The graven images of their gods (elohim) shall you burn with fire; you shalt not desire the silver or gold that is on them, nor take it unto you, lest you be snared therein; for it is an abomination to יהוה your God (YHWH Eloheikha).

26 Neither shalt you bring an abomination into your house, lest you be a cursed thing like it; but you shalt utterly detest it, and you shalt utterly abhor it; for it is a cursed thing.

8 All the commandments which I command you this day shall you observe to do, that you may live, and multiply, and go in and possess the land which יהוה sware unto your fathers.

2 And you shalt remember all the way which יהוה your God (YHWH Eloheikha) led you these forty years in the wilderness, to humble you, and to prove you, to know what was in your heart, whether you wouldest keep His commandments, or not.

3 And He humbled you, and suffered you to hunger, and fed you with manna, which you knewest not, neither did your fathers know; that He might make you know that man doth not live by bread only, but by every word that proceedeth out of the mouth of יהוה doth man live.

4 Your raiment waxed not old upon you, neither did your foot swell, these forty years.

5 You shalt also consider in your heart, that, as a man chasteneth his son, so יהוה your God (YHWH Eloheikha) chasteneth you.

6 Therefore you shalt keep the commandments of יהוה your God (YHWH Eloheikha), to walk in His ways, and to fear Him.

7 For יהוה your God (YHWH Eloheikha) bringeth you into a good land, a land of brooks of water, of fountains and depths that spring out of valleys and hills;

8 A land of wheat, and barley, and vines, and fig trees, and pomegranates; a land of oil olive, and honey;

9 A land wherein you shalt eat bread without scarceness, you shalt not lack any thing in it; a land whose stones are iron, and out of whose hills you mayest dig brass.

10 When you have eaten and art full, then you shalt bless יהוה your God (YHWH Eloheikha) for the good land which He hath given you.

11 Beware that you forget not יהוה your God (YHWH Eloheikha), in not keeping His commandments, and His judgments, and His statutes, which I command you this day,

12 Lest when you have eaten and are full, and have built goodly houses, and dwelt therein;

13 And when your herds and your flocks multiply, and your silver and your gold is multiplied, and all that you have is multiplied;

14 Then your heart be lifted up, and you forget יהוה your God (YHWH Eloheikha), which brought you forth out of the land of Egypt (Mitsrayim), from the house of bondage;

15 Who led you through that great and terrible wilderness, wherein were fiery serpents, and scorpions, and drought, where there was no water; who brought you forth water out of the rock of flint;

16 Who fed you in the wilderness with manna, which your fathers knew not, that He might humble you, and that He might prove you, to do you good at your latter end;

17 And you say in your heart, 'My power and the might of mine hand hath gotten me this wealth.'

18 But you shalt remember יהוה your God (YHWH Eloheikha), for it is He that giveth you power to get wealth, that He may establish His covenant which He sware unto your fathers, as

it is this day.

19 And it shall be, if you do at all forget יהוה your God (YHWH Eloheikha), and walk after other gods (elohim), and serve them, and worship them, I testify against you this day that you shall surely perish.

20 As the nations which יהוה destroyeth before your face, so shall you perish, because you would not be obedient unto the voice of יהוה your God (YHWH Eloheikhem).

9 Hear, O Yisrael: You are to pass over Jordan (Yarden) this day, to go in to possess nations greater and mightier than yourself, cities great and fenced up to heaven,

2 A people great and tall, the children of the Anakims, whom you knowest, and of whom you have heard say, 'Who can stand before the children of Anak?'

3 Understand therefore this day, that יהוה your God (YHWH Eloheikha) is He who goeth over before you; as a consuming fire He shall destroy them, and He shall bring them down before your face; so shalt you drive them out, and destroy them quickly, as יהוה hath said unto you.

4 Speak not you in your heart, after that יהוה your God (YHWH Eloheikha) hath cast them out from before you, saying, 'Because of my righteousness יהוה hath brought me in to possess this land'; but for the wickedness of these nations יהוה doth drive them out from before you.

5 Not for your righteousness, or for the uprightness of your heart, dost you go to possess their land, but for the wickedness of these nations יהוה your God (YHWH Eloheikha) doth drive them out from before you, and that He may perform the word which יהוה sware unto your fathers, Avraham, Isaac (Yitschaq), and Jacob (Yaaqov).

6 Understand therefore, that יהוה your God (YHWH Eloheikha) giveth you not this good land to possess it because of your righteousness, for you are a stiffnecked people.

7 Remember, and forget not, how you provokedst יהוה your God (YHWH Eloheikha) to wrath in the wilderness; from the day that you didst depart out of the land of Egypt (Mitsrayim), until you came unto this place, you have been rebellious against יהוה.

8 Also in Horeb (Chorev) you provoked יהוה to wrath, so that יהוה was angry with you to have destroyed you.

9 When I went up into the mountain to receive the tablets of stone, the tablets of the covenant which יהוה made with you, then I abode in the mountain forty days and forty nights, I neither ate bread nor drink water.

10 And יהוה delivered unto me two tablets of stone written with the finger of God (Elohim); and on them was written according to all the words, which יהוה spake with you in the mountain out of the midst of the fire in the day of the assembly.

11 And it came to pass at the end of forty days and forty nights, that יהוה gave me the two tablets of stone, the tablets of the covenant.

12 And יהוה said unto me, 'Arise, get you down quickly from hence; for your people whom you have brought forth out of Egypt (Mitsrayim) have corrupted themselves; they have quickly turned aside out of the way which I commanded them; they have made them a molten image.'

13 Furthermore יהוה spake unto me, saying, 'I have seen this people, and, behold, they are stiffnecked people.

14 Let me alone, that I may destroy them, and blot out their name from under heaven; and I will make of you a nation mightier and greater than they.'

15 So I turned and came down from the mountain, and the mountain burned with fire; and the two tablets of the covenant were in my two hands.

16 And I looked, and, behold, you had sinned against יהוה your God (YHWH Eloheikha), and had made you a molten calf; you had turned aside quickly out of the way which יהוה had commanded you.

17 And I took the two tablets, and cast them out of my two hands, and broke them before your eyes.

18 And I fell down before יהוה, as at the first, forty days and forty nights; I did neither eat bread, nor drink water, because of all your sins which you sinned, in doing wickedly in the sight of יהוה, to provoke Him to anger.

19 For I was afraid of the anger and hot displeasure, wherewith יהוה was wroth against you to destroy you. But יהוה hearkened unto me at that time also.

20 And יהוה was very angry with Aaron (Aharon) to have destroyed him; and I prayed for Aaron (Aharon) also the same time.

21 And I took your sin, the calf which you had made, and burnt it with fire, and stamped it, and ground it very small, even until it was as small as dust; and I cast the dust thereof into the brook that descended out of the mountain.

22 And at Taberah, and at Massah, and at Qivrot-Hattaavah, you provoked יהוה to wrath.

23 Likewise when יהוה sent you from Qadesh Barnea, saying, 'Go up and possess the land which I have given you; then you rebelled against the commandment of יהוה your God (YHWH Eloheikha), and you believed Him not, nor hearkened to His voice.

24 You have been rebellious against יהוה from the day that I knew you.

25 Thus I fell down before יהוה forty days and forty nights, as I fell down at the first; because יהוה had said He would destroy you.

26 I prayed therefore unto יהוה, and said, 'O Lord (Adonai) יהוה, destroy not Your people and Your inheritance, whom You have redeemed through Your greatness, whom You have brought forth out of Egypt (Mitsrayim) with a mighty hand.

27 Remember Your servants, Avraham, Isaac (Yitschaq), and Jacob (Yaaqov); look not unto the stubbornness of this people, nor to their wickedness, nor to their sin;

28 Lest the land whence You broughtest us out say, "Because יהוה was not able to bring them into the land which He promised them, and because He hated them, He hath brought them out to slay them in the wilderness."

29 Yet they are Your people and Your inheritance, whom You broughtest out by Your mighty power and by Your outstretched arm.'

10 At that time יהוה said unto me, 'Hew you two tablets of stone like unto the first, and come up unto Me into the mountain, and make you an ark of wood.

2 And I will write on the tablets the words that were in the first tablets which you brakest, and you shalt put them in the ark.

3 And I made an ark of shittim wood, and hewed two tablets of stone like unto the first, and went up into the mount, having the two tablets in mine hand.

4 And He wrote on the tablets, according to the first writing, the ten commandments, which יהוה spake unto you in the mount out of the midst of the fire in the day of the assembly; and

יהוה gave them unto me.

5 And I turned myself and came down from the mountain, and put the tablets in the ark which I had made; and there they be, as יהוה commanded me.

6 And the children of Yisrael took their journey from Beeroth of the children of Yaakan to Mosera; there Aaron (Aharon) died, and there he was buried; and Eleazar his son ministered as priest (kohen) in his stead.

7 From thence they journeyed unto Gudgodah; and from Gudgodah to Yotbath, a land of rivers of waters.

8 At that time יהוה separated the tribe of Lewi, to bear the ark of the covenant of יהוה, to stand before יהוה to minister unto Him, and to bless in His name, unto this day.

9 Wherefore Lewi hath no part nor inheritance with his brethren; יהוה is his inheritance, according as יהוה your God (YHWH Eloheikha) promised him.

10 And I stayed in the mountain according to the first time, forty days and forty nights; and יהוה hearkened unto me at that time also, and יהוה would not destroy you.

11 And יהוה said unto me, Arise, take your journey before the people, that they may go in and possess the land, which I sware unto their fathers to give unto them.'

12 And now, Yisrael, what doth יהוה your God (YHWH Eloheikha) require of you, but to fear יהוה your God (YHWH Eloheikha), to walk in all His ways, and to love Him, and to serve יהוה your God (YHWH Eloheikha) with all your heart and with all your soul,

13 To keep the commandments of יהוה, and His statutes, which I command you this day for your good?

14 Behold, the heaven and the heaven of heavens is יהוה's your God (YHWH Eloheikha), the earth also, with all that therein is.

15 Only יהוה had a delight in your fathers to love them, and He chose their seed after them, even you above all people, as it is this day.

16 Circumcise therefore the foreskin of your heart, and be no more stiffnecked.

17 For יהוה your God (YHWH Eloheikhem) is [B9]Supreme God (Elohei haElohim) and [B14]Supreme Lord (Adonei haAdonim), the great, the mighty and the awesome God (El), who regardeth not persons, nor taketh bribe.

18 He doth execute the judgment of the fatherless and widow, and loveth the stranger, in giving him food and raiment.

19 Love you therefore the stranger, for you were strangers in the land of Egypt (Mitsrayim).

20 You shalt fear יהוה your God (YHWH Eloheikha); Him shalt you serve, and to Him shalt you cleave, and swear by His name.

21 He is your praise, and He is your God (Elohim), that hath done for you these great and awesome things, which your eyes have seen.

22 Your fathers went down into Egypt (Mitsrayim) with threescore and ten persons; and now יהוה your hath made you as the stars of heaven for multitude.

11 Therefore you shalt love יהוה your God (YHWH Eloheikha), and keep His charge, and His statutes, and His judgments, and His commandments, always.

2 And know you this day, for I speak not with your children who have not known, and who have not seen the chastisement of יהוה your God (YHWH Eloheikha), His greatness, His mighty hand, and His outstretched arm,

3 And His miracles, and His acts, which He did in the midst of Egypt (Mitsrayim) unto Pharaoh (Paroh) the king of Egypt (Mitsrayim), and unto all his land;

4 And what He did unto the army of Egypt (Mitsrayim), unto their horses, and to their chariots; how He made the water of the Red sea to overflow them as they pursued after you, and how יהוה hath destroyed them unto this day;

5 And what He did unto you in the wilderness, until you came into this place;

6 And what He did unto Dathan and Abiram, the sons of Eliav, the son of Reuven; how the earth opened her mouth, and swallowed them up, and their households, and their tents, and all the substance that was in their possession, in the midst of all Yisrael;

7 But your eyes have seen all the great acts of יהוה which He did.

8 Therefore shall you keep all the commandments which I command you this day, that you may be strong, and go in and possess the land, whither you go to possess it;

9 And that you may prolong your days in the land, which יהוה sware unto your fathers to give unto them and to their seed, a land that floweth with milk and honey.

10 For the land, whither you goest in to possess it, is not as the land of Egypt (Mitsrayim), from whence you came out, where you sowedst your seed, and wateredst it with your foot, as a garden of herbs;

11 But the land, whither you go to possess it, is a land of hills and valleys, and drinketh water of the rain of heaven;

12 A land which יהוה your God (YHWH Eloheikha) careth for; the eyes of יהוה your God (YHWH Eloheikha) are always upon it, from the beginning of the year even unto the end of the year.

13 And it shall come to pass, if you shall hearken diligently unto My commandments which I command you this day, to love יהוה your God (YHWH Eloheikha), and to serve Him with all your heart and with all your soul,

14 That I will give you the rain of your land in his due season, the first rain and the latter rain, that you mayest gather in your corn, and your wine, and your oil.

15 And I will send grass in your fields for your cattle, that you mayest eat and be full.

16 Take heed to yourselves, that your heart be not deceived, and you turn aside, and serve other gods (elohim), and worship them;

17 And then יהוה's wrath be kindled against you, and He shut up the heaven, that there be no rain, and that the land yield not her fruit; and lest you perish quickly from off the good land which יהוה giveth you.

18 Therefore shall you lay up these my words in your heart and in your soul, and bind them for a sign upon your hand, that they may be as frontlets between your eyes.

19 And you shall teach them your children, speaking of them when you sittest in your house, and when you walkest by the way, when you liest down, and when you risest up.

20 And you shalt write them upon the door posts of your house, and upon your gates;

21 That your days may be multiplied, and the days of your children, in the land which יהוה sware unto your fathers to give them, as the days of heaven upon the earth.

22 For if you shall diligently keep all these commandments which I command you, to do them, to love יהוה your God (YHWH Eloheikha), to walk in all His ways, and to cleave unto Him;

23 Then will יהוה drive out all these nations

from before you, and you shall possess greater nations and mightier than yourselves.

24 Every place whereon the soles of your feet shall tread shall be yours; from the wilderness and Lebanon, from the river, the river Euphrates, even unto the uttermost sea shall your coast be.

25 There shall no man be able to stand before you; for יהוה your God (YHWH Eloheikhem) shall lay the fear of you and the dread of you upon all the land that you shall tread upon, as He hath said unto you.

26 Behold, I set before you this day a blessing and a curse:

27 A blessing, if you obey the commandments of יהוה your God (YHWH Eloheikhem), which I command you this day;

28 And a curse, if you will not obey the commandments of יהוה your God (YHWH Eloheikhem), but turn aside out of the way which I command you this day, to go after other gods (elohim), which you have not known.

29 And it shall come to pass, when יהוה your God (YHWH Eloheikha) hath brought you in unto the land whither you goest to possess it, that you shalt put the blessing upon Mount Gerizim, and the curse upon Mount Ebal.

30 Are they not on the other side Jordan (Yarden), by the way where the sun goeth down, in the land of the Canaanites, which dwell in the champaign opposit Gilgal, besides the plains of Moreh?

31 For you shall pass over Jordan (Yarden) to go in to possess the land which יהוה your God (YHWH Eloheikhem) giveth you, and you shall possess it, and dwell therein.

32 And you shall observe to do all the statutes and judgments which I set before you this day."

12 "These are the statutes and judgments, which you shall observe to do in the land, which יהוה God (Elohim) of your fathers giveth you to possess it, all the days that you live upon the earth.

2 You shall utterly destroy all the places, wherein the nations which you shall possess served their gods (elohim), upon the high mountains, and upon the hills, and under every green tree.

3 And you shall overthrow their altars, and break their pillars, and burn their Asherahs (Asherim) with fire; and you shall hew down the graven images of their gods (elohim), and destroy the names of them out of that place.

4 You shall not do so unto יהוה your God (YHWH Eloheikhem).

5 But unto the place which יהוה your God (YHWH Eloheikhem) shall choose out of all your tribes to put His name there, even unto His habitation shall you seek, and thither you shalt come.

6 And thither you shall bring your burnt offerings, and your sacrifices, and your tithes, and heave offerings of your hand, and your vows, and your freewill offerings, and the firstlings of your herds and of your flocks.

7 And there you shall eat before יהוה your God (YHWH Eloheikhem), and you shall rejoice in all that you put your hand unto, you and your households, wherein יהוה your God (YHWH Eloheikha) hath blessed you.

8 You shall not do after all the things that we do here this day, every man whatsoever is right in his own eyes.

9 For you are not as yet come to the rest and to the inheritance, which יהוה your God (YHWH Eloheikha) giveth you.

10 But when you go over Jordan (Yarden), and dwell in the land which יהוה your God (YHWH Eloheikhem) giveth you to inherit, and when He giveth you rest from all your enemies round about, so that you dwell in safety;

11 Then there shall be a place which יהוה your God (YHWH Eloheikhem) shall choose to cause His name to dwell there; thither shall you bring all that I command you; your burnt offerings, and your sacrifices, your tithes, and the heave offering of your hand, and all your choice vows which you vow unto יהוה.

12 And you shall rejoice before יהוה your God (YHWH Eloheikhem), you, and your sons, and your daughters, and your menservants, and your maidservants, and the Lewite that is within your gates; forasmuch as He hath no part nor inheritance with you.

13 Take heed to yourself that you offer not your burnt offerings in every place that you seest;

14 But in the place which יהוה shall choose in one of your tribes, there you shalt offer your burnt offerings, and there you shalt do all that I command you.

15 Notwithstanding you mayest kill and eat flesh in all your gates, whatsoever your soul lusteth after, according to the blessing of יהוה your God (YHWH Eloheikha) which He hath

given you; the unclean and the clean may eat thereof, as of the roebuck, and as of the hart.

16 Only you shall not eat the blood; you shall pour it upon the earth as water.

17 You mayest not eat within your gates the tithe of your corn, or of your wine, or of your oil, or the firstlings of your herds or of your flock, nor any of your vows which you vowest, nor your freewill offerings, or heave offering of your hand.

18 But you must eat them before יהוה your God (YHWH Eloheikha) in the place which יהוה your God (YHWH Eloheikha) shall choose, you, and your son, and your daughter, and your manservant, and your maidservant, and the Lewite that is within your gates; and you shalt rejoice before יהוה your God (YHWH Eloheikha) in all that you puttest your hands unto.

19 Take heed to yourself that you forsake not the Lewite as long as you livest upon the earth.

20 When יהוה your God (YHWH Eloheikha) shall enlarge your border, as He hath promised you, and you shalt say, I will eat flesh, because your soul longeth to eat flesh; you mayest eat flesh, whatsoever your soul lusteth after.

21 If the place which יהוה your God (YHWH Eloheikha) hath chosen to put His name there be too far from you, then you shalt kill of your herd and of your flock, which יהוה hath given you, as I have commanded you, and you shalt eat in your gates whatsoever your soul lusteth after.

22 Even as the roebuck and the hart are eaten, so you shalt eat them; the unclean and the clean shall eat of them alike.

23 Only be sure that you eat not the blood, for the blood is the life; and you mayest not eat the life with the flesh.

24 You shalt not eat it; you shalt pour it upon the earth as water.

25 You shalt not eat it; that it may go well with you, and with your children after you, when you shalt do that which is right in the sight of יהוה.

26 Only your holy things which you have, and your vows, you shalt take, and go unto the place which יהוה shall choose.

27 And you shalt offer your burnt offerings, the flesh and the blood, upon the altar of יהוה your God (YHWH Eloheikha); and the blood of your sacrifices shall be poured out upon the altar of יהוה your God (YHWH Eloheikha), and you

shalt eat the flesh.

28 Observe and hear all these words which I command you, that it may go well with you, and with your children after you forever, when you doest that which is good and right in the sight of יהוה your God (YHWH Eloheikha).

29 When יהוה your God (YHWH Eloheikha) shall cut off the nations from before you, whither you goest to possess them, and you succeedest them, and dwellest in their land;

30 Take heeds to yourself that you be not snared by following them, after that they be destroyed from before you; and that you enquire not after their gods (elohim), saying, 'How did these nations serve their gods (elohim)? Even so will I do likewise.'

31 You shalt not do so unto יהוה your God (YHWH Eloheikha); for every abomination to יהוה, which he hateth, have they done unto their gods (elohim); for even their sons and their daughters they have burnt in the fire to their gods (elohim).

32 What thing soever I command you, observe to do it; you shalt not add thereto, nor diminish from it.

13 If there arise among you a prophet, or a dreamer of dreams, and giveth you a sign or a wonder,

2 And the sign or the wonder come to pass, whereof he spake unto you, saying, 'Let us go after other gods (elohim), which you have not known, and let us serve them';

3 You shalt not hearken unto the words of that prophet, or that dreamer of dreams, for יהוה your God (YHWH Eloheikhem) proveth you, to know whether you love יהוה your God (YHWH Eloheikhem) with all your heart and with all your soul.

4 You shall walk after יהוה your God (YHWH Eloheikhem), and fear Him, and keep His commandments, and obey His voice, and you shall serve Him, and cleave unto Him.

5 And that prophet, or that dreamer of dreams, shall be put to death, because he hath spoken to turn you away from יהוה your God (YHWH Eloheikhem), which brought you out of the land of Egypt (Mitsrayim), and redeemed you out of the house of bondage, to thrust you out of the way which יהוה your God (YHWH Eloheikhem) commanded you to walk in. So shalt you put the evil away from the midst of you.

6 If your brother, the son of your mother, or your son, or your daughter, or the wife of your bosom, or your friend, which is as your own soul, entice you secretly, saying, 'Let us go and serve other gods (elohim)', which you have not known, you, nor your fathers;

7 Namely, of the gods (elohim) of the people which are round about you, near unto you, or far off from you, from the one end of the earth even unto the other end of the earth;

8 You shalt not consent unto him, nor hearken unto him; neither shall your eye pity him, neither shalt you spare, neither shalt you conceal him;

9 But you shalt surely kill him; your hand shall be first upon him to put him to death, and afterwards the hand of all the people.

10 And you shalt stone him with stones that he dies, because he hath sought to thrust you away from יהוה your God (YHWH Eloheikha), which brought you out of the land of Egypt (Mitsrayim), from the house of bondage.

11 And all Yisrael shall hear, and fear, and shall do no more any such wickedness as this is among you.

12 If you shalt hear say in one of your cities, which יהוה your God (YHWH Eloheikha) hath given you to dwell there, saying,

13 'Certain men, the scoundrel children, are gone out from among you, and have withdrawn the inhabitants of their city, saying, "Let us go and serve other gods (elohim)", which you have not known';

14 Then shalt you enquire, and make search, and ask diligently; and, behold, if it be truth, and the thing certain, that such abomination is wrought among you;

15 You shalt surely smite the inhabitants of that city with the edge of the sword, destroying it utterly, and all that is therein, and the cattle thereof, with the edge of the sword.

16 And you shalt gather all the spoil of it into the midst of the street thereof, and shalt burn with fire the city, and all the spoil thereof every whit, for יהוה your God (YHWH Eloheikha); and it shall be a heap forever; it shall not be built again.

17 And there shall cleave nought of the cursed thing to your hand, that יהוה may turn from the fierceness of His anger, and shew you mercy, and have compassion upon you, and multiply you, as He hath sworn unto your fathers;

18 When you shalt hearken to the voice of יהוה

your God (YHWH Eloheikha), to keep all His commandments which I command you this day, to do that which is right in the eyes of יהוה your God (YHWH Eloheikha).

14 You are the children of יהוה your God (YHWH Eloheikhem); you shall not cut yourselves, nor make any baldness between your eyes for the dead.

2 For you are a holy people unto יהוה your God (YHWH Eloheikha), and יהוה hath chosen you to be a peculiar people unto Himself, above all the nations that are upon the earth.

3 You shalt not eat any abominable thing.

4 These are the beasts which you shall eat: the ox, the sheep, and the goat,

5 The hart, and the roebuck, and the fallow deer, and the wild goat, and the pygarg, and the wild ox, and the chamois.

6 And every beast that parteth the hoof, and cleaveth the cleft into two claws, and cheweth the cud among the beasts, that you shall eat.

7 Nevertheless these you shall not eat of them that chew the cud, or of them that divide the cloven hoof; as the camel, and the hare, and the coney: for they chew the cud, but divide not the hoof; therefore they are unclean unto you.

8 And the swine, because it divideth the hoof, yet cheweth not the cud, it is unclean unto you; you shall not eat of their flesh, nor touch their dead carcase.

9 These you shall eat of all that are in the waters: all that have fins and scales shall you eat;

10 And whatsoever hath not fins and scales you may not eat; it is unclean unto you.

11 Of all clean birds you shall eat.

12 But these are they of which you shall not eat: the eagle, and the ossifrage, and the ospray,

13 And the glede, and the kite, and the vulture after its kind,

14 And every raven after its kind,

15 And the owl, and the night hawk, and the cuckow, and the hawk after its kind,

16 The little owl, and the great owl, and the swan,

17 And the pelican, and the gier eagle, and the cormorant,

18 And the stork, and the heron after her kind, and the lapwing, and the bat.

19 And every creeping thing that flieth is unclean unto you; they shall not be eaten.

20 But of all clean fowls you may eat.

21 You shall not eat of any thing that dieth of itself; you shalt give it unto the stranger that is in your gates, that he may eat it; or you mayest sell it unto an alien; for you are a holy people unto יהוה your God (YHWH Eloheikha). You shalt not seethe a kid in his mother's milk.

22 You shalt truly tithe all the increase of your seed, that the field bringeth forth year by year.

23 And you shalt eat before יהוה your God (YHWH Eloheikha), in the place which He shall choose to place His name there, the tithe of your corn, of your wine, and of your oil, and the firstlings of your herds and of your flocks; that you mayest learn to fear יהוה your God (YHWH Eloheikha) always.

24 And if the way be too long for you, so that you are not able to carry it; or if the place be too far from you, which יהוה your God (YHWH Eloheikha) shall choose to set His name there, when יהוה your God (YHWH Eloheikha) hath blessed you;

25 Then shalt you turn it into money, and bind up the money in your hand, and shalt go unto the place which יהוה your God (YHWH Eloheikha) shall choose.

26 And you shalt bestow that money for whatsoever your soul lusteth after, for oxen, or for sheep, or for wine, or for strong drink, or for whatsoever your soul desireth; and you shalt eat there before יהוה your God (YHWH Eloheikha), and you shalt rejoice, you, and your household,

27 And the Lewite that is within your gates; you shalt not forsake him; for he hath no part nor inheritance with you.

28 At the end of three years you shalt bring forth all the tithe of your increase the same year, and shalt lay it up within your gates.

29 And the Lewite, (because he hath no part nor inheritance with you,) and the stranger, and the fatherless, and the widow, which are within your gates, shall come, and shall eat and be satisfied, that יהוה your God (YHWH Eloheikha) may bless you in all the work of your hand which you doest."

15 "At the end of every seven years you shalt make a [B26]release (shemittah).

2 And this is the manner of the release (shemittah): Every creditor that lendeth ought unto his neighbour shall release it; he shall not exact it of his neighbour, or of his brother, because [B27]release of יהוה (shemittah le-YHWH)

has been proclaimed.

3 Of a foreigner you mayest exact it again; but that which is your with your brother your hand shall release;

4 Save when there shall be no poor among you; for יהוה shall greatly bless you in the land which יהוה your God (YHWH Eloheikha) giveth you for an inheritance to possess it;

5 Only if you carefully hearken unto the voice of יהוה your God (YHWH Eloheikha), to observe to do all these commandments which I command you this day.

6 For יהוה your God (YHWH Eloheikha) blesseth you, as He promised you; and you shalt lend unto many nations, but you shalt not borrow; and you shalt reign over many nations, but they shall not reign over you.

7 If there be among you a poor man of one of your brethren within any of your gates in your land which יהוה your God (YHWH Eloheikha) giveth you, you shalt not harden your heart, nor shut your hand from your poor brother;

8 But you shalt open your hand wide unto him, and shalt surely lend him sufficient for his need, in that which he wanteth.

9 Beware that there be not a thought in your wicked heart, saying, 'The seventh year, year of the release (shemittah), is at hand; and your eye be evil against your poor brother, and you givest him nought; and he cry unto יהוה against you, and it be sin unto you.

10 You shalt surely give him, and your heart shall not be grieved when you givest unto him, because that for this thing יהוה your God (YHWH Eloheikha) shall bless you in all your works, and in all that you puttest your hand unto.

11 For the poor shall never cease out of the land; therefore I command you, saying, 'You shalt open your hand wide unto your brother, to your poor, and to your needy, in your land.'

12 And if your brother, a Hebrew (Ivri) man, or a Hebrew (Ivri) woman, be sold unto you, and serve you six years; then in the seventh year you shalt let him go free from you.

13 And when you sendest him out free from you, you shalt not let him go away empty;

14 You shalt furnish him liberally out of your flock, and out of your floor, and out of your winepress; of that wherewith יהוה your God (YHWH Eloheikha) hath blessed you you shalt

give unto him.

15 And you shalt remember that you wast a bondman in the land of Egypt (Mitsrayim), and יהוה your God (YHWH Eloheikha) redeemed you; therefore I command you this thing today.

16 And it shall be, if he says unto you, 'I will not go away from you', because he loveth you and your house, because he is well with you;

17 Then you shalt take an aul, and thrust it through his ear unto the door, and he shall be your servant forever. And also unto your maidservant you shalt do likewise.

18 It shall not seem hard unto you, when you sendest him away free from you; for he hath been worth a double hired servant to you, in serving you six years: and יהוה your God (YHWH Eloheikha) shall bless you in all that you doest.

19 All the firstling males that come of your herd and of your flock you shalt sanctify unto יהוה your God (YHWH Eloheikha); you shalt do no work with the firstling of your bullock, nor shear the firstling of your sheep.

20 You shalt eat it before יהוה your God (YHWH Eloheikha) year by year in the place which יהוה shall choose, you and your household.

21 And if there be any blemish therein, as if it be lame, or blind, or have any ill blemish, you shalt not sacrifice it unto יהוה your God (YHWH Eloheikha).

22 You shalt eat it within your gates: the unclean and the clean person shall eat it alike, as the roebuck, and as the hart.

23 Only you shalt not eat the blood thereof; you shalt pour it upon the ground as water."

16 "Observe the month of Aviv, and keep the [B19]Passover (Pesach) unto יהוה your God (YHWH Eloheikha), for in the month of Aviv יהוה your God (YHWH Eloheikha) brought you forth out of Egypt (Mitsrayim) by night.

2 You shalt therefore sacrifice the [B19]passover lamb (pesach) unto יהוה your God (YHWH Eloheikha), of the flock and the herd, in the place which יהוה shall choose to place His name there.

3 You shalt eat no leavened bread with it; seven days shalt you eat unleaven bread (matstsah) therewith, even the bread of affliction; for you camest forth out of the land of Egypt (Mitsrayim) in haste: that you mayest remember the day when you camest forth out of the land of Egypt (Mitsrayim) all the days of your life.

4 And there shall be no leavened bread seen with you in all your coast seven days; neither shall there any thing of the flesh, which you sacrificedst the first day at even, remain all night until the morning.

5 You mayest not sacrifice the passover (pesach) within any of your gates, which יהוה your God (YHWH Eloheikha) giveth you:

6 But at the place which יהוה your God (YHWH Eloheikha) shall choose to place His name in, there you shalt sacrifice the passover (pesach) at even, at the going down of the sun, at the season that you camest forth out of Egypt (Mitsrayim).

7 And you shalt roast and eat it in the place which יהוה your God (YHWH Eloheikha) shall choose, and you shalt turn in the morning, and go unto your tents.

8 Six days you shalt eat unleaven bread (matstsah); and on the seventh day shall be a solemn assembly to יהוה your God (YHWH Eloheikha); you shalt do no work therein.

9 Seven weeks shalt you number unto you; begin to number the seven weeks from such time as you beginnest to put the sickle to the corn.

10 And you shalt keep the [B21]Feast of Weeks (Chag Shavuot) unto יהוה your God (YHWH Eloheikha) with a tribute of a freewill offering of your hand, which you shalt give unto יהוה your God (YHWH Eloheikha), according as יהוה your God (YHWH Eloheikha) hath blessed you.

11 And you shalt rejoice before יהוה your God (YHWH Eloheikha), you, and your son, and your daughter, and your manservant, and your maidservant, and the Lewite that is within your gates, and the stranger, and the fatherless, and the widow, that are among you, in the place which יהוה your God (YHWH Eloheikha) hath chosen to place His name there.

12 And you shalt remember that you wast a bondman in Egypt (Mitsrayim), and you shalt observe and do these statutes.

13 You shalt observe the feast of tabernacles seven days, after that you have gathered in your corn and your wine;

14 And you shalt rejoice in your feast, you, and your son, and your daughter, and your manservant, and your maidservant, and the Lewite, the stranger, and the fatherless, and the widow, that are within your gates.

15 Seven days shalt you keep a solemn feast

unto יהוה your God (YHWH Eloheikha) in the place which יהוה shall choose, because יהוה your God (YHWH Eloheikha) shall bless you in all your increase, and in all the works of your hands, therefore you shalt surely rejoice.

16 Three times in a year shall all your males appear before יהוה your God (YHWH Eloheikha) in the place which he shall choose; at the [B20]Feast of Unleavened Bread (Chag HaMatzot), and on the [B21]Feast of Weeks (Chag Shavuot), and at the [B24]Feast of Tabernacles (Chag Sukkot); and they shall not appear before יהוה empty.

17 Every man shall give as he is able, according to the blessing of יהוה your God (YHWH Eloheikha) which He hath given you.

18 Judges and officers shalt you make you in all your gates, which יהוה your God (YHWH Eloheikha) giveth you, throughout your tribes, and they shall judge the people with just judgment.

19 You shalt not wrest judgment; you shalt not respect persons, neither take a gift; for a gift doth blind the eyes of the wise, and pervert the words of the righteous.

20 That which is altogether just shalt you follow, that you mayest live, and inherit the land which יהוה your God (YHWH Eloheikha) giveth you.

21 You shalt not plant you a grove of any trees near unto the altar of יהוה your God (YHWH Eloheikha), which you shalt make you.

22 Neither shalt you set you up any image; which יהוה your God (YHWH Eloheikha) hateth.

17 You shalt not sacrifice unto יהוה your God (YHWH Eloheikha) any bullock, or sheep, wherein is blemish, or any defect, for that is an abomination unto יהוה your God (YHWH Eloheikha).

2 If there be found among you, within any of your gates which יהוה your God (YHWH Eloheikha) giveth you, man or woman, that hath wrought wickedness in the sight of יהוה your God (YHWH Eloheikha), in transgressing His covenant,

3 And hath gone and served other gods (elohim), and worshipped them, either the sun, or moon, or any of the host of heaven, which I have not commanded;

4 And it be told you, and you have heard of it, and enquired diligently, and, behold, it be true,

and the thing certain, that such abomination is wrought in Yisrael;

5 Then shalt you bring forth that man or that woman, which have committed that wicked thing, unto your gates, even that man or that woman, and shalt stone them with stones, till they die.

6 At the mouth of two witnesses, or three witnesses, shall he that is worthy of death be put to death; but at the mouth of one witness he shall not be put to death.

7 The hands of the witnesses shall be first upon him to put him to death, and afterward the hands of all the people. So you shalt put the evil away from among you.

8 If there arise a matter too hard for you in judgment, between blood and blood, between plea and plea, and between stroke and stroke, being matters of controversy within your gates; then shalt you arise, and get you up into the place which יהוה your God (YHWH Eloheikha) shall choose;

9 And you shalt come unto the priests (kohanim) the Levites (Lewiyim), and unto the judge that shall be in those days, and enquire; and they shall shew you the sentence of judgment.

10 And you shalt do according to the sentence, which they of that place which יהוה shall choose shall shew you; and you shalt observe to do according to all that they inform you.

11 According to the sentence of the law (torah) which they shall teach you, and according to the judgment which they shall tell you, you shalt do; you shalt not decline from the sentence which they shall shew you, to the right hand, nor to the left.

12 And the man that will do presumptuously, and will not hearken unto the priest (kohen) that standeth to minister there before יהוה your God (YHWH Eloheikha), or unto the judge, even that man shall die; and you shalt put away the evil from Yisrael.

13 And all the people shall hear, and fear, and do no more presumptuously.

14 When you are come unto the land which יהוה your God (YHWH Eloheikha) giveth you, and shalt possess it, and shalt dwell therein, and shalt say, 'I will set a king over me, like as all the nations that are about me';

15 You shalt in any wise set him king over you, whom יהוה your God (YHWH Eloheikha) shall

choose: one from among your brethren shalt you set king over you; you mayest not set a stranger over you, which is not your brother.

16 But he shall not multiply horses to himself, nor cause the people to return to Egypt (Mitsrayim), to the end that he should multiply horses; forasmuch as יהוה hath said unto you, You shall henceforth return no more that way.

17 Neither shall he multiply wives to himself, that his heart turn not away; neither shall he greatly multiply to himself silver and gold.

18 And it shall be, when he sitteth upon the throne of his kingdom, that he shall write him a copy of this law (torah) in a book out of that which is before the priests (kohanim) the Levites (Lewiyim).

19 And it shall be with him, and he shall read therein all the days of his life; that he may learn to fear יהוה his God (Elohim), to keep all the words of this law (torah) and these statutes, to do them,

20 That his heart be not lifted up above his brethren, and that he turns not aside from the commandment, to the right hand, or to the left, to the end that he may prolong his days in his kingdom, he, and his children, in the midst of Yisrael.

18 The priests (kohanim) the Levites (Lewiyim), and all the tribe of Lewi, shall have no part nor inheritance with Yisrael; they shall eat the offerings of יהוה made by fire, and his inheritance.

2 Therefore shall they have no inheritance among their brethren; יהוה is their inheritance, as he hath said unto them.

3 And this shall be the priest (kohen)'s due from the people, from them that offer a sacrifice, whether it be ox or sheep; and they shall give unto the priest (kohen) the shoulder, and the two cheeks, and the maw.

4 The firstfruit also of your corn, of your wine, and of your oil, and the first of the fleece of your sheep, shalt you give him.

5 For יהוה your God (YHWH Eloheikha) hath chosen him out of all your tribes, to stand to minister in the name of יהוה, him and his sons forever.

6 And if a Lewite come from any of your gates out of all Yisrael, where he sojourned, and come with all the desire of his mind unto the place which יהוה shall choose;

7 Then he shall minister in the name of יהוה his God (Elohim), as all his brethren the Levites (Lewiyim) do, which stand there before יהוה.

8 They shall have like portions to eat, beside that which cometh of the sale of his patrimony.

9 When you are come into the land which יהוה your God (YHWH Eloheikha) giveth you, you shalt not learn to do after the abominations of those nations.

10 There shall not be found among you any one that maketh his son or his daughter to pass through the fire, or that useth divination, or an observer of times, or an enchanter, or a witch,

11 Or a charmer, or a consulter with familiar spirits, or a wizard, or a necromancer.

12 For all that do these things are an abomination unto יהוה: and because of these abominations יהוה your God (YHWH Eloheikha) doth drive them out from before you.

13 You shalt be perfect with יהוה your God (YHWH Eloheikha).

14 For these nations, which you shalt possess, hearkened unto observers of times, and unto diviners: but as for you, יהוה your God (YHWH Eloheikha) hath not suffered you so to do.

15 יהוה your God (YHWH Eloheikha) will raise up unto you a Prophet from the midst of you, of your brethren, like unto me; unto him you shall hearken;

16 According to all that you desiredst of יהוה your God (YHWH Eloheikha) in Horeb (Chorev) in the day of the assembly, saying, 'Let me not hear again the voice of יהוה my God (YHWH Elohai), neither let me see this great fire any more, that I die not.'

17 And יהוה said unto me, 'They have well spoken that which they have spoken.

18 I will raise them up a Prophet from among their brethren, like unto you, and will put My words in His mouth; and He shall speak unto them all that I shall command Him.

19 And it shall come to pass, that whosoever will not hearken unto My words which He shall speak in My name, I will require it of him.

20 But the prophet, which shall presume to speak a word in My name, which I have not commanded him to speak, or that shall speak in the name of other gods (elohim), even that prophet shall die.'

21 And if you say in your heart, 'How shall we know the word which יהוה hath not spoken?'

22 When a prophet speaketh in the name of יהוה, if the thing follows not, nor come to pass, that is the thing which יהוה hath not spoken, but the prophet hath spoken it presumptuously; you shalt not be afraid of him."

19 "When יהוה your God (YHWH Eloheikha) hath cut off the nations, whose land יהוה your God (YHWH Eloheikha) giveth you, and you succeedest them, and dwellest in their cities, and in their houses;

2 You shalt separate three cities for you in the midst of your land, which יהוה your God (YHWH Eloheikha) giveth you to possess it.

3 You shalt prepare you a way, and divide the coasts of your land, which יהוה your God (YHWH Eloheikha) giveth you to inherit, into three parts, that every slayer may flee thither.

4 And this is the case of the slayer, which shall flee thither, that he may live: Whoso killeth his neighbour ignorantly, whom he hated not in time past;

5 As when a man goeth into the wood with his neighbour to hew wood, and his hand fetcheth a stroke with the axe to cut down the tree, and the head slippeth from the helve, and lighteth upon his neighbour, that he dies; he shall flee unto one of those cities, and live;

6 Lest the avenger of the blood pursue the slayer, while his heart is hot, and overtake him, because the way is long, and slay him; whereas he was not worthy of death, inasmuch as he hated him not in time past.

7 Wherefore I command you, saying, 'You shalt separate three cities for you.'

8 And if יהוה your God (YHWH Eloheikha) enlarge your coast, as He hath sworn unto your fathers, and give you all the land which He promised to give unto your fathers;

9 If you shalt keep all these commandments to do them, which I command you this day, to love יהוה your God (YHWH Eloheikha), and to walk ever in His ways; then shalt you add three cities more for you, besides these three,

10 That innocent blood be not shed in your land, which יהוה your God (YHWH Eloheikha) giveth you for an inheritance, and so blood be upon you.

11 But if any man hates his neighbour, and lie in wait for him, and rise up against him, and smite him mortally that he dies, and fleeth into one of these cities;

12 Then the elders of his city shall send and fetch him thence, and deliver him into the hand of the avenger of blood, that he may die.

13 Your eye shall not pity him, but you shalt put away the guilt of innocent blood from Yisrael, that it may go well with you.

14 You shalt not remove your neighbour's landmark, which they of old time have set in your inheritance, which you shalt inherit in the land that יהוה your God (YHWH Eloheikha) giveth you to possess it.

15 One witness shall not rise up against a man for any iniquity, or for any sin, in any sin that he sinneth: at the mouth of two witnesses, or at the mouth of three witnesses, shall the matter be established.

16 If a false witness rises up against any man to testify against him that which is wrong,

17 Then both the men, between whom the controversy is, shall stand before יהוה, before the priests (kohanim) and the judges, which shall be in those days.

18 And the judges shall make diligent inquisition: and, behold, if the witness be a false witness, and hath testified falsely against his brother,

19 Then shall you do unto him, as he had thought to have done unto his brother; so shalt you put the evil away from among you.

20 And those which remain shall hear, and fear, and shall henceforth commit no more any such evil among you.

21 And your eye shall not pity; but life shall go for life, eye for eye, tooth for tooth, hand for hand, foot for foot."

20 "When you goest out to battle against your enemies, and seest horses, and chariots, and a people more than you, be not afraid of them; for יהוה your God (YHWH Eloheikha) is with you, which brought you up out of the land of Egypt (Mitsrayim).

2 And it shall be, when you are come near unto the battle, that the priest (kohen) shall approach and speak unto the people,

3 And shall say unto them, 'Hear, O Yisrael, you approach this day unto battle against your enemies; let not your hearts faint, fear not, and do not tremble, neither be you terrified because of them;

4 For יהוה your God (YHWH Eloheikha) is He that goeth with you, to fight for you against your

enemies, to save you.'

5 And the officers shall speak unto the people, saying: 'What man is there that hath built a new house, and hath not dedicated it? Let him go and return to his house, lest he die in the battle, and another man dedicate it.

6 And what man is he that hath planted a vineyard, and hath not yet eaten of it? Let him also go and return unto his house, lest he die in the battle, and another man eat of it.

7 And what man is there that hath betrothed a wife, and hath not taken her? Let him go and return unto his house, lest he die in the battle, and another man take her.'

8 And the officers shall speak further unto the people, and they shall say, 'What man is there that is fearful and fainthearted? Let him go and return unto his house, lest his brethren's heart faint as well as his heart.'

9 And it shall be, when the officers have made an end of speaking unto the people, that they shall make captains of the armies to lead the people.

10 When you comest near unto a city to fight against it, then proclaim peace unto it.

11 And it shall be, if it makes you answer of peace, and open unto you, then it shall be, that all the people that is found therein shall be tributaries unto you, and they shall serve you.

12 And if it will make no peace with you, but will make war against you, then you shalt besiege it.

13 And when יהוה your God (YHWH Eloheikha) hath delivered it into your hands, you shalt smite every male thereof with the edge of the sword.

14 But the women, and the little ones, and the cattle, and all that is in the city, even all the spoil thereof, shalt you take unto yourself; and you shalt eat the spoil of your enemies, which יהוה your God (YHWH Eloheikha) hath given you.

15 Thus shalt you do unto all the cities which are very far off from you, which are not of the cities of these nations.

16 But of the cities of these people, which יהוה your God (YHWH Eloheikha) doth give you for an inheritance, you shalt save alive nothing that breatheth;

17 But you shalt utterly destroy them; namely, the Hittites, and the Amorites, the Canaanites, and the Perizzites, the Hivites, and the Yevusis;

as יהוה your God (YHWH Eloheikha) hath commanded you,

18 That they teach you not to do after all their abominations, which they have done unto their gods (elohim); so should you sin against יהוה your God (YHWH Eloheikhem).

19 When you shalt besiege a city a long time, in making war against it to take it, you shalt not destroy the trees thereof by forcing an axe against them; for you mayest eat of them, and you shalt not cut them down (for the tree of the field is man's life) to employ them in the siege.

20 Only the trees which you knowest that they be not trees for meat, you shalt destroy and cut them down; and you shalt build bulwarks against the city that maketh war with you, until it be subdued."

21 If one be found slain in the land which יהוה your God (YHWH Eloheikha) giveth you to possess it, lying in the field, and it be not known who hath slain him;

2 Then your elders and your judges shall come forth, and they shall measure unto the cities which are round about him that is slain.

3 And it shall be, that the city which is next unto the slain man, even the elders of that city shall take a heifer, which hath not been wrought with, and which hath not drawn in the yoke;

4 And the elders of that city shall bring down the heifer unto a rough valley, which is neither eared nor sown, and shall strike off the heifer's neck there in the valley.

5 And the priests (kohanim) the sons of Lewi shall come near; for them יהוה your God (YHWH Eloheikha) hath chosen to minister unto him, and to bless in the name of יהוה; and by their word shall every controversy and every stroke be settled.

6 And all the elders of that city, that are next unto the slain man, shall wash their hands over the heifer that is beheaded in the valley:

7 And they shall answer and say, 'Our hands have not shed this blood, neither have our eyes seen it.

8 Be merciful, O יהוה, unto Your people Yisrael, whom you have redeemed, and lay not innocent blood unto Your people of Yisrael's charge.' And the blood shall be forgiven them.

9 So shalt you put away the guilt of innocent blood from among you, when you shalt do that which is right in the sight of יהוה.

10 When you goest forth to war against your enemies, and יהוה your God (YHWH Eloheikha) hath delivered them into your hands, and you have taken them captive,

11 And seest among the captives a beautiful woman, and hast a desire unto her, that you wouldest have her to your wife;

12 Then you shalt bring her home to your house; and she shall shave her head, and pare her nails;

13 And she shall put the raiment of her captivity from off her, and shall remain in your house, and bewail her father and her mother a full month; and after that you shalt go in unto her, and be her husband, and she shall be your wife.

14 And it shall be, if you have no delight in her, then you shalt let her go whither she will; but you shalt not sell her at all for money, you shalt not make merchandise of her, because you have humbled her.

15 If a man has two wives, one beloved, and another hated, and they have born him children, both the beloved and the hated; and if the firstborn son be hers that was hated;

16 Then it shall be, when he maketh his sons to inherit that which he hath, that he may not make the son of the beloved firstborn before the son of the hated, which is indeed the firstborn.

17 But he shall acknowledge the son of the hated for the firstborn, by giving him a double portion of all that he hath, for he is the beginning of his strength; the right of the firstborn is his.

18 If a man has a stubborn and rebellious son, which will not obey the voice of his father, or the voice of his mother, and that, when they have chastened him, will not hearken unto them;

19 Then shall his father and his mother lay hold on him, and bring him out unto the elders of his city, and unto the gate of his place;

20 And they shall say unto the elders of his city, 'This our son is stubborn and rebellious, he will not obey our voice; he is a glutton, and a drunkard.'

21 And all the men of his city shall stone him with stones, that he dies: so shalt you put evil away from among you; and all Yisrael shall hear, and fear.

22 And if a man has committed a sin worthy of death, and he be to be put to death, and you hang him on a tree;

23 His body shall not remain all night upon the tree, but you shalt in any wise bury him that day; (for he that is hanged is accursed of God (Elohim)); that your land be not defiled, which יהוה your God (YHWH Eloheikha) giveth you for an inheritance."

22 "You shalt not see your brother's ox or his sheep go astray, and hide yourself from them; you shalt in any case bring them again unto your brother.

2 And if your brother be not near unto you, or if you know him not, then you shalt bring it unto your own house, and it shall be with you until your brother seek after it, and you shalt restore it to him again.

3 In like manner shalt you do with his ass; and so shalt you do with his raiment; and with all lost thing of your brother's, which he hath lost, and you have found, shalt you do likewise; you mayest not hide yourself.

4 You shalt not see your brother's ass or his ox fall down by the way, and hide yourself from them; you shalt surely help him to lift them up again.

5 The woman shall not wear that which pertaineth unto a man, neither shall a man put on a woman's garment, for all that do so are abomination unto יהוה your God (YHWH Eloheikha).

6 If a bird's nest chance to be before you in the way in any tree, or on the ground, whether they be young ones, or eggs, and the dam sitting upon the young, or upon the eggs, you shalt not take the dam with the young;

7 But you shalt in any wise let the dam go, and take the young to you; that it may be well with you, and that you mayest prolong your days.

8 When you buildest a new house, then you shalt make a battlement for your roof, that you bring not blood upon your house, if any man falls from thence.

9 You shalt not sow your vineyard with divers seeds, lest the fruit of your seed which you have sown, and the fruit of your vineyard, be defiled.

10 You shalt not plow with an ox and an ass together.

11 You shalt not wear a garment of divers sorts, as of woollen and linen together.

12 You shalt make you fringes upon the four quarters of your vesture, wherewith you coverest yourself.

13 If any man takes a wife, and go in unto her, and hate her,

14 And give occasions of speech against her, and bring up an evil name upon her, and say, 'I took this woman, and when I came to her, I found her not a virgin,'

15 Then shall the father of the damsel, and her mother, take and bring forth the tokens of the damsel's virginity unto the elders of the city in the gate.

16 And the damsel's father shall say unto the elders, I gave my daughter unto this man to wife, and he hateth her;

17 And, behold, he hath given occasions of speech against her, saying, I found not your daughter a maid; and yet these are the tokens of my daughter's virginity. And they shall spread the cloth before the elders of the city.

18 And the elders of that city shall take that man and chastise him;

19 And they shall fine him in a hundred shekels of silver, and give them unto the father of the damsel, because he hath brought up an evil name upon a virgin of Yisrael; and she shall be his wife; he may not put her away all his days.

20 But if this thing be true, and the tokens of virginity be not found for the damsel;

21 Then they shall bring out the damsel to the door of her father's house, and the men of her city shall stone her with stones that she dies, because she hath wrought folly in Yisrael, to play the whore in her father's house; so shalt you put evil away from among you.

22 If a man be found lying with a woman married to a husband, then they shall both of them die, both the man that lay with the woman, and the woman: so shalt you put away evil from Yisrael.

23 If a damsel that is a virgin be betrothed unto a husband, and a man find her in the city, and lie with her;

24 Then you shall bring them both out unto the gate of that city, and you shall stone them with stones that they die; the damsel, because she cried not, being in the city; and the man, because he hath humbled his neighbour's wife; so you shalt put away evil from among you.

25 But if a man finds a betrothed damsel in the field, and the man force her, and lie with her; then the man only that lay with her shall die;

26 But unto the damsel you shalt do nothing; there is in the damsel no sin worthy of death, for as when a man riseth against his neighbour, and slayeth him, even so is this matter;

27 For he found her in the field, and the betrothed damsel cried, and there was none to save her.

28 If a man finds a damsel that is a virgin, which is not betrothed, and lay hold on her, and lie with her, and they be found;

29 Then the man that lay with her shall give unto the damsel's father fifty shekels of silver, and she shall be his wife; because he hath humbled her, he may not put her away all his days.

30 A man shall not take his father's wife, nor discover his father's skirt."

23 "He that is wounded in the stones, or hath his privy member cut off, shall not enter into the congregation of יהוה.

2 A bastard shall not enter into the congregation of יהוה; even to his tenth generation shall he not enter into the congregation of יהוה.

3 An Ammonite or Moabite shall not enter into the congregation of יהוה; even to their tenth generation shall they not enter into the congregation of יהוה forever;

4 Because they met you not with bread and with water in the way, when you came forth out of Egypt (Mitsrayim); and because they hired against you Balaam the son of Beor of Pethor of Mesopotamia, to curse you.

5 Nevertheless יהוה your God (YHWH Eloheikha) would not hearken unto Balaam; but יהוה your God (YHWH Eloheikha) turned the curse into a blessing unto you, because יהוה your God (YHWH Eloheikha) loved you.

6 You shalt not seek their peace nor their prosperity all your days forever.

7 You shalt not abhor an Edomite, for he is your brother; you shalt not abhor an Egyptian (Mitsri), because you wast a stranger in his land.

8 The children that are begotten of them shall enter into the congregation of יהוה in their third generation.

9 When the army goeth forth against your enemies, then keep you from every wicked thing.

10 If there be among you any man, that is not clean by reason of uncleanness that chanceth him by night, then shall he go abroad out of the camp, he shall not come within the camp.

11 But it shall be, when evening cometh on, he shall wash himself with water; and when the sun is down, he shall come into the camp again.

12 You shalt have a place also outside the camp, whither you shalt go forth abroad;

13 And you shalt have a paddle upon your weapon; and it shall be, when you wilt ease yourself abroad, you shalt dig therewith, and shalt turn back and cover that which cometh from you.

14 For יהוה your God (YHWH Eloheikha) walketh in the midst of your camp, to deliver you, and to give up your enemies before you; therefore shall your camp be holy, that he see no unclean thing in you, and turn away from you.

15 You shalt not deliver unto his master the servant which is escaped from his master unto you.

16 He shall dwell with you, even among you, in that place which he shall choose in one of your gates, where it liketh him best; you shalt not oppress him.

17 There shall be no whore of the daughters of Yisrael, nor a sodomite of the sons of Yisrael.

18 You shalt not bring the hire of a whore, or the price of a dog, into the house of יהוה your God (YHWH Eloheikha) for any vow, for even both these are abomination unto יהוה your God (YHWH Eloheikha).

19 You shalt not lend upon usury to your brother; usury of money, usury of victuals, usury of any thing that is lent upon usury.

20 Unto a stranger you mayest lend upon usury; but unto your brother you shalt not lend upon usury, that יהוה your God (YHWH Eloheikha) may bless you in all that you settest your hand to in the land whither you goest to possess it.

21 When you shalt vow a vow unto יהוה your God (YHWH Eloheikha), you shalt not slack to pay it; for יהוה your God (YHWH Eloheikha) will surely require it of you, and it would be sin in you.

22 But if you shalt forbear to vow, it shall be no sin in you.

23 That which is gone out of your lips you shalt keep and perform; even a freewill offering, according as you have vowed unto יהוה your God (YHWH Eloheikha), which you have promised with your mouth.

24 When you comest into your neighbour's vineyard, then you mayest eat grapes your fill at your own pleasure; but you shalt not put any in your vessel.

25 When you comest into the standing corn of your neighbour, then you mayest pluck the ears

with your hand; but you shalt not move a sickle unto your neighbour's standing corn.

24 When a man hath taken a wife, and married her, and it come to pass that she finds no favor in his eyes, because he hath found some uncleanness in her, then let him write her a bill of divorcement, and give it in her hand, and send her out of his house.

2 And when she is departed out of his house, she may go and be another man's wife.

3 And if the latter husband hates her, and write her a bill of divorcement, and giveth it in her hand, and sendeth her out of his house; or if the latter husband dies, which took her to be his wife;

4 Her former husband, which sent her away, may not take her again to be his wife, after that she is defiled; for that is abomination before יהוה; and you shalt not cause the land to sin, which יהוה your God (YHWH Eloheikha) giveth you for an inheritance.

5 When a man hath taken a new wife, he shall not go out to war, neither shall he be charged with any business; but he shall be free at home one year, and shall cheer up his wife which he hath taken.

6 No man shall take the nether or the upper millstone to pledge, for he taketh a man's life to pledge.

7 If a man be found stealing any of his brethren of the children of Yisrael, and maketh merchandise of him, or selleth him; then that thief shall die; and you shalt put evil away from among you.

8 Take heed in the plague of leprosy, that you observe diligently, and do according to all that the priests (kohanim) the Levites (Lewiyim) shall teach you; as I commanded them, so you shall observe to do.

9 Remember what יהוה your God (YHWH Eloheikha) did unto Miryam by the way, after that you were come forth out of Egypt (Mitsrayim).

10 When you dost lend your brother any thing, you shalt not go into his house to fetch his pledge.

11 You shalt stand abroad, and the man to whom you dost lend shall bring out the pledge abroad unto you.

12 And if the man be poor, you shalt not sleep with his pledge.

13 In any case you shalt deliver him the pledge again when the sun goeth down, that he may sleep in his own raiment, and bless you; and it shall be righteousness unto you before יהוה your God (YHWH Eloheikha).

14 You shalt not oppress a hired servant that is poor and needy, whether he be of your brethren, or of your strangers that are in your land within your gates.

15 At his day you shalt give him his hire, neither shall the sun go down upon it; for he is poor and setteth his heart upon it; lest he cry against you unto יהוה, and it be sin unto you.

16 The fathers shall not be put to death for the children, neither shall the children be put to death for the fathers; every man shall be put to death for his own sin.

17 You shalt not pervert the judgment of the stranger, nor of the fatherless; nor take a widow's raiment to pledge.

18 But you shalt remember that you wast a bondman in Egypt (Mitsrayim), and יהוה your God (YHWH Eloheikha) redeemed you thence; therefore I command you to do this thing.

19 When you cuttest down your harvest in your field, and have forgot a sheaf in the field, you shalt not go again to fetch it; it shall be for the stranger, for the fatherless, and for the widow, that יהוה your God (YHWH Eloheikha) may bless you in all the work of your hands.

20 When you beatest your olive tree, you shalt not go over the boughs again; it shall be for the stranger, for the fatherless, and for the widow.

21 When you gatherest the grapes of your vineyard, you shalt not glean it afterward; it shall be for the stranger, for the fatherless, and for the widow.

22 And you shalt remember that you wast a bondman in the land of Egypt (Mitsrayim); therefore I command you to do this thing."

25 "If there be a controversy between men, and they come unto judgment, that the judges may judge them; then they shall justify the righteous, and condemn the wicked.

2 And it shall be, if the wicked man be worthy to be beaten, that the judge shall cause him to lie down, and to be beaten before his face, according to his fault, by a certain number.

3 Forty stripes he may give him, and not exceed; lest, if he should exceed, and beat him above these with many stripes, then your brother should seem vile unto you.

4 You shalt not muzzle the ox when he treadeth out the corn.

5 If brethren dwell together, and one of them die, and have no child, the wife of the dead shall not marry outside the family unto a stranger; her husband's brother shall go in unto her, and take her to him to wife, and perform the duty of a husband's brother unto her.

6 And it shall be, that the firstborn which she beareth shall succeed in the name of his brother which is dead, that his name be not put out of Yisrael.

7 And if the man like not to take his brother's wife, then let his brother's wife go up to the gate unto the elders, and say, 'My husband's brother refuseth to raise up unto his brother a name in Yisrael, he will not perform the duty of my husband's brother.'

8 Then the elders of his city shall call him, and speak unto him; and if he stands to it, and say, 'I like not to take her,'

9 Then shall his brother's wife come unto him in the presence of the elders, and loose his shoe from off his foot, and spit in his face, and shall answer and say, 'So shall it be done unto that man that will not build up his brother's house.'

10 And his name shall be called in Yisrael, 'The house of him that hath his shoe loosed.'

11 When men strive together one with another, and the wife of the one draweth near for to deliver her husband out of the hand of him that smiteth him, and putteth forth her hand, and taketh him by the secrets;

12 Then you shalt cut off her hand, your eye shall not pity her.

13 You shalt not have in your bag divers weights, a great and a small.

14 You shalt not have in your house divers measures, a great and a small.

15 But you shalt have a perfect and just weight, a perfect and just measure shalt you have, that your days may be lengthened in the land which יהוה your God (YHWH Eloheikha) giveth you.

16 For all that do such things, and all that do unrighteously, are an abomination unto יהוה your God (YHWH Eloheikha).

17 Remember what Amalek did unto you by the way, when you were come forth out of Egypt (Mitsrayim);

18 How he met you by the way, and smote

the hindmost of you, even all that were feeble behind you, when you wast faint and weary; and he feared not God (Elohim).

19 Therefore it shall be, when יהוה your God (YHWH Eloheikha) hath given you rest from all your enemies round about, in the land which יהוה your God (YHWH Eloheikha) giveth you for an inheritance to possess it, that you shalt blot out the remembrance of Amalek from under heaven; you shalt not forget it."

26 "And it shall be, when you come in unto the land which יהוה your God (YHWH Eloheikha) giveth you for an inheritance, and possessest it, and dwellest therein;

2 That you shalt take of the first of all the fruit of the earth, which you shalt bring of your land that יהוה your God (YHWH Eloheikha) giveth you, and shalt put it in a basket, and shalt go unto the place which יהוה your God (YHWH Eloheikha) shall choose to place His name there.

3 And you shalt go unto the priest (kohen) that shall be in those days, and say unto him, 'I profess this day unto יהוה your God (YHWH Eloheikha), that I am come unto the country which יהוה sware unto our fathers for to give us.'

4 And the priest (kohen) shall take the basket out of your hand, and set it down before the altar of יהוה your God (YHWH Eloheikha).

5 And you shalt speak and say before יהוה your God (YHWH Eloheikha): 'A Syrian (Arammi) ready to perish was my father, and he went down into Egypt (Mitsrayim), and sojourned there with a few, and became there a nation, great, mighty, and populous.

6 And the Egyptians (Mitsrayim) evil entreated us, and afflicted us, and laid upon us hard bondage:

7 And when we cried unto יהוה God (Elohim) of our fathers, יהוה heard our voice, and looked on our affliction, and our labour, and our oppression.

8 And יהוה brought us forth out of Egypt (Mitsrayim) with a mighty hand, and with an outstretched arm, and with great terribleness, and with signs, and with wonders.

9 And He hath brought us into this place, and hath given us this land, "a land that floweth with milk and honey";

10 And now, behold, I have brought the firstfruits of the land, which you, O יהוה, have given me. And you shalt set it before יהוה your God (YHWH Eloheikha), and worship before יהוה your God (YHWH Eloheikha).

11 And you shalt rejoice in every good thing which יהוה your God (YHWH Eloheikha) hath given unto you, and unto your house, you, and the Lewite, and the stranger that is among you.

12 When you have made an end of tithing all the tithes of your increase the third year, which is the year of tithing, and have given it unto the Lewite, the stranger, the fatherless, and the widow, that they may eat within your gates, and be filled;

13 Then you shalt say before יהוה your God (YHWH Eloheikha), I have brought away the hallowed things out of mine house, and also have given them unto the Lewite, and unto the stranger, to the fatherless, and to the widow, according to all Your commandments which You have commanded me: 'I have not transgressed Your commandments, neither have I forgotten them.

14 I have not eaten thereof in my mourning, neither have I taken away ought thereof for any unclean use, nor given ought thereof for the dead; but I have hearkened to the voice of יהוה my God (YHWH Elohai), and have done according to all that You have commanded me.

15 Look down from Your holy habitation, from heaven, and bless Your people Yisrael, and the land which You have given us, as you swarest unto our fathers, "a land that floweth with milk and honey."'

16 This day יהוה your God (YHWH Eloheikha) hath commanded you to do these statutes and judgments: you shalt therefore keep and do them with all your heart, and with all your soul.

17 You have avouched יהוה this day to be your God (YHWH Eloheikha), and to walk in His ways, and to keep His statutes, and His commandments, and His judgments, and to hearken unto His voice.

18 And יהוה hath avouched you this day to be His peculiar people, as He hath promised you, and that you shouldest keep all His commandments;

19 And to make you high above all nations which He hath made, in praise, and in name, and in honor; and that you mayest be a holy people unto יהוה your God (YHWH Eloheikha), as He hath spoken."

27 And Moses (Mosheh) with the elders of Yisrael commanded the people, saying: "Keep all the commandments which I command you this day.

2 And it shall be on the day when you shall pass over Jordan (Yarden) unto the land which יהוה your God (YHWH Eloheikha) giveth you, that you shalt set you up great stones, and plaister them with plaister.

3 And you shalt write upon them all the words of this law (torah), when you are passed over, that you mayest go in unto the land which יהוה your God (YHWH Eloheikha) giveth you, 'a land that floweth with milk and honey', as יהוה God (Elohim) of your fathers hath promised you.

4 Therefore it shall be when you be gone over Jordan (Yarden), that you shall set up these stones, which I command you this day, in Mount Ebal, and you shalt plaister them with plaister.

5 And there shalt you build an altar unto יהוה your God (YHWH Eloheikha), an altar of stones; you shalt not lift up any iron tool upon them.

6 You shalt build the altar of יהוה your God (YHWH Eloheikha) of whole stones; and you shalt offer burnt offerings thereon unto יהוה your God (YHWH Eloheikha).

7 And you shalt offer peace offerings, and shalt eat there, and rejoice before יהוה your God (YHWH Eloheikha).

8 And you shalt write upon the stones all the words of this law (torah) very plainly.

9 And Moses (Mosheh) and the priests (kohanim) the Levites (Lewiyim) spake unto all Yisrael, saying, "Take heed, and hearken, O Yisrael: This day you are become the people of יהוה your God (YHWH Eloheikha).

10 You shalt therefore obey the voice of יהוה your God (YHWH Eloheikha), and do His commandments and His statutes, which I command you this day."

11 And Moses (Mosheh) charged the people the same day, saying,

12 'These shall stand upon Mount Gerizim to bless the people, when you are come over Jordan (Yarden): Shimon, and Lewi, and Judah (Yehudah), and Yissaskhar, and Joseph (Yosef), and Binyamin;

13 And these shall stand upon Mount Ebal to curse: Reuven, Gad, and Asher, and Zevulun, Dan, and Naftali.

14 And the Levites (Lewiyim) shall speak, and say unto all the men of Yisrael with a loud voice:

15 'Cursed be the man that maketh any graven or molten image, an abomination unto יהוה, the work of the hands of the craftsman, and putteth it in a secret place.' And all the people shall answer and say, 'So be it (Amen)!'

16 'Cursed be he that setteth light by his father or his mother.' And all the people shall say, 'So be it (Amen)!'

17 'Cursed be he that removeth his neighbour's landmark.' And all the people shall say, 'So be it (Amen)!'

18 'Cursed be he that maketh the blind to wander out of the way.' And all the people shall say, 'So be it (Amen)!'

19 'Cursed be he that perverteth the judgment of the stranger, fatherless, and widow.' And all the people shall say, 'So be it (Amen)!'

20 Cursed be he that lieth with his father's wife; because he uncovereth his father's skirt.' And all the people shall say, 'So be it (Amen)!'

21 'Cursed be he that lieth with any manner of beast.' And all the people shall say, 'So be it (Amen)!'

22 Cursed be he that lieth with his sister, the daughter of his father, or the daughter of his mother.' And all the people shall say, 'So be it (Amen)!'

23 'Cursed be he that lieth with his mother in law.' And all the people shall say, 'So be it (Amen)!'

24 'Cursed be he that smiteth his neighbour secretly.' And all the people shall say, 'So be it (Amen)!'

25 Cursed be he that taketh reward to slay an innocent person. And all the people shall say, 'So be it (Amen)!'

26 'Cursed be he that confirmeth not all the words of this law (torah) to do them.' And all the people shall say, 'So be it (Amen)!'

28 "And it shall come to pass, if you shalt hearken diligently unto the voice of יהוה your God (YHWH Eloheikha), to observe and to do all His commandments which I command you this day, that יהוה your God (YHWH Eloheikha) will set you on high above all nations of the earth.

2 And all these blessings shall come on you, and overtake you, if you shalt hearken unto the voice of יהוה your God (YHWH Eloheikha):

3 Blessed shalt you be in the city, and blessed shalt you be in the field.

4 Blessed shall be the fruit of your body, and the fruit of your ground, and the fruit of your cattle, the increase of your kine, and the flocks of your sheep.

5 Blessed shall be your basket and your store.

6 Blessed shalt you be when you comest in, and blessed shalt you be when you goest out.

7 יהוה shall cause your enemies that rise up against you to be smitten before your face; they shall come out against you one way, and flee before you seven ways.

8 יהוה shall command the blessing upon you in your storehouses, and in all that you settest your hand unto; and he shall bless you in the land which יהוה your God (YHWH Eloheikha) giveth you.

9 יהוה shall establish you a holy people unto Himself, as He hath sworn unto you, if you shalt keep the commandments of יהוה your God (YHWH Eloheikha), and walk in His ways.

10 And all people of the earth shall see that you are called by the name of יהוה; and they shall be afraid of you.

11 And יהוה shall make you plenteous in goods, in the fruit of your body, and in the fruit of your cattle, and in the fruit of your ground, in the land which יהוה sware unto your fathers to give you.

12 יהוה shall open unto you His good treasure, the heaven to give the rain unto your land in his season, and to bless all the work of your hand: and you shalt lend unto many nations, and you shalt not borrow.

13 And יהוה shall make you the head, and not the tail; and you shalt be above only, and you shalt not be beneath; if that you hearken unto the commandments of יהוה your God (YHWH Eloheikha), which I command you this day, to observe and to do them:

14 And you shalt not go aside from any of the words which I command you this day, to the right hand, or to the left, to go after other gods (elohim) to serve them.

15 But it shall come to pass, if you wilt not hearken unto the voice of יהוה your God (YHWH Eloheikha), to observe to do all His commandments and His statutes which I command you this day; that all these curses shall come upon you, and overtake you;

16 Cursed shalt you be in the city, and cursed shalt you be in the field.

17 Cursed shall be your basket and your store.

18 Cursed shall be the fruit of your body, and the fruit of your land, the increase of your kine, and the flocks of your sheep.

19 Cursed shalt you be when you comest in, and cursed shalt you be when you goest out.

20 יהוה shall send upon you cursing, vexation, and rebuke, in all that you settest your hand unto for to do, until you be destroyed, and until you perish quickly; because of the wickedness of your doings, whereby you have forsaken me.

21 יהוה shall make the pestilence cleave unto you, until He has consumed you from off the land, whither you goest to possess it.

22 יהוה shall smite you with a consumption, and with a fever, and with an inflammation, and with an extreme burning, and with the sword, and with blasting, and with mildew; and they shall pursue you until you perish.

23 And your heaven that is over your head shall be brass, and the earth that is under you shall be iron.

24 יהוה shall make the rain of your land powder and dust; from heaven shall it come down upon you, until you be destroyed.

25 יהוה shall cause you to be smitten before your enemies; you shalt go out one way against them, and flee seven ways before them; and shalt be removed into all the kingdoms of the earth.

26 And your carcase shall be meat unto all fowls of the air, and unto the beasts of the earth, and no man shall fray them away.

27 יהוה will smite you with the botch of Egypt (Mitsrayim), and with the emerods, and with the scab, and with the itch, whereof you canst not be healed.

28 יהוה shall smite you with madness, and blindness, and astonishment of heart:

29 And you shalt grope at noonday, as the blind gropeth in darkness, and you shalt not prosper in your ways; and you shalt be only oppressed and spoiled evermore, and no man shall save you.

30 You shalt betroth a wife, and another man shall lie with her; you shalt build a house, and you shalt not dwell therein; you shalt plant a vineyard, and shalt not gather the grapes thereof.

31 Your ox shall be slain before your eyes, and you shalt not eat thereof; your ass shall be violently taken away from before your face, and

shall not be restored to you; your sheep shall be given unto your enemies, and you shalt have none to rescue them.

32 Your sons and your daughters shall be given unto another people, and your eyes shall look, and fail with longing for them all the day long; and there shall be no might in your hand.

33 The fruit of your land, and all your labours, shall a nation which you knowest not eat up; and you shalt be only oppressed and crushed always;

34 So that you shalt be mad for the sight of your eyes which you shalt see.

35 יהוה shall smite you in the knees, and in the legs, with a sore botch that cannot be healed, from the sole of your foot unto the top of your head.

36 יהוה shall bring you, and your king which you shalt set over you, unto a nation which neither you nor your fathers have known; and there shalt you serve other gods (elohim), wood and stone.

37 And you shalt become an astonishment, a proverb, and a byword, among all nations whither יהוה shall lead you.

38 You shalt carry much seed out into the field, and shalt gather but little in; for the locust shall consume it.

39 You shalt plant vineyards, and dress them, but shalt neither drink of the wine, nor gather the grapes; for the worms shall eat them.

40 You shalt have olive trees throughout all your coasts, but you shalt not anoint yourself with the oil; for your olive shall cast his fruit.

41 You shalt beget sons and daughters, but you shalt not enjoy them; for they shall go into captivity.

42 All your trees and fruit of your land shall the locust consume.

43 The stranger that is within you shall get up above you very high; and you shalt come down very low.

44 He shall lend to you, and you shalt not lend to him; he shall be the head, and you shalt be the tail.

45 Moreover all these curses shall come upon you, and shall pursue you, and overtake you, till you be destroyed, because you hearkenedst not unto the voice of יהוה your God (YHWH Eloheikha), to keep His commandments and His statutes which He commanded you.

46 And they shall be upon you for a sign and for a wonder, and upon your seed forever.

47 Because you servedst not יהוה your God (YHWH Eloheikha) with joyfulness, and with gladness of heart, for the abundance of all things;

48 Therefore shalt you serve your enemies which יהוה shall send against you, in hunger, and in thirst, and in nakedness, and in want of all things; and he shall put a yoke of iron upon your neck, until he has destroyed you.

49 יהוה shall bring a nation against you from far, from the end of the earth, as swift as the eagle flieth, a nation whose tongue you shalt not understand;

50 A nation of fierce countenance, which shall not regard the person of the old, nor shew favor to the young.

51 And he shall eat the fruit of your cattle, and the fruit of your land, until you be destroyed; which also shall not leave you either corn, wine, or oil, or the increase of your kine, or flocks of your sheep, until he has destroyed you.

52 And he shall besiege you in all your gates, until your high and fenced walls come down, wherein you trustedst, throughout all your land; and he shall besiege you in all your gates throughout all your land, which יהוה your God (YHWH Eloheikha) hath given you.

53 And you shalt eat the fruit of your own body, the flesh of your sons and of your daughters, which יהוה your God (YHWH Eloheikha) hath given you, in the siege, and in the straitness, wherewith your enemies shall distress you.

54 So that the man that is tender among you, and very delicate, his eye shall be evil toward his brother, and toward the wife of his bosom, and toward the remnant of his children which he shall leave;

55 So that he will not give to any of them of the flesh of his children whom he shall eat, because he hath nothing left him in the siege, and in the straitness, wherewith your enemies shall distress you in all your gates.

56 The tender and delicate woman among you, which would not adventure to set the sole of her foot upon the ground for delicateness and tenderness, her eye shall be evil toward the husband of her bosom, and toward her son, and toward her daughter,

57 And toward her young one that cometh out

from between her feet, and toward her children which she shall bear; for she shall eat them for want of all things secretly in the siege and straitness, wherewith your enemy shall distress you in your gates.

58 If you wilt not observe to do all the words of this law (torah) that are written in this book, that you mayest fear this glorious and awesome name, יהוה, your God (Eloheikha).

59 Then יהוה will make your plagues extraordinary, and the plagues of your seed, great plagues, and of long continuance, and sore sicknesses, and of long continuance.

60 Moreover He will bring upon you all the diseases of Egypt (Mitsrayim), which you wast afraid of; and they shall cleave unto you.

61 Also every sickness, and every plague, which is not written in the book of this law (torah), them will יהוה bring upon you, until you be destroyed.

62 And you shall be left few in number, whereas you were as the stars of heaven for multitude; because you wouldest not obey the voice of יהוה your God (YHWH Eloheikha).

63 And it shall come to pass, that as יהוה rejoiced over you to do you good, and to multiply you; so יהוה will rejoice over you to destroy you, and to bring you to nought; and you shall be plucked from off the land whither you goest to possess it.

64 And יהוה shall scatter you among all people, from the one end of the earth even unto the other; and there you shalt serve other gods (elohim), which neither you nor your fathers have known, even wood and stone.

65 And among these nations shalt you find no ease, neither shall the sole of your foot have rest: but יהוה shall give you there a trembling heart, and failing of eyes, and sorrow of mind.

66 And your life shall hang in doubt before you; and you shalt fear day and night, and shalt have none assurance of your life.

67 In the morning you shalt say, 'O how I wish it was even! And at even you shalt say, 'O how I wish it was morning!' for the fear of your heart wherewith you shalt fear, and for the sight of your eyes which you shalt see.

68 And יהוה shall bring you into Egypt (Mitsrayim) again with ships, by the way whereof I spake unto you, 'you shalt see it no more again.' And there you shall be sold unto your enemies for bondmen and bondwomen, and no man shall buy you."

29 These are the words of the covenant, which יהוה commanded Moses (Mosheh) to make with the children of Yisrael in the land of Moav, besides the covenant which He made with them in Horeb (Chorev).

2 And Moses (Mosheh) called unto all Yisrael, and said unto them: "You have seen all that יהוה did before your eyes in the land of Egypt (Mitsrayim) unto Pharaoh (Paroh), and unto all his servants, and unto all his land;

3 The great temptations which your eyes have seen, the signs, and those great miracles;

4 Yet יהוה hath not given you a heart to perceive, and eyes to see, and ears to hear, unto this day.

5 And I have led you forty years in the wilderness; your clothes are not waxen old upon you, and your shoe is not waxen old upon your foot.

6 You have not eaten bread, neither have you drunk wine or strong drink, that you might know that I am יהוה, your God (Eloheikhem).

7 And when you came unto this place, Sihon the king of Heshbon, and Og the king of Bashan, came out against us unto battle, and we smote them.

8 And we took their land, and gave it for an inheritance unto the Reubenites (Reuveni), and to the Gadites, and to the half tribe of Menashsheh.

9 Keep therefore the words of this covenant, and do them, that you may prosper in all that you do.

10 You stand this day all of you before יהוה your God (YHWH Eloheikha); your captains of your tribes, your elders, and your officers, with all the men of Yisrael,

11 Your little ones, your wives, and your stranger that is in your camp, from the hewer of your wood unto the drawer of your water,

12 That you shouldest enter into covenant with יהוה your God (YHWH Eloheikha), and into His oath, which יהוה your God (YHWH Eloheikha) maketh with you this day,

13 That He may establish you today for a people unto Himself, and that He may be unto you a God (Elohim), as He hath said unto you, and as He hath sworn unto your fathers, to Avraham, to Isaac (Yitschaq), and to Jacob (Yaaqov).

14 Neither with you only do I make this covenant and this oath;

15 But with him that standeth here with us this day before יהוה our God (YHWH Eloheinu),

and also with him that is not here with us this day;

16 (For you know how we have dwelt in the land of Egypt (Mitsrayim); and how we came through the nations which you passed by;

17 And you have seen their abominations, and their idols, wood and stone, silver and gold, which were among them;)

18 Lest there should be among you man, or woman, or family, or tribe, whose heart turneth away this day from יהוה our God (YHWH Eloheinu), to go and serve the gods (elohim) of these nations; lest there should be among you a root that beareth gall and wormwood;

19 And it come to pass, when he heareth the words of this curse, that he blesses himself in his heart, saying, 'I shall have peace, though I walk in the imagination of mine heart', to add drunkenness to thirst.

20 יהוה will not spare him, but then the anger of יהוה and His jealousy shall smoke against that man, and all the curses that are written in this book shall lie upon him, and יהוה shall blot out his name from under heaven.

21 And יהוה shall separate him unto evil out of all the tribes of Yisrael, according to all the curses of the covenant that are written in this B28bbook of the law (sefer hatorah),

22 So that the generation to come of your children that shall rise up after you, and the stranger that shall come from a far land, shall say, when they see the plagues of that land, and the sicknesses which יהוה hath laid upon it;

23 And that the whole land thereof is brimstone, and salt, and burning, that it is not sown, nor beareth, nor any grass groweth therein, like the overthrow of Sodom, and Gomorrah, Admah, and Zeboim, which יהוה overthrew in His anger, and in His wrath.'

24 All nations shall say, 'Wherefore hath יהוה done thus unto this land? What meaneth the heat of this great anger?'

25 Then men shall say: 'Because they have forsaken the covenant of יהוה God (Elohim) of their fathers, which He made with them when He brought them forth out of the land of Egypt (Mitsrayim);

26 For they went and served other gods (elohim), and worshipped them, gods (elohim) whom they knew not, and whom He had not given unto them.

27 And the anger of יהוה was kindled against this land, to bring upon it all the curses that are written in this book.

28 'And יהוה rooted them out of their land in anger, and in wrath, and in great indignation, and cast them into another land, as it is this day.'

29 "The secret things belong unto יהוה our God (YHWH Eloheinu), but those things which are revealed belong unto us and to our children forever, that we may do all the words of this law (torah)."

30 "And it shall come to pass, when all these things are come upon you, the blessing and the curse, which I have set before you, and you shalt call them to mind among all the nations, whither יהוה your God (YHWH Eloheikha) hath driven you,

2 And shalt return unto יהוה your God (YHWH Eloheikha), and shalt obey His voice according to all that I command you this day, you and your children, with all your heart, and with all your soul,

3 That then יהוה your God (YHWH Eloheikha) will turn your captivity, and have compassion upon you, and will return and gather you from all the nations, whither יהוה your God (YHWH Eloheikha) hath scattered you.

4 If any of you be driven out unto the outmost parts of heaven, from thence will יהוה your God (YHWH Eloheikha) gather you, and from thence will He fetch you.

5 And יהוה your God (YHWH Eloheikha) will bring you into the land which your fathers possessed, and you shalt possess it; and He will do you good, and multiply you above your fathers.

6 And יהוה your God (YHWH Eloheikha) will circumcise your heart, and the heart of your seed, to love יהוה your God (YHWH Eloheikha) with all your heart, and with all your soul, that you mayest live.

7 And יהוה your God (YHWH Eloheikha) will put all these curses upon your enemies, and on them that hate you, which persecuted you.

8 And you shalt return and obey the voice of יהוה, and do all His commandments which I command you this day.

9 And יהוה your God (YHWH Eloheikha) will make you plenteous in every work of your hand, in the fruit of your body, and in the fruit of your cattle, and in the fruit of your land, for good; for

יהוה will again rejoice over you for good, as He rejoiced over your fathers.

10 If you shalt hearken unto the voice of יהוה your God (YHWH Eloheikha), to keep His commandments and His statutes which are written in this book of the law (sefer hatorah), and if you turn unto יהוה your God (YHWH Eloheikha) with all your heart, and with all your soul.

11 For this commandment which I command you this day, it is not hidden from you, neither is it far off.

12 It is not in heaven, that you shouldest say, 'Who shall go up for us to heaven, and bring it unto us, that we may hear it, and do it?'

13 Neither is it beyond the sea, that you shouldest say, 'Who shall go over the sea for us, and bring it unto us, that we may hear it, and do it?'

14 But the word is very near unto you, in your mouth, and in your heart, that you mayest do it.

15 See, I have set before you this day life and good, and death and evil;

16 In that I command you this day to love יהוה your God (YHWH Eloheikha), to walk in His ways, and to keep His commandments and His statutes and His judgments, that you mayest live and multiply; and יהוה your God (YHWH Eloheikha) shall bless you in the land whither you goest to possess it.

17 But if your heart turns away, so that you wilt not hear, but shalt be drawn away, and worship other gods (elohim), and serve them;

18 I denounce unto you this day, that you shall surely perish, and that you shall not prolong your days upon the land, whither you passest over Jordan (Yarden) to go to possess it.

19 I call heaven and earth to record this day against you, that I have set before you life and death, blessing and cursing; therefore choose life, that both you and your seed may live;

20 That you mayest love יהוה your God (YHWH Eloheikha), and that you mayest obey His voice, and that you mayest cleave unto Him, for He is your life, and the length of your days; that you mayest dwell in the land which יהוה sware unto your fathers, to Avraham, to Isaac (Yitschaq), and to Jacob (Yaaqov), to give them."

31 And Moses (Mosheh) went and spake these words unto all Yisrael.

2 And he said unto them: "I am a hundred and twenty years old this day; I can no more go out and come in; also יהוה hath said unto me, 'You

shalt not go over this Jordan (Yarden).'

3 יהוה your God (YHWH Eloheikha), He will go over before you, and He will destroy these nations from before you, and you shalt possess them; and Joshua (Yehoshua), he shall go over before you, as יהוה hath said.

4 And יהוה shall do unto them as He did to Sihon and to Og, kings of the Amorites, and unto the land of them, whom He destroyed.

5 And יהוה shall give them up before your face, that you may do unto them according unto all the commandments which I have commanded you.

6 Be strong and of a good courage, fear not, nor be afraid of them; for יהוה your God (YHWH Eloheikha), He it is that doth go with you; He will not fail you, nor forsake you."

7 And Moses (Mosheh) called unto Joshua (Yehoshua), and said unto him in the sight of all Yisrael, "Be strong and of a good courage, for you must go with this people unto the land which יהוה hath sworn unto their fathers to give them; and you shalt cause them to inherit it.

8 And יהוה, He it is that doth go before you; He will be with you, He will not fail you, neither forsake you; fear not, neither be dismayed."

9 And Moses (Mosheh) wrote this law (torah), and delivered it unto the priests (kohanim) the sons of Lewi, who bare the ark of the covenant of יהוה, and unto all the elders of Yisrael.

10 And Moses (Mosheh) commanded them, saying: "At the end of every seven years, in the solemnity of the year of release (shemittah), in the Feast of Tabernacles (Chag Sukkot),

11 When all Yisrael is come to appear before יהוה your God (YHWH Eloheikha) in the place which He shall choose, you shalt read this law (torah) before all Yisrael in their hearing.

12 Gather the people together, men, and women, and children, and your stranger that is within your gates, that they may hear, and that they may learn, and fear יהוה your God (YHWH Eloheikha), and observe to do all the words of this law (torah).

13 And that their children, who have not known anything, may hear, and learn to fear יהוה your God (YHWH Eloheikhem), as long as you live in the land whither you go over Jordan (Yarden) to possess it.

14 And יהוה said unto Moses (Mosheh), "Behold, your days approach that you must die;

call Joshua (Yehoshua), and present yourselves in the tabernacle of the congregation, that I may give him an order." And Moses (Mosheh) and Joshua (Yehoshua) went, and presented themselves in the tabernacle of the congregation.

15 And יהוה appeared in the tabernacle in a pillar of a cloud; and the pillar of the cloud stood over the door of the tabernacle.

16 And יהוה said unto Moses (Mosheh), "Behold, you shalt sleep with your fathers; and this people will rise up, and go a whoring after the gods (elohim) of the strangers of the land, whither they go to be among them, and will forsake Me, and break My covenant which I have made with them.

17 Then My anger shall be kindled against them in that day, and I will forsake them, and I will hide My face from them, and they shall be devoured, and many evils and troubles shall befall them; so that they will say in that day, 'Are not these evils come upon us, because our God (Elohim) is not among us?'

18 And I will surely hide My face in that day for all the evils which they shall have wrought, in that they are turned unto other gods (elohim).

19 Now therefore write you this song for you, and teach it the children of Yisrael; put it in their mouths, that this song may be a witness for Me against the children of Yisrael.

20 For when I shall have brought them into the land which I sware unto their fathers, that floweth with milk and honey; and they shall have eaten and filled themselves, and waxen fat; then will they turn unto other gods (elohim), and serve them, and provoke Me, and break My covenant.

21 And it shall come to pass, when many evils and troubles are befallen them, that this song shall testify against them as a witness; for it shall not be forgotten out of the mouths of their seed; for I know their imagination which they go about, even now, before I have brought them into the land which I sware.

22 Moses (Mosheh) therefore wrote this song the same day, and taught it the children of Yisrael.

23 And he gave Joshua (Yehoshua) the son of Nun an order, and said, "Be strong and of a good courage, for you shalt bring the children of Yisrael into the land which I sware unto them, and I will be with you.

24 And it came to pass, when Moses (Mosheh) had made an end of writing the words of this law (torah) in a book, until they were finished,

25 That Moses (Mosheh) commanded the Levites (Lewiyim), who bare the ark of the covenant of יהוה, saying:

26 "Take this book of the law (sefer hatorah), and put it in the side of the ark of the covenant of יהוה your God (YHWH Eloheikhem), that it may be there for a witness against you.

27 For I know your rebellion, and your stiff neck; behold, while I am yet alive with you this day, you have been rebellious against יהוה; and how much more after my death?

28 Gather unto me all the elders of your tribes, and your officers, that I may speak these words in their ears, and call heaven and earth to record against them.

29 For I know that after my death you will utterly corrupt yourselves, and turn aside from the way which I have commanded you; and evil will befall you in the latter days; because you will do evil in the sight of יהוה, to provoke Him to anger through the work of your hands."

30 And Moses (Mosheh) spake in the ears of all the congregation of Yisrael the words of this song, until they were ended.

32 "Give ear, O you heavens, and I will speak; and hear, O earth, the words of my mouth.

2 My doctrine shall drop as the rain, my speech shall distil as the dew, as the small rain upon the tender herb, and as the showers upon the grass.

3 For I will proclaim the name of יהוה. Ascribe you greatness unto our God (Elohim).

4 He is the Rock, His work is perfect; for all His ways are justice; a God (Elohim) of truth and without injustice, righteous and upright is He.

5 They have corrupted themselves, their spot is not the spot of His children; they are a perverse and crooked generation.

6 Do you thus requite יהוה, O foolish people and unwise? Is not He your Father that hath bought you? Hath He not made you, and established you?

7 Remember the days of old, consider the years of many generations. Ask your father, and he will shew you; your elders, and they will tell you:

8 When Most High (Elyon) divided to the nations their inheritance, when He separated the sons of Adam, He set the bounds of the

people according to the number of the children of Yisrael.

9 For יהוה's portion is His people; Jacob (Yaaqov) is the lot of His inheritance.

10 He found him in a desert land, and in the waste howling wilderness; He led him about, He instructed him, He kept him as the apple of His eye.

11 As an eagle stirreth up her nest, fluttereth over her young, spreadeth abroad her wings, taketh them, beareth them on her wings;

12 So יהוי alone did lead him, and there was no strange god with him.

13 He made him ride on the high places of the earth, that he might eat the increase of the fields; and He made him to suck honey out of the rock, and oil out of the flinty rock;

14 Butter of kine, and milk of sheep, with fat of lambs, and rams of the breed of Bashan, and goats, with the fat of kidneys of wheat; and you didst drink the pure blood of the grape.

15 But Yeshurun waxed fat, and kicked; you are waxen fat, you are grown thick, you are covered with fatness; then he forsook B5aGod (Eloah) who made him, and lightly esteemed the Rock of his salvation.

16 They provoked Him to jealousy with strange gods (elohim), with abominations provoked they Him to anger.

17 They sacrificed unto devils, not to God (Eloah); to gods (elohim) whom they knew not, to new gods (elohim) that came newly up, whom your fathers feared not.

18 Of the Rock that begat you you are unmindful, and have forgotten God (Elohim) who formed you.

19 And when יהוי saw it, He abhorred them, because of the provoking of His sons, and of His daughters.

20 And He said: 'I will hide My face from them, I will see what their end shall be, for they are a perverse generation, children in whom is no faith.

21 They have moved Me to jealousy with that which is not God (Elohim); they have provoked Me to anger with their vanities; and I will move them to jealousy with those who are not a people; I will provoke them to anger with a foolish nation.

22 For a fire is kindled in Mine anger, and shall burn unto the lowest B32hell (sheol), and shall

consume the earth with her increase, and set on fire the foundations of the mountains.

23 I will heap mischiefs upon them; I will spend Mine arrows upon them.

24 They shall be burnt with hunger, and devoured with burning heat, and with bitter destruction; I will also send the teeth of beasts upon them, with the poison of serpents of the dust.

25 Outside, the sword and inside the terror, shall destroy both the young man and the virgin, the suckling also with the man of gray hairs.

26 I said, "I would scatter them into corners, I would make the remembrance of them to cease from among men";

27 Were it not that I feared the wrath of the enemy, lest their adversaries should behave themselves strangely, and lest they should say, "Our hand is high, and יהוי hath not done all this."'

28 For they are a nation void of counsel, neither is there any understanding in them.

29 O that they were wise, that they understood this, that they would consider their latter end!

30 How should one chase a thousand, and two put ten thousand to flight, except their Rock had sold them, and יהוי had shut them up?

31 For their rock is not as our Rock, even our enemies themselves being judges.

32 For their vine is of the vine of Sodom, and of the fields of Gomorrah: their grapes are grapes of gall, their clusters are bitter:

33 Their wine is the poison of dragons, and the cruel venom of asps.

34 'Is not this laid up in store with Me, and sealed up among My treasures?

35 To Me belongeth vengeance, and recompence; their foot shall slide in due time; for the day of their disaster is at hand, and the things that shall come upon them make haste.'

36 For יהוי shall judge His people, and have compassion for His servants, when He seeth that their power is gone, and there is none shut up, or left.

37 And He shall say: "Where are their gods (elohim), their rock in whom they trusted,

38 Who did eat the fat of their sacrifices, and drank the wine of their drink offerings? Let them rise up and help you, and be your protection.

39 See now that I, even I, am He, and there is

no God (Elohim) besides Me. I kill, and I make alive; I wound, and I heal; neither is there any that can deliver out of My hand.

40 For I lift up My hand to heaven, and say, "As I live forever,

41 If I whet My glittering sword, and Mine hand take hold on judgment; I will render vengeance to Mine enemies, and will repay those who hate Me.

42 I will make Mine arrows drunk with blood, and My sword shall devour flesh; and that with the blood of the slain and of the captives, from the beginning of revenges upon the enemy.'"

43 Rejoice, O you nations, with His people; for He will avenge the blood of His servants, and will render vengeance to His adversaries, and will be merciful unto His land, and to His people."

44 And Moses (Mosheh) came and spake all the words of this song in the ears of the people, he, and A32Joshua (Hoshea) the son of Nun.

45 And Moses (Mosheh) made an end of speaking all these words to all Yisrael;

46 And he said unto them: "Set your hearts unto all the words which I testify among you this day, which you shall command your children to observe to do, all the words of this teaching.

47 For it is not a vain thing for you; because it is your life; and through this thing you shall prolong your days in the land, whither you go over Jordan (Yarden) to possess it."

48 And יהוה spake unto Moses (Mosheh) that selfsame day, saying:

49 "Get you up into this mountain Avarim, unto Mount Nebo, which is in the land of Moav, that is opposite Yericho; and behold the land of Canaan, which I give unto the children of Yisrael for a possession;

50 And die in the mountain whither you goest up, and be gathered unto your people; as Aaron (Aharon) your brother died in Mount Hor, and was gathered unto his people;

51 Because you trespassed against Me among the children of Yisrael at the waters of Meribah-Qadesh, in the wilderness of Zin, because you sanctified Me not in the midst of the children of Yisrael.

52 Yet you shalt see the land before you; but you shalt not go thither unto the land which I give the children of Yisrael."

33 And this is the blessing, wherewith Moses (Mosheh) the man of God (Elohim)

blessed the children of Yisrael before his death.

2 And he said: "יהוה came from Sinai, and rose up from Seir unto them; He shined forth from Mount Paran, and He came with ten thousands of holy ones; from His right hand went a fiery law for them.

3 Yea, He loved the people; all His holy ones are in Your hand; and they sat down at Your feet; every one shall receive of Your words.

4 Moses (Mosheh) commanded us a B28aTorah, as the inheritance of the congregation of Jacob (Yaaqov).

5 And he was king in Yeshurun, when the heads of the people and the tribes of Yisrael were gathered together.

6 Let Reuven live, and not die; and let not his men be few.

7 And this is the blessing of Judah (Yehudah), and he said: "Hear, יהוה, the voice of Judah (Yehudah), and bring him unto his people; let his hands be sufficient for him; and be You a help to him from his enemies."

8 And of Lewi he said: "Let your Perfection (Tummim) and your Lights (Urim) be with your holy man, whom you didst prove at Massah, and with whom you didst strive at the waters of Meribah;

9 Who said unto his father and to his mother, 'I have not seen him'; neither did he acknowledge his brethren, nor knew his own children; for they have observed Your word, and kept Your covenant.

10 They shall teach Jacob (Yaaqov) Your judgments, and Yisrael Your Torah; they shall put incense before You, and whole burnt sacrifice upon Your altar.

11 Bless his substance, יהוה, and accept the work of his hands; smite through the loins of them that rise against him, and of those who hate him, that they rise not again."

12 And of Binyamin he said: "The beloved of יהוה shall dwell in safety by Him; and יהוה shall cover him all the day long, and he shall dwell between His shoulders."

13 And of Joseph (Yosef) he said: "Blessed of יהוה be his land, for the precious things of heaven, for the dew, and for the deep that coucheth beneath,

14 And for the precious fruits brought forth by the sun, and for the precious things put forth by the moon,

15 And for the chief things of the ancient mountains, and for the precious things of the lasting hills,

16 And for the precious things of the earth and fulness thereof, and for the good will of him that dwelt in the bush; let the blessing come upon the head of Joseph (Yosef), and upon the top of the head of him that was separated from his brethren.

17 His glory is like the firstling of his bullock, and his horns are like the horns of unicorns; with them he shall push the people together to the ends of the earth; and they are the multitude of Efrayim, and they are the thousands of Menashsheh."

18 And of Zevulun he said: "Rejoice, Zevulun, in your going out; and, Yissaskhar, in your tents.

19 They shall call the people unto the mountain; there they shall offer sacrifices of righteousness; for they shall suck of the abundance of the seas, and of treasures hid in the sand."

20 And of Gad he said: "Blessed be he that enlargeth Gad; he dwelleth as a lion, and teareth the arm with the crown of the head.

21 And he provided the first part for himself, because there, in a portion of the lawgiver, was he seated; and he came with the heads of the people, he executed the justice of יהוה, and His judgments with Yisrael."

22 And of Dan he said: "Dan is a lion's whelp; he shall leap from Bashan."

23 And of Naftali he said: "O Naftali, satisfied with favor, and full with the blessing of יהוה; possess you the west and the south."

24 And of Asher he said: "Let Asher be blessed with children; let him be acceptable to his brethren, and let him dip his foot in oil.

25 Your shoes shall be iron and brass; and as your days, so shall your strength be.

26 There is none like unto God (El) of Yeshurun, who rideth upon the heaven in your help, and in His excellency on the sky.

27 The eternal God (Elohim) is your refuge, and underneath are the everlasting arms; and He shall thrust out the enemy from before you; and shall say, 'Destroy them!'

28 Yisrael then shall dwell in safety alone; the fountain of Jacob (Yaaqov) shall be upon a land of corn and wine; also his heavens shall drop down dew.

29 Happy are you, O Yisrael; who is like unto you, O people saved by יהוה, the shield of your help, and who is the sword of your excellency! And your enemies shall be found liars unto you; and you shalt tread upon their high places."

34 And Moses (Mosheh) went up from the plains of Moav unto the mountain of Nebo, to the top of Pisgah, that is opposite Yericho. And יהוה shewed him all the land of Gilad, unto Dan,

2 And all Naftali, and the land of Efrayim, and Menashsheh, and all the land of Judah (Yehudah), unto the utmost sea,

3 And the south, and the plain of the valley of Yericho, the city of palm trees, unto Zoar.

4 And יהוה said unto him, "This is the land which I sware unto Avraham, unto Isaac (Yitschaq), and unto Jacob (Yaaqov), saying, 'I will give it unto your seed'; I have caused you to see it with your eyes, but you shalt not go over thither."

5 So Moses (Mosheh) the servant of יהוה died there in the land of Moav, according to the word of יהוה.

6 And He buried him in a valley in the land of Moav, opposite Beit-Peor; but no man knoweth of his sepulchre unto this day.

7 And Moses (Mosheh) was a hundred and twenty years old when he died; his eye was not dim, nor his natural force abated.

8 And the children of Yisrael wept for Moses (Mosheh) in the plains of Moav thirty days; so the days of weeping and mourning for Moses (Mosheh) were ended.

9 And Joshua (Yehoshua) the son of Nun was full of the spirit of wisdom; for Moses (Mosheh) had laid his hands upon him; and the children of Yisrael hearkened unto him, and did as יהוה commanded Moses (Mosheh).

10 And there arose not a prophet since in Yisrael like unto Moses (Mosheh), whom יהוה knew face to face,

11 In all the signs and the wonders, which יהוה sent him to do in the land of Egypt (Mitsrayim) to Pharaoh (Paroh), and to all his servants, and to all his land,

12 And in all that mighty hand, and in all the great terror which Moses (Mosheh) shewed in the sight of all Yisrael.

JOSHUA
YEHOSHUA יְהוֹשֻׁעַ
(YHWH is Salvation)

1 Now after the death of Moses (Mosheh) the servant of יהוה, it came to pass, that יהוה spake unto ᴬ³²Joshua (Yehoshua) the son of Nun, Moses (Mosheh)'s minister, saying,

2 "Moses (Mosheh) My servant is dead; now therefore arise, go over this Jordan (Yarden), you, and all this people, unto the land which I do give to them, even to the children of Yisrael.

3 Every place that the sole of your foot shall tread upon, that have I given unto you, as I said unto Moses (Mosheh).

4 From the wilderness and this Lebanon even unto the great river, the river Euphrates, all the land of the Hittites, and unto the great sea toward the going down of the sun, shall be your coast.

5 There shall not any man be able to stand before you all the days of your life: as I was with Moses (Mosheh), so I will be with you; I will not fail you, nor forsake you.

6 Be strong and of a good courage; for unto this people shalt you divide for an inheritance the land, which I sware unto their fathers to give them.

7 Only be you strong and very courageous, that you mayest observe to do according to all the law (torah) which Moses (Mosheh) My servant commanded you; turn not from it to the right hand or to the left, that you mayest prosper whithersoever you goest.

8 This book of the law (sefer hatorah) shall not depart out of your mouth; but you shalt meditate therein day and night, that you mayest observe to do according to all that is written therein; for then you shalt make your way prosperous, and then you shalt have good success.

9 Have not I commanded you? Be strong and of a good courage; be not afraid, neither be you dismayed: for יהוה your God (YHWH Eloheikha) is with you whithersoever you goest."

10 Then Joshua (Yehoshua) commanded the officers of the people, saying,

11 Pass through the camp, and command the people, saying, 'Prepare you victuals; for within three days you shall pass over this Jordan (Yarden), to go in to possess the land, which יהוה your God (YHWH Eloheikhem) giveth you to possess it.'"

12 And to the Reubenites (Reuveni), and to the Gadites, and to half the tribe of Menashsheh, spake Joshua (Yehoshua), saying,

13 "Remember the word which Moses (Mosheh) the servant of יהוה commanded you, saying, יהוה your God (YHWH Eloheikhem) hath given you rest, and hath given you this land.

14 Your wives, your little ones, and your cattle, shall remain in the land which Moses (Mosheh) gave you on this side Jordan (Yarden); but you shall pass before your brethren armed, all the mighty men of valour, and help them;

15 Until יהוה have given your brethren rest, as He hath given you, and they also have possessed the land which יהוה your God (YHWH Eloheikhem) giveth them: then you shall return unto the land of your possession, and enjoy it, which Moses (Mosheh) יהוה's servant gave you on this side Jordan (Yarden) toward the sunrising."

16 And they answered Joshua (Yehoshua), saying, "All that you commandest us we will do, and whithersoever you sendest us, we will go.

17 According as we hearkened unto Moses (Mosheh) in all things, so will we hearken unto you. Only יהוה your God (YHWH Eloheikhem) be with you, as He was with Moses (Mosheh).

18 Whosoever he be that doth rebel against your commandment, and will not hearken unto your words in all that you commandest him, he shall be put to death. Only be strong and of a good courage."

2 And Joshua (Yehoshua) the son of Nun sent out of Shittim two men to spy secretly, saying, "Go view the land, even Yericho." And they went, and came into a harlot's house, named Rachav, and lodged there.

2 And it was told the king of Yericho, saying, "Behold, there came men in hither tonight of the children of Yisrael to search out the country."

3 And the king of Yericho sent unto Rachav, saying, "Bring forth the men that have come to you, who have entered into your house, for they have come to search out all the country."

4 And the woman took the two men, and hid them, and said thus, "There came men unto me, but I knew not whence they were.

5 And it came to pass about the time of shutting

of the gate, when it was dark, that the men went out; whither the men went I knew not; pursue after them quickly, for you shall overtake them."

6 But she had brought them up to the roof of the house, and hid them with the stalks of flax, which she had laid in order upon the roof.

7 And the men pursued after them the way to Jordan (Yarden) unto the fords; and as soon as they which pursued after them were gone out, they shut the gate.

8 And before they were laid down, she came up unto them upon the roof;

9 And she said unto the men, "I know that יהוה hath given you the land, and that your terror is fallen upon us, and that all the inhabitants of the land faint because of you.

10 For we have heard how יהוה dried up the water of the Red sea for you, when you came out of Egypt (Mitsrayim); and what you did unto the two kings of the Amorites, that were on the other side Jordan (Yarden), Sihon and Og, whom you utterly destroyed.

11 And as soon as we had heard these things, our hearts did melt, neither did there remain any more courage in any man, because of you, for יהוה your God (YHWH Eloheikhem), He is God (Elohim) in heaven above, and on earth beneath.

12 Now therefore, please swear unto me by יהוה, since I have shewed you kindness, that you will also shew kindness unto my father's house, and give me a true token;

13 And that you will save alive my father, and my mother, and my brethren, and my sisters, and all that they have, and deliver our lives from death."

14 And the men answered her, "Our life for yours, if you utter not this our business. And it shall be, when יהוה hath given us the land, that we will deal kindly and truly with you."

15 Then she let them down by a cord through the window; for her house was upon the town wall, and she dwelt upon the wall.

16 And she said unto them, "Get you to the mountain, lest the pursuers meet you; and hide yourselves there three days, until the pursuers be returned. And afterward may you go your way."

17 And the men said unto her, "We will be blameless of this your oath which you have made us swear.

18 Behold, when we come into the land, you shalt bind this line of scarlet thread in the window which you didst let us down by; and you shalt bring your father, and your mother, and your brethren, and all your father's household, home unto you.

19 And it shall be, that whosoever shall go out of the doors of your house into the street, his blood shall be upon his head, and we will be guiltless; and whosoever shall be with you in the house, his blood shall be on our head, if any hand be upon him.

20 And if you utter this our business, then we will be quit of your oath which you have made us to swear."

21 And she said, "According unto your words, so be it." And she sent them away, and they departed; and she bound the scarlet line in the window.

22 And they went, and came unto the mountain, and abode there three days, until the pursuers were returned; and the pursuers sought them throughout all the way, but found them not.

23 So the two men returned, and descended from the mountain, and passed over, and came to Joshua (Yehoshua) the son of Nun, and told him all things that befell them.

24 And they said unto Joshua (Yehoshua), "Truly יהוה hath delivered into our hands all the land; for even all the inhabitants of the country do faint because of us."

3 And Joshua (Yehoshua) rose early in the morning; and they removed from Shittim, and came to Jordan (Yarden), he and all the children of Yisrael, and lodged there before they passed over.

2 And it came to pass after three days, that the officers went through the camp;

3 And they commanded the people, saying, "When you see the ark of the covenant of יהוה your God (YHWH Eloheikhem), and the priests (kohanim) the Levites (Lewiyim) bearing it, then you shall remove from your place, and go after it.

4 Yet there shall be a space between you and it, about two thousand cubits by measure; come not near unto it, that you may know the way by which you must go, for you have not passed this way before."

5 And Joshua (Yehoshua) said unto the people: "Sanctify yourselves, for tomorrow יהוה will do wonders among you."

6 And Joshua (Yehoshua) spake unto the priests

(kohanim), saying, "Take up the ark of the covenant, and pass over before the people." And they took up the ark of the covenant, and went before the people.

7 And יהוה said unto Joshua (Yehoshua), "This day will I begin to magnify you in the sight of all Yisrael, that they may know that, as I was with Moses (Mosheh), so I will be with you.

8 And you shalt command the priests (kohanim) that bear the ark of the covenant, saying, 'When you are come to the brink of the water of Jordan (Yarden), you shall stand still in Jordan (Yarden).'"

9 And Joshua (Yehoshua) said unto the children of Yisrael, "Come hither, and hear the words of יהוה your God (YHWH Eloheikhem)."

10 And Joshua (Yehoshua) said, "Hereby you shall know that the [B2]living God (El chai) is among you, and that He will without fail drive out from before you the Canaanites, and the Hittites, and the Hivites, and the Perizzites, and the Girgashites, and the Amorites, and the Yevusis:

11 "Behold, the ark of the covenant of the [12]Lord (Adonai) of all the earth passeth over before you into Jordan (Yarden).

12 Now therefore take you twelve men out of the tribes of Yisrael, out of every tribe a man.

13 And it shall come to pass, as soon as the soles of the feet of the priests (kohanim) that bear the ark of יהוה, the Lord (Adonai) of all the earth, shall rest in the waters of Jordan (Yarden), that the waters of Jordan (Yarden) shall be cut off from the waters that come down from above; and they shall stand upon a heap."

14 And it came to pass, when the people removed from their tents, to pass over Jordan (Yarden), and the priests (kohanim) bearing the ark of the covenant before the people;

15 And as they that bare the ark were come unto Jordan (Yarden), and the feet of the priests (kohanim) that bare the ark were dipped in the brim of the water, (for Yarden overfloweth all his banks all the time of harvest,)

16 That the waters which came down from above stood and rose up upon a heap very far from the city Adam, that is beside Zaretan; and those that came down toward the sea of the plain, even the salt sea, failed, and were cut off; and the people passed over right against Yericho.

17 And the priests (kohanim) that bare the ark

of the covenant of יהוה stood firm on dry ground in the midst of Jordan (Yarden), and all the Yisraelis passed over on dry ground, until all the people were passed clean over Jordan (Yarden).

4 And it came to pass, when all the people had completely passed over Jordan (Yarden), that יהוה spake unto Joshua (Yehoshua), saying:

2 "Take you twelve men out of the people, out of every tribe a man,

3 And command you them, saying, 'Take you hence out of the midst of Jordan (Yarden), out of the place where the priests' (kohanim) feet stood firm, twelve stones, and you shall carry them over with you, and leave them in the lodging place, where you shall lodge this night.'"

4 Then Joshua (Yehoshua) called the twelve men, whom he had prepared of the children of Yisrael, out of every tribe a man;

5 And Joshua (Yehoshua) said unto them: "Pass over before the ark of יהוה your God (YHWH Eloheikhem) into the midst of Jordan (Yarden), and take you up every man of you a stone upon his shoulder, according unto the number of the tribes of the children of Yisrael,

6 That this may be a sign among you, that when your children ask their fathers in time to come, saying, 'What mean you by these stones?'

7 Then you shall answer them, That the waters of Jordan (Yarden) were cut off before the ark of the covenant of יהוה; when it passed over Jordan (Yarden), the waters of Jordan (Yarden) were cut off; and these stones shall be for a memorial unto the children of Yisrael forever."

8 And the children of Yisrael did so as Joshua (Yehoshua) commanded, and took up twelve stones out of the midst of Jordan (Yarden), as יהוה spake unto Joshua (Yehoshua), according to the number of the tribes of the children of Yisrael, and carried them over with them unto the place where they lodged, and laid them down there.

9 And Joshua (Yehoshua) set up twelve stones in the midst of Jordan (Yarden), in the place where the feet of the priests (kohanim) which bare the ark of the covenant stood; and they are there unto this day.

10 For the priests (kohanim) which bare the ark stood in the midst of Jordan (Yarden), until every thing was finished that יהוה commanded Joshua (Yehoshua) to speak unto the people,

according to all that Moses (Mosheh) commanded Joshua (Yehoshua); and the people hasted and passed over.

11 And it came to pass, when all the people were clean passed over, that the ark of יהוה passed over, and the priests (kohanim), in the presence of the people.

12 And the children of Reuven, and the children of Gad, and half the tribe of Menashsheh, passed over armed before the children of Yisrael, as Moses (Mosheh) spake unto them.

13 About forty thousand prepared for war passed over before יהוה unto battle, to the plains of Yericho.

14 On that day יהוה magnified Joshua (Yehoshua) in the sight of all Yisrael; and they feared him, as they feared Moses (Mosheh), all the days of his life.

15 And יהוה spake unto Joshua (Yehoshua), saying,

16 Command the priests (kohanim) that bear the ark of the testimony, that they come up out of Jordan (Yarden)."

17 Joshua (Yehoshua) therefore commanded the priests (kohanim), saying, "Come you up out of Jordan (Yarden)."

18 And it came to pass, when the priests (kohanim) that bare the ark of the covenant of יהוה were come up out of the midst of Jordan (Yarden), and the soles of the priests' (kohanim) feet were lifted up unto the dry land, that the waters of Jordan (Yarden) returned unto their place, and flowed over all his banks, as they did before.

19 And the people came up out of Jordan (Yarden) on the tenth day of the first month, and encamped in Gilgal, in the east border of Yericho.

20 And those twelve stones, which they took out of Jordan (Yarden), did Joshua (Yehoshua) pitch in Gilgal.

21 And he spake unto the children of Yisrael, saying: 'When your children shall ask their fathers in time to come, saying, 'What mean these stones?'

22 Then you shall let your children know, saying, 'Yisrael came over this Jordan (Yarden) on dry land';

23 For יהוה your God (YHWH Eloheikhem) dried up the waters of Jordan (Yarden) from before you, until you were passed over, as יהוה

your God (YHWH Eloheikhem) did to the Red sea, which He dried up from before us, until we were gone over,

24 That all the people of the earth might know the hand of יהוה, that it is mighty; that you might fear יהוה your God (YHWH Eloheikhem) forever."

5 And it came to pass, when all the kings of the Amorites, which were on the side of Jordan (Yarden) westward, and all the kings of the Canaanites, which were by the sea, heard that יהוה had dried up the waters of Jordan (Yarden) from before the children of Yisrael, until we were passed over, that their heart melted, neither was there spirit in them any more, because of the children of Yisrael.

2 At that time יהוה said unto Joshua (Yehoshua), "Make you sharp knives, and circumcise again the children of Yisrael the second time."

3 And Joshua (Yehoshua) made him sharp knives, and circumcised the children of Yisrael at the hill of the foreskins.

4 And this is the cause why Joshua (Yehoshua) did circumcise: All the people that came out of Egypt (Mitsrayim), that were males, even all the men of war, died in the wilderness by the way, after they came out of Egypt (Mitsrayim).

5 Now all the people that came out were circumcised, but all the people that were born in the wilderness by the way as they came forth out of Egypt (Mitsrayim), them they had not circumcised.

6 For the children of Yisrael walked forty years in the wilderness, till all the people that were men of war, which came out of Egypt (Mitsrayim), were consumed, because they obeyed not the voice of יהוה; unto whom יהוה sware that He would not shew them the land, which יהוה sware unto their fathers that He would give us, "a land that floweth with milk and honey."

7 And their children, whom He raised up in their stead, them Joshua (Yehoshua) circumcised; for they were uncircumcised, because they had not circumcised them by the way.

8 And it came to pass, when they had done circumcising all the people, that they abode in their places in the camp, till they were whole.

9 And יהוה said unto Joshua (Yehoshua), "This day have I rolled away the reproach of Egypt (Mitsrayim) from off you." Wherefore the name

of the place is called Gilgal unto this day.

10 And the children of Yisrael encamped in Gilgal, and kept the Passover (Pesach) on the fourteenth day of the month at even in the plains of Yericho.

11 And they did eat of the old corn of the land on the next day after the Passover (Pesach), unleavened cakes (matstsot), and parched corn in the selfsame day.

12 And the manna ceased on the next day after they had eaten of the old corn of the land; neither had the children of Yisrael manna any more; but they did eat of the fruit of the land of Canaan that year.

13 And it came to pass, when Joshua (Yehoshua) was by Yericho, that he lifted up his eyes and looked, and, behold, there stood a man opposite him with his sword drawn in his hand; and Joshua (Yehoshua) went unto him, and said unto him, "Are you for us, or for our adversaries?"

14 And he said, "Nay, but as captain of the host of יהוה have I now come. And Joshua (Yehoshua) fell on his face to the earth, and did worship, and said unto him, "What saith my lord (adoni) unto his servant?"

15 And the captain of יהוה's host (tsava) said unto Joshua (Yehoshua), "Loose your shoe from off your foot; for the place whereon you standest is holy." And Joshua (Yehoshua) did so.

6 Now Yericho was straitly shut up because of the children of Yisrael; none went out, and none came in.

2 And יהוה said unto Joshua (Yehoshua): "See, I have given into your hand Yericho, and the king thereof, and the mighty men of valour.

3 And you shall compass the city, all you men of war, and go round about the city once. Thus shalt you do six days.

4 And seven priests (kohanim) shall bear before the ark seven trumpets of rams' horns; and the seventh day you shall compass the city seven times, and the priests (kohanim) shall blow with the trumpets.

5 And it shall come to pass, that when they make a long blast with the ram's horn, and when you hear the sound of the trumpet, all the people shall shout with a great shout; and the wall of the city shall fall down flat, and the people shall ascend up every man straight before him."

6 And Joshua (Yehoshua) the son of Nun called the priests (kohanim), and said unto them,

"Take up the ark of the covenant, and let seven priests (kohanim) bear seven trumpets of rams' horns before the ark of יהוה."

7 And he said unto the people, "Pass on, and compass the city, and let him that is armed pass on before the ark of יהוה."

8 And it came to pass, when Joshua (Yehoshua) had spoken unto the people, that the seven priests (kohanim) bearing the seven trumpets of rams' horns passed on before יהוה, and blew with the trumpets; and the ark of the covenant of יהוה followed them.

9 And the armed men went before the priests (kohanim) that blew with the trumpets, and the rereward came after the ark, the priests (kohanim) going on, and blowing with the trumpets.

10 And Joshua (Yehoshua) had commanded the people, saying, "You shall not shout, nor make any noise with your voice, neither shall any word proceed out of your mouth, until the day I bid you shout; then shall you shout."

11 So the ark of יהוה compassed the city, going about it once; and they came into the camp, and lodged in the camp.

12 And Joshua (Yehoshua) rose early in the morning, and the priests (kohanim) took up the ark of יהוה.

13 And seven priests (kohanim) bearing seven trumpets of rams' horns before the ark of יהוה went on continually, and blew with the trumpets; and the armed men went before them; but the rereward came after the ark of יהוה, the priests (kohanim) going on, and blowing with the trumpets.

14 And the second day they compassed the city once, and returned into the camp; so they did six days.

15 And it came to pass on the seventh day, that they rose early about the dawning of the day, and compassed the city after the same manner seven times: only on that day they compassed the city seven times.

16 And it came to pass at the seventh time, when the priests (kohanim) blew with the trumpets, Joshua (Yehoshua) said unto the people: "Shout, for יהוה hath given you the city!

17 And the city shall be accursed, even it, and all that are therein, to יהוה; only Rachav the harlot shall live, she and all that are with her in the house, because she hid the messengers that

we sent.

18 And you, in any wise keep yourselves from the accursed thing, lest you make yourselves accursed, when you take of the accursed thing, and make the camp of Yisrael a curse, and trouble it.

19 But all the silver, and gold, and vessels of brass and iron, are consecrated unto יהוה; they shall come into the treasury of יהוה."

20 So the people shouted when the priests (kohanim) blew with the ram's horn (shofarot): and it came to pass, when the people heard the sound of the shofar, and the people shouted with a great shout, that the wall fell down flat, so that the people went up into the city, every man straight before him, and they took the city.

21 And they utterly destroyed all that was in the city, both man and woman, young and old, and ox, and sheep, and ass, with the edge of the sword.

22 But Joshua (Yehoshua) had said unto the two men that had spied out the country, "Go into the harlot's house, and bring out thence the woman, and all that she hath, as you sware unto her."

23 And the young men that were spies went in, and brought out Rachav, and her father, and her mother, and her brethren, and all that she had; and they brought out all her kindred, and left them outside the camp of Yisrael.

24 And they burnt the city with fire, and all that was therein; only the silver, and the gold, and the vessels of brass and of iron, they put into the treasury of the house of יהוה.

25 And Joshua (Yehoshua) saved Rachav the harlot alive, and her father's household, and all that she had; and she dwelleth in Yisrael even unto this day; because she hid the messengers, which Joshua (Yehoshua) sent to spy out Yericho.

26 And Joshua (Yehoshua) adjured them at that time, saying, "Cursed be the man before יהוה, that riseth up and buildeth this city Yericho; he shall lay the foundation thereof in his firstborn, and in his youngest son shall he set up the gates of it."

27 So יהוה was with Joshua (Yehoshua); and his fame was throughout all the country.

7 But the children of Yisrael committed a trespass in the accursed thing; for Achan, the son of Carmi, the son of Zabdi, the son of Zerah, of the tribe of Judah (Yehudah), took of the

accursed thing; and the anger of יהוה was kindled against the children of Yisrael.

2 And Joshua (Yehoshua) sent men from Yericho to Ai, which is beside Beit Aven, on the east side of Bethel (Beit-El), and spake unto them, saying, "Go up and view the country." And the men went up and viewed Ai.

3 And they returned to Joshua (Yeho-shua), and said unto him, "Let not all the people go up; but let about two or three thousand men go up and smite Ai; and make not all the people to labour thither; for they are but few."

4 So there went up thither of the people about three thousand men; and they fled before the men of Ai.

5 And the men of Ai smote of them about thirty and six men; for they chased them from before the gate even unto Shebarim, and smote them in the going down; wherefore the hearts of the people melted, and became as water.

6 And Joshua (Yehoshua) rent his clothes, and fell to the earth upon his face before the ark of יהוה until the eventide, he and the elders of Yisrael, and put dust upon their heads.

7 And Joshua (Yehoshua) said, "Alas, O Lord (Adonai) יהוה, wherefore have you at all brought this people over Jordan (Yarden), to deliver us into the hand of the Amorites, to destroy us? If only we had been content, and dwelt on the other side Jordan (Yarden)!

8 O Lord (Adonai), what shall I say, when Yisrael turneth their backs before their enemies!

9 For the Canaanites and all the inhabitants of the land shall hear of it, and shall environ us round, and cut off our name from the earth; and what wilt You do unto Your great name?"

10 And יהוה said unto Joshua (Yehoshua), "Get you up; wherefore liest you thus upon your face?

11 Yisrael hath sinned, and they have also transgressed My covenant which I commanded them; for they have even taken of the accursed thing, and have also stolen, and dissembled also, and they have put it even among their own stuff.

12 Therefore the children of Yisrael could not stand before their enemies, but turned their backs before their enemies, because they were accursed; neither will I be with you any more, except you destroy the accursed from among you.

13 Up, sanctify the people, and say, 'Sanctify yourselves against tomorrow; for thus saith יהוה

God of Israel (Elohei Yisrael): "There is an accursed thing in the midst of you, O Yisrael; you canst not stand before your enemies, until you take away the accursed thing from among you."

14 'In the morning therefore you shall be brought according to your tribes; and it shall be, that the tribe which יהוה taketh shall come according to the families thereof; and the family which יהוה shall take shall come by households; and the household which יהוה shall take shall come man by man.

15 And it shall be, that he that is taken with the accursed thing shall be burnt with fire, he and all that he hath; because he hath transgressed the covenant of יהוה, and because he hath wrought folly in Yisrael.'"

16 So Joshua (Yehoshua) rose up early in the morning, and brought Yisrael by their tribes; and the tribe of Judah (Yehudah) was taken;

17 And he brought the family of Judah (Yehudah); and he took the family of the Zarhites; and he brought the family of the Zarhites man by man; and Zabdi was taken.

18 And he brought his household man by man; and Achan, the son of Carmi, the son of Zabdi, the son of Zerah, of the tribe of Judah (Yehudah), was taken.

19 And Joshua (Yehoshua) said unto Achan, "My son, please give glory to יהוה God of Israel (Elohei Yisrael), and make confession unto Him; and tell me now what you have done; hide it not from me."

20 And Achan answered Joshua (Yehoshua), and said, "Indeed I have sinned against יהוה God of Israel (Elohei Yisrael), and thus and thus have I done.

21 When I saw among the spoils a goodly Babylonish garment, and two hundred shekels of silver, and a wedge of gold of fifty shekels weight, then I coveted them, and took them; and, behold, they are hiddden in the earth in the midst of my tent, and the silver under it."

22 So Joshua (Yehoshua) sent messengers, and they ran unto the tent; and, behold, it was hiddden in his tent, and the silver under it.

23 And they took them out of the midst of the tent, and brought them unto Joshua (Yehoshua), and unto all the children of Yisrael, and laid them out before יהוה.

24 And Joshua (Yehoshua), and all Yisrael with him, took Achan the son of Zerah, and the silver, and the garment, and the wedge of gold, and his sons, and his daughters, and his oxen, and his asses, and his sheep, and his tent, and all that he had; and they brought them unto the valley of Achor.

25 And Joshua (Yehoshua) said, "Why have you troubled us? יהוה shall trouble you this day." And all Yisrael stoned him with stones, and burned them with fire, after they had stoned them with stones.

26 And they raised over him a great heap of stones unto this day. So יהוה turned from the fierceness of His anger. Wherefore the name of that place was called the Valley of Achor, unto this day.

8 And יהוה said unto Joshua (Yehoshua), "Fear not, nor be you dismayed; take all the people of war with you, and arise, go up to Ai; see, I have given into your hand the king of Ai, and his people, and his city, and his land.

2 And you shalt do to Ai and her king as you didst unto Yericho and her king: only the spoil thereof, and the cattle thereof, shall you take for a prey unto yourselves; lay you an ambush for the city behind it."

3 So Joshua (Yehoshua) arose, and all the people of war, to go up against Ai; and Joshua (Yehoshua) chose out thirty thousand mighty men of valour, and sent them away by night.

4 And he commanded them, saying: "Behold, you shall lie in wait against the city, even behind the city; go not very far from the city, but be you all ready.

5 And I, and all the people that are with me, will approach unto the city; and it shall come to pass, when they come out against us, as at the first, that we will flee before them,

6 (For they will come out after us) till we have drawn them from the city; for they will say, 'They flee before us, as at the first'; therefore we will flee before them.

7 Then you shall rise up from the ambush, and seize upon the city; for יהוה your God (YHWH Eloheikhem) will deliver it into your hand.

8 And it shall be, when you have taken the city, that you shall set the city on fire; according to the commandment of יהוה shall you do. See, I have commanded you."

9 Joshua (Yehoshua) therefore sent them forth: and they went to lie in ambush, and abode

between Bethel (Beit-El) and Ai, on the west side of Ai; but Joshua (Yehoshua) lodged that night among the people.

10 And Joshua (Yehoshua) rose up early in the morning, and numbered the people, and went up, he and the elders of Yisrael, before the people to Ai.

11 And all the people, even the people of war that were with him, went up, and drew near, and came before the city, and pitched on the north side of Ai. Now there was a valley between them and Ai.

12 And he took about five thousand men, and set them to lie in ambush between Bethel (Beit-El) and Ai, on the west side of the city.

13 And when they had set the people, even all the army that was on the north of the city, and their liers in wait on the west of the city, Joshua (Yehoshua) went that night into the midst of the valley.

14 And it came to pass, when the king of Ai saw it, that they hasted and rose up early, and the men of the city went out against Yisrael to battle, he and all his people, at a time appointed, before the plain; but he wist not that there were liers in ambush against him behind the city.

15 And Joshua (Yehoshua) and all Yisrael made as if they were beaten before them, and fled by the way of the wilderness.

16 And all the people that were in Ai were called together to pursue after them; and they pursued after Joshua (Yehoshua), and were drawn away from the city.

17 And there was not a man left in Ai or Bethel (Beit-El), that went not out after Yisrael; and they left the city open, and pursued after Yisrael.

18 And יהוה said unto Joshua (Yehoshua), "Stretch out the spear that is in your hand toward Ai; for I will give it into your hand. And Joshua (Yehoshua) stretched out the spear that he had in his hand toward the city.

19 And the ambush arose quickly out of their place, and they ran as soon as he had stretched out his hand: and they entered into the city, and took it, and hasted and set the city on fire.

20 And when the men of Ai looked behind them, they saw, and, behold, the smoke of the city ascended up to heaven, and they had no power to flee this way or that way: and the people that fled to the wilderness turned back upon the pursuers.

21 And when Joshua (Yehoshua) and all Yisrael saw that the ambush had taken the city, and that the smoke of the city ascended, then they turned again, and slew the men of Ai.

22 And the other issued out of the city against them; so they were in the midst of Yisrael, some on this side, and some on that side: and they smote them, so that they let none of them remain or escape.

23 And the king of Ai they took alive, and brought him to Joshua (Yehoshua).

24 And it came to pass, when Yisrael had made an end of slaying all the inhabitants of Ai in the field, in the wilderness wherein they chased them, and when they were all fallen on the edge of the sword, until they were consumed, that all the Yisraelis returned unto Ai, and smote it with the edge of the sword.

25 And so it was, that all that fell that day, both of men and women, were twelve thousand, even all the men of Ai.

26 For Joshua (Yehoshua) drew not his hand back, wherewith he stretched out the spear, until he had utterly destroyed all the inhabitants of Ai.

27 Only the cattle and the spoil of that city Yisrael took for a prey unto themselves, according unto the word of יהוה which He commanded Joshua (Yehoshua).

28 And Joshua (Yehoshua) burnt Ai, and made it a heap forever, even a desolation unto this day.

29 And the king of Ai he hanged on a tree until eventide: and as soon as the sun was down, Joshua (Yehoshua) commanded that they should take his carcase down from the tree, and cast it at the entering of the gate of the city, and raise thereon a great heap of stones, that remaineth unto this day.

30 Then Joshua (Yehoshua) built an altar unto יהוה God of Israel (Elohei Yisrael) in Mount Ebal,

31 As Moses (Mosheh) the servant of יהוה commanded the children of Yisrael, as [B28b]it is written in the book of the law (sefer hatorah) by Moses, an altar of whole stones, over which no man hath lift up any iron; and they offered thereon burnt offerings unto יהוה, and sacrificed peace offerings.

32 And he wrote there upon the stones a copy of the law (torah) which Moses (Mosheh) had written in the presence of the children of

Yisrael.

33 And all Yisrael, and their elders, and officers, and their judges, stood on this side the ark and on that side before the priests (kohanim) the Levites (Lewiyim), who bare the ark of the covenant of יהוה, as well the stranger, as he that was born among them; half of them opposite Mount Gerizim, and half of them opposite Mount Ebal; as Moses (Mosheh) the servant of יהוה had commanded before, that they should bless the people of Yisrael.

34 And afterward he read all the words of the law (torah), the blessings and cursings, according to all that is written in the book of the law (sefer hatorah).

35 There was not a word of all that Moses (Mosheh) commanded, which Joshua (Yehoshua) read not before all the congregation of Yisrael, with the women, and the little ones, and the strangers that were conversant among them.

9 And it came to pass, when all the kings which were on this side Jordan (Yarden), in the hills, and in the valleys, and in all the coasts of the great sea opposite Lebanon, the Hittite, and the Amorite, the Canaanite, the Perizzite, the Hivite, and the Jebusite (Yevusi), heard thereof;

2 That they gathered themselves together, to fight with Joshua (Yehoshua) and with Yisrael, with one accord.

3 And when the inhabitants of Giveon heard what Joshua (Yehoshua) had done unto Yericho and to Ai,

4 They did work craftily, and went and made as if they had been ambassadors, and took old sacks upon their asses, and wine bottles, old, and rent, and bound up;

5 And old shoes and clouted upon their feet, and old garments upon them; and all the bread of their provision was dry and mouldy.

6 And they went to Joshua (Yehoshua) unto the camp at Gilgal, and said unto him, and to the men of Yisrael, "We have come from a far country; now therefore make you a league with us.

7 And the men of Yisrael said unto the Hivites, "Perhaps you dwell among us; and how shall we make a league with you?"

8 And they said unto Joshua (Yehoshua), "We are your servants." And Joshua (Yehoshua) said

unto them, "Who are you? And from whence come you?"

9 And they said unto him: "From a very far country your servants have come because of the name of יהוה your God (YHWH Eloheikha); for we have heard the fame of him, and all that he did in Egypt (Mitsrayim),

10 And all that he did to the two kings of the Amorites, that were beyond Jordan (Yarden), to Sihon king of Heshbon, and to Og king of Bashan, who was at Ashtaroth.

11 Wherefore our elders and all the inhabitants of our country spake to us, saying, 'Take victuals with you for the journey, and go to meet them, and say unto them, "We are your servants; therefore now make you a league with us.'"

12 This our bread we took hot for our provision out of our houses on the day we came forth to go unto you; but now, behold, it is dry, and it is mouldy.

13 And these bottles of wine, which we filled, were new; and, behold, they be rent; and these our garments and our shoes are become old by reason of the very long journey."

14 And the men took of their victuals, and asked not counsel at the mouth of יהוה.

15 And Joshua (Yehoshua) made peace with them, and made a league with them, to let them live: and the princes of the congregation sware unto them.

16 And it came to pass at the end of three days after they had made a league with them, that they heard that they were their neighbours, and that they dwelt among them.

17 And the children of Yisrael journeyed, and came unto their cities on the third day. Now their cities were Giveon, and Chephirah, and Beeroth, and Qiryat-Yearim.

18 And the children of Yisrael smote them not, because the princes of the congregation had sworn unto them by יהוה God of Israel (Elohei Yisrael). And all the congregation murmured against the princes.

19 But all the princes said unto all the congregation, "We have sworn unto them by יהוה God of Israel (Elohei Yisrael); now therefore we may not touch them.

20 This we will do to them; we will even let them live, lest wrath be upon us, because of the oath which we sware unto them."

21 And the princes said unto them, "Let them

live; but let them be hewers of wood and drawers of water unto all the congregation; as the princes had promised them."

22 And Joshua (Yehoshua) called for them, and he spake unto them, saying, "Wherefore have you beguiled us, saying, 'We are very far from you;' when you dwell among us?

23 Now therefore you are cursed, and there shall none of you be freed from being bondmen, and hewers of wood and drawers of water for the house of my God (Elohim)."

24 And they answered Joshua (Yehoshua), and said, "Because it was certainly told your servants, how that יהוה your God (YHWH Eloheikha) commanded His servant Moses (Mosheh) to give you all the land, and to destroy all the inhabitants of the land from before you, therefore we were sore afraid of our lives because of you, and have done this thing.

25 And now, behold, we are in your hand; as it seemeth good and right unto you to do unto us, do."

26 And so did he unto them, and delivered them out of the hand of the children of Yisrael, that they slew them not.

27 And Joshua (Yehoshua) made them that day hewers of wood and drawers of water for the congregation, and for the altar of יהוה, even unto this day, in the place which He should choose.

10 Now it came to pass, when Adoni-Zedek king of Jerusalem (Yerushalayim) had heard how Joshua (Yehoshua) had taken Ai, and had utterly destroyed it; as he had done to Yericho and her king, so he had done to Ai and her king; and how the inhabitants of Giveon had made peace with Yisrael, and were among them;

2 That they feared greatly, because Giveon was a great city, as one of the royal cities, and because it was greater than Ai, and all the men thereof were mighty.

3 Wherefore Adoni-Zedek king of Jerusalem (Yerushalayim) sent unto Hoham king of Hebron, and unto Piram king of Yarmut, and unto Yafiya king of Lachish, and unto Debir king of Eglon, saying,

4 Come up unto me, and help me, that we may smite Giveon, for it hath made peace with Joshua (Yehoshua) and with the children of Yisrael.

5 Therefore the five kings of the Amorites, the king of Jerusalem (Yerushalayim), the king of Hebron, the king of Yarmut, the king of Lachish, the king of Eglon, gathered themselves together, and went up, they and all their hosts, and encamped before Giveon, and made war against it.

6 And the men of Giveon sent unto Joshua (Yehoshua) to the camp to Gilgal, saying, Slack not your hand from your servants; come up to us quickly, and save us, and help us; for all the kings of the Amorites that dwell in the mountains are gathered together against us.

7 So Joshua (Yehoshua) ascended from Gilgal, he, and all the people of war with him, and all the mighty men of valour.

8 And יהוה said unto Joshua (Yehoshua), "Fear them not, for I have delivered them into your hand; there shall not a man of them stand before you."

9 Joshua (Yehoshua) therefore came unto them suddenly, and went up from Gilgal all night.

10 And יהוה discomfited them before Yisrael, and slew them with a great slaughter at Giveon, and chased them along the way that goeth up to Beit-Choron, and smote them to Azekah, and unto Makkedah.

11 And it came to pass, as they fled from before Yisrael, and were in the going down to Beit-Choron, that יהוה cast down great stones from heaven upon them unto Azekah, and they died; they were more which died with hailstones than they whom the children of Yisrael slew with the sword.

12 Then spake Joshua (Yehoshua) to יהוה in the day when יהוה delivered up the Amorites before the children of Yisrael, and he said in the sight of Yisrael: "Sun, stand you still upon Giveon; and you, Moon, in the valley of Ayalon."

13 And the sun stood still, and the moon stayed, until the people had avenged themselves upon their enemies. Is not this written in the book of Yashar? So the sun stood still in the midst of heaven, and hasted not to go down about a whole day.

14 And there was no day like that before it or after it, that יהוה hearkened unto the voice of a man; for יהוה fought for Yisrael.

15 And Joshua (Yehoshua) returned, and all Yisrael with him, unto the camp to Gilgal.

16 But these five kings fled, and hid themselves in a cave at Makkedah.

17 And it was told Joshua (Yehoshua), saying, "The five kings are found hid in a cave at Makkedah."

18 And Joshua (Yehoshua) said, "Roll great stones upon the mouth of the cave, and set men by it for to keep them.

19 And stay you not, but pursue after your enemies, and smite the hindmost of them; allow them not to enter into their cities, for יהוה your God (YHWH Eloheikhem) hath delivered them into your hand."

20 And it came to pass, when Joshua (Yehoshua) and the children of Yisrael had made an end of slaying them with a very great slaughter, till they were consumed, that the rest which remained of them entered into fenced cities.

21 And all the people returned to the camp to Joshua (Yehoshua) at Makkedah in peace: none moved his tongue against any of the children of Yisrael.

22 Then said Joshua (Yehoshua), "Open the mouth of the cave, and bring out those five kings unto me out of the cave."

23 And they did so, and brought forth those five kings unto him out of the cave, the king of Jerusalem (Yerushalayim), the king of Hebron, the king of Yarmut, the king of Lachish, and the king of Eglon.

24 And it came to pass, when they brought out those kings unto Joshua (Yehoshua), that Joshua (Yehoshua) called for all the men of Yisrael, and said unto the captains of the men of war which went with him, "Come near, put your feet upon the necks of these kings." And they came near, and put their feet upon the necks of them.

25 And Joshua (Yehoshua) said unto them, "Fear not, nor be dismayed, be strong and of good courage, for thus shall יהוה do to all your enemies against whom you fight."

26 And afterward Joshua (Yehoshua) smote them, and slew them, and hanged them on five trees; and they were hanging upon the trees until the evening.

27 And it came to pass at the time of the going down of the sun, that Joshua (Yehoshua) commanded, and they took them down off the trees, and cast them into the cave wherein they had been hidden, and laid great stones in the cave's mouth, which remain until this very day.

28 And that day Joshua (Yehoshua) took Makkedah, and smote it with the edge of the sword, and the king thereof he utterly destroyed, them, and all the souls that were therein; he let none remain, and he did to the king of Makkedah as he did unto the king of Yericho.

29 Then Joshua (Yehoshua) passed from Makkedah, and all Yisrael with him, unto Libnah, and fought against Libnah.

30 And יהוה delivered it also, and the king thereof, into the hand of Yisrael; and he smote it with the edge of the sword, and all the souls that were therein; he let none remain in it; but did unto the king thereof as he did unto the king of Yericho.

31 And Joshua (Yehoshua) passed from Libnah, and all Yisrael with him, unto Lachish, and encamped against it, and fought against it.

32 And יהוה delivered Lachish into the hand of Yisrael, which took it on the second day, and smote it with the edge of the sword, and all the souls that were therein, according to all that he had done to Libnah.

33 Then Horam king of Gezer came up to help Lachish; and Joshua (Yehoshua) smote him and his people, until he had left him none remaining.

34 And from Lachish Joshua (Yehoshua) passed unto Eglon, and all Yisrael with him; and they encamped against it, and fought against it.

35 And they took it on that day, and smote it with the edge of the sword, and all the souls that were therein he utterly destroyed that day, according to all that he had done to Lachish.

36 And Joshua (Yehoshua) went up from Eglon, and all Yisrael with him, unto Hebron; and they fought against it.

37 And they took it, and smote it with the edge of the sword, and the king thereof, and all the cities thereof, and all the souls that were therein; he left none remaining, according to all that he had done to Eglon; but destroyed it utterly, and all the souls that were therein.

38 And Joshua (Yehoshua) returned, and all Yisrael with him, to Debir; and fought against it.

39 And he took it, and the king thereof, and all the cities thereof; and they smote them with the edge of the sword, and utterly destroyed all the souls that were therein; he left none remaining; as he had done to Hebron, so he did to Debir, and to the king thereof; as he had done also to Libnah, and to her king.

40 So Joshua (Yehoshua) smote all the country of the hills, and of the south, and of the vale, and

of the springs, and all their kings; he left none remaining, but utterly destroyed all that breathed, as יהוה God of Israel (Elohei Yisrael) commanded.

41 And Joshua (Yehoshua) smote them from Qadesh Barnea even unto Gaza (Azzah), and all the country of Goshen, even unto Giveon.

42 And all these kings and their land did Joshua (Yehoshua) take at one time, because יהוה God of Israel (Elohei Yisrael) fought for Yisrael.

43 And Joshua (Yehoshua) returned, and all Yisrael with him, unto the camp to Gilgal.

11 And it came to pass, when Yavin king of Hazor had heard those things, that he sent to Yovav king of Madon, and to the king of Shimron, and to the king of Achshaph,

2 And to the kings that were on the north of the mountains, and of the plains south of Chinneroth, and in the valley, and in the borders of Dor on the west,

3 And to the Canaanite on the east and on the west, and to the Amorite, and the Hittite, and the Perizzite, and the Yevusi in the mountains, and to the Hivite under Hermon in the land of Mizpeh.

4 And they went out, they and all their hosts with them, much people, even as the sand that is upon the sea shore in multitude, with horses and chariots very many.

5 And when all these kings were met together, they came and pitched together at the waters of Merom, to fight against Yisrael.

6 And יהוה said unto Joshua (Yehoshua), "Be not afraid because of them, for tomorrow about this time will I deliver them up all slain before Yisrael. You shalt hough their horses, and burn their chariots with fire."

7 So Joshua (Yehoshua) came, and all the people of war with him, against them by the waters of Merom suddenly; and they fell upon them.

8 And יהוה delivered them into the hand of Yisrael, who smote them, and chased them unto great Zidon, and unto Misrephothmaim, and unto the valley of Mizpeh eastward; and they smote them, until they left them none remaining.

9 And Joshua (Yehoshua) did unto them as יהוה bade him: he houghed their horses, and burnt their chariots with fire.

10 And Joshua (Yehoshua) at that time turned back, and took Hazor, and smote the king thereof with the sword; for Hazor beforetime was the head of all those kingdoms.

11 And they smote all the souls that were therein with the edge of the sword, utterly destroying them; there was not any left to breathe; and he burnt Hazor with fire.

12 And all the cities of those kings, and all the kings of them, did Joshua (Yehoshua) take, and smote them with the edge of the sword, and he utterly destroyed them, as Moses (Mosheh) the servant of יהוה commanded.

13 But as for the cities that stood still in their strength, Yisrael burned none of them, save Hazor only; that did Joshua (Yehoshua) burn.

14 And all the spoil of these cities, and the cattle, the children of Yisrael took for a prey unto themselves; but every man they smote with the edge of the sword, until they had destroyed them, neither left they any to breathe.

15 As יהוה commanded Moses (Mosheh) His servant, so did Moses (Mosheh) command Joshua (Yehoshua), and so did Joshua (Yehoshua); he left nothing undone of all that יהוה commanded Moses (Mosheh).

16 So Joshua (Yehoshua) took all that land, the hills, and all the south country, and all the land of Goshen, and the valley, and the plain, and the mountain of Yisrael, and the valley of the same;

17 Even from the Mount Halak, that goeth up to Seir, even unto Baalgad in the valley of Lebanon under Mount Hermon; and all their kings he took, and smote them, and slew them.

18 Joshua (Yehoshua) made war a long time with all those kings.

19 There was not a city that made peace with the children of Yisrael, save the Hivites the inhabitants of Giveon; all other they took in battle.

20 For it was of יהוה to harden their hearts, that they should come against Yisrael in battle, that He might destroy them utterly, and that they might have no favor, but that He might destroy them, as יהוה commanded Moses (Mosheh).

21 And at that time came Joshua (Yehoshua), and cut off the Anakims from the mountains, from Hebron, from Debir, from Anab, and from all the mountains of Judah (Yehudah), and from all the mountains of Yisrael; Joshua (Yehoshua) destroyed them utterly with their cities.

22 There was none of the Anakims left in the land of the children of Yisrael; only in Gaza (Azzah), in Gath, and in Ashdod, there

remained.

23 So Joshua (Yehoshua) took the whole land, according to all that יהוה said unto Moses (Mosheh); and Joshua (Yehoshua) gave it for an inheritance unto Yisrael according to their divisions by their tribes. And the land rested from war.

12 Now these are the kings of the land, which the children of Yisrael smote, and possessed their land on the other side Jordan (Yarden) toward the rising of the sun, from the river Arnon unto Mount Hermon, and all the plain on the east:

2 Sihon king of the Amorites, who dwelt in Heshbon, and ruled from Aroer, which is upon the bank of the river Arnon, and from the middle of the river, and from half Gilad, even unto the river Yabok, which is the border of the children of Ammon;

3 And from the plain to the sea of Chinneroth on the east, and unto the sea of the plain, even the salt sea on the east, the way to Beit-Yeshimot; and from the south, under Ashdothpisgah;

4 And the coast of Og king of Bashan, which was of the remnant of the giants, that dwelt at Ashtaroth and at Edrei,

5 And reigned in mount Hermon, and in Salcah, and in all Bashan, unto the border of the Geshurites and the Maachathites, and half Gilad, the border of Sihon king of Heshbon.

6 Them did Moses (Mosheh) the servant of יהוה and the children of Yisrael smite; and Moses (Mosheh) the servant of יהוה gave it for a possession unto the Reubenites (Reuveni), and the Gadites, and the half tribe of Menashsheh.

7 And these are the kings of the country which Joshua (Yehoshua) and the children of Yisrael smote on this side Jordan (Yarden) on the west, from Baalgad in the valley of Lebanon even unto the mount Halak, that goeth up to Seir; which Joshua (Yehoshua) gave unto the tribes of Yisrael for a possession according to their divisions;

8 In the mountains, and in the valleys, and in the plains, and in the springs, and in the wilderness, and in the south country; the Hittites, the Amorites, and the Canaanites, the Perizzites, the Hivites, and the Yevusis:

9 The king of Yericho, one; the king of Ai, which is beside Bethel (Beit-El), one;

10 The king of Jerusalem (Yerushalayim), one;

the king of Hebron, one;

11 The king of Yarmut, one; the king of Lachish, one;

12 The king of Eglon, one; the king of Gezer, one;

13 The king of Debir, one; the king of Geder, one;

14 The king of Hormah, one; the king of Arad, one;

15 The king of Libnah, one; the king of Adullam, one;

16 The king of Makkedah, one; the king of Bethel (Beit-El), one;

17 The king of Tappuah, one; the king of Hepher, one;

18 The king of Aphek, one; the king of Lasharon, one;

19 The king of Madon, one; the king of Hazor, one;

20 The king of Shimronmeron, one; the king of Achshaph, one;

21 The king of Taanach, one; the king of Megiddo, one;

22 The king of Kedesh, one; the king of Yokneam of Carmel, one;

23 The king of Dor in the coast of Dor, one; the king of the nations of Gilgal, one;

24 The king of Tirzah, one: all the kings thirty-one.

13 Now Joshua (Yehoshua) was old and stricken in years; and יהוה said unto him: "You are old and stricken in years, and there remaineth yet very much land to be possessed.

2 This is the land that yet remaineth: all the borders of the Philistines, and all Geshuri,

3 From Sihor, which is before Egypt (Mitsrayim), even unto the borders of Ekron northward, which is counted to the Canaanite; five lords (seranim) of the Philistines; the Gazathites, and the Ashdothites, the Eshkalonites, the Gittites, and the Ekronites; also the Avites;

4 From the south, all the land of the Canaanites, and Mearah that is beside the Sidonians, unto Aphek, to the borders of the Amorites;

5 And the land of the Giblites, and all Lebanon, toward the sunrising, from Baalgad under Mount Hermon unto the entering into Hamath.

6 All the inhabitants of the hill country from Lebanon unto Misrephothmaim, and all the Sidonians, them will I drive out from before the children of Yisrael; only divide you it by lot unto the Yisraelis for an inheritance, as I have

commanded you.

7 Now therefore divide this land for an inheritance unto the nine tribes, and the half tribe of Menashsheh,

8 With whom the Reubenites (Reuveni) and the Gadites have received their inheritance, which Moses (Mosheh) gave them, beyond Jordan (Yarden) eastward, even as Moses (Mosheh) the servant of יהוה gave them:

9 From Aroer, that is upon the bank of the river Arnon, and the city that is in the midst of the river, and all the plain of Medeba unto Dibon;

10 And all the cities of Sihon king of the Amorites, which reigned in Heshbon, unto the border of the children of Ammon;

11 And Gilad, and the border of the Geshurites and Maachathites, and all Mount Hermon, and all Bashan unto Salcah;

12 All the kingdom of Og in Bashan, which reigned in Ashtaroth and in Edrei, who remained of the remnant of the giants; for these did Moses (Mosheh) smite, and cast them out.

13 Nevertheless the children of Yisrael expelled not the Geshurites, nor the Maachathites, but the Geshurites and the Maachathites dwell among the Yisraelis until this day.

14 Only unto the tribe of Lewi he gave none inheritance; the sacrifices of יהוה God of Israel (Elohei Yisrael) made by fire are their inheritance, as He said unto them.

15 And Moses (Mosheh) gave unto the tribe of the children of Reuven inheritance according to their families.

16 And their coast was from Aroer, that is on the bank of the river Arnon, and the city that is in the midst of the river, and all the plain by Medeba;

17 Heshbon, and all her cities that are in the plain; Dibon, and Bamothbaal, and Bethbaalmeon,

18 And Yahazah, and Kedemoth, and Mephaath,

19 And Qiryathaim, and Sibmah, and Zarethshahar in the mount of the valley,

20 And Beit-Peor, and Ashdothpisgah, and Beit-Yeshimot,

21 And all the cities of the plain, and all the kingdom of Sihon king of the Amorites, which reigned in Heshbon, whom Moses (Mosheh) smote with the princes of Midian, Evi, and Rekem, and Zur, and Hur, and Reba, which were dukes of Sihon, dwelling in the country.

22 Balaam also the son of Beor, the soothsayer,

did the children of Yisrael slay with the sword among them that were slain by them.

23 And the border of the children of Reuven was Jordan (Yarden), and the border thereof. This was the inheritance of the children of Reuven after their families, the cities and the villages thereof.

24 And Moses (Mosheh) gave inheritance unto the tribe of Gad, even unto the children of Gad according to their families.

25 And their coast was Yazer, and all the cities of Gilad, and half the land of the children of Ammon, unto Aroer that is before Rabbah;

26 And from Heshbon unto Ramathmizpeh, and Betonim; and from Mahanaim unto the border of Debir;

27 And in the valley, Betharam, and Bethnimrah, and Sukkot, and Zaphon, the rest of the kingdom of Sihon king of Heshbon, Jordan (Yarden) and his border, even unto the edge of the sea of Chinnereth on the other side Jordan (Yarden) eastward.

28 This is the inheritance of the children of Gad after their families, the cities, and their villages.

29 And Moses (Mosheh) gave inheritance unto the half tribe of Menashsheh; and this was the possession of the half tribe of the children of Menashsheh by their families.

30 And their coast was from Mahanaim, all Bashan, all the kingdom of Og king of Bashan, and all the towns of Yair, which are in Bashan, threescore (sixty) cities;

31 And half Gilad, and Ashtaroth, and Edrei, cities of the kingdom of Og in Bashan, were pertaining unto the children of Machir the son of Menashsheh, even to the one half of the children of Machir by their families.

32 These are the countries which Moses (Mosheh) did distribute for inheritance in the plains of Moav, on the other side Jordan (Yarden), by Yericho, eastward.

33 But unto the tribe of Lewi Moses (Mosheh) gave not any inheritance; יהוה God of Israel (Elohei Yisrael) was their inheritance, as He said unto them.

14 And these are the countries which the children of Yisrael inherited in the land of Canaan, which Eleazar the priest (kohen), and Joshua (Yehoshua) the son of Nun, and the heads of the fathers of the tribes of the children of Yisrael, distributed for inheritance to them.

2 By lot was their inheritance, as יהוה commanded by the hand of Moses (Mosheh), for the nine tribes, and for the half tribe.

3 For Moses (Mosheh) had given the inheritance of two tribes and a half tribe on the other side Jordan (Yarden); but unto the Levites (Lewiyim) he gave none inheritance among them.

4 For the children of Joseph (Yosef) were two tribes, Menashsheh and Efrayim; therefore they gave no part unto the Levites (Lewiyim) in the land, save cities to dwell in, with their suburbs for their cattle and for their substance.

5 As יהוה commanded Moses (Mosheh), so the children of Yisrael did, and they divided the land.

6 Then the children of Judah (Yehudah) came unto Joshua (Yehoshua) in Gilgal; and Caleb the son of Yefunneh the Kenezite said unto him, "You knowest the thing that יהוה said unto Moses (Mosheh) the man of God (Elohim) concerning me and you in Qadesh Barnea.

7 Forty years old was I when Moses (Mosheh) the servant of יהוה sent me from Qadesh Barnea to espy out the land; and I brought him word again as it was in mine heart.

8 Nevertheless my brethren that went up with me made the heart of the people melt; but I wholly followed יהוה my God (YHWH Elohai).

9 And Moses (Mosheh) sware on that day, saying, 'Surely the land whereon your feet have trodden shall be your inheritance, and your children's forever, because you have wholly followed יהוה my God (YHWH Elohai).'

10 And now, behold, יהוה hath kept me alive, as He said, these forty and five years, even since יהוה spake this word unto Moses (Mosheh), while the children of Yisrael wandered in the wilderness; and now, behold, I am this day fourscore (eighty) and five years old.

11 As yet I am as strong this day as I was in the day that Moses (Mosheh) sent me: as my strength was then, even so is my strength now, for war, both to go out, and to come in.

12 Now therefore give me this mountain, whereof יהוה spake in that day; for you heardest in that day how the Anakims were there, and that the cities were great and fenced; if so be יהוה will be with me, then I shall be able to drive them out, as יהוה said.

13 And Joshua (Yehoshua) blessed him, and gave unto Caleb the son of Yefunneh Hebron for an inheritance.

14 Hebron therefore became the inheritance of Caleb the son of Yefunneh the Kenezite unto this day, because that he wholly followed יהוה God of Israel (Elohei Yisrael).

15 And the name of Hebron before was Qiryat-Arba; which Arba was a great man among the Anakims. And the land had rest from war.

15 This then was the lot of the tribe of the children of Judah (Yehudah) by their families; even to the border of Edom the wilderness of Zin southward was the uttermost part of the south coast.

2 And their south border was from the shore of the salt sea, from the bay that looketh southward.

3 And it went out to the south side to Maalehacrabbim, and passed along to Zin, and ascended up on the south side unto Qadesh Barnea, and passed along to Hezron, and went up to Adar, and fetched a compass to Karkaa.

4 From thence it passed toward Azmon, and went out unto the river of Egypt (Mitsrayim); and the goings out of that coast were at the sea: this shall be your south coast.

5 And the east border was the salt sea, even unto the end of Jordan (Yarden). And their border in the north quarter was from the bay of the sea at the uttermost part of Jordan (Yarden).

6 And the border went up to Beit-Hogla, and passed along by the north of Beit-Aravah; and the border went up to the stone of Bohan the son of Reuven.

7 And the border went up toward Debir from the valley of Achor, and so northward, looking toward Gilgal, that is before the going up to Adummim, which is on the south side of the river; and the border passed toward the waters of Enshemesh, and the goings out thereof were at En Rogel.

8 And the border went up by the valley of the son of Hinnom unto the south side of the Yevusi; the same is Jerusalem (Yerushalayim); and the border went up to the top of the mountain that lieth before the valley of Hinnom westward, which is at the end of the valley of the giants northward.

9 And the border was drawn from the top of the hill unto the fountain of the water of Nephtoah, and went out to the cities of Mount Ephron; and the border was drawn to Baalah, which is Qiryat-Yearim.

10 And the border compassed from Baalah westward unto mount Seir, and passed along unto the side of Mount Yearim, which is Chesalon, on the north side, and went down to Beit-Shemesh, and passed on to Timnah.

11 And the border went out unto the side of Ekron northward; and the border was drawn to Shicron, and passed along to Mount Baalah, and went out unto Yavneel; and the goings out of the border were at the sea.

12 And the west border was to the great sea, and the coast thereof. This is the coast of the children of Judah (Yehudah) round about according to their families.

13 And unto Caleb the son of Yefunneh he gave a part among the children of Judah (Yehudah), according to the commandment of יהוה to Joshua (Yehoshua), even the city of Arba the father of Anak, which city is Hebron.

14 And Caleb drove thence the three sons of Anak, Sheshai, and Ahiman, and Talmai, the children of Anak.

15 And he went up thence to the inhabitants of Debir; and the name of Debir before was Qiryat-Sepher.

16 And Caleb said, "He that smiteth Kirjathsepher, and taketh it, to him will I give Achsah my daughter to wife."

17 And Othniel the son of Kenaz, the brother of Caleb, took it; and he gave him Achsah his daughter to wife.

18 And it came to pass, as she came unto him, that she moved him to ask of her father a field; and she lighted off her ass; and Caleb said unto her, "What you want?"

19 Who answered, "Give me a blessing; for you have given me a south land; give me also springs of water." And he gave her the upper springs, and the nether springs.

20 This is the inheritance of the tribe of the children of Judah (Yehudah) according to their families:

21 And the uttermost cities of the tribe of the children of Judah (Yehudah) toward the coast of Edom southward were Kabzeel, and Eder, and Yagur,

22 And Kinah, and Dimonah, and Adadah,

23 And Kedesh, and Hazor, and Ithnan,

24 Ziph, and Telem, and Bealoth,

25 And Hazor, Hadattah, and Kerioth, and Hezron, which is Hazor,

26 Amam, and Shema, and Moladah,

27 And Hazargaddah, and Heshmon, and Bethpalet,

28 And Hazarshual, and Beer-Sheva, and Bizyothyah,

29 Baalah, and Iim, and Azem,

30 And Eltolad, and Chesil, and Hormah,

31 And Ziklag, and Madmannah, and Sansannah,

32 And Lebaoth, and Shilhim, and Ain, and Rimmon: all the cities are twenty and nine, with their villages:

33 And in the valley, Eshtaol, and Zoreah, and Ashnah,

34 And ZaNoach, and Engannim, Tappuah, and Enam,

35 Yarmut, and Adullam, Socoh, and Azekah,

36 And Sharaim, and Adithaim, and Gederah, and Gederothaim: fourteen cities with their villages:

37 Zenan, and Hadashah, and Migdalgad,

38 And Dilean, and Mizpeh, and Yoktheel,

39 Lachish, and Bozkath, and Eglon,

40 And Cabbon, and Lahmam, and Kithlish,

41 And Gederoth, Beit-Dagon, and Naamah, and Makkedah: sixteen cities with their villages:

42 Libnah, and Ether, and Ashan,

43 And Yiftah, and Ashnah, and Nezib,

44 And Keilah, and Achzib, and Mareshah: nine cities with their villages;

45 Ekron, with her towns and her villages;

46 From Ekron even unto the sea, all that lay near Ashdod, with their villages;

47 Ashdod with her towns and her villages, Gaza (Azzah) with her towns and her villages, unto the river of Egypt (Mitsrayim), and the great sea, and the border thereof.

48 And in the mountains, Shamir, and Yattir, and Socoh,

49 And Dannah, and Qiryat-sannah, which is Debir,

50 And Anab, and Eshtemoh, and Anim,

51 And Goshen, and Holon, and Giloh: eleven cities with their villages;

52 Arab, and Dumah, and Eshean,

53 And Yanum, and Beit-Tappuach, and Aphekah,

54 And Humtah, and Qiryat-Arba, which is Hebron, and Zior: nine cities with their villages;

55 Maon, Carmel, and Ziph, and Yutah,

56 And Yizreel, and Yokdeam, and ZaNoach,

57 Cain, Gibeah, and Timnah; ten cities with their villages:

58 Halhul, Bethzur, and Gedor,

59 And Maarath, and Bethanoth, and Eltekon; six cities with their villages:

60 Qiryat-Baal, which is Qiryat-Yearim, and Rabbah; two cities with their villages:

61 In the wilderness, Beit-Aravah, Middin, and Secacah,

62 And Nibshan, and the city of Salt, and Engedi; six cities with their villages.

63 As for the Yevusis the inhabitants of Jerusalem (Yerushalayim), the children of Judah (Yehudah) could not drive them out; but the Yevusis dwell with the children of Judah (Yehudah) at Jerusalem (Yerushalayim) unto this day.

16 And the lot of the children of Joseph (Yosef) fell from Jordan (Yarden) by Yericho, unto the water of Yericho on the east, to the wilderness that goeth up from Yericho throughout Mount Bethel (Beit-El),

2 And goeth out from Bethel (Beit-El) to Luz, and passeth along unto the borders of Archi to Ataroth,

3 And goeth down westward to the coast of Yafleti, unto the coast of Beit-Choron the nether, and to Gezer; and the goings out thereof are at the sea.

4 So the children of Joseph (Yosef), Menashsheh and Efrayim, took their inheritance.

5 And the border of the children of Efrayim according to their families was thus; even the border of their inheritance on the east side was Atarothaddar, unto Beit-Choron the upper;

6 And the border went out toward the sea to Michmethah on the north side; and the border went about eastward unto Taanathshiloh, and passed by it on the east to Yanohah;

7 And it went down from Yanohah to Ataroth, and to Naarath, and came to Yericho, and went out at Jordan (Yarden).

8 The border went out from Tappuah westward unto the river Kanah; and the goings out thereof were at the sea. This is the inheritance of the tribe of the children of Efrayim by their families.

9 And the separate cities for the children of Efrayim were among the inheritance of the children of Menashsheh, all the cities with their villages.

10 And they drave not out the Canaanites that dwelt in Gezer; but the Canaanites dwell among the Efrayimites unto this day, and serve under tribute.

17 There was also a lot for the tribe of Menashsheh; for he was the firstborn of Joseph (Yosef); for Machir the firstborn of Menashsheh, the father of Gilad: because he was a man of war, therefore he had Gilad and Bashan.

2 There was also a lot for the rest of the children of Menashsheh by their families; for the children of Abiezer, and for the children of Helek, and for the children of Asriel, and for the children of Shechem, and for the children of Hepher, and for the children of Shemida; these were the male children of Menashsheh the son of Joseph (Yosef) by their families.

3 But Zelophehad, the son of Hepher, the son of Gilad, the son of Machir, the son of Menashsheh, had no sons, but daughters; and these are the names of his daughters, Mahlah, and Noach, Hoglah, Milcah, and Tirzah.

4 And they came near before Eleazar the priest (kohen), and before Joshua (Yehoshua) the son of Nun, and before the princes, saying, "יהוה commanded Moses (Mosheh) to give us an inheritance among our brethren." Therefore according to the command-ment of יהוה he gave them an inheritance among the brethren of their father.

5 And there fell ten portions to Menashsheh, beside the land of Gilad and Bashan, which were on the other side Jordan (Yarden);

6 Because the daughters of Menashsheh had an inheritance among his sons: and the rest of Menashsheh's sons had the land of Gilad.

7 And the coast of Menashsheh was from Asher to Michmethah, that lieth before Shechem; and the border went along on the right hand unto the inhabitants of Entappuah.

8 Now Menashsheh had the land of Tappuah, but Tappuah on the border of Menashsheh belonged to the children of Efrayim;

9 And the coast descended unto the river Kanah, southward of the river; these cities of Efrayim are among the cities of Menashsheh; the coast of Menashsheh also was on the north side of the river, and the outgoings of it was at the sea:

10 Southward it was Efrayim's, and northward it was Menashsheh's, and the sea is his border;

and they met together in Asher on the north, and in Yissaskhar on the east.

11 And Menashsheh had in Yissaskhar and in Asher Beit-Shan and her towns, and Ibleam and her towns, and the inhabitants of Dor and her towns, and the inhabitants of Endor and her towns, and the inhabitants of Taanach and her towns, and the inhabitants of Megiddo and her towns, even three countries.

12 Yet the children of Menashsheh could not drive out the inhabitants of those cities; but the Canaanites would dwell in that land.

13 Yet it came to pass, when the children of Yisrael were waxen strong, that they put the Canaanites to tribute; but did not utterly drive them out.

14 And the children of Joseph (Yosef) spake unto Joshua (Yehoshua), saying, "Why have you given me but one lot and one portion to inherit, seeing I am a great people, forasmuch as יהוה hath blessed us thus far?"

15 And Joshua (Yehoshua) answered them, "If you be a great people, then get you up to the wood country, and cut down for yourself there in the land of the Perizzites and of the giants, if mount Efrayim be too narrow for you."

16 And the children of Joseph (Yosef) said, "The hill is not enough for us; and all the Canaanites that dwell in the land of the valley have chariots of iron, both they who are of Beit-Shean and her towns, and they who are of the valley of Yizreel."

17 And Joshua (Yehoshua) spake unto the house of Joseph (Yosef), even to Efrayim and to Menashsheh, saying, "You are a great people, and have great power; you shalt not have one lot only;

18 But the mountain shall be yours; for it is a wood, and you shalt cut it down; and the outgoings of it shall be yours; for you shalt drive out the Canaanites, though they have iron chariots, and though they be strong."

18 And the whole congregation of the children of Yisrael assembled together at Shiloh, and set up the tabernacle of the congregation there. And the land was subdued before them.

2 And there remained among the children of Yisrael seven tribes, which had not yet received their inheritance.

3 And Joshua (Yehoshua) said unto the children of Yisrael: "How long are you slack to go to

possess the land, which יהוה God (Elohim) of your fathers hath given you?

4 Give out from among you three men for each tribe; and I will send them, and they shall rise, and go through the land, and describe it according to the inheritance of them; and they shall come again to me.

5 And they shall divide it into seven parts: Judah (Yehudah) shall abide in their coast on the south, and the house of Joseph (Yosef) shall abide in their coasts on the north.

6 You shall therefore describe the land into seven parts, and bring the description hither to me, that I may cast lots for you here before יהוה our God (YHWH Eloheinu).

7 But the Levites (Lewiyim) have no part among you; for the priesthood of יהוה is their inheritance; and Gad, and Reuven, and half the tribe of Menashsheh, have received their inheritance beyond Jordan (Yarden) on the east, which Moses (Mosheh) the servant of יהוה gave them."

8 And the men arose, and went away: and Joshua (Yehoshua) charged them that went to describe the land, saying, "Go and walk through the land, and describe it, and come again to me, that I may here cast lots for you before יהוה in Shiloh."

9 And the men went and passed through the land, and described it by cities into seven parts in a book, and came again to Joshua (Yehoshua) to the camp at Shiloh.

10 And Joshua (Yehoshua) cast lots for them in Shiloh before יהוה: and there Joshua (Yehoshua) divided the land unto the children of Yisrael according to their divisions.

11 And the lot of the tribe of the children of Binyamin came up according to their families: and the coast of their lot came forth between the children of Judah (Yehudah) and the children of Joseph (Yosef).

12 And their border on the north side was from Jordan (Yarden); and the border went up to the side of Yericho on the north side, and went up through the mountains westward; and the goings out thereof were at the wilderness of Beit Aven.

13 And the border went over from thence toward Luz, to the side of Luz, which is Bethel (Beit-El), southward; and the border descended to Atarothadar, near the hill that lieth on the

south side of the nether Beit-Choron.

14 And the border was drawn thence, and compassed the corner of the sea southward, from the hill that lieth before Beit-Choron southward; and the goings out thereof were at Qiryat-Baal, which is Qiryat-Yearim, a city of the children of Judah (Yehudah): this was the west quarter.

15 And the south quarter was from the end of Qiryat-Yearim, and the border went out on the west, and went out to the well of waters of Nephtoah:

16 And the border came down to the end of the mountain that lieth before the valley of the son of Hinnom, and which is in the valley of the giants on the north, and descended to the valley of Hinnom, to the side of Yevusi on the south, and descended to En Rogel,

17 And was drawn from the north, and went forth to Enshemesh, and went forth toward Geliloth, which is opposite the going up of Adummim, and descended to the stone of Bohan the son of Reuven,

18 And passed along toward the side opposite Aravah northward, and went down unto Aravah:

19 And the border passed along to the side of Bethhoglah northward: and the outgoings of the border were at the north bay of the salt sea at the south end of Jordan (Yarden); this was the south coast.

20 And Jordan (Yarden) was the border of it on the east side. This was the inheritance of the children of Binyamin, by the coasts thereof round about, according to their families.

21 Now the cities of the tribe of the children of Binyamin according to their families were Yericho, and Bethhoglah, and the valley of Keziz,

22 And Beit-Aravah, and Zemaraim, and Bethel (Beit-El),

23 And Avim, and Parah, and Ophrah,

24 And Chepharhaammonai, and Ophni, and Gaba; twelve cities with their villages;

25 Giveon, and Ramah, and Beeroth,

26 And Mizpeh, and Chephirah, and Mozah,

27 And Rekem, and Irpeel, and Taralah,

28 And Zelah, Eleph, and Yevusi, which is Jerusalem (Yerushalayim), Gibeath, and Qiryat; fourteen cities with their villages. This is the inheritance of the children of Binyamin according to their families.

19 And the second lot came forth to Shimon, even for the tribe of the children of Shimon according to their families; and their inheritance was within the inheritance of the children of Judah (Yehudah).

2 And they had in their inheritance Beer-Sheva, or Sheva, and Moladah,

3 And Hazarshual, and Balah, and Azem,

4 And Eltolad, and Bethul, and Hormah,

5 And Ziklag, and Beit-Markavot, and Hazarsusah,

6 And Bethlebaoth, and Sharuhen; thirteen cities and their villages;

7 Ain, Remmon, and Ether, and Ashan; four cities and their villages;

8 And all the villages that were round about these cities to Baalathbeer, Ramath of the south. This is the inheritance of the tribe of the children of Shimon according to their families.

9 Out of the portion of the children of Judah (Yehudah) was the inheritance of the children of Shimon; for the part of the children of Judah (Yehudah) was too much for them; therefore the children of Shimon had their inheritance within the inheritance of them.

10 And the third lot came up for the children of Zevulun according to their families; and the border of their inheritance was unto Sarid.

11 And their border went up toward the sea, and Maralah, and reached to Dabbasheth, and reached to the river that is before Yokneam;

12 And turned from Sarid eastward toward the sunrising unto the border of Chislothtabor, and then goeth out to Daberath, and goeth up to Yafiya,

13 And from thence passeth on along on the east to Gittahhepher, to Ittahkazin, and goeth out to Remmonmethoar to Neah;

14 And the border compasseth it on the north side to Hannathon; and the outgoings thereof are in the valley of Yiftahel.

15 And Kattath, and Nahallal, and Shimron, and Idalah, and Bethlehem (Beit-Lechem); twelve cities with their villages.

16 This is the inheritance of the children of Zevulun according to their families, these cities with their villages.

17 And the fourth lot came out to Yissaskhar, for the children of Yissaskhar according to their families.

18 And their border was toward Yizreel, and

Chesulloth, and Shunem,

19 And Hapharaim, and Shion, and Anaharath,

20 And Rabbith, and Kishion, and Abez,

21 And Remeth, and Engannim, and Enhaddah, and Beit-Patstsets;

22 And the coast reacheth to Tabor, and Shahazimah, and Beit-Shemesh; and the outgoings of their border were at Jordan (Yarden): sixteen cities with their villages.

23 This is the inheritance of the tribe of the children of Yissaskhar according to their families, the cities and their villages.

24 And the fifth lot came out for the tribe of the children of Asher according to their families.

25 And their border was Helkath, and Hali, and Beten, and Achshaph,

26 And Alammelech, and Amad, and Misheal; and reacheth to Carmel westward, and to Shihorlibnath;

27 And turneth toward the sunrising to Bethdagon, and reacheth to Zevulun, and to the valley of Yiftahel toward the north side of Bethemek, and Neiel, and goeth out to Cabul on the left hand,

28 And Hebron, and Rehob, and Hammon, and Kanah, even unto great Zidon;

29 And then the coast turneth to Ramah, and to the strong city Tyre; and the coast turneth to Hosah; and the outgoings thereof are at the sea from the coast to Achzib.

30 Ummah also, and Aphek, and Rehob: twenty and two cities with their villages.

31 This is the inheritance of the tribe of the children of Asher according to their families, these cities with their villages.

32 The sixth lot came out to the children of Naftali, even for the children of Naftali according to their families.

33 And their coast was from Heleph, from Allon to Zaanannim, and Adami, Nekeb, and Yavneel, unto Lakum; and the outgoings thereof were at Jordan (Yarden).

34 And then the coast turneth westward to Aznothtabor, and goeth out from thence to Hukkok, and reacheth to Zevulun on the south side, and reacheth to Asher on the west side, and to Judah (Yehudah) upon Jordan (Yarden) toward the sunrising.

35 And the fenced cities are Ziddim, Zer, and Hammath, Rakkath, and Chinnereth,

36 And Adamah, and Ramah, and Hazor,

37 And Kedesh, and Edrei, and Enhazor,

38 And Iron, and Migdalel, Horem, and Beit-Anat, and Beit-Shemesh; nineteen cities with their villages.

39 This is the inheritance of the tribe of the children of Naftali according to their families, the cities and their villages.

40 And the seventh lot came out for the tribe of the children of Dan according to their families.

41 And the coast of their inheritance was Zorah, and Eshtaol, and Irshemesh,

42 And Shaalabbin, and Ayalon, and Yetlah,

43 And Elon, and Thimnathah, and Ekron,

44 And Eltekeh, and Gibbethon, and Baalath,

45 And Yehud, and Beneberak, and Gathrimmon,

46 And Meyarkon, and Rakkon, with the border before Yafo.

47 And the coast of the children of Dan went out too little for them; therefore the children of Dan went up to fight against Leshem, and took it, and smote it with the edge of the sword, and possessed it, and dwelt therein, and called Leshem, Dan, after the name of Dan their father.

48 This is the inheritance of the tribe of the children of Dan according to their families, these cities with their villages.

49 When they had made an end of dividing the land for inheritance by their coasts, the children of Yisrael gave an inheritance to Joshua (Yehoshua) the son of Nun among them.

50 According to the word of יהוה they gave him the city which he asked, even Timnathserah in Mount Efrayim; and he built the city, and dwelt therein.

51 These are the inheritances, which Eleazar the priest (kohen), and Joshua (Yehoshua) the son of Nun, and the heads of the fathers of the tribes of the children of Yisrael, divided for an inheritance by lot in Shiloh before יהוה, at the door of the tabernacle of the congregation. So they made an end of dividing the country.

20 יהוה also spake unto Joshua (Yehoshua), saying,

2 "Speak to the children of Yisrael, saying, Appoint out for yourselves cities of refuge, whereof I spake unto you by the hand of Moses (Mosheh);

3 That the slayer that killeth any person unawares and unwittingly may flee thither; and they shall be your refuge from the avenger

of blood.

4 And when he that doth flee unto one of those cities shall stand at the entering of the gate of the city, and shall declare his cause in the ears of the elders of that city, they shall take him into the city unto them, and give him a place, that he may dwell among them.

5 And if the avenger of blood pursues after him, then they shall not deliver the slayer up into his hand; because he smote his neighbour unwittingly, and hated him not beforetime.

6 And he shall dwell in that city, until he stands before the congregation for judgment, and until the death of the high priest (kohen hagadol) that shall be in those days: then shall the slayer return, and come unto his own city, and unto his own house, unto the city from whence he fled.

7 And they appointed Kedesh in Galilee in mount Naftali, and Shechem in mount Efrayim, and Qiryat-Arba, which is Hebron, in the mountain of Judah (Yehudah).

8 And on the other side Jordan (Yarden) by Yericho eastward, they assigned Bezer in the wilderness upon the plain out of the tribe of Reuven, and Ramot in Gilad out of the tribe of Gad, and Golan in Bashan out of the tribe of Menashsheh.

9 These were the cities appointed for all the children of Yisrael, and for the stranger that sojourneth among them, that whosoever killeth any person at unawares might flee thither, and not die by the hand of the avenger of blood, until he stood before the congregation.

21 Then came near the heads of the fathers of the Levites (Lewiyim) unto Eleazar the priest (kohen), and unto Joshua (Yehoshua) the son of Nun, and unto the heads of the fathers of the tribes of the children of Yisrael;

2 And they spake unto them at Shiloh in the land of Canaan, saying, "יהוה commanded by the hand of Moses (Mosheh) to give us cities to dwell in, with the suburbs thereof for our cattle."

3 And the children of Yisrael gave unto the Levites (Lewiyim) out of their inheritance, at the commandment of יהוה, these cities and their suburbs.

4 And the lot came out for the families of the Kohathites: and the children of Aaron (Aharon) the priest (kohen), which were of the Levites (Lewiyim), had by lot out of the tribe of Judah (Yehudah), and out of the tribe of Shimon, and

out of the tribe of Binyamin, thirteen cities.

5 And the rest of the children of Kohath had by lot out of the families of the tribe of Efrayim, and out of the tribe of Dan, and out of the half tribe of Menashsheh, ten cities.

6 And the children of Gershon had by lot out of the families of the tribe of Yissaskhar, and out of the tribe of Asher, and out of the tribe of Naftali, and out of the half tribe of Menashsheh in Bashan, thirteen cities.

7 The children of Merari by their families had out of the tribe of Reuven, and out of the tribe of Gad, and out of the tribe of Zevulun, twelve cities.

8 And the children of Yisrael gave by lot unto the Levites (Lewiyim) these cities with their suburbs, as יהוה commanded by the hand of Moses (Mosheh).

9 And they gave out of the tribe of the children of Judah (Yehudah), and out of the tribe of the children of Shimon, these cities which are here mentioned by name,

10 Which the children of Aaron (Aharon), being of the families of the Kohathites, who were of the children of Lewi, had: for theirs was the first lot.

11 And they gave them the city of Arba the father of Anak, which city is Hebron, in the hill country of Judah (Yehudah), with the suburbs thereof round about it.

12 But the fields of the city, and the villages thereof, gave they to Caleb the son of Yefunneh for his possession.

13 Thus they gave to the children of Aaron (Aharon) the priest (kohen) Hebron with her suburbs, to be a city of refuge for the slayer; and Libnah with her suburbs,

14 And Yattir with her suburbs, and Eshtemoa with her suburbs,

15 And Holon with her suburbs, and Debir with her suburbs,

16 And Ain with her suburbs, and Yutah with her suburbs, and Beit-Shemesh with her suburbs: nine cities out of those two tribes.

17 And out of the tribe of Binyamin, Giveon with her suburbs, Geba with her suburbs,

18 Anathoth with her suburbs, and Almon with her suburbs: four cities.

19 All the cities of the children of Aaron (Aharon), the priests (kohanim), were thirteen cities with their suburbs.

20 And the families of the children of Kohath, the Levites (Lewiyim) which remained of the children of Kohath, even they had the cities of their lot out of the tribe of Efrayim.

21 For they gave them Shechem with her suburbs in mount Efrayim, to be a city of refuge for the slayer; and Gezer with her suburbs,

22 And Kibzaim with her suburbs, and Beit-Choron with her suburbs: four cities.

23 And out of the tribe of Dan, Eltekeh with her suburbs, Gibbethon with her suburbs,

24 Aiyalon with her suburbs, Gathrimmon with her suburbs: four cities.

25 And out of the half tribe of Menashsheh, Tanach with her suburbs, and Gathrimmon with her suburbs: two cities.

26 All the cities were ten with their suburbs for the families of the children of Kohath that remained.

27 And unto the children of Gershon, of the families of the Levites (Lewiyim), out of the other half tribe of Menashsheh they gave Golan in Bashan with her suburbs, to be a city of refuge for the slayer; and Beeshterah with her suburbs: two cities.

28 And out of the tribe of Yissaskhar, Kishon with her suburbs, Dabareh with her suburbs,

29 Yarmut with her suburbs, Engannim with her suburbs: four cities.

30 And out of the tribe of Asher, Mishal with her suburbs, Abdon with her suburbs,

31 Helkath with her suburbs, and Rehob with her suburbs: four cities.

32 And out of the tribe of Naftali, Kedesh in Galilee with her suburbs, to be a city of refuge for the slayer; and Hammothdor with her suburbs, and Kartan with her suburbs: three cities.

33 All the cities of the Gershonites according to their families were thirteen cities with their suburbs.

34 And unto the families of the children of Merari, the rest of the Levites (Lewiyim), out of the tribe of Zevulun, Yokneam with her suburbs, and Kartah with her suburbs,

35 Dimnah with her suburbs, Nahalal with her suburbs: four cities.

36 And out of the tribe of Reuven, Bezer with her suburbs, and Yahazah with her suburbs,

37 Kedemoth with her suburbs, and Mephaath with her suburbs: four cities.

38 And out of the tribe of Gad, Ramot in Gilad with her suburbs, to be a city of refuge for the slayer; and Mahanaim with her suburbs,

39 Heshbon with her suburbs, Yazer with her suburbs: four cities in all.

40 So all the cities for the children of Merari by their families, which were remaining of the families of the Levites (Lewiyim), were by their lot twelve cities.

41 All the cities of the Levites (Lewiyim) within the possession of the children of Yisrael were forty and eight cities with their suburbs.

42 These cities were every one with their suburbs round about them; thus were all these cities.

43 And יהוה gave unto Yisrael all the land which He sware to give unto their fathers; and they possessed it, and dwelt therein.

44 And יהוה gave them rest round about, according to all that He sware unto their fathers; and there stood not a man of all their enemies before them; יהוה delivered all their enemies into their hand.

45 There failed not ought of any good thing which יהוה had spoken unto the house of Yisrael. All came to pass.

22 Then Joshua (Yehoshua) called the Reubenites (Reuveni), and the Gadites, and the half tribe of Menashsheh,

2 And said unto them: "You have kept all that Moses (Mosheh) the servant of יהוה commanded you, and have obeyed my voice in all that I commanded you.

3 You have not left your brethren these many days unto this day, but have kept the charge of the commandment of יהוה your God (YHWH Eloheikhem).

4 And now יהוה your God (YHWH Eloheikhem) hath given rest unto your brethren, as He promised them; therefore now return you, and get you unto your tents, and unto the land of your possession, which Moses (Mosheh) the servant of יהוה gave you on the other side Jordan (Yarden).

5 But take diligent heed to do the commandment and the Torah, which Moses (Mosheh) the servant of יהוה charged you, to love יהוה your God (YHWH Eloheikhem), and to walk in all His ways, and to keep His commandments, and to cleave unto Him, and to serve Him with all your heart and with all your soul."

6 So Joshua (Yehoshua) blessed them, and sent them away; and they went unto their tents.

7 Now to the one half of the tribe of Menashsheh Moses (Mosheh) had given possession in Bashan; but unto the other half thereof gave Joshua (Yehoshua) among their brethren on this side Jordan (Yarden) westward. And when Joshua (Yehoshua) sent them away also unto their tents, then he blessed them,

8 And he spake unto them, saying, "Return with much riches unto your tents, and with very much cattle, with silver, and with gold, and with brass, and with iron, and with very much raiment: divide the spoil of your enemies with your brethren."

9 And the children of Reuven and the children of Gad and the half tribe of Menashsheh returned, and departed from the children of Yisrael out of Shiloh, which is in the land of Canaan, to go unto the country of Gilad, to the land of their possession, whereof they were possessed, according to the word of יהוה by the hand of Moses (Mosheh).

10 And when they came unto the borders of Jordan (Yarden), that are in the land of Canaan, the children of Reuven and the children of Gad and the half tribe of Menashsheh built there an altar by Jordan (Yarden), a great altar to see to.

11 And the children of Yisrael heard say, "Behold, the children of Reuven and the children of Gad and the half tribe of Menashsheh have built an altar opposite the land of Canaan, in the borders of Jordan (Yarden), at the passage of the children of Yisrael."

12 And when the children of Yisrael heard of it, the whole congregation of the children of Yisrael gathered themselves together at Shiloh, to go up to war against them.

13 And the children of Yisrael sent unto the children of Reuven, and to the children of Gad, and to the half tribe of Menashsheh, into the land of Gilad, Phinehas the son of Eleazar the priest (kohen),

14 And with him ten princes, of each chief house a prince throughout all the tribes of Yisrael; and each one was a head of the house of their fathers among the thousands of Yisrael.

15 And they came unto the children of Reuven, and to the children of Gad, and to the half tribe of Menashsheh, unto the land of Gilad, and they spake with them, saying,

16 Thus saith the whole congregation of יהוה: "What trespass is this that you have committed against the God of Israel (Elohei Yisrael), to turn away this day from following יהוה, in that you have builded you an altar, that you might rebel this day against יהוה?

17 Is the iniquity of Peor too little for us, from which we are not cleansed until this day, although there was a plague in the congregation of יהוה,

18 But that you must turn away this day from following יהוה? And it will be, seeing you rebel today against יהוה, that tomorrow He will be wroth with the whole congregation of Yisrael.

19 Notwithstanding, if the land of your possession be unclean, then pass you over unto the land of the possession of יהוה, wherein יהוה's tabernacle dwelleth, and take possession among us; but rebel not against יהוה, nor rebel against us, in building you an altar beside the altar of יהוה our God (YHWH Eloheinu).

20 Did not Achan the son of Zerah commit a trespass in the accursed thing, and wrath fell on all the congregation of Yisrael? And that man perished not alone in his iniquity.'"

21 Then the children of Reuven and the children of Gad and the half tribe of Menashsheh answered, and said unto the heads of the thousands of Yisrael,

22 The [B5c]Mighty One (El), God יהוה (Elohim YHWH); the Mighty One (El), God יהוה (Elohim YHWH)! He knoweth, and Yisrael he shall know; if it be in rebellion, or if in transgression against יהוה, save us not this day.

23 If we have built us an altar to turn from following יהוה, or if to offer thereon burnt offering or meat offering, or if to offer peace offerings thereon, let יהוה Himself require it;

24 And if we have not rather done it for fear of this thing, saying, 'In time to come your children might speak unto our children, saying, "What have you to do with יהוה God of Israel (Elohei Yisrael)?

25 For יהוה hath made Jordan (Yarden) a border between us and you, you children of Reuven and children of Gad; you have no part in יהוה." So shall your children make our children cease from fearing יהוה.'

26 Therefore we said, 'Let us now prepare to build us an altar, not for burnt offering, nor for sacrifice,

27 But that it may be a witness between us, and you, and our generations after us, that we might do the service of יהוה before him with our burnt offerings, and with our sacrifices, and with our peace offerings; that your children may not say to our children in time to come, you have no part in יהוה.'"

28 Therefore said we, that it shall be, when they should so say to us or to our generations in time to come, that we may say again, Behold the pattern of the altar of יהוה, which our fathers made, not for burnt offerings, nor for sacrifices; but it is a witness between us and you.'

29 God (Elohim) forbid that we should rebel against יהוה, and turn this day from following יהוה, to build an altar for burnt offerings, for meat offerings, or for sacrifices, beside the altar of יהוה our God (YHWH Eloheinu) that is before His tabernacle."

30 And when Phinehas the priest (kohen), and the princes of the congregation and heads of the thousands of Yisrael which were with him, heard the words that the children of Reuven and the children of Gad and the children of Menashsheh spake, it pleased them.

31 And Phinehas the son of Eleazar the priest (kohen) said unto the children of Reuven, and to the children of Gad, and to the children of Menashsheh, "This day we perceive that יהוה is among us, because you have not committed this trespass against יהוה. Now you have delivered the children of Yisrael out of the hand of יהוה."

32 And Phinehas the son of Eleazar the priest (kohen), and the princes, returned from the children of Reuven, and from the children of Gad, out of the land of Gilad, unto the land of Canaan, to the children of Yisrael, and brought them word again.

33 And the thing pleased the children of Yisrael; and the children of Yisrael blessed God (Elohim), and did not intend to go up against them in battle, to destroy the land wherein the children of Reuven and Gad dwelt.

34 And the children of Reuven and the children of Gad called the altar Witness (Ed), "For it shall be a witness between us that יהוה is God (Elohim)."

23 And it came to pass a long time after that יהוה had given rest unto Yisrael from all their enemies round about, that Joshua (Yehoshua) waxed old and stricken in age.

2 And Joshua (Yehoshua) called for all Yisrael, and for their elders, and for their heads, and for their judges, and for their officers, and said unto them: "I am old and stricken in age.

3 And you have seen all that יהוה your God (YHWH Eloheikhem) hath done unto all these nations because of you; for יהוה your God (YHWH Eloheikhem) is He that hath fought for you.

4 Behold, I have divided unto you by lot these nations that remain, to be an inheritance for your tribes, from Jordan (Yarden), with all the nations that I have cut off, even unto the great sea westward.

5 And יהוה your God (YHWH Eloheikhem), He shall expel them from before you, and drive them from out of your sight; and you shall possess their land, as יהוה your God (YHWH Eloheikhem) hath promised unto you.

6 Be you therefore very courageous to keep and to do all that is [B28b]written in the book of the law (sefer hatorah) by Moses (Mosheh), that you turn not aside therefrom to the right hand or to the left;

7 That you come not among these nations, these that remain among you; neither make mention of the name of their gods (elohim), nor cause to swear by them, neither serve them, nor bow yourselves unto them:

8 But cleave unto יהוה your God (YHWH Eloheikhem), as you have done unto this day.

9 For יהוה hath driven out from before you great nations and strong; but as for you, no man hath been able to stand before you unto this day.

10 One man of you shall chase a thousand; for יהוה your God (YHWH Eloheikhem), He it is that fighteth for you, as He hath promised you.

11 Take good heed therefore unto yourselves, that you love יהוה your God (YHWH Eloheikhem).

12 Else if you do in any wise go back, and cleave unto the remnant of these nations, even these that remain among you, and shall make marriages with them, and go in unto them, and they to you;

13 Know for a certainty that יהוה your God (YHWH Eloheikhem) will no more drive out any of these nations from before you; but they shall be snares and traps unto you, and scourges in your sides, and thorns in your eyes, until you perish from off this good land which יהוה your

God (YHWH Eloheikhem) hath given you.

14 And, behold, this day I am going the way of all the earth; and you know in all your hearts and in all your souls, that not one thing hath failed of all the good things which יהוה your God (YHWH Eloheikhem) spake concerning you; all are come to pass unto you, and not one thing hath failed thereof.

15 Therefore it shall come to pass, that as all good things are come upon you, which יהוה your God (YHWH Eloheikhem) promised you; so shall יהוה bring upon you all evil things, until He has destroyed you from off this good land which יהוה your God (YHWH Eloheikhem) hath given you.

16 When you have transgressed the covenant of יהוה your God (YHWH Eloheikhem), which He commanded you, and have gone and served other gods (elohim), and bowed yourselves to them; then shall the anger of יהוה be kindled against you, and you shall perish quickly from off the good land which He hath given unto you."

24 And Joshua (Yehoshua) gather-ed all the tribes of Yisrael to Shechem, and called for the elders of Yisrael, and for their heads, and for their judges, and for their officers; and they presented themselves before God (Elohim).

2 And Joshua (Yehoshua) said unto all the people, "Thus saith יהוה God of Israel (Elohei Yisrael): 'Your fathers dwelt on the other side of the flood in old time, even Terah, the father of Avraham, and the father of Nachor; and they served other gods (elohim).

3 And I took your father Avraham from the other side of the flood, and led him throughout all the land of Canaan, and multiplied his seed, and gave him Isaac (Yitschaq).

4 And I gave unto Isaac (Yitschaq), Jacob (Yaaqov) and Esaw; and I gave unto Esaw mount Seir, to possess it; but Jacob (Yaaqov) and his children went down into Egypt (Mitsrayim).

5 I sent Moses (Mosheh) also and Aaron (Aharon), and I plagued Egypt (Mitsrayim), according to that which I did among them; and afterward I brought you out.

6 And I brought your fathers out of Egypt (Mitsrayim); and you came unto the sea; and the Egyptians (Mitsrayim) pursued after your fathers with chariots and horsemen unto the Red sea.

7 And when they cried unto יהוה, He put darkness between you and the Egyptians (Mitsrayim), and brought the sea upon them, and covered them; and your eyes have seen what I have done in Egypt (Mitsrayim); and you dwelt in the wilderness a long season.

8 And I brought you into the land of the Amorites, which dwelt on the other side Jordan (Yarden); and they fought with you; and I gave them into your hand, that you might possess their land; and I destroyed them from before you.

9 Then Balak the son of Zippor, king of Moav, arose and warred against Yisrael, and sent and called Balaam the son of Beor to curse you;

10 But I would not hearken unto Balaam; therefore he blessed you still; so I delivered you out of his hand.

11 And you went over Jordan (Yarden), and came unto Yericho; and the men of Yericho fought against you, the Amorites, and the Perizzites, and the Canaanites, and the Hittites, and the Girgashites, the Hivites, and the Yevusis; and I delivered them into your hand.

12 And I sent the hornet before you, which drave them out from before you, even the two kings of the Amorites; but not with your sword, nor with your bow.

13 And I have given you a land for which you did not labour, and cities which you built not, and you dwell in them; of the vineyards and oliveyards which you planted not do you eat.'

14 Now therefore fear יהוה, and serve Him in sincerity and in truth; and put away the gods (elohim) which your fathers served on the other side of the flood, and in Egypt (Mitsrayim); and serve you יהוה!

15 And if it seems evil unto you to serve יהוה, choose you this day whom you will serve; whether the gods (elohim) which your fathers served that were on the other side of the flood, or the gods (elohim) of the Amorites, in whose land you dwell; but as for me and my house, we will serve יהוה."

16 And the people answered and said: "God (Elohim) forbid that we should forsake יהוה, to serve other gods (elohim);

17 For יהוה our God (YHWH Eloheinu), He it is that brought us up and our fathers out of the land of Egypt (Mitsrayim), from the house of bondage, and which did those great signs in our sight, and preserved us in all the way wherein we went, and among all the people through

whom we passed.

18 And יהוה drave out from before us all the people, even the Amorites which dwelt in the land; therefore will we also serve יהוה; for He is our God (Elohim)."

19 And Joshua (Yehoshua) said unto the people, "You cannot serve יהוה, for He is a holy God (Elohim); He is a jealous God (El); He will not forgive your transgressions nor your sins.

20 If you forsake יהוה, and serve strange gods (elohim), then He will turn and do you hurt, and consume you, after that He hath done you good."

21 And the people said unto Joshua (Yehoshua), "Nay; but we will serve יהוה!"

22 And Joshua (Yehoshua) said unto the people, "You are witnesses against yourselves that you have chosen you יהוה, to serve Him." And they said, "We are witnesses."

23 "Now therefore put away," said he, "the strange gods (elohim) which are among you, and incline your heart unto יהוה God of Israel (Elohei Yisrael)."

24 And the people said unto Joshua (Yehoshua), "יהוה our God (YHWH Eloheinu) will we serve, and His voice will we obey."

25 So Joshua (Yehoshua) made a covenant with the people that day, and set them a statute and an ordinance in Shechem.

26 And Joshua (Yehoshua) wrote these words in the book of the torah (sefer hatorah) of God (Elohim), and took a great stone, and set it up there under an oak, that was by the sanctuary of יהוה.

27 And Joshua (Yehoshua) said unto all the people, "Behold, this stone shall be a witness unto us; for it hath heard all the words of יהוה which He spake unto us; it shall be therefore a witness unto you, lest you deny your God (Elohim)."

28 So Joshua (Yehoshua) let the people depart, every man unto his inheritance.

29 And it came to pass after these things, that Joshua (Yehoshua) the son of Nun, the servant of יהוה, died, being a hundred and ten years old.

30 And they buried him in the border of his inheritance in Timnathserah, which is in Mount Efrayim, on the north side of the hill of Gaash.

31 And Yisrael served יהוה all the days of Joshua (Yehoshua), and all the days of the elders that overlived Joshua (Yehoshua), and which had known all the works of יהוה, that He had done for Yisrael.

32 And the bones of Joseph (Yosef), which the children of Yisrael brought up out of Egypt (Mitsrayim), buried they in Shechem, in a parcel of ground which Jacob (Yaaqov) bought of the sons of Hamor the father of Shechem for a hundred pieces of silver; and it became the inheritance of the children of Joseph (Yosef).

33 And Eleazar the son of Aaron (Aharon) died; and they buried him in a hill that pertained to Phinehas his son, which was given him in Mount Efrayim.

JUDGES
SHOFETIM שֹׁפְטִים
(Book of Judges)

1 Now after the death of Joshua (Yehoshua) it came to pass, that the children of Yisrael asked יהוה, saying, "Who shall go up for us against the Canaanites first, to fight against them?"

2 And יהוה said, "Judah (Yehudah) shall go up; behold, I have delivered the land into his hand."

3 And Judah (Yehudah) said unto Shimon his brother, "Come up with me into my lot, that we may fight against the Canaanites; and I likewise will go with you into your lot." So Shimon went with him.

4 And Judah (Yehudah) went up; and יהוה delivered the Canaanites and the Perizzites into their hand; and they slew of them in Bezek ten thousand men.

5 And they found Adoni-Bezek in Bezek; and they fought against him, and they slew the Canaanites and the Perizzites.

6 But Adoni-Bezek fled; and they pursued after him, and caught him, and cut off his thumbs and his great toes.

7 And Adoni-Bezek said, "Threescore and ten kings, having their thumbs and their great toes cut off, gathered their meat under my table; as I have done, so God (Elohim) hath requited me." And they brought him to Jerusalem (Yerushalayim), and there he died.

8 Now the children of Judah (Yehudah) had fought against Jerusalem (Yerushalayim), and had taken it, and smitten it with the edge of the sword, and set the city on fire.

9 And afterward the children of Judah (Yehudah) went down to fight against the Canaanites, that dwelt in the mountain, and in the south, and in the valley.

10 And Judah (Yehudah) went against the Canaanites that dwelt in Hebron; (now the name of Hebron before was Qiryat-Arba;) and they slew Sheshai, and Ahiman, and Talmai.

11 And from thence he went against the inhabitants of Debir; and the name of Debir before was Qiryat-Sepher:

12 And Caleb said, "He that smiteth Qiryat-Sepher, and taketh it, to him will I give Achsah my daughter as wife."

13 And Othniel the son of Kenaz, Caleb's younger brother, took it: and he gave him Achsah his daughter to wife.

14 And it came to pass, when she came to him, that she moved him to ask of her father a field; and she lighted from off her ass; and Caleb said unto her, "What you wish?"

15 And she said unto him, "Give me a blessing; for you have given me a south land; give me also springs of water." And Caleb gave her the upper springs and the nether springs.

16 And the children of the Kenite, Moses (Mosheh)' father in law, went up out of the city of palm trees with the children of Judah (Yehudah) into the wilderness of Judah (Yehudah), which lieth in the south of Arad; and they went and dwelt among the people.

17 And Judah (Yehudah) went with Shimon his brother, and they slew the Canaanites that inhabited Zephath, and utterly destroyed it. And the name of the city was called Hormah.

18 Also Judah (Yehudah) took Gaza (Azzah) with the coast thereof, and Askelon with the coast thereof, and Ekron with the coast thereof.

19 And יהוה was with Judah (Yehudah); and he drave out the inhabitants of the mountain; but could not drive out the inhabitants of the valley, because they had chariots of iron.

20 And they gave Hebron unto Caleb, as Moses (Mosheh) said; and he expelled thence the three sons of Anak.

21 And the children of Binyamin did not drive out the Yevusis that inhabited Jerusalem (Yerushalayim); but the Yevusis dwell with the children of Binyamin in Jerusalem (Yerushalayim) unto this day.

22 And the house of Joseph (Yosef), they also went up against Bethel (Beit-El); and יהוה was with them.

23 And the house of Joseph (Yosef) sent to descry Bethel (Beit-El). (Now the name of the city before was Luz.)

24 And the spies saw a man come forth out of the city, and they said unto him, "Shew us, we pray you, the entrance into the city, and we will shew you mercy."

25 And when he shewed them the entrance into the city, they smote the city with the edge of the sword; but they let go the man and all his family.

26 And the man went into the land of the Hittites, and built a city, and called the name

thereof Luz; which is the name thereof unto this day.

27 Neither did Menashsheh drive out the inhabitants of Beit-Shan and her towns, nor Taanach and her towns, nor the inhabitants of Dor and her towns, nor the inhabitants of Ibleam and her towns, nor the inhabitants of Megiddo and her towns; but the Canaanites would dwell in that land.

28 And it came to pass, when Yisrael was strong, that they put the Canaanites to tribute, and did not utterly drive them out.

29 Neither did Efrayim drive out the Canaanites that dwelt in Gezer; but the Canaanites dwelt in Gezer among them.

30 Neither did Zevulun drive out the inhabitants of Kitron, nor the inhabitants of Nahalol; but the Canaanites dwelt among them, and became tributaries.

31 Neither did Asher drive out the inhabitants of Accho, nor the inhabitants of Zidon, nor of Ahlab, nor of Achzib, nor of Helbah, nor of Aphik, nor of Rehob.

32 But the Asherites dwelt among the Canaanites, the inhabitants of the land; for they did not drive them out.

33 Neither did Naftali drive out the inhabitants of Beit-Shemesh, nor the inhabitants of Beit-Anat; but he dwelt among the Canaanites, the inhabitants of the land; nevertheless the inhabitants of Beit-Shemesh and of Beit-Anat became tributaries unto them.

34 And the Amorites forced the children of Dan into the mountain: for they would not allow them to come down to the valley;

35 But the Amorites would dwell in mount Heres in Ayalon, and in Shaalbim; yet the hand of the house of Joseph (Yosef) prevailed, so that they became tributaries.

36 And the coast of the Amorites was from the going up to Akrabbim, from the rock, and upward.

2 And an angel of יהוה came up from Gilgal to Bochim, and said: "I made you to go up out of Egypt (Mitsrayim), and have brought you unto the land which I sware unto your fathers; and I said, 'I will never break My covenant with you.

2 And you shall make no league with the inhabitants of this land; you shall throw down their altars.' But you have not obeyed My voice.

Why have you done this?

3 Wherefore I also said, I will not drive them out from before you; but they shall be as thorns in your sides, and their gods (elohim) shall be a snare unto you.'"

4 And it came to pass, when the angel of יהוה spake these words unto all the children of Yisrael, that the people lifted up their voice, and wept.

5 And they called the name of that place Bochim; and they sacrificed there unto יהוה.

6 And when Joshua (Yehoshua) had let the people go, the children of Yisrael went every man unto his inheritance to possess the land.

7 And the people served יהוה all the days of Joshua (Yehoshua), and all the days of the elders that outlived Joshua (Yehoshua), who had seen all the great works of יהוה, that He did for Yisrael.

8 And Joshua (Yehoshua) the son of Nun, the servant of יהוה, died, being a hundred and ten years old.

9 And they buried him in the border of his inheritance in Timnathheres, in the mount of Efrayim, on the north side of the hill Gaash.

10 And also all that generation were gathered unto their fathers; and there arose another generation after them, which knew not יהוה, nor yet the works which He had done for Yisrael.

11 And the children of Yisrael did evil in the sight of יהוה, and served the [B33c]Baals (Baalim);

12 And they forsook יהוה God (Elohim) of their fathers, who brought them out of the land of Egypt (Mitsrayim), and followed other gods (elohim), of the gods (elohim) of the people that were round about them, and bowed themselves unto them, and provoked יהוה to anger.

13 And they forsook יהוה, and served the [B33b]Baal and Ashtaroth.

14 And the anger of יהוה was hot against Yisrael, and He delivered them into the hands of spoilers that spoiled them, and He sold them into the hands of their enemies round about, so that they could not any longer stand before their enemies.

15 Whithersoever they went out, the hand of יהוה was against them for evil, as יהוה had said, and as יהוה had sworn unto them; and they were greatly distressed.

16 Nevertheless יהוה raised up judges, who delivered them out of the hand of those that spoiled them.

17 And yet they would not hearken unto their judges, but they went a whoring after other gods (elohim), and bowed themselves unto them; they turned quickly out of the way which their fathers walked in, obeying the commandments of יהוה; but they did not so.

18 And when יהוה raised them up judges, then יהוה was with the judge, and delivered them out of the hand of their enemies all the days of the judge; for יהוה was moved to pity because of their groanings by reason of them that oppressed them and vexed them.

19 And it came to pass, when the judge was dead, that they returned, and corrupted themselves more than their fathers, in following other gods (elohim) to serve them, and to bow down unto them; they ceased not from their own doings, nor from their stubborn way.

20 And the anger of יהוה was hot against Yisrael; and He said, "Because that this people hath transgressed My covenant which I commanded their fathers, and have not hearkened unto My voice;

21 I also will not henceforth drive out any from before them of the nations which Joshua (Yehoshua) left when he died;

22 That through them I may prove Yisrael, whether they will keep the way of יהוה to walk therein, as their fathers did keep it, or not."

23 Therefore יהוה left those nations, without driving them out hastily; neither delivered He them into the hand of Joshua (Yehoshua).

3 Now these are the nations which יהוה left, to prove Yisrael by them, even as many of Yisrael as had not known all the wars of Canaan;

2 Only that the generations of the children of Yisrael might know, to teach them war, at the least such as before knew nothing thereof;

3 Namely, five lords (seranim) of the Philistines, and all the Canaanites, and the Sidonians, and the Hivites that dwelt in Mount Lebanon, from Mount Baal-Chermon unto the entering in of Hamath.

4 And they were to prove Yisrael by them, to know whether they would hearken unto the commandments of יהוה, which He commanded their fathers by the hand of Moses (Mosheh).

5 And the children of Yisrael dwelt among the Canaanites, Hittites, and Amorites, and Perizzites, and Hivites, and Yevusis:

6 And they took their daughters to be their wives, and gave their daughters to their sons, and served their gods (elohim).

7 And the children of Yisrael did evil in the sight of יהוה, and forgat יהוה their God (YHWH Eloheihem), and served [B33c]Baals (Baalim) and [B34b]Asherahs (Asherot).

8 Therefore the anger of יהוה was hot against Yisrael, and He sold them into the hand of Chushanrishathaim king of Mesopotamia; and the children of Yisrael served Chushanrishathaim eight years.

9 And when the children of Yisrael cried unto יהוה, יהוה raised up a deliverer to the children of Yisrael, who delivered them, even Othniel the son of Kenaz, Caleb's younger brother.

10 And the Spirit of יהוה came upon him, and he judged Yisrael, and went out to war; and יהוה delivered Chushanrishathaim king of Mesopotamia into his hand; and his hand prevailed against Chushanrishathaim.

11 And the land had rest forty years. And Othniel the son of Kenaz died.

12 And the children of Yisrael did evil again in the sight of יהוה; and יהוה strengthened Eglon the king of Moav against Yisrael, because they had done evil in the sight of יהוה.

13 And he gathered unto him the children of Ammon and Amalek, and went and smote Yisrael, and possessed the city of palm trees.

14 So the children of Yisrael served Eglon the king of Moav eighteen years.

15 But when the children of Yisrael cried unto יהוה, יהוה raised them up a deliverer, Ehud the son of Gera, a Binyamin, a man lefthanded; and by him the children of Yisrael sent a present unto Eglon the king of Moav.

16 But Ehud made him a dagger which had two edges, of a cubit length; and he did gird it under his raiment upon his right thigh.

17 And he brought the present unto Eglon king of Moav; and Eglon was a very fat man.

18 And when he had made an end to offer the present, he sent away the people that bare the present.

19 But he himself turned again from the quarries that were by Gilgal, and said, "I have a secret errand unto you, O king." He said, "Keep silence!" And all that stood by him went out from him.

20 And Ehud came unto him; and he was sitting in a summer parlour, which he had for himself

alone. And Ehud said, "I have a message from God (Elohim) unto you." And he arose out of his seat.

21 And Ehud put forth his left hand, and took the dagger from his right thigh, and thrust it into his belly.

22 And the haft also went in after the blade; and the fat closed upon the blade, so that he could not draw the dagger out of his belly; and the dirt came out.

23 Then Ehud went forth through the porch, and shut the doors of the parlour upon him, and locked them.

24 When he was gone out, his servants came; and when they saw that, behold, the doors of the parlour were locked, they said, "Surely he covereth his feet (relieving himself) in his summer chamber.

25 And they tarried till they were ashamed; and, behold, he opened not the doors of the parlour; therefore they took a key, and opened them; and, behold, their lord (adon) was fallen down dead on the earth.

26 And Ehud escaped while they tarried, and passed beyond the quarries, and escaped unto Seirath.

27 And it came to pass, when he was come, that he blew a shofar in the mountain of Efrayim, and the children of Yisrael went down with him from the mount, and he before them.

28 And he said unto them, "Follow after me, for יהוה hath delivered your enemies the Moavites into your hand." And they went down after him, and took the fords of Jordan (Yarden) toward Moav, and suffered not a man to pass over.

29 And they slew of Moav at that time about ten thousand men, all lusty, and all men of valour; and there escaped not a man.

30 So Moav was subdued that day under the hand of Yisrael. And the land had rest fourscore years.

31 And after him was Shamgar the son of Anath, which slew of the Philistines six hundred men with an ox goad; and he also delivered Yisrael.

4 And the children of Yisrael again did evil in the sight of יהוה, when Ehud was dead.

2 And יהוה sold them into the hand of Yavin king of Canaan, that reigned in Hazor; the captain of whose army was Sisera, who dwelt in Harosheth of the Gentiles (Goyim).

3 And the children of Yisrael cried unto יהוה;

for he had nine hundred chariots of iron; and twenty years he mightily oppressed the children of Yisrael.

4 And Deborah, a prophetess (neviah), the wife of Lapidoth, she judged Yisrael at that time.

5 And she dwelt under the palm tree of Deborah between Ramah and Bethel (Beit-El) in Mount Efrayim; and the children of Yisrael came up to her for judgment.

6 And she sent and called Barak the son of Abinoam out of Kedeshnaphtali, and said unto him, "Hath not יהוה God of Israel (Elohei Yisrael) commanded," saying, 'Go and draw toward Mount Tabor, and take with you ten thousand men of the children of Naftali and of the children of Zevulun?

7 And I will draw unto you to the river Kishon Sisera, the captain of Yavin's army, with his chariots and his multitude; and I will deliver him into your hand.'?"

8 And Barak said unto her, "If you wilt go with me, then I will go; but if you wilt not go with me, then I will not go."

9 And she said, "I will surely go with you; notwithstanding the journey that you takest shall not be for your honor; for יהוה shall sell Sisera into the hand of a woman." And Deborah arose, and went with Barak to Kedesh.

10 And Barak called Zevulun and Naftali to Kedesh; and he went up with ten thousand men at his feet: and Deborah went up with him.

11 Now Heber the Kenite, which was of the children of Hobab the father in law of Moses (Mosheh), had severed himself from the Kenites, and pitched his tent unto the plain of Zaanaim, which is by Kedesh.

12 And they shewed Sisera that Barak the son of Abinoam was gone up to Mount Tabor.

13 And Sisera gathered together all his chariots, even nine hundred chariots of iron, and all the people that were with him, from Harosheth of the Gentiles (Goyim) unto the river of Kishon.

14 And Deborah said unto Barak, "Up! For this is the day in which יהוה hath delivered Sisera into your hand. Has not יהוה gone out before you?" So Barak went down from Mount Tabor, and ten thousand men after him.

15 And יהוה discomfited Sisera, and all his chariots, and all his army, with the edge of the sword before Barak; so that Sisera lighted down off his chariot, and fled away on his feet.

16 But Barak pursued after the chariots, and after the army, unto Harosheth of the Gentiles (Goyim); and all the army of Sisera fell upon the edge of the sword; and there was not a man left.

17 Howbeit Sisera fled away on his feet to the tent of Yael the wife of Heber the Kenite; for there was peace between Yavin the king of Hazor and the house of Heber the Kenite.

18 And Yael went out to meet Sisera, and said unto him, "Turn in, my lord (adoni), turn in to me; fear not. And when he had turned in unto her into the tent, she covered him with a mantle.

19 And he said unto her, "Please give me a little water to drink; for I am thirsty." And she opened a bottle of milk, and gave him drink, and covered him.

20 Again he said unto her, "Stand in the door of the tent, and it shall be, when any man doth come and enquire of you, and say, 'Is there any man here?' that you shalt say, 'No.'"

21 Then Yael Heber's wife took a nail of the tent, and took a hammer in her hand, and went softly unto him, and smote the nail into his temples, and fastened it into the ground: for he was fast asleep and weary. So he died.

22 And, behold, as Barak pursued Sisera, Yael came out to meet him, and said unto him, "Come, and I will shew you the man whom you seekest." And when he came into her tent, behold, Sisera lay dead, and the nail was in his temples.

23 So God (Elohim) subdued on that day Yavin the king of Canaan before the children of Yisrael.

24 And the hand of the children of Yisrael prospered, and prevailed against Yavin the king of Canaan, until they had destroyed Yavin king of Canaan.

5 Then sang Deborah and Barak the son of Abinoam on that day, saying:

2 "Praise You יהוה for the avenging of Yisrael, when the people willingly offered themselves.

3 Hear, O you kings; give ear, O you princes; I, even I, will sing unto יהוה; I will sing praise to יהוה God of Israel (Elohei Yisrael).

4 יהוה, when you wentest out of Seir, when you marchedst out of the field of Edom, the earth trembled, and the heavens dropped, the clouds also dropped water.

5 The mountains melted from before יהוה, even that Sinai from before יהוה God of Israel (Elohei

Yisrael).

6 In the days of Shamgar the son of Anath, in the days of Yael, the highways were unoccupied, and the travellers walked through byways.

7 The inhabitants of the villages ceased, they ceased in Yisrael, until that I Deborah arose, that I arose a mother in Yisrael.

8 They chose new gods (elohim); then was war in the gates. Was there a shield or spear seen among forty thousand in Yisrael?

9 My heart is toward the governors of Yisrael, that offered themselves willingly among the people. Bless You יהוה.

10 Speak, you that ride on white asses, you that sit in judgment, and walk by the way.

11 They that are delivered from the noise of archers in the places of drawing water, there shall they rehearse the righteous acts of יהוה, even the righteous acts toward the inhabitants of His villages in Yisrael; then shall the people of יהוה go down to the gates.

12 Awake, awake, Deborah! Awake, awake, utter a song! Arise, Barak, and lead your captivity captive, you son of Abinoam.

13 Then He made him that remaineth have dominion over the nobles among the people; יהוה made me have dominion over the mighty.

14 Out of Efrayim was there a root of them against Amalek; after you, Binyamin, among your people; out of Machir came down governors, and out of Zevulun they that handle the pen of the writer.

15 And the princes of Yissaskhar were with Deborah; even Yissaskhar, and also Barak; he was sent on foot into the valley. For the divisions of Reuven there were great thoughts of heart.

16 Why abodest you among the sheepfolds, to hear the bleatings of the flocks? For the divisions of Reuven there were great searchings of heart.

17 Gilad abode beyond Jordan (Yarden); and why did Dan remain in ships? Asher continued on the sea shore, and abode in his breaches.

18 Zevulun and Naftali were a people that jeoparded their lives unto the death in the high places of the field.

19 The kings came and fought, then fought the kings of Canaan in Taanach by the waters of Megiddo; they took no gain of money.

20 They fought from heaven; the stars in their courses fought against Sisera.

21 The river of Kishon swept them away, that ancient river, the river Kishon. O my soul, you have trodden down strength.

22 Then were the horsehoofs broken by the means of the pransings, the pransings of their mighty ones.

23 'Curse you Meroz,' said the angel of יהוה, 'curse you bitterly the inhabitants thereof; because they came not to the help of יהוה, to the help of יהוה against the mighty.'

24 Blessed above women shall Yael the wife of Heber the Kenite be, blessed shall she be above women in the tent.

25 He asked water, and she gave him milk; she brought forth butter in a lordly dish.

26 She put her hand to the nail, and her right hand to the workmen's hammer; and with the hammer she smote Sisera, she smote off his head, when she had pierced and stricken through his temples.

27 At her feet he bowed, he fell, he lay down: at her feet he bowed, he fell; where he bowed, there he fell down dead.

28 The mother of Sisera looked out at a window, and cried through the lattice, 'Why is his chariot so long in coming? why tarry the wheels of his chariots?'

29 Her wise ladies answered her, yea, she returned answer to herself,

30 'Have they not sped? have they not divided the prey; to every man a damsel or two; to Sisera a prey of divers colours, a prey of divers colours of needlework, of divers colours of needlework on both sides, meet for the necks of them that take the spoil?'

31 So let all your enemies perish, O יהוה; but let them that love Him be as the sun when he goeth forth in his might." And the land had rest forty years.

6 And the children of Yisrael did evil in the sight of יהוה; and יהוה delivered them into the hand of Midian seven years.

2 And the hand of Midian prevailed against Yisrael; and because of the Midianites the children of Yisrael made them the dens which are in the mountains, and caves, and strong holds.

3 And so it was, when Yisrael had sown, that the Midianites came up, and the Amalekites, and the children of the east, even they came up against them;

4 And they encamped against them, and destroyed the increase of the earth, till you come unto Gaza (Azzah), and left no sustenance for Yisrael, neither sheep, nor ox, nor ass.

5 For they came up with their cattle and their tents, and they came as grasshoppers for multitude; for both they and their camels were without number; and they entered into the land to destroy it.

6 And Yisrael was greatly impoverished because of the Midianites; and the children of Yisrael cried unto יהוה.

7 And it came to pass, when the children of Yisrael cried unto יהוה because of the Midianites,

8 That יהוה sent a prophet unto the children of Yisrael, who said unto them, "Thus saith יהוה God of Israel (Elohei Yisrael): 'I brought you up from Egypt (Mitsrayim), and brought you forth out of the house of bondage;

9 And I delivered you out of the hand of the Egyptians (Mitsrayim), and out of the hand of all that oppressed you, and drave them out from before you, and gave you their land;

10 And I said unto you, "I am יהוה your God (YHWH Eloheikhem); fear not the gods (elohim) of the Amorites, in whose land you dwell; but you have not obeyed My voice."'"

11 And there came an angel of יהוה, and sat under an oak which was in Ophrah, that pertained unto Yoash the Abiezrite; and his son Gideon threshed wheat by the winepress, to hide it from the Midianites.

12 And the angel of יהוה appeared unto him, and said unto him, "יהוה is with you, you mighty man of valour."

13 And Gideon said unto him, "Oh my lord (adoni), if יהוה be with us, why then is all this befallen us? And where are all His miracles which our fathers told us of, saying, 'Did not יהוה bring us up from Egypt (Mitsrayim)?' But now יהוה hath forsaken us, and delivered us into the hands of the Midianites."

14 And יהוה looked upon him, and said, "Go in this your might, and you shalt save Yisrael from the hand of the Midianites; have not I sent you?"

15 And he said unto Him, "Oh my Lord (Adonai), how shall I save Yisrael? Behold, my family is poor in Menashsheh, and I am the least in my father's house."

16 And יהוה said unto him, "Surely I will be with you, and you shalt smite the Midianites as

one man."

17 And he said unto Him, "If now I have found grace in Your sight, then shew me a sign that You talkest with me.

18 Depart not hence, please, until I come unto You, and bring forth my present, and set it before You." And He said, "I will tarry until you come again."

19 And Gideon went in, and made ready a kid, and unleavened cakes (matstsot) of an ephah of flour; the flesh he put in a basket, and he put the broth in a pot, and brought it out unto him under the oak, and presented it.

20 And the angel of God (Elohim) said unto him, "Take the flesh and the unleavened cakes (matstsot), and lay them upon this rock, and pour out the broth." And he did so.

21 Then the angel of יהוה put forth the end of the staff that was in his hand, and touched the flesh and the unleavened cakes (matstsot); and there rose up fire out of the rock, and consumed the flesh and the unleavened cakes (matstsot). Then the angel of יהוה departed out of his sight.

22 And when Gideon perceived that he was an angel of יהוה, Gideon said, "Alas, O יהוה God (Elohim)! Because I have seen an angel of יהוה face to face."

23 And יהוה said unto him, "Peace be unto you; fear not, you shalt not die."

24 Then Gideon built an altar there unto יהוה, and called it [A5]"יהוה Shalom (YHWH Is Peace)". Unto this day it is yet in Ophrah of the Abiezrites.

25 And it came to pass the same night, that יהוה said unto him, "Take your father's young bullock, even the second bullock of seven years old, and throw down the altar of the Baal that your father hath, and cut down the [B34a]Asherah that is by it;

26 And build an altar unto יהוה your God (YHWH Eloheikha) upon the top of this rock, in the ordered place, and take the second bullock, and offer a burnt sacrifice with the wood of the Asherah which you shalt cut down.

27 Then Gideon took ten men of his servants, and did as יהוה had said unto him; and so it was, because he feared his father's household, and the men of the city, that he could not do it by day, that he did it by night.

28 And when the men of the city arose early in the morning, behold, the altar of the Baal was cast down, and the Asherah was cut down that was by it, and the second bullock was offered upon the altar that was built.

29 And they said one to another, "Who hath done this thing?" And when they enquired and asked, they said, "Gideon the son of Yoash hath done this thing."

30 Then the men of the city said unto Yoash, "Bring out your son, that he may die, because he hath cast down the altar of the Baal, and because he hath cut down the Asherah that was by it."

31 And Yoash said unto all that stood against him, "Will you plead for the Baal? Will you save him? He that will plead for him, let him be put to death whilst it is yet morning; if he is a god (elohim), let him plead for himself, because one hath cast down his altar!"

32 Therefore on that day he called him Yerubaal, saying, "Let the Baal plead against him, because he hath thrown down his altar."

33 Then all the Midianites and the Amalekites and the children of the east were gathered together, and went over, and pitched in the valley of Yizreel.

34 But the Spirit (Ruach) of יהוה came upon Gideon, and he blew a shofar; and Abiezer was gathered after him.

35 And he sent messengers throughout all Menashsheh, who also was gathered after him; and he sent messengers unto Asher, and unto Zevulun, and unto Naftali; and they came up to meet them.

36 And Gideon said unto God (Elohim), "If You wilt save Yisrael by mine hand, as You have said,

37 "Behold, I will put a fleece of wool in the floor; and if the dew be on the fleece only, and it be dry upon all the earth, then shall I know that You wilt save Yisrael by mine hand, as You have said."

38 And it was so; for he rose up early on the next day, and thrust the fleece together, and wringed the dew out of the fleece, a bowl full of water.

39 And Gideon said unto God (Elohim), "Let not Your anger be hot against me, and I will speak but this once; please let me prove, but this once with the fleece; let it now be dry only upon the fleece, and upon all the ground let there be dew."

40 And God (Elohim) did so that night; as it was

dry upon the fleece only, and there was dew on all the ground.

7 Then Yerubaal, who is Gideon, and all the people that were with him, rose up early, and pitched beside the well of Harod; so that the army of the Midianites were on the north side of them, by the hill of Moreh, in the valley.

2 And יהוה said unto Gideon, "The people that are with you are too many for me to give the Midianites into their hands, lest Yisrael vaunt themselves against me, saying, 'Mine own hand hath saved me.'

3 Now therefore go to, proclaim in the ears of the people, saying, 'Whosoever is fearful and afraid, let him return and depart early from Mount Gilad.'" And there returned of the people twenty and two thousand; and there remained ten thousand.

4 And יהוה said unto Gideon, "The people are yet too many; bring them down unto the water, and I will test them for you there; and it shall be, that of whom I say unto you, 'This shall go with you,' the same shall go with you; and of whomsoever I say unto you, 'This shall not go with you,' the same shall not go."

5 So he brought down the people unto the water; and יהוה said unto Gideon, "Every one that lappeth of the water with his tongue, as a dog lappeth, him shalt you set by himself; likewise every one that boweth down upon his knees to drink."

6 And the number of them that lapped, putting their hand to their mouth, were three hundred men; but all the rest of the people bowed down upon their knees to drink water.

7 And יהוה said unto Gideon, "By the three hundred men that lapped will I save you, and deliver the Midianites into your hand; and let all the other people go every man unto his place."

8 So the people took victuals in their hand, and their ram's horn (shofarot); and he sent all the rest of Yisrael every man unto his tent, and retained those three hundred men; and the camp of Midian was beneath him in the valley.

9 And it came to pass the same night, that יהוה said unto him, "Arise, get you down unto the camp, for I have delivered it into your hand.

10 But if you fear to go down, go you with Phurah your servant down to the camp;

11 And you shalt hear what they say; and afterward shall your hands be strengthened to go down unto the camp." Then went he down with Phurah his servant unto the outside of the armed men that were in the camp.

12 And the Midianites and the Amalekites and all the children of the east lay along in the valley like grasshoppers for multitude; and their camels were without number, as the sand by the sea side for multitude.

13 And when Gideon was come, behold, there was a man that told a dream unto his fellow, and said, "Behold, I dreamed a dream, and, behold, a cake of barley bread tumbled into the camp of Midian, and came unto a tent, and smote it that it fell, and overturned it, that the tent lay along."

14 And his fellow answered and said, "This is nothing else except the sword of Gideon the son of Yoash, a man of Yisrael; for into his hand hath God (Elohim) delivered Midian, and all the camp."

15 And it was so, when Gideon heard the telling of the dream, and the interpretation thereof, that he worshipped, and returned into the camp of Yisrael, and said, "Arise, for יהוה hath delivered into your hand the camp of Midian."

16 And he divided the three hundred men into three companies, and he put a shofar in every man's hand, with empty pitchers, and lamps within the pitchers.

17 And he said unto them, "Look on me, and do likewise; and, behold, when I come to the outside of the camp, it shall be that, as I do, so shall you do:

18 When I blow with a shofar, I and all that are with me, then blow you the ram's horn (shofarot) also on every side of all the camp, and say, 'The sword of יהוה, and of Gideon!'"

19 So Gideon, and the hundred men that were with him, came unto the outside of the camp in the beginning of the middle watch; and they had but newly set the watch; and they blew the ram's horn (shofarot), and broke the pitchers that were in their hands.

20 And the three companies blew the ram's horns (shofarot), and broke the pitchers, and held the lamps in their left hands, and the ram's horn (shofarot) in their right hands to blow withal; and they cried, "The sword of יהוה, and of Gideon!"

21 And they stood every man in his place round about the camp; and all the army ran, and cried, and fled.

22 And the three hundred blew the ram's horns (shofarot), and יהוה set every man's sword against his fellow, even throughout all the camp; and the army fled to Beit-Shittah in Zererath, and to the border of Abelmeholah, unto Tabbath.

23 And the men of Yisrael gathered themselves together out of Naftali, and out of Asher, and out of all Menashsheh, and pursued after the Midianites.

24 And Gideon sent messengers throughout all Mount Efrayim, saying, "Come down against the Midianites, and take before them the waters unto Beit-Barah and Jordan (Yarden)." Then all the men of Efrayim gathered themselves together, and took the waters unto Beit-Barah and Jordan (Yarden).

25 And they took two princes of the Midianites, Oreb and Zeeb; and they slew Oreb upon the rock Oreb, and Zeeb they slew at the winepress of Zeeb, and pursued Midian, and brought the heads of Oreb and Zeeb to Gideon on the other side Jordan (Yarden).

8 And the men of Efrayim said unto him, "Why have you served us thus, that you calledst us not, when you wentest to fight with the Midianites?" And they did chide with him sharply.

2 And he said unto them, "What have I done now in comparison of you? Is not the gleaning of the grapes of Efrayim better than the vintage of Abiezer?

3 God (Elohim) hath delivered into your hands the princes of Midian, Oreb and Zeeb; and what was I able to do in comparison of you?" Then their anger was abated toward him, when he had said that.

4 And Gideon came to Jordan (Yarden), and passed over, he, and the three hundred men that were with him, faint, yet pursuing them.

5 And he said unto the men of Sukkot, "Please give loaves of bread unto the people that follow me; for they be faint, and I am pursuing after Zebah and Zalmunna, kings of Midian."

6 And the princes of Sukkot said, "Are the hands of Zebah and Zalmunna now in your hand, that we should give bread unto your army?"

7 And Gideon said, "Therefore when יהוה hath delivered Zebah and Zalmunna into mine hand, then I will tear your flesh with the thorns of the wilderness and with briers."

8 And he went up thence to Penuel, and spake unto them likewise; and the men of Penuel answered him as the men of Sukkot had answered him.

9 And he spake also unto the men of Penuel, saying, "When I come again in peace, I will break down this tower!"

10 Now Zebah and Zalmunna were in Karkor, and their hosts with them, about fifteen thousand men, all that were left of all the hosts of the children of the east; for there fell a hundred and twenty thousand men that drew sword.

11 And Gideon went up by the way of them that dwelt in tents on the east of Nobah and Yogbehah, and smote the camp; for the camp was secure.

12 And when Zebah and Zalmunna fled, he pursued after them, and took the two kings of Midian, Zebah and Zalmunna, and discomfited all the army.

13 And Gideon the son of Yoash returned from battle before the sun was up,

14 And caught a young man of the men of Sukkot, and enquired of him; and he described unto him the princes of Sukkot, and the elders thereof, even threescore and seventeen men.

15 And he came unto the men of Sukkot, and said, "Behold Zebah and Zalmunna, with whom you did upbraid me, saying, 'Are the hands of Zebah and Zalmunna now in your hand, that we should give bread unto your men that are weary?'"

16 And he took the elders of the city, and thorns of the wilderness and briers, and with them he taught the men of Sukkot.

17 And he beat down the tower of Penuel, and slew the men of the city.

18 Then said he unto Zebah and Zalmunna, "What manner of men were they whom you slew at Tabor?" And they answered, "As you are, so were they; each one resembled the children of a king."

19 And he said, "They were my brethren, the sons of my mother; as יהוה liveth, if you had saved them alive, I would not slay you."

20 And he said unto Yeter his firstborn, "Up, and slay them." But the youth drew not his sword; for he feared, because he was yet a youth.

21 Then Zebah and Zalmunna said, "Rise you, and fall upon us; for as the man is, so is his strength." And Gideon arose, and slew Zebah and Zalmunna, and took away the ornaments

that were on their camels' necks.

22 Then the men of Yisrael said unto Gideon, "Rule you over us, both you, and your son, and your son's son also; for you have delivered us from the hand of Midian."

23 And Gideon said unto them, "I will not rule over you, nor shall my son rule over you; יהוה shall rule over you."

24 And Gideon said unto them, "I would desire a request of you, that you would give me every man the earrings of his prey." (For they had golden earrings, because they were Ishmaelites (Yishmaelim))

25 And they answered, "We will willingly give them." And they spread a garment, and did cast therein every man the earrings of his prey.

26 And the weight of the golden earrings that he requested was a thousand and seven hundred shekels of gold; beside ornaments, and collars, and purple raiment that was on the kings of Midian, and besides the chains that were about their camels' necks.

27 And Gideon made an ephod thereof, and put it in his city, even in Ophrah; and all Yisrael went thither a whoring after it; which thing became a snare unto Gideon, and to his house.

28 Thus was Midian subdued before the children of Yisrael, so that they lifted up their heads no more. And the country was in quietness forty years in the days of Gideon.

29 And Yerubaal the son of Yoash went and dwelt in his own house.

30 And Gideon had threescore and ten sons (seventy) of his body begotten; for he had many wives.

31 And his concubine that was in Shechem, she also bare him a son, whose name he called Abimelech (Avimelekh).

32 And Gideon the son of Yoash died in a good old age, and was buried in the sepulchre of Yoash his father, in Ophrah of the Abiezrites.

33 And it came to pass, as soon as Gideon was dead, that the children of Yisrael turned again, and went a whoring after Baals (Baalim), and made [33e]Baal-Berit ("Lord of Covenant") their god (elohim).

34 And the children of Yisrael remembered not יהוה their God (YHWH Eloheihem), who had delivered them out of the hands of all their enemies on every side;

35 Nor shewed they kindness to the house of Yerubaal, namely, Gideon, according to all the goodness which he had shewed unto Yisrael.

9 And Abimelech (Avimelekh) the son of Yerubaal went to Shechem unto his mother's brethren, and communed with them, and with all the family of the house of his mother's father, saying,

2 "Please speak in the ears of all the men of Shechem: 'Which is better for you, either that all the sons of Yerubaal, which are threescore and ten persons, reign over you, or that one reign over you?' Remember also that I am your bone and your flesh."

3 And his mother's brethren spake of him in the ears of all the men of Shechem all these words; and their hearts inclined to follow Abimelech (Avimelekh); for they said, "He is our brother."

4 And they gave him threescore and ten pieces of silver out of the house of Baal-Berit (Lord of Covenant), wherewith Abimelech (Avimelekh) hired vain and reckless persons, who followed him.

5 And he went unto his father's house at Ophrah, and slew his brethren the sons of Yerubaal, being threescore and ten persons, upon one stone; notwithstanding yet Yotam the youngest son of Yerubaal was left; for he hid himself.

6 And all the men of Shechem gathered together, and all the house of Millo, and went, and made Abimelech (Avimelekh) king, by the plain of the pillar that was in Shechem.

7 And when they told it to Yotam, he went and stood in the top of Mount Gerizim, and lifted up his voice, and cried, and said unto them: "Hearken unto me, you men of Shechem, that God (Elohim) may hearken unto you!

8 The trees went forth on a time to anoint a king over them; and they said unto the olive tree, 'Reign you over us!'

9 But the olive tree said unto them, 'Should I leave my fatness, wherewith by me they honor God (Elohim) and man, and go to be promoted over the trees?'

10 And the trees said to the fig tree, 'Come you, and reign over us!'

11 But the fig tree said unto them, 'Should I forsake my sweetness, and my good fruit, and go to be promoted over the trees?'

12 Then said the trees unto the vine, 'Come you, and reign over us!'

13 And the vine said unto them, 'Should I leave

my wine, which cheereth God (Elohim) and man, and go to be promoted over the trees?'

14 Then said all the trees unto the bramble, 'Come you, and reign over us!'

15 And the bramble said unto the trees, 'If in truth you anoint me king over you, then come and put your trust in my shadow; and if not, let fire come out of the bramble, and devour the cedars of Lebanon!'

16 Now therefore, if you have done truly and sincerely, in that you have made Abimelech (Avimelekh) king, and if you have dealt well with Yerubaal and his house, and have done unto him according to the deserving of his hands;

17 (For my father fought for you, and adventured his life far, and delivered you out of the hand of Midian;

18 And you have risen up against my father's house this day, and have slain his sons, threescore and ten (seventy) persons, upon one stone, and have made Abimelech (Avimelekh), the son of his maidservant, king over the men of Shechem, because he is your brother;)

19 If you then have dealt truly and sincerely with Yerubaal and with his house this day, then rejoice you in Abimelech (Avimelekh), and let him also rejoice in you.

20 But if not, let fire come out from Abimelech (Avimelekh), and devour the men of Shechem, and the house of Millo; and let fire come out from the men of Shechem, and from the house of Millo, and devour Abimelech (Avimelekh)."

21 And Yotam ran away, and fled, and went to Beer, and dwelt there, for fear of Abimelech (Avimelekh) his brother.

22 When Abimelech (Avimelekh) had reigned three years over Yisrael,

23 Then God (Elohim) sent an evil spirit between Abimelech (Avimelekh) and the men of Shechem; and the men of Shechem dealt treacherously with Abimelech (Avimelekh),

24 That the cruelty done to the threescore and ten sons of Yerubaal might come, and their blood be laid upon Abimelech (Avimelekh) their brother, which slew them; and upon the men of Shechem, which aided him in the killing of his brethren.

25 And the men of Shechem set liers in wait for him in the top of the mountains, and they robbed all that came along that way by them;

and it was told Abimelech (Avimelekh).

26 And Gaal the son of Ebed came with his brethren, and went over to Shechem; and the men of Shechem put their confidence in him.

27 And they went out into the fields, and gathered their vineyards, and trode the grapes, and made merry, and went into the house of their god (elohim), and did eat and drink, and cursed Abimelech (Avimelekh).

28 And Gaal the son of Ebed said, "Who is Abimelech (Avimelekh), and who is Shechem, that we should serve him? Is not he the son of Yerubaal? And Zebul his officer? Serve the men of Hamor the father of Shechem, for why should we serve him?

29 And if only this people were under my hand! Then would I remove Abimelech (Avimelekh)." And he said to Abimelech (Avimelekh), "Increase your army, and come out!"

30 And when Zebul the ruler of the city heard the words of Gaal the son of Ebed, his anger was kindled.

31 And he sent messengers unto Abimelech (Avimelekh) privily, saying, "Behold, Gaal the son of Ebed and his brethren be come to Shechem; and, behold, they fortify the city against you.

32 Now therefore up by night, you and the people that is with you, and lie in wait in the field.

33 And it shall be, that in the morning, as soon as the sun is up, you shalt rise early, and set upon the city; and, behold, when he and the people that is with him come out against you, then mayest you do to them as you shalt find occasion."

34 And Abimelech (Avimelekh) rose up, and all the people that were with him, by night, and they laid wait against Shechem in four companies.

35 And Gaal the son of Ebed went out, and stood in the entering of the gate of the city; and Abimelech (Avimelekh) rose up, and the people that were with him, from lying in wait.

36 And when Gaal saw the people, he said to Zebul, "Behold, there come people down from the top of the mountains." And Zebul said unto him, "You seest the shadow of the mountains as if they were men."

37 And Gaal spake again, and said, "See there come people down by the middle of the land, and another company come along by the plain

of Meonenim."

38 Then said Zebul unto him, "Where is now your mouth, wherewith you saidst, 'Who is Abimelech (Avimelekh), that we should serve him?' Is not this the people that you have despised? Go out now, and fight with them."

39 And Gaal went out before the men of Shechem, and fought with Abimelech (Avimelekh).

40 And Abimelech (Avimelekh) chased him, and he fled before him, and many were overthrown and wounded, even unto the entering of the gate.

41 And Abimelech (Avimelekh) dwelt at Arumah; and Zebul thrust out Gaal and his brethren, that they should not dwell in Shechem.

42 And it came to pass on the next day, that the people went out into the field; and they told Abimelech (Avimelekh).

43 And he took the people, and divided them into three companies, and laid wait in the field, and looked, and, behold, the people were come forth out of the city; and he rose up against them, and smote them.

44 And Abimelech (Avimelekh), and the company that was with him, rushed forward, and stood in the entering of the gate of the city; and the two other companies ran upon all the people that were in the fields, and slew them.

45 And Abimelech (Avimelekh) fought against the city all that day; and he took the city, and slew the people that was therein, and beat down the city, and sowed it with salt.

46 And when all the men of the tower of Shechem heard that, they entered into a hold of the house of the El-Berit.

47 And it was told Abimelech (Avimelekh), that all the men of the tower of Shechem were gathered together.

48 And Abimelech (Avimelekh) gat him up to Mount Zalmon, he and all the people that were with him; and Abimelech (Avimelekh) took an axe in his hand, and cut down a bough from the trees, and took it, and laid it on his shoulder, and said unto the people that were with him, "What you have seen me do, make haste, and do as I have done."

49 And all the people likewise cut down every man his bough, and followed Abimelech (Avimelekh), and put them to the hold, and set the hold on fire upon them; so that all the men of the tower of Shechem died also, about a thousand men and women.

50 Then went Abimelech (Avimelekh) to Thebez, and encamped against Thebez, and took it.

51 But there was a strong tower within the city, and thither fled all the men and women, and all they of the city, and shut it to them, and gat them up to the top of the tower.

52 And Abimelech (Avimelekh) came unto the tower, and fought against it, and went hard unto the door of the tower to burn it with fire.

53 And a certain woman cast a piece of a millstone upon Abimelech's head, and all to broke his skull.

54 Then he called hastily unto the young man his armourbearer, and said unto him, "Draw your sword, and slay me, that men say not of me, 'A women slew him.'" And his young man thrust him through, and he died.

55 And when the men of Yisrael saw that Abimelech (Avimelekh) was dead, they departed every man unto his place.

56 Thus God (Elohim) rendered the wickedness of Abimelech (Avimelekh), which he did unto his father, in slaying his seventy brethren.

57 And all the evil of the men of Shechem did God (Elohim) render upon their heads; and upon them came the curse of Yotam the son of Yerubaal.

10 And after Abimelech (Avimelekh) there arose to defend Yisrael Tola the son of Puah, the son of Dodo, a man of Yissaskhar; and he dwelt in Shamir in Mount Efrayim.

2 And he judged Yisrael twenty and three years, and died, and was buried in Shamir.

3 And after him arose Yair, a Giladite, and judged Yisrael twenty and two years.

4 And he had thirty sons that rode on thirty ass colts, and they had thirty cities, which are called Chawwot Yair unto this day, which are in the land of Gilad.

5 And Yair died, and was buried in Camon.

6 And the children of Yisrael did evil again in the sight of יהוה, and served Baalim, and Ashtaroth, and the gods (elohim) of Syria (Aram), and the gods (elohim) of Zidon, and the gods (elohim) of Moav, and the gods (elohim) of the children of Ammon, and the gods (elohim) of the Philistines, and forsook יהוה, and served not Him.

7 And the anger of יהוה was hot against Yisrael, and He sold them into the hands of the

Philistines, and into the hands of the children of Ammon.

8 And that year they vexed and oppressed the children of Yisrael; eighteen years, all the children of Yisrael that were on the other side Jordan (Yarden) in the land of the Amorites, which is in Gilad.

9 Moreover the children of Ammon passed over Jordan (Yarden) to fight also against Judah (Yehudah), and against Binyamin, and against the house of Efrayim; so that Yisrael was sore distressed.

10 And the children of Yisrael cried unto יהוה, saying, "We have sinned against you, both because we have forsaken our God (Elohim), and also served Baals (Baalim)!"

11 And יהוה said unto the children of Yisrael, "Did not I deliver you from the Egyptians (Mitsrayim), and from the Amorites, from the children of Ammon, and from the Philistines?

12 The Zidonians also, and the Amalekites, and the Maonites, did oppress you; and you cried to Me, and I delivered you out of their hand.

13 Yet you have forsaken Me, and served other gods (elohim); wherefore I will deliver you no more.

14 Go and cry unto the gods (elohim) which you have chosen; let them deliver you in the time of your tribulation."

15 And the children of Yisrael said unto יהוה, "We have sinned; do You unto us whatsoever seemeth good unto You; only please deliver us this day."

16 And they put away the strange gods (elohim) from among them, and served יהוה; and His soul was grieved for the misery of Yisrael.

17 Then the children of Ammon were gathered together, and encamped in Gilad. And the children of Yisrael assembled themselves together, and encamped in Mizpeh.

18 And the people and princes of Gilad said one to another, "What man is he that will begin to fight against the children of Ammon? He shall be head over all the inhabitants of Gilad."

11 Now Yiftach the Giladite was a mighty man of valour, and he was the son of a harlot; and Gilad begat Yiftach.

2 And Gilad's wife bare him sons; and his wife's sons grew up, and they thrust out Yiftach, and said unto him, You shalt not inherit in our father's house; for you are the son of a strange woman.

3 Then Yiftach fled from his brethren, and dwelt in the land of Tob; and there were gathered vain men to Yiftach, and went out with him.

4 And it came to pass in process of time, that the children of Ammon made war against Yisrael.

5 And it was so, that when the children of Ammon made war against Yisrael, the elders of Gilad went to fetch Yiftach out of the land of Tob.

6 And they said unto Yiftach, "Come, and be our captain, that we may fight with the children of Ammon."

7 And Yiftach said unto the elders of Gilad, "Did not you hate me, and expel me out of my father's house? And why are you come unto me now when you are in distress?"

8 And the elders of Gilad said unto Yiftach, "Therefore we turn again to you now, that you mayest go with us, and fight against the children of Ammon, and be our head over all the inhabitants of Gilad."

9 And Yiftach said unto the elders of Gilad, "If you bring me home again to fight against the children of Ammon, and יהוה deliver them before me, shall I be your head?"

10 And the elders of Gilad said unto Yiftach, "יהוה be witness between us, if we do not so according to your words."

11 Then Yiftach went with the elders of Gilad, and the people made him head and captain over them; and Yiftach uttered all his words before יהוה in Mizpeh.

12 And Yiftach sent messengers unto the king of the children of Ammon, saying, "What have you to do with me, that you are come against me to fight in my land?"

13 And the king of the children of Ammon answered unto the messengers of Yiftach, "Because Yisrael took away my land, when they came up out of Egypt (Mitsrayim), from Arnon even unto Yabok, and unto Jordan (Yarden). Now therefore restore those lands again peaceably."

14 And Yiftach sent messengers again unto the king of the children of Ammon;

15 And said unto him, "Thus saith Yiftach: 'Yisrael took not away the land of Moav, nor the land of the children of Ammon;

16 But when Yisrael came up from Egypt (Mitsrayim), and walked through the wilderness

unto the Red sea, and came to Qadesh;

17 Then Yisrael sent messengers unto the king of Edom, saying, "Please let me pass through your land." But the king of Edom would not hearken thereto. And in like manner they sent unto the king of Moav; but he would not consent; and Yisrael abode in Qadesh.

18 Then they went along through the wilderness, and compassed the land of Edom, and the land of Moav, and came by the east side of the land of Moav, and pitched on the other side of Arnon, but came not within the border of Moav; for Arnon was the border of Moav.

19 And Yisrael sent messengers unto Sihon king of the Amorites, the king of Heshbon; and Yisrael said unto him, "Please let us pass through your land into my place."

20 But Sihon trusted not Yisrael to pass through his coast; but Sihon gathered all his people together, and pitched in Yahaz, and fought against Yisrael.

21 And יהוה God of Israel (Elohei Yisrael) delivered Sihon and all his people into the hand of Yisrael, and they smote them; so Yisrael possessed all the land of the Amorites, the inhabitants of that country.

22 And they possessed all the coasts of the Amorites, from Arnon even unto Yabok, and from the wilderness even unto Jordan (Yarden).

23 So now יהוה God of Israel (Elohei Yisrael) hath dispossessed the Amorites from before his people Yisrael, and shouldest you possess it?

24 Wilt not you possess that which Chemosh your God (Elohim) giveth you to possess? So whomsoever יהוה our God (YHWH Eloheinu) shall drive out from before us, them will we possess.

25 And now are you any thing better than Balak the son of Zippor, king of Moav? Did he ever strive against Yisrael, or did he ever fight against them,

26 While Yisrael dwelt in Heshbon and her towns, and in Aroer and her towns, and in all the cities that be along by the coasts of Arnon, three hundred years? Why therefore did you not recover them within that time?

27 Wherefore I have not sinned against you, but you doest me wrong to war against me. יהוה the Judge be judge this day between the children of Yisrael and the children of Ammon.'"

28 Howbeit the king of the children of Ammon

hearkened not unto the words of Yiftach which he sent him.

29 Then the Spirit of יהוה came upon Yiftach, and he passed over Gilad, and Menashsheh, and passed over Mizpeh of Gilad, and from Mizpeh of Gilad he passed over unto the children of Ammon.

30 And Yiftach vowed a vow unto יהוה, and said, "If you shalt without fail deliver the children of Ammon into mine hands,

31 Then it shall be, that whatsoever cometh forth of the doors of my house to meet me, when I return in peace from the children of Ammon, shall surely be יהוה's, and I will offer it up for a burnt offering."

32 So Yiftach passed over unto the children of Ammon to fight against them; and יהוה delivered them into his hands.

33 And he smote them from Aroer, even till you come to Minnith, even twenty cities, and unto the plain of the vineyards, with a very great slaughter. Thus the children of Ammon were subdued before the children of Yisrael.

34 And Yiftach came to Mizpeh unto his house, and, behold, his daughter came out to meet him with timbrels and with dances; and she was his only child; besides her he had neither son nor daughter.

35 And it came to pass, when he saw her, that he rent his clothes, and said, "Alas, my daughter! You have brought me very low, and you are one of them that trouble me; for I have opened my mouth unto יהוה, and I cannot go back."

36 And she said unto him, "My father, if you have opened your mouth unto יהוה, do to me according to that which hath proceeded out of your mouth; forasmuch as יהוה hath taken vengeance for you of your enemies, even of the children of Ammon."

37 And she said unto her father, "Let this thing be done for me; let me alone two months, that I may go up and down upon the mountains, and bewail my virginity, I and my fellows."

38 And he said, "Go." And he sent her away for two months; and she went with her companions, and bewailed her virginity upon the mountains.

39 And it came to pass at the end of two months, that she returned unto her father, who did with her according to his vow which he had vowed; and she knew no man. And it was a custom in Yisrael,

40 That the daughters of Yisrael went yearly to lament the daughter of Yiftach the Giladite four days in a year.

12 And the men of Efrayim gathered themselves together, and went northward, and said unto Yiftach, "Wherefore passedst you over to fight against the children of Ammon, and didst not call us to go with you? We will burn your house upon you with fire."

2 And Yiftach said unto them, "I and my people were at great strife with the children of Ammon; and when I called you, you delivered me not out of their hands.

3 And when I saw that you delivered me not, I put my life in my hands, and passed opposite the children of Ammon, and יהוה delivered them into my hand; wherefore then are you come up unto me this day, to fight against me?"

4 Then Yiftach gathered together all the men of Gilad, and fought with Efrayim; and the men of Gilad smote Efrayim, because they said, "You Giladites are fugitives of Efrayim among the Efrayimites, and among the Manassites."

5 And the Giladites took the passages of Jordan (Yarden) before the Efrayimites; and it was so, that when those Efrayimites which were escaped said, "Let me go over," that the men of Gilad said unto him, "Are you an Efrayimite?" If he said, "Nay,"

6 Then said they unto him, "Say now 'Shibbolet'" But he said "Sibbolet" for he could not frame to pronounce it right. Then they took him, and slew him at the passages of Jordan (Yarden); and there fell at that time of the Efrayimites forty and two thousand.

7 And Yiftach judged Yisrael six years. Then died Yiftach the Giladite, and was buried in one of the cities of Gilad.

8 And after him Ibzan of Bethlehem (Beit-Lechem) judged Yisrael.

9 And he had thirty sons, and thirty daughters, whom he sent abroad, and took in thirty daughters from abroad for his sons. And he judged Yisrael seven years.

10 Then died Ibzan, and was buried at Bethlehem (Beit-Lechem).

11 And after him Elon, a Zebulonite, judged Yisrael; and he judged Yisrael ten years.

12 And Elon the Zevulonite died, and was buried in Ayalon in the country of Zevulun.

13 And after him Abdon the son of Hillel, a Pirathonite, judged Yisrael.

14 And he had forty sons and thirty nephews, that rode on threescore and ten ass colts; and he judged Yisrael eight years.

15 And Abdon the son of Hillel the Pirathonite died, and was buried in Pirathon in the land of Efrayim, in the mount of the Amalekites.

13 And the children of Yisrael did evil again in the sight of יהוה; and יהוה delivered them into the hand of the Philistines forty years.

2 And there was a certain man of Zorah, of the family of the Danites, whose name was Manoach; and his wife was barren, and bare not.

3 And the angel of יהוה appeared unto the woman, and said unto her, "Behold now, you are barren, and bearest not; but you shalt conceive, and bear a son.

4 Now therefore please beware and drink not wine nor strong drink, and eat not any unclean thing.

5 For, behold, you shalt conceive, and bear a son; and no razor shall come on his head; for the child shall be a Nazarite (Nazir) unto God (Elohim) from the womb; and he shall begin to deliver Yisrael out of the hand of the Philistines.

6 Then the woman came and told her husband, saying, "A man of God (Elohim) came unto me, and his countenance was like the countenance of an angel of God (Elohim), very awesome; but I asked him not whence he was, neither told he me his name;

7 But he said unto me, 'Behold, you shalt conceive, and bear a son; and now drink no wine nor strong drink, neither eat any unclean thing; for the child shall be a Nazarite (Nazir) to God (Elohim) from the womb to the day of his death.'"

8 Then Manoach intreated יהוה, and said, "O my Lord (Adonai), let the man of God (Elohim) which you didst send come again unto us, and teach us what we shall do unto the child that shall be born."

9 And God (Elohim) hearkened to the voice of Manoach; and the angel of God (Elohim) came again unto the woman as she sat in the field; but Manoach her husband was not with her.

10 And the woman made haste, and ran, and shewed her husband, and said unto him, "Behold, the man hath appeared unto me, that came unto me the other day."

11 And Manoach arose, and went after his wife,

and came to the man, and said unto him, "Are you the man that spakest unto the woman?" And he said, "I am."

12 And Manoach said, "Now let your words come to pass. How shall we order the child, and how shall we do unto him?"

13 And the angel of יהוה said unto Manoach, "Of all that I said unto the woman let her beware.

14 She may not eat of any thing that cometh of the vine, neither let her drink wine or strong drink, nor eat any unclean thing; all that I commanded her let her observe."

15 And Manoach said unto the angel of יהוה, "Please let us detain you, until we shall have made ready a kid for you."

16 And the angel of יהוה said unto Manoach, "Though you detain me, I will not eat of your food; and if you wilt offer a burnt offering, you must offer it unto יהוה." (For Manoach knew not that he was an angel of יהוה.)

17 And Manoach said unto the angel of יהוה, "What is your name, that when your sayings come to pass we may do you honor?"

18 And the angel of יהוה said unto him, "[B42]Why askest you thus after my name, seeing it is wonderful?"

19 So Manoach took a kid with a meat offering, and offered it upon a rock unto יהוה: and the angel did wonderously; and Manoach and his wife looked on.

20 For it came to pass, when the flame went up toward heaven from off the altar, that the angel of יהוה ascended in the flame of the altar. And Manoach and his wife looked on it, and fell on their faces to the ground.

21 But the angel of יהוה did no more appear to Manoach and to his wife. Then Manoach knew that he was an angel of יהוה.

22 And Manoach said unto his wife, "We shall surely die, because we have seen God (Elohim)."

23 But his wife said unto him, "If יהוה had desired to kill us, He would not have received a burnt offering and a meat offering at our hands, neither would He have shewed us all these things, nor would as at this time have told us such things as these."

24 And the woman bare a son, and called his name Samson; and the child grew, and יהוה blessed him.

25 And the Spirit of יהוה began to move him at times in the camp of Dan between Zorah and Eshtaol.

14 And Samson went down to Timnath, and saw a woman in Timnath of the daughters of the Philistines.

2 And he came up, and told his father and his mother, and said, "I have seen a woman in Timnath of the daughters of the Philistines; now therefore get her for me as wife."

3 Then his father and his mother said unto him, "Is there no woman among the daughters of your brethren, or among all my people, that you goest to take a wife of the uncircumcised Philistines?" And Samson said unto his father, "Get her for me; for she pleaseth me well."

4 But his father and his mother knew not that it was of יהוה, that he sought an occasion against the Philistines; for at that time the Philistines had dominion over Yisrael.

5 Then went Samson down, and his father and his mother, to Timnath, and came to the vineyards of Timnath; and, behold, a young lion roared against him.

6 And the Spirit of יהוה came mightily upon him, and he rent him as he would have rent a kid, and he had nothing in his hand; but he told not his father or his mother what he had done.

7 And he went down, and talked with the woman; and she pleased Samson well.

8 And after a time he returned to take her, and he turned aside to see the carcase of the lion; and, behold, there was a swarm of bees and honey in the carcase of the lion.

9 And he took thereof in his hands, and went on eating, and came to his father and mother, and he gave them, and they did eat; but he told not them that he had taken the honey out of the carcase of the lion.

10 So his father went down unto the woman: and Samson made there a feast; for so used the young men to do.

11 And it came to pass, when they saw him, that they brought thirty companions to be with him.

12 And Samson said unto them, I will now put forth a riddle unto you; if you can certainly declare it me within the seven days of the feast, and find it out, then I will give you thirty sheets and thirty changes of garments:

13 But if you cannot declare it me, then shall you give me thirty sheets and thirty changes of garments. And they said unto him, "Put forth

your riddle, that we may hear it."

14 And he said unto them, "Out of the eater came forth meat, and out of the strong came forth sweetness." And they could not in three days expound the riddle.

15 And it came to pass on the seventh day, that they said unto Samson's wife, "Entice your husband, that he may declare unto us the riddle, lest we burn you and your father's house with fire; have you called us to take that we have? Is it not so?"

16 And Samson's wife wept before him, and said, "You dost but hate me, and lovest me not; you have put forth a riddle unto the children of my people, and have not told it me." And he said unto her, "Behold, I have not told it my father nor my mother, and shall I tell it you?"

17 And she wept before him the seven days, while their feast lasted: and it came to pass on the seventh day, that he told her, because she lay sore upon him; and she told the riddle to the children of her people.

18 And the men of the city said unto him on the seventh day before the sun went down, "What is sweeter than honey? And what is stronger than a lion?" And he said unto them," If you had not plowed with my heifer, you had not found out my riddle!"

19 And the Spirit of יהוה came upon him, and he went down to Ashkelon, and slew thirty men of them, and took their spoil, and gave changes of garments unto them which expounded the riddle. And his anger was kindled, and he went up to his father's house.

20 But Samson's wife was given to his companion, who had been his best man.

15 But it came to pass within a while after, in the time of wheat harvest, that Samson visited his wife with a kid; and he said, "I will go in to my wife into the chamber." But her father would not allow him to go in.

2 And her father said, "I verily thought that you hadst utterly hated her; therefore I gave her to your companion; Is not her younger sister fairer than she? Please take her, instead of her."

3 And Samson said concerning them, "Now shall I be more blameless than the Philistines, though I do them a displeasure."

4 And Samson went and caught three hundred foxes, and took firebrands, and turned tail to tail, and put a firebrand in the midst between two tails.

5 And when he had set the brands on fire, he let them go into the standing corn of the Philistines, and burnt up both the shocks, and also the standing corn, with the vineyards and olives.

6 Then the Philistines said, "Who hath done this?" And they answered, "Samson, the son in law of the Timnite, because he had taken his wife, and given her to his companion." And the Philistines came up, and burnt her and her father with fire.

7 And Samson said unto them, "Though you have done this, yet will I be avenged of you, and after that I will cease."

8 And he smote them hip and thigh with a great slaughter; and he went down and dwelt in the top of the rock Etam.

9 Then the Philistines went up, and pitched in Judah (Yehudah), and spread themselves in Lehi.

10 And the men of Judah (Yehudah) said, "Why are you come up against us?" And they answered, "To bind Samson are we come up, to do to him as he hath done to us."

11 Then three thousand men of Judah (Yehudah) went to the top of the rock Etam, and said to Samson, "Knowest you not that the Philistines are rulers over us? What is this that you have done unto us?" And he said unto them, "As they did unto me, so have I done unto them."

12 And they said unto him, "We are come down to bind you, that we may deliver you into the hand of the Philistines." And Samson said unto them, "Swear unto me, that you will not fall upon me yourselves."

13 And they spake unto him, saying, "No, but we will bind you fast, and deliver you into their hand; but surely we will not kill you." And they bound him with two new cords, and brought him up from the rock.

14 And when he came unto Lehi, the Philistines shouted against him; and the Spirit of יהוה came mightily upon him, and the cords that were upon his arms became as flax that was burnt with fire, and his bands loosed from off his hands.

15 And he found a new jawbone of an ass, and put forth his hand, and took it, and slew a thousand men therewith.

16 And Samson said: "With the jawbone of an

ass, heaps upon heaps, with the jaw of an ass have I slain a thousand men."

17 And it came to pass, when he had made an end of speaking, that he cast away the jawbone out of his hand, and called that place Ramathlehi.

18 And he was sore athirst, and called on יהוה, and said, "You have given this great deliverance into the hand of your servant: and now shall I die for thirst, and fall into the hand of the uncircumcised?"

19 But God (Elohim) clave a hollow place that was in the jaw, and there came water thereout; and when he had drunk, his spirit came again, and he revived; wherefore he called the name thereof Enhakkore, which is in Lehi unto this day.

20 And he judged Yisrael in the days of the Philistines twenty years.

16 Then went Samson to Gaza (Azzah), and saw there a harlot, and went in unto her.

2 And it was told the Gazites, saying, "Samson is come hither." And they compassed him in, and laid wait for him all night in the gate of the city, and were quiet all the night, saying, "In the morning, when it is day, we shall kill him."

3 And Samson lay till midnight, and arose at midnight, and took the doors of the gate of the city, and the two posts, and went away with them, bar and all, and put them upon his shoulders, and carried them up to the top of a hill that is before Hebron.

4 And it came to pass afterward, that he loved a woman in the valley of Sorek, whose name was Delilah.

5 And the lords (seranim) of the Philis-tines came up unto her, and said unto her, "Entice him, and see wherein his great strength lieth, and by what means we may prevail against him, that we may bind him to afflict him; and we will give you every one of us eleven hundred pieces of silver."

6 And Delilah said to Samson, "Please tell me wherein your great strength lieth, and wherewith you mightest be bound to afflict you."

7 And Samson said unto her, "If they bind me with seven green withs that were never dried, then shall I be weak, and be as another man."

8 Then the lords (seranim) of the Philistines brought up to her seven green withs which had not been dried, and she bound him with them.

9 Now there were men lying in wait, abiding with her in the chamber. And she said unto him, "The Philistines be upon you, Samson." And he broke the withs, as a thread of tow is broken when it toucheth the fire. So his strength was not known.

10 And Delilah said unto Samson, "Behold, you have mocked me, and told me lies; now please tell me wherewith you mightest be bound."

11 And he said unto her, "If they bind me fast with new ropes that never were occupied, then shall I be weak, and be as another man."

12 Delilah therefore took new ropes, and bound him therewith, and said unto him, "The Philistines be upon you, Samson." And there were liers in wait abiding in the chamber. And he broke them from off his arms like a thread.

13 And Delilah said unto Samson, "Until now you have mocked me, and told me lies; tell me wherewith you mightest be bound." And he said unto her, "If you weavest the seven locks of my head with the web."

14 And she fastened it with the pin, and said unto him, "The Philistines be upon you, Samson." And he awaked out of his sleep, and went away with the pin of the beam, and with the web.

15 And she said unto him, "How canst you say, I love you, when your heart is not with me? You have mocked me these three times, and hast not told me wherein your great strength lieth."

16 And it came to pass, when she pressed him daily with her words, and urged him, so that his soul was vexed unto death;

17 That he told her all his heart, and said unto her, "There hath not come a razor upon mine head; for I have been a Nazarite (Nazir) unto God (Elohim) from my mother's womb; if I be shaven, then my strength will go from me, and I shall become weak, and be like any other man."

18 And when Delilah saw that he had told her all his heart, she sent and called for the lords (seranim) of the Philistines, saying, "Come up this once, for he hath shewed me all his heart." Then the lords (seranim) of the Philistines came up unto her, and brought money in their hand.

19 And she made him sleep upon her knees; and she called for a man, and she caused him to shave off the seven locks of his head; and she began to afflict him, and his strength went from him.

20 And she said, "The Philistines be upon you, Samson." And he awoke out of his sleep, and

said, "I will go out as at other times before, and shake myself." And he knew not that יהוה had departed from him.

21 But the Philistines took him, and put out his eyes, and brought him down to Gaza (Azzah), and bound him with fetters of brass; and he did grind in the prison house.

22 Howbeit the hair of his head began to grow again after he was shaven.

23 Then the lords (seranim) of the Philistines gathered them together for to offer a great sacrifice unto Dagon their god (elohim), and to rejoice; for they said: "Our god (elohim) hath delivered Samson our enemy into our hand."

24 And when the people saw him, they praised their god (elohim); for they said: "Our god (elohim) hath delivered into our hands our enemy, and the destroyer of our country, who slew many of us."

25 And it came to pass, when their hearts were merry, that they said, "Call for Samson, that he may make us sport. And they called for Samson out of the prison house; and he made them sport; and they set him between the pillars.

26 And Samson said unto the lad that held him by the hand, "Allow me that I may feel the pillars whereupon the house standeth, that I may lean upon them."

27 Now the house was full of men and women; and all the lords (seranim) of the Philistines were there; and there were upon the roof about three thousand men and women, that beheld while Samson made sport.

28 And Samson called unto יהוה, and said, "O Lord (Adonai) יהוה, remember me please and strengthen me please, only this once, O God (Elohim), that I may be at once avenged of the Philistines for my two eyes."

29 And Samson took hold of the two middle pillars upon which the house stood, and on which it was borne up, of the one with his right hand, and of the other with his left.

30 And Samson said, "Let me die with the Philistines!" And he bowed himself with all his might; and the house fell upon the lords (seranim), and upon all the people that were therein. So the dead which he slew at his death were more than they which he slew in his life.

31 Then his brethren and all the house of his father came down, and took him, and brought him up, and buried him between Zorah and Eshtaol in the buryingplace of Manoach his father. And he judged Yisrael twenty years.

17 And there was a man of Mount Efrayim, whose name was Mikhayehu.

2 And he said unto his mother, "The eleven hundred shekels of silver that were taken from you, about which you cursedst, and spakest of also in mine ears, behold, the silver is with me; I took it." And his mother said, "Blessed be you of יהוה, my son."

3 And when he had restored the eleven hundred shekels of silver to his mother, his mother said, "I had wholly dedicated the silver unto יהוה from my hand for my son, to make a graven image and a molten image; now therefore I will restore it unto you."

4 Yet he restored the money unto his mother; and his mother took two hundred shekels of silver, and gave them to the founder, who made thereof a graven image and a molten image; and they were in the house of Mikhayehu.

5 And the man Mikhah had a house of gods (elohim), and made an ephod, and teraphim, and consecrated one of his sons, who became his priest (kohen).

6 In those days there was no king in Yisrael, but every man did that which was right in his own eyes.

7 And there was a young man out of Bethlehem (Beit-Lechem) in Yehudah of the family of Judah (Yehudah), who was a Lewite, and he sojourned there.

8 And the man departed out of the city from Bethlehem (Beit-Lechem) in Yehudah to sojourn where he could find a place; and he came to Mount Efrayim to the house of Mikhah, as he journeyed.

9 And Mikhah said unto him, "Whence comest you?" And he said unto him, "I am a Lewite of Bethlehem (Beit-Lechem) in Yehudah, and I go to sojourn where I may find a place."

10 And Mikhah said unto him, "Dwell with me, and be unto me a father and a priest (kohen), and I will give you ten shekels of silver by the year, and a suit of apparel, and your victuals." So the Lewite went in.

11 And the Lewite was content to dwell with the man; and the young man was unto him as one of his sons.

12 And Mikhah consecrated the Lewite; and the young man became his priest (kohen), and was

in the house of Mikhah.

13 Then said Mikhah, "Now know I that יהוה will do me good, seeing I have a Lewite as my priest (kohen)."

18 In those days there was no king in Yisrael; and in those days the tribe of the Danites sought them an inheritance to dwell in; for unto that day all their inheritance had not fallen unto them among the tribes of Yisrael.

2 And the children of Dan sent of their family five men from their coasts, men of valour, from Zorah, and from Eshtaol, to spy out the land, and to search it; and they said unto them, "Go, search the land." And they came to Mount Efrayim, to the house of Mikhah, they lodged there."

3 When they were by the house of Mikhah, they knew the voice of the young man the Lewite; and they turned in thither, and said unto him, "Who brought you hither? And what makest you in this place? And what have you here?"

4 And he said unto them, "Thus and thus dealeth Mikhah with me, and hath hired me, and I am his priest (kohen)."

5 And they said unto him, "Please ask counsel of God (Elohim), that we may know whether our way which we go shall be prosperous."

6 And the priest (kohen) said unto them, "Go in peace; before יהוה is your way wherein you go.

7 Then the five men departed, and came to Laish, and saw the people that were therein, how they dwelt careless, after the manner of the Zidonians, quiet and secure; and there was no magistrate in the land, that might put them to shame in any thing; and they were far from the Zidonians, and had no business with any man.

8 And they came unto their brethren to Zorah and Eshtaol; and their brethren said unto them, "What say you?"

9 And they said, "Arise, that we may go up against them; for we have seen the land, and, behold, it is very good; and are you still? Be not slothful to go, and to enter to possess the land.

10 When you go, you shall come unto a people secure, and to a large land; for God (Elohim) hath given it into your hands; a place where there is no want of any thing that is in the earth."

11 And there went from thence of the family of the Danites, out of Zorah and out of Eshtaol, six hundred men appointed with weapons of war.

12 And they went up, and pitched in Qiryat-Yearim, in Judah (Yehudah): wherefore they called that place Mahanehdan unto this day; behold, it is behind Qiryat-Yearim.

13 And they passed thence unto Mount Efrayim, and came unto the house of Mikhah.

14 Then answered the five men that went to spy out the country of Laish, and said unto their brethren, "Do you know that there is in these houses an ephod, and teraphim, and a graven image, and a molten image? Now therefore consider what you have to do."

15 And they turned thitherward, and came to the house of the young man the Lewite, even unto the house of Mikhah, and saluted him.

16 And the six hundred men appointed with their weapons of war, who were of the children of Dan, stood by the entering of the gate.

17 And the five men that went to spy out the land went up, and came in thither, and took the graven image, and the ephod, and the teraphim, and the molten image; and the priest (kohen) stood in the entering of the gate with the six hundred men that were appointed with weapons of war.

18 And these went into Mikhah's house, and fetched the carved image, the ephod, and the teraphim, and the molten image. Then said the priest (kohen) unto them, "What do you?"

19 And they said unto him, "Hold your peace, lay your hand upon your mouth, and go with us, and be to us a father and a priest (kohen); is it better for you to be a priest (kohen) unto the house of one man, or that you be a priest (kohen) unto a tribe and a family in Yisrael?

20 And the priest (kohen)'s heart was glad, and he took the ephod, and the teraphim, and the graven image, and went in the midst of the people.

21 So they turned and departed, and put the little ones and the cattle and the carriage before them.

22 And when they were a good way from the house of Mikhah, the men that were in the houses near to Mikhah's house were gathered together, and overtook the children of Dan.

23 And they cried unto the children of Dan. And they turned their faces, and said unto Mikhah, "What aileth you, that you have gathered such a company?"

24 And he said, "You have taken away my gods (elohim) which I made, and the priest (kohen),

and you are gone away; and what have I more? And what is this that you say unto me, 'What aileth you?'"

25 And the children of Dan said unto him, "Let not your voice be heard among us, lest angry fellows run upon you, and you lose your life, with the lives of your household!"

26 And the children of Dan went their way; and when Mikhah saw that they were too strong for him, he turned and went back unto his house.

27 And they took the things which Mikhah had made, and the priest (kohen) which he had, and came unto Laish, unto a people that were at quiet and secure; and they smote them with the edge of the sword, and burnt the city with fire.

28 And there was no deliverer, because it was far from Zidon, and they had no business with any man; and it was in the valley that lieth by Beit-Rechov. And they built a city, and dwelt therein.

29 And they called the name of the city Dan, after the name of Dan their father, who was born unto Yisrael; howbeit the name of the city was Laish at the first.

30 And the children of Dan set up the graven image; and Jonathan (Yehonatan), the son of Gershom, the son of Menashsheh, he and his sons were priests (kohanim) to the tribe of Dan until the day of the captivity of the land.

31 And they set them up Mikhah's graven image, which he made, all the time that the house of God (Elohim) was in Shiloh.

19 And it came to pass in those days, when there was no king in Yisrael, that there was a certain Lewite sojourning on the side of mount Efrayim, who took to him a concubine out of Bethlehem (Beit-Lechem) in Judah (Yehudah).

2 And his concubine played the whore against him, and went away from him unto her father's house to Bethlehem (Beit-Lechem) in Judah (Yehudah), and was there four whole months.

3 And her husband arose, and went after her, to speak friendly unto her, and to bring her again, having his servant with him, and a couple of asses; and she brought him into her father's house; and when the father of the damsel saw him, he rejoiced to meet him.

4 And his father in law, the damsel's father, retained him; and he abode with him three days; so they did eat and drink, and lodged there.

5 And it came to pass on the fourth day, when they arose early in the morning, that he rose up to depart; and the damsel's father said unto his son in law, "Comfort your heart with a morsel of bread, and afterward go your way."

6 And they sat down, and did eat and drink both of them together; for the damsel's father had said unto the man, "Please be content and tarry all night, and let your heart be merry."

7 And when the man rose up to depart, his father in law urged him; therefore he lodged there again.

8 And he arose early in the morning on the fifth day to depart; and the damsel's father said, "Please comfort your heart". And they tarried until afternoon, and they did eat both of them.

9 And when the man rose up to depart, he, and his concubine, and his servant, his father in law, the damsel's father, said unto him, "Behold, now the day draweth toward evening, please tarry all night; behold, the day groweth to an end, lodge here, that your heart may be merry; and tomorrow get you early on your way, that you mayest go home."

10 But the man would not tarry that night, but he rose up and departed, and came opposite Yevus, which is Jerusalem (Yerushalayim); and there were with him two asses saddled, his concubine also was with him.

11 And when they were by Yevus, the day was far spent; and the servant said unto his master, "Please come and let us turn in into this city of the Yevusi, and lodge in it."

12 And his master said unto him, "We will not turn aside hither into the city of a stranger, that is not of the children of Yisrael; we will pass over to Gibeah."

13 And he said unto his servant, "Come, and let us draw near to one of these places to lodge all night, in Gibeah, or in Ramah."

14 And they passed on and went their way; and the sun went down upon them when they were by Gibeah, which belongeth to Binyamin.

15 And they turned aside thither, to go in and to lodge in Gibeah; and when he went in, he sat him down in a street of the city; for there was no man that took them into his house to lodging.

16 And, behold, there came an old man from his work out of the field at even, which was also of mount Efrayim; and he sojourned in Gibeah; but the men of the place were Benjamites

(Benyemini).

17 And when he had lifted up his eyes, he saw a wayfaring man in the street of the city: and the old man said, "Whither goest you? and whence comest you?"

18 And he said unto him, "We are passing from Bethlehem (Beit-Lechem) in Yehudah toward the side of Mount Efrayim; from thence am I. And I went to Bethlehem (Beit-Lechem) in Yehudah, but I am now going to the house of יהוה; and there is no man that receiveth me to house.

19 Yet there is both straw and provender for our asses; and there is bread and wine also for me, and for your handmaid, and for the young man who is with your servants; there is no want of any thing."

20 And the old man said, "Peace be with you; howsoever let all your wants lie upon me; only lodge not in the street."

21 So he brought him into his house, and gave provender unto the asses: and they washed their feet, and did eat and drink.

22 Now as they were making their hearts merry, behold, the men of the city, certain scoundrel (beliyaal) sons, beset the house round about, and beat at the door, and spake to the master of the house, the old man, saying, "Bring forth the man that came into your house, that we may know him."

23 And the man, the master of the house, went out unto them, and said unto them, "Nay, my brethren, nay, please do not so wickedly; seeing that this man is come into mine house, do not this folly.

24 Behold, here is my daughter a maiden, and his concubine; them I will bring out now, and humble you them, and do with them what seemeth good unto you; but unto this man do not so vile a thing."

25 But the men would not hearken to him; so the man took his concubine, and brought her forth unto them; and they knew her, and abused her all the night until the morning; and when the day began to spring, they let her go.

26 Then came the woman in the dawning of the day, and fell down at the door of the man's house where her lord (adon) was, till it was light.

27 And her lord (adon) rose up in the morning, and opened the doors of the house, and went out to go his way; and, behold, the woman his concubine was fallen down at the door of the house, and her hands were upon the threshold.

28 And he said unto her, "Up, and let us be going." But none answered. Then the man took her up upon an ass, and the man rose up, and gat him unto his place.

29 And when he was come into his house, he took a knife, and laid hold on his concubine, and divided her, together with her bones, into twelve pieces, and sent her into all the coasts of Yisrael.

30 And it was so, that all who saw it said, "There was no such deed done nor seen from the day that the children of Yisrael came up out of the land of Egypt (Mitsrayim) unto this day; consider of it, take advice, and speak your minds."

20 Then all the children of Yisrael went out, and the congregation was gathered together as one man, from Dan even to Beer-Sheva, with the land of Gilad, unto יהוה in Mizpeh.

2 And the chief of all the people, even of all the tribes of Yisrael, presented themselves in the assembly of the people of God (Elohim), four hundred thousand footmen that drew sword.

3 (Now the children of Binyamin heard that the children of Yisrael were gone up to Mizpeh.) Then said the children of Yisrael, "Tell us, how was this wickedness?"

4 And the Lewite, the husband of the woman that was slain, answered and said, "I came into Gibeah that belongeth to Binyamin, I and my concubine, to lodge.

5 And the men of Gibeah rose against me, and beset the house round about upon me by night, and thought to have slain me; and my concubine have they forced, that she is dead.

6 And I took my concubine, and cut her in pieces, and sent her throughout all the country of the inheritance of Yisrael; for they have committed lewdness and folly in Yisrael.

7 Behold, you are all children of Yisrael; give here your advice and counsel.

8 And all the people arose as one man, saying, "We will not any of us go to his tent, neither will we any of us turn into his house.

9 But now this shall be the thing which we will do to Gibeah; we will go up by lot against it;

10 And we will take ten men of a hundred throughout all the tribes of Yisrael, and a hundred of a thousand, and a thousand out of

ten thousand, to fetch victual for the people, that they may do, when they come to Gibeah of Binyamin, according to all the folly that they have wrought in Yisrael."

11 So all the men of Yisrael were gathered against the city, knit together as one man.

12 And the tribes of Yisrael sent men through all the tribe of Binyamin, saying, "What wickedness is this that is done among you?

13 Now therefore deliver us the men, the scoundrel (beliyaal) children, which are in Gibeah, that we may put them to death, and put away evil from Yisrael!" But the children of Binyamin would not hearken to the voice of their brethren the children of Yisrael.

14 But the children of Binyamin gathered themselves together out of the cities unto Gibeah, to go out to battle against the children of Yisrael.

15 And the children of Binyamin were numbered at that time out of the cities twenty and six thousand men that drew sword, besides the inhabitants of Gibeah, which were numbered seven hundred chosen men.

16 Among all this people there were seven hundred chosen men lefthanded; every one could sling stones at a hair breadth, and not miss.

17 And the men of Yisrael, beside Binyamin, were numbered four hundred thousand men that drew sword; all these were men of war.

18 And the children of Yisrael arose, and went up to the house of God (Elohim), and asked counsel of God (Elohim), and said, "Which of us shall go up first to the battle against the children of Binyamin?" And יהוה said, "Judah (Yehudah) shall go up first."

19 And the children of Yisrael rose up in the morning, and encamped against Gibeah.

20 And the men of Yisrael went out to battle against Binyamin; and the men of Yisrael put themselves in array to fight against them at Gibeah.

21 And the children of Binyamin came forth out of Gibeah, and destroyed down to the ground of the Yisraelis that day twenty and two thousand men.

22 And the people the men of Yisrael encouraged themselves, and set their battle again in array in the place where they put themselves in array the first day.

23 (And the children of Yisrael went up and wept before יהוה until even, and asked counsel of יהוה, saying, "Shall I go up again to battle against the children of Binyamin my brother?" And יהוה said, "Go up against him.")

24 And the children of Yisrael came near against the children of Binyamin the second day.

25 And Binyamin went forth against them out of Gibeah the second day, and destroyed down to the ground of the children of Yisrael again eighteen thousand men; all these drew the sword.

26 Then all the children of Yisrael, and all the people, went up, and came unto the house of God (Elohim), and wept, and sat there before יהוה, and fasted that day until even, and offered burnt offerings and peace offerings before יהוה.

27 And the children of Yisrael enquired of יהוה, (for the ark of the covenant of God (Elohim) was there in those days,

28 And Phinehas, the son of Eleazar, the son of Aaron (Aharon), stood before it in those days,) saying, "Shall I yet again go out to battle against the children of Binyamin my brother, or shall I cease?" And יהוה said, "Go up, for tomorrow I will deliver them into your hand."

29 And Yisrael set liers in wait round about Gibeah.

30 And the children of Yisrael went up against the children of Binyamin on the third day, and put themselves in array against Gibeah, as at other times.

31 And the children of Benjamin (Binyamin) went out against the people, and were drawn away from the city; and they began to smite of the people, and kill, as at other times, in the highways, of which one goeth up to the house of God (Elohim), and the other to Gibeah in the field, about thirty men of Yisrael.

32 And the children of Benjamin (Binyamin) said, "They are smitten down before us, as at the first." But the children of Yisrael said, "Let us flee, and draw them from the city unto the highways."

33 And all the men of Yisrael rose up out of their place, and put themselves in array at Baaltamar; and the liers in wait of Yisrael came forth out of their places, even out of the meadows of Gibeah.

34 And there came against Gibeah ten thousand chosen men out of all Yisrael, and the battle was sore; but they knew not that evil was near them.

35 And יהוה smote Benjamin (Binyamin) before Yisrael; and the children of Yisrael destroyed of the Benjamites (Ben-yemini) that day twenty and five thousand and a hundred men: all these drew the sword.

36 So the children of Benjamin (Binyamin) saw that they were smitten; for the men of Yisrael gave place to the Benjamites (Ben-yemini), because they trusted unto the liers in wait which they had set beside Gibeah.

37 And the liers in wait hasted, and rushed upon Gibeah; and the liers in wait drew themselves along, and smote all the city with the edge of the sword.

38 Now there was an appointed sign between the men of Yisrael and the liers in wait, that they should make a great flame with smoke rise up out of the city.

39 And when the men of Yisrael retired in the battle, Benjamin (Binyamin) began to smite and kill of the men of Yisrael about thirty persons; for they said, "Surely they are smitten down before us, as in the first battle."

40 But when the flame began to arise up out of the city with a pillar of smoke, the Benjamites (Benyemini) looked behind them, and, behold, the flame of the city ascended up to heaven.

41 And when the men of Yisrael turned again, the men of Benjamin (Binyamin) were amazed; for they saw that disaster (raah) was come upon them.

42 Therefore they turned their backs before the men of Yisrael unto the way of the wilderness; but the battle overtook them; and them which came out of the cities they destroyed in the midst of them.

43 Thus they inclosed the Benjamites (Benyemini) round about, and chased them, and trode them down with ease opposite Gibeah toward the sunrising.

44 And there fell of Benjamin (Binyamin) eighteen thousand men; all these were men of valour.

45 And they turned and fled toward the wilderness unto the rock of Rimmon; and they gleaned of them in the highways five thousand men; and pursued hard after them unto Gidom, and slew two thousand men of them.

46 So that all which fell that day of Benjamin (Binyamin) were twenty and five thousand men that drew the sword; all these were men of valour.

47 But six hundred men turned and fled to the wilderness unto the rock Rimmon, and abode in the rock Rimmon four months.

48 And the men of Yisrael turned again upon the children of Benjamin (Binyamin), and smote them with the edge of the sword, as well the men of every city, as the beast, and all that came to hand; also they set on fire all the cities that they came to.

21 Now the men of Yisrael had sworn in Mizpeh, saying, "There shall not any of us give his daughter unto Benjamin (Binyamin) as wife."

2 And the people came to the house of God (Elohim), and abode there till even before God (Elohim), and lifted up their voices, and wept sore;

3 And said, "O יהוה God of Israel (Elohei Yisrael), why is this come to pass in Yisrael, that there should be today one tribe lacking in Yisrael?"

4 And it came to pass on the next day, that the people rose early, and built there an altar, and offered burnt offerings and peace offerings.

5 And the children of Yisrael said, "Who is there among all the tribes of Yisrael that came not up with the congregation unto יהוה?" For they had made a great oath concerning him that came not up to יהוה to Mizpeh, saying, "He shall surely be put to death."

6 And the children of Yisrael repented them for Benjamin (Binyamin) their brother, and said, "There is one tribe cut off from Yisrael this day."

7 How shall we do for wives for them that remain, seeing we have sworn by יהוה that we will not give them of our daughters as wives?"

8 And they said, "What one is there of the tribes of Yisrael that came not up to Mizpeh to יהוה?" And, behold, there came none to the camp from Yavesh-Gilad to the assembly.

9 For the people were numbered, and, behold, there were none of the inhabitants of Yavesh-Gilad there.

10 And the congregation sent thither twelve thousand men of the valiantest, and commanded them, saying, "Go and smite the inhabitants of Yavesh-Gilad with the edge of the sword, with the women and the children.

11 And this is the thing that you shall do: You

shall utterly destroy every male, and every woman that hath lain by man."

12 And they found among the inhabitants of Yavesh-Gilad four hundred young virgins, that had known no man by lying with any male; and they brought them unto the camp to Shiloh, which is in the land of Canaan.

13 And the whole congregation sent some to speak to the children of Benjamin (Binyamin) that were in the rock Rimmon, and to call peaceably unto them.

14 And Benjamin (Binyamin) came again at that time; and they gave them wives which they had saved alive of the women of Yavesh-Gilad; and yet so they sufficed them not.

15 And the people repented them for Benjamin (Binyamin), because that יהוה had made a breach in the tribes of Yisrael.

16 Then the elders of the congregation said, "How shall we do for wives for them that remain, seeing the women are destroyed out of Benjamin (Binyamin)?"

17 And they said, "There must be an inheritance for them that be escaped of Benjamin (Binyamin), that a tribe be not destroyed out of Yisrael.

18 Howbeit we may not give them wives of our daughters; for the children of Yisrael have sworn, saying, 'Cursed be he that giveth a wife to Benjamin (Binyamin).'"

19 Then they said, "Behold, there is a Feast of יהוה in Shiloh yearly in a place which is on the north side of Bethel (Beit-El), on the east side of the highway that goeth up from Bethel (Beit-El) to Shechem, and on the south of Lebonah."

20 Therefore they commanded the children of Benjamin (Binyamin), saying, "Go and lie in wait in the vineyards;

21 And see, and, behold, if the daughters of Shiloh come out to dance in dances, then come you out of the vineyards, and catch you every man his wife of the daughters of Shiloh, and go to the land of Benjamin (Binyamin).

22 And it shall be, when their fathers or their brethren come unto us to complain, that we will say unto them, 'Be favorable unto them for our sakes, because we reserved not to each man his wife in the war; for you did not give unto them at this time, that you should be guilty.'"

23 And the children of Benjamin (Binyamin) did so, and took them wives, according to their number, of them that danced, whom they caught; and they went and returned unto their inheritance, and repaired the cities, and dwelt in them.

24 And the children of Yisrael departed thence at that time, every man to his tribe and to his family, and they went out from thence every man to his inheritance.

25 In those days there was no king in Yisrael; every man did that which was right in his own eyes.

RUTH
רוּת RUT
(Friend)

1 Now it came to pass in the days when the judges ruled, that there was a famine in the land. And a certain man of Bethlehem (Beit-Lechem) in Yehudah went to sojourn in the country of Moav, he, and his wife, and his two sons.

2 And the name of the man was Elimelech, and the name of his wife Naomi, and the name of his two sons Mahlon and Chilion, Ephrathites of Bethlehem (Beit-Lechem) in Yehudah. And they came into the country of Moav, and continued there.

3 And Elimelech Naomi's husband died; and she was left, and her two sons.

4 And they took them wives of the women of Moav; the name of the one was Orpah, and the name of the other Ruth; and they dwelled there about ten years.

5 And Mahlon and Chilion died also both of them; and the woman was left of her two sons and her husband.

6 Then she arose with her daughters in law, that she might return from the country of Moav; for she had heard in the country of Moav how that יהוה had visited His people in giving them bread.

7 Wherefore she went forth out of the place where she was, and her two daughters in law with her; and they went on the way to return unto the land of Judah (Yehudah).

8 And Naomi said unto her two daughters in law, "Go, return each to her mother's house. יהוה deal kindly with you, as you have dealt with the dead, and with me.

9 יהוה grant you that you may find rest, each of you in the house of her husband. Then she kissed them; and they lifted up their voice, and wept.

10 And they said unto her, "Surely we will return with you unto your people."

11 And Naomi said, "Turn back, my daughters; why will you go with me? Are there yet any more sons in my womb, that they may be your husbands?

12 Turn back, my daughters, go your way; for I am too old to have a husband. If I should say,

I have hope, if I should have a husband also tonight, and should also bear sons;

13 Would you tarry for them till they were grown? Would you stay for them from having husbands? Nay, my daughters; for it grieveth me much for your sakes that the hand of יהוה is gone out against me!"

14 And they lifted up their voice, and wept again; and Orpah kissed her mother in law; but Ruth clave unto her.

15 And she said, "Behold, your sister in law is gone back unto her people, and unto her gods (elohim); return you after your sister in law."

16 And Ruth said: "Intreat me not to leave you, or to return from following after you; for whither you goest, I will go; and where you lodgest, I will lodge; your people shall be my people, and your God (Elohim) my God (Elohim).

17 Where you diest, will I die, and there will I be buried; יהוה do so to me, and more also, if ought but death part you and me."

18 When she saw that she was stedfastly minded to go with her, then she left speaking unto her.

19 So they two went until they came to Bethlehem (Beit-Lechem). And it came to pass, when they were come to Bethlehem (Beit-Lechem), that all the city was moved about them, and they said, "Is this Naomi?"

20 And she said unto them, "Call me not Naomi (my delight), call me Mara (bitterness), for Almighty hath dealt very bitterly with me.

21 I went out full, and יהוה hath brought me home again empty; why then call you me Naomi, seeing יהוה hath testified against me, and Almighty hath afflicted me?"

22 So Naomi returned, and Ruth the Moavitess, her daughter in law, with her, which returned out of the country of Moav; and they came to Bethlehem (Beit-Lechem) in the beginning of barley harvest.

2 And Naomi had a kinsman of her husband's, a mighty man of wealth, of the family of Elimelech; and his name was Boaz.

2 And Ruth the Moavitess said unto Naomi, "Let me now go to the field, and glean ears of corn after him in whose sight I shall find grace." And she said unto her, "Go, my daughter."

3 And she went, and came, and gleaned in the field after the reapers; and her hap was to light on a part of the field belonging unto Boaz, who was of the kindred of Elimelech.

4 And, behold, Boaz came from Bethlehem (Beit-Lechem), and said unto the reapers, "יהוה be with you." And they answered him, "יהוה bless you."

5 Then said Boaz unto his servant that was set over the reapers, "Whose damsel is this?"

6 And the servant that was set over the reapers answered and said, "It is the Moavitish damsel that came back with Naomi out of the country of Moav.

7 And she said, 'Please let me glean and gather after the reapers among the sheaves.' So she came, and hath continued even from the morning until now, that she tarried a little in the house."

8 Then said Boaz unto Ruth, "Hearest you not, my daughter? Go not to glean in another field, neither go from hence, but abide here fast by my maidens.

9 Let your eyes be on the field that they do reap, and go you after them; have I not charged the young men that they shall not touch you? And when you are athirst, go unto the vessels, and drink of that which the young men have drawn."

10 Then she fell on her face, and bowed herself to the ground, and said unto him, "Why have I found grace in your eyes, that you shouldest take knowledge of me, seeing I am a stranger?"

11 And Boaz answered and said unto her, "It hath fully been shewed me, all that you have done unto your mother in law since the death of your husband; and how you have left your father and your mother, and the land of your nativity, and art come unto a people whom you knewest not before.

12 יהוה recompense your work, and a full reward be given you of יהוה God of Israel (Elohei Yisrael), under whose wings you are come to seek refuge."

13 Then she said, "Let me find favor in your sight, my lord (adoni); for that you have comforted me, and for that you have spoken friendly unto your handmaid, though I be not like unto one of your handmaidens."

14 And Boaz said unto her, "At mealtime come you hither, and eat of the bread, and dip your morsel in the vinegar." And she sat beside the reapers; and he reached her parched corn, and she did eat, and was sufficed, and left.

15 And when she was risen up to glean, Boaz commanded his young men, saying, "Let her glean even among the sheaves, and reproach her not.

16 And let fall also some of the handfuls of purpose for her, and leave them, that she may glean them, and rebuke her not."

17 So she gleaned in the field until even, and beat out that she had gleaned; and it was about an ephah of barley.

18 And she took it up, and went into the city; and her mother in law saw what she had gleaned; and she brought forth, and gave to her that she had reserved after she was sufficed.

19 And her mother in law said unto her, "Where have you gleaned today? and where wroughtest you? Blessed be he that did take knowledge of you." And she shewed her mother in law with whom she had wrought, and said, "The man's name with whom I wrought today is Boaz."

20 And Naomi said unto her daughter in law, "Blessed be he of יהוה, who hath not left off his kindness to the living and to the dead." And Naomi said unto her, "The man is near of kin unto us, one of our next kinsmen."

21 And Ruth the Moavitess said, "He said unto me also, 'You shalt keep fast by my young men, until they have ended all my harvest.'"

22 And Naomi said unto Ruth her daughter in law, "It is good, my daughter, that you go out with his maidens, that they meet you not in any other field."

23 So she kept fast by the maidens of Boaz to glean unto the end of barley harvest and of wheat harvest; and dwelt with her mother in law.

3 Then Naomi her mother in law said unto her, "My daughter, shall I not seek rest for you, that it may be well with you?

2 And now is not Boaz of our kindred, with whose maidens you wast? Behold, he winnoweth barley tonight in the threshingfloor.

3 Wash yourself therefore, and anoint you, and put your raiment upon you, and get you down to the floor: but make not yourself known unto the man, until he shall have done eating and drinking.

4 And it shall be, when he lieth down, that you shalt mark the place where he shall lie, and you shalt go in, and uncover his feet, and lay you down; and he will tell you what you shalt do."

5 And she said unto her, "All that you sayest unto me I will do."

6 And she went down unto the floor, and did

according to all that her mother in law bade her.

7 And when Boaz had eaten and drunk, and his heart was merry, he went to lie down at the end of the heap of corn; and she came softly, and uncovered his feet, and laid her down.

8 And it came to pass at midnight, that the man was afraid, and turned himself; and, behold, a woman lay at his feet.

9 And he said, "Who are you?" And she answered, "I am Ruth your handmaid; spread therefore your skirt over your handmaid; for you are a near kinsman."

10 And he said, "Blessed be you of יהוה, my daughter; for you have shewed more kindness in the latter end than at the beginning, inasmuch as you followedst not young men, whether poor or rich.

11 And now, my daughter, fear not; I will do to you all that you require; for all the city of my people doth know that you are a virtuous woman.

12 And now it is true that I am your near kinsman; howbeit there is a kinsman nearer than I.

13 Tarry this night, and it shall be in the morning, that if he will perform unto you the part of a kinsman, well; let him do the kinsman's part; but if he will not do the part of a kinsman to you, then will I do the part of a kinsman to you, as יהוה liveth! Lie down until the morning."

14 And she lay at his feet until the morning: and she rose up before one could know another. And he said, "Let it not be known that a woman came into the floor."

15 Also he said, "Bring the vail that you have upon you, and hold it." And when she held it, he measured six measures of barley, and laid it on her; and she went into the city.

16 And when she came to her mother in law, she said, "Who are you, my daughter?" And she told her all that the man had done to her.

17 And she said, "These six measures of barley gave he me; for he said to me, 'Go not empty unto your mother in law.'"

18 Then said she, "Sit still, my daughter, until you know how the matter will fall; for the man will not be in rest, until he has finished the thing this day."

4 Then went Boaz up to the gate, and sat him down there; and, behold, the kinsman of whom Boaz spake came by; unto whom he said,

"Ho, such a one! 'Turn aside, sit down here.'" And he turned aside, and sat down.

2 And he took ten men of the elders of the city, and said, "Sit you down here." And they sat down.

3 And he said unto the kinsman, "Naomi, who has come back out of the country of Moav, selleth a parcel of land, which was our brother Elimelech's.

4 And I thought to advertise you, saying, 'Buy it before the inhabitants, and before the elders of my people. If you wilt redeem it, redeem it; but if you wilt not redeem it, then tell me, that I may know; for there is none to redeem it besides you; and I am after you.'" And he said, "I will redeem it."

5 Then said Boaz, "What day you buyest the field of the hand of Naomi, you must buy it also of Ruth the Moavitess, the wife of the dead, to raise up the name of the dead upon his inheritance."

6 And the kinsman said, "I cannot redeem it for myself, lest I mar mine own inheritance; redeem you my right to yourself; for I cannot redeem it."

7 Now this was the manner in former time in Yisrael concerning redeeming and concerning changing, for to confirm all things; a man plucked off his shoe, and gave it to his neighbor; and this was a testimony in Yisrael.

8 Therefore the kinsman said unto Boaz, "Buy it for you." So he drew off his shoe.

9 And Boaz said unto the elders, and unto all the people, "You are witnesses this day, that I have bought all that was Elimelech's, and all that was Chilion's and Mahlon's, of the hand of Naomi.

10 Moreover Ruth the Moavitess, the wife of Mahlon, have I purchased to be my wife, to raise up the name of the dead upon his inheritance, that the name of the dead be not cut off from among his brethren, and from the gate of his place; you are witnesses this day."

11 And all the people that were in the gate, and the elders, said, "We are witnesses. יהוה make the woman that is come into your house like Rachel and like Leah, which two did build the house of Yisrael; and do you worthily in Ephratah, and be famous in Bethlehem (Beit-Lechem).

12 And let your house be like the house of Pharez, whom Tamar bare unto Judah

(Yehudah), of the seed which יהוה shall give you of this young woman."

13 So Boaz took Ruth, and she was his wife; and when he went in unto her, יהוה gave her conception, and she bare a son.

14 And the women said unto Naomi, "Blessed be יהוה, which hath not left you this day without a kinsman, that his name may be famous in Yisrael!

15 And he shall be unto you a restorer of your life, and a nourisher of your old age; for your daughter in law, which loveth you, which is better to you than seven sons, hath born him."

16 And Naomi took the child, and laid it in her bosom, and became nurse unto it.

17 And the women her neighbours gave it a name, saying, "There is a son born to Naomi." And they called his name Oved. He is the father of [A34]Jesse (Yishai), the father of Dawid.

18 Now these are the generations of Pharez: Pharez begat Hezron,

19 And Hezron begat Ram, and Ram begat Amminadab,

20 And Amminadab begat Nahshon, and Nahshon begat Salmon,

21 And Salmon begat Boaz, and Boaz begat Oved,

22 And Oved begat Jesse (Yishai), and Jesse (Yishai) begat [A35]Dawid.

1 SAMUEL
SHEMUEL 1 שְׁמוּאֵל א
(El has Heard)

1 Now there was a certain man of Ramathaimzophim, of Mount Efrayim, and his name was Elkanah, the son of Yerocham, the son of Elihu, the son of Tohu, the son of Zuph, an Ephrathite.

2 And he had two wives; the name of the one was Hannah, and the name of the other Peninnah; and Peninnah had children, but Hannah had no children.

3 And this man went up out of his city yearly to worship and to sacrifice unto [A8a]יהוה of hosts (YHWH Tsevaot) in Shiloh. And the two sons of Eli, Hophni and Phinehas, the priests (kohanim) of יהוה, were there.

4 And when the time was that Elkanah offered, he gave to Peninnah his wife, and to all her sons and her daughters, portions.

5 But unto Hannah he gave a worthy portion; for he loved Hannah; but יהוה had shut up her womb.

6 And her adversary also provoked her sore, for to make her fret, because יהוה had shut up her womb.

7 And as he did so year by year, when she went up to the house of יהוה, so she provoked her; therefore she wept, and did not eat.

8 Then said Elkanah her husband to her, "Hannah, why weepest you? And why eatest you not? And why is your heart grieved? Am not I better to you than ten sons?"

9 So Hannah rose up after they had eaten in Shiloh, and after they had drunk. Now Eli the priest (kohen) sat upon a seat by a post of the temple of יהוה.

10 And she was in bitterness of soul, and prayed unto יהוה, and wept sore.

11 And she vowed a vow, and said, "O יהוה of hosts (YHWH Tsevaot), if You wilt indeed look on the affliction of Your handmaid, and remember me, and not forget Your handmaid, but wilt give unto Your handmaid a man child, then I will give him unto יהוה all the days of his life, and there shall no razor come upon his head."

12 And it came to pass, as she continued praying before יהוה, that Eli marked her mouth.

13 Now Hannah, she spake in her heart; only her lips moved, but her voice was not heard; therefore Eli thought she had been drunken.

14 And Eli said unto her, "How long wilt you be drunken? Put away your wine from you."

15 And Hannah answered and said, "No, my lord (adoni), I am a woman of a sorrowful spirit. I have drunk neither wine nor strong drink, but have poured out my soul before יהוה.

16 Count not your handmaid for a scoundrel (beliyaal) daughter; for out of the abundance of my complaint and grief have I spoken until now."

17 Then Eli answered and said, "Go in peace; and the God of Israel (Elohei Yisrael) grant you your petition that you have asked of Him."

18 And she said, "Let your handmaid find grace in your sight." So the woman went her way, and did eat, and her countenance was no more sad.

19 And they rose up in the morning early, and worshipped before יהוה, and returned, and came to their house to Ramah; and Elkanah knew Hannah his wife; and יהוה remembered her.

20 Wherefore it came to pass, when the time was come about after Hannah had conceived, that she bare a son, and called his name [A36]Samuel (Shemuel), saying, "Because I have asked him of יהוה."

21 And the man Elkanah, and all his house, went up to offer unto יהוה the yearly sacrifice, and his vow.

22 But Hannah went not up; for she said unto her husband, "I will not go up until the child be weaned, and then I will bring him, that he may appear before יהוה, and there abide forever."

23 And Elkanah her husband said unto her, "Do what seemeth you good; tarry until you have weaned him; only יהוה establish His word." So the woman abode, and gave her son suck until she weaned him.

24 And when she had weaned him, she took him up with her, with three bullocks, and one ephah of flour, and a bottle of wine, and brought him unto the house of יהוה in Shiloh; and the child was young.

25 And they slew a bullock, and brought the child to Eli.

26 And she said, "Oh my lord (adoni), as your soul liveth, my lord (adoni), I am the woman that stood by you here, praying unto יהוה.

27 For this child I prayed; and יהוה hath given

me my petition which I asked of Him.

28 Therefore also I have lent him to יהוה; as long as he liveth he shall be lent to יהוה." And he worshipped יהוה there.

2 And Hannah prayed, and said, "My heart rejoiceth in יהוה, mine horn is exalted in יהוה; my mouth is enlarged over mine enemies; because I rejoice in Your salvation.

2 There is none holy as יהוה, for there is none besides You; nor is there any Rock like our God (Elohim).

3 Talk no more so exceeding proudly; let not arrogancy come out of your mouth, for יהוה is a God (Elohim) of knowledge, and by Him actions are weighed.

4 The bows of the mighty men are broken, and they that stumbled are girded with strength.

5 They that were full have hired out themselves for bread; and they that were hungry ceased; so that the barren hath born seven; and she that hath many children are waxed feeble.

6 יהוה killeth, and maketh alive; He bringeth down to the [B32]grave (sheol), and bringeth up.

7 יהוה maketh poor, and maketh rich; He bringeth low, and lifteth up.

8 He raiseth up the poor out of the dust, and lifteth up the beggar from the dunghill, to set them among princes, and to make them inherit the throne of glory; for the pillars of the earth are יהוה's, and He hath set the world upon them.

9 He will keep the feet of His [B31b]faithful ones (chasidim), and the wicked shall be silent in darkness; for by strength shall no man prevail.

10 The adversaries of יהוה shall be broken to pieces; out of heaven shall He thunder upon them; יהוה shall judge the ends of the earth; and He shall give strength unto His king, and exalt the horn of His anointed (mashiach)."

11 And Elkanah went to Ramah to his house. And the child did minister unto יהוה before Eli the priest (kohen).

12 Now the sons of Eli were scoundrel sons (beliyaal); they knew not יהוה.

13 And the priests' (kohanim) custom with the people was, that, when any man offered sacrifice, the priest (kohen)'s servant came, while the flesh was in seething, with a fleshhook of three teeth in his hand;

14 And he struck it into the pan, or kettle, or caldron, or pot; all that the fleshhook brought up the priest (kohen) took for himself. So they did in Shiloh unto all the Yisraelites that came thither.

15 Also before they burnt the fat, the priest (kohen)'s servant came, and said to the man that sacrificed, "Give flesh to roast for the priest (kohen); for he will not have sodden flesh of you, but raw."

16 And if any man said unto him, "Let them not fail to burn the fat presently, and then take as much as your soul desireth;" then he would answer him, "Nay, but you shalt give it me now; and if not, I will take it by force."

17 Wherefore the sin of the young men was very great before יהוה; for men abhorred the offering of יהוה.

18 But Shemuel ministered before יהוה, being a child, girded with a linen ephod.

19 Moreover his mother made him a little coat, and brought it to him from year to year, when she came up with her husband to offer the yearly sacrifice.

20 And Eli blessed Elkanah and his wife, and said, "יהוה give you seed of this woman for the loan which is lent to יהוה." And they went unto their own home.

21 And יהוה visited Hannah, so that she conceived, and bare three sons and two daughters. And the child Shemuel grew before יהוה.

22 Now Eli was very old, and heard all that his sons did unto all Yisrael; and how they lay with the women that assembled at the door of the tabernacle of the congregation.

23 And he said unto them, "Why do you such things? For I hear of your evil dealings by all this people.

24 Nay, my sons; for it is no good report that I hear; you make יהוה's people to transgress.

25 If one man sins against another, the judge shall judge him; but if a man sins against יהוה, who shall intreat for him?" Notwithstanding they hearkened not unto the voice of their father, because יהוה would slay them.

26 And the child Shemuel grew on, and was in favor both with יהוה, and also with men.

27 And there came a man of God (Elohim) unto Eli, and said unto him, "Thus saith יהוה: 'Did I plainly appear unto the house of your father, when they were in Egypt (Mitsrayim) in Pharaoh (Paroh)'s house?

28 And did I choose him out of all the tribes of

Yisrael to be My priest (kohen), to offer upon Mine altar, to burn incense, to wear an ephod before Me? And did I give unto the house of your father all the offerings made by fire of the children of Yisrael?

29 Wherefore kick you at My sacrifice and at Mine offering, which I have commanded in My habitation; and honourest your sons above Me, to make yourselves fat with the chiefest of all the offerings of Yisrael My people?'

30 Wherefore יהוה God of Israel (Elohei Yisrael) saith: 'I said indeed that your house, and the house of your father, should walk before Me forever'; but now יהוה saith: 'Be it far from Me; for them that honor Me I will honor, and they that despise Me shall be lightly esteemed.

31 Behold, the days come, that I will cut off your arm, and the arm of your father's house, that there shall not be an old man in your house.

32 And you shalt see an enemy in My habitation, in all the wealth which God (Elohim) shall give Yisrael; and there shall not be an old man in your house forever.

33 And the man of yours, whom I shall not cut off from Mine altar, shall be to consume your eyes, and to grieve your heart; and all the increase of your house shall die in the flower of their age.

34 And this shall be a sign unto you, that shall come upon your two sons, on Hophni and Phinehas; in one day they shall die both of them.

35 And I will raise Me up a faithful priest (kohen), that shall do according to that which is in Mine heart and in My mind: and I will build him a sure house; and he shall walk before Mine anointed forever.

36 And it shall come to pass, that every one that is left in your house shall come and crouch to him for a piece of silver and a morsel of bread, and shall say, "Please put me into one of the priests' offices (kehunnah), that I may eat a piece of bread."'"

3 And the child Shemuel ministered unto יהוה before Eli. And the word of יהוה was precious in those days; there was no open vision (chazon).

2 And it came to pass at that time, when Eli was laid down in his place, and his eyes began to wax dim, that he could not see;

3 And ere the lamp of God (Elohim) went out in the temple of יהוה, where the ark of God (Elohim) was, and Shemuel was laid down to sleep;

4 That יהוה called Shemuel; and he answered, "Here am I."

5 And he ran unto Eli, and said, "Here am I; for you calledst me." And he said, "I called not; lie down again." And he went and lay down.

6 And יהוה called yet again, "Shemuel!" And Shemuel arose and went to Eli, and said, "Here am I; for you didst call me." And he answered, "I called not, my son; lie down again."

7 Now Shemuel did not yet know יהוה, nor was the word of יהוה yet revealed unto him.

8 And יהוה called Shemuel again the third time. And he arose and went to Eli, and said, "Here am I; for you didst call me." And Eli perceived that יהוה had called the child.

9 Therefore Eli said unto Shemuel, "Go, lie down; and it shall be, if He call you, that you shalt say, 'Speak, יהוה; for Your servant heareth.'" So Shemuel went and lay down in his place.

10 And יהוה came, and stood, and called as at other times, "Shemuel! Shemuel!" Then Shemuel answered, "Speak, for Your servant heareth."

11 And יהוה said to Shemuel, "Behold, I will do a thing in Yisrael, at which both the ears of every one that heareth it shall tingle.

12 In that day I will perform against Eli all things which I have spoken concerning his house; when I begin, I will also make an end.

13 For I have told him that I will judge his house forever for the iniquity which he knoweth; because his sons made themselves vile, and he restrained them not.

14 And therefore I have sworn unto the house of Eli, that the iniquity of Eli's house shall not be purged with sacrifice nor offering forever."

15 And Shemuel lay until the morning, and opened the doors of the house of יהוה. And Shemuel feared to shew Eli the vision.

16 Then Eli called Shemuel, and said, "Shemuel, my son!" And he answered, "Here am I."

17 And he said, "What is the thing that יהוה hath said unto you? Please hide it not from me. God (Elohim) do so to you, and more also, if you hide any thing from me of all the things that He said unto you."

18 And Shemuel told him everything, and hid nothing from him. And he said, "It is יהוה; let Him do what seemeth Him good."

19 And Shemuel grew, and יהוה was with him, and did let none of His words fall to the ground.
20 And all Yisrael from Dan even to Beer-Sheva knew that Shemuel was established to be a prophet of יהוה.
21 And יהוה appeared again in Shiloh; for יהוה revealed Himself to Shemuel in Shiloh by the word of יהוה.

4 And the word of Shemuel came to all Yisrael. Now Yisrael went out against the Philistines to battle, and pitched beside Ebenezer; and the Philistines pitched in Aphek.
2 And the Philistines put themselves in array against Yisrael; and when they joined battle, Yisrael was smitten before the Philistines; and they slew of the army in the field about four thousand men.
3 And when the people were come into the camp, the elders of Yisrael said, "Why hath יהוה smitten us today before the Philistines? Let us fetch the ark of the covenant of יהוה out of Shiloh unto us, that, when it cometh among us, it may save us out of the hand of our enemies."
4 So the people sent to Shiloh, that they might bring from thence the ark of the covenant of יהוה of hosts (YHWH Tsevaot), who dwelleth between the cherubims (keruvim); and the two sons of Eli, Hophni and Phinehas, were there with the ark of the covenant of God (Elohim).
5 And when the ark of the covenant of יהוה came into the camp, all Yisrael shouted with a great shout, so that the earth rang again.
6 And when the Philistines heard the noise of the shout, they said, "What meaneth the noise of this great shout in the camp of the Hebrews (Ivrim)? And they understood that the ark of יהוה was come into the camp.
7 And the Philistines were afraid, for they said, "God (Elohim) has come into the camp." And they said, "Woe unto us! For there hath not been such a thing happened before.
8 Woe unto us! Who shall deliver us out of the hand of these great gods (elohim)? These are the gods (elohim) that smote the Egyptians (Mitsrayim) with all the plagues in the wilderness.
9 Be strong, and behave yourselves like men, O you Philistines, that you be not servants unto the Hebrews (Ivrim), as they have been to you; behave yourselves like men, and fight!"
10 And the Philistines fought, and Yisrael was smitten, and they fled every man into his tent; and there was a very great slaughter; for there fell of Yisrael thirty thousand footmen.
11 And the ark of God (Elohim) was taken; and the two sons of Eli, Hophni and Phinehas, were slain.
12 And there ran a man of Benjamin (Binyamin) out of the army, and came to Shiloh the same day with his clothes rent, and with earth upon his head.
13 And when he came, behold, Eli sat upon a seat by the wayside watching; for his heart trembled for the ark of God (Elohim). And when the man came into the city, and told it, all the city cried out.
14 And when Eli heard the noise of the crying, he said, "What meaneth the noise of this tumult?" And the man came in hastily, and told Eli.
15 Now Eli was ninety and eight years old; and his eyes were dim, that he could not see.
16 And the man said unto Eli, "I am he that came out of the army, and I fled today out of the army." And he said, "How did things go, my son?"
17 And the messenger answered and said, "Yisrael has fled before the Philistines, and there hath been also a great slaughter among the people, and your two sons also, Hophni and Phinehas, are dead, and the ark of God (Elohim) is taken."
18 And it came to pass, when he made mention of the ark of God (Elohim), that he fell from off the seat backward by the side of the gate, and his neck broke, and he died; for he was an old man, and heavy. And he had judged Yisrael forty years.
19 And his daughter in law, Phinehas's wife, was with child, near to be delivered: and when she heard the tidings that the ark of God (Elohim) was taken, and that her father in law and her husband were dead, she bowed herself and travailed; for her pains came upon her.
20 And about the time of her death the women that stood by her said unto her, "Fear not; for you have born a son." But she answered not, nor did she regard it.
21 And she named the child Ichabod, saying, "The glory has departed from Yisrael, because the ark of God (Elohim) was taken, and because of her father in law and her husband."
22 And she said, "The glory has departed from

Yisrael; for the ark of God (Elohim) was taken."

5 And the Philistines took the ark of God (Elohim), and brought it from Ebenezer unto Ashdod.

2 When the Philistines took the ark of God (Elohim), they brought it into the house of Dagon, and set it by Dagon.

3 And when they of Ashdod arose early on the next day, behold, Dagon was fallen upon his face to the earth before the ark of יהוה. And they took Dagon, and set him in his place again.

4 And when they arose early on the next day morning, behold, Dagon was fallen upon his face to the ground before the ark of יהוה; and the head of Dagon and both the palms of his hands were cut off upon the threshold; only the stump of Dagon was left to him.

5 Therefore neither the priests (kohanim) of Dagon, nor any that come into Dagon's house, tread on the threshold of Dagon in Ashdod unto this day.

6 But the hand of יהוה was heavy upon them of Ashdod, and He destroyed them, and smote them with emerods, even Ashdod and the coasts thereof.

7 And when the men of Ashdod saw that it was so, they said, "The ark of the God of Israel (Elohei Yisrael) shall not abide with us; for His hand is sore upon us, and upon Dagon our god (eloheinu).

8 They sent therefore and gathered all the lords (seranim) of the Philistines unto them, and said, "What shall we do with the ark of the God of Israel (Elohei Yisrael)?" And they answered, "Let the ark of the God of Israel (Elohei Yisrael) be carried about unto Gath." And they carried the ark of the God of Israel (Elohei Yisrael) about thither.

9 And it was so, that, after they had carried it about, the hand of יהוה was against the city with a very great destruction; and He smote the men of the city, both small and great, and they had emerods in their secret parts.

10 Therefore they sent the ark of God (Elohim) to Ekron. And it came to pass, as the ark of God (Elohim) came to Ekron, that the Ekronites cried out, saying, "They have brought about the ark of the God of Israel (Elohei Yisrael) to us, to slay us and our people."

11 So they sent and gathered together all the lords (seranim) of the Philistines, and said,

"Send away the ark of the God of Israel (Elohei Yisrael), and let it go again to its own place, that it slays us not, and our people." For there was a deadly destruction throughout all the city; the hand of God (Elohim) was very heavy there.

12 And the men that died not were smitten with the emerods; and the cry of the city went up to heaven.

6 And the ark of יהוה was in the country of the Philistines seven months.

2 And the Philistines called for the priests (kohanim) and the diviners, saying, "What shall we do to the ark of יהוה? Tell us wherewith we shall send it to its place."

3 And they said, "If you send away the ark of the God of Israel (Elohei Yisrael), send it not empty; but in any wise return Him a trespass offering; then you shall be healed, and it shall be known to you why His hand is not removed from you."

4 Then said they, "What shall be the trespass offering which we shall return to Him?" They answered, "Five golden emerods, and five golden mice, according to the number of the lords (seranim) of the Philistines; for one plague was on you all, and on your lords (seranim).

5 Wherefore you shall make images of your emerods, and images of your mice that mar the land; and you shall give glory unto the God of Israel (Elohei Yisrael); peradventure He will lighten His hand from off you, and from off your gods (elohim), and from off your land.

6 Wherefore then do you harden your hearts, as the Egyptians (Mitsrayim) and Pharaoh (Paroh) hardened their hearts? When He had wrought wonderfully among them, did they not let the people go, and they departed?

7 Now therefore make a new cart, and take two milch kine, on which there hath come no yoke, and tie the kine to the cart, and bring their calves home from them.

8 And take the ark of יהוה, and lay it upon the cart; and put the jewels of gold, which you return Him for a trespass offering, in a coffer by the side thereof; and send it away, that it may go.

9 And see, if it goeth up by the way of his own coast to Beit-Shemesh, then he hath done us this great evil; but if not, then we shall know that it is not His hand that smote us; it was a chance that happened to us."

10 And the men did so; and took two milch

kine, and tied them to the cart, and shut up their calves at home.

11 And they laid the ark of יהוה upon the cart, and the coffer with the mice of gold and the images of their emerods.

12 And the kine took the straight way to the way of Beit-Shemesh, and went along the highway, lowing as they went, and turned not aside to the right hand or to the left; and the lords (seranim) of the Philistines went after them unto the border of Beit-Shemesh.

13 And they of Beit-Shemesh were reaping their wheat harvest in the valley; and they lifted up their eyes, and saw the ark, and rejoiced to see it.

14 And the cart came into the field of Joshua (Yehoshua), a Beit-Shemite, and stood there, where there was a great stone; and they clave the wood of the cart, and offered the kine a burnt offering unto יהוה.

15 And the Levites (Lewiyim) took down the ark of יהוה, and the coffer that was with it, wherein the jewels of gold were, and put them on the great stone; and the men of Beit-Shemesh offered burnt offerings and sacrificed sacrifices the same day unto יהוה.

16 And when the five lords (seranim) of the Philistines had seen it, they returned to Ekron the same day.

17 And these are the golden emerods which the Philistines returned for a trespass offering unto יהוה: for Ashdod one, for Gaza (Azzah) one, for Askelon one, for Gath one, for Ekron one;

18 And the golden mice, according to the number of all the cities of the Philistines belonging to the five lords (seranim), both of fenced cities, and of country villages, even unto the great stone of Avel, whereon they set down the ark of יהוה, which stone remaineth unto this day in the field of Joshua (Yehoshua), the Beit-Shemite.

19 And He smote the men of Beit-Shemesh, because they had looked into the ark of יהוה, even He smote of the people fifty thousand and threescore and ten men; and the people lamented, because יהוה had smitten many of the people with a great slaughter.

20 And the men of Beit-Shemesh said, "Who is able to stand before this holy God (Elohim) יהוה? And to whom shall He go up from us?"

21 And they sent messengers to the inhabitants of Qiryat-Yearim, saying, "The Philistines have brought again the ark of יהוה; come you down, and fetch it up to you."

7 And the men of Qiryat-Yearim came, and fetched up the ark of יהוה, and brought it into the house of Abinadab in the hill, and sanctified Eleazar his son to keep the ark of יהוה.

2 And it came to pass, while the ark abode in Qiryat-Yearim, that the time was long; for it was twenty years: and all the house of Yisrael lamented after יהוה.

3 And Shemuel spake unto all the house of Yisrael, saying, "If you do return unto יהוה with all your hearts, then put away the strange gods (elohim) and Ashtaroth from among you, and prepare your hearts unto יהוה, and serve Him only; and He will deliver you out of the hand of the Philistines.

4 Then the children of Yisrael did put away Baals (Baalim) and Ashtaroth, and served יהוה only."

5 And Shemuel said, "Gather all Yisrael to Mizpeh, and I will pray for you unto יהוה."

6 And they gathered together to Mizpeh, and drew water, and poured it out before יהוה, and fasted on that day, and said there, "We have sinned against יהוה." And Shemuel judged the children of Yisrael in Mizpeh.

7 And when the Philistines heard that the children of Yisrael were gathered together to Mizpeh, the lords (seranim) of the Philistines went up against Yisrael. And when the children of Yisrael heard it, they were afraid of the Philistines.

8 And the children of Yisrael said to Shemuel, "Cease not to cry unto יהוה our God (YHWH Eloheinu) for us, that He will save us out of the hand of the Philistines."

9 And Shemuel took a sucking lamb, and offered it for a burnt offering wholly unto יהוה; and Shemuel cried unto יהוה for Yisrael; and יהוה heard him.

10 And as Shemuel was offering up the burnt offering, the Philistines drew near to battle against Yisrael; but יהוה thundered with a great thunder on that day upon the Philistines, and discomfited them; and they were smitten before Yisrael.

11 And the men of Yisrael went out of Mizpeh, and pursued the Philistines, and smote them, until they came under Bethcar.

12 Then Shemuel took a stone, and set it

between Mizpeh and Shen, and called the name of it Ebenezer, saying, "Thus far hath יהוה helped us."

13 So the Philistines were subdued, and they came no more into the coast of Yisrael; and the hand of יהוה was against the Philistines all the days of Shemuel.

14 And the cities which the Philistines had taken from Yisrael were restored to Yisrael, from Ekron even unto Gath; and the coasts thereof did Yisrael deliver out of the hands of the Philistines. And there was peace between Yisrael and the Amorites.

15 And Shemuel judged Yisrael all the days of his life.

16 And he went from year to year in circuit to Bethel (Beit-El), and Gilgal, and Mizpeh, and judged Yisrael in all those places.

17 And his return was to Ramah; for there was his house; and there he judged Yisrael; and there he built an altar unto יהוה.

8 And it came to pass, when Shemuel was old, that he made his sons judges over Yisrael.

2 Now the name of his firstborn was Yoel; and the name of his second, Aviyah; they were judges in Beer-Sheva.

3 And his sons walked not in his ways, but turned aside after lucre, and took bribes, and perverted judgment.

4 Then all the elders of Yisrael gathered themselves together, and came to Shemuel unto Ramah,

5 And said unto him, "Behold, you are old, and your sons walk not in your ways. Now make us a king to judge us like all the nations.

6 But the thing displeased Shemuel, when they said, "Give us a king to judge us." And Shemuel prayed unto יהוה.

7 And יהוה said unto Shemuel, "Hearken unto the voice of the people in all that they say unto you; for they have not rejected you, but they have rejected Me, that I should not reign over them.

8 According to all the works which they have done since the day that I brought them up out of Egypt (Mitsrayim) even unto this day, wherewith they have forsaken Me, and served other gods (elohim), so do they also unto you.

9 Now therefore hearken unto their voice; howbeit yet protest solemnly unto them, and shew them the manner of the king that shall reign over them."

10 And Shemuel told all the words of יהוה unto the people that asked of him a king.

11 And He said, "This will be the manner of the king that shall reign over you: He will take your sons, and appoint them for himself, for his chariots, and to be his horsemen; and some shall run before his chariots.

12 And he will appoint him captains over thousands, and captains over fifties; and will set them to ear his ground, and to reap his harvest, and to make his instruments of war, and instruments of his chariots.

13 And he will take your daughters to be confectionaries, and to be cooks, and to be bakers.

14 And he will take your fields, and your vineyards, and your oliveyards, even the best of them, and give them to his servants.

15 And he will take the tenth of your seed, and of your vineyards, and give to his officers, and to his servants.

16 And he will take your menservants, and your maidservants, and your goodliest young men, and your asses, and put them to his work.

17 He will take the tenth of your sheep: and you shall be his servants.

18 And you shall cry out in that day because of your king which you shall have chosen you; and יהוה will not hear you in that day."

19 Nevertheless the people refused to obey the voice of Shemuel; and they said, "Nay; but we will have a king over us;

20 That we also may be like all the nations; and that our king may judge us, and go out before us, and fight our battles.

21 And Shemuel heard all the words of the people, and he rehearsed them in the ears of יהוה.

22 And יהוה said to Shemuel, "Hearken unto their voice, and make them a king." And Shemuel said unto the men of Yisrael, "Go you every man unto his city."

9 Now there was a man of Benjamin (Binyamin), whose name was Kish, the son of Abiel, the son of Zeror, the son of Bechorath, the son of Aphiah, a Benjamite (Ben-Yemini), a mighty man of power.

2 And he had a son, whose name was Shaul, a choice young man, and a goodly; and there was not among the children of Yisrael a goodlier

person than he; from his shoulders and upward he was higher than any of the people.

3 And the asses of Kish Shaul's father were lost. And Kish said to Shaul his son, "Take now one of the servants with you, and arise, go seek the asses."

4 And he passed through mount Efrayim, and passed through the land of Shalisha, but they found them not; then they passed through the land of Shalim, and there they were not; and he passed through the land of the Benjamites (Ben-yemini), but they found them not.

5 And when they were come to the land of Zuph, Shaul said to his servant that was with him, "Come, and let us return; lest my father leave caring for the asses, and take thought for us."

6 And he said unto him, "Behold now, there is in this city a man of God (Elohim), and he is an honorable man; all that he saith cometh surely to pass: now let us go thither; perhaps he can shew us our way that we should go."

7 Then said Shaul to his servant, "But, behold, if we go, what shall we bring the man? For the bread is spent in our vessels, and there is not a present to bring to the man of God (Elohim); what have we?"

8 And the servant answered Shaul again, and said, "Behold, I have here at hand the fourth part of a shekel of silver; that will I give to the man of God (Elohim), to tell us our way."

9 (Beforetime in Yisrael, when a man went to enquire of God (Elohim), thus he spake, "Come, and let us go to the seer; for he that is now called a prophet was beforetime called a seer.)

10 Then said Shaul to his servant, "Well said; come, let us go." So they went unto the city where the man of God (Elohim) was.

11 And as they went up the hill to the city, they found young maidens going out to draw water, and said unto them, "Is the seer here?"

12 And they answered them, and said, "He is; behold, he is before you; make haste now, for he came today to the city; for there is a sacrifice of the people today in the high place.

13 As soon as you be come into the city, you shall straightway find him, before he goes up to the high place to eat; for the people will not eat until he come, because he doth bless the sacrifice; and afterwards they eat that be bidden. Now therefore get up; for about this time you shall find him."

14 And they went up into the city; and when they were come into the city, behold, Shemuel came out against them, for to go up to the high place.

15 Now יהוה had told Shemuel in his ear a day before Shaul came, saying,

16 "Tomorrow about this time I will send you a man out of the land of Benjamin (Binyamin), and you shalt anoint him to be captain over My people Yisrael, that he may save My people out of the hand of the Philistines; for I have looked upon My people, because their cry has come unto Me."

17 And when Shemuel saw Shaul, יהוה said unto him, "Behold the man whom I spake to you of! This same shall reign over My people."

18 Then Shaul drew near to Shemuel in the gate, and said, "Please tell me where the seer's house is."

19 And Shemuel answered Shaul, and said, "I am the seer; go up before me unto the high place; for you shall eat with me today, and tomorrow I will let you go, and will tell you all that is in your heart.

20 And as for your asses that were lost three days ago, set not your mind on them; for they are found. And on whom is all the desire of Yisrael? Is it not on you, and on all your father's house?"

21 And Shaul answered and said, "Am not I a Benjamin (Binyamin), of the smallest of the tribes of Yisrael? And my family the least of all the families of the tribe of Benjamin (Binyamin)? Why then speakest you so to me?"

22 And Shemuel took Shaul and his servant, and brought them into the parlour, and made them sit in the chiefest place among them that were bidden, which were about thirty persons.

23 And Shemuel said unto the cook, "Bring the portion which I gave you, of which I said unto you, 'Set it by you;"

24 And the cook took up the shoulder, and that which was upon it, and set it before Shaul. And Shemuel said, "Behold that which is left! Set it before you, and eat: for unto this time hath it been kept for you since I said, I have invited the people." So Shaul did eat with Shemuel that day.

25 And when they were come down from the high place into the city, Shemuel communed with Shaul upon the top of the house.

26 And they arose early; and it came to pass

about the spring of the day, that Shemuel called Shaul to the top of the house, saying, "Up, that I may send you away." And Shaul arose, and they went out both of them, he and Shemuel, abroad. 27 And as they were going down to the end of the city, Shemuel said to Shaul, "Bid the servant pass on before us, (and he passed on,) but stand you still a while, that I may shew you the word of God (Elohim)."

10 Then Shemuel took a vial of oil, and poured it upon his head, and kissed him, and said, "Is it not because יהוה hath anointed you to be captain over His inheritance?

2 When you are departed from me today, then you shalt find two men by Rachel's sepulchre in the border of Benjamin (Binyamin) at Zelzah; and they will say unto you, 'The asses which you wentest to seek are found; and, behold, your father hath left the care of the asses, and sorroweth for you, saying, "What shall I do for my son?"'

3 Then shalt you go on forward from thence, and you shalt come to the plain of Tabor, and there shall meet you three men going up to God (Elohim) to Bethel (Beit-El), one carrying three kids, and another carrying three loaves of bread, and another carrying a bottle of wine.

4 And they will salute you, and give you two loaves of bread; which you shalt receive of their hands.

5 After that you shalt come to the hill of God (Elohim), where is the garrison of the Philistines; and it shall come to pass, when you are come thither to the city, that you shalt meet a company of prophets coming down from the high place with a psaltery, and a tabret, and a pipe, and a harp, before them; and they shall prophesy.

6 And the Spirit of יהוה will come upon you, and you shalt prophesy with them, and shalt be turned into another man.

7 And let it be, when these signs are come unto you, that you do as occasion serve you; for God (Elohim) is with you.

8 And you shalt go down before me to Gilgal; and, behold, I will come down unto you, to offer burnt offerings, and to sacrifice sacrifices of peace offerings: seven days shalt you tarry, till I come to you, and shew you what you shalt do."

9 And it was so, that when he had turned his back to go from Shemuel, God (Elohim) gave him another heart; and all those signs came to pass that day.

10 And when they came thither to the hill, behold, a company of prophets met him; and the Spirit of God (Elohim) came upon him, and he prophesied among them.

11 And it came to pass, when all that knew him beforetime saw that, behold, he prophesied among the prophets, then the people said one to another, "What is this that is come unto the son of Kish? Is Shaul also among the prophets?"

12 And one of the same place answered and said, "But who is their father?" Therefore it became a proverb: "Is Shaul also among the prophets?"

13 And when he had made an end of prophesying, he came to the high place.

14 And Shaul's uncle said unto him and to his servant, "Whither went you?" And he said, "To seek the asses; and when we saw that they were no where, we came to Shemuel."

15 And Shaul's uncle said, "Please tell me what Shemuel said unto you."

16 And Shaul said unto his uncle, "He told us plainly that the asses were found." But of the matter of the kingdom, whereof Shemuel spake, he told him not.

17 And Shemuel called the people together unto יהוה to Mizpeh;

18 And said unto the children of Yisrael, "Thus saith יהוה God of Israel (Elohei Yisrael): 'I brought up Yisrael out of Egypt (Mitsrayim), and delivered you out of the hand of the Egyptians (Mitsrayim), and out of the hand of all kingdoms, and of them that oppressed you.'

19 And you have this day rejected your God (Elohim), who Himself saved you out of all your adversities and your tribulations; and you have said unto Him, 'Nay, but set a king over us!' Now therefore present yourselves before יהוה by your tribes, and by your clans."

20 And when Shemuel had caused all the tribes of Yisrael to come near, the tribe of Benjamin (Binyamin) was taken.

21 When he had caused the tribe of Benjamin (Binyamin) to come near by their families, the family of Matri was taken, and Shaul the son of Kish was taken; and when they sought him, he could not be found.

22 Therefore they enquired of יהוה further, if the man should yet come thither. And יהוה

answered, "Behold, he hath hid himself among the stuff."

23 And they ran and fetched him thence; and when he stood among the people, he was higher than any of the people from his shoulders and upward.

24 And Shemuel said to all the people, "See you him whom יהוה hath chosen, that there is none like Him among all the people?" And all the people shouted, and said, "Long live the king!"

25 Then Shemuel told the people the manner of the kingdom, and wrote it in a book, and laid it up before יהוה. And Shemuel sent all the people away, every man to his house.

26 And Shaul also went home to Gibeah; and there went with him a band of men, whose hearts God (Elohim) had touched.

27 But the scoundrel (beliyaal) children said, "How shall this man save us?" And they despised him, and brought him no presents. But he held his peace.

11 Then Nahash the Ammonite came up, and encamped against Yavesh-Gilad; and all the men of Yavesh said unto Nahash, "Make a covenant with us, and we will serve you."

2 And Nahash the Ammonite answered them, "On this condition will I make a covenant with you, that I may thrust out all your right eyes, and lay it for a reproach upon all Yisrael."

3 And the elders of Yavesh said unto him, "Give us seven days' respite, that we may send messengers unto all the coasts of Yisrael. And then, if there be no man to save us, we will come out to you."

4 Then came the messengers to Gibeah of Shaul, and told the tidings in the ears of the people; and all the people lifted up their voices, and wept.

5 And, behold, Shaul came after the herd out of the field; and Shaul said, "What aileth the people that they weep?" And they told him the tidings of the men of Yavesh.

6 And the Spirit of God (Elohim) came upon Shaul when he heard those tidings, and his anger was kindled greatly.

7 And he took a yoke of oxen, and hewed them in pieces, and sent them throughout all the coasts of Yisrael by the hands of messengers, saying, "Whosoever cometh not forth after Shaul and after Shemuel, so shall it be done unto his oxen." And the fear of יהוה fell on the people, and they came out with one consent.

8 And when he numbered them in Bezek, the children of Yisrael were three hundred thousand, and the men of Judah (Yehudah) thirty thousand.

9 And they said unto the messengers that came, "Thus shall you say unto the men of Yavesh-Gilad: 'Tomorrow, by that time the sun be hot, you shall have help.'" And the messengers came and shewed it to the men of Yavesh; and they were glad.

10 Therefore the men of Yavesh said, "Tomorrow we will come out unto you, and you shall do with us all that seemeth good unto you."

11 And it was so on the next day, that Shaul put the people in three companies; and they came into the midst of the camp in the morning watch, and slew the Ammonites until the heat of the day. And it came to pass, that they who remained were scattered, so that two of them were not left together.

12 And the people said unto Shemuel, "Who is he that said, 'Shall Shaul reign over us?' Bring the men, that we may put them to death."

13 And Shaul said, "There shall not a man be put to death this day; for today יהוה hath wrought salvation in Yisrael."

14 Then said Shemuel to the people, "Come, and let us go to Gilgal, and renew the kingdom there."

15 And all the people went to Gilgal; and there they made Shaul king before יהוה in Gilgal; and there they sacrificed sacrifices of peace offerings before יהוה; and there Shaul and all the men of Yisrael rejoiced greatly.

12 And Shemuel said unto all Yisrael: "Behold, I have hearkened unto your voice in all that you said unto me, and have made a king over you.

2 And now, behold, the king walketh before you; and I am old and grayheaded; and, behold, my sons are with you: and I have walked before you from my childhood unto this day.

3 Behold, here I am. Witness against me before יהוה, and before His anointed (mashiach); Whose ox have I taken? Or whose ass have I taken? Or whom have I defrauded? Whom have I oppressed? Or of whose hand have I received any bribe to blind mine eyes therewith? And I will restore it you."

4 And they said, "You have not defrauded us, nor oppressed us, neither have you taken

anything of any man's hand."

5 And he said unto them, "יהוה is witness against you, and His anointed (mashiach) is witness this day, that you have not found anything in my hand." And they answered, "He is witness."

6 And Shemuel said unto the people, "It is יהוה that advanced Moses (Mosheh) and Aaron (Aharon), and that brought your fathers up out of the land of Egypt (Mitsrayim).

7 Now therefore stand still, that I may reason with you before יהוה of all the righteous acts of יהוה, which He did to you and to your fathers:

8 When Jacob (Yaaqov) was come into Egypt (Mitsrayim), and your fathers cried unto יהוה, then יהוה sent Moses (Mosheh) and Aaron (Aharon), which brought forth your fathers out of Egypt (Mitsrayim), and made them dwell in this place.

9 And when they forgat יהוה their God (YHWH Eloheihem), He sold them into the hand of Sisera, captain of the army of Hazor, and into the hand of the Philistines, and into the hand of the king of Moav, and they fought against them.

10 And they cried unto יהוה, and said, 'We have sinned, because we have forsaken יהוה, and have served [34]Baals (Baalim) and Ashtaroth; but now deliver us out of the hand of our enemies, and we will serve You.'

11 And יהוה sent Yerubaal, and Bedan, and Yiftach, and Shemuel, and delivered you out of the hand of your enemies on every side, and you dwelled safe.

12 And when you saw that Nahash the king of the children of Ammon came against you, you said unto me, 'Nay, but a king shall reign over us,' when יהוה your God (YHWH Eloheikhem) was your King.

13 Now therefore behold the king whom you have chosen, and whom you have desired! And, behold, יהוה hath set a king over you.

14 If you will fear יהוה, and serve Him, and obey His voice, and not rebel against the commandment of יהוה, then shall both you and also the king that reigneth over you continue following יהוה your God (YHWH Eloheikhem);

15 But if you will not obey the voice of יהוה, but rebel against the commandment of יהוה, then shall the hand of יהוה be against you, as it was against your fathers.

16 Now therefore stand and see this great thing, which יהוה will do before your eyes:

17 Is it not wheat harvest today? I will call unto יהוה, and He shall send thunder and rain; that you may perceive and see that your wickedness is great, which you have done in the sight of יהוה, in asking for yourselves a king."

18 So Shemuel called unto יהוה; and יהוה sent thunder and rain that day; and all the people greatly feared יהוה and Shemuel.

19 And all the people said unto Shemuel, "Pray for your servants unto יהוה your God (YHWH Eloheikha), that we die not; for we have added unto all our sins this evil, to ask for ourselves a king."

20 And Shemuel said unto the people, "Fear not. You have done all this wickedness; yet turn not aside from following יהוה, but serve יהוה with all your heart;

21 And turn you not aside; for then should you go after vain things, which cannot profit nor deliver; for they are vain.

22 For יהוה will not forsake His people for His great name's sake, because it hath pleased יהוה to make you His people.

23 Moreover as for me, God (Elohim) forbid that I should sin against יהוה in ceasing to pray for you; but I will teach you the good and the right way.

24 Only fear יהוה, and serve Him in truth with all your heart; for consider how great things He hath done for you.

25 But if you shall still do wickedly, you shall be consumed, both you and your king."

13 Shaul reigned one year; and when he had reigned two years over Yisrael,

2 Shaul chose him three thousand men of Yisrael; whereof two thousand were with Shaul in Michmash and in Mount Bethel (Beit-El), and a thousand were with Jonathan (Yehonatan) in Gibeah of Benjamin (Binyamin); and the rest of the people he sent every man to his tent.

3 And Jonathan (Yehonatan) smote the garrison of the Philistines that was in Geba, and the Philistines heard of it. And Shaul blew the trumpet throughout all the land, saying, "Let the Hebrews (Ivrim) hear!"

4 And all Yisrael heard say that Shaul had smitten a garrison of the Philistines, and that Yisrael also was had in abomination with the Philistines. And the people were called together after Shaul to Gilgal.

5 And the Philistines gathered themselves together to fight with Yisrael, thirty thousand chariots, and six thousand horsemen, and people as the sand which is on the sea shore in multitude; and they came up, and pitched in Michmash, eastward from Beit Aven.

6 When the men of Yisrael saw that they were in a strait, (for the people were distressed,) then the people did hide themselves in caves, and in thickets, and in rocks, and in high places, and in pits.

7 And some of the Hebrews (Ivrim) went over Jordan (Yarden) to the land of Gad and Gilad. As for Shaul, he was yet in Gilgal, and all the people followed him trembling.

8 And he tarried seven days, according to the set time that Shemuel had appointed. But Shemuel came not to Gilgal; and the people were scattered from him.

9 And Shaul said, "Bring hither a burnt offering to me, and peace offerings. And he offered the burnt offering."

10 And it came to pass, that as soon as he had made an end of offering the burnt offering, behold, Shemuel came; and Shaul went out to meet him, that he might salute him.

11 And Shemuel said, "What have you done?" And Shaul said, "Because I saw that the people were scattered from me, and that you camest not within the days appointed, and that the Philistines gathered themselves together at Michmash;

12 Therefore said I, 'The Philistines will come down now upon me to Gilgal, and I have not made supplication unto יהוה.' I forced myself therefore, and offered a burnt offering."

13 And Shemuel said to Shaul, "You have done foolishly; you have not kept the commandment of יהוה your God (YHWH Eloheikha), which He commanded you; for now would יהוה have established your kingdom upon Yisrael forever.

14 But now your kingdom shall not continue. יהוה hath sought Him a man after His own heart, and יהוה hath commanded him to be captain over His people, because you have not kept that which יהוה commanded you."

15 And Shemuel arose, and gat him up from Gilgal unto Gibeah of Benjamin (Binyamin). And Shaul numbered the people that were present with him, about six hundred men.

16 And Shaul, and Jonathan (Yehonatan) his son, and the people that were present with them, abode in Gibeah of Benjamin (Binyamin); but the Philistines encamped in Michmash.

17 And the spoilers came out of the camp of the Philistines in three companies; one company turned unto the way that leadeth to Ophrah, unto the land of Shual;

18 And another company turned the way to Beit-Choron; and another company turned to the way of the border that looketh to the valley of Zeboim toward the wilderness.

19 Now there was no smith found throughout all the land of Yisrael, for the Philistines said, "Lest the Hebrews (Ivrim) make them swords or spears;

20 But all the Yisraelites went down to the Philistines, to sharpen every man his share, and his coulter, and his axe, and his mattock.

21 Yet they had a file for the mattocks, and for the coulters, and for the forks, and for the axes, and to sharpen the goads.

22 So it came to pass in the day of battle, that there was neither sword nor spear found in the hand of any of the people that were with Shaul and Jonathan (Yehonatan); but with Shaul and with Jonathan (Yehonatan) his son was there found.

23 And the garrison of the Philistines went out to the passage of Michmash.

14 Now it came to pass upon a day, that Jonathan (Yehonatan) the son of Shaul said unto the young man that bare his armour, "Come, and let us go over to the Philistines' garrison, that is on the other side." But he told not his father.

2 And Shaul tarried in the uttermost part of Gibeah under a pomegranate tree which is in Migron; and the people that were with him were about six hundred men;

3 And Achiyah, the son of Ahitub, Ichabod's brother, the son of Phinehas, the son of Eli, יהוה's priest (kohen) in Shiloh, wearing an ephod. And the people knew not that Jonathan (Yehonatan) was gone.

4 And between the passages, by which Jonathan (Yehonatan) sought to go over unto the Philistines' garrison, there was a sharp rock on the one side, and a sharp rock on the other side; and the name of the one was Bozez, and the name of the other Seneh.

5 The forefront of the one was situated

northward opposite Michmash, and the other southward opposite Gibeah.

6 And Jonathan (Yehonatan) said to the young man that bare his armour, "Come, and let us go over unto the garrison of these uncircumcised; it may be that יהוה will work for us; for there is no restraint to יהוה to save by many or by few."

7 And his armourbearer said unto him, "Do all that is in your heart. Turn you; behold, I am with you according to your heart."

8 Then said Jonathan (Yehonatan), "Behold, we will pass over unto these men, and we will discover ourselves unto them.

9 If they say thus unto us, 'Tarry until we come to you,' then we will stand still in our place, and will not go up unto them.

10 But if they say thus, 'Come up unto us,' then we will go up; for יהוה hath delivered them into our hand; and this shall be a sign unto us."

11 And both of them discovered themselves unto the garrison of the Philistines; and the Philistines said, "Behold, the Hebrews (Ivrim) come forth out of the holes where they have hidden themselves."

12 And the men of the garrison answered Jonathan (Yehonatan) and his armourbearer, and said, "Come up to us, and we will shew you a thing." And Jonathan (Yehonatan) said unto his armourbearer, "Come up after me, for יהוה hath delivered them into the hand of Yisrael."

13 And Jonathan (Yehonatan) climbed up upon his hands and upon his feet, and his armourbearer after him; and they fell before Jonathan (Yehonatan); and his armourbearer slew after him.

14 And that first slaughter, which Jonathan (Yehonatan) and his armourbearer made, was about twenty men, within as it was a half acre of land, which a yoke of oxen might plow.

15 And there was trembling in the camp, in the field, and among all the people; the garrison, and the spoilers, they also trembled, and the earth quaked; so it was a very great trembling.

16 And the watchmen of Shaul in Gibeah of Benjamin (Binyamin) looked; and, behold, the multitude melted away, and they went on beating down one another.

17 Then said Shaul unto the people that were with him, "Number now, and see who is gone from us." And when they had numbered, behold, Jonathan (Yehonatan) and his armourbearer were not there.

18 And Shaul said unto Achiyah, "Bring hither the ark of God (Elohim)." For the ark of God (Elohim) was at that time with the children of Yisrael.

19 And it came to pass, while Shaul talked unto the priest (kohen), that the noise that was in the camp of the Philistines went on and increased: and Shaul said unto the priest (kohen), "Withdraw your hand."

20 And Shaul and all the people that were with him assembled themselves, and they came to the battle; and, behold, every man's sword was against his fellow, and there was a very great discomfiture.

21 Moreover the Hebrews (Ivrim) that were with the Philistines before that time, which went up with them into the camp from the country round about, even they also turned to be with the Yisraelites that were with Shaul and Jonathan (Yehonatan).

22 Likewise all the men of Yisrael which had hid themselves in mount Efrayim, when they heard that the Philistines fled, even they also followed hard after them in the battle.

23 So יהוה saved Yisrael that day; and the battle passed over unto Beit Aven.

24 And the men of Yisrael were distressed that day, for Shaul had adjured the people, saying, "Cursed be the man that eateth any food until evening, that I may be avenged on mine enemies." So none of the people tasted any food.

25 And all they of the land came to a wood; and there was honey upon the ground.

26 And when the people were come into the wood, behold, the honey dropped; but no man put his hand to his mouth, for the people feared the oath.

27 But Jonathan (Yehonatan) heard not when his father charged the people with the oath; wherefore he put forth the end of the rod that was in his hand, and dipped it in a honeycomb, and put his hand to his mouth; and his eyes were enlightened.

28 Then answered one of the people, and said, "Your father straitly charged the people with an oath, saying, 'Cursed be the man that eateth any food this day.'" And the people were faint.

29 Then said Jonathan (Yehonatan), "My father hath troubled the land. Please see, how mine eyes have been enlightened, because I tasted a

little of this honey.

30 How much more, if haply the people had eaten freely today of the spoil of their enemies which they found? For had there not been now a much greater slaughter among the Philistines?"

31 And they smote the Philistines that day from Michmash to Aiyalon; and the people were very faint.

32 And the people flew upon the spoil, and took sheep, and oxen, and calves, and slew them on the ground; and the people did eat them with the blood.

33 Then they told Shaul, saying, "Behold, the people sin against יהוה, in that they eat with the blood!" And he said, "You have transgressed; roll a great stone unto me this day."

34 And Shaul said, "Disperse yourselves among the people, and say unto them, 'Bring me hither every man his ox, and every man his sheep, and slay them here, and eat; and sin not against יהוה in eating with the blood.'" And all the people brought every man his ox with him that night, and slew them there.

35 And Shaul built an altar unto יהוה; the same was the first altar that he built unto יהוה.

36 And Shaul said, "Let us go down after the Philistines by night, and spoil them until the morning light, and let us not leave a man of them." And they said, "Do whatsoever seemeth good unto you." Then said the priest (kohen), "Let us draw near hither unto God (Elohim)."

37 And Shaul asked counsel of God (Elohim), "Shall I go down after the Philistines? Wilt you deliver them into the hand of Yisrael?" But He answered him not that day.

38 And Shaul said, "Draw you near hither, all the chief of the people; and know and see wherein this sin hath been this day.

39 For, as יהוה liveth, which saveth Yisrael, though it be in Jonathan (Yehonatan) my son, he shall surely die." But there was not a man among all the people that answered him.

40 Then said he unto all Yisrael, "Be you on one side, and I and Jonathan (Yehonatan) my son will be on the other side". And the people said unto Shaul, "Do what seemeth good unto you."

41 Therefore Shaul said unto יהוה God of Israel (Elohei Yisrael), "Give a perfect lot." And Shaul and Jonathan (Yehonatan) were taken; but the people escaped.

42 And Shaul said, "Cast lots between me and Jonathan (Yehonatan) my son." And Jonathan (Yehonatan) was taken.

43 Then Shaul said to Jonathan (Yehonatan), "Tell me what you have done." And Jonathan (Yehonatan) told him, and said, "I did but taste a little honey with the end of the rod that was in mine hand, and, behold, I must die!"

44 And Shaul answered, "God (Elohim) do so and more also; for you shalt surely die, Jonathan (Yehonatan)."

45 And the people said unto Shaul, "Shall Jonathan (Yehonatan) die, who hath wrought this great salvation in Yisrael? God (Elohim) forbid! As יהוה liveth, there shall not one hair of his head fall to the ground; for he hath wrought with God (Elohim) this day." So the people rescued Jonathan (Yehonatan), that he died not.

46 Then Shaul went up from following the Philistines; and the Philistines went to their own place.

47 So Shaul took the kingdom over Yisrael, and fought against all his enemies on every side, against Moav, and against the children of Ammon, and against Edom, and against the kings of Zobah, and against the Philistines; and whithersoever he turned himself, he vexed them.

48 And he gathered an army, and smote the Amalekites, and delivered Yisrael out of the hands of them that spoiled them.

49 Now the sons of Shaul were Jonathan (Yehonatan), and Ishui, and Melchishua; and the names of his two daughters were these; the name of the firstborn Merab, and the name of the younger Michal.

50 And the name of Shaul's wife was Ahinoam, the daughter of Ahimaaz: and the name of the captain of his army was Abner, the son of Ner, Shaul's uncle.

51 And Kish was the father of Shaul; and Ner the father of Abner was the son of Abiel.

52 And there was sore war against the Philistines all the days of Shaul; and when Shaul saw any strong man, or any valiant man, he took him unto him.

15 Shemuel also said unto Shaul, "יהוה sent me to anoint you to be king over His people, over Yisrael. Now therefore hearken you unto the voice of the words of יהוה.

2 Thus saith יהוה of hosts (YHWH Tsevaot): 'I remember that which Amalek did to Yisrael,

how he laid wait for him in the way, when he came up from Egypt (Mitsrayim).

3 Now go and smite Amalek, and utterly destroy all that they have, and spare them not; but slay both man and woman, infant and suckling, ox and sheep, camel and ass.

4 And Shaul gathered the people together, and numbered them in Telaim, two hundred thousand footmen, and ten thousand men of Judah (Yehudah).

5 And Shaul came to a city of Amalek, and laid wait in the valley.

6 And Shaul said unto the Kenites, "Go, depart, get you down from among the Amalekites, lest I destroy you with them; for you shewed kindness to all the children of Yisrael, when they came up out of Egypt (Mitsrayim)." So the Kenites departed from among the Amalekites.

7 And Shaul smote the Amalekites from Havilah until you comest to Shur, that is opposite Egypt (Mitsrayim).

8 And he took Agag the king of the Amalekites alive, and utterly destroyed all the people with the edge of the sword.

9 But Shaul and the people spared Agag, and the best of the sheep, and of the oxen, and of the fatlings, and the lambs, and all that was good, and would not utterly destroy them: but every thing that was vile and refuse, that they destroyed utterly.

10 Then came the word of יהוה unto Shemuel, saying,

11 I greatly regret that I have set up Shaul as king, for he has turned back from following Me, and hath not performed My commandments." And it grieved Shemuel; and he cried unto יהוה all night.

12 And when Shemuel rose early to meet Shaul in the morning, it was told Shemuel, saying, "Shaul came to Carmel, and, behold, he set him up a place, and is gone about, and passed on, and gone down to Gilgal."

13 And Shemuel came to Shaul; and Shaul said unto him, "Blessed be you of יהוה! I have performed the commandment of יהוה."

14 And Shemuel said, "What meaneth then this bleating of the sheep in mine ears, and the lowing of the oxen which I hear?"

15 And Shaul said, "They have brought them from the Amalekites; for the people spared the best of the sheep and of the oxen, to sacrifice unto יהוה your God (YHWH Eloheikha); and the rest we have utterly destroyed."

16 Then Shemuel said unto Shaul, "Stay, and I will tell you what יהוה hath said to me this night." And he said unto him, "Say on."

17 And Shemuel said, "When you wast little in your own sight, wast you not made the head of the tribes of Yisrael, and יהוה anointed you king over Yisrael?

18 And יהוה sent you on a journey, and said, 'Go and utterly destroy the sinners the Amalekites, and fight against them until they be consumed.'

19 Wherefore then didst you not obey the voice of יהוה, but didst fly upon the spoil, and didst evil in the sight of יהוה?"

20 And Shaul said unto Shemuel, "Yea, I have obeyed the voice of יהוה, and have gone the way which יהוה sent me, and have brought Agag the king of Amalek, and have utterly destroyed the Amalekites.

21 But the people took of the spoil, sheep and oxen, the chief of the things which should have been utterly destroyed, to sacrifice unto יהוה your God (YHWH Eloheikha) in Gilgal."

22 And Shemuel said, "Hath יהוה as great delight in burnt offerings and sacrifices, as in obeying the voice of יהוה? Behold, to obey is better than sacrifice, and to hearken than the fat of rams.

23 For rebellion is as the sin of witchcraft, and stubbornness is as iniquity and idolatry. Because you have rejected the word of יהוה, He hath also rejected you from being king."

24 And Shaul said unto Shemuel, "I have sinned; for I have transgressed the commandment of יהוה, and your words; because I feared the people, and obeyed their voice.

25 Now therefore, please pardon my sin, and turn again with me, that I may worship יהוה."

26 And Shemuel said unto Shaul, "I will not return with you; for you have rejected the word of יהוה, and יהוה hath rejected you from being king over Yisrael."

27 And as Shemuel turned about to go away, he laid hold upon the skirt of his mantle, and it rent.

28 And Shemuel said unto him, "יהוה hath rent the kingdom of Yisrael from you this day, and hath given it to a neighbour of yours, that is better than you.

29 And also the Strength of Yisrael will not lie nor repent; for He is not a man, that He should

repent.

30 Then he said, "I have sinned; yet honor me now, please, before the elders of my people, and before Yisrael, and turn again with me, that I may worship יהוה your God (YHWH Eloheikha)."

31 So Shemuel turned again after Shaul; and Shaul worshipped יהוה.

32 Then said Shemuel, "Bring you hither to me Agag the king of the Amalekites." And Agag came unto him delicately. And Agag said, "Surely the bitterness of death is past."

33 And Shemuel said, "As your sword hath made women childless, so shall your mother be childless among women." And Shemuel hewed Agag in pieces before יהוה in Gilgal.

34 Then Shemuel went to Ramah; and Shaul went up to his house to Gibeah of Shaul.

35 And Shemuel came no more to see Shaul until the day of his death; nevertheless Shemuel mourned for Shaul; and יהוה regretted that He had made Shaul king over Yisrael.

16 And יהוה said unto Shemuel, "How long wilt you mourn for Shaul, seeing I have rejected him from reigning over Yisrael? Fill your horn with oil, and go, I will send you to Jesse (Yishai) the Bethlehemite; for I have provided Me a king among his sons.

2 And Shemuel said, "How can I go? If Shaul hear it, he will kill me." And יהוה said, "Take a heifer with you, and say, I am come to sacrifice to יהוה."

3 And call Jesse (Yishai) to the sacrifice, and I will shew you what you shalt do; and you shalt anoint unto Me him whom I name unto you."

4 And Shemuel did that which יהוה spake, and came to Bethlehem (Beit-Lechem). And the elders of the town trembled at his coming, and said, "Comest you peaceably?"

5 And he said, "Peaceably; I am come to sacrifice unto יהוה. Sanctify yourselves, and come with me to the sacrifice." And he sanctified Jesse (Yishai) and his sons, and called them to the sacrifice.

6 And it came to pass, when they were come, that he looked on Eliav, and said, "Surely יהוה's anointed is before him."

7 But יהוה said unto Shemuel, "Look not on his countenance, or on the height of his stature; because I have refused him; for יהוה seeth not as man seeth; for man looketh on the outward appearance, but יהוה looketh on the heart."

8 Then Jesse (Yishai) called Abinadab, and made him pass before Shemuel. And he said, "Neither hath יהוה chosen this."

9 Then Jesse (Yishai) made Shammah to pass by. And he said, "Neither hath יהוה chosen this."

10 Again, Jesse (Yishai) made seven of his sons to pass before Shemuel. And Shemuel said unto Jesse (Yishai), "יהוה hath not chosen these."

11 And Shemuel said unto Jesse (Yishai), "Are here all your children?" And he said, "There remaineth yet the youngest, and, behold, he keepeth the sheep." And Shemuel said unto Jesse (Yishai), "Send and fetch him; for we will not sit down till he come hither."

12 And he sent, and brought him in. Now he was ruddy, and withal of a beautiful countenance, and goodly to look to. And יהוה said, "Arise, anoint him; for this is he!"

13 Then Shemuel took the horn of oil, and anointed him in the midst of his brethren; and the Spirit of יהוה came upon Dawid from that day forward. So Shemuel rose up, and went to Ramah.

14 But the Spirit of יהוה departed from Shaul, and an evil spirit from יהוה troubled him.

15 And Shaul's servants said unto him, "Behold now, an evil spirit from God (Elohim) troubleth you.

16 Let our lord (adon) now command your servants, who are before you, to seek out a man, who is a cunning player on a harp; and it shall come to pass, when the evil spirit from God (Elohim) is upon you, that he shall play with his hand, and you shalt be well."

17 And Shaul said unto his servants, "Provide me now a man that can play well, and bring him to me."

18 Then answered one of the servants, and said, "Behold, I have seen a son of Jesse (Yishai) the Bethlehemite, that is cunning in playing, and a mighty valiant man, and a man of war, and prudent in matters, and a comely person, and יהוה is with him."

19 Wherefore Shaul sent messengers unto Jesse (Yishai), and said, "Send me Dawid your son, which is with the sheep."

20 And Jesse (Yishai) took an ass laden with bread, and a bottle of wine, and a kid, and sent them by Dawid his son unto Shaul.

21 And Dawid came to Shaul, and stood before

him; and he loved him greatly; and he became his armourbearer.

22 And Shaul sent to Jesse (Yishai), saying, "Please let Dawid stand before me; for he hath found favor in my sight."

23 And it came to pass, when the evil spirit from God (Elohim) was upon Shaul, that Dawid took a harp, and played with his hand. So Shaul was refreshed, and was well, and the evil spirit departed from him.

17 Now the Philistines gathered together their armies to battle, and were gathered together at Shochoh, which belongeth to Judah (Yehudah), and pitched between Shochoh and Azekah, in Ephes-dammim.

2 And Shaul and the men of Yisrael were gathered together, and pitched by the valley of Elah, and set the battle in array against the Philistines.

3 And the Philistines stood on a mountain on the one side, and Yisrael stood on a mountain on the other side; and there was a valley between them.

4 And there went out a champion out of the camp of the Philistines, named Goliath, of Gath, whose height was six cubits and a span.

5 And he had a helmet of brass upon his head, and he was armed with a coat of mail; and the weight of the coat was five thousand shekels of brass.

6 And he had greaves of brass upon his legs, and a target of brass between his shoulders.

7 And the staff of his spear was like a weaver's beam; and his spear's head weighed six hundred shekels of iron; and one bearing a shield went before him.

8 And he stood and cried unto the armies of Yisrael, and said unto them, "Why are you come out to set your battle in array? Am not I a Philistine, and you servants to Shaul? Choose you a man for you, and let him come down to me.

9 If he be able to fight with me, and to kill me, then will we be your servants: but if I prevail against him, and kill him, then shall you be our servants, and serve us."

10 And the Philistine said, "I defy the armies of Yisrael this day; give me a man, that we may fight together."

11 When Shaul and all Yisrael heard those words of the Philistine, they were dismayed, and greatly afraid.

12 Now Dawid was the son of that Ephrathite of Bethlehem (Beit-Lechem) in Yehudah, whose name was Jesse (Yishai); and he had eight sons; and the man went among men for an old man in the days of Shaul.

13 And the three eldest sons of Jesse (Yishai) went and followed Shaul to the battle; and the names of his three sons that went to the battle were Eliav the firstborn, and next unto him Abinadab, and the third Shammah.

14 And Dawid was the youngest; and the three eldest followed Shaul.

15 But Dawid went and returned from Shaul to feed his father's sheep at Bethlehem (Beit-Lechem).

16 And the Philistine drew near morning and evening, and presented himself forty days.

17 And Jesse (Yishai) said unto Dawid his son, "Take now for your brethren an ephah of this parched corn, and these ten loaves, and run to the camp to your brethren;

18 And carry these ten cheeses unto the captain of their thousand, and look how your brethren fare, and take their pledge."

19 Now Shaul, and they, and all the men of Yisrael, were in the valley of Elah, fighting with the Philistines.

20 And Dawid rose up early in the morning, and left the sheep with a keeper, and took, and went, as Jesse (Yishai) had commanded him; and he came to the trench, as the army was going forth to the fight, and shouted for the battle.

21 For Yisrael and the Philistines had put the battle in array, army against army.

22 And Dawid left his carriage in the hand of the keeper of the carriage, and ran into the army, and came and saluted his brethren.

23 And as he talked with them, behold, there came up the champion, the Philistine of Gath, Goliath by name, out of the armies of the Philistines, and spake according to the same words: and Dawid heard them.

24 And all the men of Yisrael, when they saw the man, fled from him, and were sore afraid.

25 And the men of Yisrael said, "Have you seen this man that is come up? Surely to defy Yisrael is he come up; and it shall be, that the man who killeth him, the king will enrich him with great riches, and will give him his daughter, and make his father's house free in Yisrael."

26 And Dawid spake to the men that stood by him, saying, "What shall be done to the man that killeth this Philistine, and taketh away the reproach from Yisrael? For who is this uncircumcised Philistine, that he should defy the armies of the living God (Elohim chayim)?"

27 And the people answered him after this manner, saying, "So shall it be done to the man who killeth him."

28 And Eliav his eldest brother heard when he spake unto the men; and Eliav's anger was kindled against Dawid, and he said, "Why camest you down hither? And with whom have you left those few sheep in the wilderness? I know your pride, and the naughtiness of your heart; for you are come down that you mightest see the battle."

29 And Dawid said, "What have I now done? Is there not a cause?"

30 And he turned from him toward another, and spake after the same manner; and the people answered him again after the former manner.

31 And when the words were heard which Dawid spake, they rehearsed them before Shaul; and he sent for him.

32 And Dawid said to Shaul, "Let no man's heart fail because of him; your servant will go and fight with this Philistine."

33 And Shaul said to Dawid, "You are not able to go against this Philistine to fight with him; for you are but a youth, and he a man of war from his youth."

34 And Dawid said unto Shaul, "Your servant kept his father's sheep, and there came a lion, and a bear, and took a lamb out of the flock;

35 And I went out after him, and smote him, and delivered it out of his mouth: and when he arose against me, I caught him by his beard, and smote him, and slew him.

36 Your servant slew both the lion and the bear; and this uncircumcised Philistine shall be as one of them, seeing he hath defied the armies of the living God (Elohim chayim)."

37 Dawid said moreover, יהוה that delivered me out of the paw of the lion, and out of the paw of the bear, he will deliver me out of the hand of this Philistine. And Shaul said unto Dawid, "Go, and יהוה be with you."

38 And Shaul armed Dawid with his armour, and he put a helmet of brass upon his head; also he armed him with a coat of mail.

39 And Dawid girded his sword upon his armour, and he assayed to go; for he had not proved it. And Dawid said unto Shaul, "I cannot go with these; for I have not proved them." And Dawid put them off.

40 And he took his staff in his hand, and chose him five smooth stones out of the brook, and put them in a shepherd's bag which he had, even in a scrip; and his sling was in his hand; and he drew near to the Philistine.

41 And the Philistine came on and drew near unto Dawid; and the man that bare the shield went before him.

42 And when the Philistine looked about, and saw Dawid, he disdained him; for he was but a youth, and ruddy, and of a fair countenance.

43 And the Philistine said unto Dawid, "Am I a dog, that you comest to me with staves?" And the Philistine cursed Dawid by his gods (elohim).

44 And the Philistine said to Dawid, "Come to me, and I will give your flesh unto the fowls of the air, and to the beasts of the field."

45 Then said Dawid to the Philistine, "You comest to me with a sword, and with a spear, and with a shield; but I come to you in the name of יהוה of hosts (YHWH Tsevaot), the God (Elohim) of the armies of Yisrael, whom you have defied.

46 This day will יהוה deliver you into mine hand; and I will smite you, and take your head from you; and I will give the carcases of the army of the Philistines this day unto the fowls of the air, and to the wild beasts of the earth; that all the earth may know that there is a God (Elohim) in Yisrael.

47 And all this assembly shall know that יהוה saveth not with sword and spear; for the battle is יהוה's, and He will give you into our hands."

48 And it came to pass, when the Philistine arose, and came and drew near to meet Dawid, that Dawid hasted, and ran toward the army to meet the Philistine.

49 And Dawid put his hand in his bag, and took thence a stone, and slang it, and smote the Philistine in his forehead, that the stone sunk into his forehead; and he fell upon his face to the earth.

50 So Dawid prevailed over the Philistine with a sling and with a stone, and smote the Philistine, and slew him; but there was no sword in the

hand of Dawid.

51 Therefore Dawid ran, and stood upon the Philistine, and took his sword, and drew it out of the sheath thereof, and slew him, and cut off his head therewith. And when the Philistines saw their champion was dead, they fled.

52 And the men of Yisrael and of Judah (Yehudah) arose, and shouted, and pursued the Philistines, until you come to the valley, and to the gates of Ekron. And the wounded of the Philistines fell down by the way to Shaaraim, even unto Gath, and unto Ekron.

53 And the children of Yisrael returned from chasing after the Philistines, and they spoiled their tents.

54 And Dawid took the head of the Philistine, and brought it to Jerusalem (Yerushalayim); but he put his armour in his tent.

55 And when Shaul saw Dawid go forth against the Philistine, he said unto Abner, the captain of the army, "Abner, whose son is this youth?" And Abner said, "As your soul liveth, O king, I do not know."

56 And the king said, "Enquire you whose son the stripling is."

57 And as Dawid returned from the slaughter of the Philistine, Abner took him, and brought him before Shaul with the head of the Philistine in his hand.

58 And Shaul said to him, "Whose son are you, you young man?" And Dawid answered, "I am the son of your servant Jesse (Yishai) the Bethlehemite."

18 And it came to pass, when he had made an end of speaking unto Shaul, that the soul of Jonathan (Yehonatan) was knit with the soul of Dawid, and Jonathan (Yehonatan) loved him as his own soul.

2 And Shaul took him that day, and would let him go no more home to his father's house.

3 Then Jonathan (Yehonatan) and Dawid made a covenant, because he loved him as his own soul.

4 And Jonathan (Yehonatan) stripped himself of the robe that was upon him, and gave it to Dawid, and his garments, even to his sword, and to his bow, and to his girdle.

5 And Dawid went out whithersoever Shaul sent him, and behaved himself wisely; and Shaul set him over the men of war, and he was accepted in the sight of all the people, and also in the sight of Shaul's servants.

6 And it came to pass as they came, when Dawid was returned from the slaughter of the Philistine, that the women came out of all cities of Yisrael, singing and dancing, to meet king Shaul, with tabrets, with joy, and with instruments of musick.

7 And the women answered one another as they played, and said: "Shaul hath slain his thousands, and Dawid his ten thousands."

8 And Shaul was very wroth, and the saying displeased him; and he said, "They have ascribed unto Dawid ten thousands, and to me they have ascribed but thousands; and what can he has more but the kingdom?"

9 And Shaul eyed Dawid from that day and forward.

10 And it came to pass on the next day, that the evil spirit from God (Elohim) came upon Shaul, and he prophesied in the midst of the house; and Dawid played with his hand, as at other times; and there was a javelin in Shaul's hand.

11 And Shaul cast the javelin; for he said, "I will smite Dawid even to the wall with it." And Dawid avoided out of his presence twice.

12 And Shaul was afraid of Dawid, because יהוה was with him, and was departed from Shaul.

13 Therefore Shaul removed him from him, and made him his captain over a thousand; and he went out and came in before the people.

14 And Dawid behaved himself wisely in all his ways; and יהוה was with him.

15 Wherefore when Shaul saw that he behaved himself very wisely, he was afraid of him.

16 But all Yisrael and Judah (Yehudah) loved Dawid, because he went out and came in before them.

17 And Shaul said to Dawid, "Behold my elder daughter Merab, her will I give you to wife; only be you valiant for me, and fight יהוה's battles." For Shaul said, "Let not mine hand be upon him, but let the hand of the Philistines be upon him."

18 And Dawid said unto Shaul, "Who am I? And what is my life, or my father's family in Yisrael, that I should be son in law to the king?"

19 But it came to pass at the time when Merab Shaul's daughter should have been given to Dawid, that she was given unto Adriel the Meholathite to wife.

20 And Michal Shaul's daughter loved Dawid;

and they told Shaul, and the thing pleased him.

21 And Shaul said, "I will give him her, that she may be a snare to him, and that the hand of the Philistines may be against him." Wherefore Shaul said to Dawid, "You shalt this day be my son in law in the one of the twain."

22 And Shaul commanded his servants, saying, "Commune with Dawid secretly, and say, 'Behold, the king hath delight in you, and all his servants love you; now therefore be the king's son in law.'"

23 And Shaul's servants spake those words in the ears of Dawid. And Dawid said, "Seemeth it to you a light thing to be a king's son in law, seeing that I am a poor man, and lightly esteemed?"

24 And the servants of Shaul told him, saying, "On this manner spake Dawid."

25 And Shaul said, "Thus shall you say to Dawid: 'The king desireth not any dowry, but a hundred foreskins of the Philistines, to be avenged of the king's enemies.' But Shaul thought to make Dawid fall by the hand of the Philistines.

26 And when his servants told Dawid these words, it pleased Dawid well to be the king's son in law; and the days were not expired.

27 Wherefore Dawid arose and went, he and his men, and slew of the Philistines two hundred men; and Dawid brought their foreskins, and they gave them in full tale to the king, that he might be the king's son in law. And Shaul gave him Michal his daughter to wife.

28 And Shaul saw and knew that יהוה was with Dawid, and that Michal Shaul's daughter loved him.

29 And Shaul was yet the more afraid of Dawid; and Shaul became Dawid's enemy continually.

30 Then the princes of the Philistines went forth; and it came to pass, after they went forth, that Dawid behaved himself more wisely than all the servants of Shaul; so that his name was highly esteemed.

19 And Shaul spake to Jonathan (Yehonatan) his son, and to all his servants, that they should kill Dawid.

2 But Jonathan (Yehonatan) Shaul's son delighted much in Dawid; and Jonathan (Yehonatan) told Dawid, saying, "Shaul my father seeketh to kill you; now therefore, please take heed to yourself until the morning, and abide in a secret place, and hide yourself.

3 And I will go out and stand beside my father in the field where you are, and I will commune with my father of you; and what I see, that I will tell you."

4 And Jonathan (Yehonatan) spake good of Dawid unto Shaul his father, and said unto him, "Let not the king sin against his servant, against Dawid; because he hath not sinned against you, and because his works have been to you-ward very good.

5 For he did put his life in his hand, and slew the Philistine, and יהוה wrought a great salvation for all Yisrael. You sawest it, and didst rejoice; wherefore then wilt you sin against innocent blood, to slay Dawid without a cause?"

6 And Shaul hearkened unto the voice of Jonathan (Yehonatan); and Shaul sware, "As יהוה liveth, he shall not be slain."

7 And Jonathan (Yehonatan) called Dawid, and Jonathan (Yehonatan) shewed him all those things. And Jonathan (Yehonatan) brought Dawid to Shaul, and he was in his presence, as in times past.

8 And there was war again; and Dawid went out, and fought with the Philistines, and slew them with a great slaughter; and they fled from him.

9 And the evil spirit from יהוה was upon Shaul, as he sat in his house with his javelin in his hand; and Dawid played with his hand.

10 And Shaul sought to smite Dawid even to the wall with the javelin; but he slipped away out of Shaul's presence, and he smote the javelin into the wall; and Dawid fled, and escaped that night.

11 Shaul also sent messengers unto Dawid's house, to watch him, and to slay him in the morning; and Michal Dawid's wife told him, saying, "If you save not your life tonight, tomorrow you shalt be slain."

12 So Michal let Dawid down through a window; and he went, and fled, and escaped.

13 And Michal took an image, and laid it in the bed, and put a pillow of goats' hair for his bolster, and covered it with a cloth.

14 And when Shaul sent messengers to take Dawid, she said, "He is sick."

15 And Shaul sent the messengers again to see Dawid, saying, "Bring him up to me in the bed, that I may slay him."

16 And when the messengers were come in,

behold, there was an image in the bed, with a pillow of goats' hair for his bolster.

17 And Shaul said unto Michal, "Why have you deceived me so, and sent away mine enemy, that he is escaped?" And Michal answered Shaul, "He said unto me, 'Let me go! Why should I kill you?'"

18 So Dawid fled, and escaped, and came to Shemuel to Ramah, and told him all that Shaul had done to him. And he and Shemuel went and dwelt in Naioth.

19 And it was told Shaul, saying, "Behold, Dawid is at Naioth in Ramah!"

20 And Shaul sent messengers to take Dawid: and when they saw the company of the prophets prophesying, and Shemuel standing as appointed over them, the Spirit of God (Elohim) was upon the messengers of Shaul, and they also prophesied.

21 And when it was told Shaul, he sent other messengers, and they prophesied likewise. And Shaul sent messengers again the third time, and they prophesied also.

22 Then went he also to Ramah, and came to a great well that is in Sechu; and he asked and said, "Where are Shemuel and Dawid?" And one said, "Behold, they be at Naioth in Ramah."

23 And he went thither to Naioth in Ramah; and the Spirit of God (Elohim) was upon him also, and he went on, and prophesied, until he came to Naioth in Ramah.

24 And he stripped off his clothes also, and prophesied before Shemuel in like manner, and lay down naked all that day and all that night. Wherefore they say, "Is Shaul also among the prophets?"

20 And Dawid fled from Naioth in Ramah, and came and said before Jonathan (Yehonatan), "What have I done? What is mine iniquity? And what is my sin before your father, that he seeketh my life?"

2 And he said unto him, "God (Elohim) forbid; you shalt not die. Behold, my father will do nothing either great or small, but that he will shew it me; and why should my father hide this thing from me? It is not so."

3 And Dawid sware moreover, and said, "Your father certainly knoweth that I have found grace in your eyes; and he saith, 'Let not Jonathan (Yehonatan) know this, lest he be grieved;' but truly as יהוה liveth, and as your soul liveth, there

is but a step between me and death."

4 Then said Jonathan (Yehonatan) unto Dawid, "Whatsoever your soul desireth, I will even do it for you."

5 And Dawid said unto Jonathan (Yehonatan), "Behold, tomorrow is the New Moon, and I should not fail to sit with the king to eat; but let me go, that I may hide myself in the field unto the third day at even.

6 If your father at all miss me, then say, 'Dawid earnestly asked leave of me that he might run to Bethlehem (Beit-Lechem) his city, for there is a yearly sacrifice there for all the family.'

7 If he says thus: 'It is well,' your servant shall have peace; but if he be very wroth, then be sure that evil is determined by him.

8 Therefore you shalt deal kindly with your servant; for you have brought your servant into a covenant of יהוה with you; notwithstanding, if there be in me iniquity, slay me yourself; for why shouldest you bring me to your father?"

9 And Jonathan (Yehonatan) said, "Far be it from you! For if I knew certainly that evil was determined by my father to come upon you, then would not I tell it you?"

10 Then said Dawid to Jonathan (Yehonatan), "Who shall tell me? Or what if your father answers you roughly?"

11 And Jonathan (Yehonatan) said unto Dawid, "Come, and let us go out into the field." And they went out both of them into the field.

12 And Jonathan (Yehonatan) said unto Dawid: "O יהוה God of Israel (Elohei Yisrael), when I have sounded my father about tomorrow any time, or the third day, and, behold, if there be good toward Dawid, and I then send not unto you, and shew it you;

13 יהוה do so and much more to Jonathan (Yehonatan): but if it please my father to do you evil, then I will shew it you, and send you away, that you mayest go in peace; and יהוה be with you, as He hath been with my father.

14 And you shalt not only while yet I live shew me the kindness of יהוה, that I die not;

15 But also you shalt not cut off your kindness from my house forever; no, not when יהוה hath cut off the enemies of Dawid every one from the face of the earth."

16 So Jonathan (Yehonatan) made a covenant with the house of Dawid, saying, "Let יהוה even require it at the hand of Dawid's enemies."

17 And Jonathan (Yehonatan) caused Dawid to swear again, because he loved him; for he loved him as he loved his own soul.

18 Then Jonathan (Yehonatan) said to Dawid, "Tomorrow is the new moon: and you shalt be missed, because your seat will be empty.

19 And when you have stayed three days, then you shalt go down quickly, and come to the place where you didst hide yourself when the business was in hand, and shalt remain by the stone Ezel.

20 And I will shoot three arrows on the side thereof, as though I shot at a mark.

21 And, behold, I will send a lad, saying, 'Go, find out the arrows.' If I expressly say unto the lad, 'Behold, the arrows are on this side of you, take them; then come you;' for there is peace to you, and no hurt; as יהוה liveth.

22 But if I say thus unto the young man, 'Behold, the arrows are beyond you;' go your way; for יהוה hath sent you away.

23 And as touching the matter which you and I have spoken of, behold, יהוה be between you and me forever."

24 So Dawid hid himself in the field: and when the New Moon was come, the king sat him down to eat meat.

25 And the king sat upon his seat, as at other times, even upon a seat by the wall; and Jonathan (Yehonatan) arose, and Abner sat by Shaul's side, and Dawid's place was empty.

26 Nevertheless Shaul spake not any thing that day; for he thought, "Something hath befallen him, he is not clean; surely he is not clean."

27 And it came to pass on the next day, which was the second day of the month, that Dawid's place was empty: and Shaul said unto Jonathan (Yehonatan) his son, "Wherefore cometh not the son of Jesse (Yishai) to meat, neither yesterday, nor today?"

28 And Jonathan (Yehonatan) answered Shaul, "Dawid earnestly asked leave of me to go to Bethlehem (Beit-Lechem).

29 And he said, 'Please let me go; for our family hath a sacrifice in the city; and my brother, he hath commanded me to be there; and now, if I have found favor in your eyes, please let me get away, and see my brethren.' Therefore he cometh not unto the king's table."

30 Then Shaul's anger was kindled against Jonathan (Yehonatan), and he said unto him,

"You son of the perverse rebellious woman! Do not I know that you have chosen the son of Jesse (Yishai) to your own shame, and unto the shame of your mother's nakedness?

31 For as long as the son of Jesse (Yishai) liveth upon the ground, you shalt not be established, nor your kingdom. Wherefore now send and fetch him unto me, for he shall surely die."

32 And Jonathan (Yehonatan) answered Shaul his father, and said unto him, "Why shall he be slain? What hath he done?"

33 And Shaul cast a javelin at him to smite him; whereby Jonathan (Yehonatan) knew that it was determined of his father to slay Dawid.

34 So Jonathan (Yehonatan) arose from the table in fierce anger, and did eat no meat the second day of the month; for he was grieved for Dawid, because his father had done him shame.

35 And it came to pass in the morning, that Jonathan (Yehonatan) went out into the field at the time appointed with Dawid, and a little lad with him.

36 And he said unto his lad, "Run, find out now the arrows which I shoot." And as the lad ran, he shot an arrow beyond him.

37 And when the lad was come to the place of the arrow which Jonathan (Yehonatan) had shot, Jonathan (Yehonatan) cried after the lad, and said, "Is not the arrow beyond you?"

38 And Jonathan (Yehonatan) cried after the lad, "Make speed, haste, stay not." And Jonathan (Yehonatan)'s lad gathered up the arrows, and came to his master.

39 But the lad knew not anything; only Jonathan (Yehonatan) and Dawid knew the matter.

40 And Jonathan (Yehonatan) gave his artillery unto his lad, and said unto him, "Go, carry them to the city."

41 And as soon as the lad was gone, Dawid arose out of a place toward the south, and fell on his face to the ground, and bowed himself three times; and they kissed one another, and wept one with another, but Dawid more so.

42 And Jonathan (Yehonatan) said to Dawid, "Go in peace, forasmuch as we have sworn both of us in the name of יהוה, saying, 'יהוה be between me and you, and between my seed and your seed forever.'" And he arose and departed; and Jonathan (Yehonatan) went into the city.

21 Then came Dawid to Nob to Ahimelech the priest (kohen); and Ahimelech

was afraid at the meeting of Dawid, and said unto him, "Why are you alone, and no man with you?"

2 And Dawid said unto Ahimelech the priest (kohen), "The king hath commanded me a business, and hath said unto me, 'Let no man know anything of the business whereabout I send you, and what I have commanded you.' And I have appointed my servants to such and such a place.

3 Now therefore what is under your hand? Give me five loaves of bread in mine hand, or what there is present."

4 And the priest (kohen) answered Dawid, and said, "There is no common bread under mine hand, but there is hallowed bread; if the young men have kept themselves at least from women."

5 And Dawid answered the priest (kohen), and said unto him, "Of a truth women have been kept from us about these three days, since I came out, and the vessels of the young men are holy, and the bread is in a manner common, yea, though it was sanctified this day in the vessel."

6 So the priest (kohen) gave him hallowed bread; for there was no bread there but the shewbread, that was taken from before יהוה, to put hot bread in the day when it was taken away.

7 Now a certain man of the servants of Shaul was there that day, detained before יהוה; and his name was Doeg, an Edomite, the chiefest of the herdmen that belonged to Shaul.

8 And Dawid said unto Ahimelech, "And is there not here under your hand spear or sword? For I have neither brought my sword nor my weapons with me, because the king's business required haste."

9 And the priest (kohen) said, "The sword of Goliath the Philistine, whom you slewest in the valley of Elah, behold, it is here wrapped in a cloth behind the ephod; if you wilt take that, take it; for there is no other save that here." And Dawid said, "There is none like that; give it me."

10 And Dawid arose, and fled that day for fear of Shaul, and went to Achish the king of Gath.

11 And the servants of Achish said unto him, "Is not this Dawid the king of the land? Did they not sing one to another of him in dances, saying: 'Shaul hath slain his thousands, and Dawid his ten thousands'?"

12 And Dawid laid up these words in his heart, and was sore afraid of Achish the king of Gath.

13 And he changed his behaviour before them, and feigned himself mad in their hands, and scrabbled on the doors of the gate, and let his spittle fall down upon his beard.

14 Then said Achish unto his servants, "Behold, you see the man is mad; wherefore then have you brought him to me?

15 Have I need of mad men, that you have brought this fellow to play the mad man in my presence? Shall this fellow come into my house?"

22 Dawid therefore departed thence, and escaped to the cave Adullam; and when his brethren and all his father's house heard it, they went down thither to him.

2 And every one that was in distress, and every one that was in debt, and every one that was discontented, gathered themselves unto him; and he became a captain over them; and there were with him about four hundred men.

3 And Dawid went thence to Mizpeh of Moav; and he said unto the king of Moav, "Please let my father and my mother come forth, and be with you, till I know what God (Elohim) will do for me."

4 And he brought them before the king of Moav; and they dwelt with him all the while that Dawid was in the hold.

5 And the prophet Gad said unto Dawid, "Abide not in the hold; depart, and get you into the land of Judah (Yehudah)." Then Dawid departed, and came into the forest of Hareth.

6 When Shaul heard that Dawid was discovered, and the men that were with him, (now Shaul abode in Gibeah under a tree in Ramah, having his spear in his hand, and all his servants were standing about him;)

7 Then Shaul said unto his servants that stood about him, "Hear now, you Benjamites (Ben-yemini)! Will the son of Jesse (Yishai) give every one of you fields and vineyards, and make you all captains of thousands, and captains of hundreds;

8 That all of you have conspired against me, and there is none that sheweth me that my son hath made a league with the son of Jesse (Yishai), and there is none of you that is sorry for me, or sheweth unto me that my son hath stirred up my servant against me, to lie in wait, as at

this day?"

9 Then answered Doeg the Edomite, who was set over the servants of Shaul, and said, "I saw the son of Jesse (Yishai) coming to Nob, to Ahimelech the son of Ahitub.

10 And he enquired of יהוה for him, and gave him victuals, and gave him the sword of Goliath the Philistine."

11 Then the king sent to call Ahimelech the priest (kohen), the son of Ahitub, and all his father's house, the priests (kohanim) that were in Nob; and they came all of them to the king.

12 And Shaul said, "Hear now, you son of Ahitub!" And he answered, "Here I am, my lord (adoni)."

13 And Shaul said unto him, "Why have you conspired against me, you and the son of Jesse (Yishai), in that you have given him bread, and a sword, and hast enquired of God (Elohim) for him, that he should rise against me, to lie in wait, as at this day?"

14 Then Ahimelech answered the king, and said, "And who is so faithful among all your servants as Dawid, which is the king's son in law, and goeth at your bidding, and is honourable in your house?

15 Did I then begin to enquire of God (Elohim) for him? Be it far from me; let not the king impute any thing unto his servant, nor to all the house of my father; for your servant knew nothing of all this, less or more."

16 And the king said, "You shalt surely die, Ahimelech, you, and all your father's house."

17 And the king said unto the footmen that stood about him, "Turn, and slay the priests (kohanim) of יהוה; because their hand also is with Dawid, and because they knew when he fled, and did not shew it to me." But the servants of the king would not put forth their hand to fall upon the priests (kohanim) of יהוה.

18 And the king said to Doeg, "Turn you, and fall upon the priests (kohanim)." And Doeg the Edomite turned, and he fell upon the priests (kohanim), and slew on that day fourscore and five persons that did wear a linen ephod.

19 And Nob, the city of the priests (kohanim), smote he with the edge of the sword, both men and women, children and sucklings, and oxen, and asses, and sheep, with the edge of the sword.

20 And one of the sons of Ahimelech the son of Ahitub, named Aviyahthar, escaped, and fled after Dawid.

21 And Aviyahthar shewed Dawid that Shaul had slain יהוה's priests (kohanim).

22 And Dawid said unto Aviyahthar, "I knew it that day, when Doeg the Edomite was there, that he would surely tell Shaul; I have occasioned the death of all the persons of your father's house.

23 Abide you with me; fear not, for he that seeketh my life seeketh your life; but with me you shalt be in safeguard."

23 Then they told Dawid, saying, "Behold, the Philistines fight against Keilah, and they rob the threshingfloors."

2 Therefore Dawid enquired of יהוה, saying, "Shall I go and smite these Philistines? And יהוה said unto Dawid, Go, and smite the Philistines, and save Keilah."

3 And Dawid's men said unto him, "Behold, we be afraid here in Judah (Yehudah); how much more then if we come to Keilah against the armies of the Philistines?

4 Then Dawid enquired of יהוה yet again. And יהוה answered him and said, "Arise, go down to Keilah; for I will deliver the Philistines into your hand."

5 So Dawid and his men went to Keilah, and fought with the Philistines, and brought away their cattle, and smote them with a great slaughter. So Dawid saved the inhabitants of Keilah.

6 And it came to pass, when Aviyahthar the son of Ahimelech fled to Dawid to Keilah, that he came down with an ephod in his hand.

7 And it was told Shaul that Dawid was come to Keilah. And Shaul said, "God (Elohim) hath delivered him into mine hand; for he is shut in, by entering into a town that hath gates and bars."

8 And Shaul called all the people together to war, to go down to Keilah, to besiege Dawid and his men.

9 And Dawid knew that Shaul secretly practised mischief against him; and he said to Aviyahthar the priest (kohen), "Bring hither the ephod."

10 Then said Dawid, "O יהוה God of Israel (Elohei Yisrael), your servant hath certainly heard that Shaul seeketh to come to Keilah, to destroy the city for my sake.

11 Will the men of Keilah deliver me up into his hand? Will Shaul come down, as Your servant hath heard? O יהוה God of Israel (Elohei

Yisrael), I beseech you, tell Your servant." And יהוה said, "He will come down."

12 Then said Dawid, "Will the men of Keilah deliver me and my men into the hand of Shaul?" And יהוה said, "They will deliver you up."

13 Then Dawid and his men, which were about six hundred, arose and departed out of Keilah, and went whithersoever they could go. And it was told Shaul that Dawid was escaped from Keilah; and he forbare to go forth.

14 And Dawid abode in the wilderness in strong holds, and remained in a mountain in the wilderness of Ziph. And Shaul sought him every day, but God (Elohim) delivered him not into his hand.

15 And Dawid saw that Shaul was come out to seek his life; and Dawid was in the wilderness of Ziph in a wood.

16 And Jonathan (Yehonatan) Shaul's son arose, and went to Dawid into the wood, and strengthened his hand in God (Elohim).

17 And he said unto him, "Fear not, for the hand of Shaul my father shall not find you; and you shalt be king over Yisrael, and I shall be next unto you; and that also Shaul my father knoweth."

18 And they two made a covenant before יהוה; and Dawid abode in the wood, and Jonathan (Yehonatan) went to his house.

19 Then came up the Ziphites to Shaul to Gibeah, saying, "Doth not Dawid hide himself with us in strong holds in the wood, in the hill of Hachilah, which is on the south of Yeshimon?

20 Now therefore, O king, come down according to all the desire of your soul to come down; and our part shall be to deliver him into the king's hand."

21 And Shaul said, "Blessed be you of יהוה, for you have compassion on me.

22 Go, I pray you, prepare yet, and know and see his place where his haunt is, and who hath seen him there; for it is told me that he dealeth very subtilly.

23 See therefore, and take knowledge of all the lurking places where he hideth himself, and come you again to me with the certainty, and I will go with you; and it shall come to pass, if he be in the land, that I will search him out throughout all the thousands of Judah (Yehudah)."

24 And they arose, and went to Ziph before Shaul; but Dawid and his men were in the wilderness of Maon, in the plain on the south of Yeshimon.

25 Shaul also and his men went to seek him. And they told Dawid; wherefore he came down into a rock, and abode in the wilderness of Maon. And when Shaul heard that, he pursued after Dawid in the wilderness of Maon.

26 And Shaul went on this side of the mountain, and Dawid and his men on that side of the mountain; and Dawid made haste to get away for fear of Shaul; for Shaul and his men compassed Dawid and his men round about to take them.

27 But there came a messenger unto Shaul, saying, "Haste you, and come; for the Philistines have invaded the land!"

28 Wherefore Shaul returned from pursuing after Dawid, and went against the Philistines; therefore they called that place 'the Rock of Escapes' (Sela Hammachleqot).

29 And Dawid went up from thence, and dwelt in strong holds at Engedi.

24 And it came to pass, when Shaul returned from following the Philistines, that it was told him, saying, "Behold, Dawid is in the wilderness of Engedi."

2 Then Shaul took three thousand chosen men out of all Yisrael, and went to seek Dawid and his men upon the rocks of the wild goats.

3 And he came to the sheepcotes by the way, where was a cave; and Shaul went in to cover his feet; and Dawid and his men remained in the sides of the cave.

4 And the men of Dawid said unto him, "Behold the day of which יהוה said unto you, 'Behold, I will deliver your enemy into your hand, that you mayest do to him as it shall seem good unto you.'" Then Dawid arose, and cut off the skirt of Shaul's robe privily.

5 And it came to pass afterward, that Dawid's heart smote him, because he had cut off Shaul's skirt.

6 And he said unto his men, "יהוה forbid that I should do this thing unto my master, יהוה's anointed, to stretch forth mine hand against him, seeing he is the anointed of יהוה."

7 So Dawid stayed his servants with these words, and suffered them not to rise against Shaul. But Shaul rose up out of the cave, and went on his way.

8 Dawid also arose afterward, and went out of

the cave, and cried after Shaul, saying, "My lord (Adoni) the king." And when Shaul looked behind him, Dawid stooped with his face to the earth, and bowed himself.

9 And Dawid said to Shaul: "Why hearest you men's words, saying, 'Behold, Dawid seeketh your hurt'?

10 Behold, this day your eyes have seen how that יהוה had delivered you today into mine hand in the cave; and some bade me kill you: but mine eye spared you; and I said, 'I will not put forth mine hand against my lord (adoni); for he is יהוה's anointed (mashiach).'

11 Moreover, my father, see! Yea, see the skirt of your robe in my hand; for in that I cut off the skirt of your robe, and killed you not, know you and see that there is neither evil nor transgression in mine hand, and I have not sinned against you; yet you huntest my soul to take it.

12 יהוה judge between me and you, and יהוה avenge me of you; but mine hand shall not be upon you.

13 As saith the proverb of the ancients, Wickedness proceedeth from the wicked; but mine hand shall not be upon you.

14 After whom is the king of Yisrael come out? After whom dost you pursue? After a dead dog, after a flea.

15 יהוה therefore be judge, and judge between me and you, and see, and plead my cause, and deliver me out of your hand.

16 And it came to pass, when Dawid had made an end of speaking these words unto Shaul, that Shaul said, "Is this your voice, my son Dawid?" And Shaul lifted up his voice, and wept.

17 And he said to Dawid, "You are more righteous than I; for you have rewarded me good, whereas I have rewarded you evil.

18 And you have shewed this day how that you have dealt well with me; forasmuch as when יהוה had delivered me into your hand, you killedst me not.

19 For if a man finds his enemy, will he let him go well away? Therefore may יהוה reward you good for that you have done unto me this day.

20 And now, behold, I know well that you shalt surely be king, and that the kingdom of Yisrael shall be established in your hand.

21 Swear now therefore unto me by יהוה, that you wilt not cut off my seed after me, and that

you wilt not destroy my name out of my father's house."

22 And Dawid sware unto Shaul. And Shaul went home; but Dawid and his men gat them up unto the stronghold.

25 And Shemuel died; and all the Yisraelites were gathered together, and lamented him, and buried him in his house at Ramah. And Dawid arose, and went down to the wilderness of Paran.

2 And there was a man in Maon, whose possessions were in Carmel; and the man was very great, and he had three thousand sheep, and a thousand goats; and he was shearing his sheep in Carmel.

3 Now the name of the man was Naval; and the name of his wife Avigail; and she was a woman of good understanding, and of a beautiful countenance; but the man was churlish and evil in his doings; and he was of the house of Caleb.

4 And Dawid heard in the wilderness that Naval did shear his sheep.

5 And Dawid sent out ten young men, and Dawid said unto the young men, "Get you up to Carmel, and go to Naval, and greet him in my name.

6 And thus shall you say to him that liveth in prosperity, 'Peace be both to you, and peace be to your house, and peace be unto all that you have!

7 And now I have heard that you have shearers; now your shepherds which were with us, we hurt them not, neither was there anything missing unto them, all the while they were in Carmel.

8 Ask your young men, and they will shew you. Wherefore let the young men find favor in your eyes; for we come in a good day: Please give whatsoever cometh to your hand unto your servants, and to your son Dawid.'"

9 And when Dawid's young men came, they spake to Naval according to all those words in the name of Dawid, and ceased.

10 And Naval answered Dawid's servants, and said, "Who is Dawid? And who is the son of Jesse (Yishai)? There be many servants now a days that break away every man from his master.

11 Shall I then take my bread, and my water, and my flesh that I have killed for my shearers, and give it unto men, whom I know not whence

they be?"

12 So Dawid's young men turned their way, and went again, and came and told him all those sayings.

13 And Dawid said unto his men, "Gird you on every man his sword. And they girded on every man his sword; and Dawid also girded on his sword; and there went up after Dawid about four hundred men; and two hundred abode by the stuff.

14 But one of the young men told Avigail, Naval's wife, saying, "Behold, Dawid sent messengers out of the wilderness to salute our master; and he railed on them.

15 But the men were very good unto us, and we were not hurt, neither missed we any thing, as long as we were conversant with them, when we were in the fields.

16 They were a wall unto us both by night and day, all the while we were with them keeping the sheep.

17 Now therefore know and consider what you wilt do; for evil is determined against our master, and against all his household; for he is such a scoundrel (beliyaal) son, that a man cannot speak to him."

18 Then Avigail made haste, and took two hundred loaves, and two bottles of wine, and five sheep ready dressed, and five measures of parched corn, and a hundred clusters of raisins, and two hundred cakes of figs, and laid them on asses.

19 And she said unto her servants, "Go on before me; behold, I come after you." But she told not her husband Naval.

20 And it was so, as she rode on the ass, that she came down by the covert of the hill, and, behold, Dawid and his men came down against her; and she met them.

21 Now Dawid had said, "Surely in vain have I kept all that this fellow hath in the wilderness, so that nothing was missed of all that pertained unto him: and he hath requited me evil for good.

22 So and more also do God (Elohim) unto the enemies of Dawid, if I leave of all that pertain to him by the morning light any that pisseth against the wall."

23 And when Avigail saw Dawid, she hasted, and lighted off the ass, and fell before Dawid on her face, and bowed herself to the ground,

24 And fell at his feet, and said: "Upon me,

my lord (adoni), upon me let this iniquity be; and please let your handmaid speak in your audience, and hear the words of your handmaid.

25 Please let not my lord (adoni) regard this scoundrel (beliyaal) man, Naval, for as his name is, so is he; Naval is his name, and folly is with him. But I, your handmaid saw not the young men of my lord (adoni), whom you didst send.

26 Now therefore, my lord (adoni), as יהוה liveth, and as your soul liveth, seeing יהוה hath withholden you from coming to shed blood, and from avenging yourself with your own hand, now let your enemies, and they that seek evil to my lord (adoni), be as Naval.

27 And now this blessing which your handmaid hath brought unto my lord (adoni), let it even be given unto the young men that follow my lord (adoni).

28 Please forgive the trespass of your handmaid; for יהוה will certainly make my lord (adoni) a sure house; because my lord (adoni) fighteth the battles of יהוה, and evil hath not been found in you all your days.

29 Yet a man is risen to pursue you, and to seek your soul; but the soul of my lord (adoni) shall be bound in the bundle of life with יהוה your God (YHWH Eloheikha); and the souls of your enemies, them shall he sling out, as out of the middle of a sling.

30 And it shall come to pass, when יהוה shall have done to my lord (adoni) according to all the good that he hath spoken concerning you, and shall have appointed you ruler over Yisrael;

31 That this shall be no grief unto you, nor offence of heart unto my lord (adoni), either that you have shed blood causeless, or that my lord (adoni) hath avenged himself; but when יהוה shall have dealt well with my lord (adoni), then remember your handmaid."

32 And Dawid said to Avigail: "Blessed be יהוה God of Israel (Elohei Yisrael), which sent you this day to meet me!

33 And blessed be your advice, and blessed be you, which hast kept me this day from coming to shed blood, and from avenging myself with mine own hand.

34 For in very deed, as יהוה God of Israel (Elohei Yisrael) liveth, which hath kept me back from hurting you, except you hadst hasted and come to meet me, surely there had not been left unto Naval by the morning light any that pisseth

against the wall."

35 So Dawid received of her hand that which she had brought him, and said unto her, "Go up in peace to your house; see, I have hearkened to your voice, and have accepted your person."

36 And Avigail came to Naval; and, behold, he held a feast in his house, like the feast of a king; and Naval's heart was merry within him, for he was very drunken: wherefore she told him nothing, less or more, until the morning light.

37 But it came to pass in the morning, when the wine was gone out of Naval, and his wife had told him these things, that his heart died within him, and he became as a stone.

38 And it came to pass about ten days after, that יהוה smote Naval, that he died.

39 And when Dawid heard that Naval was dead, he said, "Blessed be יהוה, that hath pleaded the cause of my reproach from the hand of Naval, and hath kept His servant from evil; for יהוה hath returned the wickedness of Naval upon his own head." And Dawid sent and communed with Avigail, to take her to him to wife.

40 And when the servants of Dawid were come to Avigail to Carmel, they spake unto her, saying, "Dawid sent us unto you, to take you to him to wife."

41 And she arose, and bowed herself on her face to the earth, and said, "Behold, let your handmaid be a servant to wash the feet of the servants of my lord (adoni)."

42 And Avigail hasted, and arose, and rode upon an ass, with five damsels of hers that went after her; and she went after the messengers of Dawid, and became his wife.

43 Dawid also took Ahinoam of Yizreel; and they were also both of them his wives.

44 But Shaul had given Michal his daughter, Dawid's wife, to Phalti the son of Laish, which was of Gallim.

26 And the Ziphites came unto Shaul to Gibeah, saying, "Doth not Dawid hide himself in the hill of Hachilah, which is before Yeshimon?"

2 Then Shaul arose, and went down to the wilderness of Ziph, having three thousand chosen men of Yisrael with him, to seek Dawid in the wilderness of Ziph.

3 And Shaul pitched in the hill of Hachilah, which is before Yeshimon, by the way. But Dawid abode in the wilderness, and he saw that Shaul came after him into the wilderness.

4 Dawid therefore sent out spies, and understood that Shaul was come in very deed.

5 And Dawid arose, and came to the place where Shaul had pitched: and Dawid beheld the place where Shaul lay, and Abner the son of Ner, the captain of his army: and Shaul lay in the trench, and the people pitched round about him.

6 Then answered Dawid and said to Ahimelech the Hittite, and to Avishai the son of Zeruyah, brother to Yoav, saying, "Who will go down with me to Shaul to the camp?" And Avishai said, "I will go down with you."

7 So Dawid and Avishai came to the people by night; and, behold, Shaul lay sleeping within the trench, and his spear stuck in the ground at his bolster; but Abner and the people lay round about him.

8 Then said Avishai to Dawid, "God (Elohim) hath delivered your enemy into your hand this day; now therefore let me smite him, please, with the spear even to the earth at once, and I will not smite him the second time!"

9 And Dawid said to Avishai, "Destroy him not; for who can stretch forth his hand against יהוה's anointed, and be guiltless?"

10 Dawid said furthermore, "As יהוה liveth, יהוה shall smite him; or his day shall come to die; or he shall descend into battle, and perish.

11 יהוה forbid that I should stretch forth mine hand against יהוה's anointed; but please, take you now the spear that is at his bolster, and the cruse of water, and let us go."

12 So Dawid took the spear and the cruse of water from Shaul's bolster; and they gat them away, and no man saw it, nor knew it, neither awaked; for they were all asleep, because a deep sleep from יהוה was fallen upon them.

13 Then Dawid went over to the other side, and stood on the top of a hill afar off; a great space being between them:

14 And Dawid cried to the people, and to Abner the son of Ner, saying, "Answerest you not, Abner?" Then Abner answered and said, "Who are you that criest to the king?"

15 And Dawid said to Abner, "Art not you a valiant man? And who is like to you in Yisrael? Wherefore then have you not kept your lord (adon) the king? For there came one of the people in to destroy the king your lord (adon).

16 This thing is not good that you have done. As

יהוה liveth, you are worthy to die, because you have not kept your master, יהוה's anointed (mashiach). And now see where the king's spear is, and the cruse of water that was at his bolster."

17 And Shaul knew Dawid's voice, and said, "Is this your voice, my son Dawid?" And Dawid said, "It is my voice, my lord (adoni), O king."

18 And he said, "Why doth my lord (adoni) thus pursue after his servant? For what have I done? Or what evil is in mine hand?

19 Now therefore, please let my lord (adoni) the king hears the words of his servant: If יהוה have stirred you up against me, let him accept an offering; but if they be the children of men, cursed be they before יהוה; for they have driven me out this day from abiding in the inheritance of יהוה, saying, 'Go, serve other gods (elohim).'

20 Now therefore, let not my blood fall to the earth before the face of יהוה; for the king of Yisrael is come out to seek a flea, as when one doth hunt a partridge in the mountains.

21 Then said Shaul, "I have sinned. Return, my son Dawid; for I will no more do you harm, because my soul was precious in your eyes this day. Behold, I have played the fool, and have erred exceedingly."

22 And Dawid answered and said, "Behold the king's spear! And let one of the young men come over and fetch it.

23 May יהוה render to every man His righteousness and His faithfulness; for יהוה delivered you into my hand today, but I would not stretch forth mine hand against יהוה's anointed (mashiach).

24 And, behold, as your life was much set by this day in mine eyes, so let my life be much set by in the eyes of יהוה, and let Him deliver me out of all tribulation."

25 Then Shaul said to Dawid, "Blessed be you, my son Dawid! You shalt both do great things, and also shalt still prevail. So Dawid went on his way, and Shaul returned to his place.

27 And Dawid said in his heart, "I shall now perish one day by the hand of Shaul; there is nothing better for me than that I should speedily escape into the land of the Philistines; and Shaul shall despair of me, to seek me any more in any coast of Yisrael; so shall I escape out of his hand."

2 And Dawid arose, and he passed over with the six hundred men that were with him unto Achish, the son of Maoch, king of Gath.

3 And Dawid dwelt with Achish at Gath, he and his men, every man with his household, even Dawid with his two wives, Ahinoam the Yizreelitess, and Avigail the Carmelitess, Naval's wife.

4 And it was told Shaul that Dawid was fled to Gath; and he sought no more again for him.

5 And Dawid said unto Achish, "If I have now found grace in your eyes, let them give me a place in some town in the country, that I may dwell there; for why should your servant dwell in the royal city with you?"

6 Then Achish gave him Ziklag that day; wherefore Ziklag pertaineth unto the kings of Judah (Yehudah) unto this day.

7 And the time that Dawid dwelt in the country of the Philistines was a full year and four months.

8 And Dawid and his men went up, and invaded the Geshurites, and the Gezrites, and the Amalekites; for those nations were of old the inhabitants of the land, as you goest to Shur, even unto the land of Egypt (Mitsrayim).

9 And Dawid smote the land, and left neither man nor woman alive, and took away the sheep, and the oxen, and the asses, and the camels, and the apparel, and returned, and came to Achish.

10 And Achish said, "Whither have you made a road today?" And Dawid said, "Against the south of Judah (Yehudah), and against the south of the Yerachmeelites, and against the south of the Kenites."

11 And Dawid saved neither man nor woman alive, to bring tidings to Gath, saying, "Lest they should tell on us, saying, 'So did Dawid.'" And so will be his manner all the while he dwelleth in the country of the Philistines.

12 And Achish believed Dawid, saying, "He hath made his people Yisrael utterly to abhor him; therefore he shall be my servant forever."

28 And it came to pass in those days, that the Philistines gathered their armies together for warfare, to fight with Yisrael. And Achish said unto Dawid, "Know you assuredly, that you shalt go out with me to battle, you and your men."

2 And Dawid said to Achish, "Surely you shalt know what your servant can do." And Achish said to Dawid, "Therefore will I make you keeper of mine head forever."

3 Now Shemuel was dead, and all Yisrael had lamented him, and buried him in Ramah, even in his own city. And Shaul had put away those that had familiar spirits, and the wizards, out of the land.

4 And the Philistines gathered themselves together, and came and pitched in Shunem; and Shaul gathered all Yisrael together, and they pitched in Gilboa.

5 And when Shaul saw the army of the Philistines, he was afraid, and his heart greatly trembled.

6 And when Shaul enquired of יהוה, יהוה answered him not, neither by dreams, nor by Urim, nor by prophets.

7 Then said Shaul unto his servants, "Seek me a woman that hath a familiar spirit, that I may go to her, and enquire of her." And his servants said to him, "Behold, there is a woman that hath a familiar spirit at En Dor."

8 And Shaul disguised himself, and put on other raiment, and he went, and two men with him, and they came to the woman by night; and he said, "Please, divine unto me by the familiar spirit, and bring him up for me, whom I shall name unto you."

9 And the woman said unto him, "Behold, you knowest what Shaul hath done, how he hath cut off those that have familiar spirits, and the wizards, out of the land: wherefore then layest you a snare for my life, to cause me to die?"

10 And Shaul sware to her by יהוה, saying, "As יהוה liveth, there shall no punishment happen to you for this thing."

11 Then said the woman, "Whom shall I bring up unto you?" And he said, "Bring up Shemuel for me."

12 And when the woman saw Shemuel, she cried with a loud voice: and the woman spake to Shaul, saying, "Why have you deceived me? For you are Shaul."

13 And the king said unto her, "Be not afraid; for what sawest you?" And the woman said unto Shaul, "I saw divine being (elohim) ascending out of the earth."

14 And he said unto her, "What form is he of?" And she said, "An old man cometh up; and he is covered with a mantle." And Shaul perceived that it was Shemuel, and he stooped with his face to the ground, and bowed himself.

15 And Shemuel said to Shaul, "Why have you disquieted me, to bring me up?" And Shaul answered, "I am sore distressed; for the Philistines make war against me, and God (Elohim) is departed from me, and answereth me no more, neither by prophets, nor by dreams; therefore I have called you, that you mayest make known unto me what I shall do."

16 Then said Shemuel, "Why then dost you ask of me, seeing יהוה is departed from you, and is become your enemy?

17 And יהוה hath done to him, as he spake by me; for יהוה hath rent the kingdom out of your hand, and given it to your neighbour, even to Dawid;

18 Because you obeyedst not the voice of יהוה, nor executedst His fierce wrath upon Amalek, therefore hath יהוה done this thing unto you this day.

19 Moreover יהוה will also deliver Yisrael with you into the hand of the Philistines; and tomorrow shalt you and your sons be with me; יהוה also shall deliver the army of Yisrael into the hand of the Philistines."

20 Then Shaul fell straightway all along on the earth, and was sore afraid, because of the words of Shemuel; and there was no strength in him; for he had eaten no food all the day, nor all the night.

21 And the woman came unto Shaul, and saw that he was sore troubled, and said unto him, "Behold, your handmaid hath obeyed your voice, and I have put my life in my hand, and have hearkened unto your words which you spakest unto me.

22 Now therefore, please hearken you also unto the voice of your handmaid, and let me set a morsel of bread before you; and eat, that you mayest have strength, when you goest on your way."

23 But he refused, and said, "I will not eat." But his servants, together with the woman, compelled him; and he hearkened unto their voice. So he arose from the earth, and sat upon the bed.

24 And the woman had a fat calf in the house; and she hasted, and killed it, and took flour, and kneaded it, and did bake unleaven bread (matstsah) thereof.

25 And she brought it before Shaul, and before his servants; and they did eat. Then they rose up, and went away that night.

29 Now the Philistines gathered together all their armies to Aphek; and the Yisraelites pitched by a fountain which is in Yizreel.

2 And the lords (seranim) of the Philistines passed on by hundreds, and by thousands; but Dawid and his men passed on in the rereward with Achish.

3 Then said the princes of the Philistines, "What do these Hebrews (Ivrim) here? And Achish said unto the princes of the Philistines, "Is not this Dawid, the servant of Shaul the king of Yisrael, who hath been with me these days, or these years, and I have found no fault in him since he fell unto me unto this day?"

4 And the princes of the Philistines were wroth with him; and the princes of the Philistines said unto him, "Make this fellow return, that he may go again to his place which you have appointed him, and let him not go down with us to battle, lest in the battle he be an adversary to us; for wherewith should he reconcile himself unto his master? should it not be with the heads of these men?

5 Is not this Dawid, of whom they sang one to another in dances, saying: 'Shaul slew his thousands, and Dawid his multitude'?"

6 Then Achish called Dawid, and said unto him, "Surely, as יהוה liveth, you have been upright, and your going out and your coming in with me in the army is good in my sight; for I have not found evil in you since the day of your coming unto me unto this day; nevertheless the lords favor you not.

7 Wherefore now return, and go in peace, that you displease not the lords (seranim) of the Philistines."

8 And Dawid said unto Achish, "But what have I done? And what have you found in your servant so long as I have been with you unto this day, that I may not go fight against the enemies of my lord (adoni) the king?"

9 And Achish answered and said to Dawid, "I know that you are good in my sight, as an angel of God (Elohim); notwithstanding the princes of the Philistines have said, 'He shall not go up with us to the battle.

10 Wherefore now rise up early in the morning with your master's servants that are come with you; and as soon as you be up early in the morning, and have light, depart.

11 So Dawid and his men rose up early to depart in the morning, to return into the land of the Philistines. And the Philistines went up to Yizreel.

30 And it came to pass, when Dawid and his men were come to Ziklag on the third day, that the Amalekites had invaded the south, and Ziklag, and smitten Ziklag, and burned it with fire;

2 And had taken the women captives, that were therein; they slew not any, either great or small, but carried them away, and went on their way.

3 So Dawid and his men came to the city, and, behold, it was burned with fire; and their wives, and their sons, and their daughters, were taken captives.

4 Then Dawid and the people that were with him lifted up their voice and wept, until they had no more power to weep.

5 And Dawid's two wives were taken captives, Ahinoam the Yizreelitess, and Avigail the wife of Naval the Carmelite.

6 And Dawid was greatly distressed; for the people spake of stoning him, because the soul of all the people was grieved, every man for his sons and for his daughters; but Dawid encouraged himself in יהוה his God (Elohim).

7 And Dawid said to Aviyahthar the priest (kohen), "Ahimelech's son, please bring me hither the ephod." And Aviyahthar brought thither the ephod to Dawid.

8 And Dawid enquired at יהוה, saying, "Shall I pursue after this troop? Shall I overtake them?" And he answered him, "Pursue, for you shalt surely overtake them, and without fail recover all."

9 So Dawid went, he and the six hundred men that were with him, and came to the Brook Besor, where those that were left behind stayed.

10 But Dawid pursued, he and four hundred men; for two hundred abode behind, which were so faint that they could not go over the Brook Besor.

11 And they found an Egyptian (Mitsri) in the field, and brought him to Dawid, and gave him bread, and he did eat; and they made him drink water;

12 And they gave him a piece of a cake of figs, and two clusters of raisins; and when he had eaten, his spirit came again to him; for he had eaten no bread, nor drunk any water, three days and three nights.

13 And Dawid said unto him, "To whom belongest you? And whence are you?" And he said, "I am a young man of Egypt (Mitsrayim), servant to an Amalekite; and my master left me, because three days agone I fell sick.

14 We made an invasion upon the south of the Cherethites, and upon the coast which belongeth to Judah (Yehudah), and upon the south of Caleb; and we burned Ziklag with fire."

15 And Dawid said to him, "Canst you bring me down to this company?" And he said, "Swear unto me by God (Elohim), that you wilt neither kill me, nor deliver me into the hands of my master, and I will bring you down to this company."

16 And when he had brought him down, behold, they were spread abroad upon all the earth, eating and drinking, and dancing, because of all the great spoil that they had taken out of the land of the Philistines, and out of the land of Judah (Yehudah).

17 And Dawid smote them from the twilight even unto the evening of the next day; and there escaped not a man of them, save four hundred young men, which rode upon camels, and fled.

18 And Dawid recovered all that the Amalekites had carried away; and Dawid rescued his two wives.

19 And there was nothing lacking to them, neither small nor great, neither sons nor daughters, neither spoil, nor any thing that they had taken to them: Dawid recovered all.

20 And Dawid took all the flocks and the herds, which they drave before those other cattle, and said, "This is Dawid's spoil."

21 And Dawid came to the two hundred men, which were so faint that they could not follow Dawid, whom they had made also to abide at the Brook Besor; and they went forth to meet Dawid, and to meet the people that were with him; and when Dawid came near to the people, he saluted them.

22 Then answered all the wicked men and scoundrel (beliyaal) men, of those that went with Dawid, and said, "Because they went not with us, we will not give them ought of the spoil that we have recovered, save to every man his wife and his children, that they may lead them away, and depart."

23 Then said Dawid, "You shall not do so, my brethren, with that which יהוה hath given us, who hath preserved us, and delivered the company that came against us into our hand.

24 For who will hearken unto you in this matter? But as his part is that goeth down to the battle, so shall his part be that tarrieth by the stuff; they shall part alike."

25 And it was so from that day forward, that he made it a statute and an ordinance for Yisrael unto this day.

26 And when Dawid came to Ziklag, he sent of the spoil unto the elders of Judah (Yehudah), even to his friends, saying, "Behold a present for you of the spoil of the enemies of יהוה;"

27 To them who were in Bethel (Beit-El), and to them who were in south Ramot, and to them who were in Yattir,

28 And to them who were in Aroer, and to them who were in Siphmoth, and to them who were in Eshtemoa,

29 And to them who were in Rachal, and to them who were in the cities of the Yerachmeelites, and to them which were in the cities of the Kenites,

30 And to them who were in Hormah, and to them who were in Chorashan, and to them who were in Athach,

31 And to them who were in Hebron, and to all the places where Dawid himself and his men had frequently visited.

31 Now the Philistines fought against Yisrael; and the men of Yisrael fled from before the Philistines, and fell down slain in Mount Gilboa.

2 And the Philistines followed hard upon Shaul and upon his sons; and the Philistines slew Jonathan (Yehonatan), and Abinadab, and Malchishua, Shaul's sons.

3 And the battle went sore against Shaul, and the archers hit him; and he was sore wounded of the archers.

4 Then said Shaul unto his armourbearer, "Draw your sword, and thrust me through therewith; lest these uncircumcised come and thrust me through, and abuse me." But his armourbearer would not; for he was sore afraid. Therefore Shaul took a sword, and fell upon it.

5 And when his armourbearer saw that Shaul was dead, he fell likewise upon his sword, and died with him.

6 So Shaul died, and his three sons, and his armourbearer, and all his men, that same day

together.

7 And when the men of Yisrael that were on the other side of the valley, and they that were on the other side Jordan (Yarden), saw that the men of Yisrael fled, and that Shaul and his sons were dead, they forsook the cities, and fled; and the Philistines came and dwelt in them.

8 And it came to pass on the next day, when the Philistines came to strip the slain, that they found Shaul and his three sons fallen in Mount Gilboa.

9 And they cut off his head, and stripped off his armour, and sent into the land of the Philistines round about, to publish it in the house of their idols, and among the people.

10 And they put his armour in the house of Ashtaroth; and they fastened his body to the wall of Beit-Shan.

11 And when the inhabitants of Yavesh-Gilad heard of that which the Philistines had done to Shaul;

12 All the valiant men arose, and went all night, and took the body of Shaul and the bodies of his sons from the wall of Beit-Shan, and came to Yavesh, and burnt them there.

13 And they took their bones, and buried them under a tree at Yavesh, and fasted seven days.

2 SAMUEL
SHEMUEL 2 שְׁמוּאֵל ב
(El has Heard)

1 Now it came to pass after the death of Shaul, when Dawid was returned from the slaughter of the Amalekites, and Dawid had abode two days in Ziklag;

2 It came even to pass on the third day, that, behold, a man came out of the camp from Shaul with his clothes rent, and earth upon his head; and so it was, when he came to Dawid, that he fell to the earth, and prostrated himself.

3 And Dawid said unto him, "From whence comest you?" And he said unto him, "Out of the camp of Yisrael am I escaped."

4 And Dawid said unto him, "How went the matter? Please tell me." And he answered, "That the people are fled from the battle, and many of the people also are fallen and dead; and Shaul and Jonathan (Yehonatan) his son are dead also."

5 And Dawid said unto the young man that told him, "How knowest you that Shaul and Jonathan (Yehonatan) his son be dead?"

6 And the young man that told him said, "As I happened by chance upon mount Gilboa, behold, Shaul leaned upon his spear; and, behold, the chariots and horsemen followed hard after him.

7 And when he looked behind him, he saw me, and called unto me. And I answered, 'Here am I.'

8 And he said unto me, 'Who are you?' And I answered him, 'I am an Amalekite.'

9 He said unto me again, 'Please stand over me, and slay me; for anguish is come upon me, because my life is yet whole in me.'

10 So I stood upon him, and slew him, because I was sure that he could not live after that he was fallen; and I took the crown that was upon his head, and the bracelet that was on his arm, and have brought them hither unto my lord (adoni)."

11 Then Dawid took hold on his clothes, and rent them; and likewise all the men that were with him.

12 And they mourned, and wept, and fasted until even, for Shaul, and for Jonathan (Yehonatan) his son, and for the people of יהוה, and for the house of Yisrael; because they were fallen by the sword.

13 And Dawid said unto the young man that told him, "Whence are you?" And he answered, "I am the son of a stranger, an Amalekite."

14 And Dawid said unto him, "How wast you not afraid to stretch forth your hand to destroy יהוה's anointed?"

15 And Dawid called one of the young men, and said, "Go near, and fall upon him!" And he smote him that he died.

16 And Dawid said unto him, "Your blood be upon your head; for your mouth hath testified against you, saying, 'I have slain יהוה's anointed (mashiach).'"

17 And Dawid lamented with this lamentation over Shaul and over Jonathan (Yehonatan) his son;

18 Also he bade them teach the children of Judah (Yehudah) the bow; behold, it is written in the Book of Yashar:

19 The beauty of Yisrael is slain upon your high places! How are the mighty fallen!

20 Tell it not in Gath, publish it not in the streets of Askelon; lest the daughters of the Philistines rejoice, lest the daughters of the uncircumcised triumph.

21 You, mountains of Gilboa, let there be no dew, neither let there be rain, upon you, nor fields of offerings; for there the shield of the mighty is vilely cast away, the shield of Shaul, as though he had not been anointed with oil.

22 From the blood of the slain, from the fat of the mighty, the bow of Jonathan (Yehonatan) turned not back, and the sword of Shaul returned not empty.

23 Shaul and Jonathan (Yehonatan) were lovely and pleasant in their lives, and in their death they were not divided; they were swifter than eagles, they were stronger than lions.

24 You daughters of Yisrael, weep over Shaul, who clothed you in scarlet, with other delights, who put on ornaments of gold upon your apparel.

25 How are the mighty fallen in the midst of the battle! O Jonathan (Yehonatan), you wast slain in your high places.

26 I am distressed for you, my brother Jonathan (Yehonatan); very pleasant have you been unto me; your love to me was wonderful, passing the love of women.

27 How are the mighty fallen, and the weapons of war perished!"

2 And it came to pass after this, that Dawid enquired of יהוה, saying, "Shall I go up into any of the cities of Judah (Yehudah)?" And יהוה said unto him, "Go up." And Dawid said, "Whither shall I go up?" And He said, "Unto Hebron."

2 So Dawid went up thither, and his two wives also, Ahinoam the Yizreelitess, and Avigail Naval's wife the Carmelite.

3 And his men that were with him did Dawid bring up, every man with his household; and they dwelt in the cities of Hebron.

4 And the men of Judah (Yehudah) came, and there they anointed Dawid king over the house of Judah (Yehudah). And they told Dawid, saying, "That the men of Yavesh-Gilad were they that buried Shaul."

5 And Dawid sent messengers unto the men of Yavesh-Gilad, and said unto them, "Blessed be you of יהוה, that you have shewed this kindness unto your lord (adon), even unto Shaul, and have buried him.

6 And now יהוה shew kindness and truth unto you; and I also will requite you this kindness, because you have done this thing.

7 Therefore now let your hands be strengthened, and be you valiant; for your master Shaul is dead, and also the house of Judah (Yehudah) have anointed me king over them."

8 But Abner the son of Ner, captain of Shaul's army, took Ishbosheth the son of Shaul, and brought him over to Mahanaim;

9 And made him king over Gilad, and over the Ashurites, and over Yizreel, and over Efrayim, and over Benjamin (Binyamin), and over all Yisrael.

10 Ishbosheth Shaul's son was forty years old when he began to reign over Yisrael, and reigned two years. But the house of Judah (Yehudah) followed Dawid.

11 And the time that Dawid was king in Hebron over the house of Judah (Yehudah) was seven years and six months.

12 And Abner the son of Ner, and the servants of Ishbosheth the son of Shaul, went out from Mahanaim to Giveon.

13 And Yoav the son of Tseruyah, and the servants of Dawid, went out, and met together by the pool of Giveon; and they sat down, the one on the one side of the pool, and the other on the other side of the pool.

14 And Abner said to Yoav, "Let the young men now arise, and play before us." And Yoav said, "Let them arise."

15 Then there arose and went over by number twelve of Benjamin (Binyamin), which pertained to Ishbosheth the son of Shaul, and twelve of the servants of Dawid.

16 And they caught every one his fellow by the head, and thrust his sword in his fellow's side; so they fell down together; wherefore that place was called Helkathhazzurim, which is in Giveon.

17 And there was a very sore battle that day; and Abner was beaten, and the men of Yisrael, before the servants of Dawid.

18 And there were three sons of Tseruyah there, Yoav, and Avishai, and Asahel: and Asahel was as light of foot as a wild roe.

19 And Asahel pursued after Abner; and in going he turned not to the right hand nor to the left from following Abner.

20 Then Abner looked behind him, and said, "Are you Asahel?" And he answered, "I am."

21 And Abner said to him, "Turn you aside to your right hand or to your left, and lay you hold on one of the young men, and take you his armour." But Asahel would not turn aside from following of him.

22 And Abner said again to Asahel, "Turn you aside from following me; wherefore should I smite you to the ground? How then should I hold up my face to Yoav your brother?"

23 Howbeit he refused to turn aside; wherefore Abner with the hinder end of the spear smote him under the fifth rib, that the spear came out behind him; and he fell down there, and died in the same place; and it came to pass, that as many as came to the place where Asahel fell down and died stood still.

24 Yoav also and Avishai pursued after Abner; and the sun went down when they were come to the hill of Ammah, that lieth before Giah by the way of the wilderness of Giveon.

25 And the children of Benjamin (Binyamin) gathered themselves together after Abner, and became one troop, and stood on the top of a hill.

26 Then Abner called to Yoav, and said, "Shall the sword devour forever? Knowest you not that it will be bitterness in the latter end? How long shall it be then, ere you bid the people return from following their brethren?"

27 And Yoav said, "As God (Elohim) liveth, unless you hadst spoken, surely then in the morning the people had gone up every one from following his brother."

28 So Yoav blew a trumpet, and all the people stood still, and pursued after Yisrael no more, neither fought they any more.

29 And Abner and his men walked all that night through the plain, and passed over Jordan (Yarden), and went through all Bithron, and they came to Mahanaim.

30 And Yoav returned from following Abner; and when he had gathered all the people together, there lacked of Dawid's servants nineteen men and Asahel.

31 But the servants of Dawid had smitten of Benjamin (Binyamin), and of Abner's men, so that three hundred and threescore men died.

32 And they took up Asahel, and buried him in the sepulchre of his father, which was in Bethlehem (Beit-Lechem). And Yoav and his men went all night, and they came to Hebron at break of day.

3 Now there was long war between the house of Shaul and the house of Dawid; but Dawid waxed stronger and stronger, and the house of Shaul waxed weaker and weaker.

2 And unto Dawid were sons born in Hebron; and his firstborn was Amnon, of Ahinoam the Yizreelitess;

3 And his second, Chileab, of Avigail the wife of Naval the Carmelite; and the third, Avshalom the son of Maacah the daughter of Talmai king of Geshur;

4 And the fourth, Adoniyah the son of Haggith; and the fifth, Shefatyah the son of Abital;

5 And the sixth, Ithream, by Eglah Dawid's wife. These were born to Dawid in Hebron.

6 And it came to pass, while there was war between the house of Shaul and the house of Dawid, that Abner made himself strong for the house of Shaul.

7 And Shaul had a concubine, whose name was Rizpah, the daughter of Ayah; and Ishbosheth said to Abner, "Why have you gone in unto my father's concubine?"

8 Then was Abner very wroth for the words of Ishbosheth, and said, "Am I a dog's head, which against Judah (Yehudah) do shew kindness this day unto the house of Shaul your father, to his brethren, and to his friends, and have not delivered you into the hand of Dawid, that you chargest me today with a fault concerning this woman?

9 So do God (Elohim) to Abner, and more also, except, as יהוה hath sworn to Dawid, even so I do to him;

10 To translate the kingdom from the house of Shaul, and to set up the throne of Dawid over Yisrael and over Judah (Yehudah), from Dan even to Beer-Sheva."

11 And he could not answer Abner a word again, because he feared him.

12 And Abner sent messengers to Dawid on his behalf, saying, "Whose is the land?" Saying also, "Make your league with me, and, behold, my hand shall be with you, to bring about all Yisrael unto you."

13 And he said, "Well, I will make a league with you; but one thing I require of you, that is, you shalt not see my face, except you first bring Michal Shaul's daughter, when you comest to see my face."

14 And Dawid sent messengers to Ishbosheth Shaul's son, saying, "Deliver me my wife Michal, which I espoused to me for a hundred foreskins of the Philistines."

15 And Ishbosheth sent, and took her from her husband, even from Phaltiel the son of Laish.

16 And her husband went with her along weeping behind her to Bahurim. Then said Abner unto him, "Go, return!" And he returned.

17 And Abner had communication with the elders of Yisrael, saying, "You sought for Dawid in times past to be king over you.

18 Now then do it, for יהוה hath spoken of Dawid, saying, 'By the hand of My servant Dawid I will save My people Yisrael out of the hand of the Philistines, and out of the hand of all their enemies.'"

19 And Abner also spake in the ears of Benjamin (Binyamin); and Abner went also to speak in the ears of Dawid in Hebron all that seemed good to Yisrael, and that seemed good to the whole house of Benjamin (Binyamin).

20 So Abner came to Dawid to Hebron, and twenty men with him. And Dawid made Abner and the men that were with him a feast.

21 And Abner said unto Dawid, "I will arise and go, and will gather all Yisrael unto my lord (adoni) the king, that they may make a league with you, and that you mayest reign over all that

your heart desireth." And Dawid sent Abner away; and he went in peace.

22 And, behold, the servants of Dawid and Yoav came from pursuing a troop, and brought in a great spoil with them: but Abner was not with Dawid in Hebron; for he had sent him away, and he was gone in peace.

23 When Yoav and all the army that was with him were come, they told Yoav, saying, "Abner the son of Ner came to the king, and he hath sent him away, and he is gone in peace."

24 Then Yoav came to the king, and said, "What have you done? Behold, Abner came unto you; why is it that you have sent him away, and he is quite gone?

25 You knowest Abner the son of Ner, that he came to deceive you, and to know your going out and your coming in, and to know all that you doest."

26 And when Yoav was come out from Dawid, he sent messengers after Abner, which brought him again from the well of Sirah; but Dawid knew it not.

27 And when Abner was returned to Hebron, Yoav took him aside in the gate to speak with him quietly, and smote him there under the fifth rib, that he died, for the blood of Asahel his brother.

28 And afterward when Dawid heard it, he said, "I and my kingdom are guiltless before יהוה forever from the blood of Abner the son of Ner.

29 Let it rest on the head of Yoav, and on all his father's house; and let there not fail from the house of Yoav one that hath an issue, or that is a leper, or that leaneth on a staff, or that falleth on the sword, or that lacketh bread."

30 So Yoav and Avishai his brother slew Abner, because he had slain their brother Asahel at Giveon in the battle.

31 And Dawid said to Yoav, and to all the people that were with him, "Rend your clothes, and gird you with sackcloth, and mourn before Abner." And king Dawid himself followed the bier.

32 And they buried Abner in Hebron; and the king lifted up his voice, and wept at the grave of Abner; and all the people wept.

33 And the king lamented over Abner, and said: "Died Abner as a fool dieth?

34 Your hands were not bound, nor your feet put into fetters: as a man falleth before wicked men, so fellest you." And all the people wept

again over him.

35 And when all the people came to cause Dawid to eat meat while it was yet day, Dawid sware, saying, "So do God (Elohim) to me, and more also, if I taste bread, or anything else, till the sun be down!"

36 And all the people took notice of it, and it pleased them: as whatsoever the king did please all the people.

37 For all the people and all Yisrael understood that day that it was not of the king to slay Abner the son of Ner.

38 And the king said unto his servants, "Know you not that there is a prince and a great man fallen this day in Yisrael?

39 And I am this day weak, though anointed king; and these men the sons of Tseruyah be too hard for me. יהוה shall reward the doer of evil according to his wickedness."

4 And when Shaul's son heard that Abner was dead in Hebron, his hands were feeble, and all the Yisraelis were troubled.

2 And Shaul's son had two men that were captains of bands; the name of the one was Baanah, and the name of the other Rechab, the sons of Rimmon a Beerothite, of the children of Benjamin (Binyamin). (For Beeroth also was reckoned to Benjamin (Binyamin);

3 And the Beerothites fled to Gittaim, and were sojourners there until this day.)

4 And Jonathan (Yehonatan), Shaul's son, had a son that was lame of his feet. He was five years old when the tidings came of Shaul and Jonathan (Yehonatan) out of Yizreel, and his nurse took him up, and fled; and it came to pass, as she made haste to flee, that he fell, and became lame. And his name was Mephibosheth.

5 And the sons of Rimmon the Beerothite, Rechab and Baanah, went, and came about the heat of the day to the house of Ishbosheth, who lay on a bed at noon.

6 And they came thither into the midst of the house, as though they would have fetched wheat; and they smote him under the fifth rib; and Rechab and Baanah his brother escaped.

7 For when they came into the house, he lay on his bed in his bedchamber, and they smote him, and slew him, and beheaded him, and took his head, and gat them away through the plain all night.

8 And they brought the head of Ishbosheth unto

Dawid to Hebron, and said to the king, "Behold the head of Ishbosheth the son of Shaul your enemy, who sought your life; and יהוה hath avenged my lord (adoni) the king this day of Shaul, and of his seed."

9 And Dawid answered Rechab and Baanah his brother, the sons of Rimmon the Beerothite, and said unto them, "As יהוה liveth, who hath redeemed my soul out of all adversity,

10 When one told me, saying, 'Behold, Shaul is dead,' thinking to have brought good tidings, I took hold of him, and slew him in Ziklag, who thought that I would have given him a reward for his tidings.

11 How much more, when wicked men have slain a righteous person in his own house upon his bed? Shall I not therefore now require his blood of your hand, and take you away from the earth?"

12 And Dawid commanded his young men, and they slew them, and cut off their hands and their feet, and hanged them up over the pool in Hebron. But they took the head of Ishbosheth, and buried it in the sepulchre of Abner in Hebron.

5 Then came all the tribes of Yisrael to Dawid unto Hebron, and spake, saying, "Behold, we are your bone and your flesh.

2 Also in time past, when Shaul was king over us, you wast he that leddest out and broughtest in Yisrael; and יהוה said to you, 'You shalt feed my people Yisrael, and you shalt be a captain over Yisrael.'"

3 So all the elders of Yisrael came to the king to Hebron; and king Dawid made a league with them in Hebron before יהוה. And they anointed Dawid king over Yisrael.

4 Dawid was thirty years old when he began to reign, and he reigned forty years.

5 In Hebron he reigned over Judah (Yehudah) seven years and six months; and in Jerusalem (Yerushalayim) he reigned thirty and three years over all Yisrael and Judah (Yehudah).

6 And the king and his men went to Jerusalem (Yerushalayim) unto the Yevusis, the inhabitants of the land, who spake unto Dawid, saying, "Except you take away the blind and the lame, you shalt not come in hither;" thinking, "Dawid cannot come in hither."

7 Nevertheless Dawid took the strong hold of Zion (Tsiyon); the same is the city of Dawid.

8 And Dawid said on that day, "Whosoever getteth up to the gutter, and smiteth the Yevusis, and the lame and the blind, that are hated of Dawid's soul, he shall be chief and captain." Wherefore they said, "The blind and the lame shall not come into the house."

9 So Dawid dwelt in the fort, and called it the city of Dawid. And Dawid built round about from Millo and inward.

10 And Dawid went on, and grew great, and יהוה God of hosts (Elohei Tsevaot) was with him.

11 And Hiram king of Tyre sent messengers to Dawid, and cedar trees, and carpenters, and masons; and they built Dawid a house.

12 And Dawid perceived that יהוה had established him king over Yisrael, and that He had exalted His kingdom for His people Yisrael's sake.

13 And Dawid took him more concubines and wives out of Jerusalem (Yerushalayim), after he was come from Hebron. And there were yet sons and daughters born to Dawid.

14 And these be the names of those that were born unto him in Jerusalem (Yerushalayim): Shammua, and Shobab, and Nathan, and Solomon (Shelomoh),

15 Ibhar also, and Elishua, and Nepheg, and Yafiya,

16 And Elishama, and Eliada, and Eliphalet.

17 But when the Philistines heard that they had anointed Dawid king over Yisrael, all the Philistines came up to seek Dawid; and Dawid heard of it, and went down to the hold.

18 The Philistines also came and spread themselves in the valley of Rephaim.

19 And Dawid enquired of יהוה, saying, "Shall I go up to the Philistines? Wilt you deliver them into mine hand?" And יהוה said unto Dawid, "Go up, for I will doubtless deliver the Philistines into your hand."

20 And Dawid came to Baal Perazim, and Dawid smote them there, and said, "יהוה hath broken forth upon mine enemies before me, as the breach of waters." Therefore he called the name of that place Baal Perazim.

21 And there they left their images, and Dawid and his men burned them.

22 And the Philistines came up yet again, and spread themselves in the valley of Rephaim.

23 And when Dawid enquired of יהוה, he said, "You shalt not go up; but fetch a compass behind

them, and come upon them opposite the mulberry trees.

24 And let it be, when you hearest the sound of a going in the tops of the mulberry trees, that then you shalt bestir yourself; for then shall יהוה go out before you, to smite the army of the Philistines."

25 And Dawid did so, as יהוה had commanded him; and smote the Philistines from Geba until you come to Gazer.

6 Again, Dawid gathered together all the chosen men of Yisrael, thirty thousand.

2 And Dawid arose, and went with all the people that were with him from Baale of Judah (Yehudah), to bring up from thence the ark of God (Elohim), whose name is called by the name of יהוה of hosts (YHWH Tsevaot) who dwelleth between the cherubims (keruvim).

3 And they set the ark of God (Elohim) upon a new cart, and brought it out of the house of Abinadab that was in Gibeah; and Uzzah and Ahio, the sons of Abinadab, drave the new cart.

4 And they brought it out of the house of Abinadab which was at Gibeah, accompanying the ark of God (Elohim); and Ahio went before the ark.

5 And Dawid and all the house of Yisrael played before יהוה on all manner of instruments made of fir wood, even on harps, and on psalteries, and on timbrels, and on cornets, and on cymbals.

6 And when they came to Nachon's threshingfloor, Uzzah put forth his hand to the ark of God (Elohim), and took hold of it; for the oxen shook it.

7 And the anger of יהוה was kindled against Uzzah; and God (Elohim) smote him there for his error; and there he died by the ark of God (Elohim).

8 And Dawid was displeased, because יהוה had made a breach upon Uzzah; and he called the name of the place Perezuzzah to this day.

9 And Dawid was afraid of יהוה that day, and said, "How shall the ark of יהוה come to me?"

10 So Dawid would not remove the ark of יהוה unto him into the city of Dawid; but Dawid carried it aside into the house of Oved-Edom the Gittite.

11 And the ark of יהוה continued in the house of Oved-Edom the Gittite three months; and יהוה blessed Oved-Edom, and all his household.

12 And it was told king Dawid, saying, "יהוה hath blessed the house of Oved-Edom, and all that pertaineth unto him, because of the ark of God (Elohim)." So Dawid went and brought up the ark of God (Elohim) from the house of Oved-Edom into the city of Dawid with gladness.

13 And it was so, that when they that bare the ark of יהוה had gone six paces, he sacrificed oxen and fatlings.

14 And Dawid danced before יהוה with all his might; and Dawid was girded with a linen ephod.

15 So Dawid and all the house of Yisrael brought up the ark of יהוה with shouting, and with the sound of the shofar.

16 And as the ark of יהוה came into the city of Dawid, Michal Shaul's daughter looked through a window, and saw King Dawid leaping and dancing before יהוה; and she despised him in her heart.

17 And they brought in the ark of יהוה, and set it in his place, in the midst of the tabernacle that Dawid had pitched for it; and Dawid offered burnt offerings and peace offerings before יהוה.

18 And as soon as Dawid had made an end of offering burnt offerings and peace offerings, he blessed the people in the name of יהוה Tsevaot.

19 And he dealt among all the people, even among the whole multitude of Yisrael, as well to the women as men, to every one a cake of bread, and a good piece of flesh, and a flagon of wine. So all the people departed every one to his house.

20 Then Dawid returned to bless his household. And Michal the daughter of Shaul came out to meet Dawid, and said, "How glorious was the king of Yisrael today, who uncovered himself today in the eyes of the handmaids of his servants, as one of the vain fellows shamelessly uncovereth himself!"

21 And Dawid said unto Michal, "It was before יהוה, who chose me before your father, and before all his house, to appoint me ruler over the people of יהוה, over Yisrael; therefore will I play before יהוה.

22 And I will yet be more vile than thus, and will be base in mine own sight; and of the maidservants which you have spoken of, of them shall I be had in honor."

23 Therefore Michal the daughter of Shaul had no child unto the day of her death.

7 And it came to pass, when the king sat in his house, and יהוה had given him rest round about from all his enemies;

2 That the king said unto Nathan the prophet, "See now, I dwell in a house of cedar, but the ark of God (Elohim) dwelleth within curtains."

3 And Nathan said to the king, "Go, do all that is in your heart; for יהוה is with you."

4 And it came to pass that night, that the word of יהוה came unto Nathan, saying,

5 "Go and tell My servant Dawid,' Thus saith יהוה: "Shalt you build a house for Me to dwell in?

6 Whereas I have not dwelt in any house since the time that I brought up the children of Yisrael out of Egypt (Mitsrayim), even to this day, but have walked in a tent and in a tabernacle.

7 In all the places wherein I have walked with all the children of Yisrael spake I a word with any of the tribes of Yisrael, whom I commanded to feed My people Yisrael, saying, 'Why build you not Me a house of cedar?'"

8 Now therefore so shalt you say unto My servant Dawid, 'Thus saith יהוה of hosts (YHWH Tsevaot): "I took you from the sheepcote, from following the sheep, to be ruler over My people, over Yisrael.

9 And I was with you whithersoever you wentest, and have cut off all your enemies out of your sight, and have made you a great name, like unto the name of the great men that are in the earth.

10 Moreover I will appoint a place for My people Yisrael, and will plant them, that they may dwell in a place of their own, and move no more; neither shall the children of wickedness afflict them any more, as beforetime,

11 And as since the time that I commanded judges to be over My people Yisrael, and have caused you to rest from all your enemies. Also יהוה telleth you that He will make you a house.

12 And when your days be fulfilled, and you shalt sleep with your fathers, I will set up your seed after you, which shall proceed out of your bowels, and I will establish his kingdom.

13 He shall build a house for My name, and I will stablish the throne of his kingdom forever.

14 I will be His father, and he shall be My son. If he commits iniquity, I will chasten him with the rod of men, and with the stripes of the children of men:

15 But My mercy shall not depart away from him, as I took it from Shaul, whom I put away before you.

16 And your house and your kingdom shall be established forever before you; your throne shall be established forever.""'

17 According to all these words, and according to all this vision, so did Nathan speak unto Dawid.

18 Then went King Dawid in, and sat before יהוה, and he said, "Who am I, O Lord (Adonai) יהוה? And what is my house, that You have brought me hitherto?

19 And this was yet a small thing in Your sight, O Lord (Adonai) יהוה; but You have spoken also of Your servant's house for a great while to come. And is this the manner of man, O Lord (Adonai) יהוה?

20 And what can Dawid say more unto You? For You, Lord (Adonai) יהוה, knowest Your servant.

21 For Your word's sake, and according to Your own heart, have You done all these great things, to make Your servant know them.

22 Wherefore You are great, O Lord (Adonai) יהוה; for there is none like You, neither is there any God (Elohim) besides You, according to all that we have heard with our ears.

23 And what one nation in the earth is like Your people, even like Yisrael, whom God (Elohim) went to redeem for a people to Himself, and to make Him a name, and to do for you great and awesome things, for Your land, before Your people, which You redeemedst to You from Egypt (Mitsrayim), from the nations and their gods (elohim)?

24 For You have confirmed to Yourself Your people Yisrael to be a people unto You forever; and You, יהוה, art become their God (Elohim).

25 And now, O יהוה God (Elohim), the word that You have spoken concerning Your servant, and concerning his house, establish it forever, and do as You have said.

26 And let Your name be magnified forever, saying, 'יהוה of hosts (YHWH Tsevaot) is the God (Elohim) over Yisrael; and let the house of Your servant Dawid be established before You.

27 For You, O יהוה of hosts (YHWH Tsevaot), God of Israel (Elohei Yisrael), hast revealed to Your servant, saying, 'I will build You a house.' Therefore hath Your servant found in his heart to pray this prayer unto You.

28 And now, O Lord (Adonai) יהוה, You are that

God (Elohim), and Your words be true, and You have promised this goodness unto Your servant.

29 Therefore now let it please You to bless the house of Your servant, that it may continue forever before You; for You, O Lord (Adonai) יהוה, hast spoken it; and with Your blessing let the house of Your servant be blessed forever."

8 And after this it came to pass, that Dawid smote the Philistines, and subdued them; and Dawid took Methegammah out of the hand of the Philistines.

2 And he smote Moav, and measured them with a line, casting them down to the ground; even with two lines measured he to put to death, and with one full line to keep alive. And so the Moavites became Dawid's servants, and brought gifts.

3 Dawid smote also Hadadezer, the son of Rehob, king of Zobah, as he went to recover his border at the river Euphrates.

4 And Dawid took from him a thousand chariots, and seven hundred horsemen, and twenty thousand footmen: and Dawid houghed all the chariot horses, but reserved of them for a hundred chariots.

5 And when the Syrians (Arammim) of Damascus (Dammeseq) came to succour Hadadezer king of Zobah, Dawid slew of the Syrians (Arammim) two and twenty thousand men.

6 Then Dawid put garrisons in Syria (Aram) of Damascus (Dammeseq); and the Syrians (Arammim) became servants to Dawid, and brought gifts. And יהוה preserved Dawid whithersoever he went.

7 And Dawid took the shields of gold that were on the servants of Hadadezer, and brought them to Jerusalem (Yerushalayim).

8 And from Betah, and from Berothai, cities of Hadadezer, King Dawid took exceeding much brass.

9 When Toi king of Hamath heard that Dawid had smitten all the army of Hadadezer,

10 Then Toi sent Yoram his son unto King Dawid, to salute him, and to bless him, because he had fought against Hadadezer, and smitten him; for Hadadezer had wars with Toi. And Yoram brought with him vessels of silver, and vessels of gold, and vessels of brass.

11 Which also King Dawid did dedicate unto יהוה, with the silver and gold that he had

dedicated of all nations which he subdued;

12 Of Syria (Aram), and of Moav, and of the children of Ammon, and of the Philistines, and of Amalek, and of the spoil of Hadadezer, son of Rehob, king of Zobah.

13 And Dawid gat him a name when he returned from smiting the Syrians (Arammim) in the valley of salt, being eighteen thousand men.

14 And he put garrisons in Edom; throughout all Edom put he garrisons, and all they of Edom became Dawid's servants. And יהוה preserved Dawid whithersoever he went.

15 And Dawid reigned over all Yisrael; and Dawid executed judgment and justice unto all his people.

16 And Yoav the son of Tseruyah was over the army; and Yehoshafat the son of Ahilud was recorder;

17 And Zadok the son of Ahitub, and Ahimelech the son of Aviyahthar, were the priests (kohanim); and Serayah was the scribe;

18 And Benayah the son of Yehoyada was over both the Cherethites and the Pelethites; and Dawid's sons were chief rulers.

9 And Dawid said, "Is there yet any that is left of the house of Shaul, that I may shew him kindness for Jonathan (Yehonatan)'s sake?"

2 And there was of the house of Shaul a servant whose name was Ziba. "And when they had called him unto Dawid, the king said unto him, "Are you Ziba?" And he said, "Your servant is he."

3 And the king said, "Is there not yet any of the house of Shaul, that I may shew the kindness of God (Elohim) unto him?" And Ziba said unto the king, "Jonathan (Yehonatan) hath yet a son, who is lame on his feet."

4 And the king said unto him, "Where is he?" And Ziba said unto the king, "Behold, he is in the house of Machir, the son of Ammiel, in Lodebar."

5 Then King Dawid sent, and fetched him out of the house of Machir, the son of Ammiel, from Lodebar.

6 Now when Mephibosheth, the son of Jonathan (Yehonatan), the son of Shaul, was come unto Dawid, he fell on his face, and did reverence. And Dawid said, "Mephibosheth." And he answered, "Behold your servant!"

7 And Dawid said unto him, "Fear not, for I will surely shew you kindness for Jonathan

(Yehonatan) your father's sake, and will restore you all the land of Shaul your father; and you shalt eat bread at my table continually."

8 And he bowed himself, and said, "What is your servant, that you shouldest look upon such a dead dog as I am?"

9 Then the king called to Ziba, Shaul's servant, and said unto him, "I have given unto your master's son all that pertained to Shaul and to all his house.

10 You therefore, and your sons, and your servants, shall till the land for him, and you shalt bring in the fruits, that your master's son may have food to eat; but Mephibosheth your master's son shall eat bread always at my table." Now Ziba had fifteen sons and twenty servants.

11 Then said Ziba unto the king, "According to all that my lord (adoni) the king hath commanded his servant, so shall your servant do. As for Mephibosheth," said the king, "he shall eat at my table, as one of the king's sons."

12 And Mephibosheth had a young son, whose name was Micha. And all that dwelt in the house of Ziba were servants unto Mephibosheth.

13 So Mephibosheth dwelt in Jerusalem (Yerushalayim), for he did eat continually at the king's table; and was lame on both his feet.

10 And it came to pass after this, that the king of the children of Ammon died, and Hanun his son reigned in his stead.

2 Then said Dawid, "I will shew kindness unto Hanun the son of Nahash, as his father shewed kindness unto me." And Dawid sent to comfort him by the hand of his servants for his father. And Dawid's servants came into the land of the children of Ammon.

3 And the princes of the children of Ammon said unto Hanun their lord (adon), "Thinkest you that Dawid doth honor your father, that he hath sent comforters unto you? Hath not Dawid rather sent his servants unto you, to search the city, and to spy it out, and to overthrow it?"

4 Wherefore Hanun took Dawid's servants, and shaved off the one half of their beards, and cut off their garments in the middle, even to their buttocks, and sent them away.

5 When they told it unto Dawid, he sent to meet them, because the men were greatly ashamed; and the king said, "Tarry at Yericho until your beards be grown, and then return."

6 And when the children of Ammon saw that they stank before Dawid, the children of Ammon sent and hired the Syrians (Arammim) of Bethrehob, and the Syrians (Arammim) of Zoba, twenty thousand footmen, and of King Maacah a thousand men, and of Ish-Tov twelve thousand men.

7 And when Dawid heard of it, he sent Yoav, and all the army of the mighty men.

8 And the children of Ammon came out, and put the battle in array at the entering in of the gate; and the Syrians (Arammim) of Zoba, and of Rehob, and Ish-Tov, and Maacah, were by themselves in the field.

9 When Yoav saw that the front of the battle was against him before and behind, he chose of all the choice men of Yisrael, and put them in array against the Syrians (Arammim).

10 And the rest of the people he delivered into the hand of Avishai his brother, that he might put them in array against the children of Ammon.

11 And he said, "If the Syrians (Arammim) be too strong for me, then you shalt help me: but if the children of Ammon be too strong for you, then I will come and help you.

12 Be of good courage, and let us play the men for our people, and for the cities of our God (Elohim); and יהוה do that which seemeth Him good."

13 And Yoav drew near, and the people that were with him, unto the battle against the Syrians (Arammim); and they fled before him.

14 And when the children of Ammon saw that the Syrians (Arammim) were fled, then fled they also before Avishai, and entered into the city. So Yoav returned from the children of Ammon, and came to Jerusalem (Yerushalayim).

15 And when the Syrian (Arammi) saw that they were smitten before Yisrael, they gathered themselves together.

16 And Hadarezer sent, and brought out the Syrias (Aram) that were beyond the river; and they came to Helam; and Shobach the captain of the army of Hadarezer went before them.

17 And when it was told Dawid, he gathered all Yisrael together, and passed over Jordan (Yarden), and came to Helam. And the Syrians (Arammim) set themselves in array against Dawid, and fought with him.

18 And the Syrians (Arammim) fled before Yisrael; and Dawid slew the men of seven hundred chariots of the Syrians (Arammim),

and forty thousand horsemen, and smote Shobach the captain of their army, who died there.

19 And when all the kings that were servants to Hadarezer saw that they were smitten before Yisrael, they made peace with Yisrael, and served them. So the Syrians (Arammim) feared to help the children of Ammon anymore.

11 And it came to pass, after the year was expired, at the time when kings go forth to battle, that Dawid sent Yoav, and his servants with him, and all Yisrael; and they destroyed the children of Ammon, and besieged Rabbah. But Dawid tarried still at Jerusalem (Yerushalayim). 2 And it came to pass in an eveningtide, that Dawid arose from off his bed, and walked upon the roof of the king's house; and from the roof he saw a woman washing herself; and the woman was very beautiful to look upon.

3 And Dawid sent and enquired after the woman. And one said, "Is not this Bat-Sheva, the daughter of Eliam, the wife of Uriyah the Hittite?"

4 And Dawid sent messengers, and took her; and she came in unto him, and he lay with her; for she was purified from her uncleanness; and she returned unto her house.

5 And the woman conceived, and sent and told Dawid, and said, "I am with child."

6 And Dawid sent to Yoav, saying, "Send me Uriyah the Hittite." And Yoav sent Uriyah to Dawid.

7 And when Uriyah was come unto him, Dawid demanded of him how Yoav did, and how the people did, and how the war prospered.

8 And Dawid said to Uriyah Uriyah, "Go down to your house, and wash your feet." And Uriyah departed out of the king's house, and there followed him a mess of meat from the king.

9 But Uriyah slept at the door of the king's house with all the servants of his lord (adon), and went not down to his house.

10 And when they had told Dawid, saying, "Uriyah went not down unto his house," Dawid said unto Uriyah, "Camest you not from your journey? Why then didst you not go down unto your house?"

11 And Uriyah said unto Dawid, "The ark, and Yisrael, and Judah (Yehudah), abide in tents; and my lord (adoni) Yoav, and the servants of my lord (adoni), are encamped in the open fields; shall I then go into mine house, to eat and to drink, and to lie with my wife? As you livest, and as your soul liveth, I will not do this thing."

12 And Dawid said to Uriyah, "Tarry here today also, and tomorrow I will let you depart." So Uriyah abode in Jerusalem (Yerushalayim) that day, and the next day.

13 And when Dawid had called him, he did eat and drink before him; and he made him drunk: and at even he went out to lie on his bed with the servants of his lord (adon), but went not down to his house.

14 And it came to pass in the morning, that Dawid wrote a letter to Yoav, and sent it by the hand of Uriyah.

15 And he wrote in the letter, saying, "Set you Uriyah in the forefront of the hottest battle, and retire you from him, that he may be smitten, and die."

16 And it came to pass, when Yoav observed the city, that he assigned Uriyah unto a place where he knew that valiant men were.

17 And the men of the city went out, and fought with Yoav; and there fell some of the people of the servants of Dawid; and Uriyah the Hittite died also.

18 Then Yoav sent and told Dawid all the things concerning the war;

19 And charged the messenger, saying, "When you have made an end of telling the matters of the war unto the king,

20 And if so be that the king's wrath arises, and he say unto you: 'Wherefore approached you so near unto the city when you did fight? Knew you not that they would shoot from the wall?

21 Who smote Abimelech (Avimelekh) the son of Yerubeshet? Did not a woman cast a piece of a millstone upon him from the wall, that he died in Thebez? Why went you near the wall?' Then say you, 'Your servant Uriyah the Hittite is dead also.'"

22 So the messenger went, and came and shewed Dawid all that Yoav had sent him for.

23 And the messenger said unto Dawid, "Surely the men prevailed against us, and came out unto us into the field, and we were upon them even unto the entering of the gate.

24 And the shooters shot from off the wall upon your servants; and some of the king's servants be dead, and your servant Uriyah the Hittite is dead also."

25 Then Dawid said unto the messenger, "Thus shalt you say unto Yoav: 'Let not this thing displease you, for the sword devoureth one as well as another; make your battle more strong against the city, and overthrow it.' So encourage you him."

26 And when the wife of Uriyah heard that Uriyah her husband was dead, she mourned for her husband.

27 And when the mourning was past, Dawid sent and fetched her to his house, and she became his wife, and bare him a son. But the thing that Dawid had done displeased יהוה.

12 And יהוה sent Nathan unto Dawid. And he came unto him, and said unto him, "There were two men in one city; the one rich, and the other poor.

2 The rich man had exceeding many flocks and herds.

3 But the poor man had nothing, save one little ewe lamb, which he had bought and nourished up; and it grew up together with him, and with his children; it did eat of his own meat, and drank of his own cup, and lay in his bosom, and was unto him as a daughter.

4 And there came a traveller unto the rich man, and he spared to take of his own flock and of his own herd, to dress for the wayfaring man that was come unto him; but took the poor man's lamb, and dressed it for the man that was come to him."

5 And Dawid's anger was greatly kindled against the man; and he said to Nathan, "As יהוה liveth, the man that hath done this thing shall surely die!

6 And he shall restore the lamb fourfold, because he did this thing, and because he had no pity."

7 And Nathan said to Dawid, "You are the man. Thus saith יהוה God of Israel (Elohei Yisrael): 'I anointed you king over Yisrael, and I delivered you out of the hand of Shaul;

8 And I gave you your master's house, and your master's wives into your bosom, and gave you the house of Yisrael and of Judah (Yehudah); and if that had been too little, I would moreover have given unto you such and such things.

9 Wherefore have you despised the commandment of יהוה, to do evil in His sight? You have killed Uriyah the Hittite with the sword, and hast taken his wife to be your wife, and hast slain him with the sword of the children of Ammon.

10 Now therefore the sword shall never depart from your house; because you have despised Me, and hast taken the wife of Uriyah the Hittite to be your wife.'

11 Thus saith יהוה: 'Behold, I will raise up evil against you out of your own house, and I will take your wives before your eyes, and give them unto your neighbour, and he shall lie with your wives in the sight of this sun.

12 For you didst it secretly; but I will do this thing before all Yisrael, and before the sun.'"

13 And Dawid said unto Nathan, "I have sinned against יהוה. And Nathan said unto Dawid," יהוה also hath put away your sin; you shalt not die.

14 Howbeit, because by this deed you have given great occasion to the enemies of יהוה to blaspheme, the child also that is born unto you shall surely die."

15 And Nathan departed unto his house. And יהוה struck the child that Uriyah's wife bare unto Dawid, and it was very sick.

16 Dawid therefore besought God (Elohim) for the child; and Dawid fasted, and went in, and lay all night upon the earth.

17 And the elders of his house arose, and went to him, to raise him up from the earth; but he would not, neither did he eat bread with them.

18 And it came to pass on the seventh day, that the child died. And the servants of Dawid feared to tell him that the child was dead; for they said, "Behold, while the child was yet alive, we spake unto him, and he would not hearken unto our voice; how will he then vex himself, if we tell him that the child is dead?"

19 But when Dawid saw that his servants whispered, Dawid perceived that the child was dead; therefore Dawid said unto his servants, "Is the child dead?" And they said, "He is dead."

20 Then Dawid arose from the earth, and washed, and anointed himself, and changed his apparel, and came into the house of יהוה, and worshipped; then he came to his own house; and when he required, they set food before him, and he did eat.

21 Then said his servants unto him, "What thing is this that you have done? You didst fast and weep for the child, while it was alive; but when the child was dead, you didst rise and eat food."

22 And he said, "While the child was yet alive, I fasted and wept; for I said, 'Who can tell whether יהוה will be gracious to me, that the child may live?'

23 But now he is dead, why should I fast? Can I bring him back again? I shall go to him, but he shall not return to me."

24 And Dawid comforted Bat-Sheva his wife, and went in unto her, and lay with her; and she bare a son, and he called his name ^A39^Solomon (Shelomoh); and יהוה loved him.

25 And he sent by the hand of Nathan the prophet; and he called his name ^A37^Yedidyah (beloved of Yahwah), because of יהוה.

26 And Yoav fought against Rabbah of the children of Ammon, and took the royal city.

27 And Yoav sent messengers to Dawid, and said, "I have fought against Rabbah, and have taken the city of waters.

28 Now therefore gather the rest of the people together, and encamp against the city, and take it; lest I take the city, and it be called after my name."

29 And Dawid gathered all the people together, and went to Rabbah, and fought against it, and took it.

30 And he took their king's crown from off his head, the weight whereof was a talent of gold with the precious stones; and it was set on Dawid's head. And he brought forth the spoil of the city in great abundance.

31 And he brought forth the people that were therein, and put them under saws, and under harrows of iron, and under axes of iron, and made them pass through the brickkiln; and thus did he unto all the cities of the children of Ammon. So Dawid and all the people returned unto Jerusalem (Yerushalayim).

13 And it came to pass after this, that Avshalom the son of Dawid had a fair sister, whose name was Tamar; and Amnon the son of Dawid loved her.

2 And Amnon was so vexed, that he fell sick for his sister Tamar; for she was a virgin; and Amnon thought it hard for him to do any thing to her.

3 But Amnon had a friend, whose name was Yonadav, the son of Shimeah Dawid's brother; and Yonadav was a very subtil man.

4 And he said unto him, "Why are you, being the king's son, lean from day to day? Wilt you not tell me?" And Amnon said unto him, "I love Tamar, my brother Avshalom's sister."

5 And Yonadav said unto him, "Lay you down on your bed, and make yourself sick; and when your father cometh to see you, say unto him, 'Please let my sister Tamar come, and give me meat, and dress the meat in my sight, that I may see it, and eat it at her hand.'"

6 So Amnon lay down, and made himself sick; and when the king was come to see him, Amnon said unto the king, 'Please let Tamar my sister come, and make me a couple of cakes in my sight, that I may eat at her hand.'"

7 Then Dawid sent home to Tamar, saying, "Go now to your brother Amnon's house, and dress him food."

8 So Tamar went to her brother Amnon's house; and he was laid down. And she took flour, and kneaded it, and made cakes in his sight, and did bake the cakes.

9 And she took a pan, and poured them out before him; but he refused to eat. And Amnon said, Have out all men from me. And they went out every man from him.

10 And Amnon said unto Tamar, "Bring the food into the chamber, that I may eat of your hand." And Tamar took the cakes which she had made, and brought them into the chamber to Amnon her brother.

11 And when she had brought them unto him to eat, he took hold of her, and said unto her, "Come lie with me, my sister."

12 And she answered him, "Nay, my brother, do not force me; for no such thing ought to be done in Yisrael; do not you this folly!

13 And I, whither shall I cause my shame to go? And as for you, you shalt be as one of the fools in Yisrael. Now therefore, please speak unto the king; for he will not withhold me from you."

14 Howbeit he would not hearken unto her voice; but, being stronger than she, forced her, and lay with her.

15 Then Amnon hated her exceedingly; so that the hatred wherewith he hated her was greater than the love wherewith he had loved her. And Amnon said unto her, "Arise, be gone."

16 And she said unto him, "There is no cause; this evil in sending me away is greater than the other that you didst unto me." But he would not hearken unto her.

17 Then he called his servant that ministered

unto him, and said, "Put now this woman out from me, and bolt the door after her."

18 And she had a garment of divers colours upon her; for with such robes were the king's daughters that were virgins apparelled. Then his servant brought her out, and bolted the door after her.

19 And Tamar put ashes on her head, and rent her garment of divers colours that was on her, and laid her hand on her head, and went on crying.

20 And Avshalom her brother said unto her, "Hath Amnon your brother been with you? But hold now your peace, my sister; he is your brother; regard not this thing." So Tamar remained desolate in her brother Avshalom's house.

21 But when King Dawid heard of all these things, he was very wroth.

22 And Avshalom spake unto his brother Amnon neither good nor bad; for Avshalom hated Amnon, because he had forced his sister Tamar.

23 And it came to pass after two full years, that Avshalom had sheepshearers in Baalhazor, which is beside Efrayim; and Avshalom invited all the king's sons.

24 And Avshalom came to the king, and said, "Behold now, your servant hath sheepshearers; let the king, I beseech you, and his servants go with your servant."

25 And the king said to Avshalom, "Nay, my son, let us not all now go, lest we be chargeable unto you." And he pressed him; howbeit he would not go, but blessed him.

26 Then said Avshalom, "If not, please let my brother Amnon go with us." And the king said unto him, "Why should he go with you?"

27 But Avshalom pressed him, that he let Amnon and all the king's sons go with him.

28 Now Avshalom had commanded his servants, saying, "Mark you now when Amnon's heart is merry with wine, and when I say unto you, 'Smite Amnon!' then kill him, fear not; have not I commanded you? Be courageous, and be valiant."

29 And the servants of Avshalom did unto Amnon as Avshalom had commanded. Then all the king's sons arose, and every man gat him up upon his mule, and fled.

30 And it came to pass, while they were in the way, that tidings came to Dawid, saying, "Avshalom hath slain all the king's sons, and there is not one of them left!"

31 Then the king arose, and tare his garments, and lay on the earth; and all his servants stood by with their clothes rent.

32 And Yonadav, the son of Shimeah Dawid's brother, answered and said, "Let not my lord (adoni) suppose that they have slain all the young men the king's sons; for Amnon only is dead; for by the appointment of Avshalom this hath been determined from the day that he forced his sister Tamar.

33 Now therefore let not my lord (adoni) the king takes the thing to his heart, to think that all the king's sons are dead; for Amnon only is dead."

34 But Avshalom fled. And the young man that kept the watch lifted up his eyes, and looked, and, behold, there came much people by the way of the hill side behind him.

35 And Yonadav said unto the king, "Behold, the king's sons come; as your servant said, so it is."

36 And it came to pass, as soon as he had made an end of speaking, that, behold, the king's sons came, and lifted up their voice and wept; and the king also and all his servants wept very sore.

37 But Avshalom fled, and went to Talmai, the son of Ammihud, king of Geshur. And Dawid mourned for his son every day.

38 So Avshalom fled, and went to Geshur, and was there three years.

39 And the soul of king Dawid longed to go forth unto Avshalom; for he was comforted concerning Amnon, seeing he was dead.

14 Now Yoav the son of Tseruyah perceived that the king's heart was toward Avshalom.

2 And Yoav sent to Tekoah, and fetched thence a wise woman, and said unto her, "Please feign yourself to be a mourner, and put on now mourning apparel, and anoint not yourself with oil, but be as a woman that had a long time mourned for the dead.

3 And come to the king, and speak on this manner unto him." So Yoav put the words in her mouth.

4 And when the woman of Tekoah spake to the king, she fell on her face to the ground, and did obeisance, and said, "Help, O king!"

5 And the king said unto her, "What aileth

you?" And she answered, "I am indeed a widow woman, and mine husband is dead.

6 And your handmaid had two sons, and they two strove together in the field, and there was none to part them, but the one smote the other, and slew him.

7 And, behold, the whole family is risen against your handmaid, and they said, 'Deliver him that smote his brother, that we may kill him, for the life of his brother whom he slew; and we will destroy the heir also.' And so they shall quench my coal which is left, and shall not leave to my husband neither name nor remainder upon the earth."

8 And the king said unto the woman, "Go to your house, and I will give charge concerning you."

9 And the woman of Tekoah said unto the king, "My lord (Adoni), O king, the iniquity be on me, and on my father's house; and the king and his throne be guiltless."

10 And the king said, "Whosoever saith ought unto you, bring him to me, and he shall not touch you any more."

11 Then said she, "Please let the king remember יהוה your God (YHWH Eloheikha), that you wouldest not allow the revengers of blood to destroy anymore, lest they destroy my son." And he said, "As יהוה liveth, there shall not one hair of your son fall to the earth."

12 Then the woman said, "Let your handmaid, please speak one word unto my lord (adoni) the king." And he said, "Say on."

13 And the woman said: "Why then have you thought such a thing against the people of God (Elohim)? For the king doth speak this thing as one which is faulty, in that the king doth not fetch home again his banished.

14 For we must needs die, and are as water spilt on the ground, which cannot be gathered up again; neither doth God (Elohim) respect any person; yet doth he devises means, that his banished be not expelled from him.

15 Now therefore that I am come to speak of this thing unto my lord (adoni) the king, it is because the people have made me afraid; and your handmaid said, 'I will now speak unto the king; it may be that the king will perform the request of his handmaid.

16 For the king will hear, to deliver his handmaid out of the hand of the man that would destroy me and my son together out of the inheritance of God (Elohim).'

17 Then your handmaid said, 'The word of my lord (adoni) the king shall now be comfortable; for as an angel of God (Elohim), so is my lord (adoni) the king to discern good and bad; therefore יהוה your God (YHWH Eloheikha) will be with you.'"

18 Then the king answered and said unto the woman, "Please hide not from me the thing that I shall ask you." And the woman said, "Let my lord (adoni) the king now speaks."

19 And the king said, "Is not the hand of Yoav with you in all this?" And the woman answered and said, "As your soul liveth, my lord (adoni) the king, none can turn to the right hand or to the left from ought that my lord (adoni) the king hath spoken; for your servant Yoav, he bade me, and he put all these words in the mouth of your handmaid.

20 To fetch about this form of speech hath your servant Yoav done this thing; and my lord (adoni) is wise, according to the wisdom of an angel of God (Elohim), to know all things that are in the earth."

21 And the king said unto Yoav, "Behold now, I have done this thing; go therefore, bring the young man Avshalom again."

22 And Yoav fell to the ground on his face, and bowed himself, and thanked the king; and Yoav said, "Today your servant knoweth that I have found grace in your sight, my lord (adoni), O king, in that the king hath fulfilled the request of his servant."

23 So Yoav arose and went to Geshur, and brought Avshalom to Jerusalem (Yerushalayim).

24 And the king said, "Let him turn to his own house, and let him not see my face." So Avshalom returned to his own house, and saw not the king's face.

25 But in all Yisrael there was none to be so much praised as Avshalom for his beauty; from the sole of his foot even to the crown of his head there was no blemish in him.

26 And when he polled his head, (for it was at every year's end that he polled it, because the hair was heavy on him, therefore he polled it;) he weighed the hair of his head at two hundred shekels after the king's weight.

27 And unto Avshalom there were born three sons, and one daughter, whose name was Tamar: she was a woman of a fair countenance.

28 So Avshalom dwelt two full years in Jerusalem (Yerushalayim), and saw not the king's face.

29 Therefore Avshalom sent for Yoav, to have sent him to the king; but he would not come to him; and when he sent again the second time, he would not come.

30 Therefore he said unto his servants, "See, Yoav's field is near mine, and he hath barley there; go and set it on fire." And Avshalom's servants set the field on fire.

31 Then Yoav arose, and came to Avshalom unto his house, and said unto him, "Wherefore have your servants set my field on fire?"

32 And Avshalom answered Yoav, "Behold, I sent unto you, saying, 'Come hither, that I may send you to the king, to say, "Why am I come from Geshur? it had been good for me to have been there still."' Now therefore let me see the king's face; and if there be any iniquity in me, let him kill me."

33 So Yoav came to the king, and told him; and when he had called for Avshalom, he came to the king, and bowed himself on his face to the ground before the king; and the king kissed Avshalom.

15 And it came to pass after this, that Avshalom prepared him chariots and horses, and fifty men to run before him.

2 And Avshalom rose up early, and stood beside the way of the gate; and it was so, that when any man that had a controversy came to the king for judgment, then Avshalom called unto him, and said, "Of what city are you?" And he said, "Your servant is of one of the tribes of Yisrael."

3 And Avshalom said unto him, "See, your matters are good and right; but there is no man deputed of the king to hear you."

4 Avshalom said moreover, "Oh that I were made judge in the land, that every man who hath any suit or cause might come unto me, and I would do him justice."

5 And it was so, that when any man came near to him to do him obeisance, he put forth his hand, and took him, and kissed him.

6 And on this manner did Avshalom to all Yisrael that came to the king for judgment; so Avshalom stole the hearts of the men of Yisrael.

7 And it came to pass after forty years, that Avshalom said unto the king, "Please let me go and pay my vow, which I have vowed unto יהוה,

in Hebron.

8 For your servant vowed a vow while I abode at Geshur in Syria (Aram), saying, 'If יהוה shall bring me again indeed to Jerusalem (Yerushalayim), then I will serve יהוה.'"

9 And the king said unto him, "Go in peace." So he arose, and went to Hebron.

10 But Avshalom sent spies throughout all the tribes of Yisrael, saying, "As soon as you hear the sound of the shofar, then you shall say, 'Avshalom reigneth in Hebron!'"

11 And with Avshalom went two hundred men out of Jerusalem (Yerushalayim), that were called; and they went in their simplicity, and they knew not any thing.

12 And Avshalom sent for Ahithophel the Gilonite, Dawid's counsellor, from his city, even from Giloh, while he offered sacrifices. And the conspiracy was strong; for the people increased continually with Avshalom.

13 And there came a messenger to Dawid, saying, "The hearts of the men of Yisrael are after Avshalom."

14 And Dawid said unto all his servants that were with him at Jerusalem (Yerushalayim), "Arise, and let us flee; for we shall not else escape from Avshalom; make speed to depart, lest he overtake us suddenly, and bring evil upon us, and smite the city with the edge of the sword."

15 And the king's servants said unto the king, "Behold, your servants are ready to do whatsoever my lord (adoni) the king shall appoint."

16 And the king went forth, and all his household after him. And the king left ten women, which were concubines, to keep the house.

17 And the king went forth, and all the people after him, and tarried in a place that was far off.

18 And all his servants passed on beside him; and all the Cherethites, and all the Pelethites, and all the Gittites, six hundred men which came after him from Gath, passed on before the king.

19 Then said the king to Ittai the Gittite, "Why goest you also with us? Return to your place, and abide with the king; for you are a stranger, and also an exile.

20 Whereas you camest but yesterday, should I this day make you go up and down with us? Seeing I go whither I may, return you, and

take back your brethren; mercy and truth be with you."

21 And Ittai answered the king, and said, "As יהוה liveth, and as my lord (adoni) the king liveth, surely in what place my lord (adoni) the king shall be, whether in death or life, even there also will your servant be."

22 And Dawid said to Ittai, "Go and pass over." And Ittai the Gittite passed over, and all his men, and all the little ones that were with him.

23 And all the country wept with a loud voice, and all the people passed over; the king also himself passed over the brook Kidron, and all the people passed over, toward the way of the wilderness.

24 And behold Zadok also, and all the Levites (Lewiyim) were with him, bearing the ark of the covenant of God (Elohim); and they set down the ark of God (Elohim); and Aviyahthar went up, until all the people had done passing out of the city.

25 And the king said unto Zadok, "Carry back the ark of God (Elohim) into the city; if I shall find favor in the eyes of יהוה, He will bring me again, and shew me both it, and His habitation.

26 But if He thus say, 'I have no delight in you;' behold, here am I, let Him do to me as seemeth good unto Him."

27 The king said also unto Zadok the priest (kohen), "Art not you a seer? Return into the city in peace, and your two sons with you, Ahimaaz your son, and Jonathan (Yehonatan) the son of Aviyahthar.

28 See, I will tarry in the plain of the wilderness, until there come word from you to certify me."

29 Zadok therefore and Aviyahthar carried the ark of God (Elohim) again to Jerusalem (Yerushalayim); and they tarried there.

30 And Dawid went up by the ascent of mount Olivet, and wept as he went up, and had his head covered, and he went barefoot; and all the people that was with him covered every man his head, and they went up, weeping as they went up.

31 And one told Dawid, saying, "Ahithophel is among the conspirators with Avshalom." And Dawid said, "O יהוה, please turn the counsel of Ahithophel into foolishness!"

32 And it came to pass, that when Dawid was come to the top of the mount, where he worshipped God (Elohim), behold, Hushai the Archite came to meet him with his coat rent, and earth upon his head.

33 Unto whom Dawid said, "If you passest on with me, then you shalt be a burden unto me.

34 But if you return to the city, and say unto Avshalom, 'I will be your servant, O king; as I have been your father's servant hitherto, so will I now also be your servant,' then mayest you for me defeat the counsel of Ahithophel.

35 And have you not there with you Zadok and Aviyahthar the priests (kohanim)? Therefore it shall be, that what thing soever you shalt hear out of the king's house, you shalt tell it to Zadok and Aviyahthar the priests (kohanim).

36 Behold, they have there with them their two sons, Ahimaaz Zadok's son, and Jonathan (Yehonatan) Aviyah-thar's son; and by them you shall send unto me every thing that you can hear."

37 So Hushai Dawid's friend came into the city, and Avshalom came into Jerusalem (Yerushalayim).

16 And when Dawid was a little past the top of the hill, behold, Ziba the servant of Mephibosheth met him, with a couple of asses saddled, and upon them two hundred loaves of bread, and a hundred bunches of raisins, and a hundred of summer fruits, and a bottle of wine.

2 And the king said unto Ziba, "What meanest you by these?" And Ziba said, "The asses be for the king's household to ride on; and the bread and summer fruit for the young men to eat; and the wine, that such as be faint in the wilderness may drink."

3 And the king said, "And where is your master's son?" And Ziba said unto the king, "Behold, he abideth at Jerusalem (Yerushalayim); for he said, 'Today shall the house of Yisrael restore me the kingdom of my father.'"

4 Then said the king to Ziba, "Behold, your are all that pertained unto Mephibosheth." And Ziba said, "I humbly beseech you that I may find grace in your sight, my lord (adoni), O king!"

5 And when King Dawid came to Bahurim, behold, thence came out a man of the family of the house of Shaul, whose name was Shimei, the son of Gera; he came forth, and cursed still as he came.

6 And he cast stones at Dawid, and at all the servants of king Dawid; and all the people and

all the mighty men were on his right hand and on his left.

7 And thus said Shimei when he cursed: 'Come out! Come out, you bloody man, and you worthless man!

8 יהוה hath returned upon you all the blood of the house of Shaul, in whose stead you have reigned; and יהוה hath delivered the kingdom into the hand of Avshalom your son; and, behold, you are taken in your mischief, because you are a bloody man!"

9 Then said Avishai the son of Tseruyah unto the king, "Why should this dead dog curse my lord (adoni) the king? Please let me go over and take off his head!"

10 And the king said, "What have I to do with you, you sons of Tseruyah? So let him curse, because יהוה hath said unto him, 'Curse Dawid.' Who shall then say, 'Why have you done so?'"

11 And Dawid said to Avishai, and to all his servants, "Behold, my son, which came forth of my bowels, seeketh my life; how much more now may this Benjamin (Binyamin) do it? Let him alone, and let him curse; for יהוה hath bidden him.

12 It may be that יהוה will look on mine affliction, and that יהוה will requite me good for his cursing this day."

13 And as Dawid and his men went by the way, Shimei went along on the hill's side opposite him, and cursed as he went, and threw stones at him, and cast dust.

14 And the king, and all the people that were with him, came weary, and refreshed themselves there.

15 And Avshalom, and all the people the men of Yisrael, came to Jerusalem (Yerushalayim), and Ahithophel with him.

16 And it came to pass, when Hushai the Archite, Dawid's friend, was come unto Avshalom, that Hushai said unto Avshalom, "Long live the king! Long live the king!"

17 And Avshalom said to Hushai, "Is this your kindness to your friend? Why wentest you not with your friend?"

18 And Hushai said unto Avshalom, "Nay, but whom יהוה, and this people, and all the men of Yisrael, choose, his will I be, and with him will I abide.

19 And again, whom should I serve? Should I not serve in the presence of his son? As I have served in your father's presence, so will I be in your presence."

20 Then said Avshalom to Ahithophel, "Give counsel among you what we shall do."

21 And Ahithophel said unto Avshalom, "Go in unto your father's concubines, which he hath left to keep the house; and all Yisrael shall hear that you are abhorred of your father; then shall the hands of all that are with you be strong."

22 So they spread Avshalom a tent upon the top of the house; and Avshalom went in unto his father's concubines in the sight of all Yisrael.

23 And the counsel of Ahithophel, which he counselled in those days, was as if a man had enquired at the oracle of God (Elohim); so was all the counsel of Ahithophel both with Dawid and with Avshalom.

17 Moreover Ahithophel said unto Avshalom, "Let me now choose out twelve thousand men, and I will arise and pursue after Dawid this night.

2 And I will come upon him while he is weary and weak handed, and will make him afraid; and all the people that are with him shall flee; and I will smite the king only.

3 And I will bring back all the people unto you; the man whom you seekest is as if all returned; so all the people shall be in peace."

4 And the saying pleased Avshalom well, and all the elders of Yisrael.

5 Then said Avshalom, "Call now Hushai the Archite also, and let us hear likewise what he saith."

6 And when Hushai was come to Avshalom, Avshalom spake unto him, saying, "Ahithophel hath spoken after this manner; shall we do after his saying? If not; speak you."

7 And Hushai said unto Avshalom: "The counsel that Ahithophel hath given is not good at this time."

8 For, said Hushai, "you knowest your father and his men, that they be mighty men, and they be chafed in their minds, as a bear robbed of her whelps in the field; and your father is a man of war, and will not lodge with the people.

9 Behold, he is hid now in some pit, or in some other place; and it will come to pass, when some of them be overthrown at the first, that whosoever heareth it will say, 'There is a slaughter among the people that follow Avshalom.'

10 And he also that is valiant, whose heart is as the heart of a lion, shall utterly melt: for all Yisrael knoweth that your father is a mighty man, and they which be with him are valiant men.

11 Therefore I counsel that all Yisrael be generally gathered unto you, from Dan even to Beer-Sheva, as the sand that is by the sea for multitude; and that you go to battle in your own person.

12 So shall we come upon him in some place where he shall be found, and we will light upon him as the dew falleth on the ground; and of him and of all the men that are with him there shall not be left so much as one.

13 Moreover, if he be gotten into a city, then shall all Yisrael bring ropes to that city, and we will draw it into the river, until there be not one small stone found there."

14 And Avshalom and all the men of Yisrael said, "The counsel of Hushai the Archite is better than the counsel of Ahithophel." For יהוה had appointed to defeat the good counsel of Ahithophel, to the intent that יהוה might bring evil upon Avshalom.

15 Then said Hushai unto Zadok and to Aviyahthar the priests (kohanim), Thus and thus did Ahithophel counsel Avshalom and the elders of Yisrael; and thus and thus have I counselled.

16 Now therefore send quickly, and tell Dawid, saying, 'Lodge not this night in the plains of the wilderness, but speedily pass over; lest the king be swallowed up, and all the people that are with him.'"

17 Now Jonathan (Yehonatan) and Ahimaaz stayed by En Rogel; for they might not be seen to come into the city; and a wench went and told them; and they went and told King Dawid. 18 Nevertheless a lad saw them, and told Avshalom; but they went both of them away quickly, and came to a man's house in Bahurim, which had a well in his court; whither they went down.

19 And the woman took and spread a covering over the well's mouth, and spread ground corn thereon; and the thing was not known.

20 And when Avshalom's servants came to the woman to the house, they said, "Where is Ahimaaz and Jonathan (Yehonatan)?" And the woman said unto them, "They be gone over the brook of water." And when they had sought and could not find them, they returned to Jerusalem (Yerushalayim).

21 And it came to pass, after they were departed, that they came up out of the well, and went and told King Dawid, and said unto Dawid, "Arise, and pass quickly over the water; for thus hath Ahithophel counselled against you."

22 Then Dawid arose, and all the people that were with him, and they passed over Jordan (Yarden): by the morning light there lacked not one of them that was not gone over Jordan (Yarden).

23 And when Ahithophel saw that his counsel was not followed, he saddled his ass, and arose, and gat him home to his house, to his city, and put his household in order, and hanged himself, and died, and was buried in the sepulchre of his father.

24 Then Dawid came to Mahanaim. And Avshalom passed over Jordan (Yarden), he and all the men of Yisrael with him.

25 And Avshalom made Amasa captain of the army instead of Yoav: which Amasa was a man's son, whose name was Ithra an Yisraeli, that went in to Avigail the daughter of Nahash, sister to Tseruyah Yoav's mother.

26 So Yisrael and Avshalom pitched in the land of Gilad.

27 And it came to pass, when Dawid was come to Mahanaim, that Shobi the son of Nahash of Rabbah of the children of Ammon, and Machir the son of Ammiel of Lodebar, and Barzillai the Giladite of Rogelim,

28 Brought beds, and basons, and earthen vessels, and wheat, and barley, and flour, and parched corn, and beans, and lentiles, and parched pulse,

29 And honey, and butter, and sheep, and cheese of kine, for Dawid, and for the people that were with him, to eat; for they said, "The people is hungry, and weary, and thirsty, in the wilderness."

18 And Dawid numbered the people that were with him, and set captains of thousands and captains of hundreds over them.

2 And Dawid sent forth a third part of the people under the hand of Yoav, and a third part under the hand of Avishai the son of Tseruyah, Yoav's brother, and a third part under the hand of Ittai the Gittite. And the king said unto the people,

"I will surely go forth with you myself also."

3 But the people answered, "You shalt not go forth; for if we flee away, they will not care for us; neither if half of us die, will they care for us. Bbut now you are worth ten thousand of us; therefore now it is better that you succour us out of the city."

4 And the king said unto them, "What seemeth you best I will do." And the king stood by the gate side, and all the people came out by hundreds and by thousands.

5 And the king commanded Yoav and Avishai and Ittai, saying, "Deal gently for my sake with the young man, even with Avshalom." And all the people heard when the king gave all the captains charge concerning Avshalom.

6 So the people went out into the field against Yisrael; and the battle was in the wood of Efrayim;

7 Where the people of Yisrael were slain before the servants of Dawid, and there was there a great slaughter that day of twenty thousand men.

8 For the battle was there scattered over the face of all the country: and the wood devoured more people that day than the sword devoured.

9 And Avshalom met the servants of Dawid. And Avshalom rode upon a mule, and the mule went under the thick boughs of a great oak, and his head caught hold of the oak, and he was taken up between the heaven and the earth; and the mule that was under him went away.

10 And a certain man saw it, and told Yoav, and said, "Behold, I saw Avshalom hanged in an oak!"

11 And Yoav said unto the man that told him, "And, behold, you sawest him, and why didst you not smite him there to the ground? And I would have given you ten shekels of silver, and a girdle."

12 And the man said unto Yoav, "Though I should receive a thousand shekels of silver in mine hand, yet would I not put forth mine hand against the king's son; for in our hearing the king charged you and Avishai and Ittai, saying, 'Beware that none touch the young man Avshalom!"

13 Otherwise I should have wrought falsehood against mine own life: for there is no matter hid from the king, and you yourself wouldest have set yourself against me."

14 Then said Yoav, "I may not tarry thus with you." And he took three darts in his hand, and thrust them through the heart of Avshalom, while he was yet alive in the midst of the oak.

15 And ten young men that bare Yoav's armour compassed about and smote Avshalom, and slew him.

16 And Yoav blew the shofar, and the people returned from pursuing after Yisrael; for Yoav held back the people.

17 And they took Avshalom, and cast him into a great pit in the wood, and laid a very great heap of stones upon him; and all Yisrael fled every one to his tent.

18 Now Avshalom in his lifetime had taken and reared up for himself a pillar, which is in the king's dale; for he said, "I have no son to keep my name in remembrance." And he called the pillar after his own name; and it is called unto this day: Avshalom's Monument.

19 Then said Ahimaaz the son of Zadok, "Let me now run, and bear the king tidings, how that יהוה hath avenged him of his enemies."

20 And Yoav said unto him, "You shalt not bear tidings this day, but you shalt bear tidings another day; but this day you shalt bear no tidings, because the king's son is dead."

21 Then said Yoav to Kushi, "Go tell the king what you have seen." And Kushi bowed himself unto Yoav, and ran.

22 Then said Ahimaaz the son of Zadok yet again to Yoav, "But howsoever, let me, I pray you, also run after Kushi." And Yoav said, "Why wilt you run, my son, seeing that you have no tidings ready?"

23 "But howsoever," said he, "let me run." And he said unto him, "Run." Then Ahimaaz ran by the way of the plain, and overran Kushi.

24 And Dawid sat between the two gates; and the watchman went up to the roof over the gate unto the wall, and lifted up his eyes, and looked, and behold a man running alone.

25 And the watchman cried, and told the king. And the king said, "If he be alone, there is tidings in his mouth." And he came apace, and drew near.

26 And the watchman saw another man running: and the watchman called unto the porter, and said, "Behold another man running alone!" And the king said, "He also bringeth tidings."

27 And the watchman said, "Me thinketh the running of the foremost is like the running

of Ahimaaz the son of Zadok." And the king said, "He is a good man, and cometh with good tidings."

28 And Ahimaaz called, and said unto the king, "All is well!" And he fell down to the earth upon his face before the king, and said, "Blessed be יהוה your God (YHWH Eloheikha), who hath delivered up the men that lifted up their hand against my lord (adoni) the king."

29 And the king said, "Is the young man Avshalom safe?" And Ahimaaz answered, "When Yoav sent the king's servant, and me your servant, I saw a great tumult, but I knew not what it was."

30 And the king said unto him, "Turn aside, and stand here." And he turned aside, and stood still.

31 And, behold, Kushi came; and Kushi said, "Tidings, my lord (adoni) the king; for יהוה hath avenged you this day of all them that rose up against you.

32 And the king said unto Kushi, "Is the young man Avshalom safe?" And Kushi answered, "The enemies of my lord (adoni) the king, and all that rise against you to do you harm (B36raah), be as that young man is!"

33 And the king was much moved, and went up to the chamber over the gate, and wept; and as he went, thus he said: "O my son Avshalom, my son, my son Avshalom! If only I had died for you, O Avshalom, my son, my son!"

19 And it was told Yoav, "Behold, the king weepeth and mourneth for Avshalom."

2 And the victory that day was turned into mourning unto all the people; for the people heard say that day how the king was grieved for his son.

3 And the people gat them by stealth that day into the city, as people being ashamed steal away when they flee in battle.

4 But the king covered his face, and the king cried with a loud voice, "O my son Avshalom, O Avshalom, my son, my son!"

5 And Yoav came into the house to the king, and said, "You have shamed this day the faces of all your servants, which this day have saved your life, and the lives of your sons and of your daughters, and the lives of your wives, and the lives of your concubines;

6 In that you lovest your enemies, and hatest your friends. For you have declared this day, that you regardest neither princes nor servants;

for this day I perceive, that if Avshalom had lived, and all we had died this day, then it had pleased you well.

7 Now therefore arise, go forth, and speak comfortably unto your servants: for I swear by יהוה, if you go not forth, there will not tarry one with you this night; and that will be worse unto you than all the evil that befell you from your youth until now."

8 Then the king arose, and sat in the gate. And they told unto all the people, saying, "Behold, the king doth sit in the gate." And all the people came before the king; for Yisrael had fled every man to his tent.

9 And all the people were at strife throughout all the tribes of Yisrael, saying, "The king saved us out of the hand of our enemies, and he delivered us out of the hand of the Philistines; and now he is fled out of the land for Avshalom.

10 And Avshalom, whom we anointed over us, is dead in battle. Now therefore why speak you not a word of bringing the king back?"

11 And king Dawid sent to Zadok and to Aviyahthar the priests (kohanim), saying, "Speak unto the elders of Judah (Yehudah), saying, 'Why are you the last to bring the king back to his house? Seeing the speech of all Yisrael is come to the king, even to his house.

12 You are my brethren, you are my bones and my flesh. Why then are you the last to bring back the king?'

13 And say you to Amasa, 'Are you not of my bone, and of my flesh? God (Elohim) do so to me, and more also, if you be not captain of the army before me continually in the room of Yoav.'"

14 And he bowed the heart of all the men of Judah (Yehudah), even as the heart of one man; so that they sent this word unto the king: "Return you, and all your servants!"

15 So the king returned, and came to Jordan (Yarden). And Judah (Yehudah) came to Gilgal, to go to meet the king, to conduct the king over Jordan (Yarden).

16 And Shimei the son of Gera, a Benjamin (Binyamin), which was of Bahurim, hasted and came down with the men of Judah (Yehudah) to meet King Dawid.

17 And there were a thousand men of Benjamin (Binyamin) with him, and Ziba the servant of the house of Shaul, and his fifteen sons and his

twenty servants with him; and they went over Jordan (Yarden) before the king.

18 And there went over a ferry boat to carry over the king's household, and to do what he thought good. And Shimei the son of Gera fell down before the king, as he was come over Jordan (Yarden);

19 And said unto the king, "Let not my lord (adoni) impute iniquity unto me, neither do you remember that which your servant did perversely the day that my lord (adoni) the king went out of Jerusalem (Yerushalayim), that the king should take it to his heart.

20 For your servant doth know that I have sinned; therefore, behold, I am come the first this day of all the house of Joseph (Yosef) to go down to meet my lord (adoni) the king."

21 But Avishai the son of Tseruyah answered and said, "Shall not Shimei be put to death for this, because he cursed יהוה's anointed?"

22 And Dawid said, "What have I to do with you, you sons of Tseruyah, that you should this day be adversaries unto me? Shall there any man be put to death this day in Yisrael? For do not I know that I am this day king over Yisrael?"

23 Therefore the king said unto Shimei, "You shalt not die." And the king sware unto him.

24 And Mephibosheth the son of Shaul came down to meet the king, and had neither dressed his feet, nor trimmed his beard, nor washed his clothes, from the day the king departed until the day he came again in peace.

25 And it came to pass, when he was come to Jerusalem (Yerushalayim) to meet the king, that the king said unto him, "Why wentest not you with me, Mephibosheth?"

26 And he answered, "My lord (Adoni), O king, my servant deceived me; for your servant said, 'I will saddle me an ass, that I may ride thereon, and go to the king,' because your servant is lame.

27 And he hath slandered your servant unto my lord (adoni) the king; but my lord (adoni) the king is as an angel of God (Elohim). Do therefore what is good in your eyes.

28 For all of my father's house were but dead men before my lord (adoni) the king: yet didst you set your servant among them that did eat at your own table. What right therefore have I yet to cry any more unto the king?"

29 And the king said unto him, "Why speakest you any more of your matters?" I have said, 'You and Ziba divide the land.'"

30 And Mephibosheth said unto the king, "Yea, let him take all, forasmuch as my lord (adoni) the king is come again in peace unto his own house."

31 And Barzillai the Giladite came down from Rogelim, and went over Jordan (Yarden) with the king, to conduct him over Jordan (Yarden).

32 Now Barzillai was a very aged man, even fourscore years old; and he had provided the king of sustenance while he lay at Mahanaim; for he was a very great man.

33 And the king said unto Barzillai, "Come you over with me, and I will feed you with me in Jerusalem (Yerushalayim)."

34 And Barzillai said unto the king, "How long have I to live, that I should go up with the king unto Jerusalem (Yerushalayim)?

35 I am this day fourscore years old; and can I discern between good and evil? Can your servant taste what I eat or what I drink? Can I hear any more the voice of singing men and singing women? Wherefore then should your servant be yet a burden unto my lord (adoni) the king?

36 Your servant will go a little way over Jordan (Yarden) with the king; and why should the king recompense it me with such a reward?

37 Let your servant, I pray you, turn back again, that I may die in mine own city, and be buried by the grave of my father and of my mother. But behold your servant Chimham; let him go over with my lord (adoni) the king; and do to him what shall seem good unto you."

38 And the king answered, "Chimham shall go over with me, and I will do to him that which shall seem good unto you; and whatsoever you shalt require of me, that will I do for you."

39 And all the people went over Jordan (Yarden). And when the king was come over, the king kissed Barzillai, and blessed him; and he returned unto his own place.

40 Then the king went on to Gilgal, and Chimham went on with him; and all the people of Judah (Yehudah) conducted the king, and also half the people of Yisrael.

41 And, behold, all the men of Yisrael came to the king, and said unto the king, "Why have our brethren the men of Judah (Yehudah) stolen you away, and have brought the king, and his

household, and all Dawid's men with him, over Jordan (Yarden)?"

42 And all the men of Judah (Yehudah) answered the men of Yisrael, "Because the king is near of kin to us; wherefore then be you angry for this matter? Have we eaten at all of the king's cost? Or hath he given us any gift?"

43 And the men of Yisrael answered the men of Judah (Yehudah), and said, "We have ten parts in the king, and we have also more right in Dawid than you; why then did you despise us, that our advice should not be first had in bringing back our king?" And the words of the men of Judah (Yehudah) were fiercer than the words of the men of Yisrael.

20 And there happened to be there a scoundrel (beliyaal) man, whose name was Sheva, the son of Bichri, a Benjamin (Binyamin); and he blew a shofar, and said: "We have no part in Dawid, neither have we inheritance in the son of Jesse (Yishai); every man to his tents, O Yisrael.

2 So every man of Yisrael went up from after Dawid, and followed Sheva the son of Bichri; but the men of Judah (Yehudah) clave unto their king, from Jordan (Yarden) even to Jerusalem (Yerushalayim).

3 And Dawid came to his house at Jerusalem (Yerushalayim); and the king took the ten women his concubines, whom he had left to keep the house, and put them in ward, and fed them, but went not in unto them. So they were shut up unto the day of their death, living in widowhood.

4 Then said the king to Amasa, "Assemble me the men of Judah (Yehudah) within three days, and be you here present."

5 So Amasa went to assemble the men of Judah (Yehudah); but he tarried longer than the set time which he had appointed him.

6 And Dawid said to Avishai, "Now shall Sheva the son of Bichri do us more harm than did Avshalom; take you your lord (adon)'s servants, and pursue after him, lest he get him fenced cities, and escape us."

7 And there went out after him Yoav's men, and the Cherethites, and the Pelethites, and all the mighty men: and they went out of Jerusalem (Yerushalayim), to pursue after Sheva the son of Bichri.

8 When they were at the great stone which is in Giveon, Amasa went before them. And Yoav's garment that he had put on was girded unto him, and upon it a girdle with a sword fastened upon his loins in the sheath thereof; and as he went forth it fell out.

9 And Yoav said to Amasa, "Are you in health, my brother?" And Yoav took Amasa by the beard with the right hand to kiss him.

10 But Amasa took no heed to the sword that was in Yoav's hand; so he smote him therewith in the fifth rib, and shed out his bowels to the ground, and struck him not again; and he died. So Yoav and Avishai his brother pursued after Sheva the son of Bichri.

11 And one of Yoav's men stood by him, and said, "He that favoureth Yoav, and he that is for Dawid, let him go after Yoav!"

12 And Amasa wallowed in blood in the midst of the highway. And when the man saw that all the people stood still, he removed Amasa out of the highway into the field, and cast a cloth upon him, when he saw that every one that came by him stood still.

13 When he was removed out of the highway, all the people went on after Yoav, to pursue after Sheva the son of Bichri.

14 And he went through all the tribes of Yisrael unto Avel, and to Bethmaachah, and all the Berites; and they were gathered together, and went also after him.

15 And they came and besieged him in Avel of Bethmaachah, and they cast up a bank against the city, and it stood in the trench; and all the people that were with Yoav battered the wall, to throw it down.

16 Then cried a wise woman out of the city, "Hear, hear! Please say unto Yoav, 'Come near hither, that I may speak with you.'"

17 And when he was come near unto her, the woman said, "Are you Yoav?" And he answered, "I am he." Then she said unto him, "Hear the words of your handmaid." And he answered, "I do hear."

18 Then she spake, saying, "They were wont to speak in old time, saying, 'They shall surely ask counsel at Avel,' and so they ended the matter.

19 I am one of them that are peaceable and faithful in Yisrael; you seekest to destroy a city and a mother in Yisrael: why wilt you swallow up the inheritance of יהוה?"

20 And Yoav answered and said, "Far be it,

far be it from me, that I should swallow up or destroy!

21 The matter is not so; but a man of mount Efrayim, Sheva the son of Bichri by name, hath lifted up his hand against the king, even against Dawid: deliver him only, and I will depart from the city." And the woman said unto Yoav, "Behold, his head shall be thrown to you over the wall."

22 Then the woman went unto all the people in her wisdom. And they cut off the head of Sheva the son of Bichri, and cast it out to Yoav. And he blew a shofar, and they retired from the city, every man to his tent. And Yoav returned to Jerusalem (Yerushalayim) unto the king.

23 Now Yoav was over all the army of Yisrael; and Benayah the son of Yehoyada was over the Cherethites and over the Pelethites;

24 And Adoram was over the tribute; and Yehoshafat the son of Ahilud was recorder;

25 And Sheva was scribe; and Zadok and Aviyahthar were the priests (kohanim);

26 And Ira also the Yairite was a chief ruler about Dawid.

21 Then there was a famine in the days of Dawid three years, year after year; and Dawid enquired of יהוה. And יהוה answered, "It is for Shaul, and for his bloody house, because he slew the Giveonites."

2 And the king called the Giveonites, and said unto them; (now the Giveonites were not of the children of Yisrael, but of the remnant of the Amorites; and the children of Yisrael had sworn unto them; and Shaul sought to slay them in his zeal to the children of Yisrael and Judah (Yehudah).)

3 Wherefore Dawid said unto the Giveonites, "What shall I do for you? and wherewith shall I make the atonement, that you may bless the inheritance of יהוה?"

4 And the Giveonites said unto him, "We will have no silver nor gold of Shaul, nor of his house; neither for us shalt you kill any man in Yisrael." And he said, "What you shall say, that will I do for you."

5 And they answered the king, "The man that consumed us, and that devised against us that we should be destroyed from remaining in any of the coasts of Yisrael,

6 Let seven men of his sons be delivered unto us, and we will hang them up unto יהוה in Gibeah of Shaul, whom יהוה did choose." And the king said, "I will give them."

7 But the king spared Mephibosheth, the son of Jonathan (Yehonatan) the son of Shaul, because of יהוה's oath that was between them, between Dawid and Jonathan (Yehonatan) the son of Shaul.

8 But the king took the two sons of Rizpah the daughter of Ayah, whom she bare unto Shaul, Armoni and Mephibosheth; and the five sons of Michal the daughter of Shaul, whom she brought up for Adriel the son of Barzillai the Meholathite;

9 And he delivered them into the hands of the Giveonites, and they hanged them in the hill before יהוה; and they fell all seven together, and were put to death in the days of harvest, in the first days, in the beginning of barley harvest.

10 And Rizpah the daughter of Ayah took sackcloth, and spread it for her upon the rock, from the beginning of harvest until water dropped upon them out of heaven, and suffered neither the birds of the air to rest on them by day, nor the beasts of the field by night.

11 And it was told Dawid what Rizpah the daughter of Ayah, the concubine of Shaul, had done.

12 And Dawid went and took the bones of Shaul and the bones of Jonathan (Yehonatan) his son from the men of Yavesh-Gilad, which had stolen them from the street of Bethshan, where the Philistines had hanged them, when the Philistines had slain Shaul in Gilboa.

13 And he brought up from thence the bones of Shaul and the bones of Jonathan (Yehonatan) his son; and they gathered the bones of them that were hanged.

14 And the bones of Shaul and Jonathan (Yehonatan) his son buried they in the country of Benjamin (Binyamin) in Zelah, in the sepulchre of Kish his father; and they performed all that the king commanded. And after that God (Elohim) was intreated for the land.

15 Moreover the Philistines had yet war again with Yisrael; and Dawid went down, and his servants with him, and fought against the Philistines; and Dawid waxed faint.

16 And Ishbibenob, which was of the sons of the giant, the weight of whose spear weighed three hundred shekels of brass in weight, he being girded with a new sword, thought to have

slain Dawid.

17 But Avishai the son of Tseruyah succoured him, and smote the Philistine, and killed him. Then the men of Dawid sware unto him, saying, "You shalt go no more out with us to battle, that you quench not the light of Yisrael."

18 And it came to pass after this, that there was again a battle with the Philistines at Gob; then Sibbechai the Hushathite slew Saph, which was of the sons of the giant.

19 And there was again a battle in Gob with the Philistines, where Elhanan the son of Yaarey-Oregim, a Bethlehemite, slew the brother of Goliath the Gittite, the staff of whose spear was like a weaver's beam.

20 And there was yet a battle in Gath, where was a man of great stature, that had on every hand six fingers, and on every foot six toes, four and twenty in number; and he also was born to the giant.

21 And when he defied Yisrael, Jonathan (Yehonatan) the son of Shimea the brother of Dawid slew him.

22 These four were born to the giant in Gath, and fell by the hand of Dawid, and by the hand of his servants.

22 And Dawid spake unto יהוה the words of this song in the day that יהוה had delivered him out of the hand of all his enemies, and out of the hand of Shaul.

2 And he said, "יהוה is my rock, and my fortress, and my deliverer;

3 My God (Elohim), my rock; in Him will I trust; He is my shield, and the horn of my salvation, my high tower, and my refuge, my Savior; You savest me from violence.

4 I will call on יהוה, who is worthy to be praised; so shall I be saved from mine enemies.

5 When the waves of death compassed me, the floods of ungodly men made me afraid;

6 The sorrows of hell (sheol) compassed me about; the snares of death prevented me;

7 In my distress I called upon יהוה, and cried to my God (Elohim); and He did hear my voice out of His temple, and my cry did enter into His ears.

8 Then the earth shook and trembled; the foundations of heaven moved and shook, because He was wroth.

9 There went up a smoke out of His nostrils, and fire out of His mouth devoured; coals were kindled by it.

10 He bowed the heavens also, and came down; and darkness was under His feet.

11 And He rode upon a cherub (keruv), and did fly; and He was seen upon the wings of the wind.

12 And He made darkness pavilions round about Him, dark waters, and thick clouds of the skies.

13 Through the brightness before Him were coals of fire kindled.

14 יהוה thundered from heaven, and יהוה Most High (Elyon) uttered His voice.

15 And He sent out arrows, and scattered them; lightning, and discomfited them.

16 And the channels of the sea appeared, the foundations of the world were discovered, at the rebuking of יהוה, at the blast of the breath of His nostrils.

17 He sent from above, He took me; He drew me out of many waters;

18 He delivered me from my strong enemy, and from them that hated me: for they were too strong for me.

19 They prevented me in the day of my disaster; but יהוה was my stay.

20 He brought me forth also into a large place; He delivered me, because He delighted in me.

21 יהוה rewarded me according to my righteousness; according to the cleanness of my hands hath He recompensed me.

22 For I have kept the ways of יהוה, and have not wickedly departed from my God (Elohim).

23 For all His judgments were before me; and as for His statutes, I did not depart from them.

24 I was also upright before Him, and have kept myself from mine iniquity.

25 Therefore יהוה hath recompensed me according to my righteousness; according to my cleanness in His eye sight.

26 With the merciful You wilt shew Yourself merciful, and with the upright man You wilt shew Yourself upright.

27 With the pure You wilt shew Yourself pure; and with the perverse You wilt shew Yourself unsavoury.

28 And the afflicted people You wilt save; but Your eyes are upon the haughty, that You mayest bring them down.

29 For You are my lamp, O יהוה; and יהוה will lighten my darkness.

30 For by You I have run through a troop; by my God (Elohim) have I leaped over a wall.

31 As for God (Elohim), His way is perfect; the word of יהוה is proven; He is a buckler to all them that trust in Him.

32 For who is God (Elohim), except יהוה? And who is a Rock, except our God (Elohim)?

33 God (Elohim) is my strength and power; and He maketh my way perfect.

34 He maketh my feet like hinds' feet; and setteth me upon my high places.

35 He teacheth my hands to war; so that a bow of steel is broken by mine arms.

36 You have also given me the shield of Your salvation; and Your gentleness hath made me great.

37 You have enlarged my steps under me; so that my feet did not slip.

38 I have pursued mine enemies, and destroyed them; and turned not again until I had consumed them.

39 And I have consumed them, and wounded them, that they could not arise; yea, they are fallen under my feet.

40 For You have girded me with strength to battle; them that rose up against me have You subdued under me.

41 You have also given me the necks of mine enemies, that I might destroy them that hate me.

42 They looked, but there was none to save; even unto יהוה, but He answered them not.

43 Then did I beat them as small as the dust of the earth, I did stamp them as the mire of the street, and did spread them abroad.

44 You also hast delivered me from the strivings of my people; You have kept me to be head of the heathen; a people which I knew not shall serve me.

45 Strangers shall submit themselves unto me; as soon as they hear, they shall be obedient unto me.

46 Strangers shall fade away, and they shall be afraid out of their close places.

47 יהוה liveth; and blessed be my Rock; and exalted be the God (Elohim) of the Rock of my salvation.

48 It is God (Elohim) that avengeth me, and that bringeth down the people under me,

49 And that bringeth me forth from mine enemies; You also hast lifted me up on high above them that rose up against me; You have delivered me from the violent man.

50 Therefore I will give thanks unto you, O יהוה, among the nations, and I will sing praises unto Your name.

51 He is the tower of salvation for His king; and sheweth mercy to His anointed (mashiach), unto Dawid, and to his seed forevermore."

23 Now these be the last words of Dawid. Dawid the son of Jesse (Yishai) said, and the man who was raised up on high, the anointed (mashiach) of the God (Elohim) of Jacob (Yaaqov), and the sweet psalmist of Yisrael, said:

2 "The Spirit of יהוה spake by me, and His word was in my tongue.

3 The God of Israel (Elohei Yisrael) said, the Rock of Yisrael spake to me: 'He that ruleth over men must be just, ruling in the fear of God (Elohim).

4 And he shall be as the light of the morning, when the sun riseth, even a morning without clouds; as the tender grass springing out of the earth by clear shining after rain.

5 Although my house be not so with God (Elohim); yet He hath made with me an everlasting covenant, ordered in all things, and sure; for this is all my salvation, and all my desire, although He make it not to grow.

6 But the scoundrel (beliyaal) sons shall be all of them as thorns thrust away, because they cannot be taken with hands.

7 But the man that shall touch them must be fenced with iron and the staff of a spear; and they shall be utterly burned with fire in the same place."

8 These be the names of the mighty men whom Dawid had: The Tachmonite that sat in the seat, chief among the captains; the same was Adino the Eznite: he lifted up his spear against eight hundred, whom he slew at one time.

9 And after him was Eleazar the son of Dodo the Ahohite, one of the three mighty men with Dawid, when they defied the Philistines that were there gathered together to battle, and the men of Yisrael were gone away:

10 He arose, and smote the Philistines until his hand was weary, and his hand clave unto the sword: and יהוה wrought a great victory that day; and the people returned after him only to spoil.

11 And after him was Shammah the son of Agee

the Hararite. And the Philistines were gathered together into a troop, where was a piece of ground full of lentils; and the people fled from the Philistines.

12 But he stood in the midst of the ground, and defended it, and slew the Philistines; and יהוה wrought a great victory.

13 And three of the thirty chief went down, and came to Dawid in the harvest time unto the cave of Adullam: and the troop of the Philistines pitched in the valley of Rephaim.

14 And Dawid was then in a hold, and the garrison of the Philistines was then in Bethlehem (Beit-Lechem).

15 And Dawid longed, and said, "Oh that one would give me drink of the water of the well of Bethlehem (Beit-Lechem), which is by the gate!"

16 And the three mighty men broke through the camp of the Philistines, and drew water out of the well of Bethlehem (Beit-Lechem), that was by the gate, and took it, and brought it to Dawid; nevertheless he would not drink thereof, but poured it out unto יהוה.

17 And he said, "Be it far from me, O יהוה, that I should do this; is not this the blood of the men that went in jeopardy of their lives?" Therefore he would not drink it. These things did these three mighty men.

18 And Avishai, the brother of Yoav, the son of Tseruyah, was chief among three. And he lifted up his spear against three hundred, and slew them, and had the name among three.

19 Was he not most honourable of three? Therefore he was their captain: howbeit he attained not unto the first three.

20 And Benayah the son of Yehoyada, the son of a valiant man, of Kabzeel, who had done many acts, he slew two lionlike men of Moav; he went down also and slew a lion in the midst of a pit in time of snow.

21 And he slew an Egyptian (Mitsri), a goodly man; and the Egyptian (Mitsri) had a spear in his hand; but he went down to him with a staff, and plucked the spear out of the Egyptian (Mitsri)'s hand, and slew him with his own spear.

22 These things did Benayah the son of Yehoyada, and had the name among three mighty men.

23 He was more honourable than the thirty, but he attained not to the first three. And Dawid set him over his guard.

24 Asahel the brother of Yoav was one of the thirty; Elhanan the son of Dodo of Bethlehem (Beit-Lechem),

25 Shammah the Harodite, Elika the Harodite,

26 Helez the Paltite, Ira the son of Ikkesh the Tekoite,

27 Abiezer the Anethothite, Mebunnai the Hushathite,

28 Zalmon the Ahohite, Maharai the Netophathite,

29 Heleb the son of Baanah, a Netophathite, Ittai the son of Ribai out of Gibeah of the children of Benjamin (Binyamin),

30 Benayah the Pirathonite, Hiddai of the brooks of Gaash,

31 Aviyahlbon the Arbathite, Azma-veth the Barhumite,

32 Eliahba the Shaalbonite, of the sons of Yashen, Jonathan (Yehonatan),

33 Shammah the Hararite, Ahiam the son of Sharar the Hararite,

34 Eliphelet the son of Ahasbai, the son of the Maachathite, Eliam the son of Ahithophel the Gilonite,

35 Hezrai the Carmelite, Paarai the Arbite,

36 Igal the son of Nathan of Zobah, Bani the Gadite,

37 Zelek the Ammonite, Naharai the Beerothite, armourbearer to Yoav the son of Tseruyah,

38 Ira an Ithrite, Gareb an Ithrite,

39 Uriyah the Hittite: thirty-seven in all.

24

And again the anger of יהוה was kindled against Yisrael, and He moved Dawid against them to say, "Go, number Yisrael and Judah (Yehudah)."

2 For the king said to Yoav the captain of the army, who was with him, "Go now through all the tribes of Yisrael, from Dan even to Beer-Sheva, and number you the people, that I may know the number of the people."

3 And Yoav said unto the king, "Now יהוה your God (YHWH Eloheikha) add unto the people, how many soever they be, a hundredfold, and that the eyes of my lord (adoni) the king may see it; but why doth my lord (adoni) the king delight in this thing?"

4 Notwithstanding the king's word prevailed against Yoav, and against the captains of the army. And Yoav and the captains of the army

went out from the presence of the king, to number the people of Yisrael.

5 And they passed over Jordan (Yarden), and pitched in Aroer, on the right side of the city that lieth in the midst of the river of Gad, and toward Yazer.

6 Then they came to Gilad, and to the land of Tahtimhodshi; and they came to Danjaan, and about to Zidon,

7 And came to the strong hold of Tyre, and to all the cities of the Hivites, and of the Canaanites; and they went out to the south of Judah (Yehudah), even to Beer-Sheva.

8 So when they had gone through all the land, they came to Jerusalem (Yerushalayim) at the end of nine months and twenty days.

9 And Yoav gave up the sum of the number of the people unto the king: and there were in Yisrael eight hundred thousand valiant men that drew the sword; and the men of Judah (Yehudah) were five hundred thousand men.

10 And Dawid's heart smote him after that he had numbered the people. And Dawid said unto יהוה, "I have sinned greatly in that I have done; and now, I beseech you, O יהוה, take away the iniquity of your servant; for I have done very foolishly."

11 For when Dawid was up in the morning, the word of יהוה came unto the prophet Gad, Dawid's seer, saying,

12 "Go and say unto Dawid, 'Thus saith יהוה: "I offer you three things; choose you one of them, that I may do it unto you."'"

13 So Gad came to Dawid, and told him, and said unto him, "Shall seven years of famine come unto you in your land? Or wilt you flee three months before your enemies, while they pursue you? Or that there be three days' pestilence in your land? Now advise, and see what answer I shall return to him that sent me."

14 And Dawid said unto Gad, "I am in a great strait; let us fall now into the hand of יהוה; for his mercies are great; and let me not fall into the hand of man."

15 So יהוה sent a pestilence upon Yisrael from the morning even to the time appointed; and there died of the people from Dan even to Beer-Sheva seventy thousand men.

16 And when the angel stretched out his hand upon Jerusalem (Yerushalayim) to destroy it, יהוה regretted of the evil, and said to the angel that destroyed the people, "It is enough; restrain now Your hand." And the angel of יהוה was by the threshingplace of Araunah the Yevusi.

17 And Dawid spake unto יהוה when he saw the angel that smote the people, and said, "Behold, I have sinned, and I have done wickedly; but these sheep, what have they done? Let your hand, I pray you, be against me, and against my father's house."

18 And Gad came that day to Dawid, and said unto him, "Go up, rear an altar unto יהוה in the threshingfloor of Araunah the Jebusite (Yevusi)."

19 And Dawid, according to the saying of Gad, went up as יהוה commanded.

20 And Araunah looked, and saw the king and his servants coming on toward him; and Araunah went out, and bowed himself before the king on his face upon the ground.

21 And Araunah said, "Why is my lord (adoni) the king come to his servant?" And Dawid said, "To buy the threshingfloor of you, to build an altar unto יהוה, that the plague may be stayed from the people."

22 And Araunah said unto Dawid, "Let my lord (adoni) the king takes and offer up what seemeth good unto him; behold, here be oxen for burnt sacrifice, and threshing instruments and other instruments of the oxen for wood.

23 All these things did Araunah, as a king, give unto the king." And Araunah said unto the king, "May יהוה your God (YHWH Eloheikha) accept you."

24 And the king said unto Araunah, "Nay, but I will surely buy it of you at a price; neither will I offer burnt offerings unto יהוה my God (YHWH Elohai) of that which doth cost me nothing." So Dawid bought the threshingfloor and the oxen for fifty shekels of silver.

25 And Dawid built there an altar unto יהוה, and offered burnt offerings and peace offerings. So יהוה was intreated for the land, and the plague was stayed from Yisrael.

1 KINGS
MELAKHIM 1 א מְלָכִים
(First Kings)

1 Now King Dawid was old and stricken in years; and they covered him with clothes, but he gat no heat.

2 Wherefore his servants said unto him, "Let there be sought for my lord (adoni) the king a young virgin; and let her stand before the king, and let her cherish him, and let her lie in your bosom, that my lord (adoni) the king may get heat."

3 So they sought for a fair damsel throughout all the coasts of Yisrael, and found Abishag a Shunammite, and brought her to the king.

4 And the damsel was very fair, and cherished the king, and ministered to him; but the king knew her not.

5 Then Adoniyah the son of Haggith exalted himself, saying, "I will be king"; and he prepared him chariots and horsemen, and fifty men to run before him.

6 And his father had not displeased him at any time in saying, "Why have you done so?" And he also was a very goodly man; and his mother bare him after Avshalom.

7 And he conferred with Yoav the son of Tseruyah, and with Aviyahthar the priest (kohen); and they following Adoniyah helped him.

8 But Zadok the priest (kohen), and Benayah the son of Yehoyada, and Nathan the prophet, and Shimei, and Rei, and the mighty men which belonged to Dawid, were not with Adoniyah.

9 And Adoniyah slew sheep and oxen and fat cattle by the stone of Zoheleth, which is by En Rogel, and called all his brethren the king's sons, and all the men of Judah (Yehudah) the king's servants.

10 But Nathan the prophet, and Benayah, and the mighty men, and Solomon (Shelomoh) his brother, he called not.

11 Wherefore Nathan spake unto Bat-Sheva the mother of Solomon (Shelomoh), saying, "Have you not heard that Adoniyah the son of Haggith doth reign, and Dawid our lord (adon) knoweth it not?

12 Now therefore come, let me, I pray you, give you counsel, that you mayest save your own life, and the life of your son Solomon (Shelomoh).

13 Go and get you in unto King Dawid, and say unto him, 'Didst not you, my lord (adoni), O king, swear unto your handmaid, saying, "Assuredly Solomon (Shelomoh) your son shall reign after me, and he shall sit upon my throne?" Why then doth Adoniyah reign?'

14 Behold, while you yet talkest there with the king, I also will come in after you, and confirm your words."

15 And Bat-Sheva went in unto the king into the chamber; and the king was very old; and Abishag the Shunammite ministered unto the king.

16 And Bat-Sheva bowed, and prostrated herself unto the king. And the king said, "What wouldest you?"

17 And she said unto him, "My lord (Adoni), you swarest by יהוה your God (YHWH Eloheikha) unto your handmaid, saying, 'Assuredly Solomon (Shelomoh) your son shall reign after me, and he shall sit upon my throne.'

18 And now, behold, Adoniyah reigneth; and now, my lord (adoni) the king, you knowest it not.

19 And he hath slain oxen and fat cattle and sheep in abundance, and hath called all the sons of the king, and Aviyahthar the priest (kohen), and Yoav the captain of the army; but Solomon (Shelomoh) your servant hath he not called.

20 And you, my lord (adoni), O king, the eyes of all Yisrael are upon you, that you shouldest tell them who shall sit on the throne of my lord (adoni) the king after him.

21 Otherwise it shall come to pass, when my lord (adoni) the king shall sleep with his fathers, that I and my son Solomon (Shelomoh) shall be counted offenders."

22 And, behold, while she yet talked with the king, Nathan the prophet also came in.

23 And they told the king, saying, "Behold Nathan the prophet." And when he was come in before the king, he bowed himself before the king with his face to the ground.

24 And Nathan said, "My lord (Adoni), O king, have you said, 'Adoniyah shall reign after me, and he shall sit upon my throne'?

25 For he is gone down this day, and hath slain oxen and fat cattle and sheep in abundance, and hath called all the king's sons, and the captains of the army, and Aviyahthar the priest (kohen); and, behold, they eat and drink before him, and

say, 'Long live King Adoniyah!'

26 But me, even me your servant, and Zadok the priest (kohen), and Benayah the son of Yehoyada, and your servant Solomon (Shelomoh), hath he not called.

27 Is this thing done by my lord (adoni) the king, and you have not shewed it unto your servant, who should sit on the throne of my lord (adoni) the king after him?"

28 Then King Dawid answered and said, "Call Bat-Sheva to me." And she came into the king's presence, and stood before the king.

29 And the king sware, and said, "As יהוה liveth, that hath redeemed my soul out of all distress,

30 Even as I sware unto you by יהוה God of Israel (Elohei Yisrael), saying, 'Assuredly Solomon (Shelo-moh) your son shall reign after me, and he shall sit upon my throne in my stead'; even so will I certainly do this day."

31 Then Bat-Sheva bowed with her face to the earth, and did reverence to the king, and said, "Let my lord (adoni) King Dawid live forever!"

32 And King Dawid said, "Call to me Zadok the priest (kohen), and Nathan the prophet, and Benayah the son of Yehoyada." And they came before the king.

33 The king also said unto them, "Take with you the servants of your lord (adon), and cause Solomon (Shelomoh) my son to ride upon mine own mule, and bring him down to Gihon:

34 And let Zadok the priest (kohen) and Nathan the prophet anoints him there king over Yisrael: and blow you with the shofar, and say, 'Long live King Solomon (Shelomoh)!'

35 Then you shall come up after him, that he may come and sit upon my throne; for he shall be king in my stead; and I have appointed him to be ruler over Yisrael and over Judah (Yehudah)."

36 And Benayah the son of Yehoyada answered the king, and said, "Amen! May יהוה God of my lord (Elohei adoni) the king says so too.

37 As יהוה hath been with my lord (adoni) the king, even so be he with Solomon (Shelomoh), and make his throne greater than the throne of my lord (adoni) King Dawid."

38 So Zadok the priest (kohen), and Nathan the prophet, and Benayah the son of Yehoyada, and the Cherethites, and the Pelethites, went down, and caused Solomon (Shelomoh) to ride upon King Dawid's mule, and brought him to Gihon.

39 And Zadok the priest (kohen) took a horn of oil out of the tabernacle, and anointed Solomon (Shelomoh). And they blew the shofar; and all the people said, "Long live King Solomon (Shelomoh)!"

40 And all the people came up after him, and the people piped with pipes, and rejoiced with great joy, so that the earth rent with the sound of them.

41 And Adoniyah and all the guests that were with him heard it as they had made an end of eating. And when Yoav heard the sound of the shofar, he said, "Wherefore is this noise of the city being in an uproar?"

42 And while he yet spake, behold, [A38]Yonatan the son of Aviyahthar the priest (kohen) came; and Adoniyah said unto him, "Come in, for you are a valiant man, and bringest good tidings."

43 And Jonathan (Yehonatan) answered and said to Adoniyah, "Verily our lord (adoneinu) King Dawid hath made Solomon (Shelomoh) king."

44 And the king hath sent with him Zadok the priest (kohen), and Nathan the prophet, and Benayah the son of Yehoyada, and the Cherethites, and the Pelethites, and they have caused him to ride upon the king's mule.

45 And Zadok the priest (kohen) and Nathan the prophet has anointed him king in Gihon; and they are come up from thence rejoicing, so that the city rang again. This is the noise that you have heard.

46 And also Solomon (Shelomoh) sitteth on the throne of the kingdom.

47 And moreover the king's servants came to bless our lord (adon) King Dawid, saying, 'God (Elohim) make the name of Solomon (Shelomoh) better than your name, and make his throne greater than your throne.' And the king bowed himself upon the bed.

48 And also thus said the king, 'Blessed be יהוה God of Israel (Elohei Yisrael), which hath given one to sit on my throne this day, mine eyes even seeing it.'"

49 And all the guests that were with Adoniyah were afraid, and rose up, and went every man his way.

50 And Adoniyah feared because of Solomon (Shelomoh), and arose, and went, and caught hold on the horns of the altar.

51 And it was told Solomon (Shelomoh), saying,

"Behold, Adoniyah feareth King Solomon (Shelomoh); for, behold, he hath caught hold on the horns of the altar, saying, 'Let King Solomon (Shelomoh) swear unto me today that he will not slay his servant with the sword.'"

52 And Solomon (Shelomoh) said, "If he will shew himself a worthy man, there shall not a hair of him fall to the earth; but if wickedness shall be found in him, he shall die."

53 So King Solomon (Shelomoh) sent, and they brought him down from the altar. And he came and bowed himself to King Solomon (Shelomoh); and Solomon (Shelomoh) said unto him, "Go to your house."

2 Now the days of Dawid drew near that he should die; and he charged Solomon (Shelomoh) his son, saying:

2 "I go the way of all the earth; be you strong therefore, and shew yourself a man;

3 And keep the charge of יהוה your God (YHWH Eloheikha), to walk in His ways, to keep His statutes, and His commandments, and His judgments, and His testimonies, as B28cit is written in the Torah by Moses (Mosheh), that you mayest prosper in all that you doest, and whithersoever you turnest yourself;

4 That יהוה may continue His word which He spake concerning me, saying, 'If your children take heed to their way, to walk before Me in truth with all their heart and with all their soul, there shall not fail you' (said He) 'a man on the throne of Yisrael.'

5 Moreover you knowest also what Yoav the son of Tseruyah did to me, and what he did to the two captains of the hosts of Yisrael, unto Abner the son of Ner, and unto Amasa the son of Yether, whom he slew, and shed the blood of war in peace, and put the blood of war upon his girdle that was about his loins, and in his shoes that were on his feet.

6 Do therefore according to your wisdom, and let not his hoar head go down to the grave in peace.

7 But shew kindness unto the sons of Barzillai the Giladite, and let them be of those that eat at your table; for so they came to me when I fled because of Avshalom your brother.

8 And, behold, you have with you Shimei the son of Gera, a Benjamin (Binyamin) of Bahurim, which cursed me with a grievous curse in the day when I went to Mahanaim; but

he came down to meet me at Jordan (Yarden), and I sware to him by יהוה, saying, 'I will not put you to death with the sword.'

9 Now therefore hold him not guiltless: for you are a wise man, and knowest what you oughtest to do unto him; but his hoar head bring you down to the grave with blood."

10 So Dawid slept with his fathers, and was buried in the city of Dawid.

11 And the days that Dawid reigned over Yisrael were forty years; seven years reigned he in Hebron, and thirty and three years reigned he in Jerusalem (Yerushalayim).

12 Then sat Solomon (Shelomoh) upon the throne of Dawid his father; and his kingdom was established greatly.

13 And Adoniyah the son of Haggith came to Bat-Sheva the mother of Solomon (Shelomoh). And she said, "Comest you peaceably?" And he said, "Peaceably."

14 He said moreover, "I have somewhat to say unto you." And she said, "Say on."

15 And he said, "You knowest that the kingdom was mine, and that all Yisrael set their faces on me, that I should reign; howbeit the kingdom is turned about, and is become my brother's; for it was his from יהוה.

16 And now I ask one petition of you, deny me not." And she said unto him, "Say on."

17 And he said, "Please speak unto Solomon (Shelomoh) the king, (for he will not say you nay,) that he gives me Abishag the Shunammite as wife."

18 And Bat-Sheva said, "Well, I will speak for you unto the king."

19 Bat-Sheva therefore went unto King Solomon (Shelomoh), to speak unto him for Adoniyah. And the king rose up to meet her, and bowed himself unto her, and sat down on his throne, and caused a seat to be set for the king's mother; and she sat on his right hand.

20 Then she said, "I desire one small petition of you; please do not refuse me." And the king said unto her, "Ask on, my mother; for I will not refuse you."

21 And she said, "Let Abishag the Shunammite be given to Adoniyah your brother as wife."

22 And King Solomon (Shelomoh) answered and said unto his mother, "And why dost you ask Abishag the Shunammite for Adoniyah? Ask for him the kingdom also; for he is mine

elder brother; even for him, and for Aviyahthar the priest (kohen), and for Yoav the son of Tseruyah."

23 Then King Solomon (Shelomoh) sware by יהוה, saying, "May God (Elohim) do so to me, and more also, if Adoniyah have not spoken this word against his own life!

24 Now therefore, as יהוה liveth, which hath established me, and set me on the throne of Dawid my father, and who hath made me a house, as he promised, Adoniyah shall be put to death this day!"

25 And King Solomon (Shelomoh) sent by the hand of Benayah the son of Yehoyada; and he fell upon him that he died.

26 And unto Aviyahthar the priest (kohen) said the king, "Get you to Anathoth, unto your own fields; for you are worthy of death; but I will not at this time put you to death, because you barest the ark of Lord (Adonai) יהוה before Dawid my father, and because you have been afflicted in all wherein my father was afflicted."

27 So Solomon (Shelomoh) thrust out Aviyahthar from being priest (kohen) unto יהוה; that he might fulfil the word of יהוה, which he spake concerning the house of Eli in Shiloh.

28 Then tidings came to Yoav; for Yoav had turned after Adoniyah, though he turned not after Avshalom. And Yoav fled unto the tabernacle of יהוה, and caught hold on the horns of the altar.

29 And it was told King Solomon (Shelomoh) that Yoav was fled unto the tabernacle of יהוה; and, behold, he is by the altar. Then Solomon (Shelomoh) sent Benayah the son of Yehoyada, saying, "Go, fall upon him."

30 And Benayah came to the tabernacle of יהוה, and said unto him, "Thus saith the king, 'Come forth.'" And he said, "Nay; but I will die here." And Benayah brought the king word again, saying, "Thus said Yoav, and thus he answered me."

31 And the king said unto him, "Do as he hath said, and fall upon him, and bury him; that you mayest take away the innocent blood, which Yoav shed, from me, and from the house of my father.

32 And יהוה shall return his blood upon his own head, who fell upon two men more righteous and better than he, and slew them with the sword--Abner the son of Ner, captain of the

army of Yisrael, and Amasa the son of Yether, captain of the army of Judah (Yehudah); without my father Dawid knowing it.

33 Their blood shall therefore return upon the head of Yoav, and upon the head of his seed forever; but upon Dawid, and upon his seed, and upon his house, and upon his throne, shall there be peace forever from יהוה."

34 So Benayah the son of Yehoyada went up, and fell upon him, and slew him; and he was buried in his own house in the wilderness.

35 And the king put Benayah the son of Yehoyada in his room over the army: and Zadok the priest (kohen) did the king put in the room of Aviyahthar.

36 And the king sent and called for Shimei, and said unto him, "Build you a house in Jerusalem (Yerushalayim), and dwell there, and go not forth thence any whither.

37 For it shall be, that on the day you goest out, and passest over the brook Kidron, you shalt know for certain that you shalt surely die; your blood shall be upon your own head."

38 And Shimei said unto the king, "The saying is good; as my lord (adoni) the king hath said, so will your servant do." And Shimei dwelt in Jerusalem (Yerushalayim) many days.

39 And it came to pass at the end of three years, that two of the servants of Shimei ran away unto Achish son of Maachah king of Gath. And they told Shimei, saying, "Behold, your servants be in Gath!"

40 And Shimei arose, and saddled his ass, and went to Gath to Achish to seek his servants; and Shimei went, and brought his servants from Gath.

41 And it was told Solomon (Shelomoh) that Shimei had gone from Jerusalem (Yerushalayim) to Gath, and was come again.

42 And the king sent and called for Shimei, and said unto him, "Did I not make you to swear by יהוה, and protested unto you, saying, 'Know for a certain, on the day you goest out, and walkest abroad any whither, that you shalt surely die?' And you saidst unto me, 'The word that I have heard is good.'

43 Why then have you not kept the oath of יהוה, and the commandment that I have charged you with?"

44 The king said moreover to Shimei, "You knowest all the wickedness which your heart is

privy to, that you didst to Dawid my father; therefore יהוה shall return your wickedness upon your own head.

45 And King Solomon (Shelomoh) shall be blessed, and the throne of Dawid shall be established before יהוה forever."

46 So the king commanded Benayah the son of Yehoyada; which went out, and fell upon him, that he died. And the kingdom was established in the hand of Solomon (Shelomoh).

3 And Solomon (Shelomoh) made affinity with Pharaoh (Paroh) king of Egypt (Mitsrayim), and took Pharaoh (Paroh)'s daughter, and brought her into the city of Dawid, until he had made an end of building his own house, and the house of יהוה, and the wall of Jerusalem (Yerushalayim) round about.

2 Only the people sacrificed in high places, because there was no house built unto the name of יהוה, until those days.

3 And Solomon (Shelomoh) loved יהוה, walking in the statutes of Dawid his father; except that he sacrificed and burnt incense in high places.

4 And the king went to Giveon to sacrifice there; for that was the great high place; a thousand burnt offerings did Solomon (Shelomoh) offer upon that altar.

5 In Giveon יהוה appeared to Solomon (Shelomoh) in a dream by night; and God (Elohim) said, "Ask what I shall give you."

6 And Solomon (Shelomoh) said: "You have shewed unto Your servant Dawid my father great mercy, according as he walked before You in truth, and in righteousness, and in uprightness of heart with You; and You have kept for him this great kindness, that You have given him a son to sit on his throne, as it is this day.

7 And now, O יהוה my God (YHWH Elohai), You have made Your servant king instead of Dawid my father; and I am but a little child; I know not how to go out or come in.

8 And Your servant is in the midst of Your people which You have chosen, a great people, that cannot be numbered nor counted for multitude.

9 Give therefore Your servant an understanding heart to judge Your people, that I may discern between good and bad; for who is able to judge this Yours so great a people?"

10 And the speech pleased the Lord (Adonai), that Solomon (Shelomoh) had asked this thing.

11 And God (Elohim) said unto him: "Because you have asked this thing, and hast not asked for yourself long life; neither hast asked riches for yourself, nor hast asked the life of your enemies; but hast asked for yourself understanding to discern justice,

12 Behold, I have done according to your words; behold, I have given you a wise and an understanding heart; so that there was none like you before you, neither after you shall any arise like unto you.

13 And I have also given you that which you have not asked, both riches, and honor; so that there shall not be any among the kings like unto you all your days.

14 And if you wilt walk in My ways, to keep My statutes and My commandments, as your father Dawid did walk, then I will lengthen your days."

15 And Solomon (Shelomoh) awoke; and, behold, it was a dream. And he came to Jerusalem (Yerushalayim), and stood before the ark of the covenant of יהוה, and offered up burnt offerings, and offered peace offerings, and made a feast to all his servants.

16 Then came there two women, that were harlots, unto the king, and stood before him.

17 And the one woman said, "O my lord (adoni), I and this woman dwell in one house; and I was delivered of a child with her in the house.

18 And it came to pass the third day after that I was delivered, that this woman was delivered also; and we were together; there was no stranger with us in the house, save we two in the house.

19 And this woman's child died in the night; because she overlaid it.

20 And she arose at midnight, and took my son from beside me, while your handmaid slept, and laid it in her bosom, and laid her dead child in my bosom.

21 And when I rose in the morning to give my child suck, behold, it was dead; but when I had considered it in the morning, behold, it was not my son, which I did bear."

22 And the other woman said, "Nay, but the living is my son, and the dead is your son." And this said, "No, but the dead is your son, and the living is my son." Thus they spake before the king.

23 Then said the king, "The one saith, 'This is my son that liveth, and your son is the dead;' and the other saith, 'Nay, but your son is the dead, and my son is the living.'"

24 And the king said, "Bring me a sword." And they brought a sword before the king.

25 And the king said, "Divide the living child in two, and give half to the one, and half to the other."

26 Then spake the woman whose the living child was unto the king, for her bowels yearned upon her son, and she said, "O my lord (adoni), give her the living child, and in no wise slay it." But the other said, "Let it be neither mine nor yours, but divide it."

27 Then the king answered and said, "Give her the living child, and in no wise slay it; she is the mother thereof."

28 And all Yisrael heard of the judgment which the king had judged; and they feared the king; for they saw that the wisdom of God (Elohim) was in him, to do judgment.

4 So King Solomon (Shelomoh) was king over all Yisrael.

2 And these were the princes whom he had: Azaryahu the son of Zadok the priest (kohen),

3 Elihoreph and Achiyah, the sons of Shisha, scribes; Yehoshafat the son of Ahilud, the recorder.

4 And Benayah the son of Yehoyada was over the army; and Zadok and Aviyahthar were the priests (kohanim);

5 And Azaryahu the son of Nathan was over the officers; and Zabud the son of Nathan was principal officer, and the king's friend;

6 And Ahishar was over the household; and Adoniram the son of Abda was over the tribute.

7 And Solomon (Shelomoh) had twelve officers over all Yisrael, which provided victuals for the king and his household; each man his month in a year made provision.

8 And these are their names: The son of Hur, in Mount Efrayim:

9 The son of Dekar, in Makaz, and in Shaalbim, and Beit-Shemesh, and Elon Beit Chanan;

10 The son of Hesed, in Aruboth; to him pertained Sochoh, and all the land of Hepher;

11 The son of Abinadab, in all the region of Dor; who had Taphath the daughter of Solomon (Shelomoh) as wife:

12 Baana the son of Ahilud; to him pertained Taanach and Megiddo, and all Beit-Shean, which is by Zartanah beneath Yizreel, from Beit-Shean to Avelmeholah, even unto the place that is beyond Yokmeam;

13 The son of Geber, in Ramot-Gilad; to him pertained the towns of Yair the son of Menashsheh, which are in Gilad; to him also pertained the region of Argob, which is in Bashan, threescore (sixty) great cities with walls and brasen bars;

14 Ahinadab the son of Iddo had Mahanaim;

15 Ahimaaz was in Naftali; he also took Basmath the daughter of Solomon (Shelomoh) as wife;

16 Baanah the son of Hushai was in Asher and in Aloth;

17 Yehoshafat the son of Paruah, in Yissaskhar;

18 Shimei the son of Ela, in Benjamin (Binyamin);

19 Geber the son of Uri was in the country of Gilad, in the country of Sihon king of the Amorites, and of Og king of Bashan; and he was the only officer which was in the land.

20 Judah (Yehudah) and Yisrael were many, as the sand which is by the sea in multitude, eating and drinking, and making merry.

21 And Solomon (Shelomoh) reigned over all kingdoms from the river unto the land of the Philistines, and unto the border of Egypt (Mitsrayim); they brought presents, and served Solomon (Shelomoh) all the days of his life.

22 And Solomon (Shelomoh)'s provision for one day was thirty measures of fine flour, and threescore measures of meal,

23 Ten fat oxen, and twenty oxen out of the pastures, and a hundred sheep, beside harts, and roebucks, and fallowdeer, and fatted fowl.

24 For he had dominion over all the region on this side the river, from Tiphsah even to Azzah, over all the kings on this side the river; and he had peace on all sides round about him.

25 And Judah (Yehudah) and Yisrael dwelt safely, every man under his vine and under his fig tree, from Dan even to Beer-Sheva, all the days of Solomon (Shelomoh).

26 And Solomon (Shelomoh) had forty thousand stalls of horses for his chariots, and twelve thousand horsemen.

27 And those officers provided victual for King Solomon (Shelomoh), and for all that came unto King Solomon (Shelomoh)'s table, every man in

his month; they lacked nothing.

28 Barley also and straw for the horses and dromedaries brought they unto the place where the officers were, every man according to his charge.

29 And God (Elohim) gave Solomon (Shelomoh) wisdom and understanding exceeding much, and largeness of heart, even as the sand that is on the sea shore.

30 And Solomon (Shelomoh)'s wisdom excelled the wisdom of all the children of the east country, and all the wisdom of Egypt (Mitsrayim).

31 For he was wiser than all men; than Ethan the Ezrahite, and Heman, and Chalcol, and Darda, the sons of Mahol: and his fame was in all nations round about.

32 And he spake three thousand proverbs; and his songs were a thousand and five.

33 And he spake of trees, from the cedar tree that is in Lebanon even unto the hyssop that springeth out of the wall; he spake also of beasts, and of fowl, and of creeping things, and of fishes.

34 And there came of all people to hear the wisdom of Solomon (Shelomoh), from all kings of the earth, who had heard of his wisdom.

5 And Hiram king of Tyre sent his servants unto Solomon (Shelomoh), for he had heard that they had anointed him king in the room of his father; for Hiram was ever a lover of Dawid.

2 And Solomon (Shelomoh) sent to Hiram, saying:

3 "You knowest how that Dawid my father could not build a house unto the name of יהוה his God (Elohim) for the wars which were about him on every side, until יהוה put them under the soles of his feet.

4 But now יהוה my God (YHWH Elohai) hath given me rest on every side, so that there is neither adversary nor evil occurrent.

5 And, behold, I purpose to build a house unto the name of יהוה my God (YHWH Elohai), as יהוה spake unto Dawid my father, saying, 'Your son, whom I will set upon your throne in your room, he shall build a house unto My name.'

6 Now therefore command you that they hew me cedar trees out of Lebanon; and my servants shall be with your servants; and unto you will I give hire for your servants according to all that you shalt appoint; for you knowest that there is not among us any that can skill to hew timber like unto the Sidonians."

7 And it came to pass, when Hiram heard the words of Solomon (Shelomoh), that he rejoiced greatly, and said, "Blessed be יהוה this day, which hath given unto Dawid a wise son over this great people!"

8 And Hiram sent to Solomon (Shelomoh), saying: "I have considered the things which you sentest to me for; and I will do all your desire concerning timber of cedar, and concerning timber of fir.

9 My servants shall bring them down from Lebanon unto the sea; and I will convey them by sea in floats unto the place that you shalt appoint me, and will cause them to be discharged there, and you shalt receive them; and you shalt accomplish my desire, in giving food for my household."

10 So Hiram gave Solomon (Shelomoh) cedar trees and fir trees according to all his desire.

11 And Solomon (Shelomoh) gave Hiram twenty thousand measures of wheat for food to his household, and twenty measures of pure oil; thus gave Solomon (Shelomoh) to Hiram year by year.

12 And יהוה gave Solomon (Shelomoh) wisdom, as He promised him: and there was peace between Hiram and Solomon (Shelomoh); and they two made a league together.

13 And King Solomon (Shelomoh) raised a levy out of all Yisrael; and the levy was thirty thousand men.

14 And he sent them to Lebanon, ten thousand a month by courses; a month they were in Lebanon, and two months at home; and Adoniram was over the levy.

15 And Solomon (Shelomoh) had threescore and ten thousand that bare burdens, and fourscore thousand hewers in the mountains;

16 Beside the chief of Solomon (Shelomoh)'s officers who were over the work, three thousand and three hundred, who ruled over the people that wrought in the work.

17 And the king commanded, and they brought great stones, costly stones, and hewed stones, to lay the foundation of the house.

18 And Solomon (Shelomoh)'s builders and Hiram's builders did hew them, and the stonesquarers; so they prepared timber and stones to build the house.

6 And it came to pass in the four hundred and eightieth year after the children of Yisrael

were come out of the land of Egypt (Mitsrayim), in the fourth year of Solomon (Shelomoh)'s reign over Yisrael, in the Month Zif, which is the second month, that he began to build the house of יהוה.

2 And the house which King Solomon (Shelomoh) built for יהוה, the length thereof was threescore cubits, and the breadth thereof twenty cubits, and the height thereof thirty cubits.

3 And the porch before the temple of the house, twenty cubits was the length thereof, according to the breadth of the house; and ten cubits was the breadth thereof before the house.

4 And for the house he made windows of narrow lights.

5 And against the wall of the house he built chambers round about, against the walls of the house round about, both of the temple and of the oracle; and he made chambers round about.

6 The nethermost chamber was five cubits broad, and the middle was six cubits broad, and the third was seven cubits broad; for outside in the wall of the house he made narrowed rests round about, that the beams should not be fastened in the walls of the house.

7 And the house, when it was in building, was built of stone made ready before it was brought thither; so that there was neither hammer nor axe nor any tool of iron heard in the house, while it was in building.

8 The door for the middle chamber was in the right side of the house; and they went up with winding stairs into the middle chamber, and out of the middle into the third.

9 So he built the house, and finished it; and covered the house with beams and boards of cedar.

10 And then he built chambers against all the house, five cubits high; and they rested on the house with timber of cedar.

11 And the word of יהוה came to Solomon (Shelomoh), saying:

12 "Concerning this house which you are in building, if you wilt walk in My statutes, and execute My judgments, and keep all My commandments to walk in them; then will I perform My word with you, which I spake unto Dawid your father.

13 And I will dwell among the children of Yisrael, and will not forsake My people Yisrael."

14 So Solomon (Shelomoh) built the house, and finished it.

15 And he built the walls of the house within with boards of cedar, both the floor of the house, and the walls of the ceiling; and he covered them on the inside with wood, and covered the floor of the house with planks of fir.

16 And he built twenty cubits on the sides of the house, both the floor and the walls with boards of cedar; he even built them for it within, even for the oracle, even for the most holy place.

17 And the house, that is, the temple before it, was forty cubits long.

18 And the cedar of the house within was carved with knops and open flowers; all was cedar; there was no stone seen.

19 And the oracle he prepared in the house within, to set there the ark of the covenant of יהוה.

20 And the oracle in the forepart was twenty cubits in length, and twenty cubits in breadth, and twenty cubits in the height thereof; and he overlaid it with pure gold; and so covered the altar which was of cedar.

21 So Solomon (Shelomoh) overlaid the house within with pure gold: and he made a partition by the chains of gold before the oracle; and he overlaid it with gold.

22 And the whole house he overlaid with gold, until he had finished all the house; also the whole altar that was by the oracle he overlaid with gold.

23 And within the oracle he made two cherubims (keruvim) of olive tree, each ten cubits high.

24 And five cubits was the one wing of the cherub (keruv), and five cubits the other wing of the cherub (keruv); from the uttermost part of the one wing unto the uttermost part of the other were ten cubits.

25 And the other cherub (keruv) was ten cubits; both the cherubims (keruvim) were of one measure and one size.

26 The height of the one cherub (keruv) was ten cubits, and so was it of the other cherub (keruv).

27 And he set the cherubims (keruvim) within the inner house; and they stretched forth the wings of the cherubims (keruvim), so that the wing of the one touched the one wall, and the wing of the other cherub (keruv) touched the other wall; and their wings touched one another in the midst of the house.

28 And he overlaid the cherubims (keruvim) with gold.

29 And he carved all the walls of the house round about with carved figures of cherubims (keruvim) and palm trees and open flowers, within and outside.

30 And the floor of the house he overlaid with gold, within and outside.

31 And for the entering of the oracle he made doors of olive tree; the lintel and side posts were a fifth part of the wall.

32 The two doors also were of olive tree; and he carved upon them carvings of cherubims (keruvim) and palm trees and open flowers, and overlaid them with gold, and spread gold upon the cherubims (keruvim), and upon the palm trees.

33 So also made he for the door of the temple posts of olive tree, a fourth part of the wall.

34 And the two doors were of fir tree; the two leaves of the one door were folding, and the two leaves of the other door were folding.

35 And he carved thereon cherubims (keruvim) and palm trees and open flowers; and covered them with gold fitted upon the carved work.

36 And he built the inner court with three rows of hewed stone, and a row of cedar beams.

37 In the fourth year was the foundation of the house of יהוה laid, in the Month Ziw.

38 And in the eleventh year, in the month Bul, which is the eighth month, was the house finished throughout all the parts thereof, and according to all the fashion of it. So was he seven years in building it.

7 But Solomon (Shelomoh) was building his own house thirteen years, and he finished all his house.

2 He built also the house of the forest of Lebanon; the length thereof was a hundred cubits, and the breadth thereof fifty cubits, and the height thereof thirty cubits, upon four rows of cedar pillars, with cedar beams upon the pillars.

3 And it was covered with cedar above upon the beams, that lay on forty-five pillars, fifteen in a row.

4 And there were windows in three rows, and light was against light in three ranks.

5 And all the doors and posts were square, with the windows; and light was against light in three ranks.

6 And he made a porch of pillars; the length thereof was fifty cubits, and the breadth thereof thirty cubits; and the porch was before them; and the other pillars and the thick beam were before them.

7 Then he made a porch for the throne where he might judge, even the porch of judgment; and it was covered with cedar from one side of the floor to the other.

8 And his house where he dwelt had another court within the porch, which was of the like work. Solomon (Shelomoh) made also a house for Pharaoh (Paroh)'s daughter, whom he had taken to wife, like unto this porch.

9 All these were of costly stones, according to the measures of hewed stones, sawed with saws, within and outside, even from the foundation unto the coping, and so on the outside toward the great court.

10 And the foundation was of costly stones, even great stones, stones of ten cubits, and stones of eight cubits.

11 And above were costly stones, after the measures of hewed stones, and cedars.

12 And the great court round about was with three rows of hewed stones, and a row of cedar beams, both for the inner court of the house of יהוה, and for the porch of the house.

13 And King Solomon (Shelomoh) sent and fetched Hiram out of Tyre.

14 He was a widow's son of the tribe of Naftali, and his father was a man of Tyre, a worker in brass; and he was filled with wisdom, and understanding, and cunning to work all works in brass. And he came to King Solomon (Shelomoh), and wrought all his work.

15 For he cast two pillars of brass, of eighteen cubits high apiece; and a line of twelve cubits did compass either of them about.

16 And he made two chapiters of molten brass, to set upon the tops of the pillars; the height of the one chapiter was five cubits, and the height of the other chapiter was five cubits.

17 And nets of checker work, and wreaths of chain work, for the chapiters which were upon the top of the pillars; seven for the one chapiter, and seven for the other chapiter.

18 And he made the pillars, and two rows round about upon the one network, to cover the chapiters that were upon the top, with pomegranates; and so did he for the other chapiter.

19 And the chapiters that were upon the top of the pillars were of lily work in the porch, four cubits.

20 And the chapiters upon the two pillars had pomegranates also above, opposite the belly which was by the network; and the pomegranates were two hundred in rows round about upon the other chapiter.

21 And he set up the pillars in the porch of the temple; and he set up the right pillar, and called the name thereof Yakhin; and he set up the left pillar, and called the name thereof Boaz.

22 And upon the top of the pillars was lily work; so was the work of the pillars finished.

23 And he made a molten sea, ten cubits from the one brim to the other; it was round all about, and his height was five cubits; and a line of thirty cubits did compass it round about.

24 And under the brim of it round about there were knops compassing it, ten in a cubit, compassing the sea round about; the knops were cast in two rows, when it was cast.

25 It stood upon twelve oxen, three looking toward the north, and three looking toward the west, and three looking toward the south, and three looking toward the east; and the sea was set above upon them, and all their hinder parts were inward.

26 And it was a hand breadth thick, and the brim thereof was wrought like the brim of a cup, with flowers of lilies; it contained two thousand baths.

27 And he made ten bases of brass; four cubits was the length of one base, and four cubits the breadth thereof, and three cubits the height of it.

28 And the work of the bases was on this manner; they had borders, and the borders were between the ledges:

29 And on the borders that were between the ledges were lions, oxen, and cherubims (keruvim); and upon the ledges there was a base above; and beneath the lions and oxen were certain additions made of thin work.

30 And every base had four brasen wheels, and plates of brass; and the four corners thereof had undersetters; under the laver were undersetters molten, at the side of every addition.

31 And the mouth of it within the chapiter and above was a cubit; but the mouth thereof was round after the work of the base, a cubit and a half; and also upon the mouth of it was gravings with their borders, foursquare, not round.

32 And under the borders were four wheels; and the axletrees of the wheels were joined to the base; and the height of a wheel was a cubit and half a cubit.

33 And the work of the wheels was like the work of a chariot wheel; their axletrees, and their naves, and their felloes, and their spokes, were all molten.

34 And there were four undersetters to the four corners of one base; and the undersetters were of the very base itself.

35 And in the top of the base was there a round compass of half a cubit high; and on the top of the base the ledges thereof and the borders thereof were of the same.

36 For on the plates of the ledges thereof, and on the borders thereof, he graved cherubims (keruvim), lions, and palm trees, according to the proportion of every one, and additions round about.

37 After this manner he made the ten bases; all of them had one casting, one measure, and one size.

38 Then made he ten lavers of brass; one laver contained forty baths; and every laver was four cubits; and upon every one of the ten bases one laver.

39 And he put five bases on the right side of the house, and five on the left side of the house; and he set the sea on the right side of the house eastward opposite the south.

40 And Hiram made the lavers, and the shovels, and the basons. So Hiram made an end of doing all the work that he made King Solomon (Shelomoh) for the house of יהוה:

41 The two pillars, and the two bowls of the chapiters that were on the top of the two pillars; and the two networks, to cover the two bowls of the chapiters which were upon the top of the pillars;

42 And four hundred pomegranates for the two networks, even two rows of pomegranates for one network, to cover the two bowls of the chapiters that were upon the pillars;

43 And the ten bases, and ten lavers on the bases;

44 And one sea, and twelve oxen under the sea;

45 And the pots, and the shovels, and the basons; and all these vessels, which Hiram made to King Solomon (Shelomoh) for the house of יהוה,

were of bright brass.

46 In the plain of Jordan (Yarden) did the king cast them, in the clay ground between Sukkot and Zarthan.

47 And Solomon (Shelomoh) left all the vessels unweighed, because they were exceeding many; neither was the weight of the brass found out.

48 And Solomon (Shelomoh) made all the vessels that pertained unto the house of יהוה; the altar of gold, and the table of gold, whereupon the shewbread was,

49 And the candlesticks (menorot) of pure gold, five on the right side, and five on the left, before the oracle, with the flowers, and the lamps, and the tongs of gold,

50 And the bowls, and the snuffers, and the basons, and the spoons, and the censers of pure gold; and the hinges of gold, both for the doors of the inner house, the most holy place, and for the doors of the house, to wit, of the temple.

51 So was ended all the work that King Solomon (Shelomoh) made for the house of יהוה. And Solomon (Shelomoh) brought in the things which Dawid his father had dedicated; even the silver, and the gold, and the vessels, did he put among the treasures of the house of יהוה.

8 Then Solomon (Shelomoh) assembled the elders of Yisrael, and all the heads of the tribes, the chief of the fathers of the children of Yisrael, unto King Solomon (Shelomoh) in Jerusalem (Yerushalayim), that they might bring up the ark of the covenant of יהוה out of the city of Dawid, which is Zion (Tsiyon).

2 And all the men of Yisrael assembled themselves unto King Solomon (Shelomoh) at the feast in the month Ethanim, which is the seventh month.

3 And all the elders of Yisrael came, and the priests (kohanim) took up the ark.

4 And they brought up the ark of יהוה, and the tabernacle of the congregation, and all the holy vessels that were in the tabernacle, even those did the priests (kohanim) and the Levites (Lewiyim) bring up.

5 And King Solomon (Shelomoh), and all the congregation of Yisrael, that were assembled unto him, were with him before the ark, sacrificing sheep and oxen, that could not be told nor numbered for multitude.

6 And the priests (kohanim) brought in the ark of the covenant of יהוה unto his place, into the oracle of the house, to the most holy place, even under the wings of the cherubims (keruvim).

7 For the cherubims (keruvim) spread forth their two wings over the place of the ark, and the cherubims (keruvim) covered the ark and the staves thereof above.

8 And they drew out the staves, that the ends of the staves were seen out in the holy place before the oracle, and they were not seen outside; and there they are unto this day.

9 There was nothing in the ark save the two tables of stone, which Moses (Mosheh) put there at Horeb, when יהוה made a covenant with the children of Yisrael, when they came out of the land of Egypt (Mitsrayim).

10 And it came to pass, when the priests (kohanim) were come out of the holy place, that the cloud filled the house of יהוה,

11 So that the priests (kohanim) could not stand to minister because of the cloud; for the glory of יהוה had filled the house of יהוה.

12 Then spake Solomon (Shelomoh): "יהוה said that he would dwell in the thick darkness.

13 I have surely built you a house to dwell in, a settled place for you to abide in forever."

14 And the king turned his face about, and blessed all the congregation of Yisrael; (and all the congregation of Yisrael stood;)

15 And he said: "Blessed be יהוה God of Israel (Elohei Yisrael), who spake with His mouth unto Dawid my father, and hath with His hand fulfilled it, saying,

16 'Since the day that I brought forth My people Yisrael out of Egypt (Mitsrayim), I chose no city out of all the tribes of Yisrael to build a house, that My name might be therein; but I chose Dawid to be over My people Yisrael.'

17 And it was in the heart of Dawid my father to build a house for the name of יהוה God of Israel (Elohei Yisrael).

18 And יהוה said unto Dawid my father, 'Whereas it was in your heart to build a house unto My name, you didst well that it was in your heart.

19 Nevertheless you shalt not build the house; but your son that shall come forth out of your loins, he shall build the house unto My name.'

20 And יהוה hath performed His word that He spake, and I am risen up in the room of Dawid my father, and sit on the throne of Yisrael, as יהוה promised, and have built a house for the

name of יהוה God of Israel (Elohei Yisrael).

21 And I have set there a place for the ark, wherein is the covenant of יהוה, which He made with our fathers, when He brought them out of the land of Egypt (Mitsrayim)."

22 And Solomon (Shelomoh) stood before the altar of יהוה in the presence of all the congregation of Yisrael, and spread forth his hands toward heaven;

23 And he said: "יהוה God of Israel (Elohei Yisrael), there is no God (Elohim) like You, in heaven above, or on earth beneath, who keepest covenant and mercy with Your servants that walk before You with all their heart.

24 Who hast kept with Your servant Dawid my father that you promisedst him. You spakest also with Your mouth, and hast fulfilled it with Your hand, as it is this day.

25 Therefore now, יהוה God of Israel (Elohei Yisrael), keep with Your servant Dawid my father that You promisedst him, saying, 'There shall not fail you a man in My sight to sit on the throne of Yisrael; so that your children take heed to their way, that they walk before Me as you have walked before Me.'

26 And now, O God of Israel (Elohei Yisrael), I pray, Your word be confirmed, which You spakest unto Your servant Dawid my father.

27 But will God (Elohim) indeed dwell on the earth? Behold, the heaven and heaven of heavens cannot contain You; how much less this house that I have builded?

28 Yet have You respect unto the prayer of Your servant, and to his supplication, O יהוה my God (YHWH Elohai), to hearken unto the cry and to the prayer, which Your servant prayeth before You today;

29 That Your eyes may be open toward this house night and day, even toward the place of which You have said, 'My name shall be there,' that You mayest hearken unto the prayer which Your servant shall make toward this place.

30 And hearken You to the supplication of Your servant, and of Your people Yisrael, when they shall pray toward this place; and hear You in heaven Your dwelling place; and when You hearest, forgive.

31 If any man trespass against his neighbour, and an oath be laid upon him to cause him to swear, and the oath come before Your altar in this house;

32 Then hear You in heaven, and do, and judge Your servants, condemning the wicked, to bring his way upon his head; and justifying the righteous, to give him according to his righteousness.

33 When Your people Yisrael be smitten down before the enemy, because they have sinned against You, and shall turn again to You, and confess Your name, and pray, and make supplication unto You in this house;

34 Then hear You in heaven, and forgive the sin of Your people Yisrael, and bring them again unto the land which You gavest unto their fathers.

35 When heaven is shut up, and there is no rain, because they have sinned against you; if they pray toward this place, and confess Your name, and turn from their sin, when You afflictest them:

36 Then hear You in heaven, and forgive the sin of Your servants, and of Your people Yisrael, that You teach them the good way wherein they should walk, and give rain upon Your land, which You have given to Your people for an inheritance.

37 If there be in the land famine, if there be pestilence, blasting, mildew, locust, or if there be caterpiller; if their enemy besiege them in the land of their cities; whatsoever plague, whatsoever sickness there be;

38 What prayer and supplication soever be made by any man, or by all Your people Yisrael, which shall know every man the plague of his own heart, and spread forth his hands toward this house:

39 Then hear You in heaven Your dwelling place, and forgive, and do, and give to every man according to his ways, whose heart You knowest; (for You, even You only, knowest the hearts of all the children of men;)

40 That they may fear You all the days that they live in the land which You gavest unto our fathers.

41 Moreover concerning a stranger, that is not of Your people Yisrael, but cometh out of a far country for Your name's sake;

42 (For they shall hear of Your great name, and of Your strong hand, and of Your outstretched arm;) when he shall come and pray toward this house;

43 Hear You in heaven Your dwelling place, and

do according to all that the stranger calleth to You for, that all people of the earth may know Your name, to fear You, as do Your people Yisrael; and that they may know that this house, which I have builded, is called by Your name.

44 If Your people go out to battle against their enemy, whithersoever You shalt send them, and shall pray unto יהוה toward the city which You have chosen, and toward the house that I have built for Your name;

45 Then hear You in heaven their prayer and their supplication, and maintain their cause.

46 If they sin against You, (for there is no man that sinneth not,) and You be angry with them, and deliver them to the enemy, so that they carry them away captives unto the land of the enemy, far or near;

47 Yet if they shall bethink themselves in the land whither they were carried captives, and repent, and make supplication unto You in the land of them that carried them captives, saying, 'We have sinned, and have done perversely, we have committed wickedness';

48 And so return unto You with all their heart, and with all their soul, in the land of their enemies, which led them away captive, and pray unto You toward their land, which You gavest unto their fathers, the city which You have chosen, and the house which I have built for Your name;

49 Then hear You their prayer and their supplication in heaven Your dwelling place, and maintain their cause,

50 And forgive Your people that have sinned against You, and all their transgressions wherein they have transgressed against You, and give them compassion before them who carried them captive, that they may have compassion on them;

51 For they be Your people, and Your inheritance, whom You broughtest forth out of Egypt (Mitsrayim), from the midst of the furnace of iron;

52 That Your eyes may be open unto the supplication of Your servant, and unto the supplication of Your people Yisrael, to hearken unto them in all that they call for unto You.

53 For You didst separate them from among all the people of the earth, to be Your inheritance, as You spakest by the hand of Moses (Mosheh) Your servant, when You broughtest our fathers out of Egypt (Mitsrayim), O Lord (Adonai) יהוה."

54 And it was so, that when Solomon (Shelomoh) had made an end of praying all this prayer and supplication unto יהוה, he arose from before the altar of יהוה, from kneeling on his knees with his hands spread up to heaven.

55 And he stood, and blessed all the congregation of Yisrael with a loud voice, saying:

56 "Blessed be יהוה, Who hath given rest unto His people Yisrael, according to all that He promised; there hath not failed one word of all His good promise, which He promised by the hand of Moses (Mosheh) His servant.

57 יהוה our God (YHWH Eloheinu) be with us, as He was with our fathers; let Him not leave us, nor forsake us;

58 That He may incline our hearts unto Him, to walk in all His ways, and to keep His commandments, and His statutes, and His judgments, which He commanded our fathers.

59 And let these my words, wherewith I have made supplication before יהוה, be near unto יהוה our God (YHWH Eloheinu) day and night, that He maintain the cause of His servant, and the cause of His people Yisrael at all times, as the matter shall require,

60 That all the people of the earth may know that יהוה is God (Elohim), and that there is none else.

61 Let your heart therefore be perfect with יהוה our God (YHWH Eloheinu), to walk in His statutes, and to keep His commandments, as at this day."

62 And the king, and all Yisrael with him, offered sacrifice before יהוה.

63 And Solomon (Shelomoh) offered a sacrifice of peace offerings, which he offered unto יהוה, two and twenty thousand oxen, and a hundred and twenty thousand sheep. So the king and all the children of Yisrael dedicated the house of יהוה.

64 The same day did the king hallow the middle of the court that was before the house of יהוה; for there he offered burnt offerings, and meat offerings, and the fat of the peace offerings; because the brasen altar that was before יהוה was too little to receive the burnt offerings, and meat offerings, and the fat of the peace offerings.

65 And at that time Solomon (Shelomoh) held a feast, and all Yisrael with him, a great

congregation, from the entering in of Hamath unto the river of Egypt (Mitsrayim), before יהוה our God (YHWH Eloheinu), seven days and seven days, even fourteen days.

66 On the eighth day he sent the people away; and they blessed the king, and went unto their tents joyful and glad of heart for all the goodness that יהוה had done for Dawid His servant, and for Yisrael His people.

9 And it came to pass, when Solomon (Shelomoh) had finished the building of the house of יהוה, and the king's house, and all Solomon (Shelomoh)'s desire which he was pleased to do,

2 That יהוה appeared to Solomon (Shelomoh) the second time, as He had appeared unto Him at Giveon.

3 And יהוה said unto him: "I have heard your prayer and your supplication, that you have made before Me; I have hallowed this house, which you have built, to put My name there forever; and Mine eyes and Mine heart shall be there perpetually.

4 And if you wilt walk before Me, as Dawid your father walked, in integrity of heart, and in uprightness, to do according to all that I have commanded you, and wilt keep My statutes and My judgments,

5 Then I will establish the throne of your kingdom upon Yisrael forever, as I promised to Dawid your father, saying, 'There shall not fail you a man upon the throne of Yisrael.'

6 But if you shall at all turn from following Me, you or your children, and will not keep My commandments and My statutes which I have set before you, but go and serve other gods (elohim), and worship them,

7 Then will I cut off Yisrael out of the land which I have given them; and this house, which I have hallowed for my name, will I cast out of my sight; and Yisrael shall be a proverb and a byword among all people.

8 And at this house, which is high, every one that passeth by it shall be astonished, and shall hiss; and they shall say, 'Why hath יהוה done thus unto this land, and to this house?'

9 And they shall answer, 'Because they forsook יהוה their God (YHWH Eloheihem), who brought forth their fathers out of the land of Egypt (Mitsrayim), and have taken hold upon other gods (elohim), and have worshipped them,

and served them; therefore hath יהוה brought upon them all this disaster (raah).'"

10 And it came to pass at the end of twenty years, when Solomon (Shelomoh) had built the two houses, the house of יהוה, and the king's house,

11 (Now Hiram the king of Tyre had furnished Solomon (Shelomoh) with cedar trees and fir trees, and with gold, according to all his desire,) that then King Solomon (Shelomoh) gave Hiram twenty cities in the land of Galilee.

12 And Hiram came out from Tyre to see the cities which Solomon (Shelomoh) had given him; and they pleased him not.

13 And he said, "What cities are these which you have given me, my brother?" And he called them the land of Cabul unto this day.

14 And Hiram sent to the king sixscore talents of gold.

15 And this is the reason of the levy which King Solomon (Shelomoh) raised; for to build the house of יהוה, and his own house, and Millo, and the wall of Jerusalem (Yerushalayim), and Hazor, and Megiddo, and Gezer.

16 For Pharaoh (Paroh) king of Egypt (Mitsrayim) had gone up, and taken Gezer, and burnt it with fire, and slain the Canaanites that dwelt in the city, and given it for a present unto his daughter, Solomon (Shelomoh)'s wife.

17 And Solomon (Shelomoh) built Gezer, and Beit-Choron the nether,

18 And Baalath, and Tadmor in the wilderness, in the land,

19 And all the cities of store that Solomon (Shelomoh) had, and cities for his chariots, and cities for his horsemen, and that which Solomon (Shelomoh) desired to build in Jerusalem (Yerushalayim), and in Lebanon, and in all the land of his dominion.

20 And all the people that were left of the Amorites, Hittites, Perizzites, Hivites, and Yevusis, which were not of the children of Yisrael,

21 Their children that were left after them in the land, whom the children of Yisrael also were not able utterly to destroy, upon those did Solomon (Shelomoh) levy a tribute of bondservice unto this day.

22 But of the children of Yisrael did Solomon (Shelomoh) make no bondmen; but they were men of war, and his servants, and his princes,

and his captains, and rulers of his chariots, and his horsemen.

23 These were the chief of the officers that were over Solomon (Shelomoh)'s work, five hundred and fifty, which bare rule over the people that wrought in the work.

24 But Pharaoh (Paroh)'s daughter came up out of the city of Dawid unto her house which Solomon (Shelomoh) had built for her; then did he build Millo.

25 And three times in a year did Solomon (Shelomoh) offer burnt offerings and peace offerings upon the altar which he built unto יהוה, and he burnt incense upon the altar that was before יהוה. So he finished the house.

26 And King Solomon (Shelomoh) made a navy of ships in Eziongeber, which is beside Eloth, on the shore of the Red sea, in the land of Edom.

27 And Hiram sent in the navy his servants, shipmen that had knowledge of the sea, with the servants of Solomon (Shelomoh).

28 And they came to Ophir, and fetched from thence gold, four hundred and twenty talents, and brought it to King Solomon (Shelomoh).

10 And when the queen of Sheba heard of the fame of Solomon (Shelomoh) concerning the name of יהוה, she came to prove him with hard questions.

2 And she came to Jerusalem (Yerushalayim) with a very great train, with camels that bare spices, and very much gold, and precious stones; and when she was come to Solomon (Shelomoh), she communed with him of all that was in her heart.

3 And Solomon (Shelomoh) told her all her questions; there was not any thing hid from the king, which he told her not.

4 And when the queen of Sheba had seen all Solomon (Shelomoh)'s wisdom, and the house that he had built,

5 And the meat of his table, and the sitting of his servants, and the attendance of his ministers, and their apparel, and his cupbearers, and his ascent by which he went up unto the house of יהוה; there was no more spirit in her.

6 And she said to the king: "It was a true report that I heard in mine own land of your acts and of your wisdom.

7 Howbeit I believed not the words, until I came, and mine eyes had seen it; and, behold, the half was not told me; your wisdom and prosperity

exceedeth the fame which I heard.

8 Happy are your men, happy are these your servants, who stand continually before you, and that hear your wisdom!

9 Blessed be יהוה your God (YHWH Eloheikha), Who delighted in you, to set you on the throne of Yisrael; because יהוה loved Yisrael forever, therefore made He you king, to do justice and righteousness."

10 And she gave the king a hundred and twenty talents of gold, and of spices very great store, and precious stones. There came no more such abundance of spices as these which the queen of Sheva gave to King Solomon (Shelomoh).

11 And the navy also of Hiram, that brought gold from Ophir, brought in from Ophir great plenty of almug trees, and precious stones.

12 And the king made of the almug trees pillars for the house of יהוה, and for the king's house, harps also and psalteries for singers; there came no such almug trees, nor were seen unto this day.

13 And King Solomon (Shelomoh) gave unto the queen of Sheva all her desire, whatsoever she asked, besides that which Solomon (Shelomoh) gave her of his royal bounty. So she turned and went to her own country, she and her servants.

14 Now the weight of gold that came to Solomon (Shelomoh) in one year was six hundred threescore and six talents of gold,

15 Besides that he had of the merchantmen, and of the traffick of the spice merchants, and of all the kings of Arabia, and of the governors of the country.

16 And King Solomon (Shelomoh) made two hundred targets of beaten gold; six hundred shekels of gold went to one target.

17 And he made three hundred shields of beaten gold; three pounds of gold went to one shield; and the king put them in the house of the forest of Lebanon.

18 Moreover the king made a great throne of ivory, and overlaid it with the best gold.

19 The throne had six steps, and the top of the throne was round behind; and there were stays on either side on the place of the seat, and two lions stood beside the stays.

20 And twelve lions stood there on the one side and on the other upon the six steps; there was not the like made in any kingdom.

21 And all King Solomon (Shelomoh)'s drinking vessels were of gold, and all the vessels of the

house of the forest of Lebanon were of pure gold; none were of silver; it was nothing accounted of in the days of Solomon (Shelomoh).

22 For the king had at sea a navy of Tharshish with the navy of Hiram: once in three years came the navy of Tharshish, bringing gold, and silver, ivory, and apes, and peacocks.

23 So King Solomon (Shelomoh) exceeded all the kings of the earth for riches and for wisdom.

24 And all the earth sought to Solomon (Shelomoh), to hear his wisdom, which God (Elohim) had put in his heart.

25 And they brought every man his present, vessels of silver, and vessels of gold, and garments, and armour, and spices, horses, and mules, a rate year by year.

26 And Solomon (Shelomoh) gathered together chariots and horsemen; and he had a thousand and four hundred chariots, and twelve thousand horsemen, whom he bestowed in the cities for chariots, and with the king at Jerusalem (Yerushalayim).

27 And the king made silver to be in Jerusalem (Yerushalayim) as stones, and cedars made he to be as the sycomore trees that are in the vale, for abundance.

28 And Solomon (Shelomoh) had horses brought out of Egypt (Mitsrayim), and linen yarn; the king's merchants received the linen yarn at a price.

29 And a chariot came up and went out of Egypt (Mitsrayim) for six hundred shekels of silver, and a horse for a hundred and fifty; and so for all the kings of the Hittites, and for the kings of Syria (Aram), did they bring them out by their means.

11 But King Solomon (Shelomoh) loved many strange women, together with the daughter of Pharaoh (Paroh), women of the Moavites, Ammonites, Edomites, Zidonians, and Hittites;

2 Of the nations concerning which יהוה said unto the children of Yisrael, "You shall not go in to them, neither shall they come in unto you; for surely they will turn away your heart after their gods (elohim)." Solomon (Shelomoh) clave unto these in love.

3 And he had seven hundred wives, princesses, and three hundred concubines; and his wives turned away his heart.

4 For it came to pass, when Solomon (Shelomoh) was old, that his wives turned away his heart after other gods (elohim); and his heart was not perfect with יהוה his God (Elohim), as was the heart of Dawid his father.

5 For Solomon (Shelomoh) went after Ashtoreth the goddess of the Zidonians, and after Milcom the abomination of the Ammonites.

6 And Solomon (Shelomoh) did evil in the sight of יהוה, and went not fully after יהוה, as did Dawid his father.

7 Then did Solomon (Shelomoh) build a high place for Chemosh, the abomination of Moav, in the hill that is before Jerusalem (Yerushalayim), and for Molech, the abomination of the children of Ammon.

8 And likewise did he for all his strange wives, who burnt incense and sacrificed unto their gods (elohim).

9 And יהוה was angry with Solomon (Shelomoh), because his heart had turned from יהוה God of Israel (Elohei Yisrael), who had appeared unto him twice,

10 And had commanded him concerning this thing, that he should not go after other gods (elohim); but he kept not that which יהוה commanded.

11 Wherefore יהוה said unto Solomon (Shelomoh), "Forasmuch as this is done of you, and you have not kept My covenant and My statutes, which I have commanded you, I will surely rend the kingdom from you, and will give it to your servant.

12 Notwithstanding in your days I will not do it for Dawid your father's sake; but I will rend it out of the hand of your son.

13 Howbeit I will not rend away all the kingdom; but will give one tribe to your son for Dawid My servant's sake, and for Jerusalem (Yerushalayim)'s sake which I have chosen.

14 And יהוה stirred up an adversary unto Solomon (Shelomoh), Hadad the Edomite; he was of the king's seed in Edom.

15 For it came to pass, when Dawid was in Edom, and Yoav the captain of the army was gone up to bury the slain, after he had smitten every male in Edom;

16 (For six months did Yoav remain there with all Yisrael, until he had cut off every male in Edom)

17 That Hadad fled, he and certain Edomites of his father's servants with him, to go into Egypt

(Mitsrayim); Hadad being yet a little child.

18 And they arose out of Midian, and came to Paran; and they took men with them out of Paran, and they came to Egypt (Mitsrayim), unto Pharaoh (Paroh) king of Egypt (Mitsrayim); who gave him a house, and appointed him victuals, and gave him land.

19 And Hadad found great favor in the sight of Pharaoh (Paroh), so that he gave him as wife the sister of his own wife, the sister of Tahpenes the queen.

20 And the sister of Tahpenes bare him Genubath his son, whom Tahpenes weaned in Pharaoh (Paroh)'s house; and Genubath was in Pharaoh (Paroh)'s household among the sons of Pharaoh (Paroh).

21 And when Hadad heard in Egypt (Mitsrayim) that Dawid slept (rested) with his fathers, and that Yoav the captain of the army was dead, Hadad said to Pharaoh (Paroh), "Let me depart, that I may go to mine own country."

22 Then Pharaoh (Paroh) said unto him, "But what have you lacked with me, that, behold, you seekest to go to your own country?" And he answered, "Nothing; howbeit let me go in any wise."

23 And God (Elohim) stirred him up another adversary, Rezon the son of Eliadah, who fled from his lord (adon) Hadadezer king of Zobah.

24 And he gathered men unto him, and became captain over a band, when Dawid slew them of Zobah; and they went to Damascus (Dammeseq), and dwelt therein, and reigned in Damascus (Dammeseq).

25 And he was an adversary to Yisrael all the days of Solomon (Shelomoh), besides the mischief that Hadad did; and he abhorred Yisrael, and reigned over Syria (Aram).

26 And ^A45Jeroboam (Yarovam) the son of Nevat, an Ephrathite of Zereda, Solomon (Shelomoh)'s servant, whose mother's name was Zeruah, a widow woman, even he lifted up his hand against the king.

27 And this was the cause that he lifted up his hand against the king; Solomon (Shelomoh) built Millo, and repaired the breaches of the city of Dawid his father.

28 And the man Jeroboam (Yarovam) was a mighty man of valour; and Solomon (Shelomoh) seeing the young man that he was industrious, he made him ruler over all the charge of the house of Joseph (Yosef).

29 And it came to pass at that time when Yarovam went out of Jerusalem (Yerushalayim), that the prophet Achiyah the Shilonite found him in the way; and he had clothed himself with a new garment; and they two were alone in the field.

30 And Achiyah caught the new garment that was on him, and rent it in twelve pieces.

31 And he said to Jeroboam (Yarovam), "Take you ten pieces, for thus saith יהוה, the God of Israel (Elohei Yisrael): 'Behold, I will rend the kingdom out of the hand of Solomon (Shelomoh), and will give ten tribes to you;'

32 (But he shall have one tribe for my servant Dawid's sake, and for Jerusalem (Yerushalayim)'s sake, the city which I have chosen out of all the tribes of Yisrael;)

33 Because that they have forsaken Me, and have worshipped Ashtoreth the goddess of the Zidonians, Chemosh the god (elohim) of the Moavites, and Milcom the god (elohim) of the children of Ammon, and have not walked in My ways, to do that which is right in Mine eyes, and to keep My statutes and My judgments, as did Dawid his father.

34 Howbeit I will not take the whole kingdom out of his hand, but I will make him prince all the days of his life for Dawid My servant's sake, whom I chose, because he kept My commandments and My statutes;

35 But I will take the kingdom out of his son's hand, and will give it unto you, even ten tribes.

36 And unto his son will I give one tribe, that Dawid My servant may have a light alway before Me in Jerusalem (Yerushalayim), the city which I have chosen Me to put My name there.

37 And I will take you, and you shalt reign according to all that your soul desireth, and shalt be king over Yisrael.

38 And it shall be, if you wilt hearken unto all that I command you, and wilt walk in My ways, and do that is right in My sight, to keep My statutes and My commandments, as Dawid My servant did; that I will be with you, and build you a sure house, as I built for Dawid, and will give Yisrael unto you.

39 And I will for this, afflict the seed of Dawid, but not forever.'"

40 Solomon (Shelomoh) sought therefore to kill Yarovam. And Jeroboam (Yarovam)

arose, and fled into Egypt (Mitsrayim), unto Shishak king of Egypt (Mitsrayim), and was in Egypt (Mitsrayim) until the death of Solomon (Shelomoh).

41 And the rest of the acts of Solomon (Shelomoh), and all that he did, and his wisdom, are they not written in the book of the acts of Solomon (Shelomoh)?

42 And the time that Solomon (Shelomoh) reigned in Jerusalem (Yerushalayim) over all Yisrael was forty years.

43 And Solomon (Shelomoh) slept (rested) with his fathers, and was buried in the city of Dawid his father; and ^A40Rehoboam (Rechavam) his son reigned in his stead.

12 And Rehoboam (Rechavam) went to Shechem; for all Yisrael had come to Shechem to make him king.

2 And it came to pass, when Yarovam the son of Nevat, who was yet in Egypt (Mitsrayim), heard of it, (for he had fled from the presence of King Solomon (Shelomoh), and Yarovam dwelt in Egypt (Mitsrayim);)

3 That they sent and called him. And Yarovam and all the congregation of Yisrael came, and spake unto Rehoboam (Rechavam), saying,

4 "Your father made our yoke grievous; now therefore make you the grievous service of your father, and his heavy yoke which he put upon us, lighter, and we will serve you."

5 And he said unto them, "Depart yet for three days, then come again to me." And the people departed.

6 And King Rehoboam (Rechavam) consulted with the old men, that stood before Solomon (Shelomoh) his father while he yet lived, and said, "How do you advise that I may answer this people?"

7 And they spake unto him, saying, "If you wilt be a servant unto this people this day, and wilt serve them, and answer them, and speak good words to them, then they will be your servants forever."

8 But he forsook the counsel of the old men, which they had given him, and consulted with the young men that were grown up with him, and who stood before him.

9 And he said unto them, "What counsel give you that we may answer this people, who have spoken to me, saying, 'Make the yoke which your father did put upon us lighter'?"

10 And the young men that were grown up with him spake unto him, saying, "Thus shalt you speak unto this people that spake unto you, saying, 'Your father made our yoke heavy, but make you it lighter unto us'; thus shalt you say unto them: 'My little finger shall be thicker than my father's loins!

11 And now whereas my father did lade you with a heavy yoke, I will add to your yoke; my father hath chastised you with whips, but I will chastise you with scorpions!'"

12 So Jeroboam (Yarovam) and all the people came to Rehoboam (Rechavam) the third day, as the king had appointed, saying, "Come to me again the third day."

13 And the king answered the people roughly, and forsook the old men's counsel that they gave him;

14 And spake to them after the counsel of the young men, saying, "My father made your yoke heavy, and I will add to your yoke; my father also chastised you with whips, but I will chastise you with scorpions!"

15 Wherefore the king hearkened not unto the people; for the cause was from יהוה, that he might perform his saying, which יהוה spake by Achiyah the Shilonite unto Jeroboam (Yarovam) the son of Nevat.

16 So when all Yisrael saw that the king hearkened not unto them, the people answered the king, saying: "What portion have we in Dawid? Neither have we inheritance in the son of Jesse (Yishai). To your tents, O Yisrael! Now see to your own house, Dawid." So Yisrael departed unto their tents.

17 But as for the children of Yisrael who dwelt in the cities of Judah (Yehudah), Rehoboam (Rechavam) reigned over them.

18 Then King Rehoboam (Rechavam) sent Adoram, who was over the tribute; and all Yisrael stoned him with stones, that he died. Therefore King Rehoboam (Rechavam) made speed to get him up to his chariot, to flee to Jerusalem (Yerushalayim).

19 So Yisrael rebelled against the house of Dawid unto this day.

20 And it came to pass, when all Yisrael heard that Yarovam was come again, that they sent and called him unto the congregation, and made him king over all Yisrael; there was none that followed the house of Dawid, but the tribe of

Judah (Yehudah) only.

21 And when Rehoboam (Rechavam) was come to Jerusalem (Yerushalayim), he assembled all the house of Judah (Yehudah), with the tribe of Benjamin (Binyamin), a hundred and fourscore thousand chosen men, who were warriors, to fight against the house of Yisrael, to bring the kingdom again to Rehoboam (Rechavam) the son of Solomon (Shelomoh).

22 But the word of God (Elohim) came unto Shemayah the man of God (Elohim), saying,

23 "Speak unto Rehoboam (Rechavam), the son of Solomon (Shelomoh), king of Judah (Yehudah), and unto all the house of Judah (Yehudah) and Benjamin (Binyamin), and to the remnant of the people, saying,

24 'Thus saith יהוה: "You shall not go up, nor fight against your brethren the children of Yisrael; return every man to his house, for this thing is from Me."' They hearkened therefore to the word of יהוה, and returned to depart, according to the word of יהוה.

25 Then Jeroboam (Yarovam) built Shechem in Mount Efrayim, and dwelt therein; and went out from thence, and built Penuel.

26 And Yarovam said in his heart, "Now shall the kingdom return to the house of Dawid;

27 If this people go up to do sacrifice in the house of יהוה at Jerusalem (Yerushalayim), then shall the heart of this people turn again unto their lord (adon), even unto Rehoboam (Rechavam) king of Judah (Yehudah), and they shall kill me, and go again to Rehoboam (Rechavam) king of Judah (Yehudah)."

28 Whereupon the king took counsel, and made two calves of gold, and said unto them, "It is too much for you to go up to Jerusalem (Yerushalayim). Behold your God (Elohim), O Yisrael, who brought you up out of the land of Egypt (Mitsrayim)!"

29 And he set the one in Bethel (Beit-El), and the other put he in Dan.

30 And this thing became a sin; for the people went to worship before the one, even unto Dan.

31 And he made a house of high places, and made priests (kohanim) of the lowest of the people, who were not of the sons of Lewi.

32 And Jeroboam (Yarovam) ordained a feast in the eighth month, on the fifteenth day of the month, like unto the feast that is in Judah (Yehudah), and he offered upon the altar. So did he in Bethel (Beit-El), sacrificing unto the calves that he had made; and he placed in Bethel (Beit-El) the priests (kohanim) of the high places which he had made.

33 So he offered upon the altar which he had made in Bethel (Beit-El) the fifteenth day of the eighth month, even in the month which he had devised of his own heart; and ordained a feast unto the children of Yisrael; and he offered upon the altar, and burnt incense.

13 And, behold, there came a man of God (Elohim) out of Judah (Yehudah) by the word of יהוה unto Bethel (Beit-El); and Jeroboam (Yarovam) stood by the altar to burn incense.

2 And he cried against the altar in the word of יהוה, and said, "O altar, altar, thus saith יהוה: 'Behold, a child shall be born unto the house of Dawid, A41Josiah (Yoshiyahu) by name; and upon you shall he offer the priests (kohanim) of the high places that burn incense upon you, and men's bones shall be burnt upon you.'"

3 And he gave a sign the same day, saying, "This is the sign which יהוה hath spoken: Behold, the altar shall be rent, and the ashes that are upon it shall be poured out."

4 And it came to pass, when king Yarovam heard the saying of the man of God (Elohim), which had cried against the altar in Bethel (Beit-El), that he put forth his hand from the altar, saying, "Lay hold on him." And his hand, which he put forth against him, dried up, so that he could not pull it in again to him.

5 The altar also was rent, and the ashes poured out from the altar, according to the sign which the man of God (Elohim) had given by the word of יהוה.

6 And the king answered and said unto the man of God (Elohim), "Intreat now the face of יהוה your God (YHWH Eloheikha), and pray for me, that my hand may be restored me again." And the man of God (Elohim) besought יהוה, and the king's hand was restored him again, and became as it was before.

7 And the king said unto the man of God (Elohim), "Come home with me, and refresh yourself, and I will give you a reward."

8 And the man of God (Elohim) said unto the king, "If you wilt give me half your house, I will not go in with you, neither will I eat bread nor drink water in this place;

9 For so was it charged me by the word of יהוה, saying, 'Eat no bread, nor drink water, nor turn again by the same way that you camest.'"

10 So he went another way, and returned not by the way that he came to Bethel (Beit-El).

11 Now there dwelt an old prophet in Bethel (Beit-El); and his sons came and told him all the works that the man of God (Elohim) had done that day in Bethel (Beit-El); the words which he had spoken unto the king, them they told also to their father.

12 And their father said unto them, "What way went he?" For his sons had seen what way the man of God (Elohim) went, which came from Judah (Yehudah).

13 And he said unto his sons, "Saddle me the ass." So they saddled him the ass; and he rode thereon,

14 And went after the man of God (Elohim), and found him sitting under an oak; and he said unto him, "Are you the man of God (Elohim) that camest from Judah (Yehudah)?" And he said, "I am."

15 Then he said unto him, "Come home with me, and eat bread."

16 And he said, "I may not return with you, nor go in with you; neither will I eat bread nor drink water with you in this place;

17 For it was said to me by the word of יהוה, 'You shalt eat no bread nor drink water there, nor turn again to go by the way that you camest.'"

18 He said unto him, "I am a prophet also as you are; and an angel spake unto me by the word of יהוה, saying, 'Bring him back with you into your house, that he may eat bread and drink water.' But he lied unto him.

19 So he went back with him, and did eat bread in his house, and drank water.

20 And it came to pass, as they sat at the table, that the word of יהוה came unto the prophet that brought him back;

21 And he cried unto the man of God (Elohim) that came from Judah (Yehudah), saying, "Thus saith יהוה: 'Forasmuch as you have disobeyed the mouth of יהוה, and hast not kept the commandment which יהוה your God (YHWH Eloheikha) commanded you,

22 But camest back, and hast eaten bread and drunk water in the place, of the which יהוה did say to you, "Eat no bread, and drink no water;"

your carcase shall not come unto the sepulchre of your fathers.'"

23 And it came to pass, after he had eaten bread, and after he had drunk, that he saddled for him the ass, for the prophet whom he had brought back.

24 And when he was gone, a lion met him by the way, and slew him; and his carcase was cast in the way, and the ass stood by it, the lion also stood by the carcase.

25 And, behold, men passed by, and saw the carcase cast in the way, and the lion standing by the carcase; and they came and told it in the city where the old prophet dwelt.

26 And when the prophet that brought him back from the way heard thereof, he said, "It is the man of God (Elohim), who was disobedient unto the word of יהוה; therefore יהוה hath delivered him unto the lion, which hath torn him, and slain him, according to the word of יהוה, which he spake unto him."

27 And he spake to his sons, saying, "Saddle me the ass." And they saddled him.

28 And he went and found his carcase cast in the way, and the ass and the lion standing by the carcase; the lion had not eaten the carcase, nor torn the ass.

29 And the prophet took up the carcase of the man of God (Elohim), and laid it upon the ass, and brought it back; and the old prophet came to the city, to mourn and to bury him.

30 And he laid his carcase in his own grave; and they mourned over him, saying, "Alas, my brother!"

31 And it came to pass, after he had buried him, that he spake to his sons, saying, "When I am dead, then bury me in the sepulchre wherein the man of God (Elohim) is buried; lay my bones beside his bones;

32 For the saying which he cried by the word of יהוה against the altar in Bethel (Beit-El), and against all the houses of the high places which are in the cities of Samaria (Shomeron), shall surely come to pass.

33 After this thing Jeroboam (Yarovam) returned not from his evil way, but made again of the lowest of the people priests (kohanim) of the high places; whosoever would, he consecrated him, and he became one of the priests (kohanim) of the high places.

34 And this thing became sin unto the house of

Jeroboam (Yarovam), even to cut it off, and to destroy it from off the face of the earth.

14 At that time Aviyah the son of Yarovam fell sick.

2 And Jeroboam (Yarovam) said to his wife, "Please arise, and disguise yourself, that you be not known to be the wife of Jeroboam (Yarovam); and get you to Shiloh. Behold, there is Achiyah the prophet, who told me that I should be king over this people.

3 And take with you ten loaves, and cracknels, and a cruse of honey, and go to him; he shall tell you what shall become of the child.

4 And Jeroboam (Yarovam)'s wife did so, and arose, and went to Shiloh, and came to the house of Achiyah. But Achiyah could not see; for his eyes were set by reason of his age.

5 And יהוה said unto Achiyah, "Behold, the wife of Yarovam cometh to ask a thing of you for her son; for he is sick. Thus and thus shalt you say unto her; for it shall be, when she cometh in, that she shall feign herself to be another woman."

6 And it was so, when Achiyah heard the sound of her feet, as she came in at the door, that he said, "Come in, you wife of Yarovam; why feignest you yourself to be another person? I have been sent for you with heavy tidings (bad news).

7 Go, tell Yarovam, 'Thus saith יהוה God of Israel (Elohei Yisrael): 'Forasmuch as I exalted you from among the people, and made you prince over My people Yisrael,

8 And rent the kingdom away from the house of Dawid, and gave it you; and yet you have not been as My servant Dawid, who kept My commandments, and who followed Me with all his heart, to do that only which was right in Mine eyes;

9 But hast done evil above all that were before you; for you have gone and made you other gods (elohim), and molten images, to provoke Me to anger, and hast cast Me behind your back;

10 Therefore, behold, I will bring disaster (raah) upon the house of Jeroboam (Yarovam), and will cut off from Jeroboam (Yarovam) him that pisseth against the wall (every male), and him that is shut up and free in Yisrael, and will take away the remnant of the house of Yarovam, as a man taketh away dung, till it be all gone.

11 Him that dieth of Yarovam in the city shall the dogs eat; and him that dieth in the field shall the fowls of the air eat; for יהוה hath spoken it!'"

12 Arise you therefore, get you to your own house; and when your feet enter into the city, the child shall die.

13 And all Yisrael shall mourn for him, and bury him; for he only of Jeroboam (Yarovam) shall come to the grave, because in him there is found some good thing toward יהוה God of Israel (Elohei Yisrael) in the house of Yarovam.

14 Moreover יהוה shall raise Him up a king over Yisrael, who shall cut off the house of Jeroboam (Yarovam) that day; but what? Even now!

15 For יהוה shall smite Yisrael, as a reed is shaken in the water, and He shall root up Yisrael out of this good land, which He gave to their fathers, and shall scatter them beyond the river, because they have made their Asherah, provoking יהוה to anger.

16 And He shall give Yisrael up because of the sins of Jeroboam (Yarovam), who did sin, and who made Yisrael to sin."

17 And Jeroboam (Yarovam)'s wife arose, and departed, and came to Tirzah; and when she came to the threshold of the door, the child died;

18 And they buried him; and all Yisrael mourned for him, according to the word of יהוה, which He spake by the hand of His servant Achiyah the prophet.

19 And the rest of the acts of Jeroboam (Yarovam), how he warred, and how he reigned, behold, they are written in the book of the Chronicles of the kings of Yisrael.

20 And the days which Jeroboam (Yarovam) reigned were two and twenty years; and he slept with his fathers, and Nadav his son reigned in his stead.

21 And Rehoboam (Rechavam) the son of Solomon (Shelomoh) reigned in Yehudah. Rehoboam (Rechavam) was forty and one years old when he began to reign, and he reigned seventeen years in Jerusalem (Yerushalayim), the city which יהוה did choose out of all the tribes of Yisrael, to put His name there. His mother's name was Naamah an Ammonitess.

22 And Judah (Yehudah) did evil in the sight of יהוה, and they provoked Him to jealousy with their sins which they had committed, above all that their fathers had done.

23 For they also built them high places, and images, and Asherah, on every high hill, and

under every green tree.

24 And there were also sodomites (male cult prostitutes) in the land; and they did according to all the abominations of the nations which יהוה cast out before the children of Yisrael.

25 And it came to pass in the fifth year of King Rehoboam (Rechavam), that Shishak king of Egypt (Mitsrayim) came up against Jerusalem (Yerushalayim).

26 And he took away the treasures of the house of יהוה, and the treasures of the king's house; he even took away all: and he took away all the shields of gold which Solomon (Shelomoh) had made.

27 And King Rehoboam (Rechavam) made in their stead brasen shields, and committed them unto the hands of the chief of the guard, which kept the door of the king's house.

28 And it was so, when the king went into the house of יהוה, that the guard bare them, and brought them back into the guard chamber.

29 Now the rest of the acts of Rehoboam (Rechavam), and all that he did, are they not written in the book of the Chronicles of the kings of Judah (Yehudah)?

30 And there was war between Rehoboam (Rechavam) and Jeroboam (Yarovam) all their days.

31 And Rehoboam (Rechavam) slept with his fathers, and was buried with his fathers in the city of Dawid. His mother's name was Naamah an Ammonitess. And Aviyam his son reigned in his stead.

15 Now in the eighteenth year of King Yarovam the son of Nevat reigned Aviyam over Judah (Yehudah).

2 Three years reigned he in Jerusalem (Yerushalayim). His mother's name was Maachah, the daughter of Avishalom.

3 And he walked in all the sins of his father, which he had done before him; and his heart was not perfect with יהוה his God (Elohim), as the heart of Dawid his father.

4 Nevertheless for Dawid's sake did יהוה his God (Elohim) give him a lamp in Jerusalem (Yerushalayim), to set up his son after him, and to establish Jerusalem (Yerushalayim);

5 Because Dawid did that which was right in the eyes of יהוה, and turned not aside from any thing that He commanded him all the days of his life, except only in the matter of Uriyah the

Hittite.

6 And there was war between Rehoboam (Rechavam) and Jeroboam (Yarovam) all the days of his life.

7 Now the rest of the acts of Aviyam, and all that he did, are they not written in the book of the chronicles of the kings of Judah (Yehudah)? And there was war between Aviyam and Jeroboam (Yarovam).

8 And Aviyam slept with his fathers; and they buried him in the city of Dawid; and Asa his son reigned in his stead.

9 And in the twentieth year of Yarovam king of Yisrael reigned Asa over Judah (Yehudah).

10 And forty and one years reigned he in Jerusalem (Yerushalayim). His mother's name was Maachah, the daughter of Avishalom.

11 And Asa did that which was right in the eyes of יהוה, as did Dawid his father.

12 And he took away the sodomites (male cult prostitutes) out of the land, and removed all the idols that his fathers had made.

13 And also Maachah his mother, even her he removed from being queen, because she had made an idol as Asherah; and Asa destroyed her idol, and burnt it by the brook Kidron.

14 But the high places were not removed; nevertheless Asa's heart was perfect with יהוה all his days.

15 And he brought in the things which his father had dedicated, and the things which himself had dedicated, into the house of יהוה, silver, and gold, and vessels.

16 And there was war between Asa and Baasha king of Yisrael all their days.

17 And Baasha king of Yisrael went up against Judah (Yehudah), and built Ramah, that he might not allow any to go out or come in to Asa king of Judah (Yehudah).

18 Then Asa took all the silver and the gold that were left in the treasures of the house of יהוה, and the treasures of the king's house, and delivered them into the hand of his servants; and king Asa sent them to Benhadad, the son of Tabrimon, the son of Hezion, king of Syria (Aram), that dwelt at Damascus (Dammeseq), saying,

19 There is a league between me and you, and between my father and your father. Behold, I have sent unto you a present of silver and gold; come and break your league with Baasha king

of Yisrael, that he may depart from me.

20 So Benhadad hearkened unto king Asa, and sent the captains of the hosts which he had against the cities of Yisrael, and smote Iyon, and Dan, and Avelbethmaachah, and all Cinneroth, with all the land of Naftali.

21 And it came to pass, when Baasha heard thereof, that he left off building of Ramah, and dwelt in Tirzah.

22 Then King Asa made a proclamation throughout all Judah (Yehudah); none was exempted; and they took away the stones of Ramah, and the timber thereof, wherewith Baasha had builded; and King Asa built with them Geba of Benjamin (Binyamin), and Mizpah.

23 The rest of all the acts of Asa, and all his might, and all that he did, and the cities which he built, are they not written in the book of the Chronicles of the kings of Judah (Yehudah)? Nevertheless in the time of his old age he was diseased in his feet.

24 And Asa slept with his fathers, and was buried with his fathers in the city of Dawid his father; and Yehoshafat his son reigned in his stead.

25 And Nadav the son of Jeroboam (Yarovam) began to reign over Yisrael in the second year of Asa king of Judah (Yehudah), and reigned over Yisrael two years.

26 And he did evil in the sight of יהוה, and walked in the way of his father, and in his sin wherewith he made Yisrael to sin.

27 And Baasha the son of Achiyah, of the house of Yissaskhar, conspired against him; and Baasha smote him at Gibbethon, which belonged to the Philistines; for Nadav and all Yisrael laid siege to Gibbethon.

28 Even in the third year of Asa king of Judah (Yehudah) did Baasha slay him, and reigned in his stead.

29 And it came to pass, when he reigned, that he smote all the house of Yarovam; he left not to Jeroboam (Yarovam) any that breathed, until he had destroyed him, according unto the saying of יהוה, which He spake by His servant Achiyah the Shilonite;

30 Because of the sins of Jeroboam (Yarovam) which he sinned, and which he made Yisrael sin, by his provocation wherewith he provoked יהוה God of Israel (Elohei Yisrael) to anger.

31 Now the rest of the acts of Nadav, and all that he did, are they not written in the book of the Chronicles of the kings of Yisrael?

32 And there was war between Asa and Baasha king of Yisrael all their days.

33 In the third year of Asa king of Judah (Yehudah) began Baasha the son of Achiyah to reign over all Yisrael in Tirzah, twenty and four years.

34 And he did evil in the sight of יהוה, and walked in the way of Jeroboam (Yarovam), and in his sin wherewith he made Yisrael to sin.

16 Then the word of יהוה came to Yehu the son of Hanani against Baasha, saying:

2 "Forasmuch as I exalted you out of the dust, and made you prince over My people Yisrael; and you have walked in the way of Jeroboam (Yarovam), and hast made My people Yisrael to sin, to provoke Me to anger with their sins;

3 Behold, I will take away the posterity of Baasha, and the posterity of his house; and will make your house like the house of Jeroboam (Yarovam) the son of Nevat.

4 Him that dieth of Baasha in the city shall the dogs eat; and him that dieth of his in the fields shall the fowls of the air eat."

5 Now the rest of the acts of Baasha, and what he did, and his might, are they not written in the book of the Chronicles of the kings of Yisrael?

6 So Baasha slept with his fathers, and was buried in Tirzah; and Ela his son reigned in his stead.

7 And also by the hand of the prophet Yehu the son of Hanani came the word of יהוה against Baasha, and against his house, even for all the evil that he did in the sight of יהוה, in provoking Him to anger with the work of his hands, in being like the house of Jeroboam (Yarovam) and because he killed him.

8 In the twenty and sixth year of Asa king of Judah (Yehudah) began Elah the son of Baasha to reign over Yisrael in Tirzah, two years.

9 And his servant Zimri, captain of half his chariots, conspired against him, as he was in Tirzah, drinking himself drunk in the house of Arza steward of his house in Tirzah.

10 And Zimri went in and smote him, and killed him, in the twenty and seventh year of Asa king of Judah (Yehudah), and reigned in his stead.

11 And it came to pass, when he began to reign, as soon as he sat on his throne, that he slew all

the house of Baasha; he left him not one that pisseth against a wall (not a single male), neither of his kinsfolks, nor of his friends.

12 Thus did Zimri destroy all the house of Baasha, according to the word of יהוה, which He spake against Baasha by Yehu the prophet,

13 For all the sins of Baasha, and the sins of Elah his son, by which they sinned, and by which they made Yisrael to sin, in provoking יהוה God of Israel (Elohei Yisrael) to anger with their vanities (idols).

14 Now the rest of the acts of Elah, and all that he did, are they not written in the book of the Chronicles of the kings of Yisrael?

15 In the twenty and seventh year of Asa king of Judah (Yehudah) did Zimri reign seven days in Tirzah. And the people were encamped against Gibbethon, which belonged to the Philistines.

16 And the people that were encamped heard say, Zimri hath conspired, and hath also slain the king; wherefore all Yisrael made Omri, the captain of the army, king over Yisrael that day in the camp.

17 And Omri went up from Gibbethon, and all Yisrael with him, and they besieged Tirzah.

18 And it came to pass, when Zimri saw that the city was taken, that he went into the palace of the king's house, and burnt the king's house over him with fire, and died,

19 For his sins which he sinned in doing evil in the sight of יהוה, in walking in the way of Jeroboam (Yarovam), and in his sin which he did, to make Yisrael to sin.

20 Now the rest of the acts of Zimri, and his treason that he wrought, are they not written in the book of the Chronicles of the kings of Yisrael?

21 Then were the people of Yisrael divided into two parts: half of the people followed Tibni the son of Ginath, to make him king; and half followed Omri.

22 But the people that followed Omri prevailed against the people that followed Tibni the son of Ginath; so Tibni died, and Omri reigned.

23 In the thirty and first year of Asa king of Judah (Yehudah) began Omri to reign over Yisrael, twelve years; six years reigned he in Tirzah.

24 And he bought the hill Samaria (Shomeron) of Shemer for two talents of silver, and built on the hill, and called the name of the city which he built, after the name of Shemer, owner of the hill, Samaria (Shomeron).

25 But Omri wrought evil in the eyes of יהוה, and did worse than all that were before him.

26 For he walked in all the way of Jeroboam (Yarovam) the son of Nevat, and in his sin wherewith he made Yisrael to sin, to provoke יהוה God of Israel (Elohei Yisrael) to anger with their vanities (idols).

27 Now the rest of the acts of Omri which he did, and his might that he shewed, are they not written in the book of the Chronicles of the kings of Yisrael?

28 So Omri slept with his fathers, and was buried in Samaria (Shomeron); and Achav his son reigned in his stead.

29 And in the thirty and eighth year of Asa king of Judah (Yehudah) began Achav the son of Omri to reign over Yisrael; and Achav the son of Omri reigned over Yisrael in Samaria (Shomeron) twenty and two years.

30 And Achav the son of Omri did evil in the sight of יהוה above all that were before him.

31 And it came to pass, as if it had been a light thing for him to walk in the sins of Yarovam the son of Nevat, that he took as wife [A42] Jezebel (Iyzevel) the daughter of Ethbaal king of the Zidonians, and went and served the Baal, and worshipped him.

32 And he reared up an altar for the Baal in the house of the Baal, which he had built in Samaria (Shomeron).

33 And Achav made an Asherah; and Achav did more to provoke יהוה God of Israel (Elohei Yisrael) to anger than all the kings of Yisrael that were before him.

34 In his days did Hiel the Bethelite (Beit haEli) build Yericho. He laid the foundation thereof in Aviram his firstborn, and set up the gates thereof in his youngest son Segub, according to the word of יהוה, which He spake by Joshua (Yehoshua) the son of Nun.

17 And [A43] Elijah (Eliyahu) the Tishbite, who was of the inhabitants of Gilad, said unto Achav, "As יהוה God of Israel (Elohei Yisrael) liveth, before whom I stand, there shall not be dew nor rain these years, but according to my word."

2 And the word of יהוה came unto him, saying,

3 "Get you hence, and turn you eastward, and hide yourself by the brook Cherith, that is

before Jordan (Yarden).

4 And it shall be, that you shalt drink of the brook; and I have commanded the ravens to feed you there."

5 So he went and did according unto the word of יהוה; for he went and dwelt by the brook Cherith, that is before Jordan (Yarden).

6 And the ravens brought him bread and meat in the morning, and bread and meat in the evening; and he drank of the brook.

7 And it came to pass after a while, that the brook dried up, because there had been no rain in the land.

8 And the word of יהוה came unto him, saying,

9 "Arise, get you to Zarephath, which belongeth to Zidon, and dwell there. Behold, I have commanded a widow woman there to sustain you."

10 So he arose and went to Zarephath. And when he came to the gate of the city, behold, the widow woman was there gathering of sticks; and he called to her, and said, "Please fetch me a little water in a vessel, that I may drink."

11 And as she was going to fetch it, he called to her, and said, "Please bring me a morsel of bread in your hand."

12 And she said, "As יהוה your God (YHWH Eloheikha) liveth, I have not a cake, but a handful of meal in a barrel, and a little oil in a cruse; and, behold, I am gathering two sticks, that I may go in and dress it for me and my son, that we may eat it, and die."

13 And Elijah (Eliyahu) said unto her, "Fear not; go and do as you have said; but make me thereof a little cake first, and bring it unto me, and afterward make for you and for your son.

14 For thus saith יהוה God of Israel (Elohei Yisrael): 'The barrel of meal shall not waste, neither shall the cruse of oil fail, until the day that יהוה sendeth rain upon the earth.'"

15 And she went and did according to the saying of Elijah (Eliyahu); and she, and he, and her house, did eat many days.

16 And the barrel of meal wasted not, neither did the cruse of oil fail, according to the word of יהוה, which He spake by Elijah (Eliyahu).

17 And it came to pass after these things, that the son of the woman, the mistress of the house, fell sick; and his sickness was so sore, that there was no breath left in him.

18 And she said unto Elijah (Eliyahu), "What have I to do with you, O you man of God (Elohim)? Are you come unto me to call my sin to remembrance, and to slay my son?"

19 And he said unto her, "Give me your son." And he took him out of her bosom, and carried him up into a loft, where he abode, and laid him upon his own bed.

20 And he cried unto יהוה, and said, "O יהוה my God (YHWH Elohai), have You also brought evil (misery) upon the widow with whom I sojourn, by slaying her son?"

21 And he stretched himself upon the child three times, and cried unto יהוה, and said, "O יהוה my God (YHWH Elohai), I pray you (please), let this child's soul come into him again."

22 And יהוה heard the voice of Elijah (Eliyahu); and the soul of the child came into him again, and he revived.

23 And Elijah (Eliyahu) took the child, and brought him down out of the chamber into the house, and delivered him unto his mother; and Elijah (Eliyahu) said, "See, your son liveth!"

24 And the woman said to Elijah (Eliyahu), "Now by this I know that you are a man of God (Elohim), and that the word of יהוה in your mouth is truth."

18 And it came to pass after many days, that the word of יהוה came to Elijah (Eliyahu) in the third year, saying, "Go, shew yourself unto Achav; and I will send rain upon the earth."

2 And Elijah (Eliyahu) went to shew himself unto Achav. And there was a sore famine in Samaria (Shomeron).

3 And Achav called [A58]Obadiah (Ovadyahu), who was the governor of his house. (Now Ovadyah feared יהוה greatly;

4 For it was so, when Jezebel (Iyzevel) cut off the prophets of יהוה, that Ovadyahu took a hundred prophets, and hid them by fifty in a cave, and fed them with bread and water.)

5 And Achav said unto Ovadyahu, "Go into the land, unto all fountains of water, and unto all brooks; perhaps we may find grass to save the horses and mules alive, that we lose not all the beasts."

6 So they divided the land between them to pass throughout it; Achav went one way by himself, and Ovadyahu went another way by himself.

7 And as Ovadyahu was on the way, behold, Elijah (Eliyahu) met him; and he knew him, and

fell on his face, and said, "Are you that my lord (adoni) Elijah (Eliyahu)?"

8 And he answered him, "I am; go, tell your lord (adon), 'Behold, Elijah (Eliyahu) is here.'"

9 And he said, "What have I sinned, that you wouldest deliver your servant into the hand of Achav, to slay me?

10 As יהוה your God (YHWH Eloheikha) liveth, there is no nation or kingdom, whither my lord (adoni) hath not sent to seek you; and when they said, 'He is not there;' he took an oath of the kingdom and nation, that they found you not.

11 And now you sayest, 'Go, tell your lord (adon), "Behold, Elijah (Eliyahu) is here"'!

12 And it shall come to pass, as soon as I am gone from you, that the Spirit of יהוה shall carry you whither I know not; and so when I come and tell Achav, and he cannot find you, he shall slay me; but I your servant fear יהוה from my youth.

13 Was it not told my lord (adoni) what I did when Jezebel (Iyzevel) slew the prophets of יהוה, how I hid a hundred men of יהוה's prophets by fifty in a cave, and fed them with bread and water?

14 And now you sayest, 'Go, tell your lord (adon), "Behold, Elijah (Eliyahu) is here!"' and he shall slay me."

15 And Elijah (Eliyahu) said, "As יהוה of hosts (YHWH Tsevaot) liveth, before whom I stand, I will surely shew myself unto him today."

16 So Ovadyahu went to meet Achav, and told him; and Achav went to meet Elijah (Eliyahu).

17 And it came to pass, when Achav saw Elijah (Eliyahu), that Achav said unto him, "Are you he that troubleth Yisrael?"

18 And he answered, "I have not troubled Yisrael; but you, and your father's house, in that you have forsaken the commandments of יהוה, and you have followed the Baals (Baalim).

19 Now therefore send, and gather to me all Yisrael unto Mount Carmel, and the prophets of the Baal four hundred and fifty, and the prophets of the Asherah four hundred, who eat at Jezebel (Iyzevel)'s table."

20 So Achav sent unto all the children of Yisrael, and gathered the prophets together unto Mount Carmel.

21 And Elijah (Eliyahu) came unto all the people, and said, "How long halt you between two opinions? If יהוה is God (Elohim), follow Him; but if Baal (Lord), then follow him." And

the people answered him not a word.

22 Then said Elijah (Eliyahu) unto the people, "I, even I only, remain a prophet of יהוה; but the Baal's prophets are four hundred and fifty men.

23 Let them therefore give us two bullocks; and let them choose one bullock for themselves, and cut it in pieces, and lay it on wood, and put no fire under; and I will dress the other bullock, and lay it on wood, and put no fire under;

24 And call you on the name of your god (elohim) and I will call on the name of יהוה; and the God (Elohim) that answereth by fire, He is the God (Elohim). And all the people answered and said, "It is well spoken."

25 And Elijah (Eliyahu) said unto the prophets of the Baal, "Choose you one bullock for yourselves, and dress it first; for you are many; and call on the name of your god (elohim), but put no fire under.

26 And they took the bullock which was given them, and they dressed it, and called on the name of the Baal from morning even until noon, saying, "O Baal, hear us." But there was no voice, nor any that answered. And they leaped upon the altar which was made.

27 And it came to pass at noon, that Elijah (Eliyahu) mocked them, and said, "Cry aloud, for he is God (Elohim); either he is talking, or he is pursuing, or he is in a journey, or perhaps he sleepeth, and must be awakened."

28 And they cried aloud, and cut themselves after their manner with knives and lancets, till the blood gushed out upon them.

29 And it came to pass, when midday was past, and they prophesied until the time of the offering of the evening sacrifice, that there was neither voice, nor any to answer, nor any that regarded.

30 And Elijah (Eliyahu) said unto all the people, "Come near unto me." And all the people came near unto him. And he repaired the altar of יהוה that was broken down.

31 And Elijah (Eliyahu) took twelve stones, according to the number of the tribes of the sons of Jacob (Yaaqov), unto whom the word of יהוה came, saying, "Yisrael shall be your name."

32 And with the stones he built an altar in the name of יהוה; and he made a trench about the altar, as great as would contain two measures of seed.

33 And he put the wood in order, and cut the

bullock in pieces, and laid him on the wood, and said, "Fill four barrels with water, and pour it on the burnt sacrifice, and on the wood."

34 And he said, "Do it the second time." And they did it the second time. And he said, "Do it the third time." And they did it the third time.

35 And the water ran round about the altar; and he filled the trench also with water.

36 And it came to pass at the time of the offering of the evening sacrifice, that Elijah (Eliyahu) the prophet came near, and said, "יהוה God of (Elohei) Avraham, Isaac (Yitschaq), and of Yisrael, let it be known this day that You are God (Elohim) in Yisrael, and that I am Your servant, and that I have done all these things at Your word.

37 Hear me, O יהוה, hear me, that this people may know that You are יהוה the God (Elohim), and that You have turned their heart back again."

38 Then the fire of יהוה fell, and consumed the burnt sacrifice, and the wood, and the stones, and the dust, and licked up the water that was in the trench.

39 And when all the people saw it, they fell on their faces; and they said, "יהוה, He is the God (Elohim)! יהוה, He is the God (Elohim)!"

40 And Elijah (Eliyahu) said unto them, "Take the prophets of the Baal; let not one of them escape." And they took them; and Elijah (Eliyahu) brought them down to the brook Kishon, and slew them there.

41 And Elijah (Eliyahu) said unto Achav, "Get you up, eat and drink; for there is a sound of abundance of rain."

42 So Achav went up to eat and to drink. And Elijah (Eliyahu) went up to the top of Carmel; and he cast himself down upon the earth, and put his face between his knees,

43 And said to his servant, "Go up now, look toward the sea." And he went up, and looked, and said, "There is nothing." And he said, "Go again seven times."

44 And it came to pass at the seventh time, that he said, "Behold, there ariseth a little cloud out of the sea, like a man's hand." And he said, "Go up, say unto Achav, 'Prepare your chariot, and get you down, that the rain stops you not.'"

45 And it came to pass in the mean while, that the heaven was black with clouds and wind, and there was a great rain. And Achav rode, and went to Yizreel.

46 And the hand of יהוה was on Elijah (Eliyahu); and he girded up his loins, and ran before Achav to the entrance of Yizreel.

19 And Achav told Jezebel (Iyzevel) all that Elijah (Eliyahu) had done, and withal how he had slain all the prophets with the sword.

2 Then Jezebel (Iyzevel) sent a messenger unto Elijah (Eliyahu), saying, "So let the gods (elohim) do to me, and more also, if I make not your life as the life of one of them by tomorrow about this time."

3 And when he saw that, he arose, and went for his life, and came to Beer-Sheva, which belongeth to Judah (Yehudah), and left his servant there.

4 But he himself went a day's journey into the wilderness, and came and sat down under a juniper tree; and he requested for himself that he might die; and said, "It is enough! Now, O יהוה, take away my life; for I am not better than my fathers."

5 And as he lay and slept under a juniper tree, behold, then an angel touched him, and said unto him, "Arise and eat."

6 And he looked, and, behold, there was a cake baken on the coals, and a cruse of water at his head. And he did eat and drink, and laid him down again.

7 And the angel of יהוה came again the second time, and touched him, and said, "Arise and eat, because the journey is too great for you."

8 And he arose, and did eat and drink, and went in the strength of that food forty days and forty nights unto Horeb the mount of God (Elohim).

9 And he came thither unto a cave, and lodged there; and, behold, the word of יהוה came to him, and He said unto him, "What doest you here, Elijah (Eliyahu)?"

10 And he said, "I have been very zealous for A8b יהוה God of hosts (YHWH Elohei Tsevaot); for the children of Yisrael have forsaken Your covenant, thrown down Your altars, and slain Your prophets with the sword; and I, even I only, am left; and they seek my life, to take it away."

11 And He said, "Go forth, and stand upon the mount before יהוה." And, behold, יהוה passed by, and a great and strong wind rent the mountains, and broke in pieces the rocks before יהוה; but יהוה was not in the wind; and after the

wind an earthquake; but יהוה was not in the earthquake;

12 And after the earthquake a fire; but יהוה was not in the fire; and after the fire a still small voice.

13 And it was so, when Elijah (Eliyahu) heard it, that he wrapped his face in his mantle, and went out, and stood in the entering in of the cave. And, behold, there came a voice unto him, and said, "What doest you here, Elijah (Eliyahu)?"

14 And he said, "I have been very zealous for יהוה God of hosts (YHWH Elohei Tsevaot), because the children of Yisrael have forsaken Your covenant, thrown down Your altars, and slain Your prophets with the sword; and I, even I only, am left; and they seek my life, to take it away."

15 And יהוה said unto him, "Go, return on your way to the wilderness of Damascus (Dammeseq); and when you comest, anoint Hazael to be king over Syria (Aram).

16 And Yehu the son of Nimshi shalt you anoint to be king over Yisrael; and Elisha the son of Shaphat of Avelmeholah shalt you anoint to be prophet in your room.

17 And it shall come to pass, that him that escapeth the sword of Hazael shall Yehu slay; and him that escapeth from the sword of Yehu shall Elisha slay.

18 Yet I have left Me seven thousand in Yisrael, all the knees which have not bowed unto the Baal, and every mouth which hath not kissed him."

19 So he departed thence, and found Elisha the son of Shaphat, who was plowing with twelve yokes of oxen before him, and he with the twelfth; and Elijah (Eliyahu) passed by him, and cast his mantle upon him.

20 And he left the oxen, and ran after Elijah (Eliyahu), and said, "Please let me, kiss my father and my mother, and then I will follow you." And he said unto him, "Go back again, for what have I done to you?"

21 And he returned back from him, and took a yoke of oxen, and slew them, and boiled their flesh with the instruments of the oxen, and gave unto the people, and they did eat. Then he arose, and went after Elijah (Eliyahu), and ministered unto him.

20 And Benhadad the king of Syria (Aram) gathered all his army together; and there were thirty and two kings with him, and horses, and chariots; and he went up and besieged Samaria (Shomeron), and warred against it.

2 And he sent messengers to Achav king of Yisrael into the city, and said unto him, "Thus saith Benhadad:

3 'Your silver and your gold is mine; your wives also and your children, even the goodliest, are mine.'"

4 And the king of Yisrael answered and said, "My lord (Adoni), O king, according to your saying, I am yours, and all that I have."

5 And the messengers came again, and said, "Thus speaketh Benhadad, saying, 'Although I have sent unto you, saying, "You shalt deliver me your silver, and your gold, and your wives, and your children;"

6 Yet I will send my servants unto you tomorrow about this time, and they shall search your house, and the houses of your servants; and it shall be, that whatsoever is pleasant in your eyes, they shall put it in their hand, and take it away."

7 Then the king of Yisrael called all the elders of the land, and said, "Please mark, and see how this man seeketh mischief; for he sent unto me for my wives, and for my children, and for my silver, and for my gold; and I denied him not."

8 And all the elders and all the people said unto him, "Hearken not unto him, nor consent."

9 Wherefore he said unto the messengers of Benhadad, "Tell my lord (adoni) the king: 'All that you didst send for to your servant at the first I will do; but this thing I may not do.'" And the messengers departed, and brought him word again.

10 And Benhadad sent unto him, and said, "The gods (elohim) do so unto me, and more also, if the dust of Samaria (Shomeron) shall suffice for handfuls for all the people that follow me."

11 And the king of Yisrael answered and said, "Tell him: 'Let not him that girdeth on his harness boast himself as he that putteth it off.'"

12 And it came to pass, when Benhadad heard this message, as he was drinking, he and the kings in the pavilions, that he said unto his servants, "Set yourselves in array." And they set themselves in array against the city.

13 And, behold, there came a prophet unto Achav king of Yisrael, saying, "Thus saith יהוה: 'Have you seen all this great multitude? Behold, I will deliver it into your hand this day; and you

shalt know that I am יהוה.'"

14 And Achav said, "By whom?" And he said, "Thus saith יהוה: 'Even by the young men of the princes of the provinces.'" Then he said, "Who shall order the battle?" And he answered, "You!"

15 Then he numbered the young men of the princes of the provinces, and they were two hundred and thirty two; and after them he numbered all the people, even all the children of Yisrael, being seven thousand.

16 And they went out at noon. But Benhadad was drinking himself drunk in the pavilions, he and the kings, the thirty and two kings that helped him.

17 And the young men of the princes of the provinces went out first; and Benhadad sent out, and they told him, saying, "There are men come out of Samaria (Shomeron)."

18 And he said, "Whether they be come out for peace, take them alive; or whether they be come out for war, take them alive."

19 So these young men of the princes of the provinces came out of the city, and the army which followed them.

20 And they slew every one his man; and the Syrians (Arammim) fled; and Yisrael pursued them; and Benhadad the king of Syria (Aram) escaped on a horse with the horsemen.

21 And the king of Yisrael went out, and smote the horses and chariots, and slew the Syrians (Arammim) with a great slaughter.

22 And the prophet came to the king of Yisrael, and said unto him, "Go, strengthen yourself, and mark, and see what you doest; for at the return of the year, the king of Syria (Aram) will come up against you."

23 And the servants of the king of Syria (Aram) said unto him, "Their God (Elohim) are God (Elohim) of the hills; therefore they were stronger than we; but let us fight against them in the plain, and surely we shall be stronger than they.

24 And do this thing: Take the kings away, every man out of his place, and put captains in their rooms;

25 And number you an army, like the army that you have lost, horse for horse, and chariot for chariot; and we will fight against them in the plain, and surely we shall be stronger than they." And he hearkened unto their voice, and did so.

26 And it came to pass at the return of the year, that Benhadad numbered the Syrians (Aramim), and went up to Aphek, to fight against Yisrael.

27 And the children of Yisrael were numbered, and were all present, and went against them; and the children of Yisrael pitched before them like two little flocks of kids; but the Syrians (Arammim) filled the country.

28 And there came a man of God (Elohim), and spake unto the king of Yisrael, and said, "Thus saith יהוה: 'Because the Syrians (Arammim) have said, "יהוה is God (Elohim) of the hills, but He is not God (Elohim) of the valleys," therefore will I deliver all this great multitude into your hand, and you shall know that I am יהוה.'"

29 And they pitched one opposite the other seven days. And so it was, that in the seventh day the battle was joined; and the children of Yisrael slew of the Syrians (Arammim) a hundred thousand footmen in one day.

30 But the rest fled to Aphek, into the city; and there a wall fell upon twenty and seven thousand of the men that were left. And Benhadad fled, and came into the city, into an inner chamber.

31 And his servants said unto him, "Behold now, we have heard that the kings of the house of Yisrael are merciful kings; please let us put sackcloth on our loins, and ropes upon our heads, and go out to the king of Yisrael; perhaps he will save your life.

32 So they girded sackcloth on their loins, and put ropes on their heads, and came to the king of Yisrael, and said, "Your servant Benhadad saith: 'Please let me live.'" And he said, "Is he yet alive? He is my brother."

33 Now the men did diligently observe whether anything would come from him, and did hastily catch it; and they said, "Your brother Benhadad." Then he said, "Go you, bring him." Then Benhadad came forth to him; and he caused him to come up into the chariot.

34 And Benhadad said unto him, "The cities, which my father took from your father, I will restore; and you shalt make streets for you in Damascus (Dammeseq), as my father made in Samaria (Shomeron)." Then said Achav, "I will send you away with this covenant." So he made a covenant with him, and sent him away.

35 And a certain man of the sons of the prophets said unto his neighbour in the word of יהוה, "Smite me, please." But the man refused to

smite him.

36 Then said he unto him, "Because you have not obeyed the voice of יהוה, behold, as soon as you are departed from me, a lion shall slay you." And as soon as he was departed from him, a lion found him, and slew him.

37 Then he found another man, and said, "Smite me, please." And the man smote him, so that in smiting he wounded him.

38 So the prophet departed, and waited for the king by the way, and disguised himself with ashes upon his face.

39 And as the king passed by, he cried unto the king; and he said, "Your servant went out into the midst of the battle; and, behold, a man turned aside, and brought a man unto me, and said, 'Guard this man; if by any means he be missing, then shall your life be for his life, or else you shalt pay a talent of silver.'

40 And as your servant was busy here and there, he was gone. And the king of Yisrael said unto him, "So shall your judgment be; yourself hast decided it."

41 And he hasted, and took the ashes away from his face; and the king of Yisrael discerned him that he was of the prophets.

42 And he said unto him, "Thus saith יהוה: 'Because you have let go out of your hand a man whom I appointed to utter destruction, therefore your life shall go for his life, and your people for his people.'"

43 And the king of Yisrael went to his house heavy and displeased, and came to Samaria (Shomeron).

21 And it came to pass after these things, that Naboth the Yizreelite had a vineyard, which was in Yizreel, hard by the palace of Achav king of Samaria (Shomeron).

2 And Achav spake unto Naboth, saying, "Give me your vineyard, that I may have it for a garden of herbs, because it is near unto my house; and I will give you for it a better vineyard than it; or, if it seems good to you, I will give you the worth of it in money."

3 And Naboth said to Achav, "יהוה forbid it me, that I should give the inheritance of my fathers unto you."

4 And Achav came into his house heavy and displeased because of the word which Naboth the Yizreelite had spoken to him; for he had said, "I will not give you the inheritance of my fathers." And he laid him down upon his bed, and turned away his face, and would eat no bread.

5 But Jezebel (Iyzevel) his wife came to him, and said unto him, "Why is your spirit so sad, that you eatest no bread?"

6 And he said unto her, "Because I spake unto Naboth the Yizreelite, and said unto him, 'Give me your vineyard for money; or else, if it please you, I will give you another vineyard for it;' and he answered: 'I will not give you my vineyard.'"

7 And Jezebel (Iyzevel) his wife said unto him, "Dost you now govern the kingdom of Yisrael? Arise, and eat bread, and let your heart be merry. I will give you the vineyard of Naboth the Yizreelite."

8 So she wrote letters in Achav's name, and sealed them with his seal, and sent the letters unto the elders and to the nobles that were in his city, dwelling with Naboth.

9 And she wrote in the letters, saying, "Proclaim a fast, and set Naboth on high among the people;

10 And set two men, scoundrel (beliyaal) sons, before him, to bear witness against him, saying: 'You didst blaspheme God (Elohim) and the king.' And then carry him out, and stone him, that he may die."

11 And the men of his city, even the elders and the nobles who were the inhabitants in his city, did as Jezebel (Iyzevel) had sent unto them, and as it was written in the letters which she had sent unto them.

12 They proclaimed a fast, and set Naboth on high among the people.

13 And there came in two men, scoundrel (beliyaal) children, and sat before him; and the scoundrel (beliyaal) men witnessed against him, even against Naboth, in the presence of the people, saying, "Naboth did blaspheme God (Elohim) and the king." Then they carried him forth out of the city, and stoned him with stones, that he died.

14 Then they sent to Jezebel (Iyzevel), saying, "Naboth is stoned, and is dead."

15 And it came to pass, when Jezebel (Iyzevel) heard that Naboth was stoned, and was dead, that Jezebel (Iyzevel) said to Achav, "Arise, take possession of the vineyard of Naboth the Yizreelite, which he refused to give you for money; for Naboth is not alive, but dead."

16 And it came to pass, when Achav heard that

Naboth was dead, that Achav rose up to go down to the vineyard of Naboth the Yizreelite, to take possession of it.

17 And the word of יהוה came to Elijah (Eliyahu) the Tishbite, saying,

18 "Arise, go down to meet Achav king of Yisrael, which is in Samaria (Shomeron). Behold, he is in the vineyard of Naboth, whither he is gone down to possess it.

19 And you shalt speak unto him, saying: 'Thus saith יהוה, "Have you killed, and also taken possession?" And you shalt speak unto him, saying: 'Thus saith יהוה: "In the place where dogs licked the blood of Naboth shall dogs lick your blood, even yours."'"

20 And Achav said to Elijah (Eliyahu), "Have you found me, O mine enemy?" And he answered, "I have found you, because you have sold yourself to work evil in the sight of יהוה.

21 Behold, I will bring evil upon you, and will take away your posterity, and will cut off from Achav him that pisseth against the wall (every male), and him that is shut up and free in Yisrael,

22 And will make your house like the house of Yarovam the son of Nevat, and like the house of Baasha the son of Achiyah, for the provocation wherewith you have provoked Me to anger, and made Yisrael to sin.

23 And of Jezebel (Iyzevel) also spake יהוה, saying, 'The dogs shall eat Jezebel (Iyzevel) by the wall of Yizreel.'

24 Him that dieth of Achav in the city the dogs shall eat; and him that dieth in the field shall the fowls of the air eat."

25 But there was none like unto Achav, who did sell himself to work wickedness in the sight of יהוה, whom Jezebel (Iyzevel) his wife stirred up.

26 And he did very abominably in following idols, according to all things as did the Amorites, whom יהוה cast out before the children of Yisrael.

27 And it came to pass, when Achav heard those words, that he rent his clothes, and put sackcloth upon his flesh, and fasted, and lay in sackcloth, and went softly.

28 And the word of יהוה came to Elijah (Eliyahu) the Tishbite, saying,

29 "Seest you how Achav humbleth himself before Me? Because he humbleth himself before Me, I will not bring the disaster (raah) in his days; but in his son's days will I bring the disaster (raah) upon his house."

22 And they continued three years without war between Syria (Aram) and Yisrael.

2 And it came to pass in the third year, that Yehoshafat the king of Judah (Yehudah) came down to the king of Yisrael.

3 And the king of Yisrael said unto his servants, "Know you that Ramot in Gilad is ours, and we be still, and take it not out of the hand of the king of Syria (Aram)?"

4 And he said unto Yehoshafat, "Wilt you go with me to battle to Ramot-Gilad?" And Yehoshafat said to the king of Yisrael," I am as you are, my people as your people, my horses as your horses."

5 And Yehoshafat said unto the king of Yisrael, "Enquire, please, at the word of יהוה today."

6 Then the king of Yisrael gathered the prophets together, about four hundred men, and said unto them, "Shall I go against Ramot-Gilad to battle, or shall I forbear?" And they said, "Go up, for the Lord (Adonai) shall deliver it into the hand of the king."

7 And Yehoshafat said, "Is there not here a prophet of יהוה besides, that we might enquire of him?"

8 And the king of Yisrael said unto Yehoshafat, "There is yet one man, Mikhayahu the son of Imlah, by whom we may enquire of יהוה; but I hate him, for he doth not prophesy good concerning me, but evil." And Yehoshafat said, "Let not the king say so."

9 Then the king of Yisrael called an officer, and said, "Hasten hither Mikhayahu the son of Imlah."

10 And the king of Yisrael and Yehoshafat the king of Judah (Yehudah) sat each on his throne, having put on their robes, in a void place in the entrance of the gate of Samaria (Shomeron); and all the prophets prophesied before them.

11 And Tsidkiyahu the son of Chenaanah made him horns of iron; and he said, "Thus saith יהוה: 'With these shalt you push the Syrians (Arammim), until you have consumed them.'"

12 And all the prophets prophesied so, saying, "Go up to Ramot-Gilad, and prosper; for יהוה shall deliver it into the king's hand."

13 And the messenger that was gone to call Mikhayahu spake unto him, saying, "Behold now, the words of the prophets declare good

unto the king with one mouth; let your word, please, be like the word of one of them, and speak that which is good."

14 And Mikhayahu said, "As יהוה liveth, what יהוה saith unto me, that will I speak."

15 So he came to the king. And the king said unto him, "Mikhayahu, shall we go against Ramot-Gilad to battle, or shall we forbear?" And he answered him, "Go, and prosper; for יהוה shall deliver it into the hand of the king."

16 And the king said unto him, "How many times shall I adjure you that you tell me nothing but that which is true in the name of יהוה?"

17 And he said, "I saw all Yisrael scattered upon the hills, as sheep that have not a shepherd; and יהוה said: 'These have no master; let them return every man to his house in peace.'"

18 And the king of Yisrael said unto Yehoshafat, "Did I not tell you that he would prophesy no good concerning me, but evil?"

19 And he said, "Hear you therefore the word of יהוה: I saw יהוה sitting on His throne, and all the host of heaven standing by Him on His right hand and on his left.

20 And יהוה said, 'Who shall persuade Achav, that he may go up and fall at Ramot-Gilad?' And one said on this manner, and another said on that manner.

21 And there came forth a spirit, and stood before יהוה, and said, 'I will persuade him.'

22 And יהוה said unto him, 'How?' And he said, 'I will go forth, and I will be a lying spirit in the mouth of all his prophets.' And He said, 'You shalt persuade him, and prevail also; go forth, and do so.'

23 Now therefore, behold, יהוה hath put a lying spirit in the mouth of all these your prophets, and יהוה hath proclaimed disaster over you."

24 But Tsidkiyahu the son of Chenaanah went near, and smote Mikhayahu on the cheek, and said, "Which way went the Spirit of יהוה from me to speak unto you?"

25 And Mikhayahu said, "Behold, you shalt see in that day, when you shalt go into an inner chamber to hide yourself."

26 And the king of Yisrael said, "Take Mikhayahu, and carry him back unto Amon the governor of the city, and to Yoash the king's son;

27 And say, 'Thus saith the king: "Put this fellow in the prison, and feed him with bread of affliction and with water of affliction, until I come in peace."'"

28 And Mikhayahu said, "If you return at all in peace, יהוה hath not spoken by me." And he said, "Hearken, O people, every one of you."

29 So the king of Yisrael and Yehoshafat the king of Judah (Yehudah) went up to Ramot-Gilad.

30 And the king of Yisrael said unto Yehoshafat, "I will disguise myself, and enter into the battle; but put you on your robes." And the king of Yisrael disguised himself, and went into the battle.

31 But the king of Syria (Aram) commanded his thirty and two captains that had rule over his chariots, saying, "Fight neither with small nor great, except only with the king of Yisrael."

32 And it came to pass, when the captains of the chariots saw Yehoshafat, that they said, "Surely it is the king of Yisrael." And they turned aside to fight against him; and Yehoshafat cried out.

33 And it came to pass, when the captains of the chariots perceived that it was not the king of Yisrael, that they turned back from pursuing him.

34 And a certain man drew a bow at a venture, and smote the king of Yisrael between the joints of the harness; wherefore he said unto the driver of his chariot, "Turn your hand, and carry me out of the camp; for I am wounded."

35 And the battle increased that day; and the king was stayed up in his chariot against the Syrians (Arammim), and died at even; and the blood ran out of the wound into the midst of the chariot.

36 And there went a proclamation throughout the army about the going down of the sun, saying, "Every man to his city, and every man to his own country."

37 So the king died, and was brought to Samaria (Shomeron); and they buried the king in Samaria (Shomeron).

38 And one washed the chariot in the pool of Samaria (Shomeron); and the dogs licked up his blood; and they washed his armour; according unto the word of יהוה which he spake.

39 Now the rest of the acts of Achav, and all that he did, and the ivory house which he made, and all the cities that he built, are they not written in the book of the Chronicles of the kings of Yisrael?

40 So Achav slept with his fathers; and Achazyah his son reigned in his stead.

41 And Yehoshafat the son of Asa began to reign over Judah (Yehudah) in the fourth year of Achav king of Yisrael.

42 Yehoshafat was thirty and five years old when he began to reign; and he reigned twenty and five years in Jerusalem (Yerushalayim). His mother's name was Azubah the daughter of Shilhi.

43 And he walked in all the ways of Asa his father; he turned not aside from it, doing that which was right in the eyes of יהוה; nevertheless the high places were not taken away; for the people offered and burnt incense yet in the high places.

44 And Yehoshafat made peace with the king of Yisrael.

45 Now the rest of the acts of Yehoshafat, and his might that he shewed, and how he warred, are they not written in the book of the Chronicles of the kings of Judah (Yehudah)?

46 And the remnant of the sodomites (male cult prostitutes), who remained in the days of his father Asa, he took out of the land.

47 There was then no king in Edom; a deputy was king.

48 Yehoshafat made ships of Tharshish to go to Ophir for gold; but they went not, for the ships were broken at Eziongeber.

49 Then said Achazyah the son of Achav unto Yehoshafat, "Let my servants go with your servants in the ships." But Yehoshafat would not.

50 And Yehoshafat slept (rested) with his fathers, and was buried with his fathers in the city of Dawid his father; and Yehoram his son reigned in his stead.

51 Achazyah the son of Achav began to reign over Yisrael in Samaria (Shomeron) the seventeenth year of Yehoshafat king of Judah (Yehudah), and reigned two years over Yisrael.

52 And he did evil in the sight of יהוה, and walked in the way of his father, and in the way of his mother, and in the way of Jeroboam (Yarovam) the son of Nevat, who made Yisrael to sin;

53 For he served the Baal, and worshipped him, and provoked to anger יהוה God of Israel (Elohei Yisrael), according to all that his father had done.

2 KINGS
מְלָכִים ב MELAKHIM 2
(Second Kings)

1 Then Moav rebelled against Yisrael after the death of Achav.

2 And Achazyah fell down through a lattice in his upper chamber that was in Samaria (Shomeron), and was sick; and he sent messengers, and said unto them, "Go, enquire of Baalzebub (Baal-Zevuv) the god (elohim) of Ekron whether I shall recover of this disease.

3 But the angel of יהוה said to [A43]Eliyah the Tishbite, "Arise, go up to meet the messengers of the king of Samaria (Shomeron), and say unto them, 'Is it not because there is not a God (Elohim) in Yisrael, that you go to enquire of Baal-Zevuv the god (elohim) of Ekron?'

4 Now therefore thus saith יהוה: 'You shalt not come down from that bed on which you are gone up, but shalt surely die.'" And Eliyah departed.

5 And when the messengers turned back unto him, he said unto them, "Why are you now turned back?"

6 And they said unto him, "There came a man up to meet us, and said unto us, 'Go, turn again unto the king that sent you, and say unto him, "Thus saith יהוה: 'Is it not because there is not a God (Elohim) in Yisrael, that you sendest to enquire of Baal-Zevuv the god (elohim) of Ekron? Therefore you shalt not come down from that bed on which you are gone up, but shalt surely die.'"'"

7 And he said unto them, "What manner of man was he who came up to meet you, and told you these words?"

8 And they answered him, "He was a hairy man, and girt with a girdle of leather about his loins." And he said, "It is Eliyah the Tishbite."

9 Then the king sent unto him a captain of fifty with his fifty. And he went up to him. And, behold, he sat on the top of a hill. And he spake unto him, "You man of God (Elohim), the king hath said, 'Come down.'"

10 And Eliyah answered and said to the captain of fifty, "If I be a man of God (Elohim), then let fire come down from heaven, and consume you and your fifty." And there came down fire from heaven, and consumed him and his fifty.

11 Again also he sent unto him another captain of fifty with his fifty. And he answered and said unto him, "O man of God (Elohim), thus hath the king said: 'Come down quickly!'"

12 And Eliyah answered and said unto them, "If I be a man of God (Elohim), let fire come down from heaven, and consume you and your fifty." And the fire of God (Elohim) came down from heaven, and consumed him and his fifty.

13 And he sent again a captain of the third fifty with his fifty. And the third captain of fifty went up, and came and fell on his knees before Eliyah, and besought him, and said unto him: "O man of God (Elohim), please let my life and the life of these fifty your servants, be precious in your sight.

14 Behold, there came fire down from heaven, and burnt up the two captains of the former fifties with their fifties; therefore let my life now be precious in your sight."

15 And the angel of יהוה said unto Eliyah, "Go down with him; be not afraid of him." And he arose, and went down with him unto the king.

16 And he said unto him, "Thus saith יהוה: 'Forasmuch as you have sent messengers to enquire of Baal-Zevuv the god (elohim) of Ekron, is it not because there is no God (Elohim) in Yisrael to enquire of His word? Therefore you shalt not come down off that bed on which you are gone up, but shalt surely die.'"

17 So Achazyah died according to the word of יהוה which Eliyah had spoken. And Yehoram reigned in his stead in the second year of Yehoram the son of Yehoshafat king of Judah (Yehudah), because he had no son.

18 Now the rest of the acts of Achazyah which he did, are they not written in the book of the Chronicles of the kings of Yisrael?

2 And it came to pass, when יהוה would take up Eliyah into heaven by a whirlwind, that Eliyah went with Elisha from Gilgal.

2 And Eliyah said unto Elisha, "Please tarry here, for יהוה hath sent me to Bethel (Beit-El)." And Elisha said unto him, "As יהוה liveth, and as your soul liveth, I will not leave you." So they went down to Bethel (Beit-El).

3 And the sons of the prophets that were at Bethel (Beit-El) came forth to Elisha, and said unto him, "Knowest you that יהוה will take away your master from your head today?" And he said, "Yea, I know it; hold you your peace."

4 And Eliyah said unto him, "Elisha, tarry here, please; for יהוה hath sent me to Yericho." And he said, "As יהוה liveth, and as your soul liveth, I will not leave you." So they came to Yericho.

5 And the sons of the prophets that were at Yericho came to Elisha, and said unto him, "Knowest you that יהוה will take away your master from your head today?" And he answered, "Yea, I know it; hold you your peace."

6 And Eliyah said unto him, "Tarry here, please; for יהוה hath sent me to Jordan (Yarden)." And he said, "As יהוה liveth, and as your soul liveth, I will not leave you." And they two went on.

7 And fifty men of the sons of the prophets went, and stood to view afar off; and they two stood by Jordan (Yarden).

8 And Eliyah took his mantle, and wrapped it together, and smote the waters, and they were divided hither and thither, so that they two went over on dry ground.

9 And it came to pass, when they had gone over, that Eliyah said unto Elisha, "Ask what I shall do for you, before I be taken away from you." And Elisha said, "Please let a double portion of your spirit be upon me."

10 And he said, "You have asked a hard thing; nevertheless, if you see me when I am taken from you, it shall be so unto you; but if not, it shall not be so."

11 And it came to pass, as they still went on, and talked, that, behold, there appeared a chariot of fire, and horses of fire, and parted them both asunder; and Eliyah went up by a whirlwind into heaven.

12 And Elisha saw it, and he cried, "My father (Avi), my father, the chariot of Yisrael, and the horsemen thereof!" And he saw him no more; and he took hold of his own clothes, and rent them in two pieces.

13 He took up also the mantle of Eliyah that fell from him, and went back, and stood by the bank of Jordan (Yarden);

14 And he took the mantle of Eliyah that fell from him, and smote the waters, and said, "Where is יהוה God (Elohim) of Eliyah?" And when he also had smitten the waters, they parted hither and thither; and Elisha went over.

15 And when the sons of the prophets who were to view at Yericho saw him, they said, "The spirit of Eliyah doth rest on Elisha." And they

came to meet him, and bowed themselves to the ground before him.

16 And they said unto him, "Behold now, there be with your servants fifty strong men; please let them go and seek your master, lest perhaps the Spirit of יהוה hath taken him up, and cast him upon some mountain, or into some valley." And he said, "You shall not send."

17 And when they urged him till he was ashamed, he said, "Send." They sent therefore fifty men; and they sought three days, but found him not.

18 And when they came again to him, (for he tarried at Yericho,) he said unto them, "Did I not say unto you, 'Go not'?"

19 And the men of the city said unto Elisha, "Behold, please, the situation of this city is pleasant, as my lord (adoni) seeth; but the water is naught, and the ground barren."

20 And he said, "Bring me a new cruse, and put salt therein." And they brought it to him.

21 And he went forth unto the spring of the waters, and cast the salt in there, and said, "Thus saith יהוה: 'I have healed these waters; there shall not be from thence anymore death or barren land.'"

22 So the waters were healed unto this day, according to the saying of Elisha which he spake.

23 And he went up from thence unto Bethel (Beit-El); and as he was going up by the way, there came forth little children out of the city, and mocked him, and said unto him, "Go up, you bald head! Go up, you bald head!"

24 And he turned back, and looked on them, and cursed them in the name of יהוה. And there came forth two she bears out of the wood, and tare forty and two children of them.

25 And he went from thence to Mount Carmel, and from thence he returned to Samaria (Shomeron).

3 Now Yehoram the son of Achav began to reign over Yisrael in Samaria (Shomeron) the eighteenth year of Yehoshafat king of Judah (Yehudah), and reigned twelve years.

2 And he wrought evil in the sight of יהוה; but not like his father, and like his mother, for he put away the image of the Baal that his father had made.

3 Nevertheless he cleaved unto the sins of Jeroboam (Yarovam) the son of Nevat, who

made Yisrael to sin; he departed not therefrom.

4 And Mesha king of Moav was a sheepmaster, and rendered unto the king of Yisrael a hundred thousand lambs, and a hundred thousand rams, with the wool.

5 But it came to pass, when Achav was dead, that the king of Moav rebelled against the king of Yisrael.

6 And king Yehoram went out of Samaria (Shomeron) the same time, and numbered all Yisrael.

7 And he went and sent to Yehoshafat the king of Judah (Yehudah), saying, "The king of Moav hath rebelled against me; wilt you go with me against Moav to battle?" And he said, "I will go up; I am as you are, my people as your people, and my horses as your horses."

8 And he said, "Which way shall we go up?" And he answered, "The way through the wilderness of Edom."

9 So the king of Yisrael went, and the king of Judah (Yehudah), and the king of Edom; and they fetched a compass of seven days' journey; and there was no water for the army, and for the cattle that followed them.

10 And the king of Yisrael said, "Alas! For יהוה hath called these three kings together, to deliver them into the hand of Moav!"

11 But Yehoshafat said, "Is there not here a prophet of יהוה, that we may enquire of יהוה by him?" And one of the king of Yisrael's servants answered and said, "Here is Elisha the son of Shaphat, who poured water on the hands of Eliyah."

12 And Yehoshafat said, "The word of יהוה is with him." So the king of Yisrael and Yehoshafat and the king of Edom went down to him.

13 And Elisha said unto the king of Yisrael, "What have I to do with you? Get you to the prophets of your father, and to the prophets of your mother." And the king of Yisrael said unto him, "Nay, for יהוה hath called these three kings together, to deliver them into the hand of Moav."

14 And Elisha said, "As יהוה of hosts (YHWH Tsevaot) liveth, before whom I stand, surely, were it not that I regard the presence of Yehoshafat the king of Judah (Yehudah), I would not look toward you, nor see you.

15 But now bring me a minstrel." And it came to pass, when the minstrel played, that the hand of יהוה came upon him.

16 And he said, "Thus saith יהוה: 'Make this valley full of ditches.'

17 For thus saith יהוה: 'You shall not see wind, nor shall you see rain; yet that valley shall be filled with water, that you may drink, both you, and your cattle, and your beasts.'

18 And this is but a light thing in the sight of יהוה. He will deliver the Moavites also into your hand.

19 And you shall smite every fenced city, and every choice city, and shall fell every good tree, and stop all wells of water, and mar every good piece of land with stones."

20 And it came to pass in the morning, when the meat offering was offered, that, behold, there came water by the way of Edom, and the country was filled with water.

21 And when all the Moavites heard that the kings had come up to fight against them, they gathered all that were able to put on armour, and upward, and stood in the border.

22 And they rose up early in the morning, and the sun shone upon the water, and the Moavites saw the water on the other side as red as blood.

23 And they said, "This is blood; the kings are surely slain, and they have smitten one another; now therefore, Moav, to the spoil!"

24 And when they came to the camp of Yisrael, the Yisraelis rose up and smote the Moavites, so that they fled before them; but they went forward smiting the Moavites, even in their country.

25 And they beat down the cities, and on every good piece of land cast every man his stone, and filled it; and they stopped all the wells of water, and felled all the good trees; only in Kirharaseth left they the stones thereof; howbeit the slingers went about it, and smote it.

26 And when the king of Moav saw that the battle was too sore for him, he took with him seven hundred men that drew swords, to break through even unto the king of Edom; but they could not.

27 Then he took his eldest son that should have reigned in his stead, and offered him for a burnt offering upon the wall. And there was great indignation against Yisrael; and they departed from him and returned to their own land.

4 Now there cried a certain woman of the wives of the sons of the prophets unto Elisha, saying, "Your servant my husband is dead; and

you knowest that your servant did fear יהוה; and the creditor is come to take unto him my two sons to be bondmen."

2 And Elisha said unto her, "What shall I do for you? Tell me, what have you in the house?" And she said, "Your handmaid hath not anything in the house, except a pot of oil."

3 Then he said, "Go, borrow vessels abroad of all your neighbours, even empty vessels; borrow not a few.

4 And when you are come in, you shalt shut the door upon you and upon your sons, and shalt pour out into all those vessels, and you shalt set aside that which is full."

5 So she went from him, and shut the door upon her and upon her sons, who brought the vessels to her; and she poured out.

6 And it came to pass, when the vessels were full, that she said unto her son, "Bring me yet a vessel." And he said unto her, "There is not a vessel more." And the oil ceased.

7 Then she came and told the man of God (Elohim). And he said, "Go, sell the oil, and pay your debt, and live you and your children of the rest."

8 And it fell on a day, that Elisha passed to Shunem, where was a great woman; and she constrained him to eat bread. And so it was, that as oft as he passed by, he turned in thither to eat bread.

9 And she said unto her husband, "Behold now, I perceive that this is a holy man of God (Elohim), who passeth by us continually.

10 Let us make a little chamber, please, on the wall; and let us set for him there a bed, and a table, and a stool, and a candlestick (menorah); and it shall be, when he cometh to us, that he shall turn in thither."

11 And it fell on a day, that he came thither, and he turned into the chamber, and lay there.

12 And he said to Gehazi his servant, "Call this Shunammite." And when he had called her, she stood before him.

13 And he said unto him, "Say now unto her: 'Behold, you have been careful for us with all this care; what is to be done for you? Wouldest you be spoken for to the king, or to the captain of the army?'" And she answered, "I dwell among mine own people."

14 And he said, "What then is to be done for her?" And Gehazi answered, "Verily she hath

no child, and her husband is old."

15 And he said, "Call her." And when he had called her, she stood in the door.

16 And he said, "About this season, according to the time of life, you shalt embrace a son." And she said, "Nay, my lord (adoni), you man of God (Elohim), do not lie unto your handmaid."

17 And the woman conceived, and bare a son at that season that Elisha had said unto her, according to the time of life.

18 And when the child was grown, it fell on a day, that he went out to his father to the reapers.

19 And he said unto his father, "My head, my head." And he said to a lad, "Carry him to his mother."

20 And when he had taken him, and brought him to his mother, he sat on her knees till noon, and then died.

21 And she went up, and laid him on the bed of the man of God (Elohim), and shut the door upon him, and went out.

22 And she called unto her husband, and said, "Send me, please, one of the young men, and one of the asses, that I may run to the man of God (Elohim), and come again."

23 And he said, "Wherefore wilt you go to him today? It is neither New Moon, nor Shabbat." And she said, "It shall be well."

24 Then she saddled an ass, and said to her servant, "Drive, and go forward; slack not your riding for me, except I bid you."

25 So she went and came unto the man of God (Elohim) to Mount Carmel. And it came to pass, when the man of God (Elohim) saw her afar off, that he said to Gehazi his servant, "Behold, there is that Shunammite.

26 Please run now to meet her, and say unto her: 'Is it well with you? Is it well with your husband? Is it well with the child?'" And she answered, "It is well."

27 And when she came to the man of God (Elohim) to the hill, she caught him by the feet; but Gehazi came near to thrust her away. And the man of God (Elohim) said, "Let her alone, for her soul is vexed within her; and יהוה hath hid it from me, and hath not told me."

28 Then she said, "Did I desire a son of my lord (adoni)? Did I not say, 'Do not deceive me?'"

29 Then he said to Gehazi, "Gird up your loins, and take my staff in your hand, and go your way; if you meet any man, salute him not; and

if any salute you, answer him not again; and lay my staff upon the face of the child."

30 And the mother of the child said, "As יהוה liveth, and as your soul liveth, I will not leave you." And he arose, and followed her.

31 And Gehazi passed on before them, and laid the staff upon the face of the child; but there was neither voice, nor hearing. Wherefore he went again to meet him, and told him, saying, "The child is not awaked."

32 And when Elisha was come into the house, behold, the child was dead, and laid upon his bed.

33 He went in therefore, and shut the door upon them twain, and prayed unto יהוה.

34 And he went up, and lay upon the child, and put his mouth upon his mouth, and his eyes upon his eyes, and his hands upon his hands; and he stretched himself upon the child; and the flesh of the child waxed warm.

35 Then he returned, and walked in the house to and fro; and went up, and stretched himself upon him; and the child sneezed seven times, and the child opened his eyes.

36 And he called Gehazi, and said, "Call this Shunammite." So he called her. And when she was come in unto him, he said, "Take up your son."

37 Then she went in, and fell at his feet, and bowed herself to the ground, and took up her son, and went out.

38 And Elisha came again to Gilgal; and there was a dearth in the land; and the sons of the prophets were sitting before him; and he said unto his servant, "Set on the great pot, and seethe pottage for the sons of the prophets."

39 And one went out into the field to gather herbs, and found a wild vine, and gathered thereof wild gourds his lap full, and came and shred them into the pot of pottage; for they knew them not.

40 So they poured out for the men to eat. And it came to pass, as they were eating of the pottage, that they cried out, and said, "O you man of God (Elohim), there is death in the pot." And they could not eat thereof.

41 But he said, "Then bring meal." And he cast it into the pot; and he said, "Pour out for the people, that they may eat." And there was no harm in the pot.

42 And there came a man from Baalshalisha,

and brought the man of God (Elohim) bread of the firstfruits, twenty loaves of barley, and full ears of corn in the husk thereof. And he said, "Give unto the people, that they may eat."

43 And his servitor said, "What, should I set this before a hundred men?" He said again, "Give the people, that they may eat; for thus saith יהוה: 'They shall eat, and shall leave thereof.'"

44 So he set it before them, and they did eat, and left thereof, according to the word of יהוה.

5 Now Naaman, captain of the army of the king of Syria (Aram), was a great man with his master, and honourable, because by him יהוה had given deliverance unto Syria (Aram); he was also a mighty man in valour, but he was a leper.

2 And the Syrians (Arammim) had gone out by companies, and had brought away captive out of the land of Yisrael a little maid; and she waited on Naaman's wife.

3 And she said unto her mistress, "If only my lord (adoni) were with the prophet that is in Samaria (Shomeron)! For he would recover him of his leprosy."

4 And one went in, and told his lord (adon), saying, "Thus and thus said the maid that is of the land of Yisrael."

5 And the king of Syria (Aram) said, "Go now, and I will send a letter unto the king of Yisrael." And he departed, and took with him ten talents of silver, and six thousand pieces of gold, and ten changes of raiment.

6 And he brought the letter to the king of Yisrael, saying, "Now when this letter is come unto you, behold, I have therewith sent Naaman my servant to you, that you mayest recover him of his leprosy."

7 And it came to pass, when the king of Yisrael had read the letter, that he rent his clothes, and said, "Am I God (Elohim), to kill and to make alive, that this man doth send unto me to recover a man of his leprosy? Wherefore consider, please, and see how he seeketh a quarrel against me."

8 And it was so, when Elisha the man of God (Elohim) had heard that the king of Yisrael had rent his clothes, that he sent to the king, saying, "Wherefore have you rent your clothes? Let him come now to me, and he shall know that there is a prophet in Yisrael."

9 So Naaman came with his horses and with his chariot, and stood at the door of the house of Elisha.

10 And Elisha sent a messenger unto him, saying, "Go and wash in Jordan (Yarden) seven times, and your flesh shall come back to you, and you shalt be clean."

11 But Naaman was wroth, and went away, and said, "Behold, I thought, 'He will surely come out to me, and stand, and call on the name of יהוה his God (Elohim), and strike his hand over the place, and recover the leper.'

12 Are not Abana and Pharpar, rivers of Damascus (Dammeseq), better than all the waters of Yisrael? May I not wash in them, and be clean?" So he turned and went away in a rage.

13 And his servants came near, and spake unto him, and said, "My father, if the prophet had bid you do some great thing, wouldest you not have done it? How much rather then, when he saith to you, 'Wash, and be clean?'"

14 Then went he down, and dipped himself seven times in Jordan (Yarden), according to the saying of the man of God (Elohim); and his flesh came back like unto the flesh of a little child, and he was clean.

15 And he returned to the man of God (Elohim), he and all his company, and came, and stood before him; and he said, "Behold, now I know that there is no God (Elohim) in all the earth, but in Yisrael; now therefore, please, take a blessing of your servant."

16 But he said, "As יהוה liveth, before whom I stand, I will receive none." And he urged him to take it; but he refused.

17 And Naaman said, "Shall there not then, please, be given to your servant two mules' burden of earth? For your servant will henceforth offer neither burnt offering nor sacrifice unto other gods (elohim), but unto יהוה."

18 In this thing יהוה pardon your servant, that when my master goeth into the house of Rimmon to worship there, and he leaneth on my hand, and I bow myself in the house of Rimmon; when I bow down myself in the house of Rimmon, יהוה pardon your servant in this thing."

19 And he said unto him, "Go in peace." So he departed from him a little way.

20 But Gehazi, the servant of Elisha the man of God (Elohim), said, "Behold, my master hath spared Naaman this Syrian (Arammi), in not receiving at his hands that which he brought; but, as יהוה liveth, I will run after him, and take somewhat of him."

21 So Gehazi followed after Naaman. And when Naaman saw him running after him, he lighted down from the chariot to meet him, and said, "Is all well?"

22 And he said, "All is well. My master hath sent me, saying: 'Behold, even now there be come to me from Mount Efrayim two young men of the sons of the prophets. Please give them a talent of silver, and two changes of garments.'"

23 And Naaman said, "Be content, take two talents." And he urged him, and bound two talents of silver in two bags, with two changes of garments, and laid them upon two of his servants; and they bare them before him.

24 And when he came to the tower, he took them from their hand, and bestowed them in the house; and he let the men go, and they departed.

25 But he went in, and stood before his master. And Elisha said unto him, "Whence comest you, Gehazi?" And he said, "Your servant went no whither."

26 And he said unto him, "Went not mine heart with you, when the man turned again from his chariot to meet you? Is it a time to receive money, and to receive garments, and oliveyards, and vineyards, and sheep, and oxen, and menservants, and maidservants?

27 The leprosy therefore of Naaman shall cleave unto you, and unto your seed forever." And he went out from his presence a leper as white as snow.

6 And the sons of the prophets said unto Elisha, "Behold now, the place where we dwell with you is too strait for us.

2 Let us go, please, unto Jordan (Yarden), and take thence every man a beam, and let us make us a place there, where we may dwell." And he answered, "Go you."

3 And one said, "Please be content and go with your servants." And he answered, "I will go."

4 So he went with them. And when they came to Jordan (Yarden), they cut down wood.

5 But as one was felling a beam, the axe head fell into the water; and he cried, and said, "Alas, master!" For it was borrowed.

6 And the man of God (Elohim) said, "Where fell it?" And he shewed him the place. And he cut down a stick, and cast it in thither; and the iron did swim.

7 Therefore said he, "Take it up to you." And he put out his hand, and took it.

8 Then the king of Syria (Aram) warred against Yisrael, and took counsel with his servants, saying, "In such and such a place shall be my camp."

9 And the man of God (Elohim) sent unto the king of Yisrael, saying, "Beware that you pass not such a place; for thither the Syrians (Arammim) are come down."

10 And the king of Yisrael sent to the place which the man of God (Elohim) told him and warned him of, and saved himself there, not once nor twice.

11 Therefore the heart of the king of Syria (Aram) was sore troubled for this thing; and he called his servants, and said unto them, "Will you not shew me which of us is for the king of Yisrael?"

12 And one of his servants said, "None, my lord (adoni), O king, but Elisha, the prophet that is in Yisrael, telleth the king of Yisrael the words that you speakest in your bedchamber."

13 And he said, "Go and spy where he is, that I may send and fetch him." And it was told him, saying, "Behold, he is in Dothan."

14 Therefore sent he thither horses, and chariots, and a great army; and they came by night, and compassed the city about.

15 And when the servant of the man of God (Elohim) was risen early, and gone forth, behold, an army compassed the city both with horses and chariots. And his servant said unto him, "Alas, my master! What shall we do?"

16 And he answered, "Fear not, for they that be with us are more than they that be with them."

17 And Elisha prayed, and said, "יהוה, please open his eyes, that he may see." And יהוה opened the eyes of the young man; and he saw; and, behold, the mountain was full of horses and chariots of fire round about Elisha.

18 And when they came down to him, Elisha prayed unto יהוה, and said, "Smite this people, please, with blindness." And He smote them with blindness according to the word of Elisha.

19 And Elisha said unto them, "This is not the way, neither is this the city. Follow me, and I will bring you to the man whom you seek." But he led them to Samaria (Shomeron).

20 And it came to pass, when they were come into Samaria (Shomeron), that Elisha said, "יהוה, open the eyes of these men, that they may see." And יהוה opened their eyes, and they saw; and, behold, they were in the midst of Samaria (Shomeron).

21 And the king of Yisrael said unto Elisha when he saw them, "My father, shall I smite them? Shall I smite them?"

22 And he answered, "You shalt not smite them; wouldest you smite those whom you have taken captive with your sword and with your bow? Set bread and water before them, that they may eat and drink, and go to their master."

23 And he prepared great provision for them; and when they had eaten and drunk, he sent them away, and they went to their master. So the bands of Syria (Aram) came no more into the land of Yisrael.

24 And it came to pass after this, that Benhadad king of Syria (Aram) gathered all his army, and went up, and besieged Samaria (Shomeron).

25 And there was a great famine in Samaria (Shomeron); and, behold, they besieged it, until an ass's head was sold for fourscore pieces of silver, and the fourth part of a cab of dove's dung for five pieces of silver.

26 And as the king of Yisrael was passing by upon the wall, there cried a woman unto him, saying, "Help, my lord (adoni), O king."

27 And he said, "If יהוה do not help you, whence shall I help you? Out of the barnfloor, or out of the winepress?"

28 And the king said unto her, "What aileth you?" And she answered, "This woman said unto me, 'Give your son, that we may eat him today, and we will eat my son tomorrow.'

29 So we boiled my son, and did eat him; and I said unto her on the next day, 'Give your son, that we may eat him'; and she hath hid her son."

30 And it came to pass, when the king heard the words of the woman, that he rent his clothes; and he passed by upon the wall, and the people looked, and, behold, he had sackcloth within upon his flesh.

31 Then he said, "God (Elohim) do so and more also to me, if the head of Elisha the son of Shaphat shall stand on him this day."

32 But Elisha sat in his house, and the elders

sat with him; and the king sent a man from before him; but ere the messenger came to him, he said to the elders, "See you how this son of a murderer hath sent to take away mine head? Look, when the messenger cometh, shut the door, and hold him fast at the door; is not the sound of his master's feet behind him?"

33 And while he yet talked with them, behold, the messenger came down unto him; and he said, "Behold, this evil is of יהוה; what should I wait for יהוה any longer?"

7 Then Elisha said, "Hear you the word of יהוה. Thus saith יהוה: 'Tomorrow about this time shall a measure of fine flour be sold for a shekel, and two measures of barley for a shekel, in the gate of Samaria (Shomeron).'"

2 Then a lord (adon) on whose hand the king leaned answered the man of God (Elohim), and said, "Behold, if יהוה would make windows in heaven, might this thing be?" And he said, "Behold, you shalt see it with your eyes, but shalt not eat thereof."

3 And there were four leprous men at the entering in of the gate; and they said one to another, "Why sit we here until we die?

4 If we say, 'We will enter into the city,' then the famine is in the city, and we shall die there; and if we sit still here, we die also. Now therefore come, and let us fall unto the army of the Syria (Aram); if they save us alive, we shall live; and if they kill us, we shall but die."

5 And they rose up in the twilight, to go unto the camp of the Syria (Aram); and when they were come to the uttermost part of the camp of Syria (Aram), behold, there was no man there.

6 For the Lord (Adonai) had made the army of the Syrians (Arammim) to hear a noise of chariots, and a noise of horses, even the noise of a great army; and they said one to another, "Behold, the king of Yisrael hath hired against us the kings of the Hittites, and the kings of the Egyptians (Mitsrayim), to come upon us."

7 Wherefore they arose and fled in the twilight, and left their tents, and their horses, and their asses, even the camp as it was, and fled for their life.

8 And when these lepers came to the uttermost part of the camp, they went into one tent, and did eat and drink, and carried thence silver, and gold, and raiment, and went and hid it; and came again, and entered into another tent, and carried thence also, and went and hid it.

9 Then they said one to another, "We do not well; this day is a day of good tidings, and we hold our peace. If we tarry till the morning light, some mischief will come upon us. Now therefore come, that we may go and tell the king's household."

10 So they came and called unto the porter of the city; and they told them, saying, "We came to the camp of the Syria (Aram), and, behold, there was no man there, neither voice of man, but horses tied, and asses tied, and the tents as they were."

11 And he called the porters; and they told it to the king's house within.

12 And the king arose in the night, and said unto his servants, I will now shew you what the Syria (Aram) have done to us. They know that we be hungry; therefore are they gone out of the camp to hide themselves in the field, saying, "When they come out of the city, we shall catch them alive, and get into the city."

13 And one of his servants answered and said, "Please let some take five of the horses that remain, which are left in the city, (behold, they are as all the multitude of Yisrael that are left in it. Behold, I say, they are even as all the multitude of the Yisraelis that are consumed;) and let us send and see."

14 They took therefore two chariot horses; and the king sent after the army of the Syria (Aram), saying, "Go and see."

15 And they went after them unto Jordan (Yarden); and, behold, all the way was full of garments and vessels, which the Syria (Aram) had cast away in their haste. And the messengers returned, and told the king.

16 And the people went out, and spoiled the tents of the Syria (Aram). So a measure of fine flour was sold for a shekel, and two measures of barley for a shekel, according to the word of יהוה.

17 And the king appointed royal officer on whose hand he leaned to have the charge of the gate; and the people trode upon him in the gate, and he died, as the man of God (Elohim) had said, who spake when the king came down to him.

18 And it came to pass as the man of God (Elohim) had spoken to the king, saying, "Two measures of barley for a shekel, and a measure of

fine flour for a shekel, shall be tomorrow about this time in the gate of Samaria (Shomeron)."

19 And that royal officer answered the man of God (Elohim), and said, "Now, behold, if יהוה should make windows in heaven, might such a thing be?" And he said, "Behold, you shalt see it with your eyes, but shalt not eat thereof."

20 And so it fell out unto him, for the people trode upon him in the gate, and he died.

8 Then spake Elisha unto the woman, whose son he had restored to life, saying, "Arise and go, you and your household, and sojourn wheresoever you canst sojourn; for יהוה hath called for a famine; and it shall also come upon the land seven years.

2 And the woman arose, and did after the saying of the man of God (Elohim), and she went with her household, and sojourned in the land of the Philistines seven years.

3 And it came to pass at the seven years' end, that the woman returned out of the land of the Philistines; and she went forth to cry unto the king for her house and for her land.

4 And the king talked with Gehazi the servant of the man of God (Elohim), saying, "Tell me, please, all the great things that Elisha hath done."

5 And it came to pass, as he was telling the king how he had restored a dead body to life, that, behold, the woman, whose son he had restored to life, cried to the king for her house and for her land. And Gehazi said, "My lord (Adoni), O king, this is the woman, and this is her son, whom Elisha restored to life."

6 And when the king asked the woman, she told him. So the king appointed unto her a certain officer, saying, "Restore all that was hers, and all the fruits of the field since the day that she left the land, even until now."

7 And Elisha came to Damascus (Dammeseq); and Benhadad the king of Syria (Aram) was sick; and it was told him, saying, "The man of God (Elohim) is come hither."

8 And the king said unto Hazael, "Take a present in your hand, and go, meet the man of God (Elohim), and enquire of יהוה by him, saying, 'Shall I recover of this disease?'"

9 So Hazael went to meet him, and took a present with him, even of every good thing of Damascus (Dammeseq), forty camels' burden, and came and stood before him, and said,

"Your son Benhadad king of Syria (Aram) hath sent me to you, saying, 'Shall I recover of this disease?'"

10 And Elisha said unto him, "Go, say unto him, 'You mayest certainly recover.' Howbeit יהוה hath shewed me that he shall surely die."

11 And he settled his countenance stedfastly, until he was ashamed; and the man of God (Elohim) wept.

12 And Hazael said, "Why weepeth my lord (adoni)?" And he answered, "Because I know the evil that you wilt do unto the children of Yisrael: Their strongholds wilt you set on fire, and their young men wilt you slay with the sword, and wilt dash their children, and rip up their women with child."

13 And Hazael said, "But what, is your servant a dog, that he should do this great thing?" And Elisha answered, "יהוה hath shewed me that you shalt be king over Syria (Aram)."

14 So he departed from Elisha, and came to his master, who said to him, "What said Elisha to you?" And he answered, "He told me that you shouldest surely recover."

15 And it came to pass on the next day, that he took a thick cloth, and dipped it in water, and spread it on his face, so that he died; and Hazael reigned in his stead.

16 And in the fifth year of Yoram the son of Achav king of Yisrael, Yehoshafat being then king of Judah (Yehudah), Yehoram the son of Yehoshafat king of Judah (Yehudah) began to reign.

17 Thirty and two years old was he when he began to reign; and he reigned eight years in Jerusalem (Yerushalayim).

18 And he walked in the way of the kings of Yisrael, as did the house of Achav, for the daughter of Achav was his wife; and he did evil in the sight of יהוה.

19 Yet יהוה would not destroy Judah (Yehudah) for Dawid His servant's sake, as He promised him to give him always a light, and to his children.

20 In his days Edom revolted from under the hand of Judah (Yehudah), and made a king over themselves.

21 So Yoram went over to Zair, and all the chariots with him. And he rose by night, and smote the Edomites which compassed him about, and the captains of the chariots, and the

people fled into their tents.

22 Yet Edom revolted from under the hand of Judah (Yehudah) unto this day. Then Libnah revolted at the same time.

23 And the rest of the acts of Yoram, and all that he did, are they not written in the book of the Chronicles of the kings of Judah (Yehudah)?

24 And Yoram slept with his fathers, and was buried with his fathers in the city of Dawid. And Achazyah his son reigned in his stead.

25 In the twelfth year of Yoram the son of Achav king of Yisrael did Achazyah the son of Yehoram king of Judah (Yehudah) begin to reign.

26 Two and twenty years old was Achazyahu when he began to reign; and he reigned one year in Jerusalem (Yerushalayim). And his mother's name was Atalyahu, the daughter of Omri king of Yisrael.

27 And he walked in the way of the house of Achav, and did evil in the sight of יהוה, as did the house of Achav, for he was the son in law of the house of Achav.

28 And he went with Yoram the son of Achav to the war against Hazael king of Syria (Aram) in Ramot-Gilad; and the Syrians (Arammim) wounded Yoram.

29 And King Yoram went back to be healed in Yizreel of the wounds which the Syrians (Arammim) had given him at Ramah, when he fought against Hazael king of Syria (Aram). And Achazyah the son of Yehoram king of Judah (Yehudah) went down to see Yoram the son of Achav in Yizreel, because he was sick.

9 And Elisha the prophet called one of the children of the prophets, and said unto him, "Gird up your loins, and take this box of oil in your hand, and go to Ramot-Gilad.

2 And when you comest thither, look out there Yehu the son of Yehoshafat the son of Nimshi, and go in, and make him arise up from among his brethren, and carry him to an inner chamber;

3 Then take the box of oil, and pour it on his head, and say, 'Thus saith יהוה: I have anointed you king over Yisrael.'" Then open the door, and flee, and tarry not."

4 So the young man, even the young man the prophet, went to Ramot-Gilad.

5 And when he came, behold, the captains of the army were sitting; and he said, "I have an errand to you, O captain." And Yehu said, "Unto which

of all us?" And he said, "To you, O captain."

6 And he arose, and went into the house; and he poured the oil on his head, and said unto him, "Thus saith יהוה God of Israel (Elohei Yisrael): 'I have anointed you king over the people of יהוה, even over Yisrael.

7 And you shalt smite the house of Achav your master, that I may avenge the blood of my servants the prophets, and the blood of all the servants of יהוה, at the hand of Jezebel (Iyzevel).

8 For the whole house of Achav shall perish; and I will cut off from Achav him that pisseth against the wall (every male), and him that is shut up and free in Yisrael.

9 And I will make the house of Achav like the house of Yarovam the son of Nevat, and like the house of Baasha the son of Achiyah.

10 And the dogs shall eat Jezebel (Iyzevel) in the portion of Yizreel, and there shall be none to bury her.'" And he opened the door, and fled.

11 Then Yehu came forth to the servants of his lord (adon); and one said unto him, "Is all well? Wherefore came this mad fellow to you?" And he said unto them, "You know the man, and his communication."

12 And they said, "It is false! Tell us now." And he said, "Thus and thus spake he to me, saying, 'Thus saith יהוה: "I have anointed you king over Yisrael."'"

13 Then they hasted, and took every man his garment, and put it under him on the top of the stairs, and blew with ram's horn (shofarot), saying, "Yehu is king."

14 So Yehu the son of Yehoshafat the son of Nimshi conspired against Yoram. (Now Yoram had kept Ramot-Gilad, he and all Yisrael, because of Hazael king of Syria (Aram).

15 But king Yoram was returned to be healed in Yizreel of the wounds which the Syrians (Arammim) had given him, when he fought with Hazael king of Syria (Aram)). And Yehu said, "If it be your minds, then let none go forth nor escape out of the city to go to tell it in Yizreel."

16 So Yehu rode in a chariot, and went to Yizreel; for Yoram lay there. And Achazyah king of Judah (Yehudah) was come down to see Yoram.

17 And there stood a watchman on the tower in Yizreel, and he spied the company of Yehu as he came, and said, "I see a company." And Yoram said, "Take a horseman, and send to meet them,

and let him say, 'Is it peace?'"

18 So there went one on horseback to meet him, and said, "Thus saith the king, 'Is it peace?'" And Yehu said, "What have you to do with peace? Turn you behind me." And the watchman told, saying, "The messenger came to them, but he cometh not again."

19 Then he sent out a second on horseback, who came to them, and said, "Thus saith the king, 'Is it peace?'" And Yehu answered, "What have you to do with peace? Turn you behind me."

20 And the watchman told, saying, "He came even unto them, and cometh not again; and the driving is like the driving of Yehu the son of Nimshi, for he driveth furiously."

21 And Yoram said, "Make ready." And his chariot was made ready. And Yoram king of Yisrael and Achazyah king of Judah (Yehudah) went out, each in his chariot, and they went out against Yehu, and met him in the portion of Naboth the Yizreelite.

22 And it came to pass, when Yoram saw Yehu, that he said, "Is it peace, Yehu?" And he answered, "What peace, so long as the whoredoms of your mother Jezebel (Iyzevel) and her witchcrafts are so many?"

23 And Yoram turned his hands, and fled, and said to Achazyah, "There is treachery, O Achazyah."

24 And Yehu drew a bow with his full strength, and smote Yehoram between his arms, and the arrow went out at his heart, and he sunk down in his chariot.

25 Then said Yehu to Bidkar his captain, "Take up, and cast him in the portion of the field of Naboth the Yizreelite; for remember how that, when I and you rode together after Achav his father, יהוה laid this burden upon him:

26 'Surely I have seen yesterday the blood of Naboth, and the blood of his sons,' saith יהוה, 'and I will requite you in this plat,' saith יהוה. Now therefore take and cast him into the plat of ground, according to the word of יהוה."

27 But when Achazyah the king of Judah (Yehudah) saw this, he fled by the way of the garden house. And Yehu followed after him, and said, "Smite him also in the chariot." And they did so at the going up to Gur, which is by Ibleam. And he fled to Megiddo, and died there.

28 And his servants carried him in a chariot to Jerusalem (Yerushalayim), and buried him in his sepulchre with his fathers in the city of Dawid.

29 And in the eleventh year of Yoram the son of Achav began Achazyah to reign over Judah (Yehudah).

30 And when Yehu was come to Yizreel, Jezebel (Iyzevel) heard of it; and she painted her face, and tired her head, and looked out at a window.

31 And as Yehu entered in at the gate, she said, "Had Zimri peace, who slew his master?"

32 And he lifted up his face to the window, and said, "Who is on my side? Who?" And there looked out to him two or three eunuchs.

33 And he said, "Throw her down." So they threw her down; and some of her blood was sprinkled on the wall, and on the horses; and he trode her under foot.

34 And when he was come in, he did eat and drink, and said, "Go, see now this cursed woman, and bury her; for she is a king's daughter."

35 And they went to bury her, but they found no more of her than the skull, and the feet, and the palms of her hands.

36 Wherefore they came again, and told him. And he said, "This is the word of יהוה, which He spake by His servant Eliyah the Tishbite, saying, 'In the portion of Yizreel shall dogs eat the flesh of Jezebel (Iyzevel).'

37 And the carcase of Jezebel (Iyzevel) shall be as dung upon the face of the field in the portion of Yizreel; so that they shall not say, "This is Jezebel (Iyzevel)."'"

10 And Achav had seventy sons in Samaria (Shomeron). And Yehu wrote letters, and sent to Samaria (Shomeron), unto the rulers of Yizreel, to the elders, and to them that brought up Achav's children, saying:

2 "Now as soon as this letter cometh to you, seeing your master's sons are with you, and there are with you chariots and horses, a fenced city also, and armour;

3 Look even out the best and meetest of your master's sons, and set him on his father's throne, and fight for your master's house.

4 But they were exceedingly afraid, and said, "Behold, two kings stood not before him; how then shall we stand?"

5 And he that was over the house, and he that was over the city, the elders also, and the bringers up of the children, sent to Yehu, saying,

"We are your servants, and will do all that you shalt bid us; we will not make any king; do you that which is good in your eyes."

6 Then he wrote a letter the second time to them, saying, "If you be mine, and if you will hearken unto my voice, take you the heads of the men your master's sons, and come to me to Yizreel by tomorrow this time." Now the king's sons, being seventy persons, were with the great men of the city, which brought them up.

7 And it came to pass, when the letter came to them, that they took the king's sons, and slew seventy persons, and put their heads in baskets, and sent him them to Yizreel.

8 And there came a messenger, and told him, saying, "They have brought the heads of the king's sons." And he said, "Lay you them in two heaps at the entering in of the gate until the morning."

9 And it came to pass in the morning, that he went out, and stood, and said to all the people, "You be righteous. Behold, I conspired against my master, and slew him; but who slew all these?

10 Know now that there shall fall unto the earth nothing of the word of יהוה, which יהוה spake concerning the house of Achav; for יהוה hath done that which he spake by his servant Eliyah."

11 So Yehu slew all that remained of the house of Achav in Yizreel, and all his great men, and his kinsfolks, and his priests (kohanim), until he left him none remaining.

12 And he arose and departed, and came to Samaria (Shomeron). And as he was at the shearing house in the way,

13 Yehu met with the brethren of Achazyah king of Judah (Yehudah), and said, "Who are you?" And they answered, "We are the brethren of Achazyah; and we go down to salute the children of the king and the children of the queen."

14 And he said, "Take them alive." And they took them alive, and slew them at the pit of the shearing house, even two and forty men; neither left he any of them.

15 And when he was departed thence, he lighted on Yehonadav the son of Rechab coming to meet him; and he saluted him, and said to him, "Is your heart right, as my heart is with your heart?" And Yehonadav answered, "It is." "If it be, give me your hand." And he gave him

his hand; and he took him up to him into the chariot.

16 And he said, "Come with me, and see my zeal for יהוה." So they made him ride in his chariot.

17 And when he came to Samaria (Shomeron), he slew all that remained unto Achav in Samaria (Shomeron), till he had destroyed him, according to the saying of יהוה, which He spake to Eliyah.

18 And Yehu gathered all the people together, and said unto them, "Achav served the Baal a little; but Yehu shall serve him much.

19 Now therefore call unto me all the prophets of the Baal, all his servants, and all his priests (kohanim); let none be missing, for I have a great sacrifice to do to Baal; whosoever shall be missing, he shall not live." But Yehu did it in subtilty, to the intent that he might destroy the worshippers of the Baal.

20 And Yehu said, "Proclaim a solemn assembly for Baal." And they proclaimed it.

21 And Yehu sent through all Yisrael; and all the worshippers of the Baal came, so that there was not a man left that came not. And they came into the house of the Baal; and the house of the Baal was full from one end to another.

22 And he said unto him that was over the vestry, "Bring forth vestments for all the worshippers of the Baal." And he brought them forth vestments.

23 And Yehu went, and Yehonadav the son of Rechab, into the house of the Baal, and said unto the worshippers of the Baal, "Search, and look that there be here with you none of the servants of יהוה, but the worshippers of the Baal only."

24 And when they went in to offer sacrifices and burnt offerings, Yehu appointed fourscore men outside, and said, "If any of the men whom I have brought into your hands escape, he that letteth him go, his life shall be for the life of him."

25 And it came to pass, as soon as he had made an end of offering the burnt offering, that Yehu said to the guard and to the captains, "Go in, and slay them; let none come forth." And they smote them with the edge of the sword; and the guard and the captains cast them out, and went to the city of the house of the Baal.

26 And they brought forth the images out of the

house of the Baal, and burned them.

27 And they broke down the image of the Baal, and broke down the house of the Baal, and made it a draught house unto this day.

28 Thus Yehu destroyed the Baal out of Yisrael.

29 Howbeit from the sins of Yarovam the son of Nevat, who made Yisrael to sin, Yehu departed not from after them, that is, the golden calves that were in Bethel (Beit-El), and that were in Dan.

30 And יהוה said unto Yehu, "Because you have done well in executing that which is right in Mine eyes, and hast done unto the house of Achav according to all that was in Mine heart, your children of the fourth generation shall sit on the throne of Yisrael."

31 But Yehu took no heed to walk in the Torah of יהוה God of Israel (Elohei Yisrael) with all his heart; for he departed not from the sins of Yarovam, which made Yisrael to sin.

32 In those days יהוה began to cut Yisrael short; and Hazael smote them in all the coasts of Yisrael;

33 From Jordan (Yarden) eastward, all the land of Gilad, the Gadites, and the Reubenites (Reuveni), and the Menashshites, from Aroer, which is by the river Arnon, even Gilad and Bashan.

34 Now the rest of the acts of Yehu, and all that he did, and all his might, are they not written in the book of the chronicles of the kings of Yisrael?

35 And Yehu slept with his fathers; and they buried him in Samaria (Shomeron). And Yehoachaz his son reigned in his stead.

36 And the time that Yehu reigned over Yisrael in Samaria (Shomeron) was twenty-eight years.

11 And when Athalyahu the mother of Achazyah saw that her son was dead, she arose and destroyed all the seed royal.

2 But Yehosheva, the daughter of king Yoram, sister of Achazyah, took Yoash the son of Achazyah, and stole him from among the king's sons who were slain; and they hid him, even him and his nurse, in the bedchamber from Athalyahu, so that he was not slain.

3 And he was with her hid in the house of יהוה six years. And Athalyahu did reign over the land.

4 And the seventh year Yehoyada sent and fetched the rulers over hundreds, with the captains and the guard, and brought them to him into the house of יהוה, and made a covenant with them, and took an oath of them in the house of יהוה, and shewed them the king's son.

5 And he commanded them, saying, "This is the thing that you shall do: A third part of you that enter in on the Shabbat shall even be keepers of the watch of the king's house;

6 And a third part shall be at the gate of Sur; and a third part at the gate behind the guard; so shall you keep the watch of the house, that it be not broken down.

7 And two parts of all you that go forth on the Shabbat, even they shall keep the watch of the house of יהוה about the king.

8 And you shall compass the king round about, every man with his weapons in his hand; and he that cometh within the ranges, let him be slain. And be you with the king as he goeth out and as he cometh in."

9 And the captains over the hundreds did according to all things that Yehoyada the priest (kohen) commanded; and they took every man his men that were to come in on the Shabbat, with them that should go out on the Shabbat, and came to Yehoyada the priest (kohen).

10 And to the captains over hundreds did the priest (kohen) give king Dawid's spears and shields, that were in the temple of יהוה.

11 And the guard stood, every man with his weapons in his hand, round about the king, from the right corner of the temple to the left corner of the temple, along by the altar and the temple.

12 And he brought forth the king's son, and put the crown upon him, and gave him the testimony; and they made him king, and anointed him; and they clapped their hands, and said, "Long live the king!"

13 And when Athalyahu heard the noise of the guard and of the people, she came to the people into the temple of יהוה.

14 And when she looked, behold, the king stood by a pillar, as the manner was, and the princes and the trumpeters by the king, and all the people of the land rejoiced, and blew with ram's horn (shofarot); and Athalyahu rent her clothes, and cried, "Treason! Treason!"

15 But Yehoyada the priest (kohen) commanded the captains of the hundreds, the officers of the army, and said unto them, "Have her forth outside the ranges, and him that followeth her

kill with the sword." For the priest (kohen) had said, "Let her not be slain in the house of יהוה."

16 And they laid hands on her; and she went by the way by which the horses came into the king's house, and there was she slain.

17 And Yehoyada made a covenant between יהוה and the king and the people, that they should be יהוה's people; between the king also and the people.

18 And all the people of the land went into the house of the Baal, and broke it down; his altars and his images broke they in pieces thoroughly, and slew Mattan the priest (kohen) of the Baal before the altars. And the priest (kohen) appointed officers over the house of יהוה.

19 And he took the rulers over hundreds, and the captains, and the guard, and all the people of the land; and they brought down the king from the house of יהוה, and came by the way of the gate of the guard to the king's house. And he sat on the throne of the kings.

20 And all the people of the land rejoiced, and the city was in quiet; and they slew Athalyahu with the sword beside the king's house.

21 Seven years old was Yehoash when he began to reign.

12 In the seventh year of Yehu, Yehoash began to reign; and forty years reigned he in Jerusalem (Yerushalayim). His mother's name was Zibiah (Tsivyah) of Beer-Sheva.

2 And Yehoash did that which was right in the sight of יהוה all his days wherein Yehoyada the priest (kohen) instructed him.

3 But the high places were not taken away; the people still sacrificed and burnt incense in the high places.

4 And Yehoash said to the priests (kohanim), "All the money of the dedicated things that is brought into the house of יהוה, even the money of every one that passeth the account, the money that every man is set at, and all the money that cometh into any man's heart to bring into the house of יהוה,

5 Let the priests (kohanim) take it to them, every man of his acquaintance; and let them repair the breaches of the house, wheresoever any breach shall be found."

6 But it was so, that in the three and twentieth year of King Yehoash the priests (kohanim) had not repaired the breaches of the house.

7 Then King Yehoash called for Yehoyada the priest (kohen), and the other priests (kohanim), and said unto them, "Why repair you not the breaches of the house? Now therefore receive no more money of your acquaintance, but deliver it for the breaches of the house."

8 And the priests (kohanim) consented to receive no more money of the people, neither to repair the breaches of the house.

9 But Yehoyada the priest (kohen) took a chest, and bored a hole in the lid of it, and set it beside the altar, on the right side as one cometh into the house of יהוה; and the priests (kohanim) that kept the door put therein all the money that was brought into the house of יהוה.

10 And it was so, when they saw that there was much money in the chest, that the king's scribe and the high priest (kohen hagadol) came up, and they put up in bags, and told the money that was found in the house of יהוה.

11 And they gave the money, being told, into the hands of them that did the work, that had the oversight of the house of יהוה; and they laid it out to the carpenters and builders, that wrought upon the house of יהוה,

12 And to masons, and hewers of stone, and to buy timber and hewed stone to repair the breaches of the house of יהוה, and for all that was laid out for the house to repair it.

13 Howbeit there were not made for the house of יהוה bowls of silver, snuffers, basons, trumpets, any vessels of gold, or vessels of silver, of the money that was brought into the house of יהוה.

14 But they gave that to the workmen, and repaired therewith the house of יהוה.

15 Moreover they reckoned not with the men, into whose hand they delivered the money to be bestowed on workmen; for they dealt faithfully.

16 The trespass money and sin money was not brought into the house of יהוה. It was the priests'(kohanim).

17 Then Hazael king of Syria (Aram) went up, and fought against Gath, and took it; and Hazael set his face to go up to Jerusalem (Yerushalayim).

18 And Yehoash king of Judah (Yehudah) took all the hallowed things that Yehoshafat, and Yehoram, and Achazyah, his fathers, kings of Judah (Yehudah), had dedicated, and his own hallowed things, and all the gold that was found in the treasures of the house of יהוה, and in the

king's house, and sent it to Hazael king of Syria (Aram); and he went away from Jerusalem (Yerushalayim).

19 And the rest of the acts of Yoash, and all that he did, are they not written in the book of the Chronicles of the kings of Judah (Yehudah)?

20 And his servants arose, and made a conspiracy, and slew Yoash in the house of Millo, who goeth down to Silla.

21 For Yozakhar the son of Shimeath, and Yehozavad the son of Shomer, his servants, smote him, and he died; and they buried him with his fathers in the city of Dawid; and Amatsyah his son reigned in his stead.

13 In the three and twentieth year of Yoash the son of Achazyah king of Judah (Yehudah) Yehoachaz the son of Yehu began to reign over Yisrael in Samaria (Shomeron), and reigned seventeen years.

2 And he did that which was evil in the sight of יהוה, and followed the sins of Yarovam the son of Nevat, who made Yisrael to sin; he departed not therefrom.

3 And the anger of יהוה was kindled against Yisrael, and he delivered them into the hand of Hazael king of Syria (Aram), and into the hand of Benhadad the son of Hazael, all their days.

4 And Yehoachaz besought יהוה, and יהוה hearkened unto him; for he saw the oppression of Yisrael, because the king of Syria (Aram) oppressed them.

5 And יהוה gave Yisrael a savior (moshiya), so that they went out from under the hand of the Syrians (Arammim); and the children of Yisrael dwelt in their tents, as beforetime.

6 Nevertheless they departed not from the sins of the house of Jeroboam (Yarovam), who made Yisrael sin, but walked therein; and there remained the Asherah also in Samaria (Shomeron).

7 Neither did he leave of the people to Yehoachaz but fifty horsemen, and ten chariots, and ten thousand footmen; for the king of Syria (Aram) had destroyed them, and had made them like the dust by threshing.

8 Now the rest of the acts of Yehoachaz, and all that he did, and his might, are they not written in the book of the Chronicles of the kings of Yisrael?

9 And Yehoachaz slept with his fathers; and they buried him in Samaria (Shomeron); and

Yoash his son reigned in his stead.

10 In the thirty and seventh year of Yoash king of Judah (Yehudah) began Yehoash the son of Yehoachaz to reign over Yisrael in Samaria (Shomeron), and reigned sixteen years.

11 And he did that which was evil in the sight of יהוה; he departed not from all the sins of Jeroboam (Yarovam) the son of Nevat, who made Yisrael sin; but he walked therein.

12 And the rest of the acts of Yoash, and all that he did, and his might wherewith he fought against Amatsyah king of Judah (Yehudah), are they not written in the book of the Chronicles of the kings of Yisrael?

13 And Yoash slept with his fathers; and Jeroboam (Yarovam) sat upon his throne; and Yoash was buried in Samaria (Shomeron) with the kings of Yisrael.

14 Now Elisha was fallen sick of his sickness whereof he would die. And Yoash the king of Yisrael came down unto him, and wept over his face, and said, "O my father, my father, the chariot of Yisrael, and the horsemen thereof."

15 And Elisha said unto him, "Take bow and arrows." And he took unto him bow and arrows.

16 And he said to the king of Yisrael, "Put your hand upon the bow." And he put his hand upon it; and Elisha put his hands upon the king's hands.

17 And he said, "Open the window eastward." And he opened it. Then Elisha said, "Shoot." And he shot. And he said, "The arrow of יהוה's deliverance, and the arrow of deliverance from Syria (Aram); for you shalt smite the Syrians (Arammim) in Aphek, till you have consumed them."

18 And he said, "Take the arrows." And he took them. And he said unto the king of Yisrael, "Smite upon the ground." And he smote thrice, and stayed.

19 And the man of God (Elohim) was wroth with him, and said, "You shouldest have smitten five or six times; then hadst you smitten Syria (Aram) till you hadst consumed it; whereas now you shalt smite Syria (Aram) but thrice."

20 And Elisha died, and they buried him. And the bands of the Moavites invaded the land at the coming in of the year.

21 And it came to pass, as they were burying a man, that, behold, they spied a band of men; and they cast the man into the sepulchre of Elisha;

and when the man was let down, and touched the bones of Elisha, he revived, and stood up on his feet.

22 But Hazael king of Syria (Aram) oppressed Yisrael all the days of Yehoachaz.

23 And יהוה was gracious unto them, and had compassion on them, and had respect unto them, because of his covenant with Avraham, Isaac (Yitschaq), and Jacob (Yaaqov), and would not destroy them, neither cast he them from his presence as yet.

24 So Hazael king of Syria (Aram) died; and Benhadad his son reigned in his stead.

25 And Yehoash the son of Yehoachaz took again out of the hand of Benhadad the son of Hazael the cities, which he had taken out of the hand of Yehoachaz his father by war. Three times did Yoash beat him, and recovered the cities of Yisrael.

14 In the second year of Yoash son of Yehoachaz king of Yisrael reigned Amatsyah the son of Yoash king of Judah (Yehudah).

2 He was twenty and five years old when he began to reign, and reigned twenty and nine years in Jerusalem (Yerushalayim). His mother's name was Yehoaddan of Jerusalem (Yerushalayim).

3 And he did that which was right in the sight of יהוה, yet not like Dawid his father; he did according to all things as Yoash his father did.

4 Howbeit the high places were not taken away; as yet the people did sacrifice and burnt incense on the high places.

5 And it came to pass, as soon as the kingdom was confirmed in his hand, that he slew his servants who had slain the king his father.

6 But the children of the murderers he slew not, according unto that which is [B28b]written in the book of the law (sefer hatorah) by Moses (Mosheh), wherein יהוה commanded, saying, "The fathers shall not be put to death for the children, nor the children be put to death for the fathers; but every man shall be put to death for his own sin."

7 He slew of Edom in the valley of salt ten thousand, and took Selah by war, and called the name of it Yokteel unto this day.

8 Then Amatsyah sent messengers to Yehoash, the son of Yehoachaz son of Yehu, king of Yisrael, saying, "Come, let us have it out

face-to-face."

9 And Yehoash the king of Yisrael sent to Amatsyah king of Judah (Yehudah), saying, "The thistle that was in Lebanon sent to the cedar that was in Lebanon, saying, 'Give your daughter to my son as wife'; and there passed by a wild beast that was in Lebanon, and trode down the thistle.

10 You have indeed smitten Edom, and your heart hath lifted you up. Glory of this, and tarry at home; for why shouldest you meddle to your hurt, that you shouldest fall, even you, and Judah (Yehudah) with you?"

11 But Amatsyah would not hear. Therefore Yehoash king of Yisrael went up; and he and Amatsyah king of Judah (Yehudah) have it out face-to-face at Beit-Shemesh, which belongeth to Judah (Yehudah).

12 And Judah (Yehudah) was put to the worse before Yisrael; and they fled every man to their tents.

13 And Yehoash king of Yisrael took Amatsyah king of Judah (Yehudah), the son of Yehoash the son of Achazyah, at Beit-Shemesh, and came to Jerusalem (Yerushalayim), and broke down the wall of Jerusalem (Yerushalayim) from the gate of Efrayim unto the corner gate, four hundred cubits.

14 And he took all the gold and silver, and all the vessels that were found in the house of יהוה, and in the treasures of the king's house, and hostages, and returned to Samaria (Shomeron).

15 Now the rest of the acts of Yehoash which he did, and his might, and how he fought with Amatsyah king of Judah (Yehudah), are they not written in the book of the Chronicles of the kings of Yisrael?

16 And Yehoash slept with his fathers, and was buried in Samaria (Shomeron) with the kings of Yisrael; and Yarovam his son reigned in his stead.

17 And Amatsyah the son of Yoash king of Judah (Yehudah) lived after the death of Yehoash son of Yehoachaz king of Yisrael fifteen years.

18 And the rest of the acts of Amatsyah, are they not written in the book of the Chronicles of the kings of Judah (Yehudah)?

19 Now they made a conspiracy against him in Jerusalem (Yerushalayim); and he fled to Lachish; but they sent after him to Lachish, and slew him there.

20 And they brought him on horses; and he was buried at Jerusalem (Yerushalayim) with his fathers in the city of Dawid.

21 And all the people of Judah (Yehudah) took Azaryah, who was sixteen years old, and made him king instead of his father Amatsyah.

22 He built Elath, and restored it to Judah (Yehudah), after that the king slept with his fathers.

23 In the fifteenth year of Amatsyah the son of Yoash king of Judah (Yehudah) Jeroboam (Yarovam) the son of Yoash king of Yisrael began to reign in Samaria (Shomeron), and reigned forty and one years.

24 And he did that which was evil in the sight of יהוה; he departed not from all the sins of Jeroboam (Yarovam) the son of Nevat, who made Yisrael to sin.

25 He restored the coast of Yisrael from the entering of Hamath unto the sea of the plain, according to the word of יהוה God of Israel (Elohei Yisrael), which He spake by the hand of His servant Yonah, the son of Amittai, the prophet, who was of Gaththepher.

26 For יהוה saw the affliction of Yisrael, that it was very bitter; for there was not any shut up, nor any free, nor any helper for Yisrael.

27 And יהוה said not that He would blot out the name of Yisrael from under heaven; but He saved them by the hand of Jeroboam (Yarovam) the son of Yoash.

28 Now the rest of the acts of Jeroboam (Yarovam), and all that he did, and his might, how he warred, and how he recovered Damascus (Dammeseq), and Hamath, which belonged to Judah (Yehudah), for Yisrael, are they not written in the book of the Chronicles of the kings of Yisrael?

29 And Jeroboam (Yarovam) slept with his fathers, even with the kings of Yisrael; and Zekharyah his son reigned in his stead.

15 In the twenty and seventh year of Jeroboam (Yarovam) king of Yisrael began Azaryah son of Amatsyah king of Judah (Yehudah) to reign.

2 Sixteen years old was he when he began to reign, and he reigned two and fifty years in Jerusalem (Yerushalayim). His mother's name was Yekholyahu of Jerusalem (Yerushalayim).

3 And he did that which was right in the sight of יהוה, according to all that his father Amatsyah had done;

4 Except that the high places were not removed; the people sacrificed and burnt incense still on the high places.

5 And יהוה smote the king, so that he was a leper unto the day of his death, and dwelt in a several house. And Yotam the king's son was over the house, judging the people of the land.

6 And the rest of the acts of Azaryah, and all that he did, are they not written in the book of the Chronicles of the kings of Judah (Yehudah)?

7 So Azaryah slept with his fathers; and they buried him with his fathers in the city of Dawid; and Yotam his son reigned in his stead.

8 In the thirty and eighth year of Azaryah king of Judah (Yehudah) did Zekharyah the son of Jeroboam (Yarovam) reign over Yisrael in Samaria (Shomeron) six months.

9 And he did that which was evil in the sight of יהוה, as his fathers had done; he departed not from the sins of Jeroboam (Yarovam) the son of Nevat, who made Yisrael to sin.

10 And Shallum the son of Yavesh conspired against him, and smote him before the people, and slew him, and reigned in his stead.

11 And the rest of the acts of Zekharyah, behold, they are written in the book of the Chronicles of the kings of Yisrael.

12 This was the word of יהוה which He spake unto Yehu, saying, "Your sons shall sit on the throne of Yisrael unto the fourth generation." And so it came to pass.

13 Shallum the son of Yavesh began to reign in the nine and thirtieth year of Uzziyah king of Judah (Yehudah); and he reigned a full month in Samaria (Shomeron).

14 For Menahem the son of Gadi went up from Tirzah, and came to Samaria (Shomeron), and smote Shallum the son of Yavesh in Samaria (Shomeron), and slew him, and reigned in his stead.

15 And the rest of the acts of Shallum, and his conspiracy which he made, behold, they are written in the book of the Chronicles of the kings of Yisrael.

16 Then Menahem smote Tiphsah, and all that were therein, and the coasts thereof from Tirzah; because they opened not to him, therefore he smote it; and all the women therein that were with child he ripped up.

17 In the nine and thirtieth year of Azaryah king

of Judah (Yehudah) began Menahem the son of Gadi to reign over Yisrael, and reigned ten years in Samaria (Shomeron).

18 And he did that which was evil in the sight of יהוה; he departed not all his days from the sins of Jeroboam (Yarovam) the son of Nevat, who made Yisrael to sin.

19 And Pul the king of Assyria (Ashshur) came against the land; and Menahem gave Pul a thousand talents of silver, that his hand might be with him to confirm the kingdom in his hand.

20 And Menahem exacted the money of Yisrael, even of all the mighty men of wealth, of each man fifty shekels of silver, to give to the king of Assyria (Ashshur). So the king of Assyria (Ashshur) turned back, and stayed not there in the land.

21 And the rest of the acts of Menahem, and all that he did, are they not written in the book of the Chronicles of the kings of Yisrael?

22 And Menahem slept with his fathers; and Peqachyah his son reigned in his stead.

23 In the fiftieth year of Azaryah king of Judah (Yehudah) Peqachyah the son of Menahem began to reign over Yisrael in Samaria (Shomeron), and reigned two years.

24 And he did that which was evil in the sight of יהוה; he departed not from the sins of Jeroboam (Yarovam) the son of Nevat, who made Yisrael to sin.

25 But Peqach the son of Remalyahu, a captain of his, conspired against him, and smote him in Samaria (Shomeron), in the palace of the king's house, with Argob and Arieh, and with him fifty men of the Giladites; and he killed him, and reigned in his room.

26 And the rest of the acts of Peqachyah, and all that he did, behold, they are written in the book of the Chronicles of the kings of Yisrael.

27 In the two and fiftieth year of Azaryah king of Judah (Yehudah) Peqach the son of Remalyahu began to reign over Yisrael in Samaria (Shomeron), and reigned twenty years.

28 And he did that which was evil in the sight of יהוה; he departed not from the sins of Jeroboam (Yarovam) the son of Nevat, who made Yisrael to sin.

29 In the days of Peqach king of Yisrael came Tiglathpileser king of Assyria (Ashshur), and took Iyon, and Avelbethmaachah, and Yanoach, and Kedesh, and Hazor, and Gilad, and Galilee,

all the land of Naftali, and carried them captive to Assyria (Ashshur).

30 And Hoshea the son of Elah made a conspiracy against Pekah the son of Remalyahu, and smote him, and slew him, and reigned in his stead, in the twentieth year of Yotam the son of Uzziyah.

31 And the rest of the acts of Pekah, and all that he did, behold, they are written in the book of the Chronicles of the kings of Yisrael.

32 In the second year of Peqach the son of Remalyahu king of Yisrael began Yotam the son of Uzziyah king of Judah (Yehudah) to reign.

33 Five and twenty years old was he when he began to reign, and he reigned sixteen years in Jerusalem (Yerushalayim). His mother's name was Yerusha, the daughter of Zadok.

34 And he did that which was right in the sight of יהוה; he did according to all that his father Uzziyah had done.

35 Howbeit the high places were not removed; the people sacrificed and burned incense still in the high places. He built the higher gate of the house of יהוה.

36 Now the rest of the acts of Yotam, and all that he did, are they not written in the book of the Chronicles of the kings of Judah (Yehudah)?

37 In those days יהוה began to send against Judah (Yehudah) Rezin the king of Syria (Aram), and Pekah the son of Remalyahu.

38 And Yotam slept with his fathers, and was buried with his fathers in the city of Dawid his father; and Achaz his son reigned in his stead.

16 In the seventeenth year of Pekah the son of Remalyahu Achaz the son of Yotam king of Judah (Yehudah) began to reign.

2 Twenty years old was Achaz when he began to reign, and reigned sixteen years in Jerusalem (Yerushalayim), and did not that which was right in the sight of יהוה his God (Elohim), like Dawid his father.

3 But he walked in the way of the kings of Yisrael, yea, and made his son to pass through the fire, according to the abominations of the heathen, whom יהוה cast out from before the children of Yisrael.

4 And he sacrificed and burnt incense in the high places, and on the hills, and under every green tree.

5 Then Rezin king of Syria (Aram) and Peqach son of Remalyahu king of Yisrael came up to

Jerusalem (Yerushalayim) to war; and they besieged Achaz, but could not overcome him.

6 At that time Rezin king of Syria (Aram) recovered Elath to Syria (Aram), and drave the [B35]Jews (Yehudim) from Elath; and the Syrians (Arammim) came to Elath, and dwelt there unto this day.

7 So Achaz sent messengers to Tiglathpileser king of Assyria (Ashshur), saying, "I am your servant and your son; come up, and save me out of the hand of the king of Syria (Aram), and out of the hand of the king of Yisrael, who rise up against me."

8 And Achaz took the silver and gold that was found in the house of יהוה, and in the treasures of the king's house, and sent it for a present to the king of Assyria (Ashshur).

9 And the king of Assyria (Ashshur) hearkened unto him; for the king of Assyria (Ashshur) went up against Damascus (Dammeseq), and took it, and carried the people of it captive to Kir, and slew Rezin.

10 And King Achaz went to Damascus (Dammeseq) to meet Tiglathpileser king of Assyria (Ashshur), and saw an altar that was at Damascus (Dammeseq); and King Achaz sent to Uriyah the priest (kohen) the fashion of the altar, and the pattern of it, according to all the workmanship thereof.

11 And Uriyah the priest (kohen) built an altar according to all that King Achaz had sent from Damascus (Dammeseq); so Uriyah the priest (kohen) made it against King Achaz came from Damascus (Dammeseq).

12 And when the king was come from Damascus (Dammeseq), the king saw the altar; and the king approached to the altar, and offered thereon.

13 And he burnt his burnt offering and his meat offering, and poured his drink offering, and sprinkled the blood of his peace offerings, upon the altar.

14 And he brought also the brasen altar, which was before יהוה, from the forefront of the house, from between the altar and the house of יהוה, and put it on the north side of the altar.

15 And King Achaz commanded Uriyah the priest (kohen), saying, "Upon the great altar burn the morning burnt offering, and the evening meat offering, and the king's burnt sacrifice, and his meat offering, with the burnt

offering of all the people of the land, and their meat offering, and their drink offerings; and sprinkle upon it all the blood of the burnt offering, and all the blood of the sacrifice; and the brasen altar shall be for me to enquire by."

16 Thus did Uriyah the priest (kohen), according to all that King Achaz commanded.

17 And King Achaz cut off the borders of the bases, and removed the laver from off them; and took down the sea from off the brasen oxen that were under it, and put it upon a pavement of stones.

18 And the covert for the Shabbat that they had built in the house, and the king's entry outside, turned he from the house of יהוה for the king of Assyria (Ashshur).

19 Now the rest of the acts of Achaz which he did, are they not written in the book of the Chronicles of the kings of Judah (Yehudah)?

20 And Achaz slept with his fathers, and was buried with his fathers in the city of Dawid; and [A44]Hezekiah (Chizkiyahu) his son reigned in his stead.

17 In the twelfth year of Achaz king of Judah (Yehudah) began Hoshea the son of Elah to reign in Samaria (Shomeron) over Yisrael nine years.

2 And he did that which was evil in the sight of יהוה, but not as the kings of Yisrael that were before him.

3 Against him came up Shalmaneser king of Assyria (Ashshur); and Hoshea became his servant, and gave him presents.

4 And the king of Assyria (Ashshur) found conspiracy in Hoshea, for he had sent messengers to So king of Egypt (Mitsrayim), and brought no present to the king of Assyria (Ashshur), as he had done year by year; therefore the king of Assyria (Ashshur) shut him up, and bound him in prison.

5 Then the king of Assyria (Ashshur) came up throughout all the land, and went up to Samaria (Shomeron), and besieged it three years.

6 In the ninth year of Hoshea the king of Assyria (Ashshur) took Samaria (Shomeron), and carried Yisrael away into Assyria (Ashshur), and placed them in Halah and in Habor by the river of Gozan, and in the cities of the Medes.

7 For so it was, that the children of Yisrael had sinned against יהוה their God (YHWH Eloheihem), who had brought them up out of the

land of Egypt (Mitsrayim), from under the hand of Pharaoh (Paroh) king of Egypt (Mitsrayim), and had feared other gods (elohim),

8 And walked in the statutes of the heathen, whom יהוה cast out from before the children of Yisrael, and of the kings of Yisrael, which they had made.

9 And the children of Yisrael did secretly those things that were not right against יהוה their God (YHWH Eloheihem), and they built them high places in all their cities, from the tower of the watchmen to the fenced city.

10 And they set them up images and Asherim in every high hill, and under every green tree;

11 And there they burnt incense in all the high places, as did the heathen whom יהוה carried away before them; and wrought wicked things to provoke יהוה to anger;

12 For they served idols, whereof יהוה had said unto them, "You shall not do this thing."

13 Yet יהוה testified against Yisrael, and against Judah (Yehudah), by all the prophets, and by all the seers, saying, "Turn you from your evil ways, and keep My commandments and My statutes, according to all the Torah which I commanded your fathers, and which I sent to you by My servants the prophets."

14 Notwithstanding they would not hear, but hardened their necks, like to the neck of their fathers, that did not believe in יהוה their God (YHWH Eloheihem).

15 And they rejected His statutes, and His covenant that He made with their fathers, and His testimonies which He testified against them; and they followed vanity (worthless things as of idols), and became vain, and went after the heathen that were round about them, concerning whom יהוה had charged them, that they should not do like them.

16 And they left all the commandments of יהוה their God (YHWH Eloheihem), and made them molten images, even two calves, and made an Asherah, and worshipped all the host of heaven, and served the Baal.

17 And they caused their sons and their daughters to pass through the fire, and used divination and enchantments, and sold themselves to do evil in the sight of יהוה, to provoke Him to anger.

18 Therefore יהוה was very angry with Yisrael, and removed them out of His sight; there was none left but the tribe of Judah (Yehudah) only.

19 Also Judah (Yehudah) kept not the commandments of יהוה their God (YHWH Eloheihem), but walked in the statutes of Yisrael which they made.

20 And יהוה rejected all the seed of Yisrael, and afflicted them, and delivered them into the hand of spoilers, until He had cast them out of His sight.

21 For He rent Yisrael from the house of Dawid; and they made Jeroboam (Yarovam) the son of Nevat king; and Jeroboam (Yarovam) drave Yisrael from following יהוה, and made them sin a great sin.

22 For the children of Yisrael walked in all the sins of Jeroboam (Yarovam) which he did; they departed not from them;

23 Until יהוה removed Yisrael out of His sight, as He had said by all His servants the prophets. So was Yisrael carried away out of their own land to Assyria (Ashshur) unto this day.

24 And the king of Assyria (Ashshur) brought men from Babylon (Bavel), and from Cuthah, and from Ava, and from Hamath, and from Sepharvaim, and placed them in the cities of Samaria (Shomeron) instead of the children of Yisrael; and they possessed Samaria (Shomeron), and dwelt in the cities thereof.

25 And so it was at the beginning of their dwelling there, that they feared not יהוה; therefore יהוה sent lions among them, which slew some of them.

26 Wherefore they spake to the king of Assyria (Ashshur), saying, "The nations which you have removed, and placed in the cities of Samaria (Shomeron), know not the manner of the God (Elohim) of the land; therefore He hath sent lions among them, and, behold, they slay them, because they know not the manner of the God (Elohim) of the land."

27 Then the king of Assyria (Ashshur) commanded, saying, "Carry thither one of the priests (kohanim) whom you brought from thence; and let them go and dwell there, and let him teach them the manner of the God (Elohim) of the land."

28 Then one of the priests (kohanim) whom they had carried away from Samaria (Shomeron) came and dwelt in Bethel (Beit-El), and taught them how they should fear יהוה.

29 Howbeit every nation made gods (elohim) of

their own, and put them in the houses of the high places which the Samaritans (Shomeronim) had made, every nation in their cities wherein they dwelt.

30 And the men of Babylon (Bavel) made Sukkot-Benot, and the men of Cuth made Nergal, and the men of Hamath made Ashima,

31 And the Avites made Nibhaz and Tartak, and the Sepharvites burnt their children in fire to Adrammelech and Anammelech, the gods (elohim) of Sepharvaim.

32 So they feared יהוה, and made unto themselves of the lowest of them priests (kohanim) of the high places, which sacrificed for them in the houses of the high places.

33 They feared יהוה, and served their own gods (elohim), after the manner of the nations whom they carried away from thence.

34 Unto this day they do after the former manners; they fear not יהוה, neither do they after their statutes, or after their ordinances, or after the Torah and commandment which יהוה commanded the children of Jacob (Yaaqov), whom He named Yisrael;

35 With whom יהוה had made a covenant, and charged them, saying, "You shall not fear other gods (elohim), nor bow yourselves to them, nor serve them, nor sacrifice to them;

36 But יהוה, who brought you up out of the land of Egypt (Mitsrayim) with great power and an outstretched arm, Him shall you fear, and Him shall you worship, and to Him shall you do sacrifice.

37 And the statutes, and the ordinances, and the Torah, and the commandment which He wrote for you, you shall observe to do forevermore; and you shall not fear other gods (elohim).

38 And the covenant that I have made with you you shall not forget; neither shall you fear other gods (elohim).

39 But יהוה your God (YHWH Eloheikhem) you shall fear; and He shall deliver you out of the hand of all your enemies.

40 Howbeit they did not hearken, but they did after their former manner.

41 So these nations feared יהוה, yet served their graven images, both their children, and their children's children; as did their fathers, so do they unto this day.

18 Now it came to pass in the third year of Hoshea son of Elah king of Yisrael, that

Hezekiah (Chizkiyahu) the son of Achaz king of Judah (Yehudah) began to reign.

2 Twenty and five years old was he when he began to reign; and he reigned twenty and nine years in Jerusalem (Yerushalayim). His mother's name was Avi, the daughter of Zechariah (Zekharyah).

3 And he did that which was right in the sight of יהוה, according to all that Dawid his father did.

4 He removed the high places, and broke the images, and cut down the Asherah, and broke in pieces the brasen serpent that Moses (Mosheh) had made; for unto those days the children of Yisrael did burn incense to it; and he called it Nechushtan.

5 He trusted in יהוה God of Israel (Elohei Yisrael); so that after him was none like him among all the kings of Judah (Yehudah), nor any that were before him.

6 For he clave to יהוה, and departed not from following Him, but kept His commandments, which יהוה commanded Moses (Mosheh).

7 And יהוה was with him; and he prospered whithersoever he went forth; and he rebelled against the king of Assyria (Ashshur), and served him not.

8 He smote the Philistines, even unto Gaza (Azzah), and the borders thereof, from the tower of the watchmen to the fenced city.

9 And it came to pass in the fourth year of King Hezekiah (Chizkiyahu), which was the seventh year of Hoshea son of Elah king of Yisrael, that Shalmaneser king of Assyria (Ashshur) came up against Samaria (Shomeron), and besieged it.

10 And at the end of three years they took it; even in the sixth year of Hezekiah (Chizkiyahu), that is the ninth year of Hoshea king of Yisrael, Samaria (Shomeron) was taken.

11 And the king of Assyria (Ashshur) did carry away Yisrael unto Assyria (Ashshur), and put them in Halah and in Habor by the river of Gozan, and in the cities of the Medes;

12 Because they obeyed not the voice of יהוה their God (YHWH Eloheihem), but transgressed His covenant, and all that Moses (Mosheh) the servant of יהוה commanded, and would not hear them, nor do them.

13 Now in the fourteenth year of King Hezekiah (Chizkiyahu) did Senna-cherib king of Assyria (Ashshur) come up against all the fenced cities

of Judah (Yehudah), and took them.

14 And Hezekiah (Chizkiyahu) king of Judah (Yehudah) sent to the king of Assyria (Ashshur) to Lachish, saying, "I have offended; return from me, that which you puttest on me will I bear." And the king of Assyria (Ashshur) appointed unto Hezekiah (Chizkiyahu) king of Judah (Yehudah) three hundred talents of silver and thirty talents of gold.

15 And Hezekiah (Chizkiyahu) gave him all the silver that was found in the house of יהוה, and in the treasures of the king's house.

16 At that time did Hezekiah (Chizkiyahu) cut off the gold from the doors of the temple of יהוה, and from the pillars which Hezekiah (Chizkiyahu) king of Judah (Yehudah) had overlaid, and gave it to the king of Assyria (Ashshur).

17 And the king of Assyria (Ashshur) sent Tartan and Rabsaris and Rabshakeh from Lachish to king Hezekiah (Chizkiyahu) with a great army against Jerusalem (Yerushalayim). And they went up and came to Jerusalem (Yerushalayim). And when they were come up, they came and stood by the conduit of the upper pool, which is in the highway of the fuller's field.

18 And when they had called to the king, there came out to them Elyaqim the son of Chilqiyahu, who was over the household, and Shebna the scribe, and Yoach the son of Asaph the recorder.

19 And Rabshakeh said unto them, "Speak you now to Hezekiah (Chizkiyahu), 'Thus saith the great king, the king of Assyria (Ashshur): "What confidence is this wherein you trustest?

20 You sayest, (but they are but vain words,) I have counsel and strength for the war. Now on whom dost you trust, that you rebellest against me?

21 Now, behold, you trustest upon the staff of this bruised reed, even upon Egypt (Mitsrayim), on which if a man leans, it will go into his hand, and pierce it; so is Pharaoh (Paroh) king of Egypt (Mitsrayim) unto all that trust on him.

22 But if you say unto me, 'We trust in יהוה our God (YHWH Eloheinu)'; is not that He, whose high places and whose altars Hezekiah (Chizkiyahu) hath taken away, and hath said to Judah (Yehudah) and Jerusalem (Yerushalayim), 'You shall worship before this altar in Jerusalem (Yerushalayim)'?"'

23 Now therefore, please give pledges to my lord (adoni) the king of Assyria (Ashshur), and I will deliver you two thousand horses, if you be able on your part to set riders upon them.

24 How then wilt you turn away the face of one captain of the least of my master's servants, and put your trust on Egypt (Mitsrayim) for chariots and for horsemen?

25 Am I now come up without יהוה against this place to destroy it? יהוה said to me, "Go up against this land, and destroy it."

26 Then said Elyaqim the son of Hilkiah (Chilqiyahu), and Shebna, and Yoach, unto Rabshakeh, "Speak, please, to your servants in the Syrian language (Aramit); for we understand it and talk not with us in the Jews' language (Yehudit) in the ears of the people that are on the wall."

27 But Rabshakeh said unto them, "Hath my master sent me to your master, and to you, to speak these words? Hath he not sent me to the men who sit on the wall, that they may eat their own dung, and drink their own piss with you?"

28 Then Rabshakeh stood and cried with a loud voice in the Jews' language (Yehudit), and spake, saying, "Hear the word of the great king, the king of Assyria (Ashshur).

29 Thus saith the king: 'Let not Hezekiah (Chizkiyahu) deceive you; for he shall not be able to deliver you out of his hand;

30 Neither let Hezekiah (Chizkiyahu) make you trust in יהוה, saying, "יהוה will surely deliver us, and this city shall not be delivered into the hand of the king of Assyria (Ashshur)."'

31 Hearken not to Hezekiah (Chizkiyahu); for thus saith the king of Assyria (Ashshur), "Make an agreement with me by a present, and come out to me, and then eat you every man of his own vine, and every one of his fig tree, and drink you every one the waters of his cistern;

32 Until I come and take you away to a land like your own land, a land of corn and wine, a land of bread and vineyards, a land of oil olive and of honey, that you may live, and not die; and hearken not unto Hezekiah (Chizkiyahu), when he persuadeth you, saying, "יהוה will deliver us."

33 Hath any of the gods (elohim) of the nations delivered at all his land out of the hand of the king of Assyria (Ashshur)?

34 Where are the gods (elohim) of Hamath, and of Arpad? Where are the gods (elohim) of Sepharvaim, Hena, and Iwah? Have they

delivered Samaria (Shomeron) out of mine hand?

35 Who are they among all the gods (elohim) of the countries, that have delivered their country out of mine hand, that יהוה should deliver Jerusalem (Yerushalayim) out of mine hand?

36 But the people held their peace, and answered him not a word; for the king's commandment was, saying, "Answer him not."

37 Then came Elyaqim the son of Hilkiah (Chilqiyahu), which was over the household, and Shebna the scribe, and Yoach the son of Asaph the recorder, to Hezekiah (Chizkiyahu) with their clothes rent, and told him the words of Rabshakeh.

19 And it came to pass, when king Hezekiah (Chizkiyahu) heard it, that he rent his clothes, and covered himself with sackcloth, and went into the house of יהוה.

2 And he sent Elyaqim, who was over the household, and Shebna the scribe, and the elders of the priests (kohanim), covered with sackcloth, to ^A51Isaiah (Yeshayahu) the prophet the son of Amoz.

3 And they said unto him, "Thus saith Hezekiah (Chizkiyahu): 'This day is a day of trouble, and of rebuke, and blasphemy; for the children are come to the birth, and there is not strength to bring forth.

4 It may be יהוה your God (YHWH Eloheikha) will hear all the words of Rabshakeh, whom the king of Assyria (Ashshur) his master hath sent to reproach the ^B2living God (Elohim chai); and will reprove the words which יהוה your God (YHWH Eloheikha) hath heard; wherefore lift up your prayer for the remnant that are left.'

5 So the servants of King Hezekiah (Chizkiyahu) came to Isaiah (Yeshayahu).

6 And Isaiah (Yeshayahu) said unto them, "Thus shall you say to your master, 'Thus saith יהוה: "Be not afraid of the words which you have heard, with which the servants of the king of Assyria (Ashshur) have blasphemed Me.

7 Behold, I will send a blast upon him, and he shall hear a rumour, and shall return to his own land; and I will cause him to fall by the sword in his own land."'"

8 So Rabshakeh returned, and found the king of Assyria (Ashshur) warring against Libnah; for he had heard that he was departed from Lachish.

9 And when he heard say of Tirhakah king of Ethiopia (Kush), "Behold, he is come out to fight against you"; he sent messengers again unto Hezekiah (Chizkiyahu), saying,

10 "Thus shall you speak to Hezekiah (Chizkiyahu) king of Judah (Yehudah), saying: 'Let not your God (Elohim) in whom you trustest deceive you, saying, "Jerusalem (Yerushalayim) shall not be delivered into the hand of the king of Assyria (Ashshur)."

11 Behold, you have heard what the kings of Assyria (Ashshur) have done to all lands, by destroying them utterly; and shalt you be delivered?

12 Have the gods (elohim) of the nations delivered them which my fathers have destroyed; as Gozan, and Haran, and Rezeph, and the children of Eden who were in Thelasar?

13 Where is the king of Hamath, and the king of Arpad, and the king of the city of Sepharvaim, of Hena, and Ivah?'"

14 And Hezekiah (Chizkiyahu) received the letter of the hand of the messengers, and read it; and Hezekiah (Chizkiyahu) went up into the house of יהוה, and spread it before יהוה.

15 And Hezekiah (Chizkiyahu) prayed before יהוה, and said, "O יהוה God of Israel (Elohei Yisrael), who dwellest between the cherubims (keruvim), you are the God (Elohim), even You alone, of all the kingdoms of the earth; You have made heaven and earth.

16 יהוה, bow down Your ear, and hear; open, יהוה, Your eyes, and see; and hear the words of Sennacherib, who hath sent him to reproach the living God (Elohim chai).

17 Of a truth, יהוה, the kings of Assyria (Ashshur) have destroyed the nations and their lands,

18 And have cast their gods (elohim) into the fire; for they were no gods (elohim), but the work of men's hands, wood and stone; therefore they have destroyed them.

19 Now therefore, O יהוה our God (YHWH Eloheinu), I beseech you, save You us out of his hand, that all the kingdoms of the earth may know that You are יהוה God (Elohim), even You only."

20 Then Isaiah (Yeshayahu) the son of Amoz sent to Hezekiah (Chizkiyahu), saying, "Thus saith יהוה God of Israel (Elohei Yisrael): 'That which you have prayed to Me against

Sennacherib king of Assyria (Ashshur) I have heard.'

21 This is the word that יהוה hath spoken concerning him: 'The virgin the daughter of Zion (Tsiyon) hath despised you, and laughed you to scorn; the daughter of Jerusalem (Yerushalayim) hath shaken her head at you.

22 Whom have you reproached and blasphemed? And against whom have you exalted your voice, and lifted up your eyes on high? Even against the Holy One of Yisrael.

23 By your messengers you have reproached the Lord (Adonai), and hast said: "With the multitude of my chariots I am come up to the height of the mountains, to the sides of Lebanon, and will cut down the tall cedar trees thereof, and the choice fir trees thereof; and I will enter into the lodgings of his borders, and into the forest of his Carmel.

24 I have digged and drunk strange waters, and with the sole of my feet have I dried up all the rivers of besieged places."

25 Have you not heard long ago how I have done it, and of ancient times that I have formed it? Now have I brought it to pass, that you shouldest be to lay waste fenced cities into ruinous heaps.

26 Therefore their inhabitants were of small power, they were dismayed and confounded; they were as the grass of the field, and as the green herb, as the grass on the housetops, and as corn blasted before it be grown up.

27 But I know your abode, and your going out, and your coming in, and your rage against Me.

28 Because your rage against Me and your tumult is come up into Mine ears, therefore I will put My hook in your nose, and My bridle in your lips, and I will turn you back by the way by which you camest.

29 And this shall be a sign unto you, You shall eat this year such things as grow of themselves, and in the second year that which springeth of the same; and in the third year sow you, and reap, and plant vineyards, and eat the fruits thereof.

30 And the remnant that is escaped of the house of Judah (Yehudah) shall yet again take root downward, and bear fruit upward.

31 For out of Jerusalem (Yerushalayim) shall go forth a remnant, and they that escape out of Mount Zion (Tsiyon); the zeal of [A8]יהוה of hosts (YHWH Tsevaot) shall do this.'

32 Therefore thus saith יהוה concerning the king of Assyria (Ashshur): 'He shall not come into this city, nor shoot an arrow there, nor come before it with shield, nor cast a bank against it.

33 By the way that he came, by the same shall he return, and shall not come into this city, saith יהוה.

34 For I will defend this city, to save it, for Mine own sake, and for My servant Dawid's sake.'"

35 And it came to pass that night, that the angel of יהוה went out, and smote in the camp of the Assyrians a hundred fourscore and five thousand; and when they arose early in the morning, behold, they were all dead corpses.

36 So Sennacherib king of Assyria (Ashshur) departed, and went and returned, and dwelt at Nineveh.

37 And it came to pass, as he was worshipping in the house of Nisroch his god (elohim), that Adrammelech and Sharezer his sons smote him with the sword; and they escaped into the land of Armenia. And Esarhaddon his son reigned in his stead.

20 In those days was Hezekiah (Chizkiyahu) sick unto death. And the prophet Isaiah (Yeshayahu) the son of Amoz came to him, and said unto him, "Thus saith יהוה: 'Set your house in order; for you shalt die, and not live.'"

2 Then he turned his face to the wall, and prayed unto יהוה, saying,

3 "I beseech You, O יהוה, remember now how I have walked before You in truth and with a perfect heart, and have done that which is good in Your sight." And Hezekiah (Chizkiyahu) wept sore.

4 And it came to pass, afore Isaiah (Yeshayahu) was gone out into the middle court, that the word of יהוה came to him, saying,

5 "Turn again, and tell Hezekiah (Chizkiyahu) the captain of My people, 'Thus saith יהוה, the God (Elohim) of Dawid your father: "I have heard your prayer, I have seen your tears; behold, I will heal you; on the third day you shalt go up unto the house of יהוה.

6 And I will add unto your days fifteen years; and I will deliver you and this city out of the hand of the king of Assyria (Ashshur); and I will defend this city for Mine own sake, and for My servant Dawid's sake."'"

7 And Isaiah (Yeshayahu) said, "Take a lump of figs." And they took and laid it on the boil, and

he recovered.

8 And Hezekiah (Chizkiyahu) said unto Isaiah (Yeshayahu), "What shall be the sign that יהוה will heal me, and that I shall go up into the house of יהוה the third day?"

9 And Isaiah (Yeshayahu) said, "This sign shalt you have of יהוה, that יהוה will do the thing that He hath spoken: shall the shadow go forward ten degrees, or go back ten degrees?"

10 And Hezekiah (Chizkiyahu) answered, "It is a light thing for the shadow to go down ten degrees; nay, but let the shadow return backward ten degrees."

11 And Isaiah (Yeshayahu) the prophet cried unto יהוה; and He brought the shadow ten degrees backward, by which it had gone down in the dial of Achaz.

12 At that time Berodach-Baladan, the son of Baladan, king of Babylon (Bavel), sent letters and a present unto Hezekiah (Chizkiyahu); for he had heard that Hezekiah (Chizkiyahu) had been sick.

13 And Hezekiah (Chizkiyahu) hearkened unto them, and shewed them all the house of his precious things, the silver, and the gold, and the spices, and the precious ointment, and all the house of his armour, and all that was found in his treasures; there was nothing in his house, nor in all his dominion, that Hezekiah (Chizkiyahu) shewed them not.

14 Then came Isaiah (Yeshayahu) the prophet unto king Hezekiah (Chizkiyahu), and said unto him, "What said these men? And from whence came they unto you?" And Hezekiah (Chizkiyahu) said, "They are come from a far country, even from Babylon (Bavel)."

15 And he said, "What have they seen in your house?" And Hezekiah (Chizkiyahu) answered, "All the things that are in mine house have they seen; there is nothing among my treasures that I have not shewed them."

16 And Isaiah (Yeshayahu) said unto Hezekiah (Chizkiyahu), "Hear the word of יהוה:

17 'Behold, the days come, that all that is in your house, and that which your fathers have laid up in store unto this day, shall be carried into Babylon (Bavel); nothing shall be left, saith יהוה.

18 And of your sons that shall issue from you, which you shalt beget, shall they take away; and they shall be eunuchs in the palace of the king of Babylon (Bavel).'"

19 Then said Hezekiah (Chizkiyahu) unto Isaiah (Yeshayahu), "Good is the word of יהוה which you have spoken." And he said, "Is it not good, if peace and truth be in my days?"

20 And the rest of the acts of Hezekiah (Chizkiyahu), and all his might, and how he made a pool, and a conduit, and brought water into the city, are they not written in the book of the Chronicles of the kings of Judah (Yehudah)?

21 And Hezekiah (Chizkiyahu) slept with his fathers; and Menashsheh his son reigned in his stead.

21 Menashsheh was twelve years old when he began to reign, and reigned fifty and five years in Jerusalem (Yerushalayim). His mother's name was Hephzibah.

2 And he did that which was evil in the sight of יהוה, after the abominations of the heathen, whom יהוה cast out before the children of Yisrael.

3 For he built up again the high places which Hezekiah (Chizkiyahu) his father had destroyed; and he reared up altars for the Baal, and made an Asherah, as did Achav king of Yisrael; and worshipped all the host of heaven, and served them.

4 And he built altars in the house of יהוה, of which יהוה said, "In Jerusalem (Yerushalayim) will I put My name."

5 And he built altars for all the host of heaven in the two courts of the house of יהוה.

6 And he made his son pass through the fire, and observed times, and used enchantments, and dealt with familiar spirits and wizards; he wrought much wickedness in the sight of יהוה, to provoke Him to anger.

7 And he set a graven image of the Asherah that he had made in the house, of which יהוה said to Dawid, and to Solomon (Shelomoh) his son, "In this house, and in Jerusalem (Yerushalayim), which I have chosen out of all tribes of Yisrael, will I put My name forever.

8 Neither will I make the feet of Yisrael move any more out of the land which I gave their fathers; only if they will observe to do according to all that I have commanded them, and according to all the Torah that My servant Moses (Mosheh) commanded them."

9 But they hearkened not, and Menashsheh seduced them to do more evil than did the

nations whom יהוה destroyed before the children of Yisrael.

10 And יהוה spake by His servants the prophets, saying,

11 "Because Menashsheh king of Judah (Yehudah) hath done these abominations, and hath done wickedly above all that the Amorites did, which were before him, and hath made Judah (Yehudah) also to sin with his idols;

12 Therefore thus saith יהוה God of Israel (Elohei Yisrael): 'Behold, I am bringing such evil upon Jerusalem (Yerushalayim) and Judah (Yehudah), that whosoever heareth of it, both his ears shall tingle.

13 And I will stretch over Jerusalem (Yerushalayim) the line of Samaria (Shomeron), and the plummet of the house of Achav; and I will wipe Jerusalem (Yerushalayim) as a man wipeth a dish, wiping it, and turning it upside down.

14 And I will forsake the remnant of mine inheritance, and deliver them into the hand of their enemies; and they shall become a prey and a spoil to all their enemies;

15 Because they have done that which was evil in My sight, and have provoked Me to anger, since the day their fathers came forth out of Egypt (Mitsrayim), even unto this day.'"

16 Moreover Menashsheh shed innocent blood very much, till he had filled Jerusalem (Yerushalayim) from one end to another; besides his sin wherewith he made Judah (Yehudah) to sin, in doing that which was evil in the sight of יהוה.

17 Now the rest of the acts of Menashsheh, and all that he did, and his sin that he sinned, are they not written in the book of the Chronicles of the kings of Judah (Yehudah)?

18 And Menashsheh slept with his fathers, and was buried in the garden of his own house, in the garden of Uzza; and Amon his son reigned in his stead.

19 Amon was twenty and two years old when he began to reign, and he reigned two years in Jerusalem (Yerushalayim). His mother's name was Meshullemeth, the daughter of Haruz of Yotbah.

20 And he did that which was evil in the sight of יהוה, as his father Menashsheh did.

21 And he walked in all the way that his father walked in, and served the idols that his father served, and worshipped them;

22 And he forsook יהוה God (Elohim) of his fathers, and walked not in the way of יהוה.

23 And the servants of Amon conspired against him, and slew the king in his own house.

24 And the people of the land slew all them that had conspired against king Amon; and the people of the land made Josiah (Yoshiyahu) his son king in his stead.

25 Now the rest of the acts of Amon which he did, are they not written in the book of the Chronicles of the kings of Judah (Yehudah)?

26 And he was buried in his sepulchre in the garden of Uzza; and Josiah (Yoshiyahu) his son reigned in his stead.

22 Josiah (Yoshiyahu) was eight years old when he began to reign, and he reigned thirty and one years in Jerusalem (Yerushalayim). His mother's name was Yedidah, the daughter of Adayah of Boscath.

2 And he did that which was right in the sight of יהוה, and walked in all the way of Dawid his father, and turned not aside to the right hand or to the left.

3 And it came to pass in the eighteenth year of King Josiah (Yoshiyahu), that the king sent Shaphan the son of Atsalyahu, the son of Meshullam, the scribe, to the house of יהוה, saying,

4 "Go up to Chilqiyahu the high priest (kohen hagadol), that he may sum the silver which is brought into the house of יהוה, which the keepers of the door have gathered of the people.

5 And let them deliver it into the hand of the doers of the work, that have the oversight of the house of יהוה; and let them give it to the doers of the work which is in the house of יהוה, to repair the breaches of the house,

6 Unto carpenters, and builders, and masons, and to buy timber and hewn stone to repair the house.

7 Howbeit there was no reckoning made with them of the money that was delivered into their hand, because they dealt faithfully."

8 And Hilkiah (Chilqiyahu) the high priest (kohen hagadol) said unto Shaphan the scribe, "I have found the book of the law (sefer hatorah) in the house of יהוה." And Hilkiah (Chilqiyahu) gave the book to Shaphan, and he read it.

9 And Shaphan the scribe came to the king, and brought the king word again, and said, "Your

servants have gathered the money that was found in the house, and have delivered it into the hand of them that do the work, that have the oversight of the house of יהוה."

10 And Shaphan the scribe shewed the king, saying, "Hilkiah (Chilqiyahu) the priest (kohen) hath delivered me a book." And Shaphan read it before the king.

11 And it came to pass, when the king had heard the words of the book of the law (sefer hatorah), that he rent his clothes.

12 And the king commanded Hilkiah (Chilqiyahu) the priest (kohen), and Ahikam the son of Shaphan, and Achbor the son of Mikhayah, and Shaphan the scribe, and Asayah a servant of the king's, saying,

13 "Go you, enquire of יהוה for me, and for the people, and for all Judah (Yehudah), concerning the words of this book that is found; for great is the wrath of יהוה that is kindled against us, because our fathers have not hearkened unto the words of this book, to do according unto all that which is written concerning us."

14 So Hilkiah (Chilqiyahu) the priest (kohen), and Ahikam, and Achbor, and Shaphan, and Asayah, went unto Huldah the prophetess (neviah), the wife of Shallum the son of Tikvah, the son of Harhas, keeper of the wardrobe; (now she dwelt in Jerusalem (Yerushalayim) in the college;) and they communed with her.

15 And she said unto them, "Thus saith יהוה God of Israel (Elohei Yisrael): 'Tell the man that sent you to me,

16 "Thus saith יהוה: 'Behold, I will bring disaster (raah) upon this place, and upon the inhabitants thereof, even all the words of the book which the king of Judah (Yehudah) hath read;

17 Because they have forsaken Me, and have burned incense unto other gods (elohim), that they might provoke Me to anger with all the works of their hands; therefore My wrath shall be kindled against this place, and shall not be quenched.'"

18 But to the king of Judah (Yehudah) who sent you to enquire of יהוה, thus shall you say to him, 'Thus saith יהוה God of Israel (Elohei Yisrael): "As touching the words which you have heard;

19 Because your heart was tender, and you have humbled yourself before יהוה, when you heardest what I spake against this place, and

against the inhabitants thereof, that they should become a desolation and a curse, and hast rent your clothes, and wept before me; I also have heard you," saith יהוה.

20 Behold therefore, I will gather you unto your fathers, and you shalt be gathered into your grave in peace; and your eyes shall not see all the evil which I will bring upon this place. And they brought the king word again.

23 And the king sent, and they gathered unto him all the elders of Judah (Yehudah) and of Jerusalem (Yerushalayim).

2 And the king went up into the house of יהוה, and all the men of Judah (Yehudah) and all the inhabitants of Jerusalem (Yerushalayim) with him, and the priests (kohanim), and the prophets, and all the people, both small and great; and he read in their ears all the words of the book of the covenant which was found in the house of יהוה.

3 And the king stood by a pillar, and made a covenant before יהוה, to walk after יהוה, and to keep His commandments and His testimonies and His statutes with all their heart and all their soul, to perform the words of this covenant that were written in this book. And all the people stood to the covenant.

4 And the king commanded Hilkiah (Chilqiyahu) the high priest (kohen hagadol), and the priests (kohanim) of the second order, and the keepers of the door, to bring forth out of the temple of יהוה all the vessels that were made for the Baal, and for the Asherah, and for all the host of heaven; and he burned them outside Jerusalem (Yerushalayim) in the fields of Kidron, and carried the ashes of them unto Bethel (Beit-El).

5 And he put down the idolatrous priests (kohanim), whom the kings of Judah (Yehudah) had ordained to burn incense in the high places in the cities of Judah (Yehudah), and in the places round about Jerusalem (Yerushalayim); them also that burned incense unto the Baal, to the sun, and to the moon, and to the planets, and to all the host of heaven.

6 And he brought out the Asherah from the house of יהוה, outside Jerusalem (Yerushalayim), unto the Brook Kidron, and burned it at the Brook Kidron, and stamped it small to powder, and cast the powder thereof upon the graves of the children of the people.

7 And he broke down the houses of the

sodomites (male cult prostitutes), that were by the house of יהוה, where the women wove hangings for the Asherah.

8 And he brought all the priests (kohanim) out of the cities of Judah (Yehudah), and defiled the high places where the priests (kohanim) had burned incense, from Geba to Beer-Sheva, and broke down the high places of the gates that were in the entering in of the gate of Joshua (Yehoshua) the governor of the city, which were on a man's left hand at the gate of the city.

9 Nevertheless the priests (kohanim) of the high places came not up to the altar of יהוה in Jerusalem (Yerushalayim), but they did eat of the unleavened bread among their brethren.

10 And he defiled Topheth, which is in the valley of the children of Hinnom, that no man might make his son or his daughter to pass through the fire to Molech.

11 And he took away the horses that the kings of Judah (Yehudah) had given to the sun, at the entering in of the house of יהוה, by the chamber of Nathanmelech the chamberlain, which was in the suburbs, and burned the chariots of the sun with fire.

12 And the altars that were on the top of the upper chamber of Achaz, which the kings of Judah (Yehudah) had made, and the altars which Menashsheh had made in the two courts of the house of יהוה, did the king beat down, and broke them down from thence, and cast the dust of them into the Brook Kidron.

13 And the high places that were before Jerusalem (Yerushalayim), which were on the right hand of the mount of corruption, which Solomon (Shelomoh) the king of Yisrael had builded for Ashtoreth the abomination of the Zidonians, and for Chemosh the abomination of the Moavites, and for Milcom the abomination of the children of Ammon, did the king defile.

14 And he broke in pieces the images, and cut down the Asherim, and filled their places with the bones of men.

15 Moreover the altar that was at Bethel (Beit-El), and the high place which Jeroboam (Yarovam) the son of Nevat, who made Yisrael to sin, had made, both that altar and the high place he broke down, and burned the high place, and stamped it small to powder, and burned the Asherah.

16 And as Josiah (Yoshiyahu) turned himself, he spied the sepulchres that were there in the mount, and sent, and took the bones out of the sepulchres, and burned them upon the altar, and polluted it, according to the word of יהוה which the man of God (Elohim) proclaimed, who proclaimed these words.

17 Then he said, "What title is that, that I see?" And the men of the city told him, "It is the sepulchre of the man of God (Elohim), who came from Judah (Yehudah), and proclaimed these things that you have done against the altar of Bethel (Beit-El)."

18 And he said, "Let him alone; let no man move his bones." So they let his bones alone, with the bones of the prophet that came out of Samaria (Shomeron).

19 And all the houses also of the high places that were in the cities of Samaria (Shomeron), which the kings of Yisrael had made to provoke יהוה to anger, Josiah (Yoshiyahu) took away, and did to them according to all the acts that he had done in Bethel (Beit-El).

20 And he slew all the priests (kohanim) of the high places that were there upon the altars, and burned men's bones upon them, and returned to Jerusalem (Yerushalayim).

21 And the king commanded all the people, saying, "Keep the Passover (Pesach) unto יהוה your God (YHWH Eloheikhem), as it is written in the book of this covenant."

22 Surely there was not holden such a Passover (Pesach) from the days of the judges that judged Yisrael, nor in all the days of the kings of Yisrael, nor of the kings of Judah (Yehudah);

23 But in the eighteenth year of King Josiah (Yoshiyahu), wherein this Passover (Pesach) was holden to יהוה in Jerusalem (Yerushalayim).

24 Moreover the workers with familiar spirits, and the wizards, and the images, and the idols, and all the abominations that were spied in the land of Judah (Yehudah) and in Jerusalem (Yerushalayim), did Josiah (Yoshiyahu) put away, that he might perform the words of the law (torah) which were written in the book that Hilkiah (Chilqiyahu) the priest (kohen) found in the house of יהוה.

25 And like unto him was there no king before him, that turned to יהוה with all his heart, and with all his soul, and with all his might, according to all the teaching of Moses (Mosheh); neither after him arose there any like him.

26 Notwithstanding יהוה turned not from the fierceness of His great wrath, wherewith His anger was kindled against Judah (Yehudah), because of all the provocations that Menashsheh had provoked Him withal.

27 And יהוה said, "I will remove Judah (Yehudah) also out of My sight, as I have removed Yisrael, and will cast off this city Jerusalem (Yerushalayim) which I have chosen, and the house of which I said, 'My name shall be there.'"

28 Now the rest of the acts of Josiah (Yoshiyahu), and all that he did, are they not written in the book of the Chronicles of the kings of Judah (Yehudah)?

29 In his days Pharaoh (Paroh) Nekhoh king of Egypt (Mitsrayim) went up against the king of Assyria (Ashshur) to the river Euphrates; and King Josiah (Yoshiyahu) went against him; and he slew him at Megiddo, when he had seen him.

30 And his servants carried him in a chariot dead from Megiddo, and brought him to Jerusalem (Yerushalayim), and buried him in his own sepulchre. And the people of the land took Yehoachaz the son of Josiah (Yoshiyahu), and anointed him, and made him king in his father's stead.

31 Yehoachaz was twenty and three years old when he began to reign; and he reigned three months in Jerusalem (Yerushalayim). His mother's name was Hamutal, the daughter of Jeremiah (Yirmeyahu) of Libnah.

32 And he did that which was evil in the sight of יהוה, according to all that his fathers had done.

33 And Pharaoh (Paroh) Nekhoh put him in bands at Riblah in the land of Hamath, that he might not reign in Jerusalem (Yerushalayim); and put the land to a tribute of a hundred talents of silver, and a talent of gold.

34 And Pharaoh (Paroh) Nekhoh made Elyaqim the son of Josiah (Yoshiyahu) king in the room of Josiah (Yoshiyahu) his father, and turned his name to Yehoyaqim, and took Yehoachaz away; and he came to Egypt (Mitsrayim), and died there.

35 And Yehoyaqim gave the silver and the gold to Pharaoh (Paroh); but he taxed the land to give the money according to the commandment of Pharaoh (Paroh); he exacted the silver and the gold of the people of the land, of every one according to his taxation, to give it unto Pharaoh (Paroh) Nekhoh.

36 Yehoyaqim was twenty and five years old when he began to reign; and he reigned eleven years in Jerusalem (Yerushalayim). His mother's name was Zebudah, the daughter of Pedayah of Rumah.

37 And he did that which was evil in the sight of יהוה, according to all that his fathers had done.

24 In his days Nebuchadnezzar king of Babylon (Bavel) came up, and Yehoyaqim became his servant three years; then he turned and rebelled against him.

2 And יהוה sent against him bands of the Chaldees, and bands of the Syrians (Arammim), and bands of the Moavites, and bands of the children of Ammon, and sent them against Judah (Yehudah) to destroy it, according to the word of יהוה, which He spake by His servants the prophets.

3 Surely at the commandment of יהוה came this upon Judah (Yehudah), to remove them out of His sight, for the sins of Menashsheh, according to all that he did;

4 And also for the innocent blood that he shed; for he filled Jerusalem (Yerushalayim) with innocent blood; which יהוה would not pardon.

5 Now the rest of the acts of Yehoyaqim, and all that he did, are they not written in the book of the Chronicles of the kings of Judah (Yehudah)?

6 So Yehoyaqim slept with his fathers; and Yehoyaqim his son reigned in his stead.

7 And the king of Egypt (Mitsrayim) came not again anymore out of his land; for the king of Babylon (Bavel) had taken from the river of Egypt (Mitsrayim) unto the river Euphrates all that pertained to the king of Egypt (Mitsrayim).

8 Yehoyaqim was eighteen years old when he began to reign, and he reigned in Jerusalem (Yerushalayim) three months. His mother's name was Nehushta, the daughter of Elnathan of Jerusalem (Yerushalayim).

9 And he did that which was evil in the sight of יהוה, according to all that his father had done.

10 At that time the servants of Nebuchadnezzar king of Babylon (Bavel) came up against Jerusalem (Yerushalayim), and the city was besieged.

11 And Nebuchadnezzar king of Babylon (Bavel) came against the city, and his servants

did besiege it.

12 And Yehoyaqim the king of Judah (Yehudah) went out to the king of Babylon (Bavel), he, and his mother, and his servants, and his princes, and his officers; and the king of Babylon (Bavel) took him in the eighth year of his reign. 13 And he carried out thence all the treasures of the house of יהוה, and the treasures of the king's house, and cut in pieces all the vessels of gold which Solomon (Shelomoh) king of Yisrael had made in the temple of יהוה, as יהוה had said.

14 And he carried away all Jerusalem (Yerushalayim), and all the princes, and all the mighty men of valour, even ten thousand captives, and all the craftsmen and smiths; none remained, except the poorest sort of the people of the land.

15 And he carried away Yehoyaqim to Babylon (Bavel), and the king's mother, and the king's wives, and his officers, and the mighty of the land, those carried he into captivity from Jerusalem (Yerushalayim) to Babylon (Bavel).

16 And all the men of might, even seven thousand, and craftsmen and smiths a thousand, all that were strong and apt for war, even them the king of Babylon (Bavel) brought captive to Babylon (Bavel).

17 And the king of Babylon (Bavel) made Mattanyah his father's brother king in his stead, and changed his name to Zedekiah (Tsidkiyahu).

18 Zedekiah (Tsidkiyahu) was twenty and one years old when he began to reign, and he reigned eleven years in Jerusalem (Yerushalayim). His mother's name was Hamutal, the daughter of Jeremiah (Yirmeyahu) of Libnah.

19 And he did that which was evil in the sight of יהוה, according to all that Yehoyaqim had done.

20 For through the anger of יהוה it came to pass in Jerusalem (Yerushalayim) and Judah (Yehudah), until He had cast them out from His presence, that Zedekiah (Tsidkiyahu) rebelled against the king of Babylon (Bavel).

25 And it came to pass in the ninth year of his reign, in the tenth month, in the tenth day of the month, that Nebuchadnezzar king of Babylon (Bavel) came, he, and all his army, against Jerusalem (Yerushalayim), and pitched against it; and they built forts against it round about.

2 And the city was besieged unto the eleventh year of King Zedekiah (Tsidkiyahu).

3 And on the ninth day of the fourth month the famine prevailed in the city, and there was no bread for the people of the land.

4 And the city was broken up, and all the men of war fled by night by the way of the gate between two walls, which is by the king's garden; (now the Chaldees were against the city round about;) and the king went the way toward the plain.

5 And the army of the Chaldees pursued after the king, and overtook him in the plains of Yericho; and all his army were scattered from him.

6 So they took the king, and brought him up to the king of Babylon (Bavel) to Riblah; and they gave judgment upon him.

7 And they slew the sons of Zedekiah (Tsidkiyahu) before his eyes, and put out the eyes of Zedekiah (Tsidkiyahu), and bound him with fetters of brass, and carried him to Babylon (Bavel).

8 And in the fifth month, on the seventh day of the month, which is the nineteenth year of King Nebuchad-nezzar king of Babylon (Bavel), came Nebuzaradan, captain of the guard, a servant of the king of Babylon (Bavel), unto Jerusalem (Yerushalayim).

9 And he burnt the house of יהוה, and the king's house, and all the houses of Jerusalem (Yerushalayim), and every great man's house burnt he with fire.

10 And all the army of the Chaldees, that were with the captain of the guard, broke down the walls of Jerusalem (Yerushalayim) round about.

11 Now the rest of the people that were left in the city, and the fugitives that fell away to the king of Babylon (Bavel), with the remnant of the multitude, did Nebuzaradan the captain of the guard carry away.

12 But the captain of the guard left of the poor of the land to be vinedressers and husbandmen.

13 And the pillars of brass that were in the house of יהוה, and the bases, and the brasen sea that was in the house of יהוה, did the Chaldees break in pieces, and carried the brass of them to Babylon (Bavel).

14 And the pots, and the shovels, and the snuffers, and the spoons, and all the vessels of brass wherewith they ministered, took they away.

15 And the firepans, and the bowls, and such things as were of gold, in gold, and of silver, in silver, the captain of the guard took away.

16 The two pillars, one sea, and the bases which Solomon (Shelomoh) had made for the house of יהוה; the brass of all these vessels was without weight.

17 The height of the one pillar was eighteen cubits, and the chapiter upon it was brass; and the height of the chapiter three cubits; and the wreathen work, and pomegranates upon the chapiter round about, all of brass; and like unto these had the second pillar with wreathen work.

18 And the captain of the guard took Serayah the chief priest (kohen), and Zephaniah (Tsefanyahu) the second priest (kohen), and the three keepers of the door.

19 And out of the city he took an officer that was set over the men of war, and five men of them that were in the king's presence, which were found in the city, and the principal scribe of the army, which mustered the people of the land, and threescore men of the people of the land that were found in the city.

20 And Nebuzaradan captain of the guard took these, and brought them to the king of Babylon (Bavel) to Riblah.

21 And the king of Babylon (Bavel) smote them, and slew them at Riblah in the land of Hamath. So Judah (Yehudah) was carried away out of their land.

22 And as for the people that remained in the land of Judah (Yehudah), whom Nebuchadnezzar king of Babylon (Bavel) had left, even over them he made Gedalyahu the son of Ahikam, the son of Shaphan, ruler.

23 And when all the captains of the armies, they and their men, heard that the king of Babylon (Bavel) had made Gedalyahu governor, there came to Gedalyahu to Mizpah, even Yishmael the son of Netanyah, and Yochanan the son of Careah, and Serayah the son of Tanhumeth the Netophathite, and Yaazanyahu the son of a Maachathite, they and their men.

24 And Gedalyahu sware to them, and to their men, and said unto them, Fear not to be the servants of the Chaldees; dwell in the land, and serve the king of Babylon (Bavel); and it shall be well with you.

25 But it came to pass in the seventh month, that Yishmael the son of Netanyah, the son of Elishama, of the seed royal, came, and ten men with him, and smote Gedalyahu, that he died, and the Jews (Yehudim) and the Chaldees that were with him at Mizpah.

26 And all the people, both small and great, and the captains of the armies, arose, and came to Egypt (Mitsrayim) for they were afraid of the Chaldees.

27 And it came to pass in the seven and thirtieth year of the captivity of Yehoyaqim king of Judah (Yehudah), in the twelfth month, on the seven and twentieth day of the month, that Evil-Merodach king of Babylon (Bavel) in the year that he began to reign did lift up the head of Yehoyaqim king of Judah (Yehudah) out of prison;

28 And he spake kindly to him, and set his throne above the throne of the kings that were with him in Babylon (Bavel);

29 And changed his prison garments; and he did eat bread continually before him all the days of his life.

30 And his allowance was a continual allowance given him of the king, a daily rate for every day, all the days of his life.

1 CHRONICLES
DIVREY HAYAMIM 1
דִּבְרֵי הַיָּמִים א
(Annals of Time)

1 Adam, Sheth, Enosh,
2 Kenan, Mahalaleel, Jared (Yered),
3 Henoch, Methuselah, Lamech,
4 Noach, Shem, Ham, and Japheth (Yefet).
5 The sons of Japheth (Yefet): Gomer, and Magog, and Madai, and Yawan, and Tubal, and Meshech, and Tiras.
6 And the sons of Gomer: Ashchenaz, and Riphath, and Togarmah.
7 And the sons of Yawan: Elishah, and Tarshish, Kittim, and Dodanim.
8 The sons of Ham: Cush, and Mitsrayim, Put, and Canaan.
9 And the sons of Cush: Seba, and Havilah, and Sabta, and Raamah, and Sabtecha. And the sons of Raamah; Sheva, and Dedan.
10 And Cush begat Nimrod; he began to be mighty upon the earth.
11 And Mitsrayim begat Ludim, and Anamim, and Lehabim, and Naphtuhim,
12 And Pathrusim, and Casluhim, (of whom came the Philistines,) and Caphthorim.
13 And Canaan begat Zidon his firstborn, and Heth,
14 The Yevusi also, and the Amorite, and the Girgashite,
15 And the Hivite, and the Arkite, and the Sinite,
16 And the Arvadite, and the Zemarite, and the Hamathite.
17 The sons of Shem: Elam, and Asshur, and Arphaxad, and Lud, and Aram, and Uz, and Hul, and Gether, and Meshech.
18 And Arphaxad begat Shelah, and Shelah begat Eber.
19 And unto Eber were born two sons: the name of the one was Peleg, because in his days the earth was divided; and his brother's name was Yoktan.
20 And Yoktan begat Almodad, and Sheleph, and Hazarmaveth, and Yerach,
21 Hadoram also, and Uzal, and Diklah,
22 And Ebal, and Abimael, and Sheva,
23 And Ophir, and Havilah, and Yovav. All these were the sons of Yoktan.

24 Shem, Arphaxad, Shelah,
25 Eber, Peleg, Reu,
26 Serug, Nahor, Terah,
27 Avram, the same is Avraham.
28 The sons of Avraham: Isaac (Yitschaq), and Yishmael.
29 These are their generations: The firstborn of Yishmael, Nebaioth; then Kedar, and Adbeel, and Mibsam,
30 Mishma, and Dumah, Massa, Hadad, and Tema,
31 Yetur, Naphish, and Kedemah. These are the sons of Yishmael.
32 Now the sons of Keturah, Avraham's concubine: she bare Zimran, and Yokshan, and Medan, and Midian, and Ishbak, and Shuah. And the sons of Yokshan: Sheva, and Dedan.
33 And the sons of Midian: Ephah, and Epher, and Henoch, and Abida, and Eldaah. All these are the sons of Keturah.
34 And Avraham begat Isaac (Yitschaq). The sons of Isaac (Yitschaq): Esaw and Yisrael.
35 The sons of Esaw: Eliphaz, Reuel, and Yeush, and Yalam, and Korah (Qorach).
36 The sons of Eliphaz: Teman, and Omar, Zephi, and Gatam, Kenaz, and Timna, and Amalek.
37 The sons of Reuel: Nahath, Zerah, Shammah, and Mizzah.
38 And the sons of Seir: Lotan, and Shobal, and Zibeon, and Anah, and Dishon, and Ezer, and Dishan.
39 And the sons of Lotan: Hori, and Homam; and Timna was Lotan's sister.
40 The sons of Shobal: Alian, and Manahath, and Ebal, Shephi, and Onam. And the sons of Zibeon: Ayah, and Anah.
41 The sons of Anah: Dishon. And the sons of Dishon: Amram, and Eshban, and Ithran, and Cheran.
42 The sons of Ezer: Bilhan, and Zavan, and Yaakan. The sons of Dishan: Uz, and Aran.
43 Now these are the kings that reigned in the land of Edom before any king reigned over the children of Yisrael: Bela the son of Beor; and the name of his city was Dinhabah.
44 And when Bela was dead, Yovav the son of Zerah of Bozrah reigned in his stead.
45 And when Yovav was dead, Husham of the land of the Temanites reigned in his stead.
46 And when Husham was dead, Hadad the

son of Bedad, which smote Midian in the field of Moav, reigned in his stead; and the name of his city was Avith.

47 And when Hadad was dead, Samlah of Masrekah reigned in his stead.

48 And when Samlah was dead, Shaul of Rehoboth by the river reigned in his stead.

49 And when Shaul was dead, Baalhanan the son of Achbor reigned in his stead.

50 And when Baalhanan was dead, Hadad reigned in his stead; and the name of his city was Pai; and his wife's name was Mehetabel, the daughter of Matred, the daughter of Mey Zahav.

51 Hadad died also. And the dukes of Edom were: duke Timnah, duke Alyah, duke Yetet,

52 Duke Aholibamah, duke Elah, duke Pinon,

53 Duke Kenaz, duke Teman, duke Mibzar,

54 Duke Magdiel, duke Iram. These are the dukes of Edom.

2 These are the sons of Yisrael: Reuven, Shimon, Lewi, and Judah (Yehudah), Yissaskhar, and Zevulun,

2 Dan, Joseph (Yosef), and Benjamin (Binyamin), Naftali, Gad, and Asher.

3 The sons of Judah (Yehudah): Er, and Onan, and Shelah, which three were born unto him of the daughter of Shua the Canaanitess. And Er, the firstborn of Judah (Yehudah), was evil in the sight of יהוה; and He slew him.

4 And Tamar his daughter in law bare him Pharez and Zerah. All the sons of Judah (Yehudah) were five.

5 The sons of Pharez: Hezron, and Hamul.

6 And the sons of Zerah: Zimri, and Ethan, and Heman, and Calcol, and Dara; five of them in all.

7 And the sons of Carmi: Achar, the troubler of Yisrael, who transgressed in the thing accursed.

8 And the sons of Ethan: Azaryah.

9 The sons also of Hezron, that were born unto him: Yerachmeel, and Ram, and Chelubai.

10 And Ram begat Amminadab; and Amminadab begat Nahshon, prince of the children of Judah (Yehudah);

11 And Nahshon begat Salma, and Salma begat Boaz,

12 And Boaz begat Oved, and Oved begat Jesse (Yishai),

13 And Jesse (Yishai) begat his firstborn Eliav, and Avinadav the second, and Shimma the third,

14 Nethaneel the fourth, Raddai the fifth,

15 Ozem the sixth, Dawid the seventh;

16 Whose sisters were Zeruyah, and Avigail. And the sons of Zeruyah; Avishai, and Yoav, and Asahel, three.

17 And Avigail bare Amasa; and the father of Amasa was Yeter the Ismaelite (Yishmaeli).

18 And Caleb the son of Hezron begat children of Azubah his wife, and of Yeriot; her sons are these: Yesher, and Shobab, and Ardon.

19 And when Azubah was dead, Caleb took unto him Ephrath, which bare him Hur.

20 And Hur begat Uri, and Uri begat Bezaleel.

21 And afterward Hezron went in to the daughter of Machir the father of Gilad, whom he married when he was threescore years old; and she bare him Segub.

22 And Segub begat Yair, who had three and twenty cities in the land of Gilad.

23 And he took Geshur, and Aram, with the towns of Yair, from them, with Kenath, and the towns thereof, even threescore cities. All these belonged to the sons of Machir the father of Gilad.

24 And after that Hezron was dead in Calebephratah, then Aviyah Hezron's wife bare him Ashur the father of Tekoa.

25 And the sons of Yerachmeel the firstborn of Hezron were, Ram the firstborn, and Bunah, and Oren, and Ozem, and Achiyah.

26 Yerachmeel had also another wife, whose name was Atarah; she was the mother of Onam.

27 And the sons of Ram the firstborn of Yerachmeel were, Maaz, and Yamin, and Eker.

28 And the sons of Onam were, Shammai, and Yada. And the sons of Shammai; Nadav, and Abishur.

29 And the name of the wife of Abishur was Avihail, and she bare him Ahban, and Molid.

30 And the sons of Nadav: Seled, and Appaim; but Seled died without children.

31 And the sons of Appaim: Ishi. And the sons of Ishi: Sheshan. And the children of Sheshan: Ahlai.

32 And the sons of Yada the brother of Shammai: Yeter, and Yonatan; and Yeter died without children.

33 And the sons of Yonatan: Peleth, and Zaza. These were the sons of Yerachmeel.

34 Now Sheshan had no sons, but daughters.

And Sheshan had a servant, an Egyptian (Mitsri), whose name was Yarha.

35 And Sheshan gave his daughter to Yarha his servant to wife; and she bare him Attai.

36 And Attai begat Nathan, and Nathan begat Zabad,

37 And Zabad begat Ephlal, and Ephlal begat Oved,

38 And Oved begat Yehu, and Yehu begat Azaryah,

39 And Azaryah begat Helez, and Helez begat Eleasah,

40 And Eleasah begat Sisamai, and Sisamai begat Shallum,

41 And Shallum begat Yekamyah, and Yekamyah begat Elishama.

42 Now the sons of Caleb the brother of Yerachmeel were, Mesha his firstborn, who was the father of Ziph; and the sons of Mareshah the father of Hebron.

43 And the sons of Hebron: Korah (Qorach), and Tappuah, and Rekem, and Shema.

44 And Shema begat Raham, the father of Yorkoam; and Rekem begat Shammai.

45 And the son of Shammai was Maon; and Maon was the father of Bethzur.

46 And Ephah, Caleb's concubine, bare Haran, and Moza, and Gazez; and Haran begat Gazez.

47 And the sons of Yahdai: Regem, and Yotam, and Geshan, and Pelet, and Ephah, and Shaaph.

48 Maachah, Caleb's concubine, bare Sheber, and Tirhanah.

49 She bare also Shaaph the father of Madmannah, Sheva the father of Machbenah, and the father of Gibea; and the daughter of Caleb was Achsah.

50 These were the sons of Caleb the son of Hur, the firstborn of Ephratah; Shobal the father of Qiryat-Yearim,

51 Salma the father of Bethlehem (Beit-Lechem), Hareph the father of Beit-Gader.

52 And Shobal the father of Kirya-Yearim had sons; Haroeh, and half of the Manahethites.

53 And the families of Kirya-Yearim: the Ithrites, and the Puhites, and the Shumathites, and the Mishraites; of them came the Zareathites, and the Eshtaulites.

54 The sons of Salma: Bethlehem (Beit-Lechem), and the Netophathites, Ataroth, the house of Yoav, and half of the Manahethites, the Zorites.

55 And the families of the scribes which dwelt at Yabets: the Tirathites, the Shimeathites, and Suchathites. These are the Kenites that came of Hemath, the father of the house of Rechab.

3 Now these were the sons of Dawid, who were born unto him in Hebron; the firstborn Amnon, of Ahinoam the Yitsreelitess; the second Daniel, of Avigail the Carmelitess.

2 The third, Avshalom the son of Maachah the daughter of Talmai king of Geshur; the fourth, Adoniyah the son of Haggith;

3 The fifth, Shefatyah of Abital; the sixth, Ithream by Eglah his wife.

4 These six were born unto him in Hebron; and there he reigned seven years and six months, and in Jerusalem (Yerushalayim) he reigned thirty-three years.

5 And these were born unto him in Jerusalem (Yerushalayim): Shimea, and Shobab, and Nathan, and Solomon (Shelomoh), four, of Bathshua the daughter of Ammiel.

6 Ibhar also, and Elishama, and Eliphelet,

7 And Nogah, and Nepheg, and Yafiya,

8 And Elishama, and Eliada, and Eliphelet, nine.

9 These were all the sons of Dawid, besides the sons of the concubines, and Tamar their sister.

10 And Solomon (Shelomoh)'s son was Rehoboam (Rechavam), Aviyah his son, Asa his son, Yehoshafat his son,

11 Yoram his son, Achazyahu his son, Yoash his son,

12 Amazyah his son, Azaryah his son, Yotam his son,

13 Achaz his son, Hezekiah (Chizki-yahu) his son, Menashsheh his son,

14 Amon his son, Josiah (Yoshiyahu) his son.

15 And the sons of Josiah (Yoshiyahu), were, the firstborn Yochanan, the second Yehoyaqim, the third Zedekiah (Tsidkiyahu), the fourth Shallum.

16 And the sons of Yehoyaqim: Yekhonyah his son, Zedekiah (Tsidkiyahu) his son.

17 And the sons of Yekhonyah: Assir, Salathiel his son,

18 Malchiram also, and Pedayah, and Shenazar, Yekamyah, Hoshama, and Nedavyah.

19 And the sons of Pedayah were Zerubbabel and Shimei; and the sons of Zerubbabel: Meshullam, and Chananyah, and Shelomith their sister;

20 And Hashubah, and Ohel, and Verekhyah, and Chasadyah, Yushav-Chesed, five.

21 And the sons of Chananyah: Pelatyah, and A51Jeshaiah (Yeshayah); the sons of Refayah, the sons of Arnan, the sons of Obadiah (Ovadyah), the sons of Shekhanyah.

22 And the sons of Shekhanyah: Shemayah; and the sons of Shemayah: Hattush, and Igeal, and Baryah, and Nearyah, and Shaphat, six.

23 And the sons of Nearyah: Elioenai, and Hezekiah (Chizkiyahu), and Azrikam, three.

24 And the sons of Elioenai were Hodayah, and Elijahhib, and Pelayah, and Akkub, and Yochanan, and Dalayah, and Anani, seven.

4 The sons of Judah (Yehudah): Pharez, Hezron, and Carmi, and Hur, and Shobal.

2 And Reayah the son of Shobal begat Yachat; and Yachat begat Ahumai, and Lahad. These are the families of the Zorathites.

3 And these were of the father of Etam: Yitsreel, and Ishma, and Idbash; and the name of their sister was Hazelelponi;

4 And Penuel the father of Gedor, and Ezer the father of Hushah. These are the sons of Hur, the firstborn of Ephratah, the father of Bethlehem (Beit-Lechem).

5 And Ashur the father of Tekoa had two wives, Helah and Naarah.

6 And Naarah bare him Ahuzam, and Hepher, and Temeni, and Haahashtari. These were the sons of Naarah.

7 And the sons of Helah were, Zereth, and Tsochar, and Ethnan.

8 And Coz begat Anub, and Zobebah, and the families of Aharhel the son of Harum.

9 And Yabets was more honorable than his brethren; and his mother called his name Yabets, saying, "Because I bare him with sorrow."

10 And Yabets called on the God of Israel (Elohei Yisrael), saying, "Oh that You wouldest bless me indeed, and enlarge my coast, and that Your hand might be with me, and that You wouldest keep me from evil, that it may not grieve me!" And God (Elohim) granted him that which he requested.

11 And Chelub the brother of Shuah begat Mehir, who was the father of Eshton.

12 And Eshton begat Beit-Rapha, and Paseah, and Tehinnah the father of Irnahash. These are the men of Rechah.

13 And the sons of Kenaz: Othniel, and Serayah; and the sons of Othniel: Hathath.

14 And Meonothai begat Ophrah; and Serayah begat Yoav, the father of the valley of Charashim; for they were craftsmen.

15 And the sons of Caleb the son of Yefunneh: Iru, Elah, and Naam; and the sons of Elah, even Kenaz.

16 And the sons of Yehallelel: Ziph, and Ziphah, Tiria, and Asareel.

17 And the sons of Ezra were Yeter, and Mered, and Epher, and Yalon; and she bare Miryam, and Shammai, and Ishbah the father of Eshtemoa.

18 And his wife Yehudiyah bare Yered the father of Gedor, and Heber the father of Socho, and Yekutiel the father of Zanoach. And these are the sons of Bityah the daughter of Pharaoh (Paroh), whom Mered took.

19 And the sons of his wife Hodiyah the sister of Naham, the father of Keilah the Garmite, and Eshtemoa the Maachathite.

20 And the sons of Shimon were, Amnon, and Rinnah, Benhanan, and Tilon. And the sons of Ishi were, Zoheth, and Benzoheth.

21 The sons of Shelah the son of Judah (Yehudah) were Er the father of Lecah, and Laadah the father of Mareshah, and the families of the house of them that wrought fine linen, of the house of Ashbea,

22 And Yokim, and the men of Chozeba, and Yoash, and Saraph, who had the dominion in Moav, and Yashuvi-Lechem. And these are ancient things.

23 These were the potters, and those that dwelt among plants and hedges; there they dwelt with the king for his work.

24 The sons of Shimon were Nemuel, and Yamin, Yariv, Zerah, and Shaul;

25 Shallum his son, Mibsam his son, Mishma his son.

26 And the sons of Mishma: Hamuel his son, Zacchur his son, Shimei his son.

27 And Shimei had sixteen sons and six daughters; but his brethren had not many children, neither did all their family multiply, like to the children of Judah (Yehudah).

28 And they dwelt at Beer-Sheva, and Moladah, and Hazarshual,

29 And at Bilhah, and at Ezem, and at Tolad,

30 And at Bethuel, and at Hormah, and at Ziklag,

31 And at Beit-Markavot, and Hazarsusim, and

at Beit-Biri, and at Shaaraim. These were their cities unto the reign of Dawid.

32 And their villages were Etam, and Ain, Rimmon, and Tochen, and Ashan, five cities;

33 And all their villages that were round about the same cities, unto the Baal. These were their habitations, and their genealogy.

34 And Meshobab, and Yamlekh, and Yoshah the son of Amazyah,

35 And Yoel, and Yehu the son of Yoshivyah, the son of Serayah, the son of Asiel,

36 And Elioenai, and Yaakovah, and Yeshochayah, and Asayah, and Adiel, and Yesimiel, and Benayah,

37 And Ziza the son of Shiphi, the son of Allon, the son of Yedayah, the son of Shimri, the son of Shemayah;

38 These mentioned by their names were princes in their families; and the house of their fathers increased greatly.

39 And they went to the entrance of Gedor, even unto the east side of the valley, to seek pasture for their flocks.

40 And they found fat pasture and good, and the land was wide, and quiet, and peaceable; for they of Ham had dwelt there of old.

41 And these written by name came in the days of Hezekiah (Chizkiyahu) king of Judah (Yehudah), and smote their tents, and the habitations that were found there, and destroyed them utterly unto this day, and dwelt in their rooms: because there was pasture there for their flocks.

42 And some of them, even of the sons of Shimon, five hundred men, went to mount Seir, having for their captains Pelatyah, and Nearyah, and Refayah, and Uzziel, the sons of Ishi.

43 And they smote the rest of the Amalekites that were escaped, and dwelt there unto this day.

5 Now the sons of Reuven the firstborn of Yisrael - he was the firstborn; but, forasmuch as he defiled his father's bed, his birthright was given unto the sons of Joseph (Yosef) the son of Yisrael; and the genealogy is not to be reckoned after the birthright.

2 For Judah (Yehudah) prevailed above his brethren, and of him came the chief ruler; but the birthright was Joseph (Yosef)'s;

3 The sons, I say, of Reuven the firstborn of Yisrael were Hanoch, and Pallu, Hezron, and Carmi.

4 The sons of Yoel: Shemayah his son, Gog his son, Shimei his son,

5 Mikhah his son, Reayah his son, Baal his son,

6 Beerah his son, whom Tilgathpilneser king of Assyria (Ashshur) carried away captive. He was prince of the Reubenites (Reuveni).

7 And his brethren by their families, when the genealogy of their generations was reckoned, were the chief, Yeiel, and [A65]Zechariah (Zekharyahu),

8 And Bela the son of Azaz, the son of Shema, the son of Yoel, who dwelt in Aroer, even unto Nebo and Baal-Meon.

9 And eastward he inhabited unto the entering in of the wilderness from the river Euphrates, because their cattle were multiplied in the land of Gilad.

10 And in the days of Shaul they made war with the Hagarites, who fell by their hand; and they dwelt in their tents throughout all the east land of Gilad.

11 And the children of Gad dwelt opposite them, in the land of Bashan unto Salchah;

12 Yoel the chief, and Shapham the next, and Yaanai, and Shaphat in Bashan.

13 And their brethren of the house of their fathers were: Mikhael, and Meshullam, and Sheva, and Yorai, and Yakan, and Zia, and Heber, seven.

14 These are the children of Avihail the son of Huri, the son of Yaroach, the son of Gilad, the son of Mikhael, the son of Yeshishai, the son of Yahdo, the son of Buz;

15 Ahi the son of Avdiel, the son of Guni, chief of the house of their fathers.

16 And they dwelt in Gilad in Bashan, and in her towns, and in all the suburbs of Sharon, upon their borders.

17 All these were reckoned by genealogies in the days of Yotam king of Judah (Yehudah), and in the days of Jeroboam (Yarovam) king of Yisrael.

18 The sons of Reuven, and the Gadites, and half the tribe of Menashsheh, of valiant men, men able to bear buckler and sword, and to shoot with bow, and skilful in war, were four and forty thousand seven hundred and threescore, that went out to the war.

19 And they made war with vhe Hagarites, with Yetur, and Nephish, and Nodab.

20 And they were helped against them, and the

Hagarites were delivered into their hand, and all that were with them: for they cried to God (Elohim) in the battle, and he was intreated of them; because they put their trust in him.

21 And they took away their cattle; of their camels fifty thousand, and of sheep two hundred and fifty thousand, and of asses two thousand, and of men a hundred thousand.

22 For there fell down many slain, because the war was of God (Elohim). And they dwelt in their steads until the captivity.

23 And the children of the half tribe of Menashsheh dwelt in the land. They increased from Bashan unto Baal-Chermon and Senir, and unto Mount Chermon.

24 And these were the heads of the house of their fathers, even Epher, and Ishi, and Eliel, and Azriel, and Jeremiah (Yirmeyahu), and Hodavyah, and Yahdiel, mighty men of valour, famous men, and heads of the house of their fathers.

25 And they transgressed against the God (Elohim) of their fathers, and went a whoring after the gods (elohim) of the people of the land, whom God (Elohim) destroyed before them.

26 And the God of Israel (Elohei Yisrael) stirred up the spirit of Pul king of Assyria (Ashshur), and the spirit of Tilgathpilneser king of Assyria (Ashshur), and he carried them away, even the Reubenites (Reuveni), and the Gadites, and the half tribe of Menashsheh, and brought them unto Halah, and Habor, and Hara, and to the river Gozan, unto this day.

6 The sons of Lewi: Gershon, Kohath, and Merari.

2 And the sons of Kohath: Amram, Izhar, and Hebron, and Uzziel.

3 And the children of Amram: Aaron (Aharon), and Moses (Mosheh), and Miryam. The sons also of Aaron (Aharon): Nadav, and Avihu, Eleazar, and Ithamar.

4 Eleazar begat Phinehas, Phinehas begat Avishua,

5 And Avishua begat Bukki, and Bukki begat Uzzi,

6 And Uzzi begat Zerahyah, and Zerahyah begat Meraioth,

7 Meraioth begat Amaryah, and Amaryah begat Ahitub,

8 And Ahitub begat Zadok, and Zadok begat Ahimaaz,

9 And Ahimaaz begat Azaryah, and Azaryah begat Yochanan,

10 And Yochanan begat Azaryah, (he it is that executed the priest's office (kehunnah) in the temple that Solomon (Shelomoh) built in Jerusalem (Yerushalayim):)

11 And Azaryah begat Amaryah, and Amaryah begat Ahitub,

12 And Ahitub begat Zadok, and Zadok begat Shallum,

13 And Shallum begat Chilqiyah, and Chilqiyah begat Azaryah,

14 And Azaryah begat Serayah, and Serayah begat Yehotsadak,

15 And Yehotsadak went into captivity, when יהוה carried away Judah (Yehudah) and Jerusalem (Yerushalayim) by the hand of Nebuchanezzar.

16 The sons of Lewi: Gershom, Kohath, and Merari.

17 And these be the names of the sons of Gershom: Libni, and Shimei.

18 And the sons of Kohath were: Amram, and Izhar, and Hebron, and Uzziel.

19 The sons of Merari: Mahli, and Mushi. And these are the families of the Levites (Lewiyim) according to their fathers.

20 Of Gershom: Libni his son, Yachat his son, Zimmah his son,

21 Yoach his son, Iddo his son, Zerah his son, Yeaterai his son.

22 The sons of Kohath: Amminadab his son, Korah (Qorach) his son, Assir his son,

23 Elkanah his son, and Ebiasaph his son, and Assir his son,

24 Tahath his son, Uriel his son, Uzziyah his son, and Shaul his son.

25 And the sons of Elkanah: Amasai, and Ahimoth.

26 As for Elkanah, the sons of Elkanah: Zophai his son, and Nahath his son,

27 Eliav his son, Yeroham his son, Elkanah his son.

28 And the sons of Shemuel: the firstborn Vashni, and Aviyah.

29 The sons of Merari: Mahli, Libni his son, Shimei his son, Uzza his son,

30 Shimea his son, Chaggiyah his son, Asayah his son.

31 And these are they whom Dawid set over the service of song in the house of יהוה, after that

the ark had rest.

32 And they ministered before the dwelling place of the tabernacle of the congregation with singing, until Solomon (Shelomoh) had built the house of יהוה in Jerusalem (Yerushalayim); and then they waited on their office according to their order.

33 And these are they that waited with their children. Of the sons of the Kohathites: Heman a singer, the son of Yoel, the son of Shemuel,

34 The son of Elkanah, the son of Yeroham, the son of Eliel, the son of Toah,

35 The son of Zuph, the son of Elkanah, the son of Mahath, the son of Amasai,

36 The son of Elkanah, the son of Yoel, the son of Azaryah, the son of Zephaniah (Tsefanyahu),

37 The son of Tahath, the son of Assir, the son of Ebiasaph, the son of Korah (Qorach),

38 The son of Izhar, the son of Kohath, the son of Lewi, the son of Yisrael.

39 And his brother Asaph, who stood on his right hand, even Asaph the son of Berakhyah, the son of Shimea,

40 The son of Mikhael, the son of Baaseyah, the son of Malkiyah,

41 The son of Ethni, the son of Zerah, the son of Adayah,

42 The son of Ethan, the son of Zimmah, the son of Shimei,

43 The son of Yachat, the son of Gershom, the son of Lewi.

44 And their brethren the sons of Merari stood on the left hand: Ethan the son of Kishi, the son of Avdi, the son of Malluch,

45 The son of Chashavyah, the son of Amazyah, the son of Chilqiyah,

46 The son of Amzi, the son of Bani, the son of Shamer,

47 The son of Mahli, the son of Mushi, the son of Merari, the son of Lewi.

48 Their brethren also the Levites (Lewiyim) were appointed unto all manner of service of the tabernacle of the house of God (Elohim).

49 But Aaron (Aharon) and his sons offered upon the altar of the burnt offering, and on the altar of incense, and were appointed for all the work of the place most holy, and to make an atonement for Yisrael, according to all that Moses (Mosheh) the servant of God (Elohim) had commanded.

50 And these are the sons of Aaron (Aharon):

Eleazar his son, Phinehas his son, Avishua his son,

51 Bukki his son, Uzzi his son, Zerahyah his son,

52 Meraioth his son, Amaryah his son, Ahitub his son,

53 Zadok his son, Ahimaaz his son.

54 Now these are their dwelling places throughout their castles in their coasts, of the sons of Aaron (Aharon), of the families of the Kohathites, for theirs was the lot.

55 And they gave them Hebron in the land of Judah (Yehudah), and the suburbs thereof round about it.

56 But the fields of the city, and the villages thereof, they gave to Caleb the son of Yefunneh.

57 And to the sons of Aaron (Aharon) they gave the cities of Judah (Yehudah), namely: Hebron, the city of refuge, and Libnah with her suburbs, and Yattir, and Eshtemoa, with their suburbs,

58 And Hilen with her suburbs, Debir with her suburbs,

59 And Ashan with her suburbs, and Beit-Shemesh with her suburbs.

60 And out of the tribe of Benjamin (Binyamin): Geba with her suburbs, and Alemeth with her suburbs, and Anathoth with her suburbs. All their cities throughout their families were thirteen cities.

61 And unto the sons of Kohath, who were left of the family of that tribe, were cities given out of the half tribe, namely, out of the half tribe of Menashsheh, by lot, ten cities.

62 And to the sons of Gershom throughout their families out of the tribe of Yissaskhar, and out of the tribe of Asher, and out of the tribe of Naftali, and out of the tribe of Menashsheh in Bashan, thirteen cities.

63 Unto the sons of Merari were given by lot, throughout their families, out of the tribe of Reuven, and out of the tribe of Gad, and out of the tribe of Zevulun, twelve cities.

64 And the children of Yisrael gave to the Levites (Lewiyim) these cities with their suburbs.

65 And they gave by lot out of the tribe of the children of Judah (Yehudah), and out of the tribe of the children of Shimon, and out of the tribe of the children of Benjamin (Binyamin), these cities, which are called by their names.

66 And the residue of the families of the sons

of Kohath had cities of their coasts out of the tribe of Efrayim.

67 And they gave unto them, of the cities of refuge, Shechem in Mount Efrayim with her suburbs; they gave also Gezer with her suburbs,

68 And Yokmeam with her suburbs, and Beit-Choron with her suburbs,

69 And Ayalon with her suburbs, and Gathrimmon with her suburbs.

70 And out of the half tribe of Menashsheh: Aner with her suburbs, and Bileam with her suburbs, for the family of the remnant of the sons of Kohath.

71 Unto the sons of Gershom were given out of the family of the half tribe of Menashsheh, Golan in Bashan with her suburbs, and Ashtaroth with her suburbs.

72 And out of the tribe of Yissaskhar: Kedesh with her suburbs, Daberath with her suburbs,

73 And Ramot with her suburbs, and Anem with her suburbs.

74 And out of the tribe of Asher: Mashal with her suburbs, and Avdon with her suburbs,

75 And Hukok with her suburbs, and Rehob with her suburbs.

76 And out of the tribe of Naftali: Kedesh in Galilee with her suburbs, and Hammon with her suburbs, and Qiryatayim with her suburbs.

77 Unto the rest of the children of Merari were given out of the tribe of Zevulun, Rimmon with her suburbs, Tabor with her suburbs.

78 And on the other side Jordan (Yarden) by Yericho, on the east side of Jordan (Yarden), were given them out of the tribe of Reuven, Bezer in the wilderness with her suburbs, and Yahzah with her suburbs,

79 Kedemoth also with her suburbs, and Mephaath with her suburbs.

80 And out of the tribe of Gad: Ramot in Gilad with her suburbs, and Mahanaim with her suburbs,

81 And Heshbon with her suburbs, and Yazer with her suburbs.

7 Now the sons of Yissaskhar were Tola, and Puah, Yashuv, and Shimron, four.

2 And the sons of Tola: Uzzi, and Refayah, and Yeriel, and Yachmai, and Yivsam, and Shemuel, heads of their father's house, of Tola; they were valiant men of might in their generations; whose number was in the days of Dawid two and twenty thousand and six hundred.

3 And the sons of Uzz: Izrahyah; and the sons of Izrahyah: Mikhael, and Ovadyah, and Yoel, Ishyah, five. All of them chief men.

4 And with them, by their generations, after the house of their fathers, were bands of soldiers for war, six and thirty thousand men; for they had many wives and sons.

5 And their brethren among all the families of Yissaskhar were valiant men of might, reckoned in all by their genealogies fourscore and seven thousand.

6 The sons of Benjamin (Binyamin): Bela, and Becher, and Yediael, three.

7 And the sons of Bela: Ezbon, and Uzzi, and Uzziel, and Yerimot, and Iri, five; heads of the house of their fathers, mighty men of valour; and were reckoned by their genealogies twenty and two thousand and thirty and four.

8 And the sons of Becher; Zemira, and Yoash, and Eliezer, and Elioenai, and Omri, and Yerimot, and Aviyah, and Anathoth, and Alameth. All these are the sons of Becher.

9 And the number of them, after their genealogy by their generations, heads of the house of their fathers, mighty men of valour, was twenty thousand and two hundred.

10 The sons also of Yediael: Bilhan; and the sons of Bilhan: Yeush, and Benjamin (Binyamin), and Ehud, and Chenaanah, and Zethan, and Tharshish, and Ahishahar.

11 All these the sons of Yediael, by the heads of their fathers, mighty men of valour, were seventeen thousand and two hundred soldiers, fit to go out for war and battle.

12 Shuppim also, and Huppim, the children of Ir, and Hushim, the sons of Aher.

13 The sons of Naftali: Yahziel, and Guni, and Yezer, and Shallum, the sons of Bilhah.

14 The sons of Menashsheh: Ashriel, whom she bare; (but his concubine the Aramitess bare Machir the father of Gilad:

15 And Machir took as wife the sister of Huppim and Shuppim, whose sister's name was Maachah;) and the name of the second was Zelophehad; and Zelophehad had daughters.

16 And Maachah the wife of Machir bare a son, and she called his name Peresh; and the name of his brother was Sheresh; and his sons were Ulam and Rakem.

17 And the sons of Ulam: Bedan. These were the sons of Gilad, the son of Machir, the son of

Menashsheh.

18 And his sister Hammoleketh bare Ishod, and Aviezer, and Mahalah.

19 And the sons of Shemida were Ahian, and Shechem, and Likhi, and Aniam.

20 And the sons of Efrayim: Shuthelah, and Bered his son, and Tahath his son, and Eladah his son, and Tahath his son,

21 And Zabad his son, and Shuthelah his son, and Ezer, and Elead, whom the men of Gath that were born in that land slew, because they came down to take away their cattle.

22 And Efrayim their father mourned many days, and his brethren came to comfort him.

23 And when he went in to his wife, she conceived, and bare a son, and he called his name Beriyah, because it went evil with his house.

24 (And his daughter was Sherah, who built Beit-Choron the nether, and the upper, and Uzzensherah.)

25 And Rephah was his son, also Resheph, and Telah his son, and Tahan his son,

26 Laadan his son, Ammihud his son, Elishama his son,

27 Nun his son, Joshua (Yehoshua) his son.

28 And their possessions and habitations were Bethel (Beit-El) and the towns thereof, and eastward Naaran, and westward Gezer, with the towns thereof; Shechem also and the towns thereof, unto Gaza (Azzah) and the towns thereof;

29 And by the borders of the children of Menashsheh, Beit-Shan and her towns, Taanach and her towns, Megiddo and her towns, Dor and her towns. In these dwelt the children of Joseph (Yosef) the son of Yisrael.

30 The sons of Asher: Imnah, and Isuah, and Ishuai, and Beriyah, and Serah their sister.

31 And the sons of Beriyah: Heber, and Malkiel, who is the father of Birzavith.

32 And Heber begat Yaflet, and Shomer, and Hotham, and Shua their sister.

33 And the sons of Yaflet: Pasach, and Bimhal, and Ashvath. These are the children of Yaflet.

34 And the sons of Shamer: Ahi, and Rohgah, Yehubbah, and Aram.

35 And the sons of his brother Helem: Zophah, and Imna, and Shelesh, and Amal.

36 The sons of Zophah: Suah, and Harnepher, and Shual, and Beri, and Imrah,

37 Bezer, and Hod, and Shamma, and Shilshah, and Ithran, and Beera.

38 And the sons of Yeter: Yefunneh, and Pispah, and Ara.

39 And the sons of Ulla: Arah, and Haniel, and Rezia.

40 All these were the children of Asher, heads of their father's house, choice and mighty men of valour, chief of the princes. And the number throughout the genealogy of them that were apt to the war and to battle was twenty and six thousand men.

8 Now Benjamin (Binyamin) begat Bela his firstborn, Ashbel the second, and Aharah the third,

2 Nohah the fourth, and Rapha the fifth.

3 And the sons of Bela were Addar, and Gera, and Avihud,

4 And Avishua, and Naaman, and Ahoah,

5 And Gera, and Shephuphan, and Huram.

6 And these are the sons of Ehud; these are the heads of the fathers of the inhabitants of Geba, and they removed them to Manahath:

7 And Naaman, and Achiyah, and Gera, he removed them, and begat Uzza, and Ahihud.

8 And Shaharaim begat children in the country of Moav, after he had sent them away; Hushim and Baara were his wives.

9 And he begat of Hodesh his wife, Yovav, and Zibia, and Mesha, and Malkam,

10 And Yeuts, and Shachia, and Mirma. These were his sons, heads of the fathers.

11 And of Hushim he begat Avituv, and Elpaal.

12 The sons of Elpaal: Eber, and Misham, and Shamed, who built Ono, and Lod, with the towns thereof;

13 Beriyah also, and Shema, who were heads of the fathers of the inhabitants of Ayalon, who drove away the inhabitants of Gath:

14 And Ahio, Shashak, and Yeremot,

15 And Zevadyahu, and Arad, and Ader,

16 And Mikhael, and Ispah, and Yocha, the sons of Beriyah.

17 And Zevadyahu, and Meshullam, and Hezeki, and Heber,

18 Ishmerai also, and Yizliyah, and Yovav, the sons of Elpaal,

19 And Yakim, and Zikhri, and Zabdi,

20 And Elienai, and Zilthai, and Eliel,

21 And Adayah, and Berayah, and Shimrath, the sons of Shimhi;

22 And Ishpan, and Heber, and Eliel,

23 And Avdon, and Zikhri, and Hanan,

24 And Chananyah, and Elam, and Antotiyah,

25 And Yifdeyah, and Penuel, the sons of Shashak;

26 And Shamsherai, and Sheharyah, and Atalyah,

27 And Yaareshyah, and Eliyah, and Zikhri, the sons of Yeroham.

28 These were heads of the fathers, by their generations, chief men. These dwelt in Jerusalem (Yerushalayim).

29 And at Giveon dwelt the father of Giveon; whose wife's name was Maachah.

30 And his firstborn son Avdon, and Zur, and Kish, and Baal, and Nadav,

31 And Gedor, and Ahio, and Zacher.

32 And Mikloth begat Shimeah. And these also dwelt with their brethren in Jerusalem (Yerushalayim), opposite them.

33 And Ner begat Kish, and Kish begat Shaul, and Shaul begat Yonatan, and Malchishua, and Avinadav, and Eshbaal.

34 And the son of Yonatan was Meribbaal, and Meribbaal begat Mikhah.

35 And the sons of Mikhah were Pithon, and Melech, and Tarea, and Achaz.

36 And Achaz begat Yehoadah, and Yehoadah begat Alemeth, and Azmaveth, and Zimri; and Zimri begat Moza,

37 And Moza begat Binea; Rapha was his son, Eleasah his son, Azel his son.

38 And Azel had six sons, whose names are these, Azrikam, Bocheru, and Yishmael, and Shearyah, and Ovadyah, and Hanan. All these were the sons of Azel.

39 And the sons of Eshek his brother were, Ulam his firstborn, Yehush the second, and Eliphelet the third.

40 And the sons of Ulam were mighty men of valour, archers, and had many sons, and sons' sons, a hundred and fifty. All these are of the sons of Benjamin (Binyamin).

9 So all Yisrael were reckoned by genealogies; and, behold, they were written in the book of the kings of Yisrael and Judah (Yehudah), who were carried away to Babylon (Bavel) for their transgression.

2 Now the first inhabitants that dwelt in their possessions in their cities were, the Yisraelis, the priests (kohanim), Levites (Lewiyim), and the temple servants (netinim).

3 And in Jerusalem (Yerushalayim) dwelt of the children of Judah (Yehudah), and of the children of Benjamin (Binyamin), and of the children of Efrayim, and Menashsheh:

4 Uthai the son of Ammihud, the son of Omri, the son of Imri, the son of Bani, of the children of Pharez the son of Judah (Yehudah).

5 And of the Shilonites: Asayah the firstborn, and his sons.

6 And of the sons of Zerah: Yeuel, and their brethren, six hundred and ninety.

7 And of the sons of Benjamin (Binyamin): Sallu the son of Meshullam, the son of Hodavyah, the son of Hasenuah,

8 And Yivneyah the son of Yeroham, and Elah the son of Uzzi, the son of Mikhri, and Meshullam the son of Shefatyah, the son of Reuel, the son of Yivniyah;

9 And their brethren, according to their generations, nine hundred and fifty and six. All these men were chief of the fathers in the house of their fathers.

10 And of the priests (kohanim): Yedayah, and Yehoyariv, and Yakhin,

11 And Azaryah the son of Chilqiyah, the son of Meshullam, the son of Zadok, the son of Meraioth, the son of Ahitub, the ruler of the house of God (Elohim);

12 And Adayah the son of Yeroham, the son of Pashur, the son of Malkiyah, and Maasiai the son of Adiel, the son of Yachzerah, the son of Meshullam, the son of Meshillemith, the son of Immer;

13 And their brethren, heads of the house of their fathers, a thousand and seven hundred and threescore; very able men for the work of the service of the house of God (Elohim).

14 And of the Levites (Lewiyim): Shemayah the son of Hasshub, the son of Azrikam, the son of Chashavyah, of the sons of Merari;

15 And Bakbakkar, Heresh, and Galal, and Mattanyah the son of Mikhah, the son of Zikhri, the son of Asaph;

16 And Obadiah (Ovadyah) the son of Shemayah, the son of Galal, the son of Yedutun, and Verekhyah the son of Asa, the son of Elkanah, that dwelt in the villages of the Netophathites.

17 And the porters were Shallum, and Akkub, and Talmon, and Ahiman, and their brethren: Shallum was the chief;

18 Who hitherto waited in the king's gate eastward; they were porters in the companies of the children of Lewi.

19 And Shallum the son of Kore, the son of Ebiasaph, the son of Korah (Qorach), and his brethren, of the house of his father, the Korahites, were over the work of the service, keepers of the gates of the tabernacle; and their fathers, being over the host of יהוה, were keepers of the entry.

20 And Phinehas the son of Eleazar was the ruler over them in time past, and יהוה was with him.

21 And Zechariah (Zekharyahu) the son of Meshelemyah was porter of the door of the tabernacle of the congregation.

22 All these which were chosen to be porters in the gates were two hundred and twelve. These were reckoned by their genealogy in their villages, whom Dawid and Shemuel the seer did ordain in their set office.

23 So they and their children had the oversight of the gates of the house of יהוה, namely, the house of the tabernacle, by wards.

24 In four quarters were the porters, toward the east, west, north, and south.

25 And their brethren, who were in their villages, were to come after seven days from time to time with them.

26 For these Levites (Lewiyim), the four chief porters, were in their set office, and were over the chambers and treasuries of the house of God (Elohim).

27 And they lodged round about the house of God (Elohim), because the charge was upon them, and the opening thereof every morning pertained to them.

28 And certain of them had the charge of the ministering vessels, that they should bring them in and out by tale.

29 Some of them also were appointed to oversee the vessels, and all the instruments of the sanctuary, and the fine flour, and the wine, and the oil, and the frankincense, and the spices.

30 And some of the sons of the priests (kohanim) made the ointment of the spices.

31 And Mattityah, one of the Levites (Lewiyim), who was the firstborn of Shallum the Korahite, had the set office over the things that were made in the pans.

32 And other of their brethren, of the sons of the Kohathites, were over the shewbread, to prepare it every Shabbat.

33 And these are the singers, chief of the fathers of the Levites (Lewiyim), who remaining in the chambers were free; for they were employed in that work day and night.

34 These chief fathers of the Levites (Lewiyim) were chief throughout their generations; these dwelt at Jerusalem (Yerushalayim).

35 And in Giveon dwelt the father of Giveon, Yehiel, whose wife's name was Maachah.

36 And his firstborn son Avdon, then Zur, and Kish, and Baal, and Ner, and Nadav,

37 And Gedor, and Ahio, and Zechariah (Zekharyahu), and Mikloth.

38 And Mikloth begat Shimeam. And they also dwelt with their brethren at Jerusalem (Yerushalayim), opposite their brethren.

39 And Ner begat Kish; and Kish begat Shaul; and Shaul begat Yonatan, and Malchishua, and Avinadav, and Eshbaal.

40 And the son of Yonatan was Meribbaal; and Meribbaal begat Micah (Mikhah).

41 And the sons of Micah (Mikhah) were Pithon, and Melech, and Tahrea, and Achaz.

42 And Achaz begat Yarah; and Yarah begat Alemeth, and Azmaveth, and Zimri; and Zimri begat Moza;

43 And Moza begat Binea; and Refayah his son, Eleasah his son, Azel his son.

44 And Azel had six sons, whose names are these: Azrikam, Bocheru, and Yishmael, and Shearyah, and Obadiah (Ovadyah), and Hanan; these were the sons of Azel.

10 Now the Philistines fought against Yisrael; and the men of Yisrael fled from before the Philistines, and fell down slain in Mount Gilboa.

2 And the Philistines followed hard after Shaul, and after his sons; and the Philistines slew Yonatan, and Avinadav, and Malchishua, the sons of Shaul.

3 And the battle went sore against Shaul, and the archers hit him, and he was wounded of the archers.

4 Then said Shaul to his armourbearer, "Draw your sword, and thrust me through therewith; lest these uncircumcised come and abuse me." But his armourbearer would not; for he was sore afraid. So Shaul took a sword, and fell upon it.

5 And when his armourbearer saw that Shaul

was dead, he fell likewise on the sword, and died.

6 So Shaul died, and his three sons, and all his house died together.

7 And when all the men of Yisrael that were in the valley saw that they fled, and that Shaul and his sons were dead, then they forsook their cities, and fled; and the Philistines came and dwelt in them.

8 And it came to pass on the next day, when the Philistines came to strip the slain, that they found Shaul and his sons fallen in Mount Gilboa.

9 And when they had stripped him, they took his head, and his armour, and sent into the land of the Philistines round about, to carry tidings unto their idols, and to the people.

10 And they put his armour in the house of their gods (elohim), and fastened his head in the temple of Dagon.

11 And when all Yavesh-Gilad heard all that the Philistines had done to Shaul,

12 They arose, all the valiant men, and took away the body of Shaul, and the bodies of his sons, and brought them to Yavesh, and buried their bones under the oak in Yavesh, and fasted seven days.

13 So Shaul died for his transgression which he committed against יהוה, even against the word of יהוה, which he kept not, and also for asking counsel of one that had a familiar spirit, to enquire of it;

14 And enquired not of יהוה; therefore He slew him, and turned the kingdom unto Dawid the son of Jesse (Yishai).

11 Then all Yisrael gathered themselves to Dawid unto Hebron, saying, "Behold, we are your bone and your flesh.

2 And moreover in time past, even when Shaul was king, you wast he that leddest out and broughtest in Yisrael; and יהוה your God (YHWH Eloheikha) said unto you, 'You shalt feed My people Yisrael, and you shalt be ruler over My people Yisrael.'"

3 Therefore came all the elders of Yisrael to the king to Hebron; and Dawid made a covenant with them in Hebron before יהוה; and they anointed Dawid king over Yisrael, according to the word of יהוה by Shemuel.

4 And Dawid and all Yisrael went to Jerusalem (Yerushalayim), which is Yevus; where the

Yevusis were, the inhabitants of the land.

5 And the inhabitants of Yevus said to Dawid, "You shalt not come hither." Nevertheless Dawid took the castle of Zion (Tsiyon), which is the city of Dawid.

6 And Dawid said, "Whosoever smiteth the Yevusis first shall be chief and captain." So Yoav the son of Zeruyah went first up, and was chief.

7 And Dawid dwelt in the castle; therefore they called it the city of Dawid.

8 And he built the city round about, even from Millo round about; and Yoav repaired the rest of the city.

9 So Dawid waxed greater and greater, for יהוה of hosts (YHWH Tsevaot) was with him.

10 These also are the chief of the mighty men whom Dawid had, who strengthened themselves with him in his kingdom, and with all Yisrael, to make him king, according to the word of יהוה concerning Yisrael.

11 And this is the number of the mighty men whom Dawid had; Yashovam, an Hachmonite, the chief of the captains; he lifted up his spear against three hundred slain by him at one time.

12 And after him was Eleazar the son of Dodo, the Ahohite, who was one of the three mighties.

13 He was with Dawid at Pasdammim, and there the Philistines were gathered together to battle, where was a parcel of ground full of barley; and the people fled from before the Philistines.

14 And they set themselves in the midst of that parcel, and delivered it, and slew the Philistines; and יהוה saved them by a great deliverance.

15 Now three of the thirty captains went down to the rock to Dawid, into the cave of Adullam; and the army of the Philistines encamped in the valley of Rephaim.

16 And Dawid was then in the hold, and the Philistines' garrison was then at Bethlehem (Beit-Lechem).

17 And Dawid longed, and said, "Oh that one would give me drink of the water of the well of Bethlehem (Beit-Lechem), that is at the gate!"

18 And the three broke through the army of the Philistines, and drew water out of the well of Bethlehem (Beit-Lechem), that was by the gate, and took it, and brought it to Dawid; but Dawid would not drink of it, but poured it out to יהוה,

19 And said, "My God (Elohai) forbid it me, that I should do this thing; shall I drink the

blood of these men that have put their lives in jeopardy? For with the jeopardy of their lives they brought it." Therefore he would not drink it. These things did these three mightiest.

20 And Avishai the brother of Yoav, he was chief of the three; for lifting up his spear against three hundred, he slew them, and had a name among the three.

21 Of the three, he was more honourable than the two; for he was their captain; howbeit he attained not to the first three.

22 Benayah the son of Yehoyada, the son of a valiant man of Kabzeel, who had done many acts; he slew two lionlike men of Moav; also he went down and slew a lion in a pit in a snowy day.

23 And he slew an Egyptian (Mitsri), a man of great stature, five cubits high; and in the Egyptian (Mitsri)'s hand was a spear like a weaver's beam; and he went down to him with a staff, and plucked the spear out of the Egyptian (Mitsri)'s hand, and slew him with his own spear.

24 These things did Benayah the son of Yehoyada, and had the name among the three mighties.

25 Behold, he was honourable among the thirty, but attained not to the first three; and Dawid set him over his guard.

26 Also the valiant men of the armies were, Asahel the brother of Yoav, Elhanan the son of Dodo of Bethlehem (Beit-Lechem),

27 Shammoth the Harorite, Helez the Pelonite,

28 Ira the son of Ikkesh the Tekoite, Aviezer the Antothite,

29 Sibbecai the Hushathite, Ilai the Ahohite,

30 Maharai the Netophathite, Heled the son of Baanah the Netophathite,

31 Ithai the son of Ribai of Gibeah, that pertained to the children of Benjamin (Binyamin), Benayah the Pirathonite,

32 Hurai of the brooks of Gaash, Aviel the Arbathite,

33 Azmaveth the Baharumite, Eliyahba the Shaalbonite,

34 The sons of Hashem the Gizonite, Yonatan the son of Shage the Hararite,

35 Ahiam the son of Sacar the Hararite, Eliphal the son of Ur,

36 Hepher the Mecherathite, Achiyah the Pelonite,

37 Hezro the Carmelite, Naarai the son of Ezbai,

38 Yoel the brother of Nathan, Mibhar the son of Haggeri,

39 Zelek the Ammonite, Naharai the Berothite, the armourbearer of Yoav the son of Zeruyah,

40 Ira the Ithrite, Gareb the Ithrite,

41 Uriyah the Hittite, Zabad the son of Ahlai,

42 Adina the son of Shiza the Reubenite (Reuveni), a captain of the Reubenites (Reuveni), and thirty with him,

43 Hanan the son of Maachah, and Yoshafat the Mithnite,

44 Uzzia the Ashterathite, Shama and Yeiel the sons of Hothan the Aroerite,

45 Yediael the son of Shimri, and Yocha his brother, the Tizite,

46 Eliel the Mahavite, and Yerivai, and Yoshawyah, the sons of Elnaam, and Ithmah the Moavite,

47 Eliel, and Oved, and Yasiel the Mesobaite.

12 Now these are they that came to Dawid to Ziklag, while he yet kept himself close because of Shaul the son of Kish; and they were among the mighty men, helpers of the war.

2 They were armed with bows, and could use both the right hand and the left in hurling stones and shooting arrows out of a bow, even of Shaul's brethren of Benjamin (Binyamin).

3 The chief was Ahiezer, then Yoash, the sons of Shemaah the Gibeathite; and Yeziel, and Pelet, the sons of Azmaveth; and Berachah, and Yehu the Antothite,

4 And Yismayah the Giveonite, a mighty man among the thirty, and over the thirty; and Jeremiah (Yirmeyahu), and Yachaziel, and Yochanan, and Yosavad the Gederathite,

5 Eluzai, and Yerimot, and Bealyah, and Shemaryahu, and Shefatyah the Haruphite,

6 Elkanah, and Yishiyahu, and Azareel, and Yoezer, and Yashovam, the Korhites,

7 And Yoelah, and Zevadyahu, the sons of Yeroham of Gedor.

8 And of the Gadites there separated themselves unto Dawid into the hold to the wilderness men of might, and men of war fit for the battle, that could handle shield and buckler, whose faces were like the faces of lions, and were as swift as the roes upon the mountains;

9 Ezer the first, Ovadyah the second, Eliav the third,

10 Mishmannah the fourth, Jeremiah

(Yirmeyahu) the fifth,

11 Attai the sixth, Eliel the seventh,

12 Yochanan the eighth, Elzabad the ninth,

13 Jeremiah (Yirmeyahu) the tenth, Machbanai the eleventh.

14 These were of the sons of Gad, captains of the army; one of the least was over a hundred, and the greatest over a thousand.

15 These are they that went over Jordan (Yarden) in the first month, when it had overflown all his banks; and they put to flight all them of the valleys, both toward the east, and toward the west.

16 And there came of the children of Benjamin (Binyamin) and Judah (Yehudah) to the hold unto Dawid.

17 And Dawid went out to meet them, and answered and said unto them, "If you be come peaceably unto me to help me, mine heart shall be knit unto you; but if you be come to betray me to mine enemies, seeing there is no wrong in mine hands, the God (Elohim) of our fathers look thereon, and rebuke it."

18 Then the spirit came upon Amasai, who was chief of the captains, and he said, "Yours are we, Dawid, and on your side, you son of Jesse (Yishai); peace, peace be unto you, and peace be to your helpers; for your God (Elohim) helpeth you." Then Dawid received them, and made them captains of the band.

19 And there fell some of Menashsheh to Dawid, when he came with the Philistines against Shaul to battle; but they helped them not, for the lords (seranim) of the Philistines upon advisement sent him away, saying, He will fall to his master Shaul to the jeopardy of our heads.

20 As he went to Ziklag, there fell to him of Menashsheh, Adnah, and Yozavad, and Yediael, and Mikhael, and Yozavad, and Elihu, and Zilthai, captains of the thousands that were of Menashsheh.

21 And they helped Dawid against the band of the rovers; for they were all mighty men of valour, and were captains in the army.

22 For at that time day by day there came to Dawid to help him, until it was a great army, like the host of God (Elohim).

23 And these are the numbers of the bands that were ready armed to the war, and came to Dawid to Hebron, to turn the kingdom of Shaul to him, according to the word of יהוה.

24 The children of Judah (Yehudah) that bare shield and spear were six thousand and eight hundred, ready armed to the war.

25 Of the children of Shimon, mighty men of valour for the war, seven thousand and one hundred.

26 Of the children of Lewi four thousand and six hundred.

27 And Yehoyada was the leader of the Aharonites, and with him were three thousand and seven hundred;

28 And Zadok, a young man mighty of valour, and of his father's house twenty and two captains.

29 And of the children of Benjamin (Binyamin), the kindred of Shaul, three thousand; for hitherto the greatest part of them had kept the ward of the house of Shaul.

30 And of the children of Efrayim twenty thousand and eight hundred, mighty men of valour, famous throughout the house of their fathers.

31 And of the half tribe of Menashsheh eighteen thousand, who were expressed by name, to come and make Dawid king.

32 And of the children of Yissaskhar, who were men that had understanding of the times, to know what Yisrael ought to do; the heads of them were two hundred; and all their brethren were at their commandment.

33 Of Zevulun, such as went forth to battle, expert in war, with all instruments of war, fifty thousand, which could keep rank; they were not of double heart.

34 And of Naftali a thousand captains, and with them with shield and spear thirty and seven thousand.

35 And of the Danites expert in war twenty and eight thousand and six hundred.

36 And of Asher, such as went forth to battle, expert in war, forty thousand.

37 And on the other side of Jordan (Yarden), of the Reubenites (Reuveni), and the Gadites, and of the half tribe of Menashsheh, with all manner of instruments of war for the battle, a hundred and twenty thousand.

38 All these men of war, that could keep rank, came with a perfect heart to Hebron, to make Dawid king over all Yisrael; and all the rest also of Yisrael were of one heart to make Dawid king.

39 And there they were with Dawid three days, eating and drinking; for their brethren had prepared for them.

40 Moreover they that were near them, even unto Yissaskhar and Zevulun and Naftali, brought bread on asses, and on camels, and on mules, and on oxen, and meat, meal, cakes of figs, and bunches of raisins, and wine, and oil, and oxen, and sheep abundantly, for there was joy in Yisrael.

13 And Dawid consulted with the captains of thousands and hundreds, and with every leader.

2 And Dawid said unto all the congregation of Yisrael, "If it seems good unto you, and that it be of יהוה our God (YHWH Eloheinu), let us send abroad unto our brethren every where, that are left in all the land of Yisrael, and with them also to the priests (kohanim) and Levites (Lewiyim) who are in their cities and suburbs, that they may gather themselves unto us;

3 And let us bring again the ark of our God (Elohim) to us, for we enquired not at it in the days of Shaul."

4 And all the congregation said that they would do so, for the thing was right in the eyes of all the people.

5 So Dawid gathered all Yisrael together, from Shihor of Egypt (Mitsrayim) even unto the entering of Hemath, to bring the ark of God (Elohim) from Kirya-Yearim.

6 And Dawid went up, and all Yisrael, to Baalah, that is, to Qirya-Yearim, which belonged to Judah (Yehudah), to bring up thence the ark of God (Elohim) יהוה, that dwelleth between the cherubims (keruvim), whose name is called on it.

7 And they carried the ark of God (Elohim) in a new cart out of the house of Avinadav; and Uzza and Ahio drave the cart.

8 And Dawid and all Yisrael played before God (Elohim) with all their might, and with singing, and with harps, and with psalteries, and with timbrels, and with cymbals, and with ram's horn (shofarot).

9 And when they came unto the threshingfloor of Chidon, Uzza put forth his hand to hold the ark; for the oxen stumbled.

10 And the anger of יהוה was kindled against Uzza, and He smote him, because he put his hand to the ark; and there he died before God (Elohim).

11 And Dawid was displeased, because יהוה had made a breach upon Uzza; wherefore that place is called Perezuzza to this day.

12 And Dawid was afraid of God (Elohim) that day, saying, "How shall I bring the ark of God (Elohim) home to me?"

13 So Dawid brought not the ark home to himself to the city of Dawid, but carried it aside into the house of Oved-Edom the Gittite.

14 And the ark of God (Elohim) remained with the family of Oved-Edom in his house three months. And יהוה blessed the house of Oved-Edom, and all that he had.

14 Now Hiram king of Tyre sent messengers to Dawid, and timber of cedars, with masons and carpenters, to build him a house.

2 And Dawid perceived that יהוה had confirmed him king over Yisrael, for his kingdom was lifted up on high, because of his people Yisrael.

3 And Dawid took more wives at Jerusalem (Yerushalayim); and Dawid begat more sons and daughters.

4 Now these are the names of his children whom he had in Jerusalem (Yerushalayim): Shammua, and Shobab, Nathan, and Solomon (Shelomoh),

5 And Ibhar, and Elishua, and Elpalet,

6 And Nogah, and Nepheg, and Yafiya,

7 And Elishama, and Beeliada, and Eliphalet.

8 And when the Philistines heard that Dawid was anointed king over all Yisrael, all the Philistines went up to seek Dawid. And Dawid heard of it, and went out against them.

9 And the Philistines came and spread themselves in the valley of Rephaim.

10 And Dawid enquired of God (Elohim), saying, "Shall I go up against the Philistines? And wilt You deliver them into mine hand?" And יהוה said unto him, "Go up, for I will deliver them into your hand."

11 So they came up to Baal-Perazim; and Dawid smote them there. Then Dawid said, "God (Elohim) hath broken in upon mine enemies by mine hand like the breaking forth of waters." Therefore they called the name of that place Baal-Perazim.

12 And when they had left their gods (elohim) there, Dawid gave an order, and they were burned with fire.

13 And the Philistines yet again spread themselves abroad in the valley.

14 Therefore Dawid enquired again of God (Elohim); and God (Elohim) said unto him, "Go not up after them; turn away from them, and come upon them opposite the mulberry trees.

15 And it shall be, when you shalt hear a sound of going in the tops of the mulberry trees, that then you shalt go out to battle, for God (Elohim) is gone forth before you to smite the army of the Philistines."

16 Dawid therefore did as God (Elohim) commanded him; and they smote the army of the Philistines from Giveon even to Gazer.

17 And the fame of Dawid went out into all lands; and יהוה brought the fear of him upon all nations.

15 And Dawid made him houses in the city of Dawid, and prepared a place for the ark of God (Elohim), and pitched for it a tent.

2 Then Dawid said, "None ought to carry the ark of God (Elohim) but the Levites (Lewiyim), for them hath יהוה chosen to carry the ark of God (Elohim), and to minister unto Him forever."

3 And Dawid gathered all Yisrael together to Jerusalem (Yerushalayim), to bring up the ark of יהוה unto its place, which he had prepared for it.

4 And Dawid assembled the children of Aaron (Aharon), and the Levites (Lewiyim).

5 Of the sons of Kohath: Uriel the chief, and his brethren a hundred and twenty;

6 Of the sons of Merari: Asayah the chief, and his brethren two hundred and twenty;

7 Of the sons of Gershom: Yoel the chief, and his brethren a hundred and thirty;

8 Of the sons of Elizaphan: Shemayah the chief, and his brethren two hundred;

9 Of the sons of Hebron: Eliel the chief, and his brethren fourscore;

10 Of the sons of Uzziel: Amminadab the chief, and his brethren a hundred and twelve.

11 And Dawid called for Zadok and Aviathar the priests (kohanim), and for the Levites (Lewiyim), for Uriel, Asayah, and Yoel, Shemayah, and Eliel, and Amminadab,

12 And said unto them, "You are the chief of the fathers of the Levites (Lewiyim); sanctify yourselves, both you and your brethren, that you may bring up the ark of יהוה God of Israel (Elohei Yisrael) unto the place that I have prepared for it.

13 For because you did it not at the first, יהוה our God (YHWH Eloheinu) made a breach upon us, for that we sought him not after the due order."

14 So the priests (kohanim) and the Levites (Lewiyim) sanctified themselves to bring up the ark of יהוה God of Israel (Elohei Yisrael).

15 And the children of the Levites (Lewiyim) bare the ark of God (Elohim) upon their shoulders with the staves thereon, as Moses (Mosheh) commanded according to the word of יהוה.

16 And Dawid spake to the chief of the Levites (Lewiyim) to appoint their brethren to be the singers with instruments of musick, psalteries and harps and cymbals, sounding, by lifting up the voice with joy.

17 So the Levites (Lewiyim) appointed Heman the son of Yoel; and of his brethren, Asaph the son of Verekhyah; and of the sons of Merari their brethren, Ethan the son of Kushayahu;

18 And with them their brethren of the second degree, Zechariah (Zekharyahu), Ben, and Yaaziel, and Shemiramoth, and Yeiel, and Unni, Eliav, and Benayah, and Maaseyahu, and Mattityah, and Elipheleh, and Mikneyahu, and Oved-Edom, and Yeiel, the porters.

19 So the singers, Heman, Asaph, and Ethan, were appointed to sound with cymbals of brass;

20 And Zechariah (Zekharyahu), and Aziel, and Shemiramoth, and Yeiel, and Unni, and Eliav, and Maaseyahu, and Benayah, with psalteries on Alamoth;

21 And Mattityah, and Elipheleh, and Mikneyahu, and Oved-Edom, and Yeiel, and Azazyahu, with harps on the Sheminith to excel.

22 And Kenanyahu, chief of the Levites (Lewiyim), was for singing; he instructed the singing, because he was skilful.

23 And Verekhyah and Elkanah were doorkeepers for the ark.

24 And Shevanyahu, and Yehoshafat, and Nethaneel, and Amasai, and Zechariah (Zekharyahu), and Benayah, and Eliezer, the priests (kohanim), did blow with the ram's horn (shofarot) before the ark of God (Elohim); and Oved-Edom and Yechiyah were doorkeepers for the ark.

25 So Dawid, and the elders of Yisrael, and the captains over thousands, went to bring up the

ark of the covenant of יהוה out of the house of Oved-Edom with joy.

26 And it came to pass, when God (Elohim) helped the Levites (Lewiyim) that bare the ark of the covenant of יהוה, that they offered seven bullocks and seven rams.

27 And Dawid was clothed with a robe of fine linen, and all the Levites (Lewiyim) that bare the ark, and the singers, and Kenanyahu the master of the song with the singers. Dawid also had upon him an ephod of linen.

28 Thus all Yisrael brought up the ark of the covenant of יהוה with shouting, and with sound of the cornet, and with ram's horn (shofarot), and with cymbals, making a noise with psalteries and harps.

29 And it came to pass, as the ark of the covenant of יהוה came to the city of Dawid, that Michal the daughter of Shaul looking out at a window saw King Dawid dancing and playing; and she despised him in her heart.

16 So they brought the ark of God (Elohim), and set it in the midst of the tent that Dawid had pitched for it; and they offered burnt sacrifices and peace offerings before God (Elohim).

2 And when Dawid had made an end of offering the burnt offerings and the peace offerings, he blessed the people in the name of יהוה.

3 And he dealt to every one of Yisrael, both man and woman, to every one a loaf of bread, and a good piece of flesh, and a flagon of wine.

4 And he appointed certain of the Levites (Lewiyim) to minister before the ark of יהוה, and to record, and to thank and praise יהוה God of Israel (Elohei Yisrael):

5 Asaph the chief, and next to him Zechariah (Zekharyahu), Yeiel, and Shemiramoth, and Yeiel, and Mattityah, and Eliav, and Benayah, and Oved-Edom; and Yeiel with psalteries and with harps; but Asaph made a sound with cymbals;

6 Benayah also and Yachaziel the priests (kohanim) with trumpets continually before the ark of the covenant of God (Elohim).

7 Then on that day Dawid delivered first this psalm to thank יהוה into the hand of Asaph and his brethren:

8 Give thanks unto יהוה, call upon His name, make known His deeds among the people.

9 Sing unto Him, sing psalms unto Him, talk you of all His wondrous works.

10 Glory you in His holy name; let the heart of them rejoice who seek יהוה.

11 Seek יהוה and His strength, seek His face continually.

12 Remember His marvellous works that He hath done, His wonders, and the judgments of His mouth;

13 O you seed of Yisrael His servant, you children of Jacob (Yaaqov), His chosen ones.

14 He is יהוה our God (YHWH Eloheinu); His judgments are in all the earth.

15 Be you mindful always of His covenant; the word which He commanded to a thousand generations,

16 Even of the covenant which He made with Avraham, and of His oath unto Isaac (Yitzchaq);

17 And hath confirmed the same to Jacob (Yaaqov) for a law, and to Yisrael for an everlasting covenant,

18 Saying, "Unto you will I give the land of Canaan, the lot of your inheritance;"

19 When you were but few, even a few, and strangers in it.

20 And when they went from nation to nation, and from one kingdom to another people;

21 He allowed no man to do them wrong; yea, He reproved kings for their sakes,

22 Saying, "Touch not Mine anointed, and do My prophets no harm."

23 Sing unto יהוה, all the earth; shew forth from day to day His salvation.

24 Declare His glory among the nations; His marvellous works among all nations.

25 For great is יהוה, and greatly to be praised; He also is to be feared above all gods (elohim).

26 For all the gods (elohim) of the people are idols; but יהוה made the heavens.

27 Glory and honor are in His presence; strength and gladness are in His place.

28 Give unto יהוה, you kindreds of the people, give unto יהוה glory and strength.

29 Give unto יהוה the glory due unto His name; bring an offering, and come before Him; worship יהוה in the beauty of holiness.

30 Fear before Him, all the earth; the world also shall be stable, that it be not moved.

31 Let the heavens be glad, and let the earth rejoice; and let men say among the nations, יהוה reigneth.

32 Let the sea roar, and the fulness thereof; let

the fields rejoice, and all that is therein.

33 Then shall the trees of the wood sing out at the presence of יהוה, because He cometh to judge the earth.

34 O give thanks unto יהוה, for He is good; for His mercy endureth forever.

35 And say you, "Save us, O God (Elohim) of our salvation, and gather us together, and deliver us from the heathen, that we may give thanks to Your holy name, and glory in Your praise."

36 Blessed be יהוה God of Israel (Elohei Yisrael) forever and ever. And all the people said, "So be it (Amen)!" and praised יהוה.

37 So he left there before the ark of the covenant of יהוה, Asaph and his brethren, to minister before the ark continually, as every day's work required;

38 And Oved-Edom with their brethren, threescore and eight; Oved-Edom also the son of Yedutun and Hosah to be porters;

39 And Zadok the priest (kohen), and his brethren the priests (kohanim), before the tabernacle of יהוה in the high place that was at Giveon,

40 To offer burnt offerings unto יהוה upon the altar of the burnt offering continually morning and evening, and to do according to all that is written in the Torah of יהוה, which He commanded Yisrael;

41 And with them Heman and Yedutun, and the rest that were chosen, who were expressed by name, to give thanks to יהוה, because His mercy endureth forever;

42 And with them Heman and Yedutun with trumpets and cymbals for those that should make a sound, and with musical instruments of God (Elohim). And the sons of Yedutun were porters.

43 And all the people departed every man to his house; and Dawid returned to bless his house.

17 Now it came to pass, as Dawid sat in his house, that Dawid said to Nathan the prophet, "Behold, I dwell in a house of cedars, but the ark of the covenant of יהוה remaineth under curtains."

2 Then Nathan said unto Dawid, "Do all that is in your heart, for God (Elohim) is with you."

3 And it came to pass the same night, that the word of God (Elohim) came to Nathan, saying,

4 "Go and tell Dawid My servant, 'Thus saith יהוה: "You shalt not build Me a house to dwell in;

5 For I have not dwelt in a house since the day that I brought up Yisrael unto this day; but have gone from tent to tent, and from one tabernacle to another.

6 Wheresoever I have walked with all Yisrael, spake I a word to any of the judges of Yisrael, whom I commanded to feed My people, saying, 'Why have you not built Me a house of cedars?'

7 Now therefore thus shalt you say unto My servant Dawid, 'Thus saith יהוה of hosts (YHWH Tsevaot): "I took you from the sheepcote, even from following the sheep, that you shouldest be ruler over My people Yisrael;

8 And I have been with you whithersoever you have walked, and have cut off all your enemies from before you, and have made you a name like the name of the great men that are in the earth.

9 Also I will ordain a place for My people Yisrael, and will plant them, and they shall dwell in their place, and shall be moved no more; neither shall the children of wickedness waste them anymore, as at the beginning,

10 And since the time that I commanded judges to be over My people Yisrael. Moreover I will subdue all your enemies. Furthermore I tell you that יהוה will build you a house.

11 And it shall come to pass, when your days be expired that you must go to be with your fathers, that I will raise up your seed after you, who shall be of your sons; and I will establish his kingdom.

12 He shall build Me a house, and I will stablish his throne forever.

13 I will be his father, and he shall be My son; and I will not take My mercy away from him, as I took it from him that was before you;

14 But I will settle him in Mine house and in My kingdom forever; and his throne shall be established forevermore.""'

15 According to all these words, and according to all this vision, so did Nathan speak unto Dawid.

16 And Dawid the king came and sat before יהוה, and said, "Who am I, O יהוה God (Elohim), and what is mine house, that you have brought me hitherto?

17 And yet this was a small thing in your eyes, O God (Elohim); for You have also spoken of Your servant's house for a great while to come, and hast regarded me according to the estate of

a man of high degree, O God (Elohim) יהוה.

18 What can Dawid speak more to You for the honor of Your servant? For You knowest Your servant.

19 O יהוה, for Your servant's sake, and according to Your own heart, have You done all this greatness, in making known all these great things.

20 O יהוה, there is none like You, neither is there any God (Elohim) besides You, according to all that we have heard with our ears.

21 And what one nation in the earth is like Your people Yisrael, whom God (Elohim) went to redeem to be His own people, to make You a name of greatness and awesomeness, by driving out nations from before Your people, whom You have redeemed out of Egypt (Mitsrayim)?

22 For Your people Yisrael didst You make Your own people forever; and You, יהוה, becamest their God (Elohim).

23 Therefore now, יהוה, let the thing that You have spoken concerning Your servant and concerning his house be established forever, and do as You have said.

24 Let it even be established, that Your name may be magnified forever, saying, "יהוה of hosts (YHWH Tsevaot) is the God of Israel (Elohei Yisrael), even a God (Elohim) to Yisrael; and let the house of Dawid Your servant be established before You.

25 For You, O my God (Elohim), hast told Your servant that You wilt build him a house; therefore Your servant hath found in his heart to pray before You.

26 And now, יהוה, You are God (Elohim), and hast promised this goodness unto Your servant.

27 Now therefore let it please You to bless the house of Your servant, that it may be before You forever; for You blessest, O יהוה, and it shall be blessed forever."

18 Now after this it came to pass, that Dawid smote the Philistines, and subdued them, and took Gath and her towns out of the hand of the Philistines.

2 And he smote Moav; and the Moavites became Dawid's servants, and brought gifts.

3 And Dawid smote Hadarezer king of Zobah unto Hamath, as he went to stablish his dominion by the river Euphrates.

4 And Dawid took from him a thousand chariots, and seven thousand horsemen, and twenty thousand footmen; Dawid also houghed all the chariot horses, but reserved of them a hundred chariots.

5 And when the Syrians (Arammim) of Damascus (Dammeseq) came to help Hadarezer king of Zobah, Dawid slew of the Syrians (Arammim) two and twenty thousand men.

6 Then Dawid put garrisons among Syrians (Arammim) in Damascus (Dammeseq); and the Syrians (Arammim) became Dawid's servants, and brought gifts. Thus יהוה preserved Dawid whithersoever he went.

7 And Dawid took the shields of gold that were on the servants of Hadarezer, and brought them to Jerusalem (Yerushalayim).

8 Likewise from Tibhath, and from Chun, cities of Hadarezer, brought Dawid very much brass, wherewith Solomon (Shelomoh) made the brasen sea, and the pillars, and the vessels of brass.

9 Now when Tou king of Hamath heard how Dawid had smitten all the army of Hadarezer king of Zobah;

10 He sent Hadoram his son to king Dawid, to enquire of his welfare, and to congratulate him, because he had fought against Hadarezer, and smitten him; (for Hadarezer had war with Tou;) and with him all manner of vessels of gold and silver and brass.

11 Them also king Dawid dedicated unto יהוה, with the silver and the gold that he brought from all these nations; from Edom, and from Moav, and from the children of Ammon, and from the Philistines, and from Amalek.

12 Moreover Avishai the son of Zeruyah slew of the Edomites in the valley of salt eighteen thousand.

13 And he put garrisons in Edom; and all the Edomites became Dawid's servants. Thus יהוה preserved Dawid whithersoever he went.

14 So Dawid reigned over all Yisrael, and executed judgment and justice among all his people.

15 And Yoav the son of Zeruyah was over the army; and Yehoshafat the son of Ahilud, recorder.

16 And Zadok the son of Ahitub, and Abimelech (Avimelekh) the son of Aviathar, were the priests (kohanim); and Shavsha was scribe;

17 And Benayah the son of Yehoyada was over the Cherethites and the Pelethites; and the sons

of Dawid were chiefs by the king.

19 Now it came to pass after this, that Nahash the king of the children of Ammon died, and his son reigned in his stead.

2 And Dawid said, "I will shew kindness unto Hanun the son of Nahash, because his father shewed kindness to me." And Dawid sent messengers to comfort him concerning his father. So the servants of Dawid came into the land of the children of Ammon to Hanun, to comfort him.

3 But the princes of the children of Ammon said to Hanun, "Thinkest you that Dawid doth honor your father, that he hath sent comforters unto you? Are not his servants come unto you for to search, and to overthrow, and to spy out the land?"

4 Wherefore Hanun took Dawid's servants, and shaved them, and cut off their garments in the midst hard by their buttocks, and sent them away.

5 Then there went certain, and told Dawid how the men were served. And he sent to meet them, for the men were greatly ashamed. And the king said, "Tarry at Yericho until your beards be grown, and then return."

6 And when the children of Ammon saw that they had made themselves odious to Dawid, Hanun and the children of Ammon sent a thousand talents of silver to hire them chariots and horsemen out of Mesopotamia, and out of Syriamaachah (Aram-Maakhah), and out of Zobah.

7 So they hired thirty and two thousand chariots, and the king of Maachah and his people; who came and pitched before Medeba. And the children of Ammon gathered themselves together from their cities, and came to battle.

8 And when Dawid heard of it, he sent Yoav, and all the army of the mighty men.

9 And the children of Ammon came out, and put the battle in array before the gate of the city; and the kings that were come were by themselves in the field.

10 Now when Yoav saw that the battle was set against him before and behind, he chose out of all the choice of Yisrael, and put them in array against the Syrians (Arammim).

11 And the rest of the people he delivered unto the hand of Avishai his brother, and they set themselves in array against the children of Ammon.

12 And he said, "If the Syrians (Arammim) be too strong for me, then you shalt help me; but if the children of Ammon be too strong for you, then I will help you.

13 Be of good courage, and let us behave ourselves valiantly for our people, and for the cities of our God (Elohim); and let יהוה do that which is good in His sight."

14 So Yoav and the people that were with him drew near before the Syrians (Arammim) unto the battle; and they fled before him.

15 And when the children of Ammon saw that the Syrians (Arammim) were fled, they likewise fled before Avishai his brother, and entered into the city. Then Yoav came to Jerusalem (Yerushalayim).

16 And when the Syrians (Arammim) saw that they were put to the worse before Yisrael, they sent messengers, and drew forth the Syrians (Arammim) that were beyond the river; and Shophach the captain of the army of Hadarezer went before them.

17 And it was told Dawid; and he gathered all Yisrael, and passed over Jordan (Yarden), and came upon them, and set the battle in array against them. So when Dawid had put the battle in array against the Syrians (Arammim), they fought with him.

18 But the Syrians (Arammim) fled before Yisrael; and Dawid slew of the Syrians (Arammim) seven thousand men who fought in chariots, and forty thousand footmen, and killed Shophach the captain of the army.

19 And when the servants of Hadarezer saw that they were put to the worse before Yisrael, they made peace with Dawid, and became his servants; neither would the Syria (Aram) help the children of Ammon anymore.

20 And it came to pass, that after the year was expired, at the time that kings go out to battle, Yoav led forth the power of the army, and wasted the country of the children of Ammon, and came and besieged Rabbah. But Dawid tarried at Jerusalem (Yerushalayim). And Yoav smote Rabbah, and destroyed it.

2 And Dawid took the crown of their king from off his head, and found it to weigh a talent of gold, and there were precious stones in it; and it was set upon Dawid's head; and he brought also exceeding much spoil out of the city.

3 And he brought out the people that were in it, and cut them with saws, and with harrows of iron, and with axes. Even so dealt Dawid with all the cities of the children of Ammon. And Dawid and all the people returned to Jerusalem (Yerushalayim).

4 And it came to pass after this, that there arose war at Gezer with the Philistines; at which time Sibbechai the Hushathite slew Sippai, that was of the children of the giant; and they were subdued.

5 And there was war again with the Philistines; and Elhanan the son of Yair slew Lahmi the brother of Goliath the Gittite, whose spear staff was like a weaver's beam.

6 And yet again there was war at Gath, where was a man of great stature, whose fingers and toes were four and twenty, six on each hand, and six on each foot; and he also was the son of the giant.

7 But when he defied Yisrael, Yonatan the son of Shimea Dawid's brother slew him.

8 These were born unto the giant in Gath; and they fell by the hand of Dawid, and by the hand of his servants.

21 And the Satan stood up against Yisrael, and provoked Dawid to number Yisrael.

2 And Dawid said to Yoav and to the rulers of the people, "Go, number Yisrael from Beer-Sheva even to Dan; and bring the number of them to me, that I may know it."

3 And Yoav answered, "יהוה make His people a hundred times so many more as they be: but, my lord (adoni) the king, are they not all my lord (adoni)'s servants? Why then doth my lord (adoni) require this thing? Why will he be a cause of trespass to Yisrael?"

4 Nevertheless the king's word prevailed against Yoav. Wherefore Yoav departed, and went throughout all Yisrael, and came to Jerusalem (Yerushalayim).

5 And Yoav gave the sum of the number of the people unto Dawid. And all they of Yisrael were a thousand thousand and a hundred thousand men that drew sword; and Judah (Yehudah) was four hundred threescore and ten thousand men that drew sword.

6 But Lewi and Benjamin (Binyamin) counted he not among them, for the king's word was abominable to Yoav.

7 And God (Elohim) was displeased with this thing; therefore He smote Yisrael.

8 And Dawid said unto God (Elohim), "I have sinned greatly, because I have done this thing; but now, I beseech You, do away the iniquity of Your servant; for I have done very foolishly."

9 And יהוה spake unto Gad, Dawid's seer, saying,

10 "Go and tell Dawid, saying, 'Thus saith יהוה: "I offer you three things: choose you one of them, that I may do it unto you."'"

11 So Gad came to Dawid, and said unto him, "Thus saith יהוה: 'Choose you,

12 Either three years' famine; or three months to be destroyed before your foes, while that the sword of your enemies overtaketh you; or else three days the sword of יהוה, even the pestilence, in the land, and the angel of יהוה destroying throughout all the coasts of Yisrael.' Now therefore advise yourself what word I shall bring again to Him that sent me."

13 And Dawid said unto Gad, "I am in a great distress; let me fall now into the hand of יהוה, for very great are His mercies; but let me not fall into the hand of man."

14 So יהוה sent pestilence upon Yisrael; and there fell of Yisrael seventy thousand men.

15 And God (Elohim) sent an angel unto Jerusalem (Yerushalayim) to destroy it; and as he was destroying, יהוה beheld, and He regretted of the disaster (raah), and said to the angel that destroyed, "It is enough, stay now your hand." And the angel of יהוה stood by the threshingfloor of Ornan the Yevusi.

16 And Dawid lifted up his eyes, and saw the angel of יהוה stand between the earth and the heaven, having a drawn sword in his hand stretched out over Jerusalem (Yerushalayim). Then Dawid and the elders of Yisrael, who were clothed in sackcloth, fell upon their faces.

17 And Dawid said unto God (Elohim), "Is it not I that commanded the people to be numbered? Even I it is that have sinned and done evil indeed; but as for these sheep, what have they done? Let Your hand, please, O יהוה my God (YHWH Elohai), be on me, and on my father's house; but not on Your people, that they should be plagued."

18 Then the angel of יהוה commanded Gad to say to Dawid, that Dawid should go up, and set up an altar unto יהוה in the threshingfloor of Ornan the Yevusi.

19 And Dawid went up at the saying of Gad, which he spake in the name of יהוה.

20 And Ornan turned back, and saw the angel; and his four sons with him hid themselves. Now Ornan was threshing wheat.

21 And as Dawid came to Ornan, Ornan looked and saw Dawid, and went out of the threshingfloor, and bowed himself to Dawid with his face to the ground.

22 Then Dawid said to Ornan, "Grant me the place of this threshingfloor, that I may build an altar therein unto יהוה. You shalt grant it me for the full price; that the plague may be stayed from the people."

23 And Ornan said unto Dawid, "Take it to you, and let my lord (adoni) the king does that which is good in his eyes. Behold, I give you the oxen also for burnt offerings, and the threshing instruments for wood, and the wheat for the meat offering; I give it all."

24 And King Dawid said to Ornan, "Nay, but I will verily buy it for the full price; for I will not take that which is your for יהוה, nor offer burnt offerings without cost."

25 So Dawid gave to Ornan for the place six hundred shekels of gold by weight.

26 And Dawid built there an altar unto יהוה, and offered burnt offerings and peace offerings, and called upon יהוה; and He answered him from heaven by fire upon the altar of burnt offering.

27 And יהוה commanded the angel; and he put up his sword again into the sheath thereof.

28 At that time when Dawid saw that יהוה had answered him in the threshingfloor of Ornan the Yevusi, then he sacrificed there.

29 For the tabernacle of יהוה, which Moses (Mosheh) made in the wilder-ness, and the altar of the burnt offering, were at that season in the high place at Giveon.

30 But Dawid could not go before it to enquire of God (Elohim), for he was afraid because of the sword of the angel of יהוה.

22 Then Dawid said, "This is the house of יהוה God (Elohim), and this is the altar of the burnt offering for Yisrael."

2 And Dawid commanded to gather together the strangers that were in the land of Yisrael; and he set masons to hew wrought stones to build the house of God (Elohim).

3 And Dawid prepared iron in abundance for the nails for the doors of the gates, and for the joinings; and brass in abundance without weight;

4 Also cedar trees in abundance; for the Zidonians and they of Tyre brought much cedar wood to Dawid.

5 And Dawid said, "Solomon (Shelomoh) my son is young and tender, and the house that is to be builded for יהוה must be exceeding magnifical, of fame and of glory throughout all countries. I will therefore now make preparation for it. So Dawid prepared abundantly before his death.

6 Then he called for Solomon (Shelomoh) his son, and charged him to build a house for יהוה God of Israel (Elohei Yisrael).

7 And Dawid said to Solomon (Shelomoh), "My son, as for me, it was in my mind to build a house unto the name of יהוה my God (YHWH Elohai);

8 But the word of יהוה came to me, saying, 'You have shed blood abundantly, and hast made great wars; you shalt not build a house unto My name, because you have shed much blood upon the earth in My sight.

9 Behold, a son shall be born to you, who shall be a man of rest; and I will give him rest from all his enemies round about; for his name shall be Solomon (Shelomoh), and I will give peace and quietness unto Yisrael in his days.

10 He shall build a house for My name; and he shall be My son, and I will be his Father; and I will establish the throne of his kingdom over Yisrael forever.'

11 Now, my son, יהוה be with you; and prosper you, and build the house of יהוה your God (YHWH Eloheikha), as He hath said of you.

12 Only יהוה give you wisdom and understanding, and give you charge concerning Yisrael, that you mayest keep the Torah of יהוה your God (YHWH Eloheikha).

13 Then shalt you prosper, if you takest heed to fulfil the statutes and judgments which יהוה charged Moses (Mosheh) with concerning Yisrael. Be strong, and of good courage; dread not, nor be dismayed.

14 Now, behold, in my trouble I have prepared for the house of יהוה a hundred thousand talents of gold, and a thousand thousand talents of silver; and of brass and iron without weight; for it is in abundance; timber also and stone have I prepared; and you mayest add thereto.

15 Moreover there are workmen with you in abundance, hewers and workers of stone and timber, and all manner of cunning men for every manner of work.

16 Of the gold, the silver, and the brass, and the iron, there is no number. Arise therefore, and be doing, and יהוה be with you."

17 Dawid also commanded all the princes of Yisrael to help Solomon (Shelomoh) his son, saying,

18 "Is not יהוה your God (YHWH Eloheikhem) with you? And hath He not given you rest on every side? For He hath given the inhabitants of the land into mine hand; and the land is subdued before יהוה, and before His people.

19 Now set your heart and your soul to seek יהוה your God (YHWH Eloheikhem); arise therefore, and build you the sanctuary of יהוה God (Elohim), to bring the ark of the covenant of יהוה, and the holy vessels of God (Elohim), into the house that is to be built to the name of יהוה."

23 So when Dawid was old and full of days, he made Solomon (Shelomoh) his son king over Yisrael.

2 And he gathered together all the princes of Yisrael, with the priests (kohanim) and the Levites (Lewiyim).

3 Now the Levites (Lewiyim) were numbered from the age of thirty years and upward; and their number by their polls, man by man, was thirty and eight thousand.

4 Of which, twenty and four thousand were to set forward the work of the house of יהוה; and six thousand were officers and judges.

5 Moreover four thousand were porters; and four thousand praised יהוה with the instruments, "which I made," said Dawid, "to praise therewith."

6 And Dawid divided them into courses among the sons of Lewi, namely, Gershon, Kohath, and Merari.

7 Of the Gershonites were Laadan, and Shimei.

8 The sons of Laadan: the chief was Yeiel, and Zetham, and Yoel, three.

9 The sons of Shimei: Shelomith, and Haziel, and Haran, three. These were the chief of the fathers of Laadan.

10 And the sons of Shimei were, Yachat, Zina, and Yeush, and Beriyah. These four were the sons of Shimei.

11 And Yachat was the chief, and Zizah the second; but Yeush and Beriyah had not many sons; therefore they were in one reckoning, according to their father's house.

12 The sons of Kohath: Amram, Izhar, Hebron, and Uzziel, four.

13 The sons of Amram: Aaron (Aharon) and Moses (Mosheh); and Aaron (Aharon) was separated, that he should sanctify the most holy things, he and his sons forever, to burn incense before יהוה, to minister unto Him, and to bless in His name forever.

14 Now concerning Moses (Mosheh) the man of God (Elohim), his sons were named of the tribe of Lewi.

15 The sons of Moses (Mosheh) were Gershom, and Eliezer.

16 Of the sons of Gershom: Shebuel was the chief.

17 And the sons of Eliezer were Rechavyah the chief. And Eliezer had none other sons; but the sons of Rechavyah were very many.

18 Of the sons of Izhar: Shelomith the chief.

19 Of the sons of Hebron: Yeriyah the first, Amaryah the second, Yachaziel the third, and Jekameam the fourth.

20 Of the sons of Uzziel: Michah the first, and Yishiyahu the second.

21 The sons of Merari: Mahli, and Mushi. The sons of Mahli: Eleazar, and Kish.

22 And Eleazar died, and had no sons, but daughters; and their brethren the sons of Kish took them.

23 The sons of Mushi: Mahli, and Eder, and Yeremot, three.

24 These were the sons of Lewi after the house of their fathers; even the chief of the fathers, as they were counted by number of names by their polls, that did the work for the service of the house of יהוה, from the age of twenty years and upward.

25 For Dawid said, "יהוה God of Israel (Elohei Yisrael) hath given rest unto His people, that they may dwell in Jerusalem (Yerushalayim) forever;"

26 And also unto the Levites (Lewiyim); they shall no more carry the tabernacle, nor any vessels of it for the service thereof.

27 For by the last words of Dawid the Levites (Lewiyim) were numbered from twenty years old and above;

28 Because their office was to wait on the sons

412

of Aaron (Aharon) for the service of the house of יהוה, in the courts, and in the chambers, and in the purifying of all holy things, and the work of the service of the house of God (Elohim);

29 Both for the shewbread, and for the fine flour for meat offering, and for the unleavened cakes (matstsot), and for that which is baked in the pan, and for that which is fried, and for all manner of measure and size;

30 And to stand every morning to thank and praise יהוה, and likewise at even;

31 And to offer all burnt sacrifices unto יהוה on the Shabbats, on the New Moons, and on the set feasts, by number, according to the order commanded unto them, continually before יהוה;

32 And that they should keep the charge of the tabernacle of the congregation, and the charge of the holy place, and the charge of the sons of Aaron (Aharon) their brethren, in the service of the house of יהוה.

24 Now these are the divisions of the sons of Aaron (Aharon). The sons of Aaron (Aharon): Nadav, and Avihu, Eleazar, and Ithamar.

2 But Nadav and Avihu died before their father, and had no children; therefore Eleazar and Ithamar executed the priest's office (kehunnah).

3 And Dawid distributed them, both Zadok of the sons of Eleazar, and Ahimelech of the sons of Ithamar, according to their offices in their service.

4 And there were more chief men found of the sons of Eleazar than of the sons of Ithamar; and thus were they divided. Among the sons of Eleazar there were sixteen chief men of the house of their fathers, and eight among the sons of Ithamar according to the house of their fathers.

5 Thus were they divided by lot, one sort with another; for the governors of the sanctuary, and governors of the house of God (Elohim), were of the sons of Eleazar, and of the sons of Ithamar.

6 And Shemayah the son of Nethaneel the scribe, one of the Levites (Lewiyim), wrote them before the king, and the princes, and Zadok the priest (kohen), and Ahimelech the son of Aviathar, and before the chief of the fathers of the priests (kohanim) and Levites (Lewiyim); one principal household being taken for Eleazar, and one taken for Ithamar.

7 Now the first lot came forth to Yehoyariv, the second to Yedayah,

8 The third to Harim, the fourth to Seorim,

9 The fifth to Malkiyah, the sixth to Miyamin,

10 The seventh to Hakkoz, the eighth to Aviyah,

11 The ninth to Joshua (A33Yeshua), the tenth to Shekhanyah,

12 The eleventh to Elijahhib, the twelfth to Yakim,

13 The thirteenth to Huppah, the fourteenth to Yeshevav,

14 The fifteenth to Bilgah, the sixteenth to Immer,

15 The seventeenth to Hezir, the eighteenth to Aphses,

16 The nineteenth to Petachyah, the twentieth to Yechezkel,

17 The one and twentieth to Yakhin, the two and twentieth to Gamul,

18 The three and twentieth to Delayahu, the four and twentieth to Maazyahu.

19 These were the orderings of them in their service to come into the house of יהוה, according to their manner, under Aaron (Aharon) their father, as יהוה God of Israel (Elohei Yisrael) had commanded him.

20 And the rest of the sons of Lewi were these: Of the sons of Amram: Shubael; of the sons of Shubael: Yechdeyahu.

21 Concerning Rechavyah, of the sons of Rechavyah: the first was Yishshiyah.

22 Of the Izharites: Shelomoth; of the sons of Shelomoth: Yachat.

23 And the sons of Hebron: Yeriyah the first, Amaryah the second, Yachaziel the third, Yekamam the fourth.

24 Of the sons of Uzziel: Michah; of the sons of Michah: Shamir.

25 The brother of Michah was Yishshiyah; of the sons of Yishshiyah: Zechariah (Zekharyahu).

26 The sons of Merari were Mahli and Mushi; the sons of Yaazyahu: Beno.

27 The sons of Merari by Yaazyahu: Beno, and Shoham, and Zaccur, and Ibri.

28 Of Mahli came Eleazar, who had no sons.

29 Concerning Kish, the son of Kish was Yerachmeel.

30 The sons also of Mushi: Mahli, and Eder, and Yerimot. These were the sons of the Levites (Lewiyim) after the house of their fathers.

31 These likewise cast lots opposite their brethren the sons of Aaron (Aharon) in the

presence of Dawid the king, and Zadok, and Ahimelech, and the chief of the fathers of the priests (kohanim) and Levites (Lewiyim), even the principal fathers opposite their younger brethren.

25 Moreover Dawid and the captains of the army separated to the service of the sons of Asaph, and of Heman, and of Yedutun, who should prophesy with harps, with psalteries, and with cymbals; and the number of the workmen according to their service was.

2 Of the sons of Asaph: Zaccur, and Joseph (Yosef), and Netanyah, and Asarelah, the sons of Asaph under the hands of Asaph, who prophesied according to the order of the king.

3 Of Yedutun, the sons of Yedutun: Gedalyahu, and Zeri, and Isaiah (Yeshayahu), Chashavyah, and Mattityah, six, under the hands of their father Yedutun, who prophesied with a harp, to give thanks and to praise יהוה.

4 Of Heman, the sons of Heman: Bukkiyah, Mattanyah, Uzziel, Shebuel, and Yerimot, Chananyah, Hanani, Eliathah, Giddalti, and Romamtiezer, Yoshbekashah, Mallothi, Hothir, and Mahazioth.

5 All these were the sons of Heman the king's seer in the words of God (Elohim), to lift up the horn. And God (Elohim) gave to Heman fourteen sons and three daughters.

6 All these were under the hands of their father for song in the house of יהוה, with cymbals, psalteries, and harps, for the service of the house of God (Elohim), according to the king's order to Asaph, Yedutun, and Heman.

7 So the number of them, with their brethren that were instructed in the songs of יהוה, even all that were cunning, was two hundred fourscore and eight.

8 And they cast lots, ward against ward, as well the small as the great, the teacher as the scholar.

9 Now the first lot came forth for Asaph to Joseph (Yosef); the second to Gedalyahu, who with his brethren and sons were twelve;

10 The third to Zaccur, he, his sons, and his brethren, were twelve;

11 The fourth to Izri, he, his sons, and his brethren, were twelve;

12 The fifth to Netanyah, he, his sons, and his brethren, were twelve;

13 The sixth to Bukkiyah, he, his sons, and his brethren, were twelve;

14 The seventh to Yesarelah, he, his sons, and his brethren, were twelve;

15 The eighth to Isaiah (Yeshayahu), he, his sons, and his brethren, were twelve;

16 The ninth to Mattanyah, he, his sons, and his brethren, were twelve;

17 The tenth to Shimei, he, his sons, and his brethren, were twelve;

18 The eleventh to Azareel, he, his sons, and his brethren, were twelve;

19 The twelfth to Chashavyah, he, his sons, and his brethren, were twelve;

20 The thirteenth to Shubael, he, his sons, and his brethren, were twelve;

21 The fourteenth to Mattityah, he, his sons, and his brethren, were twelve;

22 The fifteenth to Yeremot, he, his sons, and his brethren, were twelve;

23 The sixteenth to Chananyah, he, his sons, and his brethren, were twelve;

24 The seventeenth to Yoshbekashah, he, his sons, and his brethren, were twelve;

25 The eighteenth to Hanani, he, his sons, and his brethren, were twelve;

26 The nineteenth to Mallothi, he, his sons, and his brethren, were twelve;

27 The twentieth to Eliathah, he, his sons, and his brethren, were twelve;

28 The one and twentieth to Hothir, he, his sons, and his brethren, were twelve;

29 The two and twentieth to Giddalti, he, his sons, and his brethren, were twelve;

30 The three and twentieth to Mahazioth, he, his sons, and his brethren, were twelve;

31 The four and twentieth to Romamtiezer, he, his sons, and his brethren, were twelve.

26 Concerning the divisions of the porters: Of the Korhites was Meshelemyah the son of Kore, of the sons of Asaph.

2 And the sons of Meshelemyah were Zechariah (Zekharyahu) the firstborn, Yediael the second, Zevadyahu the third, Yatniel the fourth,

3 Elam the fifth, Yehochanan the sixth, Elioenai the seventh.

4 Moreover the sons of Oved-Edom were Shemayah the firstborn, Yehozavad the second, Yoach the third, and Sacar the fourth, and Nethaneel the fifth,

5 Ammiel the sixth, Yissaskhar the seventh, Peulthai the eighth; for God (Elohim) blessed him.

6 Also unto Shemayah his son were sons born, that ruled throughout the house of their father; for they were mighty men of valour.

7 The sons of Shemayah: Othni, and Rephael, and Oved, Elzabad, whose brethren were strong men, Elihu, and Semakhyahu.

8 All these of the sons of Oved-Edom; they and their sons and their brethren, able men for strength for the service, were threescore and two of Oved-Edom.

9 And Meshelemyah had sons and brethren, strong men, eighteen.

10 Also Hosah, of the children of Merari, had sons; Simri the chief, (for though he was not the firstborn, yet his father made him the chief;)

11 Hilkiah (Chilqiyah) the second, Tebaliah (Tevalyahu) the third, Zechariah (Zekharyahu) the fourth; all the sons and brethren of Hosah were thirteen.

12 Among these were the divisions of the porters, even among the chief men, having wards one against another, to minister in the house of יהוה.

13 And they cast lots, as well the small as the great, according to the house of their fathers, for every gate.

14 And the lot eastward fell to Shelemyah. Then for Zechariah (Zekharyahu) his son, a wise counsellor, they cast lots; and his lot came out northward.

15 To Oved-Edom southward; and to his sons the house of Asuppim.

16 To Shuppim and Hosah the lot came forth westward, with the gate Shallecheth, by the causeway of the going up, ward against ward.

17 Eastward were six Levites (Lewiyim), northward four a day, southward four a day, and toward Asuppim two and two.

18 At Parbar westward, four at the causeway, and two at Parbar.

19 These are the divisions of the porters among the sons of Kore, and among the sons of Merari.

20 And of the Levites (Lewiyim), Achiyah was over the treasures of the house of God (Elohim), and over the treasures of the dedicated things.

21 As concerning the sons of Laadan; the sons of the Gershonite Laadan, chief fathers, even of Laadan the Gershonite, were Yeieli.

22 The sons of Yeieli: Zetham, and Yoel his brother, who were over the treasures of the house of יהוה.

23 Of the Amramites, and the Izharites, the Hebronites, and the Uzzielites;

24 And Shebuel the son of Gershom, the son of Moses (Mosheh), was ruler of the treasures.

25 And his brethren by Eliezer; Rechavyah his son, and Jeshaiah (Yeshayahu) his son, and Yoram his son, and Zichri his son, and Shelomith his son.

26 Whom Shelomith and his brethren were over all the treasures of the dedicated things, which Dawid the king, and the chief fathers, the captains over thousands and hundreds, and the captains of the army, had dedicated.

27 Out of the spoils won in battles did they dedicate to maintain the house of יהוה.

28 And all that Shemuel the seer, and Shaul the son of Kish, and Abner the son of Ner, and Yoav the son of Zeruyah, had dedicated; and whosoever had dedicated any thing, it was under the hand of Shelomith, and of his brethren.

29 Of the Izharites, Kenanyahu and his sons were for the outward business over Yisrael, for officers and judges.

30 And of the Hebronites, Chashavyah and his brethren, men of valour, a thousand and seven hundred, were officers among them of Yisrael on this side Jordan (Yarden) westward in all the business of יהוה, and in the service of the king.

31 Among the Hebronites was Jerijah (Yeriyah) the chief, even among the Hebronites, according to the generations of his fathers. In the fortieth year of the reign of Dawid they were sought for, and there were found among them mighty men of valour at Yazer of Gilad.

32 And his brethren, men of valour, were two thousand and seven hundred chief fathers, whom King Dawid made rulers over the Reubenites (Reuveni), the Gadites, and the half tribe of Menashsheh, for every matter pertaining to God (Elohim), and affairs of the king.

27 Now the children of Yisrael after their number, the chief fathers and captains of thousands and hundreds, and their officers that served the king in any matter of the courses, which came in and went out month by month throughout all the months of the year, of every course were twenty and four thousand.

2 Over the first course for the first month was Yashovam the son of Zabdiel; and in his course were twenty and four thousand.

3 Of the children of Perez was the chief of all the

captains of the army for the first month.

4 And over the course of the second month was Dodai an Ahohite, and of his course was Mikloth also the ruler: in his course likewise were twenty and four thousand.

5 The third captain of the army for the third month was Benayah the son of Yehoyada, a chief priest (kohen); and in his course were twenty and four thousand.

6 This is that Benayah, who was mighty among the thirty, and above the thirty: and in his course was Ammizabad his son.

7 The fourth captain for the fourth month was Asahel the brother of Yoav, and Zevadyahu his son after him; and in his course were twenty and four thousand.

8 The fifth captain for the fifth month was Shamhuth the Izrahite; and in his course were twenty and four thousand.

9 The sixth captain for the sixth month was Ira the son of Ikkesh the Tekoite; and in his course were twenty and four thousand.

10 The seventh captain for the seventh month was Helez the Pelonite, of the children of Efrayim; and in his course were twenty and four thousand.

11 The eighth captain for the eighth month was Sibbecai the Hushathite, of the Zarhites; and in his course were twenty and four thousand.

12 The ninth captain for the ninth month was Aviezer the Anetothite, of the Benjamites (Benyemini); and in his course were twenty and four thousand.

13 The tenth captain for the tenth month was Maharai the Netophathite, of the Zarhites; and in his course were twenty and four thousand.

14 The eleventh captain for the eleventh month was Benayah the Pirathonite, of the children of Efrayim; and in his course were twenty and four thousand.

15 The twelfth captain for the twelfth month was Heldai the Netophathite, of Othniel; and in his course were twenty and four thousand.

16 Furthermore over the tribes of Yisrael: the ruler of the Reubenites (Reuveni) was Eliezer the son of Zichri; of the Shimonites, Shefatyah the son of Maachah;

17 Of the Levites (Lewiyim), Chashavyah the son of Kemuel; of the Aharonites, Zadok;

18 Of Judah (Yehudah), Elihu, one of the brethren of Dawid; of Yissaskhar, Omri the

son of Mikhael;

19 Of Zevulun, Yishmayah the son of Ovadyah; of Naftali, Yerimot the son of Azriel;

20 Of the children of Efrayim, Hoshea the son of Azazyahu; of the half tribe of Menashsheh, Yoel the son of Pedayah;

21 Of the half tribe of Menashsheh in Gilad, Iddo the son of Zechariah (Zekharyahu); of Benjamin (Binyamin), Yaasiel the son of Abner;

22 Of Dan, Azareel the son of Yeroham. These were the princes of the tribes of Yisrael.

23 But Dawid took not the number of them from twenty years old and under, because יהוה had said He would increase Yisrael like to the stars of the heavens.

24 Yoav the son of Zeruyah began to number, but he finished not, because there fell wrath for it against Yisrael; neither was the number put in the account of the Chronicles of King Dawid.

25 And over the king's treasures was Azmaveth the son of Adiel; and over the storehouses in the fields, in the cities, and in the villages, and in the castles, was [A46]Jonathan (Yehonatan) the son of Uzziyah.

26 And over them that did the work of the field for tillage of the ground was Ezri the son of Chelub.

27 And over the vineyards was Shimei the Ramathite; over the increase of the vineyards for the wine cellars was Zabdi the Shiphmite.

28 And over the olive trees and the sycomore trees that were in the low plains was Baalhanan the Gederite; and over the cellars of oil was Yoash.

29 And over the herds that fed in Sharon was Shitrai the Sharonite; and over the herds that were in the valleys was Shaphat the son of Adlai.

30 Over the camels also was Obil the Ismaelite (Yishmaeli); and over the asses was Yechdeyahu the Meronothite;

31 And over the flocks was Yaziz the Hagerite. All these were the rulers of the substance which was King Dawid's.

32 Also Jonathan (Yehonatan) Dawid's uncle was a counsellor, a wise man, and a scribe; and Yeiel the son of Hachmoni was with the king's sons.

33 And Ahithophel was the king's counsellor; and Hushai the Archite was the king's companion.

34 And after Ahithophel was Yehoyada the son

of Benayah, and Aviathar; and the general of the king's army was Yoav.

28 And Dawid assembled all the princes of Yisrael, the princes of the tribes, and the captains of the companies that ministered to the king by course, and the captains over the thousands, and captains over the hundreds, and the stewards over all the substance and possession of the king, and of his sons, with the officers, and with the mighty men, and with all the valiant men, unto Jerusalem (Yerushalayim).

2 Then Dawid the king stood up upon his feet, and said, "Hear me, my brethren, and my people: As for me, I had in mine heart to build a house of rest for the ark of the covenant of יהוה, and for the footstool of our God (Elohim), and had made ready for the building.

3 But God (Elohim) said unto me, 'You shalt not build a house for My name, because you have been a man of war, and hast shed blood.

4 Howbeit יהוה God of Israel (Elohei Yisrael) chose me before all the house of my father to be king over Yisrael forever, for He hath chosen Judah (Yehudah) to be the ruler; and of the house of Judah (Yehudah), the house of my father; and among the sons of my father He liked me to make me king over all Yisrael.

5 And of all my sons, (for יהוה hath given me many sons,) He hath chosen Solomon (Shelomoh) my son to sit upon the throne of the kingdom of יהוה over Yisrael.

6 And He said unto me, 'Solomon (Shelomoh) your son, he shall build My house and My courts, for I have chosen him to be My son, and I will be his Father.

7 Moreover I will establish his kingdom forever, if he is steadfast to do My commandments and My judgments, as at this day.'

8 Now therefore in the sight of all Yisrael the congregation of יהוה, and in the audience of our God (Elohim), keep and seek for all the commandments of יהוה your God (YHWH Eloheikhem), that you may possess this good land, and leave it for an inheritance for your children after you forever.

9 And you, Solomon (Shelomoh) my son, know you the God (Elohim) of your father, and serve Him with a perfect heart and with a willing mind; for יהוה searcheth all hearts, and understandeth all the imaginations of the thoughts. If you seek Him, He will be found of

you; but if you forsake Him, He will cast you off forever.

10 Take heed now, for יהוה hath chosen you to build a house for the sanctuary; be strong, and do it."

11 Then Dawid gave to Solomon (Shelomoh) his son the pattern of the porch, and of the houses thereof, and of the treasuries thereof, and of the upper chambers thereof, and of the inner parlours thereof, and of the place of the mercy seat,

12 And the pattern of all that he had by the spirit, of the courts of the house of יהוה, and of all the chambers round about, of the treasuries of the house of God (Elohim), and of the treasuries of the dedicated things;

13 Also for the courses of the priests (kohanim) and the Levites (Lewiyim), and for all the work of the service of the house of יהוה, and for all the vessels of service in the house of יהוה.

14 He gave of gold by weight for things of gold, for all instruments of all manner of service; silver also for all instruments of silver by weight, for all instruments of every kind of service;

15 Even the weight for the candlesticks (menorot) of gold, and for their lamps of gold, by weight for every candlestick (menorah), and for the lamps thereof; and for the candlesticks (menorot) of silver by weight, both for the candlestick (menorah), and also for the lamps thereof, according to the use of every candlestick (menorah).

16 And by weight he gave gold for the tables of shewbread, for every table; and likewise silver for the tables of silver;

17 Also pure gold for the fleshhooks, and the bowls, and the cups; and for the golden basons he gave gold by weight for every bason; and likewise silver by weight for every bason of silver;

18 And for the altar of incense refined gold by weight; and gold for the pattern of the chariot of the cherubims (keruvim), that spread out their wings, and covered the ark of the covenant of יהוה.

19 "All this," said Dawid, "יהוה made me understand in writing by His hand upon me, even all the works of this pattern."

20 And Dawid said to Solomon (Shelomoh) his son, "Be strong and of good courage, and do it;

fear not, nor be dismayed; for יהוה God (Elohim), even my God (Elohim), will be with you; He will not fail you, nor forsake you, until you have finished all the work for the service of the house of יהוה.

21 And, behold, the courses of the priests (kohanim) and the Levites (Lewiyim), even they shall be with you for all the service of the house of God (Elohim); and there shall be with you for all manner of workmanship every willing skilful man, for any manner of service; also the princes and all the people will be wholly at your command."

29 Furthermore Dawid the king said unto all the congregation: "Solomon (Shelomoh) my son, whom alone God (Elohim) hath chosen, is yet young and tender, and the work is great, for the palace is not for man but for God (Elohim) יהוה.

2 Now I have prepared with all my might for the house of my God (Elohim) the gold for things to be made of gold, and the silver for things of silver, and the brass for things of brass, the iron for things of iron, and wood for things of wood; onyx stones, and stones to be set, glistering stones, and of divers colours, and all manner of precious stones, and marble stones in abundance.

3 Moreover, because I have set my affection to the house of my God (Elohim), I have of mine own proper good, of gold and silver, which I have given to the house of my God (Elohim), over and above all that I have prepared for the holy house,

4 Even three thousand talents of gold, of the gold of Ophir, and seven thousand talents of refined silver, to overlay the walls of the houses withal;

5 The gold for things of gold, and the silver for things of silver, and for all manner of work to be made by the hands of artificers. And who then is willing to consecrate his service this day unto יהוה?"

6 Then the chief of the fathers and princes of the tribes of Yisrael, and the captains of thousands and of hundreds, with the rulers of the king's work, offered willingly,

7 And gave for the service of the house of God (Elohim) of gold five thousand talents and ten thousand drams, and of silver ten thousand talents, and of brass eighteen thousand talents,

and one hundred thousand talents of iron.

8 And they with whom precious stones were found gave them to the treasure of the house of יהוה, by the hand of Yeiel the Gershonite.

9 Then the people rejoiced, for that they offered willingly, because with perfect heart they offered willingly to יהוה; and Dawid the king also rejoiced with great joy.

10 Wherefore Dawid blessed יהוה before all the congregation; and Dawid said, "Blessed be You, יהוה God of Israel (Elohei Yisrael) our father, forever and ever.

11 Yours, O יהוה, is the greatness, and the power, and the glory, and the victory, and the majesty; for all that is in the heavens and on the earth is Yours; Yours is the kingdom, O יהוה, and You are exalted as head above all.

12 Both riches and honor come of You, and You reignest over all; and in Your hand is power and might; and in Your hand it is to make great, and to give strength unto all.

13 Now therefore, our God (Elohim), we thank You, and praise Your glorious name.

14 But who am I, and what is my people, that we should be able to offer so willingly after this sort? For all things come of You, and of Your own have we given You.

15 For we are strangers before You, and sojourners, as were all our fathers; our days on the earth are as a shadow, and there is none abiding.

16 O יהוה our God (YHWH Eloheinu), all this store that we have prepared to build You a house for Your holy name cometh of Your hand, and is all Your own.

17 I know also, my God (Elohim), that You test the heart, and hast pleasure in uprightness. As for me, in the uprightness of mine heart I have willingly offered all these things; and now have I seen with joy Your people, who are present here, to offer willingly unto You.

18 O יהוה God (Elohim) of Avraham, Isaac (Yitschaq), and of Yisrael, our fathers, keep this forever in the imagination of the thoughts of the heart of Your people, and prepare their heart unto You.

19 And give unto Solomon (Shelomoh) my son a perfect heart, to keep Your commandments, Your testimonies, and Your statutes, and to do all these things, and to build the palace, for which I have made provision."

20 And Dawid said to all the congregation, "Now bless יהוה your God (YHWH Eloheikhem)." And all the congergation blessed יהוה God (Elohim) of their fathers, and bowed down their heads, and worshipped יהוה, and the king.

21 And they sacrificed sacrifices unto יהוה, and offered burnt offerings unto יהוה, on the next day after that day, even a thousand bullocks, a thousand rams, and a thousand lambs, with their drink offerings, and sacrifices in abundance for all Yisrael.

22 And did eat and drink before יהוה on that day with great gladness. And they made Solomon (Shelomoh) the son of Dawid king the second time, and anointed him unto יהוה to be the chief governor, and Zadok to be priest (kohen).

23 Then Solomon (Shelomoh) sat on the throne of יהוה as king instead of Dawid his father, and prospered; and all Yisrael obeyed him.

24 And all the princes, and the mighty men, and all the sons likewise of King Dawid, submitted themselves unto Solomon (Shelomoh) the king.

25 And יהוה magnified Solomon (Shelomoh) exceedingly in the sight of all Yisrael, and bestowed upon him such royal majesty as had not been on any king before him in Yisrael.

26 Thus Dawid the son of Jesse (Yishai) reigned over all Yisrael.

27 And the time that he reigned over Yisrael was forty years; seven years reigned he in Hebron, and thirty and three years reigned he in Jerusalem (Yerushalayim).

28 And he died in a good old age, full of days, riches, and honor; and Solomon (Shelomoh) his son reigned in his stead.

29 Now the acts of Dawid the king, first and last, behold, they are written in the book of Shemuel the seer, and in the book of Nathan the prophet, and in the book of Gad the seer,

30 With all his reign and his might, and the times that went over him, and over Yisrael, and over all the kingdoms of the countries.

2 CHRONICLES
DIVREY HAYAMIM 2
דִּבְרֵי הַיָּמִים ב
(Annals of Time)

1 And Solomon (Shelomoh) the son of Dawid was strengthened in his kingdom, and יהוה his God (Elohim) was with him, and magnified him exceedingly.

2 Then Solomon (Shelomoh) spake unto all Yisrael, to the captains of thousands and of hundreds, and to the judges, and to every governor in all Yisrael, the chief of the fathers.

3 So Solomon (Shelomoh), and all the congregation with him, went to the high place that was at Giveon; for there was the tabernacle of the congregation of God (Elohim), which Moses (Mosheh) the servant of יהוה had made in the wilderness.

4 But the ark of God (Elohim) had Dawid brought up from Qiryat-Yearim to the place which Dawid had prepared for it; for he had pitched a tent for it at Jerusalem (Yerushalayim).

5 Moreover the brasen altar, that Bezaleel the son of Uri, the son of Hur, had made, he put before the tabernacle of יהוה; and Solomon (Shelomoh) and the congregation sought unto it.

6 And Solomon (Shelomoh) went up thither to the brasen altar before יהוה, which was at the tabernacle of the congregation, and offered a thousand burnt offerings upon it.

7 In that night did God (Elohim) appear unto Solomon (Shelomoh), and said unto him, "Ask what I shall give you."

8 And Solomon (Shelomoh) said unto God (Elohim), "You have shewed great mercy unto Dawid my father, and hast made me to reign in his stead.

9 Now, O God (Elohim) יהוה, let Your promise unto Dawid my father be established, for You have made me king over a people like the dust of the earth in multitude.

10 Give me now wisdom and knowledge, that I may go out and come in before this people; for who can judge this Your people, that is so great?"

11 And God (Elohim) said to Solomon (Shelomoh), "Because this was in your heart, and you have not asked riches, wealth, or honor, nor the life of your enemies, neither yet hast asked long life; but hast asked wisdom and knowledge for yourself, that you mayest judge My people, over whom I have made you king;

12 Wisdom and knowledge is granted unto you; and I will give you riches, and wealth, and honor, such as none of the kings have had that have been before you, neither shall there any after you have the like.

13 Then Solomon (Shelomoh) came from his journey to the high place that was at Giveon to Jerusalem (Yerushalayim), from before the tabernacle of the congregation, and reigned over Yisrael.

14 And Solomon (Shelomoh) gathered chariots and horsemen; and he had a thousand and four hundred chariots, and twelve thousand horsemen, which he placed in the chariot cities, and with the king at Jerusalem (Yerushalayim).

15 And the king made silver and gold at Jerusalem (Yerushalayim) as plenteous as stones, and cedar trees made he as the sycomore trees that are in the vale for abundance.

16 And Solomon (Shelomoh) had horses brought out of Egypt (Mitsrayim), and linen yarn; the king's merchants received the linen yarn at a price.

17 And they fetched up, and brought forth out of Egypt (Mitsrayim) a chariot for six hundred shekels of silver, and a horse for a hundred and fifty; and so brought they out horses for all the kings of the Hittites, and for the kings of Syria (Aram), by their means.

2 And Solomon (Shelomoh) determined to build a house for the name of יהוה, and a house for his kingdom.

2 And Solomon (Shelomoh) told out threescore and ten thousand men to bear burdens, and fourscore thousand to hew in the mountain, and three thousand and six hundred to oversee them.

3 And Solomon (Shelomoh) sent to Huram the king of Tyre, saying, "As you didst deal with Dawid my father, and didst send him cedars to build him a house to dwell therein, even so deal with me.

4 Behold, I build a house to the name of יהוה my God (YHWH Elohai), to dedicate it to Him, and to burn before Him sweet incense, and for the continual shewbread, and for the burnt offerings morning and evening, on the Shabbats, and on the New Moons, and on the solemn feasts of

יהוה our God (YHWH Eloheinu). This is an ordinance forever to Yisrael.

5 And the house which I build is great, for great is our God (Elohim) above all mighty ones (elohim).

6 But who is able to build Him a house, seeing the heaven and heaven of heavens cannot contain Him? Who am I then, that I should build Him a house, except only to burn sacrifice before Him?

7 Send me now therefore a man cunning to work in gold, and in silver, and in brass, and in iron, and in purple, and crimson, and blue, and that can skill to grave with the cunning men that are with me in Judah (Yehudah) and in Jerusalem (Yerushalayim), whom Dawid my father did provide.

8 Send me also cedar trees, fir trees, and algum trees, out of Lebanon; for I know that your servants can skill to cut timber in Lebanon; and, behold, my servants shall be with your servants,

9 Even to prepare me timber in abundance; for the house which I am about to build shall be wonderful great.

10 And, behold, I will give to your servants, the hewers that cut timber, twenty thousand measures of beaten wheat, and twenty thousand measures of barley, and twenty thousand baths of wine, and twenty thousand baths of oil."

11 Then Huram the king of Tyre answered in writing, which he sent to Solomon (Shelomoh), "Because יהוה hath loved His people, He hath made you king over them."

12 Huram said moreover, "Blessed be יהוה God of Israel (Elohei Yisrael), that made heaven and earth, who hath given to Dawid the king a wise son, endued with prudence and understanding, that might build a house for יהוה, and a house for his kingdom.

13 And now I have sent a cunning man, endued with understanding, of Huram my father's,

14 The son of a woman of the daughters of Dan, and his father was a man of Tyre, skilful to work in gold, and in silver, in brass, in iron, in stone, and in timber, in purple, in blue, and in fine linen, and in crimson; also to grave any manner of graving, and to find out every device which shall be put to him, with your cunning men, and with the cunning men of my lord (adoni) Dawid your father.

15 Now therefore the wheat, and the barley, the oil, and the wine, which my lord (adoni) hath spoken of, let him send unto his servants.

16 And we will cut wood out of Lebanon, as much as you shalt need; and we will bring it to you in floats by sea to Joppa (Yafo); and you shalt carry it up to Jerusalem (Yerushalayim)."

17 And Solomon (Shelomoh) numbered all the strangers that were in the land of Yisrael, after the numbering wherewith Dawid his father had numbered them; and they were found a hundred and fifty thousand and three thousand and six hundred.

18 And he set threescore and ten thousand of them to be bearers of burdens, and fourscore thousand to be hewers in the mountain, and three thousand and six hundred overseers to set the people a work.

3 Then Solomon (Shelomoh) began to build the house of יהוה at Jerusalem (Yerushalayim) in Mount Moriyah, where יהוה appeared unto Dawid his father, in the place that Dawid had prepared in the threshingfloor of Ornan the Yevusi.

2 And he began to build in the second day of the second month, in the fourth year of his reign.

3 Now these are the things wherein Solomon (Shelomoh) was instructed for the building of the house of God (Elohim). The length by cubits after the first measure was threescore cubits, and the breadth twenty cubits.

4 And the porch that was in the front of the house, the length of it was according to the breadth of the house, twenty cubits, and the height was a hundred and twenty; and he overlaid it within with pure gold.

5 And the greater house he cieled with fir tree, which he overlaid with fine gold, and set thereon palm trees and chains.

6 And he garnished the house with precious stones for beauty; and the gold was gold of Parvaim.

7 He overlaid also the house, the beams, the posts, and the walls thereof, and the doors thereof, with gold; and graved cherubims (keruvim) on the walls.

8 And he made the most holy house, the length whereof was according to the breadth of the house, twenty cubits, and the breadth thereof twenty cubits; and he overlaid it with fine gold, amounting to six hundred talents.

9 And the weight of the nails was fifty shekels

of gold. And he overlaid the upper chambers with gold.

10 And in the most holy house he made two cherubims (keruvim) of image work, and overlaid them with gold.

11 And the wings of the cherubims (keruvim) were twenty cubits long; one wing of the one cherub (keruv) was five cubits, reaching to the wall of the house; and the other wing was likewise five cubits, reaching to the wing of the other cherub (keruv).

12 And one wing of the other cherub (keruv) was five cubits, reaching to the wall of the house; and the other wing was five cubits also, joining to the wing of the other cherub (keruv).

13 The wings of these cherubims (keruvim) spread themselves forth twenty cubits; and they stood on their feet, and their faces were inward.

14 And he made the vail of blue, and purple, and crimson, and fine linen, and wrought cherubims (keruvim) thereon.

15 Also he made before the house two pillars of thirty and five cubits high, and the chapiter that was on the top of each of them was five cubits.

16 And he made chains, as in the oracle, and put them on the heads of the pillars; and made a hundred pomegranates, and put them on the chains.

17 And he reared up the pillars before the temple, one on the right hand, and the other on the left; and called the name of that on the right hand Yakhin, and the name of that on the left Boaz.

4 Moreover he made an altar of brass, twenty cubits the length thereof, and twenty cubits the breadth thereof, and ten cubits the height thereof.

2 Also he made a molten sea of ten cubits from brim to brim, round in compass, and five cubits the height thereof; and a line of thirty cubits did compass it round about.

3 And under it was the similitude of oxen, which did compass it round about: ten in a cubit, compassing the sea round about. Two rows of oxen were cast, when it was cast.

4 It stood upon twelve oxen, three looking toward the north, and three looking toward the west, and three looking toward the south, and three looking toward the east; and the sea was set above upon them, and all their hinder parts were inward.

5 And the thickness of it was a handbreadth, and the brim of it like the work of the brim of a cup, with flowers of lilies; and it received and held three thousand baths.

6 He made also ten lavers, and put five on the right hand, and five on the left, to wash in them; such things as they offered for the burnt offering they washed in them; but the sea was for the priests (kohanim) to wash in.

7 And he made ten candlesticks (menorot) of gold according to their form, and set them in the temple, five on the right hand, and five on the left.

8 He made also ten tables, and placed them in the temple, five on the right side, and five on the left. And he made a hundred basons of gold.

9 Furthermore he made the court of the priests (kohanim), and the great court, and doors for the court, and overlaid the doors of them with brass.

10 And he set the sea on the right side of the east end, opposite the south.

11 And Huram made the pots, and the shovels, and the basons. And Huram finished the work that he was to make for King Solomon (Shelomoh) for the house of God (Elohim);

12 The two pillars, and the pommels, and the chapiters which were on the top of the two pillars, and the two wreaths to cover the two pommels of the chapiters which were on the top of the pillars;

13 And four hundred pomegranates on the two wreaths; two rows of pomegranates on each wreath, to cover the two pommels of the chapiters which were upon the pillars.

14 He made also bases, and lavers made he upon the bases;

15 One sea, and twelve oxen under it.

16 The pots also, and the shovels, and the fleshhooks, and all their instruments, did Huram his father make to King Solomon (Shelomoh) for the house of יהוה of bright brass.

17 In the plain of Jordan (Yarden) did the king cast them, in the clay ground between Sukkot and Zeredathah.

18 Thus Solomon (Shelomoh) made all these vessels in great abundance; for the weight of the brass could not be found out.

19 And Solomon (Shelomoh) made all the vessels that were for the house of God (Elohim), the golden altar also, and the tables whereon the shewbread was set;

20 Moreover the candlesticks (menorot) with their lamps, that they should burn after the manner before the oracle, of pure gold;

21 And the flowers, and the lamps, and the tongs, made he of gold, and that perfect gold;

22 And the snuffers, and the basons, and the spoons, and the censers, of pure gold; and the entry of the house, the inner doors thereof for the most holy place, and the doors of the house of the temple, were of gold.

5 Thus all the work that Solomon (Shelomoh) made for the house of יהוה was finished; and Solomon (Shelomoh) brought in all the things that Dawid his father had dedicated; and the silver, and the gold, and all the instruments, put he among the treasures of the house of God (Elohim).

2 Then Solomon (Shelomoh) assem-bled the elders of Yisrael, and all the heads of the tribes, the chief of the fathers of the children of Yisrael, unto Jerusalem (Yerushalayim), to bring up the ark of the covenant of יהוה out of the city of Dawid, which is Zion (Tsiyon).

3 Wherefore all the men of Yisrael assembled themselves unto the king in the feast which was in the seventh month.

4 And all the elders of Yisrael came; and the Levites (Lewiyim) took up the ark.

5 And they brought up the ark, and the tabernacle of the congregation, and all the holy vessels that were in the tabernacle, these did the priests (kohanim) and the Levites (Lewiyim) bring up.

6 Also King Solomon (Shelomoh), and all the congregation of Yisrael that were assembled unto him before the ark, sacrificed sheep and oxen, which could not be told nor numbered for multitude.

7 And the priests (kohanim) brought in the ark of the covenant of יהוה unto his place, to the oracle of the house, into the most holy place, even under the wings of the cherubims (keruvim).

8 For the cherubims (keruvim) spread forth their wings over the place of the ark, and the cherubims (keruvim) covered the ark and the staves thereof above.

9 And they drew out the staves of the ark, that the ends of the staves were seen from the ark before the oracle; but they were not seen outside. And there it is unto this day.

10 There was nothing in the ark save the two

tables which Moses (Mosheh) put therein at Horeb, when יהוה made a covenant with the children of Yisrael, when they came out of Egypt (Mitsrayim).

11 And it came to pass, when the priests (kohanim) were come out of the Holy Place, (for all the priests (kohanim) that were present were sanctified, and did not then wait by course;

12 Also the Levites (Lewiyim) which were the singers, all of them of Asaph, of Heman, of Yedutun, with their sons and their brethren, being arrayed in white linen, having cymbals and psalteries and harps, stood at the east end of the altar, and with them a hundred and twenty priests (kohanim) sounding with trumpets;)

13 It came even to pass, as the trumpeters and singers were as one, to make one sound to be heard in praising and thanking יהוה; and when they lifted up their voice with the trumpets and cymbals and instruments of musick, and praised יהוה, saying: "For He is good, for His mercy endureth forever," that then the house was filled with a cloud, even the house of יהוה,

14 So that the priests (kohanim) could not stand to minister by reason of the cloud; for the glory of יהוה had filled the house of God (Elohim).

6 Then said Solomon (Shelomoh), יהוה hath said that He would dwell in the thick darkness.

2 But I have built a house of habitation for You, and a place for Your dwelling forever.

3 And the king turned his face, and blessed the whole congregation of Yisrael; and all the congregation of Yisrael stood.

4 And he said, "Blessed be יהוה God of Israel (Elohei Yisrael), who hath with His hands fulfilled that which He spake with His mouth to my father Dawid, saying,

5 'Since the day that I brought forth My people out of the land of Egypt (Mitsrayim) I chose no city among all the tribes of Yisrael to build a house in, that My name might be there; neither chose I any man to be a ruler over My people Yisrael;

6 But I have chosen Jerusalem (Yerushalayim), that My name might be there; and have chosen Dawid to be over My people Yisrael.'

7 Now it was in the heart of Dawid my father to build a house for the name of יהוה God of Israel (Elohei Yisrael).

8 But יהוה said to Dawid my father, 'Forasmuch

as it was in your heart to build a house for My name, you didst well in that it was in your heart.

9 Nevertheless you shalt not build the house, but your son who shall come forth out of your loins, he shall build the house for My name.'

10 יהוה therefore hath performed His word that He hath spoken, for I am risen up in the room of Dawid my father, and am set on the throne of Yisrael, as יהוה promised, and have built the house for the name of יהוה God of Israel (Elohei Yisrael).

11 And in it have I put the ark, wherein is the covenant of יהוה, that He made with the children of Yisrael."

12 And he stood before the altar of יהוה in the presence of all the congregation of Yisrael, and spread forth his hands;

13 For Solomon (Shelomoh) had made a brasen scaffold, of five cubits long, and five cubits broad, and three cubits high, and had set it in the midst of the court: and upon it he stood, and kneeled down upon his knees before all the congregation of Yisrael, and spread forth his hands toward heaven,

14 And said, "O יהוה God of Israel (Elohei Yisrael), there is no God (Elohim) like You in the heaven, nor on the earth; which keepest covenant, and shewest mercy unto Your servants, that walk before You with all their hearts.

15 You who hast kept with Your servant Dawid my father that which You have promised him; and spakest with Your mouth, and hast fulfilled it with Your hand, as it is this day.

16 Now therefore, O יהוה God of Israel (Elohei Yisrael), keep with Your servant Dawid my father that which You have promised him, saying, 'There shall not fail you a man in My sight to sit upon the throne of Yisrael; yet so that your children take heed to their way to walk in My Torah, as you have walked before Me.'

17 Now then, O יהוה God of Israel (Elohei Yisrael), let Your word be verified, which You have spoken unto Your servant Dawid.

18 But will God (Elohim) in very deed dwell with men on the earth? Behold, heaven and the heaven of heavens cannot contain You; how much less this house which I have built!

19 Have regard therefore to the prayer of Your servant, and to his supplication, O יהוה my God (YHWH Elohai), to hearken unto the cry and the prayer which Your servant prayeth before You:

20 That Your eyes may be open upon this house day and night, upon the place whereof You have said that You wouldest put Your name there; to hearken unto the prayer which Your servant prayeth toward this place.

21 Hearken therefore unto the supplications of Your servant, and of Your people Yisrael, which they shall make toward this place; hear You from Your dwelling place, even from heaven; and when You hearest, forgive.

22 If a man sin against his neighbour, and an oath be laid upon him to make him swear, and the oath come before Your altar in this house;

23 Then hear You from heaven, and do, and judge Your servants, by requiting the wicked, by recompensing his way upon his own head; and by justifying the righteous, by giving him according to his righteousness.

24 And if Your people Yisrael be put to the worse before the enemy, because they have sinned against You; and shall return and confess Your name, and pray and make supplication before You in this house;

25 Then hear You from the heaven, and forgive the sin of Your people Yisrael, and bring them again unto the land which You gavest to them and to their fathers.

26 When the heaven is shut up, and there is no rain, because they have sinned against You; yet if they pray toward this place, and confess Your name, and turn from their sin, when You dost afflict them;

27 Then hear You from heaven, and forgive the sin of Your servants, and of Your people Yisrael, when You have taught them the good way, wherein they should walk; and send rain upon Your land, which You have given unto Your people for an inheritance.

28 If there be dearth in the land, if there be pestilence, if there be blasting, or mildew, locusts, or caterpillers; if their enemies besiege them in the cities of their land; whatsoever sore or whatsoever sickness there be;

29 Then what prayer or what supplication soever shall be made of any man, or of all Your people Yisrael, when every one shall know his own sore and his own grief, and shall spread forth his hands in this house;

30 Then hear You from heaven Your dwelling place, and forgive, and render unto every man

according unto all his ways, whose heart You knowest; (for You only knowest the hearts of the children of men),

31 That they may fear You, to walk in Your ways, so long as they live in the land which You gavest unto our fathers.

32 Moreover concerning the stranger, which is not of Your people Yisrael, but is come from a far country for Your great name's sake, and Your mighty hand, and Your outstretched arm; if they come and pray in this house;

33 Then hear You from the heaven, even from Your dwelling place, and do according to all that the stranger calleth to You for, that all people of the earth may know Your name, and fear You, as doth Your people Yisrael, and may know that this house which I have built is called by Your name.

34 If Your people go out to war against their enemies by the way that You shalt send them, and they pray unto you toward this city which You have chosen, and the house which I have built for Your name;

35 Then hear You from the heaven their prayer and their supplication, and maintain their cause.

36 If they sin against You, (for there is no man which sinneth not,) and You be angry with them, and deliver them over before their enemies, and they carry them away captives unto a land far off or near;

37 Yet if they bethink themselves in the land whither they are carried captive, and turn and pray unto you in the land of their captivity, saying, 'We have sinned, we have done amiss, and have dealt wickedly;'

38 If they return to You with all their heart and with all their soul in the land of their captivity, whither they have carried them captives, and pray toward their land, which You gavest unto their fathers, and toward the city which You have chosen, and toward the house which I have built for Your name;

39 Then hear You from the heaven, even from Your dwelling place, their prayer and their supplications, and maintain their cause, and forgive Your people who have sinned against You.

40 Now, my God (Elohim), let, I beseech You, Your eyes be open, and let Your ears be attentive unto the prayer that is made in this place.

41 Now therefore arise, O God (Elohim) יהוה,

into Your resting place, You, and the ark of Your strength. Let Your priests (kohanim), O God (Elohim) יהוה, be clothed with salvation, and let Your holy ones rejoice in goodness.

42 O God (Elohim) יהוה, turn not away the face of Your anointed; remember the mercies of Dawid Your servant."

7 Now when Solomon (Shelomoh) had made an end of praying, the fire came down from heaven, and consumed the burnt offering and the sacrifices; and the glory of יהוה filled the house.

2 And the priests (kohanim) could not enter into the house of יהוה, because the glory of יהוה had filled יהוה's house.

3 And when all the children of Yisrael saw how the fire came down, and the glory of יהוה upon the house, they bowed themselves with their faces to the ground upon the pavement, and worshipped, and praised יהוה, saying, "For He is good, for His mercy endureth forever."

4 Then the king and all the people offered sacrifices before יהוה.

5 And King Solomon (Shelomoh) offered a sacrifice of twenty and two thousand oxen, and a hundred and twenty thousand sheep; so the king and all the people dedicated the house of God (Elohim).

6 And the priests (kohanim) stood at their offices; the Levites (Lewiyim) also with instruments of musick of יהוה, which Dawid the king had made to praise יהוה, because His mercy endureth forever, when Dawid praised by their ministry; and the priests (kohanim) sounded trumpets before them, and all Yisrael stood.

7 Moreover Solomon (Shelomoh) hallowed the middle of the court that was before the house of יהוה; for there he offered burnt offerings, and the fat of the peace offerings, because the brasen altar which Solomon (Shelomoh) had made was not able to receive the burnt offerings, and the meat offerings, and the fat.

8 Also at the same time Solomon (Shelomoh) kept the feast seven days, and all Yisrael with him, a very great congregation, from the entering in of Hamath unto the river of Egypt (Mitsrayim).

9 And in the eighth day they made a solemn assembly, for they kept the dedication of the altar seven days, and the feast seven days.

10 And on the three and twentieth day of the seventh month he sent the people away into their

tents, glad and merry in heart for the goodness that יהוה had shewed unto Dawid, and to Solomon (Shelomoh), and to Yisrael His people. 11 Thus Solomon (Shelomoh) finished the house of יהוה, and the king's house; and all that came into Solomon (Shelomoh)'s heart to make in the house of יהוה, and in his own house, he prosperously effected.

12 And יהוה appeared to Solomon (Shelomoh) by night, and said unto him, "I have heard your prayer, and have chosen this place to Myself for a house of sacrifice.

13 If I shut up heaven that there be no rain, or if I command the locusts to devour the land, or if I send pestilence among My people;

14 If My people, who are called by My name, shall humble themselves, and pray, and seek My face, and turn from their wicked ways; then will I hear from heaven, and will forgive their sin, and will heal their land.

15 Now Mine eyes shall be open, and Mine ears attentive unto the prayer that is made in this place.

16 For now have I chosen and sanctified this house, that My name may be there forever; and Mine eyes and Mine heart shall be there perpetually.

17 And as for you, if you wilt walk before Me, as Dawid your father walked, and do according to all that I have commanded you, and shalt observe My statutes and My judgments;

18 Then will I establish the throne of your kingdom, according as I have covenanted with Dawid your father, saying, 'There shall not fail you a man to be ruler in Yisrael.'

19 But if you turn away, and forsake My statutes and My commandments, which I have set before you, and shall go and serve other gods (elohim), and worship them;

20 Then will I pluck them up by the roots out of My land which I have given them; and this house, which I have sanctified for My name, will I cast out of My sight, and will make it to be a proverb and a byword among all nations.

21 And this house, which is high, shall be an astonishment to every one that passeth by it; so that he shall say, 'Why hath יהוה done thus unto this land, and unto this house?'

22 And it shall be answered, 'Because they forsook יהוה God (Elohim) of their fathers, who brought them forth out of the land of Egypt

(Mitsrayim), and laid hold on other gods (elohim), and worshipped them, and served them; therefore hath He brought all this disaster (raah) upon them.'"

8 And it came to pass at the end of twenty years, wherein Solomon (Shelomoh) had built the house of יהוה, and his own house,

2 That the cities which Huram had restored to Solomon (Shelomoh), Solomon (Shelomoh) built them, and caused the children of Yisrael to dwell there.

3 And Solomon (Shelomoh) went to Hamathzobah, and prevailed against it.

4 And he built Tadmor in the wilderness, and all the store cities, which he built in Hamath.

5 Also he built Beit-Choron the upper, and Beit-Choron the nether, fenced cities, with walls, gates, and bars;

6 And Baalath, and all the store cities that Solomon (Shelomoh) had, and all the chariot cities, and the cities of the horsemen, and all that Solomon (Shelomoh) desired to build in Jerusalem (Yerushalayim), and in Lebanon, and throughout all the land of his dominion.

7 As for all the people that were left of the Hittites, and the Amorites, and the Perizzites, and the Hivites, and the Yevusis, who were not of Yisrael,

8 But of their children, who were left after them in the land, whom the children of Yisrael consumed not, them did Solomon (Shelomoh) make to pay tribute until this day.

9 But of the children of Yisrael did Solomon (Shelomoh) make no servants for his work; but they were men of war, and chief of his captains, and captains of his chariots and horsemen.

10 And these were the chief of King Solomon (Shelomoh)'s officers, even two hundred and fifty, that bare rule over the people.

11 And Solomon (Shelomoh) brought up the daughter of Pharaoh (Paroh) out of the city of Dawid unto the house that he had built for her; for he said, "My wife shall not dwell in the house of Dawid king of Yisrael, because the places are holy, whereunto the ark of יהוה hath come."

12 Then Solomon (Shelomoh) offered burnt offerings unto יהוה on the altar of יהוה, which he had built before the porch,

13 Even after a certain rate every day, offering according to the commandment of Moses

(Mosheh), on the Shabbats, and on the New Moons, and on the solemn feasts, three times in the year, even in the Feast of Unleaven Bread (Chag HaMatzot), and in the Feast of Weeks (Chag Shavuot), and in the Feast of Tabernacles (Chag Sukkot).

14 And he appointed, according to the order of Dawid his father, the courses of the priests (kohanim) to their service, and the Levites (Lewiyim) to their charges, to praise and minister before the priests (kohanim), as the duty of every day required, the porters also by their courses at every gate; for so had Dawid the man of God (Elohim) commanded.

15 And they departed not from the command of the king unto the priests (kohanim) and Levites (Lewiyim) concerning any matter, or concerning the treasures.

16 Now all the work of Solomon (Shelomoh) was prepared unto the day of the foundation of the house of יהוה, and until it was finished. So the house of יהוה was perfected.

17 Then went Solomon (Shelomoh) to Eziongeber, and to Eloth, at the sea side in the land of Edom.

18 And Huram sent him by the hands of his servants, ships and servants that had knowledge of the sea; and they went with the servants of Solomon (Shelomoh) to Ophir, and took thence four hundred and fifty talents of gold, and brought them to King Solomon (Shelomoh).

9 And when the queen of Sheva heard of the fame of Solomon (Shelomoh), she came to prove Solomon (Shelomoh) with hard questions at Jerusalem (Yerushalayim), with a very great company, and camels that bare spices, and gold in abundance, and precious stones; and when she was come to Solomon (Shelomoh), she communed with him of all that was in her heart.

2 And Solomon (Shelomoh) told her all her questions; and there was nothing hid from Solomon (Shelomoh) which he told her not.

3 And when the queen of Sheva had seen the wisdom of Solomon (Shelomoh), and the house that he had built,

4 And the food of his table, and the sitting of his servants, and the attendance of his ministers, and their apparel; his cupbearers also, and their apparel; and his ascent by which he went up into the house of יהוה; she was breathless.

5 And she said to the king, "It was a true report which I heard in mine own land of your acts, and of your wisdom.

6 Howbeit I believed not their words, until I came, and mine eyes had seen it; and, behold, the one half of the greatness of your wisdom was not told me; for you exceedest the fame that I heard.

7 Happy are your men, and happy are these your servants, who stand continually before you, and hear your wisdom.

8 Blessed be יהוה your God (YHWH Eloheikha), who delighted in you to set you on His throne, to be king for יהוה your God (YHWH Eloheikha); because your God (Elohim) loved Yisrael, to establish them forever, therefore made He you king over them, to do judgment and justice.

9 And she gave the king a hundred and twenty talents of gold, and of spices great abundance, and precious stones; neither was there any such spice as the queen of Sheva gave King Solomon (Shelomoh).

10 And the servants also of Huram, and the servants of Solomon (Shelomoh), who brought gold from Ophir, brought algum trees and precious stones.

11 And the king made of the algum trees terraces to the house of יהוה, and to the king's palace, and harps and psalteries for singers; and there were none such seen before in the land of Judah (Yehudah).

12 And King Solomon (Shelomoh) gave to the queen of Sheva all her desire, whatsoever she asked, besides that which she had brought unto the king. So she turned, and went away to her own land, she and her servants.

13 Now the weight of gold that came to Solomon (Shelomoh) in one year was six hundred and threescore and six talents of gold;

14 Besides that which chapmen and merchants brought. And all the kings of Arabia and governors of the country brought gold and silver to Solomon (Shelomoh).

15 And King Solomon (Shelomoh) made two hundred targets of beaten gold; six hundred shekels of beaten gold went to one target.

16 And three hundred shields made he of beaten gold; three hundred shekels of gold went to one shield. And the king put them in the house of the forest of Lebanon.

17 Moreover the king made a great throne of

ivory, and overlaid it with pure gold.

18 And there were six steps to the throne, with a footstool of gold, which were fastened to the throne, and stays on each side of the sitting place, and two lions standing by the stays.

19 And twelve lions stood there on the one side and on the other upon the six steps. There was not the like made in any kingdom.

20 And all the drinking vessels of King Solomon (Shelomoh) were of gold, and all the vessels of the house of the forest of Lebanon were of pure gold; none were of silver; it was not any thing accounted of in the days of Solomon (Shelomoh).

21 For the king's ships went to Tarshish with the servants of Huram; every three years once came the ships of Tarshish bringing gold, and silver, ivory, and apes, and peacocks.

22 And King Solomon (Shelomoh) passed all the kings of the earth in riches and wisdom.

23 And all the kings of the earth sought the presence of Solomon (Shelomoh), to hear his wisdom, that God (Elohim) had put in his heart.

24 And they brought every man his present, vessels of silver, and vessels of gold, and raiment, harness, and spices, horses, and mules, a rate year by year.

25 And Solomon (Shelomoh) had four thousand stalls for horses and chariots, and twelve thousand horsemen; whom he bestowed in the chariot cities, and with the king at Jerusalem (Yerushalayim).

26 And he reigned over all the kings from the river even unto the land of the Philistines, and to the border of Egypt (Mitsrayim).

27 And the king made silver in Jerusalem (Yerushalayim) as stones, and cedar trees made he as the sycomore trees that are in the low plains in abundance.

28 And they brought unto Solomon (Shelomoh) horses out of Egypt (Mitsrayim), and out of all lands.

29 Now the rest of the acts of Solomon (Shelomoh), first and last, are they not written in the book of Nathan the prophet, and in the prophecy of Achiyah the Shilonite, and in the visions of Iddo the seer against Jeroboam (Yarovam) the son of Nevat?

30 And Solomon (Shelomoh) reigned in Jerusalem (Yerushalayim) over all Yisrael forty years.

31 And Solomon (Shelomoh) slept with his fathers, and he was buried in the city of Dawid his father; and Rehoboam (Rechavam) his son reigned in his stead.

10 And Rehoboam (Rechavam) went to Shechem, for to Shechem were all Yisrael come to make him king.

2 And it came to pass, when Jeroboam (Yarovam) the son of Nevat, who was in Egypt (Mitsrayim), whither he had fled from the presence of Solomon (Shelomoh) the king, heard it, that Jeroboam (Yarovam) returned out of Egypt (Mitsrayim).

3 And they sent and called him. So Jeroboam (Yarovam) and all Yisrael came and spake to Rehoboam (Rechavam), saying,

4 "Your father made our yoke grievous; now therefore ease you somewhat the grievous servitude of your father, and his heavy yoke that he put upon us, and we will serve you."

5 And he said unto them, "Come again unto me after three days." And the people departed.

6 And King Rehoboam (Rechavam) took counsel with the old men that had stood before Solomon (Shelomoh) his father while he yet lived, saying, "What counsel give you me to return answer to this people?"

7 And they spake unto him, saying, "If you be kind to this people, and please them, and speak good words to them, they will be your servants forever."

8 But he forsook the counsel which the old men gave him, and took counsel with the young men that were brought up with him, that stood before him.

9 And he said unto them, "What advice give you that we may return answer to this people, which have spoken to me, saying, 'Ease somewhat the yoke that your father did put upon us'?"

10 And the young men that were brought up with him spake unto him, saying, "Thus shalt you answer the people that spake unto you, saying, 'Your father made our yoke heavy, but make you it somewhat lighter for us;' thus shalt you say unto them: 'My little finger shall be thicker than my father's loins.

11 For whereas my father put a heavy yoke upon you, I will put more to your yoke: my father chastised you with whips, but I will chastise you with scorpions!'"

12 So Jeroboam (Yarovam) and all the people

came to Rehoboam (Rechavam) on the third day, as the king bade, saying, "Come again to me on the third day."

13 And the king answered them roughly; and King Rehoboam (Rechavam) forsook the counsel of the old men,

14 And answered them after the advice of the young men, saying, "My father made your yoke heavy, but I will add thereto; my father chastised you with whips, but I will chastise you with scorpions."

15 So the king hearkened not unto the people; for the cause was of God (Elohim), that יהוה might perform His word, which He spake by the hand of Achiyah the Shilonite to Jeroboam (Yarovam) the son of Nevat.

16 And when all Yisrael saw that the king would not hearken unto them, the people answered the king, saying, "What portion have we in Dawid? And we have none inheritance in the son of Jesse (Yishai). Every man to your tents, O Yisrael! And now, Dawid, see to your own house!" So all Yisrael went to their tents.

17 But as for the children of Yisrael that dwelt in the cities of Judah (Yehudah), Rehoboam (Rechavam) reigned over them.

18 Then King Rehoboam (Rechavam) sent Hadoram that was over the tribute; and the children of Yisrael stoned him with stones, that he died. But King Rehoboam (Rechavam) made speed to get him up to his chariot, to flee to Jerusalem (Yerushalayim).

19 And Yisrael rebelled against the house of Dawid unto this day.

11 And when Rehoboam (Rechavam) was come to Jerusalem (Yerushalayim), he gathered of the house of Judah (Yehudah) and Benjamin (Binyamin) a hundred and fourscore thousand chosen men, who were warriors, to fight against Yisrael, that he might bring the kingdom again to Rehoboam (Rechavam).

2 But the word of יהוה came to Shemayah the man of God (Elohim), saying,

3 "Speak unto Rehoboam (Rechavam) the son of Solomon (Shelomoh), king of Judah (Yehudah), and to all Yisrael in Judah (Yehudah) and Benjamin (Binyamin), saying,

4 'Thus saith יהוה: "You shall not go up, nor fight against your brethren; return every man to his house, for this thing is done of Me."'" And they obeyed the words of יהוה, and returned

from going against Jeroboam (Yarovam).

5 And Rehoboam (Rechavam) dwelt in Jerusalem (Yerushalayim), and built cities for defence in Judah (Yehudah).

6 He built even Bethlehem (Beit-Lechem), and Etam, and Tekoa,

7 And Bethzur, and Shoco, and Adullam,

8 And Gath, and Mareshah, and Ziph,

9 And Adoraim, and Lachish, and Azekah,

10 And Zorah, and Ayalon, and Hebron, which are in Judah (Yehudah) and in Benjamin (Binyamin) fenced cities.

11 And he fortified the strong holds, and put captains in them, and store of victual, and of oil and wine.

12 And in every several city he put shields and spears, and made them exceeding strong, having Judah (Yehudah) and Benjamin (Binyamin) on his side.

13 And the priests (kohanim) and the Levites (Lewiyim) that were in all Yisrael resorted to him out of all their coasts.

14 For the Levites (Lewiyim) left their suburbs and their possession, and came to Judah (Yehudah) and Jerusalem (Yerushalayim), for Jeroboam (Yarovam) and his sons had cast them off from executing the priest's office (kehunnah) unto יהוה.

15 And he ordained him priests (kohanim) for the high places, and for the idols of goat-demons (sairim), and the calves which he had made.

16 And those out of all the tribes of Yisrael such as set their hearts to seek יהוה God of Israel (Elohei Yisrael), followed them to Jerusalem (Yerushalayim), to sacrifice unto יהוה God (Elohim) of their fathers.

17 So they strengthened the kingdom of Judah (Yehudah), and made Rehoboam (Rechavam) the son of Solomon (Shelomoh) strong, three years; for three years they walked in the way of Dawid and Solomon (Shelomoh).

18 And Rehoboam (Rechavam) took him Mahalath the daughter of Yerimot the son of Dawid as wife, and Avihail the daughter of Eliav the son of Jesse (Yishai);

19 Who bare him children: Yeush, and Shamaryah, and Zaham.

20 And after her he took Maachah the daughter of Avshalom; who bare him Aviyah, and Attai, and Ziza, and Shelomith.

21 And Rehoboam (Rechavam) loved Maachah

the daughter of Avshalom above all his wives and his concubines; (for he took eighteen wives, and threescore concubines; and begat twenty and eight sons, and threescore daughters.)

22 And Rehoboam (Rechavam) made Aviyah the son of Maachah the chief, to be ruler among his brethren; for he thought to make him king.

23 And he dealt wisely, and dispersed of all his children throughout all the countries of Judah (Yehudah) and Benjamin (Binyamin), unto every fenced city; and he gave them victual in abundance. And he desired many wives.

12 And it came to pass, when Rehoboam (Rechavam) had established the kingdom, and had strengthened himself, he forsook the Torah of יהוה, and all Yisrael with him.

2 And it came to pass, that in the fifth year of King Rehoboam (Rechavam) Shishak king of Egypt (Mitsrayim) came up against Jerusalem (Yerushalayim), because they had transgressed against יהוה,

3 With twelve hundred chariots, and threescore thousand horsemen; and the people were without number that came with him out of Egypt (Mitsrayim); the Lubims, the Sukkiims, and the Ethiopians (Kushim).

4 And he took the fenced cities which pertained to Judah (Yehudah), and came to Jerusalem (Yerushalayim).

5 Then came Shemayah the prophet to Rehoboam (Rechavam), and to the princes of Judah (Yehudah), that were gathered together to Jerusalem (Yerushalayim) because of Shishak, and said unto them, "Thus saith יהוה: 'You have forsaken Me, and therefore have I also left you in the hand of Shishak.'"

6 Whereupon the princes of Yisrael and the king humbled themselves; and they said, "יהוה is righteous."

7 And when יהוה saw that they humbled themselves, the word of יהוה came to Shemayah, saying, "They have humbled themselves; therefore I will not destroy them, but I will grant them some deliverance; and My wrath shall not be poured out upon Jerusalem (Yerushalayim) by the hand of Shishak.

8 Nevertheless they shall be his servants; that they may know My service, and the service of the kingdoms of the countries."

9 So Shishak king of Egypt (Mitsrayim) came up against Jerusalem (Yerushalayim), and took away the treasures of the house of יהוה, and the treasures of the king's house; he took all; he carried away also the shields of gold which Solomon (Shelomoh) had made.

10 Instead of which King Rehoboam (Rechavam) made shields of brass, and committed them to the hands of the chief of the guard, that kept the entrance of the king's house.

11 And when the king entered into the house of יהוה, the guard came and fetched them, and brought them again into the guard chamber.

12 And when he humbled himself, the wrath of יהוה turned from him, that He would not destroy him altogether; and also in Judah (Yehudah) things went well.

13 So King Rehoboam (Rechavam) strengthened himself in Jerusalem (Yerushalayim) and reigned, for Rehoboam (Rechavam) was forty-one years old when he began to reign, and he reigned seventeen years in Jerusalem (Yerushalayim), the city which יהוה had chosen out of all the tribes of Yisrael, to put His name there. And his mother's name was Naamah an Ammonitess.

14 And he did evil, because he prepared not his heart to seek יהוה.

15 Now the acts of Rehoboam (Rechavam), first and last, are they not written in the book of Shemayah the prophet, and of Iddo the seer concerning genealogies? And there were wars between Rehoboam (Rechavam) and Jeroboam (Yarovam) continually.

16 And Rehoboam (Rechavam) slept with his fathers, and was buried in the city of Dawid. And Aviyah his son reigned in his stead.

13 Now in the eighteenth year of King Jeroboam (Yarovam) began Aviyah to reign over Judah (Yehudah).

2 He reigned three years in Jerusalem (Yerushalayim). His mother's name was Michaiah (Mikhayahu) the daughter of Uriel of Gibeah. And there was war between Aviyah and Jeroboam (Yarovam).

3 And Aviyah set the battle in array with an army of valiant men of war, even four hundred thousand chosen men; Jeroboam (Yarovam) also set the battle in array against him with eight hundred thousand chosen men, being mighty men of valour.

4 And Aviyah stood up upon Mount Zemaraim, which is in Mount Efrayim, and said, "Hear me,

you Jeroboam (Yarovam) and all Yisrael:

5 Ought you not to know that יהוה God of Israel (Elohei Yisrael) gave the kingdom over Yisrael to Dawid forever, even to him and to his sons by a covenant of salt?

6 Yet Jeroboam (Yarovam) the son of Nevat, the servant of Solomon (Shelomoh) the son of Dawid, is risen up, and hath rebelled against his lord (adon).

7 And there are gathered unto him vain men, the scoundrel (beliyaal) children, and have strengthened themselves against Rehoboam (Rechavam) the son of Solomon (Shelomoh), when Rehoboam (Rechavam) was young and tenderhearted, and could not withstand them.

8 And now you think to withstand the kingdom of יהוה in the hand of the sons of Dawid; and you be a great multitude, and there are with you golden calves, which Jeroboam (Yarovam) made for you as gods (elohim).

9 Have you not cast out the priests (kohanim) of יהוה, the sons of Aaron (Aharon), and the Levites (Lewiyim), and have made you priests (kohanim) after the manner of the nations of other lands? So that whosoever cometh to consecrate himself with a young bullock and seven rams, the same may be a priest (kohen) of them that are no God (Elohim).

10 But as for us, יהוה is our God (Elohim), and we have not forsaken Him; and the priests (kohanim), who minister unto יהוה, are the sons of Aaron (Aharon), and the Levites (Lewiyim) wait upon their work.

11 And they burn unto יהוה every morning and every evening burnt sacrifices and sweet incense; the shewbread also set they in order upon the pure table; and the candlestick (menorah) of gold with the lamps thereof, to burn every evening; for we keep the charge of יהוה our God (YHWH Eloheinu), but you have forsaken Him.

12 And, behold, God (Elohim) Himself is with us for our captain, and His priests (kohanim) with sounding trumpets to cry alarm against you. O children of Yisrael, fight you not against יהוה God (Elohim) of your fathers; for you shall not prosper!"

13 But Jeroboam (Yarovam) caused an ambushment to come about behind them; so they were before Judah (Yehudah), and the ambushment was behind them.

14 And when Judah (Yehudah) looked back, behold, the battle was before and behind; and they cried unto יהוה, and the priests (kohanim) sounded with the trumpets.

15 Then the men of Judah (Yehudah) gave a shout; and as the men of Judah (Yehudah) shouted, it came to pass, that God (Elohim) smote Jeroboam (Yarovam) and all Yisrael before Aviyah and Judah (Yehudah).

16 And the children of Yisrael fled before Judah (Yehudah), and God (Elohim) delivered them into their hand.

17 And Aviyah and his people slew them with a great slaughter; so there fell down slain of Yisrael five hundred thousand chosen men.

18 Thus the children of Yisrael were brought under at that time, and the children of Judah (Yehudah) prevailed, because they relied upon יהוה God (Elohim) of their fathers.

19 And Aviyah pursued after Jeroboam (Yarovam), and took cities from him, Bethel (Beit-El) with the towns thereof, and Yeshanah with the towns thereof, and Ephrain with the towns thereof.

20 Neither did Jeroboam (Yarovam) recover strength again in the days of Aviyah; and יהוה struck him, and he died.

21 But Aviyah waxed mighty, and married fourteen wives, and begat twenty and two sons, and sixteen daughters.

22 And the rest of the acts of Aviyah, and his ways, and his sayings, are written in the story of the prophet Iddo.

14 So Aviyah slept with his fathers, and they buried him in the city of Dawid; and Asa his son reigned in his stead. In his days the land was quiet ten years.

2 And Asa did that which was good and right in the eyes of יהוה his God (Elohim).

3 For he took away the altars of the strange gods (elohim), and the high places, and broke down the pillars, and cut down the Asherahs (Asherim);

4 And commanded Judah (Yehudah) to seek יהוה God (Elohim) of their fathers, and to do the Torah and the commandment.

5 Also he took away out of all the cities of Judah (Yehudah) the high places and the sun-pillars; and the kingdom was quiet before him.

6 And he built fenced cities in Judah (Yehudah), for the land had rest; and he had no war in those

years, because יהוה had given him rest.

7 Therefore he said unto Judah (Yehudah), "Let us build these cities, and make about them walls, and towers, gates, and bars, while the land is yet before us, because we have sought יהוה our God (YHWH Eloheinu), we have sought Him, and He hath given us rest on every side." So they built and prospered.

8 And Asa had an army of men that bare targets and spears, out of Judah (Yehudah) three hundred thousand; and out of Benjamin (Binyamin), that bare shields and drew bows, two hundred and fourscore thousand; all these were mighty men of valour.

9 And there came out against them Zerah the Ethiopian (Kushi) with an army of a thousand thousand, and three hundred chariots; and came unto Mareshah.

10 Then Asa went out against him, and they set the battle in array in the valley of Zephathah at Mareshah.

11 And Asa cried unto יהוה his God (Elohim), and said, "יהוה, it is nothing with You to help, whether with many, or with them that have no power; help us, O יהוה our God (YHWH Eloheinu); for we rest on You, and in Your name we go against this multitude. O יהוה, You are our God (Elohim); let not man prevail against You."

12 So יהוה smote the Ethiopians (Kushim) before Asa, and before Judah (Yehudah); and the Ethiopians (Kushim) fled.

13 And Asa and the people that were with him pursued them unto Gerar. And the Ethiopians (Kushim) were overthrown, that they could not recover themselves; for they were destroyed before יהוה, and before His host; and they carried away very much spoil.

14 And they smote all the cities round about Gerar; for the fear of יהוה came upon them; and they spoiled all the cities, for there was exceeding much spoil in them.

15 They smote also the tents of cattle, and carried away sheep and camels in abundance, and returned to Jerusalem (Yerushalayim).

15 And the Spirit of God (Elohim) came upon Azaryah the son of Oded.

2 And he went out to meet Asa, and said unto him, "Hear you me, Asa, and all Judah (Yehudah) and Benjamin (Binyamin). יהוה is with you, while you be with Him; and if you seek Him, He will be found of you; but if you

forsake Him, He will forsake you.

3 Now for a long season Yisrael hath been without the true God (Elohim), and without a teaching priest (kohen), and without Torah.

4 But when they in their trouble did turn unto יהוה God of Israel (Elohei Yisrael), and sought Him, He was found of them.

5 And in those times there was no peace to him that went out, nor to him that came in, but great vexations were upon all the inhabitants of the countries.

6 And nation was destroyed of nation and city of city, for God (Elohim) did vex them with all adversity.

7 Be you strong therefore and let not your hands be weak, for your work shall be rewarded."

8 And when Asa heard these words, and the prophecy of Oded the prophet, he took courage, and put away the abominable idols out of all the land of Judah (Yehudah) and Benjamin (Binyamin), and out of the cities which he had taken from Mount Efrayim, and renewed the altar of יהוה, that was before the porch of יהוה.

9 And he gathered all Judah (Yehudah) and Benjamin (Binyamin), and the strangers with them out of Efrayim and Menashsheh, and out of Shimon; for they fell to him out of Yisrael in abundance, when they saw that יהוה his God (Elohim) was with him.

10 So they gathered themselves together at Jerusalem (Yerushalayim) in the third month, in the fifteenth year of the reign of Asa.

11 And they offered unto יהוה the same time, of the spoil which they had brought, seven hundred oxen and seven thousand sheep.

12 And they entered into a covenant to seek יהוה God (Elohim) of their fathers with all their heart and with all their soul;

13 That whosoever would not seek יהוה God of Israel (Elohei Yisrael) should be put to death, whether small or great, whether man or woman.

14 And they sware unto יהוה with a loud voice, and with shouting, and with trumpets, and with cornets.

15 And all Judah (Yehudah) rejoiced at the oat, for they had sworn with all their heart, and sought him with their whole desire; and he was found of them; and יהוה gave them rest round about.

16 And also concerning Maachah the mother of Asa the king, he removed her from being queen,

because she had made an idol as [B34a]Asherah; and Asa cut down her idol, and stamped it, and burnt it at the Brook Kidron.

17 But the high places were not taken away out of Yisrael; nevertheless the heart of Asa was perfect all his days.

18 And he brought into the house of God (Elohim) the things that his father had dedicated, and that he himself had dedicated, silver, and gold, and vessels.

19 And there was no more war unto the five and thirtieth year of the reign of Asa.

16 In the six and thirtieth year of the reign of Asa, Baasha king of Yisrael came up against Judah (Yehudah), and built Ramah, to the intent that he might let none go out or come in to Asa king of Judah (Yehudah).

2 Then Asa brought out silver and gold out of the treasures of the house of יהוה and of the king's house, and sent to Benhadad king of Syria (Aram), that dwelt at Damascus (Dammeseq), saying,

3 "There is a league between me and you, as there was between my father and your father. Behold, I have sent you silver and gold; go, break your league with Baasha king of Yisrael, that he may depart from me."

4 And Benhadad hearkened unto King Asa, and sent the captains of his armies against the cities of Yisrael; and they smote Iyon, and Dan, and Avelmaim, and all the store cities of Naftali.

5 And it came to pass, when Baasha heard it, that he left off building of Ramah, and let his work cease.

6 Then Asa the king took all Judah (Yehudah); and they carried away the stones of Ramah, and the timber thereof, wherewith Baasha was building; and he built therewith Geba and Mizpah.

7 And at that time Hanani the seer came to Asa king of Judah (Yehudah), and said unto him: "Because you have relied on the king of Syria (Aram), and not relied on יהוה your God (YHWH Eloheikha), therefore is the army of the king of Syria (Aram) escaped out of your hand.

8 Were not the Ethiopians (Kushim) and the Lubims a huge army, with very many chariots and horsemen? Yet, because you didst rely on יהוה, He delivered them into your hand.

9 For the eyes of יהוה run to and fro throughout the whole earth, to shew Himself strong on the behalf of them whose heart is perfect toward Him. Herein you have done foolishly; therefore from henceforth you shalt have wars."

10 Then Asa was wroth with the seer, and put him in a prison house; for he was in a rage with him because of this thing. And Asa oppressed some of the people the same time.

11 And, behold, the acts of Asa, first and last, behold, they are written in the book of the kings of Judah (Yehudah) and Yisrael.

12 And Asa in the thirty and ninth year of his reign was diseased in his feet, until his disease was exceeding great; yet in his disease he sought not to יהוה, but to the physicians.

13 And Asa slept with his fathers, and died in the one and fortieth year of his reign.

14 And they buried him in his own sepulchres, which he had made for himself in the city of Dawid, and laid him in the bed which was filled with sweet odours and divers kinds of spices prepared by the apothecaries' art; and they made a very great burning for him.

17 And Yehoshafat his son reigned in his stead, and strengthened himself against Yisrael.

2 And he placed forces in all the fenced cities of Judah (Yehudah), and set garrisons in the land of Judah (Yehudah), and in the cities of Efrayim, which Asa his father had taken.

3 And יהוה was with Yehoshafat, because he walked in the first ways of his father Dawid, and sought not unto Baalim;

4 But sought to יהוה God (Elohim) of his father, and walked in His commandments, and not after the doings of Yisrael.

5 Therefore יהוה established the kingdom in his hand; and all Judah (Yehudah) brought to Yehoshafat presents; and he had riches and honor in abundance.

6 And his heart was lifted up in the ways of יהוה; moreover he took away the high places and Asherim out of Judah (Yehudah).

7 Also in the third year of his reign he sent to his princes, even to Benhail, and to Obadiah (Ovadyah), and to Zechariah (Zekharyahu), and to Nethaneel, and to Mikhayahu, to teach in the cities of Judah (Yehudah).

8 And with them he sent Levites (Lewiyim), even Shemayah, and Netanyah, and Zevadyahu, and Asahel, and Shemiramoth, and Jonathan

(Yeho-natan), and Adoniyah, and Toviyahu, and Tov Adoniyah, Levites (Lewiyim); and with them Elishama and Yehoram, priests (kohanim). 9 And they taught in Judah (Yehudah), and had the book of the law (sefer hatorah) of יהוה with them, and went about throughout all the cities of Judah (Yehudah), and taught the people.

10 And the fear of יהוה fell upon all the kingdoms of the lands that were round about Judah (Yehudah), so that they made no war against Yehoshafat.

11 Also some of the Philistines brought Yehoshafat presents, and tribute silver; and the Arabians brought him flocks, seven thousand and seven hundred rams, and seven thousand and seven hundred he goats.

12 And Yehoshafat waxed great exceedingly; and he built in Judah (Yehudah) castles, and cities of store.

13 And he had much business in the cities of Judah (Yehudah); and the men of war, mighty men of valour, were in Jerusalem (Yerushalayim).

14 And these are the numbers of them according to the house of their fathers: Of Judah (Yehudah), the captains of thousands; Adnah the chief, and with him mighty men of valour three hundred thousand.

15 And next to him was Yehochanan the captain, and with him two hundred and fourscore thousand.

16 And next to him was Amasyah the son of Zichri, who willingly offered himself unto יהוה; and with him two hundred thousand mighty men of valour.

17 And of Benjamin (Binyamin): Eliada a mighty man of valour, and with him armed men with bow and shield two hundred thousand.

18 And next to him was Yehozavad, and with him a hundred and fourscore thousand ready prepared for the war.

19 These waited on the king, besides those whom the king put in the fenced cities throughout all Judah (Yehudah).

18 Now Yehoshafat had riches and honor in abundance, and joined affinity with Achav.

2 And after certain years he went down to Achav to Samaria (Shomeron). And Achav killed sheep and oxen for him in abundance, and for the people that he had with him, and persuaded him to go up with him to Ramot-Gilad.

3 And Achav king of Yisrael said unto Yehoshafat king of Judah (Yehudah), "Wilt you go up with me to Ramot-Gilad?" And he answered him, "I am as you are, and my people as your people; and we will be with you in the war."

4 And Yehoshafat said unto the king of Yisrael, "Enquire, please, at the word of יהוה today."

5 Therefore the king of Yisrael gathered together of prophets four hundred men, and said unto them, "Shall we go to Ramot-Gilad to battle, or shall I forbear?" And they said, "Go up, for God (Elohim) will deliver it into the king's hand."

6 But Yehoshafat said, "Is there not here a prophet of יהוה besides, that we might enquire of Him?"

7 And the king of Yisrael said unto Yehoshafat, "There is yet one man, by whom we may enquire of יהוה; but I hate him; for he never prophesied good unto me, but always bad; the same is Mikhayahu the son of Imla. And Yehoshafat said, "Let not the king say so."

8 And the king of Yisrael called for one of his officers, and said, "Fetch quickly Mikhayahu the son of Imla."

9 And the king of Yisrael and Yehoshafat king of Judah (Yehudah) sat either of them on his throne, clothed in their robes, and they sat in a void place at the entering in of the gate of Samaria (Shomeron); and all the prophets prophesied before them.

10 And Zedekiah (Tsidkiyahu) the son of Chenaanah had made him horns of iron, and said, "Thus saith יהוה: 'With these you shalt push Syria (Aram) until they be consumed.'"

11 And all the prophets prophesied so, saying, "Go up to Ramot-Gilad, and prosper; for יהוה shall deliver it into the hand of the king."

12 And the messenger that went to call Mikhayahu spake to him, saying, "Behold, the words of the prophets declare good to the king with one assent; please let your word therefore be like one of theirs, and speak you good."

13 And Mikhayahu said, "As יהוה liveth, even what my God (Elohim) saith, that will I speak."

14 And when he was come to the king, the king said unto him, "Mikhayahu, shall we go to Ramot-Gilad to battle, or shall I forbear?" And he said, "Go you up, and prosper, and they shall be delivered into your hand."

15 And the king said to him, "How many times

shall I adjure you that you say nothing but the truth to me in the name of יהוה?"

16 Then he said, "I did see all Yisrael scattered upon the mountains, as sheep that have no shepherd; and יהוה said, 'These have no master; let them return therefore every man to his house in peace.'"

17 And the king of Yisrael said to Yehoshafat, "Did I not tell you that he would not prophesy good unto me, but bad?"

18 Again he said, "Therefore hear the word of יהוה: I saw יהוה sitting upon His throne, and all the host of heaven standing on His right hand and on His left.

19 And יהוה said, 'Who shall entice Achav king of Yisrael, that he may go up and fall at Ramot-Gilad?' And one spake saying after this manner, and another saying after that manner.

20 Then there came out a spirit, and stood before יהוה, and said, 'I will entice him.' And יהוה said unto him, 'Wherewith?'

21 And he said, 'I will go out, and be a lying spirit in the mouth of all his prophets.' And יהוה said, 'You shalt entice him, and you shalt also prevail; go out, and do even so.'

22 Now therefore, behold, יהוה hath put a lying spirit in the mouth of these your prophets, and יהוה hath proclaimed disaster over you."

23 Then Zedekiah (Tsidkiyahu) the son of Chenaanah came near, and smote Mikhayahu upon the cheek, and said, "Which way went the Spirit of יהוה from me to speak unto you?"

24 And Mikhayahu said, "Behold, you shalt see on that day when you shalt go into an inner chamber to hide yourself."

25 Then the king of Yisrael said, "Take you Mikhayahu, and carry him back to Amon the governor of the city, and to Yoash the king's son;

26 And say, 'Thus saith the king: "Put this fellow in the prison, and feed him with bread of affliction and with water of affliction, until I return in peace."'"

27 And Mikhayahu said, "If you certainly return in peace, then hath not יהוה spoken by me." And he said, "Hearken, all you people!"

28 So the king of Yisrael and Yehoshafat the king of Judah (Yehudah) went up to Ramot-Gilad.

29 And the king of Yisrael said unto Yehoshafat, "I will disguise myself, and will go to the battle; but put you on your robes." So the king of Yisrael disguised himself; and they went to the battle.

30 Now the king of Syria (Aram) had commanded the captains of the chariots that were with him, saying, "Fight you not with small or great, except only with the king of Yisrael."

31 And it came to pass, when the captains of the chariots saw Yehoshafat, that they said, "It is the king of Yisrael." Therefore they compassed about him to fight; but Yehoshafat cried out, and יהוה helped him; and God (Elohim) moved them to depart from him.

32 For it came to pass, that, when the captains of the chariots perceived that it was not the king of Yisrael, they turned back from pursuing him.

33 And a certain man drew a bow at a venture, and smote the king of Yisrael between the joints of the harness; therefore he said to his chariot man, "Turn your hand, that you mayest carry me out of the camp, for I am wounded."

34 And the battle increased that day, howbeit the king of Yisrael stayed himself up in his chariot against the Syrians (Arammim) until the even; and about the time of the sun going down he died.

19 And Yehoshafat the king of Judah (Yehudah) returned to his house in peace to Jerusalem (Yerushalayim).

2 And Yehu the son of Hanani the seer went out to meet him, and said to king Yehoshafat, "Shouldest you help the wicked, and love them that hate יהוה? Therefore is wrath upon you from before יהוה.

3 Nevertheless there are good things found in you, in that you have taken away the Asherot out of the land, and hast prepared your heart to seek God (Elohim).

4 And Yehoshafat dwelt at Jerusalem (Yerushalayim); and he went out again through the people from Beer-Sheva to Mount Efrayim, and brought them back unto יהוה God (Elohim) of their fathers.

5 And he set judges in the land throughout all the fenced cities of Judah (Yehudah), city by city,

6 And said to the judges, "Take heed what you do, for you judge not for man, but for יהוה, who is with you in the judgment.

7 Wherefore now let the fear of יהוה be upon you; take heed and do it, for there is no iniquity with יהוה our God (YHWH Eloheinu), nor

respect of persons, nor taking of bribes."

8 Moreover in Jerusalem (Yerushalayim) did Yehoshafat set of the Levites (Lewiyim), and of the priests (kohanim), and of the chief of the fathers of Yisrael, for the judgment of יהוה, and for controversies, when they returned to Jerusalem (Yerushalayim).

9 And he charged them, saying, "Thus shall you do in the fear of יהוה, faithfully, and with a perfect heart.

10 And what cause soever shall come to you of your brethren that dwell in their cities, between blood and blood, between Torah and commandment, statutes and judgments, you shall even warn them that they trespass not against יהוה, and so wrath come upon you, and upon your brethren; this do, and you shall not trespass.

11 And, behold, Amaryah the chief priest (kohen) is over you in all matters of יהוה; and Zevadyahu the son of Yishmael, the ruler of the house of Judah (Yehudah), for all the king's matters; also the Levites (Lewiyim) shall be officers before you. Deal courageously, and יהוה shall be with the good."

20 It came to pass after this also, that the children of Moav, and the children of Ammon, and with them other besides the Ammonites, came against Yehoshafat to battle.

2 Then there came some that told Yehoshafat, saying, "There cometh a great multitude against you from beyond the sea on this side Syria (Aram); and, behold, they be in Hazazontamar, which is Engedi.

3 And Yehoshafat feared, and set himself to seek יהוה, and proclaimed a fast throughout all Judah (Yehudah).

4 And Judah (Yehudah) gathered themselves together, to ask help of יהוה; even out of all the cities of Judah (Yehudah) they came to seek יהוה.

5 And Yehoshafat stood in the congregation of Judah (Yehudah) and Jerusalem (Yerusha-layim), in the house of יהוה, before the new court,

6 And said, "O יהוה God (Elohim) of our fathers, art not You God (Elohim) in heaven? And rulest not You over all the kingdoms of the nations? And in Your hand is there not power and might, so that none is able to withstand You?

7 Art not You our God (Elohim), who didst drive out the inhabitants of this land before Your people Yisrael, and gavest it to the seed of Avraham Your friend forever?

8 And they dwelt therein, and have built You a sanctuary therein for Your name, saying,

9 'If disaster (raah) cometh upon us, as the sword, judgment, or pestilence, or famine, we stand before this house, and in Your presence, (for Your name is in this house,) and cry unto You in our affliction, then You wilt hear and help.'

10 And now, behold, the children of Ammon and Moav and Mount Seir, whom You wouldest not let Yisrael invade, when they came out of the land of Egypt (Mitsrayim), but they turned from them, and destroyed them not;

11 Behold, I say, how they reward us, to come to cast us out of Your possession, which You have given us to inherit.

12 O our God (Elohim), wilt You not judge them? For we have no might against this great company that cometh against us; neither know we what to do, but our eyes are upon You."

13 And all Judah (Yehudah) stood before יהוה, with their little ones, their wives, and their children.

14 Then upon Yachaziel the son of Zechariah (Zekharyahu), the son of Benayah, the son of Yeiel, the son of Mattanyah, a Lewite of the sons of Asaph, came the Spirit (Ruach) of יהוה in the midst of the congregation;

15 And he said, "Hearken you, all Judah (Yehudah), and you inhabitants of Jerusalem (Yerushalayim), and you King Yehoshafat! Thus saith יהוה unto you: 'Be not afraid nor dismayed by reason of this great multitude; for the battle is not yours, but God (Elohim)'s.

16 Tomorrow go you down against them. Behold, they come up by the cliff of Ziz; and you shall find them at the end of the brook, before the wilderness of Yeruel.

17 You shall not need to fight in this battle; set yourselves, stand you still, and see the salvation of יהוה with you, O Yehudah (Judah) and Yerushalayim! Fear not, nor be dismayed; tomorrow go out against them, for יהוה will be with you."

18 And Yehoshafat bowed his head with his face to the ground; and all Judah (Yehudah) and the inhabitants of Jerusalem (Yerushalayim) fell before יהוה, worshipping יהוה.

19 And the Levites (Lewiyim), of the children of the Kohathites, and of the children of the Korhites, stood up to praise יהוה God of Israel (Elohei Yisrael) with a loud voice on high.

20 And they rose early in the morning, and went forth into the wilderness of Tekoa; and as they went forth, Yehoshafat stood and said, "Hear me, O Judah (Yehudah), and you inhabitants of Jerusalem (Yerushalayim): Believe in יהוה your God (YHWH Eloheikhem), so shall you be established; believe His prophets, so shall you prosper."

21 And when he had consulted with the people, he appointed singers unto יהוה, and that should praise the beauty of holiness, as they went out before the army, and to say, "Give praise unto יהוה, for His mercy endureth forever."

22 And when they began to sing and to praise, יהוה set ambushments against the children of Ammon, Moav, and Mount Seir, who were come against Judah (Yehudah); and they were smitten.

23 For the children of Ammon and Moav stood up against the inhabitants of Mount Seir, utterly to slay and destroy them; and when they had made an end of the inhabitants of Seir, every one helped to destroy another.

24 And when Judah (Yehudah) came toward the watch tower in the wilderness, they looked unto the multitude, and, behold, they were dead bodies fallen to the earth, and none escaped.

25 And when Yehoshafat and his people came to take away the spoil of them, they found among them in abundance both riches with the dead bodies, and precious jewels, which they stripped off for themselves, more than they could carry away; and they were three days in gathering of the spoil, it was so much.

26 And on the fourth day they assembled themselves in the valley of Berakhah, for there they blessed יהוה; therefore the name of the same place was called "The Valley of Berakhah (Blessing)" unto this day.

27 Then they returned, every man of Judah (Yehudah) and Jerusalem (Yerushalayim), and Yehoshafat in the forefront of them, to go again to Jerusalem (Yerushalayim) with joy; for יהוה had made them to rejoice over their enemies.

28 And they came to Jerusalem (Yerushalayim) with psalteries and harps and trumpets unto the house of יהוה.

29 And the fear of God (Elohim) was on all the kingdoms of those countries, when they had heard that יהוה fought against the enemies of Yisrael.

30 So the realm of Yehoshafat was quiet, for his God (Elohim) gave him rest round about.

31 And Yehoshafat reigned over Judah (Yehudah); he was thirty and five years old when he began to reign, and he reigned twenty and five years in Jerusalem (Yerushalayim). His mother's name was Azubah the daughter of Shilhi.

32 And he walked in the way of Asa his father, and departed not from it, doing that which was right in the sight of יהוה.

33 Howbeit the high places were not taken away, for as yet the people had not prepared their hearts unto the God (Elohim) of their fathers.

34 Now the rest of the acts of Yehoshafat, first and last, behold, they are written in the book of Yehu the son of Hanani, who is mentioned in the book of the kings of Yisrael.

35 And after this did Yehoshafat king of Judah (Yehudah) join himself with Achazyah king of Yisrael, who did very wickedly.

36 And he joined himself with him to make ships to go to Tarshish; and they made the ships in Eziongeber.

37 Then Eliezer the son of Dodavah of Mareshah prophesied against Yehoshafat, saying, "Because you have joined yourself with Achazyah, יהוה hath broken your works." And the ships were broken, that they were not able to go to Tarshish.

21 Now Yehoshafat slept with his fathers, and was buried with his fathers in the city of Dawid. And Yehoram his son reigned in his stead.

2 And he had brethren the sons of Yehoshafat, Azaryah, and Yeiel, and Zechariah (Zekharyahu), and Azaryah, and Mikhael, and Shefatyahu; all these were the sons of Yehoshafat king of Yisrael.

3 And their father gave them great gifts of silver, and of gold, and of precious things, with fenced cities in Judah (Yehudah); but the kingdom gave he to Yehoram; because he was the firstborn.

4 Now when Yehoram was risen up to the kingdom of his father, he strengthened himself, and slew all his brethren with the sword, and divers also of the princes of Yisrael.

5 Yehoram was thirty and two years old when he began to reign, and he reigned eight years in Jerusalem (Yerushalayim).

6 And he walked in the way of the kings of Yisrael, like as did the house of Achav; for he had the daughter of Achav as wife; and he wrought that which was evil in the eyes of יהוה.

7 Howbeit יהוה would not destroy the house of Dawid, because of the covenant that He had made with Dawid, and as He promised to give a light to him and to his sons forever.

8 In his days the Edomites revolted from under the dominion of Judah (Yehudah), and made themselves a king.

9 Then Yehoram went forth with his princes, and all his chariots with him. And he rose up by night, and smote the Edomites which compassed him in, and the captains of the chariots.

10 So the Edomites revolted from under the hand of Judah (Yehudah) unto this day. The same time also did Libnah revolt from under his hand; because he had forsaken יהוה God (Elohim) of his fathers.

11 Moreover he made high places in the mountains of Judah (Yehudah), and caused the inhabitants of Jerusalem (Yerushalayim) to commit fornication, and compelled Judah (Yehudah) thereto.

12 And there came a writing to him from Eliyah the prophet, saying, "Thus saith יהוה God (Elohim) of Dawid your father: 'Because you have not walked in the ways of Yehoshafat your father, nor in the ways of Asa king of Judah (Yehudah),

13 But hast walked in the way of the kings of Yisrael, and hast made Judah (Yehudah) and the inhabitants of Jerusalem (Yerushalayim) to go a whoring, like to the whoredoms of the house of Achav, and also hast slain your brethren of your father's house, who were better than yourself;

14 Behold, with a great plague will יהוה smite your people, and your children, and your wives, and all your goods;

15 And you shalt have great sickness by disease of your bowels, until your bowels fall out by reason of the sickness day by day.

16 Moreover יהוה stirred up against Yehoram the spirit of the Philistines, and of the Arabians, that were near the Ethiopians (Kushim).

17 And they came up into Judah (Yehudah), and broke into it, and carried away all the substance that was found in the king's house, and his sons also, and his wives; so that there was never a son left him, except Yehoachaz, the youngest of his sons.

18 And after all this יהוה smote him in his bowels with an incurable disease.

19 And it came to pass, that in process of time, after the end of two years, his bowels fell out by reason of his sickness; so he died of sore diseases. And his people made no burning for him, like the burning of his fathers.

20 Thirty and two years old was he when he began to reign, and he reigned in Jerusalem (Yerushalayim) eight years, and departed without being desired. Howbeit they buried him in the city of Dawid, but not in the sepulchres of the kings.

22 And the inhabitants of Jerusalem (Yerushalayim) made Achazyah his youngest son king in his stead, for the band of men that came with the Arabians to the camp had slain all the eldest. So Achazyah the son of Yehoram king of Judah (Yehudah) reigned.

2 Forty and two years old was Achazyah when he began to reign, and he reigned one year in Jerusalem (Yerushalayim). His mother's name also was Atalyah the daughter of Omri.

3 He also walked in the ways of the house of Achav, for his mother was his counsellor to do wickedly.

4 Wherefore he did evil in the sight of יהוה like the house of Achav; for they were his counsellors after the death of his father to his destruction.

5 He walked also after their counsel, and went with Yehoram the son of Achav king of Yisrael to war against Hazael king of Syria (Aram) at Ramot-Gilad; and the Syrians (Arammim) smote Yoram.

6 And he returned to be healed in Yizreel because of the wounds which were given him at Ramah, when he fought with Hazael king of Syria (Aram). And Azaryah the son of Yehoram king of Judah (Yehudah) went down to see Yehoram the son of Achav at Yizreel, because he was sick.

7 And the destruction of Achazyah was of God (Elohim) by coming to Yoram; for when he was come, he went out with Yehoram against Yehu the son of Nimshi, whom יהוה had anointed to cut off the house of Achav.

8 And it came to pass, that, when Yehu was

executing judgment upon the house of Achav, and found the princes of Judah (Yehudah), and the sons of the brethren of Achazyah, that ministered to Achazyah, he slew them.

9 And he sought Achazyah and they caught him, (for he was hid in Samaria (Shomeron)) and brought him to Yehu; and when they had slain him, they buried him; because, said they, "He is the grandson of Yehoshafat, who sought יהוה with all his heart." So the house of Achazyah had no power to keep still the kingdom.

10 But when Atalyah the mother of Achazyah saw that her son was dead, she arose and destroyed all the seed royal of the house of Judah (Yehudah).

11 But Yehoshavat, the daughter of the king, took Yoash the son of Achazyah, and stole him from among the king's sons that were slain, and put him and his nurse in a bedchamber. So Yehoshavat, the daughter of king Yehoram, the wife of Yehoyada the priest (kohen), (for she was the sister of Achazyah,) hid him from Atalyah, so that she slew him not.

12 And he was with them hid in the house of God (Elohim) six years, and Atalyah reigned over the land.

23 And in the seventh year Yehoyada strengthened himself, and took the captains of hundreds, Azaryah the son of Yeroham, and Yishmael the son of Yehochanan, and Azaryah the son of Oved, and Maaseyahu the son of Adayah, and Elishaphat the son of Zichri, into covenant with him.

2 And they went about in Judah (Yehudah), and gathered the Levites (Lewiyim) out of all the cities of Judah (Yehudah), and the chief of the fathers of Yisrael, and they came to Jerusalem (Yerushalayim).

3 And all the congregation made a covenant with the king in the house of God (Elohim). And he said unto them, "Behold, the king's son shall reign, as יהוה hath said of the sons of Dawid.

4 This is the thing that you shall do: A third part of you entering on the Shabbat, of the priests (kohanim) and of the Levites (Lewiyim), shall be porters of the doors;

5 And a third part shall be at the king's house; and a third part at the gate of the foundation. And all the people shall be in the courts of the house of יהוה.

6 But let none come into the house of יהוה, except the priests (kohanim), and they that minister of the Levites (Lewiyim); they shall go in, for they are holy; but all the people shall keep the watch of יהוה.

7 And the Levites (Lewiyim) shall compass the king round about, every man with his weapons in his hand; and whosoever else cometh into the house, he shall be put to death; but be you with the king when he cometh in, and when he goeth out."

8 So the Levites (Lewiyim) and all Judah (Yehudah) did according to all things that Yehoyada the priest (kohen) had commanded, and took every man his men that were to come in on the Shabbat, with them that were to go out on the Shabbat; for Yehoyada the priest (kohen) dismissed not the courses.

9 Moreover Yehoyada the priest (kohen) delivered to the captains of hundreds spears, and bucklers, and shields, that had been King Dawid's, which were in the house of God (Elohim).

10 And he set all the people, every man having his weapon in his hand, from the right side of the temple to the left side of the temple, along by the altar and the temple, by the king round about.

11 Then they brought out the king's son, and put upon him the crown, and gave him the testimony, and made him king. And Yehoyada and his sons anointed him, and said, "Long live the king!"

12 Now when Atalyah heard the noise of the people running and praising the king, she came to the people into the house of יהוה.

13 And she looked, and, behold, the king stood at his pillar at the entering in, and the princes and the trumpets by the king; and all the people of the land rejoiced, and sounded with trumpets, also the singers with instruments of musick, and such as taught to sing praise. Then Atalyah rent her clothes, and said, "Treason! Treason!"

14 Then Yehoyada the priest (kohen) brought out the captains of hundreds that were set over the army, and said unto them, "Have her forth of the ranges; and whoso followeth her, let him be slain with the sword. For the priest (kohen) said, "Slay her not in the house of יהוה."

15 So they laid hands on her; and when she was come to the entering of the horse gate by the

king's house, they slew her there.

16 And Yehoyada made a covenant between him, and between all the people, and between the king, that they should be יהוה's people.

17 Then all the people went to the house of the Baal, and broke it down, and broke his altars and his images in pieces, and slew Mattan the priest (kohen) of the Baal before the altars.

18 Also Yehoyada appointed the offices of the house of יהוה by the hand of the priests (kohanim) the Levites (Lewiyim), whom Dawid had distributed in the house of יהוה, to offer the burnt offerings of יהוה, as it is written in the Torah by Moses, with rejoicing and with singing, as it was ordained by Dawid.

19 And he set the porters at the gates of the house of יהוה, that none which was unclean in anything should enter in.

20 And he took the captains of hundreds, and the nobles, and the governors of the people, and all the people of the land, and brought down the king from the house of יהוה; and they came through the high gate into the king's house, and set the king upon the throne of the kingdom.

21 And all the people of the land rejoiced; and the city was quiet, after that they had slain Atalyah with the sword.

24 Yoash was seven years old when he began to reign, and he reigned forty years in Jerusalem (Yerushalayim). His mother's name also was Tsivyah of Beer-Sheva.

2 And Yoash did that which was right in the sight of יהוה all the days of Yehoyada the priest (kohen).

3 And Yehoyada took for him two wives; and he begat sons and daughters.

4 And it came to pass after this, that Yoash was minded to repair the house of יהוה.

5 And he gathered together the priests (kohanim) and the Levites (Lewiyim), and said to them, "Go out unto the cities of Judah (Yehudah), and gather of all Yisrael money to repair the house of your God (Elohim) from year to year, and see that you hasten the matter." Howbeit the Levites (Lewiyim) hastened it not.

6 And the king called for Yehoyada the chief, and said unto him, "Why have you not required of the Levites (Lewiyim) to bring in out of Judah (Yehudah) and out of Jerusalem (Yerushalayim) the collection, according to the commandment of Moses (Mosheh) the servant

of יהוה, and of the congregation of Yisrael, for the tabernacle of witness?"

7 For the sons of Atalyah, that wicked woman, had broken up the house of God (Elohim); and also all the dedicated things of the house of יהוה did they bestow upon [34]Baalim.

8 And at the king's commandment they made a chest, and set it outside at the gate of the house of יהוה.

9 And they made a proclamation through Judah (Yehudah) and Jerusalem (Yerushalayim), to bring in to יהוה the collection that Moses (Mosheh) the servant of God (Elohim) laid upon Yisrael in the wilderness.

10 And all the princes and all the people rejoiced, and brought in, and cast into the chest, until they had made an end.

11 Now it came to pass, that at what time the chest was brought unto the king's office by the hand of the Levites (Lewiyim), and when they saw that there was much money, the king's scribe and the high priest (kohen hagadol)'s officer came and emptied the chest, and took it, and carried it to his place again. Thus they did day by day, and gathered money in abundance.

12 And the king and Yehoyada gave it to such as did the work of the service of the house of יהוה, and hired masons and carpenters to repair the house of יהוה, and also such as wrought iron and brass to mend the house of יהוה.

13 So the workmen wrought, and the work was perfected by them, and they set the house of God (Elohim) in his state, and strengthened it.

14 And when they had finished it, they brought the rest of the money before the king and Yehoyada, whereof were made vessels for the house of יהוה, even vessels to minister, and to offer withal, and spoons, and vessels of gold and silver. And they offered burnt offerings in the house of יהוה continually all the days of Yehoyada.

15 But Yehoyada waxed old, and was full of days when he died; a hundred and thirty years old was he when he died.

16 And they buried him in the city of Dawid among the kings, because he had done good in Yisrael, both toward God (Elohim), and toward his house.

17 Now after the death of Yehoyada came the princes of Judah (Yehudah), and made obeisance to the king. Then the king hearkened unto them.

18 And they left the house of יהוה God (Elohim) of their fathers, and served Asherim and idols; and wrath came upon Judah (Yehudah) and Yerushalayim for this their trespass.

19 Yet he sent prophets to them, to bring them again unto יהוה; and they testified against them, but they would not give ear.

20 And the Spirit of God (Elohim) came upon Zechariah (Zekharyahu) the son of Yehoyada the priest (kohen), who stood above the people, and said unto them, "Thus saith God (Elohim): 'Why transgress you the commandments of יהוה, that you cannot prosper? Because you have forsaken יהוה, He hath also forsaken you.'"

21 And they conspired against him, and stoned him with stones at the commandment of the king in the court of the house of יהוה.

22 Thus Yoash the king remembered not the kindness which Yehoyada his father had done to him, but slew his son. And as he was dying, he said, "יהוה look upon it, and require it."

23 And it came to pass at the end of the year, that the army of Syria (Aram) came up against him; and they came to Judah (Yehudah) and Jerusalem (Yerushalayim), and destroyed all the princes of the people from among the people, and sent all the spoil of them unto the king of Damascus (Dammeseq).

24 For the army of the Syrians (Arammim) came with a small company of men, and יהוה delivered a very great army into their hand, because they had forsaken יהוה God (Elohim) of their fathers. So they executed judgment against Yoash.

25 And when they were departed from him, (for they left him in great diseases,) his own servants conspired against him for the blood of the sons of Yehoyada the priest (kohen), and slew him on his bed, and he died; and they buried him in the city of Dawid, but they buried him not in the sepulchres of the kings.

26 And these are they that conspired against him: Zabad the son of Shimeath an Ammonitess, and Yehozavad the son of Shimrith a Moavitess.

27 Now concerning his sons, and the greatness of the burdens laid upon him, and the repairing of the house of God (Elohim), behold, they are written in the story of the book of the kings. And Amatsyah his son reigned in his stead.

25 Amatsyah was twenty and five years old when he began to reign, and he reigned twenty and nine years in Jerusalem (Yerushalayim). His mother's name was Yehoaddan of Yerushalayim.

2 And he did that which was right in the sight of יהוה, but not with a perfect heart.

3 Now it came to pass, when the kingdom was established to him, that he slew his servants that had killed the king his father.

4 But he slew not their children, but did as it is written in the Torah in the book by Moses (Mosheh), where יהוה commanded, saying, "The fathers shall not die for the children, neither shall the children die for the fathers, but every man shall die for his own sin."

5 Moreover Amatsyah gathered Judah (Yehudah) together, and made them captains over thousands, and captains over hundreds, according to the houses of their fathers, throughout all Judah (Yehudah) and Benjamin (Binyamin); and he numbered them from twenty years old and above, and found them three hundred thousand choice men, able to go forth to war, that could handle spear and shield.

6 He hired also a hundred thousand mighty men of valour out of Yisrael for a hundred talents of silver.

7 But there came a man of God (Elohim) to him, saying, "O king, let not the army of Yisrael go with you, for יהוה is not with Yisrael, nor with all the children of Efrayim.

8 But if you wilt go, do it, be strong for the battle. God (Elohim) shall make you fall before the enemy, for God (Elohim) hath power to help, and to cast down."

9 And Amatsyah said to the man of God (Elohim), "But what shall we do for the hundred talents which I have given to the army of Yisrael?" And the man of God (Elohim) answered, "יהוה is able to give you much more than this."

10 Then Amatsyah separated them, the army that was come to him out of Efrayim, to go home again; wherefore their anger was greatly kindled against Judah (Yehudah), and they returned home in great anger.

11 And Amatsyah strengthened himself, and led forth his people, and went to the valley of salt, and smote of the children of Seir ten thousand.

12 And other ten thousand left alive did the children of Judah (Yehudah) carry away captive, and brought them unto the top of the rock, and cast them down from the top of the rock, that

they all were broken in pieces.

13 But the soldiers of the army which Amatsyah sent back, that they should not go with him to battle, fell upon the cities of Judah (Yehudah), from Samaria (Shomeron) even unto Beit-Choron, and smote three thousand of them, and took much spoil.

14 Now it came to pass, after that Amatsyah was come from the slaughter of the Edomites, that he brought the gods (elohim) of the children of Seir, and set them up to be his gods (elohim), and bowed down himself before them, and burned incense unto them.

15 Wherefore the anger of יהוה was kindled against Amatsyah, and He sent unto him a prophet, who said unto him, "Why have you sought after the gods (elohim) of the people, which could not deliver their own people out of your hand?"

16 And it came to pass, as he talked with him, that the king said unto him, "Are you made of the king's counsel? Forbear; why shouldest you be smitten?" Then the prophet forbare, and said, "I know that God (Elohim) hath determined to destroy you, because you have done this, and hast not hearkened unto my counsel."

17 Then Amatsyah king of Judah (Yehudah) took advice, and sent to Yoash, the son of Yehoachaz, the son of Yehu, king of Yisrael, saying, "Come, let us face one another."

18 And Yoash king of Yisrael sent to Amatsyah king of Judah (Yehudah), saying, "The thistle that was in Lebanon sent to the cedar that was in Lebanon, saying, 'Give your daughter to my son as wife; and there passed by a wild beast that was in Lebanon, and trode down the thistle.

19 You sayest, "Behold, you have smitten the Edomites; and your heart lifteth you up to boast; abide now at home; why shouldest you meddle to your hurt, that you shouldest fall, even you, and Judah (Yehudah) with you?"

20 But Amatsyah would not hear; for it came of God (Elohim), that He might deliver them into the hand of their enemies, because they sought after the gods (elohim) of Edom.

21 So Yoash the king of Yisrael went up; and they faced one another, both he and Amatsyah king of Judah (Yehudah), at Beit-Shemesh, which belongeth to Judah (Yehudah).

22 And Judah (Yehudah) was put to the worse before Yisrael, and they fled every man to his tent.

23 And Yoash the king of Yisrael took Amatsyah king of Judah (Yehudah), the son of Yoash, the son of Yehoachaz, at Beit-Shemesh, and brought him to Jerusalem (Yerushalayim), and broke down the wall of Jerusalem (Yerushalayim) from the gate of Efrayim to the corner gate, four hundred cubits.

24 And he took all the gold and the silver, and all the vessels that were found in the house of God (Elohim) with Oved-Edom, and the treasures of the king's house, the hostages also, and returned to Samaria (Shomeron).

25 And Amatsyah the son of Yoash king of Judah (Yehudah) lived after the death of Yoash son of Yehoachaz king of Yisrael fifteen years.

26 Now the rest of the acts of Amatsyah, first and last, behold, are they not written in the book of the kings of Judah (Yehudah) and Yisrael?

27 Now after the time that Amatsyah did turn away from following יהוה they made a conspiracy against him in Jerusalem (Yerushalayim); and he fled to Lachish, but they sent to Lachish after him, and slew him there.

28 And they brought him upon horses, and buried him with his fathers in the city of Judah (Yehudah).

26 Then all the people of Judah (Yehudah) took Uzziyahu, who was sixteen years old, and made him king in the room of his father Amatsyah.

2 He built Eloth, and restored it to Judah (Yehudah), after that the king slept with his fathers.

3 Sixteen years old was Uzziyahu when he began to reign, and he reigned fifty and two years in Jerusalem (Yerushalayim). His mother's name was Yekholyah of Jerusalem (Yerushalayim).

4 And he did that which was right in the sight of יהוה, according to all that his father Amatsyah did.

5 And he sought God (Elohim) in the days of Zechariah (Zekharyahu), who had understanding in the visions of God (Elohim); and as long as he sought יהוה, God (Elohim) made him to prosper.

6 And he went forth and warred against the Philistines, and broke down the wall of Gath, and the wall of Yavneh, and the wall of Ashdod, and built cities about Ashdod, and among the Philistines.

7 And God (Elohim) helped him against the Philistines, and against the Arabians that dwelt in Gurbaal, and the Mehunims.

8 And the Ammonites gave gifts to Uzziyahu; and his name spread abroad even to the entering in of Egypt (Mitsrayim), for he strengthened himself exceedingly.

9 Moreover Uzziyahu built towers in Jerusalem (Yerushalayim) at the corner gate, and at the valley gate, and at the turning of the wall, and fortified them.

10 Also he built towers in the desert, and digged many wells, for he had much cattle, both in the low country, and in the plains; husbandmen also, and vine dressers in the mountains and in Carmel, for he loved husbandry.

11 Moreover Uzziyahu had an army of fighting men, that went out to war by bands, according to the number of their account by the hand of Yeiel the scribe and Maaseyahu the ruler, under the hand of Chananyahu, one of the king's captains.

12 The whole number of the chief of the fathers of the mighty men of valour were two thousand and six hundred.

13 And under their hand was an army, three hundred thousand and seven thousand and five hundred, that made war with mighty power, to help the king against the enemy.

14 And Uzziyahu prepared for them throughout all the army shields, and spears, and helmets, and habergeons, and bows, and slings to cast stones.

15 And he made in Jerusalem (Yerushalayim) engines, invented by cunning men, to be on the towers and upon the bulwarks, to shoot arrows and great stones withal. And his name spread far abroad, for he was marvellously helped, till he was strong.

16 But when he was strong, his heart was lifted up to his destruction, for he transgressed against יהוה his God (Elohim), and went into the temple of יהוה to burn incense upon the altar of incense.

17 And Azaryahu the priest (kohen) went in after him, and with him fourscore priests (kohanim) of יהוה, that were valiant men.

18 And they withstood Uzziyahu the king, and said unto him, "It is not for you, Uzziyahu, to burn incense unto יהוה, but for the priests (kohanim) the sons of Aaron (Aharon), that are consecrated to burn incense. Get out of the sanctuary, for you have trespassed; neither shall it be for your honor from God (Elohim) יהוה."

19 Then Uzziyahu was wroth, and had a censer in his hand to burn incense; and while he was wroth with the priests (kohanim), the leprosy even rose up in his forehead before the priests (kohanim) in the house of יהוה, from beside the incense altar.

20 And Azaryahu the chief priest (kohen), and all the priests (kohanim), looked upon him, and, behold, he was leprous in his forehead, and they thrust him out from thence; yea, himself hasted also to go out, because יהוה had smitten him.

21 And Uzziyahu the king was a leper unto the day of his death, and dwelt in a several house, being a leper; for he was cut off from the house of יהוה; and Yotam his son was over the king's house, judging the people of the land.

22 Now the rest of the acts of Uzziyahu, first and last, did Isaiah (Yeshayahu) the prophet, the son of Amoz, write.

23 So Uzziyahu slept with his fathers, and they buried him with his fathers in the field of the burial which belonged to the kings, for they said, "He is a leper." And Yotam his son reigned in his stead.

27 Yotam was twenty-five years old when he began to reign, and he reigned sixteen years in Jerusalem (Yerushalayim). His mother's name was Yerushah, the daughter of Zadok.

2 And he did that which was right in the sight of יהוה, according to all that his father Uzziyahu did; howbeit he entered not into the temple of יהוה. And the people did yet corruptly.

3 He built the high gate of the house of יהוה, and on the wall of Ophel he built much.

4 Moreover he built cities in the mountains of Judah (Yehudah), and in the forests he built castles and towers.

5 He fought also with the king of the Ammonites, and prevailed against them. And the children of Ammon gave him the same year a hundred talents of silver, and ten thousand measures of wheat, and ten thousand of barley. So much did the children of Ammon pay unto him, both the second year, and the third.

6 So Yotam became mighty, because he prepared his ways before יהוה his God (Elohim).

7 Now the rest of the acts of Yotam, and all his wars, and his ways, behold, they are written in the book of the kings of Yisrael and Judah

(Yehudah).

8 He was five and twenty years old when he began to reign, and reigned sixteen years in Jerusalem (Yerushalayim).

9 And Yotam slept with his fathers, and they buried him in the city of Dawid. And Achaz his son reigned in his stead.

28 Achaz was twenty years old when he began to reign, and he reigned sixteen years in Jerusalem (Yerushalayim); but he did not that which was right in the sight of יהוה, like Dawid his father;

2 For he walked in the ways of the kings of Yisrael, and made also molten images for the Baals (Baalim).

3 Moreover he burnt incense in the valley of the son of Hinnom, and burnt his children in the fire, after the abominations of the heathen whom יהוה had cast out before the children of Yisrael.

4 He sacrificed also and burnt incense in the high places, and on the hills, and under every green tree.

5 Wherefore יהוה his God (Elohim) delivered him into the hand of the king of Syria (Aram); and they smote him, and carried away a great multitude of them captives, and brought them to Damascus (Dammeseq). And he was also delivered into the hand of the king of Yisrael, who smote him with a great slaughter.

6 For Pekah the son of Remalyahu slew in Judah (Yehudah) a hundred and twenty thousand in one day, who were all valiant men; because they had forsaken יהוה God (Elohim) of their fathers.

7 And Zichri, a mighty man of Efrayim, slew Maaseyahu the king's son, and Azrikam the governor of the house, and Elkanah that was next to the king.

8 And the children of Yisrael carried away captive of their brethren two hundred thousand, women, sons, and daughters, and took also away much spoil from them, and brought the spoil to Samaria (Shomeron).

9 But a prophet of יהוה was there, whose name was Oded; and he went out before the army that came to Samaria (Shomeron), and said unto them, "Behold, because יהוה God (Elohim) of your fathers was wroth with Judah (Yehudah), he hath delivered them into your hand, and you have slain them in a rage that reacheth up unto heaven.

10 And now you purpose to keep under the children of Judah (Yehudah) and Jerusalem (Yerushalayim) for bondmen and bondwomen unto you; but are there not with you, even with you, sins against יהוה your God (YHWH Eloheikhem)?

11 Now hear me therefore, and deliver the captives again, which you have taken captive of your brethren, for the fierce wrath of יהוה is upon you.

12 Then certain of the heads of the children of Efrayim, Azaryah the son of Yochanan, Berekhyah the son of Meshillemoth, and Jehizkiah (Yechiz-kiyahu) the son of Shallum, and Amasa the son of Hadlai, stood up against them that came from the war,

13 And said unto them, "You shall not bring in the captives hither, for whereas we have offended against יהוה already, you intend to add more to our sins and to our trespass; for our trespass is great, and there is fierce wrath against Yisrael."

14 So the armed men left the captives and the spoil before the princes and all the congregation.

15 And the men which were expressed by name rose up, and took the captives, and with the spoil clothed all that were naked among them, and arrayed them, and shod them, and gave them to eat and to drink, and anointed them, and carried all the feeble of them upon asses, and brought them to Yericho, the city of palm trees, to their brethren; then they returned to Samaria (Shomeron).

16 At that time did king Achaz send unto the kings of Assyria (Ashshur) to help him.

17 For again the Edomites had come and smitten Judah (Yehudah), and carried away captives.

18 The Philistines also had invaded the cities of the low country, and of the south of Judah (Yehudah), and had taken Beit-Shemesh, and Ayalon, and Gederoth, and Shocho with the villages thereof, and Timnah with the villages thereof, Gimzo also and the villages thereof; and they dwelt there.

19 For יהוה brought Judah (Yehudah) low because of Achaz king of Yisrael; for he made Judah (Yehudah) naked, and transgressed sore against יהוה.

20 And Tilgathpilneser king of Assyria (Ashshur) came unto him, and distressed him, but strengthened him not.

21 For Achaz took away a portion out of the house of יהוה, and out of the house of the king, and of the princes, and gave it unto the king of Assyria (Ashshur); but he helped him not.

22 And in the time of his distress did he trespass yet more against יהוה. This is that King Achaz.

23 For he sacrificed unto the gods (elohim) of Damascus (Dammeseq), which smote him; and he said, "Because the gods (elohim) of the kings of Syria (Aram) help them, therefore will I sacrifice to them, that they may help me." But they were the ruin of him, and of all Yisrael.

24 And Achaz gathered together the vessels of the house of God (Elohim), and cut in pieces the vessels of the house of God (Elohim), and shut up the doors of the house of יהוה, and he made him altars in every corner of Jerusalem (Yerushalayim).

25 And in every several city of Judah (Yehudah) he made high places to burn incense unto other gods (elohim), and provoked to anger יהוה God (Elohim) of his fathers.

26 Now the rest of his acts and of all his ways, first and last, behold, they are written in the book of the kings of Judah (Yehudah) and Yisrael.

27 And Achaz slept with his fathers, and they buried him in the city, even in Jerusalem (Yerushalayim); but they brought him not into the sepulchres of the kings of Yisrael. And Hezekiah (Chizkiyahu) his son reigned in his stead.

29 Hezekiah (Chizkiyahu) began to reign when he was five and twenty years old, and he reigned nine and twenty years in Jerusalem (Yerushalayim). His mother's name was Aviyah, the daughter of Zechariah (Zekharyahu).

2 And he did that which was right in the sight of יהוה, according to all that Dawid his father had done.

3 He in the first year of his reign, in the first month, opened the doors of the house of יהוה, and repaired them.

4 And he brought in the priests (kohanim) and the Levites (Lewiyim), and gathered them together into the east street,

5 And said unto them, "Hear me, you Levites (Lewiyim), sanctify now yourselves, and sanctify the house of יהוה God (Elohim) of your fathers, and carry forth the filthiness out of the holy place.

6 For our fathers have trespassed, and done that which was evil in the eyes of יהוה our God (YHWH Eloheinu), and have forsaken Him, and have turned away their faces from the habitation of יהוה, and turned their backs.

7 Also they have shut up the doors of the porch, and put out the lamps, and have not burned incense nor offered burnt offerings in the holy place unto the God of Israel (Elohei Yisrael).

8 Wherefore the wrath of יהוה was upon Judah (Yehudah) and Yerushalayim, and He hath delivered them to trouble, to astonishment, and to hissing, as you see with your eyes.

9 For, behold, our fathers have fallen by the sword, and our sons and our daughters and our wives are in captivity for this.

10 Now it is in mine heart to make a covenant with יהוה God of Israel (Elohei Yisrael), that His fierce wrath may turn away from us.

11 My sons, be not now negligent; for יהוה hath chosen you to stand before Him, to serve Him, and that you should minister unto Him, and burn incense."

12 Then the Levites (Lewiyim) arose, Mahath the son of Amasai, and Yoel the son of Azaryahu, of the sons of the Kohathites; and of the sons of Merari: Kish the son of Avdi, and Azaryahu the son of Yehallelel; and of the Gershonites: Yoach the son of Zimmah, and Eden the son of Yoach;

13 And of the sons of Elizaphan: Shimri, and Yeiel; and of the sons of Asaph: Zechariah (Zekharyahu), and Mattanyah;

14 And of the sons of Heman: Yeiel, and Shimei; and of the sons of Yedutun: Shemayah, and Uzziel.

15 And they gathered their brethren, and sanctified themselves, and came, according to the commandment of the king, by the words of יהוה, to cleanse the house of יהוה.

16 And the priests (kohanim) went into the inner part of the house of יהוה, to cleanse it, and brought out all the uncleanness that they found in the temple of יהוה into the court of the house of יהוה. And the Levites (Lewiyim) took it, to carry it out abroad into the Brook Kidron.

17 Now they began on the first day of the first month to sanctify, and on the eighth day of the month came they to the porch of יהוה; so they sanctified the house of יהוה in eight days; and in the sixteenth day of the first month they made

an end.

18 Then they went in to Hezekiah (Chizkiyahu) the king, and said, "We have cleansed all the house of יהוה, and the altar of burnt offering, with all the vessels thereof, and the shewbread table, with all the vessels thereof.

19 Moreover all the vessels, which King Achaz in his reign did cast away in his transgression, have we prepared and sanctified, and, behold, they are before the altar of יהוה."

20 Then Hezekiah (Chizkiyahu) the king rose early, and gathered the rulers of the city, and went up to the house of יהוה.

21 And they brought seven bullocks, and seven rams, and seven lambs, and seven he goats, for a sin offering for the kingdom, and for the sanctuary, and for Judah (Yehudah). And he commanded the priests (kohanim) the sons of Aaron (Aharon) to offer them on the altar of יהוה.

22 So they killed the bullocks, and the priests (kohanim) received the blood, and sprinkled it on the altar; likewise, when they had killed the rams, they sprinkled the blood upon the altar; they killed also the lambs, and they sprinkled the blood upon the altar.

23 And they brought forth the he goats for the sin offering before the king and the congregation; and they laid their hands upon them.

24 And the priests (kohanim) killed them, and they made reconciliation with their blood upon the altar, to make an atonement for all Yisrael, for the king commanded that the burnt offering and the sin offering should be made for all Yisrael.

25 And he set the Levites (Lewiyim) in the house of יהוה with cymbals, with psalteries, and with harps, according to the commandment of Dawid, and of Gad the king's seer, and Nathan the prophet; for so was the commandment of יהוה by His prophets.

26 And the Levites (Lewiyim) stood with the instruments of Dawid, and the priests (kohanim) with the trumpets.

27 And Hezekiah (Chizkiyahu) commanded to offer the burnt offering upon the altar. And when the burnt offering began, the song of יהוה began also with the trumpets, and with the instruments ordained by Dawid king of Yisrael.

28 And all the congregation worshipped, and the singers sang, and the trumpeters sounded; and all this continued until the burnt offering was finished.

29 And when they had made an end of offering, the king and all that were present with him bowed themselves, and worshipped.

30 Moreover Hezekiah (Chizkiyahu) the king and the princes commanded the Levites (Lewiyim) to sing praise unto יהוה with the words of Dawid, and of Asaph the seer. And they sang praises with gladness, and they bowed their heads and worshipped.

31 Then Hezekiah (Chizkiyahu) answered and said, "Now you have consecrated yourselves unto יהוה, come near and bring sacrifices and thank offerings into the house of יהוה." And the congregation brought in sacrifices and thank offerings; and as many as were of a free heart burnt offerings.

32 And the number of the burnt offerings, which the congregation brought, was threescore and ten bullocks, a hundred rams, and two hundred lambs; all these were for a burnt offering to יהוה.

33 And the consecrated things were six hundred oxen and three thousand sheep.

34 But the priests (kohanim) were too few, so that they could not skin all the burnt offerings; wherefore their brethren the Levites (Lewiyim) did help them, till the work was ended, and until the other priests (kohanim) had sanctified themselves; for the Levites (Lewiyim) were more upright in heart to sanctify themselves than the priests (kohanim).

35 And also the burnt offerings were in abundance, with the fat of the peace offerings, and the drink offerings for every burnt offering. So the service of the house of יהוה was set in order.

36 And Hezekiah (Chizkiyahu) rejoiced, and all the people, that God (Elohim) had prepared the people; for the thing was done suddenly.

30 And Hezekiah (Chizkiyahu) sent to all Yisrael and Judah (Yehudah), and wrote letters also to Efrayim and Menashsheh, that they should come to the house of יהוה at Jerusalem (Yerushalayim), to keep the Passover (Pesach) unto יהוה God of Israel (Elohei Yisrael).

2 For the king had taken counsel, and his princes, and all the congregation in Jerusalem (Yerushalayim), to keep the Passover (Pesach)

in the second month.

3 For they could not keep it at that time, because the priests (kohanim) had not sanctified themselves sufficiently, neither had the people gathered themselves together to Jerusalem (Yerushalayim).

4 And the thing pleased the king and all the congregation.

5 So they established a decree to make proclamation throughout all Yisrael, from Beer-Sheva even to Dan, that they should come to keep the Passover (Pesach) unto יהוה God of Israel (Elohei Yisrael) at Jerusalem (Yerushalayim); for they had not done it of a long time in such sort as it was written.

6 So the posts went with the letters from the king and his princes throughout all Yisrael and Judah (Yehudah), and according to the commandment of the king, saying, "You children of Yisrael, turn again unto יהוה God (Elohim) of Avraham, Isaac (Yitschaq), and Yisrael, and He will return to the remnant of you, that are escaped out of the hand of the kings of Assyria (Ashshur).

7 And be not you like your fathers, and like your brethren, who trespassed against יהוה God (Elohim) of their fathers, who therefore gave them up to desolation, as you see.

8 Now be you not stiffnecked, as your fathers were, but yield yourselves unto יהוה, and enter into His sanctuary, which He hath sanctified forever; and serve יהוה your God (YHWH Eloheikhem), that the fierceness of His wrath may turn away from you.

9 For if you turn again unto יהוה, your brethren and your children shall find compassion before them that lead them captive, so that they shall come again into this land; for יהוה your God (YHWH Eloheikhem) is gracious and merciful, and will not turn away His face from you, if you return unto Him."

10 So the posts passed from city to city through the country of Efrayim and Menashsheh even unto Zevulun; but they laughed them to scorn, and mocked them.

11 Nevertheless divers of Asher and Menashsheh and of Zevulun humbled themselves, and came to Yerushalayim.

12 Also in Judah (Yehudah) the hand of God (Elohim) was to give them one heart to do the commandment of the king and of the princes,

by the word of יהוה.

13 And there assembled at Jerusalem (Yerushalayim) much people to keep the Feast of Unleavened Bread (Chag HaMatzot) in the second month, a very great congregation.

14 And they arose and took away the altars that were in Jerusalem (Yerushalayim), and all the altars for incense took they away, and cast them into the Brook Kidron.

15 Then they killed the Passover (Pesach) on the fourteenth day of the second month; and the priests (kohanim) and the Levites (Lewiyim) were ashamed, and sanctified themselves, and brought in the burnt offerings into the house of יהוה.

16 And they stood in their place after their manner, according to the Torah by Moses the man of God (Elohim); the priests (kohanim) sprinkled the blood, which they received of the hand of the Levites (Lewiyim).

17 For there were many in the congregation that were not sanctified; therefore the Levites (Lewiyim) had the charge of the killing of the Passover lambs (Pesachim) for every one that was not clean, to sanctify them unto יהוה.

18 For a multitude of the people, even many of Efrayim, and Menashsheh, Yissaskhar, and Zevulun, had not cleansed themselves, yet did they eat the Passover lamb (Pesach) otherwise than it was written. But Hezekiah (Chizkiyahu) prayed for them, saying, "May יהוה Who is good, pardon every one,

19 who prepareth his heart to seek God (Elohim), יהוה God (Elohim) of his fathers, though he be not cleansed according to the purification of the sanctuary."

20 And יהוה hearkened to Hezekiah (Chizkiyahu), and healed the people.

21 And the children of Yisrael that were present at Jerusalem (Yerushalayim) kept the Feast of Unleavened Bread (Chag HaMatzot) seven days with great gladness; and the Levites (Lewiyim) and the priests (kohanim) praised יהוה day by day, singing with loud instruments unto יהוה.

22 And Hezekiah (Chizkiyahu) spake comfortably unto all the Levites (Lewiyim) that taught the good knowledge of יהוה; and they did eat throughout the feast seven days, offering peace offerings, and making confession to יהוה God (Elohim) of their fathers.

23 And the whole assembly took counsel to keep

other seven days; and they kept other seven days with gladness.

24 For Hezekiah (Chizkiyahu) king of Judah (Yehudah) did give to the congregation a thousand bullocks and seven thousand sheep; and the princes gave to the congregation a thousand bullocks and ten thousand sheep; and a great number of priests (kohanim) sanctified themselves.

25 And all the congregation of Judah (Yehudah), with the priests (kohanim) and the Levites (Lewiyim), and all the congregation that came out of Yisrael, and the strangers that came out of the land of Yisrael, and that dwelt in Judah (Yehudah), rejoiced.

26 So there was great joy in Jerusalem (Yerushalayim), for since the time of Solomon (Shelomoh) the son of Dawid king of Yisrael there was not the like in Jerusalem (Yerushalayim).

27 Then the priests (kohanim) the Levites (Lewiyim) arose and blessed the people; and their voice was heard, and their prayer came up to His holy dwelling place, even unto heaven.

31 Now when all this was finished, all Yisrael that were present went out to the cities of Judah (Yehudah), and broke the pillars in pieces, and cut down the Asherim, and threw down the high places and the altars out of all Judah (Yehudah) and Benjamin (Binyamin), in Efrayim also and Menashsheh, until they had utterly destroyed them all. Then all the children of Yisrael returned, every man to his possession, into their own cities.

2 And Hezekiah (Chizkiyahu) appointed the courses of the priests (kohanim) and the Levites (Lewiyim) after their courses, every man according to his service, the priests (kohanim) and Levites (Lewiyim) for burnt offerings and for peace offerings, to minister, and to give thanks, and to praise in the gates of the tents of יהוה.

3 He appointed also the king's portion of his substance for the burnt offerings, for the morning and evening burnt offerings, and the burnt offerings for the Shabbats, and for the New Moons, and for the set feasts, as it is written in the Torah of יהוה.

4 Moreover he commanded the people that dwelt in Jerusalem (Yerushalayim) to give the portion of the priests (kohanim) and the Levites

(Lewiyim), that they might be encouraged in the Torah of יהוה.

5 And as soon as the commandment came abroad, the children of Yisrael brought in abundance the firstfruits of corn, wine, and oil, and honey, and of all the increase of the field; and the tithe of all things brought they in abundantly.

6 And concerning the children of Yisrael and Judah (Yehudah), that dwelt in the cities of Judah (Yehudah), they also brought in the tithe of oxen and sheep, and the tithe of holy things which were consecrated unto יהוה their God (YHWH Eloheihem), and laid them by heaps.

7 In the third month they began to lay the foundation of the heaps, and finished them in the seventh month.

8 And when Hezekiah (Chizkiyahu) and the princes came and saw the heaps, they blessed יהוה, and His people Yisrael.

9 Then Hezekiah (Chizkiyahu) questioned with the priests (kohanim) and the Levites (Lewiyim) concerning the heaps.

10 And Azaryahu the chief priest (kohen) of the house of Zadok answered him, and said, "Since the people began to bring the offerings into the house of יהוה, we have had enough to eat, and have left plenty; for יהוה hath blessed His people; and that which is left is this great store."

11 Then Hezekiah (Chizkiyahu) commanded to prepare chambers in the house of יהוה; and they prepared them,

12 And brought in the offerings and the tithes and the dedicated things faithfully, over which Konanyahu the Lewite was ruler, and Shimei his brother was the next.

13 And Yeiel, and Azazyahu, and Nahath, and Asahel, and Yerimot, and Yozavad, and Eliel, and Yismakhiyahu, and Mahath, and Benayah, were overseers under the hand of Konanyahu and Shimei his brother, at the commandment of Hezekiah (Chizkiyahu) the king, and Azaryahu the ruler of the house of God (Elohim).

14 And Kore the son of Imnah the Lewite, the porter toward the east, was over the freewill offerings of God (Elohim), to distribute the oblations of יהוה, and the most holy things.

15 And next to him were Eden, and Miniamin, and Joshua (Yeshua), and Shemayahu, Amaryahu, and Shekhanyahu, in the cities of the priests (kohanim), in their set office, to give

to their brethren by courses, as well to the great as to the small.

16 Besides their genealogy of males, from three years old and upward, even unto every one that entereth into the house of יהוה, his daily portion for their service in their charges according to their courses;

17 Both to the genealogy of the priests (kohanim) by the house of their fathers, and the Levites (Lewiyim) from twenty years old and upward, in their charges by their courses;

18 And to the genealogy of all their little ones, their wives, and their sons, and their daughters, through all the congregation; for in their set office they sanctified themselves in holiness.

19 Also of the sons of Aaron (Aharon) the priests (kohanim), who were in the fields of the suburbs of their cities, in every several city, the men that were expressed by name, to give portions to all the males among the priests (kohanim), and to all that were reckoned by genealogies among the Levites (Lewiyim).

20 And thus did Hezekiah (Chizkiyahu) throughout all Judah (Yehudah), and wrought that which was good and right and truth before יהוה his God (Elohim).

21 And in every work that he began in the service of the house of God (Elohim), and in the Torah, and in the commandments, to seek his God (Elohim), he did it with all his heart and prospered.

32 After these things, and the establishment thereof, Senna-cherib king of Assyria (Ashshur) came, and entered into Judah (Yehudah), and encamped against the fenced cities, and thought to win them for himself.

2 And when Hezekiah (Chizkiyahu) saw that Sennacherib was come, and that he was purposed to fight against Jerusalem (Yerushalayim),

3 He took counsel with his princes and his mighty men to stop the waters of the fountains which were outside the city; and they did help him.

4 So there was gathered much people together, who stopped all the fountains, and the brook that ran through the midst of the land, saying, "Why should the kings of Assyria (Ashshur) come, and find much water?"

5 Also he strengthened himself, and built up all the wall that was broken, and raised it up to the towers, and another wall outside, and repaired Millo in the city of Dawid, and made darts and shields in abundance.

6 And he set captains of war over the people, and gathered them together to him in the street of the gate of the city, and spake comfortably to them, saying,

7 "Be strong and courageous, be not afraid nor dismayed for the king of Assyria (Ashshur), nor for all the multitude that is with him; for there be more with us than with him.

8 With him is an arm of flesh; but with us is יהוה our God (YHWH Eloheinu) to help us, and to fight our battles." And the people rested themselves upon the words of Hezekiah (Chizkiyahu) king of Judah (Yehudah).

9 After this did Sennacherib king of Assyria (Ashshur) send his servants to Jerusalem (Yerushalayim), (but he himself laid siege against Lachish, and all his power with him,) unto Hezekiah (Chizkiyahu) king of Judah (Yehudah), and unto all Judah (Yehudah) that were at Jerusalem (Yerushalayim), saying,

10 "Thus saith Sennacherib king of Assyria (Ashshur): 'Whereon do you trust, that you abide in the siege in Jerusalem (Yerushalayim)?

11 Doth not Hezekiah (Chizkiyahu) persuade you to give over yourselves to die by famine and by thirst, saying, "יהוה our God (YHWH Eloheinu) shall deliver us out of the hand of the king of Assyria (Ashshur)?"

12 Hath not the same Hezekiah (Chizkiyahu) taken away his high places and his altars, and commanded Judah (Yehudah) and Jerusalem (Yerushalayim), saying, "You shall worship before one altar, and burn incense upon it?"

13 Know you not what I and my fathers have done unto all the people of other lands? Were the gods (elohim) of the nations of those lands any ways able to deliver their lands out of mine hand?

14 Who was there among all the gods (elohim) of those nations that my fathers utterly destroyed, that could deliver his people out of mine hand, that your God (Elohim) should be able to deliver you out of mine hand?

15 Now therefore let not Hezekiah (Chizkiyahu) deceive you, nor persuade you on this manner, neither yet believe him; for no god (eloah) of any nation or kingdom was able to deliver his people out of mine hand, and out of the hand of my fathers; how much less shall your God

(Elohim) deliver you out of mine hand?

16 And his servants spake yet more against God (Elohim) יהוה, and against His servant Hezekiah (Chizkiyahu).

17 He wrote also letters to rail on יהוה God of Israel (Elohei Yisrael), and to speak against him, saying, "As the gods (elohim) of the nations of other lands have not delivered their people out of mine hand, so shall not the God (Elohim) of Hezekiah (Chizkiyahu) deliver His people out of mine hand."

18 Then they cried with a loud voice in the Jews' (Yehudim) speech unto the people of Jerusalem (Yerushalayim) that were on the wall, to affright them, and to trouble them; that they might take the city.

19 And they spake against the God (Elohim) of Jerusalem (Yerushalayim), as against the gods (elohim) of the people of the earth, which were the work of the hands of man.

20 And for this cause Hezekiah (Chizkiyahu) the king, and the prophet Isaiah (Yeshayahu) the son of Amoz, prayed and cried to heaven.

21 And יהוה sent an angel, who cut off all the mighty men of valour, and the leaders and captains in the camp of the king of Assyria (Ashshur). So he returned with shame of face to his own land. And when he was come into the house of his god (eloah), they that came forth of his own bowels slew him there with the sword.

22 Thus יהוה saved Hezekiah (Chizkiyahu) and the inhabitants of Jerusalem (Yerushalayim) from the hand of Sennacherib the king of Assyria (Ashshur), and from the hand of all other, and guided them on every side.

23 And many brought gifts unto יהוה to Jerusalem (Yerushalayim), and presents to Hezekiah (Chizkiyahu) king of Judah (Yehudah); so that he was magnified in the sight of all nations from thenceforth.

24 In those days Hezekiah (Chizkiyahu) was sick to the death, and prayed unto יהוה; and He spake unto him, and He gave him a sign.

25 But Hezekiah (Chizkiyahu) rendered not again according to the benefit done unto him; for his heart was lifted up; therefore there was wrath upon him, and upon Judah (Yehudah) and Jerusalem (Yerushalayim).

26 Notwithstanding Hezekiah (Chizkiyahu) humbled himself for the pride of his heart, both he and the inhabitants of Jerusalem

(Yerushalayim), so that the wrath of יהוה came not upon them in the days of Hezekiah (Chizkiyahu).

27 And Hezekiah (Chizkiyahu) had exceeding much riches and honor; and he made himself treasuries for silver, and for gold, and for precious stones, and for spices, and for shields, and for all manner of pleasant jewels;

28 Storehouses also for the increase of corn, and wine, and oil; and stalls for all manner of beasts, and cotes for flocks.

29 Moreover he provided him cities, and possessions of flocks and herds in abundance, for God (Elohim) had given him substance very much.

30 This same Hezekiah (Chizkiyahu) also stopped the upper watercourse of Gihon, and brought it straight down to the west side of the city of Dawid. And Hezekiah (Chizkiyahu) prospered in all his works.

31 Howbeit in the business of the ambassadors of the princes of Babylon (Bavel), who sent unto him to enquire of the wonder that was done in the land, God (Elohim) left him, to test him, that He might know all that was in his heart.

32 Now the rest of the acts of Hezekiah (Chizkiyahu), and his goodness, behold, they are written in the vision of Isaiah (Yeshayahu) the prophet, the son of Amoz, and in the book of the kings of Judah (Yehudah) and Yisrael.

33 And Hezekiah (Chizkiyahu) slept with his fathers, and they buried him in the chiefest of the sepulchres of the sons of Dawid; and all Judah (Yehudah) and the inhabitants of Jerusalem (Yerushalayim) did him honor at his death. And Menashsheh his son reigned in his stead.

33 Menashsheh was twelve years old when he began to reign, and he reigned fifty and five years in Jerusalem (Yerushalayim);

2 But he did that which was evil in the sight of יהוה, like unto the abominations of the heathen, whom יהוה had cast out before the children of Yisrael.

3 For he built again the high places which Hezekiah (Chizkiyahu) his father had broken down, and he reared up altars for Baals (Baalim), and made Asherahs (Asherim), and worshipped all the host of heaven, and served them.

4 Also he built altars in the house of יהוה, whereof יהוה had said, "In Jerusalem (Yerushalayim) shall My name be forever."

5 And he built altars for all the host of heaven in the two courts of the house of יהוה.

6 And he caused his children to pass through the fire in the valley of the son of Hinnom; also he observed times, and used enchantments, and used witchcraft, and dealt with a familiar spirit, and with wizards; he wrought much evil in the sight of יהוה, to provoke Him to anger.

7 And he set a carved image, the idol which he had made, in the house of God (Elohim), of which God (Elohim) had said to Dawid and to Solomon (Shelomoh) his son, "In this house, and in Jerusalem (Yerushalayim), which I have chosen before all the tribes of Yisrael, will I put My name forever."

8 Neither will I anymore remove the foot of Yisrael from out of the land which I have appointed for your fathers; so that they will take heed to do all that I have commanded them, according to the whole Torah and the statutes and the ordinances by the hand of Moses (Mosheh).

9 So Menashsheh made Judah (Yehudah) and the inhabitants of Jerusalem (Yerushalayim) to err, and to do worse than the heathen, whom יהוה had destroyed before the children of Yisrael.

10 And יהוה spake to Menashsheh, and to His people, but they would not hearken.

11 Wherefore יהוה brought upon them the captains of the army of the king of Assyria (Ashshur), who took Menashsheh among the thorns, and bound him with fetters, and carried him to Babylon (Bavel).

12 And when he was in affliction, he besought יהוה his God (Elohim), and humbled himself greatly before the God (Elohim) of his fathers,

13 And prayed unto Him; and He was intreated of him, and heard his supplication, and brought him again to Jerusalem (Yerushalayim) into his kingdom. Then Menashsheh knew that יהוה He was God (Elohim).

14 Now after this he built a wall outside the city of Dawid, on the west side of Gihon, in the valley, even to the entering in at the fish gate, and compassed about Ophel, and raised it up a very great height, and put captains of war in all the fenced cities of Judah (Yehudah).

15 And he took away the strange gods (elohim), and the idol out of the house of יהוה, and all the altars that he had built in the mount of the house

of יהוה, and in Jerusalem (Yerushalayim), and cast them out of the city.

16 And he repaired the altar of יהוה, and sacrificed thereon peace offerings and thank offerings, and commanded Judah (Yehudah) to serve יהוה God of Israel (Elohei Yisrael).

17 Nevertheless the people did sacrifice still in the high places, yet unto יהוה their God (YHWH Eloheihem) only.

18 Now the rest of the acts of Menashsheh, and his prayer unto his God (Elohim), and the words of the seers that spake to him in the name of יהוה God of Israel (Elohei Yisrael), behold, they are written in the book of the kings of Yisrael.

19 His prayer also, and how God (Elohim) was intreated of him, and all his sin, and his trespass, and the places wherein he built high places, and set up Asherahs (Asherim) and graven images, before he was humbled; behold, they are written among the sayings of the seers.

20 So Menashsheh slept (rested) with his fathers, and they buried him in his own house; and Amon his son reigned in his stead.

21 Amon was two and twenty years old when he began to reign, and reigned two years in Jerusalem (Yerushalayim).

22 But he did that which was evil in the sight of יהוה, as did Menashsheh his father, for Amon sacrificed unto all the carved images which Menashsheh his father had made, and served them;

23 And humbled not himself before יהוה, as Menashsheh his father had humbled himself; but Amon trespassed more and more.

24 And his servants conspired against him, and slew him in his own house.

25 But the people of the land slew all them that had conspired against king Amon; and the people of the land made Josiah (Yoshiyahu) his son king in his stead.

34 Josiah (Yoshiyahu) was eight years old when he began to reign, and he reigned in Jerusalem (Yerushalayim) one and thirty years.

2 And he did that which was right in the sight of יהוה, and walked in the ways of Dawid his father, and declined neither to the right hand, nor to the left.

3 For in the eighth year of his reign, while he was yet young, he began to seek after the God (Elohim) of Dawid his father; and in the twelfth year he began to purge Judah (Yehudah) and

Jerusalem (Yerushalayim) from the high places, and the Asherim, and the carved images, and the molten images.

4 And they broke down the altars of the Baals (Baalim) in his presence; and the images, that were on high above them, he cut down; and the Asherahs (Asherim), and the carved images, and the molten images, he broke in pieces, and made dust of them, and strowed it upon the graves of them that had sacrificed unto them.

5 And he burnt the bones of the priests (kohanim) upon their altars, and cleansed Judah (Yehudah) and Jerusalem (Yerushalayim).

6 And so did he in the cities of Menashsheh, and Efrayim, and Shimon, even unto Naftali, with their mattocks round about.

7 And when he had broken down the altars and the Asherahs (Asherim), and had beaten the graven images into powder, and cut down all the idols throughout all the land of Yisrael, he returned to Jerusalem (Yerushalayim).

8 Now in the eighteenth year of his reign, when he had purged the land, and the house, he sent Shaphan the son of Atsalyahu, and Maaseyahu the governor of the city, and Yoach the son of Yoachaz the recorder, to repair the house of יהוה his God (Elohim).

9 And when they came to Hilkiah (Chilqiyahu) the high priest (kohen hagadol), they delivered the money that was brought into the house of God (Elohim), which the Levites (Lewiyim) that kept the doors had gathered of the hand of Menashsheh and Efrayim, and of all the remnant of Yisrael, and of all Judah (Yehudah) and Benjamin (Binyamin); and they returned to Jerusalem (Yerushalayim).

10 And they put it in the hand of the workmen that had the oversight of the house of יהוה, and they gave it to the workmen that wrought in the house of יהוה, to repair and amend the house.

11 Even to the artificers and builders gave they it, to buy hewn stone, and timber for couplings, and to floor the houses which the kings of Judah (Yehudah) had destroyed.

12 And the men did the work faithfully; and the overseers of them were Jahath (Yachat) and Obadiah (Ovadyah), the Levites (Lewiyim), of the sons of Merari; and Zechariah (Zekharyahu) and Meshullam, of the sons of the Kohathites, to set it forward; and other of the Levites (Lewiyim), all that could skill of instruments of musick.

13 Also they were over the bearers of burdens, and were overseers of all that wrought the work in any manner of service; and of the Levites (Lewiyim) there were scribes, and officers, and porters.

14 And when they brought out the money that was brought into the house of יהוה, Hilkiah (Chilqiyahu) the priest (kohen) found a book of the law (sefer hatorah) of יהוה given by Moses (Mosheh).

15 And Hilkiah (Chilqiyahu) answered and said to Shaphan the scribe, "I have found the book of the law (sefer hatorah) in the house of יהוה. And Hilkiah (Chilqiyahu) delivered the book to Shaphan.

16 And Shaphan carried the book to the king, and brought the king word back again, saying, "All that was committed to your servants, they do it."

17 And they have gathered together the money that was found in the house of יהוה, and have delivered it into the hand of the overseers, and to the hand of the workmen.

18 Then Shaphan the scribe told the king, saying, "Hilkiah (Chilqiyahu) the priest (kohen) hath given me a book." And Shaphan read it before the king.

19 And it came to pass, when the king had heard the words of the law (torah), that he rent his clothes.

20 And the king commanded Hilkiah (Chilqiyahu), and Ahikam the son of Shaphan, and Avdon the son of Mikhah, and Shaphan the scribe, and Asayah a servant of the king's, saying,

21 "Go, enquire of יהוה for me, and for them that are left in Yisrael and in Judah (Yehudah), concerning the words of the book that is found; for great is the wrath of יהוה that is poured out upon us, because our fathers have not kept the word of יהוה, to do after all that is written in this book."

22 And Hilkiah (Chilqiyahu), and they that the king had appointed, went to Huldah the prophetess (neviah), the wife of Shallum the son of Tikvath, the son of Hasrah, keeper of the wardrobe; (now she dwelt in Jerusalem (Yerushalayim) in the college;) and they spake to her to that effect.

23 And she answered them, "Thus saith יהוה

God of Israel (Elohei Yisrael): 'Tell you the man that sent you to Me,

24 Thus saith יהוה: "Behold, I will bring disaster (raah) upon this place, and upon the inhabitants thereof, even all the curses that are written in the book which they have read before the king of Judah (Yehudah),

25 Because they have forsaken Me, and have burned incense unto other gods (elohim), that they might provoke Me to anger with all the works of their hands; therefore My wrath shall be poured out upon this place, and shall not be quenched.'"

26 And as for the king of Judah (Yehudah), who sent you to enquire of יהוה, so shall you say unto him, 'Thus saith יהוה God of Israel (Elohei Yisrael) concerning the words which you have heard:

27 "Because your heart was tender, and you didst humble yourself before God (Elohim), when you heardest His words against this place, and against the inhabitants thereof, and humbledst yourself before Me, and didst rend your clothes, and weep before Me; I have even heard you also," saith יהוה.

28 "Behold, I will gather you to your fathers, and you shalt be gathered to your grave in peace, neither shall your eyes see all the disaster (raah) that I will bring upon this place, and upon the inhabitants of the same.'"'" So they brought the king word again.

29 Then the king sent and gathered together all the elders of Judah (Yehudah) and Jerusalem (Yerushalayim).

30 And the king went up into the house of יהוה, and all the men of Judah (Yehudah), and the inhabitants of Jerusalem (Yerushalayim), and the priests (kohanim), and the Levites (Lewiyim), and all the people, great and small; and he read in their ears all the words of the book of the covenant that was found in the house of יהוה.

31 And the king stood in his place, and made a covenant before יהוה, to walk after יהוה, and to keep His commandments, and His testimonies, and His statutes, with all his heart, and with all his soul, to perform the words of the covenant which are written in this book.

32 And he caused all that were present in Jerusalem (Yerushalayim) and Benjamin (Binyamin) to stand to it. And the inhabitants of Jerusalem (Yerushalayim) did according to the covenant of God (Elohim), the God (Elohim) of their fathers.

33 And Josiah (Yoshiyahu) took away all the abominations out of all the countries that pertained to the children of Yisrael, and made all that were present in Yisrael to serve, even to serve יהוה their God (YHWH Eloheihem). And all his days they departed not from following יהוה, the God (Elohim) of their fathers.

35 Moreover Josiah (Yoshiyahu) kept a Passover (Pesach) unto יהוה in Jerusalem (Yerushalayim); and they killed the Passover lamb (Pesach) on the fourteenth day of the first month.

2 And he set the priests (kohanim) in their charges, and encouraged them to the service of the house of יהוה,

3 And said unto the Levites (Lewiyim) that taught all Yisrael, which were holy unto יהוה: "Put the holy ark in the house which Solomon (Shelomoh) the son of Dawid king of Yisrael did build; it shall not be a burden upon your shoulders. Serve now יהוה your God (YHWH Eloheikhem), and His people Yisrael,

4 And prepare yourselves by the houses of your fathers, after your courses, according to the writing of Dawid king of Yisrael, and according to the writing of Solomon (Shelomoh) his son.

5 And stand in the holy place according to the divisions of the families of the fathers of your brethren the people, and after the division of the families of the Levites (Lewiyim).

6 So kill the Passover lamb (Pesach), and sanctify yourselves, and prepare your brethren, that they may do according to the word of יהוה by the hand of Moses (Mosheh)."

7 And Josiah (Yoshiyahu) gave to the people, of the flock, lambs and kids, all for the Passover (Pesach) offerings, for all that were present, to the number of thirty thousand, and three thousand bullocks; these were of the king's substance.

8 And his princes gave willingly unto the people, to the priests (kohanim), and to the Levites (Lewiyim); Hilkiah (Chilqiyahu) and Zechariah (Zekharyahu) and Yeiel, rulers of the house of God (Elohim), gave unto the priests (kohanim) for the Passover (Pesach) offerings two thousand and six hundred small cattle, and three hundred oxen.

9 Konanyahu also, and Shemayah and

Nethaneel, his brethren, and Chashavyah and Yeiel and Yozavad, chief of the Levites (Lewiyim), gave unto the Levites (Lewiyim) for Passover (Pesach) offerings five thousand small cattle, and five hundred oxen.

10 So the service was prepared, and the priests (kohanim) stood in their place, and the Levites (Lewiyim) in their courses, according to the king's commandment.

11 And they killed the Passover lamb (Pesach), and the priests (kohanim) sprinkled the blood from their hands, and the Levites (Lewiyim) skinned them.

12 And they removed the burnt offerings, that they might give according to the divisions of the families of the people, to offer unto יהוה, as it is written in the book of Moses (Mosheh). And so did they with the oxen.

13 And they roasted the Passover lamb (Pesach) with fire according to the ordinance; but the other holy offerings boiled they in pots, and in caldrons, and in pans, and divided them speedily among all the people.

14 And afterward they made ready for themselves and for the priests (kohanim), because the priests (kohanim) the sons of Aaron (Aharon) were busied in offering of burnt offerings and the fat until night; therefore the Levites (Lewiyim) prepared for themselves, and for the priests (kohanim) the sons of Aaron (Aharon).

15 And the singers the sons of Asaph were in their place, according to the commandment of Dawid, and Asaph, and Heman, and Yedutun the king's seer; and the porters waited at every gate; they might not depart from their service; for their brethren the Levites (Lewiyim) prepared for them.

16 So all the service of יהוה was prepared the same day, to keep the Passover (Pesach), and to offer burnt offerings upon the altar of יהוה, according to the commandment of King Josiah (Yoshi-yahu).

17 And the children of Yisrael that were present kept the Passover (Pesach) at that time, and the Feast of Unleavened Bread (Chag HaMatzot) seven days.

18 And there was no Passover (Pesach) like to that kept in Yisrael from the days of Shemuel the prophet; neither did all the kings of Yisrael keep such a Passover (Pesach) as Josiah (Yoshi-yahu) kept, and the priests (kohanim), and the Levites (Lewiyim), and all Judah (Yehudah) and Yisrael that were present, and the inhabitants of Jerusalem (Yerushalayim).

19 In the eighteenth year of the reign of Josiah (Yoshiyahu) was this Passover (Pesach) kept.

20 After all this, when Josiah (Yoshiyahu) had prepared the temple, Necho king of Egypt (Mitsrayim) came up to fight against Carchemish by Euphrates; and Josiah (Yoshiyahu) went out against him.

21 But he sent ambassadors to him, saying, "What have I to do with you, you king of Judah (Yehudah)? I come not against you this day, but against the house wherewith I have war, for God (Elohim) commanded me to make haste; forbear you from meddling with God (Elohim), who is with me, that he destroys you not."

22 Nevertheless Josiah (Yoshiyahu) would not turn his face from him, but disguised himself, that he might fight with him, and hearkened not unto the words of Necho from the mouth of God (Elohim), and came to fight in the valley of Megiddo.

23 And the archers shot at King Josiah (Yoshiyahu); and the king said to his servants, "Have me away, for I am sore wounded."

24 His servants therefore took him out of that chariot, and put him in the second chariot that he had; and they brought him to Jerusalem (Yerushalayim), and he died, and was buried in one of the sepulchres of his fathers. And all Judah (Yehudah) and Jerusalem (Yerushalayim) mourned for Josiah (Yoshiyahu).

25 And Jeremiah (Yirmeyahu) lamented for Josiah (Yoshiyahu); and all the singing men and the singing women spake of Josiah (Yoshiyahu) in their lamentations to this day, and made them an ordinance in Yisrael; and, behold, they are written in the Lamentations.

26 Now the rest of the acts of Josiah (Yoshiyahu), and his goodness, according to that which was written in the Torah of יהוה,

27 And his deeds, first and last, behold, they are written in the book of the kings of Yisrael and Judah (Yehudah).

36 Then the people of the land took Yehoachaz the son of Josiah (Yoshiyahu), and made him king in his father's stead in Jerusalem (Yerushalayim).

2 Yehoachaz was twenty and three years old when he began to reign, and he reigned three

months in Jerusalem (Yerushalayim).

3 And the king of Egypt (Mitsrayim) put him down at Jerusalem (Yerushalayim), and condemned the land in a hundred talents of silver and a talent of gold.

4 And the king of Egypt (Mitsrayim) made Elyaqim his brother king over Judah (Yehudah) and Jerusalem (Yerushalayim), and turned his name to Yehoyaqim. And Necho took Yehoachaz his brother, and carried him to Egypt (Mitsrayim).

5 Yehoyaqim was twenty and five years old when he began to reign, and he reigned eleven years in Jerusalem (Yerushalayim); and he did that which was evil in the sight of יהוה his God (Elohim).

6 Against him came up Nebuchanezzar king of Babylon (Bavel), and bound him in fetters, to carry him to Babylon (Bavel).

7 Nebuchanezzar also carried of the vessels of the house of יהוה to Babylon (Bavel), and put them in his temple at Babylon (Bavel).

8 Now the rest of the acts of Yehoyaqim, and his abominations which he did, and that which was found in him, behold, they are written in the book of the kings of Yisrael and Judah (Yehudah); and Yehoyakhin his son reigned in his stead.

9 Yehoyakhin was eight years old when he began to reign, and he reigned three months and ten days in Jerusalem (Yerushalayim). And he did that which was evil in the sight of יהוה.

10 And when the year was expired, King Nebuchanezzar sent, and brought him to Babylon (Bavel), with the goodly vessels of the house of יהוה, and made Zedekiah (Tsidkiyahu) his brother king over Judah (Yehudah) and Jerusalem (Yerushalayim).

11 Zedekiah (Tsidkiyahu) was one and twenty years old when he began to reign, and reigned eleven years in Jerusalem (Yerushalayim).

12 And he did that which was evil in the sight of יהוה his God (Elohim), and humbled not himself before Jeremiah (Yirmeyahu) the prophet speaking from the mouth of יהוה.

13 And he also rebelled against King Nebuchanezzar, who had made him swear by God (Elohim); but he stiffened his neck, and hardened his heart from turning unto יהוה God of Israel (Elohei Yisrael).

14 Moreover all the chief of the priests (kohanim), and the people, transgressed very

much after all the abominations of the heathen; and polluted the house of יהוה which he had hallowed in Jerusalem (Yerushalayim).

15 And יהוה God (Elohim) of their fathers sent to them by His messengers, rising up betimes, and sending; because he had compassion on His people, and on His dwelling place;

16 But they mocked the messengers of God (Elohim), and despised His words, and misused His prophets, until the wrath of יהוה arose against His people, till there was no remedy.

17 Therefore He brought upon them the king of the Chaldees, who slew their young men with the sword in the house their sanctuary, and had no young men compassion upon young man or maiden, old man, or him that stooped for age; He gave them all into his hand.

18 And all the vessels of the house of God (Elohim), great and small, and the treasures of the house of יהוה, and the treasures of the king, and of his princes; all these he brought to Babylon (Bavel).

19 And they burnt the house of God (Elohim), and broke down the wall of Jerusalem (Yerushalayim), and burnt all the palaces thereof with fire, and destroyed all the goodly vessels thereof.

20 And them that had escaped from the sword carried he away to Babylon (Bavel), where they were servants to him and his sons until the reign of the kingdom of Persia,

21 To fulfil the word of יהוה by the mouth of Jeremiah (Yirmeyahu), until the land had enjoyed her Shabbats; for as long as she lay desolate she kept Shabbat, to fulfil threescore and ten (seventy) years.

22 Now in the first year of Cyrus king of Persia, that the word of יהוה spoken by the mouth of Jeremiah (Yirmeyahu) might be accomplished, יהוה stirred up the spirit of Cyrus king of Persia, that he made a proclamation throughout all his kingdom, and put it also in writing, saying,

23 "Thus saith Cyrus king of Persia: 'All the kingdoms of the earth hath יהוה God of heaven (Elohei shamayim) given me; and He hath charged me to build Him a house in Jerusalem (Yerushalayim), which is in Judah (Yehudah). Who is there among you of all His people? יהוה his God (Elohim) be with him, and let him go up.'"

EZRA
EZRA עֶזְרָא
(Help)

1 Now in the first year of Cyrus king of Persia, that the word of יהוה by the mouth of Jeremiah (Yirmeyah) might be fulfilled, יהוה stirred up the spirit of Cyrus king of Persia, that he made a proclamation throughout all his kingdom, and put it also in writing, saying,

2 "Thus saith Cyrus king of Persia: 'יהוה God of heaven (YHWH Elohei syamayim) hath given me all the kingdoms of the earth; and He hath charged me to build Him a house at Jerusalem (Yerushalayim), which is in Judah (Yehudah).

3 Who is there among you of all His people? His God (Elohim) be with him, and let him go up to Jerusalem (Yerushalayim), which is in Judah (Yehudah), and build the house of יהוה God of Israel (Elohei Yisrael), He is the God (Elohim) who is in Jerusalem (Yerushalayim).

4 And whosoever remaineth in any place where he sojourneth, let the men of his place help him with silver, and with gold, and with goods, and with beasts, besides the freewill offering for the house of God (Elohim) that is in Jerusalem (Yerushalayim).'"

5 Then rose up the chief of the fathers of Judah (Yehudah) and Benjamin (Binyamin), and the priests (kohanim), and the Levites (Lewiyim), with all them whose spirit God (Elohim) had raised, to go up to build the house of יהוה which is in Jerusalem (Yerushalayim).

6 And all they that were about them strengthened their hands with vessels of silver, with gold, with goods, and with beasts, and with precious things, besides all that was willingly offered.

7 Also Cyrus the king brought forth the vessels of the house of יהוה, which Nebuchadnezzar had brought forth out of Jerusalem (Yerushalayim), and had put them in the house of his gods (elohim);

8 Even those did Cyrus king of Persia bring forth by the hand of Mithredath the treasurer, and numbered them unto Sheshbazzar, the prince of Judah (Yehudah).

9 And this is the number of them: thirty chargers of gold, a thousand chargers of silver, nine and twenty knives,

10 Thirty basons of gold, silver basons of a second sort four hundred and ten, and other vessels a thousand.

11 All the vessels of gold and of silver were five thousand and four hundred. All these did Sheshbazzar bring up with them of the captivity that were brought up from Babylon (Bavel) unto Jerusalem (Yerushalayim).

2 Now these are the children of the province that went up out of the captivity, of those who had been carried away, whom Nebuchanezzar the king of Babylon (Bavel) had carried away unto Babylon (Bavel), and came again unto Jerusalem (Yerushalayim) and Judah (Yehudah), every one unto his city;

2 Who came with Zerubbabel: Joshua (Yeshua), Nehemiah (Nechemyah), Serayah, Reelayah, Mordecai, Bilshan, Mispar, Bigvai, Rehum, Baanah. The number of the men of the people of Yisrael:

3 The children of Parosh, two thousand one hundred seventy and two.

4 The children of Shefatyah, three hundred seventy and two.

5 The children of Arah, seven hundred seventy and five.

6 The children of Pahathmoab, of the children of Joshua (Yeshua) and Yoav, two thousand eight hundred and twelve.

7 The children of Elam, one thousand two hundred fifty and four.

8 The children of Zattu, nine hundred forty and five.

9 The children of Zaccai, seven hundred and threescore.

10 The children of Bani, six hundred forty and two.

11 The children of Bebai, six hundred twenty and three.

12 The children of Azgad, a thousand two hundred twenty and two.

13 The children of Adonikam, six hundred sixty and six.

14 The children of Bigvai, two thousand fifty and six.

15 The children of Adin, four hundred fifty and four.

16 The children of Ater of [A44]Hezekiah (Chizkiyah), ninety and eight.

17 The children of Bezai, three hundred twenty and three.

18 The children of Yorah, one hundred and twelve.

19 The children of Hashum, two hundred twenty and three.

20 The children of Gibbar, ninety and five.

21 The children of Bethlehem (Beit-Lechem), one hundred twenty and three.

22 The men of Netophah, fifty and six.

23 The men of Anathoth, one hundred twenty and eight.

24 The children of Azmaveth, forty and two.

25 The children of Qiryat-Yearim, Chephirah, and Beeroth, seven hundred and forty and three.

26 The children of Ramah and Gaba, six hundred twenty and one.

27 The men of Michmas, one hundred twenty and two.

28 The men of Bethel (Beit-El) and Ai, two hundred twenty and three.

29 The children of Nebo, fifty and two.

30 The children of Magbish, one hundred fifty and six.

31 The children of the other Elam, one thousand two hundred fifty and four.

32 The children of Harim, three hundred and twenty.

33 The children of Lod, Hadid, and Ono, seven hundred twenty and five.

34 The children of Yericho, three hundred forty and five.

35 The children of Senaah, three thousand and six hundred and thirty.

36 The priests (kohanim): the children of Yedayah, of the house of Joshua (Yeshua), nine hundred seventy and three.

37 The children of Immer, one thousand fifty and two.

38 The children of Pashur, one thousand two hundred forty and seven.

39 The children of Harim, one thousand and seventeen.

40 The Levites (Lewiyim): the children of Joshua (Yeshua) and Kadmiel, of the children of Hodavyah, seventy and four.

41 The singers: the children of Asaph, one hundred twenty and eight.

42 The children of the porters: the children of Shallum, the children of Ater, the children of Talmon, the children of Akkub, the children of Hatita, the children of Shobai, in all a hundred thirty and nine.

43 The Nethinims: the children of Ziha, the children of Hasupha, the children of Tabbaoth,

44 The children of Keros, the children of Siaha, the children of Padon,

45 The children of Lebanah, the children of Hagabah, the children of Akkub,

46 The children of Hagab, the children of Shalmai, the children of Hanan,

47 The children of Giddel, the children of Gahar, the children of Reayah,

48 The children of Rezin, the children of Nekoda, the children of Gazzam,

49 The children of Uzza, the children of Paseah, the children of Besai,

50 The children of Asnah, the children of Mehunim, the children of Nephusim,

51 The children of Bakbuk, the children of Hakupha, the children of Harhur,

52 The children of Bazluth, the children of Mehida, the children of Harsha,

53 The children of Barkos, the children of Sisera, the children of Thamah,

54 The children of Netsiyah, the children of Hatipha.

55 The children of Solomon (Shelomoh)'s servants: the children of Sotai, the children of Sophereth, the children of Peruda,

56 The children of Yaalah, the children of Darkon, the children of Giddel,

57 The children of Shefatyah, the children of Hattil, the children of Pochereth of Zebaim, the children of Ami.

58 All the Nethinims, and the children of Solomon (Shelomoh)'s servants, were three hundred ninety and two.

59 And these were they which went up from Telmelah, Telharsa, Cherub (keruv), Addan, and Immer: but they could not shew their father's house, and their seed, whether they were of Yisrael:

60 The children of Delayahu, the children of Toviyah, the children of Nekoda, six hundred fifty and two.

61 And of the children of the priests (kohanim): the children of Chavayah, the children of Koz, the children of Barzillai, who took a wife of the daughters of Barzillai the Giladite, and was called after their name.

62 These sought their register among those that were reckoned by genealogy, but they were not found; therefore were they, as polluted, put from

the priesthood (kehunnah).

63 And the Tirshatha said unto them, that they should not eat of the most holy things, till there stood up a priest (kohen) with Urim and with Thummim.

64 The whole congregation together was forty and two thousand three hundred and threescore,

65 Besides their servants and their maids, of whom there were seven thousand three hundred thirty and seven; and there were among them two hundred singing men and singing women.

66 Their horses were seven hundred thirty and six; their mules, two hundred forty and five;

67 Their camels, four hundred thirty and five; their asses, six thousand seven hundred and twenty.

68 And some of the chief of the fathers, when they came to the house of יהוה which is at Jerusalem (Yerushalayim), offered freely for the house of God (Elohim) to set it up in its place:

69 They gave after their ability unto the treasure of the work threescore and one thousand drams of gold, and five thousand pound of silver, and one hundred priests' (kohanim) garments.

70 So the priests (kohanim), and the Levites (Lewiyim), and some of the people, and the singers, and the porters, and the Nethinims, dwelt in their cities, and all Yisrael in their cities.

3 And when the seventh month had come, and the children of Yisrael were in the cities, the people gathered themselves together as one man to Jerusalem (Yerushalayim).

2 Then stood up Joshua (Yeshua) the son of Yotsadak, and his brethren the priests (kohanim), and Zerubbabel the son of Shealtiel, and his brethren, and builded the altar of the God of Israel (Elohei Yisrael), to offer burnt offerings thereon, as it is written in the Torah by Moses (Mosheh) the man of God (Elohim).

3 And they set the altar upon his bases; for fear was upon them because of the people of those countries; and they offered burnt offerings thereon unto יהוה, even burnt offerings morning and evening.

4 They kept also the Feast of Tabernacles (Chag Sukkot), as it is written, and offered the daily burnt offerings by number, according to the custom, as the duty of every day required;

5 And afterward offered the continual burnt offering, both of the new moons, and of all the set feasts of יהוה that were consecrated, and of everyone that willingly offered a freewill offering unto יהוה.

6 From the first day of the seventh month began they to offer burnt offerings unto יהוה. But the foundation of the temple of יהוה was not yet laid.

7 They gave money also unto the masons, and to the carpenters; and meat, and drink, and oil, unto them of Zidon, and to them of Tyre, to bring cedar trees from Lebanon to the sea of Joppa (Yafo), according to the grant that they had of Cyrus king of Persia.

8 Now in the second year of their coming unto the house of God (Elohim) at Jerusalem (Yerushalayim), in the second month, began Zerubbabel the son of Shealtiel, and Joshua (Yeshua) the son of Yotsadak, and the remnant of their brethren the priests (kohanim) and the Levites (Lewiyim), and all they that were come out of the captivity unto Jerusalem (Yerushalayim); and appointed the Levites (Lewiyim), from twenty years old and upward, to set forward the work of the house of יהוה.

9 Then stood Joshua (Yeshua) with his sons and his brethren, Kadmiel and his sons, the sons of Judah (Yehudah), together, to set forward the workmen in the house of God (Elohim): the sons of Henadad, with their sons and their brethren the Levites (Lewiyim).

10 And when the builders laid the foundation of the temple of יהוה, they set the priests (kohanim) in their apparel with trumpets, and the Levites (Lewiyim) the sons of Asaph with cymbals, to praise יהוה, after the ordinance of Dawid king of Yisrael.

11 And they sang together by course in praising and giving thanks unto יהוה; because he is good, for his mercy endureth forever toward Yisrael. And all the people shouted with a great shout, when they praised יהוה, because the foundation of the house of יהוה was laid.

12 But many of the priests (kohanim) and Levites (Lewiyim) and chief of the fathers, who were ancient men, that had seen the first house, when the foundation of this house was laid before their eyes, wept with a loud voice; and many shouted aloud for joy;

13 So that the people could not discern the noise of the shout of joy from the noise of the weeping of the people; for the people shouted with a loud

shout, and the noise was heard afar off.

4 Now when the adversaries of Judah (Yehudah) and Benjamin (Binyamin) heard that the children of the captivity builded the temple unto יהוה God of (Elohei) Yisrael;

2 Then they came to Zerubbabel, and to the chief of the fathers, and said unto them, "Let us build with you, for we seek your God (Elohim), as you do; and we do sacrifice unto him since the days of Esarhaddon king of Assur, which brought us up hither."

3 But Zerubbabel, and Joshua (Yeshua), and the rest of the chief of the fathers of Yisrael, said unto them, "You have nothing to do with us to build a house unto our God (Elohim); but we ourselves together will build unto יהוה God of (Elohei) Yisrael, as King Cyrus the king of Persia hath commanded us."

4 Then the people of the land weakened the hands of the people of Judah (Yehudah), and troubled them in building,

5 And hired counsellors against them, to frustrate their purpose, all the days of Cyrus king of Persia, even until the reign of Darius king of Persia.

6 And in the reign of Ahasuerus, in the beginning of his reign, wrote they unto him an accusation against the inhabitants of Judah (Yehudah) and Jerusalem (Yerushalayim).

7 And in the days of Artaxerxes wrote Bishlam, Mithredath, Tabeel, and the rest of their companions, unto Artaxerxes king of Persia; and the writing of the letter was written in the Syrian tongue (Aramit), and inter-preted in the Syrian tongue (Aramit).

8 Rehum the chancellor and Shimshai the scribe wrote a letter against Yerushalayim to Artaxerxes the king in this sort:

9 Then wrote Rehum the chancellor, and Shimshai the scribe, and the rest of their companions; the Dinaites, the Apharsathchites, the Tarpelites, the Apharsites, the Archevites, the Babylonians, the Susanchites, the Dehavites, and the Elamites,

10 And the rest of the nations whom the great and noble Asnappar brought over, and set in the cities of Samaria (Shomeron), and the rest that are on this side the river, and at such a time.

11 This is the copy of the letter that they sent unto him, even unto Artaxerxes the king; Your servants the men on this side the river, and at such a time.

12 Be it known unto the king, that the Jews (Yehudim) which came up from you to us are come unto Yerushalayim, building the rebellious and the bad city, and have set up the walls thereof, and joined the foundations.

13 Be it known now unto the king, that, if this city be builded, and the walls set up again, then will they not pay toll, tribute, and custom, and so you shalt endamage the revenue of the kings.

14 Now because we have maintenance from the king's palace, and it was not meet for us to see the king's dishonour, therefore have we sent and certified the king;

15 That search may be made in the book of the records of your fathers; so shalt you find in the book of the records, and know that this city is a rebellious city, and hurtful unto kings and provinces, and that they have moved sedition within the same of old time: for which cause was this city destroyed.

16 We certify the king that, if this city be builded again, and the walls thereof set up, by this means you shalt have no portion on this side the river.

17 Then sent the king an answer unto Rehum the chancellor, and to Shimshai the scribe, and to the rest of their companions that dwell in Samaria (Shomeron), and unto the rest beyond the river: Peace, and at such a time.

18 The letter which you sent unto us hath been plainly read before me.

19 And I commanded, and search hath been made, and it is found that this city of old time hath made insurrection against kings, and that rebellion and sedition have been made therein.

20 There have been mighty kings also over Jerusalem (Yerushalayim), which have ruled over all countries beyond the river; and toll, tribute, and custom, was paid unto them.

21 Give you now commandment to cause these men to cease, and that this city be not builded, until another commandment shall be given from me.

22 Take heed now that you fail not to do this. Why should damage grow to the hurt of the kings?

23 Now when the copy of king Artaxerxes' letter was read before Rehum, and Shimshai the scribe, and their companions, they went up in haste to Jerusalem (Yerushalayim) unto the

Jews (Yehudim), and made them to cease by force and power.

24 Then ceased the work of the house of [B5a]God (Elah) which is at Jerusalem (Yerushalayim). So it ceased unto the second year of the reign of Darius king of Persia.

5 Then the prophets, Chaggai the prophet, and Zechariah (Zekharyah) the son of Iddo, prophesied unto the Jews (Yehudim) that were in Judah (Yehudah) and Jerusalem (Yerushalayim) in the name of the God of Israel (Elohei Yisrael), even unto them.

2 Then rose up Zerubbabel the son of Shealtiel, and Joshua (Yeshua) the son of Yotsadak, and began to build the house of God (Elohim) which is at Yerushalayim; and with them were the prophets of God (Elah) helping them.

3 At the same time came to them Tatnai, governor on this side the river, and Shetharboznai, and their companions, and said thus unto them, "Who hath commanded you to build this house, and to make up this wall?"

4 Then said we unto them after this manner, "What are the names of the men that make this building?"

5 But the eye of their God (Elah) was upon the elders of the Jews (Yehudim), that they could not cause them to cease, till the matter came to Darius; and then they returned answer by letter concerning this matter.

6 The copy of the letter that Tatnai, governor on this side the river, and Shetharboznai, and his companions the Apharsachites, which were on this side the river, sent unto Darius the king.

7 They sent a letter unto him, wherein was written thus: Unto Darius the king: All peace.

8 Be it known unto the king, that we went into the province of Judea, to the house of the great God (Elah), which is builded with great stones, and timber is laid in the walls, and this work goeth fast on, and prospereth in their hands.

9 Then asked we those elders, and said unto them thus, "Who commanded you to build this house, and to make up these walls?"

10 We asked their names also, to certify you, that we might write the names of the men that were the chief of them.

11 And thus they returned us answer, saying, "We are the servants of the God (Elah) of heaven and earth, and build the house that was builded these many years ago, which a great

king of Yisrael builded and set up.

12 But after that our fathers had provoked the God (Elah) of heaven unto wrath, he gave them into the hand of Nebuchanezzar the king of Babylon (Bavel), the Chaldean, who destroyed this house, and carried the people away into Babylon (Bavel).

13 But in the first year of Cyrus the king of Babylon (Bavel) the same king Cyrus made a decree to build this house of God (Elohim).

14 And the vessels also of gold and silver of the house of God (Elohim), which Nebuchanezzar took out of the temple that was in Jerusalem (Yerushalayim), and brought them into temple of Babylon (Bavel), those did Cyrus the king take out of the temple of Babylon (Bavel), and they were delivered unto one, whose name was Sheshbazzar, whom he had made governor;

15 And said unto him, 'Take these vessels, go, carry them into the temple that is in Jerusalem (Yerushalayim), and let the house of God (Elohim) be builded in its place.'

16 Then came the same Sheshbazzar, and laid the foundation of the house of God (Elohim) which is in Yerushalayim; and since that time even until now hath it been in building, and yet it is not finished."

17 Now therefore, if it seems good to the king, let there be search made in the king's treasure house, which is there at Babylon (Bavel), whether it be so, that a decree was made of Cyrus the king to build this house of God (Elohim) at Jerusalem (Yerushalayim), and let the king send his pleasure to us concerning this matter.

6 Then Darius the king made a decree, and search was made in the house of the rolls, where the treasures were laid up in Babylon (Bavel).

2 And there was found at Achmetha, in the palace that is in the province of the Medes, a roll, and therein was a record thus written:

3 In the first year of Cyrus the king the same Cyrus the king made a decree concerning the house of God (Elohim) at Jerusalem (Yerushalayim): "Let the house be rebuilt, the place where they offered sacrifices, and let the foundations thereof be strongly laid; the height thereof threescore cubits, and the breadth thereof threescore cubits;

4 With three rows of great stones, and a row of

new timber; and let the expenses be given out of the king's house.

5 And also let the golden and silver vessels of the house of God (Elohim), which Nebuchanezzar took forth out of the temple which is at Jerusalem (Yerushalayim), and brought unto Babylon (Bavel), be restored, and brought again unto the temple which is at Jerusalem (Yerushalayim), every one to its place, and place them in the house of God (Elohim).

6 Now therefore, Tatnai, governor beyond the river, Shetharboznai, and your companions the Apharsachites, which are beyond the river, be you far from thence.

7 Let the work of this house of God (Elohim) alone; let the governor of the Jews (Yehudim) and the elders of the Jews (Yehudim) build this house of God (Elohim) in its place.

8 Moreover I make a decree what you shall do to the elders of these Jews (Yehudim) for the building of this house of God (Elohim); that of the king's goods, even of the tribute beyond the river, forthwith expenses be given unto these men, that they be not hindered.

9 And that which they have need of, both young bullocks, and rams, and lambs, for the burnt offerings of the God (Elah) of heaven, wheat, salt, wine, and oil, according to the appointment of the priests (kohanim) which are at Jerusalem (Yerushalayim), let it be given them day by day without fail,

10 That they may offer sacrifices of sweet savours unto the God (Elah) of heaven, and pray for the life of the king, and of his sons.

11 Also I have made a decree, that whosoever shall alter this word, let timber be pulled down from his house, and being set up, let him be hanged thereon; and let his house be made a dunghill for this.

12 And the God (Elah) that hath caused his name to dwell there destroy all kings and people, that shall put to their hand to alter and to destroy this house of God (Elohim) which is at Jerusalem (Yerushalayim). I Darius have made a decree; let it be done with speed.

13 Then Tatnai, governor on this side the river, Shetharboznai, and their companions, according to that which Darius the king had sent, so they did speedily.

14 And the elders of the Jews (Yehudim) builded, and they prospered through the prophesying of Chaggai the prophet and Zechariah (Zekharyah) the son of Iddo. And they builded, and finished it, according to the commandment of the God of Israel (Elohei Yisrael), and according to the commandment of Cyrus, and Darius, and Artaxerxes king of Persia.

15 And this house was finished on the third day of the month Adar, which was in the sixth year of the reign of Darius the king.

16 And the children of Yisrael, the priests (kohanim), and the Levites (Lewiyim), and the rest of the children of the captivity, kept the dedication of this house of God (Elohim) with joy,

17 And offered at the dedication of this house of God (Elohim) a hundred bullocks, two hundred rams, four hundred lambs; and for a sin offering for all Yisrael, twelve he goats, according to the number of the tribes of Yisrael.

18 And they set the priests (kohanim) in their divisions, and the Levites (Lewiyim) in their courses, for the service of God (Elah), which is at Jerusalem (Yerushalayim); as it is written in the book of Moses (Mosheh).

19 And the children of the captivity kept the Passover (Pesach) upon the fourteenth day of the first month.

20 For the priests (kohanim) and the Levites (Lewiyim) were purified together, all of them were pure, and killed the Passover lamb (Pesach) for all the children of the captivity, and for their brethren the priests (kohanim), and for themselves.

21 And the children of Yisrael, which were come again out of captivity, and all such as had separated themselves unto them from the filthiness of the heathen of the land, to seek יהוה God of Israel (Elohei Yisrael), did eat,

22 And kept the feast of unleavened bread seven days with joy: for יהוה had made them joyful, and turned the heart of the king of Assyria (Ashshur) unto them, to strengthen their hands in the work of the house of God (Elohim), the God of Israel (Elohei Yisrael).

7 Now after these things, in the reign of Artaxerxes king of Persia, [A47]Ezra the son of Serayah, the son of Azaryah, the son of Chilqiyah,

2 The son of Shallum, the son of Zadok, the son of Ahitub,

3 The son of Amaryah, the son of Azaryah, the

son of Meraioth,

4 The son of Zerachyah, the son of Uzzi, the son of Bukki,

5 The son of Avishua, the son of Phinehas, the son of Eleazar, the son of Aaron (Aharon) the chief priest (kohen):

6 This Ezra went up from Babylon (Bavel); and he was a skilled scribe in the Torah which יהוה God of Israel (Elohei Yisrael) had given to Moses (Mosheh); and the king granted him all his request, according to the hand of יהוה his God (Elohim) upon him.

7 And there went up some of the children of Yisrael, and of the priests (kohanim), and the Levites (Lewiyim), and the singers, and the porters, and the Nethinims, unto Jerusalem (Yerushalayim), in the seventh year of Artaxerxes the king.

8 And he came to Jerusalem (Yerushalayim) in the fifth month, which was in the seventh year of the king.

9 For upon the first day of the first month began he to go up from Babylon (Bavel), and on the first day of the fifth month came he to Jerusalem (Yerushalayim), according to the good hand of his God (Elohim) upon him.

10 For Ezra had prepared his heart to seek the Torah of יהוה, and to do it, and to teach in Yisrael statutes and judgments.

11 Now this is the copy of the letter that the king Artaxerxes gave unto Ezra the priest (kohen), the scribe, even a scribe of the words of the commandments of יהוה, and of his statutes to Yisrael.

12 Artaxerxes, king of kings, unto Ezra the priest (kohen), a scribe of the decree of the God (Elah) of heaven, perfect peace, and at such a time.

13 I make a decree, that all they of the people of Yisrael, and of his priests (kohanim) and Levites (Lewiyim), in my realm, which are minded of their own freewill to go up to Jerusalem (Yerushalayim), go with you.

14 Forasmuch as you are sent of the king, and of his seven counsellors, to enquire concerning Judah (Yehudah) and Jerusalem (Yerushalayim), according to the decree of your God (Elah) which is in your hand;

15 And to carry the silver and gold, which the king and his counsellors have freely offered unto the God (Elah) of Yisrael, whose habitation is in Jerusalem (Yerushalayim),

16 And all the silver and gold that you canst find in all the province of Babylon (Bavel), with the freewill offering of the people, and of the priests (kohanim), offering willingly for the house of their God (Elah) which is in Jerusalem (Yerushalayim),

17 That you mayest buy speedily with this money bullocks, rams, lambs, with their meat offerings and their drink offerings, and offer them upon the altar of the house of your God (Elah) which is in Jerusalem (Yerushalayim).

18 And whatsoever shall seem good to you, and to your brethren, to do with the rest of the silver and the gold, that do after the will of your God (Elah).

19 The vessels also that are given you for the service of the house of your God (Elah), those deliver you before the God (Elah) of Jerusalem (Yerushalayim).

20 And whatsoever more shall be needful for the house of your God (Elah), which you shalt have occasion to bestow, bestow it out of the king's treasure house.

21 And I, even I Artaxerxes the king, do make a decree to all the treasurers which are beyond the river, that whatsoever Ezra the priest (kohen), the scribe of the decree of the God (Elah) of heaven, shall require of you, it be done speedily,

22 Unto a hundred talents of silver, and to a hundred measures of wheat, and to a hundred baths of wine, and to a hundred baths of oil, and salt without prescribing how much.

23 Whatsoever is commanded by the God (Elah) of heaven, let it be diligently done for the house of the God (Elah) of heaven; for why should there be wrath against the realm of the king and his sons?

24 Also we certify you, that touching any of the priests (kohanim) and Levites (Lewiyim), singers, porters, Nethinims, or servants of this house of God (Elah), it shall not be lawful to impose toll, tribute, or custom, upon them.

25 And you, Ezra, after the wisdom of your God (Elah), that is in your hand, set magistrates and judges, which may judge all the people that are beyond the river, all such as know the decrees of your God (Elah); and teach you them that know them not.

26 And whosoever will not do the decree of your God (Elah), and the decree of the king,

let judgment be executed speedily upon him, whether it be unto death, or to banishment, or to confiscation of goods, or to imprisonment.

27 Blessed be יהוה God (Elohim) of our fathers, which hath put such a thing as this in the king's heart, to beautify the house of יהוה which is in Jerusalem (Yerushalayim),

28 And hath extended mercy unto me before the king, and his counsellors, and before all the king's mighty princes. And I was strengthened as the hand of יהוה my God (YHWH Elohai) was upon me, and I gathered together out of Yisrael chief men to go up with me.

8 These are now the chief of their fathers, and this is the genealogy of them that went up with me from Babylon (Bavel), in the reign of Artaxerxes the king.

2 Of the sons of Phinehas: Gershom; of the sons of Ithamar: Daniel; of the sons of Dawid: Hattush.

3 Of the sons of Shekhanyah, of the sons of Pharosh: Zechariah (Zekharyah); and with him were reckoned by genealogy of the males a hundred and fifty.

4 Of the sons of Pahathmoab: Elihoenai the son of Zerachyah, and with him two hundred males.

5 Of the sons of Shekhanyah: the son of Yachaziel, and with him three hundred males.

6 Of the sons also of Adin: Ebed the son of Yonatan, and with him fifty males.

7 And of the sons of Elam: Jeshaiah (Yeshayahu) the son of Atalyah, and with him seventy males.

8 And of the sons of Shefatyah: Zevadyah the son of Mikhael, and with him fourscore males.

9 Of the sons of Yoav: Obadiah (Ovadyah) the son of Yeiel, and with him two hundred and eighteen males.

10 And of the sons of Shelomith: the son of Yosifyah, and with him a hundred and threescore males.

11 And of the sons of Bebai: Zechariah (Zekharyah) the son of Bebai, and with him twenty and eight males.

12 And of the sons of Azgad: Yochanan the son of Hakkatan, and with him a hundred and ten males.

13 And of the last sons of Adonikam, whose names are these, Eliphelet, Yeiel, and Shemayah, and with them threescore males.

14 Of the sons also of Bigvai: Uthai, and Zabbud, and with them seventy males.

15 And I gathered them together to the river that runneth to Ahava; and there abode we in tents three days: and I viewed the people, and the priests (kohanim), and found there none of the sons of Lewi.

16 Then sent I for Eliezer, for Ariel, for Shemayah, and for Elnathan, and for Yariv, and for Elnathan, and for Nathan, and for Zechariah (Zekharyah), and for Meshullam, chief men; also for Yoyariv, and for Elnathan, men of understanding.

17 And I sent them with commandment unto Iddo the chief at the place Casiphia, and I told them what they should say unto Iddo, and to his brethren the Nethinims, at the place Casiphia, that they should bring unto us ministers for the house of our God (Elohim).

18 And by the good hand of our God (Elohim) upon us they brought us a man of understanding, of the sons of Mahli, the son of Lewi, the son of Yisrael; and Sherevyah, with his sons and his brethren, eighteen;

19 And Chashavyah, and with him Jeshaiah (Yeshayahu) of the sons of Merari, his brethren and their sons, twenty;

20 Also of the Nethinims, whom Dawid and the princes had appointed for the service of the Levites (Lewiyim), two hundred and twenty Nethinims. All of them were expressed by name.

21 Then I proclaimed a fast there, at the river of Ahava, that we might afflict ourselves before our God (Elohim), to seek of him a right way for us, and for our little ones, and for all our substance.

22 For I was ashamed to require of the king a band of soldiers and horsemen to help us against the enemy in the way, because we had spoken unto the king, saying, "The hand of our God (Elohim) is upon all them for good that seek him; but his power and his wrath is against all them that forsake him."

23 So we fasted and besought our God (Elohim) for this; and he was intreated of us.

24 Then I separated twelve of the chief of the priests (kohanim), Sherevyah, Chashavyah, and ten of their brethren with them,

25 And weighed unto them the silver, and the gold, and the vessels, even the offering of the house of our God (Elohim), which the king, and his counsellors, and his princes, and all Yisrael

there present, had offered.

26 I even weighed unto their hand six hundred and fifty talents of silver, and silver vessels a hundred talents, and of gold a hundred talents;

27 Also twenty basons of gold, of a thousand drams; and two vessels of fine copper, precious as gold.

28 And I said unto them, "You are holy unto יהוה; the vessels are holy also; and the silver and the gold are a freewill offering unto יהוה God (Elohim) of your fathers.

29 Watch you, and keep them, until you weigh them before the chief of the priests (kohanim) and the Levites (Lewiyim), and chief of the fathers of Yisrael, at Jerusalem (Yerushalayim), in the chambers of the house of יהוה."

30 So took the priests (kohanim) and the Levites (Lewiyim) the weight of the silver, and the gold, and the vessels, to bring them to Jerusalem (Yerushalayim) unto the house of our God (Elohim).

31 Then we departed from the river of Ahava on the twelfth day of the first month, to go unto Jerusalem (Yerushalayim); and the hand of our God (Elohim) was upon us, and he delivered us from the hand of the enemy, and of such as lay in wait by the way.

32 And we came to Jerusalem (Yerushalayim), and abode there three days.

33 Now on the fourth day was the silver and the gold and the vessels weighed in the house of our God (Elohim) by the hand of Meremoth the son of Uriyah the priest (kohen); and with him was Eleazar the son of Phinehas; and with them was Yozavad the son of Joshua (Yeshua), and Noadyah the son of Binnui, Levites (Lewiyim);

34 By number and by weight of every one: and all the weight was written at that time.

35 Also the children of those that had been carried away, which were come out of the captivity, offered burnt offerings unto the God of Israel (Elohei Yisrael), twelve bullocks for all Yisrael, ninety and six rams, seventy and seven lambs, twelve he goats for a sin offering; all this was a burnt offering unto יהוה.

36 And they delivered the king's commissions unto the king's lieutenants, and to the governors on this side the river; and they furthered the people, and the house of God (Elohim).

9 Now when these things were done, the princes came to me, saying, The people of Yisrael, and the priests (kohanim), and the Levites (Lewiyim), have not separated themselves from the people of the lands, doing according to their abominations, even of the Canaanites, the Hittites, the Perizzites, the Yevusis, the Ammonites, the Moavites, the Egyptians (Mitsrayim), and the Amorites.

2 For they have taken of their daughters for themselves, and for their sons: so that the holy seed have mingled themselves with the people of those lands; yea, the hand of the princes and rulers hath been chief in this trespass.

3 And when I heard this thing, I rent my garment and my mantle, and plucked off the hair of my head and of my beard, and sat down astonied.

4 Then were assembled unto me every one that trembled at the words of the God of Israel (Elohei Yisrael), because of the transgression of those that had been carried away; and I sat astonied until the evening sacrifice.

5 And at the evening sacrifice I arose up from my heaviness; and having rent my garment and my mantle, I fell upon my knees, and spread out my hands unto יהוה my God (YHWH Elohai),

6 And said, "O my God (Elohim), I am ashamed and blush to lift up my face to You, my God (Elohim); for our iniquities are increased over our head, and our trespass is grown up unto the heavens.

7 Since the days of our fathers have we been in a great trespass unto this day; and for our iniquities have we, our kings, and our priests (kohanim), been delivered into the hand of the kings of the lands, to the sword, to captivity, and to a spoil, and to confusion of face, as it is this day.

8 And now for a little space grace hath been shewed from יהוה our God (YHWH Eloheinu), to leave us a remnant to escape, and to give us a nail in His holy place, that our God (Elohim) may lighten our eyes, and give us a little reviving in our bondage.

9 For we were bondmen; yet our God (Elohim) hath not forsaken us in our bondage, but hath extended mercy unto us in the sight of the kings of Persia, to give us a reviving, to set up the house of our God (Elohim), and to repair the desolations thereof, and to give us a wall in Judah (Yehudah) and in Jerusalem (Yerushalayim).

10 And now, O our God (Elohim), what shall

we say after this? For we have forsaken Your commandments,

11 Which You have commanded by Your servants the prophets, saying, 'The land, unto which you go to possess it, is an unclean land with the filthiness of the people of the lands, with their abominations, which have filled it from one end to another with their uncleanness.

12 Now therefore give not your daughters unto their sons, neither take their daughters unto your sons, nor seek their peace or their wealth forever, that you may be strong, and eat the good of the land, and leave it for an inheritance to your children forever.'

13 And after all that is come upon us for our evil deeds, and for our great trespass, seeing that you our God (Elohim) hast punished us less than our iniquities deserve, and hast given us such deliverance as this;

14 Should we again break Your commandments, and join in affinity with the people of these abominations? Wouldest not You be angry with us till You hadst consumed us, so that there should be no remnant nor escaping?

15 O יהוה God of Israel (Elohei Yisrael), You are righteous, for we remain yet escaped, as it is this day. Behold, we are before You in our trespasses, for we cannot stand before You because of this."

10 Now when Ezra had prayed, and when he had confessed, weeping and casting himself down before the house of God (Elohim), there assembled unto him out of Yisrael a very great congregation of men and women and children; for the people wept very sore.

2 And Shekhanyah the son of Yeiel, one of the sons of Elam, answered and said unto Ezra, "We have trespassed against our God (Elohim), and have taken strange wives of the people of the land; yet now there is hope in Yisrael concerning this thing.

3 Now therefore let us make a covenant with our God (Elohim) to put away all the wives, and such as are born of them, according to the counsel of my lord (adoni), and of those that tremble at the commandment of our God (Elohim); and let it be done according to the Torah.

4 Arise, for this matter belongeth unto you. We also will be with you. Be of good courage, and do it.

5 Then arose Ezra, and made the chief priests

(kohanim), the Levites (Lewiyim), and all Yisrael, to swear that they should do according to this word. And they sware.

6 Then Ezra rose up from before the house of God (Elohim), and went into the chamber of Yochanan the son of Elijahhib (Elyashiv); and when he came thither, he did eat no bread, nor drink water, for he mourned because of the transgression of them that had been carried away.

7 And they made proclamation throughout Judah (Yehudah) and Jerusalem (Yerushalayim) unto all the children of the captivity, that they should gather themselves together unto Jerusalem (Yerushalayim);

8 And that whosoever would not come within three days, according to the counsel of the princes and the elders, all his substance should be forfeited, and himself separated from the congregation of those that had been carried away.

9 Then all the men of Judah (Yehudah) and Benjamin (Binyamin) gathered themselves together unto Jerusalem (Yerushalayim) within three days. It was the ninth month, on the twentieth day of the month; and all the people sat in the street of the house of God (Elohim), trembling because of this matter, and for the great rain.

10 And Ezra the priest (kohen) stood up, and said unto them, "You have transgressed, and have taken foreign wives, to increase the trespass of Yisrael.

11 Now therefore make confession unto יהוה God (Elohim) of your fathers, and do His pleasure; and separate yourselves from the people of the land, and from the foreign wives."

12 Then all the congregation answered and said with a loud voice, "As you have said, so must we do.

13 But the people are many, and it is a time of much rain, and we are not able to stand outside, neither is this a work of one day or two, for we are many that have transgressed in this thing.

14 Let now our rulers of all the congregation stand, and let all them who have taken foreign wives in our cities come at appointed times, and with them the elders of every city, and the judges thereof, until the fierce wrath of our God (Elohim) for this matter be turned from us."

15 Only Yonatan the son of Asahel and

Yachazyah the son of Tikvah were employed about this matter; and Meshullam and Shabbethai the Lewite (Lewi) helped them.

16 And the children of the captivity did so. And Ezra the priest (kohen), with certain chief of the fathers, after the house of their fathers, and all of them by their names, were separated, and sat down in the first day of the tenth month to examine the matter.

17 And they made an end with all the men that had taken foreign wives by the first day of the first month.

18 And among the sons of the priests (kohanim) there were found that had taken foreign wives: namely, of the sons of Joshua (Yeshua) the son of Yotsadak, and his brethren: Maaseyahu, and Eliezer, and Yariv, and Gedalyahu.

19 And they gave their hands that they would put away their wives; and being guilty, they offered a ram of the flock for their trespass.

20 And of the sons of Immer: Hanani, and Zebadiah (Zevadyahu).

21 And of the sons of Harim: Maaseyahu, and Eliyah, and Shemayah, and Yeiel, and Uzziyah.

22 And of the sons of Pashur: Elioenai, Maaseyah, Yishmael, Nethaneel, Yozavad, and Elasah.

23 Also of the Levites (Lewiyim): Yozavad, and Shimei, and Qelayah, (the same is Kelita,) Petachyah, Judah (Yehudah), and Eliezer.

24 Of the singers also: Elijahhib (Eliyashiv); and of the porters: Shallum, and Telem, and Uri.

25 Moreover of Yisrael: of the sons of Parosh: Ramyah, and Yizziyah, and Malkiyah, and Miamin, and Eleazar, and Malkiyah, and Benayah.

26 And of the sons of Elam: Mattanyah, Zechariah (Zekharyah), and Yeiel, and Avdi, and Yeremot, and Eliyah.

27 And of the sons of Zattu: Elioenai, Elijahhib (Elyashiv), Mattanyah, and Yeremot, and Zabad, and Aziza.

28 Of the sons also of Bebai: Yehochanan, Chananyah, Zabbai, and Athlai.

29 And of the sons of Bani: Meshullam, Malluch, and Adayah, Yashuv, and Sheal, and Ramot.

30 And of the sons of Pahathmoab: Adna, and Chelal, Benayah, Maaseyahu, Mattanyah, Bezaleel, and Binnui, and Menashsheh.

31 And of the sons of Harim: Eliezer, Ishijah (Yishshiyah), Malkiyah, Shemayah, Shimon,

32 Benjamin (Binyamin), Malluch and Shemaryah.

33 Of the sons of Hashum: Mattenai, Mattathah, Zabad, Eliphelet, Yeremai, Menashsheh, and Shimei.

34 Of the sons of Bani: Maadai, Amram, and Uel,

35 Benayah, Bedyah, Chelluh,

36 Vanyah, Meremoth, Elijahhib,

37 Mattanyah, Mattenai, and Yaaso,

38 And Bani, and Binnui, Shimei,

39 And Shelemyah, and Nathan, and Adayah,

40 Machnadebai, Shashai, Sharai,

41 Azareel, Shelemyah, Shemaryah,

42 Shallum, Amaryah, and Joseph (Yosef).

43 Of the sons of Nebo: Yeiel, Mattityah, Zabad, Zebina, Yiddo, and Yoel, Benayah.

44 All these had taken foreign wives; and some of them had wives by whom they had children.

NEHEMIAH
NECHEMYAH נְחֶמְיָה
(Comfort of YHWH)

1 The words of [A48]Nehemiah (Nechemyah) the son of Hachalyah. And it came to pass in the month Chisleu, in the twentieth year, as I was in Shushan the palace,

2 That Hanani, one of my brethren, came, he and certain men of Judah (Yehudah); and I asked them concerning the Jews (Yehudim) who had escaped, who were left from the captivity, and concerning Jerusalem (Yerushalayim).

3 And they said unto me, "The remnant that are left of captivity there in the province are in great affliction and reproach. The wall of Jerusalem (Yerushalayim) also is broken down, and the gates thereof are burned with fire."

4 And it came to pass, when I heard these words, that I sat down and wept, and mourned certain days, and fasted, and prayed before God of the Heaven (Elohei haShamayim),

5 And said, "I beseech You, O יהוה God of the Heaven (Elohei haShamayim), the great and awesome God (El), who keepeth covenant and mercy for them who love him and observe His commandments;

6 Let Your ear now be attentive, and Your eyes open, that You mayest hear the prayer of Your servant, which I pray before You now, day and night, for the children of Yisrael Your servants, and confess the sins of the children of Yisrael, which we have sinned against You; both I and my father's house have sinned.

7 We have dealt very corruptly against You, and have not kept the commandments, nor the statutes, nor the judgments, which You commandedst Your servant Moses (Mosheh).

8 Remember, I beseech You, the word that You commandedst Your servant Moses (Mosheh), saying, 'If you transgress, I will scatter you abroad among the nations;

9 But if you turn unto Me, and keep My commandments, and do them; though there were of you cast out unto the uttermost part of the heaven, yet will I gather them from thence, and will bring them unto the place that I have chosen to set My name there.'

10 Now these are Your servants and Your people, whom You have redeemed by Your great power, and by Your strong hand.

11 O Lord (Adonai), I beseech You, let now Your ear be attentive to the prayer of Your servant, and to the prayer of Your servants, who desire to fear Your name; I pray You, prosper Your servant this day, and grant him mercy in the sight of this man." For I was the king's cupbearer.

2 And it came to pass in the month Nisan, in the twentieth year of Artaxerxes the king, that wine was before him; and I took up the wine, and gave it unto the king. Now I had not been beforetime sad in his presence.

2 Wherefore the king said unto me, "Why is your countenance sad, seeing you are not sick? This is nothing else but sorrow of heart." Then I was very sore afraid,

3 And said unto the king, "Let the king live forever! Why should not my countenance be sad, when the city, the place of my fathers' sepulchres, lieth waste, and the gates thereof are consumed with fire?"

4 Then the king said unto me, "For what dost you make request?" So I prayed to God of the Heaven (Elohei haShamayim);

5 And I said unto the king, "If it pleases the king, and if your servant has found favor in your sight, that you wouldest send me unto Judah (Yehudah), unto the city of my fathers' sepulchres, that I may build it."

6 And the king said unto me, (the queen also sitting by him,) "For how long shall your journey be? And when wilt you return?" So it pleased the king to send me; and I set him a time.

7 Moreover I said unto the king, "If it pleases the king, let letters be given me to the governors beyond the river, that they may convey me over till I come into Judah (Yehudah);

8 And a letter unto Asaph the keeper of the king's forest, that he may give me timber to make beams for the gates of the palace which appertained to the house, and for the wall of the city, and for the house that I shall enter into." And the king granted me, according to the good hand of my God (Elohim) upon me.

9 Then I came to the governors beyond the river, and gave them the king's letters. Now the king had sent captains of the army and horsemen with me.

10 When Sanballat the Horonite, and Toviyah

the servant, the Ammonite, heard of it, it grieved them exceedingly that there was come a man to seek the welfare of the children of Yisrael.

11 So I came to Jerusalem (Yerushalayim), and was there three days.

12 And I arose in the night, I and some few men with me; neither told I any man what my God (Elohim) had put in my heart to do at Jerusalem (Yerushalayim); neither was there any beast with me, except the beast that I rode upon.

13 And I went out by night by the gate of the valley, even before the dragon well, and to the dung port, and viewed the walls of Jerusalem (Yerushalayim), which were broken down, and the gates thereof were consumed with fire.

14 Then I went on to the gate of the fountain, and to the king's pool, but there was no place for the beast that was under me to pass.

15 Then went I up in the night by the brook, and viewed the wall, and turned back, and entered by the gate of the valley, and so returned.

16 And the rulers knew not whither I went, or what I did; neither had I as yet told it to the Jews (Yehudim), nor to the priests (kohanim), nor to the nobles, nor to the rulers, nor to the rest that did the work.

17 Then said I unto them, "You see the distress that we are in, how Jerusalem (Yerushalayim) lieth waste, and the gates thereof are burned with fire: come, and let us build up the wall of Jerusalem (Yerushalayim), that we be no more a reproach."

18 Then I told them of the hand of my God (Elohim) which was good upon me; as also the king's words that he had spoken unto me. And they said, "Let us rise up and build." So they strengthened their hands for this good work.

19 But when Sanballat the Horonite, and Toviyah the servant, the Ammonite, and Geshem the Arabian, heard it, they laughed us to scorn, and despised us, and said, "What is this thing that you do? Will you rebel against the king?"

20 Then answered I them, and said unto them, "The God of heaven (Elohei shamayim), He will prosper us; therefore we, His servants will arise and build; but you have no portion, nor right, nor memorial, in Jerusalem (Yerushalayim)."

3 Then Elijahhib (Elyashiv) the high priest (kohen hagadol) rose up with his brethren the priests (kohanim), and they builded the sheep gate; they sanctified it, and set up the doors of it; even unto the tower of Meah they sanctified it, unto the tower of Hananeel.

2 And next unto him builded the men of Yericho. And next to them builded Zaccur the son of Imri.

3 But the fish gate did the sons of Hassenaah build, who also laid the beams thereof, and set up the doors thereof, the locks thereof, and the bars thereof.

4 And next unto them repaired Meremoth the son of Uriyah, the son of Koz. And next unto them repaired Meshullam the son of Berekhyah, the son of Meshezabeel. And next unto them repaired Zadok the son of Baana.

5 And next unto them the Tekoites repaired; but their nobles put not their necks to the work of their Lord (Adon).

6 Moreover the old gate repaired Yehoyada the son of Paseah, and Meshullam the son of Besodyah; they laid the beams thereof, and set up the doors thereof, and the locks thereof, and the bars thereof.

7 And next unto them repaired Melatiah the Giveonite, and Yadon the Meronothite, the men of Giveon, and of Mizpah, unto the throne of the governor on this side the river.

8 Next unto him repaired Uzziel the son of Charhayah, of the goldsmiths. Next unto him also repaired Chananyah the son of one of the apothecaries, and they fortified Jerusalem (Yerushalayim) unto the broad wall.

9 And next unto them repaired Refayah the son of Hur, the ruler of the half part of Jerusalem (Yerushalayim).

10 And next unto them repaired Yedayah the son of Harumaph, even opposite his house. And next unto him repaired Hattush the son of Chashavneyah.

11 Malkiyah the son of Harim, and Hashub the son of Pahathmoab, repaired the other piece, and the tower of the furnaces.

12 And next unto him repaired Shallum the son of Halohesh, the ruler of the half part of Jerusalem (Yerushalayim), he and his daughters.

13 The valley gate repaired Hanun, and the inhabitants of Zanoach; they built it, and set up the doors thereof, the locks thereof, and the bars thereof, and a thousand cubits on the wall unto the dung gate.

14 But the dung gate repaired Malkiyah the son of Rechab, the ruler of part of Bethhaccerem; he

built it, and set up the doors thereof, the locks thereof, and the bars thereof.

15 But the gate of the fountain repaired Shallun the son of Colhozeh, the ruler of part of Mizpah; he built it, and covered it, and set up the doors thereof, the locks thereof, and the bars thereof, and the wall of the pool of Siloah by the king's garden, and unto the stairs that go down from the city of Dawid.

16 After him repaired Nehemiah (Nechemyah) the son of Azbuk, the ruler of the half part of Bethzur, unto the place opposite the sepulchres of Dawid, and to the pool that was made, and unto the house of the mighty.

17 After him repaired the Levites (Lewiyim), Rehum the son of Bani. Next unto him repaired Chashavyah, the ruler of the half part of Keilah, in his part.

18 After him repaired their brethren, Bavai the son of Henadad, the ruler of the half part of Keilah.

19 And next to him repaired Ezer the son of Joshua (Yeshua), the ruler of Mizpah, another piece opposite the going up to the armoury at the turning of the wall.

20 After him Baruch the son of Zabbai earnestly repaired the other piece, from the turning of the wall unto the door of the house of Elijahhib (Elyashiv) the high priest (kohen hagadol).

21 After him repaired Meremoth the son of Uriyah the son of Koz another piece, from the door of the house of Elijahhib (Elyashiv) even to the end of the house of Elijahhib (Elyashiv).

22 And after him repaired the priests (kohanim), the men of the plain.

23 After him repaired Benjamin (Binyamin) and Hashub opposite their house. After him repaired Azaryah the son of Maaseyah the son of Ananyah by his house.

24 After him repaired Binnui the son of Henadad another piece, from the house of Azaryah unto the turning of the wall, even unto the corner.

25 Palal the son of Uzai, opposite the turning of the wall, and the tower which lieth out from the king's high house, that was by the court of the prison. After him Pedayah the son of Parosh.

26 Moreover the Nethinims dwelt in Ophel, unto the place opposite the water gate toward the east, and the tower that lieth out.

27 After them the Tekoites repaired another piece, opposite the great tower that lieth out, even unto the wall of Ophel.

28 From above the horse gate repaired the priests (kohanim), every one opposite his house.

29 After them repaired Zadok the son of Immer opposite his house. After him repaired also Shemayah the son of Shekhanyah, the keeper of the east gate.

30 After him repaired Chananyah the son of Shelemyah, and Hanun the sixth son of Zalaph, another piece. After him repaired Meshullam the son of Berekhyah opposite his chamber.

31 After him repaired Malkiyah the goldsmith's son unto the place of the Nethinims, and of the merchants, opposite the gate Miphkad, and to the going up of the corner.

32 And between the going up of the corner unto the sheep gate repaired the goldsmiths and the merchants.

4 But it came to pass, that when Sanballat heard that we builded the wall, he was wroth, and took great indignation, and mocked the Jews (Yehudim).

2 And he spake before his brethren and the army of Samaria (Shomeron), and said, "What do these feeble Jews (Yehudim)? Will they fortify themselves? Will they sacrifice? Will they make an end in a day? Will they revive the stones out of the heaps of the rubbish which are burned?"

3 Now Toviyah the Ammonite was by him, and he said, "Even that which they build, if a fox goes up, he shall even break down their stone wall."

4 Hear, O our God (Elohim), for we are despise; and turn their reproach upon their own head, and give them for a prey in the land of captivity!

5 And cover not their iniquity, and let not their sin be blotted out from before you; for they have provoked You to anger before the builders.

6 So built we the wall, and all the wall was joined together unto the half thereof; for the people had a mind to work.

7 But it came to pass, that when Sanballat, and Toviyah, and the Arabians, and the Ammonites, and the Ashdodites, heard that the walls of Jerusalem (Yerushalayim) were made up, and that the breaches began to be stopped, then they were very wroth,

8 And conspired all of them together to come and to fight against Jerusalem (Yerushalayim), and to hinder it.

9 Nevertheless we made our prayer unto our

God (Elohim), and set a watch against them day and night, because of them.

10 And Judah (Yehudah) said, "The strength of the bearers of burdens is decayed, and there is much rubbish; so that we are not able to build the wall."

11 And our adversaries said, "They shall not know, neither see, till we come in the midst among them, and slay them, and cause the work to cease."

12 And it came to pass, that when the Jews (Yehudim) who dwelt by them came, they said unto us ten times, "From all places whence you shall return unto us they will be upon you."

13 Therefore set I in the lower places behind the wall, and on the higher places, I even set the people after their families with their swords, their spears, and their bows.

14 And I looked, and rose up, and said unto the nobles, and to the rulers, and to the rest of the people, "Be not you afraid of them; remember Adonai, Who is great and awesome, and fight for your brethren, your sons, and your daughters, your wives, and your houses."

15 And it came to pass, when our enemies heard that it was known unto us, and God (Elohim) had brought their counsel to nought, that we returned all of us to the wall, every one unto his work.

16 And it came to pass from that time forth, that the half of my servants wrought in the work, and the other half of them held both the spears, the shields, and the bows, and the habergeons; and the rulers were behind all the house of Judah (Yehudah).

17 They which builded on the wall, and they that bare burdens, with those that laded, every one with one of his hands wrought in the work, and with the other hand held a weapon.

18 For the builders, every one had his sword girded by his side, and so builded. And he that sounded the trumpet was by me.

19 And I said unto the nobles, and to the rulers, and to the rest of the people, "The work is great and large, and we are separated upon the wall, one far from another.

20 In what place therefore you hear the sound of the trumpet, resort you thither unto us; our God (Elohim) shall fight for us."

21 So we laboured in the work, and half of them held the spears from the rising of the morning till the stars appeared.

22 Likewise at the same time said I unto the people, "Let every one with his servant lodge within Yerushalayim, that in the night they may be a guard to us, and labour on the day."

23 So neither I, nor my brethren, nor my servants, nor the men of the guard which followed me, none of us put off our clothes, except that every one put them off for washing.

5 And there was a great cry of the people and of their wives against their brethren the Jews (Yehudim).

2 For there were those who said, "We, our sons, and our daughters, are many; therefore we take up corn for them, that we may eat, and live."

3 There were also some who said, "We have mortgaged our lands, vineyards, and houses, that we might buy corn, because of the famine."

4 There were also those who said, "We have borrowed money for the king's tribute, and that upon our lands and vineyards.

5 Yet now our flesh is as the flesh of our brethren, our children as their children; and, behold, we bring into bondage our sons and our daughters to be servants, and some of our daughters are brought unto bondage already; neither is it in our power to redeem them; for other men have our lands and vineyards."

6 And I was very angry when I heard their cry and these words.

7 Then I consulted with myself, and I rebuked the nobles, and the rulers, and said unto them, "You exact usury, every one of his brother." And I set a great assembly against them.

8 And I said unto them, "We according to our ability have redeemed our brethren the Jews (Yehudim), who were sold unto the heathen; and will you even sell your brethren? Or shall they be sold unto us?" Then held they their peace, and found nothing to answer.

9 Also I said, "It is not good that you do; ought you not to walk in the fear of our God (Elohim) because of the reproach of the heathen our enemies?"

10 "I likewise, and my brethren, and my servants, might exact of them money and corn. Please let us leave off this usury!

11 Please restore to them, even this day, their lands, their vineyards, their oliveyards, and their houses, also the hundredth part of the money, and of the corn, the wine, and the oil,

that you exact of them."

12 Then said they, "We will restore them, and will require nothing of them; so will we do as you sayest." Then I called the priests (kohanim), and took an oath of them, that they should do according to this promise.

13 Also I shook my lap, and said, "So God (Elohim) shake out every man from his house, and from his labour, that performeth not this promise, even thus be he shaken out, and emptied." And all the congregation said, "Amen!" and praised יהוה. And the people did according to this promise.

14 Moreover from the time that I was appointed to be their governor in the land of Judah (Yehudah), from the twentieth year even unto the two and thirtieth year of Artaxerxes the king, that is, twelve years, I and my brethren have not eaten the bread of the governor.

15 But the former governors that had been before me were chargeable unto the people, and had taken of them bread and wine, beside forty shekels of silver; yea, even their servants bare rule over the people, but so did not I, because of the fear of God (Elohim).

16 Yea, also I continued in the work of this wall, neither bought we any land; and all my servants were gathered thither unto the work.

17 Moreover there were at my table one hundred and fifty of the Jews (Yehudim) and rulers, besides those that came unto us from among the heathen that are about us.

18 Now that which was prepared for me daily was one ox and six choice sheep; also fowls were prepared for me, and once in ten days store of all sorts of wine: yet for all this required not I the bread of the governor, because the bondage was heavy upon this people.

19 Think upon me, my God (Elohim), for good, according to all that I have done for this people.

6 Now it came to pass, when Sanballat, and Toviyah, and Geshem the Arabian, and the rest of our enemies, heard that I had builded the wall, and that there was no breach left therein; (though at that time I had not set up the doors upon the gates;)

2 That Sanballat and Geshem sent unto me, saying, "Come, let us meet together in some one of the villages in the plain of Ono." But they thought to do me mischief.

3 And I sent messengers unto them, saying, "I am doing a great work, so that I cannot come down. Why should the work cease, whilst I leave it, and come down to you?"

4 Yet they sent unto me four times after this sort; and I answered them after the same manner.

5 Then sent Sanballat his servant unto me in like manner the fifth time with an open letter in his hand;

6 Wherein was written: "It is reported among the nations, and Gashmu saith it, that you and the Jews (Yehudim) think to rebel; for which cause you buildest the wall, that you mayest be their king, according to these words.

7 And you have also appointed prophets to preach of you at Jerusalem (Yerushalayim), saying, 'There is a king in Judah (Yehudah)'. And now shall it be reported to the king according to these words. Come now therefore, and let us take counsel together.

8 Then I sent unto him, saying, "There are no such things done as you sayest, but you feignest them out of your own heart."

9 For they all made us afraid, saying, "Their hands shall be weakened from the work, that it be not done." Now therefore, O God (Elohim), strengthen my hands.

10 Afterward I came unto the house of Shemayah the son of Delayah the son of Mehetabeel, who was shut up; and he said, "Let us meet together in the house of God (Elohim), within the temple, and let us shut the doors of the temple, for they will come to slay you; yea, in the night will they come to slay you."

11 And I said, "Should such a man as I flee? And who is there, that, being as I am, would go into the temple to save his life? I will not go in!"

12 And, behold, I perceived that God (Elohim) had not sent him, but that he pronounced this prophecy against me, for Toviyah and Sanballat had hired him.

13 Therefore was he hired, that I should be afraid, and do so, and sin, and that they might have matter for an evil report, that they might reproach me.

14 My God (Elohai), think You upon Toviyah and Sanballat according to these their works, and on the prophetess (neviah) Noadyah, and the rest of the prophets, that would have put me in fear.

15 So the wall was finished in the twenty-fifth day of the month Elul, in fifty-two days.

16 And it came to pass, that when all our enemies heard thereof, and all the heathen that were about us saw these things, they were much cast down in their own eyes; for they perceived that this work was wrought of our God (Elohim).

17 Moreover in those days the nobles of Judah (Yehudah) sent many letters unto Toviyah, and the letters of Toviyah came unto them.

18 For there were many in Judah (Yehudah) sworn unto him, because he was the son in law of Shekhanyah the son of Arah; and his son Yochanan had taken the daughter of Meshullam the son of Berekhyah.

19 Also they reported his good deeds before me, and uttered my words to him. And Toviyah sent letters to put me in fear.

7 Now it came to pass, when the wall was built, and I had set up the doors, and the porters and the singers and the Levites (Lewiyim) were appointed,

2 That I gave my brother Hanani, and Chananyah the ruler of the palace, charge over Jerusalem (Yerushalayim), for he was a faithful man, and feared God (Elohim) above many.

3 And I said unto them, "Let not the gates of Jerusalem (Yerushalayim) be opened until the sun be hot; and while they stand by, let them shut the doors, and bar them; and appoint watches of the inhabitants of Jerusalem (Yerushalayim), every one in his watch, and every one to be opposite his house."

4 Now the city was large and great, but the people were few therein, and the houses were not rebuilt.

5 And my God (Elohim) put into mine heart to gather together the nobles, and the rulers, and the people, that they might be reckoned by genealogy. And I found a register of the genealogy of them who came up at the first, and found written therein:

6 These are the children of the province, that went up out of the captivity, of those that had been carried away, whom Nebuchanezzar the king of Babylon (Bavel) had carried away, and came again to Jerusalem (Yerushalayim) and to Judah (Yehudah), every one unto his city;

7 Who came with Zerubbabel, Joshua (Yeshua), Nehemiah (Nechemyah), Azaryah, Raamyah, Nahamani, Mordecai, Bilshan, Mispereth, Bigvai, Nehum, Baanah. The number, I say, of the men of the people of Yisrael was this:

8 The children of Parosh, two thousand one hundred seventy and two.

9 The children of Shefatyah, three hundred seventy and two.

10 The children of Arah, six hundred fifty and two.

11 The children of Pahathmoab, of the children of Joshua (Yeshua) and Yoav, two thousand and eight hundred and eighteen.

12 The children of Elam, one thousand two hundred fifty and four.

13 The children of Zattu, eight hundred forty and five.

14 The children of Zaccai, seven hundred and threescore.

15 The children of Binnui, six hundred forty and eight.

16 The children of Bebai, six hundred twenty and eight.

17 The children of Azgad, two thousand three hundred twenty and two.

18 The children of Adonikam, six hundred threescore and seven.

19 The children of Bigvai, two thousand threescore and seven.

20 The children of Adin, six hundred fifty and five.

21 The children of Ater of Hezekiah (Chizkiyah), ninety and eight.

22 The children of Hashum, three hundred twenty and eight.

23 The children of Bezai, three hundred twenty and four.

24 The children of Hariph, a hundred and twelve.

25 The children of Giveon, ninety and five.

26 The men of Bethlehem (Beit-Lechem) and Netophah, one hundred fourscore and eight.

27 The men of Anathoth, one hundred twenty and eight.

28 The men of Bethazmaveth, forty and two.

29 The men of Qiryat-Yearim, Chephirah, and Beeroth, seven hundred forty and three.

30 The men of Ramah and Geba, six hundred twenty and one.

31 The men of Michmas, one hundred and twenty and two.

32 The men of Bethel (Beit-El) and Ai, one hundred twenty and three.

33 The men of the other Nebo, fifty and two.

34 The children of the other Elam, one thousand

two hundred fifty and four.

35 The children of Harim, three hundred and twenty.

36 The children of Yericho, three hundred forty and five.

37 The children of Lod, Hadid, and Ono, seven hundred twenty and one.

38 The children of Senaah, three thousand nine hundred and thirty.

39 The priests (kohanim): the children of Yedayah, of the house of Joshua (Yeshua), nine hundred seventy and three.

40 The children of Immer, one thousand fifty and two.

41 The children of Pashur, one thousand two hundred forty and seven.

42 The children of Harim, one thousand and seventeen.

43 The Levites (Lewiyim): the children of Joshua (Yeshua), of Kadmiel, and of the children of Hodevah, seventy and four.

44 The singers: the children of Asaph, one hundred forty and eight.

45 The porters: the children of Shallum, the children of Ater, the children of Talmon, the children of Akkub, the children of Hatita, the children of Shobai, one hundred thirty and eight.

46 The Nethinims: the children of Ziha, the children of Hashupha, the children of Tabbaoth,

47 The children of Keros, the children of Sia, the children of Padon,

48 The children of Lebana, the children of Hagaba, the children of Shalmai,

49 The children of Hanan, the children of Giddel, the children of Gahar,

50 The children of Reayah, the children of Rezin, the children of Nekoda,

51 The children of Gazzam, the children of Uzza, the children of Phaseah,

52 The children of Besai, the children of Meunim, the children of Nephishesim,

53 The children of Bakbuk, the children of Hakupha, the children of Harhur,

54 The children of Bazlith, the children of Mehida, the children of Harsha,

55 The children of Barkos, the children of Sisera, the children of Tamah,

56 The children of Netsiyah, the children of Hatipha.

57 The children of Solomon (Shelomoh)'s

servants: the children of Sotai, the children of Sophereth, the children of Perida,

58 The children of Yaala, the children of Darkon, the children of Giddel,

59 The children of Shefatyah, the children of Hattil, the children of Pochereth of Zebaim, the children of Amon.

60 All the Nethinims, and the children of Solomon (Shelomoh)'s servants, were three hundred ninety and two.

61 And these were they which went up also from Telmelah, Telharesha, Cherub (Keruv), Addon, and Immer: but they could not shew their father's house, nor their seed, whether they were of Yisrael.

62 The children of Delayah, the children of Toviyah, the children of Nekoda, six hundred forty and two.

63 And of the priests (kohanim): the children of Chavayah, the children of Koz, the children of Barzillai, which took one of the daughters of Barzillai the Giladite to wife, and was called after their name.

64 These sought their register among those that were reckoned by genealogy, but it was not found; therefore were they, as polluted, put from the priesthood.

65 And the Tirshatha said unto them, that they should not eat of the most holy things, till there stood up a priest (kohen) with Urim and Thummim.

66 The whole congregation together was forty and two thousand three hundred and threescore,

67 Beside their manservants and their maidservants, of whom there were seven thousand three hundred thirty and seven; and they had two hundred forty and five singing men and singing women.

68 Their horses, seven hundred thirty and six; their mules, two hundred forty and five;

69 Their camels, four hundred thirty and five; six thousand seven hundred and twenty asses.

70 And some of the chief of the fathers gave unto the work. The Tirshatha gave to the treasure one thousand drams of gold, fifty basons, five hundred and thirty priests' (kohanim) garments.

71 And some of the chief of the fathers gave to the treasure of the work twenty thousand drams of gold, and two thousand and two hundred pounds of silver.

72 And that which the rest of the people gave

was twenty thousand drams of gold, and two thousand pounds of silver, and threescore and seven priests' (kohanim) garments.

73 So the priests (kohanim), and the Levites (Lewiyim), and the porters, and the singers, and some of the people, and the Nethinims, and all Yisrael, dwelt in their cities; and when the seventh month came, the children of Yisrael were in their cities.

8 And all the people gathered themselves together as one man into the street that was before the water gate; and they spake unto Ezra the scribe to bring the book of the law (sefer hatorah), which יהוה had commanded to Yisrael by Moses (Mosheh).

2 And Ezra the priest (kohen) brought the Torah before the congregation both of men and women, and all that could hear with understanding, upon the first day of the seventh month.

3 And he read therein before the street that was before the water gate from the morning until midday, before the men and the women, and those that could understand; and the ears of all the people were attentive unto the book of the law (sefer hatorah).

4 And Ezra the scribe stood upon a pulpit of wood, which they had made for the purpose; and beside him stood Mattityah, and Shema, and Anayah, and Uriyah, and Hilkiah (Chilqiyah), and Maaseyah, on his right hand; and on his left hand, Pedayah, and Mishael, and Malkiyah, and Hashum, and Hashbadana, Zechariah (Zekharyah), and Meshullam.

5 And Ezra opened the book in the sight of all the people; (for he was above all the people;) and when he opened it, all the people stood up:

6 And Ezra blessed יהוה, the great God (Elohim). And all the people answered, "Amen, Amen!" with lifting up their hands; and they bowed their heads, and worshipped יהוה with their faces to the ground.

7 Also Joshua (Yeshua), and Bani, and Sherevyah, Yamin, Akkub, Shabbethai, Hodiyah, Maaseyah, Kelita, Azaryah, Yozavad, Hanan, Pelayah, and the Levites (Lewiyim), caused the people to understand the Torah; and the people stood in their place.

8 So they read in the book in the law (sefer hatorah) of God (Elohim) distinctly, and gave the sense, and caused them to understand the reading.

9 And Nehemiah (Nechemyah), who is the Tirshatha, and Ezra the priest (kohen) the scribe, and the Levites (Lewiyim) who taught the people, said unto all the people, "This day is holy unto יהוה your God (YHWH Eloheikhem); mourn not, nor weep." For all the people wept, when they heard the words of the Torah.

10 Then he said unto them, "Go your way, eat the richly prepared food, and drink the sweet, and send portions unto them for whom nothing is prepared, for this day is holy unto our Lord (Adonai); neither be you sorry; for the joy of יהוה is your strength."

11 So the Levites (Lewiyim) quieted all the people, saying, "Hold your peace, for the day is holy; neither be you grieved."

12 And all the people went their way to eat, and to drink, and to send portions, and to make great mirth, because they had understood the words that were declared unto them.

13 And on the second day were gathered together the chief of the fathers of all the people, the priests (kohanim), and the Levites (Lewiyim), unto Ezra the scribe, even to understand the words of the Torah.

14 And they found written in the Torah which יהוה had commanded by Moses (Mosheh), that the children of Yisrael should dwell in booths (sukkot) in the feast of the seventh month;

15 And that they should publish and proclaim in all their cities, and in Jerusalem (Yerushalayim), saying, "Go forth unto the mount, and fetch olive branches, and pine branches, and myrtle branches, and palm branches, and branches of thick trees, to make booths, as it is written."

16 So the people went forth, and brought them, and made themselves booths, every one upon the roof of his house, and in their courts, and in the courts of the house of God (Elohim), and in the street of the water gate, and in the street of the gate of Efrayim.

17 And all the congregation of them that were come again out of the captivity made booths (sukkot), and sat under the booths (sukkot); for since the days of Joshua (Yeshua) the son of Nun unto that day had not the children of Yisrael done so. And there was very great gladness.

18 Also day by day, from the first day unto the last day, he read in the book of the law (sefer hatorah) of God (Elohim). And they kept the

feast seven days; and on the eighth day was a solemn assembly, according unto the manner.

9 Now in the twenty-fourth day of this month the children of Yisrael were assembled with fasting, and with sackclothes, and earth upon them.

2 And the seed of Yisrael separated themselves from all strangers, and stood and confessed their sins, and the iniquities of their fathers.

3 And they stood up in their place, and read in the book of the law (sefer hatorah) of יהוה their God (YHWH Eloheihem) one fourth part of the day; and another fourth part they confessed, and worshipped יהוה their God (YHWH Eloheihem).

4 Then stood up upon the stairs, of the Levites (Lewiyim), Joshua (Yeshua), and Bani, Kadmiel, Shevanyah, Bunni, Sherevyah, Bani, and Chenani, and cried with a loud voice unto יהוה their God (YHWH Eloheihem).

5 Then the Levites (Lewiyim), Joshua (Yeshua), and Kadmiel, Bani, Chashavneyah, Sherevyah, Hodiyah, Shevanyah, and Petachyah, said, "Stand up and bless יהוה your God (YHWH Eloheikhem) forever and ever; and blessed be Your glorious name, which is exalted above all blessing and praise!

6 You, even You, art יהוה alone; You have made heaven, the heaven of heavens, with all their host, the earth, and all things that are therein, the seas, and all that is therein, and You preservest them all; and the host of heaven worshippeth You.

7 You are יהוה the God (Elohim), who didst choose Avram, and broughtest him forth out of Ur of the Chaldees, and gavest him the name of Avraham;

8 And foundest his heart faithful before You, and madest a covenant with him to give the land of the Canaanites, the Hittites, the Amorites, and the Perizzites, and the Yevusis, and the Girgashites, to give it, I say, to his seed, and hast performed Your words, for You are righteous.

9 And didst see the affliction of our fathers in Egypt (Mitsrayim), and heardest their cry by the Red sea;

10 And shewedst signs and wonders upon Pharaoh (Paroh), and on all his servants, and on all the people of his land; for You knewest that they dealt proudly against them. So didst You get Yourself a name, as it is this day.

11 And You didst divide the sea before them, so

that they went through the midst of the sea on the dry land; and their persecutors You threwest into the deeps, as a stone into the mighty waters.

12 Moreover You leddest them in the day by a cloudy pillar; and in the night by a pillar of fire, to give them light in the way wherein they should go.

13 You camest down also upon Mount Sinai, and spakest with them from heaven, and gavest them right judgments, and true teachings (torot), good statutes and commandments;

14 And madest known unto them Your holy Shabbat, and commandedst them precepts, statutes, and Torah, by the hand of Moses (Mosheh) Your servant;

15 And gavest them bread from heaven for their hunger, and broughtest forth water for them out of the rock for their thirst, and promisedst them that they should go in to possess the land which You hadst sworn to give them.

16 But they and our fathers dealt proudly, and hardened their necks, and hearkened not to Your commandments,

17 And refused to obey, neither were mindful of Your wonders that You didst among them; but hardened their necks, and in their rebellion appointed a captain to return to their bondag. But You are a God (Eloah) ready to pardon, gracious and merciful, slow to anger, and of great kindness, and forsookest them not.

18 Yea, when they had made them a molten calf, and said, 'This is your God (Elohim) that brought you up out of Egypt (Mitsrayim)', and had wrought great provocations;

19 Yet You in Your manifold mercies forsookest them not in the wilderness; the pillar of the cloud departed not from them by day, to lead them in the way; neither the pillar of fire by night, to shew them light, and the way wherein they should go.

20 You gavest also Your good Spirit (Ruach) to instruct them, and withheldest not Your manna from their mouth, and gavest them water for their thirst.

21 Yea, forty years didst You sustain them in the wilderness, so that they lacked nothing; their clothes waxed not old, and their feet swelled not.

22 Moreover You gavest them kingdoms and nations, and didst divide them into corners. So they possessed the land of Sihon, and the land of the king of Heshbon, and the land of Og king

of Bashan.

23 Their children also multipliedst You as the stars of heaven, and broughtest them into the land, concerning which You hadst promised to their fathers, that they should go in to possess it.

24 So the children went in and possessed the land, and you subduedst before them the inhabitants of the land, the Canaanites, and gavest them into their hands, with their kings, and the people of the land, that they might do with them as they would.

25 And they took strong cities, and a fat land, and possessed houses full of all goods, wells digged, vineyards, and oliveyards, and fruit trees in abundance; so they did eat, and were filled, and became fat, and delighted themselves in Your great goodness.

26 Nevertheless they were disobedient, and rebelled against You, and cast Your Torah behind their backs, and slew Your prophets which testified against them to turn them to You, and they wrought great provocations.

27 Therefore You deliveredst them into the hand of their enemies, who vexed them; and in the time of their trouble, when they cried unto You, You heardest them from heaven; and according to Your manifold mercies You gavest them saviours, who saved them out of the hand of their enemies.

28 But after they had rest, they did evil again before You; therefore leftest You them in the hand of their enemies, so that they had the dominion over them; yet when they returned, and cried unto You, You heardest them from heaven; and many times didst You deliver them according to Your mercies;

29 And testifiedst against them, that You mightest bring them again unto Your Torah; yet they dealt proudly, and hearkened not unto Your commandments, but sinned against Your judgments, (which if a man does, he shall live in them;) and withdrew the shoulder, and hardened their neck, and would not hear.

30 Yet many years didst You forbear them, and testifiedst against them by Your Spirit (Ruach) in Your prophets; yet would they not give ear; therefore gavest You them into the hand of the people of the lands.

31 Nevertheless for Your great mercies' sake You didst not utterly consume them, nor forsake them; for You are a gracious and merciful God (Elohim).

32 Now therefore, our God (Elohim), the great, the mighty, and the awesome God (El), who keepest covenant and mercy, let not all the trouble seem little before You, that hath come upon us, on our kings, on our princes, and on our priests (kohanim), and on our prophets, and on our fathers, and on all Your people, since the time of the kings of Assyria (Ashshur) unto this day.

33 Howbeit You are just in all that is brought upon us, for You have done right, but we have done wickedly.

34 Neither have our kings, our princes, our priests (kohanim), nor our fathers, kept Your Torah, nor hearkened unto Your commandments and Your testimonies, wherewith You didst testify against them.

35 For they have not served You in their kingdom, and in Your great goodness that You gavest them, and in the large and fat land which You gavest before them, neither turned they from their wicked works.

36 Behold, we are servants this day, and for the land that You gavest unto our fathers to eat the fruit thereof and the good thereof, behold, we are servants in it.

37 And it yieldeth much increase unto the kings whom you have set over us because of our sins; also they have dominion over our bodies, and over our cattle, at their pleasure, and we are in great distress.

38 And because of all this we make a sure covenant, and write it; and our princes, Levites (Lewiyim), and priests (kohanim), seal unto it."

10 Now those that sealed were, Nehemiah (Nechemyah), the Tirshatha, the son of Hachalyah, and Tsidkiyah,

2 Serayah, Azaryah, Jeremiah (Yirmeyah),

3 Pashur, Amaryah, Malkiyah,

4 Hattush, Shevanyah, Malluch,

5 Harim, Meremoth, Ovadyah,

6 Daniel, Ginnethon, Baruch,

7 Meshullam, Aviyah, Miyamin,

8 Maazyahu, Bilgai, Shemayah. These were the priests (kohanim).

9 And the Levites (Lewiyim): both Joshua (Yeshua) the son of Azanyah, Binnui of the sons of Henadad, Kadmiel;

10 And their brethren, Shevanyah, Hodiyah, Kelita, Pelayah, Hanan,

11 Micha, Rehob, Chashavyah,

12 Zaccur, Sherevyah, Shevanyah,

13 Hodiyah, Bani, Beninu.

14 The chief of the people: Parosh, Pahathmoab, Elam, Zatthu, Bani,

15 Bunni, Azgad, Bebai,

16 Adoniyah, Bigvai, Adin,

17 Ater, Hezekiah (Chizkiyah), Azzur,

18 Hodiyah, Hashum, Bezai,

19 Hariph, Anathoth, Nebai,

20 Magpiash, Meshullam, Hezir,

21 Meshezabeel, Zadok, Yaddua,

22 Pelatyah, Hanan, Anayah,

23 Hoshea, Chananyah, Hashub,

24 Hallohesh, Pileha, Shobek,

25 Rehum, Hashabnah, Maaseyah,

26 And Achiyah, Hanan, Anan,

27 Malluch, Harim, Baanah.

28 And the rest of the people, the priests (kohanim), the Levites (Lewiyim), the porters, the singers, the Nethinims, and all they that had separated themselves from the people of the lands unto the Torah of God (Elohim), their wives, their sons, and their daughters, every one having knowledge, and having understanding;

29 They clave to their brethren, their nobles, and entered into a curse, and into an oath, to walk in the Torah of God (Elohim), which was given by Moses (Mosheh) the servant of God (Elohim), and to observe and do all the commandments of יהוה our Lord (YHWH Adoneinu), and His judgments and His statutes;

30 And that we would not give our daughters unto the people of the land, nor take their daughters for our sons:

31 And if the people of the land bring ware or any victuals on the Shabbat day to sell, that we would not buy it of them on the Shabbat, or on the holy day; and that we would leave the seventh year, and the exaction of every debt.

32 Also we made ordinances for us, to charge ourselves yearly with the third part of a shekel for the service of the house of our God (Elohim);

33 For the shewbread, and for the continual meat offering, and for the continual burnt offering, of the Shabbats, of the new moons, for the set feasts, and for the holy things, and for the sin offerings to make an atonement for Yisrael, and for all the work of the house of our God (Elohim).

34 And we cast the lots among the priests (kohanim), the Levites (Lewiyim), and the people, for the wood offering, to bring it into the house of our God (Elohim), after the houses of our fathers, at times appointed year by year, to burn upon the altar of יהוה our God (YHWH Eloheinu), as it is written in the Torah;

35 And to bring the firstfruits of our ground, and the firstfruits of all fruit of all trees, year by year, unto the house of יהוה;

36 Also the firstborn of our sons, and of our cattle, as it is written in the Torah, and the firstlings of our herds and of our flocks, to bring to the house of our God (Elohim), unto the priests (kohanim) that minister in the house of our God (Elohim);

37 And that we should bring the firstfruits of our dough, and our offerings, and the fruit of all manner of trees, of wine and of oil, unto the priests (kohanim), to the chambers of the house of our God (Elohim); and the tithes of our ground unto the Levites (Lewiyim), that the same Levites (Lewiyim) might have the tithes in all the cities of our tillage.

38 And the priest (kohen) the son of Aaron (Aharon) shall be with the Levites (Lewiyim), when the Levites (Lewiyim) take tithes; and the Levites (Lewiyim) shall bring up the tithe of the tithes unto the house of our God (Elohim), to the chambers, into the treasure house.

39 For the children of Yisrael and the children of Lewi shall bring the offering of the corn, of the new wine, and the oil, unto the chambers, where are the vessels of the sanctuary, and the priests (kohanim) that minister, and the porters, and the singers; and we will not forsake the house of our God (Elohim).

11 And the rulers of the people dwelt at Jerusalem (Yerushalayim); the rest of the people also cast lots, to bring one of ten to dwell in Jerusalem (Yerushalayim) the holy city, and nine parts to dwell in other cities.

2 And the people blessed all the men, that willingly offered themselves to dwell at Jerusalem (Yerushalayim).

3 Now these are the chief of the province that dwelt in Jerusalem (Yerushalayim), but in the cities of Judah (Yehudah) dwelt every one in his possession in their cities, Yisrael, the priests (kohanim), and the Levites (Lewiyim), and the Nethinims, and the children of Solomon (Shelomoh)'s servants.

4 And at Jerusalem (Yerushalayim) dwelt certain of the children of Judah (Yehudah), and of the children of Benjamin (Binyamin). Of the children of Judah (Yehudah); Atayah the son of Uzziyah, the son of Zechariah (Zekharyah), the son of Amaryah, the son of Shefatyah, the son of Mahalaleel, of the children of Perez;

5 And Maaseyah the son of Baruch, the son of Colhozeh, the son of Chazayah, the son of Adayah, the son of Yoyariv, the son of Zechariah (Zekharyah), the son of Shiloni.

6 All the sons of Perez that dwelt at Jerusalem (Yerushalayim) were four hundred threescore and eight valiant men.

7 And these are the sons of Benjamin (Binyamin); Sallu the son of Meshullam, the son of Yoed, the son of Pedayah, the son of Kolayah, the son of Maaseyah, the son of Itiel, the son of Jeshaiah (Yeshayah).

8 And after him Gabbai, Sallai, nine hundred twenty and eight.

9 And Yoel the son of Zichri was their overseer; and Judah (Yehudah) the son of Senuah was second over the city.

10 Of the priests (kohanim): Yedayah the son of Yoyariv, Yakhin.

11 Serayah the son of Hilkiah (Chilqiyah), the son of Meshullam, the son of Zadok, the son of Meraioth, the son of Ahitub, was the ruler of the house of God (Elohim).

12 And their brethren that did the work of the house were eight hundred twenty and two; and Adayah the son of Yeroham, the son of Pelalyah, the son of Amzi, the son of Zechariah (Zekharyah), the son of Pashur, the son of Malkiyah,

13 And his brethren, chief of the fathers, two hundred forty and two; and Amashai the son of Azareel, the son of Ahasai, the son of Meshillemoth, the son of Immer,

14 And their brethren, mighty men of valour, a hundred twenty and eight; and their overseer was Zabdiel, the son of one of the great men.

15 Also of the Levites (Lewiyim): Shemayah the son of Hashub, the son of Azrikam, the son of Chashavyah, the son of Bunni;

16 And Shabbethai and Yozavad, of the chief of the Levites (Lewiyim), had the oversight of the outward business of the house of God (Elohim).

17 And Mattanyah the son of Micha, the son of Zabdi, the son of Asaph, was the principal to begin the thanksgiving in prayer; and Bakbukyah the second among his brethren, and Abda the son of Shammua, the son of Galal, the son of Yedutun.

18 All the Levites (Lewiyim) in the holy city were two hundred fourscore and four.

19 Moreover the porters, Akkub, Talmon, and their brethren that kept the gates, were a hundred seventy and two.

20 And the residue of Yisrael, of the priests (kohanim), and the Levites (Lewiyim), were in all the cities of Judah (Yehudah), every one in his inheritance.

21 But the Nethinims dwelt in Ophel. And Ziha and Gispa were over the Nethinims.

22 The overseer also of the Levites (Lewiyim) at Jerusalem (Yerushalayim) was Uzzi the son of Bani, the son of Chashavyah, the son of Mattanyah, the son of Micha. Of the sons of Asaph, the singers were over the business of the house of God (Elohim).

23 For it was the king's commandment concerning them, that a certain portion should be for the singers, due for every day.

24 And Petachyah the son of Meshezabeel, of the children of Zerah the son of Judah (Yehudah), was at the king's hand in all matters concerning the people.

25 And for the villages, with their fields, some of the children of Judah (Yehudah) dwelt at Qiryat-Arba, and in the villages thereof, and at Dibon, and in the villages thereof, and at Yekavtseel, and in the villages thereof,

26 And at Joshua (Yeshua), and at Moladah, and at Bethphelet,

27 And at Hazarshual, and at Beer-Sheva, and in the villages thereof,

28 And at Ziklag, and at Mekonah, and in the villages thereof,

29 And at Enrimmon, and at Zareah, and at Yarmut,

30 Zanoach, Adullam, and in their villages, at Lachish, and the fields thereof, at Azekah, and in the villages thereof. And they dwelt from Beer-Sheva unto the valley of Hinnom.

31 The children also of Benjamin (Binyamin) from Geba dwelt at Michmash, and Aya, and Bethel (Beit-El), and in their villages,

32 And at Anathoth, Nob, Ananyah,

33 Hazor, Ramah, Gittaim,

34 Hadid, Zeboim, Neballat,

35 Lod, and Ono, the valley of craftsmen.

36 And of the Levites (Lewiyim) were divisions in Judah (Yehudah), and in Benjamin (Binyamin).

12 Now these are the priests (kohanim) and the Levites (Lewiyim) that went up with Zerubbabel the son of Shealtiel, and Joshua (Yeshua): Serayah, Jeremiah (Yirmeyah), Ezra,

2 Amaryah, Malluch, Hattush,

3 Shekhanyah, Rehum, Meremoth,

4 Iddo, Ginnetho, Aviyah,

5 Miamin, Maadiah, Bilgah,

6 Shemayah, and Yoyariv, Yedayah,

7 Sallu, Amok, Hilkiah (Chilqiyah), Yedayah. These were the chief of the priests (kohanim) and of their brethren in the days of Joshua (Yeshua).

8 Moreover the Levites (Lewiyim): Joshua (Yeshua), Binnui, Kadmiel, Sherevyah, Judah (Yehudah), and Mattanyah, which was over the thanksgiving, he and his brethren.

9 Also Bakbukyah and Unni, their brethren, were opposite them in the watches.

10 And Joshua (Yeshua) begat Yoyakim, Yoyakim also begat Elijahhib, and Elijahhib (Elyashiv) begat Yoyada,

11 And Yoyada begat Yonatan, and Yonatan begat Yaddua.

12 And in the days of Yoyakim were priests (kohanim), the chief of the fathers: of Serayah, Merayah; of Jeremiah (Yirmeyah), Chananyah;

13 Of Ezra, Meshullam; of Amaryah, Yehochanan;

14 Of Melicu, Yonatan; of Shevanyah, Joseph (Yosef);

15 Of Harim, Adna; of Meraioth, Helkai;

16 Of Iddo, Zechariah (Zekharyah); of Ginnethon, Meshullam;

17 Of Aviyah, Zichri; of Miniamin, of Moadyah, Piltai;

18 Of Bilgah, Shammua; of Shemayah, Jonathan (Yehonatan);

19 And of Yoyariv, Mattenai; of Yedayah, Uzzi;

20 Of Sallai, Kallai; of Amok, Eber;

21 Of Hilkiah (Chilqiyah), Chashavyah; of Yedayah, Nethaneel.

22 The Levites (Lewiyim) in the days of Elijahhib (Elyashiv), Yoyada, and Yochanan, and Yaddua, were recorded chief of the fathers; also the priests (kohanim), to the reign of Darius the Persian.

23 The sons of Lewi, the chief of the fathers, were written in the book of the chronicles, even until the days of Yochanan the son of Elijahhib (Elyashiv).

24 And the chief of the Levites (Lewiyim): Chashavyah, Sherevyah, and Joshua (Yeshua) the son of Kadmiel, with their brethren opposite them, to praise and to give thanks, according to the commandment of Dawid the man of God (Elohim), ward opposite ward.

25 Mattanyah, and Bakbukyah, Obadiah (Ovadyah), Meshullam, Talmon, Akkub, were porters keeping the ward at the thresholds of the gates.

26 These were in the days of Yoyakim the son of Joshua (Yeshua), the son of Yotsadak, and in the days of Nehemiah (Nechemyah) the governor, and of Ezra the priest (kohen), the scribe.

27 And at the dedication of the wall of Jerusalem (Yerushalayim) they sought the Levites (Lewiyim) out of all their places, to bring them to Jerusalem (Yerushalayim), to keep the dedication with gladness, both with thanks-givings, and with singing, with cymbals, psalteries, and with harps.

28 And the sons of the singers gathered themselves together, both out of the plain country round about Jeruselam (Yerushalayim), and from the villages of Netophathi;

29 Also from the house of Gilgal, and out of the fields of Geba and Azmaveth; for the singers had builded them villages round about Yerushalayim.

30 And the priests (kohanim) and the Levites (Lewiyim) purified themselves, and purified the people, and the gates, and the wall.

31 Then I brought up the princes of Judah (Yehudah) upon the wall, and appointed two great companies of them that gave thanks, whereof one went on the right hand upon the wall toward the dung gate;

32 And after them went Hoshayah, and half of the princes of Judah (Yehudah),

33 And Azaryah, Ezra, and Meshullam,

34 Judah (Yehudah), and Benjamin (Binyamin), and Shemayah, and Jeremiah (Yirmeyah),

35 And certain of the priests' (kohanim) sons with trumpets; namely, Zechariah (Zekharyah) the son of Yonatan, the son of Shemayah, the son of Mattanyah, the son of Mikhayah, the son of Zaccur, the son of Asaph;

36 And his brethren, Shemayah, and Azarael, Milalai, Gilalai, Maai, Nethaneel, and Judah (Yehudah), Hanani, with the musical instruments of Dawid the man of God (Elohim), and Ezra the scribe before them.

37 And at the fountain gate, which was opposite them, they went up by the stairs of the city of Dawid, at the going up of the wall, above the house of Dawid, even unto the water gate eastward.

38 And the other company of them that gave thanks went opposite them, and I after them, and the half of the people upon the wall, from beyond the tower of the furnaces even unto the broad wall;

39 And from above the gate of Efrayim, and above the old gate, and above the fish gate, and the tower of Hananeel, and the tower of Meah, even unto the sheep gate; and they stood still in the prison gate.

40 So stood the two companies of them that gave thanks in the house of God (Elohim), and I, and the half of the rulers with me:

41 And the priests (kohanim), Elyaqim, Maaseyah, Miniamin, Mikhayah, Elioenai, Zechariah (Zekharyah), and Chananyah, with trumpets;

42 And Maaseyah, and Shemayah, and Eleazar, and Uzzi, and Yehochanan, and Malkiyah, and Elam, and Ezer. And the singers sang loud, with Yizrachyah their overseer.

43 Also that day they offered great sacrifices, and rejoiced, for God (Elohim) had made them rejoice with great joy; the wives also and the children rejoiced, so that the joy of Jerusalem (Yerushalayim) was heard even afar off.

44 And at that time were some appointed over the chambers for the treasures, for the offerings, for the firstfruits, and for the tithes, to gather into them out of the fields of the cities the portions required by the law (torah) for the priests (kohanim) and Levites (Lewiyim); for Judah (Yehudah) rejoiced for the priests (kohanim) and for the Levites (Lewiyim) that waited.

45 And both the singers and the porters kept the ward of their God (Elohim), and the ward of the purification, according to the commandment of Dawid, and of Solomon (Shelomoh) his son.

46 For in the days of Dawid and Asaph of old there were chief of the singers, and songs of praise and thanksgiving unto God (Elohim).

47 And all Yisrael in the days of Zerubbabel, and in the days of Nehemiah (Nechemyah), gave the portions of the singers and the porters, every day his portion; and they sanctified holy things unto the Levites (Lewiyim); and the Levites (Lewiyim) sanctified them unto the children of Aaron (Aharon).

13 On that day they read in the book of Moses (Mosheh) in the audience of the people; and therein was found written, that the Ammonite and the Moavite should not come into the congregation of God (Elohim) forever;

2 Because they met not the children of Yisrael with bread and with water, but hired Balaam against them, that he should curse them; howbeit our God (Elohim) turned the curse into a blessing.

3 Now it came to pass, when they had heard the Torah, that they separated from Yisrael all the mixed multitude.

4 And before this, Elijahhib (Elyashiv) the priest (kohen), having the oversight of the chamber of the house of our God (Elohim), was allied unto Toviyah.

5 And he had prepared for him a great chamber, where aforetime they laid the meat offerings, the frankincense, and the vessels, and the tithes of the corn, the new wine, and the oil, which was commanded to be given to the Levites (Lewiyim), and the singers, and the porters; and the offerings of the priests (kohanim).

6 But in all this time was not I at Jerusalem (Yerushalayim), for in the two and thirtieth year of Artaxerxes king of Babylon (Bavel) came I unto the king, and after certain days obtained I leave of the king;

7 And I came to Jerusalem (Yerushalayim), and understood of the evil that Elijahhib did for Toviyah, in preparing him a chamber in the courts of the house of God (Elohim).

8 And it grieved me sore; therefore I cast forth all the household stuff of Toviyah out of the chamber.

9 Then I commanded, and they cleansed the chambers; and thither brought I again the vessels of the house of God (Elohim), with the meat offering and the frankincense.

10 And I perceived that the portions of the Levites (Lewiyim) had not been given them; for the Levites (Lewiyim) and the singers, that

did the work, were fled every one to his field.

11 Then contended I with the rulers, and said, "Why is the house of God (Elohim) forsaken?" And I gathered them together, and set them in their place.

12 Then brought all Judah (Yehudah) the tithe of the corn and the new wine and the oil unto the treasuries.

13 And I made treasurers over the treasuries, Shelemyah the priest (kohen), and Zadok the scribe, and of the Levites (Lewiyim), Pedayah; and next to them was Hanan the son of Zaccur, the son of Mattanyah; for they were counted faithful, and their office was to distribute unto their brethren.

14 Remember me, O my God (Elohim), concerning this, and wipe not out my good deeds that I have done for the house of my God (Elohim), and for the offices thereof.

15 In those days saw I in Judah (Yehudah) some treading wine presses on the Shabbat, and bringing in sheaves, and lading asses; as also wine, grapes, and figs, and all manner of burdens, which they brought into Jerusalem (Yerushalayim) on the Shabbat day; and I testified against them in the day wherein they sold victuals.

16 There dwelt men of Tyre also therein, which brought fish, and all manner of ware, and sold on the Shabbat unto the children of Judah (Yehudah), and in Jerusalem (Yerushalayim).

17 Then I contended with the nobles of Judah (Yehudah), and said unto them, "What evil thing is this that you do, and profane the Shabbat day?

18 Did not your fathers thus, and did not our God (Elohim) bring all this evil upon us, and upon this city? Yet you bring more wrath upon Yisrael by profaning the Shabbat."

19 And it came to pass, that when the gates of Jerusalem (Yerushalayim) began to be dark before the Shabbat, I commanded that the gates should be shut, and charged that they should not be opened till after the Shabbat; and some of my servants set I at the gates, that there should no burden be brought in on the Shabbat day.

20 So the merchants and sellers of all kind of ware lodged outside Jerusalem (Yerushalayim) once or twice.

21 Then I testified against them, and said unto them, Why lodge you about the wall? If you do so again, I will lay hands on you. From that time forth came they no more on the Shabbat.

22 And I commanded the Levites (Lewiyim) that they should cleanse themselves, and that they should come and keep the gates, to sanctify the Shabbat day. Remember me, O my God (Elohim), concerning this also, and spare me according to the greatness of Your mercy.

23 In those days also saw I, Jews (Yehudim) that had married wives of Ashdod, of Ammon, and of Moav;

24 And their children spake half in the speech of Ashdod, and could not speak in the Jews' language (Yehudit), but according to the language of each people.

25 And I contended with them, and cursed them, and smote certain of them, and plucked off their hair, and made them swear by God (Elohim), saying, "You shall not give your daughters unto their sons, nor take their daughters unto your sons, or for yourselves.

26 Did not Solomon (Shelomoh) king of Yisrael sin by these things? Yet among many nations was there no king like him, who was beloved of his God (Elohim), and God (Elohim) made him king over all Yisrael; nevertheless even him did foreign women cause to sin.

27 Shall we then hearken unto you to do all this great evil, to transgress against our God (Elohim) in marrying foreign wives?"

28 And one of the sons of Yoyada, the son of Elijahhib (Elyashiv) the high priest (kohen hagadol), was son in law to Sanballat the Horonite; therefore I chased him away from me.

29 Remember them, O my God (Elohim), because they have defiled the priesthood (kehunnah), and the covenant of the priesthood, and of the Levites (Lewiyim).

30 Thus cleansed I them from all strangers, and appointed the wards of the priests (kohanim) and the Levites (Lewiyim), every one in his business;

31 And for the wood offering, at times appointed, and for the firstfruits. Remember me, O my God (Elohim), for good.

ESTHER
HADASSAH הֲדַסָּה
(Myrtle Tree)

1 Now it came to pass in the days of Ahasuerus, (this is Ahasuerus who reigned, from India even unto Ethiopia (Kush), over one hundred and seven and twenty provinces;)

2 That in those days, when the king Ahasuerus sat on the throne of his kingdom, which was in Shushan the palace,

3 In the third year of his reign, he made a feast unto all his princes and his servants; the power of Persia and Media, the nobles and princes of the provinces, being before him;

4 When he shewed the riches of his glorious kingdom and the honor of his excellent majesty many days, even a hundred and fourscore days.

5 And when these days were expired, the king made a feast unto all the people that were present in Shushan the palace, both unto great and small, seven days, in the court of the garden of the king's palace;

6 Where were white, green, and blue, hangings, fastened with cords of fine linen and purple to silver rings and pillars of marble; the beds were of gold and silver, upon a pavement of red, and blue, and white, and black, marble.

7 And they gave them drink in vessels of gold, (the vessels being diverse one from another,) and royal wine in abundance, according to the state of the king.

8 And the drinking was according to the decree; none did compel; for so the king had appointed to all the officers of his house, that they should do according to every man's pleasure.

9 Also Vashti the queen made a feast for the women in the royal house which belonged to King Ahasuerus.

10 On the seventh day, when the heart of the king was merry with wine, he commanded Mehuman, Biztha, Harbona, Bigtha, and Abagtha, Zethar, and Carcas, the seven chamberlains that served in the presence of Ahasuerus the king,

11 To bring Vashti the queen before the king with the crown royal, to shew the people and the princes her beauty; for she was fair to look on.

12 But the queen Vashti refused to come at the king's commandment by his chamberlains; therefore was the king very wroth, and his anger burned in him.

13 Then the king said to the wise men, who knew the times, (for so was the king's manner toward all that knew decree and judgment;

14 And the next unto him was Carshena, Shethar, Admatha, Tarshish, Meres, Marsena, and Memucan, the seven princes of Persia and Media, which saw the king's face, and who sat the first in the kingdom;)

15 "What shall we do unto the queen Vashti according to decree, because she hath not performed the commandment of the King Ahasuerus by the chamberlains?"

16 And Memucan answered before the king and the princes: "Vashti the queen hath not done wrong to the king only, but also to all the princes, and to all the people that are in all the provinces of the King Ahasuerus.

17 For this deed of the queen shall come abroad unto all women, so that they shall despise their husbands in their eyes, when it shall be reported, 'The King Ahasuerus commanded Vashti the queen to be brought in before him, but she came not.'

18 Likewise shall the ladies of Persia and Media say this day unto all the king's princes, who have heard of the deed of the queen. Thus shall there arise too much contempt and wrath.

19 If it please the king, let there go a royal commandment from him, and let it be written among the decrees of the Persians and the Medes, that it be not altered, that Vashti come no more before King Ahasuerus; and let the king give her royal estate unto another that is better than she.

20 And when the king's decree which he shall make shall be published throughout all his empire, (for it is great), all the wives shall give to their husbands honor, both to great and small."

21 And the saying pleased the king and the princes; and the king did according to the word of Memucan.

22 For he sent letters into all the king's provinces, into every province according to the writing thereof, and to every people after their language, that every man should bear rule in his own house, and that it should be published according to the language of every people.

2 After these things, when the wrath of King Ahasuerus was appeased, he remembered Vashti, and what she had done, and what was decreed against her.

2 Then said the king's servants that ministered unto him, "Let there be fair young virgins sought for the king;

3 And let the king appoint officers in all the provinces of his kingdom, that they may gather together all the fair young virgins unto Shushan the palace, to the house of the women, unto the custody of Hege the king's chamberlain, keeper of the women; and let their things for purification be given them.

4 And let the maiden which pleaseth the king be queen instead of Vashti. And the thing pleased the king; and he did so.

5 Now in Shushan the palace there was a certain [B35]Jew (Yehudi), whose name was Mordecai, the son of Yair, the son of Shimei, the son of Kish, a Benjamin (Binyamin).

6 Who had been carried away from Jerusalem (Yerushalayim) with the captivity which had been carried away with Yekhanyah king of Judah (Yehudah), whom Nebuchanezzar the king of Babylon (Bavel) had carried away.

7 And he brought up [A49]Esther (Hadassah), that is, Esther, his uncle's daughter, for she had neither father nor mother, and the maid was fair and beautiful; whom Mordecai, when her father and mother were dead, took for his own daughter.

8 So it came to pass, when the king's commandment and his decree was heard, and when many maidens were gathered together unto Shushan the palace, to the custody of Hegai, that Esther (Hadassah) was brought also unto the king's house, to the custody of Hegai, keeper of the women.

9 And the maiden pleased him, and she obtained kindness of him; and he speedily gave her her things for purification, with such things as belonged to her, and seven maidens, which were meet to be given her, out of the king's house; and he preferred her and her maids unto the best place of the house of the women.

10 Esther (Hadassah) had not shewed her people nor her kindred, for Mordecai had charged her that she should not shew it.

11 And Mordecai walked every day before the court of the women's house, to know how Esther (Hadassah) did, and what should become of her.

12 Now when every maid's turn was come to go in to King Ahasuerus, after that she had been twelve months, according to the manner of the women, (for so were the days of their purifications accomplished, to wit, six months with oil of myrrh, and six months with sweet odours, and with other things for the purifying of the women;)

13 Then thus came every maiden unto the king; whatsoever she desired was given her to go with her out of the house of the women unto the king's house.

14 In the evening she went, and on the next day she returned into the second house of the women, to the custody of Shaashgaz, the king's chamberlain, who kept the concubines; she came in unto the king no more, except the king delighted in her, and that she was called by name.

15 Now when the turn of Esther (Hadassah), the daughter of Avihail the uncle of Mordecai, who had taken her for his daughter, was come to go in unto the king, she required nothing but what Hegai the king's chamberlain, the keeper of the women, appointed. And Esther (Hadassah) obtained favor in the sight of all them that looked upon her.

16 So Esther (Hadassah) was taken unto King Ahasuerus into his house royal in the tenth month, which is the month Tebeth, in the seventh year of his reign.

17 And the king loved Esther (Hadassah) above all the women, and she obtained grace and favor in his sight more than all the virgins; so that he set the royal crown upon her head, and made her queen instead of Vashti.

18 Then the king made a great feast unto all his princes and his servants, even Esther (Hadassah)'s feast; and he made a release to the provinces, and gave gifts, according to the state of the king.

19 And when the virgins were gathered together the second time, then Mordecai sat in the king's gate.

20 Esther (Hadassah) had not yet shewed her kindred nor her people; as Mordecai had charged her, for Esther (Hadassah) did the commandment of Mordecai, like as when she was brought up with him.

21 In those days, while Mordecai sat in the

king's gate, two of the king's chamberlains, Bigthan and Teresh, of those who kept the door, were wroth, and sought to lay hand on the King Ahasuerus.

22 And the thing was known to Mordecai, who told it unto Esther (Hadassah) the queen; and Esther (Hadassah) certified the king thereof in Mordecai's name.

23 And when inquisition was made of the matter, it was found out; therefore they were both hanged on a tree; and it was written in the book of the Chronicles before the king.

3 After these things did King Ahasuerus promote Haman the son of Hammedatha the Agagite, and advanced him, and set his seat above all the princes that were with him.

2 And all the king's servants, that were in the king's gate, bowed, and reverenced Haman; for the king had so commanded concerning him. But Mordecai bowed not, nor did him reverence.

3 Then the king's servants, who were in the king's gate, said unto Mordecai, "Why transgressest you the king's commandment?"

4 Now it came to pass, when they spake daily unto him, and he hearkened not unto them, that they told Haman, to see whether Mordecai's matters would stand; for he had told them that he was a Yehudi.

5 And when Haman saw that Mordecai bowed not, nor did him reverence, then was Haman full of wrath.

6 And he thought scorn to lay hands on Mordecai alone, for they had shewed him the people of Mordecai; wherefore Haman sought to destroy all the Jews (Yehudim) that were throughout the whole kingdom of Ahasuerus, even the people of Mordecai.

7 In the first month, that is, the month Nisan, in the twelfth year of King Ahasuerus, they cast Pur, that is, the lot, before Haman from day to day, and from month to month, to the twelfth month, that is, the month Adar.

8 And Haman said unto King Ahasuerus, "There is a certain people scattered abroad and dispersed among the people in all the provinces of your kingdom; and their decrees are diverse from all people; neither keep they the king's decrees; therefore it is not for the king's profit to allow them.

9 If it please the king, let it be written that they may be destroyed: and I will pay ten thousand talents of silver to the hands of those that have the charge of the business, to bring it into the king's treasuries."

10 And the king took his ring from his hand, and gave it unto Haman the son of Hammedatha the Agagite, the Jews' (Yehudim) enemy.

11 And the king said unto Haman, "The silver is given to you, the people also, to do with them as it seemeth good to you."

12 Then were the king's scribes called on the thirteenth day of the first month, and there was written according to all that Haman had commanded unto the king's lieutenants, and to the governors that were over every province, and to the rulers of every people of every province according to the writing thereof, and to every people after their language; in the name of King Ahasuerus was it written, and sealed with the king's ring.

13 And the letters were sent by posts into all the king's provinces, to destroy, to kill, and to cause to perish, all Jews (Yehudim), both young and old, little children and women, in one day, even upon the thirteenth day of the twelfth month, which is the month Adar, and to take the spoil of them for a prey.

14 The copy of the writing for a commandment to be given in every province was published unto all people, that they should be ready against that day.

15 The posts went out, being hastened by the king's command, and the decree was given in Shushan the palace. And the king and Haman sat down to drink; but the city Shushan was perplexed.

4 When Mordecai perceived all that was done, Mordecai rent his clothes, and put on sackcloth with ashes, and went out into the midst of the city, and cried with a loud and a bitter cry;

2 And came even before the king's gate, for none might enter into the king's gate clothed with sackcloth.

3 And in every province, whithersoever the king's command and his decree came, there was great mourning among the Jews (Yehudim), and fasting, and weeping, and wailing; and many lay in sackcloth and ashes.

4 So Esther (Hadassah)'s maids and her chamberlains came and told it her. Then was the queen exceedingly grieved; and she sent

raiment to clothe Mordecai, and to take away his sackcloth from him, but he received it not.

5 Then called Esther (Hadassah) for Hatach, one of the king's chamberlains, whom he had appointed to attend upon her, and gave him a commandment to Mordecai, to know what it was, and why it was.

6 So Hatach went forth to Mordecai unto the street of the city, which was before the king's gate.

7 And Mordecai told him of all that had happened unto him, and of the sum of the money that Haman had promised to pay to the king's treasuries for the Jews (Yehudim), to destroy them.

8 Also he gave him the copy of the writing of the decree that was given at Shushan to destroy them, to shew it unto Esther (Hadassah), and to declare it unto her, and to charge her that she should go in unto the king, to make supplication unto him, and to make request before him for her people.

9 And Hatach came and told Esther (Hadassah) the words of Mordecai.

10 Again Esther (Hadassah) spake unto Hatach, and gave him command unto Mordecai.

11 All the king's servants, and the people of the king's provinces, do know, that whosoever, whether man or woman, shall come unto the king into the inner court, who is not called, there is one decree of his to put him to death, except such to whom the king shall hold out the golden sceptre, that he may live: but I have not been called to come in unto the king these thirty days.

12 And they told to Mordecai Esther (Hadassah)'s words.

13 Then Mordecai commanded to answer Esther (Hadassah), Think not with yourself that you shalt escape in the king's house, more than all the Jews (Yehudim).

14 For if you altogether holdest your peace at this time, then shall there enlargement and deliverance arise to the Jews (Yehudim) from another place; but you and your father's house shall be destroyed: and who knoweth whether you are come to the kingdom for such a time as this?

15 Then Esther (Hadassah) bade them return Mordecai this answer:

16 "Go, gather together all the Jews (Yehudim) that are present in Shushan, and fast you for me, and neither eat nor drink three days, night or day. I also and my maidens will fast likewise; and so will I go in unto the king, which is not according to the decree; and if I perish, I perish!"

17 So Mordecai went his way, and did according to all that Esther (Hadassah) had commanded him.

5 Now it came to pass on the third day, that Esther (Hadassah) put on her royal apparel, and stood in the inner court of the king's house, opposite the king's house; and the king sat upon his royal throne in the royal house, opposite the gate of the house.

2 And it was so, when the king saw Esther (Hadassah) the queen standing in the court, that she obtained favor in his sight; and the king held out to Esther (Hadassah) the golden sceptre that was in his hand. So Esther (Hadassah) drew near, and touched the top of the sceptre.

3 Then said the king unto her, "What wilt you, Queen Esther (Hadassah)? And what is your request? It shall be even given you to the half of the kingdom!"

4 And Esther (Hadassah) answered, "If it seems good unto the king, let the king and Haman come this day unto the banquet that I have prepared for him."

5 Then the king said, "Cause Haman to make haste, that he may do as Esther (Hadassah) hath said." So the king and Haman came to the banquet that Esther (Hadassah) had prepared.

6 And the king said unto Esther (Hadassah) at the banquet of wine, "What is your petition? And it shall be granted you; and what is your request? Even to the half of the kingdom it shall be performed."

7 Then answered Esther (Hadassah), and said, "My petition and my request is:

8 If I have found favor in the sight of the king, and if it please the king to grant my petition, and to perform my request, let the king and Haman come to the banquet that I shall prepare for them, and I will do tomorrow as the king hath said."

9 Then went Haman forth that day joyful and with a glad heart; but when Haman saw Mordecai in the king's gate, that he stood not up, nor moved for him, he was full of indignation against Mordecai.

10 Nevertheless Haman refrained himself; and when he came home, he sent and called for his friends, and Zeresh his wife.

11 And Haman told them of the glory of his riches, and the multitude of his children, and all the things wherein the king had promoted him, and how he had advanced him above the princes and servants of the king.

12 Haman said moreover, "Yea, Esther (Hadassah) the queen did let no man come in with the king unto the banquet that she had prepared but myself; and tomorrow am I invited unto her also with the king.

13 Yet all this availeth me nothing, so long as I see Mordecai the Jew (Yehudi) sitting at the king's gate."

14 Then said Zeresh his wife and all his friends unto him, "Let a gallow be made of fifty cubits high, and tomorrow speak you unto the king that Mordecai may be hanged thereon: then go you in merrily with the king unto the banquet." And the thing pleased Haman; and he caused the gallows to be made.

6 On that night could not the king sleep, and he commanded to bring the book of records of the Chronicles; and they were read before the king.

2 And it was found written, that Mordecai had told of Bigthana and Teresh, two of the king's chamberlains, the keepers of the door, who sought to lay hand on the King Ahasuerus.

3 And the king said, "What honor and dignity hath been done to Mordecai for this?" Then said the king's servants that ministered unto him, "There is nothing done for him."

4 And the king said, "Who is in the court?" Now Haman was come into the outward court of the king's house, to speak unto the king to hang Mordecai on the gallows that he had prepared for him.

5 And the king's servants said unto him, "Behold, Haman standeth in the court." And the king said, "Let him come in."

6 So Haman came in. And the king said unto him, "What shall be done unto the man whom the king delighteth to honor?" Now Haman thought in his heart, "To whom would the king delight to do honor more than to myself?"

7 And Haman answered the king, "For the man whom the king delighteth to honor,

8 Let the royal apparel be brought which the king useth to wear, and the horse that the king rideth upon, and the crown royal which is set upon his head.

9 And let this apparel and horse be delivered to the hand of one of the king's most noble princes, that they may array the man withal whom the king delighteth to honor, and bring him on horseback through the street of the city, and proclaim before him: "Thus shall it be done to the man whom the king delighteth to honor!"

10 Then the king said to Haman, "Make haste, and take the apparel and the horse, as you have said, and do even so to Mordecai the Jew (Yehudi), that sitteth at the king's gate. Let nothing fail of all that you have spoken."

11 Then took Haman the apparel and the horse, and arrayed Mordecai, and brought him on horseback through the street of the city, and proclaimed before him, "Thus shall it be done unto the man whom the king delighteth to honor."

12 And Mordecai came again to the king's gate. But Haman hasted to his house mourning, and having his head covered.

13 And Haman told Zeresh his wife and all his friends every thing that had befallen him. Then said his wise men and Zeresh his wife unto him, "If Mordecai be of the seed of the Jews (Yehudim), before whom you have begun to fall, you shalt not prevail against him, but shalt surely fall before him."

14 And while they were yet talking with him, came the king's chamberlains, and hasted to bring Haman unto the banquet that Esther (Hadassah) had prepared.

7 So the king and Haman came to banquet with Esther (Hadassah) the queen.

2 And the king said again unto Esther (Hadassah) on the second day at the banquet of wine, "What is your petition, Queen Esther (Hadassah)? And it shall be granted you; and what is your request? And it shall be performed, even to the half of the kingdom."

3 Then Esther (Hadassah) the queen answered and said, "If I have found favor in your sight, O king, and if it pleases the king, let my life be given me at my petition, and my people at my request;

4 For we are sold, I and my people, to be destroyed, to be slain, and to perish. But if we had been sold for bondmen and bondwomen, I

had held my tongue, although the enemy could not countervail the king's damage."

5 Then the King Ahasuerus answered and said unto Esther (Hadassah) the queen, "Who is he, and where is he, that durst presume in his heart to do so?"

6 And Esther (Hadassah) said, "The adversary and enemy is this wicked Haman!" Then Haman was afraid before the king and the queen.

7 And the king arising from the banquet of wine in his wrath went into the palace garden; and Haman stood up to make request for his life to Esther (Hadassah) the queen, for he saw that there was evil determined against him by the king.

8 Then the king returned out of the palace garden into the place of the banquet of wine; and Haman was fallen upon the bed whereon Esther (Hadassah) was. Then said the king, "Will he force the queen also before me in the house?" As the word went out of the king's mouth, they covered Haman's face.

9 And Harbonah, one of the chamberlains, said before the king, "Behold also, the gallows fifty cubits high, which Haman had made for Mordecai, who had spoken good for the king, standeth in the house of Haman." Then the king said, "Hang him thereon!"

10 So they hanged Haman on the gallows that he had prepared for Mordecai. Then was the king's wrath pacified.

8 On that day did the King Ahasuerus give the house of Haman the Jews' (Yehudim) enemy unto Esther (Hadassah) the queen. And Mordecai came before the king, for Esther (Hadassah) had told what he was unto her.

2 And the king took off his ring, which he had taken from Haman, and gave it unto Mordecai. And Esther (Hadassah) set Mordecai over the house of Haman.

3 And Esther (Hadassah) spake yet again before the king, and fell down at his feet, and besought him with tears to put away the mischief of Haman the Agagite, and his device that he had devised against the Jews (Yehudim).

4 Then the king held out the golden sceptre toward Esther (Hadassah). So Esther (Hadassah) arose, and stood before the king,

5 And said, "If it pleases the king, and if I have found favor in his sight, and the thing seem right before the king, and I be pleasing in his eyes,

let it be written to reverse the letters devised by Haman the son of Hammedatha the Agagite, which he wrote to destroy the Jews (Yehudim) which are in all the king's provinces.

6 For how can I endure to see the evil that shall come unto my people? or how can I endure to see the destruction of my kindred?"

7 Then the King Ahasuerus said unto Esther (Hadassah) the queen and to Mordecai the Yehudi, "Behold, I have given Esther (Hadassah) the house of Haman, and him they have hanged upon the gallows, because he laid his hand upon the Jews (Yehudim).

8 Write you also for the Jews (Yehudim), as it liketh you, in the king's name, and seal it with the king's ring; for the writing which is written in the king's name, and sealed with the king's ring, may no man reverse."

9 Then were the king's scribes called at that time in the third month, that is, the month Sivan, on the three and twentieth day thereof; and it was written according to all that Mordecai commanded unto the Jews (Yehudim), and to the lieutenants, and the deputies and rulers of the provinces which are from India unto Ethiopia (Kush), a hundred twenty and seven provinces, unto every province according to the writing thereof, and unto every people after their language, and to the Jews (Yehudim) according to their writing, and according to their language.

10 And he wrote in the king Ahasuerus's name, and sealed it with the king's ring, and sent letters by posts on horseback, and riders on mules, camels, and young dromedaries.

11 Wherein the king granted the Jews (Yehudim) which were in every city to gather themselves together, and to stand for their life, to destroy, to slay, and to cause to perish, all the power of the people and province that would assault them, both little ones and women, and to take the spoil of them for a prey,

12 Upon one day in all the provinces of King Ahasuerus, namely, upon the thirteenth day of the twelfth month, which is the month Adar.

13 The copy of the writing for a commandment to be given in every province was published unto all people, and that the Jews (Yehudim) should be ready against that day to avenge themselves on their enemies.

14 So the posts that rode upon mules and camels

went out, being hastened and pressed on by the king's command. And the decree was given at Shushan the palace.

15 And Mordecai went out from the presence of the king in royal apparel of blue and white, and with a great crown of gold, and with a garment of fine linen and purple; and the city of Shushan rejoiced and was glad.

16 The Jews (Yehudim) had light, and gladness, and joy, and honor.

17 And in every province, and in every city, whithersoever the king's command and his decree came, the Jews (Yehudim) had joy and gladness, a feast and a good day. And many of the people of the land became Jews (Yehudim), for the fear of the Jews (Yehudim) fell upon them.

9 Now in the twelfth month, that is, the month Adar, on the thirteenth day of the same, when the king's commandment and his decree drew near to be put in execution, in the day that the enemies of the Jews (Yehudim) hoped to have power over them, (though it was turned to the contrary, that the Jews (Yehudim) had rule over them that hated them;)

2 The Jews (Yehudim) gathered themselves together in their cities throughout all the provinces of the king Ahasuerus, to lay hand on such as sought their hurt; and no man could withstand them; for the fear of them fell upon all people.

3 And all the rulers of the provinces, and the lieutenants, and the deputies, and officers of the king, helped the Jews (Yehudim), because the fear of Mordecai fell upon them.

4 For Mordecai was great in the king's house, and his fame went out throughout all the provinces; for this man Mordecai waxed greater and greater.

5 Thus the Jews (Yehudim) smote all their enemies with the stroke of the sword, and slaughter, and destruction, and did what they would unto those that hated them.

6 And in Shushan the palace the Jews (Yehudim) slew and destroyed five hundred men.

7 And Parshandatha, and Dalphon, and Aspatha,

8 And Poratha, and Adalia, and Aridatha,

9 And Parmashta, and Arisai, and Aridai, and Vayezata,

10 The ten sons of Haman the son of Hammedatha, the enemy of the Jews (Yehudim),

slew they; but on the spoil laid they not their hand.

11 On that day the number of those that were slain in Shushan the palace was brought before the king.

12 And the king said unto Esther (Hadassah) the queen, "The Jews (Yehudim) have slain and destroyed five hundred men in Shushan the palace, and the ten sons of Haman; what have they done in the rest of the king's provinces? Now what is your petition? And it shall be granted you; or what is your request further? And it shall be done."

13 Then said Esther (Hadassah), "If it pleases the king, let it be granted to the Jews (Yehudim) who are in Shushan to do tomorrow also according unto this day's decree, and let Haman's ten sons be hanged upon the gallows."

14 And the king commanded it so to be done; and the decree was given at Shushan; and they hanged Haman's ten sons.

15 For the Jews (Yehudim) who were in Shushan gathered themselves together on the fourteenth day also of the month Adar, and slew three hundred men at Shushan, but on the prey they laid not their hand.

16 But the other Jews (Yehudim) who were in the king's provinces gathered themselves together, and stood for their lives, and had rest from their enemies, and slew of their foes seventy and five thousand, but they laid not their hands on the prey,

17 On the thirteenth day of the month Adar; and on the fourteenth day of the same rested they, and made it a day of feasting and gladness.

18 But the Jews (Yehudim) that were at Shushan assembled together on the thirteenth day thereof, and on the fourteenth thereof; and on the fifteenth day of the same they rested, and made it a day of feasting and gladness.

19 Therefore the Jews (Yehudim) of the villages, that dwelt in the unwalled towns, made the fourteenth day of the month Adar a day of gladness and feasting, and a good day, and of sending portions one to another.

20 And Mordecai wrote these things, and sent letters unto all the Jews (Yehudim) that were in all the provinces of the King Ahasuerus, both near and far,

21 To stablish this among them, that they should keep the fourteenth day of the month Adar, and

the fifteenth day of the same, yearly,

22 As the days wherein the Jews (Yehudim) rested from their enemies, and the month which was turned unto them from sorrow to joy, and from mourning into a good day; that they should make them days of feasting and joy, and of sending portions one to another, and gifts to the poor.

23 And the Jews (Yehudim) undertook to do as they had begun, and as Mordecai had written unto them;

24 Because Haman the son of Hammedatha, the Agagite, the enemy of all the Jews (Yehudim), had devised against the Jews (Yehudim) to destroy them, and had cast Pur, that is, the lot, to consume them, and to destroy them;

25 But when Esther (Hadassah) came before the king, he commanded by letters that his wicked device, which he devised against the Jews (Yehudim), should return upon his own head, and that he and his sons should be hanged on the gallows.

26 Wherefore they called these days Purim after the name of Pur. Therefore for all the words of this letter, and of that which they had seen concerning this matter, and which had come unto them,

27 The Jews (Yehudim) ordained, and took upon them, and upon their seed, and upon all such as joined themselves unto them, so as it should not fail, that they would keep these two days according to their writing, and according to their appointed time every year;

28 And that these days should be remembered and kept throughout every generation, every family, every province, and every city; and that these days of Purim should not fail from among the Jews (Yehudim), nor the memorial of them perish from their seed.

29 Then Esther (Hadassah) the queen, the daughter of Avihail, and Mordecai the Yehudi, wrote with all authority, to confirm this second letter of Purim.

30 And he sent the letters unto all the Jews (Yehudim), to the hundred twenty and seven provinces of the kingdom of Ahasuerus, with words of peace and truth,

31 To confirm these days of Purim in their times appointed, according as Mordecai the Jew (Yehudi) and Esther (Hadassah) the queen had enjoined them, and as they had decreed for themselves and for their seed, the matters of the fastings and their cry.

32 And the decree of Esther (Hadassah) confirmed these matters of Purim; and it was written in the book.

10 And the King Ahasuerus laid a tribute upon the land, and upon the isles of the sea.

2 And all the acts of his power and of his might, and the declaration of the greatness of Mordecai, whereunto the king advanced him, are they not written in the book of the Chronicles of the Kings of Media and Persia?

3 For Mordecai the Yehudi was next unto King Ahasuerus, and great among the Jews (Yehudim), and accepted of the multitude of his brethren, seeking the wealth of his people, and speaking peace to all his seed.

JOB
IYOV אִיּוֹב
(Persecuted One)

1 There was a man in the land of Uz, whose name was [A50]Job (Iyov); and that man was perfect and upright, and one that feared God (Elohim), and shunned evil.

2 And there were born unto him seven sons and three daughters.

3 His substance also was seven thousand sheep, and three thousand camels, and five hundred yoke of oxen, and five hundred she asses, and a very great household; so that this man was the greatest of all the men of the east.

4 And his sons went and feasted in their houses, every one his day; and sent and called for their three sisters to eat and to drink with them.

5 And it was so, when the days of their feasting were gone about, that Job (Iyov) sent and sanctified them, and rose up early in the morning, and offered burnt offerings according to the number of them all, for Job (Iyov) said, "It may be that my sons have sinned, and cursed God (Elohim) in their hearts." Thus did Job (Iyov) continually.

6 Now there was a day when the sons of God (Elohim) came to present themselves before יהוה, and Satan came also among them.

7 And יהוה said unto the Satan, "Whence comest you?" Then the Satan answered יהוה, and said, "From going to and fro in the earth, and from walking up and down in it."

8 And יהוה said unto the Satan, "Have you considered My servant Job (Iyov), that there is none like him in the earth, a perfect and an upright man, one that feareth God (Elohim), and shunned evil?

9 Then the Satan answered יהוה, and said, "Doth Job (Iyov) fear God (Elohim) for nothing?

10 Have not You made a hedge about him, and about his house, and about all that he hath on every side? You have blessed the work of his hands, and his substance is increased in the land.

11 But put forth Your hand now, and touch all that he hath, and he will curse You to Your face!"

12 And יהוה said unto the Satan, "Behold, all that he hath is in your power; only upon himself put not forth your hand." So the Satan went forth from the presence of יהוה.

13 And there was a day when his sons and his daughters were eating and drinking wine in their eldest brother's house;

14 And there came a messenger unto Job (Iyov), and said, "The oxen were plowing, and the asses feeding beside them;

15 And the Sabeans fell upon them, and took them away; yea, they have slain the servants with the edge of the sword; and I only am escaped alone to tell you.

16 While he was yet speaking, there came also another, and said, "The fire of God (Elohim) is fallen from heaven, and hath burned up the sheep, and the servants, and consumed them; and I only am escaped alone to tell you!"

17 While he was yet speaking, there came also another, and said, The Chaldeans made out three bands, and fell upon the camels, and have carried them away, yea, and slain the servants with the edge of the sword; and I only am escaped alone to tell you!"

18 While he was yet speaking, there came also another, and said, "Your sons and your daughters were eating and drinking wine in their eldest brother's house;

19 And, behold, there came a great wind from the wilderness, and smote the four corners of the house, and it fell upon the young men, and they are dead; and I only am escaped alone to tell you!"

20 Then Job (Iyov) arose, and rent his mantle, and shaved his head, and fell down upon the ground, and worshipped,

21 And said, "Naked came I out of my mother's womb, and naked shall I return thither. יהוה gave, and יהוה hath taken away; blessed be the name of יהוה."

22 In all this Job (Iyov) sinned not, nor charged God (Elohim) foolishly.

2 Again there was a day when the sons of God (Elohim) came to present themselves before יהוה, and the Satan came also among them to present himself before יהוה.

2 And יהוה said unto the Satan, "From whence comest you?" And the Satan answered יהוה, and said, "From going to and fro in the earth, and from walking up and down in it."

3 And יהוה said unto the Satan, "Have you considered my servant Job (Iyov), that there is

none like him in the earth, a perfect and an upright man, one that feareth God (Elohim), and shunned evil? And still he holdeth fast his integrity, although you movedst Me against him, to destroy him without cause."

4 And the Satan answered יהוה, and said, "Skin for skin, yea, all that a man hath will he give for his life.

5 But put forth Your hand now, and touch his bone and his flesh, and he will curse You to Your face!"

6 And יהוה said unto the Satan, "Behold, he is in your hand, but preserve his life."

7 So went the Satan forth from the presence of יהוה, and smote Job (Iyov) with sore boils from the sole of his foot unto his crown.

8 And he took him a potsherd to scrape himself withal; and he sat down among the ashes.

9 Then said his wife unto him, "Dost you still retain your integrity? Curse God (Elohim), and die!"

10 But he said unto her, "You speakest as one of the foolish women speaketh. What? Shall we receive good at the hand of God (Elohim), and shall we not receive disaster (raah)?" In all this Job (Iyov) did not sin with his lips.

11 Now when Job (Iyov)'s three friends heard of all this disaster (raah) that was come upon him, they came every one from his own place; Eliphaz the Temanite, and Bildad the Shuhite, and Zophar the Naamathite; for they had made an appointment together to come to mourn with him and to comfort him.

12 And when they lifted up their eyes afar off, and knew him not, they lifted up their voice, and wept; and they rent every one his mantle, and sprinkled dust upon their heads toward heaven.

13 So they sat down with him upon the ground seven days and seven nights, and none spake a word unto him, for they saw that his grief was very great.

3 After this opened Job (Iyov) his mouth, and cursed his day.

2 And Job (Iyov) spake, and said,

3 "Let the day perish wherein I was born, and the night in which it was said, 'There is a man child conceived.'

4 Let that day be darkness; let not God (Eloah) regard it from above, neither let the light shine upon it.

5 Let darkness and the shadow of death stain

it; let a cloud dwell upon it; let the blackness of the day terrify it.

6 As for that night, let darkness seize upon it; let it not be joined unto the days of the year, let it not come into the number of the months.

7 Behold, let that night be solitary, let no joyful voice come therein.

8 Let them curse it that curse the day, who are ready to raise up their mourning.

9 Let the stars of the twilight thereof be dark; let it look for light, but have none; neither let it see the dawning of the day;

10 Because it shut not up the doors of my mother's womb, nor hid sorrow from mine eyes.

11 Why died I not from the womb? Why did I not give up the spirit when I came out of the belly?

12 Why did the knees prevent me? Or why the breasts that I should suck?

13 For now should I have lain still and been quiet, I should have slept: then had I been at rest,

14 With kings and counsellors of the earth, which built desolate places for themselves;

15 Or with princes that had gold, who filled their houses with silver;

16 Or as a hidden untimely birth I had not been; as infants who never saw light.

17 There the wicked cease from troubling; and there the weary be at rest.

18 There the prisoners rest together; they hear not the voice of the oppressor.

19 The small and great are there; and the servant is free from his master.

20 Wherefore is light given to him that is in misery, and life unto the bitter in soul;

21 Which long for death, but it cometh not; and dig for it more than for hid treasures;

22 Which rejoice exceedingly, and are glad, when they can find the grave?

23 Why is light given to a man whose way is hid, and whom God (Eloah) hath hedged in?

24 For my sighing cometh before I eat, and my roarings are poured out like the waters.

25 For the thing which I greatly feared is come upon me, and that which I was afraid of is come unto me.

26 I was not in safety, neither had I rest, neither was I quiet; yet trouble came."

4 Then Eliphaz the Temanite answered and said:

2 "If we assay to commune with you, wilt you

be grieved? But who can withhold himself from speaking?

3 Behold, you have instructed many, and you have strengthened the weak hands.

4 Your words have upholden him that was falling, and you have strengthened the feeble knees.

5 But now it is come upon you, and you faintest; it toucheth you, and you are troubled.

6 Is not this your fear, your confidence, your hope, and the uprightness of your ways?

7 Please remember, who ever perished, being innocent? Or where were the righteous cut off?

8 Even as I have seen, they that plow iniquity, and sow wickedness, reap the same.

9 By the blast of God (Eloah) they perish, and by the breath of his nostrils are they consumed.

10 The roaring of the lion, and the voice of the fierce lion, and the teeth of the young lions, are broken.

11 The old lion perisheth for lack of prey, and the stout lion's whelps are scattered abroad.

12 Now a thing was secretly brought to me, and mine ear received a little thereof.

13 In thoughts from the visions of the night, when deep sleep falleth on men,

14 Fear came upon me, and trembling, which made all my bones to shake.

15 Then a spirit passed before my face; the hair of my flesh stood up.

16 It stood still, but I could not discern the form thereof; an image was before mine eyes, there was silence, and I heard a voice, saying,

17 'Can mortal man be more just than God (Eloah)? Can a man be more pure than his Maker?

18 Behold, He put no trust in His servants; and His angels He charged with folly;

19 How much less in them that dwell in houses of clay, whose foundation is in the dust, which are crushed before the moth?

20 They are destroyed from morning to evening; they perish forever without any regarding it.

21 Doth not their excellency which is in them go away? They die, even without wisdom.'

5 Call now, if there be any that will answer you; and to which of the B31aholy ones (qadoshim) wilt you turn?

2 For wrath killeth the foolish man, and envy slayeth the silly one.

3 I have seen the foolish taking root, but

suddenly I cursed his habitation.

4 His children are far from safety, and they are crushed in the gate, neither is there any to deliver them.

5 Whose harvest the hungry eateth up, and taketh it even out of the thorns, and the robber swalloweth up their substance.

6 Although affliction cometh not forth of the dust, neither doth trouble spring out of the ground;

7 Yet man is born unto trouble, as the sparks fly upward.

8 I would seek unto God (El), and unto God (Elohim) would I commit my cause,

9 Who doeth great things and unsearchable; marvellous things without number;

10 Who giveth rain upon the earth, and sendeth waters upon the fields;

11 To set up on high those that be low; that those who mourn may be exalted to safety.

12 He disappointeth the devices of the crafty, so that their hands cannot perform their enterprise.

13 He taketh the wise in their own craftiness; and the counsel of the perverse is carried headlong.

14 They meet with darkness in the daytime, and grope in the noonday as in the night.

15 But he saveth the poor from the sword, from their mouth, and from the hand of the mighty.

16 So the poor hath hope, and iniquity stoppeth her mouth.

17 Behold, happy is the man whom God (Eloah) correcteth; therefore despise not you the chastening of the Almighty (Shaddai)

18 For He maketh sore, and bindeth up; He woundeth, and His hands make whole.

19 He shall deliver you in six troubles; yea, in seven there shall no evil touch you.

20 In famine he shall redeem you from death; and in war from the power of the sword.

21 You shalt be hid from the scourge of the tongue; neither shalt you be afraid of destruction when it cometh.

22 At destruction and famine you shalt laugh; neither shalt you be afraid of the beasts of the earth.

23 For you shalt be in league with the stones of the field; and the beasts of the field shall be at peace with you.

24 And you shalt know that your tabernacle shall be in peace; and you shalt visit your

habitation, and shalt not sin.

25 You shalt know also that your seed shall be great, and your offspring as the grass of the earth.

26 You shalt come to your grave in a full age, like as a shock of corn cometh in in his season.

27 Behold this, we have searched it, so it is; hear it, and know you it for your good."

6 But Job (Iyov) answered and said,

2 "Oh that my grief was throughly weighed, and my disaster laid in the balances together!

3 For now it would be heavier than the sand of the sea; therefore my words are swallowed up.

4 For the arrows of the Almighty (Shaddai) are within me, the poison whereof drinketh up my spirit; the terrors of God (Eloah) do set themselves in array against me.

5 Doth the wild ass bray when he hath grass? Or loweth the ox over his fodder?

6 Can that which is unsavoury be eaten without salt? Or is there any taste in the white of an egg?

7 The things that my soul refused to touch are as my sorrowful meat.

8 Oh that I might have my request; and that God (Eloah) would grant me the thing that I long for!

9 Even that it would please God (Eloah) to destroy me; that He would let loose His hand, and cut me off!

10 Then should I yet have comfort; yea, I would harden myself in sorrow: let Him not spare; for I have not concealed the words of the Holy One.

11 What is my strength, that I should hope? And what is mine end, that I should prolong my life?

12 Is my strength the strength of stones? Or is my flesh of brass?

13 Is not my help in me? And is wisdom driven quite from me?

14 To him that is afflicted pity should be shewed from his friend; but he forsaketh the fear of the Almighty (Shaddai).

15 My brethren have dealt deceitfully as a brook, and as the stream of brooks they pass away;

16 Which are blackish by reason of the ice, and wherein the snow is hid:

17 What time they wax warm, they vanish; when it is hot, they are consumed out of their place.

18 The paths of their way are turned aside; they go to nothing, and perish.

19 The troops of Tema looked, the companies of Sheva waited for them.

20 They were confounded because they had hoped; they came thither, and were ashamed.

21 For now you are nothing; you see my casting down, and are afraid.

22 Did I say, 'Bring unto me'? Or, 'Give a reward for me of your substance'?

23 Or, 'Deliver me from the enemy's hand'? Or, 'Redeem me from the hand of the mighty'?

24 Teach me, and I will hold my tongue: and cause me to understand wherein I have erred.

25 How forcible are right words! But what doth your arguing reprove?

26 Do you imagine to reprove words, and the speeches of one that is desperate, which are as wind?

27 Yea, you overwhelm the fatherless, and you dig a pit for your friend.

28 Now therefore be content, look upon me; for it is evident unto you if I lie.

29 Please return, let it not be iniquity; yea, return again, my righteousness is in it.

30 Is there iniquity in my tongue? Cannot my taste discern perverse things?

7 Is there not an appointed time to man upon earth? Are not his days also like the days of a hireling?

2 As a servant earnestly desireth the shadow, and as a hireling looketh for the reward of his work;

3 So am I made to possess months of vanity, and wearisome nights are appointed to me.

4 When I lie down, I say, 'When shall I arise, and the night be gone'? And I am full of tossings to and fro unto the dawning of the day.

5 My flesh is clothed with worms and clods of dust; my skin is broken, and become loathsome.

6 My days are swifter than a weaver's shuttle, and are spent without hope.

7 O remember that my life is wind; mine eye shall no more see good.

8 The eye of him that hath seen me shall see me no more; your eyes are upon me, and I am not.

9 As the cloud is consumed and vanisheth away; so he that goeth down to the grave shall come up no more.

10 He shall return no more to his house, neither shall his place know him any more.

11 Therefore I will not refrain my mouth; I will speak in the anguish of my spirit; I will complain in the bitterness of my soul.

12 Am I a sea, or a whale, that you settest a watch over me?

13 When I say, 'My bed shall comfort me, my couch shall ease my complaint';

14 Then you scarest me with dreams, and terrifiest me through visions,

15 So that my soul chooseth strangling, and death rather than my life.

16 I loathe it; I would not live always; let me alone, for my days are vanity.

17 What is man, that you shouldest magnify him? And that you shouldest set your heart upon him?

18 And that you shouldest visit him every morning, and try him every moment?

19 How long wilt you not depart from me, nor let me alone till I swallow down my spittle?

20 I have sinned; what shall I do unto You, O You preserver of men? Why have You set me as a mark against you, so that I am a burden to myself?

21 And why dost You not pardon my transgression, and take away mine iniquity? For now shall I sleep in the dust; and You shalt seek me in the morning, but I shall not be."

8 Then answered Bildad the Shuhite, and said, 2 "How long wilt you speak these things? And how long shall the words of your mouth be like a strong wind?

3 Doth God (El) pervert judgment? Or doth the Almighty pervert justice?

4 If your children have sinned against him, and he has cast them away for their transgression;

5 If you wouldest seek unto God (El) betimes, and make your supplication to the Almighty;

6 If you wert pure and upright; surely now He would awake for you, and make the habitation of your righteousness prosperous.

7 Though your beginning was small, yet your latter end should greatly increase.

8 For enquire, I pray you, of the former age, and prepare yourself to the search of their fathers:

9 (For we are but of yesterday, and know nothing, because our days upon earth are a shadow.)

10 Shall not they teach you, and tell you, and utter words out of their heart?

11 Can the rush grow up without mire? can the flag grow without water?

12 Whilst it is yet in his greenness, and not cut down, it withereth before any other herb.

13 So are the paths of all that forget God (El); and the hypocrite's hope shall perish,

14 Whose hope shall be cut off, and whose trust shall be a spider's web.

15 He shall lean upon his house, but it shall not stand; he shall hold it fast, but it shall not endure.

16 He is green before the sun, and his branch shooteth forth in his garden.

17 His roots are wrapped about the heap, and seeth the place of stones.

18 If he destroys him from his place, then it shall deny him, saying, 'I have not seen you.'

19 Behold, this is the joy of his way, and out of the earth shall others grow.

20 Behold, God (El) will not cast away a perfect man, neither will He help the evil doers.

21 Till He fill your mouth with laughing, and your lips with rejoicing.

22 They that hate you shall be clothed with shame; and the dwelling place of the wicked shall come to nothing."

9 Then Job (Iyov) answered and said, 2 "I know it is so of a truth, but how should man be just with God (El)?

3 If he will contend with Him, he cannot answer Him one of a thousand.

4 He is wise in heart, and mighty in strength; who hath hardened himself against Him, and hath prospered?

5 Who removeth the mountains, and they know not; who overturneth them in His anger.

6 Who shaketh the earth out of her place, and the pillars thereof tremble.

7 Who commandeth the sun, and it riseth not; and sealeth up the stars.

8 Who alone spreadeth out the heavens, and treadeth upon the waves of the sea.

9 Who maketh Arcturus, Orion, and Pleiades, and the chambers of the south.

10 Who doeth great things past finding out; yea, and wonders without number.

11 Behold, He goeth by me, and I see Him not; He passeth on also, but I perceive Him not.

12 Behold, He taketh away, who can hinder Him? Who will say unto Him, 'What doest You?'

13 If God (Eloah) will not withdraw His anger, the proud helpers do stoop under Him.

14 How much less shall I answer Him, and choose out my words to reason with Him?

15 Whom, though I was righteous, yet would

I not answer, but I would make supplication to my Judge.

16 If I had called, and He had answered me; yet would I not believe that He had hearkened unto my voice.

17 For He breaketh me with a tempest, and multiplieth my wounds without cause.

18 He will not allow me to take my breath, but filleth me with bitterness.

19 If I speak of strength, behold, He is strong: and if of judgment, who shall set me a time to plead?

20 If I justify myself, mine own mouth shall condemn me; if I say, 'I am perfect', it shall also prove me perverse.

21 Though I was perfect, yet would I not know my soul; I would despise my life.

22 This is one thing, therefore I said it, 'He destroyeth the perfect and the wicked.'

23 If the scourge slays suddenly, He will laugh at the trial of the innocent.

24 The earth is given into the hand of the wicked: He covereth the faces of the judges thereof; if not, where, and who is He?

25 Now my days are swifter than a post; they flee away, they see no good.

26 They are passed away as the swift ships; as the eagle that hasteth to the prey.

27 If I say, 'I will forget my complaint, I will leave off my heaviness, and comfort myself,'

28 I am afraid of all my sorrows, I know that You wilt not hold me innocent.

29 If I be wicked, why then labor I in vain?

30 If I wash myself with snow water, and make my hands never so clean;

31 Yet shalt You plunge me in the ditch, and mine own clothes shall abhor me.

32 For He is not a man, as I am, that I should answer Him, and we should come together in judgment.

33 Neither is there any daysman betwixt us, that might lay his hand upon us both.

34 Let Him take his rod away from me, and let not His fear terrify me;

35 Then would I speak, and not fear Him, but it is not so with me.

10 My soul is weary of my life; I will leave my complaint upon myself; I will speak in the bitterness of my soul.

2 I will say unto God (Eloah), 'Do not condemn me; shew me wherefore You contendest with me.

3 Is it good unto You that You shouldest oppress, that You shouldest despise the work of Your hands, and shine upon the counsel of the wicked?

4 Have You eyes of flesh? Or seest You as man seeth?

5 Are Your days as the days of man? Are Your years as man's days,

6 That You enquirest after mine iniquity, and searchest after my sin?

7 You knowest that I am not wicked; and there is none that can deliver out of Your hand.

8 Your hands have made me and fashioned me together round about; yet You dost destroy me.

9 Remember, I beseech You, that You have made me as the clay; and wilt You bring me into dust again?

10 Have You not poured me out as milk, and curdled me like cheese?

11 You have clothed me with skin and flesh, and hast fenced me with bones and sinews.

12 You have granted me life and favor, and Your visitation hath preserved my spirit.

13 And these things have You hid in Your heart; I know that this is with You:

14 If I sin, then You markest me, and You wilt not acquit me from mine iniquity.

15 If I be wicked, woe unto me; and if I be righteous, yet will I not lift up my head. I am full of confusion; therefore see You mine affliction;

16 For it increaseth. You huntest me as a fierce lion, and again You shewest Yourself marvellous upon me.

17 You renewest Your witnesses against me, and increasest Your indignation upon me; changes and war are against me.

18 Wherefore then have You brought me forth out of the womb? Oh would that I had given up the spirit (died), and no eye had seen me!

19 I should have been as though I had not been; I should have been carried from the womb to the grave.

20 Are not my days few? Cease then, and let me alone, that I may take comfort a little,

21 Before I go whence I shall not return, even to the land of darkness and the shadow of death;

22 A land of darkness, as darkness itself; and of the shadow of death, without any order, and where the light is as darkness.'"

11 Then answered Zophar the Naamathite, and said,

2 "Should not the multitude of words be answered? And should a man full of talk be justified?

3 Should your lies make men hold their peace? And when you mockest, shall no man make you ashamed?

4 For you have said, 'My doctrine is pure, and I am clean in your eyes.'

5 But oh that God (Eloah) would speak, and open His lips against you;

6 And that He would shew you the secrets of wisdom, that they are double to that which is! Know therefore that God (Eloah) exacteth of you less than your iniquity deserveth.

7 Canst you by searching find out God (Eloah)? Canst you find out the Almighty unto perfection?

8 It is as high as heaven; what canst you do? Deeper than hell (sheol); what canst you know?

9 The measure thereof is longer than the earth, and broader than the sea.

10 If He cut off, and shut up, or gather together, then who can hinder Him?

11 For He knoweth vain men; He seeth wickedness also; will He not then consider it?

12 For vain man would be wise, though man be born like a wild ass's colt.

13 If you prepare your heart, and stretch out your hands toward Him;

14 If iniquity be in your hand, put it far away, and let not wickedness dwell in your tabernacles.

15 For then shalt you lift up your face without spot; yea, you shalt be stedfast, and shalt not fear;

16 Because you shalt forget your misery, and remember it as waters that pass away,

17 And your age shall be clearer than the noonday; you shalt shine forth, you shalt be as the morning.

18 And you shalt be secure, because there is hope; yea, you shalt dig about you, and you shalt take your rest in safety.

19 Also you shalt lie down, and none shall make you afraid; yea, many shall make suit unto you.

20 But the eyes of the wicked shall fail, and they shall not escape, and their hope shall be as the giving up of the spirit!"

12 And Job (Iyov) answered and said:

2 "No doubt but you are the people, and wisdom shall die with you!

3 But I have understanding as well as you; I am not inferior to you; yea, who knoweth not such things as these?

4 I am as one mocked of his neighbour, who calleth upon God (Eloah), and He answereth him; the just upright man is laughed to scorn.

5 He that is ready to slip with his feet is as a lamp despised in the thought of him that is at ease.

6 The tabernacles of robbers prosper, and they that provoke God (El) are secure; into whose hand God (Eloah) bringeth abundantly.

7 But ask now the beasts, and they shall teach you; and the fowls of the air, and they shall tell you;

8 Or speak to the earth, and it shall teach you; and the fishes of the sea shall declare unto you.

9 Who knoweth not in all these that the hand of יהוה hath wrought this?

10 In whose hand is the soul of every living thing, and the breath of all mankind.

11 Doth not the ear test words? And the mouth tastes his food?

12 With the ancient is wisdom; and in length of days understanding.

13 With Him is wisdom and strength, He hath counsel and understanding.

14 Behold, He breaketh down, and it cannot be built again; He shutteth up a man, and there can be no opening.

15 Behold, He withholdeth the waters, and they dry up; also He sendeth them out, and they overturn the earth.

16 With Him is strength and wisdom; the deceived and the deceiver are His.

17 He leadeth counsellors away spoiled, and maketh the judges fools.

18 He looseth the bond of kings, and girdeth their loins with a girdle.

19 He leadeth princes away spoiled, and overthroweth the mighty.

20 He removeth away the speech of the trusty, and taketh away the understanding of the aged.

21 He poureth contempt upon princes, and weakeneth the strength of the mighty.

22 He discovereth deep things out of darkness, and bringeth out to light the shadow of death.

23 He increaseth the nations, and destroyeth them; He enlargeth the nations, and straiteneth them again.

24 He taketh away the heart of the chief of the people of the earth, and causeth them to wander

in a wilderness where there is no way.

25 They grope in the dark without light, and He maketh them to stagger like a drunken man.

13 Behold, mine eye hath seen all this, mine ear hath heard and understood it.

2 What you know, the same do I know also: I am not inferior unto you.

3 Surely I would speak to the Almighty (Shaddai), and I desire to reason with God (El).

4 But you are forgers of lies, you are all physicians of no value.

5 O that you would altogether hold your peace! and it should be your wisdom.

6 Hear now my reasoning, and hearken to the pleadings of my lips.

7 Will you speak wickedly for God (El)? And talk deceitfully for Him?

8 Will you accept his person? Will you contend for God (El)?

9 Is it good that He should search you out? Or as one man mocketh another, do you so mock Him?

10 He will surely reprove you, if you do secretly accept persons.

11 Shall not His excellency make you afraid? And His dread fall upon you?

12 Your remembrances are like unto ashes, your bodies to bodies of clay.

13 Hold your peace, let me alone, that I may speak, and let come on me what will.

14 Wherefore do I take my flesh in my teeth, and put my life in mine hand?

15 Though He slay me, yet will I trust in Him; but I will maintain mine own ways before Him.

16 He also shall be my salvation, for a hypocrite shall not come before Him.

17 Hear diligently my speech, and my declaration with your ears.

18 Behold now, I have ordered my cause; I know that I shall be justified.

19 Who is he that will plead with me? For now, if I hold my tongue, I shall give up the spirit.

20 Only do not two things unto me, then will I not hide myself from You.

21 Withdraw Your hand far from me, and let not Your dread make me afraid.

22 Then call You, and I will answer; or let me speak, and answer You me.

23 How many are mine iniquities and sins? Make me to know my transgression and my sin.

24 Wherefore hidest You Your face, and holdest me for Your enemy?

25 Wilt You break a leaf driven to and fro? And wilt You pursue the dry stubble?

26 For You writest bitter things against me, and makest me to possess the iniquities of my youth.

27 You puttest my feet also in the stocks, and lookest narrowly unto all my paths; You settest a print upon the heels of my feet.

28 And he, as a rotten thing, consumeth, as a garment that is moth eaten.

14 Man that is born of a woman is of few days, and full of trouble.

2 He cometh forth like a flower, and is cut down; he fleeth also as a shadow, and continueth not.

3 And dost You open Your eyes upon such a one, and bringest me into judgment with You?

4 Who can bring a clean thing out of an unclean? Not one.

5 Seeing his days are determined, the number of his months are with You, You have appointed his bounds that he cannot pass;

6 Turn from him, that he may rest, till he shall accomplish, as a hireling, his day.

7 For there is hope of a tree, if it be cut down, that it will sprout again, and that the tender branch thereof will not cease.

8 Though the root thereof wax old in the earth, and the stock thereof die in the ground;

9 Yet through the scent of water it will bud, and bring forth boughs like a plant.

10 But man dieth, and wasteth away; yea, man giveth up the spirit, and where is he?

11 As the waters fail from the sea, and the flood decayeth and drieth up,

12 So man lieth down, and riseth not; till the heavens be no more, they shall not awake, nor be raised out of their sleep.

13 O that you wouldest hide me in the grave, that you wouldest keep me secret, until your wrath be past, that you wouldest appoint me a set time, and remember me!

14 If a man die, shall he live again? All the days of my appointed time will I wait, till my change come.

15 You shalt call, and I will answer you: You wilt have a desire to the work of Your hands.

16 For now You numberest my steps; dost You not watch over my sin?

17 My transgression is sealed up in a bag, and You sewest up mine iniquity.

18 And surely the mountain falling cometh to nought, and the rock is removed out of his place.

19 The water wears away the stones; You washest away the things which grow out of the dust of the earth; and You destroyest the hope of man.

20 You prevailest forever against him, and he passeth; You changest his countenance, and sendest him away.

21 His sons come to honor, and he knoweth it not; and they are brought low, but he perceiveth it not of them.

22 But his flesh upon him shall have pain, and his soul within him shall mourn."

15 Then answered Eliphaz the Temanite, and said:

2 "Should a wise man utter vain knowledge, and fill his belly with the east wind?

3 Should he reason with unprofitable talk? Or with speeches wherewith he can do no good?

4 Yea, you castest off fear, and restrainest prayer before God (El).

5 For your mouth uttereth your iniquity, and you choosest the tongue of the crafty.

6 Your own mouth condemneth you, and not I: yea, your own lips testify against you.

7 Are you the first man that was born? or wast you made before the hills?

8 Have you heard the secret of God (Eloah)? And dost you restrain wisdom to yourself?

9 What knowest you, that we know not? What understandest you, which is not in us?

10 With us are both the grayheaded and very aged men, much elder than your father.

11 Are the consolations of God (El) small with you? Is there any secret thing with you?

12 Why doth your heart carry you away? And what do your eyes wink at,

13 That you turnest your spirit against God (El), and lettest such words go out of your mouth?

14 What is man, that he should be clean? And he which is born of a woman, that he should be righteous?

15 Behold, he putteth no trust in his saints; yea, the heavens are not clean in his sight.

16 How much more abominable and filthy is man, which drinketh iniquity like water?

17 I will shew you, hear me; and that which I have seen I will declare;

18 Which wise men have told from their fathers, and have not hid it:

19 Unto whom alone the earth was given, and no stranger passed among them.

20 The wicked man travaileth with pain all his days, and the number of years is hidden to the oppressor.

21 A dreadful sound is in his ears; in prosperity the destroyer shall come upon him.

22 He believeth not that he shall return out of darkness, and he is waited for of the sword.

23 He wandereth abroad for bread, saying, 'Where is it?' He knoweth that the day of darkness is ready at his hand.

24 Trouble and anguish shall make him afraid; they shall prevail against him, as a king ready to the battle.

25 For he stretcheth out his hand against God (El), and strengtheneth himself against the Almighty.

26 He runneth upon him, even on his neck, upon the thick bosses of his bucklers;

27 Because he covereth his face with his fatness, and maketh collops of fat on his flanks.

28 And he dwelleth in desolate cities, and in houses which no man inhabiteth, which are ready to become heaps.

29 He shall not be rich, neither shall his substance continue, neither shall he prolong the perfection thereof upon the earth.

30 He shall not depart out of darkness; the flame shall dry up his branches, and by the breath of his mouth shall he go away.

31 Let not him that is deceived trust in vanity: for vanity shall be his recompence.

32 It shall be accomplished before his time, and his branch shall not be green.

33 He shall shake off his unripe grape as the vine, and shall cast off his flower as the olive.

34 For the congregation of hypocrites shall be desolate, and fire shall consume the tabernacles of bribery.

35 They conceive mischief, and bring forth vanity, and their belly prepareth deceit."

16 Then Job (Iyov) answered and said:

2 "I have heard many such thing; miserable comforters are you all!

3 Shall vain words have an end? Or what emboldeneth you that you answerest?

4 I also could speak as you do, if your soul were in my soul's stead, I could heap up words against you, and shake mine head at you.

5 But I would strengthen you with my mouth, and the moving of my lips should relief your grief.

6 Though I speak, my grief is not relieved; and though I forbear, how am I eased?

7 But now he hath made me weary; You have made desolate all my company.

8 And You have filled me with wrinkles, which is a witness against me; and my leanness rising up in me beareth witness to my face.

9 He teareth me in his wrath, who hateth me; he gnasheth upon me with his teeth; mine enemy sharpeneth his eyes upon me.

10 They have gaped upon me with their mouth; they have smitten me upon the cheek reproachfully; they have gathered themselves together against me.

11 God (El) hath delivered me to the unjust, and turned me over into the hands of the wicked.

12 I was at ease, but He hath broken me asunder; He hath also taken me by my neck, and shaken me to pieces, and set me up for His mark.

13 His archers compass me round about, He cleaveth my reins asunder, and doth not spare; He poureth out my gall upon the ground.

14 He breaketh me with breach upon breach, He runneth upon me like a giant.

15 I have sewed sackcloth upon my skin, and defiled my horn in the dust.

16 My face is foul with weeping, and on my eyelids is the shadow of death;

17 Not for any injustice in mine hands; also my prayer is pure.

18 O earth, cover not you my blood, and let my cry have no place.

19 Also now, behold, my witness is in heaven, and my record is on high.

20 My friends scorn me, but mine eye poureth out tears unto God (Eloah).

21 O that one might plead for a man with God (Eloah), as a man pleadeth for his neighbour!

22 When a few years are come, then I shall go the way whence I shall not return.

17 My breath is corrupt, my days are extinct, the graves are ready for me.

2 Are there not mockers with me? And doth not mine eye continues in their provocation?

3 Lay down now, put me in a surety with You; who is he that will strike hands with me?

4 For you have hid their heart from understanding; therefore shalt You not exalt them.

5 He that speaketh flattery to his friends, even the eyes of his children shall fail.

6 He hath made me also a byword of the people; and aforetime I was as a tabret.

7 Mine eye also is dim by reason of sorrow, and all my members are as a shadow.

8 Upright men shall be astonied at this, and the innocent shall stir up himself against the hypocrite.

9 The righteous also shall hold on his way, and he that hath clean hands shall be stronger and stronger.

10 But as for you all, do you return, and come now, for I cannot find one wise man among you.

11 My days are past, my purposes are broken off, even the thoughts of my heart.

12 They change the night into day; the light is short because of darkness.

13 If I wait, the grave is mine house; I have made my bed in the darkness.

14 I have said to corruption, 'You are my father'; to the worm, 'You are my mother, and my sister.'

15 And where is now my hope? As for my hope, who shall see it?

16 They shall go down to the bars of the pit, when our rest together is in the dust.''

18 Then answered Bildad the Shuhite, and said:

2 ''How long will it be ere you make an end of words? Mark, and afterwards we will speak.

3 Wherefore are we counted as beasts, and reputed vile in your sight?

4 He teareth himself in his anger; shall the earth be forsaken for you? And shall the rock be removed out of his place?

5 Yea, the light of the wicked shall be put out, and the spark of his fire shall not shine.

6 The light shall be dark in his tabernacle, and his candle shall be put out with him.

7 The steps of his strength shall be straitened, and his own counsel shall cast him down.

8 For he is cast into a net by his own feet, and he walketh upon a snare.

9 The gin shall take him by the heel, and the robber shall prevail against him.

10 The snare is laid for him in the ground, and a trap for him in the way.

11 Terrors shall make him afraid on every side, and shall drive him to his feet.

12 His strength shall be hungerbitten, and destruction shall be ready at his side.

13 It shall devour the strength of his skin; even the firstborn of death shall devour his strength.

14 His confidence shall be rooted out of his tabernacle, and it shall bring him to the king of terrors.

15 It shall dwell in his tabernacle, because it is none of his; brimstone shall be scattered upon his habitation.

16 His roots shall be dried up beneath, and above shall his branch be cut off.

17 His remembrance shall perish from the earth, and he shall have no name in the street.

18 He shall be driven from light into darkness, and chased out of the world.

19 He shall neither have son nor nephew among his people, nor any remaining in his dwellings.

20 They that come after him shall be astonied at his day, as they that went before were affrighted.

21 Surely such are the dwellings of the wicked, and this is the place of him that knoweth not God (El)."

19 Then Job (Iyov) answered and said:
2 "How long will you vex my soul, and break me in pieces with words?

3 These ten times have you reproached me: you are not ashamed that you make yourselves strange to me.

4 And be it indeed that I have erred, mine error remaineth with myself.

5 If indeed you will magnify yourselves against me, and plead against me my reproach;

6 Know now that God (Eloah) hath overthrown me, and hath compassed me with His net.

7 Behold, I cry out of wrong, but I am not heard; I cry aloud, but there is no judgment.

8 He hath fenced up my way that I cannot pass, and He hath set darkness in my paths.

9 He hath stripped me of my glory, and taken the crown from my head.

10 He hath destroyed me on every side, and I am gone; and mine hope hath He removed like a tree.

11 He hath also kindled His wrath against me, and He counteth me unto Him as one of His enemies.

12 His troops come together, and raise up their way against me, and encamp round about my tabernacle.

13 He hath put my brethren far from me, and mine acquaintance are verily estranged from me.

14 My kinsfolk has failed, and my familiar friends have forgotten me.

15 They that dwell in mine house, and my maids, count me for a stranger; I am an alien in their sight.

16 I called my servant, and he gave me no answer; I intreated him with my mouth.

17 My breath is strange to my wife, though I intreated for the children's sake of mine own body.

18 Yea, young children despised me; I arose, and they spake against me.

19 All my inward friends abhorred me, and they whom I loved are turned against me.

20 My bone cleaveth to my skin and to my flesh, and I am escaped with the skin of my teeth.

21 Have pity upon me, have pity upon me, O you my friends; for the hand of God (Eloah) hath touched me.

22 Why do you persecute me as God (El), and are not satisfied with my flesh?

23 Oh that my words were now written! Oh that they were printed in a book!

24 That they were graven with an iron pen and lead in the rock forever!

25 For I know that my redeemer liveth, and that He shall stand at the latter day upon the earth;

26 And though after my skin worms destroy this body, yet in my flesh shall I see God (Eloah),

27 Whom I shall see for myself, and mine eyes shall behold, and not another; though my reins be consumed within me.

28 But you should say, 'Why persecute we him', seeing the root of the matter is found in me?

29 Be you afraid of the sword; for wrath bringeth the punishments of the sword, that you may know there is a judgment."

20 Then answered Zophar the Naamathite, and said:
2 "Therefore do my thoughts cause me to answer, and for this I make haste.

3 I have heard the check of my reproach, and the spirit of my understanding causeth me to answer.

4 Knowest you not this of old, since man was placed upon earth,

5 That the triumphing of the wicked is short, and the joy of the hypocrite but for a moment?

6 Though his excellency mounts up to the heavens, and his head reach unto the clouds;

7 Yet he shall perish forever like his own dung; they which have seen him shall say, 'Where is he?'

8 He shall fly away as a dream, and shall not be found; yea, he shall be chased away as a vision of the night.

9 The eye also which saw him shall see him no more; neither shall his place any more behold him.

10 His children shall seek to please the poor, and his hands shall restore their goods.

11 His bones are full of the sin of his youth, which shall lie down with him in the dust.

12 Though wickedness be sweet in his mouth, though he hides it under his tongue;

13 Though he spares it, and forsake it not; but keep it still within his mouth,

14 Yet his meat in his bowels is turned, it is the gall of asps within him.

15 He hath swallowed down riches, and he shall vomit them up again; God (El) shall cast them out of his belly.

16 He shall suck the poison of asps; the viper's tongue shall slay him.

17 He shall not see the rivers, the floods, the brooks of honey and butter.

18 That which he laboured for shall he restore, and shall not swallow it down; according to his substance shall the restitution be, and he shall not rejoice therein.

19 Because he hath oppressed and hath forsaken the poor; because he hath violently taken away a house which he builded not;

20 Surely he shall not feel quietness in his belly, he shall not save of that which he desired.

21 There shall none of his meat be left; therefore shall no man look for his goods.

22 In the fulness of his sufficiency he shall be in straits; every hand of the wicked shall come upon him.

23 When he is about to fill his belly, God (El) shall cast the fury of His wrath upon him, and shall rain it upon him while he is eating.

24 He shall flee from the iron weapon, and the bow of steel shall strike him through.

25 It is drawn, and cometh out of the body; yea, the glittering sword cometh out of his gall; terrors are upon him.

26 All darkness shall be hidden in his secret places; a fire not blown shall consume him; it shall go ill with him that is left in his tabernacle.

27 The heaven shall reveal his iniquity; and the earth shall rise up against him.

28 The increase of his house shall depart, and his goods shall flow away in the day of his wrath.

29 This is the portion of a wicked man from God (Elohim), and the heritage appointed unto him by God (El)."

21 But Job (Iyov) answered and said:

2 "Hear diligently my speech, and let this be your consolations.

3 Bear with me that I may speak; and after that I have spoken, mock on.

4 As for me, is my complaint to man? And if it was so, why should not my spirit be troubled?

5 Mark me, and be astonished, and lay your hand upon your mouth.

6 Even when I remember I am afraid, and trembling taketh hold on my flesh.

7 Wherefore do the wicked live, become old, yea, are mighty in power?

8 Their seed is established in their sight with them, and their offspring before their eyes.

9 Their houses are safe from fear, neither is the rod of God (Eloah) upon them.

10 Their bull gendereth, and faileth not; their cow calveth, and casteth not her calf.

11 They send forth their little ones like a flock, and their children dance.

12 They take the timbrel and harp, and rejoice at the sound of the organ.

13 They spend their days in wealth, and in a moment go down to the grave.

14 Therefore they say unto God (El), 'Depart from us, for we desire not the knowledge of Your ways.

15 What is the Almighty, that we should serve Him? And what profit should we have, if we pray unto Him?'

16 Lo, their good is not in their hand: the counsel of the wicked is far from me.

17 How oft is the candle of the wicked put out! And how oft cometh their destruction upon them! God (El) distributeth sorrows in His anger.

18 They are as stubble before the wind, and as chaff that the storm carrieth away.

19 God (Eloah) layeth up His iniquity for His children: He rewardeth him, and he shall know it.

20 His eyes shall see his destruction, and he shall drink of the wrath of the Almighty.

21 For what pleasure hath he in his house after him, when the number of his months is cut off

in the midst?

22 Shall any teach God (El) knowledge, seeing He judgeth those that are on high?

23 One dieth in his full strength, being wholly at ease and quiet.

24 His breasts are full of milk, and his bones are moistened with marrow.

25 And another dieth in the bitterness of his soul, and never eateth with pleasure.

26 They shall lie down alike in the dust, and the worms shall cover them.

27 Behold, I know your thoughts, and the devices which you wrongfully imagine against me.

28 For you say, 'Where is the house of the prince? And where are the dwelling places of the wicked?'

29 Have you not asked them that go by the way? And do you not know their tokens,

30 That the wicked is reserved to the day of destruction? They shall be brought forth to the day of wrath.

31 Who shall declare his way to his face? And who shall repay him what he hath done?

32 Yet shall he be brought to the grave, and shall remain in the tomb.

33 The clods of the valley shall be sweet unto him, and every man shall draw after him, as there are innumerable before him.

34 How then comfort you me in vain, seeing in your answers there remaineth falsehood?"

22 Then Eliphaz the Temanite answered and said:

2 "Can a man be profitable unto God (El), as he that is wise may be profitable unto himself?

3 Is it any pleasure to the Almighty, that you are righteous? Or is it gain to him, that you makest your ways perfect?

4 Will He reprove you for fear of you? will He enter with you into judgment?

5 Is not your wickedness great? And your iniquities infinite?

6 For you have taken a pledge from your brother for nothing, and stripped the naked of their clothing.

7 You have not given water to the weary to drink, and you have withholden bread from the hungry.

8 But as for the mighty man, he had the earth; and the honourable man dwelt in it.

9 You have sent widows away empty, and the arms of the fatherless have been broken.

10 Therefore snares are round about you, and sudden fear troubleth you;

11 Or darkness, that you canst not see; and abundance of waters cover you.

12 Is not God (Eloah) in the height of heaven? And behold the height of the stars, how high they are!

13 And you sayest, 'How doth God (El) know? Can He judge through the dark cloud?'

14 Thick clouds are a covering to Him, that He seeth not; and He walketh in the circuit of heaven.

15 Have you marked the old way which wicked men have trodden?

16 Who were cut down out of time, whose foundation was overflown with a flood;

17 Who said unto God (El), 'Depart from us; and what can the Almighty do for them?'

18 Yet he filled their houses with good things; but the counsel of the wicked is far from me.

19 The righteous see it, and are glad; and the innocent laugh them to scorn.

20 Whereas our substance is not cut down, but the remnant of them the fire consumeth.

21 Acquaint now yourself with him, and be at peace; thereby good shall come unto you.

22 Receive, please, the instruction from His mouth, and lay up His words in your heart.

23 If you return to the Almighty, you shalt be built up, you shalt put away iniquity far from your tabernacles.

24 Then shalt you lay up gold as dust, and the gold of Ophir as the stones of the brooks.

25 Yea, the Almighty shall be your defence, and you shalt have plenty of silver.

26 For then shalt you have your delight in the Almighty, and shalt lift up your face unto God (Eloah).

27 You shalt make your prayer unto Him, and He shall hear you, and you shalt pay your vows.

28 You shalt also decree a thing, and it shall be established unto you; and the light shall shine upon your ways.

29 When men are cast down, then you shalt say, 'There is lifting up'; and He shall save the humble person.

30 He delivers even the unclean. So shall you be delivered by the cleanness of your hands."

23 Then Job (Iyov) answered and said:
2 "Even today is my complaint bitter; my stroke is heavier than my groaning.

3 Oh that I knew where I might find Him! That I might come even to His seat!

4 I would order my cause before Him, and fill my mouth with arguments.

5 I would know the words which He would answer me, and understand what He would say unto me.

6 Will He plead against me with His great power? No; but He would put strength in me.

7 There the righteous might dispute with Him; so should I be delivered forever from my Judge.

8 Behold, I go forward, but He is not there; and backward, but I cannot perceive Him;

9 On the left hand, where He doth work, but I cannot behold Him; He hideth Himself on the right hand, that I cannot see Him.

10 But He knoweth the way that I take: when He hath tried me, I shall come forth as gold.

11 My foot hath held His steps, His way have I kept, and not declined.

12 Neither have I gone back from the commandment of His lips; I have esteemed the words of His mouth more than my necessary food.

13 But He is in one mind, and who can turn Him? And what His soul desireth, even that He doeth.

14 For He performeth the thing that is appointed for me, and many such things are with Him.

15 Therefore am I troubled at His presence; when I consider, I am afraid of Him.

16 For God (El) maketh my heart soft, and the Almighty troubleth me;

17 Because I was not cut off before the darkness, neither hath He covered the darkness from my face.

24 Why, seeing times are not hidden from the Almighty, do they that know Him not see His days?

2 Some remove the landmarks; they violently take away flocks, and feed thereof.

3 They drive away the ass of the fatherless, they take the widow's ox for a pledge.

4 They turn the needy out of the way; the poor of the earth hide themselves together.

5 Behold, as wild asses in the desert, go they forth to their work; rising betimes for a prey; the wilderness yieldeth food for them and for their children.

6 They reap every one his corn in the field; and they gather the vintage of the wicked.

7 They cause the naked to lodge without clothing, that they have no covering in the cold.

8 They are wet with the showers of the mountains, and embrace the rock for want of a shelter.

9 They pluck the fatherless from the breast, and take a pledge of the poor.

10 They cause him to go naked without clothing, and they take away the sheaf from the hungry;

11 Which make oil within their walls, and tread their winepresses, and suffer thirst.

12 Men groan from out of the city, and the soul of the wounded crieth out; yet God (Eloah) layeth not folly to them.

13 They are of those that rebel against the light; they know not the ways thereof, nor abide in the paths thereof.

14 The murderer rising with the light killeth the poor and needy, and in the night is as a thief.

15 The eye also of the adulterer waiteth for the twilight, saying, 'No eye shall see me'; and disguiseth his face.

16 In the dark they dig through houses, which they had marked for themselves in the daytime; they know not the light.

17 For the morning is to them even as the shadow of death; if one knows them, they are in the terrors of the shadow of death.

18 He is swift as the waters; their portion is cursed in the earth; he beholdeth not the way of the vineyards.

19 Drought and heat consume the snow waters; so doth the grave those which have sinned.

20 The womb shall forget him; the worm shall feed sweetly on him; he shall be no more remembered; and wickedness shall be broken as a tree.

21 He evil entreateth the barren that beareth not; and doeth not good to the widow.

22 He draweth also the mighty with his power: he riseth up, and no man is sure of life.

23 Though it be given him to be in safety, whereon he resteth; yet his eyes are upon their ways.

24 They are exalted for a little while, but are gone and brought low; they are taken out of the way as all other, and cut off as the tops of the ears of corn.

25 And if it be not so now, who will make me a liar, and make my speech nothing worth?"

25 Then answered Bildad the Shuhite, and said:

2 "Dominion and fear are with Him, He maketh peace in His high places.

3 Is there any number of His armies? And upon whom doth not His light arises?

4 How then can man be justified with God (El)? Or how can he be clean that is born of a woman?

5 Behold even to the moon, and it shineth not; yea, the stars are not pure in His sight.

6 How much less man, that is a worm? And the son of man, who is a worm?"

26 But Job (Iyov) answered and said:

2 "How have you helped him that is without power? How savest you the arm that hath no strength?

3 How have you counselled him that hath no wisdom? And how have you plentifully declared the thing as it is?

4 To whom have you uttered words? And whose spirit came from you?

5 Dead things are formed from under the waters, and the inhabitants thereof.

6 Hell (Sheol) is naked before him, and destruction hath no covering.

7 He stretcheth out the north over the empty place, and hangeth the earth upon nothing.

8 He bindeth up the waters in his thick clouds; and the cloud is not rent under them.

9 He holdeth back the face of His throne, and spreadeth His cloud upon it.

10 He hath compassed the waters with bounds, until the day and night come to an end.

11 The pillars of heaven tremble and are astonished at His reproof.

12 He divideth the sea with His power, and by His understanding He smiteth through the proud.

13 By His Spirit (Ruach) He hath garnished the heavens; His hand hath formed the crooked serpent.

14 Behold, these are parts of His ways, but how little a portion is heard of Him? But the thunder of His power who can understand?"

27 Moreover Job (Iyov) continued his parable, and said:

2 "As God (El) liveth, who hath taken away my judgment; and the Almighty, who hath vexed my soul;

3 That while my spirit is in me, and the breath of God (Eloah) is in my nostrils;

4 My lips shall not speak wickedness, nor my tongue utter deceit.

5 Far be it from me that I should justify you; till I die I will not remove mine integrity from me.

6 My righteousness I hold fast, and will not let it go; my heart shall not reproach me so long as I live.

7 Let mine enemy be as the wicked, and he that riseth up against me as the unrighteous.

8 For what is the hope of the hypocrite, though he hath gained, when God (Eloah) taketh away his soul?

9 Will God (El) hear his cry when trouble cometh upon him?

10 Will he delight himself in the Almighty? Will he always call upon God (Eloah)?

11 I will teach you by the hand of God (El); that which is with the Almighty will I not conceal.

12 Behold, all you yourselves have seen it; why then are you thus altogether vain?

13 This is the portion of a wicked man with God (El), and the heritage of oppressors, which they shall receive of the Almighty:

14 If his children be multiplied, it is for the sword; and his offspring shall not be satisfied with bread.

15 Those that remain of him shall be buried in death; and his widows shall not weep.

16 Though he heaps up silver as the dust, and prepare raiment as the clay;

17 He may prepare it, but the just shall put it on, and the innocent shall divide the silver.

18 He buildeth his house as a moth, and as a booth that the keeper maketh.

19 The rich man shall lie down, but he shall not be gathered; he openeth his eyes, and he is not.

20 Terrors take hold on him as waters, a tempest stealeth him away in the night.

21 The east wind carrieth him away, and he departeth; and as a storm hurleth him out of his place.

22 For God (El) shall cast upon him, and not spare; he would fain flee out of his hand.

23 Men shall clap their hands at him, and shall hiss him out of his place.

28 Surely there is a vein for the silver, and a place for gold where they fine it.

2 Iron is taken out of the earth, and brass is molten out of the stone.

3 He setteth an end to darkness, and searcheth out all perfection; the stones of darkness, and

the shadow of death.

4 The flood breaketh out from the inhabitant; even the waters forgotten of the foot; they are dried up, they are gone away from men.

5 As for the earth, out of it cometh bread; and under it is turned up as it was fire.

6 The stones of it are the place of sapphires: and it hath dust of gold.

7 There is a path which no fowl knoweth, and which the vulture's eye hath not seen:

8 The lion's whelps have not trodden it, nor the fierce lion passed by it.

9 He putteth forth his hand upon the rock; he overturneth the mountains by the roots.

10 He cutteth out rivers among the rocks; and his eye seeth every precious thing.

11 He bindeth the floods from overflowing; and the thing that is hid bringeth he forth to light.

12 But where shall wisdom be found? And where is the place of understanding?

13 Man knoweth not the price thereof; neither is it found in the land of the living.

14 The depth saith, 'It is not in me'; and the sea saith, 'It is not with me.'

15 It cannot be gotten for gold, neither shall silver be weighed for the price thereof.

16 It cannot be valued with the gold of Ophir, with the precious onyx, or the sapphire.

17 The gold and the crystal cannot equal it; and the exchange of it shall not be for jewels of fine gold.

18 No mention shall be made of coral, or of pearls; for the price of wisdom is above rubies.

19 The topaz of Ethiopia (Kush) shall not equal it, neither shall it be valued with pure gold.

20 Whence then cometh wisdom? And where is the place of understanding?

21 Seeing it is hid from the eyes of all living, and kept close from the fowls of the air.

22 Destruction and Death say, 'We have heard the fame thereof with our ears.'

23 God (Elohim) understandeth the way thereof, and He knoweth the place thereof.

24 For He looketh to the ends of the earth, and seeth under the whole heaven;

25 To make the weight for the winds; and He weigheth the waters by measure.

26 When He made a decree for the rain, and a way for the lightning of the thunder:

27 Then did He see it, and declare it; He prepared it, yea, and searched it out.

28 And unto man He said, 'Behold, the fear of the Lord (Adonai), that is wisdom; and to depart from evil is understanding.'"

29 Moreover Job (Iyov) continued his parable, and said:

2 "Oh that I was as in months past, as in the days when God (Eloah) preserved me;

3 When His candle shined upon my head, and when by His light I walked through darkness;

4 As I was in the days of my youth, when the secret of God (Eloah) was upon my tabernacle;

5 When the Almighty was yet with me, when my children were about me;

6 When I washed my steps with butter, and the rock poured me out rivers of oil;

7 When I went out to the gate through the city, when I prepared my seat in the street!

8 The young men saw me, and hid themselves; and the aged arose, and stood up.

9 The princes refrained talking, and laid their hand on their mouth.

10 The nobles held their peace, and their tongue cleaved to the roof of their mouth.

11 When the ear heard me, then it blessed me; and when the eye saw me, it gave witness to me:

12 Because I delivered the poor that cried, and the fatherless, and him that had none to help him.

13 The blessing of him that was ready to perish came upon me; and I caused the widow's heart to sing for joy.

14 I put on righteousness, and it clothed me; my judgment was as a robe and a diadem.

15 I was eyes to the blind, and feet was I to the lame.

16 I was a father to the poor; and the cause which I knew not I searched out.

17 And I broke the jaws of the wicked, and plucked the spoil out of his teeth.

18 Then I said, 'I shall die in my nest, and I shall multiply my days as the sand.

19 My root was spread out by the waters, and the dew lay all night upon my branch.

20 My glory was fresh in me, and my bow was renewed in my hand.'

21 Unto me men gave ear, and waited, and kept silence at my counsel.

22 After my words they spake not again; and my speech dropped upon them.

23 And they waited for me as for the rain; and they opened their mouth wide as for the latter

rain.

24 If I laughed on them, they believed it not; and the light of my countenance they cast not down.

25 I chose out their way, and sat chief, and dwelt as a king in the army, as one that comforteth the mourners.

30 But now they that are younger than I have me in derision, whose fathers I would have disdained to have set with the dogs of my flock.

2 Yea, whereto might the strength of their hands profit me, in whom old age was perished?

3 For want and famine they were solitary; fleeing into the wilderness in former time desolate and waste.

4 Who cut up mallows by the bushes, and juniper roots for their food.

5 They were driven forth from among men, (they cried after them as after a thief;)

6 To dwell in the clifts of the valleys, in caves of the earth, and in the rocks.

7 Among the bushes they brayed; under the nettles they were gathered together.

8 They were children of fools, yea, children of base men; they were viler than the earth.

9 And now am I their song, yea, I am their byword.

10 They abhor me, they flee far from me, and spare not to spit in my face.

11 Because he hath loosed my cord, and afflicted me, they have also let loose the bridle before me.

12 Upon my right hand rise the youth; they push away my feet, and they raise up against me the ways of their destruction.

13 They mar my path, they set forward my disaster, they have no helper.

14 They came upon me as a wide breaking in of waters; in the desolation they rolled themselves upon me.

15 Terrors are turned upon me; they pursue my soul as the wind: and my welfare passeth away as a cloud.

16 And now my soul is poured out upon me; the days of affliction have taken hold upon me.

17 My bones are pierced in me in the night season, and my sinews take no rest.

18 By the great force of my disease is my garment changed; it bindeth me about as the collar of my coat.

19 He hath cast me into the mire, and I am become like dust and ashes.

20 I cry unto you, and you dost not hear me; I stand up, and you regardest me not.

21 You are become cruel to me: with your strong hand you opposest yourself against me.

22 You liftest me up to the wind; you causest me to ride upon it, and dissolvest my substance.

23 For I know that you wilt bring me to death, and to the house appointed for all living.

24 Howbeit he will not stretch out his hand to the grave, though they cry in his destruction.

25 Did not I weep for him that was in trouble? was not my soul grieved for the poor?

26 When I looked for good, then evil came unto me; and when I waited for light, there came darkness.

27 My bowels boiled, and rested not; the days of affliction prevented me.

28 I went mourning without the sun; I stood up, and I cried in the congregation.

29 I am a brother to dragons, and a companion to owls.

30 My skin is black upon me, and my bones are burned with heat.

31 My harp also is turned to mourning, and my organ into the voice of them that weep.

31 I made a covenant with mine eyes; why then should I think upon a maid?

2 For what portion of God (Eloah) is there from above? And what inheritance of the Almighty from on high?

3 Is not destruction to the wicked? And a strange punishment to the workers of iniquity?

4 Doth not He see my ways, and count all my steps?

5 If I have walked with vanity, or if my foot hath hasted to deceit;

6 Let me be weighed in an even balance, that God (Eloah) may know mine integrity.

7 If my step hath turned out of the way, and mine heart walked after mine eyes, and if any blot hath cleaved to mine hands;

8 Then let me sow, and let another eat; yea, let my offspring be rooted out.

9 If mine heart have been deceived by a woman, or if I have laid wait at my neighbour's door;

10 Then let my wife grind unto another, and let others bow down upon her.

11 For this is a heinous crime; yea, it is an iniquity to be punished by the judges.

12 For it is a fire that consumeth to destruction, and would root out all mine increase.

13 If I did despise the cause of my manservant or of my maidservant, when they contended with me;

14 What then shall I do when God (El) riseth up? And when He visiteth, what shall I answer Him?

15 Did not He that made me in the womb make Him? And did not the same One fashion us in the womb?

16 If I have withheld the poor from their desire, or have caused the eyes of the widow to fail;

17 Or have eaten my morsel myself alone, and the fatherless hath not eaten thereof;

18 (For from my youth he was brought up with me, as with a father, and I have guided her from my mother's womb;)

19 If I have seen any perish for want of clothing, or any poor without covering;

20 If his loins have not blessed me, and if he were not warmed with the fleece of my sheep;

21 If I have lifted up my hand against the fatherless, when I saw my help in the gate;

22 Then let mine arm fall from my shoulder blade, and mine arm be broken from the bone.

23 For destruction from God (El) was a terror to me, and by reason of His majesty I could not endure.

24 If I have made gold my hope, or have said to the fine gold, You are my confidence;

25 If I rejoiced because my wealth was great, and because mine hand had gotten much;

26 If I beheld the sun when it shined, or the moon walking in brightness;

27 And my heart hath been secretly enticed, or my mouth hath kissed my hand;

28 This also were an iniquity to be punished by the judge, for I should have denied the God (El) that is above.

29 If I rejoiced at the destruction of him that hated me, or lifted up myself when evil found him.

30 Neither have I allowed my mouth to sin by wishing a curse to his soul.

31 If the men of my tabernacle said not, 'Oh that we had of his flesh! We cannot be satisfied.'

32 The stranger did not lodge in the street, but I opened my doors to the traveller.

33 If I covered my transgressions as Adam, by hiding mine iniquity in my bosom,

34 Did I fear a great multitude, or did the contempt of families terrify me, that I kept silence, and went not out of the door?

35 Oh that one would hear me! Behold, my desire is, that the Almighty would answer me, and that mine adversary had written a book.

36 Surely I would take it upon my shoulder, and bind it as a crown to me.

37 I would declare unto Him the number of my steps; as a prince would I go near unto Him.

38 If my land cry against me, or that the furrows likewise thereof complain;

39 If I have eaten the fruits thereof without money, or have caused the owners thereof to lose their life:

40 Let thistles grow instead of wheat, and cockle instead of barley. The words of Job (Iyov) are ended.

32 So these three men ceased to answer Job (Iyov), because he was righteous in his own eyes.

2 Then was kindled the wrath of Elihu the son of Barachel the Buzite, of the kindred of Ram; against Job (Iyov) was his wrath kindled, because he justified himself rather than God (Elohim).

3 Also against his three friends was his wrath kindled, because they had found no answer, and yet had condemned Job (Iyov).

4 Now Elihu had waited till Job (Iyov) had spoken, because they were elder than he.

5 When Elihu saw that there was no answer in the mouth of these three men, then his wrath was kindled.

6 And Elihu the son of Barachel the Buzite answered and said: "I am young, and you are very old; wherefore I was afraid, and durst not shew you mine opinion.

7 I said, 'Days should speak, and multitude of years should teach wisdom.'

8 But there is a spirit in man; and the inspiration of the Almighty giveth them understanding.

9 Great men are not always wise: neither do the aged understand judgment.

10 Therefore I said, 'Hearken to me; I also will shew mine opinion.'

11 Behold, I waited for your words; I gave ear to your reasons, whilst you searched out what to say.

12 Yea, I attended unto you, and, behold, there was none of you that convinced Job (Iyov), or that answered his words:

13 Lest you should say, 'We have found out wisdom'; God (El) thrusteth him down, not man.

14 Now he hath not directed his words against me; neither will I answer him with your speeches.

15 They were amazed, they answered no more: they left off speaking.

16 When I had waited, (for they spake not, but stood still, and answered no more;)

17 I said, I will answer also my part, I also will shew mine opinion.

18 For I am full of matter, the spirit within me constraineth me.

19 Behold, my belly is as wine which hath no vent; it is ready to burst like new bottles.

20 I will speak, that I may be refreshed; I will open my lips and answer.

21 Let me not, I pray, show partiality to any man, neither let me give flattering titles unto man.

22 For I know not to give flattering titles; in so doing my Maker would soon take me away.

33 Wherefore, Job (Iyov), please hear my speeches, and hearken to all my words.

2 Behold, now I have opened my mouth, my tongue hath spoken in my mouth.

3 My words shall be of the uprightness of my heart; and my lips shall utter knowledge clearly.

4 The Spirit (Ruach) of God (El) hath made me, and the breath of the Almighty hath given me life.

5 If you canst answer me, set your words in order before me, stand up.

6 Behold, I am according to your wish in God (El)'s stead; I also am formed out of the clay.

7 Behold, my terror shall not make you afraid, neither shall my hand be heavy upon you.

8 Surely you have spoken in mine hearing, and I have heard the voice of your words, saying,

9 'I am clean without transgression, I am innocent; neither is there iniquity in me.

10 Behold, he findeth occasions against me, he counteth me for his enemy,

11 He putteth my feet in the stocks, He marketh all my paths.'

12 Behold, in this you are not just: I will answer you, that God (Eloah) is greater than man.

13 Why dost you strive against Him? For He giveth not account of any of His matters.

14 For God (El) speaketh once, yea twice, yet man perceiveth it not.

15 In a dream, in a vision of the night, when deep sleep falleth upon men, in slumberings upon the bed;

16 Then He openeth the ears of men, and sealeth their instruction,

17 That He may withdraw man from his purpose, and hide pride from man.

18 He keepeth back his soul from the pit, and his life from perishing by the sword.

19 He is chastened also with pain upon his bed, and the multitude of his bones with strong pain,

20 So that his life abhorreth bread, and his soul dainty meat.

21 His flesh is consumed away, that it cannot be seen; and his bones that were not seen stick out.

22 Yea, his soul draweth near unto the grave, and his life to the destroyers.

23 If there be a messenger with him, an interpreter, one among a thousand, to shew unto man his uprightness:

24 Then He is gracious unto him, and saith, 'Deliver him from going down to the pit; I have found a ransom';

25 His flesh shall be fresher than a child's; he shall return to the days of his youth.

26 He shall pray unto God (Eloah), and He will be favourable unto him; and he shall see His face with joy, for He will render unto man His righteousness.

27 He looketh upon men, and if any say, I have sinned, and perverted that which was right, and it profited me not;

28 He will deliver his soul from going into the pit, and his life shall see the light.

29 Lo, all these things worketh God (El) oftentimes with man,

30 To bring back his soul from the pit, to be enlightened with the light of the living.

31 Mark well, O Job (Iyov), hearken unto me: hold your peace, and I will speak.

32 If you have any thing to say, answer me; speak, for I desire to justify you.

33 If not, hearken unto me; hold your peace, and I shall teach you wisdom."

34 Furthermore Elihu answered and said: 2 "Hear my words, O you wise men; and give ear unto me, you that have knowledge.

3 For the ear trieth words, as the mouth tasteth meat.

4 Let us choose to us judgment; let us know among ourselves what is good.

5 For Job (Iyov) hath said, 'I am righteous, but God (El) hath taken away my justice;

6 Should I lie against my right? My wound is

incurable without transgression.'

7 What man is like Job (Iyov), who drinketh up scorning like water?

8 Which goeth in company with the workers of iniquity, and walketh with wicked men.

9 For he hath said, 'It profiteth a man nothing that he should delight himself with God (Elohim).'

10 Therefore hearken unto me, you men of understanding: far be it from God (El), that he should do wickedness; and from the Almighty, that he should commit iniquity.

11 For the work of a man shall He render unto him, and cause every man to find according to his ways.

12 Yea, surely God (El) will not do wickedly, neither will the Almighty pervert justice.

13 Who hath given Him a charge over the earth? Or who hath disposed the whole world?

14 If He set His heart upon man, if He gather unto Himself His Spirit and His breath;

15 All flesh shall perish together, and man shall turn again unto dust.

16 If now you have understanding, hear this; hearken to the voice of my words:

17 Shall even he that hateth right govern? And wilt you condemn Him that is most just?

18 Is it fit to say to a king, 'Scoundrel one (Beliyaal)!' And to nobles, 'Wicked ones (Rasha)!'?

19 How much less to Him that accepteth not the persons of princes, nor regardeth the rich more than the poor? For they all are the work of His hands.

20 In a moment shall they die, and the people shall be troubled at midnight, and pass away; and the mighty shall be taken away without hand.

21 For His eyes are upon the ways of man, and He seeth all his goings.

22 There is no darkness, nor shadow of death, where the workers of iniquity may hide themselves.

23 For He will not lay upon man more than right; that he should enter into judgment with God (El).

24 He shall break in pieces mighty men without number, and set others in their stead.

25 Therefore He knoweth their works, and He overturneth them in the night, so that they are destroyed.

26 He striketh them as wicked men in the open sight of others;

27 Because they turned back from Him, and would not consider any of His ways,

28 So that they cause the cry of the poor to come unto Him, and He heareth the cry of the afflicted.

29 When He giveth quietness, who then can make trouble? And when He hideth His face, who then can behold Him? Whether it be done against a nation, or against a man only;

30 That the hypocrite reign not, lest the people be ensnared.

31 Surely it is meet to be said unto God (El), I have borne chastisement, I will not offend anymore;

32 That which I see not teach You me; if I have done iniquity, I will do no more.

33 Should it be according to your mind? He will recompense it, whether you refuse, or whether you choose; and not I; therefore speak what you knowest.

34 Let men of understanding tell me, and let a wise man hearken unto me:

35 'Job (Iyov) hath spoken without knowledge, and his words were without wisdom.'

36 My desire is that Job (Iyov) may be tried unto the end because of his answers for wicked men!

37 For he addeth rebellion unto his sin, he clappeth his hands among us, and multiplieth his words against God (El)."

35 Elihu spake moreover, and said:

2 "Thinkest you this to be right, that you saidst, 'My righteousness is more than God (El)'s'?

3 For you saidst, 'What advantage will it be unto you? And, 'What profit shall I have, if I be cleansed from my sin?'

4 I will answer you, and your companions with you.

5 Look unto the heavens, and see; and behold the clouds which are higher than you.

6 If you sinnest, what doest you against Him? Or if your transgressions be multiplied, what doest you unto Him?

7 If you be righteous, what givest you Him? Or what receiveth He of your hand?

8 Your wickedness may hurt a man as you are; and your righteousness may profit the son of man.

9 By reason of the multitude of oppressions

they make the oppressed to cry; they cry out by reason of the arm of the mighty.

10 But none saith, 'Where is God (Eloah) my Maker, who giveth songs in the night;

11 Who teacheth us more than the beasts of the earth, and maketh us wiser than the fowls of heaven?'

12 There they cry, but none giveth answer, because of the pride of evil men.

13 Surely God (El) will not hear vanity, neither will the Almighty regard it.

14 Although you sayest you shalt not see Him, yet judgment is before Him; therefore trust you in Him.

15 But now, because it is not so, He hath visited in His anger; yet He knoweth it not in great extremity.

16 Therefore doth Job (Iyov) open his mouth in vain; he multiplieth words without knowledge.

36 Elihu also proceeded, and said, 2 "Bear with me a little, and I will shew you that I have yet to speak on God (Eloah)'s behalf.

3 I will fetch my knowledge from afar, and will ascribe righteousness to my Maker.

4 For truly my words shall not be false; he that is perfect in knowledge is with you.

5 Behold, God (El) is mighty, and despiseth not any; He is mighty in strength and wisdom.

6 He preserveth not the life of the wicked, but giveth right to the poor.

7 He withdraweth not His eyes from the righteous; but with kings are they on the throne; yea, He doth establish them forever, and they are exalted.

8 And if they be bound in fetters, and be holden in cords of affliction;

9 Then He sheweth them their work, and their transgressions that they have exceeded.

10 He openeth also their ear to discipline, and commandeth that they return from iniquity.

11 If they obey and serve Him, they shall spend their days in prosperity, and their years in pleasures.

12 But if they obey not, they shall perish by the sword, and they shall die without knowledge.

13 But the hypocrites in heart heap up wrath; they cry not when He bindeth them.

14 They die in youth, and their life is among the unclean.

15 He delivereth the poor in his affliction, and

openeth their ears in oppression.

16 Even so would He has removed you out of the strait into a broad place, where there is no straitness; and that which should be set on your table should be full of fatness.

17 But you have fulfilled the judgment of the wicked; judgment and justice take hold on you.

18 Because there is wrath, beware lest He take you away with His stroke; then a great ransom cannot deliver you.

19 Will He esteem your riches? No, not gold, nor all the forces of strength.

20 Desire not the night, when people are cut off in their place.

21 Take heed, regard not iniquity, for this have you chosen rather than affliction.

22 Behold, God (El) exalteth by His power; who teacheth like Him?

23 Who hath enjoined Him His way? Or who can say, 'You have wrought iniquity?'

24 Remember that you magnify His work, which men behold.

25 Every man may see it; man may behold it afar off.

26 Behold, God (El) is great, and we know Him not, neither can the number of His years be searched out.

27 For He maketh small the drops of water; they pour down rain according to the vapour thereof,

28 Which the clouds do drop and distil upon man abundantly.

29 Also can any understand the spreadings of the clouds, or the noise of His tabernacle?

30 Behold, He spreadeth His light upon it, and covereth the bottom of the sea.

31 For by them judgeth He the people; He giveth food in abundance.

32 With clouds He covereth the light; and commandeth it not to shine by the cloud that cometh betwixt.

33 The noise thereof sheweth concerning it, the cattle also concerning the vapour.

37 At this also my heart trembleth, and is moved out of his place.

2 Hear attentively the noise of His voice, and the sound that goeth out of His mouth.

3 He directeth it under the whole heaven, and His lightning unto the ends of the earth.

4 After it a voice roareth; He thundereth with the voice of His excellency; and He will not stay them when His voice is heard.

5 God (El) thundereth marvellously with His voice; great things doeth He, which we cannot comprehend.

6 For He saith to the snow, 'Be you on the earth'; likewise to the small rain, and to the great rain of His strength.

7 He sealeth up the hand of every man; that all men may know His work.

8 Then the beasts go into dens, and remain in their places.

9 Out of the south cometh the whirlwind; and cold out of the north.

10 By the breath of God (El) frost is given; and the breadth of the waters is straitened.

11 Also by watering He wearieth the thick cloud; He scattereth His bright cloud:

12 And it is turned round about by His counsels, that they may do whatsoever He commandeth them upon the face of the world in the earth.

13 He causeth it to come, whether for correction, or for His land, or for mercy.

14 Hearken unto this, O Job (Iyov); stand still, and consider the wondrous works of God (El).

15 Dost you know when God (Eloah) disposed them, and caused the light of His cloud to shine?

16 Dost you know the balancings of the clouds, the wondrous works of Him which is perfect in knowledge?

17 How your garments are warm, when He quieteth the earth by the south wind?

18 Have you with Him spread out the sky, which is strong, and as a molten looking glass?

19 Teach us what we shall say unto Him; for we cannot order our speech by reason of darkness.

20 Shall it be told Him that I speak? If a man speaks, surely he shall be swallowed up.

21 And now men see not the bright light which is in the clouds; but the wind passeth, and cleanseth them.

22 Fair weather cometh out of the north: with God (Eloah) is awesome majesty.

23 Touching the Almighty, we cannot find Him out; He is excellent in power, and in judgment, and in plenty of justice; He will not afflict.

24 Men do therefore fear Him; He consider no men who think they are wise of heart."

38 Then יהוה answered Job (Iyov) out of the whirlwind, and said:

2 "Who is this that darkeneth counsel by words without knowledge?

3 Gird up now your loins like a man; for I will demand of you, and answer you Me.

4 Where wast you when I laid the foundations of the earth? Declare, if you have understanding.

5 Who hath laid the measures thereof, if you knowest? Or who hath stretched the line upon it?

6 Whereupon are the foundations thereof fastened? Or who laid the corner stone thereof;

7 When the morning stars sang together, and all the sons of God (Elohim) shouted for joy?

8 Or who shut up the sea with doors, when it broke forth, as if it had issued out of the womb?

9 When I made the cloud the garment thereof, and thick darkness a swaddlingband for it,

10 And broke up for it My decreed place, and set bars and doors,

11 And said, 'Hitherto shalt you come, but no further; and here shall your proud waves be stayed!'

12 Have you commanded the morning since your days; and caused the dayspring to know his place,

13 That it might take hold of the ends of the earth, that the wicked might be shaken out of it?

14 It is turned as clay to the seal; and they stand as a garment.

15 And from the wicked their light is withholden, and the high arm shall be broken.

16 Have you entered into the springs of the sea? Or have you walked in the search of the depth?

17 Have the gates of death been opened unto you? Or have you seen the doors of the shadow of death?

18 Have you perceived the breadth of the earth? Declare if you knowest it all.

19 Where is the way where light dwelleth? And as for darkness, where is the place thereof,

20 That you shouldest take it to the bound thereof, and that you shouldest know the paths to the house thereof?

21 Knowest you it, because you wast then born? Or because the number of your days is great?

22 Have you entered into the treasures of the snow? Or have you seen the treasures of the hail,

23 Which I have reserved against the time of trouble, against the day of battle and war?

24 By what way is the light parted, which scattereth the east wind upon the earth?

25 Who hath divided a watercourse for the overflowing of waters, or a way for the lightning of thunder;

26 To cause it to rain on the earth, where no man is; on the wilderness, wherein there is no man;

27 To satisfy the desolate and waste ground; and to cause the bud of the tender herb to spring forth?

28 Hath the rain a father? Or who hath begotten the drops of dew?

29 Out of whose womb came the ice? And the hoary frost of heaven, who hath gendered it?

30 The waters are hid as with a stone, and the face of the deep is frozen.

31 Canst you bind the sweet influences of Pleiades, or loose the bands of Orion?

32 Canst you bring forth Mazzaroth in his season? Or canst you guide Arcturus with his sons?

33 Knowest you the ordinances of heaven? Canst you set the dominion thereof in the earth?

34 Canst you lift up your voice to the clouds, that abundance of waters may cover you?

35 Canst you send lightnings, that they may go, and say unto you, 'Here we are!'?

36 Who hath put wisdom in the inward parts? Or who hath given understanding to the heart?

37 Who can number the clouds in wisdom? Or who can stay the bottles of heaven,

38 When the dust groweth into hardness, and the clods cleave fast together?

39 Wilt you hunt the prey for the lion? or fill the appetite of the young lions,

40 When they couch in their dens, and abide in the covert to lie in wait?

41 Who provideth for the raven his food? When his young ones cry unto God (El), they wander for lack of food?

39 Knowest you the time when the wild goats of the rock bring forth? Or canst you mark when the hinds do calve?

2 Canst you number the months that they fulfil? Or knowest you the time when they bring forth?

3 They bow themselves, they bring forth their young ones, they cast out their sorrows.

4 Their young ones are in good liking, they grow up with corn; they go forth, and return not unto them.

5 Who hath sent out the wild ass free? Or who hath loosed the bands of the wild ass?

6 Whose house I have made the wilderness, and the barren land his dwellings.

7 He scorneth the multitude of the city, neither regardeth he the crying of the driver.

8 The range of the mountains is his pasture, and he searcheth after every green thing.

9 Will the unicorn be willing to serve you, or abide by your crib?

10 Canst you bind the unicorn with his band in the furrow? Or will he harrow the valleys after you?

11 Wilt you trust him, because his strength is great? Or wilt you leave your labour to him?

12 Wilt you believe him, that he will bring home your seed, and gather it into your barn?

13 Gavest you the goodly wings unto the peacocks? Or wings and feathers unto the ostrich?

14 Which leaveth her eggs in the earth, and warmeth them in dust,

15 And forgetteth that the foot may crush them, or that the wild beast may break them.

16 She is hardened against her young ones, as though they were not hers; her labour is in vain without fear;

17 Because God (Eloah) hath deprived her of wisdom, neither hath he imparted to her understanding.

18 What time she lifteth up herself on high, she scorneth the horse and his rider.

19 Have you given the horse strength? Have you clothed his neck with thunder?

20 Canst you make him afraid as a grasshopper? His majestic snorting strikes terror.

21 He paweth in the valley, and rejoiceth in his strength; he goeth on to meet the armed men.

22 He mocketh at fear, and is not affrighted; neither turneth he back from the sword.

23 The quiver rattleth against him, the glittering spear and the shield.

24 He swalloweth the ground with fierceness and rage; neither believeth he that it is the sound of the trumpet.

25 He saith among the trumpets, 'Ha, ha; and he smelleth the battle afar off, the thunder of the captains, and the shouting.

26 Doth the hawk fly by your wisdom, and stretch her wings toward the south?

27 Doth the eagle mounts up at your command, and make her nest on high?

28 She dwelleth and abideth on the rock, upon the crag of the rock, and the strong place.

29 From thence she seeketh the prey, and her eyes behold afar off.

30 Her young ones also suck up blood; and

where the slain are, there is she."

40 Moreover יהוה answered Job (Iyov), and said:

2 "Shall he that contendeth with the Almighty instruct Him? He that reproveth God (Eloah), let him answer it."

3 Then Job (Iyov) answered יהוה, and said:

4 "Behold, I am vile; what shall I answer You? I will lay mine hand upon my mouth.

5 Once have I spoken; but I will not answer; yea, twice; but I will proceed no further.

6 Then answered יהוה unto Job (Iyov) out of the whirlwind, and said,

7 Gird up your loins now like a man; I will demand of you, and declare you unto Me.

8 Wilt you also disannul My judgment? Wilt you condemn Me, that you mayest be righteous?

9 Have you an arm like God (El)? Or canst you thunder with a voice like Him?

10 Deck yourself now with majesty and excellency; and array yourself with glory and beauty.

11 Cast abroad the rage of your wrath; and behold every one that is proud, and abase him.

12 Look on every one that is proud, and bring him low; and tread down the wicked in their place.

13 Hide them in the dust together; and bind their faces in secret.

14 Then will I also confess unto you that your own right hand can save you.

15 Behold now, Behemot, which I made along with you; he eateth grass as an ox.

16 Behold now, his strength is in his loins, and his force is in the navel of his belly.

17 He moveth his tail like a cedar; the sinews of his stones are wrapped together.

18 His bones are as strong pieces of brass; his bones are like bars of iron.

19 He is the chief of the ways of God (El); He who made him can make His sword to approach unto him.

20 Surely the mountains bring him forth food, where all the beasts of the field play.

21 He lieth under the shady trees, in the covert of the reed, and fens.

22 The shady trees cover him with their shadow; the willows of the brook compass him about.

23 Behold, he drinketh up a river, and hasteth not; he trusteth that he can draw up Jordan (Yarden) into his mouth.

24 He taketh it with his eyes; his nose pierceth through snares.

41 Can you draw out leviathan with an hook? Or his tongue with a cord which you lettest down?

2 Can you put a hook into his nose? or bore his jaw through with a thorn?

3 Will he make many supplications unto you? Will he speak soft words unto you?

4 Will he make a covenant with you? Wilt you take him for a servant forever?

5 Wilt you play with him as with a bird? Or wilt you bind him for your maidens?

6 Shall the companions make a banquet of him? Shall they part him among the merchants?

7 Can you fill his skin with barbed irons? Or his head with fish spears?

8 Lay your hand upon him, remember the battle, do no more.

9 Behold, the hope of him is in vain; shall not one be cast down even at the sight of him?

10 None is so fierce that dare stir him up; who then is able to stand before Me?

11 Who hath prevented Me, that I should repay him? Whatsoever is under the whole heaven is Mine.

12 I will not conceal his parts, nor his power, nor his comely proportion.

13 Who can discover the face of his garment? Or who can come to him with his double bridle?

14 Who can open the doors of his face? His teeth are terrible round about.

15 His scales are his pride, shut up together as with a close seal.

16 One is so near to another, that no air can come between them.

17 They are joined one to another, they stick together, that they cannot be sundered.

18 By his neesings a light doth shine, and his eyes are like the eyelids of the morning.

19 Out of his mouth go burning lamps, and sparks of fire leap out.

20 Out of his nostrils goeth smoke, as out of a seething pot or caldron.

21 His breath kindleth coals, and a flame goeth out of his mouth.

22 In his neck remaineth strength, and sorrow is turned into joy before him.

23 The flakes of his flesh are joined together; they are firm in themselves; they cannot be moved.

24 His heart is as firm as a stone; yea, as hard as a piece of the nether millstone.

25 When he raiseth up himself, the mighty are afraid; by reason of breakings they purify themselves.

26 The sword of him that layeth at him cannot hold; the spear, the dart, nor the habergeon.

27 He esteemeth iron as straw, and brass as rotten wood.

28 The arrow cannot make him flee; slingstones are turned with him into stubble.

29 Darts are counted as stubble; he laugheth at the shaking of a spear.

30 Sharp stones are under him; he spreadeth sharp pointed things upon the mire.

31 He maketh the deep to boil like a pot; He maketh the sea like a pot of ointment.

32 He maketh a path to shine after him; one would think the deep to be hoary.

33 Upon earth there is not his like, who is made without fear.

34 He beholdeth all high things; he is a king over all the children of pride.”

42 Then Job (Iyov) answered יהוה, and said: 2 “I know that You can do every thing, and that no thought can be withholden from You.

3 ‘Who is He that hideth counsel without knowledge?’ Therefore have I uttered that I understood not; things too wonderful for me, which I knew not.

4 Hear, I beseech You, and I will speak: ‘I will demand of You, and declare You unto me.

5 I have heard of You by the hearing of the ear; but now mine eye seeth You.

6 Wherefore I abhor myself, and repent in dust and ashes.

7 And it was so, that after יהוה had spoken these words unto Job (Iyov), יהוה said to Eliphaz the Temanite, “My wrath is kindled against you, and against your two friends; for you have not spoken of Me the thing that is right, as My

servant Job (Iyov) hath.

8 Therefore take unto you now seven bullocks and seven rams, and go to My servant Job (Iyov), and offer up for yourselves a burnt offering; and My servant Job (Iyov) shall pray for you. For him will I accept, lest I deal with you after your folly, in that you have not spoken of Me the thing which is right, like My servant Job (Iyov).”

9 So Eliphaz the Temanite and Bildad the Shuhite and Zophar the Naamathite went, and did according as יהוה commanded them: יהוה also accepted Job (Iyov).

10 And יהוה turned the captivity of Job (Iyov), when he prayed for his friends; also יהוה gave Job (Iyov) twice as much as he had before.

11 Then came there unto him all his brethren, and all his sisters, and all they that had been of his acquaintance before, and did eat bread with him in his house; and they bemoaned him, and comforted him over all the disaster (raah) that יהוה had brought upon him; every man also gave him a piece of money, and every one an earring of gold.

12 So יהוה blessed the latter end of Job (Iyov) more than his beginning; for he had fourteen thousand sheep, and six thousand camels, and a thousand yoke of oxen, and a thousand she asses.

13 He had also seven sons and three daughters.

14 And he called the name of the first, Yemima; and the name of the second, Kezia; and the name of the third, Kerenhappuch.

15 And in all the land were no women found so fair as the daughters of Job (Iyov); and their father gave them inheritance among their brethren.

16 After this lived Job (Iyov) a hundred and forty years, and saw his sons, and his sons’ sons, even four generations.

17 So Job (Iyov) died, being old and full of days.

PSALMS
TEHILLIM תְּהִלִּים
(Book of Psalms)

1 Blessed is the man that walketh not in the counsel of the wicked, nor standeth in the way of sinners, nor sitteth in the seat of the scornful.

2 But his delight is in the Torah of יהוה; and in His Torah doth he meditates day and night.

3 And he shall be like a tree planted by the rivers of water, that bringeth forth his fruit in his season; his leaf also shall not wither; and whatsoever he doeth shall prosper.

4 The wicked are not so, but are like the chaff which the wind driveth away.

5 Therefore the wicked shall not stand in the judgment, nor sinners in the congregation of the righteous.

6 For יהוה knoweth the way of the righteous; but the way of the wicked shall perish.

2 Why do the heathens rage, and the people imagine a vain thing?

2 The kings of the earth set themselves, and the rulers take counsel together, against יהוה, and against His anointed (mashiach), saying:

3 "Let us break their bands asunder, and cast away their cords from us."

4 He that sitteth in the heavens shall laugh; the Lord (Adonai) shall have them in derision.

5 Then shall He speak unto them in His wrath, and vex them in His sore displeasure:

6 "Yet have I set My King upon My holy hill of Zion (Tsiyon)."

7 "I will declare the decree: יהוה hath said unto Me, 'You are My [B47]Son (My Humanity); this day have I begotten you.'

8 Ask of Me, and I shall give you the nations for your inheritance, and the uttermost parts of the earth for your possession.

9 You shalt break them with a rod of iron; you shalt dash them in pieces like a potter's vessel.'"

10 Be wise now therefore, O you kings; be instructed, you judges of the earth.

11 Serve יהוה with fear, and rejoice with trembling.

12 Kiss the [B47]Son (Humanity of El), lest He be angry, and you perish from the way, when His wrath is kindled but a little. Blessed are all they that put their trust in Him.

3 A Psalm of Dawid, when he fled from Avshalom his son.

1 יהוה, how are they increased that trouble me! Many are they that rise up against me.

2 Many there be which say of my soul, "There is no help for him in God (Elohim)." Selah.

3 But You, O יהוה, are a shield for me; my glory, and the lifter up of mine head.

4 I cried unto יהוה with my voice, and He heard me out of His holy hill. Selah.

5 I laid me down and slept; I awaked; for יהוה sustained me.

6 I will not be afraid of ten thousands of people, that have set themselves against me round about.

7 Arise, O יהוה; save me, O my God (Elohim)! For You have smitten all mine enemies upon the cheek bone; You have broken the teeth of the wicked.

8 Salvation belongth unto יהוה. Your blessing is upon Your people. Selah.

4 To the chief Musician on Neginoth, A Psalm of Dawid.

1 Hear me when I call, O God (Elohim) of my righteousness! You have enlarged me when I was in distress; have mercy upon me, and hear my prayer.

2 O you sons of men, how long will you turn my glory into shame? How long will you love vanity, and seek after leasing? Selah.

3 But know that יהוה hath set apart him that is holy (chasid) for Himself; יהוה will hear when I call unto Him.

4 Stand in awe, and sin not; commune with your own heart upon your bed, and be still. Selah.

5 Offer the sacrifices of righteousness, and put your trust in יהוה.

6 There be many that say, "Who will shew us any good?" יהוה, lift You up the light of Your countenance upon us.

7 You have put gladness in my heart, more than in the time that their corn and their wine increased.

8 I will both lay me down in peace, and sleep; for You, יהוה, only makest me dwell in safety.

5 To the chief musician upon Nehiloth, A Psalm of Dawid.

1 Give ear to my words, O יהוה, consider my meditation.

2 Hearken unto the voice of my cry, my King, and my God (Elohim), for unto You will I pray.

3 My voice shalt You hear in the morning, O

יהוה; in the morning will I direct my prayer unto You, and will look up.

4 For You are not a God (El) who hath pleasure in wickedness; neither shall evil dwell with You.

5 The foolish shall not stand in Your sight; You hatest all workers of iniquity.

6 You shalt destroy them that speak leasing; יהוה will abhor the bloody and deceitful man.

7 But as for me, I will come into Your house in the multitude of Your mercy; and in Your fear will I worship toward Your holy temple.

8 Lead me, O יהוה, in Your righteousness because of mine enemies; make Your way straight before my face.

9 For there is no faithfulness in their mouth; their inward part is very wickedness; their throat is an open sepulchre; they flatter with their tongue.

10 Destroy them, O God (Elohim); let them fall by their own counsels; cast them out in the multitude of their transgressions, for they have rebelled against You.

11 But let all those that put their trust in You rejoice; let them ever shout for joy, because You defendest them; let them also who love Your name be joyful in You.

12 For You, יהוה, wilt bless the righteous; with favor wilt You compass him as with a shield.

6 To the chief Musician on Neginoth upon Sheminith, A Psalm of Dawid.

1 O יהוה, rebuke me not in Your anger, neither chasten me in Your hot displeasure.

2 Have mercy upon me, O יהוה; for I am weak; O יהוה, heal me; for my bones are vexed.

3 My soul is also sore vexed; but You, O יהוה, how long?

4 Return, O יהוה, deliver my soul! Oh save me for Your mercies' sake.

5 For in death there is no remembrance of You; in the grave (sheol) who shall give You thanks?

6 I am weary with my groaning; all the night makes I my bed to swim; I water my couch with my tears.

7 Mine eye is consumed because of grief; it waxeth old because of all mine enemies.

8 Depart from me, all you workers of iniquity; for יהוה hath heard the voice of my weeping.

9 יהוה hath heard my supplication; יהוה will receive my prayer.

10 Let all mine enemies be ashamed and sore vexed; let them return and be ashamed suddenly.

7 Shiggaion of Dawid, which he sang unto יהוה, concerning the words of Cush the Benjamite (Ben-yemini).

1 O יהוה my God (YHWH Elohai), in You do I put my trust; save me from all them who persecute me, and deliver me;

2 Lest he tear my soul like a lion, rending it in pieces, while there is none to deliver.

3 O יהוה my God (YHWH Elohai), if I have done this; if there be iniquity in my hands;

4 If I have rewarded evil unto him that was at peace with me; (yea, I have delivered him that without cause is mine enemy;)

5 Let the enemy persecute my soul, and take it; yea, let him tread down my life upon the earth, and lay mine honor in the dust. Selah.

6 Arise, O יהוה, in Your anger, lift up Yourself because of the rage of mine enemies; and awake for me to the judgment that You have commanded.

7 So shall the congregation of the people compass You about; for their sakes therefore return You on high.

8 יהוה shall judge the people; judge me, O יהוה, according to my righteousness, and according to mine integrity that is in me.

9 Oh let the wickedness of the wicked come to an end; but establish the just; for the righteous God (Elohim) trieth the hearts and reins.

10 My defence is of God (Elohim), who saveth the upright in heart.

11 God (Elohim) judgeth the righteous, and God (El) is angry with the wicked every day.

12 If he repents not, He will whet His sword; He hath bent His bow, and made it ready.

13 He hath also prepared for him the instruments of death; He ordaineth His arrows against the persecutors.

14 Behold, he travaileth with iniquity, and hath conceived mischief, and brought forth falsehood.

15 He made a pit, and digged it, and is fallen into the ditch which he made.

16 His mischief shall return upon his own head, and his violent dealing shall come down upon his own pate.

17 I will praise יהוה according to His righteousness; and will sing praise to the name of יהוה Most High (Elyon).

8 To the chief Musician upon Gittith, A Psalm of Dawid.

1 O יהוה our Lord (YHWH Adoneinu), how excellent is Your name in all the earth! Who hast set Your glory above the heavens.

2 Out of the mouth of babes and sucklings have You ordained strength because of Your enemies, that You mightest still the enemy and the avenger.

3 When I consider Your heavens, the work of Your fingers, the moon and the stars, which You have ordained;

4 What is man, that You are mindful of him? And the son of man, that You visitest him?

5 For You have made him a little lower than the angels, and hast crowned him with glory and honor.

6 You madest him to have dominion over the works of Your hands; You have put all things under his feet;

7 All sheep and oxen, yea, and the beasts of the field;

8 The fowl of the air, and the fish of the sea, and whatsoever passeth through the paths of the seas.

9 O יהוה our Lord (YHWH Adoneinu), how excellent is Your name in all the earth!

To the chief Musician upon Muthlabben, A Psalm of Dawid.

9 1 I will praise You, O יהוה, with my whole heart; I will shew forth all Your marvellous works.

2 I will be glad and rejoice in You; I will sing praise to Your name, O You Most High (Elyon).

3 When mine enemies are turned back, they shall fall and perish at Your presence.

4 For You have maintained my right and my cause; You satest on the throne judging right.

5 You have rebuked the nations, You have destroyed the wicked, You have put out their name forever and ever.

6 O You enemy, destructions are come to a perpetual end; and You have destroyed cities; their memorial is perished with them.

7 But יהוה shall endure forever; He hath prepared His throne for judgment.

8 And He shall judge the world in righteousness, He shall minister judgment to the people in uprightness.

9 יהוה also will be a refuge for the oppressed, a refuge in times of trouble.

10 And they that know Your name will put their trust in You, for You, יהוה, hast not forsaken them that seek You.

11 Sing praises to יהוה, who dwelleth in Zion (Tsiyon); declare among the people His doings.

12 When He maketh inquisition for blood, He remembereth them; He forgetteth not the cry of the humble.

13 Have mercy upon me, O יהוה; consider my trouble which I suffer of them that hate me, You that liftest me up from the gates of death;

14 That I may shew forth all Your praise in the gates of the daughter of Zion (Tsiyon); I will rejoice in Your salvation.

15 The nations are sunk down in the pit that they made; in the net which they hid is their own foot taken.

16 יהוה is known by the judgment which He executeth; the wicked is snared in the work of his own hands. Higgayon. Selah.

17 The wicked shall return to hell (sheol), and all the nations that forget God (Elohim).

18 For the needy shall not always be forgotten; the expectation of the poor shall not perish forever.

19 Arise, O יהוה; let not man prevail; let the nations be judged in Your sight.

20 Put them in fear, O יהוה, that the nations may know themselves to be but men. Selah.

10 Why standest You afar off, O יהוה? Why hidest You Yourself in times of trouble?

2 The wicked in his pride doth persecute the poor; let them be taken in the devices that they have imagined.

3 For the wicked boasteth of his heart's desire, and blesseth the covetous, whom יהוה abhorreth.

4 The wicked, through the pride of his countenance, will not seek after God (Elohim); God (Elohim) is not in all his thoughts.

5 His ways are always grievous; Your judgments are far above out of his sight; as for all his enemies, he puffeth at them.

6 He hath said in his heart, I shall not be moved, for I shall never be in adversity.

7 His mouth is full of cursing and deceit and fraud; under his tongue is mischief and vanity.

8 He sitteth in the lurking places of the villages; in the secret places doth he murder the innocent; his eyes are privily set against the poor.

9 He lieth in wait secretly as a lion in his den; he lieth in wait to catch the poor; he doth catch the poor, when he draweth him into his net.

10 He croucheth, and humbleth himself, that the poor may fall by his strong ones.

11 He hath said in his heart, God (Elohim) hath forgotten; He hideth His face; He will never see it.

12 Arise, O יהוה! O God (Elohim), lift up Your hand; forget not the humble.

13 Wherefore doth the wicked contemn God (Elohim)? He hath said in his heart,' You wilt not require it.'

14 You have seen it, for You beholdest mischief and spite, to requite it with Your hand; the poor committeth himself unto You; You are the helper of the fatherless.

15 Break You the arm of the wicked and the evil man; seek out his wickedness till You find none.

16 יהוה is King forever and ever; the heathen are perished out of His land.

17 יהוה, You have heard the desire of the humble; You wilt prepare their heart, You wilt cause Your ear to hear;

18 To do justice for the fatherless and the oppressed, that the man of the earth may no more oppress.

11 To the chief Musician, A Psalm of Dawid.
1 In יהוה put I my trust; how say you to my soul, "Flee as a bird to your mountain"?

2 For, behold, the wicked bend their bow, they make ready their arrow upon the string, that they may privily shoot at the upright in heart.

3 If the foundations be destroyed, what can the righteous do?

4 יהוה is in His holy temple, יהוה's throne is in heaven; His eyes behold, His eyelids test the children of men.

5 יהוה proves the righteous; but the wicked and him that loveth violence His soul hateth.

6 Upon the wicked He shall rain snares, fire and brimstone, and a horrible tempest; this shall be the portion of their cup.

7 For the righteous יהוה loveth righteousness; His countenance doth behold the upright.

12 To the chief Musician upon Sheminith, A Psalm of Dawid.
1 Help, יהוה, for the godly man (chasid) ceaseth; for the faithful fail from among the children of men.

2 They speak vanity every one with his neighbor; with flattering lips and with a double heart do they speak.

3 יהוה shall cut off all flattering lips, and the tongue that speaketh proud things,

4 Who have said, "With our tongue will we prevail; our lips are our own; who is lord (adon) over us?

5 For the oppression of the poor, for the sighing of the needy, now will I arise, saith יהוה; I will set him in safety from him that puffeth at him.

6 The words of יהוה are pure words; as silver tried in a furnace of earth, purified seven times.

7 You shalt keep them, O יהוה, You shalt preserve them from this generation forever.

8 The wicked walk on every side, when the vilest men are exalted.

13 To the chief Musician, A Psalm of Dawid.
1 How long wilt You forget me, O יהוה? Forever? How long wilt You hide Your face from me?

2 How long shall I take counsel in my soul, having sorrow in my heart daily? How long shall mine enemy be exalted over me?

3 Consider and hear me, O יהוה my God (YHWH Elohai); lighten mine eyes, lest I sleep the sleep of death;

4 Lest mine enemy say, "I have prevailed against him"; and those that trouble me rejoice when I am moved.

5 But I have trusted in Your mercy; my heart shall rejoice in Your salvation.

6 I will sing unto יהוה, because He hath dealt bountifully with me.

14 To the chief Musician, A Psalm of Dawid.
1 The fool hath said in his heart, "There is no God (Elohim)." They are corrupt, they have done abominable works, there is none that doeth good.

2 יהוה looked down from heaven upon the children of men, to see if there were any that did understand, and seek God (Elohim).

3 They have all gone aside, they have all together become filthy; there is none that doeth good, no, not one.

4 Have all the workers of iniquity no knowledge? Who eat up my people as they eat bread, and call not upon יהוה.

5 There were they in great fear, for God (Elohim) is in the generation of the righteous.

6 You have shamed the counsel of the poor, because יהוה is his refuge.

7 Oh that the salvation of Yisrael would come out of Zion (Tsiyon)! When יהוה bringeth back the captivity of His people, Jacob (Yaaqov) shall rejoice, and Yisrael shall be glad.

15 A Psalm of Dawid.
1 יהוה, who shall abide in Your tabernacle? Who shall dwell in Your holy hill?

2 He that walketh uprightly, and worketh righteousness, and speaketh the truth in his heart.

3 He that backbiteth not with his tongue, nor doeth evil to his neighbour, nor taketh up a reproach against his neighbour.

4 In whose eyes a vile person is contemned, but he honoureth them that fear יהוה. He who sweareth to his own hurt, and changeth not.

5 He who putteth not out his money to usury, nor taketh reward against the innocent. He who doeth these things shall never be moved.

16 Michtam of Dawid.
1 Preserve me, O God (Elohim), for in You do I put my trust.

2 O my soul, you have said unto יהוה, "You are my Lord (Adonai); my goodness is nothing apart from You;"

3 But to the holy ones who are on the earth, and to the excellent, in whom is all my delight.

4 Their sorrows shall be multiplied that hasten after another god; their drink offerings of blood will I not offer, nor take up their names into my lips.

5 יהוה is the portion of mine inheritance and of my cup; You maintainest my lot.

6 The lines are fallen unto me in pleasant places; yea, I have a goodly heritage.

7 I will bless יהוה, who hath given me counsel; my reins also instruct me in the night seasons.

8 I have set יהוה always before me, because He is at my right hand, I shall not be moved.

9 Therefore my heart is glad, and my glory rejoiceth; my flesh also shall rest in hope.

10 For You wilt not leave my soul in hell (sheol); neither wilt You allow Your Holy One to see destruction.

11 You wilt shew me the path of life; in Your presence is fullness of joy; at Your right hand there are pleasures forevermore.

17 A Prayer of Dawid.
1 Hear the right, O יהוה, attend unto my cry, give ear unto my prayer, that goeth not out of feigned lips.

2 Let my sentence come forth from your presence; let your eyes behold the things that are equal.

3 You have proved mine heart; You have visited me in the night; You have tested me, and shalt find nothing; I am purposed that my mouth shall not transgress.

4 Concerning the works of men, by the word of your lips I have kept me from the paths of the destroyer.

5 Hold up my goings in Your paths, that my footsteps slip not.

6 I have called upon You, for You wilt hear me, O God (Elohim); incline Your ear unto me, and hear my speech.

7 Shew Your marvellous loving-kindness, O You who savest by Your right hand them who put their trust in You from those that rise up against them.

8 Keep me as the apple of the eye, hide me under the shadow of Your wings,

9 From the wicked who oppress me, from my deadly enemies, who compass me about.

10 They are inclosed in their own fat; with their mouth they speak proudly.

11 They have now compassed us in our steps; they have set their eyes bowing down to the earth;

12 Like as a lion that is greedy of his prey, and as it was a young lion lurking in secret places.

13 Arise, O יהוה, disappoint him, cast him down; deliver my soul from the wicked, with Your sword;

14 From men with Your hand, O יהוה, from men of the world, who have their portion in this life, and whose belly you fillest with Your hid treasure; they are full of children, and leave the rest of their substance to their babes.

15 As for me, I will behold Your face in righteousness; I shall be satisfied, when I awake, with Your likeness.

18 To the chief Musician, A Psalm of Dawid, the servant of יהוה, who spake unto יהוה the words of this song in the day that יהוה delivered him from the hand of all his enemies, and from the hand of Shaul; And he said:

1 I will love You, O יהוה, my strength.

2 יהוה is my rock, and my fortress, and my deliverer; my God (Eli), my strength, in whom I will trust; my buckler, and the horn of my salvation, and my high tower.

3 I will call upon יהוה, who is worthy to be praised; so shall I be saved from mine enemies.

4 The sorrows of death compassed me, and the floods of wickedness made me afraid.

5 The sorrows of death compassed me about; the snares of death prevented me.

6 In my distress I called upon יהוה, and cried unto my God (Elohim); He heard my voice out of His temple, and my cry came before Him, even into His ears.

7 Then the earth shook and trembled; the foundations also of the hills moved and were shaken, because He was wroth.

8 There went up a smoke out of His nostrils, and fire out of His mouth devoured; coals were kindled by it.

9 He bowed the heavens also, and came down; and darkness was under His feet.

10 And He rode upon a cherub (keruv), and did fly; yea, He did fly upon the wings of the wind.

11 He made darkness His secret place; His pavilion round about Him were dark waters and thick clouds of the skies.

12 At the brightness that was before him His thick clouds passed, hail stones and coals of fire.

13 יהוה also thundered in the heavens, and the Most High (Elyon) gave His voice; hail stones and coals of fire.

14 Yea, He sent out His arrows, and scattered them; and He shot out lightnings, and discomfited them.

15 Then the channels of waters were seen, and the foundations of the world were discovered at Your rebuke, O יהוה, at the blast of the breath of Your nostrils.

16 He sent from above, He took me, He drew me out of many waters.

17 He delivered me from my strong enemy, and from them which hated me; for they were too strong for me.

18 They prevented me in the day of my disaster, but יהוה was my support.

19 He brought me forth also into a large place; He delivered me, because He delighted in me.

20 יהוה rewarded me according to my righteousness; according to the cleanness of my hands hath He recompensed me.

21 For I have kept the ways of יהוה, and have not wickedly departed from my God (Elohim).

22 For all His judgments were before me, and I did not put away His statutes from me.

23 I was also upright before Him, and I kept myself from mine iniquity.

24 Therefore hath יהוה recompensed me according to my righteousness, according to the cleanness of my hands in His eyesight.

25 With the merciful You wilt shew Yourself merciful; with an upright man You wilt shew Yourself upright;

26 With the pure You wilt shew Yourself pure; and with the perverse You wilt shew Yourself perverse.

27 For You wilt save the afflicted people; but wilt bring down haughty looks.

28 For You wilt light my candle; יהוה my God (YHWH Elohai) will enlighten my darkness.

29 For by You I have run through a troop; and by my God (Elohim) have I leaped over a wall.

30 As for God (Elohim), His way is perfect; the word of יהוה is proven; He is a buckler to all those who trust in Him.

31 For who is God (Eloah) except יהוה? Or who is a Rock except our God (Elohim)?

32 It is God (Elohim) who girdeth me with strength, and maketh my way perfect.

33 He maketh my feet like hinds' feet, and setteth me upon my high places.

34 He teacheth my hands to war, so that a bow of steel is broken by mine arms.

35 You have also given me the shield of Your salvation; and Your right hand hath holden me up, and Your gentleness hath made me great.

36 You have enlarged my steps under me, that my feet did not slip.

37 I have pursued mine enemies, and overtaken them; neither did I turn again till they were consumed.

38 I have wounded them that they were not able to rise; they are fallen under my feet.

39 For You have girded me with strength unto the battle; You have subdued under me those that rose up against me.

40 You have also given me the necks of mine enemies; that I might destroy them that hate me.

41 They cried, but there was none to save them; even unto יהוה, but He answered them not.

42 Then did I beat them small as the dust before the wind; I did cast them out as the dirt in the streets.

43 You have delivered me from the strivings of the people; and You have made me the head of the heathen; a people whom I have not known shall serve me.

44 As soon as they hear of me, they shall obey me; the strangers shall submit themselves

unto me.

45 The strangers shall fade away, and be afraid out of their close places.

46 יהוה liveth; and blessed be my Rock; and let the God (Elohim) of my salvation be exalted.

47 It is God (El) that avengeth me, and subdueth the people under me.

48 He delivereth me from mine enemies; yea, You liftest me up above those that rise up against me; You have delivered me from the violent man.

49 Therefore will I give thanks unto You, O יהוה, among the heathen, and sing praises unto Your name.

50 Great deliverance giveth He to His king; and sheweth mercy to His anointed (mashiach), to Dawid, and to His seed forevermore.

19 To the chief Musician, A Psalm of Dawid. 1 The heavens declare the glory of God (Elohim); and the firmament sheweth His handywork.

2 Day unto day uttereth speech, and night unto night sheweth knowledge.

3 There is no speech nor language, where their voice is not heard.

4 Their line is gone out through all the earth, and their words to the end of the world. In them hath He set a tabernacle for the sun,

5 Which is as a bridegroom coming out of His chamber, and rejoiceth as a strong man to run a race.

6 His going forth is from the end of the heaven, and His circuit unto the ends of it; and there is nothing hid from the heat thereof.

7 The Torah of יהוה is perfect, converting the soul; the testimony of יהוה is sure, making wise the simple.

8 The statutes of יהוה are right, rejoicing the heart; the commandment of יהוה is pure, enlightening the eyes.

9 The fear of יהוה is clean, enduring forever; the judgments of יהוה are true and righteous altogether.

10 More to be desired are they than gold, yea, than much fine gold; sweeter also than honey and the honeycomb.

11 Moreover by them is Your servant warned; and in keeping of them there is great reward.

12 Who can understand his errors? cleanse You me from secret faults.

13 Keep back Your servant also from presumptuous sins; let them not have dominion over me; then shall I be upright, and I shall be innocent from the great transgression.

14 Let the words of my mouth, and the meditation of my heart, be acceptable in Your sight, O יהוה, my strength, and my redeemer.

20 To the chief Musician, A Psalm of Dawid. 1 יהוה hear you in the day of trouble; the name of the God (Elohim) of Jacob (Yaaqov) defend you;

2 Send you help from the sanctuary, and strengthen you out of Zion (Tsiyon);

3 Remember all your offerings, and accept your burnt sacrifice; Selah.

4 Grant you according to your own heart, and fulfil all your counsel.

5 We will rejoice in Your salvation, and in the name of our God (Elohim) we will set up our banners! יהוה fulfil all your petitions.

6 Now know I that יהוה saveth His anointed (mashiach); He will hear him from His holy heaven with the saving strength of His right hand.

7 Some trust in chariots, and some in horses; but we will remember the name of יהוה our God (YHWH Eloheinu).

8 They are brought down and fallen, but we are risen, and stand upright.

9 Save, יהוה! Let the King hear us when we call.

21 To the chief Musician, A Psalm of Dawid. 1 The king shall joy in Your strength, O יהוה; and in Your salvation how greatly shall he rejoice!

2 You have given him his heart's desire, and hast not withholden the request of his lips. Selah.

3 For You preventest him with the blessings of goodness; You settest a crown of pure gold on his head.

4 He asked life of you, and you gavest it him, even length of days forever and ever.

5 His glory is great in Your salvation; honor and majesty have You laid upon him.

6 For You have made him most blessed forever; You have made him exceeding glad with Your countenance.

7 For the king trusteth in יהוה, and through the mercy of the Most High (Elyon) he shall not be moved.

8 Your hand shall find out all Your enemies; Your right hand shall find out those who hate You.

9 You shalt make them as a fiery oven in the time of Your anger; יהוה shall swallow them up in His wrath, and the fire shall devour them.

10 Their fruit shalt You destroy from the earth, and their seed from among the children of men.

11 For they intended evil against You; they imagined a mischievous device, which they are not able to perform.

12 Therefore shalt You make them turn their back, when You shalt make ready Your arrows upon Your strings against the face of them.

13 Be You exalted, יהוה, in Your own strength; so will we sing and praise Your power.

22 To the chief Musician upon Aiyeleth Shahar, A Psalm of Dawid.

1 My God (Eli), my God (Eli), why have You forsaken Me? Why art You so far from helping Me, and from the words of My roaring?

2 O My God (Elohai), I cry in the daytime, but You hearest not; and in the night season, and am not silent.

3 But You are holy, O You who inhabitest the praises of Yisrael.

4 Our fathers trusted in You; they trusted, and You didst deliver them.

5 They cried unto You, and were delivered; they trusted in You, and were not confounded.

6 But I am a worm, and no man; a reproach of men, and despised of the people.

7 All they who see Me laugh Me to scorn; they shoot out the lip, they shake the head, saying,

8 He trusted on יהוה that He would deliver Him; let Him deliver Him, seeing He delighted in Him.

9 But You are He who took Me out of the womb; You didst make Me hope when I was upon My mother's breasts.

10 I was cast upon You from the womb; You are My God (Eli) from My mother's belly.

11 Be not far from Me, for trouble is near; for there is none to help.

12 Many bulls have compassed Me; strong bulls of Bashan have beset Me round.

13 They gaped upon Me with their mouths, as a ravening and a roaring lion.

14 I am poured out like water, and all My bones are out of joint; My heart is like wax; it is melted in the midst of My bowels.

15 My strength is dried up like a potsherd; and My tongue cleaveth to My jaws; and You have brought Me into the dust of death.

16 For dogs have compassed Me; the assembly of the wicked have inclosed Me; they pierced My hands and My feet.

17 I may tell all My bones; they look and stare upon Me.

18 They part My garments among them, and cast lots upon My vesture.

19 But be not You far from Me, O יהוה; O My strength, haste You to help Me.

20 Deliver My soul from the sword; My only soul from the power of the dog.

21 Save me from the lion's mouth, for You have heard Me from the horns of the unicorns.

22 I will declare Your name unto My brethren; in the midst of the congregation will I praise You.

23 You who fear יהוה, praise Him; all you the seed of Jacob (Yaaqov), glorify Him; and fear Him, all you the seed of Yisrael.

24 For He hath not despised nor abhorred the affliction of the afflicted; neither hath He hid His face from Him; but when He cried unto Him, He heard.

25 My praise shall be of You in the great congregation; I will pay My vows before them that fear Him.

26 The meek shall eat and be satisfied; they shall praise יהוה who seek Him; your heart shall live forever.

27 All the ends of the world shall remember and turn unto יהוה; and all the kindreds of the nations shall worship before You.

28 For the kingdom is יהוה's; and He is the governor among the nations.

29 All they that be fat upon earth shall eat and worship; all they who go down to the dust shall bow before Him; and none can keep alive his own soul.

30 A seed shall serve Him; it shall be accounted to the Lord (Adonai) for a generation.

31 They shall come, and shall declare His righteousness unto a people who shall be born, that He hath done this.

23 A Psalm of Dawid.

1 יהוה is my Shepherd; I shall not want.

2 He maketh me to lie down in green pastures. He leadeth me beside the still waters.

3 He restoreth my soul; He leadeth me in the paths of righteousness for His name's sake.

4 Yea, though I walk through the valley of the shadow of death, I will fear no evil; for You are with me; Your rod and Your staff they

comfort me.

5 You preparest a table before me in the presence of mine enemies; You anointest my head with oil; my cup runneth over.

6 Surely goodness and mercy shall follow me all the days of my life; and I will dwell in the house of יהוה forever.

24 A Psalm of Dawid.
1 The earth is יהוה's, and the fullness thereof; the world, and they that dwell therein.

2 For He hath founded it upon the seas, and established it upon the floods.

3 Who shall ascend into the hill of יהוה? Or who shall stand in His holy place?

4 He who hath clean hands, and a pure heart; who hath not lifted up His soul unto vanity, nor sworn deceitfully.

5 He shall receive the blessing from יהוה, and righteousness from the God (Elohim) of his salvation.

6 This is the generation of them who seek Him, who seek Your face, O Jacob (Yaaqov). Selah.

7 Lift up your heads, O you gates; and be you lift up, you everlasting doors; and the King of glory shall come in.

8 Who is this King of glory? יהוה strong and mighty, יהוה mighty in battle.

9 Lift up your heads, O you gates; even lift them up, you everlasting doors; and the King of glory shall come in.

10 Who is this King of glory? יהוה of hosts (YHWH Tsevaot), He is the King of glory. Selah.

25 A Psalm of Dawid.
1 Unto You, O יהוה, do I lift up my soul.

2 O my God (Elohim), I trust in You; let me not be ashamed, let not mine enemies triumph over me.

3 Yea, let none who wait on You be ashamed; let them be ashamed who transgress without cause.

4 Shew me Your ways, O יהוה; teach me Your paths.

5 Lead me in Your truth, and teach me; for You are the God (Elohim) of my salvation; on You do I wait all the day.

6 Remember, O יהוה, Your tender mercies and Your lovingkindnesses; for they have been ever of old.

7 Remember not the sins of my youth, nor my transgressions; according to Your mercy remember You me for Your goodness' sake, O

יהוה.

8 Good and upright is יהוה; therefore will He teach sinners in the way.

9 The meek will He guide in judgment; and the meek will He teach His way.

10 All the paths of יהוה are mercy and truth unto such as keep His covenant and His testimonies.

11 For Your name's sake, O יהוה, pardon mine iniquity, for it is great.

12 What man is he that feareth יהוה? Him shall He teach in the way that he shall choose.

13 His soul shall dwell at ease, and his seed shall inherit the earth.

14 The secret of יהוה is with them that fear Him; and He will shew them His covenant.

15 Mine eyes are ever toward יהוה; for He shall pluck my feet out of the net.

16 Turn You unto me, and have mercy upon me; for I am desolate and afflicted.

17 The troubles of my heart are enlarged; O bring You me out of my distresses.

18 Look upon mine affliction and my pain; and forgive all my sins.

19 Consider mine enemies; for they are many; and they hate me with cruel hatred.

20 O keep my soul, and deliver me; let me not be ashamed; for I put my trust in You.

21 Let integrity and uprightness preserve me; for I wait on You.

22 Redeem Yisrael, O God (Elohim), out of all his troubles.

26 A Psalm of Dawid.
1 Judge me, O יהוה; for I have walked in mine integrity; I have trusted also in יהוה; therefore I shall not slide.

2 Examine me, O יהוה, and prove me; try my reins and my heart.

3 For Your lovingkindness is before mine eyes; and I have walked in Your truth.

4 I have not sat with vain persons, neither will I go in with dissemblers.

5 I have hated the congregation of evil doers; and will not sit with the wicked.

6 I will wash mine hands in innocency; so will I compass Your altar, O יהוה,

7 That I may publish with the voice of thanksgiving, and tell of all Your wondrous works.

8 יהוה, I have loved the habitation of Your house, and the place where Your honor dwelleth.

9 Gather not my soul with sinners, nor my life

with bloody men;

10 In whose hands is mischief, and their right hand is full of bribes.

11 But as for me, I will walk in mine integrity; redeem me, and be merciful unto me.

12 My foot standeth in an even place; in the congregations will I bless יהוה.

27 A Psalm of Dawid.
1 יהוה is my light and my salvation; whom shall I fear? יהוה is the strength of my life; of whom shall I be afraid?

2 When the wicked, even mine enemies and my foes, came upon me to eat up my flesh, they stumbled and fell.

3 Though an army should encamp against me, my heart shall not fear; though war should rise against me, in this will I be confident.

4 One thing have I desired of יהוה, that will I seek after; that I may dwell in the house of יהוה all the days of my life, to behold the beauty of יהוה, and to enquire in His temple.

5 For in the time of trouble He shall hide me in His pavilion; in the secret of His tabernacle shall He hide me; He shall set me up upon a rock.

6 And now shall mine head be lifted up above mine enemies round about me: therefore will I offer in His tabernacle sacrifices of joy; I will sing, yea, I will sing praises unto יהוה.

7 Hear, O יהוה, when I cry with my voice; have mercy also upon me, and answer me.

8 When You saidst, "Seek you My face"; my heart said unto You, "Your face, יהוה, will I seek."

9 Hide not Your face far from me; put not Your servant away in anger; You have been my help; leave me not, neither forsake me, O God (Elohim) of my salvation.

10 When my father and my mother forsake me, then יהוה will take me up.

11 Teach me Your way, O יהוה, and lead me in a plain path, because of mine enemies.

12 Deliver me not over unto the will of mine enemies: for false witnesses are risen up against me, and such as breathe out cruelty.

13 I had fainted, unless I had believed to see the goodness of יהוה in the land of the living.

14 Wait on יהוה; be of good courage, and He shall strengthen your heart; wait, I say, on יהוה.

28 A Psalm of Dawid.
1 Unto You will I cry, O יהוה my Rock;

be not silent to me; lest, if You be silent to me, I become like them that go down into the pit.

2 Hear the voice of my supplications, when I cry unto You, when I lift up my hands toward Your holy oracle.

3 Draw me not away with the wicked, and with the workers of iniquity, which speak peace to their neighbours, but mischief is in their hearts.

4 Give them according to their deeds, and according to the wickedness of their endeavours: give them after the work of their hands; render to them their desert.

5 Because they regard not the works of יהוה, nor the operation of His hands, He shall destroy them, and not build them up.

6 Blessed be יהוה, because He hath heard the voice of my supplications.

7 יהוה is my strength and my shield; my heart trusted in Him, and I am helped; therefore my heart greatly rejoiceth; and with my song will I praise Him.

8 יהוה is their strength, and He is the saving strength of His anointed (mashiach).

9 Save Your people, and bless Your inheritance: feed them also, and lift them up forever.

29 A Psalm of Dawid.
1 Give unto יהוה, O you mighty, give unto יהוה glory and strength.

2 Give unto יהוה the glory due unto His name; worship יהוה in the beauty of holiness.

3 The voice of יהוה is upon the waters; the God (El) of glory thundereth; יהוה is upon many waters.

4 The voice of יהוה is powerful; the voice of יהוה is full of majesty.

5 The voice of יהוה breaketh the cedars; yea, יהוה breaketh the cedars of Lebanon.

6 He maketh them also to skip like a calf; Lebanon and Sirion like a young unicorn.

7 The voice of יהוה divideth the flames of fire.

8 The voice of יהוה shaketh the wilderness; יהוה shaketh the wilderness of Qadesh.

9 The voice of יהוה maketh the hinds to calve, and discovereth the forests; and in His temple doth every one speaks of His glory.

10 יהוה sitteth upon the flood; yea, יהוה sitteth King forever.

11 יהוה will give strength unto His people; יהוה will bless His people with peace.

30 A Psalm and Song at the dedication of the house of Dawid.

1 I will extol You, O יהוה, for You have lifted me up, and hast not made my foes to rejoice over me.

2 O יהוה my God (YHWH Elohai), I cried unto You, and You have healed me.

3 O יהוה, You have brought up my soul from the grave (sheol); You have kept me alive, that I should not go down to the pit.

4 Sing unto יהוה, O you holy ones of His, and give thanks at the remembrance of His holiness.

5 For His anger endureth but a moment; in His favor is life; weeping may endure for a night, but joy cometh in the morning.

6 And in my prosperity I said, "I shall never be moved."

7 יהוה, by Your favor You have made my mountain to stand strong; You didst hide Your face, and I was troubled.

8 I cried to You, O יהוה; and unto יהוה I made supplication.

9 What profit is there in my blood, when I go down to the pit? Shall the dust praise You? Shall it declare Your truth?

10 Hear, O יהוה, and have mercy upon me; יהוה, be You my helper.

11 You have turned for me my mourning into dancing; You have put off my sackcloth, and girded me with gladness;

12 To the end that my glory may sing praise to You, and not be silent. O יהוה my God (YHWH Elohai), I will give thanks unto You forever.

31 To the chief Musician, A Psalm of Dawid. 1 In You, O יהוה, do I put my trust; let me never be ashamed; deliver me in Your righteousness.

2 Bow down Your ear to me; deliver me speedily; be You my strong rock, for a house of defence to save me.

3 For You are my rock and my fortress; therefore for Your name's sake lead me, and guide me.

4 Pull me out of the net that they have laid privily for me, for You are my strength.

5 Into Your hand I commit my spirit; You have redeemed me, O יהוה God (El) of truth.

6 I have hated them who regard lying vanities, but I trust in יהוה.

7 I will be glad and rejoice in Your mercy, for You have considered my trouble; You have known my soul in adversities;

8 And hast not shut me up into the hand of the enemy; You have set my feet in a large room.

9 Have mercy upon me, O יהוה, for I am in trouble; mine eye is consumed with grief, yea, my soul and my belly.

10 For my life is spent with grief, and my years with sighing; my strength faileth because of mine iniquity, and my bones are consumed.

11 I was a reproach among all mine enemies, but especially among my neighbours, and a fear to mine acquaintance; those who did see me outside fled from me.

12 I am forgotten as a dead man out of mind; I am like a broken vessel.

13 For I have heard the slander of many; fear was on every side; while they took counsel together against me, they devised to take away my life.

14 But I trusted in You, O יהוה; I said, "You are my God (Elohim)."

15 My times are in Your hand; deliver me from the hand of mine enemies, and from them that persecute me.

16 Make Your face to shine upon Your servant; save me for Your mercies' sake.

17 Let me not be ashamed, O יהוה, for I have called upon You; let the wicked be ashamed, and let them be silent in the grave (sheol).

18 Let the lying lips be put to silence; which speak grievous things proudly and contemptuously against the righteous.

19 Oh how great is Your goodness, which You have laid up for them that fear You; which You have wrought for them that trust in You before the sons of men!

20 You shalt hide them in the secret of Your presence from the pride of man; You shalt keep them secretly in a pavilion from the strife of tongues.

21 Blessed be יהוה, for he hath shewed me His marvellous kindness in a strong city.

22 For I said in my haste, "I am cut off from before Your eyes"; nevertheless You heardest the voice of my supplications when I cried unto You.

23 O love יהוה, all you His holy ones, for יהוה preserveth the faithful, and plentifully repays the proud doer.

24 Be of good courage, and He shall strengthen your heart, all you who hope in יהוה.

32 A Psalm of Dawid, Maskil. 1 Blessed is he whose transgression is forgiven, whose sin is covered.

2 Blessed is the man unto whom יהוה imputeth not iniquity, and in whose spirit there is no guile.

3 When I kept silence, my bones waxed old through my roaring all the day long.

4 For day and night Your hand was heavy upon me; my moisture is turned into the drought of summer. Selah.

5 I acknowledged my sin unto You, and mine iniquity have I not hid. I said, "I will confess my transgressions unto יהוה," and You forgavest the iniquity of my sin. Selah.

6 For this shall every one who is faithfuly pray unto You in a time when You mayest be found; surely in the floods of great waters they shall not come near unto him.

7 You are my hiding place; You shalt preserve me from trouble; You shalt compass me about with songs of deliverance. Selah.

8 I will instruct you and teach you in the way which you shalt go; I will guide you with Mine eye.

9 Be you not as the horse, or as the mule, which have no understanding; whose mouth must be held in with bit and bridle, lest they come near unto you.

10 Many sorrows shall be to the wicked; but he who trusteth in יהוה, mercy shall compass him about.

11 Be glad in יהוה, and rejoice, you righteous: and shout for joy, all you that are upright in heart.

33 Rejoice in יהוה, O you righteous; for praise is comely for the upright.

2 Praise יהוה with harp; sing unto Him with the psaltery and an instrument of ten strings.

3 Sing unto Him a new song; play skilfully with a loud noise.

4 For the word of יהוה is right; and all His works are done in truth.

5 He loveth righteousness and justice; the earth is full of the goodness of יהוה.

6 By the word of יהוה were the heavens made; and all the host of them by the breath of His mouth.

7 He gathereth the waters of the sea together as a heap; He layeth up the depth in storehouses.

8 Let all the earth fear יהוה; let all the inhabitants of the world stand in awe of Him.

9 For He spake, and it was done; He commanded, and it stood fast.

10 יהוה bringeth the counsel of the nations to nothing; He maketh the devices of the people of none effect.

11 The counsel of יהוה standeth forever, the thoughts of His heart to all generations.

12 Blessed is the nation whose God (Elohim) is יהוה; and the people whom He hath chosen for His own inheritance.

13 יהוה looketh from heaven; He beholdeth all the sons of men.

14 From the place of His habitation He looketh upon all the inhabitants of the earth.

15 He fashioneth their hearts alike; He considereth all their works.

16 There is no king saved by the multitude of an army; a mighty man is not delivered by much strength.

17 A horse is a vain thing for safety; neither shall He deliver any by His great strength.

18 Behold, the eye of יהוה is upon them that fear Him, upon them that hope in His mercy;

19 To deliver their soul from death, and to keep them alive in famine.

20 Our soul waiteth for יהוה; He is our help and our shield.

21 For our heart shall rejoice in Him, because we have trusted in His holy name.

22 Let Your mercy, O יהוה, be upon us, according as we hope in You.

34 A Psalm of Dawid, when he changed his behaviour before Abimelech (Avimelekh); who drove him away, and he departed.

1 I will bless יהוה at all times; His praise shall continually be in my mouth.

2 My soul shall make her boast in יהוה; the humble shall hear thereof, and be glad.

3 O magnify יהוה with me, and let us exalt His name together.

4 I sought יהוה, and He heard me, and delivered me from all my fears.

5 They looked unto him, and were lightened; and their faces were not ashamed.

6 This poor man cried, and יהוה heard him, and saved him out of all his troubles.

7 The angel of יהוה encampeth round about those who fear him, and delivereth them.

8 O taste and see that יהוה is good; blessed is the man that trusteth in Him.

9 O fear יהוה, you His holy ones (qadoshim), for there is no want to those who fear him.

10 The young lions do lack, and suffer hunger, but those who seek יהוה shall not want any good thing.

11 Come, you children, hearken unto me; I will teach you the fear of יהוה.

12 What man is he that desireth life, and loveth many days, that he may see good?

13 Keep your tongue from evil, and your lips from speaking guile.

14 Depart from evil, and do good; seek peace, and pursue it.

15 The eyes of יהוה are upon the righteous, and His ears are open unto their cry.

16 The face of יהוה is against those who do evil, to cut off the remembrance of them from the earth.

17 The righteous cry, and יהוה heareth, and delivereth them out of all their troubles.

18 יהוה is near unto those who are of a broken heart; and saveth such as be of a contrite spirit.

19 Many are the afflictions of the righteous, but יהוה delivereth him out of them all.

20 He keepeth all His bones, not one of them is broken.

21 Evil shall slay the wicked; and those who hate the righteous shall be desolate.

22 יהוה redeemeth the soul of His servants; and none of those who trust in Him shall be desolate.

35 A Psalm of Dawid.
1 Plead my cause, O יהוה, with those who strive with me; fight against those who fight against me.

2 Take hold of shield and buckler, and stand up for mine help.

3 Draw out also the spear, and stop the way against those who persecute me; say unto my soul, I am your salvation.

4 Let them be confounded and put to shame who seek after my soul; let them be turned back and brought to confusion who devise my hurt.

5 Let them be as chaff before the wind; and let the angel of יהוה chase them.

6 Let their way be dark and slippery; and let the angel of יהוה persecute them.

7 For without cause have they hid for me their net in a pit, which without cause they have digged for my soul.

8 Let destruction come upon him at unawares; and let his net that he hath hid catch himself; into that very destruction let him fall.

9 And my soul shall be joyful in יהוה; it shall rejoice in His salvation.

10 All my bones shall say, "יהוה, who is like unto You, who deliverest the poor from him who is too strong for him, yea, the poor and the needy from him who spoileth him?

11 False witnesses did rise up; they laid to my charge things that I knew not.

12 They rewarded me evil for good to the spoiling of my soul.

13 But as for me, when they were sick, my clothing was sackcloth; I humbled my soul with fasting; and my prayer returned into mine own bosom.

14 I behaved myself as though he had been my friend or brother; I bowed down heavily, as one who mourneth for his mother.

15 But in mine adversity they rejoiced, and gathered themselves together; yea, the abjects gathered themselves together against me, and I knew it not; they did tear me, and ceased not;

16 With hypocritical mockers in feasts, they gnashed upon me with their teeth.

17 My Lord (Adonai), how long wilt You look on? Rescue my soul from their destructions, my only soul from the lions.

18 I will give you thanks in the great congregation; I will praise You among many people.

19 Let not those who are mine enemies wrongfully rejoice over me: neither let them wink with the eye who hate me without a cause.

20 For they speak not peace, but they devise deceitful matters against them that are quiet in the land.

21 Yea, they opened their mouth wide against me, and said, "Aha, aha, our eye hath seen it."

22 This You have seen, O יהוה; keep not silence; O Lord (Adonai), be not far from me.

23 Stir up Yourself, and awake to my judgment, even unto my cause, my God (Elohim) and my Lord (Adonai).

24 Judge me, O יהוה my God (YHWH Elohai), according to Your righteousness; and let them not rejoice over me.

25 Let them not say in their hearts, Ah, so would we have it; let them not say, "We have swallowed him up."

26 Let them be ashamed and brought to confusion together who rejoice at mine hurt; let them be clothed with shame and dishonour who magnify themselves against me.

27 Let them shout for joy, and be glad, who favor my righteous cause; yea, let them say continually, "Let יהוה be magnified, who hath pleasure in the prosperity of His servant."

28 And my tongue shall speak of Your righteousness and of Your praise all the day long.

36 To the chief Musician, A Psalm of Dawid the servant of יהוה.

1 The transgression of the wicked saith within my heart, that there is no fear of God (Elohim) before his eyes.

2 For he flattereth himself in his own eyes, until his iniquity be found to be hateful.

3 The words of his mouth are iniquity and deceit; he hath left off to be wise, and to do good.

4 He deviseth mischief upon his bed; he setteth himself in a way that is not good; he abhorreth not evil.

5 Your mercy, O יהוה, is in the heavens; and Your faithfulness reacheth unto the clouds.

6 Your righteousness is like the great mountains; Your judgments are a great deep; O יהוה, You preservest man and beast.

7 How excellent is Your loving-kindness, O God (Elohim)! Therefore the children of men put their trust under the shadow of Your wings.

8 They shall be abundantly satisfied with the fatness of Your house; and You shalt make them drink of the river of Your pleasures.

9 For with You is the fountain of life; in Your light shall we see light.

10 O continue Your lovingkindness unto them that know You; and Your righteousness to the upright in heart.

11 Let not the foot of pride come against me, and let not the hand of the wicked remove me.

12 There are the workers of iniquity fallen; they are cast down, and shall not be able to rise.

37 A Psalm of Dawid.
1 Fret not yourself because of evildoers, neither be you envious against the workers of iniquity.

2 For they shall soon be cut down like the grass, and wither as the green herb.

3 Trust in יהוה, and do good; so shalt you dwell in the land, and verily you shalt be fed.

4 Delight yourself also in יהוה; and He shall give you the desires of your heart.

5 Commit your way unto יהוה; trust also in Him; and He shall bring it to pass.

6 And He shall bring forth your righteousness as the light, and your judgment as the noonday.

7 Rest in יהוה, and wait patiently for Him; fret not yourself because of him who prospereth in his way, because of the man who bringeth wicked devices to pass.

8 Cease from anger, and forsake wrath; fret not yourself in any wise to do evil.

9 For evildoers shall be cut off; but those that wait upon יהוה, they shall inherit the earth.

10 For yet a little while, and the wicked shall not be; yea, you shalt diligently consider his place, and it shall not be.

11 But the meek shall inherit the earth; and shall delight themselves in the abundance of peace.

12 The wicked plotteth against the just, and gnasheth upon him with his teeth.

13 My Lord (Adonai) shall laugh at him, for He seeth that his day is coming.

14 The wicked have drawn out the sword, and have bent their bow, to cast down the poor and needy, and to slay such as be of upright conversation.

15 Their sword shall enter into their own heart, and their bows shall be broken.

16 A little that a righteous man hath is better than the riches of many wicked.

17 For the arms of the wicked shall be broken, but יהוה upholdeth the righteous.

18 יהוה knoweth the days of the upright; and their inheritance shall be forever.

19 They shall not be ashamed in the evil time; and in the days of famine they shall be satisfied.

20 But the wicked shall perish, and the enemies of יהוה shall be as the fat of lambs; they shall consume; into smoke shall they consume away.

21 The wicked borroweth, and payeth not again; but the righteous sheweth mercy, and giveth.

22 For such as be blessed of Him shall inherit the earth; and they that be cursed of Him shall be cut off.

23 The steps of a good man are ordered by יהוה, and He delighteth in his way.

24 Though he falls, he shall not be utterly cast dow; for יהוה upholdeth him with His hand.

25 I have been young, and now am old; yet have I not seen the righteous forsaken, nor his seed begging bread.

26 He is ever merciful, and lendeth; and his seed is blessed.

27 Depart from evil, and do good; and dwell forevermore.

28 For יהוה loveth judgment, and forsaketh not His holy ones; they are preserved forever, but the seed of the wicked shall be cut off.

29 The righteous shall inherit the land, and dwell therein forever.

30 The mouth of the righteous speaketh wisdom, and his tongue talketh of judgment.

31 The Torah of his God (Elohim) is in his heart; none of his steps shall slide.

32 The wicked watcheth the righteous, and seeketh to slay him.

33 יהוה will not leave him in his hand, nor condemn him when he is judged.

34 Wait on יהוה, and keep His way, and He shall exalt you to inherit the land; when the wicked are cut off, You shalt see it.

35 I have seen the wicked in great power, and spreading himself like a green bay tree.

36 Yet he passed away, and, behold, he was not; yea, I sought him, but he could not be found.

37 Mark the perfect man, and behold the upright; for the end of that man is peace.

38 But the transgressors shall be destroyed together; the end of the wicked shall be cut off.

39 But the salvation of the righteous is of יהוה; He is their strength in the time of trouble.

40 And יהוה shall help them, and deliver them; He shall deliver them from the wicked, and save them, because they trust in Him.

38 A Psalm of Dawid, to bring to remembrance.

1 O יהוה, rebuke me not in Your wrath; nor chasten me in Your hot displeasure.

2 For Your arrows stick fast in me, and Your hand presseth me sore.

3 There is no soundness in my flesh because of Your anger; neither is there any rest in my bones because of my sin.

4 For mine iniquities are gone over mine head; as a heavy burden they are too heavy for me.

5 My wounds stink and are corrupt because of my foolishness.

6 I am troubled; I am bowed down greatly; I go mourning all the day long.

7 For my loins are filled with a loathsome disease; and there is no soundness in my flesh.

8 I am feeble and sore broken; I have roared by reason of the disquietness of my heart.

9 My Lord (Adonai), all my desire is before

You; and my groaning is not hidden from You.

10 My heart panteth, my strength faileth me; as for the light of mine eyes, it also is gone from me.

11 My love ones and my friends stand aloof from my plague; and my kinsmen stand afar off.

12 They also that seek after my life lay snares for me; and they that seek my hurt speak mischievous things, and imagine deceits all the day long.

13 But I, as a deaf man, heard not; and I was as a dumb man that openeth not his mouth.

14 Thus I was as a man that heareth not, and in whose mouth are no reproofs.

15 For in You, O יהוה, do I hope; You wilt hear, O Lord my God (Adonai Elohai).

16 For I said, "Hear me, lest otherwise they should rejoice over me; when my foot slippeth, they magnify themselves against me."

17 For I am ready to halt, and my sorrow is continually before me.

18 For I will declare mine iniquity; I will be sorry for my sin.

19 But mine enemies are lively, and they are strong; and they that hate me wrongfully are multiplied.

20 They also that render evil for good are mine adversaries; because I follow the thing that good is.

21 Forsake me not, O יהוה; my God (Elohai), be not far from me.

22 Make haste to help me, O Lord (Adonai) my deliverance.

39 To the chief Musician, even to Yedutun. A Psalm of Dawid.

1 I said, "I will take heed to my ways, that I sin not with my tongue; I will keep my mouth with a bridle, while the wicked is before me."

2 I was dumb with silence, I held my peace, even from good; and my sorrow was stirred.

3 My heart was hot within me, while I was musing the fire burned; then spake I with my tongue,

4 יהוה, make me to know mine end, and the measure of my days, what it is; that I may know how frail I am.

5 Behold, You have made my days as a handbreadth, and mine age is as nothing before You; verily every man at his best state is altogether vanity. Selah.

6 Surely every man walketh about like shadow;

surely they are disquieted in vain; he heapeth up riches, and knoweth not who shall gather them.

7 And now, my Lord (Adonai), what wait I for? My hope is in You.

8 Deliver me from all my transgressions; make me not the reproach of the foolish.

9 I was dumb, I opened not my mouth; because You didst it.

10 Remove Your plague away from me; I am consumed by the blow of Your hand.

11 When You with rebukes dost correct man for iniquity, You makest his beauty to consume away like a moth; surely every man is vanity. Selah.

12 Hear my prayer, O יהוה, and give ear unto my cry; hold not Your peace at my tears; for I am a stranger with You, and a sojourner, as all my fathers were.

13 O spare me, that I may recover strength, before I go away, and be no more.

40 To the chief Musician, A Psalm of Dawid. 1 I waited patiently for יהוה; and He inclined unto me, and heard my cry.

2 He brought me up also out of a horrible pit, out of the miry clay, and set my feet upon a rock, and established my goings.

3 And He hath put a new song in my mouth, even praise unto our God (Elohim); many shall see it, and fear, and shall trust in יהוה.

4 Blessed is that man who maketh יהוה his trust, and respecteth not the proud, nor such as turn aside to lies.

5 Many, O יהוה my God (YHWH Elohai), are Your wonderful works which You have done, and Your thoughts which are toward us; they cannot be reckoned up in order unto You; if I would declare and speak of them, they are more than can be numbered.

6 Sacrifice and offering You didst not desire; mine ears have You opened; burnt offering and sin offering have You not required.

7 Then said I, "Behold, I come; in the volume of the book it is written of me,

8 I delight to do Your will, O my God (Elohim); yea, Your Torah is within my heart."

9 I have preached righteousness in the great congregation; behold, I have not refrained my lips, O יהוה, You knowest.

10 I have not hidden Your righteousness within my heart; I have declared Your faithfulness and Your salvation; I have not concealed Your lovingkindness and Your truth from the great congregation.

11 Withhold not You Your tender mercies from me, O יהוה; let Your lovingkindness and Your truth continually preserve me.

12 For innumerable evils have compassed me about; mine iniquities have taken hold upon me, so that I am not able to look up; they are more than the hairs of mine head; therefore my heart faileth me.

13 Be pleased, O יהוה, to deliver me; O יהוה, make haste to help me.

14 Let them be ashamed and confounded together who seek after my soul to destroy it; let them be driven backward and put to shame that wish me evil.

15 Let them be desolate for a reward of their shame that say unto me, "Aha, aha!"

16 Let all those who seek You rejoice and be glad in You; let such as love Your salvation say continually, "יהוה be magnified!"

17 But I am poor and needy; yet my Lord (Adonai) thinketh upon me; You are my help and my deliverer; make no tarrying, O my God (Elohim).

41 To the chief Musician, A Psalm of Dawid. 1 Blessed is he who considereth the poor; יהוה will deliver him in time of trouble.

2 יהוה will preserve him, and keep him alive; and he shall be blessed upon the earth; and You wilt not deliver him unto the will of his enemies.

3 יהוה will strengthen him upon the bed of languishing; You wilt make all his bed in his sickness.

4 I said, "יהוה, be merciful unto me; heal my soul, for I have sinned against You."

5 Mine enemies speak evil of me: "When shall he die, and his name perish?"

6 And if he come to see me, he speaketh vanity; his heart gathereth iniquity to itself; when he goeth abroad, he telleth it.

7 All that hate me whisper together against me; against me do they devise my hurt.

8 "An evil disease", say they, "cleaveth fast unto him; and now that he lieth he shall rise up no more."

9 Yea, mine own familiar friend, in whom I trusted, which did eat of my bread, hath lifted up his heel against me.

10 But You, O יהוה, be merciful unto me, and raise me up, that I may requite them.

11 By this I know that You favourest me, because mine enemy doth not triumph over me.
12 And as for me, You upholdest me in mine integrity, and settest me before Your face forever.
13 Blessed be יהוה God of Israel (Elohei Yisrael) from everlasting, and to everlasting! Amen, and Amen.

42 To the chief Musician, Maskil, for the sons of Korah (Qorach).

1 As the deer panteth after the water brooks, so panteth my soul after You, O God (Elohim).
2 My soul thirsteth for God (Elohim), for the living God (El chai); when shall I come and appear before God (Elohim)?
3 My tears have been my food day and night, while they continually say unto me, "Where is your God (Elohim)?"
4 When I remember these things, I pour out my soul in me; for I had gone with the multitude, I went with them to the house of God (Elohim), with the voice of joy and praise, with a multitude that kept a feast.
5 Why are you cast down, O my soul? And why are you disquieted in me? Hope you in God (Elohim), for I shall yet praise Him for the help of His countenance.
6 O my God (Elohim), my soul is cast down within me; therefore will I remember You from the land of Jordan (Yarden), and of the Hermonites, from the hill Mizar.
7 Deep calleth unto deep at the noise of Your waterspouts; all Your waves and Your billows are gone over me.
8 Yet יהוה will command His lovingkindness in the daytime, and in the night His song shall be with me, and my prayer unto the God (El) of my life.
9 I will say unto God (Elohim) my Rock, "Why have You forgotten me? Why go I mourning because of the oppression of the enemy?"
10 As with a sword in my bones, mine enemies reproach me; while they say daily unto me, "Where is your God (Elohim)?"
11 Why are you cast down, O my soul? And why are you disquieted within me? Hope you in God (Elohim), for I shall yet praise Him, who is the health of my countenance, and my God (Elohim).

43 Judge me, O God (Elohim), and plead my cause against a wicked nation; O deliver me from the deceitful and unjust man!
2 For You are the God (Elohim) of my strength; why dost You cast me off? Why go I mourning because of the oppression of the enemy?
3 O send out Your light and Your truth; let them lead me; let them bring me unto Your holy hill, and to Your tabernacles.
4 Then will I go unto the altar of God (Elohim), unto God (El) my exceeding joy; yea, upon the harp will I praise you, O God my God (Elohim Elohai).
5 Why are you cast down, O my soul? And why are you disquieted within me? Hope in God (Elohim), for I shall yet praise Him, who is the health of my countenance, and my God (Elohim).

44 To the chief Musician for the sons of Korah (Qorach), Maskil.
1 We have heard with our ears, O God (Elohim), our fathers have told us, what work You didst in their days, in the times of old.
2 How You didst drive out the heathen with Your hand, and plantedst them; how You didst afflict the people, and cast them out.
3 For they got not the land in possession by their own sword, neither did their own arm save them; but Your right hand, and Your arm, and the light of Your countenance, because You hadst a favor unto them.
4 You are my King, O God (Elohim); command deliverances for Jacob (Yaaqov).
5 Through You will we push down our enemies; through Your name will we tread them under that rise up against us.
6 For I will not trust in my bow, neither shall my sword save me.
7 But You have saved us from our enemies, and have put them to shame that hated us.
8 In God (Elohim) we boast all the day long, and praise Your name forever. Selah.
9 But You have cast off, and put us to shame; and goest not forth with our armies.
10 You makest us to turn back from the enemy; and those who hate us spoil for themselves.
11 You have given us like sheep appointed for food; and have scattered us among the heathen.
12 You sellest Your people for nought, and dost not increase Your wealth by their price.
13 You makest us a reproach to our neighbours, a scorn and a derision to them that are round about us.

14 You makest us a byword among the heathens, a shaking of the head among the people.

15 My confusion is continually before me, and the shame of my face hath covered me,

16 For the voice of him that reproacheth and blasphemeth; by reason of the enemy and avenger.

17 All this is come upon us; yet have we not forgotten You, neither have we dealt falsely in Your covenant.

18 Our heart is not turned back, neither have our steps declined from Your way;

19 Though You have sore broken us in the place of dragons, and covered us with the shadow of death.

20 If we have forgotten the name of our God (Elohim), or stretched out our hands to a strange god (elohim);

21 Shall not God (Elohim) search this out? For He knoweth the secrets of the heart.

22 Yea, for Your sake are we killed all the day long; we are counted as sheep for the slaughter.

23 Awake, why sleepest You, O Lord (Adonai)? Arise, cast us not off forever.

24 Wherefore hidest You Your face, and forgettest our affliction and our oppression?

25 For our soul is bowed down to the dust; our belly cleaveth unto the earth.

26 Arise for our help, and redeem us for Your mercies' sake.

45 To the chief Musician upon Shoshannim, for the sons of Korah (Qorach), Maskil, A Song of loves.

1 My heart is inditing a good matter; I speak of the things which I have made touching the king; my tongue is the pen of a ready writer.

2 You are fairer than the children of men; grace is poured into your lips; therefore God (Elohim) hath blessed you forever.

3 Gird Your sword upon Your thigh, O most mighty, with Your glory and Your majesty.

4 And in Your majesty ride prosperously because of truth and meekness and righteousness; and Your right hand shall teach You awesome things.

5 Your arrows are sharp in the heart of the king's enemies; whereby the people fall under You.

6 Your throne, O God (Elohim), is forever and ever; the sceptre of Your kingdom is a right sceptre.

7 You lovest righteousness, and hatest wickedness; therefore God (Elohim), your God (Elohim), hath anointed you with the oil of gladness above your fellows.

8 All your garments smell of myrrh, and aloes, and cassia, out of the ivory palaces, whereby they have made You glad.

9 Kings' daughters were among Your honourable women; upon Your right hand did stand the queen in gold of Ophir.

10 Hearken, O daughter, and consider, and incline your ear; forget also your own people, and your father's house;

11 So shall the king greatly desire your beauty, for he is your lord; so honor you him.

12 And the daughter of Tyre shall be there with a gift; even the rich among the people shall intreat Your favor.

13 The king's daughter is all glorious within; her clothing is of wrought gold.

14 She shall be brought unto the king in raiment of needlework; the virgins her companions that follow her shall be brought unto You.

15 With gladness and rejoicing shall they be brought; they shall enter into the king's palace.

16 Instead of your fathers shall be your children, whom you mayest make princes in all the earth.

17 I will make Your name to be remembered in all generations; therefore shall the people praise You forever and ever.

46 To the chief Musician for the sons of Korah (Qorach), A Song upon Alamoth.

1 God (Elohim) is our refuge and strength, a very present help in trouble.

2 Therefore will not we fear, though the earth be removed, and though the mountains be carried into the midst of the sea;

3 Though the waters thereof roar and be troubled, though the mountains shake with the swelling thereof. Selah.

4 There is a river, the streams whereof shall make glad the city of God (Elohim), the holy place of the tabernacles of the Most High (Elyon).

5 God (Elohim) is in the midst of her; she shall not be moved: God (Elohim) shall help her, and that right early.

6 The nations raged, the kingdoms were moved: He uttered His voice, the earth melted.

7 יהוה of hosts (YHWH Tsevaot) is with us; the God (Elohim) of Jacob (Yaaqov) is our refuge. Selah.

8 Come, behold the works of יהוה, what desolations He hath made in the earth.

9 He maketh wars to cease unto the end of the earth; He breaketh the bow, and cutteth the spear in two; He burneth the chariot in the fire.

10 Be still, and know that I am God (Elohim); I will be exalted among the nations, I will be exalted in the earth.

11 יהוה of hosts (YHWH Tsevaot) is with us; the God (Elohim) of Jacob (Yaaqov) is our refuge. Selah.

47 To the chief Musician, A Psalm for the sons of Korah (Qorach).

1 O clap your hands, all you people; shout unto God (Elohim) with the voice of triumph.

2 For יהוה Most High (Elyon) is awesome; He is a great King over all the earth.

3 He shall subdue the people under us, and the nations under our feet.

4 He shall choose our inheritance for us, the excellency of Jacob (Yaaqov) whom He loved. Selah.

5 God (Elohim) is gone up with a shout, יהוה with the sound of a trumpet.

6 Sing praises to God (Elohim), sing praises; sing praises unto our King, sing praises.

7 For God (Elohim) is the King of all the earth; sing you praises with understanding.

8 God (Elohim) reigneth over the nations; God (Elohim) sitteth upon the throne of His holiness.

9 The princes of the people are gathered together, even the people of the God (Elohim) of Avraham; for the shields of the earth belong unto God (Elohim); He is greatly exalted.

48 A Song and Psalm for the sons of Korah (Qorach).

1 Great is יהוה, and greatly to be praised in the city of our God (Elohim), in the mountain of His holiness.

2 Beautiful for situation, the joy of the whole earth, is Mount Zion (Tsiyon), on the sides of the north, the city of the great King.

3 God (Elohim) is known in her palaces for a refuge.

4 For, behold, the kings were assembled, they passed by together.

5 They saw it, and so they marvelled; they were troubled, and hasted away.

6 Fear took hold upon them there, and pain, as of a woman in travail.

7 You breakest the ships of Tarshish with an east wind.

8 As we have heard, so have we seen in the city of יהוה of Host (YHWH Tsevaot), in the city of our God (Elohim); God (Elohim) will establish it forever. Selah.

9 We have thought of Your lovingkindness, O God (Elohim), in the midst of Your temple.

10 According to Your name, O God (Elohim), so is Your praise unto the ends of the earth; Your right hand is full of righteousness.

11 Let Mount Zion (Tsiyon) rejoice, let the daughters of Judah (Yehudah) be glad, because of Your judgments.

12 Walk about Zion (Tsiyon), and go round about her; tell the towers thereof.

13 Mark you well her bulwarks, consider her palaces; that you may tell it to the generation following.

14 For this God (Elohim) is our God (Elohim) forever and ever; He will be our guide even unto death.

49 To the chief Musician, A Psalm for the sons of Korah (Qorach).

1 Hear this, all you people; give ear, all you inhabitants of the world;

2 Both low and high, rich and poor, together.

3 My mouth shall speak of wisdom; and the meditation of my heart shall be of understanding.

4 I will incline mine ear to a parable; I will open my dark saying upon the harp.

5 Wherefore should I fear in the days of evil, when the iniquity of my heels shall compass me about?

6 They that trust in their wealth, and boast themselves in the multitude of their riches;

7 None of them can by any means redeem his brother, nor give to God (Elohim) a ransom for him;

8 (For the redemption of their soul is precious, and it ceaseth forever;)

9 That he should still live forever, and not see destruction.

10 For He seeth that wise men die, likewise the fool and the brutish person perish, and leave their wealth to others.

11 Their inward thought is, that their houses shall continue forever, and their dwelling places to all generations; they call their lands after their own names.

12 Nevertheless man being in honor abideth not; he is like the beasts that perish.

13 This their way is their folly; yet their posterity approves their sayings. Selah.

14 Like sheep they are laid in the grave (sheol); death shall feed on them; and the upright shall have dominion over them in the morning; and their beauty shall consume in the grave (sheol) from their dwelling.

15 But God (Elohim) will redeem my soul from the power of the sheol, for He shall receive me. Selah.

16 Be not you afraid when one is made rich, when the glory of his house is increased;

17 For when he dieth he shall carry nothing away; His glory shall not descend after him.

18 Though while he lives he blessed his soul; and men will praise you, when you doest well to yourself.

19 He shall go to the generation of his fathers; they shall never see light.

20 Man who is in honor, and understandeth not, is like the beasts that perish.

50 A Psalm of Asaph.
1 The Mighty One (El), God (Elohim) יהוה hath spoken, and called the earth from the rising of the sun unto the going down thereof.

2 Out of Zion (Tsiyon), the perfection of beauty, God (Elohim) hath shined.

3 Our God (Elohim) shall come, and shall not keep silence; a fire shall devour before Him, and it shall be very tempestuous round about Him.

4 He shall call to the heavens from above, and to the earth, that He may judge His people.

5 Gather my holy ones together unto me; those that have made a covenant with me by sacrifice.

6 And the heavens shall declare His righteousness, for God (Elohim) is Judge Himself. Selah.

7 Hear, O My people, and I will speak; O Yisrael, and I will testify against you: I am God (Elohim), your God (Elohim).

8 I will not reprove you for your sacrifices or your burnt offerings, to have been continually before Me.

9 I will take no bullock out of your house, nor he goats out of your folds.

10 For every beast of the forest is Mine, and the cattle upon a thousand hills.

11 I know all the fowls of the mountains; and the wild beasts of the field are Mine.

12 If I was hungry, I would not tell you; for the world is Mine, and the fullness thereof.

13 Will I eat the flesh of bulls, or drink the blood of goats?

14 Offer unto God (Elohim) thanksgiving; and pay your vows unto the Most High (Elyon);

15 And call upon Me in the day of trouble; I will deliver you, and you shalt glorify Me.

16 But unto the wicked, God (Elohim) saith, "What have you to do to declare My statutes, or that you shouldest take My covenant in your mouth?

17 Seeing you hatest instruction, and castest My words behind you.

18 When you sawest a thief, then you consentedst with him, and have been partaker with adulterers.

19 You givest your mouth to evil, and your tongue frameth deceit.

20 You sittest and speakest against your brother; you slanderest your own mother's son.

21 These things have you done, and I kept silence; you thoughtest that I was altogether such a one as yourself: but I will reprove you, and set them in order before your eyes.

22 Now consider this, you that forget God (Eloah), lest I tear you in pieces, and there be none to deliver.

23 Whoso offereth praise glorifieth Me; and to him who ordereth his conversation aright will I shew the salvation of God (Elohim)."

51 To the chief Musician, A Psalm of Dawid, when Nathan the prophet came unto him, after he had gone in to Bat-Sheva.

1 Have mercy upon me, O God (Elohim), according to Your lovingkindness; according unto the multitude of Your tender mercies blot out my transgressions.

2 Wash me throughly from mine iniquity, and cleanse me from my sin.

3 For I acknowledge my transgressions; and my sin is ever before me.

4 Against You, You only, have I sinned, and done this evil in Your sight; that You mightest be justified when You speakest, and be clear when You judgest.

5 Behold, I was shapen in iniquity; and in sin did my mother conceive me.

6 Behold, You desirest truth in the inward parts; and in the hidden part You shalt make me to know wisdom.

7 Purge me with hyssop, and I shall be clean; wash me, and I shall be whiter than snow.

8 Make me to hear joy and gladness; that the bones which You have broken may rejoice.

9 Hide Your face from my sins, and blot out all mine iniquities.

10 Create in me a clean heart, O God (Elohim); and renew a right spirit within me.

11 Cast me not away from Your presence; and take not Your B62bHoly Spirit (Ruach haQodesh) from me.

12 Restore unto me the joy of Your salvation; and uphold me with Your noble Spirit.

13 Then will I teach transgressors Your ways; and sinners shall be converted unto You.

14 Deliver me from bloodguiltiness, O God (Elohim), You God (Elohim) of my salvation; and my tongue shall sing aloud of Your righteousness.

15 O Lord (Adonai), open You my lips; and my mouth shall shew forth Your praise.

16 For You desirest not sacrifice; else would I give it; You delightest not in burnt offering.

17 The sacrifices of God (Elohim) are a broken spirit; a broken and a contrite heart, O God (Elohim), You wilt not despise.

18 Do good in Your good pleasure unto Zion (Tsiyon); build You the walls of Jerusalem (Yerushalayim).

19 Then shalt You be pleased with the sacrifices of righteousness, with burnt offering and whole burnt offering; then shall they offer bullocks upon Your altar.

52 To the chief Musician, Maskil, A Psalm of Dawid, when Doeg the Edomite came and told Shaul, and said unto him, Dawid is come to the house of Ahimelech.

1 Why boastest you yourself in mischief, O mighty man? The goodness of God (El) endureth continually.

2 Your tongue deviseth mischiefs; like a sharp razor, working deceitfully.

3 You lovest evil more than good; and lying rather than to speak righteousness. Selah.

4 You lovest all devouring words, O you deceitful tongue.

5 God (El) shall likewise destroy you forever, He shall take you away, and pluck you out of your dwelling place, and root you out of the land of the living. Selah.

6 The righteous also shall see, and fear, and shall laugh at him;

7 Behold, this is the man that made not God

(Elohim) his strength, but trusted in the abundance of his riches, and strengthened himself in his wickedness.

8 But I am like a green olive tree in the house of God (Elohim); I trust in the mercy of God (Elohim) forever and ever.

9 I will praise You forever, because You have done it; and I will wait on Your name; for it is good before Your faithful ones (chasidim).

53 To the chief Musician upon Mahalath, Maskil, A Psalm of Dawid.

1 The fool hath said in his heart, "There is no God (Elohim)." Corrupt are they, and have done abominable iniquity; there is none that doeth good.

2 God (Elohim) looked down from heaven upon the children of men, to see if there were any who did understand, who did seek God (Elohim).

3 Every one of them has gone back; they are altogether become filthy; there is none that doeth good, no, not one.

4 Have the workers of iniquity no knowledge? Who eat up my people as they eat bread; they have not called upon God (Elohim).

5 There were they in great fear, where no fear was; for God (Elohim) hath scattered the bones of him that encampeth against you. You have put them to shame, because God (Elohim) hath despised them.

6 Oh that the salvation of Yisrael would come out of Zion (Tsiyon)! When God (Elohim) bringeth back the captivity of His people, Jacob (Yaaqov) shall rejoice, and Yisrael shall be glad.

54 To the chief Musician on Neginoth, Maskil, A Psalm of Dawid. When the Ziphims came and said to Shaul, "Doth not Dawid hide himself with us?"

1 Save me, O God (Elohim), by Your name, and judge me by Your strength.

2 Hear my prayer, O God (Elohim); give ear to the words of my mouth.

3 For strangers are risen up against me, and oppressors seek after my soul; they have not set God (Elohim) before them. Selah.

4 Behold, God (Elohim) is mine helper; the Lord (Adonai) is with those who uphold my soul.

5 He shall reward evil unto mine enemies; cut them off in Your truth.

6 I will freely sacrifice unto You; I will praise Your name, O יהוה, for it is good.

7 For He hath delivered me out of all trouble;

and mine eye hath seen His desire upon mine enemies.

55 To the chief Musician on Neginoth, Maskil, A Psalm of Dawid.

1 Give ear to my prayer, O God (Elohim); and hide not Yourself from my supplication.

2 Attend unto me, and hear me; I mourn in my complaint, and make a noise;

3 Because of the voice of the enemy, because of the oppression of the wicked; for they cast iniquity upon me, and in wrath they hate me.

4 My heart is sore pained within me; and the terrors of death are fallen upon me.

5 Fearfulness and trembling have come upon me, and horror hath overwhelmed me.

6 And I said, "Oh, if only I had wings like a dove! For then would I fly away, and be at rest.

7 Behold, then would I wander far off, and remain in the wilderness. Selah.

8 I would hasten my escape from the windy storm and tempest.

9 Destroy, O Lord (Adonai), and divide their tongues; for I have seen violence and strife in the city.

10 Day and night they go about it upon the walls thereof; mischief also and sorrow are in the midst of it.

11 Wickedness is in the midst thereof; deceit and guile depart not from her streets.

12 For it was not an enemy that reproached me; then I could have borne it; neither was it he that hated me that did magnify himself against me; then I would have hidden myself from him.

13 But it was you, a man mine equal, my guide, and mine acquaintance.

14 We took sweet counsel together, and walked unto the house of God (Elohim) in company.

15 Let death seize upon them, and let them go down quick into sheol, for wickedness is in their dwellings, and among them.

16 As for me, I will call upon God (Elohim); and יהוה shall save me.

17 Evening, and morning, and at noon, will I pray, and cry aloud; and He shall hear my voice.

18 He hath delivered my soul in peace from the battle that was against me, for there were many with me.

19 God (El) shall hear, and afflict them, even he that abideth of old. Selah. Because they have no changes, therefore they fear not God (Elohim).

20 He hath put forth his hands against such as be at peace with him; he hath broken his covenant.

21 The words of his mouth were smoother than butter, but war was in his heart; his words were softer than oil, yet were they drawn swords.

22 Cast your burden upon יהוה, and He shall sustain you; He shall never allow the righteous to be moved.

23 But You, O God (Elohim), shalt bring them down into the pit of destruction; bloody and deceitful men shall not live out half their days; but I will trust in You.

56 To the chief Musician upon 'Silent dove from afar (Yonath-elem-rechokim)', Michtam of Dawid, when the Philistines took him in Gath.

1 Be merciful unto me, O God (Elohim); for man would swallow me up; he fighting daily oppresseth me.

2 Mine enemies would daily swallow me up, for they be many that fight against me, O You Most High (Elyon).

3 When I am afraid, I will trust in You.

4 In God (Elohim) I will praise His word, in God (Elohim) I have put my trust; I will not fear what flesh can do unto me.

5 Every day they wrest my words; all their thoughts are against me for evil.

6 They gather themselves together, they hide themselves, they mark my steps, when they wait for my soul.

7 Shall they escape by iniquity? In Your anger cast down the people, O God (Elohim).

8 You tellest my wanderings; put You my tears into Your bottle; are they not in Your book?

9 When I cry unto You, then shall mine enemies turn back; this I know; for God (Elohim) is for me.

10 In God (Elohim) will I praise His word; in יהוה will I praise His word.

11 In God (Elohim) have I put my trust; I will not be afraid what man can do unto me.

12 Your vows are upon me, O God (Elohim); I will render praises unto You.

13 For You have delivered my soul from death; wilt not You deliver my feet from falling, that I may walk before God (Elohim) in the light of the living?

57 To the chief Musician, Altaschith, Michtam of Dawid, when he fled from Shaul in the cave.

1 Be merciful unto me, O God (Elohim), be merciful unto me, for my soul trusteth in You;

yea, in the shadow of Your wings will I make my refuge, until these calamities be overpast.

2 I will cry unto God (Elohim) Most High (Elyon); unto God (El) that performeth all things for me.

3 He shall send from heaven, and save me from the reproach of him that would swallow me up. Selah. God (Elohim) shall send forth His mercy and His truth.

4 My soul is among lions; and I lie even among them that are set on fire, even the sons of men, whose teeth are spears and arrows, and their tongue a sharp sword.

5 Be You exalted, O God (Elohim), above the heavens; let Your glory be above all the earth.

6 They have prepared a net for my steps; my soul is bowed down; they have digged a pit before me, into the midst whereof they are fallen themselves. Selah.

7 My heart is fixed, O God (Elohim), my heart is fixed; I will sing and give praise.

8 Awake up, my glory; awake, psaltery and harp; I myself will awake early.

9 I will praise You, O Lord (Adonai), among the people; I will sing unto You among the nations.

10 For Your mercy is great unto the heavens, and Your truth unto the clouds.

11 Be You exalted, O God (Elohim), above the heavens; let Your glory be above all the earth.

58 To the chief Musician, Altaschith, Michtam of Dawid.

1 Do you indeed speak righteousness, O congregation? Do you judge uprightly, O you sons of men?

2 Yea, in heart you work wickedness; you weigh the violence of your hands in the earth.

3 The wicked are estranged from the womb; they go astray as soon as they be born, speaking lies.

4 Their poison is like the poison of a serpent; they are like the deaf adder that stoppeth her ear;

5 Which will not hearken to the voice of charmers, charming never so wisely.

6 Break their teeth, O God (Elohim), in their mouth; break out the great teeth of the young lions, O יהוה.

7 Let them melt away as waters which run continually; when he bendeth his bow to shoot his arrows, let them be as cut in pieces.

8 As a snail which melteth, let every one of them pass away; like the untimely birth of a woman,

that they may not see the sun.

9 Before your pots can feel the thorns, He shall take them away as with a whirlwind, both living, and in His wrath.

10 The righteous shall rejoice when he seeth the vengeance; he shall wash his feet in the blood of the wicked.

11 So that a man shall say, "Verily there is a reward for the righteous; verily he is a God (Elohim) who judgeth in the earth."

59 To the chief Musician, Altaschith, Michtam of Dawid;

When Shaul sent, and they watched the house to kill him.

1 Deliver me from mine enemies, O my God (Elohim); defend me from them that rise up against me.

2 Deliver me from the workers of iniquity, and save me from bloody men.

3 For, behold, they lie in wait for my soul; the mighty are gathered against me; not for my transgression, nor for my sin, O יהוה.

4 They run and prepare themselves without my fault; awake to help me, and behold.

5 You therefore, O יהוה God of hosts (Elohei Tsevaot), the God of Israel (Elohei Yisrael), awake to visit all the nations; be not merciful to any wicked transgressors. Selah.

6 They return at evening; they make a noise like a dog, and go round about the city.

7 Behold, they belch out with their mouth; swords are in their lips, for say they, "who doth hear?"

8 But You, O יהוה, shalt laugh at them; You shalt have all the nations in derision.

9 Because of his strength will I wait upon You; for God (Elohim) is my defence.

10 The God (Elohim) of my mercy shall meet me; God (Elohim) shall let me see my desire upon mine enemies.

11 Slay them not, lest my people forget; scatter them by Your power; and bring them down, O Lord (Adonai) our shield.

12 For the sin of their mouth and the words of their lips let them even be taken in their pride; and for cursing and lying which they speak.

13 Consume them in wrath, consume them, that they may not be; and let them know that God (Elohim) ruleth in Jacob (Yaaqov) unto the ends of the earth. Selah.

14 And at evening let them return; and let them

make a noise like a dog, and go round about the city.

15 Let them wander up and down for meat, and grudge if they be not satisfied.

16 But I will sing of Your power; yea, I will sing aloud of Your mercy in the morning; for You have been my defence and refuge in the day of my trouble.

17 Unto You, O my strength, will I sing; for God (Elohim) is my defence, and the God (Elohim) of my mercy.

60 To the chief Musician upon Shushaneduth, Michtam of Dawid, to teach; when he strove with Aramnaharaim and with Aramzobah, when Yoav returned, and smote of Edom in the valley of salt twelve thousand.

1 O God (Elohim), You have cast us off, You have scattered us, You have been displeased; O turn Yourself to us again.

2 You have made the earth to tremble; You have broken it; heal the breaches thereof, for it shaketh.

3 You have shewed Your people hard things; You have made us to drink the wine of astonishment.

4 You have given a banner to them that fear You, that it may be displayed because of the truth. Selah.

5 That Your beloved may be delivered; save with Your right hand, and hear me.

6 God (Elohim) hath spoken in His holiness; I will rejoice, I will divide Shechem, and measure out the valley of Sukkot.

7 Gilad is mine, and Menashsheh is mine; Efrayim also is the strength of mine head; Judah (Yehudah) is my lawgiver;

8 Moav is my washpot; over Edom will I cast out my shoe; Philistia, triumph you because of me.

9 Who will bring me into the strong city? Who will lead me into Edom?

10 Wilt not You, O God (Elohim), which hadst cast us off? And You, O God (Elohim), who didst not go out with our armies?

11 Give us help from trouble, for vain is the help of man.

12 Through God (Elohim) we shall do valiantly, for He it is that shall tread down our enemies.

61 To the chief Musician upon Neginah, A Psalm of Dawid.

1 Hear my cry, O God (Elohim); attend unto my prayer.

2 From the end of the earth will I cry unto You, when my heart is overwhelmed; lead me to the rock that is higher than I.

3 For You have been a shelter for me, and a strong tower from the enemy.

4 I will abide in Your tabernacle forever; I will trust in the covert of Your wings. Selah.

5 For You, O God (Elohim), have heard my vows; You have given me the heritage of those who fear Your name.

6 You wilt prolong the king's life; and his years as many generations.

7 He shall abide before God (Elohim) forever; O prepare mercy and truth, which may preserve him.

8 So will I sing praise unto Your name forever, that I may daily perform my vows.

62 To the chief Musician, to Yedutun, A Psalm of Dawid.

1 Truly my soul waiteth upon God (Elohim); from Him cometh my salvation.

2 He only is my rock and my salvation; He is my defence; I shall not be greatly moved.

3 How long will you imagine mischief against a man? You shall be slain all of you; as a bowing wall shall you be, and as a tottering fence.

4 They only consult to cast him down from his excellency; they delight in lies; they bless with their mouth, but they curse inwardly. Selah.

5 My soul, wait only upon God (Elohim); for my expectation is from Him.

6 He only is my rock and my salvation; He is my defence; I shall not be moved.

7 In God (Elohim) is my salvation and my glory; the rock of my strength, and my refuge, is in God (Elohim).

8 Trust in Him at all times; you people, pour out your heart before Him; God (Elohim) is a refuge for us. Selah.

9 Surely men of low degree are vanity, and men of high degree are a lie; to be laid in the balance, they are altogether lighter than vanity.

10 Trust not in oppression, and become not vain in robbery; if riches increase, set not your heart upon them.

11 God (Elohim) hath spoken once; twice have I heard this; that power belongeth unto God (Elohim).

12 Also unto You, O Lord (Adonai), belongeth mercy; for You renderest to every man according

to his work.

63 A Psalm of Dawid, when he was in the wilderness of Judah (Yehudah).

1 O God (Elohim), You are my God (Eli); early will I seek You; my soul thirsteth for You, my flesh longeth for You in a dry and thirsty land, where no water is;

2 To see Your power and Your glory, so as I have seen You in the sanctuary.

3 Because Your lovingkindness is better than life, my lips shall praise You.

4 Thus will I bless You while I live; I will lift up my hands in Your name.

5 My soul shall be satisfied as with marrow and fatness; and my mouth shall praise you with joyful lips;

6 When I remember you upon my bed, and meditate on You in the night watches.

7 Because You have been my help, therefore in the shadow of Your wings will I rejoice.

8 My soul followeth hard after You; Your right hand upholdeth me.

9 But those who seek my soul, to destroy it, shall go into the lower parts of the earth.

10 They shall fall by the sword; they shall be a portion for foxes.

11 But the king shall rejoice in God (Elohim); every one who sweareth by Him shall glory; but the mouth of those who speak lies shall be stopped.

64 To the chief Musician, A Psalm of Dawid.

1 Hear my voice, O God (Elohim), in my prayer; preserve my life from fear of the enemy.

2 Hide me from the secret counsel of the wicked; from the insurrection of the workers of iniquity;

3 Who sharpen their tongue like a sword, and bend their bows to shoot their arrows, even bitter words,

4 That they may shoot in secret at the perfect; suddenly do they shoot at him, and fear not.

5 They encourage themselves in an evil matter; they commune of laying snares privily; they say, "Who shall see them?"

6 They search out iniquities; they accomplish a diligent search; both the inward thought of every one of them, and the heart, is deep.

7 But God (Elohim) shall shoot at them with an arrow; suddenly shall they be wounded.

8 So they shall make their own tongue to fall upon themselves; all that see them shall flee away.

9 And all men shall fear, and shall declare the work of God (Elohim); for they shall wisely consider of His doing.

10 The righteous shall be glad in יהוה, and shall trust in Him; and all the upright in heart shall glory.

65 To the chief Musician, A Psalm and Song of Dawid.

1 Praise waiteth for You, O God (Elohim), in Zion (Tsiyon); and unto You shall the vow be performed.

2 O You that hearest prayer, unto You shall all flesh come.

3 Iniquities prevail against me; as for our transgressions, You shalt purge them away.

4 Blessed is the man whom You choosest, and causest to approach unto You, that he may dwell in Your courts; we shall be satisfied with the goodness of Your house, even of Your holy temple.

5 By awesome deeds in righteousness wilt You answer us, O God (Elohim) of our salvation; who art the confidence of all the ends of the earth, and of them that are afar off upon the sea;

6 Which by His strength setteth fast the mountains; being girded with power;

7 Which stilleth the noise of the seas, the noise of their waves, and the tumult of the people.

8 They also that dwell in the uttermost parts are afraid at Your tokens; You makest the outgoings of the morning and evening to rejoice.

9 You visitest the earth, and waterest it; You greatly enrichest it with the river of God (Elohim), which is full of water; You preparest them corn, when You have so provided for it.

10 You waterest the ridges thereof abundantly, You settlest the furrows thereof; You makest it soft with showers; You blessest the springing thereof.

11 You crownest the year with Your goodness; and Your paths drop fatness.

12 They drop upon the pastures of the wilderness, and the little hills rejoice on every side.

13 The pastures are clothed with flocks; the valleys also are covered over with corn; they shout for joy, they also sing.

66 To the chief Musician, A Song or Psalm.

1 Make a joyful shout unto God (Elohim), all you lands;

2 Sing forth the honor of His name; make His

praise glorious.

3 Say unto God (Elohim), "How awesome art You in Your works!" Through the greatness of Your power shall Your enemies submit themselves unto You.

4 All the earth shall worship You, and shall sing unto You; they shall sing to Your name. Selah.

5 Come and see the works of God (Elohim); He is awesome in His doing toward the children of men.

6 He turned the sea into dry land; they went through the flood on foot; there did we rejoice in Him.

7 He ruleth by His power forever; His eyes behold the nations; let not the rebellious exalt themselves. Selah.

8 O bless our God (Elohim), you people, and make the voice of His praise to be heard,

9 Which holdeth our soul in life, and allow not our feet to be moved.

10 For You, O God (Elohim), have proved us; You have tried us, as silver is tried.

11 You broughtest us into the net; You laidst affliction upon our loins.

12 You have caused men to ride over our heads; we went through fire and through water; but You broughtest us out into a wealthy place.

13 I will go into Your house with burnt offerings; I will pay You my vows,

14 Which my lips have uttered, and my mouth hath spoken, when I was in trouble.

15 I will offer unto You burnt sacrifices of fatlings, with the incense of rams; I will offer bullocks with goats. Selah.

16 Come and hear, all you that fear God (Elohim), and I will declare what He hath done for my soul.

17 I cried unto Him with my mouth, and He was extolled with my tongue.

18 If I regard iniquity in my heart, the Lord (Adonai) will not hear me:

19 But verily God (Elohim) hath heard me; He hath attended to the voice of my prayer.

20 Blessed be God (Elohim), who hath not turned away my prayer, nor His mercy from me.

67 To the chief Musician on Neginoth, A Psalm or Song.

1 God (Elohim) be merciful unto us, and bless us; and cause His face to shine upon us; Selah.

2 That Your way may be known upon earth, Your saving health among all nations.

3 Let the people praise You, O God (Elohim); let all the people praise You.

4 O let the nations be glad and sing for joy, for You shalt judge the people righteously, and govern the nations upon earth. Selah.

5 Let the people praise You, O God (Elohim); let all the people praise You.

6 Then shall the earth yield her increase; and God (Elohim), even our own God (Elohim), shall bless us.

7 God (Elohim) shall bless us; and all the ends of the earth shall fear Him.

68 To the chief Musician, A Psalm or Song of Dawid.

1 Let God (Elohim) arise, let His enemies be scattered; let them also who hate Him flee before Him.

2 As smoke is driven away, so drive them away; as wax melteth before the fire, so let the wicked perish at the presence of God (Elohim).

3 But let the righteous be glad; let them rejoice before God (Elohim); yea, let them exceedingly rejoice.

4 Sing unto God (Elohim), sing praises to His name; extol Him that rideth upon the heavens by His name יה (Yah), and rejoice before Him.

5 A father of the fatherless, and a judge of the widows, is God (Elohim) in His holy habitation.

6 God (Elohim) setteth the solitary in families; He bringeth out those who are bound with chains, but the rebellious dwell in a dry land.

7 O God (Elohim), when You wentest forth before Your people, when You didst march through the wilderness; Selah.

8 The earth shook, the heavens also dropped at the presence of God (Elohim); even Sinai itself was moved at the presence of God (Elohim), the God of Israel (Elohei Yisrael).

9 You, O God (Elohim), didst send a plentiful rain, whereby You didst confirm Your inheritance, when it was weary.

10 Your congregation hath dwelt therein; You, O God (Elohim), have prepared of Your goodness for the poor.

11 My Lord (Adonai) gave the word; great was the company of those who proclaimed it.

12 Kings of armies did flee apace; and she who tarried at home divided the spoil.

13 Though you have lien among the pots, yet shall you be as the wings of a dove covered with silver, and her feathers with yellow gold.

14 When the Almighty scattered kings in it, it was white as snow in Salmon.

15 The hill of God (Elohim) is as the hill of Bashan; a high hill as the hill of Bashan.

16 Why leap you, you high hills? This is the hill which God (Elohim) desireth to dwell in; yea, יהוה will dwell in it forever.

17 The chariots of God (Elohim) are twenty thousand, even thousands of angels; the Lord (Adonai) is among them, as in Sinai, in the holy place.

18 You have ascended on high, You have led captivity captive; You have received gifts for men; yea, for the rebellious also, that יה (Yah), God (Elohim) might dwell among them.

19 Blessed be the Lord (Adonai), Who daily loadeth us with benefits, the God (El) of our salvation. Selah.

20 He who is our God (El) is the God (Elohim) of salvation; and unto the Lord (Adonai) יהוה belong the issues from death.

21 But God (Elohim) shall wound the head of His enemies, and the hairy scalp of such a one as goeth on still in his trespasses.

22 My Lord (Adonai) said, "I will bring again from Bashan, I will bring My people again from the depths of the sea,

23 That your foot may be dipped in the blood of your enemies, and the tongue of your dogs in the same."

24 They have seen Your goings, O God (Elohim); even the goings of my God (Eli), my King, in the sanctuary.

25 The singers went before, the players on instruments followed after; among them were the damsels playing with timbrels.

26 Bless you God (Elohim) in the congregations, יהוה, from the fountain of Yisrael.

27 There is little Benjamin (Binyamin) with their ruler, the princes of Judah (Yehudah) and their council, the princes of Zevulun, and the princes of Naftali.

28 Your God (Elohim) hath commanded your strength; strengthen, O God (Elohim), that which You have wrought for us.

29 Because of Your temple at Jerusalem (Yerushalayim) shall kings bring presents unto You.

30 Rebuke the company of spearmen, the multitude of the bulls, with the calves of the people, till every one submits himself with pieces of silver; scatter You the people that delight in war.

31 Princes shall come out of Egypt (Mitsrayim); Ethiopia (Kush) shall soon stretch out her hands unto God (Elohim).

32 Sing unto God (Elohim), you kingdoms of the earth; O sing praises unto the Lord (Adonai); Selah.

33 To Him who rideth upon the heaven of heavens, which were of old; Behold, He doth send out His voice, and that a mighty voice.

34 Ascribe you strength unto God (Elohim); His excellency is over Yisrael, and His strength is in the clouds.

35 O God (Elohim), You are awesome out of Your holy places; the God of Israel (Elohei Yisrael) is He who giveth strength and power unto His people. Blessed be God (Elohim).

69 To the chief Musician upon Shoshannim, A Psalm of Dawid.

1 Save me, O God (Elohim); for the waters have come in unto my soul.

2 I sink in deep mire, where there is no standing; I have come into deep waters, where the floods overflow me.

3 I am weary of my crying; my throat is dried; mine eyes fail while I wait for my God (Elohim).

4 They who hate me without a cause are more than the hairs of mine head; they who would destroy me, being mine enemies wrongfully, are mighty; then I restored that which I took not away.

5 O God (Elohim), You knowest my foolishness; and my sins are not hid from You.

6 Let not those who wait on You, O Lord (Adonai) יהוה of hosts (YHWH Tsevaot), be ashamed for my sake; let not those who seek You be confounded for my sake, O God of Israel (Elohei Yisrael).

7 Because for Your sake I have borne reproach; shame hath covered my face.

8 I have become a stranger unto my brethren, and an alien unto my mother's children.

9 For the zeal of Your house hath eaten me up; and the reproaches of them that reproached You are fallen upon me.

10 When I wept, and chastened my soul with fasting, that was to my reproach.

11 I made sackcloth also my garment; and I became a proverb to them.

12 They that sit in the gate speak against me;

and I was the song of the drunkards.

13 But as for me, my prayer is unto You, O יהוה, in an acceptable time; O God (Elohim), in the multitude of Your mercy hear me, in the truth of Your salvation.

14 Deliver me out of the mire, and let me not sink; let me be delivered from them that hate me, and out of the deep waters.

15 Let not the waterflood overflow me, neither let the deep swallow me up, and let not the pit shut her mouth upon me.

16 Hear me, O יהוה, for Your lovingkindness is good; turn unto me according to the multitude of Your tender mercies.

17 And hide not Your face from Your servant; for I am in trouble; hear me speedily.

18 Draw near unto my soul, and redeem it; deliver me because of mine enemies.

19 You have known my reproach, and my shame, and my dishonor; mine adversaries are all before You.

20 Reproach hath broken my heart; and I am full of heaviness; and I looked for some to take pity, but there was none; and for comforters, but I found none.

21 They gave me also gall for my meat; and in my thirst they gave me vinegar to drink.

22 Let their table become a snare before them: and that which should have been for their welfare, let it become a trap.

23 Let their eyes be darkened, that they see not; and make their loins continually to shake.

24 Pour out Your indignation upon them, and let Your wrathful anger take hold of them.

25 Let their habitation be desolate; and let none dwell in their tents.

26 For they persecute him whom You have smitten; and they talk to the grief of those whom You have wounded.

27 Add iniquity unto their iniquity; and let them not come into Your righteousness.

28 Let them be blotted out of the book of the living, and not be written with the righteous.

29 But I am poor and sorrowful; let Your salvation, O God (Elohim), set me up on high.

30 I will praise the name of God (Elohim) with a song, and will magnify Him with thanksgiving.

31 This also shall please יהוה better than an ox or bullock that hath horns and hoofs.

32 The humble shall see this, and be glad; and your heart shall live who seek God (Elohim).

33 For יהוה heareth the poor, and despiseth not His prisoners.

34 Let the heaven and earth praise Him, the seas, and every thing that moveth therein.

35 For God (Elohim) will save Zion (Tsiyon), and will build the cities of Judah (Yehudah), that they may dwell there, and have it in possession.

36 The seed also of His servants shall inherit it; and those who love His name shall dwell therein.

70 To the chief Musician, A Psalm of Dawid, to bring to remembrance.

1 Make haste, O God (Elohim), to deliver me; make haste to help me, O יהוה.

2 Let them be ashamed and confounded who seek after my soul; let them be turned backward, and put to confusion, that desire my hurt.

3 Let them be turned back for a reward of their shame who say, "Aha, aha!"

4 Let all those who seek You rejoice and be glad in You; and let such as love Your salvation say continually, "Let God (Elohim) be magnified!"

5 But I am poor and needy; make haste unto me, O God (Elohim); You are my help and my deliverer; O יהוה, make no tarrying.

71 In You, O יהוה, do I put my trust; let me never be put to confusion.

2 Deliver me in Your righteousness, and cause me to escape; incline Your ear unto me, and save me.

3 Be You my strong habitation, whereunto I may continually resort; You have given commandment to save me; for You are my rock and my fortress.

4 Deliver me, O my God (Elohim), out of the hand of the wicked, out of the hand of the unrighteous and cruel man.

5 For You are my hope, O Lord (Adonai) יהוה; You are my trust from my youth.

6 By You have I been holden up from the womb; You are He who took me out of my mother's bowels. My praise shall be continually of You.

7 I am as a wonder unto many, but You are my strong refuge.

8 Let my mouth be filled with Your praise and with Your honor all the day.

9 Cast me not off in the time of old age; forsake me not when my strength faileth.

10 For mine enemies speak against me; and they that lay wait for my soul take counsel together,

11 Saying, "God (Elohim) hath forsaken him;

persecute and take him; for there is none to deliver him."

12 O God (Elohim), be not far from me; O my God (Elohim), make haste to help me!

13 Let them be confounded and consumed that are adversaries to my soul; let them be covered with reproach and dishonour that seek my hurt.

14 But I will hope continually, and will yet praise You more and more.

15 My mouth shall shew forth Your righteousness and Your salvation all the day; for I know not the numbers thereof.

16 I will go in the strength of Lord (Adonai) יהוה; I will make mention of Your righteousness, even of Yours only.

17 O God (Elohim), You have taught me from my youth; and to this day have I declared Your wondrous works.

18 Now also when I am old and grayheaded, O God (Elohim), forsake me not; until I have shewed Your strength unto this generation, and Your power to every one that is to come.

19 Your righteousness also, O God (Elohim), is very high, who have done great things; O God (Elohim), who is like unto You!

20 You, who have shewed me great and sore troubles, shalt quicken me again, and shalt bring me up again from the depths of the earth.

21 You shalt increase my greatness, and comfort me on every side.

22 I will also praise You with the psaltery, even Your truth, O my God (Elohim); unto You will I sing with the harp, O You Holy One of Yisrael.

23 My lips shall greatly rejoice when I sing unto You; and my soul, which You have redeemed.

24 My tongue also shall talk of Your righteousness all the day long, for they are confounded, for they are brought unto shame, who seek my hurt.

72 A Psalm for Solomon (Shelomoh).
1 Give the king Your judgments, O God (Elohim), and Your righteousness unto the king's son.

2 He shall judge Your people with righteousness, and Your poor with judgment.

3 The mountains shall bring peace to the people, and the little hills, by righteousness.

4 He shall judge the poor of the people, he shall save the children of the needy, and shall break in pieces the oppressor.

5 They shall fear You as long as the sun and moon endure, throughout all generations.

6 He shall come down like rain upon the mown grass; as showers that water the earth.

7 In his days shall the righteous flourish; and abundance of peace so long as the moon endureth.

8 He shall have dominion also from sea to sea, and from the river unto the ends of the earth.

9 They that dwell in the wilderness shall bow before him; and his enemies shall lick the dust.

10 The kings of Tarshish and of the isles shall bring presents; the kings of Sheva and Seva shall offer gifts.

11 Yea, all kings shall fall down before him: all nations shall serve him.

12 For he shall deliver the needy when he crieth; the poor also, and him that hath no helper.

13 He shall spare the poor and needy, and shall save the souls of the needy.

14 He shall redeem their soul from deceit and violence; and precious shall their blood be in his sight.

15 And he shall live, and to him shall be given of the gold of Sheva; prayer also shall be made for him continually; and daily shall he be praised.

16 There shall be a handful of corn in the earth upon the top of the mountains; the fruit thereof shall shake like Lebanon; and they of the city shall flourish like grass of the earth.

17 His name shall endure forever; His name shall be continued as long as the sun; and men shall be blessed in Him. All nations shall call Him blessed.

18 Blessed be God (Elohim) יהוה, the God of Israel (Elohei Yisrael), who only doeth wondrous things.

19 And blessed be His glorious name forever; and let the whole earth be filled with His glory; So be it (Amen), and so be it (Amen).

20 The prayers of Dawid the son of Jesse (Yishai) are ended.

73 A Psalm of Asaph.
1 Truly God (Elohim) is good to Yisrael, even to such as are of a clean heart.

2 But as for me, my feet were almost gone; my steps had well near slipped.

3 For I was envious at the foolish, when I saw the prosperity of the wicked.

4 For there are no bands in their death; but their strength is firm.

5 They are not in trouble as other men; neither

are they plagued like other men.

6 Therefore pride compasseth them about as a chain; violence covereth them as a garment.

7 Their eyes stand out with fatness; they have more than heart could wish.

8 They are corrupt, and speak wickedly concerning oppression; they speak loftily.

9 They set their mouth against the heavens, and their tongue walketh through the earth.

10 Therefore his people return hither: and waters of a full cup are wrung out to them.

11 And they say, "How doth God (Elohim) know?" And is there knowledge in the Most High (Elyon)?

12 Behold, these are the wicked, who prosper in the world; they increase in riches.

13 Verily I have cleansed my heart in vain, and washed my hands in innocency.

14 For all the day long have I been plagued, and chastened every morning.

15 If I say, I will speak thus; behold, I should offend against the generation of Your children.

16 When I thought to know this, it was too painful for me;

17 Until I went into the sanctuary of God (El); then understood I their end.

18 Surely You didst set them in slippery places; You castedst them down into destruction.

19 How are they brought into desolation, as in a moment! They are utterly consumed with terrors.

20 As a dream when one awaketh; so, O Lord (Adonai), when You awakest, You shalt despise their image.

21 Thus my heart was grieved, and I was pricked in my reins.

22 So foolish was I, and ignorant; I was as a beast before You.

23 Nevertheless I am continually with You; You have holden me by my right hand.

24 You shalt guide me with Your counsel, and afterward receive me to glory.

25 Whom have I in heaven but You? And there is none upon earth that I desire besides You.

26 My flesh and my heart faileth; but God (Elohim) is the strength of my heart, and my portion forever.

27 For, behold, those who are far from you shall perish; You have destroyed all those who go a whoring from You.

28 But it is good for me to draw near to God (Elohim); I have put my trust in Lord (Adonai) יהוה, that I may declare all Your works.

74 Poem (Maskil) of Asaph.
1 O God (Elohim), why have You cast us off forever? Why doth Your anger smoke against the sheep of Your pasture?

2 Remember Your congregation, which You have purchased of old; the rod of Your inheritance, which You have redeemed; this Mount Zion (Tsiyon), wherein You have dwelt.

3 Lift up Your feet unto the perpetual desolations; even all that the enemy hath done wickedly in the sanctuary.

4 Your enemies roar in the midst of Your congregations; they set up their ensigns for signs.

5 A man was famous according as he had lifted up axes upon the thick trees.

6 But now they break down the carved work thereof at once with axes and hammers.

7 They have cast fire into Your sanctuary, they have defiled by casting down the dwelling place of Your name to the ground.

8 They said in their hearts, "Let us destroy them together." They have burned up all the synagogues of God (El) in the land.

9 We see not our signs; there is no more any prophet; nor is there among us any who knoweth how long.

10 O God (Elohim), how long shall the adversary reproach? Shall the enemy blaspheme Your name forever?

11 Why withdrawest You Your hand, even Your right hand? Pluck it out of Your bosom.

12 For God (Elohim) is my King of old, working salvation in the midst of the earth.

13 You didst divide the sea by Your strength; You brakest the heads of the dragons in the waters.

14 You brakest the heads of leviathan in pieces, and gavest him to be meat to the people inhabiting the wilderness.

15 You didst cleave the fountain and the flood; You driedst up mighty rivers.

16 The day is Yours, the night also is Yours; You have prepared the light and the sun.

17 You have set all the borders of the earth: You have made summer and winter.

18 Remember this, that the enemy hath reproached, O יהוה, and that the foolish people have blasphemed Your name.

19 O deliver not the soul of Your turtledove unto the multitude of the wicked; forget not the congregation of Your poor forever.

20 Have respect unto the covenant; for the dark places of the earth are full of the habitations of cruelty.

21 O let not the oppressed return ashamed; let the poor and needy praise Your name.

22 Arise, O God (Elohim), plead Your own cause; remember how the foolish man reproacheth You daily.

23 Forget not the voice of Your enemies; the tumult of those that rise up against You increaseth continually.

75 To the chief Musician, Altaschith, A Psalm or Song of Asaph.

1 Unto You, O God (Elohim), do we give thanks, unto You do we give thanks; for that Your name is near Your wondrous works declare.

2 "When I shall receive the congregation I will judge uprightly.

3 The earth and all the inhabitants thereof are dissolved; I bear up the pillars of it. Selah.

4 I said unto the fools, 'Deal not foolishly'; and to the wicked, 'Lift not up the horn;

5 Lift not up your horn on high: speak not with a stiff neck.'"

6 For promotion cometh neither from the east, nor from the west, nor from the south.

7 But God (Elohim) is the Judge: He putteth down one, and setteth up another.

8 For in the hand of יהוה there is a cup, and the wine is red; it is full of mixture; and He poureth out of the same: but the dregs thereof, all the wicked of the earth shall wring them out, and drink them.

9 But I will declare forever; I will sing praises to the God (Elohim) of Jacob (Yaaqov).

10 "All the horns of the wicked also will I cut off; but the horns of the righteous shall be exalted."

76 To the chief Musician on Neginoth, A Psalm or Song of Asaph.

1 In Judah (Yehudah) is God (Elohim) known: His name is great in Yisrael.

2 In Shalem also is His tabernacle, and His dwelling place in Zion (Tsiyon).

3 There broke He the arrows of the bow, the shield, and the sword, and the battle. Selah.

4 You are more glorious and excellent than the mountains of prey.

5 The stouthearted are spoiled, they have slept their sleep; and none of the men of might have found their hands.

6 At Your rebuke, O God (Elohim) of Jacob (Yaaqov), both the chariot and horse are cast into a dead sleep.

7 You, even You, art to be feared; and who may stand in Your sight when once You are angry?

8 You didst cause judgment to be heard from heaven; the earth feared, and was still,

9 When God (Elohim) arose to judgment, to save all the meek of the earth. Selah.

10 Surely the wrath of man shall praise You; the remainder of wrath shalt You restrain.

11 Vow, and pay unto יהוה your God (YHWH Eloheikhem); let all that be round about Him bring presents unto Him who ought to be feared.

12 He shall cut off the spirit of princes; He is awesome to the kings of the earth.

77 To the chief Musician, to Yedutun, A Psalm of Asaph.

1 I cried unto God (Elohim) with my voice, unto God (Elohim) with my voice; and He gave ear unto me.

2 In the day of my trouble I sought my Lord (Adonai); my hand was stretched out in the night, and weary not; my soul refused to be comforted.

3 I remembered God (Elohim), and was troubled; I complained, and my spirit was overwhelmed. Selah.

4 You holdest mine eyes waking: I am so troubled that I cannot speak.

5 I have considered the days of old, the years of ancient times.

6 I call to remembrance my song in the night; I commune with mine own heart; and my spirit made diligent search.

7 Will my Lord (Adonai) cast off forever? And will He be favourable no more?

8 Has His mercy ceased forever? Doth His promise fails forevermore?

9 Hath God (El) forgotten to be gracious? Hath He in anger shut up His tender mercies? Selah.

10 And I said, "This is my infirmity; but I will remember the years of the right hand of the Most High (Elyon)."

11 I will remember the works of יה (Yah); surely I will remember Your wonders of old.

12 I will meditate also of all Your work, and talk of Your doings.

13 Your way, O God (Elohim), is in the sanctuary; who is so great a God (El) as our God (Elohim)?

14 You are the God (El) that doest wonders: You have declared Your strength among the people.

15 You have with Your arm redeemed Your people, the sons of Jacob (Yaaqov) and Joseph (Yosef). Selah.

16 The waters saw You, O God (Elohim), the waters saw You; they were afraid; the depths also were troubled.

17 The clouds poured out water; the skies sent out a sound; Your arrows also went abroad.

18 The voice of Your thunder was in the heaven; the lightnings lightened the world; the earth trembled and shook.

19 Your way is in the sea, and Your path in the great waters, and Your footsteps are not known.

20 You leddest Your people like a flock by the hand of Moses (Mosheh) and Aaron (Aharon).

78 A Poem (Maskil) of Asaph.
1 Give ear, O my people, to my teaching; incline your ears to the words of my mouth.

2 I will open my mouth in a parable; I will utter dark sayings of old;

3 Which we have heard and known, and our fathers have told us.

4 We will not hide them from their children, shewing to the generation to come the praises of יהוה, and His strength, and His wonderful works that He hath done.

5 For He established a testimony in Jacob (Yaaqov), and appointed a Torah in Yisrael, which He commanded our fathers, that they should make them known to their children;

6 That the generation to come might know them, even the children which should be born; who should arise and declare them to their children;

7 That they might set their hope in God (Elohim), and not forget the works of God (El), but keep His commandments;

8 And might not be as their fathers, a stubborn and rebellious generation; a generation that set not their heart aright, and whose spirit was not stedfast with God (El).

9 The children of Efrayim, being armed, and carrying bows, turned back in the day of battle.

10 They kept not the covenant of God (Elohim), and refused to walk in His Torah;

11 And forgot His works, and His wonders that He had shewed them.

12 Marvellous things did He in the sight of their fathers, in the land of Egypt (Mitsrayim), in the field of Zoan.

13 He divided the sea, and caused them to pass through; and He made the waters to stand as a heap.

14 In the daytime also he led them with a cloud, and all the night with a light of fire.

15 He clave the rocks in the wilderness, and gave them drink as out of the great depths.

16 He brought streams also out of the rock, and caused waters to run down like rivers.

17 And they sinned yet more against Him by provoking the Most High (Elyon) in the wilderness.

18 And they tempted God (El) in their heart by asking meat for their lust.

19 Yea, they spake against God (Elohim); they said, "Can God (El) furnish a table in the wilderness?

20 Behold, He smote the rock, that the waters gushed out, and the streams overflowed; can He give bread also? can He provide flesh for His people?"

21 Therefore יהוה heard this, and was wroth; so a fire was kindled against Jacob (Yaaqov), and anger also came up against Yisrael;

22 Because they believed not in God (Elohim), and trusted not in His salvation.

23 Though He had commanded the clouds from above, and opened the doors of heaven,

24 And had rained down manna upon them to eat, and had given them of the corn of heaven.

25 Man did eat angels' food; He sent them food to the full.

26 He caused an east wind to blow in the heaven; and by His power He brought in the south wind.

27 He rained flesh also upon them as dust, and feathered fowls like as the sand of the sea;

28 And He let it fall in the midst of their camp, round about their habitations.

29 So they did eat, and were well filled, for He gave them their own desire;

30 They were not estranged from their lust. But while their meat was yet in their mouths,

31 The wrath of God (Elohim) came upon them, and slew the fattest of them, and smote down the chosen men of Yisrael.

32 For all this they sinned still, and believed not for his wondrous works.

33 Therefore their days did He consume in

vanity, and their years in trouble.

34 When He slew them, then they sought Him; and they returned and enquired early after God (El).

35 And they remembered that God (Elohim) was their Rock, and the Most High God (El Elyon) their Redeemer.

36 Nevertheless they did flatter Him with their mouth, and they lied unto Him with their tongues.

37 For their heart was not right with Him, neither were they stedfast in His covenant.

38 But He, being full of compassion, forgave their iniquity, and destroyed them not; yea, many a time turned He His anger away, and did not stir up all His wrath.

39 For He remembered that they were but flesh; a wind that passeth away, and cometh not again.

40 How oft did they provoke Him in the wilderness, and grieve Him in the desert!

41 Yea, they turned back and tempted God (El), and limited the Holy One of Yisrael.

42 They remembered not His hand, nor the day when He delivered them from the enemy.

43 How He had wrought His signs in Egypt (Mitsrayim), and His wonders in the field of Zoan;

44 And had turned their rivers into blood; and their floods, that they could not drink.

45 He sent divers sorts of flies among them, which devoured them; and frogs, which destroyed them.

46 He gave also their increase unto the caterpiller, and their labour unto the locust.

47 He destroyed their vines with hail, and their sycomore trees with frost.

48 He gave up their cattle also to the hail, and their flocks to hot thunderbolts.

49 He cast upon them the fierceness of His anger, wrath, and indignation, and trouble, by sending evil angels among them.

50 He made a way to His anger; He spared not their soul from death, but gave their life over to the pestilence;

51 And smote all the firstborn in Egypt (Mitsrayim); the chief of their strength in the tabernacles of Ham.

52 But made His own people to go forth like sheep, and guided them in the wilderness like a flock.

53 And He led them on safely, so that they feared not; but the sea overwhelmed their enemies.

54 And He brought them to the border of His sanctuary, even to this mountain, which His right hand had purchased.

55 He cast out the heathens also before them, and divided them an inheritance by line, and made the tribes of Yisrael to dwell in their tents.

56 Yet they tempted and provoked the Most High God (Elohim Elyon), and kept not His testimonies,

57 But turned back, and dealt unfaithfully like their fathers: they were turned aside like a deceitful bow.

58 For they provoked Him to anger with their high places, and moved Him to jealousy with their graven images.

59 When God (Elohim) heard this, He was wroth, and greatly abhorred Yisrael,

60 So that He forsook the tabernacle of Shiloh, the tent which He placed among men;

61 And delivered His strength into captivity, and His glory into the enemy's hand.

62 He gave His people over also unto the sword; and was wroth with His inheritance.

63 The fire consumed their young men; and their maidens were not given to marriage.

64 Their priests (kohanim) fell by the sword; and their widows made no lamentation.

65 Then the Lord (Adonai) awaked as one out of sleep, and like a mighty man that shouteth by reason of wine.

66 And He smote His enemies in the hinder parts; He put them to a perpetual reproach.

67 Moreover He refused the tabernacle of Joseph (Yosef), and chose not the tribe of Efrayim,

68 But chose the tribe of Judah (Yehudah), the Mount Zion (Tsiyon) which He loved.

69 And He built His sanctuary like high palaces, like the earth which He hath established forever.

70 He chose Dawid also His servant, and took Him from the sheepfolds;

71 From following the ewes great with young He brought Him to feed Jacob (Yaaqov) His people, and Yisrael His inheritance.

72 So He fed them according to the integrity of His heart; and guided them by the skilfulness of His hands.

79 A Psalm of Asaph.

1 O God (Elohim), the heathens are come into Your inheritance; Your holy temple have they defiled; they have laid Jerusalem

(Yerushalayim) on heaps.

2 The dead bodies of Your servants have they given to be meat unto the fowls of the heaven, the flesh of Your faithful ones (chasidim) unto the beasts of the earth.

3 Their blood have they shed like water round about Jerusalem (Yerushalayim); and there was none to bury them.

4 We are become a reproach to our neighbours, a scorn and derision to them that are round about us.

5 How long, יהוה? Wilt You be angry forever? Shall Your jealousy burn like fire?

6 Pour out Your wrath upon the heathens that have not known you, and upon the kingdoms that have not called upon Your name.

7 For they have devoured Jacob (Yaaqov), and laid waste his dwelling place.

8 O remember not against us former iniquities; let Your tender mercies speedily prevent us, for we are brought very low.

9 Help us, O God (Elohim) of our salvation, for the glory of Your name; and deliver us, and purge away our sins, for Your name's sake.

10 Wherefore should the heathen say, "Where is their God (Elohim)?" Let Him be known among the heathens in our sight by the revenging of the blood of Your servants which is shed.

11 Let the sighing of the prisoner come before You; according to the greatness of Your power preserve You those that are appointed to die;

12 And render unto our neighbours sevenfold into their bosom their reproach, wherewith they have reproached You, O Lord (Adonai).

13 So we Your people and sheep of Your pasture will give You thanks forever; we will shew forth Your praise to all generations.

80 To the chief Musician upon Shoshannimeduth, A Psalm of Asaph.

1 Give ear, O Shepherd of Yisrael, You that leadest Joseph (Yosef) like a flock; You that dwellest between the cherubims (keruvim), shine forth.

2 Before Efrayim and Benjamin (Binyamin) and Menashsheh stir up Your strength, and come and save us.

3 Restore us, O God (Elohim), and cause Your face to shine; and we shall be saved.

4 O יהוה God of hosts (Elohei Tsevaot), how long wilt You be angry against the prayer of Your people?

5 You feedest them with the bread of tears; and givest them tears to drink in great measure.

6 You makest us a strife unto our neighbours; and our enemies laugh among themselves.

7 Restore us, O God of hosts (Elohei Tsevaot), and cause Your face to shine; and we shall be saved.

8 You have brought a vine out of Egypt (Mitsrayim); You have cast out the heathens, and planted it.

9 You preparedst room before it, and didst cause it to take deep root, and it filled the land.

10 The hills were covered with the shadow of it, and the boughs thereof were like the goodly cedars.

11 She sent out her boughs unto the sea, and her branches unto the river.

12 Why have You then broken down her hedges, so that all they which pass by the way do pluck her?

13 The boar out of the wood doth waste it, and the wild beast of the field doth devour it.

14 Return, we beseech You, O God of hosts (Elohei Tsevaot); look down from heaven, and behold, and visit this vine;

15 And the vineyard which Your right hand hath planted, and the branch that You madest strong for Yourself.

16 It is burned with fire, it is cut down; they perish at the rebuke of Your countenance.

17 Let Your hand be upon the man of Your right hand, upon the Son of man (haMashiach) whom You madest strong for Yourself.

18 So will not we go back from You; quicken us, and we will call upon Your name.

19 Turn us again, O יהוה God of hosts (YHWH Elohei Tsevaot), cause Your face to shine; and we shall be saved.

81 To the chief Musician upon Gittith, A Psalm of Asaph.

1 Sing aloud unto God (Elohim) our strength; make a joyful noise unto the God (Elohim) of Jacob (Yaaqov).

2 Take a psalm, and bring hither the timbrel, the pleasant harp with the psaltery.

3 Blow up the trumpet in the new moon, in the time appointed, on our solemn feast day.

4 For this was a statute for Yisrael, and an ordinance of the God (Elohim) of Jacob (Yaaqov).

5 This he ordained in Joseph (Yosef) for a

testimony, when he went out through the land of Egypt (Mitsrayim); where I heard a language that I understood not.

6 "I relieved his shoulder from the burden; his hands were delivered from the pots.

7 You calledst in trouble, and I delivered you; I answered you in the secret place of thunder; I proved you at the waters of Meribah. Selah.

8 Hear, O My people, and I will testify unto you; O Yisrael, if you wilt hearken unto Me;

9 There shall no strange ᴮ⁵ᵇgod (el) be in you; neither shalt you worship any foreign god (el).

10 I am יהוה your God (YHWH Eloheikha), Who brought you out of the land of Egypt (Mitsrayim); open your mouth wide, and I will fill it.

11 But My people would not hearken to My voice; and Yisrael would have none of Me.

12 So I gave them up unto their own hearts' lust; and they walked in their own counsels.

13 Oh that My people had hearkened unto Me, and Yisrael had walked in My ways!

14 I should soon have subdued their enemies, and turned My hand against their adversaries.

15 The haters of יהוה should have submitted themselves unto Him, but their time should have endured forever.

16 He should have fed them also with the finest of the wheat; and with honey out of the rock should I have satisfied you."

82 A Psalm of Asaph.
1 God (Elohim) standeth in the congregation of the judges (ᴮ¹ᵇelohim); He judgeth among the judges (elohim).

2 How long will you judge unjustly, and accept the persons of the wicked? Selah.

3 Defend the poor and fatherless; do justice to the afflicted and needy.

4 Deliver the poor and needy; rid them out of the hand of the wicked.

5 They know not, neither will they understand; they walk on in darkness; all the foundations of the earth are out of course.

6 I have said, "You are judges (elohim); and all of you are children of the Most High (Elyon).

7 But you shall die like men, and fall like one of the princes."

8 Arise, O God (Elohim), judge the earth; for You shalt inherit all nations.

83 A Song or Psalm of Asaph.
1 Keep not You silence, O God (Elohim);

hold not Your peace, and be not still, O God (El)!

2 For, behold, Your enemies make a tumult; and they that hate You have lifted up the head.

3 They have taken crafty counsel against Your people, and consulted against Your hidden ones.

4 They have said, "Come, and let us cut them off from being a nation; that the name of Yisrael may be no more in remembrance."

5 For they have consulted together with one consent; they are confederate against You:

6 The tabernacles of Edom, and the Ishmaelites; of Moav, and the Hagarenes;

7 Gebal, and Ammon, and Amalek; the Philistines with the inhabitants of Tyre;

8 Assur also is joined with them; they have holpen the children of Lot. Selah.

9 Do unto them as unto the Midianites; as to Sisera, as to Yavin, at the Brook of Kison,

10 Who perished at Endor; they became as dung for the earth.

11 Make their nobles like Oreb, and like Zeeb; yea, all their princes as Zebah, and as Zalmunna,

12 Who said, "Let us take to ourselves the houses of God (Elohim) in possession."

13 O my God (Elohim), make them like a wheel; as the stubble before the wind.

14 As the fire burneth a wood, and as the flame setteth the mountains on fire;

15 So persecute them with Your tempest, and make them afraid with Your storm.

16 Fill their faces with shame; that they may seek Your name, O יהוה.

17 Let them be confounded and troubled forever; yea, let them be put to shame, and perish,

18 That men may know that You, whose name alone is יהוה, art the Most High (Elyon) over all the earth.

84 To the chief Musician upon Gittith, A Psalm for the sons of Korah (Qorach).
1 How lovely are Your tabernacles, O יהוה of hosts (YHWH Tsevaot)!

2 My soul longeth, yea, even fainteth for the courts of יהוה; my heart and my flesh crieth out for the living God (El chai).

3 Yea, the sparrow hath found a house, and the swallow a nest for herself, where she may lay her young, even your altars, O יהוה of hosts (YHWH Tsevaot), my King, and my God (Elohim).

4 Blessed are they that dwell in Your house; they will be still praising You. Selah.

5 Blessed is the man whose strength is in You; in whose heart are the ways of them.

6 Who passing through the valley of Baca make it a well; the rain also filleth the pools.

7 They go from strength to strength, every one of them in Zion (Tsiyon) appeareth before God (Elohim).

8 O יהוה God of hosts (Elohei Tsevaot), hear my prayer; give ear, O God (Elohim) of Jacob (Yaaqov). Selah.

9 Behold, O God (Elohim) our shield, and look upon the face of Your anointed (mashiach).

10 For a day in Your courts is better than a thousand. I had rather be a doorkeeper in the house of my God (Elohim), than to dwell in the tents of wickedness.

11 For יהוה God (Elohim) is a sun and shield; יהוה will give grace and glory; no good thing will He withhold from them that walk uprightly.

12 O יהוה of hosts (YHWH Tsevaot), blessed is the man that trusteth in You.

85 To the chief Musician, A Psalm for the sons of Korah (Qorach). יהוה, You have been favourable unto Your land; You have brought back the captivity of Jacob (Yaaqov).

2 You have forgiven the iniquity of Your people, You have covered all their sin. Selah.

3 You have taken away all Your wrath; You have turned Yourself from the fierceness of Your anger.

4 Turn us, O God (Elohim) of our salvation, and cause Your anger toward us to cease.

5 Wilt You be angry with us forever? Wilt You draw out Your anger to all generations?

6 Wilt You not revive us again, that Your people may rejoice in You?

7 Shew us Your mercy, O יהוה, and grant us Your salvation.

8 I will hear what God (El) יהוה will speak, for He will speak peace unto His people, and to His faithful ones (chasidim); but let them not turn again to folly.

9 Surely His salvation is near them that fear Him; that glory may dwell in our land.

10 Mercy and truth are met together; righteousness and peace have kissed each other.

11 Truth shall spring out of the earth; and righteousness shall look down from heaven.

12 Yea, יהוה shall give that which is good; and our land shall yield her increase.

13 Righteousness shall go before Him; and shall set us in the way of His steps.

86 A Prayer of Dawid.
1 Bow down Your ear, O יהוה, hear me; for I am poor and needy.

2 Preserve my soul, for I am holy; O You my God (Elohim), save Your servant who trusteth in You.

3 Be merciful unto me, O Lord (Adonai), for I cry unto You daily.

4 Rejoice the soul of Your servant, for unto You, O Lord (Adonai), do I lift up my soul.

5 For You, my Lord (Adonai), art good, and ready to forgive; and plenteous in mercy unto all them that call upon You.

6 Give ear, O יהוה, unto my prayer; and attend to the voice of my supplications.

7 In the day of my trouble I will call upon You, for You wilt answer me.

8 Among the elohim there is none like unto You, O Lord (Adonai); neither are there any works like unto Your works.

9 All nations whom You have made shall come and worship before You, O Lord (Adonai); and shall glorify Your name.

10 For You are great, and doest wondrous things; You are God (Elohim) alone.

11 Teach me Your way, O יהוה; I will walk in Your truth; unite my heart to fear Your name.

12 I will praise You, O Lord my God (Adonai Elohai), with all my heart; and I will glorify Your name forevermore.

13 For great is Your mercy toward me; and You have delivered my soul from the lowest hell (sheol).

14 O God (Elohim), the proud are risen against me, and the assemblies of violent men have sought after my soul; and have not set You before them.

15 But You, O Lord (Adonai), art a God (Elohim) full of compassion, and gracious, longsuffering, and plenteous in mercy and truth.

16 O turn unto me, and have mercy upon me; give Your strength unto Your servant, and save the son of Your handmaid.

17 Shew me a token for good; that they which hate me may see it, and be ashamed, because You, יהוה, have holpen me, and comforted me.

87 A Psalm or Song for the sons of Korah (Qorach).
1 His foundation is in the holy mountains.

2 יהוה loveth the gates of Zion (Tsiyon) more

than all the dwellings of Jacob (Yaaqov).

3 Glorious things are spoken of You, O city of God (Elohim). Selah.

4 "I will make mention of Rachav and Babylon (Bavel) to those who know Me: behold Philistia, and Tyre, with Ethiopia (Kush);' this man was born there.'"

5 And of Zion (Tsiyon) it shall be said, "This and that man was born in her; and the Most High (Elyon) Himself shall establish her."

6 יהוה shall count, when He writeth up the people: "This man was born there." Selah.

7 As well the singers as the players on instruments say, "All my springs are in You."

88 A Song or Psalm for the sons of Korah (Qorach), to the chief Musician upon Mahalath Leannoth, Maskil of Heman the Ezrahite.

1 O יהוה God (Elohim) of my salvation, I have cried day and night before You;

2 Let my prayer come before You; incline Your ear unto my cry;

3 For my soul is full of troubles: and my life draweth near unto the grave (sheol).

4 I am counted with them that go down into the pit; I am as a man that hath no strength;

5 Free among the dead, like the slain that lie in the grave, whom You rememberest no more: and they are cut off from Your hand.

6 You have laid me in the lowest pit, in darkness, in the deeps.

7 Your wrath lieth hard upon me, and You have afflicted me with all Your waves. Selah.

8 You have put away mine acquaintance far from me; You have made me an abomination unto them; I am shut up, and I cannot come forth.

9 Mine eye mourneth by reason of affliction. יהוה, I have called daily upon You, I have stretched out my hands unto You.

10 Wilt You shew wonders to the dead? Shall the dead arise and praise You? Selah.

11 Shall Your lovingkindness be declared in the grave? Or Your faithfulness in destruction?

12 Shall Your wonders be known in the dark? And Your righteousness in the land of forgetfulness?

13 But unto You have I cried, O יהוה; and in the morning shall my prayer prevent You.

14 יהוה, why castest You off my soul? Why hidest You Your face from me?

15 I am afflicted and ready to die from my youth up; while I suffer Your terrors I am distracted.

16 Your fierce wrath goeth over me; Your terrors have cut me off.

17 They came round about me daily like water; they compassed me about together.

18 Loved one and friend have You put far from me, and mine acquaintance into darkness.

89 A Poem of Ethan the Ezrahite.
1 I will sing of the mercies of יהוה forever; with my mouth will I make known Your faithfulness to all generations.

2 For I have said, "Mercy shall be built up forever; Your faithfulness shalt You establish in the very heavens."

3 "I have made a covenant with My chosen, I have sworn unto Dawid My servant:

4 'Your seed will I establish forever, and build up your throne to all generations.'" Selah.

5 And the heavens shall praise Your wonders, O יהוה; Your faithfulness also in the congregation of the holy ones (qadoshim).

6 For who in the heaven can be compared unto יהוה? Who among the sons of the mighty can be likened unto יהוה?

7 God (El) is greatly to be feared in the assembly of the holy ones (qadoshim), and to be in reverance of all them that are about Him.

8 O יהוה God of hosts (YHWH Elohei Tsevaot), Who is a strong יה (Yah) like unto You? Or to Your faithfulness round about You?

9 You rulest the raging of the sea; when the waves thereof arise, You stillest them.

10 You have broken Rachav in pieces, as one that is slain; You have scattered Your enemies with Your strong arm.

11 The heavens are Yours, the earth also is Yours; as for the world and the fullness thereof, You have founded them.

12 The north and the south You have created them; Tabor and Hermon shall rejoice in Your name.

13 You have a mighty arm; strong is Your hand, and high is Your right hand.

14 Justice and judgment are the habitation of Your throne; mercy and truth shall go before Your face.

15 Blessed is the people that know the joyful sound; they shall walk, O יהוה, in the light of Your countenance.

16 In Your name shall they rejoice all the day;

and in Your righteousness shall they be exalted.

17 For You are the glory of their strength; and in Your favor our horn shall be exalted.

18 For יהוה is our defence; and the Holy One of Yisrael is our King.

19 Then You spakest in vision to Your holy one, and saidst, I have laid help upon one that is mighty; I have exalted one chosen out of the people.

20 I have found Dawid My servant; with My holy oil have I anointed him;

21 With whom My hand shall be established; Mine arm also shall strengthen him.

22 The enemy shall not exact upon him; nor the son of wickedness afflict him.

23 And I will beat down his foes before his face, and plague those who hate him.

24 But My faithfulness and My mercy shall be with him; and in My name shall his horn be exalted.

25 I will set his hand also in the sea, and his right hand in the rivers.

26 He shall cry unto me, 'You are my Father (Avi), my God (Eli), and the rock of my salvation.'

27 Also I will make him my firstborn, higher than the kings of the earth.

28 My mercy will I keep for him forevermore, and My covenant shall stand fast with him.

29 His seed also will I make to endure forever, and his throne as the days of heaven.

30 If his children forsake My Torah, and walk not in My judgments;

31 If they break My statutes, and keep not My commandments;

32 Then will I visit their transgression with the rod, and their iniquity with stripes.

33 Nevertheless My lovingkindness will I not utterly take from him, nor allow My faithfulness to fail.

34 My covenant will I not break, nor alter the thing that is gone out of My lips.

35 Once have I sworn by My holiness that I will not lie unto Dawid.

36 His seed shall endure forever, and his throne as the sun before Me.

37 It shall be established forever as the moon, and as a faithful witness in heaven. Selah.

38 But You have cast off and abhorred, You have been wroth with Your anointed (mashiach).

39 You have made void the covenant of Your servant; You have profaned his crown by casting it to the ground.

40 You have broken down all his hedges; You have brought his strong holds to ruin.

41 All that pass by the way spoil him: he is a reproach to his neighbours.

42 You have set up the right hand of his adversaries; You have made all his enemies to rejoice.

43 You have also turned the edge of his sword, and have not made him to stand in the battle.

44 You have made his glory to cease, and cast his throne down to the ground.

45 The days of his youth have You shortened; You have covered him with shame. Selah.

46 How long, יהוה? Wilt You hide Yourself forever? Shall Your wrath burn like fire?

47 Remember how short my time is; wherefore have You made all men in vain?

48 What man is he who liveth, and shall not see death? Shall he deliver his soul from the hand of the grave (sheol)? Selah.

49 My Lord (Adonai), where are Your former lovingkindnesses, which You swarest unto Dawid in Your truth?

50 Remember, my Lord (Adonai), the reproach of Your servants; how I do bear in my bosom the reproach of all the mighty people;

51 Wherewith Your enemies have reproached, O יהוה; wherewith they have reproached the footsteps of Your anointed (mashiach).

52 Blessed be יהוה forevermore. So be it (Amen), and so be it (Amen).

90 A Prayer of Moses (Mosheh) the man of God (Elohim).

1 My Lord (Adonai), You have been our dwelling place in all generations.

2 Before the mountains were brought forth, or ever You hadst formed the earth and the world, even from everlasting to everlasting, You are God (El).

3 You turnest man to destruction; and sayest, "Repent, you children of men."

4 For a thousand years in Your sight are but as yesterday when it is past, and as a watch in the night.

5 You carriest them away as with a flood; they are as a sleep; in the morning they are like grass which groweth up.

6 In the morning it flourisheth, and groweth up; in the evening it is cut down, and withereth.

7 For we are consumed by Your anger, and by Your wrath are we troubled.

8 You have set our iniquities before You, our secret sins in the light of Your countenance.

9 For all our days are passed away in Your wrath; we spend our years as a tale that is told.

10 The days of our years are threescore years and ten; and if by reason of strength they be fourscore years, yet is their strength labour and sorrow; for it is soon cut off, and we fly away.

11 Who knoweth the power of Your anger? Even according to Your fear, so is Your wrath.

12 So teach us to number our days, that we may apply our hearts unto wisdom.

13 Return, O יהוה, how long? And let it regret you concerning Your servants.

14 O satisfy us early with Your mercy; that we may rejoice and be glad all our days.

15 Make us glad according to the days wherein You have afflicted us, and the years wherein we have seen evil.

16 Let Your work appears unto Your servants, and Your glory unto their children.

17 And let the beauty of יהוה our God (YHWH Eloheinu) be upon us; and establish You the work of our hands upon us; yea, the work of our hands establishes You it.

91 He who dwelleth in the secret place of the Most High (Elyon) shall abide under the shadow of the Almighty.

2 I will say of יהוה, He is my refuge and my fortress; my God (Elohim), in Him will I trust.

3 Surely He shall deliver you from the snare of the fowler, and from the noisome pestilence.

4 He shall cover you with His feathers, and under His wings shalt you trust; His truth shall be your shield and buckler.

5 You shalt not be afraid for the terror by night; nor for the arrow that flieth by day;

6 Nor for the pestilence that walketh in darkness; nor for the destruction that wasteth at noonday.

7 A thousand shall fall at your side, and ten thousand at your right hand; but it shall not come near you.

8 Only with your eyes shalt you behold and see the reward of the wicked.

9 Because you have made יהוה, who is my refuge, even the Most High (Elyon), your habitation;

10 There shall no evil befall you, neither shall any plague come near your dwelling.

11 For He shall give His angels charge over you, to keep you in all your ways.

12 They shall bear you up in their hands, lest you dash your foot against a stone.

13 You shalt tread upon the lion and adder; the young lion and the dragon shalt you trample under feet.

14 Because he hath set his love upon Me, therefore will I deliver him; I will set him on high, because he hath known My name.

15 He shall call upon Me, and I will answer him; I will be with him in trouble; I will deliver him, and honor him.

16 With long life will I satisfy him, and shew him My salvation.

92 A Psalm or Song for the Shabbat day.
1 It is a good thing to give thanks unto יהוה, and to sing praises unto your name, O Most High (Elyon);

2 To shew forth Your lovingkindness in the morning, and Your faithfulness every night,

3 Upon an instrument of ten strings, and upon the psaltery; upon the harp with a solemn sound.

4 For You, יהוה, have made me glad through Your work; I will triumph in the works of Your hands. .

5 O יהוה, how great are Your works! And Your thoughts are very deep.

6 A brutish man knoweth not; neither doth a fool understands this.

7 When the wicked spring as the grass, and when all the workers of iniquity do flourish; it is that they shall be destroyed forever.

8 But You, יהוה, are Most High (Elyon) forevermore.

9 For, behold, Your enemies, O יהוה, for, behold, Your enemies shall perish; all the workers of iniquity shall be scattered.

10 But my horn shalt You exalt like the horn of a unicorn; I shall be anointed with fresh oil.

11 Mine eye also shall see my desire on mine enemies, and mine ears shall hear my desire of the wicked that rise up against me.

12 The righteous shall flourish like the palm tree; he shall grow like a cedar in Lebanon.

13 Those that be planted in the house of יהוה shall flourish in the courts of our God (Elohim).

14 They shall still bring forth fruit in old age; they shall be fat and flourishing;

15 To shew that יהוה is upright; He is my rock, and there is no unrighteousness in Him.

93 יהוה reigneth, He is clothed with majesty; יהוה is clothed with strength, wherewith He hath girded Himself. The world also is established, that it cannot be moved.

2 Your throne is established of old; You are from everlasting.

3 The floods have lifted up, O יהוי, the floods have lifted up their voice; the floods lift up their waves.

4 יהוה on high is mightier than the noise of many waters, yea, than the mighty waves of the sea.

5 Your testimonies are very sure; holiness becometh Your house, O יהוה, forever.

94 O יהוה, God (El) to Whom vengeance belongeth; O God (El), to Whom vengeance belongeth, shew Yourself.

2 Lift up Yourself, You judge of the earth; render a reward to the proud.

3 יהוה, how long shall the wicked, how long shall the wicked triumph?

4 How long shall they utter and speak hard things? And all the workers of iniquity boast themselves?

5 They break in pieces Your people, O יהוי, and afflict Your heritage.

6 They slay the widow and the stranger, and murder the fatherless.

7 Yet they say, יהוה shall not see, neither shall the God (Elohim) of Jacob (Yaaqov) regard it.

8 Understand, you brutish among the people; and you fools, when will you be wise?

9 He who planted the ear, shall He not hear? He who formed the eye, shall He not see?

10 He who chastiseth the nations, shall not He correct? He who teacheth man knowledge, shall not He know?

11 יהוה knoweth the thoughts of man, that they are vanity.

12 Blessed is the man whom You chastenest, O יה (Yah) and teachest him out of Your Torah;

13 That You mayest give him rest from the days of adversity, until the pit be digged for the wicked.

14 For יהוה will not cast off His people, neither will He forsake His inheritance.

15 But judgment shall return unto righteousness; and all the upright in heart shall follow it.

16 Who will rise up for me against the evildoers? Or who will stand up for me against the workers of iniquity?

17 Unless יהוה had been my help, my soul had almost dwelt in silence.

18 When I said, "My foot slippeth"; Your mercy, O יהוה, held me up.

19 In the multitude of my thoughts within me Your comforts delight my soul.

20 Shall the throne of iniquity have fellowship with You, which frameth mischief by an ordinance?

21 They gather themselves together against the soul of the righteous, and condemn the innocent blood.

22 But יהוה is my defence; and my God (Elohim) is the rock of my refuge.

23 And He shall bring upon them their own iniquity, and shall cut them off in their own wickedness; yea, יהוה our God (YHWH Eloheinu) shall cut them off.

95 O come, let us sing unto יהוה; let us make a joyful noise to the rock of our salvation.

2 Let us come before His presence with thanksgiving, and make a joyful noise unto Him with psalms.

3 For יהוה is a great God (El), and a great King above all rulers ([B1b]elohim).

4 In His hand are the deep places of the earth; the strength of the hills is His also.

5 The sea is His, and He made it; and His hands formed the dry land.

6 O come, let us worship and bow down; let us kneel before יהוה our Maker.

7 For He is our God (Elohim); and we are the people of His pasture, and the sheep of His hand. Today if you will hear His voice:

8 "Harden not your heart, as in the provocation, and as in the day of temptation in the wilderness;

9 When your fathers tempted Me, proved Me, and saw My work.

10 Forty years long was I grieved with this generation, and said, 'It is a people who do err in their heart, and they have not known My ways.'

11 Unto whom I sware in My wrath that they should not enter into My rest."

96 O sing unto יהוה a new song; sing unto יהוה, all the earth.

2 Sing unto יהוה, bless His name; shew forth His salvation from day to day.

3 Declare His glory among the nations, His wonders among all people.

4 For יהוה is great, and greatly to be praised; He is to be feared above all gods (elohim).

5 For all the gods (elohim) of the nations are

idols, but יהוה made the heavens.

6 Honor and majesty are before Him; strength and beauty are in His sanctuary.

7 Give unto יהוה, O you kindreds of the people, give unto יהוה glory and strength.

8 Give unto יהוה the glory due unto His name; bring an offering, and come into His courts.

9 O worship יהוה in the beauty of holiness; fear before Him, all the earth.

10 Say among the nations that יהוה reigneth; the world also shall be established that it shall not be moved; He shall judge the people righteously.

11 Let the heavens rejoice, and let the earth be glad; let the sea roar, and the fullness thereof.

12 Let the field be joyful, and all that is therein; then shall all the trees of the wood rejoice

13 before יהוה, for He cometh, for He cometh to judge the earth; He shall judge the world with righteousness, and the people with His truth.

97 יהוה reigneth; let the earth rejoice; let the multitude of isles be glad thereof.

2 Clouds and darkness are round about Him; righteousness and judgment are the habitation of His throne.

3 A fire goeth before Him, and burneth up His enemies round about.

4 His lightnings enlightened the world; the earth saw, and trembled.

5 The hills melted like wax at the presence of יהוה, at the presence of the Lord (Adonai) of the whole earth.

6 The heavens declare His righteousness, and all the people see His glory.

7 Confounded be all those who serve graven images, that boast themselves of idols; worship Him, all you mighty ones (Blbelohim).

8 Zion (Tsiyon) heard, and was glad; and the daughters of Judah (Yehudah) rejoiced because of Your judgments, O יהוה.

9 For You, יהוה, art high above all the earth; You are exalted far above all mighty ones (elohim).

10 You who love יהוה, hate evil; He preserveth the souls of His faithful ones (chasidim); He delivereth them out of the hand of the wicked.

11 Light is sown for the righteous, and gladness for the upright in heart.

12 Rejoice in יהוה, you righteous; and give thanks at the remembrance of His holiness.

98 A Psalm.
1 O sing unto יהוה a new song; for He hath done marvellous things; His right hand,

and His holy arm, hath gotten Him the victory.

2 יהוה hath made known His salvation; His righteousness hath He openly shewed in the sight of the nations.

3 He hath remembered His mercy and His truth toward the house of Yisrael; all the ends of the earth have seen the salvation of our God (Elohim).

4 Make a joyful noise unto יהוה, all the earth; make a loud noise, and rejoice, and sing praise.

5 Sing unto יהוה with the harp; with the harp, and the voice of a psalm.

6 With trumpets and sound of cornet make a joyful noise before יהוה, the King.

7 Let the sea roar, and the fullness thereof; the world, and they that dwell therein.

8 Let the floods clap their hands; let the hills be joyful together before יהוה,

9 For He cometh to judge the earth; with righteousness shall He judge the world, and the people with equity.

99 יהוה reigneth; let the people tremble; He sitteth between the cherubims (keruvim); let the earth be moved.

2 יהוה is great in Zion (Tsiyon); and He is high above all the people.

3 Let them praise Your great and awesome name; for it is holy.

4 The king's strength also loveth judgment; You dost establish equity, You executest judgment and righteousness in Jacob (Yaaqov).

5 Exalt you יהוה our God (YHWH Eloheinu), and worship at His footstool; for He is holy.

6 Moses (Mosheh) and Aaron (Aharon) among His priests (kohanim), and Shemuel among them that call upon His name; they called upon יהוה, and He answered them.

7 He spake unto them in the cloudy pillar: they kept His testimonies, and the ordinance that He gave them.

8 You answeredst them, O יהוה our God (YHWH Eloheinu); You wast a God (Elohim) that forgavest them, though You tookest vengeance of their inventions.

9 Exalt יהוה our God (YHWH Eloheinu), and worship at His holy hill; for יהוה our God (YHWH Eloheinu) is holy.

100 A Psalm of praise.
1 Make a joyful noise unto יהוה, all you lands.

2 Serve יהוה with gladness; come before His

presence with singing.

3 Know you that יהוה He is God (Elohim); it is He who hath made us, and not we ourselves; we are His people, and the sheep of His pasture.

4 Enter into His gates with thanksgiving, and into His courts with praise; be thankful unto Him, and bless His name.

5 For יהוה is good; His mercy is everlasting; and His truth endureth to all generations.

101 A Psalm of Dawid.
1 I will sing of mercy and judgment; unto You, O יהוה, will I sing.

2 I will behave myself wisely in a perfect way. O when wilt You come unto me? I will walk within my house with a perfect heart.

3 I will set no wicked thing before mine eyes; I hate the work of them that turn aside; it shall not cleave to me.

4 A perverse heart shall depart from me; I will not know a wicked person.

5 Whoso privily slandereth his neighbour, him will I cut off; him who hath a high look and a proud heart will not I suffer.

6 Mine eyes shall be upon the faithful of the land, that they may dwell with me; he who walketh in a perfect way, he shall serve me.

7 He who worketh deceit shall not dwell within my house; he who telleth lies shall not tarry in my sight.

8 I will early destroy all the wicked of the land; that I may cut off all wicked doers from the city of יהוה.

102 A Prayer of the afflicted, when he is overwhelmed, and poureth out his complaint before יהוה.
1 Hear my prayer, O יהוה, and let my cry come unto You.

2 Hide not Your face from me in the day when I am in trouble; incline Your ear unto me: in the day when I call answer me speedily.

3 For my days are consumed like smoke, and my bones are burned as a hearth.

4 My heart is smitten, and withered like grass; so that I forget to eat my bread.

5 By reason of the voice of my groaning my bones cleave to my skin.

6 I am like a pelican of the wilderness; I am like an owl of the desert.

7 I watch, and am as a sparrow alone upon the house top.

8 Mine enemies reproach me all the day;

and they that are mad against me are sworn against me.

9 For I have eaten ashes like bread, and mingled my drink with weeping,

10 Because of Your indignation and Your wrath; for You have lifted me up, and cast me down.

11 My days are like a shadow that declineth; and I am withered like grass.

12 But You, O יהוה, shalt endure forever; and Your remembrance unto all generations.

13 You shalt arise, and have mercy upon Zion (Tsiyon), for the time to favor her, yea, the set time, is come.

14 For Your servants take pleasure in her stones, and favor the dust thereof.

15 So the nations shall fear the name of יהוה, and all the kings of the earth Your glory.

16 When יהוה shall build up Zion (Tsiyon), he shall appear in His glory.

17 He will regard the prayer of the destitute, and not despise their prayer.

18 This shall be written for the generation to come; and the people which shall be created shall praise יהוה.

19 For He hath looked down from the height of His sanctuary; from heaven did יהוה behold the earth;

20 To hear the groaning of the prisoner; to loose those that are appointed to death;

21 To declare the name of יהוה in Zion (Tsiyon), and His praise in Jerusalem (Yerushalayim);

22 When the people are gathered together, and the kingdoms, to serve יהוה.

23 He weakened my strength in the way; He shortened my days.

24 I said, "O my God (Elohim), take me not away in the midst of my days; Your years are throughout all generations.

25 Of old have You laid the foundation of the earth; and the heavens are the work of Your hands.

26 They shall perish, but You shalt endure; yea, all of them shall wax old like a garment; as a vesture shalt You change them, and they shall be changed.

27 But You are the same, and Your years shall have no end.

28 The children of Your servants shall continue, and their seed shall be established before You."

103 A Psalm of Dawid.
1 Bless יהוה, O my soul; and all that is

within me, bless His holy name.

2 Bless יהוה, O my soul, and forget not all His benefits:

3 Who forgiveth all your iniquities; Who healeth all your diseases;

4 Who redeemeth your life from destruction; Who crowneth you with lovingkindness and tender mercies;

5 Who satisfieth your mouth with good things; so that your youth is renewed like the eagle's.

6 יהוה executeth righteousness and judgment for all that are oppressed.

7 He made known His ways unto Moses (Mosheh), His acts unto the children of Yisrael.

8 יהוה is merciful and gracious, slow to anger, and plenteous in mercy.

9 He will not always strive; nor will He keep His anger forever.

10 He hath not dealt with us after our sins; nor repay us according to our iniquities.

11 For as the heaven is high above the earth, so great is His mercy toward those who fear Him.

12 As far as the east is from the west, so far hath He removed our transgressions from us.

13 Like as a father pitieth his children, so יהוה pitieth them that fear Him.

14 For He knoweth our frame; He remembereth that we are dust.

15 As for man, his days are as grass; as a flower of the field, so he flourisheth.

16 For the wind passeth over it, and it is gone; and the place thereof shall know it no more.

17 But the mercy of יהוה is from everlasting to everlasting upon them that fear Him, and His righteousness unto children's children;

18 To such as keep His covenant, and to those that remember His commandments to do them.

19 יהוה hath prepared His throne in the heavens; and His kingdom ruleth over all.

20 Bless יהוה, you His angels, that excel in strength, that do His commandments, hearkening unto the voice of His word.

21 Bless you יהוה, all you His hosts; you ministers of His, that do His pleasure.

22 Bless יהוה, all His works in all places of His dominion. Bless יהוה, O my soul.

104 Bless יהוה, O my soul. O יהוה my God (YHWH Elohai), You are very great; You are clothed with honor and majesty,

2 Who coverest Yourself with light as with a garment, who stretchest out the heavens like a curtain,

3 Who layeth the beams of His chambers in the waters; Who maketh the clouds His chariot; Who walketh upon the wings of the wind,

4 Who maketh His angels spirits; His ministers a flaming fire,

5 Who laid the foundations of the earth, that it should not be removed forever.

6 You coveredst it with the deep as with a garment; the waters stood above the mountains.

7 At Your rebuke they fled; at the voice of Your thunder they hasted away.

8 They go up by the mountains; they go down by the valleys unto the place which You have founded for them.

9 You have set a bound that they may not pass over; that they turn not again to cover the earth.

10 He sendeth the springs into the valleys, which run among the hills.

11 They give drink to every beast of the field; the wild asses quench their thirst.

12 By them shall the fowls of the heaven have their habitation, which sing among the branches.

13 He watereth the hills from his chambers; the earth is satisfied with the fruit of Your works.

14 He causeth the grass to grow for the cattle, and herb for the service of man, that he may bring forth food out of the earth;

15 And wine that maketh glad the heart of man, and oil to make his face to shine, and bread which strengtheneth man's heart.

16 The trees of יהוה are full of sap; the cedars of Lebanon, which He hath planted;

17 Where the birds make their nests: as for the stork, the fir trees are her house.

18 The high hills are a refuge for the wild goats; and the rocks for the conies.

19 He appointed the moon for seasons; the sun knoweth His going down.

20 You makest darkness, and it is night; wherein all the beasts of the forest do creep forth.

21 The young lions roar after their prey, and seek their meat from God (Elohim).

22 The sun ariseth, they gather themselves together, and lay them down in their dens.

23 Man goeth forth unto his work and to his labour until the evening.

24 O יהוה, how manifold are Your works! In wisdom have You made them all; the earth is full of Your riches.

25 So is this great and wide sea, wherein are

things creeping innumerable, both small and great beasts.

26 There go the ships; there is that leviathan, whom You have made to play therein.

27 These wait all upon You; that You mayest give them their meat in due season.

28 That You givest them they gather; You openest Your hand, they are filled with good.

29 You hidest Your face, they are troubled; You takest away their breath, they die, and return to their dust.

30 You sendest forth Your spirit, they are created; and You renewest the face of the earth.

31 The glory of יהוה shall endure forever; יהוה shall rejoice in His works.

32 He looketh on the earth, and it trembleth; he toucheth the hills, and they smoke.

33 I will sing unto יהוה as long as I live; I will sing praise to my God (Elohim) while I have my being.

34 My meditation of Him shall be sweet; I will be glad in יהוה.

35 Let the sinners be consumed out of the earth, and let the wicked be no more. Bless You יהוה, O my soul. Praise You יה (B43Halelu Yah).

105 O give thanks unto יהוה; call upon His name; make known His deeds among the people.

2 Sing unto Him, sing psalms unto Him; talk you of all His wondrous works.

3 Glory you in His holy name; let the heart of them rejoice that seek יהוה.

4 Seek יהוה, and His strength; seek His face evermore.

5 Remember His marvellous works that He hath done; His wonders, and the judgments of His mouth;

6 O you seed of Avraham His servant, you children of Jacob (Yaaqov) His chosen.

7 He is יהוה our God (YHWH Eloheinu); His judgments are in all the earth.

8 He hath remembered His covenant forever, the word which He commanded to a thousand generations.

9 Which covenant He made with Avraham, and His oath unto Isaac (Yitschaq);

10 And confirmed the same unto Jacob (Yaaqov) for an ordinance, and to Yisrael for an everlasting covenant:

11 Saying, "Unto You will I give the land of Canaan, the lot of your inheritance,"

12 When they were but a few men in number; yea, very few, and strangers in it.

13 When they went from one nation to another, from one kingdom to another people;

14 He permitted no man to do them wrong; yea, He reproved kings for their sakes;

15 Saying, "Touch not Mine anointed, and do My prophets no harm."

16 Moreover He called for a famine upon the land; He broke the whole staff of bread.

17 He sent a man before them, even Joseph (Yosef), who was sold as a slave;

18 Whose feet they hurt with fetters, He was laid in iron,

19 Until the time that His word came; the word of יהוה tested him.

20 The king sent and loosed him; even the ruler of the people, and let him go free.

21 He made him master (adon) of his house, and ruler of all his substance;

22 To bind his princes at his pleasure; and teach his senators wisdom.

23 Yisrael also came into Egypt (Mitsrayim); and Jacob (Yaaqov) sojourned in the land of Ham.

24 And He increased His people greatly; and made them stronger than their enemies.

25 He turned their heart to hate His people, to deal subtilly with His servants.

26 He sent Moses (Mosheh) His servant; and Aaron (Aharon) whom He had chosen.

27 They shewed His signs among them, and wonders in the land of Ham.

28 He sent darkness, and made it dark; and they rebelled not against His word.

29 He turned their waters into blood, and slew their fish.

30 Their land brought forth frogs in abundance, in the chambers of their kings.

31 He spake, and there came divers sorts of flies, and lice in all their coasts.

32 He gave them hail for rain, and flaming fire in their land.

33 He smote their vines also and their fig trees; and broke the trees of their coasts.

34 He spake, and the locusts came, and caterpillers, and that without number,

35 And did eat up all the herbs in their land, and devoured the fruit of their ground.

36 He smote also all the firstborn in their land, the chief of all their strength.

37 He brought them forth also with silver and gold; and there was not one feeble person among their tribes.

38 Egypt (Mitsrayim) was glad when they departed, for the fear of them fell upon them.

39 He spread a cloud for a covering; and fire to give light in the night.

40 The people asked, and He brought quails, and satisfied them with the bread of heaven.

41 He opened the rock, and the waters gushed out; they ran in the dry places like a river.

42 For He remembered His holy promise, and Avraham His servant.

43 And He brought forth His people with joy, and His chosen with gladness:

44 And gave them the lands of the heathens; and they inherited the labour of the people;

45 That they might observe His statutes, and keep His Torah. Praise You יה (Halelu Yah)!

106 Praise You יה (Halelu Yah)! O give thanks unto יהוה, for He is good; for His mercy endureth forever.

2 Who can utter the mighty acts of יהוה? Who can shew forth all His praise?

3 Blessed are they that keep judgment, and He that doeth righteousness at all times.

4 Remember me, O יהוה, with the favor that You bearest unto Your people; O visit me with Your salvation;

5 That I may see the good of Your chosen, that I may rejoice in the gladness of Your nation, that I may glory with Your inheritance.

6 We have sinned with our fathers, we have committed iniquity, we have done wickedly.

7 Our fathers understood not Your wonders in Egypt (Mitsrayim); they remembered not the multitude of Your mercies; but provoked Him at the sea, even at the Red sea.

8 Nevertheless He saved them for His name's sake, that He might make His mighty power to be known.

9 He rebuked the Red sea also, and it was dried up; so He led them through the depths, as through the wilderness.

10 And He saved them from the hand of Him that hated them, and redeemed them from the hand of the enemy.

11 And the waters covered their enemies; there was not one of them left.

12 Then believed they His words; they sang His praise.

13 They soon forgat His works; they waited not for His counsel,

14 But lusted exceedingly in the wilderness, and tempted God (El) in the desert.

15 And He gave them their request; but sent leanness into their soul.

16 They envied Moses (Mosheh) also in the camp, and Aaron (Aharon) the holy one of יהוה.

17 The earth opened and swallowed up Dathan, and covered the company of Aviram.

18 And a fire was kindled in their company; the flame burned up the wicked.

19 They made a calf in Horeb, and worshipped the molten image.

20 Thus they changed their glory into the similitude of an ox that eateth grass.

21 They forgot God (El) their Savior (Moshia), Who had done great things in Egypt (Mitsrayim);

22 Wondrous works in the land of Ham, and awesome things by the Red sea.

23 Therefore He said that He would destroy them, had not Moses (Mosheh) His chosen stood before Him in the breach, to turn away His wrath, lest He should destroy them.

24 Yea, they despised the pleasant land, they believed not His word,

25 But murmured in their tents, and hearkened not unto the voice of יהוה.

26 Therefore He lifted up His hand against them, to overthrow them in the wilderness,

27 To overthrow their seed also among the nations, and to scatter them in the lands.

28 They joined themselves also unto Baalpeor, and ate the sacrifices of the dead.

29 Thus they provoked Him to anger with their inventions; and the plague broke in upon them.

30 Then stood up Phinehas, and executed judgment; and so the plague was stayed.

31 And that was counted unto Him for righteousness unto all generations forevermore.

32 They angered Him also at the waters of strife, so that it went ill with Moses (Mosheh) for their sakes;

33 Because they provoked His spirit, so that He spake unadvisedly with His lips.

34 They did not destroy the nations, concerning whom יהוה commanded them,

35 But were mingled among the heathens, and learned their works.

36 And they served their idols, which were a

snare unto them.

37 Yea, they sacrificed their sons and their daughters unto devils,

38 And shed innocent blood, even the blood of their sons and of their daughters, whom they sacrificed unto the idols of Canaan; and the land was polluted with blood.

39 Thus were they defiled with their own works, and went a whoring with their own inventions.

40 Therefore was the wrath of יהוה kindled against His people, insomuch that He abhorred His own inheritance.

41 And He gave them into the hand of the heathen; and they that hated them ruled over them.

42 Their enemies also oppressed them, and they were brought into subjection under their hand.

43 Many times did He deliver them; but they provoked Him with their counsel, and were brought low for their iniquity.

44 Nevertheless He regarded their affliction, when He heard their cry;

45 And He remembered for them His covenant, and relented according to the multitude of His mercies.

46 He made them also to be pitied of all those that carried them captives.

47 Save us, O יהוה our God (YHWH Eloheinu), and gather us from among the heathen, to give thanks unto Your holy name, and to triumph in Your praise.

48 Blessed be יהוה God of Israel (Elohei Yisrael) from everlasting to everlasting; and let all the people say, "So be it (Amen)!" Praise You יה (Halelu Yah)!

107

O give thanks unto יהוה, for He is good; for His mercy endureth forever.

2 Let the redeemed of יהוה say so, whom He hath redeemed from the hand of the enemy;

3 And gathered them out of the lands, from the east, and from the west, from the north, and from the south.

4 They wandered in the wilderness in a solitary way; they found no city to dwell in.

5 Hungry and thirsty, their soul fainted in them.

6 Then they cried unto יהוה in their trouble, and He delivered them out of their distresses.

7 And He led them forth by the right way, that they might go to a city of habitation.

8 Oh that men would praise יהוה for His goodness, and for His wonderful works to the children of men!

9 For He satisfieth the longing soul, and filleth the hungry soul with goodness.

10 Such as sit in darkness and in the shadow of death, being bound in affliction and iron;

11 Because they rebelled against the words of God (El), and contemned the counsel of the Most High (Elyon);

12 Therefore He brought down their heart with labour; they fell down, and there was none to help.

13 Then they cried unto יהוה in their trouble, and He saved them out of their distresses.

14 He brought them out of darkness and the shadow of death, and broke their bands in sunder.

15 Oh that men would praise יהוה for His goodness, and for His wonderful works to the children of men!

16 For He hath broken the gates of brass, and cut the bars of iron in sunder.

17 Fools because of their transgression, and because of their iniquities, are afflicted.

18 Their soul abhorreth all manner of meat; and they draw near unto the gates of death.

19 Then they cry unto יהוה in their trouble, and He saveth them out of their distresses.

20 He sent His word, and healed them, and delivered them from their destructions.

21 Oh that men would praise יהוה for His goodness, and for His wonderful works to the children of men!

22 And let them sacrifice the sacrifices of thanksgiving, and declare His works with rejoicing.

23 They that go down to the sea in ships, that do business in great waters;

24 These see the works of יהוה, and His wonders in the deep.

25 For He commandeth, and raiseth the stormy wind, which lifteth up the waves thereof.

26 They mount up to the heaven, they go down again to the depths; their soul is melted because of trouble.

27 They reel to and fro, and stagger like a drunken man, and are at their wits' end.

28 Then they cry unto יהוה in their trouble, and He bringeth them out of their distresses.

29 He maketh the storm a calm, so that the waves thereof are still.

30 Then are they glad because they be quiet;

so He bringeth them unto their desired haven.

31 Oh that men would praise יהוה for His goodness, and for His wonderful works to the children of men!

32 Let them exalt Him also in the congregation of the people, and praise Him in the assembly of the elders.

33 He turneth rivers into a wilderness, and the watersprings into dry ground;

34 A fruitful land into barrenness, for the wickedness of them that dwell therein.

35 He turneth the wilderness into a standing water, and dry ground into watersprings.

36 And there He maketh the hungry to dwell, that they may prepare a city for habitation;

37 And sow the fields, and plant vineyards, which may yield fruits of increase.

38 He blesseth them also, so that they are multiplied greatly; and let not their cattle to decrease.

39 Again, they are minished and brought low through oppression, affliction, and sorrow.

40 He poureth contempt upon princes, and causeth them to wander in the wilderness, where there is no way.

41 Yet setteth He the poor on high from affliction, and maketh him families like a flock.

42 The righteous shall see it, and rejoice; and all iniquity shall stop her mouth.

43 Whoso is wise, and will observe these things, even they shall understand the lovingkindness of יהוה.

108 A Song or Psalm of Dawid.
1 O God (Elohim), my heart is fixed; I will sing and give praise, even with my glory.

2 Awake, psaltery and harp; I myself will awake early.

3 I will praise You, O יהוה, among the people; and I will sing praises unto You among the nations.

4 For Your mercy is great above the heavens; and Your truth reacheth unto the clouds.

5 Be You exalted, O God (Elohim), above the heavens; and Your glory above all the earth;

6 That Your beloved may be delivered, save with Your right hand, and answer me.

7 God (Elohim) hath spoken in His holiness; I will rejoice, I will divide Shechem, and measure out the valley of Sukkot.

8 Gilad is Mine; Menashsheh is Mine; Efrayim also is the strength of Mine head; Judah (Yehudah) is My lawgiver;

9 Moav is My washpot; over Edom will I cast out My shoe; over Philistia will I triumph.

10 Who will bring me into the strong city? Who will lead me into Edom?

11 Wilt not You, O God (Elohim), Who have cast us off? And wilt not You, O God (Elohim), go forth with our hosts?

12 Give us help from trouble, for vain is the help of man.

13 Through God (Elohim) we shall do valiantly, for He it is that shall tread down our enemies.

109 To the chief Musician, A Psalm of Dawid.
1 Hold not Your peace, O God (Elohim) of my praise;

2 For the mouth of the wicked and the mouth of the deceitful are opened against me; they have spoken against me with a lying tongue.

3 They compassed me about also with words of hatred; and fought against me without a cause.

4 In return for my love they are my adversaries, but I give myself unto prayer.

5 And they have rewarded me evil for good, and hatred for my love.

6 Set You a wicked man over him; and let the Satan stand at his right hand.

7 When he shall be judged, let him be condemned; and let his prayer become sin.

8 Let his days be few; and let another take his office.

9 Let his children be fatherless, and his wife a widow.

10 Let his children be continually vagabonds, and beg; let them seek their bread also out of their desolate places.

11 Let the extortioner catch all that he hath; and let the strangers spoil his labour.

12 Let there be none to extend mercy unto him: neither let there be any to favor his fatherless children.

13 Let his posterity be cut off; and in the generation following let their name be blotted out.

14 Let the iniquity of his fathers be remembered with יהוה; and let not the sin of his mother be blotted out.

15 Let them be before יהוה continually, that He may cut off the memory of them from the earth.

16 Because that He remembered not to shew mercy, but persecuted the poor and needy man, that He might even slay the broken in heart.

17 As he loved cursing, so let it come unto him; as he delighted not in blessing, so let it be far from him.

18 As he clothed himself with cursing like as with his garment, so let it come into his bowels like water, and like oil into his bones.

19 Let it be unto him as the garment which covereth him, and for a girdle wherewith he is girded continually.

20 Let this be the reward of mine adversaries from יהוה, and of them that speak evil against my soul.

21 But deal with me, O Lord (Adonai) יהוה, for Your name's sake; because Your mercy is good, deliver me.

22 For I am poor and needy, and my heart is wounded within me.

23 I am gone like the shadow when it declineth; I am tossed up and down as the locust.

24 My knees are weak through fasting; and my flesh faileth of fatness.

25 I became also a reproach unto them; when they looked upon me they shaked their heads.

26 Help me, O יהוה my God (YHWH Elohai); O save me according to Your mercy,

27 That they may know that this is Your hand; that You, יהוה, have done it.

28 Let them curse, but bless You; when they arise, let them be ashamed; but let Your servant rejoice.

29 Let mine adversaries be clothed with shame, and let them cover themselves with their own confusion, as with a mantle.

30 I will greatly praise יהוה with my mouth; yea, I will praise Him among the multitude.

31 For He shall stand at the right hand of the poor, to save him from those that condemn his soul.

110 A Psalm of Dawid. 1 יהוה said unto my Lord (Adoni), "Sit You at My right hand, until I make Your enemies Your footstool."

2 יהוה shall send the rod of Your strength out of Zion (Tsiyon); rule You in the midst of Your enemies.

3 Your people shall be willing in the day of Your power, in the beauties of holiness from the womb of the morning; You have the dew of Your youth.

4 יהוה hath sworn, and will not regret, "You are a Priest (Kohen) forever after the order of Melchizedek (Malki-Tsedek)."

5 My Lord (Adonai) at Your right hand shall strike through kings in the day of His wrath.

6 He shall judge among the nations, He shall fill the places with the dead bodies; He shall wound the heads over many countries.

7 He shall drink of the brook in the way; therefore shall He lift up the head.

111 Praise You י (Halelu Yah)! I will praise יהוה with my whole heart, in the assembly of the upright, and in the congregation.

2 The works of יהוה are great, sought out of all those who have pleasure therein.

3 His work is honorable and glorious; and His righteousness endureth forever.

4 He hath made His wonderful works to be remembered; יהוה is gracious and full of compassion.

5 He hath given meat unto them that fear Him; He will ever be mindful of His covenant.

6 He hath shewed His people the power of His works, that He may give them the heritage of the nations.

7 The works of His hands are verity and judgment; all His commandments are sure.

8 They stand fast forever and ever, and are done in truth and uprightness.

9 He sent redemption unto His people; He hath commanded His covenant forever; holy and reverend is His name.

10 The fear of יהוה is the beginning of wisdom; a good understanding has all those who do His commandments. His praise endureth forever.

112 Praise You י (Halelu Yah)! Blessed is the man who feareth יהוה, who delighteth greatly in His commandments.

2 His seed shall be mighty upon earth; the generation of the upright shall be blessed.

3 Wealth and riches shall be in His house; and His righteousness endureth forever.

4 Unto the upright there ariseth light in the darkness; He is gracious, and full of compassion, and righteous.

5 A good man sheweth favor, and lendeth; he will guide his affairs with discretion.

6 Surely he shall not be moved forever; the righteous shall be in everlasting remembrance.

7 He shall not be afraid of evil tidings; his heart is fixed, trusting in יהוה.

8 His heart is established, he shall not be afraid, until he sees his desire upon his enemies.

9 He hath dispersed, He hath given to the poor; His righteousness endureth forever; His horn shall be exalted with honor.

10 The wicked shall see it, and be grieved; he shall gnash with his teeth, and melt away; the desire of the wicked shall perish.

113 Praise You יה (Halelu Yah)! Praise, O you servants of יהוה, praise the name of יהוה.

2 Blessed be the name of יהוה from this time forth and forevermore.

3 From the rising of the sun unto the going down of the same יהוה's name is to be praised.

4 יהוה is high above all nations, and His glory above the heavens.

5 Who is like unto יהוה our God (YHWH Eloheinu), who dwelleth on high,

6 Who humbleth himself to behold the things that are in heaven, and in the earth!

7 He raiseth up the poor out of the dust, and lifteth the needy out of the dunghill;

8 That He may set Him with princes, even with the princes of His people.

9 He maketh the barren woman to keep house, and to be a joyful mother of children. Praise You יה (Halelu Yah)!

114 When Yisrael went out of Egypt (Mitsrayim), the house of Jacob (Yaaqov) from a people of strange language;

2 Judah (Yehudah) was His sanctuary, and Yisrael His dominion.

3 The sea saw it, and fled; Jordan (Yarden) was driven back.

4 The mountains skipped like rams, and the little hills like lambs.

5 What ailed you, O you sea, that you fleddest? You Jordan (Yarden), that you wast driven back?

6 You mountains, that you skipped like rams; and you little hills, like lambs?

7 Tremble, you earth, at the presence of B13the Lord (Adon), at the presence of the God (Eloah) of Jacob (Yaaqov);

8 Which turned the rock into a standing water, the flint into a fountain of waters.

115 Not unto us, O יהוה, not unto us, but unto Your name give glory, for Your mercy, and for Your truth's sake.

2 Wherefore should the heathen say, "Where is now their God (Elohim)?"

3 But our God (Elohim) is in the heavens; He hath done whatsoever He hath pleased.

4 Their idols are silver and gold, the work of men's hands.

5 They have mouths, but they speak not; eyes have they, but they see not;

6 They have ears, but they hear not; noses have they, but they smell not;

7 They have hands, but they handle not; feet have they, but they walk not; nor speak they through their throat.

8 Those who make them are like unto them; so is every one that trusteth in them.

9 O Yisrael, trust you in יהוה; He is their help and their shield.

10 O house of Aaron (Aharon), trust in יהוה; He is their help and their shield.

11 You who fear יהוה, trust in יהוה; He is their help and their shield.

12 יהוה hath been mindful of us; He will bless us; He will bless the house of Yisrael; He will bless the house of Aaron (Aharon).

13 He will bless those who fear יהוה, both small and great.

14 יהוה shall increase you more and more, you and your children.

15 You are blessed of יהוה Who made heaven and earth.

16 The heaven, even the heavens, are יהוה's; but the earth hath He given to the children of men.

17 The dead praise not יהוה, neither any that go down into silence.

18 But we will bless יהוה from this time forth and forevermore. Praise You יה (Halelu Yah)!

116 I love יהוה, because He hath heard my voice and my supplications.

2 Because He hath inclined His ear unto me, therefore will I call upon Him as long as I live.

3 The sorrows of death compassed me, and the pains of sheol gat hold upon me: I found trouble and sorrow.

4 Then called I upon the name of יהוה; O יהוה, I beseech You, deliver my soul.

5 Gracious is יהוה, and righteous; yea, our God (Elohim) is merciful.

6 יהוה preserveth the simple; I was brought low, and He helped me.

7 Return unto Your rest, O my soul; for יהוה hath dealt bountifully with you.

8 For You have delivered my soul from death, mine eyes from tears, and my feet from falling.

9 I will walk before יהוה in the land of the living.

10 I believed, therefore have I spoken: "I was

greatly afflicted."

11 I said in my haste, "All men are liars."

12 What shall I render unto יהוה for all His benefits toward me?

13 I will take the cup of salvation, and call upon the name of יהוה.

14 I will pay my vows unto יהוה now in the presence of all his people.

15 Precious in the sight of יהוה is the death of His faithful ones (chasidim).

16 O יהוה, truly I am Your servant; I am Your servant, and the son of Your handmaid; You have loosed my bonds.

17 I will offer to You the sacrifice of thanksgiving, and will call upon the name of יהוה.

18 I will pay my vows unto יהוה now in the presence of all His people,

19 In the courts of יהוה's house, in the midst of you, O Jerusalem (Yerushalayim). Praise You יה (Halelu Yah)!

117 O praise יהוה, all you nations; praise Him, all you people.

2 For His merciful kindness is great toward us; and the truth of יהוה endureth forever. Praise You יה (Halelu Yah)!

118 O give thanks unto יהוה; for He is good, because His mercy endureth forever.

2 Let Yisrael now say, "His mercy endureth forever."

3 Let the house of Aaron (Aharon) now say, "His mercy endureth forever."

4 Let them now that fear יהוה say, "His mercy endureth forever."

5 I called upon יהוה in distress; יהוה answered me, and set me in a large place.

6 יהוה is on my side; I will not fear. What can man do unto me?

7 יהוה taketh my part with them that help me; therefore shall I see my desire upon them that hate me.

8 It is better to trust in יהוה than to put confidence in man.

9 It is better to trust in יהוה than to put confidence in princes.

10 All nations compassed me about, but in the name of יהוה will I destroy them.

11 They compassed me about; yea, they compassed me about, but in the name of יהוה I will destroy them.

12 They compassed me about like bees; they are quenched as the fire of thorns, for in the name

of יהוה I will destroy them.

13 You have thrust sore at me that I might fall, but יהוה helped me.

14 יהוה is my strength and song, and is become my salvation.

15 The voice of rejoicing and salvation is in the tabernacles of the righteous; the right hand of יהוה doeth valiantly.

16 The right hand of יהוה is exalted; the right hand of יהוה doeth valiantly.

17 I shall not die, but live, and declare the works of יהוה.

18 יהוה hath chastened me sore, but he hath not given me over unto death.

19 Open to me the gates of righteousness; I will go into them, and I will praise יהוה.

20 This gate of יהוה, into which the righteous shall enter.

21 I will praise You, for You have heard me, and art become my salvation.

22 The stone which the builders refused is become the head stone of the corner.

23 This is יהוה's doing; it is marvellous in our eyes.

24 This is the day which יהוה hath made; we will rejoice and be glad in it.

25 Save now, I beseech You, O יהוה; O יהוה, I beseech You, send now prosperity.

26 Blessed is He who cometh in the name of יהוה; we have blessed You out of the house of יהוה.

27 God (El) is יהוה, who hath shewed us light; bind the sacrifice with cords, even unto the horns of the altar.

28 You are my God (Eli), and I will praise You; You are my God (Elohim), I will exalt You.

29 O give thanks unto יהוה, for He is good; for His mercy endureth forever.

119 ALEF א

1 Blessed are the undefiled in the way, who walk in the Torah of יהוה.

2 Blessed are they that keep His testimonies, and that seek Him with the whole heart.

3 They also do no iniquity; they walk in His ways.

4 You have commanded us to keep Your precepts diligently.

5 O that my ways were directed to keep Your statutes!

6 Then shall I not be ashamed, when I have

respect unto all Your commandments.

7 I will praise You with uprightness of heart, when I shall have learned Your righteous judgments.

8 I will keep Your statutes; O forsake me not utterly.

BET ב

9 Wherewithal shall a young man cleanse his way? By taking heed thereto according to Your word.

10 With my whole heart have I sought You; O let me not wander from Your commandments.

11 Your word have I hid in mine heart, that I might not sin against You.

12 Blessed art You, O יהוה; teach me Your statutes.

13 With my lips have I declared all the judgments of Your mouth.

14 I have rejoiced in the way of Your testimonies, as much as in all riches.

15 I will meditate in Your precepts, and have respect unto Your ways.

16 I will delight myself in Your statutes; I will not forget Your word.

GIMEL ג

17 Deal bountifully with Your servant, that I may live, and keep Your word.

18 Open You mine eyes, that I may behold wondrous things out of Your Torah.

19 I am a stranger in the earth; hide not Your commandments from me.

20 My soul breaketh for the longing that it hath unto Your judgments at all times.

21 You have rebuked the proud that are cursed, which do err from Your commandments.

22 Remove from me reproach and contempt; for I have kept Your testimonies.

23 Princes also did sit and speak against me; but Your servant did meditate in Your statutes.

24 Your testimonies also are my delight and my counsellors.

DALET ד

25 My soul cleaveth unto the dust; quicken You me according to Your word.

26 I have declared my ways, and You heardest me; teach me Your statutes.

27 Make me to understand the way of Your precepts; so shall I talk of Your wondrous works.

28 My soul melteth for heaviness; strengthen

You me according unto Your word.

29 Remove from me the way of lying, and grant me Your Torah graciously.

30 I have chosen the way of truth; Your judgments have I laid before me.

31 I have cleaved unto Your testimonies; O יהוה, put me not to shame.

32 I will run the way of Your commandments, when You shalt enlarge my heart.

HEY ה

33 Teach me, O יהוה, the way of Your statutes; and I shall keep it unto the end.

34 Give me understanding, and I shall keep Your Torah; yea, I shall observe it with my whole heart.

35 Make me to go in the path of Your commandments; for therein do I delight.

36 Incline my heart unto Your testimonies, and not to covetousness.

37 Turn away mine eyes from beholding vanity; and quicken You me in Your way.

38 Establish Your word unto Your servant, who is devoted to Your fear.

39 Turn away my reproach which I fear, for Your judgments are good.

40 Behold, I have longed after Your precepts; quicken me in Your righteousness.

WAW ו

41 Let Your mercies come also unto me, O יהוה, even Your salvation, according to Your word.

42 So shall I have wherewith to answer him that reproacheth me, for I trust in Your word.

43 And take not the word of truth utterly out of my mouth, for I have hoped in Your judgments.

44 So shall I keep Your Torah continually forever and ever.

45 And I will walk at liberty, for I seek Your precepts.

46 I will speak of Your testimonies also before kings, and will not be ashamed.

47 And I will delight myself in Your commandments, which I have loved.

48 My hands also will I lift up unto Your commandments, which I have loved; and I will meditate in Your statutes.

ZAYIN ז

49 Remember the word unto Your servant, upon which You have caused me to hope.

50 This is my comfort in my affliction, for Your word hath quickened me.

51 The proud have had me greatly in derision; yet have I not declined from Your Torah.

52 I remembered Your judgments of old, O יהוה; and have comforted myself.

53 Horror hath taken hold upon me because of the wicked that forsake Your Torah.

54 Your statutes have been my songs in the house of my pilgrimage.

55 I have remembered Your name, O יהוה, in the night, and have kept Your Torah.

56 This I had, because I kept Your precepts.

CHET ח

57 You are my portion, O יהוה; I have said that I would keep Your words.

58 I intreated Your favor with my whole heart; be merciful unto me according to Your word.

59 I thought on my ways, and turned my feet unto Your testimonies.

60 I made haste, and delayed not to keep Your commandments.

61 The bands of the wicked have robbed me, but I have not forgotten Your Torah.

62 At midnight I will rise to give thanks unto you because of Your righteous judgments.

63 I am a companion of all them that fear You, and of them that keep Your precepts.

64 The earth, O יהוה, is full of Your mercy; teach me Your statutes.

TET ט

65 You have dealt well with Your servant, O יהוה, according unto Your word.

66 Teach me good judgment and knowledge, for I have believed Your commandments.

67 Before I was afflicted I went astray, but now have I kept Your word.

68 You are good, and doest good; teach me Your statutes.

69 The proud have forged a lie against me: but I will keep Your precepts with my whole heart.

70 Their heart is as fat as grease, but I delight in Your Torah.

71 It is good for me that I have been afflicted; that I might learn Your statutes.

72 The Torah of Your mouth is better unto me than thousands of gold and silver.

YOD י

73 Your hands have made me and fashioned me; give me understanding, that I may learn Your commandments.

74 They that fear You will be glad when they see

me, because I have hoped in Your word.

75 I know, O יהוה, that Your judgments are right, and that You in faithfulness have afflicted me.

76 Please let Your merciful kindness be for my comfort, according to Your word unto Your servant.

77 Let Your tender mercies come unto me, that I may live; for Your Torah is my delight.

78 Let the proud be ashamed, for they dealt perversely with me without a cause; but I will meditate in Your precepts.

79 Let those that fear You turn unto me, and those that have known Your testimonies.

80 Let my heart be sound in Your statutes, that I be not ashamed.

KAF כ

81 My soul fainteth for Your salvation, but I hope in Your word.

82 Mine eyes fail for Your word, saying, "When wilt You comfort me?"

83 For I am become like a bottle in the smoke; yet do I not forget Your statutes.

84 How many are the days of Your servant? When wilt You execute judgment on them that persecute me?

85 The proud have digged pits for me, which are not after Your Torah.

86 All Your commandments are faithful; they persecute me wrongfully; help You me.

87 They had almost consumed me upon earth; but I forsook not Your precepts.

88 Quicken me after Your loving-kindness; so shall I keep the testimony of Your mouth.

LAMED ל

89 For ever, O יהוה, Your word is settled in heaven.

90 Your faithfulness is unto all generation; You have established the earth, and it abideth.

91 They continue this day according to Your ordinances, for all are Your servants.

92 Unless Your Torah had been my delights, I should then have perished in mine affliction.

93 I will never forget Your precepts, for with them You have quickened me.

94 I am Yours, save me; for I have sought Your precepts.

95 The wicked have waited for me to destroy me, but I will consider Your testimonies.

96 I have seen an end of all perfection, but Your

commandment is exceeding broad.

MEM מ

97 O how love I Your Torah! It is my meditation all the day.

98 You through Your commandments have made me wiser than mine enemies; for they are ever with me.

99 I have more understanding than all my teachers, for Your testimonies are my meditation.

100 I understand more than the ancients, because I keep Your precepts.

101 I have refrained my feet from every evil way, that I might keep Your word.

102 I have not departed from Your judgments, for You have taught me.

103 How sweet are Your words unto my taste! Yea, sweeter than honey to my mouth!

104 Through Your precepts I get understanding; therefore I hate every false way.

NUN נ

105 Your word is a lamp unto my feet, and a light unto my path.

106 I have sworn, and I will perform it, that I will keep Your righteous judgments.

107 I am afflicted very much; quicken me, O יהוה, according unto Your word.

108 Accept, I beseech You, the freewill offerings of my mouth, O יהוה, and teach me your judgments.

109 My soul is continually in my hand; yet do I not forget Your Torah.

110 The wicked have laid a snare for me; yet I erred not from Your precepts.

111 Your testimonies have I taken as a heritage forever, for they are the rejoicing of my heart.

112 I have inclined mine heart to perform Your statutes alway, even unto the end.

SAMEKH ס

113 I hate vain thoughts, but Your Torah do I love.

114 You are my hiding place and my shield: I hope in Your word.

115 Depart from me, you evildoers, for I will keep the commandments of my God (Elohim).

116 Uphold me according unto Your word, that I may live; and let me not be ashamed of my hope.

117 Hold You me up, and I shall be safe; and I will have respect unto Your statutes continually.

118 You have trodden down all them that err from Your statutes; for their deceit is falsehood.

119 You puttest away all the wicked of the earth like dross; therefore I love Your testimonies.

120 My flesh trembleth for fear of You; and I am afraid of Your judgments.

AYIN ע

121 I have done judgment and justice; leave me not to mine oppressors.

122 Be surety for Your servant for good; let not the proud oppress me.

123 Mine eyes fail for Your salvation, and for the word of Your righteousness.

124 Deal with Your servant according unto Your mercy, and teach me Your statutes.

125 I am Your servant; give me understanding, that I may know Your testimonies.

126 It is time for You, יהוה, to act; for they have made void Your Torah.

127 Therefore I love Your commandments above gold; yea, above fine gold.

128 Therefore I esteem all Your precepts concerning all things to be right; and I hate every false way.

PEH פ

129 Your testimonies are wonderful; therefore doth my soul keep them.

130 The entrance of Your words giveth light; it giveth understanding unto the simple.

131 I opened my mouth, and panted, for I longed for Your commandments.

132 Look You upon me, and be merciful unto me, as You usest to do unto those that love Your name.

133 Order my steps in Your word; and let not any iniquity have dominion over me.

134 Deliver me from the oppression of man; so will I keep Your precepts.

135 Make Your face to shine upon Your servant; and teach me Your statutes.

136 Rivers of waters run down mine eyes, because they keep not Your Torah.

TSADI צ

137 Righteous art You, O יהוה, and upright are Your judgments.

138 Your testimonies that You have commanded are righteous and very faithful.

139 My zeal hath consumed me, because mine enemies have forgotten Your words.

140 Your word is very pure; therefore Your servant loveth it.

141 I am small and despised; yet do not I forget Your precepts.

142 Your righteousness is an everlasting righteousness, and Your Torah is the truth.

143 Trouble and anguish have taken hold on me; yet Your commandments are my delights.

144 The righteousness of Your testimonies is everlasting; give me understanding, and I shall live.

QOF ק

145 I cried with my whole heart; hear me, O יהוה; I will keep Your statutes.

146 I cried unto You; save me, and I shall keep Your testimonies.

147 I prevented the dawning of the morning, and cried; I hoped in Your word.

148 Mine eyes prevent the night watches, that I might meditate in Your word.

149 Hear my voice according unto Your lovingkindness; O יהוה, quicken me according to Your judgment.

150 They draw near that follow after mischief; they are far from Your Torah.

151 You are near, O יהוה; and all Your commandments are truth.

152 Concerning Your testimonies, I have known of old that You have founded them forever.

RESH ר

153 Consider mine affliction, and deliver me, for I do not forget Your Torah.

154 Plead my cause, and deliver me; quicken me according to Your word.

155 Salvation is far from the wicked, for they seek not Your statutes.

156 Great are Your tender mercies, O יהוה; quicken me according to Your judgments.

157 Many are my persecutors and mine enemies; yet do I not decline from Your testimonies.

158 I beheld the transgressors, and was grieved, because they kept not Your word.

159 Consider how I love Your precepts: quicken me, O יהוה, according to Your lovingkindness.

160 Your word is true from the beginning; and every one of Your righteous judgments endureth forever.

SHIN ש

161 Princes have persecuted me without a cause, but my heart standeth in awe of Your word.

162 I rejoice at Your word, as one that findeth great spoil.

163 I hate and abhor lying, but Your Torah do I love.

164 Seven times a day do I praise You because of Your righteous judgments.

165 Great peace have they which love Your Torah; and nothing shall offend them.

166 יהוה, I have hoped for Your salvation, and done Your commandments.

167 My soul hath kept Your testimonies; and I love them exceed-ingly.

168 I have kept Your precepts and Your testimonies, for all my ways are before You.

TAV ת

169 Let my cry come near before You, O יהוה; give me understanding according to Your word.

170 Let my supplication come before you; deliver me according to Your word.

171 My lips shall utter praise, when You have taught me Your statutes.

172 My tongue shall speak of Your word, for all Your commandments are righteousness.

173 Let Your hand help me, for I have chosen Your precepts.

174 I have longed for Your salvation, O יהוה; and Your Torah is my delight.

175 Let my soul live, and it shall praise you; and let Your judgments help me.

176 I have gone astray like a lost sheep; seek Your servant; for I do not forget Your commandments.

120 A Song of degrees.
1 In my distress I cried unto יהוה, and He heard me.

2 Deliver my soul, O יהוה, from lying lips, and from a deceitful tongue.

3 What shall be given unto you? Or what shall be done unto you, you false tongue?

4 Sharp arrows of the mighty, with coals of juniper.

5 Woe is me, that I sojourn in Mesech, that I dwell in the tents of Kedar!

6 My soul hath long dwelt with him who hateth peace.

7 I am for peace, but when I speak, they are for war.

121 A Song of degrees.
1 I will lift up mine eyes unto the hills, from whence cometh my help.

2 My help cometh from יהוה, who made heaven and earth.

3 He will not allow your foot to be moved; He who keepeth you will not slumber.

4 Behold, He who keepeth Yisrael shall neither slumber nor sleep.

5 יהוה is your keeper; יהוה is your shade upon your right hand.

6 The sun shall not smite you by day, nor the moon by night.

7 יהוה shall preserve you from all evil; He shall preserve your soul.

8 יהוה shall preserve your going out and your coming in from this time forth, and even forevermore.

122

A Song of degrees of Dawid.

1 I was glad when they said unto me, "Let us go into the house of יהוה."

2 Our feet shall stand within Your gates, O Jerusalem (Yerushalayim).

3 Jerusalem (Yerushalayim) is built as a city that is compact together;

4 Whither the tribes go up, the tribes of יה (Yah), unto the testimony of Yisrael, to give thanks unto the name of יהוה.

5 For there are set thrones of judgment, the thrones of the house of Dawid.

6 Pray for the peace of Jerusalem (Yerushalayim): "They shall prosper who love You.

7 Peace be within your walls, and prosperity within your palaces."

8 For my brethren and companions' sakes, I will now say, "Peace be within you."

9 Because of the house of יהוה our God (YHWH Eloheinu) I will seek Your good.

123

A Song of degrees.

1 Unto You lift I up mine eyes, O You that dwellest in the heavens.

2 Behold, as the eyes of servants look unto the hand of their masters, and as the eyes of a maiden unto the hand of her mistress; so our eyes wait upon יהוה our God (YHWH Eloheinu), until that He has mercy upon us.

3 Have mercy upon us, O יהוה, have mercy upon us! For we are exceedingly filled with contempt.

4 Our soul is exceedingly filled with the scorning of those that are at ease, and with the contempt of the proud.

124

A Song of degrees of Dawid.

1 "If it had not been יהוה who was on our side, now may Yisrael say;

2 If it had not been יהוה who was on our side, when men rose up against us;

3 Then they had swallowed us up quick, when their wrath was kindled against us;

4 Then the waters had overwhelmed us, the stream had gone over our soul:

5 Then the proud waters had gone over our soul."

6 Blessed be יהוה, who hath not given us as a prey to their teeth.

7 Our soul is escaped as a bird out of the snare of the fowlers; the snare is broken, and we are escaped.

8 Our help is in the name of יהוה, who made heaven and earth.

125

A Song of degrees.

1 Those who trust in יהוה shall be as Mount Zion (Tsiyon), which cannot be removed, but abideth forever.

2 As the mountains are round about Jerusalem (Yerushalayim), so יהוה is round about His people from henceforth even forever.

3 For the rod of the wicked shall not rest upon the lot of the righteous; lest the righteous put forth their hands unto iniquity.

4 Do good, O יהוה, unto those who are good, and to those who are upright in their hearts.

5 As for such as turn aside unto their crooked ways, יהוה shall lead them forth with the workers of iniquity; but peace shall be upon Yisrael.

126

A Song of degrees.

1 When יהוה turned again the captivity of Zion (Tsiyon), we were like those who dream.

2 Then was our mouth filled with laughter, and our tongue with singing; then said they among the nations, יהוה hath done great things for them.

3 יהוה hath done great things for us; whereof we are glad.

4 Turn back our captivity, O יהוה, as the streams in the south.

5 They that sow in tears shall reap in joy.

6 He that goeth forth and weepeth, bearing precious seed, shall doubtless come again with rejoicing, bringing his sheaves with him.

127

A Song of degrees for Solomon (Shelomoh).

1 Unless יהוה build the house, they labor in vain who build it; unless יהוה keep the city, the watchman waketh but in vain.

2 It is vain for you to rise up early, to sit up late, to eat the bread of sorrows; for so He giveth His

beloved sleep.

3 Behold, children are a heritage of יהוה; and the fruit of the womb is His reward.

4 As arrows are in the hand of a mighty man; so are children of the youth.

5 Happy is the man that hath his quiver full of them; they shall not be ashamed, but they shall speak with the enemies in the gate.

128 A Song of degrees.

1 Blessed is every one that feareth יהוה; that walketh in His ways.

2 For you shalt eat the labour of your hands; happy shalt you be, and it shall be well with you.

3 Your wife shall be as a fruitful vine by the sides of your house; your children like olive plants round about your table.

4 Behold, that thus shall the man be blessed who feareth יהוה.

5 יהוה shall bless you out of Zion (Tsiyon); and you shalt see the good of Jerusalem (Yerushalayim) all the days of your life.

6 Yea, you shalt see your children's children, and peace upon Yisrael.

129 A Song of degrees.

1 "Many a time have they afflicted me from my youth," may Yisrael now say:

2 "Many a time have they afflicted me from my youth; yet they have not prevailed against me.

3 The plowers plowed upon my back; they made long their furrows."

4 יהוה is righteous; He hath cut in pieces the cords of the wicked.

5 Let them all be confounded and turned back that hate Zion (Tsiyon).

6 Let them be as the grass upon the housetops, which withereth afore it groweth up;

7 Wherewith the mower filleth not his hand; nor he that bindeth sheaves his bosom.

8 Neither do they which go by say, "The blessing of יהוה be upon you; we bless you in the name of יהוה!"

130 A Song of degrees.

1 Out of the depths have I cried unto You, O יהוה.

2 the Lord (Adonai), hear my voice; let Your ears be attentive to the voice of my supplications.

3 If You, יה (Yah), shouldest mark iniquities, O Lord (Adonai), who shall stand?

4 But there is forgiveness with You, that You mayest be feared.

5 I wait for יהוה, my soul doth wait, and in His word do I hope.

6 My soul waiteth for the Lord (Adonai) more than they that watch for the morning; I say, more than those who watch for the morning.

7 Let Yisrael hope in יהוה: For with יהוה there is mercy, and with Him is plenteous redemption.

8 And He shall redeem Yisrael from all His iniquities.

131 A Song of degrees of Dawid.

1 יהוה, my heart is not haughty, nor mine eyes lofty; neither do I exercise myself in great matters, or in things too high for me.

2 Surely I have behaved and quieted myself, as a child that is weaned of his mother my soul is even as a weaned child.

3 Let Yisrael hope in יהוה from henceforth and forever.

132 A Song of degrees.

1 יהוה, remember Dawid, and all his afflictions;

2 How he sware unto יהוה, and vowed unto the mighty of Jacob (Yaaqov);

3 Surely I will not come into the tabernacle of my house, nor go up into my bed;

4 I will not give sleep to mine eyes, or slumber to mine eyelids,

5 Until I find out a place for יהוה, a habitation for the mighty of Jacob (Yaaqov).

6 Behold, we heard of it at Ephratah; we found it in the fields of the wood.

7 We will go into His tabernacles; we will worship at His footstool.

8 Arise, O יהוה, into Your rest; You, and the ark of Your strength.

9 Let Your priests (kohanim) be clothed with righteousness; and let Your faithful ones (chasidim) shout for joy.

10 For your servant Dawid's sake turn not away the face of Your anointed (mashiach).

11 יהוה hath sworn in truth unto Dawid; He will not turn from it: "Of the fruit of your body will I set upon your throne.

12 If your children will keep My covenant and My testimony that I shall teach them, their children shall also sit upon your throne forevermore."

13 For יהוה hath chosen Zion (Tsiyon); He hath desired it for His habitation.

14 This is my rest forever; here will I dwell, for I have desired it.

15 I will abundantly bless her provision; I will

satisfy her poor with bread.

16 I will also clothe her priests (kohanim) with salvation: and her faithful ones (chasidim) shall shout aloud for joy.

17 There will I make the horn of Dawid to bud; I have ordained a lamp for mine anointed (mashiach).

18 His enemies will I clothe with shame, but upon himself shall his crown flourish.

133 A Song of degrees of Dawid. 1 Behold, how good and how pleasant it is for brethren to dwell together in unity!

2 It is like the precious ointment upon the head, that ran down upon the beard, even Aaron (Aharon)'s beard, that went down to the skirts of his garments.

3 As the dew of Hermon, and as the dew that descended upon the mountains of Zion (Tsiyon); for there יהוה commanded the blessing, even life forevermore.

134 A Song of degrees. 1 Behold, bless you יהוה, all you servants of יהוה, who by night stand in the house of יהוה.

2 Lift up your hands in the sanctuary, and bless יהוה.

3 יהוה who made heavens and earth bless you out of Zion (Tsiyon).

135 Praise You יה (Halelu Yah)! Praise You the name of יהוה; praise Him, O you servants of יהוה.

2 You that stand in the house of יהוה, in the courts of the house of our God (Elohim),

3 Praise You יה (Halelu Yah), for יהוה is good; sing praises unto His name; for it is pleasant.

4 For יהוה hath chosen Jacob (Yaaqov) unto Himself, and Yisrael for His peculiar treasure.

5 For I know that יהוה is great, and that our Lord (Adonai) is above all mighty ones (elohim).

6 Whatsoever יהוה pleased, that did He in heaven, and in earth, in the seas, and all deep places.

7 He causeth the vapours to ascend from the ends of the earth; He maketh lightnings for the rain; He bringeth the wind out of His treasuries.

8 Who smote the firstborn of Egypt (Mitsrayim), both of man and beast.

9 Who sent tokens and wonders into the midst of you, O Egypt (Mitsrayim), upon Pharaoh (Paroh), and upon all His servants.

10 Who smote great nations, and slew mighty kings;

11 Sihon king of the Amorites, and Og king of Bashan, and all the kingdoms of Canaan;

12 And gave their land for a heritage, a heritage unto Yisrael His people.

13 Your name, O יהוה, endureth forever; and Your memorial, O יהוה, throughout all generations.

14 For יהוה will judge His people, and He will have compassion concerning His servants.

15 The idols of the heathen are silver and gold, the work of men's hands.

16 They have mouths, but they speak not; eyes have they, but they see not;

17 They have ears, but they hear not; neither is there any breath in their mouths.

18 Those who make them are like unto them; so is every one who trusteth in them.

19 Bless יהוה, O house of Yisrael; bless יהוה, O house of Aaron (Aharon);

20 Bless יהוה, O house of Lewi; you who fear יהוה, bless יהוה.

21 Blessed be יהוה out of Zion (Tsiyon), Who dwelleth at Yerushalayim. Praise You יה (Halelu Yah).

136 1 O give thanks unto יהוה, for He is good; for His mercy endureth forever.

2 O give thanks unto the [B9]Supreme God (Elohei ha-Elohim), for His mercy endureth forever.

3 O give thanks to the [B14]Supreme Lord (Adonei haAdonim), for His mercy endureth forever.

4 To Him who alone doeth great wonders, for His mercy endureth forever;

5 To Him who by wisdom made the heavens, for His mercy endureth forever;

6 To Him that stretched out the earth above the waters, for His mercy endureth forever;

7 To Him who made great lights, for His mercy endureth forever.

8 The sun to rule by day, for His mercy endureth forever;

9 The moon and stars to rule by night, for His mercy endureth forever.

10 To Him who smote Egypt (Mitsrayim) in their firstborn, for His mercy endureth forever;

11 And brought out Yisrael from among them, for His mercy endureth forever;

12 With a strong hand, and with an outstretched arm, for His mercy endureth forever;

13 To Him who divided the Red sea into parts, for His mercy endureth forever;

14 And made Yisrael to pass through the midst of it, for His mercy endureth forever;

15 But overthrew Pharaoh (Paroh) and his army in the Red sea, for His mercy endureth forever;

16 To Him who led His people through the wilderness, for His mercy endureth forever;

17 To Him which smote great kings: for His mercy endureth forever:

18 And slew famous kings, for His mercy endureth forever;

19 Sihon king of the Amorites, for His mercy endureth forever;

20 And Og the king of Bashan, for His mercy endureth forever;

21 And gave their land for a heritage, for His mercy endureth forever;

22 Even a heritage unto Yisrael His servant, for His mercy endureth forever;

23 Who remembered us in our low estate, for His mercy endureth forever;

24 And hath redeemed us from our enemies, for His mercy endureth forever;

25 Who giveth food to all flesh, for His mercy endureth forever.

26 O give thanks unto the God of Heaven (El ha-Shamayim), for His mercy endureth forever.

137 By the rivers of Babylon (Bavel), there we sat down, yea, we wept, when we remembered Zion (Tsiyon).

2 We hanged our harps upon the willows in the midst thereof.

3 For there they that carried us away captive required of us a song; and they that wasted us required of us mirth, saying, "Sing us one of the songs of Zion (Tsiyon)!"

4 How shall we sing יהוה's song in a strange land?

5 If I forget You, O Jerusalem (Yerushalayim), let my right hand forget her cunning.

6 If I do not remember You, let my tongue cleave to the roof of my mouth; if I prefer not Jerusalem (Yerushalayim) above my chief joy.

7 Remember, O יהוה, the children of Edom in the day of Jerusalem (Yerushalayim); who said, "Rase it, rase it, even to the foundation thereof!"

8 O daughter of Babylon (Bavel), who art to be destroyed; happy shall he be, who rewardeth you as you have served us!

9 Happy shall he be, who taketh and dasheth Your little ones against the rock.

138 A Psalm of Dawid.
1 I will praise You with my whole heart; before rulers (elohim) will I sing praise unto You.

2 I will worship toward Your holy temple, and praise Your name for Your lovingkindness and for Your truth: for You have magnified Your word above all Your name.

3 In the day when I cried, You answeredst me and strengthenedst me with strength in my soul.

4 All the kings of the earth shall praise You, O יהוה, when they hear the words of Your mouth.

5 Yea, they shall sing in the ways of יהוה, for great is the glory of יהוה.

6 Though יהוה be high, yet hath He respect unto the lowly, but the proud He knoweth afar off.

7 Though I walk in the midst of trouble, You wilt revive me; You shalt stretch forth Your hand against the wrath of mine enemies, and Your right hand shall save me.

8 יהוה will perfect that which concerneth me; Your mercy, O יהוה, endureth forever; forsake not the works of Your own hands.

139 To the chief Musician, A Psalm of Dawid.
1 O יהוה, You have searched me, and known me.

2 You knowest my downsitting and mine uprising, You understandest my thought afar off.

3 You compassest my path and my lying down, and art acquainted with all my ways.

4 For there is not a word in my tongue, but, behold, O יהוה, You knowest it altogether.

5 You have beset me behind and before, and laid Your hand upon me.

6 Such knowledge is too wonderful for me; it is high, I cannot attain unto it.

7 Whither shall I go from Your spirit? Or whither shall I flee from Your presence?

8 If I ascend up into heaven, You are there; if I make my bed in sheol, behold, You are there.

9 If I take the wings of the morning, and dwell in the uttermost parts of the sea;

10 Even there shall Your hand lead me, and Your right hand shall hold me.

11 If I say, "Surely the darkness shall cover me;" even the night shall be light about me.

12 Yea, the darkness hideth not from you; but the night shineth as the day; the darkness and the light are both alike to You.

13 For You have possessed my reins; You have covered me in my mother's womb.

14 I will praise You, for I am fearfully and wonderfully made; marvellous are Your works; and that my soul knoweth right well.

15 My substance was not hidden from You, when I was made in secret, and curiously wrought in the lowest parts of the earth.

16 Your eyes did see my substance, yet being unperfect; and in Your book all my members were written, which in continuance were fashioned, when as yet there was none of them.

17 How precious also are Your thoughts unto me, O God (El)! How great is the sum of them!

18 If I should count them, they are more in number than the sand; when I awake, I am still with You.

19 Surely You wilt slay the wicked, O God (Eloah); depart from me therefore, you bloody men.

20 For they speak against You wickedly, and Your enemies take Your name in vain.

21 Do not I hate them, O יהוה, that hate You? And am not I grieved with those that rise up against You?

22 I hate them with perfect hatred; I count them mine enemies.

23 Search me, O God (El), and know my heart; try me, and know my anxious thoughts;

24 And see if there be any wicked way in me, and lead me in the way everlasting.

140 To the chief Musician, A Psalm of Dawid.

1 Deliver me, O יהוה, from the evil man; preserve me from the violent man;

2 Who imagine mischiefs in their heart; continually are they gathered together for war.

3 They have sharpened their tongues like a serpent; adders' poison is under their lips. Selah.

4 Keep me, O יהוה, from the hands of the wicked; preserve me from the violent man; who have purposed to overthrow my goings.

5 The proud have hid a snare for me, and cords; they have spread a net by the wayside; they have set gins for me. Selah.

6 I said unto יהוה, "You are my God (Elohim); hear the voice of my supplications, O יהוה.

7 O יהוה my Lord (Adonai), strength of my salvation, You have covered my head in the day of battle.

8 Grant not, O יהוה, the desires of the wicked; further not his wicked device; lest they exalt

themselves. Selah.

9 As for the head of those that compass me about, let the mischief of their own lips cover them.

10 Let burning coals fall upon them; let them be cast into the fire; into deep pits, that they rise not up again.

11 Let not an evil speaker be established in the earth; evil shall hunt the violent man to overthrow him.

12 I know that יהוה will maintain the cause of the afflicted, and the right of the poor.

13 Surely the righteous shall give thanks unto Your name; the upright shall dwell in Your presence.

141 A Psalm of Dawid.

1 יהוה, I cry unto You; make haste unto me; give ear unto my voice, when I cry unto You.

2 Let my prayer be set forth before You as incense; and the lifting up of my hands as the evening sacrifice.

3 Set a watch, O יהוה, before my mouth; keep the door of my lips.

4 Incline not my heart to any evil thing, to practise wicked works with men that work iniquity; and let me not eat of their dainties.

5 Let the righteous smite me; it shall be a kindness; and let him reprove me; it shall be an excellent oil, which shall not break my head, for yet my prayer also shall be in their calamities.

6 When their judges are overthrown in stony places, they shall hear my words; for they are sweet.

7 Our bones are scattered at the grave's mouth, as when one cutteth and cleaveth wood upon the earth.

8 But mine eyes are unto you, O יהוה my Lord (Adonai); in You is my trust; leave not my soul destitute.

9 Keep me from the snares which they have laid for me, and the gins of the workers of iniquity.

10 Let the wicked fall into their own nets, whilst that I withal escape.

142 Maskil of Dawid: A Prayer when he was in the cave.

1 I cried unto יהוה with my voice; with my voice unto יהוה did I make my supplication.

2 I poured out my complaint before him; I shewed before him my trouble.

3 When my spirit was overwhelmed within me, then You knewest my path. In the way wherein

I walked have they privily laid a snare for me.

4 I looked on my right hand, and beheld, but there was no man that would know me: refuge failed me; no man cared for my soul.

5 I cried unto You, O יהוה: I said, "You are my refuge and my portion in the land of the living.

6 Attend unto my cry; for I am brought very low; deliver me from my persecutors; for they are stronger than I.

7 Bring my soul out of prison, that I may praise Your name; the righteous shall compass me about, for You shalt deal bountifully with me."

143
A Psalm of Dawid.

1 Hear my prayer, O יהוה, give ear to my supplications; in Your faithfulness answer me, and in Your righteousness.

2 And enter not into judgment with Your servant, for in Your sight shall no man living be justified.

3 For the enemy hath persecuted my soul; he hath smitten my life down to the ground; he hath made me to dwell in darkness, as those that have been long dead.

4 Therefore is my spirit overwhelmed within me; my heart within me is desolate.

5 I remember the days of old; I meditate on all your works; I muse on the work of your hands.

6 I stretch forth my hands unto You; my soul thirsteth after You, as a thirsty land. Selah.

7 Hear me speedily, O יהוה; my spirit faileth; hide not Your face from me, lest I be like unto them that go down into the pit.

8 Cause me to hear Your lovingkindness in the morning, for in You do I trust; cause me to know the way wherein I should walk; for I lift up my soul unto You.

9 Deliver me, O יהוה, from mine enemies; I flee unto You to hide me.

10 Teach me to do Your will, for You are my God (Elohim); Your Spirit is good; lead me into the land of uprightness.

11 Quicken me, O יהוה, for Your name's sake; for Your righteousness' sake bring my soul out of trouble.

12 And of Your mercy cut off mine enemies, and destroy all them that afflict my soul; for I am Your servant.

144
A Psalm of Dawid.

1 Blessed be יהוה my strength, who teacheth my hands to war, and my fingers to fight;

2 My goodness, and my fortress; my high tower, and my deliverer; my shield, and He in whom I trust; who subdueth my people under me.

3 יהוה, what is man, that You takest knowledge of him! Or the son of man, that You makest account of him!

4 Man is like to vanity; his days are as a shadow that passeth away.

5 Bow Your heavens, O יהוה, and come down; touch the mountains, and they shall smoke.

6 Cast forth lightning, and scatter them; shoot out your arrows, and destroy them.

7 Send Your hand from above; rid me, and deliver me out of great waters, from the hand of strange children;

8 Whose mouth speaketh vanity, and their right hand is a right hand of falsehood.

9 I will sing a new song unto You, O God (Elohim); upon a psaltery and an instrument of ten strings will I sing praises unto You.

10 It is He who giveth salvation unto kings; who delivereth Dawid His servant from the hurtful sword.

11 Rid me, and deliver me from the hand of strange children, whose mouth speaketh vanity, and their right hand is a right hand of falsehood;

12 That our sons may be as plants grown up in their youth, that our daughters may be as corner stones, polished after the similitude of a palace;

13 That our garners may be full, affording all manner of store; that our sheep may bring forth thousands and ten thousands in our streets;

14 That our oxen may be strong to labour; that there be no breaking in, nor going out; that there be no complaining in our streets.

15 Happy is that people, that is in such a case; yea, happy is that people, whose God (Elohim) is יהוה.

145
Dawid's Psalm of praise.

1 I will extol You, my God (Elohim), O King; and I will bless Your name forever and ever.

2 Every day will I bless You; and I will praise Your name forever and ever.

3 Great is יהוה, and greatly to be praised; and His greatness is unsearchable.

4 One generation shall praise Your works to another, and shall declare Your mighty acts.

5 I will speak of the glorious honor of Your majesty, and of Your wondrous works.

6 And men shall speak of the might of Your

awesome acts; and I will declare Your greatness.

7 They shall abundantly utter the memory of Your great goodness, and shall sing of Your righteousness.

8 יהוה is gracious, and full of compassion; slow to anger, and of great mercy.

9 יהוה is good to all; and His tender mercies are over all His works.

10 All Your works shall praise You, O יהוה; and Your faithful ones (chasidim) shall bless You.

11 They shall speak of the glory of Your kingdom, and talk of Your power;

12 To make known to the sons of men His mighty acts, and the glorious majesty of His kingdom.

13 Your kingdom is an everlasting kingdom, and Your dominion endureth throughout all generations.

14 יהוה upholdeth all that fall, and raiseth up all those that be bowed down.

15 The eyes of all wait upon You; and You givest them their food in due season.

16 You openest Your hand, and satisfiest the desire of every living thing.

17 יהוה is righteous in all His ways, and holy in all His works.

18 יהוה is near unto all them that call upon Him, to all that call upon Him in truth.

19 He will fulfil the desire of them that fear Him; He also will hear their cry, and will save them.

20 יהוה preserveth all them that love Him; but all the wicked will He destroy.

21 My mouth shall speak the praise of יהוה; and let all flesh bless His holy name forever and ever.

146

1 Praise You יה (Halelu Yah)! Praise יהוה, O my soul.

2 While I live will I praise יהוה; I will sing praises unto my God (Elohim) while I have my being.

3 Put not your trust in princes, nor in the son of man, in whom there is no help.

4 His breath goeth forth, he returneth to his earth; in that very day his thoughts perish.

5 Happy is he that hath the God (Elohim) of Jacob (Yaaqov) for his help, whose hope is in יהוה his God (Elohim);

6 Who made heavens, and earth, the sea, and all that therein is; who keepeth truth forever,

7 Who executeth judgment for the oppressed; who giveth food to the hungry. יהוה looseth the prisoners.

8 יהוה openeth the eyes of the blind. יהוה raiseth them that are bowed down; יהוה loveth the righteous.

9 יהוה preserveth the strangers; He relieveth the fatherless and widow; but the way of the wicked He turneth upside down.

10 יהוה shall reign forever, even your God (Elohim), O Zion (Tsiyon), unto all generations. Praise You יה (Halelu Yah)!

147

1 Praise You יה (Halelu Yah)! For it is good to sing praises unto our God (Elohim); for it is pleasant; and praise is beautiful.

2 יהוה doth build up Jerusalem (Yerushalayim); He gathereth together the outcasts of Yisrael.

3 He healeth the broken in heart, and bindeth up their wounds.

4 He telleth the number of the stars; He calleth them all by their names.

5 Great is our Lord (Adonai), and of great power; His understanding is infinite.

6 יהוה lifteth up the meek; He casteth the wicked down to the ground.

7 Sing unto יהוה with thanksgiving; sing praise upon the harp unto our God (Elohim);

8 Who covereth the heaven with clouds, who prepareth rain for the earth, who maketh grass to grow upon the mountains.

9 He giveth to the beast his food, and to the young ravens which cry.

10 He delighteth not in the strength of the horse; He taketh not pleasure in the legs of a man.

11 יהוה taketh pleasure in them that fear Him, in those that hope in His mercy.

12 Praise יהוה, O Jerusalem (Yerushalayim); praise your God (Elohim), O Zion (Tsiyon).

13 For He hath strengthened the bars of your gates; He hath blessed your children within you.

14 He maketh peace in your borders, and filleth you with the finest of the wheat.

15 He sendeth forth His commandment upon earth; His word runneth very swiftly.

16 He giveth snow like wool; He scattereth the hoarfrost like ashes.

17 He casteth forth His ice like morsels; who can stand before His cold?

18 He sendeth out His word, and melteth them; He causeth His wind to blow, and the waters flow.

19 He sheweth His word unto Jacob (Yaaqov), His statutes and His judgments unto Yisrael.

20 He hath not dealt so with any nation; and as for His judgments, they have not known them. Praise You יה (Halelu Yah)!

148 Praise You יה (Halelu Yah)! Praise You יהוה from the heavens; praise Him in the heights.

2 Praise You Him, all His angels; praise you Him, all His hosts.

3 Praise You Him, sun and moon; praise Him, all you stars of light.

4 Praise Him, you heavens of heavens, and you waters that be above the heavens.

5 Let them praise the name of יהוה; for He commanded, and they were created.

6 He hath also established them forever and ever; He hath made a decree which shall not pass.

7 Praise יהוה from the earth, you dragons, and all deeps;

8 Fire, and hail; snow, and vapour; stormy wind fulfilling his word:

9 Mountains, and all hills; fruitful trees, and all cedars;

10 Beasts, and all cattle; creeping things, and flying fowl;

11 Kings of the earth, and all people; princes, and all judges of the earth;

12 Both young men, and maidens; old men, and children.

13 Let them praise the name of יהוה, for His name alone is excellent; His glory is above the earth and heaven.

14 He also exalteth the horn of His people, the praise of all his faithful ones (chasidim); even of the children of Yisrael, a people near unto him. Praise You יה (Halelu Yah)!

149 Praise You יה (Halelu Yah)! Sing unto יהוה a new song, and His praise in the congregation of faithful ones (chasidim).

2 Let Yisrael rejoice in Him that made Him; let the children of Zion (Tsiyon) be joyful in their King.

3 Let them praise His name in the dance; let them sing praises unto Him with the timbrel and harp.

4 For יהוה taketh pleasure in His people; He will beautify the meek with salvation.

5 Let the faithful ones (chasidim) be joyful in glory; let them sing aloud upon their beds.

6 Let the high praises of God (Elohim) be in their mouth, and a two-edged sword in their hand;

7 To execute vengeance upon the nations, and punishments upon the people;

8 To bind their with chains, and their nobles with fetters of iron;

9 To execute upon them the judgment written; this honor have all His faithful ones (chasidim). Praise You יה (Halelu Yah)!

150 Praise You יה (Halelu Yah)! Praise God (El) in His sanctuary; praise Him in the firmament of His power.

2 Praise Him for His mighty acts; praise Him according to His excellent greatness.

3 Praise Him with the sound of the trumpet; praise Him with the psaltery and harp.

4 Praise Him with the timbrel and dance; praise Him with stringed instruments and organs.

5 Praise Him upon the loud cymbals; praise Him upon the high sounding cymbals.

6 Let every thing that hath breath praise יה (Yah). Praise You יה (Halelu Yah)!

PROVERBS
MISHLEI מִשְׁלֵי
(Book of Proverbs)

1 The proverbs of Solomon (Shelomoh) the son of Dawid, king of Yisrael;

2 To know wisdom and instruction; to perceive the words of understanding;

3 To receive the instruction of wisdom, justice, and judgment, and equity;

4 To give subtilty to the simple, to the young man knowledge and discretion.

5 A wise man will hear, and will increase learning; and a man of understanding shall attain unto wise counsels.

6 To understand a proverb, and the interpretation; the words of the wise, and their dark sayings.

7 The fear of יהוה is the beginning of knowledge, but fools despise wisdom and instruction.

8 My son, hear the instruction of your father, and forsake not the teaching of your mother.

9 For they shall be an ornament of grace unto your head, and chains about your neck.

10 My son, if sinners entice you, consent you not.

11 If they say, "Come with us, let us lay wait for blood, let us lurk privily for the innocent without cause;

12 Let us swallow them up alive as the grave; and whole, as those that go down into the pit;

13 We shall find all precious substance, we shall fill our houses with spoil:

14 Cast in your lot among us; let us all have one purse";

15 My son, walk not you in the way with them; refrain your foot from their path;

16 For their feet run to evil, and make haste to shed blood.

17 Surely in vain the net is spread in the sight of any bird.

18 And they lay wait for their own blood; they lurk privily for their own lives.

19 So are the ways of every one that is greedy of gain; which taketh away the life of the owners thereof.

20 Wisdom crieth outside; she uttereth her voice in the streets.

21 She crieth in the chief place of concourse, in the openings of the gates; in the city she uttereth her words, saying,

22 "How long, you simple ones, will you love simplicity? And the scorners delight in their scorning, and fools hate knowledge?

23 Turn you at my reproof; behold, I will pour out my spirit unto you, I will make known my words unto you.

24 Because I have called, and you refused; I have stretched out my hand, and no man regarded;

25 But you have set at nought all my counsel, and would none of my reproof.

26 I also will laugh at your disaster; I will mock when your fear cometh;

27 When your fear cometh as desolation, and your destruction cometh as a whirlwind; when distress and anguish cometh upon you.

28 Then shall they call upon me, but I will not answer; they shall seek me early, but they shall not find me:

29 For that they hated knowledge, and did not choose the fear of יהוה;

30 They would accept none of my counsel; they despised all my reproof.

31 Therefore shall they eat of the fruit of their own way, and be filled with their own devices.

32 For the turning away of the simple shall slay them, and the prosperity of fools shall destroy them.

33 But whoso hearkeneth unto me shall dwell safely, and shall be quiet from fear of evil."

2 My son, if you wilt receive my words, and hide my commandments with you;

2 So that you incline your ear unto wisdom, and apply your heart to understanding;

3 Yea, if you criest after knowledge, and liftest up your voice for understanding;

4 If you seekest her as silver, and searchest for her as for hid treasures;

5 Then shalt you understand the fear of יהוה, and find the knowledge of God (Elohim).

6 For יהוה giveth wisdom: out of his mouth cometh knowledge and understanding.

7 He layeth up sound wisdom for the righteous; he is a buckler to them that walk uprightly.

8 He keepeth the paths of judgment, and preserveth the way of His faithful ones (chadisim).

9 Then shalt you understand righteousness, and judgment, and equity; yea, every good path.

10 When wisdom entereth into your heart, and knowledge is pleasant unto your soul;

11 Discretion shall preserve you, understanding shall keep you;

12 To deliver you from the way of the evil man, from the man that speaketh perverse things;

13 Who leave the paths of uprightness, to walk in the ways of darkness;

14 Who rejoice to do evil, and delight in the frowardness of the wicked;

15 Whose ways are crooked, and they perverse in their paths;

16 To deliver you from the strange woman, even from the stranger which flattereth with her words;

17 Which forsaketh the guide of her youth, and forgetteth the covenant of her God (Elohim).

18 For her house inclineth unto death, and her paths unto the dead.

19 None that go unto her return again, neither take they hold of the paths of life.

20 That you mayest walk in the way of good men, and keep the paths of the righteous.

21 For the upright shall dwell in the land, and the perfect shall remain in it.

22 But the wicked shall be cut off from the earth, and the transgressors shall be rooted out of it.

3 My children, forget not my teaching; but let your heart keep my commandments:

2 For length of days, and long life, and peace, shall they add to you.

3 Let not mercy and truth forsake you; bind them about your neck; write them upon the table of your heart;

4 So shalt you find favor and good understanding in the sight of God (Elohim) and man.

5 Trust in יהוה with all your heart; and lean not unto your own understanding.

6 In all your ways acknowledge Him, and He shall direct your paths.

7 Be not wise in your own eyes; fear יהוה, and depart from evil.

8 It shall be health to your navel, and marrow to your bones.

9 Honour יהוה with your substance, and with the firstfruits of all your increase:

10 So shall your barns be filled with plenty, and your presses shall burst out with new wine.

11 My children, despise not the chastening of יהוה; neither be weary of His correction;

12 For whom יהוה loveth He correcteth; even as a father, the son in whom he delighteth.

13 Happy is the man that findeth wisdom, and the man that getteth understanding.

14 For the merchandise of it is better than the merchandise of silver, and the gain thereof than fine gold.

15 She is more precious than rubies; and all the things you canst desire are not to be compared unto her.

16 Length of days is in her right hand; and in her left hand riches and honor.

17 Her ways are ways of pleasantness, and all her paths are peace.

18 She is a tree of life to them that lay hold upon her; and happy is every one that retaineth her.

19 יהוה by wisdom hath founded the earth; by understanding hath He established the heavens.

20 By His knowledge the depths are broken up, and the clouds drop down the dew.

21 My children, let not them depart from your eyes; keep sound wisdom and discretion;

22 So shall they be life unto your soul, and grace to your neck.

23 Then shalt you walk in your way safely, and your foot shall not stumble.

24 When you liest down, you shalt not be afraid; yea, you shalt lie down, and your sleep shall be sweet.

25 Be not afraid of sudden fear, neither of the desolation of the wicked, when it cometh.

26 For יהוה shall be your confidence, and shall keep your foot from being taken.

27 Withhold not good from them to whom it is due, when it is in the power of your hand to do it.

28 Say not unto your neighbour, "Go, and come again, and tomorrow I will give;" when you have it by you.

29 Devise not evil against your neighbour, seeing he dwelleth securely by you.

30 Strive not with a man without cause, if he has done you no harm.

31 Envy you not the oppressor, and choose none of his ways.

32 For the perverse is abomination to יהוה, but His secret is with the righteous.

33 The curse of יהוה is in the house of the wicked, but He blesseth the habitation of the just.

34 Surely He scorneth the scorners: but He giveth grace unto the lowly.

35 The wise shall inherit glory, but shame shall be the promotion of fools.

4 Hear, you children, the instruction of a father, and attend to know understanding.

2 For I give you good doctrine, forsake you not my teaching.

3 For I was my father's son, tender and only beloved in the sight of my mother.

4 He taught me also, and said unto me, "Let your heart retain my words; keep my commandments, and live.

5 Get wisdom, get understanding: forget it not; neither decline from the words of my mouth.

6 Forsake her not, and she shall preserve you; love her, and she shall keep you.

7 Wisdom is the principal thing; therefore get wisdom; and with all your getting get understanding.

8 Exalt her, and she shall promote you; she shall bring you to honor, when you dost embrace her.

9 She shall give to your head an ornament of grace; a crown of glory shall she deliver to you."

10 Hear, O my son, and receive my sayings; and the years of your life shall be many.

11 I have taught you in the way of wisdom; I have led you in right paths.

12 When you goest, your steps shall not be straitened; and when you runnest, you shalt not stumble.

13 Take fast hold of instruction; let her not go; keep her; for she is your life.

14 Enter not into the path of the wicked, and go not in the way of evil men.

15 Avoid it, pass not by it, turn from it, and pass away.

16 For they sleep not, except they have done mischief; and their sleep is taken away, unless they cause some to fall.

17 For they eat the bread of wickedness, and drink the wine of violence.

18 But the path of the just is as the shining light, that shineth more and more unto the perfect day.

19 The way of the wicked is as darkness: they know not at what they stumble.

20 My son, attend to my words; incline your ear unto my sayings.

21 Let them not depart from your eyes; keep them in the midst of your heart.

22 For they are life unto those that find them, and health to all their flesh.

23 Keep your heart with all diligence; for out of it are the issues of life.

24 Put away from you a perverse mouth, and perverse lips put far from you.

25 Let your eyes look right on, and let your eyelids look straight before you.

26 Ponder the path of your feet, and let all your ways be established.

27 Turn not to the right hand nor to the left; remove your foot from evil.

5 My son, attend unto my wisdom, and bow your ear to my understanding,

2 That you mayest regard discretion, and that your lips may keep knowledge.

3 For the lips of a strange woman drop as a honeycomb, and her mouth is smoother than oil;

4 But her end is bitter as wormwood, sharp as a two-edged sword.

5 Her feet go down to death; her steps take hold on sheol.

6 Lest you shouldest ponder the path of life, her ways are moveable, that you canst not know them.

7 Hear me now therefore, O you children, and depart not from the words of my mouth.

8 Remove your way far from her, and come not near the door of her house;

9 Lest you give your honor unto others, and your years unto the cruel;

10 Lest strangers be filled with your wealth; and your labours be in the house of a stranger;

11 And you mourn at the last, when your flesh and your body are consumed,

12 And say, "How have I hated instruction, and my heart despised reproof;

13 And have not obeyed the voice of my teachers, nor inclined mine ear to those who instructed me!

14 I was almost in all evil in the midst of the congregation and assembly."

15 Drink waters out of your own cistern, and running waters out of your own well.

16 Let your fountains be dispersed abroad, and rivers of waters in the streets.

17 Let them be only your own, and not strangers with you.

18 Let your fountain be blessed; and rejoice with the wife of your youth.

19 Let her be as the loving hind and pleasant roe; let her breasts satisfy you at all times; and be you ravished always with her love.

20 And why wilt you, my son, be ravished with a strange woman, and embrace the bosom of a stranger?

21 For the ways of man are before the eyes of יהוה, and He pondereth all his goings.

22 His own iniquities shall take the wicked himself, and he shall be holden with the cords of his sins.

23 He shall die without instruction; and in the greatness of his folly he shall go astray.

6 My son, if you be surety for your friend, if you have stricken your hand with a stranger,

2 You are snared with the words of your mouth, you are taken with the words of your mouth.

3 Do this now, my son, and deliver yourself, when you are come into the hand of your friend; go, humble yourself, and make sure your friend.

4 Give not sleep to your eyes, nor slumber to your eyelids.

5 Deliver yourself as a roe from the hand of the hunter, and as a bird from the hand of the fowler.

6 Go to the ant, you sluggard; consider her ways, and be wise;

7 Which having no guide, overseer, or ruler,

8 Provideth her food in the summer, and gathereth her supplies in the harvest.

9 How long wilt you sleep, O sluggard? When wilt you arise out of your sleep?

10 Yet a little sleep, a little slumber, a little folding of the hands to sleep;

11 So shall your poverty come as one that travelleth, and your want as an armed man.

12 A naughty person, a wicked man, walketh with a perverse mouth.

13 He winketh with his eyes, he speaketh with his feet, he teacheth with his fingers;

14 Frowardness is in his heart, he deviseth mischief continually; he soweth discord.

15 Therefore shall his disaster come suddenly; suddenly shall he be broken without remedy.

16 These six things doth יהוה hate; yea, seven are an abomination unto him;

17 A proud look, a lying tongue, and hands that shed innocent blood,

18 A heart that deviseth wicked imaginations, feet that be swift in running to mischief,

19 A false witness who speaketh lies, and he who soweth discord among brethren.

20 My son, keep your father's command, and forsake not the teaching of your mother;

21 Bind them continually upon your heart, and tie them about your neck.

22 When you goest, it shall lead you; when you sleepest, it shall keep you; and when you awakest, it shall talk with you.

23 For the commandment is a lamp; and the Torah is light; and reproofs of instruction are the way of life;

24 To keep you from the evil woman, from the flattery of the tongue of a strange woman.

25 Lust not after her beauty in your heart; neither let her take you with her eyelids.

26 For by means of a whorish woman a man is brought to a piece of bread; and the adulteress will hunt for the precious life.

27 Can a man take fire in his bosom, and his clothes not be burned?

28 Can one go upon hot coals, and his feet not be burned?

29 So he that goeth in to his neighbour's wife; whosoever toucheth her shall not be innocent.

30 Men do not despise a thief, if he steals to satisfy his soul when he is hungry;

31 But if he be found, he shall restore sevenfold; he shall give all the substance of his house.

32 But whoso committeth adultery with a woman lacketh understanding; he who doeth it destroyeth his own soul.

33 A wound and dishonor shall he get; and his reproach shall not be wiped away.

34 For jealousy is the rage of a man; therefore he will not spare in the day of vengeance.

35 He will not regard any ransom; neither will he rest content, though you givest many gifts.

7 My son, keep my words, and lay up my commands with you.

2 Keep my commands, and live; and my teaching as the apple of your eye.

3 Bind them upon your fingers, write them upon the table of your heart.

4 Say unto wisdom, "You are my sister"; and call understanding your kinswoman,

5 That they may keep you from the strange woman, from the stranger which flattereth with her words.

6 For at the window of my house I looked through my casement,

7 And beheld among the simple ones, I discerned among the youths, a young man voids of understanding,

8 Passing through the street near her corner; and he went the way to her house,

9 In the twilight, in the evening, in the black and dark night;

10 And, behold, there met him a woman with

the attire of a harlot, and subtil of heart.

11 (She is loud and stubborn; her feet abide not in her house;

12 Now is she outside, now in the streets, and lieth in wait at every corner.)

13 So she caught him, and kissed him, and with an impudent face said unto him,

14 I have peace offerings with me; this day have I payed my vows.

15 Therefore came I forth to meet you, diligently to seek your face, and I have found you.

16 I have decked my bed with coverings of tapestry, with carved works, with fine linen of Egypt (Mitsrayim).

17 I have perfumed my bed with myrrh, aloes, and cinnamon.

18 Come, let us take our fill of love until the morning; let us solace ourselves with loves.

19 For the goodman is not at home, he is gone a long journey;

20 He hath taken a bag of money with him, and will come home at the day appointed.

21 With her much fair speech she caused him to yield, with the flattering of her lips she forced him.

22 He goeth after her straightway, as an ox goeth to the slaughter, or as a fool to the correction of the stocks;

23 Till a dart strike through his liver; as a bird hasteth to the snare, and knoweth not that it is for his life.

24 Hearken unto me now therefore, O you children, and attend to the words of my mouth.

25 Let not your heart decline to her ways, go not astray in her paths.

26 For she hath cast down many wounded; yea, many strong men have been slain by her.

27 Her house is the way to sheol, going down to the chambers of death.

8 Doth not wisdom cry? And understanding put forth her voice?

2 She standeth in the top of high places, by the way in the places of the paths.

3 She crieth at the gates, at the entry of the city, at the coming in at the doors.

4 Unto you, O men, I call; and my voice is to the sons of man.

5 O you simple, understand wisdom; and, you fools, be you of an understanding heart.

6 Hear, for I will speak of excellent things; and the opening of my lips shall be right things.

7 For my mouth shall speak truth; and wickedness is an abomination to my lips.

8 All the words of my mouth are in righteousness; there is nothing perverse or perverse in them.

9 They are all plain to him that understandeth, and right to them that find knowledge.

10 Receive my instruction, and not silver; and knowledge rather than choice gold.

11 For wisdom is better than rubies; and all the things that may be desired are not to be compared to it.

12 I, wisdom dwell with prudence, and find out knowledge of witty inventions.

13 The fear of יהוה is to hate evil; pride, and arrogancy, and the evil way, and the perverse mouth, do I hate.

14 Counsel is mine, and sound wisdom; I am understanding; I have strength.

15 By me reign, and princes decree justice.

16 By me princes rule, and nobles, even all the judges of the earth.

17 I love them that love me; and those that seek me early shall find me.

18 Riches and honor are with me; yea, durable riches and righteousness.

19 My fruit is better than gold, yea, than fine gold; and my revenue than choice silver.

20 I lead in the way of righteousness, in the midst of the paths of judgment;

21 That I may cause those that love me to inherit substance; and I will fill their treasures.

22 יהוה possessed me in the beginning of His way, before His works of old.

23 I was set up from everlasting, from the beginning, or ever the earth was.

24 When there were no depths, I was brought forth; when there were no fountains abounding with water.

25 Before the mountains were settled, before the hills was I brought forth;

26 While as yet He had not made the earth, nor the fields, nor the highest part of the dust of the world.

27 When He prepared the heavens, I was there; when He set a compass upon the face of the depth;

28 When He established the clouds above; when He strengthened the fountains of the deep;

29 When He gave to the sea His decree, that the waters should not pass His commandment; when He appointed the foundations of the earth;

30 Then I was by him, as one brought up with Him; and I was daily His delight, rejoicing always before Him;

31 Rejoicing in the habitable part of His earth; and my delights were with the sons of men.

32 Now therefore hearken unto me, O you children, for blessed are they that keep my ways.

33 Hear instruction, and be wise, and refuse it not.

34 Blessed is the man that heareth Me, watching daily at my gates, waiting at the posts of my doors.

35 For whoso findeth Me findeth life, and shall obtain favor of יהוה.

36 But he that sinneth against me wrongeth his own soul; all they that hate me love death.

9 Wisdom hath built her house, she hath hewn out her seven pillars;

2 She hath killed her beasts; she hath mingled her wine; she hath also furnished her table.

3 She hath sent forth her maidens; she crieth upon the highest places of the city,

4 Whoso is simple, let him turn in hither; as for him that wanteth understanding, she saith to him,

5 "Come, eat of my bread, and drink of the wine which I have mingled.

6 Forsake the foolish, and live; and go in the way of understanding.

7 He who reproveth a scorner getteth to himself shame; and he who rebuketh a wicked man getteth himself a blot.

8 Reprove not a scorner, lest he hate you; rebuke a wise man, and he will love you.

9 Give instruction to a wise man, and he will be yet wiser; teach a just man, and he will increase in learning.

10 The fear of יהוה is the beginning of wisdom; and the knowledge of the holy is understanding.

11 For by me your days shall be multiplied, and the years of your life shall be increased.

12 If you be wise, you shalt be wise for yourself; but if you scornest, you alone shalt bear it."

13 A foolish woman is clamorous; she is simple, and knoweth nothing.

14 For she sitteth at the door of her house, on a seat in the high places of the city,

15 To call passengers who go right on their ways;

16 Whoso is simple, let him turn in hither; and as for him who wanteth understanding, she saith

to him,

17 Stolen waters are sweet, and bread eaten in secret is pleasant.

18 But he knoweth not that the dead are there; and that her guests are in the depths of hell (sheol).

10 The proverbs of Solomon (Shelomoh). A wise son maketh a glad father; but a foolish son is the heaviness of his mother.

2 Treasures of wickedness profit nothing; but righteousness delivereth from death.

3 יהוה will not allow the soul of the righteous to famish; but he casteth away the substance of the wicked.

4 He becometh poor that dealeth with a slack hand; but the hand of the diligent maketh rich.

5 He that gathereth in summer is a wise son, but he that sleepeth in harvest is a son that causeth shame.

6 Blessings are upon the head of the just, but violence covereth the mouth of the wicked.

7 The memory of the just is blessed, but the name of the wicked shall rot.

8 The wise in heart will receive commandments, but a prating fool shall fall.

9 He that walketh uprightly walketh surely, but he that perverteth his ways shall be known.

10 He that winketh with the eye causeth sorrow, but a prating fool shall fall.

11 The mouth of a righteous man is a well of life, but violence covereth the mouth of the wicked.

12 Hatred stirreth up strifes, but love covereth all sins.

13 In the lips of him that hath understanding wisdom is found, but a rod is for the back of him that is void of understanding.

14 Wise men lay up knowledge, but the mouth of the foolish is near destruction.

15 The rich man's wealth is his strong city; the destruction of the poor is their poverty.

16 The labour of the righteous tendeth to life; the fruit of the wicked to sin.

17 He is in the way of life that keepeth instruction, but he that refuseth reproof erreth.

18 He that hideth hatred with lying lips, and he that uttereth a slander, is a fool.

19 In the multitude of words there wanteth not sin, but he that refraineth his lips is wise.

20 The tongue of the just is as choice silver, the heart of the wicked is little worth.

21 The lips of the righteous feed many, but fools

die for want of wisdom.

22 The blessing of יהוה, it maketh rich, and he addeth no sorrow with it.

23 It is as sport to a fool to do mischief, but a man of understanding hath wisdom.

24 The fear of the wicked, it shall come upon him, but the desire of the righteous shall be granted.

25 As the whirlwind passeth, so is the wicked no more, but the righteous is an everlasting foundation.

26 As vinegar to the teeth, and as smoke to the eyes, so is the sluggard to them that send him.

27 The fear of יהוה prolongeth days, but the years of the wicked shall be shortened.

28 The hope of the righteous shall be gladness, but the expectation of the wicked shall perish.

29 The way of יהוה is strength to the upright, but destruction shall be to the workers of iniquity.

30 The righteous shall never be removed, but the wicked shall not inhabit the earth.

31 The mouth of the just bringeth forth wisdom, but the perverse tongue shall be cut out.

32 The lips of the righteous know what is acceptable, but the mouth of the wicked speaketh frowardness.

11 A false balance is abomination to יהוה, but a just weight is His delight.

2 When pride cometh, then cometh shame, but with the humble is wisdom.

3 The integrity of the upright shall guide them, but the perverseness of transgressors shall destroy them.

4 Riches profit not in the day of wrath, but righteousness delivereth from death.

5 The righteousness of the perfect shall direct his way, but the wicked shall fall by his own wickedness.

6 The righteousness of the upright shall deliver them, but transgressors shall be taken in their own naughtiness.

7 When a wicked man dieth, his expectation shall perish, and the hope of unjust men perisheth.

8 The righteous is delivered out of trouble, and the wicked cometh in his stead.

9 A hypocrite with his mouth destroyeth his neighbor, but through knowledge shall the just be delivered.

10 When it goeth well with the righteous, the city rejoiceth; and when the wicked perish, there is shouting.

11 By the blessing of the upright the city is exalted, but it is overthrown by the mouth of the wicked.

12 He that is void of wisdom despiseth his neighbor, but a man of understanding holdeth his peace.

13 A talebearer revealeth secrets, but he that is of a faithful spirit concealeth the matter.

14 Where no counsel is, the people fall; but in the multitude of counsellors there is safety.

15 He that is surety for a stranger shall smart for it; and he that hateth suretiship is sure.

16 A gracious woman retaineth honor; and strong men retain riches.

17 The merciful man doeth good to his own soul, but he that is cruel troubleth his own flesh.

18 The wicked worketh a deceitful work, but to him that soweth righteousness shall be a sure reward.

19 As righteousness tendeth to life; so he that pursueth evil pursueth it to his own death.

20 They that are of a perverse heart are abomination to יהוה, but such as are upright in their way are His delight.

21 Though hand join in hand, the wicked shall not be unpunished; but the seed of the righteous shall be delivered.

22 As a jewel of gold in a swine's snout, so is a fair woman which is without discretion.

23 The desire of the righteous is only good, but the expectation of the wicked is wrath.

24 There is that scattereth, and yet increaseth; and there is that withholdeth more than is meet, but it tendeth to poverty.

25 The liberal soul shall be made fat, and he that watereth shall be watered also himself.

26 He that withholdeth corn, the people shall curse him, but blessing shall be upon the head of him that selleth it.

27 He that diligently seeketh good procureth favor, but he that seeketh mischief, it shall come unto him.

28 He that trusteth in his riches shall fall, but the righteous shall flourish as a branch.

29 He that troubleth his own house shall inherit the wind; and the fool shall be servant to the wise of heart.

30 The fruit of the righteous is a tree of life; and he that winneth souls is wise.

31 Behold, the righteous shall be recompensed

in the earth; how much more the wicked and the sinner.

12 Whoso loveth instruction loveth knowledge, but he that hateth reproof is brutish.

2 A good man obtaineth favor of יהוה, but a man of wicked devices will He condemn.

3 A man shall not be established by wickedness, but the root of the righteous shall not be moved.

4 A virtuous woman is a crown to her husband, but she that maketh ashamed is as rottenness in his bones.

5 The thoughts of the righteous are right, but the counsels of the wicked are deceit.

6 The words of the wicked are to lie in wait for blood, but the mouth of the upright shall deliver them.

7 The wicked are overthrown, and are not, but the house of the righteous shall stand.

8 A man shall be commended according to his wisdom, but he that is of a perverse heart shall be despised.

9 He that is despised, and hath a servant, is better than he that honoreth himself, and lacketh bread.

10 A righteous man regardeth the life of his beast, but the tender mercies of the wicked are cruel.

11 He that tilleth his land shall be satisfied with bread, but he that followeth vain persons is void of understanding.

12 The wicked desireth the net of evil men, but the root of the righteous yieldeth fruit.

13 The wicked is snared by the transgression of his lips, but the just shall come out of trouble.

14 A man shall be satisfied with good by the fruit of his mouth, and the recompence of a man's hands shall be rendered unto him.

15 The way of a fool is right in his own eyes, but he that hearkeneth unto counsel is wise.

16 A fool's wrath is presently known: but a prudent man covereth shame.

17 He that speaketh truth sheweth forth righteousness, but a false witness deceit.

18 There is that speaketh like the piercings of a sword, but the tongue of the wise is health.

19 The lip of truth shall be established forever, but a lying tongue is but for a moment.

20 Deceit is in the heart of them that imagine evil, but to the counsellors of peace is joy.

21 There shall no evil happen to the just, but the wicked shall be filled with mischief.

22 Lying lips are abomination to יהוה: but they that deal truly are his delight.

23 A prudent man concealeth knowledge, but the heart of fools proclaimeth foolishness.

24 The hand of the diligent shall bear rule, but the slothful shall be under tribute.

25 Heaviness in the heart of man maketh it stoop, but a good word maketh it glad.

26 The righteous is more excellent than his neighbor, but the way of the wicked seduceth them.

27 The slothful man roasteth not that which he took in hunting, but the substance of a diligent man is precious.

28 In the way of righteousness is life; and in the pathway thereof there is no death.

13 A wise son heareth his father's instruction, but a scorner heareth not rebuke.

2 A man shall eat good by the fruit of his mouth, but the soul of the transgressors shall eat violence.

3 He that keepeth his mouth keepeth his life, but he that openeth wide his lips shall have destruction.

4 The soul of the sluggard desireth, and hath nothing, but the soul of the diligent shall be made fat.

5 A righteous man hateth lying: but a wicked man is loathsome, and cometh to shame.

6 Righteousness keepeth him that is upright in the way, but wickedness overthroweth the sinner.

7 There is that maketh himself rich, yet hath nothing; there is that maketh himself poor, yet hath great riches.

8 The ransom of a man's life are his riches, but the poor heareth not rebuke.

9 The light of the righteous rejoiceth: but the lamp of the wicked shall be put out.

10 Only by pride cometh contention, but with the well advised is wisdom.

11 Wealth gotten by vanity shall be diminished, but he that gathereth by labour shall increase.

12 Hope deferred maketh the heart sick, but when the desire cometh, it is a tree of life.

13 Whoso despiseth the word shall be destroyed, but he that feareth the commandment shall be rewarded.

14 The teaching of the wise is a fountain of life, to depart from the snares of death.

15 Good understanding giveth favor, but the way of transgressors is hard.

16 Every prudent man dealeth with knowledge, but a fool layeth open his folly.

17 A wicked messenger falleth into mischief, but a faithful ambassador is health.

18 Poverty and shame shall be to him that refuseth instruction, but he that regardeth reproof shall be honoured.

19 The desire accomplished is sweet to the soul, but it is abomination to fools to depart from evil.

20 He that walketh with wise men shall be wise, but a companion of fools shall be destroyed.

21 Evil pursueth sinners, but to the righteous good shall be repayed.

22 A good man leaveth an inheritance to his children's children; and the wealth of the sinner is laid up for the just.

23 Much food is in the tillage of the poor, but there is that is destroyed for want of judgment.

24 He that spareth his rod hateth his son, but he that loveth him chasteneth him betimes.

25 The righteous eateth to the satisfying of his soul, but the belly of the wicked shall want.

14 Every wise woman buildeth her house; but the foolish plucketh it down with her hands.

2 He who walketh in his uprightness feareth יהוה; but he who is perverse in his ways despiseth Him.

3 In the mouth of the foolish is a rod of pride, but the lips of the wise shall preserve them.

4 Where no oxen are, the crib is clean; but much increase is by the strength of the ox.

5 A faithful witness will not lie, but a false witness will utter lies.

6 A scorner seeketh wisdom, and findeth it not, but knowledge is easy unto him that understandeth.

7 Go from the presence of a foolish man, when you perceivest not in him the lips of knowledge.

8 The wisdom of the prudent is to understand his way, but the folly of fools is deceit.

9 Fools make a mock at sin, but among the righteous there is favor.

10 The heart knoweth his own bitterness; and a stranger doth not intermeddle with his joy.

11 The house of the wicked shall be overthrown, but the tabernacle of the upright shall flourish.

12 There is a way which seemeth right unto a man, but the end thereof are the ways of death.

13 Even in laughter the heart is sorrowful; and the end of that mirth is heaviness.

14 The backslider in heart shall be filled with his own ways; and a good man shall be satisfied from himself.

15 The simple believeth every word, but the prudent man looketh well to his going.

16 A wise man feareth, and departeth from evil, but the fool rageth, and is confident.

17 He that is soon angry dealeth foolishly; and a man of wicked devices is hated.

18 The simple inherit folly, but the prudent are crowned with knowledge.

19 The evil bow before the good; and the wicked at the gates of the righteous.

20 The poor is hated even of his own neighbor, but the rich hath many friends.

21 He that despiseth his neighbour sinneth, but he that hath mercy on the poor, happy is he.

22 Do they not err that devise evil? But mercy and truth shall be to them that devise good.

23 In all labour there is profit, but the talk of the lips tendeth only to penury.

24 The crown of the wise is their riches, but the foolishness of fools is folly.

25 A true witness delivereth souls, but a deceitful witness speaketh lies.

26 In the fear of יהוה is strong confidence; and his children shall have a place of refuge.

27 The fear of יהוה is a fountain of life, to depart from the snares of death.

28 In the multitude of people is the king's honor, but in the want of people is the destruction of the prince.

29 He that is slow to wrath is of great understanding, but he that is hasty of spirit exalteth folly.

30 A sound heart is the life of the flesh, but envy the rottenness of the bones.

31 He that oppresseth the poor reproacheth his Maker, but he that honoreth him hath mercy on the poor.

32 The wicked is driven away in his wickedness, but the righteous hath hope in his death.

33 Wisdom resteth in the heart of him that hath understanding, but that which is in the midst of fools is made known.

34 Righteousness exalteth a nation, but sin is a reproach to any people.

35 The king's favor is toward a wise servant,

but his wrath is against him that causeth shame.

15 A soft answer turneth away wrath, but grievous words stir up anger.

2 The tongue of the wise useth knowledge aright, but the mouth of fools poureth out foolishness.

3 The eyes of יהוה are in every place, beholding the evil and the good.

4 A wholesome tongue is a tree of life, but perverseness therein is a breach in the spirit.

5 A fool despiseth his father's instruction, but he that regardeth reproof is prudent.

6 In the house of the righteous is much treasure, but in the revenues of the wicked is trouble.

7 The lips of the wise disperse knowledge, but the heart of the foolish doeth not so.

8 The sacrifice of the wicked is an abomination to יהוה, but the prayer of the upright is His delight.

9 The way of the wicked is an abomination unto יהוה, but He loveth him that followeth after righteousness.

10 Correction is grievous unto him that forsaketh the way, and he that hateth reproof shall die.

11 Hell (Sheol) and destruction (Avaddon) are before יהוה; how much more then the hearts of the children of men?

12 A scorner loveth not one that reproveth him, nor will he go unto the wise.

13 A merry heart maketh a cheerful countenance, but by sorrow of the heart the spirit is broken.

14 The heart of him that hath understanding seeketh knowledge, but the mouth of fools feedeth on foolishness.

15 All the days of the afflicted are evil, but he that is of a merry heart hath a continual feast.

16 Better is little with the fear of יהוה than great treasure and trouble therewith.

17 Better is a dinner of herbs where love is, than a stalled ox and hatred therewith.

18 A wrathful man stirreth up strife, but he that is slow to anger appeaseth strife.

19 The way of the slothful man is as a hedge of thorns, but the way of the righteous is made plain.

20 A wise son maketh a glad father, but a foolish man despiseth his mother.

21 Folly is joy to him that is destitute of wisdom, but a man of understanding walketh uprightly.

22 Without counsel purposes are disappointed,

but in the multitude of counsellors they are established.

23 A man hath joy by the answer of his mouth, and a word spoken in due season, how good is it!

24 The way of life is above to the wise, that he may depart from sheol beneath.

25 יהוה will destroy the house of the proud, but he will establish the border of the widow.

26 The thoughts of the wicked are an abomination to יהוה, but the words of the pure are pleasant words.

27 He that is greedy of gain troubleth his own house, but he that hateth gifts shall live.

28 The heart of the righteous studieth to answer, but the mouth of the wicked poureth out evil things.

29 יהוה is far from the wicked, but He heareth the prayer of the righteous.

30 The light of the eyes rejoiceth the heart, and a good report maketh the bones fat.

31 The ear that heareth the reproof of life abideth among the wise.

32 He that refuseth instruction despiseth his own soul, but He that heareth reproof getteth understanding.

33 The fear of יהוה is the instruction of wisdom, and before honor is humility.

16 The preparations of the heart in man, and the answer of the tongue, is from יהוה.

2 All the ways of a man are clean in his own eyes; but יהוה weigheth the spirits.

3 Commit your works unto יהוה, and your thoughts shall be established.

4 יהוה hath made all things for Himself; yea, even the wicked for the day of evil.

5 Everyone who is proud in heart is an abomination to יהוה; though hand join in hand, he shall not be unpunished.

6 By mercy and truth iniquity is purged; and by the fear of יהוה men depart from evil.

7 When a man's ways please יהוה, He maketh even His enemies to be at peace with him.

8 Better is a little with righteousness than great revenues without right.

9 A man's heart deviseth his way, but יהוה directeth his steps.

10 A divine sentence is in the lips of the king; his mouth transgresseth not in judgment.

11 A just weight and balance are יהוה's; all the weights of the bag are his work.

12 It is an abomination to kings to commit

wickedness, for the throne is established by righteousness.

13 Righteous lips are the delight of kings; and they love him that speaketh right.

14 The wrath of a king is as messengers of death, but a wise man will pacify it.

15 In the light of the king's countenance is life; and his favor is as a cloud of the latter rain.

16 How much better is it to get wisdom than gold! And to get understanding rather to be chosen than silver!

17 The highway of the upright is to depart from evil; he that keepeth His way preserveth his soul.

18 Pride goeth before destruction, and a haughty spirit before a fall.

19 Better it is to be of a humble spirit with the lowly, than to divide the spoil with the proud.

20 He that handleth a matter wisely shall find good; and whoso trusteth in יהוה, happy is he.

21 The wise in heart shall be called prudent; and the sweetness of the lips increaseth learning.

22 Understanding is a wellspring of life unto him that hath it; but the instruction of fools is folly.

23 The heart of the wise teacheth his mouth, and addeth learning to his lips.

24 Pleasant words are as a honeycomb, sweet to the soul, and health to the bones.

25 There is a way that seemeth right unto a man, but the end thereof are the ways of death.

26 He that laboureth laboureth for himself, for his mouth craveth it of him.

27 A wicked man diggeth up evil, and in his lips there is as a burning fire.

28 A perverse man soweth strife: and a whisperer separateth chief friends.

29 A violent man enticeth his neighbour, and leadeth him into the way that is not good.

30 He shutteth his eyes to devise perverse things; moving his lips he bringeth evil to pass.

31 The hoary head is a crown of glory, if it be found in the way of righteousness.

32 He that is slow to anger is better than the mighty; and he that ruleth his spirit than he that taketh a city.

33 The lot is cast into the lap, but the whole disposing thereof is of יהוה.

17 Better is a dry morsel, and quietness therewith, than a house full of sacrifices with strife.

2 A wise servant shall have rule over a son that causeth shame, and shall have part of the inheritance among the brethren.

3 The fining pot is for silver, and the furnace for gold, but יהוה trieth the hearts.

4 A wicked doer giveth heed to false lips; and a liar giveth ear to a naughty tongue.

5 Whoso mocketh the poor reproacheth his Maker; and he that is glad at calamities shall not be unpunished.

6 Children's children are the crown of old men; and the glory of children are their fathers.

7 Excellent speech becometh not a fool; much less do lying lips a prince.

8 A gift is as a precious stone in the eyes of him that hath it; whithersoever it turneth, it prospereth.

9 He that covereth a transgression seeketh love, but he that repeateth a matter separateth very friends.

10 A reproof entereth more into a wise man than a hundred stripes into a fool.

11 An evil man seeketh only rebellion; therefore a cruel messenger shall be sent against him.

12 Let a bear robbed of her whelps meet a man, rather than a fool in his folly.

13 Whoso rewardeth evil for good, evil shall not depart from his house.

14 The beginning of strife is as when one letteth out water; therefore leave off contention, before it be meddled with.

15 He that justifieth the wicked, and he that condemneth the just, even they both are abomination to יהוה.

16 Wherefore is there a price in the hand of a fool to get wisdom, seeing he hath no heart to it?

17 A friend loveth at all times, and a brother is born for adversity.

18 A man void of understanding striketh hands, and becometh surety in the presence of his friend.

19 He loveth transgression that loveth strife; and he that exalteth his gate seeketh destruction.

20 He that hath a perverse heart findeth no good; and he that hath a perverse tongue falleth into mischief.

21 He that begetteth a fool doeth it to his sorrow; and the father of a fool hath no joy.

22 A merry heart doeth good like a medicine, but a broken spirit drieth the bones.

23 A wicked man taketh a gift out of the bosom

to pervert the ways of judgment.

24 Wisdom is before him that hath understanding, but the eyes of a fool are in the ends of the earth.

25 A foolish son is a grief to his father, and bitterness to her that bare him.

26 Also to punish the just is not good, nor to strike princes for equity.

27 He that hath knowledge spareth his words, and a man of understanding is of an excellent spirit.

28 Even a fool, when he holdeth his peace, is counted wise; and he that shutteth his lips is esteemed a man of understanding.

18 Through desire a man, having separated himself, seeketh and intermeddleth with all wisdom.

2 A fool hath no delight in understanding, but that his heart may discover itself.

3 When the wicked cometh, then cometh also contempt, and with ignominy reproach.

4 The words of a man's mouth are as deep waters, and the wellspring of wisdom as a flowing brook.

5 It is not good to accept the person of the wicked, to overthrow the righteous in judgment.

6 A fool's lips enter into contention, and his mouth calleth for strokes.

7 A fool's mouth is his destruction, and his lips are the snare of his soul.

8 The words of a talebearer are as wounds, and they go down into the innermost parts of the belly.

9 He also that is slothful in his work is brother to him that is a great waster.

10 The name of יהוה is a strong tower; the righteous runneth into it, and is safe.

11 The rich man's wealth is his strong city, and as a high wall in his own conceit.

12 Before destruction the heart of man is haughty, and before honor is humility.

13 He that answereth a matter before he heareth it, it is folly and shame unto him.

14 The spirit of a man will sustain his infirmity; but a wounded spirit who can bear?

15 The heart of the prudent getteth knowledge; and the ear of the wise seeketh knowledge.

16 A man's gift maketh room for him, and bringeth him before great men.

17 He that is first in his own cause seemeth just; but his neighbour cometh and searcheth him.

18 The lot causeth contentions to cease, and parteth between the mighty.

19 A brother offended is harder to be won than a strong city, and their contentions are like the bars of a castle.

20 A man's belly shall be satisfied with the fruit of his mouth; and with the increase of his lips shall he be filled.

21 Death and life are in the power of the tongue: and they that love it shall eat the fruit thereof.

22 Whoso findeth a wife findeth a good thing, and obtaineth favor of יהוה.

23 The poor useth intreaties, but the rich answereth roughly.

24 A man that hath friends must shew himself friendly; and there is a friend that sticketh closer than a brother.

19 Better is the poor that walketh in his integrity, than he that is perverse in his lips, and is a fool.

2 Also, that the soul to be without knowledge, it is not good; and he that hasteth with his feet sinneth.

3 The foolishness of man perverteth his way, and his heart fretteth against יהוה.

4 Wealth maketh many friends, but the poor is separated from his neighbour.

5 A false witness shall not be unpunished, and he that speaketh lies shall not escape.

6 Many will intreat the favor of the prince, and every man is a friend to him that giveth gifts.

7 All the brethren of the poor do hate him: how much more do his friends go far from him? He pursueth them with words, yet they are wanting to him.

8 He that getteth wisdom loveth his own soul; he that keepeth understanding shall find good.

9 A false witness shall not be unpunished, and he that speaketh lies shall perish.

10 Delight is not seemly for a fool, much less for a servant to have rule over princes.

11 The discretion of a man deferreth his anger, and it is his glory to pass over a transgression.

12 The king's wrath is as the roaring of a lion, but his favor is as dew upon the grass.

13 A foolish son is the disaster of his father; and the contentions of a wife are a continual dropping.

14 House and riches are the inheritance of fathers; and a prudent wife is from יהוה.

15 Slothfulness casteth into a deep sleep, and an

idle soul shall suffer hunger.

16 He that keepeth the commandment keepeth his own soul, but he that despiseth his ways shall die.

17 He that hath pity upon the poor lendeth unto יהוה, and that which he hath given will he pay him again.

18 Chasten your son while there is hope, and let not your soul spare for his crying.

19 A man of great wrath shall suffer punishment, for if you deliver him, yet you must do it again.

20 Hear counsel, and receive instruction, that you mayest be wise in your latter end.

21 There are many devices in a man's heart; nevertheless the counsel of יהוה, that shall stand.

22 The desire of a man is his kindness, and a poor man is better than a liar.

23 The fear of יהוה tendeth to life; and he that hath it shall abide satisfied; he shall not be visited with evil.

24 A slothful man hideth his hand in his bosom, and will not so much as bring it to his mouth again.

25 Smite a scorner, and the simple will beware, and reprove one that hath understanding, and he will understand knowledge.

26 He that wasteth his father, and chaseth away his mother, is a son that causeth shame, and bringeth reproach.

27 Cease, my son, to hear the instruction that causeth to err from the words of knowledge.

28 A scoundrel (beliyaal) witness scorneth judgment, and the mouth of the wicked devoureth iniquity.

29 Judgments are prepared for scorners, and stripes for the back of fools.

20 Wine is a mocker, strong drink is raging; and whosoever is deceived thereby is not wise.

2 The fear of a king is as the roaring of a lion; whoso provoketh him to anger sinneth against his own soul.

3 It is an honor for a man to cease from strife, but every fool will be meddling.

4 The sluggard will not plow by reason of the cold; therefore shall he beg in harvest, and have nothing.

5 Counsel in the heart of man is like deep water; but a man of understanding will draw it out.

6 Most men will proclaim every one his own

goodness, but a faithful man who can find?

7 The just man walketh in his integrity; his children are blessed after him.

8 A king that sitteth in the throne of judgment scattereth away all evil with his eyes.

9 Who can say, I have made my heart clean, I am pure from my sin?

10 Divers weights, and divers measures, both of them are alike abomination to יהוה.

11 Even a child is known by his doings, whether his work be pure, and whether it be right.

12 The hearing ear, and the seeing eye, יהוה hath made even both of them.

13 Do not love sleep, lest you come to poverty; open your eyes, and you shalt be satisfied with bread.

14 "Bad, bad!", saith the buyer; but when he has gone his way, then he boasteth.

15 There is gold, and a multitude of rubies, but the lips of knowledge are a precious jewel.

16 Take his garment that is surety for a stranger; and take a pledge of him for a strange woman.

17 Bread of deceit is sweet to a man, but afterwards his mouth shall be filled with gravel.

18 Every purpose is established by counsel; and with good advice make war.

19 He that goeth about as a talebearer revealeth secrets; therefore meddle not with him that flattereth with his lips.

20 Whoso curseth his father or his mother, his lamp shall be put out in obscure darkness.

21 An inheritance may be gotten hastily at the beginning, but the end thereof shall not be blessed.

22 Say not you, I will recompense evil, but wait on יהוה, and he shall save you.

23 Divers weights are an abomination unto יהוה; and a false balance is not good.

24 Man's goings are of יהוה; how can a man then understand his own way?

25 It is a snare to the man who devoureth that which is holy, and after vows to make enquiry.

26 A wise king scattereth the wicked, and bringeth the wheel over them.

27 The spirit of man is the candle of יהוה, searching all the inward parts of the belly.

28 Mercy and truth preserve the king; and his throne is upholden by mercy.

29 The glory of young men is their strength; and the beauty of old men is the gray head.

30 The blueness of a wound cleanseth away

evil; so do stripes the inward parts of the belly.

21 The king's heart is in the hand of יהוה, as the rivers of water; He turneth it whithersoever He will.

2 Every way of a man is right in his own eyes, but יהוה pondereth the hearts.

3 To do justice and judgment is more acceptable to יהוה than sacrifice.

4 A high look, and a proud heart, and the plowing of the wicked, is sin.

5 The thoughts of the diligent tend only to plenteousness, but of every one that is hasty only to want.

6 The getting of treasures by a lying tongue is a vanity tossed to and fro of them that seek death.

7 The robbery of the wicked shall destroy them, because they refuse to do judgment.

8 The way of man is perverse and strange, but as for the pure, his work is right.

9 It is better to dwell in a corner of the housetop, than with a brawling woman in a wide house.

10 The soul of the wicked desireth evil; his neighbour findeth no favor in his eyes.

11 When the scorner is punished, the simple is made wise; and when the wise is instructed, he receiveth knowledge.

12 The righteous one wisely considereth the house of the wicked; but overthroweth the wicked for their wickedness.

13 Whoso stoppeth his ears at the cry of the poor, he also shall cry himself, but shall not be heard.

14 A gift in secret pacifieth anger; and a reward in the bosom strong wrath.

15 It is joy to the just to do judgment, but destruction shall be to the workers of iniquity.

16 The man that wandereth out of the way of understanding shall remain in the congregation of the dead.

17 He that loveth pleasure shall be a poor man; he that loveth wine and oil shall not be rich.

18 The wicked shall be a ransom for the righteous, and the transgressor for the upright.

19 It is better to dwell in the wilderness, than with a contentious and an angry woman.

20 There is treasure to be desired and oil in the dwelling of the wise, but a foolish man spendeth it up.

21 He that followeth after righteousness and mercy findeth life, righteousness, and honor.

22 A wise man scaleth the city of the mighty, and casteth down the strength of the confidence thereof.

23 Whoso keepeth his mouth and his tongue keepeth his soul from troubles.

24 Proud and haughty scorner is his name, who dealeth in proud wrath.

25 The desire of the slothful killeth him, for his hands refuse to labour.

26 He coveteth greedily all the day long, but the righteous giveth and spareth not.

27 The sacrifice of the wicked is abomination; how much more, when he bringeth it with a wicked mind?

28 A false witness shall perish, but the man that heareth speaketh constantly.

29 A wicked man hardeneth his face, but as for the upright, he directeth his way.

30 There is no wisdom nor understanding nor counsel against יהוה.

31 The horse is prepared against the day of battle, but safety is of יהוה.

22 A good name is rather to be chosen than great riches, and loving favor rather than silver and gold.

2 The rich and poor meet together; יהוה is the Maker of them all.

3 A prudent man foreseeth the evil, and hideth himself, but the simple pass on, and are punished.

4 By humility and the fear of יהוה are riches, and honor, and life.

5 Thorns and snares are in the way of the perverse; he that doth keep his soul shall be far from them.

6 Train up a child in the way he should go; and when he is old, he will not depart from it.

7 The rich ruleth over the poor, and the borrower is servant to the lender.

8 He that soweth iniquity shall reap vanity; and the rod of his anger shall fail.

9 He that hath a bountiful eye shall be blessed, for he giveth of his bread to the poor.

10 Cast out the scorner, and contention shall go out; yea, strife and reproach shall cease.

11 He that loveth pureness of heart, for the grace of his lips the king shall be his friend.

12 The eyes of יהוה preserve knowledge, and He overthroweth the words of the transgressor.

13 The slothful man saith, "There is a lion outside, I shall be slain in the streets!"

14 The mouth of strange women is a deep pit;

he that is abhorred of יהוה shall fall therein.

15 Foolishness is bound in the heart of a child, but the rod of correction shall drive it far from him.

16 He that oppresseth the poor to increase his riches, and he that giveth to the rich, shall surely come to want.

17 Bow down your ear, and hear the words of the wise, and apply your heart unto my knowledge.

18 For it is a pleasant thing if you keep them within you; they shall withal be fitted in your lips,

19 That your trust may be in יהוה, I have made known to you this day, even to you.

20 Have not I written to you excellent things in counsels and knowledge,

21 That I might make you know the certainty of the words of truth, that you mightest answer the words of truth to them that send unto you?

22 Rob not the poor, because he is poor, nor oppress the afflicted in the gate;

23 For יהוה will plead their cause, and spoil the soul of those that spoiled them.

24 Make no friendship with an angry man; and with a furious man you shalt not go,

25 Lest you learn his ways, and get a snare to your soul.

26 Be not you one of them that strike hands, or of them that are sureties for debts.

27 If you have nothing to pay, why should he take away your bed from under you?

28 Remove not the ancient landmark, which your fathers have set.

29 Seest you a man diligent in his business? He shall stand before kings; he shall not stand before mean men.

23 When you sittest to eat with a ruler, consider diligently what is before you;

2 And put a knife to your throat, if you be a man given to appetite.

3 Be not desirous of his dainties, for they are deceitful meat.

4 Labour not to be rich; cease from your own wisdom.

5 Wilt you set your eyes upon that which is not? For riches certainly make themselves wings; they fly away as an eagle toward heaven.

6 Eat you not the bread of him that hath an evil eye, nor desire you his dainty meats;

7 For as he thinketh in his heart, so is he. "Eat and drink", saith he to you, but his heart is not

with you.

8 The morsel which you have eaten shalt you vomit up, and lose your sweet words.

9 Speak not in the ears of a fool, for he will despise the wisdom of your words.

10 Remove not the old landmark, and enter not into the fields of the fatherless;

11 For their Redeemer is mighty; He shall plead their cause with you.

12 Apply your heart unto instruction, and your ears to the words of knowledge.

13 Withhold not correction from the child, for if you beatest him with the rod, he shall not die.

14 You shalt beat him with the rod, and shalt deliver his soul from sheol.

15 My son, if your heart be wise, my heart shall rejoice, even mine.

16 Yea, my reins shall rejoice, when your lips speak right things.

17 Let not your heart envy sinners, but be you in the fear of יהוה all the day long.

18 For surely there is an end; and your expectation shall not be cut off.

19 Hear you, my son, and be wise, and guide your heart in the way.

20 Be not among winebibbers; among riotous eaters of flesh;

21 For the drunkard and the glutton shall come to poverty; and drowsiness shall clothe a man with rags.

22 Hearken unto your father that begat you, and despise not your mother when she is old.

23 Buy the truth, and sell it not; also wisdom, and instruction, and understanding.

24 The father of the righteous shall greatly rejoice; and he that begetteth a wise child shall have joy of him.

25 Your father and your mother shall be glad, and she that bare you shall rejoice.

26 My son, give me your heart, and let your eyes observe my ways.

27 For a whore is a deep ditch; and a strange woman is a narrow pit.

28 She also lieth in wait as for a prey, and increaseth the transgressors among men.

29 Who hath woe? Who hath sorrow? Who hath contentions? Who hath babbling? Who hath wounds without cause? Who hath redness of eyes?

30 They that tarry long at the wine; they that go to seek mixed wine.

31 Look not you upon the wine when it is red, when it giveth his colour in the cup, when it moveth itself aright.

32 At the last it biteth like a serpent, and stingeth like an adder.

33 Your eyes shall behold strange women, and your heart shall utter perverse things.

34 Yea, you shalt be as he that lieth down in the midst of the sea, or as he that lieth upon the top of a mast.

35 They have stricken me, shalt you say, and I was not sick; they have beaten me, and I felt it not; when shall I awake? I will seek it yet again.

24 Be not you envious against evil men, neither desire to be with them.

2 For their heart studieth destruction, and their lips talk of mischief.

3 Through wisdom is a house built; and by understanding it is established:

4 And by knowledge shall the chambers be filled with all precious and pleasant riches.

5 A wise man is strong; yea, a man of knowledge increaseth strength.

6 For by wise counsel you shalt make your war, and in multitude of counsellors there is safety.

7 Wisdom is too high for a fool; he openeth not his mouth in the gate.

8 He that deviseth to do evil shall be called a mischievous person.

9 The thought of foolishness is sin, and the scorner is an abomination to men.

10 If you faint in the day of adversity, your strength is small.

11 If you forbear to deliver them that are drawn unto death, and those that are ready to be slain;

12 If you sayest, "Behold, we knew it not"; doth not he that pondereth the heart considers it? And he that keepeth your soul, doth not he knows it? And shall not he render to every man according to his works?

13 My son, eat you honey, because it is good; and the honeycomb, which is sweet to your taste;

14 So shall the knowledge of wisdom be unto your soul; when you have found it, then there shall be a reward, and your expectation shall not be cut off.

15 Lay not wait, O wicked man, against the dwelling of the righteous; spoil not his resting place;

16 For a just man falleth seven times, and riseth up again, but the wicked shall fall into mischief.

17 Rejoice not when your enemy falleth, and let not your heart be glad when he stumbleth;

18 Lest יהוה see it, and it displease him, and he turn away his wrath from him.

19 Fret not yourself because of evil men, neither be you envious at the wicked;

20 For there shall be no reward to the evil man; the candle of the wicked shall be put out.

21 My son, fear you יהוה and the king; and meddle not with them that are given to change;

22 For their disaster shall rise suddenly; and who knoweth the ruin of them both?

23 These things also belong to the wise. It is not good to have respect of persons in judgment.

24 He that saith unto the wicked, "You are righteous"; him shall the people curse, nations shall abhor him:

25 But to them that rebuke him shall be delight, and a good blessing shall come upon them.

26 Every man shall kiss his lips that giveth a right answer.

27 Prepare your work outside, and make it fit for yourself in the field; and afterwards build your house.

28 Be not a witness against your neighbour without cause; and deceive not with your lips.

29 Say not, "I will do so to him as he hath done to me; I will render to the man according to his work."

30 I went by the field of the slothful, and by the vineyard of the man void of understanding;

31 And, behold, it was all grown over with thorns, and nettles had covered the face thereof, and the stone wall thereof was broken down.

32 Then I saw, and considered it well; I looked upon it, and received instruction.

33 Yet a little sleep, a little slumber, a little folding of the hands to sleep;

34 So shall your poverty come as one that travelleth, and your want as an armed man.

25 These are also proverbs of Solomon (Shelomoh), which the men of Hezekiah (Chizkiyah) king of Judah (Yehudah) copied out.

2 It is the glory of God (Elohim) to conceal a thing, but the honor of kings is to search out a matter.

3 The heaven for height, and the earth for depth, and the heart of kings is unsearchable.

4 Take away the dross from the silver, and there shall come forth a vessel for the finer.

5 Take away the wicked from before the king, and his throne shall be established in righteousness.

6 Put not forth yourself in the presence of the king, and stand not in the place of great men;

7 For better it is that it be said unto you, "Come up hither"; than that you shouldest be put lower in the presence of the prince whom your eyes have seen.

8 Go not forth hastily to strive, lest you know not what to do in the end thereof, when your neighbour hath put you to shame.

9 Debate your cause with your neighbour himself; and discover not a secret to another:

10 Lest he that heareth it put you to shame, and your infamy turn not away.

11 A word fitly spoken is like apples of gold in pictures of silver.

12 As an earring of gold, and an ornament of fine gold, so is a wise reprover upon an obedient ear.

13 As the cold of snow in the time of harvest, so is a faithful messenger to them that send him, for he refresheth the soul of his masters.

14 Whoso boasteth himself of a false gift is like clouds and wind without rain.

15 By long forbearing is a prince persuaded, and a soft tongue breaketh the bone.

16 Have you found honey? Eat so much as is sufficient for you, lest you be filled therewith, and vomit it.

17 Withdraw your foot from your neighbour's house; lest he be weary of you, and so hate you.

18 A man that beareth false witness against his neighbour is a maul, and a sword, and a sharp arrow.

19 Confidence in an unfaithful man in time of trouble is like a broken tooth, and a foot out of joint.

20 As he that taketh away a garment in cold weather, and as vinegar upon nitre, so is he that singeth songs to a heavy heart.

21 If your enemy be hungry, give him bread to eat; and if he be thirsty, give him water to drink:

22 For you shalt heap coals of fire upon his head, and יהוה shall reward you.

23 The north wind driveth away rain; so doth an angry countenance a backbiting tongue.

24 It is better to dwell in the corner of the housetop, than with a brawling woman and in a wide house.

25 As cold waters to a thirsty soul, so is good news from a far country.

26 A righteous man falling down before the wicked is as a troubled fountain, and a corrupt spring.

27 It is not good to eat much honey; so for men to search their own glory is not glory.

28 He that hath no rule over his own spirit is like a city that is broken down, and without walls.

26 As snow in summer, and as rain in harvest, so honor is not seemly for a fool.

2 As the bird by wandering, as the swallow by flying, so the curse causeless shall not come.

3 A whip for the horse, a bridle for the ass, and a rod for the fool's back.

4 Answer not a fool according to his folly, lest you also be like unto him.

5 Answer a fool according to his folly, lest he be wise in his own conceit.

6 He that sendeth a message by the hand of a fool cutteth off the feet, and drinketh damage.

7 The legs of the lame are not equal: so is a parable in the mouth of fools.

8 As he that bindeth a stone in a sling, so is he that giveth honor to a fool.

9 As a thorn goeth up into the hand of a drunkard, so is a parable in the mouth of fools.

10 The great that formed all things both rewardeth the fool, and rewardeth transgressors.

11 As a dog returneth to his vomit, so a fool returneth to his folly.

12 Seest you a man wise in his own conceit? There is more hope of a fool than of him.

13 The slothful man saith, "There is a lion in the way; a lion is in the streets."

14 As the door turneth upon his hinges, so doth the slothful upon his bed.

15 The slothful hideth his hand in his bosom; it grieveth him to bring it again to his mouth.

16 The sluggard is wiser in his own conceit than seven men that can render a reason.

17 He that passeth by, and meddleth with strife belonging not to him, is like one that taketh a dog by the ears.

18 As a mad man who casteth firebrands, arrows, and death,

19 So is the man that deceiveth his neighbour, and saith, Am not I in sport?

20 Where no wood is, there the fire goeth out; so where there is no talebearer, the strife ceaseth.

21 As coals are to burning coals, and wood to

fire; so is a contentious man to kindle strife.

22 The words of a talebearer are as wounds, and they go down into the innermost parts of the belly.

23 Burning lips and a wicked heart are like a potsherd covered with silver dross.

24 He that hateth dissembleth with his lips, and layeth up deceit within him;

25 When he speaketh fair, believe him not, for there are seven abominations in his heart.

26 Whose hatred is covered by deceit, his wickedness shall be shewed before the whole congregation.

27 Whoso diggeth a pit shall fall therein; and he that rolleth a stone, it will return upon him.

28 A lying tongue hateth those that are afflicted by it, and a flattering mouth worketh ruin.

27 Boast not yourself of tomorrow, for you knowest not what a day may bring forth.

2 Let another man praise you, and not your own mouth; a stranger, and not your own lips.

3 A stone is heavy, and the sand weighty, but a fool's wrath is heavier than them both.

4 Wrath is cruel, and anger is outrageous, but who is able to stand before envy?

5 Open rebuke is better than secret love.

6 Faithful are the wounds of a friend, but the kisses of an enemy are deceitful.

7 The full soul loatheth a honeycomb; but to the hungry soul every bitter thing is sweet.

8 As a bird that wandereth from her nest, so is a man that wandereth from his place.

9 Ointment and perfume rejoice the heart: so doth the sweetness of a man's friend by hearty counsel.

10 Your own friend, and your father's friend, forsake not, nor go into your brother's house in the day of your disaster; for better is a neighbour that is near than a brother far off.

11 My son, be wise, and make my heart glad, that I may answer him that reproacheth me.

12 A prudent man foreseeth the evil, and hideth himself; but the simple pass on, and are punished.

13 Take his garment that is surety for a stranger, and take a pledge of him for a strange woman.

14 He that blesseth his friend with a loud voice, rising early in the morning, it shall be counted a curse to him.

15 A continual dropping in a very rainy day and a contentious woman are alike.

16 Whosoever hideth her hideth the wind, and the ointment of his right hand, which bewrayeth itself.

17 Iron sharpeneth iron, so a man sharpeneth the countenance of his friend.

18 Whoso keepeth the fig tree shall eat the fruit thereof; so he that waiteth on his master shall be honoured.

19 As in water face answereth to face, so the heart of man to man.

20 Sheol and destruction are never full; so the eyes of man are never satisfied.

21 As the fining pot for silver, and the furnace for gold; so is a man to his praise.

22 Though you shouldest bray a fool in a mortar among wheat with a pestle, yet will not his foolishness depart from him.

23 Be you diligent to know the state of your flocks, and look well to your herds.

24 For riches are not forever, and doth the crown endures to every generation?

25 The hay appeareth, and the tender grass sheweth itself, and herbs of the mountains are gathered.

26 The lambs are for your clothing, and the goats are the price of the field.

27 And you shalt have goats' milk enough for your food, for the food of your household, and for the maintenance for your maidens.

28 The wicked flee when no man pursueth, but the righteous are bold as a lion.

2 For the transgression of a land many are the princes thereof, but by a man of understanding and knowledge the state thereof shall be prolonged.

3 A poor man that oppresseth the poor is like a sweeping rain which leaveth no food.

4 They that forsake the Torah praise the wicked, but such as keep the Torah contend with them.

5 Evil men understand not judgment, but they that seek יהוה understand all things.

6 Better is the poor that walketh in his uprightness, than he that is perverse in his ways, though he be rich.

7 Whoso keepeth the Torah is a wise son; but he that is a companion of riotous men shameth his father.

8 He that by usury and unjust gain increaseth his substance, he shall gather it for him that will pity the poor.

9 He that turneth away his ear from hearing the

Torah, even his prayer shall be abomination.

10 Whoso causeth the righteous to go astray in an evil way, he shall fall himself into his own pit, but the upright shall have good things in possession.

11 The rich man is wise in his own conceit, but the poor that hath understanding searcheth him out.

12 When righteous men do rejoice, there is great glory; but when the wicked rise, a man is hidden.

13 He that covereth his sins shall not prosper, but whoso confesseth and forsaketh them shall have mercy.

14 Happy is the man that feareth always, but he that hardeneth his heart shall fall into mischief.

15 As a roaring lion, and a ranging bear; so is a wicked ruler over the poor people.

16 The prince that lack understanding is also a great oppressor, but he that hateth covetousness shall prolong his days.

17 A man that doeth violence to the blood of any person shall flee to the pit; let no man stay him.

18 Whoso walketh uprightly shall be saved, but he that is perverse in his ways shall fall at once.

19 He that tilleth his land shall have plenty of bread, but he that followeth after vain persons shall have poverty enough.

20 A faithful man shall abound with blessings, but he that maketh haste to be rich shall not be innocent.

21 To have respect of persons is not good, because for a piece of bread that man will transgress.

22 He that hasteth to be rich hath an evil eye, and considereth not that poverty shall come upon him.

23 He that rebuketh a man afterwards shall find more favor than he that flattereth with the tongue.

24 Whoso robbeth his father or his mother, and saith, "It is no transgression"; the same is the companion of a destroyer.

25 He that is of a proud heart stirreth up strife, but he that putteth his trust in יהוה shall be prosperous.

26 He that trusteth in his own heart is a fool, but whoso walketh wisely, he shall be delivered.

27 He that giveth unto the poor shall not lack, but he that hideth his eyes shall have many a curse.

28 When the wicked rise, men hide themselves, but when they perish, the righteous increase.

29 He, that being often reproved hardeneth his neck, shall suddenly be destroyed, and that without remedy.

2 When the righteous are in authority, the people rejoice, but when the wicked beareth rule, the people mourn.

3 Whoso loveth wisdom rejoiceth his father: but he that keepeth company with harlots spendeth his substance.

4 The king by judgment establisheth the land, but he that receiveth gifts overthroweth it.

5 A man that flattereth his neighbour spreadeth a net for his feet.

6 In the transgression of an evil man there is a snare, but the righteous doth sing and rejoice.

7 The righteous considereth the cause of the poor, but the wicked regardeth not to know it.

8 Scornful men bring a city into a snare, but wise men turn away wrath.

9 If a wise man contendeth with a foolish man, whether he rage or laugh, there is no rest.

10 The bloodthirsty hate the upright, but the just seek his soul.

11 A fool uttereth all his mind, but a wise man keepeth it in till afterwards.

12 If a ruler hearken to lies, all his servants are wicked.

13 The poor and the deceitful man have this in common: יהוה lighteneth both their eyes.

14 The king that faithfully judgeth the poor, his throne shall be established forever.

15 The rod and reproof give wisdom, but a child left to himself bringeth his mother to shame.

16 When the wicked are multiplied, transgression increaseth, but the righteous shall see their fall.

17 Correct your son, and he shall give you rest; yea, he shall give delight unto your soul.

18 Where there is no vision, the people perish, but he that keepeth the Torah, happy is he.

19 A servant will not be corrected by words, for though he understands he will not answer.

20 Seest you a man that is hasty in his words? There is more hope of a fool than of him.

21 He that delicately bringeth up his servant from a child shall have him become his son at the length.

22 An angry man stirreth up strife, and a furious man aboundeth in transgression.

23 A man's pride shall bring him low, but honor shall uphold the humble in spirit.

24 Whoso is partner with a thief hateth his own soul; he heareth cursing, and bewrayeth it not.

25 The fear of man bringeth a snare, but whoso putteth his trust in יהוה shall be safe.

26 Many seek the ruler's favor, but every man's judgment cometh from יהוה.

27 An unjust man is an abomination to the just; and he that is upright in the way is abomination to the wicked.

30 The words of Agur the son of Yakeh, even the prophecy; the man spake unto Ithiel, even unto Ithiel and Ucal,

2 Surely I am more brutish than any man, and have not the understanding of a man.

3 I neither learned wisdom, nor have the knowledge of the holy.

4 Who hath ascended up into heaven, or descended? Who hath gathered the wind in His fists? Who hath bound the waters in a garment? Who hath established all the ends of the earth? What is His name, and what is His [B47]Son (Humanity)'s name, if you can tell?

5 Every word of God (Eloah) is pure; He is a shield unto them that put their trust in Him.

6 Add you not unto His words, lest He reprove you, and you be found a liar.

7 Two things have I required of You; deny me them not before I die:

8 Remove far from me vanity and lies; give me neither poverty nor riches; feed me with food convenient for me;

9 Lest I be full, and deny You, and say, "Who is יהוה?" Or lest I be poor, and steal, and take the name of my God (Elohim) in vain.

10 Accuse not a servant unto his master, lest he curse you, and you be found guilty.

11 There is a generation that curseth their father, and doth not bless their mother.

12 There is a generation that are pure in their own eyes, and yet is not washed from their filthiness.

13 There is a generation, O how lofty are their eyes! And their eyelids are lifted up.

14 There is a generation, whose teeth are as swords, and their jaw teeth as knives, to devour the poor from off the earth, and the needy from among men.

15 The horseleach hath two daughters, crying, "Give! Give!" There are three things that are never satisfied, yea, four things say not, "It is enough."

16 The grave, and the barren womb; the earth that is not filled with water; and the fire that saith not, It is enough.

17 The eye that mocketh at his father, and despiseth to obey his mother, the ravens of the valley shall pick it out, and the young eagles shall eat it.

18 There be three things which are too wonderful for me, yea, four which I know not:

19 The way of an eagle in the air; the way of a serpent upon a rock; the way of a ship in the midst of the sea; and the way of a man with a maid.

20 Such is the way of an adulterous woman; she eateth, and wipeth her mouth, and saith, "I have done no wickedness."

21 For three things the earth is disquieted, and for four which it cannot bear:

22 For a servant when he reigneth; and a fool when he is filled with meat;

23 For an odious woman when she is married; and a handmaid that is heir to her mistress.

24 There be four things which are little upon the earth, but they are exceeding wise:

25 The ants are a people not strong, yet they prepare their meat in the summer;

26 The conies are but a feeble folk, yet make they their houses in the rocks;

27 The locusts have no king, yet go they forth all of them by bands;

28 The spider taketh hold with her hands, and is in kings' palaces.

29 There be three things which go well, yea, four are comely in going:

30 A lion which is strongest among beasts, and turneth not away for any;

31 A greyhound; a he goat also; and a king, against whom there is no rising up.

32 If you have done foolishly in lifting up yourself, or if you have thought evil, lay your hand upon your mouth.

33 Surely the churning of milk bringeth forth butter, and the wringing of the nose bringeth forth blood: so the forcing of wrath bringeth forth strife.

31 The words of king Lemuel, the prophecy that his mother taught him.

2 What, my son? And what, the son of my womb? And what, the son of my vows?

3 Give not your strength unto women, nor your ways to that which destroyeth kings.

4 It is not for kings, O Lemuel, it is not for kings to drink wine; nor for princes strong drink;

5 Lest they drink, and forget the decree, and pervert the judgment of any of the afflicted.

6 Give strong drink unto him that is ready to perish, and wine unto those that be of heavy hearts.

7 Let him drink, and forget his poverty, and remember his misery no more.

8 Open your mouth for the dumb in the cause of all such as are appointed to destruction.

9 Open your mouth, judge righteously, and plead the cause of the poor and needy.

10 Who can find a virtuous woman? for her price is far above rubies.

11 The heart of her husband doth safely trust in her, so that he shall have no need of spoil.

12 She will do him good and not evil all the days of her life.

13 She seeketh wool, and flax, and worketh willingly with her hands.

14 She is like the merchants' ships; she bringeth her food from afar.

15 She riseth also while it is yet night, and giveth meat to her household, and a portion to her maidens.

16 She considereth a field, and buyeth it: with the fruit of her hands she planteth a vineyard.

17 She girdeth her loins with strength, and strengtheneth her arms.

18 She perceiveth that her merchandise is good; her candle goeth not out by night.

19 She layeth her hands to the spindle, and her hands hold the distaff.

20 She stretcheth out her hand to the poor; yea, she reacheth forth her hands to the needy.

21 She is not afraid of the snow for her household, for all her household are clothed with scarlet.

22 She maketh herself coverings of tapestry; her clothing is silk and purple.

23 Her husband is known in the gates, when he sitteth among the elders of the land.

24 She maketh fine linen, and selleth it; and delivereth girdles unto the merchant.

25 Strength and honor are her clothing; and she shall rejoice in time to come.

26 She openeth her mouth with wisdom, and in her tongue is the teaching of kindness.

27 She looketh well to the ways of her household, and eateth not the bread of idleness.

28 Her children arise up, and call her blessed; her husband also, and he praiseth her:

29 "Many daughters have done virtuously, but you excellest them all.

30 Favour is deceitful, and beauty is vain, but a woman that feareth יהוה, she shall be praised."

31 Give her of the fruit of her hands, and let her own works praise her in the gates.

ECCLESIASTES
QOHELET קֹהֶלֶת
(Preacher)

1 The words of the Preacher, the son of Dawid, king in Jerusalem (Yerushalayim).

2 "Vanity of vanities!" saith the Preacher; "Vanity of vanities, all is vanity!"

3 What profit hath a man of all his labour which he taketh under the sun?

4 One generation passeth away, and another generation cometh: but the earth abideth forever.

5 The sun also ariseth, and the sun goeth down, and hasteth to his place where he arose.

6 The wind goeth toward the south, and turneth about unto the north; it whirleth about continually, and the wind returneth again according to his circuits.

7 All the rivers run into the sea; yet the sea is not full; unto the place from whence the rivers come, thither they return again.

8 All things are full of labour; man cannot utter it. The eye is not satisfied with seeing, nor the ear filled with hearing.

9 The thing that hath been, it is that which shall be; and that which is done is that which shall be done, and there is no new thing under the sun.

10 Is there any thing whereof it may be said, "See, this is new?" It hath been already of old time, which was before us.

11 There is no remembrance of former things; neither shall there be any remembrance of things that are to come with those that shall come after.

12 I the Preacher was king over Yisrael in Jerusalem (Yerushalayim).

13 And I gave my heart to seek and search out by wisdom concerning all things that are done under heaven: this sore travail hath God (Elohim) given to the sons of man to be exercised therewith.

14 I have seen all the works that are done under the sun; and, behold, all is vanity and vexation of spirit.

15 That which is crooked cannot be made straight, and that which is wanting cannot be numbered.

16 I communed with mine own heart, saying, "Behold, I am come to great estate, and have gotten more wisdom than all they that have been before me in Jerusalem (Yerushalayim); yea, my heart had great experience of wisdom and knowledge."

17 And I gave my heart to know wisdom, and to know madness and folly. I perceived that this also is vexation of spirit.

18 For in much wisdom is much grief, and he that increaseth knowledge increaseth sorrow.

2 I said in mine heart, "Come now, I will prove you with mirth, therefore enjoy pleasure"; and, behold, this also is vanity.

2 I said of laughter, "It is mad"; and of mirth, What doeth it?

3 I sought in mine heart to give myself unto wine, yet acquainting mine heart with wisdom; and to lay hold on folly, till I might see what was that good for the sons of men, which they should do under the heaven all the days of their life.

4 I made me great works; I built me houses; I planted me vineyards:

5 I made me gardens and orchards, and I planted trees in them of all kind of fruits.

6 I made me pools of water, to water therewith the wood that bringeth forth trees.

7 I got me servants and maidens, and had servants born in my house; also I had great possessions of great and small cattle above all that were in Jerusalem (Yerushalayim) before me.

8 I gathered me also silver and gold, and the peculiar treasure of kings and of the provinces. I gat me men singers and women singers, and the delights of the sons of men, as musical instruments, and that of all sorts.

9 So I was great, and increased more than all that were before me in Jerusalem (Yerushalayim). Also my wisdom remained with me.

10 And whatsoever mine eyes desired I kept not from them, I withheld not my heart from any joy, for my heart rejoiced in all my labour; and this was my portion of all my labour.

11 Then I looked on all the works that my hands had wrought, and on the labour that I had laboured to do; and, behold, all was vanity and vexation of spirit, and there was no profit under the sun.

12 And I turned myself to behold wisdom, and madness, and folly; for what can the man do that cometh after the king? Even that which hath been already done.

13 Then I saw that wisdom excelleth folly, as far as light excelleth darkness.

14 The wise man's eyes are in his head; but the

fool walketh in darkness; and I myself perceived also that one event happeneth to them all.

15 Then said I in my heart, "As it happeneth to the fool, so it happeneth even to me; and why was I then more wise?" Then I said in my heart, "This also is vanity."

16 For there is no remembrance of the wise more than of the fool forever; seeing that which now is in the days to come shall all be forgotten. And how dieth the wise man? As the fool.

17 Therefore I hated life; because the work that is wrought under the sun is grievous unto me: for all is vanity and vexation of spirit.

18 Yea, I hated all my labour which I had taken under the sun: because I should leave it unto the man that shall be after me.

19 And who knoweth whether he shall be a wise man or a fool? Yet shall he has rule over all my labour wherein I have laboured, and wherein I have shewed myself wise under the sun. This is also vanity.

20 Therefore I went about to cause my heart to despair of all the labour which I took under the sun.

21 For there is a man whose labour is in wisdom, and in knowledge, and in equity; yet to a man that hath not laboured therein shall he leave it for his portion. This also is vanity and a great evil.

22 For what hath man of all his labour, and of the vexation of his heart, wherein he hath laboured under the sun?

23 For all his days are sorrows, and his travail grief; yea, his heart taketh not rest in the night. This is also vanity.

24 There is nothing better for a man, than that he should eat and drink, and that he should make his soul enjoy good in his labour. This also I saw, that it was from the hand of God (Elohim).

25 For who can eat, or who else can hasten hereunto, more than I?

26 For God (Elohim) giveth to a man that is good in His sight wisdom, and knowledge, and joy; but to the sinner He giveth travail, to gather and to heap up, that he may give to him that is good before God (Elohim). This also is vanity and vexation of spirit.

3 To every thing there is a season, and a time to every purpose under the heaven:

2 A time to be born, and a time to die; a time to plant, and a time to pluck up that which is planted;

3 A time to kill, and a time to heal; a time to break down, and a time to build up;

4 A time to weep, and a time to laugh; a time to mourn, and a time to dance;

5 A time to cast away stones, and a time to gather stones together; a time to embrace, and a time to refrain from embracing;

6 A time to get, and a time to lose; a time to keep, and a time to cast away;

7 A time to rend, and a time to sew; a time to keep silence, and a time to speak;

8 A time to love, and a time to hate; a time of war, and a time of peace.

9 What profit hath he that worketh in that wherein he laboureth?

10 I have seen the travail, which God (Elohim) hath given to the sons of men to be exercised in it.

11 He hath made every thing beautiful in his time; also He hath set the world in their heart, so that no man can find out the work that God (Elohim) maketh from the beginning to the end.

12 I know that there is no good in them, but for a man to rejoice, and to do good in his life.

13 And also that every man should eat and drink, and enjoy the good of all his labour, it is the gift of God (Elohim).

14 I know that, whatsoever God (Elohim) doeth, it shall be forever. Nothing can be put to it, nor any thing taken from it; and God (Elohim) doeth it, that men should fear before Him.

15 That which hath been is now; and that which is to be hath already been; and God (Elohim) requireth that which is past.

16 And moreover I saw under the sun the place of judgment, that wickedness was there; and the place of righteousness, that iniquity was there.

17 I said in mine heart, "God (Elohim) shall judge the righteous and the wicked, for there is a time there for every purpose and for every work."

18 I said in mine heart concerning the estate of the sons of men, "God (Elohim) might manifest them, and that they might see that they themselves are beasts."

19 For that which befalleth the sons of men befalleth beasts; even one thing befalleth them: as the one dieth, so dieth the other; yea, they have all one breath; so that a man hath no

preeminence above a beast, for all is vanity.

20 All go unto one place; all are of the dust, and all turn to dust again.

21 Who knoweth the spirit of man that goeth upward, and the spirit of the beast that goeth downward to the earth?

22 Wherefore I perceive that there is nothing better, than that a man should rejoice in his own works; for that is his portion; for who shall bring him to see what shall be after him?

4 So I returned, and considered all the oppressions that are done under the sun; and behold the tears of such as were oppressed, and they had no comforter; and on the side of their oppressors there was power; but they had no comforter.

2 Wherefore I praised the dead which are already dead more than the living which are yet alive.

3 Yea, better is he than both they, who hath not yet been, who hath not seen the evil work that is done under the sun.

4 Again, I considered all travail, and every right work, that for this a man is envied of his neighbour. This is also vanity and vexation of spirit.

5 The fool foldeth his hands together, and eateth his own flesh.

6 Better is a handful with quietness, than both the hands full with travail and vexation of spirit.

7 Then I returned, and I saw vanity under the sun.

8 There is one alone, and there is not a second; yea, he hath neither child nor brother: yet is there no end of all his labour; neither is his eye satisfied with riches; neither saith he, "For whom do I labour, and bereave my soul of good?" This is also vanity, yea, it is a sore travail.

9 Two are better than one, because they have a good reward for their labour.

10 For if they fall, the one will lift up his fellow; but woe to him that is alone when he falleth, for he hath not another to help him up.

11 Again, if two lie together, then they have heat; but how can one be warm alone?

12 And if one prevails against him, two shall withstand him; and a threefold cord is not quickly broken.

13 Better is a poor and a wise child than an old and foolish king, who will no more be admonished.

14 For out of prison he cometh to reign; whereas also he that is born in his kingdom becometh poor.

15 I considered all the living which walk under the sun, with the second child that shall stand up in his stead.

16 There is no end of all the people, even of all that have been before them; they also that come after shall not rejoice in him. Surely this also is vanity and vexation of spirit.

5 Keep your foot when you goest to the house of God (Elohim), and be more ready to hear, than to give the sacrifice of fools, for they consider not that they do evil.

2 Be not rash with your mouth, and let not your heart be hasty to utter any thing before God (Elohim); for God (Elohim) is in heaven, and you upon earth; therefore let your words be few.

3 For a dream cometh through the multitude of business; and a fool's voice is known by multitude of words.

4 When you vowest a vow unto God (Elohim), defer not to pay it; for He hath no pleasure in fools: pay that which you have vowed.

5 Better is it that you shouldest not vow, than that you shouldest vow and not pay.

6 Let not your mouth to cause your flesh to sin; neither say you before the angel, that it was an error; wherefore should God (Elohim) be angry at your voice, and destroy the work of your hands?

7 For in the multitude of dreams and many words there are also divers vanities, but fear you God (Elohim).

8 If you seest the oppression of the poor, and violent perverting of judgment and justice in a province, marvel not at the matter; for he that is higher than the highest regardeth; and there be higher than they.

9 Moreover the profit of the earth is for all: the king himself is served by the field.

10 He that loveth silver shall not be satisfied with silver; nor he that loveth abundance with increase; this is also vanity.

11 When goods increase, they are increased that eat them; and what good is there to the owners thereof, saving the beholding of them with their eyes?

12 The sleep of a labouring man is sweet, whether he eat little or much; but the abundance

of the rich will not allow him to sleep.

13 There is a sore evil (^{B36}raah) which I have seen under the sun, namely, riches kept for the owners thereof to their hurt.

14 But those riches perish by evil travail; and he begetteth a son, and there is nothing in his hand.

15 As he came forth of his mother's womb, naked shall he return to go as he came, and shall take nothing of his labour, which he may carry away in his hand.

16 And this also is a sore evil, that in all points as he came, so shall he go; and what profit hath he that hath laboured for the wind?

17 All his days also he eateth in darkness, and he hath much sorrow and wrath with his sickness.

18 Behold that which I have seen; it is good and comely for one to eat and to drink, and to enjoy the good of all his labour that he taketh under the sun all the days of his life, which God (Elohim) giveth him, for it is his portion.

19 Every man also to whom God (Elohim) hath given riches and wealth, and hath given him power to eat thereof, and to take his portion, and to rejoice in his labour; this is the gift of God (Elohim).

20 For he shall not much remember the days of his life, because God (Elohim) answereth him in the joy of his heart.

6 There is an evil which I have seen under the sun, and it is common among men:

2 A man to whom God (Elohim) hath given riches, wealth, and honor, so that he wanteth nothing for his soul of all that he desireth, yet God (Elohim) giveth him not power to eat thereof, but a stranger eateth it. This is vanity, and it is an evil disease.

3 If a man begets a hundred children, and live many years, so that the days of his years be many, and his soul be not filled with good, and also that he has no burial; I say, that an untimely birth is better than he.

4 For he cometh in with vanity, and departeth in darkness, and his name shall be covered with darkness.

5 Moreover he hath not seen the sun, nor known anything, this hath more rest than the other.

6 Yea, though he lives a thousand years twice told, yet hath he seen no good. Do not all go to one place?

7 All the labour of man is for his mouth, and yet the appetite is not filled.

8 For what hath the wise more than the fool? What hath the poor, that knoweth to walk before the living?

9 Better is the sight of the eyes than the wandering of the desire. This is also vanity and vexation of spirit.

10 That which hath been is named already, and it is known that it is man; neither may he contend with him that is mightier than he.

11 Seeing there be many things that increase vanity, what is man the better?

12 For who knoweth what is good for man in this life, all the days of his vain life which he spendeth as a shadow? For who can tell a man what shall be after him under the sun?

7 A good name is better than precious ointment; and the day of death than the day of one's birth.

2 It is better to go to the house of mourning, than to go to the house of feasting: for that is the end of all men; and the living will lay it to his heart.

3 Sorrow is better than laughter, for by the sadness of the countenance the heart is made better.

4 The heart of the wise is in the house of mourning, but the heart of fools is in the house of mirth.

5 It is better to hear the rebuke of the wise, than for a man to hear the song of fools.

6 For as the crackling of thorns under a pot, so is the laughter of the fool: this also is vanity.

7 Surely oppression maketh a wise man mad; and a gift destroyeth the heart.

8 Better is the end of a thing than the beginning thereof; and the patient in spirit is better than the proud in spirit.

9 Be not hasty in your spirit to be angry, for anger resteth in the bosom of fools.

10 Say not you, "What is the cause that the former days were better than these? For you dost not enquire wisely concerning this.

11 Wisdom is good with an inheritance: and by it there is profit to them that see the sun.

12 For wisdom is a defence, and money is a defence: but the excellency of knowledge is, that wisdom giveth life to them that have it.

13 Consider the work of God (Elohim); for who can make that straight, which He hath made crooked?

14 In the day of prosperity be joyful, but in the

day of adversity consider: God (Elohim) also hath set the one opposite the other, to the end that man should find nothing after him.

15 All things have I seen in the days of my vanity: there is a just man that perisheth in his righteousness, and there is a wicked man that prolongeth his life in his wickedness.

16 Be not righteous over much; neither make yourself over wise; why shouldest you destroy yourself?

17 Be not over much wicked, neither be you foolish: why shouldest you die before your time?

18 It is good that you shouldest take hold of this; yea, also from this withdraw not your hand; for he that feareth God (Elohim) shall come forth of them all.

19 Wisdom strengtheneth the wise more than ten mighty men which are in the city.

20 For there is not a just man upon earth, that doeth good, and sinneth not.

21 Also take no heed unto all words that are spoken; lest you hear your servant curse you.

22 For oftentimes also your own heart knoweth that you yourself likewise hast cursed others.

23 All this have I proved by wisdom. I said, "I will be wise"; but it was far from me.

24 That which is far off, and exceeding deep, who can find it out?

25 I applied mine heart to know, and to search, and to seek out wisdom, and the reason of things, and to know the wickedness of folly, even of foolishness and madness;

26 And I find more bitter than death the woman, whose heart is snares and nets, and her hands as bands: whoso pleaseth God (Elohim) shall escape from her; but the sinner shall be taken by her.

27 "Behold, this have I found", saith the preacher, counting one by one, to find out the account,

28 Which yet my soul seeketh, but I find not; one man among a thousand have I found, but a woman among all those have I not found.

29 Behold, this only have I found, that God (Elohim) hath made man upright, but they have sought out many inventions."

8 Who is as the wise man? And who knoweth the interpretation of a thing? A man's wisdom maketh his face to shine, and the boldness of his face shall be changed.

2 I counsel you to keep the king's commandment, and that in regard of the oath of God (Elohim).

3 Be not hasty to go out of his sight; stand not in an evil thing, for he doeth whatsoever pleaseth him.

4 Where the word of a king is, there is power; and who may say unto him, What doest you?

5 Whoso keepeth the commandment shall feel no evil thing; and a wise man's heart discerneth both time and judgment.

6 Because to every purpose there is time and judgment, therefore the misery of man is great upon him.

7 For he knoweth not that which shall be; for who can tell him when it shall be?

8 There is no man that hath power over the spirit to retain the spirit; neither hath he power in the day of death; and there is no discharge in that war; neither shall wickedness deliver those that are given to it.

9 All this have I seen, and applied my heart unto every work that is done under the sun; there is a time wherein one man ruleth over another to his own hurt.

10 And so I saw the wicked buried, who had come and gone from the place of the holy, and they were forgotten in the city where they had so done. This is also vanity.

11 Because sentence against an evil work is not executed speedily, therefore the heart of the sons of men is fully set in them to do evil.

12 Though a sinner does evil a hundred times, and his days be prolonged, yet surely I know that it shall be well with them that fear God (Elohim), which fear before Him.

13 But it shall not be well with the wicked, neither shall he prolong his days, which are as a shadow, because he feareth not before God (Elohim).

14 There is a vanity which is done upon the earth; that there be just men, unto whom it happeneth according to the work of the wicked; again, there be wicked men, to whom it happeneth according to the work of the righteous. I said that this also is vanity.

15 Then I commended mirth, because a man hath no better thing under the sun, than to eat, and to drink, and to be merry; for that shall abide with him of his labour the days of his life, which God (Elohim) giveth him under the sun.

16 When I applied mine heart to know wisdom, and to see the business that is done upon the

earth; (for also there is that neither day nor night seeth sleep with his eyes;)

17 Then I beheld all the work of God (Elohim), that a man cannot find out the work that is done under the sun, because though a man labour to seek it out, yet he shall not find it; yea further; though a wise man thinks to know it, yet shall he not be able to find it.

9 For all this I considered in my heart even to declare all this: that the righteous, and the wise, and their works, are in the hand of God (Elohim); no man knoweth either love or hatred by all that is before them.

2 All things come alike to all; there is one event to the righteous, and to the wicked; to the good and to the clean, and to the unclean; to him that sacrificeth, and to him that sacrificeth not: as is the good, so is the sinner; and he that sweareth, as he that feareth an oath.

3 This is an evil among all things that are done under the sun, that there is one event unto all. Yea, also the heart of the sons of men is full of evil, and madness is in their heart while they live, and after that they go to the dead.

4 For to him that is joined to all the living there is hope, for a living dog is better than a dead lion.

5 For the living know that they shall die; but the dead know not any thing, neither have they any more a reward, for the memory of them is forgotten.

6 Also their love, and their hatred, and their envy, is now perished; neither have they any more a portion forever in any thing that is done under the sun.

7 Go your way, eat your bread with joy, and drink your wine with a merry heart; for God (Elohim) now accepteth your works.

8 Let your garments be always white; and let your head lack no ointment.

9 Live joyfully with the wife whom you lovest all the days of the life of your vanity, which He hath given you under the sun, all the days of your vanity; for that is your portion in this life, and in your labour which you takest under the sun.

10 Whatsoever your hand findeth to do, do it with your might; for there is no work, nor device, nor knowledge, nor wisdom, in the grave, whither you goest.

11 I returned, and saw under the sun, that the race is not to the swift, nor the battle to the strong, neither yet bread to the wise, nor yet riches to men of understanding, nor yet favor to men of skill; but time and chance happeneth to them all.

12 For man also knoweth not his time; as the fishes that are taken in an evil net, and as the birds that are caught in the snare; so are the sons of men snared in an evil time, when it falleth suddenly upon them.

13 This wisdom have I seen also under the sun, and it seemed great unto me:

14 There was a little city, and few men within it; and there came a great king against it, and besieged it, and built great bulwarks against it.

15 Now there was found in it a poor wise man, and he by his wisdom delivered the city; yet no man remembered that same poor man.

16 Then said I, "Wisdom is better than strength; nevertheless the poor man's wisdom is despised, and his words are not heard.

17 The words of wise men are heard in quiet more than the cry of him that ruleth among fools.

18 Wisdom is better than weapons of war; but one sinner destroyeth much good.

10 Dead flies cause the ointment of the apothecary to send forth a stinking savour; so doth a little folly him that is in reputation for wisdom and honor.

2 A wise man's heart is at his right hand, but a fool's heart at his left.

3 Yea also, when he that is a fool walketh by the way, his wisdom faileth him, and he saith to every one that he is a fool.

4 If the spirit of the ruler rises up against you, leave not your place; for yielding pacifieth great offences.

5 There is an evil which I have seen under the sun, as an error which proceedeth from the ruler:

6 Folly is set in great dignity, and the rich sit in low place.

7 I have seen servants upon horses, and princes walking as servants upon the earth.

8 He that diggeth a pit shall fall into it; and whoso breaketh an hedge, a serpent shall bite him.

9 Whoso removeth stones shall be hurt therewith; and he that cleaveth wood shall be endangered thereby.

10 If the iron be blunt, and he does not whet the edge, then must he put to more strength; but wisdom is profitable to direct.

11 Surely the serpent will bite without enchantment; and a babbler is no better.

12 The words of a wise man's mouth are gracious; but the lips of a fool will swallow up himself.

13 The beginning of the words of his mouth is foolishness; and the end of his talk is mischievous madness.

14 A fool also is full of words. A man cannot tell what shall be; and what shall be after him, who can tell him?

15 The labour of the foolish wearieth every one of them, because he knoweth not how to go to the city.

16 Woe to you, O land, when your king is a child, and your princes eat in the morning!

17 Blessed are you, O land, when your king is the son of nobles, and your princes eat in due season, for strength, and not for drunkenness!

18 By much slothfulness the building decayeth; and through idleness of the hands the house droppeth through.

19 A feast is made for laughter, and wine maketh merry; but money answereth all things.

20 Curse not the king, no not in your thought; and curse not the rich in your bedchamber; for a bird of the air shall carry the voice, and that which hath wings shall tell the matter.

11 Cast your bread upon the waters, for you shalt find it after many days.

2 Give a portion to seven, and also to eight, for you knowest not what evil shall be upon the earth.

3 If the clouds be full of rain, they empty themselves upon the earth; and if the tree fall toward the south, or toward the north, in the place where the tree falleth, there it shall be.

4 He that observeth the wind shall not sow; and he that regardeth the clouds shall not reap.

5 As you knowest not what is the way of the spirit, nor how the bones do grow in the womb of her that is with child; even so you knowest not the works of God (Elohim) who maketh all.

6 In the morning sow your seed, and in the evening withhold not your hand; for you knowest not whether shall prosper, either this or that, or whether they both shall be alike good.

7 Truly the light is sweet, and a pleasant thing it is for the eyes to behold the sun;

8 But if a man lives many years, and rejoices in them all; yet let him remember the days of darkness; for they shall be many. All that cometh is vanity.

9 Rejoice, O young man, in your youth; and let your heart cheer you in the days of your youth, and walk in the ways of your heart, and in the sight of your eyes; but know you, that for all these things God (Elohim) will bring you into judgment.

10 Therefore remove sorrow from your heart, and put away evil from your flesh, for childhood and youth are vanity.

12 Remember now your Creator in the days of your youth, while the evil days come not, nor the years draw near, when you shalt say, "I have no pleasure in them":

2 While the sun, or the light, or the moon, or the stars, be not darkened, nor the clouds return after the rain;

3 In the day when the keepers of the house shall tremble, and the strong men shall bow themselves, and the grinders cease because they are few, and those that look out of the windows be darkened,

4 And the doors shall be shut in the streets, when the sound of the grinding is low, and he shall rise up at the voice of the bird, and all the daughters of musick shall be brought low;

5 Also when they shall be afraid of that which is high, and fears shall be in the way, and the almond tree shall flourish, and the grasshopper shall be a burden, and desire shall fail; because man goeth to his long home, and the mourners go about the streets.

6 Or ever the silver cord be loosed, or the golden bowl be broken, or the pitcher be broken at the fountain, or the wheel broken at the cistern.

7 Then shall the dust return to the earth as it was; and the spirit shall return unto God (Elohim) who gave it.

8 "Vanity of vanities," saith the Preacher. "All is vanity!"

9 And moreover, because the preacher was wise, he still taught the people knowledge; yea, he gave good heed, and sought out, and set in order many proverbs.

10 The Preacher sought to find out acceptable words; and that which was written was upright, even words of truth.

11 The words of the wise are as goads, and as nails fastened by the masters of assemblies, which are given from one shepherd.

12 And further, by these, my son, be admonished; of making many books there is no end; and much study is a weariness of the flesh.

13 Let us hear the conclusion of the whole matter: Fear God (Elohim), and keep His commandments, for this is the whole duty of man.

14 For God (Elohim) shall bring every work into judgment, with every secret thing, whether it be good, or whether it be evil.

SONG OF SONGS
SHIR HASHIRIM
סירישַה ריש

1 The song of songs, which is Solomon (Shelomoh)'s.

2 Let him kiss me with the kisses of his mouth, for your love is better than wine.

3 Because of the savour of your good ointments Your name is as ointment poured forth, therefore do the virgins love you.

4 Draw me, we will run after you; the king hath brought me into his chambers. We will be glad and rejoice in you, we will remember your love more than wine; the upright loves you.

5 I am black, but comely, O you daughters of Jerusalem (Yerushalayim), as the tents of Kedar, as the curtains of Solomon (Shelomoh).

6 Look not upon me, because I am black, because the sun hath looked upon me. My mother's children were angry with me; they made me the keeper of the vineyards, but mine own vineyard have I not kept.

7 Tell me, O you whom my soul loveth, where you feedest, where you makest your flock to rest at noon; for why should I be as one that turneth aside by the flocks of your companions?

8 If you know not, O you fairest among women, go your way forth by the footsteps of the flock, and feed your kids beside the shepherds' tents.

9 I have compared you, O my love, to a company of horses in Pharaoh (Paroh)'s chariots.

10 Your cheeks are comely with rows of jewels, your neck with chains of gold.

11 We will make you borders of gold with studs of silver.

12 While the king sitteth at his table, my spikenard sendeth forth the smell thereof.

13 A bundle of myrrh is my beloved unto me; he shall lie all night betwixt my breasts.

14 My beloved is unto me as a cluster of camphire in the vineyards of Engedi.

15 Behold, you are fair, my love; behold, you are fair; you have doves' eyes.

16 Behold, you are fair, my beloved, yea, pleasant; also our bed is green.

17 The beams of our house are cedar, and our rafters of fir.

2 I am the rose of Sharon, and the lily of the valleys.

2 As the lily among thorns, so is my love among the daughters.

3 As the apple tree among the trees of the wood, so is my beloved among the sons. I sat down under his shadow with great delight, and his fruit was sweet to my taste.

4 He brought me to the banqueting house, and his banner over me was love.

5 Stay me with flagons, comfort me with apples, for I am lovesick.

6 His left hand is under my head, and his right hand doth embrace me.

7 I charge you, O you daughters of Jerusalem (Yerushalayim), by the roes, and by the hinds of the field, that you stir not up, nor awake my love, till he please.

8 The voice of my beloved! Behold, he cometh leaping upon the mountains, skipping upon the hills.

9 My beloved is like a roe or a young hart; behold, he standeth behind our wall, he looketh forth at the windows, shewing himself through the lattice.

10 My beloved spake, and said unto me, "Rise up, my love, my fair one, and come away.

11 For, behold, the winter is past, the rain is over and gone;

12 The flowers appear on the earth; the time of the singing of birds is come, and the voice of the turtle is heard in our land;

13 The fig tree putteth forth her green figs, and the vines with the tender grape give a good smell. Arise, my love, my fair one, and come away.

14 O my dove, that art in the clefts of the rock, in the secret places of the stairs, let me see your countenance, let me hear your voice; for sweet is your voice, and your countenance is comely."

15 Take us the foxes, the little foxes, that spoil the vines; for our vines have tender grapes.

16 My beloved is mine, and I am his; he feedeth among the lilies.

17 Until the day break, and the shadows flee away, turn, my beloved, and be you like a roe or a young hart upon the mountains of Bether.

3 By night on my bed I sought him whom my soul loveth. I sought him, but I found him not.

2 I will rise now, and go about the city in the streets, and in the broad ways I will seek him whom my soul loveth. I sought him, but I found

him not.

3 The watchmen that go about the city found me: to whom I said, "Saw you him whom my soul loveth?"

4 It was but a little that I passed from them, but I found him whom my soul loveth; I held him, and would not let him go, until I had brought him into my mother's house, and into the chamber of her that conceived me.

5 I charge you, O you daughters of Jerusalem (Yerushalayim), by the roes, and by the hinds of the field, that you stir not up, nor awake my love, till he please.

6 Who is this that cometh out of the wilderness like pillars of smoke, perfumed with myrrh and frankincense, with all powders of the merchant?

7 Behold his bed, which is Solomon (Shelomoh)'s; threescore valiant men are about it, of the valiant of Yisrael.

8 They all hold swords, being expert in war: every man hath his sword upon his thigh because of fear in the night.

9 King Solomon (Shelomoh) made himself a chariot of the wood of Lebanon.

10 He made the pillars thereof of silver, the bottom thereof of gold, the covering of it of purple, the midst thereof being paved with love, for the daughters of Jerusalem (Yerushalayim).

11 Go forth, O you daughters of Zion (Tsiyon), and behold king Solomon (Shelomoh) with the crown wherewith his mother crowned him in the day of his espousals, and in the day of the gladness of his heart.

4 Behold, you are fair, my love; behold, you are fair; you have doves' eyes within your locks; your hair is as a flock of goats, that appear from Mount Gilad.

2 Your teeth are like a flock of sheep that are even shorn, which came up from the washing; whereof every one bear twins, and none is barren among them.

3 Your lips are like a thread of scarlet, and your speech is comely; your temples are like a piece of a pomegranate within your locks.

4 Your neck is like the tower of Dawid builded for an armoury, whereon there hang a thousand bucklers, all shields of mighty men.

5 Your two breasts are like two young roes that are twins, which feed among the lilies.

6 Until the day break, and the shadows flee away, I will get me to the mountain of myrrh,

and to the hill of frankincense.

7 You are all fair, my love; there is no spot in you.

8 Come with me from Lebanon, my spouse, with me from Lebanon; look from the top of Amana, from the top of Shenir and Hermon, from the lions' dens, from the mountains of the leopards.

9 You have ravished my heart, my sister, my spouse; you have ravished my heart with one of your eyes, with one chain of your neck.

10 How fair is your love, my sister, my spouse! How much better is your love than wine! And the smell of your ointments than all spices!

11 Your lips, O my spouse, drop as the honeycomb; honey and milk are under your tongue; and the smell of your garments is like the smell of Lebanon.

12 A garden inclosed is my sister, my spouse; a spring shut up, a fountain sealed.

13 Your plants are an orchard of pomegranates, with pleasant fruits; camphire, with spikenard,

14 Spikenard and saffron; calamus and cinnamon, with all trees of frankincense; myrrh and aloes, with all the chief spices;

15 A fountain of gardens, a well of living waters, and streams from Lebanon.

16 Awake, O north wind; and come, you south; blow upon my garden, that the spices thereof may flow out. Let my beloved come into his garden, and eat his pleasant fruits.

5 I am come into my garden, my sister, my spouse; I have gathered my myrrh with my spice; I have eaten my honeycomb with my honey; I have drunk my wine with my milk: eat, O friends; drink, yea, drink abundantly, O beloved.

2 I sleep, but my heart waketh: it is the voice of my beloved that knocketh, saying, Open to me, my sister, my love, my dove, my undefiled; for my head is filled with dew, and my locks with the drops of the night.

3 I have put off my coat; how shall I put it on? I have washed my feet; how shall I defile them?

4 My beloved put in his hand by the hole of the door, and my bowels were moved for him.

5 I rose up to open to my beloved; and my hands dropped with myrrh, and my fingers with sweet smelling myrrh, upon the handles of the lock.

6 I opened to my beloved; but my beloved had withdrawn himself, and was gone: my soul

failed when he spake. I sought him, but I could not find him; I called him, but he gave me no answer.

7 The watchmen that went about the city found me, they smote me, they wounded me; the keepers of the walls took away my veil from me.

8 I charge you, O daughters of Jerusalem (Yerushalayim), if you find my beloved, that you tell him, that I am lovesick.

9 What is your beloved more than another beloved, O you fairest among women? What is your beloved more than another beloved, that you dost so charge us?

10 My beloved is white and ruddy, the chiefest among ten thousand.

11 His head is as the most fine gold, his locks are bushy, and black as a raven.

12 His eyes are as the eyes of doves by the rivers of waters, washed with milk, and fitly set.

13 His cheeks are as a bed of spices, as sweet flowers; his lips like lilies, dropping sweet smelling myrrh.

14 His hands are as gold rings set with the beryl. His belly is as bright ivory overlaid with sapphires.

15 His legs are as pillars of marble, set upon sockets of fine gold. His countenance is as Lebanon, excellent as the cedars.

16 His mouth is most sweet, yea, he is altogether lovely. This is my beloved, and this is my friend, O daughters of Jerusalem (Yerushalayim).

6 Whither is your beloved gone, O you fairest among women? Whither is your beloved turned aside? That we may seek him with you.

2 My beloved is gone down into his garden, to the beds of spices, to feed in the gardens, and to gather lilies.

3 I am my beloved's, and my beloved is mine; he feedeth among the lilies.

4 You are beautiful, O my love, as Tirzah, comely as Jerusalem (Yerushalayim), awesome as an army with banners.

5 Turn away your eyes from me, for they have overcome me; your hair is as a flock of goats that appear from Gilad.

6 Your teeth are as a flock of sheep which go up from the washing, whereof every one beareth twins, and there is not one barren among them.

7 As a piece of a pomegranate are your temples within your locks.

8 There are threescore queens, and fourscore concubines, and virgins without number.

9 My dove, my undefiled is but one; she is the only one of her mother, she is the choice one of her that bare her. The daughters saw her, and blessed her; yea, the queens and the concubines, and they praised her.

10 Who is she that looketh forth as the morning, fair as the moon, clear as the sun, and awesome as an army with banners?

11 I went down into the garden of nuts to see the fruits of the valley, and to see whether the vine flourished, and the pomegranates budded.

12 Or ever I was aware, my soul made me like the chariots of Amminadib.

13 Return, return, O Shulamite; return, return, that we may look upon you. What will you see in the Shulamite? As it was the company of two armies.

7 How beautiful are your feet with shoes, O prince's daughter! The joints of your thighs are like jewels, the work of the hands of a cunning workman.

2 Your navel is like a round goblet, which wanteth not liquor: your belly is like a heap of wheat set about with lilies.

3 Your two breasts are like two young roes that are twins.

4 Your neck is as a tower of ivory; your eyes like the fishpools in Heshbon, by the gate of Bathrabbim; your nose is as the tower of Lebanon which looketh toward Damascus (Dammeseq).

5 Your head upon you is like Carmel, and the hair of your head like purple; the king is held in the galleries.

6 How fair and how pleasant are you, O love, for delights!

7 This your stature is like to a palm tree, and your breasts to clusters of grapes.

8 I said, I will go up to the palm tree, I will take hold of the boughs thereof: now also your breasts shall be as clusters of the vine, and the smell of your nose like apples;

9 And the roof of your mouth like the best wine for my beloved, that goeth down sweetly, causing the lips of those that are asleep to speak.

10 I am my beloved's, and his desire is toward me.

11 Come, my beloved, let us go forth into the field; let us lodge in the villages.

12 Let us get up early to the vineyards; let us see

if the vine flourish, whether the tender grape appear, and the pomegranates bud forth: there will I give you my loves.

13 The mandrakes give a smell, and at our gates are all manner of pleasant fruits, new and old, which I have laid up for you, O my beloved.

8 O that you wert as my brother, that sucked the breasts of my mother! When I should find you outside, I would kiss you; yea, I should not be despised.

2 I would lead you, and bring you into my mother's house, who would instruct me: I would cause you to drink of spiced wine of the juice of my pomegranate.

3 His left hand should be under my head, and his right hand should embrace me.

4 I charge you, O daughters of Jerusalem (Yerushalayim), that you stir not up, nor awake my love, until he please.

5 Who is this that cometh up from the wilderness, leaning upon her beloved? I raised you up under the apple tree; there your mother brought you forth; there she brought you forth that bare you.

6 Set me as a seal upon your heart, as a seal upon your arm; for love is strong as death; jealousy is cruel as the grave; the coals thereof are coals of fire, which hath a most vehement flame.

7 Many waters cannot quench love, neither can the floods drown it: if a man would give all the substance of his house for love, it would utterly be contemned.

8 We have a little sister, and she hath no breasts. What shall we do for our sister in the day when she shall be spoken for?

9 If she be a wall, we will build upon her a palace of silver; and if she be a door, we will inclose her with boards of cedar.

10 I am a wall, and my breasts like towers; then was I in his eyes as one that found favor.

11 Solomon (Shelomoh) had a vineyard at Baal Hamon; he let out the vineyard unto keepers; every one for the fruit thereof was to bring a thousand pieces of silver.

12 My vineyard, which is mine, is before me. You, O Solomon (Shelomoh), must have a thousand, and those that keep the fruit thereof two hundred.

13 You that dwellest in the gardens, the companions hearken to your voice; cause me to hear it.

14 Make haste, my beloved, and be you like to a roe or to a young hart upon the mountains of spices.

ISAIAH
YESHAYAHU יְשַׁעְיָהוּ
(YHWH is Salvation)

1 The vision of [A51]Isaiah (Yeshayahu) the son of Amoz, which he saw concerning Judah (Yehudah) and Jerusalem (Yerushalayim) in the days of Uzziyahu, Yotam, Achaz, and Hezekiah (Chizqiyahu), kings of Judah (Yehudah).

2 Hear, O heavens, and give ear, O earth; for יהוה hath spoken: "I have nourished and brought up children, and they have rebelled against Me.

3 The ox knoweth his owner, and the ass his master's crib; but Yisrael doth not know, My people doth not consider."

4 Ah sinful nation, a people laden with iniquity, a seed of evildoers, children that are corrupters; they have forsaken יהוה, they have provoked the Holy One of Yisrael unto anger, they are gone away backward.

5 Why should you be stricken any more? You will revolt more and more: the whole head is sick, and the whole heart faint.

6 From the sole of the foot even unto the head there is no soundness in it; but wounds, and bruises, and putrifying sores: they have not been closed, neither bound up, neither mollified with ointment.

7 Your country is desolate, your cities are burned with fire; your land, strangers devour it in your presence, and it is desolate, as overthrown by strangers.

8 And the daughter of Zion (Tsiyon) is left as a cottage in a vineyard, as a lodge in a garden of cucumbers, as a besieged city.

9 Except יהוה of hosts (YHWH Tsevaot) had left unto us a very small remnant, we should have been as Sodom, and we should have been like unto Gomorrah.

10 Hear the word of יהוה, you rulers of Sodom; give ear unto the Torah of our God (Elohim), you people of Gomorrah:

11 "To what purpose is the multitude of your sacrifices unto Me?" saith יהוה. "I am full of the burnt offerings of rams, and the fat of fed beasts; and I delight not in the blood of bullocks, or of lambs, or of he goats.

12 When you come to appear before Me, who hath required this at your hand, to tread My courts?

13 Bring no more vain oblations; incense is an abomination unto Me; the New Moon and Shabbat, the calling of assemblies, I cannot endure with; it is iniquity, even the solemn meeting.

14 Your New Moons and your appointed feasts My soul hateth; they are a trouble unto Me; I am weary to bear them.

15 And when you spread forth your hands, I will hide Mine eyes from you; yea, when you make many prayers, I will not hear; your hands are full of blood.

16 Wash you, make you clean; put away the evil of your doings from before Mine eyes; cease to do evil;

17 Learn to do well; seek justice, relieve the oppressed, judge the fatherless, plead for the widow.

18 "Come now, and let us reason together," saith יהוה, "Though your sins be as scarlet, they shall be as white as snow; though they be red like crimson, they shall be as wool.

19 If you be willing and obedient, you shall eat the good of the land;

20 But if you refuse and rebel, you shall be devoured with the sword"; for the mouth of יהוה hath spoken it.

21 How is the faithful city become a harlot! It was full of judgment; righteousness lodged in it; but now murderers.

22 Your silver is become dross, your wine mixed with water.

23 Your princes are rebellious, and companions of thieves; every one loveth gifts, and followeth after rewards: they judge not the fatherless, neither doth the cause of the widow come unto them.

24 Therefore saith Lord (Adon) [A8]יהוה of hosts (YHWH Tsevaot), the Mighty One of Yisrael, "Ah, I will ease Me of Mine adversaries, and avenge Me of Mine enemies.

25 And I will turn My hand upon you, and purely purge away your dross, and take away all your tin.

26 And I will restore your judges as at the first, and your counsellors as at the beginning. Afterward you shalt be called the city of righteousness, the faithful city."

27 Zion (Tsiyon) shall be redeemed with judgment, and her converts with righteousness.

28 And the destruction of the transgressors and

of the sinners shall be together, and they that forsake יהוה shall be consumed.

29 For they shall be ashamed of the oaks which you have desired, and you shall be confounded for the gardens that you have chosen.

30 For you shall be as an oak whose leaf fadeth, and as a garden that hath no water.

31 And the strong shall be as tow, and the maker of it as a spark, and they shall both burn together, and none shall quench them.

2 The word that Isaiah (Yeshayahu) the son of Amoz saw concerning Judah (Yehudah) and Jerusalem (Yerushalayim).

2 And it shall come to pass in the last days, that the mountain of יהוה's house shall be established in the top of the mountains, and shall be exalted above the hills; and all nations shall flow unto it.

3 And many people shall go and say, "Come you, and let us go up to the mountain of יהוה, to the house of the God (Elohim) of Jacob (Yaaqov); and He will teach us of His ways, and we will walk in His paths." For out of Zion (Tsiyon) shall go forth the Torah, and the word of יהוה from Jerusalem (Yerushalayim).

4 And He shall judge among the nations, and shall rebuke many people; and they shall beat their swords into plowshares, and their spears into pruning hooks; nation shall not lift up sword against nation, neither shall they learn war any more.

5 O house of Jacob (Yaaqov), come you, and let us walk in the light of יהוה.

6 Therefore You have forsaken Your people the house of Jacob (Yaaqov), because they be replenished from the east, and are soothsayers like the Philistines, and they please themselves in the children of strangers.

7 Their land also is full of silver and gold, neither is there any end of their treasures; their land is also full of horses, neither is there any end of their chariots.

8 Their land also is full of idols; they worship the work of their own hands, that which their own fingers have made.

9 And the mean man boweth down, and the great man humbleth himself; therefore forgive them not.

10 Enter into the rock, and hide you in the dust, for fear of יהוה, and for the glory of His majesty.

11 The lofty looks of man shall be humbled, and the haughtiness of men shall be bowed down,

and יהוה alone shall be exalted in that day.

12 For the day of יהוה of hosts (YHWH Tsevaot) shall be upon every one that is proud and lofty, and upon every one that is lifted up; and he shall be brought low;

13 And upon all the cedars of Lebanon, that are high and lifted up, and upon all the oaks of Bashan;

14 And upon all the high mountains, and upon all the hills that are lifted up,

15 And upon every high tower, and upon every fenced wall,

16 And upon all the ships of Tarshish, and upon all pleasant pictures.

17 And the loftiness of man shall be bowed down, and the haughtiness of men shall be made low; and יהוה alone shall be exalted in that day.

18 And the idols He shall utterly abolish.

19 And they shall go into the holes of the rocks, and into the caves of the earth, for fear of יהוה, and for the glory of His majesty, when He ariseth to shake terribly the earth.

20 In that day a man shall cast his idols of silver, and his idols of gold, which they made each one for himself to worship, to the moles and to the bats;

21 To go into the clefts of the rocks, and into the tops of the ragged rocks, for fear of יהוה, and for the glory of His majesty, when He ariseth to shake terribly the earth.

22 Cease you from man, whose breath is in his nostrils; for wherein is he to be accounted of?

3 For, behold, the Lord יהוה of hosts (Adonai YHWH Tsevaot), doth take away from Jerusalem (Yerushalayim) and from Judah (Yehudah) the stay and the staff, the whole stay of bread, and the whole stay of water,

2 The mighty man, and the man of war, the judge, and the prophet, and the prudent, and the ancient,

3 The captain of fifty, and the honourable man, and the counsellor, and the cunning artificer, and the eloquent orator.

4 "And I will give children to be their princes, and babes shall rule over them.

5 And the people shall be oppressed, every one by another, and every one by his neighbor; the child shall behave himself proudly against the ancient, and the base against the honorable."

6 When a man shall take hold of his brother of the house of his father, saying, "You have

clothing, be you our ruler, and let this ruin be under your hand;"

7 In that day shall he swear, saying, "I will not be a healer, for in my house is neither bread nor clothing; make me not a ruler of the people."

8 For Jerusalem (Yerushalayim) is ruined, and Judah (Yehudah) is fallen, because their tongue and their doings are against יהוה, to provoke the eyes of His glory.

9 The shew of their countenance doth witness against them; and they declare their sin as Sodom, they hide it not. Woe unto their soul! For they have rewarded evil unto themselves.

10 Say you to the righteous, that it shall be well with him, for they shall eat the fruit of their doings.

11 Woe unto the wicked! It shall be ill with him, for the reward of his hands shall be given him.

12 As for My people, children are their oppressors, and women rule over them. O My people, those who lead you cause you to err, and destroy the way of your paths."

13 יהוה standeth up to plead, and standeth to judge the people.

14 יהוה will enter into judgment with the ancients of His people, and the princes thereof: "For you have eaten up the vineyard; the spoil of the poor is in your houses.

15 What mean you that you beat My people to pieces, and grind the faces of the poor?" saith Lord יהוה of hosts (Adonai YHWH Tsevaot).

16 Moreover יהוה saith: "Because the daughters of Zion (Tsiyon) are haughty, and walk with stretched forth necks and wanton eyes, walking and mincing as they go, and making a tinkling with their feet;

17 Therefore the Lord (Adonai) will smite with a scab the crown of the head of the daughters of Zion (Tsiyon), and יהוה will discover their secret parts."

18 In that day the Lord (Adonai) will take away the bravery of their tinkling ornaments about their feet, and their cauls, and their round tires like the moon,

19 The chains, and the bracelets, and the mufflers,

20 The bonnets, and the ornaments of the legs, and the headbands, and the tablets, and the earrings,

21 The rings, and nose jewels,

22 The changeable suits of apparel, and the

mantles, and the wimples, and the crisping pins,

23 The glasses, and the fine linen, and the hoods, and the vails.

24 And it shall come to pass, that instead of sweet smell there shall be stink; and instead of a girdle a rent; and instead of well set hair baldness; and instead of a stomacher a girding of sackcloth; and burning instead of beauty.

25 Your men shall fall by the sword, and your mighty in the war.

26 And her gates shall lament and mourn; and she being desolate shall sit upon the ground.

4 And in that day seven women shall take hold of one man, saying, "We will eat our own bread, and wear our own apparel; only let us be called by your name, to take away our reproach."

2 In that day shall the branch of יהוה be beautiful and glorious, and the fruit of the earth shall be excellent and comely for them that are escaped of Yisrael.

3 And it shall come to pass, that he that is left in Zion (Tsiyon), and he that remaineth in Jerusalem (Yerushalayim), shall be called holy, even every one that is written among the living in Jerusalem (Yerushalayim);

4 When the Lord (Adonai) shall have washed away the filth of the daughters of Zion (Tsiyon), and shall have purged the blood of Jerusalem (Yerushalayim) from the midst thereof by the spirit of judgment, and by the spirit of burning.

5 And יהוה will create upon every dwelling place of Mount Zion (Tsiyon), and upon her assemblies, a cloud and smoke by day, and the shining of a flaming fire by night; for upon all the glory shall be a defence.

6 And there shall be a tabernacle for a shadow in the daytime from the heat, and for a place of refuge, and for a covert from storm and from rain.

5 Now will I sing to my wellbeloved a song of my beloved touching his vineyard. My wellbeloved hath a vineyard in a very fruitful hill.

2 And he fenced it, and gathered out the stones thereof, and planted it with the choicest vine, and built a tower in the midst of it, and also made a winepress therein; and he looked that it should bring forth grapes, and it brought forth wild grapes.

3 And now, O inhabitants of Jerusalem

(Yerushalayim), and men of Judah (Yehudah), judge, please, betwixt Me and My vineyard.

4 What could have been done more to my vineyard, that I have not done in it? Wherefore, when I looked that it should bring forth grapes, brought it forth wild grapes?

5 And now, I will tell you what I will do to My vineyard: I will take away the hedge thereof, and it shall be eaten up; and break down the wall thereof, and it shall be trodden down.

6 And I will lay it waste; it shall not be pruned, nor digged, but there shall come up briers and thorns. I will also command the clouds that they rain no rain upon it."

7 For the vineyard of יהוה of hosts (YHWH Tsevaot) is the house of Yisrael, and the men of Judah (Yehudah) His pleasant plant; and He looked for judgment, but behold oppression; for righteousness, but behold a cry.

8 Woe unto them that join house to house, that lay field to field, till there be no place, that they may be placed alone in the midst of the earth!

9 In mine ears said יהוה of hosts (YHWH Tsevaot), "Of a truth many houses shall be desolate, even great and fair, without inhabitant.

10 Yea, ten acres of vineyard shall yield one bath, and the seed of a homer shall yield an ephah."

11 Woe unto them that rise up early in the morning, that they may follow strong drink; that continue until night, till wine inflame them!

12 And the harp, and the viol, the tabret, and pipe, and wine, are in their feasts; but they regard not the work of יהוה, neither consider the operation of His hands.

13 Therefore My people are gone into captivity, because they have no knowledge; and their honourable men are famished, and their multitude dried up with thirst.

14 Therefore sheol hath enlarged herself, and opened her mouth without measure; and their glory, and their multitude, and their pomp, and he that rejoiceth, shall descend into it.

15 And the mean man shall be brought down, and the mighty man shall be humbled, and the eyes of the lofty shall be humbled;

16 But יהוה of hosts (YHWH Tsevaot) shall be exalted in judgment, and God (El) that is holy shall be sanctified in righteousness.

17 Then shall the lambs feed after their manner, and the waste places of the fat ones shall strangers eat.

18 Woe unto them that draw iniquity with cords of vanity, and sin as it was with a cart rope,

19 That say, "Let him make speed, and hasten his work, that we may see it; and let the counsel of the Holy One of Yisrael draw near and come, that we may know it!"

20 Woe unto them that call evil good, and good evil; that put darkness for light, and light for darkness; that put bitter for sweet, and sweet for bitter!

21 Woe unto them that are wise in their own eyes, and prudent in their own sight!

22 Woe unto them that are mighty to drink wine, and men of strength to mingle strong drink;

23 Which justify the wicked for reward, and take away the righteousness of the righteous from him!

24 Therefore as the fire devoureth the stubble, and the flame consumeth the chaff, so their root shall be as rottenness, and their blossom shall go up as dust; because they have cast away the Torah of יהוה of hosts (YHWH Tsevaot), and despised the word of the Holy One of Yisrael.

25 Therefore is the anger of יהוה kindled against His people, and He hath stretched forth His hand against them, and hath smitten them; and the hills did tremble, and their carcases were torn in the midst of the streets. For all this His anger is not turned away, but His hand is stretched out still.

26 And He will lift up an ensign to the nations from far, and will hiss unto them from the end of the earth; and, behold, they shall come with speed swiftly.

27 None shall be weary nor stumble among them; none shall slumber nor sleep; neither shall the girdle of their loins be loosed, nor the latchet of their shoes be broken;

28 Whose arrows are sharp, and all their bows bent, their horses' hoofs shall be counted like flint, and their wheels like a whirlwind:

29 Their roaring shall be like a lion, they shall roar like young lions; yea, they shall roar, and lay hold of the prey, and shall carry it away safe, and none shall deliver it.

30 And in that day they shall roar against them like the roaring of the sea: and if one look unto the land, behold darkness and sorrow, and the light is darkened in the heavens thereof.

6 In the year that King Uzziyahu died I saw also the Lord (Adonai) sitting upon a throne,

high and lifted up, and His train filled the temple.

2 Above it stood the seraphim: each one had six wings; with twain he covered his face, and with twain he covered his feet, and with twain he did fly.

3 And one cried unto another, and said: "Holy, holy, holy, is יהוה of hosts (YHWH Tsevaot); the whole earth is full of His glory!"

4 And the posts of the door moved at the voice of him that cried, and the house was filled with smoke.

5 Then said I, "Woe is me! For I am undone; because I am a man of unclean lips, and I dwell in the midst of a people of unclean lips; for mine eyes have seen the King, יהוה of hosts (YHWH Tsevaot)."

6 Then flew one of the seraphim unto me, having a live coal in his hand, which he had taken with the tongs from off the altar:

7 And he laid it upon my mouth, and said: "Behold, this hath touched your lips; and your iniquity is taken away, and your sin purged."

8 Also I heard the voice of the Lord (Adonai), saying: "Whom shall I send, and who will go for us?" Then said I, "Here am I; send me."

9 And He said, "Go, and tell this people, 'Hear you indeed, but understand not; and see you indeed, but perceive not.'

10 Make the heart of this people fat, and make their ears heavy, and shut their eyes; lest they see with their eyes, and hear with their ears, and understand with their heart, and convert, and be healed."

11 Then said I, "Lord (Adonai), how long?" And He answered: "Until the cities be wasted without inhabitant, and the houses without man, and the land be utterly desolate,

12 And יהוה have removed men far away, and there be a great forsaking in the midst of the land.

13 But yet in it shall be a tenth, and it shall return, and shall be eaten; as a teil tree, and as an oak, whose substance is in them, when they cast their leaves. So the holy seed shall be the substance thereof."

7 And it came to pass in the days of Achaz the son of Yotam, the son of Uzziyahu, king of Judah (Yehudah), that Rezin the king of Syria (Aram), and Pekah the son of Remalyahu, king of Yisrael, went up toward Jerusalem

(Yerushalayim) to war against it, but could not prevail against it.

2 And it was told the house of Dawid, saying, "Syria (Aram) is confederate with Efrayim." And his heart was moved, and the heart of his people, as the trees of the wood are moved with the wind.

3 Then said יהוה unto Isaiah (Yeshayahu), "Go forth now to meet Achaz, you, and Shear-Yashuv your son, at the end of the conduit of the upper pool in the highway of the fuller's field;

4 And say unto him: 'Take heed, and be quiet; fear not, neither be fainthearted for the two tails of these smoking firebrands, for the fierce anger of Rezin with Syria (Aram), and of the son of Remalyahu.

5 Because Syria (Aram), Efrayim, and the son of Remalyahu, have taken evil counsel against you, saying,

6 "Let us go up against Judah (Yehudah), and vex it, and let us make a breach therein for us, and set a king in the midst of it, even the son of Tabeal".

7 Thus saith Lord (Adonai) יהוה: "It shall not stand, neither shall it come to pass.

8 For the head of Syria (Aram) is Damascus (Dammeseq), and the head of Damascus (Dammeseq) is Rezin; and within threescore and five years shall Efrayim be broken, that it be not a people.

9 And the head of Efrayim is Samaria (Shomeron), and the head of Samaria (Shomeron) is Remalyahu's son. If you will not believe, surely you shall not be established."'"

10 Moreover יהוה spake again unto Achaz, saying,

11 "Ask you a sign of יהוה your God (YHWH Eloheikha); ask it either in the depth, or in the height above."

12 But Achaz said, "I will not ask, nor will I test יהוה."

13 And he said, "Hear you now, O house of Dawid; Is it a small thing for you to weary men, but will you weary my God (Elohim) also?

14 Therefore Lord (Adonai) Himself shall give you a sign: Behold, a virgin shall conceive, and bear a son, and shall call His name "God is with us ([B48]Immanu El)".

15 Butter and honey shall He eat, that He may know to refuse the evil, and choose the good.

16 For before the child shall know to refuse the

evil, and choose the good, the land that you abhorrest shall be forsaken of both her kings.

17 יהוה shall bring upon you, and upon your people, and upon your father's house, days that have not come, from the day that Efrayim departed from Judah (Yehudah); even the king of Assyria (Ashshur)."

18 And it shall come to pass in that day, that יהוה shall hiss for the fly that is in the uttermost part of the rivers of Egypt (Mitsrayim), and for the bee that is in the land of Assyria (Ashshur).

19 And they shall come, and shall rest all of them in the desolate valleys, and in the holes of the rocks, and upon all thorns, and upon all bushes.

20 In the same day shall the Lord (Adonai) shave with a razor that is hired, namely, by them beyond the river, by the king of Assyria (Ashshur), the head, and the hair of the feet; and it shall also consume the beard.

21 And it shall come to pass in that day, that a man shall nourish a young cow, and two sheep;

22 And it shall come to pass, for the abundance of milk that they shall give he shall eat butter; for butter and honey shall everyone eat that is left in the land.

23 And it shall come to pass in that day, that every place shall be, where there were a thousand vines at a thousand silverlings, it shall even be for briers and thorns.

24 With arrows and with bows shall men come thither; because all the land shall become briers and thorns.

25 And on all hills that shall be digged with the mattock, there shall not come thither the fear of briers and thorns; but it shall be for the sending forth of oxen, and for the treading of lesser cattle.

8 Moreover יהוה said unto me, "Take you a great roll, and write in it with a man's pen concerning Maher-Shalal-Chash-Baz.

2 And I took unto me faithful witnesses to record, Uriyah the priest (kohen), and Zechariah (Zekharyahu) the son of Yeberekhyahu."

3 And I went unto the prophetess (neviah); and she conceived, and bare a son. Then said יהוה to me, "Call his name Maher Shalal Chash Baz;

4 For before the child shall have knowledge to cry, 'My father (Avi),' and 'My mother (Emmi),' the riches of Damascus (Dammeseq) and the spoil of Samaria (Shomeron) shall be taken away before the king of Assyria (Ashshur)."

5 יהוה spake also unto me again, saying:

6 "Forasmuch as this people refuseth the waters of Shiloah that go softly, and rejoice in Rezin and Remalyahu's son;

7 Now therefore, behold, the Lord (Adonai) bringeth up upon them the waters of the river, strong and many, even the king of Assyria (Ashshur), and all his glory; and he shall come up over all his channels, and go over all his banks.

8 And he shall pass through Judah (Yehudah); he shall overflow and go over, he shall reach even to the neck; and the stretching out of his wings shall fill the breadth of your land. [48]God is with us (Immanu El)!

9 Associate yourselves, O you people, and you shall be broken in pieces; and give ear, all you of far countries. Gird yourselves, and you shall be broken in pieces; gird yourselves, and you shall be broken in pieces.

10 Take counsel together, and it shall come to nought; speak the word, and it shall not stand, for God is with us (Immanu El).

11 For יהוה spake thus to me with a strong hand, and instructed me that I should not walk in the way of this people, saying:

12 "Say you not, 'A confederacy,' to all them to whom this people shall say, 'A confederacy'; nor fear you their fear, nor be afraid.

13 יהוה of hosts (YHWH Tsevaot) - sanctify Him! And let Him be your fear, and let Him be your dread.

14 And He shall be for a sanctuary; but for a stone of stumbling and for a rock of offence to both the houses of Yisrael, for a gin and for a snare to the inhabitants of Jerusalem (Yerushalayim).

15 And many among them shall stumble, and fall, and be broken, and be snared, and be taken."

16 Bind up the testimony, seal the teaching among my disciples.

17 And I will wait upon יהוה, that hideth His face from the house of Jacob (Yaaqov), and I will look for Him.

18 Behold, I and the children whom יהוה hath given me are for signs and for wonders in Yisrael from יהוה of hosts (YHWH Tsevaot), who dwelleth in Mount Zion (Tsiyon).

19 And when they shall say unto you, "Seek

unto them that have familiar spirits, and unto wizards that peep, and that mutter;" should not a people seek unto their God (Elohim)? For the living to the dead?

20 To the teaching and to the testimony; if they speak not according to this word, it is because there is no light in them.

21 And they shall pass through it, hardly bestead and hungry; and it shall come to pass, that when they shall be hungry, they shall fret themselves, and curse their king and their God (Elohim), and look upward.

22 And they shall look unto the earth; and behold trouble and darkness, dimness of anguish; and they shall be driven to darkness.

9 Nevertheless the dimness shall not be such as was in her vexation, when at the first he lightly afflicted the land of Zevulun and the land of Naftali, and afterward did more grievously afflict her by the way of the sea, beyond Jordan (Yarden), in Galilee of the nations.

2 The people that walked in darkness have seen a great light: they that dwell in the land of the shadow of death, upon them hath the light shined.

3 You have multiplied the nation, and not increased the joy: they joy before you according to the joy in harvest, and as men rejoice when they divide the spoil.

4 For you have broken the yoke of his burden, and the staff of his shoulder, the rod of his oppressor, as in the day of Midian.

5 For every battle of the warrior is with confused noise, and garments rolled in blood; but this shall be with burning and fuel of fire.

6 For unto us a Child is born, unto us a [B47]Son (Humanity) is given; and the government shall be upon His shoulder; and His name shall be called Wonderful, Counselor, Mighty God (El), Everlasting Father, Prince of Peace.

7 Of the increase of His government and peace there shall be no end, upon the throne of Dawid, and upon his kingdom, to order it, and to establish it with judgment and with justice from henceforth even forever. The zeal of יהוה of hosts (YHWH Tsevaot) will perform this.

8 The Lord (Adonai) sent a word into Jacob (Yaaqov), and it hath lighted upon Yisrael.

9 And all the people shall know, even Efrayim and the inhabitant of Samaria (Shomeron), that say in the pride and stoutness of heart,

10 The bricks are fallen down, but we will build with hewn stones; the sycomores are cut down, but we will change them into cedars.

11 Therefore יהוה shall set up the adversaries of Rezin against him, and join his enemies together;

12 The Syrians (Arammim) before, and the Philistines behind; and they shall devour Yisrael with open mouth. For all this His anger is not turned away, but His hand is stretched out still.

13 For the people turneth not unto Him that smiteth them, neither do they seek יהוה of hosts (YHWH Tsevaot).

14 Therefore יהוה will cut off from Yisrael head and tail, branch and rush, in one day.

15 The ancient and honourable, he is the head; and the prophet that teacheth lies, he is the tail.

16 For the leaders of this people cause them to err; and they that are led of them are destroyed.

17 Therefore the Lord (Adonai) shall have no joy in their young men, neither shall have mercy on their fatherless and widows: for every one is a hypocrite and an evildoer, and every mouth speaketh folly. For all this His anger is not turned away, but His hand is stretched out still.

18 For wickedness burneth as the fire; it shall devour the briers and thorns, and shall kindle in the thickets of the forest, and they shall mount up like the lifting up of smoke.

19 Through the wrath of יהוה of hosts (YHWH Tsevaot) is the land darkened, and the people shall be as the fuel of the fire; no man shall spare his brother.

20 And he shall snatch on the right hand, and be hungry; and he shall eat on the left hand, and they shall not be satisfied; they shall eat every man the flesh of his own arm.

21 Menashsheh, Efrayim; and Efrayim, Menashsheh; and they together shall be against Judah (Yehudah); for all this His anger is not turned away, but His hand is stretched out still.

10 Woe unto them that decree unrighteous decrees, and that write grievousness which they have prescribed;

2 To turn aside the needy from judgment, and to take away the right from the poor of My people, that widows may be their prey, and that they may rob the fatherless!

3 And what will you do in the day of visitation, and in the desolation which shall come from far? To whom will you flee for help? And where

will you leave your glory?

4 Without Me they shall bow down under the prisoners, and they shall fall under the slain." For all this His anger is not turned away, but His hand is stretched out still.

5 "O Assyrian (Ashshur), the rod of Mine anger, and the staff in their hand is Mine indignation.

6 I will send him against a hypocritical nation, and against the people of My wrath will I give him a charge, to take the spoil, and to take the prey, and to tread them down like the mire of the streets.

7 Howbeit he meaneth not so, nor doth his heart think so; but it is in his heart to destroy and cut off nations not a few.

8 For he saith, 'Are not my princes altogether kings?

9 Is not Calno as Carchemish? Is not Hamath as Arpad? Is not Samaria (Shomeron) as Damascus (Dammeseq)?

10 As my hand hath found the kingdoms of the idols, and whose graven images did excel them of Jerusalem (Yerushalayim) and of Samaria (Shomeron);

11 Shall I not, as I have done unto Samaria (Shomeron) and her idols, so do to Jerusalem (Yerushalayim) and her idols?'"

12 Wherefore it shall come to pass, that when the Lord (Adonai) hath performed His whole work upon Mount Zion (Tsiyon) and on Jerusalem (Yerushalayim), "I will punish the fruit of the stout heart of the king of Assyria (Ashshur), and the glory of his high looks."

13 For he saith: "By the strength of my hand I have done it, and by my wisdom; for I am prudent: and I have removed the bounds of the people, and have robbed their treasures, and I have put down the inhabitants like a valiant man.

14 And my hand hath found as a nest the riches of the people; and as one gathereth eggs that are left, have I gathered all the earth; and there was none that moved the wing, or opened the mouth, or peeped."

15 Shall the axe boast itself against him that heweth therewith? Or shall the saw magnify itself against him that shaketh it? As if the rod should shake itself against them that lift it up, or as if the staff should lift up itself, as if it was no wood.

16 Therefore shall the Lord (Adonai), יהוה of hosts (YHWH Tsevaot) send among his fat ones

leanness; and under his glory He shall kindle a burning like the burning of a fire.

17 And the light of Yisrael shall be for a fire, and his Holy One for a flame; and it shall burn and devour his thorns and his briers in one day;

18 And shall consume the glory of his forest, and of his fruitful field, both soul and body; and they shall be as when a standardbearer fainteth.

19 And the rest of the trees of his forest shall be few, that a child may write them.

20 And it shall come to pass in that day, that the remnant of Yisrael, and such as are escaped of the house of Jacob (Yaaqov), shall no more again stay upon him that smote them; but shall stay upon יהוה, the Holy One of Yisrael, in truth.

21 The remnant shall return, even the remnant of Jacob (Yaaqov), unto the mighty God (El).

22 For though Your people Yisrael be as the sand of the sea, yet a remnant of them shall return: the consumption decreed shall overflow with righteousness.

23 For Lord יהוה of hosts (Adonai YHWH Tsevaot) shall make a consumption, even determined, in the midst of all the land.

24 Therefore thus saith Lord יהוה of hosts (Adonai YHWH Tsevaot): "O My people that dwellest in Zion (Tsiyon), be not afraid of the Assyrian (Ashshur); he shall smite you with a rod, and shall lift up his staff against you, after the manner of Egypt (Mitsrayim).

25 For yet a very little while, and the indignation shall cease, and Mine anger in their destruction."

26 And יהוה of hosts (YHWH Tsevaot) shall stir up a scourge for him according to the slaughter of Midian at the rock of Oreb; and as His rod was upon the sea, so shall He lift it up after the manner of Egypt (Mitsrayim).

27 And it shall come to pass in that day, that his burden shall be taken away from off your shoulder, and his yoke from off your neck, and the yoke shall be destroyed because of the anointing.

28 He is come to Aiath, he is passed to Migron; at Michmash he hath laid up his carriages:

29 They are gone over the passage; they have taken up their lodging at Geba; Ramah is afraid; Gibeah of Shaul is fled.

30 Lift up your voice, O daughter of Gallim! Cause it to be heard unto Laish, O poor Anathoth!

31 Madmenah is removed; the inhabitants of

Gebim gather themselves to flee.

32 As yet shall he remain at Nob that day: he shall shake his hand against the mount of the daughter of Zion (Tsiyon), the hill of Jerusalem (Yerushalayim).

33 Behold, the Lord (Adonai), יהוה of hosts (YHWH Tsevaot) shall lop the bough with terror; and the high ones of stature shall be hewn down, and the haughty shall be humbled.

34 And He shall cut down the thickets of the forest with iron, and Lebanon shall fall by a mighty one.

11 And there shall come forth a rod out of the stem of Jesse (Yishai), and a Branch shall grow out of his roots.

2 And the Spirit of יהוה shall rest upon Him, the Spirit of wisdom and understanding, the Spirit of counsel and might, the Spirit of knowledge and of the fear of יהוה.

3 And shall make Him of quick understanding in the fear of יהוה; and He shall not judge after the sight of His eyes, neither reprove after the hearing of His ears;

4 But with righteousness shall He judge the poor, and reprove with equity for the meek of the earth; and He shall smite the earth with the rod of His mouth, and with the breath of His lips shall He slay the wicked.

5 And righteousness shall be the girdle of His loins, and faithfulness the girdle of His reins.

6 "The wolf also shall dwell with the lamb, and the leopard shall lie down with the kid; and the calf and the young lion and the fatling together; and a little child shall lead them.

7 And the cow and the bear shall feed; their young ones shall lie down together; and the lion shall eat straw like the ox.

8 And the sucking child shall play on the hole of the asp, and the weaned child shall put his hand on the cockatrice's den.

9 They shall not hurt nor destroy in all my holy mountain, for the earth shall be full of the knowledge of יהוה, as the waters cover the sea.

10 And in that day there shall be a root of Jesse (Yishai), who shall stand for an ensign of the people; to Him shall the Gentiles (Goyim) seek; and His rest shall be glorious."

11 And it shall come to pass in that day, that the Lord (Adonai) shall set His hand again the second time to recover the remnant of His people, who shall be left, from Assyria (Ashshur), and from Egypt (Mitsrayim), and from Pathros, and from Cush, and from Elam, and from Shinar, and from Hamath, and from the islands of the sea.

12 And He shall set up an ensign for the nations, and shall assemble the outcasts of Yisrael, and gather together the dispersed of Judah (Yehudah) from the four corners of the earth.

13 The envy also of Efrayim shall depart, and the adversaries of Judah (Yehudah) shall be cut off; Efrayim shall not envy Judah (Yehudah), and Judah (Yehudah) shall not vex Efrayim.

14 But they shall fly upon the shoulders of the Philistines toward the west; they shall spoil them of the east together; they shall lay their hand upon Edom and Moav; and the children of Ammon shall obey them.

15 And יהוה shall utterly destroy the tongue of the Egyptian (Mitsri) sea; and with His mighty wind shall He shake His hand over the river, and shall smite it in the seven streams, and make men go over dryshod.

16 And there shall be a highway for the remnant of His people, who shall be left, from Assyria (Ashshur); like as it was to Yisrael in the day that He came up out of the land of Egypt (Mitsrayim).

12 And in that day you shalt say, "O יהוה, I will praise You; though You wast angry with me, Your anger is turned away, and You comfortedst me.

2 Behold, God (El) is my salvation; I will trust, and not be afraid; 'For יה (Yah), יהוה is my strength and my song; He also has become my salvation.'"

3 Therefore with joy shall you draw water out of the wells of salvation.

4 And in that day shall you say: "Praise יהוה, call upon His name, declare His doings among the people, make mention that His name is exalted.

5 Sing unto יהוה, for He hath done excellent things; this is known in all the earth.

6 Cry out and shout, you inhabitant of Zion (Tsiyon); for great is the Holy One of Yisrael in the midst of you!"

13 The burden of Babylon (Bavel), which Isaiah (Yeshayahu) the son of Amoz did see.

2 Lift you up a banner upon the high mountain, exalt the voice unto them, shake the hand, that

they may go into the gates of the nobles.

3 I have commanded My sanctified ones, I have also called My mighty ones for Mine anger, even them that rejoice in My highness.

4 The noise of a multitude in the mountains, like as of a great people; a tumultuous noise of the kingdoms of nations gathered together: יהוה of hosts (YHWH Tsevaot) mustereth the host of the battle.

5 They come from a far country, from the end of heaven, even יהוה, and the weapons of His indignation, to destroy the whole land.

6 Howl you; for the day of יהוה is at hand; it shall come as a destruction from the Almighty.

7 Therefore shall all hands be faint, and every man's heart shall melt;

8 And they shall be afraid: pangs and sorrows shall take hold of them; they shall be in pain as a woman that travaileth; they shall be amazed one at another; their faces shall be as flames.

9 Behold, the day of יהוה cometh, cruel both with wrath and fierce anger, to lay the land desolate; and He shall destroy the sinners thereof out of it.

10 For the stars of heaven and the constellations thereof shall not give their light; the sun shall be darkened in his going forth, and the moon shall not cause her light to shine.

11 And I will punish the world for their evil, and the wicked for their iniquity; and I will cause the arrogancy of the proud to cease, and will lay low the haughtiness of the terrible.

12 I will make a man more precious than fine gold; even a man than the golden wedge of Ophir.

13 Therefore I will shake the heavens, and the earth shall remove out of her place, in the wrath of יהוה of hosts (YHWH Tsevaot), and in the day of His fierce anger.

14 And it shall be as the chased roe, and as a sheep that no man taketh up: they shall every man turn to his own people, and flee every one into his own land.

15 Every one that is found shall be thrust through; and every one that is joined unto them shall fall by the sword.

16 Their children also shall be dashed to pieces before their eyes; their houses shall be spoiled, and their wives ravished.

17 "Behold, I will stir up the Medes against them, which shall not regard silver; and as for gold, they shall not delight in it.

18 Their bows also shall dash the young men to pieces; and they shall have no pity on the fruit of the womb; their eye shall not spare children.

19 And Babylon (Bavel), the glory of kingdoms, the beauty of the Chaldees' excellency, shall be as when God (Elohim) overthrew Sodom and Gomorrah.

20 It shall never be inhabited, neither shall it be dwelt in from generation to generation; nor shall the Arabian pitch tent there; neither shall the shepherds make their fold there.

21 But wild beasts of the desert shall lie there; and their houses shall be full of doleful creatures; and owls shall dwell there, and satyrs shall dance there.

22 And the wild beasts of the islands shall cry in their desolate houses, and dragons in their pleasant palaces: and her time is near to come, and her days shall not be prolonged."

14 For יהוה will have mercy on Jacob (Yaaqov), and will yet choose Yisrael, and set them in their own land; and the strangers shall be joined with them, and they shall cleave to the house of Jacob (Yaaqov).

2 And the people shall take them, and bring them to their place; and the house of Yisrael shall possess them in the land of יהוה for servants and handmaids; and they shall take them captives, whose captives they were; and they shall rule over their oppressors.

3 And it shall come to pass in the day that יהוה shall give you rest from your sorrow, and from your fear, and from the hard bondage wherein you wast made to serve,

4 That you shalt take up this proverb against the king of Babylon (Bavel), and say: "How hath the oppressor ceased! The golden city ceased!

5 יהוה hath broken the staff of the wicked, and the sceptre of the rulers.

6 He who smote the people in wrath with a continual stroke, he that ruled the nations in anger, is persecuted, and none hindereth.

7 The whole earth is at rest, and is quiet; they break forth into singing.

8 Yea, the fir trees rejoice at you, and the cedars of Lebanon, saying, 'Since you are laid down, no feller is come up against us.'

9 Hell (Sheol) from beneath is moved for you to meet you at your coming; it stirreth up the dead for you, even all the chief ones of the earth; it

hath raised up from their thrones all the kings of the nations.

10 All they shall speak and say unto you: 'Are you also become weak as we? Are you become like unto us?

11 Your pomp is brought down to the sheol, and the noise of your viols; the worm is spread under you, and the worms cover you.'

12 How are you fallen from heaven, O Lucifer (Heylel), son of the morning! How are you cut down to the ground, which didst weaken the nations!

13 For you have said in your heart: 'I will ascend into heaven, I will exalt my throne above the stars of God (El); I will sit also upon the mount of the congregation, in the sides of the north;

14 I will ascend above the heights of the clouds; I will be like the Most High (Elyon).'

15 Yet you shalt be brought down to hell (sheol), to the sides of the pit.

16 They that see you shall narrowly look upon you, and consider you, saying: 'Is this the man that made the earth to tremble, that did shake kingdoms;

17 That made the world as a wilderness, and destroyed the cities thereof; that opened not the house of his prisoners?'

18 All the kings of the nations, even all of them, lie in glory, every one in his own house.

19 But you are cast out of your grave like an abominable branch, and as the raiment of those that are slain, thrust through with a sword, that go down to the stones of the pit; as a carcase trodden under feet.

20 You shalt not be joined with them in burial, because you have destroyed your land, and slain your people; the seed of evildoers shall never be renowned.

21 Prepare slaughter for his children for the iniquity of their fathers; that they do not rise, nor possess the land, nor fill the face of the world with cities."

22 "For I will rise up against them," saith יהוה of hosts (YHWH Tsevaot), "And cut off from Babylon (Bavel) the name, and remnant, and son, and nephew," saith יהוה.

23 I will also make it a possession for the bittern, and pools of water: and I will sweep it with the besom of destruction, saith יהוה of hosts (YHWH Tsevaot).

24 יהוה of hosts (YHWH Tsevaot) hath sworn,

saying, "Surely as I have thought, so shall it come to pass; and as I have purposed, so shall it stand;

25 That I will break the Assyrian (Ashshur) in my land, and upon my mountains tread him under foot: then shall his yoke depart from off them, and his burden depart from off their shoulders.

26 This is the purpose that is purposed upon the whole earth; and this is the hand that is stretched out upon all the nations.

27 For יהוה of hosts (YHWH Tsevaot) hath purposed, and who shall disannul it? And His hand is stretched out, and who shall turn it back?"

28 In the year that King Achaz died was this burden.

29 Rejoice not you, whole Palestina (Peleshet), because the rod of him that smote you is broken; for out of the serpent's root shall come forth a cockatrice, and his fruit shall be a fiery flying serpent.

30 And the firstborn of the poor shall feed, and the needy shall lie down in safety; and I will kill your root with famine, and he shall slay your remnant.

31 Howl, O gate; cry, O city; you, whole Palestina (Peleshet), art dissolved; for there shall come from the north a smoke, and none shall be alone in his appointed times."

32 What shall one then answer the messengers of the nation? That יהוה hath founded Zion (Tsiyon), and the poor of His people shall trust in it.

15 The burden of Moav. Because in the night Ar of Moav is laid waste, and brought to silence; because in the night Kir of Moav is laid waste, and brought to silence;

2 He is gone up to the temple (bayit), and to Dibon, the high places, to weep. Moav shall howl over Nebo, and over Medeba; on all their heads shall be baldness, and every beard cut off.

3 In their streets they shall gird themselves with sackcloth; on the tops of their houses, and in their streets, every one shall howl, weeping abundantly.

4 And Heshbon and Elealeh shall cry; their voice shall be heard even unto Yahats; therefore the armed soldiers of Moav shall cry out; his life shall be grievous unto him.

5 My heart shall cry out for Moav; his fugitives

shall flee unto Zoar, a heifer of three years old; for by the mounting up of Luhith with weeping shall they go it up; for in the way of Horonaim they shall raise up a cry of destruction.

6 For the waters of Nimrim shall be desolate, for the hay is withered away, the grass faileth, there is no green thing.

7 Therefore the abundance they have gotten, and that which they have laid up, shall they carry away to the brook of the willows.

8 For the cry is gone round about the borders of Moav; the howling thereof unto Eglaim, and the howling thereof unto Beerelim.

9 For the waters of Dimon shall be full of blood; for I will bring more upon Dimon, lions upon him that escapeth of Moav, and upon the remnant of the land.

16 Send you the lamb to the ruler of the land from Sela to the wilderness, unto the mount of the daughter of Zion (Tsiyon).

2 For it shall be, that, as a wandering bird cast out of the nest, so the daughters of Moav shall be at the fords of Arnon.

3 "Take counsel, execute judgment; make your shadow as the night in the midst of the noonday; hide the outcasts; bewray not him that wandereth.

4 Let mine outcasts dwell with you, Moav; be you a covert to them from the face of the spoiler; for the extortioner is at an end, the spoiler ceaseth, the oppressors are consumed out of the land.

5 And in mercy shall the throne be established; and he shall sit upon it in truth in the tabernacle of Dawid, judging, and seeking judgment, and hasting righteousness."

6 We have heard of the pride of Moav; he is very proud; even of his haughtiness, and his pride, and his wrath; but his lies shall not be so.

7 Therefore shall Moav howl for Moav, every one shall howl; for the foundations of Kirhareseth shall you mourn; surely they are stricken.

8 For the fields of Heshbon languish, and the vine of Sibmah: the lords of the heathen have broken down the principal plants thereof, they are come even unto Yazer, they wandered through the wilderness. Her branches are stretched out, they are gone over the sea.

9 Therefore I will bewail with the weeping of Yazer the vine of Sibmah; I will water you with my tears, O Heshbon, and Elealeh; for the shouting for your summer fruits and for your harvest is fallen.

10 And gladness is taken away, and joy out of the plentiful field; and in the vineyards there shall be no singing, neither shall there be shouting; the treaders shall tread out no wine in their presses; I have made their vintage shouting to cease.

11 Wherefore my bowels shall sound like a harp for Moav, and mine inward parts for Kirharesh.

12 And it shall come to pass, when it is seen that Moav is weary on the high place, that he shall come to his sanctuary to pray; but he shall not prevail.

13 This is the word that יהוה hath spoken concerning Moav since that time.

14 But now יהוה hath spoken, saying, "Within three years, as the years of a hireling, and the glory of Moav shall be contemned, with all that great multitude; and the remnant shall be very small and feeble."

17 The burden of Damascus (Dammeseq). "Behold, Damas-cus (Dammeseq) is taken away from being a city, and it shall be a ruinous heap.

2 The cities of Aroer are forsaken; they shall be for flocks, which shall lie down, and none shall make them afraid.

3 The fortress also shall cease from Efrayim, and the kingdom from Damascus (Dammeseq), and the remnant of Syria (Aram); they shall be as the glory of the children of Yisrael," saith יהוה of hosts (YHWH Tsevaot).

4 "And in that day it shall come to pass, that the glory of Jacob (Yaaqov) shall be made thin, and the fatness of his flesh shall wax lean.

5 And it shall be as when the harvestman gathereth the corn, and reapeth the ears with his arm; and it shall be as he that gathereth ears in the valley of Rephaim.

6 Yet gleaning grapes shall be left in it, as the shaking of an olive tree, two or three berries in the top of the uppermost bough, four or five in the outmost fruitful branches thereof," saith יהוה God of Israel (Elohei Yisrael).

7 At that day shall a man look to his Maker, and his eyes shall have respect to the Holy One of Yisrael.

8 And he shall not look to the altars, the work of his hands, neither shall respect that which

his fingers have made, either the Asherim, or the sun-pillars.

9 In that day shall his strong cities be as a forsaken bough, and an uppermost branch, which they left because of the children of Yisrael; and there shall be desolation.

10 Because you have forgotten the God (Elohim) of your salvation, and hast not been mindful of the rock of your strength, therefore shalt you plant pleasant plants, and shalt set it with strange slips.

11 In the day shalt you make your plant to grow, and in the morning shalt you make your seed to flourish; but the harvest shall be a heap in the day of grief and of desperate sorrow.

12 Woe to the multitude of many people, which make a noise like the noise of the seas; and to the rushing of nations, that make a rushing like the rushing of mighty waters!

13 The nations shall rush like the rushing of many waters; but God (Elohim) shall rebuke them, and they shall flee far off, and shall be chased as the chaff of the mountains before the wind, and like a rolling thing before the whirlwind.

14 And behold at eveningtide trouble; and before the morning he is not. This is the portion of them that spoil us, and the lot of them that rob us.

18 Woe to the land shadowing with wings, which is beyond the rivers of Ethiopia (Kush);

2 That sendeth ambassadors by the sea, even in vessels of bulrushes upon the waters, saying, "Go, you swift messengers, to a nation scattered and peeled, to a people feared from their beginning and until now; a nation meted out and trodden down, whose land the rivers have spoiled!"

3 All you inhabitants of the world, and dwellers on the earth, see you, when he lifteth up an ensign on the mountains; and when he bloweth a trumpet, hear you.

4 For so יהוה said unto me, "I will take My rest, and I will consider in My dwelling place like a clear heat upon herbs, and like a cloud of dew in the heat of harvest."

5 For afore the harvest, when the bud is perfect, and the sour grape is ripening in the flower, he shall both cut off the sprigs with pruning hooks, and take away and cut down the branches.

6 They shall be left together unto the fowls of the mountains, and to the beasts of the earth: and the fowls shall summer upon them, and all the beasts of the earth shall winter upon them.

7 In that time shall the present be brought unto יהוה of hosts (YHWH Tsevaot) of a people scattered and peeled, and from a people feared from their beginning and until now; a nation meted out and trodden under foot, whose land the rivers have spoiled, to the place of the name of יהוה of hosts (YHWH Tsevaot), the Mount Zion (Tsiyon).

19 The burden of Egypt (Mitsrayim). Behold, יהוה rideth upon a swift cloud, and shall come into Egypt (Mitsrayim): and the idols of Egypt (Mitsrayim) shall be moved at His presence, and the heart of Egypt (Mitsrayim) shall melt in the midst of it.

2 And I will set the Egyptians (Mitsrayim) against the Egyptians (Mitsrayim); and they shall fight every one against his brother, and every one against his neighbour; city against city, and kingdom against kingdom.

3 And the spirit of Egypt (Mitsrayim) shall fail in the midst thereof; and I will destroy the counsel thereof; and they shall seek to the idols, and to the charmers, and to them that have familiar spirits, and to the wizards.

4 And the Egyptians (Mitsrayim) will I give over into the hand of a cruel lord (adon); and a fierce king shall rule over them, saith the Lord (Adonai), יהוה of hosts (YHWH Tsevaot).

5 And the waters shall fail from the sea, and the river shall be wasted and dried up.

6 And they shall turn the rivers far away; and the brooks of defence shall be emptied and dried up; the reeds and flags shall wither.

7 The paper reeds by the brooks, by the mouth of the brooks, and every thing sown by the brooks, shall wither, be driven away, and be no more.

8 The fishers also shall mourn, and all they that cast angle into the brooks shall lament, and they that spread nets upon the waters shall languish.

9 Moreover they that work in fine flax, and they that weave networks, shall be confounded.

10 And they shall be broken in the purposes thereof, all that make sluices and ponds for fish.

11 Surely the princes of Zoan are fools, the counsel of the wise counsellors of Pharaoh (Paroh) is become brutish. How say you unto

Pharaoh (Paroh), I am the son of the wise, the son of ancient kings?

12 Where are they? Where are your wise men? And let them tell you now, and let them know what יהוה of hosts (YHWH Tsevaot) hath purposed upon Egypt (Mitsrayim).

13 The princes of Zoan are become fools, the princes of Noph are deceived; they have also seduced Egypt (Mitsrayim), even they that are the stay of the tribes thereof.

14 יהוה hath mingled a perverse spirit in the midst thereof; and they have caused Egypt (Mitsrayim) to err in every work thereof, as a drunken man staggereth in his vomit.

15 Neither shall there be any work for Egypt (Mitsrayim), which the head or tail, branch or rush, may do.

16 In that day shall Egypt (Mitsrayim) be like unto women; and it shall be afraid and fear because of the shaking of the hand of יהוה of hosts (YHWH Tsevaot), which He shaketh over it.

17 And the land of Judah (Yehudah) shall be a terror unto Egypt (Mitsrayim), every one that maketh mention thereof shall be afraid in himself, because of the counsel of יהוה of hosts (YHWH Tsevaot), which He hath determined against it.

18 In that day shall five cities in the land of Egypt (Mitsrayim) speak the language of Canaan, and swear to יהוה of hosts (YHWH Tsevaot); one shall be called, The City of Destruction.

19 In that day shall there be an altar to יהוה in the midst of the land of Egypt (Mitsrayim), and a pillar at the border thereof to יהוה.

20 And it shall be for a sign and for a witness unto יהוה of hosts (YHWH Tsevaot) in the land of Egypt (Mitsrayim); for they shall cry unto יהוה because of the oppressors, and He shall send them a Savior, and a great one, and He shall deliver them.

21 And יהוה shall be known to Egypt (Mitsrayim), and the Egyptians (Mitsrayim) shall know יהוה in that day, and shall do sacrifice and oblation; yea, they shall vow a vow unto יהוה, and perform it.

22 And יהוה shall smite Egypt (Mitsrayim); He shall smite and heal it; and they shall return even to יהוה, and He shall be intreated of them, and shall heal them.

23 In that day shall there be a highway out of Egypt (Mitsrayim) to Assyria (Ashshur), and the Assyrian (Ashshur) shall come into Egypt (Mitsrayim), and the Egyptians (Mitsrayim) into Assyria (Ashshur), and the Egyptians (Mitsrayim) shall serve with the Assyria (Ashshur).

24 In that day shall Yisrael be the third with Egypt (Mitsrayim) and with Assyria (Ashshur), even a blessing in the midst of the land,

25 Whom יהוה of hosts (YHWH Tsevaot) shall bless, saying, "Blessed be Egypt (Mitsrayim) My people, and Assyria (Ashshur) the work of My hands, and Yisrael Mine inheritance."

20 In the year that Tartan came unto Ashdod, (when Sargon the king of Assyria (Ashshur) sent him,) and fought against Ashdod, and took it;

2 At the same time spake יהוה by Isaiah (Yeshayahu) the son of Amoz, saying, "Go and loose the sackcloth from off your loins, and put off your shoe from your foot." And he did so, walking naked and barefoot.

3 And יהוה said, "Like as My servant Isaiah (Yeshayahu) hath walked naked and barefoot three years for a sign and wonder upon Egypt (Mitsrayim) and upon Ethiopia (Kush);

4 So shall the king of Assyria (Ashshur) lead away the Egyptians (Mitsrayim) prisoners, and the Ethiopians (Kushim) captives, young and old, naked and barefoot, even with their buttocks uncovered, to the shame of Egypt (Mitsrayim).

5 And they shall be afraid and ashamed of Ethiopia (Kush) their expectation, and of Egypt (Mitsrayim) their glory.

6 And the inhabitant of this isle shall say in that day, 'Behold, such is our expectation, whither we flee for help to be delivered from the king of Assyria (Ashshur); and how shall we escape?'"

21 The burden of the desert of the sea. As whirlwinds in the south pass through; so it cometh from the desert, from a fearsome land.

2 A grievous vision is declared unto me; the treacherous dealer dealeth treacherously, and the spoiler spoileth. Go up, O Elam; besiege, O Media; all the sighing thereof have I made to cease.

3 Therefore are my loins filled with pain: pangs have taken hold upon me, as the pangs of a woman that travaileth: I was bowed down at the

hearing of it; I was dismayed at the seeing of it.
4 My heart panted, fearfulness affrighted me;
the night of my pleasure hath he turned into
fear unto me.
5 Prepare the table, watch in the watchtower,
eat, drink. Arise, you princes, and anoint the
shield.
6 For thus hath the Lord (Adonai) said unto me;
"Go, set a watchman, let him declare what he
seeth."
7 And he saw a chariot with a couple of
horsemen, a chariot of asses, and a chariot of
camels; and he hearkened diligently with much
heed.
8 And he cried, "A lion, my Lord (Adonai)! I
stand continually upon the watchtower in the
daytime, and I am set in my ward whole nights;
9 And, behold, here cometh a chariot of men,
with a couple of horsemen. And he answered
and said, "Babylon (Bavel) is fallen, is fallen;
and all the graven images of her gods (elohim)
He hath broken unto the ground."
10 O my threshing, and the corn of my floor:
that which I have heard of יהוה of hosts (YHWH
Tsevaot), the God of Israel (Elohei Yisrael),
have I declared unto you.
11 The burden of Dumah. He calleth to me out of
Seir, "Watchman, what of the night? Watchman,
what of the night?"
12 The watchman said, "The morning cometh,
and also the night; if you will enquire, enquire
you; return, come back!"
13 The burden upon Arabia. In the forest in
Arabia shall you lodge, O you travelling
companies of Dedanim.
14 The inhabitants of the land of Tema brought
water to him that was thirsty, they prevented
with their bread him that fled.
15 For they fled from the swords, from the
drawn sword, and from the bent bow, and from
the grievousness of war.
16 For thus hath the Lord (Adonai) said unto
me: "Within a year, according to the years of
a hireling, and all the glory of Kedar shall fail;
17 And the residue of the number of archers, the
mighty men of the children of Kedar, shall be
diminished; for יהוה God of Israel (Elohei
Yisrael) hath spoken it."

22 The burden of the valley of vision. What
aileth you now, that you are wholly gone
up to the housetops?

2 You that art full of stirs, a tumultuous city, a
joyous city; your slain men are not slain with the
sword, nor dead in battle.
3 All your rulers are fled together, they are
bound by the archers; all that are found in you
are bound together, which have fled from far.
4 Therefore said I, "Look away from me; I will
weep bitterly, labour not to comfort me, because
of the spoiling of the daughter of my people."
5 For it is a day of trouble, and of treading down,
and of perplexity by Lord יהוה of hosts (Adonai
YHWH Tsevaot) in the valley of vision,
breaking down the walls, and of crying to the
mountains.
6 And Elam bare the quiver with chariots of men
and horsemen, and Kir uncovered the shield.
7 And it shall come to pass, that your choicest
valleys shall be full of chariots, and the
horsemen shall set themselves in array at the
gate.
8 And he discovered the covering of Judah
(Yehudah), and you didst look in that day to the
armour of the house of the forest.
9 You have seen also the breaches of the city of
Dawid, that they are many; and you gathered
together the waters of the lower pool.
10 And you have numbered the houses of
Jerusalem (Yerushalayim), and the houses have
you broken down to fortify the wall.
11 You made also a ditch between the two walls
for the water of the old pool: but you have not
looked unto the Maker thereof, neither had
respect unto Him that fashioned it long ago.
12 And in that day did Lord יהוה of hosts
(Adonai YHWH Tsevaot) call to weeping, and
to mourning, and to baldness, and to girding
with sackcloth.
13 And behold joy and gladness, slaying oxen,
and killing sheep, eating flesh, and drinking
wine: "Let us eat and drink; for tomorrow we
shall die!"
14 And it was revealed in mine ears by יהוה of
hosts (YHWH Tsevaot), "Surely this iniquity
shall not be purged from you till you die," saith
Lord יהוה of hosts (Adonai YHWH Tsevaot).
15 Thus saith Lord יהוה of hosts (Adonai HWH
Tsevaot): "Go, get you unto this treasurer, even
unto Shebna, which is over the house, and say:
16 'What have you here? And whom have you
here, that you have hewed you out a sepulchre
here, as he that heweth him out a sepulchre on

high, and that graveth an habitation for himself in a rock?

17 Behold, יהוה will carry you away with a mighty captivity, and will surely cover you.

18 He will surely violently turn and toss you like a ball into a large country: there shalt you die, and there the chariots of your glory shall be the shame of your lord (adon)'s house.

19 And I will drive you from your station, and from your state shall he pull you down.

20 And it shall come to pass in that day, that I will call my servant Elyaqim the son of Hilkiah (Chilqiyahu);

21 And I will clothe him with your robe, and strengthen him with your girdle, and I will commit your government into his hand; and he shall be a father to the inhabitants of Jerusalem (Yerushalayim), and to the house of Judah (Yehudah).

22 And the key of the house of Dawid will I lay upon his shoulder; so he shall open, and none shall shut; and he shall shut, and none shall open.

23 And I will fasten him as a nail in a sure place; and he shall be for a glorious throne to his father's house.

24 And they shall hang upon him all the glory of his father's house, the offspring and the issue, all vessels of small quantity, from the vessels of cups, even to all the vessels of flagons.

25 'In that day,' saith יהוה of hosts (YHWH Tsevaot), 'shall the nail that is fastened in the sure place be removed, and be cut down, and fall; and the burden that was upon it shall be cut off; for יהוה hath spoken it.'"

23 The burden of Tyre. Howl, you ships of Tarshish; for it is laid waste, so that there is no house, no entering in; from the land of Chittim it is revealed to them.

2 Be still, you inhabitants of the isle; you whom the merchants of Zidon, that pass over the sea, have replenished.

3 And by great waters the seed of Sihor, the harvest of the river, is her revenue; and she is a mart of nations.

4 Be you ashamed, O Zidon; for the sea hath spoken, even the strength of the sea, saying, "I travail not, nor bring forth children, neither do I nourish up young men, nor bring up virgins."

5 As at the report concerning Egypt (Mitsrayim), so shall they be sorely pained at the report of Tyre.

6 Pass you over to Tarshish; howl, you inhabitants of the isle.

7 Is this your joyous city, whose antiquity is of ancient days? Her own feet shall carry her afar off to sojourn.

8 Who hath taken this counsel against Tyre, the crowning city, whose merchants are princes, whose traffickers are the honourable of the earth?

9 יהוה of hosts (YHWH Tsevaot) hath purposed it, to stain the pride of all glory, and to bring into contempt all the honourable of the earth.

10 Pass through your land as a river, O daughter of Tarshish; there is no more strength.

11 He stretched out His hand over the sea, He shook the kingdoms; יהוה hath given a commandment against the merchant city, to destroy the strong holds thereof.

12 And He said, "You shalt no more rejoice, O you oppressed virgin, daughter of Zidon. Arise, pass over to Chittim; there also shalt you have no rest."

13 Behold the land of the Chaldeans; this people was not, till the Assyrian (Ashshur) founded it for them that dwell in the wilderness. They set up the towers thereof, they raised up the palaces thereof; and he brought it to ruin.

14 Howl, you ships of Tarshish; for your strength is laid waste.

15 And it shall come to pass in that day, that Tyre shall be forgotten seventy years, according to the days of one king. After the end of seventy years it will happen to Tyre as in the song of the harlot:

16 "Take a harp, go about the city, you harlot that hast been forgotten; make sweet melody, sing many songs, that you mayest be remembered."

17 And it shall come to pass after the end of seventy years, that יהוה will visit Tyre, and she shall turn to her hire, and shall commit fornication with all the kingdoms of the world upon the face of the earth.

18 And her merchandise and her hire shall be set apart for יהוה; it shall not be treasured nor laid up; for her merchandise shall be for them that dwell before יהוה, to eat sufficiently, and for durable clothing.

24 Behold, יהוה maketh the earth empty, and maketh it waste, and turneth it upside down, and scattereth abroad the inhabitants thereof.

2 And it shall be, as with the people, so with the priest (kohen); as with the servant, so with his master; as with the maid, so with her mistress; as with the buyer, so with the seller; as with the lender, so with the borrower; as with the taker of usury, so with the giver of usury to him.

3 The land shall be utterly emptied, and utterly spoiled, for יהוה hath spoken this word.

4 The earth mourneth and fadeth away, the world languisheth and fadeth away, the haughty people of the earth do languish.

5 The earth also is defiled under the inhabitants thereof; because they have transgressed the law (torah), changed the ordinance, broken the everlasting covenant.

6 Therefore hath the curse devoured the earth, and they that dwell therein are desolate. Therefore the inhabitants of the earth are burned, and few men left.

7 The new wine mourneth, the vine languisheth, all the merryhearted do sigh.

8 The mirth of tabrets ceaseth, the noise of them that rejoice endeth, the joy of the harp ceaseth.

9 They shall not drink wine with a song; strong drink shall be bitter to them that drink it.

10 The city of confusion is broken down; every house is shut up, that no man may come in.

11 There is a crying for wine in the streets; all joy is darkened, the mirth of the land is gone.

12 In the city is left desolation, and the gate is smitten with destruction.

13 When thus it shall be in the midst of the land among the people, there shall be as the shaking of an olive tree, and as the gleaning grapes when the vintage is done.

14 They shall lift up their voice, they shall sing for the majesty of יהוה, they shall cry aloud from the sea.

15 Wherefore glorify you יהוה in the fires, even the name of יהוה God of Israel (Elohei Yisrael) in the isles of the sea.

16 From the uttermost part of the earth have we heard songs, even glory to the righteous. But I said, "My leanness, my leanness, woe unto me! The treacherous dealers have dealt treacherously; yea, the treacherous dealers have dealt very treacherously."

17 Fear, and the pit, and the snare, are upon you, O inhabitant of the earth.

18 And it shall come to pass, that he who fleeth from the noise of the fear shall fall into the pit; and he that cometh up out of the midst of the pit shall be taken in the snare; for the windows from on high are open, and the foundations of the earth do shake.

19 The earth is utterly broken down, the earth is clean dissolved, the earth is moved exceedingly.

20 The earth shall reel to and fro like a drunkard, and shall be removed like a cottage; and the transgression thereof shall be heavy upon it; and it shall fall, and not rise again.

21 And it shall come to pass in that day, that יהוה shall punish the host of the high ones that are on high, and the kings of the earth upon the earth.

22 And they shall be gathered together, as prisoners are gathered in the pit, and shall be shut up in the prison, and after many days shall they be visited.

23 Then the moon shall be confounded, and the sun ashamed, when יהוה of hosts (YHWH Tsevaot) shall reign in Mount Zion (Tsiyon), and in Jerusalem (Yerushalayim), and before His ancients gloriously.

25 O יהוה, You are my God (Elohim); I will exalt You, I will praise Your name; for You have done wonderful things; Your counsels of old are faithfulness and truth.

2 For You have made of a city a heap; of a defenced city a ruin; a palace of strangers to be no city; it shall never be built.

3 Therefore shall the strong people glorify You, the city of the awesome nations shall fear You.

4 For you have been a strength to the poor, a strength to the needy in his distress, a refuge from the storm, a shadow from the heat, when the blast of the terrible ones is as a storm against the wall.

5 You shalt bring down the noise of strangers, as the heat in a dry place; even the heat with the shadow of a cloud; the branch of the terrible ones shall be brought low.

6 And in this mountain shall יהוה of hosts (YHWH Tsevaot) make unto all people a feast of fat things, a feast of wines on the lees, of fat things full of marrow, of wines on the lees well refined.

7 And He will destroy in this mountain the face of the covering cast over all people, and the vail that is spread over all nations.

8 He will swallow up death in victory; and Lord (Adonai) יהוה will wipe away tears from off all

faces; and the rebuke of His people shall He take away from off all the earth; for יהוה hath spoken it.

9 And it shall be said in that day: "Behold, this is our God (Elohim); we have waited for Him, and He will save us. This is יהוה; we have waited for Him, we will be glad and rejoice in His salvation."

10 For in this mountain shall the hand of יהוה rest, and Moav shall be trodden down under Him, even as straw is trodden down for the dunghill.

11 And He shall spread forth His hands in the midst of them, as he that swimmeth spreadeth forth his hands to swim; and He shall bring down their pride together with the spoils of their hands.

12 And the fortress of the high fort of your walls shall he bring down, lay low, and bring to the ground, even to the dust.

26 In that day shall this song be sung in the land of Judah (Yehudah): "We have a strong city; He sets up walls and bulwarks for safety.

2 Open you the gates, that the righteous nation which keepeth the truth may enter in.

3 You wilt keep him in perfect peace, whose mind is stayed on You, because he trusteth in You.

4 Trust you in יהוה forever, for in יה (Yah), יהוה is everlasting strength.

5 For He bringeth down them that dwell on high; the lofty city, He layeth it low; He layeth it low, even to the ground; He bringeth it even to the dust.

6 The foot shall tread it down, even the feet of the poor, and the steps of the needy."

7 The way of the just is uprightness; You, most upright, dost weigh the path of the just.

8 Yea, in the way of Your judgments, O יהוה, have we waited for You; the desire of our soul is to Your name, and to the remembrance of You.

9 With my soul have I desired You in the night; yea, with my spirit within me will I seek You early; for when Your judgments are in the earth, the inhabitants of the world will learn righteousness.

10 Let favor be shewed to the wicked, yet will he not learn righteousness; in the land of uprightness will he deal unjustly, and will not

behold the majesty of יהוה.

11 יהוה, when Your hand is lifted up, they will not see; but they shall see, and be ashamed for their envy at the people; yea, the fire of Your enemies shall devour them.

12 יהוה, You wilt ordain peace for us, for You also hast wrought all our works in us.

13 O יהוה our God (YHWH Eloheinu), other [B13]lords (adonim) besides You have had dominion over us; but by You only will we make mention of Your name.

14 They are dead, they shall not live; they are deceased, they shall not rise; therefore have You visited and destroyed them, and made all their memory to perish.

15 You have increased the nation, O יהוה, You have increased the nation; You are glorified; You hadst removed it far unto all the ends of the earth.

16 יהוה, in trouble have they visited You, they poured out a prayer when Your chastening was upon them.

17 Like as a woman with child, that draweth near the time of her delivery, is in pain, and crieth out in her pangs; so have we been in Your sight, O יהוה.

18 We have been with child, we have been in pain, we have as it was brought forth wind; we have not wrought any deliverance in the earth; neither have the inhabitants of the world fallen.

19 Your dead men shall live, together with my dead body shall they arise. Awake and sing, you that dwell in dust; for your dew is as the dew of herbs, and the earth shall cast out the dead.

20 Come, my people, enter you into your chambers, and shut your doors about you; hide yourself as it was for a little moment, until the indignation be overpast.

21 For, behold, יהוה cometh out of His place to punish the inhabitants of the earth for their iniquity; the earth also shall disclose her blood, and shall no more cover her slain.

27 In that day יהוה with His sore and great and strong sword shall punish leviathan the piercing serpent, even leviathan that crooked serpent; and He shall slay the dragon that is in the sea.

2 In that day sing you unto her, "A vineyard of red wine.

3 I יהוה do keep it; I will water it every moment; lest any hurt it, I will keep it night and day.

4 Fury is not in Me; who would set the briers and thorns against Me in battle? I would go through them, I would burn them together.

5 Or let him take hold of My strength, that he may make peace with Me; and he shall make peace with Me."

6 He shall cause them that come of Jacob (Yaaqov) to take root; Yisrael shall blossom and bud, and fill the face of the world with fruit.

7 Hath He smitten him, as He smote those that smote him? Or is he slain according to the slaughter of them that are slain by Him?

8 In measure, when it shooteth forth, You wilt debate with it; he stayeth his rough wind in the day of the east wind.

9 By this therefore shall the iniquity of Jacob (Yaaqov) be purged; and this is all the fruit to take away his sin; when he maketh all the stones of the altar as chalkstones that are beaten in sunder, the Asherim and sun-pillars shall not stand up.

10 Yet the defenced city shall be desolate, and the habitation forsaken, and left like a wilderness; there shall the calf feed, and there shall he lie down, and consume the branches thereof.

11 When the boughs thereof are withered, they shall be broken off; the women come, and set them on fire; for it is a people of no understanding; therefore He that made them will not have mercy on them, and He that formed them will shew them no favor.

12 And it shall come to pass in that day, that יהוה shall beat off from the channel of the river unto the stream of Egypt (Mitsrayim), and you shall be gathered one by one, O you children of Yisrael.

13 And it shall come to pass in that day, that the great trumpet shall be blown, and they shall come which were ready to perish in the land of Assyria (Ashshur), and the outcasts in the land of Egypt (Mitsrayim), and shall worship יהוה in the holy mount at Jerusalem (Yerushalayim).

28 Woe to the crown of pride, to the drunkards of Efrayim, whose glorious beauty is a fading flower, which are on the head of the fat valleys of them that are overcome with wine!

2 Behold, the Lord (Adonai) hath a mighty and strong one, which as a tempest of hail and a destroying storm, as a flood of mighty waters overflowing, shall cast down to the earth with the hand.

3 The crown of pride, the drunkards of Efrayim, shall be trodden under feet:

4 And the glorious beauty, which is on the head of the fat valley, shall be a fading flower, and as the hasty fruit before the summer; which when he that looketh upon it seeth, while it is yet in his hand he eateth it up.

5 In that day shall יהוה of hosts (YHWH Tsevaot) be for a crown of glory, and for a diadem of beauty, unto the residue of His people,

6 And for a spirit of judgment to him that sitteth in judgment, and for strength to them that turn the battle to the gate.

7 But they also have erred through wine, and through strong drink are out of the way; the priest (kohen) and the prophet have erred through strong drink, they are swallowed up of wine, they are out of the way through strong drink; they err in vision, they stumble in judgment.

8 For all tables are full of vomit and filthiness, so that there is no place clean.

9 "Whom shall He teach knowledge? and whom shall He make to understand doctrine? Them that are weaned from the milk, and drawn from the breasts.

10 For precept must be upon precept, precept upon precept; line upon line, line upon line; here a little, and there a little."

11 For with stammering lips and another tongue will He speak to this people.

12 To whom He said, "This is the rest wherewith you may cause the weary to rest; and this is the refreshing"; yet they would not hear.

13 But the word of יהוה was unto them precept upon precept, precept upon precept; line upon line, line upon line; here a little, and there a little; that they might go, and fall backward, and be broken, and snared, and taken.

14 Wherefore hear the word of יהוה, "you scornful men, that rule this people which is in Jerusalem (Yerushalayim).

15 Because you have said, "We have made a covenant with death, and with sheol are we at agreement; when the overflowing scourge shall pass through, it shall not come unto us; for we have made lies our refuge, and under falsehood have we hid ourselves."

16 Therefore thus saith Lord (Adonai) יהוה, "Behold, I lay in Zion (Tsiyon) for a foundation a stone, a tried stone, a precious corner stone, a sure foundation. He that believeth shall not make haste.

17 Judgment also will I lay to the line, and righteousness to the plummet; and the hail shall sweep away the refuge of lies, and the waters shall overflow the hiding place.

18 And your covenant with death shall be disannulled, and your agreement with sheol shall not stand; when the overflowing scourge shall pass through, then you shall be trodden down by it.

19 From the time that it goeth forth it shall take you; for morning by morning shall it pass over, by day and by night; and it shall be a terror just to understand the report."

20 For the bed is shorter than that a man can stretch himself on it; and the covering narrower than that he can wrap himself in it.

21 For יהוה shall rise up as in Mount Perazim, He shall be wroth as in the Valley of Giveon, that He may do His work, His strange work; and bring to pass His act, His extraordinary act.

22 Now therefore be you not mockers, lest your bands be made strong; for I have heard from Lord יהוה of hosts (Adonai YHWH Tsevaot) a consump-tion, even determined upon the whole earth.

23 Give you ear, and hear my voice; hearken, and hear my speech.

24 Doth the plowman plow all day to sow? Doth he open and break the clods of his ground?

25 When he hath made plain the face thereof, doth he not cast abroad the fitches, and scatter the cummin, and cast in the principal wheat and the appointed barley and the rie in their place?

26 For his God (Elohim) doth instruct him to discretion, and doth teach him.

27 For the fitches are not threshed with a threshing instrument, neither is a cart wheel turned about upon the cummin; but the fitches are beaten out with a staff, and the cummin with a rod.

28 Bread corn is bruised; because he will not ever be threshing it, nor break it with the wheel of his cart, nor bruise it with his horsemen.

29 This also cometh forth from יהוה of hosts (YHWH Tsevaot), who is wonderful in counsel, and excellent in wisdom.

29 "Woe to Ariel, to Ariel, the city where Dawid dwelt! Add you year to year; let them kill sacrifices.

2 Yet I will distress Ariel, and there shall be heaviness and sorrow: and it shall be unto me as Ariel.

3 And I will camp against you round about, and will lay siege against you with a mount, and I will raise forts against you.

4 And you shalt be brought down, and shalt speak out of the ground, and your speech shall be low out of the dust, and your voice shall be, as of one that hath a familiar spirit, out of the ground, and your speech shall whisper out of the dust.

5 Moreover the multitude of your strangers shall be like small dust, and the multitude of the terrible ones shall be as chaff that passeth away; yea, it shall be at an instant suddenly.

6 You shalt be visited of יהוה of hosts (YHWH Tsevaot) with thunder, and with earthquake, and great noise, with storm and tempest, and the flame of devouring fire.

7 And the multitude of all the nations that fight against Ariel, even all that fight against her and her munition, and that distress her, shall be as a dream of a night vision.

8 It shall even be as when a hungry man dreameth, and, behold, he eateth; but he awaketh, and his soul is empty; or as when a thirsty man dreameth, and, behold, he drinketh; but he awaketh, and, behold, he is faint, and his soul hath appetite; so shall the multitude of all the nations be, that fight against Mount Zion (Tsiyon)."

9 Stay yourselves, and wonder; cry you out, and cry; they are drunken, but not with wine; they stagger, but not with strong drink.

10 For יהוה hath poured out upon you the spirit of deep sleep, and hath closed your eyes; the prophets and your rulers, the seers hath He covered.

11 And the vision of all is become unto you as the words of a book that is sealed, which men deliver to one that is learned, saying, "Read this, please;" and he saith, "I cannot, for it is sealed."

12 And the book is delivered to him that is not learned, saying, "Read this, please"; and he saith, "I am not literate."

13 Wherefore the Lord (Adonai) said,

"Forasmuch as this people draw near Me with their mouth, and with their lips do honor Me, but have removed their heart far from Me, and their fear toward Me is taught by the precept of men;

14 Therefore, behold, I will proceed to do a marvellous work among this people, even a marvellous work and a wonder: for the wisdom of their wise men shall perish, and the understanding of their prudent men shall be hidden."

15 Woe unto them that seek deep to hide their counsel from יהוה, and their works are in the dark, and they say, "Who seeth us?" and "Who knoweth us?"

16 Surely your turning of things upside down shall be esteemed as the potter's clay; for shall the work say of Him that made it, "He made me not?" Or shall the thing framed say of Him that framed it, "He had no understanding?"

17 Is it not yet a very little while, and Lebanon shall be turned into a fruitful field, and the fruitful field shall be esteemed as a forest?

18 And in that day shall the deaf hear the words of the book, and the eyes of the blind shall see out of obscurity, and out of darkness.

19 The meek also shall increase their joy in יהוה, and the poor among men shall rejoice in the Holy One of Yisrael.

20 For the terrible one is brought to nought, and the scorner is consumed, and all that watch for iniquity are cut off:

21 That make a man an offender for a word, and lay a snare for him that reproveth in the gate, and turn aside the just for a thing of nought.

22 Therefore thus saith יהוה, who redeemed Avraham, concerning the house of Jacob (Yaaqov): "Jacob (Yaaqov) shall not now be ashamed, neither shall his face now wax pale.

23 But when he seeth his children, the work of Mine hands, in the midst of him, they shall sanctify My name, and sanctify the Holy One of Jacob (Yaaqov), and shall fear the God of Israel (Elohei Yisrael).

24 They also that erred in spirit shall come to understanding, and they that murmured shall learn doctrine."

30 "Woe to the rebellious children," saith יהוה, "that take counsel, but not of Me; and that cover with a covering, but not of My spirit, that they may add sin to sin;

2 That walk to go down into Egypt (Mitsrayim), and have not asked at My mouth; to strengthen themselves in the strength of Pharaoh (Paroh), and to trust in the shadow of Egypt (Mitsrayim)!

3 Therefore shall the strength of Pharaoh (Paroh) be your shame, and the trust in the shadow of Egypt (Mitsrayim) your confusion.

4 For his princes were at Zoan, and his ambassadors came to Hanes.

5 They were all ashamed of a people that could not profit them, nor be a help nor profit, but a shame, and also a reproach.

6 The burden of the beasts of the south; into the land of trouble and anguish, from whence come the young and old lion, the viper and fiery flying serpent, they will carry their riches upon the shoulders of young asses, and their treasures upon the bunches of camels, to a people that shall not profit them.

7 For the Egyptians (Mitsrayim) shall help in vain, and to no purpose; therefore have I called her 'strength that has been exterminated (rahav hem-shebet).'

8 Now go, write it before them in a table, and note it in a book, that it may be for the time to come forever and ever;

9 That this is a rebellious people, lying children, children that will not hear the Torah of יהוה;

10 Which say to the seers, "See not;" and to the prophets, "Prophesy not unto us right things, speak unto us smooth things, prophesy deceits.

11 Get you out of the way, turn aside out of the path, cause the Holy One of Yisrael to cease from before us."

12 Wherefore thus saith the Holy One of Yisrael: "Because you despise this word, and trust in oppression and perverseness, and stay thereon,

13 Therefore this iniquity shall be to you as a breach ready to fall, swelling out in a high wall, whose breaking cometh suddenly at an instant.

14 And He shall break it as the breaking of the potters' vessel that is broken in pieces; He shall not spare; so that there shall not be found in the bursting of it a sherd to take fire from the hearth, or to take water from the cistern.

15 For thus saith Lord (Adonai) יהוה, the Holy One of Yisrael: "In returning and rest shall you be saved; in quietness and in confidence shall be your strength;" and you would not.

16 But you said, "No, for we will flee upon horses; therefore shall you flee; and, We will

ride upon the swift; therefore shall they that pursue you be swift.

17 One thousand shall flee at the rebuke of one; at the rebuke of five shall you flee: till you be left as a beacon upon the top of a mountain, and as an ensign on a hill.

18 And therefore will יהוה wait, that He may be gracious unto you, and therefore will He be exalted, that He may have mercy upon you; for יהוה is a God (Elohim) of justice; blessed are all they that wait for Him.

19 For the people shall dwell in Zion (Tsiyon) at Jerusalem (Yerushalayim): you shalt weep no more. He will be very gracious unto you at the voice of your cry; when He shall hear it, He will answer you.

20 And though the Lord (Adonai) give you the bread of adversity, and the water of affliction, yet shall not your teachers be removed into a corner any more, but your eyes shall see your teachers.

21 And your ears shall hear a word behind you, saying, "This is the way, walk you in it," when you turn to the right hand, and when you turn to the left.

22 You shall defile also the covering of your graven images of silver, and the ornament of your molten images of gold; you shalt cast them away as a menstruous cloth; you shalt say unto it, "Get you out of here!"

23 Then shall He give the rain of your seed, that you shalt sow the ground withal; and bread of the increase of the earth, and it shall be fat and plenteous. In that day shall your cattle feed in large pastures.

24 The oxen likewise and the young asses that ear the ground shall eat clean provender, which hath been winnowed with the shovel and with the fan.

25 And there shall be upon every high mountain, and upon every high hill, rivers and streams of waters in the day of the great slaughter, when the towers fall.

26 Moreover the light of the moon shall be as the light of the sun, and the light of the sun shall be sevenfold, as the light of seven days, in the day that יהוה bindeth up the breach of His people, and healeth the stroke of their wound.

27 Behold, the name of יהוה cometh from far, burning with His anger, and the burden thereof is heavy; His lips are full of indignation, and His tongue as a devouring fire;

28 And His breath, as an overflowing stream, shall reach to the midst of the neck, to sift the nations with the sieve of vanity; and there shall be a bridle in the jaws of the people, causing them to err.

29 You shall have a song, as in the night when a holy solemnity is kept; and gladness of heart, as when one goeth with a pipe to come into the mountain of יהוה, to the Rock of Yisrael.

30 And יהוה shall cause His glorious voice to be heard, and shall shew the lighting down of His arm, with the indignation of His anger, and with the flame of a devouring fire, with scattering, and tempest, and hailstones.

31 For through the voice of יהוה shall the Assyrian (Ashshur) be beaten down, which smote with a rod.

32 And in every place where the grounded staff shall pass, which יהוה shall lay upon him, it shall be with tabrets and harps: and in battles of shaking will He fight with it.

33 For Tophet is ordained of old; yea, for the king it is prepared. He hath made it deep and large; the pile thereof is fire and much wood; the breath of יהוה, like a stream of brimstone, doth kindle it.

31 Woe to them that go down to Egypt (Mitsrayim) for help; and stay on horses, and trust in chariots, because they are many; and in horsemen, because they are very strong; but they look not unto the Holy One of Yisrael, neither seek יהוה!

2 Yet He also is wise, and will bring evil, and will not call back His words; but will arise against the house of the evildoers, and against the help of them that work iniquity.

3 Now the Egyptians (Mitsrayim) are men, and not God (Elohim); and their horses flesh, and not spirit. When יהוה shall stretch out His hand, both he that helpeth shall fall, and he that is holpen shall fall down, and they all shall fail together.

4 For thus hath יהוה spoken unto me, "Like as the lion and the young lion roaring on his prey, when a multitude of shepherds is called forth against him, he will not be afraid of their voice, nor abase himself for the noise of them; so shall יהוה of hosts (YHWH Tsevaot) come down to fight for Mount Zion (Tsiyon), and for the hill thereof.

5 As birds flying, so will יהוה of hosts (YHWH Tsevaot) defend Jerusalem (Yerushalayim); defending also He will deliver it; and passing over He will preserve it."

6 Turn you unto Him from whom the children of Yisrael have deeply revolted.

7 For in that day every man shall cast away his idols of silver, and his idols of gold, which your own hands have made unto you for a sin.

8 "Then shall the Assyrian (Ashshur) fall with the sword, not of a mighty man; and the sword, not of a mean man, shall devour him; but he shall flee from the sword, and his young men shall be discomfited.

9 And he shall pass over to his strong hold for fear, and his princes shall be afraid of the ensign," saith יהוה, whose fire is in Zion (Tsiyon), and His furnace in Jerusalem (Yerushalayim).

32 Behold, a king shall reign in righteousness, and princes shall rule in judgment.

2 And a man shall be as a hiding place from the wind, and a covert from the tempest; as rivers of water in a dry place, as the shadow of a great rock in a weary land.

3 And the eyes of them that see shall not be dim, and the ears of them that hear shall hearken.

4 The heart also of the rash shall understand knowledge, and the tongue of the stammerers shall be ready to speak plainly.

5 The vile person shall be no more called liberal, nor the churl said to be bountiful.

6 For the vile person will speak villany, and his heart will work iniquity, to practise hypocrisy, and to utter error against יהוה, to make empty the soul of the hungry, and he will cause the drink of the thirsty to fail.

7 The instruments also of the churl are evil: he deviseth wicked devices to destroy the poor with lying words, even when the needy speaketh right.

8 But the liberal deviseth liberal things; and by liberal things shall he stand.

9 Rise up, you women that are at ease; hear my voice, you careless daughters; give ear unto my speech.

10 Many days and years shall you be troubled, you careless women; for the vintage shall fail, the gathering shall not come.

11 Tremble, you women that are at ease; be troubled, you careless ones; strip you, and make you bare, and gird sackcloth upon your loins.

12 They shall lament for the teats, for the pleasant fields, for the fruitful vine.

13 Upon the land of my people shall come up thorns and briers; yea, upon all the houses of joy in the joyous city;

14 Because the palaces shall be forsaken; the multitude of the city shall be left; the forts and towers shall be for dens forever, a joy of wild asses, a pasture of flocks;

15 Until the Spirit be poured upon us from on high, and the wilderness be a fruitful field, and the fruitful field be counted for a forest.

16 Then judgment shall dwell in the wilderness, and righteousness remain in the fruitful field.

17 And the work of righteousness shall be peace; and the effect of righteousness quietness and assurance forever.

18 And my people shall dwell in a peaceable habitation, and in sure dwellings, and in quiet resting places;

19 When it shall hail, coming down on the forest; and the city shall be low in a low place.

20 Blessed are you that sow beside all waters, that send forth thither the feet of the ox and the ass.

33 Woe to you that spoilest, and you wast not spoiled; and dealest treacherously, and they dealt not treacherously with you! When you shalt cease to spoil, you shalt be spoiled; and when you shalt make an end to deal treacherously, they shall deal treacherously with you.

2 O יהוה, be gracious unto us; we have waited for You; be You their arm every morning, our salvation also in the time of trouble.

3 At the noise of the tumult the people fled; at the lifting up of Yourself the nations were scattered.

4 And your spoil shall be gathered like the gathering of the caterpiller: as the running to and fro of locusts shall he run upon them.

5 יהוה is exalted, for He dwelleth on high; He hath filled Zion (Tsiyon) with judgment and righteousness.

6 And wisdom and knowledge shall be the stability of your times, and strength of salvation; the fear of יהוה is his treasure.

7 Behold, their valiant ones shall cry outside, the ambassadors of peace shall weep bitterly.

8 The highways lie waste, the wayfaring man

ceaseth. He hath broken the covenant, He hath despised the cities, He regardeth no man.

9 The earth mourneth and languisheth, Lebanon is ashamed and hewn down: Sharon is like a wilderness; and Bashan and Carmel shake off their fruits.

10 "Now will I rise," saith יהוה; "Now will I be exalted; now will I lift up Myself.

11 You shall conceive chaff, you shall bring forth stubble; your breath, as fire, shall devour you.

12 And the people shall be as the burnings of lime: as thorns cut up shall they be burned in the fire.

13 Hear, you that are far off, what I have done; and, you that are near, acknowledge My might."

14 The sinners in Zion (Tsiyon) are afraid; fearfulness hath surprised the hypocrites. "Who among us shall dwell with the devouring fire? Who among us shall dwell with everlasting burnings?"

15 He that walketh righteously, and speaketh uprightly; he that despiseth the gain of oppressions, that shaketh his hands from holding of bribes, that stoppeth his ears from hearing of blood, and shutteth his eyes from seeing evil:

16 He shall dwell on high: his place of defence shall be the munitions of rocks: bread shall be given him; his waters shall be sure.

17 Your eyes shall see the King in His beauty; they shall behold the land that is very far off.

18 Your heart shall meditate terror: "Where is the scribe? Where is the receiver? Where is he that counted the towers?"

19 You shalt not see a fierce people, a people of a deeper speech than you canst perceive; of a stammering tongue, that you canst not understand.

20 Look upon Zion (Tsiyon), the city of our appointed feasts. Your eyes shall see Jerusalem (Yerushalayim) a quiet habitation, a tabernacle that shall not be taken down; not one of the stakes thereof shall ever be removed, neither shall any of the cords thereof be broken.

21 But there the glorious יהוה will be unto us a place of broad rivers and streams; wherein shall go no galley with oars, neither shall gallant ship pass thereby.

22 For יהוה is our Judge, יהוה is our lawgiver, יהוה is our King; He will save us.

23 Your tacklings are loosed; they could not well strengthen their mast, they could not spread the sail; then is the prey of a great spoil divided; the lame takes the prey.

24 And the inhabitant shall not say, "I am sick"; the people that dwell therein shall be forgiven their iniquity.

34 Come near, you nations, to hear; and hearken, you people! Let the earth hear, and all that is therein; the world, and all things that come forth of it.

2 For the indignation of יהוה is upon all nations, and His fury upon all their armies; He hath utterly destroyed them, He hath delivered them to the slaughter.

3 Their slain also shall be cast out, and their stink shall come up out of their carcases, and the mountains shall be melted with their blood.

4 And all the host of heaven shall be dissolved, and the heavens shall be rolled together as a scroll; and all their host shall fall down, as the leaf falleth off from the vine, and as a falling fig from the fig tree.

5 For My sword shall be bathed in heaven; behold, it shall come down upon Idumea, and upon the people of My curse, to judgment.

6 The sword of יהוה is filled with blood, it is made fat with fatness, and with the blood of lambs and goats, with the fat of the kidneys of rams; for יהוה hath a sacrifice in Bozrah, and a great slaughter in the land of Idumea.

7 And the unicorns shall come down with them, and the bullocks with the bulls; and their land shall be soaked with blood, and their dust made fat with fatness.

8 For it is the day of יהוה's vengeance, and the year of recompences for the controversy of Zion (Tsiyon).

9 And the streams thereof shall be turned into pitch, and the dust thereof into brimstone, and the land thereof shall become burning pitch.

10 It shall not be quenched night nor day; the smoke thereof shall go up forever. From generation to generation it shall lie waste; none shall pass through it forever and ever.

11 But the cormorant and the bittern shall possess it; the owl also and the raven shall dwell in it. And he shall stretch out upon it the line of confusion, and the stones of emptiness.

12 They shall call the nobles thereof to the kingdom, but none shall be there, and all her princes shall be nothing.

13 And thorns shall come up in her palaces, nettles and brambles in the fortresses thereof; and it shall be a habitation of dragons, and a court for owls.

14 The wild beasts of the desert shall also meet with the wild beasts of the island, and the satyr shall cry to his fellow; the screech owl also shall rest there, and find for herself a place of rest.

15 There shall the great owl make her nest, and lay, and hatch, and gather under her shadow; there shall the vultures also be gathered, every one with her mate.

16 "Seek you out of the book of יהוה, and read; no one of these shall fail, none shall want her mate; for His mouth it hath commanded, and His Spirit it hath gathered them.

17 And He hath cast the lot for them, and His hand hath divided it unto them by line; they shall possess it forever, from generation to generation shall they dwell therein."

35 The wilderness and the solitary place shall be glad for them; and the desert shall rejoice, and blossom as the rose.

2 It shall blossom abundantly, and rejoice even with joy and singing; the glory of Lebanon shall be given unto it, the excellency of Carmel and Sharon, they shall see the glory of יהוה, and the excellency of our God (Elohim).

3 Strengthen you the weak hands, and confirm the feeble knees.

4 Say to them that are of a fearful heart, "Be strong, fear not; behold, your God (Elohim) will come with vengeance, even God (Elohim) with a recompence; He will come and save you."

5 Then the eyes of the blind shall be opened, and the ears of the deaf shall be unstopped.

6 Then shall the lame man leap as a hart, and the tongue of the dumb sing: for in the wilderness shall waters break out, and streams in the desert.

7 And the parched ground shall become a pool, and the thirsty land springs of water; in the habitation of dragons, where each lay, shall be grass with reeds and rushes.

8 And a highway shall be there, and a way, and it shall be called The Way of Holiness; the unclean shall not pass over it; but it shall be for those who walks the way, though fools, shall not err therein.

9 No lion shall be there, nor any ravenous beast shall go up thereon, it shall not be found there; but the redeemed shall walk there;

10 And the ransomed of יהוה shall return, and come to Zion (Tsiyon) with songs and everlasting joy upon their heads; they shall obtain joy and gladness, and sorrow and sighing shall flee away.

36 Now it came to pass in the fourteenth year of King Hezekiah (Chizqiyahu), that Senna-cherib king of Assyria (Ashshur) came up against all the defenced cities of Judah (Yehudah), and took them.

2 And the king of Assyria (Ashshur) sent Rabshakeh from Lachish to Jerusalem (Yerushalayim) unto King Hezekiah (Chizqiyahu) with a great army. And he stood by the conduit of the upper pool in the highway of the fuller's field.

3 Then came forth unto him Elyaqim, Hilkiah (Chilqiyahu)'s son, who was over the house, and Shebna the scribe, and Yoach, Asaph's son, the recorder.

4 And Rabshakeh said unto them, "Say you now to Hezekiah (Chizqiyahu), 'Thus saith the great king, the king of Assyria (Ashshur): "What confidence is this wherein you trustest?

5 "I say, sayest you, (but they are but vain words) I have counsel and strength for war. Now on whom dost you trust, that you rebellest against me?

6 Behold, you trustest in the staff of this broken reed, on Egypt (Mitsrayim); whereon if a man leans, it will go into his hand, and pierce it; so is Pharaoh (Paroh) king of Egypt (Mitsrayim) to all that trust in him.

7 But if you say to me, 'We trust in יהוה our God (YHWH Eloheinu);' is it not he, whose high places and whose altars Hezekiah (Chizqiyahu) hath taken away, and said to Judah (Yehudah) and to Jerusalem (Yerushalayim), 'You shall worship before this altar'?"'

8 Now therefore give pledges, I pray you, to my master the king of Assyria (Ashshur), and I will give you two thousand horses, if you be able on your part to set riders upon them!

9 How then wilt you turn away the face of one captain of the least of my master's servants, and put your trust on Egypt (Mitsrayim) for chariots and for horsemen?

10 And am I now come up without יהוה against this land to destroy it? יהוה said unto me, 'Go up against this land, and destroy it.'"

11 Then said Elyaqim and Shebna and Yoach

unto Rabshakeh, "Please speak unto your servants in the Syrian language (Aramit); for we understand it; and speak not to us in the Jews' language (Yehudit), in the ears of the people that are on the wall."

12 But Rabshakeh said, "Hath my master sent me to your master and to you to speak these words? Hath he not sent me to the men that sit upon the wall, that they may eat their own dung, and drink their own piss with you?"

13 Then Rabshakeh stood, and cried with a loud voice in the Jews' language (Yehudit), and said, "Hear you the words of the great king, the king of Assyria (Ashshur)!

14 Thus saith the king, 'Let not Hezekiah (Chizqiyahu) deceive you; for he shall not be able to deliver you.

15 Nor let Hezekiah (Chizqiyahu) make you trust in יהוה, saying, "יהוה will surely deliver us; this city shall not be delivered into the hand of the king of Assyria (Ashshur).'"

16 Hearken not to Hezekiah (Chizqiyahu); for thus saith the king of Assyria (Ashshur): 'Make an agreement with me by a present, and come out to me: and eat you every one of his vine, and every one of his fig tree, and drink you every one the waters of his own cistern;

17 Until I come and take you away to a land like your own land, a land of corn and wine, a land of bread and vineyards.

18 Beware lest Hezekiah (Chizqiyahu) persuade you, saying, "יהוה will deliver us. Hath any of the gods (elohim) of the nations delivered his land out of the hand of the king of Assyria (Ashshur)?

19 Where are the gods (elohim) of Hamath and Arphad? Where are the gods (elohim) of Sepharvaim? And have they delivered Samaria (Shomeron) out of my hand?'"

20 Who are they among all the gods (elohim) of these lands, that have delivered their land out of my hand, that יהוה should deliver Jerusalem (Yerushalayim) out of my hand?

21 But they held their peace, and answered him not a word; for the king's commandment was, saying, "Answer him not."

22 Then came Elyaqim, the son of Hilkiah (Chilqiyahu), that was over the household, and Shebna the scribe, and Yoach, the son of Asaph, the recorder, to Hezekiah (Chizqiyahu) with their clothes rent, and told him the words of Rabshakeh.

37 And it came to pass, when king Hezekiah (Chizqiyahu) heard it, that he rent his clothes, and covered himself with sackcloth, and went into the house of יהוה.

2 And he sent Elyaqim, who was over the household, and Shebna the scribe, and the elders of the priests (kohanim) covered with sackcloth, unto Isaiah (Yeshayahu) the prophet the son of Amoz.

3 And they said unto him, "Thus saith Hezekiah (Chizqiyahu): 'This day is a day of trouble, and of rebuke, and of blasphemy; for the children are come to the birth, and there is not strength to bring forth.

4 It may be יהוה your God (YHWH Eloheikha) will hear the words of Rabshakeh, whom the king of Assyria (Ashshur) his master hath sent to reproach the living God (Elohim Chai), and will reprove the words which יהוה your God (YHWH Eloheikha) hath heard; wherefore lift up your prayer for the remnant that is left.

5 So the servants of King Hezekiah (Chizqiyahu) came to Isaiah (Yeshayahu).'"

6 And Isaiah (Yeshayahu) said unto them, "Thus shall you say unto your master, 'Thus saith יהוה: "Be not afraid of the words that you have heard, wherewith the servants of the king of Assyria (Ashshur) have blasphemed Me.

7 Behold, I will send a blast upon him, and he shall hear a rumour, and return to his own land; and I will cause him to fall by the sword in his own land."'"

8 So Rabshakeh returned, and found the king of Assyria (Ashshur) warring against Libnah; for he had heard that he was departed from Lachish.

9 And he heard say concerning Tirhakah king of Ethiopia (Kush), "He is come forth to make war with you." And when he heard it, he sent messengers to Hezekiah (Chizqiyahu), saying,

10 "Thus shall you speak to Hezekiah (Chizqiyahu) king of Judah (Yehudah), saying, 'Let not your God (Elohim), in whom you trustest, deceive you, saying, "Jerusalem (Yerushalayim) shall not be given into the hand of the king of Assyria (Ashshur)."

11 Behold, you have heard what the kings of Assyria (Ashshur) have done to all lands by destroying them utterly; and shalt you be delivered?

12 Have the gods (elohim) of the nations delivered them which my fathers have destroyed, as Gozan, and Haran, and Rezeph, and the children of Eden which were in Telassar?

13 Where is the king of Hamath, and the king of Arphad, and the king of the city of Sepharvaim, Hena, and Ivah?"'

14 And Hezekiah (Chizqiyahu) received the letter from the hand of the messengers, and read it; and Hezekiah (Chizqiyahu) went up unto the house of יהוה, and spread it before יהוה.

15 And Hezekiah (Chizqiyahu) prayed unto יהוה, saying:

16 O יהוה of hosts (YHWH Tsevaot), God of Israel (Elohei Yisrael), that dwellest between the cherubims (keruvim), You are the God (Elohim), even You alone, of all the kingdoms of the earth. You have made heaven and earth.

17 Incline Your ear, O יהוה, and hear; open Your eyes, O יהוה, and see; and hear all the words of Sennacherib, which hath sent to reproach the living God (Elohim chai).

18 Of a truth, יהוה, the kings of Assyria (Ashshur) have laid waste all the nations, and their countries,

19 And have cast their gods (elohim) into the fire, for they were not God (Elohim), but the work of men's hands, wood and stone; therefore they have destroyed them.

20 Now therefore, O יהוה our God (YHWH Eloheinu), save us from his hand, that all the kingdoms of the earth may know that You are יהוה, even You only."

21 Then Isaiah (Yeshayahu) the son of Amoz sent unto Hezekiah (Yechizqiyahu), saying, "Thus saith יהוה God of Israel (Elohei Yisrael), 'Whereas you have prayed to Me against Sennacherib king of Assyria (Ashshur),

22 This is the word which יהוה hath spoken concerning him: "The virgin, the daughter of Zion (Tsiyon), hath despised you, and laughed you to scorn; the daughter of Jerusalem (Yerushalayim) hath shaken her head at you!

23 Whom have you reproached and blasphemed? And against whom have you exalted your voice, and lifted up your eyes on high? Even against the Holy One of Yisrael.

24 By your servants have you reproached the Lord (Adonai), and hast said, 'By the multitude of my chariots am I come up to the height of the mountains, to the sides of Lebanon; and I will cut down the tall cedars thereof, and the choice fir trees thereof; and I will enter into the height of his border, and the forest of his Carmel.

25 I have digged, and drunk water; and with the sole of my feet have I dried up all the rivers of the besieged places.'

26 Have you not heard long ago, how I have done it; and of ancient times, that I have formed it? Now have I brought it to pass, that you shouldest be to lay waste defenced cities into ruinous heaps.

27 Therefore their inhabitants were of small power, they were dismayed and confounded; they were as the grass of the field, and as the green herb, as the grass on the housetops, and as corn blasted before it be grown up.

28 But I know your abode, and your going out, and your coming in, and your rage against Me.

29 Because your rage against Me, and your tumult, is come up into Mine ears, therefore will I put My hook in your nose, and My bridle in your lips, and I will turn you back by the way by which you camest."'

30 And this shall be a sign unto you, You shall eat this year such as groweth of itself; and the second year that which springeth of the same: and in the third year sow you, and reap, and plant vineyards, and eat the fruit thereof.

31 And the remnant that is escaped of the house of Judah (Yehudah) shall again take root downward, and bear fruit upward.

32 For out of Jerusalem (Yerushalayim) shall go forth a remnant, and they that escape out of Mount Zion (Tsiyon); the zeal of יהוה of hosts (YHWH Tsevaot) shall do this.

33 Therefore thus saith יהוה concerning the king of Assyria (Ashshur): 'He shall not come into this city, nor shoot an arrow there, nor come before it with shields, nor cast a bank against it.

34 By the way that he came, by the same shall he return, and shall not come into this city,' saith יהוה.

35 For I will defend this city to save it for Mine own sake, and for My servant Dawid's sake.'"

36 Then the angel of יהוה went forth, and smote in the camp of the Assyrians (Ashshur) a hundred and fourscore and five thousand: and when they arose early in the morning, behold, they were all dead corpses.

37 So Sennacherib king of Assyria (Ashshur) departed, and went and returned, and dwelt at

Nineveh.

38 And it came to pass, as he was worshipping in the house of Nisroch his god (eloah), that Adrammelech and Sharezer his sons smote him with the sword; and they escaped into the land of Armenia; and Esarhaddon his son reigned in his stead.

38 In those days was Hezekiah (Chizqiyahu) sick unto death. And Isaiah (Yeshayahu) the prophet the son of Amoz came unto him, and said unto him, "Thus saith יהוה: 'Set your house in order, for you shalt die, and not live.'"

2 Then Hezekiah (Chizqiyahu) turned his face toward the wall, and prayed unto יהוה,

3 And said, "Remember now, O יהוה, I beseech You, how I have walked before You in truth and with a perfect heart, and have done that which is good in Your sight. And Hezekiah (Chizqiyahu) wept sore.

4 Then came the word of יהוה to Isaiah (Yeshayahu), saying,

5 "Go, and say to Hezekiah (Chizqiyahu), 'Thus saith יהוה, the God (Elohim) of Dawid your father: "I have heard your prayer, I have seen your tears: behold, I will add unto your days fifteen years.

6 And I will deliver you and this city out of the hand of the king of Assyria (Ashshur); and I will defend this city."'

7 And this shall be a sign unto you from יהוה, that יהוה will do this thing that He hath spoken:

8 Behold, I will bring again the shadow of the degrees, which is gone down in the sun dial of Achaz, ten degrees backward." So the sun returned ten degrees, by which degrees it was gone down.

9 The writing of Hezekiah (Chizqiyahu) king of Judah (Yehudah), when he had been sick, and was recovered of his sickness:

10 I said, "In the cutting off of my days, I shall go to the gates of the sheol; I am deprived of the residue of my years."

11 I said, "I shall not see יה (Yah), יה (Yah) in the land of the living; I shall behold man no more with the inhabitants of the world.

12 Mine age is departed, and is removed from me as a shepherd's tent; I have cut off like a weaver my life. He will cut me off with pining sickness; from day even tonight wilt You make an end of me.

13 I reckoned till morning, that, as a lion, so will he break all my bones; from day even tonight wilt You make an end of me.

14 Like a crane or a swallow, so did I chatter; I did mourn as a dove mine eyes fail with looking upward. O יהוה, I am oppressed; undertake for me!

15 "What shall I say? He hath both spoken unto me, and Himself hath done it. I shall go softly all my years in the bitterness of my soul.

16 O Lord (Adonai), by these things men live, and in all these things is the life of my spirit; so wilt You recover me, and make me to live.

17 Behold, for peace I had great bitterness; but You have in love to my soul delivered it from the pit of corruption; for You have cast all my sins behind Your back.

18 For the sheol cannot praise You, death can not celebrate You; they that go down into the pit cannot hope for Your truth.

19 The living, the living, he shall praise You, as I do this day; the father to the children shall make known Your truth.

20 יהוה was ready to save me; therefore we will sing my songs to the stringed instruments all the days of our life in the house of יהוה."

21 For Isaiah (Yeshayahu) had said, "Let them take a lump of figs, and lay it for a plaister upon the boil, and he shall recover."

22 Hezekiah (Chizqiyahu) also had said, "What is the sign that I shall go up to the house of יהוה?"

39 At that time Merodach-Baladan, the son of Baladan, king of Babylon (Bavel), sent letters and a present to Hezekiah (Chizqiyahu); for he had heard that he had been sick, and was recovered.

2 And Hezekiah (Chizqiyahu) was glad of them, and shewed them the house of his precious things, the silver, and the gold, and the spices, and the precious ointment, and all the house of his armour, and all that was found in his treasures; there was nothing in his house, nor in all his dominion, that Hezekiah (Chizqiyahu) shewed them not.

3 Then came Isaiah (Yeshayahu) the prophet unto king Hezekiah (Chizqiyahu), and said unto him, "What said these men? And from whence came they unto you?" And Hezekiah (Chizqiyahu) said, "They are come from a far country unto me, even from Babylon (Bavel)."

4 Then said he, "What have they seen in your

house?" And Hezekiah (Chizqiyahu) answered, "All that is in mine house have they seen; there is nothing among my treasures that I have not shewed them."

5 Then said Isaiah (Yeshayahu) to Hezekiah (Chizqiyahu), "Hear the word of יהוה of hosts (YHWH Tsevaot):

6 'Behold, the days come, that all that is in your house, and that which your fathers have laid up in store until this day, shall be carried to Babylon (Bavel); nothing shall be left,' saith יהוה.

7 'And of your sons that shall issue from you, which you shalt beget, shall they take away; and they shall be eunuchs in the palace of the king of Babylon (Bavel).'"

8 Then said Hezekiah (Chizqiyahu) to Isaiah (Yeshayahu), "Good is the word of יהוה which you have spoken!" He said moreover, "For there shall be peace and truth in my days."

40 "Comfort you, comfort you My people!" saith your God (Elohim).

2 Speak you comfortably to Jerusalem (Yerushalayim), and cry unto her, that her warfare is accomplished, that her iniquity is pardoned; for she hath received of יהוה's hand double for all her sins.

3 B49The voice of him that crieth in the wilderness, "Prepare you the way of יהוה (Yahwah, YHWH), make straight in the desert a highway for our God (Elohim)."

4 Every valley shall be exalted, and every mountain and hill shall be made low; and the crooked shall be made straight, and the rough places plain;

5 And the glory of יהוה shall be revealed, and all flesh shall see it together; for the mouth of יהוה hath spoken it."

6 The voice said, "Cry out!" And he said, "What shall I cry? All flesh is grass, and all the goodliness thereof is as the flower of the field:

7 The grass withereth, the flower fadeth, because the breath (ruach) of יהוה bloweth upon it; surely the people is grass.

8 The grass withereth, the flower fadeth; but the word of our God (Elohim) shall stand forever."

9 O Zion (Tsiyon), that bringest good tidings, get you up into the high mountain; O Jerusalem (Yerushalayim), that bringest good tidings, lift up your voice with strength; lift it up, be not afraid; say unto the cities of Judah (Yehudah),

"Behold your God (Elohim)!"

10 Behold, Lord (Adonai) יהוה will come with strong hand, and His arm shall rule for Him: behold, His reward is with Him, and His work before Him.

11 He shall feed His flock like a shepherd: He shall gather the lambs with His arm, and carry them in His bosom, and shall gently lead those that are with young.

12 Who hath measured the waters in the hollow of His hand, and meted out heaven with the span, and comprehended the dust of the earth in a measure, and weighed the mountains in scales, and the hills in a balance?

13 Who hath directed the Spirit of יהוה (Ruach YHWH) or being His counsellor hath taught Him?

14 With whom took He counsel, and who instructed Him, and taught Him in the path of judgment, and taught Him knowledge, and shewed to Him the way of understanding?

15 Behold, the nations are as a drop of a bucket, and are counted as the small dust of the balance; behold, He taketh up the isles as a very little thing.

16 And Lebanon is not sufficient to burn, nor the beasts thereof sufficient for a burnt offering.

17 All nations before Him are as nothing; and they are counted to Him less than nothing, and vanity.

18 To whom then will you liken God (Elohim)? Or what likeness will you compare unto Him?

19 The workman melteth a graven image, and the goldsmith spreadeth it over with gold, and casteth silver chains.

20 He that is so impoverished that he hath no oblation chooseth a tree that will not rot; he seeketh unto him a cunning workman to prepare a graven image, that shall not be moved.

21 Have you not known? Have you not heard? Hath it not been told you from the beginning? Have you not understood from the foundations of the earth?

22 It is He that sitteth upon the circle of the earth, and the inhabitants thereof are as grasshoppers; that stretcheth out the heavens as a curtain, and spreadeth them out as a tent to dwell in:

23 That bringeth the princes to nothing; He maketh the judges of the earth as vanity.

24 Yea, they shall not be planted; yea, they shall not be sown: yea, their stock shall not take root

in the earth: and he shall also blow upon them, and they shall wither, and the whirlwind shall take them away as stubble.

25 "To whom then will you liken me, or shall I be equal?" saith the Holy One.

26 Lift up your eyes on high, and behold who hath created these things, that bringeth out their host by number: He calleth them all by names by the greatness of His might, for that He is strong in power; not one faileth.

27 Why sayest you, O Jacob (Yaaqov), and speakest, O Yisrael: "My way is hidden from יהוה, and my judgment is passed over from my God (Elohim)?"

28 Have you not known? Have you not heard, that God of Everlasting (Elohei Olam), יהוה, the Creator of the ends of the earth, fainteth not, neither is weary? There is no searching of His understanding.

29 He giveth power to the faint; and to them that have no might He increaseth strength.

30 Even the youths shall faint and be weary, and the young men shall utterly fall;

31 But they that wait upon יהוה shall renew their strength; they shall mount up with wings as eagles; they shall run, and not be weary; and they shall walk, and not faint.

41 "Keep silence before Me, O islands; and let the people renew their strength; let them come near; then let them speak: let us come near together to judgment.

2 Who raised up the righteous man from the east, called him to His foot, gave the nations before him, and made him rule over kings? He gave them as the dust to his sword, and as driven stubble to his bow.

3 He pursued them, and passed safely; even by the way that he had not gone with his feet.

4 Who hath wrought and done it, calling the generations from the beginning? 'I יהוה, the first, and with the last; I am He.'"

5 The isles saw it, and feared; the ends of the earth were afraid, drew near, and came.

6 They helped every one his neighbour; and every one said to his brother, "Be of good courage!"

7 So the carpenter encouraged the goldsmith, and he that smootheth with the hammer, him that smote the anvil, saying, "It is ready for the sodering"; and he fastened it with nails, that it should not be moved.

8 But you, Yisrael, art My servant, Jacob (Yaaqov) whom I have chosen, the seed of Avraham My friend.

9 You whom I have taken from the ends of the earth, and called you from the chief men thereof, and said unto you, 'You are My servant; I have chosen you, and not cast you away;

10 Fear you not, for I am with you; be not dismayed, for I am your God (Elohim): I will strengthen you; yea, I will help you; yea, I will uphold you with the right hand of My righteousness.'

11 Behold, all they that were incensed against you shall be ashamed and confounded; they shall be as nothing; and they that strive with you shall perish.

12 You shalt seek them, and shalt not find them, even them that contended with you; they that war against you shall be as nothing, and as a thing of nought.

13 For I יהוה your God (YHWH Eloheikha) will hold your right hand, saying unto you, 'Fear not, I will help you.'

14 "Fear not, you worm Jacob (Yaaqov), and you men of Yisrael; I will help you," saith יהוה, and your Redeemer, the Holy One of Yisrael.

15 Behold, I will make you a new sharp threshing instrument having teeth; you shalt thresh the mountains, and beat them small, and shalt make the hills as chaff.

16 You shalt fan them, and the wind shall carry them away, and the whirlwind shall scatter them; and you shalt rejoice in יהוה, and shalt glory in the Holy One of Yisrael.

17 When the poor and needy seek water, and there is none, and their tongue faileth for thirst, I יהוה will hear them, I the God of Israel (Elohei Yisrael) will not forsake them.

18 I will open rivers in high places, and fountains in the midst of the valleys; I will make the wilderness a pool of water, and the dry land springs of water.

19 I will plant in the wilderness the cedar, the shittah tree, and the myrtle, and the oil tree; I will set in the desert the fir tree, and the pine, and the box tree together,

20 That they may see, and know, and consider, and understand together, that the hand of יהוה hath done this, and the Holy One of Yisrael hath created it.

21 "Present your case," saith יהוה. "Bring forth

your strong reasons," saith the King of Jacob (Yaaqov).

22 "Let them bring them forth, and shew us what shall happen; let them shew the former things, what they be, that we may consider them, and know the latter end of them; or declare us things for to come.

23 Shew the things that are to come hereafter, that we may know that you are God (Elohim); yea, do good, or do evil, that we may be dismayed, and behold it together.

24 Behold, you are of nothing, and your work of nought; an abomination is he that chooseth you.

25 I have raised up one from the north, and he shall come; from the rising of the sun shall he call upon My name; and he shall come upon princes as upon morter, and as the potter treadeth clay.

26 Who hath declared from the beginning, that we may know? And beforetime, that we may say, 'He is righteous?' Yea, there is none that sheweth, yea, there is none that declareth, yea, there is none that heareth your words.

27 The first shall say to Zion (Tsiyon), 'Behold, there they are; and I will give to Jerusalem (Yerushalayim) one that bringeth good tidings.

28 For I beheld, and there was no man; even among them, and there was no counsellor, that, when I asked of them, could answer a word.

29 Behold, they are all vanity; their works are nothing; their molten images are wind and confusion.

42 Behold My Servant, whom I uphold; Mine Elect, in whom My soul delighteth; I have put My Spirit upon Him: He shall bring forth judgment to the nations.

2 He shall not cry, nor lift up, nor cause His voice to be heard in the street.

3 A bruised reed shall He not break, and the smoking flax shall He not quench; He shall bring forth judgment unto truth.

4 He shall not fail nor be discouraged, till He have set judgment in the earth; and the isles shall wait for His Torah."

5 Thus saith God (El) יהוה, He that created the heavens, and stretched them out; He that spread forth the earth, and that who cometh out of it; He that giveth breath unto the people upon it, and Spirit to them that walk therein:

6 "I יהוה have called you in righteousness, and will hold your hand, and will keep you, and give

you for a covenant of the people, for a light of the nations;

7 To open the blind eyes, to bring out the prisoners from the prison, and them that sit in darkness out of the prison house.

8 I am יהוה, that is My name; and My glory will I not give to another, neither My praise to graven images.

9 Behold, the former things are come to pass, and new things do I declare; before they spring forth I tell you of them."

10 Sing unto יהוה a new song, and His praise from the end of the earth, you that go down to the sea, and all that is therein; the isles, and the inhabitants thereof.

11 Let the wilderness and the cities thereof lift up their voice, the villages that Kedar doth inhabit. Let the inhabitants of the rock sing, let them shout from the top of the mountains.

12 Let them give glory unto יהוה, and declare His praise in the islands.

13 יהוה shall go forth as a mighty man, He shall stir up jealousy like a man of war. He shall cry, yea, roar; He shall prevail against His enemies.

14 "I have long time holden My peace; I have been still, and refrained Myself; now will I cry like a travailing woman; I will destroy and devour at once.

15 I will make waste mountains and hills, and dry up all their herbs; and I will make the rivers islands, and I will dry up the pools.

16 And I will bring the blind by a way that they knew not; I will lead them in paths that they have not known. I will make darkness light before them, and crooked things straight. These things will I do unto them, and not forsake them.

17 They shall be turned back, they shall be greatly ashamed, that trust in graven images, that say to the molten images, 'You are our gods (elohim).'

18 Hear, you deaf; and look, you blind, that you may see.

19 Who is blind, but My servant? Or deaf, as My messenger that I sent? Who is blind as he who is at peace, and blind as יהוה's servant?

20 Seeing many things, but you observest not; opening the ears, but he heareth not."

21 יהוה is well pleased for His righteousness' sake; He will magnify the [B28a]Law (Torah), and make it honourable.

22 But this is a people robbed and spoiled; they

are all of them snared in holes, and they are hidden in prison houses; they are for a prey, and none delivereth; for a spoil, and none saith, "Restore!"

23 Who among you will give ear to this? Who will hearken and hear for the time to come?

24 Who gave Jacob (Yaaqov) for a spoil, and Yisrael to the robbers? Did not יהוה, He against whom we have sinned? For they would not walk in His ways, neither were they obedient unto His Torah.

25 Therefore He hath poured upon him the fury of His anger, and the strength of battle; and it hath set him on fire round about, yet he knew not; and it burned him, yet he laid it not to heart.

43 But now thus saith יהוה that created you, O Jacob (Yaaqov), and He that formed you, O Yisrael: "Fear not, for I have redeemed you, I have called you by your name; you are Mine.

2 When you passest through the waters, I will be with you; and through the rivers, they shall not overflow you; when you walkest through the fire, you shalt not be burned; neither shall the flame kindle upon you.

3 For I am יהוה your God (YHWH Eloheikha), the Holy One of Yisrael, your Savior; I gave Egypt (Mitsrayim) for your ransom, Ethiopia (Kush) and Seva for you.

4 Since you wast precious in My sight, you have been honourable, and I have loved you; therefore will I give men for you, and people for your life.

5 Fear not, for I am with you; I will bring your seed from the east, and gather you from the west;

6 I will say to the north, 'Give them up!" and to the south, 'Keep not them back!' Bring My sons from far, and My daughters from the ends of the earth;

7 Every one who is called by My name, for I have created him for My glory, I have formed him; yea, I have made him."

8 Bring forth the blind people that have eyes, and the deaf that have ears.

9 Let all the nations be gathered together, and let the people be assembled: who among them can declare this, and shew us former things? Let them bring forth their witnesses, that they may be justified; or let them hear, and say, "It is truth."

10 "You are My witnesses," saith יהוה, "And My servant whom I have chosen, that you may know and believe Me, and understand that I am He; before Me there was no God (El) formed, nor shall there be after Me.

11 I, even I, am יהוה; and besides Me there is no Savior.

12 I have declared, and have saved, and I have shewed, when there was no foreign god (el) among you; therefore you are My witnesses," saith יהוה, "that I am God (El)."

13 Yea, before the day was, I am He; and there is none that can deliver out of My hand; I will work, and who shall let it?"

14 Thus saith יהוה, Your Redeemer, the Holy One of Yisrael: "For your sake I have sent to Babylon (Bavel), and have brought down all their nobles, and the Chaldeans, whose cry is in the ships.

15 I am יהוה, your Holy One, the Creator of Yisrael, your King."

16 Thus saith יהוה, Who maketh a way in the sea, and a path in the mighty waters;

17 Who bringeth forth the chariot and horse, the army and the power; they shall lie down together, they shall not rise; they are extinct, they are quenched as tow.

18 "Remember you not the former things, neither consider the things of old.

19 Behold, I will do a new thing; now it shall spring forth; shall you not know it? I will even make a way in the wilderness, and rivers in the desert.

20 The beast of the field shall honor Me, the dragons and the owls; because I give waters in the wilderness, and rivers in the desert, to give drink to My people, My chosen.

21 This people have I formed for Myself; they shall shew forth My praise.

22 But you have not called upon Me, O Jacob (Yaaqov); but you have been weary of Me, O Yisrael.

23 You have not brought Me the small cattle of your burnt offerings; neither have you honoured Me with your sacrifices. I have not caused you to serve with an offering, nor wearied you with incense.

24 You have bought Me no sweet cane with money, neither have you filled Me with the fat of your sacrifices; but you have made Me to serve with your sins, you have wearied Me with

your iniquities.

25 I, even I, am He that blotteth out your transgressions for Mine own sake, and will not remember your sins.

26 Put Me in remembrance; let us plead together; declare you, that you mayest be justified.

27 Your first father hath sinned, and your teachers have transgressed against Me.

28 Therefore I have profaned the princes of the sanctuary, and have given Jacob (Yaaqov) to the curse, and Yisrael to reproaches.

44 "Yet now hear, O Jacob (Yaaqov) My servant; and Yisrael, whom I have chosen:

2 Thus saith יהוה that made you, and formed you from the womb, who will help you: 'Fear not, O Jacob (Yaaqov), My servant; and you, Yeshurun, whom I have chosen.

3 For I will pour water upon him that is thirsty, and floods upon the dry ground; I will pour My Spirit upon your seed, and My blessing upon your offspring:

4 And they shall spring up as among the grass, as willows by the water courses.'

5 One shall say, 'I am יהוה's;' and another shall call himself by the name of Jacob (Yaaqov); and another shall subscribe on his hand: 'יהוה's', and surname himself by the name of Yisrael.

6 Thus saith יהוה the King of Yisrael and his Redeemer, יהוה of hosts (YHWH Tsevaot): 'I am the First, and I am the Last; and besides Me there is no God (Elohim).

7 And who, as I, shall call, and shall declare it, and set it in order for Me, since I appointed the ancient people? And the things that are coming, and shall come, let them shew unto them.

8 Fear you not, neither be afraid; have not I told you from that time, and have declared it? You are even My witnesses. Is there a God (Eloah) besides Me? Yea, there is no Rock; I know not any.'"

9 They that make a graven image are all of them vanity; and their delectable things shall not profit; and they are their own witnesses; they see not, nor know; that they may be ashamed.

10 Who hath formed a god (el), or molten a graven image that is profitable for nothing?

11 Behold, all his fellows shall be ashamed; and the workmen, they are of men; let them all be gathered together, let them stand up; yet they shall fear, and they shall be ashamed together.

12 The smith with the tongs both worketh in the coals, and fashioneth it with hammers, and worketh it with the strength of his arms; yea, he is hungry, and his strength faileth; he drinketh no water, and is faint.

13 The carpenter stretcheth out his rule; he marketh it out with a line; he fitteth it with planes, and he marketh it out with the compass, and maketh it after the figure of a man, according to the beauty of a man; that it may remain in the house.

14 He heweth him down cedars, and taketh the cypress and the oak, which he strengtheneth for himself among the trees of the forest; he planteth an ash, and the rain doth nourish it.

15 Then shall it be for a man to burn; for he will take thereof, and warm himself; yea, he kindleth it, and baketh bread; yea, he maketh a god, and worshippeth it; he maketh it a graven image, and falleth down thereto.

16 He burneth part thereof in the fire; with part thereof he eateth flesh; he roasteth roast, and is satisfied; yea, he warmeth himself, and saith, "Aha, I am warm, I have seen the fire."

17 And the residue thereof he maketh a god, even his graven image; he falleth down unto it, and worshippeth it, and prayeth unto it, and saith, "Deliver me; for you are my god (el)."

18 They have not known nor understood; for He hath shut their eyes, that they cannot see; and their hearts, that they cannot understand.

19 And none considereth in his heart, neither is there knowledge nor understanding to say, "I have burned part of it in the fire; yea, also I have baked bread upon the coals thereof; I have roasted flesh, and eaten it; and shall I make the residue thereof an abomination? Shall I fall down to the stock of a tree?"

20 He feedeth on ashes; a deceived heart hath turned him aside, that he cannot deliver his soul, nor say, "Is there not a lie in my right hand?"

21 "Remember these, O Jacob (Yaaqov) and Yisrael; for you are My servant. I have formed you; you are My servant; O Yisrael, you shalt not be forgotten of Me!

22 I have blotted out, as a thick cloud, your transgressions, and, as a cloud, your sins. Return unto Me, for I have redeemed you."

23 Sing, O you heavens; for יהוה hath done it! Shout, you lower parts of the earth: break forth into singing, you mountains, O forest, and every

tree therein; for יהוה hath redeemed Jacob (Yaaqov), and glorified Himself in Yisrael.

24 Thus saith יהוה, your Redeemer, and He that formed you from the womb: "I am יהוה that maketh all things; that stretcheth forth the heavens alone; that spreadeth abroad the earth by Myself;

25 That frustrateth the tokens of the liars, and maketh diviners mad; that turneth wise men backward, and maketh their knowledge foolish;

26 That confirmeth the word of His servant, and performeth the counsel of His messengers; that saith to Jerusalem (Yerushalayim), 'You shalt be inhabited;' and to the cities of Judah (Yehudah), 'You shall be built,' and I will raise up the decayed places thereof;

27 That saith to the deep, 'Be dry, and I will dry up your rivers';

28 That saith of Cyrus, 'He is My shepherd, and shall perform all My pleasure; even saying to Yerushalayim, "You shalt be built;" and to the temple, "Your foundation shall be laid."'

45 "Thus saith יהוה to His anointed (mashiach), to Cyrus, whose right hand I have holden, to subdue nations before him; and I will loose the loins of kings, to open before him the two leaved gates; and the gates shall not be shut:

2 'I will go before you, and make the crooked places straight; I will break in pieces the gates of brass, and cut in sunder the bars of iron.

3 And I will give you the treasures of darkness, and hidden riches of secret places, that you mayest know that I, יהוה, who call you by your name, am the God of Israel (Elohei Yisrael).

4 For Jacob (Yaaqov) My servant's sake, and Yisrael Mine elect, I have even called you by your name: I have surnamed you, though you have not known Me.

5 I am יהוה, and there is none else, there is no God (Elohim) besides Me. I girded you, though you have not known Me,

6 That they may know from the rising of the sun, and from the west, that there is none besides Me. I am יהוה, and there is none else.

7 I form the light, and create darkness: I make peace, and create disaster (raah); I יהוה do all these things.'

8 "Drop down, you heavens, from above, and let the skies pour down righteousness; let the earth open, and let them bring forth salvation, and let righteousness spring up together; I יהוה have created it.

9 "Woe unto him that striveth with his Maker! Let the potsherd strive with the potsherds of the earth. Shall the clay say to him that fashioneth it, 'What makest you?' Or your work, 'He hath no hands?'

10 Woe unto him that saith unto his father, 'What begettest you?' Or to the woman, 'What have you brought forth?'"

11 Thus saith יהוה, the Holy One of Yisrael, and his Maker: 'Ask Me of things to come concerning My sons, and concerning the work of My hands command you Me.

12 I have made the earth, and created man upon it: I, even My hands, have stretched out the heavens, and all their host have I commanded.

13 I have raised him up in righteousness, and I will direct all his ways; he shall build My city, and he shall let go My captives, not for price nor reward, saith יהוה of hosts (YHWH Tsevaot).

14 Thus saith יהוה: "The labour of Egypt (Mitsrayim), and merchandise of Ethiopia (Kush) and of the Sabeans, men of stature, shall come over unto you, and they shall be yours; they shall come after you; in chains they shall come over, and they shall fall down unto you, they shall make supplication unto you, saying, 'Surely God (El) is in you; and there is none else, no other God (Elohim).'"

15 Verily You are a God (El) that hidest Yourself, O God of Israel (Elohei Yisrael), the Savior.

16 They shall be ashamed, and also confounded, all of them; they shall go to confusion together that are makers of idols.

17 But Yisrael shall be saved in יהוה with an everlasting salvation; you shall not be ashamed nor confounded world without end.

18 For thus saith יהוה who created the heavens; God (Elohim) Himself who formed the earth and made it; He hath established it, He created it not in vain, He formed it to be inhabited: "I am יהוה, and there is none else.

19 I have not spoken in secret, in a dark place of the earth; I said not unto the seed of Jacob (Yaaqov), 'Seek you Me in vain'; I יהוה speak righteousness, I declare things that are right.

20 Assemble yourselves and come; draw near together, you that are escaped of the nations. They have no knowledge that set up the wood of their graven image, and pray unto a god (el)

that cannot save.

21 Tell you, and bring them near; yea, let them take counsel together. Who hath declared this from ancient time? Who hath told it from that time? Have not I יהוה? And there is no God (Elohim) else besides Me; a just God (El tzadik) and a Savior; there is none besides Me.

22 Look unto Me, and be you saved, all the ends of the earth; for I am God (El), and there is none else.

23 I have sworn by Myself, the word is gone out of My mouth in righteousness, and shall not return, that unto Me every knee shall bow, every tongue shall swear.

24 'Surely,' shall one say, 'in יהוה have I righteousness and strength; even to Him shall men come; and all that are incensed against Him shall be ashamed.

25 In יהוה shall all the seed of Yisrael be justified, and shall glory.'"

46 Bel boweth down, Nebo stoopeth, their idols were upon the beasts, and upon the cattle; your carriages were heavy loaden; they are a burden to the weary beast.

2 They stoop, they bow down together; they could not deliver the burden, but themselves are gone into captivity.

3 "Hearken unto Me, O house of Jacob (Yaaqov), and all the remnant of the house of Yisrael, who are borne by Me from the belly, who are carried from the womb:

4 And even to your old age I am He; and even to hoar hairs will I carry you! I have made, and I will bear; even I will carry, and will deliver you.

5 To whom will you liken Me, and make Me equal, and compare Me, that we may be like?

6 They lavish gold out of the bag, and weigh silver in the balance, and hire a goldsmith; and he maketh it a god (el); they fall down, yea, they worship.

7 They bear him upon the shoulder, they carry him, and set him in his place, and he standeth; from his place shall he not remove: yea, one shall cry unto him, yet can he not answer, nor save him out of his trouble.

8 Remember this, and shew yourselves men: bring it again to mind, O you transgressors.

9 Remember the former things of old; for I am God (El), and there is none else; I am God (Elohim), and there is none like Me,

10 Declaring the end from the beginning, and from ancient times the things that are not yet done, saying, 'My counsel shall stand, and I will do all My pleasure,'

11 Calling a ravenous bird from the east, the man that executeth My counsel from a far country; yea, I have spoken it, I will also bring it to pass; I have purposed it, I will also do it.

12 Hearken unto Me, you stouthearted, that are far from righteousness:

13 I bring near My righteousness; it shall not be far off, and My salvation shall not tarry; and I will place salvation in Zion (Tsiyon) for Yisrael My glory.

47 "Come down, and sit in the dust, O virgin daughter of Babylon (Bavel), sit on the ground; there is no throne, O daughter of the Chaldeans! for you shalt no more be called tender and delicate.

2 Take the millstones, and grind meal. Uncover your locks, make bare the leg, uncover the thigh, pass over the rivers.

3 Your nakedness shall be uncovered, yea, your shame shall be seen; I will take vengeance, and I will not meet you as a man."

4 As for our Redeemer, יהוה of hosts (YHWH Tsevaot) is His name, the Holy One of Yisrael.

5 "Sit you silent, and get you into darkness, O daughter of the Chaldeans; for you shalt no more be called, The lady of kingdoms.

6 I was wroth with My people, I have polluted Mine inheritance, and given them into your hand; you didst shew them no mercy; upon the ancient have you very heavily laid your yoke.

7 And you saidst, 'I shall be a lady forever,' so that you didst not lay these things to your heart, neither didst remember the latter end of it.

8 Therefore hear now this, you that art given to pleasures, that dwellest carelessly, that sayest in your heart, 'I am, and none else besides me; I shall not sit as a widow, neither shall I know the loss of children';

9 But these two things shall come to you in a moment in one day: the loss of children, and widowhood. They shall come upon you in their perfection for the multitude of your sorceries, and for the great abundance of your enchantments.

10 For you have trusted in your wickedness; you have said, 'None seeth me'; Your wisdom and your knowledge, it hath perverted you; and you have said in your heart, 'I am, and none else

besides me.'

11 Therefore shall evil come upon you; you shalt not know from whence it riseth. And mischief shall fall upon you; you shalt not be able to put it off: and desolation shall come upon you suddenly, which you shalt not know.

12 "Stand now with your enchantments, and with the multitude of your sorceries, wherein you have laboured from your youth; if so be you shalt be able to profit, if so be you mayest prevail.

13 You are wearied in the multitude of your counsels. Let now the astrologers, the stargazers, the monthly prognosticators, stand up, and save you from these things that shall come upon you.

14 Behold, they shall be as stubble; the fire shall burn them; they shall not deliver themselves from the power of the flame; there shall not be a coal to warm at, nor fire to sit before it.

15 Thus shall they be unto you with whom you have laboured, even your merchants, from your youth; they shall wander every one to his quarter; none shall save you.

48 Hear you this, O house of Jacob (Yaaqov), who are called by the name of Yisrael, and are come forth out of the waters of Judah (Yehudah), which swear by the name of יהוה, and make mention of the God of Israel (Elohei Yisrael), but not in truth, nor in righteousness.

2 For they call themselves of the holy city, and stay themselves upon the God of Israel (Elohei Yisrael); יהוה of hosts (YHWH Tsevaot) is His name.

3 I have declared the former things from the beginning; and they went forth out of My mouth, and I shewed them; I did them suddenly, and they came to pass.

4 Because I knew that you are obstinate, and your neck is an iron sinew, and your brow brass;

5 I have even from the beginning declared it to you; before it came to pass I shewed it you; lest you shouldest say, 'Mine idol hath done them, and my graven image, and my molten image, hath commanded them.'

6 "You have heard, see all this; and will not you declare it? I have shewed you new things from this time, even hidden things, and you didst not know them.

7 They are created now, and not from the beginning; even before the day when you heardest them not; lest you shouldest say,

'Behold, I knew them.'

8 Yea, you heardest not; yea, you knewest not; yea, from that time that your ear was not opened; for I knew that you wouldest deal very treacherously, and wast called a transgressor from the womb.

9 "For My name's sake will I defer Mine anger, and for My praise will I refrain for you, that I cut you not off.

10 Behold, I have refined you, but not with silver; I have chosen you in the furnace of affliction.

11 For Mine own sake, even for Mine own sake, will I do it; for how should My name be polluted? And I will not give My glory unto another.

12 Hearken unto Me, O Jacob (Yaaqov) and Yisrael, My called: I am He, I am the First, I also am the Last.

13 Mine hand also hath laid the foundation of the earth, and My right hand hath spanned the heavens; when I call unto them, they stand up together.

14 All you, assemble yourselves, and hear; which among them hath declared these things? יהוה hath loved him; he will do His pleasure on Babylon (Bavel), and His arm shall be on the Chaldeans.

15 I, even I, have spoken; yea, I have called him; I have brought him, and he shall make his way prosperous.

16 Come you near unto me, hear you this: I have not spoken in secret from the beginning; from the time that it was, there am I. And now, Lord (Adonai) יהוה and His Spirit hath sent me."

17 Thus saith יהוה, your Redeemer, the Holy One of Yisrael: "I am יהוה your God (YHWH Eloheikha) Who teacheth you to profit, Who leadeth you by the way that you shouldest go.

18 O that you hadst hearkened to My commandments! Then had your peace been as a river, and your righteousness as the waves of the sea.

19 Your seed also had been as the sand, and the offspring of your bowels like the gravel thereof; his name should not have been cut off nor destroyed from before Me."

20 Go you forth of Babylon (Bavel), flee you from the Chaldeans! With a voice of singing declare you, tell this, utter it even to the end of the earth; say you, "יהוה hath redeemed His

servant Jacob (Yaaqov)."

21 And they thirsted not when He led them through the deserts; He caused the waters to flow out of the rock for them: He clave the rock also, and the waters gushed out.

22 "There is no peace," saith יהוה, "unto the wicked."

49 "Listen, O isles, unto me; and hearken, you people, from far; יהוה hath called me from the womb; from the bowels of my mother hath He made mention of my name.

2 And He hath made my mouth like a sharp sword; in the shadow of His hand hath He hid me, and made me a polished shaft; in His quiver hath He hid me."

3 And He said unto me, 'You are my servant, O Yisrael, in whom I will be glorified.'

4 Then I said, 'I have laboured in vain, I have spent my strength for nought, and in vain; yet surely my judgment is with יהוה, and my work with my God (Elohim).'"

5 And now, saith יהוה that formed me from the womb to be His servant, to bring Jacob (Yaaqov) again to Him, "Though Yisrael be not gathered, yet shall I be glorious in the eyes of יהוה, and my God (Elohim) shall be my strength.

6 And He said, 'It is a light thing that you shouldest be My servant to raise up the tribes of Jacob (Yaaqov), and to restore the preserved of Yisrael; I will also give you for a light to the nations, that you mayest be My salvation unto the end of the earth.'"

7 Thus saith יהוה, the Redeemer of Yisrael, and his Holy One, to Him whom man despiseth, to Him whom the nation abhorreth, to a Servant of rulers: "Kings shall see and arise, princes also shall worship, because of יהוה who is faithful, and the Holy One of Yisrael, and He shall choose You."

8 Thus saith יהוה: "In an acceptable time have I heard You, and in a day of salvation have I helped You; and I will preserve You, and give You for a covenant of the people, to establish the earth, to cause to inherit the desolate heritages;

9 That You mayest say to the prisoners, 'Go forth,' to them that are in darkness, 'Shew yourselves.' "They shall feed in the ways, and their pastures shall be in all high places.

10 They shall not hunger nor thirst; neither shall the heat nor sun smite them; for He who hath mercy on them shall lead them, even by the springs of water shall He guide them.

11 And I will make all My mountains a way, and My highways shall be exalted.

12 Behold, these shall come from far; and, behold, these from the north and from the west; and these from the land of Sinim.

13 Sing, O heavens; and be joyful, O earth; and break forth into singing, O mountains; for יהוה hath comforted His people, and will have mercy upon His afflicted.

14 But Zion (Tsiyon) said, "יהוה hath forsaken me, and my Lord (Adonai) hath forgotten me."

15 "Can a woman forget her sucking child, that she should not have compassion on the son of her womb? Yea, they may forget, yet will I not forget you.

16 Behold, I have engraved you upon the palms of My hands; your walls are continually before Me.

17 Your children shall make haste; your destroyers and they that made you waste shall go forth of you.

18 Lift up your eyes round about, and behold; all these gather themselves together, and come to you. As I live," saith יהוה, "You shalt surely clothe you with them all, as with an ornament, and bind them on you, as a bride doeth.

19 "For your waste and your desolate places, and the land of your destruction, shall even now be too narrow by reason of the inhabitants, and they that swallowed you up shall be far away.

20 The children which you shalt have, after you have lost the other, shall say again in your ears, 'The place is too small for me; give place to me that I may dwell.'

21 Then shalt you say in your heart, 'Who hath begotten me these, seeing I have lost my children, and am desolate, a captive, and removing to and fro? And who hath brought up these? Behold, I was left alone; these, where had they been?'"

22 Thus saith Lord (Adonai) יהוה, "Behold, I will lift up Mine hand to the nations, and set up My standard to the people; and they shall bring your sons in their arms, and your daughters shall be carried upon their shoulders;

23 And kings shall be your nursing fathers, and their queens your nursing mothers; they shall bow down to you with their face toward the earth, and lick up the dust of your feet; and you shalt know that I am יהוה, for they shall not be

ashamed that wait for Me."

24 Shall the prey be taken from the mighty, or the lawful captive delivered?

25 But thus saith יהוה: "Even the captives of the mighty shall be taken away, and the prey of the terrible shall be delivered; for I will contend with him that contendeth with you, and I will save your children.

26 And I will feed them that oppress you with their own flesh; and they shall be drunken with their own blood, as with sweet wine; and all flesh shall know that I יהוה am your Savior and your Redeemer, the Mighty One of Jacob (Yaaqov)."

50 Thus saith יהוה: "Where is the bill of your mother's divorcement, whom I have put away? Or which of My creditors is it to whom I have sold you? Behold, for your iniquities have you sold yourselves, and for your transgressions is your mother put away.

2 Wherefore, when I came, was there no man? When I called, was there none to answer? Is My hand shortened at all, that it cannot redeem? Or have I no power to deliver? Behold, at My rebuke I dry up the sea, I make the rivers a wilderness; their fish stinketh, because there is no water, and dieth for thirst.

3 I clothe the heavens with blackness, and I make sackcloth their covering."

4 "Lord (Adonai) יהוה hath given Me the tongue of the learned, that I should know how to speak a word in season to him that is weary. He wakeneth morning by morning, He wakeneth Mine ear to hear as the learned.

5 Lord (Adonai) יהוה hath opened Mine ear; and I was not rebellious, nor turned away back.

6 I gave My back to the smiters, and My cheeks to them that plucked off the hair; I hid not My face from shame and spitting.

7 For Lord (Adonai) יהוה will help Me; therefore shall I not be confounded; therefore have I set My face like a flint, and I know that I shall not be ashamed.

8 He is near that justifieth Me; who will contend with Me? Let us stand together; who is Mine adversary? Let him come near to Me.

9 Behold, Lord (Adonai) יהוה will help Me; who is he that shall condemn Me? Behold, they all shall wax old as a garment; the moth shall eat them up.

10 Who is among you that feareth יהוה, that

obeyeth the voice of His servant, that walketh in darkness, and hath no light? Let him trust in the name of יהוה, and stay upon his God (Elohim).

11 Behold, all you that kindle a fire, that compass yourselves about with sparks: walk in the light of your fire, and in the sparks that you have kindled. This shall you have of mine hand; you shall lie down in sorrow.

51 Hearken to Me, you that follow after righteousness, you that seek יהוה; look unto the rock whence you are hewn, and to the hole of the pit whence you are digged.

2 Look unto Avraham your father, and unto Sarah that bare you; for I called him alone, and blessed him, and increased him."

3 For יהוה shall comfort Zion (Tsiyon); He will comfort all her waste places; and He will make her wilderness like Eden, and her desert like the garden of יהוה; joy and gladness shall be found therein, thanksgiving, and the voice of melody.

4 Hearken unto Me, My people; and give ear unto Me, O My nation; for a Torah shall proceed from Me, and I will make My judgment to rest for a light of the people.

5 My righteousness is near; My salvation is gone forth, and Mine arms shall judge the people; the isles shall wait upon Me, and on Mine arm shall they trust.

6 Lift up your eyes to the heavens, and look upon the earth beneath; for the heavens shall vanish away like smoke, and the earth shall wax old like a garment, and they that dwell therein shall die in like manner; but My salvation shall be forever, and My righteousness shall not be abolished.

7 "Hearken unto Me, you that know righteousness, the people in whose heart is My Torah; fear you not the reproach of men, neither be you afraid of their revilings.

8 For the moth shall eat them up like a garment, and the worm shall eat them like wool; but My righteousness shall be forever, and My salvation from generation to generation."

9 Awake, awake, put on strength, O arm of יהוה! Awake, as in the ancient days, in the generations of old. Was it not You that hath cut Rachav, and wounded the dragon (tannin)?

10 Was it not You that hath dried the sea, the waters of the great deep; that hath made the depths of the sea a way for the ransomed to

pass over?

11 Therefore the redeemed of יהוה shall return, and come with singing unto Zion (Tsiyon); and everlasting joy shall be upon their head; they shall obtain gladness and joy; and sorrow and mourning shall flee away.

12 "I, even I, am he that comforteth you: who are you, that you shouldest be afraid of a man that shall die, and of the son of man who shall be made as grass;

13 And forgettest יהוה your Maker, that hath stretched forth the heavens, and laid the foundations of the earth; and hast feared continually every day because of the fury of the oppressor, as if he were ready to destroy? And where is the fury of the oppressor?

14 The captive exile hasteneth that he may be loosed, and that he should not die in the pit, nor that his bread should fail.

15 But I am יהוה your God (YHWH Eloheikha), that divided the sea, whose waves roared; יהוה of hosts (YHWH Tsevaot) is His name.

16 And I have put My words in your mouth, and I have covered you in the shadow of Mine hand, that I may plant the heavens, and lay the foundations of the earth, and say unto Zion (Tsiyon), 'You are My people.'"

17 Awake, awake, stand up, O Jerusalem (Yerushalayim), which hast drunk at the hand of יהוה the cup of His fury; you have drunken the dregs of the cup of trembling, and wrung them out.

18 There is none to guide her among all the sons whom she hath brought forth; nor is there any that taketh her by the hand of all the sons that she hath brought up.

19 These two things are come unto you; who shall be sorry for you? Desolation, and destruction, and the famine, and the sword; by whom shall I comfort you?

20 Your sons have fainted, they lie at the head of all the streets, as a wild bull in a net: they are full of the fury of יהוה, the rebuke of your God (Elohim).

21 Therefore hear now this, you afflicted, and drunken, but not with wine:

22 Thus saith your Lord (Adonai) יהוה, and your God (Elohim) that pleadeth the cause of His people: "Behold, I have taken out of your hand the cup of trembling, even the dregs of the cup of My fury; you shalt no more drink it again.

23 But I will put it into the hand of them that afflict you; who have said to your soul, 'Bow down, that we may go over.' And you have laid your body as the ground, and as the street, to them that went over."

52 Awake, awake; put on your strength, O Zion (Tsiyon); put on your beautiful garments, O Jerusalem (Yerushalayim), the holy city! For henceforth there shall no more come into you the uncircumcised and the unclean.

2 Shake yourself from the dust; arise, and sit down, O Jerusalem (Yerushalayim); loose yourself from the bands of your neck, O captive daughter of Zion (Tsiyon)!

3 For thus saith יהוה: "You have sold yourselves for nought; and you shall be redeemed without money."

4 For thus saith Lord (Adonai) יהוה: "My people went down aforetime into Egypt (Mitsrayim) to sojourn there; and the Assyrian (Ashshur) oppressed them without cause.

5 Now therefore, what have I here," saith יהוה, "that My people is taken away for nothing? They that rule over them make them to howl," saith יהוה, "And My name continually every day is blasphemed.

6 Therefore My people shall know My name; therefore they shall know in that day that I am He who doth speak: 'Behold, it is I.'"

7 How beautiful upon the mountains are the feet of him who bringeth good tidings, who proclaims peace; that bringeth good tidings of good, who proclaims salvation; who saith unto Zion (Tsiyon), "Your God (Elohim) reigneth!"

8 Your watchmen shall lift up the voice; with the voice together shall they sing; for they shall see eye to eye, when יהוה shall bring again Zion (Tsiyon).

9 Break forth into joy, sing together, you waste places of Jerusalem (Yerushalayim); for יהוה hath comforted His people, He hath redeemed Jerusalem (Yerushalayim).

10 יהוה hath made bare His holy arm in the eyes of all the nations; and all the ends of the earth shall see the salvation of our God (Elohim).

11 Depart you, depart you, go you out from thence, touch no unclean thing; go you out of the midst of her; be you clean, that bear the vessels of יהוה.

12 For you shall not go out with haste, nor go by flight; for יהוה will go before you; and the God

of Israel (Elohei Yisrael) will be your rereward.

13 Behold, My Servant shall deal prudently, He shall be exalted and extolled, and be very high.

14 As many were astonied at you; His visage was so marred more than any man, and His form more than the sons of men.

15 So shall He sprinkle many nations; the kings shall shut their mouths at Him, for that which had not been told them shall they see; and that which they had not heard shall they consider.

53 Who hath believed our report? And to whom is the arm of יהוה revealed?

2 For He shall grow up before Him as a tender plant, and as a root out of a dry ground. He hath no form nor comeliness; and when we shall see Him, there is no beauty that we should desire Him.

3 He is despised and rejected of men; a man of sorrows, and acquainted with grief; and we hid as it was our faces from Him; He was despised, and we esteemed Him not.

4 Surely He hath borne our griefs, and carried our sorrows; yet we did esteem Him stricken, smitten of God (Elohim), and afflicted.

5 But He was wounded for our transgressions, He was bruised for our iniquities; the chastisement of our peace was upon Him; and by His stripes we are healed.

6 All we like sheep have gone astray; we have turned every one to his own way; and יהוה hath laid on Him the iniquity of us all.

7 He was oppressed, and He was afflicted, yet He opened not His mouth; He is brought as a lamb to the slaughter, and as a sheep before her shearers is dumb, so He openeth not His mouth.

8 He was taken from prison and from judgment, and who shall declare His generation? For He was cut off out of the land of the living; for the transgression of My people was He stricken.

9 And He made His grave with the wicked, and with the rich in His death; because He had done no violence, neither was any deceit in His mouth.

10 Yet it pleased יהוה to bruise Him; He hath put Him to grief; when you shalt make His soul an offering for sin, He shall see His seed, He shall prolong His days, and the pleasure of יהוה shall prosper in His hand.

11 He shall see of the travail of His soul, and shall be satisfied; by His knowledge shall My righteous servant justify many; for He shall bear their iniquities.

12 Therefore will I divide Him a portion with the great, and He shall divide the spoil with the strong; because He hath poured out His soul unto death; and He was numbered with the transgressors; and He bare the sin of many, and made intercession for the transgressors.

54 "Sing, O barren, you that didst not bear; break forth into singing, and cry aloud, you that didst not travail with child; for more are the children of the desolate than the children of the married wife," saith יהוה.

2 "Enlarge the place of your tent, and let them stretch forth the curtains of your habitations; spare not, lengthen your cords, and strengthen your stakes;

3 For you shalt break forth on the right hand and on the left; and your seed shall inherit the nations, and make the desolate cities to be inhabited.

4 "Fear not, for you shalt not be ashamed; nor be you confounded; for you shalt not be put to shame; for you shalt forget the shame of your youth, and shalt not remember the reproach of your widowhood anymore.

5 For your Maker is your B33fhusband (baal); יהוה of hosts (YHWH Tsevaot) is His name; and your Redeemer the Holy One of Yisrael; the God (Elohim) of the whole earth shall He be called.

6 For יהוה hath called you as a woman forsaken and grieved in spirit, and a wife of youth, when you wast refused," saith your God (Elohim).

7 "For a small moment have I forsaken you; but with great mercies will I gather you.

8 In a little wrath I hid My face from you for a moment; but with everlasting kindness will I have mercy on you," saith יהוה your Redeemer.

9 For this is as the waters of Noach unto Me; for as I have sworn that the waters of Noach should no more go over the earth; so have I sworn that I would not be wroth with you, nor rebuke you.

10 For the mountains shall depart, and the hills be removed; but My kindness shall not depart from you, neither shall the covenant of My peace be removed, saith יהוה that hath mercy on you.

11 O you afflicted, tossed with tempest, and not comforted, behold, I will lay your stones with fair colours, and lay your foundations with sapphires.

12 And I will make your windows of agates, and your gates of carbuncles, and all your borders of pleasant stones.

13 And all your children shall be taught of יהוה; and great shall be the peace of your children.

14 In righteousness shalt you be established; you shalt be far from oppression, for you shalt not fear; and from terror; for it shall not come near you.

15 Behold, they shall surely gather together, but not by Me; whosoever shall gather together against you shall fall for your sake.

16 "Behold, I have created the smith that bloweth the coals in the fire, and that bringeth forth an instrument for his work; and I have created the waster to destroy.

17 No weapon that is formed against you shall prosper; and every tongue that shall rise against you in judgment you shalt condemn. This is the heritage of the servants of יהוה, and their righteousness is of Me," saith יהוה.

55 "Ho! Every one that thirsteth, come you to the waters, and he that hath no money; come you, buy, and eat; yea, come, buy wine and milk without money and without price.

2 Wherefore do you spend money for that which is not bread? And your labour for that which satisfieth not? Hearken diligently unto Me, and eat you that which is good, and let your soul delight itself in fatness.

3 Incline your ear, and come unto Me. Hear, and your soul shall live; and I will make an everlasting covenant with you, even the sure mercies of Dawid.

4 Behold, I have given him for a witness to the people, a leader and commander to the people.

5 Behold, you shalt call a nation that you knowest not, and nations that knew not you shall run unto you because of יהוה your God (YHWH Eloheikha), and for the Holy One of Yisrael; for He hath glorified you."

6 Seek you יהוה while He may be found, call you upon Him while He is near.

7 Let the wicked forsake his way, and the unrighteous man his thoughts: and let him return unto יהוה, and He will have mercy upon him; and to our God (Elohim), for He will abundantly pardon.

8 "For My thoughts are not your thoughts, nor are your ways My ways," saith יהוה.

9 "For as the heavens are higher than the earth,

so are My ways higher than your ways, and My thoughts than your thoughts.

10 For as the rain cometh down, and the snow from heaven, and returneth not thither, but watereth the earth, and maketh it brings forth and bud, that it may give seed to the sower, and bread to the eater,

11 So shall My word be that goeth forth out of My mouth; it shall not return unto Me void, but it shall accomplish that which I please, and it shall prosper in the thing whereto I sent it.

12 For you shall go out with joy, and be led forth with peace; the mountains and the hills shall break forth before you into singing, and all the trees of the field shall clap their hands.

13 Instead of the thorn shall come up the fir tree, and instead of the brier shall come up the myrtle tree; and it shall be to יהוה for a name, for an everlasting sign that shall not be cut off."

56 Thus saith יהוה, "Keep you justice, and do righteousness, for My salvation is near to come, and My righteousness to be revealed.

2 Blessed is the man that doeth this, and the son of man that layeth hold on it; that keepeth the Shabbat from polluting it, and keepeth his hand from doing any evil."

3 Neither let the son of the stranger, that hath joined himself to יהוה, speak, saying, "יהוה hath utterly separated me from His people"; nor let the eunuch say, "Behold, I am a dry tree."

4 For thus saith יהוה: "Unto the eunuchs that keep My Shabbats, and choose the things that please Me, and take hold of My covenant;

5 Even unto them will I give in Mine house and within My walls a place and a name better than of sons and of daughters; I will give them an everlasting name, that shall not be cut off.

6 Also the sons of the stranger, that join themselves to יהוה, to serve Him, and to love the name of יהוה, to be His servants, every one that keepeth the Shabbat from polluting it, and taketh hold of My covenant;

7 Even them will I bring to My holy mountain, and make them joyful in My house of prayer; their burnt offerings and their sacrifices shall be accepted upon Mine altar; for Mine house shall be called a house of prayer for all peoples."

8 Lord (Adonai) יהוה who gathereth the outcasts of Yisrael saith, "Yet will I gather others to him, besides those that are gathered unto him."

9 All you beasts of the field, come to devour,

yea, all you beasts in the forest.

10 His watchmen are blind; they are all ignorant, they are all dumb dogs, they cannot bark; sleeping, lying down, loving to slumber.

11 Yea, they are greedy dogs which can never have enough, and they are shepherds that cannot understand: they all look to their own way, every one for his gain, from his quarter.

12 "Come you," say they, "I will fetch wine, and we will fill ourselves with strong drink; and tomorrow shall be as this day, and much more abundant."

57 The righteous perisheth, and no man layeth it to heart; and merciful men are taken away, none considering that the righteous is taken away from the evil to come.

2 He shall enter into peace; they shall rest in their beds, each one walking in his uprightness.

3 "But draw near hither, you sons of the sorceress, the seed of the adulterer and the whore!

4 Against whom do you sport yourselves? Against whom make you a wide mouth, and draw out the tongue? Are you not children of transgression, a seed of falsehood,

5 Enflaming yourselves with idols under every green tree, slaying the children in the valleys under the clifts of the rocks?

6 Among the smooth stones of the stream is your portion; they, they are your lot: even to them have you poured a drink offering, you have offered a meat offering. Should I receive comfort in these?

7 Upon a lofty and high mountain have you set your bed; even thither wentest you up to offer sacrifice.

8 Behind the doors also and the posts have you set up your remembrance; for you have discovered yourself to another than Me, and art gone up; you have enlarged your bed, and made you a covenant with them; you lovedst their bed where you sawest it.

9 And you wentest to the king with ointment, and didst increase your perfumes, and didst send your messengers far off, and didst debase yourself even unto sheol.

10 You are wearied in the greatness of your way; yet saidst you not, 'There is no hope.' You have found the life of your hand; therefore you wast not grieved.

11 "And of whom have you been afraid or feared, that you have lied, and hast not remembered

Me, nor laid it to your heart? Have not I held My peace even of old, and you fearest Me not?

12 I will declare your righteousness, and your works; for they shall not profit you.

13 When you criest, let your companies deliver you; but the wind shall carry them all away; vanity shall take them: but he that putteth his trust in Me shall possess the land, and shall inherit My holy mountain."

14 And shall say, "Cast you up, cast you up, prepare the way, take up the stumblingblock out of the way of My people."

15 For thus saith the high and lofty One that inhabiteth eternity, whose name is Holy; I dwell in the high and holy place, with him also that is of a contrite and humble spirit, to revive the spirit of the humble, and to revive the heart of the contrite ones.

16 For I will not contend forever, neither will I be always wroth; for the spirit should fail before Me, and the souls which I have made.

17 For the iniquity of his covetousness was I wroth, and smote him; I hid Me, and was wroth, and he went on frowardly in the way of his heart.

18 I have seen his ways, and will heal him: I will lead him also, and restore comforts unto him and to his mourners.

19 "I create the fruit of the lips; Peace, peace to him that is far off, and to him that is near," saith יהוה, "And I will heal him."

20 But the wicked are like the troubled sea, when it cannot rest, whose waters cast up mire and dirt.

21 "There is no peace," saith my God (Elohim), "for the wicked."

58 "Cry aloud, spare not, lift up your voice like a trumpet, and shew My people their transgression, and the house of Jacob (Yaaqov) their sins.

2 Yet they seek Me daily, and delight to know My ways, as a nation that did righteousness, and forsook not the ordinance of their God (Elohim); they ask of Me the ordinances of justice; they take delight in approaching to God (Elohim).

3 Wherefore have we fasted, say they, and you seest not? Wherefore have we afflicted our soul, and you takest no knowledge? Behold, in the day of your fast you find pleasure, and exact all your labours.

4 Behold, you fast for strife and debate, and to smite with the fist of wickedness. You shall not

fast as you do this day, to make your voice to be heard on high.

5 Is it such a fast that I have chosen? A day for a man to afflict his soul? Is it to bow down his head as a bulrush, and to spread sackcloth and ashes under him? Wilt you call this a fast, and an acceptable day to יהוה?

6 Is not this the fast that I have chosen? To loose the bands of wickedness, to undo the heavy burdens, and to let the oppressed go free, and that you break every yoke?

7 Is it not to deal your bread to the hungry, and that you bring the poor that are cast out to your house? When you seest the naked, that you cover him; and that you hide not yourself from your own flesh?

8 Then shall your light break forth as the morning, and your health shall spring forth speedily; and your righteousness shall go before you; the glory of יהוה shall be your rear guard.

9 Then shalt you call, and יהוה shall answer; you shalt cry, and He shall say, 'Here I am.' If you take away from the midst of you the yoke, the putting forth of the finger, and speaking vanity;

10 And if you draw out your soul to the hungry, and satisfy the afflicted soul; then shall your light rise in obscurity, and your darkness be as the noonday.

11 And יהוה shall guide you continually, and satisfy your soul in drought, and make fat your bones: and you shalt be like a watered garden, and like a spring of water, whose waters fail not.

12 And they that shall be of you shall build the old waste places; you shalt raise up the foundations of many generations; and you shalt be called, The Repairer of the Breach and The Restorer of Paths to dwell in."

13 If you turn away your foot from the Shabbat, from doing your pleasure on My holy day; and call the Shabbat a delight, the holy of יהוה, honorable; and shalt honor Him, not doing your own ways, nor finding your own pleasure, nor speaking your own words,

14 Then shalt you delight yourself in יהוה; and I will cause you to ride upon the high places of the earth, and feed you with the heritage of Jacob (Yaaqov) your father; for the mouth of יהוה hath spoken it."

59 Behold, יהוה's hand is not shortened, that it cannot save; nor His ear heavy, that it cannot hear.

2 But your iniquities have separated between you and your God (Elohim), and your sins have hidden His face from you, that He will not hear.

3 For your hands are defiled with blood, and your fingers with iniquity; your lips have spoken lies, your tongue hath muttered perverseness.

4 None calleth for justice, nor any pleadeth for truth; they trust in vanity, and speak lies; they conceive mischief, and bring forth iniquity.

5 They hatch cockatrice's eggs, and weave the spider's web; he that eateth of their eggs dieth, and that which is crushed breaketh out into a viper.

6 Their webs shall not become garments, neither shall they cover themselves with their works; their works are works of iniquity, and the act of violence is in their hands.

7 Their feet run to evil, and they make haste to shed innocent blood; their thoughts are thoughts of iniquity; wasting and destruction are in their paths.

8 The way of peace they know not; and there is no justice in their goings; they have made them crooked paths: whosoever goeth therein shall not know peace.

9 Therefore is judgment far from us, neither doth justice overtake us: we wait for light, but behold obscurity; for brightness, but we walk in darkness.

10 We grope for the wall like the blind, and we grope as if we had no eyes; we stumble at noonday as in the night; we are in desolate places as dead men.

11 We roar all like bears, and mourn sore like doves; we look for judgment, but there is none; for salvation, but it is far off from us.

12 For our transgressions are multiplied before you, and our sins testify against us; for our transgressions are with us; and as for our iniquities, we know them;

13 In transgressing and lying against יהוה, and departing away from our God (Elohim), speaking oppression and revolt, conceiving and uttering from the heart words of falsehood.

14 And judgment is turned away backward, and justice standeth afar off; for truth is fallen in the street, and equity cannot enter.

15 Yea, truth faileth; and he that departeth from evil maketh himself a prey; and יהוה saw it, and it displeased Him that there was no justice.

16 And He saw that there was no man, and

wondered that there was no intercessor; therefore His arm brought salvation unto Him; and His righteousness, it sustained Him.

17 For He put on righteousness as a breastplate, and a helmet of salvation upon His head; and He put on the garments of vengeance for clothing, and was clad with zeal as a cloke.

18 According to their deeds, accordingly He will repay, fury to His adversaries, recompence to His enemies; to the islands He will repay recompence.

19 So shall they fear the name of יהוה from the west, and His glory from the rising of the sun. When the enemy shall come in like a flood, the Spirit of יהוה shall lift up a standard against him.

20 "And the Redeemer shall come to Zion (Tsiyon), and unto them that turn from transgression in Jacob (Yaaqov)," saith יהוה.

21 "As for Me, this is My covenant with them," saith יהוה: My spirit that is upon you, and My words which I have put in your mouth, shall not depart out of your mouth, nor out of the mouth of your seed, nor out of the mouth of your descendants' descendants," saith יהוה, "from henceforth and forever."

60 Arise, shine; for your light is come, and the glory of יהוה is risen upon you.

2 For, behold, the darkness shall cover the earth, and gross darkness the people; but יהוה shall arise upon you, and His glory shall be seen upon you.

3 And the nations shall come to your light, and kings to the brightness of your rising.

4 "Lift up your eyes round about, and see; all they gather themselves together, they come to you; your sons shall come from far, and your daughters shall be nursed at your side.

5 Then you shalt see, and flow together, and your heart shall fear, and be enlarged; because the abundance of the sea shall be converted unto you, the forces of the nations shall come unto you.

6 The multitude of camels shall cover you, the dromedaries of Midian and Ephah; all they from Sheva shall come; they shall bring gold and incense; and they shall shew forth the praises of יהוה.

7 All the flocks of Kedar shall be gathered together unto you, the rams of Nebaioth shall minister unto you; they shall come up with acceptance on Mine altar, and I will glorify the house of My glory.

8 Who are these that fly as a cloud, and as the doves to their windows?

9 Surely the isles shall wait for me, and the ships of Tarshish first, to bring your sons from far, their silver and their gold with them, unto the name of יהוה your God (YHWH Eloheikha), and to the Holy One of Yisrael, because He hath glorified you.

10 And the sons of strangers shall build up your walls, and their kings shall minister unto you; for in my wrath I smote you, but in my favor have I had mercy on you.

11 Therefore your gates shall be open continually; they shall not be shut day nor night; that men may bring unto you the forces of the nations, and that their kings may be brought.

12 For the nation and kingdom that will not serve you shall perish; yea, those nations shall be utterly wasted.

13 The glory of Lebanon shall come unto you, the fir tree, the pine tree, and the box together, to beautify the place of My sanctuary; and I will make the place of My feet glorious.

14 The sons also of them that afflicted you shall come bending unto you; and all they that despised you shall bow themselves down at the soles of your feet; and they shall call you: The City of יהוה, The Zion (Tsiyon) of the Holy One of Yisrael.

15 Whereas you have been forsaken and hated, so that no man went through you, I will make you an eternal excellency, a joy of many generations.

16 You shalt also suck the milk of the nations, and shalt suck the breast of kings; and you shalt know that I יהוה am your Savior and your Redeemer, the Mighty One of Jacob (Yaaqov).

17 For brass I will bring gold, and for iron I will bring silver, and for wood brass, and for stones iron. I will also make your officers peace, and your exactors righteousness.

18 Violence shall no more be heard in your land, wasting nor destruction within your borders; but you shalt call your walls Salvation (Yeshuah), and your gates Praise (Tehillah).

19 "The sun shall be no more your light by day; nor for brightness shall the moon give light unto you; but יהוה shall be unto you an everlasting light, and your God (Elohim) your glory.

20 Your sun shall no more go down; neither

shall your moon withdraw itself; for יהוה shall be your everlasting light, and the days of your mourning shall be ended.

21 Your people also shall be all righteous; they shall inherit the land forever, the branch of My planting, the work of My hands, that I may be glorified.

22 A little one shall become a thousand, and a small one a strong nation. I, יהוה will hasten it in its time."

61 "Spirit of Lord יהוה (Ruach Adonai YHWH) is upon Me, because יהוה hath anointed Me to preach good tidings unto the meek; He hath sent Me to bind up the brokenhearted, to proclaim liberty to the captives, and the opening of the prison to them that are bound;

2 To proclaim the acceptable year of יהוה, and the day of vengeance of our God (Elohim); to comfort all who mourn;

3 To appoint unto them that mourn in Zion (Tsiyon), to give unto them beauty for ashes, the oil of joy for mourning, the garment of praise for the spirit of heaviness; that they might be called trees of righteousness, the planting of יהוה, that He might be glorified.

4 And they shall build the old wastes, they shall raise up the former desolations, and they shall repair the waste cities, the desolations of many generations.

5 And strangers shall stand and feed your flocks, and the sons of the alien shall be your plowmen and your vinedressers.

6 But you shall be named the priests (kohanim) of יהוה, men shall call you the ministers of our God (Elohim); you shall eat the riches of the nations, and in their glory shall you boast yourselves.

7 For your shame you shall have double; and for confusion they shall rejoice in their portion. Therefore in their land they shall possess the double; everlasting joy shall be unto them.

8 "For I, יהוה love justice, I hate robbery for burnt offering; and I will direct their work in truth, and I will make an everlasting covenant with them.

9 And their seed shall be known among the nations, and their offspring among the people; all that see them shall acknowledge them, that they are the seed which יהוה hath blessed."

10 I will greatly rejoice in יהוה, my soul shall be joyful in my God (Elohim); for He hath clothed me with the garments of salvation, He hath covered me with the robe of righteousness, as a bridegroom decketh Himself with ornaments, and as a bride adorneth herself with her jewels.

11 For as the earth bringeth forth her bud, and as the garden causeth the things that are sown in it to spring forth; so Lord (Adonai) יהוה will cause righteousness and praise to spring forth before all the nations.

62 For Zion (Tsiyon)'s sake will I not hold My peace, and for Jerusalem (Yerushalayim)'s sake I will not rest, until the righteousness thereof go forth as brightness, and the salvation thereof as a lamp that burneth.

2 And the nations shall see your righteousness, and all kings your glory; and you shalt be called by a new name, which the mouth of יהוה shall name.

3 You shalt also be a crown of glory in the hand of יהוה, and a royal diadem in the hand of your God (Elohim).

4 You shalt no more be termed 'Forsaken (Azuvah)'; neither shall your land anymore be termed 'Desolate (Shemamah)'; but you shalt be called 'My delight is in her (Cheftsi Bahh)', and your land 'Married (Beulah)'; for יהוה delighteth in you, and your land shall be married.

5 For as a young man marrieth a virgin, so shall your sons marry you; and as the bridegroom rejoiceth over the bride, so shall your God (Elohim) rejoice over you.

6 I have set watchmen upon your walls, O Jerusalem (Yerushalayim), which shall never hold their peace day nor night; you that make mention of יהוה, keep not silence,

7 And give Him no rest, till He establishes, and till He makes Jerusalem (Yerushalayim) a praise in the earth.

8 יהוה hath sworn by His right hand, and by the arm of His strength: "Surely I will no more give your corn to be meat for your enemies; and the sons of the stranger shall not drink your wine, for which you have labored;

9 But they that have gathered it shall eat it, and praise יהוה; and they that have brought it together shall drink it in the courts of My holiness."

10 Go through, go through the gates! Prepare you the way of the people; cast up, cast up the highway! Gather out the stones; lift up a

standard for the people.

11 Behold, יהוה hath proclaimed unto the end of the world: "Say you to the daughter of Zion (Tsiyon), 'Behold, your salvation cometh; behold, His reward is with Him, and His work before Him.'"

12 And they shall call them, 'The Holy People, The Redeemed of יהוה'; and you shalt be called 'Sought Out, A City Not Forsaken'.

63 Who is this who cometh from Edom, with dyed garments from Bozrah? This who is glorious in His apparel, travelling in the greatness of His strength? I who speak in righteousness, mighty to save.

2 Wherefore art You red in Your apparel, and Your garments like him that treadeth in the winefat?

3 I have trodden the winepress alone; and of the people there was none with me; for I will tread them in mine anger, and trample them in My fury; and their blood shall be sprinkled upon My garments, and I will stain all My raiment.

4 For the day of vengeance is in Mine heart, and the year of My redeemed is come.

5 And I looked, and there was none to help; and I wondered that there was none to uphold; therefore Mine own arm brought salvation unto Me; and My fury, it upheld Me.

6 And I will tread down the people in Mine anger, and make them drunk in My fury, and I will bring down their strength to the earth.

7 I will mention the lovingkindnesses of יהוה, and the praises of יהוה, according to all that יהוה hath bestowed on us, and the great goodness toward the house of Yisrael, which He hath bestowed on them according to His mercies, and according to the multitude of His lovingkindnesses.

8 For He said, "Surely they are My people, children that will not lie." So He was their Savior.

9 In all their affliction He was afflicted, and the angel of His presence saved them; in His love and in His pity He redeemed them; and He bare them, and carried them all the days of old.

10 But they rebelled, and vexed His Holy Spirit; therefore He was turned to be their enemy, and He fought against them.

11 Then He remembered the days of old, Moses (Mosheh), and His people, saying: "Where is He that brought them up out of the sea with the shepherd of His flock? Where is He that put His Holy Spirit within him?

12 That led them by the right hand of Moses (Mosheh) with His glorious arm, dividing the water before them, to make Himself an everlasting name?

13 That led them through the deep, as a horse in the wilderness, that they should not stumble?"

14 As a beast goeth down into the valley, the Spirit of יהוה caused him to rest; so didst You lead Your people, to make Yourself a glorious name.

15 Look down from heaven, and behold from the habitation of Your holiness and of Your glory: where is Your zeal and Your strength, the sounding of Your bowels and of Your mercies toward me? Are they restrained?

16 Doubtless You are our Father, though Avraham be ignorant of us, and Yisrael acknowledge us not; You, O יהוה, are our Father, our Redeemer; Your name is from everlasting.

17 O יהוה, why have You made us to err from Your ways, and hardened our heart from Your fear? Return for Your servants' sake, the tribes of Your inheritance.

18 The people of Your holiness have possessed it but a little while; our adversaries have trodden down Your sanctuary.

19 We are Yours; you never barest rule over them; they were not called by Your name.

64 Oh that You wouldest rend the heavens, that You wouldest come down, that the mountains might flow down at Your presence,

2 As when the melting fire burneth, the fire causeth the waters to boil, to make Your name known to Your adversaries, that the nations may tremble at Your presence!

3 When You didst awesome things which we looked not for, You camest down, the mountains flowed down at Your presence.

4 For since the beginning of the world men have not heard, nor perceived by the ear, nor hath the eye seen, O God (Elohim), besides You, who acts for the one who waiteth for Him.

5 You meetest him that rejoiceth and worketh righteousness, those that remember You in Your ways; behold, You are wroth; for we have sinned; in those is continuance, and we shall be saved.

6 But we are all as an unclean thing, and all our righteousnesses are as filthy rags; and we all do

fade as a leaf; and our iniquities, like the wind, have taken us away.

7 And there is none that calleth upon Your name, that stirreth up himself to take hold of You; for You have hid Your face from us, and hast consumed us, because of our iniquities.

8 But now, O יהוה, You are our Father; we are the clay, and You our Potter; and we all are the work of Your hand.

9 Be not wroth very sore, O יהוה, neither remember iniquity forever; behold, see, we beseech You, we are all Your people.

10 Your holy cities are a wilderness, Zion (Tsiyon) is a wilderness, Jerusalem (Yerushalayim) a desolation.

11 Our holy and our beautiful house, where our fathers praised You, is burned up with fire; and all our pleasant things are laid waste.

12 Wilt You refrain Yourself for these things, O יהוה? Wilt You hold Your peace, and afflict us very severely?

65 "I am sought of them that asked not for Me; I am found of them that sought Me not. I said, 'Here I am, here I am,' unto a nation that was not called by My name.

2 I have spread out My hands all the day unto a rebellious people, who walketh in a way that was not good, after their own thoughts;

3 A people that provoketh Me to anger continually to My face; that sacrificeth in gardens, and burneth incense upon altars of brick;

4 Who remain among the graves, and lodge in the monuments, who eat swine's flesh, and broth of abominable things is in their vessels;

5 Who say, 'Stand by yourself, come not near to me; for I am holier than you!' These are a smoke in My nostrils, a fire that burneth all the day.

6 Behold, it is written before Me: I will not keep silence, but will recompense, even recompense into their bosom,

7 Your iniquities, and the iniquities of your fathers together," saith יהוה, "who have burned incense upon the mountains, and blasphemed Me upon the hills; therefore will I measure their former work into their bosom."

8 Thus saith יהוה, "As the new wine is found in the cluster, and one saith, 'Destroy it not; for a blessing is in it,' so will I do for My servants' sakes, that I may not destroy them all.

9 And I will bring forth seeds out of Jacob

(Yaaqov), and out of Judah (Yehudah) an inheritor of My mountains; and Mine elect shall inherit it, and My servants shall dwell there.

10 And Sharon shall be a fold of flocks, and the valley of Achor a place for the herds to lie down in, for My people that have sought Me.

11 But you are they that forsake יהוה, that forget My holy mountain, that prepare a table for that troop, and that furnish the drink offering unto that number.

12 Therefore will I number you to the sword, and you shall all bow down to the slaughter; because when I called, you did not answer; when I spake, you did not hear; but did evil before Mine eyes, and did choose that wherein I delighted not."

13 Therefore thus saith Lord (Adonai) יהוה: "Behold, My servants shall eat, but you shall be hungry; behold, My servants shall drink, but you shall be thirsty; behold, My servants shall rejoice, but you shall be ashamed;

14 Behold, My servants shall sing for joy of heart, but you shall cry for sorrow of heart, and shall howl for vexation of spirit.

15 And you shall leave your name for a curse unto My chosen, for Lord (Adonai) יהוה shall slay you, and call His servants by another name;

16 That he who blesseth himself in the earth shall bless himself in the God (Elohim) of truth; and he that sweareth in the earth shall swear by the God (Elohim) of truth; because the former troubles are forgotten, and because they are hid from Mine eyes.

17 For, behold, I create new heavens and a new earth; and the former shall not be remembered, nor come into mind.

18 But be you glad and rejoice forever in that which I create; for, behold, I create Jerusalem (Yerushalayim) a rejoicing, and her people a joy.

19 And I will rejoice in Jerusalem (Yerushalayim), and joy in My people; and the voice of weeping shall be no more heard in her, nor the voice of crying.

20 "There shall be no more thence an infant of days, nor an old man that hath not filled his days; for the child shall die a hundred years old; but the sinner being a hundred years old shall be accursed.

21 And they shall build houses, and inhabit them; and they shall plant vineyards, and eat the fruit of them.

22 They shall not build, and another inhabit; they shall not plant, and another eat; for as the days of a tree are the days of My people, and Mine elect shall long enjoy the work of their hands.

23 They shall not labour in vain, nor bring forth for trouble; for they are the seed of the blessed of יהוה, and their offspring with them.

24 And it shall come to pass, that before they call, I will answer; and while they are yet speaking, I will hear.

25 The wolf and the lamb shall feed together, and the lion shall eat straw like the bullock; and dust shall be the serpent's food. They shall not hurt nor destroy in all My holy mountain," saith יהוה.

66 Thus saith יהוה: "The heaven is My throne, and the earth is My footstool; where is the house that you build unto Me? And where is the place of My rest?

2 For all those things hath Mine hand made, and all those things have been," saith יהוה; "But to this man will I look, even to him that is poor and of a contrite spirit, and trembleth at My word.

3 "He that killeth an ox is as if he slew a man; he that sacrificeth a lamb, as if he cut off a dog's neck; he that offereth an oblation, as if he offered swine's blood; he that burneth incense, as if he blessed an idol. Yea, they have chosen their own ways, and their soul delighteth in their abominations.

4 I also will choose their delusions, and will bring their fears upon them; because when I called, none did answer; when I spake, they did not hear; but they did evil before Mine eyes, and chose that in which I delighted not."

5 Hear the word of יהוה, you that tremble at His word; Your brethren that hated you, that cast you out for My name's sake, said, 'Let יהוה be glorified, that we may see your joy.' But they shall be put to shame."

6 A voice of noise from the city, a voice from the temple, a voice of יהוה who rendereth recompence to His enemies.

7 "Before she travailed, she brought forth; before her pain came, she was delivered of a man child.

8 Who hath heard such a thing? Who hath seen such things? Shall the earth be made to bring forth in one day? Or shall a nation be born at once? For as soon as Zion (Tsiyon) travailed, she brought forth her children.

9 Shall I bring to the birth, and not cause to bring forth?" saith יהוה. "Shall I cause to bring forth, and shut the womb?" saith your God (Elohim).

10 Rejoice you with Jerusalem (Yerushalayim), and be glad with her, all you that love her; rejoice for joy with her, all you that mourn for her;

11 That you may suck, and be satisfied with the breasts of her consolations; that you may milk out, and be delighted with the abundance of her glory."

12 For thus saith יהוה: "Behold, I will extend peace to her like a river, and the glory of the nations like a flowing stream; then shall you suck, you shall be borne upon her sides, and be dandled upon her knees.

13 As one whom his mother comforteth, so will I comfort you; and you shall be comforted in Yerushalayim."

14 And when you see this, your heart shall rejoice, and your bones shall flourish like an herb; and the hand of יהוה shall be known toward His servants, and His indignation toward His enemies.

15 For, behold, יהוה will come with fire, and with His chariots like a whirlwind, to render His anger with fury, and His rebuke with flames of fire.

16 For by fire and by His sword will יהוה plead with all flesh; and the slain of יהוה shall be many.

17 "They that sanctify themselves, and purify themselves in the gardens behind one tree in the midst, eating swine's flesh, and the abomination, and the mouse, shall be consumed together," saith יהוה.

18 For I know their works and their thoughts. It shall come, that I will gather all nations and tongues; and they shall come, and see My glory.

19 "And I will set a sign among them, and I will send those that escape of them unto the nations, to Tarshish, Pul, and Lud, that draw the bow, to Tubal, and Yawan, to the isles afar off, that have not heard My fame, neither have seen My glory; and they shall declare My glory among the nations.

20 And they shall bring all your brethren for an offering unto יהוה out of all nations upon horses, and in chariots, and in litters, and upon mules, and upon swift beasts, to My holy mountain Jerusalem (Yerushalayim)," saith יהוה, "as the

children of Yisrael bring an offering in a clean vessel into the house of יהוה.

21 And I will also take of them for priests (kohanim) and for Levites (Lewiyim)," saith יהוה.

22 "For as the new heavens and the new earth, which I will make, shall remain before Me," saith יהוה, "So shall your seed and your name remain.

23 And it shall come to pass, that from one New Moon to another, and from one Shabbat to another, shall all flesh come to worship before Me," saith יהוה.

24 And they shall go forth, and look upon the carcases of the men that have transgressed against Me; for their worm shall not die, neither shall their fire be quenched; and they shall be an abhorring unto all flesh."

JEREMIAH
YIRMEYAHU יִרְמְיָהוּ
(YHWH will exalt)

1 The words of [A52]Jeremiah (Yirmeyahu) the son of Hilkiah (Chilqiyahu), of the priests (kohanim) that were in Anathoth in the land of Benjamin (Binyamin),

2 To whom the word of יהוה came in the days of Josiah (Yoshiyahu) the son of Amon king of Judah (Yehudah), in the thirteenth year of his reign.

3 It came also in the days of Yehoyaqim the son of Josiah (Yoshiyahu) king of Judah (Yehudah), unto the end of the eleventh year of Zedekiah (Tsidqiyahu) the son of Josiah (Yoshiyahu) king of Judah (Yehudah), unto the carrying away of Jerusalem (Yerushalayim) captive in the fifth month.

4 Then the word of יהוה came unto me, saying:

5 "Before I formed you in the belly I knew you; and before you camest forth out of the womb I sanctified you, and I ordained you a prophet unto the nations."

6 Then said I: "Ah, Lord (Adonai) יהוה! Behold, I cannot speak, for I am a child."

7 But יהוה said unto me, "Say not, 'I am a child,' for you shalt go to all that I shall send you, and whatsoever I command you you shalt speak.

8 Be not afraid of their faces, for I am with you to deliver you," saith יהוה.

9 Then יהוה put forth His hand, and touched my mouth. And יהוה said unto me: "Behold, I have put My words in your mouth.

10 See, I have this day set you over the nations and over the kingdoms, to root out, and to pull down, and to destroy, and to throw down, to build, and to plant."

11 Moreover the word of יהוה came unto me, saying, "Jeremiah (Yirmeyahu), what seest you?" And I said, "I see a rod of an almond tree."

12 Then said יהוה unto me, "You have well seen, for I will hasten My word to perform it."

13 And the word of יהוה came unto me the second time, saying, "What seest you?" And I said, "I see a seething pot; and the face thereof is toward the north."

14 Then יהוה said unto me, "Out of the north an evil shall break forth upon all the inhabitants of the land.

15 For, behold, I will call all the families of the kingdoms of the north," saith יהוה; "and they shall come, and they shall set every one his throne at the entering of the gates of Jerusalem (Yerushalayim), and against all the walls thereof round about, and against all the cities of Judah (Yehudah).

16 And I will utter My judgments against them touching all their wickedness, who have forsaken Me, and have burned incense unto other gods (elohim), and worshipped the works of their own hands.

17 You therefore gird up your loins, and arise, and speak unto them all that I command you. Be not dismayed at their faces, lest I confound you before them.

18 For, behold, I have made you this day a defenced city, and an iron pillar, and brasen walls against the whole land, against the kings of Judah (Yehudah), against the princes thereof, against the priests (kohanim) thereof, and against the people of the land.

19 And they shall fight against you; but they shall not prevail against you; for I am with you," saith יהוה, "to deliver you."

2 Moreover the word of יהוה came to me, saying,

2 "Go and cry in the ears of Jerusalem (Yerushalayim), saying, 'Thus saith יהוה: I remember you, the kindness of your youth, the love of your espousals, when you wentest after Me in the wilderness, in a land that was not sown.

3 Yisrael was holiness unto יהוה, and the firstfruits of His increase; all that devour Him shall offend; evil shall come upon them," saith יהוה.'"

4 Hear you the word of יהוה, O house of Jacob (Yaaqov), and all the families of the house of Yisrael.

5 Thus saith יהוה, 'What iniquity have your fathers found in Me, that they are gone far from Me, and have walked after vanity, and are become vain?

6 Neither said they, 'Where is יהוה that brought us up out of the land of Egypt (Mitsrayim), that led us through the wilderness, through a land of deserts and of pits, through a land of drought, and of the shadow of death, through a land that no man passed through, and where no man

dwelt?'

7 And I brought you into a plentiful country, to eat the fruit thereof and the goodness thereof; but when you entered, you defiled My land, and made Mine heritage an abomination.

8 The priests (kohanim) said not, 'Where is יהוה?' And they that handle the Torah knew Me not; the pastors also transgressed against Me, and the prophets prophesied by the Baal, and walked after things that do not profit.

9 "Wherefore I will yet plead with you," saith יהוה, "And with your children's children will I plead.

10 For pass over the isles of Chittim, and see; and send unto Kedar, and consider diligently, and see if there be such a thing.

11 Hath a nation exchanged its gods (elohim), which are yet not *true* God (Elohim)? But My people have exchanged their glory for that which doth not profit.

12 Be astonished, O you heavens, at this, and be horribly afraid, be you very desolate," saith יהוה.

13 "For My people have committed two evils; they have forsaken Me the fountain of living waters, and hewed themselves cisterns, broken cisterns, that can hold no water.

14 "Is Yisrael a servant? Is he a homeborn slave? Why is he spoiled?

15 The young lions roared upon him, and yelled, and they made his land waste; his cities are burned without inhabitant.

16 Also the children of Noph and Tahapanes have broken the crown of your head.

17 Have you not procured this unto yourself, in that you have forsaken יהוה your God (YHWH Eloheikha), when He led you by the way?

18 And now what have you to do in the way of Egypt (Mitsrayim), to drink the waters of Sihor? Or what have you to do in the way of Assyria (Ashshur), to drink the waters of the river?

19 Your own wickedness shall correct you, and your backslidings shall reprove you; know therefore and see that it is an evil thing and bitter, that you have forsaken יהוה your God (Elohim), and that My fear is not in you," saith Lord יהוה of hosts (Adonai YHWH Tsevaot).

20 For of old time I have broken your yoke, and burst your bands; and you saidst, 'I will not transgress'; when upon every high hill and under every green tree you wanderest, playing the harlot.

21 Yet I had planted you a noble vine, wholly a right seed. How then are you turned into the degenerate plant of a strange vine unto Me?

22 For though you wash you with nitre, and take you much soap, yet your iniquity is marked before Me," saith Lord (Adonai) יהוה.

23 "How canst you say, 'I am not polluted, I have not gone after Baals (Baalim)? See your way in the valley, know what you have done. You are a swift dromedary traversing her ways;

24 A wild ass used to the wilderness, that snuffeth up the wind at her pleasure; in her occasion who can turn her away? All they that seek her will not weary themselves; in her month they shall find her.

25 Withhold your foot from being unshod, and your throat from thirst: but you saidst, 'There is no hope. No! For I have loved strangers, and after them will I go.'

26 As the thief is ashamed when he is found, so is the house of Yisrael ashamed; they, their kings, their princes, and their priests (kohanim), and their prophets,

27 Saying to a stock, 'You are my father'; and to a stone, 'You have brought me forth.' For they have turned their back unto Me, and not their face; but in the time of their trouble they will say, 'Arise, and save us.'

28 But where are your gods (elohim) that you have made yourselves? Let them arise, if they can save you in the time of your trouble; for according to the number of your cities are your gods (elohim), O Judah (Yehudah).

29 "Wherefore will you plead with Me? You all have transgressed against Me," saith יהוה.

30 "In vain have I smitten your children; they received no correction; your own sword hath devoured your prophets, like a destroying lion.

31 O generation, see you the word of יהוה. Have I been a wilderness unto Yisrael? A land of darkness? Wherefore say My people, 'We will roam; we will come no more unto You'?

32 Can a maid forget her ornaments, or a bride her attire? Yet My people have forgotten Me days without number.

33 "Why trimmest you your way to seek love? Therefore have you also taught the wicked ones your ways.

34 Also in your skirts is found the blood of the

souls of the poor innocents; I have not found it by secret search, but upon all these.

35 Yet you sayest, 'Because I am innocent, surely His anger shall turn from me.' Behold, I will plead with you, because you sayest, 'I have not sinned.'

36 Why gaddest you about so much to change your way? You also shalt be ashamed of Egypt (Mitsrayim), as you wast ashamed of Assyria (Ashshur).

37 Yea, you shalt go forth from him, and your hands upon your head; for יהוה hath rejected your confidences, and you shalt not prosper in them.

3 They say, 'If a man put away his wife, and she go from him, and become another man's, shall he return unto her again?' Shall not that land be greatly polluted? But you have played the harlot with many lovers; yet return again to Me," saith יהוה.

2 "Lift up your eyes unto the high places, and see: where you have not been lien with. In the ways have you sat for them, as the Arabian in the wilderness; and you have polluted the land with your whoredoms and with your wickedness.

3 Therefore the showers have been withholden, and there hath been no latter rain; and you hadst a whore's forehead, you refusedst to be ashamed.

4 Wilt you not from this time cry unto Me, 'My Father (Avi), You are the guide of my youth?'

5 Will He reserve His anger forever? Will He keep it to the end? Behold, You have spoken and done evil things as You couldest."

6 יהוה said also unto me in the days of Josiah (Yoshiyahu) the king: "Have you seen that which backsliding Yisrael hath done? She is gone up upon every high mountain and under every green tree, and there hath played the harlot.

7 And I said after she had done all these things, 'Return you unto Me.' But she returned not. And her treacherous sister Judah (Yehudah) saw it.

8 And I saw, when for all the causes whereby backsliding Yisrael committed adultery I had put her away, and given her a bill of divorce; yet her treacherous sister Judah (Yehudah) feared not, but went and played the harlot also.

9 And it came to pass through the lightness of her whoredom, that she defiled the land, and committed adultery with stones and with stocks.

10 And yet for all this her treacherous sister Judah (Yehudah) hath not turned unto Me with her whole heart, but feignedly," saith יהוה.

11 And יהוה said unto me, "The backsliding Yisrael hath justified herself more than treacherous Judah (Yehudah).

12 Go and proclaim these words toward the north, and say, 'Return, you backsliding Yisrael,' saith יהוה; 'and I will not cause Mine anger to fall upon you; for I am merciful,' saith יהוה, 'and I will not keep anger forever.

13 Only acknowledge your iniquity, that you have transgressed against יהוה your God (YHWH Eloheikha), and hast scattered your ways to the strangers under every green tree, and you have not obeyed My voice,' saith יהוה.

14 "Return, O backsliding children," saith יהוה; "for I am married unto you; and I will take you one of a city, and two of a family, and I will bring you to Zion (Tsiyon).

15 And I will give you pastors according to Mine heart, which shall feed you with knowledge and understanding.

16 And it shall come to pass, when you be multiplied and increased in the land, in those days," saith יהוה, "they shall say no more, 'The ark of the covenant of יהוה.' Neither shall it come to mind; nor shall they remember it; neither shall they visit it; neither shall that be done anymore.

17 At that time they shall call Jerusalem (Yerushalayim) the throne of יהוה; and all the nations shall be gathered unto it, to the name of יהוה, to Jerusalem (Yerushalayim); neither shall they walk any more after the imagination of their evil heart.

18 In those days the house of Judah (Yehudah) shall walk with the house of Yisrael, and they shall come together out of the land of the north to the land that I have given for an inheritance unto your fathers.

19 But I said, 'How shall I put you among the children, and give you a pleasant land, a goodly heritage of the hosts of nations?'" And I said: 'You shalt call Me, "My Father (Avi);" and shalt not turn away from Me.'

20 Surely as a wife treacherously departeth from her husband, so have you dealt treacherously with Me, O house of Yisrael, saith

יהוה.

21 A voice was heard upon the high places, weeping and supplications of the children of Yisrael; for they have perverted their way, and they have forgotten יהוה their God (YHWH Eloheihem).

22 "Return, you backsliding children, and I will heal your backslidings." "Behold, we come unto you, for you are יהוה our God (YHWH Eloheinu).

23 Truly in vain is salvation hoped for from the hills, and from the multitude of mountains; truly in יהוה our God (YHWH Eloheinu) is the salvation of Yisrael.

24 For shame hath devoured the labour of our fathers from our youth; their flocks and their herds, their sons and their daughters.

25 We lie down in our shame, and our confusion covereth us; for we have sinned against יהוה our God (YHWH Eloheinu), we and our fathers, from our youth even unto this day, and have not obeyed the voice of יהוה our God (YHWH Eloheinu)."

4 "If you wilt return, O Yisrael," saith יהוה, "return unto Me; and if you wilt put away your abominations out of My sight, then shalt you not remove.

2 And you shalt swear, 'יהוה liveth, in truth, in judgment, and in righteousness; and the nations shall bless themselves in Him, and in Him shall they glory."

3 For thus saith יהוה to the men of Judah (Yehudah) and Jerusalem (Yerushalayim): "Break up your fallow ground, and sow not among thorns.

4 Circumcise yourselves to יהוה, and take away the foreskins of your heart, you men of Judah (Yehudah) and inhabitants of Jerusalem (Yerushalayim); lest My fury come forth like fire, and burn that none can quench it, because of the evil of your doings."

5 Declare you in Judah (Yehudah), and publish in Jerusalem (Yerushalayim), and say: "Blow you the trumpet in the land: cry, gather together, and say, 'Assemble yourselves, and let us go into the defenced cities.'

6 Set up the standard toward Zion (Tsiyon): retire, stay not; for I will bring evil from the north, and a great destruction."

7 The lion is come up from his thicket, and the destroyer of the nations is on his way, He is gone

forth from his place to make your land desolate; and your cities shall be laid waste, without an inhabitant.

8 For this gird you with sackcloth, lament and howl; for the fierce anger of יהוה is not turned back from us.

9 "And it shall come to pass at that day," saith יהוה, "that the heart of the king shall perish, and the heart of the princes; and the priests (kohanim) shall be astonished, and the prophets shall wonder."

10 Then said I, "Ah, Lord (Adonai) יהוה! Surely You have greatly deceived this people and Jerusalem (Yerushalayim), saying, 'You shall have peace;' whereas the sword reacheth unto the soul."

11 At that time shall it be said to this people and to Jerusalem (Yerushalayim), "A dry wind of the high places in the wilderness toward the daughter of My people, not to fan, nor to cleanse,

12 Even a full wind from those places shall come unto Me; now also will I give judgments against them."

13 "Behold, he shall come up as clouds, and his chariots shall be as a whirlwind; his horses are swifter than eagles. Woe unto us! For we are spoiled."

14 O Jerusalem (Yerushalayim), wash your heart from wickedness, that you mayest be saved. How long shall your vain thoughts lodge within you?

15 For a voice declareth from Dan, and publisheth affliction from Mount Efrayim:

16 "Make you mention to the nations; behold, publish against Jerusalem (Yerushalayim), that watchers come from a far country, and give out their voice against the cities of Judah (Yehudah).

17 As keepers of a field, are they against her round about; because she hath been rebellious against Me," saith יהוה.

18 "Your way and your doings have procured these things unto you; this is your wickedness, because it is bitter, because it reacheth unto your heart."

19 My bowels, my bowels! I am pained at my very heart; my heart maketh a noise in me; I cannot hold my peace, because you have heard, O my soul, the sound of the trumpet, the alarm of war.

20 Destruction upon destruction is cried; for

the whole land is spoiled; suddenly are my tents spoiled, and my curtains in a moment.

21 How long shall I see the standard, and hear the sound of the trumpet?

22 "For My people is foolish, they have not known Me; they are sottish children, and they have none understanding; they are wise to do evil, but to do good they have no knowledge."

23 I beheld the earth, and, behold, it was without form, and void; and the heavens, and they had no light.

24 I beheld the mountains, and, behold, they trembled, and all the hills moved lightly.

25 I beheld, and, behold, there was no man, and all the birds of the heavens were fled.

26 I beheld, and, behold, the fruitful place was a wilderness, and all the cities thereof were broken down at the presence of יהוה, and by His fierce anger.

27 For thus hath יהוה said: "The whole land shall be desolate; yet will I not make a full end.

28 For this shall the earth mourn, and the heavens above be black; because I have spoken it, I have purposed it, and will not repent, neither will I turn back from it.

29 The whole city shall flee for the noise of the horsemen and bowmen; they shall go into thickets, and climb up upon the rocks; every city shall be forsaken, and not a man dwells therein.

30 And when you are spoiled, what wilt you do? Though you clothest yourself with crimson, though you deckest you with ornaments of gold, though you rentest your face with painting, in vain shalt you make yourself fair; your lovers will despise you, they will seek your life.

31 For I have heard a voice as of a woman in travail, and the anguish as of her that bringeth forth her first child, the voice of the daughter of Zion (Tsiyon), that bewaileth herself, that spreadeth her hands, saying, 'Woe is me now, for my soul is wearied because of murderers!'

5 Run you to and fro through the streets of Jerusalem (Yerushalayim), and see now, and know, and seek in the broad places thereof, if you can find a man, if there be any that executeth judgment, that seeketh the truth; and I will pardon it.

2 And though they say, 'יהוה liveth;' surely they swear falsely."

3 O יהוה, are not Your eyes upon the truth? You have stricken them, but they have not grieved; You have consumed them, but they have refused to receive correction; they have made their faces harder than a rock; they have refused to turn back.

4 Therefore I said, "Surely these are poor; they are foolish; for they know not the way of יהוה, nor the judgment of their God (Elohim).

5 I will get me unto the great men, and will speak unto them; for they have known the way of יהוה, and the judgment of their God (Elohim)." But these have altogether broken the yoke, and burst the bonds.

6 Wherefore a lion out of the forest shall slay them, and a wolf of the evenings shall spoil them, a leopard shall watch over their cities; every one that goeth out thence shall be torn in pieces; because their transgressions are many, and their backslidings are increased.

7 "How shall I pardon you for this? Your children have forsaken Me, and sworn by them that are not God (Elohim); when I had fed them to the full, they then committed adultery, and assembled themselves by troops in the harlots' houses.

8 They were as fed horses in the morning; every one neighed after his neighbour's wife.

9 Shall I not visit for these things?" saith יהוה. "And shall not My soul be avenged on such a nation as this?

10 Go you up upon her walls, and destroy; but make not a full end; take away her battlements, for they are not יהוה's.

11 For the house of Yisrael and the house of Judah (Yehudah) have dealt very treacherously against Me," saith יהוה.

12 They have belied יהוה, and said, "It is not He; neither shall evil come upon us; neither shall we see sword nor famine:

13 And the prophets shall become wind, and the word is not in them; thus shall it be done unto them."

14 Wherefore thus saith יהוה God of hosts (YHWH Elohei Tsevaot): "Because you speak this word, behold, I will make My words in your mouth fire, and this people wood, and it shall devour them.

15 Lo, I will bring a nation upon you from far, O house of Yisrael," saith יהוה. "It is a mighty nation, it is an ancient nation, a nation whose language you knowest not, neither understandest

what they say.

16 Their quiver is as an open sepulchre, they are all mighty men.

17 And they shall eat up your harvest, and your bread, which your sons and your daughters should eat; they shall eat up your flocks and your herds; they shall eat up your vines and your fig trees; they shall impoverish your fenced cities, wherein you trustedst, with the sword.

18 "Nevertheless in those days," saith יהוה, "I will not make a full end with you.

19 And it shall come to pass, when you shall say, 'Wherefore doeth יהוה our God (YHWH Eloheinu) all these things unto us?' Then shalt you answer them, 'Like as you have forsaken Me, and served foreign gods (elohim) in your land, so shall you serve strangers in a land that is not yours.'

20 Declare this in the house of Jacob (Yaaqov), and proclaim it in Judah (Yehudah), saying,

21 'Hear now this, O foolish people, and without understanding; who have eyes, and see not; who have ears, and hear not:

22 Fear you not Me?' saith יהוה. "Will you not tremble at My presence, who have placed the sand for the bound of the sea by a perpetual decree, that it cannot pass it; and though the waves thereof toss themselves, yet can they not prevail; though they roar, yet can they not pass over it?

23 But this people hath a revolting and a rebellious heart; they are revolted and gone.

24 Neither say they in their heart, "Let us now fear יהוה our God (YHWH Eloheinu), that giveth rain, both the former and the latter, in his season. He reserveth unto us the appointed weeks of the harvest."

25 Your iniquities have turned away these things, and your sins have withholden good things from you.

26 'For among My people are found wicked men; they lay wait, as he that setteth snares; they set a trap, they catch men.

27 As a cage is full of birds, so are their houses full of deceit; therefore they are become great, and waxen rich.

28 They are waxen fat, they shine; yea, they overpass the deeds of the wicked: they judge not the cause, the cause of the fatherless, yet they prosper; and the right of the needy do they not judge.

29 'Shall I not visit for these things?' saith יהוה. 'Shall not My soul be avenged on such a nation as this?'

30 An appalling and horrible thing is committed in the land:

31 The prophets prophesy falsely, and the priests (kohanim) bear rule by their means; and My people love to have it so; and what will you do in the end thereof?

6 "O you children of Benjamin (Binyamin), gather yourselves to flee out of the midst of Jerusalem (Yerushalayim)! And blow the shofar in Tekoa, and set up a sign of fire in Beit-Haccerem; for evil appeareth out of the north, and great destruction.

2 I have likened the daughter of Zion (Tsiyon) to a comely and delicate woman.

3 The shepherds with their flocks shall come unto her; they shall pitch their tents against her round about; they shall feed every one in his place."

4 "Prepare you war against her; arise, and let us go up at noon. Woe unto us! For the day goeth away, for the shadows of the evening are stretched out.

5 Arise, and let us go by night, and let us destroy her palaces."

6 For thus hath יהוה of hosts (YHWH Tsevaot) said: "Hew you down trees, and cast a mount against Jerusalem (Yerushalayim): this is the city to be visited; she is wholly oppression in the midst of her.

7 As a fountain casteth out her waters, so she casteth out her wickedness; violence and spoil is heard in her; before Me continually is grief and wounds.

8 Be you instructed, O Jerusalem (Yerushalayim), lest My soul depart from you; lest I make you desolate, a land not inhabited."

9 Thus saith יהוה of hosts (YHWH Tsevaot): "They shall throughly glean the remnant of Yisrael as a vine; turn back your hand as a grapegatherer into the baskets."

10 To whom shall I speak, and give warning, that they may hear? Behold, their ear is uncircumcised, and they cannot hearken: behold, the word of יהוה is unto them a reproach; they have no delight in it.

11 Therefore I am full of the fury of יהוה; I am weary with holding in. "I will pour it out upon the children abroad, and upon the assembly of

young men together: for even the husband with the wife shall be taken, the aged with him that is full of days.

12 And their houses shall be turned unto others, with their fields and wives together; for I will stretch out My hand upon the inhabitants of the land," saith יהוה.

13 "For from the least of them even unto the greatest of them every one is given to covetousness; and from the prophet even unto the priest (kohen) every one dealeth falsely.

14 They have healed also the hurt of the daughter of My people slightly, saying, 'Peace, peace!' when there is no peace.

15 Were they ashamed when they had committed abomination? Nay, they were not at all ashamed, neither could they blush. Therefore they shall fall among them that fall; at the time that I visit them they shall be cast down," saith יהוה.

16 Thus saith יהוה: "Stand you in the ways, and see, and ask for the old paths, where is the good way, and walk therein, and you shall find rest for your souls. But they said, 'We will not walk therein.'

17 Also I set watchmen over you, saying, 'Hearken to the sound of the shofar.' But they said, 'We will not hearken.'

18 Therefore hear, you nations, and know, O congregation, what is among them.

19 Hear, O earth: behold, I will bring evil upon this people, even the fruit of their thoughts, because they have not hearkened unto My words, nor to My Torah, but rejected it.

20 To what purpose cometh there to Me incense from Sheva, and the sweet cane from a far country? Your burnt offerings are not acceptable, nor your sacrifices sweet unto Me."

21 Therefore thus saith יהוה: "Behold, I will lay stumblingblocks before this people, and the fathers and the sons together shall fall upon them. The neighbour and his friend shall perish."

22 Thus saith יהוה, Behold, a people cometh from the north country, and a great nation shall be raised from the sides of the earth.

23 They shall lay hold on bow and spear; they are cruel, and have no mercy; their voice roareth like the sea; and they ride upon horses, set in array as men for war against you, O daughter of Zion (Tsiyon)."

24 We have heard the fame thereof; our hands wax feeble: anguish hath taken hold of us, and pain, as of a woman in travail.

25 Go not forth into the field, nor walk by the way; for the sword of the enemy and fear is on every side.

26 O daughter of My people, gird you with sackcloth, and wallow yourself in ashes: make you mourning, as for an only son, most bitter lamentation; for the spoiler shall suddenly come upon us.

27 I have set you for a tower and a fortress among My people, that you mayest know and try their way.

28 They are all grievous revolters, walking with slanders. They are brass and iron; they are all corrupters.

29 The bellows are burned, the lead is consumed of the fire; the founder melteth in vain, for the wicked are not plucked away.

30 Reprobate silver shall men call them, because יהוה hath rejected them."

7 The word that came to Jeremiah (Yirmeyahu) from יהוה, saying,

2 "Stand in the gate of יהוה's house, and proclaim there this word, and say, 'Hear the word of יהוה, all you of Judah (Yehudah), that enter in at these gates to worship יהוה!'"

3 Thus saith יהוה of hosts (YHWH Tsevaot), the God of Israel (Elohei Yisrael): "Amend your ways and your doings, and I will cause you to dwell in this place.

4 Trust you not in lying words, saying, 'The temple of יהוה, the temple of יהוה, the temple of יהוה, are these.'

5 For if you throughly amend your ways and your doings; if you throughly execute judgment between a man and his neighbour;

6 If you oppress not the stranger, the fatherless, and the widow, and shed not innocent blood in this place, neither walk after other gods (elohim) to your hurt;

7 Then will I cause you to dwell in this place, in the land that I gave to your fathers, forever and ever.

8 Behold, you trust in lying words, that cannot profit.

9 Will you steal, murder, and commit adultery, and swear falsely, and burn incense unto the Baal, and walk after other gods (elohim) whom you know not;

10 And come and stand before Me in this house,

which is called by My name, and say, 'We are delivered to do all these abominations'?

11 Is this house, which is called by My name, become a den of robbers in your eyes? Behold, even I have seen it," saith יהוה.

12 But go you now unto My place which was in Shiloh, where I set My name at the first, and see what I did to it for the wickedness of My people Yisrael.

13 "And now, because you have done all these works," saith יהוה, "and I spake unto you, rising up early and speaking, but you heard not; and I called you, but you answered not;

14 Therefore will I do unto this house, which is called by My name, wherein you trust, and unto the place which I gave to you and to your fathers, as I have done to Shiloh.

15 And I will cast you out of My sight, as I have cast out all your brethren, even the whole seed of Efrayim.

16 Therefore pray not you for this people, neither lift up cry nor prayer for them, neither make intercession to Me; for I will not hear you.

17 Seest you not what they do in the cities of Judah (Yehudah) and in the streets of Jerusalem (Yerushalayim)?

18 The children gather wood, and the fathers kindle the fire, and the women knead their dough, to make cakes to the queen of heaven, and to pour out drink offerings unto other gods (elohim), that they may provoke Me to anger.

19 "Do they provoke Me to anger?" saith יהוה; do they not provoke themselves to the confusion of their own faces?"

20 Therefore thus saith Lord (Adonai) יהוה: "Behold, Mine anger and My fury shall be poured out upon this place, upon man, and upon beast, and upon the trees of the field, and upon the fruit of the ground; and it shall burn, and shall not be quenched."

21 Thus saith יהוה of hosts (YHWH Tsevaot), the God of Israel (Elohei Yisrael): "Put your burnt offerings unto your sacrifices, and eat flesh.

22 For I spake not unto your fathers, nor commanded them in the day that I brought them out of the land of Egypt (Mitsrayim), concerning burnt offerings or sacrifices:

23 But this thing commanded I them, saying, 'Obey My voice, and I will be your God (Elohim), and you shall be My people; and walk you in all the ways that I have commanded you, that it may be well unto you.'

24 But they hearkened not, nor inclined their ear, but walked in the counsels and in the imagination of their evil heart, and went backward, and not forward.

25 Since the day that your fathers came forth out of the land of Egypt (Mitsrayim) unto this day I have even sent unto you all My servants the prophets, daily rising up early and sending them;

26 Yet they hearkened not unto Me, nor inclined their ear, but hardened their neck; they did worse than their fathers.

27 Therefore you shalt speak all these words unto them; but they will not hearken to you; you shalt also call unto them; but they will not answer you.

28 But you shalt say unto them, 'This is a nation that obeyeth not the voice of יהוה their God (YHWH Eloheihem), nor receiveth correction; truth is perished, and is cut off from their mouth.

29 Cut off your hair, O Jerusalem (Yerushalayim), and cast it away, and take up a lamentation on high places; for יהוה hath rejected and forsaken the generation of His wrath.'

30 "For the children of Judah (Yehudah) have done evil in My sight," saith יהוה. "They have set their abominations in the house which is called by My name, to pollute it.

31 And they have built the high places of Tophet, which is in the valley of the son of Hinnom, to burn their sons and their daughters in the fire; which I commanded them not, neither came it into My heart.

32 Therefore, behold, the days come," saith יהוה, "that it shall no more be called Tophet, nor the valley of the son of Hinnom, but the valley of slaughter; for they shall bury in Tophet, till there be no place.

33 And the carcases of this people shall be meat for the fowls of the heaven, and for the beasts of the earth; and none shall fray them away.

34 Then will I cause to cease from the cities of Judah (Yehudah), and from the streets of Jerusalem (Yerushalayim), the voice of mirth, and the voice of gladness, the voice of the bridegroom, and the voice of the bride; for the land shall be desolate."

8 "At that time," saith יהוה, "they shall bring out the bones of the kings of Judah (Yehudah), and the bones of his princes, and the bones of the priests (kohanim), and the bones of the prophets, and the bones of the inhabitants of Jerusalem (Yerushalayim), out of their graves:

2 And they shall spread them before the sun, and the moon, and all the host of heaven, whom they have loved, and whom they have served, and after whom they have walked, and whom they have sought, and whom they have worshipped. They shall not be gathered, nor be buried; they shall be for dung upon the face of the earth.

3 And death shall be chosen rather than life by all the residue of them that remain of this evil family, which remain in all the places whither I have driven them," saith יהוה of hosts (YHWH Tsevaot).

4 Moreover you shalt say unto them, 'Thus saith יהוה: "Shall they fall, and not arise? Shall he turn away, and not turn back?

5 Why then is this people of Jerusalem (Yerushalayim) slidden back by a perpetual backsliding? They hold fast deceit, they refuse to turn back.

6 I hearkened and heard, but they spake not aright; no man repented of his wickedness, saying, 'What have I done?' Every one turned to his course, as the horse rusheth into the battle.

7 Yea, the stork in the heaven knoweth her appointed times; and the turtle and the crane and the swallow observe the time of their coming; but My people know not the judgment of יהוה.

8 How do you say, 'We are wise, and the Torah of יהוה is with us'? Behold, certainly in vain made he it; the pen of the scribes is in vain.

9 The wise men are ashamed, they are dismayed and taken. Behold, they have rejected the word of יהוה; and what wisdom is in them?

10 Therefore will I give their wives unto others, and their fields to them that shall inherit them; for every one from the least even unto the greatest is given to covetousness, from the prophet even unto the priest (kohen) everyone dealeth falsely.

11 For they have healed the hurt of the daughter of My people slightly, saying, 'Peace, peace!' when there is no peace.

12 Were they ashamed when they had committed abomination? Nay, they were not at all ashamed, neither could they blush; therefore shall they fall among them that fall; in the time of their visitation they shall be cast down," saith יהוה.

13 "I will surely consume them," saith יהוה. "There shall be no grapes on the vine, nor figs on the fig tree, and the leaf shall fade; and the things that I have given them shall pass away from them.""""

14 "Why do we sit still? Assemble yourselves, and let us enter into the defenced cities, and let us be silent there; for יהוה our God (YHWH Eloheinu) hath put us to silence, and given us water of gall to drink, because we have sinned against יהוה.

15 We looked for peace, but no good came; and for a time of health, and behold trouble!

16 The snorting of his horses was heard from Dan. The whole land trembled at the sound of the neighing of his strong ones; for they are come, and have devoured the land, and all that is in it; the city, and those that dwell therein."

17 "For, behold, I will send serpents, cockatrices, among you, which will not be charmed, and they shall bite you," saith יהוה.

18 When I would comfort myself against sorrow, my heart is faint in me.

19 Behold the voice of the cry of the daughter of my people because of them that dwell in a far country: "Is not יהוה in Zion (Tsiyon)? Is not her king in her?" "Why have they provoked Me to anger with their graven images, and with foreign idols?"

20 "The harvest is past, the summer is ended, and we are not saved!"

21 For the hurt of the daughter of my people am I hurt; I am mourning; astonishment hath taken hold on me.

22 Is there no balm in Gilad; is there no physician there? Why then is not the health of the daughter of my people recovered?

9 Oh that my head were waters, and mine eyes a fountain of tears, that I might weep day and night for the slain of the daughter of my people!

2 Oh that I had in the wilderness a lodging place of wayfaring men; that I might leave my people, and go from them! For they be all adulterers, an assembly of treacherous men.

3 "And they bend their tongues like their bow for lies; but they are not valiant for the truth upon the earth; for they proceed from evil to evil, and they know not Me," saith יהוה.

4 "Take you heed every one of his neighbour, and trust you not in any brother; for every brother will utterly supplant, and every neighbour will walk with slanders.

5 And they will deceive every one his neighbour, and will not speak the truth; they have taught their tongue to speak lies, and weary themselves to commit iniquity.

6 Your habitation is in the midst of deceit; through deceit they refuse to know Me," saith יהוה.

7 Therefore thus saith יהוה of hosts (YHWH Tsevaot): "Behold, I will melt them, and try them; for how shall I do for the daughter of My people?

8 Their tongue is as an arrow shot out; it speaketh deceit; one speaketh peaceably to his neighbour with his mouth, but in heart he layeth his wait.

9 Shall I not visit them for these things?" saith יהוה. "Shall not My soul be avenged on such a nation as this?"

10 For the mountains will I take up a weeping and wailing, and for the habitations of the wilderness a lamentation, because they are burned up, so that none can pass through them; neither can men hear the voice of the cattle; both the fowl of the heavens and the beast are fled; they are gone.

11 "And I will make Jerusalem (Yerushalayim) heaps, and a den of dragons; and I will make the cities of Judah (Yehudah) desolate, without an inhabitant."

12 Who is the wise man, that may understand this? And who is he to whom the mouth of יהוה hath spoken, that he may declare it, for what the land perisheth and is burned up like a wilderness, that none passeth through?

13 And יהוה saith, "Because they have forsaken My Torah which I set before them, and have not obeyed My voice, neither walked therein;

14 But have walked after the imagination of their own heart, and after Baals (Baalim), which their fathers taught them;"

15 Therefore thus saith יהוה of hosts (YHWH Tsevaot), the God of Israel (Elohei Yisrael): "Behold, I will feed them, even this people, with wormwood, and give them water of gall to drink.

16 I will scatter them also among the heathen, whom neither they nor their fathers have known:

and I will send a sword after them, till I have consumed them."

17 Thus saith יהוה of hosts (YHWH Tsevaot): "Consider you, and call for the mourning women, that they may come; and send for cunning women, that they may come;

18 And let them make haste, and take up a wailing for us, that our eyes may run down with tears, and our eyelids gush out with waters.

19 For a voice of wailing is heard out of Zion (Tsiyon): 'How are we spoiled! We are greatly confounded, because we have forsaken the land, because our dwellings have cast us out.'"

20 Yet hear the word of יהוה, O you women, and let your ear receive the word of His mouth, and teach your daughters wailing, and every one her neighbour lamentation.

21 For death is come up into our windows, and is entered into our palaces, to cut off the children from outside, and the young men from the streets!

22 Speak, "Thus saith יהוה: 'Even the carcases of men shall fall as dung upon the open field, and as the handful after the harvestman, and none shall gather them.'"

23 Thus saith יהוה: "Let not the wise man glory in his wisdom, neither let the mighty man glory in his might, let not the rich man glory in his riches;

24 But let him that glorieth glory in this, that he understandeth and knoweth Me, that I am יהוה who exercise lovingkindness, judgment, and righteousness in the earth; for in these things I delight," saith יהוה.

25 "Behold, the days come," saith יהוה, "that I will punish all those who are circumcised with the uncircumcised;

26 Egypt (Mitsrayim), and Judah (Yehudah), and Edom, and the children of Ammon, and Moav, and all that are in the utmost corners, that dwell in the wilderness; for all these nations are uncircumcised, and all the house of Yisrael are uncircumcised in the heart."

10 Hear you the word which יהוה speaketh unto you, O house of Yisrael.

2 Thus saith יהוה: "Learn not the way of the heathen, and be not dismayed at the signs of heaven; for the heathen are dismayed at them.

3 For the customs of the people are vain, for one cutteth a tree out of the forest, the work of the hands of the workman, with the axe.

4 They deck it with silver and with gold; they fasten it with nails and with hammers, that it moves not.

5 They are upright as the palm tree, but speak not; they must be carried, because they cannot go. Be not afraid of them; for they cannot do evil, neither also is it in them to do good."

6 Forasmuch as there is none like unto You, O יהוה; You are great, and Your name is great in might.

7 Who would not fear You, O King of nations? For it is Your rightful due, forasmuch as among all the wise men of the nations, and in all their kingdoms, there is none like unto You.

8 But they are altogether brutish and foolish; the wood is a doctrine of vanities.

9 Silver spread into plates is brought from Tarshish, and gold from Uphaz, the work of the workman, and of the hands of the founder; blue and purple is their clothing; they are all the work of cunning men.

10 But יהוה is the true God (Elohim), He is the living God (Elohim chayim), and an everlasting King; at His wrath the earth shall tremble, and the nations shall not be able to abide His indignation.

11 Thus shall you say unto them: "The gods (elohim) that have not made the heavens and the earth, even they shall perish from the earth, and from under these heavens."

12 He hath made the earth by His power, He hath established the world by His wisdom, and hath stretched out the heavens by His discretion.

13 When He uttereth His voice, there is a multitude of waters in the heavens: "And He causeth the vapours to ascend from the ends of the earth; He maketh lightnings with rain, and bringeth forth the wind out of His treasures."

14 Every man is brutish in his knowledge; every founder is confounded by the graven image; for his molten image is falsehood, and there is no breath in them.

15 They are vanity, and the work of errors; in the time of their visitation they shall perish.

16 The portion of Jacob (Yaaqov) is not like them, for He is the Maker of all things; and Yisrael is the tribe of His inheritance: יהוה of hosts (YHWH Tsevaot) is His name.

17 Gather up your wares out of the land, O inhabitant of the fortress!

18 For thus saith יהוה: "Behold, I will sling out the inhabitants of the land at this once, and will distress them, that they may find it so."

19 Woe is me for my hurt! My wound is grievous; but I said, "Truly this is a grief, and I must bear it."

20 My tabernacle is spoiled, and all my cords are broken; my children are gone forth of me, and they are not; there is none to stretch forth my tent any more, and to set up my curtains.

21 For the pastors are become brutish, and have not sought יהוה; therefore they shall not prosper, and all their flocks shall be scattered.

22 Behold, the noise of the bruit is come, and a great commotion out of the north country, to make the cities of Judah (Yehudah) desolate, and a den of dragons (tannim).

23 O יהוה, I know that the way of man is not in himself; it is not in man that walketh to direct his steps.

24 O יהוה, correct me, but with justice; not in Your anger, lest You bring me to nothing.

25 Pour out Your fury upon the heathen that know You not, and upon the families that call not on Your name; for they have eaten up Jacob (Yaaqov), and devoured him, and consumed him, and have made his habitation desolate.

11 The word that came to Jeremiah (Yirmeyahu) from יהוה, saying,

2 "Hear you the words of this covenant, and speak unto the men of Judah (Yehudah), and to the inhabitants of Jerusalem (Yerushalayim);

3 And say you unto them, 'Thus saith יהוה God of Israel (Elohei Yisrael): "Cursed be the man that obeyeth not the words of this covenant,

4 Which I commanded your fathers in the day that I brought them forth out of the land of Egypt (Mitsrayim), from the iron furnace, saying, 'Obey My voice, and do them, according to all which I command you; so shall you be My people, and I will be your God (Elohim),'

5 That I may perform the oath which I have sworn unto your fathers, to give them a land flowing with milk and honey, as it is this day.""" Then answered I, and said, "So be it, O יהוה."

6 Then יהוה said unto me, "Proclaim all these words in the cities of Judah (Yehudah), and in the streets of Jerusalem (Yerushalayim), saying, 'Hear you the words of this covenant, and do them.

7 For I earnestly protested unto your fathers in the day that I brought them up out of the land

of Egypt (Mitsrayim), even unto this day, rising early and protesting, saying, "Obey My voice." 8 Yet they obeyed not, nor inclined their ear, but walked every one in the imagination of their evil heart; therefore I will bring upon them all the words of this covenant, which I commanded them to do, but they did them not.'"

9 And יהוה said unto me, "A conspiracy is found among the men of Judah (Yehudah), and among the inhabitants of Jerusalem (Yerushalayim).

10 They are turned back to the iniquities of their forefathers, which refused to hear my words; and they went after other gods (elohim) to serve them: the house of Yisrael and the house of Judah (Yehudah) have broken My covenant which I made with their fathers."

11 Therefore thus saith יהוה: "Behold, I will bring evil upon them, which they shall not be able to escape; and though they shall cry unto Me, I will not hearken unto them.

12 Then shall the cities of Judah (Yehudah) and inhabitants of Jerusalem (Yerushalayim) go, and cry unto the gods (elohim) unto whom they offer incense; but they shall not save them at all in the time of their trouble.

13 For according to the number of your cities were your gods (elohim), O Judah (Yehudah); and according to the number of the streets of Jerusalem (Yerushalayim) have you set up altars to that shameful thing, even altars to burn incense unto the Baal.

14 Therefore pray not you for this people, neither lift up a cry or prayer for them, for I will not hear them in the time that they cry unto Me for their trouble.

15 What hath My beloved to do in Mine house, seeing she hath wrought lewdness with many, and the holy flesh is passed from you? When you doest evil, then you rejoicest.

16 יהוה called your name, 'A green olive tree, fair, and of goodly fruit;' with the noise of a great tumult He hath kindled fire upon it, and the branches of it are broken.

17 For יהוה of hosts (YHWH Tsevaot), who planted you, hath pronounced evil against you, for the evil of the house of Yisrael and of the house of Judah (Yehudah), which they have done against themselves to provoke Me to anger in offering incense unto the Baal."

18 And יהוה hath given me knowledge of it, and I know it; then You shewedst me their doings.

19 But I was like a lamb or an ox that is brought to the slaughter; and I knew not that they had devised devices against me, saying, "Let us destroy the tree with the fruit thereof, and let us cut him off from the land of the living, that his name may be no more remembered."

20 But, O יהוה of hosts (YHWH Tsevaot), that judgest righteously, that triest the reins and the heart, let me see Your vengeance on them, for unto You have I revealed my cause.

21 Therefore thus saith יהוה of the men of Anathoth, that seek your life, saying, 'Prophesy not in the name of יהוה, that you die not by our hand';

22 Therefore thus saith יהוה of hosts (YHWH Tsevaot): 'Behold, I will punish them; the young men shall die by the sword; their sons and their daughters shall die by famine;

23 And there shall be no remnant of them; for I will bring evil upon the men of Anathoth, even the year of their visitation.'"

12 Righteous art You, O יהוה, when I plead with You; yet let me talk with You of Your judgments. Wherefore doth the way of the wicked prosper? Wherefore are all they happy that deal very treacherously?

2 You have planted them, yea, they have taken root; they grow, yea, they bring forth fruit. You are near in their mouth, and far from their reins.

3 But You, O יהוה, knowest me; You have seen me, and tested mine heart toward You. Pull them out like sheep for the slaughter, and prepare them for the day of slaughter.

4 How long shall the land mourn, and the herbs of every field wither, for the wickedness of them that dwell therein? The beasts are consumed, and the birds; because they said, "He shall not see our last end."

5 "If you have run with the footmen, and they have wearied you, then how canst you contend with horses? And if in the land of peace, wherein you trustedst, they wearied you, then how wilt you do in the swelling of Jordan (Yarden)?

6 For even your brethren, and the house of your father, even they have dealt treacherously with you; yea, they have called a multitude after you; believe them not, though they speak fair words unto you.

7 I have forsaken mine house, I have left mine heritage; I have given the dearly beloved of my soul into the hand of her enemies.

8 Mine heritage is unto me as a lion in the forest; it crieth out against me; therefore have I hated it.

9 Mine heritage is unto me as a speckled bird, the birds round about are against her; come you, assemble all the beasts of the field, come to devour!

10 Many pastors have destroyed my vineyard, they have trodden my portion under foot, they have made my pleasant portion a desolate wilderness.

11 They have made it desolate, and being desolate it mourneth unto me; the whole land is made desolate, because no man layeth it to heart.

12 The spoilers are come upon all high places through the wilderness, for the sword of יהוה shall devour from the one end of the land even to the other end of the land; no flesh shall have peace.

13 They have sown wheat, but shall reap thorns; they have put themselves to pain, but shall not profit; and they shall be ashamed of your revenues because of the fierce anger of יהוה."

14 Thus saith יהוה: "Against all Mine evil neighbours, who touch the inheritance which I have caused My people Yisrael to inherit; behold, I will pluck them out of their land, and pluck out the house of Judah (Yehudah) from among them.

15 And it shall come to pass, after that I have plucked them out I will return, and have compassion on them, and will bring them again, every man to his heritage, and every man to his land.

16 And it shall come to pass, if they will diligently learn the ways of My people, to swear by My name, 'יהוה liveth;' as they taught My people to swear by the Baal, then shall they be built in the midst of My people.

17 But if they will not obey, I will utterly pluck up and destroy that nation," saith יהוה.

13 Thus saith יהוה unto me: "Go and get you a linen girdle, and put it upon your loins, and put it not in water."

2 So I got a girdle according to the word of יהוה, and put it on my loins.

3 And the word of יהוה came unto me the second time, saying,

4 "Take the girdle that you have got, which is upon your loins, and arise, go to Euphrates, and hide it there in a hole of the rock."

5 So I went, and hid it by Euphrates, as יהוה commanded me.

6 And it came to pass after many days, that יהוה said unto me, "Arise, go to Euphrates, and take the girdle from thence, which I commanded you to hide there."

7 Then I went to Euphrates, and digged, and took the girdle from the place where I had hidden it: and, behold, the girdle was marred, it was profitable for nothing.

8 "Then the word of יהוה came unto me, saying,

9 Thus saith יהוה: 'After this manner will I mar the pride of Judah (Yehudah), and the great pride of Jerusalem (Yerushalayim).

10 This evil people, who refuse to hear My words, who walk in the imagination of their heart, and walk after other gods (elohim), to serve them, and to worship them, shall even be as this girdle, which is good for nothing.

11 For as the girdle cleaveth to the loins of a man, so have I caused to cleave unto Me the whole house of Yisrael and the whole house of Judah (Yehudah),' saith יהוה, 'that they might be unto Me for a people, and for a name, and for praise, and for glory; but they would not hear.'

12 Therefore you shalt speak unto them this word: 'Thus saith יהוה God of Israel (Elohei Yisrael): "Every bottle shall be filled with wine."' And they shall say unto you, 'Do we not certainly know that every bottle shall be filled with wine?'

13 Then shalt you say unto them, 'Thus saith יהוה: "Behold, I will fill all the inhabitants of this land, even the kings that sit upon Dawid's throne, and the priests (kohanim), and the prophets, and all the inhabitants of Jerusalem (Yerushalayim), with drunkenness!

14 And I will dash them one against another, even the fathers and the sons together," saith יהוה. "I will not pity, nor spare, nor have mercy, but destroy them."'"

15 Hear you, and give ear: Be not proud, for יהוה hath spoken.

16 Give glory to יהוה your God (YHWH Eloheikhem), before He causes darkness, and before your feet stumble upon the dark mountains, and, while you look for light, He turns it into the shadow of death, and makes it gross darkness.

17 But if you will not hear it, my soul shall weep in secret places for your pride; and mine eye

shall weep sore, and run down with tears, because יהוה's flock is carried away captive.

18 Say unto the king and to the queen, "Humble yourselves, sit down, for your principalities shall come down, even the crown of your glory."

19 The cities of the south shall be shut up, and none shall open them: Judah (Yehudah) shall be carried away captive all of it, it shall be wholly carried away captive.

20 Lift up your eyes, and behold them that come from the north: where is the flock that was given you, your beautiful flock?

21 What wilt you say when He shall punish you? For you have taught them to be captains, and as chief over you; shall not sorrows take you, as a woman in travail?

22 And if you say in your heart, "Wherefore come these things upon me?" For the greatness of your iniquity are your skirts discovered, and your heels made bare.

23 Can the Ethiopian (Kushi) change his skin, or the leopard his spots? Then may you also do good, that are accustomed to do evil.

24 "Therefore will I scatter them as the stubble that passeth away by the wind of the wilderness.

25 This is your lot, the portion of your measures from Me," saith יהוה; "Because you have forgotten Me, and trusted in falsehood.

26 Therefore will I discover your skirts upon your face, that your shame may appear.

27 I have seen your adulteries, and your neighings, the lewdness of your whoredom, and your abominations on the hills in the fields. Woe unto you, O Jerusalem (Yerushalayim)! Wilt you not be made clean? When shall it once be?"

14 The word of יהוה that came to Jeremiah (Yirmeyahu) concern -ing the drought:

2 "Judah (Yehudah) mourneth, and the gates thereof languish; they are black unto the ground; and the cry of Jerusalem (Yerushalayim) is gone up.

3 And their nobles have sent their little ones to the waters; they came to the pits, and found no water; they returned with their vessels empty; they were ashamed and confounded, and covered their heads.

4 Because the ground is chapt, for there was no rain in the earth, the plowmen were ashamed, they covered their heads.

5 Yea, the hind also calved in the field, and forsook it, because there was no grass.

6 And the wild asses did stand in the high places, they snuffed up the wind like dragons; their eyes did fail, because there was no grass."

7 O יהוה, though our iniquities testify against us, do you it for Your name's sake; for our backslidings are many; we have sinned against You.

8 O the hope of Yisrael, the savior thereof in time of trouble, why shouldest you be as a stranger in the land, and as a wayfaring man that turneth aside to tarry for a night?

9 Why shouldest you be as a man astonied, as a mighty man that cannot save? Yet You, O יהוה, art in the midst of us, and we are called by Your name; leave us not!

10 Thus saith יהוה unto this people: "Thus have they loved to wander, they have not refrained their feet, therefore יהוה doth not accept them; He will now remember their iniquity, and visit their sins."

11 Then said יהוה unto me, "Pray not for this people for their good.

12 When they fast, I will not hear their cry; and when they offer burnt offering and an oblation, I will not accept them; but I will consume them by the sword, and by the famine, and by the pestilence."

13 Then said I, "Ah, Lord (Adonai) יהוה! Behold, the prophets say unto them, 'You shall not see the sword, neither shall you have famine, but I will give you assured peace in this place.'"

14 Then יהוה said unto me, "The prophets prophesy lies in My name: I sent them not, neither have I commanded them, neither spake unto them; they prophesy unto you a false vision and divination, and a thing of nought, and the deceit of their heart.

15 Therefore thus saith יהוה "Concerning the prophets that prophesy in My name, and I sent them not, yet they say, 'Sword and famine shall not be in this land'; by sword and famine shall those prophets be consumed!

16 And the people to whom they prophesy shall be cast out in the streets of Jerusalem (Yerushalayim) because of the famine and the sword; and they shall have none to bury them, them, their wives, nor their sons, nor their daughters; for I will pour their wickedness upon them.'

17 Therefore you shalt say this word unto them:

'Let mine eyes run down with tears night and day, and let them not cease; for the virgin daughter of my people is broken with a great breach, with a very grievous blow.

18 If I go forth into the field, then behold the slain with the sword! And if I enter into the city, then behold them that are sick with famine! Yea, both the prophet and the priest (kohen) go about into a land that they know not.'"

19 Have you utterly rejected Judah (Yehudah)? Hath your soul lothed Zion (Tsiyon)? Why have You smitten us, and there is no healing for us? We looked for peace, and there is no good; and for the time of healing, and behold trouble!

20 We acknowledge, O יהוה, our wickedness, and the iniquity of our fathers; for we have sinned against You.

21 Do not abhor us for Your name's sake, do not disgrace the throne of Your glory. Remember, break not Your covenant with us.

22 Are there any among the vanities of the nations that can cause rain? Or can the heavens give showers? Art not You He, O יהוה our God (YHWH Eloheinu)? Therefore we will wait upon You, for You have made all these things.

15 Then said יהוה unto me, "Though Moses (Mosheh) and Shemuel stood before me, yet My mind could not be toward this people; cast them out of My sight, and let them go forth.

2 And it shall come to pass, if they say unto you, 'Whither shall we go forth?' Then you shalt tell them, 'Thus saith יהוה: "Such as are for death, to death; and such as are for the sword, to the sword; and such as are for the famine, to the famine; and such as are for the captivity, to the captivity."'

3 "And I will appoint over them four kinds," saith יהוה: "the sword to slay, and the dogs to tear, and the fowls of the sky, and the beasts of the earth, to devour and destroy.

4 And I will cause them to be removed into all kingdoms of the earth, because of Menashsheh the son of Hezekiah (Chizqiyahu) king of Judah (Yehudah), for that which he did in Jerusalem (Yerushalayim).

5 For who shall have pity upon you, O Jerusalem (Yerushalayim)? Or who shall bemoan you? Or who shall go aside to ask how you doest?

6 You have forsaken Me," saith יהוה, "You are gone backward. Therefore will I stretch out My hand against you, and destroy you; I am weary of relenting!

7 And I will fan them with a fan in the gates of the land; I will bereave them of children, I will destroy My people, since they return not from their ways.

8 Their widows are increased to me above the sand of the seas; I have brought upon them against the mother of the young men a spoiler at noonday; I have caused him to fall upon it suddenly, and terrors upon the city.

9 She that hath borne seven languisheth; she hath given up the spirit; her sun is gone down while it was yet day; she hath been ashamed and confounded. And the residue of them will I deliver to the sword before their enemies," saith יהוה.

10 Woe is me, my mother, that you have borne me a man of strife and a man of contention to the whole earth! I have neither lent on usury, nor men have lent to me on usury; yet every one of them doth curse me.

11 יהוה said: "Verily it shall be well with your remnant; verily I will cause the enemy to entreat you well in the time of evil and in the time of affliction.

12 Shall iron break the northern iron and the steel?

13 Your substance and your treasures will I give to the spoil without price, and that for all your sins, even in all your territories.

14 And I will make you to pass with your enemies into a land which you knowest not; for a fire is kindled in mine anger, which shall burn upon you."

15 O יהוה, you knowest; remember me, and visit me, and revenge me of my persecutors; take me not away in Your longsuffering; know that for Your sake I have suffered rebuke.

16 Your words were found, and I did eat them; and Your word was unto me the joy and rejoicing of mine heart; for I am called by Your name, O יהוה God of hosts (YHWH Elohei Tsevaot).

17 I sat not in the assembly of the mockers, nor rejoiced; I sat alone because of Your hand, for You have filled me with indignation.

18 Why is my pain perpetual, and my wound incurable, which refuseth to be healed? Wilt you be altogether unto me as a liar, and as waters that fail?

19 Therefore thus saith יהוה: "If you return, then will I bring you again, and you shalt stand

before Me; and if you take forth the precious from the vile, you shalt be as My mouth. Let them return unto you; but return not you unto them.

20 And I will make you unto this people a fenced brasen wall; and they shall fight against you, but they shall not prevail against you; for I am with you to save you and to deliver you," saith יהוה.

21 "And I will deliver you out of the hand of the wicked, and I will redeem you out of the hand of the terrible."

16 The word of יהוה came also unto me, saying,

2 "You shalt not take a wife, neither shalt you have sons or daughters in this place."

3 For thus saith יהוה concerning the sons and concerning the daughters that are born in this place, and concerning their mothers that bare them, and concerning their fathers that begat them in this land.

4 They shall die of grievous deaths; they shall not be lamented; neither shall they be buried; but they shall be as dung upon the face of the earth; and they shall be consumed by the sword, and by famine; and their carcases shall be meat for the fowls of sky, and for the beasts of the earth."

5 For thus saith יהוה: "Enter not into the house of mourning, neither go to lament nor bemoan them, for I have taken away My peace from this people," saith יהוה, "even loving-kindness and mercies."

6 "Both the great and the small shall die in this land. They shall not be buried, neither shall men lament for them, nor cut themselves, nor make themselves bald for them.

7 Nor shall men tear themselves for them in mourning, to comfort them for the dead; neither shall men give them the cup of consolation to drink for their father or for their mother.

8 You shalt not also go into the house of feasting, to sit with them to eat and to drink."

9 For thus saith יהוה of hosts (YHWH Tsevaot), the God of Israel (Elohei Yisrael): "Behold, I will cause to cease out of this place in your eyes, and in your days, the voice of mirth, and the voice of gladness, the voice of the bridegroom, and the voice of the bride.

10 And it shall come to pass, when you shalt shew this people all these words, and they shall

say unto you, 'Wherefore hath יהוה pronounced all this great evil against us? Or what is our iniquity? Or what is our sin that we have committed against יהוה our God (YHWH Eloheinu)?'

11 Then shalt you say unto them, 'Because your fathers have forsaken Me,' saith יהוה; 'and have walked after other gods (elohim), and have served them, and have worshipped them, and have forsaken Me, and have not kept My Torah.

12 And you have done worse than your fathers; for, behold, you walk every one after the imagination of his evil heart, that they may not hearken unto Me:

13 Therefore will I cast you out of this land into a land that you know not, neither you nor your fathers; and there shall you serve other gods (elohim) day and night; where I will not shew you favor.'

14 Therefore, behold, the days come," saith יהוה, "that it shall no more be said, 'יהוה liveth, who brought up the children of Yisrael out of the land of Egypt (Mitsrayim),'

15 But, 'יהוה liveth, that brought up the children of Yisrael from the land of the north, and from all the lands whither he had driven them.' And I will bring them again into their land that I gave unto their fathers.

16 "Behold, I will send for many fishermen," saith יהוה, "and they shall fish them; and after will I send for many hunters, and they shall hunt them from every mountain, and from every hill, and out of the holes of the rocks.

17 "For Mine eyes are upon all their ways: they are not hid from My face, neither is their iniquity hid from Mine eyes.

18 And first I will recompense their iniquity and their sin double; because they have defiled My land, they have filled Mine inheritance with the carcases of their detestable and abominable idols."

19 O יהוה, my strength, and my fortress, and my refuge in the day of affliction, the nations shall come unto you from the ends of the earth, and shall say, "Surely our fathers have inherited lies, vanity, and things wherein there is no profit."

20 Shall a man make ⁴gods (elohim) unto himself, and they are not God (Elohim)?

21 Therefore, behold, I will this once cause them to know, I will cause them to know Mine hand and My might; and they shall know that

My name is יהוה.

17

"The sin of Judah (Yehudah) is written with a pen of iron, and with the point of a diamond; it is engraved upon the table of their heart, and upon the horns of your altars;

2 Whilst their children remember their altars and their Asherim by the green trees upon the high hills.

3 O My mountain in the field, I will give your substance and all your treasures to the spoil, and your high places for sin, throughout all your borders.

4 And you, even yourself, shalt discontinue from your heritage that I gave you; and I will cause you to serve your enemies in the land which you knowest not; for you have kindled a fire in Mine anger, which shall burn forever."

5 Thus saith יהוה: "Cursed be the man that trusteth in man, and maketh flesh his arm, and whose heart departeth from יהוה.

6 For he shall be like the heath in the desert, and shall not see when good cometh; but shall inhabit the parched places in the wilderness, in a salt land and not inhabited.

7 Blessed is the man that trusteth in יהוה, and whose hope is יהוה.

8 For he shall be as a tree planted by the waters, and that spreadeth out her roots by the river, and shall not see when heat cometh, but her leaf shall be green; and shall not be careful in the year of drought, neither shall cease from yielding fruit.

9 The heart is deceitful above all things, and desperately wicked; who can know it?

10 I, יהוה search the heart, I try the reins, even to give every man according to his ways, and according to the fruit of his doings.

11 As the partridge sitteth on eggs, and hatcheth them not; so he that getteth riches, and not by right, shall leave them in the midst of his days, and at his end shall be a fool."

12 A glorious high throne from the beginning is the place of our sanctuary.

13 O יהוה, the hope of Yisrael, all that forsake You shall be ashamed. "And those who depart from Me shall be written in the earth, because they have forsaken יהוה, the fountain of living waters."

14 Heal me, O יהוה, and I shall be healed; save me, and I shall be saved, for You are my praise.

15 Behold, they say unto me, "Where is the word of יהוה? Let it come now."

16 As for me, I have not hastened from being a pastor to follow you; neither have I desired the woeful day; You knowest; that which came out of my lips was right before You.

17 Be not a terror unto me: You are my hope in the day of evil.

18 Let them be confounded that persecute me, but let not me be confounded; let them be dismayed, but let not me be dismayed; bring upon them the day of evil, and destroy them with double destruction!

19 Thus said יהוה unto me: "Go and stand in the gate of the children of the people, whereby the kings of Judah (Yehudah) come in, and by the which they go out, and in all the gates of Jerusalem (Yerushalayim);

20 And say unto them, 'Hear you the word of יהוה, you kings of Judah (Yehudah), and all Judah (Yehudah), and all the inhabitants of Jerusalem (Yerushalayim), that enter in by these gates.

21 'Thus saith יהוה: "Take heed to yourselves, and bear no burden on the Shabbat day, nor bring it in by the gates of Jerusalem (Yerushalayim);

22 Neither carry forth a burden out of your houses on the Shabbat, nor do you any work, but hallow you the Shabbat, as I commanded your fathers.

23 But they obeyed not, neither inclined their ear, but made their neck stiff, that they might not hear, nor receive instruction.

24 And it shall come to pass, if you diligently hearken unto Me, saith יהוה, to bring in no burden through the gates of this city on the Shabbat day, but hallow the Shabbat day, to do no work therein;

25 Then shall there enter into the gates of this city kings and princes sitting upon the throne of Dawid, riding in chariots and on horses, they, and their princes, the men of Judah (Yehudah), and the inhabitants of Jerusalem (Yerushalayim); and this city shall remain forever.

26 And they shall come from the cities of Judah (Yehudah), and from the places about Jerusalem (Yerushalayim), and from the land of Benjamin (Binyamin), and from the plain, and from the mountains, and from the south, bringing burnt offerings, and sacrifices, and meat offerings,

and incense, and bringing sacrifices of praise, unto the house of יהוה.

27 But if you will not hearken unto Me to hallow the Shabbat, and not to bear a burden, even entering in at the gates of Jerusalem (Yerushalayim) on the Shabbat; then will I kindle a fire in the gates thereof, and it shall devour the palaces of Jerusalem (Yerushalayim), and it shall not be quenched."'"

18 The word which came to Jeremiah (Yirmeyahu) from יהוה, saying:

2 "Arise, and go down to the potter's house, and there I will cause you to hear My words."

3 Then I went down to the potter's house, and, behold, he wrought a work on the wheels.

4 And the vessel that he made of clay was marred in the hand of the potter: so he made it again another vessel, as seemed good to the potter to make it.

5 Then the word of יהוה came to me, saying:

6 "O house of Yisrael, cannot I do with you as this potter?" saith יהוה. "Behold, as the clay is in the potter's hand, so are you in Mine hand, O house of Yisrael.

7 At what instant I shall speak concerning a nation, and concerning a kingdom, to pluck up, and to pull down, and to destroy it;

8 If that nation, against whom I have pronounced, turn from their evil, I will regret of the disaster (raah) that I thought to do unto them.

9 And at what instant I shall speak concerning a nation, and concerning a kingdom, to build and to plant it;

10 If it does evil in My sight, that it obeys not My voice, then I will regret of the good, wherewith I said I would benefit them.

11 Now therefore go to, speak to the men of Judah (Yehudah), and to the inhabitants of Jerusalem (Yerushalayim), saying, 'Thus saith יהוה: "Behold, I frame disaster (raah) against you, and devise a plan against you. Return you now every one from his evil way, and make your ways and your doings good."'"

12 And they said, "There is no hope; but we will walk after our own devices, and we will every one does the imagination of his evil heart."

13 Therefore thus saith יהוה: "Ask you now among the nations, who hath heard such things; the virgin of Yisrael hath done a very horrible thing.

14 Will a man leave the snow of Lebanon which cometh from the rock of the field? Or shall the cold flowing waters that come from another place be forsaken?

15 Because My people hath forgotten Me, they have burned incense to vanity, and they have caused them to stumble in their ways from the ancient paths, to walk in paths, in a way not cast up;

16 To make their land desolate, and a perpetual hissing; every one that passeth thereby shall be astonished, and wag his head.

17 I will scatter them as with an east wind before the enemy; I will shew them the back, and not the face, in the day of their disaster.

18 Then said they, "Come, and let us devise devices against Jeremiah (Yirmeyahu); for the law (torah) shall not perish from the priest (kohen), nor counsel from the wise, nor the word from the prophet. Come, and let us smite him with the tongue, and let us not give heed to any of his words."

19 Give heed to me, O יהוה, and hearken to the voice of them that contend with me!

20 Shall evil be recompensed for good? For they have digged a pit for my soul. Remember that I stood before you to speak good for them, and to turn away Your wrath from them.

21 Therefore deliver up their children to the famine, and pour out their blood by the force of the sword; and let their wives be bereaved of their children, and be widows; and let their men be put to death; let their young men be slain by the sword in battle.

22 Let a cry be heard from their houses, when you shalt bring a troop suddenly upon them; for they have digged a pit to take me, and hid snares for my feet.

23 Yet, יהוה, You knowest all their counsel against me to slay me; forgive not their iniquity, neither blot out their sin from Your sight, but let them be overthrown before You; deal thus with them in the time of Your anger.

19 Thus saith יהוה: "Go and get a potter's earthen bottle, and take of the ancients of the people, and of the ancients of the priests (kohanim);

2 And go forth unto the valley of the son of Hinnom, which is by the entry of the east gate, and proclaim there the words that I shall tell you,

3 And say, 'Hear you the word of יהוה, O kings of Judah (Yehudah), and inhabitants of

Jerusalem (Yerushalayim). Thus saith יהוה of hosts (YHWH Tsevaot), the God of Israel (Elohei Yisrael): "Behold, I will bring disaster (raah) upon this place, that whosoever heareth, his ears shall tingle.

4 Because they have forsaken Me, and have estranged this place, and have burned incense in it unto other gods (elohim), whom neither they nor their fathers have known, nor the kings of Judah (Yehudah), and have filled this place with the blood of innocents;

5 They have built also the high places of the Baal, to burn their sons with fire for burnt offerings unto the Baal, which I commanded not, nor spake it, neither came it into My mind,

6 Therefore, behold, the days come, saith יהוה, that this place shall no more be called Tophet, nor The Valley of Ben-Hinnom, but The Valley of Slaughter.

7 And I will make void the counsel of Judah (Yehudah) and Jerusalem (Yerushalayim) in this place; and I will cause them to fall by the sword before their enemies, and by the hands of them that seek their lives: and their carcases will I give to be meat for the fowls of the sky, and for the beasts of the earth.

8 And I will make this city desolate, and a hissing; every one that passeth thereby shall be astonished and hiss because of all the plagues thereof.

9 And I will cause them to eat the flesh of their sons and the flesh of their daughters, and they shall eat every one the flesh of his friend in the siege and straitness, wherewith their enemies, and they that seek their lives, shall straiten them.'"

10 Then shalt you break the bottle in the sight of the men that go with you,

11 And shalt say unto them, 'Thus saith יהוה of hosts (YHWH Tsevaot): "Even so will I break this people and this city, as one breaketh a potter's vessel, that cannot be made whole again; and they shall bury them in Tophet, till there be no place to bury.

12 Thus will I do unto this place," saith יהוה, "and to the inhabitants thereof, and even make this city as Tophet.

13 And the houses of Jerusalem (Yerushalayim), and the houses of the kings of Judah (Yehudah), shall be defiled as the place of Tophet, because of all the houses upon whose roofs they have burned incense unto all the host of heaven, and have poured out drink offerings unto other gods (elohim).""'

14 Then came Jeremiah (Yirmeyahu) from Tophet, whither יהוה had sent him to prophesy; and he stood in the court of יהוה's house; and said to all the people,

15 "Thus saith יהוה of hosts (YHWH Tsevaot), the God of Israel (Elohei Yisrael): 'Behold, I will bring upon this city and upon all her towns all the disaster (raah) that I have pronounced against it, because they have hardened their necks, that they might not hear My words.'"

20 Now Pashur the son of Immer the priest (kohen), who was also chief governor in the house of יהוה, heard that Jeremiah (Yirmeyahu) prophesied these things.

2 Then Pashur smote Jeremiah (Yirmeyahu) the prophet, and put him in the stocks that were in the high gate of Benjamin (Binyamin), which was by the house of יהוה.

3 And it came to pass on the next day, that Pashur brought forth Jeremiah (Yirmeyahu) out of the stocks. Then said Jeremiah (Yirmeyahu) unto him, "יהוה hath not called your name Pashur, but Magormissabib.

4 For thus saith יהוה: "Behold, I will make you a terror to yourself, and to all your friends; and they shall fall by the sword of their enemies, and your eyes shall behold it; and I will give all Judah (Yehudah) into the hand of the king of Babylon (Bavel), and he shall carry them captive into Babylon (Bavel), and shall slay them with the sword.

5 Moreover I will deliver all the strength of this city, and all the labours thereof, and all the precious things thereof, and all the treasures of the kings of Judah (Yehudah) will I give into the hand of their enemies, which shall spoil them, and take them, and carry them to Babylon (Bavel).

6 And you, Pashur, and all that dwell in your house shall go into captivity; and you shalt come to Babylon (Bavel), and there you shalt die, and shalt be buried there, you, and all your friends, to whom you have prophesied lies.'"

7 O יהוה, You have enticed me, and I was enticed: You are stronger than I, and hast prevailed; I am in derision daily, every one mocketh me.

8 For since I spake, I cried out, "I cried violence

and spoil!" Because the word of יהוה was made a reproach unto me, and a derision, daily.

9 Then I said, "I will not make mention of Him, nor speak any more in His name." But His word was in mine heart as a burning fire shut up in my bones, and I was weary with forbearing, and I could not stay.

10 For I heard the defaming of many: "Fear on every side!" "Report," say they, "and we will report it." All my familiars watched for my halting, saying, "Perhaps he will be enticed, and we shall prevail against him, and we shall take our revenge on him."

11 But יהוה is with me as a mighty, awesome One; therefore my persecutors shall stumble, and they shall not prevail; they shall be greatly ashamed; for they shall not prosper; their everlasting confusion shall never be forgotten.

12 But, O יהוה of hosts (YHWH Tsevaot), that triest the righteous, and seest the reins and the heart, let me see Your vengeance on them; for unto You have I opened my cause.

13 Sing unto יהוה! Praise You יהוה, for He hath delivered the soul of the poor from the hand of evildoers.

14 Cursed be the day wherein I was born! Let not the day wherein my mother bare me be blessed.

15 Cursed be the man who brought tidings to my father, saying, "A man child is born unto you"; making him very glad.

16 And let that man be as the cities which יהוה overthrew, and regretted not; and let him hear the cry in the morning, and the shouting at noontide;

17 Because he slew me not from the womb; or that my mother might have been my grave, and her womb to be always great with me.

18 Wherefore came I forth out of the womb to see labour and sorrow, that my days should be consumed with shame?

21 The word which came unto Jeremiah (Yirmeyahu) from יהוה, when King Zedekiah (Tsidqiyahu) sent unto him Pashur the son of Malkiyah, and Zephaniah (Tsefanyah) the son of Maaseyah the priest (kohen), saying,

2 "Enquire, please, of יהוה for us; for Nebuchadnezzar king of Babylon (Bavel) maketh war against us; if so be that יהוה will deal with us according to all His wondrous works, that he may go up from us."

3 Then said Jeremiah (Yirmeyahu) unto them, "Thus shall you say to Zedekiah (Tsidqiyahu);

4 Thus saith יהוה God of Israel (Elohei Yisrael): "Behold, I will turn back the weapons of war that are in your hands, wherewith you fight against the king of Babylon (Bavel), and against the Chaldeans, which besiege you outside the walls, and I will assemble them into the midst of this city.

5 And I myself will fight against you with an outstretched hand and with a strong arm, even in anger, and in fury, and in great wrath.

6 And I will smite the inhabitants of this city, both man and beast; they shall die of a great pestilence.

7 "And afterward," saith יהוה, "I will deliver Zedekiah (Tsidqiyahu) king of Judah (Yehudah), and his servants, and the people, and such as are left in this city from the pestilence, from the sword, and from the famine, into the hand of Nebuchadnezzar king of Babylon (Bavel), and into the hand of their enemies, and into the hand of those that seek their life; and he shall smite them with the edge of the sword; he shall not spare them, neither have pity, nor have mercy.

8 And unto this people you shalt say, 'Thus saith יהוה: "Behold, I set before you the way of life, and the way of death.

9 "He that abideth in this city shall die by the sword, and by the famine, and by the pestilence; but he that goeth out, and falleth to the Chaldeans that besiege you, he shall live, and his life shall be unto him for a prey.

10 For I have set My face against this city for adversity, and not for good," saith יהוה. "It shall be given into the hand of the king of Babylon (Bavel), and he shall burn it with fire."'

11 "And touching the house of the king of Judah (Yehudah), say, 'Hear you the word of יהוה;

12 O house of Dawid, thus saith יהוה: "Execute judgment in the morning, and deliver him that is spoiled out of the hand of the oppressor, lest My fury go out like fire, and burn that none can quench it, because of the evil of your doings.

13 Behold, I am against you, O inhabitant of the valley, and rock of the plain," saith יהוה, "Who say, 'Who shall come down against us? Or who shall enter into our habitations?'

14 But I will punish you according to the fruit of your doings, saith יהוה; "and I will kindle a fire in the forest thereof, and it shall devour all things round about it."'"

22 Thus saith יהוה: "Go down to the house of the king of Judah (Yehudah), and speak there this word,

2 And say, 'Hear the word of יהוה, O king of Judah (Yehudah), that sittest upon the throne of Dawid, you, and your servants, and your people that enter in by these gates!

3 Thus saith יהוה: "Execute you judgment and righteousness, and deliver the spoiled out of the hand of the oppressor; and do no wrong, do no violence to the stranger, the fatherless, nor the widow, neither shed innocent blood in this place.

4 For if you do this thing indeed, then shall there enter in by the gates of this house kings sitting upon the throne of Dawid, riding in chariots and on horses, he, and his servants, and his people.

5 But if you will not hear these words, I swear by Myself," saith יהוה, "that this house shall become a desolation.""'

6 For thus saith יהוה unto the king's house of Judah (Yehudah): "You are as Gilad unto Me, and the head of Lebanon; yet surely I will make you a wilderness, and cities which are not inhabited.

7 And I will prepare destroyers against you, every one with his weapons: and they shall cut down your choice cedars, and cast them into the fire.

8 And many nations shall pass by this city, and they shall say every man to his neighbour, 'Wherefore hath יהוה done thus unto this great city?'

9 Then they shall answer, 'Because they have forsaken the covenant of יהוה their God (YHWH Eloheihem), and worshipped other gods (elohim), and served them.'"

10 Weep you not for the dead, neither bemoan him; but weep sore for him that goeth away; for he shall return no more, nor see his native country.

11 For thus saith יהוה touching Shallum the son of Josiah (Yoshiyahu) king of Judah (Yehudah), who reigned instead of Josiah (Yoshiyahu) his father, who went forth out of this place: "He shall not return thither any more,

12 But he shall die in the place whither they have led him captive, and shall see this land no more.

13 Woe unto him that buildeth his house by unrighteousness, and his chambers by wrong;

that useth his neighbour's service without wages, and giveth him not for his work;

14 That saith, 'I will build me a wide house and large chambers, and cutteth him out windows; and it is cieled with cedar, and painted with vermilion.'

15 Shalt you reign, because you closest yourself in cedar? Did not your father eat and drink, and do judgment and justice, and then it was well with him?

16 He judged the cause of the poor and needy; then it was well with him; was not this to know Me?" saith יהוה.

17 But your eyes and your heart are not but for your covetousness, and for to shed innocent blood, and for oppression, and for violence, to do it."

18 Therefore thus saith יהוה concerning Yehoyaqim the son of Josiah (Yoshiyahu) king of Judah (Yehudah); They shall not lament for him, saying, 'Ah my brother!' Or, 'Ah sister!' They shall not lament for him, saying, 'Ah master!' or, 'Ah his glory!'

19 He shall be buried with the burial of an ass, drawn and cast forth beyond the gates of Jerusalem (Yerushalayim).

20 Go up to Lebanon, and cry; and lift up your voice in Bashan, and cry from the passages; for all your lovers are destroyed.

21 I spake unto you in your prosperity; but you saidst,' I will not hear.' This hath been your manner from your youth, that you obeyedst not My voice.

22 The wind shall eat up all your pastors, and your lovers shall go into captivity; surely then shalt you be ashamed and confounded for all your wickedness.

23 O inhabitant of Lebanon, that makest your nest in the cedars, how gracious shalt you be when pangs come upon you, the pain as of a woman in travail!

24 "As I live," saith יהוה, "though Konyahu the son of Yehoyaqim king of Judah (Yehudah) were the signet upon My right hand, yet would I pluck you thence;

25 And I will give you into the hand of them that seek your life, and into the hand of them whose face you fearest, even into the hand of Nebuchadnezzar king of Babylon (Bavel), and into the hand of the Chaldeans.

26 And I will cast you out, and your mother that

bare you, into another country, where you were not born; and there shall you die.

27 But to the land whereunto they desire to return, thither shall they not return.

28 Is this man Konyahu a despised broken idol? Is he a vessel wherein is no pleasure? Wherefore are they cast out, he and his seed, and are cast into a land which they know not?

29 O earth, earth, earth, hear the word of יהוה!

30 Thus saith יהוה: "Write you this man childless, a man that shall not prosper in his days; for no man of his seed shall prosper, sitting upon the throne of Dawid, and ruling any more in Judah (Yehudah).'"

23 Woe be unto the pastors that destroy and scatter the sheep of My pasture!" saith יהוה.

2 Therefore thus saith יהוה God of Israel (Elohei Yisrael) against the pastors that feed My people: "You have scattered My flock, and driven them away, and have not visited them; behold, I will visit upon you the evil of your doings," saith יהוה.

3 "And I will gather the remnant of My flock out of all countries whither I have driven them, and will bring them again to their folds; and they shall be fruitful and increase.

4 And I will set up shepherds over them which shall feed them; and they shall fear no more, nor be dismayed, neither shall they be lacking," saith יהוה.

5 "Behold, the days come," saith יהוה, "that I will raise unto Dawid a righteous [B44]Branch (Tsemach), and a King shall reign and prosper, and shall execute judgment and justice in the earth.

6 In his days Judah (Yehudah) shall be saved, and Yisrael shall dwell safely; and this is His name whereby He shall be called [A6"]יהוה Tsidqenu (YHWH Our Righteousness)".

7 "Therefore, behold, the days come," saith יהוה, "that they shall no more say, 'יהוה liveth, who brought up the children of Yisrael out of the land of Egypt (Mitsrayim);'

8 But, 'יהוה liveth, who brought up and who led the seed of the house of Yisrael out of the north country, and from all countries whither I had driven them; and they shall dwell in their own land."

9 Mine heart within me is broken because of the prophets; all my bones shake; I am like a drunken man, and like a man whom wine hath overcome, because of יהוה, and because of the words of His holiness.

10 For the land is full of adulterers; for because of swearing the land mourneth; the pleasant places of the wilderness are dried up, and their course is evil, and their force is not right.

11 For both prophet and priest (kohen) are profane; yea, in My house have I found their wickedness," saith יהוה.

12 Wherefore their way shall be unto them as slippery ways in the darkness: they shall be driven on, and fall therein; for I will bring disaster (raah) upon them, even the year of their visitation," saith יהוה.

13 And I have seen folly in the prophets of Samaria (Shomeron); they prophesied in the Baal, and caused My people Yisrael to err.

14 I have seen also in the prophets of Jerusalem (Yerushalayim) a horrible thing: they commit adultery, and walk in lies; they strengthen also the hands of evildoers, that none doth return from his wickedness. They are all of them unto Me as Sodom, and the inhabitants thereof as Gomorrah.

15 Therefore thus saith יהוה of hosts (YHWH Tsevaot) concerning the prophets: "Behold, I will feed them with wormwood, and make them drink the water of gall; for from the prophets of Jerusalem (Yerushalayim) is profaneness gone forth into all the land.'"

16 Thus saith יהוה of hosts (YHWH Tsevaot): "Hearken not unto the words of the prophets that prophesy unto you; they make you vain; they speak a vision of their own heart, and not out of the mouth of יהוה.

17 They say still unto them that despise Me, 'יהוה hath said, "You shall have peace"'; and they say unto every one that walketh after the imagination of his own heart, 'No evil shall come upon you.'"

18 For who hath stood in the counsel of יהוה, and hath perceived and heard His word? Who hath marked His word, and heard it?

19 Behold, a whirlwind of יהוה is gone forth in fury, even a grievous whirlwind; it shall fall grievously upon the head of the wicked.

20 The anger of יהוה shall not return, until He have executed, and till He have performed the thoughts of His heart; in the latter days you shall consider it perfectly.

21 I have not sent these prophets, yet they ran. I have not spoken to them, yet they prophesied.

22 But if they had stood in My counsel, and had caused My people to hear My words, then they should have turned them from their evil way, and from the evil of their doings.

23 "Am I a God (Elohim) at hand," saith יהוה, "And not a God (Elohim) afar off?

24 Can any hide himself in secret places that I shall not see him?" saith יהוה; "Do not I fill heaven and earth?" saith יהוה.

25 I have heard what the prophets said, that prophesy lies in My name, saying, 'I have dreamed, I have dreamed!'

26 "How long shall this be in the heart of the prophets that prophesy lies? Yea, they are prophets of the deceit of their own heart;

27 Who think to cause My people to forget My name by their dreams which they tell every man to his neighbour, as their fathers have forgotten My name for the Baal.

28 The prophet that hath a dream, let him tell a dream; and he that hath My word, let him speak My word faithfully. What is the chaff to the wheat?" saith יהוה.

29 "Is not My word like as a fire?" saith יהוה, "And like a hammer that breaketh the rock in pieces?

30 "Therefore, behold, I am against the prophets," saith יהוה, "that steal My words every one from his neighbour.

31 Behold, I am against the prophets," saith יהוה, "who use their tongues, and say, 'He saith.'

32 "Behold, I am against them that prophesy false dreams," saith יהוה, "and do tell them, and cause My people to err by their lies, and by their lightness; yet I sent them not, nor commanded them; therefore they shall not profit this people at all," saith יהוה.

33 "And when this people, or the prophet, or a priest (kohen), shall ask you, saying, 'What is the burden of יהוה?' You shalt then say unto them, 'What burden?' I will even forsake you," saith יהוה.

34 And as for the prophet, and the priest (kohen), and the people, that shall say, 'The burden of יהוה!' I will even punish that man and his house.

35 Thus shall you say every one to his neighbour, and every one to his brother, 'What hath יהוה answered?' and, 'What hath יהוה spoken?'

36 And the burden of יהוה shall you mention no more; for every man's word shall be his burden; for you have perverted the words of the living God (Elohim chayim), of יהוה of hosts (YHWH Tsevaot) our God (Elohim).

37 Thus shalt you say to the prophet, 'What hath יהוה answered you?' And, 'What hath יהוה spoken?'

38 But since you say, 'The burden of יהוה!' Therefore thus saith יהוה: 'Because you say this word, "The burden of יהוה!" and I have sent unto you, saying, "You shall not say, 'The burden of יהוה!'"'

39 Therefore, behold, I, even I, will utterly forget you, and I will forsake you, and the city that I gave you and your fathers, and cast you out of My presence.

40 And I will bring an everlasting reproach upon you, and a perpetual shame, which shall not be forgotten.'"

24 יהוה shewed me, and, behold, two baskets of figs were set before the temple of יהוה, after that Nebuchadnezzar king of Babylon (Bavel) had carried away captive Yekhonyah the son of Yehoyaqim king of Judah (Yehudah), and the princes of Judah (Yehudah), with the carpenters and smiths, from Jerusalem (Yerushalayim), and had brought them to Babylon (Bavel).

2 One basket had very good figs, even like the figs that are first ripe; and the other basket had very naughty figs, which could not be eaten, they were so bad."

3 Then said יהוה unto me, "What seest you, Jeremiah (Yirmeyahu)?" And I said, "Figs; the good figs, very good; and the bad, very bad, that cannot be eaten, they are so bad."

4 Again the word of יהוה came unto me, saying,

5 "Thus saith יהוה, the God of Israel (Elohei Yisrael): 'Like these good figs, so will I acknowledge them that are carried away captive of Judah (Yehudah), whom I have sent out of this place into the land of the Chaldeans for their good.

6 For I will set Mine eyes upon them for good, and I will bring them again to this land; and I will build them, and not pull them down; and I will plant them, and not pluck them up.

7 And I will give them a heart to know Me, that I am יהוה; and they shall be My people, and I will be their God (Elohim), for they shall return unto Me with their whole heart.

8 And as the bad figs, which cannot be eaten, they are so bad'; surely thus saith יהוה, 'So will I give Zedekiah (Tsidqiyahu) the king of Judah (Yehudah), and his princes, and the residue of Jerusalem (Yerushalayim), that remain in this land, and them that dwell in the land of Egypt (Mitsrayim).

9 And I will deliver them to be removed into all the kingdoms of the earth for their hurt, to be a reproach and a proverb, a taunt and a curse, in all places whither I shall drive them.

10 And I will send the sword, the famine, and the pestilence, among them, till they be consumed from off the land that I gave unto them and to their fathers.'"

25 The word that came to Jeremiah (Yirmeyahu) concerning all the people of Judah (Yehudah) in the fourth year of Yehoyaqim the son of Josiah (Yoshiyahu) king of Judah (Yehudah), that was the first year of Nebuchadnezzar king of Babylon (Bavel),

2 which Jeremiah (Yirmeyahu) the prophet spake unto all the people of Judah (Yehudah), and to all the inhabitants of Jerusalem (Yerushalayim), saying:

3 "From the thirteenth year of Josiah (Yoshiyahu) the son of Amon king of Judah (Yehudah), even unto this day, that is the three and twentieth year, the word of יהוה hath come unto me, and I have spoken unto you, rising early and speaking; but you have not hearkened.

4 And יהוה hath sent unto you all His servants the prophets, rising early and sending them; but you have not hearkened, nor inclined your ear to hear.

5 They said, 'Turn you again now every one from his evil way, and from the evil of your doings, and dwell in the land that יהוה hath given unto you and to your fathers forever and ever.

6 And go not after other gods (elohim) to serve them, and to worship them, and provoke Me not to anger with the works of your hands; and I will do you no hurt.'

7 "Yet you have not hearkened unto me," saith יהוה, "that you might provoke Me to anger with the works of your hands to your own hurt.

8 Therefore thus saith יהוה of hosts (YHWH Tsevaot): 'Because you have not heard My words,

9 'Behold, I will send and take all the families

of the north,' saith יהוה, and Nebuchadnezzar the king of Babylon (Bavel), My servant, and will bring them against this land, and against the inhabitants thereof, and against all these nations round about, and will utterly destroy them, and make them an astonishment, and a hissing, and perpetual desolations.

10 Moreover I will take from them the voice of mirth, and the voice of gladness, the voice of the bridegroom, and the voice of the bride, the sound of the millstones, and the light of the candle.

11 And this whole land shall be a desolation, and an astonishment; and these nations shall serve the king of Babylon (Bavel) seventy years.

12 'And it shall come to pass, when seventy years are accomplished, that I will punish the king of Babylon (Bavel), and that nation,' saith יהוה, 'for their iniquity', and the land of the Chaldeans, and will make it perpetual desolations.

13 And I will bring upon that land all My words which I have pronounced against it, even all that is written in this book, which Jeremiah (Yirmeyahu) hath prophesied against all the nations.

14 For many nations and great kings shall serve themselves of them also; and I will recompense them according to their deeds, and according to the works of their own hands.'"

15 For thus saith יהוה God of Israel (Elohei Yisrael) unto me: "Take the wine cup of this fury at My hand, and cause all the nations, to whom I send you, to drink it.

16 And they shall drink, and be moved, and be mad, because of the sword that I will send among them."

17 Then took I the cup at יהוה's hand, and made all the nations to drink, unto whom יהוה had sent me:

18 Jerusalem (Yerushalayim), and the cities of Judah (Yehudah), and the kings thereof, and the princes thereof, to make them a desolation, an astonishment, a hissing, and a curse; as it is this day;

19 Pharaoh (Paroh) king of Egypt (Mitsrayim), and his servants, and his princes, and all his people;

20 And all the mingled people, and all the kings of the land of Uz, and all the kings of the land of the Philistines, and Ashkelon, and Azzah, and

Ekron, and the remnant of Ashdod,

21 Edom, and Moav, and the children of Ammon,

22 And all the kings of Tyrus, and all the kings of Zidon, and the kings of the isles which are beyond the sea,

23 Dedan, and Tema, and Buz, and all that are in the utmost corners,

24 And all the kings of Arabia, and all the kings of the mingled people that dwell in the desert,

25 And all the kings of Zimri, and all the kings of Elam, and all the kings of the Medes,

26 And all the kings of the north, far and near, one with another, and all the kingdoms of the world, which are upon the face of the earth; and the king of Sheshach shall drink after them.

27 Therefore you shalt say unto them, 'Thus saith יהוה of hosts (YHWH Tsevaot), the God of Israel (Elohei Yisrael): "Drink, and be drunken, and spue, and fall, and rise no more, because of the sword which I will send among you."'

28 And it shall be, if they refuse to take the cup at your hand to drink, then shalt you say unto them, 'Thus saith יהוה of hosts (YHWH Tsevaot): "You shall certainly drink!

29 For, behold, I begin to bring evil on the city which is called by My name, and should you be utterly unpunished? You shall not be unpunished, for I will call for a sword upon all the inhabitants of the earth," saith יהוה of hosts (YHWH Tsevaot).'

30 Therefore prophesy you against them all these words, and say unto them: 'יהוה shall roar from on high, and utter His voice from His holy habitation; He shall mightily roar upon His habitation; He shall give a shout, as they that tread the grapes, against all the inhabitants of the earth.

31 A noise shall come even to the ends of the earth; for יהוה hath a controversy with the nations, He will plead with all flesh; He will give them that are wicked to the sword,' saith יהוה."

32 Thus saith יהוה of hosts (YHWH Tsevaot): "Behold, evil shall go forth from nation to nation, and a great whirlwind shall be raised up from the coasts of the earth.

33 And the slain of יהוה shall be at that day from one end of the earth even unto the other end of the earth; they shall not be lamented, neither gathered, nor buried; they shall be dung upon the ground.

34 Howl, you shepherds, and cry; and wallow yourselves in the ashes, you principal of the flock; for the days of your slaughter and of your dispersions are accomplished; and you shall fall like a pleasant vessel.

35 And the shepherds shall have no way to flee, nor the principal of the flock to escape.

36 A voice of the cry of the shepherds, and a howling of the principal of the flock, shall be heard; for יהוה hath spoiled their pasture.

37 And the peaceable habitations are cut down because of the fierce anger of יהוה.

38 He hath forsaken his covert, as the lion; for their land is desolate because of the fierceness of the oppressor, and because of His fierce anger."

26 In the beginning of the reign of Yehoyaqim the son of Josiah (Yoshiyahu) king of Judah (Yehudah) came this word from יהוה, saying,

2 "Thus saith יהוה: "Stand in the court of יהוה's house, and speak unto all the cities of Judah (Yehudah), who come to worship in יהוה's house, all the words that I command you to speak unto them; diminish not a word.

3 If so be they will hearken, and turn every man from his evil (raah) way, that I may regret of the disaster (raah), which I purpose to do unto them because of the evil of their doings.

4 And you shalt say unto them, 'Thus saith יהוה: "If you will not hearken to Me, to walk in My Torah, which I have set before you,

5 To hearken to the words of My servants the prophets, whom I sent unto you, both rising up early, and sending them, but you have not hearkened;

6 Then will I make this house like Shiloh, and will make this city a curse to all the nations of the earth.""

7 So the priests (kohanim) and the prophets and all the people heard Jeremiah (Yirmeyahu) speaking these words in the house of יהוה.

8 Now it came to pass, when Jeremiah (Yirmeyahu) had made an end of speaking all that יהוה had commanded him to speak unto all the people, that the priests (kohanim) and the prophets and all the people took him, saying, "You shalt surely die!

9 Why have you prophesied in the name of יהוה, saying, 'This house shall be like Shiloh, and this

city shall be desolate without an inhabitant'?" And all the people were gathered against Jeremiah (Yirmeyahu) in the house of יהוה.

10 When the princes of Judah (Yehudah) heard these things, then they came up from the king's house unto the house of יהוה, and sat down in the entry of the new gate of יהוה's house.

11 Then spake the priests (kohanim) and the prophets unto the princes and to all the people, saying, "This man is worthy to die; for he hath prophesied against this city, as you have heard with your ears."

12 Then spake Jeremiah (Yirmeyahu) unto all the princes and to all the people, saying, "יהוה sent me to prophesy against this house and against this city all the words that you have heard.

13 Therefore now amend your ways and your doings, and obey the voice of יהוה your God (YHWH Eloheikhem); and יהוה will regret of the disaster (raah) that He hath pronounced against you.

14 As for me, behold, I am in your hand; do with me as seemeth good and meet unto you.

15 But know you for certain, that if you put me to death, you shall surely bring innocent blood upon yourselves, and upon this city, and upon the inhabitants thereof; for of a truth יהוה hath sent me unto you to speak all these words in your ears."

16 Then said the princes and all the people unto the priests (kohanim) and to the prophets: "This man is not worthy to die: for he hath spoken to us in the name of יהוה our God (YHWH Eloheinu)."

17 Then rose up certain of the elders of the land, and spake to all the assembly of the people, saying:

18 Mikhah the Morasthite prophesied in the days of Hezekiah (Chizqiyahu) king of Judah (Yehudah), and spake to all the people of Judah (Yehudah), saying, Thus saith יהוה of hosts (YHWH Tsevaot): "Zion (Tsiyon) shall be plowed like a field, and Jerusalem (Yerushalayim) shall become heaps, and the mountain of the house as the high places of a forest.'"

19 Did Hezekiah (Chizqiyahu) king of Judah (Yehudah) and all Judah (Yehudah) put him at all to death? Did he not fear יהוה, and besought יהוה, and יהוה regretted of the disaster (raah)

which He had pronounced against them? Thus might we procure great evil against our souls."

20 And there was also a man that prophesied in the name of יהוה, Uriyahu the son of Shemayahu of Qiryat-Yearim, who prophesied against this city and against this land according to all the words of Jeremiah (Yirmeyahu).

21 And when Yehoyaqim the king, with all his mighty men, and all the princes, heard his words, the king sought to put him to death: but when Uriyahu heard it, he was afraid, and fled, and went into Egypt (Mitsrayim);

22 And Yehoyaqim the king sent men into Egypt (Mitsrayim): namely, Elnathan the son of Achbor, and certain men with him into Egypt (Mitsrayim).

23 And they fetched forth Uriyahu out of Egypt (Mitsrayim), and brought him unto Yehoyaqim the king; who slew him with the sword, and cast his dead body into the graves of the common people.

24 Nevertheless the hand of Ahikam the son of Shaphan was with Jeremiah (Yirmeyahu), that they should not give him into the hand of the people to put him to death.

27 In the beginning of the reign of Yehoyaqim the son of Josiah (Yoshiyahu) king of Judah (Yehudah) came this word unto Jeremiah (Yirmeyahu) from יהוה, saying,

2 "Thus saith יהוה to me: "Make you bonds and yokes, and put them upon your neck,

3 And send them to the king of Edom, and to the king of Moav, and to the king of the Ammonites, and to the king of Tyrus, and to the king of Zidon, by the hand of the messengers who come to Jerusalem (Yerushalayim) unto Zedekiah (Tsidqiyahu) king of Judah (Yehudah);

4 And command them to say unto their masters, Thus saith יהוה of hosts (YHWH Tsevaot), the God of Israel (Elohei Yisrael); Thus shall you say unto your masters:

5 I have made the earth, the man and the beast that are upon the ground, by My great power and by My outstretched arm, and have given it unto whom it seemed meet unto Me.

6 And now have I given all these lands into the hand of Nebuchadnezzar the king of Babylon (Bavel), My servant; and the beasts of the field have I given him also to serve him.

7 And all nations shall serve him, and his son, and his son's son, until the very time of his land

come; and then many nations and great kings shall serve themselves of him.

8 'And it shall come to pass, that the nation and kingdom which will not serve the same Nebuchadnezzar the king of Babylon (Bavel), and that will not put their neck under the yoke of the king of Babylon (Bavel), that nation will I punish,' saith יהוה, 'with the sword, and with the famine, and with the pestilence, until I have consumed them by his hand.

9 Therefore hearken not you to your prophets, nor to your diviners, nor to your dreamers, nor to your enchanters, nor to your sorcerers, who speak unto you, saying, "You shall not serve the king of Babylon (Bavel)."

10 For they prophesy a lie unto you, to remove you far from your land; and that I should drive you out, and you should perish.

11 'But the nations that bring their neck under the yoke of the king of Babylon (Bavel), and serve him, those will I let remain still in their own land,' saith יהוה; 'and they shall till it, and dwell therein.'"

12 I spake also to Zedekiah (Tsidqiyahu) king of Judah (Yehudah) according to all these words, saying, "Bring your necks under the yoke of the king of Babylon (Bavel), and serve him and his people, and live!

13 Why will you die, you and your people, by the sword, by the famine, and by the pestilence, as יהוה hath spoken against the nation that will not serve the king of Babylon (Bavel)?

14 Therefore hearken not unto the words of the prophets that speak unto you, saying, 'You shall not serve the king of Babylon (Bavel),' for they prophesy a lie unto you;

15 "For I have not sent them," saith יהוה, "yet they prophesy a lie in My name; that I might drive you out, and that you might perish, you, and the prophets that prophesy unto you."

16 Also I spake to the priests (kohanim) and to all this people, saying, Thus saith יהוה: 'Hearken not to the words of your prophets that prophesy unto you, saying, "Behold, the vessels of יהוה's house shall now shortly be brought again from Babylon (Bavel)"; for they prophesy a lie unto you.

17 'Hearken not unto them; serve the king of Babylon (Bavel), and live! Wherefore should this city be laid waste?

18 But if they be prophets, and if the word of

יהוה be with them, let them now make intercession to יהוה of hosts (YHWH Tsevaot), that the vessels which are left in the house of יהוה, and in the house of the king of Judah (Yehudah), and at Jerusalem (Yerushalayim), go not to Babylon (Bavel).'

19 "For thus saith יהוה of hosts (YHWH Tsevaot) concerning the pillars, and concerning the sea, and concerning the bases, and concerning the residue of the vessels that remain in this city,

20 Which Nebuchadnezzar king of Babylon (Bavel) took not, when he carried away captive Yekhonyah the son of Yehoyaqim king of Judah (Yehudah) from Jerusalem (Yerushalayim) to Babylon (Bavel), and all the nobles of Judah (Yehudah) and Jerusalem (Yerushalayim);

21 Yea, thus saith יהוה of hosts (YHWH Tsevaot), the God of Israel (Elohei Yisrael), concerning the vessels that remain in the house of יהוה, and in the house of the king of Judah (Yehudah) and of Jerusalem (Yerushalayim):

22 'They shall be carried to Babylon (Bavel), and there shall they be until the day that I visit them,' saith יהוה. 'Then will I bring them up, and restore them to this place.'"

28 And it came to pass the same year, in the beginning of the reign of Zedekiah (Tsidqiyahu) king of Judah (Yehudah), in the fourth year, and in the fifth month, that Chananyah the son of Azur the prophet, which was of Giveon, spake unto me in the house of יהוה, in the presence of the priests (kohanim) and of all the people, saying,

2 "Thus speaketh יהוה of hosts (YHWH Tsevaot), the God of Israel (Elohei Yisrael), saying: 'I have broken the yoke of the king of Babylon (Bavel).

3 Within two full years will I bring again into this place all the vessels of יהוה's house, that Nebuchadnezzar king of Babylon (Bavel) took away from this place, and carried them to Babylon (Bavel).'"

4 And I will bring again to this place Yekhonyah the son of Yehoyaqim king of Judah (Yehudah), with all the captives of Judah (Yehudah), that went into Babylon (Bavel),' saith יהוה, 'for I will break the yoke of the king of Babylon (Bavel).'"

5 Then the prophet Jeremiah (Yirmeyahu) said unto the prophet Chananyah in the presence of the priests (kohanim), and in the presence of all

the people that stood in the house of יהוה,

6 Even the prophet Jeremiah (Yirmeyahu) said, "Amen! יהוה do so; יהוה perform your words which you have prophesied, to bring again the vessels of יהוה's house, and all that is carried away captive, from Babylon (Bavel) into this place.

7 Nevertheless hear you now this word that I speak in your ears, and in the ears of all the people:

8 The prophets that have been before me and before you of old prophesied both against many countries, and against great kingdoms, of war, and of evil, and of pestilence.

9 The prophet which prophesieth of peace, when the word of the prophet shall come to pass, then shall the prophet be known, that יהוה hath truly sent him."

10 Then Chananyah the prophet took the yoke from off the prophet Jeremiah (Yirmeyahu)'s neck, and broke it.

11 And Chananyah spake in the presence of all the people, saying, "Thus saith יהוה: 'Even so will I break the yoke of Nebuchadnezzar king of Babylon (Bavel) from the neck of all nations within the space of two full years.' "And the prophet Jeremiah (Yirmeyahu) went his way.

12 Then the word of יהוה came unto Jeremiah (Yirmeyahu) the prophet, after that Chananyah the prophet had broken the yoke from off the neck of the prophet Jeremiah (Yirmeyahu), saying,

13 Go and tell Chananyah, saying, 'Thus saith יהוה: "You have broken the yokes of wood; but you shalt make for them yokes of iron."

14 For thus saith יהוה of hosts (YHWH Tsevaot), the God of Israel (Elohei Yisrael); I have put a yoke of iron upon the neck of all these nations, that they may serve Nebuchadnezzar king of Babylon (Bavel); and they shall serve him; and I have given him the beasts of the field also.""'

15 Then said the prophet Jeremiah (Yirmeyahu) unto Chananyah the prophet, "Hear now, Chananyah; יהוה hath not sent you, but you makest this people to trust in a lie.

16 Therefore thus saith יהוה: 'Behold, I will cast you from off the face of the earth. This year you shalt die, because you have taught rebellion against יהוה.'"

17 So Chananyah the prophet died the same year in the seventh month.

29 Now these are the words of the letter that Jeremiah (Yirmeyahu) the prophet sent from Jerusalem (Yerushalayim) unto the residue of the elders which were carried away captives, and to the priests (kohanim), and to the prophets, and to all the people whom Nebuchadnezzar had carried away captive from Jerusalem (Yerushalayim) to Babylon (Bavel);

2 (After that Yekhonyah the king, and the queen, and the officials, the princes of Judah (Yehudah) and Jerusalem (Yerushalayim), and the carpenters, and the smiths, were departed from Jerusalem (Yerushalayim);)

3 By the hand of Elasah the son of Shaphan, and Gemaryah the son of Chilqiyahu, (whom Zedekiah (Tsidqiyahu) king of Judah (Yehudah) sent unto Babylon (Bavel) to Nebuchadnezzar king of Babylon (Bavel)) saying,

4 Thus saith יהוה of hosts (YHWH Tsevaot), the God of Israel (Elohei Yisrael), unto all that are carried away captives, whom I have caused to be carried away from Jerusalem (Yerushalayim) unto Babylon (Bavel):

5 Build you houses, and dwell in them; and plant gardens, and eat the fruit of them;

6 Take you wives, and beget sons and daughters; and take wives for your sons, and give your daughters to husbands, that they may bear sons and daughters; that you may be increased there, and not diminished.

7 And seek the peace of the city whither I have caused you to be carried away captives, and pray unto יהוה for it; for in the peace thereof shall you have peace.

8 For thus saith יהוה of hosts (YHWH Tsevaot), the God of Israel (Elohei Yisrael): 'Let not your prophets and your diviners, that be in the midst of you, deceive you, neither hearken to your dreams which you cause to be dreamed.

9 For they prophesy falsely unto you in My name; I have not sent them,' saith יהוה.

10 For thus saith יהוה: 'That after seventy years be accomplished at Babylon (Bavel) I will visit you, and perform My good word toward you, in causing you to return to this place.

11 For I know the thoughts that I think toward you,' saith יהוה, 'thoughts of peace, and not of evil, to give you an expected end.

12 Then shall you call upon Me, and you shall go and pray unto Me, and I will hearken unto you.

13 And you shall seek Me, and find Me, when

you shall search for Me with all your heart.

14 And I will be found of you,' saith יהוה; 'and I will turn away your captivity, and I will gather you from all the nations, and from all the places whither I have driven you,' saith יהוה; 'and I will bring you again into the place whence I caused you to be carried away captive.'

15 Because you have said, "יהוה hath raised us up prophets in Babylon (Bavel)."

16 Know that thus saith יהוה of the king that sitteth upon the throne of Dawid, and of all the people that dwelleth in this city, and of your brethren that are not gone forth with you into captivity;

17 Thus saith יהוה of hosts (YHWH Tsevaot): 'Behold, I will send upon them the sword, the famine, and the pestilence, and will make them like vile figs, that cannot be eaten, they are so bad.

18 And I will persecute them with the sword, with the famine, and with the pestilence, and will deliver them to be removed to all the kingdoms of the earth, to be a curse, and an astonishment, and a hissing, and a reproach, among all the nations whither I have driven them:

19 Because they have not hearkened to My words,' saith יהוה, 'which I sent unto them by My servants the prophets, rising up early and sending them; but you would not hear,' saith יהוה.

20 Hear you therefore the word of יהוה, all you of the captivity, whom I have sent from Jerusalem (Yerushalayim) to Babylon (Bavel):

21 Thus saith יהוה of hosts (YHWH Tsevaot), the God of Israel (Elohei Yisrael), of Achav the son of Qolayah, and of Zedekiah (Tsidqiyahu) the son of Maaseyah, which prophesy a lie unto you in My name; Behold, I will deliver them into the hand of Nebuchadnezzar king of Babylon (Bavel); and he shall slay them before your eyes;

22 And of them shall be taken up a curse by all the captivity of Judah (Yehudah) which are in Babylon (Bavel), saying, "יהוה make you like Zedekiah (Tsidqiyahu) and like Achav, whom the king of Babylon (Bavel) roasted in the fire";

23 Because they have committed villany in Yisrael, and have committed adultery with their neighbours' wives, and have spoken lying words in My name, which I have not commanded them; even I know, and am a witness, saith יהוה.

24 Thus shalt you also speak to Shemayahu the Nehelamite, saying:

25 "Thus speaketh יהוה of hosts (YHWH Tsevaot), the God of Israel (Elohei Yisrael), saying: 'Because you have sent letters in your name unto all the people that are at Jerusalem (Yerushalayim), and to Zephaniah (Tsefanyah) the son of Maaseyah the priest (kohen), and to all the priests (kohanim), saying,

26 "יהוה hath made you priest (kohen) in the stead of Yehoyada the priest (kohen), that you should be officers in the house of יהוה, for every man that is mad, and maketh himself a prophet, that you shouldest put him in prison, and in the stocks.

27 Now therefore why have you not reproved Jeremiah (Yirmeyahu) of Anathoth, which maketh himself a prophet to you?

28 For therefore he sent unto us in Babylon (Bavel), saying, 'This capti-vity is long; build you houses, and dwell in them; and plant gardens, and eat the fruit of them.'"

29 And Zephaniah (Tsefanyah) the priest (kohen) read this letter in the ears of Jeremiah (Yirmeyahu) the prophet.

30 Then came the word of יהוה unto Jeremiah (Yirmeyahu), saying:

31 "Send to all them of the captivity, saying, 'Thus saith יהוה concerning Shemayahu the Nehelamite: "Because that Shemayahu hath prophesied unto you, and I sent him not, and he caused you to trust in a lie,"

32 Therefore thus saith יהוה: "Behold, I will punish Shemayahu the Nehelamite, and his seed: he shall not have a man to dwell among this people; neither shall he behold the good that I will do for My people," saith יהוה, "because he hath taught rebellion against יהוה."'"

30 The word that came to Jeremiah (Yirmeyahu) from יהוה, saying,

2 "Thus speaketh יהוה God of Israel (Elohei Yisrael), saying: 'Write you all the words that I have spoken unto you in a book.

3 'For, behold, the days come,' saith יהוה, 'that I will bring again the captivity of My people Yisrael and Judah (Yehudah),' saith יהוה. 'And I will cause them to return to the land that I gave to their fathers, and they shall possess it.'"

4 And these are the words that יהוה spake concerning Yisrael and concerning Judah

(Yehudah).

5 "For thus saith יהוה: 'We have heard a voice of trembling, of fear, and not of peace.

6 Ask you now, and see whether a man doth travail with child? Wherefore do I see every man with his hands on his loins, as a woman in travail, and all faces are turned into paleness?

7 Alas! For that day is great, so that none is like it; it is even the time of Jacob (Yaaqov)'s trouble; but he shall be saved out of it.

8 'For it shall come to pass in that day,' saith יהוה of hosts (YHWH Tsevaot), 'that I will break his yoke from off your neck, and will burst your bonds, and strangers shall no more serve themselves of him:

9 But they shall serve יהוה their God (YHWH Eloheihem), and Dawid their king, whom I will raise up unto them.

10 'Therefore fear you not, O My servant Jacob (Yaaqov),' saith יהוה, nor be dismayed, O Yisrael; for, behold, I will save you from afar, and your seed from the land of their captivity; and Jacob (Yaaqov) shall return, and shall be in rest, and be quiet, and none shall make him afraid.

11 For I am with you,' saith יהוה, 'to save you; though I make a full end of all nations whither I have scattered you, yet will I not make a full end of you; but I will correct you in measure, and will not leave you altogether unpunished.'

12 "For thus saith יהוה: 'Your bruise is incurable, and your wound is grievous.

13 There is none to plead your cause, that you mayest be bound up; you have no healing medicines.

14 All your lovers have forgotten you; they seek you not; for I have wounded you with the wound of an enemy, with the chastisement of a cruel one, for the multitude of your iniquity; because your sins were increased.

15 Why criest you for your affliction? Your sorrow is incurable for the multitude of your iniquity; because your sins were increased, I have done these things unto you.

16 Therefore all they that devour you shall be devoured; and all your adversaries, every one of them, shall go into captivity; and they that spoil you shall be a spoil, and all that prey upon you will I give for a prey.

17 For I will restore health unto you, and I will heal you of your wounds,' saith יהוה, 'Because they called you an outcast, saying: "This is Zion (Tsiyon), whom no man seeketh after."'

18 Thus saith יהוה: "Behold, I will bring again the captivity of Jacob (Yaaqov)'s tents, and have mercy on his dwellingplaces; and the city shall be builded upon her own heap, and the palace shall remain after the manner thereof.

19 And out of them shall proceed thanksgiving and the voice of them that make merry; and I will multiply them, and they shall not be few; I will also glorify them, and they shall not be small.

20 Their children also shall be as aforetime, and their congregation shall be established before Me; and I will punish all that oppress them.

21 And their nobles shall be of themselves, and their governor shall proceed from the midst of them; and I will cause him to draw near, and he shall approach unto Me; for who is this that engaged his heart to approach unto Me?' saith יהוה.

22 'And you shall be My people, and I will be your God (Elohim).'"

23 Behold, the whirlwind of יהוה goeth forth with fury, a continuing whirlwind; it shall fall with pain upon the head of the wicked.

24 The fierce anger of יהוה shall not return, until He have done it, and until He have performed the intents of His heart; in the latter days you shall consider it.

31 "At the same time," saith יהוה, "will I be the God (Elohim) of all the families of Yisrael, and they shall be My people."

2 Thus saith יהוה: "The people who were left of the sword found grace in the wilderness; even Yisrael, when I went to cause him to rest."

3 יהוה hath appeared of old unto me, saying: "Yea, I have loved you with an everlasting love; therefore with lovingkindness have I drawn you.

4 Again I will build you, and you shalt be built, O virgin of Yisrael: you shalt again be adorned with your tabrets, and shalt go forth in the dances of them that make merry.

5 You shalt yet plant vines upon the mountains of Samaria (Shomeron); the planters shall plant, and shall eat them as common things.

6 For there shall be a day, that the watchmen upon the Mount Efrayim shall cry, 'Arise you, and let us go up to Zion (Tsiyon) unto יהוה our God (YHWH Eloheinu).'"

7 For thus saith יהוה: "Sing with gladness for

Jacob (Yaaqov), and shout among the chief of the nations; proclaim, praise, and say, 'O יהוה, save Your people, the remnant of Yisrael!'

8 Behold, I will bring them from the north country, and gather them from the coasts of the earth, and with them the blind and the lame, the woman with child and her that travaileth with child together; a great company shall return thither.

9 They shall come with weeping, and with supplications will I lead them. I will cause them to walk by the rivers of waters in a straight way, wherein they shall not stumble; for I am a Father to Yisrael, and Efrayim is My firstborn.

10 "Hear the word of יהוה, O you nations, and declare it in the isles afar off, and say, 'He that scattered Yisrael will gather him, and keep him, as a shepherd doth his flock.'

11 For יהוה hath redeemed Jacob (Yaaqov), and ransomed him from the hand of him that was stronger than he.

12 Therefore they shall come and sing in the height of Zion (Tsiyon), and shall flow together to the goodness of יהוה, for wheat, and for wine, and for oil, and for the young of the flock and of the herd; and their soul shall be as a watered garden; and they shall not sorrow any more at all.

13 Then shall the virgin rejoice in the dance, both young men and old together; for I will turn their mourning into joy, and will comfort them, and make them rejoice from their sorrow.

14 And I will satiate the soul of the priests (kohanim) with fatness, and My people shall be satisfied with My goodness," saith יהוה.

15 Thus saith יהוה: "A voice was heard in Ramah, lamentation, and bitter weeping; Rahel weeping for her children refused to be comforted for her children, because they were no more"

16 Thus saith יהוה: "Refrain your voice from weeping, and your eyes from tears; for your work shall be rewarded," saith יהוה, "And they shall come again from the land of the enemy.

17 And there is hope in your end," saith יהוה, "that your children shall come again to their own border.

18 I have surely heard Efrayim bemoaning himself thus: "You have chastised me, and I was chastised, as a bullock unaccustomed to the yoke; turn you me, and I shall be turned; for You are יהוה my God (YHWH Elohai).

19 Surely after that I was turned, I repented; and after that I was instructed, I smote upon my thigh; I was ashamed, yea, even confounded, because I did bear the reproach of my youth.'

20 "Is Efrayim My dear son? Is he a pleasant child? For since I spake against him, I do earnestly remember him still; therefore My bowels are troubled for him; I will surely have mercy upon him," saith יהוה.

21 "Set you up waymarks, make you high heaps; set your heart toward the highway, even the way which you wentest; turn back, O virgin of Yisrael, turn back to these your cities.

22 How long wilt you go about, O you backsliding daughter? For יהוה hath created a new thing in the earth: A woman shall compass a man."

23 Thus saith יהוה of hosts (YHWH Tsevaot), the God of Israel (Elohei Yisrael): "As yet they shall use this speech in the land of Judah (Yehudah) and in the cities thereof, when I shall bring again their captivity; יהוה bless you, O habitation of justice, and mountain of holiness!'

24 And there shall dwell in Judah (Yehudah) itself, and in all the cities thereof together, husbandmen, and they that go forth with flocks.

25 "For I have satiated the weary soul, and I have replenished every sorrowful soul."

26 Upon this I awaked, and beheld; and my sleep was sweet unto me.

27 "Behold, the days come," saith יהוה, "that I will sow the house of Yisrael and the house of Judah (Yehudah) with the seed of man, and with the seed of beast.

28 And it shall come to pass, that like as I have watched over them, to pluck up, and to break down, and to throw down, and to destroy, and to afflict; so will I watch over them, to build, and to plant," saith יהוה.

29 In those days they shall say no more: 'The fathers have eaten a sour grape, and the children's teeth are set on edge.'

30 "But every one shall die for his own iniquity; every man that eateth the sour grape, his teeth shall be set on edge.

31 "Behold, the days come," saith יהוה, "that I will make a new covenant with the house of Yisrael, and with the house of Judah (Yehudah);

32 Not according to the covenant that I made with their fathers in the day that I took them by the hand to bring them out of the land of Egypt

(Mitsrayim); which My covenant they broke, although I was a [B33f]husband (baal) unto them," saith יהוה;

33 "But this shall be the covenant that I will make with the house of Yisrael: After those days, saith יהוה, I will put My Torah in their inward parts, and write it in their hearts; and will be their God (Elohim), and they shall be My people.

34 And they shall teach no more every man his neighbour, and every man his brother, saying, 'Know יהוה,' for they shall all know Me, from the least of them unto the greatest of them," saith יהוה. "For I will forgive their iniquity, and I will remember their sin no more."

35 Thus saith יהוה, who giveth the sun for a light by day, and the ordinances of the moon and of the stars for a light by night, who divideth the sea when the waves thereof roar; יהוה of hosts (YHWH Tsevaot) is His name:

36 "If those ordinances depart from before Me," saith יהוה, "then the seed of Yisrael also shall cease from being a nation before Me forever."

37 Thus saith יהוה: "If heaven above can be measured, and the foundations of the earth searched out beneath, I will also cast off all the seed of Yisrael for all that they have done," saith יהוה.

38 "Behold, the days come," saith יהוה, "that the city shall be built to יהוה from the tower of Hananeel unto the gate of the corner.

39 And the measuring line shall yet go forth opposite it upon the hill Gareb, and shall compass about to Goath.

40 "And the whole valley of the dead bodies, and of the ashes, and all the fields unto the brook of Kidron, unto the corner of the horse gate toward the east, shall be holy unto יהוה. It shall not be plucked up, nor thrown down any more forever."

32 The word that came to Jeremiah (Yirmeyahu) from יהוה in the tenth year of Zedekiah (Tsidqiyahu) king of Judah (Yehudah), which was the eighteenth year of Nebuchad-nezzar.

2 For then the king of Babylon (Bavel)'s army besieged Yerushalayim; and Jeremiah (Yirmeyahu) the prophet was shut up in the court of the prison, which was in the king of Judah (Yehudah)'s house.

3 For Zedekiah (Tsidqiyahu) king of Judah (Yehudah) had shut him up, saying, "Wherefore dost you prophesy, and say, 'Thus saith יהוה, "Behold, I will give this city into the hand of the king of Babylon (Bavel), and he shall take it;

4 And Zedekiah (Tsidqiyahu) king of Judah (Yehudah) shall not escape out of the hand of the Chaldeans, but shall surely be delivered into the hand of the king of Babylon (Bavel), and shall speak with him mouth to mouth, and his eyes shall behold his eyes;

5 And he shall lead Zedekiah (Tsidqiyahu) to Babylon (Bavel), and there shall he be until I visit him," saith יהוה; "though you fight with the Chaldeans, you shall not prosper.""'

6 And Jeremiah (Yirmeyahu) said, "The word of יהוה came unto me, saying,

7 'Behold, Hanameel the son of Shallum your uncle shall come unto you, saying, "Buy you my field that is in Anathoth, for the right of redemption is yours to buy it.'"

8 So Hanameel mine uncle's son came to me in the court of the prison according to the word of יהוה, and said unto me, 'Please buy my field that is in Anathoth, which is in the country of Benjamin (Binyamin); for the right of inheritance is yours, and the redemption is yours; buy it for yourself.' Then I knew that this was the word of יהוה.

9 And I bought the field of Hanameel my uncle's son, that was in Anathoth, and weighed him the money, even seventeen shekels of silver.

10 And I subscribed the evidence, and sealed it, and took witnesses, and weighed him the money in the balances.

11 So I took the evidence of the purchase, both that which was sealed according to the commandment and custom, and that which was open;

12 And I gave the evidence of the purchase unto Baruch the son of Neriyah, the son of Maaseyah, in the sight of Hanameel mine uncle's son, and in the presence of the witnesses that subscribed the book of the purchase, before all the Jews (Yehudim) that sat in the court of the prison.

13 And I charged Baruch before them, saying,

14 'Thus saith יהוה of hosts (YHWH Tsevaot), the God of Israel (Elohei Yisrael): "Take these evidences, this evidence of the purchase, both which is sealed, and this evidence which is open; and put them in an earthen vessel, that they may continue many days."

15 'For thus saith יהוה of hosts (YHWH Tsevaot), the God of Israel (Elohei Yisrael): "Houses and fields and vineyards shall be possessed again in this land."'

16 Now when I had delivered the evidence of the purchase unto Baruch the son of Neriyah, I prayed unto יהוה, saying:

17 'Ah Lord (Adonai) יהוה! Behold, You have made the heaven and the earth by Your great power and outstretched arm, and there is nothing too hard for You;

18 You shewest lovingkindness unto thousands, and recompensest the iniquity of the fathers into the bosom of their children after them; the great the mighty God (El), יהוה of hosts (YHWH Tsevaot) is His name,

19 Great in counsel, and mighty in work; for Your eyes are open upon all the ways of the sons of men; to give every one according to his ways, and according to the fruit of his doings.

20 Which hast set signs and wonders in the land of Egypt (Mitsrayim), even unto this day, and in Yisrael, and among other men; and hast made Yourself a name, as at this day;

21 And hast brought forth Your people Yisrael out of the land of Egypt (Mitsrayim) with signs, and with wonders, and with a strong hand, and with an outstretched arm, and with great terror;

22 And hast given them this land, which You didst swear to their fathers to give them, "a land flowing with milk and honey."

23 And they came in, and possessed it; but they obeyed not Your voice, neither walked in Your Torah; they have done nothing of all that You commandedst them to do; therefore You have caused all this disaster (raah) to come upon them.

24 Behold the mounts, they are come unto the city to take it; and the city is given into the hand of the Chaldeans, that fight against it, because of the sword, and of the famine, and of the pestilence; and what You have spoken is come to pass; and, behold, You seest it.

25 And You have said unto me, O Lord (Adonai) יהוה, "Buy you the field for money, and take witnesses"! For the city is given into the hand of the Chaldeans.'"

26 Then came the word of יהוה unto Jeremiah (Yirmeyahu), saying,

27 "Behold, I am יהוה, the God (Elohim) of all flesh. Is there any thing too hard for Me?"

28 Therefore thus saith יהוה: "Behold, I will give this city into the hand of the Chaldeans, and into the hand of Nebuchadnezzar king of Babylon (Bavel), and he shall take it.

29 And the Chaldeans, that fight against this city, shall come and set fire on this city, and burn it with the houses, upon whose roofs they have offered incense unto the Baal, and poured out drink offerings unto other gods (elohim), to provoke Me to anger;

30 For the children of Yisrael and the children of Judah (Yehudah) have only done evil before Me from their youth; for the children of Yisrael have only provoked Me to anger with the work of their hands," saith יהוה.

31 For this city hath been to Me as a provocation of Mine anger and of My fury from the day that they built it even unto this day; that I should remove it from before My face,

32 Because of all the evil of the children of Yisrael and of the children of Judah (Yehudah), which they have done to provoke Me to anger, they, their kings, their princes, their priests (kohanim), and their prophets, and the men of Judah (Yehudah), and the inhabitants of Jerusalem (Yerushalayim).

33 And they have turned unto Me the back, and not the face; though I taught them, rising up early and teaching them, yet they have not hearkened to receive instruction.

34 But they set their abominations in the house, which is called by My name, to defile it.

35 And they built the high places of the Baal, which are in the valley of the son of Hinnom, to cause their sons and their daughters to pass through the fire unto Molech; which I commanded them not, neither came it into my mind, that they should do this abomination, to cause Judah (Yehudah) to sin.

36 And now therefore thus saith יהוה, the God of Israel (Elohei Yisrael), concerning this city, whereof you say, 'It shall be delivered into the hand of the king of Babylon (Bavel) by the sword, and by the famine, and by the pestilence':

37 'Behold, I will gather them out of all countries, whither I have driven them in Mine anger, and in My fury, and in great wrath; and I will bring them again unto this place, and I will cause them to dwell safely.

38 And they shall be My people, and I will be their God (Elohim);

39 And I will give them one heart, and one way, that they may fear Me forever, for the good of them, and of their children after them.

40 And I will make an everlasting covenant with them, that I will not turn away from them, to do them good; but I will put My fear in their hearts, that they shall not depart from Me.

41 Yea, I will rejoice over them to do them good, and I will plant them in this land assuredly with My whole heart and with My whole soul.'

42 "For thus saith יהוה: 'Like as I have brought all this great evil upon this people, so will I bring upon them all the good that I have promised them.

43 And fields shall be bought in this land, whereof you say, "It is desolate without man or beast; it is given into the hand of the Chaldeans."

44 Men shall buy fields for money, and subscribe evidences, and seal them, and take witnesses in the land of Benjamin (Binyamin), and in the places about Jerusalem (Yerushalayim), and in the cities of Judah (Yehudah), and in the cities of the mountains, and in the cities of the valley, and in the cities of the south; for I will cause their captivity to return,' saith יהוה."

33 Moreover the word of יהוה came unto Jeremiah (Yirmeyahu) the second time, while he was yet shut up in the court of the prison, saying,

2 "Thus saith יהוה the Maker thereof, יהוה who formed it, to establish it; יהוה is His name:

3 'Call unto Me, and I will answer you, and shew you great and mighty things, which you knowest not.'

4 "For thus saith יהוה, the God of Israel (Elohei Yisrael), concerning the houses of this city, and concerning the houses of the kings of Judah (Yehudah), which are thrown down by the mounts, and by the sword:

5 'They come to fight with the Chaldeans, but it is to fill them with the dead bodies of men, whom I have slain in Mine anger and in My fury, and for all whose wickedness I have hidden My face from this city.

6 Behold, I will bring it health and cure, and I will cure them, and will reveal unto them the abundance of peace and truth.

7 And I will cause the captivity of Judah (Yehudah) and the captivity of Yisrael to return, and will build them, as at the first.

8 And I will cleanse them from all their iniquity, whereby they have sinned against Me; and I will pardon all their iniquities, whereby they have sinned, and whereby they have transgressed against Me.

9 'And it shall be to Me a name of joy, a praise and an honor before all the nations of the earth, which shall hear all the good that I do unto them; and they shall fear and tremble for all the goodness and for all the prosperity that I procure unto it.'

10 "Thus saith יהוה: 'Again there shall be heard in this place, which you say shall be desolate without man and without beast, even in the cities of Judah (Yehudah), and in the streets of Jerusalem (Yerushalayim), that are desolate, without man, and without inhabitant, and without beast,

11 'The voice of joy, and the voice of gladness, the voice of the bridegroom, and the voice of the bride, the voice of them that shall say: "Praise יהוה of hosts (YHWH Tsevaot), for יהוה is good; for His mercy endureth forever." And of them that shall bring the sacrifice of praise into the house of יהוה. For I will cause to return the captivity of the land, as at the first,' saith יהוה.

12 "Thus saith יהוה of hosts (YHWH Tsevaot): Again in this place, which is desolate without man and without beast, and in all the cities thereof, shall be an habitation of shepherds causing their flocks to lie down.

13 'In the cities of the mountains, in the cities of the vale, and in the cities of the south, and in the land of Benjamin (Binyamin), and in the places about Jerusalem (Yerushalayim), and in the cities of Judah (Yehudah), shall the flocks pass again under the hands of him that telleth them,' saith יהוה.

14 'Behold, the days come,' saith יהוה, 'that I will perform that good thing which I have promised unto the house of Yisrael and to the house of Judah (Yehudah):

15 'In those days, and at that time, will I cause the Branch of righteousness to grow up unto Dawid; and he shall execute judgment and righteousness in the land.

16 In those days shall Judah (Yehudah) be saved, and Jerusalem (Yerushalayim) shall dwell safely. And this is the name wherewith she shall be called, A6יהוה Tsidqenu (YHWH Our Righteousness).

17 For thus saith יהוה: 'Dawid shall never want

a man to sit upon the throne of the house of Yisrael;

18 Neither shall the priests (kohanim) the Levites (Lewiyim) want a man before me to offer burnt offerings, and to kindle meat offerings, and to do sacrifice continually.'"

19 And the word of יהוה came unto Jeremiah (Yirmeyahu), saying,

20 "Thus saith יהוה: 'If you can break My covenant of the day, and My covenant of the night, and that there should not be day and night in their season;

21 Then may also My covenant be broken with Dawid My servant, that he should not have a son to reign upon his throne; and with the Levites (Lewiyim) the priests (kohanim), My ministers.

22 'As the host of heaven cannot be numbered, nor the sand of the sea measured; so will I multiply the seed of Dawid My servant, and the Levites (Lewiyim) that minister unto Me.'"

23 Moreover the word of יהוה came to Jeremiah (Yirmeyahu), saying,

24 Considerest you not what this people have spoken, saying, 'The two families which יהוה hath chosen, He hath even cast them off'? Thus they have despised My people, that they should be no more a nation before them.

25 Thus saith יהוה: 'If My covenant be not with day and night, and if I have not appointed the ordinances of heaven and earth;

26 Then will I cast away the seed of Jacob (Yaaqov), and Dawid My servant, so that I will not take any of his seed to be rulers over the seed of Avraham, Isaac, and Jacob (Yaaqov). For I will cause their captivity to return, and have mercy on them.'"

34 The word which came unto Jeremiah (Yirmeyahu) from יהוה, when Nebuchadnezzar king of Babylon (Bavel), and all his army, and all the kingdoms of the earth of his dominion, and all the people, fought against Jerusalem (Yerushalayim), and against all the cities thereof, saying,

2 "Thus saith יהוה, the God of Israel (Elohei Yisrael): 'Go and speak to Zedekiah (Tsidqiyahu) king of Judah (Yehudah), and tell him, "Thus saith יהוה: 'Behold, I will give this city into the hand of the king of Babylon (Bavel), and he shall burn it with fire.

3 And you shalt not escape out of his hand, but shalt surely be taken, and delivered into his hand; and your eyes shall behold the eyes of the king of Babylon (Bavel), and he shall speak with you mouth to mouth, and you shalt go to Babylon (Bavel).'"'

4 Yet hear the word of יהוה, O Zedekiah (Tsidqiyahu) king of Judah (Yehudah)! Thus saith יהוה of you: 'You shalt not die by the sword;

5 But you shalt die in peace; and with the burnings of your fathers, the former kings who were before you, so shall they burn odours for you; and they will lament you, saying, "Ah lord (adon)!" For I have pronounced the word," saith יהוה.

6 Then Jeremiah (Yirmeyahu) the prophet spake all these words unto Zedekiah (Tsidqiyahu) king of Judah (Yehudah) in Jerusalem (Yerushalayim),

7 When the king of Babylon (Bavel)'s army fought against Jerusalem (Yerushalayim), and against all the cities of Judah (Yehudah) that were left, against Lachish, and against Azekah; for these defenced cities remained of the cities of Judah (Yehudah).

8 This is the word that came unto Jeremiah (Yirmeyahu) from יהוה, after that the king Zedekiah (Tsidqiyahu) had made a covenant with all the people which were at Jerusalem (Yerushalayim), to proclaim liberty unto them:

9 That every man should let his manservant, and every man his maidservant, being a Hebrew or a Hebrewess (Ivri), go free; that none should serve himself of them, of a Jew (Yehudi) his brother.

10 Now when all the princes, and all the people, which had entered into the covenant, heard that every one should let his manservant, and every one his maidservant, go free, that none should serve themselves of them any more, then they obeyed, and let them go.

11 But afterward they turned, and caused the servants and the handmaids, whom they had let go free, to return, and brought them into subjection for servants and for handmaids.

12 Therefore the word of יהוה came to Jeremiah (Yirmeyahu) from יהוה, saying,

13 "Thus saith יהוה, the God of Israel (Elohei Yisrael): 'I made a covenant with your fathers in the day that I brought them forth out of the land of Egypt (Mitsrayim), out of the house of bondmen, saying,

14 "At the end of seven years let you go every man his brother a Hebrew (Ivri), which hath been sold unto you; and when he hath served you six years, you shalt let him go free from you." But your fathers hearkened not unto Me, neither inclined their ear.

15 And you were now turned, and had done right in My sight, in proclaiming liberty every man to his neighbour; and you had made a covenant before Me in the house which is called by My name.

16 'But you turned and polluted My name, and caused every man his servant, and every man his handmaid, whom you had set at liberty at their pleasure, to return, and brought them into subjection, to be unto you for servants and for handmaids.'

17 "Therefore thus saith יהוה: 'You have not hearkened unto Me, in proclaiming liberty, every one to his brother, and every man to his neighbor. Behold, I proclaim a liberty for you,' saith יהוה, 'to the sword, to the pestilence, and to the famine! And I will make you to be removed into all the kingdoms of the earth.

18 And I will give the men that have transgressed My covenant, which have not performed the words of the covenant which they had made before Me, when they cut the calf in twain, and passed between the parts thereof,

19 The princes of Judah (Yehudah), and the princes of Jerusalem (Yerushalayim), the officials, and the priests (kohanim), and all the people of the land, which passed between the parts of the calf;

20 I will even give them into the hand of their enemies, and into the hand of them that seek their life; and their dead bodies shall be for meat unto the fowls of the sky, and to the beasts of the earth.

21 And Zedekiah (Tsidqiyahu) king of Judah (Yehudah) and his princes will I give into the hand of their enemies, and into the hand of them that seek their life, and into the hand of the king of Babylon (Bavel)'s army, which are gone up from you.

22 Behold, I will command,' saith יהוה, 'and cause them to return to this city; and they shall fight against it, and take it, and burn it with fire; and I will make the cities of Judah (Yehudah) a desolation without an inhabitant.'"

35 The word which came unto Jeremiah (Yirmeyahu) from יהוה in the days of Yehoyaqim the son of Josiah (Yoshiyahu) king of Judah (Yehudah), saying,

2 "Go unto the house of the Rechabites, and speak unto them, and bring them into the house of יהוה, into one of the chambers, and give them wine to drink."

3 Then I took Yaanzanyah the son of Jeremiah (Yirmeyahu), the son of Chavatsinyah, and his brethren, and all his sons, and the whole house of the Rechabites;

4 And I brought them into the house of יהוה, into the chamber of the sons of Hanan, the son of Yigdalyahu, a man of God (Elohim), which was by the chamber of the princes, which was above the chamber of Maaseyah the son of Shallum, the keeper of the door:

5 And I set before the sons of the house of the Rechabites pots full of wine, and cups, and I said unto them, "Drink wine."

6 But they said, "We will drink no wine, for Yonadav the son of Rechab our father commanded us, saying, 'You shall drink no wine, neither you, nor your sons forever.

7 Neither shall you build house, nor sow seed, nor plant vineyard, nor have any: but all your days you shall dwell in tents; that you may live many days in the land where you be strangers.'

8 "Thus have we obeyed the voice of Yonadav the son of Rechab our father in all that he hath charged us, to drink no wine all our days, we, our wives, our sons, nor our daughters;

9 Nor to build houses for us to dwell in: neither have we vineyard, nor field, nor seed.

10 But we have dwelt in tents, and have obeyed, and done according to all that Yonadav our father commanded us.

11 But it came to pass, when Nebuchadnezzar king of Babylon (Bavel) came up into the land, that we said, 'Come, and let us go to Jerusalem (Yerushalayim) for fear of the army of the Chaldeans, and for fear of the army of the Syria (Aram).' so we dwell at Jerusalem (Yerushalayim)."

12 Then came the word of יהוה unto Jeremiah (Yirmeyahu), saying,

13 "Thus saith יהוה of hosts (YHWH Tsevaot), the God of Israel (Elohei Yisrael): 'Go and tell the men of Judah (Yehudah) and the inhabitants of Jerusalem (Yerushalayim), "Will you not

receive instruction to hearken to My words?" saith יהוה.

14 "The words of Yonadav the son of Rechab, that he commanded his sons not to drink wine, are performed; for unto this day they drink none, but obey their father's commandment. Notwithstanding I have spoken unto you, rising early and speaking; but you hearkened not unto Me.

15 "I have sent also unto you all My servants the prophets, rising up early and sending them, saying, 'Turn you now every man from his evil way, and amend your doings, and go not after other gods (elohim) to serve them, and you shall dwell in the land which I have given to you and to your fathers.' But you have not inclined your ear, nor hearkened unto Me.

16 "Because the sons of Yonadav the son of Rechab have performed the commandment of their father, which he commanded them; but this people hath not hearkened unto Me'"

17 "Therefore thus saith יהוה God of hosts (YHWH Elohei Tsevaot), the God of Israel (Elohei Yisrael); Behold, I will bring upon Judah (Yehudah) and upon all the inhabitants of Jerusalem (Yerushalayim) all the evil that I have pronounced against them; because I have spoken unto them, but they have not heard; and I have called unto them, but they have not answered.'"

18 And Jeremiah (Yirmeyahu) said unto the house of the Rechabites, "Thus saith יהוה of hosts (YHWH Tsevaot), the God of Israel (Elohei Yisrael): 'Because you have obeyed the commandment of Yonadav your father, and kept all his precepts, and done according unto all that he hath commanded you;

19 'Therefore thus saith יהוה of hosts (YHWH Tsevaot), the God of Israel (Elohei Yisrael): Yonadav the son of Rechab shall not lack a man to stand before Me forever.'""

36 And it came to pass in the fourth year of Yehoyaqim the son of Josiah (Yoshiyahu) king of Judah (Yehudah), that this word came unto Jeremiah (Yirmeyahu) from יהוה, saying,

2 "Take you a roll of a book, and write therein all the words that I have spoken unto you against Yisrael, and against Judah (Yehudah), and against all the nations, from the day I spake unto you, from the days of Josiah (Yoshiyahu), even unto this day.

3 It may be that the house of Judah (Yehudah) will hear all the evil which I purpose to do unto them; that they may return every man from his evil way; that I may forgive their iniquity and their sin."

4 Then Jeremiah (Yirmeyahu) called Baruch the son of Neriyah; and Baruch wrote from the mouth of Jeremiah (Yirmeyahu) all the words of יהוה, which he had spoken unto him, upon a roll of a book.

5 And Jeremiah (Yirmeyahu) commanded Baruch, saying, "I am shut up; I cannot go into the house of יהוה.

6 Therefore go you, and read in the roll, which you have written from my mouth, the words of יהוה in the ears of the people in יהוה's house upon the fasting day: and also you shalt read them in the ears of all Judah (Yehudah) that come out of their cities.

7 It may be they will present their supplication before יהוה, and will return every one from his evil way; for great is the anger and the fury that יהוה hath pronounced against this people."

8 And Baruch the son of Neriyah did according to all that Jeremiah (Yirmeyahu) the prophet commanded him, reading in the book the words of יהוה in יהוה's house.

9 And it came to pass in the fifth year of Yehoyaqim the son of Josiah (Yoshiyahu) king of Judah (Yehudah), in the ninth month, that they proclaimed a fast before יהוה to all the people in Jerusalem (Yerushalayim), and to all the people that came from the cities of Judah (Yehudah) unto Jerusalem (Yerushalayim).

10 Then read Baruch in the book the words of Jeremiah (Yirmeyahu) in the house of יהוה, in the chamber of Gemaryah the son of Shaphan the scribe, in the higher court, at the entry of the new gate of יהוה's house, in the ears of all the people.

11 When Mikhayehu the son of Gemaryah, the son of Shaphan, had heard out of the book all the words of יהוה,

12 Then he went down into the king's house, into the scribe's chamber: and, behold, all the princes sat there, even Elishama the scribe, and Delayahu the son of Shemayahu, and Elnathan the son of Achbor, and Gemaryah the son of Shaphan, and Zedekiah (Tsidqi-yahu) the son of Chananyah, and all the princes.

13 Then Mikhayehu declared unto them all the

words that he had heard, when Baruch read the book in the ears of the people.

14 Therefore all the princes sent Yehudi the son of Netanyahu, the son of Shelemyahu, the son of Kushi, unto Baruch, saying, "Take in your hand the roll wherein you have read in the ears of the people, and come." So Baruch the son of Neriyah took the roll in his hand, and came unto them.

15 And they said unto him, "Sit down now, and read it in our ears." So Baruch read it in their ears.

16 Now it came to pass, when they had heard all the words, they were afraid both one and other, and said unto Baruch, "We will surely tell the king of all these words."

17 And they asked Baruch, saying, "Tell us now, how didst you write all these words at his mouth?"

18 Then Baruch answered them, "He pronounced all these words unto me with his mouth, and I wrote them with ink in the book."

19 Then said the princes unto Baruch, "Go, hide you, you and Jeremiah (Yirmeyahu); and let no man know where you be."

20 And they went in to the king into the court, but they laid up the roll in the chamber of Elishama the scribe, and told all the words in the ears of the king.

21 So the king sent Yehudi to fetch the roll: and he took it out of Elishama the scribe's chamber. And Yehudi read it in the ears of the king, and in the ears of all the princes which stood beside the king.

22 Now the king sat in the winterhouse in the ninth month; and there was a fire on the hearth burning before him.

23 And it came to pass, that when Yehudi had read three or four leaves, he cut it with the penknife, and cast it into the fire that was on the hearth, until all the roll was consumed in the fire that was on the hearth.

24 Yet they were not afraid, nor rent their garments, neither the king, nor any of his servants that heard all these words.

25 Nevertheless Elnathan and Delayahu and Gemaryah had made intercession to the king that he would not burn the roll; but he would not hear them.

26 But the king commanded Yerachmeel the son of Hammelech, and Serayahu the son of Azriel, and Shelemyahu the son of Abdeel, to take Baruch the scribe and Jeremiah (Yirmeyahu) the prophet; but יהוה hid them.

27 Then the word of יהוה came to Jeremiah (Yirmeyahu), after that the king had burned the roll, and the words which Baruch wrote at the mouth of Jeremiah (Yirmeyahu), saying:

28 "Take you again another roll, and write in it all the former words that were in the first roll, which Yehoyaqim the king of Judah (Yehudah) hath burned.

29 And you shalt say to Yehoyaqim king of Judah (Yehudah), 'Thus saith יהוה: "You have burned this roll, saying, 'Why have you written therein, saying that the king of Babylon (Bavel) shall certainly come and destroy this land, and shall cause to cease from thence man and beast?'"

30 Therefore thus saith יהוה of Yehoyaqim king of Judah (Yehudah); He shall have none to sit upon the throne of Dawid; and his dead body shall be cast out in the day to the heat, and in the night to the frost.

31 And I will punish him and his seed and his servants for their iniquity; and I will bring upon them, and upon the inhabitants of Jerusalem (Yerushalayim), and upon the men of Judah (Yehudah), all the evil that I have pronounced against them; but they hearkened not.'"''

32 Then took Jeremiah (Yirmeyahu) another roll, and gave it to Baruch the scribe, the son of Neriyah; who wrote therein from the mouth of Jeremiah (Yirmeyahu) all the words of the book which Yehoyaqim king of Judah (Yehudah) had burned in the fire; and there were added besides unto them many like words.

37 And King Zedekiah (Tsidqi-yahu) the son of Josiah (Yoshiyahu) reigned instead of Konyahu the son of Yehoyaqim, whom Nebuchadnezzar king of Babylon (Bavel) made king in the land of Judah (Yehudah).

2 But neither he, nor his servants, nor the people of the land, did hearken unto the words of יהוה, which He spake by the prophet Jeremiah (Yirmeyahu).

3 And Zedekiah (Tsidqiyahu) the king sent Yehukhal the son of Shelemyahu and Zephaniah (Tsefanyah) the son of Maaseyah the priest (kohen) to the prophet Jeremiah (Yirmeyahu), saying, "Pray now unto יהוה our God (YHWH Eloheinu) for us."

26 Then you shalt say unto them, 'I presented my supplication before the king, that he would not cause me to return to Jonathan (Yehonatan)'s house, to die there.'"

27 Then came all the princes unto Jeremiah (Yirmeyahu), and asked him; and he told them according to all these words that the king had commanded. So they left off speaking with him; for the matter was not perceived.

28 So Jeremiah (Yirmeyahu) abode in the court of the prison until the day that Jerusalem (Yerushalayim) was taken; and he was there when Jerusalem (Yerushalayim) was taken.

39 In the ninth year of Zedekiah (Tsidqiyahu) king of Judah (Yehudah), in the tenth month, came Nebuchadnezzar king of Babylon (Bavel) and all his army against Jerusalem (Yerushalayim), and they besieged it.

2 And in the eleventh year of Zedekiah (Tsidqiyahu), in the fourth month, the ninth day of the month, the city was broken up.

3 And all the princes of the king of Babylon (Bavel) came in, and sat in the middle gate, even Nergalsharezer, Samgarnebo, Sarsechim, Rabsaris, Nergalsharezer, Rabmag, with all the residue of the princes of the king of Babylon (Bavel).

4 And it came to pass, that when Zedekiah (Tsidqiyahu) the king of Judah (Yehudah) saw them, and all the men of war, then they fled, and went forth out of the city by night, by the way of the king's garden, by the gate betwixt the two walls: and he went out the way of the plain.

5 But the Chaldeans' army pursued after them, and overtook Zedekiah (Tsidqiyahu) in the plains of Yericho; and when they had taken him, they brought him up to Nebuchadnezzar king of Babylon (Bavel) to Riblah in the land of Hamath, where he gave judgment upon him.

6 Then the king of Babylon (Bavel) slew the sons of Zedekiah (Tsidqi-yahu) in Riblah before his eyes; also the king of Babylon (Bavel) slew all the nobles of Judah (Yehudah).

7 Moreover he put out Zedekiah (Tsidqiyahu)'s eyes, and bound him with chains, to carry him to Babylon (Bavel).

8 And the Chaldeans burned the king's house, and the houses of the people, with fire, and broke down the walls of Jerusalem (Yerushalayim).

9 Then Nebuzaradan the captain of the guard carried away captive into Babylon (Bavel) the remnant of the people that remained in the city, and those that fell away, that fell to him, with the rest of the people that remained.

10 But Nebuzaradan the captain of the guard left of the poor of the people, which had nothing, in the land of Judah (Yehudah), and gave them vineyards and fields at the same time.

11 Now Nebuchadnezzar king of Babylon (Bavel) gave charge concerning Jeremiah (Yirmeyahu) to Nebuzaradan the captain of the guard, saying,

12 "Take him, and look well to him, and do him no harm; but do unto him even as he shall say unto you."

13 So Nebuzaradan the captain of the guard sent, and Nebushasban, Rabsaris, and Nergalsharezer, Rabmag, and all the king of Babylon (Bavel)'s princes;

14 Even they sent, and took Jeremiah (Yirmeyahu) out of the court of the prison, and committed him unto Gedalyahu the son of Ahikam the son of Shaphan, that he should carry him home. So he dwelt among the people.

15 Now the word of יהוה came unto Jeremiah (Yirmeyahu), while he was shut up in the court of the prison, saying,

16 "Go and speak to Ebedmelech the Ethiopian (Kushi), saying, 'Thus saith יהוה of hosts (YHWH Tsevaot), the God of Israel (Elohei Yisrael): "Behold, I will bring My words upon this city for evil, and not for good; and they shall be accomplished in that day before you.

17 But I will deliver you in that day," saith יהוה, "and you shalt not be given into the hand of the men of whom you are afraid.

18 For I will surely deliver you, and you shalt not fall by the sword, but your life shall be for a prey unto you, because you have put your trust in Me," saith יהוה.'"

40 The word that came to Jeremiah (Yirmeyahu) from יהוה, after that Nebuzaradan the captain of the guard had let him go from Ramah, when he had taken him being bound in chains among all that were carried away captive of Jerusalem (Yerushalayim) and Judah (Yehudah), which were carried away captive unto Babylon (Bavel).

2 And the captain of the guard took Jeremiah (Yirmeyahu), and said unto him: "יהוה your God (YHWH Eloheikha) hath pronounced this evil upon this place.

3 Now יהוה hath brought it, and done according as He hath said, because you have sinned against יהוה, and have not obeyed His voice, therefore this thing is come upon you.

4 And now, behold, I loose you this day from the chains which were upon your hand. If it seems good unto you to come with me into Babylon (Bavel), come; and I will look well unto you; but if it seems ill unto you to come with me into Babylon (Bavel), forbear. Behold, all the land is before you; whither it seemeth good and convenient for you to go, thither go."

5 Now while he was not yet gone back, he said, "Go back also to Gedalyahu the son of Ahikam the son of Shaphan, whom the king of Babylon (Bavel) hath made governor over the cities of Judah (Yehudah), and dwell with him among the people; or go wheresoever it seemeth convenient unto you to go." So the captain of the guard gave him victuals and a reward, and let him go.

6 Then went Jeremiah (Yirmeyahu) unto Gedalyahu the son of Ahikam to Mizpah; and dwelt with him among the people that were left in the land.

7 Now when all the captains of the forces which were in the fields, even they and their men, heard that the king of Babylon (Bavel) had made Gedalyahu the son of Ahikam governor in the land, and had committed unto him men, and women, and children, and of the poor of the land, of them that were not carried away captive to Babylon (Bavel);

8 Then they came to Gedalyahu to Mizpah, even Yishmael the son of Netanyahu, and Yochanan and Jonathan (Yehonatan) the sons of Kareah, and Serayahu the son of Tanhumeth, and the sons of Ephai the Netophathite, and Yezanyahu the son of a Maachathite, they and their men.

9 And Gedalyahu the son of Ahikam the son of Shaphan sware unto them and to their men, saying, "Fear not to serve the Chaldeans; dwell in the land, and serve the king of Babylon (Bavel), and it shall be well with you.

10 As for me, behold, I will dwell at Mizpah to serve the Chaldeans, which will come unto us; but you, gather you wine, and summer fruits, and oil, and put them in your vessels, and dwell in your cities that you have taken."

11 Likewise when all the Jews (Yehudim) that were in Moav, and among the Ammonites, and in Edom, and that were in all the countries, heard that the king of Babylon (Bavel) had left a remnant of Judah (Yehudah), and that he had set over them Gedalyahu the son of Ahikam the son of Shaphan;

12 Even all the Jews (Yehudim) returned out of all places whither they were driven, and came to the land of Judah (Yehudah), to Gedalyahu, unto Mizpah, and gathered wine and summer fruits very much.

13 Moreover Yochanan the son of Kareah, and all the captains of the forces that were in the fields, came to Gedalyahu to Mizpah,

14 And said unto him, "Dost you certainly know that Baalis the king of the Ammonites hath sent Yishmael the son of Netanyahu to slay you?" But Gedalyahu the son of Ahikam believed them not.

15 Then Yochanan the son of Kareah spake to Gedalyahu in Mizpah secretly, saying, "Let me go, please, and I will slay Yishmael the son of Netanyahu, and no man shall know it; wherefore should he slay you, that all the Jews (Yehudim) who are gathered unto you should be scattered, and the remnant in Judah (Yehudah) perish?"

16 But Gedalyahu the son of Ahikam said unto Yochanan the son of Kareah, "You shalt not do this thing, for you speakest falsely of Yishmael."

41 Now it came to pass in the seventh month, that Yishmael the son of Netanyahu the son of Elishama, of the seed royal, and the princes of the king, even ten men with him, came unto Gedalyahu the son of Ahikam to Mizpah; and there they did eat bread together in Mizpah.

2 Then arose Yishmael the son of Netanyahu, and the ten men that were with him, and smote Gedalyahu the son of Ahikam the son of Shaphan with the sword, and slew him, whom the king of Babylon (Bavel) had made governor over the land.

3 Yishmael also slew all the Jews (Yehudim) that were with him, even with Gedalyahu, at Mizpah, and the Chaldeans that were found there, and the men of war.

4 And it came to pass the second day after he had slain Gedalyahu, and no man knew it,

5 That there came certain from Shechem, from Shiloh, and from Samaria (Shomeron), even fourscore men, having their beards shaven, and their clothes rent, and having cut themselves, with offerings and incense in their hand, to

bring them to the house of יהוה.

6 And Yishmael the son of Netanyahu went forth from Mizpah to meet them, weeping all along as he went; and it came to pass, as he met them, he said unto them, "Come to Gedalyahu the son of Ahikam."

7 And it was so, when they came into the midst of the city, that Yishmael the son of Netanyahu slew them, and cast them into the midst of the pit, he, and the men that were with him.

8 But ten men were found among them that said unto Yishmael, "Slay us not, for we have treasures in the field, of wheat, and of barley, and of oil, and of honey." So he forbare, and slew them not among their brethren.

9 Now the pit wherein Yishmael had cast all the dead bodies of the men, whom he had slain because of Gedalyahu, was it which Asa the king had made for fear of Baasha king of Yisrael; and Yishmael the son of Netanyahu filled it with them that were slain.

10 Then Yishmael carried away captive all the residue of the people that were in Mizpah, even the king's daughters, and all the people that remained in Mizpah, whom Nebuzaradan the captain of the guard had committed to Gedalyahu the son of Ahikam; and Yishmael the son of Netanyahu carried them away captive, and departed to go over to the Ammonites.

11 But when Yochanan the son of Kareah, and all the captains of the forces that were with him, heard of all the evil that Yishmael the son of Netanyahu had done,

12 Then they took all the men, and went to fight with Yishmael the son of Netanyahu, and found him by the great waters that are in Giveon.

13 Now it came to pass, that when all the people which were with Yishmael saw Yochanan the son of Kareah, and all the captains of the forces that were with him, then they were glad.

14 So all the people that Yishmael had carried away captive from Mizpah cast about and returned, and went unto Yochanan the son of Kareah.

15 But Yishmael the son of Netanyahu escaped from Yochanan with eight men, and went to the Ammonites.

16 Then took Yochanan the son of Kareah, and all the captains of the forces that were with him, all the remnant of the people whom he had recovered from Yishmael the son of Netanyahu,

from Mizpah, after that he had slain Gedalyahu the son of Ahikam, even mighty men of war, and the women, and the children, and the eunuchs, whom he had brought again from Giveon:

17 And they departed, and dwelt in the habitation of Chimham, which is by Bethlehem (Beit-Lechem), to go to enter into Egypt (Mitsrayim),

18 Because of the Chaldeans; for they were afraid of them, because Yishmael the son of Netanyahu had slain Gedalyahu the son of Ahikam, whom the king of Babylon (Bavel) made governor in the land.

42 Then all the captains of the forces, and Yochanan the son of Kareah, and Yezanyahu the son of Hoshayah, and all the people from the least even unto the greatest, came near,

2 And said unto Jeremiah (Yirmeyahu) the prophet, "We beseech you, let our supplication be accepted before you, and pray for us unto יהוה your God (YHWH Eloheikha), even for all this remnant; (for we are left but a few of many, as your eyes do behold us,)

3 That יהוה your God (YHWH Eloheikha) may shew us the way wherein we may walk, and the thing that we may do."

4 Then Jeremiah (Yirmeyahu) the prophet said unto them, "I have heard you; behold, I will pray unto יהוה your God (YHWH Eloheikhem) according to your words; and it shall come to pass, that whatsoever thing יהוה shall answer you, I will declare it unto you; I will keep nothing back from you."

5 Then they said to Jeremiah (Yirmeyahu), "יהוה be a true and faithful witness between us, if we do not even according to all things for which יהוה your God (YHWH Eloheikha) shall send you to us.

6 Whether it be good, or whether it be evil, we will obey the voice of יהוה our God (YHWH Eloheinu), to whom we send you; that it may be well with us, when we obey the voice of יהוה our God (YHWH Eloheinu)."

7 And it came to pass after ten days, that the word of יהוה came unto Jeremiah (Yirmeyahu).

8 Then called he Yochanan the son of Kareah, and all the captains of the forces which were with him, and all the people from the least even to the greatest,

9 And said unto them, "Thus saith יהוה, the God of Israel (Elohei Yisrael), unto whom you sent

me to present your supplication before Him:

10 'If you will still abide in this land, then will I build you, and not pull you down, and I will plant you, and not pluck you up; for I regret of the evil that I have done unto you.

11 'Be not afraid of the king of Babylon (Bavel), of whom you are afraid; be not afraid of him,' saith יהוה, 'for I am with you to save you, and to deliver you from his hand.'

12 And I will shew mercies unto you, that he may have mercy upon you, and cause you to return to your own land.

13 But if you say, 'We will not dwell in this land', nor obey the voice of יהוה your God (YHWH Eloheikhem),

14 Saying, 'No, but we will go into the land of Egypt (Mitsrayim), where we shall see no war, nor hear the sound of the trumpet, nor have hunger of bread; and there will we dwell.'

15 And now therefore hear the word of יהוה, you remnant of Judah (Yehudah)! Thus saith יהוה of hosts (YHWH Tsevaot), the God of Israel (Elohei Yisrael): 'If you wholly set your faces to enter into Egypt (Mitsrayim), and go to sojourn there;

16 Then it shall come to pass, that the sword, which you feared, shall overtake you there in the land of Egypt (Mitsrayim), and the famine, whereof you were afraid, shall follow close after you there in Egypt (Mitsrayim); and there you shall die.

17 So shall it be with all the men that set their faces to go into Egypt (Mitsrayim) to sojourn there. They shall die by the sword, by the famine, and by the pestilence: and none of them shall remain or escape from the evil that I will bring upon them.'

18 For thus saith יהוה of hosts (YHWH Tsevaot), the God of Israel (Elohei Yisrael): 'As Mine anger and My fury hath been poured forth upon the inhabitants of Jerusalem (Yerushalayim); so shall My fury be poured forth upon you, when you shall enter into Egypt (Mitsrayim): and you shall be an execration, and an astonishment, and a curse, and a reproach; and you shall see this place no more.'

19 יהוה hath said concerning you, O you remnant of Judah (Yehudah), 'Go you not into Egypt (Mitsrayim)!' Know certainly that I have admonished you this day.

20 For you dissembled in your hearts, when you sent me unto יהוה your God (YHWH Eloheikhem), saying, 'Pray for us unto יהוה our God (YHWH Eloheinu); and according unto all that יהוה our God (YHWH Eloheinu) shall say, so declare unto us, and we will do it.'

21 And now I have this day declared it to you, but you have not obeyed the voice of יהוה your God (YHWH Eloheikhem), nor any thing for which He hath sent me unto you.

22 Now therefore know certainly that you shall die by the sword, by the famine, and by the pestilence, in the place whither you desire to go and to sojourn."

43 And it came to pass, that when Jeremiah (Yirmeyahu) had made an end of speaking unto all the people all the words of יהוה their God (YHWH Eloheihem), for which יהוה their God (YHWH Eloheihem) had sent him to them, even all these words,

2 Then spake Azaryah the son of Hoshayah, and Yochanan the son of Kareah, and all the proud men, saying unto Jeremiah (Yirmeyahu), "You speakest falsely! יהוה our God (YHWH Eloheinu) hath not sent you to say, 'Go not into Egypt (Mitsrayim) to sojourn there.'

3 But Baruch the son of Neriyah setteth you on against us, for to deliver us into the hand of the Chaldeans, that they might put us to death, and carry us away captives into Babylon (Bavel)."

4 So Yochanan the son of Kareah, and all the captains of the forces, and all the people, obeyed not the voice of יהוה, to dwell in the land of Judah (Yehudah).

5 But Yochanan the son of Kareah, and all the captains of the forces, took all the remnant of Judah (Yehudah), that were returned from all nations, whither they had been driven, to dwell in the land of Judah (Yehudah);

6 Even men, and women, and children, and the king's daughters, and every person that Nebuzaradan the captain of the guard had left with Gedalyahu the son of Ahikam the son of Shaphan, and Jeremiah (Yirmeyahu) the prophet, and Baruch the son of Neriyah.

7 So they came into the land of Egypt (Mitsrayim), for they obeyed not the voice of יהוה; thus came they even to Tahpanhes.

8 Then came the word of יהוה unto Jeremiah (Yirmeyahu) in Tahpanhes, saying,

9 "Take great stones in your hand, and hide them in the clay in the brickkiln, which is at the

entry of Pharaoh (Paroh)'s house in Tahpanhes, in the sight of the men of Judah (Yehudah);

10 And say unto them, 'Thus saith יהוה of hosts (YHWH Tsevaot), the God of Israel (Elohei Yisrael): "Behold, I will send and take Nebuchadnezzar the king of Babylon (Bavel), My servant, and will set his throne upon these stones that I have hid; and he shall spread his royal pavilion over them.

11 And when he cometh, he shall smite the land of Egypt (Mitsrayim), and deliver such as are for death to death; and such as are for captivity to captivity; and such as are for the sword to the sword.

12 And I will kindle a fire in the houses of the gods (elohim) of Egypt (Mitsrayim); and he shall burn them, and carry them away captives; and he shall array himself with the land of Egypt (Mitsrayim), as a shepherd putteth on his garment; and he shall go forth from thence in peace.

13 He shall break also the images of Beit-Shemesh, that is in the land of Egypt (Mitsrayim); and the houses of the gods (elohim) of the Egyptians (Mitsrayim) shall he burn with fire."'"

44 The word that came to Jeremiah (Yirmeyahu) concerning all the Jews (Yehudim) which dwell in the land of Egypt (Mitsrayim), which dwell at Migdol, and at Tahpanhes, and at Noph, and in the country of Pathros, saying,

2 "Thus saith יהוה of hosts (YHWH Tsevaot), the God of Israel (Elohei Yisrael): 'You have seen all the evil that I have brought upon Jerusalem (Yerushalayim), and upon all the cities of Judah (Yehudah); and, behold, this day they are a desolation, and no man dwelleth therein,

3 Because of their wickedness which they have committed to provoke Me to anger, in that they went to burn incense, and to serve other gods (elohim), whom they knew not, neither they, you, nor your fathers.

4 Howbeit I sent unto you all my servants the prophets, rising early and sending them, saying, "Oh, do not this abominable thing that I hate!"

5 But they hearkened not, nor inclined their ear to turn from their wickedness, to burn no incense unto other gods (elohim).

6 Wherefore My fury and Mine anger was poured forth, and was kindled in the cities of Judah (Yehudah) and in the streets of Jerusalem (Yerushalayim); and they are wasted and desolate, as at this day.'

7 Therefore now thus saith יהוה, God of hosts (YHWH Elohei Tsevaot), the God of Israel (Elohei Yisrael): 'Wherefore commit you this great evil against your souls, to cut off from you man and woman, child and suckling, out of Judah (Yehudah), to leave you none to remain;

8 In that you provoke Me unto wrath with the works of your hands, burning incense unto other gods (elohim) in the land of Egypt (Mitsrayim), whither you be gone to dwell, that you might cut yourselves off, and that you might be a curse and a reproach among all the nations of the earth?

9 Have you forgotten the wickedness of your fathers, and the wickedness of the kings of Judah (Yehudah), and the wickedness of their wives, and your own wickedness, and the wickedness of your wives, which they have committed in the land of Judah (Yehudah), and in the streets of Jerusalem (Yerushalayim)?

10 They are not humbled even unto this day, neither have they feared, nor walked in My Torah, nor in My statutes, that I set before you and before your fathers.'

11 Therefore thus saith יהוה of hosts (YHWH Tsevaot), the God of Israel (Elohei Yisrael); Behold, I will set My face against you for evil, and to cut off all Judah (Yehudah).

12 And I will take the remnant of Judah (Yehudah), that have set their faces to go into the land of Egypt (Mitsrayim) to sojourn there, and they shall all be consumed, and fall in the land of Egypt (Mitsrayim); they shall even be consumed by the sword and by the famine: they shall die, from the least even unto the greatest, by the sword and by the famine; and they shall be an execration, and an astonishment, and a curse, and a reproach!

13 For I will punish them that dwell in the land of Egypt (Mitsrayim), as I have punished Jerusalem (Yerushalayim), by the sword, by the famine, and by the pestilence:

14 So that none of the remnant of Judah (Yehudah), which are gone into the land of Egypt (Mitsrayim) to sojourn there, shall escape or remain, that they should return into the land of Judah (Yehudah), to which they have a desire

to return to dwell there; for none shall return but such as shall escape.'"

15 Then all the men which knew that their wives had burned incense unto other gods (elohim), and all the women that stood by, a great multitude, even all the people that dwelt in the land of Egypt (Mitsrayim), in Pathros, answered Jeremiah (Yirmeyahu), saying:

16 "As for the word that you have spoken unto us in the name of יהוה, we will not hearken unto you!

17 But we will certainly do whatsoever thing goeth forth out of our own mouth, to burn incense unto the queen of heaven, and to pour out drink offerings unto her, as we have done, we, and our fathers, our kings, and our princes, in the cities of Judah (Yehudah), and in the streets of Jerusalem (Yerushalayim): for then had we plenty of victuals, and were well, and saw no evil.

18 But since we left off to burn incense to the queen of heaven, and to pour out drink offerings unto her, we have wanted all things, and have been consumed by the sword and by the famine."

19 "And when we burned incense to the queen of heaven, and poured out drink offerings unto her, did we make her cakes to worship her, and pour out drink offerings unto her, without our husbands?"

20 Then Jeremiah (Yirmeyahu) said unto all the people, to the men, and to the women, and to all the people who had given him that answer, saying:

21 "The incense that you burned in the cities of Judah (Yehudah), and in the streets of Jerusalem (Yerushalayim), you, and your fathers, your kings, and your princes, and the people of the land, did not יהוה remember them, and came it not into His mind?

22 So that יהוה could no longer bear, because of the evil of your doings, and because of the abominations which you have committed; therefore is your land a desolation, and an astonishment, and a curse, without an inhabitant, as at this day.

23 Because you have burned incense, and because you have sinned against יהוה, and have not obeyed the voice of יהוה, nor walked in His Torah, nor in His statutes, nor in His testimonies; therefore this evil is happened unto you, as at this day."

24 Moreover Jeremiah (Yirmeyahu) said unto all the people, and to all the women, "Hear the word of יהוה, all Judah (Yehudah) that are in the land of Egypt (Mitsrayim)!

25 Thus saith יהוה of hosts (YHWH Tsevaot), the God of Israel (Elohei Yisrael), saying: 'You and your wives have both spoken with your mouths, and fulfilled with your hand, saying, "We will surely perform our vows that we have vowed, to burn incense to the queen of heaven, and to pour out drink offerings unto her." You will surely accomplish your vows, and surely perform your vows!

26 Therefore hear you the word of יהוה, all Judah (Yehudah) that dwell in the land of Egypt (Mitsrayim): 'Behold, I have sworn by My great name,' saith יהוה, 'that My name shall no more be named in the mouth of any man of Judah (Yehudah) in all the land of Egypt (Mitsrayim), saying, "Lord (Adonai) יהוה liveth."

27 Behold, I will watch over them for evil, and not for good; and all the men of Judah (Yehudah) that are in the land of Egypt (Mitsrayim) shall be consumed by the sword and by the famine, until there be an end of them.

28 Yet a small number that escape the sword shall return out of the land of Egypt (Mitsrayim) into the land of Judah (Yehudah), and all the remnant of Judah (Yehudah), that are gone into the land of Egypt (Mitsrayim) to sojourn there, shall know whose words shall stand, mine, or theirs.

29 'And this shall be a sign unto you,' saith יהוה, 'that I will punish you in this place, that you may know that My words shall surely stand against you for disaster (raah).'

30 Thus saith יהוה: "Behold, I will give Pharaohhophra (Paroh Chofra) king of Egypt (Mitsrayim) into the hand of his enemies, and into the hand of them that seek his life; as I gave Zedekiah (Tsidqiyahu) king of Judah (Yehudah) into the hand of Nebuchadnezzar king of Babylon (Bavel), his enemy, and that sought his life.'"

45 The word that Jeremiah (Yirmeyahu) the prophet spake unto Baruch the son of Neriyah, when he had written these words in a book at the mouth of Jeremiah (Yirmeyahu), in the fourth year of Yehoyaqim the son of Josiah (Yoshiyahu) king of Judah (Yehudah), saying,

2 "Thus saith יהוה, the God of Israel (Elohei Yisrael), unto you, O Baruch:

3 You didst say, "Woe is me now! For יהוה hath added grief to my sorrow; I fainted in my sighing, and I find no rest.""

4 Thus shalt you say unto him, יהוה saith thus: "Behold, that which I have built will I break down, and that which I have planted I will pluck up, even this whole land.

5 And seekest you great things for yourself? Seek them not; for, behold, I will bring disaster (raah) upon all flesh," saith יהוה; "but your life will I give unto you for a prey in all places whither you goest.""

46

The word of יהוה which came to Jeremiah (Yirmeyahu) the prophet against the nations;

2 Against Egypt (Mitsrayim), against the army of Pharaoh (Paroh)necho king of Egypt (Mitsrayim), which was by the river Euphrates in Carchemish, which Nebuchadnezzar king of Babylon (Bavel) smote in the fourth year of Yehoyaqim the son of Josiah (Yoshiyahu) king of Judah (Yehudah):

3 "Order you the buckler and shield, and draw near to battle!

4 Harness the horses; and get up, you horsemen, and stand forth with your helmets; furbish the spears, and put on the armor!

5 Wherefore have I seen them dismayed and turned away back? And their mighty ones are beaten down, and are fled apace, and look not back; for fear was round about," saith יהוה.

6 Let not the swift flee away, nor the mighty man escape; they shall stumble, and fall toward the north by the river Euphrates.

7 Who is this that cometh up as a flood, whose waters are moved as the rivers?

8 Egypt (Mitsrayim) riseth up like a flood, and his waters are moved like the rivers; and he saith, 'I will go up, and will cover the earth; I will destroy the city and the inhabitants thereof.'

9 Come up, you horses; and rage, you chariots; and let the mighty men come forth: The Ethiopians (Kushim) and the Libyans, that handle the shield; and the Lydians, that handle and bend the bow.

10 For this is the day of Lord (Adonai) יהוה of hosts (YHWH Tsevaot), a day of vengeance, that He may avenge Him of His adversaries; and the sword shall devour, and it shall be satiate and made drunk with their blood; for Lord (Adonai) יהוה of hosts (YHWH Tsevaot) hath a sacrifice in the north country by the river Euphrates.

11 Go up into Gilad, and take balm, O virgin, the daughter of Egypt (Mitsrayim); in vain shalt you use many medicines; for you shalt not be cured.

12 The nations have heard of your shame, and your cry hath filled the land; for the mighty man hath stumbled against the mighty, and they are fallen both together."

13 The word that יהוה spake to Jeremiah (Yirmeyahu) the prophet, how Nebuchadnezzar king of Babylon (Bavel) should come and smite the land of Egypt (Mitsrayim).

14 Declare you in Egypt (Mitsrayim), and proclaim in Migdol, and proclaim in Noph and in Tahpanhes; say you, 'Stand fast, and prepare you; for the sword shall devour round about you.'

15 Why are your valiant men swept away? They stood not, because יהוה did drive them.

16 He made many to fall, yea, one fell upon another; and they said, 'Arise! Let us go again to our own people, and to the land of our nativity, from the oppressing sword.'

17 They did cry there, 'Pharaoh (Paroh) king of Egypt (Mitsrayim) is but a noise; he hath passed the time appointed!'

18 "As I live," saith the King, whose name is יהוה of hosts (YHWH Tsevaot), "Surely as Tabor is among the mountains, and as Carmel by the sea, so shall he come.

19 O you daughter dwelling in Egypt (Mitsrayim), furnish yourself to go into captivity: for Noph shall be waste and desolate without an inhabitant.

20 Egypt (Mitsrayim) is like a very fair heifer, but destruction cometh; it cometh out of the north.

21 Also her hired men are in the midst of her like fatted bullocks; for they also are turned back, and are fled away together; they did not stand, because the day of their disaster was come upon them, and the time of their visitation.

22 The voice thereof shall go like a serpent; for they shall march with an army, and come against her with axes, as hewers of wood.

23 "They shall cut down her forest," saith יהוה, "though it cannot be searched; because they are

more than the grasshoppers, and are innumerable.

24 The daughter of Egypt (Mitsrayim) shall be confounded; she shall be delivered into the hand of the people of the north."

25 יהוה of hosts (YHWH Tsevaot), the God of Israel (Elohei Yisrael), saith: "Behold, I will punish the multitude of No, and Pharaoh (Paroh), and Egypt (Mitsrayim), with their gods (elohim), and their kings; even Pharaoh (Paroh), and all them that trust in him.

26 And I will deliver them into the hand of those that seek their lives, and into the hand of Nebuchadnezzar king of Babylon (Bavel), and into the hand of his servants; and afterward it shall be inhabited, as in the days of old," saith יהוה.

27 But fear not you, O My servant Jacob (Yaaqov), and be not dismayed, O Yisrael; for, behold, I will save you from afar off, and your seed from the land of their captivity; and Jacob (Yaaqov) shall return, and be in rest and at ease, and none shall make him afraid.

28 Fear you not, O Jacob (Yaaqov) My servant," saith יהוה, "for I am with you; for I will make a full end of all the nations whither I have driven you, but I will not make a full end of you, but correct you in measure; yet will I not leave you wholly unpunished."

47 The word of יהוה that came to Jeremiah (Yirmeyahu) the prophet against the Philistines, before that Pharaoh (Paroh) smote Gaza (Azzah).

2 Thus saith יהוה: "Behold, waters rise up out of the north, and shall be an overflowing flood, and shall overflow the land, and all that is therein; the city, and them that dwell therein; then the men shall cry, and all the inhabitants of the land shall howl.

3 At the noise of the stamping of the hoofs of his strong horses, at the rushing of his chariots, and at the rumbling of his wheels, the fathers shall not look back to their children for feebleness of hands;

4 Because of the day that cometh to spoil all the Philistines, and to cut off from Tyrus and Zidon every helper that remaineth; for יהוה will spoil the Philistines, the remnant of the country of Caphtor.

5 Baldness is come upon Gaza (Azzah); Ashkelon is cut off with the remnant of their

valley. How long wilt you cut yourself?

6 O you sword of יהוה, how long until you be quiet? Put up yourself into your scabbard, rest, and be still!

7 How can it be quiet, seeing יהוה hath given it a charge against Ashkelon, and against the sea shore? There hath He appointed it."

48 Against Moav thus saith יהוה of hosts (YHWH Tsevaot), the God of Israel (Elohei Yisrael): "Woe unto Nebo! For it is spoiled, Qiryatayim is confounded and taken; Misgab is confounded and dismayed.

2 There shall be no more praise of Moav; in Heshbon they have devised evil against it: 'Come, and let us cut it off from being a nation.' Also you shalt be cut down, O Madmen! The sword shall pursue you;

3 A voice of crying shall be from Horonaim, spoiling and great destruction!

4 Moav is destroyed; her little ones have caused a cry to be heard;

5 For in the going up of Luhith continual weeping shall go up; for in the going down of Horonaim the enemies have heard a cry of destruction.

6 Flee, save your lives! And be like the heath in the wilderness.

7 For because you have trusted in your works and in your treasures, you shalt also be taken; and Chemosh shall go forth into captivity with his priests (kohanim) and his princes together.

8 And the spoiler shall come upon every city, and no city shall escape; the valley also shall perish, and the plain shall be destroyed, as יהוה hath spoken.

9 Give wings unto Moav, that it may flee and get away; for the cities thereof shall be desolate, without any to dwell therein.

10 Cursed be he that doeth the work of יהוה deceitfully, and cursed be he that keepeth back his sword from blood.

11 Moav hath been at ease from his youth, and he hath settled on his lees, and hath not been emptied from vessel to vessel, neither hath he gone into captivity; therefore his taste remained in him, and his scent is not changed.

12 "Therefore, behold, the days come," saith יהוה, "that I will send unto him wanderers, that shall cause him to wander, and shall empty his vessels, and break their bottles.

13 And Moav shall be ashamed of Chemosh,

as the house of Yisrael was ashamed of Bethel (Beit-El) their confidence.

14 How say you, 'We are mighty and strong men for the war'?

15 Moav is spoiled, and gone up out of her cities, and His chosen young men are gone down to the slaughter," saith the King, whose name is יהוה of hosts (YHWH Tsevaot).

16 The disaster of Moav is near to come, and his affliction hasteth fast.

17 All you that are about him, bemoan him; and all you that know his name, say, 'How is the strong staff broken, and the beautiful rod!'

18 You daughter that dost inhabit Dibon, come down from your glory, and sit in thirst; for the spoiler of Moav shall come upon you, and he shall destroy your strong holds.

19 O inhabitant of Aroer, stand by the way, and espy; ask him that fleeth, and her that escapeth, and say, 'What is done?'

20 Moav is confounded; for it is broken down; howl and cry; tell you it in Arnon, that Moav is spoiled,

21 And judgment is come upon the plain country; upon Holon, and upon Yahatsah, and upon Mephaath,

22 And upon Dibon, and upon Nebo, and upon Beit-Diblathaim,

23 And upon Qiryatayim, and upon Beit-Gamul, and upon Beit-Meon,

24 And upon Kerioth, and upon Bozrah, and upon all the cities of the land of Moav, far or near.

25 The horn of Moav is cut off, and his arm is broken," saith יהוה.

26 Make you him drunken, for he magnified himself against יהוה: Moav also shall wallow in his vomit, and he also shall be in derision.

27 For was not Yisrael a derision unto you? Was he found among thieves? For since you spakest of him, you skippedst for joy.

28 O you that dwell in Moav, leave the cities, and dwell in the rock, and be like the dove that maketh her nest in the sides of the hole's mouth.

29 We have heard the pride of Moav, (he is exceeding proud) his loftiness, and his arrogancy, and his pride, and the haughtiness of his heart."

30 "I know his wrath," saith יהוה, "but it shall not be so; his lies shall not so effect it.

31 Therefore will I howl for Moav, and I will cry out for all Moav; Mine heart shall mourn for the men of Kirheres.

32 O vine of Sibmah, I will weep for you with the weeping of Yazer; your plants are gone over the sea, they reach even to the sea of Yazer; the spoiler is fallen upon your summer fruits and upon your vintage.

33 And joy and gladness is taken from the plentiful field, and from the land of Moav; and I have caused wine to fail from the winepresses; none shall tread with shouting; their shouting shall be no shouting.

34 From the cry of Heshbon even unto Elealeh, and even unto Yahats, have they uttered their voice, from Zoar even unto Horonaim, as a heifer of three years old: for the waters also of Nimrim shall be desolate.

35 "Moreover I will cause to cease in Moav," saith יהוה, "him that offereth in the high places, and him that burneth incense to his gods (elohim).

36 Therefore Mine heart shall sound for Moav like pipes, and Mine heart shall sound like pipes for the men of Kirheres, because the riches that he hath gotten are perished.

37 For every head shall be bald, and every beard clipped: upon all the hands shall be cuttings, and upon the loins sackcloth.

38 There shall be lamentation generally upon all the housetops of Moav, and in the streets thereof; for I have broken Moav like a vessel wherein is no pleasure," saith יהוה.

39 They shall howl, saying: 'How is it broken down! How hath Moav turned the back with shame! So shall Moav be a derision and a dismaying to all them about him.'"

40 For thus saith יהוה: "Behold, he shall fly as an eagle, and shall spread his wings over Moav.

41 Kerioth is taken, and the strong holds are surprised, and the mighty men's hearts in Moav at that day shall be as the heart of a woman in her pangs.

42 And Moav shall be destroyed from being a people, because he hath magnified himself against יהוה.

43 Fear, and the pit, and the snare, shall be upon you, O inhabitant of Moav," saith יהוה.

44 "He that fleeth from the fear shall fall into the pit; and he that getteth up out of the pit shall be taken in the snare; for I will bring upon it, even upon Moav, the year of their visitation,"

saith יהוה.

45 They that fled stood under the shadow of Heshbon because of the force; but a fire shall come forth out of Heshbon, and a flame from the midst of Sihon, and shall devour the corner of Moav, and the crown of the head of the tumultuous ones.

46 Woe be unto you, O Moav! the people of Chemosh perisheth; for your sons are taken captives, and your daughters captives.

47 "Yet will I bring again the captivity of Moav in the latter days," saith יהוה. Thus far is the judgment of Moav.

49 Concerning the Ammonites, thus saith יהוה: "Hath Yisrael no sons? Hath he no heir? Why then doth their king inherits Gad, and his people dwell in his cities?

2 Therefore, behold, the days come," saith יהוה, "that I will cause an alarm of war to be heard in Rabbah of the Ammonites; and it shall be a desolate heap, and her daughters shall be burned with fire; then shall Yisrael be heir unto them that were his heirs," saith יהוה.

3 Howl, O Heshbon, for Ai is spoiled! Cry, you daughters of Rabbah, gird you with sackcloth; lament, and run to and fro by the hedges; for their king shall go into captivity, and his priests (kohanim) and his princes together.

4 Wherefore gloriest you in the valleys, your flowing valley, O backsliding daughter who trusted in her treasures, saying, 'Who shall come unto me?'

5 Behold, I will bring a fear upon you," saith Lord (Adonai) יהוה of hosts (YHWH Tsevaot), "from all those that be about you; and you shall be driven out every man right forth; and none shall gather up him that wandereth.

6 And afterward I will bring again the captivity of the children of Ammon," saith יהוה.

7 Concerning Edom, thus saith יהוה of hosts (YHWH Tsevaot): "Is wisdom no more in Teman? Is counsel perished from the prudent? Is their wisdom vanished?

8 Flee you, turn back, dwell deep, O inhabitants of Dedan; for I will bring the disaster of Esaw upon him, the time that I will visit him.

9 If grapegatherers come to you, would they not leave some gleaning grapes? If thieves by night, they will destroy till they have enough.

10 But I have made Esaw bare, I have uncovered his secret places, and he shall not be able to hide

himself; his seed is spoiled, and his brethren, and his neighbours, and he is not.

11 Leave your fatherless children, I will preserve them alive; and let your widows trust in Me."

12 For thus saith יהוה; "Behold, they whose judgment was not to drink of the cup have assuredly drunken; and are you he that shall altogether go unpunished? You shalt not go unpunished, but you shalt surely drink of it.

13 "For I have sworn by Myself," saith יהוה: "that Bozrah shall become a desolation, a reproach, a waste, and a curse; and all the cities thereof shall be perpetual wastes."

14 I have heard a news from יהוה, and an ambassador is sent unto the nations, saying: "Gather you together, and come against her, and rise up to the battle!

15 For, behold, I will make you small among the heathen, and despised among men.

16 Your terribleness hath deceived you, and the pride of your heart, O you that dwellest in the clefts of the rock, that holdest the height of the hill! Though you shouldest make your nest as high as the eagle, I will bring you down from thence," saith יהוה.

17 Also Edom shall be a desolation; every one that goeth by it shall be astonished, and shall hiss at all the plagues thereof.

18 As in the overthrow of Sodom and Gomorrah and the neighbour cities thereof," saith יהוה, "no man shall abide there, neither shall a son of man dwell in it.

19 Behold, he shall come up like a lion from the swelling of Jordan (Yarden) against the habitation of the strong; but I will suddenly make him run away from her; and who is a chosen man, that I may appoint over her? For who is like Me? And who will appoint Me the time? And who is that shepherd that will stand before Me?"

20 Therefore hear the counsel of יהוה, that He hath taken against Edom; and His purposes, that He hath purposed against the inhabitants of Teman: Surely the least of the flock shall draw them out; surely He shall make their habitations desolate with them.

21 The earth is moved at the noise of their fall; at the cry the noise thereof was heard in the Red sea.

22 Behold, he shall come up and fly as the eagle, and spread his wings over Bozrah; and

at that day shall the heart of the mighty men of Edom be as the heart of a woman in her pangs.

23 Concerning Damascus (Dammeseq). "Hamath is confounded, and Arpad, for they have heard evil tidings; they are fainthearted; there is sorrow on the sea; it cannot be quiet.

24 Damascus (Dammeseq) is waxed feeble, and turneth herself to flee, and fear hath seized on her: anguish and sorrows have taken her, as a woman in travail.

25 How is the city of praise not left, the city of My joy!

26 Therefore her young men shall fall in her streets, and all the men of war shall be cut off in that day," saith יהוה of hosts (YHWH Tsevaot).

27 "And I will kindle a fire in the wall of Damascus (Dammeseq), and it shall consume the palaces of Ben-Hadad."

28 Concerning Kedar, and concerning the kingdoms of Hazor, which Nebuchadnezzar king of Babylon (Bavel) shall smite, thus saith יהוה: "Arise you, go up to Kedar, and spoil the men of the east!

29 Their tents and their flocks shall they take away; they shall take to themselves their curtains, and all their vessels, and their camels; and they shall cry unto them, Fear is on every side!'

30 "Flee, get you far off, dwell deep, O you inhabitants of Hazor," saith יהוה. "For Nebuchadnezzar king of Babylon (Bavel) hath taken counsel against you, and hath conceived a purpose against you.

31 Arise, get you up unto the wealthy nation, that dwelleth without care," saith יהוה, "which have neither gates nor bars, which dwell alone.

32 And their camels shall be a booty, and the multitude of their cattle a spoil: and I will scatter into all winds them that are in the utmost corners; and I will bring their disaster from all sides thereof," saith יהוה.

33 "And Hazor shall be a dwelling for dragons, and a desolation forever: there shall no man abide there, nor any son of man dwell in it."

34 The word of יהוה that came to Jeremiah (Yirmeyahu) the prophet against Elam in the beginning of the reign of Zedekiah (Tsidqiyahu) king of Judah (Yehudah), saying,

35 "Thus saith יהוה of hosts (YHWH Tsevaot): 'Behold, I will break the bow of Elam, the chief of their might.

36 And upon Elam will I bring the four winds from the four quarters of heaven, and will scatter them toward all those winds; and there shall be no nation whither the outcasts of Elam shall not come.

37 For I will cause Elam to be dismayed before their enemies, and before them that seek their life; and I will bring evil upon them, even My fierce anger,' saith יהוה; 'and I will send the sword after them, till I have consumed them:

38 And I will set My throne in Elam, and will destroy from thence the king and the princes,' saith יהוה.

39 But it shall come to pass in the latter days, that I will bring again the captivity of Elam,' saith יהוה."

50 The word that יהוה spake against Babylon (Bavel) and against the land of the Chaldeans by Jeremiah (Yirmeyahu) the prophet.

2 "Declare you among the nations, and proclaim, and set up a standard; proclaim, and conceal not; say, 'Babylon (Bavel) is taken, Bel is confounded, Merodach is broken in pieces; her images are confounded, her idols are broken in pieces.'

3 For out of the north there cometh up a nation against her, which shall make her land desolate, and none shall dwell therein; they shall remove, they shall depart, both man and beast.

4 "In those days, and in that time," saith יהוה, "the children of Yisrael shall come, they and the children of Judah (Yehudah) together, going and weeping; they shall go, and seek יהוה their God (YHWH Eloheihem).

5 They shall ask the way to Zion (Tsiyon) with their faces thitherward, saying, 'Come, and let us join ourselves to יהוה in a perpetual covenant that shall not be forgotten.'

6 My people hath been lost sheep; their shepherds have caused them to go astray, they have turned them away on the mountains; they have gone from mountain to hill, they have forgotten their restingplace.

7 All that found them have devoured them: and their adversaries said, 'We offend not, because they have sinned against יהוה, the habitation of justice, even יהוה, the hope of their fathers.'

8 Remove out of the midst of Babylon (Bavel), and go forth out of the land of the Chaldeans,

and be as the he goats before the flocks.

9 For, behold, I will raise and cause to come up against Babylon (Bavel) an assembly of great nations from the north country; and they shall set themselves in array against her; from thence she shall be taken. Their arrows shall be as of a mighty expert man; none shall return in vain.

10 And Chaldea shall be a spoil; all that spoil her shall be satisfied," saith יהוה.

11 Because you were glad, because you rejoiced, O you destroyers of Mine heritage, because you are grown fat as the heifer at grass, and bellow as bulls;

12 Your mother shall be sore confounded; she that bare you shall be ashamed. Behold, the hindermost of the nations shall be a wilderness, a dry land, and a desert.

13 Because of the wrath of יהוה it shall not be inhabited, but it shall be wholly desolate; every one that goeth by Babylon (Bavel) shall be astonished, and hiss at all her plagues.

14 Put yourselves in array against Babylon (Bavel) round about; all you that bend the bow, shoot at her, spare no arrows, for she hath sinned against יהוה.

15 Shout against her round about; she hath given her hand; her foundations are fallen, her walls are thrown down, for it is the vengeance of יהוה; take vengeance upon her; as she hath done, do unto her.

16 Cut off the sower from Babylon (Bavel), and him that handleth the sickle in the time of harvest; for fear of the oppressing sword they shall turn every one to his people, and they shall flee every one to his own land.

17 Yisrael is a scattered sheep; the lions have driven him away. First the king of Assyria (Ashshur) hath devoured him; and last this Nebuchadnezzar king of Babylon (Bavel) hath broken his bones."

18 Therefore thus saith יהוה of hosts (YHWH Tsevaot), the God of Israel (Elohei Yisrael): "Behold, I will punish the king of Babylon (Bavel) and his land, as I have punished the king of Assyria (Ashshur).

19 And I will bring Yisrael again to his habitation, and he shall feed on Carmel and Bashan, and his soul shall be satisfied upon Mount Efrayim and Gilad.

20 In those days, and in that time," saith יהוה, "the iniquity of Yisrael shall be sought for, and

there shall be none; and the sins of Judah (Yehudah), and they shall not be found; for I will pardon them whom I reserve.

21 "Go up against the land of Merathaim, even against it, and against the inhabitants of Pekod. Waste and utterly destroy after them," saith יהוה, "and do according to all that I have commanded you.

22 A sound of battle is in the land, and of great destruction.

23 How is the hammer of the whole earth cut asunder and broken! How is Babylon (Bavel) become a desolation among the nations!

24 I have laid a snare for you; and you are also taken, O Babylon (Bavel), and you wast not aware; you are found, and also caught, because you have striven against יהוה.

25 יהוה hath opened His armoury, and hath brought forth the weapons of His indignation: for this is the work of the Lord (Adonai) יהוה of hosts (YHWH Tsevaot) in the land of the Chaldeans.

26 Come against her from the utmost border, open her storehouses; cast her up as heaps, and destroy her utterly; let nothing of her be left.

27 Slay all her bullocks; let them go down to the slaughter: woe unto them! for their day is come, the time of their visitation.

28 The voice of them that flee and escape out of the land of Babylon (Bavel), to declare in Zion (Tsiyon) the vengeance of יהוה our God (YHWH Eloheinu), the vengeance of His temple.

29 Call together the archers against Babylon (Bavel); all you that bend the bow, camp against it round about; let none thereof escape; recompense her according to her work; according to all that she hath done, do unto her; for she hath been proud against יהוה, against the Holy One of Yisrael.

30 Therefore shall her young men fall in the streets, and all her men of war shall be cut off in that day," saith יהוה.

31 "Behold, I am against you, O you most proud," saith Lord (Adonai) יהוה of hosts (YHWH Tsevaot); "for your day is come, the time that I will visit you.

32 And the most proud shall stumble and fall, and none shall raise him up; and I will kindle a fire in his cities, and it shall devour all round about him."

33 Thus saith יהוה of hosts (YHWH Tsevaot):

"The children of Yisrael and the children of Judah (Yehudah) were oppressed together: and all that took them captives held them fast; they refused to let them go.

34 Their Redeemer is strong; יהוה of hosts (YHWH Tsevaot) is His name. He shall throughly plead their cause, that He may give rest to the land, and disquiet the inhabitants of Babylon (Bavel).

35 "A sword is upon the Chaldeans," saith יהוה, "and upon the inhabitants of Babylon (Bavel), and upon her princes, and upon her wise men.

36 A sword is upon the liars; and they shall dote: a sword is upon her mighty men; and they shall be dismayed.

37 A sword is upon their horses, and upon their chariots, and upon all the mingled people that are in the midst of her; and they shall become as women; a sword is upon her treasures; and they shall be robbed.

38 A drought is upon her waters; and they shall be dried up; for it is the land of graven images, and they are mad upon their idols.

39 Therefore the wild beasts of the desert with the wild beasts of the islands shall dwell there, and the owls shall dwell therein; and it shall be no more inhabited forever; nor shall it be dwelt in from generation to generation.

40 As God (Elohim) overthrew Sodom and Gomorrah and the neighbour cities thereof," saith יהוה, "so shall no man abide there, neither shall any son of man dwell therein.

41 Behold, a people shall come from the north, and a great nation, and many kings shall be raised up from the coasts of the earth.

42 They shall hold the bow and the lance; they are cruel, and will not shew mercy; their voice shall roar like the sea, and they shall ride upon horses, every one put in array, like a man to the battle, against you, O daughter of Babylon (Bavel).

43 The king of Babylon (Bavel) hath heard the report of them, and his hands waxed feeble; anguish took hold of him, and pangs as of a woman in travail.

44 Behold, he shall come up like a lion from the swelling of Jordan (Yarden) unto the habitation of the strong; but I will make them suddenly run away from her; and who is a chosen man, that I may appoint over her? For who is like Me? And who will appoint Me the time? And who is that shepherd that will stand before Me?"

45 Therefore hear you the counsel of יהוה, that He hath taken against Babylon (Bavel); and His purposes, that He hath purposed against the land of the Chaldeans: Surely the least of the flock shall draw them out; surely He shall make their habitation desolate with them.

46 At the noise of the taking of Babylon (Bavel) the earth is moved, and the cry is heard among the nations.

51 Thus saith יהוה: "Behold, I will raise up against Babylon (Bavel), and against them that dwell in the midst of them that rise up against Me, a destroying wind.

2 And will send unto Babylon (Bavel) fanners, that shall fan her, and shall empty her land; for in the day of trouble they shall be against her round about.

3 Against him that bendeth let the archer bend his bow, and against him that lifteth himself up in his armor; and spare you not her young men; destroy you utterly all her army.

4 Thus the slain shall fall in the land of the Chaldeans, and they that are thrust through in her streets.

5 For Yisrael hath not been forsaken, nor Judah (Yehudah) of his God (Elohim), יהוה of hosts (YHWH Tsevaot); though their land was filled with sin against the Holy One of Yisrael."

6 Flee out of the midst of Babylon (Bavel), and deliver every man his soul: be not cut off in her iniquity; for this is the time of יהוה's vengeance; He will render unto her a recompence.

7 Babylon (Bavel) hath been a golden cup in יהוה's hand, that made all the earth drunken. The nations have drunken of her wine; therefore the nations are mad.

8 Babylon (Bavel) is suddenly fallen and destroyed; howl for her; take balm for her pain, if so be she may be healed.

9 We would have healed Babylon (Bavel), but she is not healed; forsake her, and let us go every one into his own country; for her judgment reacheth unto heaven, and is lifted up even to the skies.

10 יהוה hath brought forth our righteousness. Come, and let us declare in Zion (Tsiyon) the work of יהוה our God (YHWH Eloheinu).

11 Make bright the arrows; gather the shields! יהוה hath raised up the spirit of the kings of the Medes; for His device is against Babylon

(Bavel), to destroy it, because it is the vengeance of יהוה, the vengeance of His temple.

12 Set up the standard upon the walls of Babylon (Bavel), make the watch strong, set up the watchmen, prepare the ambushes; for יהוה hath both devised and done that which He spake against the inhabitants of Babylon (Bavel).

13 O you that dwellest upon many waters, abundant in treasures, your end is come, and the measure of your covetousness.

14 יהוה of hosts (YHWH Tsevaot) hath sworn by Himself, saying: "Surely I will fill you with men, as with caterpillers; and they shall lift up a shout against you."

15 He hath made the earth by His power, He hath established the world by His wisdom, and hath stretched out the heaven by His understanding.

16 When He uttereth His voice, there is a multitude of waters in the heavens; and He causeth the vapours to ascend from the ends of the earth; He maketh lightnings with rain, and bringeth forth the wind out of His treasures.

17 Every man is brutish by his knowledge; every founder is confounded by the graven image: for his molten image is falsehood, and there is no breath in them.

18 They are vanity, the work of errors: in the time of their visitation they shall perish.

19 The portion of Jacob (Yaaqov) is not like them; for He is the Maker of all things, and the tribe of His inheritance. יהוה of hosts (YHWH Tsevaot) is His name.

20 You are My battle axe and weapons of war: for with you will I break in pieces the nations, and with you will I destroy kingdoms;

21 And with you will I break in pieces the horse and his rider; and with you will I break in pieces the chariot and his rider;

22 With you also will I break in pieces man and woman; and with you will I break in pieces old and young; and with you will I break in pieces the young man and the maid;

23 I will also break in pieces with you the shepherd and his flock; and with you will I break in pieces the husbandman and his yoke of oxen; and with you will I break in pieces captains and rulers.

24 "And I will render unto Babylon (Bavel) and to all the inhabitants of Chaldea all their evil that they have done in Zion (Tsiyon) in your sight," saith יהוה.

25 "Behold, I am against you, O destroying mountain," saith יהוה, "who destroyest all the earth: and I will stretch out Mine hand upon you, and roll you down from the rocks, and will make you a burnt mountain.

26 And they shall not take of you a stone for a corner, nor a stone for foundations; but you shalt be desolate forever," saith יהוה.

27 Set you up a standard in the land, blow the trumpet among the nations, prepare the nations against her, call together against her the kingdoms of Ararat, Minni, and Ashchenaz; appoint a captain against her; cause the horses to come up as the rough caterpillers.

28 Prepare against her the nations with the kings of the Medes, the captains thereof, and all the rulers thereof, and all the land of his dominion.

29 And the land shall tremble and sorrow; for every purpose of יהוה shall be performed against Babylon (Bavel), to make the land of Babylon (Bavel) a desolation without an inhabitant.

30 The mighty men of Babylon (Bavel) have forborn to fight, they have remained in their holds; their might hath failed; they became as women; they have burned her dwelling places; her bars are broken.

31 One post shall run to meet another, and one messenger to meet another, to shew the king of Babylon (Bavel) that his city is taken at one end,

32 And that the passages are stopped, and the reeds they have burned with fire, and the men of war are affrighted.

33 For thus saith יהוה of hosts (YHWH Tsevaot), the God of Israel (Elohei Yisrael): "The daughter of Babylon (Bavel) is like a threshingfloor, it is time to thresh her: yet a little while, and the time of her harvest shall come."

34 Nebuchadnezzar the king of Babylon (Bavel) hath devoured me, he hath crushed me, he hath made me an empty vessel, he hath swallowed me up like a dragon, he hath filled his belly with my delicates, he hath cast me out.

35 "The violence done to me and to my flesh be upon Babylon (Bavel)," shall the inhabitant of Zion (Tsiyon) say; "and my blood upon the inhabitants of Chaldea," shall Jerusalem (Yerushalayim) say.

36 Therefore thus saith יהוה: "Behold, I will

plead your cause, and take vengeance for you; and I will dry up her sea, and make her springs dry.

37 And Babylon (Bavel) shall become heaps, a dwellingplace for dragons, an astonishment, and a hissing, without an inhabitant.

38 They shall roar together like lions: they shall yell as lions' whelps.

39 In their heat I will make their feasts, and I will make them drunken, that they may rejoice, and sleep a perpetual sleep, and not wake," saith יהוה.

40 I will bring them down like lambs to the slaughter, like rams with he goats.

41 "How is Sheshach taken! And how is the praise of the whole earth surprised! How is Babylon (Bavel) become an astonishment among the nations!

42 The sea is come up upon Babylon (Bavel): she is covered with the multitude of the waves thereof.

43 Her cities are a desolation, a dry land, and a wilderness, a land wherein no man dwelleth, neither doth any son of man passes thereby.

44 And I will punish Bel in Babylon (Bavel), and I will bring forth out of his mouth that which he hath swallowed up; and the nations shall not flow together any more unto him; yea, the wall of Babylon (Bavel) shall fall.

45 My people, go you out of the midst of her, and deliver you every man his soul from the fierce anger of יהוה.

46 And lest your heart faint, and you fear for the rumour that shall be heard in the land; a rumour shall both come one year, and after that in another year shall come a rumour, and violence in the land, ruler against ruler.

47 Therefore, behold, the days come, that I will do judgment upon the graven images of Babylon (Bavel); and her whole land shall be confounded, and all her slain shall fall in the midst of her.

48 Then the heaven and the earth, and all that is therein, shall sing for Babylon (Bavel); for the spoilers shall come unto her from the north," saith יהוה.

49 As Babylon (Bavel) hath caused the slain of Yisrael to fall, so at Babylon (Bavel) shall fall the slain of all the earth.

50 You that have escaped the sword, go away, stand not still! Remember יהוה afar off, and let Jerusalem (Yerushalayim) come into your mind.

51 We are confounded, because we have heard reproach. Shame hath covered our faces, for strangers are come into the sanctuaries of יהוה's house.

52 "Wherefore, behold, the days come," saith יהוה, "that I will do judgment upon her graven images: and through all her land the wounded shall groan.

53 Though Babylon (Bavel) should mount up to heaven, and though she should fortify the height of her strength, yet from Me shall spoilers come unto her," saith יהוה.

54 A sound of a cry cometh from Babylon (Bavel), and great destruction from the land of the Chaldeans:

55 Because יהוה hath spoiled Babylon (Bavel), and destroyed out of her the great voice; when her waves do roar like great waters, a noise of their voice is uttered,

56 Because the spoiler is come upon her, even upon Babylon (Bavel), and her mighty men are taken, every one of their bows is broken; for יהוה God (Elohim) of recompences shall surely requite.

57 "And I will make drunk her princes, and her wise men, her captains, and her rulers, and her mighty men; and they shall sleep a perpetual sleep, and not wake," saith the King, whose name is יהוה of hosts (YHWH Tsevaot).

58 Thus saith יהוה of hosts (YHWH Tsevaot): "The broad walls of Babylon (Bavel) shall be utterly broken, and her high gates shall be burned with fire; and the people shall labour in vain, and the folk in the fire, and they shall be weary."

59 The word which Jeremiah (Yirmeyahu) the prophet commanded Serayahu the son of Neriyah, the son of Maaseyah, when he went with Zedekiah (Tsidqiyahu) the king of Judah (Yehudah) into Babylon (Bavel) in the fourth year of his reign. And this Serayahu was a quiet prince.

60 So Jeremiah (Yirmeyahu) wrote in a book all the evil that should come upon Babylon (Bavel), even all these words that are written against Babylon (Bavel).

61 And Jeremiah (Yirmeyahu) said to Serayahu, "When you comest to Babylon (Bavel), and shalt see, and shalt read all these words;

62 Then shalt you say, 'O יהוה, You have spoken against this place, to cut it off, that none shall remain in it, neither man nor beast, but that it shall be desolate forever.'

63 And it shall be, when you have made an end of reading this book, that you shalt bind a stone to it, and cast it into the midst of Euphrates:

64 And you shalt say, 'Thus shall Babylon (Bavel) sink, and shall not rise from the evil that I will bring upon her. And they shall be weary.'" Thus far are the words of Jeremiah (Yirmeyahu).

52 Zedekiah (Tsidqiyahu) was one and twenty years old when he began to reign, and he reigned eleven years in Jerusalem (Yerushalayim). And his mother's name was Hamutal the daughter of Jeremiah (Yirmeyahu) of Libnah.

2 And he did that which was evil in the eyes of יהוה, according to all that Yehoyaqim had done.

3 For through the anger of יהוה it came to pass in Jerusalem (Yerushalayim) and Judah (Yehudah), till he had cast them out from his presence, that Zedekiah (Tsidqiyahu) rebelled against the king of Babylon (Bavel).

4 And it came to pass in the ninth year of his reign, in the tenth month, in the tenth day of the month, that Nebuchadnezzar king of Babylon (Bavel) came, he and all his army, against Jerusalem (Yerushalayim), and pitched against it, and built forts against it round about.

5 So the city was besieged unto the eleventh year of King Zedekiah (Tsidqiyahu).

6 And in the fourth month, in the ninth day of the month, the famine was sore in the city, so that there was no bread for the people of the land.

7 Then the city was broken up, and all the men of war fled, and went forth out of the city by night by the way of the gate between the two walls, which was by the king's garden; (now the Chaldeans were by the city round about;) and they went by the way of the plain.

8 But the army of the Chaldeans pursued after the king, and overtook Zedekiah (Tsidqiyahu) in the plains of Yericho; and all his army was scattered from him.

9 Then they took the king, and carried him up unto the king of Babylon (Bavel) to Riblah in the land of Hamath; where he gave judgment upon him.

10 And the king of Babylon (Bavel) slew the sons of Zedekiah (Tsidqiyahu) before his eyes; he slew also all the princes of Judah (Yehudah) in Riblah.

11 Then he put out the eyes of Zedekiah (Tsidqiyahu); and the king of Babylon (Bavel) bound him in chains, and carried him to Babylon (Bavel), and put him in prison till the day of his death.

12 Now in the fifth month, in the tenth day of the month, which was the nineteenth year of Nebuchadnezzar king of Babylon (Bavel), came Nebuzaradan, captain of the guard, who served the king of Babylon (Bavel), into Jerusalem (Yerushalayim),

13 And burned the house of יהוה, and the king's house; and all the houses of Jerusalem (Yerushalayim), and all the houses of the great men, burned he with fire.

14 And all the army of the Chaldeans, that were with the captain of the guard, broke down all the walls of Jerusalem (Yerushalayim) round about.

15 Then Nebuzaradan the captain of the guard carried away captive certain of the poor of the people, and the residue of the people that remained in the city, and those that fell away, that fell to the king of Babylon (Bavel), and the rest of the multitude.

16 But Nebuzaradan the captain of the guard left certain of the poor of the land for vinedressers and for husbandmen.

17 Also the pillars of brass that were in the house of יהוה, and the bases, and the brasen sea that was in the house of יהוה, the Chaldeans broke, and carried all the brass of them to Babylon (Bavel).

18 The caldrons also, and the shovels, and the snuffers, and the bowls, and the spoons, and all the vessels of brass wherewith they ministered, took they away.

19 And the basons, and the firepans, and the bowls, and the caldrons, and the candlesticks, and the spoons, and the cups; that which was of gold in gold, and that which was of silver in silver, took the captain of the guard away.

20 The two pillars, one sea, and twelve brasen bulls that were under the bases, which king Solomon (Shelomoh) had made in the house of יהוה; the brass of all these vessels was without weight.

21 And concerning the pillars, the height of one

pillar was eighteen cubits; and a fillet of twelve cubits did compass it; and the thickness thereof was four fingers; it was hollow.

22 And a chapiter of brass was upon it; and the height of one chapiter was five cubits, with network and pomegranates upon the chapiters round about, all of brass. The second pillar also and the pomegranates were like unto these.

23 And there were ninety and six pomegranates on a side; and all the pomegranates upon the network were a hundred round about.

24 And the captain of the guard took Serayahu the chief priest (kohen), and Zephaniah (Tsefanyah) the second priest (kohen), and the three keepers of the door.

25 He took also out of the city a eunuch, which had the charge of the men of war; and seven men of them that were near the king's person, which were found in the city; and the principal scribe of the army, who mustered the people of the land; and threescore men of the people of the land, that were found in the midst of the city.

26 So Nebuzaradan the captain of the guard took them, and brought them to the king of Babylon (Bavel) to Riblah.

27 And the king of Babylon (Bavel) smote them, and put them to death in Riblah in the land of Hamath. Thus Judah (Yehudah) was carried away captive out of his own land.

28 This is the people whom Nebuchadnezzar carried away captive: in the seventh year, three thousand and twenty-three Jews (Yehudim);

29 In the eighteenth year of Nebuchadnezzar he carried away captive from Jerusalem (Yerushalayim) eight hundred thirty-two persons;

30 In the three and twentieth year of Nebuchadnezzar, Nebuzaradan the captain of the guard carried away captive of the Jews (Yehudim) seven hundred forty-five persons; all the persons were four thousand and six hundred.

31 And it came to pass in the seven and thirtieth year of the captivity of Yehoyakhin king of Judah (Yehudah), in the twelfth month, in the five and twentieth day of the month, that Ewil-Merodach king of Babylon (Bavel) in the first year of his reign lifted up the head of Yehoyakhin king of Judah (Yehudah), and brought him forth out of prison,

32 And spake kindly unto him, and set his throne above the throne of the kings that were with him in Babylon (Bavel),

33 And changed his prison garments; and he did continually eat bread before him all the days of his life.

34 And for his diet, there was a continual diet given him of the king of Babylon (Bavel), every day a portion until the day of his death, all the days of his life.

LAMENTATION
EYKAH אֵיכָה
(How)

1 How doth the city Jerusalem (Yerushalayim) sit solitary, that was full of people! How is she become as a widow! She that was great among the nations, and princess among the provinces, how is she become tributary!

2 She weepeth sore in the night, and her tears are on her cheeks. Among all her lovers (political allies) she hath none to comfort her; all her friends have dealt treacherously with her, they are become her enemies.

3 Judah (Yehudah) is gone into captivity because of affliction, and because of great servitude; she dwelleth among the heathen, she findeth no rest; all her persecutors overtook her between the straits.

4 The ways of Zion (Tsiyon) do mourn, because none come to the solemn feasts; all her gates are desolate; her kohanim sigh, her virgins are afflicted, and she is in bitterness.

5 Her adversaries are the chief, her enemies prosper; for יהוה hath afflicted her for the multitude of her transgressions; her children are gone into captivity before the enemy.

6 And from the daughter of Zion (Tsiyon) all her beauty is departed; her princes are become like harts that find no pasture, and they are gone without strength before the pursuer.

7 Jerusalem (Yerushalayim) remem-bered in the days of her affliction and of her miseries all her pleasant things that she had in the days of old, when her people fell into the hand of the enemy, and none did help her; the adversaries saw her, and did mock at her sabbaths.

8 Jerusalem (Yerushalayim) hath grievously sinned; therefore she is removed. All that honoured her despise her, because they have seen her nakedness; yea, she sigheth, and turneth backward.

9 Her filthiness is in her skirts; she remembereth not her last end; therefore she came down astonish-ingly; she had no comforter. "O יהוה, behold my affliction, for the enemy hath magnified himself!"

10 The adversary hath spread out his hand upon all her pleasant things: for she hath seen that the heathen entered into her sanctuary, whom You didst command that they should not enter into Your congregation.

11 All her people sigh, they seek bread; they have given their pleasant things for meat to relieve the soul; see, O יהוה, and consider; for I am become vile.

12 Is it nothing to you, all you that pass by? Behold, and see if there be any sorrow like unto my sorrow, which is done unto me, wherewith יהוה hath afflicted me in the day of His fierce anger.

13 From above hath He sent fire into my bones, and it prevaileth against them. He hath spread a net for my feet, He hath turned me back; He hath made me desolate and faint all the day.

14 The yoke of my transgressions is bound by His hand; they are wreathed, and come up upon my neck. He hath made my strength to fall, my Lord (Adonai) hath delivered me into their hands, from whom I am not able to rise up.

15 The Lord (Adonai) hath trodden under foot all my mighty men in the midst of me; He hath called an assembly against me to crush my young men; the Lord (Adonai) hath trodden the virgin, the daughter of Judah (Yehudah), as in a winepress.

16 "For these things I weep; mine eye, mine eye runneth down with water, because the comforter that should relieve my soul is far from me. My children are desolate, because the enemy prevailed."

17 Zion (Tsiyon) spreadeth forth her hands, and there is none to comfort her. יהוה hath commanded concerning Jacob (Yaaqov), that his adversaries should be round about him; Jerusalem (Yerushalayim) is as a menstruous woman among them.

18 יהוה is righteous, for I have rebelled against His commandment. Please hear, all people, and behold my sorrow; my virgins and my young men are gone into captivity.

19 I (Yerushalayim) called for my lovers (political allies), but they deceived me; my priests (kohanim) and mine elders gave up the spirit (breathed their last) in the city, while they sought their food to restore their souls.

20 Behold, O יהוה, for I am in distress; my bowels are troubled; mine heart is turned within me; for I have grievously rebelled. Abroad the sword bereaveth, at home there is as death.

21 They have heard that I sigh; there is none to

comfort me: all mine enemies have heard of my trouble; they are glad that You have done it. You wilt bring the day that You have called, and they shall be like unto me.

22 Let all their wickedness come before You; and do unto them, as You have done unto me for all my transgressions, for my sighs are many, and my heart is faint."

2 How hath the Lord (Adonai) covered the daughter of Zion (Tsiyon) with a cloud in His anger, and cast down from heaven unto the earth the beauty of Yisrael, and remembered not His footstool in the day of His anger!

2 The Lord (Adonai) hath swallowed up all the habitations of Jacob (Yaaqov), and hath not pitied. He hath thrown down in His wrath the strong holds of the daughter of Judah (Yehudah); He hath brought them down to the ground; He hath polluted the kingdom and the princes thereof.

3 He hath cut off in His fierce anger all the horn of Yisrael; He hath drawn back His right hand from before the enemy, and He burned against Jacob (Yaaqov) like a flaming fire, which devoureth round about.

4 He hath bent His bow like an enemy. He stood with His right hand as an adversary, and slew all that were pleasant to the eye in the tabernacle of the daughter of Zion (Tsiyon); He poured out His fury like fire.

5 The Lord (Adonai) was as an enemy; He hath swallowed up Yisrael, He hath swallowed up all her palaces. He hath destroyed His strong holds, and hath increased in the daughter of Judah (Yehudah) mourning and lamentation.

6 And He hath violently taken away his tabernacle, as if it was of a garden; He hath destroyed His places of the assembly; יהוה hath caused the solemn feasts and Shabbats to be forgotten in Zion (Tsiyon), and hath despised in the indignation of His anger the king and the priest (kohen).

7 The Lord (Adonai) hath cast off His altar, He hath abhorred His sanctuary, He hath given up into the hand of the enemy the walls of her palaces; they have made a noise in the house of יהוה, as in the day of a solemn feast.

8 יהוה hath purposed to destroy the wall of the daughter of Zion (Tsiyon). He hath stretched out a line, He hath not withdrawn His hand from destroying; therefore He made the rampart and the wall to lament; they languished together.

9 Her gates are sunk into the ground; He hath destroyed and broken her bars; her king and her princes are among the nations; the Torah is no more; her prophets also find no vision from יהוה.

10 The elders of the daughter of Zion (Tsiyon) sit upon the ground, and keep silence; they have cast up dust upon their heads; they have girded themselves with sackcloth; the virgins of Jerusalem (Yerushalayim) hang down their heads to the ground.

11 Mine eyes do fail with tears, my bowels are troubled, my liver is poured upon the earth, for the destruction of the daughter of my people, because the children and the sucklings swoon in the streets of the city.

12 They say to their mothers, "Where is corn and wine?" When they swooned as the wounded in the streets of the city, when their soul was poured out into their mothers' bosom.

13 What thing shall I take to witness for you? What thing shall I liken to you, O daughter of Jerusalem (Yerushalayim)? What shall I equal to you, that I may comfort you, O virgin daughter of Zion (Tsiyon)? For your breach is great like the sea: who can heal you?

14 Your prophets have seen vain and foolish things for you; and they have not discovered your iniquity, to turn away your captivity; but have seen for you false burdens and causes of banishment.

15 All that pass by clap their hands at you; they hiss and wag their head at the daughter of Jerusalem (Yerushalayim), saying, "Is this the city that men call 'The perfection of beauty, the joy of the whole earth'?"

16 All your enemies have opened their mouth against you; they hiss and gnash the teeth. They say, "We have swallowed her up; certainly this is the day that we looked for; we have found, we have seen it."

17 יהוה hath done that which He had devised; He hath fulfilled His word that He had commanded in the days of old. He hath thrown down, and hath not pitied; and He hath caused your enemy to rejoice over you, He hath set up the horn of your adversaries.

18 Their heart cried unto the Lord (Adonai), "O wall of the daughter of Zion (Tsiyon), let tears run down like a river day and night; give

Yourself no rest; let not the apple of Your eye cease.

19 Arise, cry out in the night; in the beginning of the watches pour out your heart like water before the face of the Lord (Adonai); lift up your hands toward Him for the life of your young children, that faint for hunger in the top of every street."

20 "Behold, O יהוה, and consider to whom You have done this. Shall the women eat their fruit, and children of a span long? Shall the priest (kohen) and the prophet be slain in the sanctuary of the Lord (Adonai)?

21 The young and the old lie on the ground in the streets; my virgins and my young men are fallen by the sword. You have slain them in the day of Your anger; you have killed, and not pitied.

22 You have called as in a solemn day my terrors round about, so that in the day of יהוה's anger none escaped nor remained; those that I have swaddled and brought up hath mine enemy consumed."

3 I am the man that hath seen affliction by the rod of His wrath.

2 He hath led me, and brought me into darkness, but not into light.

3 Surely against me is He turned; he turneth His hand against me all the day.

4 My flesh and my skin hath He made old; He hath broken my bones.

5 He hath builded against me, and compassed me with gall and travail.

6 He hath set me in dark places, as they that be dead of old.

7 He hath hedged me about, that I cannot get out. He hath made my chain heavy.

8 Also when I cry and shout, He shutteth out my prayer.

9 He hath inclosed my ways with hewn stone, He hath made my paths crooked.

10 He was unto me as a bear lying in wait, and as a lion in secret places.

11 He hath turned aside my ways, and pulled me in pieces. He hath made me desolate.

12 He hath bent His bow, and set me as a mark for the arrow.

13 He hath caused the arrows of His quiver to enter into my reins.

14 I was a derision to all my people; and their song all the day.

15 He hath filled me with bitterness, He hath made me drunken with wormwood.

16 He hath also broken my teeth with gravel stones, He hath covered me with ashes.

17 And You have removed my soul far off from peace; I forgat prosperity.

18 And I said, "My strength and my hope is perished from יהוה."

19 Remembering mine affliction and my misery, the wormwood and the gall.

20 My soul hath them still in remembrance, and is humbled in me.

21 This I recall to my mind, therefore have I hope.

22 It is of יהוה's mercies that we are not consumed, because His compassions fail not.

23 They are new every morning; great is Your faithfulness.

24 "יהוה is my portion," saith my soul; "therefore will I hope in Him!"

25 יהוה is good unto them that wait for Him, to the soul that seeketh Him.

26 It is good that a man should both hope and quietly wait for the salvation of יהוה.

27 It is good for a man that he bears the yoke in his youth.

28 He sitteth alone and keepeth silence, because He hath borne it upon him.

29 He putteth his mouth in the dust; if so be there may be hope.

30 He giveth his cheek to him that smiteth him; he is filled full with reproach.

31 For the Lord (Adonai) will not cast off forever;

32 But though He causes grief, yet will He have compassion according to the multitude of His mercies.

33 For He doth not afflict willingly nor grieve the children of men.

34 To crush under His feet all the prisoners of the earth,

35 To turn aside the right of a man before the face of the Most High (Elyon),

36 To subvert a man in his cause, the Lord (Adonai) approveth not.

37 Who is he that saith, and it cometh to pass, when the Lord (Adonai) commandeth it not?

38 Out of the mouth of the Most High proceedeth not evil and good?

39 Wherefore doth a living man complain, a man for the punishment of his sins?

40 Let us search and try our ways, and turn back to יהוה.

41 Let us lift up our heart with our hands unto God (Elohim) in the heavens.

42 We have transgressed and have rebelled; You have not pardoned.

43 You have covered with anger, and persecuted us; You have slain, You have not pitied.

44 You have covered Yourself with a cloud, that our prayer should not pass through.

45 You have made us as the offscouring and refuse in the midst of the people.

46 All our enemies have opened their mouths against us.

47 Fear and a snare is come upon us, desolation and destruction.

48 Mine eye runneth down with rivers of water for the destruction of the daughter of my people.

49 Mine eye trickleth down, and ceaseth not, without any intermission,

50 Till יהוה look down, and behold from heaven.

51 Mine eye affecteth mine heart because of all the daughters of my city.

52 Mine enemies chased me sore, like a bird, without cause.

53 They have cut off my life in the dungeon, and cast a stone upon me.

54 Waters flowed over mine head; then I said, "I am cut off."

55 I called upon Your name, O יהוה, out of the low dungeon.

56 You have heard my voice: "Hide not Your ear at my breathing, at my cry."

57 You drewest near in the day that I called upon You, You saidst, "Fear not!"

58 O Lord (Adonai), You have pleaded the causes of my soul; You have redeemed my life.

59 O יהוה, You have seen my wrong; judge You my cause.

60 You have seen all their vengeance and all their imaginations against me.

61 You have heard their reproach, O יהוה, and all their imaginations against me;

62 The lips of those that rose up against me, and their device against me all the day.

63 Behold their sitting down, and their rising up; I am their musick.

64 Render unto them a recompence, O יהוה, according to the work of their hands.

65 Give them sorrow of heart; Your curse unto them.

66 Persecute and destroy them in anger from under the heavens of יהוה.

4 How is the gold become dim! How is the most fine gold changed! The stones of the sanctuary are poured out in the top of every street.

2 The precious sons of Zion (Tsiyon), comparable to fine gold, how are they esteemed as earthen pitchers, the work of the hands of the potter!

3 Even the sea monsters draw out the breast, they give suck to their young ones; the daughter of my people is become cruel, like the ostriches in the wilderness.

4 The tongue of the sucking child cleaveth to the roof of his mouth for thirst; the young children ask bread, and no man breaketh it unto them.

5 They that did feed delicately are desolate in the streets; they that were brought up in scarlet embrace dunghills.

6 For the punishment of the iniquity of the daughter of my people is greater than the punishment of the sin of Sodom, that was overthrown as in a moment, and no hands stayed on her.

7 Her Nazarites (Nazirim) were purer than snow, they were whiter than milk, they were more ruddy in body than rubies, their polishing was of sapphire.

8 Their visage is blacker than a coal; they are not known in the streets; their skin cleaveth to their bones; it is withered, it is become like a stick.

9 They that be slain with the sword are better than they that be slain with hunger; for these pine away, stricken through for want of the fruits of the field.

10 The hands of the pitiful women have cooked their own children; they were their food in the destruction of the daughter of my people.

11 יהוה hath accomplished His fury; He hath poured out His fierce anger, and hath kindled a fire in Zion (Tsiyon), and it hath devoured the foundations thereof.

12 The kings of the earth, and all the inhabitants of the world, would not have believed that the adversary and the enemy should have entered into the gates of Jerusalem (Yerushalayim).

13 For the sins of her prophets, and the iniquities of her priests (kohanim), that have shed the blood of the just in the midst of her,

14 They have wandered as blind men in the

streets, they have polluted themselves with blood, so that men could not touch their garments.

15 They cried unto them, "Depart you; it is unclean; depart, depart, touch not!" When they fled away and wandered, they said among the heathen, "They shall no more sojourn there."

16 The anger of יהוה hath divided them; He will no more regard them; they respected not the persons of the kohanim, they favoured not the elders.

17 As for us, our eyes as yet failed for our vain help; in our watching we have watched for a nation that could not save us.

18 They hunt our steps, that we cannot go in our streets; our end is near, our days are fulfilled; for our end is come.

19 Our persecutors are swifter than the eagles of the heaven; they pursued us upon the mountains, they laid wait for us in the wilderness.

20 The breath of our nostrils, the anointed of יהוה, was taken in their pits, of whom we said, "Under His shadow we shall live among the nations."

21 Rejoice and be glad, O daughter of Edom, that dwellest in the land of Uz; the cup also shall pass through unto you; you shalt be drunken, and shalt make yourself naked.

22 The punishment of your iniquity is accomplished, O daughter of Zion (Tsiyon); He will no more carry you away into captivity. He will visit your iniquity, O daughter of Edom; He will discover your sins!

5 Remember, O יהוה, what is come upon us; consider, and behold our reproach!

2 Our inheritance is turned to strangers, our houses to aliens.

3 We are orphans and fatherless, our mothers are as widows.

4 We have drunken our water for money; our wood is sold unto us.

5 Our necks are under persecution; we labour, and have no rest.

6 We have given the hand to the Egyptians (Mitsrayim), and to the Assyrians, to be satisfied with bread.

7 Our fathers have sinned, and are not; and we have borne their iniquities.

8 Servants have ruled over us; there is none that doth deliver us out of their hand.

9 We gat our bread with the peril of our lives because of the sword of the wilderness.

10 Our skin was black like an oven because of the terrible famine.

11 They ravished the women in Zion (Tsiyon), and the maids in the cities of Judah (Yehudah).

12 Princes are hanged up by their hand; the faces of elders were not honoured.

13 They took the young men to grind, and the children fell under the wood.

14 The elders have ceased from the gate, the young men from their musick.

15 The joy of our heart is ceased; our dance is turned into mourning.

16 The crown is fallen from our head. Woe unto us, that we have sinned!

17 For this our heart is faint; for these things our eyes are dim.

18 Because of the mountain of Zion (Tsiyon), which is desolate, the foxes walk upon it.

19 You, O יהוה, remainest forever; Your throne from generation to generation.

20 Wherefore dost You forget us forever, and forsake us so long time?

21 Turn us back unto You, O יהוה, and we shall be turned back; renew our days as of old.

22 But You have utterly rejected us; You are very wroth against us.

EZEKIEL
YECHEZQEL יְחֶזְקֵאל
(El Strengthens)

1 Now it came to pass in the thirtieth year, in the fourth month, in the fifth day of the month, as I was among the captives by the river of Chebar, that the heavens were opened, and I saw visions of God (Elohim).

2 In the fifth day of the month, which was the fifth year of King Yehoyakhin's captivity,

3 The word of יהוה came expressly unto A53Ezekiel (Yechezqel) the priest (kohen), the son of Buzi, in the land of the Chaldeans by the river Chebar; and the hand of יהוה was there upon him.

4 And I looked, and, behold, a whirlwind came out of the north, a great cloud, and a fire infolding itself, and a brightness was about it, and out of the midst thereof as the colour of amber, out of the midst of the fire.

5 Also out of the midst thereof came the likeness of four living creatures. And this was their appearance; they had the likeness of a man.

6 And every one had four faces, and every one had four wings.

7 And their feet were straight feet; and the sole of their feet was like the sole of a calf's foot; and they sparkled like the colour of burnished brass.

8 And they had the hands of a man under their wings on their four sides; and they four had their faces and their wings.

9 Their wings were joined one to another; they turned not when they went; they went every one straight forward.

10 As for the likeness of their faces, they four had the face of a man, and the face of a lion, on the right side; and they four had the face of an ox on the left side; they four also had the face of an eagle.

11 Thus were their faces, and their wings were stretched upward; two wings of every one was joined one to another, and two covered their bodies.

12 And they went every one straight forward; whither the spirit was to go, they went; and they turned not when they went.

13 As for the likeness of the living creatures, their appearance was like burning coals of fire, and like the appearance of lamps; it went up and down among the living creatures; and the fire was bright, and out of the fire went forth lightning.

14 And the living creatures ran and returned as the appearance of a flash of lightning.

15 Now as I beheld the living creatures, behold one wheel upon the earth by the living creatures, with his four faces.

16 The appearance of the wheels and their work was like unto the colour of a beryl; and they four had one likeness; and their appearance and their work was as it was a wheel in the middle of a wheel.

17 When they went, they went upon their four sides; and they turned not when they went.

18 As for their rings, they were so high that they were dreadful; and their rings were full of eyes round about them four.

19 And when the living creatures went, the wheels went by them; and when the living creatures were lifted up from the earth, the wheels were lifted up.

20 Whithersoever the spirit was to go, they went, thither was their spirit to go; and the wheels were lifted up opposite them, for the spirit of the living creature was in the wheels.

21 When those went, these went; and when those stood, these stood; and when those were lifted up from the earth, the wheels were lifted up opposite them, for the spirit of the living creature was in the wheels.

22 And the likeness of the firmament upon the heads of the living creature was as the colour of the terrible crystal, stretched forth over their heads above.

23 And under the firmament were their wings straight, the one toward the other; every one had two, which covered on this side, and every one had two, which covered on that side, their bodies.

24 And when they went, I heard the noise of their wings, like the noise of great waters, as the voice of the Almighty, the voice of speech, as the noise of an army; when they stood, they let down their wings.

25 And there was a voice from the firmament that was over their heads, when they stood, and had let down their wings.

26 And above the firmament that was over their heads was the likeness of a throne, as the appearance of a sapphire stone; and upon the

likeness of the throne was the likeness as the appearance of a man above upon it.

27 And I saw as the colour of amber, as the appearance of fire round about within it, from the appearance of his loins even upward, and from the appearance of his loins even downward, I saw as it was the appearance of fire, and it had brightness round about.

28 As the appearance of the bow that is in the cloud in the day of rain, so was the appearance of the brightness round about. This was the appearance of the likeness of the glory of יהוה. And when I saw it, I fell upon my face, and I heard a voice of one that spake.

2 And He said unto me: "Son of man, stand upon your feet, and I will speak unto you."

2 And the Spirit (Ruach) entered into me when He spake unto me, and set me upon my feet, that I heard Him that spake unto me.

3 And He said unto me: "Son of man, I send you to the children of Yisrael, to a rebellious nation that hath rebelled against Me; they and their fathers have transgressed against Me, even unto this very day.

4 For they are impudent children and stiffhearted. I do send you unto them; and you shalt say unto them, 'Thus saith Lord (Adonai) יהוה.'

5 And they, whether they will hear, or whether they will forbear, (for they are a rebellious house,) yet shall know that there hath been a prophet among them.

6 And you, son of man, be not afraid of them, neither be afraid of their words, though briers and thorns be with you, and you dost dwell among scorpions; be not afraid of their words, nor be dismayed at their looks, though they be a rebellious house.

7 And you shalt speak My words unto them, whether they will hear, or whether they will forbear, for they are most rebellious.

8 But you, son of man, hear what I say unto you; be not you rebellious like that rebellious house; open your mouth, and eat that I give you."

9 And when I looked, behold, a hand was sent unto me; and, behold, a roll of a book was therein;

10 And He spread it before me; and it was written inside and outside; and there was written therein lamentations, and mourning, and woe.

3 Moreover He said unto me: "Son of man, eat that you findest; eat this roll, and go speak

unto the house of Yisrael."

2 So I opened my mouth, and He caused me to eat that roll.

3 And He said unto me: "Son of man, cause your belly to eat, and fill your bowels with this roll that I give you." Then did I eat it; and it was in my mouth as honey for sweetness.

4 And He said unto me: "Son of man, go, get you unto the house of Yisrael, and speak with My words unto them.

5 For you are not sent to a people of a strange speech and of a hard language, but to the house of Yisrael;

6 Not to many people of a strange speech and of a hard language, whose words you canst not understand. Surely, had I sent you to them, they would have hearkened unto you.

7 But the house of Yisrael will not hearken unto you; for they will not hearken unto Me; for all the house of Yisrael are impudent and hardhearted.

8 Behold, I have made your face strong against their faces, and your forehead strong against their foreheads.

9 As an adamant harder than flint have I made your forehead; fear them not, neither be dismayed at their looks, though they be a rebellious house."

10 Moreover He said unto me, "Son of man, all My words that I shall speak unto you receive in your heart, and hear with your ears.

11 And go, get you to them of the captivity, unto the children of your people, and speak unto them, and tell them, 'Thus saith Lord (Adonai) יהוה,' whether they will hear, or whether they will forbear."

12 Then the Spirit (Ruach) took me up, and I heard behind me a voice of a great rushing, saying: "Blessed be the glory of יהוה from His place."

13 I heard also the noise of the wings of the living creatures that touched one another, and the noise of the wheels opposite them, and a noise of a great rushing.

14 So the Spirit (Ruach) lifted me up, and took me away, and I went in bitterness, in the heat of my spirit; but the hand of יהוה was strong upon me.

15 Then I came to them of the captivity at Telabib, that dwelt by the river of Chebar, and I sat where they sat, and remained there

astonished among them seven days.

16 And it came to pass at the end of seven days, that the word of יהוה came unto me, saying:

17 "Son of man, I have made you a watchman unto the house of Yisrael; therefore hear the word at My mouth, and give them warning from Me.

18 When I say unto the wicked, 'You shalt surely die;' and you givest him not warning, nor speakest to warn the wicked from his wicked way, to save his life; the same wicked man shall die in his iniquity; but his blood will I require at your hand.

19 Yet if you warn the wicked, and he turn not from his wickedness, nor from his wicked way, he shall die in his iniquity; but you have delivered your soul.

20 Again, when a righteous man doth turn from his righteousness, and commit iniquity, and I lay a stumblingblock before him, he shall die: because you have not given him warning, he shall die in his sin, and his righteousness which he hath done shall not be remembered; but his blood will I require at your hand.

21 Nevertheless if you warn the righteous man, that the righteous sin not, and he doth not sin, he shall surely live, because he is warned; also you have delivered your soul."

22 And the hand of יהוה was there upon me; and He said unto me, "Arise, go forth into the plain, and I will there talk with you."

23 Then I arose, and went forth into the plain; and, behold, the glory of יהוה stood there, as the glory which I saw by the river of Chebar; and I fell on my face.

24 Then the Spirit (Ruach) entered into me, and set me upon my feet, and spake with me, and said unto me: "Go, shut yourself within your house.

25 But you, O son of man, behold, they shall put bands upon you, and shall bind you with them, and you shalt not go out among them.

26 And I will make your tongue cleave to the roof of your mouth, that you shalt be dumb, and shalt not be to them a reprover, for they are a rebellious house.

27 But when I speak with you, I will open your mouth, and you shalt say unto them, 'Thus saith Lord (Adonai) יהוה.' He that heareth, let him hear; and he that forbeareth, let him forbear; for they are a rebellious house.

4 You also, son of man, take you a tile, and lay it before you, and pourtray upon it the city, Jerusalem (Yerushalayim).

2 And lay siege against it, and build a fort against it, and cast a mount against it; set the camp also against it, and set battering rams against it round about.

3 Moreover take you unto you an iron pan, and set it for a wall of iron between you and the city; and set your face against it, and it shall be besieged, and you shalt lay siege against it. This shall be a sign to the house of Yisrael.

4 Lie you also upon your left side, and lay the iniquity of the house of Yisrael upon it; according to the number of the days that you shalt lie upon it you shalt bear their iniquity.

5 For I have laid upon you the years of their iniquity, according to the number of the days, three hundred and ninety days; so shalt you bear the iniquity of the house of Yisrael.

6 And when you have accomplished them, lie again on your right side, and you shalt bear the iniquity of the house of Judah (Yehudah) forty days. I have appointed you each day for a year.

7 Therefore you shalt set your face toward the siege of Jerusalem (Yerushalayim), and your arm shall be uncovered, and you shalt prophesy against it.

8 And, behold, I will lay bands upon you, and you shalt not turn you from one side to another, till you have ended the days of your siege.

9 Take you also unto you wheat, and barley, and beans, and lentiles, and millet, and fitches, and put them in one vessel, and make you bread thereof, according to the number of the days that you shalt lie upon your side, three hundred and ninety days shalt you eat thereof.

10 And your meat which you shalt eat shall be by weight, twenty shekels a day; from time to time shalt you eat it.

11 You shalt drink also water by measure, the sixth part of a hin; from time to time shalt you drink.

12 And you shalt eat it as barley cakes, and you shalt bake it with dung that cometh out of man, in their sight.

13 And יהוה said, "Even thus shall the children of Yisrael eat their defiled bread among the nations, whither I will drive them."

14 Then said I, "Ah Lord (Adonai) יהוה! Behold, my soul hath not been polluted; for from my

youth up even till now have I not eaten of that which dieth of itself, or is torn in pieces; neither came there abominable flesh into my mouth."

15 Then He said unto me, "Behold, I have given you cow's dung for man's dung, and you shalt prepare your bread therewith."

16 Moreover He said unto me, "Son of man, behold, I will break the staff of bread in Jerusalem (Yerushalayim); and they shall eat bread by weight, and with care; and they shall drink water by measure, and with astonishment,

17 That they may want bread and water, and be astonied one with another, and consume away for their iniquity.

5 "And you, son of man, take you a sharp knife, take you a barber's razor, and cause it to pass upon your head and upon your beard; then take you balances to weigh, and divide the hair.

2 You shalt burn with fire a third part in the midst of the city, when the days of the siege are fulfilled; and you shalt take a third part, and smite about it with a knife; and a third pare you shalt scatter in the wind; and I will draw out a sword after them.

3 You shalt also take thereof a few in number, and bind them in your skirts.

4 Then take of them again, and cast them into the midst of the fire, and burn them in the fire; for thereof shall a fire come forth into all the house of Yisrael.

5 Thus saith Lord (Adonai) יהוה: 'This is Jerusalem (Yerushalayim); I have set it in the midst of the nations and countries that are round about her.

6 And she hath changed My judgments into wickedness more than the nations, and My statutes more than the countries that are round about her; for they have refused My judgments and My statutes, they have not walked in them.'

7 Therefore thus saith Lord (Adonai) יהוה; 'Because you multiplied more than the nations that are round about you, and have not walked in My statutes, neither have kept My judgments, neither have done according to the judgments of the nations that are round about you;'

8 Therefore thus saith Lord (Adonai) יהוה: 'Behold, I, even I, am against you, and will execute judgments in the midst of you in the sight of the nations.

9 And I will do in you that which I have not

done, and whereunto I will not do any more the like, because of all your abominations.

10 Therefore the fathers shall eat the sons in the midst of you, and the sons shall eat their fathers; and I will execute judgments in you, and the whole remnant of you will I scatter into all the winds.

11 Wherefore, as I live,' saith Lord (Adonai) יהוה, 'Surely, because you have defiled My sanctuary with all your detestable things, and with all your abominations, therefore will I also diminish you; neither shall Mine eye spare, neither will I have any pity.

12 A third part of you shall die with the pestilence, and with famine shall they be consumed in the midst of you; and a third part shall fall by the sword round about you; and I will scatter a third part into all the winds, and I will draw out a sword after them.

13 Thus shall Mine anger be accomplished, and I will cause My fury to rest upon them, and I will be comforted; and they shall know that I יהוה have spoken it in My zeal, when I have accomplished My fury in them.

14 Moreover I will make you waste, and a reproach among the nations that are round about you, in the sight of all that pass by.

15 So it shall be a reproach and a taunt, an instruction and an astonishment unto the nations that are round about you, when I shall execute judgments in you in anger and in fury and in furious rebukes. I יהוה have spoken it.

16 When I shall send upon them the evil arrows of famine, which shall be for their destruction, and which I will send to destroy you: and I will increase the famine upon you, and will break your staff of bread.

17 So will I send upon you famine and evil beasts, and they shall bereave you; and pestilence and blood shall pass through you; and I will bring the sword upon you. I, יהוה have spoken it.'"

6 And the word of יהוה came unto me, saying:
2 "Son of man, set your face toward the mountains of Yisrael, and prophesy against them,

3 And say, 'You mountains of Yisrael, hear the word of Lord (Adonai) יהוה; Thus saith Lord (Adonai) יהוה to the mountains, and to the hills, to the rivers, and to the valleys; Behold, I, even I, will bring a sword upon you, and I will destroy

your high places.

4 And your altars shall be desolate, and your images shall be broken; and I will cast down your slain men before your idols.

5 And I will lay the dead carcases of the children of Yisrael before their idols; and I will scatter your bones round about your altars.

6 In all your dwellingplaces the cities shall be laid waste, and the high places shall be desolate; that your altars may be laid waste and made desolate, and your idols may be broken and cease, and your images may be cut down, and your works may be abolished.

7 And the slain shall fall in the midst of you, and you shall know that I am יהוה.

8 Yet will I leave a remnant, that you may have some that shall escape the sword among the nations, when you shall be scattered through the countries.

9 And they that escape of you shall remember Me among the nations whither they shall be carried captives, because I am broken with their whorish heart, which hath departed from Me, and with their eyes, which go a whoring after their idols; and they shall lothe themselves for the evils which they have committed in all their abominations.

10 And they shall know that I am יהוה, and that I have not said in vain that I would do this evil unto them."

11 Thus saith Lord (Adonai) יהוה: "Smite with your hand, and stamp with your foot, and say, 'Alas for all the evil abominations of the house of Yisrael! For they shall fall by the sword, by the famine, and by the pestilence.

12 He that is far off shall die of the pestilence; and he that is near shall fall by the sword; and he that remaineth and is besieged shall die by the famine. Thus will I accomplish My fury upon them.

13 Then shall you know that I am יהוה, when their slain men shall be among their idols round about their altars, upon every high hill, in all the tops of the mountains, and under every green tree, and under every thick oak, the place where they did offer sweet savour to all their idols.

14 So will I stretch out My hand upon them, and make the land desolate, yea, more desolate than the wilderness toward Diblath, in all their habitations; and they shall know that I am יהוה.'"

7 Moreover the word of יהוה came unto me, saying,

2 "Also, you son of man, thus saith Lord (Adonai) יהוה unto the land of Yisrael: 'An end! The end is come upon the four corners of the land.

3 Now is the end come upon you, and I will send Mine anger upon you, and will judge you according to your ways, and will recompense upon you all your abominations.

4 And Mine eye shall not spare you, neither will I have pity; but I will recompense your ways upon you, and your abominations shall be in the midst of you; and you shall know that I am יהוה.'

5 Thus saith Lord (Adonai) יהוה: 'A disaster (raah), an only disaster (raah), behold, is coming.

6 An end is coming, the end has come; it watcheth for you; behold, it has come.

7 The doom has come unto you, O you that dwellest in the land; the time has come, the day of trouble is near, and tumult rather than joyful shouting in the mountains.

8 Now will I shortly pour out My fury upon you, and accomplish Mine anger upon you; and I will judge you according to your ways, and will recompense you for all your abominations.

9 And Mine eye shall not spare, neither will I have pity; I will recompense you according to your ways and your abominations that are in the midst of you; and you shall know that I am יהוה that smiteth.

10 Behold the day! Behold, it is coming; the doom has gone forth; the rod hath blossomed, pride hath budded.

11 Violence has risen up into a rod of wickedness; none of them shall remain, nor of their multitude, nor of any of theirs; nor shall there be wailing for them.

12 The time is come, the day draweth near; let not the buyer rejoice, nor the seller mourn, for wrath is upon all the multitude thereof.

13 For the seller shall not return to that which is sold, although they were yet alive; for the vision is touching the whole multitude thereof, which shall not return; neither shall any strengthen himself in the iniquity of his life.

14 They have blown the trumpet, even to make all ready; but none goeth to the battle; for My wrath is upon all the multitude thereof.

15 The sword is outside, and the pestilence and the famine within; he that is in the field shall die with the sword; and he that is in the city, famine and pestilence shall devour him.

16 But they that escape of them shall escape, and shall be on the mountains like doves of the valleys, all of them mourning, every one for his iniquity.

17 All hands shall be feeble, and all knees shall be weak as water.

18 They shall also gird themselves with sackcloth, and horror shall cover them; and shame shall be upon all faces, and baldness upon all their heads.

19 They shall cast their silver in the strects, and their gold shall be removed; their silver and their gold shall not be able to deliver them in the day of the wrath of יהוה; they shall not satisfy their souls, nor fill their bowels, because it is the stumblingblock of their iniquity.

20 As for the beauty of his ornament, he set it in majesty: but they made the images of their abominations and of their detestable things therein; therefore have I set it far from them.

21 And I will give it into the hands of the strangers for a prey, and to the wicked of the earth for a spoil; and they shall pollute it.

22 My face will I turn also from them, and they shall pollute My secret place; for the robbers shall enter into it, and defile it.

23 Make a chain, for the land is full of bloody crimes, and the city is full of violence.

24 Wherefore I will bring the worst of the nations, and they shall possess their houses; I will also make the pomp of the strong to cease; and their holy places shall be defiled.

25 Destruction cometh; and they shall seek peace, and there shall be none.

26 Mischief shall come upon mischief, and rumour shall be upon rumour; then shall they seek a vision of the prophet; but the law (torah) shall perish from the priest (kohen), and counsel from the ancients.

27 The king shall mourn, and the prince shall be clothed with desolation, and the hands of the people of the land will trembled. I will do unto them after their way, and according to their deserts will I judge them; and they shall know that I am יהוה.'"

8 And it came to pass in the sixth year, in the sixth month, in the fifth day of the month, as I sat in mine house, and the elders of Judah (Yehudah) sat before me, that the hand of Lord (Adonai) יהוה fell there upon me.

2 Then I beheld, and behold a likeness as the appearance of fire; from the appearance of His loins even downward, fire; and from His loins even upward, as the appearance of brightness, as the colour of amber.

3 And He put forth the form of a hand, and took me by a lock of mine head; and the Spirit (Ruach) lifted me up between the earth and the heaven, and brought me in the visions of God (Elohim) to Jerusalem (Yerushalayim), to the door of the inner gate that looketh toward the north; where was the seat of the image of jealousy, which provoketh to jealousy.

4 And, behold, the glory of the God of Israel (Elohei Yisrael) was there, according to the vision that I saw in the plain.

5 Then said He unto me, "Son of man, lift up your eyes now the way toward the north." So I lifted up mine eyes the way toward the north, and behold northward at the gate of the altar this image of jealousy in the entry.

6 He said furthermore unto me, "Son of man, seest you what they do? Even the great abominations that the house of Yisrael committeth here, that I should go far off from My sanctuary? But turn you yet again, and you shalt see greater abominations."

7 And He brought me to the door of the court; and when I looked, behold a hole in the wall.

8 Then said He unto me, "Son of man, dig now in the wall"; and when I had digged in the wall, behold a door.

9 And He said unto me, "Go in, and behold the wicked abominations that they do here."

10 So I went in and saw; and behold every form of creeping things, and abominable beasts, and all the idols of the house of Yisrael, pourtrayed upon the wall round about.

11 And there stood before them seventy men of the ancients of the house of Yisrael, and in the midst of them stood Yaanzanyah the son of Shaphan, with every man his censer in his hand; and a thick cloud of incense went up.

12 Then said He unto me, "Son of man, have you seen what the ancients of the house of Yisrael do in the dark, every man in the chambers of his imagery? For they say, 'יהוה seeth us not; יהוה hath forsaken the earth.'"

13 He said also unto me, "Turn you yet again, and you shalt see greater abominations that they do."

14 Then He brought me to the door of the gate of יהוה's house which was toward the north;

and, behold, there sat women weeping for Tammuz.

15 Then said He unto me, "Have you seen this, O son of man? Turn you yet again, and you shalt see greater abominations than these."

16 And He brought me into the inner court of יהוה's house, and, behold, at the door of the temple of יהוה, between the porch and the altar, were about five and twenty men, with their backs toward the temple of יהוה, and their faces toward the east; and they worshipped the sun toward the east.

17 Then He said unto me, "Have you seen this, O son of man? Is it a light thing to the house of Judah (Yehudah) that they commit the abominations which they commit here? For they have filled the land with violence, and have returned to provoke Me to anger; and, behold, they put the branch to their nose.

18 Therefore will I also deal in fury. Mine eye shall not spare, nor will I have pity; and though they cry in Mine ears with a loud voice, yet will I not hear them."

9 He cried also in mine ears with a loud voice, saying, "Cause them that have charge over the city to draw near, even every man with his destroying weapon in his hand."

2 And, behold, six men came from the way of the higher gate, which lieth toward the north, and every man a slaughter weapon in his hand; and one man among them was clothed with linen, with a writer's inkhorn by his side; and they went in, and stood beside the brasen altar.

3 And the glory of the God of Israel (Elohei Yisrael) was gone up from the cherub (keruv), whereupon he was, to the threshold of the house. And he called to the man clothed with linen, which had the writer's inkhorn by his side;

4 And יהוה said unto him, "Go through the midst of the city, through the midst of Jerusalem (Yerushalayim), and set a mark upon the foreheads of the men that sigh and that cry for all the abominations that be done in the midst thereof."

5 And to the others He said in mine hearing, "Go you after him through the city, and smite; let not your eye spare, neither have you pity;

6 Slay utterly old and young, both maids, and little children, and women; but come not near any man upon whom is the mark; and begin at My sanctuary." Then they began at the ancient men which were before the house.

7 And He said unto them, "Defile the house, and fill the courts with the slain. Go you forth!" And they went forth, and slew in the city.

8 And it came to pass, while they were slaying them, and I was left, that I fell upon my face, and cried, and said, "Ah Lord (Adonai) יהוה! Wilt you destroy all the residue of Yisrael in Your pouring out of Your fury upon Jerusalem (Yerushalayim)?"

9 Then said He unto me, "The iniquity of the house of Yisrael and Judah (Yehudah) is exceeding great, and the land is full of blood, and the city full of perverseness; for they say, 'יהוה hath forsaken the earth, and יהוה seeth not!'

10 And as for Me also, Mine eye shall not spare, neither will I have pity, but I will recompense their way upon their head."

11 And, behold, the man clothed with linen, which had the inkhorn by his side, reported the matter, saying, "I have done as You have commanded me."

10 Then I looked, and, behold, in the firmament that was above the head of the cherubims (keruvim) there appeared over them as it was a sapphire stone, as the appearance of the likeness of a throne.

2 And He spake unto the man clothed with linen, and said, "Go in between the wheels, even under the cherub (keruv), and fill your hand with coals of fire from between the cherubims (keruvim), and scatter them over the city." And he went in in my sight.

3 Now the cherubims (keruvim) stood on the right side of the house, when the man went in; and the cloud filled the inner court.

4 Then the glory of יהוה went up from the cherub (keruv), and stood over the threshold of the house; and the house was filled with the cloud, and the court was full of the brightness of יהוה's glory.

5 And the sound of the cherubims (keruvim)'s wings was heard even to the outer court, as the voice of the Almighty God (Elohim) when He speaketh.

6 And it came to pass, that when He had commanded the man clothed with linen, saying, "Take fire from between the wheels, from between the cherubims (keruvim); then he went in, and stood beside the wheels.

7 And one cherub (keruv) stretched forth his hand from between the cherubims (keruvim)

unto the fire that was between the cherubims (keruvim), and took thereof, and put it into the hands of him that was clothed with linen: who took it, and went out.

8 And there appeared in the cherubims (keruvim) the form of a man's hand under their wings.

9 And when I looked, behold the four wheels by the cherubims (keruvim), one wheel by one cherub (keruv), and another wheel by another cherub (keruv); and the appearance of the wheels was as the colour of a beryl stone.

10 And as for their appearances, they four had one likeness, as if a wheel had been in the midst of a wheel.

11 When they went, they went upon their four sides; they turned not as they went, but to the place whither the head looked they followed it; they turned not as they went.

12 And their whole body, and their backs, and their hands, and their wings, and the wheels, were full of eyes round about, even the wheels that they four had.

13 As for the wheels, it was cried unto them in my hearing, O wheel.

14 And every one had four faces: the first face was the face of a cherub (keruv), and the second face was the face of a man, and the third the face of a lion, and the fourth the face of an eagle.

15 And the cherubims (keruvim) were lifted up. This is the living creature that I saw by the river of Chebar.

16 And when the cherubims (keruvim) went, the wheels went by them; and when the cherubims (keruvim) lifted up their wings to mount up from the earth, the same wheels also turned not from beside them.

17 When they stood, these stood; and when they were lifted up, these lifted up themselves also; for the spirit of the living creature was in them.

18 Then the glory of יהוה departed from off the threshold of the house, and stood over the cherubims (keruvim).

19 And the cherubims (keruvim) lifted up their wings, and mounted up from the earth in my sight: when they went out, the wheels also were beside them, and every one stood at the door of the east gate of יהוה's house; and the glory of the God of Israel (Elohei Yisrael) was over them above.

20 This is the living creature that I saw under the God of Israel (Elohei Yisrael) by the river of Chebar; and I knew that they were the cherubims (keruvim).

21 Every one had four faces apiece, and every one four wings; and the likeness of the hands of a man was under their wings.

22 And the likeness of their faces was the same faces which I saw by the river of Chebar, their appearances and themselves; they went every one straight forward.

11 Moreover the Spirit (Ruach) lifted me up, and brought me unto the east gate of יהוה's house, which looketh eastward; and behold at the door of the gate five and twenty men; among whom I saw Yaanzanyah the son of Azur, and Pelatyahu the son of Benayahu, princes of the people.

2 Then said He unto me, "Son of man, these are the men that devise mischief, and give wicked counsel in this city,

3 Who say, 'It is not near; let us build houses; this city is the caldron, and we be the flesh.'

4 Therefore prophesy against them, prophesy, O son of man."

5 And the Spirit (Ruach) of יהוה fell upon me, and said unto me, "Speak! 'Thus saith יהוה: "Thus have you said, O house of Yisrael; for I know the things that come into your mind, every one of them.

6 You have multiplied your slain in this city, and you have filled the streets thereof with the slain."

7 'Therefore thus saith Lord (Adonai) יהוה: "Your slain whom you have laid in the midst of it, they are the flesh, and this city is the caldron; but I will bring you forth out of the midst of it.

8 You have feared the sword; and I will bring a sword upon you," saith Lord (Adonai) יהוה.

9 And I will bring you out of the midst thereof, and deliver you into the hands of strangers, and will execute judgments among you.

10 You shall fall by the sword; I will judge you in the border of Yisrael; and you shall know that I am יהוה.

11 This city shall not be your caldron, neither shall you be the flesh in the midst thereof; but I will judge you in the border of Yisrael.

12 And you shall know that I am יהוה; for you have not walked in My statutes, neither executed My judgments, but have done after the manners of the nations that are round about you.""'"

13 And it came to pass, when I prophesied, that Pelatyahu the son of Benayahu died. Then fell I down upon my face, and cried with a loud voice, and said, "Ah Lord (Adonai) יהוה! Wilt You make a full end of the remnant of Yisrael?"

14 Again the word of יהוה came unto me, saying,

15 "Son of man, your brethren, even your brethren, the men of your kindred, and all the house of Yisrael wholly, are they unto whom the inhabitants of Jerusalem (Yerushalayim) have said, 'Get you far from יהוה; unto us is this land given in possession.'

16 Therefore say, 'Thus saith Lord (Adonai) יהוה: "Although I have cast them far off among the nations, and although I have scattered them among the countries, yet will I be to them as a little sanctuary in the countries where they shall come."'

17 Therefore say, 'Thus saith Lord (Adonai) יהוה: "I will even gather you from the people, and assemble you out of the countries where you have been scattered, and I will give you the land of Yisrael."'

18 And they shall come thither, and they shall take away all the detestable things thereof and all the abominations thereof from thence.

19 And I will give them one heart, and I will put a new spirit within you; and I will take the stony heart out of their flesh, and will give them a heart of flesh,

20 That they may walk in My statutes, and keep Mine ordinances, and do them; and they shall be My people, and I will be their God (Elohim).

21 But as for them whose heart walketh after the heart of their detestable things and their abominations, I will recompense their way upon their own heads, saith Lord (Adonai) יהוה.

22 Then did the cherubims (keruvim) lift up their wings, and the wheels beside them; and the glory of the God of Israel (Elohei Yisrael) was over them above.

23 And the glory of יהוה went up from the midst of the city, and stood upon the mountain which is on the east side of the city.

24 Afterwards the Spirit (Ruach) took me up, and brought me in a vision by the Spirit of God (Ruach Elohim) into Chaldea, to them of the captivity. So the vision that I had seen went up from me.

25 Then I spake unto them of the captivity all the things that יהוה had shewed me.

12 The word of יהוה also came unto me, saying,

2 "Son of man, you dwellest in the midst of a rebellious house, which have eyes to see, and see not; they have ears to hear, and hear not; for they are a rebellious house.

3 Therefore, you son of man, prepare stuff for removing, and remove by day in their sight; and you shalt remove from your place to another place in their sight; it maybe they will consider, though they be a rebellious house.

4 Then shalt you bring forth your stuff by day in their sight, as stuff for removing; and you shalt go forth at even in their sight, as they that go forth into captivity.

5 Dig you through the wall in their sight, and carry out thereby.

6 In their sight shalt you bear it upon your shoulders, and carry it forth in the twilight; you shalt cover your face, that you see not the ground; for I have set you for a sign unto the house of Yisrael."

7 And I did so as I was commanded; I brought forth my stuff by day, as stuff for captivity, and in the even I digged through the wall with mine hand; I brought it forth in the twilight, and I bare it upon my shoulder in their sight.

8 And in the morning came the word of יהוה unto me, saying,

9 "Son of man, hath not the house of Yisrael, the rebellious house, said unto you, 'What doest you?'

10 Say you unto them, 'Thus saith Lord (Adonai) יהוה: "This burden concerneth the prince in Jerusalem (Yerushalayim), and all the house of Yisrael that are among them."'

11 Say, 'I am your sign; like as I have done, so shall it be done unto them; they shall remove and go into captivity.'

12 And the prince that is among them shall bear upon his shoulder in the twilight, and shall go forth; they shall dig through the wall to carry out thereby; he shall cover his face, that he sees not the ground with his eyes.

13 My net also will I spread upon him, and he shall be taken in My snare; and I will bring him to Babylon (Bavel) to the land of the Chaldeans; yet shall he not see it, though he shall die there.

14 And I will scatter toward every wind all that are about him to help him, and all his bands; and I will draw out the sword after them.

15 And they shall know that I am יהוה, when I shall scatter them among the nations, and disperse them in the countries.

16 But I will leave a few men of them from the sword, from the famine, and from the pestilence; that they may declare all their abominations among the nations whither they come; and they shall know that I am יהוה."

17 Moreover the word of יהוה came to me, saying,

18 "Son of man, eat your bread with quaking, and drink your water with trembling and with carefulness;

19 And say unto the people of the land, 'Thus saith Lord (Adonai) יהוה of the inhabitants of Jerusalem (Yerushalayim), and of the land of Yisrael: "They shall eat their bread with carefulness, and drink their water with astonishment, that her land may be desolate from all that is therein, because of the violence of all them that dwell therein.

20 And the cities that are inhabited shall be laid waste, and the land shall be desolate; and you shall know that I am יהוה."'"

21 And the word of יהוה came unto me, saying,

22 "Son of man, what is that proverb that you have in the land of Yisrael, saying, 'The days are prolonged, and every vision faileth'?

23 Tell them therefore, 'Thus saith Lord (Adonai) יהוה: "I will make this proverb to cease, and they shall no more use it as a proverb in Yisrael."' But say unto them, "The days are at hand, and the effect of every vision.

24 For there shall be no more any vain vision nor flattering divination within the house of Yisrael.

25 For I am יהוה. I will speak, and the word that I shall speak shall come to pass; it shall be no more prolonged; for in your days, O rebellious house, will I say the word, and will perform it," saith Lord (Adonai) יהוה.'"

26 Again the word of יהוה came to me, saying,

27 "Son of man, behold, they of the house of Yisrael say, 'The vision that he seeth is for many days to come, and he prophesieth of the times that are far off.'

28 Therefore say unto them, 'Thus saith Lord (Adonai) יהוה: "There shall none of My words be prolonged any more, but the word which I have spoken shall be done," saith Lord (Adonai) יהוה.'"

13

And the word of יהוה came unto me, saying,

2 "Son of man, prophesy against the prophets of Yisrael that prophesy, and say you unto them that prophesy out of their own hearts, 'Hear you the word of יהוה!'"

3 Thus saith Lord (Adonai) יהוה; Woe unto the foolish prophets, that follow their own spirit, and have seen nothing!

4 O Yisrael, your prophets are like the foxes in the deserts.

5 You have not gone up into the gaps, neither made up the hedge for the house of Yisrael to stand in the battle in the day of יהוה.

6 They have seen vanity and lying divination, saying, 'Thus saith יהוה; but יהוה hath not sent them; and they have made others to hope that they would confirm the word.

7 Have you not seen a vain vision, and have you not spoken a lying divination, whereas you say, 'יהוה saith it;' albeit I have not spoken?"

8 Therefore thus saith Lord (Adonai) יהוה: "Because you have spoken vanity, and seen lies, therefore, behold, I am against you," saith Lord (Adonai) יהוה.

9 And Mine hand shall be upon the prophets that see vanity, and that divine lies; they shall not be in the assembly of My people, neither shall they be written in the writing of the house of Yisrael, nor shall they enter into the land of Yisrael; and you shall know that I am Lord (Adonai) יהוה.

10 Because, even because they have seduced My people, saying, 'Peace (Shalom)!' when there was no peace; and one built up a wall, and, behold, others daubed it with untempered morter;

11 Say unto them which daub it with untempered morter, that it shall fall; there shall be an overflowing shower; and you, O great hailstones, shall fall; and a stormy wind shall rend it.

12 Behold, when the wall is fallen, shall it not be said unto you, 'Where is the daubing wherewith you have daubed it?'"

13 Therefore thus saith Lord (Adonai) יהוה: "I will even rend it with a stormy wind in my fury; and there shall be an overflowing shower in Mine anger, and great hailstones in My fury to consume it.

14 So will I break down the wall that you have daubed with untempered morter, and bring it

down to the ground, so that the foundation thereof shall be discovered, and it shall fall, and you shall be consumed in the midst thereof; and you shall know that I am יהוה.

15 Thus will I accomplish My wrath upon the wall, and upon them that have daubed it with untempered morter, and will say unto you, 'The wall is no more, nor they that daubed it;

16 the prophets of Yisrael which prophesy concerning Yerushalayim, and who see visions of peace for her, and there is no peace,'" saith Lord (Adonai) יהוה.

17 Likewise, you son of man, set your face against the daughters of your people, who prophesy out of their own heart; and prophesy you against them,

18 And say, 'Thus saith Lord (Adonai) יהוה: "Woe to the women that sew pillows to all armholes, and make kerchiefs upon the head of every stature to hunt souls! Will you hunt the souls of My people, and will you save the souls alive that come unto you?

19 And will you pollute Me among My people for handfuls of barley and for pieces of bread, to slay the souls that should not die, and to save the souls alive that should not live, by your lying to My people that hear your lies?"

20 Wherefore thus saith Lord (Adonai) יהוה: "Behold, I am against your pillows, wherewith you there hunt the souls to make them fly, and I will tear them from your arms, and will let the souls go, even the souls that you hunt to make them fly.

21 Your kerchiefs also will I tear, and deliver My people out of your hand, and they shall be no more in your hand to be hunted; and you shall know that I am יהוה.

22 Because with lies you have made the heart of the righteous sad, whom I have not made sad; and strengthened the hands of the wicked, that he should not return from his wicked way, by promising him life.

23 Therefore you shall see no more vanity, nor divine divinations; for I will deliver My people out of your hand, and you shall know that I am יהוה.'"

14 Then came certain of the elders of Yisrael unto me, and sat before me.

2 And the word of יהוה came unto me, saying,

3 "Son of man, these men have set up their idols in their heart, and put the stumblingblock of their iniquity before their face; should I be enquired of at all by them?

4 Therefore speak unto them, and say unto them, 'Thus saith Lord (Adonai) יהוה: "Every man of the house of Yisrael that setteth up his idols in his heart, and putteth the stumblingblock of his iniquity before his face, and cometh to the prophet; I יהוה will answer him that cometh according to the multitude of his idols;

5 That I may take the house of Yisrael in their own heart, because they are all estranged from Me through their idols."'

6 Therefore say unto the house of Yisrael, 'Thus saith Lord (Adonai) יהוה: "Repent, and turn yourselves from your idols; and turn away your faces from all your abominations.

7 For every one of the house of Yisrael, or of the stranger that sojourneth in Yisrael, which separateth himself from Me, and setteth up his idols in his heart, and putteth the stumblingblock of his iniquity before his face, and cometh to a prophet to enquire of him concerning Me, I יהוה will answer him by Myself.

8 And I will set my face against that man, and will make him a sign and a proverb, and I will cut him off from the midst of My people; and you shall know that I am יהוה.

9 And if the prophet be deceived when he hath spoken a thing, I יהוה have deceived that prophet, and I will stretch out My hand upon him, and will destroy him from the midst of My people Yisrael.

10 And they shall bear the punishment of their iniquity: the punishment of the prophet shall be even as the punishment of him that seeketh unto him,

11 That the house of Yisrael may go no more astray from Me, neither be polluted any more with all their transgressions; but that they may be My people, and I may be their God (Elohim)," saith Lord (Adonai) יהוה.'"

12 The word of יהוה came again to me, saying:

13 "Son of man, when the land sinneth against Me by trespassing grievously, then will I stretch out Mine hand upon it, and will break the staff of the bread thereof, and will send famine upon it, and will cut off man and beast from it:

14 "Though these three men, Noach, Daniel, and Job (Iyov), were in it, they should deliver but their own souls by their righteousness," saith Lord (Adonai) יהוה.

15 If I cause noisome beasts to pass through the land, and they spoil it, so that it be desolate, that no man may pass through because of the beasts:

16 "Though these three men were in it, as I live," saith Lord (Adonai) יהוה, "they shall deliver neither sons nor daughters; they only shall be delivered, but the land shall be desolate.

17 Or if I bring a sword upon that land, and say, 'Sword, go through the land;' so that I cut off man and beast from it:

18 "Though these three men were in it, as I live," saith Lord (Adonai) יהוה, "they shall deliver neither sons nor daughters, but they only shall be delivered themselves.

19 Or if I send a pestilence into that land, and pour out My fury upon it in blood, to cut off from it man and beast,

20 "Though Noach, Daniel, and Job (Iyov), were in it, as I live," saith Lord (Adonai) יהוה, "they shall deliver neither son nor daughter; they shall but deliver their own souls by their righteousness."

21 For thus saith Lord (Adonai) יהוה: "How much more when I send My four sore judgments upon Jerusalem (Yerushalayim), the sword, and the famine, and the noisome beast, and the pestilence, to cut off from it man and beast?

22 Yet, behold, therein shall be left a remnant that shall be brought forth, both sons and daughters; behold, they shall come forth unto you, and you shall see their way and their doings; and you shall be comforted concerning the evil that I have brought upon Jerusalem (Yerushalayim), even concerning all that I have brought upon it.

23 And they shall comfort you, when you see their ways and their doings; and you shall know that I have not done without cause all that I have done in it," saith Lord (Adonai) יהוה.

15 And the word of יהוה came unto me, saying,

2 "Son of man, how is the vine tree better than any tree, or than a branch which is among the trees of the forest?

3 Shall wood be taken thereof to do any work? Or will men take a pin of it to hang any vessel thereon?

4 Behold, it is cast into the fire for fuel; the fire devoureth both the ends of it, and the midst of it is burned. Is it meet for any work?

5 Behold, when it was whole, it was meet for no work; how much less shall it be meet yet for any work, when the fire hath devoured it, and it is burned?

6 Therefore thus saith Lord (Adonai) יהוה: 'As the vine tree among the trees of the forest, which I have given to the fire for fuel, so will I give the inhabitants of Jerusalem (Yerushalayim);

7 And I will set My face against them; they shall go out from one fire, and another fire shall devour them; and you shall know that I am יהוה, when I set My face against them.

8 'And I will make the land desolate, because they have committed a trespass,' saith Lord (Adonai) יהוה.' "

16 Again the word of יהוה came unto me, saying,

2 "Son of man, cause Jerusalem (Yerushalayim) to know her abomi-nations,

3 And say, 'Thus saith Lord (Adonai) יהוה unto Jerusalem (Yerushalayim): "Your birth and your nativity is of the land of Canaan; your father was an Amorite, and your mother a Hittite.

4 And as for your nativity, in the day you wast born your navel was not cut, neither wast you washed in water to supple you; you wast not salted at all, nor swaddled at all.

5 None eye pitied you, to do any of these unto you, to have compassion upon you; but you wast cast out in the open field, to the lothing of your person, in the day that you wast born.

6 And when I passed by you, and saw you polluted in your own blood, I said unto you when you wast in your blood, 'Live!' Yea, I said unto you when you wast in your blood, 'Live!'

7 I have caused you to multiply as the bud of the field, and you have increased and waxen great, and you are come to excellent ornaments: your breasts are fashioned, and your hair is grown, whereas you wast naked and bare.

8 Now when I passed by you, and looked upon you, behold, your time was the time of love; and I spread My Wing over you, and covered your nakedness; yea, I sware unto you, and entered into a covenant with you," saith Lord (Adonai) יהוה, "and you becamest Mine."

9 Then washed I you with water; yea, I throughly washed away your blood from you, and I anointed you with oil.

10 I clothed you also with broidered work, and

shod you with badgers' skin, and I girded you about with fine linen, and I covered you with silk.

11 I decked you also with ornaments, and I put bracelets upon your hands, and a chain on your neck.

12 And I put a jewel on your forehead, and earrings in your ears, and a beautiful crown upon your head.

13 Thus wast you decked with gold and silver; and your raiment was of fine linen, and silk, and broidered work; you didst eat fine flour, and honey, and oil; and you wast exceeding beautiful, and you didst prosper into a kingdom.

14 And your renown went forth among the nations for your beauty, for it was perfect through My splendor, which I had put upon you," saith Lord (Adonai) יהוה.

15 But you didst trust in your own beauty, and playedst the harlot because of your renown, and pouredst out your fornications on every one that passed by; his it was.

16 And of your garments you didst take, and deckedst your high places with divers colours, and playedst the harlot thereupon; the like things shall not come, neither shall it be so.

17 You have also taken your fair jewels of My gold and of My silver, which I had given you, and madest to yourself images of men, and didst commit whoredom with them,

18 And tookest your broidered garments, and coveredst them; and you have set Mine oil and Mine incense before them.

19 My meat also which I gave you, fine flour, and oil, and honey, wherewith I fed you, you have even set it before them for a sweet savour; and thus it was," saith Lord (Adonai) יהוה.

20 Moreover you have taken your sons and your daughters, whom you have borne unto Me, and these have you sacrificed unto them to be devoured. Is this of your whoredoms a small matter,

21 That you have slain My children, and delivered them to cause them to pass through the fire for them?

22 And in all your abominations and your whoredoms you have not remembered the days of your youth, when you wast naked and bare, and wast polluted in your blood.

23 And it came to pass after all your wickedness, ('Woe, woe unto you!' saith Adonai יהוה,)

24 'That you have also built unto you an eminent place, and hast made you a high place in every street.

25 You have built your high place at every head of the way, and hast made your beauty to be abhorred, and hast opened your feet to every one that passed by, and multiplied your whoredoms.

26 You have also committed fornication with the Egyptians (Mitsrayim) your neighbours, great of flesh; and hast increased your whoredoms, to provoke Me to anger.

27 Behold, therefore I have stretched out My hand over you, and have diminished your ordinary food, and delivered you unto the will of them that hate you, the daughters of the Philistines, which are ashamed of your lewd way.

28 You have played the whore also with the Assyrians, because you wast unsatiable; yea, you have played the harlot with them, and yet couldest not be satisfied.

29 You have moreover multiplied your fornication in the land of Canaan unto Chaldea; and yet you wast not satisfied herewith.

30 How weak is your heart, saith Lord (Adonai) יהוה, seeing you doest all these things, the work of an imperious whorish woman;

31 In that you buildest your eminent place in the head of every way, and makest your high place in every street; and hast not been as a harlot, in that you scornest hire;

32 But as a wife that committeth adultery, which taketh strangers instead of her husband!

33 They give gifts to all whores: but you givest your gifts to all your lovers, and hirest them, that they may come unto you on every side for your whoredom.

34 And the contrary is in you from other women in your whoredoms, whereas none followeth you to commit whoredoms; and in that you givest a reward, and no reward is given unto you, therefore you are contrary."

35 Wherefore, O harlot, hear the word of יהוה!

36 Thus saith Lord (Adonai) יהוה; Because your filthiness was poured out, and your nakedness discovered through your whoredoms with your lovers, and with all the idols of your abominations, and by the blood of your children, which you didst give unto them;

37 Behold, therefore I will gather all your

lovers, with whom you have taken pleasure, and all them that you have loved, with all them that you have hated; I will even gather them round about against you, and will discover your nakedness unto them, that they may see all your nakedness.

38 And I will judge you, as women that break wedlock and shed blood are judged; and I will give you blood in fury and jealousy.

39 And I will also give you into their hand, and they shall throw down your eminent place, and shall break down your high places: they shall strip you also of your clothes, and shall take your fair jewels, and leave you naked and bare.

40 They shall also bring up a company against you, and they shall stone you with stones, and thrust you through with their swords.

41 And they shall burn your houses with fire, and execute judgments upon you in the sight of many women: and I will cause you to cease from playing the harlot, and you also shalt give no hire any more.

42 So will I make My fury toward you to rest, and My jealousy shall depart from you, and I will be quiet, and will be no more angry.

43 "Because you have not remembered the days of your youth, but hast fretted Me in all these things; behold, therefore I also will recompense your way upon your head," saith Lord (Adonai) יהוה. "And you shalt not commit this lewdness above all your abominations.

44 Behold, every one that useth proverbs shall use this proverb against you, saying: 'As is the mother, so is her daughter!'

45 You are your mother's daughter, that loatheth her husband and her children; and you are the sister of your sisters, which lothed their husbands and their children; your mother was a Hittite, and your father an Amorite.

46 And your elder sister is Samaria (Shomeron), she and her daughters that dwell at your left hand; and your younger sister, that dwelleth at your right hand, is Sodom and her daughters.

47 Yet have you not walked after their ways, nor done after their abominations; but, as if that were a very little thing, you wast corrupted more than they in all your ways.

48 "As I live," saith Lord (Adonai) יהוה, "Sodom your sister hath not done, she nor her daughters, as you have done, you and your daughters.

49 Behold, this was the iniquity of your sister

Sodom: pride, fullness of bread, and abundance of idleness was in her and in her daughters, neither did she strengthen the hand of the poor and needy.

50 And they were haughty, and committed abomination before Me; therefore I took them away as I saw good.

51 Neither hath Samaria (Shomeron) committed half of your sins; but you have multiplied your abominations more than they, and hast justified your sisters in all your abominations which you have done.

52 You also, which hast judged your sisters, bear your own shame for your sins that you have committed more abominable than they; they are more righteous than you; yea, be you confounded also, and bear your shame, in that you have justified your sisters.

53 When I shall bring again their captivity, the captivity of Sodom and her daughters, and the captivity of Samaria (Shomeron) and her daughters, then will I bring again the captivity of your captives in the midst of them,

54 That you mayest bear your own shame, and mayest be confounded in all that you have done, in that you are a comfort unto them.

55 When your sisters, Sodom and her daughters, shall return to their former estate, and Samaria (Shomeron) and her daughters shall return to their former estate, then you and your daughters shall return to your former estate.

56 For your sister Sodom was not mentioned by your mouth in the day of your pride,

57 Before your wickedness was discovered, as at the time of your reproach of the daughters of Syria (Aram), and all that are round about her, the daughters of the Philistines, which despise you round about.

58 You have borne your lewdness and your abominations," saith יהוה.

59 For thus saith Lord (Adonai) יהוה: "I will even deal with you as you have done, which hast despised the oath in breaking the covenant.

60 Nevertheless I will remember My covenant with you in the days of your youth, and I will establish unto you an everlasting covenant.

61 Then you shalt remember your ways, and be ashamed, when you shalt receive your sisters, your elder and your younger: and I will give them unto you for daughters, but not by your covenant.

62 And I will establish My covenant with you; and you shalt know that I am יהוה,

63 That you mayest remember, and be confounded, and never open your mouth any more because of your shame, when I am pacified toward you for all that you have done," saith Lord (Adonai) יהוה.

17 And the word of יהוה came unto me, saying,

2 "Son of man, put forth a riddle, and speak a parable unto the house of Yisrael;

3 And say, 'Thus saith Lord (Adonai) יהוה: "A great eagle with great wings, longwinged, full of feathers, which had divers colours, came unto Lebanon, and took the highest branch of the cedar.

4 He cropped off the top of his young twigs, and carried it into a land of traffick; he set it in a city of merchants.

5 He took also of the seed of the land, and planted it in a fruitful field; he placed it by great waters, and set it as a willow tree.

6 And it grew, and became a spreading vine of low stature, whose branches turned toward him, and the roots thereof were under him; so it became a vine, and brought forth branches, and shot forth sprigs.

7 There was also another great eagle with great wings and many feathers; and, behold, this vine did bend her roots toward him, and shot forth her branches toward him, that he might water it by the furrows of her plantation.

8 It was planted in a good soil by great waters, that it might bring forth branches, and that it might bear fruit, that it might be a goodly vine."'

9 Say you, 'Thus saith Lord (Adonai) יהוה; Shall it prosper? Shall he not pull up the roots thereof, and cut off the fruit thereof, that it withers? It shall wither in all the leaves of her spring, even without great power or many people to pluck it up by the roots thereof.

10 Yea, behold, being planted, shall it prosper? Shall it not utterly wither, when the east wind toucheth it? It shall wither in the furrows where it grew."'"

11 Moreover the word of יהוה came unto me, saying,

12 Say now to the rebellious house: 'Know you not what these things mean? Tell them, Behold, the king of Babylon (Bavel) is come to Jerusalem (Yerushalayim), and hath taken the king thereof, and the princes thereof, and led

them with him to Babylon (Bavel);

13 And hath taken of the king's seed, and made a covenant with him, and hath taken an oath of him; he hath also taken the mighty of the land,

14 That the kingdom might be base, that it might not lift itself up, but that by keeping of his covenant it might stand.

15 But he rebelled against him in sending his ambassadors into Egypt (Mitsrayim), that they might give him horses and much people. Shall he prosper? Shall he escape that doeth such things? Or shall he break the covenant, and be delivered?

16 'As I live,' saith Lord (Adonai) יהוה, surely in the place where the king dwelleth that made him king, whose oath he despised, and whose covenant he broke, even with him in the midst of Babylon (Bavel) he shall die.

17 Nor shall Pharaoh (Paroh) with his mighty army and great company make for him in the war, by casting up mounts, and building forts, to cut off many persons;

18 Seeing he despised the oath by breaking the covenant, when, behold, he had given his hand, and hath done all these things, he shall not escape.'"

19 Therefore thus saith Lord (Adonai) יהוה; As I live, surely Mine oath that he hath despised, and My covenant that he hath broken, even it will I recompense upon his own head.

20 And I will spread My net upon him, and he shall be taken in My snare, and I will bring him to Babylon (Bavel), and will plead with him there for his trespass that he hath trespassed against Me.

21 And all his fugitives with all his bands shall fall by the sword, and they that remain shall be scattered toward all winds; and you shall know that I יהוה have spoken it."

22 Thus saith Lord (Adonai) יהוה: "I will also take of the highest branch of the high cedar, and will set it; I will crop off from the top of his young twigs a tender one, and will plant it upon a high mountain and eminent.

23 In the mountain of the height of Yisrael will I plant it; and it shall bring forth boughs, and bear fruit, and be a goodly cedar; and under it shall dwell all fowl of every wing; in the shadow of the branches thereof shall they dwell.

24 And all the trees of the field shall know that I יהוה have brought down the high tree, have

exalted the low tree, have dried up the green tree, and have made the dry tree to flourish; I יהוה have spoken and have done it."

18 The word of יהוה came unto me again, saying,

2 "What mean you, that you use this proverb concerning the land of Yisrael, saying: 'The fathers have eaten sour grapes, and the children's teeth are set on edge'?

3 "As I live," saith Lord (Adonai) יהוה, "you shall not have occasion any more to use this proverb in Yisrael.

4 Behold, all souls are Mine; as the soul of the father, so also the soul of the son is Mine; the soul that sinneth, it shall die.

5 But if a man be just, and do that which is lawful and right,

6 And hath not eaten upon the mountains, neither hath lifted up his eyes to the idols of the house of Yisrael, neither hath defiled his neighbour's wife, neither hath come near to a menstruous woman,

7 And hath not oppressed any, but hath restored to the debtor his pledge, hath spoiled none by violence, hath given his bread to the hungry, and hath covered the naked with a garment;

8 He that hath not given forth upon usury, neither hath taken any increase, that hath withdrawn his hand from iniquity, hath executed true judgment between man and man,

9 Hath walked in My statutes, and hath kept My judgments, to deal truly; he is just, he shall surely live!" saith Lord (Adonai) יהוה.

10 If he begets a son that is a robber, a shedder of blood, and that doeth the like to any one of these things,

11 And that doeth not any of those duties, but even hath eaten upon the mountains, and defiled his neighbour's wife,

12 Hath oppressed the poor and needy, hath spoiled by violence, hath not restored the pledge, and hath lifted up his eyes to the idols, hath committed abomination,

13 Hath given forth upon usury, and hath taken increase; shall he then live? He shall not live; he hath done all these abominations; he shall surely die; his blood shall be upon him.

14 Now, behold, if he begets a son, that seeth all his father's sins which he hath done, and considereth, and doeth not such like,

15 That hath not eaten upon the mountains,

neither hath lifted up his eyes to the idols of the house of Yisrael, hath not defiled his neighbour's wife,

16 Neither hath oppressed any, hath not withholden the pledge, neither hath spoiled by violence, but hath given his bread to the hungry, and hath covered the naked with a garment,

17 That hath taken off his hand from the poor, that hath not received usury nor increase, hath executed my judgments, hath walked in my statutes; he shall not die for the iniquity of his father, he shall surely live!

18 As for his father, because he cruelly oppressed, spoiled his brother by violence, and did that which is not good among his people, behold, even he shall die in his iniquity.

19 Yet say you, 'Why? doth not the son bears the iniquity of the father?' When the son hath done that which is lawful and right, and hath kept all My statutes, and hath done them, he shall surely live.

20 The soul that sinneth, it shall die. The son shall not bear the iniquity of the father, nor shall the father bear the iniquity of the son; the righteousness of the righteous shall be upon him, and the wickedness of the wicked shall be upon him.

21 But if the wicked will turn from all his sins that he hath committed, and keep all My statutes, and do that which is lawful and right, he shall surely live, he shall not die.

22 All his transgressions that he hath committed, they shall not be mentioned unto him: in his righteousness that he hath done he shall live.

23 "Have I any pleasure at all that the wicked should die?" saith Lord (Adonai) יהוה, "and not that he should return from his ways, and live?

24 But when the righteous turneth away from his righteousness, and committeth iniquity, and doeth according to all the abominations that the wicked man doeth, shall he live? All his righteousness that he hath done shall not be mentioned; in his trespass that he hath trespassed, and in his sin that he hath sinned, in them shall he die.

25 Yet you say, 'The way of Lord (Adonai) is not fair.' Hear now, O house of Yisrael; Is not my way equal? Are not your ways unequal?

26 When a righteous man turneth away from his righteousness, and committeth iniquity, and dieth in them; for his iniquity that he hath done

shall he die.

27 Again, when the wicked man turneth away from his wickedness that he hath committed, and doeth that which is lawful and right, he shall save his soul alive.

28 Because he considereth, and turneth away from all his transgressions that he hath committed, he shall surely live, he shall not die.

29 Yet saith the house of Yisrael, 'The way of Lord (Adonai) is not fair.' O house of Yisrael, are not my ways fair? Are not your ways unfair?

30 "Therefore I will judge you, O house of Yisrael, every one according to his ways," saith Lord (Adonai) יהוה. "Repent, and turn yourselves from all your transgressions; so iniquity shall not be your ruin.

31 Cast away from you all your transgressions, whereby you have transgressed; and make you a new heart and a new spirit, for why will you die, O house of Yisrael?

32 "For I have no pleasure in the death of him that dieth," saith Lord (Adonai) יהוה. "Wherefore turn yourselves, and live you!"

19 "Moreover take you up a lamentation for the princes of Yisrael,

2 And say: 'What is your mother? A lioness; she lay down among lions, she nourished her whelps among young lions.

3 And she brought up one of her whelps; it became a young lion, and it learned to catch the prey; it devoured men.

4 The nations also heard of him; he was taken in their pit, and they brought him with chains unto the land of Egypt (Mitsrayim).

5 Now when she saw that she had waited, and her hope was lost, then she took another of her whelps, and made him a young lion.

6 And he went up and down among the lions, he became a young lion, and learned to catch the prey, and devoured men.

7 And he knew their desolate palaces, and he laid waste their cities; and the land was desolate, and the fullness thereof, by the noise of his roaring.

8 Then the nations set against him on every side from the provinces, and spread their net over him; he was taken in their pit.

9 And they put him in ward in chains, and brought him to the king of Babylon (Bavel); they brought him into holds, that his voice should no more be heard upon the mountains

of Yisrael.

10 Your mother is like a vine in your blood, planted by the waters: she was fruitful and full of branches by reason of many waters.

11 And she had strong rods for the sceptres of them that bare rule, and her stature was exalted among the thick branches, and she appeared in her height with the multitude of her branches.

12 But she was plucked up in fury, she was cast down to the ground, and the east wind dried up her fruit; her strong rods were broken and withered; the fire consumed them.

13 And now she is planted in the wilderness, in a dry and thirsty ground.

14 And fire is gone out of a rod of her branches, which hath devoured her fruit, so that she hath no strong rod to be a sceptre to rule.'" This is a lamentation, and shall be for a lamentation.

20 And it came to pass in the seventh year, in the fifth month, the tenth day of the month, that certain of the elders of Yisrael came to enquire of יהוה, and sat before me.

2 Then came the word of יהוה unto me, saying,

3 "Son of man, speak unto the elders of Yisrael, and say unto them, 'Thus saith Lord (Adonai) יהוה: "Are you come to enquire of Me? As I live," saith Lord (Adonai) יהוה, "I will not be enquired of by you."'

4 Wilt you judge them, son of man, wilt you judge them? Cause them to know the abominations of their fathers:

5 And say unto them, 'Thus saith Lord (Adonai) יהוה: "On the day when I chose Yisrael, and lifted up mine hand unto the seed of the house of Jacob (Yaaqov), and made Myself known unto them in the land of Egypt (Mitsrayim), when I lifted up Mine hand unto them, saying, 'I am יהוה your God (YHWH Eloheikhem).'

6 On that day that I lifted up Mine hand unto them, to bring them forth of the land of Egypt (Mitsrayim) into a land that I had espied for them, 'flowing with milk and honey,' which is the glory of all lands.

7 Then said I unto them, 'Cast you away every man the abominations of his eyes, and defile not yourselves with the idols of Egypt (Mitsrayim): I am יהוה your God (YHWH Eloheikhem).'

8 But they rebelled against Me, and would not hearken unto Me; they did not every man cast away the abominations of their eyes, neither did they forsake the idols of Egypt (Mitsrayim);

then I said, 'I will pour out My fury upon them, to accomplish My anger against them in the midst of the land of Egypt (Mitsrayim).'

9 But I wrought for My name's sake, that it should not be polluted before the nations, among whom they were, in whose sight I made Myself known unto them, in bringing them forth out of the land of Egypt (Mitsrayim).

10 Wherefore I caused them to go forth out of the land of Egypt (Mitsrayim), and brought them into the wilderness.

11 And I gave them My statutes, and shewed them My judgments, 'which if a man does, he shall even live in them.'

12 Moreover also I gave them My Shabbats, to be a sign between Me and them, that they might know that I am יהוה that sanctify them.

13 But the house of Yisrael rebelled against Me in the wilderness; they walked not in My statutes, and they despised My judgments, 'which if a man does, he shall even live by them;' and My Shabbats they greatly polluted; then I said, I would pour out My fury upon them in the wilderness, to consume them.

14 But I wrought for My name's sake, that it should not be polluted before the nations, in whose sight I brought them out.

15 Yet also I lifted up My hand unto them in the wilderness, that I would not bring them into the land which I had given them, flowing with milk and honey, which is the glory of all lands;

16 Because they despised My judgments, and walked not in My statutes, but polluted My Shabbats; for their heart went after their idols.

17 Nevertheless Mine eye spared them from destroying them, neither did I make an end of them in the wilderness.

18 But I said unto their children in the wilderness, 'Walk you not in the statutes of your fathers, neither observe their judgments, nor defile yourselves with their idols.

19 I am יהוה your God (YHWH Eloheikhem); walk in My statutes, and keep My judgments, and do them;

20 And hallow My Shabbats; and they shall be a sign between Me and you, that you may know that I am יהוה your God (YHWH Eloheikhem).'

21 Notwithstanding the children rebelled against Me; they walked not in My statutes, neither kept My judgments to do them, which if a man do, he shall even live in them; they

polluted My Shabbats: then I said I would pour out My fury upon them, to accomplish My anger against them in the wilderness.

22 Nevertheless I withdrew Mine hand, and wrought for My name's sake, that it should not be polluted in the sight of the nations, in whose sight I brought them forth.

23 I lifted up Mine hand unto them also in the wilderness, that I would scatter them among the nations, and disperse them through the countries;

24 Because they had not executed My judgments, but had despised My statutes, and had polluted My Shabbats, and their eyes were after their fathers' idols.

25 Wherefore I gave them also statutes that were not good, and judgments whereby they should not live;

26 And I polluted them in their own gifts, in that they caused to pass through the fire all that openeth the womb, that I might make them desolate, to the end that they might know that I am יהוה.

27 Therefore, son of man, speak unto the house of Yisrael, and say unto them, 'Thus saith Lord (Adonai) יהוה: "Yet in this your fathers have blasphemed Me, in that they have committed a trespass against Me.

28 For when I had brought them into the land, for the which I lifted up Mine hand to give it to them, then they saw every high hill, and all the thick trees, and they offered there their sacrifices, and there they presented the provocation of their offering; there also they made their sweet savour, and poured out there their drink offerings.

29 Then I said unto them, 'What is the high place whereunto you go?' And the name thereof is called Bamah unto this day.'"

30 Wherefore say unto the house of Yisrael, 'Thus saith Lord (Adonai) יהוה: "Are you polluted after the manner of your fathers? And commit you whoredom after their abominations?

31 For when you offer your gifts, when you make your sons to pass through the fire, you pollute yourselves with all your idols, even unto this day; and shall I be enquired of by you, O house of Yisrael? As I live," saith Lord (Adonai) יהוה, "I will not be enquired of by you.

32 And that which cometh into your mind shall not be at all, that you say, 'We will be as the

nations, as the families of the countries, to serve wood and stone.'

33 "As I live," saith Lord (Adonai) יהוה, "surely with a mighty hand, and with an outstretched arm, and with fury poured out, will I rule over you:

34 And I will bring you out from the people, and will gather you out of the countries wherein you are scattered, with a mighty hand, and with an outstretched arm, and with fury poured out.

35 And I will bring you into the wilderness of the people, and there will I plead with you face to face.

36 Like as I pleaded with your fathers in the wilderness of the land of Egypt (Mitsrayim), so will I plead with you," saith Lord (Adonai) יהוה.

37 "And I will cause you to pass under the rod, and I will bring you into the bond of the covenant;

38 And I will purge out from among you the rebels, and them that transgress against me; I will bring them forth out of the country where they sojourn, and they shall not enter into the land of Yisrael; and you shall know that I am יהוה.

39 As for you, O house of Yisrael," thus saith Lord (Adonai) יהוה: "Go you, serve you every one his idols, and hereafter also, if you will not hearken unto Me; but pollute you My holy name no more with your gifts, and with your idols.

40 For in Mine holy mountain, in the mountain of the height of Yisrael," saith Lord (Adonai) יהוה, "there shall all the house of Yisrael, all of them in the land, serve Me; there will I accept them, and there will I require your offerings, and the firstfruits of your oblations, with all your holy things.

41 I will accept you with your sweet savour, when I bring you out from the people, and gather you out of the countries wherein you have been scattered; and I will be sanctified in you before the nations.

42 And you shall know that I am יהוה, when I shall bring you into the land of Yisrael, into the country for the which I lifted up mine hand to give it to your fathers.

43 And there shall you remember your ways, and all your doings, wherein you have been defiled; and you shall lothe yourselves in your own sight for all your evils that you have committed.

44 And you shall know that I am יהוה, when I have wrought with you for My name's sake, not according to your wicked ways, nor according to your corrupt doings, O you house of Yisrael," saith Lord (Adonai) יהוה.'"

45 Moreover the word of יהוה came unto me, saying,

46 "Son of man, set your face toward the south, and drop your word toward the south, and prophesy against the forest of the south field;

47 And say to the forest of the south, 'Hear the word of יהוה. 'Thus saith Lord (Adonai) יהוה: "Behold, I will kindle a fire in you, and it shall devour every green tree in you, and every dry tree; the flaming flame shall not be quenched, and all faces from the south to the north shall be burned therein.

48 And all flesh shall see that I יהוה have kindled it; it shall not be quenched."

49 Then said I, "Ah Lord (Adonai) יהוה! They say of me, 'Doth he not speak parables?'"

21 And the word of יהוה came unto me, saying,

2 "Son of man, set your face toward Jerusalem (Yerushalayim), and drop your word toward the holy places, and prophesy against the land of Yisrael;

3 And say to the land of Yisrael, 'Thus saith יהוה: "Behold, I am against you, and will draw forth My sword out of his sheath, and will cut off from you the righteous and the wicked.

4 Seeing then that I will cut off from you the righteous and the wicked, therefore shall My sword go forth out of his sheath against all flesh from the south to the north,

5 That all flesh may know that I יהוה have drawn forth My sword out of his sheath; it shall not return anymore."'

6 Sigh therefore, you son of man, with the breaking of your loins; and with bitterness sigh before their eyes.

7 And it shall be, when they say unto you, Wherefore sighest you? That you shalt answer, For the tidings; because it cometh; and every heart shall melt, and all hands shall be feeble, and every spirit shall faint, and all knees shall be weak as water. Behold, it cometh, and shall be brought to pass,' saith Lord (Adonai) יהוה."

8 Again the word of יהוה came unto me, saying,

9 "Son of man, prophesy, and say, 'Thus saith יהוה, "Say: 'A sword, a sword is sharpened, and also furbished!

10 It is sharpened to make a sore slaughter; it

is furbished that it may glitter: should we then make mirth? It contemneth the rod of My son, as every tree.

11 And he hath given it to be furbished, that it may be handled; this sword is sharpened, and it is furbished, to give it into the hand of the slayer.'

12 Cry and howl, son of man; for it shall be upon My people, it shall be upon all the princes of Yisrael. Terrors by reason of the sword shall be upon My people; smite therefore upon your thigh.

13 Because it is a trial, and what if the sword contemns even the rod? It shall be no more, saith Lord (Adonai) יהוה.

14 You therefore, son of man, prophesy, and smite your hands together, and let the sword be doubled the third time, the sword of the slain; it is the sword of the great men that are slain, which entereth into their privy chambers.

15 I have set the point of the sword against all their gates, that their heart may faint, and their ruins be multiplied. Ah! It is made bright, it is wrapped up for the slaughter;

16 Go you one way or other, either on the right hand, or on the left, whithersoever your face is set.

17 I will also smite Mine hands together, and I will cause My fury to rest; I יהוה have said it."

18 The word of יהוה came unto me again, saying:

19 "Also, you son of man, appoint you two ways, that the sword of the king of Babylon (Bavel) may come; both twain shall come forth out of one land; and choose you a place, choose it at the head of the way to the city.

20 Appoint a way, that the sword may come to Rabbath of the Ammonites, and to Judah (Yehudah) in Yerushalayim the defenced.

21 For the king of Babylon (Bavel) stood at the parting of the way, at the head of the two ways, to use divination; he made his arrows bright, he consulted with images, he looked in the liver.

22 At his right hand was the divination for Jerusalem (Yerushalayim), to appoint captains, to open the mouth in the slaughter, to lift up the voice with shouting, to appoint battering rams against the gates, to cast a mount, and to build a fort.

23 And it shall be unto them as a false divination in their sight, to them that have sworn oaths; but

he will call to remembrance the iniquity, that they may be taken.

24 Therefore thus saith Lord (Adonai) יהוה: 'Because you have made your iniquity to be remembered, in that your transgressions are discovered, so that in all your doings your sins do appear; because, I say, that you are come to remembrance, you shall be taken with the hand.

25 'And you, profane wicked prince of Yisrael, whose day is come, when iniquity shall have an end,'

26 Thus saith Lord (Adonai) יהוה: 'Remove the diadem, and take off the crown; this shall not be the same; exalt him that is low, and abase him that is high.

27 I will overturn, overturn, overturn, it; and it shall be no more, until he come whose right it is; and I will give it him.'

28 "And you, son of man, prophesy and say, 'Thus saith Lord (Adonai) יהוה concerning the Ammonites, and concerning their reproach;' even say you: 'The sword, the sword is drawn; for the slaughter it is furbished, to consume because of the glittering;

29 Whiles they see vanity unto you, whiles they divine a lie unto you, to bring you upon the necks of them that are slain, of the wicked, whose day is come, when their iniquity shall have an end.

30 Shall I cause it to return into his sheath? I will judge you in the place where you wast created, in the land of your nativity.

31 And I will pour out mine indignation upon you, I will blow against you in the fire of My wrath, and deliver you into the hand of brutish men, and skilful to destroy.

32 You shalt be for fuel to the fire; your blood shall be in the midst of the land; you shalt be no more remembered; for I יהוה have spoken it.'"

22 Moreover the word of יהוה came unto me, saying,

2 "Now, you son of man, wilt you judge, wilt you judge the bloody city? Yea, you shalt shew her all her abominations.

3 Then say you, 'Thus saith Lord (Adonai) יהוה: "The city sheddeth blood in the midst of it, that her time may come, and maketh idols against herself to defile herself.

4 You are become guilty in your blood that you have shed; and hast defiled yourself in your idols which you have made; and you have

caused your days to draw near, and art come even unto your years; therefore have I made you a reproach unto the nations, and a mocking to all countries.

5 Those that be near, and those that be far from you, shall mock you, which art infamous and much vexed.

6 Behold, the princes of Yisrael: every one in you have used their power to shed blood.

7 In you have they set light by father and mother; in the midst of you have they dealt by oppression with the stranger; in you have they vexed the fatherless and the widow.

8 You have despised Mine holy things, and hast profaned My Shabbats.

9 In you are men that carry tales to shed blood; and in you they eat upon the mountains; in the midst of you they commit lewdness.

10 In you have they discovered their fathers' nakedness; in you have they humbled her that was set apart for pollution.

11 And one hath committed abomination with his neighbour's wife; and another hath lewdly defiled his daughter in law; and another in you hath humbled his sister, his father's daughter.

12 In you have they taken gifts to shed blood; you have taken usury and increase, and you have greedily gained of your neighbours by extortion, and hast forgotten Me," saith Lord (Adonai) יהוה.

13 "Behold, therefore I have smitten Mine hand at your dishonest gain which you have made, and at your blood which hath been in the midst of you.

14 Can your heart endure, or can your hands be strong, in the days that I shall deal with you? I יהוה have spoken it, and will do it.

15 And I will scatter you among the nations, and disperse you in the countries, and will consume your filthiness out of you.

16 And you shalt take your inheritance in yourself in the sight of the nations, and you shalt know that I am יהוה.""""

17 And the word of יהוה came unto me, saying,

18 "Son of man, the house of Yisrael is to Me become dross; all they are brass, and tin, and iron, and lead, in the midst of the furnace; they are even the dross of silver.

19 Therefore thus saith Lord (Adonai) יהוה: 'Because you are all become dross, behold, therefore I will gather you into the midst of Jerusalem (Yerushalayim).

20 As they gather silver, and brass, and iron, and lead, and tin, into the midst of the furnace, to blow the fire upon it, to melt it; so will I gather you in Mine anger and in My fury, and I will leave you there, and melt you.

21 Yea, I will gather you, and blow upon you in the fire of My wrath, and you shall be melted in the midst thereof.

22 As silver is melted in the midst of the furnace, so shall you be melted in the midst thereof; and you shall know that I יהוה have poured out My fury upon you.'"

23 And the word of יהוה came unto me, saying,

24 "Son of man, say unto her: 'You are the land that is not cleansed, nor rained upon in the day of indignation.'

25 There is a conspiracy of her prophets in the midst thereof, like a roaring lion ravening the prey; they have devoured souls; they have taken the treasure and precious things; they have made her many widows in the midst thereof.

26 Her kohanim have violated My Torah, and have profaned Mine holy things; they have put no difference between the holy and profane, neither have they shewed difference between the unclean and the clean, and have hid their eyes from My Shabbats, and I am profaned among them.

27 Her princes in the midst thereof are like wolves ravening the prey, to shed blood, and to destroy souls, to get dishonest gain.

28 And her prophets have daubed them with untempered morter, seeing vanity (false vision), and divining lies unto them, saying, 'Thus saith Lord (Adonai) יהוה,' when יהוה hath not spoken.

29 The people of the land have used oppression, and exercised robbery, and have vexed the poor and needy; yea, they have oppressed the stranger wrongfully.

30 And I sought for a man among them, that should make up the hedge, and stand in the gap before Me for the land, that I should not destroy it; but I found none.

31 Therefore have I poured out Mine indignation upon them; I have consumed them with the fire of My wrath; their own way have I recompensed upon their heads," saith Lord (Adonai) יהוה.

23 The word of יהוה came again unto me, saying:

2 "Son of man, there were two women, the

daughters of one mother:

3 And they committed whoredoms in Egypt (Mitsrayim); they committed whoredoms in their youth; there were their breasts pressed, and there they bruised the teats of their virginity.

4 And the names of them were Aholah the elder, and Aholibah her sister; and they were mine, and they bare sons and daughters. Thus were their names: Samaria (Shomeron) is Aholah, and Jerusalem (Yerushalayim) Aholivah.

5 And Aholah played the harlot when she was Mine; and she doted on her lovers (allies), on the Ashshur (Assyrians) her neighbours,

6 Which were clothed with blue, captains and rulers, all of them desirable young men, horsemen riding upon horses.

7 Thus she committed her whoredoms with them, with all them that were the chosen men of Assyria (Ashshur), and with all on whom she lusted; with all their idols she defiled herself.

8 Neither left she her whoredoms brought from Egypt (Mitsrayim); for in her youth they lay with her, and they bruised the breasts of her virginity, and poured their whoredom upon her.

9 Wherefore I have delivered her into the hand of her lovers (allies), into the hand of the Assyrians (Ashshur), upon whom she lusted.

10 These discovered her nakedness; they took her sons and her daughters, and slew her with the sword; and she became famous among women; for they had executed judgment upon her.

11 And when her sister Aholibah saw this, she was more corrupt in her inordinate love than she, and in her whoredoms more than her sister in her whoredoms.

12 She doted upon the men of Assyrians (Ashshur) her neighbours, captains and rulers clothed most gorgeously, horsemen riding upon horses, all of them desirable young men.

13 Then I saw that she was defiled, that they took both one way,

14 And that she increased her whoredoms; for when she saw men pourtrayed upon the wall, the images of the Chaldeans pourtrayed with vermilion,

15 Girded with girdles upon their loins, exceeding in dyed attire upon their heads, all of them princes to look to, after the manner of the men of Babylonians (Bavel) of Chaldea, the land of their nativity.

16 And as soon as she saw them with her eyes, she doted upon them, and sent messengers unto them into Chaldea.

17 And the men of Babylonians (Bavel) came to her into the bed of love, and they defiled her with their whoredom, and she was polluted with them, and her mind was alienated from them.

18 So she discovered her whoredoms, and discovered her nakedness; then My mind was alienated from her, like as My mind was alienated from her sister.

19 Yet she multiplied her whoredoms, in calling to remembrance the days of her youth, wherein she had played the harlot in the land of Egypt (Mitsrayim).

20 For she doted upon their paramours, whose flesh is as the flesh of asses, and whose issue is like the issue of horses.

21 Thus you calledst to remembrance the lewdness of your youth, in bruising your teats by the Egyptians (Mitsrayim) for the paps of your youth.

22 Therefore, O Aholibah, thus saith Lord (Adonai) יהוה: 'Behold, I will raise up your lovers (allies) against you, from whom your mind is alienated, and I will bring them against you on every side;

23 The men of Babylonians (Bavel), and all the Chaldeans, Pekod, and Shoa, and Koa, and all the men of Assyrians (Ashshur) with them; all of them desirable young men, captains and rulers, great lords and renowned, all of them riding upon horses.

24 And they shall come against you with chariots, wagons, and wheels, and with an assembly of people, which shall set against you buckler and shield and helmet round about; and I will set judgment before them, and they shall judge you according to their judgments.

25 And I will set My jealousy against you, and they shall deal furiously with you; they shall take away your nose and your ears; and your remnant shall fall by the sword; they shall take your sons and your daughters; and your residue shall be devoured by the fire.

26 They shall also strip you out of your clothes, and take away your fair jewels.

27 Thus will I make your lewdness to cease from you, and your whoredom brought from the land of Egypt (Mitsrayim); so that you shalt not lift up your eyes unto them, nor remember Egypt (Mitsrayim) any more.

28 For thus saith Lord (Adonai) יהוה: 'Behold, I will deliver you into the hand of them whom you hatest, into the hand of them from whom your mind is alienated:

29 And they shall deal with you hatefully, and shall take away all your labour, and shall leave you naked and bare: and the nakedness of your whoredoms shall be discovered, both your lewdness and your whoredoms.

30 I will do these things unto you, because you have gone a whoring after the nations, and because you are polluted with their idols.

31 You have walked in the way of your sister; therefore will I give her cup into your hand.'

32 Thus saith Lord (Adonai) יהוה: 'You shalt drink of your sister's cup deep and large: you shalt be laughed to scorn and had in derision; it containeth much.

33 You shalt be filled with drunkenness and sorrow, with the cup of astonishment and desolation, with the cup of your sister Samaria (Shomeron).

34 You shalt even drink it and suck it out, and you shalt break the sherds thereof, and pluck off your own breasts; for I have spoken it,' saith Lord (Adonai) יהוה.

35 Therefore thus saith Lord (Adonai) יהוה: 'Because you have forgotten Me, and cast Me behind your back, therefore bear you also your lewdness and your whoredoms.'"

36 יהוה said moreover unto me: "Son of man, wilt you judge Aholah and Aholibah? Yea, declare unto them their abominations;

37 That they have committed adultery, and blood is in their hands, and with their idols have they committed adultery, and have also caused their sons, whom they bare unto Me, to pass for them through the fire, to devour them.

38 Moreover this they have done unto me: They have defiled My sanctuary in the same day, and have profaned My Shabbats.

39 For when they had slain their children to their idols, then they came the same day into My sanctuary to profane it; and, behold, thus have they done in the midst of Mine house.

40 And furthermore, that you have sent for men to come from far, unto whom a messenger was sent; and, behold, they came; for whom you didst wash yourself, paintedst your eyes, and deckedst yourself with ornaments,

41 And satest upon a stately bed, and a table prepared before it, whereupon you have set Mine incense and Mine oil.

42 And a voice of a multitude being at ease was with her; and with the men of the common sort were brought Sabeans from the wilderness, which put bracelets upon their hands, and beautiful crowns upon their heads.

43 Then said I unto her that was old in adulteries, 'Will they now commit whoredoms with her, and she with them?'

44 Yet they went in unto her, as they go in unto a woman that playeth the harlot; so went they in unto Aholah and unto Aholibah, the lewd women.

45 And the righteous men, they shall judge them after the manner of adulteresses, and after the manner of women that shed blood; because they are adulteresses, and blood is in their hands.

46 For thus saith Lord (Adonai) יהוה: 'I will bring up a company upon them, and will give them to be removed and spoiled.

47 And the company shall stone them with stones, and dispatch them with their swords; they shall slay their sons and their daughters, and burn up their houses with fire.

48 Thus will I cause lewdness to cease out of the land, that all women may be taught not to do after your lewdness.

49 And they shall recompense your lewdness upon you, and you shall bear the sins of your idols; and you shall know that I am Lord (Adonai) יהוה.'"

24 Again in the ninth year, in the tenth month, in the tenth day of the month, the word of יהוה came unto me, saying,

2 "Son of man, write you the name of the day, even of this same day: the king of Babylon (Bavel) set himself against Jerusalem (Yerushalayim) this same day;

3 And utter a parable unto the rebellious house, and say unto them, 'Thus saith Lord (Adonai) יהוה: "Set on a pot, set it on, and also pour water into it.

4 Gather the pieces thereof into it, even every good piece, the thigh, and the shoulder; fill it with the choice bones.

5 Take the choice of the flock, and burn also the bones under it, and make it boil well, and let them seethe the bones of it therein."

6 Wherefore thus saith Lord (Adonai) יהוה: "Woe to the bloody city, to the pot whose scum

is therein, and whose scum is not gone out of it! Bring it out piece by piece; let no lot fall upon it.

7 For her blood is in the midst of her; she set it upon the top of a rock; she poured it not upon the ground, to cover it with dust;

8 That it might cause fury to come up to take vengeance; I have set her blood upon the top of a rock, that it should not be covered."

9 Therefore thus saith Lord (Adonai) יהוה: "Woe to the bloody city! I will even make the pile for fire great.

10 Heap on wood, kindle the fire, consume the flesh, and spice it well, and let the bones be burned.

11 Then set it empty upon the coals thereof, that the brass of it may be hot, and may burn, and that the filthiness of it may be molten in it, that the scum of it may be consumed.

12 She hath wearied herself with lies, and her great scum went not forth out of her. Her scum shall be in the fire.

13 In your filthiness is lewdness, because I have purged you, and you wast not purged, you shalt not be purged from your filthiness anymore, till I have caused My fury to rest upon you.

14 I, יהוה have spoken it; it shall come to pass, and I will do it; I will not go back, neither will I spare, neither will I regret; according to your ways, and according to your doings, shall they judge you," saith Lord (Adonai) יהוה.'"

15 Also the word of יהוה came unto me, saying,

16 "Son of man, behold, I take away from you the desire of your eyes with a stroke; yet neither shalt you mourn nor weep, neither shall your tears run down.

17 Forbear to cry, make no mourning for the dead, bind the tire of your head upon you, and put on your shoes upon your feet, and cover not your lips, and eat not the bread of men."

18 So I spake unto the people in the morning: and at even my wife died; and I did in the morning as I was commanded.

19 And the people said unto me, "Wilt you not tell us what these things are to us, that you doest so?"

20 Then I answered them, "The word of יהוה came unto me, saying,

21 'Speak unto the house of Yisrael, "Thus saith Lord (Adonai) יהוה: 'Behold, I will profane My sanctuary, the excellency of your strength, the desire of your eyes, and that which your soul

pitieth; and your sons and your daughters whom you have left shall fall by the sword.

22 And you shall do as I have done; you shall not cover your lips, nor eat the bread of men.

23 And your tires shall be upon your heads, and your shoes upon your feet; you shall not mourn nor weep; but you shall pine away for your iniquities, and mourn one toward another.

24 Thus Ezekiel (Yechezqel) is unto you a sign; according to all that he hath done shall you do; and when this cometh, you shall know that I am Lord (Adonai) יהוה.'"

25 Also, you son of man, shall it not be in the day when I take from them their strength, the joy of their glory, the desire of their eyes, and that whereupon they set their minds, their sons and their daughters,

26 That he that escapeth in that day shall come unto you, to cause you to hear it with your ears?

27 In that day shall your mouth be opened to him who has escaped, and you shalt speak, and be no more dumb; and you shalt be a sign unto them; and they shall know that I am יהוה.'"

25 The word of יהוה came again unto me, saying,

2 "Son of man, set your face against the Ammonites, and prophesy against them;

3 And say unto the Ammonites, 'Hear the word of Lord (Adonai) יהוה! Thus saith Lord (Adonai) יהוה: "Because you saidst, 'Aha!', against My sanctuary, when it was profaned; and against the land of Yisrael, when it was desolate; and against the house of Judah (Yehudah), when they went into captivity;

4 Behold, therefore I will deliver you to the men of the east for a possession, and they shall set their palaces in you, and make their dwellings in you; they shall eat your fruit, and they shall drink your milk.

5 And I will make Rabbah (Amman, capital city of Ammonites) a stable for camels, and the Ammonites a couchingplace for flocks; and you shall know that I am יהוה."

6 For thus saith Lord (Adonai) יהוה: "Because you have clapped your hands, and stamped with the feet, and rejoiced in heart with all your despite against the land of Yisrael;

7 Behold, therefore I will stretch out Mine hand upon you, and will deliver you for a spoil to the nations; and I will cut you off from the people, and I will cause you to perish out of the

countries: I will destroy you; and you shalt know that I am יהוה."

8 Thus saith Lord (Adonai) יהוה: "Because that Moav and Seir do say, Behold, the house of Judah (Yehudah) is like unto all the nations;'

9 Therefore, behold, I will open the side of Moav from the cities, from his cities which are on his frontiers, the glory of the country, Beit ha-Yeshimot, Baal-Meon, and Qiryata-yim,

10 Unto the men of the east with the Ammonites, and will give them in possession, that the Ammonites may not be remembered among the nations.

11 And I will execute judgments upon Moav; and they shall know that I am יהוה."

12 Thus saith Lord (Adonai) יהוה: "Because that Edom hath dealt against the house of Judah (Yehudah) by taking vengeance, and hath greatly offended, and revenged himself upon them;"

13 Therefore thus saith Lord (Adonai) יהוה: "I will also stretch out Mine hand upon Edom, and will cut off man and beast from it; and I will make it desolate from Teman; and they of Dedan shall fall by the sword.

14 And I will lay My vengeance upon Edom by the hand of My people Yisrael; and they shall do in Edom according to Mine anger and according to My fury; and they shall know My vengeance," saith Lord (Adonai) יהוה.

15 Thus saith Lord (Adonai) יהוה: "Because the Philistines have dealt by revenge, and have taken vengeance with a despiteful heart, to destroy it for the old hatred;"

16 Therefore thus saith Lord (Adonai) יהוה: "Behold, I will stretch out Mine hand upon the Philistines, and I will cut off the Cherethims, and destroy the remnant of the sea coast.

17 And I will execute great vengeance upon them with furious rebukes; and they shall know that I am יהוה, when I shall lay My vengeance upon them."""

26 And it came to pass in the eleventh year, in the first day of the month, that the word of יהוה came unto me, saying,

2 "Son of man, because that Tyrus hath said against Jerusalem (Yerushalayim), 'Aha! She is broken that was the gates of the people: she is turned unto Me; I shall be replenished, now she is laid waste;'

3 Therefore thus saith Lord (Adonai) יהוה:

'Behold, I am against you, O Tyrus, and will cause many nations to come up against you, as the sea causeth his waves to come up.

4 And they shall destroy the walls of Tyrus, and break down her towers; I will also scrape her dust from her, and make her like the top of a rock.

5 It shall be a place for the spreading of nets in the midst of the sea, for I have spoken it,' saith Lord (Adonai) יהוה; 'and it shall become a spoil to the nations.

6 And her daughters which are in the field shall be slain by the sword; and they shall know that I am יהוה.'

7 For thus saith Lord (Adonai) יהוה: 'Behold, I will bring upon Tyrus Nebuchadnezzar king of Babylon (Bavel), a king of kings, from the north, with horses, and with chariots, and with horsemen, and companies, and much people.

8 He shall slay with the sword your daughters in the field; and he shall make a fort against you, and cast a mount against you, and lift up the buckler against you.

9 And he shall set engines of war against your walls, and with his axes he shall break down your towers.

10 By reason of the abundance of his horses their dust shall cover you; your walls shall shake at the noise of the horsemen, and of the wheels, and of the chariots, when he shall enter into your gates, as men enter into a city wherein is made a breach.

11 With the hoofs of his horses shall he tread down all your streets; he shall slay your people by the sword, and your strong garrisons shall go down to the ground.

12 And they shall make a spoil of your riches, and make a prey of your merchandise; and they shall break down your walls, and destroy your pleasant houses; and they shall lay your stones and your timber and your dust in the midst of the water.

13 And I will cause the noise of your songs to cease; and the sound of your harps shall be no more heard.

14 And I will make you like the top of a rock; you shalt be a place to spread nets upon; you shalt be built no more, for I יהוה have spoken it,' saith Lord (Adonai) יהוה.

15 Thus saith Lord (Adonai) יהוה to Tyrus: 'Shall not the isles shake at the sound of your

fall, when the wounded cry, when the slaughter is made in the midst of you?

16 Then all the princes of the sea shall come down from their thrones, and lay away their robes, and put off their broidered garments; they shall clothe themselves with trembling; they shall sit upon the ground, and shall tremble at every moment, and be astonished at you.

17 And they shall take up a lamentation for you, and say to you: 'How are you destroyed, that wast inhabited of seafaring men, the renowned city, which wast strong in the sea, she and her inhabitants, which cause their terror to be on all that haunt it!

18 Now shall the isles tremble in the day of your fall; yea, the isles that are in the sea shall be troubled at your departure.'"

19 For thus saith Lord (Adonai) יהוה: 'When I shall make you a desolate city, like the cities that are not inhabited; when I shall bring up the deep upon you, and great waters shall cover you;

20 When I shall bring you down with them that descend into the pit, with the people of old time, and shall set you in the low parts of the earth, in places desolate of old, with them that go down to the pit, that you be not inhabited; and I shall set glory in the land of the living;

21 I will make you a terror, and you shalt be no more; though you be sought for, yet shalt you never be found again,' saith Lord (Adonai) יהוה."

27 The word of יהוה came again unto me, saying,

2 "Now, you son of man, take up a lamentation for Tyrus;

3 And say unto Tyrus, 'O you that art situate at the entry of the sea, which art a merchant of the people for many isles, thus saith Lord (Adonai) יהוה: "O Tyrus, you have said, 'I am of perfect beauty.'

4 Your borders are in the midst of the seas, your builders have perfected your beauty.'

5 They have made all your ship boards of fir trees of Senir; they have taken cedars from Lebanon to make masts for you.

6 Of the oaks of Bashan have they made your oars; the company of the Ashurites have made your benches of ivory, brought out of the isles of Chittim.

7 Fine linen with broidered work from Egypt (Mitsrayim) was that which you spreadest forth to be your sail; blue and purple from the isles of Elishah was that which covered you.

8 The inhabitants of Zidon and Arvad were your mariners; your wise men, O Tyrus, that were in you, were your pilots.

9 The ancients of Gebal and the wise men thereof were in you your calkers; all the ships of the sea with their mariners were in you to occupy your merchandise.

10 They of Persia and of Lud and of Phut were in your army, your men of war; they hanged the shield and helmet in you; they set forth your splendor.

11 The men of Arvad with your army were upon your walls round about, and the Gammadims were in your towers: they hanged their shields upon your walls round about; they have made your beauty perfect.

12 Tarshish was your merchant by reason of the multitude of all kind of riches; with silver, iron, tin, and lead, they traded in your fairs.

13 Yawan, Tubal, and Meshech, they were your merchants; they traded the persons of men and vessels of brass in your market.

14 They of the house of Togarmah traded in your fairs with horses and horsemen and mules.

15 The men of Dedan were your merchants; many isles were the merchandise of your hand; they brought you for a present horns of ivory and ebony.

16 Syria (Aram) was your merchant by reason of the multitude of the wares of your making; they occupied in your fairs with emeralds, purple, and broidered work, and fine linen, and coral, and agate.

17 Judah (Yehudah), and the land of Yisrael, they were your merchants: they traded in your market wheat of Minnith, and Pannag, and honey, and oil, and balm.

18 Damascus (Dammeseq) was your merchant in the multitude of the wares of your making, for the multitude of all riches; in the wine of Helbon, and white wool.

19 Dan also and Yawan going to and fro occupied in your fairs: bright iron, cassia, and calamus, were in your market.

20 Dedan was your merchant in precious clothes for chariots.

21 Arabia, and all the princes of Kedar, they occupied with you in lambs, and rams, and goats; in these were they your merchants.

22 The merchants of Sheva and Raamah, they were your merchants; they occupied in your fairs with chief of all spices, and with all precious stones, and gold.

23 Haran, and Canneh, and Eden, the merchants of Sheva, Asshur, and Chilmad, were your merchants.

24 These were your merchants in all sorts of things, in blue clothes, and broidered work, and in chests of rich apparel, bound with cords, and made of cedar, among your merchandise.

25 The ships of Tarshish did sing of you in your market; and you wast replenished, and made very glorious in the midst of the seas.

26 Your rowers have brought you into great waters; the east wind hath broken you in the midst of the seas.

27 Your riches, and your fairs, your merchandise, your mariners, and your pilots, your calkers, and the occupiers of your merchandise, and all your men of war, that are in you, and in all your company which is in the midst of you, shall fall into the midst of the seas in the day of your ruin.

28 The suburbs shall shake at the sound of the cry of your pilots.

29 And all that handle the oar, the mariners, and all the pilots of the sea, shall come down from their ships, they shall stand upon the land;

30 And shall cause their voice to be heard against you, and shall cry bitterly, and shall cast up dust upon their heads, they shall wallow themselves in the ashes;

31 And they shall make themselves utterly bald for you, and gird them with sackcloth, and they shall weep for you with bitterness of heart and bitter wailing.

32 And in their wailing they shall take up a lamentation for you, and lament over you, saying, 'What city is like Tyrus, like the destroyed in the midst of the sea?

33 When your wares went forth out of the seas, you filledst many people; you didst enrich the kings of the earth with the multitude of your riches and of your merchandise.

34 In the time when you shalt be broken by the seas in the depths of the waters your merchandise and all your company in the midst of you shall fall.

35 All the inhabitants of the isles shall be astonished at you, and their kings shall be sore afraid, they shall be troubled in their countenance.

36 The merchants among the people shall hiss at you; you shalt be a terror, and never shalt be any more."''"

28 The word of יהוה came again unto me, saying,

2 "Son of man, say unto the prince of Tyrus, 'Thus saith Lord (Adonai) יהוה: "Because your heart is lifted up, and you have said, 'I am God (El), I sit in the seat of God (Elohim), in the midst of the sea,' yet you are a man, and not God (El), though you set your heart as the heart of God (Elohim).

3 Behold, you are wiser than Daniel; there is no secret that they can hide from you;

4 With your wisdom and with your understanding you have gotten you riches, and hast gotten gold and silver into your treasures;

5 By your great wisdom and by your traffick have you increased your riches, and your heart is lifted up because of your riches;"

6 Therefore thus saith Lord (Adonai) יהוה: "Because you have set your heart as the heart of God (Elohim);

7 Behold, therefore I will bring strangers upon you, the terrible of the nations; and they shall draw their swords against the beauty of your wisdom, and they shall defile your brightness.

8 They shall bring you down to the pit, and you shalt die the deaths of them that are slain in the midst of the seas.

9 Wilt you yet say before him that slayeth you, 'I am God (Elohim)'? But you shalt be a man, and not God (Elohim), in the hand of him that slayeth you.

10 You shalt die the deaths of the uncircumcised by the hand of strangers, for I have spoken it," saith Lord (Adonai) יהוה.

11 Moreover the word of יהוה came unto me, saying,

12 "Son of man, take up a lamentation upon the king of Tyrus, and say unto him, 'Thus saith Lord (Adonai) יהוה: "You sealest up the sum, full of wisdom, and perfect in beauty.

13 You have been in Eden the garden of God (Elohim); every precious stone was your covering: the sardius, topaz, and the diamond, the beryl, the onyx, and the jasper, the sapphire, the emerald, and the carbuncle, and gold. The workmanship of your tabrets and of your pipes was prepared in you in the day that you wast

created.

14 You are the anointed cherub (keruv) that covereth; and I have set you so; you wast upon the holy mountain of God (Elohim); you have walked up and down in the midst of the stones of fire.

15 You wast perfect in your ways from the day that you wast created, till iniquity was found in you.

16 By the multitude of your merchandise they have filled the midst of you with violence, and you have sinned; therefore I will cast you as profane out of the mountain of God (Elohim); and I will destroy you, O covering cherub (keruv), from the midst of the stones of fire.

17 Your heart was lifted up because of your beauty, you have corrupted your wisdom by reason of your brightness: I will cast you to the ground, I will lay you before kings, that they may behold you.

18 You have defiled your sanctuaries by the multitude of your iniquities, by the iniquity of your traffick; therefore will I bring forth a fire from the midst of you, it shall devour you, and I will bring you to ashes upon the earth in the sight of all them that behold you.

19 All they that know you among the people shall be astonished at you; you shalt be a terror, and never shalt you be any more.

20 Again the word of יהוה came unto me, saying,

21 "Son of man, set your face against Zidon, and prophesy against it,

22 And say, 'Thus saith Lord (Adonai) יהוה: "Behold, I am against you, O Zidon; and I will be glorified in the midst of you; and they shall know that I am יהוה, when I shall have executed judgments in her, and shall be sanctified in her.

23 For I will send pestilence upon her, and blood into her streets; and the wounded shall be judged in the midst of her by the sword upon her on every side; and they shall know that I am יהוה.

24 And there shall be no more a pricking brier unto the house of Yisrael, nor any grieving thorn of all that are round about them, that despised them; and they shall know that I am Lord (Adonai) יהוה."

25 Thus saith Lord (Adonai) יהוה: "When I shall have gathered the house of Yisrael from the people among whom they are scattered, and shall be sanctified in them in the sight of the nations, then shall they dwell in their land that I have given to My servant Jacob (Yaaqov).

26 And they shall dwell safely therein, and shall build houses, and plant vineyards; yea, they shall dwell with confidence, when I have executed judgments upon all those that despise them round about them; and they shall know that I am יהוה their God (YHWH Eloheihem).""'"

29 In the tenth year, in the tenth month, in the twelfth day of the month, the word of יהוה came unto me, saying,

2 "Son of man, set your face against Pharaoh (Paroh) king of Egypt (Mitsrayim), and prophesy against him, and against all Egypt (Mitsrayim):

3 Speak, and say, 'Thus saith Lord (Adonai) יהוה: "Behold, I am against you, Pharaoh (Paroh) king of Egypt (Mitsrayim), the great dragon (tannim) that lieth in the midst of his rivers, who hath said, 'My river is mine own, and I have made it for myself.'

4 But I will put hooks in your jaws, and I will cause the fish of your rivers to stick unto your scales, and I will bring you up out of the midst of your rivers, and all the fish of your rivers shall stick unto your scales.

5 And I will leave you thrown into the wilderness, you and all the fish of your rivers; you shalt fall upon the open fields; you shalt not be brought together, nor gathered. I have given you for meat to the beasts of the field and to the fowls of the sky.

6 And all the inhabitants of Egypt (Mitsrayim) shall know that I am יהוה, because they have been a staff of reed to the house of Yisrael.

7 When they took hold of you by your hand, you didst break, and rend all their shoulder; and when they leaned upon you, you brakest, and madest all their loins to be at a stand."

8 Therefore thus saith Lord (Adonai) יהוה: "Behold, I will bring a sword upon you, and cut off man and beast out of you.

9 And the land of Egypt (Mitsrayim) shall be desolate and waste; and they shall know that I am יהוה, because he hath said, 'The river is mine, and I have made it.'

10 Behold, therefore I am against you, and against your rivers, and I will make the land of Egypt (Mitsrayim) utterly waste and desolate, from the tower of Syene even unto the border of Ethiopia (Kush).

11 No foot of man shall pass through it, nor foot of beast shall pass through it, neither shall it be inhabited forty years.

12 And I will make the land of Egypt (Mitsrayim) desolate in the midst of the countries that are desolate, and her cities among the cities that are laid waste shall be desolate forty years; and I will scatter the Egyptians (Mitsrayim) among the nations, and will disperse them through the countries."

13 Yet thus saith Lord (Adonai) יהוה: "At the end of forty years will I gather the Egyptians (Mitsrayim) from the people whither they were scattered.

14 And I will bring again the captivity of Egypt (Mitsrayim), and will cause them to return into the land of Pathros, into the land of their habitation; and they shall be there a base kingdom.

15 It shall be the basest of the kingdoms; neither shall it exalt itself any more above the nations; for I will diminish them, that they shall no more rule over the nations.

16 And it shall be no more the confidence of the house of Yisrael, which bringeth their iniquity to remembrance, when they shall look after them; but they shall know that I am Lord (Adonai) יהוה.

17 And it came to pass in the seven and twentieth year, in the first month, in the first day of the month, the word of יהוה came unto me, saying,

18 "Son of man, Nebuchadnezzar king of Babylon (Bavel) caused his army to serve a great service against Tyrus; every head was made bald, and every shoulder was peeled; yet had he no wages, nor his army, for Tyrus, for the service that he had served against it.

19 Therefore thus saith Lord (Adonai) יהוה: 'Behold, I will give the land of Egypt (Mitsrayim) unto Nebuchad-nezzar king of Babylon (Bavel); and he shall take her multitude, and take her spoil, and take her prey; and it shall be the wages for his army.

20 I have given him the land of Egypt (Mitsrayim) for his labour wherewith he served against it, because they wrought for Me,' saith Lord (Adonai) יהוה.

21 In that day will I cause the horn of the house of Yisrael to bud forth, and I will give you the opening of the mouth in the midst of them; and they shall know that I am יהוה.'"

30The word of יהוה came again unto me, saying,

2 "Son of man, prophesy and say, 'Thus saith Lord (Adonai) יהוה: "Howl you, 'Woe worth the day!'

3 For the day is near, even the day of יהוה is near, a cloudy day; it shall be the time of the nations.

4 And the sword shall come upon Egypt (Mitsrayim), and great pain shall be in Ethiopia (Kush), when the slain shall fall in Egypt (Mitsrayim), and they shall take away her multitude, and her foundations shall be broken down.

5 Ethiopia (Kush), and Libya, and Lydia, and all the mingled people, and Chub, and the men of the land that is in league, shall fall with them by the sword."

6 Thus saith יהוה: "They also that uphold Egypt (Mitsrayim) shall fall; and the pride of her power shall come down: from the tower of Syene shall they fall in it by the sword," saith Lord (Adonai) יהוה.

7 And they shall be desolate in the midst of the countries that are desolate, and her cities shall be in the midst of the cities that are wasted.

8 And they shall know that I am יהוה, when I have set a fire in Egypt (Mitsrayim), and when all her helpers shall be destroyed.

9 In that day shall messengers go forth from Me in ships to make the careless Ethiopians (Kushim) afraid, and great pain shall come upon them, as in the day of Egypt (Mitsrayim); for, behold, it cometh."

10 Thus saith Lord (Adonai) יהוה: "I will also make the multitude of Egypt (Mitsrayim) to cease by the hand of Nebuchadnezzar king of Babylon (Bavel).

11 He and his people with him, the terrible of the nations, shall be brought to destroy the land; and they shall draw their swords against Egypt (Mitsrayim), and fill the land with the slain.

12 And I will make the rivers dry, and sell the land into the hand of the wicked; and I will make the land waste, and all that is therein, by the hand of strangers. I יהוה have spoken it."

13 Thus saith Lord (Adonai) יהוה: "I will also destroy the idols, and I will cause their images to cease out of Noph; and there shall be no more a prince of the land of Egypt (Mitsrayim); and I will put a fear in the land of Egypt (Mitsrayim).

14 And I will make Pathros desolate, and will set fire in Zoan, and will execute judgments in No.

15 And I will pour My fury upon Sin (Ciyn), the strength of Egypt (Mitsrayim); and I will cut off the multitude of No.

16 And I will set fire in Egypt (Mitsrayim); sin shall have great pain, and No shall be rent asunder, and Noph shall have distresses daily.

17 The young men of Aven and of Pibeseth shall fall by the sword; and these cities shall go into captivity.

18 At Tehaphnehes also the day shall be darkened, when I shall break there the yokes of Egypt (Mitsrayim); and the pomp of her strength shall cease in her: as for her, a cloud shall cover her, and her daughters shall go into captivity.

19 Thus will I execute judgments in Egypt (Mitsrayim); and they shall know that I am יהוה.'"""

20 And it came to pass in the eleventh year, in the first month, in the seventh day of the month, that the word of יהוה came unto me, saying,

21 "Son of man, I have broken the arm of Pharaoh (Paroh) king of Egypt (Mitsrayim); and, behold, it shall not be bound up to be healed, to put a roller to bind it, to make it strong to hold the sword.

22 Therefore thus saith Lord (Adonai) יהוה: 'Behold, I am against Pharaoh (Paroh) king of Egypt (Mitsrayim), and will break his arms, the strong, and that which was broken; and I will cause the sword to fall out of his hand.

23 And I will scatter the Egyptians (Mitsrayim) among the nations, and will disperse them through the countries.

24 And I will strengthen the arms of the king of Babylon (Bavel), and put my sword in his hand; but I will break Pharaoh (Paroh)'s arms, and he shall groan before him with the groanings of a deadly wounded man.

25 But I will strengthen the arms of the king of Babylon (Bavel), and the arms of Pharaoh (Paroh) shall fall down; and they shall know that I am יהוה, when I shall put My sword into the hand of the king of Babylon (Bavel), and he shall stretch it out upon the land of Egypt (Mitsrayim).

26 And I will scatter the Egyptians (Mitsrayim) among the nations, and disperse them among the countries; and they shall know that I am יהוה.'"

31 And it came to pass in the eleventh year, in the third month, in the first day of the month, that the word of יהוה came unto me, saying,

2 "Son of man, speak unto Pharaoh (Paroh) king of Egypt (Mitsrayim), and to his multitude: 'Whom are you like in your greatness?

3 Behold, the Assyrian (Ashshur) was a cedar in Lebanon with fair branches, and with a shadowing shroud, and of a high stature; and his top was among the thick boughs.

4 The waters made him great, the deep set him up on high with her rivers running round about his plants, and sent out her little rivers unto all the trees of the field.

5 Therefore his height was exalted above all the trees of the field, and his boughs were multiplied, and his branches became long because of the multitude of waters, when he shot forth.

6 All the fowls of heaven made their nests in his boughs, and under his branches did all the beasts of the field bring forth their young, and under his shadow dwelt all great nations.

7 Thus was he fair in his greatness, in the length of his branches, for his root was by great waters.

8 The cedars in the garden of God (Elohim) could not hide him; the fir trees were not like his boughs, and the chesnut trees were not like his branches; nor any tree in the garden of God (Elohim) was like unto him in his beauty.

9 I have made him fair by the multitude of his branches; so that all the trees of Eden, that were in the garden of God (Elohim), envied him.'

10 Therefore thus saith Lord (Adonai) יהוה: 'Because you have lifted up yourself in height, and he hath shot up his top among the thick boughs, and his heart is lifted up in his height;

11 I have therefore delivered him into the hand of the mighty one of the nations; he shall surely deal with him: I have driven him out for his wickedness.

12 And strangers, the terrible of the nations, have cut him off, and have left him: upon the mountains and in all the valleys his branches are fallen, and his boughs are broken by all the rivers of the land; and all the people of the earth are gone down from his shadow, and have left him.

13 Upon his ruin shall all the fowls of the sky remain, and all the beasts of the field shall be upon his branches;

14 To the end that none of all the trees by the waters exalt themselves for their height, neither shoot up their top among the thick boughs, neither their trees stand up in their height, all that drink water. 'For they are all delivered unto death, to the nether parts of the earth, in the midst of the children of men, with them that go down to the pit.'

15 Thus saith Lord (Adonai) יהוה: 'In the day when he went down to the grave (sheol) I caused a mourning. I covered the deep for him, and I restrained the floods thereof, and the great waters were stayed: and I caused Lebanon to mourn for him, and all the trees of the field fainted for him.

16 I made the nations to shake at the sound of his fall, when I cast him down to sheol with them that descend into the pit; and all the trees of Eden, the choice and best of Lebanon, all that drink water, shall be comforted in the nether parts of the earth.

17 They also went down into sheol with him unto them that be slain with the sword; and they that were his arm, that dwelt under his shadow in the midst of the nations.

18 To whom are you thus like in glory and in greatness among the trees of Eden? Yet shalt you be brought down with the trees of Eden unto the nether parts of the earth; you shalt lie in the midst of the uncircumcised with them that be slain by the sword. This is Pharaoh (Paroh) and all his multitude,' saith Lord (Adonai) יהוה."

32 And it came to pass in the twelfth year, in the twelfth month, in the first day of the month, that the word of יהוה came unto me, saying,

2 "Son of man, take up a lamentation for Pharaoh (Paroh) king of Egypt (Mitsrayim), and say unto him, 'You are like a young lion of the nations, and you are as a whale in the seas; and you camest forth with your rivers, and troubledst the waters with your feet, and fouledst their rivers.'

3 Thus saith Lord (Adonai) יהוה: 'I will therefore spread out My net over you with a company of many people; and they shall bring you up in My net.

4 Then will I leave you upon the land, I will cast you forth upon the open field, and will cause all the fowls of the sky to remain upon you, and I will fill the beasts of the whole earth with you.

5 And I will lay your flesh upon the mountains, and fill the valleys with your height.

6 I will also water with your blood the land wherein you swimmest, even to the mountains; and the rivers shall be full of you.

7 And when I shall put you out, I will cover the heaven, and make the stars thereof dark; I will cover the sun with a cloud, and the moon shall not give her light.

8 All the bright lights of heaven will I make dark over you, and set darkness upon your land,' saith Lord (Adonai) יהוה.

9 I will also vex the hearts of many people, when I shall bring your destruction among the nations, into the countries which you have not known.

10 Yea, I will make many people amazed at you, and their kings shall be horribly afraid for you, when I shall brandish My sword before them; and they shall tremble at every moment, every man for his own life, in the day of your fall.'

11 For thus saith Lord (Adonai) יהוה: 'The sword of the king of Babylon (Bavel) shall come upon you.

12 By the swords of the mighty will I cause your multitude to fall, the terrible of the nations, all of them; and they shall spoil the pomp of Egypt (Mitsrayim), and all the multitude thereof shall be destroyed.

13 I will destroy also all the beasts thereof from beside the great waters; neither shall the foot of man trouble them any more, nor the hoofs of beasts trouble them.

14 Then will I make their waters deep, and cause their rivers to run like oil,' saith Lord (Adonai) יהוה.

15 When I shall make the land of Egypt (Mitsrayim) desolate, and the country shall be destitute of that whereof it was full, when I shall smite all them that dwell therein, then shall they know that I am יהוה.

16 This is the lamentation wherewith they shall lament her; the daughters of the nations shall lament her; they shall lament for her, even for Egypt (Mitsrayim), and for all her multitude, saith Lord (Adonai) יהוה."

17 It came to pass also in the twelfth year, in the fifteenth day of the month, that the word of יהוה

came unto me, saying:

18 "Son of man, wail for the multitude of Egypt (Mitsrayim), and cast them down, even her, and the daughters of the famous nations, unto the nether parts of the earth, with them that go down into the pit:

19 Whom dost you pass in beauty? Go down, and be you laid with the uncircumcised.'

20 They shall fall in the midst of them that are slain by the sword; she is delivered to the sword; draw her and all her multitudes.

21 The strong among the mighty shall speak to him out of the midst of sheol with them that help him: 'They are gone down, they lie uncircumcised, slain by the sword.'

22 Assyria (Asshur) is there and all her company; his graves are about him; all of them slain, fallen by the sword;

23 Whose graves are set in the sides of the pit, and her company is round about her grave; all of them slain, fallen by the sword, which caused terror in the land of the living.

24 There is Elam and all her multitude round about her grave, all of them slain, fallen by the sword, which are gone down uncircumcised into the nether parts of the earth, which caused their terror in the land of the living; yet have they borne their shame with them that go down to the pit.

25 They have set her a bed in the midst of the slain with all her multitude; her graves are round about him; all of them uncircumcised, slain by the sword; though their terror was caused in the land of the living, yet have they borne their shame with them that go down to the pit; he is put in the midst of them that be slain.

26 There is Meshech, Tubal, and all her multitude; her graves are round about him; all of them uncircumcised, slain by the sword, though they caused their terror in the land of the living.

27 And they shall not lie with the mighty that are fallen of the uncircumcised, who are gone down to hell (sheol) with their weapons of war; and they have laid their swords under their heads, but their iniquities shall be upon their bones, though they were the terror of the mighty in the land of the living.

28 Yea, you shalt be broken in the midst of the uncircumcised, and shalt lie with them that are slain with the sword.

29 There is Edom, her kings, and all her princes, which with their might are laid by them that were slain by the sword; they shall lie with the uncircumcised, and with them that go down to the pit.

30 There be the princes of the north, all of them, and all the Zidonians, which are gone down with the slain; with their terror they are ashamed of their might; and they lie uncircumcised with them that be slain by the sword, and bear their shame with them that go down to the pit.

31 Pharaoh (Paroh) shall see them, and shall be comforted over all his multitude, even Pharaoh (Paroh) and all his army slain by the sword," saith Lord (Adonai) יהוה.

32 For I have caused My terror in the land of the living; and he shall be laid in the midst of the uncircumcised with them that are slain with the sword, even Pharaoh (Paroh) and all his multitude," saith Lord (Adonai) יהוה.

33 Again the word of יהוה came unto me, saying,

2 "Son of man, speak to the children of your people, and say unto them: 'When I bring the sword upon a land, if the people of the land take a man of their coasts, and set him for their watchman.

3 If when he seeth the sword come upon the land, he blows the trumpet, and warn the people;

4 Then whosoever heareth the sound of the trumpet, and taketh not warning; if the sword come, and take him away, his blood shall be upon his own head.

5 He heard the sound of the trumpet, and took not warning; his blood shall be upon him. But he that taketh warning shall deliver his soul.

6 But if the watchman sees the sword come, and blow not the trumpet, and the people be not warned; if the sword come, and take any person from among them, he is taken away in his iniquity; but his blood will I require at the watchman's hand.'

7 So you, O son of man, I have set you a watchman unto the house of Yisrael; therefore you shalt hear the word at My mouth, and warn them from Me.

8 When I say unto the wicked, 'O wicked man, you shalt surely die; if you dost not speak to warn the wicked from his way, that wicked man shall die in his iniquity; but his blood will I require at your hand.

9 Nevertheless, if you warn the wicked of his

way to turn from it; if he does not turn from his way, he shall die in his iniquity; but you have delivered your soul.

10 Therefore, O you son of man, speak unto the house of Yisrael: 'Thus you speak, saying, "If our transgressions and our sins be upon us, and we pine away in them, how should we then live?"'

11 "Say unto them: 'As I live,' saith Lord (Adonai) יהוה, 'I have no pleasure in the death of the wicked; but that the wicked turn from his way and live; turn you, turn you from your evil ways; for why will you die, O house of Yisrael?'

12 "Therefore, you son of man, say unto the children of your people: 'The righteousness of the righteous shall not deliver him in the day of his transgression; as for the wickedness of the wicked, he shall not fall thereby in the day that he turneth from his wickedness; neither shall the righteous be able to live for his righteousness in the day that he sinneth.'

13 When I shall say to the righteous, that he shall surely live; if he trusts to his own righteousness, and commit iniquity, all his righteousnesses shall not be remembered; but for his iniquity that he hath committed, he shall die for it.

14 Again, when I say unto the wicked, 'You shalt surely die;' if he turns from his sin, and do that which is lawful and right;

15 If the wicked restore the pledge, give again that he had robbed, walk in the statutes of life, without committing iniquity; he shall surely live, he shall not die.

16 None of his sins that he hath committed shall be mentioned unto him: he hath done that which is lawful and right; he shall surely live.

17 Yet the children of your people say, 'The way of the Lord (Adonai) is not equal,' but as for them, their way is not equal.

18 When the righteous turneth from his righteousness, and committeth iniquity, he shall even die thereby.

19 But if the wicked turn from his wickedness, and do that which is lawful and right, he shall live thereby.

20 Yet you say, 'The way of the Lord (Adonai) is not equal.' O you house of Yisrael, I will judge you every one after his ways."

21 And it came to pass in the twelfth year of our captivity, in the tenth month, in the fifth day of the month, that one that had escaped out of Jerusalem (Yerushalayim) came unto me, saying, 'The city is smitten.'

22 Now the hand of יהוה was upon me in the evening, before he that was escaped came; and had opened my mouth, until He came to me in the morning; and my mouth was opened, and I was no more dumb.

23 Then the word of יהוה came unto me, saying:

24 "Son of man, they that inhabit those wastes of the land of Yisrael speak, saying, 'Avraham was one, and he inherited the land; but we are many; the land is given us for inheritance.'

25 Wherefore say unto them, 'Thus saith Lord (Adonai) יהוה: "You eat with the blood, and lift up your eyes toward your idols, and shed blood; and shall you possess the land?

26 You stand upon your sword, you work abomination, and you defile every one his neighbour's wife: and shall you possess the land?

27 Say you thus unto them, 'Thus saith Lord (Adonai) יהוה: "As I live, surely they that are in the wastes shall fall by the sword, and him that is in the open field will I give to the beasts to be devoured, and they that be in the forts and in the caves shall die of the pestilence.

28 For I will lay the land most desolate, and the pomp of her strength shall cease; and the mountains of Yisrael shall be desolate, that none shall pass through.

29 Then shall they know that I am יהוה, when I have laid the land most desolate because of all their abominations which they have committed.'"

30 Also, you son of man, the children of your people still are talking against you by the walls and in the doors of the houses, and speak one to another, every one to his brother, saying, 'Please come, and hear what is the word that cometh forth from יהוה.'

31 And they come unto you as the people cometh, and they sit before you as My people, and they hear your words, but they will not do them; for with their mouth they shew much love, but their heart goeth after their covetousness.

32 And, behold, you are unto them as a very lovely song of one that hath a pleasant voice, and can play well on an instrument; for they hear your words, but they do them not.

33 And when this cometh to pass, (behold, it will come,) then shall they know that a prophet

hath been among them."

34 And the word of יהוה came unto me, saying,

2 "Son of man, prophesy against the shepherds of Yisrael, prophesy, and say unto them, 'Thus saith Lord (Adonai) יהוה unto the shepherds: "Woe be to the shepherds of Yisrael that do feed themselves! Should not the shepherds feed the flocks?

3 You eat the fat, and you clothe you with the wool, you kill them that are fed; but you feed not the flock.

4 The diseased have you not strengthened, neither have you healed that which was sick, neither have you bound up that which was broken, neither have you brought again that which was driven away, neither have you sought that which was lost; but with force and with cruelty have you ruled them.

5 And they were scattered, because there is no shepherd; and they became meat to all the beasts of the field, when they were scattered.

6 My sheep wandered through all the mountains, and upon every high hill; yea, my flock was scattered upon all the face of the earth, and none did search or seek after them."

7 Therefore, you shepherds, hear the word of יהוה:

8 "As I live," saith Lord (Adonai) יהוה, "surely because My flock became a prey, and My flock became meat to every beast of the field, because there was no shepherd, neither did My shepherds search for My flock, but the shepherds fed themselves, and fed not My flock."

9 Therefore, O you shepherds, hear the word of יהוה:

10 Thus saith Lord (Adonai) יהוה: "Behold, I am against the shepherds; and I will require My flock at their hand, and cause them to cease from feeding the flock; neither shall the shepherds feed themselves any more; for I will deliver My flock from their mouth, that they may not be meat for them."

11 'For thus saith Lord (Adonai) יהוה: "Behold, I, even I, will both search My sheep, and seek them out.

12 As a shepherd seeketh out his flock in the day that he is among his sheep that are scattered; so will I seek out My sheep, and will deliver them out of all places where they have been scattered in the cloudy and dark day.

13 And I will bring them out from the people, and gather them from the countries, and will bring them to their own land, and feed them upon the mountains of Yisrael by the rivers, and in all the inhabited places of the country.

14 I will feed them in a good pasture, and upon the high mountains of Yisrael shall their fold be; there shall they lie in a good fold, and in a fat pasture shall they feed upon the mountains of Yisrael.

15 I will feed My flock, and I will cause them to lie down," saith Lord (Adonai) יהוה.

16 "I will seek that which was lost, and bring again that which was driven away, and will bind up that which was broken, and will strengthen that which was sick; but I will destroy the fat and the strong; I will feed them with judgment."

17 And as for you, O My flock, thus saith Lord (Adonai) יהוה: "Behold, I judge between cattle and cattle, between the rams and the he goats.

18 Seemeth it a small thing unto you to have eaten up the good pasture, but you must tread down with your feet the residue of your pastures? And to have drunk of the deep waters, but you must foul the residue with your feet?

19 And as for My flock, they eat that which you have trodden with your feet; and they drink that which you have fouled with your feet."

20 Therefore thus saith Lord (Adonai) יהוה unto them: "Behold, I, even I, will judge between the fat cattle and between the lean cattle.

21 Because you have thrust with side and with shoulder, and pushed all the diseased with your horns, till you have scattered them abroad;

22 Therefore will I save My flock, and they shall no more be a prey; and I will judge between cattle and cattle.

23 And I will set up one shepherd over them, and he shall feed them, even My servant Dawid; he shall feed them, and he shall be their shepherd.

24 And I יהוה will be their God (Elohim), and My servant Dawid a prince among them; I יהוה have spoken it.

25 And I will make with them a covenant of peace, and will cause the evil beasts to cease out of the land; and they shall dwell safely in the wilderness, and sleep in the woods.

26 And I will make them and the places round about my hill a blessing; and I will cause the shower to come down in his season; there shall be showers of blessing.

27 And the tree of the field shall yield her fruit, and the earth shall yield her increase, and they shall be safe in their land, and shall know that I am יהוה, when I have broken the bands of their yoke, and delivered them out of the hand of those that served themselves of them.

28 And they shall no more be a prey to the nations, neither shall the beast of the land devour them; but they shall dwell safely, and none shall make them afraid.

29 And I will raise up for them a plant of renown, and they shall be no more consumed with hunger in the land, neither bear the shame of the nations any more.

30 Thus shall they know that I יהוה their God (YHWH Eloheihem) am with them, and that they, even the house of Yisrael, are My people," saith Lord (Adonai) יהוה.'"

31 "And you My flock, the flock of My pasture, are men, and I am your God (Elohim)," saith Lord (Adonai) יהוה.'"

35 Moreover the word of יהוה came unto me, saying,

2 "Son of man, set your face against Mount Seir, and prophesy against it,

3 And say unto it, 'Thus saith Lord (Adonai) יהוה: "Behold, O Mount Seir, I am against you, and I will stretch out Mine hand against you, and I will make you most desolate.

4 I will lay your cities waste, and you shalt be desolate, and you shalt know that I am יהוה.

5 Because you have had a perpetual hatred, and hast shed the blood of the children of Yisrael by the force of the sword in the time of their disaster, in the time that their iniquity had an end;

6 "Therefore, as I live," saith Lord (Adonai) יהוה, "I will prepare you unto blood, and blood shall pursue you; sith you have not hated blood, even blood shall pursue you.

7 Thus will I make Mount Seir most desolate, and cut off from it him that passeth out and him that returneth.

8 And I will fill his mountains with his slain men; in your hills, and in your valleys, and in all your rivers, shall they fall that are slain with the sword.

9 I will make you perpetual desolations, and your cities shall not return; and you shall know that I am יהוה.

10 Because you have said, 'These two nations and these two countries shall be mine, and we will possess it;' whereas יהוה was there;

11 "Therefore, as I live," saith Lord (Adonai) יהוה, "I will even do according to your anger, and according to your envy which you have used out of your hatred against them; and I will make Myself known among them, when I have judged you.

12 And you shalt know that I am יהוה, and that I have heard all your blasphemies which you have spoken against the mountains of Yisrael, saying, 'They are laid desolate, they are given us to consume.'

13 Thus with your mouth you have boasted against Me, and have multiplied your words against Me: I have heard them."

14 Thus saith Lord (Adonai) יהוה: "When the whole earth rejoiceth, I will make you desolate.

15 As you didst rejoice at the inheritance of the house of Yisrael, because it was desolate, so will I do unto you; you shalt be desolate, O Mount Seir, and all Idumea, even all of it! And they shall know that I am יהוה.'"

36 "Also, you son of man, prophesy unto the mountains of Yisrael, and say, 'You mountains of Yisrael, hear the word of יהוה:

2 Thus saith Lord (Adonai) יהוה: "Because the enemy hath said against you, 'Aha! Even the ancient high places are ours in possession;'"

3 Therefore prophesy and say, 'Thus saith Lord (Adonai) יהוה: "Because they have made you desolate, and swallowed you up on every side, that you might be a possession unto the residue of the nations, and you are taken up in the lips of talkers, and are an infamy of the people;"

4 Therefore, you mountains of Yisrael, hear the word of Lord (Adonai) יהוה: Thus saith Lord (Adonai) יהוה to the mountains, and to the hills, to the rivers, and to the valleys, to the desolate wastes, and to the cities that are forsaken, which became a prey and derision to the residue of the nations that are round about;

5 Therefore thus saith Lord (Adonai) יהוה: "Surely in the fire of My jealousy have I spoken against the residue of the nations, and against all Idumea, which have appointed My land into their possession with the joy of all their heart, with despiteful minds, to cast it out for a prey.'"

6 Prophesy therefore concerning the land of Yisrael, and say unto the mountains, and to the hills, to the rivers, and to the valleys, 'Thus

saith Lord (Adonai) יהוה: "Behold, I have spoken in My jealousy and in My fury, because you have borne the shame of the nations."

7 Therefore thus saith Lord (Adonai) יהוה: "I have lifted up Mine hand, Surely the nations that are about you, they shall bear their shame.

8 But you, O mountains of Yisrael, you shall shoot forth your branches, and yield your fruit to My people of Yisrael; for they are at hand to come.

9 For, behold, I am for you, and I will turn unto you, and you shall be tilled and sown.

10 And I will multiply men upon you, all the house of Yisrael, even all of it; and the cities shall be inhabited, and the wastes shall be builded.

11 And I will multiply upon you man and beast; and they shall increase and bring fruit; and I will settle you after your old estates, and will do better unto you than at your beginnings; and you shall know that I am יהוה.

12 Yea, I will cause men to walk upon you, even My people Yisrael; and they shall possess you, and you shalt be their inheritance, and you shalt no more henceforth bereave them of men."

13 Thus saith Lord (Adonai) יהוה: "Because they say unto you, 'You land devourest up men, and hast bereaved your nations;'

14 Therefore you shalt devour men no more, neither bereave your nations any more," saith Lord (Adonai) יהוה.

15 "Neither will I cause men to hear in you the shame of the nations any more, neither shalt you bear the reproach of the people any more, neither shalt you cause your nations to fall any more," saith Lord (Adonai) יהוה.'"

16 Moreover the word of יהוה came unto me, saying:

17 "Son of man, when the house of Yisrael dwelt in their own land, they defiled it by their own way and by their doings; their way was before Me as the uncleanness of a removed woman.

18 Wherefore I poured My fury upon them for the blood that they had shed upon the land, and for their idols wherewith they had polluted it.

19 And I scattered them among the nations, and they were dispersed through the countries; according to their way and according to their doings I judged them.

20 And when they entered unto the nations, whither they went, they profaned My holy name, when they said to them, 'These are the people of יהוה, and are gone forth out of his land.'

21 But I had pity for Mine holy name, which the house of Yisrael had profaned among the nations, whither they went.

22 Therefore say unto the house of Yisrael, 'Thus saith Lord (Adonai) יהוה: "I do not this for your sakes, O house of Yisrael, but for Mine holy name's sake, which you have profaned among the nations, whither you went.

23 And I will sanctify My great name, which was profaned among the nations, which you have profaned in the midst of them; and the nations shall know that I am יהוה," saith Lord (Adonai) יהוה, "when I shall be sanctified in you before their eyes.

24 For I will take you from among the nations, and gather you out of all countries, and will bring you into your own land.

25 Then will I sprinkle clean water upon you, and you shall be clean; from all your filthiness, and from all your idols, will I cleanse you.

26 A new heart also will I give you, and a new spirit will I put within you; and I will take away the stony heart out of your flesh, and I will give you a heart of flesh.

27 And I will put My Spirit (Ruchi) within you, and cause you to walk in My statutes, and you shall keep My judgments, and do them.

28 And you shall dwell in the land that I gave to your fathers; and you shall be My people, and I will be your God (Elohim).

29 I will also save you from all your uncleannesses; and I will call for the corn, and will increase it, and lay no famine upon you.

30 And I will multiply the fruit of the tree, and the increase of the field, that you shall receive no more reproach of famine among the nations.

31 Then shall you remember your own evil ways, and your doings that were not good, and shall lothe yourselves in your own sight for your iniquities and for your abominations.

32 Not for your sakes do I this," saith Lord (Adonai) יהוה, "be it known unto you; be ashamed and confounded for your own ways, O house of Yisrael!"

33 Thus saith Lord (Adonai) יהוה: "In the day that I shall have cleansed you from all your iniquities I will also cause you to dwell in the cities, and the wastes shall be builded.

34 And the desolate land shall be tilled, whereas it lay desolate in the sight of all that passed by.

35 And they shall say, 'This land that was desolate is become like the garden of Eden; and the waste and desolate and ruined cities are become fenced, and are inhabited.'

36 Then the nations that are left round about you shall know that I יהוה build the ruined places, and plant that that was desolate. I, יהוה have spoken it, and I will do it."

37 Thus saith Lord (Adonai) יהוה: "I will yet for this be enquired of by the house of Yisrael, to do it for them: I will increase them with men like a flock.

38 As the holy flock, as the flock of Jerusalem (Yerushalayim) in her solemn feasts; so shall the waste cities be filled with flocks of men; and they shall know that I am יהוה.""""

37 The hand of יהוה was upon me, and carried me out in the Spirit (Ruach) of יהוה, and set me down in the midst of the valley which was full of bones,

2 And caused me to pass by them round about; and, behold, there were very many in the open valley; and, behold, they were very dry.

3 And He said unto me, "Son of man, can these bones live?" And I answered, "O Lord (Adonai) יהוה, You knowest."

4 Again He said unto me, "Prophesy upon these bones, and say unto them, 'O you dry bones, hear the word of יהוה.

5 Thus saith Lord (Adonai) יהוה unto these bones: "Behold, I will cause breath to enter into you, and you shall live.

6 And I will lay sinews upon you, and will bring up flesh upon you, and cover you with skin, and put breath in you, and you shall live; and you shall know that I am יהוה.""""

7 So I prophesied as I was command-ed; and as I prophesied, there was a noise, and behold a shaking, and the bones came together, bone to its bone.

8 And when I beheld, behold, the sinews and the flesh came up upon them, and the skin covered them above; but there was no breath in them.

9 Then said he unto me, "Prophesy unto the wind, prophesy, son of man, and say to the wind, 'Thus saith Lord (Adonai) יהוה: "Come from the four winds, O breath, and breathe upon these slain, that they may live.""""

10 So I prophesied as he commanded me, and the breath came into them, and they lived, and stood up upon their feet, an exceeding great army.

11 Then he said unto me, "Son of man, these bones are the whole house of Yisrael. Behold, they say, 'Our bones are dried, and our hope is lost; we are cut off for our parts.'

12 Therefore prophesy and say unto them, 'Thus saith Lord (Adonai) יהוה: "Behold, O My people, I will open your graves, and cause you to come up out of your graves, and bring you into the land of Yisrael.

13 And you shall know that I am יהוה, when I have opened your graves, O My people, and brought you up out of your graves,

14 And shall put My Spirit in you, and you shall live, and I shall place you in your own land; then shall you know that I יהוה have spoken it, and performed it," saith יהוה.

15 The word of יהוה came again unto me, saying,

16 "Moreover, you son of man, take you one stick, and write upon it, 'For Judah (Yehudah), and for the children of Yisrael his companions.' Then take another stick, and write upon it, 'For Joseph (Yosef), the stick of Efrayim, and for all the house of Yisrael his companions.'

17 And join them one to another into one stick; and they shall become one in your hand.

18 And when the children of your people shall speak unto you, saying, 'Wilt you not shew us what you meanest by these?'

19 Say unto them: "Thus saith Lord (Adonai) יהוה: "Behold, I will take the stick of Joseph (Yosef), which is in the hand of Efrayim, and the tribes of Yisrael his fellows, and will put them with him, with the stick of Judah (Yehudah), and make them one stick, and they shall be one in Mine hand.'"

20 And the sticks whereon you writest shall be in your hand before their eyes.

21 And say unto them, 'Thus saith Lord (Adonai) יהוה: "Behold, I will take the children of Yisrael from among the nations, whither they be gone, and will gather them on every side, and bring them into their own land;

22 And I will make them one nation in the land upon the mountains of Yisrael; and one king shall be king to them all; and they shall be no more two nations, neither shall they be divided into two kingdoms any more at all;

23 Neither shall they defile themselves any more with their idols, nor with their detestable things, nor with any of their transgressions; but I will save them out of all their dwellingplaces, wherein they have sinned, and will cleanse them; so shall they be My people, and I will be their God (Elohim).

24 And Dawid My servant shall be king over them; and they all shall have one shepherd; they shall also walk in My judgments, and observe My statutes, and do them.

25 And they shall dwell in the land that I have given unto Jacob (Yaaqov) My servant, wherein your fathers have dwelt; and they shall dwell therein, even they, and their children, and their children's children forever; and My servant Dawid shall be their prince forever.

26 Moreover I will make a covenant of peace with them; it shall be an everlasting covenant with them; and I will place them, and multiply them, and will set My sanctuary in the midst of them forevermore.

27 My tabernacle also shall be with them; yea, I will be their God (Elohim), and they shall be My people.

28 And the nations shall know that I יהוה do sanctify Yisrael, when My sanctuary shall be in the midst of them forevermore.""""

38 And the word of יהוה came unto me, saying,

2 "Son of man, set your face against Gog, the land of Magog, the chief prince of Meshech and Tubal, and prophesy against him,

3 And say, 'Thus saith Lord (Adonai) יהוה: "Behold, I am against you, O Gog, the chief prince of Meshech and Tubal.

4 And I will turn you back, and put hooks into your jaws, and I will bring you forth, and all your army, horses and horsemen, all of them clothed with all sorts of armour, even a great company with bucklers and shields, all of them handling swords.

5 Iran (Persia, Paras), Ethiopia (Kush), and Libya (Put) with them; all of them with shield and helmet;

6 Gomer, and all his bands; the house of Togarmah of the north quarters, and all his bands; and many people with you.

7 Be you prepared, and prepare for yourself, you, and all your company that are assembled unto you, and be you a guard unto them.

8 After many days you shalt be visited; in the latter years you shalt come into the land that is brought back from the sword, and is gathered out of many people, against the mountains of Yisrael, which have been always waste; but it is brought forth out of the nations, and they shall dwell safely all of them.

9 You shalt ascend and come like a storm, you shalt be like a cloud to cover the land, you, and all your bands, and many people with you."

10 Thus saith Lord (Adonai) יהוה: "It shall also come to pass, that at the same time shall things come into your mind, and you shalt think an evil thought:

11 And you shalt say, 'I will go up to the land of unwalled villages; I will go to them that are at rest, that dwell safely, all of them dwelling without walls, and having neither bars nor gates,'

12 To take a spoil, and to take a prey; to turn your hand upon the desolate places that are now inhabited, and upon the people that are gathered out of the nations, which have gotten cattle and goods, that dwell in the midst of the land.

13 Sheva, and Dedan, and the merchants of Tarshish, with all the young lions thereof, shall say unto you, Are you come to take a spoil? Have you gathered your company to take a prey? To carry away silver and gold, to take away cattle and goods, to take a great spoil?'"

14 Therefore, son of man, prophesy and say unto Gog, 'Thus saith Lord (Adonai) יהוה: "In that day when My people of Yisrael dwelleth safely, shalt you not know it?

15 And you shalt come from your place out of the north parts, you, and many people with you, all of them riding upon horses, a great company, and a mighty army.

16 And you shalt come up against My people of Yisrael, as a cloud to cover the land; it shall be in the latter days, and I will bring you against My land, that the nations may know Me, when I shall be sanctified in you, O Gog, before their eyes."

17 Thus saith Lord (Adonai) יהוה: "Are you he of whom I have spoken in old time by My servants the prophets of Yisrael, which prophesied in those days many years that I would bring you against them?

18 And it shall come to pass at the same time when Gog shall come against the land of

Yisrael," saith Lord (Adonai) יהוה, "that My fury shall come up in My face.

19 For in My jealousy and in the fire of My wrath have I spoken: 'Surely in that day there shall be a great shaking in the land of Yisrael;

20 So that the fishes of the sea, and the fowls of the heaven, and the beasts of the field, and all creeping things that creep upon the earth, and all the men that are upon the face of the earth, shall shake at my presence, and the mountains shall be thrown down, and the steep places shall fall, and every wall shall fall to the ground.'

21 "And I will call for a sword against him throughout all My mountains," saith Lord (Adonai) יהוה. "Every man's sword shall be against his brother.

22 And I will plead against him with pestilence and with blood; and I will rain upon him, and upon his bands, and upon the many people that are with him, an overflowing rain, and great hailstones, fire, and brimstone.

23 Thus will I magnify Myself, and sanctify Myself; and I will be known in the eyes of many nations, and they shall know that I am יהוה.'"

39 "Therefore, you Son of man, prophesy against Gog, and say, 'Thus saith Lord (Adonai) יהוה: "Behold, I am against you, O Gog, the chief prince of Meshech and Tubal;

2 And I will turn you back, and leave but the sixth part of you, and will cause you to come up from the north parts, and will bring you upon the mountains of Yisrael.

3 And I will smite your bow out of your left hand, and will cause your arrows to fall out of your right hand.

4 You shalt fall upon the mountains of Yisrael, you, and all your bands, and the people that is with you; I will give you unto the ravenous birds of every sort, and to the beasts of the field to be devoured.

5 You shalt fall upon the open field; for I have spoken it," saith Lord (Adonai) יהוה.

6 "And I will send a fire on Magog, and among them that dwell carelessly in the isles; and they shall know that I am יהוה.

7 So will I make My holy name known in the midst of My people Yisrael; and I will not let them pollute My holy name any more; and the nations shall know that I am יהוה, the Holy One in Yisrael.

8 Behold, it is come, and it is done," saith Lord

(Adonai) יהוה. "This is the day whereof I have spoken.

9 And they that dwell in the cities of Yisrael shall go forth, and shall set on fire and burn the weapons, both the shields and the bucklers, the bows and the arrows, and the handstaves, and the spears, and they shall burn them with fire seven years.

10 So that they shall take no wood out of the field, neither cut down any out of the forests; for they shall burn the weapons with fire; and they shall spoil those that spoiled them, and rob those that robbed them," saith Lord (Adonai) יהוה.

11 "And it shall come to pass in that day, that I will give unto Gog a place there of graves in Yisrael, the valley of the passengers on the east of the sea: and it shall stop the noses of the passengers: and there shall they bury Gog and all his multitude; and they shall call it 'The Valley of Hamon Gog'.

12 And seven months shall the house of Yisrael be burying of them, that they may cleanse the land.

13 Yea, all the people of the land shall bury them; and it shall be to them a renown the day that I shall be glorified," saith Lord (Adonai) יהוה.

14 "And they shall sever out men of continual employment, passing through the land to bury with the passengers those that remain upon the face of the earth, to cleanse it; after the end of seven months shall they search.

15 And the passengers that pass through the land, when any seeth a man's bone, then shall he set up a sign by it, till the buriers have buried it in the valley of Hamon Gog.

16 And also the name of the city shall be Hamonah. Thus shall they cleanse the land.'"

17 "And, you son of man, thus saith Lord (Adonai) יהוה: 'Speak unto every feathered fowl, and to every beast of the field: "Assemble yourselves, and come; gather yourselves on every side to My sacrifice that I do sacrifice for you, even a great sacrifice upon the mountains of Yisrael, that you may eat flesh, and drink blood.

18 You shall eat the flesh of the mighty, and drink the blood of the princes of the earth, of rams, of lambs, and of goats, of bullocks, all of them fatlings of Bashan.

19 And you shall eat fat till you be full, and drink blood till you be drunken, of My sacrifice which I have sacrificed for you.

20 Thus you shall be filled at My table with horses and chariots, with mighty men, and with all men of war," saith Lord (Adonai) יהוה.

21 "And I will set My glory among the nations, and all the nations shall see My judgment that I have executed, and My hand that I have laid upon them.

22 So the house of Yisrael shall know that I am יהוה their God (YHWH Eloheihem) from that day and forward.

23 And the nations shall know that the house of Yisrael went into captivity for their iniquity; because they trespassed against Me, therefore hid I My face from them, and gave them into the hand of their enemies; so fell they all by the sword.

24 According to their uncleanness and according to their transgressions have I done unto them, and hid My face from them.'"

25 "Therefore thus saith Lord (Adonai) יהוה: 'Now will I bring again the captivity of Jacob (Yaaqov), and have mercy upon the whole house of Yisrael, and will be jealous for My holy name;

26 After that they have borne their shame, and all their trespasses whereby they have trespassed against me, when they dwelt safely in their land, and none made them afraid.

27 When I have brought them again from the people, and gathered them out of their enemies' lands, and am sanctified in them in the sight of many nations;

28 Then shall they know that I am יהוה their God (YHWH Eloheihem), which caused them to be led into captivity among the nations, but I have gathered them unto their own land, and have left none of them any more there.

29 Neither will I hide My face any more from them; for I have poured out My Spirit (Ruchi) upon the house of Yisrael,' saith Lord (Adonai) יהוה."

40 In the five and twentieth year of our captivity, in the beginning of the year, in the tenth day of the month, in the fourteenth year after that the city was smitten, in the selfsame day the hand of יהוה was upon me, and brought me thither.

2 In the visions of God (Elohim) brought He me into the land of Yisrael, and set me upon a very high mountain, by which was as the frame of a city on the south.

3 And He brought me thither, and, behold, there was a man, whose appearance was like the appearance of brass, with a line of flax in his hand, and a measuring reed; and he stood in the gate.

4 And the man said unto me, "Son of man, behold with your eyes, and hear with your ears, and set your heart upon all that I shall shew you; for to the intent that I might shew them unto you are you brought hither; declare all that you seest to the house of Yisrael."

5 And behold a wall on the outside of the house round about, and in the man's hand a measuring reed of six cubits long by the cubit and a hand breadth; so he measured the breadth of the building, one reed; and the height, one reed.

6 Then came he unto the gate which looketh toward the east, and went up the stairs thereof, and measured the threshold of the gate, which was one reed broad; and the other threshold of the gate, which was one reed broad.

7 And every little chamber was one reed long, and one reed broad; and between the little chambers were five cubits; and the threshold of the gate by the porch of the gate within was one reed.

8 He measured also the porch of the gate within, one reed.

9 Then measured he the porch of the gate, eight cubits; and the posts thereof, two cubits; and the porch of the gate was inward.

10 And the little chambers of the gate eastward were three on this side, and three on that side; they three were of one measure; and the posts had one measure on this side and on that side.

11 And he measured the breadth of the entry of the gate, ten cubits; and the length of the gate, thirteen cubits.

12 The space also before the little chambers was one cubit on this side, and the space was one cubit on that side; and the little chambers were six cubits on this side, and six cubits on that side.

13 He measured then the gate from the roof of one little chamber to the roof of another: the breadth was five and twenty cubits, door against door.

14 He made also posts of threescore cubits, even

unto the post of the court round about the gate.

15 And from the face of the gate of the entrance unto the face of the porch of the inner gate were fifty cubits.

16 And there were narrow windows to the little chambers, and to their posts within the gate round about, and likewise to the arches; and windows were round about inward; and upon each post were palm trees.

17 Then brought he me into the outward court, and, behold, there were chambers, and a pavement made for the court round about; thirty chambers were upon the pavement.

18 And the pavement by the side of the gates opposite the length of the gates was the lower pavement.

19 Then he measured the breadth from the forefront of the lower gate unto the forefront of the inner court outside, a hundred cubits eastward and northward.

20 And the gate of the outward court that looked toward the north, he measured the length thereof, and the breadth thereof.

21 And the little chambers thereof were three on this side and three on that side; and the posts thereof and the arches thereof were after the measure of the first gate; the length thereof was fifty cubits, and the breadth five and twenty cubits.

22 And their windows, and their arches, and their palm trees, were after the measure of the gate that looketh toward the east; and they went up unto it by seven steps; and the arches thereof were before them.

23 And the gate of the inner court was opposite the gate toward the north, and toward the east; and he measured from gate to gate a hundred cubits.

24 After that he brought me toward the south, and behold a gate toward the south: and he measured the posts thereof and the arches thereof according to these measures.

25 And there were windows in it and in the arches thereof round about, like those windows; the length was fifty cubits, and the breadth five and twenty cubits.

26 And there were seven steps to go up to it, and the arches thereof were before them; and it had palm trees, one on this side, and another on that side, upon the posts thereof.

27 And there was a gate in the inner court toward the south; and he measured from gate to gate toward the south a hundred cubits.

28 And he brought me to the inner court by the south gate; and he measured the south gate according to these measures;

29 And the little chambers thereof, and the posts thereof, and the arches thereof, according to these measures; and there were windows in it and in the arches thereof round about; it was fifty cubits long, and five and twenty cubits broad.

30 And the arches round about were five and twenty cubits long, and five cubits broad.

31 And the arches thereof were toward the utter court; and palm trees were upon the posts thereof; and the going up to it had eight steps.

32 And he brought me into the inner court toward the east; and he measured the gate according to these measures.

33 And the little chambers thereof, and the posts thereof, and the arches thereof, were according to these measures; and there were windows therein and in the arches thereof round about: it was fifty cubits long, and five and twenty cubits broad.

34 And the arches thereof were toward the outward court; and palm trees were upon the posts thereof, on this side, and on that side; and the going up to it had eight steps.

35 And he brought me to the north gate, and measured it according to these measures;

36 The little chambers thereof, the posts thereof, and the arches thereof, and the windows to it round about; the length was fifty cubits, and the breadth five and twenty cubits.

37 And the posts thereof were toward the utter court; and palm trees were upon the posts thereof, on this side, and on that side; and the going up to it had eight steps.

38 And the chambers and the entries thereof were by the posts of the gates, where they washed the burnt offering.

39 And in the porch of the gate were two tables on this side, and two tables on that side, to slay thereon the burnt offering and the sin offering and the trespass offering.

40 And at the outer side, as one goeth up to the entry of the north gate, were two tables; and on the other side, which was at the porch of the gate, were two tables.

41 Four tables were on this side, and four tables

on that side, by the side of the gate; eight tables, whereupon they slew their sacrifices.

42 And the four tables were of hewn stone for the burnt offering, of a cubit and a half long, and a cubit and a half broad, and one cubit high: whereupon also they laid the instruments wherewith they slew the burnt offering and the sacrifice.

43 And within were hooks, a hand broad, fastened round about; and upon the tables was the flesh of the offering.

44 And outside the inner gate were the chambers of the singers in the inner court, which was at the side of the north gate; and their prospect was toward the south: one at the side of the east gate having the prospect toward the north.

45 And he said unto me, "This chamber, whose prospect is toward the south, is for the priests (kohanim), the keepers of the charge of the house.

46 And the chamber whose prospect is toward the north is for the priests (kohanim), the keepers of the charge of the altar; these are the sons of Zadok among the sons of Lewi, who come near to יהוה to minister unto Him."

47 So he measured the court, a hundred cubits long, and a hundred cubits broad, foursquare; and the altar that was before the house.

48 And he brought me to the porch of the house, and measured each post of the porch, five cubits on this side, and five cubits on that side; and the breadth of the gate was three cubits on this side, and three cubits on that side.

49 The length of the porch was twenty cubits, and the breadth eleven cubits; and he brought me by the steps whereby they went up to it; and there were pillars by the posts, one on this side, and another on that side.

41

Afterward he brought me to the temple, and measured the posts, six cubits broad on the one side, and six cubits broad on the other side, which was the breadth of the tabernacle.

2 And the breadth of the door was ten cubits; and the sides of the door were five cubits on the one side, and five cubits on the other side; and he measured the length thereof, forty cubits; and the breadth, twenty cubits.

3 Then went he inward, and measured the post of the door, two cubits; and the door, six cubits; and the breadth of the door, seven cubits.

4 So he measured the length thereof, twenty cubits; and the breadth, twenty cubits, before the temple; and he said unto me, "This is the most holy place."

5 After he measured the wall of the house, six cubits; and the breadth of every side chamber, four cubits, round about the house on every side.

6 And the side chambers were three, one over another, and thirty in order; and they entered into the wall which was of the house for the side chambers round about, that they might have hold, but they had not hold in the wall of the house.

7 And there was an enlarging, and a winding about still upward to the side chambers, for the winding about of the house went still upward round about the house; therefore the breadth of the house was still upward, and so increased from the lowest chamber to the highest by the midst.

8 I saw also the height of the house round about; the foundations of the side chambers were a full reed of six great cubits.

9 The thickness of the outer wall, which was for the side chamber, was five cubits; and that which was left was the place of the side chambers that were within.

10 And between the chambers was the wideness of twenty cubits round about the house on every side.

11 And the doors of the side chambers were toward the place that was left, one door toward the north, and another door toward the south: and the breadth of the place that was left was five cubits round about.

12 Now the building that was before the separate place at the end toward the west was seventy cubits broad; and the wall of the building was five cubits thick round about, and the length thereof ninety cubits.

13 So he measured the house, a hundred cubits long; and the separate place, and the building, with the walls thereof, a hundred cubits long;

14 Also the breadth of the face of the house, and of the separate place toward the east, a hundred cubits.

15 And he measured the length of the building opposite the separate place which was behind it, and the galleries thereof on the one side and on the other side, a hundred cubits, with the inner temple, and the porches of the court;

16 The door posts, and the narrow windows, and

the galleries round about on their three stories, opposite the door, cieled with wood round about, and from the ground up to the windows, and the windows were covered;

17 To that above the door, even unto the inner house, and outside, and by all the wall round about inside and outside, by measure.

18 And it was made with cherubims (keruvim) and palm trees, so that a palm tree was between a cherub (keruv) and a cherub (keruv); and every cherub (keruv) had two faces;

19 So that the face of a man was toward the palm tree on the one side, and the face of a young lion toward the palm tree on the other side; it was made through all the house round about.

20 From the ground unto above the door were cherubims (keruvim) and palm trees made, and on the wall of the temple.

21 The posts of the temple were squared, and the face of the sanctuary; the appearance of the one as the appearance of the other.

22 The altar of wood was three cubits high, and the length thereof two cubits; and the corners thereof, and the length thereof, and the walls thereof, were of wood: and he said unto me, "This is the table that is before יהוה."

23 And the temple and the sanctuary had two doors.

24 And the doors had two leaves apiece, two turning leaves; two leaves for the one door, and two leaves for the other door.

25 And there were made on them, on the doors of the temple, cherubims (keruvim) and palm trees, like as were made upon the walls; and there were thick planks upon the face of the porch outside.

26 And there were narrow windows and palm trees on the one side and on the other side, on the sides of the porch, and upon the side chambers of the house, and thick planks.

42 Then he brought me forth into the utter court, the way toward the north: and he brought me into the chamber that was opposite the separate place, and which was before the building toward the north.

2 Before the length of a hundred cubits was the north door, and the breadth was fifty cubits.

3 Over against the twenty cubits which were for the inner court, and opposite the pavement which was for the utter court, was gallery against gallery in three stories.

4 And before the chambers was a walk of ten cubits breadth inward, a way of one cubit; and their doors toward the north.

5 Now the upper chambers were shorter: for the galleries were higher than these, than the lower, and than the middlemost of the building.

6 For they were in three stories, but had not pillars as the pillars of the courts; therefore the building was straitened more than the lowest and the middlemost from the ground.

7 And the wall that was outside opposite the chambers, toward the utter court on the forepart of the chambers, the length thereof was fifty cubits.

8 For the length of the chambers that were in the utter court was fifty cubits; and, behold, before the temple were a hundred cubits.

9 And from under these chambers was the entry on the east side, as one goeth into them from the utter court.

10 The chambers were in the thickness of the wall of the court toward the east, opposite the separate place, and opposite the building.

11 And the way before them was like the appearance of the chambers which were toward the north, as long as they, and as broad as they; and all their goings out were both according to their fashions, and according to their doors.

12 And according to the doors of the chambers that were toward the south was a door in the head of the way, even the way directly before the wall toward the east, as one entereth into them.

13 Then said he unto me, "The north chambers and the south chambers, which are before the separate place, they be holy chambers, where the kohanim that approach unto יהוה shall eat the most holy things; there shall they lay the most holy things, and the meat offering, and the sin offering, and the trespass offering; for the place is holy.

14 When the kohanim enter therein, then shall they not go out of the holy place into the utter court, but there they shall lay their garments wherein they minister; for they are holy; and shall put on other garments, and shall approach to those things which are for the people."

15 Now when he had made an end of measuring the inner house, he brought me forth toward the gate whose prospect is toward the east, and

measured it round about.

16 He measured the east side with the measuring reed, five hundred reeds, with the measuring reed round about.

17 He measured the north side, five hundred reeds, with the measuring reed round about.

18 He measured the south side, five hundred reeds, with the measuring reed.

19 He turned about to the west side, and measured five hundred reeds with the measuring reed.

20 He measured it by the four sides; it had a wall round about, five hundred reeds long, and five hundred broad, to make a separation between the sanctuary and the profane place.

43 Afterward he brought me to the gate, even the gate that looketh toward the east:

2 And, behold, the glory of the God of Israel (Elohei Yisrael) came from the way of the east: and his voice was like a noise of many waters: and the earth shined with his glory.

3 And it was according to the appearance of the vision which I saw, even according to the vision that I saw when I came to destroy the city; and the visions were like the vision that I saw by the river Chebar; and I fell upon my face.

4 And the glory of יהוה came into the house by the way of the gate whose prospect is toward the east.

5 So the Spirit (Ruach) took me up, and brought me into the inner court; and, behold, the glory of יהוה filled the house.

6 And I heard Him speaking unto me out of the house; and the man stood by me.

7 And He said unto me, "Son of man, the place of My throne, and the place of the soles of My feet, where I will dwell in the midst of the children of Yisrael forever, and My holy name, shall the house of Yisrael no more defile, neither they, nor their kings, by their whoredom, nor by the carcases of their kings in their high places.

8 In their setting of their threshold by My thresholds, and their post by My posts, and the wall between Me and them, they have even defiled My holy name by their abominations that they have committed; wherefore I have consumed them in Mine anger.

9 Now let them put away their whoredom, and the carcases of their kings, far from Me, and I will dwell in the midst of them forever.

10 You son of man, shew the house to the house of Yisrael, that they may be ashamed of their iniquities; and let them measure the pattern.

11 And if they be ashamed of all that they have done, shew them the form of the house, and the fashion thereof, and the goings out thereof, and the comings in thereof, and all the forms thereof, and all the ordinances thereof, and all the forms thereof, and all the laws thereof; and write it in their sight, that they may keep the whole form thereof, and all the ordinances thereof, and do them.

12 This is the instruction (torah) for the house: Upon the top of the mountain the whole limit thereof round about shall be most holy. Behold, this is the instruction (torah) of the house.

13 And these are the measures of the altar after the cubits: The cubit is a cubit and a hand breadth; even the bottom shall be a cubit, and the breadth a cubit, and the border thereof by the edge thereof round about shall be a span; and this shall be the higher place of the altar.

14 And from the bottom upon the ground even to the lower settle shall be two cubits, and the breadth one cubit; and from the lesser settle even to the greater settle shall be four cubits, and the breadth one cubit.

15 So the altar shall be four cubits; and from the altar and upward shall be four horns.

16 And the altar shall be twelve cubits long, twelve broad, square in the four squares thereof.

17 And the settle shall be fourteen cubits long and fourteen broad in the four squares thereof; and the border about it shall be half a cubit; and the bottom thereof shall be a cubit about; and his stairs shall look toward the east."

18 And He said unto me, "Son of man, thus saith Lord (Adonai) יהוה: 'These are the ordinances of the altar in the day when they shall make it, to offer burnt offerings thereon, and to sprinkle blood thereon.

19 And you shalt give to the priests (kohanim) the Levites (Lewiyim) that be of the seed of Zadok, which approach unto me, to minister unto Me,' saith Lord (Adonai) יהוה, 'a young bullock for a sin offering.'

20 'And you shalt take of the blood thereof, and put it on the four horns of it, and on the four corners of the settle, and upon the border round about; thus shalt you cleanse and purge it.

21 You shalt take the bullock also of the sin offering, and he shall burn it in the appointed

place of the house, outside the sanctuary.

22 And on the second day you shalt offer a kid of the goats without blemish for a sin offering; and they shall cleanse the altar, as they did cleanse it with the bullock.

23 When you have made an end of cleansing it, you shalt offer a young bullock without blemish, and a ram out of the flock without blemish.

24 And you shalt offer them before יהוה, and the priests (kohanim) shall cast salt upon them, and they shall offer them up for a burnt offering unto יהוה.

25 Seven days shalt you prepare every day a goat for a sin offering; they shall also prepare a young bullock, and a ram out of the flock, without blemish.

26 Seven days shall they purge the altar and purify it; and they shall consecrate themselves.

27 And when these days are expired, it shall be, that upon the eighth day, and so forward, the priests (kohanim) shall make your burnt offerings upon the altar, and your peace offerings; and I will accept you,' saith Lord (Adonai) יהוה."

44 Then He brought me back the way of the gate of the outward sanctuary which looketh toward the east; and it was shut.

2 Then said יהוה unto me, "This gate shall be shut, it shall not be opened, and no man shall enter in by it, because יהוה, the God of Israel (Elohei Yisrael), hath entered in by it, therefore it shall be shut.

3 It is for the prince; the prince, he shall sit in it to eat bread before יהוה; he shall enter by the way of the porch of that gate, and shall go out by the way of the same."

4 Then brought He me the way of the north gate before the house; and I looked, and, behold, the glory of יהוה filled the house of יהוה; and I fell upon my face.

5 And יהוה said unto me, "Son of man, mark well, and behold with your eyes, and hear with your ears all that I say unto you concerning all the ordinances of the house of יהוה, and all the instructions (torot) thereof; and mark well the entering in of the house, with every going forth of the sanctuary.

6 And you shalt say to the rebellious, even to the house of Yisrael, 'Thus saith Lord (Adonai) יהוה: "O you house of Yisrael, let it suffice you of all your abominations,

7 In that you have brought into My sanctuary strangers, uncircumcised in heart, and uncircumcised in flesh, to be in My sanctuary, to pollute it, even My house, when you offer My bread, the fat and the blood, and they have broken My covenant because of all your abominations.

8 And you have not kept the charge of Mine holy things; but you have set keepers of My charge in My sanctuary for yourselves."

9 Thus saith Lord (Adonai) יהוה: "No stranger, uncircumcised in heart, nor uncircumcised in flesh, shall enter into My sanctuary, of any stranger that is among the children of Yisrael.

10 And the Levites (Lewiyim) that are gone away far from Me, when Yisrael went astray, which went astray away from Me after their idols; they shall even bear their iniquity.

11 Yet they shall be ministers in My sanctuary, having charge at the gates of the house, and ministering to the house; they shall slay the burnt offering and the sacrifice for the people, and they shall stand before them to minister unto them.

12 Because they ministered unto them before their idols, and caused the house of Yisrael to fall into iniquity; therefore have I lifted up Mine hand against them," saith Lord (Adonai) יהוה, "and they shall bear their iniquity.

13 And they shall not come near unto Me, to do the office of a priest (kohen) unto Me, nor to come near to any of My holy things, in the most holy place; but they shall bear their shame, and their abominations which they have committed.

14 But I will make them keepers of the charge of the house, for all the service thereof, and for all that shall be done therein.

15 But the priests (kohanim) the Levites (Lewiyim), the sons of Zadok, that kept the charge of My sanctuary when the children of Yisrael went astray from Me, they shall come near to Me to minister unto Me, and they shall stand before Me to offer unto Me the fat and the blood," saith Lord (Adonai) יהוה:

16 "They shall enter into My sanctuary, and they shall come near to My table, to minister unto Me, and they shall keep My charge.

17 And it shall come to pass, that when they enter in at the gates of the inner court, they shall be clothed with linen garments; and no wool shall come upon them, whiles they minister in

the gates of the inner court, and within.

18 They shall have linen bonnets upon their heads, and shall have linen breeches upon their loins; they shall not gird themselves with any thing that causeth sweat.

19 And when they go forth into the utter court, even into the utter court to the people, they shall put off their garments wherein they ministered, and lay them in the holy chambers, and they shall put on other garments; and they shall not sanctify the people with their garments.

20 Neither shall they shave their heads, nor allow their locks to grow long; they shall only poll their heads.

21 Neither shall any priest (kohen) drink wine, when they enter into the inner court.

22 Neither shall they take for their wives a widow, nor her that is put away; but they shall take maidens of the seed of the house of Yisrael, or a widow that had a kohen before.

23 And they shall teach My people the difference between the holy and profane, and cause them to discern between the unclean and the clean.

24 And in controversy they shall stand in judgment; and they shall judge it according to My judgments; and they shall keep My laws (torot) and My statutes in all Mine assemblies; and they shall hallow My Shabbats.

25 And they shall come at no dead person to defile themselves; but for father, or for mother, or for son, or for daughter, for brother, or for sister that hath had no husband, they may defile themselves.

26 And after he is cleansed, they shall reckon unto him seven days.

27 And in the day that he goeth into the sanctuary, unto the inner court, to minister in the sanctuary, he shall offer his sin offering," saith Lord (Adonai) יהוה.

28 And it shall be unto them for an inheritance. I am their inheritance; and you shall give them no possession in Yisrael; I am their possession.

29 They shall eat the meat offering, and the sin offering, and the trespass offering; and every dedicated thing in Yisrael shall be theirs.

30 And the first of all the firstfruits of all things, and every oblation of all, of every sort of your oblations, shall be the priest (kohen)'s; you shall also give unto the priest (kohen) the first of your dough, that he may cause the blessing to rest in your house.

31 The priests (kohanim) shall not eat of any thing that is dead of itself, or torn, whether it be fowl or beast.

45 "Moreover, when you shall divide by lot the land for inheritance, you shall offer an oblation unto יהוה, an holy portion of the land; the length shall be the length of five and twenty thousand reeds, and the breadth shall be ten thousand. This shall be holy in all the borders thereof round about.

2 Of this there shall be for the sanctuary five hundred in length, with five hundred in breadth, square round about; and fifty cubits round about for the suburbs thereof.

3 And of this measure shalt you measure the length of five and twenty thousand, and the breadth of ten thousand: and in it shall be the sanctuary and the most holy place.

4 The holy portion of the land shall be for the priests (kohanim) the ministers of the sanctuary, which shall come near to minister unto יהוה; and it shall be a place for their houses, and a holy place for the sanctuary.

5 And the five and twenty thousand of length, and the ten thousand of breadth, shall also the Levites (Lewiyim), the ministers of the house, have for themselves, for a possession for twenty chambers.

6 And you shall appoint the possession of the city five thousand broad, and five and twenty thousand long, opposite the oblation of the holy portion; it shall be for the whole house of Yisrael.

7 And a portion shall be for the prince on the one side and on the other side of the oblation of the holy portion, and of the possession of the city, before the oblation of the holy portion, and before the possession of the city, from the west side westward, and from the east side eastward; and the length shall be opposite one of the portions, from the west border unto the east border.

8 In the land shall be his possession in Yisrael; and My princes shall no more oppress My people; and the rest of the land shall they give to the house of Yisrael according to their tribes."

9 Thus saith Lord (Adonai) יהוה: "Let it suffice you, O princes of Yisrael; remove violence and spoil, and execute judgment and justice, take away your exactions from My people," saith Lord (Adonai) יהוה.

10 "You shall have just balances, and a just ephah, and a just bath.

11 The ephah and the bath shall be of one measure, that the bath may contain the tenth part of a homer, and the ephah the tenth part of a homer: the measure thereof shall be after the homer.

12 And the shekel shall be twenty gerahs: twenty shekels, five and twenty shekels, fifteen shekels, shall be your maneh.

13 This is the oblation that you shall offer; the sixth part of an ephah of a homer of wheat, and you shall give the sixth part of an ephah of a homer of barley.

14 Concerning the ordinance of oil, the bath of oil, you shall offer the tenth part of a bath out of the cor, which is a homer of ten baths; for ten baths are a homer.

15 And one lamb out of the flock, out of two hundred, out of the fat pastures of Yisrael; for a meat offering, and for a burnt offering, and for peace offerings, to make reconciliation for them," saith Lord (Adonai) יהוה.

16 "All the people of the land shall give this oblation for the prince in Yisrael.

17 And it shall be the prince's part to give burnt offerings, and meat offerings, and drink offerings, in the Feasts, and in the New Moons, and in the Shabbats, in all solemnities of the house of Yisrael. He shall prepare the sin offering, and the meat offering, and the burnt offering, and the peace offerings, to make reconciliation for the house of Yisrael."

18 Thus saith Lord (Adonai) יהוה: "In the first month, in the first day of the month, you shalt take a young bullock without blemish, and cleanse the sanctuary:

19 And the priest (kohen) shall take of the blood of the sin offering, and put it upon the posts of the house, and upon the four corners of the settle of the altar, and upon the posts of the gate of the inner court.

20 And so you shalt do the seventh day of the month for every one that erreth, and for him that is simple; so shall you reconcile the house.

21 In the first month, in the fourteenth day of the month, you shall have the Pesach, a feast of seven days; unleavened bread shall be eaten.

22 And upon that day shall the prince prepare for himself and for all the people of the land a bullock for a sin offering.

23 And seven days of the feast he shall prepare a burnt offering to יהוה, seven bullocks and seven rams without blemish daily the seven days; and a kid of the goats daily for a sin offering.

24 And he shall prepare a meat offering of an ephah for a bullock, and an ephah for a ram, and an hin of oil for an ephah.

25 In the seventh month, in the fifteenth day of the month, shall he do the like in the feast of the seven days, according to the sin offering, according to the burnt offering, and according to the meat offering, and according to the oil."

46 Thus saith Lord (Adonai) יהוה: "The gate of the inner court that looketh toward the east shall be shut the six working days; but on the Shabbat it shall be opened, and in the day of the New Moon it shall be opened.

2 And the prince shall enter by the way of the porch of that gate outside, and shall stand by the post of the gate, and the priests (kohanim) shall prepare his burnt offering and his peace offerings, and he shall worship at the threshold of the gate; then he shall go forth; but the gate shall not be shut until the evening.

3 Likewise the people of the land shall worship at the door of this gate before יהוה in the Shabbats and in the New Moons.

4 And the burnt offering that the prince shall offer unto יהוה in the Shabbat day shall be six lambs without blemish, and a ram without blemish.

5 And the meat offering shall be an ephah for a ram, and the meat offering for the lambs as he shall be able to give, and a hin of oil to an ephah.

6 And in the day of the new moon it shall be a young bullock without blemish, and six lambs, and a ram; they shall be without blemish.

7 And he shall prepare a meat offering, an ephah for a bullock, and an ephah for a ram, and for the lambs according as his hand shall attain unto, and a hin of oil to an ephah.

8 And when the prince shall enter, he shall go in by the way of the porch of that gate, and he shall go forth by the way thereof.

9 But when the people of the land shall come before יהוה in the solemn feasts, he that entereth in by the way of the north gate to worship shall go out by the way of the south gate; and he that entereth by the way of the south gate shall go forth by the way of the north gate; he shall not

return by the way of the gate whereby he came in, but shall go forth opposite it.

10 And the prince in the midst of them, when they go in, shall go in; and when they go forth, shall go forth.

11 And in the feasts and in the solemnities the meat offering shall be an ephah to a bullock, and an ephah to a ram, and to the lambs as he is able to give, and a hin of oil to an ephah.

12 Now when the prince shall prepare a voluntary burnt offering or peace offerings voluntarily unto יהוה, one shall then open him the gate that looketh toward the east, and he shall prepare his burnt offering and his peace offerings, as he did on the Shabbat day; then he shall go forth; and after his going forth one shall shut the gate.

13 You shalt daily prepare a burnt offering unto יהוה of a lamb of the first year without blemish; you shalt prepare it every morning.

14 And you shalt prepare a meat offering for it every morning, the sixth part of an ephah, and the third part of an hin of oil, to temper with the fine flour; a meat offering continually by a perpetual ordinance unto יהוה.

15 Thus shall they prepare the lamb, and the meat offering, and the oil, every morning for a continual burnt offering."

16 Thus saith Lord (Adonai) יהוה: "If the prince gives a gift unto any of his sons, the inheritance thereof shall be his sons'; it shall be their possession by inheritance.

17 But if he gives a gift of his inheritance to one of his servants, then it shall be his to the year of liberty; after it shall return to the prince; but his inheritance shall be his sons' for them.

18 Moreover the prince shall not take of the people's inheritance by oppression, to thrust them out of their possession; but he shall give his sons inheritance out of his own possession; that my people be not scattered every man from his possession.""""

19 After he brought me through the entry, which was at the side of the gate, into the holy chambers of the priests (kohanim), which looked toward the north; and, behold, there was a place on the two sides westward.

20 Then said he unto me, "This is the place where the kohanim shall boil the trespass offering and the sin offering, where they shall bake the meat offering; that they bear them not

out into the utter court, to sanctify the people.

21 Then he brought me forth into the utter court, and caused me to pass by the four corners of the court; and, behold, in every corner of the court there was a court.

22 In the four corners of the court there were courts joined of forty cubits long and thirty broad; these four corners were of one measure.

23 And there was a row of building round about in them, round about them four, and it was made with boiling places under the rows round about.

24 Then said he unto me, "These are the places of them that boil, where the ministers of the house shall boil the sacrifice of the people."

47 Afterward he brought me again unto the door of the house; and, behold, waters issued out from under the threshold of the house eastward: for the forefront of the house stood toward the east, and the waters came down from under from the right side of the house, at the south side of the altar.

2 Then brought he me out of the way of the gate northward, and led me about the way outside unto the utter gate by the way that looketh eastward; and, behold, there ran out waters on the right side.

3 And when the man that had the line in his hand went forth eastward, he measured a thousand cubits, and he brought me through the waters; the waters were to the ankles.

4 Again he measured a thousand, and brought me through the waters; the waters were to the knees. Again he measured a thousand, and brought me through; the waters were to the loins.

5 Afterward he measured a thousand; and it was a river that I could not pass over; for the waters were risen, waters to swim in, a river that could not be passed over.

6 And he said unto me, "Son of man, have you seen this?" Then he brought me, and caused me to return to the brink of the river.

7 Now when I had returned, behold, at the bank of the river were very many trees on the one side and on the other.

8 Then said he unto me: "These waters issue out toward the east country, and go down into the desert, and go into the sea: which being brought forth into the sea, the waters shall be healed.

9 And it shall come to pass, that every thing that liveth, which moveth, whithersoever the rivers

shall come, shall live; and there shall be a very great multitude of fish, because these waters shall come thither; for they shall be healed; and every thing shall live whither the river cometh. 10 And it shall come to pass, that the fishers shall stand upon it from Engedi even unto Eneglaim; they shall be a place to spread forth nets; their fish shall be according to their kinds, as the fish of the great sea, exceeding many.

11 But the miry places thereof and the marishes thereof shall not be healed; they shall be given to salt.

12 And by the river upon the bank thereof, on this side and on that side, shall grow all trees for meat, whose leaf shall not fade, neither shall the fruit thereof be consumed; it shall bring forth new fruit according to his months, because their waters they issued out of the sanctuary; and the fruit thereof shall be for meat, and the leaf thereof for medicine."

13 Thus saith Lord (Adonai) יהוה: "This shall be the border, whereby you shall inherit the land according to the twelve tribes of Yisrael. Joseph (Yosef) shall have two portions.

14 And you shall inherit it, one as well as another: concerning the which I lifted up mine hand to give it unto your fathers; and this land shall fall unto you for inheritance.

15 And this shall be the border of the land toward the north side, from the great sea, the way of Hethlon, as men go to Zedad;

16 Hamath, Berothah, Sibraim, which is between the border of Damascus (Dammeseq) and the border of Hamath; Hazarhatticon, which is by the coast of Hauran.

17 And the border from the sea shall be Hazarenan, the border of Damascus (Dammeseq), and the north northward, and the border of Hamath. And this is the north side.

18 And the east side you shall measure from Hauran, and from Damascus (Dammeseq), and from Gilad, and from the land of Yisrael by Jordan (Yarden), from the border unto the east sea. And this is the east side.

19 And the south side southward, from Tamar even to the waters of strife in Qadesh, the river to the great sea. And this is the south side southward.

20 The west side also shall be the great sea from the border, till a man come opposite Hamath. This is the west side.

21 So shall you divide this land unto you according to the tribes of Yisrael.

22 And it shall come to pass, that you shall divide it by lot for an inheritance unto you, and to the strangers that sojourn among you, which shall beget children among you; and they shall be unto you as born in the country among the children of Yisrael; they shall have inheritance with you among the tribes of Yisrael.

23 And it shall come to pass, that in what tribe the stranger sojourneth, there shall you give him his inheritance," saith Lord (Adonai) יהוה.

48 Now these are the names of the tribes. From the north end to the coast of the way of Hethlon, as one goeth to Hamath, Hazarenan, the border of Damascus (Dammeseq) northward, to the coast of Hamath; for these are his sides east and west; a portion for Dan.

2 And by the border of Dan, from the east side unto the west side, a portion for Asher.

3 And by the border of Asher, from the east side even unto the west side, a portion for Naftali.

4 And by the border of Naftali, from the east side unto the west side, a portion for Menashsheh.

5 And by the border of Menashsheh, from the east side unto the west side, a portion for Efrayim.

6 And by the border of Efrayim, from the east side even unto the west side, a portion for Reuven.

7 And by the border of Reuven, from the east side unto the west side, a portion for Judah (Yehudah).

8 And by the border of Judah (Yehudah), from the east side unto the west side, shall be the offering which you shall offer of five and twenty thousand reeds in breadth, and in length as one of the other parts, from the east side unto the west side; and the sanctuary shall be in the midst of it.

9 The oblation that you shall offer unto יהוה shall be of five and twenty thousand in length, and of ten thousand in breadth.

10 And for them, even for the kohanim, shall be this holy oblation; toward the north five and twenty thousand in length, and toward the west ten thousand in breadth, and toward the east ten thousand in breadth, and toward the south five and twenty thousand in length; and the sanctuary of יהוה shall be in the midst thereof.

11 It shall be for the priests (kohanim) that

are sanctified of the sons of Zadok; who have kept My charge, who went not astray when the children of Yisrael went astray, as the Levites (Lewiyim) went astray.

12 And this oblation of the land that is offered shall be unto them a thing most holy by the border of the Levites (Lewiyim).

13 And opposite the border of the kohanim the Levites (Lewiyim) shall have five and twenty thousand in length, and ten thousand in breadth; all the length shall be five and twenty thousand, and the breadth ten thousand.

14 And they shall not sell of it, neither exchange, nor alienate the firstfruits of the land; for it is holy unto יהוה.

15 And the five thousand, that are left in the breadth opposite the five and twenty thousand, shall be a profane place for the city, for dwelling, and for suburbs; and the city shall be in the midst thereof.

16 And these shall be the measures thereof; the north side four thousand and five hundred, and the south side four thousand and five hundred, and on the east side four thousand and five hundred, and the west side four thousand and five hundred.

17 And the suburbs of the city shall be toward the north two hundred and fifty, and toward the south two hundred and fifty, and toward the east two hundred and fifty, and toward the west two hundred and fifty.

18 And the residue in length opposite the oblation of the holy portion shall be ten thousand eastward, and ten thousand westward; and it shall be opposite the oblation of the holy portion; and the increase thereof shall be for food unto them that serve the city.

19 And they that serve the city shall serve it out of all the tribes of Yisrael.

20 All the oblation shall be five and twenty thousand by five and twenty thousand: you shall offer the holy oblation foursquare, with the possession of the city.

21 And the residue shall be for the prince, on the one side and on the other of the holy oblation, and of the possession of the city, opposite the five and twenty thousand of the oblation toward the east border, and westward opposite the five and twenty thousand toward the west border, opposite the portions for the prince; and it shall be the holy oblation; and the sanctuary of the house shall be in the midst thereof.

22 Moreover from the possession of the Levites (Lewiyim), and from the possession of the city, being in the midst of that which is the prince's, between the border of Judah (Yehudah) and the border of Benjamin (Binyamin), shall be for the prince.

23 As for the rest of the tribes, from the east side unto the west side, Benjamin (Binyamin) shall have a portion.

24 And by the border of Benjamin (Binyamin), from the east side unto the west side, Shimon shall have a portion.

25 And by the border of Shimon, from the east side unto the west side, Yissaskhar a portion.

26 And by the border of Yissaskhar, from the east side unto the west side, Zevulun a portion.

27 And by the border of Zevulun, from the east side unto the west side, Gad a portion.

28 And by the border of Gad, at the south side southward, the border shall be even from Tamar unto the waters of strife in Qadesh, and to the river toward the great sea.

29 This is the land which you shall divide by lot unto the tribes of Yisrael for inheritance, and these are their portions," saith Lord (Adonai) יהוה.

30 And these are the goings out of the city on the north side, four thousand and five hundred measures.

31 And the gates of the city shall be after the names of the tribes of Yisrael; three gates northward; one gate of Reuven, one gate of Judah (Yehudah), one gate of Lewi;

32 And at the east side four thousand and five hundred; and three gates; and one gate of Joseph (Yosef), one gate of Benjamin (Binyamin), one gate of Dan;

33 And at the south side four thousand and five hundred measures; and three gates; one gate of Shimon, one gate of Yissaskhar, one gate of Zevulun;

34 At the west side four thousand and five hundred, with their three gates; one gate of Gad, one gate of Asher, one gate of Naftali.

35 It was round about eighteen thousand measures; and the name of the city from that day shall be: [A7]"יהוה Shammah (YHWH Is There)".

DANIEL
DANIYEL דָּנִיֵאל
(El is my Judge)

1 In the third year of the reign of Yehoyaqim king of Judah (Yehudah) came Nebuchadnezzar king of Babylon (Bavel) unto Jerusalem (Yerushalayim), and besieged it.

2 And the Lord (Adonai) gave Yehoyaqim king of Judah (Yehudah) into his hand, with part of the vessels of the house of God (Elohim); which he carried into the land of Shinar to the house of his god (el); and he brought the vessels into the treasure house of his god (el).

3 And the king spake unto Ashpenaz the master of his eunuchs, that he should bring certain of the children of Yisrael, and of the king's seed, and of the princes;

4 Children in whom was no blemish, but well favoured, and skilful in all wisdom, and cunning in knowledge, and understanding science, and such as had ability in them to stand in the king's palace, and whom they might teach the learning and the tongue of the Chaldeans.

5 And the king appointed them a daily provision of the king's meat, and of the wine which he drank; so nourishing them three years, that at the end thereof they might stand before the king.

6 Now among these were of the children of Judah (Yehudah); A54Daniel, Chananyah, Mishael, and Azaryah,

7 Unto whom the prince of the eunuchs gave names: for he gave unto Daniel the name of Belteshazzar; and to Chananyah, of Shadrach; and to Mishael, of Meshach; and to Azaryah, of Abednego.

8 But Daniel purposed in his heart that he would not defile himself with the portion of the king's meat, nor with the wine which he drank; therefore he requested of the prince of the eunuchs that he might not defile himself.

9 Now God (Elohim) had brought Daniel into favor and tender love with the prince of the eunuchs.

10 And the prince of the eunuchs said unto Daniel, "I fear my lord (adoni) the king, who hath appointed your meat and your drink; for why should he see your faces worse liking than the children which are of your sort? Then shall you make me endanger my head to the king."

11 Then said Daniel to Melzar, whom the prince of the eunuchs had set over Daniel, Chananyah, Mishael, and Azaryah,

12 "Prove your servants, I beseech you, ten days; and let them give us pulse to eat, and water to drink.

13 Then let our countenances be looked upon before you, and the countenance of the children that eat of the portion of the king's meat; and as you seest, deal with your servants."

14 So he consented to them in this matter, and proved them ten days.

15 And at the end of ten days their countenances appeared fairer and fatter in flesh than all the children which did eat the portion of the king's meat.

16 Thus Melzar took away the portion of their meat, and the wine that they should drink; and gave them pulse.

17 As for these four children, God (Elohim) gave them knowledge and skill in all learning and wisdom; and Daniel had understanding in all visions and dreams.

18 Now at the end of the days that the king had said he should bring them in, then the prince of the eunuchs brought them in before Nebuchadnezzar.

19 And the king communed with them; and among them all was found none like Daniel, Chananyah, Mishael, and Azaryah; therefore stood they before the king.

20 And in all matters of wisdom and understanding, that the king enquired of them, he found them ten times better than all the magicians and astrologers that were in all his realm.

21 And Daniel continued even unto the first year of King Cyrus.

2 And in the second year of the reign of Nebuchadnezzar, Nebuchadnezzar dreamed dreams, wherewith his spirit was troubled, and his sleep broke from him.

2 Then the king commanded to call the magicians, and the astrologers, and the sorcerers, and the Chaldeans, for to shew the king his dreams. So they came and stood before the king.

3 And the king said unto them, I have dreamed a dream, and my spirit was troubled to know the dream.

4 Then spake the Chaldeans to the king in

Syriack (Aramit), "O king, live forever; tell your servants the dream, and we will shew the interpretation."

5 The king answered and said to the Chaldeans, "The thing is gone from me; if you will not make known unto me the dream, with the interpretation thereof, you shall be cut in pieces, and your houses shall be made a dunghill.

6 But if you shew the dream, and the interpretation thereof, you shall receive of me gifts and rewards and great honor; therefore shew me the dream, and the interpretation thereof."

7 They answered again and said, "Let the king tell his servants the dream, and we will shew the interpretation of it."

8 The king answered and said, "I know of certainty that you would gain the time, because you see the thing is gone from me.

9 But if you will not make known unto me the dream, there is but one decree for you; for you have prepared lying and corrupt words to speak before me, till the time be changed; therefore tell me the dream, and I shall know that you can shew me the interpretation thereof.

10 The Chaldeans answered before the king, and said, "There is not a man upon the earth that can shew the king's matter; therefore there is no king, lord (adon), nor ruler, that asked such things at any magician, or astrologer, or Chaldean.

11 And it is a rare thing that the king requireth, and there is none other that can shew it before the king, except the gods (elohim), whose dwelling is not with flesh."

12 For this cause the king was angry and very furious, and commanded to destroy all the wise men of Babylon (Bavel).

13 And the decree went forth that the wise men should be slain; and they sought Daniel and his fellows to be slain.

14 Then Daniel answered with counsel and wisdom to Arioch the captain of the king's guard, which was gone forth to slay the wise men of Babylon (Bavel);

15 He answered and said to Arioch the king's captain, "Why is the decree so hasty from the king?" Then Arioch made the thing known to Daniel.

16 Then Daniel went in, and desired of the king that he would give him time, and that he would shew the king the interpretation.

17 Then Daniel went to his house, and made the thing known to Chananyah, Mishael, and Azaryah, his companions,

18 That they would desire mercies of the [B5a]God (Elah) of heaven concerning this secret; that Daniel and his fellows should not perish with the rest of the wise men of Babylon (Bavel).

19 Then was the secret revealed unto Daniel in a night vision. Then Daniel blessed the God (Elah) of heaven.

20 Daniel answered and said: "Blessed be the name of God (Elah) forever and ever, for wisdom and might are His.

21 And He changeth the times and the seasons: He removeth kings, and setteth up kings; He giveth wisdom unto the wise, and knowledge to them that know understanding.

22 He revealeth the deep and secret things; He knoweth what is in the darkness, and the light dwelleth with him.

23 I thank You, and praise You, O You God (Elah) of my fathers, who hast given me wisdom and might, and hast made known unto me now what we desired of You; for You have now made known unto us the king's matter."

24 Therefore Daniel went in unto Arioch, whom the king had ordained to destroy the wise men of Babylon (Bavel); he went and said thus unto him: "Destroy not the wise men of Babylon (Bavel); bring me in before the king, and I will shew unto the king the interpretation."

25 Then Arioch brought in Daniel before the king in haste, and said thus unto him, "I have found a man of the captives of Judah (Yehudah), that will make known unto the king the interpretation."

26 The king answered and said to Daniel, whose name was Belteshazzar, "Are you able to make known unto me the dream which I have seen, and the interpretation thereof?"

27 Daniel answered in the presence of the king, and said, "The secret which the king hath demanded cannot the wise men, the astrologers, the magicians, the soothsayers, shew unto the king.

28 But there is a God (Elah) in heaven that revealeth secrets, and maketh known to the King Nebuchadnezzar what shall be in the latter days. Your dream, and the visions of your head upon your bed, are these;

29 As for you, O king, your thoughts came into your mind upon your bed, what should come to pass hereafter; and he that revealeth secrets maketh known to you what shall come to pass.

30 But as for me, this secret is not revealed to me for any wisdom that I have more than any living, but for their sakes that shall make known the interpretation to the king, and that you mightest know the thoughts of your heart.

31 You, O king, sawest, and behold a great image. This great image, whose brightness was excellent, stood before you; and the form thereof was awesome.

32 This image's head was of fine gold, his breast and his arms of silver, his belly and his thighs of brass,

33 His legs of iron, his feet part of iron and part of clay.

34 You sawest till that a stone was cut out without hands, which smote the image upon his feet that were of iron and clay, and broke them to pieces.

35 Then was the iron, the clay, the brass, the silver, and the gold, broken to pieces together, and became like the chaff of the summer threshingfloors; and the wind carried them away, that no place was found for them; and the stone that smote the image became a great mountain, and filled the whole earth.

36 This is the dream; and we will tell the interpretation thereof before the king.

37 You, O king, art a king of kings; for the God (Elah) of heaven hath given you a kingdom, power, and strength, and glory.

38 And wheresoever the children of men dwell, the beasts of the field and the fowls of the sky hath He given into your hand, and hath made you ruler over them all. You are this head of gold.

39 And after you shall arise another kingdom inferior to you, and another third kingdom of brass, which shall bear rule over all the earth.

40 And the fourth kingdom shall be strong as iron; forasmuch as iron breaketh in pieces and subdueth all things; and as iron that breaketh all these, shall it break in pieces and bruise.

41 And whereas you sawest the feet and toes, part of potters' clay, and part of iron, the kingdom shall be divided; but there shall be in it of the strength of the iron, forasmuch as you sawest the iron mixed with miry clay.

42 And as the toes of the feet were part of iron, and part of clay, so the kingdom shall be partly strong, and partly broken.

43 And whereas you sawest iron mixed with miry clay, they shall mingle themselves with the seed of men; but they shall not cleave one to another, even as iron is not mixed with clay.

44 And in the days of these kings shall the God (Elah) of heaven set up a kingdom, which shall never be destroyed; and the kingdom shall not be left to other people, but it shall break in pieces and consume all these kingdoms, and it shall stand forever.

45 Forasmuch as you sawest that the stone was cut out of the mountain without hands, and that it broke in pieces the iron, the brass, the clay, the silver, and the gold; the great God (Elah) hath made known to the king what shall come to pass hereafter; and the dream is certain, and the interpretation thereof sure."

46 Then the king Nebuchadnezzar fell upon his face, and worshipped Daniel, and commanded that they should offer an oblation and sweet odours unto him.

47 The king answered unto Daniel, and said, "Of a truth it is, that your God (Elah) is the [B9]Supreme God (Elah Elahin), and the Lord of kings (Supreme King), and a revealer of secrets, seeing you couldest reveal this secret."

48 Then the king made Daniel a great man, and gave him many great gifts, and made him ruler over the whole province of Babylon (Bavel), and chief of the governors over all the wise men of Babylon (Bavel).

49 Then Daniel requested of the king, and he set Shadrach, Meshach, and Abednego, over the affairs of the province of Babylon (Bavel); but Daniel sat in the gate of the king.

3 Nebuchadnezzar the king made an image of gold, whose height was threescore cubits, and the breadth thereof six cubits; he set it up in the plain of Dura, in the province of Babylon (Bavel).

2 Then Nebuchadnezzar the king sent to gather together the princes, the governors, and the captains, the judges, the treasurers, the counsellors, the sheriffs, and all the rulers of the provinces, to come to the dedication of the image which Nebuchadnezzar the king had set up.

3 Then the princes, the governors, and captains, the judges, the treasurers, the counsellors, the

sheriffs, and all the rulers of the provinces, were gathered together unto the dedication of the image that Nebuchadnezzar the king had set up; and they stood before the image that Nebuchadnezzar had set up.

4 Then a herald cried aloud: "To you it is commanded, O people, nations, and languages, 5 That at what time you hear the sound of the cornet, flute, harp, sackbut, psaltery, dulcimer, and all kinds of musick, you fall down and worship the golden image that Nebuchadnezzar the king hath set up.

6 And whoso falleth not down and worshippeth shall the same hour be cast into the midst of a burning fiery furnace."

7 Therefore at that time, when all the people heard the sound of the cornet, flute, harp, sackbut, psaltery, and all kinds of musick, all the people, the nations, and the languages, fell down and worshipped the golden image that Nebuchadnezzar the king had set up.

8 Wherefore at that time certain Chaldeans came near, and accused the Jews (Yehudim).

9 They spake and said to the king Nebuchadnezzar, "O king, live forever!

10 You, O king, hast made a decree, that every man that shall hear the sound of the cornet, flute, harp, sackbut, psaltery, and dulcimer, and all kinds of musick, shall fall down and worship the golden image:

11 And whoso falleth not down and worshippeth, that he should be cast into the midst of a burning fiery furnace.

12 There are certain Jews (Yehudim) whom you have set over the affairs of the province of Babylon (Bavel), Shadrach, Meshach, and Abednego; these men, O king, have not regarded you; they serve not your gods (elahin), nor worship the golden image which you have set up."

13 Then Nebuchadnezzar in his rage and fury commanded to bring Shadrach, Meshach, and Abednego. Then they brought these men before the king.

14 Nebuchadnezzar spake and said unto them, "Is it true, O Shadrach, Meshach, and Abednego, do not you serve my gods (elah), nor worship the golden image which I have set up? 15 Now if you be ready that at what time you hear the sound of the cornet, flute, harp, sackbut, psaltery, and dulcimer, and all kinds of

musick, you fall down and worship the image which I have made. Well, but if you worship not, you shall be cast the same hour into the midst of a burning fiery furnace; and who is that God (Elah) that shall deliver you out of my hands?"

16 Shadrach, Meshach, and Abednego, answered and said to the king, "O Nebuchadnezzar, we are not careful to answer you in this matter.

17 If it be so, our God (Elah) whom we serve is able to deliver us from the burning fiery furnace, and He will deliver us out of your hand, O king.

18 But if not, be it known unto you, O king, that we will not serve your gods (elohim), nor worship the golden image which you have set up."

19 Then was Nebuchadnezzar full of fury, and the form of his visage was changed against Shadrach, Meshach, and Abednego; therefore he spake, and commanded that they should heat the furnace one seven times more than it was wont to be heated.

20 And he commanded the most mighty men that were in his army to bind Shadrach, Meshach, and Abednego, and to cast them into the burning fiery furnace.

21 Then these men were bound in their coats, their hosen, and their hats, and their other garments, and were cast into the midst of the burning fiery furnace.

22 Therefore because the king's commandment was urgent, and the furnace exceeding hot, the flame of the fire slew those men that took up Shadrach, Meshach, and Abednego.

23 And these three men, Shadrach, Meshach, and Abednego, fell down bound into the midst of the burning fiery furnace.

24 Then Nebuchadnezzar the king was astonied, and rose up in haste, and spake, and said unto his counsellors, "Did not we cast three men bound into the midst of the fire?" They answered and said unto the king, "True, O king."

25 He answered and said, "Behold, I see four men loose, walking in the midst of the fire, and they have no hurt; and the form of the fourth is like the B47Humanity of El (YHWH)"

26 Then Nebuchadnezzar came near to the mouth of the burning fiery furnace, and spake, and said, "Shadrach, Meshach, and Abednego, you servants of the B6aMost High God (Elaha Illaahi), come forth, and come hither." Then

Shadrach, Meshach, and Abednego, came forth of the midst of the fire.

27 And the princes, governors, and captains, and the king's counsellors, being gathered together, saw these men, upon whose bodies the fire had no power, nor was a hair of their head singed, neither were their coats changed, nor the smell of fire had passed on them.

28 Then Nebuchadnezzar spake, and said, "Blessed be the God (Elah) of Shadrach, Meshach, and Abednego, who hath sent His angel, and delivered His servants that trusted in Him, and have changed the king's word, and yielded their bodies, that they might not serve nor worship any god, except their own God (Elah).

29 Therefore I make a decree: "That every people, nation, and language, which speak any thing amiss against the God (Elah) of Shadrach, Meshach, and Abednego, shall be cut in pieces, and their houses shall be made a dunghill; because there is no other God (Elah) that can deliver after this sort."

30 Then the king promoted Shadrach, Meshach, and Abednego, in the province of Babylon (Bavel).

4 Nebuchadnezzar the king, unto all people, nations, and languages, that dwell in all the earth: Peace be multiplied unto you.

2 I thought it good to shew the signs and wonders that the Most High God (Elaha Illaahi) hath wrought toward me.

3 How great are His signs! And how mighty are His wonders! His kingdom is an everlasting kingdom, and His dominion is from generation to generation.

4 I, Nebuchadnezzar was at rest in mine house, and flourishing in my palace.

5 I saw a dream which made me afraid, and the thoughts upon my bed and the visions of my head troubled me.

6 Therefore made I a decree to bring in all the wise men of Babylon (Bavel) before me, that they might make known unto me the interpretation of the dream.

7 Then came in the magicians, the astrologers, the Chaldeans, and the soothsayers; and I told the dream before them; but they did not make known unto me the interpretation thereof.

8 But at the last Daniel came in before me, whose name was Belteshazzar, according to the name of my god (elah), and in whom is the Spirit (Ruach) of the Holy God; and before him I told the dream, saying,

9 "O Belteshazzar, master of the magicians, because I know that the Spirit of the Holy God is in you, and no secret troubleth you, tell me the visions of my dream that I have seen, and the interpretation thereof.

10 Thus were the visions of mine head in my bed; I saw, and behold a tree in the midst of the earth, and the height thereof was great.

11 The tree grew, and was strong, and the height thereof reached unto heaven, and the sight thereof to the end of all the earth.

12 The leaves thereof were fair, and the fruit thereof much, and in it was meat for all; the beasts of the field had shadow under it, and the fowls of the sky dwelt in the boughs thereof, and all flesh was fed of it.

13 I saw in the visions of my head upon my bed, and, behold, a watcher and a holy one came down from heaven;

14 He cried aloud, and said thus: 'Hew down the tree, and cut off his branches, shake off his leaves, and scatter his fruit. Let the beasts get away from under it, and the fowls from his branches.

15 Nevertheless leave the stump of his roots in the earth, even with a band of iron and brass, in the tender grass of the field; and let it be wet with the dew of heaven, and let his portion be with the beasts in the grass of the earth;

16 Let his heart be changed from man's, and let a beast's heart be given unto him; and let seven times pass over him.

17 This matter is by the decree of the watchers, and the demand by the word of the holy ones; to the intent that the living may know that the [B6b]Most High (Illaahi) ruleth in the kingdom of men, and giveth it to whomsoever he will, and setteth up over it the basest of men.'

18 This dream I King Nebuchadnezzar have seen. Now you, O Belteshazzar, declare the interpretation thereof, forasmuch as all the wise men of my kingdom are not able to make known unto me the interpretation; but you are able; for the Spirit of the Holy God is in you."

19 Then Daniel, whose name was Belteshazzar, was astonied for one hour, and his thoughts troubled him. The king spake, and said, Belteshazzar, let not the dream, or the

interpretation thereof, trouble you. Belteshazzar answered and said, "My lord (Adoni), the dream be to them that hate you, and the interpretation thereof to your enemies.

20 The tree that you sawest, which grew, and was strong, whose height reached unto the heaven, and the sight thereof to all the earth;

21 Whose leaves were fair, and the fruit thereof much, and in it was meat for all; under which the beasts of the field dwelt, and upon whose branches the fowls of the sky had their habitation;

22 It is you, O king, that art grown and become strong; for your greatness is grown, and reacheth unto heaven, and your dominion to the end of the earth.

23 And whereas the king saw a watcher and an holy one coming down from heaven, and saying, 'Hew the tree down, and destroy it; yet leave the stump of the roots thereof in the earth, even with a band of iron and brass, in the tender grass of the field; and let it be wet with the dew of heaven, and let his portion be with the beasts of the field, till seven times pass over him';

24 This is the interpretation, O king, and this is the decree of the Most High (Illaahi), which is come upon my lord (adoni) the king,

25 That they shall drive you from men, and your dwelling shall be with the beasts of the field, and they shall make you to eat grass as oxen, and they shall wet you with the dew of heaven, and seven times shall pass over you, till you know that the Most High (Illaahi) ruleth in the kingdom of men, and giveth it to whomsoever He will.

26 And whereas they commanded to leave the stump of the tree roots; your kingdom shall be sure unto you, after that you shalt have known that the heavens do rule.

27 Wherefore, O king, let my counsel be acceptable unto you, and break off your sins by righteousness, and your iniquities by shewing mercy to the poor; if it may be a lengthening of your tranquillity."

28 All this came upon the king Nebuchadnezzar.

29 At the end of twelve months he walked in the palace of the kingdom of Babylon (Bavel).

30 The king spake, and said, "Is not this great Babylon (Bavel), that I have built for the house of the kingdom by the might of my power, and for the honor of my majesty?"

31 While the word was in the king's mouth, there fell a voice from heaven, saying: "O King Nebuchadnezzar, to you it is spoken: "The kingdom has departed from you!

32 And they shall drive you from men, and your dwelling shall be with the beasts of the field: they shall make you to eat grass as oxen, and seven times shall pass over you, until you know that the Most High (Illaahi) ruleth in the kingdom of men, and giveth it to whomsoever He will."

33 The same hour was the thing fulfilled upon Nebuchadnezzar; and he was driven from men, and did eat grass as oxen, and his body was wet with the dew of heaven, till his hairs were grown like eagles' feathers, and his nails like birds' claws.

34 And at the end of the days I Nebuchadnezzar lifted up mine eyes unto heaven, and mine understanding returned unto me, and I blessed the Most High (Illaahi), and I praised and honoured Him that liveth forever, whose dominion is an everlasting dominion, and His kingdom is from generation to generation:

35 And all the inhabitants of the earth are reputed as nothing; and He doeth according to His will in the army of heaven, and among the inhabitants of the earth: and none can stay His hand, or say unto Him, "What doest You?"

36 At the same time my reason returned unto me; and for the glory of my kingdom, mine honor and brightness returned unto me; and my counsellors and my lords sought unto me; and I was established in my kingdom, and excellent majesty was added unto me.

37 Now I, Nebuchadnezzar praise and extol and honor the King of heaven, all whose works are truth, and His ways justice. And those that walk in pride He is able to abase.

5 Belshazzar the king made a great feast to a thousand of his nobles, and drank wine before the thousand.

2 Belshazzar, while he tasted the wine, commanded to bring the golden and silver vessels which his father Nebuchadnezzar had taken out of the temple which was in Jerusalem (Yerushalayim); that the king, and his princes, his wives, and his concubines, might drink therein.

3 Then they brought the golden vessels that were taken out of the temple of the house of God

(Elah) which was at Jerusalem (Yerushalayim); and the king, and his princes, his wives, and his concubines, drank in them.

4 They drank wine, and praised the gods (elohim) of gold, and of silver, of brass, of iron, of wood, and of stone.

5 In the same hour came forth fingers of a man's hand, and wrote opposite the candlestick upon the plaister of the wall of the king's palace; and the king saw the part of the hand that wrote.

6 Then the king's countenance was changed, and his thoughts troubled him, so that the joints of his loins were loosed, and his knees smote one against another.

7 The king cried aloud to bring in the astrologers, the Chaldeans, and the soothsayers. And the king spake, and said to the wise men of Babylon (Bavel), "Whosoever shall read this writing, and shew me the interpretation thereof, shall be clothed with scarlet, and have a chain of gold about his neck, and shall be the third ruler in the kingdom."

8 Then came in all the king's wise men, but they could not read the writing, nor make known to the king the interpretation thereof.

9 Then was King Belshazzar greatly troubled, and his countenance was changed in him, and his nobles were astonied.

10 Now the queen, by reason of the words of the king and his nobles, came into the banquet house; and the queen spake and said, "O king, live forever! Let not your thoughts trouble you, nor let your countenance be changed.

11 There is a man in your kingdom, in whom is the Spirit (Ruach) of the Holy God; and in the days of your father light and understanding and wisdom, like the wisdom of the God (Elahin), was found in him; whom the King Nebuchadnezzar your father, the king, I say, your father, made master of the magicians, astrologers, Chaldeans, and soothsayers;

12 Forasmuch as an excellent spirit, and knowledge, and understanding, interpreting of dreams, and shewing of hard sentences, and dissolving of doubts, were found in the same Daniel, whom the king named Belteshazzar; now let Daniel be called, and he will shew the interpretation.

13 Then was Daniel brought in before the king. And the king spake and said unto Daniel, "Are you that Daniel, which art of the children of the captivity of Judah (Yehudah), whom the king my father brought out of Judah (Yehudah)?

14 I have even heard of you, that the Spirit of God (Ruach Elahin) is in you, and that light and understanding and excellent wisdom is found in you.

15 And now the wise men, the astrologers, have been brought in before me, that they should read this writing, and make known unto me the interpretation thereof, but they could not shew the interpretation of the thing.

16 And I have heard of you, that you canst make interpretations, and dissolve doubts; now if you canst read the writing, and make known to me the interpretation thereof, you shalt be clothed with scarlet, and have a chain of gold about your neck, and shalt be the third ruler in the kingdom."

17 Then Daniel answered and said before the king, "Let your gifts be to yourself, and give your rewards to another; yet I will read the writing unto the king, and make known to him the interpretation.

18 O you king, the [6d]Most High God (Elaha Illaahi) gave Nebuchadnezzar your father a kingdom, and majesty, and glory, and honor.

19 And for the majesty that he gave him, all people, nations, and languages, trembled and feared before him; whom he would he slew; and whom he would he kept alive; and whom he would he set up; and whom he would he put down.

20 But when his heart was lifted up, and his mind hardened in pride, he was deposed from his kingly throne, and they took his glory from him.

21 And he was driven from the sons of men; and his heart was made like the beasts, and his dwelling was with the wild asses; they fed him with grass like oxen, and his body was wet with the dew of heaven; till he knew that the Most High God (Elaha Illaahi) ruled in the kingdom of men, and that He appointeth over it whomsoever He will.

22 And you his son, O Belshazzar, hast not humbled your heart, though you knewest all this;

23 But hast lifted up yourself against Lord (Adon) of heaven; and they have brought the vessels of his house before you, and you, and your lords, your wives, and your concubines, have drunk

wine in them; and you have praised the gods (elah) of silver, and gold, of brass, iron, wood, and stone, which see not, nor hear, nor know; and the God (Elah) in whose hand your breath is, and whose are all your ways, have you not glorified;

24 Then was the part of the hand sent from him; and this writing was written.

25 And this is the inscription that was written: Mene! Mene! Teqel, Ufarsin.

26 This is the interpretation of the message: Mene: God (Elah) hath numbered your kingdom, and finished it;

27 Teqel: You are weighed in the balances, and art found wanting;

28 Peres: Your kingdom is divided, and given to the Medes and Persians."

29 Then commanded Belshazzar, and they clothed Daniel with scarlet, and put a chain of gold about his neck, and made a proclamation concerning him, that he should be the third ruler in the kingdom.

30 In that night was Belshazzar the king of the Chaldeans slain.

31 And Darius the Median took the kingdom, being about threescore and two years old.

6 It pleased Darius to set over the kingdom a hundred and twenty princes, which should be over the whole kingdom;

2 And over these three presidents; of whom Daniel was first, that the princes might give accounts unto them, and the king should have no damage.

3 Then this Daniel was preferred above the presidents and princes, because an excellent spirit was in him; and the king thought to set him over the whole realm.

4 Then the presidents and princes sought to find occasion against Daniel concerning the kingdom; but they could find none occasion nor fault; forasmuch as he was faithful, nor was there any error or fault found in him.

5 Then said these men, "We shall not find any occasion against this Daniel, except we find it against him concerning the decree of his God (Elah).

6 Then these presidents and princes assembled together to the king, and said thus unto him, King Darius, live forever.

7 All the presidents of the kingdom, the governors, and the princes, the counsellors, and the captains, have consulted together to establish a royal statute, and to make a firm decree, that whosoever shall ask a petition of any God (Elah) or man for thirty days, save of you, O king, he shall be cast into the den of lions.

8 Now, O king, establish the decree, and sign the writing, that it be not changed, according to the decree of the Medes and Persians, which altereth not.

9 Wherefore King Darius signed the writing and the decree.

10 Now when Daniel knew that the writing was signed, he went into his house; and his windows being open in his chamber toward Jerusalem (Yerushalayim), he kneeled upon his knees three times a day, and prayed, and gave thanks before his God (Elah), as he did beforetime.

11 Then these men assembled, and found Daniel praying and making supplication before his God (Elah).

12 Then they came near, and spake before the king concerning the king's decree: "Have you not signed a decree, that every man that shall ask a petition of any God (Elah) or man within thirty days, save of you, O king, shall be cast into the den of lions? The king answered and said, "The thing is true, according to the decree of the Medes and Persians, which altereth not."

13 Then answered they and said before the king, "That Daniel, which is of the children of the captivity of Judah (Yehudah), regardeth not you, O king, nor the decree that you have signed, but maketh his petition three times a day."

14 Then the king, when he heard these words, was sore displeased with himself, and set his heart on Daniel to deliver him; and he laboured till the going down of the sun to deliver him.

15 Then these men assembled unto the king, and said unto the king, "Know, O king, that the law of the Medes and Persians is, that no decree nor statute which the king establisheth may be changed."

16 Then the king commanded, and they brought Daniel, and cast him into the den of lions. Now the king spake and said unto Daniel, "Your God (Elah) whom you servest continually, He will deliver you."

17 And a stone was brought, and laid upon the mouth of the den; and the king sealed it with his own signet, and with the signet of his lords; that the purpose might not be changed concerning

Daniel.

18 Then the king went to his palace, and passed the night fasting; neither were instruments of musick brought before him; and his sleep went from him.

19 Then the king arose very early in the morning, and went in haste unto the den of lions.

20 And when he came to the den, he cried with a lamentable voice unto Daniel; and the king spake and said to Daniel, "O Daniel, servant of the [B2]living God (Elah chaiya), is your God (Elah), whom you servest continually, able to deliver you from the lions?"

21 Then said Daniel unto the king, "O king, live forever!

22 [B5a]My God (Elahi) hath sent His angel, and hath shut the lions' mouths, that they have not hurt me; forasmuch as before Him innocency was found in me; and also before you, O king, have I done no hurt."

23 Then was the king exceeding glad for him, and commanded that they should take Daniel up out of the den. So Daniel was taken up out of the den, and no manner of hurt was found upon him, because he believed in his God (Elah).

24 And the king commanded, and they brought those men which had accused Daniel, and they cast them into the den of lions, them, their children, and their wives; and the lions had the mastery of them, and broke all their bones in pieces or ever they came at the bottom of the den.

25 Then King Darius wrote unto all people, nations, and languages, that dwell in all the earth: Peace be multiplied unto you.

26 I make a decree, that in every dominion of my kingdom men tremble and fear before the God (Elah) of Daniel; for He is the living God (Elah chaiya) and stedfast forever, and His kingdom that which shall not be destroyed, and His dominion shall be even unto the end.

27 He delivereth and rescueth, and He worketh signs and wonders in heaven and in earth, who hath delivered Daniel from the power of the lions.

28 So this Daniel prospered in the reign of Darius, and in the reign of Cyrus the Persian.

7 In the first year of Belshazzar king of Babylon (Bavel) Daniel had a dream and visions of his head upon his bed: then he wrote the dream, and told the sum of the matters.

2 Daniel spake and said, "I saw in my vision by night, and, behold, the four winds of the heaven strove upon the great sea.

3 And four great beasts came up from the sea, diverse one from another.

4 The first was like a lion, and had eagle's wings; I beheld till the wings thereof were plucked, and it was lifted up from the earth, and made stand upon the feet as a man, and a man's heart was given to it.

5 And behold another beast, a second, like to a bear, and it raised up itself on one side, and it had three ribs in the mouth of it between the teeth of it; and they said thus unto it: 'Arise, devour much flesh!'

6 After this I beheld, and behold another, like a leopard, which had upon the back of it four wings of a fowl; the beast had also four heads; and dominion was given to it.

7 After this I saw in the night visions, and behold a fourth beast, dreadful and terrible, and strong exceedingly; and it had great iron teeth; it devoured and broke in pieces, and stamped the residue with the feet of it; and it was diverse from all the beasts that were before it; and it had ten horns.

8 I considered the horns, and, behold, there came up among them another little horn, before whom there were three of the first horns plucked up by the roots: and, behold, in this horn were eyes like the eyes of man, and a mouth speaking great things.

9 I beheld till the thrones were cast down, and the Ancient of Days did sit, whose garment was white as snow, and the hair of His head like the pure wool; His throne was like the fiery flame, and His wheels as burning fire.

10 A fiery stream issued and came forth from before Him; thousand thousands ministered unto Him, and ten thousand times ten thousand stood before Him; the judgment was set, and the books were opened.

11 I beheld then because of the voice of the great words which the horn spake; I beheld even till the beast was slain, and his body destroyed, and given to the burning flame.

12 As concerning the rest of the beasts, they had their dominion taken away; yet their lives were prolonged for a season and time.

13 I saw in the night visions, and, behold, one like the Son of man (haMashiach) came with

the clouds of heaven, and came to the Ancient of Days, and they brought Him near before Him.
14 And there was given Him dominion, and glory, and a kingdom, that all people, nations, and languages, should serve Him. His dominion is an everlasting dominion, which shall not pass away, and His kingdom that which shall not be destroyed.
15 I, Daniel was grieved in my spirit in the midst of my body, and the visions of my head troubled me.
16 I came near unto one of them that stood by, and asked him the truth of all this. So he told me, and made me know the interpretation of the things.
17 'These great beasts, which are four, are four kings, which shall arise out of the earth.
18 But the holy ones of the Most High shall take the kingdom, and possess the kingdom forever, even forever and ever.'
19 Then I would know the truth of the fourth beast, which was diverse from all the others, exceeding dreadful, whose teeth were of iron, and his nails of brass; which devoured, broke in pieces, and stamped the residue with his feet;
20 And of the ten horns that were in his head, and of the other which came up, and before whom three fell; even of that horn that had eyes, and a mouth that spake very great things, whose look was more stout than his fellows.
21 "I beheld, and the same horn made war with the holy ones, and prevailed against them;
22 Until the Ancient of Days came, and judgment was given to the holy ones of the Most High; and the time came that the holy ones possessed the kingdom.
23 Thus he said: 'The fourth beast shall be the fourth kingdom upon earth, which shall be diverse from all kingdoms, and shall devour the whole earth, and shall tread it down, and break it in pieces.
24 And the ten horns out of this kingdom are ten kings that shall arise; and another shall rise after them; and he shall be diverse from the first, and he shall subdue three kings.
25 And he shall speak great words against the Most High, and shall wear out the holy ones of the Most High, and think to change times and law; and they shall be given into his hand until a time and times and the dividing of time.
26 But the judgment shall sit, and they shall take

away his dominion, to consume and to destroy it unto the end.
27 And the kingdom and dominion, and the greatness of the kingdom under the whole heaven, shall be given to the people of the holy ones of the Most High, whose kingdom is an everlasting kingdom, and all dominions shall serve and obey Him.'
28 This is the end of the matter. As for me Daniel, my cogitations much troubled me, and my countenance changed in me; but I kept the matter in my heart."

8 In the third year of the reign of King Belshazzar a vision appeared unto me, even unto me Daniel, after that which appeared unto me at the first.
2 And I saw in a vision; and it came to pass, when I saw, that I was at Shushan in the palace, which is in the province of Elam; and I saw in a vision, and I was by the river of Ulai.
3 Then I lifted up mine eyes, and saw, and, behold, there stood before the river a ram which had two horns: and the two horns were high; but one was higher than the other, and the higher came up last.
4 I saw the ram pushing westward, and northward, and southward; so that no beasts might stand before him, neither was there any that could deliver out of his hand; but he did according to his will, and became great.
5 And as I was considering, behold, an he goat came from the west on the face of the whole earth, and touched not the ground: and the goat had a notable horn between his eyes.
6 And he came to the ram that had two horns, which I had seen standing before the river, and ran unto him in the fury of his power.
7 And I saw him come close unto the ram, and he was moved with choler against him, and smote the ram, and broke his two horns; and there was no power in the ram to stand before him, but he cast him down to the ground, and stamped upon him; and there was none that could deliver the ram out of his hand.
8 Therefore the he goat waxed very great; and when he was strong, the great horn was broken; and for it came up four notable ones toward the four winds of heaven.
9 And out of one of them came forth a little horn, which waxed exceeding great, toward the south, and toward the east, and toward the

pleasant land.

10 And it waxed great, even to the host of heaven; and it cast down some of the host and of the stars to the ground, and stamped upon them.

11 Yea, he magnified himself even to the prince of the host, and by him the daily sacrifice was taken away, and the place of his sanctuary was cast down.

12 And a host was given him against the daily sacrifice by reason of transgression, and it cast down the truth to the ground; and it practised, and prospered.

13 Then I heard one saint speaking, and another holy one said unto that certain holy one who spake, "How long shall be the vision concerning the daily sacrifice, and the transgression of desolation, to give both the sanctuary and the host to be trodden under foot?"

14 And he said unto me, "Unto two thousand and three hundred days; then shall the sanctuary be cleansed."

15 And it came to pass, when I, even I Daniel, had seen the vision, and sought for the meaning, then, behold, there stood before me as the appearance of a man.

16 And I heard a man's voice between the banks of Ulai, which called, and said, "Gavriel, make this man to understand the vision."

17 So he came near where I stood; and when he came, I was afraid, and fell upon my face; but he said unto me, "Understand, O son of man, for at the time of the end shall be the vision."

18 Now as he was speaking with me, I was in a deep sleep on my face toward the ground; but he touched me, and set me upright.

19 And he said, "Behold, I will make you know what shall be in the last end of the indignation, for at the time appointed the end shall be.

20 The ram which you sawest having two horns are the kings of Media and Persia.

21 And the rough goat is the king of Greece (Yawan); and the great horn that is between his eyes is the first king.

22 Now that being broken, whereas four stood up for it, four kingdoms shall stand up out of the nation, but not in his power.

23 And in the latter time of their kingdom, when the transgressors are come to the full, a king of fierce countenance, and understanding dark sentences, shall stand up.

24 And his power shall be mighty, but not by his own power; and he shall destroy wonderfully, and shall prosper, and practise, and shall destroy the mighty and the holy people.

25 And through his policy also he shall cause craft to prosper in his hand; and he shall magnify himself in his heart, and by peace shall destroy many; he shall also stand up against the Prince of princes; but he shall be broken without hand.

26 And the vision of the evening and the morning which was told is true; wherefore shut you up the vision, for it shall be for many days."

27 And I, Daniel fainted, and was sick certain days; afterward I rose up, and did the king's business; and I was astonished at the vision, but none understood it.

9 In the first year of Darius the son of Ahasuerus, of the seed of the Medes, which was made king over the realm of the Chaldeans;

2 In the first year of his reign I, Daniel understood by books the number of the years, whereof the word of יהוה came to Jeremiah (Yirmeyahu) the prophet, that he would accomplish seventy years in the desolations of Jerusalem (Yerushalayim).

3 And I set my face unto the Lord God (Adonai Elohim), to seek by prayer and supplications, with fasting, and sackcloth, and ashes.

4 And I prayed unto יהוה my God (YHWH Elohai), and made my confession, and said, "O Lord (Adonai), the great and awesome God (El), keeping the covenant and mercy to them that love Him, and to them that keep His commandments;

5 We have sinned, and have committed iniquity, and have done wickedly, and have rebelled, even by departing from Your precepts and from Your judgments.

6 Neither have we hearkened unto Your servants the prophets, who spake in Your name to our kings, our princes, and our fathers, and to all the people of the land.

7 O Lord (Adonai), righteousness belongeth unto You, but unto us confusion of faces, as at this day; to the men of Judah (Yehudah), and to the inhabitants of Jerusalem (Yerushalayim), and unto all Yisrael, that are near, and that are far off, through all the countries whither you have driven them, because of their trespass that they have trespassed against You.

8 O Lord (Adonai), to us belongeth confusion of face, to our kings, to our princes, and to our

fathers, because we have sinned against You.

9 To the Lord our God (Adonai Eloheinu) belong mercies and forgivenesses, though we have rebelled against Him;

10 Neither have we obeyed the voice of יהוה our God (YHWH Eloheinu), to walk in His Torah, which He set before us by His servants the prophets.

11 Yea, all Yisrael have transgressed Your Torah, even by departing, that they might not obey Your voice; therefore the curse is poured upon us, and the oath that is written in the Torah by Moses (Mosheh) the servant of God (Elohim), because we have sinned against Him.

12 And He hath confirmed His words, which He spake against us, and against our judges who judged us, by bringing upon us a great disaster (raah), for under the whole heaven hath not been done as hath been done upon Jerusalem (Yerushalayim).

13 As it is written in the Torah by Moses (Mosheh), all this disaster (raah) has come upon us; yet made we not our prayer before יהוה our God (YHWH Eloheinu), that we might turn from our iniquities, and understand Your truth.

14 Therefore hath יהוה watched upon the evil, and brought it upon us; for יהוה our God (YHWH Eloheinu) is righteous in all His works which He doeth; for we obeyed not His voice.

15 And now, O Lord our God (Adonai Eloheinu), who hast brought Your people forth out of the land of Egypt (Mitsrayim) with a mighty hand, and hast gotten You renown, as at this day; we have sinned, we have done wickedly.

16 O Lord (Adonai), according to all Your righteousness, I beseech You, let Your anger and Your fury be turned away from Your city Jerusalem (Yerushalayim), Your holy mountain; because for our sins, and for the iniquities of our fathers, Jerusalem (Yerushalayim) and Your people are become a reproach to all who are around us.

17 Now therefore, O our God (Elohim), hear the prayer of Your servant, and his supplications, and cause Your face to shine upon Your sanctuary that is desolate, for the Lord (Adonai)'s sake.

18 O my God (Elohim), incline Your ear, and hear; open Your eyes, and behold our desolations, and the city which is called by Your name; for we do not present our supplications before You for our righteousnesses, but for Your great mercies.

19 O my Lord (Adonai), hear; O my Lord (Adonai), forgive; O my Lord (Adonai), hearken and do; defer not, for Your own sake, O my God (Elohim); for Your city and Your people are called by Your name."

20 And whiles I was speaking, and praying, and confessing my sin and the sin of my people Yisrael, and presenting my supplication before יהוה my God (YHWH Elohai) for the holy mountain of my God (Elohim);

21 Yea, whiles I was speaking in prayer, even the man Gavriel, whom I had seen in the vision at the beginning, being caused to fly swiftly, touched me about the time of the evening oblation.

22 And he informed me, and talked with me, and said, "O Daniel, I have now come forth to give you skill and understanding.

23 At the beginning of your supplications the commandment came forth, and I am come to shew you; for you are greatly beloved; therefore understand the matter, and consider the vision.

24 Seventy weeks are determined upon your people and upon your holy city, to finish the transgression, and to make an end of sins, and to make reconciliation for iniquity, and to bring in everlasting righteousness, and to seal up the vision and prophecy, and to anoint the Most Holy.

25 Know therefore and understand, that from the going forth of the commandment to restore and to build Jerusalem (Yerushalayim) unto Messiah (B45Mashiach) the Prince shall be seven weeks, and threescore and two weeks (sixty-two weeks): the street shall be built again, and the wall, even in troublous times.

26 And after threescore and two weeks shall Messiah (Mashiach) be cut off, but not for Himself; and the people of the prince that shall come shall destroy the city and the sanctuary; and the end thereof shall be with a flood, and unto the end of the war desolations are determined.

27 And he shall confirm the covenant with many for one week; and in the midst of the week he shall cause the sacrifice and the oblation to cease, and for the overspreading of abominations he shall make it desolate, even until the consummation, and that determined shall be poured upon the desolate.

10 In the third year of Cyrus king of Persia a thing was revealed unto Daniel, whose name was called Belteshazzar; and the thing was true, but the time appointed was long; and he understood the thing, and had understanding of the vision.

2 In those days I, Daniel was mourning three full weeks.

3 I ate no pleasant bread, neither came flesh nor wine in my mouth, neither did I anoint myself at all, till three whole weeks were fulfilled.

4 And in the four and twentieth day of the first month, as I was by the side of the great river, which is Hiddekel;

5 Then I lifted up mine eyes, and looked, and behold a certain man clothed in linen, whose loins were girded with fine gold of Uphaz!

6 His body also was like the beryl, and his face as the appearance of lightning, and his eyes as lamps of fire, and his arms and his feet like in colour to polished brass, and the voice of his words like the voice of a multitude.

7 And I, Daniel alone saw the vision, for the men that were with me saw not the vision; but a great quaking fell upon them, so that they fled to hide themselves.

8 Therefore I was left alone, and saw this great vision, and there remained no strength in me; for my comeliness was turned in me into frailty, and I retained no strength.

9 Yet heard I the voice of his words; and when I heard the voice of his words, then was I in a deep sleep on my face, and my face toward the ground.

10 And, behold, a hand touched me, which set me upon my knees and upon the palms of my hands.

11 And he said unto me, "O Daniel, a man greatly beloved, understand the words that I speak unto you, and stand upright; for unto you am I now sent." And when he had spoken this word unto me, I stood trembling.

12 Then said he unto me, "Fear not, Daniel, for from the first day that you didst set your heart to understand, and to chasten yourself before your God (Elohim), your words were heard, and I have come for your words.

13 But the prince of the kingdom of Persia withstood me one and twenty days; but, behold, Mikhael, one of the chief princes, came to help me; and I remained there with the kings of Persia.

14 Now I am come to make you understand what shall befall your people in the latter days; for yet the vision is for many days.

15 And when he had spoken such words unto me, I set my face toward the ground, and I became dumb.

16 And, behold, one like the similitude of the sons of men touched my lips; then I opened my mouth, and spake, and said unto him that stood before me, "O my lord (adoni), by the vision my sorrows are turned upon me, and I have retained no strength."

17 For how can such servant of my lord (adoni) talk with this my lord (adoni)? For as for me, straightway there remained no strength in me, neither is there breath left in me.

18 Then there came again and touched me one like the appearance of a man, and he strengthened me,

19 And said, "O man greatly beloved, fear not; peace be unto you, be strong, yea, be strong." And when he had spoken unto me, I was strengthened, and said, "Let my lord (adoni) speak; for you have strengthened me."

20 Then said he, "Knowest you wherefore I come unto you? And now will I return to fight with the prince of Persia; and when I have gone forth, behold, the prince of Greece (Yawan) shall come.

21 But I will shew you that which is noted in the scripture of truth; and there is none that holdeth with me in these things, but Mikhael your prince.

11 Also I, in the first year of Darius the Mede, even I, stood to confirm and to strengthen him.

2 And now will I shew you the truth. Behold, there shall stand up yet three kings in Persia; and the fourth shall be far richer than they all; and by his strength through his riches he shall stir up all against the realm of Grecia.

3 And a mighty king shall stand up, that shall rule with great dominion, and do according to his will.

4 And when he shall stand up, his kingdom shall be broken, and shall be divided toward the four winds of heaven; and not to his posterity, nor according to his dominion which he ruled; for his kingdom shall be plucked up, even for others beside those.

5 And the king of the south shall be strong, and one of his princes; and he shall be strong above him, and have dominion; his dominion shall be a great dominion.

6 And in the end of years they shall join themselves together; for the king's daughter of the south shall come to the king of the north to make an agreement; but she shall not retain the power of the arm; neither shall he stand, nor his arm; but she shall be given up, and they that brought her, and he that begat her, and he that strengthened her in these times.

7 But out of a branch of her roots shall one stand up in his estate, which shall come with an army, and shall enter into the fortress of the king of the north, and shall deal against them, and shall prevail.

8 And shall also carry captives into Egypt (Mitsrayim) their gods (elohim), with their princes, and with their precious vessels of silver and of gold; and he shall continue more years than the king of the north.

9 So the king of the south shall come into his kingdom, and shall return into his own land.

10 But his sons shall be stirred up, and shall assemble a multitude of great forces; and one shall certainly come, and overflow, and pass through; then shall he return, and be stirred up, even to his fortress.

11 And the king of the south shall be moved with choler, and shall come forth and fight with him, even with the king of the north; and he shall set forth a great multitude; but the multitude shall be given into his hand.

12 And when he hath taken away the multitude, his heart shall be lifted up; and he shall cast down many ten thousands; but he shall not be strengthened by it.

13 For the king of the north shall return, and shall set forth a multitude greater than the former, and shall certainly come after certain years with a great army and with much riches.

14 And in those times there shall many stand up against the king of the south; also the robbers of your people shall exalt themselves to establish the vision; but they shall fall.

15 So the king of the north shall come, and cast up a mount, and take the most fenced cities; and the arms of the south shall not withstand, neither his chosen people, neither shall there be any strength to withstand.

16 But he that cometh against him shall do according to his own will, and none shall stand before him; and he shall stand in the glorious land, which by his hand shall be consumed.

17 He shall also set his face to enter with the strength of his whole kingdom, and upright ones with him; thus shall he do: and he shall give him the daughter of women, corrupting her: but she shall not stand on his side, neither be for him.

18 After this shall he turn his face unto the isles, and shall take many; but a prince for his own behalf shall cause the reproach offered by him to cease; without his own reproach he shall cause it to turn upon him.

19 Then he shall turn his face toward the fort of his own land; but he shall stumble and fall, and not be found.

20 Then shall stand up in his estate a raiser of taxes in the glory of the kingdom; but within few days he shall be destroyed, neither in anger, nor in battle.

21 And in his estate shall stand up a vile person, to whom they shall not give the honor of the kingdom; but he shall come in peaceably, and obtain the kingdom by flatteries.

22 And with the arms of a flood shall they be overflown from before him, and shall be broken; yea, also the prince of the covenant.

23 And after the league made with him he shall work deceitfully; for he shall come up, and shall become strong with a small people.

24 He shall enter peaceably even upon the fattest places of the province; and he shall do that which his fathers have not done, nor his fathers' fathers; he shall scatter among them the prey, and spoil, and riches; yea, and he shall forecast his devices against the strong holds, even for a time.

25 And he shall stir up his power and his courage against the king of the south with a great army; and the king of the south shall be stirred up to battle with a very great and mighty army; but he shall not stand; for they shall forecast devices against him.

26 Yea, they that feed of the portion of his meat shall destroy him, and his army shall overflow; and many shall fall down slain.

27 And both these kings' hearts shall be to do mischief, and they shall speak lies at one table; but it shall not prosper; for yet the end shall be at the time appointed.

28 Then shall he return into his land with great riches; and his heart shall be against the holy covenant; and he shall do exploits, and return to his own land.

29 At the time appointed he shall return, and come toward the south; but it shall not be as the former, or as the latter.

30 For the ships of Chittim shall come against him; therefore he shall be grieved, and return, and have indignation against the holy covenant; so shall he do; he shall even return, and have intelligence with them that forsake the holy covenant.

31 And arms shall stand on his part, and they shall pollute the sanctuary of strength, and shall take away the daily sacrifice, and they shall place the abomination that maketh desolate.

32 And such as do wickedly against the covenant shall he corrupt by flatteries; but the people that do know their God (Elohim) shall be strong, and do exploits.

33 And they that understand among the people shall instruct many; yet they shall fall by the sword, and by flame, by captivity, and by spoil, many days.

34 Now when they shall fall, they shall be holpen with a little help; but many shall cleave to them with flatteries.

35 And some of them of understanding shall fall, to try them, and to purge, and to make them white, even to the time of the end, because it is yet for a time appointed.

36 And the king shall do according to his will; and he shall exalt himself, and magnify himself above every rulers ([B1b]elohim), and shall speak marvellous things against the [B9]Supreme God (Elohei haElohim), and shall prosper till the indignation be accomplished, for what has been determined shall be done.

37 Neither shall he regard the God (Elohim) of his fathers, nor the desire of women, nor regard any rulers (elohim); for he shall magnify himself above all.

38 But in his estate shall he honor the god of forces; and a god whom his fathers knew not shall he honor with gold, and silver, and with precious stones, and pleasant things.

39 Thus shall he do in the most strong holds with a strange god, whom he shall acknowledge and increase with glory; and he shall cause them to rule over many, and shall divide the land for gain.

40 And at the time of the end shall the king of the south push at him; and the king of the north shall come against him like a whirlwind, with chariots, and with horsemen, and with many ships; and he shall enter into the countries, and shall overflow and pass over.

41 He shall enter also into the glorious land, and many countries shall be overthrown; but these shall escape out of his hand: Edom, and Moav, and the chief of the children of Ammon.

42 He shall stretch forth his hand also upon the countries; and the land of Egypt (Mitsrayim) shall not escape.

43 But he shall have power over the treasures of gold and of silver, and over all the precious things of Egypt (Mitsrayim); and the Libyans and the Ethiopians (Kushim) shall be at his steps.

44 But tidings out of the east and out of the north shall trouble him; therefore he shall go forth with great fury to destroy, and utterly to make away many.

45 And he shall plant the tabernacles of his palace between the seas in the glorious holy mountain; yet he shall come to his end, and none shall help him.

12 And at that time shall Mikhael stand up, the great prince which standeth for the children of your people; and there shall be a time of trouble, such as never was since there was a nation even to that same time; and at that time your people shall be delivered, every one that shall be found written in the book.

2 And many of them that sleep in the dust of the earth shall awake, some to everlasting life, and some to shame and everlasting contempt.

3 And they that be wise shall shine as the brightness of the firmament; and they that turn many to righteousness as the stars forever and ever.

4 But you, O Daniel, shut up the words, and seal the book, even to the time of the end; many shall run to and fro, and knowledge shall be increased.

5 Then I, Daniel looked, and, behold, there stood other two, the one on this side of the bank of the river, and the other on that side of the bank of the river.

6 And one said to the man clothed in linen, who was upon the waters of the river, "How long

shall it be to the end of these wonders?"

7 And I heard the man clothed in linen, which was upon the waters of the river, when he held up his right hand and his left hand unto heaven, and sware by him that liveth forever that it shall be for a time, times, and a half; and when he shall have accomplished to scatter the power of the holy people, all these things shall be finished.

8 And I heard, but I understood not; then said I, "O my lord (adoni), what shall be the end of these things?"

9 And he said, "Go your way, Daniel, for the words are closed up and sealed till the time of the end.

10 Many shall be purified, and made white, and refined; but the wicked shall do wickedly; and none of the wicked shall understand; but the wise shall understand.

11 And from the time that the daily sacrifice shall be taken away, and the abomination that maketh desolate set up, there shall be a thousand two hundred and ninety days.

12 Blessed is he that waiteth, and cometh to the thousand three hundred and five and thirty days.

13 But go you your way till the end be; for you shalt rest, and stand for your allotted portion at the end of the days."

HOSEA
HOSHEA הוֹשֵׁעַ
(Salvation)

1 The word of יהוה that came unto [A55]Hoshea, the son of Beeri, in the days of Uzziyahu, Yotam, Achaz, and Hezekiah (Chizqiyahu), kings of Judah (Yehudah), and in the days of Jeroboam (Yarovam) the son of Yoash, king of Yisrael.

2 The beginning of the word of יהוה by Hoshea. And יהוה said to Hoshea: "Go, take unto you a wife of whoredoms and children of whoredoms: for the land hath committed great whoredom, departing from יהוה.

3 So he went and took Gomer the daughter of Diblaim; who conceived, and bare him a son.

4 And יהוה said unto him, "Call his name Yizreel; for yet a little while, and I will avenge the blood of Yizreel upon the house of Yehu, and will cause to cease the kingdom of the house of Yisrael.

5 And it shall come to pass at that day, that I will break the bow of Yisrael in the valley of Yizreel.

6 And she conceived again, and bare a daughter. And God (Elohim) said unto him, "Call her name Lo-Ruhamah, for I will no more have mercy upon the house of Yisrael, but I will utterly take them away.

7 But I will have mercy upon the house of Judah (Yehudah), and will save them by יהוה their God (YHWH Eloheihem), and will not save them by bow, nor by sword, nor by battle, by horses, nor by horsemen."

8 Now when she had weaned Lo-Ruhamah, she conceived, and bare a son.

9 Then said God (Elohim): "Call his name Lo-Ammi, for you are not My people, and I will not become your God (Elohim).

10 Yet the number of the children of Yisrael shall be as the sand of the sea, which cannot be measured nor numbered; and it shall come to pass, that in the place where it was said unto them, 'You are not My people,' there it shall be said unto them, 'You are the sons of the living God (El chai).'

11 Then shall the children of Judah (Yehudah) and the children of Yisrael be gathered together, and appoint themselves one head, and they shall come up out of the land; for great shall be the day of Yizreel!

2 Say you unto your brethren, 'My people (Ammi)'; and to your sisters, 'Mercy is shown (Ruhamah)'.

2 Contend with your mother, contend; for she is not my wife, neither am I her husband; let her therefore put away her whoredoms out of her sight, and her adulteries from between her breasts;

3 Lest I strip her naked, and set her as in the day that she was born, and make her as a wilderness, and set her like a dry land, and slay her with thirst.

4 And I will not have mercy upon her children; for they be the children of whoredoms.

5 For their mother hath played the harlot; she that conceived them hath done shamefully; for she said, 'I will go after my lovers, that give me my bread and my water, my wool and my flax, mine oil and my drink.

6 Therefore, behold, I will hedge up your way with thorns, and make a wall, that she shall not find her paths.

7 And she shall follow after her lovers, but she shall not overtake them; and she shall seek them, but shall not find them. Then shall she say, 'I will go and return to my first husband; for then was it better with me than now.'

8 For she did not know that I gave her corn, and wine, and oil, and multiplied her silver and gold, which they prepared for the Baal.

9 Therefore will I return, and take away my corn in the time thereof, and my wine in the season thereof, and will recover my wool and my flax given to cover her nakedness.

10 And now will I discover her lewdness in the sight of her lovers, and none shall deliver her out of Mine hand.

11 I will also cause all her mirth to cease, her feast days, her New Moons, and her Shabbats, and all her solemn feasts.

12 And I will destroy her vines and her fig trees, whereof she hath said, 'These are my rewards that my lovers have given me.' And I will make them a forest, and the beasts of the field shall eat them.

13 And I will visit upon her the days of the Baals (Baalim), wherein she burned incense to them, and she decked herself with her earrings and her jewels, and she went after her lovers,

and forgat me," saith יהוה.

14 Therefore, behold, I will allure her, and bring her into the wilderness, and speak comfortably unto her.

15 And I will give her her vineyards from thence, and the valley of Achor for a door of hope; and she shall sing there, as in the days of her youth, and as in the day when she came up out of the land of Egypt (Mitsrayim).

16 "And it shall be at that day," saith יהוה, "that you shalt call Me 'Ishi (My Husband)'; and shalt call Me no more ʻB33eBaali (My Lord)',

17 For I will take away the names of the Baals (Baalim) out of her mouth, and they shall no more be remembered by their name.

18 And in that day will I make a covenant for them with the beasts of the field, and with the fowls of sky, and with the creeping things of the ground; and I will break the bow and the sword and the battle out of the earth, and will make them to lie down safely.

19 And I will betroth you unto Me forever; yea, I will betroth you unto Me in righteousness, and in judgment, and in lovingkindness, and in mercies.

20 I will even betroth you unto Me in faithfulness; and you shalt know יהוה.

21 And it shall come to pass in that day, I will hear," saith יהוה, I will hear the heavens, and they shall hear the earth;

22 And the earth shall hear the corn, and the wine, and the oil; and they shall hear Yizreel.

23 And I will sow her unto Me in the earth; and I will have mercy upon her that had not obtained mercy; and I will say to them who were not My people, 'You are My people!' And they shall say, 'You are my God (Elohim)!'"

3 Then said יהוה unto me, "Go yet, love a woman beloved of her friend, yet an adulteress, according to the love of יהוה toward the children of Yisrael, who look to other gods (elohim), and love flagons of wine."

2 So I bought her to me for fifteen pieces of silver, and for a homer of barley, and a half homer of barley.

3 And I said unto her, "You shalt abide for me many days; you shalt not play the harlot, and you shalt not be for another man; so will I also be for you."

4 For the children of Yisrael shall abide many days without a king, and without a prince, and

without a sacrifice, and without an image, and without an ephod, and without teraphim.

5 Afterward shall the children of Yisrael return, and seek יהוה their God (YHWH Eloheihem), and Dawid their king; and shall fear יהוה and His goodness in the latter days.

4 Hear the word of יהוה, you children of Yisrael, for יהוה hath a controversy with the inhabitants of the land, because there is no truth, nor mercy, nor knowledge of God (Elohim) in the land.

2 By swearing, and lying, and killing, and stealing, and committing adultery, they break out, and blood toucheth blood.

3 Therefore shall the land mourn, and every one that dwelleth therein shall languish, with the beasts of the field, and with the fowls of sky; yea, the fishes of the sea also shall be taken away.

4 Yet let no man strive, nor reprove another, for your people are as they that strive with the kohen.

5 Therefore shalt you fall in the day, and the prophet also shall fall with you in the night, and I will destroy your mother.

6 My people are destroyed for lack of knowledge; because you have rejected knowledge, I will also reject you, that you shalt be no priest (kohen) to Me; seeing you have forgotten the Torah of your God (Elohim), I will also forget your children.

7 As they were increased, so they sinned against Me; therefore will I change their glory into shame.

8 They eat up the sin of My people, and they set their heart on their iniquity.

9 And there shall be, like people, like priest (kohen); and I will punish them for their ways, and reward them their doings.

10 For they shall eat, and not have enough; they shall commit whoredom, and shall not increase; because they have left off to take heed to יהוה.

11 Whoredom and wine and new wine take away the heart.

12 My people ask counsel at their stocks, and their staff declareth unto them; for the spirit of whoredoms hath caused them to err, and they have gone a whoring from under their God (Elohim).

13 They sacrifice upon the tops of the mountains, and burn incense upon the hills, under oaks and poplars and elms, because the shadow thereof

is good; therefore your daughters shall commit whoredom, and your spouses shall commit adultery.

14 I will not punish your daughters when they commit whoredom, nor your spouses when they commit adultery; for themselves are separated with whores, and they sacrifice with harlots; therefore the people that doth not understand shall fall.

15 Though you, Yisrael, play the harlot, yet let not Judah (Yehudah) offend; and come not you unto Gilgal, neither go you up to House of Vanity (Beit Awen), nor swear, 'יהוה liveth'.

16 For Yisrael slideth back as a backsliding heifer; now יהוה will feed them as a lamb in a large place.

17 Efrayim is joined to idols; let him alone.

18 Their drink is sour; they have committed whoredom continually; her rulers dearly love shame.

19 The wind hath bound her up in her wings, and they shall be ashamed because of their sacrifices.

5 "Hear you this, O priests (kohanim); and hearken, you house of Yisrael; and give you ear, O house of the king; for judgment is toward you, because you have been a snare on Mizpah, and a net spread upon Tabor.

2 And the revolters are profound to make slaughter, though I have been a rebuker of them all.

3 I know Efrayim, and Yisrael is not hid from Me; for now, O Efrayim, you committest whoredom, and Yisrael is defiled.

4 They will not frame their doings to turn unto their God (Elohim); for the spirit of whoredoms is in the midst of them, and they have not known יהוה.

5 And the pride of Yisrael doth testify to his face; therefore shall Yisrael and Efrayim fall in their iniquity; Judah (Yehudah) also shall fall with them.

6 They shall go with their flocks and with their herds to seek יהוה; but they shall not find Him; He hath withdrawn Himself from them.

7 They have dealt treacherously against יהוה, for they have begotten strange children. Now shall New Moon devour them with their portions.

8 Blow you the shofar in Gibeah, and the trumpet in Ramah; cry aloud at Beit Awen, 'Behind you, O Benjamin (Binyamin)!'

9 Efrayim shall be desolate in the day of rebuke;

among the tribes of Yisrael have I made known that which shall surely be.

10 The princes of Judah (Yehudah) were like them that remove the bound; therefore I will pour out My wrath upon them like water.

11 Efrayim is oppressed and broken in judgment, because he willingly walked after the commandment.

12 Therefore will I be unto Efrayim as a moth, and to the house of Judah (Yehudah) as rottenness.

13 When Efrayim saw his sickness, and Judah (Yehudah) saw his wound, then went Efrayim to the Assyrian (Ashshur), and sent to King Yarev; yet could he not heal you, nor cure you of your wound.

14 For I will be unto Efrayim as a lion, and as a young lion to the house of Judah (Yehudah). I, even I, will tear and go away; I will take away, and none shall rescue him.

15 I will go and return to My place, till they acknowledge their offence, and seek My face; in their affliction they will seek Me early."

6 'Come, and let us return unto יהוה; for He hath torn, and He will heal us; He hath smitten, and He will bind us up.

2 After two days will He revive us; on the third day He will raise us up, and we shall live in His sight.

3 Then shall we know, if we follow on to know יהוה. His going forth is prepared as the morning; and He shall come unto us as the rain, as the latter and former rain unto the earth.'

4 "O Efrayim, what shall I do unto you? O Judah (Yehudah), what shall I do unto you? For your goodness is as a morning cloud, and as the early dew it goeth away.

5 Therefore have I hewed them by the prophets; I have slain them by the words of My mouth; and your judgments are as the light that goeth forth.

6 For I desired mercy, and not sacrifice; and the knowledge of God (Elohim) more than burnt offerings.

7 But they like men have transgressed the covenant; there have they dealt treacherously against Me.

8 Gilad is a city of them that work iniquity, and is polluted with blood.

9 And as troops of robbers wait for a man, so the company of priests (kohanim) murder in

the way by consent; for they commit lewdness.

10 I have seen a horrible thing in the house of Yisrael; there is the whoredom of Efrayim, Yisrael is defiled.

11 Also, O Judah (Yehudah), he hath set a harvest for you, when I returned the captivity of My people."

7 "When I would have healed Yisrael, then the iniquity of Efrayim was uncovered, and the wickedness of Samaria (Shomeron); for they commit falsehood; and the thief cometh in, and the troop of robbers spoileth outside.

2 And they consider not in their hearts that I remember all their wickedness; now their own doings have beset them about; they are before My face.

3 They make the king glad with their wickedness, and the princes with their lies.

4 They are all adulterers, as an oven heated by the baker, who ceaseth from raising after he hath kneaded the dough, until it be leavened.

5 In the day of our king the princes have made him sick with bottles of wine; he stretched out his hand with scorners.

6 For they have made ready their heart like an oven, while they lie in wait; their baker sleepeth all the night; in the morning it burneth as a flaming fire.

7 They are all hot as an oven, and have devoured their judges; all their kings are fallen; there is none among them that calleth unto Me.

8 Efrayim, he hath mixed himself among the people; Efrayim is a cake not turned.

9 Strangers have devoured his strength, and he knoweth it not; yea, gray hairs are here and there upon him, yet he knoweth not.

10 And the pride of Yisrael testifieth to his face; and they do not return to יהוה their God (YHWH Eloheihem), nor seek him for all this.

11 Efrayim also is like a silly dove without heart; they call to Egypt (Mitsrayim), they go to Assyria (Ashshur).

12 When they shall go, I will spread my net upon them; I will bring them down as the fowls of the sky; I will chastise them, as their congregation hath heard.

13 Woe unto them! For they have fled from Me; destruction unto them! Because they have transgressed against Me; though I have redeemed them, yet they have spoken lies against Me.

14 And they have not cried unto Me with their heart, when they howled upon their beds; they assemble themselves for corn and wine, and they rebel against Me.

15 Though I have bound and strengthened their arms, yet do they imagine mischief against Me.

16 They return, but not upward; they are like a deceitful bow; their princes shall fall by the sword for the rage of their tongue; this shall be their derision in the land of Egypt (Mitsrayim)."

8 "Set the shofar to your mouth. He shall come as an eagle against the house of יהוה, because they have transgressed My covenant, and trespassed against My Torah.

2 Yisrael shall cry unto Me, 'My God (Elohim), we know You!'

3 Yisrael hath cast off the thing that is good; the enemy shall pursue him.

4 They have set up kings, but not by Me; they have made princes, and I knew it not; of their silver and their gold have they made them idols, that they may be cut off.

5 Your calf, O Samaria (Shomeron), hath cast you off; Mine anger is kindled against them; how long will it be ere they attain to innocency?

6 For from Yisrael was it also; the workman made it; therefore it is not God (Elohim); but the calf of Samaria (Shomeron) shall be broken in pieces.

7 For they have sown the wind, and they shall reap the whirlwind; it hath no stalk; the bud shall yield no meal; if so be it yield, the strangers shall swallow it up.

8 Yisrael is swallowed up; now shall they be among the nations as a vessel wherein is no pleasure.

9 For they are gone up to Assyria (Ashshur), a wild ass alone by himself; Efrayim hath hired lovers.

10 Yea, though they have hired among the nations, now will I gather them, and they shall sorrow a little for the burden of the king of princes.

11 Because Efrayim hath made many altars to sin, altars shall be unto him to sin.

12 I have written to him the great things of My Torah, but they were counted as a strange thing.

13 They sacrifice flesh for the sacrifices of Mine offerings, and eat it; but יהוה accepteth them not; now will He remember their iniquity, and visit their sins; they shall return to Egypt

(Mitsrayim).

14 For Yisrael hath forgotten his Maker, and buildeth temples; and Judah (Yehudah) hath multiplied fenced cities; but I will send a fire upon his cities, and it shall devour the palaces thereof."

9 Rejoice not, O Yisrael, for joy, as other people, for you have gone a whoring from your God (Elohim). You have loved a reward upon every cornfloor.

2 The floor and the winepress shall not feed them, and the new wine shall fail in her.

3 They shall not dwell in יהוה's land; but Efrayim shall return to Egypt (Mitsrayim), and they shall eat unclean things in Assyria (Ashshur).

4 They shall not offer wine offerings to יהוה, neither shall they be pleasing unto him: their sacrifices shall be unto them as the bread of mourners; all that eat thereof shall be polluted. For their bread for their soul shall not come into the house of יהוה.

5 What will you do in the solemn day, and in the day of the feast of יהוה?

6 For, behold, they are gone because of destruction. Egypt (Mitsrayim) shall gather them up, Memphis shall bury them; the pleasant places for their silver, nettles shall possess them; thorns shall be in their tabernacles.

7 The days of visitation are come, the days of recompence are come; Yisrael shall know it; the prophet is a fool, the spiritual man is mad, for the multitude of your iniquity, and the great hatred.

8 The watchman of Efrayim was with my God (Elohim); but the prophet is a snare of a fowler in all his ways, and hatred in the house of his God (Elohim).

9 They have deeply corrupted themselves, as in the days of Gibeah; therefore He will remember their iniquity, He will visit their sins.

10 "I found Yisrael like grapes in the wilderness; I saw your fathers as the firstripe in the fig tree at her first time; but they went to Baal-Peor, and separated themselves unto that shame; and their abominations were according as they loved.

11 As for Efrayim, their glory shall fly away like a bird, from the birth, and from the womb, and from the conception.

12 Though they bring up their children, yet will I bereave them, that there shall not be a man left; yea, woe also to them when I depart from

them!

13 Efrayim, as I saw Tyrus, is planted in a pleasant place; but Efrayim shall bring forth his children to the murderer."

14 Give them, O יהוה; what wilt You give? Give them a miscarrying womb and dry breasts.

15 "All their wickedness is in Gilgal; for there I hated them; for the wickedness of their doings I will drive them out of Mine house, I will love them no more. All their princes are revolters.

16 Efrayim is smitten, their root is dried up, they shall bear no fruit; yea, though they bring forth, yet will I slay even the beloved fruit of their womb."

17 My God (Elohim) will cast them away, because they did not hearken unto him; and they shall be wanderers among the nations.

10 Yisrael is an empty vine, he bringeth forth fruit unto himself; according to the multitude of his fruit he hath increased the altars; according to the goodness of his land they have made goodly images.

2 Their heart is divided; now shall they be found faulty. He shall break down their altars, he shall spoil their images.

3 For now they shall say, "We have no king, because we feared not יהוה; what then should a king do to us?"

4 They have spoken words, swearing falsely in making a covenant; thus judgment springeth up as hemlock in the furrows of the field.

5 The inhabitants of Samaria (Shomeron) shall fear because of the calves of Beit Aven; for the people thereof shall mourn over it, and the priests (kohanim) thereof that rejoiced on it, for the glory thereof, because it is departed from it.

6 It shall be also carried unto Assyria (Ashshur) for a present to king Yarev; Efrayim shall receive shame, and Yisrael shall be ashamed of his own counsel.

7 As for Samaria (Shomeron), her king is cut off as the foam upon the water.

8 The high places also of Aven, the sin of Yisrael, shall be destroyed; the thorn and the thistle shall come up on their altars; and they shall say to the mountains, "Cover us!" And to the hills, "Fall on us!"

9 "O Yisrael, you have sinned from the days of Gibeah. There they stood; the battle in Gibeah against the children of iniquity did not overtake them.

10 It is in My desire that I should chastise them; and the people shall be gathered against them, when they shall bind themselves in their two furrows.

11 And Efrayim is as a heifer that is taught, and loveth to tread out the corn; but I passed over upon her fair neck: I will make Efrayim to ride; Judah (Yehudah) shall plow, and Jacob (Yaaqov) shall break his clods."

12 Sow to yourselves in righteousness, reap in mercy; break up your fallow ground, for it is time to seek יהוה, till He come and rain righteousness upon you.

13 You have plowed wickedness, you have reaped iniquity; you have eaten the fruit of lies; because you didst trust in your way, in the multitude of your mighty men.

14 Therefore shall a tumult arise among your people, and all your fortresses shall be spoiled, as Shalman spoiled Beit-Arvel in the day of battle; the mother was dashed in pieces upon her children.

15 So shall Bethel (Beit-El) do unto you because of your great wickedness. In a morning shall the king of Yisrael utterly be cut off!

11 "When Yisrael was a child (young nation), I loved him, and called My son (people) out of Egypt (Mitsrayim).

2 As they called them, so they went from them; they sacrificed unto Baals (Baalim), and burned incense to graven images.

3 I taught Efrayim also to go, taking them by their arms; but they knew not that I healed them.

4 I drew them with cords of a man, with bands of love: and I was to them as they that take off the yoke on their jaws, and I laid meat unto them.

5 He shall not return into the land of Egypt (Mitsrayim), but the Assyrian (Ashshur) shall be his king, because they refused to return.

6 And the sword shall abide on his cities, and shall consume his branches, and devour them, because of their own counsels.

7 And My people are bent to backsliding from Me; though they called them to the Most High, none at all would exalt Him.

8 How shall I give you up, Efrayim? How shall I deliver you, Yisrael? How shall I make you as Admah? How shall I set you as Zeboim? Mine heart is turned within Me, My compassions are kindled together.

9 I will not execute the fierceness of Mine anger, I will not return to destroy Efrayim; for I am God (Elohim), and not man; the Holy One in the midst of you; and I will not enter into the city.

10 They shall walk after יהוה; he shall roar like a lion; when he shall roar, then the children shall tremble from the west.

11 They shall tremble as a bird out of Egypt (Mitsrayim), and as a dove out of the land of Assyria (Ashshur). And I will place them in their houses," saith יהוה.

12 Efrayim compasseth Me about with lies, and the house of Yisrael with deceit; but Judah (Yehudah) yet ruleth with God (Elohim), and is faithful with the holy ones.

12 Efrayim feedeth on wind, and followeth after the east wind; he daily increaseth lies and desolation; and they do make a covenant with the Assyrians, and oil is carried into Egypt (Mitsrayim).

2 יהוה hath also a controversy with Judah (Yehudah), and will punish Jacob (Yaaqov) according to his ways; according to his doings will He recompense him.

3 He took his brother by the heel in the womb, and by his strength he had power with God (Elohim).

4 Yea, he had power over the angel, and prevailed; he wept, and made supplication unto him; he found Him in Bethel (Beit-El), and there He spake with us;

5 That is יהוה God of hosts (YHWH Elohei Tsevaot); יהוה is His memorial!

6 Therefore turn you to your God (Elohim); keep mercy and judgment, and wait on your God (Elohim) continually.

7 He is a merchant, the balances of deceit are in his hand; he loveth to oppress.

8 And Efrayim said, "Yet I am become rich, I have found me out substance; in all my labors they shall find none iniquity in me that were sin."

9 "And I that am יהוה your God (YHWH Eloheikha) from the land of Egypt (Mitsrayim) will yet make you to dwell in tabernacles, as in the days of the solemn feast.

10 I have also spoken by the prophets, and I have multiplied visions, and used similitudes, by the ministry of the prophets."

11 Is there iniquity in Gilad? Surely they are

vanity; they sacrifice bullocks in Gilgal; yea, their altars are as heaps in the furrows of the fields.

12 And Jacob (Yaaqov) fled into the country of Syria (Aram), and Yisrael served for a wife, and for a wife he kept sheep.

13 And by a prophet יהוה brought Yisrael out of Egypt (Mitsrayim), and by a prophet was he preserved.

14 Efrayim provoked Him to anger most bitterly; therefore shall He leave his blood upon him, and his reproach shall his Lord (Adonai) return unto him.

13 When Efrayim spake trembling, he exalted himself in Yisrael; but when he offended in the Baal, he died.

2 And now they sin more and more, and have made them molten images of their silver, and idols according to their own understanding, all of it the work of the craftsmen; they say of them, "Let the men that sacrifice kiss the calves."

3 Therefore they shall be as the morning cloud, and as the early dew that passeth away, as the chaff that is driven with the whirlwind out of the floor, and as the smoke out of the chimney.

4 "Yet I am יהוה your God (YHWH Eloheikha) from the land of Egypt (Mitsrayim), and you shalt know no God (Elohim) but Me; for there is no Savior besides Me.

5 I did know you in the wilderness, in the land of great drought.

6 According to their pasture, so were they filled; they were filled, and their heart was exalted; therefore have they forgotten Me.

7 Therefore I will be unto them as a lion; as a leopard by the way will I observe them;

8 I will meet them as a bear that is bereaved of her whelps, and will rend the caul of their heart, and there will I devour them like a lion; the wild beast shall tear them.

9 O Yisrael, you have destroyed yourself; but in Me is your help.

10 I will be your king; where is any other that may save you in all your cities? And your judges of whom you saidst, 'Give me a king and princes?'

11 I gave you a king in Mine anger, and took him away in My wrath.

12 The iniquity of Efrayim is bound up; his sin is stored up.

13 The sorrows of a travailing woman shall come upon him; he is an unwise son; for he should not stay long in the place of the breaking forth of children.

14 I will ransom them from the power of the grave (sheol); I will redeem them from death. O Death, I will be your plagues! O Grave (sheol), I will be your destruction! Compassion shall be hidden from Mine eyes.

15 Though he be fruitful among his brethren, an east wind shall come, the wind of יהוה shall come up from the wilderness, and his spring shall become dry, and his fountain shall be dried up; he shall spoil the treasure of all pleasant vessels.

16 Samaria (Shomeron) shall become desolate; for she hath rebelled against her God (Elohim); they shall fall by the sword; their infants shall be dashed in pieces, and their women with child shall be ripped up.

14 O Yisrael, return unto יהוה your God (YHWH Eloheikha); for you have fallen by your iniquity.

2 Take with you words, and turn to יהוה; say unto Him, "Take away all iniquity, and receive us graciously; so will we render the calves of our lips.

3 Asshur (Assyria) shall not save us; we will not ride upon horses; neither will we say anymore to the work of our hands, 'Our gods (elohim)'; for in You the fatherless findeth mercy.'"

4 I will heal their backsliding, I will love them freely; for Mine anger is turned away from him.

5 I will be as the dew unto Yisrael; he shall grow as the lily, and cast forth his roots as Lebanon.

6 His branches shall spread, and his beauty shall be as the olive tree, and his smell as Lebanon.

7 They that dwell under his shadow shall return; they shall revive as the corn, and grow as the vine; the scent thereof shall be as the wine of Lebanon.

8 Efrayim shall say, 'What have I to do any more with idols?' I have heard him, and observed him; I am like a green fir tree. From Me is your fruit found."

9 Who is wise, and he shall understand these things? Prudent, and he shall know them? For the ways of יהוה are right, and the just shall walk in them; but the transgressors shall fall therein.

JOEL
YOEL יוֹאֵל
(YHWH is El)

1 The word of יהוה that came to [A56]Joel (Yoel) the son of Pethuel.

2 Hear this, you old men, and give ear, all you inhabitants of the land. Hath this been in your days, or even in the days of your fathers?

3 Tell you your children of it, and let your children tell their children, and their children another generation.

4 That which the palmerworm hath left hath the locust eaten; and that which the locust hath left hath the cankerworm eaten; and that which the cankerworm hath left hath the caterpiller eaten.

5 Awake, you drunkards, and weep; and howl, all you drinkers of wine, because of the new wine; for it is cut off from your mouth.

6 For a nation is come up upon my land, strong, and without number, whose teeth are the teeth of a lion, and he hath the cheek teeth of a great lion.

7 He hath laid my vine waste, and barked my fig tree; he hath made it clean bare, and cast it away; the branches thereof are made white.

8 Lament like a virgin girded with sackcloth for the husband of her youth.

9 The meat offering and the drink offering is cut off from the house of יהוה; the priests (kohanim), יהוה's ministers, mourn.

10 The field is wasted; the land mourneth, for the corn is wasted; the new wine is dried up, the oil languisheth.

11 Be you ashamed, O you husbandmen; howl, O you vinedressers, for the wheat and for the barley; because the harvest of the field is perished.

12 The vine is dried up, and the fig tree languisheth; the pomegranate tree, the palm tree also, and the apple tree, even all the trees of the field, are withered; because joy has withered away from the sons of men.

13 Gird yourselves, and lament, you priests (kohanim); howl, you ministers of the altar; come, lie all night in sackcloth, you ministers of my God (Elohim); for the meat offering and the drink offering is withholden from the house of your God (Elohim).

14 Sanctify you a fast, call a solemn assembly, gather the elders and all the inhabitants of the land into the house of יהוה your God (YHWH Eloheikhem), and cry unto יהוה,

15 Alas for the day! For the day of יהוה is at hand, and as a destruction from the Almighty shall it come.

16 Is not the meat cut off before our eyes, yea, joy and gladness from the house of our God (Elohim)?

17 The seed is rotten under their clods, the garners are laid desolate, the barns are broken down; for the corn is withered.

18 How do the beasts groan! the herds of cattle are perplexed, because they have no pasture; yea, the flocks of sheep are made desolate.

19 O יהוה, to You will I cry; for the fire hath devoured the pastures of the wilderness, and the flame hath burned all the trees of the field.

20 The beasts of the field cry also unto You, for the rivers of waters are dried up, and the fire hath devoured the pastures of the wilderness.

2 Blow you the trumpet in Zion (Tsiyon), and sound an alarm in my holy mountain; let all the inhabitants of the land tremble, for the day of יהוה cometh, for it is near at hand;

2 A day of darkness and of gloominess, a day of clouds and of thick darkness, as the morning spread upon the mountains; a great people and a strong; there hath not been ever the like, neither shall be any more after it, even to the years of many generations.

3 A fire devoureth before them; and behind them a flame burneth; the land is as the garden of Eden before them, and behind them a desolate wilderness; yea, and nothing shall escape them.

4 The appearance of them is as the appearance of horses; and as horsemen, so shall they run.

5 Like the noise of chariots on the tops of mountains shall they leap, like the noise of a flame of fire that devoureth the stubble, as a strong people set in battle array.

6 Before their face the people shall be much pained; all faces shall gather blackness.

7 They shall run like mighty men; they shall climb the wall like men of war; and they shall march every one on his ways, and they shall not break their ranks:

8 Neither shall one thrust another; they shall walk every one in his path; and when they fall upon the sword, they shall not be wounded.

9 They shall run to and fro in the city; they shall

run upon the wall, they shall climb up upon the houses; they shall enter in at the windows like a thief.

10 The earth shall quake before them; the heavens shall tremble; the sun and the moon shall be dark, and the stars shall withdraw their shining;

11 And יהוה shall utter His voice before His army, for His camp is very great; for He is strong who executeth His word; for the day of יהוה is great and very terrible; and who can abide it?

12 Therefore also now, saith יהוה, turn you even to Me with all your heart, and with fasting, and with weeping, and with mourning;

13 And rend your heart, and not your garments, and turn unto יהוה your God (YHWH Eloheikhem), for he is gracious and merciful, slow to anger, and of great kindness, and regret of the disaster (raah).

14 Who knoweth if he will return and repent, and leave a blessing behind him; even a meat offering and a drink offering unto יהוה your God (YHWH Eloheikhem)?

15 Blow the shofar in Zion (Tsiyon), sanctify a fast, call a solemn assembly;

16 Gather the people, sanctify the congregation, assemble the elders, gather the children, and those that suck the breasts; let the bridegroom go forth of his chamber, and the bride out of her closet.

17 Let the priests (kohanim), the ministers of יהוה, weep between the porch and the altar, and let them say, "Spare Your people, O יהוה, and give not Your heritage to reproach, that the heathen should rule over them; wherefore should they say among the people, 'Where is their God (Elohim)?'"

18 Then will יהוה be jealous for His land, and pity His people.

19 Yea, יהוה will answer and say unto His people, "Behold, I will send you corn, and wine, and oil, and you shall be satisfied therewith; and I will no more make you a reproach among the heathen;

20 But I will remove far off from you the northern army, and will drive him into a land barren and desolate, with his face toward the east sea, and his hinder part toward the utmost sea, and his stink shall come up, and his ill savour shall come up, because he hath done great things.

21 Fear not, O land; be glad and rejoice, for יהוה will do great things.

22 Be not afraid, you beasts of the field; for the pastures of the wilderness do spring, for the tree beareth her fruit, the fig tree and the vine do yield their strength.

23 Be glad then, you children of Zion (Tsiyon), and rejoice in יהוה your God (YHWH Eloheikhem); for He hath given you the former rain moderately, and He will cause to come down for you the rain, the former rain, and the latter rain in the first month.

24 And the floors shall be full of wheat, and the fats shall overflow with wine and oil.

25 And I will restore to you the years that the locust hath eaten, the cankerworm, and the caterpiller, and the palmerworm, My great army which I sent among you.

26 And you shall eat in plenty, and be satisfied, and praise the name of יהוה your God (YHWH Eloheikhem), that hath dealt wondrously with you; and My people shall never be ashamed.

27 And you shall know that I am in the midst of Yisrael, and that I am יהוה your God (YHWH Eloheikhem), and none else; and My people shall never be ashamed.

28 And it shall come to pass afterward, that I will pour out My Spirit upon all flesh; and your sons and your daughters shall prophesy, your old men shall dream dreams, your young men shall see visions:

29 And also upon the servants and upon the handmaids in those days will I pour out My Spirit.

30 And I will shew wonders in the heavens and in the earth, blood, and fire, and pillars of smoke.

31 The sun shall be turned into darkness, and the moon into blood, before the great and the awesome day of יהוה come.

32 And it shall come to pass, that whosoever shall call on the name of יהוה shall be delivered; for in Mount Zion (Tsiyon) and in Jerusalem (Yerushalayim) shall be deliverance, as יהוה hath said, and in the remnant whom יהוה shall call.

3 For, behold, in those days, and in that time, when I shall bring again the captivity of Judah (Yehudah) and Jerusalem (Yerushalayim),

2 I will also gather all nations, and will bring

them down into the valley of Yehoshafat, and will plead with them there for My people and for My heritage Yisrael, whom they have scattered among the nations, and parted My land.

3 And they have cast lots for My people; and have given a boy for a harlot, and sold a girl for wine, that they might drink.

4 Yea, and what have you to do with Me, O Tyre, and Zidon, and all the coasts of Palestine? Will you render Me a recompence? And if you recompense Me, swiftly and speedily will I return your recompence upon your own head;

5 Because you have taken My silver and My gold, and have carried into your temples My goodly pleasant things;

6 The children also of Judah (Yehudah) and the children of Jerusalem (Yerushalayim) have you sold unto the Grecians, that you might remove them far from their border.

7 Behold, I will raise them out of the place whither you have sold them, and will return your recompence upon your own head.

8 And I will sell your sons and your daughters into the hand of the children of Judah (Yehudah), and they shall sell them to the Sabeans, to a people far off: for יהוה hath spoken it.

9 Proclaim you this among the nations: "Prepare war! Wake up the mighty men, let all the men of war draw near; let them come up;

10 Beat your plowshares into swords, and your pruninghooks into spears; let the weak say, 'I am strong.'"

11 Assemble yourselves, and come, all you nations, and gather yourselves together round about; thither cause Your mighty ones to come down, O יהוה.

12 Let the nations be wakened, and come up to the valley of Yehoshafat, for there will I sit to judge all the heathen round about.

13 Put you in the sickle, for the harvest is ripe; come, get you down, for the press is full, the fats overflow; for their wickedness is great.

14 Multitudes, multitudes in the valley of decision, for the day of יהוה is near in the valley of decision.

15 The sun and the moon shall be darkened, and the stars shall withdraw their shining.

16 יהוה also shall roar out of Zion (Tsiyon), and utter His voice from Jerusalem (Yerushalayim); and the heavens and the earth shall shake; but יהוה will be the hope of His people, and the strength of the children of Yisrael.

17 So shall you know that I am יהוה your God (YHWH Eloheikhem) dwelling in Zion (Tsiyon), My holy mountain; then shall Jerusalem (Yerushalayim) be holy, and there shall no strangers pass through her any more.

18 And it shall come to pass in that day, that the mountains shall drop down new wine, and the hills shall flow with milk, and all the rivers of Judah (Yehudah) shall flow with waters, and a fountain shall come forth of the house of יהוה, and shall water the valley of Shittim.

19 Egypt (Mitsrayim) shall be a desolation, and Edom shall be a desolate wilderness, for the violence against the children of Judah (Yehudah), because they have shed innocent blood in their land.

20 But Judah (Yehudah) shall dwell forever, and Jerusalem (Yerushalayim) from generation to generation.

21 For I will cleanse their blood that I have not cleansed; for יהוה dwelleth in Zion (Tsiyon)."

AMOS
עָמוֹס AMOS
(Burden Bearer)

1 The words of [A57]Amos, who was among the herdmen of Tekoa, which he saw concerning Yisrael in the days of Uzziyahu king of Judah (Yehudah), and in the days of Jeroboam (Yarovam) the son of Yoash king of Yisrael, two years before the earthquake.

2 And he said, "יהוה will roar from Zion (Tsiyon), and utter His voice from Jerusalem (Yerushalayim); and the habitations of the shepherds shall mourn, and the top of Carmel shall wither."

3 Thus saith יהוה: "For three transgressions of Damascus (Dammeseq), and for four, I will not turn away the punishment thereof; because they have threshed Gilad with threshing instruments of iron;

4 But I will send a fire into the house of Hazael, which shall devour the palaces of Ben-Hadad.

5 I will break also the bar of Damascus (Dammeseq), and cut off the inhabitant from the plain of Aven, and him that holdeth the sceptre from the house of Eden; and the people of Syria (Aram) shall go into captivity unto Kir," saith יהוה.

6 Thus saith יהוה: "For three transgressions of Gaza (Azzah), and for four, I will not turn away the punishment thereof; because they carried away captive the whole captivity, to deliver them up to Edom;

7 But I will send a fire on the wall of Gaza (Azzah), which shall devour the palaces thereof;

8 And I will cut off the inhabitant from Ashdod, and him that holdeth the sceptre from Ashkelon, and I will turn Mine hand against Ekron; and the remnant of the Philistines shall perish," saith Lord (Adonai) יהוה.

9 Thus saith יהוה: "For three transgressions of Tyrus, and for four, I will not turn away the punishment thereof, because they delivered up the whole captivity to Edom, and remembered not the brotherly covenant;

10 But I will send a fire on the wall of Tyrus, which shall devour the palaces thereof."

11 Thus saith יהוה: "For three transgressions of Edom, and for four, I will not turn away the punishment thereof; because he did pursue his brother with the sword, and did cast off all pity, and his anger did tear perpetually, and he kept his wrath forever;

12 But I will send a fire upon Teman, which shall devour the palaces of Bozrah."

13 Thus saith יהוה: "For three transgressions of the children of Ammon, and for four, I will not turn away the punishment thereof; because they have ripped up the women with child of Gilad, that they might enlarge their border;

14 But I will kindle a fire in the wall of Rabbah, and it shall devour the palaces thereof, with shouting in the day of battle, with a tempest in the day of the whirlwind;

15 And their king shall go into captivity, he and his princes together," saith יהוה.

2 Thus saith יהוה: "For three transgressions of Moav, and for four, I will not turn away the punishment thereof, because he burned the bones of the king of Edom into lime;

2 But I will send a fire upon Moav, and it shall devour the palaces of Kerioth; and Moav shall die with tumult, with shouting, and with the sound of the shofar.

3 And I will cut off the judge from the midst thereof, and will slay all the princes thereof with him," saith יהוה.

4 Thus saith יהוה: "For three transgressions of Judah (Yehudah), and for four, I will not turn away the punishment thereof, because they have despised the Torah of יהוה, and have not kept His commandments, and their lies caused them to err, after the which their fathers have walked;

5 But I will send a fire upon Judah (Yehudah), and it shall devour the palaces of Jerusalem (Yerushalayim).

6 Thus saith יהוה: "For three transgressions of Yisrael, and for four, I will not turn away the punishment thereof, because they sold the righteous for silver, and the poor for a pair of shoes,

7 That pant after the dust of the earth on the head of the poor, and turn aside the way of the meek; and a man and his father will go in unto the same maid, to profane My holy name;

8 And they lay themselves down upon clothes laid to pledge by every altar, and they drink the wine of the condemned in the house of their god.

9 Yet destroyed I the Amorite before them, whose height was like the height of the cedars, and he was strong as the oaks; yet I destroyed

his fruit from above, and his roots from beneath.

10 Also I brought you up from the land of Egypt (Mitsrayim), and led you forty years through the wilderness, to possess the land of the Amorite.

11 And I raised up of your sons for prophets, and of your young men for Nazarites (Nazirim). Is it not even thus, O you children of Yisrael?" saith יהוה.

12 "But you gave the Nazarites (Nazirim) wine to drink; and commanded the prophets, saying, 'Prophesy not!'.

13 Behold, I am pressed under you, as a cart is pressed that is full of sheaves.

14 Therefore the flight shall perish from the swift, and the strong shall not strengthen his force, neither shall the mighty deliver himself;

15 Neither shall he stand that handleth the bow; and he that is swift of foot shall not deliver himself; neither shall he that rideth the horse deliver himself.

16 And he that is courageous among the mighty shall flee away naked in that day", saith יהוה.

3 Hear this word that יהוה hath spoken against you, O children of Yisrael, against the whole family which I brought up from the land of Egypt (Mitsrayim), saying:

2 "You only have I known of all the families of the earth; therefore I will punish you for all your iniquities."

3 Can two walks together, except they be agreed?

4 Will a lion roar in the forest, when he hath no prey? Will a young lion cry out of his den, if he has taken nothing?

5 Can a bird fall in a snare upon the earth, where no gin is for him? Shall one take up a snare from the earth, and have taken nothing at all?

6 Shall a trumpet be blown in the city, and the people not be afraid? Shall there be disaster (raah) in a city, and יהוה hath not done it?

7 Surely Lord (Adonai) יהוה will do nothing, but He revealeth His secret unto His servants the prophets.

8 The lion hath roared, who will not fear? Lord (Adonai) יהוה hath spoken, who can but prophesy?

9 "Publish in the palaces at Ashdod, and in the palaces in the land of Egypt (Mitsrayim), and say: 'Assemble yourselves upon the mountains of Samaria (Shomeron); and behold the great tumults in the midst thereof, and the oppressed in the midst thereof.

10 For they know not to do right', saith יהוה, who store up violence and robbery in their palaces.

11 Therefore thus saith Lord (Adonai) יהוה: "An adversary there shall be even round about the land; and he shall bring down your strength from you, and your palaces shall be plundered."

12 Thus saith יהוה: "As the shepherd taketh out of the mouth of the lion two legs, or a piece of an ear; so shall the children of Yisrael be taken out that dwell in Samaria (Shomeron) in the corner of a bed, and in Damascus (Dammeseq) in a couch!

13 Hear you, and testify in the house of Jacob (Yaaqov)," saith Lord (Adonai) יהוה, God of hosts (Elohei Tsevaot),

14 That in the day that I shall visit the transgressions of Yisrael upon him I will also visit the altars of Bethel (Beit-El); and the horns of the altar shall be cut off, and fall to the ground.

15 And I will smite the winter house with the summer house; and the houses of ivory shall perish, and the great houses shall have an end," saith יהוה.

4 Hear this word, you kine (women) of Bashan, that are in the mountain of Samaria (Shomeron), who oppress the poor, who crush the needy, who say to their masters (husbands), "Bring, and let us drink."

2 Lord (Adonai) יהוה hath sworn by His holiness, that, behold, the days shall come upon you, that He will take you away with hooks, and your posterity with fishhooks.

3 And you shall go out at the breaches, every cow (women) at that which is before her; and you shall cast them into the palace," saith יהוה.

4 "Come to Bethel (Beit-El), and transgress; at Gilgal multiply transgression; and bring your sacrifices every morning, and your tithes after three years;

5 And offer a sacrifice of thanksgiving with leaven, and proclaim and publish the free offerings, for this liketh you, O you children of Yisrael," saith Lord (Adonai) יהוה.

6 "And I also have given you cleanness of teeth in all your cities, and want of bread in all your places; yet have you not returned unto Me," saith יהוה.

7 "And also I have withholden the rain from

you, when there were yet three months to the harvest; and I caused it to rain upon one city, and caused it not to rain upon another city; one piece was rained upon, and the piece whereupon it rained not withered.

8 So two or three cities wandered unto one city, to drink water; but they were not satisfied; yet have you not returned unto me," saith יהוה.

9 "I have smitten you with blasting and mildew; when your gardens and your vineyards and your fig trees and your olive trees increased, the palmerworm devoured them; yet have you not returned unto Me," saith יהוה.

10 "I have sent among you the pestilence after the manner of Egypt (Mitsrayim); your young men have I slain with the sword, and have taken away your horses; and I have made the stink of your camps to come up unto your nostrils; yet have you not returned unto Me," saith יהוה.

11 "I have overthrown some of you, as God (Elohim) overthrew Sodom and Gomorrah, and you were as a firebrand plucked out of the burning; yet have you not returned unto Me," saith יהוה.

12 "Therefore thus will I do unto you, O Yisrael; and because I will do this unto you, prepare to meet your God (Elohim), O Yisrael!"

13 For, behold, He Who formeth the mountains, and createth the wind, and declareth unto man what is His thought, that maketh the morning darkness, and treadeth upon the high places of the earth, יהוה God of hosts (YHWH Elohei Tsevaot) is His name.

5 Hear you this word which I take up against you, even a lamentation, O house of Yisrael:

2 The virgin of Yisrael is fallen; she shall no more rise. She is forsaken upon her land; there is none to raise her up.

3 For thus saith Lord (Adonai) יהוה: "The city that went out by a thousand shall leave a hundred, and that which went forth by a hundred shall leave ten, to the house of Yisrael!"

4 For thus saith יהוה unto the house of Yisrael: "Seek you Me, and you shall live;

5 But seek not Bethel (Beit-El), nor enter into Gilgal, and pass not to Beer-Sheva; for Gilgal shall surely go into captivity, and Bethel (Beit-El) shall come to nothing.

6 Seek יהוה, and you shall live; lest he break out like fire in the house of Joseph (Yosef), and devour it, and there be none to quench it in Bethel (Beit-El).

7 You who turn judgment to wormwood, and leave off righteousness in the earth!"

8 Seek Him who maketh the seven stars and Orion, and turneth the shadow of death into the morning, and maketh the day dark with night; who calleth for the waters of the sea, and poureth them out upon the face of the earth: יהוה is His name.

9 He who causes destruction against the strong, so that the destruction shall come against the fortress.

10 They hate him who rebuketh in the gate, and they abhor him who speaketh uprightly.

11 Forasmuch therefore as your treading is upon the poor, and you take from him burdens of wheat; you have built houses of hewn stone, but you shall not dwell in them; you have planted pleasant vineyards, but you shall not drink wine of them.

12 For I know your manifold transgressions and your mighty sins; they afflict the just, they take a bribe, and they turn aside the poor in the gate from their right.

13 Therefore the prudent shall keep silence in that time, for it is an evil time.

14 Seek good, and not evil, that you may live; and so יהוה God of hosts (YHWH Elohei Tsevaot), shall be with you, as you have spoken.

15 Hate the evil, and love the good, and establish judgment in the gate; it may be that יהוה God of hosts (YHWH Elohei Tsevaot) will be gracious unto the remnant of Joseph (Yosef).

16 Therefore יהוה God of hosts (YHWH Elohei Tsevaot), the Lord (Adonai), saith thus: "Wailing shall be in all streets; and they shall say in all the highways, 'Alas! Alas!' And they shall call the husbandman to mourning, and such as are skilful of lamentation to wailing.

17 And in all vineyards shall be wailing, for I will pass through you," saith יהוה.

18 Woe unto you that desire the day of יהוה! To what end is it for you? The day of יהוה is darkness, and not light.

19 As if a man did flee from a lion, and a bear met him; or went into the house, and leaned his hand on the wall, and a serpent bit him.

20 Shall not the day of יהוה be darkness, and not light? Even very dark, and no brightness in it?

21 I hate, I despise your feast days, and I will not smell in your solemn assemblies.

22 Though you offer Me burnt offerings and your meat offerings, I will not accept them; nor will I regard the peace offerings of your fat beasts.

23 Take you away from Me the noise of your songs, for I will not hear the melody of your harps.

24 But let judgment run down as waters, and righteousness as a mighty stream.

25 Have you offered unto Me sacrifices and offerings in the wilderness forty years, O house of Yisrael?

26 But you have borne the tabernacle of your Moloch and Chiun your images, the star of your god, which you made to yourselves.

27 Therefore will I cause you to go into captivity beyond Damascus (Dammeseq)," saith the God of hosts (Elohei Tsevaot), Whose name is יהוה.

6 Woe to them that are at ease in Zion (Tsiyon), and trust in the mountain of Samaria (Shomeron), which are named chief of the nations, to whom the house of Yisrael came!

2 Pass you unto Calneh, and see; and from thence go you to Hamath the great; then go down to Gath of the Philistines; be they better than these kingdoms? Or their territory greater than your territory?

3 You that put far away the evil day, and cause the seat of violence to come near;

4 That lie upon beds of ivory, and stretch themselves upon their couches, and eat the lambs out of the flock, and the calves out of the midst of the stall;

5 That chant to the sound of the viol, and invent to themselves instruments of musick, like Dawid;

6 That drink wine in bowls, and anoint themselves with the chief ointments, but they are not grieved for the affliction of Joseph (Yosef).

7 Therefore now shall they go captive with the first that go captive, and the banquet of them that stretched themselves shall be removed.

8 Lord (Adonai) יהוה hath sworn by Himself, saith יהוה God of hosts (YHWH Elohei Tsevaot): "I abhor the excellency of Jacob (Yaaqov), and hate his palaces; therefore will I deliver up the city with all that is therein."

9 And it shall come to pass, if there remain ten men in one house, that they shall die.

10 And a man's uncle shall take him up, and he that burneth him, to bring out the bones out of the house, and shall say unto him that is by the sides of the house, "Is there yet any with you?" And he shall say, "No." Then shall he say, "Hold your tongue, for we must not make mention of the name of יהוה."

11 For, behold, יהוה commandeth, and He will smite the great house with breaches, and the little house with clefts.

12 Shall horses run upon the rock? Will one plow there with oxen? For you have turned judgment into gall, and the fruit of righteousness into wormwood (bitterness);

13 You who rejoice in worthless thing (lo debar), who say, "Have we not taken Qarnayim by our own strength?

14 But, behold, I will raise up against you a nation, O house of Yisrael," saith יהוה God of hosts (YHWH Elohei Tsevaot); and they shall afflict you from the entrance of Hemath unto the river of the wilderness.

7 Thus hath Lord (Adonai) יהוה shewed unto me: Behold, He formed grasshoppers in the beginning of the shooting up of the latter growth; and, behold, it was the latter growth after the king's mowings.

2 And it came to pass, that when they had made an end of eating the grass of the land, then I said: "O Lord (Adonai) יהוה, forgive, I beseech you; by whom shall Jacob (Yaaqov) arise, for he is small?

3 יהוה regretted for this. "It shall not be," saith יהוה.

4 Thus hath Lord (Adonai) יהוה shewed unto me: and, behold, Lord (Adonai) יהוה called to contend by fire, and it devoured the great deep, and did eat up a part.

5 Then said I, "O Lord (Adonai) יהוה, cease, I beseech you; by whom shall Jacob (Yaaqov) arise, for he is small?"

6 יהוה regretted for this. "This also shall not be," saith Lord (Adonai) יהוה.

7 Thus He shewed me; and, behold, the Lord (Adonai) stood upon a wall made by a plumbline, with a plumbline in His hand.

8 And יהוה said unto me, "Amos, what seest you?" And I said, "A plumbline." Then said the Lord (Adonai), "Behold, I will set a plumbline in the midst of My people Yisrael; I will not again pass by them anymore.

9 And the high places of Isaac (Yitschaq) shall

be desolate, and the sanctuaries of Yisrael shall be laid waste; and I will rise against the house of Jeroboam (Yarovam) with the sword.

10 Then Amazyah the kohen of Bethel (Beit-El) sent to Jeroboam (Yarovam) king of Yisrael, saying, "Amos hath conspired against you in the midst of the house of Yisrael; the land is not able to bear all his words.

11 For thus Amos saith: 'Jeroboam (Yarovam) shall die by the sword, and Yisrael shall surely be led away captive out of their own land.'"

12 Also Amazyah said unto Amos, "O you seer, go, flee you away into the land of Judah (Yehudah), and there eat bread, and prophesy there;

13 But prophesy not again anymore at Bethel (Beit-El), for it is the king's chapel, and it is the king's court."

14 Then answered Amos, and said to Amazyah: "I was no prophet, nor was I a prophet's son; but I was an herdman, and a gatherer of sycamore fruit.

15 And יהוה took me as I followed the flock, and יהוה said unto me, 'Go, prophesy unto My people Yisrael.'

16 Now therefore hear you the word of יהוה: you sayest, 'Prophesy not against Yisrael, and drop not your word against the house of Isaac (Yitschaq).'

17 Therefore thus saith יהוה: 'Your wife shall be a harlot in the city, and your sons and your daughters shall fall by the sword, and your land shall be divided by line; and you shalt die in a polluted land; and Yisrael shall surely go into captivity forth of his land.'"

8 Thus hath Lord (Adonai) יהוה shewed unto me: and behold a basket of summer fruit.

2 And He said, "Amos, what seest you?" And I said, "A basket of summer fruit." Then said יהוה unto me, "The end has come upon My people of Yisrael; I will not again pass by them anymore.

3 And the songs of the temple shall be howlings in that day," saith Lord (Adonai) יהוה; "there shall be many dead bodies in every place; they shall cast them forth with silence."

4 Hear this, O you that swallow up the needy, even to make the poor of the land to fail,

5 Saying: "When will the New Moon be gone, that we may sell corn? And the Shabbat, that we may set forth wheat, making the ephah small, and the shekel great, and falsifying the balances by deceit,

6 That we may buy the poor for silver, and the needy for a pair of shoes; yea, and sell the refuse of the wheat?"

7 יהוה hath sworn by the excellency of Jacob (Yaaqov): "Surely I will never forget any of their works.

8 Shall not the land tremble for this, and every one mourns that dwelleth therein? And it shall rise up wholly as a flood; and it shall be cast out and drowned, as by the flood of Egypt (Mitsrayim).

9 And it shall come to pass in that day," saith Lord (Adonai) יהוה, that I will cause the sun to go down at noon, and I will darken the earth in the clear day;

10 And I will turn your feasts into mourning, and all your songs into lamentation; and I will bring up sackcloth upon all loins, and baldness upon every head; and I will make it as the mourning of an only son, and the end thereof as a bitter day.

11 "Behold, the days come," saith Lord (Adonai) יהוה, "That I will send a famine in the land, not a famine of bread, nor a thirst for water, but of hearing the words of יהוה;

12 And they shall wander from sea to sea, and from the north even to the east, they shall run to and fro to seek the word of יהוה, and shall not find it.

13 In that day shall the fair virgins and young men faint for thirst.

14 They that swear by the sin of Samaria (Shomeron), and say, 'Your God (Elohim), O Dan, liveth!' and, 'The manner of Beer-Sheva liveth; even they shall fall, and never rise up again."

9 I saw the Lord (Adonai) standing upon the altar; and He said, "Smite the lintel of the door, that the posts may shake; and cut them in the head, all of them; and I will slay the last of them with the sword; he that fleeth of them shall not flee away, and he that escapeth of them shall not be delivered.

2 Though they dig into hell (sheol), thence shall Mine hand take them; though they climb up to heaven, thence will I bring them down;

3 And though they hide themselves in the top of Carmel, I will search and take them out thence; and though they be hidden from My sight in the bottom of the sea, thence will I command the

serpent, and he shall bite them;

4 And though they go into captivity before their enemies, thence will I command the sword, and it shall slay them; and I will set Mine eyes upon them for evil, and not for good.

5 And Lord (Adonai) יהוה of hosts (YHWH Tsevaot) is He who toucheth the land, and it shall melt, and all that dwell therein shall mourn; and it shall rise up wholly like a flood; and shall be drowned, as by the flood of Egypt (Mitsrayim).

6 It is He that buildeth His stories in the heaven, and hath founded His troop in the earth; He who calleth for the waters of the sea, and poureth them out upon the face of the earth: יהוה is His name.

7 "Are you not as children of the Ethiopians (Kushim) unto Me, O children of Yisrael?" saith יהוה. "Have not I brought up Yisrael out of the land of Egypt (Mitsrayim)? And the Philistines from Caphtor, and the Syrians (Arammim) from Kir?

8 Behold, the eyes of Lord (Adonai) יהוה are upon the sinful kingdom, and I will destroy it from off the face of the earth; except that I will not utterly destroy the house of Jacob (Yaaqov)," saith יהוה.

9 "For, behold, I will command, and I will sift the house of Yisrael among all nations, like as corn is sifted in a sieve, yet shall not the least grain fall upon the earth.

10 All the sinners of My people shall die by the sword, who say, 'The disaster (raah) shall not overtake nor prevent us.'

11 In that day will I raise up the tabernacle of Dawid that is fallen, and close up the breaches thereof; and I will raise up his ruins, and I will build it as in the days of old;

12 That they may possess the remnant of Edom, and of all the nations, which are called by My name," saith יהוה that doeth this.

13 "Behold, the days come," saith יהוה, "that the plowman shall overtake the reaper, and the treader of grapes him that soweth seed; and the mountains shall drop sweet wine, and all the hills shall melt.

14 And I will bring again the captivity of My people of Yisrael, and they shall build the waste cities, and inhabit them; and they shall plant vineyards, and drink the wine thereof; they shall also make gardens, and eat the fruit of them.

15 And I will plant them upon their land, and they shall no more be pulled up out of their land which I have given them," saith יהוה your God (YHWH Eloheikha).

OBADIAH
OVADYAH עֹבַדְיָה
(Servant of YHWH)

1 The vision of [A58]Obadiah (Ovadyah). Thus saith Lord (Adonai) יהוה concerning Edom: We have heard a report from יהוה, and an ambassador is sent among the nations saying, "Arise you, and let us rise up against her in battle":

2 "Behold, I have made you small among the nations; you are greatly despised.

3 The pride of your heart hath deceived you, you that dwellest in the clefts of the rock, whose habitation is high; that saith in his heart, 'Who shall bring me down to the ground?'

4 Though you exalt yourself as the eagle, and though you set your nest among the stars, thence will I bring you down," saith יהוה.

5 If thieves came to you, if robbers by night, (how are you cut off!) would they not have stolen till they had enough? If the grapegatherers came to you, would they not leave some grapes?

6 How are the things of Esaw searched out! How are his hidden things sought out.

7 All the men of your confederacy have brought you even to the border; the men that were at peace with you have deceived you, and prevailed against you; they that eat your bread have laid a wound under you; there is none understanding in him.

8 "Shall I not in that day," saith יהוה, "even destroy the wise men out of Edom, and understanding out of the mount of Esaw?

9 And your mighty men, O Teman, shall be dismayed, to the end that every one of the mount of Esaw may be cut off by slaughter.

10 For your violence against your brother Jacob (Yaaqov) shame shall cover you, and you shalt be cut off forever.

11 In the day that you stoodest on the other side, in the day that the strangers carried away captive his forces, and foreigners entered into his gates, and cast lots upon Jerusalem (Yerushalayim), even you wast as one of them.

12 But you shouldest not have looked on the day of your brother in the day that he became a stranger; neither shouldest you have rejoiced over the children of Judah (Yehudah) in the day of their destruction; nor shouldest you have spoken proudly in the day of distress.

13 You shouldest not have entered into the gate of My people in the day of their disaster; yea, you shouldest not have looked on their affliction in the day of their disaster, nor have laid hands on their substance in the day of their disaster;

14 Neither shouldest you have stood in the stakeway, to cut off those of his that did escape; nor shouldest you have delivered up those of his that did remain in the day of distress.

15 "For the day of יהוה is near upon all the nations; as you have done, it shall be done unto you; your reward shall return upon your own head.

16 For as you have drunk upon My holy mountain, so shall all the nations drink continually, yea, they shall drink, and they shall swallow down, and they shall be as though they had not been.

17 But upon Mount Zion (Tsiyon) shall be deliverance, and there shall be holiness; and the house of Jacob (Yaaqov) shall possess their possessions.

18 And the house of Jacob (Yaaqov) shall be a fire, and the house of Joseph (Yosef) a flame, and the house of Esaw for stubble, and they shall kindle in them, and devour them; and there shall not be any remaining of the house of Esaw," for יהוה hath spoken it.

19 And they of the south shall possess the mount of Esaw; and they of the plain the Philistines; and they shall possess the fields of Efrayim, and the fields of Samaria (Shomeron); and Benjamin (Binyamin) shall possess Gilad.

20 And the captivity of this host of the children of Yisrael shall possess that of the Canaanites, even unto Zarephath; and the captivity of Jerusalem (Yerushalayim), which is in Sepharad, shall possess the cities of the south.

21 And saviors shall come up on Mount Zion (Tsiyon) to judge the mount of Esaw; and the kingdom shall be יהוה's.

JONAH
YONAH יוֹנָה
(Dove)

1 Now the word of יהוה came unto [A59]Jonah (Yonah) the son of Amittai, saying,

2 "Arise, go to Nineveh, that great city, and cry against it; for their wickedness has come up before Me.

3 But Yonah rose up to flee unto Tarshish from the presence of יהוה, and went down to Joppa (Yafo); and he found a ship going to Tarshish; so he paid the fare thereof, and went down into it, to go with them unto Tarshish from the presence of יהוה.

4 But יהוה sent out a great wind into the sea, and there was a mighty tempest in the sea, so that the ship was like to be broken.

5 Then the mariners were afraid, and cried every man unto his god, and cast forth the wares that were in the ship into the sea, to lighten it of them. But Yonah was gone down into the sides of the ship; and he lay, and was fast asleep.

6 So the shipmaster came to him, and said unto him, "What meanest you, O sleeper? Arise, call upon your God (Elohim), if so be that God (Elohim) will think upon us, that we perish not."

7 And they said every one to his fellow, "Come, and let us cast lots, that we may know for whose cause this evil is upon us." So they cast lots, and the lot fell upon Yonah.

8 Then said they unto him, "Please tell us, for whose cause this disaster (raah) is upon us? What is your occupation? And whence comest you? What is your country? And of what people are you?"

9 And he said unto them, "I am a Hebrew (Ivri); and I fear יהוה, God of the Heaven (Elohei haShamayim), who hath made the sea and the dry land.

10 Then were the men exceedingly afraid, and said unto him, "Why have you done this?" For the men knew that he fled from the presence of יהוה, because he had told them.

11 Then said they unto him, "What shall we do unto you, that the sea may be calm unto us? For the sea wrought, and was tempestuous."

12 And he said unto them, "Take me up, and cast me forth into the sea; so shall the sea be calm unto you; for I know that for my sake this great tempest is upon you."

13 Nevertheless the men rowed hard to bring it to the land; but they could not, for the sea wrought, and was tempestuous against them.

14 Wherefore they cried unto יהוה, and said, "We beseech You, O יהוה, we beseech You, let us not perish for this man's life, and lay not upon us innocent blood; for You, O יהוה, hast done as it pleased You.

15 So they took up Yonah, and cast him forth into the sea, and the sea ceased from her raging.

16 Then the men feared יהוה exceedingly, and offered a sacrifice unto יהוה, and made vows.

17 Now יהוה had prepared a great fish to swallow up Yonah. And Yonah was in the belly of the fish three days and three nights.

2 Then Yonah prayed unto יהוה his God (Elohim) out of the fish's belly,

2 And said, "I cried by reason of mine affliction unto יהוה, and He heard me; out of the belly of hell (sheol) cried I, and You heardest my voice.

3 For You hadst cast me into the deep, in the midst of the seas; and the floods compassed me about; all your billows and your waves passed over me."

4 Then I said, "I am cast out of Your sight; yet I will look again toward Your holy temple.

5 The waters compassed me about, even to the soul; the depth closed me round about, the weeds were wrapped about my head.

6 I went down to the bottoms of the mountains; the earth with her bars was about me forever; yet have You brought up my life from corruption, O יהוה my God (YHWH Elohai).

7 When my soul fainted within me I remembered יהוה; and my prayer came in unto You, into Your holy temple.

8 They that observe lying vanities forsake their own mercy.

9 But I will sacrifice unto You with the voice of thanksgiving; I will pay that what I have vowed. Salvation (Yeshuah) is of יהוה."

10 And יהוה spake unto the fish, and it vomited out Yonah upon the dry land.

3 And the word of יהוה came unto Yonah the second time, saying,

2 "Arise, go unto Nineveh, that great city, and preach unto it the preaching that I bid you."

3 So Yonah arose, and went unto Nineveh, according to the word of יהוה. Now Nineveh was an exceeding great city of three days'

journey.

4 And Yonah began to enter into the city a day's journey, and he cried, and said, "Yet forty days, and Nineveh shall be overthrown."

5 So the people of Nineveh believed God (Elohim), and proclaimed a fast, and put on sackcloth, from the greatest of them even to the least of them.

6 For word came unto the king of Nineveh, and he arose from his throne, and he laid his robe from him, and covered him with sackcloth, and sat in ashes.

7 And he caused it to be proclaimed and published through Nineveh by the decree of the king and his nobles, saying, "Let neither man nor beast, herd nor flock, taste anything; let them not feed, nor drink water;

8 But let man and beast be covered with sackcloth, and cry mightily unto God (Elohim); yea, let them turn every one from his evil way, and from the violence that is in their hands.

9 Who can tell if God (Elohim) will turn and regret, and turn away from His fierce anger, that we perish not?

10 And God (Elohim) saw their works, that they turned from their evil way; and God (Elohim) regretted of the disaster (raah), that He had said that he would do unto them; and He did it not.

4 But it displeased Yonah exceedingly, and he was very angry.

2 And he prayed unto יהוה, and said, "Please, O יהוה, was not this my saying, when I was yet in my country? Therefore I fled before unto Tarshish; for I knew that You are a gracious God (Elohim), and merciful, slow to anger, and of great kindness, and regretted of the disaster (raah).

3 Therefore now, O יהוה, take, I beseech You, my life from me; for it is better for me to die than to live!"

4 Then said יהוה, "Doest you well to be angry?"

5 So Yonah went out of the city, and sat on the east side of the city, and there made him a booth, and sat under it in the shadow, till he might see what would become of the city.

6 And God (Elohim) יהוה prepared a gourd, and made it to come up over Yonah, that it might be a shadow over his head, to deliver him from his grief. So Yonah was exceeding glad of the gourd.

7 But God (Elohim) prepared a worm when the morning rose the next day, and it smote the gourd that it withered.

8 And it came to pass, when the sun did arise, that God (Elohim) prepared a vehement east wind; and the sun beat upon the head of Yonah, that he fainted, and wished in himself to die, and said, "It is better for me to die than to live."

9 And God (Elohim) said to Yonah, "Doest you well to be angry for the gourd?" And he said, "I do well to be angry, even unto death."

10 Then said יהוה, "You have had pity on the gourd, for which you have not labored, neither madest it grows; which came up in a night, and perished in a night.

11 And should not I spare Nineveh, that great city, wherein are more than sixscore thousand persons that cannot discern between their right hand and their left hand; and also much cattle?"

MICAH
MIKHAH מִיכָה
(Who is like YHWH)

1 The word of יהוה that came to [A60]Micah (Mikhah) the Morasthite in the days of Yotam, Achaz, and Hezekiah (Chizqiyahu), kings of Judah (Yehudah), which he saw concerning Samaria (Shomeron) and Jerusalem (Yerushalayim).

2 Hear, all you people; hearken, O earth, and all that therein is; and let Lord (Adonai) יהוה be witness against you, the Lord (Adonai) from His holy temple.

3 For, behold, יהוה cometh forth out of His place, and will come down, and tread upon the high places of the earth.

4 And the mountains shall be molten under Him, and the valleys shall be cleft, as wax before the fire, and as the waters that are poured down a steep place.

5 For the transgression of Jacob (Yaaqov) is all this, and for the sins of the house of Yisrael. What is the transgression of Jacob (Yaaqov)? Is it not Samaria (Shomeron)? And what are the high places of Judah (Yehudah)? Are they not Jerusalem (Yerushalayim)?

6 Therefore I will make Samaria (Shomeron) as a heap of the field, and as plantings of a vineyard; and I will pour down the stones thereof into the valley, and I will discover the foundations thereof.

7 And all the graven images thereof shall be beaten to pieces, and all the hires thereof shall be burned with the fire, and all the idols thereof will I lay desolate; for she gathered it of the hire of a harlot, and they shall return to the hire of a harlot.

8 Therefore I will wail and howl, I will go stripped and naked; I will make a wailing like the dragons, and mourning as the owls.

9 For her wound is incurable; for it is come unto Judah (Yehudah); he is come unto the gate of My people, even to Jerusalem (Yerushalayim).

10 Declare you it not at Gath, weep you not at all; in the house of Aphrah roll yourself in the dust.

11 Pass you away, you inhabitant of Saphir, having your shame naked; the inhabitant of Zaanan came not forth in the mourning of Bethezel; he shall receive of you his standing.

12 For the inhabitant of Maroth waited carefully for good, but disaster (raah) came down from יהוה unto the gate of Jerusalem (Yerushalayim).

13 O you inhabitant of Lachish, bind the chariot to the swift beast; she is the beginning of the sin to the daughter of Zion (Tsiyon), for the transgressions of Yisrael were found in you.

14 Therefore shalt you give presents to Moreshethgath; the houses of Achzib shall be a lie to the kings of Yisrael.

15 Yet will I bring an heir unto you, O inhabitant of Mareshah; he shall come unto Adullam the glory of Yisrael.

16 Make you bald, and poll you for your delicate children; enlarge your baldness as the eagle; for they are gone into captivity from you.

2 Woe to them that devise iniquity, and work evil upon their beds! When the morning is light, they practise it, because it is in the power of their hand.

2 And they covet fields, and take them by violence; and houses, and take them away; so they oppress a man and his house, even a man and his heritage.

3 Therefore thus saith יהוה: "Behold, against this family do I devise a disaster (raah), from which you shall not remove your necks; nor shall you go haughtily; for this time is evil.

4 In that day shall one take up a parable against you, and lament with a doleful lamentation, and say, 'We be utterly destroyed; He hath changed the portion of my people; how hath He removed it from me! Turning away He hath divided our fields.'"

5 Therefore you shalt have none that shall cast a cord by lot in the congregation of יהוה.

6 "Prophesy you not", say they to them that prophesy; they shall not prophesy to them, that they shall not take shame.

7 O you who art named the house of Jacob (Yaaqov): "Is the Spirit of יהוה straitened? Are these His doings?' Do not My words do good to him that walketh uprightly?

8 Even of late My people is risen up as an enemy; you pull off the robe with the garment from them that pass by securely as men averse from war.

9 The women of My people have you cast out from their pleasant houses; from their children have you taken away My glory forever.

10 Arise you and depart, for this is not your rest;

because it is polluted, it shall destroy you, even with a sore destruction.

11 If a man walking in the spirit and falsehood do lie, saying, 'I will prophesy unto you of wine and of strong drink;' he shall even be the spokeman of this people.

12 I will surely assemble, O Jacob (Yaaqov), all of you; I will surely gather the remnant of Yisrael; I will put them together as the sheep of Bozrah, as the flock in the midst of their fold; they shall make great noise by reason of the multitude of men.

13 The breaker is come up before them; they have broken up, and have passed through the gate, and are gone out by it; and their king shall pass before them, and יהוה on the head of them."

3 And I said, "Hear, please, O heads of Jacob (Yaaqov), and you princes of the house of Yisrael: Is it not for you to know justice?

2 Who hate the good, and love the evil; who pluck off their skin from off them, and their flesh from off their bones;

3 Who also eat the flesh of my people, and flay their skin from off them; and they break their bones, and chop them in pieces, as for the pot, and as flesh within the caldron."

4 Then shall they cry unto יהוה, but He will not hear them: He will even hide His face from them at that time, as they have behaved themselves ill in their doings.

5 Thus saith יהוה concerning the prophets that make my people err, that bite with their teeth, and cry, "Peace"; and he that putteth not into their mouths, they even prepare war against him:

6 "Therefore night shall be unto you, that you shall not have a vision; and it shall be dark unto you, that you shall not divine; and the sun shall go down over the prophets, and the day shall be dark over them.

7 Then shall the seers be ashamed, and the diviners confounded: yea, they shall all cover their lips; for there is no answer of God (Elohim)."

8 But truly I am full of power by the Spirit of יהוה, and of justice, and of might, to declare unto Jacob (Yaaqov) his transgression, and to Yisrael his sin.

9 Hear this, please, you heads of the house of Jacob (Yaaqov), and princes of the house of Yisrael, that abhor judgment, and pervert all equity.

10 They build up Zion (Tsiyon) with blood, and

Jerusalem (Yerushalayim) with iniquity.

11 The heads thereof judge for reward, and the kohanim thereof teach for hire, and the prophets thereof divine for money: yet will they lean upon יהוה, and say, "Is not יהוה among us? None evil can come upon us."

12 Therefore shall Zion (Tsiyon) for your sake be plowed as a field, and Jerusalem (Yerushalayim) shall become heaps, and the mountain of the house as the high places of the forest.

4 But in the last days it shall come to pass, that the mountain of the house of יהוה shall be established in the top of the mountains, and it shall be exalted above the hills; and people shall flow unto it.

2 And many nations shall come, and say, "Come, and let us go up to the mountain of יהוה, and to the house of the God (Elohim) of Jacob (Yaaqov); and He will teach us of His ways, and we will walk in His paths." For the Torah shall go forth of Zion (Tsiyon), and the word of יהוה from Jerusalem (Yerushalayim).

3 And He shall judge among many people, and rebuke strong nations afar off; and they shall beat their swords into plowshares, and their spears into pruning hooks; nation shall not lift up a sword against nation, neither shall they learn war anymore.

4 But they shall sit every man under his vine and under his fig tree; and none shall make them afraid, for the mouth of יהוה of hosts (YHWH Tsevaot) hath spoken it.

5 For all people will walk every one in the name of his god (elohim), but we will walk in the name of יהוה (YHWH) our God (Eloheinu) forever and ever.

6 "In that day," saith יהוה, "will I assemble her that halteth, and I will gather her that is driven out, and her that I have afflicted;

7 And I will make her that halted a remnant, and her that was cast far off a strong nation; and יהוה shall reign over them in Mount Zion (Tsiyon) from henceforth, even forever.

8 And you, O tower of the flock, the strong hold of the daughter of Zion (Tsiyon), unto you shall it come, even the first dominion; the kingdom shall come to the daughter of Yerushalayim."

9 Now why dost you cry out aloud? Is there no king in you? Is your counsellor perished? For pangs have taken you as a woman in travail.

10 Be in pain, and labour to bring forth, O

daughter of Zion (Tsiyon), like a woman in travail; for now shalt you go forth out of the city, and you shalt dwell in the field, and you shalt go even to Babylon (Bavel). There shalt you be delivered; there יהוה shall redeem you from the hand of your enemies.

11 Now also many nations are gathered against you, that say, "Let her be defiled, and let our eye look upon Zion (Tsiyon)."

12 But they know not the thoughts of יהוה, neither understand they his counsel; for he shall gather them as the sheaves into the floor.

13 Arise and thresh, O daughter of Zion (Tsiyon); for I will make your horn iron, and I will make your hoofs brass; and you shalt beat in pieces many people; and I will consecrate their gain unto יהוה, and their substance unto the Lord (Adonai) of the whole earth."

5 Now gather yourself in troops, O daughter of troops; he hath laid siege against us; they shall smite the judge of Yisrael with a rod upon the cheek.

2 "But you, Bethlehem (Beit-Lechem) Efratah, though you be little among the thousands of Judah (Yehudah), yet out of you shall he come forth unto Me that is to be ruler in Yisrael; whose goings forth have been from of old, from everlasting.

3 Therefore will He give them up, until the time that she which travaileth hath brought forth; then the remnant of his brethren shall return unto the children of Yisrael.

4 And he shall stand and feed in the strength of יהוה, in the majesty of the name of יהוה his God (Elohim); and they shall abide, for now shall He be great unto the ends of the earth.

5 And this man shall be the peace, when the Assyrian (Ashshur) shall come into our land; and when he shall tread in our palaces, then shall we raise against him seven shepherds, and eight principal men.

6 And they shall waste the land of Assyria (Ashshur) with the sword, and the land of Nimrod in the entrances thereof; thus shall He deliver us from the Assyrian (Ashshur), when he cometh into our land, and when he treadeth within our borders.

7 And the remnant of Jacob (Yaaqov) shall be in the midst of many people as a dew from יהוה, as the showers upon the grass, that tarrieth not for man, nor waiteth for the sons of men.

8 And the remnant of Jacob (Yaaqov) shall be among the nations in the midst of many people as a lion among the beasts of the forest, as a young lion among the flocks of sheep; who, if he go through, both treadeth down, and teareth in pieces, and none can deliver.

9 Your hand shall be lifted up upon your adversaries, and all your enemies shall be cut off.

10 "And it shall come to pass in that day," saith יהוה, "that I will cut off your horses out of the midst of you, and I will destroy your chariots.

11 And I will cut off the cities of your land, and throw down all your strong holds.

12 And I will cut off witchcrafts out of your hand; and you shalt have no more soothsayers.

13 Your graven images also will I cut off, and your standing pillar out of the midst of you; and you shalt no more worship the work of your hands.

14 And I will pluck up your Asherim out of the midst of you; so will I destroy your cities.

15 And I will execute vengeance in anger and fury upon the nations which have not obeyed."

6 Hear you now what יהוה saith: "Arise, contend you before the mountains, and let the hills hear your voice.

2 Hear you, O mountains, יהוה's controversy, and you strong foundations of the earth; for יהוה hath a controversy with His people, and He will plead with Yisrael.

3 O My people, what have I done unto you? And wherein have I wearied you? Testify against Me.

4 For I brought you up out of the land of Egypt (Mitsrayim), and redeemed you out of the house of servants; and I sent before you Moses (Mosheh), Aaron (Aharon), and Miryam.

5 O My people, remember now what Balak king of Moav consulted, and what Balaam the son of Beor answered him from Shittim unto Gilga, that you may know the righteousness of יהוה."

6 Wherewith shall I come before יהוה, and bow myself before the God (Elohim) on high? Shall I come before Him with burnt offerings, with calves of a year old?

7 Will יהוה be pleased with thousands of rams, or with ten thousands of rivers of oil? Shall I give my firstborn for my transgression, the fruit of my body for the sin of my soul?

8 He hath shewed you, O man, what is good; and what doth יהוה require of you, but to do justly, and to love mercy, and to walk humbly with

your God (Elohim)?

9 יהוה's voice crieth unto the city, and the man of wisdom shall see Your name: "Hear, O tribe, and who hath appointed it?

10 Are there yet the treasures of wickedness in the house of the wicked, and the scant measure that is abominable?

11 Shall I count them pure with the wicked balances, and with the bag of deceitful weights?

12 For the rich men thereof are full of violence, and the inhabitants thereof have spoken lies, and their tongue is deceitful in their mouth.

13 Therefore also will I make you sick in smiting you, in making you desolate because of your sins.

14 You shalt eat, but not be satisfied; and your casting down shall be in the midst of you; and you shalt take hold, but shalt not deliver; and that which you deliverest will I give up to the sword.

15 You shalt sow, but you shalt not reap; you shalt tread the olives, but you shalt not anoint you with oil; and sweet wine, but shalt not drink wine.

16 For the statutes of Omri are kept, and all the works of the house of Achav, and you walk in their counsels, that I should make you a desolation, and the inhabitants thereof a hissing; therefore you shall bear the reproach of My people."

7 Woe is me! For I am as when they have gathered the summer fruits, as the grapegleanings of the vintage; there is no cluster to eat; my soul desired the firstripe fruit.

2 The good man has perished out of the earth; and there is none upright among men; they all lie in wait for blood; they hunt every man his brother with a net.

3 That they may do evil with both hands earnestly, the prince asketh, and the judge asketh for a reward; and the great man, he uttereth his mischievous desire; so they wrap it up.

4 The best of them is as a brier; the most upright is sharper than a thorn hedge; the day of your watchmen and your visitation cometh; now shall be their perplexity.

5 Trust you not in a friend, put you not confidence in a guide; keep the doors of your mouth from her that lieth in your bosom.

6 For the son dishonoureth the father, the daughter riseth up against her mother, the daughter in law against her mother in law; a man's enemies are the men of his own house.

7 Therefore I will look unto יהוה; I will wait for the God (Elohim) of my salvation; my God (Elohim) will hear me.

8 Rejoice not against me, O mine enemy; when I fall, I shall arise; when I sit in darkness, יהוה shall be a light unto me.

9 I will bear the indignation of יהוה, because I have sinned against Him, until He plead my cause, and execute judgment for me. He will bring me forth to the light, and I shall behold His righteousness.

10 Then she that is mine enemy shall see it, and shame shall cover her which said unto me, "Where is יהוה your God (YHWH Eloheikha)?" Mine eyes shall behold her; now shall she be trodden down as the mire of the streets.

11 In the day that your walls are to be built, in that day shall the decree be far removed.

12 In that day also he shall come even to you from Assyria (Ashshur), and from the fortified cities, and from the fortress even to the river, and from sea to sea, and from mountain to mountain.

13 Notwithstanding the land shall be desolate because of them that dwell therein, for the fruit of their doings.

14 Feed your people with your rod, the flock of your heritage, which dwell solitarily in the wood, in the midst of Carmel; let them feed in Bashan and Gilad, as in the days of old.

15 "According to the days of your coming out of the land of Egypt (Mitsrayim) will I shew unto him marvellous things."

16 The nations shall see and be confounded at all their might; they shall lay their hand upon their mouth, their ears shall be deaf.

17 They shall lick the dust like a serpent, they shall move out of their holes like worms of the earth; they shall be afraid of יהוה our God (YHWH Eloheinu), and shall fear because of you.

18 Who is a God (Elohim) like unto You, that pardoneth iniquity, and passeth by the transgression of the remnant of His heritage? He retaineth not His anger forever, because He delighteth in mercy.

19 He will turn again, He will have compassion upon us; He will subdue our iniquities; and You wilt cast all their sins into the depths of the sea.

20 You wilt perform the truth to Jacob (Yaaqov), and the mercy to Avraham, which You have sworn unto our fathers from the days of old.

NAHUM
NACHUM נַחוּם
(Comforter)

1 The burden of Nineveh. The book of the vision of [A61]Nahum (Nachum) the Elkoshite.
2 God (El) is jealous, and יהוה revengeth; יהוה revengeth, and is furious; יהוה will take vengeance on His adversaries, and He reserveth wrath for His enemies.
3 יהוה is slow to anger, and great in power, and will not at all acquit the wicked; יהוה hath His way in the whirlwind and in the storm, and the clouds are the dust of His feet.
4 He rebuketh the sea, and maketh it dry, and drieth up all the rivers. Bashan languisheth, and Carmel, and the flower of Lebanon languisheth.
5 The mountains quake at Him, and the hills melt, and the earth is burned at His presence, yea, the world, and all that dwell therein.
6 Who can stand before His indignation? And who can abide in the fierceness of His anger? His fury is poured out like fire, and the rocks are thrown down by Him.
7 יהוה is good, a strong hold in the day of trouble; and He knoweth them that trust in Him.
8 But with an overrunning flood He will make an utter end of the place thereof, and darkness shall pursue His enemies.
9 What do you device against יהוה? He will make an utter end; affliction shall not rise up the second time.
10 For while they be folden together as thorns, and while they are drunken as drunkards, they shall be devoured as stubble fully dry.
11 There is one come out of you, that plots evil against יהוה, a wicked counsellor.
12 Thus saith יהוה: "Though they be quiet, and likewise many, yet thus shall they be cut down, when he shall pass through. Though I have afflicted you, I will afflict you no more;
13 For now will I break his yoke from off you, and will burst your bonds apart."
14 And יהוה hath given a commandment concerning you: "That no more of your name be sown; out of the house of your gods (elohim) will I cut off the graven image and the molten image; I will make your grave; for you are vile."
15 Behold upon the mountains the feet of him that bringeth good tidings, that publisheth

peace! O Judah (Yehudah), keep your solemn feasts, perform your vows; for the wicked shall no more pass through you; he is utterly cut off.
2 He that dasheth in pieces has come up before your face; keep the munition, watch the way, make your loins strong, fortify your power mightily.
2 For יהוה hath turned away the excellency of Jacob (Yaaqov), as the excellency of Yisrael; for the emptiers have emptied them out, and marred their vine branches.
3 The shield of His mighty men is made red, the valiant men are in scarlet; the chariots shall be with flaming torches in the day of his preparation, and the fir trees shall be terribly shaken.
4 The chariots shall rage in the streets, they shall justle one against another in the broad ways; they shall seem like torches, they shall run like the lightnings.
5 He shall recount his worthies; they shall stumble in their walk; they shall make haste to the wall thereof, and the defence shall be prepared.
6 The gates of the rivers shall be opened, and the palace shall be dissolved.
7 And Huzzab shall be led away captive, she shall be brought up, and her maids shall lead her as with the voice of doves, tabering upon their breasts.
8 But Nineveh is of old like a pool of water; yet they shall flee away. Stand, stand, shall they cry; but none shall look back.
9 Take you the spoil of silver, take the spoil of gold; for there is none end of the store and glory out of all the pleasant furniture.
10 She is empty, and void, and waste: and the heart melteth, and the knees smite together, and much pain is in all loins, and the faces of them all gather blackness.
11 Where is the dwelling of the lions, and the feedingplace of the young lions, where the lion, even the old lion, walked, and the lion's whelp, and none made them afraid?
12 The lion did tear in pieces enough for his whelps, and strangled for his lionesses, and filled his holes with prey, and his dens with ravin.
13 "Behold, I am against you," saith יהוה of hosts (YHWH Tsevaot), "and I will burn her chariots in the smoke, and the sword shall

devour your young lions: and I will cut off your prey from the earth, and the voice of your messengers shall no more be heard."

3 Woe to the bloody city! It is all full of lies and robbery; the prey departeth not;

2 The noise of a whip, and the noise of the rattling of the wheels, and of the pransing horses, and of the jumping chariots.

3 The horseman lifteth up both the bright sword and the glittering spear; and there is a multitude of slain, and a great number of carcases; and there is none end of their corpses; they stumble upon their corpses;

4 Because of the multitude of the whoredoms of the wellfavoured harlot, the mistress of witchcrafts, that selleth nations through her whoredoms, and families through her witchcrafts.

5 "Behold, I am against you," saith יהוה of hosts (YHWH Tsevaot); "And I will discover your skirts upon your face, and I will shew the nations your nakedness, and the kingdoms your shame.

6 And I will cast abominable filth upon you, and make you vile, and will set you as a gazingstock.

7 And it shall come to pass, that all they that look upon you shall flee from you, and say, 'Nineveh is laid waste; who will bemoan her?' Whence shall I seek comforters for you?"

8 Are you better than No-Amon, that was situate among the rivers, that had the waters round about it, whose rampart was the sea, and her wall was from the sea?

9 Ethiopia (Kush) and Egypt (Mitsrayim) were her strength, and it was infinite; Put and Lubim were your helpers.

10 Yet was she carried away, she went into captivity; her young children also were dashed in pieces at the top of all the streets; and they cast lots for her honourable men, and all her great men were bound in chains.

11 You also shalt be drunken; you shalt be hidden, you also shalt seek strength because of the enemy.

12 All your strong holds shall be like fig trees with the firstripe figs; if they be shaken, they shall even fall into the mouth of the eater.

13 Behold, your people in the midst of you are women! The gates of your land shall be set wide open unto your enemies; the fire shall devour your bars.

14 Draw you waters for the siege, fortify your strong holds! Go into clay, and tread the morter, make strong the brickkiln.

15 There shall the fire devour you; the sword shall cut you off, it shall eat you up like the cankerworm; make yourself many as the cankerworm, make yourself many as the locusts.

16 You have multiplied your merchants above the stars of heaven; the cankerworm spoileth, and flieth away.

17 Your crowned are as the locusts, and your captains as the great grasshoppers, which camp in the hedges in the cold day, but when the sun ariseth they flee away, and their place is not known where they are.

18 Your shepherds slumber, O king of Assyria (Ashshur); your nobles shall dwell in the dust; your people is scattered upon the mountains, and no man gathereth them.

19 There is no healing of your bruise; your wound is grievous; all that hear the bruit of you shall clap the hands over you, for upon whom hath not your wickedness passed continually?

HABAKKUK
CHAVAQQUQ חֲבַקּוּק
(Embrace)

1 The burden which [A62]Habakkuk (Chavaqquq) the prophet did see.

2 O יהוה, how long shall I cry, and You wilt not hear! Even cry out unto You of violence, and You wilt not save!

3 Why dost You shew me iniquity, and cause me to behold grievance? For spoiling and violence are before me; and there are that raise up strife and contention.

4 Therefore the Torah is slacked, and justice doth never go forth; for the wicked doth compass about the righteous; therefore perverse judgment proceedeth.

5 Behold you among the nations, and regard, and wonder marvelously; for I will work a work in your days, which you will not believe, though it be told you.

6 For, behold I raise up the Chaldeans, that bitter and hasty nation, which shall march through the breadth of the land, to possess the dwelling places that are not theirs.

7 They are terrible and dreadful; their judgment and their dignity shall proceed of themselves.

8 Their horses also are swifter than the leopards, and are more fierce than the evening wolves; and their horsemen shall spread themselves, and their horsemen shall come from far; they shall fly as the eagle that hasteth to eat.

9 They shall come all for violence; their faces shall sup up as the east wind, and they shall gather the captivity as the sand.

10 And they shall scoff at the kings, and the princes shall be a scorn unto them; they shall deride every strong hold, for they shall heap dust, and take it.

11 Then shall his mind change, and he shall pass over, and offend, imputing this his power unto his god.

12 Are you not from everlasting, O יהוה my God (YHWH Elohai), Mine Holy One? We shall not die. O יהוה, You have ordained them for judgment; and, O Rock, You have established them for correction.

13 You are of purer eyes than to behold evil, and canst not look on iniquity; wherefore lookest You upon them that deal treacherously, and holdest Your tongue when the wicked devoureth the man that is more righteous than he?

14 And makest men as the fishes of the sea, as the creeping things, that have no ruler over them?

15 They take up all of them with the angle, they catch them in their net, and gather them in their drag; therefore they rejoice and are glad.

16 Therefore they sacrifice unto their net, and burn incense unto their drag; because by them their portion is fat, and their food plenteous.

17 Shall they therefore empty their net, and not spare continually to slay the nations?

2 I will stand upon my watch, and set me upon the tower, and will watch to see what he will say unto me, and what I shall answer when I am reproved.

2 And יהוה answered me, and said: "Write the vision, and make it plain upon tablets, that he may run that readeth it.

3 For the vision is yet for an appointed time, but at the end it shall speak, and not lie; though it tarry, wait for it; because it will surely come, it will not tarry.

4 Behold, his soul which is lifted up is not upright in him; but the just shall live by his faith.

5 Yea also, because he transgresseth by wine, he is a proud man, neither keepeth at home, who enlargeth his desire as sheol, and is as death, and cannot be satisfied, but gathereth unto him all nations, and heapeth unto him all people.

6 Shall not all these take up a parable against him, and a taunting proverb against him, and say, 'Woe to him that increaseth that which is not his! How long? And to him that ladeth himself with thick clay!'

7 Shall they not rise up suddenly that shall bite you, and awake that shall vex you, and you shalt be for booties unto them?

8 Because you have plundered many nations, all the remnant of the people shall plunder you, because of men's blood, and for the violence of the land, of the city, and of all that dwell therein.

9 Woe to him that coveteth an evil covetousness to his house, that he may set his nest on high, that he may be delivered from the power of evil!

10 You have consulted shame to your house by cutting off many people, and hast sinned against your soul.

11 For the stone shall cry out of the wall, and the beam out of the timber shall answer it.

12 Woe to him that buildeth a town with blood, and stablisheth a city by iniquity!

13 Behold, is it not of יהוה of hosts (YHWH Tsevaot) that the people shall labour in the very fire, and the people shall weary themselves for very vanity?

14 For the earth shall be filled with the knowledge of the glory of יהוה, as the waters cover the sea.

15 Woe unto him that giveth his neighbour drink, that puttest your bottle to him, and makest him drunken also, that you mayest look on their nakedness!

16 You are filled with shame for glory; drink you also, and let your foreskin be uncovered; the cup of יהוה's right hand shall be turned unto you, and shameful spewing shall be on your glory.

17 For the violence of Lebanon shall cover you, and the spoil of beasts, which made them afraid, because of men's blood, and for the violence of the land, of the city, and of all that dwell therein.

18 What profiteth the graven image that the maker thereof hath graven it; the molten image, and a teacher of lies, that the maker of his work trusteth therein, to make dumb idols?

19 Woe unto him that saith to the wood, 'Awake!' to the dumb stone, 'Arise, it shall teach!' Behold, it is laid over with gold and silver, and there is no breath at all in the midst of it.

20 But יהוה is in His holy temple; let all the earth keep silence before Him."

3 A prayer of Habakkuk (Chavaqquq) the prophet upon Shigionoth.

2 O יהוה, I have heard Your speech, and was afraid; O יהוה, revive Your work in the midst of the years, in the midst of the years make known; in wrath remember mercy.

3 God (Eloah) came from Teman, and the Holy One from Mount Paran. Selah. His glory covered the heavens, and the earth was full of His praise.

4 And His brightness was as the light; He had horns coming out of His hand; and there was the hiding of His power.

5 Before him went the pestilence, and burning coals went forth at his feet.

6 He stood, and measured the earth; he beheld, and drove asunder the nations; and the everlasting mountains were scattered, the perpetual hills did bow; His ways are everlasting.

7 I saw the tents of Cushan in affliction; and the curtains of the land of Midian did tremble.

8 Was יהוה displeased against the rivers? Was Your anger against the rivers? Was Your wrath against the sea, that You didst ride upon Your horses and Your chariots of salvation?

9 Your bow was made quite naked, according to the oaths of the tribes, even your word. Selah. You didst cleave the earth with rivers.

10 The mountains saw You, and they trembled; the overflowing of the water passed by; the deep uttered his voice, and lifted up his hands on high.

11 The sun and moon stood still in their habitation; at the light of Your arrows they went, and at the shining of Your glittering spear.

12 You didst march through the land in indignation, You didst thresh the nations in anger.

13 You wentest forth for the salvation of Your people, even for salvation with Your Anointed; You woundedst the head out of the house of the wicked, by discovering the foundation unto the neck. Selah.

14 You didst strike through with his staves the head of his villages; they came out as a whirlwind to scatter me; their rejoicing was as to devour the poor secretly.

15 You didst walk through the sea with your horses, through the heap of great waters.

16 When I heard, my belly trembled; my lips quivered at the voice; rottenness entered into my bones, and I trembled in myself, that I might rest in the day of trouble; when he cometh up unto the people, he will invade them with his troops.

17 Although the fig tree shall not blossom, neither shall fruit be in the vines; the labour of the olive shall fail, and the fields shall yield no meat; the flock shall be cut off from the fold, and there shall be no herd in the stalls;

18 Yet I will exult in יהוה, I will rejoice in the God (Elohim) of my salvation.

19 God (Elohim) יהוה is my strength, and He will make my feet like hinds' feet, and He will make me to walk upon mine high places. To the chief singer on my stringed instruments.

ZEPHANIAH
TSEFANYAH צְפַנְיָה
(YHWH has Protected)

1 The word of יהוה which came unto [A63]Zephaniah (Tsefanyah) the son of Kushi, the son of Gedalyah, the son of Amaryah, the son of Chizqiyah, in the days of Josiah (Yoshiyahu) the son of Amon, king of Judah (Yehudah).

2 I will utterly consume all things from off the land, saith יהוה.

3 I will consume man and beast; I will consume the fowls of the sky, and the fishes of the sea, and the stumblingblocks with the wicked; and I will cut off man from off the land, saith יהוה.

4 I will also stretch out Mine hand upon Judah (Yehudah), and upon all the inhabitants of Jerusalem (Yerushalayim); and I will cut off the remnant of the Baal from this place, and the name of the Chemarims with the kohanim;

5 And them that worship the host of heaven upon the housetops; and them that worship and that swear by יהוה and yet swear by Milkom (god of the Ammonites);

6 And them that are turned back from יהוה; and those that have not sought יהוה, nor enquired for him.

7 Hold your peace at the presence of Lord (Adonai) יהוה, for the day of יהוה is at hand; for יהוה hath prepared a sacrifice, He hath bid His guests.

8 And it shall come to pass in the day of יהוה's sacrifice, that I will punish the princes, and the king's children, and all such as are clothed with strange apparel.

9 In the same day also will I punish all those that leap on the threshold, which fill their masters' houses with violence and deceit.

10 And it shall come to pass in that day, saith יהוה, that there shall be the noise of a cry from the fish gate, and a howling from the second, and a great crashing from the hills.

11 Howl, you inhabitants of Maktesh, for all the merchant people are cut down; all they that bear silver are cut off.

12 And it shall come to pass at that time, that I will search Jerusalem (Yerushalayim) with candles, and punish the men that are settled on their lees, that say in their heart, יהוה will not

do good, neither will He do evil.

13 Therefore their goods shall become a booty, and their houses a desolation: they shall also build houses, but not inhabit them; and they shall plant vineyards, but not drink the wine thereof.

14 The great day of יהוה is near, it is near, and hasteth greatly, even the voice of the day of יהוה, the mighty man shall cry there bitterly.

15 That day is a day of wrath, a day of trouble and distress, a day of wasteness and desolation, a day of darkness and gloominess, a day of clouds and thick darkness,

16 A day of the trumpet and alarm against the fenced cities, and against the high towers.

17 And I will bring distress upon men, that they shall walk like blind men, because they have sinned against יהוה; and their blood shall be poured out as dust, and their flesh as the dung.

18 Neither their silver nor their gold shall be able to deliver them in the day of יהוה's wrath; but the whole land shall be devoured by the fire of His jealousy, for He shall make even a speedy riddance of all them that dwell in the land.

2 Gather yourselves together, yea, gather together, O nation not desired;

2 Before the decree bring forth, before the day pass as the chaff, before the fierce anger of יהוה come upon you, before the day of יהוה's anger come upon you.

3 Seek you יהוה, all you meek of the earth, who have wrought His judgment; seek righteousness, seek meekness; it may be you shall be hidden in the day of יהוה's anger.

4 For Gaza (Azzah) shall be forsaken, and Ashkelon a desolation; they shall drive out Ashdod at the noon day, and Ekron shall be rooted up.

5 Woe unto the inhabitants of the sea coast, the nation of the Cherethites! The word of יהוה is against you; O Canaan, the land of the Philistines: "I will even destroy you, that there shall be no inhabitant."

6 And the sea coast shall be dwellings and cottages for shepherds, and folds for flocks.

7 And the coast shall be for the remnant of the house of Judah (Yehudah); they shall feed thereupon; in the houses of Ashkelon shall they lie down in the evening, for יהוה their God (YHWH Eloheihem) shall visit them, and turn away their captivity.

8 I have heard the reproach of Moav, and the revilings of the children of Ammon, whereby they have reproached My people, and magnified themselves against their border.

9 "Therefore as I live," saith יהוה of hosts (YHWH Tsevaot), the God of Israel (Elohei Yisrael), "Surely Moav shall be as Sodom, and the children of Ammon as Gomorrah, even the breeding of nettles, and saltpits, and a perpetual desolation; the residue of My people shall spoil them, and the remnant of My people shall possess them."

10 This shall they have for their pride, because they have reproached and magnified themselves against the people of יהוה of hosts (YHWH Tsevaot).

11 יהוה will be terrible unto them; for He will famish all the gods (elohim) of the earth; and men shall worship Him, every one from his place, even all the isles of the nations.

12 "You Ethiopians (Kushim) also, you shall be slain by My sword."

13 And He will stretch out His hand against the north, and destroy Assyria (Ashshur); and will make Nineveh a desolation, and dry like a wilderness.

14 And flocks shall lie down in the midst of her, all the beasts of the nations; both the cormorant and the bittern shall lodge in the upper lintels of it; their voice shall sing in the windows; desolation shall be in the thresholds, for He shall uncover the cedar work.

15 This is the rejoicing city that dwelt carelessly, that said in her heart, "I am, and there is none besides me;" how is she become a desolation, a place for beasts to lie down in! Every one that passeth by her shall hiss, and wag his hand.

3 Woe to her that is filthy and polluted, to the oppressing city!

2 She obeyed not the voice; she received not correction; she trusted not in יהוה; she drew not near to her God (Elohim).

3 Her princes within her are roaring lions; her judges are evening wolves; they gnaw not the bones till tomorrow.

4 Her prophets are light and treacherous persons; her kohanim have polluted the sanctuary, they have done violence to the Torah.

5 The just יהוה is in the midst thereof; He will not do iniquity. Every morning doth He bring His judgment to light, He faileth not; but the unjust knoweth no shame.

6 "I have cut off the nations; their towers are desolate; I made their streets waste, that none passeth by; their cities are destroyed, so that there is no man, that there is none inhabitant.

7 I said, 'Surely you wilt fear Me, you wilt receive instruction'; so their dwelling should not be cut off, howsoever I punished them; but they rose early, and corrupted all their doings.

8 "Therefore wait you upon Me," saith יהוה, "until the day that I rise up to the prey, for My determination is to gather the nations, that I may assemble the kingdoms, to pour upon them Mine indignation, even all My fierce anger; for all the earth shall be devoured with the fire of My jealousy.

9 For then will I turn (restore) to the people a pure language, that they may all call upon the name of יהוה (YHWH), and serve with one consent.

10 From beyond the rivers of Ethiopia (Kush) My suppliants, even the daughter of My dispersed, shall bring Mine offering.

11 In that day shalt you not be ashamed for all your doings, wherein you have transgressed against me; for then I will take away out of the midst of you them that rejoice in your pride, and you shalt no more be haughty because of My holy mountain.

12 I will also leave in the midst of you an afflicted and poor people, and they shall trust in the name of יהוה.

13 The remnant of Yisrael shall not do iniquity, nor speak lies; neither shall a deceitful tongue be found in their mouth, for they shall feed and lie down, and none shall make them afraid."

14 Sing, O daughter of Zion (Tsiyon); shout, O Yisrael; be glad and rejoice with all the heart, O daughter of Jerusalem (Yerushalayim).

15 יהוה hath taken away your judgments, He hath cast out your enemy; the king of Yisrael, even יהוה, is in the midst of you; you shalt not see disaster (raah) any more.

16 In that day it shall be said to Jerusalem (Yerushalayim), "Fear you not;" and to Zion (Tsiyon), "Let not your hands be slack."

17 יהוה your God (YHWH Eloheikha) in the midst of you is mighty; He will save, He will rejoice over you with joy; He will rest in His love, He will rejoice over you with singing."

18 "I will gather them that are sorrowful for the

solemn assembly, who are of you, to whom the reproach of it was a burden.

19 Behold, at that time I will undo all that afflict you; and I will save her that halteth, and gather her that was driven out; and I will get them praise and fame in every land where they have been put to shame.

20 At that time will I bring you again, even in the time that I gather you, for I will make you a name and a praise among all people of the earth, when I turn back your captivity before your eyes," saith יהוה.

HAGGAI
CHAGGAI חַגַּי
(Festive)

1 In the second year of Darius the king, in the sixth month, in the first day of the month, came the word of יהוה by [A64]Haggai (Chaggai) the prophet unto Zerubbabel the son of Shealtiel, governor of Judah (Yehudah), and to Joshua (Yehoshua) the son of Yehotsadaq, the high priest (kohen hagadol), saying,

2 "Thus speaketh יהוה of hosts (YHWH Tsevaot), saying: 'This people say, "The time is not come, the time that יהוה's house should be built."'"

3 Then came the word of יהוה by Chaggai the prophet, saying,

4 "Is it time for you, O you, to dwell in your cieled houses, and this house lie waste?"

5 Now therefore thus saith יהוה of hosts (YHWH Tsevaot): "Consider your ways.

6 You have sown much, and bring in little; you eat, but you have not enough; you drink, but you are not filled with drink; you clothe you, but there is none warm; and he that earneth wages earneth wages to put it into a bag with holes."

7 Thus saith יהוה of hosts (YHWH Tsevaot): "Consider your ways.

8 Go up to the mountain, and bring wood, and build the house; and I will take pleasure in it, and I will be glorified," saith יהוה.

9 You looked for much, and, behold, it came to little; and when you brought it home, I did blow upon it. Why?" saith יהוה of hosts (YHWH Tsevaot). "Because of Mine house that is waste, and you run every man unto his own house.

10 Therefore the heaven over you is stayed from dew, and the earth is stayed from her fruit.

11 And I called for a drought upon the land, and upon the mountains, and upon the corn, and upon the new wine, and upon the oil, and upon that which the ground bringeth forth, and upon men, and upon cattle, and upon all the labour of the hands."

12 Then Zerubbabel the son of Shealtiel, and Joshua (Yehoshua) the son of Yehotsadaq, the high priest (kohen hagadol), with all the remnant of the people, obeyed the voice of יהוה their God (YHWH Eloheihem), and the words of Chaggai the prophet, as יהוה their God (YHWH Eloheihem) had sent him, and the people did fear before יהוה.

13 Then spake Chaggai, יהוה's messenger in יהוה's message unto the people, saying, "I am with you," saith יהוה.

14 And יהוה stirred up the spirit of Zerubbabel the son of Shealtiel, governor of Judah (Yehudah), and the spirit of Joshua (Yehoshua) the son of Yehotsadaq the high priest, and the spirit of all the remnant of the people; and they came and did work in the house of יהוה of hosts (YHWH Tsevaot), their God (Elohim),

15 In the four and twentieth day of the sixth month, in the second year of Darius the king.

2 In the seventh month, in the one and twentieth day of the month, came the word of יהוה by the prophet Chaggai, saying:

2 "Speak now to Zerubbabel the son of Shealtiel, governor of Judah (Yehudah), and to Joshua (Yehoshua) the son of Yehotsadaq, the high priest, and to the residue of the people, saying:

3 "Who is left among you that saw this house in her first glory? And how do you see it now? Is it not in your eyes in comparison of it as nothing?

4 'Yet now be strong, O Zerubbabel,' saith יהוה; 'and be strong, O Joshua (Yehoshua), son of Yehotsadaq, the high priest (kohen hagadol); and be strong, all you people of the land,' saith יהוה, 'and work, for I am with you,' saith יהוה of hosts (YHWH Tsevaot):

5 'According to the word that I covenanted with you when you came out of Egypt (Mitsrayim), so My Spirit remaineth among you; fear you not!'

6 For thus saith יהוה of hosts (YHWH Tsevaot): "Yet once, it is a little while, and I will shake the heavens, and the earth, and the sea, and the dry land;

7 'And I will shake all nations, and the desire of all nations shall come: and I will fill this house with glory, saith יהוה of hosts (YHWH Tsevaot).

8 The silver is Mine, and the gold is Mine,' saith יהוה of hosts (YHWH Tsevaot).

9 'The glory of this latter house shall be greater than of the former,' saith יהוה of hosts (YHWH Tsevaot); 'and in this place will I give peace,' saith יהוה of hosts (YHWH Tsevaot)."

10 In the four and twentieth day of the ninth month, in the second year of Darius, came the word of יהוה by Chaggai the prophet, saying,

11 "Thus saith יהוה of hosts (YHWH Tsevaot): 'Ask now the priests (kohanim) concerning the

law (torah), saying,

12 "If one bear holy flesh in the edge of his garment, and with his edge do touch bread, or pottage, or wine, or oil, or any meat, shall it be holy?"'" And the priests (kohanim) answered and said, "No."

13 Then said Chaggai, "If one that is unclean by a dead body touch any of these, shall it be unclean?" And the priests (kohanim) answered and said, "It shall be unclean."

14 Then answered Chaggai, and said, 'So is this people, and so is this nation before Me,' saith יהוה; 'and so is every work of their hands; and that which they offer there is unclean.

15 And now, I pray you, consider from this day and upward, from before a stone was laid upon a stone in the temple of יהוה;

16 Since those days were, when one came to a heap of twenty measures, there were but ten; when one came to the pressfat for to draw out fifty vessels out of the press, there were but twenty.

17 I smote you with blasting and with mildew and with hail in all the labours of your hands; yet you turned not to Me,' saith יהוה.

18 Consider now from this day and upward, from the four and twentieth day of the ninth month, even from the day that the foundation of יהוה's temple was laid, consider it:

19 Is the seed yet in the barn? Yea, as yet the vine, and the fig tree, and the pomegranate, and the olive tree, hath not brought forth; from this day will I bless you.'"

20 And again the word of יהוה came unto Chaggai in the four and twentieth day of the month, saying:

21 'Speak to Zerubbabel, governor of Judah (Yehudah), saying: 'I will shake the heavens and the earth;

22 And I will overthrow the throne of kingdoms, and I will destroy the strength of the kingdoms of the nations; and I will overthrow the chariots, and those that ride in them; and the horses and their riders shall come down, every one by the sword of his brother.

23 'In that day,' saith יהוה of hosts (YHWH Tsevaot), 'will I take you, O Zerubbabel, My servant, the son of Shealtiel,' saith יהוה, 'and will make you as a signet; for I have chosen you,' saith יהוה of hosts (YHWH Tsevaot)."

ZECHARIAH
ZEKHARYAH זְכַרְיָה
(YHWH Remembers)

1 In the eighth month, in the second year of Darius, came the word of יהוה unto A65Zechariah (Zekharyah), the son of Berekhyah, the son of Iddo the prophet, saying,

2 "יהוה hath been sore displeased with your fathers.

3 Therefore say you unto them, 'Thus saith יהוה of hosts (YHWH Tsevaot): 'Return you unto Me,' saith יהוה of hosts (YHWH Tsevaot), 'and I will return unto you,' saith יהוה of hosts (YHWH Tsevaot).

4 Be you not as your fathers, unto whom the former prophets have cried, saying, 'Thus saith יהוה of hosts (YHWH Tsevaot): "Turn you now from your evil ways, and from your evil doings."' But they did not hear, nor hearken unto Me," saith יהוה.

5 "Your fathers, where are they? And the prophets, do they live forever?

6 But My words and My statutes, which I commanded My servants the prophets, did they not take hold of your fathers?" "And they returned and said: 'Like as יהוה of hosts (YHWH Tsevaot) thought to do unto us, according to our ways, and according to our doings, so hath He dealt with us.'"'"

7 Upon the four and twentieth day of the eleventh month, which is the month Sebat, in the second year of Darius, came the word of יהוה unto Zechariah (Zekharyah), the son of Berekhyah, the son of Iddo the prophet, saying:

8 "I saw by night, and behold a man riding upon a red horse, and he stood among the myrtle trees that were in the bottom; and behind him were there red horses, speckled, and white."

9 Then said I, "O my lord (adoni), what are these?" And the angel that talked with me said unto me, "I will shew you what these be."

10 And the man that stood among the myrtle trees answered and said, "These are they whom יהוה hath sent to walk to and fro through the earth."

11 And they answered the angel of יהוה that stood among the myrtle trees, and said, "We have walked to and fro through the earth, and, behold, all the earth sitteth still, and is at rest."

12 Then the angel of יהוה answered and said, "O יהוה of hosts (YHWH Tsevaot), how long wilt You not have mercy on Jerusalem (Yerushalayim) and on the cities of Judah (Yehudah), against which You have had indignation these threescore and ten years?"

13 And יהוה answered the angel that talked with me with good words and comfortable words.

14 So the angel that communed with me said unto me, "Proclaim you, saying, 'Thus saith יהוה of hosts (YHWH Tsevaot): "I am zealous for Jerusalem (Yerushalayim) and for Zion (Tsiyon) with a great zeal.

15 And I am very sore displeased with the nations that are at ease; for I was but a little displeased, and they helped forward the affliction."

16 Therefore thus saith יהוה: "I am returned to Jerusalem (Yerushalayim) with mercies; My house shall be built in it," saith יהוה of hosts (YHWH Tsevaot), "and a line shall be stretched forth upon Jerusalem (Yerushalayim).""

17 "Proclaim yet, saying, 'Thus saith יהוה of hosts (YHWH Tsevaot): "My cities through prosperity shall yet be spread abroad; and יהוה shall yet comfort Zion (Tsiyon), and shall yet choose Jerusalem (Yerushalayim)."'"

18 Then lifted I up mine eyes, and saw, and behold four horns.

19 And I said unto the angel that talked with me, "What be these?" And he answered me, "These are the horns which have scattered Judah (Yehudah), Yisrael, and Jerusalem (Yerushalayim)."

20 And יהוה shewed me four carpenters.

21 Then said I, "What come these to do?" And he spake, saying, "These are the horns which have scattered Judah (Yehudah), so that no man did lift up his head: but these are come to fray them, to cast out the horns of the Gentiles (Goyim), which lifted up their horn over the land of Judah (Yehudah) to scatter it."

2 I lifted up mine eyes again, and looked, and behold a man with a measuring line in his hand.

2 Then said I, "Whither goest you?" And he said unto me, "To measure Jerusalem (Yerushalayim), to see what is the breadth thereof, and what is the length thereof."

3 And, behold, the angel that talked with me went forth, and another angel went out to meet him,

4 And said unto him, "Run, speak to this young man, saying, 'Yerushalayim shall be inhabited as towns without walls for the multitude of men and cattle therein.

5 'For I,' saith יהוה, 'will be unto her a wall of fire round about, and will be the glory in the midst of her.'"

6 "Ho, ho, come forth, and flee from the land of the north," saith יהוה; "for I have spread you abroad as the four winds of the heaven," saith יהוה.

7 Deliver yourself, O Zion (Tsiyon), that dwellest with the daughter of Babylon (Bavel).

8 For thus saith יהוה of hosts (YHWH Tsevaot): "After the glory hath He sent Me unto the nations which spoiled you; for he that toucheth you toucheth the apple of His eye.

9 For, behold, I will shake Mine hand upon them, and they shall be a spoil to their servants; and you shall know that יהוה of hosts (YHWH Tsevaot) hath sent Me.

10 "Sing and rejoice, O daughter of Zion (Tsiyon); for, behold, I come, and I will dwell in the midst of you," saith יהוה.

11 "And many nations shall be joined to יהוה in that day, and shall be My people; and I will dwell in the midst of you, and you shalt know that יהוה of hosts (YHWH Tsevaot) hath sent Me unto you.

12 And יהוה shall inherit Judah (Yehudah) His portion in the holy land, and shall choose Jerusalem (Yerushalayim) again.

13 Be silent, O all flesh, before יהוה, for He is raised up out of His holy habitation!"

3 And he shewed me Joshua (Yehoshua) the high priest (kohen hagadol) standing before the angel of יהוה, and the Satan standing at his right hand to resist him.

2 And יהוה said unto the Satan, "יהוה rebuke you, O Satan! Indeed יהוה that hath chosen Jerusalem (Yerushalayim) rebuke you! Is not this a brand plucked out of the fire?"

3 Now Joshua (Yehoshua) was clothed with filthy garments, and stood before the angel.

4 And he answered and spake unto those that stood before him, saying, "Take away the filthy garments from him." And unto him he said, "Behold, I have caused your iniquity to pass from you, and I will clothe you with change of raiment."

5 And I said, "Let them set a fair mitre upon his head." So they set a fair mitre upon his head,

and clothed him with garments. And the angel of יהוה stood by.

6 And the angel of יהוה protested unto Joshua (Yehoshua), saying,

7 "Thus saith יהוה of hosts (YHWH Tsevaot): 'If you wilt walk in My ways, and if you wilt keep My charge, then you shalt also judge My house, and shalt also keep My courts, and I will give you places to walk among these that stand by.

8 Hear now, O Joshua (Yehoshua) the high priest (kohen hagadol), you, and your fellows that sit before you, for they are men wondered at; for, behold, I will bring forth My servant the B44Branch (Tsemach).

9 For behold the stone that I have laid before Joshua (Yehoshua); upon one stone shall be seven eyes. Behold, I will engrave the graving thereof,' saith יהוה of hosts (YHWH Tsevaot), 'and I will remove the iniquity of that land in one day.'

10 'In that day,' saith יהוה of hosts (YHWH Tsevaot), 'shall you call every man his neighbour under the vine and under the fig tree.'"

4 And the angel that talked with me came again, and waked me, as a man that is wakened out of his sleep,

2 And said unto me, "What seest you?" And I said, "I have looked, and behold a candlestick (menorah) all of gold, with a bowl upon the top of it, and his seven lamps thereon, and seven pipes to the seven lamps, which are upon the top thereof."

3 And two olive trees by it, one upon the right side of the bowl, and the other upon the left side thereof.

4 So I answered and spake to the angel that talked with me, saying, "What are these, my lord (adoni)?

5 Then the angel that talked with me answered and said unto me, "Knowest you not what these be?" And I said, "No, my lord (adoni)."

6 Then he answered and spake unto me, saying, "This is the word of יהוה unto Zerubbabel, saying: 'Not by might, nor by power, but by My Spirit,' saith יהוה of hosts (YHWH Tsevaot).

7 'Who are you, O great mountain? Before Zerubbabel you shalt become a plain! And he shall bring forth the headstone thereof with shoutings, crying, "Grace, grace unto it!"'"

8 Moreover the word of יהוה came unto me,

saying,

9 "The hands of Zerubbabel have laid the foundation of this house; his hands shall also finish it; and you shalt know that יהוה of hosts (YHWH Tsevaot) hath sent me unto you.

10 For who hath despised the day of small things? For they shall rejoice, and shall see the plummet in the hand of Zerubbabel with those seven; they are the eyes of יהוה, which run to and fro through the whole earth."

11 Then answered I, and said unto him, "What are these two olive trees upon the right side of the candlestick (menorah) and upon the left side thereof?"

12 And I answered again, and said unto him, "What be these two olive branches which through the two golden pipes empty the golden oil out of themselves?"

13 And he answered me and said, "Knowest you not what these be?" And I said, "No, my lord (adoni)."

14 Then said he, "These are the two anointed ones, that stand by the Lord (Adonai) of the whole earth."

5 Then I turned, and lifted up mine eyes, and looked, and behold a flying roll.

2 And he said unto me, "What seest you?" And I answered, "I see a flying roll; the length thereof is twenty cubits, and the breadth thereof ten cubits."

3 Then said he unto me, "This is the curse that goeth forth over the face of the whole earth: 'For every one that stealeth shall be cut off as on this side according to it; and every one that sweareth shall be cut off as on that side according to it."

4 "I will bring it forth," saith יהוה of hosts (YHWH Tsevaot); "and it shall enter into the house of the thief, and into the house of him that sweareth falsely by My name. It shall remain in the midst of his house, and shall consume it with the timber thereof and the stones thereof."

5 Then the angel that talked with me went forth, and said unto me, "Lift up now your eyes, and see what is this that goeth forth."

6 And I said, "What is it?" And he said, "This is an ephah that goeth forth." He said moreover, "This is their resemblance through all the earth.

7 And, behold, there was lifted up a talent of lead; and this is a woman that sitteth in the midst of the ephah."

8 And he said, "This is wickedness. And he cast it into the midst of the ephah; and he cast the weight of lead upon the mouth thereof.

9 Then lifted I up mine eyes, and looked, and, behold, there came out two women, and the wind was in their wings; for they had wings like the wings of a stork, and they lifted up the ephah between the earth and the heaven.

10 Then said I to the angel that talked with me, "Whither do these bear the ephah?"

11 And he said unto me, "To build it a house in the land of Shinar; and it shall be established, and set there upon her own base."

6 And I turned, and lifted up mine eyes, and looked, and, behold, there came four chariots out from between two mountains; and the mountains were mountains of brass.

2 In the first chariot were red horses; and in the second chariot black horses;

3 And in the third chariot white horses; and in the fourth chariot grisled and bay horses.

4 Then I answered and said unto the angel that talked with me, "What are these, my lord (adoni)?"

5 And the angel answered and said unto me, "These are the four spirits of the heavens, who go forth from standing before the Lord (Adonai) of all the earth.

6 The black horses which are therein go forth into the north country; and the white go forth after them; and the grisled go forth toward the south country."

7 And the bay went forth, and sought to go that they might walk to and fro through the earth. And he said, "Go, walk to and fro through the earth." So they walked to and fro through the earth.

8 Then cried He upon me, and spake unto me, saying, "Behold, these that go toward the north country have quieted My spirit in the north country."

9 And the word of יהוה came unto me, saying:

10 "Take of them of the captivity, even of Heldai, of Toviyah, and of Yedayah, which are come from Babylon (Bavel), and come you the same day, and go into the house of Josiah (Yoshiyahu) the son of Zephaniah (Tsefanyah);

11 Then take silver and gold, and make crowns, and set them upon the head of Joshua (Yehoshua) the son of Yehotsadaq, the high priest (kohen hagadol);

12 And speak unto him, saying, 'Thus speaketh

יהוה of hosts (YHWH Tsevaot), saying: "Behold the man whose name is [B44]Branch (Tsemach); and He shall sprout up from His place, and He shall build the temple of יהוה;

13 Yes, He shall build the temple of יהוה; and He shall bear the glory, and shall sit and rule upon His throne; and He shall be a priest (kohen) upon His throne; and the counsel of peace shall be between them both.

14 And the crowns shall be to Helem, and to Toviyah, and to Yedayah, and to Hen the son of Zephaniah (Tsefanyah), for a memorial in the temple of יהוה.

15 And they that are far off shall come and build in the temple of יהוה, and you shall know that יהוה of hosts (YHWH Tsevaot) hath sent me unto you. And this shall come to pass, if you will diligently obey the voice of יהוה your God (YHWH Eloheikhem)."

7 And it came to pass in the fourth year of King Darius, that the word of יהוה came unto Zechariah (Zekharyah) in the fourth day of the ninth month, even in Chisleu;

2 When they had sent unto the house of God (El), Sherezer and Regem-melech, and their men, to pray before יהוה,

3 And to speak unto the kohanim who were in the house of יהוה of hosts (YHWH Tsevaot), and to the prophets, saying, "Should I weep in the fifth month, separating myself, as I have done these so many years?"

4 Then came the word of יהוה of hosts (YHWH Tsevaot) unto me, saying,

5 "Speak unto all the people of the land, and to the kohanim, saying: 'When you fasted and mourned in the fifth and seventh month, even those seventy years, did you at all fast unto Me, even to Me?

6 And when you did eat, and when you did drink, did not you eat for yourselves, and drink for yourselves?

7 Should you not hear the words which יהוה hath cried by the former prophets, when Jerusalem (Yerushalayim) was inhabited and in prosperity, and the cities thereof round about her, when men inhabited the south and the plain?'"

8 And the word of יהוה came unto Zechariah (Zekharyah), saying,

9 "Thus speaketh יהוה of hosts (YHWH Tsevaot), saying: 'Execute true justice, and shew mercy and compassions every man to his brother.'

10 And oppress not the widow, nor the fatherless, the stranger, nor the poor; and let none of you imagine evil against his brother in your heart.

11 But they refused to hearken, and pulled away the shoulder, and stopped their ears, that they should not hear.

12 Yea, they made their hearts as an adamant stone, lest they should hear the Torah, and the words which יהוה of hosts (YHWH Tsevaot) hath sent in His Spirit (Ruach) by the former prophets; therefore came a great wrath from יהוה of hosts (YHWH Tsevaot).

13 "Therefore it is come to pass, that as he cried, and they would not hear; so they cried, and I would not hear," saith יהוה of hosts (YHWH Tsevaot).

14 "But I scattered them with a whirlwind among all the nations whom they knew not. Thus the land was desolate after them, that no man passed through nor returned; for they laid the pleasant land desolate."

8 Again the word of יהוה of hosts (YHWH Tsevaot) came to me, saying,

2 "Thus saith יהוה of hosts (YHWH Tsevaot): 'I was zealous for Zion (Tsiyon) with great zeal, and I was zealous for her with great fury.'

3 Thus saith יהוה: 'I am returned unto Zion (Tsiyon), and will dwell in the midst of Jerusalem (Yerushalayim); and Jerusalem (Yerushalayim) shall be called a city of truth; and the mountain of יהוה of hosts (YHWH Tsevaot) the holy mountain.'

4 Thus saith יהוה of hosts (YHWH Tsevaot): 'There shall yet old men and old women dwell in the streets of Jerusalem (Yerushalayim), and every man with his staff in his hand for very age.

5 And the streets of the city shall be full of boys and girls playing in the streets thereof.'

6 Thus saith יהוה of hosts (YHWH Tsevaot): If it be marvellous in the eyes of the remnant of this people in these days, should it also be marvellous in Mine eyes? saith יהוה of hosts (YHWH Tsevaot).

7 Thus saith יהוה of hosts (YHWH Tsevaot): 'Behold, I will save My people from the east country, and from the west country;

8 And I will bring them, and they shall dwell in the midst of Jerusalem (Yerushalayim); and they shall be My people, and I will be their God (Elohim), in truth and in righteousness.'

9 Thus saith יהוה of hosts (YHWH Tsevaot): 'Let your hands be strong, you that hear in these days these words by the mouth of the prophets, which were in the day that the foundation of the house of יהוה of hosts (YHWH Tsevaot) was laid, that the temple might be built.

10 For before these days there was no hire for man, nor any hire for beast; neither was there any peace to him that went out or came in because of the affliction; for I set all men every one against his neighbour.

11 But now I will not be unto the residue of this people as in the former days,' saith יהוה of hosts (YHWH Tsevaot).

12 For the seed shall be prosperous; the vine shall give her fruit, and the ground shall give her increase, and the heavens shall give their dew; and I will cause the remnant of this people to possess all these things.

13 And it shall come to pass, that as you were a curse among the nations, O house of Judah (Yehudah), and house of Yisrael; so will I save you, and you shall be a blessing. Fear not, but let your hands be strong.'

14 For thus saith יהוה of hosts (YHWH Tsevaot): 'As I thought to punish you, when your fathers provoked Me to wrath,' saith יהוה of hosts (YHWH Tsevaot), and I regretted not;

15 So again have I thought in these days to do well unto Jerusalem (Yerushalayim) and to the house of Judah (Yehudah); fear you not.

16 These are the things that you shall do; Speak you every man the truth to his neighbour; execute the judgment of truth and peace in your gates;

17 And let none of you imagine evil in your hearts against his neighbour; and love no false oath; for all these are things that I hate,' saith יהוה.''

18 And the word of יהוה of hosts (YHWH Tsevaot) came unto me, saying,

19 "Thus saith יהוה of hosts (YHWH Tsevaot): 'The fast of the fourth month, and the fast of the fifth, and the fast of the seventh, and the fast of the tenth, shall be to the house of Judah (Yehudah) joy and gladness, and cheerful feasts; therefore love the truth and peace.'

20 Thus saith יהוה of hosts (YHWH Tsevaot): 'It shall yet come to pass, that there shall come people, and the inhabitants of many cities;

21 And the inhabitants of one city shall go to another, saying, "Let us go speedily to pray before יהוה, and to seek יהוה of hosts (YHWH Tsevaot); I will go also."

22 Yea, many people and strong nations shall come to seek יהוה of hosts (YHWH Tsevaot) in Yerushalayim, and to pray before יהוה.'

23 Thus saith יהוה of hosts (YHWH Tsevaot): 'In those days it shall come to pass, that ten men shall take hold out of all languages of the nations, even shall take hold of the skirt of him that is a Jew (Yehudi), saying, "We will go with you, for we have heard that God (Elohim) is with you."''"

9 The burden of the word of יהוה in the land of Hadrach, and Damascus (Dammeseq) shall be the rest thereof; when the eyes of man, as of all the tribes of Yisrael, shall be toward יהוה.

2 And Hamath also shall border thereby; Tyrus, and Zidon, though it be very wise.

3 And Tyrus did build herself a strong hold, and heaped up silver as the dust, and fine gold as the mire of the streets.

4 Behold, the Lord (Adonai) will cast her out, and He will smite her power in the sea; and she shall be devoured with fire.

5 Ashkelon shall see it, and fear; Gaza (Azzah) also shall see it, and be very sorrowful, and Ekron; for her expectation shall be ashamed; and the king shall perish from Gaza (Azzah), and Ashkelon shall not be inhabited.

6 And a bastard shall dwell in Ashdod, and I will cut off the pride of the Philistines.

7 And I will take away his blood out of his mouth, and his abominations from between his teeth: but he that remaineth, even he, shall be for our God (Elohim), and he shall be as a governor in Judah (Yehudah), and Ekron as a Jebusite (Yevusi).

8 And I will encamp about mine house because of the army, because of him that passeth by, and because of him that returneth: and no oppressor shall pass through them any more; for now have I seen with mine eyes.

9 Rejoice greatly, O daughter of Zion (Tsiyon); shout, O daughter of Jerusalem (Yerushalayim); behold, your King cometh unto you; he is just, and having salvation; lowly, and riding upon an ass, and upon a colt the foal of an ass.

10 And I will cut off the chariot from Efrayim, and the horse from Jerusalem (Yerushalayim), and the battle bow shall be cut off; and he shall

speak peace unto the nations; and his dominion shall be from sea even to sea, and from the river even to the ends of the earth.

11 As for you also, by the blood of your covenant I have sent forth your prisoners out of the pit wherein is no water.

12 Turn you to the strong hold, you prisoners of hope; even today do I declare that I will render double unto you;

13 When I have bent Judah (Yehudah) for me, filled the bow with Efrayim, and raised up your sons, O Zion (Tsiyon), against your sons, O Greece, and made you as the sword of a mighty man.

14 And יהוה shall be seen over them, and His arrow shall go forth as the lightning; and Lord (Adonai) יהוה shall blow the trumpet, and shall go with whirlwinds of the south.

15 יהוה of hosts (YHWH Tsevaot) shall defend them; and they shall devour, and subdue with sling stones; and they shall drink, and make a noise as through wine; and they shall be filled like bowls, and as the corners of the altar.

16 And יהוה their God (YHWH Eloheihem) shall save them in that day as the flock of His people; for they shall be as the stones of a crown, lifted up as an ensign upon His land.

17 For how great is His goodness, and how great is His beauty! Corn shall make the young men cheerful, and new wine the maids.

10 Ask you of יהוה rain in the time of the latter rain; so יהוה shall make bright clouds, and give them showers of rain, to every one grass in the field.

2 For the idols have spoken vanity, and the diviners have seen a lie, and have told false dreams; they comfort in vain; therefore they went their way as a flock, they were troubled, because there was no shepherd.

3 Mine anger was kindled against the shepherds, and I punished the goats; for יהוה of hosts (YHWH Tsevaot) hath visited His flock the house of Judah (Yehudah), and hath made them as His goodly horse in the battle.

4 Out of him came forth the corner, out of him the nail, out of him the battle bow, out of him every oppressor together.

5 And they shall be as mighty men, which tread down their enemies in the mire of the streets in the battle; and they shall fight, because יהוה is with them, and the riders on horses shall be confounded.

6 And I will strengthen the house of Judah (Yehudah), and I will save the house of Joseph (Yosef), and I will bring them back to place them; for I have mercy upon them; and they shall be as though I had not cast them off, for I am יהוה their God (YHWH Eloheihem), and will hear them.

7 And they of Efrayim shall be like a mighty man, and their heart shall rejoice as through wine; yea, their children shall see it, and be glad; their heart shall rejoice in יהוה.

8 I will hiss for them, and gather them; for I have redeemed them; and they shall increase as they have increased.

9 And I will sow them among the people, and they shall remember Me in far countries; and they shall live with their children, and turn back.

10 I will bring them back also out of the land of Egypt (Mitsrayim), and gather them out of Assyria (Ashshur); and I will bring them into the land of Gilad and Lebanon; and place shall not be found for them.

11 And he shall pass through the sea with affliction, and shall smite the waves in the sea, and all the deeps of the river shall dry up; and the pride of Assyria (Ashshur) shall be brought down, and the sceptre of Egypt (Mitsrayim) shall depart away.

12 "And I will strengthen them in יהוה; and they shall walk up and down in His name," saith יהוה.

11 Open your doors, O Lebanon, that the fire may devour your cedars.

2 Howl, fir tree; for the cedar is fallen; because the mighty are spoiled. Howl, O you oaks of Bashan; for the forest of the vintage is come down.

3 There is a voice of the howling of the shepherds; for their glory is spoiled. A voice of the roaring of young lions, for the pride of Jordan (Yarden) is spoiled.

4 Thus saith יהוה my God (YHWH Elohai): "Feed the flock of the slaughter;

5 Whose possessors slay them, and hold themselves not guilty; and they that sell them say, 'Blessed be יהוה, for I am rich'; and their own shepherds pity them not.

6 For I will no more pity the inhabitants of the land," saith יהוה. "But, behold, I will deliver the men every one into his neighbour's hand, and

into the hand of his king; and they shall smite the land, and out of their hand I will not deliver them."

7 And I will feed the flock of slaughter, even you, O poor of the flock. And I took unto me two staves: the one I called 'Pleasantness (Noam)', and the other I called 'Bonds (Chovalim)'; and I fed the flock.

8 Three shepherds also I cut off in one month; and my soul lothed them, and their soul also abhorred me.

9 Then said I, "I will not feed you; whichever is dying, let it dies, whichever is to be cut off, let it be cut off; and let the rest eat every one the flesh of another."

10 And I took my staff, Pleasantness (Noam), and cut it in two, that I might break My covenant which I had made with all the people.

11 And it was broken in that day; and so the poor of the flock that waited upon Me knew that it was the word of יהוה.

12 And I said unto them, "If you think good, give me my price; and if not, forbear." So they weighed for my price thirty pieces of silver.

13 And יהוה said unto me, "Cast it unto the potter"; a goodly price that I was prised at by them. And I took the thirty pieces of silver, and cast them to the potter in the house of יהוה.

14 Then I cut in two mine other staff, Bonds (Chovalim), that I might break the brotherhood between Judah (Yehudah) and Yisrael.

15 And יהוה said unto me, "Take unto you yet the instruments of a foolish shepherd.

16 For, behold, I will raise up a shepherd in the land, which shall not visit those that be cut off, neither shall seek the young one, nor heal that that is broken, nor feed that that standeth still; but he shall eat the flesh of the fat, and tear their claws in pieces.

17 Woe to the worthless shepherd that leaveth the flock! The sword shall be upon his arm, and upon his right eye; his arm shall be clean dried up, and his right eye shall be utterly darkened.

12 The burden of the word of יהוה for Yisrael. Thus saith יהוה, who stretcheth forth the heavens, and layeth the foundation of the earth, and formeth the spirit of man within Him.

2 Behold, I will make Jerusalem (Yerushalayim) a cup of trembling unto all the people round about, when they shall be in the siege both against Judah (Yehudah) and against Jerusalem

(Yerushalayim).

3 And in that day will I make Jerusalem (Yerushalayim) a burdensome stone for all people; all that burden themselves with it shall be cut in pieces, though all the people of the earth be gathered together against it.

4 "In that day," saith יהוה, "I will smite every horse with astonishment, and his rider with madness; and I will open Mine eyes upon the house of Judah (Yehudah), and will smite every horse of the people with blindness.

5 And the governors of Judah (Yehudah) shall say in their heart, 'The inhabitants of Jerusalem (Yerushalayim) shall be my strength in יהוה of hosts their God (YHWH Tsevaot Eloheihem)'

6 In that day will I make the governors of Judah (Yehudah) like a hearth of fire among the wood, and like a torch of fire in a sheaf; and they shall devour all the people round about, on the right hand and on the left; and Jerusalem (Yerushalayim) shall be inhabited again in her own place, even in Jerusalem (Yerushalayim).

7 יהוה also shall save the tents of Judah (Yehudah) first, that the glory of the house of Dawid and the glory of the inhabitants of Jerusalem (Yerushalayim) do not magnify themselves against Judah (Yehudah).

8 In that day shall יהוה defend the inhabitants of Jerusalem (Yerushalayim); and he that is feeble among them at that day shall be as Dawid; and the house of Dawid shall be as God (Elohim), as the angel of יהוה before them.

9 And it shall come to pass in that day, that I will seek to destroy all the nations that come against Jerusalem (Yerushalayim).

10 And I will pour upon the house of Dawid, and upon the inhabitants of Jerusalem (Yerushalayim), the Spirit (Ruach) of grace and of supplications; and they shall look upon Me whom they have pierced, and they shall mourn for Him, as one mourneth for his only son, and shall be in bitterness for Him, as one that is in bitterness for his firstborn.

11 In that day shall there be a great mourning in Jerusalem (Yerushalayim), as the mourning of Hadadrimmon in the valley of Megiddon.

12 And the land shall mourn, every family apart; the family of the house of Dawid apart, and their wives apart; the family of the house of Nathan apart, and their wives apart;

13 The family of the house of Lewi apart, and

their wives apart; the family of Shimei apart, and their wives apart;

14 All the families that remain, every family apart, and their wives apart."

13 "In that day there shall be a fountain opened to the house of Dawid and to the inhabitants of Jerusalem (Yerushalayim) for sin and for uncleanness.

2 "And it shall come to pass in that day," saith יהוה of hosts (YHWH Tsevaot), "that I will cut off the names of the idols out of the land, and they shall no more be remembered; and also I will cause the prophets and the unclean spirit to pass out of the land.

3 And it shall come to pass, that when any shall yet prophesy, then his father and his mother that begat him shall say unto him, 'You shalt not live; for you speakest lies in the name of יהוה.' And his father and his mother that begat him shall thrust him through when he prophesieth.

4 And it shall come to pass in that day, that the prophets shall be ashamed every one of his vision, when he hath prophesied; neither shall they wear a rough garment to deceive.

5 But he shall say, 'I am no prophet, I am a husbandman; for man taught me to keep cattle from my youth.'

6 And one shall say unto him, 'What are these wounds in your hands?' Then he shall answer, 'Those with which I was wounded in the house of my friends.'

7 "Awake, O sword, against My Shepherd, and against the Man that is My fellow," saith יהוה of hosts (YHWH Tsevaot). "Smite the Shepherd (Roeh), and the sheep shall be scattered; and I will turn Mine hand upon the little ones.

8 And it shall come to pass, that in all the land," saith יהוה, two parts therein shall be cut off and die; but the third shall be left therein:

9 And I will bring the third part through the fire, and will refine them as silver is refined, and will try them as gold is tried; they shall call on My name, and I will hear them; I will say, 'This is My people'; and they shall say, 'יהוה is my God (Elohim).'"

14 Behold, the day of יהוה cometh, and your spoil shall be divided in the midst of you.

2 For I will gather all nations against Jerusalem (Yerushalayim) to battle; and the city shall be taken, and the houses rifled, and the women ravished; and half of the city shall go forth into captivity, and the residue of the people shall not be cut off from the city.

3 Then shall יהוה go forth, and fight against those nations, as when He fought in the day of battle.

4 And His feet shall stand in that day upon the Mount of Olives, which is before Jerusalem (Yerushalayim) on the east, and the Mount of Olives shall cleave in the midst thereof toward the east and toward the west, and there shall be a very great valley; and half of the mountain shall remove toward the north, and half of it toward the south.

5 And you shall flee to the valley of the mountains; for the valley of the mountains shall reach unto Azal; yea, you shall flee, like as you fled from before the earthquake in the days of Uzziyah king of Judah (Yehudah); and יהוה my God (YHWH Elohai) shall come, and all the holy ones with You.

6 And it shall come to pass in that day, that the light shall not be clear, nor dark.

7 But it shall be one day which shall be known to יהוה, not day, nor night; but it shall come to pass, that at evening time it shall be light.

8 And it shall be in that day, that living waters shall go out from Jerusalem (Yerushalayim); half of them toward the former sea, and half of them toward the hinder sea; in summer and in winter shall it be.

9 And יהוה shall be King over all the earth. In that day shall there be one יהוה, and His name one.

10 All the land shall be turned as a plain from Geba to Rimmon south of Jerusalem (Yerushalayim); and it shall be lifted up, and inhabited in her place, from Benjamin (Binyamin)'s gate unto the place of the first gate, unto the corner gate, and from the tower of Hananeel unto the king's winepresses.

11 And men shall dwell in it, and there shall be no more utter destruction; but Jerusalem (Yerushalayim) shall be safely inhabited.

12 And this shall be the plague wherewith יהוה will smite all the people that have fought against Jerusalem (Yerushalayim). Their flesh shall consume away while they stand upon their feet, and their eyes shall consume away in their holes, and their tongue shall consume away in their mouth.

13 And it shall come to pass in that day, that a great tumult from יהוה shall be among them;

and they shall lay hold every one on the hand of his neighbour, and his hand shall rise up against the hand of his neighbour.

14 And Judah (Yehudah) also shall fight at Jerusalem (Yerushalayim); and the wealth of all the nations round about shall be gathered together, gold, and silver, and apparel, in great abundance.

15 And so shall be the plague of the horse, of the mule, of the camel, and of the ass, and of all the beasts that shall be in these tents, as this plague.

16 And it shall come to pass, that every one that is left of all the nations which came against Jerusalem (Yerushalayim) shall even go up from year to year to worship the King, יהוה of hosts (YHWH Tsevaot), and to keep the Feast of Tabernacles (Chag Sukkot).

17 And it shall be, that whoso will not come up of all the families of the earth unto Jerusalem (Yerushalayim) to worship the King, יהוה of hosts (YHWH Tsevaot), even upon them shall be no rain.

18 And if the family of Egypt (Mitsrayim) go not up, and come not, that have no rain; there shall be the plague, wherewith יהוה will smite the nations that come not up to keep the Feast of Tabernacles (Chag Sukkot).

19 This shall be the punishment of Egypt (Mitsrayim), and the punishment of all nations that come not up to keep the Feast of Tabernacles (Chag Sukkot).

20 In that day shall there be upon the bells of the horses: "Holiness unto YHWH (Qodesh la-YHWH)"; and the pots in יהוה's house shall be like the bowls before the altar.

21 Yea, every pot in Jerusalem (Yerushalayim) and in Judah (Yehudah) shall be consecrated unto יהוה of hosts (YHWH Tsevaot); and all they that sacrifice shall come and take of them, and seethe therein; and in that day there shall be no more the Canaanite in the house of יהוה of hosts (YHWH Tsevaot).

MALACHI
MALAKHI מַלְאָכִי
(My Messenger)

1 The burden of the word of יהוה to Yisrael by [A66]Malachi (Malakhi).

2 "I have loved you," saith יהוה. "Yet you say, 'Wherein have You loved us?' "Was not Esaw, Jacob (Yaaqov)'s brother?" saith יהוה; "yet I loved Jacob (Yaaqov),

3 And Esaw I have hated, and laid his mountains and his heritage waste for the dragons of the wilderness."

4 Whereas Edom saith, "We are impoverished, but we will return and build the desolate places." Thus saith יהוה of hosts (YHWH Tsevaot): "They shall build, but I will throw down; and they shall call them, The border of wickedness, and the people against whom יהוה hath indignation forever.

5 And your eyes shall see, and you shall say, 'יהוה will be magnified from the border of Yisrael.'

6 A son honoureth his father, and a servant his master; if then I be a Father, where is Mine honor? And if I be a Master (Adon), where is My fear? saith יהוה of hosts (YHWH Tsevaot) unto you, O priests (kohanim), that despise My name. And you say, 'Wherein have we despised Your name?'

7 You offer polluted bread upon Mine altar; and you say, 'Wherein have we polluted You?' In that you say, 'The table of יהוה is contemptible.'

8 And if you offer the blind for sacrifice, is it not evil? And if you offer the lame and sick, is it not evil? Offer it now unto your governor, will he be pleased with you, or accept your person?" saith יהוה of hosts (YHWH Tsevaot).

9 "And now, please, beseech God (El) that He will be gracious unto us. This hath been by your means; will He regard your persons?" saith יהוה of hosts (YHWH Tsevaot).

10 "Who is there even among you that would shut the doors for nothing? Neither do you kindle fire on Mine altar for nought. I have no pleasure in you," saith יהוה of hosts (YHWH Tsevaot), "Nor will I accept an offering at your hand.

11 For from the rising of the sun even unto the going down of the same My name shall be great among the nations; and in every place incense shall be offered unto My name, and a pure offering; for My name shall be great among the nations," saith יהוה of hosts (YHWH Tsevaot).

12 "But you have profaned it, in that you say, 'The table of יהוה is polluted; and the fruit thereof, even his meat, is contemptible.'

13 You said also, 'Behold, what a weariness is it!' And you have snuffed at it," saith יהוה of hosts (YHWH Tsevaot); "And you brought that which was torn, and the lame, and the sick; thus you brought an offering; should I accept this of your hand?" saith יהוה.

14 "But cursed be the deceiver, which hath in his flock a male, and voweth, and sacrificeth unto the Lord (Adonai) a corrupt thing; for I am a great King," saith יהוה of hosts (YHWH Tsevaot), "And My name is feared among the nations."

2 "And now, O you priests (kohanim), this commandment is for you.

2 If you will not hear, and if you will not lay it to heart, to give glory unto My name," saith יהוה of hosts (YHWH Tsevaot), "I will even send a curse upon you, and I will curse your blessings; yea, I have cursed them already, because you do not lay it to heart.

3 Behold, I will corrupt your seed, and spread dung upon your faces, even the dung of your solemn feasts; and one shall take you away with it.

4 And you shall know that I have sent this commandment unto you, that My covenant might be with Lewi," saith יהוה of hosts (YHWH Tsevaot).

5 "My covenant was with him of life and peace; and I gave them to him for the fear wherewith he feared Me, and was reverent before My name.

6 The Torah of truth was in his mouth, and iniquity was not found in his lips: he walked with Me in peace and equity, and did turn many away from iniquity.

7 For the priest (kohen)'s lips should keep knowledge, and they should seek the Torah at his mouth; for he is the messenger of יהוה of hosts (YHWH Tsevaot).

8 But you are departed out of the way; you have caused many to stumble at the Torah; you have corrupted the covenant of Lewi," saith יהוה of hosts (YHWH Tsevaot).

9 Therefore have I also made you contemptible and base before all the people, according as you

have not kept My ways, but have been partial in the Torah.

10 Have we not all one Father (Av)? Hath not one God (El) created us? Why do we deal treacherously every man against his brother, by profaning the covenant of our fathers?

11 Judah (Yehudah) hath dealt treacherously, and an abomination is committed in Yisrael and in Jerusalem (Yerushalayim); for Judah (Yehudah) hath profaned the holiness of יהוה which he loved, and hath married the daughter of a strange god.

12 יהוה will cut off the man that doeth this, the master and the scholar, out of the tabernacles of Jacob (Yaaqov), and him that offereth an offering unto יהוה of hosts (YHWH Tsevaot).

13 And this have you done again: covering the altar of יהוה with tears, with weeping, and with crying out, insomuch that he regardeth not the offering any more, or receiveth it with good will at your hand.

14 Yet you say, "Wherefore?" Because יהוה hath been witness between you and the wife of your youth, against whom you have dealt treacherously; yet is she your companion, and the wife of your covenant.

15 And did not He make one? Yet had He the remnant of the Spirit (Ruach). And wherefore one? That he might seek a godly seed. Therefore take heed to your spirit, and let none deal treacherously against the wife of his youth.

16 "For יהוה, the God of Israel (Elohei Yisrael), saith that He hateth putting away; for one covereth violence with his garment," saith יהוה of hosts (YHWH Tsevaot); therefore take heed to your spirit, that you deal not treacherously."

17 You have wearied יהוה with your words. Yet you say, "Wherein have we wearied him?" When you say, "Every one that doeth evil is good in the sight of יהוה, and He delighteth in them;" or, "Where is the God (Elohim) of justice?"

3 "Behold, I will send My messenger, and he shall prepare the way before Me; and the Lord (Adon) whom you seek, shall suddenly come to His temple, even the messenger of the covenant, whom you delight in; behold, He shall come," saith יהוה of hosts (YHWH Tsevaot).

2 "But who may abide the day of His coming? And who shall stand when He appeareth? For He is like a refiner's fire, and like fullers' soap;

3 And He shall sit as a refiner and purifier of silver; and He shall purify the sons of Lewi, and purge them as gold and silver, that they may offer unto יהוה an offering in righteousness.

4 Then shall the offering of Judah (Yehudah) and Jerusalem (Yerushalayim) be pleasant unto יהוה, as in the days of old, and as in former years.

5 And I will come near to you to judgment; and I will be a swift witness against the sorcerers, and against the adulterers, and against false swearers, and against those that oppress the hireling in his wages, the widow, and the fatherless, and that turn aside the stranger from his right, and fear not Me," saith יהוה of hosts (YHWH Tsevaot).

6 "For I am יהוה, I change not; therefore you sons of Jacob (Yaaqov) are not consumed.

7 Even from the days of your fathers you are gone away from mine ordinances, and have not kept them. Return unto Me, and I will return unto you," saith יהוה of hosts (YHWH Tsevaot). "But you said, 'Wherein shall we return?'

8 "Will a man rob God (Elohim)? Yet you have robbed Me. But you say, 'Wherein have we robbed You?' In tithes and offerings.

9 You are cursed with a curse, for you have robbed Me, even this whole nation.

10 Bring you all the tithes into the storehouse, that there may be meat in Mine house, and prove Me now herewith," saith יהוה of hosts (YHWH Tsevaot), "If I will not open you the windows of heaven, and pour you out a blessing, that there shall not be room enough to receive it.

11 And I will rebuke the devourer for your sakes, and he shall not destroy the fruits of your ground; nor shall your vine cast her fruit before the time in the field," saith יהוה of hosts (YHWH Tsevaot).

12 "And all nations shall call you blessed, for you shall be a delightsome land," saith יהוה of hosts (YHWH Tsevaot).

13 "Your words have been stout against Me," saith יהוה. "Yet you say, 'What have we spoken against You?'

14 You have said, 'It is vain to serve God (Elohim); and what profit is it that we have kept His ordinance, and that we have walked mournfully before יהוה of hosts (YHWH Tsevaot)?

15 And now we call the proud happy; yea, they

that work wickedness are set up; yea, they that tempt God (Elohim) are even delivered.'"

16 Then those who feared יהוה spake often one to another; and יהוה hearkened, and heard it, and a book of remembrance was written before Him for those who feared יהוה, and who thought upon His name.

17 "And they shall be Mine," saith יהוה of hosts (YHWH Tsevaot), "On that day when I make up My jewels; and I will spare them, as a man spareth his own son that serveth him."

18 Then shall you return, and discern between the righteous and the wicked, between him that serveth God (Elohim) and him that serveth Him not.

4 "For, behold, the day cometh, that shall burn as an oven; and all the proud, yea, and all that do wickedly, shall be stubble; and the day that cometh shall burn them up," saith יהוה of hosts (YHWH Tsevaot), "that it shall leave them neither root nor branch.

2 But unto you that fear My name shall the sun of righteousness arise with healing in its wings; and you shall go forth, and grow up as calves of the stall.

3 And you shall tread down the wicked; for they shall be ashes under the soles of your feet in the day that I shall do this," saith יהוה of hosts (YHWH Tsevaot).

4 "Remember you the teaching of Moses (torat Mosheh) My servant, which I commanded unto him in Horeb for all Yisrael, with the statutes and judgments.

5 Behold, I will send you Eliyah the prophet before the coming of the great and dreadful day of יהוה.

6 And he shall turn the heart of the fathers to the children, and the heart of the children to their fathers, lest I come and smite the earth with a curse."

NEW
BLOOD COVENANT

דַּס־הַבְּרִית
חֲדָשָׁה

Dam haBerit
Chadashah

MATTHEW
MATTIYAHU מַתִּתְיָהוּ
(Gospel of Matthew)

1 The book of the generation of [A1]Yahwah [B45]haMashiach, the son (descendant) of Dawid, the son (descendant) of [A11]Avraham.

2 Avraham begat [A12]Isaac (Yitschaq); and Isaac (Yitschaq) begat Jacob (Yaaqov); and [A14]Jacob (Yaaqov) begat [A19]Judah (Yehudah) and his brethren;

3 And Judah (Yehudah) begat Phares (Perets) and Zara of Thamar; and Phares (Perets) begat Esrom (Chetsron); and Esrom (Chetsron) begat Aram;

4 And Aram begat Aminadab; and Aminadab begat Naasson; and Naasson begat Salmon;

5 And Salmon begat Boaz of Rachab; and Boaz begat Obed of Ruth; and Obed begat [A34]Jesse (Yishai);

6 And Jesse (Yishai) begat Dawid the king; and Dawid the king begat [A39]Solomon (Shelomoh) of her that had been the wife of Urias (Uriyah);

7 And Solomon (Shelomoh) begat [A40]Roboam (Rechavam); and Roboam (Rechavam) begat Abia (Aviyah); and Abia (Aviyah) begat Asa;

8 And Asa begat Josaphat (Yehoshafat); and Josaphat (Yehoshafat) begat Yoram; and Yoram begat Orias (Uzziyah);

9 And Orias (Uzziyah) begat Joatham (Yotam); and Joatham (Yotam) begat Achaz; and Achaz begat [A44]Hezekiah (Chizqiyahu);

10 And Hezekiah (Chizqiyahu) begat [A28]Manasseh (Menashsheh); and Manasseh (Menashsheh) begat Amon; and Amon begat Josias (Yoshiyahu);

11 And Josias (Yoshiyahu) begat Jechonias (Yekonyah) and his brethren, about the time they were carried away to Babylon (Bavel);

12 And after they were brought to Babylon (Bavel), Jechonias (Yekonyah) begat Shealtiel; and Shealtiel begat Zerubbabel;

13 And Zerubbabel begat Avihud; and Avihud begat Eliakim; and Eliakim begat Azzur;

14 And Azzur begat Sadoc; and Sadoc begat Achim; and Achim begat Eliud;

15 And Eliud begat Eleazar; and Eleazar begat Mattan; and Mattan begat Jacob (Yaaqov);

16 And Jacob (Yaaqov) begat [A26]Joseph (Yosef) the husband of Mary (Miryam), of whom was born [A1]Yahwah (YHWH), who is called the Messiah (haMashiach).

17 So all the generations from Avraham to Dawid are fourteen generations; and from Dawid until the carrying away into Babylon (Bavel) are fourteen generations; and from the carrying away into Babylon (Bavel) unto Messiah (Mashiach) are fourteen generations.

18 Now the birth of Yahwah haMashiach was on this wise: When as His mother Mary (Miryam) was espoused to Joseph (Yosef), before they came together, she was found with child of the Holy Spirit (Ruach haQodesh).

19 Then Joseph (Yosef) her husband, being a just man, and not willing to make her a public example, was minded to put her away privily.

20 But while he thought on these things, behold, the angel of [A1]יהוה appeared unto him in a dream, saying, "Joseph (Yosef), you son (descendant) of Dawid, fear not to take unto you Mary (Miryam) your wife; for that which is conceived in her is of the Holy Spirit (Ruach haQodesh).

21 And she shall bring forth a son, and you shalt call His name [A1]Yahwah (YHWH); for He shall save His people from their sins.

22 Now all this was done, that it might be fulfilled which was spoken of יהוה by the prophet, saying,

23 "Behold, a virgin shall be with child, and shall bring forth a son, and they shall call His name "[B48]Immanu El", which is being interpreted: "God with us." – *Isa. 7:14, 9:6*

24 Then Joseph (Yosef) being raised from sleep did as the angel of יהוה had bidden him, and took unto him his wife,

25 And knew her not till she had brought forth her firstborn son; and he called His name Yahwah (YHWH).

2 Now when Yahwah was born in Bethlehem (Beit-Lechem) of Judah (Yehudah) in the days of Herod the king, behold, there came wise men from the east to Jerusalem (Yerushalayim),

2 Saying, "Where is He that is born King of the Jews (Yehudim)? For we have seen His star in the east, and are come to worship Him."

3 When Herod the king had heard these things, he was troubled, and all Jerusalem (Yerushalayim) with him.

4 And when he had gathered all the chief priests (kohanim) and scribes of the people together,

he demanded of them where the Messiah (haMashiach) should be born.

5 And they said unto him, "In Bethlehem (Beit-Lechem) of Judah (Yehudah), for thus it is written by the prophet:

6 'And you Bethlehem (Beit-Lechem), in the land of Judah (Yehudah), art not the least among the rulers of Judah (Yehudah); for out of you shall come a Ruler, that shall rule My people Yisrael.'" – *Mic.5:2*

7 Then Herod, when he had privily called the wise men, enquired of them diligently what time the star appeared.

8 And he sent them to Bethlehem (Beit-Lechem), and said, "Go and search diligently for the young Child (haMashiach); and when you have found Him, bring me word again, that I may come and worship Him also."

9 When they had heard the king, they departed; and, behold, the star, which they saw in the east, went before them, till it came and stood over where the young Child (haMashiach) was.

10 When they saw the star, they rejoiced with exceeding great joy.

11 And when they were come into the house, they saw the young Child (haMashiach) with Mary (Miryam) His mother, and fell down, and worshipped Him; and when they had opened their treasures, they presented unto Him gifts; gold, and frankincense, and myrrh.

12 And being divinely warned in a dream that they should not return to Herod, they departed into their own country another way.

13 And when they were departed, behold, the angel of יהוה appeareth to Joseph (Yosef) in a dream, saying, "Arise, and take the young Child (haMashiach) and His mother, and flee into Egypt (Mitsrayim), and be you there until I bring you word; for Herod will seek the young Child (haMashiach) to destroy Him."

14 When he arose, he took the young Child (haMashiach) and His mother by night, and departed into Egypt (Mitsrayim);

15 And was there until the death of Herod, that it might be fulfilled which was spoken of יהוה by the prophet, saying, "Out of Egypt (Mitsrayim) have I called My son (people)." – *Hos.11:1*

16 Then Herod, when he saw that he was mocked of the wise men, was exceeding wroth, and sent forth, and slew all the children that were in Bethlehem (Beit-Lechem), and in all the coasts thereof, from two years old and under, according to the time which he had diligently enquired of the wise men.

17 Then was fulfilled that which was spoken by [A52]Jeremiah (Yirmeyahu) the prophet, saying,

18 "In Rama was there a voice heard, lamentation, and weeping, and great mourning, Rachel weeping for her children, and would not be comforted, because they are no more." – *Jer.31:15*

19 But when Herod was dead, behold, an angel of יהוה appeareth in a dream to Joseph (Yosef) in Egypt (Mitsrayim),

20 Saying, "Arise, and take the young Child (haMashiach) and His mother, and go into the land of Yisrael, for they are dead who sought the young Child (haMashiach)'s life."

21 And he arose, and took the young Child (haMashiach) and His mother, and came into the land of Yisrael.

22 But when he heard that Archelaus did reign in Judah (Yehudah) in the room of his father Herod, he was afraid to go thither; notwithstanding, being warned in a dream, he turned aside into the parts of Galilee.

23 And he came and dwelt in a city called Nazareth, that it might be fulfilled which was spoken by the prophets, "He shall be called a Nazarene."

3 In those days came [A67]John the Baptist (Yochanan haMatvil), preaching in the wilderness of Judah (Yehudah),

2 And saying, "Repent you, for the kingdom of heaven is at hand!"

3 For this is he that was spoken of by the prophet [A51]Isaiah (Yeshayahu), saying, [B49]"The voice of one crying in the wilderness, 'Prepare you the way of יהוה (Yahwah, YHWH), make His paths straight.'" – *Isa.40:3, Mark 1:3, Luke 3:4*

4 And the same John (Yochanan) had his raiment of camel's hair, and a leathern girdle about his loins; and his meat was locusts and wild honey.

5 Then went out to him Jerusalem (Yerushalayim), and all Judah (Yehudah), and all the region round about Jordan (Yarden),

6 And were baptized of him in Jordan (Yarden), confessing their sins.

7 But when he saw many of the [B50]Pharisees and [B51]Sadducees come to his [B52]baptism, he said

unto them, "O generation of vipers, who hath warned you to flee from the wrath to come?

8 Bring forth therefore fruits meet for repentance;

9 And think not to say within yourselves, 'We have Avraham to our father;' for I say unto you, that [B1a]God (Elohim) is able of these stones to raise up children unto Avraham.

10 And now also the axe is laid unto the root of the trees; therefore every tree which bringeth not forth good fruit is hewn down, and cast into the fire.

11 I indeed baptize you with water unto repentance; but He that cometh after me is mightier than I, whose shoes I am not worthy to bear; He shall baptize you with the Holy Spirit (Ruach haQodesh), and with fire;

12 Whose winnowing fan is in His hand, and He will throughly purge His floor, and gather His wheat into the garner; but He will burn up the chaff with unquenchable fire.

13 Then cometh Yahwah from Galilee to Jordan (Yarden) unto John (Yochanan), to be baptized of him.

14 But John (Yochanan) forbad Him, saying, "I have need to be baptized of you, and comest You to me?"

15 And Yahwah answering said unto him, "Let it to be so now, for thus it becometh us to fulfil all righteousness." Then he let Him.

16 And Yahwah, when He was baptized, went up straightway out of the water; and, behold, the heavens were opened unto Him, and He saw the Spirit of God (Ruach Elohim) descending like a dove, and lighting upon Him.

17 And behold [B53]a voice from heaven, saying, "This is My beloved [B47]Son (Humanity) in whom I am well pleased."

4 Then was Yahwah led up of the Spirit into the wilderness to be tempted of the devil.

2 And when He had fasted forty days and forty nights, He was afterward an hungred.

3 And when the tempter came to Him, he said, "If You be the [B47]Humanity of El (YHWH), command that these stones be made bread."

4 But He answered and said, "It is written, 'Man shall not live by bread alone, but by every word that proceedeth out of the mouth of יהוה.' – Deu. 8:3

5 Then the devil taketh Him up into the holy city, and setteth Him on a pinnacle of the temple,

6 And saith unto Him, "If You be the Humanity of El (YHWH), cast Yourself down; for it is written, 'He shall give His angels charge concerning you; and in their hands they shall bear you up, lest at any time you dash your foot against a stone.' – Psa. 91:1-2

7 Yahwah said unto him, "It is written again, 'You shalt not tempt יהוה your God (YHWH Eloheikhem).' – Deu. 6:16

8 Again, the devil taketh Him up into an exceeding high mountain, and sheweth Him all the kingdoms of the world, and the glory of them;

9 And saith unto him, "All these things will I give You, if You wilt fall down and worship me."

10 Then saith Yahwah unto him, "Get you away, Satan! For it is written, 'You shalt worship יהוה your God (YHWH Eloheikha), and Him only shalt you serve.'" – Deu.6:13-14

11 Then the devil leaveth Him, and, behold, angels came and ministered unto Him.

12 Now when Yahwah had heard that John (Yochanan) was cast into prison, He departed into Galilee;

13 And leaving Nazareth, He came and dwelt in Capernaum, which is upon the sea coast, in the borders of Zabulon and Nephthalim;

14 That it might be fulfilled which was spoken by Isaiah (Yeshayahu) the prophet, saying,

15 "The land of Zabulon (Zevulun), and the land of Nephthalim, by the way of the sea, beyond Jordan (Yarden), Galilee of the nations: – Isa.9:1

16 The people who sat in darkness saw great light; and to them who sat in the region and shadow of death light is sprung up." – Isa.9:2

17 From that time Yahwah began to preach, and to say, "Repent, for the kingdom of heaven is at hand."

18 And Yahwah, walking by the sea of Galilee, saw two brethren, Shimon called Peter (Kefa), and Andrew his brother, casting a net into the sea; for they were fishermen.

19 And He saith unto them, "Follow Me, and I will make you fishers of men."

20 And they straightway left their nets, and followed Him.

21 And going on from thence, He saw other two brethren, Jacob son of Zebedee (Yaaqov Ben-Zavdai), and John (Yochanan) his brother, in a ship with Zebedee (Zavdai) their father, mending their nets; and He called them.

22 And they immediately left the ship and their father, and followed Him.

23 And Yahwah went about all Galilee, teaching in their synagogues, and preaching the gospel (good news) of the kingdom, and healing all manner of sickness and all manner of disease among the people.

24 And his fame went throughout all Syria (Aram); and they brought unto him all sick people that were taken with divers diseases and torments, and those who were possessed with devils, and those who were lunatick, and those that had the palsy; and He healed them.

25 And there followed Him great multitudes of people from Galilee, and from Decapolis, and from Jerusalem (Yerushalayim), and from Judah (Yehudah), and from beyond Jordan (Yarden).

5 And seeing the multitudes, He went up into a mountain; and when He was set, His disciples came unto Him.

2 And He opened His mouth, and taught them, saying,

3 "Blessed are the poor in spirit, for theirs is the kingdom of heaven.

4 Blessed are they that mourn, for they shall be comforted.

5 Blessed are the meek, for they shall inherit the earth.

6 Blessed are they who do hunger and thirst after righteousness, for they shall be filled.

7 Blessed are the merciful, for they shall obtain mercy.

8 Blessed are the pure in heart, for they shall see God (Elohim, יהוה (YHWH)).

9 Blessed are the peacemakers, for they shall be called the children of God (Elohim, יהוה (YHWH)).

10 Blessed are they who are persecuted for righteousness' sake, for theirs is the kingdom of heaven.

11 Blessed are you, when men shall revile you, and persecute you, and shall say all manner of evil against you falsely, for My sake.

12 Rejoice, and be exceeding glad, for great is your reward in heaven, for so persecuted they the prophets who were before you.

13 You are the salt of the earth, but if the salt has lost its savour, wherewith shall it be salted? It is thenceforth good for nothing, but to be cast out, and to be trodden under foot of men.

14 You are the light of the world. A city that is set on a hill cannot be hidden.

15 Neither do men light a candle, and put it under a bushel, but on a candlestick; and it giveth light unto all that are in the house.

16 Let your light so shine before men, that they may see your good works, and glorify your Father who is in heaven.

17 Think not that I came to destroy the [B28d]Torah or the Prophets (Nevi'im). I did not come to destroy, but to fulfil.

18 For verily I say unto you, till heaven and earth pass away, one jot or one tittle shall in no wise pass from the Torah, till all be fulfilled.

19 Whosoever therefore shall break one of these least commandments, and shall teach men so, he shall be called the least in the kingdom of heaven; but whosoever shall do and teach them, the same shall be called great in the kingdom of heaven.

20 For I say unto you, that except your righteousness shall exceed the righteousness of the scribes and Pharisees, you shall in no case enter into the kingdom of heaven.

21 You have heard that it was said by them of old time, 'You shalt not kill; and whosoever shall kill shall be in danger of the judgment;

22 But I say unto you, that whosoever is angry with his brother without a cause shall be in danger of the judgment: and whosoever shall say to his brother, '[B54]Rhaka (You empty-headed)' shall be in danger of the [B55]council (Sanhedrin); but whosoever shall say, 'You fool' shall be in danger of [B56]hell fire (gehenna).

23 Therefore if you bring your gift to the altar, and there rememberest that your brother hath something against you;

24 Leave there your gift before the altar, and go your way; first be reconciled to your brother, and then come and offer your gift.

25 Agree with your adversary quickly, whiles you are in the way with him; lest at any time the adversary deliver you to the judge, and the judge deliver you to the officer, and you be cast into prison.

26 Verily I say unto you, you shalt by no means come out thence, till you have paid the uttermost farthing.

27 You have heard that it was said by them of old time, 'You shalt not commit adultery.'

28 But I say unto you, that whosoever looketh

on a woman to lust after her hath committed adultery with her already in his heart.

29 And if your right eye offends you, pluck it out, and cast it from you; for it is profitable for you that one of your members should perish, and not that your whole body should be cast into hell.

30 And if your right hand offends you, cut it off, and cast it from you; for it is profitable for you that one of your members should perish, and not that your whole body should be cast into hell (gehenna).

31 It hath been said, 'Whosoever shall put away his wife, let him give her a writing of divorcement.'

32 But I say unto you, that whosoever shall put away his wife, except for the cause of fornication (sexual immorality), causeth her to commit adultery; and whosoever shall marry her that is divorced committeth adultery.

33 Again, you have heard that it hath been said by them of old time, 'You shalt not swear falsely yourself, but shalt perform unto יהוה your oaths.' – Lev 19:12, Num.30:2

34 But I say unto you, swear not at all: neither by heaven, for it is God (Elohim)'s throne;

35 Nor by the earth, for it is His footstool; neither by Jerusalem (Yerushalayim); for it is the city of the great King.

36 Neither shalt you swear by your head, because you canst not make one hair white or black.

37 But let your communication be, 'Yes, yes'; 'No, no'; for whatsoever is more than these cometh of evil.

38 You have heard that it hath been said, 'An eye for an eye, and a tooth for a tooth';

39 But I say unto you, that you resist not evil; but whosoever shall smite you on your right cheek, turn to him the other also.

40 And if any man will sue you at the law, and take away your coat, let him have your cloke also.

41 And whosoever shall compel you to go a mile, go with him twain.

42 Give to him that asketh you, and from him that would borrow of you turn not you away.

43 You have heard that it hath been said, 'You shalt love your neighbour, and hate your enemy.'

44 But I say unto you, 'Love your enemies, bless them that curse you, do good to them that hate you, and pray for them who despitefully use you, and persecute you;

45 That you may be the children of your Father who is in heaven; for He maketh His sun to rise on the evil and on the good, and sendeth rain on the just and on the unjust.

46 For if you love them who love you, what reward have you? Do not even the tax collectors do the same?

47 And if you salute your brethren only, what do you more than others? Do not even the tax collectors do so?

48 Be you therefore perfect, even as your Father who is in heaven is perfect.

6 Take heed that you do not your alms before men, to be seen of them; otherwise you have no reward of your Father who is in heaven.

2 Therefore when you doest your alms, do not sound a trumpet before you, as the hypocrites do in the synagogues and in the streets, that they may have glory of men. Verily I say unto you, they have their reward.

3 But when you doest alms, let not your left hand know what your right hand doeth;

4 That your alms may be in secret; and your Father who seeth in secret Himself shall reward you openly.

5 And when you prayest, you shalt not be as the hypocrites are; for they love to pray standing in the synagogues and in the corners of the streets, that they may be seen of men. Verily I say unto you, they have their reward.

6 But you, when you prayest, enter into your closet, and when you have shut your door, pray to your Father who is in secret; and your Father who seeth in secret shall reward you openly.

7 But when you pray, use not vain repetitions, as the heathen do; for they think that they shall be heard for their much speaking.

8 Be not you therefore like unto them; for your Father knoweth what things you have need of, before you ask Him.

9 After this manner therefore pray you: Our Father who art in heaven, Hallowed be Your name.

10 Your kingdom come. Your will be done on earth, as it is in heaven.

11 Give us this day our daily bread.

12 And forgive us our debts, as we forgive our debtors.

13 And lead us not into temptation, but deliver

us from evil; for Yours is the kingdom, and the power, and the glory, forever. So be it (Amen).

14 For if you forgive men their trespasses, your heavenly Father will also forgive you;

15 But if you forgive not men their trespasses, neither will your Father forgive your trespasses.

16 Moreover when you fast, be not, as the hypocrites, of a sad countenance; for they disfigure their faces, that they may appear unto men to fast. Verily I say unto you, they have their reward.

17 But you, when you fastest, anoint your head, and wash your face;

18 That you appear not unto men to fast, but unto your Father who is in secret; and your Father, who seeth in secret, shall reward you openly.

19 Lay not up for yourselves treasures upon earth, where moth and rust doth corrupt, and where thieves break through and steal;

20 But lay up for yourselves treasures in heaven, where neither moth nor rust doth corrupt, and where thieves do not break through nor steal;

21 For where your treasure is, there will your heart be also.

22 The light of the body is the eye. If therefore your eye be clear, your whole body shall be full of light.

23 But if your eye be bad, your whole body shall be full of darkness. If therefore the light that is in you be darkness, how great is that darkness!

24 No man can serve two masters; for either he will hate the one, and love the other; or else he will hold to the one, and despise the other. You cannot serve God (Elohim) and mammon.

25 Therefore I say unto you, take no thought for your life, what you shall eat, or what you shall drink; nor yet for your body, what you shall put on. Is not the life more than food, and the body than raiment?

26 Behold the fowls of the air; for they sow not, neither do they reap, nor gather into barns; yet your heavenly Father feedeth them. Are you not much better than they?

27 Which of you by taking thought can add one cubit unto his stature?

28 And why take you thought for raiment? Consider the lilies of the field, how they grow; they toil not, neither do they spin;

29 And yet I say unto you, that even Solomon (Shelomoh) in all his glory was not arrayed like one of these.

30 Wherefore, if God (Elohim) so clothe the grass of the field, which today is, and tomorrow is cast into the oven, shall He not much more clothe you, O you of little faith?

31 Therefore take no thought, saying, 'What shall we eat?' Or, 'What shall we drink?' Or, 'Wherewithal shall we be clothed?'

32 (For after all these things do the Gentiles (Goyim) seek;) for your heavenly Father knoweth that you have need of all these things.

33 But seek you first the kingdom of God (Elohim, יהוה (YHWH)), and His righteousness; and all these things shall be added unto you.

34 Take therefore no thought for tomorrow, for tomorrow shall take thought for the things of itself. Sufficient unto the day is its own trouble.

7 Judge not, that you be not judged.

2 For with what judgment you judge, you shall be judged; and with what measure you use, it shall be measured back to you.

3 And why beholdest you the mote that is in your brother's eye, but considerest not the beam that is in your own eye?

4 Or how wilt you say to your brother, 'Let me pull out the mote out of your eye;' and, behold, a beam is in your own eye?

5 You hypocrite! First cast out the beam out of your own eye; and then shalt you see clearly to cast out the mote out of your brother's eye.

6 Give not that which is holy unto the dogs, neither cast you your pearls before swine, lest they trample them under their feet, and turn again and rend you.

7 Ask, and it shall be given you; seek, and you shall find; knock, and it shall be opened unto you;

8 For every one that asketh receiveth; and he that seeketh findeth; and to him that knocketh it shall be opened.

9 Or what man is there of you, whom if his son ask bread, will he give him a stone?

10 Or if he asks a fish, will he give him a serpent?

11 If you then, being evil, know how to give good gifts unto your children, how much more shall your Father who is in heaven give good things to them that ask him?

12 Therefore all things whatsoever you would that men should do to you, do you even so to them; for this is the [B28d]Torah and the Prophets

(Nevi'im).

13 Enter you in at the strait gate; for wide is the gate, and broad is the way, that leadeth to destruction, and many there be who go in thereat;

14 Because strait is the gate, and narrow is the way, which leadeth unto life, and few there be that find it.

15 Beware of false prophets, who come to you in sheep's clothing, but inwardly they are ravening wolves.

16 You shall know them by their fruits. Do men gather grapes of thorns, or figs of thistles?

17 Even so every good tree bringeth forth good fruit; but a corrupt tree bringeth forth bad fruit.

18 A good tree cannot bring forth bad fruit, neither can a corrupt tree bring forth good fruit.

19 Every tree that bringeth not forth good fruit is hewn down, and cast into the fire.

20 Wherefore by their fruits you shall know them.

21 Not every one that saith unto Me, 'Lord (Adonai), Lord (Adonai),' shall enter into the kingdom of heaven; but he that doeth the will of My Father who is in heaven.

22 Many will say to Me in that day, 'Lord (Adonai), Lord (Adonai), have we not prophesied in Your name? And in Your name have cast out devils? And in Your name done many wonderful works?'

23 And then will I profess unto them, 'I never knew you; depart from Me, you that work iniquity!'

24 Therefore whosoever heareth these sayings of Mine, and doeth them, I will liken him unto a wise man, who built his house upon a rock:

25 And the rain descended, and the floods came, and the winds blew, and beat upon that house; and it fell not; for it was founded upon a rock.

26 And every one that heareth these sayings of Mine, and doeth them not, shall be likened unto a foolish man, who built his house upon the sand:

27 And the rain descended, and the floods came, and the winds blew, and beat upon that house; and it fell; and great was the fall of it."

28 And it came to pass, when Yahwah had ended these sayings, the people were astonished at His teaching;

29 For He taught them as one having authority, and not as the scribes.

8 When He has come down from the mountain, great multitudes followed Him.

2 And, behold, there came a leper and worshipped Him, saying, "Lord (Adonai), if You wilt, You canst make me clean."

3 And Yahwah put forth His hand, and touched him, saying, "I will; be you clean." And immediately his leprosy was cleansed.

4 And Yahwah saith unto him, "See you tell no man; but go your way, shew yourself to the priest (kohen), and offer the gift that Moses (Mosheh) commanded, for a testimony unto them."

5 And when Yahweh has entered into Capernaum, there came unto Him a centurion, beseeching Him,

6 And saying, "Lord (Adonai), my servant lieth at home sick of the palsy, grievously tormented.

7 And Yahwah saith unto him, "I will come and heal him."

8 The centurion answered and said, "Lord (Adonai), I am not worthy that You shouldest come under my roof; but speak the word only, and my servant shall be healed.

9 For I am a man under authority, having soldiers under me; and I say to this man, 'Go!' and he goeth; and to another, 'Come!' and he cometh; and to my servant, 'Do this!' and he doeth it.

10 When Yahwah heard it, He marvelled, and said to them that followed, "Verily I say unto you, I have not found so great faith, no, not in Yisrael."

11 And I say unto you, that many shall come from the east and west, and shall sit down with Avraham, and Isaac (Yitschaq), and Jacob (Yaaqov), in the kingdom of heaven.

12 But the children of the kingdom shall be cast out into outer darkness. There shall be weeping and gnashing of teeth.

13 And Yahwah said unto the centurion, "Go your way; and as you have believed, so be it done unto you." And his servant was healed in the selfsame hour.

14 And when Yahwah had come into Peter (Kefa)'s house, He saw his wife's mother, laid and sick of a fever.

15 And He touched her hand, and the fever left her; and she arose, and ministered unto them.

16 When the even had come, they brought unto

Him many that were possessed with devils; and He cast out the spirits with His word, and healed all that were sick;

17 That it might be fulfilled which was spoken by Isaiah (Yeshayahu) the prophet, saying, "He Himself took our infirmities, and bare our sicknesses." – *Isa. 53:4*

18 Now when Yahwah saw great multitudes about Him, He gave commandment to depart unto the other side.

19 And a certain scribe came, and said unto Him, "Teacher (Rabbi), I will follow You whithersoever You goest."

20 And Yahwah saith unto him, "The foxes have holes, and the birds of the air have nests; but the Son of man (haMashiach) hath not where to lay His head."

21 And another of His disciples said unto Him, "Lord (Adonai), let me first to go and bury my father."

22 But Yahwah said unto him, "Follow Me; and let the dead bury their dead."

23 And when He has entered into a ship, His disciples followed Him.

24 And, behold, there arose a great tempest in the sea, insomuch that the ship was covered with the waves; but He was asleep.

25 And His disciples came to Him, and awoke Him, saying, "Lord (Adonai), save us; we are perishing!"

26 And He saith unto them, "Why are you fearful, O you of little faith?" Then He arose, and rebuked the winds and the sea; and there was a great calm.

27 But the men marvelled, saying, "What manner of man is this, that even the winds and the sea obey Him!"

28 And when He had come to the other side into the country of the Gergesenes, there met Him two possessed with devils, coming out of the tombs, exceeding fierce, so that no man might pass by that way.

29 And, behold, they cried out, saying, "What have we to do with You, Yahwah, You [B47]Humanity of El (YHWH)? Art You come here to torment us before the time?"

30 And there was a good way off from them a herd of many swine feeding.

31 So the devils besought Him, saying, "If You cast us out, let us to go away into the herd of swine."

32 And He said unto them, "Go!" And when they were come out, they went into the herd of swine; and, behold, the whole herd of swine ran violently down a steep place into the sea, and perished in the waters.

33 And they that kept them fled, and went their ways into the city, and told everything, and what was befallen to the possessed of the devils.

34 And, behold, the whole city came out to meet Yahwah; and when they saw Him, they besought Him that He would depart out of their district.

9 And He entered into a ship, and passed over, and came into His own city.

2 And, behold, they brought to Him a man sick of the palsy, lying on a bed. And Yahwah seeing their faith, said unto the sick of the palsy: "Son, be of good cheer; your sins be forgiven you."

3 And, behold, certain of the scribes said within themselves, "This Man blasphemeth."

4 And Yahwah knowing their thoughts said, "Why think you evil in your hearts?

5 For whether is easier, to say, 'Your sins be forgiven you;' or to say, 'Arise, and walk?'

6 But that you may know that the Son of man (haMashiach) hath power on earth to forgive sins;" (then saith He to the sick of the palsy,) "Arise, take up your bed, and go unto your house."

7 And he arose, and departed to his house.

8 But when the multitudes saw it, they marvelled, and glorified God (Elohim, יהוה (YHWH)), who had given such power unto men.

9 And as Yahwah passed forth from there, He saw a man, named [A68]Matthew (Mattityahu), sitting at the receipt of custom; and He saith unto him, "Follow Me!" And he arose, and followed Him.

10 And it came to pass, as Yahwah sat at meal in the house, behold, many tax collectors and sinners came and sat down with Him and His disciples.

11 And when the Pharisees saw it, they said unto His disciples, "Why eateth your Teacher (Rabbi) with tax collectors and sinners?

12 But when Yahwah heard that, He said unto them, "They that be whole need not a physician, but they that are sick.

13 But go you and learn what that meaneth: 'I will have mercy, and not sacrifice;' for I did not come to call the righteous, but sinners to

repentance."

14 Then came to Him the disciples of John (Yochanan), saying, "Why do we and the Pharisees fast often, but Your disciples fast not?"

15 And Yahwah said unto them, "Can the children of the bridechamber mourn, as long as the bridegroom is with them? But the days will come, when the bridegroom shall be taken from them, and then shall they fast.

16 No man putteth a piece of new cloth unto an old garment, for that which is put in to fill it up taketh from the garment, and the rent is made worse.

17 Neither do men put new wine into old bottles; else the bottles break, and the wine runneth out, and the bottles perish; but they put new wine into new bottles, and both are preserved."

18 While He spake these things unto them, behold, there came a certain ruler, and worshipped Him, saying, "My daughter is even now dead; but come and lay Your hand upon her, and she shall live."

19 And Yahwah arose, and followed him, and so did His disciples.

20 And, behold, a woman, who was diseased with an issue of blood twelve years, came behind Him, and touched the tassel (tsitsit) of His garment;

21 For she said within herself, "If I may but touch His garment, I shall be whole."

22 But Yahwah turned Him about, and when He saw her, He said, "Daughter, be of good comfort; your faith hath made you whole." And the woman was made whole from that hour.

23 And when Yahwah came into the ruler's house, and saw the minstrels and the people making a noise,

24 He said unto them, "Give place, for the maid is not dead, but sleepeth." And they laughed Him to scorn.

25 But when the people were put forth, He went in, and took her by the hand, and the maid arose.

26 And the fame hereof went abroad into all that land.

27 And when Yahwah departed thence, two blind men followed Him, crying, and saying, "You son (descendant) of Dawid, have mercy on us."

28 And when He had come into the house, the blind men came to Him; and Yahwah saith unto them, "Believe you that I am able to do this?"

They said unto Him, "Yes, Lord (Adonai)."

29 Then touched He their eyes, saying, "According to your faith be it unto you."

30 And their eyes were opened; and Yahwah straitly charged them, saying, "See that no man know it."

31 But they, when they were departed, spread abroad His fame in all that country.

32 As they went out, behold, they brought to Him a dumb man possessed with a devil.

33 And when the devil was cast out, the dumb spake; and the multitudes marvelled, saying, "It was never so seen in Yisrael."

34 But the Pharisees said, "He casteth out devils through the prince of the devils."

35 And Yahwah went about all the cities and villages, teaching in their synagogues, and preaching the gospel (good news) of the kingdom, and healing every sickness and every disease among the people.

36 But when He saw the multitudes, He was moved with compassion on them, because they fainted, and were scattered abroad, as sheep having no shepherd.

37 Then saith He unto His disciples, "The harvest truly is plenteous, but the labourers are few;

38 Pray you therefore Lord (Adon) of the harvest, that He will send forth labourers into His harvest."

10 And when He had called unto Him His twelve disciples, He gave them power against unclean spirits, to cast them out, and to heal all manner of sickness and all manner of disease.

2 Now the names of the twelve apostles are these: The first, Shimon, who is called Peter (Kefa), and Andrew his brother; James son of Zebedee (Yaaqov Ben-Zavdai), and John (Yochanan) his brother;

3 Philip, and Bartholomew (Bar-Talmai); Thomas, and Matthew (Mattityahu) the tax collector; James the son of Alphaeus (Yaaqov Ben-Chalfai), and Lebbaeus, whose surname was Thaddaeus (Taddai);

4 Shimon the Canaanite (Zealot), and Judah Iscariot (Yehudah Ishqeriot), who betrayed Him.

5 These twelve, Yahwah sent forth, and commanded them, saying, "Go not into the way of the Gentiles (Goyim), and into any city of the Samaritans enter you not;

6 But go rather to the lost sheep of the house of Yisrael.

7 And as you go, preach, saying, "The kingdom of heaven is at hand.

8 Heal the sick, cleanse the lepers, raise the dead, cast out devils; freely you have received, freely give.

9 Provide neither gold, nor silver, nor brass in your purses,

10 Nor scrip for your journey, neither two coats, neither shoes, nor yet staves; for the workman is worthy of his food.

11 And into whatsoever city or town you shall enter, enquire who in it is worthy; and there abide till you go thence.

12 And when you come into a house, greet it.

13 And if the house be worthy, let your peace come upon it; but if it be not worthy, let your peace return to you.

14 And whosoever shall not receive you, nor hear your words, when you depart out of that house or city, shake off the dust of your feet.

15 Verily I say unto you, it shall be more tolerable for the land of Sodom and Gomorrah in the day of judgment, than for that city.

16 Behold, I send you forth as sheep in the midst of wolves; be you therefore wise as serpents, and harmless as doves.

17 But beware of men, for they will deliver you up to the councils (Sanhedrins), and they will scourge you in their synagogues;

18 And you shall be brought before governors and kings for My sake, for a testimony against them and the nations.

19 But when they deliver you up, take no thought how or what you shall speak, for it shall be given you in that same hour what you shall speak.

20 For it is not you that speak, but the Spirit of your Father who speaketh in you.

21 And the brother shall deliver up the brother to death, and the father the child; and the children shall rise up against their parents, and cause them to be put to death.

22 And you shall be hated of all men for My name's sake; but he that endureth to the end shall be saved.

23 But when they persecute you in this city, flee you into another; for verily I say unto you, you shall not have gone over the cities of Yisrael, till the Son of man (haMashiach) comes.

24 The disciple (talmid) is not above his teacher (rabbi), nor the servant above his master (adon).

25 It is enough for the disciple (talmid) that he be as his teacher (rabbi), and the servant as his master (adon). If they have called the master of the house Beelzebub (Baal-Zebub), how much more shall they call them of his household?

26 Fear them not therefore, for there is nothing covered, that shall not be revealed; and hidden, that shall not be known.

27 What I tell you in darkness, that speak you in light; and what you hear in the ear, that preach you upon the housetops.

28 And fear not them who kill the body, but are not able to kill the soul; but rather fear him who is able to destroy both soul and body in hell (gehenna).

29 Are not two sparrows sold for a copper coin? And not one of them shall fall on the ground apart from your Father.

30 But the very hairs of your head are all numbered.

31 Fear you not therefore, you are of more value than many sparrows.

32 Whosoever therefore shall confess Me before men, him will I confess also before My Father who is in heaven.

33 But whosoever shall deny Me before men, him will I also deny before My Father who is in heaven.

34 Think not that I have come to send peace on earth; I came not to send peace, but a sword.

35 For I have come to set a man at variance against his father, and the daughter against her mother, and the daughter in law against her mother in law. – Mic.7:6

36 And a man's foes shall be they of his own household.

37 He that loveth father or mother more than Me is not worthy of Me; and he that loveth son or daughter more than Me is not worthy of Me.

38 And he that taketh not his stake, and followeth after Me, is not worthy of Me.

39 He that findeth his life shall lose it; and he that loseth his life for My sake shall find it.

40 He that receiveth you receiveth Me, and he that receiveth Me receiveth Him that sent Me.

41 He that receiveth a prophet in the name of a prophet shall receive a prophet's reward; and he that receiveth a righteous man in the name of a righteous man shall receive a righteous man's

reward.

42 And whosoever shall give to drink unto one of these little ones a cup of cold water only in the name of a disciple, verily I say unto you, he shall in no wise lose his reward."

11 And it came to pass, when Yahwah had made an end of commanding His twelve disciples, He departed from there to teach and to preach in their cities.

2 Now when John (Yochanan) had heard in the prison the works of the Messiah (haMashiach), he sent two of his disciples,

3 And said unto Him, "Art You He that should come, or do we look for another?

4 Yahwah answered and said unto them, "Go and shew John (Yochanan) again those things which you do hear and see:

5 The blind receives their sight, and the lame walk, the lepers are cleansed, and the deaf hear, the dead are raised up, and the poor have the gospel (good news) preached to them.

6 And blessed is he, whosoever shall not be offended in Me."

7 And as they departed, Yahwah began to say unto the multitudes concerning John (Yochanan): "What went you out into the wilderness to see? A reed shaken with the wind?

8 But what went you out for to see? A man clothed in soft raiment? Behold, they that wear soft clothing are in kings' houses.

9 But what went you out for to see? A prophet? Yes, I say unto you, and more than a prophet.

10 For this is He, of whom it is written: 'Behold, I send My messenger before Your face, who shall prepare Your way before You.' – *Mal 3:1*

11 Verily I say unto you, among them that are born of women there hath not risen a greater than John the Baptist (Yochanan haMatvil); notwithstanding he that is least in the kingdom of heaven is greater than he.

12 And from the days of John the Baptist (Yochanan haMatvil) until now the kingdom of heaven suffereth violence, and the violent take it by force.

13 For all the Prophets (Nevi'im) and the Torah prophesied until John (Yochanan).

14 And if you will receive it, this is [A43]Elias (Eliyah), who was about to come.

15 He that hath ears to hear, let him hear.

16 But whereunto shall I liken this generation? It is like unto children sitting in the markets, and calling unto their fellows,

17 And saying, 'We have piped unto you, and you have not danced; we have mourned unto you, and you have not lamented.'

18 For John (Yochanan) came neither eating nor drinking, and they say, 'He hath a devil.'

19 The Son of man (haMashiach) came eating and drinking, and they say, 'Behold a man gluttonous, and a winebibber, a friend of tax collectors and sinners!' But wisdom is justified of her children."

20 Then began He to upbraid the cities wherein most of His mighty works were done, because they repented not:

21 Woe unto you, Chorazin! Woe unto you, Bethsaida! For if the mighty works, which were done in you, had been done in Tyre and Sidon, they would have repented long ago in sackcloth and ashes.

22 But I say unto you, it shall be more tolerable for Tyre and Sidon at the day of judgment, than for you.

23 And you, Capernaum, who exalted yourself unto heaven, shalt be brought down to [B32]Hades (sheol), for if the mighty works, which have been done in you, had been done in Sodom, it would have remained until this day. – *Isa. 14:13, 15*

24 But I say unto you, that it shall be more tolerable for the land of Sodom in the day of judgment, than for you."

25 At that time Yahwah answered and said, "I thank You, O Father, Lord (Adon) of heaven and earth, because You have hid these things from the wise and prudent, and hast revealed them unto babes.

26 Even so, Father; for so it seemed good in Your sight.

27 All things are delivered unto Me of My Father; and no man knoweth the [B47]Son (Humanity of El (YHWH)), but the Father; neither knoweth any man the Father, except the [B47]Son, and he to whomsoever the [B47]Son wills to reveal Him.

28 Come unto Me, all you that labour and are heavy laden, and I will give you rest.

29 Take My yoke upon you, and learn of Me; for I am meek and lowly in heart; and you shall find rest unto your souls.

30 For My yoke is easy, and My burden is light."

12 At that time Yahwah went on the [B18]Shabbat through the grainfields; and

His disciples were hungry, and began to pluck the heads of grain, and to eat.

2 But when the Pharisees saw it, they said unto Him, "Behold, Your disciples do that which is not lawful to do upon the Shabbat.

3 But He said unto them, "Have you not read what Dawid did, when he was hungry, and they that were with him;

4 How he entered into the house of God (Elohim), and did eat the shewbread, which was not lawful for him to eat, neither for them who were with him, but only for the priests (kohanim)?

5 Or have you not read in the Torah, how that on the Shabbat the priests (kohanim) in the temple profane the Shabbat, and are blameless?

6 But I say unto you, that in this place is one greater than the temple.

7 But if you had known what this meaneth, I will have mercy, and not sacrifice, you would not have condemned the guiltless.

8 For the Son of man (haMashiach) is Lord of the Sabbath (Adon haShabbat)."

9 And when He had departed from there, He went into their synagogue.

10 And, behold, there was a man who had his hand withered. And they asked Him, saying, "Is it lawful to heal on the Shabbat?" that they might accuse Him.

11 And He said unto them, "What man shall there be among you, that shall have one sheep, and if it falls into a pit on the Shabbat, will he not lay hold on it, and lift it out?

12 How much then is a man better than a sheep? Therefore it is lawful to do good on the Shabbat."

13 Then saith He to the man, "Stretch forth your hand." And he stretched it forth; and it was restored whole, like as the other.

14 Then the Pharisees went out, and held a council against Him, how they might destroy Him.

15 But when Yahwah knew it, He withdrew Himself from there; and great multitudes followed Him, and He healed them all;

16 And charged them that they should not make Him known;

17 That it might be fulfilled which was spoken by Isaiah (Yeshayahu) the prophet, saying,

18 "Behold My Servant, whom I have chosen; My beloved, in whom My soul is well pleased; I will put My Spirit upon Him, and He shall shew judgment to the nations. – *Isa. 42:1*

19 He shall not strive, nor cry; neither shall any man hear His voice in the streets. – *Isa. 42:2*

20 A bruised reed shall He not break, and smoking flax shall He not quench, till He send forth justice unto victory. – *Isa 42:3*

21 And in His name shall the nations trust.

22 Then was brought unto Him one possessed with a devil, blind, and dumb: and He healed him, insomuch that the blind and dumb both spake and saw.

23 And all the people were amazed, and said, "Is not this the son (descendant) of Dawid?"

24 But when the Pharisees heard it, they said, "This fellow doth not cast out devils, but by Beelzebul (Baal-Zebub) the prince of the devils.

25 And Yahwah knew their thoughts, and said unto them, "Every kingdom divided against itself is brought to desolation; and every city or house divided against itself shall not stand.

26 And if Satan cast out Satan, he is divided against himself; how shall then his kingdom stand?

27 And if I by Beelzebul (Baal-Zebub) cast out devils, by whom do your children cast them out? Therefore they shall be your judges.

28 But if I cast out devils by the Spirit of God (Ruach Elohim), then the kingdom of God (Elohim, יהוה (YHWH)) has come unto you.

29 Or else how can one enter into a strong man's house, and spoil his goods, except he first binds the strong man? And then he will spoil his house.

30 He that is not with Me is against Me; and he that gathereth not with Me scattereth abroad.

31 Therefore I say unto you, all manner of sin and blasphemy shall be forgiven unto men; but the blasphemy against the Spirit (Ruach) shall not be forgiven unto men.

32 And whosoever speaketh a word against the son of man, it shall be forgiven him; but whosoever speaketh against the Holy Spirit (Ruach haQodesh), it shall not be forgiven him, neither in this world, neither in the world to come.

33 Either make the tree good, and his fruit good; or else make the tree corrupt, and his fruit corrupt; for the tree is known by its fruit.

34 O generation of vipers, how can you, being evil, speak good things? For out of the

abundance of the heart the mouth speaketh.

35 A good man out of the good treasure of the heart bringeth forth good things; and an evil man out of the evil treasure bringeth forth evil things.

36 But I say unto you, that every idle word that men shall speak, they shall give account thereof in the day of judgment.

37 For by your words you shalt be justified, and by your words you shalt be condemned."

38 Then certain of the scribes and of the Pharisees answered, saying, "Teacher (Rabbi), we wish to see a sign from you."

39 But He answered and said unto them, "An evil and adulterous generation seeketh after a sign; and there shall no sign be given to it, but the sign of the prophet Yonah;

40 For as Yonah was three days and three nights in the whale's belly; so shall the Son of man (haMashiach) be three days and three nights in the heart of the earth. – *Jon. 1:17*

41 The men of Nineveh shall rise in judgment with this generation, and shall condemn it; because they repented at the preaching of Yonah; and, behold, a greater than Yonah is here.

42 The queen of the south shall rise up in the judgment with this generation, and shall condemn it; for she came from the uttermost parts of the earth to hear the wisdom of Solomon (Shelomoh); and, behold, a greater than Solomon (Shelomoh) is here.

43 When the unclean spirit is gone out of a man, he walketh through dry places, seeking rest, and findeth none.

44 Then he saith, 'I will return into my house from where I came out;' and when he is come, he findeth it empty, swept, and garnished.

45 Then goeth he, and taketh with himself seven other spirits more wicked than himself, and they enter in and dwell there; and the last state of that man is worse than the first. Even so shall it be also unto this wicked generation.

46 While He yet talked to the people, behold, His mother and His brethren stood outside, desiring to speak with Him.

47 Then one said unto Him, "Behold, Your mother and Your brethren stand outside, desiring to speak with You."

48 But He answered and said unto him that told Him, "Who is My mother? And who are My brethren?"

49 And He stretched forth His hand toward His disciples, and said, "Behold My mother and My brethren!

50 For whosoever shall do the will of My Father who is in heaven, the same is My brother, and sister, and mother."

13 The same day went Yahwah out of the house, and sat by the sea side.

2 And great multitudes were gathered together unto Him, so that He went into a ship, and sat; and the whole multitude stood on the shore.

3 And He spake many things unto them in parables, saying, "Behold, a sower went forth to sow;

4 And when he sowed, some seeds fell by the way side, and the fowls came and devoured them up:

5 Some fell upon stony places, where they had not much earth; and forthwith they sprung up, because they had no deepness of earth.

6 And when the sun was up, they were scorched; and because they had no root, they withered away.

7 And some fell among thorns; and the thorns sprung up, and choked them:

8 But other fell into good ground, and brought forth fruit, some a hundredfold, some sixtyfold, some thirtyfold.

9 Who hath ears to hear, let him hear."

10 And the disciples came, and said unto Him, "Why speakest You unto them in parables?"

11 He answered and said unto them, "Because it is given unto you to know the mysteries of the kingdom of heaven, but to them it is not given.

12 For whosoever hath, to him shall be given, and he shall have more abundance; but whosoever hath not, from him shall be taken away even that he hath.

13 Therefore speak I to them in parables; because they seeing see not; and hearing they hear not, neither do they understand.

14 And in them is fulfilled the prophecy of Isaiah (Yeshayahu), who saith: 'By hearing you shall hear, and shall not understand; and seeing you shall see, and shall not perceive; – *Isa. 6:9*

15 For this people's heart is waxed gross, and their ears are dull of hearing, and their eyes they have closed; lest at any time they should see with their eyes, and hear with their ears, and should understand with their heart, and should

be converted, and I should heal them.' – *Isa.6:10*

16 But blessed are your eyes, for they see; and your ears, for they hear.

17 For verily I say unto you, that many prophets and righteous men have desired to see those things which you see, and have not seen them; and to hear those things which you hear, and have not heard them.

18 Hear you therefore the parable of the sower.

19 When any one heareth the word of the kingdom, and understandeth it not, then cometh the wicked one, and catcheth away that which was sown in his heart. This is he who received seed by the way side.

20 But he that received the seed into stony places, the same is he that heareth the word, and anon with joy receiveth it;

21 Yet hath he not root in himself, but dureth for a while; for when tribulation or persecution ariseth because of the word, by and by he is offended.

22 He also that received seed among the thorns is he that heareth the word; and the care of this world, and the deceitfulness of riches, choke the word, and he becometh unfruitful.

23 But he that received seed into the good ground is he that heareth the word, and understandeth it; which also beareth fruit, and bringeth forth, some a hundredfold, some sixty, some thirty."

24 Another parable put He forth unto them, saying, "The kingdom of heaven is likened unto a man who sowed good seed in his field;

25 But while men slept, his enemy came and sowed tares among the wheat, and went his way.

26 But when the blade was sprung up, and brought forth fruit, then appeared the tares also.

27 So the servants of the householder came and said unto him, 'Sir, didst not you sow good seed in your field? From whence then hath it tares?'

28 He said unto them, 'An enemy hath done this.' The servants said unto him, 'Wilt you then let us go and gather them up?'

29 But he said, 'No; lest while you gather up the tares, you root up also the wheat with them.

30 Let both grow together until the harvest: and in the time of harvest I will say to the reapers, "Gather you together first the tares, and bind them in bundles to burn them; but gather the wheat into my barn."''

31 Another parable put He forth unto them, saying, "The kingdom of heaven is like to a grain of mustard seed, which a man took, and sowed in his field,

32 Which indeed is the least of all seeds; but when it is grown, it is the greatest among herbs, and becometh a tree, so that the birds of the air come and lodge in the branches thereof."

33 Another parable spake He unto them; "The kingdom of heaven is like unto leaven, which a woman took, and hid in three measures of meal, till the whole was leavened."

34 All these things spake Yahwah unto the multitude in parables; and without a parable spake He not unto them;

35 That it might be fulfilled which was spoken by the prophet, saying, "I will open My mouth in parables; I will utter things which have been kept secret from the foundation of the world." – *Psa.78:2*

36 Then Yahwah sent the multitude away, and went into the house; and His disciples came unto Him, saying, "Declare unto us the parable of the tares of the field."

37 He answered and said unto them, "He that soweth the good seed is the Son of man (haMashiach);

38 The field is the world; the good seed are the children of the kingdom; but the tares are the children of the wicked one;

39 The enemy that sowed them is the devil; the harvest is the end of the world; and the reapers are the angels.

40 As therefore the tares are gathered and burned in the fire; so shall it be in the end of this world.

41 The Son of man (haMashiach) shall send forth His angels, and they shall gather out of His kingdom all things that offend, and them who do iniquity;

42 And shall cast them into a furnace of fire; there shall be wailing and gnashing of teeth.

43 Then shall the righteous shine forth as the sun in the kingdom of their Father. Who hath ears to hear, let him hear.

44 Again, the kingdom of heaven is like unto treasure hidden in a field; which when a man hath found, he hideth, and for joy thereof goeth and selleth all that he hath, and buyeth that field.

45 Again, the kingdom of heaven is like unto a merchant man, seeking goodly pearls,

46 Who, when he had found one pearl of great price, went and sold all that he had, and

bought it.

47 Again, the kingdom of heaven is like unto a net, that was cast into the sea, and gathered of every kind,

48 Which, when it was full, they drew to shore, and sat down, and gathered the good into vessels, but cast the bad away.

49 So shall it be at the end of the world: the angels shall come forth, and separate the wicked from among the just,

50 And shall cast them into the furnace of fire; there shall be wailing and gnashing of teeth."

51 Yahwah saith unto them, "Have you understood all these things?" They say unto Him, "Yes, Lord (Adonai)."

52 Then said He unto them, "Therefore every scribe who is instructed unto the kingdom of heaven is like unto a man that is a householder, who bringeth forth out of his treasure things new and old."

53 And it came to pass, that when Yahwah had finished these parables, He departed from there.

54 And when He had come into His own country, He taught them in their synagogue, insomuch that they were astonished, and said, "Where hath this man this wisdom, and these mighty works?

55 Is not this the carpenter's son? Is not His mother called Mary (Miryam)? And His brethren, James (Yaaqov), and Joseph (Yosef), and Shimon, and Judah (Yehudah)?

56 And His sisters, are they not all with us? Where then hath this man all these things?"

57 And they were offended in Him. But Yahwah said unto them, "A prophet is not without honor, except in his own country, and in his own house."

58 And He did not many mighty works there because of their unbelief.

14 At that time Herod the tetrarch heard of the fame of Yahwah,

2 And said unto his servants, "This is John the Baptist (Yochanan haMatvil); he is risen from the dead; and therefore mighty works do shew forth themselves in him."

3 For Herod had laid hold on John (Yochanan), and bound him, and put him in prison for Herodias' sake, his brother Philip's wife.

4 For John (Yochanan) said unto him, "It is not lawful for you to have her."

5 And when he would have put him to death,

he feared the multitude, because they counted him as a prophet.

6 But when Herod's birthday was celebrated, the daughter of Herodias danced before them, and pleased Herod.

7 Whereupon he promised with an oath to give her whatsoever she would ask.

8 And she, being before instructed of her mother, said, "Give me here John the Baptist (Yochanan haMatvil)'s head in a charger."

9 And the king was sorry; nevertheless for the oath's sake, and them who sat with him at meat, he commanded it to be given her.

10 And he sent, and beheaded John (Yochanan) in the prison.

11 And his head was brought in a charger, and given to the damsel; and she brought it to her mother.

12 And his disciples came, and took up the body, and buried it, and went and told Yahwah.

13 When Yahwah heard of it, He departed from there by ship into a desert place apart; and when the people had heard thereof, they followed Him on foot out of the cities.

14 And Yahwah went forth, and saw a great multitude, and was moved with compassion toward them, and He healed their sick.

15 And when it was evening, His disciples came to Him, saying, "This is a desert place, and the time is now past; send the multitude away, that they may go into the villages, and buy themselves victuals."

16 But Yahwah said unto them, "They need not depart; give you them to eat."

17 And they say unto Him, "We have here but five loaves, and two fishes."

18 He said, "Bring them here to Me."

19 And He commanded the multitude to sit down on the grass, and took the five loaves, and the two fishes, and looking up to heaven, He blessed, and broke, and gave the loaves to His disciples, and the disciples to the multitude.

20 And they did all eat, and were filled; and they took up of the fragments that remained twelve baskets full.

21 And they that had eaten were about five thousand men, besides women and children.

22 And straightway Yahwah constrained His disciples to get into a ship, and to go before Him unto the other side, while He sent the multitudes away.

23 And when He had sent the multitudes away, He went up into a mountain apart to pray; and when the evening had come, He was there alone.

24 But the ship was now in the midst of the sea, tossed with waves; for the wind was contrary.

25 And in the fourth watch of the night Yahwah went unto them, walking on the sea.

26 And when the disciples saw Him walking on the sea, they were troubled, saying, "It is a spirit (ghost)!" And they cried out for fear.

27 But straightway Yahwah spake unto them, saying, "Be of good cheer; it is I; be not afraid."

28 And Peter (Kefa) answered Him and said, "Lord (Adonai), if it be You, bid me come unto You on the water."

29 And He said, "Come!" And when Peter (Kefa) had come down out of the ship, he walked on the water, to go to Yahwah.

30 But when he saw the wind boisterous, he was afraid; and beginning to sink, he cried, saying, "Lord (Adonai), save me!"

31 And immediately Yahwah stretched forth His hand, and caught him, and said unto him, "O you of little faith, wherefore didst you doubt?"

32 And when they had come into the ship, the wind ceased.

33 Then they that were in the ship came and worshipped Him, saying, "Of a truth you are the [B47]Humanity of El (YHWH)."

34 And when they had gone over, they came into the land of Gennesaret.

35 And when the men of that place had knowledge of him, they sent out into all that country round about, and brought unto him all that were diseased;

36 And besought Him that they might only touch the hem of His garment; and as many as touched were made perfectly whole.

15 Then came to Yahwah scribes and Pharisees, who were of Jerusalem (Yerushalayim), saying,

2 "Why do your disciples transgress the tradition of the elders? For they wash not their hands when they eat bread.

3 But He answered and said unto them, "Why do you also transgress the commandment of God (Elohim) by your tradition?

4 For יהוה your God (Elohim) commanded, saying, 'Honor your father and mother; and, 'He that curseth father or mother, let him die the death.' – *Deut. 5:16, Exo. 21:17*

5 But you say, 'Whosoever shall say to his father or his mother, "It is a gift (given to the temple of God), whatsoever you mightest be profited by me;"

6 And he shall be free from honoring his father or his mother;' Thus have you made the commandment of God (Elohim) of none effect by your tradition.

7 You hypocrites, well did Isaiah (Yeshayahu) prophesy of you, saying,

8 'This people draweth near unto Me with their mouth, and honoureth Me with their lips; but their heart is far from Me. – *Isa. 29:3*

9 But in vain they do worship Me, teaching as doctrines the commandments of men.'" – *Isa. 29:3*

10 And He called the multitude, and said unto them, "Hear, and understand:

11 Not that which goeth into the mouth defileth a man; but that which cometh out of the mouth, this defileth a man."

12 Then came His disciples, and said unto Him, "Knowest You that the Pharisees were offended, after they heard this saying?"

13 But He answered and said, "Every plant, which My heavenly Father hath not planted, shall be rooted up.

14 Let them alone; they be blind leaders of the blind. And if the blind lead the blind, both shall fall into the ditch."

15 Then answered Peter (Kefa) and said unto Him, "Declare unto us this parable."

16 And Yahwah said, "Are you also yet without understanding?

17 Do not you yet understand, that whatsoever entereth in at the mouth goeth into the belly, and is cast out into the draught?

18 But those things which proceed out of the mouth come forth from the heart; and they defile the man.

19 For out of the heart proceed evil thoughts, murders, adulteries, fornications, thefts, false witness, blasphemies.

20 These are the things which defile a man; but to eat with unwashen hands defileth not a man."

21 Then Yahwah went from there, and departed into the coasts of Tyre and Sidon.

22 And, behold, a woman of Canaan came out of the same coasts, and cried unto Him, saying, "Have mercy on me, O Lord (Adonai), You son (descendant) of Dawid; my daughter is

grievously vexed with a devil.

23 But He answered her not a word. And His disciples came and besought Him, saying, "Send her away; for she crieth after us."

24 But he answered and said, "I am not sent but unto the lost sheep of the house of Yisrael."

25 Then came she and worshipped him, saying, "Lord (Adonai), help me!"

26 But He answered and said, "It is not right to take the children's bread, and to cast it to dogs."

27 And she said, "Yes, Lord (Adonai); yet the dogs eat of the crumbs which fall from their masters' table."

28 Then Yahwah answered and said unto her, "O woman, great is your faith; be it unto you even as you wilt." And her daughter was made whole from that very hour.

29 And Yahwah departed from there, and came near unto the sea of Galilee; and went up into a mountain, and sat down there.

30 And great multitudes came unto Him, having with them those that were lame, blind, dumb, maimed, and many others, and cast them down at Yahwah's feet; and He healed them.

31 Insomuch that the multitude wondered, when they saw the dumb to speak, the maimed to be whole, the lame to walk, and the blind to see; and they glorified the God (Elohim) of Yisrael.

32 Then Yahwah called His disciples unto Him, and said, "I have compassion on the multitude, because they continue with Me now three days, and have nothing to eat; and I will not send them away fasting, lest they faint on the way."

33 And His disciples say unto Him, "Where should we have so much bread in the wilderness, as to fill so great a multitude?"

34 And Yahwah saith unto them, "How many loaves have you?" And they said, "Seven, and a few little fishes."

35 And He commanded the multitude to sit down on the ground.

36 And He took the seven loaves and the fishes, and gave thanks, and broke them, and gave to His disciples, and the disciples to the multitude.

37 And they did all eat, and were filled; and they took up of the broken pieces that was left seven baskets full.

38 And they that did eat were four thousand men, besides women and children.

39 And He sent away the multitude, and took ship, and came into the coasts of Magdala.

16 The Pharisees also with the Sadducees came, and testing Him, asked that He would shew them a sign from heaven.

2 He answered and said unto them, "When it is evening, you say, 'It will be fair weather; for the sky is red.'

3 And in the morning, 'It will be foul weather today, for the sky is red and lowring.' O you hypocrites, you can discern the face of the sky; but can you not discern the signs of the times?

4 A wicked and adulterous generation seeketh after a sign; and there shall no sign be given unto it, but the sign of the prophet Yonah." And He left them, and departed.

5 And when His disciples had come to the other side, they had forgotten to take bread.

6 Then Yahwah said unto them, "Take heed and beware of the leaven of the Pharisees and of the Sadducees."

7 And they reasoned among themselves, saying, "It is because we have taken no bread."

8 Which when Yahwah perceived, He said unto them, "O you of little faith, why reason you among yourselves, because you have brought no bread?

9 Do you not yet understand, neither remember the five loaves of the five thousand, and how many baskets you took up?

10 Neither the seven loaves of the four thousand, and how many baskets you took up?

11 How is it that you do not understand that I spake it not to you concerning bread, that you should beware of the leaven of the Pharisees and of the Sadducees?"

12 Then understood they how that He bade them not beware of the leaven of bread, but of the doctrine of the Pharisees and of the Sadducees.

13 When Yahwah came into the coasts of Caesarea Philippi, He asked His disciples, saying, "Whom do men say that I the Son of man (haMashiach), am?"

14 And they said, "Some say that You are John the Baptist (Yochanan haMatvil); some, Elijah (Eliyahu); and others, Jeremiah (Yirmeyahu), or one of the prophets.

15 He saith unto them, "But whom say you that I am?"

16 And Shimon Peter (Kefa) answered and said, "You are the Messiah (haMashiach), the [B47]Humanity of the [B2]living God (Elohim chayim)

17 And Yahwah answered and said unto him, "Blessed are you, Simon son of Jonah (Shimon Bar-Yonah); for flesh and blood hath not revealed it unto you, but My Father who is in heaven.

18 And I say also unto you, that you are Peter (Kefa), and upon this rock I will build My B61assembly; and the gates of Hades shall not prevail against it.

19 And I will give unto you the keys of the kingdom of heaven; and whatsoever you shalt bind on earth shall be bound in heaven; and whatsoever you shalt loose on earth shall be loosed in heaven."

20 Then charged He His disciples that they should tell no man that He is the Messiah (haMashiach).

21 From that time forth began Yahwah to shew unto His disciples, how that He must go unto Jerusalem (Yerushalayim), and suffer many things of the elders and chief priests (kohanim) and scribes, and be killed, and be raised again the third day.

22 Then Peter (Kefa) took Him, and began to rebuke Him, saying, "Be it far from You, Lord (Adonai); this shall not be unto You!"

23 But He turned, and said unto Peter (Kefa), "Get you behind Me, Satan! you are an offence unto Me; for you savourest not the things that be of God (Elohim), but those that be of men."

24 Then said Yahwah unto His disciples, "If any man will come after Me, let him deny himself, and take up his stake, and follow Me.

25 For whosoever will save his life shall lose it; and whosoever will lose his life for My sake shall find it.

26 For what is a man profited, if he shall gain the whole world, and lose his own soul? Or what shall a man give in exchange for his soul?

27 For the Son of man (haMashiach) shall come in the glory of His Father with His angels; and then He shall reward every man according to his works.

28 Verily I say unto you, 'There be some standing here, who shall not taste of death, till they see the Son of man (haMashiach) coming in His kingdom."

17 And after six days Yahwah taketh Peter (Kefa), James (Yaaqov), and John (Yochanan) his brother, and bringeth them up into a high mountain apart,

2 And was transfigured before them; and His face did shine as the sun, and His raiment was white as the light.

3 And, behold, there appeared unto them Moses (Mosheh) and Elijah (Eliyahu) talking with Him.

4 Then answered Peter (Kefa), and said unto Yahwah, "Lord (Adonai), it is good for us to be here; if You wilt, let us make here three tabernacles; one for You, and one for Moses (Mosheh), and one for Elijah (Eliyahu)."

5 While he yet spake, behold, a bright cloud overshadowed them; and behold a voice out of the cloud, who said, "This is My beloved B47Son (Humanity), in whom I am well pleased; hear you Him!"

6 And when the disciples heard it, they fell on their face, and were sore afraid.

7 And Yahwah came and touched them, and said, "Arise, and be not afraid."

8 And when they had lifted up their eyes, they saw no man, except Yahwah only.

9 And as they came down from the mountain, Yahwah charged them, saying, "Tell the vision to no man, until the Son of man (haMashiach) be risen again from the dead.

10 And His disciples asked Him, saying, "Why then say the scribes that Elijah (Eliyahu) must first come?"

11 And Yahwah answered and said unto them, "Elijah (Eliyahu) truly shall first come, and restore all things.

12 But I say unto you, that Elijah (Eliyahu) has come already, and they knew him not, but have done unto him whatsoever they wished. Likewise shall also the Son of man (haMashiach) suffer of them."

13 Then the disciples understood that He spake unto them of John the Baptist (Yochanan haMatvil).

14 And when they had come to the multitude, there came to Him a certain man, kneeling down to Him, and saying,

15 "Lord (Adonai), have mercy on my son; for he is lunatick, and sore vexed; for ofttimes he falleth into the fire, and often into the water.

16 And I brought him to your disciples, and they could not cure him."

17 Then Yahwah answered and said, "O faithless and perverse generation, how long shall I be with you? How long shall I bear with you? Bring

him here to Me."

18 And Yahwah rebuked the devil; and he departed out of him; and the child was cured from that very hour.

19 Then came the disciples to Yahwah privately, and said, "Why could not we cast him out?"

20 And Yahwah said unto them, "Because of your unbelief; for verily I say unto you, if you have faith as a grain of mustard seed, you shall say unto this mountain, 'Remove hence to yonder place;' and it shall remove; and nothing shall be impossible unto you.

21 Howbeit this kind goeth not out but by prayer and fasting."

22 And while they abode in Galilee, Yahwah said unto them, "The Son of man (haMashiach) shall be betrayed into the hands of men;

23 And they shall kill Him, and the third day He shall be raised again." And they were exceeding sorry.

24 And when they had come to Capernaum, they that received tribute money (temple tax) came to Peter (Kefa), and said, "Doth not your Teacher (Rabbi) pay tribute (temple tax)?"

25 He saith, "Yes." And when he had come into the house, Yahwah prevented him, saying, "What thinkest you, Shimon? Of whom do the kings of the earth take custom or tribute (temple tax)? Of their own children, or of strangers?"

26 Peter (Kefa) saith unto Him, "Of strangers." Yahwah saith unto him, "Then are the children free.

27 However, lest we should offend them, go you to the sea, and cast a hook, and take up the fish that first cometh up; and when you have opened his mouth, you shalt find a piece of money; that take, and give unto them for Me and you."

18 At the same time came the disciples unto Yahwah, saying, "Who is the greatest in the kingdom of heaven?"

2 And Yahwah called a little child unto him, and set him in the midst of them,

3 And said, "Verily I say unto you, except you be converted, and become as little children, you shall not enter into the kingdom of heaven.

4 Whosoever therefore shall humble himself as this little child, the same is greatest in the kingdom of heaven.

5 And whoso shall receive one such little child in My name receiveth Me.

6 But whoso shall offend one of these little ones

who believe in Me, it was better for him that a millstone was hanged about his neck, and that he be drowned in the depth of the sea.

7 Woe unto the world because of offences! For it must needs be that offences come; but woe to that man by whom the offence cometh!

8 Therefore if your hand or your foot offend you, cut them off, and cast them from you; it is better for you to enter into life halt or maimed, rather than having two hands or two feet to be cast into everlasting fire.

9 And if your eye offends you, pluck it out, and cast it from you: it is better for you to enter into life with one eye, rather than having two eyes to be cast into hell fire (gehenna).

10 Take heed that you despise not one of these little ones; for I say unto you, that in heaven their angels do always behold the face of My Father who is in heaven.

11 For the Son of man (haMashiach) is come to save that which was lost.

12 How think you? If a man has a hundred sheep, and one of them be gone astray, doth he not leaves the ninety and nine, and goeth into the mountains, and seeketh that which is gone astray?

13 And if so be that he finds it, verily I say unto you, he rejoiceth more of that sheep, than of the ninety and nine which went not astray.

14 Even so it is not the will of your Father who is in heaven, that one of these little ones should perish.

15 Moreover if your brother shall trespass against you, go and tell him his fault between you and him alone; if he shall hear you, you have gained your brother.

16 But if he will not hear you, then take with you one or two more, that 'in the mouth of two or three witnesses every word may be established.'

17 And if he shall neglect to hear them, tell it unto the assembly; but if he neglects to hear the assembly, let him be unto you like a heathen man and a tax collector.

18 Verily I say unto you, whatsoever you shall bind on earth shall be bound in heaven; and whatsoever you shall loose on earth shall be loosed in heaven.

19 Again I say unto you, that if two of you shall agree on earth as touching anything that they shall ask, it shall be done for them of My Father who is in heaven.

20 For where two or three are gathered together in My name, there am I in the midst of them."

21 Then came Peter (Kefa) to him, and said, "Lord (Adonai), how often shall my brother sin against me, and I forgive him? Till seven times?"

22 Yahwah saith unto him, "I say not unto you, until seven times; but until seventy times seven.

23 Therefore is the kingdom of heaven likened unto a certain king, who would take account of his servants.

24 And when he had begun to reckon, one was brought unto him, who owed him ten thousand talents.

25 But forasmuch as he had not to pay, his master commanded him to be sold, and his wife, and children, and all that he had, and payment to be made.

26 The servant therefore fell down, and worshipped him, saying, 'Master, have patience with me, and I will pay you all.'

27 Then the master of that servant was moved with compassion, and loosed him, and forgave him the debt.

28 But the same servant went out, and found one of his fellowservants, who owed him a hundred pence; and he laid hands on him, and took him by the throat, saying, 'Pay me that you owest.'

29 And his fellowservant fell down at his feet, and besought him, saying, 'Have patience with me, and I will pay you all.'

30 And he would not, but went and cast him into prison, till he should pay the debt.

31 So when his fellowservants saw what was done, they were very sorry, and came and told unto their master all that was done.

32 Then his master after that he had called him, said unto him, 'O you wicked servant, I forgave you all that debt, because you begged me.

33 Shouldest not you also have had compassion on your fellowservant, even as I had pity on you?'

34 And his master was wroth, and delivered him to the tormentors, till he should pay all that was due unto him.

35 So likewise shall My heavenly Father do also unto you, if you from your hearts forgive not every one his brother their trespasses."

19 And it came to pass, that when Yahwah had finished these sayings, He departed from Galilee, and came into the coasts of Judah

(Yehudah) beyond Jordan (Yarden);

2 And great multitudes followed Him; and He healed them there.

3 The Pharisees also came unto Him, testing him, and saying unto Him, "Is it lawful for a man to put away his wife for every cause?"

4 And He answered and said unto them, "Have you not read, that He who made them at the beginning made them male and female, – *Gen. 1:27, 5:2*

5 And said, 'For this cause shall a man leave father and mother, and shall cleave to his wife; and they twain shall be one flesh? – *Gen. 2:24*

6 Therefore they are no more twain, but one flesh. What therefore Elohim hath joined together, let not man separate."

7 They say unto Him, "Why did Moses (Mosheh) then command to give a writing of divorcement, and to put her away?" – *Deut. 24:1, 24:3*

8 He saith unto them, "Moses (Mosheh), because of the hardness of your hearts let you to put away your wives, but from the beginning it was not so.

9 And I say unto you, 'Whosoever shall put away his wife, except it be for fornication (sexual immorality) and shall marry another, committeth adultery; and whoso marrieth her who is put away doth commit adultery!"

10 His disciples say unto Him, "If the case of the man be so with his wife, it is not good to marry."

11 But He said unto them, "Not everyone receives this saying, except they to whom it has been given;

12 For there are some eunuchs, who were so born from their mother's womb; and there are some eunuchs, who were made eunuchs of men; and there were eunuchs, who have made themselves eunuchs for the kingdom of heaven's sake. He that is able to receive it, let him receive it."

13 Then were there brought unto Him little children, that He should put his hands on them, and pray; and the disciples rebuked them.

14 But Yahwah said, "Let little children, and forbid them not to come unto Me; for of such is the kingdom of heaven."

15 And He laid his hands on them, and departed from there.

16 And, behold, one came and said unto Him, "Good Teacher (Rabbi), what good thing shall I do, that I may have eternal life?"

17 And He said unto him, "Why callest you Me good? There is none good but One, that is, God (Elohim); but if you wish to enter into life, keep the commandments."

18 He saith unto Him, "Which?" Yahwah said, "'You shalt do no murder,' 'You shalt not commit adultery,' 'You shalt not steal,' 'You shalt not bear false witness,'

19 'Honour your father and your mother;' and, 'You shalt love your neighbour as yourself.'"

20 The young man saith unto Him, "All these things have I kept from my youth up; what lack I yet?"

21 Yahwah said unto him, "If you wilt be perfect, go and sell that you have, and give to the poor, and you shalt have treasure in heaven; and come and follow Me."

22 But when the young man heard that saying, he went away sorrowful; for he had great possessions.

23 Then said Yahwah unto His disciples, "Verily I say unto you, that a rich man shall hardly enter into the kingdom of heaven.

24 And again I say unto you, "It is easier for a camel to go through the eye of a needle, than for a rich man to enter into the kingdom of God (Elohim, יהוה (YHWH))."

25 When His disciples heard it, they were exceedingly amazed, saying, "Who then can be saved?"

26 But Yahwah beheld them, and said unto them, "With men this is impossible; but with God (Elohim) all things are possible."

27 Then answered Peter (Kefa) and said unto Him, "Behold, we have forsaken all, and followed you; what shall we have therefore?"

28 And Yahwah said unto them, "Verily I say unto you, that you who have followed Me, in the regeneration when the Son of man (haMashiach) shall sit in the throne of His glory, you also shall sit upon twelve thrones, judging the twelve tribes of Yisrael."

29 And every one that hath forsaken houses, or brethren, or sisters, or father, or mother, or wife, or children, or lands, for My name's sake, shall receive a hundredfold, and shall inherit everlasting life.

30 But many that are first shall be last; and the last shall be first.

20 For the kingdom of heaven is like unto a man that is a householder, who went out early in the morning to hire labourers into his vineyard.

2 And when he had agreed with the labourers for a penny a day, he sent them into his vineyard.

3 And he went out about the third hour, and saw others standing idle in the marketplace,

4 And said unto them: "Go you also into the vineyard, and whatsoever is right I will give you." And they went their way.

5 Again he went out about the sixth and ninth hour, and did likewise.

6 And about the eleventh hour he went out, and found others standing idle, and saith unto them, "Why stand you here all the day idle?"

7 They say unto him, "Because no man hath hired us." He saith unto them, "Go you also into the vineyard; and whatsoever is right, that shall you receive."

8 So when even was come, the lord (owner) of the vineyard saith unto his steward, "Call the labourers, and give them their hire, beginning from the last unto the first."

9 And when they came that were hired about the eleventh hour, they received every man a penny.

10 But when the first came, they supposed that they should have received more; and they likewise received every man a penny.

11 And when they had received it, they murmured against the goodman of the house,

12 Saying, "These last have wrought but one hour, and you have made them equal unto us, who have borne the burden and heat of the day."

13 But he answered one of them, and said, "Friend, I do you no wrong; didst not you agree with me for a penny?"

14 Take that your is, and go your way; I will give unto this last, even as unto you.

15 Is it not lawful for me to do what I will with mine own? Is your eye evil, because I am good?"

16 So the last shall be first, and the first last; for many be called, but few chosen.

17 And Yahwah going up to Jerusalem (Yerushalayim) took the twelve disciples apart in the way, and said unto them,

18 "Behold, we go up to Jerusalem (Yerushalayim); and the Son of man (haMashiach) shall be betrayed unto the chief priests (kohanim) and unto the scribes, and they shall condemn Him to death,

19 And shall deliver Him to the Gentiles

(Goyim) to mock, and to scourge, and to crucify Him; and the third day He shall rise again."

20 Then came to Him the mother of Zebedee (Zavdai)'s children with her sons, worshipping Him, and requesting a certain thing of Him.

21 And He said unto her, "What wilt you?" She saith unto Him, "Grant that these my two sons may sit, the one on your right hand, and the other on the left, in Your kingdom."

22 But Yahwah answered and said, "You know not what you ask. Are you able to drink of the cup that I shall drink of, and to be baptized with the baptism that I am baptized with?" They say unto Him, "We are able."

23 And He saith unto them, "You shall drink indeed of My cup, and be baptized with the baptism that I am baptized with; but to sit on My right hand, and on My left, is not Mine to give, but it shall be given to them for whom it is prepared of My Father."

24 And when the ten heard it, they were moved with indignation against the two brethren.

25 But Yahwah called them unto Him, and said, "You know that the rulers of the Gentiles (Goyim) exercise dominion over them, and they that are great exercise authority upon them.

26 But it shall not be so among you, but whosoever will be great among you, let him be your servant;

27 And whosoever will be chief among you, let him be your slave;

28 Even as the Son of man (haMashiach) came not to be served unto, but to serve, and to give His life a ransom for many."

29 And as they departed from Yericho, a great multitude followed Him.

30 And, behold, two blind men sitting by the way side, when they heard that Yahwah passed by, cried out, saying, "Have mercy on us, O Lord (Adonai), You son (descendant) of Dawid."

31 And the multitude rebuked them, because they should hold their peace, but they cried the more, saying, "Have mercy on us, O Lord (Adonai), You son (descendant) of Dawid!"

32 And Yahwah stood still, and called them, and said, "What will you that I shall do unto you?"

33 They say unto Him, "Lord (Adonai), that our eyes may be opened."

34 So Yahwah had compassion on them, and touched their eyes; and immediately their eyes received sight, and they followed Him.

21 And when they drew near unto Jerusalem (Yerushalayim), and had come to Bethphage, unto the Mount of Olives, then sent Yahwah two disciples,

2 Saying unto them, "Go into the village opposite you, and straightway you shall find an ass tied, and a colt with her; loose them, and bring them unto Me.

3 And if any man says anything unto you, you shall say, the Lord (Adonai) hath need of them; and straightway he will send them."

4 All this was done, that it might be fulfilled which was spoken by the prophet [A65]Zechariah (Zekharyah), saying:

5 "Tell you the daughter of Zion (Tsiyon), 'Behold, your King cometh unto you, meek, and sitting upon an ass, and a colt the foal of an ass.'" – Zec. 9:9

6 And the disciples went, and did as Yahwah commanded them,

7 And brought the ass, and the colt, and put on them their clothes, and they set him thereon.

8 And a very great multitude spread their garments on the road; others cut down branches from the trees, and strawed them in the way.

9 And the multitudes that went before, and that followed, cried, saying, "[B57]Hosanna to the son (descendant) of Dawid: 'Blessed is He that cometh in the name of יהוה (YHWH, Yahwah)!' Hosanna in the highest." – Psa. 118:25, 26

10 And when He had come into Jerusalem (Yerushalayim), all the city was moved, saying, "Who is this?"

11 And the multitude said, "This is Yahwah (YHWH) the prophet of Nazareth of Galilee.

12 And Yahwah went into the temple of God (Elohim), and cast out all them that sold and bought in the temple, and overthrew the tables of the moneychangers, and the seats of them that sold doves,

13 And said unto them, "It is written, 'My house shall be called the house of prayer;' but you have made it 'a den of thieves.'" – Isa. 56:7, Jer. 7:11

14 And the blind and the lame came to Him in the temple; and He healed them.

15 And when the chief priests (kohanim) and scribes saw the wonderful things that He did, and the children crying in the temple, and saying, "Hosanna to the son (descendant) of Dawid!" they were sore displeased,

16 And said unto Him, "Hearest You what these

say?" And Yahwah saith unto them, "Yes. Have you never read, 'Out of the mouth of babes and sucklings You have perfected praise'?" – *Psa. 8:2*

17 And He left them, and went out of the city into Bethany; and He lodged there.

18 Now in the morning as He returned into the city, He hungered.

19 And when He saw a fig tree in the way, He came to it, and found nothing thereon, but leaves only, and said unto it, "Let no fruit grow on you henceforward forever." And presently the fig tree withered away.

20 And when the disciples saw it, they marvelled, saying, "How soon is the fig tree withered away!"

21 Yahwah answered and said unto them, "Verily I say unto you, if you have faith, and doubt not, you shall not only do this which is done to the fig tree, but also if you shall say unto this mountain, 'Be you removed, and be you cast into the sea;' it shall be done.

22 And all things, whatsoever you shall ask in prayer, believing, you shall receive."

23 And when He had come into the temple, the chief priests (kohanim) and the elders of the people came unto Him as He was teaching, and said, "By what authority doest You these things? And who gave You this authority?"

24 And Yahwah answered and said unto them, "I also will ask you one thing, which if you tell Me, I in like wise will tell you by what authority I do these things.

25 The baptism of John (Yochanan), where was it? From heaven, or of men?" And they reasoned with themselves, saying, "If we shall say, 'From heaven;' He will say unto us, 'Why did you not then believe Him?'

26 But if we shall say, 'Of men;' we fear the people; for all hold John (Yochanan) as a prophet.

27 And they answered Yahwah, and said, "We cannot tell." And He said unto them, "Neither tell I you by what authority I do these things.

28 But what think you? A certain man had two sons; and he came to the first, and said, 'Son, go work today in my vineyard.'

29 He answered and said, 'I will not;' but afterward he repented, and went.

30 And he came to the second, and said likewise. And he answered and said, 'I go, sir;'

and went not.

31 Whether of them twain did the will of his father?" They say unto him, "The first." Yahwah saith unto them, "Verily I say unto you, that the tax collectors and the harlots go into the kingdom of God (Elohim, יהוה (YHWH)) before you;

32 For John (Yochanan) came unto you in the way of righteousness, and you believed him not, but the tax collectors and the harlots believed him; and you, when you had seen it, repented not afterward, that you might believe him.

33 Hear another parable: There was a certain householder, who planted a vineyard, and hedged it round about, and digged a winepress in it, and built a tower, and let it out to husbandmen, and went into a far country.

34 And when the time of the fruit drew near, he sent his servants to the husbandmen, that they might receive the fruits of it.

35 And the husbandmen took his servants, and beat one, and killed another, and stoned another.

36 Again, he sent other servants more than the first; and they did unto them likewise.

37 But last of all he sent unto them his son, saying, 'They will reverence my son.'

38 But when the husbandmen saw the son, they said among themselves, 'This is the heir; come, let us kill him, and let us seize on his inheritance.'

39 And they caught him, and cast him out of the vineyard, and slew him.

40 When the owner therefore of the vineyard cometh, what will he do unto those husbandmen?"

41 They say unto Him, "He will miserably destroy those wicked men, and will let out his vineyard unto other husbandmen, who shall render him the fruits in their seasons."

42 Yahwah saith unto them, "Did you never read in the scriptures, 'The stone which the builders rejected, the same is become the head of the corner'; this is יהוה (YHWH)'s doing, and it is marvellous in our eyes? – *Psa.118:22*

43 Therefore say I unto you, 'The kingdom of God (Elohim, יהוה (YHWH)) shall be taken from you, and given to a nation bringing forth the fruits thereof.

44 And whosoever shall fall on this stone shall be broken; but on whomsoever it shall fall, it will grind him to powder.'"

45 And when the chief priests (kohanim) and Pharisees had heard His parables, they perceived that He spake of them.

46 But when they sought to lay hands on Him, they feared the multitude, because they took Him for a prophet.

22 And Yahwah answered and spake unto them again by parables, and said,

2 "The kingdom of heaven is like unto a certain king, who made a marriage for his son,

3 And sent forth his servants to call them that were bidden to the wedding; and they would not come.

4 Again, he sent forth other servants, saying, 'Tell them who are bidden, "Behold, I have prepared my dinner; my oxen and my fatlings are killed, and all things are ready. Come unto the marriage."'

5 But they made light of it, and went their ways, one to his farm, another to his merchandise;

6 And the remnant took his servants, and entreated them spitefully, and slew them.

7 But when the king heard thereof, he was wroth; and he sent forth his armies, and destroyed those murderers, and burned up their city.

8 Then saith he to his servants, 'The wedding is ready, but they who were bidden were not worthy.

9 Go you therefore into the highways, and as many as you shall find, bid to the marriage.'

10 So those servants went out into the highways, and gathered together all as many as they found, both bad and good; and the wedding was furnished with guests.

11 And when the king came in to see the guests, he saw there a man who had not on a wedding garment.

12 And he saith unto him, 'Friend, how camest you in here not having a wedding garment?' And he was speechless.

13 Then said the king to the servants, 'Bind him hand and foot, and take him away, and cast him into outer darkness; there shall be weeping and gnashing of teeth.'

14 For many are called, but few are chosen."

15 Then went the Pharisees, and took counsel how they might entangle Him in His talk.

16 And they sent out unto Him their disciples with the Herodians, saying, "Teacher (Rabbi), we know that You are true, and teachest the way of God (Elohim) in truth, neither carest You for any man; for You regardest not the person of men.

17 Tell us therefore, what thinkest You? Is it lawful to give tribute (poll-tax) unto Caesar (Roman Emperor), or not?"

18 But Yahwah perceived their wickedness, and said, "Why test you Me, you hypocrites?

19 Shew Me the tribute (poll tax) money." And they brought unto Him a penny.

20 And He saith unto them, "Whose is this image and superscription?"

21 They say unto Him, Caesar's. Then saith He unto them, "Render therefore unto Caesar the things which are Caesar's; and unto God (Elohim) the things that are God (Elohim)'s."

22 When they had heard these words, they marvelled, and left Him, and went their way.

23 The same day came to Him the Sadducees, who say that there is no resurrection, and asked Him,

24 Saying, "Teacher (Rabbi), Mosheh said, 'If a man dies, having no children, his brother shall marry his wife, and raise up seed unto his brother.'

25 Now there were with us seven brethren: and the first, when he had married a wife, deceased, and, having no issue, left his wife unto his brother;

26 Likewise the second also, and the third, unto the seventh.

27 And last of all the woman died also.

28 Therefore in the resurrection, whose wife shall she be of the seven? For they all had her."

29 Yahwah answered and said unto them, "You do err, not knowing the scriptures, nor the power of God (Elohim).

30 For in the resurrection they neither marry, nor are given in marriage, but are as the angels of God (Elohim) in heaven.

31 But as touching the resurrection of the dead, have you not read that which was spoken unto you by יהוה, saying,

32 "I am the God (Elohim) of Avraham, and the God (Elohim) of Isaac (Yitschaq), and the God (Elohim) of Jacob (Yaaqov)"? יהוה (YHWH) is not the God (Elohim) of the dead, but of the living." – *Exo. 3:6*

33 And when the multitude heard this, they were astonished at His doctrine.

34 But when the Pharisees had heard that He had put the Sadducees to silence, they were

gathered together.

35 Then one of them, who was a lawyer, asked Him a question, testing Him, and saying,

36 "Teacher (Rabbi), which is the great commandment in the Torah?"

37 Yahwah said unto him, "You shalt love יהוה your God (YHWH Eloheikha) with all your heart, and with all your soul, and with all your mind. – *Deu. 6:5*

38 This is the first and great commandment.

39 And the second is like unto it, 'You shalt love your neighbour as yourself.' – *Lev. 19:18*

40 On these two commandments hang all the Torah and the Prophets (Nevi'im)."

41 While the Pharisees were gathered together, Yahwah asked them,

42 Saying, "What think you of the Messiah (haMashiach)? Whose son is He?" They say unto Him, "The son of Dawid."

43 He saith unto them, "How then doth Dawid in spirit call Him my Lord (Adoni), saying,

44 'יהוה said unto my Lord (Adoni), "Sit You on My right hand, till I make Your enemies Your footstool"? – *Psa. 110:1*

45 If Dawid then call Him Lord (Adon), how is He his son?"

46 And no man was able to answer Him a word, neither durst any man from that day forth ask Him any more questions.

23 Then spake Yahwah to the multitude, and to His disciples,

2 Saying, "The scribes and the Pharisees sit in Moses (Mosheh)'s seat.

3 All therefore whatsoever they bid you observe, that observe and do; but do not you after their works, for they say, and do not.

4 For they bind heavy burdens and grievous to be borne, and lay them on men's shoulders; but they themselves will not move them with one of their fingers.

5 But all their works they do for to be seen of men; they make broad their phylacteries (tefillin), and enlarge the borders of their tassels (tzitziyot),

6 And love the uppermost rooms at feasts, and the chief seats in the synagogues,

7 And greetings in the markets, and to be called of men, 'Rabbi, Rabbi'.

8 But be not you called Teacher (Rabbi); for One is your Teacher (Rabbi), the Messiah (haMashiach); and all you are brethren.

9 And call no man your father upon the earth; for One is your Father, who is in heaven.

10 Neither be you called masters; for One is your Master, the Messiah (haMashiach).

11 But he that is greatest among you shall be your servant.

12 And whosoever shall exalt himself shall be abased; and he that shall humble himself shall be exalted.

13 But woe unto you, scribes and Pharisees, hypocrites! For you shut up the kingdom of heaven against men; for you neither go in yourselves, neither allow you them that are entering to go in.

14 Woe unto you, scribes and Pharisees, hypocrites! For you devour widows' houses, and for a pretence make long prayer; therefore you shall receive greater damnation.

15 Woe unto you, scribes and Pharisees, hypocrites! For you compass sea and land to win one proselyte (convert), and when he is won, you make him twofold more the child of hell (gehenna) than yourselves.

16 Woe unto you, you blind guides, who say, 'Whosoever shall swear by the temple, it is nothing; but whosoever shall swear by the gold of the temple, he is a debtor!'

17 You fools and blind! For whether is greater, the gold, or the temple that sanctifieth the gold?

18 And, 'Whosoever shall swear by the altar, it is nothing; but whosoever sweareth by the gift that is upon it, he is guilty.'

19 You fools and blind! For whether is greater, the gift, or the altar that sanctifieth the gift?

20 Whoso therefore shall swear by the altar, sweareth by it, and by all things thereon.

21 And whoso shall swear by the temple, sweareth by it, and by Him that dwelleth therein.

22 And he that shall swear by heaven, sweareth by the throne of God (Elohim), and by Him that sitteth thereon.

23 Woe unto you, scribes and Pharisees, hypocrites! For you pay tithe of mint and anise and cummin, and have omitted the weightier matters of the Torah: judgment, mercy, and faith; these ought you to have done, and not to leave the other undone.

24 You blind guides, who strain at a gnat, and swallow a camel.

25 Woe unto you, scribes and Pharisees, hypocrites! For you make clean the outside of

the cup and of the platter, but within they are full of extortion and excess.

26 You blind Pharisee, cleanse first that which is within the cup and platter, that the outside of them may be clean also.

27 Woe unto you, scribes and Pharisees, hypocrites! For you are like unto whited sepulchres, which indeed appear beautiful outward, but are within full of dead men's bones, and of all uncleanness.

28 Even so you also outwardly appear righteous unto men, but within you are full of hypocrisy and iniquity.

29 Woe unto you, scribes and Pharisees, hypocrites! Because you build the tombs of the prophets, and garnish the sepulchres of the righteous,

30 And say, 'If we had been in the days of our fathers, we would not have been partakers with them in the blood of the prophets.'

31 Therefore you be witnesses unto yourselves, that you are the children of them who killed the prophets.

32 Fill you up then the measure of your fathers.

33 You serpents, you generation of vipers, how can you escape the damnation of hell (gehenna)?

34 Therefore, behold, I send unto you prophets, and wise men, and scribes; and some of them you shall kill and crucify; and some of them shall you scourge in your synagogues, and persecute them from city to city,

35 That upon you may come all the righteous blood shed upon the earth, from the blood of righteous Abel (Hevel) unto the blood of Zacharias son of Barachias (Zekharyah ben-Berekhyah), whom you slew between the temple and the altar.

36 Verily I say unto you, all these things shall come upon this generation.

37 O Jerusalem, Jerusalem (Yerushalayim), you that killest the prophets, and stonest them who are sent unto you, how often would I have gathered your children together, even as a hen gathereth her chickens under her wings, and you would not!

38 Behold, your house is left unto you desolate. – *Jer. 22:5*

39 For I say unto you, 'You shall not see Me henceforth, till you shall say, 'Blessed is He that cometh in the name of יהוה (YHWH, Yahwah)!'" – *Psa. 118:26*

24 And Yahwah went out, and departed from the temple; and His disciples came to Him for to show Him the buildings of the temple.

2 And Yahwah said unto them, "See you not all these things? Verily I say unto you, there shall not be left here one stone upon another, that shall not be thrown down."

3 And as He sat upon the Mount of Olives, the disciples came unto Him privately, saying, "Tell us, when shall these things be? And what shall be the sign of Your coming, and of the end of the world?"

4 And Yahwah answered and said unto them, "Take heed that no man deceives you.

5 For many shall come in My name (reputation and power), saying, 'I am the anointed one (hamashiach)'; and shall deceive many.

6 And you shall hear of wars and rumours of wars. See that you be not troubled; for all these things must come to pass, but the end is not yet.

7 For nation shall rise against nation, and kingdom against kingdom; and there shall be famines, and pestilences, and earthquakes, in divers places.

8 All these are the beginning of sorrows.

9 Then shall they deliver you up to be afflicted, and shall kill you; and you shall be hated of all nations for My name's sake.

10 And then shall many be offended, and shall betray one another, and shall hate one another.

11 And many false prophets shall rise, and shall deceive many.

12 And because iniquity shall abound, the love of many shall wax cold.

13 But he that shall endure unto the end, the same shall be saved.

14 And this gospel (good news) of the kingdom shall be preached in all the world for a witness unto all nations; and then shall the end come.

15 When you therefore shall see the abomination of desolation, spoken of by Daniel the prophet, stand in the holy place. (whoso readeth, let him understand), – *Dan .9:27, 11:31, 12:11*

16 Then let them who are in Judah (Yehudah) flee into the mountains;

17 Let him who is on the housetop not come down to take any thing out of his house;

18 Neither let him who is in the field return back to take his clothes.

19 And woe unto them that are with child, and

to them that give suck in those days!

20 But pray you that your flight be not in the winter, neither on the Shabbat;

21 For then shall be great tribulation, such as was not since the beginning of the world to this time, no, nor ever shall be.

22 And except those days should be shortened, there should no flesh be saved; but for the elect's sake those days shall be shortened.

23 Then if any man shall say unto you, 'Behold, here is the Messiah (haMashiach) or there;' believe it not.

24 For there shall arise false Messiahs (Mashiachi), and false prophets, and shall show great signs and wonders; insomuch that, if it was possible, they shall deceive the very elect.

25 Behold, I have told you before.

26 Therefore if they shall say unto you, 'Behold, He is in the desert;' go not forth; 'Behold, He is in the secret chambers;' believe it not.

27 For as the lightning cometh out of the east, and shineth even unto the west; so shall also the coming of the Son of man (haMashiach) be.

28 For wheresoever the carcase is, there will the eagles be gathered together.

29 Immediately after the tribulation of those days shall the sun be darkened, and the moon shall not give her light, and the stars shall fall from heaven, and the powers of the heavens shall be shaken; – *Isa. 13:10; Eze. 32:7; Joel 2:10, 2:31; Eze. 3:15; Hag.2:6, 21*

30 And then shall appear the sign of the Son of man (haMashiach) in heaven; and then shall all the tribes of the earth mourn, and they shall see the Son of man (haMashiach) coming in the clouds of heaven with power and great glory. – *Dan.7:13*

31 And He shall send His angels with a great sound of a trumpet, and they shall gather together His elect from the four winds, from one end of heaven to the other.

32 Now learn a parable of the fig tree: When its branch is yet tender, and putteth forth leaves, you know that summer is near.

33 So likewise you, when you shall see all these things, know that it is near, even at the doors.

34 Verily I say unto you, this generation shall not pass, till all these things be fulfilled.

35 Heaven and earth shall pass away, but My words shall not pass away. – *Mark 13:31, Luke 21:33*

36 But of that day and hour knoweth no man, no, nor the angels of heaven, but My Father only.

37 But as the days of Noe (Noach) were, so shall also the coming of the Son of man (haMashiach) be.

38 For as in the days that were before the flood they were eating and drinking, marrying and giving in marriage, until the day that Noe (Noach) entered into the ark,

39 And knew not until the flood came, and took them all away; so shall also the coming of the Son of man (haMashiach) be.

40 Then shall two be in the field; the one shall be taken, and the other left.

41 Two women shall be grinding at the mill; the one shall be taken, and the other left.

42 Watch therefore, for you know not what hour your Lord (Adonai) doth come.

43 But know this, that if the goodman of the house had known in what watch the thief would come, he would have watched, and would not have suffered his house to be broken up.

44 Therefore be you also ready, for in such an hour as you think not the Son of man (haMashiach) cometh.

45 Who then is a faithful and wise servant, whom his master hath made ruler over his household, to give them food in due season?

46 Blessed is that servant, whom his master, when he cometh shall find so doing.

47 Verily I say unto you, that he shall make him ruler over all his goods.

48 But if that evil servant shall say in his heart, 'My master delayeth his coming;'

49 And shall begin to smite his fellowservants, and to eat and drink with the drunken;

50 The master of that servant shall come in a day when he looketh not for him, and in an hour that he is not aware of,

51 And shall cut him in two, and appoint him his portion with the hypocrites; there shall be weeping and gnashing of teeth.

25 Then shall the kingdom of heaven be likened unto ten virgins, who took their lamps, and went forth to meet the bridegroom.

2 And five of them were wise, and five were foolish.

3 They that were foolish took their lamps, and took no oil with them;

4 But the wise took oil in their vessels with their lamps.

5 While the bridegroom tarried, they all slumbered and slept.

6 And at midnight there was a cry made: 'Behold, the bridegroom cometh; go you out to meet him!'

7 Then all those virgins arose, and trimmed their lamps.

8 And the foolish said unto the wise, 'Give us of your oil; for our lamps have gone out.'

9 But the wise answered, saying, 'Not so; lest there be not enough for us and you; but go you rather to them that sell, and buy for yourselves.'

10 And while they went to buy, the bridegroom came; and they that were ready went in with him to the marriage; and the door was shut.

11 Afterward came also the other virgins, saying, 'Master, master, open to us.'

12 But he answered and said, 'Verily I say unto you, I know you not.'

13 Watch therefore, for you know neither the day nor the hour wherein the Son of man (haMashiach) cometh.

14 For the kingdom of heaven is as a man travelling into a far country, who called his own servants, and delivered unto them his goods.

15 And unto one he gave five talents, to another two, and to another one; to every man according to his several ability; and straightway took his journey.

16 Then he that had received the five talents went and traded with the same, and made them other five talents.

17 And likewise he that had received two, he also gained other two.

18 But he that had received one went and digged in the earth, and hid his master's money.

19 After a long time the master of those servants cometh, and reckoneth with them.

20 And so he that had received five talents came and brought other five talents, saying, 'Master, you deliveredst unto me five talents; behold, I have gained besides them five talents more.'

21 His master said unto him, 'Well done, you good and faithful servant; you have been faithful over a few things, I will make you ruler over many things. Enter you into the joy of your master.

22 He also that had received two talents came and said, 'Master, you deliveredst unto me two talents; behold, I have gained two other talents besides them.'

23 His master said unto him, 'Well done, good and faithful servant; you have been faithful over a few things, I will make you ruler over many things. Enter you into the joy of your master.'

24 Then he that had received the one talent came and said, 'Master, I knew you that you are a hard man, reaping where you have not sown, and gathering where you have not strawed.

25 And I was afraid, and went and hid your talent in the earth. Behold, there you have that is yours.'

26 His master answered and said unto him, 'You wicked and slothful servant, you knewest that I reap where I sowed not, and gather where I have not strawed.

27 You oughtest therefore to have put my money to the exchangers, and then at my coming I should have received mine own with usury.

28 Take therefore the talent from him, and give it unto him who hath ten talents.

29 For unto every one that hath shall be given, and he shall have abundance; but from him that hath not shall be taken away even that which he hath.

30 And cast you the unprofitable servant into outer darkness; there shall be weeping and gnashing of teeth.'

31 When the Son of man (haMashiach) shall come in His glory, and all the holy angels with Him, then shall He sit upon the throne of His glory.

32 And before Him shall be gathered all nations; and He shall separate them one from another, as a shepherd divideth his sheep from the goats.

33 And He shall set the sheep on His right hand, but the goats on the left.

34 Then shall the King say unto them on His right hand, 'Come, you blessed of My Father, inherit the kingdom prepared for you from the foundation of the world:

35 For I was hungry, and you gave Me food; I was thirsty, and you gave Me drink; I was a stranger, and you took Me in;

36 Naked, and you clothed Me; I was sick, and you visited Me; I was in prison, and you came unto Me.

37 Then shall the righteous answer Him, saying, 'Lord (Adonai), when saw we You hungry, and fed You? Or thirsty, and gave You drink?

38 When saw we You a stranger, and took You in? Or naked, and clothed You?

39 Or when saw we You sick, or in prison, and came unto You?'

40 And the King shall answer and say unto them, 'Verily I say unto you, inasmuch as you have done it unto one of the least of these My brethren, you have done it unto Me.'

41 Then shall He say also unto them on the left hand, 'Depart from Me, you cursed, into everlasting fire, prepared for the devil and his angels;

42 For I was hungry, and you gave Me no food; I was thirsty, and you gave Me no drink;

43 I was a stranger, and you took Me not in; naked, and you clothed Me not; sick, and in prison, and you visited Me not.'

44 Then shall they also answer Him, saying, 'Lord (Adonai), when saw we You hungry, or thirsty, or a stranger, or naked, or sick, or in prison, and did not minister unto You?'

45 Then shall He answer them, saying, 'Verily I say unto you, inasmuch as you did it not to one of the least of these, you did it not to Me.'

46 And these shall go away into eternal punishment, but the righteous into eternal life."

26 And it came to pass, when Yahwah had finished all these sayings, He said unto His disciples,

2 "You know that after two days is the [B19]Passover (Pesach), and the Son of man (haMashiach) will be betrayed to be crucified."

3 Then assembled together the chief priests (kohanim), and the scribes, and the elders of the people, unto the palace of the high priest (kohen hagadol), who was called Caiaphas,

4 And consulted that they might take Yahwah by subtilty, and kill Him.

5 But they said, "Not on the feast day, lest there be an uproar among the people."

6 Now when Yahwah was in Bethany, in the house of Shimon the leper,

7 There came unto Him a woman having an alabaster box of very precious ointment, and poured it on His head, as He sat at meat.

8 But when His disciples saw it, they had indignation, saying, "To what purpose is this waste?

9 For this ointment might have been sold for much, and given to the poor."

10 When Yahwah understood it, He said unto them, "Why trouble you the woman? For she hath wrought a good work upon Me.

11 For you have the poor always with you; but Me you have not always.

12 For in that she hath poured this ointment on My body, she did it for My burial.

13 Verily I say unto you, wheresoever this gospel (good news) shall be preached in the whole world, there shall also this, that this woman hath done, be told for a memorial of her."

14 Then one of the twelve, called Judas Iscariot (Yehudah Ishkeriot), went unto the chief priests (kohanim),

15 And said unto them, "What will you give me, and I will deliver Him unto you?" And they covenanted with him for thirty pieces of silver. – *Zec. 11:12*

16 And from that time he sought opportunity to betray Him.

17 Now the first day of the [B20]Feast of Unleavened Bread (Chag HaMatzot) the disciples came to Yahwah, saying unto Him, "Where wilt You that we prepare for You to eat the Passover (Pesach)?

18 And He said, "Go into the city to such a man, and say unto him, 'The Teacher (Rabbi) saith, "My time is at hand; I will keep the Passover (Pesach) at your house with My disciples."'"

19 And the disciples did as Yahwah had appointed them; and they made ready the Passover (Pesach).

20 Now when the even came, He sat down with the twelve.

21 And as they did eat, He said, "Verily I say unto you, that one of you shall betray Me."

22 And they were exceeding sorrowful, and began every one of them to say unto Him, "Lord (Adonai), is it I?"

23 And He answered and said, "He that dippeth his hand with Me in the dish, the same shall betray Me."

24 The Son of man (haMashiach) goeth away as it is written of Him; but woe unto that man by whom the Son of man (haMashiach) is betrayed! It had been good for that man if he had not been born."

25 Then Judas (Yehudah), who betrayed Him, answered and said, "Teacher (Rabbi), is it I?" He said unto him, "You have said."

26 And as they were eating, Yahwah took bread, and blessed it, and broke it, and gave it to the disciples, and said, "Take, eat; this is My body."

27 And He took the cup, and gave thanks, and

gave it to them, saying, "Drink you all of it;

28 B58For this is My blood of the New Covenant (dam haBerit haChadashah), which is shed for many for the remission of sins.

29 But I say unto you, I will not drink from this time on of this fruit of the vine, until that day when I drink it new with you in My Father's kingdom."

30 And when they had sung a hymn, they went out into the Mount of Olives.

31 Then saith Yahwah unto them, "All you shall be stumbled because of Me this night, for it is written, 'I will smite the shepherd, and the sheep of the flock shall be scattered abroad. – Zec.13:7

32 But after I am risen again, I will go before you into Galilee."

33 Peter (Kefa) answered and said unto Him, "Though all men shall be stumbled because of You, yet I will never be stumbled."

34 Yahwah said unto him, "Verily I say unto you, that this night, before the cock crows, you shalt deny Me thrice."

35 Peter (Kefa) said unto Him, "Though I should die with You, yet I will not deny You." Likewise also said all the disciples.

36 Then cometh Yahwah with them unto a place called Gethsemane, and saith unto the disciples, "Sit you here, while I go and pray over there."

37 And he took with him Peter (Kefa) and the two sons of Zebedee (Zavdai), and began to be sorrowful and very heavy.

38 Then saith He unto them, "My soul is exceeding sorrowful, even unto death; tarry you here, and watch with Me."

39 And He went a little further, and fell on His face, and prayed, saying, "O My Father (Avi), if it be possible, let this cup pass from Me; nevertheless not as I will, but as You wilt."

40 And He cometh unto the disciples, and findeth them asleep, and saith unto Peter (Kefa), "What, could you not watch with Me one hour?

41 Watch and pray, that you enter not into temptation; the spirit indeed is willing, but the flesh is weak."

42 He went away again the second time, and prayed, saying, "O My Father, if this cup may not pass away from Me, except I drink it, Your will be done."

43 And He came and found them asleep again, for their eyes were heavy.

44 And He left them, and went away again, and prayed the third time, saying the same words.

45 Then cometh He to His disciples, and saith unto them, "Sleep on now, and take your rest; behold, the hour is at hand, and the Son of man (haMashiach) is betrayed into the hands of sinners.

46 Rise, let us be going; behold, he is at hand that doth betray Me."

47 And while He yet spake, behold, Judas (Yehudah), one of the twelve, came, and with him a great multitude with swords and staves, from the chief priests (kohanim) and elders of the people.

48 Now he that betrayed Him gave them a sign, saying, "Whomsoever I shall kiss, that same is He; hold Him fast."

49 And immediately he came to Yahwah, and said, "Hail (Greetings), Teacher (Rabbi)!" and kissed Him.

50 And Yahwah said unto him, "Friend, for what are you come?" Then came they, and laid hands on Yahwah, and took Him.

51 And, behold, one of them who were with Yahwah stretched out his hand, and drew his sword, and struck a servant of the high priest (kohen hagadol), and smote off his ear.

52 Then said Yahwah unto him, "Put up again your sword into its place, for all they that take the sword shall perish with the sword.

53 Thinkest you that I cannot now pray to My Father, and He shall presently give Me more than twelve legions of angels?

54 But how then shall the scriptures be fulfilled, that thus it must be?"

55 In that same hour said Yahwah to the multitudes, "Are you come out as against a thief with swords and staves for to take Me? I sat daily with you teaching in the temple, and you laid no hold on Me.

56 But all this was done, that the scriptures of the prophets might be fulfilled." Then all the disciples forsook Him, and fled.

57 And they that had laid hold on Yahwah led Him away to Caiaphas the high priest (kohen hagadol), where the scribes and the elders were assembled.

58 But Peter (Kefa) followed Him afar off unto the high priest (kohen hagadol)'s palace, and went in, and sat with the servants, to see the end.

59 Now the chief priests (kohanim), and elders, and all the council (Sanhedrin), sought false

witness against Yahwah, to put Him to death;

60 But found none; yes, though many false witnesses came, yet found they none. At the last came two false witnesses,

61 And said, "This fellow said, 'I am able to destroy the temple of God (Elohim), and to build it in three days.'"

62 And the high priest (kohen hagadol) arose, and said unto Him, "Answerest You nothing? What is it which these witness against You?"

63 But Yahwah held His peace. And the high priest (kohen hagadol) answered and said unto Him, "I adjure You by the living God (Elohim chayim), that You tell us whether You are the Messiah (haMashiach), the [B47]Humanity of El (YHWH).

64 Yahwah saith unto him, "You have said. Nevertheless I say unto you, hereafter shall you see the Son of man (haMashiach) sitting on the right hand of power, and coming in the clouds of heaven." – Dan. 7:13; Psa.110:1

65 Then the high priest (kohen hagadol) rent his clothes, saying, "He hath spoken blasphemy; what further need have we of witnesses? Behold, now you have heard His blasphemy!

66 What think you?" They answered and said, "He is guilty of death."

67 Then did they spit in His face, and buffeted Him; and others smote Him with the palms of their hands,

68 Saying, "Prophesy unto us, You the Messiah (haMashiach)! Who is he that smote You?"

69 Now Peter (Kefa) sat outside in the palace; and a damsel came unto him, saying, "You also wast with Yahwah of Galilee."

70 But he denied before them all, saying, "I know not what you sayest."

71 And when he was gone out into the porch, another maid saw him, and said unto them that were there, "This fellow was also with Yahwah of Nazareth."

72 And again he denied with an oath, I do not know the man.

73 And after a while came unto him they that stood by, and said to Peter (Kefa), "Surely you also art one of them; for your speech bewrayeth you."

74 Then began he to curse and to swear, saying, "I know not the man." And immediately the cock crew.

75 And Peter (Kefa) remembered the word of Yahwah, who said unto him, "Before the cock crows, you shalt deny Me thrice." And he went out, and wept bitterly.

27 When the morning came, all the chief priests (kohanim) and elders of the people took counsel against Yahwah to put Him to death.

2 And when they had bound Him, they led Him away, and delivered Him to Pontius Pilate the governor.

3 Then Judas (Yehudah), who had betrayed Him, when he saw that he was condemned, repented himself, and brought again the thirty pieces of silver to the chief priests (kohanim) and elders,

4 Saying, "I have sinned in that I have betrayed the innocent blood." And they said, "What is that to us? See you to that."

5 And he cast down the pieces of silver in the temple, and departed, and went and hanged himself.

6 And the chief priests (kohanim) took the silver pieces, and said, "It is not lawful for to put them into the treasury, because it is the price of blood."

7 And they took counsel, and bought with them the potter's field, to bury strangers in.

8 Therefore that field was called 'The Field of Blood' unto this day.

9 Then was fulfilled that which was spoken by Jeremy (Yirmeyahu) the prophet, saying, "And they took the thirty pieces of silver, the price of him that was valued, whom they of the children of Yisrael did value,

10 And gave them for the potter's field, as יהוה appointed me. – Zec. 11:12,13

11 And Yahwah stood before the governor; and the governor asked Him, saying, "Are You the King of the Jews (Yehudim)?" And Yahwah said unto him, "You sayest."

12 And when He was accused of the chief priests (kohanim) and elders, He answered nothing.

13 Then said Pilate unto Him, "Hearest You not how many things they witness against You?"

14 And He answered him not a word; insomuch that the governor marvelled greatly.

15 Now at that feast the governor was accustomed to release unto the people a prisoner, whom they wished.

16 And they had then a notable prisoner, called Barabbas.

17 Therefore when they were gathered together, Pilate said unto them, "Whom will you that I release unto you? Barabbas, or Yahwah who is called the Messiah (haMashiach)?"

18 For he knew that for envy they had delivered Him.

19 When he was set down on the judgment seat, his wife sent unto him, saying, "Have you nothing to do with that just Man, for I have suffered many things this day in a dream because of Him."

20 But the chief priests (kohanim) and elders persuaded the multitude that they should ask Barabbas, and destroy Yahwah.

21 The governor answered and said unto them, "Which of the two will you that I release unto you?" They said, "Barabbas!"

22 Pilate saith unto them, "What shall I do then with Yahwah who is called the Messiah (haMashiach)? They all say unto him, "Let Him be crucified."

23 And the governor said, "Why, what evil hath He done?" But they cried out the more, saying, "Let Him be crucified."

24 When Pilate saw that he could prevail nothing, but that rather a tumult was made, he took water, and washed his hands before the multitude, saying, "I am innocent of the blood of this just Person; see you to it."

25 Then answered all the people, and said, "His blood be on us, and on our children."

26 Then released he Barabbas unto them; and when he had scourged Yahwah, he delivered Him to be crucified.

27 Then the soldiers of the governor took Yahwah into the common hall, and gathered unto Him the whole band of soldiers.

28 And they stripped Him, and put on Him a scarlet robe.

29 And when they had platted a crown of thorns, they put it upon His head, and a reed in His right hand; and they bowed the knee before Him, and mocked Him, saying, "Hail, King of the Jews (Yehudim)!"

30 And they spit upon Him, and took the reed, and smote Him on the head.

31 And after that they had mocked Him, they took the robe off from Him, and put His own raiment on Him, and led Him away to crucify Him.

32 And as they came out, they found a man of Cyrene, Shimon by name; him they compelled to bear His stake.

33 And when they came unto a place called Golgotha, that is to say "a place of a skull".

34 They gave Him vinegar to drink mingled with gall; and when He had tasted thereof, He would not drink.

35 And they crucified Him, and parted His garments, casting lots, that it might be fulfilled which was spoken by the prophet: "They parted My garments among them, and upon My vesture did they cast lots. – *Psa. 22:18*

36 And sitting down they watched Him there;

37 And set up over His head His accusation written: THIS IS YAHWAH (YHWH) THE KING OF THE JEWS (YEHUDIM).

38 Then were there two thieves crucified with Him, one on the right hand, and another on the left.

39 And they that passed by reviled Him, wagging their heads, – *Psa. 22:7*

40 And saying, "You that destroyest the temple, and buildest it in three days, save Yourself. If You be the [B47]Humanity of El (YHWH), come down from the stake."

41 Likewise also the chief priests (kohanim) mocking Him, with the scribes and elders, said,

42 "He saved others; Himself He cannot save. If He be the King of Yisrael, let Him now come down from the stake, and we will believe Him.

43 He trusted in God (Elohim); let Him deliver Him now, if He will have Him; for He said, 'I am the Humanity of El (YHWH).'" – *Psa. 22:8*

44 The thieves also, who were crucified with Him, insulted Him the same way.

45 Now from the sixth hour there was darkness over all the land unto the ninth hour.

46 And about the ninth hour Yahwah cried with a loud voice, saying, "Eli, Eli, lama shavaqtani? That is to say, "My God (Eli), My God (Eli), why have You forsaken Me?" – *Psa. 22:1*

47 Some of them that stood there, when they heard that, said, "This man calleth for Elijah (Eliyahu)."

48 And straightway one of them ran, and took a spunge, and filled it with vinegar, and put it on a reed, and gave Him to drink. – *Psa. 69:21*

49 The rest said, "Let be, let us see whether Elijah (Eliyahu) will come to save Him."

50 Yahwah, when He had cried again with a loud voice, yielded up His Spirit.

51 And, behold, the veil of the temple was rent in twain from the top to the bottom; and the earth did quake, and the rocks rent;

52 And the graves were opened; and many bodies of the holy ones which slept arose,

53 And came out of the graves after His resurrection, they went into the holy city, and appeared unto many.

54 Now when the centurion, and they that were with Him, watching Yahwah, saw the earthquake, and those things that were done, they feared greatly, saying, "Truly this was the B47Humanity of El (YHWH)."

55 And many women were there beholding afar off, who followed Yahwah from Galilee, ministering unto Him;

56 Among whom was Mary (Miryam) Magdalene, and Mary (Miryam) the mother of James (Yaaqov) and Joseph (Yosef), and the mother of Zebedee (Zavdai)'s children.

57 When the even came, there came a rich man of Arimathaea, named Joseph (Yosef), who also himself was Yahwah's disciple;

58 He went to Pilate, and begged the body of Yahwah. Then Pilate commanded the body to be delivered.

59 And when Joseph (Yosef) had taken the body, he wrapped it in a clean linen cloth,

60 And laid it in his own new tomb, which he had hewn out in the rock; and he rolled a great stone to the door of the sepulchre, and departed.

61 And there was Mary (Miryam) Magdalene, and the other Mary (Miryam), sitting over against the sepulchre.

62 Now the next day, that followed the day of the preparation, the chief priests (kohanim) and Pharisees came together unto Pilate,

63 Saying, "Sir, we remember that, that deceiver said, while He was yet alive, 'After three days I will rise again.'

64 Command therefore that the sepulchre be made sure until the third day, lest His disciples come by night, and steal Him away, and say unto the people, 'He is risen from the dead;' so the last error shall be worse than the first."

65 Pilate said unto them, "You have a watch; go your way, make it as sure as you can."

66 So they went, and made the sepulchre sure, sealing the stone, and setting a watch.

28 In the end of the Shabbat, as it began to dawn toward the first day of the week, came Mary (Miryam) Magdalene and the other Mary (Miryam) to see the sepulchre.

2 And, behold, there was a great earthquake; for the angel of יהוה descended from heaven, and came and rolled back the stone from the door, and sat upon it.

3 His countenance was like lightning, and His raiment white as snow.

4 And for fear of him, the keepers shook and became as dead men.

5 And the angel answered and said unto the women, "Fear not you, for I know that you seek Yahwah, who was crucified.

6 He is not here for He is risen as He said. Come, see the place where He lay.

7 And go quickly, and tell His disciples that He is risen from the dead; and, behold, He goeth before you into Galilee; there shall you see Him. Behold, I have told you."

8 And they departed quickly from the sepulchre with fear and great joy; and did run to bring His disciples word.

9 And as they went to tell His disciples, behold, Yahwah met them, saying, "Rejoice." And they came and held Him by the feet, and worshipped Him.

10 Then said Yahwah unto them, "Be not afraid. Go tell My brethren that they go into Galilee, and there shall they see Me."

11 Now when they were going, behold, some of the watch came into the city, and shewed unto the chief priests (kohanim) all the things that were done.

12 And when they were assembled with the elders, and had taken counsel, they gave large money unto the soldiers,

13 Saying, "Say you, His disciples came by night, and stole Him away while we slept.

14 And if this come to the governor's ears, we will persuade him, and secure you."

15 So they took the money, and did as they were taught; and this saying is commonly reported among the Jews (Yehudim) until this day.

16 Then the eleven disciples went away into Galilee, into a mountain where Yahwah had appointed them.

17 And when they saw Him, they worshipped Him; but some doubted.

18 And Yahwah came and spake unto them, saying, "All power is given unto Me in heaven and on earth.

19 Go you therefore, and teach all nations, [B59]baptizing them in the name of the Father, and of the Son, and of the Holy Spirit; – *Acts 2:38*

20 Teaching them to observe all things whatsoever I have commanded you; and, behold, I am with you always, even unto the end of the world." So be it (Amen).

MARK
MARQOS מרקוס
(Gospel of [A69]Mark)

1 The beginning of the gospel (good news) of [A1]Yahwah [B45]haMashiach, the [B47]Humanity of El (YHWH);

2 As it is written in the Prophets (Nevi'im): "Behold, I send My messenger before Your face, who shall prepare Your way before You." – *Mal. 3:1*

3 "[B49]The voice of one crying in the wilderness: 'Prepare you the way of יהוה (Yahwah, YHWH), make His paths straight.'" – *Isa. 40:3, Mat. 3:3, Luke 3:4*

4 John (Yochanan) did baptize in the wilderness, and preach the baptism of repentance for the remission of sins.

5 And there went out unto him all the land of Judah (Yehudah), and they of Jerusalem (Yerushalayim), and were all baptized of him in the river of Jordan (Yarden), confessing their sins.

6 And John (Yochanan) was clothed with camel's hair, and with a girdle of a skin about his loins; and he did eat locusts and wild honey;

7 And preached, saying, "There cometh one mightier than I after me, the latchet of whose shoes I am not worthy to stoop down and unloose.

8 I indeed have baptized you with water, but He shall baptize you with the Holy Spirit (Ruach haQodesh).

9 And it came to pass in those days, that Yahwah came from Nazareth of Galilee, and was baptized of John (Yochanan) in Jordan (Yarden).

10 And straightway coming up out of the water, He saw the heavens opened, and the Spirit (Ruach) like a dove descending upon Him;

11 And there came [B53]a voice from heaven, saying, "You are My beloved [B47]Humanity, in whom I am well pleased." – *Matt 3:17, Luke 3:22*

12 And immediately the Spirit (Ruach) driveth Him into the wilderness.

13 And He was there in the wilderness forty days, tempted of Satan; and was with the wild beasts; and the angels ministered unto Him.

14 Now after that John (Yochanan) was put in prison, Yahwah came into Galilee, preaching the gospel (good news) of the kingdom of God (Elohim, יהוה (YHWH)),

15 And saying, "The time is fulfilled, and the kingdom of God (Elohim, יהוה (YHWH)) is at hand. Repent you, and believe the gospel (good news)."

16 Now as He walked by the sea of Galilee, He saw Shimon and Andrew his brother casting a net into the sea; for they were fishers.

17 And Yahwah said unto them, "Come you after Me, and I will make you to become fishers of men."

18 And straightway they forsook their nets, and followed Him.

19 And when He had gone a little further from there, He saw James the son of Zebedee (Yaaqov ben-Zavdai), and John (Yochanan) his brother, who also were in the ship mending their nets.

20 And straightway He called them; and they left their father Zebedee (Zavdai) in the ship with the hired servants, and went after Him.

21 And they went into Capernaum; and straightway on the Shabbat He entered into the synagogue, and taught.

22 And they were astonished at His doctrine (teaching); for He taught them as one that had authority, and not as the scribes.

23 And there was in their synagogue a man with an unclean spirit; and he cried out,

24 Saying, "Let us alone; what have we to do with You, You Yahwah of Nazareth? Art You come to destroy us? I know You who You are, the Holy One of God (Elohim).

25 And Yahwah rebuked him, saying, "Hold your peace, and come out of him."

26 And when the unclean spirit had torn him, and cried with a loud voice, he came out of him.

27 And they were all amazed, insomuch that they questioned among themselves, saying, "What thing is this? What new doctrine (teaching) is this? For with authority commandeth He even the unclean spirits, and they do obey Him."

28 And immediately His fame spread abroad throughout all the region round about Galilee.

29 And immediately, when they had come out of the synagogue, they entered into the house of Shimon and Andrew, with James (Yaaqov) and John (Yochanan).

30 But Shimon's wife's mother lay sick of a fever, and immediately they tell Him of her.

31 And He came and took her by the hand, and

lifted her up; and immediately the fever left her, and she served them.

32 And at even, when the sun set, they brought unto Him all that were diseased, and them that were possessed with devils.

33 And all the city was gathered together at the door.

34 And He healed many that were sick of divers diseases, and cast out many devils; and allowed not the devils to speak, because they knew Him.

35 And in the morning, rising up a great while before day, He went out, and departed into a solitary place, and there prayed.

36 And Shimon and they that were with Him followed after Him.

37 And when they had found Him, they said unto Him, "All men seek for You."

38 And He said unto them, "Let us go into the next towns, that I may preach there also; for this therefore I have come forth."

39 And He preached in their synagogues throughout all Galilee, and cast out devils.

40 And there came a leper to Him, beseeching Him, and kneeling down to Him, and saying unto Him, "If You wilt, You canst make me clean."

41 And Yahwah, moved with compassion, put forth His hand, and touched Him, and saith unto Him, "I will; be you clean."

42 And as soon as He had spoken, immediately the leprosy departed from Him, and He was cleansed.

43 And He sternly warned him, and immediately sent him away;

44 And saith unto him, "See you say nothing to any man; but go your way, show yourself to the priest (kohen), and offer for your cleansing those things which Moses (Mosheh) commanded, for a testimony unto them."

45 But he went out, and began to publish it much, and to blaze abroad the matter, insomuch that Yahwah could no more openly enter into the city, but was outside in desert places; and they came to Him from every quarter.

2 And again He entered into Capernaum after some days; and it was heard that He was in the house.

2 And straightway many were gathered together, insomuch that there was no room to receive them, no, not so much as about the door; and He preached the word unto them.

3 And they come unto Him, bringing one sick of the palsy, who was borne of four.

4 And when they could not come near unto Him because of the crowd, they uncovered the roof where He was; and when they had broken it up, they let down the bed wherein the sick of the palsy lay.

5 When Yahwah saw their faith, He said unto the sick of the palsy, "Son, your sins be forgiven you."

6 But there were certain of the scribes sitting there, and reasoning in their hearts,

7 "Why doth this man thus speak blasphemies? Who can forgive sins but God (Elohim) only?"

8 And immediately when Yahwah perceived in His spirit that they so reasoned within themselves, He said unto them, "Why reason you these things in your hearts?

9 Whether is it easier to say to the sick of the palsy, 'Your sins be forgiven you;' or to say, 'Arise, and take up your bed, and walk?'

10 But that you may know that the Son of man (haMashiach) hath power on earth to forgive sins, (He saith to the sick of the palsy,)

11 I say unto you, arise and take up your bed, and go your way into your house."

12 And immediately he arose, took up the bed, and went forth before them all; insomuch that they were all amazed, and glorified God (Elohim), saying, "We never saw it on this fashion."

13 And He went forth again by the sea side; and all the multitude resorted unto Him, and He taught them.

14 And as He passed by, He saw Lewi the son of Alphaeus sitting at the receipt of custom, and said unto him, "Follow Me." And he arose and followed Him.

15 And it came to pass, that, as Yahwah sat at meat in his house, many tax collectors and sinners sat also together with Yahwah and His disciples; for there were many, and they followed Him.

16 And when the scribes and Pharisees saw Him eat with tax collectors and sinners, they said unto His disciples, "How is it that He eateth and drinketh with tax collectors and sinners?"

17 When Yahwah heard it, He saith unto them, "They that are whole have no need of the physician, but they that are sick; I came not to call the righteous, but sinners to repentance."

18 And the disciples of John (Yochanan) and of the Pharisees used to fast; and they come and say unto Him, "Why do the disciples of John (Yochanan) and of the Pharisees fast, but Your disciples fast not?"

19 And Yahwah said unto them, "Can the children of the bridechamber fast, while the bridegroom is with them? As long as they have the bridegroom with them, they cannot fast.

20 But the days will come, when the bridegroom shall be taken away from them, and then shall they fast in those days.

21 No man also seweth a piece of new cloth on an old garment; else the new piece that filled it up taketh away from the old, and the rent is made worse.

22 And no man putteth new wine into old bottles; else the new wine doth burst the bottles, and the wine is spilled, and the bottles will be marred; but new wine must be put into new bottles."

23 And it came to pass, that He went through the grainfields on the Shabbat; and His disciples began, as they went, to pluck the heads of grain.

24 And the Pharisees said unto him, "Behold, why do they on the Shabbat that which is not lawful?"

25 And He said unto them, "Have you never read what Dawid did, when he had need, and was hungry, he, and they that were with him?

26 How he went into the house of יהוה (YHWH) in the days of Abiathar the high priest (kohen hagadol), and did eat the shewbread, which is not lawful to eat but for the priests (kohanim), and gave also to them which were with him?" – *1 Sam.21:1-6*

27 And He said unto them, "The Shabbat was made for man, and not man for the Shabbat;

28 Therefore the Son of man (haMashiach) is Lord (Adon) also of the Shabbat."

3 And He entered again into the synagogue; and there was a man there who had a withered hand.

2 And they watched Him, whether He would heal him on the Shabbat; that they might accuse Him.

3 And He saith unto the man who had the withered hand, "Stand forth."

4 And He saith unto them, "Is it lawful to do good on the Shabbat, or to do evil? To save life, or to kill?" But they held their peace.

5 And when He had looked round about on them with anger, being grieved for the hardness of their hearts, He saith unto the man, "Stretch forth your hand." And he stretched it out; and his hand was restored whole as the other.

6 And the Pharisees went forth, and straightway took counsel with the Herodians against Him, how they might destroy Him.

7 But Yahwah withdrew Himself with His disciples to the sea; and a great multitude from Galilee followed Him, and from Judah (Yehudah),

8 And from Jerusalem (Yerushalayim), and from Idumaea, and from beyond Jordan (Yarden); and they about Tyre and Sidon, a great multitude, when they had heard what great things He did, came unto Him.

9 And He spake to His disciples, that a small ship should wait on Him because of the multitude, lest they should throng Him.

10 For He had healed many; insomuch that they pressed upon Him for to touch Him, as many as had plagues.

11 And unclean spirits, when they saw Him, fell down before Him, and cried, saying, "You are the [B47]Humanity of El (YHWH)."

12 And He sternly warned them that they should not make Him known.

13 And He goeth up into a mountain, and calleth unto Him whom He would; and they came unto Him.

14 And He ordained twelve, that they should be with Him, and that He might send them forth to preach,

15 And to have power to heal sicknesses, and to cast out devils:

16 And Shimon He surnamed Peter (Kefa);

17 And James the son of Zebedee (Yaaqov ben-Zavdai), and John (Yochanan) the brother of James (Yaaqov); and He surnamed them Boanerges, which is, "The sons of Thunder":

18 And Andrew, and Philip, and Bartholomew (Bar-Talmai), and Matthew (Mattityahu), and Thomas (Toma), and James the son of Alphaeus (Yaaqov ben-Alpheus), and Thad-daeus, and Shimon the Canaanite,

19 And Judas Iscariot (Yehudah Ishkeriot) also, who betrayed Him; and they went into a house.

20 And the multitude cometh together again, so that they could not so much as eat bread.

21 And when his friends heard of it, they went

out to lay hold on him; for they said, "He is besides himself."

22 And the scribes who came down from Jerusalem (Yerushalayim) said, "He hath Beelzebul (Baal-Zebub), and by the prince of the devils casteth He out devils."

23 And He called them unto Him, and said unto them in parables, "How can Satan cast out Satan?

24 And if a kingdom be divided against itself, that kingdom cannot stand.

25 And if a house be divided against itself, that house cannot stand.

26 And if Satan rise up against himself, and be divided, he cannot stand, but hath an end.

27 No man can enter into a strong man's house, and spoil his goods, except he will first bind the strong man; and then he will spoil his house.

28 Verily I say unto you, all sins shall be forgiven unto the sons of men, and blasphemies wherewith soever they shall blaspheme;

29 But he that shall blaspheme against the Holy Spirit (Ruach haQodesh) hath never forgiveness, but is in danger of eternal damnation;"

30 Because they said, "He hath an unclean spirit."

31 There came then His brethren and His mother, and, standing outside, sent unto Him, calling Him.

32 And the multitude sat about Him, and they said unto Him, "Behold, Your mother and your brethren outside seek for You."

33 And He answered them, saying, "Who is My mother, or My brethren?"

34 And He looked round about on them which sat about Him, and said, "Behold My mother and My brethren!

35 For whosoever shall do the will of God (Elohim, יהוה (YHWH)), the same is My brother, and My sister, and mother."

4 And He began again to teach by the sea side; and there was gathered unto Him a great multitude, so that He entered into a ship, and sat in the sea; and the whole multitude was by the sea on the land.

2 And He taught them many things by parables, and said unto them in His doctrine (teaching):

3 "Hearken! Behold, there went out a sower to sow.

4 And it came to pass, as he sowed, some fell by the way side, and the fowls of the air came

and devoured it up.

5 And some fell on stony ground, where it had not much earth; and immediately it sprang up, because it had no depth of earth;

6 But when the sun was up, it was scorched; and because it had no root, it withered away.

7 And some fell among thorns, and the thorns grew up, and choked it, and it yielded no fruit.

8 And other fell on good ground, and did yield fruit that sprang up and increased; and brought forth, some thirty, and some sixty, and some a hundred."

9 And He said unto them, "He that hath ears to hear, let him hear."

10 And when He was alone, they that were about Him with the twelve asked of Him the parable.

11 And He said unto them, "Unto you it is given to know the mystery of the kingdom of God (Elohim, יהוה (YHWH)); but unto them that are outside, all these things are done in parables;

12 That seeing they may see, and not perceive; and hearing they may hear, and not understand; lest at any time they should be converted, and their sins should be forgiven them." – *Isa. 6:9*

13 And He said unto them, "Know you not this parable? And how then will you know all parables?

14 The sower soweth the word.

15 And these are they by the way side, where the word is sown; but when they have heard, Satan cometh immediately, and taketh away the word that was sown in their hearts.

16 And these are they likewise who are sown on stony ground; who, when they have heard the word, immediately receive it with gladness;

17 And have no root in themselves, and so endure but for a time: afterward, when affliction or persecution ariseth for the word's sake, immediately they are stumbled.

18 And these are they who are sown among thorns; such as hear the word,

19 And the cares of this world, and the deceitfulness of riches, and the lusts of other things entering in, choke the word, and it becometh unfruitful.

20 And these are they who are sown on good ground; such as hear the word, and receive it, and bring forth fruit, some thirtyfold, some sixty, and some a hundred."

21 And He said unto them, "Is a candle brought to be put under a bushel, or under a bed? And

not to be set on a candlestick (menorah)?

22 For there is nothing hidden, which shall not be manifested; neither was any thing kept secret, but that it should come abroad.

23 If any man has ears to hear, let him hear."

24 And He said unto them, "Take heed what you hear. With what measure you use, it shall be measured to you; and unto you that hear shall more be given.

25 For he that hath, to him shall be given; and he that hath not, from him shall be taken even that which he hath."

26 And He said, "So is the kingdom of God (Elohim, יהוה (YHWH)), as if a man should cast seed into the ground;

27 And should sleep, and rise night and day, and the seed should spring and grow up, he knoweth not how.

28 For the earth bringeth forth fruit of herself; first the blade, then the ear, after that the full corn in the ear.

29 But when the fruit is brought forth, immediately he putteth in the sickle, because the harvest is come."

30 And He said, "Whereunto shall we liken the kingdom of God (Elohim, יהוה (YHWH))? Or with what comparison shall we compare it?

31 It is like a grain of mustard seed, which, when it is sown in the earth, is less than all the seeds that be in the earth;

32 But when it is sown, it groweth up, and becometh greater than all herbs, and shooteth out great branches; so that the fowls of the air may lodge under the shadow of it."

33 And with many such parables spake He the word unto them, as they were able to hear it.

34 But without a parable spake He not unto them; and when they were alone, He expounded all things to His disciples.

35 And the same day, when the even had come, He saith unto them, "Let us pass over unto the other side."

36 And when they had sent away the multitude, they took Him even as He was in the ship. And there were also with Him other little ships.

37 And there arose a great storm of wind, and the waves beat into the ship, so that it was now full.

38 And He was in the hinder part of the ship, asleep on a pillow; and they awake Him, and say unto Him, "Teacher (Rabbi), carest You not

that we perish?"

39 And He arose, and rebuked the wind, and said unto the sea, "Peace, be still." And the wind ceased, and there was a great calm.

40 And He said unto them, "Why are you so fearful? How is it that you have no faith?"

41 And they feared exceedingly, and said one to another, "What manner of man is this, that even the wind and the sea obey Him?"

5 And they came over unto the other side of the sea, into the country of the Gadarenes.

2 And when He had come out of the ship, immediately there met Him out of the tombs a man with an unclean spirit,

3 Who had his dwelling among the tombs; and no man could bind him, no, not with chains;

4 Because that he had been often bound with fetters and chains, and the chains had been plucked apart by him, and the fetters broken in pieces: neither could any man tame him.

5 And always, night and day, he was in the mountains, and in the tombs, crying, and cutting himself with stones.

6 But when he saw Yahwah afar off, he ran and worshipped Him,

7 And cried with a loud voice, and said, "What have I to do with You, Yahwah, You [B47]Humanity of Most High God (Elyon El)? I adjure You by God (Elohim), that You torment me not."

8 For He said unto him, "Come out of the man, you unclean spirit."

9 And He asked him, "What is your name?" And he answered, saying, "My name is Legion, for we are many."

10 And he besought Him much that He would not send them away out of the country.

11 Now there was there near unto the mountains a great herd of swine feeding.

12 And all the devils besought Him, saying, "Send us into the swine, that we may enter into them."

13 And immediately Yahwah gave them permission. And the unclean spirits went out, and entered into the swine; and the herd ran violently down a steep place into the sea, (they were about two thousand;) and were choked in the sea.

14 And they that fed the swine fled, and told it in the city, and in the country. And they went out to see what it was that was done.

15 And they come to Yahwah, and see him

that was possessed with the devil, and had the legion, sitting, and clothed, and in his right mind; and they were afraid.

16 And they that saw it told them how it befell to him that was possessed with the devil, and also concerning the swine.

17 And they began to beseech Him to depart out of their coasts.

18 And when He had come into the ship, he that had been possessed with the devil besought Him that he might be with Him.

19 Howbeit Yahwah permitted him not, but saith unto him, "Go home to your friends, and tell them how great things יהוה hath done for you, and hath had compassion on you."

20 And he departed, and began to publish in Decapolis how great things Yahwah had done for him; and all men did marvel.

21 And when Yahwah had passed over again by ship unto the other side, much people gathered unto Him; and He was near unto the sea.

22 And, behold, there cometh one of the rulers of the synagogue, Yair by name; and when he saw Him, he fell at His feet,

23 And besought Him greatly, saying, "My little daughter lieth at the point of death; I pray You, come and lay your hands on her, that she may be healed; and she shall live."

24 And Yahwah went with him; and much people followed Him, and thronged Him.

25 And a certain woman, who had an issue of blood twelve years,

26 And had suffered many things of many physicians, and had spent all that she had, and was nothing bettered, but rather grew worse,

27 When she had heard of Yahwah, came in the press behind, and touched His garment.

28 For she said, "If I may touch but His clothes, I shall be whole."

29 And straightway the fountain of her blood was dried up; and she felt in her body that she was healed of that plague.

30 And Yahwah, immediately knowing in Himself that power had gone out of Him, turned Him about in the crowd, and said, "Who touched My clothes?"

31 And His disciples said unto Him, "You seest the multitude thronging You, and sayest You, 'Who touched Me?'"

32 And He looked round about to see her that had done this thing.

33 But the woman fearing and trembling, knowing what was done in her, came and fell down before Him, and told Him all the truth.

34 And He said unto her, "Daughter, your faith hath made you whole; go in peace, and be whole of your plague."

35 While He yet spake, there came from the ruler of the synagogue's house certain which said, "Your daughter is dead; why troublest you the Teacher (Rabbi) any further?"

36 As soon as Yahwah heard the word that was spoken, He saith unto the ruler of the synagogue, "Be not afraid, only believe."

37 And He permitted no man to follow Him, except Peter (Kefa), and James (Yaaqov), and John (Yochanan) the brother of James (Yaaqov).

38 And He cometh to the house of the ruler of the synagogue, and seeth the tumult, and them that wept and wailed greatly.

39 And when He had come in, He saith unto them, "Why make you this commotion, and weep? The damsel is not dead, but sleepeth."

40 And they laughed Him to scorn. But when He had put them all out, He taketh the father and the mother of the damsel, and them that were with Him, and entereth in where the damsel was lying.

41 And He took the damsel by the hand, and said unto her, "Talita, qumi!" which is, being interpreted, "Damsel, I say unto you, arise!"

42 And straightway the damsel arose, and walked; for she was of the age of twelve years. And they were astonished with a great astonishment.

43 And He warned them sternly that no man should know it; and commanded that something should be given her to eat.

6 And He went out from there, and came into His own country; and His disciples follow Him.

2 And when the Shabbat had come, He began to teach in the synagogue; and many hearing Him were astonished, saying, "From where hath this man these things? And what wisdom is this which is given unto Him, that even such mighty works are wrought by His hands?

3 Is not this the carpenter, the son of Mary (Miryam), the brother of James (Yaaqov), and Joseph (Yosef), and of Judas (Yehudah), and Shimon? And are not His sisters here with us?" And they were offended at Him.

4 But Yahwah said unto them, "A prophet is not without honour, but in His own country, and among His own kin, and in His own house."

5 And He could there do no mighty work, except that He laid His hands upon a few sick folk, and healed them.

6 And He marvelled because of their unbelief. And He went round about the villages, teaching.

7 And He called unto Him the twelve, and began to send them forth by two and two; and gave them power over unclean spirits;

8 And commanded them that they should take nothing for their journey, except a staff only; no scrip, no bread, no money in their purse;

9 But be shod with sandals; and not put on two coats.

10 And He said unto them, "In what place soever you enter into a house, there abide till you depart from that place.

11 And whosoever shall not receive you, nor hear you, when you depart there, shake off the dust under your feet for a testimony against them. Verily I say unto you, it shall be more tolerable for Sodom and Gomorrah in the day of judgment, than for that city."

12 And they went out, and preached that men should repent.

13 And they cast out many devils, and anointed with oil many that were sick, and healed them.

14 And King Herod heard of Him; (for His name was spread abroad;) and he said, "That John the Baptist (Yochanan haMatvil) was risen from the dead, and therefore mighty works do shew forth themselves in Him."

15 Others said, "That it is Elijah (Eliyahu)." And others said, "That it is a prophet, or as one of the prophets."

16 But when Herod heard thereof, he said, "It is John (Yochanan), whom I beheaded; He is risen from the dead."

17 For Herod himself had sent forth and laid hold upon John (Yochanan), and bound him in prison for Herodias' sake, his brother Philip's wife; for he had married her.

18 For John (Yochanan) had said unto Herod, "It is not lawful for you to have your brother's wife."

19 Therefore Herodias had a quarrel against him, and would have killed him, but she could not;

20 For Herod feared John (Yochanan), knowing that he was a just and holy man, and observed him; and when he heard him, he did many things, and heard him gladly.

21 And when an opportunity day had come, that Herod on his birthday made a supper to his nobles, high captains, and chief estates of Galilee;

22 And when the daughter of the said Herodias came in, and danced, and pleased Herod and them that sat with him, the king said unto the damsel, "Ask of me whatsoever you wilt, and I will give it you."

23 And he sware unto her, "Whatsoever you shalt ask of me, I will give it you, unto the half of my kingdom."

24 And she went forth, and said unto her mother, "What shall I ask?" And she said, "The head of John the Baptist (Yochanan haMatvil)."

25 And she came in straightway with haste unto the king, and asked, saying, "I will that you give me at once on a platter the head of John the Baptist (Yochanan haMatvil)."

26 And the king was exceeding sorry; yet for his oath's sake, and for their sakes who sat with him, he would not reject her.

27 And immediately the king sent an executioner, and commanded his head to be brought; and he went and beheaded him in the prison,

28 And brought his head on a platter, and gave it to the damsel; and the damsel gave it to her mother.

29 And when his disciples heard of it, they came and took up his corpse, and laid it in a tomb.

30 And the apostles gathered themselves together unto Yahwah, and told Him all things, both what they had done, and what they had taught.

31 And He said unto them, "Come you yourselves apart into a desert place, and rest a while;" for there were many coming and going, and they had no leisure so much as to eat.

32 And they departed into a desert place by ship privately.

33 And the people saw them departing, and many knew Him, and ran afoot thither out of all cities, and outwent them, and came together unto Him.

34 And Yahwah, when He came out, saw much people, and was moved with compassion toward them, because they were as sheep not having a

shepherd; and He began to teach them many things.

35 And when the day was now far spent, His disciples came unto Him, and said, "This is a desert place, and now the time is far passed.

36 Send them away, that they may go into the country round about, and into the villages, and buy themselves bread; for they have nothing to eat."

37 He answered and said unto them, "Give you them to eat." And they say unto Him, "Shall we go and buy two hundred penny worth of bread, and give them to eat?"

38 He saith unto them, "How many loaves have you? Go and see." And when they knew, they say, "Five, and two fishes."

39 And He commanded them to make all sit down by companies upon the green grass.

40 And they sat down in ranks, by hundreds, and by fifties.

41 And when He had taken the five loaves and the two fishes, He looked up to heaven, and blessed, and broke the loaves, and gave them to His disciples to set before them; and the two fishes divided He among them all.

42 And they did all eat, and were filled.

43 And they took up twelve baskets full of the fragments, and of the fishes.

44 And they that did eat of the loaves were about five thousand men.

45 And straightway He constrained His disciples to get into the ship, and to go to the other side before unto Bethsaida, while He sent away the people.

46 And when He had sent them away, He departed into a mountain to pray.

47 And when even had come, the ship was in the midst of the sea, and He alone on the land.

48 And He saw them toiling in rowing; for the wind was contrary unto them; and about the fourth watch of the night He cometh unto them, walking upon the sea, and would have passed by them.

49 But when they saw Him walking upon the sea, they supposed it had been a spirit (ghost), and cried out;

50 For they all saw Him, and were troubled. And immediately He talked with them, and saith unto them, "Be of good cheer! It is I; be not afraid."

51 And He went up unto them into the ship; and the wind ceased; and they were sore amazed in themselves beyond measure, and wondered.

52 For they considered not the miracle of the loaves, for their heart was hardened.

53 And when they had passed over, they came into the land of Gennesaret, and drew to the shore.

54 And when they had come out of the ship, straightway they recognized Him,

55 And ran through that whole region round about, and began to carry about in beds those that were sick, where they heard He was.

56 And whithersoever He entered, into villages, or cities, or country, they laid the sick in the streets, and besought him that they might touch if it was but the border of His garment; and as many as touched Him were made whole.

7 Then came together unto Him the Pharisees and certain of the scribes, who came from Jerusalem (Yerushalayim).

2 And when they saw some of His disciples eat bread with defiled, that is to say, with unwashen hands, they found fault.

3 For the Pharisees and all the Jews (Yehudim), except they wash their hands often, eat not, holding the tradition of the elders.

4 And when they come from the market, except they wash, they eat not. And many other things there be, which they have received to hold, as the washing of cups, and pots, brasen vessels, and of tables.

5 Then the Pharisees and scribes asked Him, "Why walk not Your disciples according to the tradition of the elders, but eat bread with unwashen hands?"

6 He answered and said unto them, "Well hath Isaiah (Yeshayahu) prophesied of you hypocrites, as it is written, 'This people honoureth Me with their lips, but their heart is far from Me.'

7 Howbeit in vain do they worship Me, teaching for doctrines the commandments of men. – *Isa. 29:13*

8 For laying aside the commandment of God (Elohim), you hold the tradition of men, as the washing of pots and cups; and many other such like things you do."

9 And He said unto them, "Well you reject the commandment of God (Elohim), that you may keep your own tradition.

10 For Moses (Mosheh) said, 'Honour your

father and your mother;' and, 'Whoso curseth father or mother, let him die the death;' – *Deu. 5:16, Exo. 21:17*

11 But you say, 'If a man shall say to his father or mother, "It is Korban" that is to say "a Gift", by whatsoever you mightest be profited by me; he shall be free.'

12 And you let him no more to do anything for his father or his mother;

13 Making the word of God (Elohim, יהוה (YHWH)) of none effect through your tradition, which you have delivered; and many such things do you."

14 And when He had called all the people unto Him, He said unto them, "Hearken unto Me every one of you, and understand:

15 There is nothing from outside a man, that entering into him can defile him; but the things which come out of him, those are they that defile the man.

16 If any man has ears to hear, let him hear."

17 And when He was entered into the house from the people, His disciples asked Him concerning the parable.

18 And He saith unto them, "Are you so without understanding also? Do you not perceive, that whatsoever thing from outside entereth into the man, it cannot defile him;

19 Because it entereth not into his heart, but into the belly, and goeth out into the draught, purging all foods?"

20 And He said, "That which cometh out of the man, that defileth the man.

21 For from within, out of the heart of men, proceed evil thoughts, adulteries, fornications, murders,

22 Thefts, covetousness, wickedness, deceit, lasciviousness, an evil eye, blasphemy, pride, foolishness;

23 All these evil things come from within, and defile the man."

24 And from there He arose, and went into the borders of Tyre and Sidon, and entered into a house, and would have no man know it; but He could not be hidden.

25 For a certain woman, whose young daughter had an unclean spirit, heard of Him, and came and fell at His feet.

26 The woman was a Greek, a Syrophenician by nation; and she besought Him that He would cast forth the devil out of her daughter.

27 But Yahwah said unto her, "Let the children first be filled, for it is not right to take the children's bread, and to cast it unto the dogs."

28 And she answered and said unto Him, "Yes, Lord (Adonai); yet the dogs under the table eat of the children's crumbs."

29 And He said unto her, "For this saying go your way; the devil is gone out of your daughter."

30 And when she had come to her house, she found the devil gone out, and her daughter laid upon the bed.

31 And again, departing from the coasts of Tyre and Sidon, He came unto the sea of Galilee, through the midst of the coasts of Decapolis.

32 And they bring unto Him one that was deaf, and had an impediment in his speech; and they beseech Him to put His hand upon him.

33 And He took him aside from the multitude, and put His fingers into his ears, and He spit, and touched his tongue;

34 And looking up to heaven, He sighed, and saith unto him, "Ephphatha" that is: "Be opened."

35 And straightway his ears were opened, and the string of his tongue was loosed, and he spake plain.

36 And He warned them that they should tell no man; but the more He warned them, so much the more a great deal they published it;

37 And were beyond measure astonished, saying, "He hath done all things well; He maketh both the deaf to hear, and the dumb to speak."

8 In those days the multitude being very great, and having nothing to eat, Yahwah called His disciples unto Him, and saith unto them,

2 "I have compassion on the multitude, because they have now been with Me three days, and have nothing to eat.

3 And if I send them away fasting to their own houses, they will faint by the way, for divers of them came from far."

4 And His disciples answered Him, "From where can a man satisfy these men with bread here in the wilderness?"

5 And He asked them, "How many loaves have you?" And they said, "Seven."

6 And He commanded the people to sit down on the ground; and He took the seven loaves, and gave thanks, and broke, and gave to His disciples to set before them; and they did set

them before the people.

7 And they had a few small fishes; and He blessed, and commanded to set them also before them.

8 So they did eat, and were filled; and they took up of the fragments that was left seven baskets.

9 And they that had eaten were about four thousand; and He sent them away.

10 And straightway He entered into a ship with His disciples, and came into the parts of Dalmanutha.

11 And the Pharisees came forth, and began to question with Him, seeking of Him a sign from heaven, testing Him.

12 And He sighed deeply in His spirit, and saith, "Why doth this generation seek after a sign? Verily I say unto you, there shall no sign be given unto this generation."

13 And He left them, and entering into the ship again departed to the other side.

14 Now the disciples had forgotten to take bread, neither had they in the ship with them more than one loaf.

15 And He warned them, saying, "Take heed, beware of the leaven of the Pharisees, and of the leaven of Herod."

16 And they reasoned among themselves, saying, "It is because we have no bread."

17 And when Yahwah knew it, He saith unto them, "Why reason you, because you have no bread? Perceive you not yet, neither understand? Have you your heart yet hardened?

18 Having eyes, see you not? And having ears, hear you not? And do you not remember?

19 When I broke the five loaves among five thousand, how many baskets full of fragments took you up?" They say unto Him, "Twelve."

20 "And when the seven among four thousand, how many baskets full of fragments took you up?" And they said, "Seven."

21 And He said unto them, "How is it that you do not understand?"

22 And He cometh to Bethsaida; and they bring a blind man unto Him, and besought Him to touch him.

23 And He took the blind man by the hand, and led him out of the town; and when He had spit on his eyes, and put His hands upon him, He asked him if he saw anything.

24 And he looked up, and said, "I see men as trees, walking."

25 After that He put His hands again upon his eyes, and made him look up; and he was restored, and saw every man clearly.

26 And He sent him away to his house, saying, "Neither go into the town, nor tell it to any in the town."

27 And Yahwah went out, and His disciples, into the towns of Caesarea Philippi; and on the way He asked His disciples, saying unto them, "Whom do men say that I am?"

28 And they answered, "John the Baptist (Yochanan haMatvil);" but some say, "Elijah (Eliyahu);" and others, "One of the prophets."

29 And He saith unto them, "But whom say you that I am?" And Peter (Kefa) answereth and saith unto Him, "You are the Messiah (haMashiach)."

30 And He warned them that they should tell no man of Him.

31 And He began to teach them, that the Son of man (haMashiach) must suffer many things, and be rejected of the elders, and of the chief priests (kohanim), and scribes, and be killed, and after three days rise again.

32 And He spake that saying openly. And Peter (Kefa) took Him, and began to rebuke Him.

33 But when He had turned about and looked on His disciples, He rebuked Peter (Kefa), saying, "Get you behind Me, Satan; for you savourest not the things that be of God (Elohim), but the things that be of men."

34 And when He had called the people unto Him with His disciples also, He said unto them, "Whosoever will come after Me, let him deny himself, and take up his stake, and follow Me.

35 For whosoever will save his life shall lose it; but whosoever shall lose his life for My sake and the gospel (good news)'s, the same shall save it.

36 For what shall it profit a man, if he shall gain the whole world, and lose his own soul?

37 Or what shall a man give in exchange for his soul?

38 Whosoever therefore shall be ashamed of Me and of My words in this adulterous and sinful generation; of him also shall the Son of man (haMashiach) be ashamed, when He cometh in the glory of His Father with the holy angels."

9 And He said unto them, "Verily I say unto you, that there be some of them that stand here, who shall not taste of death, till they have seen the kingdom of God (Elohim, יהוה

(YHWH)) come with power."

2 And after six days Yahwah taketh with Him Peter (Kefa), and James (Yaaqov), and John (Yochanan), and leadeth them up into a high mountain apart by themselves; and He was transfigured before them.

3 And His raiment became shining, exceeding white as snow; so as no fuller on earth can whiten them.

4 And there appeared unto them Elijah (Eliyahu) with Moses (Mosheh); and they were talking with Yahwah.

5 And Peter (Kefa) answered and said to Yahwah, "Teacher (Rabbi), it is good for us to be here; and let us make three tabernacles; one for You, and one for Moses (Mosheh), and one for Elijah (Eliyahu)."

6 For he wist not what to say; for they were sore afraid.

7 And there was a cloud that overshadowed them; and a voice came out of the cloud, saying, "This is My beloved [B47]Son (Humanity); hear Him!"

8 And suddenly, when they had looked round about, they saw no man any more, except Yahwah only with themselves.

9 And as they came down from the mountain, He warned them that they should tell no man what things they had seen, till the Son of man (haMashiach) were risen from the dead.

10 And they kept that saying with themselves, questioning one with another what the rising from the dead meant.

11 And they asked Him, saying, "Why say the scribes that Elijah (Eliyahu) must first come?"

12 And He answered and told them, "Elijah (Eliyahu) verily cometh first, and restoreth all things; and how it is written of the Son of man (haMashiach), that He must suffer many things, and be set at nought.

13 But I say unto you, that Elijah (Eliyahu) has indeed come, and they have done unto him whatsoever they desired, as it is written of him."

14 And when He came to His disciples, He saw a great multitude about them, and the scribes questioning with them.

15 And straightway all the people, when they beheld Him, were greatly amazed, and running to Him saluted Him.

16 And He asked the scribes, "What question you with them?"

17 And one of the multitudes answered and said, "Teacher (Rabbi), I have brought unto You my son, who hath a dumb spirit;

18 And wheresoever he taketh him, he teareth him; and he foameth, and gnasheth with his teeth, and pineth away; and I spake to your disciples that they should cast him out; and they could not."

19 He answereth him, and saith, "O faithless generation, how long shall I be with you? How long shall I bear with you? Bring him unto Me."

20 And they brought him unto Him; and when He saw him, straightway the spirit tare him; and he fell on the ground, and wallowed foaming.

21 And He asked his father, "How long is it ago since this came unto him?" And he said, "From childhood."

22 And ofttimes it hath cast him into the fire, and into the waters, to destroy him; but if you canst do any thing, have compassion on us, and help us."

23 Yahwah said unto him, "If you canst believe, all things are possible to him that believeth."

24 And straightway the father of the child cried out, and said with tears, "Lord (Adonai), I believe; help You mine unbelief.

25 When Yahwah saw that the people came running together, He rebuked the foul spirit, saying unto him, "You dumb and deaf spirit, I command you, come out of him, and enter no more into him."

26 And the spirit cried, and rent him sore, and came out of him; and he was as one dead; insomuch that many said, "He is dead."

27 But Yahwah took him by the hand, and lifted him up; and he arose.

28 And when He had come into the house, His disciples asked Him privately, "Why could not we cast him out?"

29 And He said unto them, "This kind can come forth by nothing, but by prayer and fasting."

30 And they departed from there, and passed through Galilee; and He did not want that any man should know it.

31 For He taught His disciples, and said unto them, "The Son of man (haMashiach) is delivered into the hands of men, and they shall kill Him; and after that He is killed, He shall rise the third day."

32 But they understood not that saying, and were afraid to ask Him.

33 And He came to Capernaum; and being in the house He asked them, "What was it that you disputed among yourselves on the way?"

34 But they held their peace, for on the way they had disputed among themselves, who should be the greatest.

35 And He sat down, and called the twelve, and saith unto them, "If any man desire to be first, the same shall be last of all, and servant of all."

36 And He took a child, and set him in the midst of them; and when he had taken him in His arms, He said unto them,

37 "Whosoever shall receive one of such children in My name, receiveth Me; and whosoever shall receive Me, receiveth not Me but Him who sent Me."

38 And John (Yochanan) answered Him, saying, "Teacher (Rabbi), we saw one casting out devils in Your name, and he followeth not us; and we forbad him, because he followeth not us."

39 But Yahwah said, "Forbid him not, for there is no man who shall do a miracle in My name, that can lightly speak evil of Me.

40 For he that is not against us is on our side.

41 For whosoever shall give you a cup of water to drink in My name, because you belong to the Messiah (haMashiach), verily I say unto you, he shall not lose his reward.

42 And whosoever shall cause one of these little ones that believe in Me to stumble, it is better for him that a millstone was hanged about his neck, and he were cast into the sea.

43 And if your hand makes you stumble, cut it off; it is better for you to enter into life maimed, than having two hands to go into hell (gehenna), into the fire that never shall be quenched;

44 Where their worm dieth not, and the fire is not quenched.

45 And if your foot causes you to stumble, cut it off: it is better for you to enter halt into life, than having two feet to be cast into hell (gehenna), into the fire that never shall be quenched;

46 Where their worm dieth not, and the fire is not quenched.

47 And if your eye causes you to stumble, pluck it out; it is better for you to enter into the kingdom of God (Elohim, יהוה (YHWH)) with one eye, than having two eyes to be cast into hell (gehenna) fire;

48 Where their worm dieth not, and the fire is not quenched.

49 For every one shall be salted with fire, and every sacrifice shall be salted with salt.

50 Salt is good; but if the salt has lost its saltness, wherewith will you season it? Have salt in yourselves, and have peace one with another."

10 And He arose from there and cometh into the coasts of Judah (Yehudah) by the farther side of Jordan (Yarden); and the people resort unto Him again; and, as He was accustomed, He taught them again.

2 And the Pharisees came to Him, and asked Him, "Is it lawful for a man to put away his wife?" testing Him.

3 And He answered and said unto them, "What did Moses (Mosheh) command you?"

4 And they said, "Moses (Mosheh) permitted to write a bill of divorcement, and to put her away." – *Deu.24:1,3*

5 And Yahwah answered and said unto them, "For the hardness of your heart he wrote you this precept.

6 But from the beginning of the creation God (Elohim) made them male and female. – *Gen. 1:27, 5:2*

7 For this cause shall a man leave his father and mother, and cleave to his wife;

8 And they twain shall be one flesh; so then they are no more twain, but one flesh. – *Gen. 2:24*

9 What therefore God (Elohim) hath joined together, let not man separate.

10 And in the house His disciples asked Him again of the same matter.

11 And He saith unto them, "Whosoever shall put away his wife, and marry another, committeth adultery against her.

12 And if a woman shall put away her husband, and be married to another, she committeth adultery."

13 And they brought young children to Him, that He should touch them; and His disciples rebuked those that brought them.

14 But when Yahwah saw it, He was much displeased, and said unto them, "Let the little children to come unto Me, and forbid them not, for of such is the kingdom of God (Elohim, יהוה (YHWH)).

15 Verily I say unto you, whosoever shall not receive the kingdom of God (Elohim, יהוה (YHWH)) as a little child, he shall not enter therein."

16 And He took them up in His arms, put His hands upon them, and blessed them.

17 And when He was gone forth into the way, there came one running, and kneeled to Him, and asked him, "Good Teacher (Rabbi), what shall I do that I may inherit eternal life?"

18 And Yahwah said unto him, "Why callest you Me good? There is none good but one, that is, God (Elohim, יהוה (YHWH)).

19 You knowest the commandments, 'Do not commit adultery, do not kill, do not steal, do not bear false witness, defraud not, honour your father and mother'.

20 And he answered and said unto Him, "Teacher (Rabbi), all these have I observed from my youth."

21 Then Yahwah beholding him loved him, and said unto him, "One thing you lackest: go your way, sell whatsoever you have, and give to the poor, and you shalt have treasure in heaven; and come, follow Me."

22 And he was sad at that saying, and went away grieved; for he had great possessions.

23 And Yahwah looked round about, and saith unto His disciples, "How hardly shall they that have riches enter into the kingdom of God (Elohim, יהוה (YHWH))!"

24 And the disciples were astonished at His words. But Yahwah answereth again, and saith unto them, "Children, how hard is it for them that trust in riches to enter into the kingdom of God (Elohim, יהוה (YHWH))!

25 It is easier for a camel to go through the eye of a needle, than for a rich man to enter into the kingdom of God (Elohim, יהוה (YHWH))."

26 And they were astonished out of measure, saying among themselves, "Who then can be saved?"

27 And Yahwah looking upon them saith, "With men it is impossible, but not with God (Elohim); for with God (Elohim) all things are possible."

28 Then Peter (Kefa) began to say unto Him, "Behold, we have left all, and have followed You."

29 And Yahwah answered and said, "Verily I say unto you, there is no man that hath left house, or brethren, or sisters, or father, or mother, or wife, or children, or lands, for My sake, and the gospel (good news)'s,

30 But he shall receive a hundredfold now in this time, houses, and brethren, and sisters, and mothers, and children, and lands, with persecutions; and in the world to come, eternal life.

31 But many that are first shall be last; and the last first."

32 And they were in the way going up to Jerusalem (Yerushalayim); and Yahwah went before them; and they were amazed; and as they followed, they were afraid. And He took again the twelve, and began to tell them what things should happen unto Him,

33 Saying, "Behold, we go up to Jerusalem (Yerushalayim); and the Son of man (haMashiach) shall be delivered unto the chief priests (kohanim), and unto the scribes; and they shall condemn Him to death, and shall deliver Him to the Gentiles (Goyim).

34 And they shall mock Him, and shall scourge Him, and shall spit upon Him, and shall kill Him; and the third day He shall rise again."

35 And James (Yaaqov) and John (Yochanan), the sons of Zebedee (Zavdai), come unto Him, saying, "Teacher (Rabbi), we wish that You shouldest do for us whatsoever we shall desire."

36 And He said unto them, "What wish you that I should do for you?"

37 They said unto Him, "Grant unto us that we may sit, one on Your right hand, and the other on Your left hand, in Your glory."

38 But Yahwah said unto them, "You know not what you ask; can you drink of the cup that I drink of? And be baptized with the baptism that I am baptized with?"

39 And they said unto Him, "We can." And Yahwah said unto them, "You shall indeed drink of the cup that I drink of; and with the baptism that I am baptized withal shall you be baptized;

40 But to sit on My right hand and on My left hand is not Mine to give; but it shall be given to them for whom it is prepared."

41 And when the ten heard it, they began to be much displeased with James (Yaaqov) and John (Yochanan).

42 But Yahwah called them to Him, and saith unto them, "You know that they who are accounted to rule over the Gentiles (Goyim) exercise lordship over them; and their great ones exercise authority upon them.

43 But so shall it not be among you; but whosoever will be great among you, shall be

your servant;

44 And whosoever of you will be the chiefest, shall be slave of all.

45 For even the Son of man (haMashiach) came not to be served unto, but to serve, and to give His life a ransom for many."

46 And they came to Yericho; and as He went out of Yericho with His disciples and a great number of people, blind Bartimaeus, the son of Timaeus, sat by the highway side begging.

47 And when He heard that it was Yahwah of Nazareth, He began to cry out, and say, "Yahwah, You son (descendant) of Dawid, have mercy on me."

48 And many warned him that he should hold his peace; but he cried the more a great deal, "You son (descendant) of Dawid, have mercy on me."

49 And Yahwah stood still, and commanded him to be called. And they call the blind man, saying unto him, "Be of good comfort, rise; He calleth you."

50 And he, casting away his garment, rose, and came to Yahwah.

51 And Yahwah answered and said unto him, "What wilt you that I should do unto you?" The blind man said unto him, "Lord (Adonai), that I might receive my sight."

52 And Yahwah said unto him, "Go your way; your faith hath made you whole." And immediately he received his sight, and followed Yahwah on the way.

11 And when they came near to Jerusalem (Yerushalayim), unto Bethphage and Bethany, at the Mount of Olives, He sendeth forth two of His disciples,

2 And saith unto them, "Go your way into the village opposite you; and as soon as you have entered into it, you shall find a colt tied, whereon never man sat; loose him, and bring him.

3 And if any man says unto you, 'Why do you this?' Say you that the Lord (Adonai) hath need of him; and straightway he will send him hither."

4 And they went their way, and found the colt tied by the door outside in a place where two ways met; and they loose him.

5 And certain of them that stood there said unto them, "What do you, loosing the colt?"

6 And they said unto them even as Yahwah had commanded; and they let them go.

7 And they brought the colt to Yahwah, and cast their garments on Him; and He sat upon him.

8 And many spread their garments on the road; and others cut down branches off the trees, and strawed them in the way.

9 And they that went before, and they that followed, cried, saying, "Hosanna! 'Blessed is He that cometh in the name of יהוה (YHWH (Yahwah))!' – *Psa.118:26, Mat.21:9*

10 Blessed be the kingdom of our forefather Dawid, that cometh in the name of יהוה (YHWH (Yahwah)); Hosanna in the highest!"

11 And Yahwah entered into Jerusalem (Yerushalayim), and into the temple; and when He had looked round about upon all things, and now the eventide was come, He went out unto Bethany with the twelve.

12 And on the next day, when they had come from Bethany, He was hungry.

13 And seeing a fig tree afar off having leaves, He came, if haply He might find any thing thereon; and when He came to it, He found nothing but leaves; for the time of figs was not yet.

14 And Yahwah answered and said unto it, "No man eat fruit of you hereafter for ever." And His disciples heard it.

15 And they come to Jerusalem (Yerushalayim); and Yahwah went into the temple, and began to cast out them that sold and bought in the temple, and overthrew the tables of the moneychangers, and the seats of them that sold doves;

16 And would not allow that any man should carry any vessel through the temple.

17 And He taught, saying unto them, "Is it not written, 'My house shall be called of all nations the house of prayer? But you have made it a den of thieves. – *Isa.56:7; Jer.7:11, Mat.21:13*

18 And the scribes and chief priests (kohanim) heard it, and sought how they might destroy Him; for they feared Him, because all the people was astonished at His doctrine (teaching).

19 And when even had come, He went out of the city.

20 And in the morning, as they passed by, they saw the fig tree dried up from the roots.

21 And [A72]Peter (Kefa) calling to remembrance saith unto Him, "Teacher (Rabbi), behold, the fig tree which You cursedst has withered away."

22 And Yahwah answering saith unto them, "Have faith in God (Elohim, יהוה (YHWH)).

23 For verily I say unto you, that whosoever shall say unto this mountain, 'Be you removed, and be you cast into the sea;' and shall not doubt in his heart, but shall believe that those things which he saith shall come to pass; he shall have whatsoever he saith.

24 Therefore I say unto you, what things soever you desire, when you pray, believe that you receive them, and you shall have them.

25 And when you stand praying, forgive, if you have anything against any; that your Father also who is in heaven may forgive you your trespasses.

26 But if you do not forgive, neither will your Father who is in heaven forgive your trespasses."

27 And they come again to Jerusalem (Yerushalayim); and as He was walking in the temple, there come to Him the chief priests (kohanim), and the scribes, and the elders,

28 And say unto Him, "By what authority doest You these things? And who gave you this authority to do these things?"

29 And Yahwah answered and said unto them, "I will also ask of you one question, and answer Me, and I will tell you by what authority I do these things.

30 The baptism of John (Yochanan), was it from heaven, or of men? Answer Me!"

31 And they reasoned with themselves, saying, "If we shall say, 'From heaven;' He will say, 'Why then did you not believe Him?'

32 But if we shall say, 'Of men;'" they feared the people; for all men counted John (Yochanan), that he was a prophet indeed.

33 And they answered and said unto Yahwah, "We cannot tell." And Yahwah answering saith unto them, "Neither do I tell you by what authority I do these things."

12 And He began to speak unto them by parables: "A certain man planted a vineyard, and set a hedge about it, and digged a place for the winefat, and built a tower, and let it out to husbandmen, and went into a far country.

2 And at the season he sent to the husbandmen a servant, that he might receive from the husbandmen of the fruit of the vineyard.

3 And they caught him, and beat him, and sent him away empty.

4 And again he sent unto them another servant; and at him they cast stones, and wounded him in the head, and sent him away shamefully handled.

5 And again he sent another; and him they killed, and many others; beating some, and killing some.

6 Having yet therefore one son, his wellbeloved, he sent him also last unto them, saying, 'They will reverence my son.'

7 But those husbandmen said among themselves, 'This is the heir; come, let us kill him, and the inheritance shall be ours.'

8 And they took him, and killed him, and cast him out of the vineyard.

9 What shall therefore the owner of the vineyard do? He will come and destroy the husbandmen, and will give the vineyard unto others.

10 And have you not read this scripture: 'The stone which the builders rejected is become the head of the corner. – Psa. 118:22

11 This was יהוה's doing, and it is marvellous in our eyes?'"

12 And they sought to lay hold on Him, but feared the people; for they knew that He had spoken the parable against them; and they left Him, and went their way.

13 And they send unto Him certain of the Pharisees and of the Herodians, to catch Him in His words.

14 And when they had come, they say unto Him, "Teacher (Rabbi), we know that You are true, and carest for no man, for You regardest not the person of men, but teachest the way of God (Elohim) in truth. Is it lawful to give tribute (poll-tax) to Caesar, or not?

15 Shall we give, or shall we not give?" But He, knowing their hypocrisy, said unto them, "Why test you Me? Bring Me a penny, that I may see it."

16 And they brought it. And He saith unto them, "Whose is this image and superscription?" And they said unto Him, "Caesar's."

17 And Yahwah answering said unto them, "Render to Caesar the things that are Caesar's, and to God (Elohim) the things that are God (Elohim)'s. And they marvelled at Him.

18 Then come unto Him the Sadducees, who say there is no resurrection; and they asked Him, saying,

19 "Teacher (Rabbi), Moses (Mosheh) wrote unto us, 'If a man's brother dies, and leave his wife behind him, and leave no children, that his brother should take his wife, and raise up seed

unto his brother.'

20 Now there were seven brethren; and the first took a wife, and dying left no seed.

21 And the second took her, and died, neither left he any seed; and the third likewise.

22 And the seven had her, and left no seed: last of all the woman died also.

23 In the resurrection therefore, when they shall rise, whose wife shall she be of them? For the seven had her as wife."

24 And Yahwah answering said unto them, "Do you not therefore err, because you know not the scriptures, neither the power of God (Elohim)?

25 For when they shall rise from the dead, they neither marry, nor are given in marriage; but are as the angels who are in heaven.

26 And as touching the dead, that they rise; have you not read in the book of Moses (Mosheh), how in the bush God (Elohim) spake unto him, saying, 'I am the God (Elohim) of Avraham, and the God (Elohim) of Isaac (Yitschaq), and the God (Elohim) of Jacob (Yaaqov)'? – *Exo.3:6, Mat.22:32*

27 He is not the God (Elohim) of the dead, but the God (Elohim) of the living; you therefore do greatly err."

28 And one of the scribes came, and having heard them reasoning together, and perceiving that He had answered them well, asked Him, "Which is the first commandment of all?"

29 And Yahwah answered him, "The first of all the commandments is, 'Hear, O Yisrael: יהוה our God (YHWH Eloheinu) יהוה is one (YHWH echad); – *Deu.6:4*

30 And you shalt love יהוה your God (YHWH Eloheikha) with all your heart, and with all your soul, and with all your mind, and with all your strength; This is the first commandment. – *Deu.6:5, Mat. 22:37*

31 And the second is like, namely this: 'You shalt love your neighbour as yourself.' There is none other commandment greater than these." – *Lev.19:18, Mat.22:39*

32 And the scribe said unto Him, "Well, Teacher (Rabbi), You have said the truth; for there is one God (Elohim); and there is none other but He;

33 And to love Him with all the heart, and with all the understanding, and with all the soul, and with all the strength, and to love his neighbour as himself, is more than all whole burnt offerings and sacrifices."

34 And when Yahwah saw that he answered discreetly, He said unto him, "You are not far from the kingdom of God (Elohim, יהוה (YHWH))." And no man after that dared ask Him any question.

35 And Yahwah answered and said, while He taught in the temple, "How say the scribes that the Messiah (haMashiach) is the son of Dawid?

36 For Dawid himself said by the Holy Spirit: 'יהוה said to my Lord (Adonai), "Sit You on My right hand, till I make Your enemies Your footstool."' – *Psa.110:1, Mat.22:44*

37 Dawid therefore himself calleth Him 'my Lord (Adonai)'; and how is He then his son?" And the common people heard Him gladly.

38 And He said unto them in His doctrine (teaching), "Beware of the scribes, who love to go in long robes, and love salutations in the marketplaces,

39 And the chief seats in the synagogues, and the uppermost rooms at feasts;

40 Who devour widows' houses, and for a pretence make long prayers; these shall receive greater damnation."

41 And Yahwah sat opposite the treasury, and beheld how the people cast money into the treasury; and many that were rich cast in much.

42 And there came a certain poor widow, and she threw in two mites, which make a farthing.

43 And He called unto Him His disciples, and saith unto them, "Verily I say unto you, that this poor widow hath cast more in, than all they who have cast into the treasury;

44 For all they did cast in of their abundance; but she of her want did cast in all that she had, even all her living."

13 And as He went out of the temple, one of His disciples saith unto Him, "Teacher (Rabbi), see what manner of stones and what buildings are here!"

2 And Yahwah answering said unto him, "Seest you these great buildings? There shall not be left one stone upon another, that shall not be thrown down."

3 And as He sat upon the Mount of Olives opposite the temple, Peter (Kefa) and James (Yaaqov) and John (Yochanan) and Andrew asked Him privately,

4 "Tell us, when shall these things be? And what shall be the sign when all these things shall be fulfilled?"

5 And Yahwah answering them began to say, "Take heed lest any man deceive you;

6 For many shall come in My name (reputation), saying, 'I am the anointed (hamashiach);' and shall deceive many.

7 And when you shall hear of wars and rumours of wars, be you not troubled; for such things must needs be; but the end shall not be yet.

8 For nation shall rise against nation, and kingdom against kingdom. And there shall be earthquakes in divers places, and there shall be famines and troubles. These are the beginnings of sorrows.

9 But take heed to yourselves, for they shall deliver you up to councils (Sanhedrins); and in the synagogues you shall be beaten; and you shall be brought before rulers and kings for My sake, for a testimony against them.

10 And the gospel (good news) must first be published among all nations.

11 But when they shall lead you, and deliver you up, take no thought beforehand what you shall speak, neither do you premeditate, but whatsoever shall be given you in that hour, that speak you; for it is not you that speak, but the Holy Spirit (Ruach haQodesh).

12 Now the brother shall betray the brother to death, and the father the son; and children shall rise up against their parents, and shall cause them to be put to death.

13 And you shall be hated of all men for My name's sake; but he that shall endure unto the end, the same shall be saved.

14 But when you shall see the abomination of desolation, spoken of by Daniel the prophet, standing where it ought not, (let him that readeth understand,) then let them that be in Judah (Yehudah) flee to the mountains. – *Dan.9:27, 11:31, 12:11*

15 And let him that is on the housetop not go down into the house, neither enter therein, to take any thing out of his house.

16 And let him that is in the field not turn back again for to take up his garment.

17 But woe to them that are with child, and to them that give suck in those days!

18 And pray you that your flight be not in the winter.

19 For in those days shall be affliction, such as was not from the beginning of the creation which God (Elohim) created unto this time, neither shall be.

20 And except that יהוה had shortened those days, no flesh should be saved; but for the elect's sake, whom He hath chosen, He hath shortened the days.

21 And then if any man shall say to you, 'Behold, here is the Messiah (haMashiach); or, 'Behold, He is there;' believe him not;

22 For false Messiahs (Mashiachi) and false prophets shall rise, and shall shew signs and wonders, to seduce, if it was possible, even the elect.

23 But take you heed; behold, I have foretold you all things.

24 But in those days, after that tribulation, the sun shall be darkened, and the moon shall not give her light,

25 And the stars of heaven shall fall, and the powers that are in heaven shall be shaken. – *Eze.32:7, Yoel 2:31*

26 And then shall they see the Son of man (haMashiach) coming in the clouds with great power and glory. – *Dan.7:13-14*

27 And then shall He send His angels, and shall gather together His elect from the four winds, from the uttermost part of the earth to the uttermost part of heaven.

28 Now learn a parable of the fig tree: When her branch is yet tender, and putteth forth leaves, you know that summer is near.

29 So you in like manner, when you shall see these things come to pass, know that it is near, even at the doors.

30 Verily I say unto you, that this generation shall not pass, till all these things be done.

31 Heaven and earth shall pass away, but My words shall not pass away.

32 But of that day and that hour knoweth no man, no, not the angels who are in heaven, neither the [B47]Son (Humanity), but the Father.

33 Take you heed, watch and pray; for you know not when the time is.

34 For the Son of man (haMashiach) is as a man taking a far journey, who left his house, and gave authority to his servants, and to every man his work, and commanded the porter to watch.

35 Watch you therefore, for you know not when the master of the house cometh, at even, or at midnight, or at the cockcrowing, or in the morning;

36 Lest coming suddenly he find you sleeping.

37 And what I say unto you I say unto all: Watch!"

14 After two days was the Passover (Pesach), and Feast of Unleavened Bread (Chag haMatzot); and the chief priests and the scribes sought how they might take Him by craft, and put Him to death.

2 But they said, "Not on the feast day, lest there be an uproar of the people."

3 And being in Bethany in the house of Shimon the leper, as He sat at meat, there came a woman having an alabaster box of ointment of spikenard very precious; and she brake the box, and poured it on His head.

4 And there were some that had indignation within themselves, and said, "Why was this waste of the ointment made?

5 For it might have been sold for more than three hundred pence, and have been given to the poor." And they murmured against her.

6 And Yahwah said, "Let her alone; why trouble you her? She hath wrought a good work on Me.

7 For you have the poor with you always, and whensoever you will you may do them good; but Me you have not always.

8 She hath done what she could; she has come beforehand to anoint My body to the burying.

9 Verily I say unto you, wheresoever this gospel (good news) shall be preached throughout the whole world, this also that she hath done shall be spoken of for a memorial of her."

10 And Judas Iscariot (Yehudah Ishkeriot), one of the twelve, went unto the chief priests (kohanim), to betray Him unto them.

11 And when they heard it, they were glad, and promised to give him money. And he sought how he might conveniently betray Him.

12 And the first day of Unleavened Bread, when they killed the Passover lamb (Pesach), His disciples said unto Him, "Where wilt You that we go and prepare that You mayest eat the Passover (Pesach)?"

13 And He sendeth forth two of His disciples, and saith unto them, "Go you into the city, and there shall meet you a man bearing a pitcher of water; follow him.

14 And wheresoever he shall go in, say you to the goodman of the house, "The Teacher (Rabbi) saith, 'Where is the guestchamber, where I shall eat the Passover (Pesach) with My disciples'?

15 And he will shew you a large upper room furnished and prepared; there make ready for us."

16 And His disciples went forth, and came into the city, and found as He had said unto them; and they made ready the Passover (Pesach).

17 And in the evening He cometh with the twelve.

18 And as they sat and did eat, Yahwah said, "Verily I say unto you, one of you who eateth with Me shall betray Me."

19 And they began to be sorrowful, and to say unto Him one by one, "Is it I?" And another said, "Is it I?"

20 And He answered and said unto them, "It is one of the twelve, that dippeth with Me in the dish.

21 The Son of man (haMashiach) indeed goeth, as it is written of Him; but woe to that man by whom the Son of man (haMashiach) is betrayed! Good was it for that man if he had never been born."

22 And as they did eat, Yahwah took bread, and blessed, and broke it, and gave to them, and said, "Take, eat; this is My body."

23 And He took the cup, and when He had given thanks, He gave it to them; and they all drank of it.

24 And He said unto them, "[B58]This is My blood, the blood of the New Covenant (dam haBerit haChadashah), which is shed for many.

25 Verily I say unto you, I will drink no more of the fruit of the vine, until that day that I drink it new in the kingdom of God (Elohim, יהוה (YHWH))."

26 And when they had sung a hymn, they went out into the Mount of Olives.

27 And Yahwah saith unto them, "All you shall be stumbled because of Me this night; for it is written: 'I will smite the shepherd, and the sheep shall be scattered.' – *Zec.13:7, Mat.26:31*

28 But after that I have risen, I will go before you into Galilee."

29 But Peter (Kefa) said unto Him, "Although all shall be offended, yet I will not."

30 And Yahwah saith unto Him, "Verily I say unto you, that this day, even in this night, before the cock crow twice, you shalt deny Me thrice."

31 But He spake the more vehemently, "If I should die with You, I will not deny You in any wise." Likewise also said they all.

32 And they came to a place which was named

Gethsemane; and He saith to His disciples, "Sit you here, while I shall pray."

33 And He taketh with him Peter (Kefa) and James (Yaaqov) and John (Yochanan), and began to be sore amazed, and to be very heavy;

34 And saith unto them, "My soul is exceeding sorrowful unto death; tarry you here, and watch."

35 And He went forward a little, and fell on the ground, and prayed that, if it was possible, the hour might pass from Him.

36 And He said, "Abba, Father, all things are possible unto You; take away this cup from Me; nevertheless not what I will, but what You wilt."

37 And He cometh, and findeth them sleeping, and saith unto Peter (Kefa), "Shimon, sleepest you? Couldest not you watch one hour?

38 Watch you and pray, lest you enter into temptation. The spirit truly is willing, but the flesh is weak."

39 And again He went away, and prayed, and spake the same words.

40 And when He returned, He found them asleep again, (for their eyes were heavy,) neither wist they what to answer Him.

41 And He cometh the third time, and saith unto them, "Sleep on now, and take your rest; it is enough, the hour has come; behold, the Son of man (haMashiach) is betrayed into the hands of sinners.

42 Rise up, let us go; behold, he that betrayeth Me is at hand."

43 And immediately, while He yet spake, cometh Judas (Yehudah), one of the twelve, and with him a great multitude with swords and staves, from the chief priests (kohanim) and the scribes and the elders.

44 And he that betrayed Him had given them a token, saying, "Whomsoever I shall kiss, that same is He; take Him, and lead Him away safely."

45 And as soon as he had come, he goeth straightway to Him, and saith, "Teacher (Rabbi), Teacher (Rabbi)!" and kissed Him.

46 And they laid their hands on Him, and took Him.

47 And one of them that stood by drew a sword, and smote a servant of the high priest (kohen hagadol), and cut off his ear.

48 And Yahwah answered and said unto them, "Are you come out, as against a thief, with swords and with staves to take Me?

49 I was daily with you in the temple teaching, and you took Me not; but the Scriptures must be fulfilled."

50 And they all forsook Him, and fled.

51 And there followed Him a certain young man, having a linen cloth cast about his naked body; and some men laid hold on him;

52 But he left the linen cloth, and fled from them naked.

53 And they led Yahwah away to the high priest (kohen hagadol); and with Him were assembled all the chief priests (kohanim) and the elders and the scribes.

54 And Peter (Kefa) followed Him afar off, even into the palace of the high priest (kohen hagadol); and he sat with the servants, and warmed himself at the fire.

55 And the chief priests (kohanim) and all the council (Sanhedrin) sought for witness against Yahwah to put Him to death; and found none.

56 For many bare false witness against Him, but their witness agreed not together.

57 And there arose certain, and bare false witness against Him, saying,

58 "We heard Him say, 'I will destroy this temple that is made with hands, and within three days I will build another made without hands.'"

59 But neither so did their witness agree together.

60 And the high priest (kohen hagadol) stood up in the midst, and asked Yahwah, saying, "Answerest You nothing? What is it which these witness against You?"

61 But He held His peace, and answered nothing. Again the high priest (kohen hagadol) asked Him, and said unto Him, "Art You the Messiah (haMashiach), the [B47]Son of the Blessed?

62 And Yahwah said, "I am; and you shall see the Son of man (haMashiach) sitting on the right hand of power, and coming in the clouds of heaven." – Dan.7:13, Psa.110:1

63 Then the high priest (kohen hagadol) rent his clothes, and saith, "What need we any further witnesses?

64 You have heard the blasphemy; what think you?" And they all condemned Him to be guilty of death.

65 And some began to spit on Him, and to cover His face, and to buffet Him, and to say unto

Him, "Prophesy!" And the servants did strike Him with the palms of their hands.

66 And as Peter (Kefa) was beneath in the palace, there cometh one of the maids of the high priest (kohen hagadol).

67 And when she saw Peter (Kefa) warming himself, she looked upon him, and said, "And you also wast with Yahwah of Nazareth."

68 But he denied, saying, "I know not, neither understand I what you sayest." And he went out into the porch; and the cock crew.

69 And a maid saw him again, and began to say to them that stood by, "This is one of them."

70 And he denied it again. And a little after, they that stood by said again to Peter (Kefa), "Surely you are one of them; for you are a Galilaean, and your speech agreeth thereto."

71 But he began to curse and to swear, saying, "I know not this man of whom you speak."

72 And the second time the cock crew. And Peter (Kefa) called to mind the word that Yahwah said unto him, "Before the cock crow twice, you shalt deny Me thrice." And when he thought thereon, he wept.

15 And straightway in the morning the chief priests (kohanim) held a consultation with the elders and scribes and the whole council (Sanhedrin), and bound Yahwah, and carried Him away, and delivered Him to Pilate.

2 And Pilate asked Him, "Art You the King of the Jews (Yehudim)?" And He answering said unto him, "You sayest it."

3 And the chief priests (kohanim) accused Him of many things, but He answered nothing.

4 And Pilate asked Him again, saying, "Answerest you nothing? Behold how many things they witness against You."

5 But Yahwah yet answered nothing; so that Pilate marvelled.

6 Now at that feast he released unto them one prisoner, whomsoever they desired.

7 And there was one named Barabbas, who lay bound with them that had made insurrection with him, who had committed murder in the insurrection.

8 And the multitude crying aloud began to desire him to do as he had ever done unto them.

9 But Pilate answered them, saying, "Will you that I release unto you the King of the Jews (Yehudim)?"

10 For he knew that the chief priests (kohanim) had delivered Him for envy.

11 But the chief priests (kohanim) moved the people, that he should rather release Barabbas unto them.

12 And Pilate answered and said again unto them, "What will you then that I shall do unto Him whom you call the King of the Jews (Yehudim)?"

13 And they cried out again, "Crucify Him!"

14 Then Pilate said unto them, "Why, what evil hath He done?" And they cried out the more exceedingly, "Crucify Him!"

15 And so Pilate, willing to content the people, released Barabbas unto them, and delivered Yahwah, when he had scourged Him, to be crucified.

16 And the soldiers led Him away into the hall, called Praetorium; and they call together the whole band.

17 And they clothed Him with purple, and platted a crown of thorns, and put it about His head,

18 And began to salute Him, "Hail, King of the Jews (Yehudim)!"

19 And they smote Him on the head with a reed, and did spit upon Him, and bowing their knees worshipped Him.

20 And when they had mocked Him, they took off the purple from Him, and put His own clothes on Him, and led Him out to crucify Him.

21 And they compel one Shimon a Cyrenian, who passed by, coming out of the country, the father of Alexander and Rufus, to bear His stake.

22 And they bring Him unto the place Golgotha, which is, being interpreted, "The place of a skull."

23 And they gave Him to drink wine mingled with myrrh, but He received it not.

24 And when they had crucified Him, they parted His garments, casting lots upon them, what every man should take. – *Psa. 22:18*

25 And it was the third hour, and they crucified Him.

26 And the superscription of His accusation was written over: THE KING OF THE JEWS (YEHUDIM).

27 And with Him they crucify two thieves; the one on His right hand, and the other on His left.

28 And the scripture was fulfilled, which saith, "And He was numbered with the

transgressors. – *Isa. 53:12*

29 And they that passed by railed on Him, wagging their heads, and saying, "Ah, You that destroyest the temple, and buildest it in three days,

30 Save Yourself, and come down from the stake!"

31 Likewise also the chief priests mocking said among themselves with the scribes, "He saved others; Himself He cannot save."

32 Let the Messiah (haMashiach) the King of Yisrael descend now from the stake, that we may see and believe." And they that were crucified with Him reviled Him.

33 And when the sixth hour was come, there was darkness over the whole land until the ninth hour.

34 And at the ninth hour Yahwah cried with a loud voice, saying, "Eli, Eli, lama sabachthani?" Which is, being interpreted: "My God, My God, why have You forsaken Me?" – *Psa. 22:1, Mat. 27:46*

35 And some of them that stood by, when they heard it, said, "Behold, He calleth Elijah (Eliyahu)."

36 And one ran and filled a spunge full of vinegar, and put it on a reed, and gave him to drink, saying, "Let alone; let us see whether Elijah (Eliyahu) will come to take Him down."

37 And Yahwah cried with a loud voice, and gave up the Spirit.

38 And the veil of the temple was rent in twain from the top to the bottom.

39 And when the centurion, who stood opposite Him, saw that He so cried out, and gave up the Spirit, he said, "Truly this man was the [B47]Humanity of El (YHWH)."

40 There were also women looking on afar off; among whom was Mary (Miryam) Magdalene, and Mary (Miryam) the mother of James (Yaaqov) the less and of Joseph (Yosef), and Salome;

41 (Who also, when He was in Galilee, followed Him, and ministered unto Him;) and many other women who came up with Him unto Jerusalem (Yerushalayim).

42 And now when the even was come, because it was the preparation, that is, the day before the Shabbat,

43 Joseph (Yosef) of Arimathaea, an honourable counsellor, who also waited for the kingdom of God (Elohim, יהוה (YHWH)) came, and went in boldly unto Pilate, and craved the body of Yahwah.

44 And Pilate marvelled if He was already dead; and calling unto him the centurion, he asked him whether He had been dead awhile.

45 And when he knew it of the centurion, he gave the body to Joseph (Yosef).

46 And he bought fine linen, and took him down, and wrapped Him in the linen, and laid Him in a sepulchre which was hewn out of a rock, and rolled a stone unto the door of the sepulchre.

47 And Mary (Miryam) Magdalene and Mary (Miryam) the mother of Joseph (Yosef) beheld where He was laid.

16 And when the Shabbat was past, Mary (Miryam) Magdalene, and Mary (Miryam) the mother of James (Yaaqov), and Salome, had bought sweet spices, that they might come and anoint Him.

2 And very early in the morning the first day of the week, they came unto the sepulchre at the rising of the sun.

3 And they said among themselves, "Who shall roll us away the stone from the door of the sepulchre?"

4 And when they looked, they saw that the stone was rolled away; for it was very great.

5 And entering into the sepulchre, they saw a young man sitting on the right side, clothed in a long white garment; and they were affrighted.

6 And he saith unto them, "Be not affrighted. You seek Yahwah of Nazareth, who was crucified; He is risen; He is not here; behold the place where they laid Him.

7 But go your way, tell His disciples and Peter (Kefa) that He goeth before you into Galilee; there shall you see Him, as He said unto you."

8 And they went out quickly, and fled from the sepulchre; for they trembled and were amazed; neither said they any thing to any man; for they were afraid.

9 Now when Yahwah was risen early the first day of the week, He appeared first to Mary (Miryam) Magdalene, out of whom He had cast seven devils.

10 And she went and told them that had been with Him, as they mourned and wept.

11 And they, when they had heard that He was alive, and had been seen of her, believed not.

12 After that He appeared in another form unto two of them, as they walked, and went into the country.

13 And they went and told it unto the residue; neither believed they them.

14 Afterward He appeared unto the eleven as they sat at meat, and upbraided them with their unbelief and hardness of heart, because they believed not them who had seen Him after He was risen.

15 And He said unto them, "Go you into all the world, and preach the gospel (good news) to every creature.

16 He that believeth and is baptized shall be saved; but he that believeth not shall be damned.

17 And these signs shall follow them that believe: In My name shall they cast out devils; they shall speak with new tongues;

18 They shall take up serpents; and if they drink any deadly thing, it shall not hurt them; they shall lay hands on the sick, and they shall recover."

19 So then after Yahwah had spoken unto them, He was received up into heaven, and sat on the right hand of God (Elohim).

20 And they went forth, and preached every where, Yahwah working with them, and confirming the word with signs following. So be it (Amen).

LUKE
LUQAS לוקס
(Gospel of [A70]Luke)

1 Forasmuch as many have taken in hand to set forth in order a declaration of those things which are most surely believed among us,

2 Even as they delivered them unto us, which from the beginning were eyewitnesses, and ministers of the word;

3 It seemed good to me also, having had perfect understanding of all things from the very first, to write unto you in order, most excellent Theophilus,

4 That you mightest know the certainty of those things, wherein you have been instructed.

5 There was in the days of Herod, the king of Judah (Yehudah), a certain priest (kohen) named Zacharias (Zekharyah), of the [B46]course of Abia (Aviyah); and his wife was of the daughters of Aaron (Aharon), and her name was Elisabeth (Elisheva).

6 And they were both righteous before God (Elohim), walking in all the commandments and ordinances of יהוה blameless.

7 And they had no child, because that Elisabeth (Elisheva) was barren, and they both were now well stricken in years.

8 And it came to pass, that while he executed the priest's office (kehunnah) before God (Elohim) in the order of his course,

9 According to the custom of the priest's office (kehunnah), his lot was to burn incense when he went into the temple of יהוה.

10 And the whole multitude of the people were praying outside at the time of incense.

11 And there appeared unto him an angel of יהוה standing on the right side of the altar of incense.

12 And when Zacharias (Zekharyah) saw him, he was troubled, and fear fell upon him.

13 But the angel said unto him, "Fear not, Zacharias (Zekharyah); for your prayer is heard; and your wife Elisabeth (Elisheva) shall bear you a son, and you shalt call his name John (Yochanan).

14 And you shalt have joy and gladness; and many shall rejoice at his birth.

15 For he shall be great in the sight of יהוה, and shall drink neither wine nor strong drink; and he shall be filled with the Holy Spirit (Ruach haQodesh), even from his mother's womb.

16 And many of the children of Yisrael shall he turn to יהוה their God (YHWH Eloheihem).

17 And he shall go before Him in the spirit and power of Elijah (Eliyahu), to turn the hearts of the fathers to the children, and the disobedient to the wisdom of the just; to make ready a people prepared for יהוה." – *Mal. 4:5-6, Isa. 40:3*

18 And Zacharias (Zekharyah) said unto the angel, "Whereby shall I know this? For I am an old man, and my wife well stricken in years."

19 And the angel answering said unto him, "I am Gavriel, that stand in the presence of God (Elohim); and am sent to speak unto you, and to shew you these glad tidings.

20 And, behold, you shalt be dumb, and not able to speak, until the day that these things shall be performed, because you believest not my words, which shall be fulfilled in their season.

21 And the people waited for Zacharias (Zekharyah), and marvelled that he tarried so long in the temple.

22 And when he came out, he could not speak unto them; and they perceived that he had seen a vision in the temple; for he beckoned unto them, and remained speechless.

23 And it came to pass, that, as soon as the days of his ministration were accomplished, he departed to his own house.

24 And after those days his wife Elisabeth (Elisheva) conceived, and hid herself five months, saying,

25 "Thus hath יהוה dealt with me in the days wherein He looked on me, to take away my reproach among men."

26 And in the sixth month the angel Gavriel was sent from God (Elohim) unto a city of Galilee, named Nazareth,

27 To a virgin espoused to a man whose name was Joseph (Yosef), of the house of Dawid; and the virgin's name was Mary (Miryam).

28 And the angel came in unto her, and said, "Hail, you that art highly favoured, יהוה is with you; blessed are you among women."

29 And when she saw him, she was troubled at his saying, and cast in her mind what manner of salutation this should be.

30 And the angel said unto her, "Fear not, Mary (Miryam); for you have found favour with God (Elohim).

31 And, behold, you shalt conceive in your womb, and bring forth a son, and shalt call His name ᴬ¹YHWH (Yahwah). – *Isa. 7:14, 9:6*

32 He shall be great, and shall be called the ᴮ⁴⁷Humanity of the Most High (Elyon) and God (Elohim) יהוה shall give unto Him the throne of His forefather Dawid.

33 And He shall reign over the house of Jacob (Yaaqov) for ever; and of His kingdom there shall be no end."

34 Then said Mary (Miryam) unto the angel, "How shall this be, seeing I know not a man?"

35 And the angel answered and said unto her, "The Holy Spirit (Ruach haQodesh) shall come upon you, and the power of the Most High (Elyon) shall overshadow you; therefore also that Holy One who shall be born of you shall be called the ᴮ⁴⁷Humanity of El (YHWH).

36 And, behold, your cousin Elisabeth (Elisheva), she hath also conceived a son in her old age; and this is the sixth month with her, who was called barren.

37 For with God (Elohim) nothing shall be impossible."

38 And Mary (Miryam) said, "Behold the handmaid of יהוה; be it unto me according to your word." And the angel departed from her.

39 And Mary (Miryam) arose in those days, and went into the hill country with haste, into a city of Judah (Yehudah);

40 And entered into the house of Zacharias (Zekharyah), and saluted Elisabeth (Elisheva).

41 And it came to pass, that, when Elisabeth (Elisheva) heard the salutation of Mary (Miryam), the babe leaped in her womb; and Elisabeth (Elisheva) was filled with the Holy Spirit (Ruach haQodesh).

42 And she spake out with a loud voice, and said, "Blessed are you among women, and blessed is the fruit of your womb!

43 And whence is this to me, that the mother of my Lord (Adonai) should come to me?

44 For, behold, as soon as the voice of your salutation sounded in mine ears, the babe leaped in my womb for joy.

45 And blessed is she that believed, for there shall be a performance of those things which were told her from יהוה."

46 And Mary (Miryam) said, "My soul doth magnify יהוה,

47 And my spirit hath rejoiced in יהוה (YHWH, Yahwah) my Savior.

48 For He hath regarded the low estate of His handmaiden; for, behold, from henceforth all generations shall call me blessed.

49 For He that is mighty hath done to me great things; and His name is holy.

50 And His mercy is on them that fear Him from generation to generation.

51 He hath shewed strength with His arm; He hath scattered the proud in the imagination of their hearts.

52 He hath put down the mighty from their seats, and exalted them of low degree.

53 He hath filled the hungry with good things; and the rich He hath sent empty away.

54 He hath helped His servant Yisrael, in remembrance of His mercy;

55 As He spake to our fathers, to Avraham, and to His seed for ever."

56 And Mary (Miryam) abode with her about three months, and returned to her own house.

57 Now Elisabeth (Elisheva)'s full time came that she should be delivered; and she brought forth a son.

58 And her neighbours and her cousins heard how יהוה had shewed great mercy upon her; and they rejoiced with her.

59 And it came to pass, that on the eighth day they came to circumcise the child; and they called him Zacharias (Zekharyah), after the name of his father.

60 And his mother answered and said, "Not so; but he shall be called John (Yochanan)."

61 And they said unto her, "There is none of your kindred that is called by this name."

62 And they made signs to his father, how he would have him called.

63 And he asked for a writing table, and wrote, saying, "His name is John (Yochanan)." And they marvelled all.

64 And his mouth was opened immediately, and his tongue loosed, and he spake, and praised God (Elohim, יהוה (YHWH)).

65 And fear came on all that dwelt round about them; and all these sayings were noised abroad throughout all the hill country of Judah (Yehudah).

66 And all they that heard them laid them up in their hearts, saying, "What manner of child shall this be?" And the hand of יהוה was with him.

67 And his father Zacharias (Zekharyah) was filled with the Holy Spirit (Ruach haQodesh), and prophesied, saying,

68 "Blessed be יהוה God (Elohim) of Yisrael; for He hath visited and redeemed His people,

69 And hath raised up a horn of salvation for us in the house of His servant Dawid; – *Psa. 132:17*

70 As He spake by the mouth of His holy prophets, who have been since the world began;

71 That we should be saved from our enemies, and from the hand of all that hate us;

72 To perform the mercy promiscd to our fathers, and to remember His holy covenant; – *Lev. 26:42*

73 The oath which He sware to our father Avraham,

74 That He would grant unto us, that we being delivered out of the hand of our enemies might serve Him without fear,

75 In holiness and righteousness before Him, all the days of our life.

76 And you, child, shalt be called the prophet of the Most High; for you shalt go before the face of יהוה (YHWH, Yahwah) to prepare His ways; – *Isa.40:3*

77 To give knowledge of salvation unto His people by the remission of their sins,

78 Through the tender mercy of our God (Elohim); whereby the dayspring from on high hath visited us,

79 To give light to them that sit in darkness and in the shadow of death, to guide our feet into the way of peace.

80 And the child grew, and waxed strong in spirit, and was in the deserts till the day of his shewing unto Yisrael.

2 And it came to pass in those days, that there went out a decree from Caesar Augustus, that all the world should be taxed.

2 (And this taxing was first made when Cyrenius was governor of Syria.)

3 And all went to be taxed, every one into his own city.

4 And Joseph (Yosef) also went up from Galilee, out of the city of Nazareth, into Judah (Yehudah), unto the city of Dawid, which is called Bethlehem (Beit-Lechem); (because he was of the house and lineage of Dawid);

5 To be taxed with Mary (Miryam) his espoused wife, being great with Child.

6 And so it was, that, while they were there, the days were accomplished that she should be delivered.

7 And she brought forth her firstborn son, and wrapped Him in swaddling clothes, and laid Him in a manger; because there was no room for them in the inn.

8 And there were in the same country shepherds abiding in the field, keeping watch over their flock by night.

9 And, behold, the angel of יהוה came upon them, and the glory of יהוה shone round about them; and they were sore afraid.

10 And the angel said unto them, "Fear not; for, behold, I bring you good tidings of great joy, which shall be to all people.

11 For unto you is born this day in the city of Dawid a Savior, who is the Messiah (B45haMashiach) Yahwah. – *Isa. 9:6*

12 And this shall be a sign unto you: You shall find the Babe wrapped in swaddling clothes, lying in a manger.

13 And suddenly there was with the angel a multitude of the heavenly host praising God (Elohim), and saying,

14 "Glory to God (Elohim) in the highest, and on earth peace, good will toward men."

15 And it came to pass, as the angels were gone away from them into heaven, the shepherds said one to another, "Let us now go even unto Bethlehem (Beit-Lechem), and see this thing which is come to pass, which יהוה hath made known unto us."

16 And they came with haste, and found Mary (Miryam), and Joseph (Yosef), and the Babe lying in a manger.

17 And when they had seen it, they made known abroad the saying which was told them concerning this Child.

18 And all they that heard it wondered at those things which were told them by the shepherds.

19 But Mary (Miryam) kept all these things, and pondered them in her heart.

20 And the shepherds returned, glorifying and praising God (Elohim) for all the things that they had heard and seen, as it was told unto them.

21 And when eight days were accomplished for the circumcising of the Child, His name was called Yahwah (YHWH), who was so named of the angel before He was conceived in the womb. – *Lev.12:3*

22 And when the days of her purification according to the teaching of Moses (torat Mosheh) were accomplished, they brought Him to Jerusalem (Yerushalayim), to present Him to יהוה;

23 As it is written in the Torah of יהוה: "Every male that openeth the womb shall be called holy to יהוה"; – *Exo. 13:2*

24 And to offer a sacrifice according to that which is said in the Torah of יהוה, "A pair of turtledoves, or two young pigeons." – *Lev.12:8*

25 And, behold, there was a man in Jerusalem (Yerushalayim), whose name was Shimon; and the same man was just and devout, waiting for the consolation of Yisrael; and the Holy Spirit (Ruach haQodesh) was upon him.

26 [B60] And it was revealed unto him by the Holy Spirit (Ruach haQodesh), that he should not see death, before he had seen the Messiah Yahwah. (et-Mashiach YHWH).

27 And he came by the Spirit into the temple; and when the parents brought in the Child, Yahwah, to do for Him after the custom of the Torah,

28 Then took he Him up in his arms, and blessed God (Elohim, יהוה (YHWH)), and said,

29 "יהוה (YHWH), now lettest You Your servant depart in peace, according to Your word;

30 For mine eyes have seen Your salvation,

31 Which You have prepared before the face of all people;

32 A light to lighten the nations, and the glory of Your people Yisrael."

33 And Joseph (Yosef) and his mother marvelled at those things which were spoken of Him.

34 And Shimon blessed them, and said unto Mary (Miryam) His mother, "Behold, this Child is set for the fall and rising again of many in Yisrael; and for a sign which shall be spoken against;

35 (Yea, a sword shall pierce through your own soul also,) that the thoughts of many hearts may be revealed.

36 And there was one Anna, a prophetess, the daughter of Phanuel, of the tribe of Aser; she was of a great age, and had lived with a husband seven years from her virginity;

37 And she was a widow of about fourscore and four (eighty-four) years, who departed not from the temple, but served God ((Elohim, יהוה (YHWH)) with fastings and prayers night and day.

38 And she coming in that instant gave thanks likewise unto יהוה, and spake of Him to all them that looked for redemption in Jerusalem (Yerushalayim).

39 And when they had performed all things according to the Torah of יהוה, they returned into Galilee, to their own city Nazareth.

40 And the Child grew, and waxed strong in spirit, filled with wisdom; and the grace of God (Elohim, יהוה (YHWH)) was upon Him.

41 Now His parents went to Jerusalem (Yerushalayim) every year at the feast of the Passover (Pesach).

42 And when He was twelve years old, they went up to Jerusalem (Yerushalayim) after the custom of the feast.

43 And when they had fulfilled the days, as they returned, the Child Yahwah tarried behind in Jerusalem (Yerushalayim); and Joseph (Yosef) and His mother knew not of it.

44 But they, supposing Him to have been in the company, went a day's journey; and they sought Him among their kinsfolk and acquaintance.

45 And when they found Him not, they turned back again to Jerusalem (Yerushalayim), seeking Him.

46 And it came to pass, that after three days they found Him in the temple, sitting in the midst of the doctors, both hearing them, and asking them questions.

47 And all that heard Him were astonished at His understanding and answers.

48 And when they saw Him, they were amazed; and His mother said unto Him, "Son, why have You thus dealt with us? Behold, Your father and I have sought You sorrowing."

49 And He said unto them, "How is it that you sought Me? Wist you not that I must be about My Father's business?"

50 And they understood not the saying which He spake unto them.

51 And He went down with them, and came to Nazareth, and was subject unto them; but His mother kept all these sayings in her heart.

52 And Yahwah increased in wisdom and stature, and in favour with God (Elohim) and man.

3 Now in the fifteenth year of the reign of Tiberius Caesar, Pontius Pilate being governor of Judah (Yehudah), and Herod

being tetrarch of Galilee, and His brother Philip tetrarch of Ituraea and of the region of Trachonitis, and Lysanias the tetrarch of Abilene,

2 Annas and Caiaphas being the high priests (kohanim), the word of God (Elohim, יהוה (YHWH)) came unto John (Yochanan) the son of Zacharias (Zekharyah) in the wilderness.

3 And he came into all the country about Jordan (Yarden), preaching the baptism of repentance for the remission of sins;

4 As it is written in the book of the words of Isaiah (Yeshayahu) the prophet, saying, "[B49]The voice of one crying in the wilderness: 'Prepare you the way of יהוה (YHWH, Yahwah), make His paths straight. – *Isa. 40:3, Mat. 3:3, Mar. 1:3*

5 Every valley shall be filled, and every mountain and hill shall be brought low; and the crooked shall be made straight, and the rough ways shall be made smooth; – *Isa. 40:4*

6 And all flesh shall see the salvation of God (Elohim, יהוה (YHWH))." – *Isa. 40:5*

7 Then said he to the multitude that came forth to be baptized of him, "O generation of vipers, who hath warned you to flee from the wrath to come?

8 Bring forth therefore fruits worthy of repentance, and begin not to say within yourselves, 'We have Avraham to our father.' For I say unto you, that God (Elohim) is able of these stones to raise up children unto Avraham.

9 And now also the axe is laid unto the root of the trees. Every tree therefore which bringeth not forth good fruit is hewn down, and cast into the fire."

10 And the people asked him, saying, "What shall we do then?"

11 He answereth and saith unto them, "He that hath two coats, let him impart to him that hath none; and he that hath food, let him do likewise."

12 Then came also tax collectors to be baptized, and said unto him, "Teacher (Rabbi), what shall we do?"

13 And he said unto them, "Exact no more than that which is appointed you."

14 And the soldiers likewise demanded of him, saying, "And what shall we do?" And he said unto them, "Do violence to no man, neither accuse any falsely; and be content with your wages."

15 And as the people were in expectation, and all men reasoned in their hearts of John (Yochanan), whether he was the Messiah (haMashiach), or not;

16 John (Yochanan) answered, saying unto them all, "I indeed baptize you with water; but one mightier than I cometh, the latchet of whose shoes I am not worthy to unloose. He shall baptize you with the Holy Spirit (Ruach haQodesh) and with fire;

17 Whose fan is in His hand, and He will throughly purge His floor, and will gather the wheat into His garner; but the chaff He will burn with fire unquenchable."

18 And many other things in his exhortation preached he unto the people.

19 But Herod the tetrarch, being reproved by him for Herodias his brother Philip's wife, and for all the evils which Herod had done,

20 Added yet this above all, that he shut up John (Yochanan) in prison.

21 Now when all the people were baptized, it came to pass, that Yahwah also being baptized, and praying, the heaven was opened,

22 And the Holy Spirit (Ruach haQodesh) descended in a bodily shape like a dove upon Him, and [B53]a voice came from heaven, who said, "You are My beloved [B47]Humanity; in You I am well pleased." – *Mat. 3:17, Mark 1:11*

23 And Yahwah Himself began to be about thirty years of age, being (as was supposed) the son of Joseph (Yosef), who was the son of Heli (Eli),

24 Who was the son of Mattat, who was the son of Lewi, who was the son of Melchi, who was the son of Yanah, who was the son of Joseph (Yosef),

25 Who was the son of Matthew (Mattityahu), who was the son of Amos, who was the son of Nachum, who was the son of Esli, who was the son of Naggai,

26 Who was the son of Maath, who was the son of Matthew (Mattityahu), who was the son of Semei, who was the son of Joseph (Yosef), who was the son of Juda (Yodah),

27 Who was the son of John (Yochanan), who was the son of Resha, who was the son of Zerubbbabel, who was the son of Shealtiel, who was the son of Neri,

28 Who was the son of Melchi, who was the son of Adi, who was the son of Cosam, who was the

son of Elmodam, who was the son of Er,

29 Who was the son of Jose (Yeshua), who was the son of Eliezer, who was the son of Jorim (Yoram), who was the son of Mattat, who was the son of Lewi,

30 Who was the son of Shimon, who was the son of Juda (Yehudah), who was the son of Joseph (Yosef), who was the son of Jonan (Yonam), who was the son of Eliakim (Elyaqim),

31 Who was the son of Melea, who was the son of Menan, who was the son of Mattattah, who was the son of Nathan, who was the son of Dawid,

32 Who was the son of Jesse (Yishai), who was the son of Obed, who was the son of Boaz, who was the son of Salmon, who was the son of Naasson,

33 Who was the son of Aminadab, who was the son of Aram, who was the son of Esrom, who was the son of Phares, who was the son of Juda (Yehudah),

34 Who was the son of Jacob (Yaaqov), who was the son of Isaac (Yitschaq), who was the son of Avraham, who was the son of Thara, who was the son of Nachor,

35 Who was the son of Saruch, who was the son of Ragau, who was the son of Phalec, who was the son of Heber, who was the son of Sala,

36 Who was the son of Kenan, who was the son of Arphaxad, who was the son of Shem, who was the son of Noe (Noach), who was the son of Lamek,

37 Who was the son of Mathusala, who was the son of Enoch (Chanok), which was the son of Jared (Yered), who was the son of Mahalalel, who was the son of Cainan,

38 Who was the son of Enosh, who was the son of Shet, who was the son of Adam, who was the son of God (Elohim).

4 And Yahwah being full of the Holy Spirit (Ruach haQodesh) returned from Jordan (Yarden), and was led by the Spirit into the wilderness,

2 Being forty days tempted of the devil. And in those days He did eat nothing; and when they were ended, He afterward hungered.

3 And the devil said unto Him, "If You be the [B47]Humanity of El (YHWH), command this stone that it be made bread."

4 And Yahwah answered him, saying, "It is written, 'That man shall not live by bread alone,

but by every word of יהוה (YHWH)'" – *Deu. 8:3*

5 And the devil, taking Him up into a high mountain, shewed unto Him all the kingdoms of the world in a moment of time.

6 And the devil said unto Him, "All this power will I give You, and the glory of them; for that is delivered unto me; and to whomsoever I will I give it.

7 If You therefore wilt worship me, all shall be Yours."

8 And Yahwah answered and said unto him, "Get you behind Me, Satan; for it is written, 'You shalt worship יהוה your God (YHWH Eloheikha), and Him only shalt you serve." – *Deu. 6:13-14, 10:20*

9 And he brought Him to Jerusalem (Yerushalayim), and set Him on a pinnacle of the temple, and said unto Him, "If You be the [B47]Humanity of El (YHWH), cast Yourself down from here;

10 For it is written, 'He shall give His angels charge over You, to keep You.

11 And in their hands they shall bear You up, lest at any time You dash Your foot against a stone.'" – *Psa. 91:1-2*

12 And Yahwah answered and said unto him, "It is said, 'You shalt not test יהוה your God (YHWH Eloheikhem).'" – *Deu. 6:16*

13 And when the devil had ended all the temptation, he departed from Him for a season.

14 And Yahwah returned in the power of the Spirit into Galilee; and there went out a fame of Him through all the region round about.

15 And He taught in their synagogues, being glorified of all.

16 And He came to Nazareth, where He had been brought up; and, as His custom was, He went into the synagogue on the Shabbat, and stood up for to read.

17 And there was delivered unto Him the book of the prophet Isaiah (Yeshayahu). And when He had opened the book, He found the place where it was written,

18 "The Spirit of יהוה (Ruach YHWH) is upon Me, because He hath anointed Me to preach the good tidings to the poor. He hath sent Me to heal the brokenhearted, to preach deliverance to the captives, and recovering of sight to the blind, to set at liberty them that are bruised, – *Isa. 61:1*

19 To preach the acceptable year of יהוה (YHWH)" – *Isa. 61:2*

20 And He closed the book, and He gave it again to the minister, and sat down. And the eyes of all them that were in the synagogue were fastened on Him.

21 And He began to say unto them, "This day is this scripture fulfilled in your ears."

22 And all bare Him witness, and wondered at the gracious words which proceeded out of His mouth. And they said, "Is not this Joseph (Yosef)'s son?"

23 And He said unto them, "You will surely say unto Me this proverb, 'Physician, heal yourself! Whatsoever we have heard done in Capernaum, do also here in Your country.'"

24 And He said, "Verily I say unto you, no prophet is accepted in his own country.

25 But I tell you of a truth, many widows were in Yisrael in the days of Elijah (Eliyahu), when the heaven was shut up three years and six months, when great famine was throughout all the land;

26 But unto none of them was Elijah (Eliyahu) sent, except unto Sarepta, a city of Sidon, unto a woman that was a widow.

27 And many lepers were in Yisrael in the time of Elisha the prophet; and none of them was cleansed, except Naaman the Syrian."

28 And all they in the synagogue, when they heard these things, were filled with wrath,

29 And rose up, and thrust Him out of the city, and led Him unto the brow of the hill whereon their city was built, that they might cast Him down headlong.

30 But He passing through the midst of them went His way,

31 And came down to Capernaum, a city of Galilee, and taught them on the Shabbats.

32 And they were astonished at His doctrine (teaching), for His word was with power.

33 And in the synagogue there was a man, who had a spirit of an unclean devil, and cried out with a loud voice,

34 Saying, "Let us alone; what have we to do with You, You Yahwah of Nazareth? Are You come to destroy us? I know You who You are; the Holy One of God (Elohim)."

35 And Yahwah rebuked him, saying, "Hold your peace, and come out of him." And when the devil had thrown him in the midst, he came out of him, and hurt him not.

36 And they were all amazed, and spake among themselves, saying, "What a word is this!" For with authority and power He commandeth the unclean spirits, and they come out.

37 And the fame of Him went out into every place of the country round about.

38 And He arose out of the synagogue, and entered into Shimon's house. And Shimon's wife's mother was taken with a great fever; and they besought Him for her.

39 And He stood over her, and rebuked the fever; and it left her; and immediately she arose and ministered unto them.

40 Now when the sun was setting, all they that had any sick with divers diseases brought them unto Him; and He laid His hands on every one of them, and healed them.

41 And devils also came out of many, crying out, and saying, "You are Messiah (Mashiach) the B47Humanity of El (YHWH)." And He rebuking them allowed them not to speak, for they knew that He was the Messiah (haMashiach).

42 And when it was day, He departed and went into a desert place; and the people sought Him, and came unto Him, and stayed Him, that He should not depart from them.

43 And He said unto them, "I must preach the kingdom of God (Elohim, יהוה (YHWH)) to other cities also, for therefore am I sent."

44 And He preached in the synagogues of Galilee.

5 And it came to pass, that, as the people pressed upon Him to hear the word of God (Elohim, יהוה (YHWH)), He stood by the lake of Gennesaret,

2 And saw two ships standing by the lake; but the fishermen had gone out of them, and were washing their nets.

3 And He entered into one of the ships, which was Shimon's, and prayed him that he would thrust out a little from the land. And He sat down, and taught the people out of the ship.

4 Now when He had left speaking, He said unto Shimon, "Launch out into the deep, and let down your nets for a catch."

5 And Shimon answering said unto Him, "Teacher (Rabbi), we have toiled all the night, and have caught nothing; nevertheless at Your word I will let down the net."

6 And when they had this done, they inclosed a great multitude of fishes, and their net broke.

7 And they beckoned unto their partners, who

were in the other ship, that they should come and help them. And they came, and filled both the ships, so that they began to sink.

8 When Shimon Peter (Kefa) saw it, he fell down at Yahwah's knees, saying, "Depart from me; for I am a sinful man, O Lord (Adonai)."

9 For he was astonished, and all that were with him, at the catch of the fishes which they had taken:

10 And so was also Jacob (Yaaqov), and John (Yochanan), the sons of Zebedee (Zavdai), who were partners with Shimon. And Yahwah said unto Shimon, "Fear not; from now on you shalt catch men."

11 And when they had brought their ships to land, they forsook all, and followed Him.

12 And it came to pass, when He was in a certain city, behold a man full of leprosy; who seeing Yahwah fell on His face and besought Him, saying, "Lord (Adonai), if You wilt, You canst make me clean."

13 And He put forth His hand, and touched him, saying, "I will; be you clean." And immediately the leprosy departed from him.

14 And He warned him to tell no man; "But go, and shew yourself to the priest (kohen), and offer for your cleansing, according as Moses (Mosheh) commanded, for a testimony unto them."

15 But so much the more went there a fame abroad of Him; and great multitudes came together to hear, and to be healed by Him of their infirmities.

16 And He withdrew Himself into the wilderness, and prayed.

17 And it came to pass on a certain day, as He was teaching, that there were Pharisees and teachers of the [B28a]Torah sitting by, who had come out of every town of Galilee, and Judah (Yehudah), and Jerusalem (Yerushalayim); and the power of יהוה (YHWH) was present to heal them.

18 And, behold, men brought in a bed a man who was taken with a palsy; and they sought means to bring him in, and to lay him before Him.

19 And when they could not find by what way they might bring him in because of the multitude, they went upon the housetop, and let him down through the tiling with his couch into the midst before Yahwah.

20 And when He saw their faith, He said unto him, "Man, your sins are forgiven you."

21 And the scribes and the Pharisees began to reason, saying, "Who is this who speaketh blasphemies? Who can forgive sins, but God (Elohim, יהוה (YHWH)) alone?

22 But when Yahwah perceived their thoughts, He answering said unto them, "What reason you in your hearts?

23 Whether is easier, to say, 'Your sins be forgiven you;' or to say, 'Rise up and walk'?

24 But that you may know that the Son of man (haMashiach) hath power upon earth to forgive sins. (He said unto the sick of the palsy) I say unto you, 'Arise, and take up your couch, and go into your house.'"

25 And immediately he rose up before them, and took up that whereon he lay, and departed to his own house, glorifying God (Elohim, יהוה (YHWH)).

26 And they were all amazed, and they glorified God (Elohim), and were filled with fear, saying, "We have seen strange things today."

27 And after these things He went forth, and saw a tax collector, named Lewi, sitting at the receipt of custom; and He said unto him, "Follow Me."

28 And he left all, rose up, and followed Him.

29 And Lewi made Him a great feast in his own house; and there was a great company of tax collectors and of others that sat down with them.

30 But their scribes and Pharisees murmured against His disciples, saying, "Why do you eat and drink with tax collectors and sinners?"

31 And Yahwah answering said unto them, "They that are whole need not a physician; but they that are sick.

32 I came not to call the righteous, but sinners to repentance."

33 And they said unto Him, "Why do the disciples of John (Yochanan) fast often, and make prayers, and likewise the disciples of the Pharisees; but You eat and drink?"

34 And He said unto them, "Can you make the children of the bridechamber fast, while the bridegroom is with them?

35 But the days will come, when the bridegroom shall be taken away from them, and then shall they fast in those days."

36 And He spake also a parable unto them: "No man putteth a piece of a new garment upon an

old; if otherwise, then both the new maketh a rent, and the piece that was taken out of the new agreeth not with the old.

37 And no man putteth new wine into old bottles; else the new wine will burst the bottles, and be spilled, and the bottles shall perish.

38 But new wine must be put into new bottles; and both are preserved.

39 No man also having drunk old wine straightway desireth new; for he saith, 'The old is better.'"

6 And it came to pass on the second Shabbat after the first, that He went through the grainfields; and His disciples plucked the heads of grain, and did eat, rubbing them in their hands.

2 And certain of the Pharisees said unto them, "Why do you that which is not lawful to do on the Shabbat?"

3 And Yahwah answering them said, "Have you not read so much as this, what Dawid did, when himself was hungry, and they who were with him;

4 How he went into the house of God (Elohim), and did take and eat the shewbread, and gave also to them that were with him; which it is not lawful to eat but for the priests (kohanim) alone?"

5 And He said unto them that: "The Son of man (haMashiach) is Lord (Adon) also of the Shabbat."

6 And it came to pass also on another Shabbat, that He entered into the synagogue and taught; and there was a man whose right hand was withered.

7 And the scribes and Pharisees watched Him, whether He would heal on the Shabbat; that they might find an accusation against Him.

8 But He knew their thoughts, and said to the man who had the withered hand, "Rise up, and stand forth in the midst." And he arose and stood forth.

9 Then said Yahwah unto them, "I will ask you one thing: Is it lawful on the Shabbat to do good, or to do evil? To save life, or to destroy it?"

10 And looking round about upon them all, He said unto the man, "Stretch forth your hand." And he did so; and his hand was restored whole as the other.

11 And they were filled with madness; and communed one with another what they might do to Yahwah.

12 And it came to pass in those days, that He went out into a mountain to pray, and continued all night in prayer to יהוה (YHWH).

13 And when it was day, He called unto Him His disciples; and of them He chose twelve, whom also He named apostles;

14 Shimon, (whom He also named Peter (Kefa), and Andrew his brother, Jacob (Yaaqov) and John (Yochanan), Philip and Bartholomew (Bar-Talmai),

15 Matthew (Mattityahu) and Thomas (Toma), James the son of Alphaeus (Yaaqov ben-Alpheus), and Shimon called Zelotes,

16 And Judas the son of James (Yehudah ben-Yaaqov), and Judas Iscariot (Yehudah Ishkeriot), who also was the traitor.

17 And He came down with them, and stood in the plain, and the company of His disciples, and a great multitude of people out of all Judah (Yehudah) and Jerusalem (Yerushalayim), and from the sea coast of Tyre and Sidon, who came to hear Him, and to be healed of their diseases;

18 And they that were vexed with unclean spirits; and they were healed.

19 And the whole multitude sought to touch Him; for there went virtue out of Him, and healed them all.

20 And He lifted up His eyes on His disciples, and said, "Blessed be you poor, for yours is the kingdom of God (Elohim, יהוה (YHWH)).

21 Blessed are you that hunger now, for you shall be filled. Blessed are you that weep now, for you shall laugh.

22 Blessed are you, when men shall hate you, and when they shall separate you from their company, and shall reproach you, and cast out your name as evil, for the Son of man (haMashiach)'s sake.

23 Rejoice you in that day, and leap for joy, for, behold, your reward is great in heaven; for in the like manner did their fathers unto the prophets.

24 But woe unto you that are rich! For you have received your consolation.

25 Woe unto you that are full! For you shall hunger. Woe unto you that laugh now! For you shall mourn and weep.

26 Woe unto you, when all men shall speak well of you! For so did their fathers to the false prophets.

27 But I say unto you who hear: 'Love your

enemies, do good to them who hate you,

28 Bless them that curse you, and pray for them who despitefully use you.

29 And unto him that smiteth you on the one cheek offer also the other; and him that taketh away your cloke forbid not to take your coat also.

30 Give to every man that asketh of you; and of him that taketh away your goods ask them not again.

31 And as you would that men should do to you, do you also to them likewise.

32 For if you love them who love you, what credit have you? For sinners also love those that love them.

33 And if you do good to them who do good to you, what credit have you? For sinners also do even the same.

34 And if you lend to them of whom you hope to receive, what credit have you? For sinners also lend to sinners, to receive as much again.

35 But love you your enemies, and do good, and lend, hoping for nothing again; and your reward shall be great, and you shall be the children of the Most High (haElyon); for He is kind unto the unthankful and to the evil.

36 Be you therefore merciful, as your Father also is merciful.

37 Judge not, and you shall not be judged; condemn not, and you shall not be condemned; forgive, and you shall be forgiven;

38 Give, and it shall be given unto you; good measure, pressed down, and shaken together, and running over, shall men give into your bosom. For with the same measure that you use, with that it shall be measured to you again."

39 And He spake a parable unto them, "Can the blind lead the blind? Shall they not both fall into the ditch?

40 The disciple is not above his master; but every one that is perfect shall be as his master.

41 And why look you the speck that is in your brother's eye, but perceivest not the beam that is in your own eye?

42 Either how canst you say to your brother, 'Brother, let me pull out the speck that is in your eye,' when you yourself see not the beam that is in your own eye? You hypocrite, cast out first the beam out of your own eye, and then shalt you see clearly to pull out the speck that is in your brother's eye.

43 For a good tree bringeth not forth corrupt fruit; neither doth a corrupt tree brings forth good fruit.

44 For every tree is known by his own fruit. For of thorns men do not gather figs, nor of a bramble bush gather they grapes.

45 A good man out of the good treasure of his heart bringeth forth that which is good; and an evil man out of the evil treasure of his heart bringeth forth that which is evil; for of the abundance of the heart his mouth speaketh.

46 And why call you Me, 'Lord (Adonai), Lord (Adonai),' and do not the things which I say?

47 Whosoever cometh to Me, and heareth My sayings, and doeth them, I will shew you to whom he is like:

48 He is like a man who built a house, and digged deep, and laid the foundation on a rock; and when the flood arose, the stream beat vehemently upon that house and could not shake it, for it was founded upon a rock.

49 But he that heareth, and doeth not, is like a man that without a foundation built a house upon the earth; against which the stream did beat vehemently, and immediately it fell; and the ruin of that house was great."

7 Now when He had ended all His sayings in the audience of the people, He entered into Capernaum.

2 And a certain centurion's servant, who was dear unto Him, was sick, and ready to die.

3 And when he heard of Yahwah, he sent unto Him the elders of the Jews (Yehudim), beseeching Him that He would come and heal His servant.

4 And when they came to Yahwah, they besought Him instantly, saying, "He was worthy for whom He should do this;

5 For he loveth our nation, and he hath built us a synagogue."

6 Then Yahwah went with them. And when He was now not far from the house, the centurion sent friends to Him, saying unto Him, "Lord (Adonai), trouble not Yourself, for I am not worthy that You shouldest enter under my roof.

7 Therefore neither thought I myself worthy to come unto You, but say in a word, and my servant shall be healed.

8 For I also am a man set under authority, having under me soldiers, and I say unto one, 'Go,' and he goeth; and to another, 'Come,' and

he cometh; and to my servant, 'Do this,' and he doeth it.'"

9 When Yahwah heard these things, He marvelled at him, and turned about, and said unto the people that followed Him, "I say unto you, I have not found so great faith, no, not in Yisrael."

10 And they that were sent, returning to the house, found the servant whole that had been sick.

11 And it came to pass the day after, that He went into a city called Nain; and many of His disciples went with Him, and much people.

12 Now when He came near to the gate of the city, behold, there was a dead man carried out, the only son of his mother, and she was a widow; and much people of the city was with her.

13 And when the Lord (Yahwah) saw her, He had compassion on her, and said unto her, "Weep not."

14 And He came and touched the bier (open coffin); and they that bare him stood still. And He said, "Young man, I say unto you, 'Arise.'"

15 And he that was dead sat up, and began to speak. And He delivered him to his mother.

16 And there came a fear on all; and they glorified God (Elohim, יהוה (YHWH)), saying, "That a great prophet is risen up among us;" and that "God (Elohim) hath visited His people."

17 And this rumour of Him went forth throughout all Judah (Yehudah), and throughout all the region round about.

18 And the disciples of John (Yochanan) shewed him of all these things.

19 And John (Yochanan) calling unto him two of his disciples sent them to Yahwah, saying, "Art You He that should come? Or look we for another?"

20 When the men had come unto Him, they said, "John (Yochanan) Baptist hath sent us unto You, saying, 'Art You He that should come? Or look we for another?'"

21 And in that same hour He cured many of their infirmities and plagues, and of evil spirits; and unto many that were blind He gave sight.

22 Then Yahwah answering said unto them, "Go your way, and tell John (Yochanan) what things you have seen and heard; how that the blind sees, the lame walk, the lepers are cleansed, the deaf hear, the dead are raised, to the poor the gospel (good news) is preached.

23 And blessed is he, whosoever shall not be offended in Me."

24 And when the messengers of John (Yochanan) had departed, He began to speak unto the people concerning John (Yochanan), "What went you out into the wilderness for to see? A reed shaken with the wind?

25 But what went you out for to see? A man clothed in soft raiment? Behold, they who are gorgeously apparelled, and live delicately, are in kings' courts.

26 But what went you out for to see? A prophet? Yea, I say unto you, and much more than a prophet.

27 This is he, of whom it is written: "Behold, I send My messenger before Your face, who shall prepare Your way before You. - *Mal. 3:1*

28 For I say unto you, 'Among those that are born of women there is not a greater prophet than John the Baptist (Yochanan haMatvil); but he that is least in the kingdom of God (Elohim, יהוה (YHWH)) is greater than he."

29 And all the people that heard Him, and the tax collectors, justified יהוה (YHWH), being baptized with the baptism of John (Yochanan).

30 But the Pharisees and lawyers rejected the counsel of יהוה (YHWH) against themselves, being not baptized of him.

31 And the Lord (Yahwah) said, "Whereunto then shall I liken the men of this generation? And to what are they like?

32 They are like unto children sitting in the marketplace, and calling one to another, and saying, 'We have piped unto you, and you have not danced; we have mourned to you, and you have not wept.'

33 For John the Baptist (Yochanan haMatvil) came neither eating bread nor drinking wine; and you say, 'He hath a devil.'

34 The Son of man (haMashiach) has come eating and drinking; and you say, 'Behold a gluttonous man, and a winebibber, a friend of tax collectors and sinners!'

35 But wisdom is justified of all her children."

36 And one of the Pharisees desired Him that He would eat with him. And He went into the Pharisee's house, and sat down to eat.

37 And, behold, a woman in the city, who was a sinner, when she knew that Yahwah sat at meat in the Pharisee's house, brought an alabaster box of ointment,

38 And stood at His feet behind Him weeping, and began to wash His feet with tears, and did wipe them with the hairs of her head, and kissed His feet, and anointed them with the ointment.

39 Now when the Pharisee who had bidden Him saw it, he spake within himself, saying, "This man, if He was a prophet, would have known who and what manner of woman this is that toucheth Him; for she is a sinner."

40 And Yahwah answering said unto him, "Shimon, I have somewhat to say unto you." And he saith, "Teacher (Rabbi), say on."

41 There was a certain creditor who had two debtors: the one owed five hundred pence, and the other fifty.

42 And when they had nothing to pay, he frankly forgave them both. Tell me therefore, which of them will love him most?"

43 Shimon answered and said, "I suppose that he, to whom he forgave most." And He said unto him, "You have rightly judged."

44 And He turned to the woman, and said unto Shimon, "Seest you this woman? I entered into your house, you gavest Me no water for My feet; but she hath washed My feet with tears, and wiped them with the hairs of her head.

45 You gavest Me no kiss, but this woman since the time I came in hath not ceased to kiss My feet.

46 My head with oil you didst not anoint, but this woman hath anointed My feet with ointment.

47 Therefore I say unto you, her sins, which are many, are forgiven; for she loved much; but to whom little is forgiven, the same loveth little."

48 And He said unto her, "Your sins are forgiven."

49 And they that sat at meat with Him began to say within themselves, "Who is this that forgiveth sins also?"

50 And He said to the woman, "Your faith hath saved you; go in peace."

8 And it came to pass afterward, that He went throughout every city and village, preaching and shewing the glad tidings of the kingdom of God (Elohim, יהוה (YHWH)); and the twelve were with Him,

2 And certain women, who had been healed of evil spirits and infirmities, Mary (Miryam) called Magdalene, out of whom went seven devils,

3 And Joanna (Yochanah) the wife of Chuza Herod's steward, and Susanna, and many others, who ministered unto Him of their substance.

4 And when much people were gathered together, and had come to Him out of every city, He spake by a parable:

5 "A sower went out to sow his seed; and as he sowed, some fell by the way side; and it was trodden down, and the fowls of the air devoured it.

6 And some fell upon a rock; and as soon as it was sprung up, it withered away, because it lacked moisture.

7 And some fell among thorns; and the thorns sprang up with it, and choked it.

8 And other fell on good ground, and sprang up, and bare fruit a hundredfold." And when He had said these things, He cried, "He that hath ears to hear, let him hear."

9 And His disciples asked Him, saying, "What might this parable be?"

10 And He said, "Unto you it is given to know the mysteries of the kingdom of God (Elohim, יהוה (YHWH)); but to others in parables; that seeing they might not see, and hearing they might not understand. – Isa. 6:9

11 Now the parable is this: The seed is the word of God (Elohim, יהוה (YHWH)).

12 Those by the way side are they that hear; then cometh the devil, and taketh away the word out of their hearts, lest they should believe and be saved.

13 They on the rock are they, who, when they hear, receive the word with joy; and these have no root, who for a while believe, and in time of temptation fall away.

14 And that which fell among thorns are they, who, when they have heard, go forth, and are choked with cares and riches and pleasures of this life, and bring no fruit to perfection.

15 But that on the good ground are they, who in an honest and good heart, having heard the word, keep it, and bring forth fruit with patience.

16 No man, when he hath lighted a candle, covereth it with a vessel, or putteth it under a bed; but setteth it on a candlestick (menorah), that they who enter in may see the light.

17 For nothing is secret, that shall not be made manifest; neither any thing hid, that shall not be known and come abroad.

18 Take heed therefore how you hear; for

whosoever hath, to him shall be given; and whosoever hath not, from him shall be taken even that which he seemeth to have."

19 Then came to Him His mother and His brethren, and could not come to Him because of the crowd.

20 And it was told Him by certain who said, "Your mother and Your brethren stand outside, desiring to see You."

21 And He answered and said unto them, "My mother and My brethren are these who hear the word of God (Elohim, יהוה (YHWH)), and do it."

22 Now it came to pass on a certain day, that He went into a ship with His disciples; and He said unto them, "Let us go over unto the other side of the lake." And they launched forth.

23 But as they sailed He fell asleep; and there came down a storm of wind on the lake; and they were filled with water, and were in jeopardy.

24 And they came to Him, and awoke Him, saying, "Teacher (Rabbi)! Teacher (Rabbi)! We perish." Then He arose, and rebuked the wind and the raging of the water; and they ceased, and there was a calm.

25 And He said unto them, "Where is your faith?" And they being afraid wondered, saying one to another, "What manner of man is this!" For He commandeth even the winds and water, and they obey Him.

26 And they arrived at the country of the Gadarenes, which is opposite Galilee.

27 And when He went forth to land, there met Him out of the city a certain man, which had devils long time, and ware no clothes, neither abode in any house, but in the tombs.

28 When he saw Yahwah, he cried out, and fell down before Him, and with a loud voice said, "What have I to do with you, Yahwah, you B47Humanity of God Most High (El Elyon)? I beseech You, torment me not."

29 (For He had commanded the unclean spirit to come out of the man. For oftentimes it had caught him: and he was kept bound with chains and in fetters; and he brake the bands, and was driven of the devil into the wilderness.)

30 And Yahwah asked him, saying, "What is your name?" And he said, "Legion," because many devils were entered into him.

31 And they besought Him that He would not command them to go out into the deep.

32 And there was there a herd of many swine feeding on the mountain; and they besought Him that He would allow them to enter into them. And He allowed them.

33 Then went the devils out of the man, and entered into the swine; and the herd ran violently down a steep place into the lake, and were choked.

34 When they that fed them saw what was done, they fled, and went and told it in the city and in the country.

35 Then they went out to see what was done; and came to Yahwah, and found the man, out of whom the devils were departed, sitting at the feet of Yahwah, clothed, and in his right mind; and they were afraid.

36 They also who saw it told them by what means he that was possessed of the devils was healed.

37 Then the whole multitude of the country of the Gadarenes round about besought Him to depart from them; for they were taken with great fear. And He went up into the ship, and returned back again.

38 Now the man out of whom the devils were departed besought Him that he might be with Him; but Yahwah sent him away, saying,

39 "Return to your own house, and shew how great things God (Elohim) hath done unto you." And he went his way, and published throughout the whole city how great things Yahwah had done unto him.

40 And it came to pass, that, when Yahwah had returned, the people gladly received Him; for they were all waiting for Him.

41 And, behold, there came a man named Yair, and he was a ruler of the synagogue; and he fell down at Yahwah's feet, and besought Him that He would come into his house;

42 For he had one only daughter, about twelve years of age, and she lay dying. But as He went the people thronged Him.

43 And a woman having an issue of blood twelve years, who had spent all her living upon physicians, neither could be healed of any,

44 Came behind Him, and touched the border of His garment; and immediately her issue of blood stanched.

45 And Yahwah said, "Who touched Me?" When all denied, Peter (Kefa) and they that were with Him said, "Teacher (Rabbi), the

multitude throng You and press You, and sayest You, "Who touched Me?"

46 And Yahwah said, "Somebody hath touched Me, for I perceive that power has gone out of Me."

47 And when the woman saw that she was not hid, she came trembling, and falling down before Him, she declared unto Him before all the people for what causes she had touched Him, and how she was healed immediately.

48 And He said unto her, "Daughter, be of good comfort; your faith hath made you whole, go in peace."

49 While He yet spake, there cometh one from the ruler of the synagogue's house, saying to him, "Your daughter is dead; trouble not the Teacher (Rabbi)."

50 But when Yahwah heard it, He answered him, saying, "Fear not; believe only, and she shall be made whole."

51 And when He came into the house, He allowed no man to go in, except Peter (Kefa), and Jacob (Yaaqov), and John (Yochanan), and the father and the mother of the maiden.

52 And all wept, and bewailed her; but He said, "Weep not; she is not dead, but sleepeth."

53 And they laughed Him to scorn, knowing that she was dead.

54 And He put them all out, and took her by the hand, and called, saying, "Maid, arise."

55 And her spirit came again, and she arose straightway; and He commanded to give her to eat.

56 And her parents were astonished; but He warned them that they should tell no man what was done."

9 Then He called His twelve disciples together, and gave them power and authority over all devils, and to cure diseases.

2 And He sent them to preach the kingdom of God (Elohim, יהוה (YHWH)), and to heal the sick.

3 And He said unto them, "Take nothing for your journey, neither staves, nor scrip, neither bread, neither money; neither have two coats apiece.

4 And whatsoever house you enter into, there abide, and thence depart.

5 And whosoever will not receive you, when you go out of that city, shake off the very dust from your feet for a testimony against them."

6 And they departed, and went through the towns, preaching the gospel (good news), and healing every where.

7 Now Herod the tetrarch heard of all that was done by Him; and He was perplexed, because that it was said of some, that John (Yochanan) was risen from the dead;

8 And of some, that Elijah (Eliyahu) had appeared; and of others, that one of the old prophets was risen again.

9 And Herod said, "John (Yochanan) have I beheaded; but who is this, of whom I hear such things?" And he desired to see Him.

10 And the apostles, when they were returned, told Him all that they had done. And He took them, and went aside privately into a desert place belonging to the city called Bethsaida.

11 And the people, when they knew it, followed Him; and He received them, and spake unto them of the kingdom of God (Elohim, יהוה (YHWH)), and healed them that had need of healing.

12 And when the day began to wear away, then came the twelve, and said unto Him, "Send the multitude away, that they may go into the towns and country round about, and lodge, and get victuals; for we are here in a desert place."

13 But He said unto them, "Give you them to eat." And they said, "We have no more but five loaves and two fishes; except we should go and buy meat for all this people."

14 For they were about five thousand men. And He said to His disciples, "Make them sit down by fifties in a company."

15 And they did so, and made them all sit down.

16 Then He took the five loaves and the two fishes, and looking up to heaven, He blessed them, and brake, and gave to the disciples to set before the multitude.

17 And they did eat, and were all filled; and there was taken up of fragments that remained to them twelve baskets.

18 And it came to pass, as He was alone praying, His disciples were with him; and He asked them, saying, "Whom say the people that I am?"

19 They answering said, "John the Baptist (Yochanan haMatvil); but some say, Elijah (Eliyahu); and others say that one of the old prophets is risen again."

20 He said unto them, "But whom say you that I am?" Peter (Kefa) answering said, "You are

the Anointed One of God (Mashiach haElohim atah).”

21 And He straitly charged them, and commanded them to tell no man that thing;

22 Saying, “The Son of man (haMashiach) must suffer many things, and be rejected of the elders and chief priests (kohanim) and scribes, and be slain, and be raised the third day.”

23 And He said to them all, “If any man will come after Me, let him deny himself, and take up his stake daily, and follow Me.

24 For whosoever will save his life shall lose it, but whosoever will lose his life for My sake, the same shall save it.

25 For what is a man advantaged, if he gains the whole world, and lose himself, or be cast away?

26 For whosoever shall be ashamed of Me and of My words, of him shall the Son of man (haMashiach) be ashamed, when He shall come in His own glory, and in His Father’s, and of the holy angels.

27 But I tell you of a truth, there be some standing here, who shall not taste of death, till they see the kingdom of God (Elohim, יהוה (YHWH)).”

28 And it came to pass about eight days after these sayings, He took Peter (Kefa) and John (Yochanan) and Jacob (Yaaqov), and went up into a mountain to pray.

29 And as He prayed, the fashion of His countenance was altered, and His raiment was white and glistering.

30 And, behold, there talked with Him two men, who were Moses (Mosheh) and Elijah (Eliyahu);

31 Who appeared in glory, and spake of His decease which He should accomplish at Jerusalem (Yerushalayim).

32 But Peter (Kefa) and they that were with him were heavy with sleep; and when they were awake, they saw His glory, and the two men that stood with Him.

33 And it came to pass, as they departed from Him, Peter (Kefa) said unto Yahwah, “Teacher (Rabbi), it is good for us to be here; and let us make three tabernacles: one for You, and one for Moses (Mosheh), and one for Elijah (Eliyahu); not knowing what he said.

34 While he thus spake, there came a cloud, and overshadowed them; and they feared as they entered into the cloud.

35 And there came a voice out of the cloud,

saying, “This is My beloved [B47]Son (Humanity); hear Him.”

36 And when the voice was past, Yahwah was found alone. And they kept it close, and told no man in those days any of those things which they had seen.

37 And it came to pass, that on the next day, when they were come down from the hill, much people met Him.

38 And, behold, a man of the company cried out, saying, “Teacher (Rabbi), I beseech You, look upon my son; for he is mine only child.

39 And, behold, a spirit taketh him, and he suddenly crieth out; and it teareth him that he foameth again, and bruising him hardly departeth from him.

40 And I besought Your disciples to cast him out; and they could not.”

41 And Yahwah answering said, “O faithless and perverse generation, how long shall I be with you, and bear with you? Bring your son hither.”

42 And as he was yet coming, the devil threw him down, and tare him. And Yahwah rebuked the unclean spirit, and healed the child, and delivered him again to his father.

43 And they were all amazed at the mighty power of God (Elohim, יהוה (YHWH). But while they wondered every one at all things which Yahwah did, He said unto His disciples,

44 “Let these sayings sink down into your ears, for the Son of man (haMashiach) shall be delivered into the hands of men.”

45 But they understood not this saying, and it was hidden from them, that they perceived it not; and they feared to ask Him of that saying.

46 Then there arose a reasoning among them, which of them should be greatest.

47 And Yahwah, perceiving the thought of their heart, took a child, and set him by Him,

48 And said unto them, “Whosoever shall receive this child in My name receiveth Me; and whosoever shall receive Me receiveth Him that sent Me. For he that is least among you all, the same shall be great.”

49 And John (Yochanan) answered and said, “Teacher (Rabbi), we saw one casting out devils in Your name; and we forbad him, because he followeth not with us.”

50 And Yahwah said unto him, “Forbid him not, for he that is not against us is for us.”

51 And it came to pass, when the time was come that He should be received up, He stedfastly set His face to go to Jerusalem (Yerushalayim),
52 And sent messengers before His face; and they went, and entered into a village of the Samaritans, to make ready for Him.
53 And they did not receive Him, because His face was as though He would go to Jerusalem (Yerushalayim).
54 And when His disciples Jacob (Yaaqov) and John (Yochanan) saw this, they said, "Lord (Adonai), wilt You that we command fire to come down from heaven, and consume them, even as Elijah (Eliyahu) did?"
55 But He turned, and rebuked them, and said, "You know not what manner of spirit you are of.
56 For the Son of man (haMashiach) did not come to destroy men's lives, but to save them." And they went to another village.
57 And it came to pass, that, as they went in the way, a certain man said unto Him, "Lord (Adonai), I will follow You whithersoever You goest."
58 And Yahwah said unto him, "Foxes have holes, and birds of the air have nests; but the Son of man (haMashiach) hath not where to lay His head."
59 And He said unto another, "Follow Me." But he said, "Lord (Adonai), let me first to go and bury my father."
60 Yahwah said unto him, "Let the dead bury their dead; but go you and preach the kingdom of God (Elohim, יהוה (YHWH))."
61 And another also said, "Lord (Adonai), I will follow You; but let me first go bid them farewell, who are at home at my house."
62 And Yahwah said unto him, "No man, having put his hand to the plough, and looking back, is fit for the kingdom of God (Elohim, יהוה (YHWH))."

10 After these things the Lord (Yahwah) appointed other seventy also, and sent them two and two before His face into every city and place, whither He Himself would come.
2 Therefore said He unto them, "The harvest truly is great, but the labourers are few; pray you therefore the Lord God (El Adon) of the Harvest (haQatsir), that He would send forth labourers into His harvest.
3 Go your ways; behold, I send you forth as lambs among wolves.

4 Carry neither purse, nor scrip, nor shoes; and salute no man by the way.
5 And into whatsoever house you enter, first say, 'Peace be to this house.'
6 And if the son of peace be there, your peace shall rest upon it; if not, it shall turn to you again.
7 And in the same house remain, eating and drinking such things as they give; for the labourer is worthy of his hire. Go not from house to house.
8 And into whatsoever city you enter, and they receive you, eat such things as are set before you;
9 And heal the sick that are therein, and say unto them, 'The kingdom of God (Elohim, יהוה (YHWH)) is come near unto you.'
10 But into whatsoever city you enter, and they receive you not, go your ways out into the streets of the same, and say,
11 'Even the very dust of your city, which cleaveth on us, we do wipe off against you; notwithstanding be you sure of this, that the kingdom of God (Elohim, יהוה (YHWH)) is come near unto you.'
12 But I say unto you, that it shall be more tolerable in that day for Sodom, than for that city.
13 Woe unto you, Chorazin! Woe unto you, Bethsaida! For if the mighty works had been done in Tyre and Sidon, which have been done in you, they had a great while ago repented, sitting in sackcloth and ashes.
14 But it shall be more tolerable for Tyre and Sidon at the judgment, than for you.
15 And you, Capernaum, which art exalted to heaven, shalt be thrust down to hell (sheol). – *Isa.14:13, 15*
16 He that heareth you heareth Me; and he that despiseth you despiseth Me; and he that despiseth Me despiseth Him that sent Me."
17 And the seventy returned again with joy, saying, "Lord (Adonai), even the devils are subject unto us through Your name."
18 And He said unto them, "I beheld Satan as lightning fall from heaven.
19 Behold, I give unto you power to tread on serpents and scorpions, and over all the power of the enemy; and nothing shall by any means hurt you.
20 Notwithstanding in this rejoice not, that the spirits are subject unto you; but rather rejoice,

because your names are written in heaven."

21 In that hour Yahwah rejoiced in Spirit, and said, "I thank You, O Father, Lord (Adon) of the heaven and the earth, that You have hid these things from the wise and prudent, and hast revealed them unto babes; even so, Father; for so it seemed good in Your sight.

22 All things are delivered to Me of My Father; and no man knoweth who the [B47]Son (Humanity of El) is, but the Father; and who the Father is, but the [B47]Son, and to him whom the [B47]Son will to reveal Him."

23 And He turned Himself unto His disciples, and said privately, "Blessed are the eyes who see the things that you see;

24 For I tell you, that many prophets and kings have desired to see those things which you see, and have not seen them; and to hear those things which you hear, and have not heard them."

25 And, behold, a certain lawyer stood up, and tested Him, saying, "Teacher (Rabbi), what shall I do to inherit eternal life?"

26 He said unto him, "What is written in the Torah? How readest you?"

27 And he answering said, "You shalt love יהוה your God (YHWH Eloheikha) with all your heart, and with all your soul, and with all your strength, and with all your mind; and your neighbour as yourself." – *Deu. 6:5, Lev. 19:18*

28 And He said unto him, "You have answered right; this do, and you shalt live."

29 But he, willing to justify himself, said unto Yahwah, "And who is my neighbour?"

30 And Yahwah answering said, "A certain man went down from Jerusalem (Yerushalayim) to Yericho, and fell among thieves, who stripped him of his raiment, and wounded him, and departed, leaving him half dead.

31 And by chance there came down a certain priest (kohen) that way; and when he saw him, he passed by on the other side.

32 And likewise a Levite (Lewi), when he was at the place, came and looked on him, and passed by on the other side.

33 But a certain Samaritan, as he journeyed, came where he was; and when he saw him, he had compassion on him,

34 And went to him, and bound up his wounds, pouring in oil and wine, and set him on his own animal, and brought him to an inn, and took care of him.

35 And on the morrow when he departed, he took out two pence, and gave them to the host, and said unto him, 'Take care of him; and whatsoever you spendest more, when I come again, I will repay you.'

36 Which now of these three, thinkest you, was neighbour unto him that fell among the thieves?"

37 And he said, "He that shewed mercy on him." Then said Yahwah unto him, "Go, and do you likewise."

38 Now it came to pass, as they went, that He entered into a certain village; and a certain woman named Martha received Him into her house.

39 And she had a sister called Mary (Miryam), who also sat at Yahwah's feet, and heard His word.

40 But Martha was cumbered about much serving, and came to Him, and said, "Lord (Adonai), dost You not care that my sister hath left me to serve alone? Bid her therefore that she helps me."

41 And Yahwah answered and said unto her, "Martha, Martha, you are careful and troubled about many things;

42 But one thing is needful; and Mary (Miryam) hath chosen that good part, which shall not be taken away from her."

11 And it came to pass, that, as He was praying in a certain place, when He ceased, one of His disciples said unto Him, "Lord (Adonai), teach us to pray, as John (Yochanan) also taught His disciples.

2 And He said unto them, "When you pray, say: 'Our Father who art in heaven, hallowed be Your name. Your kingdom come. Your will be done, as in heaven, so in earth.

3 Give us day by day our daily bread.

4 And forgive us our sins; for we also forgive every one that is indebted to us. And lead us not into temptation; but deliver us from evil."

5 And He said unto them, "Which of you shall have a friend, and shall go unto him at midnight, and say unto him, 'Friend, lend me three loaves;

6 For a friend of mine in his journey is come to me, and I have nothing to set before him?'

7 And he from within shall answer and say, 'Trouble me not; the door is now shut, and my children are with me in bed; I cannot rise and give you.'

8 I say unto you, though he will not rise and give him, because he is his friend, yet because of his importunity he will rise and give him as many as he needeth.

9 And I say unto you, ask, and it shall be given you; seek, and you shall find; knock, and it shall be opened unto you.

10 For every one that asketh receiveth; and he that seeketh findeth; and to him that knocketh it shall be opened.

11 If a son shall ask bread of any of you that is a father, will he give him a stone? Or if he asks a fish, will he for a fish give him a serpent?

12 Or if he shall ask an egg, will he offer him a scorpion?

13 If you then, being evil, know how to give good gifts unto your children; how much more shall your heavenly Father give the Holy Spirit (Ruach haQodesh) to them that ask Him?"

14 And He was casting out a devil, and it was dumb. And it came to pass, when the devil was gone out, the dumb spake; and the people wondered.

15 But some of them said, "He casteth out devils through Beelzebul (Baal Zebub) the chief of the devils."

16 And others, testing Him, sought of Him a sign from heaven.

17 But He, knowing their thoughts, said unto them, "Every kingdom divided against itself is brought to desolation; and a house divided against a house falleth.

18 If Satan also be divided against himself, how shall his kingdom stand? Because you say that I cast out devils through Beelzebul (Baal Zebub).

19 And if I by Beelzebul (Baal Zebub) cast out devils, by whom do your sons cast them out? Therefore shall they be your judges.

20 But if I with the finger of God (Elohim) cast out devils, no doubt the kingdom of God (Elohim, יהוה (YHWH)) is come upon you.

21 When a strong man armed keepeth his palace, his goods are in peace;

22 But when a stronger than he shall come upon him, and overcome him, he taketh from him all his armour wherein he trusted, and divideth his spoils.

23 He that is not with Me is against Me; and he that gathereth not with Me scattereth.

24 When the unclean spirit is gone out of a man, he walketh through dry places, seeking rest; and finding none, he saith, 'I will return unto my house whence I came out.'

25 And when he cometh, he findeth it swept and garnished.

26 Then goeth he, and taketh to him seven other spirits more wicked than himself; and they enter in, and dwell there; and the last state of that man is worse than the first."

27 And it came to pass, as He spake these things, a certain woman of the company lifted up her voice, and said unto Him, "Blessed is the womb that bare You, and the paps which You have sucked."

28 But He said, "Yea rather, blessed are they that hear the word of God (Elohim, יהוה (YHWH)), and keep it."

29 And when the people were gathered thick together, He began to say, "This is an evil generation. They seek a sign; and there shall no sign be given it, but the sign of Jonas (Yonah) the prophet.

30 For as Jonas (Yonah) was a sign unto the Ninevites, so shall also the Son of man (haMashiach) be to this generation.

31 The queen of the south shall rise up in the judgment with the men of this generation, and condemn them; for she came from the utmost parts of the earth to hear the wisdom of Solomon (Shelomoh); and, behold, a greater than Solomon (Shelomoh) is here.

32 The men of Nineve shall rise up in the judgment with this generation, and shall condemn it; for they repented at the preaching of Jonas (Yonah); and, behold, a greater than Jonas (Yonah) is here.

33 No man, when he hath lighted a candle, putteth it in a secret place, neither under a bushel, but on a candlestick (menorah), that they who come in may see the light.

34 The lamp of the body is the eye; therefore when your eye is clear, your whole body also is full of light; but when your eye is bad, your body also is full of darkness.

35 Take heed therefore that the light which is in you be not darkness.

36 If your whole body therefore be full of light, having no part dark, the whole shall be full of light, as when the bright shining of a candle doth give you light."

37 And as He spake, a certain Pharisee besought Him to dine with him; and He went in, and sat

down to meat.

38 And when the Pharisee saw it, he marvelled that He had not first washed before dinner.

39 And the Lord (Yahwah) said unto him, "Now do you Pharisees make clean the outside of the cup and the platter; but your inward part is full of ravening and wickedness.

40 You fools, did not he that made that which is outside make that which is within also?

41 But rather give alms of such things as you have; and, behold, all things are clean unto you.

42 But woe unto you, Pharisees! For you tithe mint and rue and all manner of herbs, and pass over judgment and the love of God (Elohim); these ought you to have done, and not to leave the other undone.

43 Woe unto you, Pharisees! For you love the uppermost seats in the synagogues, and greetings in the markets.

44 Woe unto you, scribes and Pharisees, hypocrites! For you are as graves which appear not, and the men that walk over them are not aware of them."

45 Then answered one of the lawyers, and said unto Him, "Teacher (Rabbi), thus saying You reproachest us also."

46 And He said, "Woe unto you also, you lawyers! For you lade men with burdens grievous to be borne, and you yourselves touch not the burdens with one of your fingers.

47 Woe unto you! For you build the sepulchres of the prophets, and your fathers killed them.

48 Truly you bear witness that you allow the deeds of your fathers; for they indeed killed them, and you build their sepulchres.

49 Therefore also said the wisdom of God (Elohim), 'I will send them prophets and apostles, and some of them they shall slay and persecute;'

50 That the blood of all the prophets, which was shed from the foundation of the world, may be required of this generation;

51 From the blood of Abel (Hevel) unto the blood of Zacharias (Zekharyah), who perished between the altar and the temple; verily I say unto you, it shall be required of this generation.

52 Woe unto you, lawyers! For you have taken away the key of knowledge; you entered not in yourselves, and them that were entering in you hindered."

53 And as He said these things unto them, the scribes and the Pharisees began to urge Him vehemently, and to provoke Him to speak of many things;

54 Laying wait for Him, and seeking to catch something out of His mouth, that they might accuse Him.

12 In the mean time, when there were gathered together an innumerable multitude of people, insomuch that they trode one upon another, He began to say unto His disciples first of all, "Beware you of the leaven of the Pharisees, which is hypocrisy.

2 For there is nothing covered, that shall not be revealed; neither hid, that shall not be known.

3 Therefore whatsoever you have spoken in darkness shall be heard in the light; and that which you have spoken in the ear in closets shall be proclaimed upon the housetops.

4 And I say unto you my friends, 'Be not afraid of them that kill the body, and after that have no more that they can do.

5 But I will forewarn you whom you shall fear: Fear Him, who after He hath killed hath power to cast into hell (sheol); yea, I say unto you, fear Him.

6 Are not five sparrows sold for two farthings, and not one of them is forgotten before God (Elohim)?

7 But even the very hairs of your head are all numbered. Fear not therefore, you are of more value than many sparrows.

8 Also I say unto you, whosoever shall confess Me before men, him shall the Son of man (haMashiach) also confess before the angels of God (Elohim);

9 But he that denieth Me before men shall be denied before the angels of God (Elohim).

10 And whosoever shall speak a word against the son of man, it shall be forgiven him; but unto him that blasphemeth against the Holy Spirit it shall not be forgiven.

11 And when they bring you unto the synagogues, and unto magistrates, and powers, take you no thought how or what thing you shall answer, or what you shall say;

12 For the Holy Spirit (Ruach haQodesh) shall teach you in the same hour what you ought to say."

13 And one of the company said unto Him, "Teacher (Rabbi), speak to my brother, that he divide the inheritance with me."

14 And He said unto him, "Man, who made Me a judge or a divider over you?"

15 And He said unto them, "Take heed, and beware of covetousness; for a man's life consisteth not in the abundance of the things which he possesseth."

16 And He spake a parable unto them, saying, "The ground of a certain rich man brought forth plentifully;

17 And he thought within himself, saying, 'What shall I do, because I have no room where to bestow my fruits?'

18 And he said, 'This will I do: I will pull down my barns, and build greater; and there will I bestow all my fruits and my goods.

19 And I will say to my soul, "Soul, you have much goods laid up for many years; take your ease, eat, drink, and be merry."'

20 But God (Elohim) said unto him, 'You fool! This night your soul shall be required of you; then whose shall those things be, which you have provided?'

21 So is he that layeth up treasure for himself, and is not rich toward God (Elohim)."

22 And He said unto His disciples, "Therefore I say unto you, take no thought for your life, what you shall eat; neither for the body, what you shall put on.

23 The life is more than food, and the body is more than raiment.

24 Consider the ravens, for they neither sow nor reap; which neither have storehouse nor barn; and God (Elohim) feedeth them; how much more are you better than the fowls?

25 And which of you with taking thought can add to his stature one cubit?

26 If you then be not able to do that thing which is least, why take you thought for the rest?

27 Consider the lilies how they grow: they toil not, they spin not; and yet I say unto you, that Solomon (Shelomoh) in all his glory was not arrayed like one of these.

28 If then God (Elohim) so clothe the grass, which is today in the field, and tomorrow is cast into the oven; how much more will He clothe you, O you of little faith?

29 And seek not you what you shall eat, or what you shall drink, neither be you of doubtful mind.

30 For all these things do the nations of the world seek after; and your Father knoweth that you have need of these things.

31 But rather seek you the kingdom of God (Elohim, יהוה (YHWH)); and all these things shall be added unto you.

32 Fear not, little flock; for it is your Father's good pleasure to give you the kingdom.

33 Sell that you have, and give alms; provide yourselves bags which wax not old, a treasure in the heavens that faileth not, where no thief approacheth, neither moth corrupteth.

34 For where your treasure is, there will your heart be also.

35 Let your loins be girded about, and your lights burning;

36 And you yourselves like unto men that wait for their master, when he will return from the wedding; that when he cometh and knocketh, they may open unto him immediately.

37 Blessed are those servants, whom the master when he cometh shall find watching; verily I say unto you, that he shall gird himself, and make them to sit down to meat, and will come forth and serve them.

38 And if he shall come in the second watch, or come in the third watch, and find them so, blessed are those servants.

39 And this know, that if the goodman of the house had known what hour the thief would come, he would have watched, and not have let his house to be broken through.

40 Be you therefore ready also, for the Son of man (haMashiach) cometh at an hour when you think not."

41 Then Peter (Kefa) said unto Him, "Lord (Adonai), speakest You this parable unto us, or even to all?"

42 And the Lord (Yahwah) said, "Who then is that faithful and wise steward, whom his master shall make ruler over his household, to give them their portion of meat in due season?

43 Blessed is that servant, whom his master when he cometh shall find so doing.

44 Of a truth I say unto you, that he will make him ruler over all that he hath.

45 But and if that servant says in his heart, 'My master delayeth his coming;' and shall begin to beat the menservants and maidens, and to eat and drink, and to be drunken;

46 The master of that servant will come in a day when he looketh not for him, and at an hour when he is not aware, and will cut him in sunder, and will appoint him his portion with

the unbelievers.

47 And that servant, who knew his master's will, and prepared not himself, neither did according to his will, shall be beaten with many stripes.

48 But he that knew not, and did commit things worthy of stripes, shall be beaten with few stripes. For unto whomsoever much is given, of him shall be much required; and to whom men have committed much, of him they will ask the more.

49 I am come to send fire on the earth; and what will I, if it be already kindled?

50 But I have a baptism to be baptized with; and how am I straitened till it be accomplished!

51 Suppose you that I am come to give peace on earth? I tell you, nay; but rather division;

52 For from henceforth there shall be five in one house divided, three against two, and two against three.

53 The father shall be divided against the son, and the son against the father; the mother against the daughter, and the daughter against the mother; the mother in law against her daughter in law, and the daughter in law against her mother in law."

54 And He said also to the people, "When you see a cloud rise out of the west, straightway you say, 'There cometh a shower;' and so it is.

55 And when you see the south wind blow, you say, 'There will be heat;' and it cometh to pass.

56 You hypocrites! You can discern the face of the sky and of the earth; but how is it that you do not discern this time?

57 Yea, and why even of yourselves judge you not what is right?

58 When you goest with your adversary to the magistrate, as you are in the way, give diligence that you mayest be delivered from him; lest he hale you to the judge, and the judge deliver you to the officer, and the officer cast you into prison.

59 I tell you, you shalt not depart thence, till you have paid the very last mite."

13 There were present at that season some that told Him of the Galilaeans, whose blood Pilate had mingled with their sacrifices.

2 And Yahwah answering said unto them, "Suppose you that these Galilaeans were sinners above all the Galilaeans, because they suffered such things?

3 I tell you, nay; but, except you repent, you shall all likewise perish.

4 Or those eighteen, upon whom the tower in Siloam fell, and slew them, think you that they were sinners above all men that dwelt in Jerusalem (Yerushalayim)?

5 I tell you, nay; but, except you repent, you shall all likewise perish."

6 He spake also this parable: "A certain man had a fig tree planted in his vineyard; and he came and sought fruit thereon, and found none.

7 Then said he unto the dresser of his vineyard, 'Behold, these three years I come seeking fruit on this fig tree, and find none; cut it down; why cumbereth it the ground?'

8 And he answering said unto him, 'Master, let it alone this year also, till I shall dig about it, and dung it;

9 And if it bears fruit, well; and if not, then after that you shalt cut it down.'"

10 And He was teaching in one of the synagogues on the Shabbat.

11 And, behold, there was a woman who had a spirit of infirmity eighteen years, and was bowed together, and could in no wise lift up herself.

12 And when Yahwah saw her, He called her to Him, and said unto her, "Woman, you are loosed from your infirmity."

13 And He laid his hands on her; and immediately she was made straight, and glorified God (Elohim).

14 And the ruler of the synagogue answered with indignation, because that Yahwah had healed on the Shabbat day, and said unto the people, "There are six days in which men ought to work; in them therefore come and be healed, and not on the Shabbat day."

15 The Lord (Adonai) then answered him, and said, "You hypocrite! Doth not each one of you on the Shabbat loose his ox or his ass from the stall, and lead him away to watering?

16 And ought not this woman, being a daughter of Avraham, whom Satan hath bound, behold, these eighteen years, be loosed from this bond on the Shabbat day?"

17 And when He had said these things, all His adversaries were ashamed; and all the people rejoiced for all the glorious things that were done by Him.

18 Then said He, "Unto what is the kingdom of God (Elohim, יהוה (YHWH)) like? And

whereunto shall I resemble it?

19 It is like a grain of mustard seed, which a man took, and cast into his garden; and it grew, and waxed a great tree; and the fowls of the air lodged in the branches of it."

20 And again He said, "Whereunto shall I liken the kingdom of God (Elohim, יהוה (YHWH))?

21 It is like leaven, which a woman took and hid in three measures of meal, till the whole was leavened."

22 And He went through the cities and villages, teaching, and journeying toward Jerusalem (Yerushalayim).

23 Then said one unto Him, "Lord (Adonai), are there few that be saved?" And He said unto them,

24 "Strive to enter in at the strait gate; for many, I say unto you, will seek to enter in, and shall not be able.

25 When once the master of the house is risen up, and hath shut to the door, and you begin to stand outside, and to knock at the door, saying, 'Lord (Adonai), Lord (Adonai), open unto us;' and He shall answer and say unto you, 'I know you not whence you are.'

26 Then shall you begin to say, 'We have eaten and drunk in Your presence, and You have taught in our streets.'

27 But He shall say, 'I tell you, I know you not whence you are; depart from Me, all you workers of iniquity.'

28 There shall be weeping and gnashing of teeth, when you shall see Avraham, and Isaac (Yitschaq), and Jacob (Yaaqov), and all the prophets, in the kingdom of God (Elohim, יהוה (YHWH)), and you yourselves thrust out.

29 And they shall come from the east, and from the west, and from the north, and from the south, and shall sit down in the kingdom of God (Elohim, יהוה (YHWH)).

30 And, behold, there are last who shall be first, and there are first who shall be last."

31 The same day there came certain of the Pharisees, saying unto Him, "Get You out, and depart hence; for Herod will kill You."

32 And He said unto them, "Go you, and tell that fox, 'Behold, I cast out devils, and I do cures today and tomorrow, and the third day I shall be perfected.'

33 Nevertheless I must walk today, and tomorrow, and the day following; for it cannot

be that a prophet perishes out of Jerusalem (Yerushalayim).

34 O Jerusalem, Jerusalem (Yerushalayim), which killest the prophets, and stonest them that are sent unto you; how often would I have gathered your children together, as a hen doth gather her brood under her wings, and you would not!

35 Behold, your house is left unto you desolate; and verily I say unto you, you shall not see Me, until the time come when you shall say, 'Blessed is He that cometh in the name of יהוה (YHWH, Yahwah).'" – *Psa. 118:26*

14 And it came to pass, as He went into the house of one of the chief Pharisees to eat bread on the Shabbat day, that they watched Him.

2 And, behold, there was a certain man before Him who had the dropsy.

3 And Yahwah answering spake unto the lawyers and Pharisees, saying, "Is it lawful to heal on the Shabbat day?"

4 And they held their peace. And He took him, and healed him, and let him go;

5 And answered them, saying, "Which of you shall have an ass or an ox fallen into a pit, and will not straightway pull him out on the Shabbat day?"

6 And they could not answer Him again to these things.

7 And He put forth a parable to those who were bidden, when He marked how they chose out the chief rooms; saying unto them,

8 "When you are bidden of any man to a wedding, sit not down in the highest room; lest a more honourable man than you be bidden of him;

9 And he that bade you and him come and say to you, 'Give this man place;' and you begin with shame to take the lowest room.

10 But when you are bidden, go and sit down in the lowest room; that when he that bade you cometh, he may say unto you, 'Friend, go up higher;' then shalt you have worship in the presence of them that sit at meat with you.

11 For whosoever exalteth himself shall be abased; and he that humbleth himself shall be exalted."

12 Then said He also to him that bade Him, "When you makest a dinner or a supper, call not your friends, nor your brethren, neither

your kinsmen, nor your rich neighbours; lest they also bid you again, and a recompence be made you.

13 But when you makest a feast, call the poor, the maimed, the lame, the blind;

14 And you shalt be blessed; for they cannot recompense you; for you shalt be recompensed at the resurrection of the just."

15 And when one of them that sat at meat with Him heard these things, he said unto Him, 'Blessed is he that shall eat bread in the kingdom of God (Elohim, יהוה (YHWH)).'

16 Then said He unto him, "A certain man made a great supper, and bade many;

17 And sent his servant at supper time to say to them that were bidden, 'Come; for all things are now ready.'

18 And they all with one consent began to make excuse. The first said unto him, 'I have bought a piece of ground, and I must needs go and see it. I pray you have me excused.'

19 And another said, 'I have bought five yokes of oxen, and I go to prove them. I pray you have me excused.'

20 And another said, 'I have married a wife, and therefore I cannot come.'

21 So that servant came, and shewed his master these things. Then the master of the house being angry said to his servant, 'Go out quickly into the streets and lanes of the city, and bring in hither the poor, and the maimed, and the halt, and the blind.'

22 And the servant said, 'Master, it is done as you have commanded, and yet there is room.'

23 And the master said unto the servant, 'Go out into the highways and hedges, and compel them to come in, that my house may be filled.

24 For I say unto you, that none of those men who were bidden shall taste of my supper.'"

25 And there went great multitudes with Him; and He turned, and said unto them,

26 "If any man come to Me, and hate (love less) not his father, and mother, and wife, and children, and brethren, and sisters, yea, and his own life also, he cannot be My disciple.

27 And whosoever doth not bear his stake, and come after Me, cannot be My disciple.

28 For which of you, intending to build a tower, sitteth not down first, and counteth the cost, whether he has sufficient to finish it?

29 Lest haply, after he hath laid the foundation, and is not able to finish it, all that behold it begin to mock him,

30 Saying, 'This man began to build, and was not able to finish.'

31 Or what king, going to make war against another king, sitteth not down first, and consulteth whether he be able with ten thousand to meet him that cometh against him with twenty thousand?

32 Or else, while the other is yet a great way off, he sendeth an ambassage, and desireth conditions of peace.

33 So likewise, whosoever he be of you that forsaketh not all that he hath, he cannot be My disciple.

34 Salt is good; but if the salt has lost its savour, wherewith shall it be seasoned?

35 It is neither fit for the land, nor yet for the dunghill; but men cast it out. He that hath ears to hear, let him hear."

15 Then drew near unto Him all the tax collectors and sinners for to hear Him.

2 And the Pharisees and scribes murmured, saying, "This man receiveth sinners, and eateth with them."

3 And He spake this parable unto them, saying,

4 "What man of you, having a hundred sheep, if he loses one of them, doth not leave the ninety and nine in the wilderness, and go after that which is lost, until he finds it?

5 And when he hath found it, he layeth it on his shoulders, rejoicing.

6 And when he cometh home, he calleth together his friends and neighbours, saying unto them, 'Rejoice with me; for I have found my sheep which was lost.'

7 I say unto you, that likewise joy shall be in heaven over one sinner that repenteth, more than over ninety and nine just persons, who need no repentance.

8 Either what woman having ten pieces of silver, if she loses one piece, doth not light a candle, and sweep the house, and seek diligently till she finds it?

9 And when she hath found it, she calleth her friends and her neighbours together, saying, 'Rejoice with me; for I have found the piece which I had lost.'

10 Likewise, I say unto you, there is joy in the presence of the angels of God (Elohim) over one sinner that repenteth."

11 And He said, "A certain man had two sons:

12 And the younger of them said to his father, 'Father, give me the portion of goods that falleth to me.' And he divided unto them his living.

13 And not many days after the younger son gathered all together, and took his journey into a far country, and there wasted his substance with riotous living.

14 And when he had spent all, there arose a mighty famine in that land; and he began to be in want.

15 And he went and joined himself to a citizen of that country; and he sent him into his fields to feed swine.

16 And he would fain have filled his belly with the husks that the swine did eat: and no man gave unto him.

17 And when he came to himself, he said, 'How many hired servants of my father's have bread enough and to spare, and I perish with hunger!

18 I will arise and go to my father, and will say unto him, "Father, I have sinned against heaven, and before you,

19 And am no more worthy to be called your son;' make me as one of your hired servants.'"

20 And he arose, and came to his father. But when he was yet a great way off, his father saw him, and had compassion, and ran, and fell on his neck, and kissed him.

21 And the son said unto him, 'Father, I have sinned against heaven, and in your sight, and am no more worthy to be called your son.'

22 But the father said to his servants, 'Bring forth the best robe, and put it on him; and put a ring on his hand, and shoes on his feet.

23 And bring hither the fatted calf, and kill it; and let us eat, and be merry:

24 For this my son was dead, and is alive again; he was lost, and is found.' And they began to be merry.

25 Now his elder son was in the field; and as he came and drew near to the house, he heard musick and dancing.

26 And he called one of the servants, and asked what these things meant.

27 And he said unto him, 'Your brother is come; and your father hath killed the fatted calf, because he hath received him safe and sound.'

28 And he was angry, and would not go in; therefore came his father out, and intreated him.

29 And he answering said to his father, 'Behold,

these many years do I serve you, neither transgressed I at any time your commandment; and yet you never gavest me a kid, that I might make merry with my friends.

30 But as soon as this your son was come, who hath devoured your living with harlots, you have killed for him the fatted calf.

31 And he said unto him, 'Son, you are ever with me, and all that I have is yours.

32 It was meet that we should make merry, and be glad; for this your brother was dead, and is alive again; and was lost, and is found.'"

16 And He said also unto His disciples: "There was a certain rich man, who had a steward; and the same was accused unto him that he had wasted his goods.

2 And he called him, and said unto him, 'How is it that I hear this of you? Give an account of your stewardship; for you mayest be no longer steward.'

3 Then the steward said within himself, 'What shall I do? For my master taketh away from me the stewardship; I cannot dig; to beg I am ashamed.

4 I am resolved what to do, that, when I am put out of the stewardship, they may receive me into their houses.'

5 So he called every one of his master's debtors unto him, and said unto the first, 'How much owest you unto my master?'

6 And he said, 'A hundred measures of oil.' And he said unto him, 'Take your bill, and sit down quickly, and write fifty.'

7 Then said he to another, 'And how much owest you?' And he said, 'A hundred measures of wheat.' And he said unto him, 'Take your bill, and write fourscore (eighty).'

8 And the master commended the unjust steward, because he had done wisely; for the children of this world are in their generation wiser than the children of light.

9 And I say unto you, 'Make to yourselves friends of the mammon of unrighteousness; that, when you fail, they may receive you into everlasting habitations.

10 He that is faithful in that which is least is faithful also in much; and he that is unjust in the least is unjust also in much.

11 If therefore you have not been faithful in the unrighteous mammon, who will commit to your trust the true riches?

12 And if you have not been faithful in that which is another man's, who shall give you that which is your own?

13 No servant can serve two masters; for either he will hate the one, and love the other; or else he will hold to the one, and despise the other. You cannot serve God (Elohim) and mammon."

14 And the Pharisees also, who were covetous, heard all these things; and they derided Him.

15 And He said unto them, "You are they who justify yourselves before men; but God (Elohim) knoweth your hearts; for that which is highly esteemed among men is abomination in the sight of God (Elohim).

16 The Torah and the Prophets (Nevi'im) were until John (Yochanan); since that time the kingdom of God (Elohim, יהוה (YHWH)) is preached, and every man presseth into it.

17 And it is easier for heaven and earth to pass, than one tittle of the [B28a]Torah to fail.

18 Whosoever putteth away his wife, and marrieth another, committeth adultery; and whosoever marrieth her that is put away from her husband committeth adultery.

19 There was a certain rich man, who was clothed in purple and fine linen, and fared sumptuously every day.

20 And there was a certain beggar named Lazarus, who was laid at his gate, full of sores,

21 And desiring to be fed with the crumbs which fell from the rich man's table; moreover the dogs came and licked his sores.

22 And it came to pass, that the beggar died, and was carried by the angels into Avraham's bosom; the rich man also died, and was buried;

23 And in hell (sheol) he lifts up his eyes, being in torments, and seeth Avraham afar off, and Lazarus in his bosom.

24 And he cried and said, 'Father Avraham, have mercy on me, and send Lazarus, that he may dip the tip of his finger in water, and cool my tongue; for I am tormented in this flame.'

25 But Avraham said, 'Son, remember that you in your lifetime receivedst your good things, and likewise Lazarus bad things; but now he is comforted, and you are tormented.

26 And beside all this, between us and you there is a great gulf fixed; so that they who would pass from hence to you cannot; neither can they pass to us, that would come from thence.'

27 Then he said, 'I pray you therefore, father,

that you wouldest send him to my father's house;

28 For I have five brethren; that he may testify unto them, lest they also come into this place of torment.'

29 Avraham saith unto him, 'They have Moses (Mosheh) and the prophets; let them hear them.'

30 And he said, 'Nay, father Avraham; but if one went unto them from the dead, they will repent.'

31 And he said unto him, 'If they hear not Moses (Mosheh) and the prophets, neither will they be persuaded, though one rose from the dead.'"

17 Then said He unto the disciples, "It is impossible but that offences will come; but woe unto him, through whom they come!

2 It were better for him that a millstone was hanged about his neck, and he cast into the sea, than that he should offend one of these little ones.

3 Take heed to yourselves. If your brother trespass against you, rebuke him; and if he repents, forgive him.

4 And if he trespasses against you seven times in a day, and seven times in a day turn again to you, saying, 'I repent;' you shalt forgive him."

5 And the apostles said unto the Lord (Yahwah), "Increase our faith."

6 And the Lord (Yahwah) said, "If you had faith as a grain of mustard seed, you might say unto this sycamine tree, 'Be you plucked up by the root, and be you planted in the sea;' and it should obey you.

7 But which of you, having a servant plowing or feeding cattle, will say unto him by and by, when he is come from the field, 'Go and sit down to meat'?

8 And will not rather say unto him, 'Make ready wherewith I may sup, and gird yourself, and serve me, till I have eaten and drunken; and afterward you shalt eat and drink'?

9 Doth he thanks that servant because he did the things that were commanded him? I trow not.

10 So likewise you, when you shall have done all those things which are commanded you, say, 'We are unprofitable servants; we have done that which was our duty to do.'"

11 And it came to pass, as He went to Jerusalem (Yerushalayim), that He passed through the midst of Samaria and Galilee.

12 And as He entered into a certain village, there met Him ten men that were lepers, who

stood afar off.

13 And they lifted up their voices, and said, "Yahwah our Teacher (Rabbi), have mercy on us."

14 And when He saw them, He said unto them, "Go shew yourselves unto the priests (kohanim)." And it came to pass, that, as they went, they were cleansed.

15 And one of them, when he saw that he was healed, turned back, and with a loud voice glorified יהוה (YHWH, Yahwah),

16 And fell down on his face at His feet, giving Him thanks; and he was a Samaritan.

17 And Yahwah answering said, "Were there not ten cleansed? But where are the nine?

18 There are not found that returned to give glory to God (Elohim), except this stranger."

19 And He said unto him, "Arise, go your way; your faith hath made you whole."

20 And when He was demanded of the Pharisees, when the kingdom of God (Elohim, יהוה (YHWH)) should come, He answered them and said, "The kingdom of God (Elohim, יהוה (YHWH)) cometh not with observation;

21 Neither shall they say, 'Behold here!' Or, 'Behold there!' For, behold, the kingdom of God (Elohim, יהוה (YHWH)) is within you."

22 And He said unto the disciples, "The days will come, when you shall desire to see one of the days of the Son of man (haMashiach), and you shall not see it.

23 And they shall say to you, 'See here!' or 'See there!' Go not after them, nor follow them.

24 For as the lightning, that lighteneth out of the one part under heaven, shineth unto the other part under heaven; so shall also the Son of man (haMashiach) be in His day.

25 But first must He suffer many things, and be rejected of this generation.

26 And as it was in the days of Noe (Noach), so shall it be also in the days of the Son of man (haMashiach).

27 They did eat, they drank, they married wives, they were given in marriage, until the day that Noe (Noach) entered into the ark, and the flood came, and destroyed them all.

28 Likewise also as it was in the days of Lot; they did eat, they drank, they bought, they sold, they planted, they builded;

29 But the same day that Lot went out of Sodom it rained fire and brimstone from heaven, and destroyed them all.

30 Even thus shall it be in the day when the Son of man (haMashiach) is revealed.

31 In that day, he who shall be upon the housetop, and his stuff in the house, let him not come down to take it away; and he that is in the field, let him likewise not return back.

32 Remember Lot's wife.

33 Whosoever shall seek to save his life shall lose it; and whosoever shall lose his life shall preserve it.

34 I tell you, in that night there shall be two men in one bed; the one shall be taken, and the other shall be left.

35 Two women shall be grinding together; the one shall be taken, and the other left.

36 Two men shall be in the field; the one shall be taken, and the other left."

37 And they answered and said unto him, "Where, Lord (Adonai)?" And He said unto them, "Wheresoever the body is, thither will the eagles be gathered together."

18 And He spake a parable unto them to this end, that men ought always to pray, and not to faint;

2 Saying: "There was in a city a judge, who feared not God (Elohim), neither regarded man;

3 And there was a widow in that city; and she came unto him, saying, 'Avenge me of mine adversary.'

4 And he would not for a while; but afterward he said within himself, 'Though I fear not God (Elohim), nor regard man;

5 Yet because this widow troubleth me, I will avenge her, lest by her continual coming she weary me.'

6 And the Lord (Yahwah) said, "Hear what the unjust judge saith.

7 And shall not God (Elohim) avenge His own elect, who cry day and night unto Him, though He bear long with them?

8 I tell you that He will avenge them speedily. Nevertheless when the Son of man (haMashiach) cometh, shall He find faith on the earth?"

9 And He spake this parable unto certain who trusted in themselves that they were righteous, and despised others:

10 "Two men went up into the temple to pray; the one a Pharisee, and the other a publican.

11 The Pharisee stood and prayed thus with himself, 'God (Elohim), I thank You, that I

am not as other men are, extortioners, unjust, adulterers, or even as this publican.

12 I fast twice in the week, I give tithes of all that I possess.'

13 And the publican, standing afar off, would not lift up so much as his eyes unto heaven, but smote upon his breast, saying, 'God (Elohim) be merciful to me a sinner.'

14 I tell you, this man went down to his house justified rather than the other; for every one that exalteth himself shall be abased; and he that humbleth himself shall be exalted."

15 And they brought unto Him also infants, that He would touch them; but when His disciples saw it, they rebuked them.

16 But Yahwah called them unto Him, and said, "Let little children to come unto Me, and forbid them not; for of such is the kingdom of God (Elohim, יהוה (YHWH)).

17 Verily I say unto you, whosoever shall not receive the kingdom of God (Elohim, יהוה (YHWH)) as a little child shall in no wise enter therein."

18 And a certain ruler asked Him, saying, "Good Teacher (Rabbi), what shall I do to inherit eternal life?"

19 And Yahwah said unto him, "Why callest you Me good? None is good, except one, that is, God (Elohim).

20 You knowest the commandments: 'Do not commit adultery, do not kill, do not steal, do not bear false witness, honour your father and your mother.'"

21 And he said, "All these have I kept from my youth up."

22 Now when Yahwah heard these things, He said unto him, "Yet lackest you one thing: sell all that you have, and distribute unto the poor, and you shalt have treasure in heaven; and come, follow Me."

23 And when he heard this, he was very sorrowful; for he was very rich.

24 And when Yahwah saw that he was very sorrowful, He said, "How hardly shall they that have riches enter into the kingdom of God (Elohim, יהוה (YHWH))!

25 For it is easier for a camel to go through a needle's eye, than for a rich man to enter into the kingdom of God (Elohim, יהוה (YHWH))."

26 And they that heard it said, "Who then can be saved?"

27 And He said, "The things which are impossible with men are possible with God (Elohim)."

28 Then Peter (Kefa) said, "Behold, we have left all, and followed you."

29 And He said unto them, "Verily I say unto you, there is no man that hath left house, or parents, or brethren, or wife, or children, for the kingdom of God (Elohim, יהוה (YHWH))'s sake,

30 Who shall not receive manifold more in this present time, and in the world to come life everlasting."

31 Then He took unto Him the twelve, and said unto them, "Behold, we go up to Jerusalem (Yerushalayim), and all things that are written by the prophets concerning the Son of man (haMashiach) shall be accomplished.

32 For He shall be delivered unto the Gentiles (Goyim), and shall be mocked, and spitefully entreated, and spitted on.

33 And they shall scourge Him, and put Him to death; and the third day He shall rise again."

34 And they understood none of these things; and this saying was hidden from them, neither knew they the things which were spoken.

35 And it came to pass, that as He was come near unto Yericho, a certain blind man sat by the way side begging;

36 And hearing the multitude pass by, he asked what it meant.

37 And they told him, that Yahwah of Nazareth passeth by.

38 And he cried, saying, "Yahwah, You son (descendant) of Dawid, have mercy on me."

39 And they who went before rebuked him, that he should hold his peace; but he cried so much the more, "You son (descendant) of Dawid, have mercy on me."

40 And Yahwah stood, and commanded him to be brought unto Him; and when he was come near, He asked him,

41 Saying, "What wilt you that I shall do unto you?" And he said, "Lord (Adonai), that I may receive my sight."

42 And Yahwah said unto him, "Receive your sight; your faith hath saved you."

43 And immediately he received his sight, and followed Him, glorifying God (Elohim); and all the people, when they saw it, gave praise unto God (Elohim).

19

And Yahwah entered and passed through Yericho.

2 And, behold, there was a man named Zacchaeus, who was the chief among the tax collectors, and he was rich.

3 And he sought to see Yahwah who He was; and could not for the press, because he was little of stature.

4 And he ran before, and climbed up into a sycomore tree to see Him; for He was to pass that way.

5 And when Yahwah came to the place, He looked up, and saw him, and said unto him, "Zacchaeus, make haste, and come down; for today I must abide at your house."

6 And he made haste, and came down, and received Him joyfully.

7 And when they saw it, they all murmured, saying, "That He was gone to be guest with a man that is a sinner."

8 And Zacchaeus stood, and said unto the Lord (Yahwah): "Behold, my Lord (Adonai), the half of my goods I give to the poor; and if I have taken any thing from any man by false accusation, I restore him fourfold."

9 And Yahwah said unto him, "This day is salvation come to this house, forsomuch as he also is a son of Avraham.

10 For the Son of man (haMashiach) has come to seek and to save that which was lost."

11 And as they heard these things, He added and spake a parable, because He was near to Jerusalem (Yerushalayim), and because they thought that the kingdom of God (Elohim, יהוה (YHWH)) should immediately appear.

12 He said therefore, "A certain nobleman went into a far country to receive for himself a kingdom, and to return.

13 And he called his ten servants, and delivered them ten pounds, and said unto them, 'Occupy till I come.'

14 But his citizens hated him, and sent a message after him, saying, 'We will not have this man to reign over us.'

15 And it came to pass, that when he was returned, having received the kingdom, then he commanded these servants to be called unto him, to whom he had given the money, that he might know how much every man had gained by trading.

16 Then came the first, saying, 'Master, your pound hath gained ten pounds.'

17 And he said unto him, 'Well, you good servant; because you have been faithful in a very little, have you authority over ten cities.'

18 And the second came, saying, 'Master, your pound hath gained five pounds.'

19 And he said likewise to him, 'Be you also over five cities.'

20 And another came, saying, 'Master, behold, here is your pound, which I have kept laid up in a napkin;

21 For I feared you, because you are an austere man; you takest up that you layedst not down, and reapest that you didst not sow.'

22 And he saith unto him, 'Out of your own mouth will I judge you, you wicked servant. You knewest that I was an austere man, taking up that I laid not down, and reaping that I did not sow;

23 Wherefore then gavest not you my money into the bank, that at my coming I might have required mine own with usury?'

24 And he said unto them that stood by, 'Take from him the pound, and give it to him that hath ten pounds.'

25 (And they said unto him, 'Lord (Master), he hath ten pounds.')

26 For I say unto you, that unto every one who hath shall be given; and from him that hath not, even that he hath shall be taken away from him.

27 But those mine enemies, who would not that I should reign over them, bring hither, and slay them before me.'"

28 And when He had thus spoken, He went before, ascending up to Jerusalem (Yerushalayim).

29 And it came to pass, when He was come near to Bethphage and Bethany, at the mount called the Mount of Olives, He sent two of His disciples,

30 Saying, "Go you into the village over against you; in the which at your entering you shall find a colt tied, whereon yet never man sat; loose him, and bring him hither.

31 And if any man asks you, 'Why do you loose him?' thus shall you say unto him, 'Because the Lord (Adonai) hath need of him.'"

32 And they that were sent went their way, and found even as He had said unto them.

33 And as they were loosing the colt, the owners thereof said unto them, "Why loose you the

colt?"

34 And they said, "The Lord (Adonai) hath need of him."

35 And they brought him to Yahwah; and they cast their garments upon the colt, and they set Yahwah thereon.

36 And as He went, they spread their clothes in the way.

37 And when He was come near, even now at the descent of the Mount of Olives, the whole multitude of the disciples began to rejoice and praise God (Elohim) with a loud voice for all the mighty works that they had seen;

38 Saying, "Blessed be the King that cometh in the name of יהוה (YHWH, Yahwah); peace in heaven, and glory in the highest." – *Psa. 118:26*

39 And some of the Pharisees from among the multitude said unto Him, "Teacher (Rabbi), rebuke Your disciples."

40 And He answered and said unto them, "I tell you that, if these should hold their peace, the stones would immediately cry out."

41 And when He was come near, He beheld the city, and wept over it,

42 Saying, "If you hadst known, even you, at least in this your day, the things which belong unto your peace! But now they are hidden from your eyes.

43 For the days shall come upon you, that your enemies shall cast a trench about you, and compass you round, and keep you in on every side,

44 And shall lay you even with the ground, and your children within you; and they shall not leave in you one stone upon another; because you knewest not the time of your visitation."

45 And He went into the temple, and began to cast out them that sold therein, and them that bought;

46 Saying unto them, "It is written: 'My house is the house of prayer; but you have made it a den of thieves.'"– *Isa. 56:7, Jer.7:11*

47 And He taught daily in the temple. But the chief priests (kohanim) and the scribes and the chief of the people sought to destroy Him,

48 And could not find what they might do; for all the people were very attentive to hear Him.

20 And it came to pass, that on one of those days, as He taught the people in the temple, and preached the gospel (good news), the chief priests (kohanim) and the scribes came

upon Him with the elders,

2 And spake unto Him, saying, "Tell us, by what authority doest You these things? Or who is he that gave You this authority?"

3 And He answered and said unto them, "I will also ask you one thing; and answer Me:

4 The baptism of John (Yochanan), was it from heaven, or of men?"

5 And they reasoned with themselves, saying, "If we shall say, 'From heaven;' He will say, 'Why then believed you Him not?'

6 But and if we say, 'Of men;' all the people will stone us; for they be persuaded that John (Yochanan) was a prophet."

7 And they answered, that they could not tell whence it was.

8 And Yahwah said unto them, "Neither tell I you by what authority I do these things."

9 Then began He to speak to the people this parable: "A certain man planted a vineyard, and let it forth to husbandmen, and went into a far country for a long time.

10 And at the season he sent a servant to the husbandmen, that they should give him of the fruit of the vineyard; but the husbandmen beat him, and sent him away empty.

11 And again he sent another servant; and they beat him also, and entreated him shamefully, and sent him away empty.

12 And again he sent a third; and they wounded him also, and cast him out.

13 Then said the master of the vineyard, 'What shall I do? I will send my beloved son; it may be they will reverence him when they see him.'

14 But when the husbandmen saw him, they reasoned among themselves, saying, 'This is the heir; come, let us kill him, that the inheritance may be ours.'

15 So they cast him out of the vineyard, and killed him. What therefore shall the master of the vineyard do unto them?

16 He shall come and destroy these husbandmen, and shall give the vineyard to others." And when they heard it, they said, "God (Elohim) forbid."

17 And He beheld them, and said, "What is this then that is written: 'The stone which the builders rejected, the same is become the head of the corner'? – *Psa. 118:22*

18 Whosoever shall fall upon that stone shall be broken; but on whomsoever it shall fall, it will grind him to powder.

19 And the chief priests (kohanim) and the scribes the same hour sought to lay hands on Him; and they feared the people; for they perceived thatHhe had spoken this parable against them.

20 And they watched Him, and sent forth spies, who should feign themselves just men, that they might take hold of His words, that so they might deliver Him unto the power and authority of the governor.

21 And they asked Him, saying, "Teacher (Rabbi), we know that You sayest and teachest rightly, neither acceptest You the person of any, but teachest the way of God (Elohim) truly.

22 Is it lawful for us to give tribute (poll-tax) unto Caesar, or no?"

23 But He perceived their craftiness, and said unto them, "Why test you Me?

24 Shew Me a penny. Whose image and superscription hath it?" They answered and said, "Caesar's."

25 And He said unto them, "Render therefore unto Caesar the things which be Caesar's, and unto God (Elohim) the things which be God (Elohim)'s."

26 And they could not take hold of His words before the people; and they marvelled at His answer, and held their peace.

27 Then came to Him certain of the Sadducees, who deny that there is any resurrection; and they asked Him,

28 Saying, "Teacher (Rabbi), Moses (Mosheh) wrote unto us, 'If any man's brother dies, having a wife, and he die without children, that his brother should take his wife, and raise up seed unto his brother.' – *Deu. 25:5*

29 There were therefore seven brethren; and the first took a wife, and died without children.

30 And the second took her to wife, and he died childless.

31 And the third took her; and in like manner the seven also; and they left no children, and died.

32 Last of all the woman died also.

33 Therefore in the resurrection whose wife of them is she? For seven had her as wife."

34 And Yahwah answering said unto them, "The children of this world marry, and are given in marriage;

35 But they who shall be accounted worthy to obtain that world, and the resurrection from the dead, neither marry, nor are given in marriage;

36 Neither can they die any more; for they are equal unto the angels; and are the children of God (Elohim), being the children of the resurrection.

37 Now that the dead are raised, even Moses (Mosheh) shewed at the bush, when he calleth יהוה (YHWH) the God (Elohim) of Avraham, and the God (Elohim) of Isaac (Yitschaq), and the God (Elohim) of Jacob (Yaaqov). – *Exo. 3:6*

38 For He is not a God (Elohim) of the dead, but of the living; for all live unto Him."

39 Then certain of the scribes answering said, "Teacher (Rabbi), You have well said."

40 And after that they durst not ask Him any question at all.

41 And He said unto them, "How say they that the Messiah (haMashiach) is Dawid's son?

42 And Dawid himself saith in the book of Psalms, 'יהוה said unto my Lord (Adoni), "Sit You on My right hand,

43 Till I make Your enemies Your footstool."' – *Psa. 110:1*

44 Dawid therefore calleth Him 'Lord (Adon)', how is He then his son?"

45 Then in the audience of all the people He said unto His disciples,

46 "Beware of the scribes, who desire to walk in long robes, and love greetings in the markets, and the highest seats in the synagogues, and the chief rooms at feasts;

47 Who devour widows' houses, and for a shew make long prayers; the same shall receive greater damnation."

21 And He looked up, and saw the rich men casting their gifts into the treasury.

2 And He saw also a certain poor widow casting in thither two mites.

3 And He said, "Of a truth I say unto you, that this poor widow hath cast in more than they all;

4 For all these have of their abundance cast in unto the offerings of God (Elohim); but she of her penury hath cast in all the living that she had."

5 And as some spake of the temple, how it was adorned with goodly stones and gifts, He said,

6 "As for these things which you behold, the days will come, in which there shall not be left one stone upon another, that shall not be thrown down."

7 And they asked Him, saying, "Teacher

(Rabbi), but when shall these things be? And what sign will there be when these things shall come to pass?"

8 And He said, "Take heed that you be not deceived; for many shall come in My name, saying, 'I am He;' and the time draweth near; go you not therefore after them.

9 But when you shall hear of wars and commotions, be not terrified; for these things must first come to pass; but the end is not by and by."

10 Then said he unto them, "Nation shall rise against nation, and kingdom against kingdom;

11 And great earthquakes shall be in divers places, and famines, and pestilences; and fearful sights and great signs shall there be from heaven.

12 But before all these, they shall lay their hands on you, and persecute you, delivering you up to the synagogues, and into prisons, being brought before kings and rulers for My name's sake.

13 And it shall turn to you for a testimony.

14 Settle it therefore in your hearts, not to meditate before what you shall answer;

15 For I will give you a mouth and wisdom, which all your adversaries shall not be able to gainsay nor resist.

16 And you shall be betrayed both by parents, and brethren, and kinsfolks, and friends; and some of you shall they cause to be put to death.

17 And you shall be hated of all men for My name's sake.

18 But there shall not a hair of your head perish.

19 In your patience possess you your souls.

20 And when you shall see Jerusalem (Yerushalayim) compassed with armies, then know that the desolation thereof is near.

21 Then let them which are in Judah (Yehudah) flee to the mountains; and let them who are in the midst of it depart out; and let not them that are in the countries enter thereinto.

22 For these be the days of vengeance, that all things which are written may be fulfilled.

23 But woe unto them that are with child, and to them that give suck, in those days! For there shall be great distress in the land, and wrath upon this people.

24 And they shall fall by the edge of the sword, and shall be led away captive into all nations; and Jerusalem (Yerushalayim) shall be trodden down of the Gentiles (Goyim), until the times of the Gentiles (Goyim) be fulfilled.

25 And there shall be signs in the sun, and in the moon, and in the stars; and upon the earth distress of nations, with perplexity; the sea and the waves roaring;

26 Men's hearts failing them for fear, and for looking after those things which are coming on the earth; for the powers of heaven shall be shaken.

27 And then shall they see the Son of man (haMashiach) coming in a cloud with power and great glory.

28 And when these things begin to come to pass, then look up, and lift up your heads; for your redemption draweth near.

29 And He spake to them a parable: "Behold the fig tree, and all the trees;

30 When they now shoot forth, you see and know of your own selves that summer is now near at hand.

31 So likewise you, when you see these things come to pass, know you that the kingdom of God (Elohim, יהוה (YHWH)) is near at hand.

32 Verily I say unto you, this generation shall not pass away, till all be fulfilled.

33 Heaven and earth shall pass away; but My words shall not pass away.

34 And take heed to yourselves, lest at any time your hearts be overcharged with surfeiting, and drunkenness, and cares of this life, and so that day come upon you unawares.

35 For as a snare shall it come on all them that dwell on the face of the whole earth.

36 Watch you therefore, and pray always, that you may be accounted worthy to escape all these things that shall come to pass, and to stand before the Son of man (haMashiach)."

37 And in the day time He was teaching in the temple; and at night He went out, and abode in the mount that is called the Mount of Olives.

38 And all the people came early in the morning to Him in the temple, for to hear Him.

22 Now the B20Feast of Unleavened Bread (Chag haMatzot) drew near, which is called the B19Passover (Pesach).

2 And the chief priests (kohanim) and scribes sought how they might kill Him, for they feared the people.

3 Then entered Satan into Judas (Yehudah) surnamed Iscariot (Ishkeriot), being of the number of the twelve.

4 And he went his way, and communed with the chief priests (kohanim) and captains, how he might betray Him unto them.

5 And they were glad, and covenanted to give him money.

6 And he promised, and sought opportunity to betray Him unto them in the absence of the multitude.

7 Then came the day of unleavened bread, when the Passover lamb (Pesach) must be killed.

8 And He sent Peter (Kefa) and John (Yochanan), saying, "Go and prepare us the Passover (Pesach), that we may eat."

9 And they said unto Him, "Where wilt you that we prepare?"

10 And He said unto them, "Behold, when you are entered into the city, there shall a man meet you, bearing a pitcher of water; follow him into the house where he entereth in.

11 And you shall say unto the goodman of the house, "Our Teacher (Rabbi) saith unto you, 'Where is the guestchamber, where I shall eat the Passover (Pesach) with My disciples?'

12 And he shall shew you a large upper room furnished; there make ready."

13 And they went, and found as He had said unto them; and they made ready the Passover (Pesach).

14 And when the hour was come, He sat down, and the twelve apostles with Him.

15 And He said unto them, "With desire I have desired to eat this Passover (Pesach) with you before I suffer;

16 For I say unto you, I will not any more eat thereof, until it be fulfilled in the kingdom of God (Elohim, יהוה (YHWH))."

17 And He took the cup, and gave thanks, and said, "Take this, and divide it among yourselves;

18 For I say unto you, I will not drink of the fruit of the vine, until the kingdom of God (Elohim, יהוה (YHWH)) shall come."

19 And He took bread, and gave thanks, and brake it, and gave unto them, saying, "This is My body which is given for you; this do in remembrance of Me."

20 Likewise also the cup after supper, saying, "This cup is the New Covenant (haBerit haChadashah) in My blood, which is shed for you.

21 But, behold, the hand of him that betrayeth Me is with Me on the table.

22 And truly the Son of man (haMashiach) goeth as it was determined; but woe unto that man by whom He is betrayed!"

23 And they began to enquire among themselves, which of them it was that should do this thing.

24 And there was also a strife among them, which of them should be accounted the greatest.

25 And He said unto them, "The kings of the Gentiles (Goyim) exercise lordship over them; and they that exercise authority upon them are called benefactors.

26 But you shall not be so; but he that is greatest among you, let him be as the younger; and he that is chief, as he that doth serve.

27 For whether is greater, he that sitteth at meat, or he that serveth? Is not he that sitteth at meat? But I am among you as he that serveth.

28 You are they who have continued with Me in My trials.

29 And I appoint unto you a kingdom, as My Father hath appointed unto Me;

30 That you may eat and drink at My table in My kingdom, and sit on thrones judging the twelve tribes of Yisrael."

31 And the Lord (Yahwah) said, "Shimon, Shimon (Peter), behold, Satan hath desired to have you, that he may sift you as wheat;

32 But I have prayed for you, that your faith fails not; and when you have converted (turned back in repentance), strengthen your brethren."

33 And he said unto Him, "My Lord (Adonai), I am ready to go with You, both into prison, and to death."

34 And He said, "I tell you, Peter (Kefa), the cock shall not crow this day, before that you shalt thrice deny that you knowest Me."

35 And He said unto them, "When I sent you without purse, and scrip, and shoes, lacked you any thing?" And they said, "Nothing."

36 Then said He unto them, "But now, he that hath a purse, let him take it, and likewise his scrip; and he that hath no sword, let him sell his garment, and buy one.

37 For I say unto you, that this that is written must yet be accomplished in Me: 'And he was reckoned among the transgressors;' for the things concerning Me have an end." – Isa. 53:12

38 And they said, "Lord (Adonai), behold, here are two swords." And He said unto them, "It is enough."

39 And He came out, and went, as He was wont,

to the Mount of Olives; and His disciples also followed Him.

40 And when He was at the place, He said unto them, "Pray that you enter not into temptation."

41 And He was withdrawn from them about a stone's cast, and kneeled down, and prayed,

42 Saying, "Father, if you be willing, remove this cup from Me; nevertheless not My will, but Yours, be done."

43 And there appeared an angel unto Him from heaven, strengthening Him.

44 And being in an agony He prayed more earnestly; and His sweat was as it was great drops of blood falling down to the ground.

45 And when He rose up from prayer, and was come to His disciples, He found them sleeping for sorrow,

46 And said unto them, "Why sleep you? Rise and pray, lest you enter into temptation."

47 And while He yet spake, behold a multitude, and he that was called Judas (Yehudah), one of the twelve, went before them, and drew near unto Yahwah to kiss Him.

48 But Yahwah said unto him, "Judas (Yehudah), betrayest you the Son of man (haMashiach) with a kiss?"

49 When they who were about Him saw what would follow, they said unto Him, "Lord (Adonai), shall we smite with the sword?"

50 And one of them smote the servant of the high priest (kohen hagadol), and cut off his right ear.

51 And Yahwah answered and said, "Permit you thus far." And He touched his ear, and healed him.

52 Then Yahwah said unto the chief priests (kohanim), and captains of the temple, and the elders, who were come to Him, "Be you come out, as against a thief, with swords and staves?

53 When I was daily with you in the temple, you stretched forth no hands against Me; but this is your hour, and the power of darkness."

54 Then took they Him, and led Him, and brought Him into the high priest (kohen hagadol)'s house. And Peter (Kefa) followed afar off.

55 And when they had kindled a fire in the midst of the hall, and were set down together, Peter (Kefa) sat down among them.

56 But a certain maid beheld him as he sat by the fire, and earnestly looked upon him, and said, "This man was also with Him."

57 And he denied Him, saying, "Woman, I know Him not."

58 And after a little while another saw him, and said, "You are also of them." And Peter (Kefa) said, "Man, I am not."

59 And about the space of one hour after another confidently affirmed, saying, "Of a truth this fellow also was with Him; for he is a Galilaean."

60 And Peter (Kefa) said, "Man, I know not what you sayest." And immediately, while he was still speaking, the cock crew.

61 And the Lord (Yahwah) turned, and looked upon Peter (Kefa). And Peter (Kefa) remembered the word of the Lord (Yahwah), how He had said unto him, "Before the cock crow, you shalt deny Me thrice."

62 And Peter (Kefa) went out, and wept bitterly.

63 And the men that held Yahwah mocked Him, and smote Him.

64 And when they had blindfolded Him, they struck Him on the face, and asked Him, saying, "Prophesy, who is it that smote You?"

65 And many other things blasphemously spake they against Him.

66 And as soon as it was day, the elders of the people and the chief priests (kohanim) and the scribes came together, and led Him into their council (Sanhedrin), saying,

67 "Are you the Messiah (haMashiach)? Tell us!" And He said unto them, "If I tell you, you will not believe.

68 And if I also ask you, you will not answer Me, nor let Me go.

69 Hereafter shall the Son of man (haMashiach) sit on the right hand of the power of God (Elohim)." – *Psa. 110:1*

70 Then said they all, "Are you then the [B47]Humanity of El (YHWH)? And He said unto them, "You say that I am."

71 And they said, "What need we any further witness? For we ourselves have heard of His own mouth."

23 And the whole multitude of them arose, and led Him unto Pilate.

2 And they began to accuse Him, saying, "We found this fellow perverting the nation, and forbidding to give tribute to Caesar, saying that He Himself is the Messiah (haMashiach) - the King!"

3 And Pilate asked Him, saying, "Art You the

King of the Jews (Yehudim)? And He answered him and said, "You sayest it."

4 Then said Pilate to the chief priests (kohanim) and to the people, "I find no fault in this Man."

5 And they were the more fierce, saying, "He stirreth up the people, teaching throughout all Jewry (Yehudah), beginning from Galilee to this place."

6 When Pilate heard of Galilee, he asked whether the Man was a Galilaean.

7 And as soon as he knew that He belonged unto Herod's jurisdiction, he sent Him to Herod, who himself also was at Jerusalem (Yerushalayim) at that time.

8 And when Herod saw Yahwah, he was exceeding glad; for he was desirous to see Him of a long season, because he had heard many things of Him; and he hoped to have seen some miracle done by Him.

9 Then he questioned with Him in many words; but He answered him nothing.

10 And the chief priests (kohanim) and scribes stood and vehemently accused Him.

11 And Herod with his men of war set Him at nought, and mocked Him, and arrayed Him in a gorgeous robe, and sent Him again to Pilate.

12 And the same day Pilate and Herod were made friends together; for before they were at enmity between themselves.

13 And Pilate, when he had called together the chief priests (kohanim) and the rulers and the people,

14 Said unto them, "You have brought this Man unto me, as one that perverteth the people; and, behold, I, having examined Him before you, have found no fault in this Man touching those things whereof you accuse Him;

15 No, nor yet Herod; for I sent you to him; and, behold, nothing worthy of death is done unto Him.

16 I will therefore chastise Him, and release Him."

17 (For of necessity he must release one unto them at the feast.)

18 And they cried out all at once, saying, "Away with this Man, and release unto us Barabbas;"

19 (Who for a certain sedition made in the city, and for murder, was cast into prison.)

20 Pilate therefore, willing to release Yahwah, spake again to them.

21 But they cried, saying, "Crucify Him, crucify Him!"

22 And he said unto them the third time, "Why, what evil hath He done? I have found no cause of death in Him; I will therefore chastise Him, and let Him go."

23 And they were instant with loud voices, requiring that He might be crucified. And the voices of them and of the chief priests (kohanim) prevailed.

24 And Pilate gave sentence that it should be as they required.

25 And he released unto them him that for sedition and murder was cast into prison, whom they had desired; but he delivered Yahwah to their will.

26 And as they led Him away, they laid hold upon one Shimon, a Cyrenian, coming out of the country, and on him they laid the stake, that he might bear it after Yahwah.

27 And there followed Him a great company of people, and of women, who also bewailed and lamented Him.

28 But Yahwah turning unto them said, "Daughters of Jerusalem (Yerushalayim), weep not for Me, but weep for yourselves, and for your children.

29 For, behold, the days are coming, in which they shall say, 'Blessed are the barren, and the wombs that never bare, and the paps which never gave suck!'

30 Then shall they begin to say to the mountains, "Fall on us!" And to the hills, "Cover us!"" – *Hos. 10:8*

31 For if they do these things in a green tree, what shall be done in the dry?"

32 And there were also two others, malefactors, led with Him to be put to death.

33 And when they were come to the place, which is called Calvary, there they crucified Him, and the malefactors, one on the right hand, and the other on the left.

34 Then said Yahwah, "Father, forgive them; for they know not what they do." And they parted His raiment, and cast lots. – *Psa. 22:18*

35 And the people stood beholding. And the rulers also with them derided him, saying, "He saved others; let Him save Himself, if He be the Messiah (haMashiach), the chosen of God (Elohim)." – *Psa. 22:8*

36 And the soldiers also mocked Him, coming to Him, and offering Him vinegar, – *Psa. 69:21*

37 And saying, "If You be the King of the Jews (Yehudim), save Yourself."

38 And a superscription also was written over Him in letters of Greek, and Latin, and Hebrew: THIS IS THE KING OF THE JEWS (YEHUDIM).

39 And one of the malefactors who were hanged railed on Him, saying, "If You be the Messiah (haMashiach), save Yourself and us."

40 But the other answering rebuked him, saying, "Dost not you fear God (Elohim), seeing you are in the same condemnation?

41 And we indeed justly; for we receive the due reward of our deeds; but this Man hath done nothing amiss."

42 And he said unto Yahwah, "My Lord (Adonai), remember me when You comest into Your kingdom."

43 And Yahwah said unto him, "Verily I say unto you, today shalt you be with Me in paradise."

44 And it was about the sixth hour, and there was a darkness over all the earth until the ninth hour.

45 And the sun was darkened, and the veil of the temple was rent in the midst.

46 And when Yahwah had cried with a loud voice, He said, "Father, into Your hands I commend My Spirit." and having said thus, He gave up His Spirit (breathed His last). – *Psa. 31:5*

47 Now when the centurion saw what was done, he glorified God (Elohim), saying, "Certainly this was a righteous Man!"

48 And all the people that came together to that sight, beholding the things which were done, smote their breasts, and returned.

49 And all His acquaintance, and the women that followed Him from Galilee, stood afar off, beholding these things.

50 And, behold, there was a man named Joseph (Yosef), a counsellor; and he was a good man, and a just.

51 (The same had not consented to the counsel and deed of them;) he was of Arimathaea, a city of the Jews (Yehudim); who also himself waited for the kingdom of God (Elohim, יהוה (YHWH)).

52 This man went unto Pilate, and begged the body of Yahwah.

53 And he took it down, and wrapped it in linen, and laid it in a sepulchre that was hewn in stone,

wherein never man before was laid.

54 And that day was the preparation, and the Shabbat drew on.

55 And the women also, who came with Him from Galilee, followed after, and beheld the sepulchre, and how His body was laid.

56 And they returned, and prepared spices and ointments; and rested the Shabbat day according to the commandment.

24 Now upon the first day of the week, very early in the morning, they came unto the sepulchre, bringing the spices which they had prepared, and certain others with them.

2 And they found the stone rolled away from the sepulchre.

3 And they entered in, and found not the body of the Lord (Adonai) Yahwah.

4 And it came to pass, as they were much perplexed thereabout, behold, two men stood by them in shining garments;

5 And as they were afraid, and bowed down their faces to the earth, they said unto them, "Why seek you the living among the dead?"

6 He is not here, but is risen; remember how He spake unto you when He was yet in Galilee,

7 Saying, "The Son of man (haMashiach) must be delivered into the hands of sinful men, and be crucified, and the third day rise again."

8 And they remembered His words,

9 And returned from the sepulchre, and told all these things unto the eleven, and to all the rest.

10 It was Mary (Miryam) Magdalene, and Joanna (Yochanah), and Mary (Miryam) the mother of Jacob (Yaaqov), and other women that were with them, who told these things unto the apostles.

11 And their words seemed to them as idle tales, and they believed them not.

12 Then arose Peter (Kefa), and ran unto the sepulchre; and stooping down, he beheld the linen clothes laid by themselves, and departed, wondering in himself at that which was come to pass.

13 And, behold, two of them went that same day to a village called Emmaus, who was from Jerusalem (Yerushalayim) about threescore furlongs.

14 And they talked together of all these things which had happened.

15 And it came to pass, that, while they communed together and reasoned, Yahwah

Himself drew near, and went with them.

16 But their eyes were holden that they should not know Him.

17 And He said unto them, "What manner of communications are these that you have one to another, as you walk, and are sad?"

18 And the one of them, whose name was Cleopas, answering said unto Him, "Art You only a stranger in Jerusalem (Yerushalayim), and hast not known the things which are come to pass there in these days?"

19 And He said unto them, "What things?" And they said unto Him, "Concerning Yahwah of Nazareth, who was a prophet mighty in deed and word before God (Elohim) and all the people;

20 And how the chief priests (kohanim) and our rulers delivered Him to be condemned to death, and have crucified Him.

21 But we trusted that it had been He who should have redeemed Yisrael; and beside all this, today is the third day since these things were done.

22 Yea, and certain women also of our company made us astonished, who were early at the sepulchre;

23 And when they found not His body, they came, saying, that they had also seen a vision of angels, who said that He was alive.

24 And certain of them who were with us went to the sepulchre, and found it even so as the women had said; but Him they saw not."

25 Then He said unto them, "O fools, and slow of heart to believe all that the prophets have spoken!

26 Ought not the Messiah (haMashiach) to have suffered these things, and to enter into His glory?"

27 And beginning at Moses (Mosheh) and all the prophets, He expounded unto them in all the scriptures the things concerning Himself.

28 And they drew near unto the village, whither they went; and He made as though He would have gone further.

29 But they constrained Him, saying, "Abide with us; for it is toward evening, and the day is far spent." And He went in to tarry with them.

30 And it came to pass, as He sat at meat with them, He took bread, and blessed it, and brake, and gave to them.

31 And their eyes were opened, and they knew Him; and He vanished out of their sight.

32 And they said one to another, "Did not our heart burn within us, while He talked with us by the way, and while He opened to us the scriptures?"

33 And they rose up the same hour, and returned to Jerusalem (Yerushalayim), and found the eleven gathered together, and them that were with them,

34 Saying, "The Lord (Yahwah) is risen indeed, and hath appeared to Shimon."

35 And they told what things were done in the way, and how He was known of them in breaking of bread.

36 And as they thus spake, Yahwah Himself stood in the midst of them, and saith unto them, "Peace be unto you."

37 But they were terrified and affrighted, and supposed that they had seen a spirit (ghost).

38 And He said unto them, "Why are you troubled? And why do thoughts arise in your hearts?

39 Behold My hands and My feet, that it is I Myself; touch Me, and see; for a spirit (ghost) hath not flesh and bones, as you see Me have."

40 And when He had thus spoken, He shewed them His hands and His feet.

41 And while they yet believed not for joy, and wondered, He said unto them, "Have you here any food?"

42 And they gave Him a piece of a broiled fish, and of a honeycomb.

43 And He took it, and did eat before them.

44 And He said unto them, "These are the words which I spake unto you, while I was yet with you, that all things must be fulfilled, which were written in the Torah, and in the Prophets, and in the Psalms, concerning Me.

45 Then opened He their understanding, that they might understand the scriptures,

46 And said unto them, "Thus it is written, and thus it behoved the Messiah (haMashiach) to suffer, and to rise from the dead the third day;

47 And that repentance and remission of sins should be preached in His name among all nations, beginning at Jerusalem (Yerushalayim).

48 And you are witnesses of these things.

49 And, behold, I send the promise of My Father upon you; but tarry you in the city of Jerusalem (Yerushalayim), until you be endued with power from on high."

50 And He led them out as far as to Bethany, and He lifted up His hands, and blessed them.
51 And it came to pass, while He blessed them, He was parted from them, and carried up into heaven.

52 And they worshipped Him, and returned to Jerusalem (Yerushalayim) with great joy;
53 And were continually in the temple, praising and blessing God (Elohim, יהוה (YHWH)). So be it (Amen).

JOHN
YOCHANAN יוֹחָנָן
(Gospel of [A71]John)

1 In the beginning was the [B61]Word (Davar), and the Word was with [B1a]God (Elohim), and the Word was God (Elohim, יהוה (YHWH)).

2 The same was in the beginning with God (Elohim).

3 All things were made by Him; and without Him was not anything made that was made.

4 In Him was life; and the life was the light of men.

5 And the light shineth in darkness; and the darkness comprehended it not.

6 There was a man sent from God (Elohim, יהוה (YHWH)), whose name was [A67]John (Yochanan).

7 The same came for a witness, to bear witness of the Light, that all men through him might believe.

8 He was not that Light, but was sent to bear witness of that Light.

9 That was the true Light, which lighteth every man that cometh into the world.

10 He was in the world, and the world was made by Him, and the world knew Him not.

11 He came unto His own, and His own received Him not.

12 But as many as received Him, to them gave He power to become the sons of God (Elohim), even to them that believe on His name,

13 Who were born, not of blood, nor of the will of the flesh, nor of the will of man, but of God (Elohim).

14 And the [B61]Word was made flesh, and dwelt among us, (and we beheld His glory, the glory as of the only begotten of the Father,) full of grace and truth. – *1 Tim. 3:16*

15 John (Yochanan) bare witness of Him, and cried, saying, "This was He of whom I spake, 'He that cometh after me is preferred before me; for He was before me.'"

16 And of His fulness have all we received, and grace for grace.

17 For the [B28a]law (torah) was given by Moses (Mosheh), but grace and truth came by Yahwah haMashiach.

18 No man hath seen God (Elohim, יהוה (YHWH)) at any time; the only begotten (one and only) [B47]Son (Humanity of El), who is in the bosom of the Father, He hath declared Him.

19 And this is the record of John (Yochanan), when the Jews (Yehudim) sent priests (kohanim) and Levites (Lewiyim) from Jerusalem (Yerushalayim) to ask him, "Who are you?"

20 And he confessed, and denied not; but confessed, "I am not the Messiah (haMashiach)."

21 And they asked him, "What then? Are you Elijah (Eliyahu)?" And he saith, "I am not." "Are you that prophet?" And he answered, "No."

22 Then said they unto him, "Who are you, that we may give an answer to them that sent us. What sayest you of yourself?"

23 He said, "I am the voice of one crying in the wilderness, 'Make straight the way of יהוה (YHWH, Yahwah),' as said the prophet Esaias (Yeshayahu)." – *Isa. 40:3, Mat, 3:3, Mark 1:3, Luke 3:4*

24 And they who were sent were of the Pharisees.

25 And they asked him, and said unto him, "Why baptizest you then, if you be not the Messiah (haMashiach), nor Elijah (Eliyahu), neither that prophet?"

26 John (Yochanan) answered them, saying, "I baptize with water, but there standeth one among you, whom you know not;

27 He it is, who coming after me is preferred before me, whose shoe's latchet I am not worthy to unloose.

28 These things were done in Bethabara beyond Jordan (Yarden), where John (Yochanan) was baptizing.

29 The next day John (Yochanan) seeth Yahwah coming unto him, and saith, "Behold the Lamb of God (Elohim, יהוה (YHWH)), who taketh away the sin of the world.

30 This is He of whom I said, "After me cometh a man who is preferred before me; for He was before me.

31 And I knew Him not; but that He should be made manifest to Yisrael, therefore am I come baptizing with water."

32 And John (Yochanan) bare record, saying, "I saw the Spirit descending from heaven like a dove, and it abode upon Him.

33 And I knew Him not; but He that sent me to baptize with water, the same said unto me, "Upon whom you shalt see the Spirit (Ruach) descending, and remaining on Him, the same is He who baptizeth with the Holy Spirit (Ruach

haQodesh).

34 And I saw, and bare record that this is the [B47]Humanity of El (YHWH).”

35 Again the next day after John (Yochanan) stood, and two of his disciples;

36 And looking upon Yahwah as He walked, he saith, “Behold the Lamb of God (Elohim, יהוה (YHWH))!”

37 And the two disciples heard him speak, and they followed Yahwah.

38 Then Yahwah turned, and saw them following, and saith unto them, “What seek you?” They said unto Him, “Rabbi, (which is to say, being interpreted, Teacher) where dwellest You?”

39 He saith unto them, “Come and see.” They came and saw where He dwelt, and abode with Him that day; for it was about the tenth hour.

40 One of the two who heard John (Yochanan) speak, and followed Him, was Andrew, Shimon Peter (Kefa)’s brother.

41 He first findeth his own brother Shimon, and saith unto him, “We have found the Messiah (haMashiach)” (which is, being interpreted, the Anointed One).

42 And he brought him to Yahwah. And when Yahwah beheld him, He said, “You are Shimon the son of Jonah (Yonah); you shalt be called [A72]Cephas (Kefa).” (which is by interpretation, “A stone”.)

43 The day following Yahwah would go forth into Galilee, and findeth Philip, and saith unto him, “Follow Me.”

44 Now Philip was of Bethsaida, the city of Andrew and Peter (Kefa).

45 Philip findeth Nathanael, and saith unto him, “We have found Him, of whom Moses (Mosheh) in the Torah, and the Prophets, did write, Yahwah of Nazareth, the son of Joseph (Yosef).”

46 And Nathanael said unto him, “Can there any good thing come out of Nazareth?” Philip saith unto him, “Come and see.”

47 Yahwah saw Nathanael coming to him, and saith of him, “Behold an Israelite (Yisraeli) indeed, in whom is no guile!”

48 Nathanael saith unto Him, “Whence knowest You me?” Yahwah answered and said unto him, “Before that Philip called you, when you wast under the fig tree, I saw you.”

49 Nathanael answered and saith unto Him,

“Teacher (Rabbi), You are the [B47]Humanity of El (YHWH); You are the King of Yisrael.”

50 Yahwah answered and said unto him, “Because I said unto you, I saw you under the fig tree, believest you? You shalt see greater things than these.”

51 And He saith unto him, “Verily, verily, I say unto you, hereafter you shall see heaven open, and the angels of God (Elohim) ascending and descending upon the Son of man (haMashiach).”

2 And the third day there was a marriage in Cana of Galilee; and the mother of Yahwah was there.

2 And both Yahwah was called, and His disciples, to the marriage.

3 And when they wanted wine, the mother of Yahwah saith unto Him, “They have no wine.”

4 Yahwah saith unto her, “Woman, what have I to do with you? Mine hour is not yet come.”

5 His mother saith unto the servants, “Whatsoever He saith unto you, do it.”

6 And there were set there six waterpots of stone, after the manner of the purifying of the Jews (Yehudim), containing two or three firkins apiece.

7 Yahwah saith unto them, “Fill the waterpots with water.” And they filled them up to the brim.

8 And He saith unto them, “Draw out now, and bear unto the governor of the feast.” And they bare it.

9 When the ruler of the feast had tasted the water that was made wine, and knew not whence it was; (but the servants who drew the water knew;) the governor of the feast called the bridegroom,

10 And saith unto him, “Every man at the beginning doth set forth good wine; and when men have well drunk, then that which is worse; but you have kept the good wine until now.”

11 This beginning of miracles did Yahwah in Cana of Galilee, and manifested forth His glory; and His disciples believed on Him.

12 After this He went down to Capernaum, He, and His mother, and His brethren, and His disciples; and they continued there not many days.

13 And the Jews’ (Yehudim) Passover (Pesach) was at hand, and Yahwah went up to Jerusalem (Yerushalayim),

14 And found in the temple those that sold oxen

928

and sheep and doves, and the changers of money sitting.

15 And when He had made a scourge of small cords, He drove them all out of the temple, and the sheep, and the oxen; and poured out the changers' money, and overthrew the tables;

16 And said unto them that sold doves, "Take these things hence; make not My Father's house a house of merchandise."

17 And His disciples remembered that it was written, "The zeal of your house hath eaten Me up." – *Psa. 69:9*

18 Then answered the Jews (Yehudim) and said unto Him, "What sign shewest You unto us, seeing that You doest these things?"

19 Yahwah answered and said unto them, "Destroy this temple (body), and in three days I will raise it up."

20 Then said the Jews (Yehudim), "Forty and six years was this temple in building, and wilt You rear it up in three days?"

21 But He spake of the temple of His body.

22 When therefore He was risen from the dead, His disciples remembered that He had said this unto them; and they believed the scripture, and the word which Yahwah had said.

23 Now when He was in Jerusalem (Yerushalayim) at the Passover (Pesach), in the feast day, many believed in His name, when they saw the miracles which He did.

24 But Yahwah did not commit Himself unto them, because He knew all men,

25 And needed not that any should testify of man; for He knew what was in man.

3 There was a man of the Pharisees, named Nicodemus, a ruler of the Jews (Yehudim).

2 The same came to Yahwah by night, and said unto Him, "Teacher (Rabbi), we know that You are a teacher come from God (Elohim), for no man can do these miracles that You doest, except God (Elohim) be with him."

3 Yahwah answered and said unto him, "Verily, verily, I say unto you, except a man be born again, he cannot see the kingdom of God (Elohim, יהוה (YHWH))."

4 Nicodemus saith unto him, "How can a man be born when he is old? Can he enter the second time into his mother's womb, and be born?"

5 Yahwah answered, "Verily, verily, I say unto you, except a man be born of water and of the Spirit (Ruach), he cannot enter into the kingdom

of God (Elohim, יהוה (YHWH)).

6 That who is born of the flesh is flesh; and that who is born of the Spirit is spirit.

7 Marvel not that I said unto you, 'You must be born again.'

8 The wind bloweth where it listeth, and you hearest the sound thereof, but canst not tell whence it cometh, and whither it goeth; so is every one that is born of the Spirit (Ruach).

9 Nicodemus answered and said unto Him, "How can these things be?"

10 Yahwah answered and said unto him, "Are you a teacher of Yisrael, and knowest not these things?

11 Verily, verily, I say unto you, we speak that we do know, and testify that we have seen; and you receive not our witness.

12 If I have told you earthly things, and you believe not, how shall you believe, if I tell you of heavenly things?

13 And no man hath ascended up to heaven, but He that came down from heaven, even the Son of man (haMashiach) who is in heaven.

14 And as Moses (Mosheh) lifted up the serpent in the wilderness, even so must the Son of man (haMashiach) be lifted up;

15 That whosoever believeth in Him should not perish, but have eternal life.

16 For God (Elohim, יהוה (YHWH)) so loved the world, that He gave His only begotten [B47]Humanity (Yahwah haMashiach), that whosoever believeth in Him should not perish, but have everlasting life.

17 For God (Elohim, יהוה (YHWH)) sent not His [B47]Humanity into the world to condemn the world; but that the world through Him might be saved.

18 He that believeth on Him is not condemned; but he that believeth not is condemned already, because he hath not believed in the name of the only begotten [B47]Humanity of El (YHWH).

19 And this is the condemnation, that light is come into the world, and men loved darkness rather than light, because their deeds were evil.

20 For every one that doeth evil hateth the light, neither cometh to the light, lest his deeds should be reproved.

21 But he that doeth truth cometh to the light, that his deeds may be made manifest, that they are wrought in God (Elohim)."

22 After these things came Yahwah and His

disciples into the land of Judah (Yehudah); and there He tarried with them, and baptized.

23 And John (Yochanan) also was baptizing in Aenon near to Salim, because there was much water there; and they came, and were baptized.

24 For John (Yochanan) was not yet cast into prison.

25 Then there arose a question between some of John (Yochanan)'s disciples and the Jews (Yehudim) about purifying.

26 And they came unto John (Yochanan), and said unto him, "Teacher (Rabbi), He that was with you beyond Jordan (Yarden), to whom you barest witness, behold, the same baptizeth, and all men come to Him."

27 John (Yochanan) answered and said, "A man can receive nothing, except it be given him from heaven.

28 You yourselves bear me witness, that I said, 'I am not the Messiah (haMashiach), but that I am sent before Him.

29 He that hath the bride is the bridegroom; but the friend of the bridegroom, who standeth and heareth him, rejoiceth greatly because of the bridegroom's voice; this my joy therefore is fulfilled.

30 He must increase, but I must decrease.

31 He that cometh from above is above all; he that is of the earth is earthly, and speaketh of the earth; He that cometh from heaven is above all.

32 And what He hath seen and heard, that He testifieth; and no man receiveth His testimony.

33 He that hath received His testimony hath set to His seal that God (Elohim, יהוה (YHWH)) is true.

34 For He whom God (Elohim, יהוה (YHWH)) hath sent speaketh the words of יהוה (YHWH); for יהוה (YHWH) giveth not the Spirit (Ruach) by measure unto Him.

35 The Father loveth the [B47]Son (Humanity of El (YHWH)), and hath given all things into His hand.

36 He that believeth on the [B47]Son (Humanity of El (YHWH)), hath everlasting life; and he that believeth not the [B47]Son shall not see life; but the wrath of God (Elohim, יהוה (YHWH)) abideth on him."

4 When therefore the Lord (Yahwah) knew how the Pharisees had heard that Yahwah made and baptized more disciples than John (Yochanan),

2 (Though Yahwah Himself baptized not, but His disciples,)

3 He left Judah (Yehudah), and departed again into Galilee.

4 And He must needs go through Samaria.

5 Then cometh He to a city of Samaria, which is called Sychar, near to the parcel of ground that Jacob (Yaaqov) gave to his son Joseph (Yosef).

6 Now Jacob (Yaaqov)'s well was there. Yahwah therefore, being wearied with His journey, sat thus on the well; and it was about the sixth hour.

7 There cometh a woman of Samaria to draw water. Yahwah saith unto her, "Give Me to drink."

8 (For His disciples were gone away unto the city to buy food.)

9 Then saith the woman of Samaria unto Him, "How is it that You, being a Jew (Yehudi), askest drink of me, who am a woman of Samaria? For the Jews (Yehudim) have no dealings with the Samaritans."

10 Yahwah answered and said unto her, "If you knewest the gift of God (Elohim), and who it is that saith to you, 'Give Me to drink;' you wouldest have asked of Him, and He would have given you living water."

11 The woman saith unto Him, "Sir, You have nothing to draw with, and the well is deep; from whence then have You that living water?

12 Are you greater than our father Jacob (Yaaqov), who gave us the well, and drank thereof himself, and his children, and his cattle?"

13 Yahwah answered and said unto her, "Whosoever drinketh of this water shall thirst again;

14 But whosoever drinketh of the water that I shall give him shall never thirst; but the water that I shall give him shall be in him a well of water springing up into everlasting life."

15 The woman saith unto him, "Sir, give me this water, that I thirst not, neither come hither to draw."

16 Yahwah saith unto her, "Go, call your husband, and come hither."

17 The woman answered and said, "I have no husband." Yahwah said unto her, "You have well said, 'I have no husband;'

18 For you have had five husbands; and he whom you now hast is not your husband; in that saidst you truly."

19 The woman saith unto Him, "Sir, I perceive that You are a prophet.

20 Our fathers worshipped in this mountain; and you say, that in Jerusalem (Yerushalayim) is the place where men ought to worship."

21 Yahwah saith unto her, "Woman, believe Me, the hour cometh, when you shall neither in this mountain, nor yet at Jerusalem (Yerushalayim), worship the Father.

22 You worship you know not what; we know what we worship; for salvation is of the Jews (Yehudim).

23 But the hour cometh, and now is, when the true worshippers shall worship the Father in spirit and in truth; for the Father seeketh such to worship Him.

24 God (Elohim) is a Spirit (Ruach); and they that worship Him must worship Him in spirit and in truth."

25 The woman saith unto Him, "I know that Messiah (Mashiach) cometh" (who is called the Anointed); when He is come, He will tell us all things."

26 Yahwah saith unto her, "I that speak unto you am He."

27 And upon this came His disciples, and marvelled that He talked with the woman; yet no man said, 'What seekest You?' Or, 'Why talkest You with her?'

28 The woman then left her waterpot, and went her way into the city, and saith to the men,

29 "Come, see a man, who told me all things that ever I did; is not this the Messiah ([B45]haMashiach)?"

30 Then they went out of the city, and came unto Him.

31 In the mean while His disciples urged Him, saying, "Teacher (Rabbi), eat."

32 But He said unto them, "I have food to eat that you know not of."

33 Therefore said the disciples one to another, "Hath any man brought Him anything to eat?"

34 Yahwah saith unto them, "My food is to do the will of Him that sent Me, and to finish His work.

35 Say not you, 'There are yet four months, and then cometh harvest?' Behold, I say unto you, lift up your eyes, and look on the fields; for they are white already to harvest.

36 And he that reapeth receiveth wages, and gathereth fruit unto life eternal; that both he that

soweth and he that reapeth may rejoice together.

37 And herein is that saying true, 'One soweth, and another reapeth.'

38 I sent you to reap that whereon you bestowed no labour; other men laboured, and you are entered into their labours."

39 And many of the Samaritans of that city believed on Him for the saying of the woman, who testified, "He told me all that ever I did."

40 So when the Samaritans were come unto Him, they besought Him that He would tarry with them; and He abode there two days.

41 And many more believed because of His own word;

42 And said unto the woman, "Now we believe, not because of your saying; for we have heard Him ourselves, and know that this is indeed the Messiah (haMashiach), the Savior of the world."

43 Now after two days He departed thence, and went into Galilee.

44 For Yahwah Himself testified, that a prophet hath no honour in his own country.

45 Then when He was come into Galilee, the Galilaeans received Him, having seen all the things that He did at Jerusalem (Yerushalayim) at the feast; for they also went unto the feast.

46 So Yahwah came again into Cana of Galilee, where He made the water wine. And there was a certain nobleman, whose son was sick at Capernaum.

47 When he heard that Yahwah was come out of Judah (Yehudah) into Galilee, he went unto Him, and besought Him that He would come down, and heal his son; for he was at the point of death.

48 Then said Yahwah unto him, "Except you see signs and wonders, you will not believe."

49 The nobleman saith unto him, "Sir, come down ere my child die."

50 Yahwah saith unto him, "Go your way; your son liveth." And the man believed the word that Yahwah had spoken unto him, and he went his way.

51 And as he was now going down, his servants met him, and told him, saying, "Your son liveth."

52 Then enquired he of them the hour when he began to amend. And they said unto him, "Yesterday at the seventh hour the fever left him."

53 So the father knew that it was at the same hour, in the which Yahwah said unto him, "Your

son liveth;" and himself believed, and his whole house.

54 This is again the second miracle that Yahwah did, when he was come out of Judah (Yehudah) into Galilee.

5 After this there was a feast of the Jews (Yehudim); and Yahwah went up to Jerusalem (Yerushalayim).

2 Now there is at Jerusalem (Yerushalayim) by the sheep market a pool, which is called in the Hebrew tongue Bethesda, having five porches.

3 In these lay a great multitude of impotent folk, of blind, halt, withered, waiting for the moving of the water.

4 For an angel went down at a certain season into the pool, and troubled the water: whosoever then first after the troubling of the water stepped in was made whole of whatsoever disease he had.

5 And a certain man was there, who had an infirmity thirty and eight years.

6 When Yahwah saw him lie, and knew that he had been now a long time in that case, He saith unto him, "Wilt you be made whole?"

7 The impotent man answered Him, "Sir, I have no man, when the water is troubled, to put me into the pool; but while I am coming, another steppeth down before me."

8 Yahwah saith unto him, "Rise, take up your bed, and walk."

9 And immediately the man was made whole, and took up his bed, and walked; and on the same day was the Shabbat.

10 The Jews (Yehudim) therefore said unto him that was cured, "It is the Shabbat day; it is not lawful for you to carry your bed."

11 He answered them, "He that made me whole, the same said unto me, 'Take up your bed, and walk.'"

12 Then asked they him, "What man is that who said unto you, 'Take up your bed, and walk?'"

13 And he that was healed wist not who it was; for Yahwah had conveyed himself away, a multitude being in that place.

14 Afterward Yahwah findeth him in the temple, and said unto him, "Behold, you are made whole; sin no more, lest a worse thing come unto you."

15 The man departed, and told the Jews (Yehudim) that it was Yahwah, who had made him whole.

16 And therefore did the Jews (Yehudim) persecute Yahwah, and sought to slay Him, because He had done these things on the Shabbat day.

17 But Yahwah answered them, "My Father worketh until now, and I work."

18 Therefore the Jews (Yehudim) sought the more to kill Him, because He not only had broken the Shabbat, but said also that God (Elohim, יהוה (YHWH)) was His Father, making Himself equal with God (Elohim).

19 Then answered Yahwah and said unto them, "Verily, verily, I say unto you, 'The [B47]Son (Humanity of El (YHWH)) can do nothing of Himself, but what He seeth the Father do; for what things soever He doeth, these also doeth the [B47]Son (Humanity of El (YHWH) likewise.

20 For the Father loveth the Son (Humanity of El (YHWH)), and sheweth Him all things that Himself doeth; and He will shew Him greater works than these, that you may marvel.

21 For as the Father raiseth up the dead, and quickeneth them; even so the Son (Humanity of El (YHWH)) quickeneth whom He will.

22 For the Father judgeth no man, but hath committed all judgment unto the Son (Humanity of El (YHWH));

23 That all men should honour the Son (Humanity of El (YHWH)), even as they honour the Father. He that honoureth not the Son (Humanity of El (YHWH)) honoureth not the Father who hath sent Him.

24 Verily, verily, I say unto you, he that heareth My word, and believeth on Him that sent Me, hath everlasting life, and shall not come into condemnation; but is passed from death unto life.

25 Verily, verily, I say unto you, 'The hour is coming, and now is, when the dead shall hear the voice of the Son (Humanity of El (YHWH)); and they that hear shall live.

26 For as the Father hath life in Himself; so hath He given to the Son (Humanity of El (YHWH)) to have life in Himself;

27 And hath given Him authority to execute judgment also, because He is the Son of man (haMashiach).

28 Marvel not at this; for the hour is coming, in which all that are in the graves shall hear His voice,

29 And shall come forth; they that have done good, unto the resurrection of life; and they

that have done evil, unto the resurrection of damnation.

30 I can of Mine own self do nothing; as I hear, I judge; and My judgment is just; because I seek not Mine own will, but the will of the Father who hath sent Me.

31 If I bear witness of Myself, My witness is not true.

32 There is another that beareth witness of Me; and I know that the witness which he witnesseth of Me is true.

33 You sent unto John (Yochanan), and he bare witness unto the truth.

34 But I receive not testimony from man; but these things I say, that you might be saved.

35 He was a burning and a shining light; and you were willing for a season to rejoice in his light.

36 But I have greater witness than that of John (Yochanan); for the works which the Father hath given Me to finish, the same works that I do, bear witness of Me, that the Father hath sent Me.

37 And the Father Himself, who hath sent Me, hath borne witness of Me. You have neither heard His voice at any time, nor seen His shape.

38 And you have not His word abiding in you; for whom He hath sent, Him you believe not.

39 Search the scriptures, for in them you think you have eternal life; and they are they which testify of Me.

40 And you will not come to Me, that you might have life.

41 I receive not honour from men.

42 But I know you, that you have not the love of God (Elohim, יהוה (YHWH)) in you.

43 I am come in My Father's name, and you receive Me not; if another shall come in his own name, him you will receive.

44 How can you believe, who receive honour one of another, and seek not the honour that cometh from God (Elohim) only?

45 Do not think that I will accuse you to the Father; there is one that accuseth you, even Moses (Mosheh), in whom you trust.

46 For had you believed Moses (Mosheh), you would have believed Me; for he wrote of Me. – *Exo. 3:14-15*

47 But if you believe not his writings, how shall you believe My words?"

6 After these things Yahwah went over the sea of Galilee, which is the sea of Tiberias.

2 And a great multitude followed Him, because they saw His miracles which He did on them that were diseased.

3 And Yahwah went up into a mountain, and there He sat with His disciples.

4 And the Passover (Pesach), a feast of the Jews (Yehudim), was near.

5 When Yahwah then lifted up His eyes, and saw a great company come unto Him, He saith unto Philip, "Whence shall we buy bread, that these may eat?"

6 And this He said to prove him; for He Himself knew what he would do.

7 Philip answered him, "Two hundred pennyworth of bread is not sufficient for them, that every one of them may take a little."

8 One of His disciples, Andrew, Shimon Peter (Kefa)'s brother, saith unto Him,

9 "There is a lad here, who hath five barley loaves, and two small fishes; but what are they among so many?"

10 And Yahwah said, "Make the men sit down." Now there was much grass in the place. So the men sat down, in number about five thousand.

11 And Yahwah took the loaves; and when He had given thanks, He distributed to the disciples, and the disciples to them that were set down; and likewise of the fishes as much as they would.

12 When they were filled, He said unto His disciples, "Gather up the fragments that remain, that nothing be lost."

13 Therefore they gathered them together, and filled twelve baskets with the fragments of the five barley loaves, which remained over and above unto them that had eaten.

14 Then those men, when they had seen the miracle that Yahwah did, said, "This is of a truth that prophet that should come into the world."

15 When Yahwah therefore perceived that they would come and take Him by force, to make Him a king, He departed again into a mountain Himself alone.

16 And when even was now come, His disciples went down unto the sea,

17 And entered into a ship, and went over the sea toward Capernaum. And it was now dark, and Yahwah was not come to them.

18 And the sea arose by reason of a great wind that blew.

19 So when they had rowed about five and

twenty or thirty furlongs, they see Yahwah walking on the sea, and drawing near unto the ship; and they were afraid.

20 But He saith unto them, "It is I; be not afraid."

21 Then they willingly received Him into the ship; and immediately the ship was at the land whither they went.

22 The day following, when the people who stood on the other side of the sea saw that there was none other boat there, except that one whereinto His disciples were entered, and that Yahwah went not with His disciples into the boat, but that His disciples were gone away alone;

23 Howbeit there came other boats from Tiberias near unto the place where they did eat bread, after that the Lord (Yahwah) had given thanks;

24 When the people therefore saw that Yahwah was not there, neither His disciples, they also took shipping, and came to Capernaum, seeking for Yahwah.

25 And when they had found Him on the other side of the sea, they said unto Him, "Teacher (Rabbi), when camest You hither?"

26 Yahwah answered them and said, "Verily, verily, I say unto you, you seek Me, not because you saw the miracles, but because you did eat of the loaves, and were filled.

27 Labour not for the food which perisheth, but for that food which endureth unto everlasting life, which the Son of man (haMashiach) shall give unto you; for Him hath God (Elohim) the Father sealed."

28 Then said they unto Him, "What shall we do, that we might work the works of God (Elohim)?"

29 Yahwah answered and said unto them, "This is the work of God (Elohim), that you believe on Him whom He hath sent."

30 They said therefore unto Him, "What sign shewest You then, that we may see, and believe You? What dost You work?

31 Our fathers did eat manna in the desert; as it is written, 'He gave them bread from heaven to eat.'" – Psa. 78:24, Neh. 9:15

32 Then Yahwah said unto them, "Verily, verily, I say unto you, Moses (Mosheh) gave you not that bread from heaven; but My Father giveth you the true bread from heaven.

33 For the bread of God (Elohim) is He who cometh down from heaven, and giveth life unto the world."

34 Then said they unto Him, "Lord (Adonai), evermore give us this bread."

35 And Yahwah said unto them, "I am the bread of life; he that cometh to Me shall never hunger; and he that believeth on Me shall never thirst.

36 But I said unto you, that you also have seen Me, and believe not.

37 All that the Father giveth Me shall come to Me; and him that cometh to Me I will in no wise cast out.

38 For I came down from heaven, not to do Mine own will, but the will of Him that sent Me.

39 And this is the Father's will who hath sent Me, that of all which He hath given Me I should lose nothing, but should raise it up again at the last day.

40 And this is the will of Him that sent Me, that every one who seeth the [B47]Son (Humanity of El (YHWH)), and believeth on Him, may have everlasting life; and I will raise him up at the last day."

41 The Jews (Yehudim) then murmured at Him, because He said, "I am the bread which came down from heaven."

42 And they said, "Is not this Yahwah, the son of Joseph (Yosef), whose father and mother we know? How is it then that He saith, "I came down from heaven?"

43 Yahwah therefore answered and said unto them, "Murmur not among yourselves.

44 No man can come to Me, except the Father who hath sent Me draw him; and I will raise him up at the last day.

45 It is written in the prophets, 'And they shall be all taught of יהוה (YHWH).' Every man therefore that hath heard, and hath learned of the Father, cometh unto Me. – Isa. 54:13

46 Not that any man hath seen the Father, except He who is of God (Elohim, יהוה (YHWH)), He hath seen the Father.

47 Verily, verily, I say unto you, he that believeth on Me hath everlasting life.

48 I am that bread of life.

49 Your fathers did eat manna in the wilderness, and are dead.

50 This is the bread which cometh down from heaven, that a man may eat thereof, and not die.

51 I am the living bread which came down from heaven; if any man eats of this bread, he shall

live forever; and the bread that I will give is My flesh, which I will give for the life of the world."

52 The Jews (Yehudim) therefore strove among themselves, saying, "How can this Man give us His flesh to eat?"

53 Then Yahwah said unto them, "Verily, verily, I say unto you, except you eat the flesh of the Son of man (haMashiach), and drink His blood, you have no life in you.

54 Whoso eateth My flesh, and drinketh My blood, hath eternal life; and I will raise him up at the last day.

55 For My flesh is food indeed, and My blood is drink indeed.

56 He that eateth My flesh, and drinketh My blood, dwelleth in Me, and I in him.

57 As the living Father hath sent Me, and I live by the Father; so he that eateth Me, even he shall live by Me.

58 This is that bread which came down from heaven; not as your fathers did eat manna, and are dead; he that eateth of this bread shall live forever."

59 These things said He in the synagogue, as He taught in Capernaum.

60 Many therefore of His disciples, when they had heard this, said, "This is a hard saying; who can hear it?"

61 When Yahwah knew in Himself that His disciples murmured at it, He said unto them, "Doth this offend you?

62 What and if you shall see the Son of man (haMashiach) ascend up where He was before?

63 It is the spirit that quickeneth; the flesh profiteth nothing; the words that I speak unto you, they are spirit, and they are life.

64 But there are some of you that believe not." For Yahwah knew from the beginning who they were that believed not, and who should betray Him.

65 And He said, "Therefore said I unto you, that no man can come unto Me, except it was given unto him of My Father."

66 From that time many of His disciples went back, and walked no more with Him.

67 Then said Yahwah unto the twelve, "Will you also go away?"

68 Then Shimon Peter (Kefa) answered Him, "Lord (Adonai), to whom shall we go? You have the words of eternal life.

69 And we believe and are sure that You are

that Messiah (Mashiach), the [B47]Humanity of the living God (Elohim)."

70 Yahwah answered them, "Have not I chosen you twelve, and one of you is a devil?"

71 He spake of Judas (Yehudah) Ishkeriot the son of Shimon; for he it was that should betray Him, being one of the twelve.

7 After these things Yahwah walked in Galilee; for He would not walk in Jewry (Yehudah), because the Jews (Yehudim) sought to kill Him.

2 Now the Jews' (Yehudim) [B24]Feast of Tabernacles (Chag Sukkot) was at hand.

3 His brethren therefore said unto Him, "Depart hence, and go into Judah (Yehudah), that Your disciples also may see the works that You doest.

4 For there is no man that doeth any thing in secret, and he himself seeketh to be known openly. If You do these things, shew Yourself to the world."

5 For neither did His brethren believe in Him.

6 Then Yahwah said unto them, "My time is not yet come; but your time is always ready.

7 The world cannot hate you; but Me it hateth, because I testify of it, that the works thereof are evil.

8 Go you up unto this feast; I go not up yet unto this feast; for My time is not yet full come."

9 When He had said these words unto them, He abode still in Galilee.

10 But when His brethren were gone up, then went He also up unto the feast, not openly, but as it was in secret.

11 Then the Jews (Yehudim) sought Him at the feast, and said, "Where is He?"

12 And there was much murmuring among the people concerning Him; for some said, "He is a good man;" others said, "Nay; but He deceiveth the people."

13 Howbeit no man spake openly of Him for fear of the Jews (Yehudim).

14 Now about the midst of the feast Yahwah went up into the temple, and taught.

15 And the Jews (Yehudim) marvelled, saying, "How knoweth this Man letters, having never learned?"

16 Yahwah answered them, and said, "My doctrine is not Mine, but His that sent Me.

17 If any man will do His will, he shall know of the doctrine, whether it be of God (Elohim, יהוה (YHWH)), or whether I speak of Myself.

18 He that speaketh of himself seeketh his own

glory; but He that seeketh His glory that sent Him, the same is true, and no unrighteousness is in Him.

19 Did not Moses (Mosheh) give you the Torah, and yet none of you keepeth the Torah? Why go you about to kill Me?"

20 The people answered and said, "You have a devil; who goeth about to kill You?"

21 Yahwah answered and said unto them, "I have done one work, and you all marvel.

22 Moses (Mosheh) therefore gave unto you circumcision; (not because it is of Moses (Mosheh), but of the fathers;) and you on the Shabbat day circumcise a man.

23 If a man on the Shabbat day receive circumcision, that the teaching of Moses (torat Mosheh) should not be broken; are you angry at Me, because I have made a man every whit whole on the Shabbat day?

24 Judge not according to the appearance, but judge righteous judgment."

25 Then said some of them of Jerusalem (Yerushalayim), "Is not this He, whom they seek to kill?

26 But, behold, He speaketh boldly, and they say nothing unto Him. Do the rulers know indeed that this is the very Messiah (Mashiach)?

27 Howbeit we know this Man whence He is; but when the Messiah (haMashiach) cometh, no man knoweth whence He is."

28 Then cried Yahwah in the temple as He taught, saying, "You both know Me, and you know whence I am; and I am not come of Myself, but He that sent Me is true, whom you know not.

29 But I know Him; for I am from Him, and He hath sent Me."

30 Then they sought to take Him; but no man laid hands on Him, because His hour was not yet come.

31 And many of the people believed on Him, and said, "When the Messiah (haMashiach) cometh, will He do more miracles than these which this Man hath done?"

32 The Pharisees heard that the people murmured such things concerning Him; and the Pharisees and the chief priests (kohanim) sent officers to take Him.

33 Then said Yahwah unto them, "Yet a little while am I with you, and then I go unto Him that sent Me.

34 You shall seek Me, and shall not find Me; and where I am, thither you cannot come."

35 Then said the Jews (Yehudim) among themselves, "Whither will He go, that we shall not find Him? Will He go unto the dispersed among the Gentiles (Goyim), and teach the Gentiles (Goyim)?

36 What manner of saying is this that He said, 'You shall seek Me, and shall not find Me; and where I am, thither you cannot come'?"

37 In the last day, that great day of the feast, Yahwah stood and cried, saying, "If any man thirst, let him come unto Me, and drink.

38 He that believeth on Me, as the Scripture hath said, out of his belly shall flow rivers of living water."

39 But this spake He of the Spirit (Ruach), which they that believe on Him should receive; for the Holy Spirit (Ruach haQodesh) was not yet given; because that Yahwah was not yet glorified.

40 Many of the people therefore, when they heard this saying, said, "Of a truth this is the Prophet."

41 Others said, "This is the Messiah (haMashiach)." But some said, "Shall the Messiah (haMashiach) come out of Galilee?

42 Hath not the Scripture said, that the Messiah (haMashiach) cometh of the seed of Dawid, and out of the town of Bethlehem (Beit-Lechem), where Dawid was?" – *Mic. 5:2*

43 So there was a division among the people because of Him.

44 And some of them would have taken Him; but no man laid hands on Him.

45 Then came the officers to the chief priests (kohanim) and Pharisees; and they said unto them, "Why have you not brought Him?"

46 The officers answered, "Never man spake like this Man."

47 Then answered them the Pharisees, "Are you also deceived?

48 Have any of the rulers or of the Pharisees believed on Him?

49 But this people who knoweth not the [B28a]law (torah) are cursed."

50 Nicodemus saith unto them, (he that came to Yahwah by night, being one of them,)

51 "Doth our law (torah) judge any man, before it hears him, and know what he doeth?"

52 They answered and said unto him, "Are you

also of Galilee? Search, and look; for out of Galilee ariseth no prophet."

53 And every man went unto his own house.

8 Yahwah went unto the Mount of Olives.

2 And early in the morning He came again into the temple, and all the people came unto Him; and He sat down, and taught them.

3 And the scribes and Pharisees brought unto Him a woman taken in adultery; and when they had set her in the midst,

4 They say unto Him, "Teacher (Rabbi), this woman was taken in adultery, in the very act.

5 Now Moses (Mosheh) in the Torah commanded us, that such should be stoned; but what sayest You?"

6 This they said, testing Him, that they might have to accuse Him. But Yahwah stooped down, and with His finger wrote on the ground, as though He heard them not.

7 So when they continued asking Him, He lifted up Himself, and said unto them, "He that is without sin among you, let him first cast a stone at her."

8 And again He stooped down, and wrote on the ground.

9 And they who heard it, being convicted by their own conscience, went out one by one, beginning at the eldest, even unto the last; and Yahwah was left alone, and the woman standing in the midst.

10 When Yahwah had lifted up Himself, and saw none but the woman, He said unto her, "Woman, where are those your accusers? Hath no man condemned you?"

11 She said, "No man, my Lord (Adonai)." And Yahwah said unto her, "Neither do I condemn you; go, and sin no more."

12 Then spake Yahwah again unto them, saying, "I am the light of the world; he that followeth Me shall not walk in darkness, but shall have the light of life."

13 The Pharisees therefore said unto Him, "You bearest record of Yourself; Your record is not true."

14 Yahwah answered and said unto them, "Though I bear record of Myself, yet My record is true; for I know whence I came, and whither I go; but you cannot tell whence I come, and whither I go.

15 You judge after the flesh; I judge no man.

16 And yet if I judge, My judgment is true; for I am not alone, but I and the Father that sent Me.

17 It is also written in your Torah, that the testimony of two men is true.

18 I am One that bear witness of Myself, and the Father that sent Me beareth witness of Me."

19 Then said they unto Him, "Where is Your Father?" Yahwah answered, "You neither know Me, nor My Father; if you had known Me, you should have known My Father also."

20 These words spake Yahwah in the treasury, as He taught in the temple; and no man laid hands on Him; for His hour was not yet come.

21 Then said Yahwah again unto them, "I go My way, and you shall seek Me, and shall die in your sins; whither I go, you cannot come."

22 Then said the Jews (Yehudim), "Will He kill Himself, because He saith, 'Whither I go, you cannot come'?"

23 And He said unto them, "You are from beneath; I am from above; you are of this world; I am not of this world.

24 I said therefore unto you, that you shall die in your sins; for if you believe not that I am He, you shall die in your sins."

25 Then said they unto Him, "Who art You?" And Yahwah saith unto them, "Even the same that I said unto you from the beginning.

26 I have many things to say and to judge of you; but He that sent Me is true; and I speak to the world those things which I have heard of Him."

27 They understood not that He spake to them of the Father.

28 Then said Yahwah unto them, "When you have lifted up the Son of man (haMashiach), then shall you know that I am He, and that I do nothing of Myself; but as My Father hath taught Me, I speak these things.

29 And He that sent Me is with Me; the Father hath not left Me alone; for I do always those things that please Him."

30 As He spake these words, many believed on Him.

31 Then said Yahwah to those Jews (Yehudim) who believed on Him, "If you continue in My word, then are you My disciples indeed;

32 And you shall know the truth, and the truth shall make you free."

33 They answered Him, "We be Avraham's seed, and were never in bondage to any man; how sayest You, 'You shall be made free'?"

34 Yahwah answered them, "Verily, verily, I say unto you, whosoever committeth sin is the servant of sin.

35 And the servant abideth not in the house forever; but the son abideth ever.

36 If the [B47]Humanity of El (YHWH) therefore shall make you free, you shall be free indeed.

37 I know that you are Avraham's seed; but you seek to kill Me, because My word hath no place in you.

38 I speak that which I have seen with My Father; and you do that which you have seen with your father."

39 They answered and said unto Him, "Avraham is our father." Yahwah saith unto them, "If you were Avraham's children, you would do the works of Avraham.

40 But now you seek to kill Me, a Man that hath told you the truth, which I have heard of God (Elohim, יהוה (YHWH)); this did not Avraham.

41 You do the deeds of your father." Then said they to Him, "We be not born of fornication; we have one Father, even God (Elohim)."

42 Yahwah said unto them, "If God (Elohim) were your Father, you would love Me; for I proceeded forth and came from God (Elohim); neither came I of Myself, but He sent Me.

43 Why do you not understand My speech? Because you cannot hear My word.

44 You are of your father the devil, and the desires of your father you will do. He was a murderer from the beginning, and abode not in the truth, because there is no truth in him. When he speaketh a lie, he speaketh of his own; for he is a liar, and the father of it.

45 And because I tell you the truth, you believe Me not.

46 Which of you convinceth Me of sin? And if I say the truth, why do you not believe Me?

47 He that is of God (Elohim) heareth יהוה (YHWH)'s words; you therefore hear them not, because you are not of God (Elohim)."

48 Then answered the Jews (Yehudim), and said unto Him, "Say we not well that You are a Samaritan, and hast a devil?"

49 Yahwah answered, "I have not a devil; but I honour My Father, and you do dishonour Me.

50 And I seek not Mine own glory; there is one that seeketh and judgeth.

51 Verily, verily, I say unto you, if a man keeps My saying, he shall never see death."

52 Then said the Jews (Yehudim) unto Him, "Now we know that You have a devil. Avraham is dead, and the prophets; and You sayest, 'If a man keeps My saying, he shall never taste of death.'

53 Art You greater than our father Avraham, who is dead? And the prophets are dead; whom makest You Yourself?"

54 Yahwah answered, "If I honour Myself, My honour is nothing; it is My Father that honoureth Me; of whom you say, that He is your God (Elohim);

55 Yet you have not known Him; but I know Him; and if I should say, I know Him not, I shall be a liar like unto you; but I know Him, and keep His saying.

56 Your father Avraham rejoiced to see My day; and he saw it, and was glad."

57 Then said the Jews (Yehudim) unto Him, "You are not yet fifty years old, and have You seen Avraham?"

58 Yahwah said unto them, "Verily, verily, I say unto you, before Avraham was, [B15b]I AM (Ehyeh)." – *Exo. 3:14*

59 Then took they up stones to cast at Him; but Yahwah hid Himself, and went out of the temple, going through the midst of them, and so passed by.

9 And as Yahwah passed by, He saw a man who was blind from his birth.

2 And His disciples asked Him, saying, "Teacher (Rabbi), who did sin, this man, or his parents, that he was born blind?"

3 Yahwah answered, "Neither hath this man sinned, nor his parents; but that the works of God (Elohim) should be made manifest in him.

4 I must work the works of Him that sent Me, while it is day; the night cometh, when no man can work.

5 As long as I am in the world, I am the light of the world."

6 When He had thus spoken, He spat on the ground, and made clay of the spittle, and He anointed the eyes of the blind man with the clay,

7 And said unto him, "Go, wash in the pool of Siloam," (which is by interpretation, Sent.) He went his way therefore, and washed, and came seeing.

8 The neighbours therefore, and they who before had seen him that he was blind, said, "Is not this he that sat and begged?"

9 Some said, "This is he;" others said, "He is like him"; but he said, "I am he."

10 Therefore said they unto him, "How were your eyes opened?"

11 He answered and said, "A man that is called Yahwah made clay, and anointed mine eyes, and said unto me, "Go to the pool of Siloam, and wash;" and I went and washed, and I received sight.

12 Then said they unto him, "Where is He?" He said, "I know not."

13 They brought to the Pharisees him that aforetime was blind.

14 And it was the Shabbat day when Yahwah made the clay, and opened his eyes.

15 Then again the Pharisees also asked him how he had received his sight. He said unto them, "He put clay upon mine eyes, and I washed, and do see."

16 Therefore said some of the Pharisees, "This Man is not of God (Elohim), because He keepeth not the Shabbat day." Others said, "How can a man that is a sinner do such miracles?" And there was a division among them.

17 They say unto the blind man again, "What sayest you of Him, that He hath opened your eyes?" He said, "He is a prophet."

18 But the Jews (Yehudim) did not believe concerning him, that he had been blind, and received his sight, until they called the parents of him that had received his sight.

19 And they asked them, saying, "Is this your son, who you say was born blind? How then doth he now see?"

20 His parents answered them and said, "We know that this is our son, and that he was born blind;

21 But by what means he now seeth, we know not; or who hath opened his eyes, we know not; he is of age; ask him; he shall speak for himself."

22 These words spake his parents, because they feared the Jews (Yehudim); for the Jews (Yehudim) had agreed already, that if any man did confess that He was the Messiah (haMashiach), he should be put out of the synagogue.

23 Therefore said his parents, "He is of age; ask him."

24 Then again called they the man that was blind, and said unto him, "Give God (Elohim) the praise; we know that this Man is a sinner."

25 He answered and said, "Whether He be a sinner or no, I know not; one thing I know, that, whereas I was blind, now I see."

26 Then said they to him again, "What did He to you? How opened He your eyes?"

27 He answered them, "I have told you already, and you did not hear; wherefore would you hear it again? Will you also be His disciples?"

28 Then they reviled him, and said, "You are His disciple; but we are Moses (Mosheh)'s disciples.

29 We know that God (Elohim) spake unto Moses (Mosheh); as for this fellow, we know not from whence He is."

30 The man answered and said unto them, "Why herein is a marvellous thing, that you know not from whence He is, and yet He hath opened mine eyes.

31 Now we know that God (Elohim) heareth not sinners; but if any man be a worshipper of God (Elohim), and doeth His will, him He heareth.

32 Since the world began was it not heard that any man opened the eyes of one that was born blind.

33 If this Man were not of God (Elohim), He could do nothing."

34 They answered and said unto him, "You wast altogether born in sins, and dost you teach us?" And they cast him out.

35 Yahwah heard that they had cast him out; and when He had found him, He said unto him, "Dost you believe on the [B47]Humanity of El (YHWH)?"

36 He answered and said, "Who is He, Lord (Adonai), that I might believe on Him?"

37 And Yahwah said unto him, "You have both seen Him, and it is He that talketh with you."

38 And he said, "My Lord (Adonai), I believe." And he worshipped Him.

39 And Yahwah said, "For judgment I am come into this world, that they who see not might see; and that they who see might be made blind."

40 And some of the Pharisees who were with Him heard these words, and said unto Him, "Are we blind also?"

41 Yahwah said unto them, "If you were blind, you should have no sin; but now you say, 'We see;' therefore your sin remaineth.

10 Verily, verily, I say unto you, he that entereth not by the door into the sheepfold, but climbeth up some other way, the same is a

thief and a robber.

2 But he that entereth in by the door is the shepherd of the sheep.

3 To him the porter openeth; and the sheep hear his voice; and he calleth his own sheep by name, and leadeth them out.

4 And when he putteth forth his own sheep, he goeth before them, and the sheep follow him; for they know his voice.

5 And a stranger will they not follow, but will flee from him; for they know not the voice of strangers."

6 This parable spake Yahwah unto them; but they understood not what things they were which He spake unto them.

7 Then said Yahwah unto them again, "Verily, verily, I say unto you, I am the door of the sheep.

8 All that ever came before Me are thieves and robbers; but the sheep did not hear them.

9 I am the door; by Me if any man enters in, he shall be saved, and shall go in and out, and find pasture.

10 The thief cometh not, but for to steal, and to kill, and to destroy; I am come that they might have life, and that they might have it more abundantly.

11 I am the good Shepherd; the good Shepherd giveth His life for the sheep.

12 But he that is a hireling, and not the shepherd, whose own the sheep are not, seeth the wolf coming, and leaveth the sheep, and fleeth; and the wolf catcheth them, and scattereth the sheep.

13 The hireling fleeth, because he is a hireling, and careth not for the sheep.

14 I am the good Shepherd, and know My sheep, and am known of Mine.

15 As the Father knoweth Me, even so know I the Father; and I lay down My life for the sheep.

16 And other sheep I have, who are not of this fold; them also I must bring, and they shall hear My voice; and there shall be one flock, and one Shepherd.

17 Therefore doth My Father love Me, because I lay down My life, that I might take it again.

18 No man taketh it from Me, but I lay it down of Myself. I have power to lay it down, and I have power to take it again. This commandment have I received of My Father."

19 There was a division therefore again among the Jews (Yehudim) for these sayings.

20 And many of them said, "He hath a devil, and is mad; why hear you Him?"

21 Others said, "These are not the words of Him that hath a devil. Can a devil open the eyes of the blind?"

22 And it was at Jerusalem (Yerushalayim) the feast of the dedication, and it was winter.

23 And Yahwah walked in the temple in Solomon (Shelomoh)'s porch.

24 Then came the Jews (Yehudim) round about Him, and said unto Him, "How long dost You make us to doubt? If You be the Messiah (haMashiach), tell us plainly.

25 Yahwah answered them, "I told you, and you believed not: the works that I do in My Father's name, they bear witness of Me.

26 But you believe not, because you are not of My sheep, as I said unto you.

27 My sheep hear My voice, and I know them, and they follow Me;

28 And I give unto them eternal life; and they shall never perish, neither shall any man pluck them out of My hand.

29 My Father, who gave them Me, is greater than all; and no man is able to pluck them out of My Father's hand.

30 I and My Father are one."

31 Then the Jews (Yehudim) took up stones again to stone Him.

32 Yahwah answered them, "Many good works have I shewed you from My Father; for which of those works do you stone Me?"

33 The Jews (Yehudim) answered Him, saying, "For a good work we stone You not; but for blasphemy; and because that You, being a man, makest Yourself God (Elohim)."

34 Yahwah answered them, "Is it not written in your Torah, 'I said, "You are judges ([B1b]elohim)'"? – *Psa. 82:6*

35 If He called them judges (elohim), unto whom the word of God (Elohim, יהוה (YHWH)) came, and the scripture cannot be broken;

36 Say you of Him, whom the Father hath sanctified, and sent into the world, 'You blasphemest;' because I said, 'I am the [B47]Humanity of El (YHWH)'?

37 If I do not the works of My Father, believe Me not.

38 But if I do, though you believe not Me, believe the works; that you may know, and believe, that the Father is in Me, and I in Him."

39 Therefore they sought again to take Him; but

He escaped out of their hand,

40 And went away again beyond Jordan (Yarden) into the place where John (Yochanan) at first baptized; and there He abode.

41 And many resorted unto Him, and said, "John (Yochanan) did no miracle; but all things that John (Yochanan) spake of this Man were true."

42 And many believed on Him there.

11 Now a certain man was sick, named Lazarus, of Bethany, the town of Mary (Miryam) and her sister Martha.

2 (It was that Mary (Miryam) who anointed the Lord (Yahwah) with ointment, and wiped His feet with her hair, whose brother Lazarus was sick.)

3 Therefore his sisters sent unto Him, saying, "My Lord (Adonai), behold, he whom You lovest is sick."

4 When Yahwah heard that, He said, "This sickness is not unto death, but for the glory of God (Elohim, יהוה (YHWH)), that the B47Humanity of El (YHWH) might be glorified thereby."

5 Now Yahwah loved Martha, and her sister, and Lazarus.

6 When He had heard therefore that he was sick, He abode two days still in the same place where he was.

7 Then after that saith He to His disciples, "Let us go into Judah (Yehudah) again."

8 His disciples say unto Him, "Teacher (Rabbi), the Jews (Yehudim) of late sought to stone You; and goest You thither again?"

9 Yahwah answered, "Are there not twelve hours in the day? If any man walks in the day, he stumbleth not, because he seeth the light of this world.

10 But if a man walks in the night, he stumbleth, because there is no light in him."

11 These things said He; and after that He saith unto them, "Our friend Lazarus sleepeth; but I go, that I may awake him out of sleep."

12 Then said His disciples, "Lord (Adonai), if he sleeps, he shall do well."

13 Howbeit Yahwah spake of his death; but they thought that he had spoken of taking of rest in sleep.

14 Then said Yahwah unto them plainly, "Lazarus is dead.

15 And I am glad for your sakes that I was not there, to the intent you may believe; nevertheless let us go unto him."

16 Then said Thomas, who is called Didymus, unto his fellowdisciples, "Let us also go, that we may die with him."

17 Then when Yahwah came, He found that he had lain in the grave four days already.

18 Now Bethany was near unto Jerusalem (Yerushalayim), about fifteen furlongs off.

19 And many of the Jews (Yehudim) came to Martha and Mary (Miryam), to comfort them concerning their brother.

20 Then Martha, as soon as she heard that Yahwah was coming, went and met Him; but Mary (Miryam) sat still in the house.

21 Then said Martha unto Yahwah, "Lord (Adonai), if You hadst been here, my brother had not died.

22 But I know, that even now, whatsoever You wilt ask of God (Elohim), God (Elohim) will give it You."

23 Yahwah saith unto her, "Your brother shall rise again."

24 Martha saith unto Him, "I know that he shall rise again in the resurrection at the last day."

25 Yahwah said unto her, "I am the resurrection, and the life; he that believeth in Me, though he were dead, yet shall he live;

26 And whosoever liveth and believeth in Me shall never die. Believest you this?"

27 She saith unto Him, "Yea, Lord (Adonai); I believe that You are the Messiah (haMashiach), B47Humanity of El (YHWH), who should come into the world."

28 And when she had so said, she went her way, and called Mary (Miryam) her sister secretly, saying, "The Teacher (Rabbi) is come, and calleth for you."

29 As soon as she heard that, she arose quickly, and came unto Him.

30 Now Yahwah was not yet come into the town, but was in that place where Martha met Him.

31 The Jews (Yehudim) then who were with her in the house, and comforted her, when they saw Mary (Miryam), that she rose up hastily and went out, followed her, saying, "She goeth unto the grave to weep there."

32 Then when Mary (Miryam) was come where Yahwah was, and saw Him, she fell down at His feet, saying unto Him, "Lord (Adonai), if You hadst been here, my brother had not died."

33 When Yahwah therefore saw her weeping, and the Jews (Yehudim) also weeping who came with her, He groaned in the spirit, and was troubled,

34 And said, "Where have you laid him?" They said unto Him, "Lord (Adonai), come and see."

35 Yahwah wept.

36 Then said the Jews (Yehudim), "Behold how He loved him!"

37 And some of them said, "Could not this Man, who opened the eyes of the blind, have caused that even this man should not have died?"

38 Yahwah therefore again groaning in Himself cometh to the grave. It was a cave, and a stone lay upon it.

39 Yahwah said, "Take you away the stone." Martha, the sister of him that was dead, saith unto Him, "Lord (Adonai), by this time he stinketh; for he hath been dead four days."

40 Yahwah saith unto her, "Said I not unto you, that, if you wouldest believe, you shouldest see the glory of God (Elohim)?"

41 Then they took away the stone from the place where the dead was laid. And Yahwah lifted up His eyes, and said, "Father, I thank You that You have heard Me.

42 And I knew that You hearest Me always; but because of the people who stand by I said it, that they may believe that You have sent Me."

43 And when He thus had spoken, He cried with a loud voice, "Lazarus, come forth."

44 And he that was dead came forth, bound hand and foot with graveclothes; and his face was bound about with a napkin. Yahwah saith unto them, "Loose him, and let him go."

45 Then many of the Jews (Yehudim) who came to Mary (Miryam), and had seen the things which Yahwah did, believed on Him.

46 But some of them went their ways to the Pharisees, and told them what things Yahwah had done.

47 Then gathered the chief priests (kohanim) and the Pharisees a council, and said, "What do we? For this Man doeth many miracles.

48 If we let Him thus alone, all men will believe on Him; and the Romans shall come and take away both our place and nation."

49 And one of them, named Caiaphas, being the high priest (kohen hagadol) that same year, said unto them, "You know nothing at all,

50 Nor consider that it is expedient for us, that one man should die for the people, and that the whole nation perishes not."

51 And this spake he not of himself: but being high priest (kohen hagadol) that year, he prophesied that Yahwah should die for that nation;

52 And not for that nation only, but that also He should gather together in one the children of God (Elohim) that were scattered abroad.

53 Then from that day forth they took counsel together for to put Him to death.

54 Yahwah therefore walked no more openly among the Jews (Yehudim); but went thence unto a country near to the wilderness, into a city called Ephraim, and there continued with His disciples.

55 And the Jews' (Yehudim) Passover (Pesach) was near at hand; and many went out of the country up to Jerusalem (Yerushalayim) before the Passover (Pesach), to purify themselves.

56 Then sought they for Yahwah, and spake among themselves, as they stood in the temple, "What think you, that He will not come to the feast?"

57 Now both the chief priests (kohanim) and the Pharisees had given a commandment, that, if any man knew where He was, he should shew it, that they might take Him.

12 Then Yahwah six days before the Passover (Pesach) came to Bethany, where Lazarus was who had been dead, whom He raised from the dead.

2 There they made Him a supper; and Martha served; but Lazarus was one of them that sat at the table with Him.

3 Then took Mary (Miryam) a pound of ointment of spikenard, very costly, and anointed the feet of Yahwah, and wiped His feet with her hair; and the house was filled with the odour of the ointment.

4 Then saith one of His disciples, Judas (Yehudah) Ishkeriot, Shimon's son, who should betray Him,

5 "Why was not this ointment sold for three hundred pence, and given to the poor?"

6 This he said, not that he cared for the poor; but because he was a thief, and had the bag, and bare what was put therein.

7 Then said Yahwah, "Let her alone; against the day of My burying hath she kept this.

8 For the poor always you have with you; but Me

you have not always."

9 Much people of the Jews (Yehudim) therefore knew that He was there; and they came not for Yahwah's sake only, but that they might see Lazarus also, whom He had raised from the dead.

10 But the chief priests (kohanim) consulted that they might put Lazarus also to death;

11 Because that by reason of him many of the Jews (Yehudim) went away, and believed on Yahwah.

12 On the next day much people that were come to the feast, when they heard that Yahwah was coming to Jerusalem (Yerushalayim),

13 Took branches of palm trees, and went forth to meet Him, and cried, "Hosanna! Blessed is the King of Yisrael that cometh in the name of יהוה (YHWH, Yahwah). – *Psa. 118:25-26*

14 And Yahwah, when He had found a young ass, sat thereon; as it is written,

15 "Fear not, daughter of Sion (Tsiyon); behold, your King cometh, sitting on an ass's colt." – *Zech. 9:9*

16 These things understood not His disciples at the first; but when Yahwah was glorified, then remembered they that these things were written of Him, and that they had done these things unto Him.

17 The people therefore that was with Him when He called Lazarus out of his grave, and raised him from the dead, bare record.

18 For this cause the people also met Him, for that they heard that He had done this miracle.

19 The Pharisees therefore said among themselves, "Perceive you how you prevail nothing? Behold, the world is gone after Him."

20 And there were certain Greeks among them that came up to worship at the feast;

21 The same came therefore to Philip, who was of Bethsaida of Galilee, and desired him, saying, "Sir, we would see Yahwah."

22 Philip cometh and telleth Andrew; and again Andrew and Philip tell Yahwah.

23 And Yahwah answered them, saying, "The hour is come, that the Son of man (haMashiach) should be glorified.

24 Verily, verily, I say unto you, except a corn of wheat fall into the ground and die, it abideth alone; but if it dies, it bringeth forth much fruit.

25 He that loveth his life shall lose it; and he that hateth his life in this world shall keep it unto life eternal.

26 If any man serves Me, let him follow Me; and where I am, there shall also My servant be; if any man serves Me, him will My Father honour.

27 Now is My soul troubled; and what shall I say? Father, save Me from this hour; but for this cause came I unto this hour.

28 Father, glorify Your name." Then came there a voice from heaven, saying, "I have both glorified it, and will glorify it again."

29 The people therefore, that stood by, and heard it, said that it thundered; others said, "An angel spake to Him."

30 Yahwah answered and said, "This voice came not because of Me, but for your sakes.

31 Now is the judgment of this world; now shall the prince of this world be cast out.

32 And I, if I be lifted up from the earth, will draw all men unto Me."

33 This He said, signifying what death He should die.

34 The people answered Him, "We have heard out of the Torah that the Messiah (haMashiach) abideth forever; and how sayest You, 'The Son of man (haMashiach) must be lifted up'? Who is this Son of man?

35 Then Yahwah said unto them, "Yet a little while is the light with you. Walk while you have the light, lest darkness come upon you; for he that walketh in darkness knoweth not whither he goeth.

36 While you have light, believe in the light, that you may be the children of light." These things spake Yahwah, and departed, and did hide Himself from them.

37 But though He had done so many miracles before them, yet they believed not on Him;

38 That the saying Isaiah (Yeshayahu) the prophet might be fulfilled, which he spake, "יהוה, who hath believed our report? And to whom hath the arm of יהוה been revealed?" – *Isa. 53:1*

39 Therefore they could not believe, because that Isaiah (Yeshayahu) said again,

40 "He hath blinded their eyes, and hardened their heart; that they should not see with their eyes, nor understand with their heart, and be converted, and I should heal them." – *Isa. 6:10*

41 These things said Isaiah (Yeshayahu), when he saw His glory, and spake of Him.

42 Nevertheless among the chief rulers also

many believed on Him; but because of the Pharisees they did not confess Him, lest they should be put out of the synagogue;

43 For they loved the praise of men more than the praise of God (Elohim)."

44 Yahwah cried and said, "He that believeth on Me, believeth not on Me, but on Him that sent Me.

45 And he that seeth Me seeth Him that sent Me.

46 I am come a light into the world, that whosoever believeth on Me should not abide in darkness.

47 And if any man hears My words, and believe not, I judge him not; for I came not to judge the world, but to save the world.

48 He that rejecteth Me, and receiveth not My words, hath one that judgeth him: the word that I have spoken, the same shall judge him in the last day.

49 For I have not spoken of Myself; but the Father who sent Me, He gave Me a commandment, what I should say, and what I should speak.

50 And I know that His commandment is life everlasting; whatsoever I speak therefore, even as the Father said unto Me, so I speak."

13 Now before the feast of the Passover (Pesach), when Yahwah knew that His hour was come that He should depart out of this world unto the Father, having loved His own which were in the world, He loved them unto the end.

2 And supper being ended, the devil having now put into the heart of Judas (Yehudah) Ishkeriot, Shimon's son, to betray Him;

3 Yahwah (haMashiach, Humanity of El) knowing that the Father had given all things into His hands, and that He was come from God (Elohim, יהוה (YHWH)) and went to God (Elohim, יהוה (YHWH));

4 He riseth from supper, and laid aside His garments; and took a towel, and girded Himself.

5 After that He poureth water into a bason, and began to wash the disciples' feet, and to wipe them with the towel wherewith He was girded.

6 Then cometh He to Shimon Peter (Kefa); and Peter (Kefa) saith unto Him, "Lord (Adonai), dost You wash My feet?"

7 Yahwah answered and said unto him, "What I do you knowest not now; but you shalt know hereafter."

8 Peter (Kefa) saith unto Him, "You shalt never wash my feet." Yahwah answered him, "If I wash you not, you have no part with Me."

9 Shimon Peter (Kefa) saith unto Him, "Lord (Adonai), not my feet only, but also my hands and my head."

10 Yahwah saith to him, "He that is washed needeth not except to wash his feet, but is clean every whit; and you are clean, but not all."

11 For He knew who should betray him; therefore said He, "You are not all clean."

12 So after He had washed their feet, and had taken His garments, and was set down again, He said unto them, "Know you what I have done to you?

13 You call Me Teacher (Rabbi) and Lord (Adon); and you say well; for so I am.

14 If I then, your Lord (Adon) and Teacher (Rabbi), have washed your feet; you also ought to wash one another's feet.

15 For I have given you an example, that you should do as I have done to you.

16 Verily, verily, I say unto you, the servant is not greater than his master; neither He that is sent greater than He that sent Him.

17 If you know these things, happy are you if you do them.

18 I speak not of you all; I know whom I have chosen; but that the scripture may be fulfilled, He that eateth bread with Me hath lifted up his heel against Me. – *Psa. 41:9*

19 Now I tell you before it come, that, when it is come to pass, you may believe that I am He.

20 Verily, verily, I say unto you, He that receiveth whomsoever I send receiveth Me; and he that receiveth Me receiveth Him that sent Me."

21 When Yahwah had thus said, He was troubled in spirit, and testified, and said, "Verily, verily, I say unto you, that one of you shall betray Me."

22 Then the disciples looked one on another, doubting of whom He spake.

23 Now there was leaning on Yahwah's bosom one of His disciples, whom Yahwah loved.

24 Shimon Peter (Kefa) therefore beckoned to Him, that he should ask who it should be of whom He spake.

25 He then lying on Yahwah's breast saith unto Him, "Lord (Adonai), who is it?"

26 Yahwah answered, "He it is, to whom I shall give a sop, when I have dipped it." And when He had dipped the sop, He gave it to Judas

(Yehudah) Ishkeriot, the son of Shimon.

27 And after the sop Satan entered into him. Then said Yahwah unto him, "That you doest, do quickly."

28 Now no man at the table knew for what intent He spake this unto him.

29 For some of them thought, because Judas (Yehudah) had the bag, that Yahwah had said unto him, "Buy those things that we have need of against the feast;" or, that he should give something to the poor.

30 He then having received the sop went immediately out; and it was night.

31 Therefore, when he was gone out, Yahwah said, "Now is the Son of man (haMashiach) glorified, and God (Elohim, יהוה (YHWH)) is glorified in Him.

32 If God (Elohim, יהוה (YHWH)) be glorified in Him (Yahwah haMashiach, Humanity of El), God (Elohim, יהוה (YHWH)) shall also glorify Him in Himself, and shall straightway glorify Him.

33 Little children, yet a little while I am with you. You shall seek Me; and as I said unto the Jews (Yehudim), 'Whither I go, you cannot come;' so now I say to you.

34 A new commandment I give unto you, that you love one another; as I have loved you, that you also love one another.

35 By this shall all men know that you are My disciples, if you have love one to another."

36 Shimon Peter (Kefa) said unto Him, "Lord (Adonai), whither goest You?" Yahwah answered him, "Whither I go, you canst not follow Me now; but you shalt follow Me afterwards."

37 Peter (Kefa) said unto Him, "Lord (Adonai), why cannot I follow You now? I will lay down my life for Your sake."

38 Yahwah answered him, "Wilt you lay down your life for My sake? Verily, verily, I say unto you, the cock shall not crow, till you have denied Me thrice.

14 Let not your heart be troubled; you believe in God (Elohim, יהוה (YHWH)), believe also in Me.

2 In My Father's house are many mansions; if it was not so, I would have told you. I go to prepare a place for you.

3 And if I go and prepare a place for you, I will come again, and receive you unto Myself; that

where I am, there you may be also.

4 And whither I go you know, and the way you know."

5 Thomas saith unto Him, "Lord (Adonai), we know not whither You goest; and how can we know the way?"

6 Yahwah saith unto him, "I am the way, the truth, and the life; no man cometh unto the Father, but by Me.

7 If you had known Me, you should have known My Father also; and from henceforth you know Him, and have seen Him."

8 Philip saith unto Him, "Lord (Adonai), shew us the Father, and it sufficeth us."

9 Yahwah saith unto him, "Have I been so long time with you, and yet have you not known Me, Philip? He that hath seen Me hath seen the Father; and how sayest you then, 'Shew us the Father?'

10 Believest you not that I am in the Father, and the Father in Me? The words that I speak unto you I speak not of Myself: but the Father that dwelleth in Me, He doeth the works.

11 Believe Me that I am in the Father, and the Father in Me; or else believe Me for the very works' sake.

12 Verily, verily, I say unto you, He that believeth on Me, the works that I do shall he do also; and greater works than these shall he do; because I go unto My Father.

13 And whatsoever you shall ask in My name, that will I do, that the Father may be glorified in the [B47]Son (Humanity of El, (YHWH)).

14 If you shall ask any thing in My name, I will do it.

15 If you love Me, keep My commandments.

16 And I will pray the Father, and He shall give you another Comforter, that He may abide with you for ever;

17 Even the Spirit of truth; whom the world cannot receive, because it seeth Him not, neither knoweth Him; but you know Him; for He dwelleth with you, and shall be in you.

18 I will not leave you comfortless; I will come to you.

19 Yet a little while, and the world seeth Me no more; but you see Me; because I live, you shall live also.

20 At that day you shall know that I am in My Father, and you in Me, and I in you.

21 He that hath My commandments, and

keepeth them, he it is that loveth Me; and he that loveth Me shall be loved of My Father, and I will love him, and will manifest Myself to him.

22 Judah (Yehudah) saith unto Him, not Ishkeriot, "Lord (Adonai), how is it that You wilt manifest Yourself unto us, and not unto the world?"

23 Yahwah answered and said unto him, "If a man loves Me, he will keep My words; and My Father will love him, and we will come unto him, and make our abode with him.

24 He that loveth Me not keepeth not My sayings; and the word which you hear is not Mine, but the Father's who sent Me.

25 These things have I spoken unto you, being yet present with you.

26 But the Comforter, who is the Holy Spirit (Ruach haQodesh), whom the Father will send in My name, He shall teach you all things, and bring all things to your remembrance, whatsoever I have said unto you.

27 Peace I leave with you, My peace I give unto you; not as the world giveth, give I unto you. Let not your heart be troubled, neither let it be afraid.

28 You have heard how I said unto you, I go away, and come again unto you. If you loved Me, you would rejoice, because I said, I go unto the Father; for My Father is greater than I.

29 And now I have told you before it come to pass, that, when it is come to pass, you might believe.

30 Hereafter I will not talk much with you; for the prince of this world cometh, and hath nothing in Me.

31 But that the world may know that I love the Father; and as the Father gave Me commandment, even so I do. Arise, let us go hence."

15 "I am the true vine, and My Father is the husbandman.

2 Every branch in Me that beareth not fruit He taketh away; and every branch that beareth fruit, He purgeth it, that it may bring forth more fruit.

3 Now you are clean through the word which I have spoken unto you.

4 Abide in Me, and I in you. As the branch cannot bear fruit of itself, except it abide in the vine; no more can you, except you abide in Me.

5 I am the vine, you are the branches. He that abideth in Me, and I in him, the same bringeth forth much fruit; for without Me you can do nothing.

6 If a man abides not in Me, he is cast forth as a branch, and is withered; and men gather them, and cast them into the fire, and they are burned.

7 If you abide in Me, and My words abide in you, you shall ask what you will, and it shall be done unto you.

8 Herein is My Father glorified, that you bear much fruit; so shall you be My disciples.

9 As the Father hath loved Me, so have I loved you: continue you in My love.

10 If you keep My commandments, you shall abide in My love; even as I have kept My Father's commandments, and abide in His love.

11 These things have I spoken unto you, that My joy might remain in you, and that your joy might be full.

12 This is My commandment, that you love one another, as I have loved you.

13 Greater love hath no man than this, that a man lay down his life for his friends.

14 You are My friends, if you do whatsoever I command you.

15 Henceforth I call you not slaves, for the slave knoweth not what his master doeth; but I have called you friends; for all things that I have heard of My Father I have made known unto you.

16 You have not chosen Me, but I have chosen you, and ordained you, that you should go and bring forth fruit, and that your fruit should remain; that whatsoever you shall ask of the Father in My name, He may give it you.

17 These things I command you, that you love one another.

18 If the world hates you, you know that it hated Me before it hated you.

19 If you were of the world, the world would love its own; but because you are not of the world, but I have chosen you out of the world, therefore the world hateth you.

20 Remember the word that I said unto you, 'The slave is not greater than his master. If they have persecuted Me, they will also persecute you; if they have kept My saying, they will keep yours also.

21 But all these things will they do unto you for My name's sake, because they know not Him that sent Me.

22 If I had not come and spoken unto them, they had not had sin; but now they have no cloke for their sin.

23 He that hateth Me hateth My Father also.

24 If I had not done among them the works which none other man did, they had not had sin; but now have they both seen and hated both Me and My Father.

25 But this cometh to pass, that the word might be fulfilled that is written in their Torah, 'They hated Me without a cause.' – *Psa. 35:19; 69:4*

26 But when the Comforter is come, whom I will send unto you from the Father, the Spirit of truth, which proceedeth from the Father, He shall testify of Me.

27 And you also shall bear witness, because you have been with Me from the beginning.

16 These things have I spoken unto you, that you should not be offended.

2 They shall put you out of the synagogues; yea, the time cometh, that whosoever killeth you will think that he doeth God (Elohim) service.

3 And these things will they do unto you, because they have not known the Father, nor Me.

4 But these things have I told you, that when the time shall come, you may remember that I told you of them. And these things I said not unto you at the beginning, because I was with you.

5 But now I go My way to Him that sent Me; and none of you asketh Me, 'Whither goest You?'

6 But because I have said these things unto you, sorrow hath filled your heart.

7 Nevertheless I tell you the truth: It is expedient for you that I go away; for if I go not away, the Comforter will not come unto you; but if I depart, I will send Him unto you.

8 And when He is come, He will reprove the world of sin, and of righteousness, and of judgment;

9 Of sin, because they believe not on Me;

10 Of righteousness, because I go to My Father, and you see Me no more;

11 Of judgment, because the prince of this world is judged.

12 I have yet many things to say unto you, but you cannot bear them now.

13 Howbeit when He, the Spirit of truth, is come, He will guide you into all truth; for He shall not speak of Himself; but whatsoever He shall hear, that shall He speak; and He will shew you things to come.

14 He shall glorify Me; for He shall receive of Mine, and shall shew it unto you.

15 All things that the Father hath are Mine; therefore said I, that He shall take of Mine, and shall shew it unto you.

16 A little while, and you shall not see Me; and again, a little while, and you shall see Me, because I go to the Father."

17 Then said some of His disciples among themselves, "What is this that He saith unto us, 'A little while, and you shall not see Me; and again, a little while, and you shall see Me;' and, 'Because I go to the Father?'"

18 They said therefore, "What is this that He saith, 'A little while?' we cannot tell what He saith.

19 Now Yahwah knew that they were desirous to ask Him, and said unto them, "Do you enquire among yourselves of that I said, 'A little while, and you shall not see Me; and again, a little while, and you shall see Me?'

20 Verily, verily, I say unto you, that you shall weep and lament, but the world shall rejoice; and you shall be sorrowful, but your sorrow shall be turned into joy.

21 A woman when she is in travail hath sorrow, because her hour is come; but as soon as she is delivered of the child, she remembereth no more the anguish, for joy that a man is born into the world.

22 And you now therefore have sorrow; but I will see you again, and your heart shall rejoice, and your joy no man taketh from you.

23 And in that day you shall ask Me nothing. Verily, verily, I say unto you, whatsoever you shall ask the Father in My name, He will give it you.

24 Hitherto have you asked nothing in My name; ask, and you shall receive, that your joy may be full.

25 These things have I spoken unto you in proverbs; but the time cometh, when I shall no more speak unto you in proverbs, but I shall shew you plainly of the Father.

26 At that day you shall ask in My name; and I say not unto you, that I will pray the Father for you;

27 For the Father Himself loveth you, because you have loved Me, and have believed that I came out from God (Elohim, יהוה (YHWH)).

28 I came forth from the Father, and am come

into the world; again, I leave the world, and go to the Father."

29 His disciples said unto Him, "Behold, now speakest You plainly, and speakest no proverb.

30 Now are we sure that You knowest all things, and needest not that any man should ask You; by this we believe that You camest forth from God (Elohim, יהוה (YHWH))"

31 Yahwah answered them, "Do you now believe?

32 Behold, the hour cometh, yea, is now come, that you shall be scattered, every man to his own, and shall leave Me alone; and yet I am not alone, because the Father is with Me.

33 These things I have spoken unto you, that in Me you might have peace. In the world you shall have tribulation; but be of good cheer; I have overcome the world."

17 These words spake Yahwah, and lifted up His eyes to heaven, and said, "Father, the hour is come; glorify Your [B47]Son (Humanity), that Your [B47]Son (Humanity) also may glorify You;

2 As You have given Him power over all flesh, that He should give eternal life to as many as You have given Him.

3 And this is life eternal, that they might know You the only true God (Elohim), and Yahwah haMashiach, whom You have sent.

4 I have glorified You on the earth. I have finished the work which You gavest Me to do.

5 And now, O Father, glorify Me with Your own self with the glory which I had with You before the world was.

6 I have manifested Your name unto the men which You gavest Me out of the world; Yours they were, and You gavest them Me; and they have kept Your word.

7 Now they have known that all things whatsoever You have given Me are of You.

8 For I have given unto them the words which You gavest Me; and they have received them, and have known surely that I came out from You, and they have believed that You didst send Me.

9 I pray for them; I pray not for the world, but for them whom You have given Me; for they are Yours.

10 And all Mine are Yours, and Yours are Mine; and I am glorified in them.

11 And now I am no more in the world, but these are in the world, and I come to You. Holy Father, keep through Your own name those whom You have given Me, that they may be one, as we are.

12 While I was with them in the world, I kept them in Your name; those that You gavest Me I have kept, and none of them is lost, but the son of perdition; that the scripture might be fulfilled.

13 And now come I to You; and these things I speak in the world, that they might have My joy fulfilled in themselves.

14 I have given them Your word; and the world hath hated them, because they are not of the world, even as I am not of the world.

15 I pray not that You shouldest take them out of the world, but that You shouldest keep them from the evil.

16 They are not of the world, even as I am not of the world.

17 Sanctify them through Your truth; Your word is truth.

18 As You have sent Me into the world, even so have I also sent them into the world.

19 And for their sakes I sanctify Myself, that they also might be sanctified through the truth.

20 Neither pray I for these alone, but for them also who shall believe on Me through their word;

21 That they all may be one; as You, Father, are in Me, and I in You, that they also may be one in Us; that the world may believe that You have sent Me.

22 And the glory which You gavest Me I have given them; that they may be one, even as We are one;

23 I in them, and You in Me, that they may be made perfect in one; and that the world may know that You have sent Me, and hast loved them, as You have loved Me.

24 Father, I will that they also, whom You have given Me, be with Me where I am; that they may behold My glory, which You have given Me; for You lovedst Me before the foundation of the world.

25 O righteous Father, the world hath not known You; but I have known You, and these have known that You have sent Me.

26 And I have declared unto them Your name, and will declare it; that the love wherewith You have loved Me may be in them, and I in them."

18 When Yahwah had spoken these words, He went forth with His disciples over the Brook Cedron, where was a garden, into the which He entered, and His disciples.

2 And Judas (Yehudah) also, who betrayed Him, knew the place; for Yahwah ofttimes resorted thither with His disciples.

3 Judas (Yehudah) then, having received a band of men and officers from the chief priests (kohanim) and Pharisees, cometh thither with lanterns and torches and weapons.

4 Yahwah therefore, knowing all things that should come upon Him, went forth, and said unto them, "Whom seek you?"

5 They answered Him, "Yahwah of Nazareth." Yahwah saith unto them, "I am He." And Judas (Yehudah) also, who betrayed Him, stood with them.

6 As soon then as He had said unto them, "I am He," they went backward, and fell to the ground.

7 Then asked He them again, "Whom seek you?" And they said, "Yahwah of Nazareth."

8 Yahwah answered, "I have told you that I am He; if therefore you seek Me, let these go their way;

9 That the saying might be fulfilled, which He spake, "Of them whom You gavest Me have I lost none."

10 Then Shimon Peter (Kefa) having a sword drew it, and smote the high priest (kohen hagadol)'s servant, and cut off his right ear. The servant's name was Malchus.

11 Then said Yahwah unto Peter (Kefa), "Put up your sword into the sheath; the cup which My Father hath given Me, shall I not drink it?"

12 Then the band and the captain and officers of the Jews (Yehudim) took Yahwah, and bound Him,

13 And led Him away to Annas first; for he was father in law to Caiaphas, who was the high priest (kohen hagadol) that same year.

14 Now Caiaphas was he, who gave counsel to the Jews (Yehudim), that it was expedient that one man should die for the people.

15 And Shimon Peter (Kefa) followed Yahwah, and so did another disciple; that disciple was known unto the high priest (kohen hagadol), and went in with Yahwah into the palace of the high priest (kohen hagadol).

16 But Peter (Kefa) stood at the door outside. Then went out that other disciple, who was known unto the high priest (kohen hagadol), and spake unto her that kept the door, and brought in Peter (Kefa).

17 Then saith the damsel that kept the door unto Peter (Kefa), "Art not you also one of this man's disciples?" He saith, "I am not."

18 And the servants and officers stood there, who had made a fire of coals; for it was cold; and they warmed themselves; and Peter (Kefa) stood with them, and warmed himself.

19 The high priest (kohen hagadol) then asked Yahwah of His disciples, and of His doctrine.

20 Yahwah answered him, "I spake openly to the world; I ever taught in the synagogue, and in the temple, whither the Jews (Yehudim) always resort; and in secret have I said nothing.

21 Why askest you Me? Ask them who heard Me, what I have said unto them; behold, they know what I said."

22 And when He had thus spoken, one of the officers who stood by struck Yahwah with the palm of his hand, saying, "Answerest You the high priest (kohen hagadol) so?"

23 Yahwah answered him, "If I have spoken evil, bear witness of the evil; but if well, why smitest you Me?"

24 Now Annas had sent Him bound unto Caiaphas the high priest (kohen hagadol).

25 And Shimon Peter (Kefa) stood and warmed himself. They said therefore unto him, "Art not you also one of His disciples?" He denied it, and said, "I am not."

26 One of the servants of the high priest (kohen hagadol), being his kinsman whose ear Peter (Kefa) cut off, saith, "Did not I see you in the garden with Him?"

27 Peter (Kefa) then denied again; and immediately the cock crew.

28 Then led they Yahwah from Caiaphas unto the hall of judgment; and it was early; and they themselves went not into the judgment hall, lest they should be defiled; but that they might eat the Passover (Pesach).

29 Pilate then went out unto them, and said, "What accusation bring you against this Man?"

30 They answered and said unto him, "If He was not a malefactor, we would not have delivered Him up unto you."

31 Then said Pilate unto them, "Take you Him, and judge Him according to your [B28a]law (torah)." The Jews (Yehudim) therefore said

unto him, "It is not lawful for us to put any man to death;"

32 That the saying of Yahwah might be fulfilled, which He spake, signifying what death He should die.

33 Then Pilate entered into the judgment hall again, and called Yahwah, and said unto Him, "Art You the King of the Jews (Yehudim)?"

34 Yahwah answered him, "Sayest you this thing of yourself, or did others tell it you of Me?"

35 Pilate answered, "Am I a Jew (Yehudi)? Your own nation and the chief priests (kohanim) have delivered You unto me. What have you done?"

36 Yahwah answered, "My kingdom is not of this world; if My kingdom was of this world, then would My servants fight, that I should not be delivered to the Jews (Yehudim); but now is My kingdom not from hence."

37 Pilate therefore said unto Him, "Art You a King then?" Yahwah answered, "You sayest that I am a King. To this end was I born, and for this cause came I into the world, that I should bear witness unto the truth. Every one that is of the truth heareth My voice."

38 Pilate saith unto Him, "What is truth?" And when he had said this, he went out again unto the Jews (Yehudim), and saith unto them, "I find in Him no fault at all.

39 But you have a custom, that I should release unto you one at the Passover (Pesach); will you therefore that I release unto you the King of the Jews (Yehudim)?"

40 Then cried they all again, saying, "Not this Man, but Barabbas!" Now Barabbas was a robber.

19 Then Pilate therefore took Yahwah, and scourged Him.

2 And the soldiers platted a crown of thorns, and put it on His head, and they put on Him a purple robe,

3 And said, "Hail, King of the Jews (Yehudim)!" And they smote Him with their hands.

4 Pilate therefore went forth again, and saith unto them, "Behold, I bring Him forth to you, that you may know that I find no fault in Him."

5 Then came Yahwah forth, wearing the crown of thorns, and the purple robe. And Pilate saith unto them, "Behold the Man!"

6 When the chief priests (kohanim) therefore and officers saw Him, they cried out, saying, "Crucify Him, crucify Him!" Pilate saith unto them, "Take you Him, and crucify Him; for I find no fault in Him."

7 The Jews (Yehudim) answered Him, "We have a law (torah), and by our law (torah) He ought to die, because He made Himself the [B47]Humanity of El (YHWH)."

8 When Pilate therefore heard that saying, he was the more afraid;

9 And went again into the judgment hall, and saith unto Yahwah, "Whence art You?" But Yahwah gave him no answer.

10 Then saith Pilate unto Him, "Speakest You not unto me? Knowest You not that I have power to crucify You, and have power to release You?"

11 Yahwah answered, "You couldest have no power at all against Me, except it was given you from above; therefore he that delivered Me unto you hath the greater sin."

12 And from thenceforth Pilate sought to release Him: but the Jews (Yehudim) cried out, saying, "If you let this Man go, you are not Caesar's friend; whosoever maketh himself a king speaketh against Caesar."

13 When Pilate therefore heard that saying, he brought Yahwah forth, and sat down in the judgment seat in a place that is called the Pavement, but in the Hebrew, Gabbatha.

14 And it was the preparation of the Passover (Pesach), and about the sixth hour; and he saith unto the Jews (Yehudim), "Behold your King!"

15 But they cried out, "Away with Him, away with Him, crucify Him!" Pilate saith unto them, "Shall I crucify your King?" The chief priests (kohanim) answered, "We have no King but Caesar."

16 Then delivered he Him therefore unto them to be crucified. And they took Yahwah, and led Him away.

17 And He bearing His stake went forth into a place called the place of a skull, which is called in the Hebrew, Golgotha;

18 Where they crucified Him, and two others with Him, on either side one, and Yahwah in the midst.

19 And Pilate wrote a title, and put it on the stake. And the writing was, "YAHWAH (YHWH) OF NAZARETH THE KING OF THE JEWS (YEHUDIM)."

20 This title then read many of the Jews (Yehudim); for the place where Yahwah was crucified was near to the city; and it was written

in Hebrew, and Greek, and Latin.

21 Then said the chief priests (kohanim) of the Jews (Yehudim) to Pilate, "Write not, 'The King of the Jews (Yehudim);' but that 'He said: "I am King of the Jews (Yehudim).""""

22 Pilate answered, "What I have written I have written."

23 Then the soldiers, when they had crucified Yahwah, took His garments, and made four parts, to every soldier a part; and also His coat. Now the coat was without seam, woven from the top throughout.

24 They said therefore among themselves, "Let us not rend it, but cast lots for it, whose it shall be; that the Scripture might be fulfilled, which saith, 'They parted My raiment among them, and for My vesture they did cast lots.' These things therefore the soldiers did. – *Psa. 22:18*

25 Now there stood by the stake of Yahwah His mother, and His mother's sister, Mary (Miryam) the wife of Cleophas, and Mary (Miryam) Magdalene.

26 When Yahwah therefore saw His mother, and the disciple standing by, whom He loved, He saith unto His mother, "Woman, behold your son!"

27 Then saith he to the disciple, "Behold your mother!" And from that hour that disciple took her unto his own home.

28 After this, Yahwah knowing that all things were now accomplished, that the Scripture might be fulfilled, saith, "I thirst."

29 Now there was set a vessel full of vinegar; and they filled a spunge with vinegar, and put it upon hyssop, and put it to His mouth.

30 When Yahwah therefore had received the vinegar, He said, "It is finished;" and He bowed His head, and gave up His spirit.

31 The Jews (Yehudim) therefore, because it was the preparation, that the bodies should not remain upon the stake on the Shabbat day, (for that Shabbat day was a high day,) besought Pilate that their legs might be broken, and that they might be taken away.

32 Then came the soldiers, and brake the legs of the first, and of the other who was crucified with Him.

33 But when they came to Yahwah, and saw that He was dead already, they brake not His legs;

34 But one of the soldiers with a spear pierced His side, and forthwith came there out blood and water.

35 And he that saw it bare record, and his record is true; and he knoweth that he saith true, that you might believe.

36 For these things were done, that the Scripture should be fulfilled, "A bone of Him shall not be broken." – *Psa. 34:20; Exo. 12:46; Num. 9:12*

37 And again another Scripture saith, "They shall look on Me (Humanity of El (YHWH)) whom they pierced." – *Zec. 12:10*

38 And after this Joseph (Yosef) of Arimathaea, being a disciple of Yahwah, but secretly for fear of the Jews (Yehudim), besought Pilate that he might take away the body of Yahwah; and Pilate gave him leave. He came therefore, and took the body of Yahwah.

39 And there came also Nicodemus, who at the first came to Yahwah by night, and brought a mixture of myrrh and aloes, about a hundred pound weight.

40 Then took they the body of Yahwah, and wound it in linen clothes with the spices, as the manner of the Jews (Yehudim) is to bury.

41 Now in the place where He was crucified there was a garden; and in the garden a new sepulchre, wherein was never man yet laid.

42 There laid they Yahwah therefore because of the Jews' (Yehudim)' preparation day; for the sepulchre was near at hand.

20 The first day of the week cometh Mary (Miryam) Magdalene early, when it was yet dark, unto the sepulchre, and seeth the stone taken away from the sepulchre.

2 Then she runneth, and cometh to Shimon Peter (Kefa), and to the other disciple, whom Yahwah loved, and saith unto them, "They have taken away the Lord (Yahwah) out of the sepulchre, and we know not where they have laid Him."

3 Peter (Kefa) therefore went forth, and that other disciple, and came to the sepulchre.

4 So they ran both together; and the other disciple did outrun Peter (Kefa), and came first to the sepulchre.

5 And he stooping down, and looking in, saw the linen clothes lying; yet went he not in.

6 Then cometh Shimon Peter (Kefa) following him, and went into the sepulchre, and seeth the linen clothes lie,

7 And the napkin, that was about His head, not lying with the linen clothes, but wrapped

together in a place by itself.

8 Then went in also that other disciple, who came first to the sepulchre, and he saw, and believed.

9 For as yet they knew not the Scripture, that He must rise again from the dead.

10 Then the disciples went away again unto their own home.

11 But Mary (Miryam) stood outside at the sepulchre weeping; and as she wept, she stooped down, and looked into the sepulchre,

12 And seeth two angels in white sitting, the one at the head, and the other at the feet, where the body of Yahwah had lain.

13 And they say unto her, "Woman, why weepest you?" She saith unto them, "Because they have taken away my Lord (Adonai), and I know not where they have laid Him."

14 And when she had thus said, she turned herself back, and saw Yahwah standing, and knew not that it was Yahwah.

15 Yahwah saith unto her, "Woman, why weepest you? Whom seekest you?" She, supposing Him to be the gardener, saith unto Him, "Sir, if you have borne Him hence, tell me where you have laid Him, and I will take Him away."

16 Yahwah saith unto her, "Mary (Miryam)." She turned herself, and saith unto Him, "Rabboni!" which is to say, "My Teacher!"

17 Yahwah saith unto her, "Touch Me not; for I am not yet ascended to My Father; but go to My brethren, and say unto them, 'I ascend unto My Father, and your Father; and to My God (Elohai), and your God (Eloheikha).'"

18 Mary (Miryam) Magdalene came and told the disciples that she had seen the Lord (Yahwah), and that He had spoken these things unto her.

19 Then the same day at evening, being the first day of the week, when the doors were shut where the disciples were assembled for fear of the Jews (Yehudim), came Yahwah and stood in the midst, and saith unto them, "Peace be unto you."

20 And when He had so said, He shewed unto them His hands and His side. Then were the disciples glad, when they saw the Lord (Yahwah).

21 Then said Yahwah to them again, "Peace be unto you; as My Father hath sent Me, even so send I you."

22 And when He had said this, He breathed on them, and saith unto them, "Receive you the Holy Spirit (Ruach haQodesh);

23 Whose soever sins you remit, they are remitted unto them; and whose soever sins you retain, they are retained."

24 But Thomas, one of the twelve, called Didymus, was not with them when Yahwah came.

25 The other disciples therefore said unto him, "We have seen the Lord (Yahwah). But he said unto them, "Except I shall see in His hands the print of the nails, and put my finger into the print of the nails, and thrust my hand into His side, I will not believe."

26 And after eight days again His disciples were inside, and Thomas with them; then came Yahwah, the doors being shut, and stood in the midst, and said, "Peace be unto you."

27 Then saith He to Thomas, "Reach hither your finger, and behold My hands; and reach hither your hand, and thrust it into My side; and be not faithless, but believing."

28 And Thomas answered and said unto Him, "My Lord (Adonai) and my God (Elohai)."

29 Yahwah saith unto him, "Thomas, because you have seen Me, you have believed; blessed are they that have not seen, and yet have believed."

30 And many other signs truly did Yahwah in the presence of His disciples, which are not written in this book;

31 But these are written, that you might believe that Yahwah (YHWH) is the Messiah (haMashiach), [B47]Humanity of El (YHWH); and that believing you might have life through His name.

21 After these things Yahwah shewed Himself again to the disciples at the sea of Tiberias; and on this wise shewed He Himself.

2 There were together Shimon Peter (Kefa), and Thomas called Didymus, and Nathanael of Cana in Galilee, and the sons of Zebedee (Zavdai), and two others of His disciples.

3 Shimon Peter (Kefa) saith unto them, "I am going fishing." They say unto him, "We also go with you." They went forth, and entered into a ship immediately; and that night they caught nothing.

4 But when the morning was now come, Yahwah stood on the shore; but the disciples knew not

that it was Yahwah.

5 Then Yahwah saith unto them, "Children, have you any food?" They answered Him, "No."

6 And He said unto them, "Cast the net on the right side of the ship, and you shall find." They cast therefore, and now they were not able to draw it for the multitude of fishes.

7 Therefore that disciple whom Yahwah loved saith unto Peter (Kefa), "It is the Lord (Yahwah). Now when Shimon Peter (Kefa) heard that it was the Lord (Yahwah), he girts his fisher's coat unto him, (for he was naked,) and did cast himself into the sea.

8 And the other disciples came in a little ship; (for they were not far from land, but as it was two hundred cubits,) dragging the net with fishes.

9 As soon then as they were come to land, they saw a fire of coals there, and fish laid thereon, and bread.

10 Yahwah saith unto them, "Bring of the fish which you have now caught."

11 Shimon Peter (Kefa) went up, and drew the net to land full of great fishes, a hundred and fifty and three; and for all there were so many, yet was not the net broken.

12 Yahwah saith unto them, "Come and dine." And none of the disciples durst ask Him, "Who are you?" knowing that it was the Lord (Yahwah).

13 Yahwah then cometh, and taketh bread, and giveth them, and fish likewise.

14 This is now the third time that Yahwah shewed Himself to His disciples, after that He was risen from the dead.

15 So when they had dined, Yahwah saith to Shimon Peter (Kefa), "Shimon, son of Jonas (Yonah), lovest you Me more than these?" He saith unto Him, "Yea, Lord (Adonai); You knowest that I love You." He saith unto him, "Feed My lambs."

16 He saith to him again the second time, "Shimon, son of Jonas (Yonah), lovest you Me?"

He saith unto him, "Yea, Lord (Adonai); You knowest that I love You." He saith unto him, "Feed My sheep."

17 He saith unto him the third time, "Shimon, son of Jonas (Yonah), lovest you Me?" Peter (Kefa) was grieved because He said unto him the third time, "Lovest you Me?" And he said unto Him, "Lord (Adonai), You knowest all things; You knowest that I love You." Yahwah saith unto him, "Feed My sheep.

18 Verily, verily, I say unto you, when you wast young, you girdedst yourself, and walkedst whither you wouldest; but when you shalt be old, you shalt stretch forth your hands, and another shall gird you, and carry you whither you wouldest not."

19 This spake He, signifying by what death he should glorify God (Elohim, יהוה (YHWH)). And when He had spoken this, He saith unto him, "Follow Me."

20 Then Peter (Kefa), turning about, seeth the disciple whom Yahwah loved following; who also leaned on His breast at supper, and said, "Lord (Adonai), who is he that betrayeth You?"

21 Peter (Kefa) seeing him saith to Yahwah, "Lord (Adonai), and what shall this man do?"

22 Yahwah saith unto him, "If I will that he tarries till I come, what is that to you? Follow you Me."

23 Then went this saying abroad among the brethren, that that disciple should not die; yet Yahwah said not unto him, that he shall not die; but, "If I will that he tarries till I come, what is that to you?"

24 This is the disciple who testifieth of these things, and wrote these things; and we know that his testimony is true.

25 And there are also many other things which Yahwah did, if they should be written every one of them, I suppose that even the world itself could not contain the books that should be written. So be it (Amen).

ACTS
MAASEH מַעֲשֵׂה
(Acts of the Apostles)

1 The former treatise have I made, O Theophilus, of all that [A1]Yahwah (haMashiach) began both to do and teach,

2 Until the day in which He was taken up, after that He through the Holy Spirit (Ruach haQodesh) had given commandments unto the apostles whom He had chosen;

3 To whom also He shewed Himself alive after His passion by many infallible proofs, being seen of them forty days, and speaking of the things pertaining to the kingdom of God (Elohim, יהוה (YHWH)).

4 And, being assembled together with them, commanded them that they should not depart from Jerusalem (Yerushalayim), but wait for the promise of the Father, which, saith He, "You have heard of Me.

5 For [A67]John (Yochanan) truly [B52]baptized with water; but you shall be baptized with the Holy Spirit (Ruach haQodesh) not many days hence."

6 When they therefore were come together, they asked of Him, saying, "Lord (Adonai), wilt You at this time restore again the kingdom to Yisrael?"

7 And He said unto them, "It is not for you to know the times or the seasons, which the Father hath put in His own power.

8 But you shall receive power, after that the Holy Spirit (Ruach haQodesh) is come upon you; and you shall be witnesses unto Me both in Jerusalem (Yerushalayim), and in all Judah (Yehudah), and in Samaria, and unto the uttermost part of the earth."

9 And when He had spoken these things, while they beheld, He was taken up; and a cloud received Him out of their sight.

10 And while they looked stedfastly toward heaven as He went up, behold, two men stood by them in white apparel;

11 Which also said, "You men of Galilee, why stand you gazing up into heaven? This same Yahwah, who is taken up from you into heaven, shall so come in like manner as you have seen Him go into heaven."

12 Then returned they unto Jerusalem (Yerushalayim) from the mount called Olivet, which is from Jerusalem (Yerushalayim) a Shabbat day's journey.

13 And when they were come in, they went up into an upper room, where abode both Peter (Kefa), and James (Yaaqov), and John (Yochanan), and Andrew, Philip, and Thomas, Bartholomew (Bar-Talmai), and Matthew (Mattityahu), James (Yaaqov) the son of Alphaeus, and Shimon Zelotes, and Judah (Yehudah) the brother of Jacob (Yaaqov).

14 These all continued with one accord in prayer and supplication, with the women, and Mary (Miryam) the mother of Yahwah, and with his brethren.

15 And in those days Peter (Kefa) stood up in the midst of the disciples, and said, (the number of names together were about a hundred and twenty,)

16 "Men and brethren, this Scripture must needs have been fulfilled, which the Holy Spirit (Ruach haQodesh) by the mouth of Dawid spake before concerning Judas (Yehudah), who was guide to them that took Yahwah.

17 For he was numbered with us, and had obtained part of this ministry."

18 (Now this man purchased a field with the reward of iniquity; and falling headlong, he burst asunder in the midst, and all his bowels gushed out.

19 And it was known unto all the dwellers at Jerusalem (Yerushalayim); insomuch as that field is called in their proper tongue, 'Aceldama' (Chaqal-Dema), that is to say, 'The field of Blood.'

20 For it is written in the book of Psalms, 'Let his habitation be desolate, and let no man dwell therein; and his bishoprick let another take.' – *Psa. 69:25; Psa. 109:8*

21 Wherefore of these men who have companied with us all the time that our Lord (Adonai) Yahwah went in and out among us,

22 Beginning from the baptism of John (Yochanan), unto that same day that He was taken up from us, must one be ordained to be a witness with us of His resurrection.

23 And they appointed two: Joseph (Yosef) called Barsabas (Bar-Sabba), who was surnamed Yustus, and Matthew (Mattityahu).

24 And they prayed, and said, "You, יהוה, who knowest the hearts of all men, shew whether of these two You have chosen,

25 That he may take part of this ministry and apostleship, from which Judas (Yehudah) by transgression fell, that he might go to his own place.

26 And they gave forth their lots; and the lot fell upon Matthew (Mattiyahu); and he was numbered with the eleven apostles.

2 And when the day of Pentecost was fully come, they were all with one accord in one place.

2 And suddenly there came a sound from heaven as of a rushing mighty wind, and it filled all the house where they were sitting.

3 And there appeared unto them cloven tongues like as of fire, and it sat upon each of them.

4 And they were all filled with the Holy Spirit (Ruach haQodesh), and began to speak with other tongues, as the Spirit gave them utterance.

5 And there were Jews (Yehudim) dwelling at Jerusalem (Yerushalayim), devout men, out of every nation under heaven.

6 Now when this was noised abroad, the multitude came together, and were confounded, because that every man heard them speak in his own language.

7 And they were all amazed and marvelled, saying one to another, "Behold, are not all these who speak Galilaeans?

8 And how hear we every man in our own tongue, wherein we were born?

9 Parthians, and Medes, and Elamites, and the dwellers in Mesopotamia, and in Judah (Yehudah), and Cappadocia, in Pontus, and Asia,

10 Phrygia, and Pamphylia, in Egypt (Mitsrayim), and in the parts of Libya about Cyrene, and strangers of Rome, Jews (Yehudim) and proselytes,

11 Cretes and Arabians, we do hear them speak in our tongues the wonderful works of God (Elohim)."

12 And they were all amazed, and were in doubt, saying one to another, "What meaneth this?"

13 Others mocking said, "These men are full of new wine."

14 But Peter (Kefa), standing up with the eleven, lifted up his voice, and said unto them, "You men of Judah (Yehudah), and all you that dwell at Jerusalem (Yerushalayim), be this known unto you, and hearken to my words:

15 For these are not drunken, as you suppose, seeing it is but the third hour of the day.

16 But this is that which was spoken by the prophet Yoel:

17 'And it shall come to pass in the last days, saith God (Elohim, יהוה (YHWH)), I will pour out of My Spirit upon all flesh; and your sons and your daughters shall prophesy, and your young men shall see visions, and your old men shall dream dreams. – Yoel 2:28

18 And on My servants and on My handmaidens I will pour out in those days of My Spirit; and they shall prophesy. – Yoel 2:29

19 And I will shew wonders in heaven above, and signs in the earth beneath; blood, and fire, and vapour of smoke.

20 The sun shall be turned into darkness, and the moon into blood, before that great and notable day of יהוה (YHWH) come. – Yoel 2:30-31

21 And it shall come to pass, that whosoever shall call on the name of יהוה (YHWH, Yahwah) shall be saved.' – Yoel 2:32

22 You men of Yisrael, hear these words: Yahwah of Nazareth, a Man approved of God (Elohim) among you by miracles and wonders and signs, which God (Elohim) did by Him in the midst of you, as you yourselves also know:

23 Him, being delivered by the determinate counsel and foreknowledge of God (Elohim), you have taken, and by wicked hands have crucified and slain;

24 Whom God (Elohim) hath raised up, having loosed the pains of death, because it was not possible that He should be holden of it.

25 For Dawid speaketh concerning Him: 'I foresaw יהוה (YHWH) always before my face, for He is on my right hand, that I should not be moved;

26 Therefore did my heart rejoice, and my tongue was glad; moreover also my flesh shall rest in hope;

27 Because You wilt not leave my soul in hell (sheol), neither wilt You let Your Holy One to see corruption.

28 You have made known to me the ways of life; You shalt make me full of joy with Your countenance.' – Psa.16:8–11

29 Men and brethren, let me freely speak unto you of the patriarch Dawid, that he is both dead and buried, and his sepulchre is with us unto this day.

30 Therefore being a prophet, and knowing that God (Elohim) had sworn with an oath to him, that of the fruit of his loins, according to the flesh, He would raise up the Messiah (haMashiach) to sit on His throne;

31 He seeing this before spake of the resurrection of the Messiah (haMashiach), that His soul was not left in hell (sheol), neither His flesh did see corruption.

32 This Yahwah hath God (Elohim) raised up, whereof we all are witnesses.

33 Therefore being by the right hand of God (Elohim) exalted, and having received of the Father the promise of the Holy Spirit, He hath shed forth this, which you now see and hear.

34 For Dawid is not ascended into the heavens; but he saith himself, "יהוה said unto my Lord (Adoni), "Sit You on My right hand,

35 Until I make Your foes Your footstool."' – *Psa. 110:1*

36 Therefore let all the house of Yisrael know assuredly, that God (Elohim) hath made that same Yahwah, whom you have crucified, both Lord (Adon) and Messiah (Mashiach).

37 Now when they heard this, they were pricked in their heart, and said unto Peter (Kefa) and to the rest of the apostles, "Men and brethren, what shall we do?"

38 B62aThen Peter (Kefa) said unto them, "Repent, and be baptized everyone of you in the name of A1Yahwah (YHWH) haMashiach for the remission of sins, and you shall receive the gift of the Holy Spirit (B62bRuach haQodesh).

39 For the promise is unto you, and to your children, and to all that are afar off, even as many as יהוה our God (YHWH Eloheinu) shall call.

40 And with many other words did he testify and exhort, saying, "Save yourselves from this perverse generation."

41 Then they that gladly received his word were baptized; and the same day there were added unto them about three thousand souls.

42 And they continued stedfastly in the apostles' doctrine and fellowship, and in breaking of bread, and in prayers.

43 And fear came upon every soul; and many wonders and signs were done by the apostles.

44 And all that believed were together, and had all things common;

45 And sold their possessions and goods, and parted them to all men, as every man had need.

46 And they, continuing daily with one accord in the temple, and breaking bread from house to house, did eat their food with gladness and singleness of heart,

47 Praising God (Elohim, יהוה (YHWH)), and having favour with all the people. And יהוה (YHWH) added to the assembly daily such as should be saved.

3 Now Peter (Kefa) and John (Yochanan) went up together into the temple at the hour of prayer, being the ninth hour.

2 And a certain man lame from his mother's womb was carried, whom they laid daily at the gate of the temple which is called Beautiful, to ask alms of them that entered into the temple;

3 Who seeing Peter (Kefa) and John (Yochanan) about to go into the temple asked an alms.

4 And Peter (Kefa), fastening his eyes upon him with John (Yochanan), said, "Look on us."

5 And he gave heed unto them, expecting to receive something of them.

6 Then Peter (Kefa) said, "Silver and gold have I none; but such as I have, give I you: In the name of Yahwah haMashiach of Nazareth rise up and walk."

7 And he took him by the right hand, and lifted him up; and immediately his feet and ancle bones received strength.

8 And he leaping up stood, and walked, and entered with them into the temple, walking, and leaping, and praising God (Elohim).

9 And all the people saw him walking and praising God (Elohim);

10 And they knew that it was he who sat for alms at the Beautiful Gate of the temple; and they were filled with wonder and amazement at that which had happened unto him.

11 And as the lame man who was healed held Peter (Kefa) and John (Yochanan), all the people ran together unto them in the porch that is called Solomon (Shelomoh)'s, greatly wondering.

12 And when Peter (Kefa) saw it, he answered unto the people, "You men of Yisrael, why marvel you at this? Or why look you so earnestly on us, as though by our own power or holiness we had made this man to walk?

13 The God (Elohim) of Avraham, and of Isaac (Yitschaq), and of Jacob (Yaaqov), the God (Elohim) of our fathers, hath glorified His B47Humanity, Yahwah; whom you delivered up,

and denied Him in the presence of Pilate, when he was determined to let Him go. – *Exo. 3:6, 15*

14 But you denied the Holy One and the Just, and desired a murderer to be granted unto you;

15 And killed the Prince of life, whom God (Elohim) hath raised from the dead; whereof we are witnesses.

16 And His name through faith in His name hath made this man strong, whom you see and know; yea, the faith which is by Him hath given him this perfect soundness in the presence of you all.

17 And now, brethren, I know that through ignorance you did it, as did also your rulers.

18 But those things, which God (Elohim, יהוה (YHWH)) before had shewed by the mouth of all His prophets, that the Messiah (haMashiach) should suffer, He hath so fulfilled.

19 Repent you therefore, and be converted, that your sins may be blotted out, when the times of refreshing shall come from the presence of יהוה (YHWH);

20 And He shall send Yahwah haMashiach, who before was preached unto you;

21 Whom the heaven must receive until the times of restitution of all things, which God (Elohim, יהוה (YHWH)) hath spoken by the mouth of all His holy prophets since the world began.

22 For Moses (Mosheh) truly said unto the fathers, "A prophet shall your God (Elohim) raise up unto you of your brethren, like unto me; Him shall you hear in all things whatsoever He shall say unto you.

23 And it shall come to pass, that every soul, who will not hear that prophet, shall be destroyed from among the people. – *Deu. 18:15–16*

24 Yea, and all the prophets from Samuel and those that follow after, as many as have spoken, have likewise foretold of these days.

25 You are the children of the prophets, and of the covenant which God (Elohim) made with our fathers, saying unto Avraham, 'And in your seed shall all the kindreds of the earth be blessed.' – *Gen. 22:18; 26:4*

26 Unto you first God (Elohim), having raised up His [B47]Humanity, Yahwah, sent Him to bless you, in turning away every one of you from his iniquities."

4 And as they spake unto the people, the priests (kohanim), and the captain of the temple, and the Sadducees, came upon them,

2 Being grieved that they taught the people, and preached through Yahwah the resurrection from the dead.

3 And they laid hands on them, and put them in hold unto the next day; for it was now eventide.

4 Howbeit many of them who heard the word believed; and the number of the men was about five thousand.

5 And it came to pass on the morrow, that their rulers, and elders, and scribes,

6 And Annas the high priest (kohen hagadol), and Caiaphas, and John (Yochanan), and Alexander, and as many as were of the kindred of the high priest (kohen hagadol), were gathered together at Jerusalem (Yerushalayim).

7 And when they had set them in the midst, they asked, "By what power, or by what name, have you done this?"

8 Then Peter (Kefa), filled with the Holy Spirit (Ruach haQodesh), said unto them, "You rulers of the people, and elders of Yisrael,

9 If we this day be examined of the good deed done to the impotent man, by what means he is made whole;

10 Be it known unto you all, and to all the people of Yisrael, that by the name of Yahwah haMashiach of Nazareth, whom you crucified, whom God (Elohim) raised from the dead, even by Him doth this man stands here before you whole.

11 This is the stone which was set at nought of you builders, which is become the head of the corner. – *Psa. 118:22*

12 Neither is there salvation in any other; for there is none other name under heaven given among men, whereby we must be saved.

13 Now when they saw the boldness of Peter (Kefa) and John (Yochanan), and perceived that they were unlearned and ignorant men, they marvelled; and they took knowledge of them, that they had been with Yahwah.

14 And beholding the man who was healed standing with them, they could say nothing against it.

15 But when they had commanded them to go aside out of the council, they conferred among themselves,

16 Saying, "What shall we do to these men? For that indeed a notable miracle hath been done by them is manifest to all them that dwell

in Jerusalem (Yerushalayim); and we cannot deny it.

17 But that it spread no further among the people, let us straitly threaten them, that they speak henceforth to no man in this name."

18 And they called them, and commanded them not to speak at all nor teach in the name of Yahwah (YHWH).

19 But Peter (Kefa) and John (Yochanan) answered and said unto them, "Whether it be right in the sight of God (Elohim) to hearken unto you more than unto God (Elohim), judge you.

20 For we cannot but speak the things which we have seen and heard."

21 So when they had further threatened them, they let them go, finding nothing how they might punish them, because of the people; for all men glorified God (Elohim) for that which was done.

22 For the man was above forty years old, on whom this miracle of healing was shewed.

23 And being let go, they went to their own company, and reported all that the chief priests (kohanim) and elders had said unto them.

24 And when they heard that, they lifted up their voice to God (Elohim) with one accord, and said, "Lord (Adonai), You are the God (El), who hast made heaven, and earth, and the sea, and all that in them is;

25 Who by the mouth of your servant Dawid hast said, 'Why did the heathen rage, and the people imagine vain things? – *Psa. 2:1*

26 The kings of the earth stood up, and the rulers were gathered together against יהוה, and against His Anointed (Mashiach). – *Psa. 2:2*

27 For of a truth against Your holy Child Yahwah, whom You have anointed, both Herod, and Pontius Pilate, with the Gentiles (Goyim), and the people of Yisrael, were gathered together,

28 For to do whatsoever Your hand and Your counsel determined before to be done.

29 And now, יהוה (YHWH) behold their threatenings; and grant unto Your servants, that with all boldness they may speak Your word,

30 By stretching forth Your hand to heal; and that signs and wonders may be done by the name of Your holy Child Yahwah (YHWH).

31 And when they had prayed, the place was shaken where they were assembled together;

and they were all filled with the Holy Spirit (Ruach haQodesh), and they spake the word of God (Elohim, יהוה (YHWH)) with boldness.

32 And the multitude of them that believed were of one heart and of one soul; neither said any of them that ought of the things which he possessed was his own; but they had all things common.

33 And with great power gave the apostles witness of the resurrection of the Lord (Adonai) Yahwah; and great grace was upon them all.

34 Neither was there any among them that lacked; for as many as were possessors of lands or houses sold them, and brought the prices of the things that were sold,

35 And laid them down at the apostles' feet: and distribution was made unto every man according as he had need.

36 And Joses (Yosef), who by the apostles was surnamed Barnabas, (which is, being interpreted, The son of consolation,) a Levite (Lewi), and of the country of Cyprus,

37 Having land, sold it, and brought the money, and laid it at the apostles' feet.

5 But a certain man named Ananias, with Sapphira his wife, sold a possession,

2 And kept back part of the price, his wife also being privy to it, and brought a certain part, and laid it at the apostles' feet.

3 But Peter (Kefa) said, Ananias, why hath Satan filled your heart to lie to the Holy Spirit (Ruach haQodesh), and to keep back part of the price of the land?

4 Whiles it remained, was it not your own? And after it was sold, was it not in your own power? Why have you conceived this thing in your heart? You have not lied unto men, but unto God (Elohim).

5 And Ananias hearing these words fell down, and gave up the spirit; and great fear came on all them that heard these things.

6 And the young men arose, wound him up, and carried him out, and buried him.

7 And it was about the space of three hours after, when his wife, not knowing what was done, came in.

8 And Peter (Kefa) answered unto her, "Tell me whether you sold the land for so much?" And she said, "Yea, for so much."

9 Then Peter (Kefa) said unto her, "How is it that you have agreed together to test the Spirit

of יהוה (Ruach YHWH)? Behold, the feet of them who have buried your husband are at the door, and shall carry you out."

10 Then fell she down straightway at his feet, and yielded up the spirit; and the young men came in, and found her dead, and, carrying her forth, buried her by her husband.

11 And great fear came upon all the assembly, and upon as many as heard these things.

12 And by the hands of the apostles were many signs and wonders wrought among the people; (and they were all with one accord in Solomon (Shelomoh)'s porch.

13 And of the rest durst no man join himself to them; but the people magnified them.

14 And believers were the more added to the Lord (YHWH), multitudes both of men and women.)

15 Insomuch that they brought forth the sick into the streets, and laid them on beds and couches, that at the least the shadow of Peter (Kefa) passing by might overshadow some of them.

16 There came also a multitude out of the cities round about unto Jerusalem (Yerushalayim), bringing sick folks, and them which were vexed with unclean spirits; and they were healed every one.

17 Then the high priest (kohen hagadol) rose up, and all they that were with him, (which is the sect of the Sadducees,) and were filled with indignation,

18 And laid their hands on the apostles, and put them in the common prison.

19 But the angel of יהוה by night opened the prison doors, and brought them forth, and said,

20 "Go, stand and speak in the temple to the people all the words of this life."

21 And when they heard that, they entered into the temple early in the morning, and taught. But the high priest (kohen hagadol) came, and they that were with him, and called the council together, and all the senate of the children of Yisrael, and sent to the prison to have them brought.

22 But when the officers came, and found them not in the prison, they returned, and told,

23 Saying, "The prison truly found we shut with all safety, and the keepers standing outside before the doors; but when we had opened, we found no man inside."

24 Now when the high priest (kohen hagadol) and the captain of the temple and the chief priests (kohanim) heard these things, they doubted of them whereunto this would grow.

25 Then came one and told them, saying, "Behold, the men whom you put in prison are standing in the temple, and teaching the people."

26 Then went the captain with the officers, and brought them without violence; for they feared the people, lest they should have been stoned.

27 And when they had brought them, they set them before the council; and the high priest (kohen hagadol) asked them,

28 Saying, "Did not we straitly command you that you should not teach in this name? And, behold, you have filled Jerusalem (Yerushalayim) with your doctrine, and intend to bring this man's blood upon us."

29 Then Peter (Kefa) and the other apostles answered and said, "We ought to obey God (Elohim) rather than men.

30 The God (Elohim) of our fathers raised up Yahwah, whom you slew and hanged on a tree.

31 Him hath God (Elohim) exalted with His right hand to be a Prince and a Savior, for to give repentance to Yisrael, and forgiveness of sins. – *Psa. 110:1*

32 And we are His witnesses of these things; and so is also the Holy Spirit (Ruach haQodesh), whom God (Elohim) hath given to them that obey Him."

33 When they heard that, they were cut to the heart, and took counsel to slay them.

34 Then stood there up one in the council (Sanhedrin), a Pharisee, named Gamaliel, a teacher of the Torah, had in reputation among all the people, and commanded to put the apostles forth a little space;

35 And said unto them, "You men of Yisrael, take heed to yourselves what you intend to do as touching these men.

36 For before these days rose up Theudas, boasting himself to be somebody; to whom a number of men, about four hundred, joined themselves; who was slain; and all, as many as obeyed him, were scattered, and brought to nought.

37 After this man rose up Judah (Yehudah) of Galilee in the days of the taxing, and drew away much people after him; he also perished; and all, even as many as obeyed him, were dispersed.

38 And now I say unto you, refrain from these men, and let them alone; for if this counsel or this work be of men, it will come to nought;

39 But if it be of God (Elohim), you cannot overthrow it; lest haply you be found even to fight against God (Elohim)."

40 And to him they agreed; and when they had called the apostles, and beaten them, they commanded that they should not speak in the name of Yahwah (YHWH), and let them go.

41 And they departed from the presence of the council (Sanhedrin), rejoicing that they were counted worthy to suffer shame for His name.

42 And daily in the temple, and in every house, they ceased not to teach and preach Yahwah haMashiach.

6 And in those days, when the number of the disciples was multiplied, there arose a murmuring of the Grecians against the Hebrews, because their widows were neglected in the daily ministration.

2 Then the twelve called the multitude of the disciples unto them, and said, "It is not reason that we should leave the word of God (Elohim, יהוה (YHWH)), and serve tables.

3 Wherefore, brethren, look you out among you seven men of honest report, full of the Holy Spirit (Ruach haQodesh) and wisdom, whom we may appoint over this business.

4 But we will give ourselves continually to prayer, and to the ministry of the word."

5 And the saying pleased the whole multitude; and they chose Stephen, a man full of faith and of the Holy Spirit (Ruach haQodesh), and Philip, and Prochorus, and Nicanor, and Timon, and Parmenas, and Nicolas a proselyte of Antioch;

6 Whom they set before the apostles; and when they had prayed, they laid their hands on them.

7 And the word of God (Elohim, יהוה (YHWH)) increased; and the number of the disciples multiplied in Jerusalem (Yerushalayim) greatly; and a great company of the priests (kohanim) were obedient to the faith.

8 And Stephen, full of faith and power, did great wonders and miracles among the people.

9 Then there arose certain of the synagogue, which is called the synagogue of the Libertines, and Cyrenians, and Alexandrians, and of them of Cilicia and of Asia, disputing with Stephen.

10 And they were not able to resist the wisdom and the spirit by which he spake.

11 Then they suborned men, who said, "We have heard him speak blasphemous words against Moses (Mosheh), and against God (Elohim)."

12 And they stirred up the people, and the elders, and the scribes, and came upon him, and caught him, and brought him to the council (Sanhedrin),

13 And set up false witnesses, who said, "This man ceaseth not to speak blasphemous words against this holy place, and the Torah;

14 For we have heard him say, that this Yahwah of Nazareth shall destroy this place, and shall change the customs which Moses (Mosheh) delivered us."

15 And all that sat in the council (Sanhedrin), looking stedfastly on him, saw his face as it had been the face of an angel.

7 Then said the high priest (kohen hagadol), "Are these things so?"

2 And he said, "Men, brethren, and fathers, hearken: The God (Elohim) of glory appeared unto our father Avraham, when he was in Mesopotamia, before he dwelt in Charran,

3 And said unto him, 'Get you out of your country, and from your kindred, and come into the land which I shall shew you.'

4 Then came he out of the land of the Chaldaeans, and dwelt in Charran; and from thence, when his father was dead, He moved him into this land, wherein you now dwell.

5 And He gave him none inheritance in it, no, not so much as to set his foot on; yet He promised that He would give it to him for a possession, and to his seed after him, when as yet he had no child.

6 And God (Elohim) spake on this wise: that his seed should sojourn in a foreign land; and that they should bring them into bondage, and entreat them evil four hundred years. – *Gen. 15:13, Eph. 2:12*

7 'And the nation to whom they shall be in bondage will I judge,' said God (Elohim); 'and after that shall they come forth, and serve Me in this place.'

8 And He gave him the covenant of circumcision; and so Avraham begat Isaac (Yitschaq), and circumcised him the eighth day; and Isaac (Yitschaq) begat Jacob (Yaaqov); and Jacob (Yaaqov) begat the twelve patriarchs.

9 And the patriarchs, moved with envy, sold Joseph (Yosef) into Egypt (Mitsrayim); but God

(Elohim) was with him,

10 And delivered him out of all his afflictions, and gave him favour and wisdom in the sight of Pharaoh king of Egypt (Mitsrayim); and He made him governor over Egypt (Mitsrayim) and all his house.

11 Now there came a dearth over all the land of Egypt (Mitsrayim) and Chanaan, and great affliction; and our fathers found no sustenance.

12 But when Jacob (Yaaqov) heard that there was corn in Egypt (Mitsrayim), he sent out our fathers first.

13 And at the second time Joseph (Yosef) was made known to his brethren; and Joseph (Yosef)'s kindred was made known unto Pharaoh.

14 Then sent Joseph (Yosef), and called his father Jacob (Yaaqov) to him, and all his kindred, threescore and fifteen souls.

15 So Jacob (Yaaqov) went down into Egypt (Mitsrayim), and died, he, and our fathers,

16 And were carried over into Sychem, and laid in the sepulchre that Avraham bought for a sum of money of the sons of Emmor the father of Sychem.

17 But when the time of the promise drew near, which God (Elohim) had sworn to Avraham, the people grew and multiplied in Egypt (Mitsrayim),

18 Till another king arose, who knew not Joseph (Yosef).

19 The same dealt subtilly with our kindred, and evil entreated our fathers, so that they cast out their young children, to the end they might not live.

20 In which time Moses (Mosheh) was born, and was exceeding fair, and nourished up in his father's house three months;

21 And when he was cast out, Pharaoh's daughter took him up, and nourished him for her own son.

22 And Moses (Mosheh) was learned in all the wisdom of the Egyptians (Mitsrayim), and was mighty in words and in deeds.

23 And when he was full forty years old, it came into his heart to visit his brethren the children of Yisrael.

24 And seeing one of them suffer wrong, he defended him, and avenged him that was oppressed, and smote the Egyptian (Mitsriy);

25 For he supposed his brethren would have understood how that God (Elohim) by his hand would deliver them; but they understood not.

26 And the next day he shewed himself unto them as they strove, and would have set them at one again, saying, 'Sirs, you are brethren; why do you wrong one to another?'

27 But he that did his neighbour wrong thrust him away, saying, 'Who made you a ruler and a judge over us?

28 Wilt you kill me, as you diddest the Egyptian (Mitsriy) yesterday?'

29 Then fled Moses (Mosheh) at this saying, and was a stranger in the land of Madian, where he begat two sons.

30 And when forty years were expired, there appeared to him in the wilderness of Mount Sina an angel of יהוה in a flame of fire in a bush.

31 When Moses (Mosheh) saw it, he wondered at the sight; and as he drew near to behold it, the voice of יהוה came unto him,

32 Saying, 'I am the God (Elohim) of your fathers, the God (Elohim) of Avraham, and the God (Elohim) of Isaac (Yitzchaq), and the God (Elohim) of Jacob (Yaaqov). Then Moses (Mosheh) trembled, and durst not behold.

33 Then said יהוה (YHWH) to him, "Put off your shoes from your feet; for the place where you standest is holy ground.

34 I have seen, I have seen the affliction of My people which is in Egypt (Mitsrayim), and I have heard their groaning, and am come down to deliver them. And now come, I will send you into Egypt (Mitsrayim)."

35 This Moses (Mosheh) whom they refused, saying, 'Who made you a ruler and a judge?' The same did יהוה (YHWH) send to be a ruler and a deliverer by the hand of the angel which appeared to him in the bush.

36 He brought them out, after that He had shewed wonders and signs in the land of Egypt (Mitsrayim), and in the Red sea, and in the wilderness forty years.

37 This is that Moses (Mosheh), which said unto the children of Yisrael, 'A prophet shall יהוה your God (Elohim) raise up unto you of your brethren, like unto me; him shall you hear.'

38 This is he, that was in the assembly in the wilderness with the angel who spake to him in the Mount Sina, and with our fathers; who received the lively oracles to give unto us;

39 To whom our fathers would not obey, but

thrust him from them, and in their hearts turned back again into Egypt (Mitsrayim),

40 Saying unto Aharon, 'Make us god (elohim) to go before us; for as for this Moses (Mosheh), who brought us out of the land of Egypt (Mitsrayim), we wot not what is become of him.

41 And they made a calf in those days, and offered sacrifice unto the idol, and rejoiced in the works of their own hands.

42 Then יהוה (YHWH) turned, and gave them up to worship the host of heaven; as it is written in the book of the prophets, 'O you house of Yisrael, have you offered to Me slain beasts and sacrifices by the space of forty years in the wilderness?

43 Yea, you took up the tabernacle of Moloch, and the star of your god Remphan, figures which you made to worship them; and I will carry you away beyond Babylon (Bavel).

44 Our fathers had the tabernacle of witness in the wilderness, as he had appointed, speaking unto Moses (Mosheh), that he should make it according to the fashion that he had seen.

45 Which also our fathers that came after brought in with ᴬ³²Joshua (Yehoshua) into the possession of the Gentiles (Goyim), whom God (Elohim) drave out before the face of our fathers, unto the days of Dawid;

46 Who found favour before יהוה (YHWH), and desired to find a tabernacle for the God (Elohim) of Jacob (Yaaqov).

47 But Solomon (Shelomoh) built him a house.

48 Howbeit the Most High dwelleth not in temples made with hands; as saith the prophet:

49 'Heaven is My throne, and earth is My footstool; what house will you build Me? saith יהוה; or what is the place of My rest?

50 Hath not My hand made all these things?'

51 You stiffnecked and uncircumcised in heart and ears, you do always resist the Holy Spirit (Ruach haQodesh); as your fathers did, so do you.

52 Which of the prophets have not your fathers persecuted? And they have slain them who shewed before of the coming of the Just One; of whom you have been now the betrayers and murderers;

53 Who have received the ᴮ²⁸ᵃTorah by the disposition of angels, and have not kept it.

54 When they heard these things, they were cut to the heart, and they gnashed on him with their teeth.

55 But he, being full of the Holy Spirit (Ruach haQodesh), looked up stedfastly into heaven, and saw the glory of God (Elohim), and Yahwah standing on the right hand of God (Elohim),

56 And said, "Behold, I see the heavens opened, and the Son of man (haMashiach) standing on the right hand of God (Elohim)."

57 Then they cried out with a loud voice, and stopped their ears, and ran upon him with one accord,

58 And cast him out of the city, and stoned him; and the witnesses laid down their clothes at a young man's feet, whose name was ᴬ⁷³Shaul.

59 And they stoned Stephen, calling upon God (Elohim), and saying, "Lord Yahwah (Adonai YHWH), receive my spirit."

60 And he kneeled down, and cried with a loud voice, "יהוה (YHWH), lay not this sin to their charge." And when he had said this, he fell asleep.

8 And Shaul was consenting unto his death. And at that time there was a great persecution against the assembly which was at Jerusalem (Yerushalayim); and they were all scattered abroad throughout the regions of Judah (Yehudah) and Samaria, except the apostles.

2 And devout men carried Stephen to his burial, and made great lamentation over him.

3 As for Shaul, he made havock of the assembly, entering into every house, and haling men and women committed them to prison.

4 Therefore they that were scattered abroad went every where preaching the word.

5 Then Philip went down to the city of Samaria, and preached the Messiah (haMashiach) unto them.

6 And the people with one accord gave heed unto those things which Philip spake, hearing and seeing the miracles which he did.

7 For unclean spirits, crying with loud voice, came out of many that were possessed with them; and many taken with palsies, and that were lame, were healed.

8 And there was great joy in that city.

9 But there was a certain man, called Shimon, who beforetime in the same city used sorcery, and bewitched the people of Samaria, giving out that himself was some great one;

10 To whom they all gave heed, from the least

to the greatest, saying, "This man is the great power of God (Elohim).

11 And to him they had regard, because that of long time he had bewitched them with sorceries.

12 But when they believed Philip preaching the things concerning the kingdom of God (Elohim, יהוה (YHWH)), and the name of Yahwah haMashiach, they were baptized, both men and women.

13 Then Shimon himself believed also; and when he was baptized, he continued with Philip, and wondered, beholding the miracles and signs which were done.

14 Now when the apostles who were at Jerusalem (Yerushalayim) heard that Samaria had received the word of God (Elohim, יהוה (YHWH)), they sent unto them Peter (Kefa) and John (Yochanan);

15 Who, when they were come down, prayed for them, that they might receive the Holy Spirit (Ruach haQodesh).

16 (For as yet he was fallen upon none of them; only they were baptized in the name of the Lord (Adonai) Yahwah.)

17 Then laid they their hands on them, and they received the Holy Spirit (Ruach haQodesh).

18 And when Shimon saw that through laying on of the apostles' hands the Holy Spirit (Ruach haQodesh) was given, he offered them money,

19 Saying, "Give me also this power, that on whomsoever I lay hands, he may receive the Holy Spirit (Ruach haQodesh).

20 But Peter (Kefa) said unto him, "Your money perishes with you, because you have thought that the gift of God (Elohim) may be purchased with money.

21 You have neither part nor lot in this matter; for your heart is not right in the sight of God (Elohim).

22 Repent therefore of this your wickedness, and pray God (Elohim), if perhaps the thought of your heart may be forgiven you.

23 For I perceive that you are in the gall of bitterness, and in the bond of iniquity."

24 Then answered Shimon, and said, "Pray you to יהוה for me, that none of these things which you have spoken come upon me."

25 And they, when they had testified and preached the word of יהוה, returned to Jerusalem (Yerushalayim), and preached the gospel (good news) in many villages of the Samaritans.

26 And the angel of יהוה spake unto Philip, saying, "Arise, and go toward the south unto the way that goeth down from Jerusalem (Yerushalayim) unto Gaza, which is desert."

27 And he arose and went; and, behold, a man of Ethiopia, a eunuch of great authority under Candace queen of the Ethiopians, who had the charge of all her treasure, and had come to Jerusalem (Yerushalayim) for to worship,

28 Was returning, and sitting in his chariot read Isaiah (Yeshayahu) the prophet.

29 Then the Spirit said unto Philip, "Go near, and join yourself to this chariot."

30 And Philip ran thither to him, and heard him read the prophet Isaiah (Yeshayahu), and said, "Understandest you what you readest?"

31 And he said, "How can I, except some man should guide me?" And he desired Philip that he would come up and sit with him.

32 The place of the Scripture which he read was this: He was led as a sheep to the slaughter; and like a lamb dumb before His shearer, so opened He not His mouth.

33 In His humiliation His judgment was taken away; and who shall declare His generation? For His life is taken from the earth." – Isa. 53:7–8

34 And the eunuch answered Philip, and said, "I pray you, of whom speaketh the prophet this? Of himself, or of some other man?"

35 Then Philip opened his mouth, and began at the same Scripture, and preached unto him Yahwah.

36 And as they went on their way, they came unto a certain water; and the eunuch said, "See, here is water; what doth hinder me to be baptized?"

37 And Philip said, "If you believest with all your heart, you mayest." And he answered and said, "I believe that Yahwah haMashiach is the [B47]Humanity of El (YHWH) .

38 And he commanded the chariot to stand still; and they went down both into the water, both Philip and the eunuch; and he baptized him.

39 And when they were come up out of the water, the Spirit of יהוה (Ruach YHWH) caught away Philip, that the eunuch saw him no more; and he went on his way rejoicing.

40 But Philip was found at Azotus; and passing through he preached in all the cities, till he came to Caesarea.

9 And Shaul, yet breathing out threatenings and slaughter against the disciples of the

Lord (Yahwah), went unto the high priest (kohen hagadol),

2 And desired of him letters to Damascus to the synagogues, that if he found any of this way, whether they were men or women, he might bring them bound unto Jerusalem (Yerushalayim).

3 And as he journeyed, he came near Damascus; and suddenly there shined round about him a light from heaven;

4 And he fell to the earth, and heard a voice saying unto him, "Shaul, Shaul, why persecutest you Me?"

5 And he said, "Who are you, Lord (Adonai)? And the Lord (Yahwah) said, "I am Yahwah whom you persecute; it is hard for you to kick against the pricks."

6 And he trembling and astonished said, "Lord (Adonai), what wilt You have me to do?" And the Lord (Yahwah) said unto him, "Arise, and go into the city, and it shall be told you what you must do."

7 And the men who journeyed with him stood speechless, hearing a voice, but seeing no man.

8 And Shaul arose from the earth; and when his eyes were opened, he saw no man; but they led him by the hand, and brought him into Damascus.

9 And he was three days without sight, and neither did eat nor drink.

10 And there was a certain disciple at Damascus, named Ananias; and to him said the Lord (Yahwah) in a vision, "Ananias." And he said, "Behold, I am here, my Lord (Adonai)."

11 And the Lord (Yahwah) said unto him, "Arise, and go into the street which is called Straight, and enquire in the house of Judah (Yehudah) for one called Shaul, of Tarsus; for, behold, he prayeth,

12 And hath seen in a vision a man named Ananias coming in, and putting his hand on him, that he might receive his sight."

13 Then Ananias answered, "Lord (Adonai), I have heard by many of this man, how much evil he hath done to your holy ones at Jerusalem (Yerushalayim):

14 And here he hath authority from the chief priests (kohanim) to bind all that call on Your name."

15 But the Lord (Yahwah) said unto him, "Go your way, for he is a chosen vessel unto Me, to bear My name before the Gentiles (Goyim), and kings, and the children of Yisrael;

16 For I will shew him how great things he must suffer for My name's sake."

17 And Ananias went his way, and entered into the house; and putting his hands on him said, "Brother Shaul, the Lord (Adonai), Yahwah, that appeared unto you in the way as you camest, hath sent me, that you mightest receive your sight, and be filled with the Holy Spirit (Ruach haQodesh).

18 And immediately there fell from his eyes as it had been scales; and he received sight forthwith, and arose, and was baptized.

19 And when he had received food, he was strengthened. Then was Shaul certain days with the disciples who were at Damascus.

20 And straightway he preached the Messiah (haMashiach) in the synagogues, that He is the [B47]Humanity of El (YHWH).

21 But all that heard him were amazed, and said: "Is not this he that destroyed them who called on this name in Jerusalem (Yerushalayim), and came hither for that intent, that he might bring them bound unto the chief priests (kohanim)?"

22 But Shaul increased the more in strength, and confounded the Jews (Yehudim) who dwelt at Damascus, proving that this is the Messiah (haMashiach).

23 And after that many days were fulfilled, the Jews (Yehudim) took counsel to kill him;

24 But their laying await was known of Shaul. And they watched the gates day and night to kill him.

25 Then the disciples took him by night, and let him down by the wall in a basket.

26 And when Shaul was come to Jerusalem (Yerushalayim), he assayed to join himself to the disciples; but they were all afraid of him, and believed not that he was a disciple.

27 But Barnabas took him, and brought him to the apostles, and declared unto them how he had seen the Lord (Yahwah) in the way, and that he had spoken to Him, and how he had preached boldly at Damascus in the name of Yahwah.

28 And he was with them coming in and going out at Jerusalem (Yerushalayim).

29 And he spake boldly in the name of the Lord Yahwah (Adonai YHWH), and disputed against the Grecians; but they went about to slay him.

30 Which when the brethren knew, they brought

him down to Caesarea, and sent him forth to Tarsus.

31 Then had the [B6l]assemblies (ekklesias) rest throughout all Judah (Yehudah) and Galilee and Samaria, and were edified; and walking in the fear of יהוה, and in the comfort of the Holy Spirit (Ruach haQodesh), were multiplied.

32 And it came to pass, as Peter (Kefa) passed throughout all quarters, he came down also to the holy ones (qadoshim) who dwelt at Lydda.

33 And there he found a certain man named Aeneas, who had kept his bed eight years, and was sick of the palsy.

34 And Peter (Kefa) said unto him, "Aeneas, Yahwah haMashiach maketh you whole; arise, and make your bed." And he arose immediately.

35 And all that dwelt at Lydda and Saron saw him, and turned to the Lord (Yahwah).

36 Now there was at Joppa (Yafo) a certain disciple named Tabitha, which by interpretation is called Dorcas; this woman was full of good works and almsdeeds which she did.

37 And it came to pass in those days, that she was sick, and died; whom when they had washed, they laid her in an upper chamber.

38 And forasmuch as Lydda was near to Joppa (Yafo), and the disciples had heard that Peter (Kefa) was there, they sent unto him two men, desiring him that he would not delay to come to them.

39 Then Peter (Kefa) arose and went with them. When he was come, they brought him into the upper chamber; and all the widows stood by him weeping, and shewing the coats and garments which Dorcas made, while she was with them.

40 But Peter (Kefa) put them all forth, and kneeled down, and prayed; and turning him to the body said, "Tabitha, arise." And she opened her eyes; and when she saw Peter (Kefa), she sat up.

41 And he gave her his hand, and lifted her up, and when he had called the holy ones and widows, presented her alive.

42 And it was known throughout all Joppa (Yafo); and many believed in the Lord (Yahwah).

43 And it came to pass, that he tarried many days in Joppa (Yafo) with one Shimon a tanner.

10 There was a certain man in Caesarea called Cornelius, a centurion of the band called the Italian band,

2 A devout man, and one that feared God (Elohim) with all his house, which gave much alms to the people, and prayed to God (Elohim) always.

3 He saw in a vision evidently about the ninth hour of the day an angel of God (Elohim) coming in to him, and saying unto him, "Cornelius."

4 And when he looked on him, he was afraid, and said, "What is it, my lord (adoni)? And he said unto him, "Your prayers and your alms are come up for a memorial before God (Elohim).

5 And now send men to Joppa (Yafo), and call for one Shimon, whose surname is Peter (Kefa);

6 He lodgeth with one Shimon a tanner, whose house is by the sea side; he shall tell you what you oughtest to do."

7 And when the angel who spake unto Cornelius was departed, he called two of his household servants, and a devout soldier of them that waited on him continually;

8 And when he had declared all these things unto them, he sent them to Joppa (Yafo).

9 On the morrow, as they went on their journey, and drew near unto the city, Peter (Kefa) went up upon the housetop to pray about the sixth hour;

10 And he became very hungry, and would have eaten; but while they made ready, he fell into a trance,

11 And saw heaven opened, and a certain vessel descending unto him, as it had been a great sheet knit at the four corners, and let down to the earth;

12 Wherein were all manner of fourfooted beasts of the earth, and wild beasts, and creeping things, and fowls of the air.

13 And there came a voice to him, "Rise, Peter (Kefa); kill, and eat."

14 But Peter (Kefa) said, "Not so, my lord (adoni); for I have never eaten any thing that is common or unclean."

15 And the voice spake unto him again the second time, "What God (Elohim) hath cleansed, that call not you common."

16 This was done thrice; and the vessel was received up again into heaven.

17 Now while Peter (Kefa) doubted in himself what this vision which he had seen should mean, behold, the men who were sent from Cornelius had made enquiry for Shimon's house, and stood before the gate,

18 And called, and asked whether Shimon, who

was surnamed Peter (Kefa), were lodged there.

19 While Peter (Kefa) thought on the vision, the Spirit said unto him, "Behold, three men seek you.

20 Arise therefore, and get you down, and go with them, doubting nothing; for I have sent them."

21 Then Peter (Kefa) went down to the men who were sent unto him from Cornelius; and said, "Behold, I am he whom you seek; what is the cause wherefore you are come?"

22 And they said, "Cornelius the centurion, a just man, and one that feareth God (Elohim), and of good report among all the nation of the Jews (Yehudim), was warned from God (Elohim) by a holy angel to send for you into his house, and to hear words of you."

23 Then called he them in, and lodged them. And on the morrow Peter (Kefa) went away with them, and certain brethren from Joppa (Yafo) accompanied him.

24 And the morrow after they entered into Caesarea. And Cornelius waited for them, and had called together his kinsmen and near friends.

25 And as Peter (Kefa) was coming in, Cornelius met him, and fell down at his feet, and worshipped him.

26 But Peter (Kefa) took him up, saying, "Stand up; I myself also am a man."

27 And as he talked with him, he went in, and found many that were come together.

28 And he said unto them, "You know how that it is an unlawful thing for a man that is a Jew (Yehudi) to keep company, or come unto one of another nation; but God (Elohim) hath shewed me that I should not call any man common or unclean.

29 Therefore came I unto you without gainsaying, as soon as I was sent for; I ask therefore for what intent you have sent for me?"

30 And Cornelius said, "Four days ago I was fasting until this hour; and at the ninth hour I prayed in my house, and, behold, a man stood before me in bright clothing,

31 And said, 'Cornelius, your prayer is heard, and your alms are had in remembrance in the sight of God (Elohim).

32 Send therefore to Joppa (Yafo), and call hither Shimon, whose surname is Peter (Kefa); he is lodged in the house of one Shimon a tanner

by the sea side; who, when he cometh, shall speak unto you.'

33 Immediately therefore I sent to you; and you have well done that you are come. Now therefore are we all here present before God (Elohim), to hear all things that are commanded you of God (Elohim)."

34 Then Peter (Kefa) opened his mouth, and said, "Of a truth I perceive that God (Elohim) is no respecter of persons;

35 But in every nation he that feareth him, and worketh righteousness, is accepted with Him.

36 The word which God (Elohim) sent unto the children of Yisrael, preaching peace by Yahwah haMashiach; (He is Lord of all;)

37 That word, I say, you know, which was published throughout all Judah (Yehudah), and began from Galilee, after the baptism which John (Yochanan) preached;

38 How God (Elohim) anointed Yahwah of Nazareth with the Holy Spirit and with power; who went about doing good, and healing all that were oppressed of the devil; for God (Elohim) was with Him.

39 And we are witnesses of all things which He did both in the land of the Jews (Yehudim), and in Jerusalem (Yerushalayim); whom they slew and hanged on a tree;

40 Him God (Elohim) raised up the third day, and shewed Him openly;

41 Not to all the people, but unto witnesses chosen before of God (Elohim), even to us, who did eat and drink with Him after He rose from the dead.

42 And He commanded us to preach unto the people, and to testify that it is He who was ordained of God (Elohim) to be the Judge of the living and the dead.

43 To Him give all the prophets witness, that through His name (YHWH, Yahwah) whosoever believeth in Him shall receive remission of sins.

44 While Peter (Kefa) yet spake these words, the Holy Spirit (Ruach haQodesh) fell on all them who heard the word.

45 And they of the circumcision who believed were astonished, as many as came with Peter (Kefa), because that on the Gentiles (Goyim) also was poured out the gift of the Holy Spirit (Ruach haQodesh).

46 For they heard them speak with tongues, and magnify God (Elohim). Then answered Peter

(Kefa),

47 "Can any man forbid water, that these should not be baptized, who have received the Holy Spirit (Ruach haQodesh) as well as we?"

48 And he commanded them to be baptized in the name of the Lord (YHWH, Yahwah). Then prayed they him to tarry certain days.

11 And the apostles and brethren that were in Judah (Yehudah) heard that the Gentiles (Goyim) had also received the word of God (Elohim, יהוה (YHWH)).

2 And when Peter (Kefa) was come up to Jerusalem (Yerushalayim), they that were of the circumcision contended with him,

3 Saying, "You wentest in to men uncircumcised, and didst eat with them."

4 But Peter (Kefa) rehearsed the matter from the beginning, and expounded it by order unto them, saying,

5 "I was in the city of Joppa (Yafo) praying; and in a trance I saw a vision: A certain vessel descend, as it had been a great sheet, let down from heaven by four corners; and it came even to me.

6 Upon the which when I had fastened mine eyes, I considered, and saw fourfooted beasts of the earth, and wild beasts, and creeping things, and fowls of the air.

7 And I heard a voice saying unto me, 'Arise, Peter (Kefa); slay and eat.'

8 But I said, 'Not so, my lord (adoni); for nothing common or unclean hath at any time entered into my mouth.'

9 But the voice answered me again from heaven, 'What God (Elohim) hath cleansed, that call not you common.'

10 And this was done three times; and all were drawn up again into heaven.

11 And, behold, immediately there were three men already come unto the house where I was, sent from Caesarea unto me.

12 And the Spirit bade me go with them, nothing doubting. Moreover these six brethren accompanied me, and we entered into the man's house.

13 And he shewed us how he had seen an angel in his house, who stood and said unto him, 'Send men to Joppa (Yafo), and call for Shimon, whose surname is Peter (Kefa);

14 Who shall tell you words, whereby you and all your house shall be saved.'

15 And as I began to speak, the Holy Spirit (Ruach haQodesh) fell on them, as on us at the beginning.

16 Then remembered I the word of the Lord (Yahwah), how that He said, 'John (Yochanan) indeed baptized with water; but you shall be baptized with the Holy Spirit (Ruach haQodesh).

17 Forasmuch then as God (Elohim) gave them the like gift as He did unto us, who believed on the Lord (Adonai) Yahwah haMashiach; what was I, that I could withstand God (Elohim)?"

18 When they heard these things, they held their peace, and glorified יהוה (YHWH), saying, "Then hath יהוה (YHWH) also to the Gentiles (Goyim) granted repentance unto life."

19 Now they who were scattered abroad upon the persecution that arose about Stephen travelled as far as Phenice, and Cyprus, and Antioch, preaching the word to none but unto the Jews (Yehudim) only.

20 And some of them were men of Cyprus and Cyrene, who, when they were come to Antioch, spake unto the Grecians, preaching the Lord Yahwah (Adonai YHWH).

21 And the hand of יהוה (YHWH) was with them; and a great number believed, and turned unto the Lord (YHWH).

22 Then tidings of these things came unto the ears of the assembly which was in Jerusalem (Yerushalayim); and they sent forth Barnabas, that he should go as far as Antioch.

23 Who, when he came, and had seen the grace of God (Elohim, יהוה (YHWH)), was glad, and exhorted them all, that with purpose of heart they would cleave unto the Lord (Yahwah).

24 For he was a good man, and full of the Holy Spirit (Ruach haQodesh) and of faith; and much people was added unto the Lord (YHWH).

25 Then departed Barnabas to Tarsus, for to seek Shaul;

26 And when he had found him, he brought him unto Antioch. And it came to pass, that a whole year they assembled themselves with the assembly, and taught much people. And the disciples were called [B64]Mashiachiyim (followers of Messiah) first in Antioch.

27 And in these days came prophets from Jerusalem (Yerushalayim) unto Antioch.

28 And there stood up one of them named Agabus, and signified by the Spirit that there should be great dearth throughout all the world;

which came to pass in the days of Claudius Caesar.

29 Then the disciples, every man according to his ability, determined to send relief unto the brethren who dwelt in Judah (Yehudah);

30 Which also they did, and sent it to the elders by the hands of Barnabas and Shaul.

12 Now about that time Herod the king stretched forth his hands to vex certain of the assembly.

2 And he killed Jacob (Yaaqov) the brother of John (Yochanan) with the sword.

3 And because he saw it pleased the Jews (Yehudim), he proceeded further to take Peter (Kefa) also. (Then were the days of unleavened bread.)

4 And when he had apprehended him, he put him in prison, and delivered him to four quaternions of soldiers to keep him; intending after B19Passover (Pesach) to bring him forth to the people.

5 Peter (Kefa) therefore was kept in prison; but prayer was made without ceasing of the assembly unto God (Elohim) for him.

6 And when Herod would have brought him forth, the same night Peter (Kefa) was sleeping between two soldiers, bound with two chains; and the keepers before the door kept the prison.

7 And, behold, the angel of יהוה came upon him, and a light shined in the prison; and he smote Peter (Kefa) on the side, and raised him up, saying, "Arise up quickly." And his chains fell off from his hands.

8 And the angel said unto him, "Gird yourself, and bind on your sandals." And so he did. And he saith unto him, "Cast your garment about you, and follow me."

9 And he went out, and followed him; and wist not that it was true which was done by the angel; but thought he saw a vision.

10 When they were past the first and the second ward, they came unto the iron gate that leadeth unto the city; which opened to them of his own accord; and they went out, and passed on through one street; and forthwith the angel departed from him.

11 And when Peter (Kefa) was come to himself, he said, "Now I know of a surety, that יהוה hath sent His angel, and hath delivered me out of the hand of Herod, and from all the expectation of the people of the Jews (Yehudim).

12 And when he had considered the thing, he came to the house of Mary (Miryam) the mother of John (Yochanan), whose surname was Mark (Marqos); where many were gathered together praying.

13 And as Peter (Kefa) knocked at the door of the gate, a damsel came to hearken, named Rhoda.

14 And when she knew Peter (Kefa)'s voice, she opened not the gate for gladness, but ran in, and told how Peter (Kefa) stood before the gate.

15 And they said unto her, "You are mad." But she constantly affirmed that it was even so. Then said they, "It is his angel."

16 But Peter (Kefa) continued knocking; and when they had opened the door, and saw him, they were astonished.

17 But he, beckoning unto them with the hand to hold their peace, declared unto them how the Lord (YHWH) had brought him out of the prison. And he said, "Go shew these things unto Jacob (Yaaqov), and to the brethren." And he departed, and went into another place.

18 Now as soon as it was day, there was no small stir among the soldiers, what was become of Peter (Kefa).

19 And when Herod had sought for him, and found him not, he examined the keepers, and commanded that they should be put to death. And he went down from Judah (Yehudah) to Caesarea, and there abode.

20 And Herod was highly displeased with them of Tyre and Sidon; but they came with one accord to him, and, having made Blastus the king's chamberlain their friend, desired peace; because their country was nourished by the king's country.

21 And upon a set day Herod, arrayed in royal apparel, sat upon his throne, and made an oration unto them.

22 And the people gave a shout, saying, "It is the voice of a god (elohim), and not of a man."

23 And immediately the angel of יהוה smote him, because he gave not יהוה (YHWH) the glory; and he was eaten of worms, and gave up the spirit.

24 But the word of God (Elohim, יהוה (YHWH)) grew and multiplied.

25 And Barnabas and Shaul returned from Jerusalem (Yerushalayim), when they had fulfilled their ministry, and took with them

John (Yochanan), whose surname was Mark.

13 Now there were in the assembly that was at Antioch certain prophets and teachers; as Barnabas, and Shimon that was called Niger, and Lucius of Cyrene, and Manaen, who had been brought up with Herod the tetrarch, and Shaul.

2 As they ministered to יהוה, and fasted, the Holy Spirit (Ruach haQodesh) said, "Separate Me Barnabas and Shaul for the work whereunto I have called them."

3 And when they had fasted and prayed, and laid their hands on them, they sent them away.

4 So they, being sent forth by the Holy Spirit (Ruach haQodesh), departed unto Seleucia; and from thence they sailed to Cyprus.

5 And when they were at Salamis, they preached the word of God (Elohim, יהוה (YHWH)) in the synagogues of the Jews (Yehudim); and they had also John (Yochanan) to their minister.

6 And when they had gone through the isle unto Paphos, they found a certain sorcerer, a false prophet, a Jew (Yehudi), whose name was Barjesus (Bar-Yeshua);

7 Who was with the deputy of the country, Sergius Paulus, a prudent man; who called for Barnabas and Shaul, and desired to hear the word of God (Elohim, יהוה (YHWH)).

8 But Elymas the sorcerer (for so is his name by interpretation) withstood them, seeking to turn away the deputy from the faith.

9 Then [A73]Shaul, (who also is called [A74]Paul,) filled with the Holy Spirit (Ruach haQodesh), set his eyes on him,

10 And said, "O full of all subtilty and all mischief, you child of the devil, you enemy of all righteousness, wilt you not cease to pervert the right ways of יהוה?" – *Prov. 10:9*

11 And now, behold, the hand of יהוה (YHWH) is upon you, and you shalt be blind, not seeing the sun for a season. And immediately there fell on him a mist and a darkness; and he went about seeking some to lead him by the hand.

12 Then the deputy, when he saw what was done, believed, being astonished at the doctrine of the Lord (Yahwah).

13 Now when Paul and his company loosed from Paphos, they came to Perga in Pamphylia; and John (Yochanan) departing from them returned to Jerusalem (Yerushalayim).

14 But when they departed from Perga, they came to Antioch in Pisidia, and went into the synagogue on the Shabbat day, and sat down.

15 And after the reading of the Torah and the Prophets (Nevi'im), the rulers of the synagogue sent unto them, saying, "You men and brethren, if you have any word of exhortation for the people, say on."

16 Then Paul stood up, and beckoning with his hand said, "Men of Yisrael, and you that fear God (Elohim), give audience.

17 The God (Elohim) of this people of Yisrael chose our fathers, and exalted the people when they dwelt as strangers in the land of Egypt (Mitsrayim), and with a high arm brought He them out of it. –*Exo.6:6; 12:51*

18 And about the time of forty years suffered He their manners in the wilderness. – *Exo. 16:35; Num. 14:34*

19 And when He had destroyed seven nations in the land of Chanaan, He divided their land to them by lot. – *Deu.7:1*

20 And after that He gave unto them judges about the space of four hundred and fifty years, until Shamuel the prophet. – *Judg. 2:16*

21 And afterward they desired a king; and God (Elohim) gave unto them Shaul the son of Cis, a man of the tribe of Benjamin (Binyamin), by the space of forty years.

22 And when He had removed him, He raised up unto them Dawid to be their king; to whom also He gave testimony, and said, 'I have found Dawid the son of Jesse (Yishai), a man after Mine own heart, who shall fulfil all My will.'

23 Of this man's seed hath God (Elohim) according to His promise raised unto Yisrael a Savior, Yahwah;

24 When John (Yochanan) had first preached before His coming the baptism of repentance to all the people of Yisrael.

25 And as John (Yochanan) fulfilled his course, he said, 'Whom think you that I am? I am not He. But, behold, there cometh One after me, whose shoes of His feet I am not worthy to loose.'

26 Men and brethren, children of the stock of Avraham, and whosoever among you feareth God (Elohim, יהוה (YHWH)), to you is the word of this salvation sent.

27 For they that dwell at Jerusalem (Yerushalayim), and their rulers, because they knew Him not, nor yet the voices of the prophets

who are read every Shabbat day, they have fulfilled them in condemning Him.

28 And though they found no cause of death in Him, yet desired they Pilate that He should be slain.

29 And when they had fulfilled all that was written of Him, they took Him down from the tree, and laid Him in a sepulchre.

30 But God (Elohim) raised Him from the dead;

31 And He was seen many days of them who came up with Him from Galilee to Jerusalem (Yerushalayim), who are His witnesses unto the people.

32 And we declare unto you glad tidings, how that the promise which was made unto the fathers,

33 God (Elohim) hath fulfilled the same unto us their children, in that He hath raised up Yahwah again; as it is also written in the second psalm: 'You are My [B47]Humanity, this day have I begotten You.' – *Psa. 2:7*

34 And as concerning that He raised Him up from the dead, now no more to return to corruption, He said on this wise, 'I will give You the sure mercies of Dawid.' – *Isa. 55:3*

35 Wherefore He saith also in another psalm: 'You shalt not allow Your Holy One to see corruption.' – *Psa. 6:10*

36 For Dawid, after he had served his own generation by the will of God (Elohim, יהוה (YHWH)), fell on sleep, and was laid unto his fathers, and saw corruption;

37 But He, whom God (Elohim) raised again, saw no corruption.

38 Be it known unto you therefore, men and brethren, that through this Man is preached unto you the forgiveness of sins;

39 And by Him all that believe are justified from all things, from which you could not be justified by the teaching of Moses (torat Mosheh).

40 Beware therefore, lest that come upon you, which is spoken of in the prophets:

41 'Behold, you despisers, and wonder, and perish; for I work a work in your days, a work which you shall in no wise believe, though a man declares it unto you.'" – *Hab.1:5*

42 And when the Jews (Yehudim) were gone out of the synagogue, the Gentiles (Goyim) besought that these words might be preached to them the next Shabbat.

43 Now when the congregation was broken up,

many of the Jews (Yehudim) and religious proselytes followed Paul and Barnabas; who, speaking to them, persuaded them to continue in the grace of God (Elohim, יהוה (YHWH)).

44 And the next Shabbat day came almost the whole city together to hear the word of God (Elohim, יהוה (YHWH)).

45 But when the Jews (Yehudim) saw the multitudes, they were filled with envy, and spake against those things which were spoken by Paul, contradicting and blaspheming.

46 Then Paul and Barnabas waxed bold, and said, "It was necessary that the word of God (Elohim, יהוה (YHWH)) should first have been spoken to you; but seeing you put it from you, and judge yourselves unworthy of everlasting life, behold, we turn to the Gentiles (Goyim).

47 For so hath יהוה commanded us, saying, 'I have set you to be a light of the Gentiles (Goyim), that you shouldest be for salvation unto the ends of the earth.' – *Isa. 49:6*

48 And when the Gentiles (Goyim) heard this, they were glad, and glorified the word of God (Elohim, יהוה (YHWH)) and as many as were ordained to eternal life believed.

49 And the word of God (Elohim, יהוה (YHWH)) was published throughout all the region.

50 But the Jews (Yehudim) stirred up the devout and honourable women, and the chief men of the city, and raised persecution against Paul and Barnabas, and expelled them out of their coasts.

51 But they shook off the dust of their feet against them, and came unto Iconium.

52 And the disciples were filled with joy, and with the Holy Spirit (Ruach haQodesh).

14 And it came to pass in Iconium, that they went both together into the synagogue of the Jews (Yehudim), and so spake, that a great multitude both of the Jews (Yehudim) and also of the Greeks believed.

2 But the unbelieving Jews (Yehudim) stirred up the Gentiles (Goyim), and made their minds evil affected against the brethren.

3 Long time therefore abode they speaking boldly in יהוה (YHWH) who gave testimony unto the word of His grace, and granted signs and wonders to be done by their hands.

4 But the multitude of the city was divided; and part held with the Jews (Yehudim), and part with the apostles.

5 And when there was an assault made both

of the Gentiles (Goyim), and also of the Jews (Yehudim) with their rulers, to use them despitefully, and to stone them,

6 They were ware of it, and fled unto Lystra and Derbe, cities of Lycaonia, and unto the region that lieth round about:

7 And there they preached the gospel (good news).

8 And there sat a certain man at Lystra, impotent in his feet, being a cripple from his mother's womb, who never had walked;

9 The same heard Paul speak; who stedfastly beholding him, and perceiving that he had faith to be healed,

10 Said with a loud voice, "Stand upright on your feet!" And he leaped and walked.

11 And when the people saw what Paul had done, they lifted up their voices, saying in the speech of Lycaonia, "The gods (elohim) are come down to us in the likeness of men."

12 And they called Barnabas, [B37]Jupiter (Zeus); and Paul, [B38]Mercurius (Hermes), because he was the chief speaker.

13 Then the priest (kohen) of Jupiter (Zeus) who was before their city, brought oxen and garlands unto the gates, and would have done sacrifice with the people.

14 Who when the apostles, Barnabas and Paul, heard of, they rent their clothes, and ran in among the people, crying out,

15 And saying, "Sirs, why do you these things? We also are men of like passions with you, and preach unto you that you should turn from these vanities unto the living God (Elohim), who made heaven, and earth, and the sea, and all things that are therein;

16 Who in times past allowed all nations to walk in their own ways.

17 Nevertheless He left not Himself without witness, in that He did good, and gave us rain from heaven, and fruitful seasons, filling our hearts with food and gladness."

18 And with these sayings scarce restrained they the people, that they had not done sacrifice unto them.

19 And there came thither certain Jews (Yehudim) from Antioch and Iconium, who persuaded the people, and, having stoned Paul, drew him out of the city, supposing he had been dead.

20 Howbeit, as the disciples stood round about him, he rose up, and came into the city; and the next day he departed with Barnabas to Derbe.

21 And when they had preached the gospel (good news) to that city, and had taught many, they returned again to Lystra, and to Iconium, and Antioch,

22 Confirming the souls of the disciples, and exhorting them to continue in the faith, and that we must through much tribulation enter into the kingdom of God (Elohim, יהוה (YHWH)).

23 And when they had ordained them elders in every assembly, and had prayed with fasting, they commended them to the Lord (Yahwah), on whom they believed.

24 And after they had passed throughout Pisidia, they came to Pamphylia.

25 And when they had preached the word in Perga, they went down into Attalia;

26 And thence sailed to Antioch, from whence they had been recommended to the grace of God (Elohim, יהוה (YHWH)) for the work which they fulfilled.

27 And when they were come, and had gathered the assembly together, they rehearsed all that God (Elohim) had done with them, and how He had opened the door of faith unto the Gentiles (Goyim).

28 And there they abode long time with the disciples.

15 And certain men who came down from Judah (Yehudah) taught the brethren, and said, "Except you be circumcised after the manner of Moses (Mosheh), you cannot be saved."

2 When therefore Paul and Barnabas had no small dissension and disputation with them, they determined that Paul and Barnabas, and certain other of them, should go up to Jerusalem (Yerushalayim) unto the apostles and elders about this question.

3 And being brought on their way by the assembly, they passed through Phenice and Samaria, declaring the conversion of the Gentiles (Goyim); and they caused great joy unto all the brethren.

4 And when they were come to Jerusalem (Yerushalayim), they were received of the assembly, and of the apostles and elders, and they declared all things that God (Elohim, יהוה (YHWH)) had done with them.

5 But there rose up certain of the sect of the

Pharisees who believed, saying, "That it was needful to circumcise them, and to command them to keep the teaching of Moses (torat Mosheh).

6 And the apostles and elders came together for to consider of this matter.

7 And when there had been much disputing, Peter (Kefa) rose up, and said unto them, "Men and brethren, you know how that a good while ago God (Elohim) made choice among us, that the Gentiles (Goyim) by my mouth should hear the word of the gospel (good news), and believe.

8 And God (Elohim), who knoweth the hearts, bare them witness, giving them the Holy Spirit (Ruach haQodesh), even as He did unto us;

9 And put no difference between us and them, purifying their hearts by faith.

10 Now therefore why tempt you God (Elohim), to put a yoke upon the neck of the disciples, who neither our fathers nor we were able to bear?

11 But we believe that through the grace of Lord (Adonai) Yahwah haMashiach we shall be saved, even as they.

12 Then all the multitude kept silence, and gave audience to Barnabas and Paul, declaring what miracles and wonders God (Elohim) had wrought among the Gentiles (Goyim) by them.

13 And after they had held their peace, James (Yaaqov) answered, saying, "Men and brethren, hearken unto me:

14 Shimon hath declared how יהוה (YHWH, Yahwah) at the first did visit the Gentiles (Goyim), to take out of them a people for His name.

15 And to this agree the words of the prophets, as it is written:

16 'After this I will return, and will build again the tabernacle of Dawid, which is fallen down; and I will build again the ruins thereof, and I will set it up; – Amos 9:11

17 That the residue of men might seek after יהוה (YHWH) even all the Gentiles (Goyim), upon whom My name is called, saith יהוה (YHWH) who doeth all these things.' – Amos 9:12

18 Known unto יהוה (YHWH) are all His works from the beginning of the world.

19 Wherefore my sentence is, that we trouble not them, who from among the Gentiles (Goyim) are turned to יהוה (YHWH);

20 But that we write unto them, that they abstain from pollutions of idols, and from fornication,

and from things strangled, and from blood.

21 For Moses (Mosheh) of old time hath in every city them that preach him, being read in the synagogues every Shabbat day."

22 Then pleased it the apostles and elders, with the whole assembly, to send chosen men of their own company to Antioch with Paul and Barnabas; namely, Judah (Yehudah) surnamed Barsabas, and Silas, chief men among the brethren;

23 And they wrote letters by them after this manner: "The apostles and elders and brethren send greeting unto the brethren who are of the Gentiles (Goyim) in Antioch and Syria and Cilicia.

24 Forasmuch as we have heard, that certain who went out from us have troubled you with words, subverting your souls, saying, 'You must be circumcised, and keep the B28alaw (torah);' to whom we gave no such commandment.

25 It seemed good unto us, being assembled with one accord, to send chosen men unto you with our beloved Barnabas and Paul,

26 Men that have hazarded their lives for the name of our Lord (Adonai) Yahwah haMashiach.

27 We have sent therefore Judah (Yehudah) and Silas, who shall also tell you the same things by mouth.

28 For it seemed good to the Holy Spirit, and to us, to lay upon you no greater burden than these necessary things:

29 That you abstain from foods offered to idols, and from blood, and from things strangled, and from fornication; from which if you keep yourselves, you shall do well. Fare you well."

30 So when they were dismissed, they came to Antioch; and when they had gathered the multitude together, they delivered the epistle;

31 Which when they had read, they rejoiced for the consolation.

32 And Judah (Yehudah) and Silas, being prophets also themselves, exhorted the brethren with many words, and confirmed them.

33 And after they had tarried there a space, they were let go in peace from the brethren unto the apostles.

34 Notwithstanding it pleased Silas to abide there still.

35 Paul also and Barnabas continued in Antioch, teaching and preaching the word of God (Elohim, יהוה (YHWH)) with many others also.

36 And some days after Paul said unto Barnabas, 'Let us go again and visit our brethren in every city where we have preached the word of יהוה (YHWH) and see how they do.

37 And Barnabas determined to take with them John (Yochanan), whose surname was Mark.

38 But Paul thought not good to take him with them, who departed from them from Pamphylia, and went not with them to the work.

39 And the contention was so sharp between them, that they departed asunder one from the other; and so Barnabas took Mark, and sailed unto Cyprus;

40 And Paul chose Silas, and departed, being recommended by the brethren unto the grace of God (Elohim, יהוה (YHWH)).

41 And he went through Syria and Cilicia, confirming the assemblies (ekklesias).

16 Then came he to Derbe and Lystra; and, behold, a certain disciple was there, named Timotheus, the son of a certain woman, who was a Jewess (Yehudit), and believed; but his father was a Greek;

2 Who was well reported of by the brethren that were at Lystra and Iconium.

3 Him would Paul have to go forth with him; and took and circumcised him because of the Jews (Yehudim) who were in those quarters; for they knew all that his father was a Greek.

4 And as they went through the cities, they delivered them the decrees for to keep, that were ordained of the apostles and elders which were at Jerusalem (Yerushalayim).

5 And so were the assemblies (ekklesias) established in the faith, and increased in number daily.

6 Now when they had gone throughout Phrygia and the region of Galatia, and were forbidden of the Holy Spirit (Ruach haQodesh) to preach the word in Asia,

7 After they were come to Mysia, they assayed to go into Bithynia; but the Spirit allowed them not.

8 And they passing by Mysia came down to Troas.

9 And a vision appeared to Paul in the night: There stood a man of Macedonia, and prayed him, saying, "Come over into Macedonia, and help us."

10 And after he had seen the vision, immediately we endeavoured to go into Macedonia, assuredly gathering that God (Elohim) had called us for to preach the gospel (good news) unto them.

11 Therefore loosing from Troas, we came with a straight course to Samothracia, and the next day to Neapolis;

12 And from thence to Philippi, which is the chief city of that part of Macedonia, and a colony; and we were in that city abiding certain days.

13 And on the Shabbat we went out of the city by a river side, where prayer was wont to be made; and we sat down, and spake unto the women who resorted thither.

14 And a certain woman named Lydia, a seller of purple, of the city of Thyatira, who worshipped God (Elohim), heard us; whose heart יהוה (YHWH) opened, that she attended unto the things which were spoken of Paul.

15 And when she was baptized, and her household, she besought us, saying, "If you have judged me to be faithful to the Lord (YHWH), come into my house, and abide there." And she constrained us.

16 And it came to pass, as we went to prayer, a certain damsel possessed with a spirit of divination met us, who brought her masters much gain by soothsaying;

17 The same followed Paul and us, and cried, saying, "These men are the servants of the Most High God (El Elyon), who shew unto us the way of salvation."

18 And this did she many days. But Paul, being grieved, turned and said to the spirit, "I command you in the name of Yahwah haMashiach to come out of her." And he came out the same hour.

19 And when her masters saw that the hope of their gains was gone, they caught Paul and Silas, and drew them into the marketplace unto the rulers,

20 And brought them to the magistrates, saying, "These men, being Jews (Yehudim), do exceedingly trouble our city,

21 And teach customs, which are not lawful for us to receive, neither to observe, being Romans."

22 And the multitude rose up together against them; and the magistrates rent off their clothes, and commanded to beat them.

23 And when they had laid many stripes upon them, they cast them into prison, charging the

jailor to keep them safely:

24 Who, having received such a charge, thrust them into the inner prison, and made their feet fast in the stocks.

25 And at midnight Paul and Silas prayed, and sang praises unto יהוה (YHWH); and the prisoners heard them.

26 And suddenly there was a great earthquake, so that the foundations of the prison were shaken; and immediately all the doors were opened, and every one's bands were loosed.

27 And the keeper of the prison awaking out of his sleep, and seeing the prison doors open, he drew out his sword, and would have killed himself, supposing that the prisoners had been fled.

28 But Paul cried with a loud voice, saying, "Do yourself no harm; for we are all here."

29 Then he called for a light, and sprang in, and came trembling, and fell down before Paul and Silas,

30 And brought them out, and said, "Sirs, what must I do to be saved?"

31 And they said, "Believe on the Lord (Adon) Yahwah haMashiach, and you shalt be saved, and your house."

32 And they spake unto him the word of God (Elohim, יהוה (YHWH)) and to all that were in his house.

33 And he took them the same hour of the night, and washed their stripes; and was baptized, he and all his, straightway.

34 And when he had brought them into his house, he set food before them, and rejoiced, believing in יהוה (YHWH) with all his house.

35 And when it was day, the magistrates sent the serjeants, saying, "Let those men go."

36 And the keeper of the prison told this saying to Paul, "The magistrates have sent to let you go; now therefore depart, and go in peace."

37 But Paul said unto them, "They have beaten us openly uncondemned, being Romans, and have cast us into prison; and now do they thrust us out privily? Nay verily; but let them come themselves and fetch us out."

38 And the serjeants told these words unto the magistrates; and they feared, when they heard that they were Romans.

39 And they came and besought them, and brought them out, and desired them to depart out of the city.

40 And they went out of the prison, and entered into the house of Lydia; and when they had seen the brethren, they comforted them, and departed.

17 Now when they had passed through Amphipolis and Apollonia, they came to Thessalonica, where was a synagogue of the Jews (Yehudim);

2 And Paul, as his manner was, went in unto them, and three Shabbat days reasoned with them out of the scriptures,

3 Opening and alleging, that the Messiah (haMashiach) must needs have suffered, and risen again from the dead; and that "This Yahwah, whom I preach unto you, is the Messiah (haMashiach)."

4 And some of them believed, and consorted with Paul and Silas; and of the devout Greeks a great multitude, and of the chief women not a few.

5 But the Jews (Yehudim) who believed not, moved with envy, took unto them certain lewd fellows of the baser sort, and gathered a company, and set all the city on an uproar, and assaulted the house of Jason, and sought to bring them out to the people.

6 And when they found them not, they drew Jason and certain brethren unto the rulers of the city, crying, "These that have turned the world upside down are come hither also;

7 Whom Jason hath received; and these all do contrary to the decrees of Caesar, saying that there is another king, Yahwah."

8 And they troubled the people and the rulers of the city, when they heard these things.

9 And when they had taken security of Jason, and of the other, they let them go.

10 And the brethren immediately sent away Paul and Silas by night unto Berea; who coming thither went into the synagogue of the Jews (Yehudim).

11 These were more noble than those in Thessalonica, in that they received the word with all readiness of mind, and searched the scriptures daily, whether those things were so.

12 Therefore many of them believed; also of honourable women who were Greeks, and of men, not a few.

13 But when the Jews (Yehudim) of Thessalonica had knowledge that the word of God (Elohim, יהוה (YHWH)) was preached of Paul at Berea,

they came thither also, and stirred up the people.

14 And then immediately the brethren sent away Paul to go as it was to the sea; but Silas and Timotheus abode there still.

15 And they that conducted Paul brought him unto Athens; and receiving a commandment unto Silas and Timotheus for to come to him with all speed, they departed.

16 Now while Paul waited for them at Athens, his spirit was stirred in him, when he saw the city wholly given to idolatry.

17 Therefore disputed he in the synagogue with the Jews (Yehudim), and with the devout persons, and in the market daily with them that met with him.

18 Then certain philosophers of the Epicureans, and of the Stoicks, encountered him. And some said, "What will this babbler say?" Other said, "He seemeth to be a setter forth of foreign god (elohim);" because he preached unto them Yahwah, and the resurrection.

19 And they took him, and brought him unto Areopagus, saying, "May we know what this new doctrine, whereof you speakest, is?

20 For you bringest certain strange things to our ears; we would know therefore what these things mean."

21 (For all the Athenians and strangers who were there spent their time in nothing else, but either to tell, or to hear some new thing.)

22 Then Paul stood in the midst of Mars' hill, and said, "You men of Athens, I perceive that in all things you are too superstitious.

23 For as I passed by, and beheld your devotions, I found an altar with this inscription, 'To The Unknown God (Elohim)' whom therefore you ignorantly worship, Him declare I unto you.

24 יהוה (YHWH) that made the world and all things therein, seeing that He is the Lord (Adonai) of heaven and earth, dwelleth not in temples made with hands;

25 Neither is worshipped with men's hands, as though He needed any thing, seeing He giveth to all life, and breath, and all things;

26 And hath made of one blood all nations of men for to dwell on all the face of the earth, and hath determined the times before appointed, and the bounds of their habitation;

27 That they should seek יהוה (YHWH), if haply they might feel after Him, and find Him, though He be not far from every one of us;

28 For in Him we live, and move, and have our being; as certain also of your own poets have said, 'For we are also His offspring.'

29 Forasmuch then as we are the offspring of God (Elohim), we ought not to think that the Godhead (Divine nature) is like unto gold, or silver, or stone, graven by art and man's device.

30 And the times of this ignorance God (Elohim, יהוה (YHWH)) winked at; but now commandeth all men every where to repent;

31 Because He hath appointed a day, in the which He will judge the world in righteousness by that Man (Yahwah haMashiach) whom He hath ordained; whereof He hath given assurance unto all men, in that He hath raised Him from the dead."

32 And when they heard of the resurrection of the dead, some mocked; and others said, "We will hear you again of this matter."

33 So Paul departed from among them.

34 Howbeit certain men clave unto him, and believed; among the which was Dionysius the Areopagite, and a woman named Damaris, and others with them.

18 After these things Paul departed from Athens, and came to Corinth;

2 And found a certain Jew (Yehudi) named Aquila, born in Pontus, lately come from Italy, with his wife Priscilla; (because that Claudius had commanded all Jews (Yehudim) to depart from Rome;) and came unto them.

3 And because he was of the same craft, he abode with them, and wrought; for by their occupation they were tentmakers.

4 And he reasoned in the synagogue every Shabbat, and persuaded the Jews (Yehudim) and the Greeks.

5 And when Silas and Timotheus were come from Macedonia, Paul was pressed in the spirit, and testified to the Jews (Yehudim) that Yahwah was the Messiah (haMashiach).

6 And when they opposed themselves, and blasphemed, he shook his raiment, and said unto them, "Your blood be upon your own heads; I am clean; from henceforth I will go unto the Gentiles (Goyim)."

7 And he departed thence, and entered into a certain man's house, named Yustus, one that worshipped God (Elohim), whose house joined hard to the synagogue.

8 And Crispus, the chief ruler of the synagogue,

believed on the Lord (Yahwah) with all his house; and many of the Corinthians hearing believed, and were baptized.

9 Then spake the Lord (Yahwah) to Paul in the night by a vision, "Be not afraid, but speak, and hold not your peace;

10 For I am with you, and no man shall set on you to hurt you; for I have much people in this city."

11 And he continued there a year and six months, teaching the word of God (Elohim, יהוה (YHWH)) among them.

12 And when Gallio was the deputy of Achaia, the Jews (Yehudim) made insurrection with one accord against Paul, and brought him to the judgment seat,

13 Saying, "This fellow persuadeth men to worship God (Elohim) contrary to the law (torah)."

14 And when Paul was now about to open his mouth, Gallio said unto the Jews (Yehudim), "If it was a matter of wrong or wicked lewdness, O you Jews (Yehudim), reason would that I should bear with you;

15 But if it be a question of words and names, and of your law (torah), look you to it; for I will be no judge of such matters."

16 And he drave them from the judgment seat.

17 Then all the Greeks took Sosthenes, the chief ruler of the synagogue, and beat him before the judgment seat. And Gallio cared for none of those things.

18 And Paul after this tarried there yet a good while, and then took his leave of the brethren, and sailed thence into Syria, and with him Priscilla and Aquila; having shorn his head in Cenchrea; for he had a vow.

19 And he came to Ephesus, and left them there; but he himself entered into the synagogue, and reasoned with the Jews (Yehudim).

20 When they desired him to tarry longer time with them, he consented not;

21 But bade them farewell, saying, "I must by all means keep this feast that cometh in Jerusalem (Yerushalayim); but I will return again unto you, if God (Elohim) will." And he sailed from Ephesus.

22 And when he had landed at Caesarea, and gone up, and saluted the assembly, he went down to Antioch.

23 And after he had spent some time there,

he departed, and went over all the country of Galatia and Phrygia in order, strengthening all the disciples.

24 And a certain Jew (Yehudi) named Apollos, born at Alexandria, an eloquent man, and mighty in the scriptures, came to Ephesus.

25 This man was instructed in the way of the Lord (YHWH); and being fervent in the spirit, he spake and taught diligently the things of the Lord (YHWH), knowing only the baptism of John (Yochanan).

26 And he began to speak boldly in the synagogue; whom when Aquila and Priscilla had heard, they took him unto them, and expounded unto him the way of יהוה (YHWH) more perfectly.

27 And when he was disposed to pass into Achaia, the brethren wrote, exhorting the disciples to receive him: who, when he was come, helped them much which had believed through grace:

28 For he mightily convinced the Jews (Yehudim), and that publicly, shewing by the scriptures that Yahwah (YHWH) was the Messiah (haMashiach).

19 And it came to pass, that, while Apollos was at Corinth, Paul having passed through the upper coasts came to Ephesus; and finding certain disciples,

2 He said unto them, "Have you received the Holy Spirit (Ruach haQodesh) since you believed?" And they said unto him, "We have not so much as heard whether there be any Holy Spirit."

3 And he said unto them, "Unto what then were you baptized?" And they said, "Unto John (Yochanan)'s baptism."

4 Then said Paul, John (Yochanan) verily baptized with the baptism of repentance, saying unto the people, that they should believe on Him who should come after him, that is, on the Messiah (haMashiah) Yahwah."

5 When they heard this, they were baptized in the name of the Lord Yahwah (Adonai YHWH).

6 And when Paul had laid his hands upon them, the Holy Spirit (Ruach haQodesh) came on them; and they spake with tongues, and prophesied.

7 And all the men were about twelve.

8 And he went into the synagogue, and spake boldly for the space of three months, disputing

and persuading the things concerning the kingdom of God (Elohim, יהוה (YHWH)).

9 But when some were hardened, and believed not, but spake evil of that way before the multitude, he departed from them, and separated the disciples, disputing daily in the school of one Tyrannus.

10 And this continued by the space of two years; so that all they who dwelt in Asia heard the word of the Lord Yahwah (Adonai YHWH), both Jews (Yehudim) and Greeks.

11 And God (Elohim) wrought special miracles by the hands of Paul;

12 So that from his body were brought unto the sick handkerchiefs or aprons, and the diseases departed from them, and the evil spirits went out of them.

13 Then certain of the vagabond Jews (Yehudim), exorcists, took upon them to call the name of the Lord Yahwah (Adonai YHWH) over those who had evil spirits, saying, "We adjure you by Yahwah whom Paul preacheth."

14 And there were seven sons of one Sceva, a Jew (Yehudi), and chief of the priests (kohanim), who did so.

15 And the evil spirit answered and said, "Yahwah I know, and Paul I know; but who are you?"

16 And the man in whom the evil spirit was leaped on them, and overcame them, and prevailed against them, so that they fled out of that house naked and wounded.

17 And this was known to all the Jews (Yehudim) and Greeks also dwelling at Ephesus; and fear fell on them all, and the name of the Lord Yahwah (Adonai YHWH) was magnified.

18 And many that believed came, and confessed, and shewed their deeds.

19 Many of them also who used curious arts brought their books together, and burned them before all men; and they counted the price of them, and found it fifty thousand pieces of silver.

20 So mightily grew the word of God (Elohim, יהוה (YHWH)) and prevailed.

21 After these things were ended, Paul purposed in the spirit, when he had passed through Macedonia and Achaia, to go to Jerusalem (Yerushalayim), saying, "After I have been there, I must also see Rome."

22 So he sent into Macedonia two of them that ministered unto him, Timotheus and Erastus; but he himself stayed in Asia for a season.

23 And the same time there arose no small stir about that way.

24 For a certain man named Demetrius, a silversmith, who made silver shrines for Diana, brought no small gain unto the craftsmen;

25 Whom he called together with the workmen of like occupation, and said, "Sirs, you know that by this craft we have our wealth.

26 Moreover you see and hear, that not alone at Ephesus, but almost throughout all Asia, this Paul hath persuaded and turned away much people, saying that they be no gods (elohim), which are made with hands;

27 So that not only this our craft is in danger to be set at nought; but also that the temple of the great goddess Diana should be despised, and her magnificence should be destroyed, whom all Asia and the world worshippeth."

28 And when they heard these sayings, they were full of wrath, and cried out, saying, "Great is Diana of the Ephesians."

29 And the whole city was filled with confusion; and having caught Gaius and Aristarchus, men of Macedonia, Paul's companions in travel, they rushed with one accord into the theatre.

30 And when Paul would have entered in unto the people, the disciples allowed him not.

31 And certain of the chief of Asia, which were his friends, sent unto him, desiring him that he would not adventure himself into the theatre.

32 Some therefore cried one thing, and some another; for the assembly was confused; and the more part knew not wherefore they were come together.

33 And they drew Alexander out of the multitude, the Jews (Yehudim) putting him forward. And Alexander beckoned with the hand, and would have made his defence unto the people.

34 But when they knew that he was a Jew (Yehudi), all with one voice about the space of two hours cried out, "Great is Diana of the Ephesians."

35 And when the townclerk had appeased the people, he said, "You men of Ephesus, what man is there that knoweth not how that the city of the Ephesians is a worshipper of the great goddess Diana, and of the image which fell down from Jupiter (Zeus)?

36 Seeing then that these things cannot be spoken against, you ought to be quiet, and to do nothing rashly.

37 For you have brought hither these men, who are neither robbers of assemblies (ekklesias), nor yet blasphemers of your goddess.

38 Wherefore if Demetrius, and the craftsmen who are with him, have a matter against any man, the courts are open, and there are deputies; let them implead one another.

39 But if you enquire any thing concerning other matters, it shall be determined in a lawful assembly.

40 For we are in danger to be called in question for this day's uproar, there being no cause whereby we may give an account of this concourse."

41 And when he had thus spoken, he dismissed the assembly.

20 And after the uproar was ceased, Paul called unto him the disciples, and embraced them, and departed for to go into Macedonia.

2 And when he had gone over those parts, and had given them much exhortation, he came into Greece,

3 And there abode three months. And when the Jews (Yehudim) laid wait for him, as he was about to sail into Syria, he purposed to return through Macedonia.

4 And there accompanied him into Asia Sopater of Berea; and of the Thessalonians, Aristarchus and Secundus; and Gaius of Derbe, and Timotheus; and of Asia, Tychicus and Trophimus.

5 These going before tarried for us at Troas.

6 And we sailed away from Philippi after the days of unleavened bread, and came unto them to Troas in five days; where we abode seven days.

7 And upon the first day of the week, when the disciples came together to break bread, Paul preached unto them, ready to depart on the morrow; and continued his speech until midnight.

8 And there were many lights in the upper chamber, where they were gathered together.

9 And there sat in a window a certain young man named Eutychus, being fallen into a deep sleep: and as Paul was long preaching, he sunk down with sleep, and fell down from the third loft, and was taken up dead.

10 And Paul went down, and fell on him, and embracing him said, "Trouble not yourselves; for his life is in him."

11 When he therefore was come up again, and had broken bread, and eaten, and talked a long while, even till break of day, so he departed.

12 And they brought the young man alive, and were not a little comforted.

13 And we went before to ship, and sailed unto Assos, there intending to take in Paul; for so had he appointed, minding himself to go afoot.

14 And when he met with us at Assos, we took him in, and came to Mitylene.

15 And we sailed thence, and came the next day over against Chios; and the next day we arrived at Samos, and tarried at Trogyllium; and the next day we came to Miletus.

16 For Paul had determined to sail by Ephesus, because he would not spend the time in Asia; for he hasted, if it was possible for him, to be at Jerusalem (Yerushalayim) the day of B21Pentecost (Chag Shavuot).

17 And from Miletus he sent to Ephesus, and called the elders of the assembly.

18 And when they were come to him, he said unto them, "You know, from the first day that I came into Asia, after what manner I have been with you at all seasons,

19 Serving the Lord (YHWH) with all humility of mind, and with many tears, and temptations, which befell me by the plotting of the Jews (Yehudim);

20 And how I kept back nothing that was profitable unto you, but have shewed you, and have taught you publickly, and from house to house,

21 Testifying both to the Jews (Yehudim), and also to the Greeks, repentance toward God (Elohim), and faith toward our Lord (Adonai) Yahwah haMashiach.

22 And now, behold, I go bound in the spirit unto Jerusalem (Yerushalayim), not knowing the things that shall befall me there;

23 Except that the Holy Spirit (Ruach haQodesh) witnesseth in every city, saying that bonds and afflictions abide me.

24 But none of these things move me, neither count I my life dear unto myself, so that I might finish my course with joy, and the ministry, which I have received of the Lord Yahwah

(Adonai YHWH), to testify the gospel (good news) of the grace of God (Elohim, יהוה (YHWH)).

25 And now, behold, I know that you all, among whom I have gone preaching the kingdom of God (Elohim, יהוה (YHWH)), shall see my face no more.

26 Wherefore I take you to record this day, that I am pure from the blood of all men.

27 For I have not shunned to declare unto you all the counsel of יהוה (YHWH).

28 Take heed therefore unto yourselves, and to all the flock, over the which the Holy Spirit (Ruach haQodesh) hath made you overseers, to feed the assembly of יהוה (YHWH), which He hath purchased with His own blood.

29 For I know this, that after my departing shall grievous wolves enter in among you, not sparing the flock.

30 Also of your own selves shall men arise, speaking perverse things, to draw away disciples after them.

31 Therefore watch, and remember, that by the space of three years I ceased not to warn every one night and day with tears.

32 And now, brethren, I commend you to יהוה (YHWH), and to the word of His grace, which is able to build you up, and to give you an inheritance among all them who are sanctified.

33 I have coveted no man's silver, or gold, or apparel.

34 Yea, you yourselves know, that these hands have ministered unto my necessities, and to them that were with me.

35 I have shewed you all things, how that so labouring you ought to support the weak, and to remember the words of the Lord Yahwah (Adonai YHWH), how He said, 'It is more blessed to give than to receive.'"

36 And when he had thus spoken, he kneeled down, and prayed with them all.

37 And they all wept sore, and fell on Paul's neck, and kissed him,

38 Sorrowing most of all for the words which he spake, that they should see his face no more. And they accompanied him unto the ship.

21 And it came to pass, that after we were gotten from them, and had launched, we came with a straight course unto Coos, and the day following unto Rhodes, and from thence unto Patara;

2 And finding a ship sailing over unto Phenicia, we went aboard, and set forth.

3 Now when we had discovered Cyprus, we left it on the left hand, and sailed into Syria, and landed at Tyre; for there the ship was to unlade her burden.

4 And finding disciples, we tarried there seven days; who said to Paul through the Spirit, that he should not go up to Jerusalem (Yerushalayim).

5 And when we had accomplished those days, we departed and went our way; and they all brought us on our way, with wives and children, till we were out of the city; and we kneeled down on the shore, and prayed.

6 And when we had taken our leave one of another, we took ship; and they returned home again.

7 And when we had finished our course from Tyre, we came to Ptolemais, and saluted the brethren, and abode with them one day.

8 And the next day we that were of Paul's company departed, and came unto Caesarea; and we entered into the house of Philip the evangelist, which was one of the seven; and abode with him.

9 And the same man had four daughters, virgins, who did prophesy.

10 And as we tarried there many days, there came down from Judah (Yehudah) a certain prophet, named Agabus.

11 And when he was come unto us, he took Paul's girdle, and bound his own hands and feet, and said, "Thus saith the Holy Spirit (Ruach haQodesh): 'So shall the Jews (Yehudim) at Jerusalem (Yerushalayim) bind the man that owneth this girdle, and shall deliver him into the hands of the Gentiles (Goyim).'

12 And when we heard these things, both we, and they of that place, besought him not to go up to Jerusalem (Yerushalayim)."

13 Then Paul answered, "What mean you to weep and to break mine heart? For I am ready not to be bound only, but also to die at Jerusalem (Yerushalayim) for the name of the Lord Yahwah (Adonai YHWH)."

14 And when he would not be persuaded, we ceased, saying, "The will of יהוה (YHWH) be done."

15 And after those days we took up our carriages, and went up to Jerusalem (Yerushalayim).

16 There went with us also certain of the

disciples of Caesarea, and brought with them one Mnason of Cyprus, an old disciple, with whom we should lodge.

17 And when we were come to Jerusalem (Yerushalayim), the brethren received us gladly.

18 And the day following Paul went in with us unto Jacob (Yaaqov); and all the elders were present.

19 And when he had saluted them, he declared particularly what things God (Elohim, יהוה (YHWH)) had wrought among the Gentiles (Goyim) by his ministry.

20 And when they heard it, they glorified יהוה (YHWH), and said unto him, "You seest, brother, how many thousands of Jews (Yehudim) there are who believe; and they are all zealous of the Torah;

21 And they are informed of you, that you teachest all the Jews (Yehudim) who are among the Gentiles (Goyim) to forsake Moses (Mosheh), saying that they ought not to circumcise their children, neither to walk after the customs.

22 What is it therefore? The multitude must needs come together; for they will hear that you are come.

23 Do therefore this that we say to you: We have four men who have a vow on them;

24 Them take, and purify yourself with them, and be at charges with them, that they may shave their heads; and all may know that those things, whereof they were informed concerning you, are nothing; but that you yourself also walkest orderly, and keepest the Torah.

25 As touching the Gentiles (Goyim) who believe, we have written and concluded that they observe no such thing, except only that they keep themselves from things offered to idols, and from blood, and from strangled, and from fornication."

26 Then Paul took the men, and the next day purifying himself with them entered into the temple, to signify the accomplishment of the days of purification, until that an offering should be offered for every one of them.

27 And when the seven days were almost ended, the Jews (Yehudim) who were of Asia, when they saw him in the temple, stirred up all the people, and laid hands on him,

28 Crying out, "Men of Yisrael, help! This is the man, that teacheth all men everywhere against the people, and the Torah, and this place; and further brought Greeks also into the temple, and hath polluted this holy place."

29 (For they had seen before with him in the city Trophimus an Ephesian, whom they supposed that Paul had brought into the temple.)

30 And all the city was moved, and the people ran together; and they took Paul, and drew him out of the temple; and forthwith the doors were shut.

31 And as they went about to kill him, tidings came unto the chief captain of the band, that all Jerusalem (Yerushalayim) was in an uproar.

32 Who immediately took soldiers and centurions, and ran down unto them; and when they saw the chief captain and the soldiers, they left beating of Paul.

33 Then the chief captain came near, and took him, and commanded him to be bound with two chains; and demanded who he was, and what he had done.

34 And some cried one thing, some another, among the multitude; and when he could not know the certainty for the tumult, he commanded him to be carried into the castle.

35 And when he came upon the stairs, so it was, that he was borne of the soldiers for the violence of the people.

36 For the multitude of the people followed after, crying, "Away with him!"

37 And as Paul was to be led into the castle, he said unto the chief captain, "May I speak unto you?" Who said, "Canst you speak Greek?

38 Art not you that Egyptian (Mitsri), who before these days madest an uproar, and leddest out into the wilderness four thousand men that were murderers?"

39 But Paul said, "I am a man who am a Jew (Yehudi) of Tarsus, a city in Cilicia, a citizen of no mean city; and, I beseech you, allow me to speak unto the people."

40 And when he had given him licence, Paul stood on the stairs, and beckoned with the hand unto the people. And when there was made a great silence, he spake unto them in the Hebrew tongue, saying,

22 "Men, brethren, and fathers, hear you my defence which I make now unto you.

2 And when they heard that he spake in the Hebrew tongue to them, they kept the more silence; and he saith:

3 "I am verily a man who am a Jew (Yehudi), born in Tarsus, a city in Cilicia, yet brought up in this city at the feet of Gamaliel, and taught according to the perfect manner of the teaching of the fathers, and was zealous toward God (Elohim), as you all are this day.

4 And I persecuted this way unto the death, binding and delivering into prisons both men and women.

5 As also the high priest (kohen hagadol) doth bear me witness, and all the estate of the elders; from whom also I received letters unto the brethren, and went to Damascus, to bring them who were there bound unto Jerusalem (Yerushalayim), for to be punished.

6 And it came to pass, that, as I made my journey, and was come near unto Damascus about noon, suddenly there shone from heaven a great light round about me.

7 And I fell unto the ground, and heard a voice saying unto me, 'Shaul, Shaul, why persecutest you Me?'

8 And I answered, 'Who art You, Lord (Adonai)?' And He said unto me, 'I am Yahwah of Nazareth, whom you persecutest.'

9 And they that were with me saw indeed the light, and were afraid; but they heard not the voice of Him that spake to me.

10 And I said, 'What shall I do, Lord (Adonai)?' And the Lord (YHWH) said unto me, 'Arise, and go into Damascus; and there it shall be told you of all things which are appointed for you to do.'

11 And when I could not see for the glory of that light, being led by the hand of them that were with me, I came into Damascus.

12 And one Ananias, a devout man according to the Torah, having a good report of all the Jews (Yehudim) who dwelt there,

13 Came unto me, and stood, and said unto me, 'Brother Shaul, receive your sight.' And the same hour I looked up upon him.

14 And he said, 'The God (Elohim) of our fathers hath chosen you, that you shouldest know His will, and see that Just One (Tzaddik), and shouldest hear the voice of His mouth.

15 For you shalt be His witness unto all men of what you have seen and heard.

16 And now why tarriest you? Arise, and be baptized, and wash away your sins, calling on the name of [A1]יהוה (YHWH, Yahwah).'

17 And it came to pass, that, when I was come again to Jerusalem (Yerushalayim), even while I prayed in the temple, I was in a trance;

18 And saw Him saying unto me, 'Make haste, and get you quickly out of Jerusalem (Yerushalayim); for they will not receive your testimony concerning Me.'

19 And I said, 'Lord (Adonai), they know that I imprisoned and beat in every synagogue them that believed on You;

20 And when the blood of Your martyr Stephen was shed, I also was standing by, and consenting unto his death, and kept the raiment of them that slew him.'

21 And He said unto me, 'Depart, for I will send you far hence unto the Gentiles (Goyim).'"

22 And they gave him audience unto this word, and then lifted up their voices, and said, "Away with such a fellow from the earth, for it is not fit that he should live."

23 And as they cried out, and cast off their clothes, and threw dust into the air,

24 The chief captain commanded him to be brought into the castle, and bade that he should be examined by scourging; that he might know wherefore they cried so against him.

25 And as they bound him with thongs, Paul said unto the centurion that stood by, "Is it lawful for you to scourge a man that is a Roman, and uncondemned?"

26 When the centurion heard that, he went and told the chief captain, saying, "Take heed what you doest, for this man is a Roman."

27 Then the chief captain came, and said unto him, "Tell me, are you a Roman?" He said, "Yea."

28 And the chief captain answered, "With a great sum obtained I this freedom." And Paul said, "But I was free born."

29 Then straightway they departed from him who should have examined him; and the chief captain also was afraid, after he knew that he was a Roman, and because he had bound him.

30 On the morrow, because he would have known the certainty wherefore he was accused of the Jews (Yehudim), he loosed him from his bands, and commanded the chief priests (kohanim) and all their council to appear, and brought Paul down, and set him before them.

23 And Paul, earnestly beholding the council, said, "Men and brethren, I have

lived in all good conscience before God (Elohim, יהוה (YHWH)) until this day."

2 And the high priest (kohen hagadol) Ananias commanded them that stood by him to smite him on the mouth.

3 Then said Paul unto him, "God (Elohim, יהוה (YHWH)) shall smite you, you whited wall; for sittest you to judge me after the Torah, and commandest me to be smitten contrary to the Torah?"

4 And they that stood by said, "Revilest you God (Elohim)'s high priest (kohen hagadol)?"

5 Then said Paul, "I wist not, brethren, that he was the high priest (kohen hagadol); for it is written: 'You shalt not speak evil of the ruler of your people.'

6 But when Paul perceived that the one part were Sadducees, and the other Pharisees, he cried out in the council, "Men and brethren, I am a Pharisee, the son of a Pharisee; of the hope and resurrection of the dead I am called in question!"

7 And when he had so said, there arose a dissension between the Pharisees and the Sadducees; and the multitude was divided.

8 For the Sadducees say that there is no resurrection, neither angel, nor spirit; but the Pharisees confess both.

9 And there arose a great cry; and the scribes that were of the Pharisees' part arose, and strove, saying, "We find no evil in this man; but if a spirit or an angel hath spoken to him, let us not fight against God (Elohim)."

10 And when there arose a great dissension, the chief captain, fearing lest Paul should have been pulled in pieces of them, commanded the soldiers to go down, and to take him by force from among them, and to bring him into the castle.

11 And the night following the Lord (Yahwah) stood by him, and said, "Be of good cheer, Paul; for as you have testified of Me in Jerusalem (Yerushalayim), so must you bear witness also at Rome."

12 And when it was day, certain of the Jews (Yehudim) banded together, and bound themselves under a curse, saying that they would neither eat nor drink till they had killed Paul.

13 And they were more than forty who had made this conspiracy.

14 And they came to the chief priests (kohanim) and elders, and said, "We have bound ourselves under a great curse, that we will eat nothing until we have slain Paul.

15 Now therefore you with the council signify to the chief captain that he brings him down unto you tomorrow, as though you would enquire something more perfectly concerning him; and we, or ever he come near, are ready to kill him."

16 And when Paul's sister's son heard of their lying in wait, he went and entered into the castle, and told Paul.

17 Then Paul called one of the centurions unto him, and said, "Bring this young man unto the chief captain; for he hath a certain thing to tell him."

18 So he took him, and brought him to the chief captain, and said, "Paul the prisoner called me unto him, and prayed me to bring this young man unto you, who hath something to say unto you."

19 Then the chief captain took him by the hand, and went with him aside privately, and asked him, "What is that you have to tell me?"

20 And he said, "The Jews (Yehudim) have agreed to desire you that you wouldest bring down Paul tomorrow into the council, as though they would enquire somewhat of him more perfectly.

21 But do not you yield unto them; for there lie in wait for him of them more than forty men, who have bound themselves with an oath, that they will neither eat nor drink till they have killed him; and now are they ready, looking for a promise from you."

22 So the chief captain then let the young man depart, and charged him, "See you tell no man that you have shewed these things to me."

23 And he called unto him two centurions, saying, "Make ready two hundred soldiers to go to Caesarea, and horsemen threescore and ten, and spearmen two hundred, at the third hour of the night;

24 And provide them beasts, that they may set Paul on, and bring him safe unto Felix the governor."

25 And he wrote a letter after this manner:

26 Claudius Lysias unto the most excellent governor Felix sendeth greeting.

27 This man was taken of the Jews (Yehudim), and should have been killed of them; then

came I with an army, and rescued him, having understood that he was a Roman.

28 And when I would have known the cause wherefore they accused him, I brought him forth into their council (Sanhedrin);

29 Whom I perceived to be accused of questions of their law (torah), but to have nothing laid to his charge worthy of death or of bonds.

30 And when it was told me how that the Jews (Yehudim) laid wait for the man, I sent straightway to you, and gave commandment to his accusers also to say before you what they had against him. Farewell.

31 Then the soldiers, as it was commanded them, took Paul, and brought him by night to Antipatris.

32 On the morrow they left the horsemen to go with him, and returned to the castle;

33 Who, when they came to Caesarea, and delivered the epistle to the governor, presented Paul also before him.

34 And when the governor had read the letter, he asked of what province he was. And when he understood that he was of Cilicia;

35 "I will hear you," said he, "when your accusers are also come." And he commanded him to be kept in Herod's judgment hall.

24 And after five days Ananias the high priest (kohen hagadol) descended with the elders, and with a certain orator named Tertullus, who informed the governor against Paul.

2 And when he was called forth, Tertullus began to accuse him, saying, "Seeing that by you we enjoy great quietness, and that very worthy deeds are done unto this nation by your providence,

3 We accept it always, and in all places, most noble Felix, with all thankfulness.

4 Notwithstanding, that I be not further tedious unto you, I pray you that you wouldest hear us of your clemency a few words.

5 For we have found this man a pestilent fellow, and a mover of sedition among all the Jews (Yehudim) throughout the world, and a ringleader of the sect of the Nazarenes;

6 Who also hath gone about to profane the temple; whom we took, and would have judged according to our law (torah).

7 But the chief captain Lysias came upon us, and with great violence took him away out of our hands,

8 Commanding his accusers to come unto you; by examining of whom yourself mayest take knowledge of all these things, whereof we accuse him.

9 And the Jews (Yehudim) also assented, saying that these things were so.

10 Then Paul, after that the governor had beckoned unto him to speak, answered, "Forasmuch as I know that you have been of many years a judge unto this nation, I do the more cheerfully answer for myself;

11 Because that you mayest understand, that there are yet but twelve days since I went up to Jerusalem (Yerushalayim) for to worship.

12 And they neither found me in the temple disputing with any man, neither raising up the people, neither in the synagogues, nor in the city.

13 Neither can they prove the things whereof they now accuse me.

14 But this I confess unto you, that after the way which they call heresy, so worship I the God (Elohim) of my fathers, believing all things which are written in the Torah and in the Prophets;

15 And have hope toward God (Elohim), which they themselves also allow, that there shall be a resurrection of the dead, both of the just and unjust.

16 And herein do I exercise myself, to have always a conscience void of offence toward God (Elohim), and toward men.

17 Now after many years I came to bring alms to my nation, and offerings.

18 Whereupon certain Jews (Yehudim) from Asia found me purified in the temple, neither with multitude, nor with tumult.

19 Who ought to have been here before you, and object, if they had ought against me.

20 Or else let these same here say, if they have found any evil doing in me, while I stood before the council,

21 Except it be for this one voice, that I cried standing among them, "Touching the resurrection of the dead I am called in question by you this day."

22 And when Felix heard these things, having more perfect knowledge of that way, he deferred them, and said, "When Lysias the chief captain shall come down, I will know the uttermost of

your matter."

23 And he commanded a centurion to keep Paul, and to let him have liberty, and that he should forbid none of his acquaintance to minister or come unto him.

24 And after certain days, when Felix came with his wife Drusilla, who was a Jewess (Yehudit), he sent for Paul, and heard him concerning the faith in the Messiah (haMashiach).

25 And as he reasoned of righteousness, temperance, and judgment to come, Felix trembled, and answered, "Go your way for this time; when I have a convenient season, I will call for you."

26 He hoped also that money should have been given him of Paul, that he might loose him; wherefore he sent for him the oftener, and communed with him.

27 But after two years Porcius Festus came into Felix' room; and Felix, willing to shew the Jews (Yehudim) a pleasure, left Paul bound.

25 Now when Festus was come into the province, after three days he ascended from Caesarea to Jerusalem (Yerushalayim).

2 Then the high priest (kohen hagadol) and the chief of the Jews (Yehudim) informed him against Paul, and besought him,

3 And desired favour against him, that he would send for him to Jerusalem (Yerushalayim), laying wait in the way to kill him.

4 But Festus answered, that Paul should be kept at Caesarea, and that he himself would depart shortly thither.

5 "Let them therefore," said he, "who among you are able, go down with me, and accuse this man, if there be any wickedness in him."

6 And when he had tarried among them more than ten days, he went down unto Caesarea; and the next day sitting on the judgment seat commanded Paul to be brought.

7 And when he was come, the Jews (Yehudim) who came down from Jerusalem (Yerushalayim) stood round about, and laid many and grievous complaints against Paul, which they could not prove.

8 While he answered for himself, "Neither against the law (torah) of the Jews (Yehudim), neither against the temple, nor yet against Caesar, have I offended any thing at all."

9 But Festus, willing to do the Jews (Yehudim) a pleasure, answered Paul, and said, "Wilt you go up to Jerusalem (Yerushalayim), and there be judged of these things before me?"

10 Then said Paul, "I stand at Caesar's judgment seat, where I ought to be judged; to the Jews (Yehudim) have I done no wrong, as you very well knowest.

11 For if I be an offender, or have committed any thing worthy of death, I refuse not to die; but if there be none of these things whereof these accuse me, no man may deliver me unto them. I appeal unto Caesar."

12 Then Festus, when he had conferred with the council, answered, "Have you appealed unto Caesar? Unto Caesar shalt you go."

13 And after certain days King Agrippa and Bernice came unto Caesarea to salute Festus.

14 And when they had been there many days, Festus declared Paul's cause unto the king, saying: "There is a certain man left in bonds by Felix;

15 About whom, when I was at Jerusalem (Yerushalayim), the chief priests (kohanim) and the elders of the Jews (Yehudim) informed me, desiring to have judgment against him.

16 To whom I answered, 'It is not the manner of the Romans to deliver any man to die, before that he which is accused have the accusers face to face, and have licence to answer for himself concerning the crime laid against him.'

17 Therefore, when they were come hither, without any delay on the morrow I sat on the judgment seat, and commanded the man to be brought forth.

18 Against whom when the accusers stood up, they brought none accusation of such things as I supposed;

19 But had certain questions against him of their own superstition, and of one, Yahwah, who was dead, whom Paul affirmed to be alive.

20 And because I doubted of such manner of questions, I asked him whether he would go to Jerusalem (Yerushalayim), and there be judged of these matters.

21 But when Paul had appealed to be reserved unto the hearing of Augustus, I commanded him to be kept till I might send him to Caesar."

22 Then Agrippa said unto Festus, "I would also hear the man myself." "Tomorrow," said he, "you shalt hear him."

23 And on the morrow, when Agrippa was come, and Bernice, with great pomp, and was

entered into the place of hearing, with the chief captains, and principal men of the city, at Festus' commandment Paul was brought forth.

24 And Festus said, "King Agrippa, and all men who are here present with us, you see this man, about whom all the multitude of the Jews (Yehudim) have dealt with me, both at Jerusalem (Yerushalayim), and also here, crying that he ought not to live any longer.

25 But when I found that he had committed nothing worthy of death, and that he himself hath appealed to Augustus, I have determined to send him.

26 Of whom I have no certain thing to write unto my lord (adoni). Wherefore I have brought him forth before you, and specially before you, O King Agrippa, that, after examination had, I might have somewhat to write.

27 For it seemeth to me unreasonable to send a prisoner, and not withal to signify the crimes laid against him."

26 Then Agrippa said unto Paul, "You are permitted to speak for yourself. Then Paul stretched forth the hand, and answered for himself:

2 "I think myself happy, King Agrippa, because I shall answer for myself this day before you touching all the things whereof I am accused of the Jews (Yehudim);

3 Especially because I know you to be expert in all customs and questions which are among the Jews (Yehudim); wherefore I beseech you to hear me patiently.

4 My manner of life from my youth, which was at the first among mine own nation at Jerusalem (Yerushalayim), know all the Jews (Yehudim);

5 Who knew me from the beginning, if they would testify, that after the most straitest sect of our religion I lived a Pharisee.

6 And now I stand and am judged for the hope of the promise made of God (Elohim, יהוה (YHWH)) unto our fathers;

7 Unto which promise our twelve tribes, instantly serving God (Elohim) day and night, hope to come. For which hope's sake, King Agrippa, I am accused of the Jews (Yehudim).

8 Why should it be thought a thing incredible with you, that God (Elohim, יהוה (YHWH))) should raise the dead?

9 I verily thought with myself, that I ought to do many things contrary to the name of Yahwah of Nazareth.

10 Which thing I also did in Jerusalem (Yerushalayim); and many of the holy ones did I shut up in prison, having received authority from the chief priests (kohanim); and when they were put to death, I gave my voice against them.

11 And I punished them often in every synagogue, and compelled them to blaspheme; and being exceedingly mad against them, I persecuted them even unto strange cities.

12 Whereupon as I went to Damascus with authority and commission from the chief priests (kohanim),

13 At midday, O king, I saw in the way a light from heaven, above the brightness of the sun, shining round about me and them who journeyed with me.

14 And when we were all fallen to the earth, I heard a voice speaking unto me, and saying in the Hebrew tongue, 'Shaul, Shaul, why persecutest you Me?' It is hard for you to kick against the pricks.

15 And I said, 'Who are you, Lord (Adonai)?' And He said, 'I am Yahwah (YHWH) whom you persecutest.

16 But rise, and stand upon your feet; for I have appeared unto you for this purpose, to make you a minister and a witness both of these things which you have seen, and of those things in the which I will appear unto you;

17 Delivering you from the people, and from the Gentiles (Goyim), unto whom now I send you,

18 To open their eyes, and to turn them from darkness to light, and from the power of Satan unto יהוה (YHWH), that they may receive forgiveness of sins, and inheritance among them which are sanctified by faith that is in Me.'

19 Whereupon, O King Agrippa, I was not disobedient unto the heavenly vision;

20 But shewed first unto them of Damascus, and at Jerusalem (Yerushalayim), and throughout all the coasts of Judah (Yehudah), and then to the Gentiles (Goyim), that they should repent and turn to יהוה (YHWH), and do works meet for repentance.

21 For these causes the Jews (Yehudim) caught me in the temple, and went about to kill me.

22 Having therefore obtained help of יהוה (YHWH), I continue unto this day, witnessing both to small and great, saying none other things than those which the prophets and Moses

(Mosheh) did say should come;

23 That the Messiah (haMashiach) should suffer, and that He should be the first that should rise from the dead, and should shew light unto the people, and to the Gentiles (Goyim)."

24 And as he thus spake for himself, Festus said with a loud voice, "Paul, you are beside yourself; much learning doth make you mad!"

25 But he said, "I am not mad, most noble Festus; but speak forth the words of truth and soberness.

26 For the king knoweth of these things, before whom also I speak freely; for I am persuaded that none of these things are hidden from him; for this thing was not done in a corner.

27 King Agrippa, believest you the prophets? I know that you believest."

28 Then Agrippa said unto Paul, "Almost you persuadest me to be a B63Mashiachi (follower of Messiah)."

29 And Paul said, "I wish that not only you, but also all that hear me this day, were both almost, and altogether such as I am, except these bonds."

30 And when he had thus spoken, the king rose up, and the governor, and Bernice, and they that sat with them.

31 And when they were gone aside, they talked between themselves, saying, "This man doeth nothing worthy of death or of bonds."

32 Then said Agrippa unto Festus, "This man might have been set at liberty, if he had not appealed unto Caesar."

27 And when it was determined that we should sail into Italy, they delivered Paul and certain other prisoners unto one named Julius (Yulios), a centurion of Augustus' band.

2 And entering into a ship of Adramyttium, we launched, meaning to sail by the coasts of Asia; one Aristarchus, a Macedonian of Thessalonica, being with us.

3 And the next day we touched at Sidon. And Julius (Yulios) courteously entreated Paul, and gave him liberty to go unto his friends to refresh himself.

4 And when we had launched from thence, we sailed under Cyprus, because the winds were contrary.

5 And when we had sailed over the sea of Cilicia and Pamphylia, we came to Myra, a city of Lycia.

6 And there the centurion found a ship of Alexandria sailing into Italy; and he put us therein.

7 And when we had sailed slowly many days, and scarce were come over against Cnidus, the wind not suffering us, we sailed under Crete, over against Salmone;

8 And, hardly passing it, came unto a place which is called 'The fair havens'; near whereunto was the city of Lasea.

9 Now when much time was spent, and when sailing was now dangerous, because the fast was now already past, Paul admonished them,

10 And said unto them, "Sirs, I perceive that this voyage will be with hurt and much damage, not only of the lading and ship, but also of our lives."

11 Nevertheless the centurion believed the master and the owner of the ship, more than those things which were spoken by Paul.

12 And because the haven was not commodious to winter in, the more part advised to depart thence also, if by any means they might attain to Phenice, and there to winter; which is a haven of Crete, and lieth toward the south west and north west.

13 And when the south wind blew softly, supposing that they had obtained their purpose, loosing thence, they sailed close by Crete.

14 But not long after there arose against it a tempestuous wind, called Euroclydon.

15 And when the ship was caught, and could not bear up into the wind, we let her drive.

16 And running under a certain island which is called Clauda, we had much work to come by the boat;

17 Which when they had taken up, they used helps, undergirding the ship; and, fearing lest they should fall into the quicksands, strake sail, and so were driven.

18 And we being exceedingly tossed with a tempest, the next day they lightened the ship;

19 And the third day we cast out with our own hands the tackling of the ship.

20 And when neither sun nor stars in many days appeared, and no small tempest lay on us, all hope that we should be saved was then taken away.

21 But after long abstinence Paul stood forth in the midst of them, and said, "Sirs, you should have hearkened unto me, and not have loosed

from Crete, and to have gained this harm and loss.

22 And now I exhort you to be of good cheer; for there shall be no loss of any man's life among you, but of the ship.

23 For there stood by me this night the angel of יהוה (YHWH), whose I am, and whom I serve,

24 Saying, 'Fear not, Paul; you must be brought before Caesar; and, behold, יהוה (YHWH) hath given you all them that sail with you.'

25 Wherefore, sirs, be of good cheer; for I believe יהוה (YHWH), that it shall be even as it was told me."

26 Howbeit we must be cast upon a certain island.

27 But when the fourteenth night was come, as we were driven up and down in Adria, about midnight the shipmen deemed that they drew near to some country;

28 And sounded, and found it twenty fathoms: and when they had gone a little further, they sounded again, and found it fifteen fathoms.

29 Then fearing lest we should have fallen upon rocks, they cast four anchors out of the stern, and wished for the day.

30 And as the shipmen were about to flee out of the ship, when they had let down the boat into the sea, under colour as though they would have cast anchors out of the foreship,

31 Paul said to the centurion and to the soldiers, "Except these abide in the ship, you cannot be saved."

32 Then the soldiers cut off the ropes of the boat, and let her fall off.

33 And while the day was coming on, Paul besought them all to take food, saying, "This day is the fourteenth day that you have tarried and continued fasting, having taken nothing.

34 Wherefore I pray you to take some food; for this is for your health; for there shall not a hair fall from the head of any of you."

35 And when he had thus spoken, he took bread, and gave thanks to God (Elohim, יהוה (YHWH)) in presence of them all; and when he had broken it, he began to eat.

36 Then were they all of good cheer, and they also took some food.

37 And we were in all in the ship two hundred threescore and sixteen souls.

38 And when they had eaten enough, they lightened the ship, and cast out the wheat into the sea.

39 And when it was day, they knew not the land; but they discovered a certain creek with a shore, into the which they were minded, if it was possible, to thrust in the ship.

40 And when they had taken up the anchors, they committed themselves unto the sea, and loosed the rudder bands, and hoised up the mainsail to the wind, and made toward shore.

41 And falling into a place where two seas met, they ran the ship aground; and the forepart stuck fast, and remained unmoveable, but the hinder part was broken with the violence of the waves.

42 And the soldiers' counsel was to kill the prisoners, lest any of them should swim out, and escape.

43 But the centurion, willing to save Paul, kept them from their purpose; and commanded that they which could swim should cast themselves first into the sea, and get to land;

44 And the rest, some on boards, and some on broken pieces of the ship. And so it came to pass, that they escaped all safe to land.

28 And when they were escaped, then they knew that the island was called Melita.

2 And the barbarous people shewed us no little kindness; for they kindled a fire, and received us every one, because of the present rain, and because of the cold.

3 And when Paul had gathered a bundle of sticks, and laid them on the fire, there came a viper out of the heat, and fastened on his hand.

4 And when the barbarians saw the venomous beast hang on his hand, they said among themselves, "No doubt this man is a murderer, whom, though he hath escaped the sea, yet vengeance suffereth not to live."

5 And he shook off the beast into the fire, and felt no harm.

6 Howbeit they looked when he should have swollen, or fallen down dead suddenly; but after they had looked a great while, and saw no harm come to him, they changed their minds, and said that he was a god (elohim).

7 In the same quarters were possessions of the chief man of the island, whose name was Publius; who received us, and lodged us three days courteously.

8 And it came to pass, that the father of Publius lay sick of a fever and of a bloody flux; to whom Paul entered in, and prayed, and laid his hands

on him, and healed him.

9 So when this was done, others also, who had diseases in the island, came, and were healed;

10 Who also honoured us with many honours; and when we departed, they laded us with such things as were necessary.

11 And after three months we departed in a ship of Alexandria, which had wintered in the isle, whose sign was Castor and Pollux.

12 And landing at Syracuse, we tarried there three days.

13 And from thence we fetched a compass, and came to Rhegium; and after one day the south wind blew, and we came the next day to Puteoli;

14 Where we found brethren, and were desired to tarry with them seven days; and so we went toward Rome.

15 And from thence, when the brethren heard of us, they came to meet us as far as Appii Forum, and The Three Taverns; whom when Paul saw, he thanked יהוה (YHWH), and took courage.

16 And when we came to Rome, the centurion delivered the prisoners to the captain of the guard; but Paul was allowed to dwell by himself with a soldier that kept him.

17 And it came to pass, that after three days Paul called the chief of the Jews (Yehudim) together; and when they were come together, he said unto them, "Men and brethren, though I have committed nothing against the people, or customs of our fathers, yet was I delivered prisoner from Jerusalem (Yerushalayim) into the hands of the Romans.

18 Who, when they had examined me, would have let me go, because there was no cause of death in me.

19 But when the Jews (Yehudim) spake against it, I was constrained to appeal unto Caesar; not that I had ought to accuse my nation of.

20 For this cause therefore have I called for you, to see you, and to speak with you; because that for the hope of Yisrael I am bound with this chain."

21 And they said unto him, "We neither received letters out of Judah (Yehudah) concerning you, neither any of the brethren that came shewed or spake any harm of you.

22 But we desire to hear of you what you thinkest; for as concerning this sect, we know that every where it is spoken against."

23 And when they had appointed him a day, there came many to him into his lodging; to whom he expounded and testified the kingdom of God (Elohim, יהוה (YHWH)), persuading them concerning Yahwah (YHWH), both out of the Torah by Moses (Torat Mosheh), and out of the Prophets, from morning till evening.

24 And some believed the things which were spoken, and some believed not.

25 And when they agreed not among themselves, they departed, after that Paul had spoken one word, "Well spake the Holy Spirit (Ruach haQodesh) by Isaiah (Yeshayahu) the prophet unto our fathers,

26 Saying, 'Go unto this people, and say, "Hearing you shall hear, and shall not understand; and seeing you shall see, and not perceive;

27 For the heart of this people is waxed gross, and their ears are dull of hearing, and their eyes have they closed; lest they should see with their eyes, and hear with their ears, and understand with their heart, and should be converted, and I should heal them.'" – Isa. 6:9–10

28 Be it known therefore unto you, that the salvation of יהוה (YHWH) is sent unto the Gentiles (Goyim), and that they will hear it."

29 And when he had said these words, the Jews (Yehudim) departed, and had great reasoning among themselves.

30 And Paul dwelt two whole years in his own hired house, and received all that came in unto him,

31 Preaching the kingdom of God (Elohim, יהוה (YHWH)), and teaching those things which concern Lord (Adonai) Yahwah haMashiach, with all confidence, no man forbidding him.

ROMANS
ROMIYIM רוֹמִיִּים
(Epistle to the Romans)

1 Paul, a servant of [A1]Yahwah [B45]haMashiach, called to be an apostle, separated unto the gospel (good news) of God (Elohim, יהוה (YHWH)),

2 (Which He had promised afore by His prophets in the holy scriptures,)

3 [B65]Concerning His [B47]Humanity (Yahwah haMashiach), [B66]who was made of the seed of Dawid according to the flesh; – *John 7:42*

4 And declared to be the [B47]Humanity of El (YHWH) with power, according to the Spirit of holiness, by the resurrection from the dead;

5 By whom we have received grace and apostleship, for obedience to the faith among all nations, for His name;

6 Among whom are you also the called of Yahwah haMashiach.

7 To all that be in Rome, beloved of God (Elohim), called to be set apart: Grace to you and peace from God (Elohim, יהוה (YHWH)) our Father, and our Lord (Adonai) Yahwah haMashiach.

8 First, I thank my God (Elohim) through Yahwah haMashiach for you all, that your faith is spoken of throughout the whole world.

9 For יהוה (YHWH) is my witness, whom I serve with my spirit in the gospel (good news) of His [B47]Humanity (Yahwah haMashiach), that without ceasing I make mention of you always in my prayers;

10 Making request, if by any means now at length I might have a prosperous journey by the will of God (Elohim, יהוה (YHWH)) to come unto you.

11 For I long to see you, that I may impart unto you some spiritual gift, to the end you may be established;

12 That is, that I may be comforted together with you by the mutual faith both of you and me.

13 Now I would not have you ignorant, brethren, that oftentimes I purposed to come unto you, (but was let hitherto) that I might have some fruit among you also, even as among other Gentiles (Goyim).

14 I am debtor both to the Greeks, and to the Barbarians; both to the wise, and to the unwise.

15 So, as much as in me is, I am ready to preach the gospel (good news) to you that are at Rome also.

16 For I am not ashamed of the gospel (good news) of the Messiah (haMashiach); for it is the power of יהוה (YHWH) unto salvation to every one that believeth; to the Jew (Yehudi) first, and also to the Greek.

17 For therein is the righteousness of God (Elohim) revealed from faith to faith; as it is written, 'The just shall live by faith.' – *Hab. 2:4*

18 For the wrath of God (Elohim, יהוה (YHWH)) is revealed from heaven against all ungodliness and unrighteousness of men, who hold the truth in unrighteousness;

19 Because that which may be known of God (Elohim) is manifest in them; for God (Elohim) hath shewed it unto them.

20 For the invisible things of Him from the creation of the world are clearly seen, being understood by the things that are made, even His eternal power and Godhead (Divine nature); so that they are without excuse;

21 Because that, when they knew יהוה (YHWH), they glorified Him not as God (Elohim), neither were thankful; but became vain in their imaginations, and their foolish heart was darkened.

22 Professing themselves to be wise, they became fools,

23 And changed the glory of the uncorruptible God (Elohim) into an image made like to corruptible man, and to birds, and fourfooted beasts, and creeping things.

24 Wherefore יהוה (YHWH) also gave them up to uncleanness through the lusts of their own hearts, to dishonour their own bodies between themselves;

25 Who changed the truth of יהוה (YHWH) into a lie, and worshipped and served the creature more than the Creator, who is blessed forever. Amen.

26 For this cause God (Elohim, יהוה (YHWH)) gave them up unto vile affections; for even their women did change the natural use into that which is against nature;

27 And likewise also the men, leaving the natural use of the woman, burned in their lust one toward another; men with men working that which is unseemly, and receiving in themselves that recompence of their error which was meet.

28 And even as they did not like to retain יהוה (YHWH) in their knowledge, יהוה (YHWH) gave them over to a reprobate mind, to do those things which are not convenient;

29 Being filled with all unrighteousness, fornication, wickedness, covetousness, maliciousness; full of envy, murder, debate, deceit, malignity; whisperers,

30 Backbiters, haters of God (Elohim, יהוה (YHWH)), despiteful, proud, boasters, inventors of evil things, disobedient to parents,

31 Without understanding, covenant-breakers, without natural affection, implacable, unmerciful;

32 Who knowing the judgment of God (Elohim), that they which commit such things are worthy of death, not only do the same, but have pleasure in them that do them.

2 Therefore you are inexcusable, O man, whosoever you are that judgest; for wherein you judgest another, you condemnest yourself; for you that judgest doest the same things.

2 But we are sure that the judgment of God (Elohim) is according to truth against them who commit such things.

3 And thinkest you this, O man, that judgest them who do such things, and doest the same, that you shalt escape the judgment of God (Elohim)?

4 Or despisest you the riches of His goodness and forbearance and longsuffering; not knowing that the goodness of God (Elohim, יהוה (YHWH)) leadeth you to repentance?

5 But after your hardness and impenitent heart treasurest up unto yourself wrath against the day of wrath and revelation of the righteous judgment of God (Elohim, יהוה (YHWH));

6 Who will render to every man according to his deeds; – Prov. 24:12

7 To them who by patient continuance in well doing seek for glory and honour and immortality, eternal life;

8 But unto them that are contentious, and do not obey the truth, but obey unrighteousness, indignation and wrath,

9 Tribulation and anguish, upon every soul of man that doeth evil, of the Jew (Yehudi) first, and also of the Gentiles (Goyim);

10 But glory, honour, and peace, to every man that worketh good, to the Jew (Yehudi) first, and also to the Gentile (Goyi);

11 For there is no respect of persons with God (Elohim).

12 For as many as have sinned outside the B28aTorah shall also perish outside the Torah; and as many as have sinned within the Torah shall be judged by the Torah;

13 (For not the hearers of the Torah are just before God (Elohim), but the doers of the Torah shall be justified.

14 For when the Gentiles (Goyim), who have not the Torah, do by nature the things contained in the Torah, these, having not the Torah, are a Torah unto themselves;

15 Who shew the work of the Torah written in their hearts, their conscience also bearing witness, and between one another, their thoughts sometimes accusing or defending them;) – Jer. 31:33

16 In the day when God (Elohim) shall judge the secrets of men by Yahwah haMashiach according to my gospel (good news).

17 Behold, you are called a Jew (Yehudi), and restest in the law (torah), and makest your boast of God (Elohim),

18 And knowest His will, and approvest the things that are more excellent, being instructed out of the Torah;

19 And are confident that you yourself are a guide of the blind, a light of them who are in darkness,

20 An instructor of the foolish, a teacher of babes, who hast the form of knowledge and of the truth in the Torah.

21 You therefore who teachest another, teachest you not yourself? You that preachest a man should not steal, dost you steal? – Exo. 20:15, Deu. 5:19

22 You that sayest a man should not commit adultery, dost you commit adultery? You that abhorrest idols, dost you commit sacrilege (idolatrous act)? – Exo. 20:14, Deu. 5:18

23 You that makest your boast of the law (torah), through breaking the law (torah) dishonourest you God (Elohim)?

24 For the name of God (Elohim, יהוה (YHWH)) is blasphemed among the Gentiles (Goyim) through you, as it is written. – Isa. 52:5, Eze. 36:20

25 For circumcision verily profiteth, if you keep the law (torah); but if you be a breaker of the law (torah), your circumcision is made

uncircumcision.

26 Therefore if the uncircumcised keeps the righteousness of the law (torah), shall not his uncircumcision be counted for circumcision?

27 And shall not uncircumcision which is by nature, if it fulfils the law (torah), judge you, who by the letter and circumcision dost transgress the law (torah)?

28 For he is not a Jew (Yehudi), who is one outwardly; neither is that circumcision, which is outward in the flesh;

29 But he is a Jew (Yehudi), who is one inwardly; and circumcision is that of the heart, in the spirit, and not in the letter; whose praise is not of men, but of God (Elohim).

3 What advantage then hath the Jew (Yehudi)? Or what profit is there of circumcision?

2 Much every way; chiefly, because that unto them were committed the oracles of God (Elohim, יהוה (YHWH)).

3 For what if some did not believe? Shall their unbelief make the faith of יהוה (YHWH) without effect?

4 God (Elohim) forbid; yea, let God (Elohim, יהוה (YHWH)) be true, but every man a liar; as it is written, 'That You mightest be justified in Your sayings, and mightest overcome when You are judged.' – *Psa. 51:4*

5 But if our unrighteousness commends the righteousness of God (Elohim), what shall we say? Is God (Elohim) unrighteous who taketh vengeance? (I speak as a man)

6 God (Elohim) forbid; for then how shall God (Elohim, יהוה (YHWH)) judge the world?

7 For if the truth of God (Elohim, יהוה (YHWH)) hath more abounded through my lie unto His glory; why yet am I also judged as a sinner?

8 And not rather, (as we be slanderously reported, and as some affirm that we say,) "Let us do evil, that good may come"? Their damnation is just.

9 What then? Are we better than they? No, in no wise; for we have before proved both Jews (Yehudim) and Gentiles (Goyim), that they are all under sin;

10 As it is written: "There is none righteous, no, not one.

11 There is none that understandeth, there is none that seeketh after God (Elohim, יהוה (YHWH)).

12 They are all gone out of the way, they are together become unprofitable; there is none that doeth good, no, not one. – *Psa. 14:1–3, 53:1–3*

13 Their throat is an open sepulchre; with their tongues they have used deceit; the poison of asps is under their lips; – *Psa. 5:9, Psa. 140:3*

14 Whose mouth is full of cursing and bitterness." – *Psa. 10:7*

15 Their feet are swift to shed blood;

16 Destruction and misery are in their ways;

17 And the way of peace have they not known: – *Isa. 59:7–8, Prov. 1:16*

18 There is no fear of God (Elohim) before their eyes." – *Psa. 36:1*

19 Now we know that what things soever the law (torah) saith, it saith to them who are under the law (torah); that every mouth may be stopped, and all the world may become guilty before God (Elohim, יהוה (YHWH)).

20 Therefore by the deeds of the law (torah); there shall no flesh be justified in His sight; for by the law (torah) is the knowledge of sin. – *Psa. 143:2*

21 But now the righteousness of God (Elohim, יהוה (YHWH)) apart from the [B28a]law (torah) is manifested, being witnessed by the [B28d]Torah and the Prophets (Nevi'im);

22 Even the righteousness of God (Elohim) which is by faith of Yahwah haMashiach unto all and upon all them that believe; for there is no difference;

23 For all have sinned, and come short of the glory of God (Elohim, יהוה (YHWH));

24 Being justified freely by His grace through the redemption that is in the Messiah (haMashiach) Yahwah;

25 Whom יהוה (YHWH) hath set forth to be a propitiation through faith in His blood, to declare His righteousness for the remission of sins that are past, through the forbearance of יהוה (YHWH);

26 To declare, I say, at this time His righteousness; that He might be just, and the justifier of him who believeth in Yahwah.

27 Where is boasting then? It is excluded. By what Torah? Of works? Nay; but by the Torah of faith.

28 Therefore we conclude that a man is justified by faith apart from the deeds of the law (torah).

29 Is He the God (Elohim) of the Jews (Yehudim) only? Is He not also of the Gentiles (Goyim)? Yes, of the Gentiles (Goyim) also;

30 Seeing it is one God (Elohim), who shall justify the circumcision by faith, and uncircumcision through faith.

31 Do we then make void the law (torah) through faith? God (Elohim) forbid; yea, we establish the law (torah).

4 What shall we say then that Avraham our father, as pertaining to the flesh, hath found?

2 For if Avraham were justified by works, he hath whereof to glory; but not before God (Elohim, יהוה (YHWH)).

3 For what saith the scripture? Avraham believed יהוה (YHWH), and it was counted unto him for righteousness. – Gen. 15:6

4 Now to him that worketh is the reward not reckoned of grace, but of debt.

5 But to him that worketh not, but believeth on Him that justifieth the ungodly, his faith is counted for righteousness.

6 Even as Dawid also describeth the blessedness of the man, unto whom God (Elohim) imputeth righteousness without works,

7 Saying, "Blessed are they whose iniquities are forgiven, and whose sins are covered.

8 Blessed is the man to whom יהוה will not impute sin. – Psa. 32:1–2

9 Cometh this blessedness then upon the circumcision only, or upon the uncircumcision also? For we say that faith was reckoned to Avraham for righteousness.

10 How was it then reckoned? When he was in circumcision, or in uncircumcision? Not in circumcision, but in uncircumcision.

11 And he received the sign of circumcision, a seal of the righteousness of the faith which he had yet being uncircumcised; that he might be the father of all them that believe, though they be not circumcised; that righteousness might be imputed unto them also;

12 And the father of circumcision to them who are not of the circumcision only, but who also walk in the steps of that faith of our father Avraham, which he had being yet uncircumcised.

13 For the promise, that he should be the heir of the world, to Avraham, or to his seed, was not through the [B28a]law (torah), but through the righteousness of faith.

14 For if they who are of the law (torah) be heirs, faith is made void, and the promise made of none effect;

15 Because the law (torah) worketh wrath (bring punishment); for where no law (torah) is, there is no transgression.

16 Therefore it is of faith, that it might be by grace; to the end the promise might be sure to all the seed; not to that only which is of the law (torah), but to that also which is of the faith of Avraham; who is the father of us all,

17 (As it is written, I have made you a father of many nations,) before him whom he believed, even God (Elohim, יהוה (YHWH)), who quickeneth the dead, and calleth those things which be not as though they were. – Gen. 17:5

18 Who against hope believed in hope, that he might become the father of many nations; according to that which was spoken, so shall your seed be. – Gen. 15:5

19 And being not weak in faith, he considered not his own body now dead, when he was about a hundred years old, neither yet the deadness of Sarah's womb;

20 He staggered not at the promise of God (Elohim) through unbelief; but was strong in faith, giving glory to יהוה (YHWH);

21 And being fully persuaded that, what He had promised, He was able also to perform.

22 And therefore it was imputed to him for righteousness." – Gen. 15:6

23 Now it was not written for his sake alone, that it was imputed to him;

24 But for us also, to whom it shall be imputed, if we believe on Him that raised up Yahwah our Lord (Adonai) from the dead;

25 Who was delivered for our offences, and was raised again for our justification.

5 Therefore being justified by faith, we have peace with God (Elohim) through our Lord (Adonai) Yahwah haMashiach;

2 By whom also we have access by faith into this grace wherein we stand, and rejoice in hope of the glory of God (Elohim, יהוה (YHWH)).

3 And not only so, but we glory in tribulations also; knowing that tribulation worketh patience;

4 And patience, proven character; and proven character, hope;

5 And hope maketh not ashamed; because the love of יהוה (YHWH) is shed abroad in our hearts by the Holy Spirit (Ruach haQodesh) which is given unto us.

6 For when we were yet without strength, in due time the Messiah (haMashiach) died for

the ungodly.

7 For scarcely for a righteous man will one die; yet peradventure for a good man some would even dare to die.

8 But God (Elohim, יהוה (YHWH)) commendeth His love toward us, in that, while we were yet sinners, the Messiah (haMashiach) died for us.

9 Much more then, being now justified by His blood, we shall be saved from wrath through Him.

10 For if, when we were enemies, we were reconciled to יהוה (YHWH) by the death of His [B47]Humanity, much more, being reconciled, we shall be saved by His life.

11 And not only so, but we also joy in God (Elohim) through our Lord (Adonai) Yahwah haMashiach, by whom we have now received the atonement.

12 Wherefore, as by one man sin entered into the world, and death by sin; and so death passed upon all men, for that all have sinned;

13 For until the [B28a]law (torah), sin was in the world; but sin is not imputed when there is no law (torah).

14 Nevertheless death reigned from Adam to Moses (Mosheh), even over them that had not sinned after the similitude of Adam's transgression, who is the figure of Him that was to come.

15 But not as the offence, so also is the free gift. For if through the offence of one many be dead, much more the grace of God (Elohim, יהו ה (YHWH)), and the gift by grace, which is by one Man, Yahwah haMashiach, hath abounded unto many.

16 And not as it was by one that sinned, so is the gift; for the judgment was by one to condemnation, but the free gift is of many offences unto justification.

17 For if by one man's offence death reigned by one; much more they who receive abundance of grace and of the gift of righteousness shall reign in life by one, Yahwah haMashiach.

18 Therefore as by the offence of one judgment came upon all men to condemnation; even so by the righteousness of one the free gift came upon all men unto justification of life.

19 For as by one man's disobedience many were made sinners, so by the obedience of one shall many be made righteous.

20 Moreover the law (torah) entered, that the offence might abound. But where sin abounded, grace did much more abound;

21 That as sin hath reigned unto death, even so might grace reign through righteousness unto eternal life by Yahwah haMashiach our Lord (Adonai).

6 What shall we say then? Shall we continue in sin, that grace may abound?

2 God (Elohim) forbid. How shall we, that are dead to sin, live any longer therein?

3 Know you not, that so many of us as were [B52]baptized into Yahwah haMashiach were baptized into His death?

4 Therefore we are buried with Him by baptism into death; that like as the Messiah (haMashiach) was raised up from the dead by the glory of the Father, even so we also should walk in newness of life.

5 For if we have been planted together in the likeness of His death, we shall be also in the likeness of His resurrection;

6 Knowing this, that our old man is crucified with Him, that the body of sin might be destroyed, that henceforth we should not serve sin.

7 For he that is dead is freed from sin.

8 Now if we be dead with the Messiah (haMashiach), we believe that we shall also live with Him;

9 Knowing that the Messiah (haMashiach) being raised from the dead dieth no more; death hath no more dominion over Him.

10 For in that He died, He died unto sin once; but in that He liveth, He liveth unto God (Elohim, יהוה (YHWH)).

11 Likewise reckon you also yourselves to be dead indeed unto sin, but alive unto God (Elohim) through Yahwah haMashiach our Lord (Adonai).

12 Let not sin therefore reign in your mortal body, that you should obey it in the lusts thereof.

13 Neither yield you your members as instruments of unrighteousness unto sin; but yield yourselves unto God (Elohim, יהוה (YHWH)), as those that are alive from the dead, and your members as instruments of righteousness unto God (Elohim, יהוה (YHWH)).

14 For sin shall not have dominion over you; for you are not under the [B28a]law (torah), but under grace.

15 What then? Shall we sin, because we are not under the law (torah), but under grace? God (Elohim) forbid.

16 Know you not, that to whom you yield yourselves servants to obey, his servants you are to whom you obey; whether of sin unto death, or of obedience unto righteousness?

17 But God (Elohim, יהוה (YHWH)) be thanked, that you were once slave of sin, but you have obeyed from the heart that form of doctrine which was delivered you.

18 Being then made free from sin, you became the servants of righteousness.

19 I speak after the manner of men because of the infirmity of your flesh; for as you have yielded your members servants to uncleanness and to iniquity unto iniquity; even so now yield your members servants to righteousness unto holiness.

20 For when you were the slaves of sin, you were free from righteousness.

21 What fruit had you then in those things whereof you are now ashamed? For the end of those things is death.

22 But now being made free from sin, and become servants to God (Elohim, יהוה (YHWH)), you have your fruit unto holiness and the end everlasting life.

23 For the wages of sin is death; but the gift of God (Elohim) is eternal life through Yahwah haMashiach our Lord (Adonai).

7 Know you not, brethren, (for I speak to them that know the [B28a]law (torah) how that the law (torah) hath dominion over a man as long as he liveth?

2 For the woman who hath a husband is bound by the law (torah) to her husband so long as he liveth; but if the husband be dead, she is loosed from the law (torah) of her husband.

3 So then if, while her husband liveth, she be married to another man, she shall be called an adulteress; but if her husband be dead, she is free from that law (torah); so that she is no adulteress, though she be married to another man.

4 Wherefore, my brethren, you also have become dead to the law (torah) by the body of the Messiah (haMashiach); that you should belong to another, to Him who is raised from the dead, that we should bring forth fruit unto God (Elohim, יהוה (YHWH)).

5 For when we were in the flesh, the motions of sins, which were by the law (torah), did work in our members to bring forth fruit unto death.

6 But now we are delivered from the law (torah), that being dead wherein we were held; that we should serve in newness of spirit, and not in the oldness of the letter.

7 What shall we say then? Is the law (torah) sin? God (Elohim) forbid. Nay, I had not known sin, but by the law (torah); for I had not known covetousness, except the Torah had said, 'You shalt not covet.' – Exo. 20:17, Deu. 5:21

8 But sin, taking occasion by the commandment, wrought in me all manner of concupiscence. For without the law (torah) sin was dead.

9 For I was alive without the law (torah) once; but when the commandment came, sin revived, and I died.

10 And the commandment, which was ordained to life, I found to be unto death.

11 For sin, taking occasion by the commandment, deceived me, and by it slew me.

12 Wherefore the [B28a]Torah is holy, and the commandment holy, and just, and good.

13 Was then that which is good made death unto me? God (Elohim) forbid. But sin, that it might appear sin, working death in me by that which is good; that sin by the commandment might become exceeding sinful.

14 For we know that the Torah is spiritual; but I am carnal, sold under sin.

15 For that which I do I allow not; for what I will, that do I not; but what I hate, that do I.

16 If then I do that which I will not, I consent unto the Torah that it is good.

17 Now then it is no more I that do it, but sin that dwelleth in me.

18 For I know that in me (that is, in my flesh,) dwelleth no good thing; for to will is present with me; but how to perform that which is good I find not.

19 For the good that I will I do not; but the evil which I will not, that I do.

20 Now if I do that I will not, it is no more I that do it, but sin that dwelleth in me.

21 I find then a law (torah), that, when I will to do good, evil is present with me.

22 For I delight in the Law (Torah) of יהוה (YHWH) after the inward man;

23 But I see another law (torah) in my members, warring against the Law (Torah) of my mind,

and bringing me into captivity to the law (torah) of sin which is in my members.

24 O wretched man that I am! Who shall deliver me from the body of this death?

25 I thank God (Elohim) through Yahwah haMashiach our Lord (Adonai). So then with the mind I myself serve the Law (Torah) of יהוה (YHWH); but with the flesh the law (torah) of sin.

8 There is therefore now no condemnation to them who are in the Messiah (haMashiach) Yahwah, who walk not after the flesh, but after the Spirit.

2 For the [B28a]Law (Torah) of the Spirit of life in the Messiah (haMashiach) Yahwah hath made me free from the law (torah) of sin and death.

3 For what the law (torah) could not do, in that it was weak through the flesh, God (Elohim, יהוה (YHWH)) sending His own [B47]Humanity (Yahwah haMashiach), in the likeness of sinful flesh, and for sin, condemned sin in the flesh;

4 That the righteousness of the Law (Torah) might be fulfilled in us, who walk not after the flesh, but after the Spirit.

5 For they that are after the flesh do mind the things of the flesh; but they that are after the Spirit the things of the Spirit.

6 For to be carnally minded is death; but to be spiritually minded is life and peace.

7 Because the carnal mind is enmity against God (Elohim); for it is not subject to the Torah of יהוה (YHWH), neither indeed can be.

8 So then they that are in the flesh cannot please God (Elohim, יהוה (YHWH)).

9 But you are not in the flesh, but in the Spirit, if so be that the Spirit of יהוה (Ruach YHWH) dwell in you. Now if any man has not the Spirit of the Messiah (haMashiach), he is none of His.

10 And if the Messiah (haMashiach) be in you, the body is dead because of sin; but the Spirit is life because of righteousness.

11 But if the Spirit of Him that raised up Yahwah from the dead dwell in you, He that raised up the Messiah (haMashiach) from the dead shall also quicken your mortal bodies by His Spirit that dwelleth in you.

12 Therefore, brethren, we are debtors, not to the flesh, to live after the flesh.

13 For if you live after the flesh, you shall die; but if you through the Spirit do mortify the deeds of the body, you shall live.

14 For as many as are led by the Spirit of יהוה (Ruach YHWH), they are the sons of God (Elohim).

15 For you have not received the spirit of bondage again to fear; but you have received the Spirit of adoption, whereby we cry, "Abba, our Father!"

16 The Spirit itself beareth witness with our spirit, that we are the children of God (Elohim);

17 And if children, then heirs; heirs of God (Elohim), and joint-heirs with the Messiah (haMashiach); if so be that we suffer with Him, that we may be also glorified together.

18 For I reckon that the sufferings of this present time are not worthy to be compared with the glory which shall be revealed in us.

19 For the earnest expectation of the creature waiteth for the manifestation of the sons of God (Elohim).

20 For the creature was made subject to vanity, not willingly, but by reason of Him who hath subjected the same in hope,

21 Because the creature itself also shall be delivered from the bondage of corruption into the glorious liberty of the children of God (Elohim).

22 For we know that the whole creation groaneth and travaileth in pain together until now.

23 And not only they, but ourselves also, who have the firstfruits of the Spirit, even we ourselves groan within ourselves, waiting for the adoption, to wit, the redemption of our body.

24 For we are saved by hope; but hope that is seen is not hope; for what a man seeth, why doth he yet hope for?

25 But if we hope for that we see not, then do we with patience wait for it.

26 Likewise the Spirit also helpeth our infirmities; for we know not what we should pray for as we ought; but the Spirit itself maketh intercession for us with groanings which cannot be uttered.

27 And He that searcheth the hearts knoweth what is the mind of the Spirit, because He maketh intercession for the holy ones according to the will of God (Elohim, יהוה (YHWH)).

28 And we know that all things work together for good to them that love God (Elohim), to them who are the called according to His purpose.

29 For whom He did foreknow, He also did predestinate to be conformed to the image of

His [B47]Humanity (Yahwah haMashiach), that He might be the firstborn among many brethren.

30 Moreover whom He did predestinate, them He also called; and whom He called, them He also justified; and whom He justified, them He also glorified.

31 What shall we then say to these things? If God (Elohim) be for us, who can be against us?

32 He that spared not His own [B47]Humanity (Yahwah haMashiach), but delivered Him up for us all, how shall He not with Him also freely give us all things?

33 Who shall lay any thing to the charge of God (Elohim)'s elect? It is God (Elohim) that justifieth.

34 Who is he that condemneth? It is the Messiah (haMashiach) that died, yea rather, that is risen again, who is even at the right hand of God (Elohim), who also maketh intercession for us.

35 Who shall separate us from the love of the Messiah (haMashiach)? Shall tribulation, or distress, or persecution, or famine, or nakedness, or peril, or sword?

36 As it is written: "For Your sake we are killed all the day long; we are accounted as sheep for the slaughter."– *Psa. 44:22*

37 Nay, in all these things we are more than conquerors through Him that loved us.

38 For I am persuaded, that neither death, nor life, nor angels, nor principalities, nor powers, nor things present, nor things to come,

39 Nor height, nor depth, nor any other creature, shall be able to separate us from the love of God (Elohim), which is in the Messiah (haMashiach) Yahwah our Lord (Adonai).

9 I say the truth in the Messiah (haMashiach), I lie not, my conscience also bearing me witness in the Holy Spirit (Ruach haQodesh),

2 That I have great heaviness and continual sorrow in my heart.

3 For I could wish that myself were accursed from the Messiah (haMashiach) for my brethren, my kinsmen according to the flesh;

4 Who are the children of Yisrael; to whom pertaineth the adoption, and the glory, and the covenants, and the giving of the [B28a]Torah, and the service of God (Elohim), and the promises;

5 Whose are the fathers, and of whom as concerning the flesh the Messiah (haMashiach) came, who is over all, יהוה (YHWH) blessed for ever. Amen.

6 Not as though the word of God (Elohim, יהוה (YHWH)) hath taken none effect. For they are not all Yisrael, who are of Yisrael;

7 Neither, because they are the seed of Avraham, are they all children; but, "In Isaac (Yitschaq) shall your seed be called." – *2 Chro. 20:7, Psa.105:6, Gen. 21:12*

8 That is, they who are the children of the flesh, these are not the children of God (Elohim); but the children of the promise are counted for the seed.

9 For this is the word of promise: "At this time will I come, and Sarah shall have a son." – *Gen. 18:14*

10 And not only this; but when Rebecca also had conceived by one, even by our father Isaac (Yitschaq);

11 (For the children being not yet born, neither having done any good or evil, that the purpose of God (Elohim) according to election might stand, not of works, but of Him that calleth;)

12 It was said unto her: "The elder shall serve the younger." – *Gen. 25:23*

13 As it is written, "Jacob (Yaaqov) have I loved, but Esaw have I hated." – *Mal. 1:2–3*

14 What shall we say then? Is there unrighteousness with God (Elohim, יהוה (YHWH))? God (Elohim) forbid.

15 For He saith to Moses (Mosheh), "I will have mercy on whom I will have mercy, and I will have compassion on whom I will have compassion." – *Exo.33:19*

16 So then it is not of him that willeth, nor of him that runneth, but of God (Elohim, יהוה (YHWH)) that sheweth mercy.

17 For the scripture saith unto Pharaoh, "Even for this same purpose have I raised you up, that I might shew My power in you, and that My name might be declared throughout all the earth." – *Exo. 9:16*

18 Therefore hath He mercy on whom He will have mercy, and whom He will He hardeneth.

19 You wilt say then unto me, "Why doth He yet find fault? For who hath resisted His will?"

20 Nay but, O man, who are you that repliest against יהוה (YHWH)? Shall the thing formed say to him that formed it, "Why have you made me thus?" – *Isa. 29:16, 45:9*

21 Hath not the potter power over the clay, of the same lump to make one vessel unto honour, and another unto dishonour?

22 What if יהוה (YHWH), willing to shew His wrath, and to make His power known, endured with much longsuffering the vessels of wrath fitted to destruction;

23 And that He might make known the riches of His glory on the vessels of mercy, which He had afore prepared unto glory,

24 Even us, whom He hath called, not of the Jews (Yehudim) only, but also of the Gentiles (Goyim)?

25 As He saith also in Osee (Hoshea): "I will call them My people, who were not My people; and her beloved, who was not beloved."

26 And it shall come to pass, that in the place where it was said unto them, "You are not My people; there shall they be called the children of the living God (Elohim)." – *Hos. 2:23, 1:10*

27 Isaiah (Yeshayahu) also crieth concerning Yisrael: "Though the number of the children of Yisrael be as the sand of the sea, a remnant shall be saved;

28 For He will finish the work, and cut it short in righteousness; because a short work will the Lord (YHWH) make upon the earth." – *Isa. 10:22–23*

29 And as Isaiah (Yeshayahu) said before: "Except יהוה of hosts (YHWH Tsevaot) had left us a seed, we had been as Sodoma, and been made like unto Gomorrha." – *Isa. 1:9*

30 What shall we say then? That the Gentiles (Goyim), who followed not after righteousness, have attained to righteousness, even the righteousness which is of faith.

31 But Yisrael, who followed after the Law (Torah) of righteousness, hath not attained to the Law (Torah) of righteousness.

32 Wherefore? Because they sought it not by faith, but as it was by the works of the law (torah). For they stumbled at that stumblingstone; – *Isa 8:14*

33 As it is written: "Behold, I lay in Sion (Tsiyon) a stumblingstone and rock of offence; and whosoever believeth on Him shall not be ashamed. – *Isa. 28:16*

10 Brethren, my heart's desire and prayer to God (Elohim, יהוה (YHWH)) for Yisrael is, that they might be saved.

2 For I bear them record that they have a zeal of God (Elohim), but not according to knowledge.

3 For they being ignorant of יהוה (YHWH)'s righteousness, and going about to establish their own righteousness, have not submitted themselves unto the righteousness of יהוה (YHWH).

4 [B67]For the goal at which the [B28a]law (torah) aims is the Messiah (haMashiach), unto righteousness to everyone that believeth in Him.

5 For Moses (Mosheh) describeth the righteousness which is of the law (torah), that the man who does those things shall attain life through them. – *Lev. 18:5*

6 But the righteousness which is of faith speaketh on this wise, "Say not in your heart, 'Who shall ascend into heaven?'" (that is, to bring the Messiah (haMashiach) down from above;)

7 Or, "Who shall descend into the deep?' (that is, to bring up the Messiah (haMashiach) again from the dead.)

8 But what saith it? "The word is near you, even in your mouth, and in your heart;" that is, the word of faith, which we preach:

9 That if you shalt confess with your mouth the Lord Yahwah (Adonai YHWH), and shalt believe in your heart that יהוה (YHWH) hath raised Him (His Humanity) from the dead, you shalt be saved.

10 For with the heart man believeth unto righteousness; and with the mouth confession is made unto salvation.

11 For the scripture saith: "Whosoever believeth on Him shall not be ashamed." – *Isa. 28:16*

12 For there is no difference between the Jew (Yehudi) and the Greek; for the same Lord (Adon) over all is rich unto all that call upon Him.

13 [B68]For "whosoever shall call upon the name of יהוה (YHWH, Yahwah) shall be saved." – *Yoel 2:32*

14 How then shall they call on Him in whom they have not believed? And how shall they believe in Him of whom they have not heard? And how shall they hear without a preacher?

15 And how shall they preach, except they be sent? As it is written: "How beautiful are the feet of them that preach the gospel (good news) of peace, and bring glad tidings of good things!" – *Isa 52:7*

16 But they have not all obeyed the gospel (good news). For Isaiah (Yeshayahu) saith, "יהוה (YHWH), who hath believed our report?" – *Isa.53:1*

17 So then faith cometh by hearing, and hearing by the word of God (Elohim, יהוה (YHWH)).

18 But I say, have they not heard? Yes verily, "Their sound went into all the earth, and their words unto the ends of the world." – *Psa. 19:4*

19 But I say, did not Yisrael know? First Moses (Mosheh) saith, "I will provoke you to jealousy by them that are no people, and by a foolish nation I will anger you." – *Deu. 32:21*

20 But Isaiah (Yeshayahu) is very bold, and saith, "I was found of them that sought Me not; I was made manifest unto them that asked not after Me." – *Isa. 65:1*

21 But to Yisrael He saith, "All day long I have stretched forth My hands unto a disobedient and gainsaying people." – *Isa. 65:2*

11 I say then, hath God (Elohim, יהוה (YHWH)) cast away His people? God (Elohim) forbid. For I also am an Yisraeli, of the seed of Avraham, of the tribe of Benjamin (Binyamin). – *2 Chro. 20:7, Psa.105:6*

2 יהוה (YHWH) hath not cast away His people whom He foreknew. Wot you not what the scripture saith of Elijah (Eliyahu)? How he maketh intercession to יהוה (YHWH) against Yisrael, saying, – *1 Sam. 12:22, Psa. 94:14*

3 "יהוה (YHWH), they have killed Your prophets, and digged down Your altars; and I am left alone, and they seek my life." – *1 Kin. 19:10, 19:14*

4 But what saith the answer of יהוה (YHWH) unto him? "I have reserved to Myself seven thousand men, who have not bowed the knee to the image of [B33b]Baal." – *1 Kin. 19:18*

5 Even so then at this present time also there is a remnant according to the election of grace.

6 And if by grace, then is it no more of works; otherwise grace is no more grace. But if it be of works, then is it no more grace; otherwise work is no more work.

7 What then? Yisrael hath not obtained that which he seeketh for; but the election hath obtained it, and the rest were blinded.

8 According as it is written: "יהוה (YHWH) hath given them the spirit of slumber, eyes that they should not see, and ears that they should not hear, unto this day." – *Deu. 29:4, Isa. 29:10*

9 And Dawid saith, "Let their table be made a snare, and a trap, and a stumblingblock, and a recompence unto them; – *Psa. 69:22*

10 Let their eyes be darkened, that they may not see, and bow down their back always." – *Psa. 69:23*

11 I say then, have they stumbled that they should fall? God (Elohim) forbid; but rather through their fall, salvation is come unto the Gentiles (Goyim), for to provoke them to jealousy. – *Deu.32:21*

12 Now if the fall of them be the riches of the world, and the diminishing of them the riches of the Gentiles (Goyim); how much more their fulness?

13 For I speak to you Gentiles (Goyim): inasmuch as I am the apostle of the Gentiles (Goyim), I magnify mine office;

14 If by any means I may provoke to emulation them who are my flesh, and might save some of them.

15 For if the casting away of them be the reconciling of the world, what shall the receiving of them be, but life from the dead?

16 For if the firstfruit be holy, the lump is also holy; and if the root be holy, so are the branches.

17 And if some of the branches be broken off, and you, being a wild olive tree, wert graffed in among them, and with them partakest of the root and fatness of the olive tree;

18 Boast not against the branches. But if you boast, you bearest not the root, but the root you.

19 You wilt say then, "The branches were broken off, that I might be graffed in."

20 Well; because of unbelief they were broken off, and you standest by faith. Be not highminded, but fear;

21 For if God (Elohim, יהוה (YHWH)) spared not the natural branches, take heed lest He also spare not you.

22 Behold therefore the goodness and severity of God (Elohim, יהוה (YHWH)); on them who fell, severity; but toward you, goodness, if you continue in His goodness; otherwise you also shalt be cut off.

23 And they also, if they abide not still in unbelief, shall be graffed in; for God (Elohim, יהוה (YHWH)) is able to graff them in again.

24 For if you wert cut out of the olive tree which is wild by nature, and wert graffed contrary to nature into a good olive tree; how much more shall these, which be the natural branches, be graffed into their own olive tree?

25 For I would not, brethren, that you should be ignorant of this mystery, lest you should be

wise in your own conceits; that blindness in part is happened to Yisrael, until the fulness of the Gentiles (Goyim) be come in.

26 And so all Yisrael shall be saved; as it is written: "There shall come out of Sion (Tsiyon) the Deliverer, and shall turn away ungodliness from Jacob (Yaaqov);

27 For this is My covenant unto them, when I shall take away their sins. – *Isa.59:20–21, 27:9*

28 As concerning the gospel (good news), they are enemies for your sakes; but as touching the election, they are beloved for the fathers' sakes.

29 For the gifts and calling of יהוה (YHWH) are without repentance.

30 For as you in times past have not believed יהוה (YHWH), yet have now obtained mercy through their unbelief;

31 Even so have these also now not believed, that through your mercy they also may obtain mercy.

32 For יהוה (YHWH) hath concluded them all in unbelief, that He might have mercy upon all.

33 O the depth of the riches both of the wisdom and knowledge of יהוה (YHWH)! How unsearchable are His judgments, and His ways past finding out!

34 For who hath known the mind of יהוה (YHWH)? Or who hath been His counsellor? – *Isa. 40:13*

35 Or who hath first given to Him, and it shall be recompensed unto him again?"

36 For of Him, and through Him, and to Him, are all things; to whom be glory for ever. Amen.

12 I beseech you therefore, brethren, by the mercies of יהוה (YHWH), that you present your bodies a living sacrifice, holy, acceptable unto יהוה (YHWH), which is your reasonable service.

2 And be not conformed to this world; but be you transformed by the renewing of your mind, that you may prove what is that good, and acceptable, and perfect, will of יהוה (YHWH).

3 For I say, through the grace given unto me, to every man that is among you, not to think of himself more highly than he ought to think; but to think soberly, according as יהוה (YHWH) hath dealt to every man the measure of faith.

4 For as we have many members in one body, and all members have not the same office (function);

5 So we, being many, are one body in the Messiah (Mashiach), and everyone members one of another.

6 Having then gifts differing according to the grace that is given to us, whether prophecy, let us prophesy according to the proportion of faith;

7 Or ministry, let us wait on our ministering; or he that teacheth, on teaching;

8 Or he that exhorteth, on exhortation; he that giveth, let him do it with simplicity; he that ruleth, with diligence; he that sheweth mercy, with cheerfulness.

9 Let love be without dissimulation. Abhor that which is evil; cleave to that which is good.

10 Be kindly affectioned one to another with brotherly love; in honour preferring one another;

11 Not slothful in business; fervent in spirit; serving יהוה (YHWH);

12 Rejoicing in hope; patient in tribulation; continuing instant in prayer;

13 Distributing to the necessity of holy ones; given to hospitality.

14 Bless them who persecute you; bless, and curse not.

15 Rejoice with them that do rejoice, and weep with them that weep.

16 Be of the same mind one toward another. Mind not high things, but condescend to men of low estate. Be not wise in your own conceits.

17 Recompense to no man evil for evil. Provide things honest in the sight of all men.

18 If it be possible, as much as lieth in you, live peaceably with all men.

19 Dearly beloved, avenge not yourselves, but rather give place unto wrath; for it is written: "Vengeance is Mine; I will repay," saith יהוה (YHWH) – *Deu. 32:41*

20 "Therefore if your enemy hungers, feed him; if he thirsts, give him drink; for in so doing you shalt heap coals of fire on his head." – *Prov. 25:21–22*

21 Be not overcome by evil, but overcome evil with good.

13 Let every soul be subject unto the higher powers. For there is no power but of God (Elohim, יהוה (YHWH)); the powers that be are ordained of יהוה (YHWH).

2 Whosoever therefore resisteth the power, resisteth the ordinance of יהוה (YHWH); and they that resist shall receive to themselves damnation.

3 For rulers are not a terror to good works, but

to the evil. Wilt you then not be afraid of the power? Do that which is good, and you shalt have praise of the same;

4 For he is the minister of יהוה (YHWH) to you for good. But if you do that which is evil, be afraid; for he beareth not the sword in vain; for he is the minister of יהוה (YHWH), a revenger to execute wrath upon him that doeth evil.

5 Wherefore you must needs be subject, not only for wrath, but also for conscience sake.

6 For for this cause pay you tribute also; for they are יהוה (YHWH)'s ministers, attending continually upon this very thing.

7 Render therefore to all their dues; tribute to whom tribute is due; custom to whom custom; fear to whom fear; honour to whom honour.

8 Owe no man anything, but to love one another; for he that loveth another hath fulfilled the Torah.

9 For this, "You shalt not commit adultery, you shalt not kill, you shalt not steal, you shalt not bear false witness, you shalt not covet;" and if there be any other commandment, it is briefly comprehended in this saying, namely, "You shalt love your neighbour as yourself." – *Exo. 20:13–17, Deu. 5:17–21, Lev. 19:18*

10 Love worketh no ill to his neighbour; therefore love is the fulfilling of the Torah.

11 And that, knowing the time, that now it is high time to awake out of sleep; for now is our salvation nearer than when we believed.

12 The night is far spent, the day is at hand; let us therefore cast off the works of darkness, and let us put on the armour of light.

13 Let us walk honestly, as in the day; not in rioting and drunkenness, not in chambering and wantonness, not in strife and envying.

14 But put you on our Lord (Adonai) Yahwah haMashiach, and make not provision for the flesh, to fulfil the lusts thereof.

14 Him that is weak in the faith receive you, but not to doubtful disputations.

2 For one believeth that he may eat all things; another, who is weak, eateth herbs.

3 Let not him that eateth despise him that eateth not; and let not him who eateth not, judge him that eateth; for יהוה (YHWH) hath received him.

4 Who are you that judgest another man's servant? To his own master he standeth or falleth. Yea, he shall be holden up; for יהוה (YHWH) is able to make him stand.

5 One man esteemeth one day above another; another esteemeth every day alike. Let every man be fully persuaded in his own mind.

6 He that regardeth the day, regardeth it unto יהוה; and he that regardeth not the day, to יהוה he doth not regard it. He that eateth, eateth to יהוה, for he giveth God (Elohim) thanks; and he that eateth not, to יהוה he eateth not, and giveth God (Elohim) thanks.

7 For none of us liveth to himself, and no man dieth to himself.

8 For whether we live, we live unto יהוה; and whether we die, we die unto יהוה; whether we live therefore, or die, we are יהוה's.

9 For to this end the Messiah (haMashiach) both died, and rose, and revived, that He might be Lord (Adon) both of the dead and living.

10 But why dost you judge your brother? Or why dost you set at nought your brother? For we shall all stand before the judgment seat of the Messiah (haMashiach).

11 For it is written, "As I live, saith יהוה (YHWH), every knee shall bow to Me, and every tongue shall confess to God (Elohim, יהוה (YHWH))." – *Isa. 45:23*

12 So then every one of us shall give account of himself to God (Elohim).

13 Let us not therefore judge one another any more; but judge this rather, that no man put a stumblingblock or an occasion to fall in his brother's way.

14 I know, and am persuaded by our Lord Yahwah (Adonai YHWH), that there is nothing unclean of itself; but to him that esteemeth any thing to be unclean, to him it is unclean.

15 But if your brother be grieved with your food, now walkest you not charitably. Destroy not him with your food, for whom the Messiah (haMashiach) died.

16 Let not then your good be evil spoken of;

17 For the kingdom of God (Elohim, יהוה (YHWH)) is not food and drink; but righteousness, and peace, and joy in the Holy Spirit (Ruach haQodesh).

18 For he that in these things serveth the Messiah (haMashiach) is acceptable to God (Elohim), and approved of men.

19 Let us therefore follow after the things which make for peace, and things wherewith one may edify another.

20 For food destroy not the work of God

(Elohim). All things indeed are pure; but it is evil for that man who eateth with offence.

21 It is good neither to eat flesh, nor to drink wine, nor any thing whereby your brother stumbleth, or is offended, or is made weak.

22 Have you faith? Have it to yourself before God (Elohim). Happy is he that condemneth not himself in that thing which he alloweth.

23 And he that doubteth is damned if he eats, because he eateth not of faith; for whatsoever is not of faith is sin.

15 We then that are strong ought to bear the infirmities of the weak, and not to please ourselves.

2 Let every one of us please his neighbour for his good to edification.

3 For even the Messiah (haMashiach) pleased not Himself; but, as it is written, "The reproaches of them that reproached You fell on me." – Psa. 69:9

4 For whatsoever things were written aforetime were written for our learning, that we through patience and comfort of the scriptures might have hope.

5 Now the God (Elohim) of patience and consolation grant you to be likeminded one toward another according to the Messiah (haMashiach) Yahwah;

6 That you may with one mind and one mouth glorify God (Elohim), the Father of our Lord (Adonai) Yahwah haMashiach.

7 Wherefore receive you one another, as the Messiah (haMashiach) also received us to the glory of God (Elohim, יהוה (YHWH)).

8 Now I say that Yahwah haMashiach was a minister of the circumcision for the truth of God (Elohim), to confirm the promises made unto the fathers;

9 And that the Gentiles (Goyim) might glorify God (Elohim, יהוה (YHWH)) for His mercy; as it is written, "For this cause I will confess to You among the Gentiles (Goyim), and sing unto Your name." – 2 Sam. 22:50, Psa. 18:49

10 And again he saith, "Rejoice, you Gentiles (Goyim), with His people." – Deu. 32:43

11 And again, "Praise יהוה (YHWH), all you Gentiles (Goyim); and laud Him, all you people." – Psa. 117:1

12 And again, Isaiah (Yeshayahu) saith, "There shall be a root of Jesse (Yishai), and He that shall rise to reign over the Gentiles (Goyim);

in Him shall the Gentiles (Goyim) trust." – Isa. 11:10

13 Now the God (Elohim) of hope fill you with all joy and peace in believing, that you may abound in hope, through the power of the Holy Spirit (Ruach haQodesh).

14 And I myself also am persuaded of you, my brethren, that you also are full of goodness, filled with all knowledge, able also to admonish one another.

15 Nevertheless, brethren, I have written the more boldly unto you in some sort, as putting you in mind, because of the grace that is given to me of God (Elohim),

16 That I should be the minister of Yahwah haMashiach to the Gentiles (Goyim), ministering the gospel (good news) of God (Elohim, יהוה (YHWH)), that the offering up of the Gentiles (Goyim) might be acceptable, being sanctified by the Holy Spirit (Ruach haQodesh).

17 I have therefore whereof I may glory through Yahwah haMashiach in those things which pertain to God (Elohim).

18 For I will not dare to speak of any of those things which the Messiah (haMashiach) hath not wrought by me, to make the Gentiles (Goyim) obedient, by word and deed,

19 Through mighty signs and wonders, by the power of the Spirit of יהוה (Ruach YHWH); so that from Jerusalem (Yerushalayim), and round about unto Illyricum, I have fully preached the gospel (good news) of the Messiah (haMashiach).

20 Yea, so have I strived to preach the gospel (good news), not where the Messiah (haMashiach) was named, lest I should build upon another man's foundation;

21 But as it is written, "To whom He was not spoken of, they shall see; and they that have not heard shall understand. – Isa. 52:15

22 For which cause also I have been much hindered from coming to you.

23 But now having no more place in these parts, and having a great desire these many years to come unto you;

24 Whensoever I take my journey into Spain, I will come to you; for I trust to see you in my journey, and to be brought on my way thitherward by you, if first I be somewhat filled with your company.

25 But now I go unto Jerusalem (Yerushalayim)

to minister unto the holy ones (qadoshim).

26 For it hath pleased them of Macedonia and Achaia to make a certain contribution for the poor holy ones (qadoshim) who are at Jerusalem (Yerushalayim).

27 It hath pleased them verily; and their debtors they are. For if the Gentiles (Goyim) have been made partakers of their spiritual things, their duty is also to minister unto them in carnal things.

28 When therefore I have performed this, and have sealed to them this fruit, I will come by you into Spain.

29 And I am sure that, when I come unto you, I shall come in the fulness of the blessing of the gospel (good news) of the Messiah (haMashiach).

30 Now I beseech you, brethren, for our Lord (Adonai) Yahwah haMashiach's sake, and for the love of the Spirit, that you strive together with me in your prayers to God (Elohim) for me;

31 That I may be delivered from them that do not believe in Judah (Yehudah); and that my service which I have for Jerusalem (Yerushalayim) may be accepted of the holy ones (qadoshim);

32 That I may come unto you with joy by the will of God (Elohim, יהוה (YHWH)), and may with you be refreshed.

33 Now the God (Elohim) of peace be with you all. So be it (Amen).

16 I commend unto you Phebe our sister, who is a servant of the assembly who is at Cenchrea;

2 That you receive her in יהוה (YHWH), as God (Elohim)'s people should, and that you assist her in whatsoever business she hath need of you; for she hath been a succourer of many, and of myself also.

3 Greet Priscilla and Aquila my helpers in the Messiah (haMashiach) Yahwah;

4 Who have for my life laid down their own necks; unto whom not only I give thanks, but also all the assemblies (ekklesias) of the Gentiles (Goyim).

5 Likewise greet the assembly that is in their house. Salute my wellbeloved Epaenetus, who is the firstfruits of Achaia unto Messiah (Mashiach).

6 Greet Mary (Miryam), who bestowed much labour on us.

7 Salute Andronicus and Yunia, my kinsmen,

and my fellowprisoners, who are of note among the apostles, who also were in our Messiah (Mashiach) before me.

8 Greet Amplias my beloved in יהוה (YHWH).

9 Salute Urbane, our helper in Mashiach, and Stachys my beloved.

10 Salute Apelles approved in the Messiah (haMashiach). Salute them who are of Aristobulus' household.

11 Salute Herodion my kinsman. Greet them that be of the household of Narcissus, who are in יהוה (YHWH).

12 Salute Tryphena and Tryphosa, who labour in the Lord (YHWH). Salute the beloved Persis, which laboured much in יהוה (YHWH).

13 Salute Rufus chosen in יהוה (YHWH), and his mother and mine.

14 Salute Asyncritus, Phlegon, Hermas, Patrobas, Hermes, and the brethren who are with them.

15 Salute Philologus, and Yulia, Nereus, and his sister, and Olympas, and all the holy ones (qadoshim) who are with them.

16 Salute one another with a holy kiss. The assemblies (ekklesias) of our Messiah (Mashiach) salute you.

17 Now I beseech you, brethren, mark them who cause divisions and offences contrary to the doctrine which you have learned and avoid them.

18 For they that are such serve not our Lord (Adonai) Yahwah haMashiach but their own belly; and by good words and fair speeches deceive the hearts of the simple.

19 For your obedience is come abroad unto all men. I am glad therefore on your behalf; but yet I would have you wise unto that which is good, and simple concerning evil.

20 And the God (Elohim) of peace shall bruise Satan under your feet shortly. The grace of our Lord (Adonai) Yahwah haMashiach be with you. So be it (Amen).

21 Timotheus my workfellow, and Lucius, and Jason (Yason), and Sosipater, my kinsmen, salute you.

22 I Tertius, who wrote this epistle, salute you in the Lord (YHWH).

23 Gaius mine host, and of the whole assembly, saluteth you. Erastus the chamberlain of the city saluteth you, and Quartus a brother.

24 The grace of our Lord (Adonai) Yahwah

haMashiach be with you all. So be it (Amen).

25 Now to him that is of power to stablish you according to my gospel (good news), and the preaching of Yahwah haMashiach, according to the revelation of the mystery, which was kept secret since the world began,

26 But now is made manifest, and by the scriptures of the prophets, according to the commandment of the everlasting God (Elohim), made known to all nations for the obedience of faith;

27 To God (Elohim) only wise, be glory through Yahwah haMashiach forever. So be it (Amen).

1 CORINTHIANS
QORINTIYIM 1 א קוֹרִנְתִּים
(First Epistle to the Corinthians)

1 Paul, called to be an apostle of [A1]Yahwah [B45]haMashiach through the will of God (Elohim, יהוה (YHWH)), and Sosthenes our brother,

2 Unto the assembly of God (Elohim) which is at Corinth, to them that are sanctified in Yahwah haMashiach, called to be the holy ones, with all that in every place call upon the name of Yahwah haMashiach our Lord (Adonai), both theirs and ours;

3 Grace be unto you, and peace, from YHWH our Father, and from Lord (Adonai) Yahwah haMashiach.

4 I thank my God (Elohim) always on your behalf, for the grace of God (Elohim, יהוה (YHWH)) which is given you by Yahwah haMashiach;

5 That in every thing you are enriched by Him, in all utterance, and in all knowledge;

6 Even as the testimony of the Messiah (haMashiach) was confirmed in you;

7 So that you come behind in no gift; waiting for the coming of our Lord (Adonai) Yahwah haMashiach;

8 Who shall also confirm you unto the end, that you may be blameless in the day of our Lord (Adonai) Yahwah haMashiach.

9 God (Elohim) is faithful, by whom you were called unto the fellowship of His [B47]Humanity, Yahwah haMashiach our Lord (Adonai).

10 Now I beseech you, brethren, by the name of our Lord (Adonai) Yahwah haMashiach, that you all speak the same thing, and that there be no divisions among you; but that you be perfectly joined together in the same mind and in the same judgment.

11 For it hath been declared unto me of you, my brethren, by them who are of the house of Chloe, that there are contentions among you.

12 Now this I say, that every one of you saith, "I am of Paul;" and "I of Apollos;" and "I of Cephas (Kefa);" and "I of the Messiah (haMashiach)."

13 Is the Messiah (haMashiach) divided? Was Paul crucified for you? Or were you baptized in the name of Paul?

14 I thank God (Elohim) that I baptized none of you, but Crispus and Gaius;

15 Lest any should say that I had baptized in mine own name.

16 And I baptized also the household of Stephanas; besides, I know not whether I baptized any other.

17 For the Messiah (haMashiach) sent me not to baptize, but to preach the gospel (good news); not with wisdom of words, lest the stake of the Messiah (haMashiach) should be made of none effect.

18 For the preaching of the stake is foolishness to them that perish; but unto us who are saved it is the power of God (Elohim, יהוה (YHWH)).

19 For it is written, "I will destroy the wisdom of the wise, and will bring to nothing the understanding of the prudent." – *Isa. 29:14*

20 Where is the wise? Where is the scribe? Where is the disputer of this world? Hath not God (Elohim) made foolish the wisdom of this world?

21 For after that in the wisdom of God (Elohim, יהוה (YHWH)) the world by wisdom knew not God (Elohim, יהוה (YHWH)), it pleased God (Elohim, יהוה (YHWH)) by the foolishness of preaching to save them that believe.

22 For the Jews (Yehudim) require a sign, and the Greeks seek after wisdom;

23 But we preach the Messiah (haMashiach) crucified, unto the Jews (Yehudim) a stumblingblock, and unto the Greeks foolishness;

24 But unto them who are called, both Jews (Yehudim) and Greeks, the Messiah (haMashiach) the power of God (Elohim, יהוה (YHWH)), and the wisdom of God (Elohim, יהוה (YHWH)).

25 Because the foolishness of God (Elohim, יהוה (YHWH)) is wiser than men; and the weakness of God (Elohim, יהוה (YHWH)) is stronger than men.

26 For you see your calling, brethren, how that not many wise men after the flesh, not many mighty, not many noble, are called;

27 But God (Elohim, יהוה (YHWH)) hath chosen the foolish things of the world to confound the wise; and God (Elohim) hath chosen the weak things of the world to confound the things which are mighty;

28 And base things of the world, and things which are despised, hath God (Elohim, יהוה

(YHWH)) chosen, yea, and things which are not, to bring to nought things that are;

29 That no flesh should glory in His presence.

30 But of Him are you in the Messiah (haMashiach) Yahwah, who of God (Elohim, יהוה (YHWH)) is made unto us wisdom, and righteousness, and sanctification, and redemption;

31 That, according as it is written, "He that glorieth, let him glory in יהוה (YHWH). – *Jer. 9:24*

2 And I, brethren, when I came to you, came not with excellency of speech or of wisdom, declaring unto you the testimony of God (Elohim, יהוה (YHWH)).

2 For I determined not to know any thing among you, except Yahwah haMashiach, and Him crucified.

3 And I was with you in weakness, and in fear, and in much trembling.

4 And my speech and my preaching was not with enticing words of man's wisdom, but in demonstration of the Spirit and of power;

5 That your faith should not stand in the wisdom of men, but in the power of God (Elohim, יהוה (YHWH)).

6 Howbeit we speak wisdom among them that are perfect; yet not the wisdom of this world, nor of the princes of this world, that come to nought;

7 But we speak the wisdom of God (Elohim, יהוה (YHWH)) in a mystery, even the hidden wisdom, which God (Elohim, יהוה (YHWH)) ordained before the world unto our glory;

8 Which none of the princes of this world knew; for had they known it, they would not have crucified the Lord (Adon) of glory.

9 But as it is written, "Eye hath not seen, nor ear heard, neither have entered into the heart of man, the things which God (Elohim) hath prepared for them that love Him." – *Isa. 64:4*

10 But God (Elohim, יהוה (YHWH)) hath revealed them unto us by His Spirit; for the Spirit searcheth all things, yea, the deep things of God (Elohim, יהוה (YHWH)).

11 For what man knoweth the things of a man, except the spirit of man which is in Him? Even so the things of God (Elohim, יהוה (YHWH)) knoweth no man, but the Spirit of יהוה (Ruach YHWH).

12 Now we have received, not the spirit of the world, but the Spirit which is of God (Elohim, יהוה (YHWH)); that we might know the things that are freely given to us of God (Elohim, יהוה (YHWH)).

13 Which things also we speak, not in the words which man's wisdom teacheth, but which the Holy Spirit (Ruach haQodesh) teacheth; comparing spiritual things with spiritual.

14 But the natural man receiveth not the things of the Spirit of יהוה (Ruach YHWH); for they are foolishness unto him; neither can he know them, because they are spiritually discerned.

15 But he that is spiritual judgeth all things, yet he himself is judged of no man.

16 For who hath known the mind of יהוה (YHWH) that He may instruct him? But we have the mind of the Messiah (haMashiach).

3 And I, brethren, could not speak unto you as unto spiritual, but as unto carnal, even as unto babes in the Messiah (haMashiach).

2 I have fed you with milk, and not with meat, for hitherto you were not able to bear it, neither yet now are you able.

3 For you are yet carnal, for whereas there is among you envying, and strife, and divisions, are you not carnal, and walk as men?

4 For while one saith, I am of Paul; and another, I am of Apollos; are you not carnal?

5 Who then is Paul, and who is Apollos, but ministers by whom you believed, even as the Lord (YHWH) gave to every man?

6 I have planted, Apollos watered; but God (Elohim) gave the increase.

7 So then neither is he that planteth any thing, neither he that watereth; but God (Elohim) that giveth the increase.

8 Now he that planteth and he that watereth are one; and every man shall receive his own reward according to his own labour.

9 For we are labourers together with God (Elohim, יהוה (YHWH)); you are God (Elohim)'s field, you are God (Elohim)'s building.

10 According to the grace of God (Elohim, יהוה (YHWH)) which is given unto me, as a wise masterbuilder, I have laid the foundation, and another buildeth thereon. But let every man take heed how he buildeth thereupon.

11 For other foundation can no man lay than that is laid, which is Yahwah haMashiach.

12 Now if any man builds upon this foundation

gold, silver, precious stones, wood, hay, stubble;

13 Every man's work shall be made manifest; for the day shall declare it, because it shall be revealed by fire; and the fire shall try every man's work of what sort it is.

14 If any man's work abides which he hath built thereupon, he shall receive a reward.

15 If any man's work shall be burned, he shall suffer loss; but he himself shall be saved; yet so as by fire.

16 Know you not that you are the temple of God (Elohim), and that the Spirit of יהוה (Ruach YHWH) dwelleth in you?

17 If any man defiles the temple of God (Elohim, יהוה (YHWH)), him shall יהוה (YHWH) destroy; for the temple of God (Elohim, יהוה (YHWH)) is holy, which temple you are.

18 Let no man deceive himself. If any man among you seemeth to be wise in this world, let him become a fool, that he may be wise.

19 For the wisdom of this world is foolishness with God (Elohim, יהוה (YHWH)). For it is written, "He taketh the wise in their own craftiness." – Job 5:13

20 And again, יהוה (YHWH) knoweth the thoughts of the wise, that they are vain.

21 Therefore let no man glory in men. For all things are yours; – Psa. 94:11

22 Whether Paul, or Apollos, or Cephas (Kefa), or the world, or life, or death, or things present, or things to come; all are yours;

23 And you are Messiah (Mashiach)'s; and the Messiah (haMashiach) is God (Elohim)'s.

4 Let a man so account of us, as of the ministers of Messiah (Mashiachim), and stewards of the mysteries of God (Elohim).

2 Moreover it is required in stewards, that a man be found faithful.

3 But with me it is a very small thing that I should be judged of you, or of man's judgment; yea, I judge not mine own self.

4 For I know nothing by myself; yet am I not hereby justified; but He that judgeth me is God (Elohim, יהוה (YHWH)).

5 Therefore judge nothing before the time, until Yahwah (YHWH) come, who both will bring to light the hidden things of darkness, and will make manifest the counsels of the hearts: and then shall every man have praise of God (Elohim).

6 And these things, brethren, I have in a figure transferred to myself and to Apollos for your sakes; that you might learn in us not to think of men above that which is written, that no one of you be puffed up for one against another.

7 For who maketh you to differ from another? And what have you that you didst not receive? Now if you didst receive it, why dost you glory, as if you hadst not received it?

8 Now you are full, now you are rich, you have reigned as kings without us; and I wish you did reign, that we also might reign with you.

9 For I think that God (Elohim) hath set forth us the apostles last, as it was appointed to death; for we are made a spectacle unto the world, and to angels, and to men.

10 We are fools for the Messiah (haMashiach)'s sake, but you are wise in Messiah (Mashiach); we are weak, but you are strong; you are honourable, but we are despised.

11 Even unto this present hour we both hunger, and thirst, and are naked, and are buffeted, and have no certain dwellingplace;

12 And labour, working with our own hands; being reviled, we bless; being persecuted, we suffer it;

13 Being defamed, we intreat; we are made as the filth of the world, and are the offscouring of all things unto this day.

14 I write not these things to shame you, but as my beloved sons I warn you.

15 For though you have ten thousand instructors in the Messiah (haMashiach), yet have you not many fathers; for in the Messiah (haMashiach) Yahwah I have begotten you through the gospel (good news).

16 Wherefore I beseech you, be you followers of me.

17 For this cause have I sent unto you Timotheus, who is my beloved son, and faithful in the Lord (YHWH), who shall bring you into remembrance of my ways which be in Messiah (Mashiach), as I teach every where in every assembly.

18 Now some are puffed up, as though I would not come to you.

19 But I will come to you shortly, if יהוה (YHWH) will, and will know, not the speech of them which are puffed up, but the power.

20 For the kingdom of God (Elohim, יהוה (YHWH)) is not in word, but in power.

21 What will you? Shall I come unto you with

a rod, or in love, and in the spirit of meekness?

5 It is reported commonly that there is fornication among you, and such fornication as is not so much as named among the Gentiles (Goyim), that one should have his father's wife.

2 And you are puffed up, and have not rather mourned, that he that hath done this deed might be taken away from among you.

3 For I verily, as absent in body, but present in spirit, have judged already, as though I was present, concerning him that hath so done this deed,

4 In the name of our Lord (Adonai) Yahwah haMashiach, when you are gathered together, and my spirit, with the power of our Lord (Adonai) Yahwah haMashiach,

5 To deliver such a one unto Satan for the destruction of the flesh, that the spirit may be saved in the day of our Lord Yahwah (Adonai YHWH).

6 Your glorying is not good. Know you not that a little leaven leaveneth the whole lump?

7 Purge out therefore the old leaven, that you may be a new lump, as you are unleavened. For even Messiah (Mashiach) our Passover lamb (Pesach) is sacrificed for us.

8 Therefore let us keep the feast, not with old leaven, neither with the leaven of malice and wickedness; but with the unleavened bread of sincerity and truth.

9 I wrote unto you in an epistle not to company with fornicators;

10 Yet not altogether with the fornicators of this world, or with the covetous, or extortioners, or with idolaters; for then must you need go out of the world.

11 But now I have written unto you not to keep company, if any man that is called a brother be a fornicator, or covetous, or an idolater, or a railer, or a drunkard, or an extortioner; with such a one no not to eat.

12 For what have I to do to judge them also that are outsider? Do not you judge them that are within?

13 But them that are outside, God (Elohim, יהוה (YHWH)) judgeth. Therefore put away from among yourselves that wicked person.

6 Dare any of you, having a matter against another, go to law before the unjust, and not before the holy ones?

2 Do you not know that the holy ones shall judge the world? And if the world shall be judged by you, are you unworthy to judge the smallest matters?

3 Know you not that we shall judge angels? How much more things that pertain to this life?

4 If then you have judgments of things pertaining to this life, set them to judge who are least esteemed in the assembly.

5 I speak to your shame. Is it so, that there is not a wise man among you? No, not one that shall be able to judge between his brethren?

6 But brother goeth to law with brother, and that before the unbelievers.

7 Now therefore there is utterly a fault among you, because you go to law one with another. Why do you not rather take wrong? Why do you not rather suffer yourselves to be defrauded?

8 Nay, you do wrong, and defraud, and that to your own brethren!

9 Know you not that the unrighteous shall not inherit the kingdom of God (Elohim, יהוה (YHWH))? Be not deceived; neither fornicators, nor idolaters, nor adulterers, nor effeminate, nor abusers of themselves with mankind,

10 Nor thieves, nor covetous, nor drunkards, nor revilers, nor extortioners, shall inherit the kingdom of God (Elohim, יהוה (YHWH)).

11 And such were some of you; but you are washed, but you are sanctified, but you are justified in the name of our Lord Yahwah (Adonai YHWH), and by the Spirit of our God (Elohim).

12 All things are lawful unto me, but all things are not expedient; all things are lawful for me, but I will not be brought under the power of any.

13 Meats for the belly, and the belly for meats; but God (Elohim) shall destroy both it and them. Now the body is not for fornication, but for the Lord (YHWH); and the Lord (YHWH) for the body.

14 And God (Elohim, יהוה (YHWH)) hath both raised up Yahwah (YHWH) and will also raise up us by His own power.

15 Know you not that your bodies are the members of Messiah (Mashiach)? Shall I then take the members of Messiah (Mashiach), and make them the members of a harlot? God (Elohim) forbid.

16 What? Know you not that he who is joined to a harlot is one body? For two, saith He, shall be one flesh.

17 But he that is joined unto the Lord (YHWH) is one spirit.

18 Flee fornication. Every sin that a man doeth is outside the body; but he that committeth fornication sinneth against his own body.

19 What? Know you not that your body is the temple of the Holy Spirit (Ruach haQodesh) which is in you, which you have of God (Elohim, יהוה (YHWH)), and you are not your own?

20 For you are bought with a price; therefore glorify יהוה (YHWH) in your body, and in your spirit, which are יהוה (YHWH)'s.

7 Now concerning the things whereof you wrote unto me: It is good for a man not to touch a woman.

2 Nevertheless, to avoid fornication, let every man have his own wife, and let every woman have her own husband.

3 Let the husband render unto the wife due benevolence; and likewise also the wife unto the husband.

4 The wife hath not power of her own body, but the husband; and likewise also the husband hath not power of his own body, but the wife.

5 Defraud you not one another, except it be with consent for a time, that you may give yourselves to fasting and prayer; and come together again, that Satan tempt you not for your incontinency.

6 But I speak this by permission, and not of commandment.

7 For I would that all men were even as I myself. But every man hath his proper gift of God (Elohim), one after this manner, and another after that.

8 I say therefore to the unmarried and widows, it is good for them if they abide even as I.

9 But if they cannot contain, let them marry; for it is better to marry than to burn.

10 And unto the married I command, yet not I, but the Lord (YHWH), let not the wife depart from her husband;

11 But and if she departs, let her remain unmarried, or be reconciled to her husband; and let not the husband put away his wife.

12 But to the rest speak I, not the Lord (YHWH). If any brother hath a wife that believeth not, and she be pleased to dwell with him, let him not put her away.

13 And the woman who hath a husband that believeth not, and if he be pleased to dwell with her, let her not leave him.

14 For the unbelieving husband is sanctified by the wife, and the unbelieving wife is sanctified by the husband; else were your children unclean; but now are they holy.

15 But if the unbelieving departs, let him depart. A brother or a sister is not under bondage in such cases; but God (Elohim) hath called us to peace.

16 For what knowest you, O wife, whether you shalt save your husband? Or how knowest you, O man, whether you shalt save your wife?

17 But as God (Elohim) hath distributed to every man, as the Lord (YHWH) hath called every one, so let him walk. And so ordain I in all assemblies (ekklesias).

18 Is any man called being circumcised? Let him not become uncircumcised. Is any called in uncircumcision? Let him not be circumcised.

19 Circumcision is nothing, and uncircumcision is nothing, but the keeping of the commandments of יהוה (YHWH).

20 Let every man abide in the same calling wherein he was called.

21 Are you called being a servant? Care not for it; but if you mayest be made free, use it rather.

22 For he that is called in the Lord (YHWH), being a servant, is the Lord (YHWH)'s freeman; likewise also he that is called, being free, is Messiah (Mashiach)'s servant.

23 You are bought with a price; be not you the servants of men.

24 Brethren, let every man, wherein he is called, therein abide with God (Elohim, יהוה (YHWH)).

25 Now concerning virgins I have no commandment of the Lord (YHWH); yet I give my judgment, as one that hath obtained mercy of the Lord (YHWH) to be faithful.

26 I suppose therefore that this is good for the present distress, I say, that it is good for a man so to be.

27 Are you bound unto a wife? Seek not to be loosed. Are you loosed from a wife? Seek not a wife.

28 But and if you marry, you have not sinned; and if a virgin marry, she hath not sinned. Nevertheless such shall have trouble in the flesh; but I spare you.

29 But this I say, brethren, the time is short; it remaineth, that both they that have wives be as though they had none;

30 And they that weep, as though they wept

not; and they that rejoice, as though they rejoiced not; and they that buy, as though they possessed not;

31 And they that use this world, as not abusing it; for the fashion of this world passeth away.

32 But I would have you without carefulness. He that is unmarried careth for the things that belong to the Lord (YHWH), how he may please the Lord (YHWH);

33 But he that is married careth for the things that are of the world, how he may please his wife.

34 There is difference also between a wife and a virgin. The unmarried woman careth for the things of the Lord (YHWH), that she may be holy both in body and in spirit; but she that is married careth for the things of the world, how she may please her husband.

35 And this I speak for your own profit; not that I may cast a snare upon you, but for that which is comely, and that you may attend upon our Lord (YHWH) without distraction.

36 But if any man thinks that he behaveth himself uncomely toward his virgin, if she passes the flower of her age, and need so require, let him do what he will, he sinneth not; let them marry.

37 Nevertheless he that standeth stedfast in his heart, having no necessity, but hath power over his own will, and hath so decreed in his heart that he will keep his virgin, doeth well.

38 So then he that giveth her in marriage doeth well; but he that giveth her not in marriage doeth better.

39 The wife is bound by the law (torah) as long as her husband liveth; but if her husband be dead, she is at liberty to be married to whom she will; only in the Lord (YHWH).

40 But she is happier if she so abides, after my judgment; and I think also that I have the Spirit of יהוה (Ruach YHWH).

8 Now as touching things offered unto idols, we know that we all have knowledge. Knowledge puffeth up, but love edifieth.

2 And if any man thinks that he knoweth any thing, he knoweth nothing yet as he ought to know.

3 But if any man loves God (Elohim, יהוה (YHWH)), the same is known of Him.

4 As concerning therefore the eating of those things that are offered in sacrifice unto idols, we know that an idol is nothing in the world, and that there is none other God (Elohim) but one.

5 For though there be that are called gods (elohim), whether in heaven or on earth, as there be gods (elohim) many, and lords (adonim) many,

6 But to us there is but one God (Elohim, יהוה (YHWH), the Father, of whom are all things, and we in Him; and one Lord (Adon) Yahwah haMashiach, by whom are all things, and we by Him.

7 Howbeit there is not in every man that knowledge; for some with conscience of the idol unto this hour eat it as a thing offered unto an idol; and their conscience being weak is defiled.

8 But food commendeth us not to God (Elohim); for neither, if we eat, are we the better; neither, if we eat not, are we the worse.

9 But take heed lest by any means this liberty of yours become a stumblingblock to them that are weak.

10 For if any man sees you who hast knowledge sit at meat in the idol's temple, shall not the conscience of him who is weak be emboldened to eat those things which are offered to idols;

11 And through your knowledge shall the weak brother perish, for whom the Messiah (haMashiach) died?

12 But when you sin so against the brethren, and wound their weak conscience, you sin against the Messiah (haMashiach).

13 Wherefore, if meat make my brother to offend, I will eat no flesh while the world standeth, lest I make my brother to offend.

9 Am I not an apostle? Am I not free? Have I not seen Yahwah haMashiach our Lord (Adonai)? Are not you my work in the Lord (YHWH)?

2 If I be not an apostle unto others, yet doubtless I am to you; for the seal of mine apostleship are you in the Lord (YHWH).

3 Mine answer to them that do examine me is this:

4 Have we not power to eat and to drink?

5 Have we not power to lead about a sister, a wife, as well as other apostles, and as the brethren of the Lord (YHWH), and Cephas (Kefa)?

6 Or I only and Barnabas, have not we power to forbear working?

7 Who goeth a warfare any time at his own

charges? Who planteth a vineyard, and eateth not of the fruit thereof? Or who feedeth a flock, and eateth not of the milk of the flock?

8 Say I these things as a man? Or saith not the Torah the same also?

9 For [B28c]it is written in the Torah by Moses (Mosheh), "You shalt not muzzle the mouth of the ox that treadeth out the corn." Doth God (Elohim) take care for oxen? – *Deu. 25:4*

10 Or saith He it altogether for our sakes? For our sakes, no doubt, this is written, that he that ploweth should plow in hope; and that he that thresheth in hope should be partaker of his hope.

11 If we have sown unto you spiritual things, is it a great thing if we shall reap your carnal things?

12 If others be partakers of this power over you, are not we rather? Nevertheless we have not used this power; but suffer all things, lest we should hinder the gospel (good news) of the Messiah (haMashiach).

13 Do you not know that they who minister about holy things live of the things of the temple? And they who wait at the altar are partakers with the altar?

14 Even so hath the Lord (YHWH) ordained that they who preach the gospel (good news) should live of the gospel (good news).

15 But I have used none of these things; neither have I written these things, that it should be so done unto me; for it was better for me to die, than that any man should make my glorying void.

16 For though I preach the gospel (good news), I have nothing to glory of; for necessity is laid upon me; yea, woe is unto me, if I preach not the gospel (good news)!

17 For if I do this thing willingly, I have a reward; but if against my will, a dispensation of the gospel (good news) is committed unto me.

18 What is my reward then? Verily that, when I preach the gospel (good news), I may make the gospel (good news) of the Messiah (haMashiach) without charge, that I abuse not my power in the gospel (good news).

19 For though I be free from all men, yet have I made myself servant unto all, that I might gain the more.

20 And unto the Jews (Yehudim) I became as a Jew (Yehudi), that I might gain the Jews (Yehudim); to them that are under the law

(torah), as under the law (torah), that I might gain them that are under the law (torah);

21 To them that are outside law (torah), as outside law (torah), being not outside law (torah) to God (Elohim), but under the law (torah) to the Messiah (haMashiach), that I might gain them that are outside law (torah).

22 To the weak became I as weak, that I might gain the weak; I am made all things to all men, that I might by all means save some.

23 And this I do for the gospel (good news)'s sake, that I might be partaker thereof with you.

24 Know you not that they who run in a race run all, but one receiveth the prize? So run, that you may obtain.

25 And every man that striveth for the mastery is temperate in all things. Now they do it to obtain a corruptible crown; but we an incorruptible.

26 I therefore so run, not as uncertainly; so fight I, not as one that beateth the air;

27 But I keep under my body, and bring it into subjection; lest that by any means, when I have preached to others, I myself should be a castaway.

10 Moreover, brethren, I would not that you should be ignorant, how that all our fathers were under the cloud, and all passed through the sea;

2 And were all baptized unto Moses (Mosheh) in the cloud and in the sea;

3 And did all eat the same spiritual food;

4 And did all drink the same spiritual drink; for they drank of that spiritual Rock that followed them; and that Rock was the Messiah (haMashiach).

5 But with many of them God (Elohim) was not well pleased; for they were overthrown in the wilderness.

6 Now these things were our examples, to the intent we should not lust after evil things, as they also lusted.

7 Neither be you idolaters, as were some of them; as it is written, "The people sat down to eat and drink, and rose up to play." – *Exo. 32:6*

8 Neither let us commit fornication, as some of them committed, and fell in one day three and twenty thousand.

9 Neither let us test the Messiah (haMashiach), as some of them also tested, and were destroyed of יהוה (YHWH) and serpents.

10 Neither murmur you, as some of them also

murmured, and were destroyed of the destroyer.

11 Now all these things happened unto them for ensamples; and they are written for our admonition, upon whom the ends of the world are come.

12 Wherefore let him that thinketh he standeth take heed lest he fall.

13 There hath no temptation taken you but such as is common to man; but God (Elohim) is faithful, who will not let you to be tempted above that you are able; but will with the temptation also make a way to escape, that you may be able to bear it.

14 Wherefore, my dearly beloved, flee from idolatry.

15 I speak as to wise men; judge you what I say.

16 The cup of blessing which we bless, is it not the communion of the blood of the Messiah (haMashiach)? The bread which we break, is it not the communion of the body of the Messiah (haMashiach)?

17 For we being many are one bread, and one body; for we are all partakers of that one bread.

18 Look at Yisrael after the flesh (physical Yisrael): Are not they who eat of the sacrifices partakers of the altar?

19 What say I then? That the idol is any thing, or that which is offered in sacrifice to idols is any thing?

20 But I say, that the things which the Gentiles (Goyim) sacrifice, they sacrifice to devils, and not to God (Elohim); and I would not that you should have fellowship with devils.

21 You cannot drink both the cup of the Lord (YHWH), and the cup of devils; you cannot be partakers of both the Lord (YHWH)'s table, and of the table of devils.

22 Do we provoke the Lord (YHWH) to jealousy? Are we stronger than He?

23 All things are lawful for me, but all things are not expedient; all things are lawful for me, but all things edify not.

24 Let no man seek his own interests, but that of the other.

25 Whatsoever is sold in the shambles, that eat, asking no question for conscience sake;

26 For the earth is יהוה (YHWH)'s, and the fulness thereof. – *Psa. 24:1, 50:12, 89:11*

27 If any of them that believe not bid you to a feast, and you be disposed to go; whatsoever is set before you, eat, asking no question for conscience sake.

28 But if any man says unto you, "This is offered in sacrifice unto idols", eat not for his sake that shewed it, and for conscience sake; for the earth is יהוה (YHWH)'s, and the fulness thereof;

29 Conscience, I say, not your own, but of the other; for why is my liberty judged of another man's conscience?

30 For if I by grace be a partaker, why am I evil spoken of for that for which I give thanks?

31 Whether therefore you eat, or drink, or whatsoever you do, do all to the glory of God (Elohim).

32 Give none offence, neither to the Jews (Yehudim), nor to the Gentiles (Goyim), nor to the assembly of God (Elohim);

33 Even as I please all men in all things, not seeking mine own profit, but the profit of many, that they may be saved.

11 Be you followers of me, even as I also am of the Messiah (haMashiach).

2 Now I praise you, brethren, that you remember me in all things, and keep the ordinances, as I delivered them to you.

3 But I would have you know, that the head of every man is the Messiah (haMashiach); and the head of the woman is the man; and the head of the Messiah (haMashiach) is God (Elohim).

4 Every man praying or prophesying, having his head covered, dishonoureth his head.

5 But every woman that prayeth or prophesieth with her head uncovered dishonoureth her head; for that is even all one as if she were shaven.

6 For if the woman be not covered, let her also be shorn; but if it be a shame for a woman to be shorn or shaven, let her be covered.

7 For a man indeed ought not to cover his head, forasmuch as he is the image and glory of God (Elohim); but the woman is the glory of the man.

8 For the man is not from the woman; but the woman from the man.

9 Neither was the man created for the woman; but the woman for the man.

10 For this cause ought the woman to have power on her head because of the angels.

11 Nevertheless neither is the man independent of the woman, neither the woman independent of the man, in the Lord (YHWH).

12 For as the woman is from the man, even so is the man also through the woman; but all things

from God (Elohim).

13 Judge in yourselves. Is it comely that a woman prays unto God (Elohim) uncovered?

14 Doth not even nature itself teach you, that, if a man has long hair, it is a shame unto him?

15 But if a woman has long hair, it is a glory to her; for her hair is given her for a covering.

16 But if any man seems to be contentious, we have no such custom, neither the assemblies (ekklesias) of God (Elohim).

17 Now in this that I declare unto you I praise you not, that you come together not for the better, but for the worse.

18 For first of all, when you come together in the assembly, I hear that there be divisions among you; and I partly believe it.

19 For there must be also heresies among you, that they who are approved may be made manifest among you.

20 When you come together therefore into one place, this is not to eat the Lord (Yahwah)'s supper.

21 For in eating every one taketh before other his own supper; and one is hungry, and another is drunken.

22 What? Have you not houses to eat and to drink in? Or despise you the assembly of God (Elohim), and shame them that have not? What shall I say to you? Shall I praise you in this? I praise you not.

23 For I have received of יהוה (YHWH) that which also I delivered unto you, that the Lord Yahwah (Adonai YHWH) the same night in which He was betrayed took bread;

24 And when He had given thanks, He brake it, and said, "Take, eat; this is My body, which is broken for you; this do in remembrance of Me."

25 After the same manner also He took the cup, when He had supped, saying, "This cup is the New Covenant (Berit haChadashah) in My blood; this do you, as often as you drink it, in remembrance of Me."

26 For as often as you eat this bread, and drink this cup, you do shew the Lord (Yahwah)'s death till He come.

27 Wherefore whosoever shall eat this bread, and drink this cup of the Lord (Yahwah), unworthily, shall be guilty of the body and blood of the Lord (Yahwah).

28 But let a man examine himself, and so let him eat of that bread, and drink of that cup.

29 For he that eateth and drinketh unworthily, eateth and drinketh damnation to himself, not discerning the Lord (Yahwah)'s body.

30 For this cause many are weak and sickly among you, and many sleep.

31 For if we would judge ourselves, we should not be judged.

32 But when we are judged, we are chastened of יהוה (YHWH) that we should not be condemned with the world.

33 Wherefore, my brethren, when you come together to eat, tarry one for another.

34 And if any man hunger, let him eat at home; that you come not together unto condemnation. And the rest will I set in order when I come.

12 Now concerning spiritual gifts, brethren, I would not have you ignorant.

2 You know that you were Gentiles (Goyim), carried away unto these dumb idols, even as you were led.

3 Wherefore I give you to understand, that no man speaking by the Spirit of יהוה (Ruach YHWH) calleth Yahwah (YHWH) accursed; and that no man can say that Yahwah (YHWH) is Lord (Adonai), but by the Holy Spirit (Ruach haQodesh).

4 Now there are diversities of gifts, but the same Spirit.

5 And there are differences of administrations, but the same Lord (Adon).

6 And there are diversities of operations, but it is the same God (Elohim) who worketh all in all.

7 But the manifestation of the Spirit is given to every man to profit withal.

8 For to one is given by the Spirit the word of wisdom; to another the word of knowledge by the same Spirit;

9 To another faith by the same Spirit; to another the gifts of healing by the same Spirit;

10 To another the working of miracles; to another prophecy; to another discerning of spirits; to another divers kinds of tongues; to another the interpretation of tongues;

11 But all these worketh that one and the selfsame Spirit, dividing to every man severally as He wills.

12 For as the body is one, and hath many members, and all the members of that one body, being many, are one body; so also is the Messiah (haMashiach).

13 For by one Spirit are we all baptized into

one body, whether we be Jews (Yehudim) or Gentiles (Goyim), whether we be bond or free; and have been all made to drink into one Spirit.

14 For the body is not one member, but many.

15 If the foot shall say, "Because I am not the hand, I am not of the body;" is it therefore not of the body?

16 And if the ear shall say, "Because I am not the eye, I am not of the body;" is it therefore not of the body?

17 If the whole body were an eye, where were the hearing? If the whole were hearing, where were the smelling?

18 But now hath God (Elohim) set the members every one of them in the body, as it hath pleased Him.

19 And if they were all one member, where were the body?

20 But now are they many members, yet but one body.

21 And the eye cannot say unto the hand, "I have no need of you;" nor again the head to the feet, "I have no need of you."

22 Nay, much more those members of the body, which seem to be more feeble, are necessary;

23 And those members of the body, which we think to be less honourable, upon these we bestow more abundant honour; and our uncomely parts have more abundant comeliness.

24 For our comely parts have no need; but God (Elohim) hath tempered the body together, having given more abundant honour to that part which lacked;

25 That there should be no schism in the body; but that the members should have the same care one for another.

26 And whether one member suffer, all the members suffer with it; or one member be honoured, all the members rejoice with it.

27 Now you are the body of the Messiah (haMashiach), and members in particular.

28 And God (Elohim) hath set some in the assembly, first apostles, secondarily prophets, thirdly teachers, after that miracles, then gifts of healings, helps, governments, diversities of tongues.

29 Are all apostles? Are all prophets? Are all teachers? Are all workers of miracles?

30 Have all the gifts of healing? Do all speak with tongues? Do all interpret?

31 But desire earnestly the best gifts; and yet shew I unto you a more excellent way.

13 Though I speak with the tongues of men and of angels, but have not love (agape), I am become as sounding brass, or a tinkling cymbal.

2 And though I have the gift of prophecy, and understand all mysteries, and all knowledge; and though I have all faith, so that I could remove mountains, but have not love (agape), I am nothing.

3 And though I bestow all my goods to feed the poor, and though I give my body to be burned, and have not love (agape), it profiteth me nothing.

4 Love (agape) suffereth long, and is kind; love envieth not; love vaunteth not itself, is not puffed up,

5 Doth not behave itself unseemly, seeketh not her own, is not easily provoked, thinketh no evil;

6 Rejoiceth not in iniquity, but rejoiceth in the truth;

7 Beareth all things, believeth all things, hopeth all things, endureth all things.

8 Love never faileth; but whether there be prophecies, they shall fail; whether there be tongues, they shall cease; whether there be knowledge, it shall vanish away.

9 For we know in part, and we prophesy in part.

10 But when that which is perfect is come, then that which is in part shall be done away.

11 When I was a child, I spake as a child, I understood as a child, I thought as a child; but when I became a man, I put away childish things.

12 For now we see through a glass, darkly; but then face to face; now I know in part; but then shall I know even as also I am known.

13 And now abideth faith, hope, love, these three; but the greatest of these is love.

14 Follow after love, and desire spiritual gifts, but rather that you may prophesy.

2 For he that speaketh in an unknown tongue speaketh not unto men, but unto God (Elohim); for no man understandeth him; howbeit in the spirit he speaketh mysteries.

3 But he that prophesieth speaketh unto men to edification, and exhortation, and comfort.

4 He that speaketh in an unknown tongue edifieth himself; but he that prophesieth edifieth the assembly.

5 I would that you all spake with tongues, but rather that you prophesied; for greater is he that prophesieth than he that speaketh with tongues, except he interprets, that the assembly may receive edifying.

6 Now, brethren, if I come unto you speaking with tongues, what shall I profit you, except I shall speak to you either by revelation, or by knowledge, or by prophesying, or by doctrine?

7 And even things without life giving sound, whether pipe or harp, except they give a distinction in the sounds, how shall it be known what is piped or harped?

8 For if the trumpet gives an uncertain sound, who shall prepare himself to the battle?

9 So likewise you, except you utter by the tongue words easy to be understood, how shall it be known what is spoken? For you shall speak into the air.

10 There are, it may be, so many kinds of voices in the world, and none of them is without signification.

11 Therefore if I know not the meaning of the voice, I shall be unto him that speaketh a barbarian, and he that speaketh shall be a barbarian unto me.

12 Even so you, forasmuch as you are zealous of spiritual gifts, seek that you may excel to the edifying of the assembly.

13 Wherefore let him that speaketh in an unknown tongue pray that he may interpret.

14 For if I pray in an unknown tongue, my spirit prayeth, but my understanding is unfruitful.

15 What is it then? I will pray with the spirit, and I will pray with the understanding also; I will sing with the spirit, and I will sing with the understanding also.

16 Else when you shalt bless with the spirit, how shall he that occupieth the room of the unlearned say "So be it (Amen)" at your giving of thanks, seeing he understandeth not what you sayest?

17 For you verily givest thanks well, but the other is not edified.

18 I thank my God (Elohim), I speak with tongues more than you all;

19 Yet in the assembly I had rather speak five words with my understanding, that by my voice I might teach others also, than ten thousand words in an unknown tongue.

20 Brethren, be not children in understanding: howbeit in malice be you children, but in understanding be men.

21 In the Torah it is written, "With men of other tongues and other lips will I speak unto this people; and yet for all that will they not hear Me," saith יהוה (YHWH). – *Isa. 28:11–12*

22 Wherefore tongues are for a sign, not to them that believe, but to them that believe not; but prophesying serveth not for them that believe not, but for them who believe.

23 If therefore the whole assembly be come together into one place, and all speak with tongues, and there come in those that are unlearned, or unbelievers, will they not say that you are mad?

24 But if all prophesy, and there come in one that believeth not, or one unlearned, he is convinced of all, he is judged of all;

25 And thus are the secrets of his heart made manifest; and so falling down on his face he will worship God (Elohim), and report that God (Elohim) is in you of a truth.

26 How is it then, brethren? When you come together, every one of you hath a psalm, hath a doctrine, hath a tongue, hath a revelation, hath an interpretation. Let all things be done unto edifying.

27 If any man speaks in an unknown tongue, let it be by two, or at the most by three, and that by course; and let one interpret.

28 But if there be no interpreter, let him keep silence in the assembly; and let him speak to himself, and to God (Elohim).

29 Let the prophets speak two or three, and let the other judge.

30 If any thing be revealed to another that sitteth by, let the first hold his peace.

31 For you may all prophesy one by one, that all may learn, and all may be comforted.

32 And the spirits of the prophets are subject to the prophets.

33 For God (Elohim, יהוה (YHWH)) is not the author of confusion, but of peace, as in all assemblies (ekklesias) of the holy ones.

34 Let your women keep silence in the assemblies (ekklesias); for it is not permitted unto them to speak; but they are commanded to be under obedience, as also saith the Torah.

35 And if they will learn any thing, let them ask their husbands at home; for it is a shame for women to speak in the assembly.

36 What? Came the word of God (Elohim, יהוה (YHWH)) out from you? Or came it unto you only?

37 If any man think himself to be a prophet, or spiritual, let him acknowledge that the things that I write unto you are the commandments of יהוה (YHWH).

38 But if any man be ignorant, let him be ignorant.

39 Wherefore, brethren, desire to prophesy, and forbid not to speak with tongues.

40 Let all things be done decently and in order.

15 Moreover, brethren, I declare unto you the gospel (good news) which I preached unto you, which also you have received, and wherein you stand;

2 By which also you are saved, if you keep in memory what I preached unto you, unless you have believed in vain.

3 For I delivered unto you first of all that which I also received, how that the Messiah (haMashiach) died for our sins according to the scriptures;

4 And that He was buried, and that He rose again the third day according to the scriptures;

5 And that He was seen of Peter (Kefa), then of the twelve.

6 After that, He was seen of above five hundred brethren at once; of whom the greater part remains unto this present, but some are fallen asleep.

7 After that, He was seen of James (Yaaqov); then of all the apostles.

8 And last of all He was seen of me also, as of one born out of due time.

9 For I am the least of the apostles, that am not meet to be called an apostle, because I persecuted the assembly of God (Elohim).

10 But by the grace of God (Elohim, יהוה (YHWH)) I am what I am; and His grace which was bestowed upon me was not in vain; but I laboured more abundantly than they all; yet not I, but the grace of God (Elohim, יהוה (YHWH)) which was with me.

11 Therefore whether it was I or they, so we preach, and so you believed.

12 Now if the Messiah (haMashiach) be preached that He rose from the dead, how say some among you that there is no resurrection of the dead?

13 But if there be no resurrection of the dead,

then is the Messiah (haMashiach) not risen;

14 And if the Messiah (haMashiach) be not risen, then is our preaching vain, and your faith is also vain.

15 Yea, and we are found false witnesses of God (Elohim, יהוה (YHWH)); because we have testified of יהוה that He raised up the Messiah (haMashiach); whom He raised not up, if so be that the dead rise not.

16 For if the dead rise not, then is not the Messiah (haMashiach) raised;

17 And if the Messiah (haMashiach) be not raised, your faith is vain; you are yet in your sins.

18 Then they also who are fallen asleep in Messiah (Mashiach) are perished.

19 If in this life only we have hope in Messiah (Mashiach), we are of all men most miserable.

20 But now is the Messiah (haMashiach) risen from the dead, and become the firstfruits of them that slept.

21 For since by man came death, by man came also the resurrection of the dead.

22 For as in Adam all die, even so in Messiah (Mashiach) shall all be made alive.

23 But every man in his own order: The Messiah (haMashiach) the firstfruits; afterward they that are Messiah (Mashiach)'s at His coming.

24 Then cometh the end, when He shall have delivered up the kingdom to God (Elohim), even the Father; when He shall have put down all rule and all authority and power.

25 For He must reign, till He hath put all enemies under His feet.

26 The last enemy that shall be destroyed is Death.

27 For He hath put all things under His feet. But when He saith, "All things are put under Him," it is manifest that He is excepted, who did put all things under Him. – *Psa. 8:6*

28 And when all things shall be subdued unto Him, then shall the [B47]Humanity of El (YHWH) also Himself be subject unto Him that put all things under Him, that God (Elohim, יהוה (YHWH)) may be all in all.

29 Else what shall they do who are baptized for the dead, if the dead rise not at all? Why are they then baptized for the dead?

30 And why stand we in jeopardy every hour?

31 I protest by your rejoicing which I have in the Messiah (haMashiach) Yahwah our Lord

(Adonai), I die daily.

32 If after the manner of men I have fought with beasts at Ephesus, what advantageth it me, if the dead rise not? Let us eat and drink; for tomorrow we die. – *Isa. 22:13, 56:12*

33 Be not deceived; evil communications corrupt good manners.

34 Awake to righteousness, and sin not; for some have not the knowledge of God (Elohim, יהוה (YHWH)). I speak this to your shame.

35 But some man will say, "How are the dead raised up? And with what body do they come?"

36 You fool, that which you sowest is not quickened, except it die;

37 And that which you sowest, you sowest not that body that shall be, but bare grain, it may chance of wheat, or of some other grain;

38 But God (Elohim) giveth it a body as it hath pleased Him, and to every seed its own body.

39 All flesh is not the same flesh; but there is one kind of flesh of men, another flesh of beasts, another of fishes, and another of birds.

40 There are also celestial bodies, and bodies terrestrial; but the glory of the celestial is one, and the glory of the terrestrial is another.

41 There is one glory of the sun, and another glory of the moon, and another glory of the stars; for one star differeth from another star in glory.

42 So also is the resurrection of the dead. It is sown in corruption; it is raised in incorruption;

43 It is sown in dishonour; it is raised in glory; it is sown in weakness; it is raised in power.

44 It is sown a natural body; it is raised a spiritual body. There is a natural body, and there is a spiritual body.

45 And so it is written, "The first man, Adam was made a living soul; the last "Adam" (haMashiach) was made a quickening spirit." – *Gen. 2:7*

46 Howbeit that was not first which is spiritual, but that which is natural; and afterward that which is spiritual.

47 The first man is of the earth, earthy; the second man is the Lord (YHWH) from heaven.

48 As is the earthy, such are they also that are earthy; and as is the heavenly, such are they also that are heavenly.

49 And as we have borne the image of the earthy, we shall also bear the image of the heavenly.

50 Now this I say, brethren, that flesh and blood cannot inherit the kingdom of God (Elohim, יהוה (YHWH); neither doth corruption inherit incorruption.

51 Behold, I shew you a mystery: We shall not all sleep, but we shall all be changed,

52 In a moment, in the twinkling of an eye, at the last trump; for the trumpet shall sound, and the dead shall be raised incorruptible, and we shall be changed.

53 For this corruptible must put on incorruption, and this mortal must put on immortality.

54 So when this corruptible shall have put on incorruption, and this mortal shall have put on immortality, then shall be brought to pass the saying that is written, "Death is swallowed up in victory." – *Isa. 25:8*

55 O Death, where is your sting? O Grave (Sheol), where is your victory?" – *Hos. 13:14*

56 The sting of death is sin; and the strength of sin is the Torah.

57 But thanks be to God (Elohim), who giveth us the victory through our Lord (Adonai) Yahwah haMashiach.

58 Therefore, my beloved brethren, be you stedfast, unmoveable, always abounding in the work of the Lord (YHWH), forasmuch as you know that your labour is not in vain in the Lord (YHWH).

16 Now concerning the collection for the holy ones, as I have given order to the assemblies (ekklesias) of Galatia, even so do you.

2 Upon the first day of the week let every one of you lay by him in store, as God (Elohim) hath prospered him, that there be no gatherings when I come.

3 And when I come, whomsoever you shall approve by your letters, them will I send to bring your liberality unto Jerusalem (Yerushalayim).

4 And if it be meet that I go also, they shall go with me.

5 Now I will come unto you, when I shall pass through Macedonia; for I do pass through Macedonia.

6 And it may be that I will abide, yea, and winter with you, that you may bring me on my journey whithersoever I go.

7 For I will not see you now by the way; but I trust to tarry a while with you, if יהוה (YHWH) permit.

8 But I will tarry at Ephesus until [B21]Pentecost

(Feast of Weeks - Chag Shavuot).

9 For a great door and effectual is opened unto me, and there are many adversaries.

10 Now if Timotheus come, see that he may be with you without fear; for he worketh the work of יהוה (YHWH) as I also do.

11 Let no man therefore despise him; but conduct him forth in peace, that he may come unto me; for I look for him with the brethren.

12 As touching our brother Apollos, I greatly desired him to come unto you with the brethren; but his will was not at all to come at this time; but he will come when he shall have convenient time.

13 Watch you, stand fast in the faith, act you like men, be strong.

14 Let all your things be done with love (agape).

15 I beseech you, brethren, (you know the house of Stephanas, that it is the firstfruits of Achaia, and that they have addicted themselves to the ministry of the holy ones,)

16 That you submit yourselves unto such, and to every one that helpeth with us, and laboureth.

17 I am glad of the coming of Stephanas and Fortunatus and Achaicus; for that which was lacking on your part they have supplied.

18 For they have refreshed my spirit and yours; therefore acknowledge you them that are such.

19 The assemblies (ekklesias) of Asia salute you. Aquila and Priscilla salute you much in the Lord (YHWH), with the assembly that is in their house.

20 All the brethren greet you. Greet you one another with a holy kiss.

21 The salutation of me Paul with mine own hand.

22 If any man loves not the Lord (Adonai) Yahwah haMashiach, let him be accursed (Anathema). Our Lord, come! (Marana ta!)

23 The grace of our Lord (Adonai) Yahwah haMashiach be with you.

24 My love (agape) be with you all in the Messiah (haMashiach) Yahwah. So be it (Amen).

2 CORINTHIANS
קוֹרִנְתִּים 2 QORINTIYIM 2 ב
(Second Epistle to the Corinthians)

1 Paul, an apostle of [A1]Yahwah [B45]haMashiach by the will of God (Elohim, יהוה (YHWH)), and [A75]Timothy our brother, unto the assembly of God (Elohim) who is at Corinth, with all the holy ones who are in all Achaia;

2 Grace be to you and peace from YHWH our Father, and from our Lord (Adonai) Yahwah haMashiach.

3 Blessed be YHWH, even the Father of our Lord (Adonai) Yahwah haMashiach, the Father of mercies, and the God (Elohim) of all comfort;

4 Who comforteth us in all our tribulation, that we may be able to comfort them who are in any trouble, by the comfort wherewith we ourselves are comforted of God (Elohim, יהוה (YHWH)).

5 For as the sufferings of the Messiah (haMashiach) abound in us, so our consolation also aboundeth by the Messiah (haMashiach).

6 And whether we be afflicted, it is for your consolation and salvation, which is effectual in the enduring of the same sufferings which we also suffer; or whether we be comforted, it is for your consolation and salvation.

7 And our hope of you is stedfast, knowing, that as you are partakers of the sufferings, so shall you be also of the consolation.

8 For we would not, brethren, have you ignorant of our trouble which came to us in Asia, that we were pressed out of measure, above strength, insomuch that we despaired even of life;

9 But we had the sentence of death in ourselves, that we should not trust in ourselves, but in God (Elohim) who raiseth the dead;

10 Who delivered us from so great a death, and doth deliver; in whom we trust that He will yet deliver us;

11 You also helping together by prayer for us, that for the gift bestowed upon us by the means of many persons thanks may be given by many on our behalf.

12 For our rejoicing is this, the testimony of our conscience, that in simplicity and godly sincerity, not with fleshly wisdom, but by the grace of God (Elohim, יהוה (YHWH)), we have had our conversation in the world, and more abundantly toward you.

13 For we write none other things unto you than what you read or acknowledge; and I trust you shall acknowledge even to the end;

14 As also you have acknowledged us in part, that we are your rejoicing, even as you also are ours in the day of our Lord Yahwah (Adonai YHWH).

15 And in this confidence I was minded to come unto you before, that you might have a second benefit;

16 And to pass by you into Macedonia, and to come again out of Macedonia unto you, and of you to be brought on my way toward Judah (Yehudah).

17 When I therefore was thus minded, did I use lightness? Or the things that I purpose, do I purpose according to the flesh, that with me there should be yea yea, and nay nay?

18 But as יהוה (YHWH) is true, our word toward you was not yea and nay.

19 For the [B47]Humanity of El, Yahwah haMashiach, who was preached among you by us, even by me and Silvanus and Timotheus, was not yea and nay, but in Him was yea.

20 For all the promises of God (Elohim) in Him are yea, and in Him Amen, unto the glory of God (Elohim, יהוה (YHWH)) by us.

21 Now He who stablisheth us with you in Messiah (Mashiach), and hath anointed us, is יהוה (YHWH);

22 Who hath also sealed us, and given the earnest of the Spirit in our hearts.

23 Moreover I call יהוה (YHWH) for a record upon my soul, that to spare you I came not as yet unto Corinth.

24 Not for that we have dominion over your faith, but are helpers of your joy; for by faith you stand.

2 But I determined this with myself, that I would not come again to you in heaviness.

2 For if I make you sorry, who is he then that maketh me glad, but the same which is made sorry by me?

3 And I wrote this same unto you, lest, when I came, I should have sorrow from them of whom I ought to rejoice; having confidence in you all, that my joy is the joy of you all.

4 For out of much affliction and anguish of heart I wrote unto you with many tears; not that you should be grieved, but that you might know the love which I have more abundantly unto you.

5 But if any have caused grief, he hath not grieved me, but in part; that I may not overcharge you all.

6 Sufficient to such a man is this punishment, which was inflicted of many.

7 So that contrariwise you ought rather to forgive him, and comfort him, lest perhaps such a one should be swallowed up with overmuch sorrow.

8 Wherefore I beseech you that you would confirm your love toward him.

9 For to this end also did I write, that I might know the proof of you, whether you be obedient in all things.

10 To whom you forgive any thing, I forgive also; for if I forgave any thing, to whom I forgave it, for your sakes forgave I it in the person of the Messiah (haMashiach);

11 Lest Satan should get an advantage of us, for we are not ignorant of his devices.

12 Furthermore, when I came to Troas to preach Messiah (Mashiach)'s gospel (good news), and a door was opened unto me of the Lord (YHWH),

13 I had no rest in my spirit, because I found not Titus my brother; but taking my leave of them, I went from thence into Macedonia.

14 Now thanks be unto God (Elohim), who always causeth us to triumph in our Messiah (Mashiach), and maketh manifest the savour of His knowledge by us in every place.

15 For we are unto God (Elohim) a sweet savour of the Messiah (haMashiach), in them that are saved, and in them that perish;

16 To the one we are the savour of death unto death; and to the other the savour of life unto life. And who is sufficient for these things?

17 For we are not as many, who corrupt the word of God (Elohim, יהוה (YHWH)); but as of sincerity, but as of God (Elohim), in the sight of God (Elohim) speak we in Messiah (Mashiach).

3 Do we begin again to commend ourselves? Or need we, as some others, epistles of commendation to you, or letters of commendation from you?

2 You are our epistle written in our hearts, known and read of all men;

3 Forasmuch as you are manifestly declared to be the epistle of the Messiah (haMashiach) ministered by us, written not with ink, but with the Spirit of the living God (Elohim); not in tables of stone, but in fleshy tables of the heart.

4 And such trust have we through our Messiah (Mashiach) toward God (Elohim);

5 Not that we are sufficient of ourselves to think any thing as of ourselves; but our sufficiency is of God (Elohim);

6 Who also hath made us able ministers of the New Covenant (Berit haChadashah); not of the letter, but of the Spirit; for the letter killeth, but the Spirit giveth life.

7 But if the ministration of death, written and engraven in stones, was glorious, so that the children of Yisrael could not stedfastly behold the face of Moses (Mosheh) for the glory of his countenance; which glory was to be done away;

8 How shall not the ministration of the Spirit be rather glorious?

9 For if the ministration of condemnation be glory, much more doth the ministration of righteousness exceeds in glory.

10 For even that which was made glorious had no glory in this respect, by reason of the glory that excelleth.

11 For if that which is done away was glorious, much more that which remaineth is glorious.

12 Seeing then that we have such hope, we use great plainness of speech;

13 And not as Moses (Mosheh), who put a vail over his face, that the children of Yisrael could not stedfastly look to the end of that which is abolished;

14 But their minds were blinded, for until this day remaineth the same vail untaken away in the reading of the Old Covenant (Berit haYeshanah); which vail is done away in Messiah (Mashiach).

15 But even unto this day, when Moses (Mosheh) is read, the vail is upon their heart.

16 Nevertheless when it shall turn to יהוה (YHWH) the vail shall be taken away. – *Exo. 34:34*

17 Now יהוה (YHWH) is that Spirit; and where the Spirit of יהוה (YHWH) is, there is liberty.

18 But we all, with open face beholding as in a glass the glory of יהוה are changed into the same image from glory to glory, even as by the Spirit of יהוה.

4 Therefore seeing we have this ministry, as we have received mercy, we faint not;

2 But have renounced the hidden things of dishonesty, not walking in craftiness, nor handling the word of God (Elohim, יהוה (YHWH)) deceitfully; but by manifestation of

the truth commending ourselves to every man's conscience in the sight of God (Elohim).

3 But if our gospel (good news) be hid, it is hid to them that are lost;

4 In whom the gods (elohim) of this world hath blinded the minds of them who believe not, lest the light of the glorious gospel (good news) of the Messiah (haMashiach), who is the image of God (Elohim, יהוה (YHWH)), should shine unto them.

5 For we preach not ourselves, but the Messiah (haMashiach) Yahwah the Lord (Adonai); and ourselves your servants for Yahwah's sake.

6 For God (Elohim), who commanded the light to shine out of darkness, hath shined in our hearts, to give the light of the knowledge of the glory of God (Elohim) in the face of Yahwah haMashiach.

7 But we have this treasure in earthen vessels, that the excellency of the power may be of God (Elohim, יהוה (YHWH)), and not of us.

8 We are troubled on every side, yet not distressed; we are perplexed, but not in despair;

9 Persecuted, but not forsaken; cast down, but not destroyed;

10 Always bearing about in the body the dying of our Lord Yahwah (Adonai YHWH), that the life also of Yahwah might be made manifest in our body.

11 For we who live are always delivered unto death for Yahwah's sake, that the life also of Yahwah might be made manifest in our mortal flesh.

12 So then death worketh in us, but life in you.

13 We having the same spirit of faith, according as it is written, "I believed, and therefore have I spoken"; we also believe, and therefore speak; – Psa.116:10

14 Knowing that He who raised up the Lord Yahwah (Adonai YHWH) shall raise up us also by Yahwah and shall present us with you.

15 For all things are for your sakes, that the abundant grace might through the thanksgiving of many redound to the glory of God (Elohim).

16 For which cause we faint not; but though our outward man perish, yet the inward man is renewed day by day.

17 For our light affliction, which is but for a moment, worketh for us a far more exceeding and eternal weight of glory;

18 While we look not at the things which are seen, but at the things which are not seen; for the things which are seen are temporal; but the things which are not seen are eternal.

5 For we know that if our earthly house of this tabernacle were dissolved, we have a building of God (Elohim), a house not made with hands, eternal in the heavens.

2 For in this we groan, earnestly desiring to be clothed upon with our house which is from heaven;

3 If so be that being clothed we shall not be found naked.

4 For we that are in this tabernacle do groan, being burdened; not for that we would be unclothed, but clothed upon, that mortality might be swallowed up of life.

5 Now He that hath wrought us for the selfsame thing is God (Elohim, יהוה (YHWH)) who also hath given unto us the earnest of the Spirit.

6 Therefore we are always confident, knowing that, whilst we are at home in the body, we are absent from the Lord (YHWH);

7 For we walk by faith, not by sight;

8 We are confident, I say, and willing rather to be absent from the body, and to be present with the Lord (YHWH).

9 Wherefore we labour, that, whether present or absent, we may be accepted of Him.

10 For we must all appear before the judgment seat of the Messiah (haMashiach); that every one may receive the things done in his body, according to that he hath done, whether it be good or bad.

11 Knowing therefore the terror of יהוה, we persuade men; but we are made manifest unto God (Elohim); and I trust also are made manifest in your consciences.

12 For we commend not ourselves again unto you, but give you occasion to glory on our behalf, that you may have somewhat to answer them who glory in appearance, and not in heart.

13 For whether we be beside ourselves, it is to God (Elohim); or whether we be sober, it is for your cause.

14 For the love of the Messiah (haMashiach) constraineth us; because we thus judge, that if one died for all, then were all dead;

15 And that He died for all, that they who live should not henceforth live unto themselves, but unto Him who died for them, and rose again.

16 Wherefore henceforth know we no man

after the flesh; yea, though we have known the Messiah (haMashiach) after the flesh, yet now henceforth know we Him no more.

17 Therefore if any man be in Messiah (Mashiach), he is a new creature; old things are passed away; behold, all things are become new.

18 And all things are of God (Elohim, יהוה (YHWH)), who hath reconciled us to Himself by Yahwah haMashiach, and hath given to us the ministry of reconciliation;

19 To wit, that יהוה (YHWH) was in Messiah (Mashiach), reconciling the world unto Himself, not imputing their trespasses unto them; and hath committed unto us the word of reconciliation.

20 Now then we are ambassadors for the Messiah (haMashiach), as though God (Elohim) did beseech you by us; we pray you in Messiah (Mashiach)'s stead, be you reconciled to God (Elohim).

21 For He hath made Him to be sin for us, who knew no sin; that we might be made the righteousness of God (Elohim) in Him.

6 We then, as workers together with Him, beseech you also that you receive not the grace of God (Elohim, יהוה (YHWH)) in vain.

2 For He saith, "I have heard you in a time accepted, and in the day of salvation have I succoured you." Behold, now is the accepted time; behold, now is the day of salvation. – *Isa. 49:8*

3 Giving no offence in any thing, that the ministry be not blamed;

4 But in all things approving ourselves as the ministers of God (Elohim), in much patience, in afflictions, in necessities, in distresses,

5 In stripes, in imprisonments, in tumults, in labours, in watchings, in fastings;

6 By pureness, by knowledge, by longsuffering, by kindness, by the Holy Spirit, by love unfeigned,

7 By the word of truth, by the power of God (Elohim, יהוה (YHWH)), by the armour of righteousness on the right hand and on the left,

8 By honour and dishonour, by evil report and good report; as deceivers, and yet true;

9 As unknown, and yet well known; as dying, and, behold, we live; as chastened, and not killed;

10 As sorrowful, yet always rejoicing; as poor, yet making many rich; as having nothing, and yet possessing all things.

11 O you Corinthians, our mouth is open unto you, our heart is enlarged.

12 You are not straitened in us, but you are straitened in your own bowels.

13 Now for a recompence in the same, (I speak as unto my children,) be you also enlarged.

14 Be you not unequally yoked together with unbelievers; for what fellowship hath righteousness with unrighteousness? And what communion hath light with darkness?

15 And what harmony hath the Messiah (haMashiach) with Beliyaal (which is an epithet of Satan)? Or what part hath he that believeth with an unbeliever?

16 And what agreement hath the temple of God (Elohim) with idols? For you are the temple of the living God (Elohim); as יהוה (YHWH) hath said, "I will dwell in them, and walk in them; and I will be their God (Elohim), and they shall be My people. – *Lev. 26:12; Exo. 6:7; Jer. 31:33, 32:38; Eze. 37:27*

17 Wherefore come out from among them, and be you separate," saith יהוה, "and touch not the unclean thing; and I will receive you, – *Isa. 52:11, Eze. 20:34, 41*

18 And will be a Father unto you, and you shall be My sons and daughters," saith [A8]יהוה of hosts (YHWH Tsevaot). – *2 Sam. 7:14, Isa. 43:6*

7 Having therefore these promises, dearly beloved, let us cleanse ourselves from all filthiness of the flesh and spirit, perfecting holiness in the fear of God (Elohim).

2 Receive us; we have wronged no man, we have corrupted no man, we have defrauded no man.

3 I speak not this to condemn you, for I have said before, that you are in our hearts to die and live with you.

4 Great is my boldness of speech toward you, great is my glorying of you; I am filled with comfort, I am exceeding joyful in all our tribulation.

5 For, when we were come into Macedonia, our flesh had no rest, but we were troubled on every side; outside were fightings, inside were fears.

6 Nevertheless God (Elohim), that comforteth those that are cast down, comforted us by the coming of Titus;

7 And not by his coming only, but by the consolation wherewith he was comforted in you, when he told us your earnest desire, your

mourning, your fervent mind toward me; so that I rejoiced the more.

8 For though I made you sorry with a letter, I do not regret, though I did regret; for I perceive that the same epistle hath made you sorry, though it was but for a season.

9 Now I rejoice, not that you were made sorry, but that you sorrowed to repentance; for you were made sorry after a godly manner, that you might receive damage by us in nothing.

10 For godly sorrow produces repentance to salvation not to be regretted of; but the sorrow of the world produces death.

11 For behold this selfsame thing, that you sorrowed after a godly sort, what carefulness it wrought in you, yea, what clearing of yourselves, yea, what indignation, yea, what fear, yea, what vehement desire, yea, what zeal, yea, what revenge! In all things you have approved yourselves to be clear in this matter.

12 Wherefore, though I wrote unto you, I did it not for his cause that had done the wrong, nor for his cause that suffered wrong, but that our care for you in the sight of God (Elohim) might appear unto you.

13 Therefore we were comforted in your comfort; yea, and exceedingly the more joyed we for the joy of Titus, because his spirit was refreshed by you all.

14 For if I have boasted any thing to him of you, I am not ashamed; but as we spake all things to you in truth, even so our boasting, which I made before Titus, is found a truth.

15 And his inward affection is more abundant toward you, whilst he remembereth the obedience of you all, how with fear and trembling you received him.

16 I rejoice therefore that I have confidence in you in all things.

8 Moreover, brethren, we do you to wit of the grace of God (Elohim, יהוה (YHWH)) bestowed on the assemblies (ekklesias) of Macedonia;

2 How that in a great trial of affliction the abundance of their joy and their deep poverty abounded unto the riches of their liberality.

3 For to their power, I bear record, yea, and beyond their power they were willing of themselves;

4 Praying us with much intreaty that we would receive the gift, and take upon us the fellowship of the ministering to the holy ones.

5 And this they did, not as we hoped, but first gave their own selves to the Lord (YHWH), and unto us by the will of God (Elohim, יהוה (YHWH)).

6 Insomuch that we desired Titus, that as he had begun, so he would also finish in you the same grace also.

7 Therefore, as you abound in every thing, in faith, and utterance, and knowledge, and in all diligence, and in your love to us, see that you abound in this grace also.

8 I speak not by commandment, but by occasion of the forwardness of others, and to prove the sincerity of your love.

9 For you know the grace of our Lord (Adonai) Yahwah haMashiach, that, though He was rich, yet for your sakes He became poor, that you through His poverty might be rich.

10 And herein I give my advice: For this is expedient for you, who have begun before, not only to do, but also to be forward a year ago.

11 Now therefore perform the doing of it; that as there was a readiness to will, so there may be a performance also out of that which you have.

12 For if there be first a willing mind, it is accepted according to that a man hath, and not according to that he hath not.

13 For I mean not that other men be eased, and you burdened;

14 But by an equality, that now at this time your abundance may be a supply for their want, that their abundance also may be a supply for your want; that there may be equality;

15 As it is written, "He that had gathered much had nothing over; and he that had gathered little had no lack." – *Exo. 16:18*

16 But thanks be to God (Elohim), who put the same earnest care into the heart of Titus for you.

17 For indeed he accepted the exhortation; but being more forward, of his own accord he went unto you.

18 And we have sent with him the brother, whose praise is in the gospel (good news) throughout all the assemblies (ekklesias);

19 And not that only, but who was also chosen of the assemblies (ekklesias) to travel with us with this grace, which is administered by us to the glory of the Lord (YHWH) Himself, and declaration of your ready mind;

20 Avoiding this, that no man should blame us

in this abundance which is administered by us;

21 Providing for honest things, not only in the sight of יהוה (YHWH) but also in the sight of men.

22 And we have sent with them our brother, whom we have oftentimes proved diligent in many things, but now much more diligent, upon the great confidence which I have in you.

23 Whether any do enquire of Titus, he is my partner and fellowhelper concerning you; or our brethren be enquired of, they are the messengers of the assemblies (ekklesias), and the glory of our Messiah (Mashiachnu).

24 Wherefore shew you to them, and before the assemblies (ekklesias), the proof of your love, and of our boasting on your behalf.

9 For as touching the ministering to the holy ones (qadoshim), it is superfluous for me to write to you:

2 For I know the forwardness of your mind, for which I boast of you to them of Macedonia, that Achaia was ready a year ago; and your zeal hath provoked very many.

3 Yet have I sent the brethren, lest our boasting of you should be in vain in this behalf; that, as I said, you may be ready:

4 Lest haply if they of Macedonia come with me, and find you unprepared, we (that we say nothing of you) should be ashamed in this same confident boasting.

5 Therefore I thought it necessary to exhort the brethren, that they would go before unto you, and make up beforehand your bounty, whereof you had notice before, that the same might be ready, as a matter of bounty, and not as of covetousness.

6 But this I say, He who soweth sparingly shall reap also sparingly; and he who soweth bountifully shall reap also bountifully.

7 Every man according as he purposeth in his heart, so let him give; not grudgingly, or of necessity; for God (Elohim) loveth a cheerful giver. – *Pro. 22:8*

8 And God (Elohim) is able to make all grace abound toward you; that you, always having all sufficiency in all things, may abound to every good work:

9 As it is written, "He hath dispersed abroad; he hath given to the poor; his righteousness remaineth for ever."–*Psa.112:9*

10 Now he that ministereth seed to the sower

both minister bread for your food, and multiply your seed sown, and increase the fruits of your righteousness;

11 Being enriched in every thing to all bountifulness, which causeth through us thanksgiving to God (Elohim).

12 For the administration of this service not only supplieth the want of the holy ones, but is abundant also by many thanksgivings unto God (Elohim);

13 Whiles by the experiment of this ministration they glorify God (Elohim) for your professed subjection unto the gospel (good news) of the Messiah (haMashiach), and for your liberal distribution unto them, and unto all men;

14 And by their prayer for you, who long after you for the exceeding grace of God (El) in you.

15 Thanks be unto God (Elohim) for His unspeakable gift.

10 Now I Paul myself beseech you by the meekness and gentleness of our Messiah (Mashiach), who in presence am base among you, but being absent am bold toward you;

2 But I beseech you, that I may not be bold when I am present with that confidence, wherewith I think to be bold against some, who think of us as if we walked according to the flesh.

3 For though we walk in the flesh, we do not war after the flesh;

4 For the weapons of our warfare are not carnal, but mighty through God (Elohim) to the pulling down of strong holds;

5 Casting down imaginations, and every high thing that exalteth itself against the knowledge of God (Elohim), and bringing into captivity every thought to the obedience of Messiah (Mashiach);

6 And having in a readiness to revenge all disobedience, when your obedience is fulfilled.

7 Do you look on things after the outward appearance? If any man trusts to himself that he is Messiah (Mashiach)'s, let him of himself think this again, that, as he is Messiah (Mashiach)'s, even so are we Messiah (Mashiach)'s.

8 For though I should boast somewhat more of our authority, which the Lord (YHWH) hath given us for edification, and not for your destruction, I should not be ashamed;

9 That I may not seem as if I would terrify you by letters.

10 For his letters, say they, are weighty and

powerful; but his bodily presence is weak, and his speech contemptible.

11 Let such a one think this, that, such as we are in word by letters when we are absent, such will we be also in deed when we are present.

12 For we dare not make ourselves of the number, or compare ourselves with some that commend themselves; but they measuring themselves by themselves, and comparing themselves among themselves, are not wise.

13 But we will not boast of things without our measure, but according to the measure of the rule which God (Elohim) hath distributed to us, a measure to reach even unto you.

14 For we stretch not ourselves beyond our measure, as though we reached not unto you; for we are come as far as to you also in preaching the gospel (good news) of the Messiah (haMashiach);

15 Not boasting of things without our measure, that is, of other men's labours; but having hope, when your faith is increased, that we shall be enlarged by you according to our rule abundantly,

16 To preach the gospel (good news) in the regions beyond you, and not to boast in another man's line of things made ready to our hand.

17 But he that glorieth, let him glory in יהוה (YHWH).

18 For not he that commendeth himself is approved, but whom יהוה (YHWH) commendeth.

11 Would that you could bear with me a little in my folly; and indeed bear with me.

2 For I am jealous over you with godly jealousy; for I have espoused you to one husband, that I may present you as a chaste virgin to the Messiah (haMashiach).

3 But I fear, lest by any means, as the serpent beguiled [A9]Eve (Chawah) through his subtilty, so your minds would be corrupted from the simplicity that is in the Messiah (haMashiach).

4 For if he that cometh preacheth another Yahwah (YHWH), whom we have not preached, or if you receive another spirit, which you have not received, or another gospel (good news), which you have not accepted, you might well bear with him.

5 For I suppose I was not a whit behind the very chiefest apostles.

6 But though I be rude in speech, yet not in knowledge; but we have been throughly made manifest among you in all things.

7 Have I committed an offence in abasing myself that you might be exalted, because I have preached to you the gospel (good news) of God (Elohim, יהוה (YHWH)) freely?

8 I robbed other assemblies (ekklesias) by taking wages from them, to do you service.

9 And when I was present with you, and wanted, I was chargeable to no man; for that which was lacking to me the brethren who came from Macedonia supplied; and in all things I have kept myself from being burdensome unto you, and so will I keep myself.

10 As the truth of the Messiah (haMashiach) is in me, no man shall stop me of this boasting in the regions of Achaia.

11 Wherefore? Because I love you not? God (Elohim) knoweth.

12 But what I do, that I will do, that I may cut off occasion from them who desire occasion; that wherein they glory, they may be found even as we.

13 For such are false apostles, deceitful workers, transforming themselves into the apostles of the Messiah (haMashiach).

14 And no marvel; for Satan himself is transformed into an angel of light.

15 Therefore it is no great thing if his ministers also be transformed as the ministers of righteousness; whose end shall be according to their works.

16 I say again, let no man think me a fool; if otherwise, yet as a fool receive me, that I may boast myself a little.

17 That which I speak, I speak it not after the Lord (YHWH), but as it was foolishly, in this confidence of boasting.

18 Seeing that many glory after the flesh, I will glory also.

19 For you suffer fools gladly, seeing you yourselves are wise.

20 For you suffer, if a man brings you into bondage, if a man devours you, if a man takes of you, if a man exalts himself, if a man smites you on the face.

21 I speak as concerning reproach, as though we had been weak. Howbeit whereinsoever any is bold, (I speak foolishly,) I am bold also.

22 Are they Hebrews (Ivrim)? So am I. Are they Yisraelim? So am I. Are they the seed of

Avraham? So am I.

23 Are they ministers of the Messiah (haMashiach)? (I speak as a fool) I am more; in labours more abundant, in stripes above measure, in prisons more frequent, in deaths often.

24 Of the Jews (Yehudim) five times received I forty stripes except one.

25 Thrice was I beaten with rods, once was I stoned, thrice I suffered shipwreck, a night and a day I have been in the deep;

26 In journeyings often, in perils of waters, in perils of robbers, in perils by mine own countrymen, in perils by the heathen, in perils in the city, in perils in the wilderness, in perils in the sea, in perils among false brethren;

27 In weariness and painfulness, in watchings often, in hunger and thirst, in fastings often, in cold and nakedness.

28 Besides those things that are external, that which cometh upon me daily, the care of all the assemblies (ekklesias).

29 Who is weak, and I am not weak? Who is offended, and I burn not?

30 If I must need glory, I will glory of the things which concern mine infirmities.

31 The God (Elohim) and Father of our Lord (Adonai) Yahwah haMashiach, who is blessed for evermore, knoweth that I lie not.

32 In Damascus the governor under Aretas the king kept the city of the Damascenes with a garrison, desirous to apprehend me;

33 And through a window in a basket was I let down by the wall, and escaped his hands.

12 It is not expedient for me doubtless to glory. I will come to visions and revelations of the Lord (YHWH).

2 I knew a man in Messiah (Mashiach) above fourteen years ago, (whether in the body, I cannot tell; or whether out of the body, I cannot tell; God (Elohim) knoweth;) such a one caught up to the third heaven.

3 And I knew such a man, (whether in the body, or out of the body, I cannot tell; God (Elohim) knoweth;)

4 How that he was caught up into paradise, and heard unspeakable words, which it is not lawful for a man to utter.

5 Of such a one will I glory; yet of myself I will not glory, but in mine infirmities.

6 For though I would desire to glory, I shall not be a fool; for I will say the truth; but now I forbear, lest any man should think of me above that which he seeth me to be, or that he heareth of me.

7 And lest I should be exalted above measure through the abundance of the revelations, there was given to me a thorn in the flesh, the messenger of Satan to buffet me, lest I should be exalted above measure.

8 For this thing I besought the Lord (YHWH) thrice, that it might depart from me.

9 And He said unto me, "My grace is sufficient for you; for My strength is made perfect in weakness." Most gladly therefore will I rather glory in my infirmities, that the power of the Messiah (haMashiach) may rest upon me.

10 Therefore I take pleasure in infirmities, in reproaches, in necessities, in persecutions, in distresses for the Messiah (haMashiach)'s sake; for when I am weak, then am I strong.

11 I am become a fool in glorying; you have compelled me; for I ought to have been commended of you; for in nothing am I behind the very chiefest apostles, though I be nothing.

12 Truly the signs of an apostle were wrought among you in all patience, in signs, and wonders, and mighty deeds.

13 For what is it wherein you were inferior to other assemblies (ekklesias), except it be that I myself was not burdensome to you? Forgive me this wrong.

14 Behold, the third time I am ready to come to you; and I will not be burdensome to you; for I seek not yours, but you; for the children ought not to lay up for the parents, but the parents for the children.

15 And I will very gladly spend and be spent for you; though the more abundantly I love you, the less I be loved.

16 But be it so, I did not burden you; nevertheless, being crafty, I caught you with guile.

17 Did I make a gain of you by any of them whom I sent unto you?

18 I desired Titus, and with him I sent a brother. Did Titus make a gain of you? Walked we not in the same spirit? Walked we not in the same steps?

19 Again, think you that we excuse ourselves unto you? We speak before God (Elohim, יהוה (YHWH)) in Messiah (Mashiach); but we do all things, dearly beloved, for your edifying.

20 For I fear, lest, when I come, I shall not find you such as I would, and that I shall be found unto you such as you would not; lest there be debates, envyings, wraths, strifes, backbitings, whisperings, swellings, tumults;

21 And lest, when I come again, my God (Elohim) will humble me among you, and that I shall bewail many who have sinned already, and have not repented of the uncleanness and fornication and lasciviousness which they have committed.

13 This is the third time I am coming to you. In the mouth of two or three witnesses shall every word be established.

2 I told you before, and foretell you, as if I were present, the second time; and being absent now I write to them who heretofore have sinned, and to all other, that, if I come again, I will not spare;

3 Since you seek a proof of the Messiah (haMashiach) speaking in me, which toward you is not weak, but is mighty in you.

4 For though He was crucified through weakness, yet He liveth by the power of God (Elohim, יהוה (YHWH)). For we also are weak in Him, but we shall live with Him by the power of God (Elohim, יהוה (YHWH)) toward you.

5 Examine yourselves, whether you be in the faith; prove your own selves. Know you not your own selves, how that Yahwah haMashiach is in you, except you be reprobates?

6 But I trust that you shall know that we are not reprobates.

7 Now I pray to God (Elohim) that you do no evil; not that we should appear approved, but that you should do that which is honest, though we be as reprobates.

8 For we can do nothing against the truth, but for the truth.

9 For we are glad, when we are weak, and you are strong: and this also we wish, even your perfection.

10 Therefore I write these things being absent, lest being present I should use sharpness, according to the power which the Lord (YHWH) hath given me to edification, and not to destruction.

11 Finally, brethren, farewell. Be perfect, be of good comfort, be of one mind, live in peace; and the God (Elohim) of love and peace shall be with you.

12 Greet one another with a holy kiss.

13 All the holy ones salute you.

14 The grace of our Lord (Adonai) Yahwah haMashiach, and the love of God (Elohim), and the communion of the Holy Spirit (Ruach haQodesh), be with you all. So be it (Amen).

GALATIANS
GALATIYIM גָּלָטִיִּים
(Epistle to the Galatians)

1 Paul, an apostle, (not of men, neither by man, but by Yahwah haMashiach, and YHWH the Father, who raised Him from the dead;)

2 And all the brethren who are with me, unto the assemblies (ekklesias) of Galatia;

3 Grace be to you and peace from YHWH the Father and our Lord (Adonai) Yahwah haMashiach,

4 Who gave Himself for our sins, that He might deliver us from this present evil world, according to the will of יהוה our Father;

5 To whom be glory for ever and ever. So be it (Amen).

6 I marvel that you are so soon removed from Him that called you by the grace of our Messiah (Mashiach) unto another gospel (good news);

7 Which is not another; but there be some that trouble you, and would pervert the gospel (good news) of the Messiah (haMashiach).

8 But even if we, or an angel from heaven, preach any other gospel (good news) unto you than that which we have preached unto you, let him be accursed.

9 As we said before, so say I now again, if any man preaches any other gospel (good news) unto you than that you have received, let him be accursed.

10 For do I now persuade men, or God (Elohim)? Or do I seek to please men? For if I yet pleased men, I should not be the servant of Messiah (Mashiach).

11 But I certify you, brethren, that the gospel (good news) which was preached of me is not after man.

12 For I neither received it of man, neither was I taught it, but by the revelation of Yahwah haMashiach.

13 For you have heard of my conversation in time past in the Jews' (Yehudim) religion, how that beyond measure I persecuted the assembly of God (Elohim), and wasted it;

14 And profited in the Jews' (Yehudim) religion above many my equals in mine own nation, being more exceedingly zealous of the traditions of my fathers.

15 But when it pleased God (Elohim), who separated me from my mother's womb, and called me by His grace,

16 To reveal His [B47]Humanity in me, that I might preach Him among the heathen; immediately I conferred not with flesh and blood;

17 Neither went I up to Jerusalem (Yerushalayim) to them who were apostles before me; but I went into Arabia, and returned again unto Damascus.

18 Then after three years I went up to Jerusalem (Yerushalayim) to see Peter (Kefa), and abode with him fifteen days.

19 But other of the apostles saw I none, except James (Yaaqov) the Lord (Yahwah)'s brother.

20 Now the things which I write unto you, behold, before God (Elohim), I lie not.

21 Afterwards I came into the regions of Syria and Cilicia;

22 And was unknown by face unto the assemblies (ekklesias) of Judah (Yehudah) which were in the Messiah (haMashiach);

23 But they had heard only, "That he who persecuted us in times past now preacheth the faith which once he destroyed."

24 And they glorified יהוה (YHWH) in me.

2 Then fourteen years after I went up again to Jerusalem (Yerushalayim) with Barnabas, and took Titus with me also.

2 And I went up by revelation, and communicated unto them that gospel (good news) which I preach among the Gentiles (Goyim), but privately to them who were of reputation, lest by any means I should run, or had run, in vain.

3 But neither Titus, who was with me, being a Greek, was compelled to be circumcised;

4 And that because of false brethren unawares brought in, who came in privily to spy out our liberty which we have in the Messiah (haMashiach) Yahwah, that they might bring us into bondage;

5 To whom we gave place by subjection, no, not for an hour; that the truth of the gospel (good news) might continue with you.

6 But of these who seemed to be somewhat, (whatsoever they were, it maketh no matter to me; God (Elohim) accepteth no man's person;) for they who seemed to be somewhat in conference added nothing to me;

7 But contrariwise, when they saw that the gospel (good news) of the uncircumcision was committed unto me, as the gospel (good news) of the circumcision was unto Peter (Kefa);

8 (For he that wrought effectually in Peter (Kefa) to the apostleship of the circumcision, the same was mighty in me toward the Gentiles (Goyim);

9 And when James (Yaaqov), Peter (Kefa), and John (Yochanan), who seemed to be pillars, perceived the grace that was given unto me, they gave to me and Barnabas the right hands of fellowship; that we should go unto the heathen, and they unto the circumcision.

10 Only they wish that we should remember the poor; the same which I also was forward to do.

11 But when Peter (Kefa) was come to Antioch, I withstood him to the face, because he was to be blamed.

12 For before that certain came from James (Yaaqov), he did eat with the Gentiles (Goyim); but when they were come, he withdrew and separated himself, fearing them who were of the circumcision.

13 And the other Jews (Yehudim) dissembled likewise with him; insomuch that Barnabas also was carried away with their dissimulation.

14 But when I saw that they walked not uprightly according to the truth of the gospel (good news), I said unto Peter (Kefa) before them all, "If you, being a Jew (Yehudi), livest after the manner of Gentiles (Goyim), and not as do the Jews (Yehudim), why compellest you the Gentiles (Goyim) to live as do the Jews (Yehudim)?

15 We who are Jews (Yehudim) by nature, and not sinners of the Gentiles (Goyim),

16 Knowing that a man is not justified by the works of the [B28a]law (torah), but by the faith of Yahwah haMashiach, even we have believed in Yahwah haMashiach, that we might be justified by the faith of the Messiah (haMashiach), and not by the works of the law (torah); for by the works of the law (torah) shall no flesh be justified.

17 But if, while we seek to be justified by the Messiah (haMashiach), we ourselves also are found sinners, is therefore Messiah (Mashiach) the minister of sin? God (Elohim) forbid.

18 For if I build again the things which I have destroyed, I make myself a transgressor.

19 For I through the law (torah) am dead to the law (torah), that I might live unto God (Elohim).

20 I am crucified with the Messiah (haMashiach); nevertheless I live; yet not I, but the Messiah (haMashiach) liveth in me; and the life which

I now live in the flesh I live by the faith of the [B47]Humanity of El (Yahwah haMashiach), who loved me, and gave Himself for me.

21 I do not frustrate the grace of God (Elohim, יהוה (YHWH)); for if righteousness come by the law (torah), then the Messiah (haMashiach) is dead in vain.

3 O foolish Galatians, who hath bewitched you, that you should not obey the truth, before whose eyes Yahwah haMashiach hath been evidently set forth, crucified among you?

2 This only would I learn of you, "Received you the Spirit by the works of the law (torah), or by the hearing of faith?

3 Are you so foolish? Having begun in the Spirit, are you now made perfect by the flesh?

4 Have you suffered so many things in vain? If it be yet in vain.

5 He therefore that ministereth to you the Spirit, and worketh miracles among you, doeth he it by the works of the law (torah), or by the hearing of faith?

6 Even as Avraham believed God (Elohim, יהוה (YHWH)), and it was accounted to him for righteousness. – Gen. 15:6

7 Know you therefore that they who are of faith, the same are the children of Avraham.

8 And the scripture, foreseeing that God (Elohim) would justify the heathen through faith, preached before the gospel (good news) unto Avraham, saying, "In you shall all nations be blessed." – Gen. 12:3

9 So then they who be of faith are blessed with faithful Avraham.

10 For as many as are of the works of the law (torah) are under the curse; for it is written, "Cursed is every one that continueth not in all things which are written in the [B28b]book of the law (sefer hatorah) to do them." – Deu. 27:26

11 But that no man is justified by the law (torah) in the sight of God (Elohim), it is evident; for, "The just shall live by faith." – Hab. 2:4

12 And the law (torah) is not of faith; but, "The man that doeth them shall live in them." – Lev. 18:5

13 The Messiah (haMashiach) hath redeemed us from the curse pronounced in the [B28a]law (torah), being made a curse for us; for it is written, "Cursed is every one that hangeth on a tree (stake);" – Deu. 21:22–23, Deu. Chp. 27, 28

14 That the blessing of Avraham might come

on the Gentiles (Goyim) through Yahwah haMashiach; that we might receive the promise of the Spirit through faith.

15 Brethren, I speak after the manner of men; though it be but a man's covenant, yet if it be confirmed, no man disannulleth, or addeth thereto.

16 Now to Avraham and his seed were the promises made. He saith not, "And to seeds," as of many; but as of one, "And to your seed," who is the Messiah (haMashiach). – *Gen. 22:18, 26:4*

17 And this I say: The [B28a]law (torah) which came into existance four hundred and thirty years later, cannot disannul the covenant (berit) that was confirmed before by God (Elohim, יהוה (YHWH)) in Messiah (Mashiach), that it should make the promise of none effect.

18 For if the inheritance be of the law (torah), it is no more of promise; but God (Elohim) gave it to Avraham by promise.

19 Wherefore then does the [B28a]law (torah) serveth? It was added because of transgressions, till the Seed should come to whom the promise was made; and it was ordained by angels in the hand of a mediator.

20 Now a mediator is not a mediator of one, but God (Elohim, יהוה (YHWH)) is one.

21 Is the law (torah) then against the promises of God (Elohim)? God (Elohim) forbid; for if there had been a law (torah) given which could have given life, verily righteousness should have been by the law (torah).

22 But the scripture hath concluded all under sin, that the promise by faith of Yahwah haMashiach might be given to them that believe. – *Rom. 4:16*

23 But before faith came, we were kept under the law (torah), shut up unto the faith which should afterwards be revealed.

24 Wherefore the law (torah) was our schoolmaster to bring us unto the Messiah (haMashiach), that we might be justified by faith.

25 But after that faith is come, we are no longer under a schoolmaster.

26 For you are all the children of God (Elohim) by faith in the Messiah (haMashiach) Yahwah.

27 For as many of you as have been baptized into the Messiah (haMashiach) have put on the Messiah (haMashiach).

28 There is neither Jew (Yehudi) nor Greek, there is neither bond nor free, there is neither male nor female; for you are all one in the Messiah (haMashiach) Yahwah.

29 And if you be Messiah (Mashiach)'s, then are you Avraham's seed, and heirs according to the promise. – *Eph. 3:6*

4 Now I say, that the heir, as long as he is a child, differeth nothing from a servant, though he be master (adon) of all;

2 But is under tutors and governors until the time appointed of the father.

3 Even so we, when we were children, were in bondage under the elements of the world;

4 But when the fulness of the time was come, God (Elohim, יהוה (YHWH)) sent forth His [B47]Humanity, made of a woman, made under the law (torah),

5 To redeem them that were under the law (torah), that we might receive the adoption of sons.

6 And because you are sons, God (Elohim, יהוה (YHWH)) hath sent forth His Spirit into your hearts, crying, "Abba, Father."

7 Wherefore you are no more a servant, but a son; and if a son, then an heir of יהוה (YHWH) through the Messiah (haMashiach).

8 Howbeit then, when you knew not God (Elohim, יהוה (YHWH)), you did service unto them which by nature are not God (Elohim).

9 But now, after that you have known God (Elohim, יהוה (YHWH)), or rather are known of God (Elohim, יהוה (YHWH)), how turn you again to the weak and beggarly elements, whereunto you desire again to be in bondage?

10 You observe days, and months, and times, and years.

11 I am afraid of you, lest I have bestowed upon you labour in vain.

12 Brethren, I beseech you, be as I am; for I am as you are; you have not injured me at all.

13 You know how through infirmity of the flesh I preached the gospel (good news) unto you at the first.

14 And my trial which was in my flesh you despised not, nor rejected; but received me as an angel of God (Elohim), even as the Messiah (haMashiach) Yahwah.

15 Where is then the blessedness you spake of? For I bear you record, that, if it had been possible, you would have plucked out your own eyes, and have given them to me.

16 Am I therefore become your enemy, because

I tell you the truth?

17 They zealously affect you, but not well; yea, they would exclude you, that you might affect them.

18 But it is good to be zealously affected always in a good thing, and not only when I am present with you.

19 My little children, of whom I travail in birth again until the Messiah (haMashiach) be formed in you,

20 I desire to be present with you now, and to change my voice; for I stand in doubt of you.

21 Tell me, you that desire to be under the B28alaw (torah), do you not hear the Torah;

22 For it is written, that Avraham had two sons, the one by a bondmaid, the other by a freewoman.

23 But he who was of the bondwoman was born after the flesh; but he of the freewoman was by promise.

24 Which things are an allegory; for these are the two covenants: the one from the Mount Sinai, which gendereth to bondage, which is Hagar.

25 For this Hagar is Mount Sinai in Arabia, and answereth to Jerusalem (Yerushalayim) which now is, and is in bondage with her children.

26 But Jerusalem (Yerushalayim) which is above is free, which is the mother of us all.

27 For it is written, "Rejoice, you barren that bearest not; break forth and cry, you that travailest not; for the desolate hath many more children than she who hath a husband." – *Isa. 54:1*

28 Now we, brethren, as Isaac (Yitschaq) was, are the children of promise.

29 But as then he that was born after the flesh persecuted him that was born after the Spirit, even so it is now.

30 Nevertheless what saith the scripture? Cast out the bondwoman and her son; for the son of the bondwoman shall not be heir with the son of the freewoman. – *Gen. 21:10*

31 So then, brethren, we are not children of the bondwoman, but of the free.

5 Stand fast therefore in the liberty wherewith the Messiah (haMashiach) hath made us free, and be not entangled again with the yoke of bondage.

2 Behold, I Paul say unto you, that if you be circumcised, the Messiah (haMashiach) shall

profit you nothing.

3 For I testify again to every man that is circumcised, that he is a debtor to do the whole B28alaw (torah).

4 The Messiah (haMashiach) is become of no effect unto you, whosoever of you are justified by the law (torah); you are fallen from grace.

5 For we through the Spirit wait for the hope of righteousness by faith.

6 For in Yahwah haMashiach neither circumcision availeth anything, nor uncircumcision; but faith which worketh by love.

7 You did run well; who did hinder you that you should not obey the truth?

8 This persuasion cometh not of Him that calleth you.

9 A little leaven leaveneth the whole lump.

10 I have confidence in you through the Lord (YHWH), that you will be none otherwise minded; but he that troubleth you shall bear his judgment, whosoever he be.

11 And I, brethren, if I yet preach circumcision, why do I yet suffer persecution? Then is the offence of the stake ceased.

12 I wish they were even cut off who trouble you.

13 For, brethren, you have been called unto liberty; only use not liberty for an occasion to the flesh, but by love serve one another.

14 For the whole of B28aTorah is fulfilled in one sentence, even in this: You shalt love your neighbour as yourself. – *Lev. 19:18, Jam. 2:8*

15 But if you bite and devour one another, take heed that you be not consumed one of another.

16 This I say then: Walk in the Spirit, and you shall not fulfil the lust of the flesh.

17 For the flesh lusteth against the Spirit, and the Spirit against the flesh; and these are contrary the one to the other; so that you cannot do the things that you would.

18 But if you be led of the Spirit, you are not under the law (torah).

19 Now the works of the flesh are manifest, which are these: Adultery, fornication, uncleanness, lasciviousness,

20 Idolatry, witchcraft, hatred, variance, emulations, wrath, strife, seditions, heresies,

21 Envyings, murders, drunkenness, revellings, and such like; of which I tell you before, as I have also told you in time past, that they who do such things shall not inherit the kingdom of God

(Elohim, יהוה (YHWH)).

22 But the fruit of the Spirit is love, joy, peace, longsuffering, gentleness, goodness, faith,

23 Meekness, temperance; nothing in the Torah stands against such thing.

24 And they that are Messiah (Mashiach)'s have crucified the flesh with the affections and lusts.

25 If we live in the Spirit, let us also walk in the Spirit.

26 Let us not be desirous of vain glory, provoking one another, envying one another.

6 Brethren, if a man be overtaken in a fault, you who are spiritual, restore such a one in the spirit of meekness; considering yourself, lest you also be tempted.

2 Bear you one another's burdens, and so fulfil the Torah of the Messiah (haMashiach).

3 For if a man think himself to be something, when he is nothing, he deceiveth himself.

4 But let every man prove his own work, and then shall he has rejoicing in himself alone, and not in another.

5 For every man shall bear his own burden.

6 Let him that is taught in the word communicate unto him that teacheth in all good things.

7 Be not deceived; God (Elohim) is not mocked; for whatsoever a man soweth, that shall he also reap.

8 For he that soweth to his flesh shall of the flesh reap corruption; but he that soweth to the Spirit shall of the Spirit reap life everlasting.

9 And let us not be weary in well doing; for in due season we shall reap, if we faint not.

10 As we have therefore opportunity, let us do good unto all men, especially unto them who are of the household of faith.

11 You see how large a letter I have written unto you with mine own hand.

12 As many as desire to make a fair shew in the flesh, they constrain you to be circumcised; only lest they should suffer persecution for the stake of the Messiah (haMashiach).

13 For neither they themselves who are circumcised keep the Torah; but desire to have you circumcised, that they may glory in your flesh.

14 But God (Elohim) forbid that I should glory, except in the stake of our Lord (Adonai) Yahwah haMashiach, by whom the world is crucified unto me, and I unto the world.

15 For in the Messiah (haMashiach) Yahwah neither circumcision availeth anything, nor uncircumcision, but a new creature.

16 And as many as walk according to this rule, peace be on them, and mercy, and upon the Yisrael of God (Elohim).

17 From henceforth let no man trouble me; for I bear in my body the marks of the Lord Yahwah (Adonai YHWH).

18 Brethren, the grace of our Lord (Adonai) Yahwah haMashiach be with your spirit. So be it (Amen).

EPHESIANS
EFISIYIM אפסיים
(Epistle to the Ephesians)

1 Paul, an apostle of Yahwah haMashiach by the will of God (Elohim, יהוה (YHWH)), to the holy ones who are at Ephesus, and to the faithful in the Messiah (haMashiach) Yahwah.

2 Grace be to you, and peace, from יהוה (YHWH)) our Father and our Lord (Adonai) Yahwah haMashiach.

3 Blessed be the God (Elohim) and Father of our Lord (Adonai) Yahwah haMashiach, who hath blessed us with all spiritual blessings in heavenly places in Messiah (Mashiach);

4 According as He hath chosen us in Him before the foundation of the world, that we should be holy and without blame before Him in love;

5 Having predestinated us unto the adoption of children by Yahwah haMashiach to Himself, according to the good pleasure of His will,

6 To the praise of the glory of His grace, wherein He hath made us accepted in the beloved.

7 In whom we have redemption through His blood, the forgiveness of sins, according to the riches of His grace;

8 Wherein He hath abounded toward us in all wisdom and prudence;

9 Having made known unto us the mystery of His will, according to His good pleasure which He hath purposed in Himself;

10 That in the dispensation of the fulness of times He might gather together in one all things in Mashiach, both which are in heaven, and which are on earth; even in Him:

11 In whom also we have obtained an inheritance, being predestinated according to the purpose of Him who worketh all things after the counsel of His own will;

12 That we should be to the praise of His glory, who first trusted in Messiah (Mashiach).

13 In whom you also trusted, after that you heard the word of truth, the gospel (good news) of your salvation; in whom also after that you believed, you were sealed with that Holy Spirit of promise,

14 Which is the earnest of our inheritance until the redemption of the purchased possession, unto the praise of His glory.

15 Wherefore I also, after I heard of your faith in our Lord Yahwah (Adonai YHWH), and love unto all the holy ones,

16 Cease not to give thanks for you, making mention of you in my prayers;

17 That the God (Elohim) of our Lord (Adonai) Yahwah haMashiach, the Father of glory, may give unto you the spirit of wisdom and revelation in the knowledge of Him;

18 The eyes of your understanding being enlightened; that you may know what is the hope of His calling, and what the riches of the glory of His inheritance in the holy ones,

19 And what is the exceeding greatness of His power toward us who believe, according to the working of His mighty power,

20 Which He wrought in Messiah (Mashiach), when He raised Him from the dead, and set Him at His own right hand in the heavenly places,

21 Far above all principality, and power, and might, and dominion, and every name that is named, not only in this world, but also in that which is to come;

22 And hath put all things under His feet, and gave Him to be the head over all things to the assembly,

23 Which is His body, the fulness of Him that filleth all in all.

2 And you hath He quickened, who were dead in trespasses and sins;

2 Wherein in time past you walked according to the course of this world, according to the prince of the power of the air, the spirit that now worketh in the children of disobedience;

3 Among whom also we all had our conversation in times past in the lusts of our flesh, fulfilling the desires of the flesh and of the mind; and were by nature the children of wrath, even as others.

4 But God (Elohim, יהוה (YHWH)) who is rich in mercy, for His great love wherewith He loved us,

5 Even when we were dead in sins, hath quickened us together with the Messiah (haMashiach), (by grace you are saved;)

6 And hath raised us up together, and made us sit together in heavenly places in the Messiah (haMashiach) Yahwah;

7 That in the ages to come He might shew the exceeding riches of His grace in His kindness toward us through the Messiah (haMashiach) Yahwah.

8 For by grace are you saved through faith; and that not of yourselves; it is the gift of God (Elohim);

9 Not of works, lest any man should boast.

10 For we are His workmanship, created in the Messiah (haMashiach) Yahwah unto good works, which God (Elohim) hath before ordained that we should walk in them.

11 Wherefore remember, that you being in time past Gentiles (Goyim) in the flesh, who are called 'the Uncircumcised' by those who are called 'the Circumcised' in the flesh made by hands;

12 That at that time you were without Messiah (Mashiach), being aliens from the commonwealth of Yisrael, and strangers from the covenants of promise, having no hope, and without God (Elohim) in the world; – *Gen. 15:13, Acts. 7:6*

13 But now in the Messiah (haMashiach) Yahwah you who sometimes were far off are made near by the blood of Messiah (Mashiach).

14 For He is our peace, who hath made both one, and hath broken down the middle wall of partition between us;

15 Having abolished in His flesh the enmity, even the teaching of commandments contained in ordinances; for to make in Himself of twain one new man, so making peace;

16 And that He might reconcile both unto יהוה (YHWH) in one body by the stake, having slain the enmity thereby;

17 And came and preached peace to you who were afar off, and to them that were near. – *Isa. 57:19*

18 For through Him we both have access by one Spirit unto the Father.

19 Now therefore you are no more strangers and foreigners, but fellowcitizens with the holy ones, and of the household of יהוה (YHWH);

20 And are built upon the foundation of the apostles and prophets, Yahwah haMashiach Himself being the chief cornerstone;

21 In whom all the building fitly framed together groweth unto a holy temple in יהוה;

22 In whom you also are builded together for a habitation of God (Elohim) through the Spirit.

3 For this cause I Paul, the prisoner of Yahwah haMashiach for you Gentiles (Goyim),

2 If you have heard of the dispensation of the grace of God (Elohim, יהוי (YHWH)) which is

given me toward you;

3 How that by revelation He made known unto me the mystery; as I wrote afore in few words,

4 Whereby, when you read, you may understand my knowledge in the mystery of the Messiah (haMashiach)

5 Which in other ages was not made known unto the sons of men, as it is now revealed unto His holy apostles and prophets by the Spirit;

6 That the Gentiles (Goyim) should be fellowheirs, and of the same body, and partakers of His promise in the Messiah (haMashiach) by the gospel (good news); – *Gal. 3:28,29*

7 Whereof I was made a minister, according to the gift of the grace of God (Elohim, יהוה (YHWH)) given unto me by the effectual working of His power.

8 Unto me, who am less than the least of all holy ones, is this grace given, that I should preach among the Gentiles (Goyim) the unsearchable riches of the Messiah (haMashiach);

9 And to make all men see what is the fellowship of the mystery, which from the beginning of the world hath been hid in God (Elohim), who created all things by Yahwah haMashiach;

10 To the intent that now unto the principalities and powers in heavenly places might be known by the assembly the manifold wisdom of God (Elohim),

11 According to the eternal purpose which He purposed in the Messiah (haMashiach) Yahwah our Lord (Adonai);

12 In whom we have boldness and access with confidence by the faith of Him.

13 Wherefore I desire that you faint not at my tribulations for you, which is your glory.

14 For this cause I bow my knees unto the Father of our Lord (Adonai) Yahwah haMashiach,

15 Of whom the whole family in heaven and earth is named,

16 That He would grant you, according to the riches of His glory, to be strengthened with might by His Spirit in the inner man;

17 That the Messiah (haMashiach) may dwell in your hearts by faith; that you, being rooted and grounded in love,

18 May be able to comprehend with all holy ones what is the breadth, and length, and depth, and height;

19 And to know the love of the Messiah (haMashiach), which passeth knowledge, that

you might be filled with all the fulness of God (Elohim, יהוה (YHWH)).

20 Now unto Him that is able to do exceeding abundantly above all that we ask or think, according to the power that worketh in us,

21 Unto Him be glory in the assembly by the Messiah (haMashiach) Yahwah throughout all ages, world without end. So be it (Amen).

4 I therefore, the prisoner of the Lord (YHWH), beseech you that you walk worthy of the vocation wherewith you are called,

2 With all lowliness and meekness, with longsuffering, forbearing one another in love;

3 Endeavouring to keep the unity of the Spirit in the bond of peace.

4 There is one body, and one Spirit, even as you are called in one hope of your calling;

5 One Lord (Adon), one faith, one baptism,

6 One God (Elohim, יהוה (YHWH)) and Father of all, who is above all, and through all, and in you all.

7 But unto every one of us is given grace according to the measure of the gift of the Messiah (haMashiach).

8 Wherefore He saith, "When He ascended up on high, He led captivity captive, and gave gifts unto men." – Psa. 68:18

9 (Now that He ascended, what is it but that He also descended first into the lower parts of the earth?

10 He that descended is the same also that ascended up far above all heavens, that He might fill all things.)

11 And He gave some, apostles; and some, prophets; and some, evangelists; and some, pastors and teachers;

12 For the perfecting of the holy ones, for the work of the ministry, for the edifying of the body of the Messiah (haMashiach).

13 Till we all come in the unity of the faith, and of the knowledge of the Humanity of El (YHWH), unto a perfect man, unto the measure of the stature of the fulness of the Messiah (haMashiach);

14 That we henceforth be no more children, tossed to and fro, and carried about with every wind of doctrine, by the sleight of men, and cunning craftiness, whereby they lie in wait to deceive;

15 But speaking the truth in love, may grow up into Him in all things, who is the head, even the Messiah (haMashiach);

16 From whom the whole body fitly joined together and compacted by that which every joint supplieth, according to the effectual working in the measure of every part, maketh increase of the body unto the edifying of itself in love.

17 This I say therefore, and testify in the Lord (YHWH), that you henceforth walk not as other Gentiles (Goyim) walk, in the vanity of their mind,

18 Having the understanding darkened, being alienated from the life of יהוה (YHWH) through the ignorance that is in them, because of the blindness of their heart;

19 Who being past feeling have given themselves over unto lasciviousness, to work all uncleanness with greediness.

20 But you have not so learned from the Messiah (haMashiach);

21 If so be that you have heard Him, and have been taught by Him, as the truth is in Yahwah;

22 That you put off concerning the former conversation the old man, which is corrupt according to the deceitful lusts;

23 And be renewed in the spirit of your mind;

24 And that you put on the new man, which after God (Elohim, יהוה (YHWH)) has created in righteousness and true holiness.

25 Wherefore putting away lying, speak every man truth with his neighbour; for we are members one of another. – Zec. 8:16

26 Be you angry, but sin not; let not the sun go down upon your wrath; – Psa. 4:4

27 Neither give place to the devil.

28 Let him that stole steal no more; but rather let him labour, working with his hands the thing which is good, that he may have to give to him that needeth.

29 Let no corrupt communication proceed out of your mouth, but that which is good to the use of edifying, that it may minister grace unto the hearers.

30 And grieve not the Holy Spirit (Ruach haQodesh) of God (Elohim, יהוה (YHWH)), whereby you are sealed unto the day of redemption.

31 Let all bitterness, and wrath, and anger, and clamour, and evil speaking, be put away from you, with all malice;

32 And be you kind one to another,

tenderhearted, forgiving one another, even as in the Messiah (haMashiach) God (Elohim, יהוה (YHWH)) hath forgiven you.

5 Be you therefore followers of God (Elohim, יהוה (YHWH)), as dear children;

2 And walk in love, as the Messiah (haMashiach) also hath loved us, and hath given Himself for us an offering and a sacrifice to יהוה (YHWH) for a sweetsmelling savour.

3 But fornication, and all uncleanness, or covetousness, let it not be once named among you, as becometh holy people;

4 Neither filthiness, nor foolish talking, nor jesting, which are not convenient; but rather giving of thanks.

5 For this you know, that no whoremonger, nor unclean person, nor covetous man, who is an idolater, hath any inheritance in the kingdom of our Messiah (Mashiach) and of יהוה (YHWH).

6 Let no man deceive you with vain words; for because of these things cometh the wrath of יהוה (YHWH) upon the children of disobedience.

7 Be not you therefore partakers with them.

8 For you were once darkness, but now are you light in the Lord (YHWH); walk as children of light,

9 For the fruit of the Spirit is in all goodness and righteousness and truth;

10 Proving what is acceptable unto the Lord (YHWH).

11 And have no fellowship with the unfruitful works of darkness, but rather reprove them.

12 For it is a shame even to speak of those things which are done of them in secret.

13 But all things that are reproved are made manifest by the light; for whatsoever doth make manifest is light.

14 Wherefore He saith, "Awake you that sleepest, and arise from the dead, and the Messiah (haMashiach) shall give you light."

15 See then that you walk circumspectly, not as fools, but as wise,

16 Redeeming the time, because the days are evil.

17 Wherefore be you not unwise, but understanding what the will of God (Elohim, יהוה (YHWH)) is.

18 And be not drunk with wine, wherein is excess; but be filled with the Spirit;

19 Speaking to yourselves in psalms and hymns and spiritual songs, singing and making melody

in your heart to יהוה (YHWH);

20 Giving thanks always for all things unto God (Elohim) and the Father in the name of our Lord (Adonai) Yahwah haMashiach;

21 Submitting yourselves one to another in the fear of God (Elohim).

22 Wives, submit yourselves unto your own husbands, as unto the Lord (YHWH).

23 For the husband is the head of the wife, even as the Messiah (haMashiach) is the head of the assembly; and He is the Savior of the body.

24 Therefore as the assembly is subject unto the Messiah (haMashiach), so let the wives be to their own husbands in every thing.

25 Husbands, love your wives, even as the Messiah (haMashiach) also loved the assembly, and gave Himself for it;

26 That He might sanctify and cleanse it with the washing of water by the word,

27 That He might present it to Himself a glorious assembly, not having spot, or wrinkle, or any such thing; but that it should be holy and without blemish.

28 So ought men to love their wives as their own bodies. He that loveth his wife loveth himself.

29 For no man ever yet hated his own flesh; but nourisheth and cherisheth it, even as the Messiah (haMashiach) doesth the assembly;

30 For we are members of His body, of His flesh, and of His bones.

31 For this cause shall a man leave his father and mother, and shall be joined unto his wife, and they two shall be one flesh.

32 This is a great mystery: but I speak concerning the Messiah (haMashiach) and the assembly.

33 Nevertheless let every one of you in particular so love his wife even as himself; and the wife sees that she reverences her husband.

6 Children, obey your parents in the Lord (YHWH); for this is right.

2 Honour your father and mother; which is the first commandment with promise;

3 That it may be well with you, and you mayest live long on the earth. – *Exo. 20:12; Deu. 5:16*

4 And, you fathers, provoke not your children to wrath; but bring them up in the nurture and admonition of the Lord (YHWH).

5 Servants, be obedient to them that are your masters according to the flesh, with fear and trembling, in singleness of your heart, as unto

Messiah (Mashiach);

6 Not with eyeservice, as menpleasers; but as the servants of the Messiah (haMashiach), doing the will of יהוה (YHWH) from the heart;

7 With good will doing service, as to the Lord (YHWH), and not to men;

8 Knowing that whatsoever good thing any man doeth, the same shall he receive of the Lord (YHWH), whether he be bond or free.

9 And, you masters (adonim), do the same things unto them, forbearing threatening; knowing that your Master (Adon) also is in heaven; neither is there respect of persons with Him.

10 Finally, my brethren, be strong in the Lord (YHWH), and in the power of His might.

11 Put on the whole armour of God (Elohim), that you may be able to stand against the wiles of the devil.

12 For we wrestle not against flesh and blood, but against principalities, against powers, against the rulers of the darkness of this world, against spiritual wickedness in high places.

13 Wherefore take unto you the whole armour of God (Elohim, יהוה (YHWH)), that you may be able to withstand in the evil day, and having done all, to stand.

14 Stand therefore, having your loins girt about with truth, and having on the breastplate of righteousness;

15 And your feet shod with the preparation of the gospel (good news) of peace;

16 Above all, taking the shield of faith, wherewith you shall be able to quench all the fiery darts of the wicked.

17 And take the helmet of salvation, and the sword of the Spirit, which is the word of God (Elohim, יהוה (YHWH));

18 Praying always with all prayer and supplication in the Spirit, and watching thereunto with all perseverance and supplication for all holy ones;

19 And for me, that utterance may be given unto me, that I may open my mouth boldly, to make known the mystery of the gospel (good news),

20 For which I am an ambassador in bonds; that therein I may speak boldly, as I ought to speak.

21 But that you also may know my affairs, and how I do, Tychicus, a beloved brother and faithful minister in the Lord (YHWH), shall make known to you all things:

22 Whom I have sent unto you for the same purpose, that you might know our affairs, and that he might comfort your hearts.

23 Peace be to the brethren, and love with faith, from YHWH the Father and the Lord (Adonai) Yahwah haMashiach.

24 Grace be with all them that love our Lord (Adonai) Yahwah haMashiach in sincerity. So be it (Amen).

PHILIPPIANS
FILIPPIYIM פִּילִפִּיִּים
(Epistle to the Philippians)

1 Paul and Timotheus, the servants of [A1]Yahwah [B45]haMashiach, to all the holy ones in the Messiah (haMashiach) Yahwah who are at Philippi, with the bishops and deacons;

2 Grace be unto you, and peace, from YHWH our Father, and from our Lord (Adonai) Yahwah haMashiach.

3 I thank my God (Elohim) upon every remembrance of you,

4 Always in every prayer of mine for you all making request with joy,

5 For your fellowship in the gospel (good news) from the first day until now;

6 Being confident of this very thing, that He who hath begun a good work in you will perform it until the day of Yahwah haMashiach;

7 Even as it is meet for me to think this of you all, because I have you in my heart; inasmuch as both in my bonds, and in the defence and confirmation of the gospel (good news), you all are partakers of my grace.

8 For God (Elohim) is my record, how greatly I long after you all in the bowels of Yahwah haMashiach.

9 And this I pray, that your love may abound yet more and more in knowledge and in all judgment;

10 That you may approve things that are excellent; that you may be sincere and without offence till the day of the Messiah (haMashiach);

11 Being filled with the fruits of righteousness, which are by Yahwah haMashiach, unto the glory and praise of יהוה (YHWH).

12 But I would you should understand, brethren, that the things which happened unto me have fallen out rather unto the furtherance of the gospel (good news);

13 So that my bonds in the Messiah (haMashiach) are manifest in all the palace, and in all other places;

14 And many of the brethren in the Lord (YHWH), waxing confident by my bonds, are much more bold to speak the word without fear.

15 Some indeed preach the Messiah (haMashiach) even of envy and strife; and some also of good will;

16 The one preaches the Messiah (haMashiach) of contention, not sincerely, supposing to add affliction to my bonds;

17 But the other of love, knowing that I am set for the defence of the gospel (good news).

18 What then? Notwithstanding, every way, whether in pretence, or in truth, Messiah (haMashiach) is preached; and I therein do rejoice, yea, and will rejoice.

19 For I know that this shall turn to my salvation through your prayer, and the supply of the Spirit of Yahwah haMashiach,

20 According to my earnest expectation and my hope, that in nothing I shall be ashamed, but that with all boldness, as always, so now also Messiah (Mashiach) shall be magnified in my body, whether it be by life, or by death.

21 For to me, life is the Messiah (haMashiach), and death is gain.

22 But if I live in the flesh, this is the fruit of my labour; yet what I shall choose I wot not.

23 For I am in a strait betwixt two, having a desire to depart, and to be with the Messiah (haMashiach); which is far better;

24 Nevertheless to abide in the flesh is more needful for you.

25 And having this confidence, I know that I shall abide and continue with you all for your furtherance and joy of faith;

26 That your rejoicing may be more abundant in Yahwah haMashiach for me by my coming to you again.

27 Only let your conversation be as it becometh the gospel (good news) of the Messiah (haMashiach); that whether I come and see you, or else be absent, I may hear of your affairs, that you stand fast in one spirit, with one mind striving together for the faith of the gospel (good news);

28 And in nothing terrified by your adversaries; which is to them an evident token of perdition, but to you of salvation, and that of God (Elohim, Elohim, יהוה (YHWH)).

29 For unto you it is given in the behalf of Messiah (Mashiach), not only to believe on Him, but also to suffer for His sake;

30 Having the same conflict which you saw in me, and now hear to be in me.

2 If there be therefore any consolation in Messiah (Mashiach), if any comfort of love, if any fellowship of the Spirit, if any bowels and mercies,

2 Fulfil you my joy, that you be likeminded, having the same love, being of one accord, of one mind.

3 Let nothing be done through strife or vainglory; but in lowliness of mind let each esteem other better than themselves.

4 Look not every man on his own things, but every man also on the things of others.

5 Let this mind be in you, which was also in the Messiah (haMashiach) Yahwah;

6 Who, being in the form of God (Elohim), thought it not robbery to be equal with God (Elohim, יהוה (YHWH));

7 But made Himself of no reputation, and took upon Him the form of a servant, and was made in the likeness of men;

8 And being found in fashion as a man, He humbled Himself, and became obedient unto death, even the death of the stake.

9 Wherefore God (Elohim, יהוה (YHWH)) also hath highly exalted Him, and given Him a name which is above every name,

10 [B69]That at the name of יהוה (YHWH) every knee should bow, of things in heaven, and things on earth, and things under the earth; – *Isa. 45:23*

11 And that every tongue should confess that Yahwah haMashiach is the Lord (Adonai), to the glory of YHWH the Father. – *Isa. 45:23*

12 Wherefore, my beloved, as you have always obeyed, not as in my presence only, but now much more in my absence, work out your own salvation with fear and trembling.

13 For it is God (Elohim, יהוה (YHWH)) who worketh in you both to will and to do of His good pleasure.

14 Do all things without murmurings and disputings;

15 That you may be blameless and harmless, the sons of God (Elohim), without rebuke, in the midst of a crooked and perverse nation, among whom you shine as lights in the world;

16 Holding forth the word of life; that I may rejoice in the day of the Messiah (haMashiach), that I have not run in vain, neither laboured in vain.

17 Yea, and if I be offered upon the sacrifice and service of your faith, I joy, and rejoice with you all.

18 For the same cause also do you joy, and rejoice with me.

19 But I trust in the Lord Yahwah (Adonai YHWH) to send Timotheus shortly unto you, that I also may be of good comfort, when I know your state.

20 For I have no man likeminded, who will naturally care for your state.

21 For all seek their own, not the things which are Yahwah haMashiach's.

22 But you know the proof of Him, that, like a son with the father, he hath served with me in the gospel (good news).

23 Him therefore I hope to send presently, so soon as I shall see how it will go with me.

24 But I trust in the Lord (YHWH) that I also myself shall come shortly.

25 Yet I supposed it necessary to send to you Epaphroditus, my brother, and companion in labour, and fellowsoldier, but your messenger, and he that ministered to my needs.

26 For he longed after you all, and was full of heaviness, because that you had heard that he had been sick.

27 For indeed he was sick near unto death; but God (Elohim, יהוה (YHWH)) had mercy on him; and not on him only, but on me also, lest I should have sorrow upon sorrow.

28 I sent him therefore the more carefully, that, when you see him again, you may rejoice, and that I may be the less sorrowful.

29 Receive him therefore in the Lord (YHWH) with all gladness; and hold such in reputation;

30 Because for the work of the Messiah (haMashiach) he was near unto death, not regarding his life, to supply your lack of service toward me.

3 Finally, my brethren, rejoice in the Lord (YHWH). To write the same things to you, to me indeed is not grievous, but for you it is safe.

2 Beware of dogs, beware of evil workers, beware of the concision.

3 For we are the circumcised, who worship God (Elohim, יהוה (YHWH)) in the Spirit, and rejoice in the Messiah (haMashiach) Yahwah, and have no confidence in the flesh;

4 Though I might also have confidence in the flesh. If any other man thinketh that he hath whereof he might trust in the flesh, I more;

5 Circumcised the eighth day, of the stock of Yisrael, of the tribe of Benjamin (Binyamin), a

Hebrew (Ivri) of the Hebrews (Ivrim); according to the law (torah), a Pharisee;

6 Concerning zeal, persecuting the assembly; according to righteousness which is in the law (torah), blameless.

7 But what things were gain to me, those I counted loss for the Messiah (haMashiach).

8 Yea doubtless, and I count all things but loss for the excellency of the knowledge of the Messiah (haMashiach) Yahwah my Lord (Adonai); for whom I have suffered the loss of all things, and do count them but dung, that I may win the Messiah (haMashiach),

9 And be found in Him, not having mine own righteousness which is of the law (torah), but that which is through the faith of the Messiah (haMashiach), the righteousness which is of God (Elohim) by faith; – Heb. 11:7

10 That I may know Him, and the power of His resurrection, and the fellowship of His sufferings, being made conformable unto His death;

11 If by any means I might attain unto the resurrection of the dead.

12 Not as though I had already attained, either were already perfect; but I follow after, if that I may apprehend that for which also I am apprehended of the Messiah (haMashiach) Yahwah.

13 Brethren, I count not myself to have apprehended; but this one thing I do, forgetting those things which are behind, and reaching forth unto those things which are before,

14 I press toward the mark for the prize of the high calling of God (Elohim) in the Messiah (haMashiach) Yahwah.

15 Let us therefore, as many as be perfect, be thus minded; and if in any thing you be otherwise minded, God (Elohim, יהוה (YHWH)) shall reveal even this unto you.

16 Nevertheless, whereto we have already attained, let us walk by the same rule, let us mind the same thing.

17 Brethren, be followers together of me, and mark them which walk so as you have us for an ensample.

18 (For many walk, of whom I have told you often, and now tell you even weeping, that they are the enemies of the stake of the Messiah (haMashiach);

19 Whose end is destruction, whose God

(Elohim) is their belly, and whose glory is in their shame, who mind earthly things.)

20 For our conversation is in heaven; from whence also we look for our Savior, our Lord (Adonai) Yahwah haMashiach;

21 Who shall change our vile body, that it may be fashioned like unto His glorious body, according to the working whereby He is able even to subdue all things unto Himself.

4 Therefore, my brethren dearly beloved and longed for, my joy and crown, so stand fast in the Lord (YHWH), my dearly beloved.

2 I beseech Euodias, and beseech Syntyche, that they be of the same mind in the Lord (YHWH).

3 And I intreat you also, true yokefellow, help those women who laboured with me in the gospel (good news), with Clement also, and with other my fellowlabourers, whose names are in the book of life.

4 Rejoice in the Lord (YHWH) always; and again I say, rejoice!

5 Let your moderation be known unto all men. The Lord (YHWH) is at hand.

6 Be anxious for nothing, but in everything by prayer and supplication with thanksgiving let your requests be made known unto God (Elohim, יהוה (YHWH)).

7 And the peace of God (Elohim, יהוה (YHWH)), which passeth all understanding, shall keep your hearts and minds through the Messiah (haMashiach) Yahwah.

8 Finally, brethren, whatsoever things are true, whatsoever things are honest, whatsoever things are just, whatsoever things are pure, whatsoever things are lovely, whatsoever things are of good report; if there be any virtue, and if there be any praise, think on these things.

9 Those things, which you have both learned, and received, and heard, and seen in me, do; and the God (Elohim) of peace shall be with you.

10 But I rejoiced in the Lord (YHWH) greatly, that now at the last your care of me hath flourished again; wherein you were also careful, but you lacked opportunity.

11 Not that I speak in respect of need; for I have learned, in whatsoever state I am, therewith to be content.

12 I know both how to be abased, and I know how to abound; everywhere and in all things I am instructed both to be full and to be hungry, both to abound and to suffer need.

13 I can do all things through the Messiah (haMashiach) who strengtheneth me.

14 Notwithstanding you have well done, that you did communicate with my affliction.

15 Now you Philippians know also, that in the beginning of the gospel (good news), when I departed from Macedonia, no assembly communicated with me as concerning giving and receiving, but you only.

16 For even in Thessalonica you sent once and again unto my necessity.

17 Not because I desire a gift; but I desire fruit that may abound to your account.

18 But I have all, and abound; I am full, having received of Epaphroditus the things which were sent from you, an odour of a sweet smell, a sacrifice acceptable, wellpleasing to God (Elohim, יהוה (YHWH)).

19 But my God (Elohim) shall supply all your need according to His riches in glory by the Messiah (haMashiach) Yahwah.

20 Now unto our God (Elohim, יהוה (YHWH)) and Father be glory for ever and ever. So be it (Amen).

21 Salute every holy ones (qadoshim) in the Messiah (haMashiach) Yahwah. The brethren who are with me greet you.

22 All the holy ones salute you, chiefly they that are of Caesar's household.

23 The grace of our Lord (Adonai) Yahwah haMashiach be with you all. So be it (Amen).

COLOSSIANS
QOLASIM קולוסים
(Epistle to the Colossians)

1 Paul, an apostle of [A1]Yahwah [B45]haMashiach by the will of God (Elohim, יהוה (YHWH)), and Timotheus our brother,

2 To the holy ones and faithful brethren in Messiah (Mashiach) who are at Colosse. Grace be unto you, and peace, from YHWH our Father and our Lord (Adonai) Yahwah haMashiach.

3 We give thanks to God (Elohim) and the Father of our Lord (Adonai) Yahwah haMashiach, praying always for you,

4 Since we heard of your faith in the Messiah (haMashiach) Yahwah, and of the love which you have to all the holy ones,

5 For the hope which is laid up for you in heaven, whereof you heard before in the word of the truth of the gospel (good news);

6 Which is come unto you, as it is in all the world; and bringeth forth fruit, as it doth also in you, since the day you heard of it, and knew the grace of God (Elohim, יהוה (YHWH)) in truth;

7 As you also learned of Epaphras our dear fellowservant, who is for you a faithful minister of Messiah (Mashiach);

8 Who also declared unto us your love in the Spirit.

9 For this cause we also, since the day we heard it, do not cease to pray for you, and to desire that you might be filled with the knowledge of His will in all wisdom and spiritual understanding;

10 That you might walk worthy of the Lord (YHWH) unto all pleasing, being fruitful in every good work, and increasing in the knowledge of God (Elohim, יהוה (YHWH));

11 Strengthened with all might, according to His glorious power, unto all patience and longsuffering with joyfulness;

12 Giving thanks unto the Father, who hath made us meet to be partakers of the inheritance of the holy ones in light;

13 Who hath delivered us from the power of darkness, and hath translated us into the kingdom of His dear [B47]Humanity;

14 In whom we have redemption through His blood, even the forgiveness of sins;

15 Who is the image of the invisible God (Elohim), the firstborn of every creature;

16 For by Him were all things created, that are in heaven, and that are in earth, visible and invisible, whether they be thrones, or dominions, or principalities, or powers; all things were created by Him, and for Him;

17 And He is before all things, and by Him all things consist.

18 And He is the head of the body, the assembly; who is the beginning, the firstborn from the dead; that in all things He might have the preeminence.

19 For it pleased the Father that in Him should all fulness dwell;

20 And, having made peace through the blood of His stake, by Him to reconcile all things unto Himself; by Him, I say, whether they be things on earth, or things in heaven.

21 And you, that were sometime alienated and enemies in your mind by wicked works, yet now hath He reconciled,

22 In the body of His flesh through death, to present you holy and unblameable and unreproveable in His sight;

23 If you continue in the faith grounded and settled, and be not moved away from the hope of the gospel (good news), which you have heard, and which was preached to every creature which is under heaven; whereof I Paul am made a minister;

24 Who now rejoice in my sufferings for you, and fill up that which is behind of the afflictions of Messiah (Mashiach) in my flesh for His body's sake, which is the assembly;

25 Whereof I am made a minister, according to the dispensation of God (Elohim) which is given to me for you, to fulfil the word of God (Elohim, יהוה (YHWH));

26 Even the mystery which hath been hid from ages and from generations, but now is made manifest to His holy ones;

27 To whom God (Elohim, יהוה (YHWH)) would make known what is the riches of the glory of this mystery among the Gentiles (Goyim); which is the Messiah (haMashiach) in you, the hope of glory;

28 Whom we preach, warning every man, and teaching every man in all wisdom; that we may present every man perfect in the Messiah (haMashiach) Yahwah;

29 Whereunto I also labour, striving according to His working, which worketh in me mightily.

2 For I would that you knew what great conflict I have for you, and for them at Laodicea, and for as many as have not seen my face in the flesh;

2 That their hearts might be comforted, being knit together in love, and unto all riches of the full assurance of understanding, to the acknowledgement of the mystery of God (Elohim, יהוה (YHWH)), and of the Father, and of the Messiah (haMashiach);

3 In whom are hid all the treasures of wisdom and knowledge.

4 And this I say, lest any man should beguile you with enticing words;

5 For though I be absent in the flesh, yet am I with you in the spirit, joying and beholding your order, and the stedfastness of your faith in Messiah (Mashiach).

6 As you have therefore received the Messiah (haMashiach) Yahwah our Lord (Adonai), so walk you in Him;

7 Rooted and built up in Him, and stablished in the faith, as you have been taught, abounding therein with thanksgiving.

8 Beware lest any man spoil you through philosophy and vain deceit, after the tradition of men, after the rudiments of the world, and not after the Messiah (haMashiach).

9 For in Him dwelleth all the fulness of the Godhead bodily.

10 And you are complete in Him, who is the head of all principality and power;

11 In whom also you are circumcised with the circumcision made without hands, in putting off the body of the sins of the flesh by the circumcision of Messiah (Mashiach);

12 Buried with Him in baptism, wherein also you are risen with Him through the faith of the operation of God (Elohim), who hath raised Him from the dead.

13 And you, being dead in your sins and the uncircumcision of your flesh, hath He quickened together with Him, having forgiven you all trespasses;

14 Blotting out the handwriting of ordinances that was against us, which was contrary to us, and took it out of the way, nailing it to the stake; – *Gal. 3:15-20*

15 And having spoiled principalities and powers, He made a shew of them openly, triumphing over them in it. – *Deut. 31:16*

16 Let no man therefore judge you in food, or in drink, or in respect of a holyday, or of the new moon, or of the Shabbat days; – *Lev. 23:1-44*

17 Which are a shadow of things to come; but the body is of Messiah (Mashiach). – *Gal. 3:16*

18 Let no man beguile you of your reward in a voluntary humility and worshipping of angels, intruding into those things which he hath not seen, vainly puffed up by his fleshly mind,

19 And not holding the Head, from which all the body by joints and bands having nourishment ministered, and knit together, increaseth with the increase of God (Elohim).

20 Wherefore if you be dead with the Messiah (haMashiach) from the rudiments of the world, why, as though living in the world, are you subject to ordinances,

21 (Touch not; taste not; handle not;

22 Which all are to perish with the using;) after the commandments and doctrines of men?

23 Which things have indeed a shew of wisdom in will worship, and humility, and neglecting of the body; not in any honour to the satisfying of the flesh.

3 If you then be risen with the Messiah (haMashiach), seek those things which are above, where the Messiah (haMashiach) sitteth on the right hand of God (Elohim).

2 Set your affection on things above, not on things on the earth.

3 For you are dead, and your life is hid with the Messiah (haMashiach) in God (Elohim).

4 When the Messiah (haMashiach), who is our life, shall appear, then shall you also appear with Him in glory.

5 Mortify therefore your members which are upon the earth: fornication, uncleanness, inordinate affection, evil concupiscence, and covetousness, which is idolatry;

6 For which things' sake the wrath of God (Elohim, יהוה (YHWH)) cometh on the children of disobedience;

7 In which you also walked some time, when you lived in them.

8 But now you also put off all these; anger, wrath, malice, blasphemy, filthy communication out of your mouth.

9 Lie not one to another, seeing that you have put off the old man with his deeds;

10 And have put on the new man, which is renewed in knowledge after the image of Him

that created him;

11 Where there is neither Greek nor Jew (Yehudi), circumcision nor uncircumcision, Barbarian, Scythian, bond nor free; but the Messiah (haMashiach) is all, and in all.

12 Put on therefore, as the elect of יהוה (YHWH), holy and beloved, bowels of mercies, kindness, humbleness of mind, meekness, longsuffering;

13 Forbearing one another, and forgiving one another, if any man has a quarrel against any; even as the Messiah (haMashiach) forgave you, so also do you.

14 And above all these things clothe yourselves with love, which is the bond of perfectness.

15 And let the peace (shalom) of God (Elohim) rule in your hearts, to which also you are called in one body; and be you thankful.

16 Let the word of the Messiah (haMashiach) dwell in you richly in all wisdom; teaching and admonishing one another in psalms and hymns and spiritual songs, singing with grace in your hearts to God (Elohim, יהוה (YHWH)).

17 And whatsoever you do in word or deed, do all in the name of the Lord Yahwah (Adonai YHWH), giving thanks to YHWH the Father by Him.

18 Wives, submit yourselves unto your own husbands, as it is fit in the Lord (YHWH).

19 Husbands, love your wives, and be not bitter against them.

20 Children, obey your parents in all things, for this is well pleasing unto the Lord (YHWH).

21 Fathers, provoke not your children to anger, lest they be discouraged.

22 Servants, obey in all things your masters according to the flesh; not with eyeservice, as menpleasers; but in singleness of heart, fearing God (Elohim, יהוה (YHWH));

23 And whatsoever you do, do it heartily, as to יהוה (YHWH) and not unto men;

24 Knowing that of יהוה (YHWH) you shall receive the reward of the inheritance; for you serve our Lord the Messiah (Adoneinu haMashiach).

25 But he that doeth wrong shall receive for the wrong which he hath done; and there is no respect of persons.

4 Masters (Adonim), give unto your servants that which is just and equal; knowing that you also have a Master (Adon) in heaven.

2 Continue in prayer, and watch in the same with thanksgiving;

3 Withal praying also for us, that God (Elohim, יהוה (YHWH)) would open unto us a door of utterance, to speak the mystery of the Messiah (haMashiach), for which I am also in bonds;

4 That I may make it manifest, as I ought to speak.

5 Walk in wisdom toward them that are outsiders, redeeming the time.

6 Let your speech be always with grace, seasoned with salt, that you may know how you ought to answer every man.

7 All my state shall Tychicus declare unto you, who is a beloved brother, and a faithful minister and fellowservant in the Lord (YHWH);

8 Whom I have sent unto you for the same purpose, that he might know your estate, and comfort your hearts;

9 With Onesimus, a faithful and beloved brother, who is one of you. They shall make known unto you all things which are done here.

10 Aristarchus my fellowprisoner saluteth you, and Marcus, sister's son to Barnabas, (touching whom you received commandments; if he comes unto you, receive him;)

11 And Joshua ([A33]Yeshua), who is called Justus, who are of the circumcised. These only are my fellowworkers unto the kingdom of God (Elohim, יהוה (YHWH)), who have been a comfort unto me.

12 Epaphras, who is one of you, a servant of the Messiah (haMashiach), saluteth you, always labouring fervently for you in prayers, that you may stand perfect and complete in all the will of God (Elohim, יהוה (YHWH)).

13 For I bear him record, that he hath a great zeal for you, and them that are in Laodicea, and them in Hierapolis.

14 Luke (Luqas), the beloved physician, and Demas, greet you.

15 Salute the brethren who are in Laodicea, and Nymphas, and the assembly who is in his house.

16 And when this epistle is read among you, cause that it be read also in the assembly of the Laodiceans; and that you likewise read the epistle from Laodicea.

17 And say to Archippus, "Take heed to the ministry which you have received in the Lord (YHWH), that you fulfil it."

18 The salutation by the hand of me Paul. Remember my bonds. Grace be with you. So be it (Amen).

1 THESSALONIANS
TASELONIQIM 1 א תֶּסָלוֹנִיקִים
(First Epistle to the Thessalonnians)

1 Paul, and Silvanus, and Timotheus, unto the assembly of the Thessalonians which is in YHWH the Father and in the Lord (Adonai) [A1]Yahwah [B45]haMashiach. Grace be unto you, and peace, from YHWH our Father, and our Lord (Adonai) Yahwah haMashiach.

2 We give thanks to God (Elohim, יהוה (YHWH)) always for you all, making mention of you in our prayers;

3 Remembering without ceasing your work of faith, and labour of love, and patience of hope in our Lord (Adonai) Yahwah haMashiach, in the sight of God (Elohim) and our Father;

4 Knowing, brethren beloved, your election of God (Elohim, יהוה (YHWH)).

5 For our gospel (good news) came not unto you in word only, but also in power, and in the Holy Spirit (Ruach haQodesh), and in much assurance; as you know what manner of men we were among you for your sake.

6 And you became followers of us, and of the Lord (YHWH), having received the word in much affliction, with joy of the Holy Spirit (Ruach haQodesh);

7 So that you were ensamples to all that believe in Macedonia and Achaia.

8 For from you sounded out the word of God (Elohim, יהוה (YHWH)) not only in Macedonia and Achaia, but also in every place your faith toward יהוה (YHWH) is spread abroad; so that we need not to speak anything.

9 For they themselves shew of us what manner of entering in we had unto you, and how you turned to יהוה (YHWH) from idols to serve the living and true God (Elohim);

10 And to wait for His [B47]Humanity from heaven, whom He raised from the dead, even Yahwah, who delivered us from the wrath to come.

2 For yourselves, brethren, know our entrance in unto you, that it was not in vain;

2 But even after that we had suffered before, and were shamefully entreated, as you know, at Philippi, we were bold in our God (Elohim) to speak unto you the gospel (good news) of God (Elohim, יהוה (YHWH)) with much contention.

3 For our exhortation was not of deceit, nor of uncleanness, nor in guile;

4 But as we were allowed of God (Elohim, יהוה (YHWH)) to be put in trust with the gospel (good news), even so we speak; not as pleasing men, but God (Elohim, יהוה (YHWH)), who trieth our hearts.

5 For neither at any time used we flattering words, as you know, nor a cloke of covetousness; God (Elohim, יהוה (YHWH)) is witness;

6 Nor of men sought we glory, neither of you, nor yet of others, when we might have been burdensome, as the apostles of the Messiah (haMashiach).

7 But we were gentle among you, even as a nurse cherisheth her children;

8 So being affectionately desirous of you, we were willing to have imparted unto you, not the gospel (good news) of God (Elohim, יהוה (YHWH)) only, but also our own souls, because you were dear unto us.

9 For you remember, brethren, our labour and travail; for labouring night and day, because we would not be chargeable unto any of you, we preached unto you the gospel (good news) of God (Elohim, יהוה (YHWH)).

10 You are witnesses, and God (Elohim, יהוה (YHWH)) also, how holily and justly and unblameably we behaved ourselves among you that believe;

11 As you know how we exhorted and comforted and charged every one of you, as a father doth his children,

12 That you would walk worthy of God (Elohim, יהוה (YHWH)), who hath called you unto His kingdom and glory.

13 For this cause also thank we God (Elohim) without ceasing, because, when you received the word of God (Elohim, יהוה (YHWH)) which you heard of us, you received it not as the word of men, but as it is in truth, the word of God (Elohim, יהוה (YHWH)), which effectually worketh also in you that believe.

14 For you, brethren, became followers of the assemblies (ekklesias) of God (Elohim) which in Judah (Yehudah) are in the Messiah (haMashiach) Yahwah; for you also have suffered like things of your own countrymen, even as they have of the Jews (Yehudim);

15 Who both killed the Lord Yahwah (Adonai YHWH), and their own prophets, and have

persecuted us; and they please not God (Elohim), and are contrary to all men;

16 Forbidding us to speak to the Gentiles (Goyim) that they might be saved, to fill up their sins always; for the wrath is come upon them to the uttermost.

17 But we, brethren, being taken from you for a short time in presence, not in heart, endeavoured the more abundantly to see your face with great desire.

18 Wherefore we would have come unto you, even I Paul, once and again; but Satan hindered us.

19 For what is our hope, or joy, or crown of rejoicing? Are not even you in the presence of our Lord (Adonai) Yahwah haMashiach at His coming?

20 For you are our glory and joy.

3 Wherefore when we could no longer forbear, we thought it good to be left at Athens alone;

2 And sent Timotheus, our brother, and minister of God (Elohim), and our fellowlabourer in the gospel (good news) of the Messiah (haMashiach), to establish you, and to comfort you concerning your faith;

3 That no man should be moved by these afflictions; for yourselves know that we are appointed thereunto.

4 For verily, when we were with you, we told you before that we should suffer tribulation; even as it came to pass, and you know.

5 For this cause, when I could no longer forbear, I sent to know your faith, lest by some means the tempter have tempted you, and our labour be in vain.

6 But now when Timotheus came from you unto us, and brought us good tidings of your faith and love, and that you have good remembrance of us always, desiring greatly to see us, as we also to see you;

7 Therefore, brethren, we were comforted over you in all our affliction and distress by your faith;

8 For now we live, if you stand fast in the Lord (YHWH).

9 For what thanks can we render to God (Elohim) again for you, for all the joy wherewith we joy for your sakes before our God (Elohim);

10 Night and day praying exceedingly that we might see your face, and might perfect that which is lacking in your faith?

11 Now God (Elohim, יהוה (YHWH)) Himself, our Father (Avinu) and our Lord (Adonai) Yahwah haMashiach, direct our way unto you.

12 And the Lord (YHWH) make you to increase and abound in love one toward another, and toward all men, even as we do toward you;

13 To the end He may stablish your hearts unblameable in holiness before God (Elohim, יהוה (YHWH)), even our Father, at the coming of our Lord (Adonai) Yahwah haMashiach with all His holy ones.

4 Furthermore then we beseech you, brethren, and exhort you by the Lord Yahwah (Adonai YHWH), that as you have received of us how you ought to walk and to please God (Elohim), so you would abound more and more.

2 For you know what commandments we gave you by the Lord Yahwah (Adonai YHWH).

3 For this is the will of God (Elohim, יהוה (YHWH)), even your sanctification, that you should abstain from fornication;

4 That every one of you should know how to possess his vessel in sanctification and honour;

5 Not in the lust of concupiscence, even as the Gentiles (Goyim) who know not God (Elohim, יהוה (YHWH));

6 That no man goes beyond and defraud his brother in any matter; because that יהוה (YHWH) is the avenger of all such, as we also have forewarned you and testified.

7 For God (Elohim, יהוה (YHWH)) hath not called us unto uncleanness, but unto holiness.

8 He therefore that despiseth, despiseth not man, but God (Elohim, יהוה (YHWH)), who hath also given unto us His holy Spirit (Ruach haQodesh).

9 But as touching brotherly love, you need not that I write unto you; for you yourselves are taught of God (Elohim) to love one another.

10 And indeed you do it toward all the brethren who are in all Macedonia; but we beseech you, brethren, that you increase more and more;

11 And that you study to be quiet, and to do your own business, and to work with your own hands, as we commanded you;

12 That you may walk honestly toward them that are outsiders, and that you may have lack of nothing.

13 But I would not have you to be ignorant, brethren, concerning them who are asleep, that you sorrow not, even as others who have no

hope.

14 For if we believe that Yahwah died and rose again, even so them also who sleep in Yahwah will God (Elohim, יהוה (YHWH)) bring with Him.

15 For this we say unto you by the word of God (Elohim, יהוה (YHWH)), that we who are alive and remain unto the coming of the Lord (YHWH) shall not prevent them who are asleep.

16 For the Lord (YHWH) Himself shall descend from heaven with a shout, with the voice of the archangel, and with the trump of God (Elohim, יהוה (YHWH)); and the dead in the Messiah (haMashiach) shall rise first;

17 Then we who are alive and remain shall be caught up together with them in the clouds, to meet the Lord (YHWH) in the air; and so shall we ever be with the Lord (YHWH).

18 Wherefore comfort one another with these words.

5 But of the times and the seasons, brethren, you have no need that I write unto you.

2 For yourselves know perfectly that the day of יהוה (YHWH) so cometh as a thief in the night.

3 For when they shall say, "Peace and safety;" then sudden destruction cometh upon them, as travail upon a woman with child; and they shall not escape.

4 But you, brethren, are not in darkness, that that day should overtake you as a thief.

5 You are all the children of light, and the children of the day; we are not of the night, nor of darkness.

6 Therefore let us not sleep, as do others; but let us watch and be sober.

7 For they that sleep sleep in the night; and they that be drunken are drunken in the night.

8 But let us, who are of the day, be sober, putting on the breastplate of faith and love; and for a helmet, the hope of salvation.

9 For God (Elohim) hath not appointed us to wrath, but to obtain salvation by our Lord (Adonai) Yahwah haMashiach,

10 Who died for us, that, whether we wake or sleep, we should live together with Him.

11 Wherefore comfort yourselves together, and edify one another, even as also you do.

12 And we beseech you, brethren, to know them who labour among you, and are over you in the Lord (YHWH), and admonish you;

13 And to esteem them very highly in love for their work's sake. And be at peace among yourselves.

14 Now we exhort you, brethren, warn them that are unruly, comfort the feebleminded, support the weak, be patient toward all men.

15 See that none render evil for evil unto any man; but ever follow that which is good, both among yourselves, and to all men.

16 Rejoice evermore.

17 Pray without ceasing.

18 In everything give thanks, for this is the will of God (Elohim, יהוה (YHWH)) in the Messiah (haMashiach) Yahwah concerning you.

19 Quench not the Spirit.

20 Despise not prophesyings.

21 Prove all things; hold fast that which is good.

22 Abstain from all appearance of evil.

23 And the very God (Elohim) of peace sanctify you wholly; and may your whole spirit and soul and body be preserved blameless unto the coming of our Lord (Adonai) Yahwah haMashiach.

24 Faithful is He that calleth you, who also will do it.

25 Brethren, pray for us.

26 Greet all the brethren with a holy kiss.

27 I charge you by the Lord (YHWH) that this epistle be read unto all the holy brethren.

28 The grace of our Lord (Adonai) Yahwah haMashiach be with you. So be it (Amen).

2 THESSALONIANS
TASELONIQIM 2 ב תַּסְלוֹנִיקִים
(Second Epistle to the Thessalonians)

1 Paul, and Silvanus, and Timotheus, unto the assembly of the Thessalonians in YHWH our Father and our Lord (Adonai) Yahwah haMashiach.

2 Grace unto you, and peace, from YHWH our Father and our Lord (Adonai) Yahwah haMashiach.

3 We are bound to thank God (Elohim, יהוה (YHWH)) always for you, brethren, as it is meet, because that your faith groweth exceedingly, and the love of every one of you all toward each other aboundeth;

4 So that we ourselves glory in you in the assemblies (ekklesias) of God (Elohim) for your patience and faith in all your persecutions and tribulations that you endure;

5 Which is a manifest token of the righteous judgment of God (Elohim, יהוה (YHWH)), that you may be counted worthy of the kingdom of God (Elohim, יהוה (YHWH)), for which you also suffer;

6 Seeing it is a righteous thing with God (Elohim, יהוה (YHWH)) to recompense tribulation to them that trouble you;

7 And to you who are troubled rest with us, when our Lord Yahwah (Adonai YHWH) shall be revealed from heaven with His mighty angels,

8 In flaming fire taking vengeance on them that know not God (Elohim, יהוה (YHWH)), and that obey not the gospel (good news) of our Lord (Adonai) Yahwah haMashiach; – *Isa. 66:15, Jer. 10:25, Psa. 79:6*

9 Who shall be punished with everlasting destruction from the presence of יהוה (YHWH), and from the glory of His power; – *Isa. 2:10,19,21*

10 When He shall come to be glorified in His holy ones, and to be admired in all them that believe (because our testimony among you was believed) in that day.

11 Wherefore also we pray always for you, that our God (Elohim) would count you worthy of this calling, and fulfil all the good pleasure of His goodness, and the work of faith with power;

12 That the name of our Lord (Adonai) Yahwah haMashiach may be glorified in you, and you in Him, according to the grace of our God (Elohim) and our Lord (Adonai) Yahwah haMashiach.

2 Now we beseech you, brethren, by the coming of our Lord (Adonai) Yahwah haMashiach, and by our gathering together unto Him,

2 That you be not soon shaken in mind, or be troubled, neither by spirit, nor by word, nor by letter as from us, as that the day of the Messiah (haMashiach) is at hand.

3 Let no man deceive you by any means; for that day shall not come, except there come a falling away first, and that man of sin be revealed, the son of perdition;

4 Who opposeth and exalteth himself above all that is called God (Elohim), or that is worshipped; so that he as God (Elohim) sitteth in the temple of God (Elohim), shewing himself that he is God (Elohim). – *Eze. 28:2*

5 Remember you not, that, when I was yet with you, I told you these things?

6 And now you know what withholdeth that he might be revealed in his time.

7 For the mystery of iniquity doth already work; only he who now letteth will let, until he be taken out of the way.

8 And then shall that wicked be revealed, whom יהוה (YHWH) shall consume with the breath of His mouth, and shall destroy with the brightness of His coming; – *Isa. 11:4*

9 Even him, whose coming is after the working of Satan with all power and signs and lying wonders, – *Isa. 2:10,19,21*

10 And with all deceivableness of unrighteousness in them that perish; because they received not the love of the truth, that they might be saved.

11 And for this cause God (Elohim, יהוה (YHWH)) shall send them strong delusion, that they should believe a lie;

12 That they all might be damned who believed not the truth, but had pleasure in unrighteousness.

13 But we are bound to give thanks always to God (Elohim) for you, brethren beloved of the Lord (YHWH), because God (Elohim, יהוה (YHWH)) hath from the beginning chosen you to salvation through sanctification of the Spirit and belief of the truth;

14 Whereunto He called you by our gospel

(good news), to the obtaining of the glory of our Lord (Adonai) Yahwah haMashiach.

15 Therefore, brethren, stand fast, and hold the traditions which you have been taught, whether by word, or our epistle.

16 Now our Lord (Adonai) Yahwah haMashiach Himself, and יהוה (YHWH), our Father, who hath loved us, and hath given us everlasting consolation and good hope through grace,

17 Comfort your hearts, and stablish you in every good word and work.

3 Finally, brethren, pray for us, that the word of God (Elohim, יהוה (YHWH)) may have free course, and be glorified, even as it is with you;

2 And that we may be delivered from unreasonable and wicked men; for all men have not faith.

3 But the Lord (YHWH) is faithful, who shall stablish you, and keep you from evil.

4 And we have confidence in the Lord (YHWH) touching you, that you both do and will do the things which we command you.

5 And the Lord (YHWH) direct your hearts into the love of God (Elohim, יהוה (YHWH)), and into the patient waiting for the Messiah (haMashiach).

6 Now we command you, brethren, in the name of our Lord (Adonai) Yahwah haMashiach, that you withdraw yourselves from every brother that walketh disorderly, and not after the tradition which he received of us.

7 For yourselves know how you ought to follow us; for we behaved not ourselves disorderly among you;

8 Neither did we eat any man's bread for nought; but wrought with labour and travail night and day, that we might not be chargeable to any of you;

9 Not because we have not power, but to make ourselves an ensample unto you to follow us.

10 For even when we were with you, this we commanded you, that if any would not work, neither should he eat.

11 For we hear that there are some which walk among you disorderly, working not at all, but are busybodies.

12 Now them that are such we command and exhort by our Lord (Adonai) Yahwah haMashiach, that with quietness they work, and eat their own bread.

13 But you, brethren, be not weary in well doing.

14 And if any man obeys not our word by this epistle, note that man, and have no company with him, that he may be ashamed.

15 Yet count him not as an enemy, but admonish him as a brother.

16 Now the Lord (Adon) of peace Himself give you peace always by all means. The Lord (YHWH) be with you all.

17 The salutation of Paul with mine own hand, which is the token in every epistle; so I write.

18 The grace of our Lord (Adonai) Yahwah haMashiach be with you all. So be it (Amen).

1 TIMOTHY
TIMOTIYOS 1 א טִימוֹתִיוֹס
(First Epistle to Timothy)

1 Paul, an apostle of Yahwah haMashiach by the commandment of יהוה (YHWH) our Savior, and our Lord (Adonai) Yahwah haMashiach, who is our hope;

2 Unto Timothy, my own son in the faith. Grace, mercy, and peace, from YHWH our Father and Yahwah haMashiach our Lord (Adonai).

3 As I besought you to abide still at Ephesus, when I went into Macedonia, that you mightest charge some that they teach no other doctrine,

4 Neither give heed to fables and endless genealogies, which minister questions, rather than godly edifying which is in faith; so do.

5 Now the goal of the commandment is love out of a pure heart, and of a good conscience, and of faith unfeigned;

6 From which some having swerved have turned aside unto vain jangling;

7 Desiring to be teachers of the law; understanding neither what they say, nor whereof they affirm.

8 But we know that the law is good, if a man uses it lawfully;

9 Knowing this, that the law is not made for a righteous man, but for the lawless and disobedient, for the ungodly and for sinners, for unholy and profane, for murderers of fathers and murderers of mothers, for manslayers,

10 For whoremongers, for them that defile themselves with mankind, for menstealers, for liars, for perjured persons, and if there be any other thing that is contrary to sound doctrine;

11 According to the glorious gospel (good news) of the blessed God (Elohim), who was committed to my trust.

12 And I thank the Messiah (haMashiach) Yahwah our Lord (Adonai), who hath enabled me, for that He counted me faithful, putting me into the ministry;

13 Who was before a blasphemer, and a persecutor, and injurious; but I obtained mercy, because I did it ignorantly in unbelief.

14 And the grace of our Lord (Adonai) was exceeding abundant with faith and love which is in the Messiah (haMashiach) Yahwah.

15 This is a faithful saying, and worthy of all acceptation, that the Messiah (haMashiach) Yahwah came into the world to save sinners; of whom I am chief.

16 Howbeit for this cause I obtained mercy, that in me first Yahwah haMashiach might shew forth all longsuffering, for a pattern to them who should hereafter believe on Him to life everlasting.

17 Now unto the King – eternal, immortal, invisible, the only wise God (Elohim), be honour and glory for ever and ever. So be it (Amen).

18 This charge I commit unto you, son Timothy, according to the prophecies which went before on you, that you by them mightest war a good warfare;

19 Holding faith, and a good conscience; which some having put away concerning faith have made shipwreck;

20 Of whom is Hymenaeus and Alexander; whom I have delivered unto Satan, that they may learn not to blaspheme.

2 I exhort therefore, that, first of all, supplications, prayers, intercessions, and giving of thanks, be made for all men;

2 For kings, and for all that are in authority; that we may lead a quiet and peaceable life in all godliness and honesty.

3 For this is good and acceptable in the sight of God (Elohim, יהוה (YHWH)) our Savior;

4 Who will for all men to be saved, and to come unto the knowledge of the truth.

5 For God (Elohim) is one, and one mediator between God (Elohim) and men, the man Yahwah haMashiach;

6 Who gave Himself a ransom for all, to be testified in due time.

7 Whereunto I am ordained a preacher, and an apostle, I speak the truth in Messiah (Mashiach), and lie not; a teacher of the Gentiles (Goyim) in faith and verity.

8 I will therefore that men pray everywhere, lifting up holy hands, without wrath and doubting.

9 In like manner also, that women adorn themselves in modest apparel, with shamefacedness and sobriety; not with broided hair, or gold, or pearls, or costly array;

10 But which becometh women professing godliness with good works.

11 Let the woman learn in silence with all

subjection.

12 But I permit not a woman to teach, nor to usurp authority over the man, but to be in silence.

13 For Adam was first formed, then Eve (Chawah).

14 And Adam was not deceived, but the woman being deceived was in the transgression.

15 Notwithstanding she shall be saved in childbearing, if they continue in faith and love and holiness with sobriety.

3 This is a true saying, "If a man desires the office of a bishop, he desireth a good work."

2 A bishop then must be blameless, the husband of one wife, vigilant, sober, of good behaviour, given to hospitality, apt to teach;

3 Not given to wine, no striker, not greedy of filthy lucre; but patient, not a brawler, not covetous;

4 One that ruleth well his own house, having his children in subjection with all gravity;

5 For if a man knows not how to rule his own house, how shall he take care of the assembly of God (Elohim)?

6 Not a novice, lest being lifted up with pride he falls into the condemnation of the devil.

7 Moreover he must have a good report of them who are outsiders; lest he falls into reproach and the snare of the devil.

8 Likewise must the deacons be of good character, not doubletongued, not given to much wine, not greedy of filthy lucre;

9 Holding the mystery of the faith in a pure conscience.

10 And let these also first be proved; then let them use the office of a deacon, being found blameless.

11 Even so must their wives be good character, not slanderers, sober, faithful in all things.

12 Let the deacons be the husbands of one wife, ruling their children and their own houses well.

13 For they that have used the office of a deacon well purchase to themselves a good degree, and great boldness in the faith which is in Yahwah haMashiach.

14 These things write I unto you, hoping to come unto you shortly;

15 But if I tarry long, that you mayest know how you oughtest to behave yourself in the house of יהוה (YHWH), which is the assembly of the living God (Elohim), the pillar and ground of

the truth.

16 And without controversy great is the mystery of godliness: God (Elohim, יהוה (YHWH)) was manifest in the flesh, justified in the Spirit, seen of angels, preached unto the Gentiles (Goyim), believed on in the world, received up into glory.

4 Now the Spirit speaketh expressly, that in the latter times some shall depart from the faith, giving heed to seducing spirits, and doctrines of devils;

2 Speaking lies in hypocrisy; having their conscience seared with a hot iron;

3 Forbidding to marry, and commanding to abstain from meats, which God (Elohim) hath created to be received with thanksgiving of them who believe and know the truth.

4 For every creature of God (Elohim) is good, and nothing to be refused, if it be received with thanksgiving;

5 For it is sanctified by the word of God (Elohim, יהוה (YHWH)) and prayer.

6 If you put the brethren in remembrance of these things, you shalt be a good minister of Yahwah haMashiach, nourished up in the words of faith and of good doctrine, whereunto you have attained.

7 But refuse profane and old wives' fables, and exercise yourself rather unto godliness.

8 For bodily exercise profiteth little; but godliness is profitable unto all things, having promise of the life that now is, and of that which is to come.

9 This is a faithful saying and worthy of all acceptation.

10 For therefore we both labour and suffer reproach, because we trust in the living God (Elohim), who is the Savior of all men, specially of those that believe.

11 These things command and teach.

12 Let no man despise your youth; but be you an example of the believers, in word, in conversation, in love, in spirit, in faith, in purity.

13 Till I come, give attendance to reading, to exhortation, to doctrine.

14 Neglect not the gift that is in you, which was given you by prophecy, with the laying on of the hands of the presbytery.

15 Meditate upon these things; give yourself wholly to them; that your profiting may appear to all.

16 Take heed unto yourself, and unto the

doctrine; continue in them; for in doing this you shalt both save yourself, and them that hear you.

5 Rebuke not an older man, but intreat him as a father; and the younger men as brethren;

2 The older women as mothers; the younger as sisters, with all purity.

3 Honour widows that are widows indeed.

4 But if any widow has children or nephews, let them learn first to shew piety at home, and to requite their parents; for that is good and acceptable before God (Elohim, יהוה (YHWH)).

5 Now she that is a widow indeed, and desolate, trusteth in יהוה (YHWH), and continueth in supplications and prayers night and day.

6 But she that liveth in pleasure is dead while she liveth.

7 And these things give in charge, that they may be blameless.

8 But if any provide not for his own, and specially for those of his own house, he hath denied the faith, and is worse than an infidel.

9 Let a widow above threescore (sixty) years old be taken into the number, having been the wife of one man,

10 Well reported of for good works; if she has brought up children, if she has lodged strangers, if she has washed the holy ones' feet, if she has relieved the afflicted, if she has diligently followed every good work.

11 But refuse the younger widows; for when they have begun to wax wanton against the Messiah (haMashiach), they will marry;

12 Having damnation, because they have cast off their first faith.

13 And withal they learn to be idle, wandering about from house to house; and not only idle, but tattlers also and busybodies, speaking things which they ought not.

14 I will therefore that the younger women marry, bear children, guide the house, give none occasion to the adversary to speak reproachfully.

15 For some are already turned aside after Satan.

16 If any man or woman that believeth have widows, let them relieve them, and let not the assembly be charged; that it may relieve them that are widows indeed.

17 Let the elders that rule well be counted worthy of double honour, especially they who labour in the word and doctrine.

18 For the scripture saith, "You shalt not muzzle the ox that treadeth out the corn." And, "The labourer is worthy of his reward." – *Deu. 25:4*

19 Receive not an accusation against an elder, but before two or three witnesses. – *Deu. 17:6; 19:15*

20 Them that sin rebuke before all, that others also may fear.

21 I charge you before God (Elohim), Yahwah haMashiach, and the elect angels, that you observe these things without preferring one before another, doing nothing by partiality.

22 Do not hurry to lay hands on man, neither be partaker of other men's sins; keep yourself pure.

23 Drink no longer water, but use a little wine for your stomach's sake and your often infirmities.

24 Some men's sins are open beforehand, going before to judgment; and some men they follow after.

25 Likewise also the good works of some are manifest beforehand; and they that are otherwise cannot be hid.

6 Let as many servants as are under the yoke count their own masters worthy of all honour, that the name of יהוה (YHWH) and His doctrine be not blasphemed.

2 And they that have believing masters, let them not despise them, because they are brethren; but rather do them service, because they are faithful and beloved, partakers of the benefit. These things teach and exhort.

3 If any man teaches otherwise, and consent not to wholesome words, even the words of our Lord (Adonai) Yahwah haMashiach, and to the doctrine which is according to godliness;

4 He is proud, knowing nothing, but doting about questions and strifes of words, whereof cometh envy, strife, railings, evil surmisings,

5 Perverse disputings of men of corrupt minds, and destitute of the truth, supposing that gain is godliness; from such withdraw yourself.

6 But godliness with contentment is great gain.

7 For we brought nothing into this world, and it is certain we can carry nothing out.

8 And having food and raiment let us be therewith content.

9 But they that will be rich fall into temptation and a snare, and into many foolish and hurtful lusts, which drown men in destruction and perdition.

10 For the love of money is the root of all evil; which while some coveted after, they have erred from the faith, and pierced themselves through with many sorrows.

11 But you, O man of God (Elohim), flee these things; and follow after righteousness, godliness, faith, love, patience, meekness.

12 Fight the good fight of faith, lay hold on eternal life, whereunto you are also called, and hast professed a good profession before many witnesses.

13 I give you charge in the sight of God (Elohim), who quickeneth all things, and before Yahwah haMashiach, who before Pontius Pilate witnessed a good confession;

14 That you keep this commandment without spot, unrebukeable, until the appearing of our Lord (Adonai) Yahwah haMashiach;

15 Which in His times He shall shew, who is the blessed and only Potentate, the King of kings, and Lord of lords (Supreme Lord);

16 Who only hath immortality, dwelling in the light which no man can approach unto; whom no man hath seen, nor can see; to whom be honour and power everlasting. So be it (Amen).

17 Charge them that are rich in this world, that they be not highminded, nor trust in uncertain riches, but in the living God (Elohim), who giveth us richly all things to enjoy;

18 That they do good, that they be rich in good works, ready to distribute, willing to communicate;

19 Laying up in store for themselves a good foundation against the time to come, that they may lay hold on eternal life.

20 O Timothy, keep that which is committed to your trust, avoiding profane and vain babblings, and oppositions of science falsely so called;

21 Which some professing have erred concerning the faith. Grace be with you. So be it (Amen).

2 TIMOTHY
TIMOTIYOS 2 ב טִימוֹתִיּוֹס
(Second Epistle to Timothy)

1 Paul, an apostle of Yahwah haMashiach by the will of God (Elohim, יהוה (YHWH)), according to the promise of life which is in the Messiah (haMashiach) Yahwah,

2 To Timothy, my dearly beloved son: Grace, mercy, and peace, from YHWH our Father and the Messiah (haMashiach) Yahwah, our Lord (Adonai).

3 I thank God (Elohim, יהוה (YHWH)), whom I serve from my forefathers with pure conscience, that without ceasing I have remembrance of you in my prayers night and day;

4 Greatly desiring to see you, being mindful of your tears, that I may be filled with joy;

5 When I call to remembrance the unfeigned faith that is in you, which dwelt first in your grandmother Lois, and your mother Eunice; and I am persuaded that in you also.

6 Wherefore I put you in remembrance that you stir up the gift of God (Elohim), which is in you by the putting on of my hands.

7 For God (Elohim, יהוה (YHWH)) hath not given us the spirit of fear; but of power, and of love, and of a sound mind.

8 Be not you therefore ashamed of the testimony of our Lord (Adonai), nor of me His prisoner; but be you partaker of the afflictions of the gospel (good news) according to the power of God (Elohim, יהוה (YHWH));

9 Who hath saved us, and called us with a holy calling, not according to our works, but according to His own purpose and grace, which was given us in the Messiah (haMashiach) Yahwah before the world began,

10 But is now made manifest by the appearing of our Savior Yahwah haMashiach, who hath abolished death, and hath brought life and immortality to light through the gospel (good news);

11 Whereunto I am appointed a preacher, and an apostle, and a teacher of the Gentiles (Goyim).

12 For which cause I also suffer these things; nevertheless I am not ashamed, for I know whom I have believed, and am persuaded that He is able to keep that which I have committed unto Him until that day.

13 Hold fast the form of sound words, which you have heard of me, in faith and love which is in the Messiah (haMashiach) Yahwah.

14 That good thing which was committed unto you keep by the Holy Spirit (Ruach haQodesh) who dwelleth in us.

15 This you knowest, that all they who are in Asia be turned away from me; of whom are Phygellus and Hermogenes.

16 The Lord (YHWH) give mercy unto the house of Onesiphorus; for he often refreshed me, and was not ashamed of my chain;

17 But, when he was in Rome, he sought me out very diligently, and found me.

18 The Lord (YHWH) grant unto him that he may find mercy of יהוה (YHWH) in that day; and in how many things he ministered unto me at Ephesus, you knowest very well.

2 You therefore, my son, be strong in the grace that is in the Messiah (haMashiach) Yahwah.

2 And the things that you have heard of me among many witnesses, the same commit you to faithful men, who shall be able to teach others also.

3 You therefore endure hardness, as a good soldier of Yahwah haMashiach.

4 No man that warreth entangleth himself with the affairs of this life; that he may please Him who hath chosen him to be a soldier.

5 And if a man also strives for masteries, yet is he not crowned, except he strives lawfully.

6 The husbandman that laboureth must be first partaker of the fruits.

7 Consider what I say; and the Lord (YHWH) give you understanding in all things.

8 Remember that Yahwah haMashiach of the seed of Dawid was raised from the dead according to my gospel (good news);

9 Wherein I suffer trouble, as an evil doer, even unto bonds; but the word of God (Elohim, יהוה (YHWH)) is not bound.

10 Therefore I endure all things for the elect's sakes, that they may also obtain the salvation which is in the Messiah (haMashiach) Yahwah with eternal glory.

11 It is a faithful saying: For if we be dead with Him, we shall also live with Him;

12 If we suffer, we shall also reign with Him; if we deny Him, He also will deny us;

13 If we believe not, yet He abideth faithful; He

cannot deny Himself.

14 Of these things put them in remembrance, charging them before the Lord (YHWH) that they strive not about words to no profit, but to the subverting of the hearers.

15 Study to shew yourself approved unto יהוה (YHWH), a workman that needeth not to be ashamed, rightly dividing the word of truth.

16 But shun profane and vain babblings; for they will increase unto more ungodliness.

17 And their word will eat as doth a canker; of whom is Hymenaeus and Philetus;

18 Who concerning the truth have erred, saying that the resurrection is past already; and overthrow the faith of some.

19 Nevertheless the foundation of God (Elohim, יהוה (YHWH)) standeth sure, having this seal: "יהוה (YHWH) knoweth them that are His." And, "Let everyone that called upon the name of the Messiah (haMashiach) depart from iniquity. – *Num. 16:5; Nah. 1:7; Num. 16:26*

20 But in a great house there are not only vessels of gold and of silver, but also of wood and of earth; and some to honour, and some to dishonour.

21 If a man therefore purge himself from these, he shall be a vessel unto honour, sanctified, and meet for the master's use, and prepared unto every good work.

22 Flee also youthful lusts; but follow righteousness, faith, love, peace, with them that call on יהוה (YHWH) out of a pure heart.

23 But avoid foolish and unlearned questions, knowing that they do gender strifes.

24 And the servant of the Lord (YHWH) must not strive; but be gentle unto all men, apt to teach, patient,

25 In meekness instructing those that oppose themselves; if יהוה (YHWH) peradventure will give them repentance to the acknowledging of the truth;

26 And that they may recover themselves out of the snare of the devil, who are taken captive by him at his will.

3 This know also, that in the last days perilous times shall come.

2 For men shall be lovers of their own selves, covetous, boasters, proud, blasphemers, disobedient to parents, unthankful, unholy,

3 Without natural affection, trucebreakers, false accusers, incontinent, fierce, despisers of those

that are good,

4 Traitors, heady, highminded, lovers of pleasures more than lovers of God (Elohim);

5 Having a form of godliness, but denying the power thereof; from such turn away.

6 For of this sort are they who creep into houses, and lead captive silly women laden with sins, led away with divers lusts,

7 Ever learning, and never able to come to the knowledge of the truth.

8 Now as Jannes and Jambres (the court magicians of Egypt) opposed Moses (Mosheh), so do these also resist the truth; men of corrupt minds, reprobate concerning the faith.

9 But they shall proceed no further, for their folly shall be manifest unto all men, as theirs also was.

10 But you have fully known my doctrine, manner of life, purpose, faith, longsuffering, love, patience,

11 Persecutions, afflictions, who came unto me at Antioch, at Iconium, at Lystra; what persecutions I endured; but out of them all the Lord (YHWH) delivered me.

12 Yea, and all that will live godly in the Messiah (haMashiach) Yahwah shall suffer persecution.

13 But evil men and seducers shall wax worse and worse, deceiving, and being deceived.

14 But continue you in the things which you have learned and hast been assured of, knowing of whom you have learned them;

15 And that from a child you have known the holy scriptures, which are able to make you wise unto salvation through faith which is in the Messiah (haMashiach) Yahwah.

16 All scripture is given by inspiration of God (Elohim, יהוה (YHWH)), and is profitable for doctrine, for reproof, for correction, for instruction in righteousness;

17 That the man of God (Elohim) may be perfect, thoroughly furnished unto all good works.

4 I charge you therefore before God (Elohim), and our Lord (Adonai) Yahwah haMashiach, who shall judge the quick and the dead at His appearing and His kingdom;

2 Preach the word; be instant in season, out of season; reprove, rebuke, exhort with all longsuffering and doctrine.

3 For the time will come when they will not endure sound doctrine; but after their own lusts shall they heap to themselves teachers, having

itching ears;

4 And they shall turn away their ears from the truth, and shall be turned unto fables.

5 But watch you in all things, endure afflictions, do the work of an evangelist, make full proof of your ministry.

6 For I am now ready to be offered, and the time of my departure is at hand.

7 I have fought a good fight, I have finished my course, I have kept the faith.

8 Henceforth there is laid up for me a crown of righteousness, which the Lord (YHWH), the righteous Judge, shall give me at that day; and not to me only, but unto all them also that love His appearing.

9 Do your diligence to come shortly unto me;

10 For Demas hath forsaken me, having loved this present world, and is departed unto Thessalonica; Crescens to Galatia, Titus unto Dalmatia.

11 Only Luke is with me. Take Mark, and bring him with you; for he is profitable to me for the ministry.

12 And Tychicus have I sent to Ephesus.

13 The cloke that I left at Troas with Carpus, when you comest, bring with you, and the books, but especially the parchments.

14 Alexander the coppersmith did me much evil; יהוה (YHWH) repay him according to his works;

15 Of whom be you ware also; for he hath greatly withstood our words.

16 At my first answer no man stood with me, but all men forsook me. I pray that it may not be laid to their charge.

17 Notwithstanding the Lord (YHWH) stood with me, and strengthened me; that by me the preaching might be fully known, and that all the Gentiles (Goyim) might hear; and I was delivered out of the mouth of the lion.

18 And the Lord (YHWH) shall deliver me from every evil work, and will preserve me unto His heavenly kingdom; to whom be glory for ever and ever. So be it (Amen).

19 Salute Prisca and Aquila, and the household of Onesiphorus.

20 Erastus abode at Corinth; but Trophimus have I left at Miletum sick.

21 Do your diligence to come before winter. Eubulus greeteth you, and Pudens, and Linus, and Claudia, and all the brethren.

22 Our Lord (Adonai) Yahwah haMashiach be with your spirit. Grace be with you. So be it (Amen).

TITUS
TITOS טִיטוֹס
(Epistle to Titus)

1 Paul, a servant of God (Elohim, יהוה (YHWH)), and an apostle of Yahwah haMashiach, according to the faith of יהוה (YHWH)'s elect, and the acknowledging of the truth which is after godliness;

2 In hope of eternal life, which יהוה (YHWH), that cannot lie, promised before the world began;

3 But hath in due times manifested His word through preaching, which is committed unto me according to the commandment of יהוה (YHWH) our Savior;

4 To Titus, mine own son after the common faith: Grace, mercy, and peace, from YHWH the Father and the Lord (Adonai) Yahwah haMashiach our Savior.

5 For this cause left I you in Crete, that you shouldest set in order the things that are wanting, and ordain elders in every city, as I had appointed you.

6 If any be blameless, the husband of one wife, having faithful children not accused of riot or unruly.

7 For a bishop must be blameless, as the steward of God (Elohim); not selfwilled, not soon angry, not given to wine, no striker, not given to filthy lucre;

8 But a lover of hospitality, a lover of good men, sober, just, holy, temperate;

9 Holding fast the faithful word as he hath been taught, that he may be able by sound doctrine both to exhort and to convince the gainsayers.

10 For there are many unruly and vain talkers and deceivers, specially they of the circumcision,

11 Whose mouths must be stopped, who subvert whole houses, teaching things which they ought not, for filthy lucre's sake.

12 One of themselves, even a prophet of their own, said, "The Cretians are always liars, evil beasts, slow bellies."

13 This witness is true. Wherefore rebuke them sharply, that they may be sound in the faith;

14 Not giving heed to Jewish (Yehudim) fables, and commandments of men, that turn from the truth.

15 Unto the pure all things are pure; but unto them that are defiled and unbelieving is nothing pure; but even their mind and conscience is defiled.

16 They profess that they know God (Elohim, יהוה (YHWH)); but in works they deny Him, being abominable, and disobedient, and unto every good work reprobate.

2 But speak you the things which become sound doctrine;

2 That the aged men be sober, grave, temperate, sound in faith, in love, in patience.

3 The aged women likewise, that they be in behaviour as becometh holiness, not false accusers, not given to much wine, teachers of good things;

4 That they may teach the young women to be sober, to love their husbands, to love their children,

5 To be discreet, chaste, keepers at home, good, obedient to their own husbands, that the word of God (Elohim, יהוה (YHWH)) be not blasphemed.

6 Young men likewise exhort to be sober minded.

7 In all things shewing yourself a pattern of good works; in doctrine shewing uncorruptness, gravity, sincerity,

8 Sound speech, that cannot be condemned; that he that is of the contrary part may be ashamed, having no evil thing to say of you.

9 Exhort servants to be obedient unto their own masters, and to please them well in all things; not answering again;

10 Not purloining, but shewing all good fidelity; that they may adorn the doctrine of יהוה (YHWH) our Savior in all things.

11 For the grace of God (Elohim, יהוה (YHWH)) that bringeth salvation hath appeared to all men,

12 Teaching us that, denying ungodliness and worldly lusts, we should live soberly, righteously, and godly, in this present world;

13 Looking for that blessed hope, and the glorious appearing of the great God (Elohim) and our Savior, Yahwah haMashiach;

14 Who gave Himself for us, that He might redeem us from all iniquity, and purify unto himself a peculiar people, zealous of good works.

15 These things speak, and exhort, and rebuke with all authority. Let no man despise you.

3 Put them in mind to be subject to principalities and powers, to obey magistrates, to be ready to every good work,

2 To speak evil of no man, to be no brawlers, but gentle, shewing all meekness unto all men.

3 For we ourselves also were sometimes foolish, disobedient, deceived, serving divers lusts and pleasures, living in malice and envy, hateful, and hating one another.

4 But when the kindness and love of יהוה (YHWH) our Savior toward man appeared,

5 Not by works of righteousness which we have done, but according to His mercy He saved us, by the washing of regeneration, and renewing of the Holy Spirit (Ruach haQodesh);

6 Which He shed on us abundantly through Yahwah haMashiach our Savior;

7 That being justified by His grace, we should be made heirs according to the hope of eternal life.

8 This is a faithful saying, and these things I will that you affirm constantly, that they who have believed in God (Elohim, יהוה (YHWH)) might be careful to maintain good works. These things are good and profitable unto men.

9 But avoid foolish questions, and genealogies, and contentions, and strivings about the law (torah); for they are unprofitable and vain.

10 Reject a man that is an heretick after the first and second admonition;

11 Knowing that he that is such is subverted, and sinneth, being condemned of himself.

12 When I shall send Artemas unto you, or Tychicus, be diligent to come unto me to Nicopolis; for I have determined there to winter.

13 Bring Zenas the lawyer and Apollos on their journey diligently, that nothing be wanting unto them.

14 And let ours also learn to maintain good works for necessary uses, that they be not unfruitful.

15 All that are with me salute you. Greet them that love us in the faith. Grace be with you all. So be it (Amen).

PHILEMON
PILEYMON פִּילֵימוֹן
(Epistle to Philemon)

1 Paul, a prisoner (for the sake) of [A1]Yahwah haMashiach, and Timothy our brother, unto Philemon our dearly beloved, and fellowlabourer,

2 And to our beloved Apphia, and Archippus our fellowsoldier, and to the assembly in your house;

3 Grace to you, and peace, from YHWH our Father and our Lord (Adonai) Yahwah haMashiach.

4 I thank my God (Elohim), making mention of you always in my prayers,

5 Hearing of your love and faith, which you have toward our Lord Yahwah (Adonai Yahwah), and toward all holy ones;

6 That the communication of your faith may become effectual by the acknowledging of every good thing which is in you in the Messiah (haMashiach) Yahwah.

7 For we have great joy and consolation in your love, because the bowels of the holy ones are refreshed by you, brother.

8 Wherefore, though I might be much bold in Messiah (Mashiach) to direct you that which is convenient,

9 Yet for love's sake I rather beseech you, being such a one as Paul the aged, and now also a prisoner (for the sake) of Yahwah haMashiach.

10 I beseech you for my son Onesimus, whom I have begotten in my bonds;

11 Which in time past was to you unprofitable, but now profitable to you and to me;

12 Whom I have sent again; you therefore receive him, that is, mine own bowels;

13 Whom I would have retained with me, that in your stead he might have ministered unto me in the bonds of the gospel (good news);

14 But without your mind would I do nothing; that your benefit should not be as it was of necessity, but willingly.

15 For perhaps he therefore departed for a season, that you shouldest receive him forever;

16 Not now as a servant, but above a servant, a brother beloved, specially to me, but how much more unto you, both in the flesh, and in the Lord (YHWH)?

17 If you count me therefore a partner, receive him as myself.

18 If he hath wronged you, or oweth you ought, put that on mine account;

19 I Paul have written it with mine own hand, I will repay it; albeit I do not say to you how you owest unto me even your own self besides.

20 Yea, brother, let me have joy of you in the Lord (YHWH); refresh my bowels in Messiah (Mashiach).

21 Having confidence in your obedience I wrote unto you, knowing that you wilt also do more than I say.

22 But withal prepare me also a lodging; for I trust that through your prayers I shall be given unto you.

23 There salute you Epaphras, my fellowprisoner in the Messiah (haMashiach) Yahwah;

24 Marcus, Aristarchus, Demas, Lucas, my fellowlabourers.

25 The grace of our Lord (Adonai) Yahwah haMashiach be with your spirit. So be it (Amen).

HEBREWS
IVRIM עִבְרִים
(Epistle to the Hebrews)

1 God (Elohim, יהוה (YHWH)), who at various times and in divers manners spake in time past unto the fathers by the prophets,

2 Hath in these last days spoken unto us by His [B47]Humanity (Yahwah haMashiach), whom He hath appointed heir of all things, by whom also He made the worlds;

3 Who being the brightness of His glory, and the express image of His person, and upholding all things by His powerful Word, when He had by Himself purged our sins, sat down on the right hand of the Majesty on high; – *Psa. 110:1*

4 Being made so much better than the angels, as He hath by inheritance obtained a more excellent name than they.

5 For unto whom of the angels said He at any time, "You are My [B47]Humanity, this day have I begotten You?" And again, "I will be to Him a father, and He shall be to Me a son? – *Psa. 2:7, 2 Sam. 7:14; 1 Chro. 17:13*

6 And again, when He bringeth in the firstbegotten into the world, He saith, "And let all the angels of God (Elohim) worship Him." – *Psa. 97:7*

7 And of the angels He saith, "Who maketh His angels spirits, and His ministers a flame of fire." – *Psa. 104:4*

8 But unto the [B47]Son (Humanity of El (YHWH)) He saith, "Your throne, O God (Elohim), is for ever and ever; a sceptre of righteousness is the sceptre of Your kingdom. – *Psa. 45:6*

9 You have loved righteousness, and hated iniquity; therefore יהוה (YHWH), your God (Elohim), hath anointed You with the oil of gladness above Your fellows." – *Psa. 45:7*

10 And, "You, Lord (Adonai) יהוה (YHWH), in the beginning hast laid the foundation of the earth; and the heavens are the works of Your hands; ." – *Psa. 102:25*

11 They shall perish; but You remainest; and they all shall wax old as doth a garment;

12 And as a vesture shalt You fold them up, and they shall be changed; but You are the same, and Your years shall not fail." – *Psa. 102:26-27*

13 But to which of the angels said He at any time, "Sit on My right hand, until I make Your enemies Your footstool?" – *Psa. 110:1*

14 Are they not all ministering spirits, sent forth to minister for them who shall be heirs of salvation?

2 Therefore we ought to give the more earnest heed to the things which we have heard, lest at any time we should let them slip.

2 For if the word spoken by angels was stedfast, and every transgression and disobedience received a just recompence of reward;

3 How shall we escape, if we neglect so great salvation; which at the first began to be spoken by the Lord (YHWH), and was confirmed unto us by them that heard Him;

4 God (Elohim, יהוה (YHWH)) also bearing them witness, both with signs and wonders, and with divers miracles, and gifts of the Holy Spirit (Ruach haQodesh), according to His own will?

5 For unto the angels hath He not put in subjection the world to come, whereof we speak.

6 But one in a certain place testified, saying, "What is man, that You are mindful of him? Or the son of man, that You visitest him?

7 You madest him a little lower than the angels; You crownedst him with glory and honour, and didst set him over the works of Your hands;

8 You have put all things in subjection under his feet. For in that He put all in subjection under him, He left nothing that is not put under him. But now we see not yet all things put under him. – *Psa. 8:4–6*

9 But we see Yahwah, who was made a little lower than the angels for the suffering of death, crowned with glory and honour; that He by the grace of God (Elohim, יהוה (YHWH)) should taste death for every man.

10 For it became Him, for whom are all things, and by whom are all things, in bringing many sons unto glory, to make the captain of their salvation perfect through sufferings.

11 For both He that sanctifieth and they who are sanctified are all of one; for which cause He is not ashamed to call them brethren,

12 Saying, "I will declare Your name unto My brethren, in the midst of the assembly will I sing praise unto You." – *Psa. 22:22*

13 And again, "I will put My trust in Him." And again, "Behold I and the children whom יהוה hath given Me." – *Isa. 8:18*

14 Forasmuch then as the children are partakers of flesh and blood, He also Himself likewise

took part of the same; that through death He might destroy him that had the power of death, that is, the devil;

15 And deliver them who through fear of death were all their lifetime subject to bondage.

16 For verily He took not on Him the nature of angels; but He took on Him the seed of Avraham. – *Isa. 41:8-9*

17 Wherefore in all things it behoved Him to be made like unto His brethren, that He might be a merciful and faithful High Priest (Kohen Gadol) in things pertaining to יהוה (YHWH), to make reconciliation for the sins of the people.

18 For in that He Himself hath suffered being tested, He is able to succour them that are tested.

3 Wherefore, holy brethren, partakers of the heavenly calling, consider the Apostle and High Priest (Kohen Gadol) of our profession, the Messiah (haMashiach) Yahwah;

2 Who was faithful to Him that appointed Him, as also Moses (Mosheh) was faithful in all his house. – *Num. 12:7*

3 For this Man was counted worthy of more glory than Moses (Mosheh), inasmuch as he who hath builded the house hath more honour than the house.

4 For every house is builded by some man; but He that built all things is God (Elohim, יהוה (YHWH)).

5 And Moses (Mosheh) verily was faithful in all his house, as a servant, for a testimony of those things which were to be spoken after;

6 But the Messiah (haMashiach) as a son (descendant) over His own house; whose house are we, if we hold fast the confidence and the rejoicing of the hope firm unto the end.

7 Wherefore as the Holy Spirit saith, "Today if you will hear His voice,

8 Harden not your hearts, as in the provocation, in the day of testing in the wilderness;

9 When your fathers tested Me, proved Me, and saw My works forty years.

10 Wherefore I was grieved with that generation, and said, 'They do always err in their heart; and they have not known My ways.'

11 So I sware in My wrath, 'They shall not enter into My rest.'" – *Psa. 95:7-11*

12 Take heed, brethren, lest there be in any of you an evil heart of unbelief, in departing from the living God (Elohim).

13 But exhort one another daily, while it is

called "Today;" lest any of you be hardened through the deceitfulness of sin.

14 For we are made partakers of Messiah (Mashiach), if we hold the beginning of our confidence stedfast unto the end;

15 While it is said, "Today if you will hear His voice, harden not your hearts, as in the provocation." – *Psa. 95:7-8*

16 For some, when they had heard, did provoke; howbeit not all that came out of Egypt (Mitsrayim) by Moses (Mosheh).

17 But with whom was He grieved forty years? Was it not with them that had sinned, whose carcases fell in the wilderness?

18 And to whom sware He that they should not enter into His rest, but to them that believed not?

19 So we see that they could not enter in because of unbelief.

4 Let us therefore fear, lest, a promise being left us of entering into His rest, any of you should seem to come short of it.

2 For unto us was the gospel (good news) preached, as well as unto them; but the word preached did not profit them, not being mixed with faith in them that heard it.

3 For we who have believed do enter into rest, as He said, "As I have sworn in My wrath, if they shall enter into My rest; although the works were finished from the foundation of the world. – *Psa. 95:11*

4 For He spake in a certain place of the seventh day on this wise, "And God (Elohim) did rest the seventh day from all His works." – *Gen. 2:2*

5 And in this place again, "If they shall enter into My rest." – *Psa. 95:11*

6 Seeing therefore it remaineth that some must enter therein, and they to whom it was first preached entered not in because of unbelief;

7 Again, He limiteth a certain day, saying in Dawid, "Today," after so long a time; as it is said, "Today if you will hear His voice, harden not your hearts." – *Psa. 95:7-8*

8 For if [A32]Joshua (Yehoshua) had given them rest, then he would not afterward have spoken of another day.

9 There remaineth therefore a rest to the people of God (Elohim).

10 For he that is entered into His rest, he also hath ceased from his own works, as God (Elohim) did from His.

11 Let us labour therefore to enter into that

rest, lest any man fall after the same example of unbelief.

12 For the word of God (Elohim, יהוה (YHWH)) is quick, and powerful, and sharper than any two-edged sword, piercing even to the dividing asunder of soul and spirit, and of the joints and marrow, and is a discerner of the thoughts and intents of the heart.

13 Neither is there any creature that is not manifest in His sight; but all things are naked and opened unto the eyes of Him with whom we have to do.

14 Seeing then that we have a great High Priest (Kohen Gadol), that is passed into the heavens, Yahwah (haMashiach) the [B47]Humanity of El, let us hold fast our profession.

15 For we have not a High Priest (Kohen Gadol) who cannot be touched with the feeling of our infirmities; but was in all points tempted like as we are, yet without sin.

16 Let us therefore come boldly unto the throne of grace, that we may obtain mercy, and find grace to help in time of need.

5 For every high priest taken from among men is ordained for men in things pertaining to God (Elohim, יהוה (YHWH)), that he may offer both gifts and sacrifices for sins;

2 Who can have compassion on the ignorant, and on them that are out of the way; for that he himself also is compassed with infirmity.

3 And by reason hereof he ought, as for the people, so also for himself, to offer for sins.

4 And no man taketh this honour unto himself, but he that is called of יהוה (YHWH), as was Aaron (Aharon).

5 So also the Messiah (haMashiach) glorified not Himself to be made a High Priest; but He that said unto Him, "You are My [B47]Humanity, today have I begotten You." – Psa. 2:7

6 As He saith also in another place, "You are a Priest (Kohen) for ever after the order of Melchisedec." – Psa. 110:4

7 Who in the days of His flesh, when He had offered up prayers and supplications with strong crying and tears unto Him that was able to save Him from death, and was heard in that He feared;

8 Though He was a son, yet learned He obedience by the things which He suffered;

9 And being made perfect, He became the author of eternal salvation unto all them that obey Him;

10 Called of יהוה (YHWH) a High Priest (Kohen Gadol) after the order of Melchisedec.

11 Of whom we have many things to say, and hard to be uttered, seeing you are dull of hearing.

12 For when for the time you ought to be teachers, you have need that one teach you again which be the first principles of the oracles of God (Elohim); and are become such as have need of milk, and not of strong meat.

13 For everyone that useth milk is unskilful in the word of righteousness; for he is a babe.

14 But strong meat belongeth to them that are of full age, even those who by reason of use have their senses exercised to discern both good and evil.

6 Therefore leaving the principles of the doctrine of the Messiah (haMashiach), let us go on unto perfection; not laying again the foundation of repentance from dead works, and of faith toward יהוה (YHWH),

2 Of the doctrine of baptisms, and of laying on of hands, and of resurrection of the dead, and of eternal judgment.

3 And this will we do, if יהוה (YHWH) permit.

4 For it is impossible for those who were once enlightened, and have tasted of the heavenly gift, and were made partakers of the Holy Spirit (Ruach haQodesh),

5 And have tasted the good word of God (Elohim, יהוה (YHWH)), and the powers of the world to come,

6 If they shall fall away, to renew them again unto repentance; seeing they crucify to themselves the [B47]Humanity of El (YHWH) afresh, and put Him to an open shame.

7 For the earth which drinketh in the rain that cometh often upon it, and bringeth forth herbs meet for them by whom it is dressed, receiveth blessing from God (Elohim);

8 But that which beareth thorns and briers is rejected, and is near unto cursing; whose end is to be burned. – Gen. 3:17–18

9 But, beloved, we are persuaded better things of you, and things that accompany salvation, though we thus speak.

10 For יהוה (YHWH) is not unrighteous to forget your work and labour of love, which you have shewed toward His name, in that you have ministered to the holy ones, and do minister.

11 And we desire that every one of you do shew the same diligence to the full assurance of hope unto the end;

12 That you be not slothful, but followers of them who through faith and patience inherit the promises.

13 For when יהוה (YHWH) made promise to Avraham, because He could swear by no greater, He sware by Himself, – *Gen. 22:16*

14 Saying, "Surely blessing I will bless you, and multiplying I will multiply you." – *Gen. 22:17*

15 And so, after he had patiently endured, he obtained the promise.

16 For men verily swear by the greater; and an oath for confirmation is to them an end of all strife.

17 Wherein יהוה (YHWH), willing more abundantly to shew unto the heirs of promise the immutability of His counsel, confirmed it by an oath;

18 That by two immutable things, in which it was impossible for יהוה (YHWH) to lie, we might have a strong consolation, who have fled for refuge to lay hold upon the hope set before us:

19 Which hope we have as an anchor of the soul, both sure and stedfast, and which entereth into that within the veil;

20 Whither the forerunner is for us entered, even Yahwah, made a High Priest forever after the order of Melchisedec. – *Psa. 110:4*

7 For this Melchisedec, king of Salem (Shalom), priest (kohen) of the Most High God (El Elyon), who met Avraham returning from the slaughter of the kings, and blessed him; 2 To whom also Avraham gave a tenth part of all; first being by interpretation king of righteousness, and after that also king of Salem (Shalom), which means, king of Peace; – *Gen. 14:17–20*

3 Without father, without mother, without descent, having neither beginning of days, nor end of life; but made like unto the son of God (Elohim); abideth a priest (kohen) continually.

4 Now consider how great this man was, unto whom even the patriarch Avraham gave the tenth of the spoils.

5 And verily they that are of the sons of Lewi, who receive the office of the priesthood (kehunnah), have a commandment to take tithes of the people according to the law (torah), that is, of their brethren, though they come out of the loins of Avraham;

6 But he whose descent is not counted from them received tithes of Avraham, and blessed him that had the promises.

7 And without all contradiction the less is blessed of the better.

8 And here men that die receive tithes; but there he receiveth them, of whom it is witnessed that he liveth.

9 And as I may so say, Lewi also, who receiveth tithes, payed tithes in Avraham.

10 For he was yet in the loins of his father, when Melchisedec met him.

11 If therefore perfection were by the Lewitical priesthood, for under it the people received the [B28a]law (torah), what further need was there that another priest (kohen) should rise after the order of Melchisedec, and not be called after the order of Aaron (Aharon)?

12 For the priesthood being changed, there is made of necessity a change also of the law (torah).

13 For he of whom these things are spoken pertaineth to another tribe, of which no man gave attendance at the altar.

14 For it is evident that our Lord (Adonai) sprang out of Judah (Yehudah); of which tribe Moses (Mosheh) spake nothing concerning priesthood (kehunnah).

15 And it is yet far more evident, for that after the similitude of Melchisedec there ariseth another Priest (Kohen),

16 Who is made, not after the law (torah) of a fleshly commandment, but after the power of an endless life.

17 For He testifieth, "You (Yahwah haMashiach) are a Priest (Kohen) for ever after the order of Melchisedec." – *Psa. 110:4*

18 For there is verily a disannulling of the commandment going before for the weakness and unprofitableness thereof.

19 For the law (torah) made nothing perfect, but the bringing in of a better hope did; by which we draw near unto God (Elohim).

20 And inasmuch as not without an oath He was made Priest (Kohen);

21 (For those priests (kohanim) were made without an oath; but this with an oath by Him that said unto Him, "יהוה sware and will not relent, "You are a Priest (Kohen) forever after the order of Melchisedec;)" – *Psa. 110:4*

22 By so much was Yahwah made a surety of a better testament.

23 And they truly were many priests (kohanim), because they were not suffered to continue by reason of death;

24 But this, because He continueth ever, hath an unchangeable priesthood.

25 Wherefore He is able also to save them to the uttermost that come unto God (Elohim) by Him, seeing He ever liveth to make intercession for them.

26 For such a High Priest (Kohen Gadol) is fitting for us, who is holy, harmless, undefiled, separate from sinners, and made higher than the heavens;

27 Who needeth not daily, as those high priests (kohanim gadolim), to offer up sacrifice, first for his own sins, and then for the people's; for this He did once, when He offered up Himself.

28 For the law (torah) maketh men high priests (kohanim gadolim) who have infirmity; but the word of the oath, which came after the law (torah), maketh the [B47]Son (Yahwah haMashiach), who is consecrated for evermore.

8 Now of the things which we have spoken this is the sum: We have such a High Priest (Kohen Gadol), who is set on the right hand of the throne of the Majesty in the heavens; – *Psa. 110:1*

2 A minister of the sanctuary, and of the true tabernacle, which יהוה (YHWH) pitched, and not man.

3 For every high priest is ordained to offer gifts and sacrifices; wherefore it is of necessity that this man have somewhat also to offer.

4 For if He was on earth, He should not be a Priest (Kohen), seeing that there are priests (kohanim) that offer gifts according to the law (torah);

5 Who serve unto the example and shadow of heavenly things, as Moses (Mosheh) was admonished of God (Elohim, יהוה (YHWH)) when he was about to make the tabernacle; for saith He, "See that you make all things according to the pattern shewed to you in the mount." – *Exo. 25:40*

6 But now hath He obtained a more excellent ministry, by how much also He is the Mediator of a better covenant, which was established upon better promises.

7 For if that first covenant had been faultless, then should no place have been sought for the second.

8 For finding fault with them, He saith, "Behold, the days come," saith יהוה, "when I will make a New Covenant (Berit Chadashah) with the house of Yisrael and with the house of Judah (Yehudah); – *Jer. 31:31*

9 Not according to the covenant that I made with their fathers in the day when I took them by the hand to lead them out of the land of Egypt (Mitsrayim); because they continued not in My covenant, and I regarded them not," saith יהוה. – *Jer. 31: 32*

10 "For this is the covenant that I will make with the house of Yisrael after those days," saith יהוה; "I will put My Torah into their mind, and write them in their hearts; and I will be to them a God (Elohim), and they shall be to Me a people; – *Jer. 31: 33*

11 And they shall not teach every man his neighbour, and every man his brother, saying, 'Know יהוה;' for all shall know Me, from the least to the greatest.

12 For I will be merciful to their unrighteousness, and their sins and their iniquities will I remember no more." – *Jer. 31: 34*

13 In that He saith, "A New Covenant (Berit Chadashah)," He hath made the first old. Now that which decayeth and waxeth old is ready to vanish away.

9 Then verily the first covenant (berit) had also ordinances of divine service, and a worldly sanctuary.

2 For there was a tabernacle made; the first, wherein was the candlestick (menorah), and the table, and the shewbread; which is called sanctuary.

3 And after the second veil, the tabernacle which is called the Holiest of all;

4 Which had the golden censer, and the ark of the covenant overlaid round about with gold, wherein was the golden pot that had manna, and Aaron (Aharon)'s rod that budded, and the tables of the covenant;

5 And over it the cherubims (keruvim) of glory shadowing the mercyseat; of which we cannot now speak particularly.

6 Now when these things were thus ordained, the priests (kohanim) went always into the first tabernacle, accomplishing the service of God (Elohim, יהוה (YHWH)).

7 But into the second went the high priest alone once every year, not without blood, which he offered for himself, and for the errors of the people;

8 The Holy Spirit (Ruach haQodesh) signifying this, that the way into the holiest of all was not yet made manifest, while as the first tabernacle was yet standing;

9 Which was a figure for the time then present, in which were offered both gifts and sacrifices, that could not make him that did the service perfect, as pertaining to the conscience;

10 Which stood only in foods and drinks, and divers washings, and carnal ordinances, imposed on them until the time of reformation.

11 But the Messiah (haMashiach) being come a High Priest of good things to come, by a greater and more perfect tabernacle, not made with hands, that is to say, not of this building;

12 Neither by the blood of goats and calves, but by His own blood He entered in once into the holy place, having obtained eternal redemption for us.

13 For if the blood of bulls and of goats, and the ashes of a heifer sprinkling the unclean, sanctifieth to the purifying of the flesh;

14 How much more shall the blood of the Messiah (haMashiach), who through the eternal Spirit offered Himself without spot to God (Elohim, יהוה (YHWH))), purge your conscience from dead works to serve the living God (Elohim)?

15 And for this cause He is the Mediator of the New Covenant (Berit Chadashah), that by means of death, for the redemption of the transgressions that were under the first covenant, they who are called might receive the promise of eternal inheritance.

16 For where a testament (covenant) is, there must also of necessity be the death of the testator.

17 For a covenant is of force after men are dead; otherwise it is of no strength at all while the testator liveth.

18 Whereupon neither the first covenant was dedicated without blood.

19 For when Moses (Mosheh) had spoken every precept to all the people according to the law (torah), he took the blood of calves and of goats, with water, and scarlet wool, and hyssop, and sprinkled both the book, and all the people,

20 Saying, "This is the blood of the covenant which יהוה (YHWH) hath enjoined unto you."

21 Moreover he sprinkled with blood both the tabernacle, and all the vessels of the ceremony.

22 And by the law (torah) almost all things are purged with blood; and without shedding of blood is no remission.

23 It was therefore necessary that the patterns of things in the heavens should be purified with these; but the heavenly things themselves with better sacrifices than these.

24 For the Messiah (haMashiach) is not entered into the holy places made with hands, which are the figures of the true; but into heaven itself, now to appear in the presence of God (Elohim, יהוה (YHWH)) for us;

25 Nor yet that He should offer Himself often, as the high priest entereth into the holy place every year with blood of others;

26 For then must He often have suffered since the foundation of the world; but now once in the end of the world hath He appeared to put away sin by the sacrifice of Himself.

27 And as it is appointed unto men once to die, but after this the judgment;

28 So the Messiah (haMashiach) was once offered to bear the sins of many; and unto them that look for Him shall He appear the second time without sin unto salvation.

10 For the [B28a]law (torah), having a shadow of good things to come, and not the very image of the things, can never with those sacrifices which they offered year by year continually make the comers thereunto perfect.

2 For then would they not have ceased to be offered? Because that the worshippers once purged should have had no more conscience of sins.

3 But in those sacrifices there is a remembrance again made of sins every year.

4 For it is not possible that the blood of bulls and of goats should take away sins.

5 Wherefore when He cometh into the world, He saith, "Sacrifice and offering You willed not, but a body have you prepared Me;

6 In burnt offerings and sacrifices for sin You have had no pleasure.

7 Then said I, 'Behold, I come (in the volume of the book it is written of me,) to do your will, O God (Elohim, יהוה (YHWH))."' – *Psa.40:6–8*

8 Above when He said, "Sacrifice and offering

and burnt offerings and offering for sin You willed not, neither hadst pleasure therein;" which are offered by the law (torah);

9 Then said He, "Behold, I come to do Your will, O God (Elohim, יהוה (YHWH))." He taketh away the first, that He may establish the second.

10 By which will we are sanctified through the offering of the body of Yahwah haMashiach once for all.

11 And every priest (kohen) standeth daily ministering and offering oftentimes the same sacrifices, which can never take away sins;

12 But this Man, after He had offered one sacrifice for sins forever, sat down on the right hand of God (Elohim);

13 From henceforth expecting till His enemies be made His footstool. – Psa.110:1

14 For by one offering He hath perfected for ever them that are sanctified.

15 Whereof the Holy Spirit (Ruach haQodesh) also is a witness to us; for after that He had said before,

16 "This is the covenant (berit) that I will make with them after those days," saith יהוה (YHWH) "I will put My Torah into their hearts, and in their minds will I write them; – Jer. 31:33

17 And their sins and iniquities will I remember no more." – Jer. 31:34

18 Now where remission of these is, there is no more offering for sin.

19 Having therefore, brethren, boldness to enter into the holiest by the blood of Yahwah,

20 By a new and living way, which He hath consecrated for us, through the veil, that is to say, His flesh;

21 And having a High Priest (Kohen Gadol) over the house of יהוה (YHWH);

22 Let us draw near with a true heart in full assurance of faith, having our hearts sprinkled from an evil conscience, and our bodies washed with pure water. – Eze. 36:25

23 Let us hold fast the profession of our faith without wavering; (for He is faithful that promised;)

24 And let us consider one another to spur unto love and to good works;

25 Not forsaking the assembling of ourselves together, as the manner of some is; but exhorting one another; and so much the more, as you see the day approaching.

26 For if we sin wilfully after that we have received the knowledge of the truth, there remaineth no more sacrifice for sins,

27 But a certain fearful looking for of judgment and fiery indignation, which shall devour the adversaries. – Isa. 26:11

28 He that despised the Torah written by Moses (Mosheh) died without mercy under two or three witnesses; – Deu. 17:6; 19:15

29 Of how much sorer punishment, suppose you, shall he be thought worthy, who hath trodden under foot the [B47]Humanity of El (YHWH), and hath counted the blood of the covenant (berit), wherewith he was sanctified, an unholy thing, and hath done despite unto the Spirit of grace? – Exo. 24:8

30 For we know Him that hath said, "Vengeance belongeth unto Me, I will recompense," saith יהוה (YHWH). And again, "יהוה (YHWH) shall judge His people." – Deu. 32:35–36

31 It is a fearful thing to fall into the hands of the living God (Elohim).

32 But call to remembrance the former days, in which, after you were illuminated, you endured a great fight of afflictions;

33 Partly, whilst you were made a gazingstock both by reproaches and afflictions; and partly, whilst you became companions of them that were so used.

34 For you had compassion of me in my bonds, and took joyfully the spoiling of your goods, knowing in yourselves that you have in heaven a better and an enduring substance.

35 Cast not away therefore your confidence, which hath great recompence of reward.

36 For you have need of patience, that, after you have done the will of God (Elohim, יהוה (YHWH)), you might receive the promise.

37 For yet a little while, and he that shall come will come, and will not tarry.

38 Now the just shall live by faith; but if any man draws back, my soul shall have no pleasure in him. – Hab. 2:3-4

39 But we are not of them who draw back unto perdition; but of them that believe to the saving of the soul.

11 Now faith is the substance of things hoped for, the evidence of things not seen. – Hab. 2:4

2 For by it the elders obtained a good report.

3 Through faith we understand that the worlds

were framed by the word of God (Elohim, יהוה (YHWH)), so that things which are seen were not made of things which do appear.

4 By faith Abel (Havel) offered unto God (Elohim) a more excellent sacrifice than Cain, by which he obtained witness that he was righteous, God (Elohim) testifying of his gifts; and by it he being dead yet speaketh.

5 By faith Enoch was translated that he should not see death; and was not found, because God (Elohim) had translated him; for before his translation he had this testimony, that he pleased God (Elohim, יהוה (YHWH)). – Gen. 5:24

6 But without faith it is impossible to please Him; for he that cometh to God (Elohim, יהוה (YHWH)) must believe that He is, and that He is a rewarder of them that diligently seek Him.

7 By faith Noah, being warned of God (Elohim, יהוה (YHWH)) of things not seen as yet, moved with fear, prepared an ark to the saving of his house; by which he condemned the world, and became heir of the righteousness which is by faith.

8 By faith Avraham, when he was called to go out into a place which he should after receive for an inheritance, obeyed; and he went out, not knowing whither he went. – Gen. 12:1

9 By faith he sojourned in the land of promise, as in a strange country, dwelling in tabernacles with Isaac (Yitschaq) and Jacob (Yaaqov), the heirs with him of the same promise;

10 For he looked for a city which hath foundations, whose builder and maker is יהוה (YHWH).

11 Through faith also Sara herself received strength to conceive seed, and was delivered of a child when she was past age, because she judged Him faithful who had promised.

12 Therefore sprang there even of one, and him as good as dead, so many as the stars of the sky in multitude, and as the sand which is by the sea shore innumerable. – Gen. 15:5–6; 22:17; 32:12; Exo. 32:13; Deu. 1:10; 10:22

13 These all died in faith, not having received the promises, but having seen them afar off, and were persuaded of them, and embraced them, and confessed that they were strangers and pilgrims on the earth. – 1 Chro. 29:15

14 For they that say such things declare plainly that they seek a country.

15 And truly, if they had been mindful of that country from whence they came out, they might have had opportunity to have returned.

16 But now they desire a better country, that is, a heavenly; wherefore יהוה (YHWH) is not ashamed to be called their God (Elohim); for He hath prepared for them a city.

17 By faith Avraham, when he was tried, offered up Isaac (Yitschaq); and he that had received the promises offered up his only begotten son,

18 Of whom it was said, "That in Isaac (Yitschaq) shall your seed be called; – Gen. 21:12

19 Accounting that God (Elohim, יהוה (YHWH)) was able to raise him up, even from the dead; from whence also he received him in a figure.

20 By faith Isaac (Yitschaq) blessed Jacob (Yaaqov) and Esau concerning things to come.

21 By faith Jacob (Yaaqov), when he was dying, blessed both the sons of Joseph (Yosef); and worshipped, leaning upon the top of his staff. – Gen. 47:31

22 By faith Joseph (Yosef), when he died, made mention of the departing of the children of Yisrael; and gave commandment concerning his bones.

23 By faith Moses (Mosheh), when he was born, was hid three months of his parents, because they saw he was a proper child; and they were not afraid of the king's commandment. – Exo. 2:2

24 By faith Moses (Mosheh), when he was come to years, refused to be called the son of Pharaoh's daughter; – Exo. 2:11

25 Choosing rather to suffer affliction with the people of God (Elohim, יהוה (YHWH)), than to enjoy the pleasures of sin for a season;

26 Esteeming the reproach of the Messiah (haMashiach) greater riches than the treasures in Egypt (Mitsrayim); for he had respect unto the recompence of the reward.

27 By faith he forsook Egypt (Mitsrayim), not fearing the wrath of the king; for he endured, as seeing Him who is invisible.

28 Through faith he kept the Passover (Pesach), and the sprinkling of blood, lest he that destroyed the firstborn should touch them.

29 By faith they passed through the Red sea as by dry land; which the Egyptians (Mitsrayim) assaying to do were drowned.

30 By faith the walls of Yericho fell down, after

they were compassed about seven days.

31 By faith the harlot Rahab perished not with them that believed not, when she had received the spies with peace.

32 And what shall I more say? For the time would fail me to tell of Gedeon, and of Barak, and of Samson, and of Jephthae (Yiftach); of Dawid also, and Shamuel, and of the prophets;

33 Who through faith subdued kingdoms, wrought righteousness, obtained promises, stopped the mouths of lions, – *Dan. 6:22*

34 Quenched the violence of fire, escaped the edge of the sword, out of weakness were made strong, waxed valiant in fight, turned to flight the armies of the aliens.

35 Women received their dead raised to life again; and others were tortured, not accepting deliverance; that they might obtain a better resurrection;

36 And others had trial of cruel mockings and scourgings, yea, moreover of bonds and imprisonment;

37 They were stoned, they were sawn asunder, were tempted, were slain with the sword; they wandered about in sheepskins and goatskins; being destitute, afflicted, tormented;

38 (Of whom the world was not worthy;) they wandered in deserts, and in mountains, and in dens and caves of the earth.

39 And these all, having obtained a good report through faith, received not the promise;

40 God (Elohim, יהוה (YHWH)) having provided some better thing for us, that they without us should not be made perfect.

12 Wherefore seeing we also are compassed about with so great a cloud of witnesses, let us lay aside every weight, and the sin which doth so easily beset us, and let us run with patience the race that is set before us,

2 Looking unto Yahwah the author and finisher of our faith; who for the joy that was set before Him endured the stake, despising the shame, and is set down at the right hand of the throne of God (Elohim, יהוה (YHWH)). – *Psa.110:1*

3 For consider Him that endured such contradiction of sinners against Himself, lest you be wearied and faint in your minds.

4 You have not yet resisted unto blood, striving against sin.

5 And you have forgotten the exhortation which speaketh unto you as unto children, "My

chiildren, despise not you the chastening of יהוה (YHWH), nor faint when you are rebuked of Him; – *Prov. 3:11*

6 For whom יהוה (YHWH) loveth He chasteneth, and scourgeth every children whom He receiveth." – *Prov. 3:12*

7 If you endure chastening, God (Elohim, יהוה (YHWH)) dealeth with you as with sons; for what son is he whom the father chasteneth not?

8 But if you be without chastisement, whereof all are partakers, then are you bastards, and not sons.

9 Furthermore we have had fathers of our flesh which corrected us, and we gave them reverence; shall we not much rather be in subjection unto the Father of spirits, and live?

10 For they verily for a few days chastened us after their own pleasure; but He for our profit, that we might be partakers of His holiness.

11 Now no chastening for the present seemeth to be joyous, but grievous; nevertheless afterward it yieldeth the peaceable fruit of righteousness unto them who are exercised thereby.

12 Wherefore lift up the hands which hang down, and the feeble knees; – *Isa. 35:3*

13 And make straight paths for your feet, lest that which is lame be turned out of the way; but let it rather be healed. – *Prov. 4:26*

14 Follow peace with all men, and holiness, without which no man shall see the Lord (YHWH);

15 Looking diligently lest any man fail of the grace of God (Elohim, יהוה (YHWH)); lest any root of bitterness springing up trouble you, and thereby many be defiled; – *Deu. 29:18*

16 Lest there be any fornicator, or profane person, as Esaw, who for one morsel of meat sold his birthright.

17 For you know how that afterward, when he would have inherited the blessing, he was rejected; for he found no place of repentance, though he sought it carefully with tears.

18 For you are not come unto the mount that might be touched, and that burned with fire, nor unto blackness, and darkness, and tempest,

19 And the sound of a trumpet, and the voice of words; which voice they that heard intreated that the word should not be spoken to them anymore;

20 For they could not endure that which was commanded, "And if so much as a beast touch

the mountain, it shall be stoned, or thrust through with a dart;" – *Exo. 19:12–13*

21 And so terrible was the sight, that Moses (Mosheh) said, "I exceedingly fear and quake;" – *Deu. 9:19*

22 But you are come unto mount Sion, and unto the city of the living God (Elohim), the heavenly Jerusalem (Yerushalayim), and to an innumerable company of angels,

23 To the general assembly and assembly of the firstborn, which are written in heaven, and to יהוה (YHWH) the Judge of all, and to the spirits of just men made perfect,

24 And to Yahwah the Mediator of the new covenant (berit chadashah), and to the blood of sprinkling, that speaketh better things than that of Abel (Havel).

25 See that you refuse not Him that speaketh. For if they escaped not who refused Him that spake on earth, much more shall not we escape, if we turn away from Him that speaketh from heaven;

26 Whose voice then shook the earth; but now He hath promised, saying, "Yet once more I shake not the earth only, but also heaven." – *Hag. 2:6, 21*

27 And this word, yet once more, signifieth the removing of those things that are shaken, as of things that are made, that those things which cannot be shaken may remain.

28 Wherefore we receiving a kingdom which cannot be moved, let us have grace, whereby we may serve God (Elohim, יהוה (YHWH)) acceptably with reverence and godly fear;

29 For our God (Elohim) is a consuming fire. – *Deu. 4:24; 9:3; Isa. 33:14*

13 Let brotherly love continue. 2 Be not forgetful to entertain strangers; for thereby some have entertained angels unawares.

3 Remember them that are in bonds, as bound with them; and them who suffer adversity, as being yourselves also in the body.

4 Marriage is honourable in all, and the bed undefiled; but whoremongers and adulterers יהוה (YHWH) will judge.

5 Let your conversation be without covetousness; and be content with such things as you have; for He hath said, "I will never leave you, nor forsake you." – *Deu. 31:6*

6 So that we may boldly say, "יהוה (YHWH) is

my helper, and I will not fear what man shall do unto me." – *Psa. 118:6*

7 Remember them who have the rule over you, who have spoken unto you the word of God (Elohim, יהוה (YHWH)); whose faith follow, considering the end of their conversation.

8 Yahwah haMashiach the same yesterday, and today, and forever.

9 Be not carried about with divers and strange doctrines. For it is a good thing that the heart be established with grace; not with meats, which have not profited them that have been occupied therein.

10 We have an altar, whereof they have no right to eat which serve the tabernacle.

11 For the bodies of those beasts, whose blood is brought into the sanctuary by the high priest for sin, are burned outside the camp.

12 Wherefore Yahwah also, that He might sanctify the people with His own blood, suffered outside the gate.

13 Let us go forth therefore unto Him outside the camp, bearing His reproach.

14 For here have we no continuing city, but we seek one to come.

15 By Him therefore let us offer the sacrifice of praise to יהוה (YHWH) continually, that is, the fruit of our lips giving thanks to His name.

16 But to do good and to communicate forget not; for with such sacrifices יהוה (YHWH) is well pleased.

17 Obey them that have the rule over you, and submit yourselves; for they watch for your souls, as they that must give account, that they may do it with joy, and not with grief; for that is unprofitable for you.

18 Pray for us, for we trust we have a good conscience, in all things willing to live honestly.

19 But I beseech you the rather to do this, that I may be restored to you the sooner.

20 Now the God (Elohim) of peace, that brought again from the dead our Lord Yahwah (Adonai YHWH), that great shepherd of the sheep, through the blood of the everlasting covenant,

21 Make you perfect in every good work to do His will, working in you that which is wellpleasing in His sight, through Yahwah haMashiach; to whom be glory for ever and ever. So be it (Amen).

22 And I beseech you, brethren, bear the word

of exhortation; for I have written a letter unto you in few words.

23 Know you that our brother Timothy is set at liberty; with whom, if he come shortly, I will see you.

24 Salute all them that have the rule over you, and all the saints. They of Italy salute you.

25 Grace be with you all. So be it (Amen).

JAMES
YAAQOV יַעֲקֹב
(Epistle of James)

1 [A76]James (Yaaqov), a servant of God (Elohim) and of the Lord (Adonai) Yahwah haMashiach, to the twelve tribes which are scattered abroad, greeting.

2 My brethren, count it all joy when you fall into divers temptations;

3 Knowing this, that the trying of your faith worketh patience.

4 But let patience have her perfect work, that you may be perfect and entire, wanting nothing.

5 If any of you lack wisdom, let him ask of God (Elohim, יהוה (YHWH)), that giveth to all men liberally, and upbraideth not; and it shall be given him.

6 But let him ask in faith, nothing wavering. For he that wavereth is like a wave of the sea driven with the wind and tossed.

7 For let not that man think that he shall receive any thing of God (Elohim, יהוה (YHWH)).

8 A double minded man is unstable in all his ways.

9 Let the brother of low degree rejoice in that he is exalted;

10 But the rich, in that he is made low; because as the flower of the grass he shall pass away.

11 For the sun is no sooner risen with a burning heat, but it withereth the grass, and the flower thereof falleth, and the grace of the fashion of it perisheth; so also shall the rich man fade away in his ways.

12 Blessed is the man that endureth temptation; for when he is tried, he shall receive the crown of life, which the Lord (YHWH) hath promised to them that love Him.

13 Let no man say when he is tempted, "I am tempted of God (Elohim);" for God (Elohim, יהוה (YHWH)) cannot be tempted with evil, neither tempteth He any man;

14 But every man is tempted, when he is drawn away of his own lust, and enticed.

15 Then when lust hath conceived, it bringeth forth sin; and sin, when it is finished, bringeth forth death.

16 Do not err, my beloved brethren.

17 Every good gift and every perfect gift is from above, and cometh down from the Father of lights, with whom is no variableness, neither shadow of turning.

18 Of His own will begat He us with the word of truth, that we should be a kind of firstfruits of His creatures.

19 Wherefore, my beloved brethren, let every man be swift to hear, slow to speak, slow to wrath;

20 For the wrath of man worketh not the righteousness of God (Elohim, יהוה (YHWH)).

21 Wherefore lay apart all filthiness and superfluity of naughtiness, and receive with meekness the engrafted word, which is able to save your souls.

22 But be you doers of the word, and not hearers only, deceiving your own selves.

23 For if any be a hearer of the word, and not a doer, he is like unto a man beholding his natural face in a glass;

24 For he beholdeth himself, and goeth his way, and straightway forgetteth what manner of man he was.

25 But whoso looketh into the perfect [B28a]Law (Torah) of liberty (which gives freedom), and continueth therein, he being not a forgetful hearer, but a doer of the work, this man shall be blessed in his deed. – *Psa. 19:7*

26 If any man among you seem to be religious, and bridleth not his tongue, but deceiveth his own heart, this man's religion is vain.

27 Pure religion and undefiled before YHWH the Father is this: "To visit the fatherless and widows in their affliction, and to keep himself unspotted from the world."

2 My brethren, have not the faith of our Lord (Adonai) Yahwah haMashiach, Lord (Adon) of glory, with respect of persons.

2 For if there come unto your assembly a man with a gold ring, in goodly apparel, and there come in also a poor man in vile raiment;

3 And you have respect to him that weareth the gay clothing, and say unto him, "Sit you here in a good place;" and say to the poor, "Stand you there, or sit here under my footstool;"

4 Are you not then partial in yourselves, and are become judges of evil thoughts?

5 Hearken, my beloved brethren, hath not God (Elohim, יהוה (YHWH)) chosen the poor of this world rich in faith, and heirs of the kingdom which He hath promised to them that love Him?

6 But you have despised the poor. Do not rich

men oppress you, and draw you before the judgment seats?

7 Do not they blaspheme that worthy name by which you are called?

8 If you fulfil the royal Law (Torah) according to the scripture, "You shalt love your neighbour as yourself," you do well; – *Lev. 19:18*

9 But if you have respect to persons (show partiality), you commit sin, and are convicted by the Law (Torah) as transgressors.

10 For whosoever shall keep the whole Law (Torah), and yet offend in one point, he is guilty of all.

11 For he that said, "Do not commit adultery," said also, "Do not kill." Now if you commit no adultery, yet if you kill, you are become a transgressor of the Law (Torah). – *Exo. 20:13, Deu. 5:17*

12 So speak you, and so do, as they that shall be judged by the Law (Torah) of liberty (which gives freedom).

13 For he shall have judgment without mercy, that hath shewed no mercy; and mercy rejoiceth against judgment.

14 What doth it profits, my brethren, though a man say he hath faith, and have not works? Can faith save him?

15 If a brother or sister be naked, and destitute of daily food,

16 And one of you say unto them, "Depart in peace, be you warmed and filled;" notwithstanding you give them not those things which are needful to the body; what doth it profits?

17 Even so faith, if it hath not works, is dead, being alone.

18 Yea, a man may say, "You have faith, and I have works; shew me your faith without your works, and I will shew you my faith by my works.

19 You believest that there is one God (Elohim); you doest well; the devils also believe, and tremble. – *Deu. 6:4*

20 But wilt you know, O vain man, that faith without works is dead?

21 Was not Avraham our father justified by works, when he had offered Isaac (Yitschaq) his son upon the altar?

22 Seest you how faith wrought with his works, and by works was faith made perfect?

23 And the scripture was fulfilled which saith,

"Avraham believed יהוה (YHWH), and it was imputed unto him for righteousness; and he was called the friend of יהוה (YHWH). – *Gen. 15:6, Isa. 41:8, 2 Chro. 20:7*

24 You see then how that by works a man is justified, and not by faith only.

25 Likewise also was not Rahab the harlot justified by works, when she had received the messengers, and had sent them out another way?

26 For as the body without the spirit is dead, so faith without works is dead also.

3 My brethren, be not many masters, knowing that we shall receive the greater condemnation.

2 For in many things we offend all. If any man offends not in word, the same is a perfect man, and able also to bridle the whole body.

3 Behold, we put bits in the horses' mouths, that they may obey us; and we turn about their whole body.

4 Behold also the ships, which though they be so great, and are driven of fierce winds, yet are they turned about with a very small helm, whithersoever the governor listeth.

5 Even so the tongue is a little member, and boasteth great things. Behold, how great a matter a little fire kindleth!

6 And the tongue is a fire, a world of iniquity; so is the tongue among our members, that it defileth the whole body, and setteth on fire the course of nature; and it is set on fire of hell.

7 For every kind of beasts, and of birds, and of serpents, and of things in the sea, is tamed, and hath been tamed of mankind;

8 But the tongue can no man tame; it is an unruly evil, full of deadly poison.

9 Therewith bless we YHWH our Father; and therewith curse we men, who are made after the similitude of God (Elohim). – *Gen 1:26-27*

10 Out of the same mouth proceedeth blessing and cursing. My brethren, these things ought not so to be.

11 Doth a fountain sends forth at the same place sweet water and bitter?

12 Can the fig tree, my brethren, bear olive berries? Either a vine, figs? So can no fountain both yield salt water and fresh.

13 Who is a wise man and endued with knowledge among you? Let him shew out of a good conversation his works with meekness of wisdom.

14 But if you have bitter envying and strife in your hearts, glory not, and lie not against the truth.

15 This wisdom descendeth not from above, but is earthly, sensual, devilish.

16 For where envying and strife is, there is confusion and every evil work.

17 But the wisdom that is from above is first pure, then peaceable, gentle, and easy to be intreated, full of mercy and good fruits, without partiality, and without hypocrisy.

18 And the fruit of righteousness is sown in peace of them that make peace.

4 From whence come wars and fightings among you? Come they not hence, even of your lusts that war in your members?

2 You lust, and have not; you kill, and desire to have, and cannot obtain; you fight and war, yet you have not, because you ask not.

3 You ask, and receive not, because you ask amiss, that you may consume it upon your lusts.

4 You adulterers and adulteresses, know you not that the friendship of the world is enmity with God (Elohim, יהוה (YHWH))? Whosoever therefore will be a friend of the world is the enemy of God (Elohim, יהוה (YHWH).

5 Do you think that the scripture saith in vain, "The spirit that dwelleth in us lusteth to envy?"

6 But He giveth more grace. Wherefore He saith, "יהוה (YHWH) resisteth the proud, but giveth grace unto the humble." – Prov. 3:34

7 Submit yourselves therefore to יהוה (YHWH). Resist the devil, and he will flee from you.

8 Draw near to יהוה (YHWH), and He will draw near to you. Cleanse your hands, you sinners; and purify your hearts, you double minded.

9 Be afflicted, and mourn, and weep; let your laughter be turned to mourning, and your joy to heaviness.

10 Humble yourselves in the sight of יהוה (YHWH) and He shall lift you up.

11 Speak not evil one of another, brethren. He that speaketh evil of his brother, and judgeth his brother, speaketh evil of the Torah, and judgeth the Torah; but if you judge the Torah, you are not a doer of the Torah, but a judge.

12 There is one giver of Torah, who is able to save and to destroy; who are you that judgest another?

13 Go to now, you that say, "Today or tomorrow we will go into such a city, and continue there a year, and buy and sell, and get gain;"

14 Whereas you know not what shall be on the morrow. For what is your life? It is even a vapour, that appeareth for a little time, and then vanisheth away.

15 For that you ought to say, "If יהוה (YHWH) will, we shall live, and do this, or that."

16 But now you rejoice in your boastings; all such rejoicing is evil.

17 Therefore to him that knoweth to do good, and doeth it not, to him it is sin.

5 Go to now, you rich men, weep and howl for your miseries that shall come upon you.

2 Your riches are corrupted, and your garments are motheaten.

3 Your gold and silver is cankered; and the rust of them shall be a witness against you, and shall eat your flesh as it was fire. You have heaped treasure together for the last days.

4 Behold, the hire of the labourers who have reaped down your fields, which is of you kept back by fraud, crieth; and the cries of them who have reaped are entered into the ears of יהוה of hosts (YHWH Tsevaot).

5 You have lived in pleasure on the earth, and been wanton; you have nourished your hearts, as in a day of slaughter.

6 You have condemned and killed the just; and he doth not resist you.

7 Be patient therefore, brethren, unto the coming of יהוה (YHWH). Behold, the husbandman waiteth for the precious fruit of the earth, and hath long patience for it, until he receives the early and latter rain. – Deu. 11:14; Jer. 5:24; Joel 2:23

8 Be you also patient; stablish your hearts; for the coming of יהוה (YHWH) draweth near.

9 Grudge not one against another, brethren, lest you be condemned; behold, the judge standeth before the door.

10 Take, my brethren, the prophets, who have spoken in the name of יהוה (YHWH), for an example of suffering affliction, and of patience.

11 Behold, we count them happy who endure. You have heard of the patience of Job (Iyov), and have seen the final outcome of the Lord (Adonai) that יהוה (YHWH) is very compassionate, and of tender mercy. – Exo. 34:6; Psa. 103:8; 111:4

12 But above all things, my brethren, swear not, neither by heaven, neither by the earth, neither

by any other oath; but let your yea be yea; and your nay, nay; lest you fall into condemnation.

13 Is any among you afflicted? Let him pray. Is any merry? Let him sing psalms.

14 Is any sick among you? Let him call for the elders of the assembly; and let them pray over him, anointing him with oil in the name of יהוה (YHWH);

15 And the prayer of faith shall save the sick, and יהוה (YHWH) shall raise him up; and if he has committed sins, they shall be forgiven him.

16 Confess your faults one to another, and pray one for another, that you may be healed. The effectual fervent prayer of a righteous man availeth much.

17 Elijah (Eliyahu) was a man subject to like passions as we are, and he prayed earnestly that it might not rain: and it rained not on the earth by the space of three years and six months.

18 And he prayed again, and the heaven gave rain, and the earth brought forth her fruit.

19 Brethren, if any of you do err from the truth, and one convert him;

20 Let him know, that he who converteth the sinner from the error of his way shall save a soul from death, and shall cover a multitude of sins. – *Prov. 10:12*

1 PETER
כֵּיפָא א KEFA 1
(First Epistle of Peter)

1 Peter (Kefa), an apostle of [A1]Yahwah haMashiach, to the strangers scattered throughout Pontus, Galatia, Cappadocia, Asia, and Bithynia,

2 Elect according to the foreknowledge of YHWH the Father, through sanctification of the Spirit, unto obedience and sprinkling of the blood of Yahwah haMashiach. Grace unto you, and peace, be multiplied.

3 Blessed be the God (Elohim) and Father of our Lord (Adonai) Yahwah haMashiach, who according to His abundant mercy hath begotten us again unto a lively hope by the resurrection of Yahwah haMashiach from the dead,

4 To an inheritance incorruptible, and undefiled, and that fadeth not away, reserved in heaven for you,

5 Who are kept by the power of God (Elohim, יהוה (YHWH)) through faith unto salvation ready to be revealed in the last time.

6 Wherein you greatly rejoice, though now for a season, if need be, you are in heaviness through manifold temptations;

7 That the trial of your faith, being much more precious than of gold that perisheth, though it be tried with fire, might be found unto praise and honour and glory at the appearing of Yahwah haMashiach;

8 Whom having not seen, you love; in whom, though now you see Him not, yet believing, you rejoice with joy unspeakable and full of glory;

9 Receiving the end of your faith, even the salvation of your souls.

10 Of which salvation the prophets have enquired and searched diligently, who prophesied of the grace that should come unto you;

11 Searching what, or what manner of time the Spirit of the Messiah (haMashiach) which was in them did signify, when it testified beforehand the sufferings of the Messiah (haMashiach), and the glory that should follow.

12 Unto whom it was revealed, that not unto themselves, but unto us they did minister the things, which are now reported unto you by them that have preached the gospel (good news) unto you with the Holy Spirit (Ruach haQodesh)

sent down from heaven; which things the angels desire to look into.

13 Wherefore gird up the loins of your mind, be sober, and hope to the end for the grace that is to be brought unto you at the revelation of Yahwah haMashiach;

14 As obedient children, not fashioning yourselves according to the former lusts in your ignorance;

15 But as He who hath called you is holy, so be you holy in all manner of conversation;

16 Because it is written, "Be you holy; for I am holy." – Lev. 11:44, 45; 19:2; 20:7

17 And if you call on the Father, who without respect of persons judgeth according to every man's work, pass the time of your sojourning here in fear;

18 Forasmuch as you know that you were not redeemed with corruptible things, as silver and gold, from your vain conversation received by tradition from your fathers;

19 But with the precious blood of the Messiah (haMashiach), as of a lamb without blemish and without spot;

20 Who verily was foreordained before the foundation of the world, but was manifest in these last times for you,

21 Who through Him do believe in God (Elohim, יהוה (YHWH)), that raised Him up from the dead, and gave Him glory; that your faith and hope might be in יהוה (YHWH).

22 Seeing you have purified your souls in obeying the truth through the Spirit unto unfeigned love of the brethren, see that you love one another with a pure heart fervently;

23 Being born again, not of corruptible seed, but of incorruptible, by the word of God (Elohim, יהוה (YHWH)), which liveth and abideth for ever.

24 For all flesh is as grass, and all the glory of man as the flower of grass. The grass withereth, and the flower thereof falleth away;

25 But the word of God (Elohim, יהוה (YHWH)) endureth forever. And this is the word which by the gospel (good news) is preached unto you. – Isa. 40:6–8

2 Wherefore laying aside all malice, and all guile, and hypocrisies, and envies, and all evil speakings,

2 As newborn babes, desire the sincere milk of the word, that you may grow thereby;

3 If so be you have tasted that the Lord (YHWH) is gracious. – *Psa. 34:8*

4 To whom coming, as unto a living stone, disallowed indeed of men, but chosen of God (Elohim, יהוה (YHWH)), and precious,

5 You also, as lively stones, are built up a spiritual house, a holy priesthood, to offer up spiritual sacrifices, acceptable to God (Elohim) by Yahwah haMashiach.

6 Wherefore also it is contained in the scripture, "Behold, I lay in Sion (Tsiyon) a chief corner stone, elect, precious; and he that believeth on Him shall not be confounded." – *Isa. 28:16*

7 Unto you therefore who believe he is precious; but unto them who be disobedient, the stone which the builders disallowed, the same is made the head of the corner, – *Psa. 118:22*

8 And a stone of stumbling, and a rock of offence, even to them who stumble at the word, being disobedient; whereunto also they were appointed. – *Isa. 8:14*

9 But you are a chosen generation, a royal priesthood, a holy nation, a peculiar people; that you should shew forth the praises of Him who hath called you out of darkness into His marvellous light; – *Isa. 43:20-21; Deu.7:6; Deu. 10:15; Exo. 19:5-6; Isa. 61:6*

10 Which in time past were not a people, but are now the people of God (Elohim, יהוה (YHWH)); who had not obtained mercy, but now have obtained mercy. – *Hos. 2:23*

11 Dearly beloved, I beseech you as strangers and pilgrims, abstain from fleshly lusts, which war against the soul; – *Gen.23:4, 47:4; Psa.39:12; 1 Chro. 29:15*

12 Having your conversation honest among the Gentiles (Goyim); that, whereas they speak against you as evildoers, they may by your good works, which they shall behold, glorify יהוה (YHWH) in the day of visitation.

13 Submit yourselves to every ordinance of man for the Lord (YHWH)'s sake; whether it be to the king, as supreme;

14 Or unto governors, as unto them that are sent by Him for the punishment of evildoers, and for the praise of them that do well.

15 For so is the will of God (Elohim, יהוה (YHWH)), that with well doing you may put to silence the ignorance of foolish men;

16 As free, and not using your liberty for a cloke of maliciousness, but as the servants of God (El).

17 Honour all men. Love the brotherhood. Fear God (El). Honour the king.

18 Servants, be subject to your masters with all fear; not only to the good and gentle, but also to the froward.

19 For this is thankworthy, if a man for conscience toward God (Elohim) endure grief, suffering wrongfully.

20 For what glory is it, if, when you be buffeted for your faults, you shall take it patiently? but if, when you do well, and suffer for it, you take it patiently, this is acceptable with God (Elohim).

21 For even hereunto were you called, because the Messiah (haMashiach) also suffered for us, leaving us an example, that you should follow His steps;

22 Who did no sin, neither was guile found in His mouth; – *Isa. 53:9*

23 Who, when He was reviled, reviled not again; when He suffered, He threatened not; but committed Himself to Him that judgeth righteously;

24 Who His own self bares our sins in His own body on the tree (stake), that we, being dead to sins, should live unto righteousness; by whose stripes you were healed. – *Isa.53:4,5,12; Deu.21:22–23*

25 For you were as sheep going astray; but are now returned unto the Shepherd and Overseer of your souls. – *Isa. 53:6*

3 Likewise, you wives, be in subjection to your own husbands; that, if any obey not the word, they also may without the word be won by the conversation of the wives;

2 While they behold your chaste conversation coupled with fear.

3 Whose adorning let it not be that outward adorning of plaiting the hair, and of wearing of gold, or of putting on of apparel;

4 But let it be the hidden man of the heart, in that which is not corruptible, even the ornament of a meek and quiet spirit, which is in the sight of God (Elohim, יהוה (YHWH)) of great price.

5 For after this manner in the old time the holy women also, who trusted in God (Elohim), adorned themselves, being in subjection unto their own husbands;

6 Even as Sarah obeyed Avraham, calling him 'my lord (adoni)'; whose daughters you are, as long as you do well, and are not afraid with any

amazement.

7 Likewise, you husbands, dwell with them according to knowledge, giving honour unto the wife, as unto the weaker vessel, and as being heirs together of the grace of life; that your prayers be not hindered.

8 Finally, be you all of one mind, having compassion one of another, love as brethren, be pitiful, be courteous;

9 Not rendering evil for evil, or railing for railing; but contrariwise blessing; knowing that you are thereunto called, that you should inherit a blessing.

10 For he that will love life, and see good days, let him refrain his tongue from evil, and his lips that they speak no guile.

11 Let him eschew (keep away from) evil, and do good; let him seek peace, and pursue it.

12 For the eyes of יהוה (YHWH) are over the righteous, and His ears are open unto their prayers; but the face of יהוה (YHWH) is against them that do evil. – *Psa. 34:12-16*

13 And who is he that will harm you, if you be followers of that which is good?

14 But and if you suffer for righteousness' sake, happy are you; and be not afraid of their terror, neither be troubled;

15 But sanctify God (Elohim, יהוה (YHWH)) in your hearts; and be ready always to give an answer to every man that asketh you a reason of the hope that is in you with meekness and fear; – *Isa. 8:12-13*

16 Having a good conscience; that, whereas they speak evil of you, as of evildoers, they may be ashamed that falsely accuse your good conversation in Messiah (Mashiach).

17 For it is better, if the will of God (Elohim, יהוה (YHWH)) be so, that you suffer for well doing, than for evil doing.

18 For the Messiah (haMashiach) also hath once suffered for sins, the just for the unjust, that He might bring us to יהוה (YHWH), being put to death in the flesh, but quickened by the Spirit;

19 By which also He went and preached unto the spirits in prison;

20 Which sometime were disobedient, when once the longsuffering of God (Elohim, יהוה (YHWH)) waited in the days of Noah, while the ark was a preparing, wherein few, that is, eight souls were saved by water.

21 The like figure whereunto even baptism doth also now save us, not the putting away of the filth of the flesh, but the answer of a good conscience toward God (Elohim) by the resurrection of Yahwah haMashiach;

22 Who is gone into heaven, and is on the right hand of God (Elohim, יהוה (YHWH)); angels and authorities and powers being made subject unto Him. – *Psa. 110:1*

4 Forasmuch then as the Messiah (haMashiach) hath suffered for us in the flesh, arm yourselves likewise with the same mind; for he that hath suffered in the flesh hath ceased from sin;

2 That he no longer should live the rest of his time in the flesh to the desires of men, but to the will of God (Elohim, יהוה (YHWH)).

3 For the time past of our life may suffice us to have wrought the will of the Gentiles (Goyim), when we walked in lasciviousness, lusts, excess of wine, revellings, banquetings, and abominable idolatries;

4 Wherein they think it strange that you run not with them to the same excess of riot, speaking evil of you;

5 Who shall give account to Him that is ready to judge the quick and the dead.

6 For this cause was the gospel (good news) preached also to them that are dead, that they might be judged according to men in the flesh, but live according to God (Elohim) in the spirit.

7 But the end of all things is at hand; be you therefore sober, and watch unto prayer.

8 And above all things have fervent love among yourselves; for love shall cover the multitude of sins. – *Prov. 10:12*

9 Be hospitable one to another without grudging.

10 As every man hath received the gift, even so minister the same one to another, as good stewards of the manifold grace of God (Elohim, יהוה (YHWH)).

11 If any man speaks, let him speak as the oracles of God (Elohim); if any man minister, let him do it as of the ability which God (Elohim) giveth; that God (Elohim) in all things may be glorified through Yahwah haMashiach, to whom be praise and dominion for ever and ever. So be it (Amen).

12 Beloved, think it not strange concerning the fiery trial which is to try you, as though some strange thing happened unto you;

13 But rejoice, inasmuch as you are partakers

of the Messiah (haMashiach)'s sufferings; that, when His glory shall be revealed, you may be glad also with exceeding joy.

14 If you be reproached for the name of the Messiah (haMashiach), happy are you; for the spirit of glory and of God (Elohim, יהוה (YHWH)) resteth upon you; on their part He is evil spoken of, but on your part He is glorified.

15 But let none of you suffer as a murderer, or as a thief, or as an evildoer, or as a busybody in other men's matters.

16 Yet if any man suffers as a follower of Messiah (Mashiach), let him not be ashamed; but let him glorify יהוה (YHWH) on this behalf.

17 For the time is come that judgment must begin at the house of יהוה (YHWH); and if it first begins at us, what shall the end be of them that obey not the gospel (good news) of God (Elohim, יהוה (YHWH))?

18 And if the righteous scarcely be saved, where shall the ungodly and the sinner appear? – *Prov. 11:31*

19 Wherefore let them that suffer according to the will of God (Elohim, יהוה (YHWH)) commit the keeping of their souls to Him in well doing, as unto a faithful Creator.

5 The elders who are among you I exhort, who am also an elder, and a witness of the sufferings of the Messiah (haMashiach), and also a partaker of the glory that shall be revealed;

2 Feed the flock of יהוה (YHWH) which is among you, taking the oversight thereof, not by constraint, but willingly; not for filthy lucre, but of a ready mind;

3 Neither as being lords over יהוה (YHWH)'s heritage, but being ensamples to the flock.

4 And when the chief Shepherd shall appear, you shall receive a crown of glory that fadeth not away.

5 Likewise, you younger, submit yourselves unto the elder. Yea, all of you be subject one to another, and be clothed with humility; for יהוה (YHWH) resisteth the proud, and giveth grace to the humble. – *Prov. 3:34*

6 Humble yourselves therefore under the mighty hand of יהוה (YHWH), that He may exalt you in due time;

7 Casting all your care upon Him; for He careth for you.

8 Be sober, be vigilant; because your adversary the devil, as a roaring lion, walketh about, seeking whom he may devour;

9 Whom resist stedfast in the faith, knowing that the same afflictions are accomplished in your brethren that are in the world.

10 But the God (Elohim) of all grace, who hath called us unto His eternal glory by Messiah (Mashiach) Yahwah, after that you have suffered a while, make you perfect, stablish, strengthen, settle you.

11 To Him be glory and dominion for ever and ever. So be it (Amen).

12 By Silvanus, a faithful brother unto you, as I suppose, I have written briefly, exhorting, and testifying that this is the true grace of God (Elohim, יהוה (YHWH)) wherein you stand.

13 The assembly that is at Babylon (Bavel), elected together with you, saluteth you; and so doth Marcus my son.

14 Greet you one another with a kiss of love. Peace be with you all that are in Messiah (Mashiach) Yahwah. So be it (Amen).

2 PETER
כֵּיפָא 2 ב KEFA 2
(Second Epistle of Peter)

1 Shimon Peter (Kefa), a servant and an apostle of [A1]Yahwah haMashiach, to them that have obtained like precious faith with us through the righteousness of God ([B1a]Elohim) and our Savior, Yahwah haMashiach.

2 Grace and peace be multiplied unto you through the knowledge of God (Elohim), and of Yahwah our Lord (Adonai),

3 According as His divine power hath given unto us all things that pertain unto life and godliness, through the knowledge of Him that hath called us to glory and virtue;

4 Whereby are given unto us exceeding great and precious promises; that by these you might be partakers of the divine nature, having escaped the corruption that is in the world through lust.

5 And besides this, giving all diligence, add to your faith virtue; and to virtue knowledge;

6 And to knowledge temperance; and to temperance patience; and to patience godliness;

7 And to godliness brotherly kindness; and to brotherly kindness love.

8 For if these things be in you, and abound, they make you that you shall neither be barren nor unfruitful in the knowledge of our Lord (Adonai) Yahwah haMashiach.

9 But he that lacketh these things is blind, and cannot see afar off, and hath forgotten that he was purged from his old sins.

10 Wherefore the rather, brethren, give diligence to make your calling and election sure; for if you do these things, you shall never fall;

11 For so an entrance shall be ministered unto you abundantly into the everlasting kingdom of our Lord (Adonai) and Savior Yahwah haMashiach.

12 Wherefore I will not be negligent to put you always in remembrance of these things, though you know them, and be established in the present truth.

13 Yea, I think it meet, as long as I am in this tabernacle, to stir you up by putting you in remembrance;

14 Knowing that shortly I must put off this my tabernacle, even as our Lord (Adonai) Yahwah haMashiach hath shewed me.

15 Moreover I will endeavour that you may be able after my decease to have these things always in remembrance.

16 For we have not followed cunningly devised fables, when we made known unto you the power and coming of our Lord (Adonai) Yahwah haMashiach, but were eyewitnesses of His majesty.

17 For He received from YHWH the Father honour and glory, when there came such a voice to Him from the excellent glory, "This is My beloved [B47]Son (Humanity), in whom I am well pleased."

18 And this voice which came from heaven we heard, when we were with Him in the holy mount.

19 We have also a more sure word of prophecy; whereunto you do well that you take heed, as unto a light that shineth in a dark place, until the day dawn, and the day star arise in your hearts;

20 Knowing this first, that no prophecy of the scripture is of any private interpretation.

21 For the prophecy came not in old time by the will of man; but holy men of God (Elohim) spake as they were moved by the Holy Spirit (Ruach haQodesh).

2 But there were false prophets also among the people, even as there shall be false teachers among you, who privily shall bring in damnable heresies, even denying the Lord (YHWH) that bought them, and bring upon themselves swift destruction.

2 And many shall follow their pernicious ways; by reason of whom the way of truth shall be evil spoken of.

3 And through covetousness shall they with feigned words make merchandise of you; whose judgment now of a long time lingereth not, and their damnation slumbereth not.

4 For if God (Elohim, יהוה (YHWH)) spared not the angels that sinned, but cast them down to hell (sheol), and delivered them into chains of darkness, to be reserved unto judgment;

5 And spared not the old world, but saved Noah the eighth person, a preacher of righteousness, bringing in the flood upon the world of the ungodly;

6 And turning the cities of Sodom and Gomorrha into ashes condemned them with an overthrow, making them an ensample unto those that after

should live ungodly;

7 And delivered just Lot, vexed with the filthy conversation of the wicked;

8 (For that righteous man dwelling among them, in seeing and hearing, vexed his righteous soul from day to day with their unlawful deeds;)

9 יהוה (YHWH) knoweth how to deliver the godly out of temptations, and to reserve the unjust unto the day of judgment to be punished;

10 But chiefly them that walk after the flesh in the lust of uncleanness, and despise government. Presumptuous are they, selfwilled, they are not afraid to speak evil of dignities.

11 Whereas angels, which are greater in power and might, bring not railing accusation against them before יהוה (YHWH).

12 But these, as natural brute beasts, made to be taken and destroyed, speak evil of the things that they understand not; and shall utterly perish in their own corruption;

13 And shall receive the reward of unrighteousness, as they that count it pleasure to riot in the day time. Spots they are and blemishes, sporting themselves with their own deceivings while they feast with you;

14 Having eyes full of adultery, and that cannot cease from sin; beguiling unstable souls: a heart they have exercised with covetous practices; cursed children;

15 Which have forsaken the right way, and are gone astray, following the way of Balaam the son of Bosor, who loved the wages of unrighteousness;

16 But was rebuked for his iniquity; the dumb ass speaking with man's voice forbad the madness of the prophet.

17 These are wells without water, clouds that are carried with a tempest; to whom the mist of darkness is reserved for ever.

18 For when they speak great swelling words of vanity, they allure through the lusts of the flesh, through much wantonness, those that were clean escaped from them who live in error.

19 While they promise them liberty, they themselves are the servants of corruption; for of whom a man is overcome, of the same is he brought in bondage.

20 For if after they have escaped the pollutions of the world through the knowledge of our Lord (Adonai) and Savior Yahwah haMashiach, they are again entangled therein, and overcome, the

latter end is worse with them than the beginning.

21 For it had been better for them not to have known the way of righteousness, than, after they have known it, to turn from the holy commandment delivered unto them.

22 But it is happened unto them according to the true proverb, "The dog is turned to his own vomit again; and the sow that was washed to her wallowing in the mire." – *Prov. 26:11*

3 This second epistle, beloved, I now write unto you; in both which I stir up your pure minds by way of remembrance;

2 That you may be mindful of the words which were spoken before by the holy prophets, and of the commandment of us the apostles of the Lord (Adonai) and Savior;

3 Knowing this first, that there shall come in the last days scoffers, walking after their own lusts,

4 And saying, "Where is the promise of His coming? For since the fathers fell asleep, all things continue as they were from the beginning of the creation.

5 For this they willingly are ignorant of, that by the word of God (Elohim, יהוה (YHWH)) the heavens were of old, and the earth standing out of the water and in the water;

6 Whereby the world that then was, being overflowed with water, perished;

7 But the heavens and the earth, which are now, by the same word are kept in store, reserved unto fire against the day of judgment and perdition of ungodly men.

8 But, beloved, be not ignorant of this one thing, that one day is with יהוה (YHWH) as a thousand years, and a thousand years as one day.

9 יהוה (YHWH) is not slack concerning His promise, as some men count slackness; but is longsuffering toward us, not willing that any should perish, but that all should come to repentance.

10 But the day of יהוה (YHWH) will come as a thief in the night; in the which the heavens shall pass away with a great noise, and the elements shall melt with fervent heat, the earth also and the works that are therein shall be burned up.

11 Seeing then that all these things shall be dissolved, what manner of persons ought you to be in all holy conversation and godliness,

12 Looking for and hasting unto the coming of the day of יהוה (YHWH), wherein the heavens being on fire shall be dissolved, and the

elements shall melt with fervent heat?

13 Nevertheless we, according to His promise, look for new heavens and a new earth, wherein dwelleth righteousness.

14 Wherefore, beloved, seeing that you look for such things, be diligent that you may be found of Him in peace, without spot, and blameless.

15 And account that the longsuffering of our Lord (Yahwah) is salvation; even as our beloved brother Paul also according to the wisdom given unto him hath written unto you;

16 As also in all his epistles, speaking in them of these things; in which are some things hard to be understood, which they that are unlearned and unstable wrest, as they do also the other scriptures, unto their own destruction.

17 You therefore, beloved, seeing you know these things before, beware lest you also, being led away with the error of the wicked, fall from your own stedfastness.

18 But grow in grace, and in the knowledge of our Lord (Adonai) and Savior Yahwah haMashiach. To Him be glory both now and forever. So be it (Amen).

1 JOHN
YOCHANAN 1 א יוֹחָנָן
(First Epistle of John)

1 That which was from the beginning, which we have heard, which we have seen with our eyes, which we have looked upon, and our hands have handled, of the Word of life;

2 (For the life was manifested, and we have seen it, and bear witness, and shew unto you that eternal life, which was with the Father, and was manifested unto us;)

3 That which we have seen and heard declare we unto you, that you also may have fellowship with us; and truly our fellowship is with the Father, and with His [B47]Humanity, [A1]Yahwah [B45]haMashiach.

4 And these things write we unto you, that your joy may be full.

5 This then is the message which we have heard of Him, and declare unto you, that God (Elohim, יהוה (YHWH)) is light, and in Him is no darkness at all.

6 If we say that we have fellowship with Him, and walk in darkness, we lie, and do not the truth;

7 But if we walk in the light, as He is in the light, we have fellowship one with another, and the blood of Yahwah haMashiach His Humanity cleanseth us from all sin.

8 If we say that we have no sin, we deceive ourselves, and the truth is not in us.

9 If we confess our sins, He is faithful and just to forgive us our sins, and to cleanse us from all unrighteousness.

10 If we say that we have not sinned, we make Him a liar, and His word is not in us.

2 My little children, these things write I unto you, that you sin not. And if any man sin, we have an advocate with the Father, Yahwah haMashiach the righteous (tsaddiq);

2 And He is the propitiation for our sins; and not for ours only, but also for the sins of the whole world.

3 And hereby we do know that we know Him, if we keep His commandments.

4 He that saith, I know Him, and keepeth not His commandments, is a liar, and the truth is not in him.

5 But whoso keepeth His word, in Him verily is the love of God (Elohim, יהוה (YHWH)) perfected; hereby know we that we are in Him.

6 He that saith he abideth in Him ought himself also so to walk, even as He walked.

7 Brethren, I write no new commandment unto you, but an old commandment which you had from the beginning. The old commandment is the word which you have heard from the beginning.

8 Again, a new commandment I write unto you, which thing is true in Him and in you, because the darkness is past, and the true light now shineth.

9 He that saith he is in the light, and hateth his brother, is in darkness even until now.

10 He that loveth his brother abideth in the light, and there is none occasion of stumbling in him.

11 But he that hateth his brother is in darkness, and walketh in darkness, and knoweth not whither he goeth, because that darkness hath blinded his eyes.

12 I write unto you, little children, because your sins are forgiven you for His name's sake.

13 I write unto you, fathers, because you have known Him that is from the beginning. I write unto you, young men, because you have overcome the wicked one. I write unto you, little children, because you have known the Father.

14 I have written unto you, fathers, because you have known Him that is from the beginning. I have written unto you, young men, because you are strong, and the word of God (Elohim, יהוה (YHWH)) abideth in you, and you have overcome the wicked one.

15 Love not the world, neither the things that are in the world. If any man loves the world, the love of the Father is not in him.

16 For all that is in the world, the lust of the flesh, and the lust of the eyes, and the pride of life, is not of the Father, but is of the world.

17 And the world passeth away, and the lust thereof; but he that doeth the will of God (Elohim, יהוה (YHWH)) abideth for ever.

18 Little children, it is the last time; and as you have heard that anti-Messiah (anti-Mashiach) shall come, even now are there many anti-Messiah (anti-Mashiach); whereby we know that it is the last time.

19 They went out from us, but they were not of us; for if they had been of us, they would no doubt have continued with us; but they went

out, that they might be made manifest that they were not all of us.

20 But you have an unction from the Holy One, and you know all things.

21 I have not written unto you because you know not the truth, but because you know it, and that no lie is of the truth.

22 Who is a liar but he that denieth that Yahwah (YHWH) is the Messiah (haMashiach)? He is anti-Messiah (anti-Mashiach), that denieth the Father and the [B47]Son (Humanity of El (YHWH)).

23 Whosoever denieth the [B47]Son (Humanity of El (YHWH)), the same hath not the Father; but he that acknowledgeth the [B47]Son hath the Father also.

24 Let that therefore abide in you, which you have heard from the beginning. If that which you have heard from the beginning shall remain in you, you also shall continue in the [B47]Son (Humanity of El (YHWH)), and in the Father.

25 And this is the promise that He hath promised us, even eternal life.

26 These things have I written unto you concerning them that seduce you.

27 But the anointing which you have received of Him abideth in you, and you need not that any man teaches you; but as the same anointing teacheth you of all things, and is truth, and is no lie, and even as it hath taught you, you shall abide in Him.

28 And now, little children, abide in Him; that, when He shall appear, we may have confidence, and not be ashamed before Him at His coming.

29 If you know that He is righteous, you know that every one that doeth righteousness is born of Him.

3 Behold, what manner of love the Father hath bestowed upon us, that we should be called the sons of God (Elohim); therefore the world knoweth us not, because it knew Him not.

2 Beloved, now are we the sons of God (Elohim), and it doth not yet appear what we shall be; but we know that, when He shall appear, we shall be like Him; for we shall see Him as He is.

3 And every man that hath this hope in Him purifieth himself, as He is pure.

4 Whosoever committeth sin transgresseth also the Torah; for sin is the transgression of the Torah.

5 And you know that He was manifested to take away our sins; and in Him is no sin.

6 Whosoever abideth in Him sinneth not; whosoever sinneth hath not seen Him, neither known Him.

7 Little children, let no man deceive you; he that doeth righteousness is righteous, even as He is righteous.

8 He that committeth sin is of the devil; for the devil sinneth from the beginning. For this purpose the [B47]Humanity of El (YHWH) was manifested, that He might destroy the works of the devil.

9 Whosoever is born of God (Elohim, יהוה (YHWH)) doth not commit sin; for His seed remaineth in him; and he cannot sin, because he is born of God (Elohim, יהוה (YHWH)).

10 Through this manifest the children of God (Elohim) and the children of the devil; whosoever doeth not righteousness is not of God (Elohim), neither he that loveth not his brother.

11 For this is the message that you heard from the beginning, that we should love one another.

12 Not as Cain, who was of that wicked one, and slew his brother. And wherefore slew he him? Because his own works were evil, and his brother's righteous.

13 Marvel not, my brethren, if the world hate you.

14 We know that we have passed from death unto life, because we love the brethren. He that loveth not his brother abideth in death.

15 Whosoever hateth his brother is a murderer; and you know that no murderer hath eternal life abiding in him.

16 Hereby perceive we the love of Yahwah (YHWH), because He laid down His life for us; and we ought to lay down our lives for the brethren.

17 But whoso hath this world's good, and seeth his brother has need, and shutteth up his bowels of compassion from him, how dwelleth the love of God (Elohim, יהוה (YHWH)) in him?

18 My little children, let us not love in word, neither in tongue; but in deed and in truth.

19 And hereby we know that we are of the truth, and shall assure our hearts before Him.

20 For if our heart condemns us, יהוה (YHWH) is greater than our heart, and knoweth all things.

21 Beloved, if our heart condemns us not, then have we confidence toward יהוה (YHWH).

22 And whatsoever we ask, we receive of Him, because we keep His commandments, and do those things that are pleasing in His sight.

23 And this is His commandment, that we should believe on the name of His Humanity, Yahwah haMashiach, and love one another, as He gave us commandment.

24 And he that keepeth His commandments dwelleth in Him, and He in him. And hereby we know that He abideth in us, by the Spirit which He hath given us.

4 Beloved, believe not every spirit, but try the spirits whether they are of God (Elohim, יהוה (YHWH)); because many false prophets are gone out into the world.

2 Hereby know you the Spirit of יהוה (Ruach YHWH): Every spirit that confesseth that Yahwah haMashiach is come in the flesh is of God (Elohim, יהוה (YHWH));

3 And every spirit that confesseth not that Yahwah haMashiach is come in the flesh is not of God (Elohim, יהוה (YHWH)); and this is that spirit of anti-Messiah (anti-Mashiach), whereof you have heard that it should come; and even now already is it in the world.

4 You are of God (Elohim, יהוה (YHWH)), little children, and have overcome them; because greater is He that is in you, than he that is in the world.

5 They are of the world; therefore speak they of the world, and the world heareth them.

6 We are of God (Elohim, יהוה (YHWH)); he that knoweth יהוה (YHWH) heareth us; he that is not of God (Elohim, יהוה (YHWH)) heareth not us. Hereby know we the Spirit of truth, and the spirit of error.

7 Beloved, let us love one another; for love is of God (Elohim, יהוה (YHWH)); and every one that loveth is born of God (Elohim, יהוה (YHWH)), and knoweth יהוה (YHWH).

8 He that loveth not knoweth not יהוה (YHWH); for God (Elohim, יהוה (YHWH)) is love.

9 In this was manifested the love of God (Elohim, יהוה (YHWH)) toward us, because that יהוה (YHWH) sent His begotten (one and only) [B47]Humanity (Yahwah haMashiach) into the world, that we might live through Him.

10 Herein is love, not that we loved יהוה (YHWH), but that He loved us, and sent His [B47]Humanity to be the propitiation for our sins.

11 Beloved, if God (Elohim, יהוה (YHWH)) so loved us, we ought also to love one another.

12 No man hath seen יהוה (YHWH's Spirit) at any time. If we love one another, יהוה (YHWH's Spirit) dwelleth in us, and His love is perfected in us.

13 Hereby know we that we dwell in Him, and He in us, because He hath given us of His Spirit.

14 And we have seen and do testify that the Father sent His [B47]Son (Humanity of El (YHWH)) to be the Savior of the world.

15 Whosoever shall confess that Yahwah is the [B47]Humanity of El, יהוה (YHWH) dwelleth in him, and he in יהוה (YHWH).

16 And we have known and believed the love that God (Elohim, יהוה (YHWH)) hath to us. יהוה (YHWH) is love; and he that dwelleth in love dwelleth in יהוה (YHWH), and יהוה (YHWH) in him.

17 Herein is our love made perfect, that we may have boldness in the day of judgment; because as He is, so are we in this world.

18 There is no fear in love, but perfect love casteth out fear; because fear hath torment. He that feareth is not made perfect in love.

19 We love Him, because He first loved us.

20 If a man says, "I love God (Elohim)," and hateth his brother, he is a liar; for he that loveth not his brother whom he hath seen, how can he love God (Elohim, יהוה (YHWH)) whom he hath not seen?

21 And this commandment have we from Him, that he who loveth God (Elohim, יהוה (YHWH)) love his brother also.

5 Whosoever believeth that Yahwah (YHWH) is the Messiah (haMashiach) is born of God (Elohim, יהוה (YHWH)); and every one that loveth Him who begat loveth Him also that is begotten of Him.

2 By this we know that we love the children of God (Elohim, יהוה (YHWH)), when we love יהוה (YHWH), and keep His commandments.

3 For this is the love of יהוה (YHWH), that we keep His commandments; and His commandments are not grievous.

4 For whatsoever is born of God (Elohim, יהוה (YHWH)) overcometh the world; and this is the victory that overcometh the world, even our faith.

5 Who is he that overcometh the world, but he that believeth that Yahwah is the [B47]Humanity of El (YHWH)?

6 This is He that came by water and blood, even Yahwah haMashiach; not by water only, but by water and blood. And it is the Spirit that beareth witness, because the Spirit is truth.

7 For there are three that bear record in heaven: the Father, the Word, and the Holy Spirit; and these three are one.

8 And there are three that bear witness on earth: the Spirit, and the water, and the blood; and these three agree in one.

9 If we receive the witness of men, the witness of God (Elohim, יהוה (YHWH)) is greater; for this is the witness of יהוה (YHWH) which He hath testified of His Humanity (Yahwah haMashiach).

10 He that believeth on the [B47]Humanity of El (YHWH) hath the witness in himself; he that believeth not God (Elohim, יהוה (YHWH)) hath made Him a liar; because he believeth not the record that God (Elohim, יהוה (YHWH)) gave of His Humanity (Yahwah haMashiach).

11 And this is the record, that God (Elohim, יהוה (YHWH)) hath given to us eternal life, and this life is in His Humanity.

12 He that hath the [B47]Humanity of El (YHWH) hath life; and he that hath not the Humanity of El (YHWH) hath not life.

13 These things have I written unto you that believe on the name of the [B47]Humanity of El (YHWH); that you may know that you have eternal life, and that you may believe on the name of the Humanity of El (YHWH).

14 And this is the confidence that we have in Him, that, if we ask any thing according to His will, He heareth us.

15 And if we know that He hears us, whatsoever we ask, we know that we have the petitions that we desired of Him.

16 If any man sees his brother sin a sin which is not unto death, he shall ask, and He shall give him life for them that sin not unto death. There is a sin unto death; I do not say that he shall pray for it.

17 All unrighteousness is sin; and there is a sin not unto death.

18 We know that whosoever is born of God (Elohim, יהוה (YHWH)) sinneth not; but he that is begotten of God (Elohim) keepeth himself, and that wicked one toucheth him not.

19 And we know that we are of God (Elohim, יהוה (YHWH)), and the whole world lieth in wickedness.

20 And we know that the [B47]Humanity of El (YHWH) is come, and hath given us an understanding, that we may know Him that is true, and we are in Him that is true, in His Humanity – Yahwah haMashiach. This is the true God (Elohim), and eternal life. – *Jer. 10:10*

21 Little children, keep yourselves from idols. So be it (Amen).

2 JOHN
YOCHANAN 2 ב יוֹחָנָן
(Second Epistle of John)

1 The elder unto the elect lady and her children, whom I love in the truth; and not I only, but also all they that have known the truth;

2 For the truth's sake, which dwelleth in us, and shall be with us forever.

3 Grace be with you, mercy, and peace, from YHWH the Father, and from our Lord (Adonai) [A1]Yahwah haMashiach, the [B47]Humanity of the Father, in truth and love.

4 I rejoiced greatly that I found of your children walking in truth, as we have received a commandment from the Father.

5 And now I beseech you, lady, not as though I wrote a new commandment unto you, but that which we had from the beginning, that we love one another.

6 And this is love, that we walk after His commandments. This is the commandment, that, as you have heard from the beginning, you should walk in it.

7 For many deceivers are entered into the world, who confess not that Yahwah haMashiach is come in the flesh. This is a deceiver and an anti-Messiah (anti-Mashiach).

8 Look to yourselves, that we lose not those things which we have wrought, but that we receive a full reward.

9 Whosoever transgresseth, and abideth not in the doctrine of the Messiah (haMashiach), hath not God (Elohim, יהוה (YHWH)). He that abideth in the doctrine of the Messiah (haMashiach), he hath both the Father and the Son (Humanity of El (YHWH)).

10 If there come any unto you, and bring not this doctrine, receive him not into your house, neither bid him peace.

11 For he that biddeth him peace is partaker of his evil deeds.

12 Having many things to write unto you, I would not write with paper and ink; but I trust to come unto you, and speak face to face, that our joy may be full.

13 The children of your elect sister greet you. So be it (Amen).

3 JOHN
YOCHANAN 3 יוֹחָנָן ג
(Third Epistle of John)

1 The elder unto the well beloved Gaius, whom I love in the truth.

2 Beloved, I wish above all things that you mayest prosper and be in health, even as your soul prospereth.

3 For I rejoiced greatly, when the brethren came and testified of the truth that is in you, even as you walkest in the truth.

4 I have no greater joy than to hear that my children walk in truth.

5 Beloved, you doest faithfully whatsoever you doest to the brethren, and to strangers;

6 Who have borne witness of your love before the assembly; whom if you bring forward on their journey after a godly sort, you shalt do well;

7 Because that for His name's sake they went forth, taking nothing of the Gentiles (Goyim).

8 We therefore ought to receive such, that we might be fellow helpers to the truth.

9 I wrote unto the assembly; but Diotrephes, who loveth to have the preeminence among them, receiveth us not.

10 Wherefore, if I come, I will remember his deeds which he doeth, prating against us with malicious words; and not content therewith, neither doth he himself receive the brethren, and forbiddeth them that would, and casteth them out of the assembly.

11 Beloved, follow not that which is evil, but that which is good. He that doeth good is of God (Elohim, יהוה (YHWH)); but he that doeth evil hath not seen God (Elohim, יהוה (YHWH)).

12 Demetrius hath good report of all men, and of the truth itself; yea, and we also bear record; and you know that our record is true.

13 I had many things to write, but I will not with ink and pen write unto you;

14 But I trust I shall shortly see you, and we shall speak face to face. Peace be to you. Our friends salute you. Greet the friends by name.

JUDE
YEHUDAH יְהוּדָה
(Epistle of Jude)

1 [A77]Jude (Yehudah), the servant of [A1]Yahwah haMashiach, and brother of James (Yaaqov), to them that are sanctified by YHWH the Father, and preserved in Yahwah haMashiach, and called;

2 Mercy unto you, and peace, and love, be multiplied.

3 Beloved, when I gave all diligence to write unto you of the common salvation, it was needful for me to write unto you, and exhort you that you should earnestly contend for the faith which was once delivered unto the saints.

4 For there are certain men crept in unawares, who were before of old ordained to this condemnation, ungodly men, turning the grace of our God (Elohim) into lasciviousness, and denying the only God (Elohim), and our Lord (Adonai) Yahwah haMashiach.

5 I will therefore put you in remembrance, though you once knew this, how that יהוה[A1] (YHWH), having saved the people out of the land of Egypt (Mitsrayim), afterward destroyed them that believed not.

6 And the angels who kept not their first estate, but left their own habitation, He hath reserved in everlasting chains under darkness unto the judgment of the great day.

7 Even as Sodom and Gomorrha, and the cities about them in like manner, giving themselves over to fornication, and going after strange flesh, are set forth for an example, suffering the vengeance of eternal fire.

8 Likewise also these filthy dreamers defile the flesh, despise dominion, and speak evil of dignities.

9 Yet Michael the archangel, when contending with the devil he disputed about the body of Moses (Mosheh), durst not bring against him a railing accusation, but said, "יהוה (YHWH) rebuke you."

10 But these speak evil of those things which they know not; but what they know naturally, as brute beasts, in those things they corrupt themselves.

11 Woe unto them! For they have gone in the way of Cain, and ran greedily after the error of Balaam for reward, and perished in the gainsaying of Core.

12 These are spots in your feasts of charity, when they feast with you, feeding themselves without fear; clouds they are without water, carried about of winds; trees whose fruit withereth, without fruit, twice dead, plucked up by the roots;

13 Raging waves of the sea, foaming out their own shame; wandering stars, to whom is reserved the blackness of darkness for ever.

14 And Enoch (Chanok) also, the seventh from Adam, prophesied of these, saying, "Behold, יהוה (Yahwah, YHWH) cometh with ten thousands of His holy ones,

15 To execute judgment upon all, and to convince all that are ungodly among them of all their ungodly deeds which they have ungodly committed, and of all their hard speeches which ungodly sinners have spoken against Him."

16 These are murmurers, complainers, walking after their own lusts; and their mouth speaketh great swelling words, having men's persons in admiration because of advantage.

17 But, beloved, remember you the words which were spoken before of the apostles of our Lord (Adonai) Yahwah haMashiach;

18 How that they told you there should be mockers in the last time, who should walk after their own ungodly lusts.

19 These be they who separate themselves, sensual, having not the Spirit.

20 But you, beloved, building up yourselves on your most holy faith, praying in the Holy Spirit (Ruach haQodesh),

21 Keep yourselves in the love of God (Elohim, יהוה (YHWH)), looking for the mercy of our Lord (Adonai) Yahwah haMashiach unto eternal life.

22 And of some have compassion, making a difference;

23 And others save with fear, pulling them out of the fire; hating even the garment spotted by the flesh.

24 Now unto Him that is able to keep you from falling, and to present you faultless before the presence of His glory with exceeding joy,

25 To the only wise God (Elohim, יהוה (YHWH)) our Savior, be glory and majesty, dominion and power, both now and ever. So be it (Amen).

REVELATION
CHAZON חָזוֹן
(Book of Revelation)

1 The Revelation of [A1]Yahwah [B45]haMashiach (Humanity of El (YHWH)), which God (Elohim, יהוה (YHWH)) gave unto Him, to shew unto His servants things which must shortly come to pass; and He sent and signified it by His angel unto His servant John (Yochanan);

2 Who bare record of the word of God (Elohim, יהוה (YHWH)), and of the testimony of Yahwah haMashiach, and of all things that he saw.

3 Blessed is he that readeth, and they that hear the words of this prophecy, and keep those things which are written therein; for the time is at hand.

4 John (Yochanan) to the seven assemblies ([B63]ekklesias) which are in Asia: Grace be unto you, and peace, from Him who is, and who was, and who is to come; and from the seven Spirits who are before His throne;

5 And from Yahwah haMashiach, who is the faithful witness, and the first begotten of the dead, and the prince of the kings of the earth. Unto Him that loved us, and washed us from our sins in His own blood,

6 And hath made us kings and priests (kohanim) unto God (Elohim) and Father; to Him be glory and dominion for ever and ever. So be it (Amen).

7 Behold, He cometh with clouds; and every eye shall see Him, and they also who pierced Him; and all kindreds of the earth shall wail because of Him. Even so, so be it (Amen). – *Dan. 7:13; Zec. 12:10–14*

8 "[B70]I am Alpha and Omega, the beginning and the ending," saith [A1] יהוה (Yahwah, YHWH), Who is, and Who was, and Who is to come, God of hosts (Elohei Tsevaot). – *Exo. 3:14, Isa. 44:6*

9 I John (Yochanan), who also am your brother, and companion in tribulation, and in the kingdom and patience of Yahwah haMashiach, was in the isle that is called Patmos, for the word of God (Elohim, יהוה (YHWH)), and for the testimony of Yahwah haMashiach.

10 I was in the Spirit on יהוה (YHWH)'s day, and heard behind me a great voice, as of a trumpet,

11 Saying, "I am Alpha and Omega, the First and the Last;" and, "What you seest, write in a book, and send it unto the seven assemblies (ekklesias) which are in Asia: unto Ephesus, and unto Smyrna, and unto Pergamos, and unto Thyatira, and unto Sardis, and unto Philadelphia, and unto Laodicea." – *Isa 41:4, 44:6, 48:12*

12 And I turned to see the voice that spake with me. And being turned, I saw seven golden candlesticks (menorot);

13 And in the midst of the seven candlesticks (menorot) one like unto the Son of man (haMashiach), clothed with a garment down to the foot, and girt about the paps with a golden girdle. – *Dan. 7:13; 10:5*

14 His head and His hairs were white like wool, as white as snow; and His eyes were as a flame of fire;

15 And His feet like unto fine brass, as if they burned in a furnace; and His voice as the sound of many waters. – *Dan. 10:6; Eze. 1:24; 43:2*

16 And He had in His right hand seven stars; and out of His mouth went a sharp two-edged sword; and His countenance was as the sun shineth in its strength.

17 And when I saw Him, I fell at His feet as dead. And He laid His right hand upon me, saying unto me, "Fear not; I am the First and the Last; – *Isa 41:4, 44:6, Isa.48:12*

18 I am He that liveth, and was dead; and, behold, I am alive for evermore, so be it (Amen); and have the keys of hell (sheol) and of death.

19 Write the things which you have seen, and the things which are, and the things which shall be hereafter;

20 The mystery of the seven stars which you sawest in My right hand, and the seven golden candlesticks (menorot). The seven stars are the angels of the seven assemblies (ekklesias); and the seven candlesticks (menorot) which you sawest are the seven assemblies (ekklesias).

2 Unto the angel of the assembly of Ephesus write: 'These things saith He that holdeth the seven stars in His right hand, who walketh in the midst of the seven golden candlesticks (menorot);

2 I know your works, and your labour, and your patience, and how you canst not bear them who are evil; and you have tried them who say they are apostles, and are not, and hast found them liars;

3 And hast borne, and hast patience, and for My name's sake hast laboured, and hast not fainted.

4 Nevertheless I have somewhat against you, because you have left your first love.

5 Remember therefore from whence you are fallen, and repent, and do the first works; or else I will come unto you quickly, and will remove your candlestick (menorah) out of its place, except you repent.

6 But this you have, that you hatest the deeds of the Nicolaitans, which I also hate.

7 He that hath an ear, let him hear what the Spirit saith unto the assemblies (ekklesias). To him that overcometh will I give to eat of the tree of life, which is in the midst of the paradise of God (Elohim, יהוה (YHWH))."'

8 And unto the angel of the assembly in Smyrna write: 'These things saith the First and the Last, who was dead, and is alive; – *Isa 41:4, 44:6, 48:12*

9 I know your works, and tribulation, and poverty, (but you are rich) and I know the blasphemy of them who say they are Jews (Yehudim), and are not, but are the synagogue of Satan.

10 Fear none of those things which you shalt suffer. Behold, the devil shall cast some of you into prison, that you may be tried; and you shall have tribulation ten days; be you faithful unto death, and I will give you a crown of life.

11 He that hath an ear, let him hear what the Spirit saith unto the assemblies (ekklesias); He that overcometh shall not be hurt of the second death."'

12 And to the angel of the assembly in Pergamos write: 'These things saith He who hath the sharp sword with two edges:

13 "I know your works, and where you dwellest, even where Satan's seat is; and you holdest fast My name, and hast not denied My faith, even in those days wherein Antipas was My faithful martyr, who was slain among you, where Satan dwelleth.

14 But I have a few things against you, because you have there them that hold the doctrine of Balaam, who taught Balac to cast a stumblingblock before the children of Yisrael, to eat things sacrificed unto idols, and to commit fornication.

15 So have you also them that hold the doctrine of the Nicolaitans, which thing I hate.

16 'Repent; or else I will come unto you quickly, and will fight against them with the sword of My mouth.

17 He that hath an ear, let him hear what the Spirit saith unto the assemblies (ekklesias). To him that overcometh will I give to eat of the hidden manna, and will give him a white stone, and in the stone a new name written, which no man knoweth except he that receiveth it."'

18 And unto the angel of the assembly in Thyatira write: 'These things saith the [B47]Humanity of El (YHWH), who hath His eyes like unto a flame of fire, and His feet are like fine brass:

19 "I know your works, and love, and service, and faith, and your patience, and your works; and the last to be more than the first.

20 Notwithstanding I have a few things against you, because you allow that woman Jezebel (Iyzevel), who calleth herself a prophetess, to teach and to seduce My servants to commit fornication, and to eat things sacrificed unto idols.

21 And I gave her space to repent of her fornication; and she repented not.

22 Behold, I will cast her into a bed, and them that commit adultery with her into great tribulation, except they repent of their deeds.

23 And I will kill her children with death; and all the assemblies (ekklesias) shall know that I am He who searcheth the reins and hearts; and I will give unto every one of you according to your works.

24 But unto you I say, and unto the rest in Thyatira, as many as have not this doctrine, and who have not known the depths of Satan, as they speak; I will put upon you none other burden.

25 But that which you have already hold fast till I come.

26 And he that overcometh, and keepeth My works unto the end, to him will I give power over the nations;

27 And he shall rule them with a rod of iron; as the vessels of a potter shall they be broken to shivers; even as I received of My Father. – *Psa. 2:8–9*

28 And I will give him the morning star.

29 He that hath an ear, let him hear what the Spirit saith unto the assemblies (ekklesias)."'

3 "And unto the angel of the assembly in Sardis write: 'These things saith He that hath the seven Spirits of יהוה (YHWH), and the seven stars: "I know your works, that you have a name (reputation) that you livest, and art dead.

2 Be watchful, and strengthen the things which remain, that are ready to die; for I have not found your works perfect before God (Elohim, יהוה (YHWH)).

3 Remember therefore how you have received and heard, and hold fast, and repent. If therefore you shalt not watch, I will come on you as a thief, and you shalt not know what hour I will come upon you.

4 You have a few names even in Sardis who have not defiled their garments; and they shall walk with Me in white, for they are worthy.

5 He that overcometh, the same shall be clothed in white raiment; and I will not blot out his name out of the book of life, but I will confess his name before My Father, and before His angels.

6 He that hath an ear, let him hear what the Spirit saith unto the assemblies (ekklesias)."'

7 "And to the angel of the assembly in Philadelphia write: 'These things saith He that is holy, He that is true, He that hath the key of Dawid, He that openeth, and no man shutteth; and shutteth, and no man openeth:

8 "I know your works. Behold, I have set before you an open door, and no man can shut it; for you have a little strength, and hast kept My word, and hast not denied My name.

9 Behold, I will make them of the synagogue of Satan, which say they are Jews (Yehudim), and are not, but do lie; behold, I will make them to come and worship before your feet, and to know that I have loved you.

10 Because you have kept the word of My patience, I also will keep you from the hour of temptation, which shall come upon all the world, to try them that dwell upon the earth.

11 Behold, I come quickly; hold that fast which you have, that no man takes your crown.

12 Him that overcometh will I make a pillar in the temple of my God (Elohim), and he shall go no more out; and I will write upon him the name of my God (Elohim), and the name of the city of my God (Elohim), which is new Jerushalem (Yerushalayim), which cometh down out of heaven from my God (Elohim); and I will write upon him my new name.

13 He that hath an ear, let him hear what the Spirit saith unto the assemblies (ekklesias)."'

14 And unto the angel of the assembly of the Laodiceans write: 'These things saith the Amen, the faithful and true witness, the beginning of the creation of God (Elohim):

15 "I know your works, that you are neither cold nor hot. I would you wert cold or hot.

16 So then because you are lukewarm, and neither cold nor hot, I will spue you out of My mouth.

17 Because you sayest, 'I am rich, and increased with goods, and have need of nothing;' and knowest not that you are wretched, and miserable, and poor, and blind, and naked;

18 I counsel you to buy of Me gold tried in the fire, that you mayest be rich; and white raiment, that you mayest be clothed, and that the shame of your nakedness does not appear; and anoint your eyes with eyesalve, that you mayest see.

19 As many as I love, I rebuke and chasten; be zealous therefore, and repent.

20 Behold, I stand at the door, and knock. If any man hears My voice, and open the door, I will come in to him, and will sup with him, and he with Me.

21 To him that overcometh will I grant to sit with Me in My throne, even as I also overcame, and am set down with My Father in His throne.

22 He that hath an ear, let him hear what the Spirit saith unto the assemblies (ekklesias)."'"

4 After this I looked, and, behold, a door was opened in heaven; and the first voice which I heard was as it was of a trumpet talking with me; which said, "Come up hither, and I will shew you things which must be hereafter.

2 And immediately I was in the spirit; and, behold, a throne was set in heaven, and one sat on the throne.

3 And He that sat was to look upon like a jasper and a sardine stone; and there was a rainbow round about the throne, in sight like unto an emerald.

4 And round about the throne were four and twenty seats; and upon the seats I saw four and twenty elders sitting, clothed in white raiment; and they had on their heads crowns of gold.

5 And out of the throne proceeded lightnings and thunderings and voices; and there were seven lamps of fire burning before the throne, which are the seven Spirits of יהוה (Ruach YHWH).

6 And before the throne there was a sea of glass like unto crystal; and in the midst of the throne, and round about the throne, were four beasts full of eyes before and behind.

7 And the first beast was like a lion, and the second beast like a calf, and the third beast had a face as a man, and the fourth beast was like a flying eagle.

8 And the four beasts had each of them six wings about him; and they were full of eyes within; and they rest not day and night, saying, 'Holy, holy, holy (qadosh), יהוה God of hosts (YHWH Elohei Tsevaot), who was, and is, and is to come.'

9 And when those beasts give glory and honour and thanks to Him that sat on the throne, who liveth for ever and ever,

10 The four and twenty elders fall down before Him that sat on the throne, and worship Him that liveth for ever and ever, and cast their crowns before the throne, saying,

11 You are worthy, O יהוה (YHWH), to receive glory and honour and power; for you have created all things, and for your pleasure they are and were created.

5 And I saw in the right hand of Him that sat on the throne a book written inside and on the back, sealed with seven seals.

2 And I saw a strong angel proclaiming with a loud voice, "Who is worthy to open the book, and to loose the seals thereof?"

3 And no man in heaven, nor on earth, neither under the earth, was able to open the book, neither to look thereon.

4 And I wept much, because no man was found worthy to open and to read the book, neither to look thereon.

5 And one of the elders saith unto me, "Weep not; behold, the Lion of the tribe of Judah (Yehudah), the Root of Dawid, hath prevailed to open the book, and to loose the seven seals thereof."

6 And I beheld, and, behold, in the midst of the throne and of the four beasts, and in the midst of the elders, stood a Lamb as it had been slain, having seven horns and seven eyes, which are the sevenfold Spirit of יהוה (Ruach YHWH) sent forth into all the earth.

7 And He came and took the book out of the right hand of Him that sat upon the throne.

8 And when He had taken the book, the four beasts and four and twenty elders fell down before the Lamb, having every one of them harps, and golden vials full of incense, which are the prayers of holy ones.

9 And they sung a new song, saying, "You are worthy to take the book, and to open the seals thereof; for You wast slain, and hast redeemed us to God (Elohim, יהוה (YHWH)) by Your blood out of every kindred, and tongue, and people, and nation;

10 And hast made us unto our God (Elohim) kings and priests (kohanim); and we shall reign on the earth."

11 And I beheld, and I heard the voice of many angels round about the throne and the beasts and the elders; and the number of them was ten thousand times ten thousand, and thousands of thousands;

12 Saying with a loud voice: "Worthy is the Lamb that was slain to receive power, and riches, and wisdom, and strength, and honour, and glory, and blessing."

13 And every creature which is in heaven, and on the earth, and under the earth, and such as are in the sea, and all that are in them, heard I saying: "Blessing, and honour, and glory, and power, be unto Him that sitteth upon the throne, and unto the Lamb forever and ever."

14 And the four beasts said, "So be it (Amen)." And the four and twenty elders fell down and worshipped Him that liveth for ever and ever.

6 And I saw when the Lamb opened one of the seals, and I heard, as it was the noise of thunder, one of the four beasts saying, "Come and see."

2 And I saw, and behold a white horse; and he that sat on him had a bow; and a crown was given unto him; and he went forth conquering, and to conquer.

3 And when he had opened the second seal, I heard the second beast say, "Come and see."

4 And there went out another horse that was red; and power was given to him that sat thereon to take peace from the earth, and that they should kill one another; and there was given unto him a great sword.

5 And when he had opened the third seal, I heard the third beast say, "Come and see." And I beheld, and behold a black horse; and he that sat on him had a pair of scales in his hand.

6 And I heard a voice in the midst of the four beasts say, "A measure of wheat for a penny, and three measures of barley for a penny; and see you hurt not the oil and the wine."

7 And when He had opened the fourth seal, I

heard the voice of the fourth beast say, "Come and see."

8 And I looked, and behold a pale horse; and his name that sat on him was Death, and Hell (Sheol) followed with him. And power was given unto them over the fourth part of the earth, to kill with sword, and with hunger, and with death, and with the beasts of the earth.

9 And when He had opened the fifth seal, I saw under the altar the souls of them that were slain for the word of God (Elohim, יהוה (YHWH)), and for the testimony which they held;

10 And they cried with a loud voice, saying, "How long, O יהוה (YHWH), holy and true, dost You not judge and avenge our blood on them that dwell on the earth?"

11 And white robes were given unto every one of them; and it was said unto them, that they should rest yet for a little season, until their fellow servants also and their brethren, that should be killed as they were, should be fulfilled.

12 And I beheld when He had opened the sixth seal, and, behold, there was a great earthquake; and the sun became black as sackcloth of hair, and the moon became as blood;

13 And the stars of heaven fell unto the earth, even as a fig tree casteth her untimely figs, when she is shaken of a mighty wind.

14 And the heaven departed as a scroll when it is rolled together; and every mountain and island were moved out of their places.

15 And the kings of the earth, and the great men, and the rich men, and the chief captains, and the mighty men, and every bondman, and every free man, hid themselves in the dens and in the rocks of the mountains;

16 And said to the mountains and rocks, "Fall on us, and hide us from the face of Him that sitteth on the throne, and from the wrath of the Lamb! – *Hos. 10:8*

17 For the great day of His wrath is come; and who shall be able to stand?"

7 And after these things I saw four angels standing on the four corners of the earth, holding the four winds of the earth, that the wind should not blow on the earth, nor on the sea, nor on any tree.

2 And I saw another angel ascending from the east, having the seal of the living God (El Chai); and he cried with a loud voice to the four angels, to whom it was given to hurt the earth and the sea,

3 Saying, "Hurt not the earth, neither the sea, nor the trees, till we have sealed the servants of our God (Elohim) in their foreheads.

4 And I heard the number of them who were sealed; and there were sealed a hundred and forty and four thousand of all the tribes of the children of Yisrael.

5 Of the tribe of [A19]Judah (Yehudah) were sealed twelve thousand. Of the tribe of [A16]Reuven were sealed twelve thousand. Of the tribe of [A22]Gad were sealed twelve thousand.

6 Of the tribe of [A23]Asher were sealed twelve thousand. Of the tribe of [A21]Nepthalim (Naftali) were sealed twelve thousand. Of the tribe of [A28]Manasseh (Menashsheh) were sealed twelve thousand.

7 Of the tribe of [A17]Shimon were sealed twelve thousand. Of the tribe of [A18]Lewi were sealed twelve thousand. Of the tribe of [A24]Issachar (Yissaskhar) were sealed twelve thousand.

8 Of the tribe of [A25]Zabulon (Zevulun) were sealed twelve thousand. Of the tribe of [A26]Joseph (Yosef) were sealed twelve thousand. Of the tribe of [A27]Benjamin (Binyamin) were sealed twelve thousand.

9 After this I beheld, and, behold, a great multitude, which no man could number, of all nations, and kindreds, and people, and tongues, stood before the throne, and before the Lamb, clothed with white robes, and palms in their hands;

10 And cried with a loud voice, saying, "Salvation to our God (Elohim) who sitteth upon the throne, and unto the Lamb."

11 And all the angels stood round about the throne, and about the elders and the four beasts, and fell before the throne on their faces, and worshipped God (Elohim, יהוה (YHWH)),

12 Saying, "So be it (Amen)! Blessing, and glory, and wisdom, and thanksgiving, and honour, and power, and might, be unto our God (Elohim) forever and ever. So be it (Amen)."

13 And one of the elders answered, saying unto me, "Who are these who are arrayed in white robes? And whence came they?"

14 And I said unto him, "Sir, you knowest." And he said to me, "These are they who came out of great tribulation, and have washed their robes, and made them white in the blood of the Lamb.

15 Therefore are they before the throne of God (Elohim, יהוה (YHWH)), and serve Him day and night in His temple; and He that sitteth on the throne shall dwell among them.

16 They shall hunger no more, neither thirst any more; neither shall the sun light on them, nor any heat. – *Isa. 49:10*

17 For the Lamb which is in the midst of the throne shall feed them, and shall lead them unto living fountains of waters; and God (Elohim, יהוה (YHWH)) shall wipe away all tears from their eyes." – *Isa.49:10; Jer. 2:13; Eze. 34:23; Psa. 23:1–2*

8 And when He had opened the seventh seal, there was silence in heaven about the space of half an hour.

2 And I saw the seven angels who stood before God (Elohim); and to them were given seven trumpets (shofarot).

3 And another angel came and stood at the altar, having a golden censer; and there was given unto him much incense, that he should offer it with the prayers of all holy ones upon the golden altar which was before the throne.

4 And the smoke of the incense, which came with the prayers of the holy ones, ascended up before God (Elohim, יהוה (YHWH)) out of the angel's hand.

5 And the angel took the censer, and filled it with fire of the altar, and cast it into the earth; and there were voices, and thunderings, and lightnings, and an earthquake.

6 And the seven angels who had the seven trumpets (shofarot) prepared themselves to sound.

7 The first angel sounded, and there followed hail and fire mingled with blood, and they were cast upon the earth; and the third part of trees was burnt up, and all green grass was burnt up.

8 And the second angel sounded, and as it was a great mountain burning with fire was cast into the sea; and the third part of the sea became blood;

9 And the third part of the creatures which were in the sea, and had life, died; and the third part of the ships were destroyed.

10 And the third angel sounded, and there fell a great star from heaven, burning as it was a lamp, and it fell upon the third part of the rivers, and upon the fountains of waters;

11 And the name of the star is called Bitterness

(Wormwood); and the third part of the waters became bitter; and many men died of the waters, because they were made bitter.

12 And the fourth angel sounded, and the third part of the sun was smitten, and the third part of the moon, and the third part of the stars; so as the third part of them was darkened, and the day shone not for a third part of it, and the night likewise.

13 And I beheld, and heard an angel flying through the midst of heaven, saying with a loud voice, "Woe, woe, woe, to the inhabiters of the earth by reason of the other voices of the trumpet (shofar) of the three angels, which are yet to sound!"

9 And the fifth angel sounded, and I saw a star fall from heaven unto the earth; and to him was given the key of the bottomless pit.

2 And he opened the bottomless pit; and there arose a smoke out of the pit, as the smoke of a great furnace; and the sun and the air were darkened by reason of the smoke of the pit.

3 And there came out of the smoke locusts upon the earth; and unto them was given power, as the scorpions of the earth have power.

4 And it was commanded them that they should not hurt the grass of the earth, neither any green thing, neither any tree; but only those men who have not the seal of יהוה (YHWH) in their foreheads.

5 And to them it was given that they should not kill them, but that they should be tormented five months; and their torment was as the torment of a scorpion, when he striketh a man.

6 And in those days shall men seek death, and shall not find it; and shall desire to die, and death shall flee from them.

7 And the shapes of the locusts were like unto horses prepared unto battle; and on their heads were as it was crowns like gold, and their faces were as the faces of men.

8 And they had hair as the hair of women, and their teeth were as the teeth of lions.

9 And they had breastplates, as it was breastplates of iron; and the sound of their wings was as the sound of chariots of many horses running to battle.

10 And they had tails like unto scorpions, and there were stings in their tails; and their power was to hurt men five months.

11 And they had a king over them, which is the

angel of the bottomless pit, whose name in the Hebrew tongue is Abaddon, but in the Greek tongue hath his name Apollyon (Destroyer).

12 One woe is past; and, behold, there come two woes more hereafter. – *Psa. 115:4–7; 135:15–17; Dan. 5:23*

13 And the sixth angel sounded, and I heard a voice from the four horns of the golden altar which is before God (Elohim, יהוה (YHWH)),

14 Saying to the sixth angel who had the trumpet (shofar), "Loose the four angels who are bound in the great river Euphrates."

15 And the four angels were loosed, who were prepared for an hour, and a day, and a month, and a year, for to slay the third part of men.

16 And the number of the army of the horsemen were two hundred thousand thousand; and I heard the number of them.

17 And thus I saw the horses in the vision, and them that sat on them, having breastplates of fire, and of jacinth, and brimstone; and the heads of the horses were as the heads of lions; and out of their mouths issued fire and smoke and brimstone.

18 By these three was the third part of men killed, by the fire, and by the smoke, and by the brimstone, which issued out of their mouths.

19 For their power is in their mouth, and in their tails; for their tails were like unto serpents, and had heads, and with them they do hurt.

20 And the rest of the men who were not killed by these plagues yet repented not of the works of their hands, that they should not worship devils, and idols of gold, and silver, and brass, and stone, and of wood; who neither can see, nor hear, nor walk;

21 Neither repented they of their murders, nor of their sorceries, nor of their fornication, nor of their thefts.

10 And I saw another mighty angel come down from heaven, clothed with a cloud; and a rainbow was upon his head, and his face was as it was the sun, and his feet as pillars of fire.

2 And he had in his hand a little book open; and he set his right foot upon the sea, and his left foot on the earth,

3 And cried with a loud voice, as when a lion roareth; and when he had cried, seven thunders uttered their voices.

4 And when the seven thunders had uttered their voices, I was about to write; and I heard a voice from heaven saying unto me, "Seal up those things which the seven thunders uttered, and write them not."

5 And the angel whom I saw stand upon the sea and upon the earth lifted up his hand to heaven,

6 And sware by Him that liveth for ever and ever, who created heaven, and the things that therein are, and the earth, and the things that therein are, and the sea, and the things which are therein, that there should be time no longer; – *Deu.32:40; Dan.12:7; Neh.9:6; Exo.20:11; Psa.146:6*

7 But in the days of the voice of the seventh angel, when he shall begin to sound, the mystery of God (Elohim, יהוה (YHWH)) should be finished, as He hath declared to His servants the prophets.

8 And the voice which I heard from heaven spake unto me again, and said, "Go and take the little book which is open in the hand of the angel which standeth upon the sea and upon the earth."

9 And I went unto the angel, and said unto him, "Give me the little book." And he said unto me, "Take it, and eat it up; and it shall make your belly bitter, but it shall be in your mouth sweet as honey."

10 And I took the little book out of the angel's hand, and ate it up; and it was in my mouth sweet as honey; and as soon as I had eaten it, my belly was bitter.

11 And he said unto me, "You must prophesy again before many peoples, and nations, and tongues, and kings."

11 And there was given me a reed like unto a rod; and the angel stood, saying, "Rise, and measure the temple of יהוה (YHWH), and the altar, and them that worship therein.

2 But the court which is outside the temple leave out, and measure it not; for it is given unto the Gentiles (Goyim); and the holy city shall they tread under foot forty and two months.

3 And I will give power unto My two witnesses, and they shall prophesy a thousand two hundred and threescore days, clothed in sackcloth."

4 These are the two olive trees, and the two candlesticks (menorot) standing before the God (Elohim) of the earth.

5 And if any man will hurt them, fire proceedeth out of their mouth, and devoureth their enemies;

and if any man will hurt them, he must in this manner be killed.

6 These have power to shut heaven, that it rains not in the days of their prophecy; and have power over waters to turn them to blood, and to smite the earth with all plagues, as often as they will.

7 And when they shall have finished their testimony, the beast that ascendeth out of the bottomless pit shall make war against them, and shall overcome them, and kill them.

8 And their dead bodies shall lie in the street of the great city, which spiritually is called Sodom and Egypt (Mitsrayim), where also our Lord (Yahwah) was crucified.

9 And they of the people and kindreds and tongues and nations shall see their dead bodies three days and a half, and shall not allow their dead bodies to be put in graves.

10 And they that dwell upon the earth shall rejoice over them, and make merry, and shall send gifts one to another; because these two prophets tormented them that dwelt on the earth.

11 And after three days and a half the Spirit of life from God (Elohim, יהוה (YHWH)) entered into them, and they stood upon their feet; and great fear fell upon them who saw them.

12 And they heard a great voice from heaven saying unto them, "Come up hither." And they ascended up to heaven in a cloud; and their enemies beheld them.

13 And the same hour was there a great earthquake, and the tenth part of the city fell, and in the earthquake were slain of men seven thousand; and the remnant were affrighted, and gave glory to the God (Elohim) of heaven.

14 The second woe is past; and, behold, the third woe cometh quickly.

15 And the seventh angel sounded; and there were great voices in heaven, saying, "The kingdoms of this world are become the kingdoms of our Lord (YHWH), and of His Messiah (Mashiach); and He shall reign for ever and ever."

16 And the four and twenty elders, who sat before God (Elohim, יהוה (YHWH)) on their seats, fell upon their faces, and worshipped God (Elohim, יהוה (YHWH)),

17 Saying, "We give you thanks, O יהוה God of hosts (YHWH Elohei Tsevaot), who art, and wast, and art to come; because You have taken

of Your great power, and hast reigned. – *Amos 3:13; 4:13*

18 And the nations were angry, and Your wrath is come, and the time of the dead, that they should be judged, and that You shouldest give reward unto Your servants the prophets, and to the holy ones, and them that fear Your name, small and great; and shouldest destroy them who destroy the earth."

19 And the temple of יהוה (YHWH) was opened in heaven, and there was seen in His temple the ark of His covenant (berit); and there were lightnings, and voices, and thunderings, and an earthquake, and great hail.

12 And there appeared a great wonder in heaven: a woman clothed with the sun, and the moon under her feet, and upon her head a crown of twelve stars;

2 And she being with child cried, travailing in birth, and pained to be delivered.

3 And there appeared another wonder in heaven: and behold a great red dragon, having seven heads and ten horns, and seven crowns upon his heads.

4 And his tail drew the third part of the stars of heaven, and did cast them to the earth; and the dragon stood before the woman who was ready to give birth, for to devour her Child as soon as it was born.

5 And she brought forth a male Child, who was to rule all nations with a rod of iron; and her Child was caught up unto God (Elohim, יהוה (YHWH)), and to His throne.

6 And the woman fled into the wilderness, where she hath a place prepared of יהוה (YHWH), that they should feed her there a thousand two hundred and threescore (1260) days.

7 And there was war in heaven: Michael and his angels fought against the dragon; and the dragon and his angels fought,

8 And prevailed not; neither was their place found any more in heaven.

9 And the great dragon was cast out, that old serpent, called the Devil, and Satan, who deceiveth the whole world; he was cast out into the earth, and his angels were cast out with him. – *Psa. 2:9*

10 And I heard a loud voice saying in heaven, "Now is come salvation, and strength, and the kingdom of our God (Elohim), and the power of

His Messiah (Mashiach); for the accuser of our brethren is cast down, who accused them before our God (Elohim) day and night.

11 And they overcame him by the blood of the Lamb, and by the word of their testimony; and they loved not their lives unto the death.

12 Therefore rejoice, you heavens, and you that dwell in them. Woe to the inhabiters of the earth and of the sea! For the devil is come down unto you, having great wrath, because he knoweth that he hath but a short time."

13 And when the dragon saw that he was cast unto the earth, he persecuted the woman who brought forth the male Child.

14 And to the woman were given two wings of a great eagle, that she might fly into the wilderness, into her place, where she is nourished for a time, and times, and half a time, from the face of the serpent. – *Dan. 7:25; 12:7*

15 And the serpent cast out of his mouth water as a flood after the woman, that he might cause her to be carried away of the flood.

16 And the earth helped the woman, and the earth opened her mouth, and swallowed up the flood which the dragon cast out of his mouth.

17 And the dragon was wroth with the woman, and went to make war with the remnant of her seed, who keep the commandments of יהוה (YHWH), and have the testimony of Yahwah haMashiach.

13 And I stood upon the sand of the sea, and saw a beast rise up out of the sea, having seven heads and ten horns, and upon his horns ten crowns, and upon his heads the name of blasphemy.

2 And the beast which I saw was like unto a leopard, and his feet were as the feet of a bear, and his mouth as the mouth of a lion; and the dragon gave him his power, and his seat, and great authority.

3 And I saw one of his heads as it was wounded to death; and his deadly wound was healed; and all the world wondered after the beast.

4 And they worshipped the dragon which gave power unto the beast; and they worshipped the beast, saying, "Who is like unto the beast? Who is able to make war with him?"

5 And there was given unto him a mouth speaking great things and blasphemies; and power was given unto him to continue forty and two months.

6 And he opened his mouth in blasphemy against יהוה (YHWH), to blaspheme His name, and His tabernacle, and them that dwell in heaven.

7 And it was given unto him to make war with the holy ones, and to overcome them; and power was given him over all kindreds, and tongues, and nations.

8 And all that dwell upon the earth shall worship him, whose names are not written in the book of life of the Lamb slain from the foundation of the world.

9 If any man has an ear, let him hear.

10 He that leadeth into captivity shall go into captivity; he that killeth with the sword must be killed with the sword. Here is the patience and the faith of the holy ones. – *Jer. 15:2, 43:11*

11 And I beheld another beast coming up out of the earth; and he had two horns like a lamb, and he spake as a dragon.

12 And he exerciseth all the power of the first beast before him, and causeth the earth and them which dwell therein to worship the first beast, whose deadly wound was healed.

13 And he doeth great wonders, so that he maketh fire come down from heaven on the earth in the sight of men,

14 And deceiveth them that dwell on the earth by the means of those miracles which he had power to do in the sight of the beast; saying to them that dwell on the earth, that they should make an image to the beast, which had the wound by a sword, and did live.

15 And he had power to give life unto the image of the beast, that the image of the beast should both speak, and cause that as many as would not worship the image of the beast should be killed.

16 And he causeth all, both small and great, rich and poor, free and bond, to receive a mark in their right hand, or in their foreheads;

17 And that no man might buy or sell, except he that had the mark, or the name of the beast, or the number of his name.

18 Here is wisdom. Let him that hath understanding count the number of the beast; for it is the number of a man; and his number is six hundred threescore and six (666).

14 And I looked, and, behold, a Lamb stood on the Mount Sion (Tsiyon), and with him a hundred forty and four thousand, having His Father's name (יהוה) written in their foreheads.

2 And I heard a voice from heaven, as the voice of many waters, and as the voice of a great thunder; and I heard the voice of harpers harping with their harps.

3 And they sung as it was a new song before the throne, and before the four beasts, and the elders; and no man could learn that song but the hundred and forty and four thousand, who were redeemed from the earth.

4 These are they who were not defiled with women; for they are virgins. These are they who follow the Lamb whithersoever He goeth. These were redeemed from among men, being the firstfruits unto יהוה (YHWH) and to the Lamb.

5 And in their mouth was found no guile; for they are without fault before the throne of God (Elohim, יהוה (YHWH)).

6 And I saw another angel fly in the midst of heaven, having the everlasting gospel (good news) to preach unto them that dwell on the earth, and to every nation, and kindred, and tongue, and people,

7 Saying with a loud voice, "Fear God (Elohim, יהוה (YHWH)), and give glory to Him; for the hour of His judgment is come; and worship Him that made heaven, and earth, and the sea, and the fountains of waters."

8 And there followed another angel, saying, "Babylon (Bavel) is fallen, is fallen, that great city, because she made all nations drink of the wine of the wrath of her fornication. – *Isa. 21:9*

9 And the third angel followed them, saying with a loud voice, "If any man worships the beast and his image, and receive his mark in his forehead, or in his hand,

10 The same shall drink of the wine of the wrath of יהוה (YHWH), which is poured out without mixture into the cup of His indignation; and he shall be tormented with fire and brimstone in the presence of the holy angels, and in the presence of the Lamb;

11 And the smoke of their torment ascendeth up for ever and ever; and they have no rest day nor night, who worship the beast and his image, and whosoever receiveth the mark of his name.

12 Here is the patience of the holy ones; here are they that keep the commandments of God (Elohim, יהוה (YHWH)) and the faith of Yahwah (YHWH).

13 And I heard a voice from heaven saying unto me, "Write: 'Blessed are the dead who die in the Lord (YHWH) from henceforth.'" "Yea," saith the Spirit, "that they may rest from their labours; and their works do follow them."

14 And I looked, and behold a white cloud, and upon the cloud sat one like the Son of man (haMashiach), having on His head a golden crown, and in His hand a sharp sickle. – *Dan. 7:13*

15 And another angel came out of the temple, crying with a loud voice to Him that sat on the cloud, "Thrust in Your sickle, and reap; for the time is come for You to reap; for the harvest of the earth is ripe."

16 And He that sat on the cloud thrust in His sickle on the earth; and the earth was reaped.

17 And another angel came out of the temple who is in heaven, he also having a sharp sickle.

18 And another angel came out from the altar, who had power over fire; and cried with a loud cry to him that had the sharp sickle, saying, "Thrust in your sharp sickle, and gather the clusters of the vine of the earth; for her grapes are fully ripe."

19 And the angel thrust in his sickle into the earth, and gathered the vine of the earth, and cast it into the great winepress of the wrath of God (Elohim, יהוה (YHWH)).

20 And the winepress was trodden outside the city, and blood came out of the winepress, even unto the horse bridles, by the space of a thousand and six hundred furlongs.

15 And I saw another sign in heaven, great and marvellous, seven angels having the seven last plagues; for in them is filled up the wrath of God (Elohim, יהוה (YHWH)).

2 And I saw as it was a sea of glass mingled with fire; and them that had gotten the victory over the beast, and over his image, and over his mark, and over the number of his name, stand on the sea of glass, having the harps of God (Elohim).

3 And they sing the song of Moses (Mosheh) the servant of יהוה (YHWH), and the song of the Lamb, saying, "Great and marvellous are Your works, יהוה God of hosts (YHWH Elohei Tsevaot); just and true are Your ways, You King of the holy ones (qadoshim).

4 Who shall not fear you, O יהוה (YHWH) and glorify Your name? For You only are holy; for all nations shall come and worship before You; for Your judgments are made manifest.

5 And after that I looked, and, behold, the temple of the tabernacle of the testimony in

heaven was opened;

6 And the seven angels came out of the temple, having the seven plagues, clothed in pure and white linen, and having their breasts girded with golden girdles.

7 And one of the four beasts gave unto the seven angels seven golden vials full of the wrath of God (Elohim, יהוה (YHWH)), who liveth for ever and ever.

8 And the temple was filled with smoke from the glory of יהוה (YHWH), and from His power; and no man was able to enter into the temple, till the seven plagues of the seven angels were fulfilled.

16 And I heard a great voice out of the temple saying to the seven angels, "Go your ways, and pour out the vials of the wrath of God (Elohim, יהוה (YHWH)) upon the earth."

2 And the first went, and poured out his vial upon the earth; and there fell a noisome and grievous sore upon the men who had the mark of the beast, and upon them who worshipped his image.

3 And the second angel poured out his vial upon the sea; and it became as the blood of a dead man; and every living soul died in the sea.

4 And the third angel poured out his vial upon the rivers and fountains of waters; and they became blood.

5 And I heard the angel of the waters say, "You are righteous, O יהוה (YHWH) Who art, and wast, and shalt be, because You have judged thus.

6 For they have shed the blood of the holy ones (qadoshim) and prophets, and you have given them blood to drink; for they are worthy."

7 And I heard another out of the altar say, "Even so, יהוה God Almighty (YHWH El Shaddai), true and righteous are Your judgments." – *Amos 3:13; 4:13*

8 And the fourth angel poured out his vial upon the sun; and power was given unto him to scorch men with fire.

9 And men were scorched with great heat, and blasphemed the name of God (Elohim, יהוה (YHWH)), who hath power over these plagues; and they repented not to give Him glory.

10 And the fifth angel poured out his vial upon the seat of the beast; and his kingdom was full of darkness; and they gnawed their tongues for pain,

11 And blasphemed the God of heaven (Elohei shamayim) because of their pains and their sores, and repented not of their deeds.

12 And the sixth angel poured out his vial upon the great river Euphrates; and the water thereof was dried up, that the way of the kings of the east might be prepared.

13 And I saw three unclean spirits like frogs come out of the mouth of the dragon, and out of the mouth of the beast, and out of the mouth of the false prophet.

14 For they are the spirits of devils, working miracles, which go forth unto the kings of the earth and of the whole world, to gather them to the battle of that great day of יהוה of hosts (YHWH Tsevaot).

15 "Behold, I come as a thief. Blessed is he that watcheth, and keepeth his garments, lest he walk naked, and they see his shame."

16 And they gathered them together into a place called in the Hebrew tongue Armageddon (Har Megiddo).

17 And the seventh angel poured out his vial into the air; and there came a great voice out of the temple of heaven, from the throne, saying, "It is done."

18 And there were voices, and thunders, and lightnings; and there was a great earthquake, such as was not since men were upon the earth, so mighty an earthquake, and so great.

19 And the great city was divided into three parts, and the cities of the nations fell; and great Babylon (Bavel) came in remembrance before God (Elohim, יהוה (YHWH)), to give unto her the cup of the wine of the fierceness of His wrath.

20 And every island fled away, and the mountains were not found.

21 And there fell upon men a great hail out of heaven, every stone about the weight of a talent; and men blasphemed God (Elohim) because of the plague of the hail; for the plague thereof was exceeding great.

17 And there came one of the seven angels who had the seven vials, and talked with me, saying unto me, "Come hither; I will shew unto you the judgment of the great whore that sitteth upon many waters;

2 With whom the kings of the earth have committed fornication, and the inhabitants of the earth have been made drunk with the wine

of her fornication."

3 So he carried me away in the spirit into the wilderness; and I saw a woman sit upon a scarlet coloured beast, full of names of blasphemy, having seven heads and ten horns.

4 And the woman was arrayed in purple and scarlet colour, and decked with gold and precious stones and pearls, having a golden cup in her hand full of abominations and filthiness of her fornication.

5 And upon her forehead was a name written, MYSTERY, BABYLON (BAVEL) THE GREAT, THE MOTHER OF HARLOTS AND ABOMINATIONS OF THE EARTH.

6 And I saw the woman drunken with the blood of the holy ones, and with the blood of the martyrs of Yahwah (YHWH); and when I saw her, I wondered with great amazement.

7 And the angel said unto me, "Wherefore didst you marvel? I will tell you the mystery of the woman, and of the beast that carrieth her, which hath the seven heads and ten horns.

8 The beast that you sawest was, and is not; and shall ascend out of the bottomless pit, and go into perdition; and they that dwell on the earth shall wonder, whose names were not written in the book of life from the foundation of the world, when they behold the beast that was, and is not, and yet is.

9 And here is the mind who hath wisdom: The seven heads are seven mountains, on which the woman sitteth.

10 And there are seven kings: five have fallen, and one is, and the other has not yet come; and when he cometh, he must continue a short space.

11 And the beast that was, and is not, he is the eighth, and is of the seven, and goeth into perdition.

12 And the ten horns which you sawest are ten kings, who have received no kingdom as yet; but receive power as kings one hour with the beast.

13 These have one mind, and shall give their power and strength unto the beast.

14 These shall make war with the Lamb, and the Lamb shall overcome them; for He is Lord of lords (Supreme Lord, Adonei haAdonim), and King of kings; and they that are with Him are called, and chosen, and faithful.

15 And he saith unto me, "The waters which you sawest, where the whore sitteth, are peoples, and multitudes, and nations, and tongues.

16 And the ten horns which you sawest upon the beast, these shall hate the whore, and shall make her desolate and naked, and shall eat her flesh, and burn her with fire.

17 For God (Elohim, יהוה (YHWH)) hath put in their hearts to fulfil His will, and to agree, and give their kingdom unto the beast, until the words of יהוה (YHWH) shall be fulfilled.

18 And the woman which you sawest is that great city, which reigneth over the kings of the earth."

18 And after these things I saw another angel come down from heaven, having great power; and the earth was lightened with his glory.

2 And he cried mightily with a strong voice, saying, "Babylon (Bavel) the great is fallen, is fallen, and has become the habitation of devils, and the hold of every foul spirit, and a cage of every unclean and hateful bird. – *Isa. 21:9*

3 For all nations have drunk of the wine of the wrath of her fornication, and the kings of the earth have committed fornication with her, and the merchants of the earth are waxed rich through the abundance of her luxury.

4 And I heard another voice from heaven, saying, "Come out of her, My people, that you be not partakers of her sins, and that you receive not of her plagues.

5 For her sins have reached unto heaven, and God (Elohim, יהוה (YHWH)) hath remembered her iniquities.

6 Reward her even as she rewarded you, and double unto her double according to her works; in the cup which she hath filled fill to her double.

7 How much she hath glorified herself, and lived luxuriously, so much torment and sorrow give her; for she saith in her heart, 'I sit as queen, and am no widow, and shall see no sorrow.'

8 Therefore shall her plagues come in one day, death, and mourning, and famine; and she shall be utterly burned with fire; for strong is God (Elohim) יהוה (YHWH) who judgeth her.

9 And the kings of the earth, who have committed fornication and lived luxuriously with her, shall bewail her, and lament for her, when they shall see the smoke of her burning,

10 Standing afar off for the fear of her torment, saying, 'Alas, alas, that great city Babylon

(Bavel), that mighty city! For in one hour is your judgment come.'

11 And the merchants of the earth shall weep and mourn over her; for no man buyeth their merchandise anymore;

12 The merchandise of gold, and silver, and precious stones, and of pearls, and fine linen, and purple, and silk, and scarlet, and all thyine wood, and all manner vessels of ivory, and all manner vessels of most precious wood, and of brass, and iron, and marble,

13 And cinnamon, and incense, and ointments, and frankincense, and wine, and oil, and fine flour, and wheat, and beasts, and sheep, and horses, and chariots, and slaves, and souls of men.

14 And the fruits that your soul lusted after are departed from you, and all things which were dainty and goodly are departed from you, and you shalt find them no more at all.

15 The merchants of these things, which were made rich by her, shall stand afar off for the fear of her torment, weeping and wailing,

16 And saying, 'Alas, alas, that great city, that was clothed in fine linen, and purple, and scarlet, and decked with gold, and precious stones, and pearls!

17 For in one hour so great riches is come to nought.' And every shipmaster, and all the company in ships, and sailors, and as many as trade by sea, stood afar off,

18 And cried when they saw the smoke of her burning, saying, 'What city is like unto this great city!'

19 And they cast dust on their heads, and cried, weeping and wailing, saying, 'Alas, alas, that great city, wherein were made rich all that had ships in the sea by reason of her costliness! For in one hour is she made desolate.'

20 Rejoice over her, you heaven, and you holy apostles and prophets; for יהוה (YHWH) hath avenged you on her.

21 And a mighty angel took up a stone like a great millstone, and cast it into the sea, saying, "Thus with violence shall that great city Babylon (Bavel) be thrown down, and shall be found no more at all.

22 And the voice of harpers, and musicians, and of pipers, and trumpeters, shall be heard no more at all in you; and no craftsman, of whatsoever craft he be, shall be found any more

in you; and the sound of a millstone shall be heard no more at all in you;

23 And the light of a candle shall shine no more at all in you; and the voice of the bridegroom and of the bride shall be heard no more at all in you; for your merchants were the great men of the earth; for by your sorceries were all nations deceived.

24 And in her was found the blood of prophets, and of the holy ones, and of all that were slain upon the earth."

19 And after these things I heard a great voice of much people in heaven, saying, "Praise You Yah (Halelu Yah)! Salvation, and glory, and honour, and power, unto יהוה our God (YHWH Eloheinu);

2 For true and righteous are His judgments; for He hath judged the great whore, who did corrupt the earth with her fornication, and hath avenged the blood of His servants at her hand.

3 And again they said, "Praise You Yah (Halelu Yah)! And her smoke rose up for ever and ever."

4 And the four and twenty elders and the four beasts fell down and worshipped יהוה (YHWH) that sat on the throne, saying, "So be it (Amen); Praise You Yah (Halelu Yah)!"

5 And a voice came out of the throne, saying, "Praise our God (Elohim), all you His servants, and you that fear Him, both small and great."

6 And I heard as it was the voice of a great multitude, and as the voice of many waters, and as the voice of mighty thunderings, saying, "Praise You Yah (Halelu Yah)! For יהוה God of hosts (YHWH Elohei Tsevaot) reigneth. – *Amos 3:13; 4:13*

7 Let us be glad and rejoice, and give honour to Him; for the marriage of the Lamb has come, and His wife hath made herself ready."

8 And to her was granted that she should be arrayed in fine linen, clean and white; for the fine linen is the righteousness of the holy ones.

9 And he saith unto me, "Write: 'Blessed are they who are called unto the marriage supper of the Lamb.'" And he saith unto me, "These are the true sayings of God (Elohim, יהוה (YHWH))."

10 And I fell at his feet to worship him. And he said unto me, "See you do it not! I am your fellowservant, and of your brethren that have the testimony of Yahwah (YHWH). Worship יהוה (YHWH), for the testimony of Yahwah

(YHWH) is the Spirit of prophecy."

11 And I saw heaven opened, and behold a white horse; and He that sat upon him was called Faithful and True, and in righteousness He doth judge and make war.

12 His eyes were as a flame of fire, and on His head were many crowns; and He had a name written, that no man knew, but He Himself.

13 And He was clothed with a vesture dipped in blood; and His name is called "The Word of God (Elohim, יהוה (YHWH))."

14 And the armies which were in heaven followed Him upon white horses, clothed in fine linen, white and clean.

15 And out of His mouth goeth a sharp sword, that with it He should smite the nations; and He shall rule them with a rod of iron; and He treadeth the winepress of the fierceness and wrath of יהוה God of hosts (YHWH Elohei Tsevaot). – *Psa. 2:9*

16 And He hath on His vesture and on His thigh a name written, KING OF KINGS, AND LORD OF LORDS (ADONEI HAADONIM).

17 And I saw an angel standing in the sun; and he cried with a loud voice, saying to all the fowls that fly in the midst of heaven, "Come and gather yourselves together unto the supper of the great God (Elohim);

18 That you may eat the flesh of kings, and the flesh of captains, and the flesh of mighty men, and the flesh of horses, and of them that sit on them, and the flesh of all men, both free and bond, both small and great."

19 And I saw the beast, and the kings of the earth, and their armies, gathered together to make war against Him that sat on the horse, and against His army.

20 And the beast was taken, and with him the false prophet that wrought miracles before him, with which he deceived them that had received the mark of the beast, and them that worshipped his image. These both were cast alive into a lake of fire burning with brimstone.

21 And the rest were slain with the sword of Him that sat upon the horse, which sword proceeded out of His mouth; and all the fowls were filled with their flesh.

20 And I saw an angel come down from heaven, having the key of the bottomless pit and a great chain in his hand.

2 And he laid hold on the dragon, that old serpent, which is the Devil, and Satan, and bound him a thousand years,

3 And cast him into the bottomless pit, and shut him up, and set a seal upon him, that he should deceive the nations no more, till the thousand years should be fulfilled; and after that he must be loosed a little season.

4 And I saw thrones, and they sat upon them, and judgment was given unto them; and I saw the souls of them that were beheaded for the witness of Yahwah (the Messiah, Humanity of El (YHWH)), and for the Word of יהוה (YHWH), and who had not worshipped the beast, neither his image, neither had received his mark upon their foreheads, or in their hands; and they lived and reigned with the Messiah (haMashiach) a thousand years.

5 But the rest of the dead lived not again until the thousand years were finished. This is the first resurrection.

6 Blessed and holy is he that hath part in the first resurrection; on such the second death hath no power, but they shall be priests (kohanim) of יהוה (YHWH) and of Messiah (Mashiach), and shall reign with Him a thousand years.

7 And when the thousand years have expired, Satan shall be loosed out of his prison,

8 And shall go out to deceive the nations which are in the four quarters of the earth, Gog and Magog, to gather them together to battle; the number of whom is as the sand of the sea. – *Eze. 38:2*

9 And they went up on the breadth of the earth, and compassed the camp of the holy ones about, and the beloved city; and fire came down from God (Elohim, יהוה (YHWH)) out of heaven, and devoured them.

10 And the devil that deceived them was cast into the lake of fire and brimstone, where the beast and the false prophet are, and shall be tormented day and night for ever and ever.

11 And I saw a great white throne, and Him that sat on it, from whose face the earth and the heaven fled away; and there was found no place for them.

12 And I saw the dead, small and great, stand before God (Elohim, יהוה (YHWH)); and the books were opened; and another book was opened, which is the book of life; and the dead were judged out of those things which were written in the books, according to their works.

13 And the sea gave up the dead which were in it; and Death and Hell (Sheol) delivered up the dead which were in them; and they were judged every man according to their works.

14 And Death and Hell (Sheol) were cast into the lake of fire. This is the second death.

15 And whosoever was not found written in the book of life was cast into the lake of fire.

21 And I saw a new heaven and a new earth, for the first heaven and the first earth were passed away; and there was no more sea.

2 And I John (Yochanan) saw the holy city, new Jerusalem (Yerushalayim), coming down from God (Elohim, יהוה (YHWH)) out of heaven, prepared as a bride adorned for her husband.

3 And I heard a great voice out of heaven saying, "Behold, the tabernacle of God (Elohim, יהוה (YHWH)) is with men, and He will dwell with them, and they shall be His people, and יהוה (YHWH) Himself shall be with them, and be their God (Elohim).

4 And יהוה (YHWH) shall wipe away all tears from their eyes; and there shall be no more death, neither sorrow, nor crying, neither shall there be any more pain; for the former things are passed away."

5 And He that sat upon the throne said, "Behold, I make all things new." And He said unto me, "Write, for these words are true and faithful."

6 And He said unto me, "It is done. I am Alpha and Omega, the Beginning and the End. I will give unto him that is athirst of the fountain of the water of life freely.

7 He that overcometh shall inherit all things; and I will be his God (Elohim), and he shall be My son.

8 But the fearful, and unbelieving, and the abominable, and murderers, and whoremongers, and sorcerers, and idolaters, and all liars, shall have their part in the lake which burneth with fire and brimstone; which is the second death."

9 And there came unto me one of the seven angels who had the seven vials full of the seven last plagues, and talked with me, saying, "Come hither, I will shew you the bride, the Lamb's wife."

10 And he carried me away in the spirit to a great and high mountain, and shewed me that great city, the holy Jerusalem (Yerushalayim), descending out of heaven from God (Elohim, יהוה (YHWH)),

11 Having the glory of God (Elohim, יהוה (YHWH)); and her light was like unto a stone most precious, even like a jasper stone, clear as crystal;

12 And had a wall great and high, and had twelve gates, and at the gates twelve angels, and names written thereon, which are the names of the twelve tribes of the children of Yisrael.

13 On the east three gates; on the north three gates; on the south three gates; and on the west three gates.

14 And the wall of the city had twelve foundations, and in them the names of the twelve apostles of the Lamb.

15 And he that talked with me had a golden reed to measure the city, and the gates thereof, and the wall thereof.

16 And the city lieth foursquare, and the length is as large as the breadth; and he measured the city with the reed, twelve thousand furlongs. The length and the breadth and the height of it are equal.

17 And he measured the wall thereof, a hundred and forty and four cubits, according to the measure of a man, that is, of the angel.

18 And the building of the wall of it was of jasper; and the city was pure gold, like unto clear glass.

19 And the foundations of the wall of the city were garnished with all manner of precious stones. The first foundation was jasper; the second, sapphire; the third, a chalcedony; the fourth, an emerald;

20 The fifth, sardonyx; the sixth, sardius; the seventh, chrysolite; the eighth, beryl; the ninth, a topaz; the tenth, a chrysoprasus; the eleventh, a jacinth; the twelfth, an amethyst.

21 And the twelve gates were twelve pearls; every several gate was of one pearl; and the street of the city was pure gold, as it was transparent glass.

22 And I saw no temple therein, for יהוה God of hosts (YHWH Elohei Tsevaot) and the Lamb are the temple of it.

23 And the city had no need of the sun, neither of the moon, to shine in it; for the glory of יהוה (YHWH) did lighten it, and the Lamb is the light thereof.

24 And the nations of them who are saved shall walk in the light of it; and the kings of the earth do bring their glory and honour into it.

25 And the gates of it shall not be shut at all by day, for there shall be no night there.

26 And they shall bring the glory and honour of the nations into it.

27 And there shall in no wise enter into it any thing that defileth, neither whatsoever worketh abomination, or maketh a lie; but those who are written in the Lamb's Book of Life.

22 And he shewed me a pure river of water of life, clear as crystal, proceeding out of the throne of יהוה (YHWH) and of the Lamb.

2 In the midst of the street of it, and on either side of the river, was there the tree of life, which bare twelve manner of fruits, and yielded her fruit every month; and the leaves of the tree were for the healing of the nations.

3 And there shall be no more curse, but the throne of יהוה (YHWH) and of the Lamb shall be in it; and His servants shall serve Him.

4 And they shall see His face; and His name shall be in their foreheads.

5 And there shall be no night there; and they need no candle, neither light of the sun; for God (Elohim) יהוה (YHWH) giveth them light; and they shall reign for ever and ever.

6 And he said unto me, "These sayings are faithful and true; and יהוה (YHWH) God (Elohim) of the holy prophets sent His angel to shew unto His servants the things which must shortly be done.

7 "Behold, I come quickly; blessed is he that keepeth the sayings of the prophecy of this book."

8 And I John (Yochanan) saw these things, and heard them. And when I had heard and seen, I fell down to worship before the feet of the angel who shewed me these things.

9 Then saith he unto me, "See you do it not, for I am your fellowservant, and of your brethren the prophets, and of them who keep the sayings of this book. Worship יהוה (YHWH)."

10 And he saith unto me, "Seal not the sayings of the prophecy of this book, for the time is at hand.

11 He that is unjust, let him be unjust still; and he who is filthy, let him be filthy still; and he that is righteous, let him be righteous still; and he that is holy, let him be holy still."

12 "And, behold, I come quickly; and My reward is with Me, to give every man according as his work shall be.

13 I am Alpha and Omega, the Beginning and the End, the First and the Last." – *Isa 41:4, 44:6, 48:12*

14 Blessed are they that do His commandments, that they may have right to the tree of life, and may enter in through the gates into the city.

15 For outside are dogs, and sorcerers, and whoremongers, and murderers, and idolaters, and whosoever loveth and maketh a lie.

16 I Yahwah (YHWH) have sent Mine angel to testify unto you these things in the assemblies (ekklesias). I am the root and the offspring of Dawid, and the bright and morning star."

17 And the Spirit and the bride say, "Come!" And let him that heareth say, "Come!" And let him that is athirst come. And whosoever will, let him take the water of life freely.

18 For I testify unto every man that heareth the words of the prophecy of this book: If any man shall add unto these things, יהוה (YHWH) shall add unto him the plagues that are written in this book.

19 And if any man shall take away from the words of the book of this prophecy, יהוה (YHWH) shall take away his part out of the book of life, and out of the holy city, and from the things which are written in this book.

20 He who testifieth these things saith, "Surely I come quickly." So be it (Amen). Even so, come, our Lord (Adonai) Yahwah haMashiach.

21 The grace of our Lord (Adonai) Yahwah haMashiach be with you all. So be it (Amen).

Name	Hebrew Block Letter	Sound	Numerical Value	Name	Hebrew Block Letter		Sound	Numerical Value
Aleph	א	Silent letter	1	Lamed	ל		L as in Luke	30
Bet	בּ	B as in Boy	2	Mem	ם	מ	M as in Mark	40
	ב	V as in View		Nun	נ	ן	N as in Noach	50
Gimmel	ג	G as in Gad	3	Samech	ס		S as in Sun	60
Dalet	ד	D as in Daniel	4	Ayin	ע		Silent letter	70
Hey	ה	H as in Heaven	5	Pey	פּ	ף	P as in Peter	80
Waw	ו	W as in Wine	6		פ		F as in Feast	
Zayin	ז	Z as in Zion	7	Tsade	צ	ץ	Ts as in NuTs	90
Chet	ח	Ch as in HatCh	8	Qof	ק		Q as in Quest	100
Tet	ט	T as in Tall	9	Resh	ר		R as in Rock	200
Yod	י	Y as in Yah	10	Shin	שׁ		Sh as in Shalom	300
Kaf	כ	K as in King	20		שׂ		S as in Sun	
	ך	Kh as in Khaf		Taw	ת		T as in Torah	400

Sign	Vowel	Sound	Name of Hebrew Niqqud Vowel
אָ or אֳ	a	a as in Abba	**Kamatz** or **qamatz** (קָמַץ) is represented by two perpendicular lines (looking like an uppercase T) underneath a letter.
אַ	a	a as in Abba	**Pataḥ** (פַּתַח) is sign represented by a horizontal line underneath a letter.
אֲ	a	a as in Abba	**ḥaṭaf pataḥ** (חֲטַף פַּתַח, "reduced *pataḥ*"). The reduced (or *haṭaf*) niqqud exist for pataḥ, qamatz, and segol which contain a shva next to it.
אִ	i	i as in big	**Hiriq** (חִירִיק) is represented by a single dot underneath the letter.
	e	ee as in bee	
אֵ	e	ay as in bay	**Tzere** (צֵירֵי) is represented by two dots ".." underneath a letter.
אֶ	e	e as in bed	**Segol** (סֶגוֹל) is represented by three dots forming an upside down equilateral triangle.
אֹ or אוֹ	o	o as in row	**Cholam** (חוֹלָם) is represented by a dot above the upper left corner of the consonant letter.
אֻ	u	u as in put	**Kubutz** (קֻבּוּץ) represent the short sound [u].
אוּ	u	u as in pool	**Shuruk** (שׁוּרוּק) represent a long [u] sound.
אְ	-	Silent / short sound	**Shva** or, in biblical Hebrew, **Shewa** is written as two vertical dots beneath a letter.

Nr.	Strong's and Scripture Reference	Hebrew Texts / Transliteration & {Phonetic Spelling}	Word(s) Written in English Bibles	Word(s) Written in יהוה Sacred Scriptures
A1	H3068 יהוה Gen. 2:4	YHWH יהוה {Yah-Wah}	the LORD, GOD	יהוה
	Exo. 6:3	YHWH יהוה {Yah-Wah}	JEHOVAH	

יהוה (yod hey waw hey) are 4-Hebrew consonant letters written in the Hebrew block letter (Hebrew letters reading from right to left), represented by the Latin script as YHWH (called the tetragrammaton, meaning four letters). יהוה (yod hey waw hey), properly read from right to left, are: Y for yod (י), H for hey (ה), W for waw (ו) and H for hey (ה). יהוה (YHWH) is pronounced YaHWaH in all languages.

יהוה is the sacred name of the God (Elohim) of Yisrael which has been translated to titles and many other names after the Hebrew Scripture was being translated to other languages. In this יהוה Sacred Scripture, the true name of God (Elohim) יהוה is restored according to the originally written word in the Hebrew Scriptures wherever title "the LORD" or "GOD" were found in English Old Testament Bibles and "the Lord" in the New Testament. Read the Preface in the front pages for further information about the sacred name of the Creator of heavens and earth, יהוה (Yahwah, YHWH).

| Mat. 1:1, 1:21 | - | Jesus | YHWH |
| Mat. 1:20 | יהוה {Yah-Wah} | The Lord | יהוה |

The true name of the Messiah (haMashiach) was revealed by God (Elohim) Himself when haMashiach (called 'the Messias/Christ/the Lord" in Christianity) spoke in John 5:43 "I am come in My Father's name, and you receive Me not; if another shall come in his own name, him you will receive."

The written Words of the original Hebrew Scriptures revealed the true name of Heavenly Father (Creator of heavens and earth) as יהוה (YHWH pronounced Yahwah), and all the prophets testified of יהוה (YHWH): the Savior (Isa.43:3); the only God (Deu. 4:35, Isa.45:5,21, 46:9); the Father (Isa. 63:16); the Son, Counselor (Holy Spirit) and Everlasting Father (Isa.9:6); the King of Yisrael, the First and the Last (Isa. 44:6); one God (Elohim) with one name (Deut 6:4, Zech. 14:9).

All the Apostles of haMashiach preached using the Scripture (known as Tanakh) during their time as there was no New Blood Covenant Scripture (known as New Testament of the English Bible) written until tens of years later after haMashiach was crucified. With that in mind, the words spoken by Apostle Peter in Act 2:21, is directly quoted from Yoel 2:32 of the Tanakh Scripture, which testified יהוה (YHWH) as the name to be delivered (saved).

Acts 2:21 (KJV):
And it shall come to pass, that whosoever shall call on the name of *the Lord*, shall be saved.
Yoel 2:32 (KJV):
And it shall come to pass, that whosoever shall call on the name of *the LORD*, shall be delivered.
Yoel 2:32 written in Hebrew with the name of יהוה (YHWH):

והיה כל אשר־יקרא בשם יהוה ימלט

Nr.	Strong's and Scripture Reference	Hebrew Texts / Transliteration & {Phonetic Spelling}	Word(s) Written in English Bibles	Word(s) Written in יהוה Sacred Scriptures
	Evidently, the true name of God (Elohim), **יהוה (YHWH)** has been removed and replaced by titles "**the LORD**" or "**GOD**" in Old Testament; and also "**the Lord**" and many other false name of God (Elohim) in the New Testament.			
	Another clear evidence that the true name of haMashiach is **יהוה (YHWH)** was given witnessed by apostle Matthew (Mat.3:3), Mark (1:3) and Luke (3:4) as they preached the prophesy of Isaiah (Yeshayahu) about prophet John the Baptist preparing the way of the Messiah (haMashiach):			
	Isa. 40:3 (KJV): "The voice of him that crieth in the wilderness: 'Prepare ye the way of _**the LORD**_, make straight in the desert a highway for our God.' **Isa. 40:3 (Hebrew Tanakh):** קול קורא במדבר פנו דרך _**יהוה**_ ישרו בערבה מסלה לאלהינו: As the original Tanakh Scripture was written in Hebrew, therefore, the correct translation of Isaiah (Yeshayahu) 40:3, Matthew (Mat.3:3), Mark (1:3) and Luke (3:4) should be: "The voice of him that crieth in the wilderness: "Prepare you the way of _יהוה_ _**(Yahwah, YHWH)**_, make straight in the desert a highway for our God (Elohim)."			
A2	H3050 יה Exo. 15:2	YH יָהּ {Yah}	LORD, Jah	Yah
	H3050 יה (Yah) is the shortened form of יהוה (YHWH), the sacred name of God (Elohim) of Yisrael. Yah was written as "Jah" and "iah" in the English bibles.			
A3	H3070 יהוה יראה Gen. 22:14	YHWH Yireh יהוה יִרְאֶה {Yah-Wah Yir-eh}	Jehovah-jireh	יהוה Yireh (YHWH Sees, YHWH Provides)
	"Jehovah-jireh" written in KJV1769 for "יהוה יראה" is appropriately transliterated to "יהוה Yireh" according to the Hebrew scriptures. "יהוה Yireh" is not another name of Adonai יהוה, but an attribute name given by Abraham for Mount Moriyah in commemoration of the interposition of the angel of יהוה who prevented the sacrifice of Isaac and provided a ram as substitute.			
A4	H3071 יהוה נסי Exo 17:15	YHWH Nissi יהוה נִסִּי {Yah-Wah Nis-see}	Jehovah-nissi	יהוה Nissi (YHWH Is My Banner)
	"Jehovah-nissi" written in KJV1769 for "יהוה נסי" is appropriately transliterated to "יהוה Nissi" according to Hebrew Scripture. "יהוה Nissi" means "YHWH Is My Banner", the name of the altar made by Mosheh to remember the victory over the Amalekites.			
A5	H3068 & H3073 יהוה שלום Judges 6:24	YHWH Shalom יהוה שָׁלוֹם {Yah-Wah Sha-lom}	Jehovah-shalom	יהוה Shalom (YHWH Is Peace)
	"יהוה שלום" (יהוה Shalom) means "YHWH is Peace". It is the name of a sacred altar built by Gideon in Ophrah.			

Nr.	Strong's and Scripture Reference	Hebrew Texts / Transliteration & {Phonetic Spelling}	Word(s) Written in English Bibles	Word(s) Written in יהוה Sacred Scriptures
A6	H3072 יהוה צדקנו Jer. 23:6, 33:16	YHWH Tsidqenu צִדְקֵנוּ יהוה {Yah-Wah Tsid-kay-noo}	THE LORD OUR RIGHTEOUS-NESS	יהוה Tsidqenu (YHWH Our Righteousness)
A7	H3074 יהוה שמה Eze. 48:35	YHWH Shammah יהוה שָׁמָּה {Yah-Wah Sham-mah}	THE LORD is there	יהוה Shammah (YHWH Is There)
A8a	H3068 & H6635 יהוה צבאות 1 Sam 1:3	YHWH Tsevaot יהוה צְבָאוֹת {Yah-Wah Tse-va-ot}	LORD of hosts	יהוה of hosts (YHWH Tsevaot)
A8b	H430 & H6635 אלהי צבאות 1 Kin. 19:10	Elohei Tsevaot אֱלֹהֵי צְבָאוֹת {E-lo-hay Tse-va-ot}	The LORD God of hosts	יהוה God of hosts (YHWH Elohei Tsevaot)
	"Tsevaot צבאות" is the plural form of "H6635 צָבָא tsava", translated in English as "hosts". It denotes יהוה in His role as Lord /Master of the heavenly hosts.			
A9	H2332 חוּה Gen. 3:20	Chawah חַוָּה {Kha-wah}	Eve	Eve (Chawah)
	Chawah is a Hebrew name which was called "Eve" in English, meaning "life or living". Chawah is Adam's wife.			
A10	H87 אברם Gen. 11:26	Avram אַבְרָם {Av-ram}	Abram	Avram
	Avram is the original name of Avraham, meaning "exalted-father".			
A11	H85 אברהם Gen. 17:5	Avraham אַבְרָהָם {Av-ra-ham}	Abraham	Avraham
	Avraham means "father of a multitude" or "chief of a multitude"; he is called a friend of יהוה and founder of Hebrew nation via Elohim's elective covenant.			
A12	H3327 יצחק Gen. 17:19	Yitschaq יִצְחָק {Yits-khak}	Isaac	Isaac (Yitschaq)
	Yitschaq is a Hebrew name which was transliterated as "Isaac" in English, the name of the son of Avraham and Sarah. Yitschaq means "he laughs".			
A13	H6215 עשׂו Gen. 25:25	Esaw עֵשָׂו {ay-saw}	Esau	Esaw
	Esaw is Hebrew name meaning "hairy"; eldest son of Yitschaq (Isaac) and Rebecca and twin brother of Yaaqov (Jacob); sold his birth-right for food when he was hungry and the divine blessing went to Yaaqov; progenitor of the Arab people.			
A14	H3290 יעקב Gen. 25:26	Yaaqov יַעֲקֹב {Ya-ak-ov}	Jacob	Jacob (Yaaqov)
	The Hebrew name of the son of Yitschaq (Isaac), grandson of Avraham, and father of the 12 patriarchs of the tribes of Yisrael. Yaaqov means "heel holder" or "supplanter".			

Nr.	Strong's and Scripture Reference	Hebrew Texts / Transliteration & {Phonetic Spelling}	Word(s) Written in English Bibles	Word(s) Written in יהוה Sacred Scriptures
A15	H3478 ישׂראל Gen. 32:28, 35:10	Yisrael יִשְׂרָאֵל{Yis-ra-ale}	Israel	Yisrael
	Yisrael means "he will rule as El"; the second name for Yaakoq given to him by Elohim after his wrestling with the angel at Peniel. Also to identify the 12 tribes (sons of Yaaqov) later to become the state of Yisrael.			
A16	H7205 ראובן Gen. 29:32, Rev. 7:5	Reuven רְאוּבֵן {Re-oo-ven}	Reuben	Reuven
	Reuben (Reuven) is the eldest son of Jacob (Yaaqov) by Leah; Reuven means "behold a son"; the tribe descended from Reuven and the territory inhabited by the tribe of Reuven.			
A17	H8095 שמעון Gen. 29:33, Rev. 7:7	Shimon שִׁמְעוֹן {Shee-mon}	Simeon	Shimon
	Simeon (Shimon) is the 2nd son of Yaaqov by his wife Leah, meaning "heard"; also, the progenitor of tribe of Shimon.			
A18	H3878 לוי Gen. 29:34, Rev. 7:7	Lewi, Lewiy לֵוִי {Lay-wee}	Levi / Levite	Lewi
	H3881 לוים Exo. 6:25	Lewiyim (pl.) לְוִיֶּם {Lay-wee-yim}	Levites	Lewites (Lewiyim)
	Lewi is the 3rd son of Jacob (Yaaqov) by Leah, meaning "joined to" and the progenitor of tribe of Lewites (Lewiyim).			
A19	H3063 יהודה Gen. 29:35, Mat. 1:1	Yehudah יְהוּדָה {Yeh-hoo-dah}	Judah, Judas	Judah (Yehudah)
	Judah (Yehudah) is the 4th son of Jacob (Yaaqov) by Leah, meaning "YHWH is praised"; the tribe descended from Yehudah the son of Yaaqov and the territory occupied by the tribe of Yehudah.			
A20	H1835 דן Gen. 30:6	Dan דָּן	Dan	Dan
	Dan is the 5th son of Jacob (Yaaqov), the 1st of Bilhah, Rachel's handmaid, meaning "judge".			
A21	H5321 נפתלי Gen. 30:8, Rev. 7:6	Naftali / Naftaliy נַפְתָּלִי {Naf-ta-lee}	Naphtali / Nepthalim	Naftali
	Naftali is the 6th son of Jacob (Yaaqov) and the 2nd by Bilhah the handmaid of Rachel, meaning "my wrestling"; the name of tribe descended from Naftali.			
A22	H1410 גד Gen. 30:11, Rev. 7:5	Gad גָּד {gawd}	Gad	Gad
	Gad is the 7th son of Jacob (Yaaqov) by Zilpah, Leah's handmaid, and full brother of Asher; meaning "a "troop"; the name of tribe descended from Gad.			

Nr.	Strong's and Scripture Reference	Hebrew Texts / Transliteration & {Phonetic Spelling}	Word(s) Written in English Bibles	Word(s) Written in יהוה Sacred Scriptures
A39	H8010 שלמה 2 Sam.12:24, Mat. 1:6	Shelomoh שְׁלֹמֹה {She-lo-moh}	Solomon	Solomon (Shelomoh)

Solomon (Hebrew: שלמה, *Shelomoh*), also called Jedidiah (Hebrew: ידידיה Yedidyah), according to the Hebrew Bible, was a fabulously wealthy and wise king of Yisrael who succeeded his father, King Dawid. The conventional dates of Solomon's reign are circa 970 to 931 BCE, normally given in alignment with the dates of Dawid's reign. He is described as the third king of the United Monarchy, which would break apart into the northern Kingdom of Yisrael and the southern Kingdom of Judah (Yehudah) shortly after his death. Following the split, his patrilineal descendants ruled over Judah (Yehudah) alone.

Solomon (Shelomoh) is the author of the Book of Proverbs and Song of Songs. Shelomoh means "peaceful" in Hebrew. The life of Solomon is primarily described in the second Book of Samuel, and by 1 Chronicles and 1 Kings.

A40	H7346 רחבעם 1 Kings 11:43	Rechavam רְחַבְעָם {Rekh-a-vam}	Rehoboam	Rehoboam (Rechavam)
	Mat. 1:7	רחבעם {Rekh-a-vam}	Roboam	Roboam (Rechavam)

Rechavam is a Hebrew name, meaning "a people has enlarged". Rechavam is the son of Shelomoh and the 1st king of Yehudah after the split up of the kingdom of Yisrael.

A41	H2977 יאשיהו or יאשיה	Yoshiyah יֹאשִׁיָּה {Yo-shee-yah} or Yoshiyahu יֹאשִׁיָּהוּ {Yo-shee-yah-oo}		
	יאשיהו 1 Kin. 13:2	Yoshiyahu יֹאשִׁיָּהוּ {Yo-shee-yah-oo}	Josiah	Josiah (Yoshiyahu)

Josiah (Yoshiyahu) is the son of Amon by Yedidah who succeeded his father to the throne of Yehudah and reigned for 31 years; his reign is noteworthy for the great revivals back to the worship of יהוה (YHWH) which he led. Yoshiyahu mean "whom יהוה (YHWH) heals".

A42	H348 אִיזֶבֶל 1 Kin. 16:31	Iyzevel אִיזֶבֶל {Ee-zeh-vel}	Jezebel	Jezebel (Iyzevel)

Iyzevel (English: Jezebel) is the Hebrew name which means "Baal exalts" or "Baal is husband/lord to" or "unchaste". Iyzevel is a queen of Yisrael, wife of Ahab, daughter of Ethbaal.

A43	H452 אליהו or אליה	Eliyah אֵלִיָּה {El-ee-yah} or Eliyahu אֵלִיָּהוּ {El-ee-yah-oo}		
	1 Kin. 17:1	Eliyahu אֵלִיָּהוּ	Elijah /	Elijah (Eliyahu)
	Mat. 11:14	Eliyahu אֵלִיָּהוּ	Elias	Elias (Eliyahu)
	2 Kin. 1:3	Eliyah אֵלִיָּה	Elijah	Elijah (Eliyah)

"H452 אליה Eliyah" means "my El is יה (Yah)" or "Eliyahu" which means "Yah, He is El (Mighty One)". Eliyah/Eliyahu is the great prophet of the reign of Ahab.

Nr.	Strong's and Scripture Reference	Hebrew Texts / Transliteration & {Phonetic Spelling}	Word(s) Written in English Bibles	Word(s) Written in יהוה Sacred Scriptures
A44	H2396 חזקיהו or חזקיה	Chizkiyah חִזְקִיָּה {Khiz-kee-yah} or Chizkiyahu חִזְקִיָּהוּ {Khiz-kee-yah-oo}		
	2 Kin.16:20, Mat. 1:9	Chizkiyahu חִזְקִיָּהוּ	Hezekiah / Ezekias	Hezekiah (Chizkiyahu)
	Ezra 2:16	Chizkiyah חִזְקִיָּה	Hezekiah	Hezekiah (Chizkiyah)
	"Hezekiah (Chizkiyah/Chizkiyahu)" is the 12th king of Judah (Yehudah), son of Ahaz and Aviyah. He is a good king in that he served יהוה (YHWH) and did away with idolatrous practices.			
A45	H3379 ירבעם 1 Kin. 11:26	Yarovam יָרָבְעָם {Ya-ro-vam}	Jeroboam	Jeroboam (Yarovam)
	Yarovam is a Hebrew name, meaning "the people will contend"; Yarovam is the first king of the northern kingdom of Yisrael when the kingdom split at the death of Shelomoh and the 10 tribes split off from Yehudah and Binyamin and the kingdom under Shelomoh's son Rechavam; idolatry was introduced at the beginning of his reign.			
A46	H3083 יהונתן 1 Chro. 27:25	Yehonatan יְהוֹנָתָן {Ye-ho-na-tan}	Jonathan / Jehonatan	Jonathan (Yehonatan)
	Yehonatan is a Hebrew name which was transliterated as "Jonathan" in English. Yehonatan means "יהוה (YHWH) has given".			
A47	H5830 עזרא Ezra 7:1	Ezra עֶזְרָא	Ezra	Ezra
	Ezra is the Hebrew name, meaning "help". He is the priest and scribe who led the reforms of the returned exiles in Yerushalayim, a co-worker with Nechemyah. Ezra continues the First Blood Covenant narrative of Second Chronicles by showing how Elohim YHWH fulfils His promises after seventy years of exile. Yisrael's "second exodus", this one from Babylon, is less impressive than the return from Egypt because only a remnant chooses to leave Babylon. Ezra relates the story of two returns from Babylon- the first led by Zerubbabel to rebuild the temple (1-6), and the second under the leadership of Ezra to rebuild the spiritual condition of the people (7-10). Sandwiched between these two accounts is a gap of nearly six decades, during which Esther (Hadassah) lives and rules as queen in Persia.			
A48	H5166 נחמיה Neh. 1:1	Nechemyah נְחֶמְיָה {Ne-khem-yah}	Nehemiah	Nehemiah (Nechemyah)

Nr.	Strong's and Scripture Reference	Hebrew Texts / Transliteration & {Phonetic Spelling}	Word(s) Written in English Bibles	Word(s) Written in יהוה Sacred Scriptures
	Nehemiah (Hebrew: Nechemyah נחמיה) means "comfort of יהוה (YHWH)." Nehemiah is the central figure of the Book of Nehemiah, which describes his work in rebuilding Yerushalayim during the Second Temple period. He was governor of Persian Judea under Artaxerxes I of Persia (465-424 BC).			
	In the 20th of Artaxerxes (445 or 444 BC), Nehemiah was cupbearer to the king. Learning that the remnant of Jews (Yehudim) in Judah (Yehudah) were in distress and that the walls of Yerushalayim were broken down, he asked the king and was granted permission to return and rebuild the city. Nehemiah defied the opposition of Yehudah's enemies on all sides, and rebuilt the shattered wall of Yerushalayim together with his countrymen in only fifty-two days.			
	He then took measures to repopulate the city and purify the Jewish (Yehudi) community, enforcing the cancellation of debt, assisting Ezra to promulgate the law (torah) written by Mosheh and enforcing the divorce of Jewish (Yehudi) men from their non-Jewish (Yehudi) wives. After ruling for 12 years as governor with justice and righteousness, Nehemiah returned to the king in Susa and then returned back to Yerushalayim, only to find that the people had fallen back into their evil ways, broke the law (torah) on Shabbat and defiled the Temple. Greatly angered, he purified the Temple and enforced the observance of the law (torah) of יהוה (YHWH) written by Mosheh.			
A49	H1919 הדסה Est. 2:7	Hadassah הֲדַסָּה {Had-as-sah}	Esther	Esther (Hadassah)
	Hadassah which means "myrtle", is the Hebrew name of Queen Esther. She is the queen of Persia, the heroine of the Book of Esther (Hadassah) - daughter of Abihail, cousin			
	and adopted daughter of Mordecai, of the tribe of Binyamin. Esther (Hadassah) was made queen by King Ahasuerus to replace divorced queen, Vashti.			
	The Book of Esther (Hadassah), also known in Hebrew as "the Scroll" (Megillah), is a book in the third section (Ketuvim – "Writings") of the Hebrew Scripture (Tanakh). יהוה (YHWH)'s hand of providence and protection for His people is evident throughout the Book of Esther. Haman's plot which brought grave danger to the Jews (Yehudim) was countered by the courage of Esther (Hadassah) and the counsel of her wise cousin Mordecai, resulting in a great deliverance. The Feast of Purim becomes an annual reminder of Elohim יהוה (YHWH)'s faithfulness for His people.			
A50	H347 איוב Job 1:1	Iyov אִיּוֹב {Ee-yov}	Job	Job (Iyov)
	Job (Hebrew: איוב Iyov) is a patriarch, the subject of the book of Job (Iyov). Iyov has two possible meaning. If derived from the Hebrew word, it means "the persecuted one". If derived from the Arabic word, it means "to come back" or "repent".			
	The Book of Job (Iyov) is a book in the Ketuvim ("Writings") section of the Hebrew Scripture (Tanakh). It tells the story of a man who loses everything - his wealth, his family, his health and he wrestles with the question: Why?			
	The book begins with a heavenly debate between יהוה (YHWH) and Satan, moves through three cycles of earthly debates between Job and his friends, and concludes with a dramatic "divine diagnosis" of Iyov's problem. In the end, Iyov acknowledges the sovereignty of God (Elohim, יהוה (YHWH)) in his life and receives back more than he had before his trials.			

Nr.	Strong's and Scripture Reference	Hebrew Texts / Transliteration & {Phonetic Spelling}	Word(s) Written in English Bibles	Word(s) Written in יהוה Sacred Scriptures
A51	H3470 ישעיה or ישעיהו	Yeshayahu יְשַׁעְיָהוּ {Ye-sha-yah-oo} or Yeshayah יְשַׁעְיָה {Ye-sha-yah}		
	2 Kings 19:2, Isa. 1:1	Yeshayahu יְשַׁעְיָהוּ	Isaiah	Isaiah (Yeshayahu)
	Mat. 3:3	Yeshayahu יְשַׁעְיָהוּ	Esaias	Isaiah (Yeshayahu)
	1 Chr. 3:21	Yeshayah יְשַׁעְיָה	Jesaiah	Isaiah (Yeshayah)

The Book of Isaiah (Yeshayahu) is like a miniature Scripture. The first thirty-nine chapters (like the thirty-nine book of the First Blood Covenant-Tanakh) narrate judgment upon immoral and idolatrous men: Judah (Yehudah) and its surrounding nations and the whole earth have sinned; that the judgment must come, for God (Elohim) cannot allow such blatant sin to go unpunished forever. Isa. 9:19 is a direct portrayal of the "wrath of יהוה (YHWH)" as it was written: "Through the wrath of יהוה of hosts (YHWH Tsevaot) is the land darkened, and the people shall be as the fuel of the fire."

The final twenty-seven chapters (like the twenty-seven book of the New Blood Covenant - Dam haBerit Chadashah) prophesied and declared a message of comfort and hope: The Messiah (haMashiach) will be coming as a Savior and Sovereign to bear a stake and to wear a crown.

A52	H3414 ירמיה or ירמיהו	Yirmeyahu יִרְמְיָהוּ {Yir-meh-yah-oo} or Yirmeyah יִרְמְיָה {Yir-meh-yah}		
	Jer. 1:1	Yirmeyahu יִרְמְיָהוּ	Jeremiah	Jeremiah Yirmeyahu)
	Mat.2:17	Yirmeyah יִרְמְיָה	Jeremy	Jeremiah (Yirmeyah)

Yirmeyahu is the prophet of יהוה (YHWH), the son of Hilkiah of the priestly family in Anathoth. Yirmeyahu means "YHWH will exalt", also called the "weeping prophet". He is the author of the prophetic book "Jeremiah (Yirmeyahu)".

Yirmeyahu was called to prophetic ministry in about 626 BC by God יהוה (YHWH) to give prophecy to Yerushalayim's destruction that would occur by invaders from the north. This was because Yisrael had been unfaithful to the Torah of the covenant and had forsaken God (Elohim) by worshipping Baal, causing יהוה (YHWH) to withdraw His blessings. He was guided by God to proclaim that the nation of Judah (Yehudah) would be faced with famine, plundered and taken captive by foreigners who would exile them to the foreign land.

In his early ministry, Yirmeyahu was preaching throughout Yisrael. He condemned idolatry and the people burning their children as offerings to Moloch, the greed of priests (kohanim) and false prophets. In tears of compassion, Yirmeyahu labors for more than forty years proclaiming a message of destruction to the stiff-necked people of Judah (Yehudah) despite being despised and persecuted by his countrymen. Through his preaching, he faithfully declares that surrender to Adonai יהוה (YHWH)'s will is the only way to escape calamity.

Nr.	Strong's and Scripture Reference	Hebrew Texts / Transliteration & {Phonetic Spelling}	Word(s) Written in English Bibles	Word(s) Written in יהוה Sacred Scriptures
A53	H3168 יחזקאל Eze. 1:3	Yechezqel יְחֶזְקֵאל {Yekh-ez-kel}	Ezekiel / Jehezekel	Ezekial (Yechezqel)

Ezekiel (Yechezqel) is a priest (kohen) and prophet in the 6th-century BCE, who ministers during the darkest days of Judah (Yehudah)'s history: the seventy-year period of Babylonian captivity. Yechezqel means "God (Elohim) Strengthens" in Hebrew. Yechezqel is indeed strengthened by Adonai יהוה (YHWH) for the prophetic ministry to which he was called.

Ezekiel (Yechezqel) is also the author of the book by his name, which reveals prophecies regarding the destruction of Yerushalayim, the restoration of the land of Yisrael, and the Millennial Temple visions. Carried to Babylon before the final assault on Yerushalayim, Yechezqel uses prophecies, parables, signs and symbols to dramatize God (Elohim)'s message to His exiled people. Yechezqel and his contemporaries like

Yirmeyahu, witnessed the fulfillment of their prophecies with the siege of Yerushalayim by the Babylonians in 589 BC.

Nr.	Strong's and Scripture Reference	Hebrew Texts / Transliteration & {Phonetic Spelling}	Word(s) Written in English Bibles	Word(s) Written in יהוה Sacred Scriptures
A54	H1840 דניאל / דנאל Dan. 1:6	Daniyel / Daniel דָּנִיֵּאל {Da-nee-yale} דָּנִאֵל {Da-nee-ale}	Daniel	Daniel

Daniyel/Daniel is the Hebrew name which means "El is my Judge". Daniel's life and ministry bridge the entire seventy-year period of Babylonian captivity. Daniel was taken into captivity by the Babylon King Nebuchadnezzar at the age of sixteen and served the king and his successors with loyalty and ability until the time of the Persian conqueror, King Cyrus. He was a noble Jewish (Yehudi) and remained faithful to God (Elohim) of Yisrael.

Daniel becomes Adonai יהוה (YHWH)'s prophetic mouthpiece to the gentile and Jewish (Yehudi) world declaring God (Elohim)'s present and eternal purpose. In both his personal adventures and prophetic visions, Daniel shows יהוה (YHWH)'s guidance, intervention, and power in the affairs of men.

Nr.	Strong's and Scripture Reference	Hebrew Texts / Transliteration & {Phonetic Spelling}	Word(s) Written in English Bibles	Word(s) Written in יהוה Sacred Scriptures
A55	H1954 הושע Hos. 1:1	Hoshea הוֹשֵׁעַ {Ho-shea}	Hosea / Oshea	Hoshea

Hoshea, whose name means "Salvation", is the 19th and last king who ministers to the northern kingdom of Yisrael (also called Efrayim, after its largest tribe). Outwardly, the nation is enjoying a time of prosperity and growth, but inwardly, moral corruption and spiritual adultery permeate the people.

The Book of Hoshea denounces the worship of gods (elohim) other than Adonai יהוה (YHWH), metaphorically comparing Yisrael's abandonment of יהוה (YHWH) to a woman being unfaithful to her husband. According to the book's narrative, the relationship between Hoshea and his unfaithful wife Gomer is comparable to the relationship between יהוה (YHWH) and His unfaithful nation of Yisrael. The eventual reconciliation of Hoshea and Gomer is treated as a hopeful metaphor for the eventual reconciliation between יהוה (YHWH) and Yisrael.

Nr.	Strong's and Scripture Reference	Hebrew Texts / Transliteration & {Phonetic Spelling}	Word(s) Written in English Bibles	Word(s) Written in יהוה Sacred Scriptures
	The prophecy of Hoshea centers around God יהוה (YHWH)'s unending love towards a sinful Yisrael. God (Elohim)'s agony was expressed over His betrayal by Yisrael. Hoshea declared that unless they repent of their sins, Adonai יהוה (YHWH) will allow their nation to be destroyed and the people will be taken captivity by Assyria.			
A56	H3100 יואל Joel 1:1	Yoel יוֹאֵל {Yo-el}	Joel	Yoel
	Yoel is the son of Pethuel and the prophet of יהוה (YHWH); also the author of the book by his name. Yoel means "יהוה (YHWH) is El". Yoel, יהוה's spokeman during the reign of Yoash (835-796 B.C.), proclaim יהוה's messages:			
	Chapter 1 mentioned the invasion of locust and a call to Elohim's people for repentance. In chapter 2, Yoel declared "The Day of יהוה (YHWH)" and calling His people to return to Him; יהוה (YHWH) has compassion and will pour out His Spirit upon His people; that whoever shall call upon the name of יהוה (YHWH) shall be delivered (saved). Joel ended his prophesies in chapter 3 by declaring יהוה (YHWH)'s judgement on Judah (Yehudah)'s enemies and how they will be destroyed. In that day, יהוה (YHWH) will bring glorious future to Judah (Yehudah); יהוה (YHWH) will be the hope for His people and the strength of the children of Yisrael.			
A57	H5986 עמוס Amos 1:1	Amos עָמוֹס {A-mos}	Amos	Amos
	Amos means "Burden-Bearer", the name derived from the Hebrew root "amas", meaning "to lift a burden, to carry". Amos prophesies during a period of national optimism in Yisrael. Business is booming and boundaries are bulging. But below the surface, greed and injustice are festering.			
	Amos prophesied during the reign of Jeroboam II, King of Yisrael and of Uzziyah of Judah (Yehudah) in the first half of the 8th century BC. His prophetic mission was in the northern kingdom. Amos was called a "shepherd" and a "dresser of sycamore trees".			
	The book of Amos opens with a historical note about the prophet, then a short oracle announcing Adonai יהוה (YHWH)'s judgment. Amos decounced the crimes against humanity committed by the gentile nations, and told Yisrael that even they have sinned and are guilty of the same crimes. There are total 9 chapters in this prophetic book which can be summarized as following:			
	1) Judgment on Yisrael's neighbouring nations 2) Judgment on Judah (Yehudah) and Yisrael 3) Yisrael's sins and God (Elohim)'s punishment 4) Yisrael has not return to Adonai יהוה (YHWH) despite His severe punishments 5) The coming of "The Day of יהוה (YHWH)"; seek יהוה (YHWH) and live righteous 6) Woe to those at ease in Zion (Tsiyon) 7) Warning visions 8) The coming of bitter mourning 9) Destruction of Yisrael and the promising restoration of the house of Dawid.			

Nr.	Strong's and Scripture Reference	Hebrew Texts / Transliteration & {Phonetic Spelling}	Word(s) Written in English Bibles	Word(s) Written in יהוה Sacred Scriptures
A58	H5662 עבדיה or עבדיהו	Ovadyah עֹבַדְיָה {O-vad-yah} or Ovadyahu עֹבַדְיָהוּ {O-vad-yah-oo}		
	עבדיה Oba. 1:1	Ovadyah עֹבַדְיָה	Obadiah	Obadiah (Ovadyah)
	עבדיהו 1 Kin. 18:3	Ovadyahu עֹבַדְיָהוּ	Obadiah	Obadiah (Ovadyahu)

Ovadyah is the prophet of God (Elohim) and the author of the book by his name. Ovadyah means "servant of YHWH". The book of Obadyah is based on a prophetic vision concerning the fall of Edom, a mountain dwelling nation whose founding father is Esaw. Obadyah described an encounter with God (Elohim), who addresses Edom's arrogance and charges them for their violent actions against their brother nation, the house of Jacob (Yaaqov).

Obadyah wrote the prophesy around 590 BCE. In judgment, God (Elohim) will wipe out the house of Esaw forever, and not even a remnant would remain. The Edomite land will be possessed by Egypt (Mitsrayim) and they will cease to exist as a people. Ovadyah declared that judgment on all the nations in "The Day of יהוה (YHWH)" is near. The children of Yisrael shall return to possess the lands and establish the kingdom of God (Elohim, יהוה (YHWH)).

| A59 | H3124 יונה Jon. 1:1 | Yonah יוֹנָה | Jonah | Yonah |

Yonah, whose name means "dove", is the son of Amittai and a native of Gath-hepher. He is the prophet of the northern kingdom of Yisrael around 8th century BCE, who prophesied during the reign of Jeroboam (Yerovam) II and whom Elohim sent also to prophecy to Nineveh.

Yonah is the central character in the Book of Yonah, in which he is called upon by Adonai יהוה (YHWH) to travel to Nineveh and warn its residents of impending divine wrath. However, Yonah fled from the presence of God (Elohim). He boarded a ship to Tarshish, but was caught in a storm and later thrown into the sea and swallowed up by a giant fish. After 3 days and 3 nights in the giant fish's belly, Yonah finally prayed to יהוה (YHWH) and agreed to pay that he has vowed. So God (Elohim) caused the fish to vomit him out of its belly and sent him to Nineveh. The people of Nineveh repented after hearing the message of Yonah.

In the New Blood Covenant, Yonah was mentioned in the gospel book of Matthew and Luke. The Messiah, Adonai YHWH made a reference to Yonah when He was asked for a sign by some of the scribes and Pharisees. Adonai YHWH said that the sign will be the sign of Yonah. Yonah restoration after 3 days and 3 nights in the giant fish's belly prefigures Yahwah haMashiach's resurrection from the death after 3 days and 3 nights in the heart of the earth. (Mat. 12:38-41, Mat. 16:4 and Luke 11:29-32.)

Nr.	Strong's and Scripture Reference	Hebrew Texts / Transliteration & {Phonetic Spelling}	Word(s) Written in English Bibles	Word(s) Written in יהוה Sacred Scriptures
A60	H4321 מכיה · Mic. 1:1	Mikhah מִיכָה {Mikh-ah}	Micah	Micah (Mikhah)

Micah (Mikhah), also called Mikhayahu in Hebrew means "Who is like YHWH?" Mikhah was called from his rustic home to be a prophet, leaves his familiar surroundings to deliver a stern message of judgment to the princes and people of Yerushalayim. He prophesied during the reigns of kings Yotam, Ahaz and Hezekiah of Judah (Yehudah).

Micah's messages were directed chiefly toward Yerushalayim. He prophesied the future destruction of Yerushalayim and Samaria, the destruction and then future restoration of Judah (Yehudah); he exposed and rebuked the people of Yehudah of their dishonesty and idolatry and corruption in government. He warned the people, of pending destruction if their ways and hearts were not changed. Through it all, יהוה (YHWH)'s righteous demands upon His people are clear: "to do justly, to love mercy, and to walk humbly with your God (Elohim)" (Mic.6:8). Yisrael's response to Micah's charges consisted of three parts: an admission of guilt, a warning of adversaries that Yisrael will rely on יהוה (YHWH) for deliverance and forgiveness, and a prayer for forgiveness and deliverance.

Micah prophesied the coming of the Messiah (haMashiach) in chapter 5. Mic. 5:2 was interpreted as a prophecy that Bethlehem (Beit-lechem), a small village south of Yerushalayim would be the birthplace of haMashiach. The fulfillment of this prophecy was mentioned in Matthew 2:1-6.

Nr.				
A61	H5151 נחוּם Nah. 1:1	Nachum נַחוּם{Nakh-oom}	Nahum	Nachum

Nachum which means "comforter", is a shortened form of Nechemyah (Comfort of YHWH). In this prophetic book, Nachum wrote about the end of the Assyrian Empire and its capital city, Nineveh in a vivid poetic style.

Adonai יהוה (YHWH) had graciously deferred His judgment on the city of Nineveh after the people had repented upon hearing the message of prophet Yonah. However, a hundred years later, Nachum proclaimed the fall and destruction of Nineveh because the Assyrians have forgotten their revival and have returned to their sinful acts of violence, idolatry, and arrogance. Nachum prophesied that Babylon will so destroy the city that no trace of it will remain. The destruction of the capital city of Assyria however, was a consolation to Judah (Yehudah) and all who live in fear of the cruelty of the Assyrians.

Nr.				
A62	H2265 חבקוק Hab. 1:1	Chavakkuk or Chavaqquq חֲבַקּוּק {Kha-vak-kuk}	Habakkuk	Habakkuk (Chavaqquq)

Chavaqquq (English: Habakkuk) is the Hebrew name derived from the verb "chavaq" which means "embrace". Chavaqquq is a prophet of Yisrael who ministers during the "death thrones" of the nation of Judah (Yehudah).

The book of Habakkuk consists of three chapters and was neatly divided into three different genres:

Nr.	Strong's and Scripture Reference	Hebrew Texts / Transliteration & {Phonetic Spelling}	Word(s) Written in English Bibles	Word(s) Written in יהוה Sacred Scriptures
	- A discussion between God (Elohim) and Habakkuk - An oracle of woe - A psalm. The first two chapters are dialog between Adonai יהוה (YHWH) and the prophet. In one of the conversations, יהוה (YHWH) told Habakkuk that the Babylonians will be His chastening rod upon the nation, because of the people's unrepentance heart.			
A63	H6846 צפניה or צפניהו	Tsefanyah צְפַנְיָה {Tse-fan-yah} or Tsefanyahu צְפַנְיָהוּ {Tse-fan-yah-oo}		
	צפניה Zep. 1:1	Tsefanyah צְפַנְיָה	Zephaniah	Zephaniah (Tsefanyah)
	צפניה 2 Kin. 25:18	Tsefanyahu צְפַנְיָהוּ	Zephaniah	Zephaniah (Tsefanyahu)
	Zephaniah (Tsefanyah) means "YHWH has hidden/protected". He is a prophet of יהוה (YHWH) in the time of King Josiah (Yoshiyahu) and the author of the book by his name. The book of Zephaniah contained three chapters, of which can be summarized in these sub-titles: 1) The coming judgment of Judah (Yehudah); 2) The Judgment on Yehudah's enemies; 3) The cleansing judgment of Adonai יהוה (YHWH) on Yerushalayim and the gentile nations. This book concluded with an announcement of hope and joy for Yisrael restoration and fullness of salvation for God (Elohim)'s people.			
A64	H2292 חגי Ezr. 5:1	Chaggai חַגַּי {Khag-gah-ee}	Haggai	Chaggai
	Chaggai means "festive/my holiday" in Hebrew and he is the author of the book by his name. Chaggai was the first of the three post-exile prophets of God (Elohim) from the Neo-Babylonian exile of the house of Judah (Yehudah) (with Zechariah, his contemporary, and Malachi, who lived about one hundred years later). Chaggai prophesy during the building of the Second Temple in Yerushalayim in 520 BCE after the return from captivity in Babylon. Chaggai's message was filled with an urgency for the people to proceed with the rebuilding of the Second Temple. He attributed a recent drought to the people's refusal to rebuild the Temple, which he sees as the key to Yerushalayim's glory. Chaggai and Zechariah exhorted the people and calls the builders to renew courage in Adonai יהוה (YHWH), renew holiness of life, and renew their faith in God (Elohim) who controls the future. Through their efforts, the work of rebuilding the temple was resumed after having suspended for eighteen years. Chaggai reported the rebuilding of the Temple began on September 7 521 BCE (Hag. 1:14-15); the book of Ezra indicates that the Temple was completed on February 25 516 BCE (Ezra 6:15). The book ended with the prediction of the downfall of kingdoms, with Zerubbabel the governor of Judah (Yehudah) chosen by Adonai יהוה (YHWH) as a signet.			

Nr.	Strong's and Scripture Reference	Hebrew Texts / Transliteration & {Phonetic Spelling}	Word(s) Written in English Bibles	Word(s) Written in יהוה Sacred Scriptures
A65	H2148 זכריהו or זכריה	Zekaryahu זְכַרְיָהוּ {Zek-ar-yah-oo} or Zekaryah זְכַרְיָה {Zek-ar-yah}		
	Zec. 1:1	Zekaryah זְכַרְיָה	Zechariah	Zechariah (Zekaryah)
	1 Chro. 5:7	Zekaryahu זְכַרְיָהוּ	Zechariah	Zechariah (Zekaryahu)

The name Zechariah (Zekaryah) means "YHWH remembers". Zekaryah is a prophet commissioned by Adonai יהוה (YHWH) with Chaggai his contemporary, to encourage the people in their unfinished responsibility of rebuilding the temple in the days of Zerubbabel. Zechariah's prophesies took place during the reign of Darius the Great in a post -exilic world after the fall of Yerushalayim in 587/6 BCE. Zechariah was specific about dating his writing (520 – 518 BC).

Zekaryah encouraged the Temple's builders to action by reminding them of the future importance of the temple, and they entered into the building project with wholehearted zeal to complete the Temple in wait for the coming of the Messiah (haMashiach).

Chapter 1-6: The book begins with a preface, which recalls the nation's history, for the purpose of presenting a solemn warning to the present generation. It's followed by a series of eight visions, which may be regarded as symbolic history of Yisrael.

Chapter 7-8: It records an encouraging address of Zechariah to the people, assuring them of God (Elohim)'s presence and blessing.

Chapter 9-11: Oracles that give an outline of the course of God's providential dealings with His people down to the time of the coming of the Messiah.

Chapter 12-14 Oracles that point out the glories that awaits Yisrael in "the latter day", the final conflicts and triumph of Adonai יהוה (YHWH)'s kingdom.

| A66 | H4401 מלאכי
Mal. 1:1 | Malakhi
מַלְאָכִי
{Mal-a-khee} | Malachi | Malakhi |

Malachi (Malakhi) means "My messenger", a prophet in the days of Nehemiah (Nechemyah) who wrote the last book of the Prophets (Nevi'im) section in the Hebrew Tanakh Scriptures.

The book of Malakhi was written to correct the lax religious and social behavior of the Israelites (Yisraeli) particularly the priests (kohanim) in post-exilic Yerushalayim. Using the question-and-answer method, Malakhi probed deeply into their problems of hypocrisy, infidelity, mixed marriages, divorce, false worship and arrogance. So sinful has the nation become that God (Elohim)'s words to the people no longer have any impact. For four hundred years after Malakhi's ringing condemnations, Adonai יהוה (YHWH) remained silent. Only with the coming of the last prophet, John the Baptist (Yochanan haMatvil) (prophesied in Mal. 3:1) did Adonai יהוה (YHWH) spoke to His people again through a prophet's voice.

Nr.	Strong's and Scripture Reference	Hebrew Texts / Transliteration & {Phonetic Spelling}	Word(s) Written in English Bibles	Word(s) Written in יהוה Sacred Scriptures
A67	G2491 Ióannés G910 Baptistes Mat. 3:1	יוחנן המטביל Yo-cha-nan ha-Mat-vil	John the Baptist	John the Baptist (Yochanan haMatvil)

John the Baptist (Yochanan haMatvil) was considered the last prophet of the First Blood Covenant, the son of Zechariah (Zekaryah) the priest (kohen) and his wife, Elisabeth. He was a Jewish (Yehudi) itinerant preacher in the early 1st century AD.

Yochanan the Baptist is a Jewish (Yehudi) ascetic who was considered the precursor or forerunner of the Messiah (haMashiach), Adonai YHWH. The work of John the Baptist fulfilled the prophesy of Isaiah concerning him which was written in Isa.40:3: The voice of him that crieth in the wilderness, "Prepare you the way of יהוה (Yahwah, YHWH) make straight in the desert a highway for our God (Elohim)." This prophesy was written also in all the three gospel books: Matthew 3:3, Mark 1:3 and Luke 3:4.

According to the Gospel of Luke, John the Baptist and Yahwah haMashiach were relatives, as it is mentioned by the angel Gavriel in Luke 1:36 that Elisabeth (mother of prophet John) was the cousin of Mary (Miriam) who gave birth to Yahwah haMashiach.

| A68 | Matthew G3156 Matthaios Mat. 9:9 | מַתִּתְיָהוּ Mat-tit-yahu | Matthew | Matthew (Mattityahu) |

Matthew is the English form of Greek name "Matthaios, which was derived from the Hebrew name מַתִּתְיָהוּ (Mattityahu), meaning "Gift of YHWH" from the roots מַתָּן (mattan) meaning "gift" and יָה (Yah). Matthew, also known with surname Lewi, was one of the twelve apostles. He was a tax collector, and the author of the first gospel in the New Blood Covenant (NT).

Matthew wrote the gospel mainly for the Jewish (Yehudi) people, to show them that Adonai Yahwah (YHWH) is truly the Messiah (haMashiach). In the gospel of Matthew (Mattityahu), Yahwah haMashiach was presented as the King of the Jews (Yehudim), the long-awaited Messiah (Mashiach) prophesied by the prophets of Adonai יהוה (YHWH). Yahwah haMashiach's geneology, baptism, teachings, and miracles all pointed to the same conclusion: Yahwah haMashiach is the prophesied King of the Jews (Yehudim), as given witnessed by all the prophets in the Nevi'im (Prophets) of Tanakh Scriptures.

| A69 | G3138 Markos | - | Mark | Mark (Marqos) |

Mark is the English form of the Latin name Markos/Marqos and Greek name Markos. Apostle Mark was the author of the second gospel in the New Blood Covenant (NT). Gospel of Mark is one of the four canonical gospels. It tells of the ministry of Yahwah haMashiach from His baptism by John the Baptist to His death and burial and the discovery of the empty tomb.

Mark portrayed Adonai Yahwah haMashiach as a servant in action, an exorcist, a healer and a miracle worker. Yahwah haMashiach is the Humanity of El (Mark 1:1, 3:11, 15:39) but He kept His identity in secret, concealing it in parables as He spoke. In the end of this gospel book, Adonai Yahwah haMashiach commissions His disciples to spread the gospel and continue His work in His power.

Nr.	Strong's and Scripture Reference	Hebrew Texts / Transliteration & {Phonetic Spelling}	Word(s) Written in English Bibles	Word(s) Written in יהוה Sacred Scriptures
A70	G3065 Loukas	-	Luke	Luke (Luqas)

Luke is the English form of Latin Lucas, from the Greek name Loukas meaning "from Lucania". Luke was a physician who travelled in the company of the apostle Paul. According to tradition, he was the author of the third canonical Gospels and Book of Acts in the New Blood Covenant (NT).

The gospel of Luke recorded the origins, birth, ministry, death, resurrection and ascension of Adonai Yahwah haMashiach. The author carefully narrated the perfect humanity of Yahwah haMashiach. He used the Gospel of Mark as a source for the narrative of Yahwah haMashiach's earthly life.

| A71 | John
John 1:15 | יוֹחָנָן
{Yo-kha-nan} | John | John (Yochanan) |

John is the English form of the Latin name Iohannes and Greek name Ioannes, which was derived from Hebrew name יוֹחָנָן (Yochanan) meaning "YHWH is gracious".

John (Yochanan) is traditionally regarded as the author of the fourth gospel and Book of Revelation. In the gospel of John, Apostle John (Yochanan) portrayed Adonai Yahwah haMashiach in His deity as the Humanity of El (YHWH). Following an extended eyewitness description of the Upper Room meal and discourse, John recorded events leading up to the resurrection.

Read also study note B47 on "Humanity of El" in Appendix II-B.

| A72 | G2786 Kephas
Mark 11:21,
John 1:42 | Kephas / Kefa
כֵּיפָא {Kay-fa} | Peter /
Cephas | Peter (Kefa) /
Cephas (Kefa) |

The name Cephas (Hebrew: כֵּיפָא Kefa, Greek: Petros, English: Peter) means "rock" in Aramaic, it's the new name given by Yahwah haMashiach to Apostle Simon Peter, also known as שמעון בר יונה Simon bar-Yonah.

| A73 | H7856 שאול
Acts 7:58 | Shaul שָׁאוּל
{Shaw-ool} | Shaul | Shaul |

Shaul was the original Hebrew name שאול (Sha'ul) of Apostle Paul, meaning "asked for, prayed for".

| A74 | G3972 Paulos
Acts 13:9 | - | Paul | Paul |

Paul the Apostle (Latin: Paulus; Greek: Paulos; and also known by his Jewish (Yehudi) name, Shaul of Tarsus (Hebrew: שאול התרסי: Sha'ūl ha-Tarsī), was an apostle who taught the gospel of Yahwah haMashiach to the first-century world. According to the New Blood Covenant (NT) "Acts of the Apostles" (known as Acts), Paul was dedicated to persecuting the early disciples of Yahwah haMashiach in the area of Yerushalayim prior to his conversion.

In the mid-30s to the mid-50s AD Paul founded several assemblies in Asia Minor and Europe. He took advantage of his status as both a Jew (Yehudi) and a Roman citizen to minister to both Jewish (Yehudi) and Roman audiences. Thirteen of the twenty-seven books in the New Blood Covenant (NT) have traditionally been attributed to Paul.

Nr.	Strong's and Scripture Reference	Hebrew Texts / Transliteration & {Phonetic Spelling}	Word(s) Written in English Bibles	Word(s) Written in יהוה Sacred Scriptures
A75	G5095 Timotheos 2 Cor 1:1	-	Timothy	Timothy
	Timothy (Greek: Timótheos, meaning "honouring God (Elohim)" or "honoured by God (Elohim)" was an early evangelist and the first bishop of Ephesus. Timothy was from the Lycaonian city of Lystra in Asia Minor, born of a Jewish (Yehudi) mother who had become a believer of Yahwah haMashiach, and a Greek father. The Apostle Paul met him during his second missionary journey and he became Paul's companion and co-worker along with Silas. The New Blood Covenant (NT) indicates that Timothy travelled with Paul the apostle, who was also his mentor. Paul entrusted him with important assignments. He is addressed as the recipient of the First and Second Epistles to Timothy.			
A76	G2385 Iakobos Jam. 1:1	-	James	James (Yaaqov)
	James is the English form of the Late Latin name Iacomus, which was derived from Greek name Iakobos; the Hebrew name is Yaaqov (transliterated in English as Jacob). Throughout James epistle to Jewish (Yehudi) believers, he integrates true faith and everyday practical experience by stressing that true faith must manifest itself in works of faith in Yahwah haMashiach.			
A77	G2455 Ioudas H3063 Yehudah Jude 1:1	Yehudah יְהוּדָה {Ye-hoo-dah}	Jude	Jude (Yehudah)
	Jude is the English form of the Greek-Latin name "Ioudas" which is called "Yehudah" in Hebrew, meaning "YHWH is Praised". At the beginning of his letter, Jude (Yehudah) spoke about believers' common salvation. He then challenged believers to contend for the faith in Yahwah haMashiach because apostasy has arosed and the false teachers have crept into the assembly, turning Yahwah's grace into unbounded license to do as they please. Jude asked reader to recall how even after Adonai יהוה (YHWH) has saved His own people out of the land of Egypt (Mitsrayim), He did not hesitate to destroy those who fell into unbelief and sins, much as He punished the angels who fell from their original state. Jude called believers to persevere in his final message and ended his epistle with a doxology.			

Nr.	Strong's and Scripture Reference	Hebrew Text / Transliteration & {Phonetic Spelling}	Word(s) Written in English Bibles	Word(s) Written in יהוה Sacred Scriptures
B1a	H430 אלהים Gen. 1:1	Elohim אֱלֹהִים {El-o-heem}	God	God (Elohim)

"Elohim" is the Hebrew title of the Creator of heavens and earth which means "Mighty One", commonly translated as "God" in all the English Bibles. The -im suffix of Elohim in Hebrew indicates the plural form i.e. many attributes of Creator.

Examples of the other suffixes of Elohim which consist of pronoun or preposition are:

i) Elohei אלֹהֵי {El-o-heh-ee} = Elohim of
ii) Elohai אלֹהַי {El-o-ha-ee} = my Elohim
iii) Eloheinu אלֹהֵינוּ {El-o-heh-ee-noo} = our Elohim
iv) Eloheika אלֹהֶיךָ {El-o-heh-ka} = thy/your Elohim
v) Eloheikem = אלֹהֵיהֶם {El-o-heh-hem} = their Elohim
vi) Elohaw = אֱלֹהָיו {El-o-haw}= his Elohim
vii) Eloheha = אֱלֹהֶיהָ {El-o-heh-ha}= her Elohim

Elohim is also found in the singular form as "El", "H426 Elah" and "H433 Eloah". Elahin (which is used in the book of Daniel 2:47) is the plural for Elah, the Aramaic word equivalent to Elohim.

B1b	H430 אלהים Gen. 31:30	elohim אֱלֹהִים {el-o-heem}	gods	gods (elohim)
	Exo. 22:20		god	god (elohim)
	Exo.18:11		gods	rulers (elohim)
	Psa. 82:1		gods	judges (elohim)
	Psa. 97:7		gods	mighty ones (elohim)

Depending on the context of the Scriptures, the Hebrew word "אלהים elohim" can have many different meanings besides rendering it as God (referring to YHWH Almighty). Below are the meanings written in the BibleWorks program:

1a) rulers, judges 1b) divine ones 1c) angels 1d) gods 2) (plural intensive - singular meaning) 2a) god, goddess 2b) godlike one 2c) works or special possessions of God 2d) the (true) God.

B2	H430 & H2416 אלהים חיים Deu. 5:26 Mat. 16:16	a) Elohim chayim אֱלֹהִים חַיִּים {E-lo-heem Khah-yeem}	living God	living God (Elohim chayim)
	אלהים חי 2 Kin. 19:4	b) Elohim chai אֱלֹהִים חַי {E-lo-eem Khah-ee}		living God (Elohim chai)
	H410 & H2416 אל חי Jos. 3:10	c) El chai אֵל חַי {El Khah-ee}		living God (El chai)

The word "חיים chayim" and "חי chai" means "living". "Elohim Chayim חיים אלהים is the Hebrew words for "living God". "El chai חי אל" was the singular form of Hebrew words used in the book of Joshua (Yehoshua) which has the same meaning.

Nr.	Strong's and Scripture Reference	Hebrew Text / Transliteration & {Phonetic Spelling}	Word(s) Written in English Bibles	Word(s) Written in יהוה Sacred Scriptures
	H426 & H2416 אלהא חיא Dan. 6:20	Elah chaiya אֱלָהָא חַיָּא {El-ah Khah-ee-ya}	living God	living God (Elah chaiya)
	In Syrian/Aramaic language (Aramit), the "living God" is called "Elah chaiya אֱלָהָא חַיָּא" which was used in the book of Daniel.			
B3	Gen. 1:26	-	Let us make mankind in our image, after our likeness	Let Us make mankind in Our image, after Our likeness.
	"Let Us make man in Our image, after Our likeness" refers to God (Elohim)'s counsel of His own will (Eph 1:11).			
B4	Gen. 1:27	Betsalmow בְּצַלְמוֹ {be-tsal-mow}	in his own image	in His own image
	"His own image" refers to the Messiah (haMashiach - Humanity of El) who was foreordained before the foundation of the world (1 Peter 1:20, Eph1:4) for which Adam and mankind were patterned after the image of the Messiah (haMashiach). "His" is singular, denotes one God (Elohim) who alone created mankind.			
B5a	H410 אל Gen. 46:3	El אֵל {ale}	God	Mighty One (El)
	H433 אלוה Deut 32:15	Eloah אֱלוֹהַּ {El-o-ah}		God (Eloah)
	H426 אלה Dan. 2:18	Elah / Elahh אֱלָהּ {El-ah} Elahin (pl.) אֱלָהִין {El-ah-in}		God (Elah)
	Dan. 6:22	Elahi אֱלָהִי {El-ah-ee}	My God	My God (Elahi)
B5b	Psa. 81:9	el	god	god (el)
	El is the transliteration of the Hebrew word אל, the singular form of "God (Elohim)" which means "Mighty One", rendered in the English Bibles as "God". El is God (Elohim) in all of His power and strength, as Elohim the Omnipotent. El is the Mighty One who knows all (first occurrence in Gen. 14:18-22) and sees all (Gen. 16:13), and that perform all things for His people (Psalm 57:2). El is a generic Semitic designation for deity. Book of Iyov (Job) and Psalms have most of the 238 occurrences of El. The small letter "el" is the translation for "god" the man-made graven image/idol. "H426 Elah" is the Syrian/Aramaic (Aramit) corresponding to "H420 El" and "H433 Eloah"; and "Elahi" is the Aramaic corresponding to "Adonai" for "my God".			
B5c	Josh. 22:22	יהוה אֵלוֹ אֱלֹהִים El Elohim YHWH	The LORD God of gods	The Mighty One (El), God יהוה (Elohim YHWH)
	This verse is retranslated according to the actual wording in Hebrew Scriptures: "El Elohim YHWH" which means "God יהוה the Mighty One".			

Nr.	Strong's and Scripture Reference	Hebrew Text / Transliteration & {Phonetic Spelling}	Word(s) Written in English Bibles	Word(s) Written in יהוה Sacred Scriptures
B6a	H410 & H5945 אל עליון Gen 14:18	El Elyon אֵל עֶלְיוֹן	most high God	Most High God (El Elyon)
	H426 &H5943 אלהא עליא Dan. 3:26	Elaha Illaahi אֱלָהָא עִלָּיָא		Most High God (Elaha Ilaahi)
B6b	H5945 עליון Num. 24:16	Elyon עֶלְיוֹן {El-yon}	most high	Most High (Elyon)
	H5943 עלי Dan. 4:17	Illaahi עִלָּי {Il-lahh-ee}		Most High (Illaahi)

a) "El Elyon אל עליון" is the Hebrew word translated as "Most High God" in English Bibles; El Elyon is not the name of God (Elohim) יהוה but an attribute name. "Elaha Illaahi אלהא עליא" is the Syrian/Aramaic equivalent of the Hebrew, El Elyon.

b) "Elyon עליון" is the Hebrew word translated as "Most High" in English. In Daniel 4:17, the Most High is written in Syrian/Aramaic language (Aramit) as "עלי Illahi".

| B7a | H7706 שדי Gen 49:25 | Shaddai שַׁדַּי {Shad-dah-ee} | Almighty | Almighty (Shaddai) |
| B7b | Gen. 17:1 | El Shaddai אֵל שַׁדַּי | God Almighty | Almighty God (El Shaddai) |

"El Shaddai אֵל שַׁדַּי" is translated in English as "Almighty God". This Hebrew title "El Shaddai" is attribute of God (El) יהוה associated with His giving of grace and ability to supply all the needs of His people. It is first used in Gen. 17:1 to show Avraham that He Who call him out could supply all of his needs.

Dr. Eli Lizorkin-Eyzenberg in his article on the topic "El Shaddai" published November 6, 2013 on Israel Institute of Biblical Studies website, suggested that "El Shaddai" should be more appropriately translated as "El All-Sufficient" based on his study on the Hebrew root words. Another translation suggested in the Concordant Old Testament was "El Who Suffices.

"El Shaddai אֵל שַׁדַּי" is not another name of יהוה, but one of the many attributes of God (El).

Reference:
https://blog.israelbiblicalstudies.com/jewish-studies/he-is-our-el-shadai-insight-by-dr-eli/

| B8 | H410 & H7210 אתה אל ראי Gen. 16:13 | Attah El Roi אַתָּה אֵל רֳאִי {At-tah El Ro-ee} | Thou God seeth me | Thou God Seeth Me (Attah El Roi) |

"H7210 ראי roi" means "sees me". "El Roi אל ראי" is not another name of Elohim יהוה but a calling for יהוה Who is an Omnipresent El.

| B9 | H430 אלהי האלהים Deu. 10:17 | Elohei haElohim אֱלֹהֵי הָאֱלֹהִים | God of gods | Supreme God (Elohei haElohim) |
| | H426 אֱלָהּ Dan 2:47 | Elah Elahin אֱלָהּ אֱלָהִין | | Supreme God (Elah Elahin) |

Nr.	Strong's and Scripture Reference	Hebrew Text / Transliteration & {Phonetic Spelling}	Word(s) Written in English Bibles	Word(s) Written in יהוה Sacred Scriptures
	Small letter "gods (elohim)" was referred to the "pagan idols/graven images"; but "elohim" could also means "mighty ones" instead of "gods". Therefore the translation of "God of gods" seems to be inappropriate since the true living Elohim יהוה cannot be the God of "gods (the pagan idols/graven images)". A more appropriate translation for the Hebrew words "Elohei haElohim אלהי האלהים" would be "Supreme God" or "God of the mighty ones" instead of "God of gods". In Daniel 2:47, the Aramaic (Aramit) words "Elah Elahin אלה אלהין" were used instead of the Hebrew.			
B10	H3068 & H6944 קדש ליהוה Exo 28:36 Exo 39:30	Qodesh la-YHWH קֹדֶשׁ לַיהוה {Ko-desh la-Yah-Wah}	HOLINESS TO THE LORD	Holiness Unto יהוה (Qodesh la-YHWH)
	The LORD in this phrase is "יהוה (YHWH)" according to the Hebrew Scriptures.			
B11	H3068 & H430 יהוה אלהיך Deu. 28:52	יהוה Eloheikha יהוה אֱלֹהֶיךָ {Yah-Wah Elo-hei-kha}	The LORD thy God	יהוה your God (YHWH Eloheikha)
	This phrase "The LORD thy God" based on the original written words in the Hebrew Scriptures can be transliterated as "יהוה Eloheikha: יהוה אלהיך"; Eloheika is Hebrew title for Elohim with suffix, meaning "thy/your God (Elohim)".			
B12	H136 אדני Gen. 15:2	Adonai אֲדֹנָי {Ad-o-na-ee}	the Lord	my Lord (Adonai)
	"H136 Adonai אדני" is a Hebrew word, meaning "my Lord/Master" or simply "Lord/Master". In Strong's Exhaustive Concordance, "H136 Adonai" is defined as: "Am emphatic form of 'adown (H113 adon); the Lord -- (my) Lord." Read B13: H113 אדון Adon. In the KJV and most other Old Testament bibles, "Adonai אדני" was translated as "the Lord", a title used for addressing God (Elohim) יהוה. Adonai is first used in Gen. 15:2: "Adonai YHWH אדני יהוה" which means "My Lord YHWH (Yahwah)". In the New Testament of the English Bibles, the translator rendered both "Adonai אדני" and "יהוה (YHWH) as "the Lord". In this יהוה Sacred Scriptures, "Adonai" is written in parenthesis besides "the Lord" according to the writing of the Hebrew Scriptures.			
B13	H113 אדון Gen 40:1	adon אָדוֹן {aw-don}	lord	lord (adon)
	אדון Psa. 114:7	Adon	the Lord	the Lord (Adon)
	אדנים Isa. 26:13	adonim אֲדֹנִים {aw-don-eem}	lords	lords (adonim)
	אדני Gen 18:12	adoni אֲדֹנִי (aw-don-ee)	my lord	my lord (adoni)

Nr.	Strong's and Scripture Reference	Hebrew Text / Transliteration & {Phonetic Spelling}	Word(s) Written in English Bibles	Word(s) Written in יהוה Sacred Scriptures
	Besides addressing the Supreme God (Elohim) יהוה with title "Adon אדון" as in Psa. 114:7, the Hebrew word "adon אדון" is also used as a title of superiority for earthly rulers or "lords/masters"; adonim is the plural of adon (lord/master).			
B14	אדני האדנים Deut 10:17	Adonei haAdonim אֲדֹנֵי הָאֲדֹנִים	Lord of lords	Supreme Lord (Adonei haAdonim)
	The Hebrew words "Adonei haAdonim" were translated in English as "Lord of lords". In this Scriptures, the words "Supreme Lord" is used.			
B15a	H1961 & H834 אהיה אשר אהיה Exo. 3:14	Ehyeh asher ehyeh אֶהְיֶה אֲשֶׁר אֶהְיֶה	I AM THAT I AM	I AM Who I AM (Ehyeh Asher Ehyeh)
	"אהיה Ehyeh" is from the Hebrew root word "H1961 היה hayah", meaning "be or become, be in existence, come to pass."			
	In the book of *Parke-Taylor, G.H. (1975) YHWH: The Divine Name in the Bible (pg. 51)*, he wrote and explained the word "Ehyeh" in verse Exo. 3:14 'I AM (Ehyeh) has sent me unto you' is the first person form of "hayah", "to be", and owing to the peculiarities of Hebrew grammar means "I am", I was", and "I will be". His explanation of "Ehyeh" in Hebrew grammar context confirmed God (Elohim) יהוה (YHWH) declaration of Himself in **Rev. 1:8: "I am Alpha and Omega, the beginning and the ending," saith יהוה (YHWH), Who is, and Who was, and Who is to come, God of hosts (Elohei Tsevaot).**			
	Thus "Ehyeh asher ehyeh" which was translated as "I AM Who I AM" could also mean "I Will Be/Become Who I Will Be/Become".			
B15b	אהיה Exo. 3:14, John 8:58	Ehyeh אֶהְיֶה {ay-yeh}	I AM	I AM (Ehyeh)
	Many believers has taken this verse: "I AM (Ehyeh) has sent me unto you" to say that "I AM" or Hebrew "Ehyeh" (some pronounce it "Ahayah") is the name of God (Elohim). This could not be true because God (Elohim) has only one holy and everlasting name: יהוה (YHWH) which was revealed in Exo. 3:15, also many other verses in the Tanakh Scriptures. Read also study notes A1 in Appendix II-A for further study about God (Elohim)'s true name.			
B16	Exo. 3:15	יהוה אלהי אברהם אלהי אבתיכם אלהי יצחק ואלהי יעקב	The LORD God of your fathers, the God of Abraham, the God of Isaac, and the God of Jacob...	יהוה, God (Elohim) of your fathers, God (Elohim) of Avraham, God (Elohim) of Yitschaq and God (Elohim) of Yaaqov...
			this *is* my name for ever, and this *is* my memorial unto all generations.	this is My name forever, and this is My memorial unto all generations.
	In verse Exo 3:15, God (Elohim) revealed His name as: "יהוה (**YHWH**)", the God (Elohim) of Avraham, Yitschaq and Yaaqov. God (Elohim) goes on to stress that His name יהוה (YHWH) is forever and is His memorial to all generations.			

Nr.	Strong's and Scripture Reference	Hebrew Text / Transliteration & {Phonetic Spelling}	Word(s) Written in English Bibles	Word(s) Written in יהוה Sacred Scriptures
B17	H7776 שבתון Exo. 16:23, Exo. 35:2	Shabbaton שַׁבָּתוֹן {Shab-ba-ton}	sabbath of rest	Shabbaton

Shabbaton is a weekly day of rest and ceasing from work, which falls on every seventh day in a week.

| B18 | H7676 שבת Exo. 16:23 | Shabbat שַׁבָּת {Shab-bat} | sabbath | Shabbat |

Shabbat is the Hebrew word, meaning "day or year of rest".

B19	H6453 פסח Exo. 12:11, Mat. 26:2	Pesach פֶּסַח {peh-sakh}	passover	Passover (Pesach)
	Exo. 12:21		passover	passover lamb (pesach)
	Acts 12:4		Easter	Passover (Pesach)

"H6453 pesach תֶּסַם" is the Hebrew word for "passover". Pesach carries a few meanings:
a) sacrifice of passover
b) animal victim of the passover
c) festival of the Pesach (Passover)

Passover (Pesach): the name given to the chief of the three great historical annual festivals of the Jews (Yehudim). It was kept in remembrance of יהוה (YHWH)'s passing over the houses of the Yisraeli (Exo. 12:13) when the first born of all the Egyptians were destroyed. (Exo. 23:15; Mark14:1; Acts12:3), because during its celebration, no leavened bread was to be eaten or even kept in the household (Exo. 12:15). The word afterwards came to denote the lamb that was slain at the feast (Mark 14:12-14; 1 Cor 5:7).

In Acts 12:4, the English bible used the word "Easter" (also called Resurrection Sunday or Pascha in Greek-Latin), a festival celebrated by the Roman Catholics and Christians to commemorate the death and resurrection of their savior Jesus Christ/Yeshua in replacement of Adonai YHWH's Passover (Pesach). The Easter is celebrated on a fixed Sunday in second or third week of April, two days after the Good Friday.

Passover (Pesach) is not the same holiday as Easter as both are not celebrated on the same way and not the same day. Passover (Pesach) is to be celebrated on the 14th day of the month of Nisan (Aviv) according to the commandment of God (Elohim) as written in the Hebrew Tanakh Scriptures (Lev. 23:5). Below is the etymology of Easter taken from a book called *"Wallis, Faith (1999). Bede: The Reckoning of Time. Liverpool University Press, p.54"* which shows proof that "Easter" is not the feast for commemorating the resurrection of our true Messiah (Mashiach) and Savior, Yahwah haMashiach.

Etymology of "Easter":
The modern English term "Easter", cognate with modern Dutch "ooster" and German "Ostern", developed from an Old English word that usually appears in the form Ēastrun, -on, or -an; but also as Ēastru, -o; and Ēastre or Ēostre. Bede provides the only documentary source for the etymology of the word, in his 'Reckoning of Time'. He wrote that Ēosturmōnaþ (Old English 'Month of Ēostre', translated in Bede's time as "Paschal month") was an English month, corresponding to April, which he says "was once called after a goddess of theirs named Ēostre, in whose honour feasts were celebrated in that month."

Nr.	Strong's and Scripture Reference	Hebrew Text / Transliteration & {Phonetic Spelling}	Word(s) Written in English Bibles	Word(s) Written in יהוה Sacred Scriptures
B20	H2282 & H4682 חג המצה Exo.12:17, Mat. 26:17	Chag haMatzot חַג הַמַצּוֹת {khag ha-mats-tsot}	feast of unleaven bread	The Feast of Unleaven Bread (Chag haMatzot)

The Feast of Unleavened Bread is the first appointment in the year designated by יהוה (YHWH) our God (Elohim) to meet with Him in a holy convocation. The festival in itself extends over seven days with the first and the last days being high Sabbaths in which no work is done and it is commenced by the Passover (Pesach) memorial on the fourteenth (14ᵗʰ) day of the first month at twilight. The instruction to observe this feast was given in relation to Passover (Pesach) and is a continuation of it:

"These are the feasts of יהוה (YHWH), holy convocations which you shall proclaim at their appointed times. On the fourteenth day of the first month at twilight is יהוה (YHWH)'s Passover. And on the fifteenth day of the same month is the Feast of Unleavened Bread to יהוה (YHWH). On the first day you shall have a holy convocation, you shall do no customary work on it. But you shall offer an offering made by fire to יהוה (YHWH) for seven days. The seventh day shall be a holy convocation; you shall do no customary work on it" (Leviticus 23: 4-8) Read also Exodus 13: 4-10; Numbers 28:16-25; Deuteronomy 16: 2-4, 8.

Passover then, is on the fourteenth day from the commencement of the new year and is eaten after twilight on that day, which is then the start of the fifteenth day and the first High Sabbath of the week of Unleavened Bread.

Reference: *https://en.wikibooks.org/wiki/Hebrew_Roots/Holy_Days/Week_of_Unleavened_Bread*

Matzah/Matstsah (pl. Matzot) is the Hebrew word for 'unleavened bread," and the feast itself is a reminder of how Elohim miraculously delivered the children of Yisrael from their Egyptian bondage. They were told to eat in a hurry and be ready at any time in the night to escape from Egypt. Since it takes time to place leaven in a batch of dough and allow it to rise, יהוה (YHWH) instructed His people to eat bread made without leaven during their Pesach (Passover) meal.

To commemorate the event, Adonai יהוה (YHWH) said, "You shall eat no leavened bread with it. Seven days you shall eat it with unleavened bread, the bread of affliction—for you came out of the land of Egypt in haste—that all the days of your life you may remember the day when you came out of the land of Egypt" (Deuteronomy 16:3; see also Exodus 12:39).

The Feast of Unleavened Bread is observed in the early spring, beginning on the 15ᵗʰ day of the Hebrew month of Nisan (may fall between March – April of Gregorian calender) which lasted for seven days.

Nr.	Strong's and Scripture Reference	Hebrew Text / Transliteration & {Phonetic Spelling}	Word(s) Written in English Bibles	Word(s) Written in יהוה Sacred Scriptures
B21	H7620 & H4682 חג שבעה Deu. 16:10	Chag Shavuot חַג שָׁבֻעוֹת {Khag Sha-voo-ot}	feast of weeks	Feast of Weeks (Chag Shavuot)
	Acts 20:16		Pentacost	Pentacost (Chag Shavuot)

"Shavuot" is the plural word for "Shavua", meaning "a period of seven (days, years), heptad, week" **Shavuot** or **Shovuos** in Ashkenazi usage; **Shavu'oth** in Sephardi and Mizrahi Hebrew (Hebrew: שבועות, lit. "Weeks"), is known as the **Feast of Weeks** in English and as Pentecost (Πεντηκοστή) in Ancient Greek. It is a Jewish (Yehudi) holiday that occurs on the sixth day of the Hebrew month of Sivan (may fall between May 14 – June 15).

Shavuot has a double significance. It marks the all-important wheat harvest in Yisrael (Exodus 34:22), and it commemorates the anniversary of the day when יהוה gave the Torah to the nation of Yisrael assembled at Mount Sinai. The holiday is one of the three Biblical pilgrimage festivals (*Shalosh Regalim*). The word Shavuot means weeks, and it marks the conclusion of the Counting of the Omer.

| B22 | H8643 תרועה Lev. 23:24, Num. 29:1 | Teruah תְּרוּעָה {Te-roo-ah} | blowing of trumpets | blowing of trumpets (Teruah) |

Teruah is a Hebrew word translated as "blowing of trumpets". The Scripture (Num. 29:1) refers to the first (1st) day of the seventh month (1 Tishrei) as "יום תְּרוּעָה Yom Teruah" which is known as "The Day of Shofar-blasts", also called "Feast of Trumpets". This feast falls on the month of Sept/Oct of Gregorian calender.

Note:

Tishrei is the first month of the civil year (which starts on 1 Tishrei) and the seventh month of the ecclesiastical year (which is equal to Nisan) in the Hebrew calender. Tishrei is a Babylonian name, an autumn month of 30 days, occurs in September- October of Gregorian calender. Before the Babylonian exile, the month was called Ethanim (1 Kings 8:2)

| B23 | H3725 & H3117 יום כפר Lev 23:27 | Yom haKippurim יוֹם הַכִּפֻּרִים {Yom ha-kip-poo-rim} | day of atonement | Day of the Atonements (Yom haKippurim) |

Day of the Atonements is the feast celebrated on the tenth (10th) day of the seventh month (Tishrei), called Yom haKippurim in Hebrew. Kippurim is the plural of Kippur (H3725 כפר Kippur) in Hebrew which means "atonement". This feast falls on the month of Sept/Oct of Gregorian calender.

| B24 | H5521 & H2282 סכה חג Lev. 23:34, John 7:2 | Chag Sukkot חַג הַסֻּכּוֹת {Khag Sook-kot} | Feast of Tabernacles | Feast of Tabernacles (Chag Sukkot) |

Sukkot is the feast celebrated on the fifteen (15th) day of the seventh month (Tishrei), known as Feast of Booths (Sukkot), also called Feast of Tabernacles or Feast of the Ingathering. This feast falls on the month of Sept/Oct of Gregorian calender.

Nr.	Strong's and Scripture Reference	Hebrew Text / Transliteration & {Phonetic Spelling}	Word(s) Written in English Bibles	Word(s) Written in יהוה Sacred Scriptures
B25	H3104 יובל Lev 25:9	Yovel יוֹבֵל{Yov-ale}	jubile	Jubilee (Yovel)

The Jubilee (Hebrew: יובל yovel) is the year at the end of seven cycles of Shemittah (Sabbatical years), and according to Biblical regulations had a special impact on the ownership and management of land in the Land of Yisrael; there is some debate whether it was the 49th year (the last year of seven sabbatical cycles, referred to as the Sabbath's Sabbath), or whether it was the following (50th) year. Jubilee deals largely with land, property, and property rights.

According to Lewiticus, slaves and prisoners would be freed, debts would be forgiven, and the mercies of YHWH would be particularly manifest.

| B26 | H8059 שמטה Deu. 15:1 | shemittah שְׁמִטָּה {she-mit-tah} | release | release (shemittah) |

"H8059 shemittah שמטה" is the Hebrew word, meaning "letting drop of exactions, temporary remitting, release (of debt)".

| B27 | H5521 & H3068 שמטה ליהוה Deu. 15:2 | shemittah le-YHWH שְׁמִטָּ ה לַיהֹוָה {she-mit-tah le-Yah-Wah} | release of the LORD | release of יהוה (shemittah le-YHWH). |

The Shabbat year (**Shemittah**, Hebrew: שמיטה literally "release") also called the Shabbatical year or sheviit (שביעית, literally "seventh") is the seventh year of the seven-year agricultural cycle mandated by the Torah for the Land of Yisrael, and still observed in the contemporary Judaism (Yehudahism).

B28a	H8451 תורה Exo. 13:9	תּוֹרָה {tow-rah}	law	Torah
	Exo. 24:12			Law (Torah)
	H8451 תורה Lev. 6:9 G3551 nomos Gal. 3:17			law (torah)

Torah (Hebrew: תורה, Greek: νόμος nomos) is the Hebrew word which means "Instruction", "Teaching" or "Law". In the Scriptures, "Torah" can be referred as: five books of Mosheh (which is the 1st of the 3-part sections of the Tanakh, also known as "Torah Scroll" or "Pentateuch"); or as God (Elohim)'s law which is eternal and that which is temporal; or simply: the teaching, instruction and law of God (Elohim).

In the English bibles, the word "torah" was commonly translated as "law" throughout the whole Old and New Testament, which need to be studied very carefully in order to correctly understand what "torah" the Scriptures actually refers to.

In this Sacred Scriptures, the word "law" is substituted with by the following words as according to the context of the Scriptures:

Nr.	Strong's and Scripture Reference	Hebrew Text / Transliteration & {Phonetic Spelling}	Word(s) Written in English Bibles	Word(s) Written in יהוה Sacred Scriptures

i) Torah
   a) Refer to the 1st-part of the 3-part sections of the Tanakh: Five books of Mosheh.
   b) Teaching, instruction and law of Adonai יהוה (YHWH) in general.
   The original Hebrew word "Torah: תורה" is used in Lev. 11:46 instead of English word "law" in order not to be misunderstood as the temporary "law (torah)" that was added because of transgressions. The Torah (teaching, instruction and law) of Adonai יהוה (YHWH) in Leviticus chapter 11 regarding the clean and unclean animals is eternal and was not "nailed to the stake".

i) Law (Torah)
   The capital-letter words "Law (Torah)" refers to the eternal Torah of Adonai יהוה (YHWH) which apostle James (Yaaqov) called it "the perfect Law (Torah) of liberty (Jam. 1:25) or the royal Law (Torah) (Jam. 2:8)". The eternal Torah of God (Elohim) is holy (Rom. 7:12) and spiritual (Rom. 7:14) and is perfect (Psa. 19:7).

ii) law (torah)
   The small-letter words "law (torah)" refers to the temporary laws (ordinances) of Adonai יהוה (YHWH) written in the Torah – the five books of Mosheh (which was commonly known as "Law of Moses/Mosaic Law" in Christianity). This "law (torah)" refers to those ordinances that regulated the priesthood, sacrifices, rituals, meat and drink offerings, feasts etc. (e.g. Exo. chapter 25, 27, 29, Lev. chapter 23). Apostle Paul taught in Galatian 3:16-17,19 that those law (torah) that existed after 430 years {*i.e. the time period between 1877 B.C when the confirmation of the covenant of Jacob (Gen. 46:2-4) was made, to 1447 B.C (cf. 1 Kings 6:1) when the Exodus took place (children of Yisrael came out of Egypt).*} was added because of transgressions till the seed should come (Gal. 3:19)" and that seed was "YHWH the Messiah (haMashiach)." The CJB (Complete Jewish Bible) translated the "law (torah)" as "the legal part of the Torah (Gal 3:17)".

Apostle Paul spoke that the law (torah) was "handwriting of ordinances that was against us, which was contrary to us, and took it out of the way, nailing it to the stake (Col. 2:14)". Apostle Paul clearly explained in his epistles, that those "law (torah)" came to an end at the stake after the death of the Messiah (haMashiach). Such law (torah) made nothing perfect (Heb. 7:19) but put those whose deeds were not of faith in the Messiah (haMashiach) but of the works of the law (torah) under the curse of the law (Gal 3:10-13) and bondage (Gal 5:1).

There could be some misunderstanding that the Ten Commandments were part of the law (torah) too. This is not true because the Ten Commandments of God (Elohim) were not written in the book of the law (sefer hatorah) by Mosheh, but were written with the finger of Adonai יהוה (YHWH) on the two tablets of stone (Exo. 31:18) and the tablets were the work of God (Elohim), and the writing was the writing of God (Elohim), graven upon the tablets (Exo. 32:16).

In order for reader to have a good knowledge and understanding of the word "Torah", an article extracted from the source of Wikipedia-the free Encyclopedia is written in Appendix III (see page number 1058) for reference.

Nr.	Strong's and Scripture Reference	Hebrew Text / Transliteration & {Phonetic Spelling}	Word(s) Written in English Bibles	Word(s) Written in יהוה Sacred Scriptures
B28b	ספר H5612 תורה H8451 Deu. 27:26	ספר התורה {Se-fer ha-to-rah}	book of the law	book of the law (sefer-hatorah)
	Jos. 8:31 Gal. 3:10	הַכָּתוּב בְּסֵפֶר תּוֹרַת מֹשֶׁה	...it is written in the book of the law of Moses	...it is written in the book of the law (sefer hatorah) by Moses (Mosheh)
	Jos. 8:32		...a copy of the law of Moses, which he wrote..	...a copy of the law (torah) which Moses (Mosheh) had written...

The "book of the law" is "sefer hatorah" in Hebrew. As it is true that the law (torah) was given by God (Elohim) and written by Mosheh, in order not to be misunderstood the law (torah) of God (Elohim) as "law of Moses", therefore, the above verses were rephrased appropriately according to the context of the Hebrew Scriptures.

| B28c | 1 Kin. 2:3
1 Cor. 9:9 | כַּכָּתוּב בְּתוֹרַת מֹשֶׁה | ...it is written in the law of Moses | ...it is written in the Torah by Moses (Mosheh) |

In 1 Kin. 2:3 and 1 Cor. 9:9, this verse is not talking about "law of Moses" but about all that's written by Moses (Mosheh) in the 1st-part of the Tanakh called Torah. Therefore, it is appropriately translated as "...it is written in the Torah by Moses (Mosheh)".

| B28d | Mat. 5:17 | | law or the prophets | Torah or the Prophets (Nevi'im) |
| | Mat. 7:12 | | law and the prophets | Torah and the Prophets (Nevi'im) |

i)   The word "Torah" should be used instead of "law" because the Messiah (haMashiach) actually refer to the first two-part of the three-part division of TaNaKh: Torah (Five books of Moses) and Prophets (Nevi'im).

ii) Mat. 5:17 "Think not that I came to destroy the Torah or the Prophets (Nevi'im). I did not come to destroy, but to fulfil." In this verse, the Messiah (haMashiach) was saying that He did not come to destroy (abolish) the Torah or the Prophets (Nevi'im) but to fulfil, meaning to accomplish the promises of God (Elohim) and make the prophesies of the prophets come to pass as written in the Torah and books of the Prophets.

| B29 | H4501 מנרה
Exo. 26:35 | menorah
מְנוֹרָה | candlestick | candlestick (menorah) |

The menorah (Hebrew: מנרה) is described in the Bible as the seven-lamp (six branches) ancient Hebrew candlestick made of pure gold and used in the portable sanctuary set up by Mosheh in the wilderness and later in the Temple in Jerusalem (Yerushalayim). Fresh olive oil of the purest quality was burned daily to light its lamps.

The menorah has been a symbol of Judaism (Yehudaism) since ancient times and is the emblem on the coat of arms of the modern state of Yisrael.

| B30 | H5139 נזיר
Num 6:2 | Nazir
נָזִיר {Na-zeer} | Nazarite | Nazarite (Nazir) |

"Nazir" is a Hebrew word meaning "consecrated or devoted one"; one who took the ascetic vow as described in Numbers 6:1-21.

Nr.	Strong's and Scripture Reference	Hebrew Text / Transliteration & {Phonetic Spelling}	Word(s) Written in English Bibles	Word(s) Written in יהוה Sacred Scriptures
B31a	קדשים Job 5:1	qadoshim (pl.) קְדֹשִׁים {qa-do-sheem}	saints	holy ones (qadoshim)
B31b	H2623 חסיד 1 Sam. 2:9	Chasidim (pl.) חֲסִידִים {kha-see-deem}	saints	faithful ones (chasidim)

The word "saint(s)" is replaced by "holy one(s)" as according to the Hebrew Scriptures:

Qadoshim קְדֹשִׁים is from original word: H6918 קָדֹשׁ Qadosh, meaning: 1) sacred, holy, Holy One, saint, set apart. Chasidim חֲסִידִים is from the original word: H2623 Chasid חָסִיד, meaning: 1) faithful, kind, godly, holy one, saint, pious.

B32	H7585 שאול Deut. 32:22	sheol שְׁאוֹל {sheh-ole}	hell	hell (sheol)
	1 Sam. 2:6	sheol	grave	grave (sheol)
	G86 hádēs Mat. 11:23	sheol	Hades	Hades (sheol)

"לואש sheol" is the Hebrew word, meaning "underworld, grave, hell, pit".

HELP Word-Studies from Strong's Concordance:

86 *hádēs* – properly, the "unseen place," referring to the (invisible) realm in which all the dead reside, i.e. the present dwelling place of all the departed (deceased); *Hades*.

B33a	H1167 בעלי Num. 21:28	Baalei בַּעֲלֵי {Ba-al-ee}	the lords	the lords (Baalei)
B33b	H1168 בעל Judg. 2:13, Rom. 11:4	Baal בָּעַל {Ba-al}	Baal	Baal
B33c	H1168 בעלים Judg. 2:11	Baalim (pl.) בְּעָלִים {Ba-al-eem}	Baalim	Baals (Baalim)
B33d	H1170 בעל ברית Judg. 8:33	Baal-Berit בַּעַל בְּרִית {Ba-al Be-rit}	Baalberith	Baal-Berit (Lord of Covenant)
B33e	H1180 בעלי Hosea 2:16	Baali בַּעֲלִי {Ba-al-ee}	Baali	Baali (My Lord)

"H1168 Baal בעל" is the supreme male divinity of the Phoenicians or Canaanites, the heathen god (elohim), which means "Lord" in Hebrew. "Baalim בעלים" is the plural form of Baal. "H1170 בעל ברית Baal-Berit" which means "Lord of Covenant" is a special diety of the Shechemite.

Nr.	Strong's and Scripture Reference	Hebrew Text / Transliteration & {Phonetic Spelling}	Word(s) Written in English Bibles	Word(s) Written in יהוה Sacred Scriptures
B33f	H1166 בעל Jer. 31:32, Isa. 54:5	baal בָּעַל{ba-al}	husband	husband (baal)
	The word "baal בעל" means owner or lord or husband. In most cases where it is used in the Old Testament, it is a general reference rather than pointing to a specific husband. However, in this verse Jer. 31:32 and in Isa. 54:5, it refers to יהוה (YHWH) as Yisrael's husband (baal). (Reference: https://www.sermonwriter.com/biblical-commentary/jeremiah-3131-34/)			
B34a	H842 אשרה Judg.6:25. 2 Chro. 15:16	Asherah אֲשֵׁרָה{Ash-ay-rah}	grove	Asherah
B34b	Judg. 3:7	Asherot (pl.) אֲשֵׁרוֹת {Ash-ay-rot}	groves	Asherahs (Asherot)
	Exo. 34:13	Asherim (pl.) אֲשֵׁרִים {Ash-ay-reem}		Asherahs (Asherim)
	Definitions from BibleWorks: Meaning: Ashera(h) = "groves (for idol worship)" 1) a Babylonian (Astarte)-Canaanite goddess (of fortune and happiness), the supposed consort of Baal, her images 1a) the goddess, goddesses 1b) her images 1c) sacred trees or poles set up near an altar. Meaning: a Phoenician goddess, also an image of the same. Reference from Easton's Bible Dictionary at www.biblestudytool.com: Heb. 'asherah, properly a wooden image, or a pillar representing Ashtoreth, a sensual Canaanitish goddess, probably usually set up in a grove (2 Kin. 21:7; 23:4). In the Revised Version the word "Asherah" (q.v.) is introduced as a proper noun, the name of the wooden symbol of a goddess, with the plurals Asherim (Exo.34:13) and Asheroth (Judg. 3:13). The LXX. have rendered asherah in 2 Chro. 15:16 by "Astarte." The Vulgate has done this also in Judg. 3:7.			
B35	H3064 יהודי Est. 2:5	Yehudi יְהוּדִי {Yeh-hoo-dee}	Jew	Jew (Yehudi)
	יהודים 2 Kin. 16:6	Yehudim (pl.) יְהוּדִים {Yeh-hoo-deem}	Jews	Jews (Yehudim)
	"Yehudi" is called "Jew" or "Jewish people" in English, which is of the tribe of Yehudah. The English term *Jew* originates in the Biblical Hebrew word *Yehudi*; *Yehudim* is the plural term for *Jews*, meaning "from the Kingdom of Judah (Yehudah)". It passed into Greek as *Ioudaios* and Latin as *Iudaeus*, which evolved into the Old French *giu* after the letter "d" was dropped. A variety of related forms are found in early English from about the year 1000, including *Iudea, Gyu, Giu, Iuu, Iuw,* and *Iew*, which eventually developed into the modern word *Jew*. Information about "Jew" from Easton's Bible Dictionary at www.biblestudytool.com:			

Nr.	Strong's and Scripture Reference	Hebrew Text / Transliteration & {Phonetic Spelling}	Word(s) Written in English Bibles	Word(s) Written in יהוה Sacred Scriptures
	The name derived from the patriarch Judah (Yehudah), at first given to one belonging to the tribe of Judah (Yehudah) or to the separate kingdom of Judah (2 Kin.16:6, 25:25; Jer.32:12 ; 38:19, 40:11, 41:3) in contradistinction from those belonging to the kingdom of the ten tribes, who were called Israelites (Yisraeli).			
	During the Captivity, and after the Restoration, the name, however, was extended to all the Hebrew nation without distinction (Est. 3:6, 10; Dan. 3:8,12; Ezra 4:12, 5:1,5). Originally this people were called Hebrews (Gen. 39:14, 40:15; Exo. 2:7, 3:18, 5:3; 1 Sam. 4:6, 4:9, etc.), but after the Exile this name fell into disuse. But Paul was styled a Hebrew (2 Cor. 11:22; Phil 3:5).			
	The history of the Jewish nation is interwoven with the history of Palestine and with the narratives of the lives of their rulers and chief men. They are now [1897] dispersed over all lands, and to this day remain a separate people, "without a king, and without a prince, and without a sacrifice, and without an image [RSV 'pillar,' marg. 'obelisk'], and without an ephod, and without teraphim" (Hosea 3:4). Till about the beginning of the present century [1800] they were everywhere greatly oppressed, and often cruelly persecuted; but now their condition is greatly improved, and they are admitted in most European countries to all the rights of free citizens. In 1860 the "Jewish disabilities" were removed, and they were admitted to a seat in the British Parliament. Their number in all is estimated at about six millions, about four millions being in Europe.			
	There are three names used in the New Testament (New Blood Covenant) to designate this people:			
	i) Jews (Yehudah), as regards their nationality, to distinguish them from Gentiles. ii) Hebrews (Ivrim), with regard to their language and education, to distinguish them from Hellenists, i.e., Jews who spoke the Greek language. iii) Israelites (Yisraeli), as respects their sacred privileges as the chosen people of God.			
B36	H7451 רע Gen 19:19	רַע ra' / רָעָה raah	evil	disaster (raah)
	Eccl. 5:13			evil (raah)
	2 Sam. 18:32			harm (raah)
	The translation of the word "raah רָעָה" has been revised according to the contexts of the Hebrew Scripture. In the Strong's Hebrew H7451: "ra'/raah" was defined as "adversity/bad/evil/calamity/harm".			
B37	G2202 Acts 14:12	Zeus	Jupiter	Jupiter (Zeus)
	Zeus, the Greek god of the sky in all its manifestations, corresponding to the Roman Jupiter and to the leading god of the native Lycaonians.			
B38	Acts 14:12	Hermes	Mercuries	Mercuries (Hermes)
	Hermes, the messenger and herald of the Greek gods, or rather the corresponding Lycaonian deity; called by the Romans Mercuries.			

Nr.	Strong's and Scripture Reference	Hebrew Text / Transliteration & {Phonetic Spelling}	Word(s) Written in English Bibles	Word(s) Written in יהוה Sacred Scriptures
B39	Exo. 6:3	ושמי יהוה לא נודעתי	by My name JEHOVAH was I not known to them.	by My name יהוה (YHWH) was I not known to them?

1) The sacred name "יהוה (YHWH pronounced Yahwah)" has been transliterated as "JEHOVAH" in KJV Bible using the Masoretic vowel point of "Adonai". Refer A1 in Appendix II-A for further information on the name of יהוה (YHWH).

2) Exo 6:3 "by My name יהוה (YHWH) was I not known to them?" is an interrogative sentence, not a statement "I was not known to them." as translated in many other English OT bibles which have led to the wrong interpretation of this verse in the Tanakh Scriptures.

| B40 | Deu. 6:4 | Shema Yisrael, YHWH Eloheinu, YHWH echad. | Hear, O Israel: The LORD our God is one LORD: | Hear, O Yisrael: יהוה our Elohim, יהוה is one. |

This verse is translated with the correct transliteration of the sacred name of יהוה (YHWH) according to the Hebrew scripture.

The Hebrew Scripture as written in Deuteronomy 6:4:

שמע ישראל יהוה אלהינו יהוה | אחד

This verse revealed that the God (Elohim) of Yisrael is one God (Elohim) with one Name: יהוה (YHWH); He is not a duality or trinity Elohim/God with two or three or many names.

| B41 | Deu. 7:21 | אֵל גָּדוֹל וְנוֹרָא El gadol wanora | a mighty God and terrible | a mighty and awesome God (El) |

This verse is translated according to the written words in Hebrew Scripture and uses the transliteration of "El אל" (Mighty One/God); "H1419 gadol גָּדוֹל" means "great/mighty" and "נוֹרָא nora" is from the original word "H3372 yara יָרָא" which means "awesome".

| B42 | H6383 פלאי Judg. 13:18 | pili פִּלְאִי {pil-ee} | ... Why askest thou thus after my name, seeing it is secret? | ... Why askest you thus after my name, seeing it is wonderful? |

The meaning of Hebrew word "H6383 פלאי pili" is: wonderful, incomprehensible, or extraordinary; secret is incorrect translation.

| B43 | H1984 הללו H3050 יה Psa. 104:35 | Halelu Yah הַלְלוּ־יָהּ {Ha-le-loo Yah} | Praise ye the LORD / Hallelujah | Praise You Yah (Halelu Yah) |

The word "הללו־יה" consists of two Hebrew words (called compound words) which are "Halelu" (הללו) and "Yah" (יה). "Halelu" means "Praise You" and "Yah" is the short form of יהוה (YHWH), thus "Halelu Yah הללו־יה" is translated as "Praise You Yah".

| B44 | H6780 צמח Jer. 23:5 Zec. 3:8, 6:12 | tsemach צֶמַח {tseh-makh} | BRANCH | Branch (Tsemach) |

Nr.	Strong's and Scripture Reference	Hebrew Text / Transliteration & {Phonetic Spelling}	Word(s) Written in English Bibles	Word(s) Written in יהוה Sacred Scriptures
	In Jer. 23:5, the "BRANCH" translated from Hebrew word "H6780 Tsemach צמח" was speaking about יהוה (YHWH) as revealed in verse 6: "יהוה our Righteousness (YHWH Tsidqenu)". In Zec.3:8, prophet Zechariah prophesied of the same "Branch (Tsemach)" who is the Messiah (haMashiach) YHWH.			
B45	H4899 משיח Dan. 9:25	Mashiach מָשִׁיחַ {Ma-shee-akh}	Messiah	Messiah (Mashiach)
	Mat.1:1, Joh. 1:41	haMashiach המשיח {ha-Ma-shee-akh}	Christ, The Messias	the Messiah (haMashiach)
	"Mashiach" which was transliterated in English as "Messias/Messiah" is a more accurate transliteration for the Hebrew word "H4899 מְשִׁיח".			

These were the meaning of "H4899 משיח Mashiach" from BibleWorks: anointed, anointed one 1a) of the Messiah (haMashiach), Messianic prince 1b) of the king of Israel 1c) of the high priest (kohen hagadol) of Yisrael 1d) of Cyrus 1e) of the patriarchs as anointed kings.

In the Book of New Covenant, God (Elohim) who manifest in the flesh (1 Tim 3:16), the Word that became flesh (John 1:14), the Humanity of El (John 1:41, Mat. 26:63) is called haMashiach המשיח (the Anointed One). The Hebrew transliteration of "haMashiach" is used instead of "Christ" (transliteration of Greek word "G5547 Christos") throughout the entire Scriptures.

i) Study about the true name of the Messiah (haMashiach)
Knowing that the Messiah (haMashiach) is God (Elohim) manifest in the flesh (1 Tim 3:16); also testified by apostle John in John 1:1 that the Word was God (Elohim) and the Word became flesh (John 1:14), the true name of the Messiah (haMashiach) who is given the Name above all names (Phili.2:9), to whom all the prophets gave witness (Acts 10:43), is thus revealed as יהוה (YHWH). Read also A1 study notes in Appendix II-A.

B46	Luke 1:5-36	-	-	-
	Luke 1:5 G7 Abia H29 Aviyah		course of Abia	course of Abia (Abiyah)

A Study about the true birth date of the Messiah (haMashiach)

The Messiah (haMashiach) was not born on the 25th December as most believers might have known this fact. Here're some Scriptural facts and study that shall reveal the true birth date/month of the Messiah (haMashiach), Adonai YHWH our Savior:

a) The birth of prophet John the Baptist was foretold to Zachariah and his wife Elisabeth (Read Luke 1:5-25)
b) The birth of the Messiah was foretold to Mary (Miriam) – Read Luke 1:26-35
c) Elisabeth was conceived after Zechariah returned home from serving in the course of Abia (Abiyah, Luke 1:5, 24). The course of Abia (Abiyah) mentioned in Luke 1:5 is the eighth of the priestly courses of ministration in the Temple (1 Chron. 24:10), and occurred, as did the others, twice a year.

Nr.	Strong's and Scripture Reference	Hebrew Text / Transliteration & {Phonetic Spelling}	Word(s) Written in English Bibles	Word(s) Written in יהוה Sacred Scriptures
	d) All the courses served together at the three great feasts, therefore the month for the two yearly ministrations of Aviyah will be seen to fall on: First ministration: 6 – 12 December (Hebrew: Chisleu) Second ministration: 13 – 19 June (Hebrew: Sevan) According to Luke 1:23-24, Elisabeth was conceived in those days after her husband, prophet Zechariah returned home upon completion of the course of Aviyah. Therefore, Elisabeth conception of John the Baptist must have falls somewhere at the end of the month of June. e) Elisabeth was in her sixth month pregnancy when angel Gabriel was sent to inform Mary (Miriam) about her conception of the Messiah. (Luke 1:26-27, 31, 36). With above Scriptural facts, the Messiah's conception by Mary (Miriam) must have been taken place in the month of December. The 9 months' pregnancy of Mary (Miriam) would put her due date in the month of September (Hebrew: Tisrei / Ethanim), the actual month for the birth of Yahwah haMashiach. There are two biblical Jewish (Yehudi) holidays which fall in the month of Tishrei: 1st Tishrei - Day of Trumpets (Yom Teruah, Lev. 23:23-32); 15th – 21st Tishrei - Feast of Tablenacle (Chag Sukkot). There were studies by different groups of believers, some believe that the Messiah (haMashiach) was born on Yom Teruah (1st Tishrei) and some believe He was born on the Feast of Sukkot (15th Tishrei). Below are the references where readers can search and study for themselves. Do pray to Adonai YHWH and allow His Holy Spirit to lead into knowing His truth. **Notes:** Tishrei is the first month of the civil year (which starts on 1 Tishrei) and the seventh month of the ecclesiastical year (which equal to 1 Nisan) in the Hebrew calender. Tishrei is a Babylonian name, an autumn month of 30 days, occurs between September - October of Gregorian calender. Before the Babylonian exile, month of Tishrei was called Ethanim (1 Kings 8:2) **References:** https://biblehub.com/sermons/auth/kitto/of_the_course_of_abia.htm http://www.angelfire.com/nv/TheOliveBranch/append179d.html https://en.wikipedia.org/wiki/Tishrei			
B47	Mat. 3:17		Son	Son (Humanity)
	Mat. 4:3		Son of God	Humanity of El (YHWH)
	Rom 1:3 John 3:16, 17	-	His Son	His Humanity

Nr.	Strong's and Scripture Reference	Hebrew Text / Transliteration & {Phonetic Spelling}	Word(s) Written in English Bibles	Word(s) Written in יהוה Sacred Scriptures
	The word "Son" refers to the Messiah (haMashiach, who was called "Christ" in Christianity), sometimes called "Son of Dawid" or Son of man. The Messiah (haMashiach) is not the second Person of God (Elohim) but is God (Elohim) יהוה (YHWH) Himself Who manifested in the flesh (1 Tim 3:16, John 1:14) to become human and dwell among mankind. In other words, God (Elohim, יהוה (YHWH)) was the "Son".			
	Therefore, in order to help readers with the correct understanding of the Oneness of God (Elohim) and His manifestation in the flesh to become the "Son", the word "Humanity" or "Humanity of El (YHWH)" is added in parenthesis to describe the word "Son". In some verses e.g. Rom. 1:3 and John 3:16, 17, the word "Son" is rendered simply as "Humanity". The phrase "Son of God" (which confused many that God (Elohim) has a Son as a second person of God, which is not true), is substituted by the phrase "Humanity of El (YHWH)" in this Scriptures.			
B48	עמנו אל Isa. 7:14	immanu el עִמָּנוּ אֵל {eem-ma-noo-ale}	Emmanuel	Immanu El
	G1694 Emmanouél Mat. 1:23			
	Prophet Isaiah (Yeshayahu) prophesied in Isa. 7:14, saying: "Behold, the virgin shall conceive and bear a Son (Humanity of El), and shall call His name "Immanu El" (the correct transliteration of Hebrew word "עמנו אל".			
	"Immanu El" is not the name of the Messiah (haMashiach) but the calling of Him as "God is with us" since God יהוה (YHWH) was manifested in the flesh (1 Tim 3:16) and dwell among men (John 4:24).			
B49	Isa. 40:3 Matt 3:3 Mark 1:3 Luke 3:4	קוֹרֵא בַמִּדְבָּר פַּנּוּ דֶּרֶךְ יהוה יַשְּׁרוּ בָּעֲרָבָה מְסִלָּה לֵאלֹהֵינוּ:	The voice of one crying in the wilderness, 'Prepare ye the way of **the LORD**, make his paths straight.'	The voice of one crying in the wilderness, 'Prepare the way of יהוה **(YHWH)**, make His paths straight.'
	Apostle Matthew, Mark and Luke gave witness to God (Elohim) יהוה (YHWH) according to the prophesy of prophet Isaiah (Yeshayahu) in the original Hebrew Scripture (Tanakh): **Isaiah (Yeshayahu) 40:3**			

קוֹרֵא בַמִּדְבָּר פַּנּוּ דֶּרֶךְ יהוה יַשְּׁרוּ בָּעֲרָבָה מְסִלָּה לֵאלֹהֵינוּ:

which were being translated as:
The voice of one crying in the wilderness, "Prepare ye the way of יהוה (YHWH), make His paths straight."

The Scripture clearly written and testified that יהוה (YHWH) is the Messiah (haMashiach) whom John the Baptist (Yochanan haMatvil) came to prepare the way for, not any other Messiah (Mashiach) with any other names!

Nr.	Strong's and Scripture Reference	Hebrew Text / Transliteration & {Phonetic Spelling}	Word(s) Written in English Bibles	Word(s) Written in יהוה Sacred Scriptures
B50	G5330 Pharisaíos Matt 3:7	-	Pharisees	Pharisees

Commentary taken from the source of Wikipedia:
The **Pharisees** were at various times a political party, a social movement, and a school of thought in the Holy Land during the time of Second Temple Judaism. After the destruction of the Second Temple in 70 CE, Pharisaic beliefs became the foundational, liturgical and ritualistic basis for Rabbinic Judaism.

Footnote from AMP Bible:
The **Pharisees** identified with the common people and had control over them. They were prominent legalistic leaders in Judaism who were experts in Mosaic Law and its rituals and traditions. They believed in the resurrection of the dead, immortality of the soul and in the existence of angels and spirits.

Nr.	Strong's and Scripture Reference	Hebrew Text / Transliteration & {Phonetic Spelling}	Word(s) Written in English Bibles	Word(s) Written in Sacred Scriptures
B51	G4523 Saddou-kaíos Matt 3:7	-	Sadducees	Sadducees

Commentary taken from the source of Wikipedia:

The **Sadducees** (Hebrew: צְדוּקִים *Tsĕḏûqîm*) were a sect or group of Jews (Yehudim) that was active in Judea (Yehudah) during the Second Temple period, starting from the second century BCE through the destruction of the Temple in 70 CE. The sect was identified by Josephus (Yosef) with the upper social and economic echelon of Judean (Yehudi) society. As a whole, the sect fulfilled various political, social, and religious roles, including maintaining the Temple.

Footnote from AMP Bible:

The **Sadducees** were aristocratic members of a priestly group (religious party) who controlled the temple. They denied the possibility of a resurrection and the existence of any spiritual beings apart from God. Although the Sadducees were in the minority, they were leaders of the Sanhedrin, controlling the Jewish High Court.

Nr.	Strong's and Scripture Reference	Hebrew Text / Transliteration & {Phonetic Spelling}	Word(s) Written in English Bibles	Word(s) Written in Sacred Scriptures
B52	G908 baptisma Matt 3:7	-	baptism	baptism
	G907 baptize Acts 2:38	-	baptized	baptized

Baptism is done for those who have sincerely repented of their sins, and in their hearts have truly believed on Yahwah haMashiach as Savior. In so doing, they declare to the world that they have died with YHWH and that they have also been raised with Him to walk in newness of life (Acts 2:38; Romans 6:4). The scriptural mode of baptism is by immersion in water (submerged completely under the water).

Nr.	Strong's and Scripture Reference	Hebrew Text / Transliteration & {Phonetic Spelling}	Word(s) Written in English Bibles	Word(s) Written in יהוה Sacred Scriptures
	The water immersion baptism of John the Baptist (Yochanan haMatvil) was baptism of repentance which was done for those living under the First Covenant (before crucifixion and resurrection of the Messiah as the Passover Lamb-Pesach). After the crucifixion and resurrection of Yahwah haMashiach, apostle Peter who has the key to the Kingdom of Heaven, preached the good news (gospel) of salvation in Acts 2:38: **Then Peter said to them, "Repent, and let everyone of you be baptized in the name of Yahwah haMashiach for the remission of sins; and you shall receive the gift of Holy Spirit."** HELPS Word-Studies in Strong's Concordance: 908 báptisma – baptism (note the -ma suffix, emphasizing it is a result, i.e. of sincere repentance.). 907 baptízō – properly, "submerge" (Souter); hence, baptize, to immerse (literally, dip under") 907 (baptízō) implies submersion ("immersion"), in contrast to 472 antexomai ("sprinkle").			
B53	Matt 3:17 Mark 1:11 Luke 3:22	-	And behold a voice from heaven, saying, 'This is My beloved Son, in whom I am well pleased.'	And behold a voice from heaven, saying, 'This is My beloved Son (Humanity of El (YHWH)), in whom I am well pleased.
	In Matt 3:17, Adonai יהוה (YHWH) the One and only God (Elohim) was speaking from heaven as the role of a Father, that He was pleased with "His beloved Son (Humanity)", meaning the human form of temple (body) that Adonai יהוה (YHWH) Himself will dwell in, to become the Son of man (haMashiach). Adonai יהוה (YHWH) is the Father and Adonai יהוה (YHWH) is the Son (haMashiach/Humanity of El) as testified by apostle John and apostle Paul also, that the Father and Son are One:- **John 10:30** "I and My Father are one." **John 14:7 – 9** "If you had known Me, you should have known My Father also; and from henceforth you know Him, and have seen Him." Philip saith unto Him, "Lord (Adonai), shew us the Father, and it sufficeth us." Yahwah saith unto him, "Have I been so long time with you, and yet have you not known me, Philip? He that hath seen Me hath seen the Father; and how sayest you then, 'Shew us the Father'? **1 Tim. 3:16** And without controversy great is the mystery of godliness: God (Elohim) was manifest in the flesh, justified in the Spirit, seen of angels, preached unto the Gentiles (Goyim), believed on in the world, received up into glory. Read also study note B47.			
B54	G4469 rhaká Mat. 5:22	-	Raca	Rhaka (You empty-headed)
	HELP Word-Studies of Strong's Concordance: 4469 rhaká (apparently related to the Aramaic term rōq, "empty") – properly, empty-headed. This term expressed contempt for a man's head, viewing him as stupid (without sense) – i.e. a "numbskull" who acts presumptuously and thoughtlessly.			

Nr.	Strong's and Scripture Reference	Hebrew Text / Transliteration & {Phonetic Spelling}	Word(s) Written in English Bibles	Word(s) Written in יהוה Sacred Scriptures
B55	G4892 synédrion Mat. 5:22	-	council	council (Sanhedrin)

HELP Word-Studies of Strong's Concordance:

4892 synédrion (from 4862 /sýn, "identified *with*" and hedra, "a convening, sitting together") – "a *council* of leading Jews (Yehudim) (Mk 13:9, Mt 10:17), or the Jewish council at Jerusalem (Yerushalayim), the Sanhedrin (Aramaic form of synedrion), the High Court, the Senate, composed of 71 members comprising members of: high-priestly families, Pharisees learned in the Torah, and a lay element of Elders".

Nr.	Strong's and Scripture Reference	Hebrew Text / Transliteration & {Phonetic Spelling}	Word(s) Written in English Bibles	Word(s) Written in יהוה Sacred Scriptures
B56	G1067 geenna Mat. 5:22	-	hell fire	hell fire (Gehenna)

Footnote from AMP bible:

Gehenna, a Greek-transliterated version of the Hebrew for Gei-Hinnom גֵּי בֶן־הִנֹּם (Valley of Hinnom), a ravine where garbage was burned continuously, located just south of Jerusalem (Yerushalayim). Often regarded in ancient times as symbolic of hell (the lake of fire), a realm reserved for the wicked. Mentioned in Mat. 5:22, 29, 30; 10:28; 18:9; 23:15, 33; Mark 9:43, 45, 47; Luke 12:5; James 3:6.

Nr.	Strong's and Scripture Reference	Hebrew Text / Transliteration & {Phonetic Spelling}	Word(s) Written in English Bibles	Word(s) Written in יהוה Sacred Scriptures
B57	Mat. 21:9	-	Hosanna to the son of Dawid: 'Blessed is He that cometh in the name of **the Lord**.' Hosanna in the highest.	Hosanna to the son (descendant) of Dawid: 'Blessed is He that cometh in the name of יהוה **(YHWH, Yahwah)**!' Hosanna in the highest.

A detail search into the original Hebrew scripture gave evidences that the title "**the Lord**" which was written in the entire New Testament had replaced the true name of God (Elohim) - יהוה (**YHWH**) wherever the Tanakh Scriptures was quoted from:

Matthew 21:9 written in Hebrew:

הושע נא לבן דוד **ברוך הבא בשם יהוה** הושע נא במרומים

Original Scripture for Psalm 118:26a written in Hebrew which was quoted in part of Mat.21:9: 'Blessed is He that cometh in the name of יהוה (YHWH, Yahwah):

ברוך הבא בשם יהוה

HELP Word-Studies of Strong's Concordance for G5614 hosanna:
5614 hōsanná – a transliteration of the Hebrew term (hôsî-âh-nā) meaning "*Oh, save now!*" or "*Please save!*"[The -na suffix in Hebrew expresses *intense emotion*.]

Nr.	Strong's and Scripture Reference	Hebrew Text / Transliteration & {Phonetic Spelling}	Word(s) Written in English Bibles	Word(s) Written in יהוה Sacred Scriptures
B58	Matt 26:28 Mark 14:24	כִּי זֶה הוּא דָמִי דַּם־הַבְּרִית הַחֲדָשָׁה	For this is the blood of the New Testament	For this is My blood of the New Covenant (dam haBerit haChadashah)

Yahwah haMashiach announced the institution of a New Blood Covenant between God (Elohim) and man. As He is both God (Elohim) and Son of man (Humanity of El), foreordained before the foundation of the world (1 Peter 1:20) to be the Lamb of God (Elohim) who takes away the sins of the world (John 1:29), He has the authority to establish a New Covenant, sealed with His own precious blood, to put away sins by the sacrifice of Himself (Hebrew 9:26).

In this New Blood Covenant, Yahwah haMashiach did it once and for all for eternal redemption (Romans 6:10, Hebrews 7:27, 9:12), replacing the First Blood Covenant that requires the shed blood of animals (Exo. 24:8) to be done over and over which are never able to strip away sins (Hebrew 10:11). In the book of Jeremiah (Yirmeyahu) chapter 31, prophet Jeremiah (Yirmeyahu) prophesied about this New Covenant which Adonai יהוה (YHWH) will made with His people:

Jeremiah (Yirmeyahu) 31:

33 But this is the covenant that I will make with the house of Yisrael: After those days, says יהוה (YHWH), I will put My Torah in their minds, and write it on their heart; I will be their God (Elohim), and they shall be My people.
34 For I will forgive their iniquity, and their sin I will remember no more.

| B59 | Matt. 28:19 | - | Baptizing them in the name of the Father, and of the Son, and of the Holy Spirit. | Baptizing them in the name (hashem) of the Father, and of the Son, and of the Holy Spirit. |

In the Book of Matthew 28:19, Yahwah haMashiach instruct His disciples to baptize believers in the name of the Father, Son and Holy Spirit which are three manifestation of the one living God (Elohim) – יהוה (YHWH) as revealed in the Scripture: Isaiah (Yeshayahu) 9:6, 45:21; Zechariah (Zekaryah) 14:1; 1 Timothy 3:16; Ephesians 4:4-6.

Matthew 28:19 is in agreement with Tanakh Scripture and Acts 2:38 where apostle Peter preached the baptism of believers in the name of יהוה (YHWH) haMashiach. Read also study notes 62a (Acts 2:38).

| B60 | Luke 2:26 | אֶת־מְשִׁיחַ יהוה et-Mashiach YHWH | And it was revealed unto him by the Holy Ghost, that he should not see death, before he had seen **the Lord's Christ.** | And it was revealed unto him by the Holy Spirit (Ruach haQodesh), that he should not see death, before he had seen **the Messiah YHWH. (et-Mashiach YHWH).** |

Luke 2:26 written in Hebrew:

וְדָבָר נִגְלָה לּוֹ בְּרוּחַ הַקֹּדֶשׁ כִּי לֹא יִרְאֶה־מָוֶת עַד־אֲשֶׁר יִרְאֶה אֶת־מְשִׁיחַ יהוה :

"אֶת־מְשִׁיחַ יהוה et-Mashiach YHWH" should be correctly transliterated as **"the Messiah YHWH"**.

Nr.	Strong's and Scripture Reference	Hebrew Text / Transliteration & {Phonetic Spelling}	Word(s) Written in English Bibles	Word(s) Written in יהוה Sacred Scriptures
B61	G3056 Logos H1697 Davar דָּבָר John 1:1	הַדָּבָר {ha-da-var}	In the beginning was the Word, and the Word was with God, and the Word was God.	In the beginning was the Word (Davar), and the Word was with God (Elohim), and the Word was God (Elohim).
	John 1:14	-	And the Word was made flesh, and dwelt among us...	And the Word was made flesh, and dwelt among us...
	Apostle John testified in John 1:1-3 about the creation of all things in the beginning by the Word (Davar) which was with God (Elohim), as recorded in Genesis chapter 1, where God (Elohim) spoke the Word and brought all His creations into existence. By the testimony of John, it was revealed to us: The Word that was made flesh, and dwelt among us (John 1:14), we knew to be the Messiah (haMashiach – Humanity of El), He is the everlasting God (Elohim) – יהוה (YHWH pronounced Yahwah) is His sacred name (Read also study note B45 in pg.1045 and A1 in pg. 1008 of Appendix II-A).			
B62a	Act 2:38	-	Then Peter said unto them, Repent, and be baptized every one of you in the name of Jesus Christ for the remission of sins, and ye shall receive the gift of the Holy Ghost.	Then Peter (Kefa) said unto them, "Repent, and be baptized every one of you in the name of Yahwah haMashiach for the remission of sins, and you shall receive the gift of the Holy Spirit (Ruach haQodesh).
	The Tanakh Scripture (First Covenant Book: Genesis to Malachi) revealed that our true living God (Elohim) is יהוה (YHWH), the God (Elohim) of Abraham (Avraham), Isaac (Yitschaq) and Jacob (Yaaqov), who alone is the God (Elohim) and Savior that can bring salvation and give remission of sins. It was also testified by apostle Peter (Kefa) in Acts 10:43: "To Him give all the prophets witness, that through His name whosoever believeth in Him shall receive remission of sins." The conclusion is: there can never be any other name, other than the name of יהוה (YHWH) that one must repent and be baptized in, for remission of sins as preached by apostle Peter (Kefa) in Acts 2:38 and Acts 4:12. Read also study note A1 and A33 in Appendix II-A for further study about the true name of God (Elohim) and Savior.			
B62b	H7307 רוּחַ H6944 קֹדֶשׁ Psa. 51:11	רוּחַ הַקֹּדֶשׁ Ruach haQodesh	Holy Spirit	Holy Spirit (Ruach haQodesh)
	G4151 peuma Acts 2:38		Holy Ghost	
	The proper translation of "Ruach haQodesh רוח הקדש" should be "the Holy Spirit". In the Wikipedia source, the definition of "ghost" was given as such: "*In folklore, a **ghost** is the soul or spirit of a dead person or animal that can appear to the living.*" Thus "H7307 רוּחַ ruach" for Greek work "peuma" is appropriately translated as "Spirit" in יהוה Sacred Scriptures.			

Nr.	Strong's and Scripture Reference	Hebrew Text / Transliteration & {Phonetic Spelling}	Word(s) Written in English Bibles	Word(s) Written in יהוה Sacred Scriptures
B63	G1577 ekklésia Mat. 16:18	-	church	assembly (ekklesia)
	Acts 9:31		churches	assemblies (ekklesias)

The Greek word "ekklesia" is defined in Strong's Concordance as "an assembly, a (religious) congregation". In this book of scriptures, the word "assembly (ekklesia)" is appropriately used instead of "church (which relates to Christianity)".

HELP Word-Studies of Strong's Concordance:

G1577 ekklēsía (from G1537 /ek, "out from and to" and G2564 /kaléō, "to call") – properly, people called out from the world and to God (Elohim), the outcome being the Assembly (the mystical body of the Messiah (haMashiach)) – i.e. the universal (total) body of believers whom God (Elohim) calls out from the world and into His eternal kingdom.

[The *English* word "*church*" comes from the Greek word *kyriakos*, "belonging to the Lord (YHWH)" (*kyrios*). 1577 /*ekklēsía* ("church") is the root of the terms "ecclesiology" and "ecclesiastical."]

B64	G5546 Acts 11:26	Mashiachiyim (pl.) מְשִׁיחִיִּים {Ma-shee-a-khee-yeem}	Christians	Mashiachiyim (followers of Messiah)
	G5546 Acts 26:28	Mashiachi מְשִׁיחָי {Ma-shee-a-khee}	Christian	Mashiachi (follower of Messiah)
B65	Rom. 1:3	עַל־דְּבַר בְּנוֹ	Concerning his Son *Jesus Christ our Lord*	Concerning His Humanity

In Rom 1:3, "*Jesus Christ our Lord*" was not written in the Greek nor Hebrew Scriptures, it was added into the translated English bibles.

The word "Son" in this Scripture is rendered as "Humanity" in order for reader to have the correct understanding that God (Elohim, יהוה (YHWH)) manifested Himself in the flesh (1 Tim 3:16) to be the Son of man (haMashiach), not to be confused as a second person of God (Elohim) by the word "His Son". Read also study note nr. B47.

| B66 | Rom. 1:3 | אֲשֶׁר יָצָא מִזֶּרַע דָּוִד לְפִי בְשָׂרוֹ | ...who was made of the seed of Dawid according to the flesh; | ...who was made of the seed of Dawid according to the flesh; |

Apostle Paul clearly taught that the [B47]Son (Humanity of El) was made of the seed of Dawid according to the flesh, which means the Messiah (haMashiach) came from descendant of Dawid through the seed of Joseph (Yosef), Mary (Miryam)'s husband.

Nr.	Strong's and Scripture Reference	Hebrew Text / Transliteration & {Phonetic Spelling}	Word(s) Written in English Bibles	Word(s) Written in יהוה Sacred Scriptures
B67	Rom. 10:4	כִּי תַכְלִית הַתּוֹרָה הוּא הַמָּשִׁיחַ לְכָל־הַמַּאֲמִין לִצְדָקָה בּוֹ׃	**For Christ is the end of the law** for righteousness to everyone that believeth.	**For the goal at which the law (torah) aims is the Messiah (haMashiach),** for righteousness to everyone that believeth.

Romans 10:4 is properly revised by obtaining references from HELP Word-Studies of Strong's Greek G5056 Telos and CJB bible version:

Rom 10:4 (CJB): For the goal at which the Torah aims is the Messiah, who offers righteousness to everyone who trusts.

HELP Word-Studies (Copyright @ 1987, 2011 by Help Ministries, Inc.)

5056 *télos* (a neuter noun) – properly, consummation (the *end-goal*, *purpose*), such as *closure* with all its *results*. [This root (*tel-*) means "reaching the *end* (aim)." It is well-illustrated with the old pirate's telescope, unfolding (extending out) one stage at a time to function at full-strength (capacity effectiveness).]

| B68 | Rom. 10:13 | כִּי־כֹל אֲשֶׁר־יִקְרָא בְּשֵׁם יהוה יִמָּלֵט | For whosoever shall call upon the name of **the Lord** shall be saved. | For whosoever shall call upon the name of יהוה **(YHWH)** shall be saved. |

Apostle Paul preached in Romans 10:13, quoting from the book of Joel (Yoel) 2:32 that whosoever shall call upon the name of יהוה (YHWH) shall be saved. The Lord is a title, not a name and as it was written in the Scriptures, believers shall be saved by calling upon the name of יהוה (YHWH), not calling upon a title "the Lord" or any other names.

| B69 | Phil. 2:10 | - | That at the name of **Jesus** every knee should bow, of things in heaven, and things on earth, and things under the earth; | That at the name of יהוה **(YHWH)** every knee should bow, of things in heaven, and things on earth, and things under the earth; |

Apostle Paul preached to the Philippians using the Tanakh Scriptures (First Covenant Book: Genesis to Malachi) and he quoted from the Book of Isaiah (Yeshayahu) chapter 45, saying in Phil. 2:9-10: "Wherefore God (Elohim) also hath highly exalted Him (haMashiach), and given Him a name which is above every name, that at the name of יהוה (YHWH) every knee should bow (Isa. 45:23), of things in heaven, and things on earth, and things under the earth; and that every tongue should confess that Yahwah haMashiach is the Lord (Adonai), to the glory of God (Elohim) the Father."

Isaiah 45:

21 Tell you, and bring them near; yea, let them take counsel together. Who hath declared this from ancient time? Who hath told it from that time? Have not I יהוה? And there is no God (Elohim) else besides Me; a just God (El tzadik) and a Savior; there is none besides Me.

Nr.	Strong's and Scripture Reference	Hebrew Text / Transliteration & {Phonetic Spelling}	Word(s) Written in English Bibles	Word(s) Written in יהוה Sacred Scriptures
	22 Look unto Me, and be you saved, all the ends of the earth; for I am God (El), and there is none else. 23 I have sworn by Myself, the word is gone out of My mouth in righteousness, and shall not return, that unto Me every knee shall bow, every tongue shall swear. The Scriptures gave indisputable evidences that יהוה (YHWH) is the name above every name of the Messiah (haMashiach) and the only God (Elohim), there is none else besides Him. Read also study notes A1 and A46.			
B70	Rev. 1:8	אָנֹכִי אָלֶף וְתָו רֹאשׁ וָסוֹף נְאֻם־יְ יהוה אֱלֹהִים אֲשֶׁר הוּא הֹוֶה וְהָיָה וְיָבוֹא אֱלֹהֵי צְבָאוֹת:	I am Alpha and Omega, the beginning and the ending, saith **the Lord**, which is, and which was, and which is to come, the Almighty.	"I am Alpha and Omega, the beginning and the ending," saith יהוה **(YHWH)**, "who is, and who was, and who is to come, God of hosts (Elohei Tsevaot)."

The Hebrew Scripture gave evidences that יהוה (YHWH) is the Lord (Adonai), יהוה (YHWH) is the Alpha and Omega, the beginning and the ending, the First and the Last.

Apostle John testified this in Revelation 1:8, the witness given by Prophet Isaiah (Yeshayahu) as written in the Book of Isaiah (Yeshayahu):

Isaiah (Yeshayahu) 41:4 (KJV)
Who hath wrought and done it, calling the generations from the beginning? 'I יהוה, the First, and with the Last; I am He.'"

מי־פעל ועשה קרא הדרות מראש אני יהוה ראשון ואת־אחרנים אני־הוא:

Isaiah (Yeshayahu) 44:6 (KJV)
Thus saith יהוה the King of Yisrael and his Redeemer, יהוה of hosts (YHWH Tsevaot): 'I am the First, and I am the Last; and besides Me there is no God (Elohim).

כה־אמר יהוה מלך־ישראל וגאלו יהוה צבאות אני ראשון ואני אחרון ומבלעדי אין אלהים:

Torah (Hebrew: תורה, «Instruction», «Teaching» or «Law») has a range of meanings. It can most specifically mean the first five books (Pentateuch or five books of Moses) of the 24 books of the Tanakh (Hebrew Bible). This is commonly known as the **Written Torah**. It can also mean the continued narrative from all the 24 books, from the Book of Genesis to the end of the Tanakh (Chronicles), and it can even mean the totality of Jewish teaching, culture, and practice, whether derived from biblical texts or later rabbinic writings. This is often known as the **Oral Torah**. Common to all these meanings, Torah consists of the origin of Jewish peoplehood: their call into being by God, their trials and tribulations, and their covenant with their God, which involves following a way of life embodied in a set of moral and religious obligations and civil laws (*halakha*). If in bound book form, it is usually printed with the rabbinic commentaries (*perushim*). If meant for liturgic purposes, it takes the form of a Torah scroll (*sefer Torah*), which contains strictly the five books of Moses.

In rabbinic literature the word *Torah* denotes both the five books (Hebrew: תורה שבכתב «Torah that is written») and the Oral Torah (תורה שבעל פה, «Torah that is spoken»). The Oral Torah consists of interpretations and amplifications which according to rabbinic tradition have been handed down from generation to generation and are now embodied in the Talmud and Midrash. Rabbinic tradition›s understanding is that all of the teachings found in the Torah (both written and oral) were given by God through the prophet Moses, some at Mount Sinai and others at the Tabernacle, and all the teachings were written down by Moses, which resulted in the Torah that exists today. According to the Midrash, the Torah was created prior to the creation of the world, and was used as the blueprint for Creation. The majority of Biblical scholars believe that the written books were a product of the Babylonian captivity (c. 6th century BCE), based on earlier written sources and oral traditions, and that it was completed with final revisions during the post-Exilic period (c. 5th century BCE). Traditionally, the words of the Torah are written on a scroll by a scribe (*sofer*) in Hebrew. A Torah portion is read publicly at least once every three days in the presence of a congregation. Reading the Torah publicly is one of the bases of Jewish communal life.

Meaning and Names

The word "Torah" in Hebrew is derived from the root ירה, which in the hif'il conjugation means 'to guide' or 'to teach' (cf. Lev 10:11). The meaning of the word is therefore "teaching", "doctrine", or "instruction"; the commonly accepted "law" gives a wrong impression. The Alexandrian Jews who translated the Septuagint used the Greek word *nomos*, meaning norm, standard, doctrine, and later "law". Greek and Latin Bibles then began the custom of calling the Pentateuch (five books of Moses) The Law. Other translational contexts in the English language include custom, theory, guidance, or system.

The term "Torah" is used in the general sense to include both Rabbinic Judaism's written law and Oral Law, serving to encompass the entire spectrum of authoritative Jewish religious teachings throughout history, including the Mishnah, the Talmud, the Midrash and more, and the inaccurate rendering of "Torah" as "Law" may be an obstacle to understanding the ideal that is summed up in the term *talmud torah* (תלמוד תורה, "study of Torah").

The earliest name for the first part of the Bible seems to have been "The Torah of Moses". This title, however, is found neither in the Torah itself, nor in the works of the pre-Exilic literary prophets. It appears in Joshua (8:31–32; 23:6) and Kings (I Kings 2:3; II Kings 14:6; 23:25), but it cannot be said to refer there to the entire corpus (according to academic Bible criticism). In contrast, there is every likelihood that its use in the post-Exilic works (Mal. 3:22; Dan. 9:11, 13; Ezra 3:2; 7:6; Neh. 8:1; II Chron. 23:18; 30:16) was intended to be comprehensive. Other early titles were "The Book of Moses" (Ezra 6:18; Neh. 13:1; II Chron. 35:12; 25:4; cf. II Kings 14:6) and "The Book of the Torah" (Neh. 8:3), which seems to be a contraction of a fuller name, "The Book of the Torah of God" (Neh. 8:8, 18; 10:29–30; cf. 9:3).

*Note: Only for reader's general knowledge regarding the meaning of Hebrew word "**Torah**". Source: Directly extracted from Wikipedia, the Free Encyclopedia; links: https://en.wikipedia.org/wiki/Torah*

1. Bible Hub Online Study Tools
   Links: https://biblehub.com/
2. e-Sword Software – the Sword of the LORD with an electronic edge
3. BibleWorks – Version 10.0.8.365
4. The Holy Bible, King James Version (KJV), 1769 Edition
5. The Holy Bible, New King James Version (NKJV) on www. Biblegateway.com
6. The Holy Bible, Complete Jewish Bible (CJB) on www.biblegateway.com
7. The Holy Bibles on Bible Gateway Search and Study Tools
   Links: https://www.biblegateway.com/
8. Halleluyah Scriptures, 7th Edition-2017
9. Wikipedia, the Free Encyclopedia
   Links: https://en.wikipedia.org/
10. Sermon Writer Biblical Commentary
    Links: https://www.sermonwriter.com/
11. Blue Letter Bible Search and Study Tools
    Links: https://www.blueletterbible.org/
12. Easton's Bible Dictionary
    Links: https://www.biblestudytool.com
13. HELP Word-Studies, Copyright @ 1987, 2011 by Help Ministries, Inc.
14. Israel Study Centre
    Links: http://www.Israelstudycentre.com
15. The Ancient Hebrew Research Centre, founded Nov 1, 1999 by Jeff A. Benner.
    Links: https://www.ancient-hebrew.org/
16. Wallis, Faith (1999). Bede: The Reckoning of Time. Liverpool University Press, p.54
17. The Course of Abia (Luke 1:5) – A study on the Messiah's true birth date
    Links: http://www.angelfire.com/nv/TheOliveBranch/append179d.html

Our Contacts:

Yahwah Apostolic Ministries
P.O. Box 132,
1271 Main Street,
Smithfield, Ohio 43948
USA

Email: yam543238@gmail.com
Facebook : https://web.facebook.com/Yahwah-Apostolic-Ministries-Ohio-619817078189119/

Printed in the USA
CPSIA information can be obtained
at www.ICGtesting.com
CBHW071450150324
5323CB00071B/756